Praise for *The Green Book*

"The most useful book in my music reference library, period." — **Mark Edwards, Program Director, WLIT-FM/Chicago**

"Indispensable for our musical research. *The Green Book* has contributed to the soundtracks of several major motion pictures." — **Margaret Ross & Marilyn Schanzer, production researchers, Universal City Studios**

"Invaluable for parody song ideas, song montages, and on-air trivia contests. It should be called the 'Gold' Book!" — **Ron "Iceman" Izenberg, writer/producer, Premiere Radio Networks**

"Not only expanded, but its graphics and layout are more user-friendly than ever. In a business where you're always trying to add an extra bit of spice and creativity, you can never have too many sources of ingenuity . . . that's why *The Green Book* is always close at hand." — **Andy Denemark, VP/Programming, United Stations Radio Networks**

"We do specials every weekend on several formats. Since the new *Green Book* arrived I have two or three program directors chasing me down the hall to get the book. Looks like I'll just have to get a couple more copies!" — **Bob McNeill, VP/Programming, Westwood One Radio Networks**

"An extremely valuable resource. There isn't anything like it. It's always been of great use to us." — **James Austin, Sr. Director of A&R/Special Projects, Rhino Records**

"If your interest in music goes deeper than the surface, you need *The Green Book*. It's a great tool, whether you're organizing your personal collection, putting together programming for broadcast, or just putting together a party tape!" — **Dave Nichols, Executive Director, Country Radio Broadcasters, Inc.**

"*The Green Book* is dangerous. Aside from its absolutely inestimable value in tracking down all manner of music information, this tome appeals to people—like Jeff Green and me—who have a lifelong tendency towards

such people can be!" — **Adam White, International Editor-in-Chief, *Billboard***

"You can't be an effective music director without this essential reference book." — **Ron Fell, Editor, *Gavin***

"The ultimate topical musical reference. It's proved endlessly useful as an idea hatchery and column catalyst." — **Ken Barnes, *Ice Magazine***

"With so many topics covered, this book is an invaluable help for radio producers looking for an original angle to their show." — **Machgiel Bakker, Editor-in-Chief, *Music & Media*, Amsterdam**

"For over 15 years—first as a radio programmer, and now as an editor/journalist—I've considered *The Green Book* to be among my most valuable reference books." — **Ron Rodrigues, Managing Editor, *Radio & Records***

"I wore the cover off my copy of the last edition...and then somebody stole it! It's one of those books you have to chain to the desk!" — **Ross Brittain, Radio & Talent, Inc.**

"It's been an absolute godsend. I frequently assemble 'thematic' music montages for on-air use, and *The Green Book* is the best tool for the job. Just what the producer ordered!" — **Mark Davis, Creative Projects Director, Kevin & Bean Morning Show, KROQ-FM/Los Angeles**

"For anyone involved in the art of communication, this book is an invaluable resource." — **Judy Massa, Director of Music, Voice Of America**

"*The Green Book* is an excellent tool. We use it all the time!" — **Dene Hallam, Program Director, KKBQ-FM/Houston**

"We find *The Green Book* to be an invaluable source of ideas and inspiration." — **Carol Holt, Pollack Media Group**

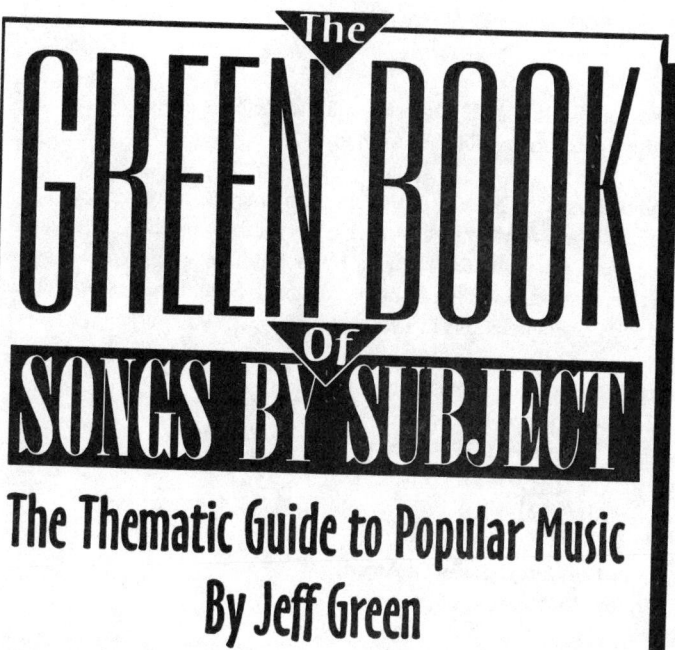

The GREEN BOOK Of SONGS BY SUBJECT

The Thematic Guide to Popular Music
By Jeff Green

4th Edition — Updated & Expanded

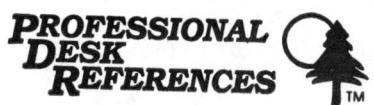

PROFESSIONAL
DESK
REFERENCES
™

The Green Book Of Songs By Subject
Fourth Edition — Updated & Expanded
by Jeff Green

Cover and book design by Mark Schlicher

Professional Desk References, Inc.
4815 Trousdale Drive, Suite 576
Nashville, Tennessee 37220-1324 USA
Phone: (615) 832-1942
Fax: (615) 331-1410

Printed In The United States Of America
First Printing: January, 1995
9 8 7 6 5 4 3 2 1

Library Of Congress Catalog Card Number: 94—69175

Publisher's Cataloging in Publication Data:

Green, Jeff.
    The Green book of songs by subject : the thematic guide to popular music / Jeff Green. — 4th ed., updated & expanded.
    p. cm.
    Includes index.
    Rev. ed. of: Green book. 3rd ed. print. c1989.
    ISBN 0-939735-05-9 (Hard)
    ISBN 0-939735-04-0 (Paper)

    1. Popular Music—Discography.   I. Green, Jeff. Green Book.
II. Title.

ML156.4.P6G73 1989   016.78242164'0266
                                      QBI94-2372

*This book is dedicated to the songwriters who
create these songs, the musicians and singers
who perform them, and the publishers and
record companies which provide them to us all.*

ACKNOWLEDGEMENTS

Many thanks to all of those in the entertainment and media industries who've helped make the Fourth Edition *Green Book* possible. Special thanks to Ken Barnes, *Billboard*, Ed Blissick and Sherry Ringler of Bookcrafters, Scott Brown and Joseph Lovett of Step 2 Software, Lisa Carlson of Upper Access Books, Andy Cohen, the Country Music Association, Norman Davis, Steve Dudugjian, Mark Edwards, Ron Fell, Film House, Ben Fong-Torres, *Gavin*, Jeff Heiman, Robert Hilburn, Sam and Stephanie Marmorstein, *Music & Media*, Robert K. Oermann, Mitchell Pindus, Dan Poynter, Jennifer Queen, *Radio & Records*, Ron Rodrigues, Jeff Rowe, Linda, Emily, Kate and Julia Schlicher, Dave Sholin, Earl Spielman, Ph.D., Dr. Roger Taylor, Lauren Virshup, Howard Watkins, Isa Watkins, Adam White, Norm Winer, and Brad Woodward.

With great appreciation to Mark Schlicher.

CONTENTS

FOREWORD

by Robert K. Oermann

Welcome to one of the most fascinating reference books ever published.

Well, that is if you're (1) a music lover, (2) a trivia buff, (3) a record collector or (4) an inveterate list maker. I am all of those things; and my spirit rejoices when I find a kindred spirit like Jeff Green.

In many ways, guys like Jeff are the backbone of popular culture research. Before any of us collect music, analyze it, write about it and make sense of it, we have to have lists. Lists map out the territory we explore. They guide us to the source material. They direct our steps.

Sometimes they take the form of discographies—who recorded what and when. Sometimes they are compendiums of radio favorites or sales champions—the charts. Sometimes they chronicle important award winners. They've been organized by artist, by era, by music style, by city/country, by value (price guides), by critics' ranking, by record company, by songwriter or even by music videos.

This list is different.

You hold in your hands the first major effort to organize the popular music of this century by topics. I cannot overstate how important and revolutionary I think *The Green Book* is. Just as the Joel Whitburn *Billboard* chart compilations, the Grammy-winners books, our various pop encyclopedias and the RIAA Gold and Platinum tallies have become part of every good working popular-music library, so *The Green Book* will take its place as an indispensable tome.

Sociologists will pore over these pages, for every song is a little window into everyday citizens' views—whether it's war, gambling, poverty, divorce, work, or crime.

Newsrooms will never be the same. Now, every carnival story has a soundtrack. So do TV and radio broadcasts about doctors, basketball, cars, nuclear energy, presidents, snow, cigarettes, dogs, guns, airplanes, food, the environment, sex, and UFO's.

Movie makers will love it. Documentary producers will mine this volume for years to come. And can you imagine what marching-band directors are going to be doing with football halftime shows once they get a load of song topics like winning, gold, fighting, party, freedom, and magic?

But best of all will be the reactions from the record collectors, the trivia nuts, the music lovers, and the list makers. All of you are in for a treat.

This is Jeff's fourth edition of *The Green Book*, and his best effort yet to corral an enormous amount of information. Perusing these pages will set your mind dancing and your memory working overtime. At one turn, you'll recall a half-forgotten oldie. At another, you'll squeal, "Ooh, he forgot my favorite moon song!"

I cherished the third edition. I am awestruck by the scope of the fourth. And this work-in-progress will increase in importance, size, and usefulness as we move from edition to edition.

But in the meantime, celebrate with me. I don't know what makes people collectors and list makers. I only know that they're marvelous obsessives and devoted chroniclers. They compile without paychecks, royalties, or advances, for their work springs from love and passion and belief.

Along with television, popular music is the most powerful artform of the late 20th century. Yet its study has developed largely outside of universities. It is knit together by amateur archivists, media workers and a loose federation of record collectors. The list makers are the bricklayers of this whole field of scholarship. I think what they do is so significant. I think they're the salt of the earth.

And I surely delight in anyone who thinks lists of songs about fire, weddings, jukeboxes, women's names, schools, summertime and roads are as nutty, fascinating, and and delightful as I do.

For stunning research and plain old fun, here's a tip of the hat from one list maker to another: Congratulations, Jeff; you've done it again.

A whole list of people are going to reap the benefits of your unique vision and herculean work. But what's more important is that work, itself. You're making a contribution. You're making a difference.

I'm awfully proud to know you.

— Robert K. Oermann
Nashville, 1994

INTRODUCTION

What is The Green Book?

The Green Book Of Songs By Subject, 4th Edition represents 16 years of music research undertaken to identify and classify over 21,000 popular songs by over 800 subjects and subcategories. With the invaluable support of leading music industry authorities, these works were culled from the recordings themselves, sheet music, trade charts, individual collections, reference books and music specialists.

The Green Book covers all genres and generations of music over the entire 20th Century, including popular standards, contemporary hits, oldies, rock, country, R&B, jazz of all styles and eras, alternative music, Broadway, folk, blues, Cajun, reggae, television themes, marching compositions, instrumentals, children's songs, novelty records—you name it, it's in here!

How To Use The Green Book

Much time and effort has been put into making the 4th Edition of *The Green Book* easy to use. With over 73,000 total individual listings, the book is divided into three sections:

The main body of the book is organized alphabetically by subject category. At the top of each page you'll find guide words to make browsing easier. At the beginning of each subject grouping is a boldface listing of the main category in CAPITAL letters, followed by subcategories, if any, in upper/lower case. All songs relating to the subcategories are grouped together with the songs relating to the main category. Notice that sometimes the subcategory is the opposite to the main category listing. This is because songwriters commonly deal with both a theme and its opposite simultaneously.

Below the category/subcategory listing you may find a *See Also:* cross—reference to other related main categories; turn to those categories for additional related songs.

Each discography consists of a boldface **Song Title**, one or more artists, each accompanied by one or more album (or single, EP, etc.) listing and a record label code.

The second section is the record label codes listing, which can be easily located by the grey bar printed in the margin. It contains each record label code used in *The Green Book*, followed by the label name.

The third section is the Subject Index, a tool for browsing the subject categories and subcategories. It also can be located by a grey bar printed in the margin. Each main category is listed with the page where it appears. Each subcategory is listed with a cross-reference (*See*), followed by the name of the corresponding main category and page number. *See Also* cross—references are listed for convenience under any main category to which they are associated.

How The Categories Were Selected

The Green Book concentrates on popular subjects and includes over 200 new themes and subcategories compared to the previous edition. There are many new categories being researched for future editions. Categories have been chosen to provide a useful mixture of general and specific, abstract and concrete subjects. It should be noted, however, that there are a few categories which I've chosen not to include due to their overly general nature.

For example, the numerous romantic themes of falling in love, commitment and togetherness, breaking up and the ensuing states of sadness, loneliness and feeling "blue" are, of course, common in songwriting. To compile comprehensive lists of songs reflecting one or more of these conditions of love could fill several volumes alone.

Please bear in mind that alphabetical listings for songs about different countries may also include songs about particular territories, such as Puerto Rico or Hong Kong. While there are many songs about certain countries or states, songs about a city in a specific country or state can be found under the "Cities" categories.

How Songs And Recordings Were Selected

The Green Book listings emphasize singles and album tracks released and still available from American record companies, and seeks to encompass the entire spectrum of music from 1900 to the present, including over 5,000 artists. Selections are chosen on the basis of popularity, production value, artist recognition, unique character and balance within each category.

Since this book has been created especially for those who work with audio production and programming, the vast majority of songs included are vocal selections. Instrumental recordings appearing in this book have been selected based on their popularity, familiar association with a particular category or to add depth to a subject of limited coverage.

The Green Book documents as many original versions as possible, although some are no longer in print. I've also endeavored to recognize recordings performed by the songwriters, even if they are not the most widely known versions of the songs they've written.

Regarding popular standards and oldies which have been widely recorded by dozens of artists, I've tried to accommodate a cross-section of the many releases available.

How the Lyrics And Songs Have Been Interpreted

Because music is such a subjective experience, varying degrees of personal interpretation must be involved to classify songs. Songwriters frequently employ metaphorical references, and as author I cannot possibly claim to determine every song's actual lyric intent by its composer, especially with certain themes such as "Baby" and "Mama" songs, for example.

Since every lyric is a potential metaphor, with the true meanings often known only by the songwriters themselves, I've aimed to highlight each song's major themes as I believe the composers apparently intended them. It should be kept in mind, however, that the lyrics of some songs bear little, if any, actual relationship to the title. As a result, many songs can be found under classifications other than the key words in the titles. Therefore, determining the usefulness of some songs will require a certain amount of individual interpretation by the reader.

Considering that my lyrical interpretations of certain songs included in this book may be inaccurate, and that the status of labels and album releases is always changing, there are bound to be errors and omissions. I regret any such misinterpretations or mistakes and appreciate learning of any distortion or falseness which can be corrected in future *Green Book* materials.

Availability of Songs And Configurations

The availability of any given recording is constantly changing. As CDs and cassettes have rapidly replaced vinyl 33-1/3 and 45 RPM formats, many titles and entire catalogs of certain artists are being repackaged, renamed, discontinued and perhaps later reissued by the original record companies or different manufacturers. The goal of *The Green Book* is to include albums that are available in as many formats as possible, with cassettes being the most common configuration, followed by CD and vinyl.

Wherever possible, *The Green Book* attempts to include the original albums and labels unless the songs currently exist only within different albums and/or released by different companies. Titles thought to have gone out of print within recent years will carry their most recently known record company imprint.

Where it has been recognized that such songs and the albums on which they appeared have remained out of print for several years, they will be identified with the "OOP" label code.

A large number of out-of-print songs are featured in *The Green Book*, including many vintage standards that were popular before modern recording techniques were established. These also will be identified with the "OOP" code.

Although few 45s are still being issued, some are included with their original or last-known imprint when no album containing that title has been located by the author.

There are many record labels identified with songs in this book which are no longer in business, but they are included to help users track down the recordings through specialist dealers, collectors and music libraries.

AUTHOR'S NOTES

Although a very serious amount of work and time was involved in the preparation of *The Green Book*, it is meant to be enjoyable as well as useful to the reader. While this book contains many landmark recordings about political strife, peace, war and other aspects of humanity, there are also categories such as insults and nonsense words (with thanks to radio and records veteran Bonnie Simmons for that idea).

What's particularly interesting is to see the sociological shifts in songwriting over the decades—specifically, the blunt frankness of lyrics in modern compositions. We've come a long way from popular standards such as "Let Me Call You Sweetheart" to George Michael's "I Want Your Sex." The focus of straightforward lyric-writing seems to be drawing to an increasingly sharper point, as the primal angst and rage commonly heard during the late '70s punk era has been more than matched by the political and emotional sensitivities brought forth in some of today's rap and alternative music.

The same attitudinal and imaging changes can be seen in names of groups. Innocent monikers such as the Mom & Dads, the Coasters and Gerry & The Pacemakers have evolved to the Trash Can Sinatras, Icepick Trotsky and Dead Youth.

These colorful transitions in the music and artists being recorded today are what make *The Green Book* a musical panorama, encompassing every possible artistic expression.

Of great significance is that there is an increasing amount of provocative material being written and recorded about contemporary issues—everything from racial prejudice, feminist issues, and homelessness to family problems such as child custody, domestic violence and alcoholism.

This new edition and forthcoming *Green Books* will continue to establish new categories along these lines whenever enough songs can be traced to create a meaningful list. Users of *The Green Book* are welcome and encouraged to submit songs, categories, interpretations and suggestions for future *Green Book* research.

LEGEND

/ =	"and the" or "and his/her"
# =	number, edition or volume in a set or series
S =	single on cassette, 12" vinyl or CD
same =	the album is the same name as the artist (used in some cases)
ST =	soundtrack recording to a motion picture
TT =	title track: the album and song have the same name (used in some cases)

Note: Where artist performances as duets are listed, unless the entire album is a collaboration between two or more artists, the first name given is the one associated with the particular album discography listed.

AFRICA, Apartheid

See Also: FREEDOM, PREJUDICE, PROTEST

2nd Movement: African Lady
Randy Weston; *Uhuru Africa/Highlife* .... (RLL)
Africa
Aldo Nova; *Subject...Aldo Nova* .... (POR)
Daryl Hall & John Oates; *Voices* ....(RCA)
Doug E. Fresh/Get Fresh Crew; *World's Greatest Entertainer* .... (REA)
John Coltrane; *Best Of-His Greatest Years* .... (MCA)
Meters; *Rejuvenation* ....(RPR)
Tony Wilson; *Catch One* .... (BRS)
Toto; *IV* ....(COL)
  Past To Present 1977-1990 ....(COL)
Africa Is For Me
Pablo Moses; *Pave The Way* .... (MGO)
Africa Talks To You-"The Asphalt Jungle"
Sly/Family Stone; *There's A Riot Goin' On* .... (EPI)
Africa Unite
Bob Marley/Wailers; *Survival* .... (ISL)
African
Peter Tosh; *Captured Live* ....(EIA)
  Equal Rights ....(COL)
African Dance
Soul II Soul; *Keep On Movin'* .... (VIA)
African Dream
Stewart Copeland; *Rhythmatist* .... (A&M)
African Flame
Herb Alpert; *Wild Romance* .... (A&M)
African Friend
Jimmy Buffett; *Son Of A Son Of A Sailor* .... (MCA)
African Night Flight
David Bowie; *Lodger* ....(RYK)
African Queen
Ali Thompson; *Take A Little Rhythm* .... (A&M)
African Ripples
Fats Waller; *Joint Is Jumpin'* ....(BLU)
  Piano Solos ....(RCA)
  Turn On The Heat: Solos ....(BLU)
African Shadow Man
Johnny Clegg & Savuka; *Shadow Man* ....(CAP)
African Summer
Herb Alpert & Hugh Masekela; *Herb Alpert & Hugh Masekela* ....(A&M)
African Sunrise
John Denver; *Dreamland Express* ....(RCA)
African Sunset
Tommy Page; *Tommy Page* .... (SIR)
African Trilogy
Neil Diamond; *Tap Root Manuscript* .... (MCA)
African Waltz
Cannonball Adderley; *African Waltz* ....(RVR)
  Original Jazz Classics-#1 ....(RVR)
African Woman
Third World; *Journey to Addis* .... (ISL)
Africano
Earth, Wind & Fire; *Gratitude* ....(COL)
  That's The Way Of The World ....(COL)
Afrika
Jonathan Butler; *Introducing* .... (JVA)
Afro Blue
Cal Tjader; *Concert By The Sea* .... (FAN)
  Greatest Hits-#1 ....(FAN)
  Monterey Concerts .... (PRS)
John Coltrane; *Afro Blue Impressions* ....(PAB)
  Best Of ....(PAB)
  Best Of-His Greatest Years ....(MCA)
Mongo Santamaria; *Afro-Roots* .... (PRS)
  Greatest Hits ....(FAN)
Apartheid
C. Chris & Rich E. Rich/Rudy Pardee; *12"* ..... (MCA)
K-9 Posse; *On A Different Tip* .... (ARI)
Peter Tosh; *Equal Rights* ....(COL)
A.F.R.I.C.A.
Stetsasonic/Rev. Jesse Jackson/Olatunji; *12"* ... (TMB)
Black Africa
Devonsquare; *Walking On Ice* .... (ATL)
Brass Band In African Chimes
Simple Minds; *45* .... (A&M)
Cowboys In Africa
Bush Tetras; *Better Late Than Never* .... (ROI)

December African Rain
Juluka; *Best Of* ....(RHY)
Dial Africa
John Coltrane & Wilbur Harden; *Africa-Savoy Sessions* .... (SAV)
  Dial Africa .... (SAV)
Echoes Of The African Forest
Saka Acquaye Ensemble; *Voices Of Africa* ..... (NON)
Exodus
Bob Marley/Wailers; *Babylon By Bus* .... (TUF)
  Exodus .... (TUF)
  Legend .... (TUF)
Free Nelson Mandela
Special AKA; *In The Studio* .... (CHR)
Gold In Africa
Tiger; *Where Was Butler?-Calypso Documentary* . (FLK)
Gone A South Africa
Yellowman & Charlie Chaplin; *Negril Chill-Live In Concert* .... (ROI)
Heart Is In Africa
Rozalla; *Everybody's Free* ....(EPI)
I Never Was To Africa
Ferron; *Shadows On A Dime* ....(LCY)
Madda Africa
Sister Breeze; *Riddym Ravings* .... (ROI)
Man From South Africa
Max Roach; *Percussion Bitter Sweet* ....(GRP)
Mbali Africa
Sadao Watanabe; *Orange Express* ....(COL)
Meeting In Afrika
Jimmy Cliff; *Give Thanx* .... (WB)
Moter-bike In Afrika
Peter Hammill; *Future Now* ....(BP)
Mother Africa
Judy Mowatt; *Welcome* ....(SHA)
Santana; *Welcome* ....(COL)
New Africa
Youssou N'Dour; *Eyes Open* .... (40)
New African Blues
Cassandra Wilson; *She Who Weeps* ....(JMT)
New African Whistler
Roger Whittaker; *Live In Concert* ....(RCA)
Out Of Africa
Deborah Franciose; *Almost Home* ....(NS)
Out Of Africa Medley
Danny Wright; *Black & White II* ....(MD)
Peace For South Africa
Oscar Peterson Trio; *Live At The Blue Note* ...... (TLR)
Peace In Liberia
Alpha Blondy; *Masada* ....(WP)
Pieces Of Africa
Boom Shaka; *Creation* .... (MOV)
Ponta De Lanca Africano (Umbabarauma)
Jorge Ben; *To Scratch That Itch-Roots Rock & Rhythm* ....(LB)
Rhymin' Wit The African Symphony
Legit Zimbabwe; *Basic Beats Sampler* ....(HOL)
Ritmo Africano
Cal Tjader; *Greatest Hits-#2* ....(FAN)
  Ritmos Calientes ....(FAN)
Sail Away
Linda Ronstadt; *Don't Cry Now* .... (ASY)
Randy Newman; *Sail Away* ....(RPR)
Scatterlings Of Africa
Johnny Clegg & Savuka; *ST/Rain Man* ....(CAP)
  Third World Child ....(CAP)
Serengeti
Cal Tjader; *Onda Va Bien* .... (CP)
Chi; *Sun Lake* ....(SA)
Cusco; *Cusco 2000* ....(HO)
Eric Marienthal; *Round Trip* ....(GRP)
Peter Seiler; *Dream Code* ....(INN)
  Flying Frames ....(INN)
  Sensitive Touch ....(INN)
Serengeti Long Walk
Stewart Copeland; *Rhythmatist* .... (A&M)
Serengeti Trail
Starr Parodi; *Change* ....(GFT)
Serengeti Walk
Dave Grusin; *Collection* ....(GRP)
  Out Of The Shadows ....(GRP)
Dave Grusin & NY/LA Dream Band; *Dave Grusin & NY/LA Dream Band* ....(GRP)

Serengeti (The Adventure)
H.M.A. Salsa/Jazz Orchestra; *California Salsa* ... (SEA)
Serengetti
Grateful Dead; *Shakedown Street* .... (ARI)
Serenghetti
Barefoot; *Barefoot* .... (GLO)
Shaka Zulu LP
Ladysmith Black Mambazo; *Various Tracks* ...... (WB)
Sorry Africa
Tony Bird; *Sorry Africa* .... (PHO)
South Africa
Cadillac Tramps; *Cadillac Tramps* .... (DD)
Gillan; *Magic* .... (MET)
Sons Of Selassie; *Changes* .... (RHY)
Zawinul Syndicate; *Lost Tribes* .... (COL)
South African Blues
Windy Rhythm Kings; *Chicago
Jazz-#2-1925-1929* .... (BIO)
South African Enlistment
Abyssinians; *Arise* .... (FL)
Star Of Africa
Gerry Mulligan & Chet Baker; *Gerry Mulligan & Chet
Baker* .... (CRS)
Stole & Sold From Africa
John McCutcheon; *Live At Wolf Trap* .... (ROU)
Storms In Africa
Enya; *Watermark* .... (RPR)
Struggle (Free South Africa)
Rochester/Easley Band; *One Minute Of Love* .... (GRM)
Sun City
Artists United Against Apartheid; *Sun City* ..... (MAN)
Taking Islands In Africa
Japan; *Gentlemen Take Polaroids* .... (BP)
Teacher (African Teacher)
Burning Spear; *Living Dub-#2* .... (HRT)
"Techno Bush" Album
Hugh Masekela; *Various Tracks* .... (ARI)
Thank You For Talking To Me, Africa
Miki Howard; *Femme Fatale* .... (GIA)
Sly/Family Stone; *Anthology* .... (EPI)
There's A Riot Goin' On .... (EPI)
Theme From "Out Of Africa"
John Barry; *ST/Out Of Africa* .... (MCA)
Thoroughly African Man
Red Clay Ramblers; *Chuckin' The Frizz* .... (FF)
Uncle Isak Goes To Africa
Tom Wasinger; *Rock Music* .... (INV)
Under African Skies
Paul Simon; *Graceland* .... (WB)
War A Africa
Jimmy Cliff; *Breakout* .... (JRS)
We Are The World
USA For Africa; *We Are The World* .... (COL)
West Africa
Willie Jackson; *West Africa* .... (MUS)
Whole World African
Ska Danks; *H.E.A.L. Civilization Vs. Technology* . (ELE)
World Is Africa
Black Uhuru; *Sinsemilla* .... (MGO)

AFTERNOON

Afternoon
Jonathan Richman/Modern Lovers; *Beserkley Years: Best
Of* .... (RHI)
Rock 'N' Roll With .... (RHI)
Afternoon Delight
Starland Vocal Band; *Starland Vocal Band* .... (WS)
Afternoon In Paris
Anita O'Day; *Night Has A Thousand Eyes* ..... (EML)
Sonny Stitt; *Genesis* .... (PRS)
Stitt/Bud Powell/J.J. Johnson .... (PRS)
Afternoon Of A Faun
Vikki Carr; *Live At The Greek Theatre* .... (COL)
Afternoon Sunshine
Edwin Starr; *Edwin Starr* .... (20)
Afternoon Tea
Kinks; *Something Else* .... (RPR)
Afternoons In Utopia
Alphaville; *Afternoons In Utopia* .... (ATL)
April Afternoon
Joan Amalbert Latin Jazz Quintet; *Hot Sauce* .... (PRS)

Arthur In The Afternoon
Liza Minnelli/Original Cast; *The Act* .... (DRG)
August Afternoon
Mulgrew Miller; *The Countdown* .... (LAN)
Every Sunday Afternoon
Bobby Short; *Celebrates Rodgers & Hart* .... (ATL)
Groovin'
Aretha Franklin; *Lady Soul* .... (ATL)
Booker T./M.G.s; *Best Of* .... (ATL)
Soul Shots-#3 Soul Twist .... (RHI)
Rascals; *Greatest Hits* .... (ATL)
Groovin' .... (RHI)
Hit Singles-1958-1977 .... (ATL)
ST/Platoon .... (ATL)
It's Been A Great Afternoon
Merle Haggard; *Greatest Hits* .... (MCA)
I'm Always On A Mountain When I Fall .... (MCA)
More Of The Best .... (RHI)
Lazy Afternoon
Barbra Streisand; *Lazy Afternoon* .... (COL)
Marlene Dietrich; *At The Cafe De Paris* .... (COL)
Patti Austin; *Real Me* .... (QUE)
Tony Bennett; *At Carnegie Hall* .... (SSP)
Forty Years-Artistry Of .... (COL)
Lazy Day
Moody Blues; *On The Threshold Of A Dream* .... (POL)
Long Afternoons
Jerry Jeff Walker; *Gypsy Songman* .... (RYK)
Man Must Carry On .... (MCA)
Louisiana Sunday Afternoon
Diane Schuur; *Collection* .... (GRP)
Talkin' 'Bout You .... (GRP)
Love In The Hot Afternoon
Gene Watson; *Best Of* .... (CAP)
Great Records Of The Decade-'70s-Country .... (CCB)
Greatest Hits .... (CCB)
November Afternoon
Dizzy Gillespie; *Composer's Concepts* .... (EMA)
James Moody; *Moving Forward* .... (NOV)
Paul Christopher; *Lavender* .... (ARY)
Ohio Afternoon
Original New York Cast; *Oil City Symphony* ... (DRG)
On A Sunday Afternoon
Lighter Shade Of Brown & Huggy Boy; *Brown &
Proud* .... (PMP)
On Rainy Afternoons
Barbra Streisand; *Wet* .... (COL)
On Saturday Afternoons In 1963
Rickie Lee Jones; *Rickie Lee Jones* .... (WB)
On Sunday Afternoon
Harptones; *Echoes Of A Rock Era* .... (RLL)
Quiet Afternoon
Paul Rebhan; *Colors* .... (CRM)
Stanley Clarke; *Live 1976-1977* .... (EPI)
School Days .... (EPI)
Rainy Afternoon
Lee Konitz; *In Rio* .... (MA)
Saturday Afternoon
Cassell Webb; *Thief Of Sadness* .... (VEN)
Jefferson Airplane; *After Bathing At Baxters* ...... (RCA)
Flight Log 1966-1976 .... (GRU)
ST/Woodstock Two .... (ATL)
Thelonius Monsters; *Next Saturday Afternoon* ... (REL)
Seattle Afternoon
Reilly & Maloney; *At Last* .... (FRK)
Summer Afternoon
Vogues; *Greatest Hits* .... (RHI)
Sunday Afternoon
Candy Dulfer; *Sax-A-Go-Go* .... (RCA)
Sunday Afternoon In The Park
Van Halen; *Fair Warning* .... (WB)
Sunny Afternoon
Kinks; *Compleat Collection-20th Anniversary* ... (CMP)
Greatest Hits-#1 .... (RHI)
Kink Kronikles .... (RPR)
Live .... (RPR)
Thursday Afternoon
Brian Eno; *Thursday Afternoon* .... (EDI)
Tuesday Afternoon
Moody Blues; *Caught Live Plus Five* .... (POL)
Days Of Future Passed .... (POL)
ST/1969 .... (POL)
This Is The .... (POL)

AIR, Breathe

See Also: ECOLOGY, WIND

Air
Incredible String Band; *Relics Of* .... (ELE)
   Weetam .... (ELE)
Original Broadway Cast; *Hair* .... (RCA)
Talking Heads; *Fear Of Music* .... (SIR)
   Name Of This Band Is Talking Heads .... (SIR)
Air Dance
Black Sabbath; *Never Say Die* .... (WB)
Air That I Breathe
Hollies; *Anthology From Original Master Tapes* ... (EPI)
   Best Of-#2 .... (EMI)
   Hollies .... (EPI)
Breath Away From Heaven
George Harrison; *Cloud Nine* .... (DKH)
Breath Of Life
Brian Setzer; *Knife Feels Like Justice* .... (AMR)
Erasure; *Chorus* .... (SIR)
Breathe
Collective Soul; *Hints Allegations And Things Left
Unsaid* .... (ATL)
Ministry; *Just Say Da-Vol. IV Of Just Say Yes* ... (SIR)
   Mind Is A Terrible Thing To Taste .... (SIR)
Pink Floyd; *Dark Side Of The Moon* .... (CAP)
   Gift Set .... (CAP)
Breathe Again
Toni Braxton; *Toni Braxton* .... (LAF)
Breathing
Fat; *Automat Hi-Life* .... (CUN)
Kate Bush; *Never For Ever* .... (EMI)
   Whole Story .... (EMI)
Sextants; *Lucky You* .... (IMG)
Breathless
Jerry Lee Lewis; *18 Original Sun Greatest Hits* ... (RHI)
   Golden Rock Hits .... (SMA)
   Oldies/Goodies-#6 .... (OSR)
   Original .... (SUN)
   Original Golden Hits #1 .... (SUN)
Mtume; *Theater Of The Mind* .... (EPI)
Quiet Riot; *Metal Health* .... (PSH)
Todd Rundgren; *Something/Anything?* .... (RHI)
Breathtaking Guy
Diana Ross/Supremes; *Anthology* .... (MOT)
   Where Did Our Love Go .... (MOT)
Marvelettes; *Anthology* .... (MOT)
Castles In The Air
Don McLean; *Best Of* .... (EMI)
   Greatest Hits-Then & Now .... (EMI)
   Tapestry .... (LIB)
Country Air
Beach Boys; *Smiley Smile/Wild Honey* .... (CAP)
Death In The Autumn Air
Michael McDermott; *620 W. Surf* .... (GIA)
Dizzy Atmosphere
Dizzy Gillespie; *Dizzy's Diamonds-Best Of Verve
Years* .... (VRV)
Oscar Peterson & Dizzy Gillespie; *Oscar Peterson &
Dizzy Gillespie* .... (PAB)
Dog Breath
Frank Zappa; *Uncle Meat* .... (BAR)
Mothers Of Invention; *Just Another Band From
L.A.* .... (BIZ)
Every Breath I Take
Gene Pitney; *Anthology* .... (RHI)
   Greatest Hits .... (EVR)
Phil Spector-1958-1961-Early Productions ..... (RHI)
   Remember When .... (GRL)
   Super Oldies Of The '60s-#5 .... (AUF)
Every Breath You Take
Police; *Singles* .... (A&M)
   Synchronicity .... (A&M)
Tammy Wynette & Sting; *Without Walls* .... (EPI)
Fresh Air
Quicksilver Messenger Service; *Anthology* .... (CAP)
Sons Of Mercury .... (RHI)
I Can't Breathe Anymore
David Gilmour; *David Gilmour* .... (COL)
I Get Out Of Breath
Turtles; *Turtle Wax-Best Of-#2* .... (RHI)

In The Air Tonight
Phil Collins; *Classic Rock 1966-1988* .... (ATL)
   Face Value .... (ATL)
   Miami Vice .... (MCA)
   Prince's Trust 10th Anniversary Party .... (A&M)
   Secret Policeman's Other Ball .... (ISL)
   Serious Hits...Live! .... (ATL)
Life In The Air Age
Be Bop Deluxe; *Live In The Air Age* .... (HAR)
   Sunburst Finish .... (HAR)
Londonderry Air
Mormon Tabernacle Choir; *Album* .... (COL)
   Greatest Hits-#2 .... (COL)
   Lord's Prayer .... (COL)
Norwegian Aire
Magical Strings; *Crossing To Skellig* .... (FF)
On The Air
Peter Gabriel; *Peter Gabriel* .... (ATL)
   Plays Live .... (GEF)
   Revisited .... (ATL)
Out Of Thin Air
Howard Jones; *Cross That Line* .... (ELE)
Room To Breathe
Daryl Hall & John Oates; *Bigger Than Both Of
Us* .... (RCA)
Downtown Science; *Downtown Science* .... (DFJ)
Scottish Air
Carl MacKenzie; *Welcome To Your Feet Again* . (ROU)
She Takes My Breath Away
Eddie Money; *Right Here* .... (COL)
Smog
Miracles; *City Of Angels* .... (TAM)
Something In The Air
Thunderclap Newman; *History Of British
Rock-#9* .... (MCA)
   Hollywood Dream .... (MCA)
   ST/Strawberry Statement .... (MCA)
Take My Breath Away
Berlin; *Best Of-1979-1988* .... (GEF)
   Count Three & Pray .... (GEF)
   ST/Top Gun .... (COL)

AIRPLANES, Airports, Flying In Planes, Pilots

See Also: BIRDS, FLYING

Air Algiers
Country Joe McDonald; *Hold On It's Coming* ... (VAN)
Air Crash Museum
Dead Milkmen; *Eat Your Paisley* .... (RES)
Airplane
Beach Boys; *Love You* .... (RPR)
Ian Gomm; *Gomm With The Wind* .... (STF)
Airport
Motors; *Approved By* .... (BP)
Smith Sisters; *Bluebird* .... (FF)
Wet Willie; *Drippin' Wet Alive* .... (CPC)
   Greatest Hits .... (CPC)
Airport Giveth
Rick Derringer; *All American Boy* .... (BS)
Amelia Earhart
Bachman-Turner Overdrive; *Rock 'n' Roll Nights* (MER)
Another Runway
Little River Band; *Diamantina Cocktail* .... (CAP)
Bennie & The Jets
Elton John; *Billboard Top Rock 'N' Roll Hits-1974* (RHI)
   Classic Rock-#1 .... (MCA)
   Goodbye Yellow Brick Road .... (POL)
   Greatest Hits .... (POL)
   Here & There .... (POL)
Bermuda Triangle
Fleetwood Mac; *Heroes Are Hard To Find* .... (RPR)
Bermuda Triangle Blues (Flight 45)
Blondie; *Plastic Letters* .... (CHR)
Biggest Airport In The World
Moe Bandy; *Best Of-#1* .... (COL)
Blues From An Airplane
Jefferson Airplane; *2400 Fulton Street-An
Anthology* .... (RCA)
   Worst Of .... (RCA)
Bomber
James Gang; *Best Of* .... (MCA)
   Rides Again .... (MCA)

Budapest By Blimp
Thomas Dolby; *Aliens Ate My Buick* .... (EMI)
Coming Into Los Angeles
Arlo Guthrie; *Best Of* .... (WB)
   Running Down The Road .... (RPR)
   ST/Woodstock .... (ATL)
Danger Zone
Crystal Gayle; *Miss The Mississippi* .... (LIB)
Kenny Loggins; *ST/Top Gun* ....(COL)
Klymaxx; *Klymaxx* .... (CON)
L.A. Posse; *They Come In All Colors* .... (ATL)
Planet Patrol; *Planet Patrol* .... (TMB)
   Tommy Boy Greatest Beats .... (TMB)
Ramones; *Too Tough To Die* .... (SIR)
Shirley Murdock; *Shirley Murdock* .... (ELE)
Deportee (Plane Wreck At Los Gatos)
Arlo Guthrie & Pete Seeger; *Together In Concert* (RPR)
Byrds; *Byrds (collection)* ....(COL)
Cisco Houston; *Greatest Songs Of Woody Guthrie* (VAN)
Gene Clark & Carla Olson; *So Rebellious A Lover* (RHI)
W. Jennings/W. Nelson/J. Cash/K. Krist.;
   Highwayman ....(COL)
Flight 309 To Tennessee
Shelly West; *West By West* .... (VVA)
Flight 602
Chicago; *3* .... (COL)
   At Carnegie Hall ....(COL)
   Group Portrait ....(COL)
Flight (505)
Rolling Stones; *Aftermath* .... (AKO)
Flyer
Saga; *Heads Or Tales* .... (POR)
Flying Down To Rio
Bobby Short; *Ertegun's N.Y. N.Y. Cabaret
Music-#5* .... (ATL)
Ghost Of Flight 401
Bob Welch; *Three Hearts* .... (OOP)
I'm Mandy Fly Me
10 CC; *Greatest Hits 1972-1978* .... (POL)
   How Dare You .... (OOP)
   Live & Let Live .... (OOP)
Jet
Paul McCartney; *Tripping The Live Fantastic* .... (CAP)
Paul McCartney/Wings; *All The Best* .... (CAP)
   Band On The Run .... (CAP)
   Wings Greatest .... (CAP)
   Wings Over America .... (COL)
Jet Airliner
Steve Miller Band; *Book Of Dreams* .... (CAP)
   Gift Set .... (CAP)
   Greatest Hits-1974-1978 .... (CAP)
   Live .... (CAP)
Jet City Woman
Queensryche; *Empire* .... (EMI)
Jet Fighter
Three O'Clock; *Sixteen Tambourines* .... (FRN)
Jet Lag
Nazareth; *Rampant* .... (A&M)
Jet Pilot
Bob Dylan; *Biograph* ....(COL)
Jet Silver & The Dolls Of Venus
Be Bop Deluxe; *Ax Victim* .... (OOP)
   Best Of-Raiding The Divine Archive .... (CAP)
Jet Song
Original Cast; *West Side Story* ....(COL)
Jets At Dawn
Be Bop Deluxe; *Axe Victim* .... (OOP)
Leaving On A Jet Plane
John Denver; *Greatest Hits-#1* .... (RCA)
   Rhymes & Reasons .... (RCA)
Kendalls; *Super Hits Country-1970s* .... (GUS)
Peter, Paul & Mary; *1700* .... (WB)
   Ten Years Together .... (WB)
Letter, The
Box Tops; *Billboard Top Rock 'N' Roll Hits-1967* (RHI)
   Cruisin'-1967 .... (INC)
   Greatest Hits .... (RHI)
   Oldies But Goodies-#12 .... (OSR)
   Rockin' '60s .... (PRY)
Joe Cocker; *Classics-#4* .... (A&M)
   Greatest Hits .... (A&M)
   Live .... (CAP)
   Mad Dogs & Englishmen .... (A&M)

Medallions; *Golden Classics* .... (CLT)
   Oldies But Goodies-#1 .... (OSR)
L.A. International Airport
Susan Raye; *Best Of* .... (CAP)
Motels & Planes
Bill Morrissey; *Standing Eight* .... (PHO)
Next Plane To London
Rose Garden; *45* .... (ATL)
Night Flight
Buddy Guy; *Complete Chess Studio Recordings* ... (CSS)
Led Zeppelin; *Physical Graffiti* .... (SS)
No Plane On Sunday
Jimmy Buffett; *Floridays* .... (MCA)
Northwest 222
Harry Chapin; *Remember When The Music* ......(DHL)
Out On The Airstrip
Urge Overkill; *Americruiser/Jesus Urge Superstar* (T&G)
Outbound Plane
Nanci Griffith; *Little Love Affairs* .... (MCA)
Suzy Bogguss; *Aces* .... (LIB)
Paper Airplanes
Seals & Crofts; *Year Of Sunday* .... (WB)
Pilot
Heart; *Bebe Le Strange* .... (EPI)
Private Plane
Husker Du; *Flip Your Wig* .... (SST)
Silver Wings
Merle Haggard; *More Of The Best* .... (RHI)
   w/Willie Nelson: Seashores Of Old Mexico ...... (EPI)
Merle Haggard/Strangers; *Okie From Muskogee* ..(CAP)
   Songs I'll Always Sing ....(CAP)
Pam Tillis; *Mama's Hungry Eyes-Merle Haggard
Tribute* .... (ARI)
Sky Pilot
Eric Burdon/Animals; *Greatest Hits* ....(MGM)
   History Of British Rock-#9 .... (RHI)
Skywriter
Jackson 5; *Anthology* .... (MOT)
Snoopy Vs. The Red Baron
Royal Guardsmen; *Best Of-#1* .... (RHI)
   Collectables Presents History Of Rock-#9 .... (CLT)
   Cruisin'-1967 .... (INC)
   Million-Dollar Memories #1 ....(RCA)
   Super Oldies/'60s-#6 ....(AUF)
Sydney From A 727
Paul Kelly/Messengers; *Comedy* .... (DD)
Take Me To The Pilot
Elton John; *11-17-70* .... (POL)
   Elton John .... (POL)
   Here & There .... (POL)
   Live In Australia w/Melbourne Symphony ...... (MCA)
Talking Airplane Disaster
Phil Ochs; *Original New Folks* .... (VAN)
Thank You, Republic Airlines
Tom Paxton; *One Million Lawyers & Other
Disasters* .... (FF)
This Flight Tonight
Joni Mitchell; *Blue* .... (RPR)
Nazareth; *Classics-#16* .... (A&M)
   Hot Tracks .... (A&M)
Trains & Boats & Planes
Billy J. Kramer/Dakotas; *Definitive Collection* .... (EMI)
   History Of British Rock-#4 .... (RHI)
Dionne Warwick; *Anthology-1962-1971* .... (RHI)
   Dionne Warwick ....(EVR)
   Greatest Hits ....(EVR)
   Hot! Live & Otherwise .... (ARI)
Trans-Atlantic Westbound Jet
Hollies; *Hollies* .... (EPI)
"Twelve O'Clock High" Theme
Original Music; *Television's Greatest Hits-#2* .....(TVT)
Twenty Flight Rock
Commander Cody/Lost Planet Airmen; *Lost In The
Ozone* .... (MCA)
   Too Much Fun-Best Of .... (MCA)
Eddie Cochran; *Greatest Hits* .... (CCB)
   Legendary Masters .... (EMI)
   On The Air .... (EMI)
Montrose; *Montrose* .... (WB)
Paul McCartney; *CHOBA B CCCP-Russian
Album* .... (CAP)
   Tripping The Live Fantastic .... (CAP)
Rolling Stones; *Still Life-American Concert 1981* ...(RS)

U.S. Air Force
Mormon Tabernacle Choir; *Stars & Stripes*
Together ....(COL)
Who's Driving Your Plane?
Rolling Stones; *Singles Collection-London Years* . (AKO)

ALCOHOL, Beer, Booze, Drinking, Getting Drunk, Wine

See Also: BARS, CRAZY, PARTY

3 Martini Lunch
Graham Parker; *Best Of-1988-1991* ....(RCA)
51 Beers
Claude King; *Hi-Tone Poppa* ....(CLT)
Alcohol
Kinks; *Everybody's In Show Biz* ....(RHI)
Greatest ....(RCA)
Muswell Hillbillies ....(RHI)
American Pie
Don McLean; *American Pie* ....(UA)
Best Of ....(EMI)
Greatest Hits Then & Now ....(EMI)
ST/Born On The Fourth Of July ....(MCA)
And Her Tears Flowed Like Wine
Stan Kenton; *Greatest Hits* ....(CAP)
Lighter Side ....(CW)
Stan Kenton & Anita O'Day; *Comprehensive
Kenton* ....(CAP)
Another Pack Of Cigarettes...
Marty Robbins; *The Performer* ....(COL)
Applejack
Dolly Parton; *Collector's* ....(RCA)
Greatest Hits ....(RCA)
Joe Morris; *Atlantic R&B 1947-1974-#1
(1947-1952)* ....(ATL)
Attack Of The Killer Beers
Murphy's Law; *Back With A Bong!* ....(PRO)
Bad Whiskey
Lightnin' Hopkins; *Low Down Dirty Blues* ....(MST)
Beer And Bones
John Michael Montgomery; *Life's A Dance* .....(ATL)
Beer Barrel Polka
Andrews Sisters; *16 Great Performances* ....(MCA)
Best Of ....(MCA)
Frankie Yankovic/Yanks; *Greatest Hits* ....(COL)
Will Glahe; *This Is-Decade Of The '30s* ....(RCA)
Beer Drinkers & Hell Raisers
ZZ Top; *Best Of* ....(WB)
Six Pack ....(WB)
Tres Hombres ....(WB)
Beer Drinkin' Song
Lacy J. Dalton; *Hot Country Rock-#2* ....(EPI)
Lacy J. Dalton ....(COL)
Beer Drinkin' Woman
Memphis Slim; *At The Gate Of Horn* ....(VJ)
Raining The Blues ....(FAN)
Big Ole Brew
Mel McDaniel; *Greatest Hits* ....(CAP)
Take Me To The Country ....(CAP)
Blame The Whiskey
Paul David Wells; *Sounds Good To Me* ....(CAP)
Blind Love & Whiskey
Little Mike/Tornadoes; *Heart Attack* ....(BLI)
Bloody Mary
Original Cast; *South Pacific* ....(COL)
Soundtrack; *South Pacific* ....(RCA)
Whitesnake; *Snakebite* ....(GEF)
Bloody Mary Morning
Willie Nelson; *Best Of Willie* ....(RCA)
Phases & Stages ....(ATL)
ST/Honeysuckle Rose ....(COL)
& Family Live ....(COL)
Blue Champagne
Manhattan Transfer; *Manhattan Transfer* ....(ATL)
Bottle Of Red Wine
Eric Clapton; *Eric Clapton* ....(RSO)
Bottle Of Wine
Jimmy Gilmer/Fireballs; *Frat Rock-#4* ....(RHI)
Son Of Frat Rock ....(RHI)
Super Hits-#1 ....(GUS)

Brand New Whiskey
Gary Stewart; *Brand New* ....(HT)
Gary's Greatest ....(HT)
Bubbles In My Beer
Bob Wills; *Sounds Of Texas* ....(CAP)
Bob Wills/Texas Playboys; *24 Great Hits* ....(POL)
Anthology-1935-1973 ....(RHI)
Willie Nelson; *Shotgun Willie* ....(ATL)
Bubbles In The Wine
Lawrence Welk; *16 Most Requested Songs* ....(COL)
Best Of ....(RAN)
California Wine
Bobby Goldsboro; *10th Anniversary Album-#2* .... (UA)
Carolina Moonshiner
Porter Wagoner; *20 Great Country Hits* ....(RCA)
Collector's ....(RCA)
Case Of You
Joni Mitchell; *Blue* ....(RPR)
Miles Of Aisles ....(RPR)
Champagne And Wine
Otis Redding; *Story* ....(ATL)
Champagne Jam
Atlanta Rhythm Section; *Are You Ready* ....(POL)
Champagne Jam ....(POL)
Champagne & Rock & Roll
Climax Blues Band; *Shine On* ....(SIR)
Cheap Seats, The
Alabama; *Cheap Seats* ....(RCA)
Cheap Tequila
Johnny Winter; *Still Alive & Well* ....(COL)
Rick Derringer; *All American Boy* ....(BS)
Cocktails For Two
Spike Jones; *Best Of* ....(RCA)
Dinner Music...For People Who Aren't... ....(RHI)
Dr. Demento Presents Greatest Novelty CD ..... (RHI)
Dr. Demento's Greatest-#1 ....(RHI)
Nipper's Greatest Hits-'40s-#1 ....(RCA)
Coors In Colorado
Ray Price; *Master Of The Art* ....(WB)
Daddy's Drinking Up Our Christmas
Commander Cody; *Hillbilly Holiday* .... (RHI)
Days Of Wine And Roses
Andy Williams; *16 Most Requested Songs* ....(COL)
Close Enough For Love ....(ATC)
Greatest Hits ....(COL)
TT/Moon River & Other Great Movie Themes ...(COL)
Dream Syndicate; *Days Of Wine & Roses* ....(SLS)
Live At Raji's ....(RES)
Frank Sinatra; *Days Of Wine & Roses/Acad. Award
Winners* ....(RPR)
Henry Mancini; *All-Time Greatest Hits-#1* ......(RCA)
Best Of ....(RCA)
Pure Gold ....(RCA)
Don't Come Home A Drinkin' (With...
Loretta Lynn; *Greatest Hits* ....(MCA)
Greatest Hits Live ....(KT)
MCA Records 30 Years Of Hits-1958-1988 ...(MCA)
Don't Drink That Wine
N.W.A.; *Efil4zaggin* ....(RUT)
Don't Drink Whiskey
Johnny Winter; *Birds Can't Row Boats* ....(RLX)
Don't Drink & Drive
James Cannings; *Music For All Seasons* ....(JC)
Don't Drive Drunk
Stevie Wonder; *ST/Woman In Red* .... (MOT)
Don't Sell Daddy Any More Whiskey
Joe Val/New England Bluegrass Boys; *Not A Word
From Home* ....(ROU)
Drink A Round To Ireland
Judy Collins; *Times Of Our Lives* ....(ELE)
Drink To Me Only With Thine Eyes
Paul Robeson; *Essential* ....(VAN)
Roger Whittaker; *Folk Songs Of Our Time* ....(RCA)
Drinking Again
Aretha Franklin; *Sings The Blues* ....(COL)
Bette Midler; *Bette Midler* ....(ATL)
Live At Last ....(ATL)
Drinking And Driving
Black Flag; *In My Head* ....(SST)
Drinking Champagne
George Strait; *Livin' It Up* ....(MCA)
Ten Strait Hits ....(MCA)
Drinking On The Job
Rainmakers; *Rainmakers* ....(MER)

Drinking Straight Whiskey
Johnny Young; *Chicago Blues* .... (ARH)
Drinkin' Beer
Jimmy Witherspoon; *Best Of* .... (PRS)
Evenin' Blues .... (PRS)
Drinkin' In My Sunday Dress
Maria McKee; *Maria McKee* .... (GEF)
Drinkin' My Baby Goodbye
Charlie Daniels Band; *Me & The Boys* .... (EPI)
Drinkin' My Baby (Off My Mind)
Eddie Rabbitt;
Number 1's .... (WB)
Best Of/Greatest Hits-II .... (WB)
Rocky Mountain Music .... (WB)
Drinkin' My Way Back Home
Gene Watson/Farewell Party Band; *Greatest Hits* (MCA)
Little By Little .... (MCA)
Texas Saturday Night .... (MCA)
Drinkin' Wine (Spo Dee O De)
Jerry Lee Lewis; *18 Original Sun Greatest Hits* ... (RHI)
Best Of Town & Country-#3 .... (GUS)
I'm On Fire .... (MER)
Milestones .... (RHI)
Original Sun Greatest Hits .... (RHI)
Stick McGhee/Buddies; *Atlantic R&B 1947-1974-#1:*
1947-1952 .... (ATL)
Soul Years .... (ATL)
Drinkin' & Dreamin'
Waylon Jennings; *Best Of* .... (RCA)
Greatest Greatest Hits .... (RCA)
Turn The Page .... (RCA)
Drinkin' & Drivin'
Johnny Paycheck; *Biggest Hits* .... (EPI)
Encore .... (EPI)
Everybody's Got a Family .... (EPI)
Drunk Again
Champion Jack Dupree; *Collectables Blues*
Collection-#1 .... (CLT)
Drunk In My Past
X; *More Fun In The New World* .... (ELE)
Drunk On The Moon
Tom Waits; *Heart Of Saturday Night* .... (ASY)
Drunken Blue Rooster
Todd Rundgren; *Todd* .... (RHI)
Drunken Butterfly
Sonic Youth; *Dirty* .... (DGC)
Drunken Hearted Boy
Allman Brothers Band; *Dreams* .... (POL)
Drunken Hearted Man
Robert Johnson; *Complete Recordings* .... (COL)
D.U.I.
Drink Small; *Round Two* .... (ICH)
Elderberry Wine
Elton John; *Don't Shoot Me I'm Only The Piano*
Player .... (POL)
Escape (Pina Colada Song)
Rupert Holmes; *Billboard Top Hits-1979* .... (RHI)
Partners In Crime .... (INF)
Feelin' Single, Seein' Double
Emmylou Harris; *Elite Hotel* .... (RPR)
Fifteen Beers
Johnny Paycheck; *Biggest Hits* .... (EPI)
Gimme A Pig Foot
Billie Holiday; *From The Original Decca Masters* (MCA)
Story .... (MCA)
Gin And Juice
Snoop Doggy Dogg; *Doggystyle* .... (DR)
God Loves A Drunk
Richard Thompson; *Rumor & Sigh* .... (CAP)
God's Own Drunk
Jimmy Buffett; *Living & Dying In 3/4 Time* ..... (MCA)
You Had To Be There .... (MCA)
Good Friends & A Bottle Of Wine
Ted Nugent; *Weekend Warriors* .... (EPI)
Hey Nineteen
Steely Dan; *Gaucho* .... (MCA)
Gold .... (MCA)
However Much I Booze
Who; *By Numbers* .... (MCA)
I Ain't Drunk, I'm Just Drinking
Albert Collins; *Genuine Houserockin' Music II* ...(ALG)

I Get A Kick Out Of You
Frank Sinatra; *Capitol Years* .... (CAP)
Main Event .... (SIN)
My One & Only Love .... (CAP)
Reprise Collection .... (RPR)
Round #1 .... (CAP)
Sinatra & Swingin' Brass .... (RPR)
I Gotta Get Drunk
Willie Nelson; *Honky Tonkin'* .... (RCA)
Live .... (RCA)
Redneck Mothers .... (RCA)
What Can You Do To Me Now? .... (RCA)
& Family Live .... (COL)
I Like Beer
Tom T. Hall; *Greatest Hits-#2* .... (MER)
In Concert .... (RCA)
If Drinkin' Don't Kill Me...
George Jones; *Anniversary-10 Years Of Hits* ...... (EPI)
I Am What I Am .... (EPI)
If I Were A Drinker
Travis Tritt; *Country Club* .... (WB)
If The River Was Whiskey
Mississippi Fred McDowell; *Great Bluesmen At*
Newport .... (VAN)
In Praise Of Drugs & Alcohol
San Francisco Mime Troupe; *Steel Town* .... (FF)
Intoxicated Rat
New Lost City Ramblers; *American Moonshine &*
Prohibition Songs .... (FLW)
I'll Drink To That
Jimmy Smith; *Off The Top* .... (ELE)
I'm Gonna Hire A Wino To Decorate...
David Frizzell; *Family's Fine But This One's All*
Mine .... (WB)
John Barleycorn
Traffic; *John Barleycorn Must Die* .... (ISL)
Jose Cuervo
Shelly West; *West By West* .... (WB)
Kentucky Moonshine
Pure Prairie League; *Takin' The Stage* .... (RCA)
Two Lane Highway .... (RCA)
Kentucky Moonshiner
Dave Van Ronk; *Inside Dave Van Ronk* .... (FAN)
George Tucker; *George Tucker* .... (ROU)
Killin' Time
Clint Black; *Killin' Time* .... (RCA)
RCA Award Winners .... (RCA)
Kisses Sweeter Than Wine
Jimmie Rodgers; *Best Of* .... (RHI)
Cruisin'-1958 .... (INC)
Weavers; *At Carnegie Hall* .... (VAN)
Best Of .... (MCA)
Greatest Hits .... (VAN)
Reunion-At Carnegie Hall-1963 .... (VAN)
Let's Go Get Stoned
Joe Cocker; *Mad Dogs & Englishmen* .... (A&M)
Ray Charles; *Anthology* .... (RHI)
Greatest Hits .... (RHI)
His Greatest Hits-#1 .... (DHL)
Little Old Wine Drinker Me
Dean Martin; *Greatest Hits-#2* .... (RPR)
Welcome To My World .... (RPR)
Mel Tillis; *Best Of* .... (MCA)
Little Rock
Collin Raye; *Extremes* .... (EPI)
Lone Star Beer & Bob Wills Music
Red Steagall; *Lone Star Beer & Bob Wills Music* (MCA)
Texas Country .... (MCA)
Lone Star State Of Mind
Don Williams; *Currents* .... (RCA)
Nanci Griffith; *Country Classics-#8-1986-1987* .. (MSP)
Lone Star State Of Mind .... (MCA)
Pat Alger/Nanci Griffith/Trisha Yearwood; *True Love &*
Other Short Stories .... (SH)
Lost In The Ozone
Commander Cody; *Lost In The Ozone* .... (MCA)
We Got A Live One Here .... (WB)
Love Hangover
Diana Ross; *20 Greatest Songs In Motown*
History-CD .... (MOT)
20/20 .... (MOT)
All The Great Hits .... (MOT)
Anthology .... (MOT)
Greatest Hits .... (MOT)

Margaritaville
Jimmy Buffett; *Changes In Latitudes...Attitudes* .. (MCA)
  Songs You Know By Heart .... (MCA)
  You Had To Be There .... (MCA)
Misery And Gin
Merle Haggard; *Back To The Barrooms* .... (MCA)
  Greatest Hits .... (MCA)
  Rainbow Stew .... (MCA)
Moonlight Cocktail
Glenn Miller; *Best Of-#2* .... (RCA)
  Complete Glen Miller/Orchestra-#8 .... (BLU)
  Memorial 1944-1969 .... (BLU)
  Nipper's Greatest Hits-'40s-#1 .... (RCA)
Rivieras; *45* .... (CLT)
  45 .... (ERI)
More Wine Waiter Please
Poor; *Who Cares* .... (550)
Mountain Dew
Charlie Daniels Band; *Volunteer Jam* .... (CPC)
Clancy Brothers; *Greatest Hits* .... (VAN)
Doc Watson; *Old Timey Concert* .... (VAN)
Eric Weissberg; *ST/Dueling Banjos From
  "Deliverance"* .... (WB)
Stanley Brothers; *Stanley Series-Vol 1-#2* .... (COP)
  Stanley Series-Vol 2-#2 .... (COP)
Munich Beer Garden
Michigan Dutchmen; *German Polka Favorites* ...... (JJ)
My Friend
Jimi Hendrix; *Cry Of Love* .... (RPR)
My Whiskey Head Buddies
Elvin Bishop; *Don't Let The Bossman Get You
  Down* .... (ALG)
My Wife, She Got Drunk
Li'l Wally; *All American Polkas* .... (JJ)
Nancy Whiskey
Ian & Sylvia; *Greatest Hits* .... (VAN)
  Ian & Sylvia .... (VAN)
Irish Rovers; *Greatest Hits* .... (MCA)
Nashville Beer Garden
Andy Badale/Beer Garden Band; *Nashville Beer
  Garden* .... (RAN)
Neon Moon
Brooks & Dunn; *Brand New Man* .... (ARI)
Night They Invented Champagne
Betty Wand/Louis Jordan/Others; *ST/Gigi* .... (SSP)
  Original Cast; *Gigi* .... (RCA)
No More Booze (On Tuesdays)
Freewheelers; *Freewheelers* .... (DGC)
No Way Jose
Ray Kennedy; *Guitar Man* .... (ATL)
Old Dogs, Children & Watermelon Wine
Tom T. Hall; *Essential Twentieth Anniversary
  Collect.* .... (MER)
  Greatest Hits-#2 .... (MER)
On Tap, In The Can, Or In The Bottle
Hank Thompson; *Country Music Hall Of Fame* . (MCA)
One Bourbon One Scotch One Beer
George Thorogood/Destroyers; *George
  Thorogood/Destroyers* .... (ROU)
  Live .... (EMI)
John Lee Hooker; *Best Of Chess Blues* .... (CSS)
  Real Folk Blues .... (CSS)
  Ultimate Collection-1948-1990 .... (RHI)
One Mint Julep
Clovers; *Down In The Alley* .... (ATL)
  Love Potion #9 .... (EMI)
Ray Charles; *His Greatest Hits-#1* .... (DHL)
Outlaws & Lone Star Beer
C.W. McCall; *& Co.* .... (POL)
Paddy Kelly's Brew
Tommy Makem; *Evening With* .... (SHA)
Pass The 40 Ounce
Jena Si Qua; *Conquest Of A Nation* .... (CNQ)
Pass The Booze
Ernest Tubb; *Retrospective-#2* .... (MSP)
Pink Cocktail For A Blue Lady
Glenn Miller/Orchestra; *Complete* .... (BLU)
  Complete-#9 .... (RCA)
Pink Elephants
Eddie Lang Blue Five/Joe Venuti; *Jazz In The
  Thirties* .... (DSQ)
Poison Whiskey
Lynyrd Skynyrd; *Pronounced Leh-nerd Skin-nerd* (MCA)

Popcorn, Pretzels & Beer Waltz
Michigan Dutchmen; *Beer & Dutchmen Polkas* ...... (JJ)
Pour Me Another Tequila
Eddie Rabbitt; *All Time Greatest Hits* .... (WB)
Power Of Positive Drinkin'
Mickey Gilley; *Biggest Hits* .... (EPI)
  Ten Years Of Hits .... (EPI)
Pretending To Be Drunk
Sparks; *Pulling Rabbits Out Of A Hat* .... (ATL)
Punch Drunk
Sade; *Promise* .... (POR)
Rather Be Sloppy Drunk
Big Joe Williams; *Dark Muddy Bottom Blues* .... (SPE)
Red Red Wine
Neil Diamond; *Hot August Night* .... (MCA)
  Classics (Early Years) .... (COL)
  Double Gold .... (BNG)
  Greatest Hits .... (BNG)
Replacements; *Pleased To Meet Me* .... (SIR)
UB40; *Labour Of Love* .... (A&M)
Red Wine & Blue Memories
Joe Stampley; *Biggest Hits* .... (EPI)
Rednecks, White Socks & Blue Ribbon Beer
Johnny Russell; *Beer Redneck Mothers* .... (RCA)
  Rednecks, White Socks & Blue Ribbon Beer ....(RCA)
Rum & Coca-Cola
Andrews Sisters; *16 Great Performances* .... (MCA)
  Best Of .... (MCA)
  Boogie Woogie Bugle Girls .... (MCA)
  Capitol Collectors Series .... (CAP)
Professor Longhair; *Last Mardi Gras* .... (ATL)
  Mardi Gras In Baton Rouge .... (RHI)
Sambuca Nights
Special EFX; *Special EFX* .... (GRP)
Same Old Wine
Loggins & Messina; *Sittin' In* .... (COL)
San Antonio Champagne
Troy Cory; *Real Country* .... (VRA)
Sangria
Tania Maria; *Come With Me* .... (CP)
  The Real Tania Maria-Wild! .... (CP)
Sangria Wine
Jerry Jeff Walker; *Best Of* .... (MCA)
  Great Gonzos .... (MCA)
  Viva Terlingua .... (MCA)
Saturday Night's Alright For Fighting
Elton John; *Goodbye Yellow Brick Road* .... (POL)
  Greatest Hits .... (POL)
  Knebworth-The Album .... (POL)
  Rock Classics .... (KT)
Who; *Two Rooms-Songs Of E. John & B. Taupin* (POL)
Scotch And Soda
Kingston Trio; *100 Proof Hits* .... (KT)
  25 Years Non-Stop .... (XER)
  Best Of .... (CAP)
  Capitol Collectors Series .... (CAP)
  Tom Dooley .... (CAP)
Manhattan Transfer; *Coming Out* .... (ATL)
Send Me No Wine
Moody Blues; *On The Threshold Of A Dream* .... (POL)
Set Up Two Glasses, Joe
Ernest Tubb/Ferlin Husky/Simon Crum; *Ernest Tubb
  Collection* .... (SO)
Set 'Em Up Joe
Vern Gosdin; *Chiseled In Stone* .... (COL)
  Greatest Country Hits/'80s-1988 .... (COL)
Show Me The Way To Go Home
Artie Shaw; *Best Of* .... (MCA)
Randy Erwin; *Back Home* .... (ROM)
Sister Moonshine
Supertramp; *Crisis? What Crisis?* .... (A&M)
Six Pack To Go
Hank Thompson; *Best Of The Best* .... (GUS)
  Capitol Collectors Series .... (CAP)
  Country Comes To Carnegie Hall .... (MCA)
  Greatest Hits-#2 .... (SO)
  Hank Thompson .... (DOT)
Snortin' Whiskey
Pat Travers Band; *Boom Boom...The Best Of* ..... (POL)
  Crash & Burn .... (POL)
Sober
Tool; *Undertow* .... (ZOO)

Stoned At The Jukebox
Hank Williams, Jr.; *Best Of* ....(CCB)
   Best Of-#1-Roots & Branches ....(MER)
   Bocephus Box-Collection-1979-1992 ....(CPC)
   Lone Wolf ....(W/C)
Straight Tequila Night
John Anderson; *Seminole Wind* ....(BNA)
   Today's Hot Country ....(KT)
Straight, No Chaser
Miles Davis; *Milestones* ....(COL)
Oscar Peterson; *Live At The North Sea Jazz*
Festival ....(PAB)
Quincy Jones/Orchestra; *Quintessence* ....(MCI)
Thelonius Monk; *Best Of* ....(BLN)
   Composer ....(COL)
   ST/Thelonius Monk-Straight No Chaser ....(COL)
Strawberry Wine
Band; *Stage Fright* ....(CAP)
Suckin' A Big Bottle Of Gin
Joe Ely; *Joe Ely* ....(MCA)
Swedish Schnapps
Charlie Parker; *Swedish Schnapps* ....(VRV)
   Verve Years-1950-1951 ....(VRV)
Sweet Cherry Wine
Tommy James/Shondells; *Anthology* ...... (RHI)
   Very Best Of ....(PRR)
Take Your Whiskey Home
Van Halen; *Women & Children First* ....(WB)
Tanqueray
Vern Gosdin; *Alone* ....(COL)
   Greatest Hits-#1 ....(COL)
   Super Hits ....(COL)
Tears Will Be The Chaser For Your Wine
Wanda Jackson; *Greatest Hits* ....(GUS)
   Rockin' In The Country-Best Of ....(RHI)
Ten Feet Tall And Bulletproof
Travis Tritt; *Ten Feet Tall And Bulletproof* ....(WB)
Tennessee Bottle
Kenny Rogers; *The Gambler* ....(EMI)
Tennessee Toddy
Marty Robbins; *Essential-1951-1982* ....(COL)
Tennessee Whiskey
David Allan Coe; *17 Greatest Hits* ....(COL)
   Biggest Hits ....(COL)
   For The Record-First 10 Years ....(COL)
   Tennessee Whiskey ....(COL)
George Jones; *By Request* ....(EPI)
   First Time Live ....(EPI)
   Greatest Country Hits/'80s-1983 ....(COL)
   Shine On ....(EPI)
   Super Hits ....(EPI)
Merle Haggard; *19 Hot Country Requests-#2* ..... (EPI)
Tennessee Whiskey & Texas Women
Rayburn Anthony; *Audiograph Alive* ...... (AUD)
   Dance Floor Crystal Ball ....(AUD)
Tequila
Champs; *Billboard Top Rock 'N' Roll Hits-1958* . (RHI)
   Cruisin'-1958 ....(INC)
   Grandson Of Frat Rock-#3 ....(RHI)
   Oldies But Goodies-#7 ....(OSR)
   Super Oldies Of The '50s-#7 ....(AUF)
Larry Carlton; *Collection* ....(GRP)
   Friends ....(MCA)
Pretenders; *Last Of The Independents* ....(SIR)
Tequila Sheila
Bobby Bare; *Biggest Hits* ....(COL)
   Encore ....(COL)
Mac Davis; *It's Hard To Be Humble* ....(CAS)
Tequila Sunrise
Alan Jackson; *Common Thread-Songs Of The*
Eagles .... (GIA)
Eagles; *Anthology* ....(ASY)
   Desperado ....(ASY)
   Their Greatest Hits-1971-1975 ....(ASY)
Fagles; *Hell Freezes Over* ....(GEF)
There Stands The Glass
Carl Smith; *Best Of* ....(CCB)
Webb Pierce; *Golden Hits* ....(PLN)
They'll All Out Of Liquor, Let's Find...
Waitresses; *Best Of* ....(POL)
This Bottle (In My Hand)
David Allan Coe & George Jones; *17 Greatest*
Hits ....(COL)
   For The Record-First 10 Years ....(COL)

This Drinkin' Will Kill Me
Dwight Yoakam; *Hillbilly Deluxe* ....(RPR)
Three Drunk Newts
Barnes & Barnes; *Dr. Demento's Dementia Royale* (RHI)
Three Drunken Maidens
Maddy Prior & Tim Hart; *Summer Solstice* ....(SHA)
Titties And Beer
Kiss; *Alive 2* ....(CAS)
   Double Platinum ....(CAS)
   Rock & Roll Over ....(CAS)
Titties N' Beer
Frank Zappa; *Baby Snakes* ....(BAR)
   In New York ....(BAR)
Tonight The Bottle Let Me Down
Brooks & Dunn; *Mama's Hungry Eyes-Merle Haggard*
Tribute ....(ARI)
Elvis Costello/Attractions; *Almost Blue* ....(COL)
Gram Parsons/Flying Burrito Brothers; *Sleepless*
Night ....(A&M)
Merle Haggard; *Swinging Doors* ....(OOP)
Too Much Blood In My Alcohol System
Cold Shot; *Salt City Blues* ....(BWV)
Two Beers Away
Moe Bandy & Joe Stampley; *Greatest Hits* ....(COL)
Two More Bottles Of Wine
Delbert McClinton; *Honky Tonkin'-I Done Me*
Some ....(ALG)
Emmylou Harris; *Honky Tonk Country* ....(WB)
   Profile-Best Of ....(WB)
   Quarter Moon In A Ten-Cent Town ....(WB)
Vintage Wine
Moody Blues; *Sur La Mer* ....(POL)
Vodka
John Coltrane; *Prestige Recordings* ....(PRS)
John Coltrane & Paul Quinichette; *Cattin' With* .. (PRS)
Vodka Frenzy
Aversion; *Fit To Be Tied* ....(RES)
Warm Beer & Cold Women
Tom Waits; *Nighthawks At The Diner* ....(ASY)
Was It Just The Wine
Vern Gosdin; *10 Years Of Greatest Hits Newly*
Recorded ....(COL)
Water Into Wine
Bruce Cockburn; *In The Falling Dark* ....(TRN)
Water With The Wine
Joan Armatrading; *Joan Armatrading* ....(A&M)
Watermelon Crawl
Tracy Byrd; *No Ordinary Man* ....(MCA)
Whalecatchers/Drunken Landlady
John Faulkner; *Kind Providence* ....(GRE)
What's Made Milwaukee Famous
Jerry Lee Lewis; *Heartbreak* ....(TOM)
   Milestones ....(RHI)
Rod Stewart; *Best Of* ....(MER)
   Storyteller-Complete Anthology-1964-1990 ......(WB)
Whiskey
Charlie Daniels Band; *Volunteer Jam* ....(CPC)
   Whiskey ....(EPI)
Loggins & Messina; *Loggins & Messina* ....(COL)
Whiskey Ain't Workin'
Travis Tritt & Marty Stuart; *It's All About To*
Change ....(WB)
Whiskey And Wimmen
John Lee Hooker; *Best Of* ....(CRS)
   Best Of ....(VJ)
   Infinite Boogie ....(RHI)
   Real Blues Brothers ....(DHL)
   World's Greatest Blues Singer ....(VJ)
Whiskey Bent & Hell Bound
Hank Williams, Jr.; *Greatest Hits* ....(WB)
   Whiskey Bent & Hell Bound ....(W/C)
Whiskey On A Sunday (Puppet Song)
Irish Rovers; *Greatest Hits* ....(MCA)
Whiskey River
Willie Nelson; *Greatest Hits & Some That Will Be* (COL)
   Shotgun Willie ....(ATL)
   ST/Honeysuckle Rose ....(COL)
   & Family Live ....(COL)
Whiskey Rock A Roller
Lynyrd Skynyrd; *Gold & Platinum* ....(MCA)
   Nuthin' Fancy ....(MCA)
   One More From The Road ....(MCA)

Whiskey Train
Procol Harum; *Best Of* .... (A&M)
   Classics-#17 .... (A&M)
   Home .... (MOB)
Whiskey, If You Were A Woman
Highway 101; *Greatest Hits* .... (WB)
   Highway 101 .... (WB)
White Lightning & Wine
Heart; *Dreamboat Annie* .... (CAP)
Why Am I Drinkin'
Merle Haggard; *Going Where The Lonely Go* ..... (EPI)
   Super Hits .... (EPI)
Why Don't We Get Drunk
Jimmy Buffett; *Boats Beaches Bars & Ballads* ... (MGR)
   Songs You Know By Heart-Greatest Hits .... (MCA)
   White Sport Coat & A Pink Crustacean .... (MCA)
   You Had To Be There-In Concert .... (MCA)
Yesterday's Wine
Merle Haggard & George Jones; *By Request* ...... (EPI)
   Greatest Country Hits/'80s-1982 .... (EPI)
   Taste Of Yesterday's Wine .... (EPI)
   Walking The Line .... (EPI)
Willie Nelson; *Best Of Willie* .... (RCA)
   Collector's .... (RCA)
   The Outlaws .... (RCA)

ANATOMY: ARMS
See Also: Other Anatomy Categories

Angel In Your Arms
Barbara Mandrell; *Country Classics-#5
(1985-1986)* .... (MCA)
   Get To The Heart .... (MCA)
Reba McEntire; *Reba McEntire* .... (MER)
Arms Of A Fool
Mel Tillis; *Best Of* .... (MGM)
   Brand New Mister Me .... (POL)
Back In My Arms Again
Diana Ross/Supremes; *25th Anniversary* .... (MOT)
   Anthology .... (MOT)
   Every Great #1 Hit .... (MOT)
   Greatest Hits .... (MOT)
   Motown Story .... (MOT)
Circle Of Your Arms
Louis Armstrong; *Louis Armstrong* .... (EVR)
Crazy Arms
Chuck Berry; *Chess Box* .... (CSS)
Jerry Lee Lewis; *18 Original Sun Greatest Hits* ... (RHI)
   Golden Rock Hits .... (SMA)
   Jerry Lee Lewis .... (RHI)
Linda Ronstadt; *Retrospective* .... (CAP)
Patsy Cline; *Last Sessions* .... (MCA)
   Portrait Of .... (MCA)
Ray Price; *Columbia Country Classics-#2* .... (COL)
   Greatest Hits .... (COL)
   Greatest Hits-#1 .... (STE)
Willie Nelson; *San Antonio Rose* .... (COL)
Embraceable You
Billie Holiday; *Body & Soul* .... (VRV)
Frank Sinatra; *Capitol Years* .... (CAP)
MGM Studio Orchestra; *ST/American In Paris* .... (SSP)
Oleta Adams; *Glory Of Gershwin Featuring Larry
Adler* .... (MER)
Sarah Vaughan; *Complete-On Mercury-#1-Great Jazz
Years* .... (MER)
Empty Arms
Stevie Ray Vaughan/Double Trouble; *The Sky Is
Crying* .... (EPI)
Fifty Miles Of Elbow Room
Iris DeMent; *Infamous Angel* .... (PHO)
   Infamous Angel .... (WB)
Norman & Nancy Blake; *Blind Dog* .... (ROU)
Red Clay Ramblers; *Twisted Laurel* .... (FF)
Full Moon & Empty Arms
Frank Sinatra; *Greatest Hits-#2* .... (COL)
Sarah Vaughan; *Slightly Classical* .... (RLL)
Heaven In Your Arms
R.J.'s Latest Arrival; *Hold On* .... (MAN)
Hold You Tight
Tara Kemp; *Tara Kemp* .... (GIA)
(I Just) Died In Your Arms
Cutting Crew; *Broadcast* .... (VIA)
   MTV-VH1 Powerplayers .... (AMR)

If Ever You're In My Arms Again
Peabo Bryson; *Straight From The Heart* .... (ELE)
In The Arms Of Cocaine
Hank Williams, Jr.; *Strong Stuff* .... (WB)
In These Arms
Bon Jovi; *Keep The Faith* .... (MER)
Into Your Arms
Lemonheads; *Come On Feel The Lemonheads* .... (ATL)
My Arms Stay Open All Night
Tanya Tucker; *Greatest Hits* .... (CAP)
Not Here In My Arms
Lisa Brokop; *Every Little Girl's Dream* .... (PAT)
Open Arms
Journey; *Escape* .... (COL)
   Greatest Hits .... (COL)
   Seems Like Yesterday-#4-Early '80s .... (KT)
   ST/Heavy Metal .... (COL)
Other Arms
Robert Plant; *Principle Of Moments* .... (EPR)
Put Your Arms Around Me, Honey
Fats Domino; *They Call Me The Fat Man* .... (EMI)
Judy Garland; *Best Of-From MGM Classic Films* (MCA)
Sammy Kaye; *Best Of* .... (MCA)
Rollin' In My Sweet Baby's Arms
Bill Monroe; *Bean Blossom* .... (MCA)
Dillard & Clark; *Fantastic Expedition Of* .... (MOB)
Flatt & Scruggs; *Golden Hits Of* .... (GUS)
Flying Burrito Brothers; *Close Encounters To The West
Coast* .... (RLX)
Ramblin' Jack Elliott; *Hard Travelin'* .... (FAN)
Tony Trischka; *Heartlands* .... (ROU)
Willie Nelson; *& Family Live* .... (COL)
Run Baby Run (Back Into My Arms)
Tremeloes; *Best Of* .... (RHI)
Run To My Lovin' Arms
Jay/Americans; *Greatest Hits* .... (EMI)
Safe In The Arms Of Love
Baillie & The Boys; *Turn The Tide* .... (RCA)
Martika; *Martika's Kitchen* .... (COL)
Take Me In Your Arms
Doobie Brothers; *Best Of* .... (WB)
   Stampede .... (WB)
Isley Brothers; *Motown Superstar Series-#6* ..... (MOT)
   Story-#1-Rockin' Soul-1959-1968 .... (RHI)
Kim Weston; *25 Hard-To-Find Motown
Classics-#3* .... (MOT)
   Every Great Motown Song-First 25 Years ...... (MOT)
   Greatest By Holland/Dozier/Holland .... (MOT)
   Motown Dance Party-#1 .... (MOT)
Take Me In Your Arms & Hold Me
Eddy Arnold; *World of Hits* .... (MGM)
Jim Reeves; *Don't Let Me Cross Over* .... (RCA)
   I Love You Because .... (RCA)
Les Paul; *Legend & The Legacy* .... (CAP)
Take Me In Your Arms & Love Me
Gladys Knight/Pips; *Anthology* .... (MOT)
   Everybody Needs Love .... (MOT)
These Arms Of Mine
Otis Redding; *Best Of* .... (ATC)
   Good To Me .... (STX)
   Story .... (ATL)
   ST/More Dirty Dancing .... (RCA)
   Very Best Of .... (RHI)
Trying To Throw Your Arms Around The...
U2; *Achtung Baby* .... (ISL)

ANATOMY: BACK
See Also: Other Anatomy Categories

Baby Scratch My Back
Slim Harpo; *Best Of* .... (RHI)
   Sound Of The Swamp: Best Of Excello-#1 ..... (RHI)
Better Watch Your Back
Daryl Hall & John Oates; *War Babies* .... (ATL)
Get Off My Back Woman
B.B. King; *Live & Well* .... (MCA)
Monkey On My Back
Aerosmith; *Pump* .... (GEF)
Inspiral Carpets; *Life* .... (ELE)
Ten Years After; *A Space In Time* .... (COL)
Monkey On Your Back
Aldo Nova; *Portrait Of* .... (EPI)
   Subject...Aldo Nova .... (POR)

Police On My Back
Clash; *On Broadway* .... (EPI)
Sandinista .... (EPI)
Ribbons Down My Back
Original Broadway Cast; *Hello Dolly!* .... (RCA)
Scratch My Back
Fabulous Thunderbirds; *Fabulous Thunderbirds* . (CHR)
Otis Redding; *Soul Album* .... (ATC)
Roxx Gang; *Things You've Never Done Before* ... (VIA)
Smoove; *Smoove With A Ruffness* .... (EW)

ANATOMY: BODY

See Also: Other Anatomy Categories

36-22-36
Bobby Bland; *Best Of-#2* .... (MCA)
Bobby Bland .... (MCA)
Here's The Man .... (MCA)
Bodies
Sex Pistols; *Never Mind The Bollocks* .... (WB)
Body Electric
Rush; *Grace Under Pressure* .... (MER)
Body Heavenly
Full Force; *Get Busy 1 Time* .... (COL)
Body Language
INXS; *INXS* .... (ATC)
Pete Townshend; *Scoop* .... (ATC)
Queen; *Hot Space* .... (HOL)
Body Slam!
Bootsy's Rubber Band; *45* .... (WB)
Body Talk
Deele; *Body Talk* .... (SLR)
Street Beat .... (SLR)
Kix; *Cool Kids* .... (ATL)
Ratt; *Dancing Undercover* .... (ATL)
Ratt & Roll 8191 .... (ATL)
ST/Golden Child .... (CAP)
Wallets; *Body Talk* .... (TT)
Body & Soul
Anita Baker; *Rhythm Of Love* .... (ELE)
Billie Holiday; *Billie Holiday* .... (COL)
Body & Soul .... (VRV)
Story #2 .... (COL)
Carly Simon; *Torch* .... (WB)
Eddie Jefferson; *Body & Soul* .... (PRS)
Jazz Singer .... (IC)
Main Man .... (IC)
Louis Armstrong; *At Symphony Hall* .... (MCA)
Musical Autobiography-#2 .... (MCA)
Story .... (COL)
Manhattan Transfer; *Best Of* .... (ATL)
Extensions .... (ATL)
Sarah Vaughan; *How Long Has This Been Going
On* .... (PAB)
Sarah Vaughan .... (EVR)
Bullet-Ridden Bodies
Accused; *Grinning Like An Undertaker* .... (NSY)
Bury My Body
Animals; *Best Of* .... (AKO)
Heartbeat/Free Your Body
Seduction; *Nothing Matters Without Love* .... (VDT)
Heavenly Bodies
Earl Thomas Conley; *Somewhere Between Right And
Wrong* .... (RCA)
Heavenly Body
Chi-Lites; *Ear Candy-#2* .... (20)
Heavenly Body .... (20)
Naked & Nude
Lou & Peter Berryman; *Cupid's Trash Truck* .... (COR)
One Hit (To The Body)
Rolling Stones; *Dirty Work* .... (RS)
Shake Your Body (Down To The Ground)
Jacksons; *Destiny* .... (EPI)
Live .... (EPI)
ST/Skatetown USA .... (COL)
Shake Your Groove Thing
Peaches & Herb; *2 Hot* .... (POL)
Billboard Top Dance Hits-1978 .... (RHI)
Disco Years-#1-1974-1978 .... (RHI)
Mega Hits Dance Classics-#2 .... (PRY)
Night At Studio 54 .... (POL)
Polydor Dance Classics .... (POL)

This Body Is A Prison
Spencer Bohren; *Live In New Orleans* .... (GSR)
Touch Me (I Want Your Body)
Samantha Fox; *Greatest Hits* .... (JVA)
Touch Me (I Want Your Body) .... (JVA)
What's The Ugliest Part Of Your Body
Mothers Of Invention; *We're Only In It For The...*/*Lumpy
Gravy* .... (RYK)
Wiggle It
2 In A Room; *S* .... (CUT)
Wrap My Body Tight
Johnny Gill; *Johnny Gill* .... (MOT)
Your Body Is An Outlaw
Mel Tillis; *Your Body Is An Outlaw* .... (ELE)
Your Body's Callin'
R. Kelly; *12 Play* .... (JVA)
Your Body's Here With Me
O'Jays; *My Favorite Person* .... (PI)

ANATOMY: FACE

*See Also: Other Anatomy Categories, EYES,
SMILE*

Angels With Dirty Faces
Tommy Dorsey; *Complete-#8* .... (RCA)
Baby Face
Al Jolson; *Story-#3* .... (MCA)
World's Greatest .... (MCA)
Bobby Darin; *Splish Splash-Best Of-#1* .... (ATL)
Kinks; *Everybody's In Show Biz* .... (RHI)
Little Richard; *Compact Command Performances* (MOT)
Greatest Hits .... (EVR)
His Greatest Hits .... (VJ)
Tutti Frutti .... (ACC)
Blonde Hair, Brown Nose
Dweezil Zappa; *Havin' A Bad Day* .... (RYK)
Cheek To Cheek
Ella Fitzgerald; *Silver Collection-Songbooks* .. (VRV)
Frank Sinatra; *Come Dance With Me* .... (CAP)
Fred Astaire; *Cheek To Cheek* .... (POE)
Irving Berlin Songbook .... (VRV)
Mundell Lowe; *Quartet* .... (RVR)
Pete Fountain; *Cheek To Cheek* .... (RAN)
Tommy Dorsey; *Irving Berlin 100th Anniversary
Collect.* .... (MCA)
Tony Bennett; *Bennett/Berlin* .... (COL)
De Bat (Fly In Me Face)
Carly Simon; *Boys In The Trees* .... (ELE)
Der Fuehrer's Face
Spike Jones; *Best Of* .... (RCA)
Eyes Without A Face
Billy Idol; *Rebel Yell* .... (CHR)
Flesheaters; *ST/Return Of The Living Dead* ..... (ENI)
Face Dances, Part 2
Pete Townshend; *All The Best Cowboys Have Chinese
Eyes* .... (ATC)
Face In The Crowd
Kinks; *Soap Opera* .... (RHI)
Lisa Lisa & Cult Jam; *Spanish Fly* .... (COL)
Michael Martin Murphey & Holly Dunn;
Americana .... (WB)
Favorite Country Duets .... (WB)
Milestones-Greatest Hits .... (WB)
Tom Petty; *Full Moon Fever* .... (MCA)
Face On The Cutting Room Floor
Nitty Gritty Dirt Band; *Live Two Five* .... (CAP)
More Great Dirt-Best Of-#2 .... (WB)
Face The Face
Pete Townshend; *White City* .... (ATC)
Who; *Join Together* .... (MCA)
Face To Face
Garth Brooks; *The Chase* .... (LIB)
First Time Ever I Saw Your Face
Roberta Flack; *Atlantic R&B-#6-(1966-1969)* ... (ATL)
Best Of .... (ATL)
First Take .... (ATL)
Freckle Song
Larry Vincent; *Dr. Demento's Greatest-#1* ...... (RHI)
Funny Face
Donna Fargo; *Super Hits/'70s-#11* .... (RHI)
Original Cast; *My One & Only* .... (ATL)

Get The Funk Out Ma Face
Brothers Johnson; *Blast* .... (A&M)
Classics-#11 .... (A&M)
Look Out For No. 1 .... (A&M)
Hide Your Face
Spade Cooley; *Columbia Historic Edition* ....(COL)
I Can't See Your Face In My Mind
Doors; *Classics* .... (ELE)
Strange Days .... (ELE)
I Just Want To See His Face
Rolling Stones; *Exile On Main Street* .... (RS)
I See Your Face Before Me
Frank Sinatra; *In The Wee Small Hours* .... (CAP)
What Is This Thing Called Love .... (CAP)
Miles Davis; *Chronicle* .... (PRS)
Green Haze .... (PRS)
I've Grown Accustomed To Her Face
Rex Harrison/Original Cast; *My Fair Lady* ......(COL)
Tony Bennett; *Big Band Bash* .... (INT)
Chicago ....(DHL)
I've Just Seen A Face
Beatles; *Help* .... (CAP)
Rubber Soul .... (CAP)
Paul McCartney; *Unplugged-Official Bootleg* ..... (CAP)
Paul McCartney/Wings; *Over America* .... (CAP)
I've Seen That Face Before
Grace Jones; *Nightclubbing* .... (ISL)
Island Life .... (ISL)
Jawbone
Band; *Gift Set* .... (CAP)
Stage Fright .... (CAP)
Jawbreaker
Judas Priest; *Defenders Of The Faith* ....(COL)
Lines On My Face
Peter Frampton; *Classics-#12* .... (A&M)
Comes Alive .... (A&M)
Frampton's Camel .... (A&M)
Lose That Long Face
Judy Garland; *A Star Is Born* ....(COL)
May The Bird Of Paradise Fly Up Your...
Harlow Wilcox/Oakies; *Cripple Cricket* .... (PLN)
Little Jimmy Dickens; *Columbia Country
Classics-#3-Americana* ....(COL)
Moon-faced, Starry-Eyed
Popular Standard; *Out of print recording* ....(OOP)
My Brave Face
Paul McCartney; *Flowers In The Dirt* .... (CAP)
Tripping The Light Fantastic-Highlights! .... (CAP)
Nancy (With The Laughing Face)
Frank Sinatra; *Sinatra's Reprise-Very Good Years* (RPR)
Sinatra's Sinatra .... (RPR)
John Coltrane; *Gentle Side Of* .... (GRP)
Tony Bennett; *Perfectly Frank* ....(COL)
New Faces
Rolling Stones; *Voodoo Lounge* .... (VIA)
Pizza Face
Barnes & Barnes; *Zabagabee-Best Of* .... (RHI)
Powder Your Face With Sunshine (Smile!)
Guy Lombardo; *Best Of* ....(CCB)
Sammy Kaye/Orchestra; *Play 22 Original Big Band
Recordings* .... (HIN)
Put On A Happy Face
Dick Van Dyke; *Broadway Magic-1960s* ....(COL)
ST/Bye Bye Birdie ....(RCA)
Dick Van Dyke/Original Cast; *Bye Bye Birdie* ...(COL)
Stevie Wonder; *With A Song In My Heart* .... (MOT)
Tony Bennett; *All-Time Greatest Hits* ....(COL)
Forty Years-Artistry Of ....(COL)
Razor Face
Elton John; *Madman Across The Water* .... (POL)
Shaddup You Face
Joe Dolce; *45* .... (MCA)
Smiling Faces Sometimes
Undisputed Truth; *Hard-To-Find Motown
Classics-#2* .... (MOT)
Soul Hits/'70s-#5 .... (RHI)
Take A Look At My Face
Michael Bolton; *The Hunger* ....(COL)
Tell Me To My Face
Dan Fogelberg & Tim Weisberg; *Twin Sons Of Different
Mothers* .... (FM)
Tonight I Shall Sleep With A Smile On...
Duke Ellington; *Black Brown & Beige* ....(BLU)
Sarah Vaughan; *Duke Ellington Songbook Two* ... (PAB)

Tripe Face Boogie
Little Feat; *Feats Don't Fail Me Now* .... (WB)
Sailin' Shoes .... (WB)
Waiting For Columbus .... (WB)
Tulip Or Turnip (Tell Me Dream Face)
Duke Ellington & Teresa Brewer; *It Don't Mean A
Thing If It Ain't Got...* ....(COL)
Two Faces
Bruce Springsteen; *Tunnel Of Love* ....(COL)
Two Faces Have I
Lou Christie; *Back To The '60s-#4* .... (DOM)
Enlightnin'ment-Best Of .... (RHI)
Written All Over Your Face
Rude Boys; *Rude Awakening* .... (ATL)
Your Smiling Face
James Taylor; *J.T.* ....(COL)
ST/FM .... (MCA)

ANATOMY: FEET
See Also: Other Anatomy Categories

Amazing Bigfoot Diet
Mojo Nixon & Skid Roper; *Frenzy* .... (IRS)
Back On My Feet Again
Babys; *Anthology* .... (CHR)
Union Jacks .... (CHR)
Furry Lewis; *Back On My Feet Again* .... (PRS)
Shake 'Em Down .... (FAN)
Randy Newman; *Good Old Boys* .... (RPR)
Barefoot In Baltimore
Strawberry Alarm Clock; *Best Of-#1* .... (BCT)
Barefoot In Beverly Hills
Grace Jones; *Inside Story* .... (MAN)
Barefoot & Pregnant
Joan Armatrading; *To The Limit* .... (A&M)
Barefootin'
Alabama; *Southern Star* ....(RCA)
Barefoot Jerry; *Barefootin'* .... (MON)
Pete Townshend; *Deep End-Live* ....(ATC)
Robert Parker; *Billboard Top R&B Hits-1966* .... (RHI)
Golden Classics .... (CLT)
Soul Shots-#1-We Got More Soul .... (RHI)
Super Oldies Of The '60s-#4 .... (AUF)
Country Boy (You Got Your Feet In L.A.)
Glen Campbell; *Best Of* .... (LIB)
Classics Collection .... (LIB)
Greatest Hits ....(CCB)
Dancin' Feet
Montrose; *Montrose* .... (WB)
Footloose
Kenny Loggins; *ST/Footloose* ....(COL)
Footprints In The Snow
Bill Monroe; *Best Of* .... (MCA)
Clarence White; *Treasures Untold* .... (VAN)
Emerson, Lake & Palmer; *Black Moon* .... (VIC)
Isley Brothers; *Complete UA Sessions* .... (EMI)
Kentucky Colonels feat. Clarence White; *Kentucky
Colonels feat. Clarence White* .... (ROU)
Has Anybody Seen Amy
John & Audrey Wiggins; *John & Audrey* .... (MER)
Head Over Heels
Accept; *Accept* .... (POR)
Go-Go's; *Greatest* .... (IRS)
Talk Show .... (IRS)
Tears For Fears; *Songs From The Big Chair* ..... (MER)
Tony Terry; *Tony Terry* .... (EPI)
Head To Toe
Lisa Lisa & Cult Jam; *Spanish Fly* ....(COL)
Knock Me Off My Feet
Stevie Wonder; *Songs In The Key Of Life* .... (MOT)
Living In The Footsteps Of Another Man
Chi-Lites; *Greatest Hits* .... (BRU)
Half A Love .... (BRU)
My Head Hurts, My Feet Stink...
Jimmy Buffett; *Havana Daydreamin'* .... (MCA)
On Your Toes
Bobby Short; *Celebrates Rodgers & Hart* .... (ATL)
One Foot, Other Foot
Original Cast; *Allegro* ....(OOP)
Ooh! My Feet!
Original Broadway Cast; *Most Happy Fella* ..... (SMC)
Popsicle Toes
Manhattan Transfer; *Coming Out* .... (ATL)

Michael Franks; *Art Of Tea* .... (RPR)
Put Your Little Foot Right Out
Myron Floren; *22 Great Accordion Classics* ..... (RAN)
Russ Morgan; *Best Of* .... (MCA)
Shoe Goes On The Other Foot Tonight
George Jones; *20 Golden Pieces Of* .... (BLD)
Stand Up On Your Own Feet
Third World; *Arise In Harmony* .... (ISL)
Tickle Toe
Count Basie; *I Like Jazz-Essence Of* ....(COL)
Count Basie/Orchestra; *Best Of-Roulette Years* ... (RLL)
Tip-Toe Through The Tulips With Me
Tiny Tim; *Dr. Demento's Greatest Novelty-#3* .... (RHI)
Silly Songs .... (KT)
Two Left Feet
Richard Thompson; *Hand Of Darkness* .... (HBL)
Watching The Dark-History Of .... (HBL)
When I'm Back On My Feet Again
Michael Bolton; *Soul Provider* ....(COL)
Your Feet's Too Big
Beatles; *45* .... (CLT)
Fats Waller; *20 Golden Pieces Of* .... (BLD)
Ain't Misbehavin' ....(RCA)
Joint Is Jumpin' ....(BLU)
Legendary Performer ....(RCA)
Original Cast; *Ain't Misbehavin'* ....(RCA)

ANATOMY: HAIR

See Also: Other Anatomy Categories

Almost Cut My Hair
Crosby, Stills, Nash & Young; *Deja Vu* .... (ATL)
Bald Head
Professor Longhair; *Crawfish Fiesta* ....(ALG)
Last Mardi Gras .... (ATL)
Bald-Headed Woman
Kinks; *You Really Got Me* .... (RHI)
Lightnin' Hopkins; *Lightnin' Sam Hopkins* ..... (ARH)
Who; *Two's Missing* .... (MCA)
Blonde Hair, Brown Nose
Dweezil Zappa; *Havin' A Bad Day* ....(RYK)
Blondes In Black Cars
Autograph; *That's The Stuff* ....(RCA)
Blondes (Have More Fun)
Rod Stewart; *Blondes (Have More Fun)* .... (WB)
Brownsville Blues (Girl I Love, She...)
Hammie Nixon; *Tappin' That Thing* ....(HW)
Camarillo Brillo
Mothers; *Apostrophe/Overnite Sensation* ....(RYK)
Don't Mess With My Ducktail
Hank C. Burnette; *Don't Mess With My Ducktail* . (SUN)
Get A Haircut
George Thorogood/Destroyers; *Haircut* .... (EMI)
Gray Haired Young Man
Don Potter; *Over The Rainbow* .... (MRR)
Hair
Cowsills; *Billboard Top Rock 'N' Roll Hits-1969* . (RHI)
Original Broadway Cast; *Hair* ....(RCA)
Haircut Song
Ray Stevens; *Greatest Hits-#2* .... (MCA)
I Have Returned .... (MCA)
Today's Country Classics-#3 .... (MCA)
I Dream Of Jeanie With Light Brown Hair
Al Jolson; *Story-#5* .... (MCA)
Joan Baez; *Diamonds & Rust* .... (A&M)
Mormon Tabernacle Choir; *Beautiful Dreamer* ...(COL)
Greatest Hits-#3 ....(COL)
Old Beloved Songs ....(COL)
I'm Gonna Wash That Man Right Outta...
Kiri Te Kanawa/Original Cast; *South Pacific* ...(COL)
Mary Martin/Original Cast; *South Pacific* ....(COL)
Mitzi Gaynor; *ST/South Pacific* ....(RCA)
Weather Girls; *Success* ....(COL)
Kinky Afro
Happy Mondays; *Pills 'N' Thrills & Bellyaches* ... (ELE)
Lend Me Your Comb
Beatles; *45* .... (CLT)
Carl Perkins; *Original Golden Hits* .... (SUN)
Original Sun Greatest Hits .... (RHI)
Long Hair Queer
Vandals; *Slippery When Ill* .... (RES)

Long Haired Country Boy
Charlie Daniels Band; *Decade Of Hits* .... (EPI)
Fire On The Mountain .... (EPI)
Me & The Boys .... (EPI)
South's Greatest Hits-#2 ....(CPC)
Truckers' Jukebox-#2 ....(COL)
Volunteer Jam-#3 & 4 .... (EPI)
Long Haired Guys From England
Too Much Joy; *Cereal Killers* .... (GIA)
Longhaired Redneck
David Allan Coe; *17 Greatest Hits* ....(COL)
For The Record-First 10 Years ....(COL)
Longhaired Redneck ....(COL)
Pencil Thin Mustache
Jimmy Buffett; *Boats Beaches Bars & Ballads* ... (MGR)
Living & Dying In 3/4 Time .... (MCA)
Songs You Know By Heart .... (MCA)
You Had To Be There .... (MCA)
Permanent Waves
Kinks; *Misfits* .... (ARI)
Red Headed Irishman
J.P. Fraley & Annadeene; *Wild Rose Of The*
Mountain .... (ROU)
Red Headed Stranger
Willie Nelson; *Red Headed Stranger* ....(COL)
San Francisco (Be Sure To Wear Some...)
Scott McKenzie; *Nuggets-#10-Folk Rock* .... (RHI)
Rock Artifacts-#3 ....(COL)
ST/Forrest Gump ....(EPX)
Summer Of Love .... (RHI)
Scarlet Ribbons
Harry Belafonte; *All-Time Greatest Hits-#1* ......(RCA)
Legendary Performer ....(RCA)
This Is ....(RCA)
Kingston Trio; *At Large/Here We Go Again!* ...(CAP)
Capitol Collectors Series ....(CAP)
Lennon Sisters; *Best Of* .... (RAN)
Les Paul; *Legend & The Legacy-#1-4* ....(CAP)
NRBQ; *Diggin' Uncle Q* .... (ROU)
Patti Page; *16 Most Requested Songs* ....(COL)
Roger Whittaker; *Classics Collections-#2* .... (LIB)
She Ain't Got No Hair
Professor Longhair; *Mardi Gras In Baton Rouge* (RHI)
Silver Haired Daddy Of Mine
Frank Yankovic; *I Wish I Was 18 Again* .... (SMA)
Sister Golden Hair
America; *Billboard Top Rock 'N' Roll Hits-1975* . (RHI)
History-Greatest Hits .... (WB)
In Concert ....(CAP)
Suicide Blonde
INXS; *Live Baby Live* .... (ATL)
X .... (ATL)
That Silver Haired Daddy Of Mine
Doc Watson; *My Dear Old Southern Home* ....(SH)
Gene Autry; *Country Music Hall Of Fame* ....(COL)
Uneasy Rider
Charlie Daniels Band; *Decade Of Hits* .... (EPI)
Homesick Heroes .... (EPI)
Super Hits/'70s-Have A Nice Day-#11 .... (RHI)
Uneasy Rider .... (EPI)
Wind Blows Her Hair
Seeds; *Nuggets-#9-Acid Rock* .... (RHI)

ANATOMY: HANDS, Fingers

See Also: Other Anatomy Categories

Bird In The Hand
Velvelettes; *25 Hard-To-Find Motown*
Classics-#3 .... (MOT)
Burning Fingers
Shawn Phillips; *Collaboration* ....(A&M)
Circle Of Hands
Uriah Heep; *Demons & Lizards* .... (MER)
Live .... (MER)
Clap Hands, Here Comes Charlie
Barbra Streisand; *ST/Funny Lady* .... (BC)
Charlie Barnet; *Big Band-1967* .... (MOB)
Clap Hands, Here Comes Charlie ....(BLU)
Complete-#6 ....(RCA)
Cold Hands From New York
Gordon Lightfoot; *United Artists Collection* ...... (EMI)
Country's In The Best Of Hands
Original Cast; *Li'l Abner* .... (COL)

Crack Pipe (Burnin' My Hand)
Coolies; *Doug (A Rock Opera & Comic Book)* .... (DB)
Daddy's Hands
Holly Dunn; *Country Love Songs* .... (WB)
Holly Dunn .... (MTM)
Devil's Right Hand
Steve Earle; *Essential* .... (MCA)
Steve Earle/Dukes; *Early Tracks* .... (EPI)
Shut Up & Die Like An Aviator .... (MCA)
Waylon Jennings; *Will The Wolf Survive* .... (MCA)
Everything You Touch
Smokey Robinson; *Love Smokey* .... (MOT)
Fingerprint File
Rolling Stones; *It's Only Rock 'N' Roll* .... (RS)
Love You Live .... (RS)
Goldfinger
Shirley Bassey; *13 Original James Bond Themes* .. (EMI)
Best Of .... (EMI)
Great Performances .... (LIB)
Greatest Hits .... (EMI)
Live At Carnegie Hall .... (UA)
ST/Goldfinger .... (UA)
Hand In Hand
BoDeans; *Home* .... (SLS)
Dire Straits; *Making Movies* .... (WB)
Elmore James; *Collectables Blues Collection-#3* .. (CLT)
Golden Classics .... (CLT)
Elvis Costello; *This Year's Model* .... (COL)
Phil Collins; *Face Value* .... (ATL)
Three O'Clock; *Arrive Without Traveling* .... (IRS)
Hand Of Fate
Rolling Stones; *Black & Blue* .... (RS)
Hand That Feeds
Aerosmith; *Draw The Line* .... (COL)
Hand That Rocks The Cradle
Glen Campbell; *Country Classics-#10-1987* .... (MCA)
Still Within The Sound Of My Voice .... (MCA)
Smiths; *Smiths* .... (SIR)
Hand To Hold On To
John Cougar Mellencamp; *American Fool* .... (RIV)
Hands Across The Table
Art Tatum; *Tatum Group Masterpieces-#4-Part 2* (PAB)
Hands To Heaven
Breathe; *All That Jazz* .... (A&M)
Healing Hands Of Time
Willie Nelson; *Healing Hands Of Time* .... (LIB)
He's Got The Whole World In His Hands
Laurie London; *45* .... (ERI)
Mormon Tabernacle Choir; *Greatest Hits-#2* .... (COL)
Odetta; *Essential* .... (VAN)
Hold An Old Friend's Hand
Rita Coolidge; *Fall Into Spring* .... (A&M)
Tiffany; *Hold An Old Friend's Hand* .... (MCA)
Hold My Hand
Hootie/Blowfish; *Cracked Rear View* .... (ATL)
Holdin' A Good Hand
Lee Greenwood; *Holdin' A Good Hand* .... (CAP)
Home In My Hand
Dave Edmunds; *Repeat When Necessary* .... (SS)
Foghat; *Best Of* .... (RHI)
Energized .... (RHI)
Live .... (RHI)
Human Hands
Elvis Costello/Attractions; *Imperial Bedroom* ....(COL)
Human Touch
Bruce Springsteen; *Human Touch* ....(COL)
Elvis Costello/Attractions; *Get Happy!* ....(RYK)
Joe Jackson; *Blaze Of Glory* ....(A&M)
Rick Springfield; *Greatest Hits* ....(RCA)
Living In Oz ....(RCA)
I Touch Myself
Divinyls; *Divinyls* .... (VIA)
I Want To Hold Your Hand
Beatles; *1962-1966* ....(CAP)
20 Greatest Hits ....(CAP)
Meet The Beatles ....(CAP)
Past Masters-#1 & 2 ....(CAP)
Lakeside; *Your Wish Is My Command* .... (SLR)
I Want To Touch You
Catherine Wheel; *Ferment* ....(FON)
Keep Your Hands To Yourself
Georgia Satellites; *Georgia Satellites* .... (ELE)
Hank Williams, Jr.; *Born To Boogie* ....(W/C)

Lay Your Hands On Me
Bon Jovi; *New Jersey* .... (MER)
Peter Gabriel; *Security* .... (GEF)
Thompson Twins; *Greatest Mixes-Best Of* .... (ARI)
Greenpeace/Rainbow Warriors .... (GEF)
Here's To Future Days .... (ARI)
ST/Perfect .... (ARI)
Lend A Helpin' Hand
Lynyrd Skynyrd; *Skynyrd's First & Last* .... (MCA)
Look Heart No Hands
Randy Travis; *Greatest Hits-#2* .... (WB)
Lord Take My Hand
Maddox Brothers & Rose; *On The Air-#1 & 2* .. (ARH)
Love Is In Control (Finger On The...)
Donna Summer; *Donna Summer* .... (GEF)
Lovely Hula Hands
101 Strings; *Sound Of Magnificence* .... (ALS)
Magic Fingers (25 Cents)
Birdsongs Of The Mesozoic; *Faultline* .... (CUN)
Man With The Golden Thumb
Jerry Reed; *Man With The Golden Thumb* ......(RCA)
My Fate Is In Your Hands
Fats Waller; *Piano Solos (1929-1941)* ....(RCA)
Rare Piano Roll Solos-#3 ....(BIO)
Turn On The Heat-Fats Waller Piano Solos ..... (BLU)
On The Other Hand
Randy Travis; *Greatest Hits-#1* .... (WB)
Storms Of Life .... (WB)
Praying Hands
Devo; *Live-Mongoloid Years* ....(RYK)
Q: Are We Not Men? A: We Are Devo! .... (WB)
Precious Lord, Take My Hand
Linda Hopkins; *How Blue Can You Get* .... (QKS)
Preservation Hall Jazz Band; *Best Of* ....(COL)
Put That Ring On My Finger
Andrews Sisters; *50th Anniversary Collection-#2* (MCA)
Woody Herman; *Best Of The Big Bands* ....(COL)
Put Your Hand In The Hand
Anne Murray; *Country* ....(CAP)
Danny's Song ....(CAP)
Snowbird ....(CAP)
Elvis Presley; *Canadian Tribute* ....(RCA)
Now ....(RCA)
Ocean; *Super Hits/'70s-Have A Nice Day-#4* .. (RHI)
Put Your Hands On The Screen
Martin Briley; *One Night With A Stranger* .... (MER)
Put Your Hands Together
O'Jays; *Live In London* .... (PI)
Ship Ahoy .... (PI)
Raise Your Hand
Bruce Springsteen/E Street Band;
Live-1975-1985 ....(COL)
Eddie Floyd; *Knock On Wood* ....(ATL)
Stax/Volt Revue-#2-Live In Paris ....(ATL)
J. Geils Band; *Blow Your Face Out* .... (ATL)
Raise Your Hands
Bon Jovi; *Slippery When Wet* .... (MER)
Reach Out And Touch
Diana Ross; *All The Great Hits* .... (MOT)
Anthology .... (MOT)
Live At Caesar's Palace .... (MOT)
Most Played Songs On America's Jukeboxes .... (MOT)
Motown Story .... (MOT)
Riding My Thumb To Mexico
Johnny Rodriguez; *40 Years Of Country*
Music-#3-1970-1979 ....(MER)
All I Ever Meant To Do .... (MER)
Desperado .... (MER)
Greatest Hits .... (MER)
Right Hand Man
Eddy Raven; *Best Of* ....(RCA)
Right Hand Man ....(RCA)
Right Hand Of God
Move; *Yeah Whatever* .... (ATL)
Right In The Palm Of Your Hand
Crystal Gayle; *Crystal* .... (EMI)
Favorites .... (LIB)
Mel McDaniel; *Countryfied* ....(CAP)
Right Left Hand
George Jones; *Greatest Country Hits/'80s-1987* ..(COL)
More Hot Country Requests-#2 .... (EPI)
Wine-Colored Glasses .... (EPI)

Ring On Her Finger, Time On Her Hands
Lee Greenwood; *Greatest Hits* .... (MCA)
   Inside Out .... (MCA)
Sable On Blond
Stevie Nicks; *Wild Heart* .... (MOD)
Shake A Hand
La Vern Baker; *Soul On Fire* .... (ATL)
Little Richard; *Fabulous* .... (SPE)
   Georgia Peach .... (SPE)
Shake And Fingerpop
Junior Walker/All-Stars; *All The Great Hits* ..... (MOT)
   Anthology .... (MOT)
   Greatest Hits .... (MOT)
   Shotgun .... (MOT)
Shake My Mother's Hand
Bill Monroe/Blue Grass Boys; *Mule Skinner Blues* (RCA)
She Put Her Hand Where My Money Was
John Lee; *Down At The Depot* .... (ROU)
Slow Hand
Conway Twitty; *Greatest Hits* ....(CCB)
   Latest Greatest Hits-#1 .... (WB)
   Number One's-Warner Bros. Years .... (WB)
Pointer Sisters; *Black & White* .... (PNT)
   Greatest Hits ....(RCA)
   Sweet & Soulful ....(RCA)
Snap Your Fingers
Ronnie Milsap; *Greatest Hits-#3* .... (RCA)
   Heart & Soul ....(RCA)
Teena Marie; *Ivory* .... (EPI)
Soul Finger
Bar-Kays; *Atlantic Rhythm & Blues-#6*
(1966-1969) .... (ATL)
   Soul Finger .... (RHI)
   Soul Shots-#3-Soul Twist .... (RHI)
   Top Of The Stax-Twenty Greatest Hits-#2 ...... (STX)
Sun In My Hand
Scorpions; *Best Of-#2* ....(RCA)
   In Trance ....(RCA)
Take My Hand
Los Lobos; *The Neighborhood* ....(SLS)
Taking My Life In Your Hands
Elvis Costello/Brodsky Quartet; *Juliet Letters* ..... (WB)
Takin' Love Into My Own Hands
Sylvester; *12 By 12-Collection* .... (MTO)
Tear In Your Hand
Tori Amos; *Little Earthquakes* .... (ATL)
Tender Moment
Lee Roy Parnell; *Love Without Mercy* .... (ARI)
This Bottle (In My Hand)
David Allan Coe & George Jones; *17 Greatest*
Hits ....(COL)
   For The Record-First 10 Years ....(COL)
Time On My Hands
Billie Holiday; *Billie Holiday* ....(COL)
   Quintessential-#8-1939-1940 ....(COL)
   Story-#2 ....(COL)
Duke Ellington; *Lullaby Of Birdland* .... (INT)
Glenn Miller; *Best Of The Big Bands* ....(COL)
Sweet Honey In The Rock; *Good News* .... (FF)
Tips Of My Fingers
Bill Anderson; *Greatest Hits-#1* .... (MCA)
   Story .... (MCA)
Eddy Arnold; *Best Of-#2* ....(RCA)
Roy Clark; *Best Of* .... (MCA)
   Greatest Hits-#1 .... (MCA)
   Yesterday When I Was Young .... (MCA)
Steve Wariner; *I Am Ready* .... (ARI)
Too Many Hands
Eagles; *One Of These Nights* .... (ASY)
Too Much Time On My Hands
Styx; *Caught In The Act* .... (A&M)
   Classics-#15 .... (A&M)
   Paradise Theatre .... (A&M)
Touch A Hand, Make A Friend
Oak Ridge Boys; *Country's Greatest Hits-#4* ..... (MSP)
   Greatest Hits-#3 .... (MCA)
   Step On Out .... (MSP)
Staple Singers; *15 Original Big Hits-#4* .... (STX)
   Chronicle .... (STX)
   Top Of The Stax-20 Greatest Hits-#2 ....(STX)
Touch Me (All Night Long)
Cathy Dennis; *Move To This* .... (POL)
Touch The Hand
Bryan Adams; *Waking Up The Neighbours* ...... (A&M)

Under My Thumb
Rolling Stones; *12 X 5* .... (AKO)
   Aftermath .... (AKO)
   Got Live If You Want It .... (AKO)
   Hot Rocks 1964-1971 .... (AKO)
   Still Life-American Concert 1981 ....(RS)
Who; *Who's Missing* ....(MCA)
White Knuckles
Elvis Costello/Attractions; *Trust* ....(RYK)
Will Jesus Wash The Bloodstains From...
Exene Cervenka; *Running Sacred* .... (RHI)
Willie & The Hand Jive
Eric Clapton; *451 Ocean Boulevard* ....(POL)
   Time Pieces-Best Of ....(POL)
George Thorogood/Destroyers; *Maverick* .... (EMI)
Johnny Otis; *All-Time Greatest Hits Of Rock &*
Roll ....(CCB)
   Capitol Years ....(CAP)
   Let The Good Times Roll ....(CAP)
World Is Changing Hands
Dave Davies; *Dave Davies* ....(RCA)
Wrapped Around Your Finger
Police; *Every Breath You Take-The Singles* ...... (A&M)
   Synchronicity .... (A&M)
You're Gonna Get Your Fingers Burned
Alan Parsons Project; *Eye In The Sky* .... (ARI)

ANATOMY: HEAD

Anotherloverholenyohead
Prince; *Parade* .... (WB)
Bald Head
Professor Longhair; *Crawfish Fiesta* ....(ALG)
   Last Mardi Gras .... (ATL)
Banging My Head Against The Moon
John David Souther; *Black Rose* .... (ASY)
Bird On My Head
David Seville; *45* .... (UA)
Bullet In The Head
Rage Against The Machine; *Rage Against The*
Machine ....(EPA)
Can't Get It Out Of My Head
Electric Light Orchestra; *Eldorado* ....(JET)
   Exposition .... (EPI)
   Greatest Hits ....(JET)
   Ole ELO ....(JET)
Crazy Baldhead
Bob Marley/Wailers; *Rastaman Vibration* ....(TUF)
   Rebel Music ....(TUF)
   Songs Of Freedom ....(TUF)
Dope Head Blues
Victoria Spivey; *News & The Blues-Telling It Like It*
Is ....(COL)
Goin' Out Of My Head
Lettermen; *All-Time Greatest Hits* ....(CAP)
   Best Of-#2 ....(CAP)
Little Anthony/Imperials; *Best Of* .... (RHI)
   EMI Legends Or Rock 'N' Roll-24 Greatest ..... (EMI)
Hard Headed Woman
Cat Stevens; *Greatest Hits* .... (A&M)
   Tea For The Tillerman .... (A&M)
Elvis Presley; *Billboard Top Rock 'N' Roll*
Hits-1958 ....(RCA)
   Number One Hits ....(RCA)
   ST/King Creole ....(RCA)
   Top Ten Hits ....(RCA)
   Worldwide 50 Gold Award Hits-#1 ....(RCA)
Head First
Babys; *Anthology* .... (CHR)
   Head First .... (CHR)
Head Games
Foreigner; *Head Games* .... (ATL)
   Records .... (ATL)
Head On
Jesus & Mary Chain; *Automatic* .... (WB)
Head Over Heels
Accept; *Accept* .... (POR)
Go-Go's; *Greatest* .... (IRS)
   Talk Show .... (IRS)
Tears For Fears; *Songs From The Big Chair* ..... (MER)
Tony Terry; *Tony Terry* .... (EPI)
Head To Toe
Lisa Lisa & Cult Jam; *Spanish Fly* ....(COL)

Headkeeper
Dave Mason; *Classic Rock-#2* .... (MCA)
    Headkeeper .... (MCA)
    It's Like You Never Left .... (COL)
    Very Best Of .... (MCA)
Headlong
Queen; *Classic Queen* .... (HOL)
    Collection .... (HOL)
    Innuendo .... (HOL)
Hold Your Head Up
Argent; *Anthology* .... (EPI)
    Encore .... (EPI)
    Rock Artifacts-#1-From The Vaults .... (COL)
    ST/Queen's Logic .... (EPI)
I Wish You Could Have Turned My Head
Oak Ridge Boys; *Bobbie Sue* .... (MCA)
(Lay Your Head On My) Pillow
Tony Toni Tone; *Sons Of Soul* .... (WIN)
Man With The Lightbulb Head
Robyn Hitchcock/Egyptians; *Fegmania* .... (SLS)
My Head Hurts, My Feet Stink...
Jimmy Buffett; *Havana Daydreamin'* .... (MCA)
My Head's In Mississippi
ZZ Top; *Greatest Hits* .... (WB)
    Recycler .... (WB)
Mystical Potato Head Groove Thing
Joe Satriani; *Flying In A Blue Dream* .... (REL)
Over My Head
Fleetwood Mac; *25 Years-The Chain* .... (WB)
    Fleetwood Mac .... (RPR)
    Greatest Hits .... (WB)
    Live .... (WB)
Potato Head Blues
Louis Armstrong; *Best Of The Decca Years-#2-The*
Composer .... (MCA)
    You Rascal You .... (POE)
Pumpkin Head
Dharma Bums; *Bliss* .... (FRN)
Put Your Head On My Shoulder
Lettermen; *All Time Greatest Hits* .... (CAP)
    Capitol Collectors Series .... (CAP)
Paul Anka; *21 Golden Hits* .... (RCA)
    30th Anniversary Collection .... (RHI)
    Oldies But Goodies-#1 .... (OSR)
    Remember Diana .... (RCA)
    Sings His Favorites .... (RCA)
Radio Head
Talking Heads; *True Stories* .... (SIR)
Raindrops Keep Fallin' On My Head
B.J. Thomas; *16 Greatest Hits* .... (TRP)
    Best Of .... (DOM)
    Greatest Hits .... (RHI)
    ST/Butch Cassidy & The Sundance Kid .... (A&M)
    ST/Forrest Gump .... (EPX)
    '70s Greatest Rock Hits-#9-#1 Hits .... (PRY)
Screaming Skull
Fleshtones; *Living Legends* .... (IRS)
Shake Your Heads
Accept; *Accept* .... (POR)
    Restless & Wild .... (POR)
Suedehead
Morrissey; *Bona Drag* .... (SIR)
    Viva Hate .... (SIR)
Two Headed Cow
Ennui; *Olive* .... (SLM)
Two Headed Dog (Red Temple Prayer)
Roky Erickson; *You're Gonna Miss Me-Best Of* .. (RES)
Two Headed Man
Lonnie Brooks; *Genuine Houserockin' Music-#3* ..(ALG)
Two Headed Sex Change
Cramps; *Look Mom No Head!* .... (RES)
Up Above My Head/Blind Bartimus
Marty Stuart & Jerry & Tammy Sullivan; *Red Hot +*
Country .... (MER)
Voices In My Head
Naked Eyes; *Best Of* .... (EMI)
Voices Inside My Head
Police; *Zenyatta Mondatta* .... (A&M)
You Go To My Head
Billie Holiday; *At Storyville* .... (BL)
    First Verve Sessions .... (VRV)
Bing Crosby; *Radio Years* .... (CRS)

Frank Sinatra; *Nice 'N' Easy* .... (CAP)
    Round #1 .... (CAP)
    Voice-The Columbia Years-1943-1952 .... (COL)
Linda Ronstadt; *For Sentimental Reasons* .... (ASY)

ANATOMY: LEGS
See Also: Other Anatomy Categories

Death On Two Legs
Queen; *Live Killers* .... (HOL)
    Night At The Opera .... (HOL)
Don't Feel My Leg
Maria Muldaur; *Maria Muldaur* .... (RPR)
Down On My Knees
Beth Nielsen Chapman; *Beth Nielsen Chapman* .. (RPR)
Bread; *Anthology* .... (ELE)
    Baby I'm A-Want You .... (ELE)
    Best Of .... (ELE)
Trisha Yearwood; *Hearts In Armor* .... (MCA)
Get A Leg Up
John Mellencamp; *Whenever We Wanted* .... (MER)
Hot Legs
Rod Stewart; *Absolutely Live* .... (WB)
    Footloose & Fancy Free .... (WB)
    Greatest Hits .... (WB)
    Storyteller-Complete Anthology-1964-1990 ...... (WB)
Just Another Thigh
Roxy Music; *Siren* .... (ATC)
Legs
ZZ Top; *Eliminator* .... (WB)
Long Legged Guitar Pickin' Man
Johnny Cash & June Carter; *Greatest Hits-#2* ....(COL)
Long Legged Hannah (From Butte, Montana)
Jesse Hunter; *A Man Like Me* .... (BNA)
Lord Of The Thighs
Aerosmith; *Classics Live* .... (COL)
    Gems .... (COL)
    Get Your Wings .... (COL)
    Live! Bootleg .... (COL)
    Pandora's Box .... (COL)
Skinny Legs & All
Joe Tex; *Billboard Top R&B Hits* .... (RHI)
    I Believe I'm Gonna Make It!-Best Of .... (RHI)
    Soul Years .... (ATL)
Televisions On My Leg
Squirrels; *What Gives?* .... (PL)
Thigh Ride
Tawatha; *Welcome To My Dream* .... (EPI)

ANATOMY: LIPS
See Also: Other Anatomy Categories

Cautious Lip
Blondie; *Plastic Letters* .... (CHR)
I Wanna Hear It From Your Lips
Eric Carmen; *Eric Carmen* .... (GEF)
Louise Mandrell; *Dreamin'* .... (RCA)
Lip Service
Elvis Costello; *This Year's Model* .... (COL)
Jimmy Buffett; *Somewhere Over China* .... (MCA)
John Astley; *Everyone Loves The Pilot Except The*
Crew .... (ATL)
Michael Franks; *Camera Never Lies* .... (WB)
Lips Like Sugar
Echo/Bunnymen; *Echo/Bunnymen* .... (SIR)
    Just Say Yes...Sire's Winter CD Sampler .... (SIR)
Lipstick On Your Collar
Connie Francis; *Very Best Of* .... (POL)
Lipstick Sunset
John Hiatt; *Bring The Family* .... (A&M)
Lipstick, Powder & Paint
Big Joe Turner; *Rhythm & Blues Years* .... (ATL)
Lyin' Comes So Easy To Your Lips
David Allan Coe; *D.A.C.* .... (COL)
Our Lips Are Sealed
Go-Go's; *Beauty & The Beat* .... (IRS)
    Greatest .... (IRS)
Read My Lips
Betsy Rose; *Sacred Ground* .... (KAL)
Duran Duran; *Liberty* .... (CAP)
Jimmy Somerville; *Singles Collection-1984-1990* .(LON)
Loverboy; *Wildside* .... (COL)

Mary Chapin Carpenter; *Hitchhiker Exampler* ....(COL)
   Hot Country Rock-#2 ....(EPI)
   State Of The Heart ....(COL)
Melba Moore; *Read My Lips* ....(CAP)
Michael Franks; *Skin Dive* ....(WB)
Talk Back Trembling Lips
Johnny Tillotson; *Cruisin'-1964* .... (INC)
These Lips Don't Know How To Say Goodbye
Doug Stone; *Doug Stone* .... (EPI)
   Greatest Country Hits/'90s-1991 ....(COL)
Forester Sisters; *Sincerely* ....(WB)
Touch Of Your Lips
Ben Webster; *Compact Jazz-Ben Webster-Verve
Years* ....(VRV)
Nat King Cole; *Nat King Cole* ....(CAP)
Tony Bennett & Bill Evans; *Tony Bennett & Bill
Evans* ....(FAN)

ANATOMY: MOUTH, Teeth, Tongue

*See Also: ANATOMY: FACE, other ANATOMY
categories, KISSING, SMILE*

All I Want For Christmas
David Seville/Chipmunks; *Christmas With The
Chipmunks-#2* .... (EMI)
Nat King Cole; *Let It Snow!-Cuddly Christmas
Classics* ....(CAP)
New Edition; *Christmas All Over The World* ....(MCA)
Ray Charles; *Spirit Of Christmas* ....(COL)
Spike Jones; *Christmas* ....(RHI)
   Dr. Demento's Greatest-#6 ....(RHI)
Big Mouth Blues
Gram Parsons; *G.P./Grievous Angel* ....(RPR)
   Gram Parsons/Fallen Angels Live 1973 ....(SIE)
Cloud On My Tongue
Tori Amos; *Under The Pink* ....(ATL)
Coming Down (Drug Tongue)
Cult; *The Cult* ....(SIR)
I Tan't Wait Till Quithmuth Day
Mel Blanc; *Christmas Comedy Classics* ....(PRY)
Kicked In The Teeth
AC/DC; *Powerage* ....(ATL)
Only Tongue Can Tell
Trash Can Sinatras; *Cake* ....(LON)
Pulling Teeth
Green Day; *Dookie* ....(RPR)
Pulling Teeth (Anesthesia)
Metallica; *Kill 'Em All* ....(ELE)
Tip Of My Tongue
Grass Roots; *Anthology-1965-1975* .... (RHI)
John Hiatt; *Bring The Family* ....(A&M)
Tommy Quickly; *History Of British Rock-#1* .....(RHI)
Tubes; *Best Of* ....(CAP)
Your Gold Teeth
Steely Dan; *Countdown To Ecstasy* ....(MCA)
Your Gold Teeth II
Steely Dan; *Katy Lied* ....(MCA)

ANATOMY: PRIVATES

See Also: Other Anatomy Categories, SEX

Baby Baby (Just A Little More Head)
2 Live Crew; *Sports Weekend-As Clean As They Wanna
Be* ....(LUK)
Big Balls
AC/DC; *Dirty Deeds Done Dirt Cheap* ....(ATL)
Big Chested Girls
Prince Charles/City Beat Band; *Stone Killers!* ....(ROI)
Boobs A Lot
Fugs; *First Album* ....(ESP)
   Fugs 4 Rounders Score ....(ESP)
   Greatest Hits-#1 ....(PVC)
Holy Modal Rounders; *Dr. Demento's Delights* ....(WB)
Boogie In Your Butt
Eddie Murphy; *45* ....(COL)
Bop Gun
Ice Cube & George Clinton; *S* ....(PRY)
Bounce Your Boobies
Rusty Warren; *Dr. Demento's Greatest-#3* ....(RHI)

Davy's Dinghy
Ruth Wallis; *Dr. Demento's Dementia Royale* .... (RHI)
   Dr. Demento's Greatest Novelties-#2 ....(RHI)
Dick In The Dirt
Sammy Hagar; *VOA* ....(GEF)
Don't Go Home With Your Hard On
Leonard Cohen; *Death Of A Ladies' Man* ....(COL)
Don't Touch Me There
Tubes; *T.R.A.S.H.* ....(A&M)
   What Do You Want From-Live ....(A&M)
   Young & Rich ....(A&M)
Don't Use Your Penis (For A Brain)
Romanovsky & Phillips; *Trouble In Paradise* .....(FRE)
Fish & Tits
Barefoot Jerry; *Barefoot Jerry's Grocery* ....(MON)
I Touch Myself
Divinyls; *Divinyls* .... (VIA)
I.L.B.T.s (I Like Big Tits)
Joe Walsh; *45* ....(WB)
   You Bought It-You Name It ....(WB)
Lemon Song
Led Zeppelin; *II* ....(ATL)
Longview
Green Day; *Dookie* ....(RPR)
Love Gun
Kiss; *Alive 2* ....(CAS)
   Double Platinum ....(CAS)
   Love Gun ....(CAS)
   Smashes Thrashes & Hits ....(MER)
More Than Seven Dwarfs In Penis-Land
Ron Geesin; *ST/The Body* ....(RES)
Muscle Of Love
Alice Cooper; *Greatest Hits* ....(WB)
   Muscle Of Love ....(MET)
My Ding-A-Ling
Chuck Berry; *Best Of The Best Of* ....(IGR)
   Billboard Top Rock 'N' Roll Hits-1972 ....(RHI)
   Chess Box ....(CSS)
   Roll Over Beethoven ....(ALL)
   Toronto Rock 'N' Roll Revival-#2 ....(ACC)
My Toot Toot
Fats Domino; *Greatest Hits* ....(MCA)
Fats Domino & Doug Kershaw; *Alligator
Stomp-#2* .... (RHI)
Rockin' Sidney; *19 Hot Country Requests-#3* ......(EPI)
   Alligator Stomp-#1 ....(RHI)
Nutted By Reality
Nick Lowe; *Pure Pop For Now People* ....(COL)
Pass The Pussy
A.T.E.E.M.; *A.T.E.E.M.* ....(SEL)
Penis Dimension
Frank Zappa; *Disconnected Synapses* .... (RHI)
Penis Envy
Uncle Bonsai; *Lonely Grain Of Corn* ....(FRK)
Penis Song (Not The Noel Coward Song)
Monty Python; *Sings* .... (VIA)
Phallic Marauder
Squadron; *Fatal Strike* ....(WAR)
Pop My Dick Song
Sloppy Seconds; *First Seven Inches...& Then
Some!* .... (TNG)
Pop That Pussy
2 Live Crew; *Sports Weekend-As Nasty As They Wanna
Be* ....(LUK)
Red Neck Friend
Jackson Browne; *For Everyman* ....(ASY)
Rocket In My Pocket
Little Feat; *Hoy-Hoy!* ....(WB)
   Time Loves A Hero ....(WB)
   Waiting For Columbus ....(WB)
Silicone Sally
Slammin' Gladys; *Slammin' Gladys* ....(PRY)
Sugar Walls
Sheena Easton; *Dance Mix* ....(EMI)
   Private Heaven ....(EMI)
Sweat Of My Balls
CB4/Daddy-O-Hi-C; *ST/CB4* .... (MCA)
Testicle Of God (& It Was Good)
Gaye Bykers On Acid; *Stewed To The Gills* ......(CRL)
Texas Tattoo
Gibson/Miller Band; *Steppin' Country* ....(COL)
   Where There's Smoke ....(EPI)
Thinking With The Wrong Head
Little Charlie/Nightcats; *Captured Live* ....(ALG)

Thrill My Gorilla
Alice Cooper; *Constrictor* .... (MCA)
Tit Photographer Blues
Fabulous Poodles; *Mirror Stars* .... (EPI)
Tits
Sparks; *Indiscreet* ....(OOP)
Titties And Beer
Kiss; *Alive 2* ....(CAS)
Double Platinum .... (CAS)
Rock & Roll Over .... (CAS)
Titties N' Beer
Frank Zappa; *Baby Snakes* ....(BAR)
In New York ....(BAR)
Titty City
Nasty Niggas; *Banned From The Planet* .... (CRI)
U Can't Touch This
Hammer; *Please Hammer Don't Hurt 'Em* ....(CAP)
Vasectomy
Limeliters; *Singing For The Fun* ....(CRS)
Wang Dang Sweet Poontang
Ted Nugent; *Cat Scratch Fever* .... (EPI)
Double Live Gonzo .... (EPI)

ANATOMY: REAR

See Also: Other Anatomy Categories, INSULTS

Asswhippin'
Fishbone; *Reality Of My Surroundings* ....(COL)
Baby Got Back
Sir Mix-A-Lot; *Mack Daddy* .... (DEF)
Backfield In Motion
Mel & Tim; *Collectables Presents-History Of Rock-#4* ....(CLT)
Oldies/Goodies-#2 .... (OSR)
Soul Shots-#2 ....(RHI)
Super Oldies/'60s-#10 .... (AUF)
Big Butt
Bobby Jimmy/Critters; *West Coast Rap-First Dynasty-#3* .... (RHI)
Big Fat Funky Booty
Spin Doctors; *Up For Grabs...Live* .... (EPA)
Butt Fuck
Human Sexual Response; *Fig. 15* .... (EAT)
Butt Naked
Charm; *Atrophy* .... (ATL)
Dr. Jeckyll & Mr. Hyde; *Champagne Of Rap* ....(PRO)
Dance Your Ass Off
Bohannon; *Dance Your Ass Off* .... (DAK)
Don't Kick Her In The Butt
Bobby Taylor & Carolyn Majors; *ST/Far Out Man* ....(CML)
Fat Bottomed Girls
Queen; *Greatest Hits* ....(HOL)
Jazz ....(HOL)
Get Off Your Ass & Jam
George Clinton/Parliament/Funkadelic; *Mothership Connection* ....(CAP)
Kick A Little
Little Texas; *Kick A Little* .... (WB)
Lyin' Ass Bitch
Fishbone; *Fishbone* ....(COL)
Meet De Boys On The Battlefront
Wild Tchoupitoulas; *Treacherous-History Of The Neville Bros.* .... (RHI)
Wild Tchoupitoulas .... (ISL)
My Ass Is On Fire
Mr. Bungle; *Mr. Bungle* .... (WB)
Rhythm (Devoted To Art Of Moving Butts)
Tribe Called Quest; *People's Instinctive Travels...* . (JVA)
Rump Shaker
Wreckx-N-Effect; *Hard Or Smooth* .... (MCA)
Shake Your Ass!
Blowfly; *Twisted World Of* ....(OPS)
Shake Your Booty
K.C./Sunshine Band; *Best Of* .... (RHI)
Greatest Hits .... (TK)
Mega Hits Dance Classics-#4 .... (PRY)
Part 3 .... (TK)
Shake Your Money Maker
Elmore James; *King Of The Slide Guitar* ....(CPC)
Fleetwood Mac; *Vintage Years* .... (SIR)
George Thorogood; *Born To Be Bad* .... (EMI)

Paul Butterfield; *Golden Butter* .... (ELE)
Paul Butterfield Blues Band .... (ELE)
Shake Your Tailfeather
Blues Brothers & Ray Charles; *ST/Blues Brothers* (ATL)
Tush
ZZ Top; *Best Of* ....(WB)
Fandango ....(WB)
Greatest Hits ....(WB)
Six Pack ....(WB)
ST/An Officer & A Gentleman .... (ISL)

ANATOMY: SHOULDER

See Also: Other Anatomy Categories

Cold On The Shoulder
Gordon Lightfoot; *Cold On The Shoulder* .... (RPR)
Gord's Gold ....(RPR)
Cry On My Shoulder
Bonnie Raitt; *Nick Of Time* ....(CAP)
Cry On Your Own Shoulder
General Public; *Hand To Mouth* .... (IRS)
Crying On Your Shoulder Again
Doug Stone; *Doug Stone* .... (EPI)
Over My Shoulder
Patty Loveless; *When Fallen Angels Fly* .... (EPI)
Put Your Head On My Shoulder
Lettermen; *All Time Greatest Hits* ....(CAP)
Capitol Collectors Series ....(CAP)
Paul Anka; *21 Golden Hits* ....(RCA)
30th Anniversary Collection .... (RHI)
Oldies But Goodies-#1 .... (OSR)
Remember Diana ....(RCA)
Sings His Favorites ....(RCA)
Rabbit On My Shoulder
P. Alsop/D. Crow/B. Phillips/H. Traum; *Silly Songs & Modern Lullabies* ....(BRR)
Sunshine On My Shoulders
John Denver; *Greatest Hits-#1* ....(RCA)
Take Me Home Country Roads & Other Hits ....(RCA)
There's A New Moon Over My Shoulder
Gene Autry; *Columbia Historic Edition* ....(COL)
Jimmie Davis; *Best Of* .... (MCA)
Country Music Hall Of Fame .... (MCA)
Golden Hits .... (PLN)
Tex Ritter; *Greatest Hits* ....(CCB)
There's A Rainbow 'Round My Shoulder
Al Jolson; *Jolson Sang 'Em* ....(BIO)
Mammy ....(POE)
Whose Shoulder Will You Cry On
Kitty Wells; *Greatest Hits-#1* ....(SO)

ANATOMY: SKIN

See Also: Other Anatomy Categories

Beauty Is Only Skin Deep
Temptations; *Anthology* .... (MOT)
Billboard Top R&B Hits-1966 .... (RHI)
Good Feeling Music/Big Chill-#1 .... (MOT)
Motown Story: First 25 Years .... (MOT)
Motown's Mustang-A Motown Video .... (MOT)
Flesh And Blood
Johnny Cash; *Biggest Hits* ....(COL)
Roxy Music; *Flesh And Blood* ....(ATC)
Flesh For Fantasy
Billy Idol; *Rebel Yell* .... (CHR)
Vital Idol .... (CHR)
In The Flesh
Blondie; *Best Of* .... (CHR)
Blondie .... (CHR)
Pink Floyd; *The Wall* ....(COL)
Roger Waters; *The Wall Live In Berlin* .... (MER)
In The Raw
Whispers; *Love Is Where You Find It* .... (SLR)
I've Got You Under My Skin
Four Seasons; *25th Anniversary Collection* .... (RHI)
Frank Sinatra; *At The Sands* ....(RPR)
Man & His Music ....(RPR)
Reprise Collection ....(RPR)
Round #1 ....(CAP)
Sinatra's Sinatra ....(RPR)
Songs For Swingin' Lovers ....(CAP)
Frank Sinatra & Bono; *Frank Sinatra Duets* ......(CAP)

Lose This Skin
Clash; *Sandinista* .... (EPI)
Mr. Skin
Spirit; *12 Dreams Of Dr. Sardonicus* .... (EPI)
Best Of .... (EPI)
Spirit Of '84 .... (MER)
Time Circle .... (EPI)
Skin I'm In
Cameo; *Machismo* .... (ATA)
Sly/Family Stone; *Fresh* .... (EPI)
Under My Skin
Dandelion; *I Think I'm Gonna Be Sick* .... (RUC)

ANATOMY: VARIOUS

See Also: Other Anatomy Categories, EYES, HEART, SEX, SMILE

Ain't Got No (I Got Life)
Original Cast; *ST/Hair* .... (RCA)
And A Bang On The Ear
Waterboys; *Fisherman's Blues* .... (ENS)
Bad Liver & A Broken Heart
Tom Waits; *Small Change* .... (ASY)
Belly Button Window
Jimi Hendrix; *Cry Of Love* .... (RPR)
Belly Up To The Bar, Boys
Debbie Reynolds; *ST/Unsinkable Molly Brown* .. (MCA)
Original Cast; *Unsinkable Molly Brown* .... (CAP)
Chest Pains
Greg "Fingers" Taylor; *Chest Pains* .... (MCA)
Death At One's Elbow
Smiths; *Strangeways Here We Come* .... (SIR)
Earache My Eye featuring Alice Bowie
Cheech & Chong; *Dr. Demento 20th Anniversary Collection* .... (RHI)
Greatest Hit .... (WB)
Wedding Album .... (WB)
Flava In Ya Ear
Craig Mack; *Funk Da World* .... (ARI)
I Love Your Guts
Elvis Hitler; *Disgraceland* .... (RES)
Jealous Bone
Patty Loveless; *Greatest Hits* .... (MCA)
Up Against My Heart .... (MCA)
Knee Deep In The Blues
Guy Mitchell; *16 Most Requested Songs* .... (COL)
Marty Robbins; *Columbia Country Classics-#2* ...(COL)
Greatest Hits .... (COL)
Lifetime Of Song-1951-1982 .... (COL)
Memphis Hip Shake
Cult; *Electric* .... (SIR)
Moon Is Still Over Her Shoulder
Michael Johnson; *Best Of* .... (RCA)
Country Love Songs .... (RCA)
That's That .... (RCA)
Wings .... (RCA)
Night In My Veins
Pretenders; *Last Of The Independents* .... (SIR)
Pencil Neck Geek
Fred Blassie; *Dr. Demento 20th Anniversary Collection* .... (RHI)
Dr. Demento's Dementia Royale .... (RHI)
Dr. Demento's Greatest-#4-1970s .... (RHI)
Physical
Olivia Newton-John; *Back To Basics-Essential Collection* ....(GEF)
Greatest Hits-#2 .... (MCA)
Physical .... (MCA)
Sat In Your Lap
Kate Bush; *The Dreaming* .... (EMI)
Whole Story .... (EMI)
Shake Your Hips
Love Sculpture; *Blues Helping* .... (AMR)
Rolling Stones; *Exile On Main Street* .... (RS)
Slim Harpo; *Best Of* .... (RHI)
Suck On The Jugular
Rolling Stones; *Voodoo Lounge* .... (VIA)
Up The Neck
Pretenders; *Pretenders* .... (SIR)
Van Gogh's Left Ear
Kenny Garrett; *Black Hope* .... (WB)

Wear My Ring Around Your Neck
Elvis Presley; *Golden Records-#2* ....(RCA)
Hits Like Never Before-Essential-#3 ....(RCA)
Top Ten Hits ....(RCA)
Worldwide 50 Gold Award Hits-#1&2 ....(RCA)
Ricky Van Shelton; *Greatest Hits Plus* ....(COL)

ANGELS

See Also: GOD, HEAVEN, HELL

And The Angels Sing
Ella Fitzgerald; *Lady Time* .... (PAB)
Angel
Aerosmith; *Permanent Vacation* .... (GEF)
Angela Winbush; *Sharp* .... (MER)
Aretha Franklin; *30 Greatest Hits* .... (ATL)
Atlanta Rhythm Section; *3rd Annual Pipe Dream* (POL)
Are You Ready .... (POL)
Bonnie Raitt; *Nine Lives* .... (WB)
Bruce Springsteen; *Greetings From Asbury Park, NJ* ....(COL)
Buffy Sainte-Marie; *Best Of-#2* .... (VAN)
Illuminations .... (VAN)
Dirt Band; *Dirt Band* .... (UA)
Elvis Presley; *Sings For Children* ....(RCA)
Fleetwood Mac; *25 Years-The Chain* .... (WB)
Heroes Are Hard To Find .... (RPR)
Tusk .... (WB)
Iguanas; *Nuevo Boogaloo* .... (MGR)
Jimi Hendrix; *Cry Of Love* .... (RPR)
Jon Secada; *Jon Secada* .... (SBK)
Madonna; *Like A Virgin* .... (SIR)
New Kids On The Block; *New Kids On The Block* ....(COL)
Poco; *Ride The Country* .... (EPI)
Pure Prairie League; *Bustin' Out* ....(RCA)
Rod Stewart; *Best Of* .... (MER)
Angel Angelina
George Strait; *Beyond The Blue Neon* .... (MCA)
Angel Baby
John Lennon; *Lennon* .... (CAP)
Menlove Ave. .... (CAP)
Rosie/Originals; *Cruisin' 1960* .... (INC)
Rock Gems-Classics From Small Label Era .... (MOT)
Super Oldies Of The '60s-#1 .... (AUF)
WCBS FM 101 History Of Rock-'60s-#1 .... (CLT)
Angel Child
Lightnin' Hopkins; *Greatest Hits* .... (PRS)
How Many More Years I Got .... (FAN)
Angel Come Home
Beach Boys; *L.A.-The Light Album* ....(CAR)
Angel Eyes
Abba; *Greatest Hits-#2* .... (ATL)
Voulez-Vous .... (ATL)
Ella Fitzgerald; *Best Of-#2* .... (MCA)
Frank Sinatra; *At The Sands* .... (RPR)
Main Event .... (RPR)
Round #1 .... (CAP)
Sings For Only The Lonely .... (CAP)
Jeff Healey Band; *See The Light* .... (ARI)
Roxy Music; *Atlantic Years 1973-1980* .... (ACO)
Manifesto .... (ATC)
Angel Flying Too Close To The Ground
Willie Nelson; *Greatest Hits & Some That Will Be* (COL)
ST/Honeysuckle Rose ....(COL)
Angel Food Cake
Siegel-Schwall Band; *Best Of* .... (VAN)
Angel From Atlanta
Reddog; *Reddog* .... (SUR)
Angel From Montgomery
Bonnie Raitt; *Streetlights* .... (WB)
Bonnie Raitt & John Prine; *Bonnie Raitt Collection* (WB)
John Prine; *John Prine* .... (ATL)
Angel In Blue
J. Geils Band; *Freeze-Frame* .... (EMI)
Angel In Disguise
Earl Thomas Conley; *Don't Make It Easy For Me* (RCA)
Greatest Hits ....(RCA)
Angel In The Sky
Rose Royce; *Strikes Again* .... (WHI)

Angel In Your Arms
Barbara Mandrell; *Country Classics-#5*
(1985-1986) .... (MCA)
Get To The Heart .... (MCA)
Reba McEntire; *Reba McEntire* .... (MER)
Angel Lady
Boz Scaggs; *Slow Dancer* .... (COL)
Angel Loose In Houston
Larry Gatlin/Gatlin Brothers; *Cookin' Up A
Storm* .... (CAP)
Angel Number Nine
Pure Prairie League; *Bustin' Out* .... (RCA)
Angel Of Harlem
U2; *ST/Rattle & Hum* .... (ISL)
Angel Of Mercy
Albert King; *Best Of Wattstax* .... (STX)
Chronicle .... (STX)
I'll Play The Blues For You .... (STX)
Masterworks .... (ATL)
New Orleans Heat .... (TOM)
Dire Straits; *Communique* .... (WB)
Angel Of The City
Robert Tepper; *No Easy Way Out* .... (SCO)
ST/Cobra .... (SCO)
Angel Of The Morning
Juice Newton; *All-Time Country Classics-#2* ..... (CAP)
Greatest Hits .... (CAP)
Greatest Hits & More .... (CAP)
Juice .... (CAP)
Merrilee Rush; *Dick Bartley's One-Hit
Wonders-'60s-#2* .... (RHI)
Mellow '60s .... (PRY)
Angel Of The Night
Angela Bofill; *Angel Of The Night* .... (GRP)
Best Of .... (ARI)
Angel Spread Your Wings
Judy Collins; *Judith* .... (ELE)
Angel Woman
Andrew Gold; *What's Wrong With This Picture* ... (ASY)
Angel You
Boz Scaggs; *Middle Man* .... (COL)
Angels
Amy Grant; *Collection* .... (A&M)
Straight Ahead .... (A&M)
BoDeans; *Love & Hope & Sex & Dreams* .... (SLS)
Heart; *Private Audition* .... (EPI)
Angels Don't Cry
Psychedelic Furs; *Midnight To Midnight* .... (COL)
Angels Don't Fall In Love
Bangles; *Different Light* .... (COL)
Angels Don't Lie
Jim Reeves; *Best Of-#4* .... (RCA)
Angels Get Lonesome Sometimes
Hank Williams, Jr.; *Early Years* .... (W/C)
One Night Stands .... (WB)
Angels Have Fallen
Kansas; *Monolith* .... (KIR)
Angels Listened In
Crests; *Greatest Hits* .... (CLT)
Super Oldies Of The '50s-#3 .... (AUF)
WCBS FM 101-History Of Rock-'50s-#2 .... (CLT)
Angels Love Bad Men
Barbara Mandrell; *Sure Feels Good* .... (EMI)
Barbara Mandrell & Waylon Jennings; *Country Duets
Two By Two* .... (CAP)
Angels Never Call
'Til Tuesday; *Welcome Home* .... (EPI)
Angels Of Atlanta
Marvin "Hannibal" Peterson; *Angels Of Atlanta* .. (ENJ)
Angels Rejoiced Last Night
Gram Parsons/Flying Burrito Brothers; *Sleepless
Nights* .... (A&M)
Angels With Dirty Faces
Tommy Dorsey; *Complete-#8* .... (RCA)
Angels & Sailors
Doors; *American Prayer* .... (ELE)
Angel's Sunday
Jim Ed Brown; *Best Of* .... (RCA)
Back Door Angels
Jethro Tull; *War Child* .... (CHR)

Blue Angel
Roy Orbison; *All-Time Greatest Hits* .... (MON)
For The Lonely-18 Greatest Hits .... (RHI)
Greatest Hits .... (MON)
In Dreams-Greatest Hits .... (VIA)
Very Best Of .... (MON)
Centerfold
J. Geils Band; *Flashback-Best Of* .... (EMI)
Freeze-Frame .... (EMI)
Showtime .... (EMI)
City Of Angels
10,000 Maniacs; *In My Tribe* .... (ELE)
Jay Ferguson; *Real Life Ain't This Way* .... (ASY)
Miracles; *City Of Angels* .... (TAM)
City Of The Angels
Journey; *Evolution* .... (COL)
Wang Chung; *ST/To Live And Die In L.A.* ...... (GEF)
Devil Or Angel
Bobby Vee; *Best Of* .... (EMI)
Golden Hits .... (LIB)
Legendary Masters .... (EMI)
Clovers; *Atlantic R&B
1947-1974-#3-(1955-1958)* .... (ATL)
Oldies But Goodies-#2 .... (OSR)
Eagle Over Angel
Brother Phelps; *Let Go* .... (ASY)
Earth Angel
Elvis Presley; *Golden Celebration* .... (RCA)
New Edition; *ST/Under The Blue Moon* .... (MCA)
Penguins; *Billboard Top Rock 'N' Roll Hits-1955* . (RHI)
Golden Classics .... (CLT)
Oldies But Goodies-#1 .... (OSR)
ST/American Graffiti .... (MCA)
Fallen Angel
Blue Oyster Cult; *Cultosaurus Erectus* .... (COL)
Debbie Gibson; *Out Of The Blue* .... (ATL)
Fallen Angel; *Go For The Ride* .... (MCA)
Poison; *Open Up And Say...Ahhh!* .... (CAP)
Robbie Robertson; *Robbie Robertson* .... (GEF)
Roger Daltrey; *Under A Raging Moon* .... (ATL)
Fallen Angels
Dio; *Sacred Heart* .... (WB)
Kris Kristofferson; *Gift Of Song* .... (POL)
Shake Hands With The Devil .... (COL)
Fools Rush In
Brook Benton; *Super Oldies!'60s-#10* .... (AUF)
Frank Sinatra/Tommy Dorsey Orchestra;
Sessions-#1 .... (RCA)
Friday's Angels
Generation X; *Valley Of The Dolls* .... (CHR)
Goodbye Angel
Fleetwood Mac; *25 Years-The Chain* .... (WB)
Got A Date With An Angel
Hal Kemp; *Best Of The Big Bands* .... (COL)
Sammy Kaye; *Best Of* .... (MCA)
Guardian Angel
Graham Parker; *Struck By Lightning* .... (RCA)
Judds; *Greatest Hits-#2* .... (RCA)
River Of Time .... (RCA)
Vels; *House Of Miracles* .... (MER)
Guardian Angels
Pearls Before Swine; *Balaklava* .... (ESP)
Best Of .... (ADE)
Heaven Must Be Missing An Angel
Tavares; *Best Of* .... (CAP)
Sky High .... (CAP)
Help Me Angel
Steve Winwood; *Talking Back To The Night* ...... (ISL)
How Do You Speak To An Angel
Popular Standard; *Out Of Print Recording* .... (OOP)
How Do You Talk To An Angel
Heights; *ST/Heights* .... (CAP)
I Can See An Angel
Patsy Cline; *20 Golden Pieces Of* .... (BLD)
Hungry For Love-Her First Recordings-#2 ...... (RHI)
Today Tomorrow & Forever .... (MCA)
I Married An Angel
George Siravo; *Heritage Of Broadway-Rodgers &
Hart* .... (BAI)
Infamous Angel
Iris DeMent; *Infamous Angel* .... (PHO)
Infamous Angel .... (WB)

It Wasn't God Who Made Honky Tonk Angels
Kitty Wells; *Greatest Hits-#1* ....(SO)
Story ....(MCA)
I'm No Angel
Gregg Allman Band; *I'm No Angel* ....(EPI)
Johnny Angel
Shelley Fabares; *Billboard Top Rock 'N' Roll Hits-1962* ....(RHI)
ST/Mermaids ....(GEF)
Let Me Be Your Angel
Stacy Lattisaw; *45* ....(COT)
Look Back In Anger
David Bowie; *Golden Years* ....(RCA)
Lodger ....(RYK)
Sound + Vision ....(RYK)
ST/Chrisiane F. ....(RCA)
The Singles-1969-1993 ....(RYK)
Midnight Angel
Barbara Mandrell; *Best Of* ....(MCA)
Midnight Angel ....(MCA)
Highway 101; *Paint The Town* ....(WB)
My Angel
Stephen Stills; *Stills* ....(COL)
Todd Rundgren/Utopia; *Oops, Wrong Planet* ..... (RHI)
My Angel Baby
Toby Beau; *Toby Beau* ....(RCA)
My Blue Angel
Aaron Tippin; *Read Between The Lines* ....(RCA)
My Special Angel
Bobby Helms; *American Graffiti-#3* ....(MCA)
Blue Ribbon Country #3 ....(ACC)
Oldies/Goodies-#14 ....(OSR)
Pop A Billy ....(MCA)
Vintage Music-Orig. Oldies/'50s-#2 ....(MCA)
Next Door To An Angel
Neil Sedaka; *All-Time Greatest Hits* ....(RCA)
Sings His Greatest Hits ....(RCA)
(Only Angels Wanna Wear My) Red Shoes
Elvis Costello; *Girls Girls Girls* ....(COL)
My Aim Is True ....(COL)
Elvis Costell/Attractions; *Best Of* ....(COL)
Overnight Angels
Ian Hunter/Mott The Hoople; *Shades Of Ian Hunter* ....(COL)
Poison Angel
Winger; *Winger* ....(ATL)
Precious Angel
Bob Dylan; *Slow Train Coming* ....(COL)
Pretty Little Angel
Crests; *Greatest Hits* ....(CLT)
Stevie Wonder; *Uptight* ....(MOT)
Pretty Little Angel Eyes
Curtis Lee; *Back To Mono-1958-1969* ....(AKO)
Million Dollar Memories-#2 ....(RCA)
Oldies But Goodies-#2 ....(OSR)
Phil Spector-The Early Years 1958-61 ....(RHI)
Rock & Roll USA-21 Favorites-#2 ....(LAU)
Return Of The Grievous Angel
Gram Parsons; *GP/Grievous Angel* ....(RPR)
Road Angel
Doobie Brothers; *What Were Once Vices Are Now Habits* ....(WB)
Rock An' Roll Angels
Whitesnake; *Saints & Sinners* ....(GEF)
Rock 'N' Roll Angel
Kentucky HeadHunters; *Pickin' On Nashville* .... (MER)
Send Me An Angel
Scorpions; *Crazy World* ....(MER)
Send Me An Angel '89
Real Life; *Send Me An Angel '89* ....(CRB)
Sent By Angels
Arc Angels; *Arc Angels* ....(DGC)
Seven Spanish Angels
Willie Nelson & Ray Charles; *19 Hot Country Requests-#3* ....(EPI)
Friendship ....(COL)
Greatest Country Hits/'80s-1985 ....(COL)
Half Nelson ....(COL)
She Talks To Angels
Black Crowes; *Shake Your Money Maker* ....(DEF)
Sleeps With Angels
Neil Young/Crazy Horse; *Sleeps With Angels* ..... (RPR)
Sweet Black Angel
Rolling Stones; *Exile On Main Street* ....(RS)

Sweet Little Angel
Buddy Guy; *Best Of The Chicago Blues* ....(VAN)
Man & The Blues ....(VAN)
B.B. King; *16 Original Big Hits* ....(FAN)
Back In The Alley ....(MCA)
Live At The Regal ....(MCA)
Live & Well ....(MCA)
Etta James; *Late Show* ....(FAN)
Rocks The House ....(CSS)
Swing Low, Sweet Chariot
Eric Clapton; *Time Pieces-Best Of* ....(POL)
Glenn Miller/Orchestra; *Moonlight Serenade* .... (RAN)
Hi-Lo's; *Suddenly It's The Hi-Lo's* ....(COL)
Jerry Garcia Acoustic Band; *Almost Acoustic* ... (GRD)
Joan Baez; *From Every Stage* ....(A&M)
Peggy Lee; *Best Of* ....(MCA)
Talking To My Angel
Melissa Etheridge; *Yes I Am* .... (ISL)
Teen Angel
Dion/Belmonts; *Everything You Always Wanted* ..(LAU)
Rock & Roll U.S.A.-21 R&R Favorites-#2 .....(LAU)
Mark Dinning; *45 On CD-#1-1956-1959* ......(MER)
Golden Years-1959 ....(DOM)
Oldies But Goodies-#7 ....(OSR)
ST/American Graffiti ....(MCA)
Teenage Tragedies ....(RHI)
Thank You For Sending Me An Angel
Talking Heads; *More Songs About Buildings & Food* ....(SIR)
There Must Be An Angel Playing With...
Eurythmics; *Be Yourself Tonight* ....(RCA)
Greatest Hits ....(ARI)
Live-1983-1989 ....(ARI)
To See An Angel Cry
Conway Twitty; *Greatest Hits-#1* ....(MCA)
#1's-#1 ....(CAP)
To See My Angel In Virginia
Livewire; *Wired* ....(ROU)
Visions Of Angels
Genesis; *Trespass* ....(MCA)
When The Fallen Angels Fly
Patty Loveless; *When Fallen Angels Fly* ....(EPI)
Wild Angel
John Mellencamp; *Nothin' Matters & What If It Did* ....(RIV)
Wild Side of Life
Freddie Fender; *Before The Next Teardrop Falls* (MCA)
Best Of ....(MCA)
Hank Thompson; *All-Time Greatest Hits* ....(CCB)
Best Of The Best Of ....(GUS)
Capitol Collectors Series ....(CAP)
Traditions In Country Music ....(CAP)
Rod Stewart; *Night On The Town* ....(WB)
You Angel You
Bob Dylan; *Biograph* ....(COL)
Bob Dylan/Band; *Planet Waves* ....(COL)
New Riders Of The Purple Sage; *Best Of* ....(COL)

ANIMALS: A

See Also: ANIMALS: GENERAL, CATS, DOGS, HORSES, PIGS, WHALES

Apeman
Kinks; *Kink Kronikles* ....(RPR)
Live-The Road ....(MCA)
Lola Vs. Powerman & The Moneygoround .....(RPR)
Apeman Hop
Ramones; *Animal Boy* ....(SIR)
Harry The Hairy Ape
Ray Stevens; *Best Of* ....(MEr)
Home On The Range
Bing Crosby; *Crooner-Columbia Years-1928-1934* ....(COL)
Boston Pops Orchestra; *Yankee Doodle Dandy* ...(RCA)
Gene Autry; *50th Anniversary* ....(REP)
Country Music Hall Of Fame ....(COL)
Neil Young; *ST/Where The Buffalo Roam* ....(BKS)
Run Like An Antelope
Phish; *Lawn Boy* ....(ELE)

ANIMALS: B

Bad Brahma Bull
Chris LeDoux; *Old Cowboy Classics* .... (CAP)
Sing Me A Song Mr. Rodeo Man .... (CAP)
Tex Ritter; *An American Legend* .... (CAP)
Best Of .... (CAP)
Bat Out Of Hell
Meatloaf; *Bat Out Of Hell* .... (EPI)
Batdance
Prince; *ST/Batman* .... (WB)
Bears
Quicksilver Messenger Service; *Anthology* ...... (CAP)
Sons Of Mercury .... (RHI)
Black Bear Road
C.W. McCall; *Greatest Hits* .... (POL)
Buffalo Gun
Michael Murphey; *Swans Against The Son* ...... (EPI)
Buffalo River Home
John Hiatt; *Perfectly Good Guitar* .... (A&M)
Buffalo Skinners
Woody Guthrie; *Cowboy Songs On Folkways* ... (FLW)
Worried Man Blues-Golden Classics-#1 .... (CLT)
Buffalo Stance
Neneh Cherry; *Raw Like Sushi* .... (VIA)
ST/Slaves Of New York .... (VIA)
De Bat (Fly In Me Face)
Carly Simon; *Boys In The Trees* .... (ELE)
Eager Beaver
Original Broadway Cast; *No Strings* .... (ANG)
Stan Kenton; *In Stereo* .... (CW)
Kenton In Hi-Fi .... (BLN)
Solo-Without His Orchestra .... (CW)
Great White Buffalo
Ted Nugent; *Double Live Gonzo* .... (EPI)
Home On The Range
Bing Crosby; *Crooner-Columbia
Years-1928-1934* .... (COL)
Boston Pops Orchestra; *Yankee Doodle Dandy* ...(RCA)
Gene Autry; *50th Anniversary* .... (REP)
Country Music Hall Of Fame .... (COL)
Neil Young; *ST/Where The Buffalo Roam* .... (BKS)
House At Pooh Corner
Loggins & Messina; *Best Of-Friends* .... (COL)
On Stage .... (COL)
Sittin' In .... (COL)
Nitty Gritty Dirt Band; *Best Of* .... (EMI)
Dirt Silver & Gold .... (OOP)
Lonely Bull
Herb Alpert/Tijuana Brass; *Classics-#1* .... (A&M)
Four-Sider .... (A&M)
Greatest Hits .... (A&M)
Lonely Bull .... (A&M)
Now That The Buffalo's Gone
Buffy Sainte-Marie; *American Child* .... (VAN)
Best Of .... (VAN)
Greatest Folksingers/'60s .... (VAN)
I'm Gonna Be A Country Child .... (VAN)
On Wisconsin/If You Want To Be A Badger
University Of Wisconsin Marching Band; *Fifth
Quarter* .... (FID)
Preacher & The Bear
Andy Griffith; *American Originals* .... (CAP)
Big Bopper; *Hellooo Baby! Best Of-1954-1959* .. (RHI)
Rufus Thomas & Carla Thomas; *Chronicle* ...... (STX)
Release The Bats
Birthday Party; *Best & Rarest* .... (MIS)
Collection .... (MIS)
Sadder & Wiser Beaver
Original Broadway Cast; *Beyond The Fringe* ..... (CAP)
Simon Smith & His Amazing Dancing Bear
Randy Newman; *Sail Away* .... (RPR)
Summer Bunnies
R. Kelly; *12 Play* .... (JVA)
Sweet As Bear Meat
Johnny Hodges Orchestra; *Used To Be Duke* ..... (VRV)
Teddy Bear Song
Barbara Fairchild; *Back To The '70s-Country* ... (DOM)
Country Superstars .... (DOM)

Teddy Bear (Let Me Be Your)
Elvis Presley; *Golden Records-#1* .... (RCA)
In Concert .... (RCA)
Number One Hits .... (RCA)
ST/Loving You .... (RCA)
Top Ten Hits .... (RCA)
Teddy Bears
Barbra Streisand; *ST/Prince Of Tides* .... (COL)
Teddy Bears' Picnic
Anne Murray; *There's A Hippo In My Tub* .... (LIB)
Frank DeVol; *Small Fry-Capitol Sings Kids Songs* (CAP)
You Can't Roller Skate In A Buffalo Herd
Roger Miller; *Best Of-#2-King Of The Road* .... (MER)
Golden Hits .... (SMA)

ANIMALS: C

Behind My Camel
Police; *Zenyatta Mondatta* .... (A&M)
Callin' All Cows
Elvin Bishop; *Juke Joint Jump* .... (CPC)
Raisin' Hell .... (CPC)
Camel
Sonny Rollins; *Don't Stop The Carnival* .... (MS)
Cattle Call
Eddy Arnold; *Best Of* .... (RCA)
Cattle Call .... (RCA)
Nipper's Greatest Hits/'50s-#1 .... (RCA)
Pure Gold .... (RCA)
Riders In The Sky; *Riders Radio Theater* .... (MCA)
Chipmunk Song
Chipmunks; *Christmas With-#1* .... (EMI)
David Seville/Chipmunks; *Billboard's Greatest Christmas
Hits* .... (RHI)
Dr. Demento Greatest Christmas CD .... (RHI)
Cowtown
Carly Simon; *Another Passenger* .... (ELE)
George Strait; *#7* .... (MCA)
Webb Pierce; *Golden Hits-#2* .... (PLN)
Cow-Cow Boogie
Ella Fitzgerald; *Best Of-#2* .... (MCA)
Freddie Slack/Ella Mae Morse; *Jukebox Saturday
Night* .... (CAP)
Judds; *Heartland* .... (RCA)
Coyote
Country Joe McDonald; *Into The Fray* .... (RGB)
Rock & Roll Music From The Planet Earth ...... (FAN)
Joni Mitchell; *Hejira* .... (ASY)
Shadows & Light .... (ASY)
/The Band; Last Waltz .... (WB)
Coyote, El
Kris Kristofferson; *Repossessed* .... (MER)
Farmer & The Cowman
Original Broadway Cast; *Oklahoma* .... (RCA)
Holy Cow
54.40; *54.40* .... (RPR)
Band; *Moondog Matinee* .... (CAP)
Lee Dorsey; *Golden Classics* .... (CLT)
New Orleans Jazz & Heritage Fest. 1976 .... (RHI)
It Must Be A Camel
Frank Zappa; *Hot Rats* .... (RYK)
Midnight At The Oasis (Camel)
Maria Muldaur; *Maria Muldaur* .... (RPR)
Super Hits/'70s-Have A Nice Day-#13 .... (RHI)
Milk Cow Blues
Aerosmith; *Draw The Line* .... (COL)
Pandora's Box .... (COL)
Bob Wills/Texas Playboys; *Best Of* .... (MCA)
Tiffany Transcriptions-#3 .... (KAL)
Eddie Cochran; *Legendary Masters* .... (EMI)
Rick Nelson; *Legendary Masters* .... (LIB)
Souvenirs .... (LIB)
Milk Cow Blues Boogie
Elvis Presley; *Complete Sun Sessions* .... (RCA)
Date With .... (RCA)
Sun Sessions .... (RCA)
Ricky Nelson; *Live In '85* .... (RHI)
Old Coyote Town
Don Williams; *Traces* .... (CAP)
One Little Coyote
Riders In The Sky; *Harmony Ranch* .... (COL)

Party Till The Cows Come Home
Elvin Bishop Group; *Bill Graham-Fillmore-Last
Days* .... (EPA)
Poor Cow
Donovan; *Troubadour-Definitive Collection* .... (EPI)
Elton John; *Reg Strikes Back* .... (MCA)
Tanita Tikaram; *Ancient Heart* .... (RPR)
Pretty Girl Milking A Cow
Judy Garland; *Best Of* .... (MCA)
One & Only .... (CAP)
Quaker's Cow
Doc Watson; *On Stage (Featuring Merle Watson)* (VAN)
Saddle The Cow
Dr. John; *Brightest Smile In Town* .... (CLE)
Sat On A Cow Polka
Li'l Wally; *Old Country Polish Polkas* .... (JJ)
Song Of The Camels
Popular Standard; *Out of print recording* .... (OOP)
There Ain't A Cow In Texas
Vassar Clements & Buddy Emmons; *Sat. Night
Shuffle-Merle Travis Celebr.* .... (SHA)
True Men Don't Kill Coyotes
Red Hot Chili Peppers; *Abbey Road E.P.* .... (EMI)
Red Hot Chili Peppers .... (EMI)
What Hits!? Best Of .... (EMI)
Two Headed Cow
Ennui; *Olive* .... (SLM)
Wild Cow Moan
Big Joe Turner & Sonny Boy Williamson; *Story Of The
Blues* .... (COL)

ANIMALS: D

Donkey Serenade
Allan Jones; *Nipper's Greatest Hits-'30s-#1* .... (RCA)
Sings Favorites .... (GLN)
ST/Radio Days .... (NOV)
Artie Shaw; *Complete-#1 (1938-1939)* .... (RCA)
This Is .... (RCA)
Home On The Range
Bing Crosby; *Crooner-Columbia
Years-1928-1934* .... (COL)
Boston Pops Orchestra; *Yankee Doodle Dandy* ... (RCA)
Gene Autry; *50th Anniversary* .... (REP)
Country Music Hall Of Fame .... (COL)
Neil Young; *ST/Where The Buffalo Roam* .... (BKS)
Man & The Donkey
Chuck Berry; *Missing Berries-Rarities-#3* .... (CSS)
One Way Donkey Ride
Sandy Denny; *Best Of* .... (HBL)
Who Knows Where The Time Goes? .... (HBL)
Ride Your Donkey
Joe Strummer; *Earthquake Weather* .... (EPI)
Run Like A Deer
Beers Family Sings; *Seasons Of Peace* .... (BIO)

ANIMALS: E

Ant & The Elephant
Chick Corea Elektric Band II; *Paint The World* .. (GRP)
Baby Elephant Walk
Henry Mancini; *All-Time Greatest Hits-#1* .... (RCA)
Pure Gold .... (RCA)
Elephant
Tanita Tikaram; *Eleven Kinds Of Loneliness* ...... (RPR)
Elephant Day Parade
Beat Farmers; *Pursuit Of Happiness* .... (CCB)
Elephant Gun
David Lee Roth; *Eat 'Em & Smile* .... (WB)
Elephant Ride
Squeeze; *Sweets From A Stranger* .... (A&M)
Elephant Song
Reilly & Maloney; *Profiles* .... (FRK)
Elephant Stone
Stone Roses; *Stone Roses* .... (SIL)
Turns Into Stone .... (SIL)
Elephant Talk
King Crimson; *Abbreviated* .... (EDI)
Compact .... (EDI)
Discipline .... (EDI)
Elephant Trainer
Liz Story; *Part Of Fortune* .... (NOV)

Elephants In Love
Jean-Luc Ponty; *Fables* .... (ATL)
Elephants & Flowers
Prince; *ST/Graffiti Bridge* .... (PAI)
Elephant's Graveyard
Boomtown Rats; *Greatest Hits* .... (COL)
Mondo Bongo .... (COL)
L'Elephant
Tom Tom Club; *Tom Tom Club* .... (SIR)
One Bad Elephant
Brian Slawson; *Distant Drums* .... (COL)
Pink Elephants
Eddie Lang Blue Five/Joe Venuti; *Jazz In The
Thirties* .... (DSQ)
Pink Elephants On Parade
Barbara Cook; *Disney Album* .... (MCA)
Psychic Elephant
Shankar; *Vision* .... (ECM)
Seeing The Elephant
Debby McClatchy/Red Clay Ramblers; *Debby
McClatchy/Red Clay Ramblers* .... (GRE)
When I See An Elephant Fly
Barbara Cook; *Disney Album* .... (MCA)
C. Edwards/J. Carmichael/H. Johnson Ch.; *Disney
Collection-#2* .... (DIS)

ANIMALS: F

Fox On The Run
George Jones; *First Time Love* .... (EPI)
Sweet; *Desolation Boulevard* .... (CAP)
Foxey Lady
Jimi Hendrix; *Essential-#2* .... (RPR)
Smash Hits .... (RPR)
ST/Jimi Plays Monterey .... (RPR)
ST/Wayne's World .... (RPR)
Jimi Hendrix Experience; *Are You Experienced?* . (RPR)
Mary's Danish; *Circa* .... (MC)
Johnny The Fox Meets Jimmy The Weed
Thin Lizzy; *Live & Dangerous* .... (WB)
Run With The Fox
Yes; *Yesyears* .... (ATC)
Twentieth Century Fox
Doors; *Doors* .... (ELE)

ANIMALS: G

Gorilla
James Taylor; *Gorilla* .... (WB)
Gorilla, You're A Desperado
Warren Zevon; *Bad Luck Streak In Dancing
School* .... (ASY)
Green Gorilla
Spirit; *Time Circle* .... (EPI)
Ground Hog
Buffy Sainte-Marie; *Best Of* .... (VAN)
Many A Mile .... (VAN)
Dillards; *Bluegrass Breakdown* .... (VAN)
Doc Watson; *Essential* .... (VAN)
New Lost City Ramblers; *20 Years Of Concert
Performances* .... (FF)
Ground Hog Blues
John Lee Hooker; *Blues-#5* .... (CSS)
House Of The Blues .... (CSS)
Lonely Goatherd
Julie Andrews; *ST/Sound Of Music* .... (RCA)
Original Cast/Mary Martin; *Sound Of Music* ..... (COL)
Papa's Billy Goat
Sarah Ogan Gunning; *Silver Dagger* .... (ROU)
Rootin' Ground Hog
K.C. Douglas; *K.C.'s Blues* .... (BV)
Shaved Gorilla
Flaming Lips; *Telepathic Surgery* .... (RES)
Ten Tall Giraffes
Liquid Pink; *Liquid Pink* .... (ATO)
Thrill My Gorilla
Alice Cooper; *Constrictor* .... (MCA)
Wild Goose Grasses In Tarrytown
Weavers; *Classics* .... (VAN)
Greatest Hits .... (VAN)

ANIMALS: GENERAL, Zoos

Animal
Bar-Kays; *Animal* .... (MER)
Def Leppard; *Hysteria* .... (MER)
Pearl Jam; *Vs.* .... (EPA)
Toto; *Past To Present 1987-1990* ....(COL)
Animal Boy
Ramones; *Animal Boy* .... (SIR)
Ramones Mania .... (SIR)
Animal Crackers
Anne Murray; *There's A Hippo In My Tub* ......(CAP)
Melanie; *Best Of* ....(BUD)
Animal Farm
Kinks; *Village Green Preservation Society* .... (RPR)
Animal House
Stephen Bishop; *ST/Animal House* .... (MCA)
Animal Instinct
Commodores; *Nightshift* .... (MOT)
Elvis Presley; *ST/Harum Scarum* ....(RCA)
Animal Magic
Belouis Some; *Animal Magic* ....(CAP)
Blow Monkeys; *Animal Magic* ....(RCA)
Peter Gabriel; *Peter Gabriel* .... (ATL)
Animal Speaks
Golden Palominos; *Visions Of Excess* .... (CEL)
Animal Trainer & The Toad
Mountain; *Best Of* ....(COL)
Animal Zoo
Spirit; *12 Dreams of Dr. Sardonicus* .... (EPI)
Best Of .... (EPI)
Animals
Talking Heads; *Fear Of Music* .... (SIR)
Animals In Jungles
China Crisis; *Working With Fire & Steel* .... (WB)
At The Zoo
Simon & Garfunkel; *Bookends* ....(COL)
Collected Works ....(COL)
Carcass
Siouxsie/Banshees; *The Scream* .... (GEF)
Don't Kill The Animals
Lene Lovich; *Animal Liberation* .... (WAX)
Lene Lovich & Nina Hagen; *Tame Yourself* ...... (RHI)
Friendly Beasts
Garth Brooks; *Beyond The Season* .... (LIB)
Peter, Paul & Mary/N.Y. Choral Society; *Holiday
Celebration* .... (WB)
Froggie Went A Courtin'
Doc Watson; *Essential* .... (VAN)
Home Again .... (VAN)
Going To The Zoo
Peter, Paul & Mary; *Peter, Paul & Mommy* .... (WB)
Pet Sematary
Ramones; *Brain Drain* .... (SIR)
Loco Live .... (SIR)
Several Species Of Small Furry Animals
Pink Floyd; *Umma Gumma* ....(CAP)
Works ....(CAP)
Shakin' The Cage
Zoo; *Shakin' The Cage* ....(CPC)
Sweet Betsy From Pike
Cisco Houston; *Cowboy Ballads* .... (FLW)
Mormon Tabernacle Choir; *This Land Is Your
Land* ....(COL)
Talk To The Animals
Sammy Davis, Jr.; *Greatest Songs* ....(CCB)
Turkey In The Straw
Stanley Brothers; *Stanley Series-Vol.1-#3* ....(COP)
Vassar Clements; *Grass Routes* .... (ROU)
Tusk
Fleetwood Mac; *25 Years-The Chain* .... (WB)
Tusk .... (WB)
Wildlife
Yellowjackets; *Four Corners* ....(MCA)
Live Wires .... (GRP)
Zooropa
U2; *Zooropa* .... (ISL)

ANIMALS: H

Attack Of The Radioactive Hamsters
Weird Al Yankovic; *ST/UHF* ....(RAR)
Don't Be A Hog
Doctor Nerve; *Armed Observation* .... (CUN)
I Am A Hog For Ya
Casey Jones; *Solid Blue* .... (ROO)
I Want A Hippopotamus For Christmas
Gayla Peevey; *Dr. Demento Greatest Christmas
CD* .... (RHI)
Dr. Demento's Greatest-#6 .... (RHI)
Three Stooges; *Christmas With* ..... (RHI)
Screamin' Night Hog
Steppenwolf; *16 Greatest Hits* .... (MCA)
Wart Hog
Ramones; *Ramones Mania* .... (SIR)
Too Tough To Die .... (SIR)
Who's Gonna Feed Them Hogs
Tom T. Hall; *Essential Twentieth Anniversary
Collect.* .... (MER)
Greatest Hits-#2 .... (MER)

ANIMALS: K

I'll Bet You A Kangaroo
Olivia Newton-John; *Don't Stop Believin'* .... (MCA)
Kangaroo
Klaxons; *How Do You Do?* .... (CRS)
Les Paul; *Legend & The Legacy-#1-4* ....(CAP)
Kangaroo Hop
Dee Clark; *Rain Drops* .... (VJ)
Tie Me Kangaroo Down Sport
Rolf Harris; *45* .... (ERI)

ANIMALS: L

Dixie Chicken (Lamb)
Little Feat; *Dixie Chicken* .... (WB)
Waiting For Columbus .... (WB)
I Am A Lion
Neil Diamond; *Tap Root Manuscript* .... (MCA)
I'm On The Lamb, But I Ain't No Sheep
Blue Oyster Cult; *Blue Oyster Cult* ....(COL)
Lamb Lies Down On Broadway
Genesis; *Lamb Lies Down On Broadway* .... (ATC)
Seconds Out .... (ATL)
Leopard Skin Pillbox Hat
Bob Dylan; *Blonde On Blonde* ....(COL)
Leopards In Love
Zummos; *Modern Marriage* .... (A&M)
Lion
Burning Spear; *Live* .... (ISL)
Man In the Hills .... (ISL)
Toto; *Isolation* ....(COL)
Lion In The Winter
Hoyt Axton; *Road Songs* .... (A&M)
Southbound .... (A&M)
Listen To The Lion
Van Morrison; *It's Too Late To Stop Now* .... (WB)
St. Dominic's Preview ....(WB)
Little Lamb
Original Cast; *Gypsy* ....(COL)
Mama Lion
David Crosby & Graham Nash; *Wind On The
Water* .... (MCA)
Mary Had A Little Lamb
Stevie Ray Vaughan/Double Trouble; *Live Alive* .. (EPI)
Texas Flood .... (EPI)
Wings; *Wings Wild Life* ....(CAP)
Ride My Llama
Neil Young/Crazy Horse; *Rust Never Sleeps* ...... (RPR)
Searching For Lambs
June Tabor; *Aqaba* .... (SHA)
Peter Bellamy; *Peter Bellamy* ....(GRE)
Someone To Watch Over Me
Ella Fitzgerald; *Sings The George & Ira Gershwin
Songbook* ....(VRV)
Elton John; *Glory Of Gershwin Featuring Larry
Adler* .... (MER)

Frank Sinatra; *Nice 'N' Easy* .... (CAP)
   The Capitol Years .... (CAP)
Jack Jones; *Gershwin Album* .... (COL)
Original Broadway Cast; *Crazy For You* .... (ANG)
Oscar Peterson; *My Favorite Instrument* .... (VRV)
Sarah Vaughan; *George Gershwin Songbook-#2* . (EMA)
Willie Nelson; *Stardust* .... (COL)
Strong Like A Lion
Roots Radics; *Forward Ever-Backwards Never* ...(HRT)
Whiffenpoof Song
Bing Crosby/Fred Waring & His Glee Club; *Bing
   Crosby's Greatest Hits* .... (MCA)
Count Basie & Mills Brothers; *16 Great
   Performances* .... (MCA)
Louis Armstrong; *Best Of* .... (MCA)
Mitch Miller; *34 All-Time Great Sing-Along
   Selections* .... (COL)
Statler Brothers; *World Of The* .... (COL)
Wimoweh (Mbube)-The Lion Sleeps Tonight
Chet Atkins; *RCA Years* .... (RCA)
Kingston Trio; *Kingston Trio/From The Hungry i* . (CAP)
Nylons; *Seamless* .... (OPE)
Pete Seeger; *Greatest Hits* .... (COL)
Tokens; *Billboard Top Rock 'N' Roll Hits-1961* .. (RHI)
   Nipper's Greatest Hits!'60s-#1 .... (RCA)
Weavers; *Greatest Hits* .... (VAN)

ANIMALS: M

And The Mouse Police Never Sleeps
Jethro Tull; *Heavy Horses* .... (CHR)
Chinese Mule Train
Spike Jones; *Best Of-#2* .... (RCA)
Erie Canal
Burl Ives; *Best Of* .... (MCA)
Weavers; *Classics* .... (VAN)
   Greatest Folksingers/'60s .... (VAN)
   Greatest Hits .... (VAN)
Everybody's Got Something To Hide...
Beatles; *White Album* .... (CAP)
Gator Tails And Monkey Ribs
Spats; *45* .... (OOP)
Hard Monkeys
Ten Years After; *A Space In Time* .... (COL)
King Kong's Monkey
Gary U.S. Bonds; *45* .... (LEG)
Mickey Mouse
Sparks; *Angst In My Pants* .... (ATL)
Mickey Mouse Alma Mater
Mouseketeers; *Disney Collection-#1* .... (DIS)
Mickey Mouse March
Aaron Neville & Dr. John; *Stay Awake-Music From
   Disney Films* .... (A&M)
Mouseketeers; *Disney Collection-#1* .... (DIS)
Mickey's Monkey
Smokey Robinson/Miracles; *Anthology* .... (MOT)
   Compact Command Performances .... (MOT)
   Greatest Hits .... (MOT)
   Motown Story-First 25 Years .... (MOT)
   Songs That Inspired 25th Anniv. Special ...... (MOT)
"Mighty Mouse" Theme
Original Music; *Television's Greatest Hits-#2* ..... (TVT)
Monkey
Fabulous Thunderbirds; *T-Bird Rhythm* .... (CHR)
George Michael; *Faith* .... (COL)
Monkey In Winter
Colourfield; *Deception* .... (CHR)
Monkey In Your Soul
Steely Dan; *Pretzel Logic* .... (MCA)
Monkey Island
J. Geils Band; *Best Of* .... (ATL)
   Monkey Island .... (ATL)
Monkey Man
Rolling Stones; *Let It Bleed* .... (AKO)
Toots/Maytals; *Live* .... (MGO)
Monkey On My Back
Aerosmith; *Pump* .... (GEF)
Inspiral Carpets; *Life* .... (ELE)
Ten Years After; *A Space In Time* .... (COL)
Monkey On Your Back
Aldo Nova; *Portrait Of* .... (EPI)
   Subject...Aldo Nova .... (POR)

Monkey See, Monkey Do
Dickies; *Second Coming* .... (ENI)
Melissa Manchester; *Help Is On The Way* .... (ARI)
Michael Franks; *Art Of Tea* .... (RPR)
Ringo Starr; *Bad Boy* .... (EPI)
Monkey Shine
Head East; *Act Yourself Up* .... (A&M)
   Live .... (A&M)
Monkey Time
Major Lance; *Back To The '60s-#3* .... (DOM)
   Groove 'N' Grind-'50s & '60s Dance Hits ...... (RHI)
   Soul Shots-'60s Soul Classics-#2 .... (RHI)
Tubes; *Best Of* .... (CAP)
Monkey & The Engineer
Grateful Dead; *Reckoning* .... (ARI)
Jesse Fuller; *Lone Cat* .... (GTJ)
Morse Moose & The Grey Goose
Wings; *London Town* .... (CAP)
Mule Skinner Blues (Blue Yodel #8)
Bill Monroe; *Bean Blossom* .... (MCA)
Dolly Parton; *Best Of* .... (RCA)
   RCA Years 1967-1986 .... (RCA)
Hank Williams, Jr.; *Living Proof-MGM
   Recordings-1963-1975* .... (MER)
Mule Train
Gene Autry; *Country Music Hall Of Fame* ....(COL)
Tennessee Ernie Ford; *16 Tons Of Boogie-Best Of* (RHI)
   Capitol Collectors Series .... (CAP)
   Great Records Of The Decade-'40s Hits ....(CCB)
Muskrat Love
America; *Hat Trick* .... (WB)
   History-Greatest Hits .... (WB)
   Live .... (WB)
Captain & Tennille; *Greatest Hits* .... (A&M)
Muskrat Ramble
Dukes Of Dixieland; *Digital Dixieland* .... (PJ)
Louis Armstrong; *Essential* .... (VAN)
   Greatest Hits .... (CCB)
McGuire Sisters; *Greatest Hits* .... (MCA)
Pete Fountain; *High Society* .... (BLU)
One Brown Mouse
Jethro Tull; *Bursting Out* .... (CHR)
   Heavy Horses .... (CHR)
One Monkey Don't Stop No Show
Big Maybelline; *Okeh R&B Story-1949-1957* .... (EPI)
Honey Cone; *Greatest Hits* .... (HDH)
Joe Tex; *Greatest Hits* .... (CCB)
   I Believe I'm Gonna Make It!-Best Of .... (RHI)
Pretty Mouse
Fluid; *Glue* .... (SP)
Rockin' The Mule
Barrence Whitfield/Savages; *Ow Ow Ow Ow* ... (ROU)
"Rocky & Bullwinkle" Theme
Original Music; *Television's Greatest Hits-#2* ..... (TVT)
Sell My Monkey
B.B. King; *Blues 'N' Jazz* .... (MCA)
   Blues 'N' Jazz/Electric B.B. King .... (MCA)
She Caught The Katy & Left Me A Mule...
Blues Brothers; *Best Of* .... (ATL)
   ST/Blues Brothers .... (ATL)
Taj Mahal; *Best Of-#1* .... (COL)
   Natch'l Blues .... (COL)
She Got A Mule Kick
Harry Crafton; *Harry Crafton* .... (CLT)
She Left Me A Mule To Ride
Big Joe Williams; *Shake Your Boogie* .... (ARH)
Shock The Monkey
Peter Gabriel; *Greenpeace* .... (A&M)
   Plays Live .... (GEF)
   Security .... (GEF)
   Shaking The Tree-16 Golden Greats .... (GEF)
Sly Mongoose
Charlie Parker; *Bebop & Bird-#2* .... (RHI)
Monty Alexander Ivory & Steel; *Jamboree* .... (CP)
Space Monkey
Patti Smith Group; *Easter* .... (ARI)
Steel Monkey
Jethro Tull; *Crest Of A Knave* .... (CHR)
Strollin' (With My Moose)
Edgar Meyer; *Sampler '88-#2* .... (MCA)
Sugar Mice
Marillion; *Clutching At Straws* .... (CAP)
   Thieving Magpie .... (CAP)

Surf Monkey
Freddie King; *Just Pickin'* .... (MBR)
Theme From "Tom & Jerry"
Henry Mancini; *ST/Tom & Jerry-The Movie* ..... (MCA)
Three Blind Mice
Van Alexander; *Small Fry-Capitol Sings Kids
Songs* ....(CAP)
Too Much Monkey Business
Chuck Berry; *Classic Oldies From The '50s &
'60s-#16* .... (MCA)
Roll Over Beethoven .... (ALL)
ST/Hail! Hail! Rock 'N' Roll .... (MCA)
Toronto Rock 'N' Roll Revival-#2 .... (ACC)
Elvis Presley; *Guitar Man* .... (RCA)
Million-Dollar Quartet .... (RCA)
ST/This Is ....(RCA)
Yardbirds; *Five Live Yardbirds* .... (RHI)
For Your Love .... (ACC)
Greatest Hits-#1-1964-1966 .... (RHI)
Tweeter & The Monkey Man
Traveling Wilburys; *#1* .... (WIL)
Two Moose In A Caboose
Stan Kenton/Orchestra;
Uncollected-#5-1945-1947 .... (HIN)

ANIMALS: P

Oh Mr. Possum
Jimmy Preston; *Jimmy Preston* .... (CLT)
Panther In Michigan
Michael Smith; *Michael Smith* .... (FF)
Porcupine
Mary's Danish; *American Standard* .... (MC)
Youth Gone Mad; *West/East* .... (MOV)
Porcupine Pie
Neil Diamond; *Hot August Night* .... (MCA)
Moods .... (MCA)
Possum Hunt
Lightnin' Hopkins; *Lost Texas Tapes-#4* .... (CLT)
Possum Up A Gum Stump
Dick Fegy; *Flatpicking Guitar Festival* .... (SHA)
Run Possum Run!
Southern Rail; *Roadwork* .... (TUR)
Shetland Pony Blues
Son House; *Delta Blues-Library Of Congress
Sessions* ....(BIO)
Theme From "The Pink Panther"
Henry Mancini; *All-Time Greatest Hits-#1* .... (RCA)
Legendary Performer ....(RCA)
Pure Gold ....(RCA)
ST/Revenge Of The Pink Panther .... (EMI)
Television's Greatest Hits-#2 .... (TVT)
Thing Called Love (Porcupine)
Bonnie Raitt; *Nick Of Time* .... (CAP)
Tony The Pony
Morrissey; *Kill Uncle* .... (SIR)

ANIMALS: R

Ben
Jackson 5; *16 Greatest Hits* .... (MOT)
Anthology .... (MOT)
Jacksons; *Live* .... (EPI)
Michael Jackson; *Anthology* .... (MOT)
Best Of .... (MOT)
Motown Superstar Series-#7 .... (MOT)
Confident Rat
Ignorance; *Confident Rat* .... (MET)
Cotton Tail
Duke Ellington; *Reminiscing In Tempo* ....(COL)
Duke Ellington & Ella Fitzgerald; *Compact Jazz-Best Of
The Big Bands* ....(VRV)
Lambert, Hendricks & Ross; *Twisted-Best Of* .... (RHI)
Wes Montgomery; *Artistry Of* .... (RVR)
Hotel Rats & Photostats
Jimmy Page; *ST/Death Wish 2* .... (SS)
Intoxicated Rat
New Lost City Ramblers; *American Moonshine &
Prohibition Songs* .... (FLW)
King Of Rats
Neighborhoods; *Neighborhoods* .... (THI)

Lone Rhinoceros
Adrian Belew; *Desire Of The Rhino King* .... (ISL)
Lone Rhino .... (ISL)
Pet Rabbit
Johnny Shines; *Traditional Delta Blues* ....(BIO)
Pressed Rat & Warthog
Cream; *Wheels Of Fire* .... (POL)
Rabbit Chase
New Lost City Ramblers; *Early
Years-1958-1962* .... (FLW)
Rabbit In A Log
Stanley Brothers; *Stanley Series-Vol. 1 & 2* .....(COP)
Rabbit In The Moon
Aztec Two-Step; *See It Was Like This...Acoustic
Retrosp.* ....(FF)
Peter Erskine; *Transition* .... (DEN)
Rabbit In The Pea Patch
Red Clay Ramblers; *Merchant's Lunch* .... (FF)
Rabbit On My Shoulder
P. Alsop/D. Crow/B. Phillips/H. Traum; *Silly Songs &
Modern Lullabies* .... (BRR)
Raccoon Straits
Cal Tjader; *San Francisco Moods* .... (FAN)
Rat Bait
Swimming Pool Q's; *Deep End* .... (DB)
Rat In The Kitchen
UB40; *Live In Moscow* ....(A&M)
Rat In The Kitchen ....(A&M)
Rat Race
Bob Marley/Wailers; *Babylon By Bus* .... (TUF)
Rastaman Vibration .... (TUF)
Rebel Music .... (TUF)
Rat Salad
Black Sabbath; *Paranoid* .... (WB)
Rat Trap
Boomtown Rats; *Greatest Hits* ....(COL)
Tonic For The Troops ....(COL)
Rats
Kinks; *Lola vs. Powerman & The Moneygoround* . (RPR)
Pearl Jam; *Vs.* .... (EPA)
Syd Barrett; *Barrett* .... (CAP)
Opel .... (CAP)
Rats In My Kitchen
Sleepy John Estes; *Legend Of* .... (DEL)
Rats In The Cellar
Aerosmith; *Gems* ....(COL)
Pandora's Box ....(COL)
Rocks ....(COL)
Rats Motel
Lord Tracy; *Deaf Gods Of Babylon* .... (UNI)
Rats & Roaches In My Kitchen
Silas Hogan; *Louisiana Blues* .... (ARH)
Rat's Eyes
Black Flag; *Slip It In* ....(SST)
Rhinocerous
Smashing Pumpkins; *Gish* ....(CRL)
Ride The Rhino
Rhino Bucket; *Rhino Bucket* .... (RPR)
Road Rats
Alice Cooper; *Lace & Whiskey* .... (WB)
Rocky Raccoon
Beatles; *Box Set* ....(CAP)
White Album ....(CAP)
Run Little Rabbit
John & Jamie Hartford; *Hartford & Hartford* ...... (FF)
Sexy Rhino
Adrian Belew; *Desire Of The Rhino King* .... (ISL)
Street Rats
Ted Nugent; *Free-For-All* .... (EPI)
Out Of Control .... (EPI)
White Rabbit
Damned; *Best Of* .... (ROA)
Machine Gun Etiquette .... (ROA)
George Benson; *Collection* .... (WB)
White Rabbit ....(CBA)
Jefferson Airplane; *2400 Fulton Street-An
Anthology* ....(RCA)
Flight Log 1966-1976 .... (GRU)
Loves You ....(RCA)
ST/Platoon-& Songs From The Era ....(ATL)
Surrealistic Pillow ....(RCA)
Worst Of ....(RCA)

ANIMALS: S

10,432 Sheep
Dris Day Quartet/Frank Comstock Orch.; *Day At The Movies* ....(COL)
And Dream Of Sheep
Kate Bush; *Hounds Of Love* ....(EMI)
Black Sheep
John Anderson; *All The People Are Talkin'* ....(WB)
Greatest Hits ....(WB)
Sam The Sham/Pharaohs; *Pharaohization! (Best Of)* ....(RHI)
Black Sheep Of The Family
Ritchie Blackmore; *Rainbow* ....(POL)
Cat's Squirrel
Cream; *Fresh Cream* ....(RSO)
Jethro Tull; *This Was* ....(CHR)
Dead Skunk
Loudon Wainwright III; *Dr. Demento's Greatest Novelties-#4* ....(RHI)
Super Hits/'70s-Have A Nice Day-#10 ....(RHI)
Last Snow Leopard
Spencer Brewer; *Emerald* ....(NAR)
Mississippi Squirrel Revival
Ray Stevens; *Country Classics-#1* ....(MCA)
Greatest Hits ....(MCA)
He Thinks He's Ray Stevens ....(MCA)
On Squirrel Hill
Ian Matthews; *Legacy-Collection Of New Folk Music* ....(WH)
Walking A Changing Line ....(WH)
Pissin' On A Skunk (No Need)
Saffire-Uppity Blues Women; *Hot Flash* ....(ALG)
Playful Squirrels
Carlos Barbosa-Lima; *Music Of The Americas* .... (CP)
"Rocky & Bullwinkle" Theme
Original Music; *Television's Greatest Hits-#2* .....(TVT)
Sable On Blond
Stevie Nicks; *Wild Heart* ....(MOD)
Sheep
Housemartins; *London 0 Hull 4* ....(ELE)
Pink Floyd; *Animals* ....(COL)
Collection Of Great Dance Songs ....(COL)
Skunk Creek
Poco; *Forgotten Trail-1969-1974* ....(EPI)
Skunk Funk
Brecker Brothers; *Collection-#1 & #2* ....(NOV)
Skunk (Sonically Speaking)
MC5; *High Times* ....(RHI)
Skunk, The Goose & The Fly
Tower Of Power; *East Bay Grease* ....(RHI)
Try Counting Sheep
Black Sheep; *A Wolf In Sheep's Clothing* ....(MER)

ANIMALS: T

Eye Of The Tiger
Survivor; *Eye Of The Tiger* ....(SCO)
Frankenstein & Other Rock Monsters ....(CBA)
Rocky Story ....(SCO)
ST/Rocky III ....(EMI)
Hold That Tiger
Popular Standard; *Out of print recording* ....(OOP)
Hunting Tigers Out In India
Bonzo Dog Band; *Best Of* ....(RHI)
Tadpoles ....(LIB)
I've Got A Tiger By The Tail
Buck Owens; *Billboard Top Country Hits-1965* .. (RHI)
Live At Carnegie Hall ....(CMF)
Rick Springfield; *Living In Oz* ....(RCA)
Paper Tiger
Painted Willie; *Relics* ....(SST)
Sue Thompson; *Collectables Presents History Of Rock-#4* ....(CLT)
Return Of The Tasmanian Tiger
John Fahey; *Live In Tasmania* ....(TAK)
Ride The Tiger
Jefferson Starship; *Dragonfly* ....(RCA)
Flight Log ....(GRU)
Gold ....(RCA)

Tiger
Fabian; *Best Of* ....(MCA)
Greatest Hits ....(EVR)
Partytime '50s ....(PRY)
Super Oldies/'50s-#7 ....(AUF)
'50s Dance Party ....(DOM)
Tiger In A Dress
Dan Reed Network; *Slam* ....(MEr)
Tiger In The Rain
Michael Franks; *Tiger In The Rain* ....(WB)
Tiger In Your Tank
Muddy Waters; *At Newport* ....(CSS)
Tiger Rag
Django Reinhardt; *Jazz Legacy* ....(IC)
Legendary ....(CRS)
Django Reinhardt & Stephane Grappelli; *Django Reinhardt & Stephane Grappelli* ....(CRS)
Les Paul & Mary Ford; *Selections From Legend & Legacy Box Set* ....(CAP)
Louis Armstrong; *Essential* ....(VAN)
Louis & The Big Bands ....(DSQ)
Mostly Blues ....(OLR)
Stardust ....(POR)
Louis Armstrong/Friends; *20 Golden Pieces Of* ..(BLD)
Mills Brothers; *22 Great Hits* ....(RAN)
Preservation Hall Jazz Band; *New Orleans-#1* ...(COL)
Tiger Rose
Robert Hunter; *Tiger Rose* ....(RYK)
Tiger Woman
Claude King; *American Originals* ....(COL)
Claude King's Best ....(GUS)
Tiger, Tiger
Barbara Tiger/Original Cast; *Apple Tree* ....(SSP)

ANIMALS: U

Unicorn
Irish Rovers; *Greatest Hits* ....(MCA)
Unicorn ....(MCA)
Vintage Music-Classic Oldies-#19 ....(MCA)

ANIMALS: W

Brother Wolf, Sister Moon
Cult; *Love* ....(SIR)
Crazed Weasel
Ricky Peterson; *Night Watch* ....(WB)
Cry Wolf
Laura Branigan; *Touch* ....(ATL)
Stevie Nicks; *Other Side Of The Mirror* ....(MOD)
Victoria Shaw; *In Full View* ....(RPR)
Dire Wolf
Grateful Dead; *Reckoning* ....(ARI)
Workingman's Dead ....(WB)
Hungry Like The Wolf
Duran Duran; *Arena* ....(CAP)
Decade ....(CAP)
Duran Duran ....(CAP)
Rio ....(CAP)
I Am The Walrus
Beatles; *1967-1970* ....(CAP)
Magical Mystery Tour ....(CAP)
Rarities ....(CAP)
Reel Music ....(CAP)
Li'l Red Riding Hood
Sam The Sham/Pharaohs; *Best Of* ....(POL)
Cruisin'-1966 ....(INC)
Pharaohization-Best Of ....(RHI)
Lonesome Roving Wolves
Rosalie Sorrels; *Lonesome Roving Wolves-Songs & Ballads Of The West* ....(GRE)
Pop Goes The Weasel
3rd Bass; *Derelicts Of Dialect* ....(DFJ)
Bing Crosby; *Where The Blue Of The Night Meets The...* ....(BIO)
Boston Pops Orchestra/Arthur Fiedler; *Forever Fiedler* ....(RCA)
Merry Macs; *Small Fry-Capitol Sings Kids Songs...* (CAP)
Pressed Rat & Warthog
Cream; *Wheels Of Fire* ....(POL)
Rock-N-Roll Weasel
Dead Serios; *Ralph Rules* ....(LGS)

Run Of The Wolf
Cris Williamson; *Wolf Moon* ....(OLI)
Run With The Wolf
Blackmore's Rainbow; *Rainbow Rising* ....(OYS)
Strolling Wolf
Creatures; *Boomerang* ....(GEF)
Theme From "Dances With Wolves"
John Barry; *Moviola* ....(EPI)
Werewolves Of London
Warren Zevon; *Excitable Boy* ....(ASY)
Quiet Normal Life-Best Of ....(ASY)
Stand In The Fire ....(ASY)
ST/Color Of Money ....(MCA)
Who's Afraid Of The Big Bad Wolf
Barbra Streisand; *Album* ....(COL)
Just For The Record ....(COL)
L.L. Cool J; *Simply Mad About The Mouse* ......(COL)
Mormon Tabernacle Choir/Columbia Symph.; *When
You Wish Upon A Star-Disney Tribute* ....(COL)
M. Moder/D. Compton/P. Colvig/Others; *Disney
Collection-#1* ....(DIS)
Wild As A Wildcat
Charlie Walker; *Golden Hits* ....(PLN)
Will The Wolf Survive
Los Lobos; *How Will The Wolf Survive* ....(SLS)
Waylon Jennings; *Country Classics-#6
(1985-1986)* ....(MSP)
New Classic Waylon ....(MCA)
Will The Wolf Survive ....(MCA)
Witch Wolf
Styx; *Best Of* ....(RCA)
Serpent ....(RCA)
You Cried Wolf
Todd Rundgren; *Anthology-1968-1985* ....(RHI)
Hermit Of Mink Hollow ....(RHI)

ART & PHOTOGRAPHY, Cameras

8 X 10
Bill Anderson; *Story* ....(MCA)
Art Decade
David Bowie; *Low* ....(RYK)
Art For Art's Sake
10 CC; *Greatest Hits 1972-78* ....(POL)
How Dare You ....(MER)
Live & Let Live ....(MER)
Art Lover
Kinks; *Give The People What They Want* ....(ARI)
Live-The Road ....(MCA)
Artist
Cat Stevens; *Back To Earth* ....(A&M)
Jeannie C. Riley; *Things Go Better With Love* ....(PLN)
Artistry In Rhythm
Stan Kenton; *Comprehensive* ....(CAP)
Greatest Hits ....(CAP)
Live In Europe ....(MER)
Road Show ....(CAP)
Summer Of '51 ....(GRL)
Artists Only
Talking Heads; *More Songs About Buildings &
Food* ....(SIR)
Name Of This Band Is Talking Heads ....(SIR)
Camera
Crosby, Stills & Nash; *After The Storm* ....(ATL)
R.E.M.; *Reckoning* ....(IRS)
Camera Eye
Rush; *Moving Pictures* ....(MER)
Camera Never Lies
Elton John; *Reg Strikes Back* ....(MCA)
Michael Franks; *Camera Never Lies* ....(WB)
Centerfold
J. Geils Band; *Flashback-Best Of* ....(EMI)
Freeze-Frame ....(EMI)
Showtime ....(EMI)
Children And Art
Original Cast; *Sunday In The Park With George* ..(RCA)
Every Picture Tells A Story
Rod Stewart; *Best Of* ....(MER)
Every Picture Tells A Story ....(MER)
Storyteller/Complete Anthology 1964-1990 ......(WB)

Eyes Of A Painter
Kate Wolf; *Close To You* ....(KAL)
Evening In Austin ....(KAL)
Gold In California (Retrospective...) ....(KAL)
Family Snapshot
Peter Gabriel; *Peter Gabriel* ....(GEF)
Plays Live ....(GEF)
Shaking The Tree-16 Golden Hits ....(GEF)
Freeze-Frame
J. Geils Band; *Flashback-Best Of* ....(EMI)
Freeze-Frame ....(EMI)
Girls On Film
Duran Duran; *Decade* ....(CAP)
Duran Duran ....(CAP)
Great Work Of Art
T.G. Sheppard; *Biggest Hits* ....(COL)
Livin' On The Edge ....(COL)
Having My Picture Taken
Boomtown Rats; *Fine Art of Surfacing* ....(COL)
Hotel Rats & Photostats
Jimmy Page; *ST/Death Wish 2* .... (SS)
I've Got A Secret Miniature Camera
Peter Murphy; *ST/Pump Up The Volume* .... (MCA)
Kodachrome
Paul Simon; *Greatest Hits* ....(COL)
Negotations & Love Songs 1971-1986 ....(WB)
There Goes Rhymin' Simon ....(WB)
Simon & Garfunkel; *Concert In Central Park* .....(WB)
Let The Picture Paint Itself
Rodney Crowell; *Let The Picture Paint Itself* ....(MCA)
Masterpiece
Atlantic Starr; *Love Crazy* ....(RPR)
Grover Washington, Jr.; *At His Best* ....(MOT)
Soul Box-#1 ....(MOT)
Temptations; *Anthology* ....(MOT)
Masterpiece ....(MOT)
Miss Emily's Picture
John Conlee; *Country Gold* ....(PRY)
Greatest Hits ....(MCA)
With Love ....(MCA)
Mona Lisa
Carl Mann; *Original Memphis Rock & Roll-#1* ...(SUN)
Sun Story ....(RHI)
Elvis Presley; *Legendary Performer-#4* ....(RCA)
Jim Reeves; *Pure Gold* ....(RCA)
Nat King Cole; *Best Of-#1* ....(CAP)
Capitol Collectors Series ....(CAP)
Story ....(CAP)
Unforgettable ....(CAP)
Neville Brothers; *Fiyo On The Bayou* ....(A&M)
Mona Lisa On Cruise Control
Dennis Robbins; *Born Ready* .... (GIA)
Mona Lisas And Mad Hatters
Elton John; *Honky Chateau* ....(POL)
Reg Strikes Back ....(MCA)
Mona Lisa's Lost Her Smile
David Allan Coe; *17 Greatest Hits* ....(COL)
19 Hot Country Requests-#2 ....(EPI)
For The Record-First 10 Years ....(COL)
Greatest Country Hits/'80s-1984 ....(COL)
Just Divorced ....(COL)
Museum
Greg Kihn Band; *Next Of Kihn* .... (BES)
Herman's Hermits; *XX-Greatest Hits* ....(AKO)
Wall Of Voodoo; *Seven Days In Sammystown* .... (IRS)
Night Of Van Gogh
Boz Scaggs; *Other Roads* ....(COL)
Old Photographs
Carlene Carter; *Two Sides To Every Woman* ......(WB)
Charley Pride; *Amazing Love* ....(RCA)
Sawyer Brown; *Somewhere In The Night* ....(LIB)
Paint A Picture Of Yourself
Harry Chapin; *Dance Band On The Titanic* ......(ELE)
Paint A Vulgar Picture
Smiths; *Strangeways Here We Come* ....(SIR)
Paint Another Picture
Darlene Love; *Paint Another Picture* ....(COL)
Paint Box
Pink Floyd; *Relics* ....(CAP)
Paint By Numbers
Al Stewart; *24 Carrots* ....(ARI)
Paint It Black
Eric Burdon/Animals; *Greatest Hits* ....(ALL)

Rolling Stones; *Aftermath* .... (AKO)
   Flashpoint .... (RS)
   Hot Rocks-1964-1971 .... (AKO)
   Singles Collection-London Years .... (AKO)
   Through The Past Darkly-Big Hits-#2 .... (AKO)
Paint Me A Picture (You Don't Have To)
Gary Lewis; *Best Of* .... (EMI)
   Greatest Hits .... (RHI)
Paint Me Back Home In Wyoming
Chris LeDoux; *Paint Me Back Home In Wyoming* . (LIB)
   Sounds Of The Western Country .... (LIB)
Paint Your Pretty Picture
Carmen McRae; *At The Great American Music*
Hall .... (BLN)
Painted Bird
Siouxsie/Banshees; *Kiss In The Dream House* .... (GEF)
   Nocturne .... (GEF)
Painted Picture
Commodores; *All The Great Hits* .... (MOT)
Painted Rhythm
Stan Kenton; *Comprehensive* .... (CAP)
   Greatest Hits .... (CAP)
   Kenton In Hi-Fi .... (BLN)
Painted, Tainted Rose
Al Martino; *Best Of* .... (CAP)
   Capitol Collectors Series .... (CAP)
Painting Box
Incredible String Band; *5000 Spirits* .... (ELE)
   Relics Of .... (ELE)
People Take Pictures Of Each Other
Kinks; *Are The Village Green Preservation Soc.* ... (RPR)
Photograph
Def Leppard; *Pyromania* .... (MER)
Ella Fitzgerald; *Ella Abraca Jobim* .... (PAB)
Ringo Starr; *Blast From Your Past* .... (CAP)
   Ringo .... (CAP)
Photograph Of You
Depeche Mode; *Broken Frame* .... (SIR)
Photographic
Depeche Mode; *Speak & Spell* .... (SIR)
Photographs & Memories
Jim Croce; *Time In A Bottle* .... (21)
   Photographs & Memories-His Greatest Hits ..... (21)
   You Don't Mess Around With Jim .... (LIF)
Picasso's Last Words
Paul McCartney/Wings; *Band On The Run* .... (CAP)
   Wings Over America .... (CAP)
Picture
Ricky Van Shelton; *Loving Proof* .... (COL)
Picture Book
Kinks; *Are The Village Green Preservation Soc.* ... (RPR)
Simply Red; *Picture Book* .... (ELE)
Picture From Life's Other Side
George Jones; *Hallelujah Weekend* .... (EPI)
Goebel Reeves; *Texas Drifter* .... (GLN)
Hank Williams; *Beyond The Sunset* .... (POL)
   Hey Good Lookin' (Dec. 1950-July 1951) ...... (POL)
Picture In My Wallet
Darrell/Oxfords; *45* .... (RLL)
Picture Of England
Sun & The Moon; *Sun & The Moon* .... (GEF)
Picture Of Love
Continentals; *Doo-Wop Era-Harlem N.Y.-40 Hits* (CLT)
Picture Of Me Without You
George Jones; *Anniversary-Ten Years Of Hits* ..... (EPI)
   Best Of .... (EPI)
   Columbia Country Classics-#4-Nashville .... (COL)
   Super Hits .... (EPI)
Lorrie Morgan; *Something In Red* .... (RCA)
Picture Of Our Love
Mickey Gilley; *Gilley* .... (EPI)
Picture On The Wall
Carter Family; *Three Generations* .... (COL)
   'Mid The Green Fields Of Virginia .... (RCA)
Picture Puzzle
Kate Wolf; *Evening In Austin* .... (KAL)
   Give Yourself To Love .... (KAL)
   Lines On The Paper .... (KAL)
Pictured Life
Scorpions; *Best Of* .... (RCA)
   Tokyo Tapes .... (RCA)
   Virgin Killer .... (RCA)
Pictures Don't Lie
Billy Ray Cyrus; *Red Hot + Country* .... (MER)

Pictures Of Bernadette
Talk Talk; *45* .... (EMI)
Pictures Of Home
Deep Purple; *Machine Head* ....(WB)
Pictures Of Lily
Pete Townshend; *Another Scoop* ....(ATC)
Who; *Magic Bus* .... (MCA)
   Meaty Beaty Big & Bouncy .... (MCA)
   Who's Better Who's Best-Very Best Of .... (MCA)
Pictures Of Matchstick Men
Camper Van Beethoven; *Edge Of Rock* ....(ERA)
   Key Lime Pie .... (VIA)
Status Quo; *History Of British Rock-#8* .... (RHI)
   Sixties Rule!-#1 .... (OW)
Pictures Of You
Cure; *Disintegration* .... (ELE)
   Mixed Up .... (ELE)
   Show .... (ELE)
Pictures (S.B.)
Statler Brothers; *Best Of* .... (MER)
Porno For Pyros
Porno For Pyros; *Porno For Pyros* ....(WB)
Porno Freak
Blowfly; *Twisted World Of* .... (OPS)
Pornography
Cure; *Cure* .... (ELE)
Portrait
Damned; *Anything* .... (MCA)
Enya; *Enya* ....(ATL)
Kansas; *Point Of Know Return* .... (KIR)
   Two For The Show .... (KIR)
Portrait In Atlanta
House Of Love; *Audience With The Mind* ....(FON)
Portrait Of Jenny
Nat King Cole; *Unforgettable* .... (CAP)
Red Garland & Ray Barretto; *Manteca* .... (PRS)
Portrait Of My Love
Dee Clark; *Best Of* .... (VJ)
Lettermen; *Best Of* ....(CAP)
Portraits Of Summer
Jim Bajor; *Gentle Images* .... (JBX)
Pretty Little Picture
Original Cast; *Funny Thing Happened On The*
Way... ....(CAP)
Stephen Sondheim; *Collector's Sondheim* ....(RCA)
Robot Portrait
Quincy Jones/Orchestra; *Quintessence* .... (MCI)
Self Portrait
Ritchie Blackmore; *Rainbow* .... (POL)
Send A Picture Of Mother
Johnny Cash; *At Folsom Prison & San Quentin* ...(COL)
Snap Shot
Slave; *Show Time* .... (COT)
Snapshot
Art Of Noise; *(Who's Afraid Of)* .... (ISL)
Sylvia; *Greatest Hits* ....(RCA)
   Snapshot ....(RCA)
Sunday In The Park With George
Original Cast; *Sunday In The Park With George* ..(RCA)
Tapestry
Carole King; *Tapestry* .... (EPI)
Tear Me Out Of The Picture
George Jones; *High-Tech Redneck* .... (MCA)
Texas Tattoo
Gibson/Miller Band; *Steppin' Country* ....(COL)
   Where There's Smoke .... (EPI)
Tit Photographer Blues
Fabulous Poodles; *Mirror Stars* .... (EPI)
Van Gogh's Left Ear
Kenny Garrett; *Black Hope* ....(WB)
Vincent
Don McLean; *American Pie* .... (EMI)
   Best Of .... (EMI)
   Greatest Hits Then & Now .... (EMI)
Visions Of Gaudi
Phil Woods; *Here's To My Lady* ....(CHE)
When I Paint My Masterpiece
Band; *Bob Dylan 30th Anniversary Concert* ......(COL)
   To Kingdom Come-Definitive Collection ....(CAP)
Bob Dylan; *Greatest Hits-#2* ....(COL)
Where Do I Fit In
Clay Walker; *Clay Walker* .... (GIA)

Wishing (If I Had A Photograph Of You)
A Flock Of Seagulls; *Best Of* .... (JVA)
Listen .... (JVA)

ASTROLOGY, Tarot
See Also: CIRCLES, FUTURE, LIFE, MAGIC,
STARS

Ace Of Swords
Alan Parsons Project; *Turn Of A Friendly Card* .. (ARI)
Ace Of Wands
Steve Hackett; *Steve Hackett* .... (CHR)
Voyage Of The Acolyte .... (CHR)
Aquarian Cycle
Lonnie Liston Smith; *Song For The Children* .....(COL)
Aquarius
Original Broadway Cast; *Hair* ....(RCA)
Aquarius/Let The Sunshine In Medley
Fifth Dimension; *Billboard Top Rock & Roll
Hits-1969* .... (RHI)
Greatest Hits On Earth .... (ARI)
ST/1969 .... (POL)
ST/Forrest Gump .... (EPX)
Aries
Supertramp; *Indelibly Stamped* .... (A&M)
Born Under A Bad Sign
Albert King; *Atlantic Blues-Guitar* .... (ATL)
Masterworks .... (ATL)
Stax Blues Masters-Blue Monday .... (STX)
Cream; *Strange Brew-Very Best Of* .... (RSO)
Wheels Of Fire .... (RSO)
Paul Butterfield Blues Band; *Live* .... (ELE)
Rita Coolidge; *Greatest Hits* .... (A&M)
Rita Coolidge .... (A&M)
Simpsons; *Sing The Blues* .... (GEF)
Born Under The Wrong Sign
Nazareth; *Close Enough For Rock 'N' Roll* ......(A&M)
Born With The Moon In Virgo
Michael Franks; *Previously Unavailable* .... (DRG)
Capricorn
Barclay James Harvest; *Eyes Of The Universe* .... (POL)
Motorhead; *No Sleep 'Til Hammersmith* .... (RR)
Overkill .... (RR)
Richard Elliot; *Initial Approach* .... (BLN)
Wayne Shorter; *Super Nova* .... (BLN)
Capricorn Kings
Lee Wright; *45* .... (PRA)
Capricorn Rising
Richard Evans; *Richard Evans* .... (A&M)
Capricorn Sister
Mother Love Bone; *Mother Love Bone* .... (STD)
Five Planets In Leo
Brew Moore Quintet; *Brew Moore Quintet* .... (FAN)
Gemini
Alan Parsons Project; *Eye In The Sky* .... (ARI)
Cannonball Adderley; *Coast To Coast* .... (MS)
In Europe-Collection-#7 ....(LAN)
Sextet-In New York ....(RVR)
Mamas & The Papas; *Papas & Mamas* .... (MCA)
Miracles; *Greatest Hits* .... (TAM)
Gemini Dream
Moody Blues; *Long Distance Voyager* .... (POL)
Voices In The Sky-Best Of ....(T/P)
Gemini Girl
David Allan Coe; *Son Of The South* ....(COL)
I Feel Lucky
Mary Chapin Carpenter; *Come On Come On* ....(COL)
I, Capricorn
Shirley Bassey; *Greatest Hits* .... (EMI)
I'm A Scorpio
Russ Ballard; *At The Third Stroke* .... (EPI)
Jesus Was a Capricorn
Kris Kristofferson; *Jesus Was a Capricorn* ....(COL)
Journey To Capricorn
Stan Kenton; *Journey Into Capricorn* ....(CW)
Leo Rising
Ronnie Montrose; *Open Fire* .... (WB)
Magic Moon
Peter Frampton; *Something's Happening* .... (A&M)
Maybe I'm A Leo
Deep Purple; *Machine Head* .... (WB)

My Aquarian
Juan Martin; *Through The Moving Window* ..... (NOV)
Pisces
Bobby Lyle; *The Genie* ....(CAP)
Lief Strand; *Zodiac* .... (INN)
Matthew McCauley; *ST/Laserium Zodiac* ....(POL)
Pisces Apple Lady
Leon Russell; *Leon Russell* .... (MCA)
Sagittarius
Burkard Schmidl; *Zodiac Symphony* .... (INN)
Scorpio
Grandmaster Flash/Furious Five; *Street Jams-Hip-Hop
From The Top-#2* .... (RHI)
Leif Strand; *Zodiac* .... (INN)
Scorpio Crew
Yellowman; *Don't Burn It Down* .... (SHA)
Scorpio Rising
10,000 Maniacs; *Wishing Chair* .... (ELE)
Army Of Lovers; *Army Of Lovers* .... (GIA)
Son Of Sagittarius
Eddie Kendricks; *Motown Superstar Series-#19* . (MOT)
Southern Cross
Ozark Mountain Daredevils; *Car Over The Lake
Album* .... (A&M)
Swinging Scorpio
Buddy Tate & Humphrey Lyttelton; *Swinging
Scorpio* ....(BL)
Tarot Woman
Richie Blackmore's Rainbow; *Rainbow Rising* .... (POL)
Taurus
Leif Strand; *Zodiac* .... (INN)
Spirit; *Spirit* .... (EPI)
Time Circle .... (EPI)
Turn Of A Friendly Card
Alan Parsons Project; *Best Of-#2* .... (ARI)
Turn Of A Friendly Card .... (ARI)
Virgo
Jose Feliciano; *And The Feeling's Good* ....(RCA)
Matthew McCauley; *ST/Laserium Zodiac* ....(POL)
Wayne Shorter; *Best Of-Blue Note Years* ...... (BLN)
Night Dreamer .... (BLN)
Virgo Clowns
Van Morrison; *His Band & Street Choir* .... (WB)
Water Sign
Gary Wright; *Light Of Smiles* .... (WB)
Parliament; *Motor-Booty Affair* .... (CAS)
Zodiac
Fatback Band; *Man With The Band* .... (SPR)
Zodiacs
Roberta Kelly; *Zodiac Lady* .... (CAS)

BABY, Being Born, Pregnant

And The Baby Never Cries
Harry Chapin; *Sniper & Other Love Songs* .... (ELE)
And The Cradle Will Rock
Van Halen; *Women & Children First* .... (WB)
Annie Had A Baby
Hank Ballard/Midnighters; *Cruisin'-1955* .... (INC)
Babies Makin' Babies
Sly/Family Stone; *Anthology* .... (EPI)
Fresh .... (EPI)
Baby Blue
Beach Boys; *L.A.-The Light Album* ....(CAR)
Echoes; *Super Oldies!'60s-#5* ....(AUF)
Gene Vincent; *Capitol Collectors Series* ....(CAP)
George Strait; *If You Ain't Lovin' (You Ain't
Livin')* .... (MCA)
Paul Butterfield; *North South* .... (RHI)
Baby Boom Baby
James Taylor; *Never Die Young* ....(COL)
Baby Doll
Bessie Smith; *Complete Recordings-#3* ....(COL)
Carlo; *La Bamba & Other Original Hits* ....(LAU)
Devo; *Total Devo* ....(ENC)
Ella Fitzgerald; *Best Of* .... (MCA)
Farmers; *Rock Angel* ....(FF)
Marvin & Johnny; *Flipped Out* .... (SPE)
Memphis Slim; *Raining The Blues* .... (FAN)
Raindogs; *Border Drive-In Theatre* ....(ATC)
Rita Remington; *Girls Girls Girls* .... (PLN)
Tony! Toni! Tone!; *Who?* ....(WNG)

Baby Doll Polka
Frank Yankovic; *America's Favorites* .... (SMA)
  One More Time .... (CRS)
Baby Driver
Simon & Garfunkel; *Bridge Over Troubled Water* (COL)
  Collected Works ....(COL)
Baby Elephant Walk
Henry Mancini; *All-Time Greatest Hits-#1* ......(RCA)
  Pure Gold ....(RCA)
Baby Face
Al Jolson; *Story-#3* ....(MCA)
  World's Greatest ....(MCA)
Bobby Darin; *Splish Splash-Best Of-#1* ......(ATL)
Kinks; *Everybody's In Show Biz* .... (RHI)
Little Richard; *Compact Command Performances* (MOT)
  Greatest Hits ....(EVR)
  His Greatest Hits .... (VJ)
  Tutti Frutti ....(ACC)
Baby Fat
Wet Willie; *Greatest Hits* ....(POL)
Baby Mine
Barbara Cook; *Disney Album* .... (MCA)
Bette Midler; *ST/Beaches* ....(ATL)
Bonnie Raitt/Was (Not Was); *Stay Awake-Various Music*
  Of Disney Films ....(A&M)
Baby Needs New Shoes
Restless Heart; *Matters Of The Heart* ....(RCA)
Baby Ruth
John Prine; *Storm Windows* ....(ASY)
Baby Sitter
Betty Wright; *Golden Classics* ....(CLT)
Harry Chapin; *Portrait Gallery* ....(ELE)
Baby Talk
Billy Idol; *Don't Stop* ....(CHR)
Jan & Dean; *Best Of* ....(EMI)
  Collectables History Of Rock-#9 ....(CLT)
  One Summer Night/Live ....(RHI)
Baby's House
Steve Miller Band; *Anthology* ....(CAP)
  Your Saving Grace ....(CAP)
Baby's Smile Woman's Kiss
Johnny Duncan; *Best Of* ....(COL)
Barefoot & Pregnant
Joan Armatrading; *To The Limit* ....(A&M)
Biggest Hurt, The
Barbara Fairchild; *The Biggest Hurt* .... (AUD)
Billie Jean
Michael Jackson; *Thriller* ....(EPI)
Billion Dollar Babies
Alice Cooper; *Alice Cooper Show* ....(WB)
  Billion Dollar Babies ....(WB)
  Greatest Hits ....(WB)
Born A Fool
Freddie Hart; *Best Of* ....(MCA)
Born A Woman
Sandy Posey; *Best Of Town & Country-#3* ....(GUS)
  Cruisin'-1966 ....(INC)
Sandy Posey/Skeeter Davis/Wanda Jackson .....(GUS)
  Super Hits-#5 ....(GUS)
  With Skeeter Davis; Best Of ....(GUS)
Born Again
Christians; *Christians* .... (ISL)
Born Again Human
B.B. King; *There Must Be A Better World*
  Somewhere ....(MCA)
Born And Raised In Compton
DJ Quik; *S* ....(PRO)
Born Country
Alabama; *Greatest Hits-#2* ....(RCA)
Born Cross-Eyed
Grateful Dead; *Anthem Of The Sun* ....(WB)
  What A Long Strange Trip It's Been ....(WB)
Born Enchanter
Fleetwood Mac; *Heroes Are Hard To Find* ....(RPR)
Born Fighter
Nick Lowe; *Basher: Best Of* ....(COL)
  Labour Of Lust ....(COL)
Born For Adventure
Styx; *Equinox* ....(A&M)
Born Free
Andy Williams; *16 Most Requested Songs* ....(COL)
  Greatest Hits ....(COL)
John Barry; *Film Music Of* ....(COL)
Matt Monro; *ST/Born Free* ....(MGM)

Roger Williams; *Best Of* .... (MCA)
  Golden Hits ....(MCA)
Born In a Prison
John & Yoko Lennon/Others; *Sometime In New York*
  City ....(CAP)
Born In America
Riot; *Born In America* ....(QUA)
Born In Chicago
George Thorogood/Destroyers; *Boogie People* ... (EMI)
Paul Butterfield Blues Band; *Golden Butter* ..... (ELE)
  Paul Butterfield Blues Band ....(ELE)
Pixies; *Rubaiyat (Elektra's 40th Anniversary)* ... (ELE)
Born In East L.A.
Cheech & Chong; *45* ....(MCA)
Born In Georgia
Tinsley Ellis; *Fanning The Flames* ....(ALG)
Born In Louisiana
Clarence "Gatemouth" Brown; *Alligator Records 20th*
  Anniversary ....(ALG)
  Standing My Ground ....(ALG)
Troy Turner; *Handful Of Aces* .... (ICH)
Born In Mississippi
Chris LeDoux; *Wild & Wooly* ....(LIB)
Born In Moscow
Vasily Shumov; *My District* ....(GC)
Born In The Fifties
Police; *Outlandos D'Amour* ....(A&M)
Born In The U.S.A.
Bruce Springsteen; *Born In The U.S.A.* ....(COL)
Bruce Springsteen/E Street Band;
  Live-1975-1985 ....(COL)
Born In The Water
Tragically Hip; *Road Apples* ....(MCA)
Born Late '58
Mott The Hoople; *Ballad Of Mott* ....(COL)
  Greatest Hits ....(COL)
Born Loose
Rod Stewart; *Footloose & Fancy Free* ....(WB)
Born On A Friday
Cleo Laine; *Born On A Friday* ....(RCA)
  Return To Carnegie ....(RCA)
Linda Hopkins; *How Blue Can You Get* ....(QKS)
Born On A Monday
Michael Quatro; *Bottom Line* ....(SPC)
Born On The Bayou
Creedence Clearwater Revival; *Bayou Country* ..(FAN)
  Chooglin' ....(FAN)
  Gold ....(FAN)
  Live In Europe ....(FAN)
  The Concert ....(FAN)
  '68-'69 ....(FAN)
Born Ready
Jesse Hunter; *A Man Like Me* ....(BNA)
Born To Be Alive
Patrick Hernandez; *Let's Dance-DJ's Collection* ..(COL)
Born To Be Bad
George Thorogood/Destroyers; *Born To Be Bad* . (EMI)
  ST/Bull Durham ....(CAP)
Runaways; *Best Of* ....(MER)
Born To Be Blue
George Shearing & Mel Torme; *Evening With* ... (CCJ)
Judds; *Greatest Hits-#2* ....(RCA)
  Love Can Build A Bridge ....(RCC)
Steve Miller; *Born 2 B Blue* ....(CAP)
Born To Be My Baby
Bon Jovi; *New Jersey* ....(MER)
Born To Be Together
Ronettes; *45* ....(CLT)
Born To Be Wild
Steppenwolf; *16 Greatest Hits* ....(MCA)
  Billboard Top Rock 'N' Roll Hits-1968 .... (RHI)
  Live ....(MCA)
  Steppenwolf ....(MCA)
  Vintage Music-Oldies-'60s-#9 & 10 ....(MCA)
Born To Be With You
Chordettes; *Best Of* .... (RHI)
  Greatest Hits ....(EVR)
  Lil' Bit Of Gold 3" CD Series .... (RHI)
Born To Boogie
Hank Williams, Jr.; *Born To Boogie* ....(W/C)
  Greatest Hits III ....(W/C)
T. Rex; *T. Rextasy: Best Of T. Rex 1970-1973* ....(WB)

Born To Cry
Dion/Belmonts; *20 Golden Classics* .... (CLT)
   24 Original Classics .... (ARI)
   Everything You've Always Wanted ....(LAU)
   More Great Hits ....(LAU)
Born To Hand-Jive
Original Broadway Cast; *Grease* .... (POL)
Soundtrack; *Grease* .... (RSO)
Born To Kill
Damned; *Damned Damned Damned* .... (FRN)
   Final Damnation .... (RES)
Gillan; *Double Trouble* .... (MET)
Born To Lose
Johnny Cash; *Johnny Cash* .... (EVR)
   Man-The World-His Music .... (SUN)
   Original .... (SUN)
   Rough Cut King Of Country Music .... (SUN)
Ray Charles; *Greatest Hits-#1* ....(DHL)
Born To Love Me
Roy Orbison; *Legendary* .... (SSP)
   Our Love Song .... (MON)
   Regeneration .... (MON)
Born To Love You
Fabulous Thunderbirds; *Walk That Walk Talk That
Talk* .... (EPA)
Karen Brooks; *Hearts On Fire* ....(WB)
Mark Collie; *Mark Collie* .... (MCA)
Michael Nesmith; *Best Of (1970-1973)* .... (RHI)
Temptations; *Temptin'* .... (MOT)
Born To Move
Creedence Clearwater Revival; *1970* .... (FAN)
   Chronicle-#2 .... (FAN)
   Pendulum .... (FAN)
Born To Rock
Quiet Riot; *Condition Critical* .... (PSH)
Born To Roll
Masta Ace, Inc.; *S* .... (DV)
Born To Run
Bruce Springsteen; *Born To Run* ....(COL)
   Chimes Of Freedom ....(COL)
Bruce Springsteen/E Street Band;
Live-1975-1985 ....(COL)
Emmylou Harris; *Cimarron* .... (WB)
   Profile 2-Best Of .... (WB)
Born To The Breed
Judy Collins; *Judith* .... (ELE)
   So Early In The Spring .... (ELE)
Born To Wander
Rare Earth; *20 Hard-To-Find Motown
Classics-#2* .... (MOT)
   Ecology .... (MOT)
   Hard-To-Find Motown Classics-#2 .... (MOT)
   Motown Superstar-#16 .... (MOT)
Born Too Late
Poni-Tails; *Orig. Classics Oldies From The
'50s-#4* .... (MCA)
Born Under A Bad Sign
Albert King; *Atlantic Blues-Guitar* .... (ATL)
   Masterworks .... (ATL)
   Stax Blues Masters-Blue Monday .... (STX)
Cream; *Strange Brew-Very Best Of* .... (RSO)
   Wheels Of Fire .... (RSO)
Paul Butterfield Blues Band; *Live* .... (ELE)
Rita Coolidge; *Greatest Hits* .... (A&M)
   Rita Coolidge .... (A&M)
Simpsons; *Sing The Blues* .... (GEF)
Born Under Punches
Talking Heads; *Remain In Light* .... (SIR)
Born Under The Wrong Sign
Nazareth; *Close Enough For Rock 'N' Roll* ...... (A&M)
Born With The Blues
Johnny Rodriguez; *Biggest Hits* .... (EPI)
Born With The Moon In Virgo
Michael Franks; *Previously Unavailable* .... (DRG)
Born Yesterday
Everly Brothers; *Born Yesterday* .... (MER)
Careless Love
Dinah Washington; *Bessie Smith Songbook* ...... (EMA)
Pete Fountain; *Mr. New Orleans* ....(MCA)
Preservation Hall Jazz Band; *When The Saints Go
Marchin' In-#3* ....(COL)
Child Is Born
Barbra Streisand; *Lazy Afternoon* ....(COL)

Kenny Burrell; *Fire Into Music-#2* ....(CBA)
   God Bless The Child ....(CBA)
   Heritage ....(VOS)
Toots Thielemans; *East Coast West Coast* .... (PRV)
Come Back As A Flower
Stevie Wonder; *Journey Through The Secret Life
Of...* .... (MOT)
Cradle Of Love
Billy Idol; *Charmed Life* .... (CHR)
   ST/Adventures Of Ford Fairlane .... (ELE)
Cry Like A Baby
Bourgeois Tagg; *Yoyo* .... (ISL)
Box Tops; *Billboard Top Rock 'N' Roll Hits-1968* (RHI)
   Greatest Hits .... (RHI)
   Super Hits-#5 .... (GUS)
   WCBS FM101-History Of Rock-'60s-#4 .... (CLT)
Flock Of Seagulls; *Dream Come True* .... (JVA)
Danny's Song
Anne Murray; *Country* .... (CAP)
   Danny's Song .... (CAP)
   Greatest Hits .... (CAP)
Loggins & Messina; *Best Of-Friends* ....(COL)
   On Stage ....(COL)
   Sittin' In ....(COL)
Dead Babies
Alice Cooper; *Killer* .... (WB)
Don't Take The Girl
Tim McGraw; *Not A Moment Too Soon* .... (CRB)
Every Night When The Sun Goes In
Jo Stafford; *Jo Plus Blues* .... (CRN)
Hand That Rocks The Cradle
Glen Campbell; *Country Classics-#10-1987* .... (MCA)
   Still Within The Sound Of My Voice .... (MCA)
Smiths; *Smiths* .... (SIR)
Having My Baby
Paul Anka; *His Best* .... (EMI)
   Live ....(COL)
   Times Of Your Life .... (UA)
He Would Be Sixteen
Michelle Wright; *Now & Then* .... (ARI)
High Hopes And Empty Pockets
Terry McBride/Ride; *Terry McBride & The Ride* (MCA)
I Was Born
Kenny Rankin; *Like A Seed* .... (LD)
I Was Born A Dreamer
Mickey Gilley; *Live At Gilley's* .... (EPI)
   ST/Tough Enough ....(LIB)
I Was Born About 10,000 Years Ago
Elvis Presley; *Now* ....(RCA)
Odetta; *Live* .... (FAN)
I Was Born When You Kissed Me
Whispers; *Excellence* .... (ALL)
   Shhhh .... (DOR)
I Wasn't Born Yesterday
Allan Clarke; *I Wasn't Born Yesterday* .... (ATL)
Daryl Hall; *Three Hearts In The Happy Ending
Machine* ....(RCA)
Safire; *I Wasn't Born Yesterday* .... (MER)
If You Don't Wanna Get Pregnant
U.T.F.O.; *Bag It & Bone It* .... (JVA)
It's A Boy
Who; *Tommy* ....(MCA)
Lullaby For The First Born
Jesse Winchester; *3rd Down 110 To Go* .... (RHI)
Mammas Don't Let Your Babies Grow Up...
Gibson Miller Band; *ST/The Cowboy Way* .... (EPI)
Waylon Jennings & Willie Nelson; *Greatest Hits* .(RCA)
   Waylon & Willie ....(RCA)
Willie Nelson; *Greatest Hits & Some That Will Be* (COL)
   ST/Electric Horseman ....(COL)
   & Family Live ....(COL)
Newborn Friend
Seal; *Seal* .... (ZTT)
Oldest Baby In The World
John Prine; *Aimless Love* .... (OB)
   Anthology-Great Days .... (RHI)
   Live .... (OB)
Papa Don't Preach
Madonna; *Immaculate Collection* .... (SIR)
   Royal Box .... (SIR)
   True Blue .... (SIR)
Pregnant Again
Loretta Lynn; *45* .... (MCA)

BABY — BARS

Pretty Baby
Al Jolson; *Story-#2* .... (MCA)
Five Satins; *45* .... (CLT)
Kool/Gang; *As One* .... (DL)
Leon Redbone; *Sugar* .... (PRV)
Ready Or Not
Jackson Browne; *For Everyman* .... (ASY)
Scream Like A Baby
David Bowie; *Scary Monsters* .... (RYK)
Shortenin' Bread
Andrews Sisters; *50th Anniversary Collection-#2* (MCA)
Sam McNeil/Dent Wimmer/Others; *Old
Originals-#2* .... (ROU)
Sonny Terry; *Folkways Years-1944-1963* ...... (FLW)
Space Baby
Tubes; *Tubes* .... (A&M)
Sweet Baby James
Highway 101; *Paint The Town* .... (WB)
James Taylor; *Greatest Hits* .... (WB)
Sweet Baby James .... (WB)
Tennessee Born & Bred
Eddie Rabbitt; *Jersey Boy* .... (LIB)
Test Tube Babies
Skids; *Scared To Dance* .... (BP)
There Is A Sucker Born Ev'ry Minute
Cy Coleman; *Presents Barnum* .... (BAI)
This Woman's Work
Kate Bush; *Sensual World* .... (COL)
ST/She's Having A Baby .... (IRS)
Triplets
F. Astaire/N. Fabray/J. Buchanan; *ST/Band
Wagon* .... (MCA)
Original Cast; *Forbidden Broadway* .... (DRG)
Unborn Heart
Dan Hill; *Real Love* .... (COL)
War Baby
"C" Company/Terry Nelson; *Wake Up America* . (PLN)
War Baby Son Of Zorro
Daryl Hall & John Oates; *War Babies* .... (ATL)
When My Baby Smiles At Me
Pete Fountain; *Best Of* .... (MCA)
Why Was I Born
Billie Holiday; *Quintessential-#3-1936-1937* .... (COL)
Elisabeth Welch; *Sings Jerome Kern* .... (RCA)
Frank Sinatra; *Voice: The Columbia
Years-1943-1952* .... (COL)
Lena Horne; *20 Golden Pieces Of* .... (BLD)
The Lady .... (DHL)
With You I'm Born Again
Billy Preston & Syreeta; *15 Of Motown's Greatest Love
Songs* .... (MOT)
Endless Love-Motown Greatest Love Songs ..... (MOT)
Hard-To-Find Motown Classics-#2 .... (MOT)
Motown Story-First 25 Years-#3 .... (MOT)
You Don't Have To Be A Baby To Cry
Ann J. Morton; *45* .... (PRA)
You Must Have Been A Beautiful Baby
Bobby Darin; *Splish Splash-Best Of-#1* .... (ATL)
Johnny Mercer; *Sings Johnny Mercer* .... (EVR)
Russ Morgan/Orchestra; *Play 22 Original Big Band
Recordings* .... (HIN)

BARS, Honky Tonks
See Also: ALCOHOL, JUKEBOX

All I Wanna Do
Sheryl Crow; *Tuesday Night Music Club* .... (A&M)
American Honky-Tonk Bar Association
Garth Brooks; *In Pieces* .... (LIB)
Another Honky Tonk Night On Broadway
David Frizzell & Shelly West; *Album* .... (WB)
Golden Duets .... (VVA)
Arkansas Road House Blues
Memphis Slim; *Traveling With The Blues* .... (STY)
Back To The Barrooms Again
Merle Haggard; *Back To The Barrooms Again* .. (MCA)
His Best .... (MCA)
Bar Room Buddies
Merle Haggard & Clint Eastwood; *ST/Bronco
Billy* .... (ELE)
Barroom Country Singer
Roger Whittaker; *Greatest Hits* .... (RCA)

Barstool Mountain
Moe Bandy; *Greatest Hits* .... (COL)
Wayne Carson; *45* .... (ELE)
Belly Up To The Bar, Boys
Debbie Reynolds; *ST/Unsinkable Molly Brown* .. (MCA)
Original Cast; *Unsinkable Molly Brown* .... (CAP)
Bright Lights & Country Music
Bill Anderson; *Greatest Hits-#1* .... (MCA)
Charleston Railroad Tavern
Bobby Bare; *This Is* .... (RCA)
"Cheers" Theme
Original Music; *Television's Greatest Hits-#3* ..... (TVT)
Close Up The Honky Tonks
Radney Foster; *Red Hot + Country* .... (MER)
Club At The End Of The Street
Elton John; *Sleeping With The Past* .... (MCA)
Country Club
Travis Tritt; *Country Club* .... (WB)
Dear John Letter Lounge
Jerry Jeff Walker; *It's A Good Night For Singin'* . (MCA)
Dim Lights Thick Smoke & Loud Loud Music
Flatt & Scruggs; *Golden Era* .... (ROU)
Flying Burrito Brothers; *Close Encounters Of The West
Coast* .... (RLX)
Farther Along-Best Of .... (A&M)
Hey Bartender
Blues Brothers; *Briefcase Full of Blues* .... (ATL)
Johnny Lee; *Greatest Hits* .... (FM)
Hey Bartender .... (WB)
Honky Tonk Country .... (WB)
Koko Taylor; *Blues Delux* .... (ALG)
Earthshaker .... (ALG)
Hong Kong Bar
Tim Buckley; *Greetings From L.A.* .... (BIZ)
Honky Tonk
Bill Doggett; *21 Number One Hits* .... (OSR)
Cruisin' 1956 .... (INC)
Rock & Roll Show .... (GUS)
Honky Tonk Amnesia
Moe Bandy; *Best Of-#1* .... (COL)
Honky Tonk Attitude
Joe Diffie; *Honky Tonk Attitude* .... (EPI)
Honky Tonk Blues
Charley Pride; *Greatest Hits* .... (RCA)
Hank Williams; *24 Of Greatest Hits* .... (POL)
40 Greatest Hits .... (POL)
Let's Turn Back The Years: 1951-1953 .... (POL)
Rare Takes & Radio Cuts .... (POL)
Huey Lewis/News; *Sports* .... (CHR)
Nitty Gritty Dirt Band; *Will The Circle Be
Unbroken* .... (EMI)
Honky Tonk Crowd
Rick Trevino; *Rick Trevino* .... (COL)
Honky Tonk Heart
Highway 101; *Greatest Hits* .... (WB)
One-O-One .... (WB)
Jim Owen; *45* .... (SUN)
Keith Whitley; *Don't Close Your Eyes* .... (RCA)
Honky Tonk Man
Dwight Yoakam; *Guitars Cadillacs Etc. Etc.* ..... (RPR)
Just Lookin' For A Hit .... (RPR)
Johnny Horton; *Columbia Country Classics-#2* ... (COL)
Marty Robbins; *Greatest Country Hits From The
Movies* .... (EPI)
Honky Tonk Merry Go Round
Patsy Cline; *20 Golden Pieces Of* .... (BLD)
Patsy Cline .... (AUF)
Today Tomorrow & Forever .... (MCA)
Try Again .... (QKS)
Walkin' Dreams-Her First Recordings-#1 ...... (RHI)
Honky Tonk Moon
Randy Travis; *Greatest Hits-#1* .... (WB)
Old 8 X 10 .... (WB)
Rosie Flores; *Once More With Feeling* .... (HT)
Honky Tonk Night Time Man
Lynyrd Skynyrd; *Street Survivors* .... (MCA)
Merle Haggard/Strangers; *Presents His 30th
Album* .... (CAP)
Songs I'll Always Sing .... (CAP)
Honky Tonk Superman
Aaron Tippin; *Call Of The Wild* .... (RCA)
Honky Tonk Toys
John Conlee; *Friday Night Blues* .... (MCA)

Honky Tonk Women
Elton John; *11-17-70* .... (POL)
Humble Pie; *Best* .... (A&M)
  Classics-#14 .... (A&M)
  Eat It .... (A&M)
Ike & Tina Turner; *Best Of* .... (EMI)
  Get Back .... (LIB)
Joe Cocker; *Mad Dogs & Englishmen* .... (A&M)
Rolling Stones; *Get Yer Ya-Ya's Out* .... (AKO)
  Hot Rocks-1964-1971 .... (AKO)
  Love You Live .... (RS)
  Through The Past Darkly-Big Hits-#2 .... (AKO)
Willie Nelson & Leon Russell; *Half Nelson* ..... (COL)

Honky Tonkin'
Hank Williams; *Rare Takes & Radio Cuts* .... (POL)
  24 Of Hank Williams Greatest Hits .... (POL)
  I Ain't Got Nothin' But Time .... (POL)
  Lovesick Blues .... (POL)
Hank Williams, Jr.; *Greatest Hits-#2* .... (E/C)
  High Notes .... (W/C)
  New Tradition Sings The Old Tradition .... (WB)

Honky Tonky Fool
Doug Supernaw; *Red & Rio Grande* .... (BNA)

Honky-Tonk Crazy
Gene Watson; *Honky-Tonk Crazy* .... (EPI)
George Strait; *Strait From The Heart* .... (MCA)

Honky-Tonk Crowd
John Anderson; *Greatest Hits-#2* .... (WB)

Honky-Tonk Heroes
Billy Joe Shaver; *Rebels Renegades & Ramblers* ... (POL)
Waylon Jennings; *Greatest Hits* .... (RCA)
  Outlaws .... (RCA)

It Wasn't God Who Made Honky Tonk Angels
Kitty Wells; *Greatest Hits-#1* .... (SO)
  Story .... (MCA)

My Second Home
Tracy Lawrence; *Alibis* .... (ATL)

Neon Moon
Brooks & Dunn; *Brand New Man* .... (ARI)

Over At Herbie's Juke Joint
Donald Brown; *People Music* .... (MUS)

O'Reilly At The Bar
Dan Hicks/Hot Licks; *Striking It Rich* .... (MCA)

Piano Has Been Drinking
Tom Waits; *Anthology* .... (ASY)
  Small Change .... (ASY)

Prop Me Up Beside The Jukebox
Joe Diffie; *Honky Tonk Attitude* .... (EPI)

Roadhouse Blues
Doors; *13* .... (ELE)
  Best Of .... (ELE)
  Classics .... (ELE)
  Greatest Hits .... (ELE)
  Morrison Hotel .... (ELE)
  ST/Doors .... (ELE)

She's Got The Rhythm (& I Got The Blues)
Alan Jackson; *Lot About Livin' (& A Little 'Bout Love* .... (ARI)

Swinging Doors
George Jones; *20 Golden Pieces Of* .... (BLD)
Merle Haggard; *Capitol Collectors Series* .... (CAP)
Merle Haggard/Strangers; *Best Of* .... (CAP)
  Okie From Muskogee .... (CAP)
  Songs I'll Always Sing .... (CAP)

Texas Honky Tonk
David Houston; *Sings Texas Honky Tonk* .... (DEL)
  Texas Country .... (DEL)

There Is A Tavern In The Town
Stan Wolowic/Polka Chips; *Million-Seller Polkas/Greatest Band...* .... (CAP)

There'll Always Be A Honky Tonk...
Randy Travis; *Honky Tonk Country* .... (WB)
  Storms Of Life .... (WB)

There'll Always Be Honky Tonks In Texas
Darrell McCall & Johnny Bush; *Hot Texas Country* (SO)

Top Hat Bar & Grille
Jim Croce; *50th Anniversary Collection* .... (SAJ)

Y'All Come Back Saloon
Oak Ridge Boys; *Collection* .... (MCA)
  Greatest Hits .... (MCA)
  Y'All Come Back Saloon .... (MCA)

BASEBALL
See Also: SPORTS

Baseball
Michael Franks; *One Bad Habit* .... (WB)

Bug, The
Dire Straits; *On Every Street* .... (WB)
Mary Chapin Carpenter; *Come On Come On* ..... (WB)

Centerfield
John Fogerty; *Centerfield* .... (WB)
  ST/Bull Durham .... (CAP)

Cheap Seats, The
Alabama; *Cheap Seats* .... (RCA)

Cooperstown
Terry Cashman; *45* .... (LIF)

Did You See Jackie Robinson Hit That...
Count Basie; *RCA Victor Blues & Rhythm Revue* .(RCA)
  & Orchestra: Baseball's Greatest Hits .... (RHI)

Dying Cub Fan's Last Request
Steve Goodman; *Baseball's Greatest Hits* .... (RHI)

D-O-D-G-E-R-S Song
Danny Kaye; *Baseball's Greatest Hits* .... (RHI)

Glory Days
Bruce Springsteen; *Born In The U.S.A.* .... (COL)

I Love Mickey
Mickey Mantle & Teresa Brewer; *Baseball's Greatest Hits* .... (RHI)

Joltin' Joe DiMaggio
Les Brown/Orchestra; *Baseball's Greatest Hits* ... (RHI)
  Words & Music Of World War II .... (COL)

Just A Friendly Game Of Baseball
Main Source; *Breaking Atoms* .... (EMI)
  ST/Boyz N The Hood .... (QUE)

Last Game Of The Season (A Blind Man...
David Geddes; *Super Hits/'70s-Have A Nice Day-#20* .... (RHI)

Life's Just A Ballgame
Womack & Womack; *Conscience* .... (ISL)

Love Is Like A Baseball Game
Intruders; *Super Hits* .... (PI)

Nolan Ryan (He's A Hero To Us All)
Jerry Jeff Walker; *Navajo Rug* .... (RYK)

Out Of Left Field
Hank Williams, Jr.; *Out Of Left Field* .... (CPC)
Percy Sledge; *Best Of* .... (ATL)
  It Tears Me Up-Best Of .... (RHI)
  Ultimate Collection-When A Man Loves... .... (ATL)

Red Sox Are Winning
Earth Opera; *Elektrock-'60s* .... (ELE)

Roundin' Third & Heading Home
Fred Koller; *Night Of The Living Fred* .... (ALC)

Say Hey (The Willie Mays Song)
Treniers; *Baseball's Greatest Hits* .... (RHI)

Shoeless Joe From Hannibal, Mo.
Original Broadway Cast; *Damn Yankees* .... (RCA)

Strike Zone
Loverboy; *Keep It Up* .... (COL)

Take Me Out To The Ball Game
Bruce Springsteen; *Baseball's Greatest Hits* .... (RHI)
Doc & Merle Watson; *Baseball's Greatest Hits* ... (RHI)
Frank Zappa; *You Can't Do That On Stage Anymore-#4* .... (RYK)

There Used To Be A Ballpark
Frank Sinatra; *Ol' Blue Eyes Is Back* .... (RPR)
  Reprise Collection .... (RPR)

Three Base Hit
Pat Martino; *Exit* .... (MUS)

Willie, Mickey & The Duke (Talkin'...)
Terry Cashman; *Baseball's Greatest Hits* .... (RHI)

BATHROOM, Bathtub, Sink

30 Years In The Bathroom
Wonderstuff; *Hup!* .... (POL)

Away Go Troubles Down The Drain
Lenny White; *Venusian Summer* .... (NEM)

Bathin' In Love Waters
Paul Kelly; *Stand On The Positive Side* .... (WB)

Bathroom Wall
Faster Pussycat; *Decline Of Western*
Civilization-#2 ....(CAP)
Faster Pussycat ....(ELE)
Bathtub
Snoop Doggy Dogg; *Doggystyle* ....(DR)
Bird Bathroom
Surf Punks; *My Beach* ....(EPI)
Dancing In The Bathtub
John Hartford; *All In The Name Of Love* ....(FF)
Don't Eat The Yellow Snow
Frank Zappa; *Apostrophe/Overnite Sensation* .....(RYK)
Enema Party
Buck Naked/Bare Bottom Boys; *Buck Naked/Bare*
Bottom Boys ....(HEY)
Enema Picnic
Dead Youth; *Intense Brutality* ....(GCI)
Fat Man In The Bathtub
Little Feat; *Dixie Chicken* ....(WB)
Waiting For Columbus ....(WB)
Germans At The Spa
Original London Cast; *Nine* ....(RCA)
I Do My Bawling In The Bathroom
David Peel/Lower East Side; *Have A Marijuana* . (ELE)
In The Girls' Room
Rick James; *Wonderful* ....(RPR)
I'm Gonna Wash That Man Right Outta...
Kiri Te Kanawa/Original Cast; *South Pacific* ....(COL)
Mary Martin/Original Cast; *South Pacific* ....(COL)
Mitzi Gaynor; *ST/South Pacific* ....(RCA)
Weather Girls; *Success* ....(COL)
Let's Talk It Over In The Ladies Room
Curtie/Boom Box; *Black Kisses* ....(RCA)
Little Bit Of Soap
Jarmels; *Collectables Presents History Of Rock-#7* (CLT)
Golden Classics ....(CLT)
Laurie Golden Oldies ....(LAU)
Million Dollar Memories-#1 ....(RCA)
Pick Hits Of The Radio Good Guys ....(LAU)
Paul Davis; *Best Of* ....(BNG)
Little Bit Of ....(BNG)
Meeting In The Ladies Room
Klymaxx; *Meeting In The Ladies Room* ....(CON)
ST/Secret Admirer ....(MCA)
Men's Room L.A.
Kinky Friedman; *Lasso From El Paso* ....(EPI)
Mirror In The Bathroom
English Beat; *I Just Can't Stop It* ....(IRS)
ST/Dance Craze ....(CHR)
What Is Beat ....(IRS)
Norwegian Wood
Beatles; *1962-1966* ....(CAP)
Box Set ....(CAP)
Love Songs ....(CAP)
Rubber Soul ....(CAP)
Outhouse Quake
Bootsauce; *Bull* ....(ISL)
Paper Toilet
Henry Threadgill; *Too Much Sugar For A Dime* .. (AXI)
Potty Train 'Em
Poet Society; *Q.D. III Soundlab* ....(QUE)
Shaving Cream
Benny Bell & Paul Wynn; *Dr. Demento's Dementia*
Royale ....(RHI)
Dr. Demento's Greatest-#1-'40s & 50s ....(RHI)
She Came In Through The Bathroom Window
Beatles; *Abbey Road* ....(CAP)
Box Set ....(CAP)
Joe Cocker; *Classics-#4* ....(A&M)
Joe Cocker ....(A&M)
Live ....(CAP)
Mad Dogs & Englishmen ....(A&M)
Shit House Shuffle
Aerosmith; *Pandora's Box* ....(COL)
Shower Me With Your Love
Surface; *2nd Wave* ....(COL)
Best Of...Nice Time 4 Lovin' ....(COL)
Power Jams-Today's Hottest Hits ....(KT)
Smokin' In The Boys' Room
Brownsville Station; *Hit Singles-1958-1977* ......(ATL)
Legends Of Rock Guitar-'70s ....(RHI)
ST/Rock & Roll High School ....(SIR)
Motley Crue; *Decade Of Decadence* ....(ELE)
Theatre Of Pain ....(ELE)

Splish Splash
Barbra Streisand; *Wet* ....(COL)
Bobby Darin; *Greatest Hits* ....(CCB)
Oldies But Goodies-#8 ....(OSR)
Splish Splash-Best Of-#1 ....(ATL)
Story ....(ATC)
Sha-Na-Na; *Having An Oldies Party With* ....(KT)
Toilet
Jeffrey Frederick/Clamtones; *Spiders In The*
Moonlight ....(ROU)
Tracy In The Bathroom Killing Thrills
Mary's Danish; *Circa* ....(MC)
Experience-Live + Foxey Lady ....(CML)
T.S.R. (Toilet Stool Rap)
Biz Markie; *I Need A Haircut* ....(CLD)
You Left The Water Running
Huey Lewis/News; *Four Chords & Several Years*
Ago ....(ELE)
Otis Redding; *Otis Redding Story* ....(ATL)

BIRDS, Fowl
See Also: FLYING

Ain't Nobody Here But Us Chickens
Louis Jordan; *Best Of* ....(MCA)
Albatross
Fleetwood Mac; *25 Years-The Chain* ....(WB)
Vintage Years ....(SIR)
Judy Collins; *Colors Of The Day-Best Of* ......(ELE)
Wildflowers ....(ELE)
Public Image, Ltd.; *Second Edition* ....(ISL)
And Your Bird Can Sing
Beatles; *Revolver* ....(CAP)
Yesterday & Today ....(CAP)
At Seventeen
Janis Ian; *Between The Lines* ....(COL)
Super Hits/'70s-Have A Nice Day-#15 ....(RHI)
Baltimore Oriole
Carmen McRae; *Greatest Of* ....(MCA)
George Harrison; *Somewhere In England* ....(DKH)
Bangkok Cockfight
Martin Denny; *Exotica-Best Of* ....(RHI)
Bird
George Jones; *Too Wild Too Long* ....(EPI)
Jerry Reed/Friends; *Bird* ....(RCA)
Greatest Hits ....(RCA)
Time; *Ice Cream Castle* ....(WB)
Bird Bathroom
Surf Punks; *My Beach* ....(EPI)
Bird Brain Baby
Mercy Dee Walton; *Back Luck 'N' Trouble* ..... (ARH)
Bird Dog
Everly Brothers; *Best Of* ....(RHI)
Billboard Top Rock 'N' Roll Hits-1958 ....(RHI)
Cadence Classics-Their 20 Greatest Hits ....(RHI)
Fabulous Style ....(RHI)
Very Best Of ....(WB)
Bird In A Gilded Cage
Joan Morris & William Bolcom; *After The Ball* . (NON)
Bird In The Hand
Velvelettes; *25 Hard-To-Find Motown*
Classics-#3 ....(MOT)
Bird Of Beauty
Stevie Wonder; *Fulfillingness' First Finale* ..... (MOT)
Bird Of Brazil
Joyce; *Music Inside* .... (VF)
Bird Of Japan
Joyce; *Music Inside* .... (VF)
Bird Of Prey
Uriah Heep; *Best Of* ....(MER)
Bird On A Wire
Johnny Cash; *American Recordings* ....(AME)
Bird On My Head
David Seville; *45* ....(UA)
Bird On The Wire
Jennifer Warnes; *Famous Blue Raincoat* ....(CYP)
Joe Cocker; *Joe Cocker* ....(A&M)
Mad Dogs & Englishmen ....(A&M)
Judy Collins; *So Early In The Spring* ....(ELE)
Who Knows Where The Time Goes ....(ELE)
Leonard Cohen; *Best Of* ....(COL)
Bird That Whistles
Joni Mitchell; *Chalk Mark In A Rain Storm* ......(GEF)

Birdbrain
Tom Buffalo; *Birdbrain* .... (BEG)
Birdhouse In Your Soul
They Might Be Giants; *Flood* .... (ELE)
Birdland
Chubby Checker; *Greatest Hits* .... (AKO)
  Greatest Hits .... (EVR)
Manhattan Transfer; *Best Of* .... (ATL)
  Extensions .... (ATL)
Quincy Jones; *Back On The Block* .... (QUE)
Birdmad Girl
Cure; *The Top* .... (SIR)
Birdman Of Alkatrash
Strawberry Alarm Clock; *45* .... (MCA)
Birds
Bette Midler; *Live At Last* .... (ATL)
Linda Ronstadt; *Linda Ronstadt* .... (CAP)
Neil Young; *After The Goldrush* .... (RPR)
Birds In My Tree
Strawberry Alarm Clock; *Best Of-#1* .... (BCT)
Birds Of A Feather
Paul Revere/Raiders; *Legend Of* .... (COL)
Tim Curry; *Best Of* .... (A&M)
Birds Of Paradise
Ed Bruce; *Tell 'Em I've Gone Crazy* .... (MCA)
Pretenders; *II* .... (SIR)
Birds Of Winter
Zamfir; *Return To Romance* .... (PHI)
Birds & The Bees
Jewel Akens; *American Graffiti-#3* .... (MCA)
  Collectables History Of Rock-#4 .... (CLT)
  Cruisin'-1965 .... (INC)
  Oldies But Goodies-#9 .... (OSR)
  Super Hits-#3 .... (GUS)
Bird-Brain Rag
Max Morath; *World Of Scott Joplin-#2* .... (VAN)
Bird's The Word
Rivingtons; *Groove 'N' Grind-'50s & '60s Dance*
Hits .... (RHI)
  Let's Dance .... (GUS)
  Super Oldies Of The '60s-#10 .... (AUF)
Black Crow
Joni Mitchell; *Hejira* .... (ASY)
  Shadows & Light .... (ASY)
Black Crow Blues
Bob Dylan; *Another Side Of* .... (COL)
Blackbird
Beatles; *Box Set* .... (CAP)
  White Album .... (CAP)
Crosby, Stills & Nash; *Crosby, Stills & Nash* ..... (ATL)
Paul McCartney; *Unplugged-The Official Bootleg* (CAP)
Paul McCartney/Wings; *Over America-#1* .... (CAP)
Blue Jay Way
Beatles; *Box Set* .... (CAP)
  Magical Mystery Tour .... (CAP)
Bluebird
Buffalo Springfield; *Again* .... (ATC)
  Classic Rock 1966-1988 .... (ATL)
  Retrospective .... (ATC)
Electric Light Orchestra; *Secret Messages* .... (JET)
Helen Reddy; *Live In London* .... (CAP)
  No Way To Treat A Lady .... (CAP)
Leon Russell; *Best Of* .... (SHE)
  Will O' The Wisp .... (SHE)
Paul McCartney/Wings; *Band On The Run* ...... (CAP)
  Over America .... (CAP)
Robin Trower; *In City Dreams* .... (CHR)
Bluebird Is Dead
Electric Light Orchestra; *Afterglow* .... (EPI)
  On The Third Day .... (JET)
Bluebird Of Happiness
Lee Andrews/Hearts; *Biggest Hits* .... (CLT)
  Gotham Recording Sessions .... (CLT)
Bluebirds Over the Mountain
Beach Boys; *Absolute Best-#2* .... (CAP)
  Friends/20/20 .... (CAP)
  Sunshine Dream .... (CAP)
  '69 .... (CAP)
Ritchie Valens; *Best Of* .... (RHI)
  History Of .... (RHI)
  Ritchie Valens .... (RHI)
Bye Bye Blackbird
Dean Martin; *Swingin' Down Yonder* .... (CAP)
Joe Cocker; *With A Little Help From My Friends* (A&M)

Liza Minnelli; *ST/Liza With A Z* .... (COL)
Miles Davis; *Ballads* .... (COL)
  Quintet/Jazz Sampler #2 .... (COL)
  'Round About Midnight .... (COL)
Cage The Songbird
Elton John; *Blue Moves* .... (MCA)
  Elton John .... (POL)
California Saga (Beaks Of Eagles)
Beach Boys; *Holland* .... (CAR)
  Ten Years Of Harmony .... (CAR)
Canary In A Coal Mine
Police; *Zenyatta Mondatta* .... (A&M)
Chicken Soup
Angel; *Helluva Band* .... (MER)
Chicken Stew Part I
Geoff Muldaur & Amos Garrett; *Geoff Muldaur & Amos*
Garrett .... (FF)
Cluckin' Hen, Going Back To Kentucky...
J.P. Fraley & Annadeene; *Wild Rose Of The*
Mountain .... (ROU)
Cry Of The Wild Goose
Frankie Laine; *Golden Hits* .... (MER)
Disco Duck
Rick Dees/Cast Of Idiots; *Original Disco Duck* .. (RSO)
Diving Duck Blues
Kingsnakes; *19 Lucky Strikes* .... (BWV)
  Salt City Blues .... (BWV)
Sleepy John Estes; *Legend Of* .... (DEL)
Taj Mahal; *Taj Mahal* .... (COL)
Dixie Chicken
Little Feat; *Dixie Chicken* .... (WB)
  Waiting For Columbus .... (WB)
Do The Bird
Dee Dee Sharp; *Let's Dance* .... (GUS)
  Rock-O-Rama-#2 .... (AKO)
Do The Funky Chicken
Rufus Thomas; *15 Original Big Hits-III* .... (STX)
  Chronicle .... (STX)
  Let's Dance .... (GUS)
Do The Funky Penguin
Rufus Thomas; *15 Original Big Hits-III* .... (STX)
  Chronicle .... (STX)
  Rufus Thomas .... (GUS)
Drunken Blue Rooster
Todd Rundgren; *Todd* .... (RHI)
Duck
Jackie Lee; *Sock Hop* .... (DHL)
  Soul Shots-#1-We Got More Soul .... (RHI)
  Super Oldies Of The '60s-#6 .... (AUF)
Olympics; *Best Of* .... (VJ)
Eagle
Abba; *Greatest Hits #2* .... (ATL)
  I Love Abba .... (ATL)
  The Album .... (ATL)
Paul Winter; *Common Ground* .... (A&M)
Waylon Jennings; *Eagle* .... (EPI)
  Greatest Country Hits/'90s-1991 .... (COL)
Eagle Never Hunts The Fly
Music Machine; *Best Of* .... (RHI)
  Nuggets-#2-Punk .... (RHI)
Eagle Over Angel
Brother Phelps; *Let Go* .... (ASY)
Eagle Will Rise Again
Alan Parsons Project; *Pyramid* .... (ARI)
Eagle & The Hawk
John Denver; *Aerie* .... (RCA)
  Evening With .... (RCA)
  Greatest Hits-#1 .... (RCA)
Eagles Fly
Sammy Hagar; *Sammy Hagar* .... (GEF)
Flamingo Express
Royaltones; *45* .... (RLL)
Flamingo (D.E.)
Duke Ellington; *Best Of* .... (CAP)
  Blanton-Webster Band .... (BLU)
  Do Nothin' Til You Hear From Me .... (INT)
Flamingos Fly
Sammy Hagar; *Nine On A Ten Scale* .... (CAP)
Van Morrison; *Period Of Transition* .... (WB)

Fly Like An Eagle
Steve Miller Band; *Fly Like An Eagle* ....(CAP)
   Gift Set ....(CAP)
   Greatest Hits ....(CAP)
   Live ....(CAP)
   ST/FM .... (MCA)
Fly Robin Fly
Silver Convention; *45* ....(OOP)
Flying Turkey Trot
R.E.O. Speedwagon; *Decade Of Rock & Roll* ......(EPI)
   Live ....(EPI)
   R.E.O. ....(EPI)
Free Bird
Lynyrd Skynyrd; *Gold & Platinum* ....(MCA)
   One More From The Road ....(MCA)
   Pronounced Leh-nerd Skin-nerd ....(MCA)
   Southern By The Grace Of God ....(MCA)
Wynonna; *Skynyrd Frynds* ....(MCA)
Golden Goose
Peter Frampton; *Somethin's Happening* ....(A&M)
Todd Rundgren; *Healing* ..... (RHI)
Golden Lark
Styx; *Man Of Miracles* ....(WDN)
Grantchester Meadows
Pink Floyd; *Umma Gumma* ....(CAP)
Gray Eagle
Taylor's Kentucky Boys; *Traditional Country Classics*
1927-1929 ....(HIS)
Great Speckled Bird
Roy Acuff; *Best Of* ....(CAP)
   Greatest Hits ....(COL)
Green Finch & Linnet Bird
Original Cast/Angela Lansbury/Len Cariou; *Sweeney
Todd* ....(RCA)
Grey Goose/Sixpenny Money
Joe Burke; *Traditional Music Of Ireland* ....(GRE)
Hey Little Bird
Buffy Sainte-Marie; *Best Of-#2* .... (VAN)
   Fire & Fleet & Candlelight .... (VAN)
High Flying Bird
Elton John; *Don't Shoot Me I'm Only The Piano
Player* ....(POL)
His Eye Is On The Sparrow
Carmen McRae; *Greatest Of* ....(MCA)
Marvin Gaye; *Musical Testament 1964-1984* ... (MOT)
Soundtrack; *Streetcar Named Desire* ....(ALL)
Hummingbird
Bob Seger; *Smokin' O.P.'s* ....(CAP)
B.B. King; *Best Of* ....(MCA)
Jimmy Page; *Outrider* ....(GEF)
Leon Russell; *Best Of* ....(MCA)
   Leon Russell ....(MCA)
Restless Heart; *Wheels* ....(RCA)
Ricky Skaggs; *Kentucky Thunder* ....(EPI)
Seals & Crofts; *Greatest Hits* ....(WB)
   Summer Breeze ....(WB)
Hunting The Wren
Steeleye Span; *Live At Last* .... (CHR)
Kentucky Bluebird
Keith Whitley; *Kentucky Bluebird* ....(RCA)
Kentucky Song Bird
Roger Whittaker; *Mirrors Of My Mind* ....(RCA)
Last Lonely Eagle
New Riders Of The Purple Sage; *Best Of* ....(COL)
   New Riders Of The Purple Sage ....(COL)
Listen To The Mocking Bird
Lester Flatt; *Lester Raymond Flatt* .... (FF)
Little Bird
Beach Boys; *Friends/20/20* ....(CAP)
Jerry Jeff Walker; *Mr. Bojangles* ....(BAI)
   Viva Terlingua ....(MCA)
Little Birdie
Joe Williams; *Happy Anniversary Charie Brown* .(GRP)
Stanley Brothers; *Stanley Brothers* ....(MEL)
   Stanley Series-#2, No. 1 ....(COP)
Little Bird, Little Bird
Original Cast; *Man Of La Mancha* ....(MCA)
Little Brown Bird
Elvin Bishop; *Raisin' Hell* ....(CPC)
Little Red Hen
Johnny Otis; *Original Johnny Otis Show* ....(SAV)
Little Red Rooster
Big Mama Thornton; *Jail* .... (VAN)

B.B. King/Muddy Waters/Big Mama Thornton; *Live At
Newport* .... (INT)
Rolling Stones; *Love You Live* ....(RS)
   Now! ....(AKO)
Sam Cooke; *Having A Party* ....(RCA)
   This Is ....(RCA)
Little Turtle Dove
Bobby Day; *Best Of* .... (RHI)
Little Wing
Derek/Dominos; *Layla* ....(RSO)
Jimi Hendrix; *Axis: Bold As Love* ....(RPR)
   Concerts ....(RPR)
   Essential-#1 & 2 ....(RPR)
   Lifelines/Jimi Hendrix Story ....(RPR)
Sting; *Nothing Like The Sun* ....(A&M)
May The Bird Of Paradise Fly Up Your...
Harlow Wilcox/Oakies; *Cripple Cricket* ....(PLN)
Little Jimmy Dickens; *Columbia Country
Classics-#3-Americana* ....(COL)
Mexican Blackbird
ZZ Top; *Fandango* ....(WB)
   Six Pack ....(WB)
Mocking Bird Hill
Patti Page; *16 Most Requested Songs* ....(COL)
   Golden Hits ....(MER)
   Greatest Hits ....(COL)
Russ Morgan; *Best Of* ....(MCA)
Mockingbird
Carly Simon; *Best Of* ....(ELE)
   Hotcakes ....(ELE)
Inez & Charlie Foxx; *Billboard Top R&B
Hits-1963* ....(RHI)
   Oldies/Goodies-#8 ....(OSR)
   Super Oldies/'60s-#4 ....(AUF)
Peter, Paul & Mary; *Peter Paul & Mommy* ....(WB)
Morse Moose & The Grey Goose
Wings; *London Town* ....(CAP)
Mother Goose
Jethro Tull; *Aqualung* ....(CHR)
My Canary Is Yellow
Chesterfield Kings; *Stop* ....(MRR)
My Song Bird
Emmylou Harris; *Quarter Moon In A Ten Cent
Town* ....(WB)
McCarters; *The Gift* ....(WB)
Night Bird Flying
Jimi Hendrix; *Cry Of Love* ....(RPR)
   Lifelines/Jimi Hendrix Story ....(RPR)
Night Owl
Carly Simon; *Best Of* ....(ELE)
   No Secrets ....(ELE)
Night Owls
Little River Band; *Greatest Hits* ....(CAP)
   Time Exposure ....(CAP)
Nightingale Sang In Berkeley Square
Harry Connick, Jr.; *We Are In Love* ....(COL)
Manhattan Transfer; *Best Of* ....(ATL)
   Mecca For Moderns ....(ATL)
Oklahoma Rooster
Backwoods Banjo; *Jes' Fine* .... (ROU)
On The Wings Of A Nightingale
Everly Brothers; *EB84* ....(MER)
Ostrich
Steppenwolf; *Born To Be Wild-History Of* ....(MCA)
   Steppenwolf ....(MCA)
Ostrich Walk
Bob Crosby Orchestra; *Bob Crosby Orchestra* ....(HIN)
Bob Scobey's Frisco Band; *Direct From San
Francisco* ....(GTJ)
Painted Bird
Siouxsie/Banshees; *Kiss In The Dream House* ....(GEF)
   Nocturne ....(GEF)
Phoenix
Cult; *Love* ....(SIR)
Dan Fogelberg; *Phoenix* ....(FM)
Wishbone Ash; *Live Dates* ....(MCA)
   Wishbone Ash ....(MCA)
Pigeon Song
America; *America* ....(WB)
Pink Flamingos
Rickie Lee Jones; *Traffic From Paradise* ....(GEF)

Poisoning Pigeons In The Park
Tom Lehrer; *Dr. Demento 20th Anniversary
Collection* .... (RHI)
  Dr. Demento Presents Greatest Novelty CD ..... (RHI)
  Evening Wasted With .... (RPR)
Pretty Flamingo
Manfred Mann; *Best Of* .... (EMI)
  History Of British Rock-#4 .... (RHI)
Rod Stewart; *Night On The Town* .... (WB)
Ragtime Nightingale
Max Morath; *Plays Best Of Scott Joplin & Other
Rags* .... (VAN)
Ragtime Oriole
Max Morath; *World Of Scott Joplin* .... (VAN)
Raven
Alan Parsons Project; *Tales Of Mystery &
Imagination* .... (MER)
Genesis; *Lamb Lies Down On Broadway* ....(ATC)
Red Bird Tennessee Waltz
Clark Kessinger & Gene Meade; *Clark Kessinger & Gene
Meade* .... (ROU)
Red Rooster
Howlin' Wolf; *Chess Box* .... (CSS)
Paula Lockheart; *It Ain't The End Of The World* ...(FF)
Road Runner
Greg Kihn Band; *With The Naked Eye* .... (BES)
Joan Jett; *Hit List* .... (BLK)
Joan Jett/Blackhearts; *Good Music* .... (BLK)
Jonathan Richman/Modern Lovers; *Beserkley Years-Best
Of* .... (RHI)
Modern Lovers; *Modern Lovers* .... (RHI)
Pretty Things; *History Of British Rock-#5* .... (RHI)
Road Runner (I'm A)
Fleetwood Mac; *Penguin* .... (RPR)
Humble Pie; *Eat It* .... (A&M)
  Smokin' .... (A&M)
Junior Walker/All-Stars; *Anthology* .... (MOT)
  Greatest Hits .... (MOT)
  Motown Superstar Series-#5 .... (MOT)
  Shotgun .... (MOT)
"Road Runner" Theme
Original Music; *Television's Greatest Hits-#2* ..... (TVT)
Rockin' Goose
Johnny/Hurricanes; *45* .... (CLT)
Rockin' Robin
Bobby Day; *Cruisin'-1958* .... (INC)
  Oldies But Goodies-#5 .... (OSR)
  Rockin' Robin .... (CLT)
  Super Oldies/'50s-#2 .... (AUF)
Michael Jackson; *Anthology* .... (MOT)
  Best Of .... (MOT)
  Got To Be There .... (MOT)
  Original Soul Of .... (MOT)
Rooster
Alice In Chains; *Dirt* ....(COL)
Rooster Blues
Lightnin' Slim; *Sound Of The Swamp-Best Of
Excello-#1* .... (RHI)
Peter Wolf; *ST/Fried Green Tomatoes* .... (MCA)
Wade Walton; *I Have To Paint My Face* .... (ARH)
Rooster Song
Fats Domino; *They Call Me The Fat Man* .... (EMI)
Rudy The Magic Crow
Swamp Zombies; *Chicken Vulture Crow* .... (DD)
Sacred Bird
Original Cast; *Miss Saigon* .... (GEF)
Shoot That Turkey
Holy Modal Rounders; *Alleged In Their Own
Time* .... (ROU)
Silver Bird
Mark Lindsay; *Super Hits/'70s-Have A Nice
Day-#4* .... (RHI)
Silver Eagle
Merle Haggard & George Jones; *Taste Of Yesterday's
Wine* .... (EPI)
Reba McEntire; *Just A Little Love* .... (MCA)
Silver Swan Rag
Scott Joplin; *Elite Syncopations* .... (BIO)
  Ragtime-#3 (early 1900s) ....(BIO)
Sister Seagull
Be Bop Deluxe; *Best Of-And The Rest Of* .... (HAR)
  Best Of-Raiding The Divine Archive .... (CAP)
  Futurama .... (HAR)
  Live In The Air Age .... (HAR)

Skunk, The Goose & The Fly
Tower Of Power; *East Bay Grease* .... (RHI)
Skybird
Neil Diamond; *Love At The Greek* ....(COL)
  ST/Jonathan Livingston Seagull ....(COL)
Skylark
Anita O'Day; *1940s-The Singers* ....(COL)
Bette Midler; *Bette Midler* ....(ATL)
Erroll Garner Trio; *Greatest Garner* ....(ATL)
Glenn Miller; *Best Of-#3* ....(RCA)
Hoagy Carmichael; *Hoagy Sings Carmichael* ..... (EMI)
  Too Marvelous For Words ....(CAP)
Linda Ronstadt; *Lush Life* ....(ASY)
Tony Bennett; *Forty Years-Artistry Of* ....(COL)
Skyline Pigeon
Elton John; *Empty Sky* .... (POL)
  Here & There .... (POL)
Snowbird
Anne Murray; *15 Of The Best* .... (LIB)
  Country ....(CAP)
  Greatest Hits ....(CAP)
  Snowbird ....(CAP)
Elvis Presley; *Canadian Tribute* ....(RCA)
  I'm 10,000 Years Old ....(RCA)
Loretta Lynn; *Coal Miner's Daughter* .... (MCA)
Songbird
Barbra Streisand; *Greatest Hits-#2* ....(COL)
  Songbird ....(COL)
Fleetwood Mac; *25 Years-The Chain* ....(WB)
  Rumours ....(WB)
Jesse Colin Young; *Songbird* ....(WB)
Kenny G; *Duotones* .... (ARI)
  Live .... (ARI)
Spread My Wings
Troop; *Attitude* .... (ATL)
Stereo Chickens
Jerry Jeff Walker; *Man Must Carry On* .... (MCA)
Stone The Crows
Original Cast; *Joseph/Amazing Technicolor
Dreamcoat* .... (MCA)
  Joseph/Amazing Technicolor Dreamcoat .... (POL)
Surfin' Bird
Pee-Wee Herman; *ST/Back To The Beach* ....(COL)
Ramones; *All The Stuff & More-#2* .... (SIR)
  Rocket To Russia .... (SIR)
Trashmen; *Collectables Presents History Of
Rock-#1* .... (CLT)
  History Of Surf Music-#2 .... (RHI)
  Monster Summer Hits-Wild Surf ....(CAP)
  ST/Full Metal Jacket ....(WB)
  Super Oldies/'60s-#11 ....(AUF)
Sweet Bird
Joni Mitchell; *Hissing Of Summer Lawns* .... (ASY)
Tastes Just Like Chicken
Scatterbrain; *Scamboogery* .... (ELE)
Tennessee Bird Walk
Blanchard & Morgan; *Super Hits-#2* .... (GUS)
Tennessee Guitars; *20 Great Hits* .... (PLN)
  Golden Guitar Hits .... (SSS)
There Ain't Nobody Here But Us Chickens
Original London Cast; *Five Guys Named Moe* ... (REL)
There'll Be Bluebirds Over The White...
Kay Kyser; *Best Of The Big Bands* ....(COL)
Thirty Dirty Birds
Red Hot Chili Peppers; *Freaky Styley* .... (EMI)
Three Little Birds
Bob Marley/Wailers; *Exodus* .... (TUF)
  Legend .... (TUF)
  Songs Of Freedom .... (TUF)
Three Ravens
Peter, Paul & Mary; *In Concert* .... (WB)
Tiny Sparrow
Peter, Paul & Mary; *Moving* .... (WB)
Tired Wings
Four Horsemen; *Nobody Said It Was Easy* .... (DEF)
Toucan's Dance
Sergio Mendes; *Arara* .... (A&M)
Turkey In The Straw
Stanley Brothers; *Stanley Series-Vol.1-#3* ....(COP)
Vassar Clements; *Grass Routes* .... (ROU)
Turkey Lurky Time
Original Cast; *Promises Promises* .... (UA)

Turtle Dovin'
Coasters; *Their Greatest Recordings-Early Years* ..(ATC)
Young Blood ....(ATL)
Coasters/Robins; *50 Coastin' Classics* .... (RHI)
Two Sparrows In A Hurricane
Tanya Tucker; *Can't Run From Yourself* ....(LIB)
Greatest Hits-1990-1992 ....(LIB)
Ugly Duckling
Danny Kaye; *45* ....(OOP)
Voice Of The Eagle
Robbie Basho; *Voice Of The Eagle* .... (VAN)
When Doves Cry
Prince; *ST/Purple Rain* ....(WB)
When The Eagle Flies
Traffic; *When The Eagle Flies* ....(ASY)
When The Red, Red Robin
Al Jolson; *Best Of* ....(MCA)
Story-#3 ....(MCA)
Louis Armstrong; *I Like Jazz-Essence Of* ....(COL)
Mitch Miller; *16 Most Requested Songs* ....(COL)
When...Swallows Come Back To Capistrano
Glenn Miller; *In The Mood* ....(POE)
Ink Spots; *Best Of* ....(MCA)
Greatest Hits ....(MCA)
Whisper To A Scream (Birds Fly)
Icicle Works; *Icicle Works* .... (ARI)
White Dove
Lynyrd Skynyrd; *First & Last* ....(MCA)
Wild Turkey
Lacy J. Dalton; *Hot Country Rock-#1* ....(EPI)
Wings Of A Dove
Bob Marley/Wailers; *Birth Of A
Legend-1963-1966* ....(EPA)
Ferlin Husky; *Billboard Top Country Hits-1960* .. (RHI)
Country Music Classics-#2-1960-1965 ....(KT)
Greatest Hits ....(CCB)
Woody Woodpecker Song
Kay Kyser; *Best Of The Big Bands* ....(COL)
Sentimental Favorites ....(COL)
Mel Blanc/Sportsmen; *Small Fry-Capitol Sings Kids
Songs* ....(CAP)
Yellow Bird
Brothers Four; *Greatest Hits* ....(COL)
Lawrence Welk; *Best Of-20 Great Hits* .... (RAN)
Mills Brothers; *16 Great Performances* ....(MCA)
22 Great Hits ....(RAN)
Cab Driver ....(RAN)
Roger Whittaker; *Greatest Hits* ....(RCA)
Yellow Raven
Scorpions; *Best Of The Ballads Hot & Slow* ......(RCA)
Virgin Killer ....(RCA)

BOOKS, Diary, Stories, Writing

All I Can Do Is Write About It
Lynyrd Skynyrd; *Gimme Back My Bullets* ... (MCA)
Autobiography
Phoebe Snow; *It Looks Like Snow* ....(COL)
Autograph
John Denver; *Greatest Hits-#3* ....(RCA)
Autumn Almanac
Kinks; *Kink Kronikles* .... (RPR)
Banjo Story
Elizabeth Cotten; *Live* .... (ARH)
Beautiful Story
Sonny & Cher; *Beat Goes On* ....(ATC)
Best Of ....(ATC)
Bedtime Story
Tammy Wynette; *Biggest Hits* ....(EPI)
First Lady Of Country Music ....(EPI)
Greatest Hits-#3 ....(EPI)
Behind The Lines
Genesis; *Duke* ....(ATL)
Three Sides Live ....(ATL)
Phil Collins; *Face Value* ....(ATL)
Book Of Dreams
Bruce Springsteen; *Lucky Town* ....(COL)
Book Of Love
Book Of Love; *Book Of Love* .... (SIR)
Fleetwood Mac; *Mirage* ....(WB)

Monotones; *American Graffiti* ....(MCA)
Bedrock-Late '50s/'60s Rock 'N' Roll ....(ALL)
Best Of Chess Rock 'N' Roll ....(CSS)
Original Golden Rock Oldies-#1 ....(SPE)
Super Oldies Of The '50s-#2 ....(AUF)
Book Of Miracles
Fleetwood Mac; *45* ....(WB)
Book Of Rules, The
Heptones; *Night Food* ....(ISL)
This Is Reggae Music-#1 ....(ISL)
Book Of Saturday
King Crimson; *Lark's Tongues In Aspic* .... (EDI)
Book Song
Fairport Convention; *Chronicles* ....(A&M)
Fairport Convention ....(A&M)
Bookends
Joe Walsh; *The Smoker You Drink The Player You
Get* ....(MCA)
Bookends Theme
Simon & Garfunkel; *Bookends* ....(COL)
Collected Works ....(COL)
Greatest Hits ....(COL)
Books I Read
Talking Heads; *'77* .... (SIR)
Both Sides Of The Story
Phil Collins; *Both Sides* ....(ATL)
Brush Up Your Shakespeare
Dick Hyman; *Cole Porter: All Through The Night* (MM)
Keenan Wynn & James Whitmore; *ST/Kiss Me
Kate* ....(MCA)
Original Cast; Kiss Me Kate ....(COL)
Camelot
Original 1982 London Cast; *Camelot* ....(VS)
Original Cast; *Camelot* ....(COL)
Richard Burton; *Broadway Magic-1960s* ....(COL)
Richard Harris; *ST/Camelot* ....(WB)
Captain Nemo
Michael Schenker; *Built To Destroy* .... (CHR)
Rock Will Never Die .... (CHR)
Close As Pages In A Book
Benny Goodman; *Best Of The Big Bands* ....(COL)
Warren Vache; *Polished Brass* ....(CCJ)
Cover Of Rolling Stone
Dr. Hook/Medicine Show; *Greatest Hits* ....(CAP)
Revisited ....(COL)
Dear Diary
Moody Blues; *On The Threshold Of A Dream* .... (POL)
This Is The ....(POL)
Death Of An Unpopular Poet
Jimmy Buffett; *White Sport Coat & A Pink
Crustacean* ....(MCA)
Diary
Bread; *Anthology* ....(ELE)
Baby I'm A Want-You ....(ELE)
Best Of ....(ELE)
Little Anthony/Imperials; *Best Of* ....(RHI)
Neil Sedaka; *All-Time Greatest Hits* ....(RCA)
Nipper's Greatest Hits-'50s-#2 ....(RCA)
Sings His Greatest Hits ....(RCA)
Diary Of A Madman
Ozzy Osbourne; *Diary Of A Madman* ....(JET)
Diary Of Horace Wimp
Electric Light Orchestra; *Discovery* ....(JET)
Diary Of My Mind
George Jones; *Alone Again* ....(EPI)
Dolphin Story
Claudia Schmidt; *Midwestern Heart* .... (FF)
Ecology Poem
Mutabaruka; *Blakk Wi Blak...k...k...* ....(SHA)
Editions Of You
Roxy Music; *For Your Pleasure...Second Album* .. (RPR)
Greatest Hits ....(ATC)
Heart Still Beating ....(RPR)
Editorial
Paul Davis; *Singer Of Songs Teller Of Tales* ......(BNG)
Southern Tracks & Fantasies ....(BNG)
Eight Line Poem
David Bowie; *Hunky Dory* ....(RYK)
Empty Pages
Air Supply; *Love & Other Bruises* ....(COL)
Traffic; *John Barleycorn Must Die* .... (ISL)
Fairy Tale
Elvis Presley; *In Concert* ....(RCA)
Pointer Sisters; *Retrospect* ....(MCA)

Rita Remington; *Country Girl Gold* .... (PLN)
Fairy Tale High
Donna Summer; *Live & More* .... (CAS)
Once Upon A Time .... (CAS)
Fairy Tales
Anita Baker; *Compositions* .... (ELE)
Rivingtons; *Liberty Years-Legends Of Rock & Roll* (EMI)
Style Council; *Cost Of Loving* .... (POL)
Fairytale Of New York
Pogues; *Essential* .... (ISL)
If I Should Fall From Grace With God .... (ISL)
Ghost Writer
Garland Jeffreys; *Ghost Writer* .... (A&M)
God's Coloring Book
Dolly Parton; *Here You Come Again* ....(RCA)
Goin' By The Book
Johnny Cash; *Mystery Of Life* .... (MER)
Goodbye Yellow Brick Road
Elton John; *Billboard Top Rock 'N' Roll Hits-1973* (RHI)
Goodbye Yellow Brick Road .... (POL)
Greatest Hits .... (POL)
Greatest Story Ever Told
Bob Weir; *Ace* .... (GRD)
Grateful Dead; *Dead Set* .... (ARI)
Hard Luck Stories
Neil Young; *Landing On Water* .... (GEF)
Richard & Linda Thompson; *Pour Down Like
Silver* ....(CTH)
Hard Luck Story
Elton John; *Rock Of The Westies* .... (POL)
Here's Where The Story Ends
Sundays; *Reading Writing & Arithmetic* .... (DGC)
I Could Write A Book
Frank Sinatra; *Voice-Columbia Years-1943-1952* (COL)
Original Cast; *Pal Joey* ....(COL)
Tony Bennett; *Rodgers & Hart Songbook* .... (DRG)
I Guess You Had To Be There
Lorrie Morgan; *Watch Me* ....(BNA)
I Love A Murder Mystery
Jerry Lewis; *Capitol Collectors Series* ....(CAP)
I Wrote The Book
Lauren Bacall; *Woman Of The Year* ....(BAY)
If You Could Read My Mind
Gordon Lightfoot; *Gord's Gold* .... (RPR)
If You Could Read My Mind .... (RPR)
Sit Down Young Stranger .... (RPR)
It Ain't Necessarily So
Aretha Franklin; *The Great-First 12 Sides* ....(COL)
Cab Calloway; *Sullivan Years-Best Of Broadway* (TVT)
Cal Tjader; *Cal Tjader Plays/Mary Stallings Sings* (FAN)
Cher; *Glory Of Gershwin Featuring Larry Adler* . (MER)
Ella Fitzgerald & Louis Armstrong; *Porgy & Bess* (VRV)
Miles Davis/Orchestra; *Porgy & Bess* ....(COL)
It Was Written In The Stars
Ella Fitzgerald; *Harold Arlen Songbook-#2* ......(VRV)
Johnny Can't Read
Don Henley; *I Can't Stand Still* .... (ASY)
Lady Writer
Dire Straits; *Communique* .... (WB)
Las Vegas Story
Gun Club; *Las Vegas Story* .... (IRS)
Life's Like Poetry
Lefty Frizzell; *Legendary* .... (MCA)
Little Black Book
Jimmy Dean; *American Originals* ....(COL)
Greatest Hits ....(COL)
Longfellow Serenade
Neil Diamond; *12 Greatest Hits-#2* ....(COL)
Love At The Greek ....(COL)
On The Way To The Sky ....(COL)
Serenade ....(COL)
Love Story
Andy Williams; *Greatest Hits-#2* ....(COL)
Love Story ....(COL)
Jethro Tull; *20 Years Of-Boxed Set* .... (CHR)
Living In The Past .... (CHR)
Johnny Mathis; *16 Most Requested Songs* ....(COL)
All-Time Greatest Hits ....(COL)
Randy Newman; *Randy Newman* ....(RPR)
Stephen Stills; *Stills* ....(COL)
Tanita Tikaram; *Sweet Keeper* ....(RPR)
Marian The Librarian
Original Broadway Cast; *Music Man* .... (ANG)
Robert Preston; *ST/Music Man* .... (WB)

Murder Story
Simple Minds; *Life In A Day* .... (VIA)
My Back Pages
Bob Dylan; *Another Side Of* ....(COL)
Greatest Hits-#2 ....(COL)
Byrds; *20 Essential Tracks From Box Set* ....(COL)
Byrds Play Dylan ....(COL)
Greatest Hits ....(COL)
Younger Than Yesterday ....(COL)
My Coloring Book
Barbra Streisand; *Greatest Hits* ....(COL)
Second Album ....(COL)
Perry Como; *This Is-#2* ....(RCA)
My Little Brown Book
Duke Ellington; *& John Coltrane* .... (MCI)
John Coltrane; *Gentle Side Of* ....(GRP)
My Little Red Book
Love; *Best Of* .... (RHI)
Elektrock-'60s .... (ELE)
Nuggets-#2-Punk .... (RHI)
My Mother's Bible
Warrior River Boys; *New Beginnings* .... (ROU)
My True Story
Jive Five; *Back Seat Jams-CD* ....(DHL)
Billboard Top R&B Hits-1961 .... (RHI)
Cruisin' 1961 .... (INC)
Greatest Hits .... (CLT)
Oldies But Goodies-#4 .... (OSR)
Never Ending Story
Limahl; *ST/Never Ending Story* .... (AMR)
Once Upon A Time
Dan Fogelberg; *Nether Lands* .... (FM)
Donna Summer; *Live & More* ....(CAS)
Once Upon A Time ....(CAS)
Frank Sinatra; *September Of My Years* .... (RPR)
Marvin Gaye & Mary Wells; *Anthology* .... (MOT)
Together .... (MOT)
Simple Minds; *In The City Of Light* .... (A&M)
Once Upon A Time ....(A&M)
Page 43
Crosby, Stills & Nash; *Crosby, Stills & Nash
(collection)* .... (ATL)
David Crosby & Graham Nash; *David Crosby &
Graham Nash* .... (ATL)
Pages Of My Mind
Ray Charles; *From The Pages Of My Mind* ....(COL)
Paperback Writer
Beatles; *1962-1966* .... (CAP)
20 Greatest Hits ....(CAP)
Box Set ....(CAP)
Hey Jude ....(CAP)
Past Masters-#2 ....(CAP)
Piano Lesson & If You Don't Mind My...
Shirley Jones; *ST/Music Man* .... (WB)
Picture Book
Kinks; *Are The Village Green Preservation Soc.* ... (RPR)
Simply Red; *Picture Book* .... (ELE)
Poem 58
Chicago; *Chicago Transit Authority* ....(COL)
Group Portrait ....(COL)
Poem For The People
Chicago; *2* ....(COL)
Poem Of Summer
J.D. Robb; *Triptyque/Other Electronic
Compositions* .... (FLW)
Poem On The Underground Wall
Simon & Garfunkel; *Collected Works* ....(COL)
Parsley Sage Rosemary & Thyme ....(COL)
Poems, Prayers & Promises
John Denver; *Evening With* ....(RCA)
Greatest Hits-#1 ....(RCA)
Poems, Prayers & Promises ....(RCA)
John Denver/Muppets; *Rocky Mountain Holiday* .(RCA)
Poetry In Motion
Johnny Tillotson; *10 Top Ten Hits-#1* ....(LAU)
American Graffiti-#3 .... (MCA)
Jukebox Classics-#1 .... (RHI)
Mellow '60s .... (PRY)
Million Dollar Memories-#2 ....(RCA)
Poetry Man
Phoebe Snow; *Best Of* ....(COL)
Phoebe Snow .... (MCA)

Poet's Heart
Kate Wolf; *Gold In*
  California-Retrospective-1975-85 ....(KAL)
  Poet's Heart ....(KAL)
Poison Pen
  Hoodoo Gurus; *Mars Needs Guitars* ....(ELE)
  Molly Hatchet; *Beatin' The Odds* ....(EPI)
Read About It
  Midnight Oil; *10-9-8-7-6-5-4-3-2-1* ....(COL)
  Scream In Blue ....(COL)
Read Between The Lines
  Aaron Tippin; *Read Between The Lines* ....(RCA)
Read It In Books
  Echo/Bunnymen; *Crocodiles* ....(SIR)
Rhymes & Reasons
  John Denver; *Evening With* ....(RCA)
  Greatest Hits ....(RCA)
  Take Me Home Country Roads & Other Hits ....(RCA)
Rhythm In My Nursery Rhymes
  Tommy Dorsey/Clambake Seven; *Music Goes Round &*
  Round ....(BLU)
Rime Of The Ancient Mariner
  Iron Maiden; *Live After Death* ....(CAP)
  Powerslave ....(CAP)
Sad Story
  Jack Scott; *Capitol Collectors Series* ....(CAP)
Same Old Story
  Billie Holiday; *Fine & Mellow* ....(CLT)
  Quintessential-#8-1939-1940 ....(COL)
  Garth Brooks; *No Fences* ....(LIB)
  Ronna Reeves; *Only The Heart* ....(MER)
  Stevie Wonder; *Journey Through Secret Life Of*
  Plants ....(MOT)
San Antonio Story
  Stephen Woodfin & Joe Vickers; *Waco* ....(SO)
Shakespeare Stole My Baby
  Eye To Eye; *Shakespeare Stole My Baby* ....(WB)
Shakespeare's Sister
  Smiths; *Louder Than Bombs* ....(SIR)
Sign Your Name
  Terence Trent D'Arby; *Introducing The Hardline*
  According To... ....(COL)
  Slow Dancin' ....(KT)
Sounds Of Silence
  Paul Simon; *Live Rhymin'* ....(COL)
  Simon & Garfunkel; *Collected Works* ....(COL)
  Concert In Central Park ....(WB)
  Greatest Hits ....(COL)
  More American Graffiti-#4 ....(MCA)
  Sounds Of Silence ....(COL)
  ST/The Graduate ....(COL)
Stories For Boys
  U2; *Boy* ....(ISL)
Stories I Tell
  Toad The Wet Sprocket; *Fear* ....(COL)
Stories Of Old
  Depeche Mode; *Some Great Reward* ....(SIR)
Stories We Could Tell
  Jimmy Buffett; *A-1-A* ....(MCA)
  John Sebastian; *Best Of* ....(RHI)
  Tom Petty/Heartbreakers; *Pack Up The*
  Plantation-Live ....(MCA)
Story Behind The Story
  Big Al Downing; *45* ....(WB)
Story Book Of Love
  Whispers; *Excellence* ....(ALL)
  Shhhh ....(DOR)
Story Goes On
  Original Broadway Cast; *Baby* ....(POL)
Story In Your Eyes
  Moody Blues; *Every Good Boy Deserves Favour* ..(POL)
  This Is The ....(POL)
Story Of A Broken Heart
  Johnny Cash; *Original* ....(SUN)
  Original Golden Hits #3 ....(SUN)
  Rough Cut King Of Country Music ....(SUN)
  The Man The World His Music ....(SUN)
Story Of A Teenager
  America; *Hearts* ....(WB)
Story Of Bo Diddley
  Animals; *Best Of* ....(AKO)
  Bo Diddley; *In The Spotlight* ....(CSS)
Story Of Love
  Desert Rose Band; *Pages Of Life* ....(MCA)

Velvetones; *45* ....(OOP)
Story Of My Life
  Don Williams; *Lovers & Best Friends* ....(MCA)
  Yellow Moon ....(MCA)
  Guitar Slim; *Legends Of Electric Blues Guitar-#1* . (RHI)
  Things That I Used To Do ....(SPE)
  Marty Robbins; *Essential-1951-1982* ....(COL)
  Greatest Hits ....(COL)
  Lifetime Of Song-1951-1982 ....(COL)
  Neil Diamond; *Headed For The Future* ....(COL)
  Unrelated Segments; *Nuggets-#11* ....(RHI)
Story Of Rock & Roll
  Turtles; *Best Of* ....(RHI)
  Chalon Road ....(RHI)
  Greatest Hits ....(RHI)
Story Untold
  Nutmegs; *Back Seat Jams* ....(DHL)
  Cruisin'-1955 ....(INC)
  Greatest Hits ....(CLT)
  Oldies But Goodies-#2 ....(OSR)
Storybook Children
  Bette Midler; *Broken Blossom* ....(ATL)
  Nancy Sinatra & Lee Hazlewood; *Fairy Tales &*
  Fantasies-Best Of ....(RHI)
Storybook Love
  Mark Knopfler & Willy DeVille; *ST/Princess Bride* (WB)
Storybook Lovers
  Four Seasons; *Who Loves You* ....(WB)
Storybook Of Love
  Rozalla; *Everybody's Free* ....(EPI)
Story's Been Told
  Third World; *Story's Been Told* ....(ISL)
Stranger Than Fiction
  Belouis Some; *Belouis Some* ....(CAP)
  Killer Dwarfs; *Method To The Madness* ....(EPI)
  Split Enz; *Mental Notes* ....(CHR)
Survival Handbook Vs. Global Extinction
  Sister Souljah; *360 Degrees Of Power* ....(EPI)
Tales From The Vienna Woods
  101 Strings Orchestra; *Best Of Johann Strauss Jr.* (ALS)
  Lawrence Welk; *22 Great Waltzes* ....(RAN)
Tales Of Brave Ulysses
  Cream; *Disraeli Gears* ....(POL)
  Eric Clapton-Crossroads ....(POL)
  Live Cream-#2 ....(POL)
Tales Of Kilimanjaro
  Carlos Santana; *Havana Moon* ....(COL)
  Santana; *Zebop* ....(COL)
Tell Me A Bedtime Story
  Norman Connors; *Remember Who You Are* ....(MOJ)
  Quincy Jones; *Sounds...& Stuff Like That* ....(A&M)
That Ain't In Any Catalog
  Mustard & Gravy; *Long Gone Daddy* ....(CLT)
That's My Story
  Collin Raye; *Extremes* ....(EPI)
Them Poems
  White Mountain Singers; *Memories-Live!* ....(FOL)
Theme From "Love Story"
  Cincinnati Pops Orchestra/Erich Kunzel; *Hollywood's*
  Greatest Hits-#1 ....(TLR)
  Francis Lai; *ST/Love Story* ....(MCA)
  Peter Nero; *Greatest Hits* ....(COL)
Theme From "Out Of Africa"
  John Barry; *ST/Out Of Africa* ....(MCA)
Tom Sawyer
  Rush; *Chronicles* ....(MER)
  Exit...Stage Left ....(MER)
  Moving Pictures ....(MER)
Tore Down A La Rimbaud
  Van Morrison; *A Sense Of Wonder* ....(MER)
Trinidad
  Eddie Money; *Playing For Keeps* ....(COL)
  Unplug It In ....(COL)
Turn Back The Pages
  Crosby, Stills & Nash; *Crosby, Stills & Nash*
  (collection) ....(ATL)
  Stephen Stills; *Stills* ....(COL)
Turn The Page
  Rush; *Hold Your Fire* ....(MER)
  Show Of Hands ....(MER)
  Terence Trent D'Arby; *Symphony Or Damn* .....(COL)
Two Fairy Tales
  Mark Lambert & Victoria Mallory; *Sondheim-Musical*
  Tribute ....(RCA)

Original Cast; *Marry Me A Little* ....(RCA)
Typewriter, The
  101 Strings Orchestra; *Strings Have Fun!* .... (ALS)
  Rochester Pops Orchestra; *Leroy Anderson's Greatest
  Hits* ....(POE)
  Rochester Pops Orchestra/Erich Kunzel; *Syncopated
  Clock* ....(POE)
U.F.O. Story
  Flaming Lips; *Telepathic Surgery* ....(RES)
Virginia Woolf
  Indigo Girls; *Rites Of Passage* ....(EPI)
Washable Ink
  John Hiatt; *Slug Line* ....(MCA)
  Y'All Caught? Ones That Got Away-1979-85 .(A&M)
  Neville Brothers; *Love Gets Strange-Songs Of John
  Hiatt* ....(RHI)
  Treacherous-History Of-1955-1985 ....(RHI)
Whale Of A Tale
  Original London Cast; *Moby Dick* ....(RCA)
Whaling Stories
  Procol Harum; *Classics-#17* ....(A&M)
  Home ....(MOB)
  Live In Concert With Edmonton Symphony .... (MOB)
Wild Billy's Circus Story
  Bruce Springsteen; *Wild The Innocent & The E Street
  Shuffle* ....(COL)
Wild Tales
  Crosby, Stills & Nash; *Crosby, Stills & Nash* .....(ATL)
Wondrous Stories
  Yes; *Classic Yes* ....(ATL)
  Going For The One ....(ATL)
  Yesshows ....(ATL)
Write Your Own Songs (Mr. Record Exec.)
  Asleep At The Wheel; *Asleep At The Wheel* .... (DOT)
  Waylon Jennings & Willie Nelson; *WW2* ....(RCA)
  Willie Nelson & Kris Kristofferson; *Music From
  "Songwriter"* ....(COL)
Writer
  UFO; *Best Of The Rest* ....(CHR)
  Mechanix ....(CHR)
Writing
  Elton John; *Capt. Fantastic & The Brown Dirt
  Cowboy* ....(POL)
  Saga; *Heads Or Tales* ....(POR)
Writing On The Wall
  Cheap Trick; *Dream Police* ....(EPI)
  George Jones; *One Woman Man* ....(EPI)
  Lene Lovich; *Stateless...Plus* ....(RHI)
  Original Broadway Cast; *Mystery Of Edwin
  Drood* ....(POL)
  Ted Nugent; *Free For All* ....(EPI)
  Triumph; *Never Surrender* ....(MCA)
Written All Over Your Face
  Rude Boys; *Rude Awakening* ....(ATL)
Written In Sand
  Santana; *Beyond Appearances* ....(COL)
Written In Stone
  Randy Travis; *Old 8 X 10* ....(WB)
Written On The Wind
  Four Aces; *20 Greatest Hits* ....(EVR)
  Best Of ....(MCA)
  Love Is A Many Splendored Thing ....(ACC)
You Can't Judge A Book By Its Cover
  Stevie Wonder; *Signed Sealed & Delivered* ....(MOT)
You Can't Judge A Book By The Cover
  Hank Williams, Jr.; *Montana Cafe* ....(CRB)
  Patti Labelle; *Patti Labelle* ....(EPI)

BRIDGES

See Also: RIVERS, ROAD

59th St. Bridge Song (Feelin' Groovy)
  Simon & Garfunkel; *Collected Works* ....(COL)
  Concert In Central Park ....(WB)
  Greatest Hits ....(COL)
  Parsley Sage Rosemary & Thyme ....(COL)
Another Bridge To Burn
  Mel Tillis; *Best Of* ....(MCA)
Bridge
  Sonny Rollins; *Bluebird Sampler* ....(BLU)
  Quartets w/Jim Hall ....(BLU)
Bridge Across Forever
  Highway 101; *Highway 101* ....(WB)

Bridge I'm Still Building On
  Vern Gosdin; *Out Of My Heart* ....(COL)
Bridge Of Caulaincourt
  Original Cast; *Irma La Douce* ....(SSP)
Bridge Of Sighs
  Robin Trower; *Best Of Hard Rock-#2* ....(MSP)
  Bridge Of Sighs ....(CHR)
Bridge Of Spies
  T'Pau; *Bridge Of Spies* ....(VIA)
Bridge On The River Kwai
  Magic Organ; *Plays Movie Themes* ....(RAN)
Bridge Over Troubled Water
  Aretha Franklin; *30 Greatest Hits* ....(ATL)
  Greatest Hits ....(ATL)
  Live At Fillmore West ....(ATL)
  Paul Simon; *Concert In The Park-August 15 1991* (WB)
  Live Rhymin' ....(WB)
  Simon & Garfunkel; *Bridge Over Troubled Water* (COL)
  Collected Works ....(COL)
  Concert In Central Park ....(WB)
  Greatest Hits ....(COL)
Bridge That Just Won't Burn
  Conway Twitty; *Number Ones* ....(MCA)
Bridge Washed Out
  Warner Mack; *Country's Greatest Hits-#3* ....(MCA)
  MCA 30 Years Of Hits 1958-1988 ....(MCA)
Bridges Burning
  Mission U.K.; *God's Own Medicine* ....(MER)
Bridges Over Borders
  Spoons; *Bridges Over Borders* ....(MER)
Bridges & Walls
  Oak Ridge Boys; *Greatest Hits 3* ....(MCA)
  Monongahela ....(MCA)
Burn Down The Bridges
  Artch; *For The Sake Of Mankind* ....(MET)
Burn That Bridge
  Jimmy Buffett; *Riddles In The Sand* ....(MCA)
Burning Bridges
  38 Special; *Bone Against Steel* ....(CHS)
  Collective Soul; *Hints Allegations And Things Left
  Unsaid* ....(ATL)
  Garth Brooks; *Ropin' The Wind* ....(CAP)
  George Jones; *Jones Country* ....(EPI)
  One Woman Man ....(EPI)
  Glen Campbell; *Greatest Hits* ....(CAP)
  Jack Scott; *Capitol Collectors Series* ....(CAP)
  Super Oldies!'60s-#6 ....(AUF)
  Mike Curb Congregation; *Super Hits!'70s-Have A Nice
  Day-#5* ....(RHI)
  Naked Eyes; *Best Of* ....(EMI)
  Pink Floyd; *Gift Set* ....(CAP)
  ST/Obscured By Clouds ....(CAP)
  Roger Miller; *King Of The Road* ....(LAS)
Chelsea Bridge
  Duke Ellington; *Blanton-Webster Band* ....(BLU)
  Concert In The Virgin Islands ....(DCO)
  Sarah Vaughan; *Duke Ellington Songbook 2* ......(PAB)
Cross Over The Bridge
  Patti Page; *Golden Hits* ....(MER)
  Greatest Hits ....(COL)
Cross That Bridge
  Status Quo; *Status Quo* ....(MER)
Gonna Burn Some Bridges
  Ray Price; *For The Good Times/I Won't Mention
  It...* ....(COL)
London Bridge
  Big Audio Dynamite; *Megatop Phoenix* ....(COL)
  Bread; *Anthology* ....(ELE)
  Best Of-#2 ....(ELE)
  Bread ....(ELE)
London Bridge Is Falling Down
  Count Basie; *Good Morning Blues* ....(MCA)
  Newtrament; *Word 2* ....(JVA)
Love Can Build A Bridge
  Judds; *Love Can Build A Bridge* ....(RCC)
Nippon Bridge
  Kim Robertson; *Angels In Disguise* ....(INV)
On London Bridge
  Jo Stafford; *International Hits* ....(CRN)
One Lane Bridge
  Kim Pensyl; *Eyes Of Wonder* ....(GRP)
Racin' Burnin' Bridges
  Ranch Romance; *Blue Blazes* ....(SH)

Ruck A Pit Bridge
Tuff; *What Comes Around Goes Around* .... (ATL)
Seven Bridges Road
Eagles; *Greatest Hits-#2* .... (ASY)
Live .... (ASY)
Steve Young; *Seven Bridges Road* .... (ROU)
Singing Bridge Of Memphis Tennessee
John Fahey; *Essential* .... (VAN)
Swinging Bridge
Jerry Douglas; *Plant Early* .... (MCA)
Sampler '89-#1 .... (MCA)
Under The Bridge
Merle Haggard; *Blue Jungle* ....(CCB)
Red Hot Chili Peppers; *Blood Sugar Sex Magik* ... (WB)
What Hits!? *Best Of* ....(EMI)
Under The Bridges Of Paris
Michel LeGrand; *LeGrand Piano* ....(COL)
Walk Softly On The Bridge
Mel Street; *Greatest Hits* ....(GRT)
Water Under The Bridge
Dan Seals; *Greatest Hits* ....(LIB)
On Arrival ....(LIB)
Olivia Newton-John; *Have You Never Been*
Mellow .... (MCA)
We'll Burn That Bridge
Brooks & Dunn; *Hard Workin' Man* .... (ARI)

BUS

See Also: ROAD, TRAVELING

Another One Rides The Bus
Weird Al Yankovic; *Dr. Demento Greatest Novelty*
Records-#5 .... (RHI)
Weird Al Yankovic ....(RAR)
Bus Driver
Muddy Waters; *Hard Again* .... (BS)
Bus Drivin' Woman
Chicago Bob; *Hit & Run Lover* .... (ICH)
Bus Dust
Count Basie; *Long Live The Chief* .... (DEN)
Bus Fare Home
Spaniels; *Heart & Soul-#2* .... (VJ)
Bus Fare To Kentucky
Skeeter Davis; *Best Of The Best Of* ....(GUS)
Bus From Amarillo
Original Cast; *Best Little Whorehouse In Texas* .. (MCA)
Bus Has Come
Jai Uttal; *Footprints* ....(TRI)
Bus Ride
Original New York Cast; *Oil City Symphony* ... (DRG)
Bus Rider
Guess Who; *At Their Best* ....(RCA)
Best Of ....(RCA)
Track Record-Collection ....(RCA)
Bus Rider Blues
Blind Boy Fuller; *1935-1940* ....(BCL)
Bus Song
Tony Gable & 206; *Tony Gable & 206* .... (HUR)
Bus Station Blues
John Lee Hooker; *Great Bluesmen At Newport* .. (VAN)
Bus Stations & Train Yards
Gutterboy; *Gutterboy* .... (MER)
Bus Stop
Hollies; *Best Of-#1* .... (EMI)
Greatest Hits .... (EPI)
History Of British Rock-#3 .... (RHI)
Bus Stop Bench
Darden Smith; *Native Soil* .... (WAT)
Bus Stop (Electric Slide)
World Class Wreckin' Cru; *Best of Electric Slide* . (SOH)
Bus Tours
George Duke; *Snapshot* ....(WB)
Bus With No Driver
Thelonius Monster; *Beautiful Mess* ....(CAP)
Does This Bus Stop At 82nd St.
Bruce Springsteen; *Greetings From Asbury Park*
N.J. ....(COL)
Frisco Depot
Mickey Newbury; *Frisco Mabel Joy* .... (ELE)
Gimme A Quarter, 25 Cents For The Bus
October Faction; *October Faction* ....(SST)
I Missed The Bus
Kris Kross; *Totally Krossed Out* .... (RUF)

I Ride This Bus
4PM; *Jackin' Boots* ....(RPR)
Kiss Me On The Bus
Replacements; *Tim* ....(SIR)
Lady Bus Driver
Ultra Head; *Cement Truck* .... (IST)
Magic Bus
Who; *Greatest Hits* ....(MCA)
Live At Leeds .... (MCA)
Magic Bus .... (MCA)
Meaty Beaty Big & Bouncy .... (MCA)
ST/Kids Are Alright .... (MCA)
Who's Last ....(MCA)
Midnight Bus
Jesse Winchester; *Third Down 110 To Go* .... (RHI)
On A Lopsided Bus
Original Cast; *Pipe Dream* ....(RCA)
One Way Bus
New Birth; *Golden Classics* ....(CLT)
Only Losers Take The Bus (Dump The Dead)
Fatima Mansions; *Viva Dead Ponies* .... (RAD)
Porcelin Bus
Pajama Slave Dancers; *Blood Sweat & Beers* ..... (RES)
Pound For A Brown On The Bus
Frank Zappa; *Electric Aunt Jemima* .... (RHI)
Uncle Meat ....(BAR)
She Came From Fort Worth
Kathy Mattea; *Willow In The Wind* .... (MER)
Pat Alger & Kathy Mattea; *True Love & Other Short*
Stories ....(SH)
Slow Bus Movin' (Howard's Beach Party)
Fishbone; *Truth & Soul* ....(COL)
Thank God & Greyhound
Roy Clark; *Best Of* ....(MCA)
Greatest Hits-#1 .... (MCA)
Live .... (MCA)
Waitin' For The Bus
ZZ Top; *Best Of* ....(WB)
Six Pack ....(WB)
Tres Hombres ....(WB)

CAPITAL PUNISHMENT

See Also: CRIME, DEATH, KILL, REBELS

Another Execution
Above The Law; *Livin' Like Hustlers* ....(RUT)
Asswhippin'
Fishbone; *Reality Of My Surroundings* ....(COL)
At The Gallows End
Candlemass; *Live* .... (MET)
Crucified
Agnostic Front; *Best Of* .... (REL)
Last Warning .... (REL)
Army Of Lovers; *Massive Luxury Overdose* ...... (GIA)
Fixx; *Ink* .... (IPA)
Dang Me
Roger Miller; *Billboard Top Rock 'N' Roll*
Hits-1964 .... (RHI)
Cruisin' 1964 .... (INC)
Golden Hits .... (SMA)
Death Row
David Allan Coe; *Penitentiary Blues* .... (SSS)
Death Sentence
Big Daddy Kane; *Prince Of Darkness* ....(CLD)
Capital Punishment; *Livin' On The Edge Of A*
Razor .... (W/I)
Electric Chair
Prince; *ST/Batman* .... (WB)
Sleepy John Estes/Tennessee Jug Busters; *Broke &*
Hungry (Ragged & Dirty Too) ....(DEL)
Electric Chair Blues
Guitar Welch; *Angola Prisoner's Blues* .... (ARH)
Electric Chair, The
SNFU; *Last Of The Big Time Suspenders* ... (CGO)
Executioner Style
Awesome Dre/Hardcore Committee; *You Can't Hold*
Me Back .... (PRY)
Gallows Pole
Leadbelly; *Leadbelly* ....(EVR)
Led Zeppelin; *3* ....(ATL)
Led Zeppelin ....(ATL)
Page & Plant; *Unledded* .... (ATL)

Gallows Song
Carl Sandburg; *Americana* .... (EVR)
Hang 'Em High
Booker T./M.G.s; *15 Original Big Hits-#4* .... (STX)
Greatest Hits .... (STX)
Van Halen; *Diver Down* .... (WB)
Hanging Song
Fairport Convention; *Babbacombe Lee* .... (A&M)
Hanging Tree
Marty Robbins; *All-Time Greatest Hits* ....(COL)
Hollywood Magic-1950s ....(COL)
Lifetime Of Song ....(COL)
Hangman
John Jacob Niles; *Best Of* ....(TRD)
Peter, Paul & Mary; *See What Tomorrow Brings* ..(WB)
Hangman Hang My Shell On A Tree
Spooky Tooth; *Spooky Two* .... (A&M)
Hangman Jury
Aerosmith; *Permanent Vacation* .... (GEF)
Hangman & Papist
Strawbs; *From The Witchwood* .... (A&M)
Hangman's Knee
Jeff Beck; *Beck-Ola* .... (EPI)
Heads Will Roll
Echo/Bunnymen; *Porcupine* .... (SIR)
Ted Nugent; *Intensities in Ten Cities* ....(EPI)
I Cheat The Hangman
Doobie Brothers; *Stampede* .... (WB)
It's Not My Cross To Bear
Allman Brothers Band; *Allman Brothers Band* ... (POL)
Beginnings .... (POL)
Dreams .... (POL)
Gregg Allman Band; *I'm No Angel* ....(EPI)
Joe Hill
Arlo Guthrie & Pete Seeger; *Together In Concert* (RPR)
Joan Baez; *Carry It On* .... (VAN)
From Every Stage .... (A&M)
One Day At A Time .... (VAN)
ST/Woodstock .... (ATL)
Soundtrack; *Carry It On* .... (VAN)
John Barleycorn
Traffic; *John Barleycorn Must Die* .... (ISL)
Nebraska
Bruce Springsteen; *Nebraska* ....(COL)
Bruce Springsteen/E Street Band;
Live-1975-1985 ....(COL)
Only A Hangman
Brownie Ford; *Stories From Mtns. Swamps &
Honky-Tonks* .... (FF)
Poor Will & The Jolly Hangman
Richard Thompson; *Guitar Vocal* ....(HBL)
Public Execution
Mouse/Traps; *Nuggets-#2* .... (RHI)
Quarterdrawing Of The Dog
Siouxsie/Banshees; *Tinderbox* .... (GEF)
Renegade
Styx; *Classics-#15* ....(A&M)
Pieces Of Eight .... (A&M)
Send Me To The 'Lectric Chair
David Bromberg; *Out Of The Blues-Best Of* .....(COL)
Wanted Dead Or Alive ....(COL)
Hoyt Axton; *Down & Out* .... (ALL)
They're Hanging Me Tonight
Marty Robbins; *Gunfighter Ballads & Trail Songs* (COL)
Tom Dooley
Doc Watson; *Doc Watson* .... (VAN)
Essential .... (VAN)
Out In The Country .... (INT)
Kingston Trio; *Capitol Collectors Series* ....(CAP)
From The Hungry i .... (CAP)
Greatest Hits ....(CCB)
Tom Dooley .... (CAP)
Troubadours Of The Folk Era-#3 .... (RHI)
Torture
Cure; *Kiss Me Kiss Me Kiss Me* .... (ELE)
Jacksons; *Victory* ....(EPI)
Replacements; *All Shook Down* .... (SIR)
Twenty-Five Minutes To Go
Johnny Cash; *At Folsom Prison & San Quentin* ...(COL)
Essential ....(COL)
True West ....(COL)
Two Years Of Torture
Lou Rawls; *At Last* .... (BLN)
Percy Mayfield; *Please Send Me Someone To Love* (INT)

Walking Down Death Row
Pete Seeger; *Dangerous Songs* ....(OOP)
When The Whip Comes Down
Rolling Stones; *Some Girls* .... (RS)
Sucking In The Seventies ....(RS)
Whip
Eddie Kendricks; *Vintage '78* .... (ARI)
Whip It
Devo; *Best Of-Greatest Hits* .... (WB)
EZ Listening Disc ....(RYK)
Freedom Of Choice .... (WB)
Last American Virgin ....(COL)
Whipping Post
Allman Brothers Band; *Allman Brothers Band* ...(POL)
At Fillmore East .... (POL)
Beginnings .... (POL)
Decade Of Hits-1969-1979 .... (POL)
Dreams .... (POL)
Road Goes On Forever .... (POL)
Frank Zappa; *Them Or Us* ....(RYK)

CARNIVALS, Amusement Parks, Circus, Clowns, Fairs, Mardi Gras, Parades
See Also: FUN, HAPPINESS, CITIES: NEW ORLEANS

76 Trombones
Original Cast; *Music Man* ....(CAP)
Arcade Queen
Rubinoos; *Back To The Drawing Board* .... (BES)
Assholes On Parade
Timbuk 3; *Best Of* .... (IRS)
At The Chicago World's Fair
Original Cast; *Show Boat* ....(RCA)
At The Fair In Pacanow
Myron Floren; *Polka Party* .... (RAN)
Before The Parade Passes By
Broadway Cast; *Hello Dolly!* ....(RCA)
Carol Channing/Original Cast; *Hello Dolly!* .....(RCA)
Being For The Benefit Of Mr. Kite
Beatles; *Box Set* ....(CAP)
Sgt. Pepper's Lonely Hearts Club Band ....(CAP)
Bourbon Street Parade
Al Hirt; *Best Of* ....(RCA)
Dukes Of Dixieland; *Digital Dixieland* .... (PJ)
Pete Fountain; *Best Of-#2* ....(MCA)
Preservation Hall Jazz Band; *New Orleans-#4* ..(COL)
Wynton Marsalis; *Standard Time-#2-Intimacy
Calling* ....(COL)
Carnaval
Santana; *Festival* ....(COL)
Moonflower ....(COL)
Sergio Mendes; *Sergio Mendes* ....(A&M)
Carney
Leon Russell; *Carney* .... (MCA)
Carnival
Eric Clapton; *No Reason To Cry* .... (RSO)
Mose Allison; *Down Home Piano* .... (PRS)
Mose Allison .... (PRS)
Simple Minds; *Real To Real Cacophony* .... (VIA)
Stomu Yamashta/Others; *Go Live From Paris* ..... (ISL)
Tito Puente; *Puente Now!* .... (CRS)
Carnival In New Orleans
Professor Longhair; *Last Mardi Gras* ....(ATL)
Carnival Is Over
Seekers; *Best Of* ....(CAP)
Carnival Of Sorts
R.E.M.; *Dead Letter Office/Chronic Town* ...... (IRS)
Carnival Of Venice
Carmen Cavallaro; *Best Of* ....(MCA)
Mantovani; *Mantovani's Italia* ....(BAI)
Carnival Song
Tim Buckley; *Best Of* .... (RHI)
Carousel
Original Cast; *Jacques Brel Is Alive & Well* ....(ATL)
Jacques Brel Is Alive & Well ....(COL)
Siouxsie/Banshees; *Peepshow* .... (GEF)
Carousel Man
Cher; *Greatest Hits* .... (MCA)
Carousel Of Love
Jane Olivor; *First Night* ....(COL)
In Concert ....(COL)

Carousel Waltz
Original Cast; *Carousel* .... (MCA)
Cathy's Clown
Everly Brothers; *Billboard Top Rock 'N' Roll
Hits-1960* .... (RHI)
  Golden Hits .... (WB)
  Reunion Concert .... (MER)
  Very Best Of .... (WB)
Reba McEntire; *Sweet Sixteen* .... (MCA)
Children In The Carousel
Mabel Mercer & Bobby Short; *At Town Hall* .... (ATL)
Circus
Erasure; *Circus* .... (SIR)
  Two Ring Circus .... (SIR)
Circus Of Heaven
Yes; *Tormato* .... (ATL)
Circus Polka
Myron Floren; *22 Great Polkas* .... (RAN)
  Great Polka Hits .... (RAN)
Clown
Conway Twitty; *Latest Greatest Hits-#1* .... (WB)
  Number One's: Warner Brothers Years .... (WB)
  Southern Comfort .... (WB)
Images; *Master Series Sampler '89* .... (CAP)
  Relative Work .... (CAP)
Clown Woman
Montrose; *Montrose* .... (WB)
Clowntime Is Over
Elvis Costello; *Girls Girls Girls* .... (COL)
  Taking Liberties .... (COL)
Elvis Costello/Attractions; *Get Happy!* .... (RYK)
Comedians
Elvis Costello/Attractions; *Goodbye Cruel World* (COL)
Roy Orbison; *Mystery Girl* .... (VIA)
  & Friends: Black & White Night-Live .... (VIA)
Coney Island Baby
Excellents; *WCBS FM101-History Of
Rock/Doo-Wop-#1* .... (CLT)
Lou Reed; *City Lights* .... (ARI)
  Walk On The Wild Side .... (RCA)
Coney Island Washboard
Mills Brothers; *22 Great Hits* .... (RAN)
  50th Anniversary .... (RAN)
Cowboys & Clowns
Billy Strange; *Great Western Themes* .... (CRS)
Ronnie Milsap; *ST/Bronco Billy* .... (ELE)
Death Of A Clown
Kinks; *Kink Kronikles* .... (RPR)
  Something Else .... (RPR)
Disney Girls
Art Garfunkel; *Breakaway* .... (COL)
Beach Boys; *Surf's Up* .... (CAR)
Captain & Tennille; *Greatest Hits* .... (A&M)
Don't Rain On My Parade
Barbra Streisand; *Greatest Hits* .... (COL)
  Live At The Forum .... (COL)
  Original Cast-Funny Girl .... (CAP)
  ST/Funny Girl .... (COL)
  & Other Musical Instruments .... (COL)
Easter Parade
Andy Russell; *Puttin' On The Ritz-Capitol Sings
Berlin* .... (CAP)
Bing Crosby; *All Time Best Of* .... (CCB)
Judy Garland & Fred Astaire; *ST/Easter Parade* .. (SSP)
Sarah Vaughan; *Complete On Mercury-#2-American
Songs* .... (MER)
Elephant Day Parade
Beat Farmers; *Pursuit Of Happiness* .... (CCB)
Elephant Trainer
Liz Story; *Part Of Fortune* .... (NOV)
Fourth Of July At A County Fair
Red Clay Ramblers; *Chuckin' The Frizz* .... (FF)
Fourth Of July, Asbury Park (Sandy)
Bruce Springsteen; *Wild The Innocent & The E Street
Shuffle* .... (COL)
Bruce Springsteen/E Street Band;
Live-1975-1985 .... (COL)
Funhouse
Kid 'N Play; *S* .... (SEL)
Here Comes The Big Parade
Harry Connick, Jr.; *She* .... (COL)
Highwire
Rolling Stones; *Flashpoint* .... (COL)
  Flashpoint & Collectibles .... (COL)

Honky Tonk Merry Go Round
Patsy Cline; *20 Golden Pieces Of* .... (BLD)
  Patsy Cline .... (AUF)
  Today Tomorrow & Forever .... (MCA)
  Try Again .... (QKS)
  Walkin' Dreams-Her First Recordings-#1 .... (RHI)
Hurdy Gurdy Man
Donovan; *Greatest Hits* .... (EPI)
  Hurdy Gurdy Man .... (EPI)
I Love A Parade
Cab Calloway; *Bessie Smith/Louis Armstrong/C.
Calloway* .... (BIO)
I Remember Coney Island
Lounge Lizards; *Lounge Lizards* .... (EDI)
Joker James
Brian Hyland; *Greatest Hits* .... (RHI)
Joker, The
Steve Miller Band; *Best Of-1968-1973* .... (CAP)
  Gift Set .... (CAP)
  Greatest Hits-1974-1978 .... (CAP)
  Live .... (CAP)
  The Joker .... (CAP)
June Parade
Vic Shine; *Far & Distant Shore* .... (RCA)
Karn Evil 9
Emerson, Lake & Palmer; *Best Of* .... (ATL)
  Brain Salad Surgery .... (ATL)
  Ladies & Gentlemen... .... (MTC)
Life Is A Carnival
Band; *Anthology-#2* .... (CAP)
  Best Of .... (CAP)
  Cahoots .... (CAP)
  Last Waltz .... (WB)
  Rock Of Ages-#1 & 2 .... (CAP)
Love Parade
Dream Academy; *Dream Academy* .... (RPR)
Magical Mystery Tour
Beatles; *1967-1970* .... (CAP)
  Magical Mystery Tour .... (CAP)
  Reel Music .... (CAP)
Mardi Gras
Gino Vannelli; *Pauper In Paradise* .... (A&M)
Original Cast; *House Of Flowers* .... (SSP)
Mardi Gras Boogie
Clifton Chenier; *In New Orleans* .... (CRS)
Mardi Gras In New Orleans
Professor Longhair; *Atlantic Rhythm & Blues-#1
(1947-52)* .... (ATL)
  New Orleans Jazz & Heritage Fest.-1976 .... (RHI)
  New Orleans Piano-Blues Originals-#2 .... (ATL)
  Rockin' Dopsie; Alligator Stomp-#2 .... (RHI)
Mardi Gras Mambo
Hawketts; *Treacherous: History Of Neville Bros.* .. (RHI)
Meet Me In St. Louis, Louis
Judy Garland; *Best Of* .... (MCA)
Merry Go Round
Buffalo Springfield; *Last Time Around* .... (ATC)
Charlie Parker; *Bird/Savoy Recordings (Master
Takes)* .... (SAV)
  Bird/Savoy Recordings (Master Takes)-#2 ...... (SAV)
  Complete Savoy Studio Sessions .... (SAV)
  Encores-#2 .... (SAV)
J.B. Summers; *Big Band Blues* .... (CLT)
  Collectables Blues Collection-#2 .... (CLT)
  & The Blues Shouters .... (CLT)
Keith Sweat; *I'll Give All My Love To You* ...... (VNT)
Neil Diamond; *And The Singer Sings His Song* .. (MCA)
  Velvet Gloves & Spit .... (MCA)
Replacements; *All Shook Down* .... (SIR)
Midnight Carnival
Chris Mars; *Horseshoes & Hand Grenades* ...... (SMA)
"Monty Python's Flying Circus" Theme
Original Music; *Television's Greatest Hits-#2* ..... (TVT)
My Carnival
Wings; *Venus & Mars* .... (CAP)
Night The Carousel Burned Down
Todd Rundgren; *Somthing/Anything?* .... (RHI)
Nobody's Gonna Rain On Our Parade
Kathy Mattea; *Walking Away A Winner* .... (MER)
On A Carousel
Hollies; *Best OF-#1* .... (EMI)
  Greatest Hits .... (EPI)
  History Of British Rock-#1-9 .... (RHI)

Opryland In Paris
Andy Badale/Beer Garden Band; *Nashville Beer
Garden* .... (RAN)
Our State Fair
Popular Standard; *Out of print recording* ....(OOP)
Paducah Parade
Bob Crosby; *Uncollected-#2-1952-1953* .... (HIN)
Palisades Park
Beach Boys; *15 Big Ones* .... (RPR)
Freddie "Boom Boom" Cannon; *14 Blooming Hits* (RHI)
  Billboard Top Rock 'N' Roll Hits-1962 .... (RHI)
  His Latest & Greatest .... (CRI)
  Memories Of The Cow Palace .... (RHI)
  Oldies But Goodies-#11-CD .... (OSR)
Ramones; *Brain Drain* .... (SIR)
Pink Elephants On Parade
Barbara Cook; *Disney Album* .... (MCA)
Planet Of The Clowns
Bruce Cockburn; *Trouble With Normal* ....(COL)
Pocket Of A Clown
Dwight Yoakam; *This Time* .... (RPR)
Rollercoaster
Echo/Bunnymen; *45* .... (SIR)
Fabulous Thunderbirds; *Walk That Walk Talk That
Talk* .... (EPA)
Jesus & Mary Chain; *Honey's Dead* .... (DEF)
Mighty Lemon Drops; *Out Of Hand* .... (SIR)
Ohio Players; *45* ....(OOP)
Roseville Fair
Nanci Griffith; *One Fair Summer Evening* .... (MCA)
Scarborough Fair
Simon & Garfunkel; *Collected Works* ....(COL)
  Concert In Central Park ....(WB)
  Greatest Hits ....(COL)
  Parsley Sage Rosemary & Thyme ....(COL)
  ST/The Graduate ....(COL)
See The Funny Little Clown
Bobby Goldsboro; *10th Anniversary Album-#1* ... (EMI)
  Greatest Hits ....(LIB)
  Honey-Best Of ....(EMI)
Send In The Clowns
Barbra Streisand; *Broadway Album* ....(COL)
Carmen McRae; *Sarah-Dedicated To You* ...... (NOV)
Frank Sinatra; *Reprise Collection* .... (RPR)
Judy Collins; *Judith* .... (ELE)
  So Early In The Spring-First 15 Years .... (ELE)
Original Cast; *Little Night Music* ....(COL)
She Moved Through The Fair
Art Garfunkel; *Watermark* ....(COL)
James Galway/Chieftains; *In Ireland* ....(RCA)
She's A Carnival
Siouxsie/Banshees; *Kiss In The Dream House* .... (GEF)
Side Show
Blue Magic; *Blue Magic* ....(ATC)
  Golden Age Of Black Music-1970-1975 .... (ATL)
  Greatest Hits ....(OMN)
  Live ....(WMO)
  Magic Of The Blue-Greatest Hits .... (CLT)
  Soul Hits/'70s-#13 .... (RHI)
Spinning Wheel
Blood, Sweat & Tears; *Blood, Sweat & Tears* ...(COL)
  Greatest Hits ....(COL)
  Rock Classics/'60s ....(COL)
State Fair
Doug Supernaw; *Deep Thoughts From A Shallow
Mind* ....(BNA)
Stayed Too Long At The Fair
Bonnie Raitt; *Give It Up* .... (WB)
Stuck In The Middle With You
Stealers Wheel; *Super Hits/'70s-Have A Nice
Day-#10* .... (RHI)
Sweethearts On Parade
Guy Lombardo; *Best Of* ....(CCB)
  Best Of ....(MCA)
Louis Armstrong; *#7-You're Drivin' Me Crazy* ...(COL)
Pete Fountain; *Pete Fountain's New Orleans* ..... (MCA)
Roy Eldridge; *Happy Time* .... (PAB)
Take Me To The Fair
ELvis Presley; *It Happened At The World's Fair* ..(RCA)
Soundtrack; *Camelot* .... (WB)
Take Me To The Mardi Gras
Paul Simon; *There Goes Rhymin' Simon* ....(WB)

Tears Of A Clown
English Beat; *I Just Can't Stop It* .... (IRS)
  What Is Beat .... (IRS)
Smokey Robinson/Miracles; *25 #1 Hits From 25
Years* .... (MOT)
  Anthology .... (MOT)
  Billboard Top Rock 'N' Roll Hits-1970 .... (RHI)
  Compact Command Performances .... (MOT)
  Endless Love-Mot. Greatest Love Songs .... (MOT)
  Tears Of A Clown .... (MOT)
Thanks For The Ride On The MerryGoRound
Andy Badale/Beer Garden Band; *Nashville Beer
Garden* .... (RAN)
That Song About The Midway
Bonnie Raitt; *Streetlights* .... (WB)
Joni Mitchell; *Clouds* .... (RPR)
Theme From "Jurassic Park"
John Williams; *ST/Jurassic Park* .... (MCA)
Then You May Take Me To The Fair
Original Cast; *Camelot* ....(COL)
Vanessa Redgrave; *ST/Camelot* ....(WB)
This Ain't Disneyland
Forever Einstein; *Opportunity Crosses The Bridge* (CUN)
Ticket To Ride
Beatles; *1962-1966* ....(CAP)
  20 Greatest Hits ....(CAP)
  At The Hollywood Bowl ....(CAP)
  Box Set ....(CAP)
  Help! ....(CAP)
  Reel Music ....(CAP)
  ST/Help! ....(CAP)
Carpenters; *Classics-#2* .... (A&M)
  From The Top ....(A&M)
  Singles-1969-1973 ....(A&M)
  Ticket To Ride ....(A&M)
  Yesterday Once More ....(A&M)
Vanilla Fudge; *Best Of* .... (ATC)
  Vanilla Fudge ....(ATC)
Tightrope
Bob Seger/Silver Bullet Band; *Like A Rock* ...... (CAP)
Electric Light Orchestra; *Afterglow* .... (EPI)
Stevie Ray Vaughan/Double Trouble; *In Step* ..... (EPI)
Tracy Nelson; *Homemade Songs* .... (FF)
Tightrope Walk
Damned; *Anything* .... (MCA)
Too Long At The Fair
Bonnie Raitt; *Give It Up* .... (WB)
Tunnel Of Love
Bruce Springsteen; *Tunnel Of Love* ....(COL)
Byrds; *Byrdmaniax* ....(COL)
Dire Straits; *Live-Alchemy* .... (WB)
  Making Movies .... (WB)
  Money For Nothing .... (WB)
  ST/Officer & A Gentleman .... (ISL)
Under The Boardwalk
Bette Midler; *ST/Beaches* .... (ATL)
Bruce Willis; *Return Of Bruno* .... (MOT)
Drifters; *16 Greatest Hits* .... (TRP)
  Atlantic R&B 1947-1974-#5 (1962-1966) ..... (ATL)
  Golden Hits .... (ATL)
  Super Oldies/'60s-#5 .... (AUF)
John Cougar Mellencamp; *45* .... (RIV)
Lynn Anderson; *What She Does Best* .... (MER)
Rickie Lee Jones; *Girl At Her Volcano* .... (WB)
Rolling Stones; *12 X 5* .... (AKO)
Untouchables; *Agent Double O Soul* .... (RES)
Virgo Clowns
Van Morrison; *His Band & Street Choir* .... (WB)
Watching The Wheels
John Lennon; *Lennon* ....(CAP)
John Lennon & Yoko Ono; *Double Fantasy* ......(CAP)
When The Circus Comes
Los Lobos; *Just Another Band From East
L.A.-Coll.* ....(SLS)
  Kiko ....(SLS)
Wild Billy's Circus Story
Bruce Springsteen; *Wild The Innocent & The E Street
Shuffle* ....(COL)
Working Without A Net
Waylon Jennings; *Country Classics-#5
(1985-1986)* .... (MCA)
  New Classic Waylon .... (MCA)
  Today's Country Classics-#2 .... (MCA)
  Will The Wolf Survive .... (MCA)

W.S. Walcott Medicine Show
Band; *Rock Of Ages-#1 & 2* .... (CAP)
   Stage Fright .... (CAP)
   To Kingdom Come-Definitive Collection .... (CAP)

CARS, Driving, Hitchhiking

See Also: CARS: CADILLAC, ROAD, ROAD
ACCIDENTS, TAXI, TRAVELING, TRUCKS

409
Beach Boys; *Best Of* .... (CAP)
   Greatest Hits .... (GUS)
   Made In The U.S.A. .... (CAP)
   Spirit Of America .... (CAP)
American Pie
Don McLean; *American Pie* .... (UA)
   Best Of .... (EMI)
   Greatest Hits Then & Now .... (EMI)
   ST/*Born On The Fourth Of July* .... (MCA)
Arrested For Driving While Blind
ZZ Top; *Six Pack* .... (WB)
   Tejas .... (WB)
Automatic Drive
Platinum Blonde; *Contact* .... (EPI)
Automobile
John Prine; *Anthology-Great Days* .... (RHI)
   Pink Cadillac .... (ASY)
N.W.A.; *Efil4zaggin* .... (RUP)
Automobile Blues
Lightnin' Hopkins; *Lightnin'* .... (PRS)
   Early Recordings-#1 .... (ARH)
   Low Down Dirty Blues .... (MST)
Automobile Noise
Blue Nile; *Walk Across The Rooftops* .... (A&M)
Baby Driver
Simon & Garfunkel; *Bridge Over Troubled Water* (COL)
   Collected Works ....(COL)
Back Seat Of My Car
Paul McCartney; *CD Gift Set* .... (CAP)
Paul & Linda McCartney; *Ram* .... (CAP)
Bad Brakes
Cat Stevens; *Back To Earth* .... (A&M)
Beep Beep
Playmates; *Dr. Demento's 20th Anniversary Coll.* (RHI)
Big Log
Robert Plant; *Principle Of Moments* .... (EPR)
Black Limousine
Rolling Stones; *Tattoo You* .... (RS)
Blondes In Black Cars
Autograph; *That's The Stuff* .... (RCA)
Brand New Car
Rolling Stones; *Voodoo Lounge* .... (VIA)
Brand New Convertible Car
Die Warzau; *Big Electric Metal Bass Face* .... (ATL)
Bug, The
Dire Straits; *On Every Street* .... (WB)
Mary Chapin Carpenter; *Come On Come On* ..... (WB)
Buick '55
Johnny/Distractions; *My Desire* .... (BRN)
Buick '59
Vernon Green/Medallions; *Best Vocal Group In Rhythm
   & Blues* ....(DTN)
   Golden Classics .... (CLT)
   Vernon Green/Medallions .... (DTN)
Burn Rubber On Me
Gap Band; *12" Collection* .... (MER)
   Gap Gold-Best Of .... (MER)
   III .... (MER)
Buy, Buy This American Car
Charlie King; *Food Phone Gas Lodging* .... (FF)
"Car 54, Where Are You?" Theme
Original Music; *Television's Greatest Hits-#2* ..... (TVT)
Car Bomb
Negativeland; *Escape From Noise* ....(SST)
Car Car
Peter, Paul & Mary; *In Concert* .... (WB)
Car On A Hill
Joni Mitchell; *Court & Spark* .... (ASY)

Car Wash
Rose Royce; *Best Of* .... (OMN)
   Billboard Top Hits-1977 .... (RHI)
   Disco Years-#1-1974-1978 .... (RHI)
   Greatest Hits ....(WHI)
Cars
Gary Numan; *Pleasure Principle* .... (ATC)
Tom Wopat; *Little Bit Closer* .... (EMI)
Cars Hiss By My Window
Doors; *L.A. Woman* .... (ELE)
Cherry Bomb
John Cougar Mellencamp; *Check It Out* .... (MER)
   Lonesome Jubilee .... (MER)
Cherry, Cherry Coupe
Beach Boys; *Little Deuce Coupe/All Summer Long* (CAP)
Chevrolet
Foghat; *Stone Blue* .... (RHI)
Jim Kweskin/Jug Band; *Greatest Hits* .... (VAN)
   Jim Kweskin/Jug Band .... (VAN)
Taj Mahal; *Best Of-#1* .... (COL)
ZZ Top; *Rio Grande Mud* .... (WB)
   Six Pack .... (WB)
Chevy Van
Sammy Johns; *Super Hits/'70s-Have A Nice
   Day-#14* .... (RHI)
Waylon Jennings; *Hangin' Tough* .... (MCA)
Crosstown Traffic
Jimi Hendrix Experience; *Electric Ladyland* ...... (RPR)
   Essential-#2 .... (RPR)
   Kiss The Sky .... (RPR)
   Smash Hits .... (RPR)
Cruisin'
Alabama; *The Touch* ....(RCA)
Michael Nesmith; *Never Stuff* .... (RHI)
Smokey Robinson; *Compact Command
   Performances* .... (MOT)
   Motown Love Songs .... (MOT)
   Motown Story: First 25 Years .... (MOT)
   Where There's Smoke .... (MOT)
Ted Nugent; *Weekend Warriors* .... (EPI)
Custom Machine
Beach Boys; *Gift Set* .... (CAP)
   Little Deuce Coupe/All Summer Long .... (CAP)
   Spirit Of America .... (CAP)
Death Alley Driver
Rainbow; *Straight Between The Eyes* .... (MER)
Detroit 442
Blondie; *Plastic Letters* .... (CHR)
Devil In A Fast Car
Sheena Easton; *Best Kept Secret* .... (EMI)
Diamonds On My Windshield
Tom Waits; *Anthology* .... (ASY)
   Heart Of Saturday Night .... (ASY)
Don't Drink & Drive
James Cannings; *Music For All Seasons* .... (JC)
Don't Drive Drunk
Stevie Wonder; ST/*Woman In Red* .... (MOT)
Drag City
Jan & Dean; *Beach Party Blasts* .... (EMI)
   Best Of .... (EMI)
   Deadman's Curve .... (EMI)
   One Summer Night/Live .... (RHI)
Drinking And Driving
Black Flag; *In My Head* ....(SST)
Drinkin' & Drivin'
Johnny Paycheck; *Biggest Hits* .... (EPI)
   Encore .... (EPI)
   Everybody's Got a Family .... (EPI)
Drive
Cars; *Greatest Hits* .... (ELE)
   Heartbeat City .... (ELE)
   MTV's Rock 'N Roll To Go .... (ELE)
Drive All Night
Bruce Springsteen; *The River* ....(COL)
Drive My Car
Beatles; *1962-1966* .... (CAP)
   Rock 'n' Roll Music-#2 .... (CAP)
   Rubber Soul .... (CAP)
   Yesterday...And Today .... (CAP)
Drive On
Johnny Cash; *American Recordings* .... (AME)
Drive South
John Hiatt; *Slow Turning* .... (A&M)
Suzy Bogguss; *Voices In The Wind* .... (LIB)

Driver's Seat
Sniff 'n' The Tears; *Fickle Heart* .... (ATL)
Drive-In
Beach Boys; *All Summer Long* .... (CAP)
Spirit Of America .... (CAP)
Drive-In Movies & Dashboard Lights
Nanci Griffith; *Storms* .... (MCA)
Driving Along
Nilsson; *Nilsson Schmilsson* .... (RCA)
Driving Sister
Mott The Hoople; *Mott* .... (COL)
Drivin' Around
Raspberries; *Best* .... (CAP)
Capitol Collectors Series .... (CAP)
Drivin' My Life Away
Eddie Rabbitt; *All Time Greatest Hits* .... (WB)
Greatest Hits-#2 .... (WB)
Horizon .... (ELE)
Number 1's .... (WB)
Ten Years Of Greatest Hits .... (CAP)
Drivin' Wheel
Albert King; *Stax Blues Masters: Blue Monday* ... (STX)
Foghat; *Best Of* .... (RHI)
Night Shift .... (RHI)
Little Junior Parker; *Best Of* .... (MCA)
Drivin' Wheel .... (MCA)
Soul Shots-#7-Urban Blues .... (RHI)
Drivin' With Your Eyes Closed
Don Henley; *Building The Perfect Beast* .... (GEF)
Drivin' & Cryin'
Steve Wariner; *Drive* .... (ARI)
D.U.I.
Drink Small; *Round Two* .... (ICH)
Easy Driver
Kenny Loggins; *Alive!* .... (COL)
Nightwatch .... (COL)
Fast Car
Tracy Chapman; *Tracy Chapman* .... (ELE)
Faster
George Harrison; *George Harrison* .... (DKH)
Four Wheel Drive
C.W. McCall; *Greatest Hits* .... (POL)
Wolf Creek Pass .... (MGM)
Four Wheels
38 Special; *38 Special* .... (A&M)
From A Buick 6
Bob Dylan; *Highway 61 Revisited* .... (COL)
Fun Fun Fun
Beach Boys; *Best Of* .... (CAP)
Endless Summer .... (CAP)
Gift Set .... (CAP)
In Concert .... (CAR)
Made In The U.S.A. .... (CAP)
Gas Station Woman
Phil Ochs; *War Is Over-Best Of* .... (A&M)
Gasoline Alley
Rod Stewart; *Absolutely Live* .... (WB)
Best Of .... (MER)
Gasoline Alley .... (MER)
Sing It Again Rod .... (MER)
Storyteller/Complete Anthology .... (WB)
Get Outta My Dreams, Get Into My Car
Billy Ocean; *Greatest Hits* .... (JVA)
ST/License To Drive .... (MCA)
Great Filling Station Holdup
Jimmy Buffett; *White Sport Coat & A Pink
Crustacean* .... (MCA)
G.T.O.
Ronny/Daytonas; *Beach Classics* ....(DHL)
Hard Drivin' Man
J. Geils Band; *Full House* .... (ATL)
J. Geils Band .... (ATL)
Heart Of Saturday Night (Looking For...)
Shawn Colvin; *Cover Girl* .... (COL)
Tom Waits; *Anthology* .... (ASY)
Heart Of Saturday Night (Looking For...) .... (ASY)
Heaven In The Back Seat
Eddie Money; *Right Here* .... (COL)
High Tech Redneck
George Jones; *High Tech Redneck* .... (MCA)

Hitchhike
Marvin Gaye; *Anthology* .... (MOT)
Good Feeling Music/Big Chill Gen.-#3-CD ..... (MOT)
Greatest Hits .... (MOT)
Super Hits .... (MOT)
Rolling Stones; *Out Of Our Heads* .... (AKO)
Hitchin' A Ride
Vanity Fare; *Collectables Presents History Of
Rock-#1* .... (CLT)
Super Hits/'70s-Have A Nice Day-#2 .... (RHI)
Super Oldies/'60s-#11 .... (AUF)
Hot Rod
Ray Charles; *Live* .... (ATL)
Hot Rod Baby
Ronny/Daytonas; *45* .... (FSB)
Hot Rod Hearts
Robbie Dupree; *Robbie Dupree* .... (ELE)
Hot Rod Lincoln
Asleep At The Wheel; *Western Standard Time* .... (EPI)
Commander Cody/Lost Planet Airmen; *Lost In The
Ozone* .... (MCA)
Super Hits/'70s-Have A Nice Day-#8 .... (RHI)
We've Got A Live One Here .... (WB)
Johnny Bond; *Best Of* .... (STR)
I Can't Drive 55
Sammy Hagar; *VOA* .... (GEF)
I Drove All Night
Cyndi Lauper; *Night To Remember* .... (EPI)
I Get Around
Beach Boys; *Best Of* .... (CAP)
Billboard Top Rock 'N' Roll Hits-1964 .... (RHI)
Endless Summer .... (CAP)
Made In The U.S.A. .... (CAP)
ST/Good Morning Vietnam .... (A&M)
I'll Be Your Chauffeur
David J; *Songs From Another Season* ....(RCA)
I'll Change Your Flat Tire, Merle
Pure Prairie League; *Two Lane Highway* ....(RCA)
I'm In Love With My Car
Queen; *Live Killers* .... (HOL)
Night At The Opera .... (HOL)
Johnny Needs A Fast Car
Chris Rea; *espresso logic* .... (EW)
Joy Ride
Rick Derringer; *All-American Boy* .... (BS)
Joyride
Roxette; *Joyride* .... (EMI)
Junk Cars
Mac McAnally; *Live & Learn* .... (MCA)
Keep It Between The Lines
Ricky Van Shelton; *Backroads* .... (COL)
Kiss Me In The Car
John Berry; *John Berry* .... (LIB)
Last Chance Texaco
Rickie Lee Jones; *Rickie Lee Jones* .... (WB)
Let It Roll
Little Feat; *Let It Roll* .... (WB)
Let Me Be Your Car
Rod Stewart; *Best Of* .... (MER)
Rod Stewart & Elton John; *Storyteller/Complete
Anthology-1964-1990* .... (WB)
Let Me Drive
Greg Holland; *Greg Holland* .... (WB)
Let's Go Ridin' In The Car
Country Joe McDonald; *Goodbye Blues* .... (FAN)
Limousine Boogie (Hey Hey Mama)
Savoy Brown; *Make Me Sweat* .... (CRS)
Limousine Driver
James Taylor; *That's Why I'm Here* .... (COL)
Limousines
Robbie Nevil; *Robbie Nevil* .... (EMI)
Little Deuce Coupe
Beach Boys; *Best Of* .... (CAP)
Concert .... (CAP)
Endless Summer .... (CAP)
Little Deuce Coupe .... (CAP)
Summer Means Fun-Calif. Surf Music .... (CAP)
Little Old Lady From Pasadena
Beach Boys; *Concert* .... (CAP)
Jan & Dean; *Best Of* .... (EMI)
Billboard Top Rock 'N' Roll Hits-1964 .... (RHI)
Deadman's Curve .... (EMI)
Surf City-Best Of .... (EMI)

Little Red Corvette
Prince; *1999* .... (WB)
London Traffic
Jam; *This Is The Modern World* .... (POL)
Long Black Limousine
Bobby Bare; *This Is* .... (RCA)
Elvis Presley; *From Elvis In Memphis* .... (RCA)
   Memphis Record .... (RCA)
Long White Car
Hipsway; *Hipsway* .... (COL)
Lord, Mr. Ford
Jerry Reed; *Best Of A Great Year-#3* .... (RCA)
   In Concert .... (RCA)
L.A. Woman
Billy Idol; *Charmed Life* .... (CHR)
Doors; *Best Of* .... (ELE)
   Greatest Hits .... (ELE)
   L.A. Woman .... (ELE)
   ST/Doors .... (ELE)
   Weird Scenes Inside The Gold Mine .... (ELE)
Magic Jewelled Limousine
Nasa; *Insha-Allah!* .... (SIR)
   ST/Wild Orchid .... (SIR)
Making Love In A Subaru
Damaskas; *Dr. Demento's Dementia Royale* ...... (RHI)
Me & Bobby McGee
Grateful Dead; *Grateful Dead* .... (WB)
Janis Joplin; *Greatest Hits* ....(COL)
   Janis ....(COL)
   Pearl ....(COL)
   Rock Classics/'70s ....(COL)
Willie Nelson; *Sings Kristofferson* ....(COL)
Mercedes Benz
Janis Joplin; *Pearl* ....(COL)
   ST/Janis ....(COL)
Mercedes Boy
Pebbles; *Pebbles* .... (MCA)
Mercury Blues
Alan Jackson; *Lot About Livin' (& A Little 'Bout Love)* .... (ARI)
Steve Miller Band; *Fly Like An Eagle* ....(CAP)
   Live ....(CAP)
Moonlight Drive
Doors; *13* .... (ELE)
   Alive She Cried .... (ELE)
   Strange Days .... (ELE)
Moonlight Drive-In
Turner Nichols; *Moonlight Drive-In* .... (BNA)
Mustang Sally
Rascals; *Greatest Hits* .... (ATL)
Wilson Pickett; *Atlantic R&B-1947-1974-#6* .... (ATL)
   Best Of .... (ATL)
   Greatest Hits .... (ATL)
   Man & A Half-Best Of .... (RHI)
   Super Hits .... (ATL)
Young Rascals; *Young Rascals* .... (RHI)
My Baby Drives A Buick
Sawyer Brown; *Buick* ....(CCB)
My Kingdom For A Car
Gene Parsons; *Melodies* .... (SIE)
Jason/Scorchers; *Thunder & Fire* .... (A&M)
Phil Ochs; *Greatest Hits* .... (A&M)
"My Mother The Car" Theme
Original Music; *Television's Greatest Hits-#2* ..... (TVT)
My Old Yellow Car
Dan Seals; *Best Of* ....(CAP)
   Classics Collection-#1 ....(CAP)
   Early Dan Seals ....(CAP)
   San Antone ....(EMI)
Lacy J. Dalton; *Blue Eyed Blues* ....(COL)
   Dream Baby ....(COL)
No Money Down
Chuck Berry; *Chess Box* ....(CSS)
John Hammond; *Best Of* .... (VAN)
   Blues Explosion .... (ATL)
No Particular Place To Go
Chuck Berry; *Best Of The Best Of* .... (GUS)
   Chess Box ....(CSS)
Nothin' But The Wheel
Patty Loveless; *Only What I Feel* .... (EPI)
Objects In The Rear View Mirror...
Meat Loaf; *Bat Out Of Hell II-Back Into Hell* ... (MCA)
Old Blue Car
Peter Case; *Peter Case* .... (GEF)

Ol' '55
Eagles; *On The Border* .... (ASY)
Tom Waits; *Anthology* .... (ASY)
One I Loved Back Then (Corvette Song)
George Jones; *19 Hot Country Requests-#3* ...... (EPI)
   Greatest Country Hits/'80s-1986 ....(COL)
   Super Hits .... (EPI)
   Who's Gonna Fill Their Shoes .... (EPI)
One More Payment
Clint Black; *Put Yourself In My Shoes* ....(RCA)
Paradise By The Dashboard Light
Meatloaf; *Bat Out Of Hell* .... (EPI)
Party In The Parking Lot
Johnny Van Zant; *Brickyard Road* .... (ATL)
Pink Thunderbird
Jeff Beck; *Crazy Legs* .... (EPI)
Pontiac
Lyle Lovett; *Pontiac* .... (MCC)
Pontiac Blues
Sonny Boy Williamson; *King Biscuit Time* .... (ARH)
Pop, Let Me Have The Car
Carl Perkins; *Restless-Columbia Recordings* ....(COL)
   Whole Lotta Shakin' ....(SSP)
Porsche
Seth Marsh; *Whole Lotta Noise* .... (JRS)
Powder Blue Mercedes Queen
Paul Revere/Raiders; *Legend Of* ....(COL)
Power Windows
Billy Falcon; *Pretty Blue World* .... (JBC)
Racing In The Street
Bruce Springsteen; *Darkness At The Edge Of Town* ....(COL)
Bruce Springsteen/E Street Band; *Live-1975-1985* ....(COL)
Ramrod
Bruce Springsteen; *The River* ....(COL)
Rearviewmirror
Pearl Jam; *Vs.* .... (EPA)
Red Chevrolet
Jimmie Dale Gilmore; *Jimmie Dale Gilmore* ...... (HT)
   Points West-New Horizons In Country .... (HT)
Rhythm From A Red Car
Hardline; *Double Eclipse* .... (MCA)
Ride My New Car With Me
Big Joe Williams; *Dark Muddy Bottom Blues* .... (SPE)
Ride On Josephine
George Thorogood/Destroyers; *George Thorogood/Destroyers* .... (ROU)
Ride To A Funeral In A V-8
Dan Pickett; *1949 Country Blues* ....(CLT)
Riding In My Car
Woody Guthrie; *Greatest Songs Of* .... (VAN)
Riding My Thumb To Mexico
Johnny Rodriguez; *40 Years Of Country Music-#3-1970-1979* .... (MER)
   All I Ever Meant To Do .... (MER)
   Desperado .... (MER)
   Greatest Hits .... (MER)
Riding With A Movie Star
L7; *Hungry For Stink* ....(SLS)
Ridin' In My Car
NRBQ; *All Hopped Up* .... (ROU)
   At Yankee Stadium .... (MER)
   Peek-A-Boo-Best Of-1969-1989 .... (RHI)
Road Beneath My Wheels
Dan Fogelberg; *Live-Greetings From The West* .... (FM)
Rockin' In The Parkin' Lot
Razzy Bailey; *Country Classics-#6-1985-1986* .. (MCA)
Rollin' In My 5.0
Vanilla Ice; *Extremely Live* .... (SBK)
Rolls Royce
Virginia Liston; *Rare Blues Of The Twenties-1924-1929* .... (HIS)
Rumbleseat
John Cougar Mellencamp; *Scarecrow* ....(RIV)
Running On Empty
Jackson Browne; *Running On Empty* .... (ASY)
Shade Tree Mechanic
Joe Louis Walker; *The Gift* .... (HT)
Z.Z. Hill; *Greatest Hits* .... (MAL)
   I'm A Blues Man .... (MAL)
She Don't Have A License To Drive Me...
Porter Wagoner; *45* .... (WB)

She Has Funny Cars
Allman Brothers Band/Second Coming; *Dreams* . (POL)
Jefferson Airplane; *2400 Fulton Street-Anthology* (RCA)
Loves You ....(RCA)
Surrealistic Pillow ....(RCA)
She Loves My Automobile
ZZ Top; *Deguello* .... (WB)
She Loves My Car
Bobby Caldwell; *August Moon* ....(SD)
Ronnie Milsap; *One More Try For Love* ....(RCA)
Shut Down
Beach Boys; *Absolute Best-#1* ....(CAP)
Endless Summer ....(CAP)
Little Deuce Coupe/All Summer Long ....(CAP)
Monster Summer Hits-Drag City ....(CAP)
Surfin' U.S.A./Surfin' Safari ....(CAP)
Silver Thunderbird
Marc Cohn; *Marc Cohn* .... (ATL)
Sitting At The Wheel
Moody Blues; *The Present* ....(POL)
Voices In The Sky-Best Of ....(T/P)
Sleeping In My Car
Roxette; *Crash! Boom! Bang!* ....(EMI)
Spirit Of America
Beach Boys; *Gift Set* ....(CAP)
Little Deuce Coupe/All Summer Long ....(CAP)
Spirit Of America ....(CAP)
Start The Car
Jude Cole; *Start The Car* ....(RPR)
Stolen Car
Bruce Springsteen; *The River* ....(COL)
Stranded In A Limousine
Paul Simon; *Greatest Hits Etc.* ....(COL)
Strangers In A Car
Marc Cohn; *Marc Cohn* .... (ATL)
Street Machine
Super Stocks; *Monster Summer Hits-Drag City* ...(CAP)
Studebaker
Riders In The Sky; *Riders Go Commercial* ...... (MCA)
Sunday Driving
Jerry Lewis; *Capitol Collectors Series* ....(CAP)
Dr. Demento's Greatest-#2-1950s .... (RHI)
Sweet Hitchhiker
Creedence Clearwater Revival; *Chronicle* .... (FAN)
Live In Europe ....(FAN)
Mardi Gras ....(FAN)
More Creedence Gold ....(FAN)
Sweet Little '66
Steve Earle/Dukes; *Exit 0* .... (MCA)
Tennessee Plates
Charlie Sexton; *ST/Thelma & Louise* .... (MCA)
John Hiatt; *Slow Turning* ....(A&M)
Testarossa
Sir Mix-A-Lot; *Mack Daddy* ....(DEF)
Texas In My Rear View Mirror
Mac Davis; *Texas In My Rear View Mirror* ...... (CAS)
Very Best & More ....(CAS)
There Ain't Nothin' Wrong With The Radio
Aaron Tippin; *Read Between The Lines* ....(RCA)
Today's Hit Country ....(KT)
This Car Of Mine
Beach Boys; *Gift Set* ....(CAP)
Spirit Of America ....(CAP)
Surfer Girl/Shut Down-#2 ....(CAP)
Thousand Miles From Nowhere
Dwight Yoakam; *This Time* ....(RPR)
Three Window Coupe
Rip Chords; *Rock Artifacts-#4-From The Vaults* ..(COL)
Thunder Road
Bruce Springsteen; *Born To Run* ....(COL)
Bruce Springsteen/E Street Band;
Live-1975-1985 ....(COL)
Too Many Drivers
Lightnin' Hopkins; *Soul Blues* .... (PRS)
Paul Butterfield's Better Days; *It All Comes Back* (RHI)
Traffic Jam
Artie Shaw; *Begin The Beguine* .... (BLU)
Ella Fitzgerald & Chick Webb; *Ella Sings Chick
Swings* ....(OLR)
James Taylor; *JT* ....(COL)
Trans Am
Neil Young/Crazy Horse; *Sleeps With Angels* ..... (RPR)

Two-Car Garage
B.J. Thomas; *19 Hot Country Requests-#2* ....(EPI)
Great American Dream ....(CI)
Greatest Country Hits/'80s-1984 ....(EPI)
T-Bird To Vegas
Albert Lee; *Speechless* .... (MCA)
Under The Light Of The Texaco
Jeff Stevens/Bullets; *Jeff Stevens/Bullets* ...... (ATL)
Lisa Stewart; *Lisa Stewart* ....(BNA)
Used Cars
Bruce Springsteen; *Nebraska* ....(COL)
Wednesday Car
Johnny Cash; *Rambler* ....(COL)
White Car In Germany
Associates; *Popera-Singles Collection* .... (SIR)
Workin' At The Car Wash Blues
Jim Croce; *50th Anniversary Collection* ....(SAJ)
Greatest Character Songs ....(LIF)
I Got A Name ....(LIF)
Photographs & Memories-His Greatest Hits ...... (21)
You Already Drove Me There
Lisa Brokop; *Every Little Girl's Dream* .... (PAT)
You Can't Catch Me
Chuck Berry; *Chess Box* .... (CSS)
Rock Rock Rock ....(CSS)
George Thorogood; *Born To Be Bad* .... (EMI)
John Lennon; *Rock 'N' Roll* ....(CAP)
Rolling Stones; *Now!* ....(AKO)
Stephen Stills; *Live* .... (ATL)
You Dream Flat Tires
Joni Mitchell; *Wild Things Run Fast* ....(GEF)
You're Still Not Safe In A Japanese Car
Jumpin' John Goldsmith; *45* .... (ATL)

CARS: CADILLAC

See Also: CARS, ROAD, ROAD ACCIDENTS,
TRAVELING, TRUCKS

Always Drive A Cadillac
Everly Brothers; *Mercury Years* .... (MER)
Big Black Cadillac Blues
Lightnin' Hopkins; *Drinkin' In The Blues-Golden
Classics-#1* ....(CLT)
Lightnin' Hopkins ....(EVR)
Black Cadillac
Catfish Hodge Band; *Eyewitness Blues* .... (ADE)
Lightnin' Hopkins; *How Many More Years I Got* .(FAN)
Brand New Cadillac
Clash; *London Calling* ....(EPI)
On Broadway ....(EPI)
Bring That Cadillac Back
Harry Crafton; *Harry Crafton* ....(CLT)
Cadillac
Bo Diddley; *Is A Gunslinger* ....(CSS)
Firm; *Mean Business* ....(ATL)
Kinks; *Compleat Collection-20th Anniversary* ... (CMP)
You Really Got Me ....(RHI)
Steve Earle/Dukes; *Early Tracks* ....(EPI)
Cadillac Assembly Line
Albert King; *Masterworks* ....(ATL)
Truckload Of Lovin' ....(TOM)
Cadillac Blues
Gary Primich; *Gary Primich* .... (AMA)
T.N.T. Tribble; *Red Hot Boogie-#2* ....(CLT)
T.N.T. Tribble ....(CLT)
Cadillac Car
Original Cast; *Dreamgirls* ....(GEF)
Cadillac Of The Skies
American Boy Choir; *Spielberg/Williams
Collaboration* ....(COL)
Cadillac Ranch
Bruce Springsteen; *The River* ....(COL)
Bruce Springsteen/E Street Band;
Live-1975-1985 ....(COL)
Nitty Gritty Dirt Band; *More Great Dirt-Best
Of-#3* .... (WB)
Plain Dirt Fashion .... (WB)
Cadillac Red
Judds; *Collection-1983-1990* ....(RCA)
River Of Time ....(RCA)
This Country's Rockin' ....(RCA)

Cadillac Style
Sammy Kershaw; *Don't Go Near The Water* .... (MER)
Cadillac Walk
Mink De Ville; *Mink De Ville* ....(CAP)
Savoire Faire ....(CAP)
Cool Daddy In A Cadillac
Elvis Hitler; *Disgraceland* .... (RES)
Daddy Never Was The Cadillac Kind
Confederate Railroad; *Notorious* ....(ATL)
Eggs & Sausage (In A Cadillac...)
Tom Waits; *Nighthawks At The Diner* ....(ASY)
Eldorado To The Moon
Michael Nesmith; *Newer Stuff* .... (RHI)
Freeway Of Love
Aretha Franklin; *Who's Zoomin' Who?* ....(ARI)
Guitars, Cadillacs
Dwight Yoakam; *Guitars Cadillacs Etc. Etc.* .....(RPR)
Just Lookin' For A Hit ....(RPR)
Long White Cadillac
Blasters; *Collection* ....(SLS)
Dave Alvin; *Romeo's Escape* ....(EPI)
Dwight Yoakam; *Just Lookin' For A Hit* ....(RPR)
Look At That Cadillac
Stray Cats; *Best Of-Rock This Town* .... (EMI)
Maybelline
Chuck Berry; *Cruisin'-1955* ....(INC)
Golden Hits ....(MER)
Greatest Hits ....(EVR)
Oldies But Goodies-#11 ....(OSR)
Super Oldies!'50s-#5 ....(AUF)
Johnny Rivers; *Anthology-1964-1977* ....(RHI)
Very Best Of ....(EMI)
My Black Cadillac
Lightnin' Hopkins; *Complete Prestige/Bluesville
Recordings* .... (BV)
Night Of The Cadillacs
L.A. Guns; *Cuts* ....(POL)
Northside Cadillac
James Cotton; *Mighty Long Time* ....(ANT)
Pink Cadillac
Bruce Springsteen; *45* ....(COL)
Natalie Cole; *Everlasting* .... (ELE)
Gotta Have House-Best Of House Music-#2 ....(PRO)
Southern Pacific; *Greatest Hits* ....(WB)
Killbilly Hill ....(WB)
Rockin' Country ....(WB)
Rainbow's Cadillac
Bruce Hornsby; *Harbor Lights* ....(RCA)
Ray's Dad Cadillac
Joni Mitchell; *Night Ride Home* ....(GEF)
Red Cadillac
Colin Winski; *Rock Therapy* ....(TAK)
Reverend Jack & His Roamin' Cadillac...
Timbuk 3; *Eden Alley* .... (IRS)
Sandpaper Cadillac
Joe Cocker; *With A Little Help From My Friends* (A&M)
She's My Cadillac
Santa Fe; *Santa Fe* ....(CIA)
Slick Black Cadillac
Quiet Riot; *Heavy Metal Memories* .... (RHI)
Metal Health ....(EPA)
Solid Gold Cadillac
Mitch Woods/Rocket 88's; *Solid Gold Cadillac* ... (BLI)
Swing Low, Sweet Cadillac
Dizzy Gillespie; *Dizzy's Diamonds-Best Of The Verve
Years* ....(VRV)
Welfare Cadillac
Gary B.B. Coleman; *Too Much Weekend* ....(ICH)

CARTOON CHARACTERS

Assorted Tracks
Carl Stallings Project; *Music From Warner Bros.
Cartoons-1936-58* ....(WB)
Batdance
Prince; *ST/Batman* ....(WB)
Bugs Bunny: Rhapsody Rabbit
Philadelphia Orchestra/Eugene Ormandy; *TV
Classics* ....(RCA)
Captain Marvel
Arnold Bean; *Cosmic Bean* ....(SSS)
Chick Corea/Return To Forever; *Light As A
Feather* ....(POL)

Check Mr. Popeye
Eddie Bo; *Carnival Time-Best Of Ric Records-#1* (ROU)
Check Mr. Popeye ....(ROU)
Southside Johnny/Asbury Jukes; *This Time It's For
Real* ....(EPI)
"Courageous Cat" Theme
Original Music; *Television's Greatest Hits-#2* .....(TVT)
Dick Tracy
Ice-T; *ST/Dick Tracy* ....(SIR)
Do The Bartman
Bart Simpson; *Simpsons Sing The Blues* ....(GEF)
"Dudley-Do-Right" Theme
Original Music; *Television's Greatest Hits-#3* .....(TVT)
"Fractured Fairy Tales" Theme
Original Music; *Television's Greatest Hits-#3* .....(TVT)
"George Of The Jungle" Theme
Original Music; *Television's Greatest Hits-#2* .....(TVT)
Honky Tonk Superman
Aaron Tippin; *Call Of The Wild* ....(RCA)
House At Pooh Corner
Loggins & Messina; *Best Of-Friends* ....(COL)
On Stage ....(COL)
Sittin' In ....(COL)
Nitty Gritty Dirt Band; *Best Of* ....(EMI)
Dirt Silver & Gold ....(OOP)
"Huckleberry Hound" Theme
Original Music; *Television's Greatest Hits-#2* .....(TVT)
I Wanna Be A Flintstone
Screaming Blue Messiahs; *Bikini Red* .... (ELE)
It's Superman
Original Cast; *Superman* ....(SSP)
I'm Popeye The Sailor Man
Billy Costello; *Dr. Demento's Greatest-#1-'40s &
Before* .... (RHI)
Jimmy Olsen's Blues
Spin Doctors; *Pocket Full Of Kryptonite* ....(EPI)
"Looney Tunes" Theme
Original Music; *Television's Greatest Hits-#2* .....(TVT)
Meet The Flintstones
B.C. 52's; *ST/The Flintstones-Music From
Bedrock* ....(MCA)
Herb Ellis & Ray Brown; *Soft Shoe* ....(CCJ)
Herb Ellis/Others; *After You've Gone* ....(CCJ)
"Merrie Melodies" Theme
Original Music; *Television's Greatest Hits-#2* .....(TVT)
Mickey Mouse
Sparks; *Angst In My Pants* ....(ATL)
Mickey Mouse Alma Mater
Mouseketeers; *Disney Collection-#1* ....(DIS)
Mickey Mouse March
Aaron Neville & Dr. John; *Stay Awake-Music From
Disney Films* ....(A&M)
Mouseketeers; *Disney Collection-#1* ....(DIS)
"Mighty Mouse" Theme
Original Music; *Television's Greatest Hits-#2* .....(TVT)
"Mr. Magoo" Theme
Original Music; *Television's Greatest Hits-#3* .....(TVT)
"Road Runner" Theme
Original Music; *Television's Greatest Hits-#2* .....(TVT)
"Rocky & Bullwinkle" Theme
Original Music; *Television's Greatest Hits-#2* .....(TVT)
Salsa Smurf
Special Request; *Tommy Boy Greatest Beats* .... (TMB)
Saturday Morning Cartoons
Sergio Salvatore; *Sergio Salvatore* ....(GRP)
"Scooby Doo" Theme
Original Music; *Television's Greatest Hits-#3* .....(TVT)
"Spiderman" Theme
Original Music; *Television's Greatest Hits-#2* .....(TVT)
Sunshine Superman
Donovan; *Greatest Hits* ....(EPI)
History Of British Rock-#5 ....(RHI)
Sunshine Superman ....(EPI)
Troubadour-Definitive Collection ....(EPI)
Superman
101 Strings Orchestra; *Superman-Music From & Other
Space Themes* ....(ALS)
Barbra Streisand; *Greatest Hits-#2* ....(COL)
Streisand Superman ....(COL)
Robyn Hitchcock/Egyptians; *Queen Elvis* ....(A&M)
R.E.M.; *10th Anniversary-These People Are Nuts* .. (IRS)
Life's Rich Pageant ....(IRS)

Superman (I Wish I Could Fly Like)
Kinks; *Come Dancing With-Best Of-1977-1986* .. (ARI)
   Low Budget .... (ARI)
Superman's Ghost
Don McLean; *Greatest Hits Then & Now* .... (EMI)
Superman's Song
Crash Test Dummies; *Ghosts That Haunt Me* .... (ARI)
Superwoman
Karyn White; *Karyn White* .... (WB)
Stevie Wonder; *Music Of My Mind* .... (MOT)
   Original Musiquarium .... (MOT)
"The Archies" Theme
Original Music; *Television's Greatest Hits-#3* ..... (TVT)
"The Flintstones" Theme
Steve Hobbs; *Escape* ....(CEX)
"The Smurfs" Theme
Original Music; *Television's Greatest Hits-#3* ..... (TVT)
Theme From "Superman"
London Symphony Orchestra/John Williams;
   ST/Superman-The Movie .... (WB)
Neil Norman; *Greatest Science Fiction Hits* .... (CRS)
Theme From "The Jetsons"
Stunners; *ST/Jetsons-The Movie* .... (MCA)
Theme From "The Pink Panther"
Henry Mancini; *All-Time Greatest Hits-#1* ....(RCA)
   Legendary Performer ....(RCA)
   Pure Gold ....(RCA)
   ST/Revenge Of The Pink Panther .... (EMI)
   Television's Greatest Hits-#2 .... (TVT)
Theme From "Tom & Jerry"
Henry Mancini; *ST/Tom & Jerry-The Movie* ..... (MCA)
"Underdog Theme"
Original Music; *Television's Greatest Hits-#2* ..... (TVT)
When The Flintstones Meet The President
Dirty Dozen Brass Band; *Louisiana Scrapbook* ...(RYK)
Woody Woodpecker Song
Kay Kyser; *Best Of The Big Bands* ....(COL)
   Sentimental Favorites ....(COL)
Mel Blanc/Sportsmen; *Small Fry-Capitol Sings Kids*
   Songs ....(CAP)
You're A Good Man, Charlie Brown
Original Cast; *You're A Good Man, Charlie*
   Brown .... (POL)

CATS

See Also: ANIMALS: A-Z

Alaska Cats
Garrison Keillor & Frederica von Stade; *Songs Of The*
   Cat ....(RCA)
Alley Cat
Bent Fabric; *45* .... (ATL)
Big Tiny Little; *Piano Memories* .... (CRS)
Alley Katz
Daryl Hall & John Oates; *Along The Red Ledge* ..(RCA)
Big Electric Cat
Adrian Belew; *Desire Of The Rhino King* .... (ISL)
Black Cat
Chris Daniels/Kings; *In Your Face* ....(FF)
Janet Jackson; *Rhythm Nation-1814* .... (A&M)
Black Cat Blues
John Lee Hooker; *...Alone* .... (SPE)
Memphis Minnie; *Hoodoo Lady-1933-1937* .....(COL)
Black Cat Bone
Albert Collins & Johnny Copeland; *Alligator Records*
   20th Anniversary Coll. ....(ALG)
Johnny Winter; *Progressive Blues Experiment* .... (OW)
Lightnin' Hopkins; *Dark Muddy Bottom Blues* ... (SPE)
   Mojo Hand-Anthologoy ....(RHI)
Lonesome Sundown; *Been Gone Too Long* .... (HT)
Roy Rogers; *Blues On The Range* .... (BLI)
Black Cat Moan
Beck, Bogert & Appice; *Beckology* .... (EPI)
   Beck, Bogert & Appice .... (EPI)
Black Cat Shuffle
Al DiMeola; *Electric Rendezvous* ....(COL)
Cat Fever
Little Feat; *Sailin' Shoes* .... (WB)
Cat Melody
Pete Townshend & Ronnie Lane; *Rough Mix* ... (MCA)

Cat People (Putting Out Fire)
David Bowie; *Let's Dance* .... (EMI)
   ST/Cat People ....(MCA)
   The Singles-1969-1993 ....(RYK)
Cat Scratch Fever
Ted Nugent; *Cat Scratch Fever* .... (EPI)
   Double Live Gonzo .... (EPI)
Cats In The Cradle
Ugly Kid Joe; *America's Least Wanted* .... (STD)
Cats Under The Stars
Jerry Garcia; *Cats Under The Stars* .... (ARI)
Catwalk
Art Of Noise; *Below The Waste* .... (CHI)
Saga; *Heads Or Tales* ....(POR)
Cat's In The Cradle
Harry Chapin; *Anthology* .... (ELE)
   Greatest Stories-Live .... (ELE)
   Verities & Balderdash .... (ELE)
Cat's In The Cupboard
Pete Townshend; *Empty Glass* .... (ATC)
Cat's Squirrel
Cream; *Fresh Cream* .... (RSO)
Jethro Tull; *This Was* .... (CHR)
China Cat Sunflower
Grateful Dead; *Aoxomoxoa* .... (WB)
   Europe '72 .... (WB)
   Without A Net .... (ARI)
Cleopatra's Cat
Spin Doctors; *Turn It Upside Down* .... (EPI)
Cool Cat
Queen; *Hot Space* ....(HOL)
Cool For Cats
Squeeze; *Classics-#25* .... (A&M)
   Cool For Cats ....(A&M)
   Single-45s & Under .... (A&M)
"Courageous Cat" Theme
Original Music; *Television's Greatest Hits-#2* .... (TVT)
Curiosity Killed The Cat
Curiosity Killed The Cat; *Keep Your Distance* .. (MER)
Dead Cat
Shelleyan Orphan; *Humroot* ....(COL)
Dead Cat Alley
Dirty White Boy; *Bad Reputation* .... (POL)
Dead Cat On The Line
Lucky Peterson; *Lucky Strikes!* ....(ALG)
Eyes Like A Cat
Little Charlie/Nightcats; *All The Way Crazy* .....(ALG)
   Captured Live ....(ALG)
Hell Cat
Scorpions; *Best Of* ....(RCA)
   Virgin Killer ....(RCA)
Honky Cat
Elton John; *Greatest Hits* .... (POL)
   Here & There .... (POL)
   Honky Chateau .... (POL)
House-Cat
Danielle Dax; *Dark Adapted Eye* .... (SIR)
Intoxicated Rat
New Lost City Ramblers; *American Moonshine &*
   Prohibition Songs .... (FLW)
Killed A Cat
Kenny Rankin; *Silver Morning* .... (LD)
Kitten On The Keys
Claude Bolling; *Original Ragtime* ....(COL)
Dick Hyman; *Flip Side Of Red Seal* ....(RCA)
   Kitten On The Keys ....(RCA)
Liberace; *16 Most Requested Songs* ....(COL)
Kitty Cat Song
Lee Dorsey; *45* .... (FSB)
Life #9
Martina McBride; *The Way That I Am* ....(RCA)
Litterbox
Meat Puppets; *Meat Puppets* ....(SST)
Mr. Mistofelees
Original Broadway Cast; *Cats* .... (GEF)
Original London Cast; *Cats* .... (GEF)
My Cat Fell In The Well (Well Well Well)
Manhattan Transfer; *Bop Doo-Wopp* .... (ATL)
My Night To Howl
Lorrie Morgan; *War Paint* .... (BNA)
Old Deuteronomy
Original Broadway Cast; *Cats* .... (GEF)
Original London Cast; *Cats* .... (GEF)

Old Gumbie Cat
Original Broadway Cast; *Cats* ....(GEF)
Pattin' That Cat
Teddy Bunn; *Rare Blues Of The
Twenties-1927-1930* ....(HIS)
Pink Pussycat
Devo; *Duty Now For The Future* ....(WB)
Rest Of-Greatest Misses ....(WB)
Pink-Eyed Pussycat
Bill Haley/Comets; *Rock Around The Country* ...(CRS)
Rockin' & Rollin' ....(ACC)
Pussy Cat Blues
Big Bill Broonzy; *Do That Guitar Rag* ....(YAZ)
Pussy Cat Song (Nyow!)
Gordon MacRae & Jo Stafford; *Capitol Sings Kids Songs
For Grown-ups* ....(CAP)
Pussycat Meow
Deee-Lite; *Infinity Within* ....(ELE)
Pussycat Moan
Katie Webster; *Alligator Records 20th Anniversary
Coll.* ....(ALG)
Put Your Cat Clothes On
Carl Perkins; *Legends Of Rock Guitar-'50s* ....(RHI)
Original Sun Greatest Hits ....(RHI)
Rambo The Cat
Dave Valentin; *Two Amigos* ....(GRP)
Savannah Russet/Jete The Dancing Cat
Jeanne Newhall; *Novice* ....(MAR)
Stray Cat Blues
Rolling Stones; *Beggar's Banquet* ....(AKO)
Get Yer Ya-Ya's Out ....(AKO)
Soundgarden; *Badmotorfinger/Somms
(Satanoscillatemy)* ....(A&M)
Stray Cat Strut
Stray Cats; *Best Of-Rock This Town* ....(EMI)
Built For Speed ....(EMI)
Rock The First-#4 ....(SAN)
Sweetest Kittens (Have The Sharpest...)
Meatmen; *Rock 'N' Roll Juggernaut* ....(CRL)
Thanks To The Cat House...
Johnny Paycheck; *Armed & Crazy* ....(EPI)
That Cat Is High
Manhattan Transfer; *Anthology-Down In Birdland* (RHI)
Manhattan Transfer ....(RHI)
Theme From "Tom & Jerry"
Henry Mancini; *ST/Tom & Jerry-The Movie* .....(MCA)
There Are No Cats In America
Nehemiah Persoff/J. Guarnieri/W. Hays; *ST/An
American Tail* ....(MCA)
This Black Cat Has 9 Lives
Louis Armstrong; *What A Wonderful World* ......(BLU)
Tom Cat Blues
Jelly Roll Morton; *Greatest Ragtime Of The
Century* ....(BIO)
Two Old Cats Like Us
Hank Williams, Jr. & Ray Charles; *Greatest
Hits-#2* ....(W/C)
Ray Charles & Hank Williams, Jr.; *Friendship* ...(COL)
Seven Spanish Angels & Other Hits ....(COL)
Walking My Cat Named Dog
Norma Tanega; *45* ....(ERI)
What's New Pussycat
Tom Jones; *London Collector-Greatest Hits* ......(LON)
Wholly Cats
Charlie Christian; *Genius Of The Electric Guitar* .(COL)
Wild Cat
UB40; *Present Arms* ....(VIA)
Year Of The Cat
Al Stewart; *Best Of* ....(ARI)
Year Of The Cat ....(ARI)
'70s Greatest Rock Hits-#5-Kickin' Back ....(PRY)
Yellow Cat
John Denver; *Rhymes & Reasons* ....(RCA)

CHAOS, Danger, Disasters, Impending Doom

*See Also: CRIME, LAW & ORDER, NUCLEAR
ENERGY, ROAD ACCIDENTS, SHIPS, WAR*

1999
Prince; *1999* ....(WB)
Abandon City
Utopia; *Oops Wrong Planet* ....(RHI)

Accidents Will Happen
Elvis Costello; *Girls Girls Girls* ....(COL)
Elvis Costello/Attractions; *Armed Forces* ....(COL)
Best Of ....(COL)
Frank Sinatra; *Rarities-Columbia Years* ....(COL)
Air Crash Museum
Dead Milkmen; *Eat Your Paisley* ....(RES)
Anarchy Divine
Fates Warning; *Best Of Metal Blade-#3* ....(MET)
No Exit ....(MET)
Anarchy In The U.K.
Megadeth; *So Far So Good So What* ....(CAP)
Sex Pistols; *Never Mind The Bollocks* ....(WB)
Anarchy-X
Queensryche; *Operation: Mindcrime* ....(EMI)
Armageddon
Aldo Nova; *Subject...Aldo Nova* ....(POR)
Planet P Project; *Planet P Project* ....(GEF)
Rush; *Hemispheres* ....(MER)
Armageddon It
Def Leppard; *Hysteria* ....(MER)
Armageddon Man
Black Flag; *Family Man* ....(SST)
Armagideon Time
Clash; *Black Market Clash* ....(EPI)
Story Of-#1 ....(EPI)
Ball Of Confusion
Temptations; *All The Million-Sellers* ....(MOT)
Anthology ....(MOT)
Compact Command Performances ....(MOT)
Greatest Hits-#2 ....(MOT)
Top 10 With A Bullet-Motown Male Groups ...(MOT)
Breakdown Dead Ahead
Boz Scaggs; *Hits* ....(COL)
Middle Man ....(COL)
California Mudslide
Lightnin' Hopkins; *Los Angeles Blues* ....(RHI)
Casey Jones
Grateful Dead; *Best Of-Skeletons From The Closet* (WB)
Bill Graham Presents Last Fillmore Days ....(EPA)
Workingman's Dead ....(WB)
Jerry Garcia Acoustic Band; *Almost Acoustic* ...(GRD)
City
Fleetwood Mac; *Mystery To Me* ....(RPR)
Crumblin' Down
John Cougar Mellencamp; *Uh-Huh* ....(RIV)
Cul De Sac
Genesis; *Duke* ....(ATL)
Van Morrison; *Veedon Fleece* ....(WB)
Dance Electric
Andre Cymone; *A.C.* ....(COL)
Pointer Sisters; *Break Out* ....(PNT)
Danger
AC/DC; *Fly On The Wall* ....(ATL)
Gorky Park; *Gorky Park* ....(MER)
Kiss; *Creatures Of The Night* ....(CAS)
Motley Crue; *Shout At The Devil* ....(ELE)
Pylon; *Hits* ....(DB)
Selecter; *Too Much Pressure* ....(CHR)
Danger Ahead
Electric Light Orchestra; *Secret Messages* ....(JET)
Tanya Tucker; *Can't Run From Yourself* ....(LIB)
Danger At My Door
Mark Chesnutt; *Too Cold At Home* ....(MCA)
Danger Heartbreak Dead Ahead
Bonnie Raitt; *Bonnie Raitt* ....(WB)
Marvelettes; *Anthology* ....(MOT)
Greatest Hits ....(MOT)
ST/Good Morning Vietnam ....(A&M)
Danger List
John Mellencamp; *American Fool* ....(RIV)
Danger Man
David Bromberg; *Wanted Dead Or Alive* ....(COL)
Danger Stranger
Drivin' N' Cryin'; *Scarred But Smareter* ....(ISL)
Danger Waters (Hold Me Tight)
Joan Baez; *In Concert* ....(VAN)
Lovesong Album ....(VAN)
Danger Zone
Crystal Gayle; *Miss The Mississippi* ....(LIB)
Kenny Loggins; *ST/Top Gun* ....(COL)
Klymaxx; *Klymaxx* ....(CON)
L.A. Posse; *They Come In All Colors* ....(ATL)

Planet Patrol; *Planet Patrol* .... (TMB)
 Tommy Boy Greatest Beats .... (TMB)
Ramones; *Too Tough To Die* .... (SIR)
Shirley Murdock; *Shirley Murdock* .... (ELE)
Dangerous
Doobie Brothers; *Brotherhood* .... (CAP)
Heaven 17; *Teddy Bear Duke & Psycho* .... (CRL)
L.L. Cool J; *Radio* .... (DFC)
Michael Jackson; *Dangerous* .... (EPI)
Monalisa Young; *ST/Allnighter* .... (CML)
Natalie Cole; *Dangerous* .... (MOD)
Roxette; *Look Sharp!* .... (EMI)
 Rock The First-#6 .... (SAN)
Who; *It's Hard* .... (MCA)
Dangerous Age
Bad Company; *Dangerous Age* .... (ATL)
Gerry Rafferty; *Right Down The Line-Best Of* .... (EMI)
Dangerous Drug
Electric Angels; *Electric Angels* .... (ATL)
Dangerous Fun
Jesse Winchester; *Best Of* .... (RHI)
 Third Down 110 To Go .... (RHI)
Dangerous Jade
Original London Cast; *Evita* .... (MCA)
Dangerous Man
Dwight Yoakam; *If There Was A Way* .... (RPR)
Dangerous Times
Cher; *Cher* .... (GEF)
Dangerous Type
Cars; *Candy-O* .... (ELE)
Dangerous Woman
Mississippi Jook Band; *Good Time Blues* .... (COL)
Dangerously Lonely
Johnny Lee; *Best Of* .... (CCB)
Danger! She's A Stranger
Five Stairsteps; *Greatest Hits* .... (CLT)
Darkness On The Edge Of Town
Bruce Springsteen; *Darkness On The Edge Of
Town* .... (COL)
Bruce Springsteen/E Street Band;
Live-1975-1985 .... (COL)
Deportee (Plane Wreck At Los Gatos)
Arlo Guthrie & Pete Seeger; *Together In Concert* (RPR)
Byrds; *Byrds (collection)* .... (COL)
Cisco Houston; *Greatest Songs Of Woody Guthrie* (VAN)
Gene Clark & Carla Olson; *So Rebellious A Lover* (RHI)
W. Jennings/W. Nelson/J. Cash/K. Krist.;
Highwayman .... (COL)
Disco Apocalypse
Jackson Browne; *Hold Out* .... (ASY)
Distant Early Warning
Rush; *Grace Under Pressure* .... (MER)
 Hear 'N Aid .... (MER)
 Show Of Hands .... (MER)
Eve Of Destruction
Barry McGuire; *Billboard Top Rock 'N' Roll
Hits-1965* .... (RHI)
 Cruisin'-1965 .... (INC)
 Good Feeling Music/Big Chill-#3 .... (MOT)
 Vintage Music-#9 & 10 .... (MCA)
Dickies; *Great Dictations (Definitive Collection)* . (A&M)
 Incredible Shrinking .... (A&M)
Turtles; *Turtle Wax-Best Of-#2* .... (RHI)
 Turtlesized .... (RHI)
Explosion In The Fairmount Mines
Blind Alfred Reed; *How Can A Poor Man Stand Such
Times...* .... (ROU)
Full Speed Ahead
John Mayall; *Best Of* .... (POL)
Going Up Against Chaos
Bruce Cockburn; *Trouble With Normal* .... (GC)
Hard Rain's Gonna Fall
Bob Dylan; *Concert For Bangla Desh* .... (CAP)
 Freewheelin' .... (COL)
 Greatest Hits-#2 .... (COL)
Bryan Ferry; *Street Life-20 Great Hits* .... (RPR)
 These Foolish Things .... (RPR)
Edie Brickell/New Bohemians; *ST/Born On The Fourth
Of July* .... (MCA)
Joan Baez; *Farewell Angelina* .... (VAN)
 First 10 Years .... (VAN)
Helter Skelter
Aerosmith; *Pandora's Box* .... (COL)

Beatles; *Box Set* .... (CAP)
 Rarities .... (CAP)
 Rock 'n' Roll Music-#2 .... (CAP)
 White Album .... (CAP)
Husker Du; *12"* .... (WB)
Motley Crue; *Shout At The Devil* .... (ELE)
Pat Benatar; *Precious Time* .... (CHR)
Siouxsie/Banshees; *Nocturne* .... (GEF)
 The Scream .... (GEF)
U2; *ST/Rattle & Hum* .... (ISL)
Here Comes The Flood
Peter Gabriel; *Peter Gabriel* .... (ATC)
 Revisited .... (ATL)
 Shaking The Tree-16 Golden Greats .... (GEF)
In The Year 2525
Zager & Evans; *Nipper's Greatest Hits-'60s-#2* ...(RCA)
It's Alright
Loggins & Messina; *Native Sons* .... (COL)
I'm Not Gonna Let It Bother Me Tonight
Atlanta Rhythm Section; *Are You Ready?* .... (POL)
 Champagne Jam .... (POL)
Keep Smiling At Trouble
Al Jolson; *Story-Rainbow 'Round My Shoulder* .. (MCA)
Tony Bennett; *Forty Years-Artistry Of* ....(COL)
Little Chicago Fire
Count Basie Orchestra; *Live At El Morocco* ...... (TLR)
Living In Danger
Ace Of Base; *The Sign* .... (ARI)
London Bridge Is Falling Down
Count Basie; *Good Morning Blues* .... (MCA)
Newtrament; *Word 2* .... (JVA)
Louisiana Flood
Paul Butterfield/Better Days; *It All Comes Back* .. (RHI)
Love Is Dangerous
Fleetwood Mac; *25 Years-The Chain* .... (WB)
Mind Disaster
Initial Shock; *Nuggets-#8* .... (RHI)
More Trouble Every Day
Frank Zappa/Mothers Of Invention; *Roxy &
Elsewhere* .... (OOP)
Nature's Way
Spirit; *12 Dreams Of Dr. Sardonicus* .... (EPI)
 Best Of .... (EPI)
 Time Circle .... (EPI)
New Orleans Is Sinking
Tragically Hip; *Up To Here* .... (MCA)
New York Mining Disaster 1941
Bee Gees; *Gold-#1* .... (POL)
 Here At Last .... (RSO)
 History Of British Rock-#8 .... (RHI)
New York Minute
Don Henley; *End Of The Innocence* .... (GEF)
Panic In Detroit
David Bowie; *Aladdin Sane* ....(RYK)
 Scary Monsters ....(RYK)
 Sound + Vision ....(RYK)
Panic In The World
Be Bop Deluxe; *Best Of & The Rest Of* ....(OOP)
 Best Of-Raiding The Divine Archive .... (CAP)
 Drastic Plastic ....(OOP)
Preservation
Kinks; *Preservation-A Play In Two Acts* .... (RHI)
Queen Of The Hours
Electric Light Orchestra; *No Answer* ....(JET)
Quicksand Jesus
Skid Row; *Slave To The Grind* .... (ATL)
Rampage
EPMD; *Business As Usual* .... (DFJ)
Red Alert
Quiet Riot; *Condition Critical* .... (PSH)
Red Garland; *Red Alert* ....(GAL)
Saxon; *Destiny* .... (ENI)
Runaway Train
Dawn Sears; *S* .... (DEC)
Elton John featuring Eric Clapton; *The One* ..... (POL)
John Stewart; *Punch The Big Guy* .... (CYP)
Rosanne Cash; *Greatest Country Hits/'80s-1988* .(COL)
 King's Record Shop .... (COL)
Soul Asylum; *Grace Dancers Union* .... (COL)
Runaway Trains
Tom Petty/Heartbreakers; *Let Me Up (I've Had
Enough)* .... (MCA)

Science Gone Too Far
Dictators; *Live-F... 'Em If They Can't Take A Joke* (ROI)
   Manifest Destiny .... (ASY)
Ship Titanic
Pink Anderson; *Gospel Blues & Street Songs* ..... (RVR)
Sinkin' In The Sea
Barefoot Jerry; *You Can't Get Off With Your Shoes
   On* .... (MON)
State Trooper
Bruce Springsteen; *Nebraska* .... (COL)
Surfin' Tragedy
Bob Vaught/Renegaids; *Original Surfin' Hits* ..... (CRS)
Breakers; *World's Worst Records* .... (RHI)
Talking Airplane Disaster
Phil Ochs; *Original New Folks* .... (VAN)
Third Rock From The Sun
Joe Diffie; *Thousand Winding...* .... (EPI)
This Wheel's On Fire
Band; *Anthology* .... (CAP)
   Music From Big Pink .... (CAP)
   Rock Of Ages-#1 & 2 .... (CAP)
Bob Dylan/Band; *Basement Tapes* .... (COL)
Byrds; *Byrds (collection)* .... (COL)
Ian & Sylvia; *Greatest Hits* .... (VAN)
Siouxsie/Banshees; *Through The Looking Glass* .. (GEF)
   Twice Upon A Time-The Singles .... (GEF)
Three Mile Island
Pinkard & Bowden; *Writers In Disguise* .... (WB)
Three Mile Smile
Aerosmith; *Night In The Ruts* .... (COL)
   Pandora's Box .... (COL)
Thunder Rolls, The
Garth Brooks; *No Fences* .... (LIB)
Tidal Wave
Sugarcubes; *Here Today Tomorrow Next Week!* .. (ELE)
Time Is Running Out
Steve Winwood; *Steve Winwood* .... (ISL)
Titanic, The
John Townley/Press Gang; *Chesapeake Sailor's
   Companion* .... (ADE)
Tragedy
Bee Gees; *Greatest* .... (POL)
   Mega Hits Dance Classics-#8 .... (PRY)
   Spirits Having Flown .... (POL)
Train Wreck On Prom Night
Pajama Slave Dancers; *Blood Sweat & Beers* ..... (RES)
Trainwreck Of Emotion
Lorrie Morgan; *Leave The Light On* .... (BNA)
Trouble's Comin' Like A Train
Mark Collie; *Mark Collie* .... (MCA)
Utter Chaos
Gerry Mulligan & Paul Desmond; *Gerry Mulligan &
   Paul Desmond* .... (FAN)
Volcano
Band; *Cahoots* .... (CAP)
Count Basie; *Essential-#2* .... (COL)
Jimmy Buffett; *Boats Beaches Bars & Ballads* ... (MGR)
   Songs You Know By Heart-Greatest Hits .... (MCA)
   Volcano .... (MCA)
Rupture; *Hardness Of The World* .... (COT)
   Slave .... (COT)
Waiting For The End Of The World
Elvis Costello; *My Aim Is True* .... (COL)
Walkaway Joe
Trisha Yearwood; *Hearts In Armor* .... (MCA)
West Virginia Mine Disaster
Betsy Rutherford; *Betsy Rutherford* .... (BIO)
Cindy Mangsen; *Long Time Traveling* .... (HOG)
When The Shit Hits The Fan
Circle Jerks; *Gig* .... (REL)
   ST/Repo Man .... (MCA)
White Riot
Clash; *Clash* .... (EPI)
   On Broadway .... (EPI)
   Story Of-#1 .... (EPI)
World Is Upside Down
Joe Higgs; *This Is Reggae Music-#1* .... (ISL)
Wreck Of The Edmund Fitzgerald
Gordon Lightfoot; *Gord's Gold-#2* .... (WB)
   Summertime Dream .... (RPR)

Wreck Of The Old '97
Johnny Cash; *At Folsom Prison & San Quentin* ...(COL)
   Man-The World-His Music .... (SUN)
   Original Golden Hits-#3 .... (SUN)
   Story Songs Of The Trains & Rivers .... (SUN)
   Superbilly .... (SUN)

CHILDREN

   *See Also: BABY, REBELS, TEENAGERS, TOYS
   & GAMES*

All God's Chillun Got Rhythm
Judy Garland; *Collector's Items-1936-1945* ..... (MCA)
All The Children Sing
Todd Rundgren; *Anthology (1968-1985)* .... (RHI)
   Hermit Of Mink Hollow .... (RHI)
Angel Child
Lightnin' Hopkins; *Greatest Hits* .... (PRS)
   How Many More Years I Got .... (FAN)
Anne Frank Story
Human Sexual Response; *Fig. 15* .... (EAT)
Another Brick In The Wall, Part 2
Pink Floyd; *Collection Of Great Dance Songs* ....(COL)
   Delicate Sound Of Thunder ....(COL)
   The Wall ....(COL)
Roger Waters; *The Wall Live In Berlin* .... (MER)
As Tears Go By
Marianne Faithfull; *Greatest Hits* .... (AKO)
   Strange Weather .... (ISL)
Rolling Stones; *Big Hits-High Tide & Green Grass* (AKO)
   December's Children .... (AKO)
   Hot Rocks 1964-1971 .... (AKO)
   Singles Collection-London Years .... (AKO)
Beautiful Child
Blow Monkeys; *She Was Only The Grocer's
   Daughter* ....(RCA)
Fleetwood Mac; *25 Years-The Chain* .... (WB)
   Tusk .... (WB)
Belfast Child
Simple Minds; *Street Fighting Years* .... (A&M)
Billy The Kid (I Miss...)
Billy Dean; *Billy Dean* .... (LIB)
Boogie Child
Bee Gees; *Boogie Child* .... (RSO)
   Child Of The World .... (RSO)
   Here At Last .... (RSO)
Boogie Chillun
John Lee Hooker; *Best Of* .... (CRS)
   Best Of .... (VJ)
   Boogie Chillun .... (FAN)
   Hooked On The Blues .... (EVR)
Child Apart
Ian & Sylvia; *Greatest Hits* .... (VAN)
Child In These Hills
Jackson Browne; *Jackson Browne* .... (ASY)
Child In Time
Deep Purple; *Deepest Purple-Very Best Of* .... (WB)
   In Rock .... (WB)
   Made In Japan .... (WB)
Child Is Born
Barbra Streisand; *Lazy Afternoon* ....(COL)
Kenny Burrell; *Fire Into Music-#2* .... (CBA)
   God Bless The Child .... (CBA)
   Heritage .... (VOS)
Toots Thielemans; *East Coast West Coast* .... (PRV)
Child Is Coming
Paul Kantner/Jefferson Starship; *Blows Against The
   Empire* ....(RCA)
Child Of Babylon
Whitesnake; *Come An' Get It* .... (GEF)
Child Of Innocence
Kansas; *Masque* .... (KIR)
Child Of Light
Deep Purple; *Deepest Purple* .... (WB)
   In Rock .... (WB)
   Made In Japan .... (WB)
Child Of Mine
Fleetwood Mac; *Bare Trees* .... (RPR)
Child Of Our Times
Barry McGuire; *45* .... (MCA)

Child Of Poverty
Paul Martin; *Country Gold* .... (PLN)
   Great Country Gold .... (PLN)
Child Of The Fifties
Statler Brothers; *Legend Goes On* .... (MER)
Child Of The Moon
Rolling Stones; *More Hot Rocks-Big Hits & Fazed*
Cookies .... (AKO)
Child Of The Wild Blue Yonder
John Hiatt; *Stolen Moments* .... (A&M)
Child Of Vision
Supertramp; *Breakfast In America* .... (A&M)
Child Support
Barbara Mandrell; *Sure Feels Good* .... (EMI)
Buck Owens; *Buck 'Em* .... (WB)
Childhood Hero
Bobby Bare; *Bare* .... (COL)
Children
America; *America* .... (WB)
Burning Spear; *Man In The Hills* .... (ISL)
EMF; *Schubert Dip* .... (CAP)
Jeannie C. Riley; *Jeannie* .... (PLN)
Joe South; *Best Of* .... (RHI)
Rex Allen, Jr.; *Country Cowboy* .... (ACC)
   Today's Generation .... (SSS)
Starship; *No Protection* .... (GRU)
Children And All That Jazz
Joan Baez; *Best Of* .... (A&M)
   Classics-#8 .... (A&M)
   Diamonds & Rust .... (A&M)
Children And Art
Original Cast; *Sunday In The Park With George* ..(RCA)
Children Children
Wings; *London Town* .... (CAP)
Children Go Where I Send Thee
Peter, Paul & Mary/N.Y. Choral Society; *Holiday*
Celebration .... (WB)
Weavers; *At Carnegie Hall* .... (VAN)
White Mountain Singers; *Best* .... (FOL)
Children In The Carousel
Mabel Mercer & Bobby Short; *At Town Hall* .... (ATL)
Children Of Darkness
Joan Baez; *Contemporary Ballad Book* .... (VAN)
Children Of Poland
Si Kahn; *Unfinished Portraits* .... (FF)
Children Of Production
Parliament; *Clones Of Dr. Funkenstein* .... (CAS)
   Live .... (CAS)
Children Of Sanchez
Chuck Mangione; *Best Of* .... (A&M)
   Children Of Sanchez .... (A&M)
   Classics-#6 .... (A&M)
   Evening Of Magic .... (A&M)
Children Of The Damned
Iron Maiden; *Live After Death (World Slavery*
Tour) .... (CAP)
   Number Of The Beast .... (CAP)
Children Of The Earth
Tower Of Power; *Bump City* .... (WB)
Children Of The Future
Steve Miller Band; *Children Of The Future* .... (CAP)
Children Of The Ghetto
Courtney Pine; *Journey To The Urge Within* .... (AND)
Philip Bailey; *Chinese Wall* .... (COL)
Children Of The Land
Styx; *45* ....(RCA)
Children Of The Night
Richard Marx; *Repeat Offender* .... (EMI)
Children Of The Revolution
Violent Femmes; *Blind Leading The Naked* ....(SLS)
Children Of The World
Amy Grant; *House Of Love* .... (A&M)
Bee Gees; *Children Of The World* .... (RSO)
   Greatest .... (RSO)
Third World; *Sense Of Purpose* .... (COL)
Wailers Band; *I.D.* .... (ATL)
Children Of The World Unite
Angela Bofill; *Angie* .... (GRP)
Children & All That Jazz
Joan Baez; *Best Of* .... (A&M)
   Classics-#8 .... (A&M)
   Diamonds & Rust .... (A&M)

Child's Claim To Fame
Buffalo Springfield; *Again* ....(ATC)
   Buffalo Springfield ....(ATC)
Child's Song
Tom Rush; *Best Of* ....(COL)
   Tom Rush ....(COL)
Daybreak (Storybook Children)
Cheryl Lynn; *Cheryl Lynn* ....(COL)
Dear Prudence
Beatles; *White Album* .... (CAP)
Siouxsie/Banshees; *Hyaena* .... (GEF)
   Nocturne .... (GEF)
Devil Comes Back To Georgia
Marc O'Connor; *Heroes* .... (WB)
Down The Road
Mac McAnally; *Knots* .... (MCA)
End Of The Innocence
Don Henley; *End Of The Innocence* .... (GEF)
Endless Cycle
Lou Reed; *New York* .... (SIR)
Eyes Of A Child
Moody Blues; *This Is The* .... (POL)
   To Our Children's Children's Children .... (POL)
Naked Eyes; *Best Of* .... (EMI)
Friday The 13th Child
David Clayton-Thomas; *Clayton* .... (MCA)
Gabriel's Mother's Hiway Ballad 16 Blues
Arlo Guthrie; *Best Of* .... (WB)
Ghetto Child
Spinners; *Best Of* .... (ATL)
God Bless The Child
Billie Holiday; *From The Original Decca Masters* (MCA)
   Greatest Hits ....(COL)
   Songbook ....(VRV)
   Story .... (MCA)
   Story-#2 ....(COL)
Blood, Sweat & Tears; *Blood, Sweat & Tears* ....(COL)
   Greatest Hits ....(COL)
Diana Ross; *ST/Lady Sings The Blues* .... (MOT)
Liza Minnelli; *4-Sider* ....(CYP)
   ST/Liza With A "Z" ....(COL)
Lou Rawls; *Best From* .... (CAP)
God Bless The Children
Loretta Lynn; *Out Of My Head & Back In My*
Bed .... (MCA)
Motley Crue; *Shout At The Devil* .... (ELE)
God's Children
Kinks; *Kink Kronikles* .... (RPR)
Goonies 'R' Good Enough
Cyndi Lauper; *ST/Goonies* .... (EPI)
Got A Letter From My Kid Today
Merle Haggard/Strangers; *Working Man Can't Get*
Nowhere Today .... (CAP)
Greatest Discovery
Elton John; *Elton John* .... (POL)
   Live In Australia w/Melbourne Symphony ...... (MCA)
Greatest Love Of All
George Benson; *Collection* .... (WB)
   ST/The Greatest .... (ARI)
   Weekend In L.A. .... (WB)
Whitney Houston; *Whitney Houston* .... (ARI)
Heaven Help Us All
Stevie Wonder; *Greatest Hits-#2* .... (MOT)
   Love Songs-20 Classic Hits .... (MOT)
   My Cherie Amour/Signed Sealed Delivered ..... (MOT)
   Signed Sealed & Delivered .... (MOT)
Hell Is For Children
Pat Benatar; *Best Shots* .... (CHR)
   Crimes Of Passion .... (CHR)
   Live From Earth .... (CHR)
   MTV's Rock & Roll To Go .... (ELE)
   ST/American Pop .... (MCA)
Hello Muddah, Hello Fadduh
Allan Sherman; *Dr. Demento Greatest Novelty CD* (RHI)
   Dr. Demento's Greatest-#3 .... (RHI)
Highway Child
Bob Seger System; *Mongrel* .... (CAP)
Honey Child
Bad Company; *Run With The Pack* .... (SS)
Honey Chile
Martha Reeves/Vandellas; *Anthology* .... (MOT)
   Compact Command Performances .... (MOT)
   Superstar Series-#11 .... (MOT)

Hot Child In The City
Nick Gilder; *Billboard Top Hits-1978* .... (RHI)
   City Nights .... (CHR)
House At Pooh Corner
Loggins & Messina; *Best Of-Friends* ....(COL)
   On Stage ....(COL)
   Sittin' In ....(COL)
Nitty Gritty Dirt Band; *Best Of* ....(EMI)
   Dirt Silver & Gold ....(OOP)
How Can I Help You Say Goodbye
Patty Loveless; *Only What I Feel* ....(EPI)
I Am A Child
Buffalo Springfield; *Buffalo Springfield* ....(ATC)
   Classic Rock 1966-1988 ....(ATL)
   Last Time Around ....(ATC)
   Retrospective ....(ATC)
   ST/Made In Heaven ....(ELE)
Neil Young; *Crazy Horse/Live Rust* ....(RPR)
   Decade ....(RPR)
I Don't Call Him Daddy
Doug Supernaw; *Red & Rio Grande* ....(BNA)
I Thought I Was A Child
Bonnie Raitt; *Takin' My Time* ....(WB)
Jackson Browne; *For Everyman* ....(ASY)
I Want A Little Girl
Joe Turner; *Atlantic Jazz-Singers* ....(ATL)
Ray Charles; *Life In Music* ....(ATL)
I Wish I Could Have Been There
John Anderson; *Solid Ground* ....(BNA)
I Won't Grow Up
Original Cast/Mary Martin; *Peter Pan* ....(RCA)
I'm Just A Kid
Daryl Hall & John Oates; *Abandoned*
   Luncheonette ....(ATL)
   Livetime ....(RCA)
Jesus Children Of America
Stevie Wonder; *Innervisions* ....(MOT)
Just Like A Woman
Bob Dylan; *At Budokan* ....(COL)
   Before The Flood ....(COL)
   Biograph ....(COL)
   Blonde On Blonde ....(COL)
   Greatest Hits ....(COL)
Byrds; *Byrds (collection)* ....(COL)
Kids Of The Baby Boom
Bellamy Brothers; *Country Rap* .... (MCA)
   Greatest Hits-#3 .... (MCA)
   MCA #1 Hits/'80s-#3 .... (MCA)
Last Child
Aerosmith; *Classics Live-#2* ....(COL)
   Greatest Hits ....(COL)
   Live Bootleg ....(COL)
   Rocks ....(COL)
Let The Children Play
Santana; *Festival* ....(COL)
   Moonflower ....(COL)
Little Child
Beatles; *Meet The* ....(CAP)
Little Children
Billy J. Kramer; *History Of British Rock-#1* ...... (RHI)
Little John Of God
Los Lobos; *The Neighborhood* ....(SLS)
Lonely Child
Styx; *Equinox* .... (A&M)
Lonely Children
Foreigner; *Double Vision* ....(ATL)
Lord Protect My Child
Bob Dylan; *Bootleg Series-#1-3-1961-1989* .....(COL)
Love Child
Diana Ross/Supremes; *Anthology* .... (MOT)
   Billboard Top Rock 'N' Roll Hits-1968 .... (RHI)
   Every Great #1 Hit .... (MOT)
   Greatest Hits-#3 .... (MOT)
   Motown Story-1st 25 Years .... (MOT)
   Motown's Biggest Pop Hits .... (MOT)
Sweet Sensation; *Love Child* ....(ATC)
Love Without End, Amen
George Strait; *Livin' It Up* .... (MCA)
   Ten Strait Hits .... (MCA)
Luka
Suzanne Vega; *Solitude Standing* .... (A&M)
March Of The Siamese Children
Original Broadway Cast; *King & I* ....(RCA)
Original Cast; *King & I* .... (MCA)

Memphis
Chuck Berry; *Chess Box* .... (CSS)
   Chuck Berry ....(AUF)
   Golden Hits .... (MER)
   Greatest Hits ....(EVR)
   St. Louis To Liverpool .... (CSS)
   ST/Hail! Hail! Rock 'N' Roll .... (MCA)
   Toronto Rock 'N' Roll Revival-#2 .... (ACC)
Joe Jackson; *ST/Mike's Murder* .... (A&M)
John Cale; *IRS Greatest Hits #2 & 3* .... (IRS)
Johnny Rivers; *Anthology-1964-1977* .... (RHI)
   Best Of ....(EMI)
Lonnie Mack; *Teen Beat-Instrumental*
   Rock-1957-1965 ....(CAP)
Mindless Child Of Motherhood
Kinks; *Kink Kronikles* ....(RPR)
Monday's Child
Cambridge Singers; *Fancies* ....(CLG)
Moonchild
Iron Maiden; *Seventh Son Of A Seventh Son* .....(CAP)
King Crimson; *In The Court Of The Crimson
   King* ....(ATL)
Shakespear's Sister; *Hormonally Yours* ....(LON)
Morning Side
Neil Diamond; *Hot August Night* .... (MCA)
   Moods .... (MCA)
Mother And Child Reunion
Paul Simon; *Live Rhymin'* ....(WB)
   Negotiations & Love Songs 1971-1986 ....(WB)
   Paul Simon ....(WB)
Motherless Child
Eric Clapton; *From The Cradle* .... (DUC)
Steve Miller Band; *Anthology* ....(CAP)
   Your Saving Grace ....(CAP)
Motherless Children
Eric Clapton; *461 Ocean Blvd.* .... (RSO)
   Crossroads ....(POL)
Nature's Child
Triumph; *Progressions Of Power* .... (MCA)
Nobody's Child
Beatles/Tony Sheridan; *In The Beginning* ....(OOP)
Electric Light Orchestra; *Eldorado* ....(JET)
Hank Williams, Jr.; *Best Of-#1-Roots & Branches* (MER)
Maria McKee; *Maria McKee* ....(GEF)
Traveling Wilburys; *Nobody's Child-Romanian Angel
   Appeal* ....(WB)
North Carolina Tune/Child Of My Heart
Liz Carroll; *Friend Indeed* ....(SHA)
October's Child
Elvin Jones; *Brother John* ....(PAJ)
Old Dogs, Children & Watermelon Wine
Tom T. Hall; *Essential Twentieth Anniversary
   Collect.* .... (MER)
   Greatest Hits-#2 .... (MER)
One Child China
Ecoteur; *Decorated Life* ....(DAL)
Only 12 Years Old
Tony Adolescent/Flower Leperds; *Dirges In The
   Dark* .... (XXX)
Only A Lad
Oingo Boingo; *10th Anniversary-These People Are
   Nuts* .... (IRS)
   Alive .... (MCA)
   Best O' .... (MCA)
   Only A Lad .... (A&M)
   Skeletons In The Closet-Best Of .... (A&M)
Only Child
Jackson Browne; *The Pretender* ....(ASY)
Ooh Child
Dino; *The Way I Am* ....(EW)
O-o-h Child
Five Stairsteps; *Greatest Hits* ....(CLT)
   Radio Active Hits-#2 ....(ACC)
   Soul Hits/'70s-#2 ....(RHI)
Spinners; *Best Of* .... (MOT)
Valerie Carter; *Just A Stone's Throw Away* ......(COL)
   ST/Over The Edge ....(WB)
Problem Child
3rd Bass; *Derelicts Of Dialect* ....(DFJ)
AC/DC; *Dirty Deeds Done Dirt Cheap* ....(ATL)
   If You Want Blood You've Got It ....(ATL)
   Let There Be Rock ....(ATC)
Damned; *Light At The End Of The Tunnel* ...... (MCA)
Graham Parker/Rumour; *Stick To Me* .... (MER)

Hanoi Rocks; *Self-Destruction Blues* .... (GEF)
Mitch Malloy; *Mitch Malloy* .... (RCA)
Royal Tramps; *Dangerous & Extremely Unhealthy* . (RL)
Puerto Rican Children
  Hilton Ruiz; *Something Grand* .... (NOV)
Puff (The Magic Dragon)
  Peter, Paul & Mary; *In Concert* .... (WB)
  Moving .... (WB)
  Peter Paul & Mommy .... (WB)
  Ten Years Together-Best Of .... (WB)
Remember The Children
  Earth, Wind & Fire; *Last Days & Time* .... (COL)
Rock 'N' Roll Children
  Dio; *Intermission* .... (WB)
  Sacred Heart .... (WB)
Roller Skating Child
  Beach Boys; *Love You* .... (CAR)
  Ten Years In Harmony .... (CAR)
Roots Of My Raising
  Merle Haggard; *Capitol Collectors Series* .... (CAP)
Runaway Child Running Wild
  Temptations; *All The Million-Sellers* .... (MOT)
  Anthology .... (MOT)
  Cloud Nine .... (MOT)
  Compact Command Performances .... (MOT)
  Greatest Hits-#2 .... (MOT)
Saturday's Child
  Monkees; *Listen To The Band* .... (RHI)
  More Greatest Hits Of .... (ARI)
Saturday's Kids
  Jam; *Setting Sons* .... (POL)
Save The Children
  Diana Ross; *Anthology* .... (MOT)
  Touch Me In The Morning .... (MOT)
  Gil Scott-Heron; *Gil ScoSave The Children-Heron* (BLU)
  Revolution Will Not Be Televised .... (FLD)
  Marvin Gaye; *Anthology* .... (MOT)
  Live At The London Palladium .... (MOT)
  Musical Testament 1964-1984 .... (MOT)
  What's Going On .... (MOT)
Save The Life Of My Child
  Simon & Garfunkel; *Bookends* .... (COL)
  Collected Works .... (COL)
See Emily Play
  David Bowie; *Pinups* .... (RYK)
  Pink Floyd; *Relics* .... (CAP)
  Works .... (CAP)
Seein' My Father In Me
  Paul Overstreet; *Sowin' Love* .... (RCA)
"Sesame Street" Theme
  Original Music; *Television's Greatest Hits-#3* ..... (TVT)
Sing Child
  Heart; *Dreamboat Annie* .... (CAP)
Six O'Clock News
  John Prine; *John Prine* .... (ATL)
Small Fry
  Georgie Fame/Annie Ross/Hoagy Carmichael; *In Hoagland* .... (DRG)
  June Christy; *Small Fry-Capitol Sings Kids Songs For Grownups* .... (CAP)
Society's Child
  Janis Ian; *45* .... (POL)
  Lou Gramm; *Past Times Behind Rock & Roll* ..... (INT)
Sometimes I Feel Like A Motherless Child
  Dave Van Ronk; *Folksinger* .... (PRS)
  Inside .... (FAN)
  Grant Green; *Feelin' The Spirit* .... (BLN)
  Iron City .... (MUS)
  Jerry Butler; *Gold* .... (VJ)
  Mormon Tabernacle Choir; *Songs Of The Civil War & Stephen Foster* .... (SMC)
  Odetta; *Essential* .... (VAN)
  O.V. Wright; *O.V. Wright* .... (MCA)
  Peter, Paul & Mary; *The Song Will Rise* .... (WB)
  Van Morrison; *Poetic Champions Compose* ...... (MER)
Space Child
  Spirit; *12 Dreams Of Dr. Sardonicus* .... (EPI)
  UFO; *Phenomenon* .... (CHR)
Starchild
  Teena Marie; *Starchild* .... (EPI)
Storybook Children
  Bette Midler; *Broken Blossom* .... (ATL)
  Nancy Sinatra & Lee Hazlewood; *Fairy Tales & Fantasies-Best Of* .... (RHI)

Sugar Mountain
  Neil Young; *Decade* .... (RPR)
  Neil Young/Crazy Horse; *Live Rust* .... (RPR)
Suicide Child
  Nuns; *Best Of Rodney On The ROQ* .... (PBO)
  Posh Hits-#1 .... (PBO)
Sweet Child O' Mine
  Guns N' Roses; *Appetite For Destruction* .... (GEF)
Teach The Gifted Children
  Lou Reed; *Between Thought & Expression-Anthology* .... (RCA)
Teach Your Children
  Crosby, Stills & Nash; *Crosby, Stills & Nash (collection)* .... (ATL)
  Crosby, Stills, Nash & Young; *Deja Vu* .... (ATL)
  Four-Way Street .... (ATL)
  So Far .... (ATL)
  ST/Wonder Years-Music From Show & Era ..... (ATL)
  Suzy Bogguss/Alison Krauss/Kathy Mattea; w/*Crosby Stills & Nash-Red Hot + Country* .... (MER)
Texas Girl At The Funeral Of Her Father
  Randy Newman; *Little Criminals* .... (WB)
Thank God For Kids
  Oak Ridge Boys; *Christmas* .... (MSP)
  Christmas For The '90s-#1 .... (LIB)
  Collection .... (MCA)
  Greatest Hits-#2 .... (MCA)
Thank Heaven For Little Girls
  Maurice Chevalier; *ST/Gigi* .... (SSP)
  Merle Haggard & Janie Fricke; *It's All In The Game* .... (EPI)
That's My Boy
  Stan Freberg; *Capitol Collectors Series* .... (CAP)
"The Brady Bunch" Theme
  Brady Bunch Kids; *It's A Sunshine Day-Best Of* . (MCA)
  Television's Greatest Hits-#2 .... (TVT)
Things Will Grow
  Sweethearts Of The Rodeo; *Rodeo Waltz* .... (SH)
Third World Child
  Johnny Clegg & Savuka; *Sounds Of Soweto* ..... (CAP)
  Third World Child .... (CAP)
This Child Needs Its Father
  Gladys Knight/Pips; *Neither One Of Us* .... (MOT)
This One's For The Children
  New Kids On The Block; *Hangin' Tough* .... (COL)
Thursday's Child
  Abbey Lincoln; *Abbey Is Blue* .... (RVR)
  A. Davis/J. Newton/A. Wadud; *Trio 2* .... (GRM)
  Barbara Lea; *Barbara Lea* .... (PRS)
  Bev Kelly; *Love Locked Out* .... (RVR)
  Chameleons UK; *Script Of The Bridge* .... (MCA)
  Tanita Tikaram; *Sweet Keeper* .... (RPR)
Toys Are Made For Little Children
  Uniques; *Golden Hits* .... (PLN)
Trouble Child
  Joni Mitchell; *Court & Spark* .... (ASY)
Tuesday's Child
  Trouble; *Run To The Light* .... (MET)
Twelve Year Old Boy
  Elmore James; *Collectables Blues Collection-#1* .. (CLT)
  Golden Classics .... (CLT)
  Sky Is Crying-History Of .... (RHI)
Two Of A Kind, Workin' On A Full House
  Garth Brooks; *No Fences* .... (LIB)
Two-Bit Man Child
  Neil Diamond; *Glory Road-1968-1972* .... (MCA)
  Velvet Gloves & Spit .... (MSP)
Vision Of A Child
  Steve Young; *Honky Tonk Man* .... (ROU)
Voodoo Child
  Voodoo Child; *Best Of Techno-#1* .... (PRO)
Voodoo Chile
  Jimi Hendrix; *Concerts* .... (RPR)
  Essential-#1 & 2 .... (RPR)
  Kiss The Sky .... (RPR)
  Lifelines/Story .... (RPR)
  Jimi Hendrix Experience; *Electric Ladyland* ...... (RPR)
  Stevie Ray Vaughan/Double Trouble; *Couldn't Stand The Weather* .... (EPI)
  Live Alive .... (EPI)
War Child
  Jethro Tull; *Repeat* .... (CHR)
  War Child .... (CHR)

We Are The World
USA For Africa; *We Are The World* ....(COL)
When I Grow Up (To Be A Man)
Beach Boys; *Absolute Best-#1* ....(CAP)
  Dance Dance Dance ....(CAP)
  Gift Set ....(CAP)
  Made In The U.S.A. ....(CAP)
  Spirit Of America ....(CAP)
When The Children Are Asleep
Original Broadway Cast; *Carousel* ....(ANG)
Original CAst; *Carousel* .... (MCA)
When The Children Cry
White Lion; *Best Of* ....(ATL)
  Pride ....(ATL)
When The Kids Get Married
Original Broadway Cast; *I Do! I Do!* ....(RCA)
Where Do The Children Play
Cat Stevens; *Classics-#24* .... (A&M)
  Footsteps In The Dark-#2 ....(A&M)
  Tea For The Tillerman ....(A&M)
Wild Child
Doors; *13* ....(ELE)
  Classics ....(ELE)
  Soft Parade ....(ELE)
Heart; *Brigade* ....(CAP)
  Rock The House "Live" ....(CAP)
Lou Reed; *Walk On The Wild Side-Best Of* ....(RCA)
Untouchables; *Wild Child* ....(MCA)
W.A.S.P.; *Head Banging Metal* ....(PRY)
  Last Command ....(CAP)
  Live...In The Raw ....(CAP)
Wild Children
Van Morrison; *Hard Nose The Highway* ....(WB)
  It's Too Late To Stop Now ....(WB)
Wild Kids
David Benoit; *Urban Daydreams* ....(GRP)

CHRISTMAS, New Year's
See Also: GOD

25th Day Of Last December
Roberta Flack; *Blue Lights In The Basement* ...... (ATL)
25th Of December
Bonnie Koloc; *You're Going To Love Yourself...* . (OVA)
Adeste Fideles (O Come All Ye Faithful)
Anne Murray; *Christmas* ....(LIB)
Bing Crosby/Andrews Sisters; *Merry Christmas* ..(MSP)
Boys Choir Of Vienna Woods; *Christmas Voices &*
Bells ....(SPM)
Don Williams; *Home For The Holidays* ....(RCA)
Donna Summer; *Christmas Spirit* ....(MER)
Ella Fitzgerald; *Christmas* ....(CAP)
Elvis Presley; *Memories Of Christmas* ....(RCA)
  Sings The Wonderful World Of Christmas ......(RCA)
Jackie Wilson; *Merry Christmas From* ....(RHI)
Joel Nava; *Tejano Country Christmas* ....(ART)
Nat King Cole; *Christmas Song* ....(CAP)
Philadelphia Orchestra/Eugene Ormandy; *Joy To The*
World ....(RCA)
  Yuletide Cheer ....(COL)
Ricky Skaggs; *Voices Of The Season* .... (EPI)
Take 6; *He Is Christmas* ....(RPR)
Vienna Boys Choir; *Christmas Festival* ....(RCA)
Wynton Marsalis/Marcus Roberts; *Acoustic*
Christmas ....(COL)
Album For The Special Olympics
Very Special Christmas; *Various Tracks* .... (A&M)
Alfie, The Christmas Tree
John Denver/Muppets; *Christmas Together* ....(RCA)
All I Want For Christmas
David Seville/Chipmunks; *Christmas With The*
Chipmunks-#2 ....(EMI)
Nat King Cole; *Let It Snow!-Cuddly Christmas*
Classics ....(CAP)
New Edition; *Christmas All Over The World* .... (MCA)
Ray Charles; *Spirit Of Christmas* ....(COL)
Spike Jones; *Christmas* ....(RHI)
  Dr. Demento's Greatest-#6 ....(RHI)
All I Want For Christmas Dear Is You
Buck Owens; *Christmas With* ....(CCB)
Travis Tritt; *Christmas-Loving Time Of The Year* ..(WB)
All I Want For Christmas Is You
Carla Thomas; *Soul Christmas* ....(ATL)

Doug Stone; *First Christmas* ....(EPI)
Foghat; *Christmas Party With Eddie G.* ....(COL)
Alone On New Year's Eve
Manhattans; *For You & Yours-Golden*
Carnival-#2 ....(CLT)
Amigos Del Mundo (Happy Christmas)
La Diferenzia; *Tejano Country Christmas* ...(ART)
And The Glory Of The Lord
Dianne Reeves; *Handel's Messiah-Soulful*
Celebration ....(WB)
Angel Like You
Doug Stone; *First Christmas* ....(EPI)
Angel Song (Glory To God In The Highest)
Lynn Anderson & Butch Baker; *Christmas On The*
General Jackson ....(MER)
Angels Cried
Alan Jackson; *Honky Tonk Christmas* .... (ARI)
Angels We Have Heard On High
Amy Grant; *Christmas Album* ....(WOR)
Andy Williams; *Christmas Present* ....(COL)
Charlie Byrd; *Christmas Album* ....(CCJ)
Commodores; *Christmas* ....(CMO)
Joan Sutherland; *Christmas Stars* ....(LON)
  Joy Of Christmas ....(LON)
Roches; *We Three Kings* ....(MSP)
Roger Williams; *Christmas Time* ....(MCA)
  Golden Christmas ....(SPM)
Tennessee Ernie Ford; *Heart Of Christmas* ....(CAP)
Another Christmas Song
Jethro Tull; *Rock Island* ....(CHR)
At The Christmas Ball
Bessie Smith; *Complete Recordings-#2* ....(COL)
  Nobody's Blues But Mine ....(COL)
Ave Maria
Carpenters; *Christmas Portrait* ....(A&M)
James Galway/Royal Philharmonic; *James Galway's*
Christmas Carol ....(RCA)
Luciano Pavarotti; *O Holy Night* ....(LON)
Mario Lanza; *Christmas With* ....(RCA)
Perry Como; *I Wish It Could Be Christmas*
Forever ....(RCA)
Renata Tebaldi; *Christmas Stars* ....(LON)
Stevie Wonder; *Motown Christmas* ....(MOT)
  Someday At Christmas ....(MOT)
Away In A Manger
Andy Williams; *Christmas Album* ....(COL)
Anne Murray; *Christmas Wishes* ....(LIB)
Ed Ames; *This Is Christmas* ....(RCA)
Emmylou Harris; *Light Of The Stable* ....(WB)
Joan Baez; *Noel* ....(VAN)
Judds; *Christmas Time With* ....(RCA)
Julie Andrews & Andre Previn; *Christmas*
Treasure ....(RCA)
Lacy J. Dalton; *Christmas For The '90s-#2* .....(LIB)
Loretta Lynn; *Country Christmas* ....(MCA)
Nat King Cole; *Christmas Song* ....(CAP)
Philadelphia Orchestra/Eugene Ormandy; *Joy To The*
World ....(RCA)
Reba McEntire; *Merry Christmas To You* ....(MSP)
  Tennessee Christmas ....(MCA)
Trisha Yearwood; *The Sweetest Gift* ....(MCA)
Back Door Santa
Bon Jovi; *Very Special Christmas* ....(A&M)
Clarence Carter; *Christmas Classics* .... (RHI)
  Snatching It Back-Best Of ....(RHI)
  Soul Christmas ....(ATL)
Blanca Navidad (White Christmas)
Freddy Fender; *Tejano Country Christmas* ....(ART)
Blue Christmas
Anne Wilson & Nancy Wilson; *Very Special*
Christmas-#2 ....(A&M)
Beach Boys; *Christmas Album* ....(CAP)
Booker T./M.G.s; *In The Christmas Spirit* ....(ATL)
Earl Thomas Conley; *Best Of Christmas* ....(RCA)
Eddy Raven; *Warner Bros. Christmas Tradition* ...(WB)
Elvis Presley; *Blue Christmas* ....(RCA)
  Christmas Album ....(RCA)
  Memories Of Christmas ....(RCA)
Ernest Tubb; *Billboard's Greatest Christmas Hits* . (RHI)
Freddy Fender; *Christmas Time In The Valley* ....(MSP)
Highway 101; *Warner Bros. Christmas*
Tradition-#2 ....(WB)
Jim Reeves; *12 Songs Of Christmas* ....(RCA)

Sawyer Brown; *Christmas Country Classics-#1* ...(CCB)
Christmas For The '90s-#1 ....(LIB)
Brahm's Bethlehem Lullaby
Nat King Cole; *Cole Christmas & Kids* ....(CAP)
Roger Whittaker; *Christmas Album* ....(RCA)
Statler Brothers; *A Christmas Present* ....(MER)
Breath Of Heaven
Donna Summer; *Christmas Spirit* ....(MER)
Bring Christmas Home
Lee Greenwood; *Christmas To Christmas* ....(MSP)
California Christmas
Hillary Kanter; *Country Christmas-#4* ....(RCA)
Candle In The Window
Alabama; *Christmas* ....(RCA)
Carol Of The Bells
Barry Manilow; *Because It's Christmas* ....(ARI)
Carpenters; *Christmas Portrait* ....(A&M)
David Benoit; *GRP Christmas Collection* ....(GRP)
David Rose; *Best Of Christmas* ....(CAP)
Forester Sisters; *Christmas Card* ....(WB)
Four Seasons; *Christmas Album* ....(RHI)
Johnny Mathis; *Christmas With* ....(COL)
Kenny Rogers; *Christmas* ....(EMI)
O'Jays; *Home For Christmas* ....(EMI)
Ronnie Milsap; *Christmas With* ....(RCA)
Soundtrack; *Home Alone* ....(COL)
Child Of Winter
Beach Boys; *45* ....(RPR)
Children Go Where I Send Thee
Peter, Paul & Mary/N.Y. Choral Society; *Holiday
Celebration* ....(WB)
Weavers; *At Carnegie Hall* ....(VAN)
White Mountain Singers; *Best* ....(FOL)
Children's Christmas Song
Diana Ross/Supremes; *Merry Christmas* ....(MOT)
Motown Christmas ....(MOT)
Chipmunk Song
Chipmunks; *Christmas With-#1* ....(EMI)
David Seville/Chipmunks; *Billboard's Greatest Christmas
Hits* ....(RHI)
Dr. Demento Greatest Christmas CD ....(RHI)
Christ Child's Lullabye
Kathy Mattea; *Good News* ....(MER)
Christ Is Born
Carpenters; *Christmas Portrait* ....(A&M)
From The Top ....(A&M)
Perry Como; *Christmas Album* ....(RCA)
Christ Time Is Here
Vince Guaraldi; *Charlie Brown Christmas* ....(FAN)
Christmas
Chuck Berry; *Back Home* ....(CSS)
Clarence "Gatemouth" Brown; *Alligator Records
Christmas Collection* ....(ALG)
Elmo & Patsy; *Grandma Got Run Over By A
Reindeer* ....(EPI)
Jim Reeves; *12 Songs Of Christmas* ....(RCA)
Who; *Tommy* ....(MCA)
Christmas Ain't Christmas, New Year's...
O'Jays; *Have A Merry Chess Christmas* ....(MSP)
Christmas As I Knew It
Johnny Cash; *Christmas Spirit* ....(COL)
Christmas At Our House
Barbara Mandrell; *Christmas At Our House* ......(MSP)
Christmas In The Country ....(MSP)
Christmas Blues
Canned Heat; *Blue Yule-Christmas Blues & R&B
Classics* ....(RHI)
Dean Martin; *Winter Romance* ....(CAP)
Willie Nelson; *Pretty Paper* ....(COL)
Christmas Card From A Hooker...
Tom Waits; *Blue Valentine* ....(ASY)
Christmas Carol
Oak Ridge Boys; *Christmas* ....(MSP)
Skip Ewing; *Following Yonder Star* ....(MSP)
Tom Lehrer; *Dr. Demento Greatest Christmas CD* (RHI)
Dr. Demento's Greatest-#6 ....(RHI)
Evening Wasted With ....(RPR)
Christmas Celebration
B.B. King; *Rhythm & Blues Christmas* ....(UA)
Christmas Collection
Alligator Records; *Various Tracks* ....(ALG)
Christmas Country Style
Statler Brothers; *Christmas Present* ....(MER)

Christmas Cowboy Style
Michael Martin Murphey; *Cowboy Christmas* .....(WB)
Christmas Day
Beach Boys; *Christmas Album* ....(CAP)
Detroit Junior; *Blue Yule-Christmas Blues & R&B
Classics* ....(RHI)
Squeeze; *Just In Time For Christmas* ....(IRS)
Christmas Eve
Billy Eckstine; *Have Yourself A Jazzy Little
Christmas* ....(VRV)
Maureen McGovern; *Christmas With* ....(COL)
Christmas Eve In My Home Town
Bobby Vinton; *Country Christmas* ....(EPI)
Kate Smith; *Christmas Album* ....(RCA)
Christmas Everyday
Kenny Rogers; *Christmas* ....(EMI)
Miracles; *Christmas With* ....(MOT)
Smokey Robinson/Miracles; *Christmas Hits* ......(MSP)
Temptations; *Christmas Card/Give Love At
Christmas-CD* ....(MOT)
Christmas In Dixie
Alabama; *Best Of Christmas* ....(RCA)
Christmas ....(RCA)
Country Christmas-#3 ....(RCA)
Christmas In My Heart
Jets; *Christmas With* ....(MSP)
Christmas In My Soul
Laura Nyro; *Christmas & The Beads Of Sweat* ...(COL)
Christmas In Prison
John Prine; *Sweet Revenge* ....(ATL)
Christmas In The Caribbean
Jimmy Buffett; *Boats Beaches Bars & Ballads* ... (MGR)
Tennessee Christmas ....(MSP)
Christmas Is A Birthday
Burl Ives; *Have A Holly Jolly Christmas* ....(MSP)
Christmas Is For Children
Glen Campbell; *Best Of Christmas* ....(CAP)
Merry Christmas ....(LIB)
Christmas Is Here
Donna Summer; *Christmas Spirit* ....(MER)
Christmas Is Paintin' The Town
Oak Ridge Boys; *Christmas* ....(MSP)
Tennessee Christmas ....(MSP)
Christmas Is The Time To Say I Love You
Billy Squier; *45* ....(CAP)
Christmas Island
Andrews Sisters/Guy Lombardo; *Billboard Greatest
Christmas Hits* ....(RHI)
Jackie Gleason; *All I Want For Christmas* ....(CAP)
Leon Redbone; *Christmas Island* ....(PRV)
Christmas Letter
Keith Whitley; *Country Christmas-#4* ....(RCA)
Season's Greetings ....(RCA)
Reba McEntire; *Merry Christmas To You* ....(MSP)
Christmas Memories
Alabama; *Christmas* ....(RCA)
Steve Wariner; *Christmas Memories* ....(MSP)
Christmas Must Be Tonight
Band; *Islands* ....(CAP)
To Kingdom Come-Definitive Collection ....(CAP)
Robbie Robertson; *ST/Scrooged* ....(A&M)
Christmas Prayer
Marty Robbins; *Christmas With* ....(COL)
Christmas Shopping
Buck Owens/Buckaroos; *Merry Hee Haw
Christmas* ....(CAP)
Christmas Song
Jethro Tull; *Living In The Past* ....(CHR)
Christmas Song (Chestnuts Roasting...)
Amy Grant; *Christmas Album* ....(WOR)
Anne Murray; *Christmas* ....(LIB)
Barbra Streisand; *Christmas Album* ....(COL)
Bing Crosby; *Sings Christmas Songs* ....(MSP)
Brenda Lee; *Tennessee Christmas* ....(MSP)
Buddy Emmons; *Christmas Sounds Of The Steel
Guitar* ....(SO)
Carpenters; *Christmas Portrait* ....(A&M)
Charlie Daniels; *Christmas Time Down South* .....(EPI)
Crystal Gayle; *Crystal Christmas* ....(WB)
Donna Summer; *Christmas Spirit* ....(MER)
Drifters; *Soul Christmas* ....(ATL)
Frank Sinatra; *Jolly Christmas From* ....(CAP)
Glen Campbell; *Merry Christmas* ....(LIB)
Herb Alpert/Tijuana Brass; *Christmas Album* ...(A&M)

James Brown; *Santa's Got A Brand New Bag* .... (RHI)
John Denver; *Rocky Mountain Christmas* ....(RCA)
Kathy Mattea; *Home For Christmas* ....(WB)
Kenny Rogers & Dolly Parton; *Once Upon A Christmas* ....(RCA)
Lee Greenwood; *Christmas To Christmas* ....(MSP)
Lou Rawls; *Merry Christmas Ho! Ho! Ho!* ....(CAP)
Luther Vandross; *Very Special Christmas-#2* .... (A&M)
Manhattan Transfer; *Christmas Album* ....(COL)
Mel Torme; *Have Yourself A Jazzy Little Christmas* ....(VRV)
Miracles; *Christmas With* ....(MOT)
Nat King Cole; *Best Of Christmas* ....(CAP)
  Billboard's Greatest Christmas Hits ....(CAP)
  Christmas Song (Chestnuts Roasting...) ....(CAP)
O'Jays; *Home For Christmas* ....(EMI)
Perry Como; *Season's Greetings* ....(RCA)
Randy Travis; *Old Time Christmas* ....(WB)
Reba McEntire; *Merry Christmas To You* ....(MSP)
Roger Whittaker; *Christmas With* ....(RCA)
Roger Williams; *Golden Christmas* ....(SPM)
Rosemary Clooney; *Magic Of Christmas* ....(SPM)
Smokey Robinson & Temptations; *Motown Christmas Album* ....(MOT)
Stevie Wonder; *Someday At Christmas* ....(MOT)
Stylistics; *Christmas* ....(AMH)
Temptations; *Give Love At Christmas* ....(MOT)
Tony Bennett; *Christmas Album* ....(COL)
Trisha Yearwood; *The Sweetest Gift* ....(MCA)
Vince Guaraldi; *Charlie Brown Christmas* ....(FAN)
Christmas Spirit
Donna Summer; *Christmas Spirit* ....(MER)
Wailers; *Bummed Out Christmas* ....(RHI)
  Rockin' Christmas-The '60s ....(RHI)
Christmas Started With A Child
Ed Bruce; *Country Christmas-#4* ....(RCA)
Christmas Time
Bryan Adams; *45* ....(A&M)
Gary Morris; *Every Christmas* ....(LIB)
Ray Charles; *Spirit Of Christmas* ....(COL)
Christmas Time In The Motor City
Was (Not Was); *Christmas Record* ....(PAS)
Christmas To Christmas
Lee Greenwood; *Christmas In The Country* ......(MSP)
  Christmas To Christmas ....(MSP)
Christmas Trail
Michael Martin Murphey; *Cowboy Christmas* .....(WB)
Christmas Waltz
Carpenters; *Christmas Portrait* ....(A&M)
Frank Sinatra; *Jolly Christmas From* ....(CAP)
Johnny Mathis; *Christmas Eve With* ....(COL)
Lettermen; *For Christmas This Year* ....(CAP)
Nancy Wilson; *Best Of Christmas* ....(CAP)
  Merry Christmas Baby-Romance & Reindeer ....(CAP)
Peggy Lee; *Christmas Carousel* ....(CAP)
Christmas Without Mary
Charley Pride; *Country Christmas-#4* ....(RCA)
Christmas (Baby, Please Come Home)
Crystals; *Christmas Gift For You From P. Spector* (RHI)
Darlene Love; *Back To Mono* ....(AKO)
  Phil Spector's Christmas Album ....(PAS)
U2; *Very Special Christmas* ....(A&M)
Closing Of The Year
Wendy & Lisa; *ST/Toys* ....(GEF)
Comin' Down The Chimney
Sonny Bono & Little Tootsie; *45* ....(SPE)
Coventry Carol
Alison Moyet; *Very Special Christmas* ....(A&M)
Anne Murray; *Christmas* ....(LIB)
Joan Baez; *Noel* ....(VAN)
John Denver; *Rocky Mountain Christmas* ....(RCA)
Royal College Of Music Chamber Choir; *Carols For Christmas-#1&2* ....(RYK)
Cowboy Christmas Ball
Michael Martin Murphey; *Cowboy Christmas* .....(WB)
C-H-R-I-S-T-M-A-S
Eddy Arnold; *Billboard's Greatest Christmas Hits* . (RHI)
Perry Como; *Sings Merry Christmas Music* ....(SPM)
Daddy's Christmas
Albert Brooks & Little Kristi; *45* ....(ASY)
Daddy's Drinking Up Our Christmas
Commander Cody; *Hillbilly Holiday* ....(RHI)

Dance Of The Sugar Plum Fairy
Boston Pops Orchestra; *Encores* ....(DGG)
  Sleigh Ride!-Classic Christmas Favorites ....(RCA)
Dead By X-Mas
Hanoi Rocks; *Self-Destruction Blues* ....(GEF)
Dear Santa-Bring Me A Man This Christmas
Weather Girls; *Success* ....(COL)
Deck The Halls
Bobby Vinton; *Great Songs Of Christmas* ....(CCB)
Christmas Children's Chorus; *#2* ....(SPM)
David Seville/Chipmunks; *Christmas With The Chipmunks-#2* ....(EMI)
Jackie Wilson; *Merry Christmas From* ....(RHI)
Mantovani; *Christmas Favorites* ....(LON)
Mario Lanza; *Christmas With* ....(RCA)
Mormon Tabernacle Choir; *Christmas Album* ....(COL)
Nat King Cole; *Christmas Song* ....(CAP)
Roger Williams; *Christmas Time* ....(MCA)
Shirley/Squirrely; *Christmas With* ....(GRT)
Trapp Family Singers; *Christmas With* ....(MSP)
Do You Hear What I Hear
Bing Crosby; *Best Of Christmas* ....(CAP)
Chet Atkins; *East Tennessee Christmas* ....(COL)
  Nashville's Greatest Christmas Hits ....(COL)
Commodores; *Christmas* ....(CMO)
Connie Scott; *Christmas In Your Heart* ....(WOR)
Gladys Knight/Pips; *Bless The House* ....(MOT)
Mahalia Jackson; *Christmas With* ....(COL)
Sonny James; *It's Christmas Time* ....(LIB)
Steve Wariner; *Christmas Memories* ....(MSP)
Vince Gill; *Let There Be Peace On Earth* ....(MCA)
Whitney Houston; *Very Special Christmas* ....(A&M)
Father Christmas
Kinks; *Come Dancing With-Best Of-1977-1986* .. (ARI)
Feliz Navidad
Jose Feliciano; *15 Especiales De* ....(GLB)
  Greatest Hits ....(RCA)
Fight On Christmas Fight On
John Fahey; *Essential* ....(VAN)
  John Fahey ....(VAN)
First Noel
Air Supply; *Christmas Album* ....(ARI)
Bing Crosby; *Christmas* ....(MSP)
Connie Francis; *Christmas In My Heart* ....(POL)
Crash Test Dummies; *Lump Of Coal* ....(FIR)
Dolly Parton; *Home For Christmas* ....(COL)
Ella Fitzgerald; *Christmas* ....(CAP)
Elvis Presley; *Elvis Christmas Classics* ....(RCA)
  Sings The Wonderful World Of Christmas ....(RCA)
Emmylou Harris; *Light Of The Stable* ....(WB)
George Howard; *GRP Christmas Collection-#2* ...(GRP)
Joe Williams; *That Holiday Feelin'* ....(VRV)
John Tesh; *Romantic Christmas* ....(GTS)
Johnny Mathis/Percy Faith & Orchestra; *Merry Christmas* ....(COL)
Kenny Rogers; *Christmas In America* ....(RPR)
Loretta Lynn; *Tennessee Christmas* ....(MSP)
Nat King Cole; *Christmas Song* ....(CAP)
Pete Seeger; *Traditional Christmas Carols* ....(FLW)
Philadelphia Orchestra/Eugene Ormandy; *Joy To The World* ....(RCA)
Roger Whittaker; *Christmas With* ....(LIB)
Suzy Bogguss; *Christmas For The '90s-#2* ....(LIB)
For Momma
Statler Brothers; *Christmas Present* ....(MER)
Forgive Me Santa
Jimmie Davis; *Best Of* ....(MCA)
  Canaan Country Christmas ....(CNN)
Shirley Caesar; *Christmasing* ....(WOR)
Friendly Beasts
Garth Brooks; *Beyond The Season* ....(LIB)
Peter, Paul & Mary/N.Y. Choral Society; *Holiday Celebration* ....(WB)
Frosty The Snowman
Beach Boys; *Christmas Album* ....(CAP)
Bing Crosby; *Christmas Classics* ....(CAP)
Conway Twitty; *Merry Twismas From C.T. & Little Friends* ....(WB)
Gene Autry; *16 Most Requested Songs Of Christmas* ....(COL)
George Strait; *Merry Christmas Strait To You* ....(MSP)
Jackson 5; *Christmas Album* ....(MOT)
Jan & Dean; *Legends Of Christmas Past-Rock & R&B* ....(EMI)

Loretta Lynn; *Christmas Without Daddy* .... (MSP)
Ray Conniff; *Yuletide Cheer* .... (COL)
Ronettes; *Phil Spector's Christmas Album* .... (PAS)
Funky Christmas
Whispers; *Happy Holidays To You* .... (SLR)
Funky New Year
Eagles; *45* .... (ELE)
Give Love On Christmas Day
Jackson 5; *Christmas Album* .... (MOT)
Johnny Gill; *Motown Christmas* .... (MOT)
New Edition; *Christmas All Over The World* .... (MCA)
Temptations; *Give Love At Christmas* .... (MOT)
Give Me Your Love For Christmas
Johnny Mathis; *Give Me Your Love For Christmas* (COL)
Go Tell It On The Mountain
Bobby Darin; *25th Day Of December* .... (ATC)
Dolly Parton; *Home For Christmas* .... (COL)
Garth Brooks; *Beyond The Season* .... (LIB)
Simon & Garfunkel; *Collected Works* .... (COL)
    Wednesday Morning 3 A.M. .... (COL)
Weavers; *On Tour* .... (VAN)
God Rest Ye Merry Gentlemen
Bing Crosby; *Merry Christmas* .... (MSP)
    Sings Christmas Songs .... (MSP)
Bobby Vinton; *Christmas All-Time Greatest
    Records-#2* .... (CCB)
Ella Fitzgerald; *Best Of Christmas* .... (CAP)
Garth Brooks; *Beyond The Season* .... (LIB)
    Christmas For The '90s-#1 .... (LIB)
Jackie Wilson; *Merry Christmas From* .... (RHI)
Kenny Rogers; *Christmas In America* .... (RPR)
Leontyne Price; *Christmas Songs* .... (LON)
Mel Torme; *Christmas Songs* .... (TLR)
Nat King Cole; *Cole Christmas & Kids* .... (CAP)
Neil Diamond; *Christmas Album* .... (COL)
Randy Travis; *An Old Time Christmas* .... (WB)
Roger Whittaker; *Tidings Of Comfort & Joy* ...... (LIB)
Smokey Robinson/Miracles; *Season For Miracles* (MOT)
Steve Wariner; *Christmas Memories* .... (MSP)
Take 6/Yellowjackets; *He Is Christmas* .... (RPR)
T-Bone Burnett; *Acoustic Christmas* .... (COL)
Good King Wenceslas
E. Power Biggs/Gregg Smith Singers; *We Wish You A
Merry Christmas* .... (COL)
Mel Torme; *Christmas Songs* .... (TLR)
Philadelphia Orchestra/Eugene Ormandy; *Joy To The
World* .... (RCA)
Roches; *We Three Kings* .... (MSP)
Stan Kenton; *Merry Christmas From Creative World
Of* .... (CAP)
Grandma Got Run Over By A Reindeer
Elmo & Patsy; *Billboard's Greatest Christmas Hits* (RHI)
    Dr. Demento Greatest Novelty CD .... (RHI)
    Dr. Demento's Greatest-#6 .... (RHI)
    Grandma Got Run Over By A Reindeer .... (EPI)
    Greatest Children's Christmas Hits .... (EPI)
Greatest Gift Of All
Kenny Rogers & Dolly Parton; *Once Upon A
Christmas* .... (RCA)
Lee Greenwood; *Christmas To Christmas* .... (MSP)
Greatest Little Christmas Ever Wuz
Ray Stevens; *Country Christmas To Remember* ... (MSP)
    Tennessee Christmas .... (MSP)
Green Christmas
Stan Freberg; *Capitol Collectors Series* .... (CAP)
    Christmas Comedy Classics .... (PRY)
    Dr. Demento Greatest Christmas CD .... (RHI)
    Dr. Demento's Greatest Novelty-#6 .... (RHI)
Greensleeves
Jeff Beck; *Truth* .... (EPI)
Olivia Newton-John; *Come On Over* .... (MCA)
Ray Conniff Singers; *Christmas* .... (COL)
Vienna Boys Choir; *Christmas Festival* .... (RCA)
Grown-Up Christmas
David Foster; *River Of Love* .... (ATL)
Happy Holidays
Alabama; *Christmas* .... (RCA)
Bing Crosby & Norman Luboff Choir; *Christmas Sing
With Bing* .... (MSP)
Happy New Year
Abba; *Super Trouper* .... (ATL)
Judy Garland; *Alone* .... (CAP)
Lightnin' Hopkins; *Blue Yule-Christmas Blues & R&B
Classics* .... (RHI)

Happy Xmas (War Is Over)
Andy Williams; *I Still Believe In Santa Claus* ..... (CCB)
John Lennon; *Lennon* .... (CAP)
    Shaved Fish .... (CAP)
Neil Diamond; *Christmas Album* .... (COL)
Hard Candy Christmas
Dolly Parton; *Best Of Christmas* .... (RCA)
    Country Christmas-#2 .... (RCA)
    Greatest Hits .... (RCA)
    Season's Greetings .... (RCA)
    ST/Best Little Whorehouse In Texas .... (MCA)
Original Cast; *Best Little Whorehouse In Texas* .. (MCA)
Hark! The Herald Angels Sing
Amy Grant; *Christmas Album* .... (WOR)
Bing Crosby; *Christmas Classics* .... (CAP)
Guy Lombardo; *Best Of Christmas* .... (CAP)
James Cleveland; *Merry Christmas* .... (SAV)
Jose Feliciano; *This Is Christmas* .... (RCA)
Marty Robbins; *Christmas Greetings From
Nashville* .... (COL)
    Country Christmas Favorites .... (COL)
    Nashville's Greatest Christmas Hits .... (COL)
Mormon Tabernacle Choir; *Joy To The World* ...(COL)
    Spirit Of Christmas .... (COL)
National Philharmonic Orchestra; *50 Songs Of
Christmas* .... (SPW)
Philadelphia Orchestra/Eugene Ormandy; *Joy To The
World* .... (RCA)
Have Yourself A Merry Little Christmas
Amy Grant; *Home For Christmas* .... (A&M)
Barbra Streisand; *Christmas Album* .... (COL)
Bing Crosby; *Christmas Classics* .... (CAP)
Buddy Emmons; *Christmas Sounds Of The Steel
Guitar* .... (SO)
Canadian Brass; *Christmas Celebration* .... (COL)
Crystal Gayle; *Crystal Christmas* .... (WB)
    Warner Bros. Records Christmas Tradition .... (WB)
David Seville/Chipmunks; *Christmas With-#2* .... (EMI)
Eddie Rabbitt; *Christmas For The '90s-#2* .... (LIB)
Frank Sinatra; *Jolly Christmas From* .... (CAP)
Jackson 5; *Christmas Album* .... (MOT)
John Scofield; *Christmas Guitars* .... (GRE)
Johnny Mathis; *Christmas With* .... (COL)
Judy Garland; *Best Of* .... (MCA)
Kenny Rogers; *Christmas In America* .... (RPR)
Kiri Te Kanawa; *Christmas With* .... (LON)
Lou Rawls; *Merry Christmas Baby-Romance &
Reindeer* .... (CAP)
Manhattan Transfer; *Christmas Album* .... (COL)
Maureen McGovern; *Christmas With* .... (COL)
Mel Torme; *ST/Home Alone* .... (COL)
O'Jays; *Home For Christmas* .... (EMI)
Pretenders; *Very Special Christmas* .... (A&M)
Tom Scott; *GRP Christmas Collection* .... (GRP)
Vanessa Williams; *Christmas Message* .... (LEC)
Head Crushing Yuletide Sing-A-Long
Mojo Nixon/Toadliquors; *Horny Holidays!* ...... (XXX)
Here Comes Santa Claus
Bob B. Soxx/Blue Jeans; *Back To
Mono-1958-1969* .... (AKO)
    Christmas Gift For You From Phil Spector ...... (RHI)
    Phil Spector's Christmas Album .... (PAS)
Doris Day; *16 Most Requested Songs Of
Christmas* .... (COL)
Elvis Presley; *Christmas Album* .... (RCA)
Gene Autry; *Billboard's Greatest Christmas Hits* .. (RHI)
    His Christmas Album .... (EVR)
    Season's Greetings From Nashville .... (COL)
Kitty Wells; *Christmas Day* .... (MSP)
Ramsey Lewis Trio; *Sound Of Christmas* .... (MSP)
Riders In The Sky; *Merry Christmas From Harmony
Ranch* .... (COL)
Spike Jones; *It's A Spike Jones Christmas* .... (RHI)
Here We Come A-Wassailing
Players; *Christmas* .... (RYK)
Ho Ho Ho-Who'd Be A Turkey At Christmas
Elton John; *Rockin' Christmas* .... (MSP)
Holly Jolly Christmas
Alan Jackson; *ST/Home Alone 2-Lost In New
York* .... (FOX)
Burl Ives; *Christmas Hits* .... (MSP)
    Have A Holly Jolly Christmas .... (MSP)

CHRISTMAS — CHRISTMAS

Holly Leaves & Christmas Trees
Elvis Presley; *Sings the Wonderful World Of Christmas* ....(RCA)
Holly & The Ivy
Bing Crosby; *Christmas Classics* ....(CAP)
Charlie Byrd; *Christmas Album* ....(CCJ)
Emily Mitchell; *Holly & The Ivy* ....(RCA)
Empire Brass; *Joy To The World-Music Of Christmas* .... (ANG)
Joan Sutherland; *Joy Of Christmas* ....(LON)
Jon Anderson; *3 Ships* ....(ELE)
Players; *Christmas* ....(RYK)
Homecoming Christmas
Alabama; *Christmas* ....(RCA)
How Would You Like To Be
Elvis Presley; *45* ....(RCA)
Howdy Doody Christmas
Howdy Doody/Fontane Sisters; *TV Family Christmas* .... (SCO)
I Believe In Father Christmas
Greg Lake; *Emerson Lake & Palmer-Works-#2* ... (ATL)
I Believe In Santa Claus
Kenny Rogers & Dolly Parton; *Once Upon A Christmas* ....(RCA)
I Believe In Santa's Cause
Statler Brothers; *Christmas Card* ....(MER)
I Found The Brains Of Santa Claus
Jason/Straptones; *Demento's Mementos* ... (PVC)
I Heard The Bells On Christmas Day
Bing Crosby; *That Christmas Feeling* ....(MSP)
Eddy Arnold; *Christmas With* ....(RCA)
Harry Belafonte; *To Wish You A Merry Christmas* (RCA)
Johnny Cash; *Christmas Spirit* ....(COL)
Classic Christmas ....(COL)
Michael Martin Murphey; *Cowboy Christmas* .....(WB)
Travis Tritt; *Christmas-Loving Time Of The Year* ..(WB)
I Like A Sleighride
Peggy Lee; *Best Of Christmas* ....(CAP)
Christmas Carousel ....(CAP)
I Only Want You For Christmas
Alan Jackson; *Honky Tonk Christmas* .... (ARI)
I Pray On Christmas
Harry Connick, Jr.; *When My Heart Finds Christmas* ....(COL)
I Saw Mommy Kissing Santa Claus
Andy Williams; *I Still Believe In Santa Claus* .....(CCB)
Impressions; *Funky Christmas* ....(COT)
Jackie Gleason; *All I Want For Christmas* ....(CAP)
Jackson 5; *Christmas Album* ....(MOT)
Motown Christmas ....(MOT)
Jimmy Boyd; *Billboard's Great Country Christmas Hits* ....(RHI)
Billboard's Greatest Christmas Hits ....(RHI)
John Cougar Mellencamp; *Very Special Christmas* ....(A&M)
Ronettes; *Back To Mono-1958-1969* ....(AKO)
Christmas Gift For You From Phil Spector ....(RHI)
Phil Spector's Christmas Album ....(PAS)
I Saw Three Ships Come Sailing In
Mannheim Steamroller; *Christmas* ....(AG)
Mario Lanza; *Christmas With* ....(RCA)
Nat King Cole; *Christmas Song* ....(CAP)
I Tan't Wait Till Quithmuth Day
Mel Blanc; *Christmas Comedy Classics* ....(PRY)
I Wanna Spend Christmas With You
Lowell Fulson; *Rhythm & Blues Christmas* ... (UA)
I Want A Hippopotamus For Christmas
Gayla Peevey; *Dr. Demento Greatest Christmas CD* ....(RHI)
Dr. Demento's Greatest-#6 ....(RHI)
Three Stooges; *Christmas With* ....(RHI)
I Want Elvis For Christmas
Holly Twins & Eddie Cochran; *Legends Of Christmas Past-Rock & R&B* ....(EMI)
I Wish It Could Be Christmas Forever
Perry Como; *I Wish It Could Be Christmas Forever* ....(RCA)
I Wonder As I Wander
Gary Morris; *Every Christmas* ....(LIB)
Mormon Tabernacle Choir; *This Land Is Your Land* ....(COL)
Peter, Paul & Mary; *Holiday Celebration* ....(WB)
Philadelphia Orchestra/Eugene Ormandy; *Sleigh Ride!-Classic Christmas Favorites* ....(RCA)

Sandi Patti; *Gift Goes On* ....(WOR)
I Won't Be Twisting This Christmas
Father Guido Sarducci; *45* ....(WB)
I Yust Go Nuts At Christmas
Yogi Yorgesson; *Christmas Kisses-Capitol Early Years* ....(CAP)
Dr. Demento Greatest Christmas CD ....(RHI)
Dr. Demento's Greatest-#6 ....(RHI)
If Every Day Was Like Christmas
Elvis Presley; *Christmas Album* ....(SPM)
Memories Of Christmas ....(RCA)
If I Get Home On Christmas Day
Elvis Presley; *Sings The Wonderful World Of Christmas* ....(RCA)
If We Make It Through December
Merle Haggard; *Christmas Gift* ....(CCB)
Eleven Winners ....(CAP)
Goin' Home For Christmas ....(EPI)
Very Best Of ....(CAP)
If You Don't Wanna See Santa Claus Cry
Alan Jackson; *Honky Tonk Christmas* .... (ARI)
In Dulci Jubilo
Michael Hedges; *Winter's Solstice III* ....(WH)
Players; *Christmas* ....(RYK)
Virgil Fox; *Christmas Album* ....(BAI)
It Came Upon A Midnight Clear
Anne Murray; *Christmas* ....(LIB)
Beausoleil; *Alligator Stomp-#4-Cajun Christmas* .. (RHI)
Frank Sinatra; *Jolly Christmas From* ....(CAP)
Guy Lombardo; *Peace On Earth* ....(CAP)
Highway 101; *Warner Bros. Records Christmas Tradition* ....(WB)
John Tesh; *Romantic Christmas* ....(GTS)
Julie Andrews & Andre Previn; *Christmas Treasure* ....(RCA)
Mahalia Jackson; *Christmas With* ....(COL)
Rosanne Cash; *Acoustic Christmas* ....(COL)
Tammy Wynette; *Country Christmas* ....(EPI)
Nashville's Greatest Christmas Hits-#2 ....(COL)
Voices Of The Season-A Capella ....(EPI)
It Doesn't Have To Be That Way
Jim Croce; *Life & Times* ....(LIF)
It Wasn't His Child
Trisha Yearwood; *The Sweetest Gift* .... (MCA)
It's Beginning To Look A Lot Like...
Bing Crosby; *All-Time Christmas Favorites-#4* ...(MSP)
Sings Christmas Songs ....(MSP)
Duke Ellington; *Take The Holiday Train* ....(SPM)
Johnny Mathis; *ST/Home Alone 2-Lost In New York* ....(FOX)
It's Christmas
John Schneider; *White Christmas* ....(SCO)
Ronnie Milsap; *Best Of Christmas* ....(RCA)
Christmas With ....(RCA)
Country Christmas-#3 ....(RCA)
It's Christmas Time
Carpenters; *Christmas Portrait* .... (A&M)
Castelles; *Rhythm & Blues Christmas-#1* ....(CLT)
Sweet Sounds Of ....(CLT)
Clifton Chenier; *King Of The Bayous* ....(ARH)
Five Keys; *Doo-Wop Christmas* ....(RHI)
Legends Of Christmas Past-Rock & R&B .... (EMI)
Marvin & Johnny; *Legends Of Christmas Past-Rock & R&B* .... (EMI)
Rockin' Christmas-'50s ....(RHI)
Smokey Robinson/Miracles; *Motown Christmas* . (MOT)
Season For Miracles ....(MOT)
It's Christmastime In Louisiana
Johnnie Allan; *Alligator Stomp-#4-Cajun Christmas* ....(RHI)
It's Gonna Be a Punk Rock Christmas
Ravers; *45* ....(ZMB)
It's Just Another New Year's Eve
Barry Manilow; *Live* .... (ARI)
I'd Like To Hitch A Ride With Santa
Andrews Sisters; *All-Time Christmas Favorites-#3* (MSP)
I'll Be Gnome For Christmas
Jethros; *Dark Side Of The Xmas Tree* ....(PFR)
I'll Be Home For Christmas
Al Green; *White Christmas* ....(WOR)
Amy Grant; *Home For Christmas* ....(A&M)
Anne Murray; *Christmas Wishes* ....(LIB)
Barbara Mandrell; *Christmas At Our House* ......(MSP)
Beach Boys; *Christmas Album* ....(CAP)

Carpenters; *Christmas Portrait* .... (A&M)
Crystal Gayle; *Crystal Christmas* .... (WB)
Dolly Parton; *Home For Christmas* .... (COL)
Donna Summer; *Christmas Spirit* .... (MER)
Duke Ellington/Orchestra; *Take The Holiday Train* .... (SPM)
Elvis Presley; *Christmas Album* .... (RCA)
Floyd Cramer; *We Wish You A Merry Christmas* .(RCA)
Forester Sisters; *Christmas Card* .... (WB)
Frank Sinatra; *Jolly Christmas From* .... (CAP)
Glen Campbell; *Merry Christmas Baby-Romance & Reindeer* .... (CAP)
Kenny Rogers; *Christmas In America* .... (RPR)
Lee Greenwood; *Christmas To Christmas* .... (MCA)
Mickey Gilley; *Christmas At Gilley's* .... (EPI)
  Nashville's Greatest Hits-#2 .... (COL)
Pat Boone; *White Christmas* .... (MSP)
Percy Faith; *Christmas Is* .... (COL)
  Christmas Melodies .... (COL)
Reba McEntire; *Christmas In The Country* ...... (MSP)
  Merry Christmas To You .... (MSP)
Ronnie Milsap; *Christmas With* .... (RCA)
Spyro Gyra; *GRP Christmas Collection-#2* .... (GRP)
Statler Brothers; *Christmas Card* .... (MER)
Suzy Bogguss; *Christmas For The '90s-#1* .... (LIB)
  Family Christmas Treasury .... (LIB)
Wayne Newton; *Christmas All-Time Greatest Records-#2* .... (CCB)
I'll Be Walking The Floor This Christmas
Ernest Tubb; *Hillbilly Holiday* .... (RHI)
I'll Be Your Santa, Baby
Rufus Thomas; *It's Christmas Time Again* .... (STX)
I'll Make Everyday Christmas
Joe Tex; *Soul Christmas* .... (ATL)
I'll Place My Order Early
Johnny Paycheck; *45* .... (LDR)
I'm A Christmas Tree
Wild Man Fischer & Dr. Demento; *Dr. Demento Greatest Christmas CD* .... (RHI)
I'm A Pleasure To Shop For
Ogden Nash; *Christmas With* .... (CAE)
I'm Christmasing With You
Patti Labelle; *Starlight Christmas* .... (MCA)
I'm Gonna Lasso Santa Claus
Brenda Lee; *Hillbilly Holiday* .... (RHI)
  Rockin' Little Christmas .... (MCA)
I've Got What You Want For Christmas
Louise Mandrell; *Country Christmas-#2* .... (RCA)
Jesus, Jesus, Rest Your Head
Trapp Family Singers; *Christmas With* .... (MSP)
Jingle Bell Boogie
Big Jack Johnson; *Blue Yule-Christmas Blues & R&B Classics* .... (RHI)
Jingle Bell Rock
Bobby Helms; *Billboard Great Country Christmas Hits* .... (RHI)
  Christmas Classics .... (RHI)
  ST/Home Alone 2-Lost In New York .... (FOX)
Booker T./M.G.s; *Cool Yule* .... (RHI)
Brenda Lee; *All-Time Christmas Favorites-#4* .... (MSP)
Chet Atkins; *East Tennessee Christmas* .... (COL)
Jambalaya Cajun Band; *Alligator Stomp-#4-Cajun Christmas* .... (RHI)
Lenny Dee; *Best Of* .... (MCA)
Neil Diamond; *Christmas Album* .... (COL)
Randy Travis; *Very Special Christmas-#2* .... (A&M)
Rick Orozco; *Tejano Country Christmas* .... (ART)
Wild Rose; *Christmas For The '90s-#1* .... (LIB)
Jingle Bells
Al Green; *White Christmas* .... (WOR)
Barbra Streisand; *Christmas Album* .... (COL)
Bing Crosby/Andrews Sisters; *Christmas All-Time Greatest Records* .... (CCB)
Booker T./M.G.s; *In The Christmas Spirit* .... (ATL)
Buck Owens; *Christmas With* .... (CCB)
Carpenters; *Christmas Portrait* .... (A&M)
Count Basie; *Yule Struttin'* .... (BLN)
Dolly Parton; *Home For Christmas* .... (COL)
Flaco Jimenez/Freddie Fender/Others; *Tejano Country Christmas* .... (ART)
Frank Sinatra & Bing Crosby; *Happy Holiday* ... (SPM)
Frankie Valli/Four Seasons; *Christmas Album* ... (RHI)
Les Paul; *Christmas Kisses-Capitol Early Years* ... (CAP)
Roger Wagner; *Caroles* .... (CAP)

Roy Rogers; *Christmas On The Range-Cowboy Classics* .... (CAP)
Spike Jones; *It's A Spike Jones Christmas* .... (RHI)
Statler Brothers; *Christmas Card* .... (MER)
Tony Bennett; *Snowfall/Christmas Album* .... (COL)
Ventures; *Christmas Album* .... (EMI)
Willie Nelson; *Pretty Paper* .... (COL)
Wynton Marsalis; *Crescent City Christmas Card* ..(COL)
Jingle Cats Medley
Jingle Cats; *Christmas Comedy Classics-#2* ...... (PRY)
Jingle Hell
Space Negros; *Dark Side Of The Xmas Tree* ..... (PFR)
Jingle Jangle
Archies; *Grooviest Hits* .... (BCT)
Penguins; *Doo Wop Christmas* .... (RHI)
Jolly Old Saint Nicholas
Eddy Arnold; *Christmas With* .... (RCA)
Michael Martin Murphey; *Cowboy Christmas* ..... (WB)
Joseph And Mary's Boy
Alabama; *Christmas* .... (RCA)
Joy To The World (Christmas)
Anne Murray; *Christmas Wishes* .... (LIB)
Billy Vaughn; *Traditional Christmas Classics* .... (MSP)
Bob Rivers Comedy Corp.; *Twisted Christmas* ... (CRI)
Boston Pops Orchestra/Arthur Fiedler; *Christmas Festival* .... (DGG)
Empire Brass; *Joy To The World* .... (ANG)
Johnny Cash; *Nashville's Greatest Christmas Hits* .(COL)
Larry Carlton; *Christmas At My House* .... (MCA)
Larry Gatlin/Gatlin Brothers; *Christmas With The Gatlins* .... (CAP)
Larry Groce/Disney Chorus; *Family Christmas* ....(DIS)
Liberace; *Christmas* .... (MSP)
Mormon Tabernacle Choir; *Joy To The World (Christmas)* .... (COL)
Pat Boone; *White Christmas* .... (MSP)
Ronnie Milsap; *Christmas With* .... (RCA)
Slim Whitman; *Country Christmas Classics* .... (LIB)
Junk Bond Christmas Blues
Elmo Shropshire; *Dr. Elmo's Twisted Christmas* .. (LAF)
Lamb Of God
Donna Summer; *Christmas Spirit* .... (MER)
Let It Snow! Let It Snow! Let It Snow!
Bing Crosby; *Christmas Classics* .... (CAP)
Carpenters; *Christmas Portrait* .... (A&M)
Charley Pride; *Country Christmas-#1* .... (RCA)
Dean Martin; *Winter Romance* .... (CAP)
Herb Alpert/Tijuana Brass; *Christmas Album* ... (A&M)
Joe Williams; *That Holiday Feelin'* .... (VRV)
Lee Greenwood; *Christmas In The Country* ...... (MSP)
  Christmas To Christmas .... (MSP)
  Country Christmas To Remember .... (MSP)
Marcus Roberts; *Merry Jazzmus* .... (NOV)
Marie Osmond; *Christmas Country Classics-#1* ... (CCB)
Miracles; *Christmas With* .... (MOT)
Mitch Miller; *Yuletide Cheer* .... (COL)
Steve Wariner; *Christmas Memories* .... (MCA)
Temptations; *Christmas Card* .... (MOT)
  Christmas Card/Give Love At Christmas .... (MOT)
Trisha Yearwood; *The Sweetest Gift* .... (MCA)
Vaughn Monroe; *Billboard's Greatest Christmas Hits* .... (RHI)
Wynton Marsalis; *Crescent City Christmas Card* ..(COL)
Let's Get It Together For Christmas
Chambers Brothers; *45* .... (COL)
Let's Make Christmas Mean Something...
James Brown; *Rockin' Christmas-The '60s* .... (RHI)
  Santa's Got A Brand New Bag .... (RHI)
Let's Make Christmas Merry, Baby
Amos Milburn; *Billboard's Greatest R&B Christmas Hits* .... (RHI)
  Legends Of Christmas Past-Rock & R&B .... (EMI)
Let's Put The 'X' Back In Christmas
Pinkard & Bowden; *P.G. 13* .... (WB)
Let's Unite The Whole World At Christmas
James Brown; *Sant's Got A Brand New Bag* .... (RHI)
Light Of The Stable
Emmylou Harris; *Light Of The Stable* .... (WB)
  Warner Bros. Records Christmas Tradition ..... (WB)
Judds; *Best Of Christmas* .... (RCA)
  Country Christmas-#3 .... (RCA)
  Season's Greetings .... (RCA)
Linus & Lucy
Vince Guaraldi; *Charlie Brown Christmas* .... (FAN)

Little Boy That Santa Forgot
Nat King Cole; *Christmas Gift Set* .... (CAP)
  Cole Christmas & Kids .... (CAP)
Little Bummer Boy
Jethros; *Dark Side Of The Xmas Tree* .... (PFR)
Little Christmas Tree
Michael Jackson; *Motown Christmas* .... (MOT)
Little Drummer Boy
Air Supply; *Christmas Album* .... (ARI)
Alexander O'Neal; *My Gift To You* .... (TAB)
Anne Murray; *Christmas Wishes* .... (CAP)
Bob Seger/Silver Bullet Band; *Very Special
Christmas* .... (A&M)
Boston Pops Orchestra/Arthur Fiedler; *Christmas
Festival* .... (RCA)
Burl Ives; *Have A Happy Jolly Christmas* .... (MSP)
David Bowie & Bing Crosby; *Bowie-The
Singles-1969-1993* .... (RYK)
Diana Ross/Supremes; *Merry Christmas* .... (MOT)
Dino; *Christmas Gift* .... (BEN)
Dolly Parton; *Home For Christmas* .... (COL)
Elvin Bishop; *Alligator Records Christmas
Collection* .... (ALG)
Emmylou Harris; *Light Of The Stable* .... (WB)
Four Seasons; *Christmas Album* .... (RHI)
Frankie Valli/Four Seasons; *Christmas Album* ... (RHI)
Gatlin Brothers; *Christmas For The '90s-#1* .... (LIB)
Hank Williams, Jr.; *Christmas Country
Classics-#1* .... (CCB)
Harry Simeone Chorale; *Best Of Christmas* ..... (SPM)
  Billboard's Greatest Christmas Hits .... (RHI)
  Little Drummer Boy .... (SPM)
Henry Mancini; *Merry Mancini Christmas* .... (RCA)
Joan Jett; *I Love Rock & Roll* .... (BW)
Joan Jett/Blackhearts; *I Love Rock 'N' Roll* ...... (BLK)
Johnny Cash; *Billboard's Great Country Christmas
Hits* .... (RHI)
Larry Carlton; *Christmas At My House* .... (MCA)
Lettermen; *For Christmas This Year* .... (CAP)
Marlene Dietrich; *Best Of Christmas* .... (CAP)
  Marlene .... (CAP)
Mormon Tabernacle Choir; *White Christmas* .... (COL)
Neil Diamond; *Christmas Album* .... (COL)
Peggy Lee; *Christmas Carousel* .... (CAP)
Restless Heart; *Home For The Holidays* .... (RCA)
Stevie Wonder; *Someday At Christmas* .... (MOT)
Stylistics; *Christmas* .... (AMH)
Temptations; *Christmas Card* .... (MOT)
  Give Love At Christmas .... (MOT)
  Motown Christmas .... (MOT)
Wynton Marsalis; *Crescent City Christmas Card* .. (COL)
Little Saint Nick
Beach Boys; *Christmas Album* .... (CAP)
  Christmas All-Time Greatest Records .... (CCB)
  Legends Of Christmas Past-Rock & R&B .... (EMI)
  Party/Stack-O-Tracks .... (CAP)
Log Cabin Home In The Sky
Michael Martin Murphey; *Cowboy Christmas* .... (WB)
Lone Star Christmas
Lee Greenwood; *Christmas To Christmas* .... (MCA)
Lonely Christmas
Ferlin Husky; *Christmas On The Range-Cowboy
Classics* .... (CAP)
Sonny Til/Orioles; *Greatest Hits* .... (CLT)
  Rhythm & Blues Christmas-#1 .... (CLT)
Lonely Night
Merle Haggard; *Goin' Home For Christmas* ...... (EPI)
Louisiana Christmas Day
Aaron Neville; *Soulful Christmas* .... (A&M)
Lo, How A Rose E'er Blooming
Beane Family; *Christmas Classics From Around The
World* .... (CRI)
John Fahey; *Christmas Guitar-#1* .... (VAR)
New York City Gay Men's Chorus; *Christmas Comes
Anew* .... (VIA)
Pete Seeger; *Traditional Christmas Carols* ...... (FLW)
Philadelphia Brass Ensemble/E. Ormandy; *Festival Of
Carols In Brass* .... (COL)
Trapp Family Singers; *Christmas With* .... (MSP)
Vienna Boys Choir; *Christmas Festival* .... (RCA)
Vienna Boys Choir & Hermann Prey; *Christmas
With* .... (RCA)
Mama's Boy
Joel Nava; *Tejano Country Christmas* .... (ART)

Man With All The Toys
Beach Boys; *Christmas Album* .... (CAP)
Mary, Did You Know?
Kathy Mattea; *Good News* .... (MER)
Mary's Boy Child
Andy Williams; *Merry Christmas* .... (COL)
Anne Murray; *Christmas* .... (LIB)
Harry Belafonte; *Billboard's Greatest Christmas
Hits* .... (RHI)
  This Is Christmas .... (RCA)
Kiri Te Kanawa; *Christmas With* .... (LON)
Mary's Sweet Smile
Statler Brothers; *Christmas Present* .... (MER)
Merry Christmas Baby
Bonnie Raitt & Charles Brown; *Very Special
Christmas-#2* .... (A&M)
Booker T./M.G.s; *Soul Christmas* .... (ATL)
Bruce Springsteen; *Very Special Christmas* ..... (A&M)
Charles Brown; *Christmas Classics* .... (RHI)
Chuck Berry; *Chess Box* .... (CSS)
  Christmas Hits .... (MSP)
  Cool Yule-Collection .... (RHI)
  Have A Merry Chess Christmas .... (CSS)
  Rockin' Little Christmas .... (MCA)
Elvis Presley; *Memories Of Christmas* .... (RCA)
  Reconsider Baby .... (RCA)
  Sings The Wonderful World Of Christmas ..... (RCA)
Ike & Tina Turner; *Best Of Cool Yule* .... (RHI)
Johnny Moore's 3 Blazers; *Billboard's Greatest R&B
Christmas Hits* .... (RHI)
Lionel Hampton/Orchestra; *Hipster's Holiday-Vocal Jazz
& R&B* .... (RHI)
Otis Redding; *Story* .... (ATL)
Poets; *Rockin' Christmas-The '60s* .... (RHI)
Merry Christmas To You From Me
Marty Robbins; *Christmas With* .... (COL)
Merry Christmas, Baby
Beach Boys; *Christmas Album* .... (CAP)
Merry Christmas, Darling
Carpenters; *Christmas Portrait* .... (A&M)
  From The Top .... (A&M)
Dino; *Christmas...A Time For Peace* .... (BEN)
Fabulous Thunderbirds; *Christmas Party With Eddie
G.* .... (COL)
Poppa Hop/Orchestra; *Blue Yule-Christmas Blues & R&B
Classics* .... (RHI)
Uniques; *Doo Wop Christmas* .... (RHI)
Merry Texas Christmas You All
Michael Martin Murphey; *Cowboy Christmas* .... (WB)
Monster Holiday
Lon Chaney; *Christmas Comedy Classics* .... (PRY)
  Legends Of Christmas Past-Rock & R&B .... (EMI)
Mrs. Santa Claus
Nat King Cole; *Cole Christmas & Kids* .... (CAP)
Mr. Mistletoe
Lynn Anderson; *Christmas Album* .... (COL)
Mr. Santa Claus
Nathaniel Mayer; *Rockin' Christmas-The '60s* .... (RHI)
My Birthday Comes On Christmas
Spike Jones; *It's A Spike Jones Christmas* .... (RHI)
My Christmas Tree
Diana Ross/Supremes; *Merry Christmas* .... (MOT)
Home Alone Children's Choir; *ST/Home Alone 2-Lost In
New York* .... (FOX)
Temptations; *Christmas Card* .... (MOT)
My Favorite Things
Andy Williams; *Merry Christmas* .... (COL)
Barbra Streisand; *Christmas Album* .... (COL)
Betty Carter; *Compact Jazz* .... (VRV)
Diana Ross/Supremes; *Merry Christmas* .... (MOT)
  Motown Christmas .... (MOT)
Herb Alpert/Tijuana Brass; *Christmas Album* ... (A&M)
John Coltrane; *Best Of* .... (ATL)
Johnny Mathis; *Give Me Your Love For Christmas* (COL)
Julie Andrews; *ST/Sound Of Music* .... (RCA)
Kenny Rogers; *Christmas* .... (EMI)
Lorrie Morgan; *Merry Christmas From London* ... (BNA)
Natividad Song
Freddy Fender; *Country Christmas To Remember* (MSP)
New Deal For Christmas
Original Broadway Cast; *Annie* .... (COL)
New Year's Day
U2; *Under A Blood Red Sky* .... (ISL)
  War .... (ISL)

Night Before Christmas
Amy Grant; *Home For Christmas* .... (A&M)
Carly Simon; *ST/This Is My Life* .... (QUE)
Gladys Knight/Pips; *Bless This House* ....(BUD)
Glen Campbell; *Merry Christmas* .... (LIB)
Stan Freberg; *Christmas Kisses-Capitol's Early
Years* ....(CAP)
White Mountain Singers; *Folk Era Christmas* .... (FOL)
No Christmas In Kentucky
Phil Ochs; *Toast To Those Who Are Gone* .... (RHI)
No Presents For Christmas
King Diamond; *Dark Sides* .... (RR)
In Concert-1987-Abigail .... (RR)
No Reservation At The Inn
Statler Brothers; *Christmas Present* .... (MER)
No Room At The Inn
Anne Murray; *Christmas* ....(LIB)
James Cleveland; *Merry Christmas* .... (SAV)
Mahalia Jackson; *Christmas With* ....(COL)
Staple Singers; *25th Day Of December* ....(FAN)
Nuttin' For Christmas
Barry Gordon; *Billboard's Greatest Christmas Hits* (RHI)
Stan Freberg; *Christmas Comedy Classcis* .... (PRY)
Dr. Demento Greatest Christmas CD .... (RHI)
Dr. Demento's Greatest-#6 .... (RHI)
O Come, O Come, Emmanuel
Bryan Duncan; *Our Christmas* ....(WOR)
Carpenters; *Christmas Portrait* .... (A&M)
Joan Baez; *Noel* .... (VAN)
Mike Reid; *Voices Of The Season-A Capella* ...... (EPI)
Mormon Tabernacle Choir; *Joy To The World* ...(COL)
Sings ....(COL)
New York Choral Artists; *O Come All ye
Faithful* .... (ANG)
Peter, Paul & Mary/N.Y. Choral Society; *Holiday
Celebration* .... (WB)
Philadelphia Orchestra/Eugene Ormandy; *Glorious
Sound Of Christmas* ....(COL)
O Holy Night
Al Green; *White Christmas* .... (WOR)
Al Hirt; *Sound Of Christmas* ....(RCA)
Anne Murray; *Christmas Wishes* ....(LIB)
Bing Crosby; *Christmas Classics* ....(CAP)
Carpenters; *Christmas Portrait* .... (A&M)
Old Fashioned Christmas .... (A&M)
Dino; *Christmas Gift* ....(BEN)
Donna Summer; *Christmas Spirit* .... (MER)
Ella Fitzgerald; *Christmas* ....(CAP)
Glen Campbell; *Christmas For The '90s-#2* ......(LIB)
Joan Baez; *Noel* .... (VAN)
John Denver; *Rocky Mountain Christmas* ....(RCA)
Larry Gatlin/Gatlin Brothers; *Christmas With* ....(CAP)
Lee Greenwood; *Christmas To Christmas* ....(MCA)
Lettermen; *For Christmas This Year* ....(CAP)
Luciano Pavarotti; *O Holy Night* ....(LON)
Miracles; *Christmas With* ....(MOT)
Mormon Tabernacle Choir; *Holly & The Ivy* .....(COL)
Joy To The World ....(COL)
Sings ....(COL)
Nat King Cole; *Christmas Song* ....(CAP)
Neil Diamond; *Christmas Album* ....(COL)
Reba McEntire; *Christmas In The Country* ....(MSP)
Merry Christmas To You ....(MSP)
Ronnie Milsap; *Christmas With* ....(RCA)
O Little Town Of Bethlehem
Bing Crosby/Others; *Christmas Sing With Bing* .. (MCA)
Bobby Vinton; *Great Songs Of Christmas* ....(CCB)
Dino; *Christmas...A Time For Peace* ....(BEN)
Dolly Parton; *Home For Christmas* ....(COL)
Elvis Presley; *Elvis Christmas Classics* ....(RCA)
Frank Sinatra; *Jolly Christmas From* ....(CAP)
Kenny Rogers; *Christmas In America* ....(RPR)
King's College Choir; *Carols From* .... (ANG)
Mario Lanza; *Christmas With* ....(RCA)
Mormon Tabernacle Choir; *Joy Of Christmas* ....(COL)
Spirit Of Christmas ....(COL)
Nat King Cole; *Peace On Earth* ....(CAP)
Philadelphia Orchestra/Eugene Ormandy; *Greatest
Christmas Hits* ....(COL)
Ray Price; *Nashville's Greatest Christmas Hits* ....(COL)
Roger Williams; *All-Time Christmas Favorites-#3* (MSP)
Oh Christmas Tree (O Tannenbaum)
David Benoit; *Christmastime* ....(BM)
Kevin Gibbs Trio; *Christmas Presence* ....(CCJ)

Leontyne Price; *Christmas Songs* ....(LON)
Mormon Tabernacle Choir; *Joy To The World* ...(COL)
Nat King Cole; *Christmas Song* ....(CAP)
Richard Clayderman; *Christmas Celebration* .....(COL)
Roger Wagner; *Caroles* ....(CAP)
Wynton Marsalis; *Crescent City Christmas Card* ..(COL)
Oh Happy Day
Edwin Hawkins Singers; *Soul Hits/'70s-#1* .... (RHI)
Super Hits-#3 ....(GUS)
Five Satins; *Sing Their Greatest Hits* ....(CLT)
Old Christmas Card
Forester Sisters; *Christmas Card* ....(WB)
Jim Reeves; *Twelve Songs Of Christmas* ....(RCA)
Mickey Gilley; *Christmas At Gilley's* .... (EPI)
Old Fashioned Christmas
Jimmie Rodgers; *Christmas With Jimmie* ....(MSP)
Statler Brothers; *Christmas Present* .... (MER)
Old Toy Trains
Billy Strange; *Railroad Man* ....(CRS)
Glen Campbell; *All-Star Country Christmas* ......(CAP)
That Christmas Feeling ....(CAP)
Statler Brothers; *Christmas Present* .... (MER)
Old Year Is Gone
Johnny Paycheck; *45* ....(LDR)
On A Snowy Christmas Night
Elvis Presley; *Sings The Wonderful World Of
Christmas* ....(RCA)
On Christmas Eve
John Hartford; *Headin' Down Into The Mystery
Below* .... (FF)
Me Oh My-How The Time Does Fly-Anthology ...(FF)
On This Christmas Night
B.J. Thomas; *On This Christmas Night* ....(LIB)
One Bright Star
John Jarvis; *Sounds Of The Season* ....(MSP)
Nicolette Larson; *Have Yourself A Merry Little
Christmas* .... (RHI)
Tennessee Christmas ....(MSP)
One Little Christmas Tree
Stevie Wonder; *Motown Christmas* .... (MOT)
Pearls In The Snow
Michael Martin Murphey; *Cowboy Christmas* ..... (WB)
Pink Christmas
Leo Kottke; *Regards From Chuck Pink* ....(PRV)
Please Come Home For Christmas
Aaron Neville; *Soulful Christmas* .... (A&M)
Bon Jovi; *Very Special Christmas-#2* .... (A&M)
Charles Brown; *Billboard Greatest Christmas Hits* (RHI)
Eagles; *45* ....(ELE)
Freddy Fender; *Country Christmas* ....(MSP)
Merry Christmas From ....(MSP)
Tejano Country Christmas ....(ART)
James Brown; *Santa's Got A Brand New Bag* .... (RHI)
John Schneider; *Tennessee Christmas* ....(MSP)
Leon Rausch; *Rausch Touch* ....(STH)
Little Johnny Taylor; *It's Christmas Time Again* .. (STX)
Sawyer Brown; *Christmas For The '90s-#2* ....(LIB)
Family Christmas Treasury ....(LIB)
Postpone Christmas
Mutabaruka; *High Times All-Star Explosion* ......(ALG)
Pretty Paper
Don McLean; *Christmas* ....(CCB)
Christmas Country Classics-#1 ....(CCB)
Freddy Fender; *Country Christmas To Remember* (MSP)
Glen Campbell; *Merry Christmas* ....(LIB)
Randy Travis; *Old Time Christmas* ....(WB)
Roy Orbison; *All-Time Greatest Hits-#2* ....(MON)
Christmas Classics ....(RHI)
Legendary ....(SSP)
Willie Nelson; *Best Of Christmas* ....(RCA)
Country Christmas-#1 ....(RCA)
Hillbilly Holiday .... (RHI)
Nashville's Greatest Christmas Hits-#2 ....(COL)
Pretty Paper ....(COL)
Reindeer Boogie
Trisha Yearwood; *The Sweetest Gift* .... (MCA)
Remember Christmas
Harry Nilsson; *Son Of Schmilsson* ....(RCA)
Ridin' Home On Christmas Eve
Michael Martin Murphey; *Cowboy Christmas* .... (WB)
Rockin' Around The Christmas Tree
Amy Grant; *Home For Christmas* .... (A&M)
Bill Haley/Comets; *Legends Of Christmas Past-Rock &
R&B* .... (EMI)

Brenda Lee; *Billboard's Greatest Christmas Hits* .. (RHI)
   Christmas Classics .... (RHI)
   Country Christmas To Remember .... (MSP)
Cajun Gold; *Alligator Stomp-#4-Cajun Christmas* (RHI)
Eddie Rabbitt; *Christmas For The '90s-#1* .... (LIB)
Forester Sisters; *Christmas Card* .... (WB)
Lynn Anderson; *Greatest Children's Christmas
Hits* ....(COL)
Ronnie Spector & Darlene Love; *Very Special
Christmas* .... (A&M)
Rockin' Little Christmas
Deborah Allen; *Country Christmas-#3* ....(RCA)
   Season's Greetings ....(RCA)
Rockin' "J" Bells
Bobby Rey; *45* .... (OSR)
Rudolph, The Red Nosed Reindeer
Al Hirt; *Sound Of Christmas* ....(RCA)
Bing Crosby; *Christmas* ....(MSP)
Burl Ives; *Have A Holly Jolly Christmas* ....(MSP)
Cadillacs; *Billboard's Greatest R&B Christmas Hits* (RHI)
Cheech & Chong; *45* .... (EOD)
Conway Twitty; *Merry Twismas From C.T. & Little
Friends* .... (WB)
Crystals; *Back To Mono-1958-1969* .... (AKO)
   Christmas Gift For You From Phil Spector ...... (RHI)
   Phil Spector's Christmas Album .... (PAS)
Dean Martin; *Best Of Christmas* ....(CAP)
   Christmas All-Time Greatest Records ....(CCB)
Dolly Parton; *Home For Christmas* ....(COL)
Ernest Tubb; *Country Christmas To Remember* ...(MSP)
Gene Autry; *16 Most Requested Songs Of
Christmas* ....(COL)
   Billboard's Greatest Christmas Hits .... (RHI)
   Greatest Children's Christmas Hits ....(COL)
Hank Thompson/Brazos Valley Boys; *Christmas On The
Range-Cowboy Classics* ....(CAP)
Jackson 5; *Christmas Album* ....(MOT)
Johnny Mathis; *Christmas With* ....(COL)
Lena Horne; *Merry Christmas Baby-Romance &
Reindeer* ....(CAP)
Merle Haggard; *Goin' Home For Christmas* .... (EPI)
Riders In The Sky; *Merry Christmas From Harmony
Ranch* ....(COL)
Spike Jones; *It's A Spike Jones Christmas* .... (RHI)
Stephanie Mills; *Christmas* ....(MCA)
Temptations; *Christmas Card* ....(MOT)
   Motown Christmas ....(MOT)
Run Rudolph Run
Bryan Adams; *Very Special Christmas* .... (A&M)
Chuck Berry; *Billboard's Greatest R&B Christmas
Hits* .... (RHI)
   Chess Box .... (CSS)
   Have A Merry Chess Christmas ....(MSP)
   Rhythm & Blues Christmas-#1 ....(CLT)
Southern Pacific; *Warner Bros. Records Christmas
Tradition* .... (WB)
Sailing Home For Christmas
Doug Stone; *First Christmas* .... (EPI)
Same Old Lang Syne
Dan Fogelberg; *Greatest Hits* .... (FM)
   Innocent Age .... (FM)
   Live-Greetings From The West .... (FM)
Santa And The Satellite
Dickie Goodman; *Dr. Demento's Greatest-#6* .... (RHI)
Santa Baby
Charmaine Neville; *Christmas In New Orleans-R&B Jazz
Gospel* ....(MG)
Eartha Kitt; *Billboard's Greatest Christmas Hits* .. (RHI)
   Hipster's Holiday-Vocal Jazz & R&B .... (RHI)
Madonna; *Very Special Christmas* .... (A&M)
Santa Claus
Throwing Muses; *Hunkpapa* .... (SIR)
Santa Claus And Popcorn
Merle Haggard; *Christmas Gift* ....(CCB)
   Goin' Home For Christmas .... (EPI)
Santa Claus Blues
Louis Armstrong & King Oliver; *Louis Armstrong &
King Oliver* .... (MS)
Walter Davis; *Cripple Clarence Lofton & Walter
Davis* ....(YAZ)
Santa Claus Came In The Spring
Benny Goodman; *Birth Of Swing* .... (BLU)

Santa Claus Goes Straight To The Ghetto
James Brown; *Christmas Classics* .... (RHI)
   Cool Yule .... (RHI)
   Santa's Got A Brand New Bag .... (RHI)
Santa Claus Is Back In Town
Dwight Yoakam; *Warner Bros. Records Christmas
Tradition* .... (WB)
Elvis Presley; *Christmas Album* ....(RCA)
   Memories Of Christmas ....(RCA)
   Sings Leiber & Stoller ....(RCA)
Trisha Yearwood; *The Sweetest Gift* ....(MCA)
Santa Claus Is Coming For Christmas...
Eddy Raven; *Country Christmas-#4* ....(RCA)
Santa Claus Is Comin' To Town
Beach Boys; *Christmas Album* ....(CAP)
Bing Crosby/Andrews Sisters; *Merry Christmas* ..(MSP)
Booker T./M.G.s; *In The Christmas Spirit* ....(ATL)
Boston Pops Orchestra/Arthur Fiedler; *Pop Goes
Christmas* ....(RCA)
   This Is Christmas ....(RCA)
Bruce Springsteen; *In Harmony 2* ....(COL)
Chipmunks; *Christmas With-#1* .... (EMI)
Crystals; *Back To Mono-1958-1969* .... (AKO)
   Phil Spector's Christmas Album .... (PAS)
David Grisman; *Acoustic Christmas* .... (ROU)
Dolly Parton; *Home For Christmas* ....(COL)
Eddie Fisher; *Christmas With* ....(MSP)
Eddy Arnold; *Christmas With* ....(RCA)
George Strait; *Christmas In The Country* ....(MSP)
   Merry Christmas Strait To You ....(MSP)
Hank Thompson/Brazos Valley Boys; *Christmas On The
Range-Cowboy Classics* ....(CAP)
Jackson 5; *Billboard's Greatest R&B Christmas
Hits* .... (RHI)
Johnny Mercer; *Christmas Kisses-Capitol's Early
Years* ....(CAP)
Loretta Lynn; *Christmas Without Daddy* ....(MSP)
Louis Armstrong & Pete Fountain; *Christmas In New
Orleans* ....(MSP)
Michael Martin Murphey; *Warner Bros. Christmas
Tradition-#2* .... (WB)
Neil Diamond; *Christmas Album* ....(COL)
Patti Page; *16 Most Requested Songs Of
Christmas* ....(COL)
Pointer Sisters; *Very Special Christmas* .... (A&M)
Randy Travis; *An Old Time Christmas* .... (WB)
Temptations; *Christmas Card* ....(MOT)
Ventures; *Christmas Album* .... (EMI)
Whispers; *Happy Holidays To You* .... (SLR)
Santa Claus Schottische
Michael Martin Murphey; *Cowboy Christmas* ..... (WB)
Santa Claus Wants Some Lovin'
Albert King; *It's Christmas Time Again* .... (STX)
Mack Rice; *It's Christmas Time Again* .... (STX)
Santa Claus & His Old Lady
Cheech & Chong; *Dr. Demento Greatests Christmas
CD* .... (RHI)
   Dr. Demento's Greatest-#6 .... (RHI)
Santa Claus (I Still Believe In You)
Alabama; *Christmas* ....(RCA)
   Season's Greetings ....(RCA)
Santa Claus' Daughter
Charlie Rich; *Complete Smash Sessions* .... (MER)
Santa Doesn't Cop Out On Dope
Martin Mull; *45* ....(CPC)
Santa Done Got Hip
Marquees; *Cool Yule* .... (RHI)
   Hipster's Holiday-Vocal Jazz & R&B .... (RHI)
Santa Looked A Lot Like Daddy
Buck Owens; *All-Star Country Christmas* ....(CAP)
   Billboard's Great Country Christmas Hits .... (RHI)
   Christmas With ....(CCB)
   Hillbilly Holiday .... (RHI)
   /Buckaroos; Merry Hee Haw Christmas ....(CAP)
Garth Brooks; *Beyond The Season* ....(LIB)
Travis Tritt; *Christmas-Loving Time Of The Year* .. (WB)
Santa Must Be Polish
Bobby Vinton; *Great Songs Of Christmas* ....(CCB)
Santa & The Kids
Charley Pride; *Country Christmas-#3* ....(RCA)
Santafly
Martin Mull; *45* ....(CPC)

Santa, Are You Coming To Atlanta
Pake McEntire; *Country Christmas-#4* ....(RCA)
  Season's Greetings ....(RCA)
Santa's Beard
Beach Boys; *Christmas Album* ....(CAP)
Santa's Got A Brand New Bag
Murphy's Law; *Best Of Times* ....(REL)
Senor Santa Claus
Jim Reeves; *Twelve Songs Of Christmas* ....(RCA)
Silent Night
Aaron Neville; *Soulful Christmas* ....(A&M)
Anne Murray; *Christmas Wishes* ....(LIB)
Baby Washington; *Legends Of Christmas Past-Rock &*
  R&B ....(EMI)
  Only Those In Love ....(CLT)
Barbra Streisand; *Christmas Album* ....(COL)
  Happening In Central Park ....(COL)
  Just For The Record ....(COL)
Be Be & Ce Ce Winans; *Christmas* ....(SPW)
Bing Crosby; *Christmas Sing With Bing* ....(MSP)
Boston Pops Orchestra/Arthur Fiedler; *Christmas*
  Festival ....(RCA)
  Pop Goes Christmas ....(RCA)
B.J. Thomas; *All Is Calm All Is Bright* ....(COL)
Carpenters; *Christmas Portrait* ....(A&M)
Connie Francis; *Christmas In My Heart* ....(POL)
Cristy Lane; *White Christmas* ....(ARR)
Dinah Washington; *Have Yourself A Jazzy Little*
Christmas ....(VRV)
Dr. John; *Have Yourself A Merry Little Christmas* (RHI)
Ella Fitzgerald; *Christmas* ....(CAP)
Elvis Presley; *Blue Christmas* ....(RCA)
  Christmas Album ....(RCA)
Emmylou Harris; *Light Of The Stable* ....(WB)
Engelbert Humperdinck; *Merry Christmas With* ...(EPI)
Frank Sinatra; *Jolly Christmas From* ....(CAP)
Garth Brooks; *Beyond The Season* ....(LIB)
  Christmas For The '90s-#2 ....(LIB)
  Family Christmas Treasury ....(LIB)
Gary Morris; *Every Christmas* ....(LIB)
Glen Campbell; *Merry Christmas* ....(LIB)
Huey "Piano" Smith/Clowns; *Best Of Cool Yule* . (RHI)
Impressions; *Funky Christmas* ....(COT)
James Galway/Royal Philharmonic; *James Galway's*
Christmas Carol ....(RCA)
Jim Hendricks; *Handcrafted Christmas* ....(BEN)
Joan Baez; *Noel* ....(VAN)
John Denver; *Rocky Mountain Christmas* ....(RCA)
John Schneider; *White Christmas* ....(SCO)
Johnny Cash; *Christmas Spirit* ....(COL)
  Classic Christmas ....(COL)
Judds; *Christmas Time With* ....(RCA)
Julie Andrews; *16 Most Requested Songs Of*
Christmas ....(COL)
Kenny Rogers & Dolly Parton; *Once Upon A*
Christmas ....(RCA)
La Diferenzia; *Tejano Country Christmas* ....(ART)
Mahalia Jackson; *Best Of* ....(KEN)
  Christmas With ....(SPM)
Mannheim Steamroller; *Christmas* ....(AG)
Mantovani; *Christmas Favorites* ....(LON)
Merle Haggard; *Christmas Gift* ....(CCB)
Michael W. Smith; *Smith* ....(WOR)
Mormon Tabernacle Choir; *Joy To The World* ...(COL)
  Sings ....(COL)
Nat King Cole; *Christmas Song* ....(CAP)
Neil Diamond; *Christmas Album* ....(COL)
Oak Ridge Boys; *Christmas* ....(MCA)
Phil Spector & Artists; *Back To*
Mono-1958-1969 ....(AKO)
Philadelphia Orchestra/Eugene Ormandy; *Joy To The*
World ....(RCA)
Reba McEntire; *Merry Christmas To You* ....(MSP)
Ronnie Milsap; *Christmas With* ....(RCA)
Sister Rosetta Tharpe; *Billboard Greatest R&B Christmas*
Hits ....(RHI)
Special EFX; *GRP Christmas Collection* ....(GRP)
Stanley Jordan; *Standards-#1* ....(BLN)
  Yule Struttin' ....(BLN)
Stevie Nicks; *Very Special Christmas* ....(A&M)
Tanya Tucker; *Country Christmas Favorites* ......(COL)
Temptations; *Christmas Card* ....(MOT)
  Motown Christmas ....(MOT)
Vienna Boys Choir; *Vienna Boys Choir* ....(RCA)

Waylon Jennings & Jessi Colter; *Best Of*
Christmas ....(RCA)
Wayne Newton; *Best Of Christmas* ....(CAP)
Wilson Phillips; *Very Special Christmas-#2* ......(A&M)
Zaca Creek; *Voices Of The Season (A Capella)* ...(EPI)
Silver Bells
Atlantic Starr; *ST/Home Alone 2-Lost In New*
York ....(FOX)
Bob Wills; *Fiddle* ....(CMF)
Booker T./M.G.s; *Soul Christmas* ....(ATL)
Brenda Lee; *Christmas* ....(WB)
Diana Ross/Supremes; *Merry Christmas* ....(MOT)
Earl Grant; *Winter Wonderland* ....(MSP)
Elvis Presley; *Memories Of Christmas* ....(RCA)
  Sings The Wonderful World Of Christmas ......(RCA)
Gary Morris; *Every Christmas* ....(LIB)
John Denver; *Rocky Mountain Christmas* ....(RCA)
Johnny Mathis/Percy Faith & Orchestra; *Merry*
Christmas ....(COL)
Judds; *Christmas Time With* ....(RCA)
Kenny Rogers; *Christmas In America* ....(RPR)
Kevin Eubanks; *GRP Christmas Collection* ....(GRP)
Lacy J. Dalton; *Christmas For The '90s-#1* ....(LIB)
Loretta Lynn; *Christmas Without Daddy* ....(MSP)
Margaret Whiting & Jimmy Wakely; *Christmas On The*
Range-Cowboy Classics ....(CAP)
Merle Haggard; *Christmas Gift* ....(CCB)
Miracles; *Christmas With* ....(MOT)
Mormon Tabernacle Choir; *White Christmas* .....(COL)
Oak Ridge Boys; *Christmas* ....(MSP)
Perry Como; *I Wish It Could Be Christmas*
Forever ....(RCA)
Ray Price; *Christmas Gift For You From* ....(SO)
Roches; *We Three Kings* ....(MSP)
Ronnie Milsap; *Christmas With* ....(RCA)
Stevie Wonder; *Someday At Christmas* .... (MOT)
Travis Tritt; *Christmas-Loving Time Of The Year* ..(WB)
Sleigh Ride
Amy Grant; *Christmas Album* ....(WOR)
Andy Williams; *16 Most Requested Songs Of*
Christmas ....(COL)
A-Strings; *Home For Christmas* ....(WB)
Boston Pops Orchestra/Arthur Fiedler; *Christmas*
Festival ....(DGG)
  Pops Go Christmas ....(RCA)
Carpenters; *Christmas Portrait* ....(A&M)
Chipmunks; *Rockin' Through The Decades* ....(EMI)
Commodores; *Christmas* ....(CMO)
Debbie Gibson; *Very Special Christmas-#2* ....(A&M)
Doc Severinsen/Tonight Show Orchestra; *Merry*
Christmas From ....(AMH)
Eddie Daniels; *GRP Christmas Collection* ....(GRP)
Jack Jones; *Christmas All-Time Greatest*
Records-#2 ....(CCB)
London Symphony Orchestra; *Christmas*
Traditions ....(SPM)
Mel Torme; *Christmas Songs* ....(TLR)
Ronettes; *Back To Mono-1958-1969* ....(AKO)
  Christmas Gift For You From Phil Spector ......(RHI)
  Phil Spector's Christmas Album ....(PAS)
Snoopy's Christmas
Royal Guardsmen; *Snoopy & His Friends* ....(LAU)
Sock It To Me Santa
Bud Logan; *Cool Yule* ....(RHI)
Some Children See Him
Dave Grusin; *GRP Christmas Collection* ....(GRP)
Debby Boone; *Home For Christmas* ....(BEN)
Evie Tornquist; *Come On Ring Those Bells* ......(WOR)
Tennessee Ernie Ford; *Star Carol* ....(CAP)
Somebody Talkin' About Jesus
Kathy Mattea; *Good News* .... (MER)
Someday At Christmas
Jackson 5; *Christmas Album* ....(MOT)
Stevie Wonder; *Christmas Classics* .... (RHI)
  Christmas Hits ....(MSP)
  Motown Christmas ....(MOT)
  Someday At Christmas ....(MOT)
Temptations; *Christmas Card* ....(MOT)
Step Into Christmas
Elton John; *Rockin' Christmas* ....(MSP)
Sweet Little Jesus Boy
Anne Murray; *Christmas* ....(LIB)
Boys Choir Of Harlem; *Christmas Carols & Sacred*
Songs ....(BLN)

Trisha Yearwood; *The Sweetest Gift* .... (MCA)
Sweetest Gift, The
Trisha Yearwood; *The Sweetest Gift* .... (MCA)
Take A Walk Through Bethlehem
Trisha Yearwood; *The Sweetest Gift* .... (MCA)
Tennessee Christmas
Alabama; *Christmas* .... (RCA)
Amy Grant; *Christmas Album* .... (WOR)
Lee Greenwood; *Christmas To Christmas* .... (MSP)
Steve Wariner; *Country Christmas To Remember* . (MSP)
Tennessee Christmas .... (MSP)
Thank God For Kids
Oak Ridge Boys; *Christmas* .... (MSP)
Christmas For The '90s-#1 .... (LIB)
Collection .... (MCA)
Greatest Hits-#2 .... (MCA)
Thank God It's Christmas
Queen; *Queen Collection* ....(HOL)
There Ain't No Santa Claus On The...
Captain Beefheart; *Spotlight Kid/Clear Spot* ...... (RPR)
There's A New Kid In Town
Kathy Mattea; *Good News* .... (MER)
Trisha Yearwood; *The Sweetest Gift* .... (MCA)
This Christmas
Alexander O'Neal; *My Gift To You* .... (TAB)
Donny Hathaway; *Best Of* ....(ATC)
Soul Christmas .... (ATL)
Gloria Estefan; *Christmas Through Your Eyes* ..... (EPI)
Jets; *Christmas With* .... (MCA)
Rula Brown; *Reggae Christmas* .... (PRO)
Stephanie Mills; *Christmas* .... (MCA)
Temptations; *Give Love At Christmas* .... (MOT)
Yutaka; *GRP Christmas Collection* .... (GRP)
This Is The Way Christmas Ought To Be
Disney Players; *Christmas Carol* .... (DIS)
Thistlehair The Christmas Bear
Alabama; *Christmas* ....(RCA)
To Heck With Ole Santa Claus
Loretta Lynn; *Country Christmas* .... (MCA)
Hillbilly Holiday .... (RHI)
Tonight Is Christmas
Alabama; *Christmas* ....(RCA)
'Twas The Night Before Christmas
Chipmunks; *TV Family Christmas* .... (SCO)
Liberace; *Best Of Music* .... (SPM)
Peter, Paul & Mary/N.Y. Choral Society; *Holiday*
Celebration .... (WB)
Wynton Marsalis; *Crescent City Christmas Card* ..(COL)
Twelve Days Of Christmas
Allan Sherman; *Christmas Comedy Classics-#2* ... (PRY)
Dr. Demento's Greatest-#6 .... (RHI)
Andrews Sisters; *Christmas* .... (MSP)
Bing Crosby; *That Christmas Feeling* .... (MSP)
Bob & Doug McKenzie; *Dr. Demento Greatest*
Christmas CD .... (RHI)
David Seville; *Christmas With The Chipmunks-#2* (EMI)
Fred Waring; *Now Is The Caroling Season* ...... (CAP)
Harry Belafonte; *Christmas Classics-#2* .... (RCA)
Joan Sutherland; *Christmas Stars* .... (LON)
Kiri Te Kanawa; *Christmas With* .... (LON)
Ray Conniff; *Christmas Carolling* .... (COL)
Twelve Days To Christmas
Original Cast; *She Loves Me* .... (POL)
Twelve Pains Of Christmas
Bob Rivers Comedy Corp.; *Twisted Christmas* ... (CRI)
Up On The House Top
Michael Jackson/Jackson 5; *45* .... (MOT)
We Have Love
Mickey Mouse (As Bob Cratchit); *Christmas Carol* (DIS)
We Need A Little Christmas
Angela Lansbury; *16 Most Requested Songs Of*
Christmas ....(COL)
Johnny Mathis; *Christmas Music With-Personal*
Collection .... (COL)
Original Cast; *Mame* ....(COL)
Percy Faith/Orchestra; *Yuletide Cheer* ....(COL)
We Three Kings Of Orient Are
Adrian Belew; *Christmas Guitars* .... (GRE)
Barbara Higbie; *Winter's Solstice* .... (WH)
Beach Boys; *Christmas Album* ....(CAP)
Gary Morris; *Every Christmas* .... (LIB)
Jimmy Smith; *Christmas Cookin'* ....(VRV)
Leontyne Price; *Christmas Stars* .... (LON)
Mannheim Steamroller; *Christmas* .... (AG)

Mojo Nixon/Toadliquors; *Horny Holidays!* ...... (XXX)
Philadelphia Orchestra/Eugene Ormandy; *Greatest*
Christmas Hits ....(COL)
Greatest Hits Of Christmas ....(RCA)
Robert Shaw Chorale; *Festival Of Carols* ....(RCA)
Wynton Marsalis; *Crescent City Christmas Card* ..(COL)
We Wish You A Merry Christmas
David Grisman; *Acoustic Christmas* .... (ROU)
Floyd Cramer; *We Wish You A Merry Christmas* .(RCA)
Mormon Tabernacle Choir; *Joy To The World* ...(COL)
Perry Como; *I Wish It Could Be Christmas*
Forever ....(RCA)
Peter, Paul & Mary/N.Y. Choral Society; *Holiday*
Celebration .... (WB)
Raffi; *Christmas Album* ....(SHO)
Tony Bennett; *Snowfall/Christmas Album* ....(COL)
Weavers; *We Wish You A Merry Christmas* ...... (MSP)
What Are You Doing New Year's Eve
Carpenters; *Old Fashioned Christmas* .... (A&M)
Gladys Knight/Pips; *That Special Time Of Year* ..(COL)
Harry Connick, Jr.; *When My Heart Finds*
Christmas ....(COL)
King Curtis; *Soul Christmas* .... (ATL)
Lena Horne; *Happy Holidays-Capitol Sings*
Christmas ....(CAP)
Lou Rawls; *Merry Christmas Ho! Ho! Ho!* ....(CAP)
Nancy Wilson; *Yesterday's Love Songs...Today's*
Blues .... (BLN)
Sonny Til/Orioles; *Doo Wop Christmas* .... (RHI)
Rhythm & Blues Christmas-#1 .... (CLT)
What Child Is This
Al Martino; *Best Of Christmas* .... (CAP)
Bing Crosby; *Christmas Classics* .... (CAP)
Boston Pops Orchestra/Arthur Fiedler; *Pop Goes*
Christmas ....(RCA)
David Benoit; *Christmastime* .... (BM)
Garth Brooks; *Beyond The Season* .... (LIB)
Glen Campbell; *Home For The Holidays* .... (BEN)
Glenn Medeiros; *Christmas Album* .... (AMH)
Harry Connick, Jr.; *When My Heart Finds*
Christmas ....(COL)
John Anderson; *Sounds Of The Season* .... (BNA)
John Denver; *Rocky Mountain High* ....(RCA)
Judds; *Christmas Time With* ....(RCA)
Kathie Lee Gifford; *It's Christmas Time* .... (WB)
Larry Coryell; *Christmas Guitars* .... (GRE)
Mormon Tabernacle Choir; *Holly & The Ivy* ....(COL)
Sings ....(COL)
Roberta Flack; *Our Christmas* .... (WOR)
Tanya Tucker; *Christmas For The '90s-#2* ...... (LIB)
Family Christmas Treasury .... (LIB)
Vanessa Williams; *Very Special Christmas-#2* ... (A&M)
Vince Gill; *Let There Be Peace On Earth* .... (MCA)
Vince Guaraldi; *Charlie Brown Christmas* .... (FAN)
What Christmas Means To Me
Al Green; *White Christmas* .... (MYR)
Paul Young; *Very Special Christmas* .... (A&M)
Stevie Wonder; *Motown Christmas* .... (MOT)
Someday At Christmas .... (MOT)
What Do The Lonely Do At Christmas
Emotions; *It's Christmas Time Again* .... (STX)
When It's Christmas Time In Texas
Rick Orozco; *Tejano Country Christmas* ....(ART)
When The Rain Turns To Snow
Lee Greenwood; *Christmas To Christmas* .... (MSP)
When The Stars Come Out For Christmas
Commodores; *Christmas* ....(CMO)
While Shepherds Watched Their Flocks
Fred Bock; *25 Piano Christmas Carols* .... (BEN)
Jim Hendricks; *20 Appalachian Christmas Carols* (BEN)
Mormon Tabernacle Choir; *Holly & The Ivy* .....(COL)
Spirit Of Christmas ....(COL)
White Christmas
Aaron Neville; *Soulful Christmas* .... (A&M)
Baby Washington; *Only Those In Love* .... (CLT)
Barbra Streisand; *Christmas Album* ....(COL)
Beach Boys; *Christmas Album* .... (CAP)
Billy Squier; *45* .... (CAP)
Bing Crosby; *Billboard's Greatest Christmas Hits* . (RHI)
Sings Christmas Songs .... (MSP)
Boston Pops Orchestra/Arthur Fiedler; *Christmas*
Treasures ....(RCA)
Boys Choir Of Harlem; *Christmas Carols & Sacred*
Songs .... (BLN)

Carpenters; *From The Top* .... (A&M)
Darlene Love; *Back To Mono-1958-1969* ..... (AKO)
  Christmas Gift For You From Phil Spector ...... (RHI)
  Phil Spector's Christmas Album .... (PAS)
Diana Ross/Supremes; *Merry Christmas* .... (MOT)
Dion; *Rock & Roll Christmas* .... (RIT)
Dolly Parton; *Christmas Classics-#1* .... (RCA)
Don McLean; *Christmas* .... (CCB)
Donna Summer; *Christmas Spirit* .... (MER)
Drifters; *Billboard's Greatest Christmas Hits* ..... (RHI)
  Christmas Classics .... (RHI)
  ST/Home Alone .... (COL)
  Their Greatest Recordings .... (ATC)
Earl Thomas Conley; *Season's Greetings* .... (RCA)
Elvis Presley; *Christmas Album* .... (RCA)
Ernest Tubb; *Billboard's Great Country Christmas*
  Hits .... (RHI)
Faron Young; *Country Christmas* .... (SO)
Frank Sinatra; *Christmas Album* .... (COL)
Garth Brooks; *Beyond The Season* .... (LIB)
George Strait; *Christmas In The Country* .... (MSP)
  Merry Christmas Strait To You .... (MSP)
Glen Campbell; *Merry Christmas* .... (LIB)
Gloria Estefan; *Christmas Through Your Eyes* ..... (EPI)
Henry Mancini; *Merry Mancini Christmas* .... (RCA)
Jackie Wilson; *Merry Christmas From* .... (RHI)
Jimmy Smith; *Christmas Cookin'* .... (VRV)
Jo Stafford; *Puttin' On The Ritz-Capitol Sings*
  Berlin .... (CAP)
Johnny Mathis; *Christmas Music Of-Personal*
  Collection .... (COL)
J. Carreras/P. Domingo/L. Pavarotti; *Christmas*
  Favorites From World's Tenors .... (SMC)
Kathie Lee Gifford; *It's Christmas Time* .... (WB)
Kenny Rogers; *Christmas* .... (EMI)
Lee Ritenour; *GRP Christmas Collection* .... (GRP)
Lena Horne; *Merry From Lena* .... (EMI)
Loretta Lynn; *Christmas Without Daddy* .... (MSP)
  Country Christmas .... (MCA)
Mel Tillis; *Christmas On The General Jackson* .. (MER)
Merle Haggard; *Christmas Present* .... (CCB)
Michael Bolton; *Timeless-Classics* .... (COL)
  Very Special Christmas-#2 .... (A&M)
Neil Diamond; *Christmas Album* .... (COL)
Oak Ridge Boys; *Christmas* .... (MSP)
Otis Redding; *Story* .... (ATL)
  Ultimate R&B Christmas .... (RIT)
Reba McEntire; *Merry Christmas To You* .... (MSP)
Roger Williams; *Golden Christmas* .... (SPM)
Statues; *Doo Wop Christmas* .... (RHI)
Stephanie Mills; *Christmas* .... (MCA)
Tony Bennett; *16 Most Requested Songs Of*
  Christmas .... (COL)
  Essence Of Christmas .... (COL)
Vince Gill; *Let There Be Peace On Earth* .... (MCA)
Wayne Newton; *Merry Christmas From* .... (CCB)
Wesley Tuttle; *Christmas On The Range-Cowboy*
  Classics .... (CAP)
White Christmas Makes Me Blue
  Randy Travis; *An Old Time Christmas* .... (WB)
  Christmas Tradition .... (WB)
Who Do You Think
  Statler Brothers; *Christmas Card* .... (MER)
Who Is This Babe
  Judds; *Christmas Time With* .... (RCA)
  Country Christmas-#4 .... (RCA)
Who Took The Merry Out Of Christmas
  Staple Singers; *Bummed Out Christmas* .... (RHI)
  Complete Stax/Volt Soul Singles-#2 .... (STX)
  It's Christmas Time Again .... (STX)
Who Would Have Thought
  Boyz II Men; *Christmas Interpretations* .... (MOT)
Whose Birthday Is Christmas
  Statler Brothers; *Christmas Present* .... (MER)
Why Christmas
  Boyz II Men; *Christmas Interpretations* .... (MOT)
Why Do The Nations So Furiously Rage
  Al Jarreau; *Handel's Messiah-Soulful Celebration* .. (WB)
Winter Wonderland
  Alexander O'Neal; *My Gift To You* .... (TAB)
  Amy Grant; *Home For Christmas* .... (A&M)
  Andrews Sisters; *Christmas* .... (MSP)
  Aretha Franklin; *Rock 'N' Roll Christmas Classics* (MFL)

Barbara Mandrell; *Christmas At Our House* ...... (MSP)
  Tennessee Christmas .... (MCA)
Bing Crosby; *Christmas Classics* .... (CAP)
Blue Notes; *Rhythm & Blues Christmas-#1* ...... (CLT)
Brenda Lee; *Jingle Bell Rock* .... (MSP)
Carnie & Wendy Wilson; *Hey Santa!* .... (SBK)
Carpenters; *Christmas Portrait* .... (A&M)
Darlene Love; *Back To Mono-1958-1969* ..... (AKO)
  Christmas Gift For You From Phil Spector ...... (RHI)
  Phil Spector's Christmas Album .... (PAS)
Eddy Arnold; *Christmas With* .... (RCA)
Elvis Presley; *Sings The Wonderful World Of*
  Christmas .... (RCA)
Eurythmics; *Very Special Christmas* .... (A&M)
Faron Young; *Country Christmas* .... (SO)
George Strait; *Merry Christmas Strait To You* .... (MSP)
Hank Crawford; *We Got A Good Thing Going* .. (KDU)
Johnny Mercer/Pied Pipers; *Merry Christmas*
  Baby-Romance & Reindeer .... (CAP)
Kathie Lee Gifford; *It's Christmas Time* .... (WB)
Kenny Rogers; *Christmas In America* .... (RPR)
London Symphony Orchestra; *Christmas*
  Traditions .... (SPM)
Merle Haggard; *Christmas Present* .... (CCB)
Randy Travis; *An Old Time Christmas* .... (WB)
Robert Goulet; *Essence Of Christmas* .... (A&M)
Roger Whittaker; *World's Most Beautiful Christmas*
  Songs .... (LIB)
Tanya Tucker; *Christmas For The '90s-#1* .... (LIB)
Travis Tritt; *Christmas-Loving Time Of The Year* .. (WB)
Wonderful Christmastime
  Wings; *Back To The Egg* .... (CAP)
Wonderful World Of Christmas
  Elvis Presley; *Sings The Wonderful World Of*
  Christmas .... (RCA)
Wreck The Halls With Boughs Of Holly
  Three Stooges; *Christmas Time With* .... (RHI)
  Dr. Demento's Greatest-#6 .... (RHI)
X-Mas Shopping Blues
  Christmas Jug Band; *Mistletoe Jam* .... (RLX)
Yah Das Ist Ein Christmas Tree
  Mel Blanc; *Christmas Comedy Classics-#2* .... (PRY)
  Christmas Kisses-CApitol's Early Years .... (CAP)
Yingle Bells
  Yogi Yorgesson; *45* .... (CAP)
Yo Ho Ho
  Klark Kent; *Just In Time For Christmas* .... (IRS)
You Are My Christmas
  Bobby Bland; *45* .... (MCA)
You Know It's Christmas
  Larry Farrow; *45* .... (CAP)
You Make It Feel Like Christmas
  Neil Diamond; *Christmas Album* .... (COL)
  Primitive .... (COL)
You're All I Want For Christmas
  Al Martino; *Merry Christmas Baby-Romance &*
  Reindeer .... (CAP)
  Bing Crosby; *Sings Christmas Songs* .... (MCA)
  That Christmas Feeling .... (MCA)
  Brook Benton; *Best Of Christmas* .... (SPM)
  Merry Christmas .... (SPM)
  Jackie Gleason; *'Tis The Season* .... (CAP)
Zat You Santa?
  Louis Armstrong; *Soul Of Christmas-#2* .... (MAL)

CIGARETTES, Smoking, Tobacco
  See Also: FIRE

90 Minute Cigarette
  John Hart; *Blue Guitar* .... (BLN)
Another Cup Of Coffee & A Cigarette
  Robbin Thompson; *Robbin Thompson* .... (NEM)
Another Pack Of Cigarettes...
  Marty Robbins; *The Performer* .... (COL)
Ashtray Blues
  Papa Charlie Jackson; *Papa Charlie Jackson* ..... (BIO)
Ashtray Heart
  Captain Beefheart; *Doc At The Radar Station* ..... (BP)
Ashtray Taxi
  Sam Chatmon; *Sam Chatmon's Advice* .... (ROU)
Can I Have A Smoke, Dude?
  Mary's Danish; *Edge Of Rock* .... (ERA)
  There Goes The Wondertruck... .... (CML)

Cigarette
Smithereens; *Especially For You* .... (ENI)
Cigarette Motel
Leaving Trains; *Kill Tunes* .... (SST)
Cigarette Of A Single Man
Squeeze; *Babylon & On* .... (A&M)
Cigarettes
City Boys; *Book Early* .... (MER)
Cigarettes & Coffee
Otis Redding; *Best Of* .... (ATC)
   Best Of .... (ATL)
   Story .... (ATL)
Cowboy Serenade (While I'm Rollin'...)
Glenn Miller/Orchestra; *Complete* .... (BLU)
Dim Lights Thick Smoke & Loud Loud Music
Flatt & Scruggs; *Golden Era* .... (ROU)
Flying Burrito Brothers; *Close Encounters Of The West*
   Coast .... (RLX)
   Farther Along-Best Of .... (A&M)
Don't Smoke In Bed
Nina Simone; *Finest Of* .... (BET)
   In Concert/I Put A Spell On You .... (MER)
Peggy Lee; *Capitol Collectors Series-#1-Early*
   Years .... (CAP)
   Greatest .... (CAP)
Flowers On The Wall
Statler Brothers; *Best Of The* .... (MER)
   Billboard Top Country Hits-1966 .... (RHI)
   Columbia Country Classics-#3 .... (COL)
   Pop Classics/'60s .... (COL)
Fool About A Cigarette
Tom Ball/Kenny Sultan; *Bloodshot Eyes* .... (FF)
Fool For A Cigarette
Ry Cooder; *Paradise & Lunch* .... (RPR)
Have A Cigar
Pink Floyd; *Wish You Were Here* .... (COL)
I'm Down To My Last Cigarette
k.d. lang; *Shadowland* .... (SIR)
Last Cigarette
Dramarama; *Live At The China Club* .... (CML)
   Stuck In Wonderamaland .... (CML)
Lipstick Traces
Amazing Rhythm Aces; *Amazing Rhythm Aces* .. (MCA)
Benny Spellman; *History Of New Orleans*
   R&B-#3-1962-1970 .... (RHI)
   It Will Stand-Minit Records 1960-1963 .... (EMI)
O'Jays; *Soul Shots-#10-More Sweet Soul* .... (RHI)
Ringo Starr; *Bad Boy* .... (POR)
Long Drag Off A Cigarette
Joe Cocker; *Civilized Man* .... (CAP)
Miles Is A Cigarette
Chris Rea; *espresso logic* .... (EW)
Nicotine Stain
Siouxsie/Banshees; *The Scream* .... (GEF)
One Paper Kid
Emmylou Harris; *Quarter Moon In A Ten-Cent*
   Town .... (WB)
Papa Rolled His Own
Tommy James/Shondells; *Crimson & Clover/Cellophane*
   Symphony .... (RHI)
Papirossen (Cigarettes)
Gordon Jenkins; *Soul Of A People* .... (BAI)
Peace Pipe
Cry Of Love; *Brother* .... (COL)
Edgar Winter; *Entrance* .... (EPI)
Pope On A Rope (Cigarette Butt)
Squirrels; *What Gives?* .... (PL)
Roll Your Own
Hoyt Axton; *Southbound* .... (A&M)
Smoke Dreams (Chesterfield Supper Club)
Benny Goodman; *Complete-#3* .... (RCA)
   This Is-#2 .... (RCA)
Mildred Bailey; *Her Greatest* .... (COL)
Smoke From Your Cigarette
Belmonts; *45* .... (CLT)
Fabulons; *Harlem Holiday-New York R&B-#7* ... (CLT)
Lillian Leach/Mellows; *45* .... (CLT)
Smoke Rings
Django Reinhardt/Quintet; *Django 1935* .... (CRS)
Glen Gray; *Best Of The Big Bands* .... (COL)
Glen Gray/Casa Loma Orchestra; *ST/Wild At*
   Heart .... (POL)
Les Paul; *Legend & The Legacy-#1-4* .... (CAP)

Smoke (La Vie En Fumer)
Tubes; *Now* .... (A&M)
   What Do You Want From-Live .... (A&M)
Smoke! Smoke! Smoke!
Commander Cody/Lost Planet Airmen; *Country*
   Casanova .... (MCA)
   Too Much Fun-Best Of .... (MCA)
   We Got A Live One .... (WB)
Doc Watson; *Red Rocking Chair* .... (FF)
Merle Travis; *Johnny Gimble's Texas Honky-Tonk*
   Hits .... (CMH)
Tex Williams; *Birth Of A Dream-Capitol's Early*
   Hits .... (CAP)
   Dr. Demento's Greatest-#1-1940s & Before .... (RHI)
Smoke-Off
Shel Silverstein; *Songs & Stories* .... (PAR)
Smoking Cigarettes & Drinking Coffee...
Marty Robbins; *Essential-1951-1982* .... (COL)
Smokin' In The Boys' Room
Brownsville Station; *Hit Singles-1958-1977* ..... (ATL)
   Legends Of Rock Guitar-'70s .... (RHI)
   ST/Rock & Roll High School .... (SIR)
Motley Crue; *Decade Of Decadence* .... (ELE)
   Theatre Of Pain .... (ELE)
Smokin' Room
Randy Brown; *Check It Out* .... (STX)
Ronnie Milsap; *Star Spangled Country* .... (RCA)
Rufus; *Rags To Rufus* .... (MCA)
Talking Cancer Blues
Dave Van Ronk; *Inside* .... (FAN)
   Van Ronk .... (FAN)
Three Cigarettes In An Ashtray
k.d. lang; *New Tradition Sings The Old Tradition* . (WB)
k.d. lang/Reclines; *Angel With A Lariat* .... (SIR)
Patsy Cline; *20 Golden Pieces Of* .... (BLD)
   Patsy Cline .... (MCA)
   Stop Look & Listen .... (MCA)
   Walkin' Dreams-Her First Recordings-#1 .... (RHI)
Tobacco Box
Cumberland Three; *Songs Of The Civil War* ..... (RHI)
Tobacco Road
Dan Seals; *I Won't Be Blue Anymore* .... (EMI)
David Lee Roth; *Eat 'Em & Smile* .... (WB)
Edgar Winter; *Collection* .... (RHI)
   Roadwork .... (EPI)
Eric Burdon/Animals; *Greatest Hits* .... (ALL)
Jefferson Airplane; *Loves You* .... (RCA)
   Takes Off .... (RCA)
John D. Loudermilk; *Rockabilly Stars-#3* .... (EPI)
Junior Wells; *Best Of The Chicago Blues* .... (VAN)
   Comin' At You .... (VAN)
Lou Rawls; *Best From* .... (CAP)
   Greatest Hits .... (CCB)
   Legendary .... (BLN)
   Live .... (CAP)
Nashville Teens; *London Collector-Rock Invasion* (LON)
Rare Earth; *Get Ready* .... (MOT)
Steve Young; *Redneck Mothers* .... (RCA)
   Solo/Live .... (WAT)
Two Cigarettes In The Dark
Alberta Hunter; *Legendary-London Sessions* ..... (DRG)
Betty Carter; *'Round Midnight* .... (ATL)
When You Wish Upon A Fag
Leon Russell & Marc Benno; *Asylum Choir-#2* . (MCA)

CIRCLES, Deja Vu, Karma, Wheels
   See Also: LIFE

Always Come Back To You
Natasha's Brother; *Always Come Back To You* ... (ATL)
And On And On
Janet Jackson; *Any Time Any Place* .... (VIA)
Around & Around
38 Special; *38 Special* .... (A&M)
Animals; *Best Of* .... (AKO)
Chuck Berry; *Berry Is On Top* .... (CSS)
   Chess Box .... (CSS)
   ST/Hail! Hail! Rock 'N' Roll .... (MCA)
Grateful Dead; *One From The Vault* .... (GRD)
   Steal Your Face .... (GRD)
Rolling Stones; *12 x 5* .... (AKO)
   Love You Live .... (RS)

Back Where I Started
Box Of Frogs; *Box Of Frogs* .... (EPI)
Big Wheels In The Moonlight
Dan Seals; *Classics Collection-#2* .... (LIB)
  Greatest Hits .... (LIB)
  Rage On .... (LIB)
California Here I Come
Al Jolson; *Best Of* .... (MCA)
Circle
Big Head Todd/Monsters; *Sister Sweetly* .... (GIA)
Sarah McLachlan; *Fumbling Towards Ecstasy* .... (ARI)
Circle Dance
Bonnie Raitt; *Longing In Their Hearts* ....(CAP)
Circle Game
Buffy Sainte-Marie; *Best Of* .... (VAN)
  Fire & Fleet & Candlelight .... (VAN)
Ian & Sylvia; *Greatest Hits* .... (VAN)
Joni Mitchell; *Ladies Of The Canyon* .... (RPR)
  Miles Of Aisles .... (ASY)
Tom Rush; *Circle Game* .... (ELE)
  Classic Rush .... (ELE)
Circle In The Sand
Belinda Carlisle; *Heaven On Earth* .... (MCA)
Circle Is Small
Gordon Lightfoot; *Back Here On Earth* .... (UA)
  Endless Wire .... (WB)
Circle Of Friends
Ray Pillow; *20 Great Hits* .... (PLN)
  People Music .... (PLN)
Circle Of Hands
Uriah Heep; *Demons & Lizards* .... (MER)
  Live .... (MER)
Circle Of Life
Elton John; *ST/The Lion King* .... (DIS)
Circle Of One
Oleta Adams; *Circle Of One* ....(FON)
Circle Of Steel
Gordon Lightfoot; *Gord's Gold* .... (RPR)
  Sundown .... (RPR)
Circle Of Your Arms
Louis Armstrong; *Louis Armstrong* .... (EVR)
Circles
Arlo Guthrie & Pete Seeger; *Precious Friend* ...... (WB)
Atlantic Starr; *Classics-#10* .... (A&M)
  Secret Lovers-Best Of .... (A&M)
Captain & Tennille; *Greatest Hits* .... (A&M)
Harry Chapin; *Sniper & Other Love Songs* .... (ELE)
Pete Townshend; *Scoop* ....(ATC)
Who; *Two's Missing* .... (MCA)
Coming Around Again
Carly Simon; *Coming Around Again* .... (ARI)
Crazy Circles
Bad Company; *Desolation Angels* .... (SS)
Cycles
Frank Sinatra; *Cycles* .... (RPR)
  Greatest Hits-#2 .... (RPR)
Deja Vu
Crosby, Stills, Nash & Young; *Deja Vu* .... (ATL)
  So Far .... (ATL)
Dionne Warwick; *Dionne* .... (ARI)
  Perfect 10 III .... (ARI)
Iron Maiden; *Somewhere In Time* ....(CAP)
Statler Brothers; *Maple Street Memories* ...... (MER)
Teena Marie; *Compact Command Performances* .. (MOT)
  Greatest Hits .... (MOT)
  Wild & Peaceful .... (MOT)
Do It Again
Beach Boys; *Best Of* .... (RPR)
  Friends/20/20 ....(CAP)
  Made In The U.S.A. ....(CAP)
Judy Garland; *At Carnegie Hall* ....(CAP)
Kinks; *Come Dancing With-Best Of 1977-1986* .. (ARI)
  Word Of Mouth .... (ARI)
New Birth; *Golden Classics* .... (CLT)
Sarah Vaughan; *George Gershwin Songbook-#1* . (EMA)
Steely Dan; *Can't Buy A Thrill* .... (MCA)
  Classic Rock-#1 .... (MCA)
  Greatest Hits .... (MCA)
  ST/FM .... (MCA)
Don't Stop To Watch The Wheels
Doobie Brothers; *Minute By Minute* .... (WB)
Eternal Circle
Bob Dylan; *Bootleg Series-#1-3-1961-1989* ......(COL)

Everybody's Everything
Santana; *Greatest Hits* ....(COL)
  Santana ....(COL)
  Viva Santana! ....(COL)
Falling Again
Don Williams; *Especially For You* .... (MCA)
  Greatest Hits .... (MCA)
  I Believe In You .... (MCA)
Falling In Love Again
Linda Ronstadt; *Lush Life* .... (ASY)
Marlene Dietrich; *Best Of* ....(COL)
  Her Complete Decca Recordings .... (MCA)
Falling In Love (Uh-Oh)
Miami Sound Machine; *Primitive Love* .... (EPI)
Feel It Again
Honeymoon Suite; *Big Prize* .... (WB)
Full Circle
Jeff Healey Band; *Hell To Pay* .... (ARI)
Going In Circles
Friends Of Distinction; *Golden Classics* .... (CLT)
  Soul Hits/'70s-#1 .... (RHI)
Gap Band; 7 .... (TE)
Luther Vandross; *Songs* .... (EPI)
Heart Like A Wheel
Linda Ronstadt; *Heart Like A Wheel* ....(CAP)
Steve Miller Band; *Circle Of Love* ....(CAP)
Here I Go Again
Force MD's; *Chillin'* .... (TMB)
Hollies; *Best Of* .... (EMI)
  Greatest Hits ....(CAP)
Robbie Nevil; *Place Like This* .... (EMI)
Smokey Robinson/Miracles; *Anthology* .... (MOT)
  Time Out For/Special Occasion .... (MOT)
Whitesnake; *Saints & Sinners* .... (GEF)
  Whitesnake .... (GEF)
Here We Go Again!
Portrait; *Portrait* ....(CAP)
Human Wheels
John Mellencamp; *Human Wheels* .... (MER)
I Get Around
Beach Boys; *Best Of* ....(CAP)
  Billboard Top Rock 'N' Roll Hits-1964 .... (RHI)
  Endless Summer ....(CAP)
  Made In The U.S.A. ....(CAP)
  ST/Good Morning Vietnam .... (A&M)
I Want To Make The World Turn Around
Steve Miller Band; *Living In The 20th Century* ...(CAP)
Instant Karma
John Lennon; *Lennon* ....(CAP)
  Live In New York City ....(CAP)
  Shaved Fish ....(CAP)
Instant Replay
Dan Hartman; *Instant Replay* .... (BS)
  Night At Studio 54 ....(CAS)
It Comes Around
Jude Cole; *Start The Car* .... (RPR)
It's Inevitable
Charlie; *Charlie* .... (MIR)
I'd Love You All Over Again
Alan Jackson; *Here In The Real World* .... (ARI)
I'll Come Back As Another Woman
Tanya Tucker; *Girls Like Me* ....(CAP)
  Greatest Hits ....(CAP)
I'm Gonna Be A Wheel Someday
Fats Domino; *Best Of* .... (EMI)
  Fats Domino .... (AUF)
  Greatest Hits .... (EVR)
  Greatest Hits .... (MCA)
  My Blue Heaven-Best Of-#1 .... (EMI)
Los Lobos; *Fine Mess* .... (MOT)
I've Been In Love Before
Cutting Crew; *Broadcast* .... (VIA)
I've Been This Way Before
Neil Diamond; *Love At The Greek* ....(COL)
  Serenade ....(COL)
(Just Like) Starting Over
John Lennon & Yoko Ono; *Double Fantasy* ...... (GEF)
Karma Chameleon
Culture Club; *Colour By Numbers* .... (VIA)
Keep Coming Back
Edie Brickell/New Bohemians; *Shooting Rubberbands At
  The Stars* .... (GEF)
Richard Marx; *Rush Street* ....(CAP)

Keep Me Turning
Pete Townshend & Ronnie Lane; *Rough Mix* ....(ATC)
King Of The Wheels
Bobby Fuller Four; *Best Of* .... (RHI)
Let's Start All Over Again
Paragons; *Best Of* ....(CLT)
Harlem Holiday-New York R&B-#4 ....(CLT)
Super Oldies Of The '50s-#4 ....(AUF)
Let's Start Love Over
Miles Jaye; *Miles* .... (ISL)
Little Old Fashioned Karma
Willie Nelson; *Tougher Than Leather* ....(COL)
Little Wheel
John Lee Hooker; *Best Of* .... (CRS)
Best Of .... (VJ)
John Lee Hooker ....(EVR)
Little Wheel Spin & Spin
Buffy Sainte-Marie; *Best Of* .... (VAN)
Little Wheel Spin & Spin .... (VAN)
Native North American Child .... (VAN)
Love Makes The World Go Round
Deon Jackson; *Golden Classics* ....(CLT)
Oldies But Goodies-#15 ....(OSR)
Soul Shots-#2-The In Crowd .... (RHI)
Super Oldies/'60s-#7 ....(AUF)
Jo Basile; *Hit Broadway Musicals* ....(AUF)
Madonna; *True Blue* ....(SIR)
Original Cast; *Me & My Girl* ....(EMI)
Me & My Girl .... (MCA)
Love Me Over Again
Don Williams; *Best Of-#3* .... (MCA)
Greatest Hits .... (MCA)
Lovers & Best Friends .... (MCA)
Love Will Lead You Back
Taylor Dayne; *Can't Fight Fate* .... (ARI)
Love Will Turn You Around
Kenny Rogers; *Love Will Turn You Around* ...... (EMI)
Twenty Greatest Hits ....(LIB)
May Be A Price To Pay
Alan Parsons Project; *Turn Of A Friendly Card* .. (ARI)
Nothin' But The Wheel
Patty Loveless; *Only What I Feel* .... (EPI)
On & On
Stephen Bishop; *Best Of Bish* .... (RHI)
Outside Of A Small Circle Of Friends
Phil Ochs; *There & Now-Live In Vancouver-1968* (RHI)
War Is Over-Best Of ....(A&M)
Over And Over
Pajama Party; *Freestyle's Greatest Hits* ....(TST)
Up All Night ....(ATL)
Over & Over
Angel; *Live Without A Net* ....(CAS)
White Hot ....(CAS)
Babys; *Babys* ....(CHR)
Black Sabbath; *Mob Rules* ....(WB)
Bobby Day; *Oldies But Goodies-#9* ....(OSR)
Rockin' Robin ....(CLT)
Super Oldies/'50s-#3 ....(AUF)
Chicago; *18* .... (FM)
Dave Clark Five; *45* ....(EPI)
Fleetwood Mac; *Live* ....(WB)
Tusk ....(WB)
Georgia Satellites; *Georgia Satellites* ....(ELE)
Joe Walsh; *But Seriously Folks* ....(ASY)
Madonna; *Like A Virgin* ....(SIR)
You Can Dance ....(SIR)
Neil Young/Crazy Horse; *Ragged Glory* ....(RPR)
Railway Children; *Recurrence* ....(VIA)
Wilson Phillips; *Wilson Phillips* ....(SBK)
Payback
Choice; *Explicit Rap* ....(PRY)
James Brown; *In Yo' Face-History Of Funk-#4* ... (RHI)
Payback Is A Mutha
Luke; *I Got Sumthin' On My Mind* ....(LUK)
Payback Is Hell
Candy Fresh; *Just The Way I Like It* ....(W/I)
Payback's A Mutha
King Tee; *Act A Fool* ....(CAP)
Rap Beginnings-#2 .... (KT)
Perfect Circle
R.E.M.; *Murmur* ....(IRS)
Piccadilly Circus
Stiff Little Fingers; *See You Up There!* ....(CRL)

Price You Pay
Bruce Springsteen; *The River* ....(COL)
Repetitive Regret
Eddie Rabbitt; *Rabbit Trax* ....(RCA)
Right Back Where We Started From
Maxine Nightingale; *Mega-Hits Dance Classics-#10* ....(PRY)
Road Beneath My Wheels
Dan Fogelberg; *Live-Greetings From The West* .... (FM)
Round And Round
4PM; *Jackin' Boots* ....(RPR)
Aerosmith; *Gems* ....(COL)
Pandora's Box ....(COL)
Toys In The Attic ....(COL)
David Bowie; *Sound + Vision* ....(RYK)
Edgar Winter; *Collection* .... (RHI)
Edgar Winter Group; *They Only Come Out At Night* .... (EPI)
Lionel Richie; *Lionel Richie* ....(MOT)
Neil Young/Crazy Horse; *Everybody Knows This Is Nowhere* ....(RPR)
New Order; *Technique* ....(QUE)
Original Cast; *Fantasticks* ....(POL)
Ratt; *Classic Rock 1966-1988* ....(ATL)
Out Of The Cellar ....(ATL)
Ratt & Roll 8191 ....(ATL)
Strawbs; *Best Of* ....(A&M)
Here & Heroine ....(A&M)
Tevin Campbell; *ST/Graffiti Bridge* ....(PAI)
T.E.V.I.N. ....(RPR)
Roundabout
Yes; *Fragile* ....(ATL)
Yessongs ....(ATL)
Yesyears ....(ATC)
Sex On Wheelz
My Life With The Thrill Kill Kult; *Sexplosion!* .. (WAX)
Silver Wheels
Bruce Cockburn; *Waiting For A Miracle (Singles 1970-87)* .... (GC)
Heart; *Bebe Le Strange* .... (EPI)
Greatest Hits/Live .... (EPI)
So It Goes
Nick Lowe; *Basher-Best Of* ....(COL)
Pure Pop For Now People ....(COL)
ST/Rock 'N' Roll High School .... (SIR)
Spinning Around Over You
Lenny Kravitz; *Spinning Around Over You* .... (VIA)
Spinning Wheel
Blood, Sweat & Tears; *Blood, Sweat & Tears* ....(COL)
Greatest Hits ....(COL)
Rock Classics/'60s ....(COL)
Starting All Over Again
Daryl Hall & John Oates; *Change Of Season* ..... (ARI)
Mel & Tim; *15 Original Big Hits-#1* ....(STX)
Top Of The Stax-Twenty Greatest Hits ....(STX)
Starting Over Again
Dolly Parton; *Dolly Dolly Dolly* ....(RCA)
Natalie Cole; *Good To Be Back* .... (ELE)
Steve Wariner; *Country Classics-#7-1986-1987* . (MCA)
Greatest Hits .... (MCA)
Life's Highway ....(MCA)
Summer's Coming Around Again
Carly Simon; *Anticipation* .... (ELE)
This Song Has No Title
Elton John; *Goodbye Yellow Brick Road* .... (POL)
This Wheel's On Fire
Band; *Anthology* ....(CAP)
Music From Big Pink ....(CAP)
Rock Of Ages-#1 & 2 ....(CAP)
Bob Dylan/Band; *Basement Tapes* ....(COL)
Byrds; *Byrds (collection)* ....(COL)
Ian & Sylvia; *Greatest Hits* ....(VAN)
Siouxsie/Banshees; *Through The Looking Glass* .. (GEF)
Twice Upon A Time-The Singles ....(GEF)
Turning Circles
Judas Priest; *Point Of Entry* ....(COL)
Turn! Turn! Turn!
Byrds; *Billboard Top Rock 'N' Roll Hits-1965* .... (RHI)
Greatest Hits ....(COL)
Original Singles-#1-1965-1967 ....(COL)
Byrds (collection) ....(COL)
ST/Forrest Gump ....(EPX)
Turn! Turn! Turn! ....(COL)

Pete Seeger; *Greatest Hits* ....(COL)
  Troubadours Of The Folk Era-#2 .... (RHI)
Under My Wheels
  Alice Cooper; *Greatest Hits* ....(WB)
  Killer ....(WB)
  Show ....(WB)
Until Your Love Comes Back Around
  RTZ; *Return To Zero* .... (GIA)
Waiting For The Tide To Turn
  Robert Cray Band; *Bad Influence* .... (HT)
Watching The Wheels
  John Lennon; *Lennon* ....(CAP)
  John Lennon & Yoko Ono; *Double Fantasy* ......(CAP)
Waterwheel
  Daryl Hall & John Oates; *Whole Oats* .... (ATL)
What Goes Around
  Gloria Estefan; *Into The Light* .... (EPI)
  Jerry Garcia; *Compliments* .... (GRD)
  Regina Belle; *Stay With Me* ....(COL)
  Ringo Starr; *Time Takes Time* .... (PRV)
Wheel
  Asleep At The Wheel; *Wheel* ....(CAP)
  Edie Brickell/New Bohemians; *Shooting Rubberbands At The Stars* ....(GEF)
  Jefferson Airplane; *Jefferson Airplane* .... (EPI)
  Jerry Garcia; *Garcia* .... (GRD)
  Utopia; *Another Live* .... (RHI)
  Anthology-1974-1985 .... (RHI)
Wheel In The Sky
  Journey; *Captured* ....(COL)
  Greatest Hits ....(COL)
  Infinity ....(COL)
Wheel Of Fortune
  Cardinals; *Atlantic R&B 1947-1974-collection* ... (ATL)
  Kay Starr; *Capitol Collectors Series* ....(CAP)
Wheel Of Life
  Rance Allen; *Straight From The Heart* .... (STX)
Wheels
  Billy Vaughn; *Greatest Hits* ....(CCB)
  Chet Atkins; *Best Of* ....(RCA)
  On The Road Live ....(RCA)
  Emmylou Harris; *Elite Hotel* .... (WB)
  Flying Burrito Brothers; *Cabin Fever* ....(RLX)
  Close Up The Honky Tonks .... (A&M)
  Farther Along-Bes Of .... (A&M)
  Gilded Palace Of Sin .... (A&M)
  Lone Justice; *Shelter* ....(GEF)
  Restless Heart; *Best Of* ....(RCA)
  Wheels ....(RCA)
Wheels Of Fortune
  Doobie Brothers; *Takin' It To The Streets* .... (WB)
Wheels Of Life
  Gino Vannelli; *Best Of* .... (A&M)
  Brother To Brother .... (A&M)
  Classics-#7 .... (A&M)
Width Of A Circle
  David Bowie; *Live* ....(RYK)
  Man Who Sold The World ....(RYK)
  ST/Ziggy Stardust-The Motion Picture ....(RCA)
Will It Go Round In Circles
  Billy Preston; *Best Of* .... (A&M)
  Billboard Top Rock 'N' Roll Hits-1973 .... (RHI)
  Soul Hits/'70s-#11 .... (RHI)
Will The Circle Be Unbroken
  Charlie Daniels Band/Friends; *Volunteer Jam #3 & #4* .... (EPI)
  Joan Baez; *Country Music Album* .... (VAN)
  First 10 Years .... (VAN)
  Nitty Gritty Dirt Band; *Will The Circle Be Unbroken* .... (EMI)
  Roy Acuff; *Best Of* ....(CCB)
  Willie Nelson; *Willie & Family Live* ....(COL)
World Turning
  Fleetwood Mac; *Fleetwood Mac* .... (RPR)
Yesterday Once More
  Carpenters; *Classics-#2* .... (A&M)
  Now & Then .... (A&M)
  Singles 1969-1973 .... (A&M)
  Yesterday Once More .... (A&M)
You Spin Me Around (Like A Record)
  Dead Or Alive; *Rip It Up* .... (EPI)
  Youthquake .... (EPI)

CITIES: A

See Also: *COUNTRIES, STATES, CITIES: ATLANTA*

Abilene
  George Hamilton IV; *Billboard Top Country Hits-1963* .... (RHI)
  Nipper's Greatest Hits-'60s-#2 ....(RCA)
  Sonny James; *American Originals* ....(COL)
  Waylon Jennings; *Outlaw Reunion-#1* .... (ARA)
Acapulco
  Neil Diamond; *Jazz Singer* ....(CAP)
Acid Annapolis
  Leon Russell; *Carney* .... (MCA)
Albuquerque
  Neil Young; *Tonight's The Night* .... (RPR)
Alexandria, VA
  Bill Jennings; *Stompin' With Bill* ....(CLT)
All Alone In Austin
  Marty Mitchell; *You Are The Sunshine Of My Life* .... (MCP)
Allentown
  Billy Joel; *Greatest Hits-#1 & 2* ....(COL)
  KOHUEPT Live In Leningrad ....(COL)
  Nylon Curtain ....(COL)
Allentown Jail
  Jo Stafford; *International Hits* ....(CRN)
  Kingston Trio; *Rediscover The* .... (FOL)
Alleys Of Austin
  Michael Murphey; *Cosmic Cowboy Souvenir* .... (A&M)
Amarillo
  Emmylou Harris; *Elite Hotel* .... (RPR)
  Neil Sedaka; *A Song* .... (RPR)
Amarillo By Morning
  George Strait; *Greatest Hits* .... (MCA)
  Strait Country/Strait From The Heart .... (MCA)
  Strait From The Heart .... (MCA)
Amsterdam
  Joan Baez; *Play Me Backwards* .... (VIA)
  John Denver; *Take Me To Tomorrow* ....(RCA)
  Original Cast; *Jacques Brel Is Alive & Well & Living...* ....(COL)
Amsterdam Dog Shit Blues
  Mojo Nixon & Skid Roper; *Enigma Variations 2* .(ENC)
Anaheim, Azusa & Cucamonga Sewing Circle
  Jan & Dean; *Best Of* .... (EMI)
  Legendary Masters .... (UA)
Ann Arbor
  John Fahey; *Visits Washington D.C.* ....(TAK)
Ann Arbor Polka
  Michigan Dutchmen; *More New Polkas* ....(JJ)
Appleton
  Webb Pierce; *45* .... (PLN)
Aspen
  Dan Fogelberg; *Captured Angel* .... (FM)
Atlantic City
  Bruce Springsteen; *Nebraska* ....(COL)
  Paul Anka; *ST/Atlantic City* .... (DRG)
  Randy Newman; *ST/Ragtime* .... (ELE)
Atlantic City Gambler
  Grace Jones; *Muse* .... (ISL)
Atlantis
  Donovan; *Barbarajagal* .... (EPI)
  Steve Kilbey; *Earthed* ....(RYK)
  Steal This Disc 2 ....(RYK)
Attica State
  John & Yoko Lennon; *Sometime In New York City* .... (CAP)
Austin
  Jeff Palmer; *Laser Wizard* ....(STS)
Avalon
  Al Jolson; *Best Of* .... (MCA)
  Jolson Sang 'Em ....(BIO)
  Story-#2 .... (MCA)
  Roxy Music; *Avalon* .... (WB)
  Heart Still Beating .... (RPR)
  Street Life-20 Great Hits .... (RPR)
Avalon My Home Town
  Mississippi John Hurt; *Best Of* .... (VAN)
Bus From Amarillo
  Original Cast; *Best Little Whorehouse In Texas* .. (MCA)

Charlie Dunn (Austin TX)
Jerry Jeff Walker; *Gypsy Songman* ....(RYK)
   Jerry Jeff Walker .... (MCA)
"E" Street Shuffle (Asbury Park)
Bruce Springsteen; *Wild The Innocent & The E Street
Shuffle* ....(COL)
Fourth Of July, Asbury Park (Sandy)
Bruce Springsteen; *Wild The Innocent & The E Street
Shuffle* ....(COL)
Bruce Springsteen/E Street Band;
Live-1975-1985 ....(COL)
Girls Of Amsterdam
Shaw Brothers; *Best Of* .... (FOL)
   Shaw Brothers Collection .... (FOL)
Goin' To Acapulco
Bob Dylan/Band; *Basement Tapes* ....(COL)
It's A Long Way From Detroit...To Austin
Buddy Harris; *45* .... (PLN)
I'm Leaving Abilene
Dede Upchurch; *45* .... (LG)
Midnight In Old Amarillo
Buddy Emmons & Ray Pennington; *Swing & Other
Things* ....(SO)
New Amsterdam
Elvis Costello; *Girls Girls Girls* ....(COL)
Elvis Costello/Attractions; *Get Happy!* ....(RYK)
She Loves Austin
Johnny Rodriguez; *Gracias* ....(CAP)
Tennessee Flat Top Box (Austin)
Johnny Cash; *Classic Cash-Hall Of Fame Series* . (MER)
   Columbia Country Classics-#3-Americana ......(COL)
   Essential ....(COL)
Rosanne Cash; *30 Years Of #1 Hits-#17* ....(COL)
   Hits-1979-1989 .... (COL)
   King's Record Shop ....(COL)
That Acapulco Gold
Rainy Daze; *Summer Of Love-#2-Turn On* .... (RHI)
Timon Of The Athens March
Duke Ellington/Boston Pops Orchestra; *Duke At
Tanglewood* ....(RCA)
Walkaway Joe (Abilene)
Trisha Yearwood; *Hearts In Armor* .... (MCA)
Way Out In Abilene
Lightnin' Hopkins; *Legacy Of The Blues-#12* ..... (CRS)
When You Leave Amarillo
Bob Wills/Texas Playboys; *For The Last Time* .... (UA)

CITIES: ATLANTA

See Also: STATES: GEORGIA

Angel From Atlanta
Reddog; *Reddog* .... (SUR)
Angels Of Atlanta
Marvin "Hannibal" Peterson; *Angels Of Atlanta* .. (ENJ)
Atlanta
Stanley Clarke & George Duke; *Project 2* ....(EPI)
Wagoneers; *Good Fortune* ....(A&M)
Atlanta Blue
Statler Brothers; *14 Country Favorites* .... (MER)
   Atlanta Blue .... (MER)
   Greatest Hits .... (MER)
Atlanta Burned Again Last Night
Atlanta; *Pictures* ....(MCA)
Atlanta Georgia Stray
Johnny Duncan; *Greatest Hits* ....(COL)
   Johnny Duncan ....(COL)
   Nice & Easy ....(COL)
Atlanta June
Pablo Cruise; *Place In The Sun* ....(A&M)
Atlanta Lady
Marty Balin; *Balin* ....(EMI)
   Balance-A Collection .... (RHI)
Atlanta Song
David Allan Coe; *Mysterious Rhinestone Cowboy* (COL)
Atlanta Special
Bukka White; *Legacy Of The Blues-#1* ....(CRS)
   Mississippi Blues ....(TAK)
Atlanta Town
Chasey Collins; *Jug Jook & Washboard Bands* ...(BCL)
Atlanta, GA
Sammy Kaye; *Dance To My Golden Favorites* ... (MCA)
Woody Herman; *Best Of The Big Bands* ....(COL)

Atlanta's Burning Down
Dickey Betts/Great Southern; *Dickey Betts/Great
Southern* .... (ARI)
Randy Howard; *All-American Redneck* ....(WB)
Back To Atlanta
David Allan Coe; *I've Got Something To Say* ....(COL)
Battle Of Atlanta
Reno & Smiley; *1983 Collector's Edition-#2* .....(GUS)
Burning Of Atlanta
Claude King; *American Originals* ....(COL)
Dark Side Of Atlanta
Dan Hill; *Best Of* .... (20)
   Frozen In The Night ....(20)
Girl From Atlanta
Benny Carter All-Star Sax Ensemble; *Over The
Rainbow* .... (MM)
Hot 'Lanta
38 Special; *Rock & Roll Strategy* ....(A&M)
Allman Brothers Band; *At The Fillmore East* ..... (POL)
   Road Goes On Forever .... (POL)
Oh Atlanta
Bad Company; *Desolation Angels* .... (SS)
Charlie Daniels Band; *Simple Man* ....(EPI)
Little Feat; *Feats Don't Fail Me Now* ....(WB)
   Waiting For Columbus ....(WB)
Sue Medley; *Sue Medley* ....(MER)
Partyin' Gal
Charlie Daniels Band; *Windows* ....(EPI)
Portrait In Atlanta
House Of Love; *Audience With The Mind* ....(FON)
Santa, Are You Coming To Atlanta
Pake McEntire; *Country Christmas-#4* ....(RCA)
   Season's Greetings ....(RCA)

CITIES: B

*See Also: CITIES: BALTIMORE, BERLIN,
BIRMINGHAM, BOSTON*

3 A.M. Somewhere Out Of Beaumont
KLF; *Chill Out* ....(WAX)
Back To Bologna
Milt Jackson/Gold Medal Winners; *Brother Jim* .. (PAB)
Baghdad Ragman
Karen Alexander; *Isn't It Always Love* ....(ASY)
Bangkok Attorney
Doves; *Affinity* ....(ELE)
Bangkok Cockfight
Martin Denny; *Exotica-Best Of* .... (RHI)
Bangkok Rain
Cult; *Ceremony* .... (SIR)
Barcelona
Juan Carlos Quintero; *Juan Carlos Quintero* .... (NVA)
Nomad; *Changing Cabins* ....(CAP)
Original Cast; *Company* ....(COL)
Spies; *Music Of Espionage* ....(TLR)
Barefoot In Beverly Hills
Grace Jones; *Inside Story* ....(MAN)
Barrytown
Steely Dan; *Pretzel Logic* ....(MCA)
Barstow Blue Eyes
Jo Jo Gunne; *Jo Jo Gunne* ....(ASY)
Baton Rouge
Bill Medley; *Sweet Thunder* .... (UA)
Beaumont Rag
Bob Wills; *Best Of-#2* .... (MCA)
   Tiffany Transcriptions-#4 ....(KAL)
   /Texas Playboys-In Concert ....(CAP)
Beautiful Downtown Burbank
Harper Valley P.T.A.; *Country Gold* ....(PLN)
Beirut
Steps Ahead; *Magnetic* .... (ELE)
Belfast
Energy Orchard; *Energy Orchard* .... (MCA)
Orbital; *Orbital* ....(FFR)
Richard Pinhas; *L'Ethique* ....(CUN)
Belfast Child
Simple Minds; *Street Fighting Years* ....(A&N
Belfast Cowboys
Pretty Things; *Silk Torpedo* .... (S:
Belfast Hornpipe
James Galway; *Greatest Hits* .... (RC/

Berkeley Woman
John Denver; *Farewell Andromeda* ....(RCA)
  John Denver ....(RCA)
"Beverly Hills, 90210" Theme
John Davis; *ST/"Beverly Hills, 90210" Theme* .... (GIA)
Biloxi
Ian Matthews; *Some Days You Eat The Bear* ..... (ELE)
Jesse Winchester; *Best Of* ....(RHI)
  Jesse Winchester ....(RHI)
Jimmy Buffett; *Changes In Latitudes...Attitudes* .. (MCA)
Bombay
Golden Earring; *Mad Love* .... (MCA)
Lawrence Welk; *Calcutta* ....(RAN)
Bristol Stomp
Dovells; *Echoes Of A Rock Era-Middle Years* .... (RLL)
  Let's Dance ....(GUS)
  Rock-A-Rama #1 ....(AKO)
Brownsville Blues (Girl I Love, She...)
Hammie Nixon; *Tappin' That Thing* ....(HW)
Brownsville Girl
Bob Dylan; *Knocked Out Loaded* ....(COL)
Brownsville Road
Peter Lang; *Prime Cuts* .... (WTR)
Brownsville Turnaround On The Tex-Mex...
KLF; *Chill Out* .... (WAX)
Budapest
Jethro Tull; *Crest Of A Knave* .... (CHR)
Budapest By Blimp
Thomas Dolby; *Aliens Ate My Buick* .... (EMI)
Buenos Aires
Original New York Cast; *Evita* .... (MCA)
Callin' Baton Rouge
Garth Brooks; *In Pieces* .... (LIB)
New Grass Revival; *Anthology* .... (LIB)
Oak Ridge Boys; *Room Service* .... (MSP)
Child Of Babylon
Whitesnake; *Come An' Get It* ....(GEF)
Going Back To Big Sur
Johnny Rivers; *Anthology-1964-1977* .... (RHI)
  Touch Of Gold .... (IMP)
Goin' To Brownsville
Ron Thompson/Resistors-Rollo Smith; *Treat Her Like
Gold/No Band Days* .... (TAK)
Ry Cooder; *Ry Cooder* .... (RPR)
Honeymoon In Beirut
Rick Springfield; *Rock Of Life* .... (RCA)
I'm Going To Brownsville
Furry Lewis; *Back On My Feet Again* .... (PRS)
  Shake 'Em On Down .... (FAN)
Ladies Night In Buffalo
David Lee Roth; *Eat 'Em & Smile* .... (WB)
Long Gone John From Bowling Green
Red Knuckles/Trailblazers; *Red
Knuckles/Trailblazers* .... (FF)
Long Legged Hannah (From Butte, Montana)
Jesse Hunter; *A Man Like Me* ....(BNA)
Louisiana Rain (Baton Rouge)
Tom Petty/Heartbreakers; *Damn The Torpedoes* . (BKS)
Man From Bowling Green
Johnny Paycheck; *Take This Job & Shove It* ...... (EPI)
Night In Buenos Aires
101 Strings Orchestra; *Best Of Latin* .... (ALS)
Off To Buffalo
Fletcher Henderson/Dixie Stompers; *Fletcher
Henderson/Dixie Stompers-1925-1928* ....(DSQ)
Miroslav Vitous; *Guardian Angels* ....(EVD)
One Night In Bangkok
Murray Head; *Chess Pieces* ....(RCA)
Original Broadway Cast; *Chess* ....(RCA)
Passage To Bangkok
Rush; *2112* .... (MER)
  Chronicles .... (MER)
  Exit...Stage Left .... (MER)
Pretty Litle Lady From Beaumont, Texas
George Jones; *One Woman Man* .... (EPI)
Richest Man In Bogota
Gil Melle; *Mindscape* ....(BLN)
Riflemen Of Bennington
Jim Burroughs; *Songs Of Rebellion* ....(AUF)
Road To Bangor
Northeast Winds; *Songs Of Ireland & The Sea* ..(FOL)
She Came From Fort Worth (Boulder)
Kathy Mattea; *WIllow In The Wind* .... (MER)

Pat Alger & Kathy Mattea; *True Love & Other Short
Stories* ....(SH)
Shuffle Off To Buffalo
Hal Kemp; *Best Of The Big Bands* ....(COL)
Original Broadway Cast; *42nd Street* ....(RCA)
Star Of Bethlehem
Emmylou Harris & Neil Young; *Duets* .... (RPR)
Neil Young; *Decade* .... (RPR)
Neil Young/Crazy Horse; *American Stars 'N'
Bars* .... (RPR)
Streets Of Bakersfield
Buck Owens; *All-Time Greatest-#1* ....(CCB)
  Collection-1959-1990 .... (RHI)
Dwight Yoakam; *Buenas Noches From A Lonely
Room* .... (RPR)
  Just Lookin' For A Hit .... (RPR)
Dwight Yoakam & Buck Owens; *Country's Greatest
Hits-#9-'80s Duets* .... (PRY)
Streets Of Belfast
Celtic Thunder; *Light Of Other Days* ....(GRE)
There Ain't No Beverly Hills In...
Shenandoah; *Long Time Comin'* ....(RCA)
Tiananmen Square
Blazing Redheads; *Crazed Women* .... (REF)
Train To Bombay
Christopher Max; *More Than Physical* .... (EMI)
Tree Grows In Burbank
Harry James; *Uncollected-#5-1943-1953* .... (HIN)

CITIES: BALTIMORE

See Also: STATES: MARYLAND

Baltimore
Drifters; *1959-1965-All-Time Greatest Hits &
More* ....(ATL)
Lyle Lovett; *Joshua Judges Ruth* ....(CRB)
Nina Simone; *Let It Be Me* ....(VRV)
Randy Newman; *Little Criminals* ....(WB)
Baltimore Oriole
Carmen McRae; *Greatest Of* .... (MCA)
George Harrison; *Somewhere In England* .... (DKH)
Barefoot In Baltimore
Strawberry Alarm Clock; *Best Of-#1* ....(BCT)
From Baltimore To Paris
Go West; *Dancing On The Couch* .... (CHR)
Girl From Baltimore
Fleshtones; *Living Legends* .... (IRS)
Hungry Heart
Bruce Springsteen; *The River* ....(COL)
Bruce Springsteen/E Street Band;
Live-1975-1985 ....(COL)
Lady Came From Baltimore
Joan Baez; *Contemporary Ballad Book* .... (VAN)
  Joan .... (VAN)
John Stewart; *Neon Beach* ....(HOM)
Tim Hardin; *Hang On To A Dream-Verve
Recordings* ....(POL)
Port Of Baltimore Blues
Gerry Mulligan & Scott Hamilton; *Soft Lights & Sweet
Music* ....(CCJ)
Raining In Baltimore
Counting Crows; *August And Everything After* .. (DGC)
Streets Of Baltimore
Bobby Bare; *This Is* ....(RCA)
Flying Burrito Brothers; *Live From Europe* ....(RLX)
Gram Parsons; *GP/Grievous Angel* .... (RPR)
  Gram Parsons/Fallen Angels Live-1973 .... (SIE)
Tomorrow Night In Baltimore
Roger Miller; *Best Of* .... (MER)
  More Golden Hits .... (SMA)
What's New In Baltimore
Frank Zappa; *Meets The Mothers Of Prevention* ..(BAR)
  You Can't Do That On Stage Anymore-#5 ......(RYK)

CITIES: BERLIN

Berlin
Lou Reed; *Berlin* .... (ARI)
  City Lights ....(RCA)
  Live .... (ARI)
Marillion; *Seasons End* ....(CAP)

Berlin To Memphis
Elvis Hitler; *Disgraceland* .... (RES)
Berlin Tonight
Bruce Cockburn; *World Of Wonders* .... (COL)
Berlin Wall
Johnny Clegg & Savuka; *Third World Child* ..... (CAP)
City Of Night (Berlin)
Peter Schilling; *Different Story (World Of Lust & Crime)* .... (ELE)
Dancing In Berlin
Berlin; *Love Life* .... (GEF)
Doing The Best That I Can
Stevie Nicks; *Other Side Of The Mirror* .... (MOD)
Party At The Berlin Wall
Root Boy Slim/Sex Change Band; *Root 6* .... (NL)
Road Movie To Berlin
They Might Be Giants; *Flood* .... (ELE)
Summer In Berlin
Alphaville; *Forever Young* .... (ATL)
There'll Be A Hot Time In...Berlin
Woody Herman; *Uncollected-& His First Herd* ... (HIN)

CITIES: BIRMINGHAM
See Also: STATES: ALABAMA

96 Miles To Birmingham
Dick Silveras; *Negro Folk Songs & Ballads* .... (STO)
All The Way To Birmingham/Roaring Mary
Celtic Thunder; *Celtic Thunder* .... (GRE)
Birmingham
Jeannie Kendall; *45* .... (MCA)
Randy Newman; *Good Old Boys* .... (RPR)
Birmingham Blues
Charlie Daniels Band; *Volunteer Jam* .... (CPC)
Night Rider .... (EPI)
Electric Light Orchestra; *Out Of The Blue* ...... (JET)
Birmingham Sunday
Joan Baez; *Contemporary Ballad Book* .... (VAN)
Joan Baez .... (VAN)
Boulder To Birmingham
Emmylou Harris; *Pieces Of The Sky* .... (RPR)
Profile .... (WB)
Down & Out In Birmingham
Pirates Of The Mississippi; *Pirates Of The Mississippi* .... (LIB)
Fifteen Miles To Birmingham
Happy & Artie Traum/Others; *Mud Acres* ...... (ROU)
From Cotton To Satin
Gene Watson; *This Dream's On Me* .... (MCA)
Johnny Paycheck; *Ake This Job & Shove It* ...... (EPI)
Going Back To Birmingham
Ten Years After; *Universal* .... (CHR)
Train To Birmingham
Kevin Welch/Overtones; *Western Beat* .... (RPR)
When Jesus Left Birmingham
John Mellencamp/Sounds Of Blackness; *Human Wheels* .... (MER)

CITIES: BOSTON
See Also: STATES: MASSACHUSETTS

Boston
Byrds; *...In The Beginning* .... (RHI)
Gene Clark; *Echoes* .... (COL)
Lori Lieberman; *Letting Go* .... (MIL)
Boston Lady
John Stewart; *Fire In The Wind* .... (RSO)
Boston Rag
Steely Dan; *Countdown To Ecstasy* .... (MCA)
Dirty Water
Standells; *Best Of* .... (RHI)
Nuggets-Classics From Psychedelic Era .... (RHI)
Super Oldies/'60s-#10 .... (AUF)
Hey Nineteen
Steely Dan; *Gaucho* .... (MCA)
Gold .... (MCA)
M.T.A.
Kingston Trio; *25 Years Non-Stop* .... (XER)
Best Of .... (CAP)
Capitol Collectors Series .... (CAP)
Scarlet Ribbons .... (CAP)
Very Best Of .... (CAP)

Please Come To Boston
Dave Loggins; *Apprentice (In A Musical Workshop)* .... (EPI)
Rock Artifacts-#2 .... (COL)
Super Hits/'70s-Have A Nice Day-#13 .... (RHI)
David Allan Coe; *17 Greatest Hits* .... (COL)
For The Record-First 10 Years .... (COL)
Joan Baez; *Best Of* .... (A&M)
Classics-#8 .... (A&M)
Railroad Lady
Jerry Jeff Walker; *A Man Must Carry On* .... (MCA)
Gypsy Songman .... (RYK)
Jimmy Buffett; *White Sport Coat & A Pink Crustacean* .... (MCA)
J.D. Crowe/New South; *My Home Ain't In The Hall Of Fame* .... (ROU)
Willie Nelson; *Greatest Hits (& Some That Will Be)* .... (COL)
To Lefty From Willie .... (COL)
Red Moon Over Boston
Romanovsky & Phillips; *Be Political Not Polite* ... (FRE)
Sandy MacIntyre's Trip To Boston
John Campbell; *Cape Breton Violin Music* ...... (ROU)
Theresa & Marie MacLellan; *Trip To Mabou Ridge* .... (ROU)
Twilight In Boston
Jonathan Richman; *I Jonathan* .... (ROU)

CITIES: C
See Also: CITIES: CHICAGO, CINCINNATI

1-900-2-COMPTON
N.W.A.; *Efil4zaggin* .... (RUP)
Anaheim, Azusa & Cucamonga Sewing Circle
Jan & Dean; *Best Of* .... (EMI)
Legendary Masters .... (UA)
April In Cambridge
Peter Walker; *Rainy Day Raga* .... (VAN)
Born And Raised In Compton
DJ Quik; *S* .... (PRO)
Burn On (Cleveland)
Randy Newman; *Sail Away* .... (RPR)
Calcutta
Lawrence Welk; *Best Of* .... (RAN)
Calcutta .... (RAN)
Camarillo Brillo
Mothers; *Apostrophe/Overnite Sensation* .... (RYK)
Charleston
Paul Whiteman/Orchestra; *Nipper's Greatest Hits-'20s* .... (RCA)
Charleston Rag
Eubie Blake; *Greatest Ragtime Of The Century* ....(BIO)
Charleston Railroad Tavern
Bobby Bare; *This Is* .... (RCA)
Charlotte's In North Carolina
Ronnie McDowell; *Country Boy's Heart* .... (EPI)
Chattanooga Choo Choo
Billy Strange; *Railroad Man* .... (CRS)
Boston Pops Orchestra/Arthur Fiedler; *Boston Pops Orchestra/Arthur Fiedler* .... (RCA)
Greatest Hits Of The '40s .... (RCA)
Glenn Miller; *Best Of* .... (RCA)
Decade Of The '40s .... (RCA)
Legendary Performer .... (RCA)
Memorial 1944-1969 .... (RCA)
Nipper's Greatest Hits-'40s .... (RCA)
Pure Gold .... (RCA)
Tuxedo Junction; *Best Of Butterfly Records* ...... (HOT)
Tuxedo Junction .... (BTF)
Chattanooga Shoe Shine Boy
Freddy Cannon; *14 Booming Hits* .... (RHI)
Chelsea Bridge
Duke Ellington; *Blanton-Webster Band* .... (BLU)
Concert In The Virgin Islands .... (DCO)
Sarah Vaughan; *Duke Ellington Songbook 2* ...... (PAB)
Chelsea Morning
Joni Mitchell; *Clouds* .... (RPR)
Neil Diamond; *Rainbow* .... (MCA)
Stones .... (MCA)
Cherry Hill Park
Billy Joe Royal; *Greatest Hits* .... (COL)
Super Hits/'70s-Have A Nice Day-#1 .... (RHI)

Cheyenne
Bluegrass Album Band; *Bluegrass Compact Disc* (ROU)
Bo Diddley; *Is A Gunslinger* .... (CSS)
Hanoi Rocks; *Bangkok Shocks-Saigon Shakes-Hanoi
Rocks* ....(GEF)
Ricky Lynn Gregg; *Ricky Lynn Gregg* .... (LIB)
Sons Of The Pioneers; *Sunset On The Range* ..... (PRR)
Cheyenne Autumn
Kansas; *Leftoverture* .... (KIR)
China Grove
Doobie Brothers; *Best Of* .... (WB)
  Captain & Me .... (WB)
  Farewell Tour .... (WB)
Chinatown
Chaka Khan; *I Feel For You* .... (WB)
Doobie Brothers; *Livin' On The Fault Line* .... (WB)
Greg Kihn; *Next Of Kihn* .... (BES)
Joe Jackson; *Night & Day* .... (A&M)
Chinatown My Chinatown
Al Jolson; *Story-#1* .... (MCA)
Louis Armstrong; *Armstrong #2* .... (EVR)
  Stardust .... (POR)
Cleveland
Martin Mull; *Sex & Violins* .... (MCA)
Cleveland Polka
Li'l Wally; *Thanks For A Wonderful Evening* .... (JJ)
Cleveland Rocks
Ian Hunter; *Shades Of* .... (CHR)
  ST/Light Of Day .... (CBA)
  You're Never Alone With A Schizophrenic ...... (CHR)
Clovis, New Mexico
Hank Williams, Jr.; *& Friends* .... (POL)
Cooperstown
Terry Cashman; *45* .... (LIF)
Copenhagen
Artie Shaw; *Best Of The Big Bands-#3* ....(COL)
Bix Beiderbecke/Chicago Cornets; *Bix
Beiderbecke/Chicago Cornets* .... (MS)
Chris LeDoux; *Songs Of Rodeo Life* .... (LIB)
Copenhagen Junkie
Chris LeDoux; *Melodies & Memories* .... (LIB)
Corpus Christi Blue
Dewayne Blackwell & Jill Hollier; *45* .... (WB)
Cowtown
Carly Simon; *Another Passenger* .... (ELE)
George Strait; *#7* .... (MCA)
Webb Pierce; *Golden Hits-#2* .... (PLN)
Down In Chihuahua
Stan Kenton; *Lighter Side* ....(CW)
Evening In Casablanca
Art Farmer Quintet; *Art Farmer Quintet* .... (PRS)
Fall Of Charleston
Tennessee Ernie Ford; *Sings Songs Of The Civil
War* ....(CAP)
Fire In Cairo
Cure; *Boys Don't Cry* .... (ELE)
F-ck Compton
Tim Dog; *S* .... (RUF)
Goin' To Cairo
Joel Mabus; *Settin' The Woods On Fire* ....(FF)
Goin' To Chattanooga
Ralph Willis; *East Coast Blues* .... (CLT)
It's A Compton Thang
Compton's Most Wanted; *It's A Compton Thang* . (ORF)
I'm Gonna Charleston Back To Charleston
Firehouse Five Plus Two; *Goes South* .... (GTJ)
Last Train To Clarksville
Monkees; *Greatest Hits* .... (ARI)
  Live 1967 .... (RHI)
  Monkees .... (ARI)
  Then & Now...Best Of .... (ARI)
Look Out Cleveland
Band; *Band* .... (CAP)
Night Boat To Cairo
Madness; *One Step Beyond* .... (SIR)
  ST/Dance Craze .... (CHR)
Pride Of Cucamonga
Grateful Dead; *From The Mars Hotel* .... (GRD)
Purple Rose Of Cairo
New Orleans Ragtime Orchestra; *New Orleans
Jazz* .... (ARH)
Raised In Compton
Compton's Most Wanted; *Straight Checkn 'Em* ...(ORF)

Relaxin' At Camarillo
Charlie Parker; *Very Best Of Bird* .... (WB)
Joe Henderson; *Relaxin' At Camarillo* .... (CTM)
Joe Pass; *Appassionato* .... (PAB)
Road To Columbus
Sally Van Meter; *All In Good Time* ....(SH)
Sail Away (Charleston Bay)
Linda Ronstadt; *Don't Cry Now* .... (ASY)
Randy Newman; *Sail Away* .... (RPR)
Shipmates In Cheyenne
Bobby Darin; *1936-1973* .... (MOT)
Shoot Out In Chinatown
Band; *Cahoots* .... (CAP)
Straight Outta Compton
N.W.A.; *Straight Outta Compton* .... (RUP)
Streets Of Calgary
Kate Wolf; *Wind Blows Wild* .... (KAL)
This Is Compton
Compton's Most Wanted; *It's A Compton Thang* . (ORF)
UFO Over Cairo
NASA; *Insha-Allah* .... (SIR)
Welcome To Chinatown
John Mellencamp; *John Cougar* ....(RIV)
When...Swallows Come Back To Capistrano
Glenn Miller; *In The Mood* .... (POE)
Ink Spots; *Best Of* .... (MCA)
  Greatest Hits .... (MCA)
Wonderful Copenhagen
Danny Kaye; *45* ....(OOP)
Dave Brubeck; *I Like Jazz-Essence Of* ....(COL)
Dave Brubeck Quartet;
  Concerts-Amsterdam/Copenhagen/Carnegie ....(COL)
  Jazz Masters-27 Classic Performances ....(COL)

CITIES: CHICAGO
See Also: STATES: ILLINOIS

2120 So. Michigan Avenue
Rolling Stones; *12 x 5* ....(LON)
At The Chicago World's Fair
Original Cast; *Show Boat* ....(RCA)
Back To Chicago
Duke Tumatoe; *Dukes Up* .... (BLI)
Styx; *Edge of The Century* .... (A&M)
Bad Bad Leroy Brown
Jim Croce; *Billboard Top Rock 'N' Roll Hits-1973* (RHI)
  Down The Highway .... (21)
  Life & Times ....(OOP)
  Photographs & Memories .... (21)
Band From Chicago
Max Creek; *Windows* ....(RLX)
Born In Chicago
George Thorogood/Destroyers; *Boogie People* ... (EMI)
Paul Butterfield Blues Band; *Golden Butter* ...... (ELE)
  Paul Butterfield Blues Band .... (ELE)
Pixies; *Rubaiyat (Elektra's 40th Anniversary)* ..... (ELE)
Chicago
Al Jolson; *Immortal* .... (MCA)
Crosby, Stills, Nash & Young; *4-Way Street* ...... (ATL)
David Crosby & Graham Nash; *Best Of* .... (MCA)
Doobie Brothers; *Doobie Brothers* ....(WB)
Graham Nash; *Songs For Beginners* .... (ATL)
Judy Garland; *At Carnegie Hall* .... (CAP)
  Hits Of .... (CAP)
Tony Bennett & Count Basie; *Echoes Of An Era-Basie
Vocal Years* .... (RLL)
Chicago Breakdown
Louis Armstrong; *Genius Of* ....(COL)
  Story #2 ....(COL)
Louis Armstrong & Earl Hines; *#4* ....(COL)
Chicago Institute
Manfred Mann's Earth Band; *Watch* .... (WB)
Chicago Send Her Home
Thelma Houston & Jerry Butler; *Two To One* ... (MOT)
Chicago Song
David Sanborn; *Change Of Heart* .... (WB)
City Of Chicago
Christy Moore; *Christy Moore* .... (ATL)
  Ride On ....(GRE)
Cold Windy City Of Chicago
Boxcar Willie; *Best Of-#1* ....(MAI)

Comin' Back To South Chicago
Jeannie & Jimmy Cheatham; *Luv In The Afternoon* .... (CCJ)
Eggplant That Ate Chicago
Dr. West's Medicine Show & Junk Band; *Dr. Demento's Greatest-#3* .... (RHI)
Going To Chicago Blues
Count Basie; *Essential-#1* .... (COL)
Jimmy Rushing; *Essential* .... (VAN)
Joe Williams; *Jazz Singers* .... (PRS)
Lambert, Hendricks & Ross; *Twisted-Best Of* .... (RHI)
Lowell Fulson; *Let's Go Get Stoned* .... (KNT)
I Wish I Was In Chicago
Original Cast; *Charlie Sent Me* .... (GLN)
In Chicago's Forest Preserve
Li'l Wally; *Polish Feelings* .... (JJ)
In The Ghetto
Elvis Presley; *From Elvis In Memphis* .... (RCA)
From Memphis To Vegas .... (RCA)
Golden Records-#5 .... (RCA)
In Person .... (RCA)
Pure Gold .... (RCA)
Top Ten Hits .... (RCA)
Mac Davis; *Greatest Hits* .... (COL)
I'm Leaving Chicago
Luther Johnson/Magic Rockers; *I Want To Groove With You* .... (BUL)
Jesus Just Left Chicago
ZZ Top; *Best Of* .... (WB)
Six-Pack .... (WB)
Tres Hombres .... (WB)
Little Chicago Fire
Count Basie Orchestra; *Live At El Morocco* ..... (TLR)
Little Joe From Chicago
Mary Lou Williams; *Best Of* .... (PAB)
Nat King Cole; *Straighten Up & Fly Right* .... (POE)
Mama Chicago
Bonnie Koloc; *With You On My Side* .... (FF)
My Kind Of Town
Frank Sinatra; *At The Sands* .... (RPR)
Main Event-Live From Madison Sq. Garden .... (RPR)
Man & His Music .... (RPR)
Reprise Collection .... (RPR)
Sinatra Reprise-The Very Good Years .... (RPR)
Night Chicago Died
Paper Lace; *Back To The '70s-#3* .... (DOM)
Super Hits/'70s-Have A Nice Day-#13 .... (RHI)
On The Southside Of Chicago
Vic Damone; *Best* .... (RCA)
Only In Chicago
Barry Manilow; *Barry* .... (ARI)
Phone Call From Chicago
Peter Himmelman; *From Strength To Strength* ..... (EPI)
Pretty Girls In Chicago Polka
Li'l Wally; *Brings Happiness To You* .... (JJ)
Sheik Of Chicago
Joe Stampley; *Greatest Hits* .... (EPI)
Streets Of Old Chicago
Carl Martin/Ted Bogan/Howard Armstrong; *That Old Gang Of Mine* .... (FF)
Sweet Chicago Home
David Bromberg; *How Late'll Ya Play 'Til* .... (FAN)
Sweet Home Chicago
Blues Brothers; *ST/Blues Brothers* .... (ATL)
Foghat; *Best Of-#2* .... (RHI)
Stone Blue .... (RHI)
Junior Parker; *Best Of* .... (MCA)
Leon Russell & Marc Benno; *Asylum Choir-#2* .. (MCA)
Magic Sam; *Live* .... (DEL)
Robert Johnson; *Complete Recordings* .... (COL)
King Of The Delta Blues Singers-#2 .... (COL)
Taj Mahal; *Recycling The Blues-Other Related Stuff* .... (COL)
Take Me Back To Chicago
Chicago; *Greatest Hits-#2* .... (COL)
Group Portrait .... (COL)
Take Me Back To Chicago .... (COL)
#11 .... (COL)
Two Years In Chicago
Robin Trower; *1st Dibs* .... (FF)
When The Levee Breaks
Led Zeppelin; *Led Zeppelin (collection)* .... (ATL)
#4 .... (ATL)

CITIES: CINCINNATI
See Also: STATES: OHIO

Cincinnati Blues
Jesse Fuller; *Brother Lowdown* .... (FAN)
Favorites .... (PRS)
Frisco Bound .... (ARH)
Ray Pennington & Buddy Emmons; *Swingin' From The '40s Through The '80s* .... (SO)
Cincinnati Daddy
Duke Ellington; *Jazz Heritage-Rockin' In Rhythm-#3* .... (MSP)
Jungle Band-Brunswick Era-#2 .... (DEC)
Cincinnati Fatback
Roogalator; *Stiff Records Box Set* .... (RHI)
Cincinnati Fireball
Johnny Burnette; *Best Of-You're Sixteen* .... (EMI)
Cincinnati Jail
Lonnie Mack; *Attack Of The Killer V* .... (ALG)
Second Sight .... (ALG)
Cincinnati Lou
Merle Travis; *Best Of* .... (RHI)
Cincinnati Rag
Jerry Douglas; *Fluxedo* .... (ROU)
Cincinnati Stomp
Big Joe Duskin; *Cincinnati Stomp* .... (ARH)
Cincinnati Underworld Woman
Bob Coleman/Cincinnati Jug Band; *Cincinnati Blues-1928-1936* .... (SB)
Cincinnati, Ohio
Bill Anderson; *Story* .... (MCA)
Connie Smith; *Best Of* .... (DOM)
Greatest Hits-#1 .... (RCA)
Cockroach That Ate Cincinnati
Possum; *Dr. Demento's Delights* .... (WB)
Rose/Arrangement; *Dr. Demento's Greatest-#4-1970s* .... (RHI)
South Of Cincinnati
Dwight Yoakam; *Guitars, Cadillacs, Etc., Etc.* .... (RPR)
Susie Cincinnati
Beach Boys; *15 Big Ones* .... (RPR)
"WKRP In Cincinnati" Theme
Steve Carlisle; *Sings WKRP* .... (MCA)

CITIES: D
See Also: CITIES: DALLAS, DENVER, DETROIT, DUBLIN

Back Home In Derry
Christy Moore; *Ride On* .... (GRE)
Spirit Of Freedom .... (GRE)
Cliffs Of Dover
Eric Johnson; *Ah Via Musicom* .... (CAP)
Davenport Blues
Bix Beiderbecke/Chicago Cornets; *Bix Beiderbecke/Chicago Cornets* .... (MS)
Ry Cooder; *Jazz* .... (WB)
Dayton Ohio 1903
Randy Newman; *Sail Away* .... (RPR)
Deadwood, South Dakota
Nanci Griffith; *One Fair Summer Evening* ...... (MCA)
Doraville
Atlanta Rhythm Section; *Are You Ready* .... (POL)
South's Greatest Hits .... (CPC)
Third Annual Pipe Dream .... (POL)
Dry Cleaner From Des Moines
Joni Mitchell; *Mingus* .... (ASY)
Shadows & Light .... (ASY)
Dubuque, Crazy Creek, & Goldrush
Robin Flower; *Green Sneakers* .... (FF)
Duke Of Dubuque
Manhattan Transfer; *Bop Doo-Wopp* .... (ATL)
Live .... (ATL)
Eight'r From Decatur
Bob Wills; *Best Of-#2* .... (MCA)
It's A Long Way To Daytona
Mel Tillis; *45* .... (ELE)
Ramona From Daytona
Dave Holladay; *Ramona From Daytona* .... (SO)

Romance In Durango
Bob Dylan; *Biograph* ....(COL)
Desire ....(COL)
Streets Of Derry
Andy Irvine & Paul Brady; *Andy Irvine & Paul
Brady* ....(GRE)
White Cliffs Of Dover
Kay Kyser/Orchestra; *16 Most Requested
Songs/'40s-#1* ....(COL)
Lee Andrews/Hearts; *Biggest Hits* ....(CLT)
Mystics; *16 Golden Classics* ....(CLT)
Righteous Brothers; *Anthology-1962-1974* .... (RHI)
Greatest Hits ....(VRV)
Rosemary Clooney; *For The Duration* ....(CCJ)

CITIES: DALLAS

See Also: STATES: TEXAS

Alice You've Made Dallas (Paradise...)
Lee Ferrell; *Hard Times* .... (TMS)
Backside Of Dallas
Jeannie C. Riley; *Greatest Hits* .... (PLN)
Things Go Better With Love .... (PLN)
Big D
Broadway Cast; *Most Happy Fella* ....(RCA)
Original Broadway Cast; *Most Happy Fella* ..... (SMC)
Cowboy Hat In Dallas
Charlie Daniels Band; *Homesick Heroes* .... (EPI)
Dallas
Alan Jackson; *Don't Rock The Jukebox* .... (ARI)
Jimmie Dale Gilmore; *Jimmie Dale Gilmore* ...... (HT)
Jimmy Buffett; *A 1 A* .... (MCA)
Joe Ely; *Must Notta Gotta Lotta* .... (MCA)
Johnny Winter; *Johnny Winter* ....(COL)
Poco; *Head Over Heels* .... (MCA)
Dallas Alice
Joe Stampley; *45* .... (MCA)
Dallas Blues
Louis Armstrong/Orchestra; *Louis & The Big
Bands* ....(DSQ)
Dallas Cowboys
Charley Pride; *45* ....(RCA)
Dallas Delight
Buck Clayton & Buddy Tate; *Kansas City Nights* . (PRS)
Dallas Doings
Duke Ellington; *Jubilee Stomp* .... (BLU)
Dallas In The Rain
Clyde Crell; *45* ....(OOP)
Dallas Rag
Dallas String Band; *Greatest Country
Blues-1927-1936-#2* .... (SB)
New Lost City Ramblers; *Early
Years-1958-1962* .... (FLW)
Dallas Rag/Maple Leaf Rag
David Bromberg; *How Late'll Ya Play 'Til* ....(FAN)
Dallas To Odessa
Lyn Childress; *Different Shade Of Country* ....(SO)
Dallas We Come From
Nemesis; *Munchies For Your Bass* ....(PRO)
Dallas, Texas
Austin Lounge Lizards; *Highway Cafe Of The
Damned* .... (WAT)
"Dallas" Theme
Original Music; *Television's Greatest Hits-#3* ..... (TVT)
Down Dallas Alley
Buckwheat Zydeco; *Taking It Home* .... (ISL)
Eyes As Big As Dallas
Randy Wagner; *45* .... (DOO)
Forth Worth & Dallas Blues
Leadbelly; *King Of The Twelve-String Guitar* .....(COL)
Legends Of The Blues-#1 ....(COL)
Goin' Through The Big D
Mark Chesnutt; *What A Way To Live* .... (DEC)
Goin' To Dallas
Lightnin' Hopkins; *Drinkin' In The Blues-Golden
Classics-#1* ....(CLT)
Lightnin' Hopkins ....(EVR)
Goin' To Dallas To See My Pony Run
Lightnin' Hopkins; *Blues In My Bottle* .... (BV)
Drinkin' In The Blues-Golden Classics-#1 ....(CLT)
Goodnight Dallas
Carlene Carter; *I Fell In Love* ....(RPR)

Hot Nite In Dallas
Moon Martin; *Shots From A Cold Nightmare* ..... (CAP)
Out Of Dallas
Jerry Giddens; *Devil's Front Door* .... (DD)
Raining In Dallas
Kelly Schoppa; *Amarillo By Morning* .... (BLR)
Saturday Night In Dallas
Kenny Seratt; *45* ....(MDJ)
South Dallas Drop
Ron "C"; "C" Ya ....(PRO)
This Ain't Dallas
Hank Williams, Jr.; *Five-O* ....(W/C)
Greatest Hits-#3 ....(W/C)
Trouble In Dallas
Regulators; *Regulators* ....(POL)

CITIES: DENVER

See Also: STATES: COLORADO

Almost Dawn In Denver
Faron Young; *Greatest Hits-#3* ....(SO)
Beautiful People Of Denver
Original Cast; *Unsinkable Molly Brown* ....(CAP)
Coming Down From Denver
Byron Berline; *Dad's Favorites* .... (ROU)
Denver
Gatlin Brothers; *Biggest Hits* ....(COL)
Larry Gatlin/Gatlin Brothers; *17 Greatest Hits* ...(COL)
Houston To Denver ....(COL)
Ronnie Milsap; *Denver* ....(FFT)
There Goes My Heart ....(FFT)
Willie Nelson; *Red-Headed Stranger* ....(COL)
Denver Blues
Tampa Red; *Great Blues Guitarists-String
Dazzlers* ....(COL)
Get Out Of Denver
Bob Seger; *Live Bullet* ....(CAP)
Seven ....(CAP)
Dave Edmunds; *Get It* .... (SS)
Gone To Denver
Waylon Jennings; *Lonesome On're & Mean* ......(RCA)
I Won't Go Back To Denver
Lynn Anderson; *What A Man My Man Is* ....(COL)
Kid From Denver
Paul Quinichette; *Kid From Denver* ....(BIO)
Lone Star State Of Mind
Don Williams; *Currents* ....(RCA)
Nanci Griffith; *Country Classics-#8-1986-1987* . .(MSP)
Lone Star State Of Mind ....(MCA)
Pat Alger/Nanci Griffith/Trisha Yearwood; *True Love &
Other Short Stories* ....(SH)
O.D.'d In Denver
Hank Williams, Jr.; *Whiskey Bent & Hell Bound* ..(W/C)
Things To Do In Denver When You're Dead
Warren Zevon; *Mr. Bad Example* .... (GIA)
This Ain't The Denver I Remember
Pirates Of The Mississippi; *Walk The Plank* ....(LIB)

CITIES: DETROIT

See Also: CARS, STATES: MICHIGAN

Born In Detroit
Rockets; *Live* ....(CAP)
Rocket Roll ....(ELE)
Christmas Time In The Motor City
Was (Not Was); *Christmas Record* .... (PAS)
Detroit
Almighty; *Blood Fire & Love* ....(POL)
J To The D; *Living On The Edge* ....(W/I)
Detroit 442
Blondie; *Plastic Letters* ....(CHR)
Detroit Blues
Blind James Campbell; *& His Nashville Street
Band* .... (ARH)
Detroit Breakdown
J. Geils Band; *Best Of* ....(ATL)
Blow Your Face Out ....(ATL)
Nightmares ....(ATL)
Detroit City
Ace Cannon; *Golden Favorites* .... (RAN)
Bill Anderson; *Best Of* ....(CCB)

Bobby Bare; *Nipper's Greatest Hits-'60s-#2* ......(RCA)
  This Is ....(RCA)
Chet Atkins; *Country Gems* ....(PRR)
Flatt & Scruggs; *20 All-Time Great Recordings* ...(COL)
Hank Williams, Jr.; *Live At Cobo Hall Detroit* ....(POL)
  Standing In The Shadows ....(POL)
Mel Tillis; *Best Of* ....(MCA)
  Live At The Sam Houston Coliseum ....(MGM)
Solomon Burke; *Home In Your Heart-Best Of* .... (RHI)
Detroit Diesel
Alvin Lee; *Detroit Diesel* .... (21)
Detroit Girls
Starz; *Live In Action* .... (MET)
  Starz .... (MET)
Detroit Oberek
Li'l Wally; *Here Comes* ....(JJ)
Detroit Rock City
Kiss; *Alive II* .... (CAS)
  Destroyer .... (CAS)
  Double Platinum .... (CAS)
  Smashes Thrashes & Hits .... (MER)
Detroit Snackbar Dreamer
Edgar Froese; *Stuntman* ....(BP)
Detroit Special
Big Bill Broonzy; *Unissued Test Pressings* .... (MLN)
Going Back To Detroit
Platters; *Double Gold* .... (MCR)
It's A Long Way From Detroit...To Austin
Buddy Harris; *45* .... (PLN)
Motor City Madhouse
Ted Nugent; *Double Live Gonzo* .... (EPI)
  Ted Nugent .... (EPI)
Motownphilly
Boyz II Men; *Cooleyhighharmony* .... (MOT)
Panic In Detroit
David Bowie; *Aladdin Sane* ....(RYK)
  Scary Monsters ....(RYK)
  Sound + Vision ....(RYK)
Passport To Detroit
Joe Strummer; *Earthquake Weather* .... (EPI)
Three Girls From Detroit
Will/Bushmen; *Will/Bushmen* .... (SBK)

CITIES: DUBLIN

See Also: COUNTRIES: IRELAND

Cockles & Mussels
Emily Mitchell; *The Irish Album* ....(RCA)
Dublin In My Tears
Fureys/Dave Arthur; *Dublin Songs* .... (AJK)
Dublin In The Rare Old Times
Garrison Brothers; *Songs & Stories* .... (BOO)
Dublin Lady
Andy M. Stewart & Manus Lunny; *Dublin Lady* .(GRE)
Dublin My Dublin
Paddy Reilly; *Dublin Songs* .... (AJK)
Dublin Saunter
Paddy Reilly; *Dublin Songs* .... (AJK)
Dublin Town
Brendan Grace; *Dublin Songs* .... (AJK)
Going Back To Dublin
Eric Bogle; *Something Of Value* ....(PHO)
Off To Dublin In The Green
Dubliners; *Best Of-Irish Favorites* ....(TRD)
Rocky Road To Dublin
Dubliners; *Dublin Songs* ....(AJK)
Saturday Night In Dublin
Michael "Jesse" Owens; *Across The Sea To*
Ireland ....(RGO)
Summer In Dublin
James Last/Orchestra; *Plays The Rose Of Tralee/Other*
Irish... ....(RGO)
Jim McCann; *Dublin Songs* ....(AJK)

CITIES: E

Asshole From El Paso
Kinky Friedman; *Lasso From El Paso* .... (EPI)
Kinky Friedman/Texas Jewboys; *Old Testaments & New*
Revelations ....(FTT)

East St. Louis Toodle oo
Duke Ellington; *Bethlehem Years-#1* .... (BET)
  Brunswick Era-#1 .... (MCA)
  Era ....(COL)
  Jazz Heritage-Beginning 1926-1928 .... (MCA)
Steely Dan; *Greatest Hits* .... (MCA)
  Pretzel Logic .... (MCA)
El Paso
Grateful Dead; *Steal Your Face* .... (GRD)
Marty Robbins; *Biggest Hits* ....(COL)
  Billboard Top Country Hits-1960 .... (RHI)
  Gunfighter Ballads & Trail Songs ....(COL)
  Radio Classics/'50s ....(COL)
El Paso Blues
Phillip Walker; *Someday You'll Have These Blues* (ALG)
El Paso City
Marty Robbins; *El Paso City* ....(COL)
  Greatest Country Hits Of The '70s ....(COL)
  Greatest Hits-#4 ....(COL)
  Lifetime Of Song (1951-1982) ....(COL)
I Left My Wallet In El Segundo
Tribe Called Quest; *People's Instinctive Travels...* . (JVA)
  Rap: Most Valuable Players .... (KT)
New East St. Louis Toodle-oo
Duke Ellington; *Reminiscing In Tempo* ....(COL)

CITIES: F

August In Forest City
Carol Montag; *Song For Carrie* .... (SLK)
Does Fort Worth Ever Cross Your Mind
George Strait; *Country Classics-#3* .... (MCA)
  Does Fort Worth Ever Cross Your Mind .... (MCA)
  Greatest Hits-#2 .... (MCA)
  MCA #1 Hits/'80s-#1 .... (MCA)
Folsom Prison Blues
Brooks & Dunn & Johnny Cash; *Red Hot +*
Country .... (MER)
Johnny Cash; *At Folsom Prison & San Quentin* ...(COL)
  Billboard Top Country Hits-1968 .... (RHI)
  Classic Cash-Hall Of Fame Series .... (MER)
  Greatest Hits #2 ....(COL)
  Original Golden Hits #1 .... (SUN)
  Superbilly .... (SUN)
Fort Lauderdale
Cannonball Adderley; *Compact Jazz* .... (EMA)
  Impacts; Wipe Out .... (OCE)
Fort Lauderdale Chamber Of Commerce
Elvis Presley; *ST/Girl Happy* ....(RCA)
Fort Smith
Brother Oswald/Charlie Collins; *That's Country* (ROU)
Fort Worth
Joe Lovano; *From The Soul* ....(BLN)
Fort Worth Hambone Blues
Johnny Gimble/Texas Swing Pioneers; *Johnny Gimble's*
Texas Honky Tonk Hits ....(CMH)
Fort Worth Jail
Tex Ritter; *Hillbilly Music...Thank God!-#1* ....(BUG)
Forth Worth & Dallas Blues
Leadbelly; *King Of The Twelve-String Guitar* .....(COL)
  Legends Of The Blues-#1 ....(COL)
Fresno Beauties
Original Cast; *Most Happy Fella* ....(RCA)
Ft. Worth Featherbed
Donnie Rohrs; *Country Music USA* .... (PC)
She Came From Fort Worth
Kathy Mattea; *Willow In The Wind* .... (MER)
Pat Alger & Kathy Mattea; *True Love & Other Short*
Stories ....(SH)
Trip To Flagstaff
Kornos; *On Seven Winds* ....(GRE)

CITIES: G

Bring Me A Shawl From Galway
Mary O'Hara; *At The Royal Festival Hall* ...... (SHA)
  Song For Ireland .... (SHA)
Galveston
Glen Campbell; *Classics Collection* ....(CAP)
  Greatest Hits .... (CAP)
  Very Best Of ....(CAP)

Gary, Indiana
Original Cast; *ST/Music Man* .... (CAP)
Robert Preston; *ST/Music Man* .... (WB)
Glendale Train
New Riders Of The Purple Sage; *Best Of* .... (COL)
New Riders Of The Purple Sage .... (COL)
Guadalajara
Desi Arnaz; *Best Of-Mambo King* .... (RCA)
Guantanamera
Sandpipers; *Greatest Hits* .... (A&M)
Mellow '60s .... (PRY)
How Are Things In Glocca Mora
Julie Andrews; *Little Bit Of Broadway* .... (COL)
Original Cast; *Finian's Rainbow* .... (RCA)
Rosemary Clooney; *Show Tunes* .... (CCJ)
I Belong To Glasgow
Jack Elliot; *Essential* .... (PRS)
Hard Travelin' .... (FAN)
Jack Elliot .... (VAN)
North Gulfport Boogie
Roosevelt Sykes; *Hard Drivin' Blues* .... (DEL)
Sunday In Genoa
101 Strings Orchestra; *30th Anniversary* .... (ALS)

CITIES: H

See Also: CITIES: HOUSTON

Back Home In Huntsville Again
Bobby Bare; *20 Great Country Hits* .... (RCA)
20 Greatest Country Hits .... (RCA)
Back To Havana
Michael Pluznick; *Cradle Of The Sun* .... (SOG)
Blues For The Hague
Joe Pass & Niels Henning Orsted Pederson; *North Sea Nights* .... (PAB)
Blues From Havana
Cal Tjader; *Latin Kick* .... (FAN)
Brush Fire In Hoboken
Chris Stamey; *It's A Wonderful Life* .... (DB)
Girl From Hiroshima
Third World; *Sense Of Purpose* .... (COL)
Harrisburg
Midnight Oil; *Red Sails In The Sunset* .... (COL)
Havana Affair
Ramones; *All The Stuff & More-#1* .... (SIR)
Ramones .... (SIR)
Havana Daydreamin'
Jimmy Buffett; *Havana Daydreamin'* .... (MCA)
You Had To Be There .... (MCA)
Havana For A Night
Mae West; *Fabulous* .... (MCA)
Havana Moon
Carlos Santana; *Havana Moon* .... (COL)
Chuck Berry; *After School Session* .... (CSS)
Chess Box .... (CSS)
Rockit .... (ATC)
Hiroshima
Todd Rundgren/Utopia; *Ra* .... (RHI)
Hiroshima Hole
Barefoot Jerry; *Barefootin'* .... (MON)
Holiday In Havana
Desi Arnaz; *Best Of-Mambo King* .... (RCA)
Honolulu
Michael Murphey; *Cosmic Cowboy Souvenir* .... (A&M)
Honolulu Lulu
Jan & Dean; *Deadman's Curve* .... (EMI)
Legendary Masters .... (EMI)
Surf City-Best Of .... (EMI)
/Bel-Air Bandits-One Summer Night .... (RHI)
Hot Springs, Arkansas
Bukka White; *Three Shades Of Blues* .... (BIO)
Let's Go To Big Houston
Papa Link Davis; *Best Of Cajun Country* .... (ERA)
New Huntsville Jail
Joe Evans & John Dilleshaw; *Early Country Music* (HIS)
Rush Hour In Hong Kong
Gil Melle; *Primitive Modern* .... (PRS)
Sheriff Of Hong Kong
Captain Beefheart; *Doc At The Radar Station* ...... (BP)
Shoeless Joe From Hannibal, Mo.
Original Broadway Cast; *Damn Yankees* .... (RCA)
Sister Havana
Urge Overkill; *Saturation* .... (GEF)

Surfin' In Harlem
Swamp Dogg; *Surfin' In Harlem* .... (VOL)
Swingtime In Honolulu
Duke Ellington/Cootie Williams/R.Cutters; *Duke's Men-Small Groups-#2* .... (COL)
This Ain't Havana
Ramones; *End Of The Century* .... (SIR)
West Helena Blues
Jimmy Cotton; *Chicago/The Blues/Today* .... (VAN)

CITIES: HOUSTON

See Also: STATES: TEXAS

Angel Loose In Houston
Larry Gatlin/Gatlin Brothers; *Cookin' Up A Storm* .... (CAP)
Heaven, Hell Or Houston
ZZ Top; *El Loco* .... (WB)
Six Pack .... (WB)
Houston
Dean Martin; *Greatest Hits* .... (RPR)
Glen Campbell; *Best Of* .... (CAP)
Johnny Copeland; *Ain't Nothin' But A Party* .... (ROU)
Texas Twister .... (ROU)
Houston Solution
Ronnie Milsap; *Stranger Things Have Happened* ..(RCA)
Houston (Means I'm One Day Closer...)
Gatlin Brothers; *19 Hot Country Requests* .... (EPI)
Larry Gatlin/Gatlin Brothers; *17 Greatest Hits* ...(COL)
Greatest Country Hits/'80s-1983 .... (COL)
Greatest Hits Encore .... (CAP)
Houston, Treat My Lady Good
Joe Stampley; *Red Wine & Blue Memories* .... (EPI)
If You Ain't Been To Houston
Lonesome Sundown; *Been Gone Too Long* .... (HT)
If You Ever Get To Houston
Mickey Newbury; *Sweet Memories* .... (MCA)
Spend Another Night In Houston
Sonny James; *Sonny's Side Of The Street* .... (MON)
Struggle Here In Houston
Juke Boy Bonner; *Life Gave Me A Dirty Deal* ... (ARH)
The Struggle .... (ARH)

CITIES: I

Girl From Ipanema
Antonio Carlos Jobim; *Antonio Carlos Jobim* ..... (WB)
Compact Jazz .... (VRV)
Ella Fitzgerald; *Ella A Nice* .... (PAB)
Montreux '75 .... (PAB)
Pablo Today-Ella Embraces A.C. Jobim .... (PAB)
Stan Getz & Astrud Gilberto; *Cruisin'-1964* ..... (INC)
Getz/Gilberto .... (VRV)
Going Back To Iuka
Albert King; *Lovejoy* .... (STX)
Koko Taylor/Blues Machine; *Live From Chicago-With The Queen* .... (ALG)
Indianapolis Blues
David Lahm; *Freal Jazz For The Folks Who Feel Jazz* .... (PAJ)
Telephone Call From Istanbul
Tom Waits; *Big Time* .... (ISL)
Frank's Wild Years-Un Operachi Romantico ..... (ISL)

CITIES: J

Back To Johnson City
J.E. Mainer's Crazy Mountaineers; *#2* .... (OT)
Don't You Hear Jerusalem Moan
Nitty Gritty Dirt Band; *Will The Circle Be Unbroken-#2* .... (UNI)
From Jerusalem To Jericho
Uncle Dave Macon; *Laugh Your Blues Away* ... (ROU)
Funkin' For Jamaica (NY)
Tom Browne; *Love Approach* .... (GRP)
Honky Tonk Women (Jackson)
Elton John; *11-17-70* .... (POL)
Humble Pie; *Best* .... (A&M)
Classics-#14 .... (A&M)
Eat It .... (A&M)

Ike & Tina Turner; *Best Of* .... (EMI)
  Get Back .... (LIB)
Joe Cocker; *Mad Dogs & Englishmen* .... (A&M)
Rolling Stones; *Get Yer Ya-Ya's Out* .... (AKO)
  Hot Rocks-1964-1971 .... (AKO)
  Love You Live .... (RS)
  Through The Past Darkly-Big Hits-#2 ...... (AKO)
Willie Nelson & Leon Russell; *Half Nelson* ..... (COL)
Jackson
Johnny Cash & June Carter; *Johnny Cash's Greatest*
  Hits .... (COL)
Nancy Sinatra & Lee Hazlewood; *Hit Years* ..... (RHI)
Jackson Ain't A Very Big Town
Tammy Wynette; *My World* .... (FFT)
Jerusalem On The Jukebox
Richard Thompson; *Amnesia* .... (CAP)
Johannesburg Woman
David Rudder; *1990* .... (SIR)
Joshua Fought The Battle Of Jericho
Elvis Presley; *His Hand In Mine* .... (RCA)
Jordanaires; *Tribute To Elvis' Favorite Spirituals* ....(SO)
New Messengers Of Happiness; *Swinging Gospel* . (ALS)
Pete Seeger; *20 Golden Pieces Of* .... (BLD)
Sister Rosetta Tharpe; *Live At The Hot Club De*
  France .... (MLN)
New Jerusalem
Tom Gavornik; *High Places* .... (AP)
Word Of Mouth Chorus; *Rivers Of Delight* ...... (NON)
Road To Jakarta
Steve Hunter; *The Deacon* .... (IRN)
Run, Come See Jerusalem
Arlo Guthrie & Pete Seeger; *Precious Friend* ...... (WB)
Train To Johannesburg
Original Cast; *Lost In The Stars* .... (MCA)
Walkin' In Jerusalem
Bill Monroe; *Country Music Hall Of Fame* ...... (MCA)
Doc Watson; *Old Timey Concert* .... (VAN)
Ricky Skaggs; *Love's Gonna Get Ya* .... (EPI)

CITIES: K

See Also: CITIES: KANSAS CITY

Funky Kingston
Toots/Maytals; *Funky Kingston* .... (ISL)
  Island Story-25th Anniversary .... (ISL)
  Live .... (MGO)
Girl From Key Biscayne
Diego Modena & Jean Philippe Audin; *Ocarina* . (PRV)
Girl From Knoxville
Dave Loggins; *Apprentice (In A Musical*
  Workshop) .... (EPI)
I've Got A Gal In Kalamazoo
Glenn Miller; *Best Of* .... (RCA)
  Decade Of The '40s .... (RCA)
  Legendary Performer-#1 & 2 .... (RCA)
  Memorial 1944-1969 .... (RCA)
  Pure Gold .... (RCA)
  Story .... (RCA)
  Unforgettable .... (RCA)
Kaplan Waltz
Nathan Abshire; *& Other Cajun Gems* .... (ARH)
Katmandu
Bob Seger; *Beautiful Loser* .... (CAP)
  Live Bullet .... (CAP)
Cat Stevens; *Classics-#24* .... (A&M)
  Footsteps In The Dark-Greatest Hits-#2 ..... (A&M)
  Mona Bone Jakon .... (A&M)
Knoxville Blues
Toulouse Engelhardt; *Toullusions* .... (BRR)
Knoxville Courthouse Blues
Hank Williams, Jr.; *Major Moves* .... (W/C)
Knoxville Girl
Cathy Fink & Duck Donald; *Cathy Fink & Duck*
  Donald .... (FF)
Jimmy Martin; *Me 'N Ole Pete* .... (IGR)
Stanley Brothers; *Stanley Series-Vol. 1-#1* ...... (COP)
Knoxville Rag
Etta Baker; *One-Dime Blues* .... (ROU)
One Sad Night In Kerrville
Tom Kell; *Sad Night* .... (WB)

CITIES: KANSAS CITY

See Also: STATES: KANSAS, MISSOURI

Blue Monday At Kansas City Red's
Cary Bell; *Blues Harp* .... (DEL)
Eternal Kansas City
Van Morrison; *Period Of Transition* .... (WB)
From K.C. To L.A.
Max Groove; *Maximum Groove* .... (OPT)
Goin' To Kansas City
Furry Lewis; *Shake 'Em On Down* .... (FAN)
Jimmy Witherspoon; *'Spoon Concerts* .... (FAN)
I'm Goin' To Kansas City
Frances Faye; *Caught In The Act-Thunderbird* ... (CRS)
Kansas City
Beatles; *Box Set* .... (CAP)
  Rock 'N' Roll Music-#1 .... (CAP)
  Super Oldies/'60s-#10 .... (AUF)
  VI .... (CAP)
Bill Haley/Comets; *Greatest Hits* .... (EVR)
Fats Domino; *Greatest Hits* .... (EVR)
Original Broadway Cast; *Oklahoma* .... (MCA)
Wilbert Harrison; *American Graffiti-#3* .... (MCA)
  Billboard Top Rock 'N' Roll Hits-1959 .... (RHI)
  Cruisin' 1959 .... (INC)
  Echoes Of A Rock Era-Middle Years .... (RLL)
  Super Oldies/'50s-#2 .... (AUF)
Kansas City Blues
Big Joe Turner; *Turns On The Blues* .... (KNT)
Janis Joplin; *ST/Janis* .... (COL)
Jo Stafford; *Jo Plus Blues* .... (CRN)
Joe Williams; *Everyday I Have The Blues* .... (SAV)
Kansas City Bomber
Phil Ochs; *War Is Over-Best Of* .... (A&M)
Kansas City Lights
Steve Wariner; *Greatest Hits* .... (RCA)
  Steve Wariner .... (RCA)
Kansas City Papa
Leadbelly; *King Of The Twelve-String Guitar* ..... (COL)
  Leadbelly .... (COL)
Kansas City Railroad Blues
Nashville Bluegrass Band; *Waitin' For The Hard Times*
  To Go .... (SH)
Kansas City Song
Buck Owens; *Collection-1959-1990* .... (RHI)
Kansas City Southern
Pure Prairie League; *Takin' The Stage* .... (RCA)
  Two Lane Highway .... (RCA)
Kansas City Star
Roger Miller; *Best Of-His Greatest Songs* .... (CCB)
  Golden Hits .... (SMA)
Kansas City Stomp
Jelly Roll Morton; *1923-1924* .... (MS)
  Jelly Roll Morton .... (BLU)
Kansas City Tango
Bud Shank & Shorty Rogers; *California Concert* (CTM)
Kansas City Woman
Little Charlie/Nightcats; *Big Break!* .... (ALG)
Kansas City Wrinkle
Count Basie/Orchestra; *ST/Listen Up-Lives Of Quincy*
  Jones .... (QUE)
Leaving Kansas City
George Jackson; *Sweet Down Home Delta Blues* (AMB)
Mobile & K.C. Line
Robert Shaw; *Ma Grinder* .... (ARH)
Powder River/Carrie's Gone To Kansas C.
Bill Shute & Lisa Null; *American Primitive* ...... (GRE)
Train From Kansas City
Shangri-Las; *Golden Hits Of* .... (MER)
We Gonna Move To Kansas City
Walter Horton; *Fine Cuts* .... (BLI)

CITIES: L

See Also: CITIES: LAS VEGAS, LONDON, LOS
ANGELES

Big Bad Bill Is Sweet William Now
Ry Cooder; *Jazz* .... (WB)
Deportee (Plane Wreck At Los Gatos)
Arlo Guthrie & Pete Seeger; *Together In Concert* (RPR)
Byrds; *Byrds (collection)* .... (COL)

Cisco Houston; *Greatest Songs Of Woody Guthrie* (VAN)
Gene Clark & Carla Olson; *So Rebellious A Lover* (RHI)
W. Jennings/W. Nelson/J. Cash/K. Krist.;
    Highwayman ....(COL)
Eight More Miles To Louisville
Eric Weissberg; *Dueling Banjos From "Deliverance"* (WB)
Mike Auldridge; *Dobro/Blues & Bluegrass* ....(TAK)
Reno & Smiley; *1983 Collector's Edition-#3* .....(GUS)
    Best Of ....(STR)
Girl From Lodi
Bola Sete; *Incomparable* ....(FAN)
Going Back To Liverpool
Jackie Lomax; *Is This What You Want?* ....(CAP)
Going Down To Liverpool
Bangles; *All Over The Place* ....(COL)
    Greatest Hits ....(COL)
Goin' Down To Laurel
Steve Forbert; *Alive On Arrival* .... (NEM)
How Far To Little Rock
Stanley Brothers; *Stanley Series-Vol. 1-#2* ....(COP)
Leaving Lexington
Fiction Brothers; *Things Are Coming My Way* ......(FF)
Leaving Of Liverpool
Clancy Brothers; *Greatest Hits* .... (VAN)
Leningrad
Billy Joel; *Storm Front* ....(COL)
Lisbon Antigua
Nelson Riddle/Orchestra; *Memories Are Made Of
    This* ....(CAP)
Little Girl From Little Rock
Original Cast; *Gentlemen Prefer Blondes* ....(SSP)
Little Rock
Collin Raye; *Extremes* ....(EPI)
Livingston Saturday Night
Jimmy Buffett; *Son Of A Son Of A Sailor* .... (MCA)
    ST/FM ....(MCA)
Lodi
Creedence Clearwater Revival; *1969* ....(FAN)
    Chronicle ....(FAN)
    Creedence Country ....(FAN)
    Green River ....(FAN)
    Live In Europe ....(FAN)
    More Creedence Gold ....(FAN)
    Travelin' Band ....(FAN)
Louisville
Jann Browne; *Tell Me Why* ....(CCB)
Louisville Lou
Johnny Mercer; *Uncollected-1944* .... (HIN)
Lovetown
Peter Gabriel; *ST/Philadelphia* ....(EPX)
Luckenbach Texas
Waylon Jennings; *Greatest Hits* ....(RCA)
    Ol' Waylon ....(RCA)
    Stars Are Out In Texas ....(RCA)
Man Of La Mancha
Original Cast; *Man Of La Mancha* .... (MCA)
Original London Cast; *Man Of La Mancha* ..... (MCA)
Streets Of Laredo
Buck Owens/Buckaroos; *Live At Carnegie Hall* .. (CMF)
Marty Robbins; *All-Time Greatest Hits* ....(COL)
    More Greatest Hits ....(COL)
    More Gunfighter Ballads & Trail Songs ....(COL)
Rex Allen; *Great American Singing Cowboys* ..... (REP)
Sunrise In La Jolla
Kilauea; *Antigua Blue* ....(BRA)

CITIES: LAS VEGAS

*See Also: GAMBLING, LUCK, STATES:
    NEVADA*

Big In Vegas
Buck Owens; *All-Time Greatest-#1* ....(CCB)
    Collection-1959-1990 ....(RHI)
    Great Records/Decade-'70s Hits-Country ....(CCB)
Goin' To Las Vegas
Suicide; *1/2 Alive* ....(ROI)
Heaven Or Las Vegas
Cocteau Twins; *Heaven Or Las Vegas* ....(CAP)
Las Vegas Basement
Julian Cope; *Peggy Suicide* ....(ISL)
Las Vegas Blues
Don Malena; *City Boy* ....(ACT)

Las Vegas Girl
Leroy Van Dyke; *45* ....(MCA)
Las Vegas Oberek
Cavaliers; *Have Polka Will Travel* ....(ACT)
Las Vegas Ramble
Happy Polkateers; *Happy Polkateers* .... (CRS)
Las Vegas Story
Gun Club; *Las Vegas Story* .... (IRS)
Las Vegas Tango
Gil Evans; *Individualism Of* ....(VRV)
Las Vegas Turnaround
Daryl Hall & John Oates; *Abandoned
    Luncheonette* ....(ATL)
    No Goodbyes ....(ATL)
Leaving Las Vegas
Sheryl Crow; *Tuesday Night Music* ....(A&M)
Mambo Las Vegas
Howard Rumsey's Lighthouse All-Stars; *Music For
    Lighthousekeeping* ....(CTM)
Ooh Las Vegas
Emmylou Harris; *Elite Hotel* ....(RPR)
Gram Parsons; *Grievous Angel* ....(RPR)
Queen Of Las Vegas
B-52's; *Whammy* ....(WB)
That Night In Las Vegas
Ennio Morricone; *ST/Bugsy* .... (EPI)
T-Bird To Vegas
Albert Lee; *Speechless* ....(MCA)
Vegas Weekend
Thelonius Monster; *Beautiful Mess* ....(CAP)
Viva Las Vegas
Elvis Presley; *ST/This Is Elvis* ....(RCA)
    Worldwide 50 Gold Award Hits-#1 & 2 ....(RCA)

CITIES: LONDON
    See Also: COUNTRIES: ENGLAND

Autumn In London Town
Norrie Paramor; *Autumn* .... (ANG)
Dark Streets Of London
Greater Than One; *Duty & Trust* .... (ROI)
Dead Girls Of London
Frank Zappa; *You Can't Do That On Stage
    Anymore-#5* ....(RYK)
Foggy Day (In London Town)
Dick Hyman; *Music Of 1937-Maybeck Recital
    Hall-#3* .... (CCJ)
Foggy Night In London Town
Fred Astaire; *45* ....(OOP)
Foggy Streets Of London
Special EFX; *Special EFX* ....(GRP)
I Love London
Tommy Page; *Tommy Page* .... (SIR)
Inner London Violence
Bad Manners; *ST/Dance Craze* .... (CHR)
Last Train To London
Electric Light Orchestra; *Box Of Their Best* ....(JET)
    Discovery ....(JET)
Leaving London
Tom Paxton; *Compleat* .... (ELE)
    Outward Bound ....(ELE)
Life In London
Pat Travers; *Boom Boom...Best Of* ....(POL)
    Putting It Straight ....(POL)
Little London Boys
Johnny Thunders; *Stations Of The Cross* .... (ROI)
London
Queensryche; *Rage For Order* .... (EMI)
Smiths; *Louder Than Bombs* ....(SIR)
    Rank .... (SIR)
London After Midnight
Wrathchild America; *Climbin' The Walls* .... (ATL)
London Belongs To Me
Saint Etienne; *Foxbase Alpha* ....(WB)
London Blues (Shoe Shiner's Drag)
Jelly Roll Morton; *1923-1924* .... (MS)
London Boys
David Bowie; *London Collector-Starting Point* ....(LON)
    Love You Till Tuesday ....(LON)
London Bridge
Big Audio Dynamite; *Megatop Phoenix* ....(COL)

Bread; *Anthology* .... (ELE)
   Best Of-#2 .... (ELE)
   Bread .... (ELE)
London Bridge Is Falling Down
   Count Basie; *Good Morning Blues* .... (MCA)
   Newtrament; *Word 2* .... (JVA)
London By Night
   Frank Sinatra; *Come Fly With Me* .... (CAP)
   Sinatra Rarities-Columbia Years .... (COL)
London Bye Ta-Ta
   David Bowie; *Sound + Vision* .... (RYK)
London Calling
   Clash; *London Calling* .... (EPI)
   On Broadway .... (EPI)
   Story Of-#1 .... (EPI)
London Gets Ready
   Oscar Peterson; *Royal Wedding Suite* .... (PAB)
London Girl
   Jam; *This Is The Modern World* .... (POL)
London Girls
   Vibrators; *Pure Mania* .... (COL)
London Homesick Blues
   David Allan Coe; *Biggest Hits* .... (COL)
   Jerry Jeff Walker; *Great Gonzos* .... (MCA)
   Viva Terlingua .... (MCA)
London In July
   Corky Hale; *Plays George Gershwin & Vernon
   Duke* .... (CRS)
London Lady
   Stranglers; *All Live & All Of The Night* .... (EPI)
   Rattus Norvegicus .... (A&M)
London Leatherboys
   Accept; *Balls To The Wall* .... (POR)
   Compilation .... (POR)
London Life
   Ian & Sylvia; *Greatest Hits* .... (VAN)
   Nashville .... (VAN)
London Luck & Love
   Daryl Hall & John Oates; *Bigger Than Both Of
   Us* .... (RCA)
London Pride
   John Williams; *Echoes Of London* .... (COL)
London Skyline
   Acoustic Alchemy; *New Edge* .... (GRP)
London Song
   Seatrain; *Marblehead Messenger* .... (OW)
London Suite
   Fats Waller; *In London* .... (DSQ)
London Town
   Donovan; *Troubadour-Definitive Collection* .... (EPI)
   James Taylor; *Dad Loves His Work* .... (COL)
   Wings; *London Town* .... (CAP)
London Traffic
   Jam; *This Is The Modern World* .... (POL)
London You're A Lady
   Pogues; *Peace & Love* .... (ISL)
Londonderry Air
   Mormon Tabernacle Choir; *Album* .... (COL)
   Greatest Hits-#2 .... (COL)
   Lord's Prayer .... (COL)
London/Old Welsh Song
   Joan Baez; *First Ten Years* .... (VAN)
London's Burning
   Clash; *Clash* .... (EPI)
   On Broadway .... (EPI)
   Story Of-#1 .... (EPI)
Next Plane To London
   Rose Garden; *45* .... (ATL)
Night In London
   Poncho Sanchez; *Chile Con Soul* .... (CP)
No Place Like London
   Original Cast/Angela Lansbury; *Sweeney Todd* ..(RCA)
On London Bridge
   Jo Stafford; *International Hits* .... (CRN)
Piccadilly
   Squeeze; *East Side Story* .... (A&M)
Piccadilly Circus
   Stiff Little Fingers; *See You Up There!* .... (CRL)
Piccadilly Palare
   Morrissey; *Bona Drag* .... (SIR)
   Kill Uncle .... (SIR)
Port London Early
   Robin Williamson/Merry Band; *American
   Stonehenge* .... (FF)

Rainy Day In London
   Boulevard; *Into The Street* .... (MCA)
Souvenir Of London
   Cleo Laine; *Born On A Friday* .... (RCA)
   Return To Carnagie .... (RCA)
Souvenir Of London (V.D.)
   Procol Harum; *Grand Hotel* .... (CHR)
Streets Of London
   Mary Hopkin; *Earth Song/Ocean Song* .... (CAP)
This Amazing London Town
   Original Broadway Cast; *The Rothschilds* .... (SMC)
Tower Of London
   ABC; *How To Be A Zillionaire* .... (MER)
Werewolves Of London
   Warren Zevon; *Excitable Boy* .... (ASY)
   Quiet Normal Life-Best Of .... (ASY)
   Stand In The Fire .... (ASY)
   ST/Color Of Money .... (MCA)
West End Girls
   Pet Shop Boys; *Disco* .... (EMI)
   Discography-Complete Singles Collection .... (EMI)
   Please .... (EMI)
Wild West End
   Dire Straits; *Dire Straits* .... (WB)
Worst Pies In London
   Original Cast; *Sweeney Todd* .... (RCA)

CITIES: LOS ANGELES

*See Also: This category for L.A. suburbs,
HOLLYWOOD, STATES: CALIFORNIA*

Ain't Nobody Straight In L.A.
   Miracles; *City Of Angels* .... (TAM)
All I Wanna Do
   Sheryl Crow; *Tuesday Night Music Club* ... (A&M)
Anaheim, Azusa & Cucamonga Sewing Circle
   Jan & Dean; *Best Of* .... (EMI)
   Legendary Masters .... (UA)
Another Nice Day In L.A.
   Eddie Money; *Right Here* .... (COL)
Back In L.A.
   B.B. King; *There Is Always One More Time* ..... (MCA)
   Neil Diamond; *Hot August Night II* .... (COL)
Beautiful Downtown Burbank
   Harper Valley P.T.A.; *Country Gold* .... (PLN)
Born In East L.A.
   Cheech & Chong; *45* .... (MCA)
Burnin' In L.A.
   Lightnin' Hopkins; *Lightnin' Sam Hopkins* ...... (ARH)
Century City
   Tom Petty/Heartbreakers; *Damn The Torpedoes* . (BKS)
City Of Angels
   Jay Ferguson; *Real Life Ain't This Way* .... (ASY)
   Miracles; *City Of Angels* .... (TAM)
City Of The Angels
   Journey; *Evolution* .... (COL)
   Wang Chung; *ST/To Live And Die In L.A.* ...... (GEF)
Coming Into Los Angeles
   Arlo Guthrie; *Best Of* .... (WB)
   Running Down The Road .... (RPR)
   ST/Woodstock .... (ATL)
Country Boy (You Got Your Feet In L.A.)
   Glen Campbell; *Best Of* .... (LIB)
   Classics Collection .... (LIB)
   Greatest Hits .... (CCB)
Electric L.A. Sunset
   Al Stewart; *Early Years* .... (OOP)
Free Fallin'
   Tom Petty; *Full Moon Fever* .... (MCA)
From K.C. To L.A.
   Max Groove; *Maximum Groove* .... (OPT)
Going To Live In L.A.
   Roger Waters; *45* .... (COL)
Honey Don't Leave L.A.
   James Taylor; *JT* .... (COL)
How Much Is It Worth To Live In L.A.
   Waylon Jennings; *New Classic Waylon* .... (MCA)
I Am...I Said
   Neil Diamond; *12 Greatest Hits* .... (MCA)
   Hot August Night .... (MCA)
   Hot August Night II .... (MCA)
   Stones .... (MCA)

I Love L.A.
Randy Newman; *Trouble In Paradise* .... (WB)
It's A Compton Thang
Compton's Most Wanted; *It's A Compton Thang* . (ORF)
Join Me In L.A.
Warren Zevon; *Warren Zevon* .... (ASY)
Ladies Of The Canyon
Joni Mitchell; *Ladies Of The Canyon* .... (RPR)
Letter To L.A.
Joe Ely; *Live At Liberty Lunch* .... (MCA)
  Lord Of The Highway .... (HT)
Life Beyond L.A.
Ambrosia; *Life Beyond L.A.* .... (WB)
Little Old Lady From Pasadena
Beach Boys; *Concert* ....(CAP)
Jan & Dean; *Best Of* .... (EMI)
  Billboard Top Rock 'N' Roll Hits-1964 .... (RHI)
  Deadman's Curve .... (EMI)
  Surf City-Best Of .... (EMI)
Livin' In South Central L.A.
South Central Posse; *We're All In The Same Gang* (WB)
Lonesome L.A. Cowboy
New Riders Of The Purple Sage; *Adventures Of Panama
Red* ....(COL)
  Midnight Moonlight .... (RLX)
Los Angelenos
Billy Joel; *Songs In The Attic* ....(COL)
  Streetlife Serenade ....(COL)
Los Angeles
Circus Of Power; *Vices* ....(RCA)
F. Machine; *Here Comes The 21st Century* .... (RPR)
X; *Dangerous-#1* .... (FRN)
  Live At The Whisky A Go-Go .... (ELE)
  Los Angeles ....(SLS)
  TT/Wild Gift ....(SLS)
Los Angeles Blues
Lightnin' Hopkins; *Los Angeles Blues* .... (RHI)
Los Angeles Boogie
Lightnin' Hopkins; *Los Angeles Blues* .... (RHI)
L.A.
Neil Young; *Time Fades Away* .... (RPR)
L.A. Breakdown
Helen Reddy; *I Don't Know How To Love Him* ..(CAP)
L.A. Connection
Rainbow; *Long Live Rock & Roll* .... (POL)
L.A. Dreams
Charlie; *Lines* .... (JNS)
L.A. Freeway
Guy Clark; *Old No. 1* ....(SH)
Jerry Jeff Walker; *Best Of* .... (MCA)
  Great Gonzos .... (MCA)
L.A. Girls
Nazareth; *Play'n' The Game* .... (A&M)
L.A. International Airport
Susan Raye; *Best Of* ....(CAP)
L.A. Lady
New Riders Of The Purple Sage; *Adventures Of Panama
Red* ....(COL)
"L.A. Law" Theme
Original Music; *Television's Greatest Hits-#3* ..... (TVT)
L.A. Mama
Jim Stafford; *Jim Stafford* .... (POL)
L.A. Serenade
Livingston Taylor; *3-Way Mirror* .... (EPI)
L.A. Sunshine
War; *Platinim Jazz* .... (BLN)
L.A. Woman
Billy Idol; *Charmed Life* .... (CHR)
Doors; *Best Of* .... (ELE)
  Greatest Hits .... (ELE)
  L.A. Woman .... (ELE)
  ST/Doors .... (ELE)
  Weird Scenes Inside The Gold Mine .... (ELE)
L.A. (My Town)
Four Tops; *Still Waters Run Deep* .... (MOT)
MacArthur Park
Andy Williams; *Greatest Hits-#2* ....(COL)
Donna Summer; *Live & More* .... (CAS)
  On The Radio-Greatest Hits-#1&2 .... (CAS)
  Summer Collection .... (CAS)
  Walk Away-Best Of 1977-1980 .... (CAS)

Richard Harris; *His Greatest Performances* ...... (MCA)
  Love Album .... (MCA)
  Tramp Shining .... (MCA)
  Vintage Music-Orig. Oldies/'50s-'60s-#13 ..... (MCA)
Waylon Jennings; *Are You Ready For The
Country* ....(RCA)
  Best Of ....(RCA)
Magic
Cars; *Greatest Hits* .... (ELE)
  Heartbeat City .... (ELE)
Marina Del Rey
George Strait; *Greatest Hits* .... (MCA)
  Strait From The Heart .... (MCA)
Men's Room L.A.
Kinky Friedman; *Lasso From El Paso* .... (EPI)
Out In L.A.
Red Hot Chili Peppers; *Red Hot Chili Peppers* ... (EMI)
Pasadena
Al Jolson; *Lullaby Of Broadway-Music Of H.
Warren* ....(PF)
Pride Of Cucamonga
Grateful Dead; *From The Mars Hotel* .... (GRD)
Raised In Compton
Compton's Most Wanted; *Straight Checkn 'Em* ...(ORF)
Redondo Beach
Patti Smith; *Horses* .... (ARI)
San Fernando
Mary McCaslin; *Sunny California* .... (MER)
Roy Orbison; *Legendary* ....(SSP)
  Rare Orbison-#2 ....(MON)
Santa Ana
Willi Jones; *Willi Jones* .... (GEF)
Santa Ana Woman
Bobs; *Songs For Tomorrow Morning* ....(KAL)
Santa Monica Pier
Christine Lavin; *Good Thing He Can't Read My
Mind* ....(PHO)
Holly Near; *Live Album* ....(RWD)
Nitty Gritty Dirt Band; *Dream* .... (UA)
She's Gone To L.A. Again
Oak Ridge Boys; *Fancy Free* .... (MCA)
So L.A.
Motels; *All Four One* ....(CAP)
  Best Of/No Vacancy ....(CAP)
South Central L.A.
Broken Homes; *Wing & A Prayer* .... (MCA)
Straight Outta Compton
N.W.A.; *Straight Outta Compton* .... (RUP)
Sunday Night In San Fernando
Mel Torme/Mel-Tones; *California Suite* .... (DCO)
Take Me To Los Angeles
Jimmy Soul; *Best Of* .... (RHI)
That's How We Do It In L.A.
Lindsey Buckingham; *Law & Order* .... (WB)
This Is Compton
Compton's Most Wanted; *It's A Compton Thang* . (ORF)
To Live And Die In L.A.
Wang Chung; *ST/To Live And Die In L.A.* .... (GEF)
Too Dumb For New York City
Waylon Jennings; *Too Dumb For N.Y. City-Too Ugly
For L.A.* .... (EPI)
Tree Grows In Burbank
Harry James; *Uncollected-#5-1943-1953* .... (HIN)
Uptown L.A.
Beau Coup; *Born & Raised (On Rock & Roll)* ... (AMH)
Walking In L.A.
Missing Persons; *Best Of* ....(CAP)
West L.A. Fadeaway
Grateful Dead; *In The Dark* .... (ARI)
You're The Reason God Made Oklahoma
David Frizzell & Shelly West; *Carryin' On The Family
Names* .... (WB)
  Country's Greatest Hits-#9-Country Duets ...... (PRY)
  Golden Duets .... (WB)

CITIES: M

*See Also: CITIES: MEMPHIS, MIAMI, MOBILE,
NEW YORK (for Manhattan)*

Angel From Montgomery
Bonnie Raitt; *Streetlights* .... (WB)
Bonnie Raitt & John Prine; *Bonnie Raitt Collection* (WB)

John Prine; *John Prine* .... (ATL)
By The Waters Of Lake Minnetonka (Mpls.)
Glenn Miller; *Best Of-#2* ....(RCA)
Glenn Miller/Orchestra; *Complete* ....(BLU)
Christmas Card From A Hooker (Mpls.)
Tom Waits; *Blue Valentine* .... (ASY)
Coast Of Marseilles
Jimmy Buffett; *Son Of A Son Of A Sailor* .... (MCA)
Fog In Monterey
Mary Black; *No Frontiers* ....(GFT)
Girl From Mill Valley
Jeff Beck Group; *Beck-Ola* .... (EPI)
Girls Of Montreal
Artie Traum; *Life On Earth* .... (ROU)
Going To Malibu
Malibooz; *Malibooz Rule* .... (RHI)
Goin' Down To Muskogee
Jim Pepper; *Comin' & Goin'* .... (AND)
Hotter Than Mojave In My Heart
Iris DeMent; *Infamous Angel* .... (WB)
I Just Wanna Stop (Montreal)
Gino Vannelli; *Best Of* ....(A&M)
  Brother To Brother ....(A&M)
  Classics-#7 ....(A&M)
It Happened In Monterey
Frank Sinatra/Nelson Riddle Orchestra; *Songs For*
Swingin' Lovers ....(CAP)
Mel Torme/Mel-Tones; *Back In Town* ....(VRV)
Macon Georgia Bad Girl
Jeannie C. Riley; *& Fancy Friends* .... (PLN)
Macon Hambone Blues
Wet Willie; *Drippin' Wet Live* ....(CPC)
Madison Blues
George Thorogood/Destroyers; *George*
Thorogood/Destroyers .... (ROU)
  Live .... (EMI)
  Steal This Disc ....(RYK)
Nighthawks; *Best Of The Blues* .... (ADE)
  Open All Nite .... (ADE)
Manchester England
Original Broadway Cast; *Hair* ....(RCA)
Marching Through Madrid
Herb Alpert/Tijuana Brass; *Classics-#1* ....(A&M)
  Featuring Herb Alpert-#2 ....(A&M)
Marina Del Rey
George Strait; *Greatest Hits* .... (MCA)
  Strait From The Heart .... (MCA)
Marrakesh Express
Crosby, Stills & Nash; *Crosby, Stills & Nash* ..... (ATL)
  Replay .... (ATL)
  Woodstock Two .... (ATL)
Memories Of Madrid
Herb Alpert/Tijuana Brass; *Classics-#1* ....(A&M)
Mendocino
Sir Douglas Quintet; *Best Of* ....(TAK)
Mexicali Blues
Bob Weir; *Ace* .... (GRD)
Grateful Dead; *Best Of-Skeletons From The Closet* (WB)
Mexicali Rose
Bing Crosby; *Best Of* ....(SSP)
Bob Wills; *Anthology* ....(COL)
Midnight In Montgomery
Alan Jackson; *Don't Rock The Jukebox* .... (ARI)
Milwaukee
Al Jarreau; *Glow* ....(RPR)
Milwaukee Blues
Red Clay Ramblers; *Merchant's Lunch* ....(FF)
Milwaukee Polka
Frank Yankovic; *America's Favorites* ....(SMA)
Frank Yankovic/Yanks; *Greatest Hits* ....(COL)
Milwaukee Waltz
Michigan Dutchmen; *W.J.R.T. TV All-Time Polkas* ..(JJ)
Milwaukee's Favorite Waltz
Li'l Wally; *America's Favorite* ....(JJ)
Minneapolis
ABC; *Alphabet City* .... (MER)
Minneapolis Twirl
Li'l Wally; *Here Comes* ....(JJ)
Montego Bay
Amazulu; *Island Story-1962-1987-25th*
Anniversary .... (ISL)
Bobby Bloom; *Super Hits/'70s-Have A Nice*
Day-#3 .... (RHI)

Monterey
Danny Gottlieb; *Aquamarine* ....(ATL)
Eric Burdon/Animals; *Greatest Hits* ....(MGM)
Tim Buckley; *Starsailor* .... (BIZ)
Monterey Mist
Modern Jazz Quartet; *Blues At Carnegie Hall* .... (ATL)
Monterrey Pen
Marc Benno; *Lost In Austin* .... (A&M)
Montevideo
Monty Alexander Quintet; *Ivory & Steel* .... (CP)
Montgomery In The Rain
Hank Williams, Jr.; *Early Years* ....(W/C)
Steve Young; *No Place To Fall* ....(RCA)
  Seven Bridges Road .... (ROU)
Montreal
Adam Ant; *Strip* .... (EPI)
Bruce Cockburn; *Further Adventure Of* .... (ISL)
Lucie Blue Tremblay; *Tendresse* ....(OLI)
Montreal Blues
Big Joe Williams; *Shake Your Boogie* .... (ARH)
Montreux
Azymuth; *Rapid Transit* .... (MS)
Montreux Blues
R. Eldridge/D. Gillespie/C. Terry; *Trumpet Kings At*
Montreux '75 .... (PAB)
Montreux Ramble
Adrian legg; *Guitars & Other Cathedrals* .... (REL)
Moonlight In Marrakesh
Otto Cesana; *#2* .... (TUD)
Moonlight Montreal
Peter White; *Reveillez-Vous* ....(CMG)
Morning Morgantown
Joni Mitchell; *Ladies Of The Canyon* ....(RPR)
Munich Beer Garden
Michigan Dutchmen; *German Polka Favorites* ...... (JJ)
My Cousin In Milwaukee
Ella Fitzgerald; *George & Ira Gershwin Songbook* (VRV)
Night Train To Madrid
Bertram Levy; *That Old Gut Feeling* .... (FF)
Okie From Muskogee
Merle Haggard/Strangers; *Best of* ....(CAP)
  Capitol Collectors Series ....(CAP)
  Country Music Classics-#3-1965-1970 .... (KT)
  Friend In California ....(EPI)
  Songs I'll Always Sing ....(CAP)
  ST/Platoon & Songs From The Era) .... (ATL)
On The Road To Mandalay
Count Basie; *Compact Jazz-Standards* ....(VRV)
Frank Sinatra; *Come Fly With Me* ....(CAP)
Punch Out At Malibu
Surf Punks; *My Beach* .... (EPI)
Rainy Day In Monterey
Joe Sample; *Carmel* .... (MCA)
  Collection ....(GRP)
Rose Of Old Monterey
Happy Polkateers; *Happy Polkateers* ....(CRS)
Sabu Visits The Twin Cities Alone
John Prine; *Bruised Orange* .... (ASY)
Somewhere South Of Macon
Marshall Chapman; *Me I'm Feeling Free* .... (EPI)
Sweet Milwaukee Rose
Andy Badale/Beer Garden Band; *Nashville Beer*
Garden .... (RAN)
What's Made Milwaukee Famous
Jerry Lee Lewis; *Heartbreak* .... (TOM)
  Milestones .... (RHI)
Rod Stewart; *Best Of* .... (MER)
  Storyteller-Complete Anthology-1964-1990 ...... (WB)
Winter In Madrid
Stan Kenton & Ann Richards; *By*
Request-#5-1953-1960 .... (CW)
Wintry Feeling (Montreal)
Anne Murray; *Country Collection* ....(LIB)
  I'll Always Love You .... (CAP)
Jesse Winchester; *Touch On The Rainy Side* ..... (RHI)

CITIES: MEMPHIS

See Also: STATES: TENNESSEE

18 Miles To Memphis
Stray Cats; *Rant 'N' Rave With* .... (AMR)
All The Way From Memphis
Contraband; *Contraband* ....(IPA)

Ian Hunter; *Shades Of* .... (CHR)
Mott The Hoople; *Ballad Of Mott* ....(COL)
   Greatest Hits ....(COL)
   Live ....(COL)
   Mott ....(COL)
Back To Memphis
   Band; *To Kingdom Come-Definitive Collection* .... (CAP)
Berlin To Memphis
   Elvis Hitler; *Disgraceland* .... (RES)
Big Train From Memphis
   John Fogerty; *Centerfield* ....(WB)
Black Velvet
   Alannah Myles; *Alannah Myles* .... (ATL)
   Robin Lee; *Black Velvet* .... (ATL)
Dixie Chicken
   Little Feat; *Dixie Chicken* .... (WB)
   Waiting For Columbus .... (WB)
Going Back To Memphis
   Muddy Waters; *Muddy Brass & Blues* .... (CSS)
Goin' To Memphis
   Carl Perkins; *Best Of-Jive After 5-1958-1978* .... (RHI)
Honky Tonk Women
   Elton John; *11-17-70* ....(POL)
   Humble Pie; *Best* ....(A&M)
     Classics-#14 ....(A&M)
     Eat It ....(A&M)
   Ike & Tina Turner; *Best Of* ....(EMI)
     Get Back ....(LIB)
   Joe Cocker; *Mad Dogs & Englishmen* ....(A&M)
   Rolling Stones; *Get Yer Ya-Ya's Out* .... (AKO)
     Hot Rocks-1964-1971 .... (AKO)
     Love You Live ....(RS)
     Through The Past Darkly-Big Hits-#2 .... (AKO)
   Willie Nelson & Leon Russell; *Half Nelson* ......(COL)
I Lost My Gal From Memphis
   New Sunshine Jazz Band; *Too Much Mustard* ....(BIO)
Katie Left Memphis
   Tangle Eye; *Roots Of The Blues* ....(NW)
Leavin' Memphis, Frisco Bound
   Jesse Fuller; *Frisco Bound* .... (ARH)
   Lone Cat ....(GTJ)
Long Way From Memphis
   Lonnie Mack; *Strike Like Lightning* ....(ALG)
Maybe It Was Memphis
   Pam Tillis; *Put Yourself In My Place* .... (ARI)
Meet Me In Memphis
   Jimmy Buffett; *Floridays* .... (MCA)
Memphis
   Chuck Berry; *Chess Box* .... (CSS)
     Chuck Berry ....(AUF)
     Golden Hits .... (MER)
     Greatest Hits ....(EVR)
     St. Louis To Liverpool .... (CSS)
     ST/Hail! Hail! Rock 'N' Roll .... (MCA)
     Toronto Rock 'N' Roll Revival-#2 .... (ACC)
   Joe Jackson; *ST/Mike's Murder* ....(A&M)
   John Cale; *IRS Greatest Hits #2 & 3* .... (IRS)
   Johnny Rivers; *Anthology-1964-1977* ....(RHI)
     Best Of .... (EMI)
   Lonnie Mack; *Teen Beat-Instrumental*
     Rock-1957-1965 ....(CAP)
Memphis Belle
   Hank Williams, Jr.; *Pure Hank* ....(W/C)
Memphis Blues
   Duke Ellington; *Black Brown & Beige* .... (BLU)
   Eubie Blake; *Memories Of You* ....(BIO)
   Nat King Cole; *Nat King Cole* ....(CAP)
   Wild Bill Davison; *Giants Of Traditional Jazz* .... (SAV)
Memphis Boogie
   Dr. Isaiah Ross; *Boogie Disease* .... (ARH)
Memphis B-K
   Sonny Little; *Black & Blue* .... (STX)
Memphis Flyer
   Neil Diamond; *You Don't Bring Me Flowers* .....(COL)
Memphis Hip Shake
   Cult; *Electric* .... (SIR)
Memphis In June
   Eddie Miller/Orchestra; *Uncollected-1944-1945* . (HIN)
   Hoagy Carmichael; *Hoagy Sings Carmichael* ..... (EMI)
     Hoagy Sings Carmichael ....(PAU)
Memphis In The Meantime
   John Hiatt; *Bring The Family* ....(A&M)
Memphis Jellyroll
   Stefan Grossman; *Yazoo Basin Boogie* ....(SHA)

Memphis Mail
   Eli Owens; *Roosevelt Holts & His Friends* .... (ARH)
Memphis Pearl
   Lucinda Williams; *Sweet Old World* ....(CML)
Memphis Queen
   Southern Pacific; *County Line* ....(WB)
Memphis Rendezvous
   Jim Horn; *Work It Out* ....(WB)
Memphis Shakedown
   Trapezoid; *Three Forks Of Cheat* ....(ROU)
Memphis Slim U.S.A.
   Memphis Slim; *Blue This Evening* ....(BL)
Memphis Soul Stew
   King Curtis; *Atlantic Jazz-Soul* .... (ATL)
     Atlantic R&B 1947-1974-#6-(1966-1969) .....(ATL)
     Best Of .... (ATL)
     Golden Soul .... (ATL)
     Live At The Fillmore West .... (ATL)
Memphis Streets
   Neil Diamond; *Glory Road-1968-1972* .... (MCA)
     Sweet Caroline .... (MCA)
Memphis Sun
   Orion; *Rockabilly* ....(SUN)
Memphis Thing
   Rob Jungklas; *Closer To The Flame* .... (MAN)
Memphis Underground
   Herbie Mann; *Best Of* .... (ATL)
     Great Moments In Jazz .... (ATL)
     Memphis Underground .... (ATL)
Memphis Yodel
   Jimmie Rodgers; *First Sessions-1927-1928* ...... (ROU)
Memphis #999
   Graveyard Train; *Graveyard Train* ....(GEF)
Memphis, Tennessee Hot Rock
   Gordon Terry; *Tennessee Hot Rock* .... (PLN)
Midnight In Memphis
   Bette Midler; *ST/The Rose* .... (ATL)
   Hoyt Axton; *Where Did The Money Go* ....(JER)
   Meri Wilson; *First Take* ....(GRT)
Music Makin' Mama From Memphis
   Hank Snow; *Best Of* ....(RCA)
My Memphis Baby
   Johnny Wiggs; *Jazz Fest Masters-Traditionalists* ....(JM)
Night Train To Memphis
   Jerry Lee Lewis; *Rare Tracks* ....(RHI)
     Taste Of Country ....(SUN)
   Roy Acuff; *Best Of* ....(CAP)
     Greatest Hits ....(COL)
One Way Ticket To Memphis
   Bobby King & Terry Evans; *Rhythm Blues Soul &*
     Grooves .... (ROU)
Queen Of Memphis
   Confederate Railroad; *Confederate Railroad* ..... (ATL)
Singing Bridge Of Memphis Tennessee
   John Fahey; *Essential* .... (VAN)
Slow Train To Memphis
   Jim Horn; *Work It Out* ....(WB)
Stuck Inside Of Mobile With The...
   Bob Dylan; *Blonde On Blonde* ....(COL)
     Greatest Hits-#2 ....(COL)
     Hard Rain ....(COL)
That's How I Got To Memphis
   Rosanne Cash; *Somewhere In The Stars* ....(COL)
   Tom T. Hall; *Greatest Hits* .... (MER)
Walking In Memphis
   Marc Cohn; *Marc Cohn* .... (ATL)
West Memphis Blues
   Sonny Boy Williamson; *King Biscuit Time* .... (ARH)
Wrong Side Of Memphis
   Matraca Berg; *Bittersweet Surrender* ....(RCA)
   Trisha Yearwood; *Hearts In Armor* .... (MCA)

CITIES: MIAMI

   See Also: STATES: FLORIDA

Dateline Miami
   Judy Nylon & Crucial; *Pal Judy* ....(ROI)
Going Back To Miami
   Blues Brothers; *Best Of* .... (ATL)
     Made In America .... (ATL)
   Wayne Cochran; *Soul Shots-#6* ....(RHI)

Mambo In Miami
Peggy Lee & George Shearing; *Beauty & The
Beat!* .... (BLN)
Miami
John Cougar Mellencamp; *John Cougar
Mellencamp* ....(COL)
Randy Newman; *Trouble In Paradise* ....(WB)
Miami 2017
Billy Joel; *Songs In The Attic* ....(COL)
Turnstiles ....(COL)
Miami Beach
Garland Jeffreys; *Escape Artist* ....(EPI)
"Miami Vice" Theme
Jan Hammer; *Escape From Television* ....(MCA)
Soundtrack Smashes-'80s ....(MCA)
ST/"Miami Vice" Theme ....(MCA)
Original Music; Television's Greatest Hits-#3 .....(TVT)
Miami, My Amy
Keith Whitley; *Greatest Hits* ....(RCA)
L.A. To Miami ....(RCA)
Star-Spangled Country ....(RCA)
Moon Over Miami
Bourbon Street Stompers; *I Like Dixieland* ....(BAI)
Vaughn Monroe; *This Is* ....(RCA)
Only In Miami
Bette Midler; *Experience The Divine-Greatest Hits* (ATL)
No Frills ....(ATL)

CITIES: MOBILE
See Also: STATES: ALABAMA

Boogie Down In Mobile Alabama
Rocky Burnette; *45* .... (AMR)
Donna From Mobile
Anne Hills; *Don't Panic (Panic Is On/Don't
Explain)* .... (HOG)
Mobile
Marcia Ball; *Gartorrhythms* .... (ROU)
Mobile Bay
Hank Crawford; *Night Beat* .... (MS)
Rex Stewart; *RCA Victor Jazz-First Half-Century* .(RCA)
Mobile Bay (Magnolia Blossoms)
Cal Smith; *Stories Of Life By* ....(SO)
Johnny Cash; *Biggest Hits* ....(COL)
Merle Haggard & George Jones; *Taste Of Yesterday's
Wine* ....(EPI)
Mobile Boogie
Hank Williams, Jr.; *Early Years* ....(W/C)
One Night Stands ....(WB)
Mobile Line
Jim Kweskin/Jug Band; *Greatest Hits* ....(VAN)
Jim Kweskin/Jug Band ....(VAN)
Troubadours Of The Folk Era-#3 ....(RHI)
Mobile & K.C. Line
Robert Shaw; *Ma Grinder* .... (ARH)
Mobile/Texas Line
Tom Rush; *Blues Songs & Ballads* ....(FAN)
Mind Ramblin' ....(PRS)
Tom Rush ....(FAN)
Stuck Inside Of Mobile With The...
Bob Dylan; *Blonde On Blonde* ....(COL)
Greatest Hits-#2 ....(COL)
Hard Rain ....(COL)
Thirty Nine Miles To Mobile
Charlie Daniels Band; *Charlie Daniels Band* .....(CAP)

CITIES: MOSCOW
See Also: COUNTRIES: RUSSIA

Born In Moscow
Vasily Shumov; *My District* .... (GC)
Midnight In Moscow
Dukes Of Dixieland; *Dixieland's Greatest Hits* ... (MCA)
Kenny Ball; *45* ....(ERI)
Mission To Moscow
Benny Goodman; *All The Cats Join In* ....(COL)
Glenn Miller; *Legendary Performer-#3* ....(RCA)
/Army-Air Force Band; This Is ....(RCA)
Moscow
Chris Cutler & Fred Frith; *Live In Moscow Prague &
Washington* .... (CUN)

Moscow Blues
Paul Horn; *Inside The Cathedral (Inside Russia)* . (KUC)
Moscow Diskow
Telex; *12"* .... (SIR)
Moscow Farewell
Ennio Morricone; *Film Music-#1* ....(VMM)
Moscow Nights
Feelies; *Crazy Rhythms* ....(A&M)
Radio Free Moscow
Jethro Tull; *Under Wraps* ....(CHR)
Roads To Moscow
Al Stewart; *Past Present Future* ....(JNS)
Suburbs Of Moscow
Kim Wilde; *Teases & Dares* ....(MCA)

CITIES: N
*See Also: CITIES: NASHVILLE, NEW ORLEANS,
NEW YORK*

Funky Nassau
Beginning Of The End; *Atlantic Rhythm & Blues
1947-74-#7* ....(ATL)
Soul Hits/'70s-#5 .... (RHI)
Going To Newport
Frankie Laine; *16 Greatest Hits* ....(TRP)
Last Train To Nuremberg
Pete Seeger; *Rainbow Race* ....(OOP)
Moon Over Naples
Billy Vaughn; *Best Of* ....(MCA)
Nagasaki
Cab Calloway; *Hi De Ho Man* ....(COL)
Fletcher Henderson/Orchestra; *Fletcher
Henderson/Orchestra* ....(ALE)
Nevada City
Lonesome Romeos; *Lonesome Romeos* ....(CCB)
New Delhi
Cannonball Adderley; *Plus* ....(RVR)
New Delhi Freight Train
Little Feat; *Time Loves A Hero* ....(WB)
Norfolk Ferry
Panama Francis; *& The Savoy Sultans* ....(CJ)
Norfolk Girls
John Townley/Press Gang; *Chesapeake Sailor's
Companion* .... (ADE)
Northfield, The Disaster
Charlie Daniels Band; *Legend Of Jesse James* ... (A&M)
Northfield, The Plan
Levon Helm; *Legend Of Jesse James* ....(A&M)
Nutbush City Limits
Bob Seger; *Beautiful Loser* ....(CAP)
Live Bullet ....(CAP)
Ike & Tina Turner; *Best Of* ....(EMI)
Proud Mary-Best Of ....(EMI)
Simply The Best ....(CAP)
Tina Turner; *Live In Europe* ....(CAP)
Shaw Of Newark
Bobby Watson; *The Inventor* ....(BLN)
Whaler Out Of New Bedford
Musical Film Score; *Whaler Out Of New Bedford* (FLW)

CITIES: NASHVILLE
See Also: STATES: TENNESSEE

16th Avenue
Lacy J. Dalton; *19 Hot Country Requests-#2* ......(EPI)
Greatest Country Hits/'80s-1982 ....(COL)
Greatest Hits ....(COL)
Down In Nashville, Tennessee
Reno & Smiley; *1983 Collector's Edition-#2* .....(GUS)
God Don't Live In Nashville, Tennessee
Randy Howard; *All-American Redneck* ....(WB)
I Wish I Was In Nashville
Mel McDaniel; *Take Me To The Country* ....(CAP)
Missing You
Little Feat; *Let It Roll* ....(WB)
Nashville
Hoyt Axton; *Southbound* ....(A&M)
Indigo Girls; *Rites Of Passage* ....(EPI)
Mason Williams; *Anthology Of The 12-String
Guitar* ....(TRD)

Ray Stevens; *Best Of* .... (BBY)
  Nashville .... (BBY)
Wind Machine; *Wind Machine-featuring Steve*
Mesple .... (SW)
Nashville 1 A.M.
  Harvey Mandel; *Cristo Redentor* .... (EDI)
Nashville Beer Garden
  Andy Badale/Beer Garden Band; *Nashville Beer*
Garden .... (RAN)
Nashville Blues
  Doc Watson; *Doc Watson* .... (VAN)
  J.D. Crowe; *J.D. Crowe/New South* .... (ROU)
  Nitty Gritty Dirt Band; *Will The Circle Be*
Unbroken .... (EMI)
Nashville Cats
  Lovin' Spoonful; *Anthology* .... (RHI)
  Hums Of ....(OOP)
Nashville Connection
  Rodney Lay & Wild West; *Rockabilly Nuggets* ... (SUN)
Nashville In The Rain
  Ginger Boatwright; *Fertile Ground* .... (FF)
Nashville Moon
  Charlie Daniels Band; *Windows* .... (EPI)
  Ronnie Milsap; *Lost In The Fifties Tonight* ....(RCA)
Nashville Nightengale
  Royal Society Jazz Orchestra; *Harlem To*
Hollywood ....(KLA)
Nashville Nights/Redneck Blues
  Pirates Of The Mississippi; *Walk The Plank* ......(CAP)
Nashville Pickin'
  Doc Watson; *Southbound* .... (VAN)
Nashville Scene
  Hank Williams, Jr.; *Five-O* ....(W/C)
Nashville Shuffle Boogie
  Mark O'Connor; *New Nashville Cats* .... (WB)
Nashville Skyline Rag
  Bob Dylan; *Nashville Skyline* ....(COL)
Nashville West
  Byrds; *Dr. Byrds & Mr. Hyde* ....(COL)
  Legends Of Country Guitar-#1 .... (RHI)
  Byrds (collection) ....(COL)
  Untitled ....(COL)
  Nashville West; *Nashville West* .... (SIE)
Nashville Women's Blues
  Bessie Smith; *Complete Recordings-#2* ....(COL)
Nashville, Tennessee
  Troy Cory; *Real Country* ....(VRA)
Nashville, Tenn. Blues
  Washboard Sam; *Blues Classics By* ....(BCL)
Nobody Eats At Linebaugh's Anymore
  John Hartford; *Me Oh My How The Time Does*
Fly-Anthology .... (FF)
Old Nashville Cowboys
  Hank Williams, Jr.; *Whiskey Bent & Hell Bound* ..(W/C)
Outside The Nashville City Limits
  Joan Baez; *Country Music Album* .... (VAN)
  Night They Drove Old Dixie Down .... (VAN)
Paddy Goes To Nashville
  Adrian Legg; *Mrs. Crowe's Blue Waltz* .... (REL)
Song A Day In Nashville
  John Sebastian; *Welcome Back* .... (RPR)
Straight Through To Nashville
  Agitpop; *Open Seasons* .... (TT)
That Was The Day
  Marianne Faithfull; *Faithless* ....(SSP)
West Nashville Boogie
  Steve Earle/Dukes; *Shut Up & Die Like An*
Aviator .... (MCA)
  The Hard Way ....(MCA)
West Nashville Grand Ballroom Gown
  Jimmy Buffett; *Living & Dying In 3/4 Time* ..... (MCA)
Wrong Side Of Memphis
  Matraca Berg; *Bittersweet Surrender* ....(RCA)
  Trisha Yearwood; *Hearts In Armor* .... (MCA)

CITIES: NEW ORLEANS, Mardi Gras

See Also: CARNIVALS, STATES: LOUISIANA

Back To New Orleans
  Lightnin' Hopkins; *Lightnin'* .... (BV)
  Lightnin' Greatest Hits .... (PRS)
  Sonny Terry & Brownie McGhee; *Back To New*
Orleans ....(FAN)

Basin Street Blues
  Louis Armstrong; *Best Of* .... (MCA)
  Jazz Heritage-Old Favorites .... (MCA)
  Satchmo: Musical Autobiography-#2 .... (MCA)
  Young Louis Armstrong ....(RCA)
Battle Of New Orleans
  Chet Atkins/Boston Pops; *Best Of* ....(RCA)
  Johnny Horton; *American Originals* ....(COL)
  Greatest Hits ....(COL)
  Radio Classics/'50s ....(COL)
  Nitty Gritty Dirt Band; *Dirt Silver & Gold* ..... (UA)
  Dream .... (UA)
  Stars & Stripes Forever .... (UA)
Big Chief From New Orleans
  Mike Bloomfield; *Between The Hard Place & The*
Ground ....(TAK)
Bourbon Street
  Elvin Bishop; *Let It Flow* ....(CPC)
Bourbon Street Parade
  Al Hirt; *Best Of* ....(RCA)
  Dukes Of Dixieland; *Digital Dixieland* .... (PJ)
  Pete Fountain; *Best Of-#2* .... (MCA)
  Preservation Hall Jazz Band; *New Orleans-#4* ...(COL)
  Wynton Marsalis; *Standard Time-#2-Intimacy*
Calling ....(COL)
Carnival In New Orleans
  Professor Longhair; *Last Mardi Gras* ....(ATL)
City Of New Orleans
  Arlo Guthrie; *Best Of* .... (WB)
  Hobo's Lullaby ....(RPR)
  Together In Concert w/Pete Seeger ....(RPR)
  HARP; *HARP* ....(RWD)
  Willie Nelson; *19 Hot Country Requests-#2* ....(EPI)
  City Of New Orleans ....(COL)
  Greatest Country Hits/'80s-#4 ....(COL)
Crescent City Crawl On The St...
  Wynton Marsalis; *ST/Tune In Tomorrow...* ....(COL)
Dixie Chicken
  Little Feat; *Dixie Chicken* .... (WB)
  Waiting For Columbus .... (WB)
Do You Know What It Means To Miss New...
  Billie Holiday; *Sing 2* .... (KNT)
  Harry Connick, Jr.; *Twenty* ....(COL)
  Louis Armstrong; *Chicago Concert 1956* ....(COL)
  Mostly Blues ....(OLR)
  Pops .... (BLU)
  Pete Fountain; *Best Of* .... (MCA)
Down Home In New Orleans
  Magic Organ; *Traveling With* .... (RAN)
Down South In New Orleans
  Band/Van Morrison; *Last Waltz* .... (WB)
Fancy
  Bobbi Gentry; *All-Time Country Classics-#1* .....(CAP)
  Reba McEntire; *Rumor Has It* .... (MCA)
Go To The Mardi Gras
  Professor Longhair; *New Orleans Party Classics* .. (RHI)
Going Back To New Orleans
  Dr. John; *Going Back To New Orleans* .... (WB)
Goin' To New Orleans
  Rockin' Tabby Thomas; *Rockin' With The Blues* (MSO)
Heart Of The Night (New Orleans)
  Poco; *Backtracks* .... (MCA)
  Legend .... (MCA)
Home To New Orleans
  Queen Ida; *Caught In The Act* .... (CRS)
Hometown New Orleans
  Champion Jack Dupree; *Forever & Ever* .... (BUL)
House Of The Rising Sun
  Animals; *Best Of* .... (AKO)
  Greatest Hits ....(ALL)
  Rip It To Shreds-Greatest Hits Live .... (IRS)
  Hank Williams, Jr.; *Hank Live* ....(W/C)
  Ronnie Milsap; *16 Greatest Hits-#2* .... (TRP)
I Love New Orleans Music
  Ronnie Milsap; *Inside* ....(RCA)
I Wish I Was In New Orleans
  Tom Waits; *Small Change* ....(ASY)
Johnny B. Goode
  Chuck Berry; *Chess Box* .... (CSS)
  Classic Rock-#2 .... (MCA)
  Greatest Hits ....(EVR)
  Roll Over Beethoven ....(ALL)
  ST/American Graffiti .... (MCA)

Elvis Presley; *From Memphis To Vegas* ....(RCA)
  In Concert ....(RCA)
Grateful Dead; *Bill Graham Presents Fillmore-Last*
  Days ....(EPA)
Johnny Winter; *Live* ....(COL)
  Second Winter ....(COL)
Mardi Gras
Gino Vannelli; *Pauper In Paradise* ....(A&M)
Original Cast; *House Of Flowers* ....(SSP)
Mardi Gras Boogie
Clifton Chenier; *In New Orleans* .... (CRS)
Mardi Gras In New Orleans
Professor Longhair; *Atlantic Rhythm & Blues-#1*
  (1947-52) ....(ATL)
  New Orleans Jazz & Heritage Fest.-1976 .... (RHI)
  New Orleans Piano-Blues Originals-#2 ....(ATL)
Rockin' Dopsie; *Alligator Stomp-#2* ....(RHI)
Mardi Gras Mambo
Hawketts; *Treacherous: History Of Neville Bros.* .. (RHI)
Moon Over Bourbon Street
Sting; *Bring On The Night* ....(A&M)
  Dream Of The Blue Turtles ....(A&M)
My Little Home Down In New Orleans
Jimmie Rodgers; *Early Years-1928-1929* ...... (ROU)
New Orleans
Elvis Presley; *ST/King Creole* ....(RCA)
Gary U.S. Bonds; *Golden Hits* ....(LAU)
  Oldies But Goodies-#7 ....(OSR)
  School Of Rock 'N' Roll-Best Of ....(RHI)
Hank Williams, Jr.; *Five-O* ....(W/C)
Neil Diamond; *Double Gold* ....(BNG)
  Feel Of ....(BNG)
  Greatest Hits ....(BNG)
Wynton Marsalis; *Marsalis Standard Time-#1* ....(COL)
New Orleans Blues
Marcus Roberts; *Alone With Three Giants* .... (NOV)
New Orleans Bump
Jelly Roll Morton; *Jazz Classics In Digital Stereo* .(ABC)
New Orleans Ceremony
Dukes Of Dixieland; *Best Of* ....(COL)
New Orleans Function
Louis Armstrong; *Of New Orleans* .... (MCA)
New Orleans Hop Scop Blues
Bessie Smith; *Complete Recordings-#4* ....(COL)
New Orleans Instrumental No. 1
R.E.M.; *Automatic For The People* ....(WB)
New Orleans Is Sinking
Tragically Hip; *Up To Here* .... (MCA)
New Orleans Joys
Butch Thompson; *New Orleans Joys* .... (DAR)
New Orleans Ladies
Louisiana's Le Roux; *Louisiana's Le Roux* ......(CAP)
  '70s Greatest Rock Hits-#4 ....(PRY)
New Orleans Low-Down
Duke Ellington/Orchestra; *Brunswick*
  Era-#1-1926-1929 .... (MCA)
New Orleans Shuffle
Johnny Otis; *Original Johnny Otis Show* ....(SAV)
New Orleans Stomp
Johnny Dodds; *South Side Chicago Jazz* .... (MCA)
New Orleans Streamline
Bukka White; *Legacy Of The Blues-#1* ....(CRS)
New Orleans Street Beat
Marlon Jordan; *The Undaunted* ....(COL)
New Orleans Waltz
Nathan Abshire; *French Blues* .... (ARH)
New Orleans Wins The War
Randy Newman; *Land Of Dreams* ....(RPR)
Pearl Of The Quarter
Steely Dan; *Countdown To Ecstasy* .... (MCA)
Planet Of New Orleans
Dire Straits; *On Every Street* ....(WB)
Proud Mary
Creedence Clearwater Revival; *1968-1969* ...... (FAN)
  Bayou Country ....(FAN)
  Chronicle ....(FAN)
  Gold ....(FAN)
  Live In Europe ....(FAN)
George Jones & Johnny Paycheck; *My Very Special*
  Guests .... (EPI)
Ike & Tina Turner; *Best Of* ....(EMI)
  EMI Legends Of Rock 'N' Roll-24 Greatest ...... (RHI)
  Greatest Hits ....(CCB)
  Soul Hits/'70s-#4 ....(RHI)

Royal Orleans
Led Zeppelin; *Presence* .... (SS)
Suite Home New Orleans
Dr. John; *Brightest Smile In Town* ....(CLE)
Take Me Back To New Orleans
Chris Barber & Dr. John; *Take Me Back To New*
  Orleans ....(BL)
Gary U.S. Bonds; *School Of Rock 'N' Roll-Best Of* (RHI)
Take Me To The Mardi Gras
Paul Simon; *There Goes Rhymin' Simon* ....(WB)
Walking To New Orleans
Fats Domino; *Fats Domino* ....(EVR)
  Greatest Hits ....(MCA)
  My Blue Heaven-Best Of-#1 ....(EMI)
  They Call Me The Fat Man ....(EMI)
Way Down Yonder In New Orleans
Freddy Cannon; *14 Blooming Hits* ....(RHI)
  Rockin' '50s ....(PRY)
Louis Armstrong; *20 Golden Pieces Of* ....(BLD)
  Greatest Hits ....(CCB)
  I Like Jazz-Essence Of ....(COL)
  Mostly Blues ....(OLR)
When The Saints Go Marching In
Al Hirt; *Best Of* ....(RCA)
  Our Man-In New Orleans ....(NOV)
Jerry Lee Lewis; *Jerry Lee Lewis* ....(RHI)
Louis Armstrong; *At The Crescendo* ....(MCA)
  Big Bands Of The Swinging Years-#1 ....(CLT)
  C'Est Si Bon ....(RHI)
  Essential ....(VAN)
  Of New Orleans ....(MCA)
Pete Fountain; *Best Of* ....(MCA)
  Down On Rampart Street ....(INT)
  Pete Fountain's New Orleans ....(MCA)
Preservation Hall Jazz Band; *Best Of* ....(COL)
Where The Blues Were Born In New Orleans
Louis Armstrong; *Pops: 1940s Small Band Sides* . (BLU)
  Sings The Blues .... (BLU)

CITIES: NEW YORK, Bronx, Brooklyn, Harlem, Manhattan, Queens, Staten Island
  See Also: STATES: NEW YORK, this category for
  Broadway

All The Critics Love U In New York
Prince; *1999* ....(WB)
Am I Ever Gonna Fall In Love In New York
Grace Jones; *Fame* .... (ISL)
Angel Of Harlem
U2; *ST/Rattle & Hum* .... (ISL)
Another Night In The Bronx
Donald D; *Notorious* ....(EPI)
Another Rainy Day In New York City
Chicago; *If You Leave Me Now* ....(COL)
  X ....(COL)
Arrival In New York
Joe Zawinul; *Zawinul* ....(ATL)
Arthur's Theme
Christopher Cross; *ST/Arthur* ....(WB)
Autumn In New York
Frank Sinatra; *Capitol Years* ....(CAP)
  Come Fly With Me ....(CAP)
  Main Event ....(SIN)
  Round #1 ....(CAP)
Sarah Vaughan; *Complete-On*
  Mercury-#2-1956-1957 ....(MER)
  Golden Hits ....(MER)
Back To Brooklyn
Prince Markie Dee/Soul Convention; *Free* ....(COL)
Back To The Apple
Count Basie/Orchestra; *ST/Hannah & Her*
  Sisters .... (MCA)
Back To The Island
Leon Russell; *Best Of* .... (MCA)
  Rock Of The '70s ....(MSP)
  Will O' The Wisp .... (MCA)
Bavarian In New York
Triumvirat; *A LaCarte* ....(CAP)
Big Apple
Tommy Dorsey/Clambake Seven; *Nipper's Greatest*
  Hits-'30s-#2 ....(RCA)

Tommy Dorsey/Orchestra; *Seventeen Number Ones* ....(RCA)
Blame It On New York City
Dramatics; *Positive State Of Mind* ....(VOL)
Boy From New York City
Ad-Libs; *Jewels-#1* ....(SSS)
Oldies But Goodies-#6 ....(OSR)
Original Golden Hits/Great Groups-#1 ....(SSS)
Original New York Rock & Roll-#1 ....(SSS)
Manhattan Transfer; *Best Of* ....(ATL)
Mecca For Moderns ....(ATL)
Broadway
Clash; *On Broadway* ....(EPI)
Sandinista ....(EPI)
Count Basie; *Essential-#3* ....(COL)
Count Basie/Orchestra; *Best Of-Roulette Years* ... (RLL)
Jack McDuff/Friends; *Color Me Blue* ....(CCJ)
Mel Torme; *Songs Of New York* ....(ATL)
Broadway Baby
Julia McKenzie; *Collector's Sondheim* ....(RCA)
Original Broadway Cast; *Follies* ....(CAP)
Broadway Ballet
Gene Kelly/Chorus; *ST/Singin' In The Rain* ....(SSP)
Broadway Fools
Branford Marsalis; *Random Abstract* ....(COL)
Broadway Hotel
Al Stewart; *Year Of The Cat* ....(ARI)
Broadway My Street
Original Broadway Cast; *70 Girls 70* ....(SMC)
Brooklyn
Cody Jameson; *45* ....(ATC)
Steely Dan; *Can't Buy A Thrill* ....(MCA)
Brooklyn Roads
Neil Diamond; *12 Greatest Hits* ....(MCA)
And The Singer Sings His Songs ....(MCA)
Velvet Gloves & Spit ....(MCA)
City
Fleetwood Mac; *Mystery To Me* ....(RPR)
Cold Hands From New York
Gordon Lightfoot; *United Artists Collection* ......(EMI)
Come Back To Brooklyn
Jimmy Roselli; *Saloon Songs-#3* ....(M&R)
Crack In New York
Culture; *Nuff Crisis!* ....(SHA)
Daddy Don't Live In That New York...
Steely Dan;
Katy Lied ....(MCA)
Do Like You Do In New York
Boz Scaggs; *Middle Man* ....(COL)
Does This Bus Stop At 82nd St.
Bruce Springsteen; *Greetings From Asbury Park N.J.* ....(COL)
Drop Me Off In Harlem
David Frishberg; *Can't Take You Nowhere* ....(FAN)
Duke Ellington; *I Like Jazz-Essence Of* ....(COL)
Ella Fitzgerald; *Essential-Great Songs* ....(VRV)
Louis Armstrong & Duke Ellington; *Complete Sessions* ....(RLL)
Echoes Of Harlem
Clark Terry Five; *Memories Of Duke* ....(PAB)
Claude Bolling; *Plays Ellington-#1* ....(COL)
Cootie Williams; *Jazz Sampler-#3* ....(COL)
Duke Ellington; *Mood Indigo* ....(POE)
Englishman In New York
Sting; *Nothing Like The Sun* ....(A&M)
Ev'ry Street's A Boulevard In Old N.Y.
Norrie Paramor; *Autumn* ....(ANG)
Eyes Of A New York Woman
B.J. Thomas; *16 Greatest Hits* ....(TRP)
Greatest Hits ....(RHI)
Fairytale Of New York
Pogues; *Essential* ....(ISL)
If I Should Fall From Grace With God ....(ISL)
First We Take Manhattan
Jennifer Warnes; *Critics Choice* ....(CYP)
Famous Blue Raincoat ....(PRV)
Leonard Cohen; *I'm Your Man* ....(COL)
R.E.M.; *I'm Your Fan-Songs Of Leonard Cohen* ..(ATL)
Forty-Five Minutes From Broadway
Mickey Finn; *Caught In The Act* ....(CRS)
From Cotton To Satin
Gene Watson; *This Dream's On Me* ....(MCA)
Johnny Paycheck; *Ake This Job & Shove It* ....(EPI)

Funky Broadway
Dyke/Blasers; *Greatest Hits* ....(OSR)
Soul Shots-#1-We Got More Soul ....(RHI)
Wilson Pickett; *Atlantic R&B 1947-74-#6* ....(ATL)
Best Of ....(ATL)
Greatest Hits ....(ATL)
Oldies/Goodies-#14 ....(OSR)
Girl From New York City
Beach Boys; *Today!/Summer Days (& Summer Nights!)* ....(CAP)
Give It Back To The Indians (New York)
Ella Fitzgerald; *Rodgers & Hart Songbook* ....(VRV)
Give My Regards To Broadway
Barry Manilow; *Showstoppers* ....(ARI)
Joel Grey; *Broadway Magic-1960s* ....(COL)
Original Cast; *George M.* ....(COL)
Go Brooklyn
Hostyle; *Get Off* ....(ATL)
Going To New York
Climax Blues Band; *FM/Live* ....(SIR)
Jimmy Reed; *At Carnegie Hall* ....(VJ)
Best Of ....(CRS)
Greatest Hits-#2 ....(KNT)
Legend-The Man ....(VJ)
Siegel-Schwall Band; *Best Of* ....(VAN)
Siegel-Schwall Band ....(VAN)
Grey Cloud Over New York
Philip Glass; *1000 Airplanes On The Roof* ....(VIA)
Ground Zero Brooklyn
Carnivore; *Retaliation* ....(RR)
Harlem
Bill Withers; *Best Of* ....(COL)
Just As I Am ....(COL)
Suicide; *1/2 Alive* ....(ROI)
Ghost Riders ....(ROI)
Harlem Blues
Cynda Williams; *ST/Mo' Better Blues* ....(COL)
Nat King Cole; *Nat King Cole* ....(CAP)
Harlem Nocturne
Mel Torme; *Songs Of New York* ....(ATL)
Viscounts; *Soul Shots-#3-Soul Twist* ....(RHI)
Harlem On My Mind
Ethel Waters; *Irving Berlin-100 Years* ....(COL)
Tim Curry; *Read By Lips* ....(A&M)
Harlem Shuffle
Bill Deal/Rhondels; *Best Of* ....(RHI)
Bob & Earl; *Cruisin' 1964* ....(INC)
Soul Shots-#1-We Got More Soul ....(RHI)
Johnny & Edgar Winter; *Together* ....(BS)
Rolling Stones; *Dirty Work* ....(RS)
Flashpoint & Collectibles ....(RS)
Heart In New York
Art Garfunkel; *Garfunkel* ....(COL)
Scissors Cut ....(COL)
Simon & Garfunkel; *Concert In Central Park* .....(WB)
Heat In Harlem
Graham Parker; *Pourin' It All Out-Mercury Years* (MER)
Graham Parker/Rumour; *Parkerilla* ....(MER)
Stick To Me ....(MER)
Hot Night In New York City
Bonnie Koloc; *With You On My Side* ....(FF)
I Am...I Said
Neil Diamond; *12 Greatest Hits* ....(MCA)
Hot August Night ....(MCA)
Hot August Night II ....(MCA)
Stones ....(MCA)
I Guess The Lord Must Be In New York C.
Nilsson; *Greatest Hits* ....(RCA)
Harry ....(RCA)
I Happen To Like New York
Bobby Short; *Live At The Cafe Carlyle* ....(ATL)
I Love New York
Bernadette Peters; *Song & Dance* ....(RCA)
I Remember Harlem
Roy Eldridge; *Roy Eldridge* ....(CRS)
In A New York Minute
Ronnie McDowell; *19 Hot Country Requests-#3* ..(EPI)
In A New York Minute ....(EPI)
Older Women & Other Greatest Hits ....(EPI)
In Brooklyn
Al Stewart; *Love Chronicles* ....(EPI)
In Old New York
Victor Herbert; *Victor Herbert* ....(ALS)

Incident On 57th Street
Bruce Springsteen; *Wild The Innocent & The E Street*
Shuffle ....(COL)
Italian From New York
Chicago; *#7* ....(COL)
I'll Take New York
Tom Waits; *Frank's Wild Years* ....(ISL)
Just Another Death In NYC
Judy Small; *One Voice In The Crowd* ....(RWD)
King Of New York
D Schoolly; *How A Black Man Feels* ....(CAP)
King Of The New York Streets
Dion; *Yo Frankie* ....(ARI)
Latin From Manhattan
Al Jolson; *Best Of* ....(MCA)
Immortal ....(MCA)
Living For The City
Stevie Wonder; *Innervisions* ....(MOT)
Original Musiquarium ....(MOT)
Lost In The Lights Of Broadway
Bernie Shanahan; *Bernie Shanahan* ....(ATL)
Lullaby Of Broadway
Andrews Sisters; *Best Of-#2* ....(MCA)
Bette Midler; *Bette Midler* ....(ATL)
Live At Last ....(ATL)
Tony Bennett; *Jazz* ....(COL)
Man From Harlem
Cab Calloway/Orchestra; *Tribute To Black*
Entertainers ....(COL)
Manhattan
Ella Fitzgerald; *Rodgers/Hart Songbook* ....(VRV)
Tony Bennett; *Rodgers & Hart Songbook* ....(DRG)
Sings 10 Rodgers & Hart Songs ....(IPV)
Manhattan Island Serenade
Leon Russell; *Carney* ....(MCA)
Manhattan Project
Rush; *Power Windows* ....(MER)
Show Of Hands ....(MER)
Manhattan Rumble
Electric Light Orchestra; *No Answer* ....(JET)
Manhattan Serenade
Popular Standard; *Out of print recording* ....(OOP)
Manhattan Spiritual
Reg Owen; *45* ....(OOP)
Moon Over Brooklyn
Anne Murray; *Somebody's Waiting* ....(CAP)
Native New Yorker
Esther Phillips; *All About* ....(MER)
Odyssey; *Nipper's Greatest Hits-'70s* ....(RCA)
New Amsterdam
Elvis Costello; *Girls Girls Girls* ....(COL)
Elvis Costello/Attractions; *Get Happy!* ....(RYK)
New York
Dreams; *Dreams* ....(COL)
Nuggetts; *N.Y.* ....(MER)
Sex Pistols; *Live At Chelmsford Top Security*
Prison ....(RES)
Never Mind The Bollocks (Here's The) ....(WB)
New York Boy
Neil Diamond; *Glory Road-1968-1972* ....(MCA)
Touching You Touching Me ....(MCA)
New York Broken Toy
Nazareth; *Expect No Mercy* ....(A&M)
New York City
Elephants Memory/Invisible Strings; *Sometime In New*
York City ....(CAP)
John Lennon; *Lennon* ....(CAP)
Live In New York City ....(CAP)
Manhattans; *Love Talk* ....(COL)
Statler Brothers; *Best Of The* ....(MER)
New York City Blues
Bonnie Koloc; *After All This Time* ....(OVA)
At Her Best ....(OVA)
Duke Ellington/Orchestra; *Carnegie Hall*
Concerts-December 1947 ....(PRS)
Jimmy Witherspoon; *Midnight Lady Called The*
Blues ....(MUS)
Yardbirds; *Best Of British Rock* ....(PRR)
New York City King Size Rosewood Bed
Charlie Daniels Band; *John Grease & Wolfman* ...(EPI)
Fire On The Mountain ....(EPI)

New York City Rhythm
Barry Manilow; *Greatest Hits-#1* ....(ARI)
Live ....(ARI)
Trying To Get The Feeling ....(ARI)
New York City Serenade
Bruce Springsteen; *Wild Innocent & The E Street*
Shuffle ....(COL)
New York City Song
Mighty High; *Mighty High* ....(MCA)
New York Girls
Kingston Trio; *Kingston Trio/From The Hungry i* .(CAP)
New York Groove
Ace Frehley; *Ace Frehley* ....(CAS)
New York Hippodrome
Detroit Concert Band; *Sousa American Bicentennial*
Collection ....(H&L)
New York Interlude
Original Broadway Cast; *Crazy For You* ....(ANG)
New York Lady
Burt Bacharach; *Classics-#23* ....(A&M)
New York Minute
Don Henley; *End Of The Innocence* ....(GEF)
"New York New York" Theme
Frank Sinatra; *Reprise Collection* ....(RPR)
Sinatra Reprise-Very Good Years ....(RPR)
Trilogy ....(RPR)
New York On My Mind
John McLaughlin; *Electric Guitarist* ....(COL)
New York Rhapsody
Hollywood Bowl Orch./G. Hines/P. Austin; *Gershwins In*
Hollywood ....(PHI)
New York Shuffle
Graham Parker/Rumour; *Parkerilla* ....(MER)
Stick To Me ....(MER)
New York Skyline
Garland Jeffreys; *Ghost Writer* ....(A&M)
Matador & More... ....(A&M)
New York State Of Mind
Barbra Streisand; *Memories* ....(COL)
Streisand Superman ....(COL)
Billy Joel; *Greatest Hits-#1 & 2-1973-1985* ......(COL)
Turnstiles ....(COL)
Carmen McRae; *Ms. Magic* ....(DHL)
New York Telephone Conversation
Lou Reed; *Transformer* ....(RCA)
Walk On The Wild Side-Best Of ....(RCA)
New York Tendaberry
Laura Nyro; *New York Tendaberry* ....(COL)
New York Willies
Barbra Streisand; *ST/Prince Of Tides* ....(COL)
New York, I Don't Know About You
Peter Allen; *Taught By Experts* ....(A&M)
New York, New York
Frank Sinatra & Tony Bennett; *Frank Sinatra*
Duets ....(CAP)
Leonard Bernstein; *Bernstein Songbook* ....(COL)
Mel Torme; *Songs Of New York* ....(ATL)
New York, New York/Sailors On The Town
Original Broadway Cast; *Jerome Robbins'*
Broadway ....(RCA)
New York's A Lonely Town
Ad-Libs; *45* ....(CLT)
Tradewinds; *Beach Classics* ....(DHL)
Original Golden Hits/Great Groups-#1 ....(SSS)
Surfin' Hits ....(RHI)
Nights On Broadway
Bee Gees; *Greatest* ....(POL)
Here At Last ....(RSO)
Main Course ....(RSO)
No Sleep Till Brooklyn
Beastie Boys; *Licensed To Ill* ....(DFJ)
N.Y.C.
Charles & Eddie; *Duophonic* ....(CAP)
Human Radio; *Human Radio* ....(COL)
Original Broadway Cast; *Annie* ....(COL)
Weather Report; *Weather Report* ....(COL)
On Broadway
Drifters; *16 Greatest Hits* ....(TRP)
Golden Hits ....(ATL)
George Benson; *Collection* ....(WB)
ST/All That Jazz ....(CAS)
Weekend In L.A. ....(WB)
On The Other Side Of Harlem
David Munyon; *Code Name: Jumper* ....(LH)

Only Living Boy In New York
Simon & Garfunkel; *Bridge Over Troubled Water* (COL)
  Collected Works ....(COL)
Peace To New York
Doug E. Fresh/Get Fresh Crew; *Doin' What I Gotta
Do* ....(BUS)
Positively 4th Street
Bob Dylan; *Biograph* ....(COL)
  Greatest Hits ....(COL)
Byrds; *Byrds (collection)* ....(COL)
  Untitled ....(COL)
Posse On Broadway
Sir Mix-A-Lot; *Rap Straight Outta The Ghetto* .... (KT)
  Swass .... (NSY)
Rage In Harlem
Little Jimmy Scott/Expressions; *ST/Rage In
Harlem* .... (SIR)
Red Cab To Manhattan
Stephen Bishop; *Best Of Bish* .... (RHI)
Reggae On Broadway
Bob Marley; *Chances Are* .... (COT)
Robinson Crusoe In New York
Silencers; *Dance To The Holy Man* ....(RCA)
Rockin' Around In N.Y.C.
Marshall Crenshaw; *Marshall Crenshaw* ....(WB)
Royal Scam
Steely Dan; *Royal Scam* .... (MCA)
Saga Of New York
Rascals; *Anthology-1965-1972* .... (RHI)
  Searching For Ecstasy-Rest Of-1969-1972 ...... (RHI)
Sally's Got A Friend In New York City
Larry McCray; *Ambition* .... (CHS)
She's A Latin From Manhattan
La Jolson; *Lullaby Of Broadway-Music Of H.
Warren* .... (PF)
Sidewalks Of New York
Cannonball Adderley & Milt Jackson; *Things Are Getting
Better* ....(RVR)
Mel Torme; *Songs Of New York* .... (ATL)
Son Of A New York Gun
Gino Vannelli; *Powerful People* .... (A&M)
South Bronx
Boogie Down Productions; *Live Hardcore
Worldwide-Paris London NYC* .... (JVA)
Spanish Harlem
Aretha Franklin; *30 Greatest Hits* .... (ATL)
  Best Of .... (ATL)
  Ten Years Of Gold .... (ATL)
Ben E. King; *Back To Mono-1958-1969* .... (AKO)
  Greatest Hits .... (ATC)
Crusaders; *At Their Best* .... (MOT)
Drifters; *Greatest Hits* .... (GUS)
Spanish Harlem Incident
Bob Dylan; *Another Side Of* ....(COL)
Byrds; *Mr. Tambourine Man* ....(COL)
  Byrds (collection) ....(COL)
Streets Of New York
Carmel Quinn/Anna McGoldrick/P. Noonan; *Let's Have
An Irish Party* ....(RGO)
Kool G Rap & D.J. Polo; *Wanted: Dead Or Alive* (CLD)
Summer Means New York
Beach Boys; *Today/Summer Days & Summer
Nights!* ....(CAP)
Sunday In New York
Mel Torme; *Songs Of New York* .... (ATL)
Sunday School To Broadway
Sammi Smith; *45* .... (ELE)
Take Me Back To Manhattan
Original Cast; *Anything Goes* .... (EPI)
Take Me Back To New York City
Si Kahn; *Unfinished Portraits* .... (FF)
Talkin' New York
Bob Dylan; *Bob Dylan* ....(COL)
That Man From New York City
Lightnin' Hopkins; *Lost Texas Tapes-#1* .... (CLT)
That's The Way We Do Things In New York
Original Cast; *Jelly's Last Jam* .... (MER)
There's A Boat Dat's Leavin' Soon For NY
Ella Fitzgerald & Louis Armstrong; *Porgy & Bess* (VRV)
Original Cast; *Porgy & Bess* .... (MCA)
There's A Broken Heart For Every...
Mel Torme; *Songs Of New York* .... (ATL)

Too Dumb For New York City
Waylon Jennings; *Too Dumb For N.Y. City-Too Ugly
For L.A.* .... (EPI)
Under The Harlem Moon
Fletcher Henderson/Orchestra; *Fletcher
Henderson/Orchestra* .... (ASV)
Underneath The Harlem Moon
Randy Newman; *12 Songs* .... (RPR)
Unique New York
John Scofield; *Grace Under Pressure* .... (BLN)
Uptown Manhattan
Budd Johnson; *Let's Swing* .... (PRS)
Michel Camilo; *On Fire* .... (EPI)
U.M.M.G. (Upper Manhattan Medical Group)
Art Farmer Quartet; *Warm Valley* .... (CCJ)
Branford Marsalis; *Trio Jeepy* ....(COL)
Duke Ellington & Dizzy Gillespie; *Jazz Party* ....(COL)

CITIES: O

Dallas To Odessa
Lyn Childress; *Different Shade Of Country* ....(SO)
Going Back To Okinawa
Ry Cooder; *Get Rhythm* ....(WB)
Goin' Back To Oakland
Isaac Scott; *S.F. Blues Festival-#2* .... (SSM)
Tom McFarland; *Travelin' With The Blues* ...... (ARH)
My Favorite Town Osaka
Shonen Knife; *712* .... (RV)
Oakland
Pooh-Man; *Life Of A Criminal* .... (JVA)
Oakland Blues
Conjure; *Music For The Texts Of Ishmael Reed* ...(PNG)
Oscar Peterson/Trumpet Kings; *Jousts* .... (PAB)
Oakland Jungle
Wild Boyz; *It Had To Be Done* .... (VOL)
Oakland Stroke
Tony! Toni! Tone!; *Revival* .... (WIN)
Tower Of Power; *Back To Oakland* .... (WB)
Oklahoma City Times
Limeliters; *Harmony!* .... (FOL)
Omaha
Counting Crows; *August And Everything After* .. (DGC)
Golden Palominos; *History-1982-1986* .... (MTR)
Moby Grape; *Very Best Of* ....(COL)
Waylon Jennings; *Taker/Tulsa & Honky Tonk
Heroes* .... (MOB)
Omaha Blues
Big Joe Williams; *Piney Woods Blues* .... (DEL)
Omaha Celebration
Pat Metheny; *Bright Size Life* .... (ECM)
Omaha Polka
Li'l Wally; *Here Comes* .... (JJ)
Omaha, Nebraska
Doug Mathews; *Legacy II* .... (HIG)
Onion Town
John Delafose/Eunice Playboys; *Stomp Down
Zydeco* .... (ROU)
Osaka
John Hicks & Elise Wood; *Luminous* ....(EVD)
Osaka Castle
Peter Erskine; *Transition* .... (DEN)
Osaka Rocka
Jeff Watson; *Lone Ranger* .... (SHR)
West Oakland Strut
Ed Kelly & Pharoah Sanders; *Ed Kelly & Pharoah
Sanders* ....(EVD)
Wild Night In Odessa
Klezmorim; *Metropolis* .... (FF)

CITIES: P

See Also: CITIES: PARIS, PHILADELPHIA

At The Fair In Pacanow
Myron Floren; *Polka Party* .... (RAN)
By The Time I Get To Phoenix
Glen Campbell; *All-Time Country Classics-#1* ...(CAP)
  Classics Collection ....(CAP)
  Greatest Hits ....(CAP)
  Live ....(CAP)
  Very Best Of ....(CAP)

Come To The Supermarket (In Old Peking)
Barbra Streisand; *Album* ....(COL)
I Wish I Was In Peoria
Max Morath; & *His Ragtime Stompers* .... (VAN)
Little Old Lady From Pasadena
Beach Boys; *Concert* ....(CAP)
Jan & Dean; *Best Of* ....(EMI)
  Billboard Top Rock 'N' Roll Hits-1964 .... (RHI)
  Deadman's Curve ....(EMI)
  Surf City-Best Of ....(EMI)
My Niece From Pittsburgh In 1992
PFS; *Illustrative Problems* ....(CUN)
Night Life In Pompeii
Earl Hines; *Earl Hines* ....(CRS)
Night Ride Out Of Phoenix
Gillan; *Future Shock* ....(MET)
O'er The Town Of Pedro
Firehouse; *Flyin' The Flannel* ....(COL)
Paducah
George Thomas; *Chocolate Dandies-1928-1933* .(DSQ)
Paducah Parade
Bob Crosby; *Uncollected-#2-1952-1953* .... (HIN)
Palm Springs Jump
Flat Foot Floogie Boys & Slim Gaillard; *1940s-The
Singers* ....(COL)
Palo Alto
Lee Konitz; *Subconscious-Lee* .... (PRS)
Palo Alto Cowboy
Reilly & Maloney; *Profiles* ....(FRK)
Paradise City
Guns N' Roses; *Appetite For Destruction* ....(GEF)
Parsons, Kansas Blues
Bob Scobey's Frisco Band & Clancy Hayes; *Bob
Scobey's Frisco Band & Clancy Hayes* .... (GTJ)
Pasadena
Al Jolson; *Lullaby Of Broadway-Music Of H.
Warren* ....(PF)
Pascagoula Run
Jimmy Buffett; *Boats Beaches Bars & Ballads* ... (MGR)
  Off To See The Lizard ....(MCA)
Peking Doll
Kazumi Watanabe/Resonance Vox; *Pandora* ... (GRM)
Peking Fling
Vassar Clements; *Vassar* ....(FF)
Peking Theme (So Little Time)
Andy Williams; *ST/55 Days At Peking* ....(VS)
Pensacola Joy
Kellis Ethridge; *Tomorrow Sky* .... (IC)
"Petticoat Junction" Theme
Flatt & Scruggs; *20 All-Time Great Recordings* ...(COL)
Original Music; *TV Theme Sing-Along Album* .... (RHI)
Phoenix City
Skatalites; *Original Club Ska* ....(HRT)
Pittsburgh
Ahmad Jamal; *Pittsburgh* ....(ATL)
Pittsburgh 1901
Mark Isham; *Sampler '86* ....(WH)
  Windham Hill-First Ten Years ....(WH)
Pittsburgh Stealers
Kendalls; *20 Favorites* ....(EPI)
Pittsburgh Town
Pete Seeger; *American Industrial Ballads* .... (FLW)
Pittsburgh, Pennsylvania
101 Strings Orchestra; *Million Seller Hits From
Mexico* ....(ALS)
Guy Mitchell; *16 Most Requested Songs* ....(COL)
Plano Texas Girl
Steve Wariner; *I Got Dreams* ....(MCA)
Playa Del Rey
Warne Marsh Quartet; *Music For Prancing* ......(VSO)
Pompeii
Peter Hammill; *Nadir's Big Chance* ....(BP)
Port Arthur Blues
Eric Thompson; *Flatpicking Guitar Festival* .... (SHA)
Savoy-Doucet Cajun Band; *Harias-Home Music* (ARH)
Port Arthur Waltz
Harry Choates; *Fiddle King Of Cajun Swing* ..... (ARH)
Porterville
Creedence Clearwater Revival; *1968-1969* ......(FAN)
  Creedence Clearwater Revival ....(FAN)
  More Creedence Gold ....(FAN)
Portland Town
Joan Baez; *In Concert* .... (VAN)
Ramblin' Jack Elliott; *Essential* .... (VAN)

Portland Woman
New Riders Of The Purple Sage; *New Riders Of The
Purple Sage* ....(COL)
  Vintage NRPS ....(RLX)
Prague
Chris Cutler & Fred Frith; *Live In Moscow Prague &
Washington* ....(CUN)
Prague In March
Hendrik Meurkens; *Sambahia* .... (CP)
Prague Spring
Legendary Pink Dots; *Shadow Weaver* ....(PIA)
Puerto Vallarta
101 Strings Orchestra; *Million Seller Hits From
Mexico* ....(ALS)
  Music From Mexico ....(ALS)
There's A Fella Waitin' In Poughkeepsie
Pied Pipers; *Capitol Collectors Series* ....(CAP)
To Portsmouth
John Townley/Press Gang; *Chesapeake-Sailor's
Companion* ....(ADE)
Town Called Paradise
Van Morrison; *No Guru No Method No Teacher* (MER)
View From Pony, Montana
Philip Aaberg; *Upright* ....(WH)

CITIES: PARIS

See Also: COUNTRIES: FRANCE

Afternoon In Paris
Anita O'Day; *Night Has A Thousand Eyes* ...... (EML)
Sonny Stitt; *Genesis* ....(PRS)
  Stitt/Bud Powell/J.J. Johnson .... (PRS)
Ah, Paree, Beautiful Girls
Millicent Martin; *Collector's Sondheim* ....(RCA)
Stephen Sondheim; *Collector's Sondheim* ....(RCA)
Alone In Paris
Alphonse Mouzon; *Best Of* .... (BSU)
  Early Spring ....(TEN)
April In Paris
Charlie Parker; *Verve Years* ....(VRV)
  With Strings ....(VRV)
Ella Fitzgerald & Oscar Peterson; *Ella & Oscar* .. (PAB)
Frank Sinatra; *Come Fly With Me* ....(CAP)
Mel Torme; *Mel Torme* ....(GLN)
Sarah Vaughan; *Complete On Mercury-#1: Great Jazz
Years* ....(MER)
  Sarah Vaughan ....(EMA)
Wynton Marsalis; *Marsalis Standard Time-#1* ....(COL)
  Perspectives: Columbia Jazz Sampler ....(COL)
Azure-Te (Paris Blues)
Frank Sinatra; *Hello Young Lovers* ....(COL)
Louis Jordan; *Five Guys Named Moe-Orig. Decca
Rec.-#2* ....(DEC)
Nat King Cole; *Nat King Cole* ....(CAP)
Original Cast; *Five Guys Named Moe* ....(COL)
Original London Cast; *Five Guys Named Moe* ... (REL)
Belles Of Paris
Beach Boys; *M.I.U. Album* ....(CAR)
Crimes Of Paris
Elvis Costello; *Girls Girls Girls* ....(COL)
Elvis Costello/Attractions; *Blood & Chocolate* ...(COL)
Evening In Paris
Stan Getz; *Artistry Of-Best Of Verve Years-#1* ...(VRV)
Free Man In Paris
Joni Mitchell; *Court & Spark* ....(ASY)
  Shadows & Light ....(ASY)
From Baltimore To Paris
Go West; *Dancing On The Couch* .... (CHR)
Going To Paris
Champion Jack Dupree; *Tricks* .... (CRS)
Goin' Back To Paris
Bill Collins; *Charmin' Billy* ....(CHT)
He Went To Paris
Jimmy Buffett; *Songs You Know By Heart-Greatest
Hits* ....(MCA)
  White Sport Coat & A Pink Crustacean .... (MCA)
  You Had To Be There ....(MCA)
How Ya Gonna Keep 'Em Down...
Eddie Cantor; *Memories* ....(MCA)
I Love Paris
Frank Sinatra; *Sings Of Love & Things* ....(CAP)
  Sings The Select Cole Porter ....(CAP)

It Wasn't Paris, It Was You
Nancy Holloway; *Songbirds* ....(BAI)
King Of Paris
Jo Stafford; *By Request* .... (CRN)
Last Mango In Paris
Jimmy Buffett; *Feeding Frenzy* .... (MCA)
   Last Mango In Paris .... (MCA)
Last Tango In Paris
Herb Alpert/Tijuana Brass; *Four Sider* .... (A&M)
   Greatest Hits-#2 .... (A&M)
Last Time I Saw Paris
Jonathan & Darlene Edwards; *Greatest Hits* ..... (CRN)
   In Paris .... (CRN)
Soundtrack; *That's Entertainment-#2* .... (MCA)
Memories Of Paris
Michael Petrucciani; *Music* .... (BLN)
Midnight In Paris
Michael Hurley/Unholy Modal Rounders; *Have
Moicy* .... (ROU)
Stephen Stills; *Illegal Stills* ....(COL)
Morning In Paris
John Lewis; *Private Concert* .... (EMA)
On The Roofs Of Paris
Ennio Morricone; *ST/Frantic* .... (ELE)
One Night In Paris
John Boswell; *Count Me In* ....(HS)
Opryland In Paris
Andy Badale/Beer Garden Band; *Nashville Beer
Garden* .... (RAN)
Paris
Elton John; *Leather Jackets* .... (MCA)
Figures On A Beach; *Standing On Ceremony* ..... (SIR)
Nicki Richards; *Naked (To The World)* .... (ATL)
Shawn Lane; *Powers Of Ten* .... (RPR)
Paris Blues
Duke Ellington/Orchestra; *Featuring Paul
Gonsalves* .... (FAN)
Milt Jackson; *Statements* .... (GRP)
Paris Calling
Shark Island; *Law Of The Order* .... (EPI)
Paris Finale
Santana; *Viva Santana!* ....(COL)
Paris In The Spring
Michel Legrand; *Legrand Piano* ....(COL)
Paris Is Burning
Dokken; *Breaking The Chains* .... (ELE)
Paris Is Paris Again
Original Cast; *Gigi* ....(RCA)
Paris Loves Lovers
Popular Standard; *Cole Porter-Centennial
Celebration* ....(RCA)
Paris Summer
Nancy Sinatra & Lee Hazlewood; *Fairy Tales &
Fantasies-Best Of* .... (RHI)
Parisian Thoroughfare
Bud Powell; *Amazing-#2* .... (BLN)
   Genius Of ....(VRV)
Clifford Brown/Max Roach/Harold Land; *Compact
Jazz-Clifford Brown* ....(VRV)
Stephane Grappelli; *Parisian Thoroughfare* ....(BL)
Paris, Tennessee
Dennis Robbins; *Man With A Plan* .... (GIA)
Tracy Lawrence; *Sticks & Stones* .... (ATL)
Play The Paris Blues
Dr. John; *It's In The Air* .... (SUM)
Poor People Of Paris
Les Baxter; *Memories Are Made Of This* ....(CAP)
Postcard From Paris
Jimmy Webb; *Suspending Disbelief* .... (ELE)
Sleeping In Paris
Rosanne Cash; *The Wheel* ....(COL)
Tango In Paris
Regina Belle; *Passion* ....(COL)
There Is Only One Paris For That
Original Cast; *Irma La Douce* .... (SMC)
There's A Place Called Paris
Mae Barnes; *Mae Barnes* .... (DSQ)
Under Paris Skies
Arthur Murray/Orchestra; *Music For
Dancing-Waltz* ....(RCA)
Gordon Jenkins; *France* ....(BAI)
Under The Bridges Of Paris
Michel LeGrand; *LeGrand Piano* ....(COL)

Whores Of Paris
Bernie Taupin; *He Who Rides The Tiger* .... (ASY)

CITIES: PHILADELPHIA
See Also: STATES: PENNSYLVANIA

Baby Do The Philly Dog
Olympics; *Official Record Album Of* .... (RHI)
Fall In Philadelphia
Daryl Hall & John Oates; *Whole Oats* .... (ATL)
Motownphilly
Boyz II Men; *Cooleyhighharmony* .... (MOT)
Off To Philadelphia
Robert White/Monte Carlo Philharmonic; *Favorite Irish
Songs Of Princess Grace* .... (VC)
Philadelphia
John O'Connor; *Songs For Our Times* ....(FF)
Magazine; *Correct Use Of Soap* .... (BP)
Mongo Santamaria; *Live At Jazz Alley* .... (CP)
Neil Young; *ST/Philadelphia* ....(COL)
Philadelphia Baby
Charlie Rich; *20 Golden Hits* .... (SUN)
   Original .... (SUN)
Philadelphia Boogie
Len McCall; *Philadelphia Boogie* .... (CLT)
Philadelphia Fillies
Del Reeves; *Super Country Hits Of The '70s* .....(GUS)
Philadelphia Freedom
Daryl Hall & John Oates; *Two Rooms-Songs Of E. John
& B. Taupin* ....(POL)
Elton John; *Billboard Top Rock 'N' Roll Hits-1975* (RHI)
   Greatest Hits-#2 ....(POL)
Philadelphia Hop
Li'l Wally; *Here Comes* ....(JJ)
Philadelphia Lawyer
Rose Maddox; *Rose Of The West Coast Country* (ARH)
   Super Hits Country-1940s ....(GUS)
Willie Nelson; *Tribute To Woody Guthrie &
Leadbelly* ....(COL)
Woody Guthrie; *Cowboy Songs On Folkways* ... (FLW)
Philadelphia Mambo
Cal Tjader; *Black Orchid* .... (FAN)
Philly Dog
Mar-Keys; *Back To Back/Mar-Keys & Booker
T/MGs* .... (ATL)
   Great Memphis Sound .... (ATL)
   Stax/Volt Revue-#1-Live In London .... (ATL)
   Super Hits-#1 .... (ATL)
Philly Freeze
Alvin Cash/Registers; *45* .... (ERI)
Philly Rag
Dan Hicks/Hot Licks; *Striking It Rich* .... (MCA)
Streets Of Philadelphia
Bruce Springsteen; *ST/Philadelphia* ....(COL)
Trees In Philadelphia
Patti Page; *Touch Of Country* .... (FFT)
Trimble's Compliments To The City Of...
Gerald Trimble; *Crosscurrents* .... (GRE)
T.S.O.P. (The Sound Of Philadelphia)
MFSB; *Ten Years Of #1 Hits* .... (PI)
   & Three Degrees-Philadelphia Classics .... (PI)
   & Three Degrees-Soul Hits/'70s-#12 .... (RHI)

CITIES: R

All Roads Lead To Rome
Stranglers; *Feline* .... (EPI)
All The Way To Richmond
Roger Whittaker; *Reflections Of Love* ....(RCA)
Arrivederci Roma
Jerry Vale; *17 Most Requested Songs* ....(COL)
   Sings The Great Italian Hits ....(COL)
Mario Lanza; *Best Of* ....(RCA)
   Legendary Performer ....(RCA)
   Legendary Tenor ....(RCA)
Dancing In Rackville, Maryland
Fred Frith; *Gravity* .... (RAL)
Fiesta In Rio
Bette Midler; *Live At Last* .... (ATL)
Flying Down To Rio
Bobby Short; *Ertegun's N.Y. N.Y. Cabaret
Music-#5* .... (ATL)

Folsom Prison Blues (Reno)
Johnny Cash; *At Folsom Prison & San Quentin* ...(COL)
Billboard Top Country Hits-1968 .... (RHI)
Classic Cash-Hall Of Fame Series .... (MER)
Greatest Hits-#2 ....(COL)
Original Golden Hits #1 .... (SUN)
Superbilly ....(SUN)
Guitar Picker From Rody, Wyoming
Joey Davis; *45* .... (MRC)
Holiday In Rio
Barney Kessel; *Barney Plays Kessel* .... (CCJ)
I Go To Rio
Pablo Cruise; *Worlds Away* ....(A&M)
Peter Allen; *It Is Time For* ....(A&M)
Taught By Experts ....(A&M)
The Best ....(A&M)
Only A Dream In Rio
James Taylor; *That's Why I'm Here* ....(COL)
Rainy Night In Rio
Susannah McCorkle; *Thanks For The Memory* ...(PAU)
Raywood Texas
Queen Ida; *Caught In The Act* .... (CRS)
Queen Ida/Zydeco Band; *In San Francisco* .... (CRS)
Redondo Beach
Patti Smith; *Horses* .... (ARI)
Reno
Doug Supernaw; *Red & Rio Grande* ....(BNA)
Reno And Me
T.G. Sheppard; *Perfect Stranger* ....(WB)
Waylon Jennings; *The Eagle* ....(EPI)
Reno Bound
Southern Pacific; *Greatest Hits* ....(WB)
Southern Pacific ....(WB)
ST/Pink Cadillac ....(WB)
Reno Burrito
Tom Collier; *Pacific Aire* .... (NEB)
Reno Waltz
Marc Savoy; *Oh What A Night* .... (ARH)
Reno, Nevada
Ian Matthews; *Circle Dance-Hokey Pokey Charity
Comp.* ....(GRE)
Mimi & Richard Farina; *Best Of* ....(VAN)
Celebrations For A Grey Day ....(VAN)
Troubadours Of The Folk Era-#1 .... (RHI)
Return To Rio
Oscar Castro-Neves; *Brazilian Scandals* .... (JVC)
Richland Woman Blues
Mississippi John Hurt; *Best Of* .... (VAN)
Richmond Cotillion
Delaware Water Gap; *Fox Follow String Band* ....(BIO)
Riding To Rio
William Orbit; *Strange Cargo* .... (IRN)
Rio
Doobie Brothers; *Takin' It To The Streets* ....(WB)
Duran Duran; *Decade* ....(CAP)
Rio ....(CAP)
Michael Nesmith; *From A Radio Engine To The Photon
Wing* ....(PA)
Newer Stuff ....(RHI)
Rio De Janeiro
Barry White; *Beware!* .... (UG)
Rio De Janeiro Blue
Nicolette Larson; *In The Nick Of Time* ....(WB)
Randy Crawford; *Secret Combination* ....(WB)
Road To Rome
PFS; *279* ....(CUN)
Roanoke
Blaine Sprouse; *Summertime* .... (ROU)
Vassar Clements/Others; *Nashville Jam* ....(FF)
Rock Island
Soundtrack; *Music Man* ....(WB)
Rock Island Line
Johnny Cash; *Story Songs Of The Trains & Rivers* (SUN)
Sun Years ....(RHI)
Vintage Years-1955-1963 ....(RHI)
Sonny Terry & Brownie McGhee; *Hootin'* ......(MUS)
Jazz Heritage ....(MCA)
Weavers; *At Carnegie Hall* ....(VAN)
Best Of ....(MCA)
Greatest Hits ....(VAN)
Rock Island Rocket
Tom Scott; *Best Of* ....(COL)
Tom Scott/L.A. Express; *Tom Cat* .... (EOD)

Rockport Sunday
Tom Rush; *Circle Game* .... (ELE)
Rockville (Don't Go Back To)
R.E.M.; *Eponymous* .... (IRS)
Reckoning .... (IRS)
Rome Is A Song
Jimmy Roselli; *More I See You* .... (M&R)
Rome Wasn't Built In A Day
Sam Cooke; *Man & His Music* ....(RCA)
Roseville Fair
Nanci Griffith; *One Fair Summer Evening* .... (MCA)
Rotterdam Blues
Dave Brubeck; *We're All Together Again* .... (ATL)
Ruins Of Richmond
Norman Blake; *Fields Of November* ....(FF)
See You In Rio
Joyce; *Music Inside* .... (VF)
Walking Back To Richmond
Dry Brance Fire Squad; *Fannin' The Flames* .... (ROU)

CITIES: S

*See Also: CITIES: SAN ANTONIO, SAN
FRANCISCO, SANTA FE, SAVANNAH, ST.
LOUIS*

Chains (Seattle)
Patty Loveless; *Greatest Hits* .... (MCA)
Honky Tonk Angel .... (MCA)
Come Back To Sorrento
Dean Martin; *All-Time Greatest Hits* ....(CCB)
Frank Sinatra; *Columbia Years-1943-1952-Complete
Rec.* ....(COL)
Dancing In Sunrise, Switzerland
Muffins; *Open City* .... (CUN)
Dear Old Stockholm
Miles Davis; *Best Of* .... (BLN)
Miles Davis Quintet; *'Round About Midnight* .....(COL)
Terence Blanchard; *Simply Stated* ....(COL)
Toots Thielemans; *East Coast West Coast* ....(PRV)
Dear Old Syracuse
Original New York Cast; *Boys From Syracuse* .. (ANG)
Do You Know The Way To San Jose
Dionne Warwick; *Anthology 1962-1971* .... (RHI)
Greatest Hits ....(EVR)
Hot! Live & Otherwise .... (ARI)
Fall Of Saigon
Original London Cast; *Miss Saigon* .... (GEF)
From Silver Lake
Jackson Browne; *Jackson Browne* .... (ASY)
Goodnight Saigon
Billy Joel; *Greatest Hits #1 & 2-1978-85* ....(COL)
KOHUEPT ....(COL)
Nylon Curtain ....(COL)
Heat Is On Is Saigon
Original London Cast; *Miss Saigon* .... (GEF)
I Lost My Sugar In Salt Lake City
Johnny Mercer; *Capitol Collectors Series* ....(CAP)
Kill Surf City
Jesus & Mary Chain; *Barbed Wire Kisses* ....(RPR)
Leaving Sedona
Don Harriss; *Elevations* ....(SA)
Like A Sunday In Salem
Gene Cotton; *No Strings Attached* ....(ARL)
Save The Dancer ....(ARL)
Little Bit South Of Saskatoon
Sonny James; *American Originals* ....(COL)
Midnight In San Juan
Earl Klugh; *Midnight In San Juan* ....(WB)
Old San Juan
Spyro Gyra; *Access All Areas* .... (MCA)
Collection ....(GRP)
Incognito ....(MCA)
Queen Of Sydney
Oregon; *Crossing* .... (ECM)
Road To Santa Rosa
Frank Chacksfield; *Mirrors* .... (STA)
Runnin' Back To Saskatoon
Guess Who; *Track Record-Collection* ....(RCA)
Sacramento
Chrysanthemum Ragtime Band; *Vol. 1* .... (OME)

Saginaw, Michigan
Lefty Frizzell; *American Originals* ....(COL)
  Billboard Top Country Hits-1964 .... (RHI)
  Columbia Country Classics-#3-Americana ......(COL)
  Greatest Hits ....(COL)
Saigon
John Prine; *Pink Cadillac* ....(ASY)
Saigon Bride
Joan Baez; *Contemporary Ballad Book* .... (VAN)
Saigon Warrior
Saul Broudy & Robin Thomas; *In Country-Americans In The Vietnam War* ....(FF)
Salt Lake City
Beach Boys; *California Girls* ....(CAP)
  Gift Set ....(CAP)
  Spirit Of America ....(CAP)
Bob Weir; *Heaven Help The Fool* .... (ARI)
Salt Lake City Blues
Eric Thompson & Alan Senauke; *Two Guitars* .....(FF)
Salt Pork, West Virginia
Louis Jordan; *Jazz Heritage-Greatest Hits-#2* .... (MCA)
Salzburg
Jean Stapleton & Eddie Lawrence; *Bells Are Ringing* ....(COL)
San Angelo
Marty Robbins; *All Around Cowboy* ....(COL)
  Essential Marty Robbins-1951-1982 ....(COL)
  More Gunfighter Ballads & Trail Songs ....(COL)
San Ber'dino
Mothers Of Invention; *One Size Fits All* ....(RYK)
San Carlos
Don Grusin; *No Borders* ....(GRP)
San Diego Serenade
Nanci Griffith; *Late Night Grande Hotel* .... (MCA)
Tom Waits; *Anthology* ....(ASY)
  Heart Of Saturday Night ....(ASY)
San Fernando
Mary McCaslin; *Sunny California* ....(MER)
Roy Orbison; *Legendary* ....(SSP)
  Rare Orbison-#2 ....(MON)
San Jacinto
Peter Gabriel; *Security* ....(GEF)
  Shaking The Tree-16 Golden Greats ....(GEF)
San Jose
Blind Snooks Eaglin; *Down Yonder (Snooks Eaglin Today)* ....(CRS)
San Miguel
Beach Boys; *10 Years Of Harmony* ....(CAR)
San Tropez
Pink Floyd; *Gift Set* ....(CAP)
  Meddle ....(CAP)
Santa Ana
Willi Jones; *Willi Jones* ....(GEF)
Santa Ana Woman
Bobs; *Songs For Tomorrow Morning* ....(KAL)
Santa Barbara
David Benoit; *This Side Up* ....(SPT)
Ronnie Milsap; *Only One Love In My Life* ....(RCA)
"Santa Barbara" Theme
Original Music; *Soap Opera's Greatest Love Themes* ....(SCO)
Santa Cruz
Dirty Dozen Brass Band; *Voodoo* ....(COL)
Ray Barretto; *Handprints* ....(CP)
Santa Lucia
Elvis Presley; *ST/Viva Las Vegas/Roustabout* .....(RCA)
Mario Lanza; *Legendary Tenor* ....(RCA)
Santa Monica Pier
Christine Lavin; *Good Thing He Can't Read My Mind* ....(PHO)
Holly Near; *Live Album* ....(RWD)
Nitty Gritty Dirt Band; *Dream* ....(UA)
Santa Rosa
Gino Vannelli; *Nightwalker* ....(ARI)
Sao Paulo
Dan Moretti; *Point Of Entry* ....(PRC)
David Amram; *No More Walls* ....(FF)
David Benoit; *Every Step Of The Way* ....(GRP)
Freddie Hubbard & Woody Shaw; *Eternal Triangle* ....(BLN)
Sausalito
Ashra; *Belle Alliance* ....(BP)
Grover Washington, Jr.; *Live At The Bijou* ......(MOT)

Mark Murphy; *Bridging A Gap* .... (MUS)
  September Ballads ....(MS)
SOS All-Stars; *Greetings From New York* ....(CMG)
Sausalito Summernight
Diesel; *Watts In A Tank* ....(REG)
Scarborough Fair
Simon & Garfunkel; *Collected Works* ....(COL)
  Concert In Central Park ....(WB)
  Greatest Hits ....(COL)
  Parsley Sage Rosemary & Thyme ....(COL)
  ST/The Graduate ....(COL)
Seattle
Bobby Sherman; *Very Best Of* .... (RES)
Perry Como; *This Is* ....(RCA)
Public Image, Ltd.; *Greatest Hits So Far* .... (VIA)
  Happy? .... (VIA)
Seattle Afternoon
Reilly & Maloney; *At Last* ....(FRK)
Seattle Ain't Bullshittin'
Sir Mix-A-Lot; *Mack Daddy* ....(DEF)
Seattle Hunch
Jelly Roll Morton; *Centennial-Complete Victor Recordings* ....(BLU)
Seattle Morning
David Benoit; *Urban Daydreams* ....(GRP)
Sedona
Freeway Philharmonic; *Car Tunes* ....(SPT)
Shanghai Breezes
John Denver; *Greatest Hits-#3* ....(RCA)
  Seasons Of The Heart ....(RCA)
Shanghai Lil
Guy Lombardo; *16 Most Requested Songs* ....(COL)
Shanghai Noodle Factory
Traffic; *Last Exit* .... (ISL)
Shanghai Shuffle
Bunny Berigan Orchestra; *Bunny Berigan Orchestra-1937-1938* .... (HIN)
Fletcher Henderson Orchestra; *1924-1941* ......(BIO)
Silverton
C.W. McCall; *Greatest Hits* ....(POL)
Sioux City Sue
Bob Wills/Texas Playboys; *Tiffany Transcriptions-#8* ....(KAL)
Gene Autry; *Country Music Hall Of Fame* ......(COL)
Jimmy C. Newman; *Cajun Cowboy* ....(PLN)
Mom & Dads; *In The Good Old Summertime* ....(CRS)
Willie Nelson & Leon Russell; *One For The Road* ....(COL)
Skatetown U.S.A.
Dave Mason; *Skatetown U.S.A.* ....(COL)
Snow In San Anselmo
Van Morrison; *Hard Nose The Highway* ....(WB)
Starkville City Jail
Johnny Cash; *At Folsom Prison & San Quentin* ...(COL)
Statesboro Blues
Allman Brothers Band; *At Fillmore East* .... (POL)
  Best Of ....(POL)
  Decade Of Hits-1969-1979 ....(POL)
  Dreams ....(POL)
  Duane Allman Anthology ....(CPC)
  Road Goes On Forever ....(POL)
Blind Willie McTell; *Early Years-1927-1932* ....(YAZ)
Charlie Daniels Band/Friends; *Volunteer Jam #3&4* ....(EPI)
Pat Travers; *Makin' Magic* ....(POL)
Taj Mahal; *Taj's Blues* ....(COL)
Still In Saigon
Charlie Daniels Band; *Decade Of Hits* .... (EPI)
  Windows ....(EPI)
Stockholm
Dave Edmunds; *Closer To The Flame* ....(CAP)
Django Reinhardt; *Immortal* ....(CRS)
New Fast Automatic Daffodils; *Body Exit Mind* . (MUT)
Stockholm Stomp
California Ramblers; *Miss Annabelle Lee-#1* ......(BIO)
Stockholm Sweetnin'
Al Jarreau; *1965* ....(BAI)
Cannonball Adderley/Orchestra; *African Waltz* ..(RVR)
Clifford Brown; *Memorial* ....(PRS)
Jon Hendricks; *Jazz-Club Vocal* ....(VRV)
Patti Austin; *Real Me* ....(QUE)
Sun City
Artists United Against Apartheid; *Sun City* .....(MAN)

Sunday Night In San Fernando
Mel Torme/Mel-Tones; *California Suite* .... (DCO)
Sweetwater Nights
Dave Grusin; *Out Of The Shadows* .... (GRP)
Sweetwater, Texas
Charlie Daniels Band; *Saddle Tramp* .... (EPI)
Sydney By Night
James Morrison; *Postcards From Down Under* ... (ATL)
Sydney From A 727
Paul Kelly/Messengers; *Comedy* .... (DD)
Syracuse
Jean Sablon; *1932-1962* .... (DRG)
Syracuse Oberek
Li'l Wally; *Here Comes* .... (JJ)
Would They Love Him Down In Shreveport
George Jones; *Hallelujah Weekend* .... (EPI)
Oak Ridge Boys; *Bobbie Sue* .... (MCA)

CITIES: SAN ANTONIO

See Also: STATES: TEXAS

Ain't No Fun To Be Alone In San Antone
Gene Watson; *Mack In The Fire* .... (WB)
China Grove
Doobie Brothers; *Best Of* .... (WB)
Captain & Me .... (WB)
Farewell Tour .... (WB)
Home In San Antone
Bob Wills/Texas Playboys; *Tiffany*
Transcriptions-#4 .... (KAL)
Texas Playboys/Leon McAuliffe; *Greatest Hits Of*
Texas .... (RHI)
San Antonio Rose Story .... (DEL)
Honky Tonk Moon (San Antonio)
Rosie Flores; *Once More With Feeling* .... (HT)
In San Antone
Dan Seals; *Early* .... (CAP)
San Antone .... (EMI)
My San Antonio Rose
Freddy Powers; *45* .... (MCA)
My Sweetheart Lives In San Antonio
Ray Duncan; *45* .... (OOP)
New San Antonio Rose
Bob Wills/Texas Playboys; *Columbia Country*
Classics-#1-Golden Age .... (COL)
Essential .... (COL)
Greatest Hits .... (CCB)
Rosa De San Antonio
Santiago Jimenez, Jr.; *Mero Mero De San*
Antonio .... (ARH)
Rose Of San Antone
Bashful Brother Oswald; *Don't Say Aloha* ...... (ROU)
San Antonio Champagne
Troy Cory; *Real Country* .... (VRA)
San Antonio Girl
Steve Earle/Dukes; *Exit 0* .... (MCA)
San Antonio Nights
Eddy Raven; *Greatest Hits* .... (WB)
San Antonio Rose
Asleep At The Wheel; *Western Standard Time* .... (EPI)
Bob Wills; *Best Of-#2* .... (MCA)
Sounds Of Texas .... (CAP)
Texas State Of Mind .... (LIB)
Floyd Cramer; *Billboard Top Country Hits-1961* . (RHI)
Country Love .... (SO)
Patsy Cline; *Story* .... (MCA)
Ricky Skaggs; *Comin' Home To Stay* .... (EPI)
Willie Nelson; *San Antonio Rose* .... (COL)
San Antonio Shout
Bob Crosby Orchestra; *Play 22 Original Big Band*
Hits .... (HIN)
San Antonio Story
Stephen Woodfin & Joe Vickers; *Waco* .... (SO)
San Antonio Stroll
Tanya Tucker; *Collection* .... (MCA)
Greatest Hits .... (MCA)
Greatest Hits Encore .... (LIB)
MCA Records 30 Years Of Hits-1958-1988 ... (MCA)
Tanya Tucker .... (MCA)
San Anton'
Thomas "Fats" Waller; *Fats Waller & His*
Rhythm-1936-1938 .... (BLU)

Walkin' Back To San Antonio
Hank Thompson; *Here's To Country Music* .... (SO)

CITIES: SAN FRANCISCO

See Also: This category for various S.F. suburbs,
STATES: CALIFORNIA

Do You Know The Way To San Jose
Dionne Warwick; *Anthology 1962-1971* .... (RHI)
Greatest Hits .... (EVR)
Hot! Live & Otherwise .... (ARI)
Frisco
John Lee Hooker; *Hooked On The Blues* .... (EVR)
Tommy O'Day; *45* .... (NTR)
Frisco Depot
Mickey Newbury; *Frisco Mabel Joy* .... (ELE)
Frisco Lines
Fred McDowell; *Blues Roots* .... (TOM)
Here In Frisco
Merle Haggard; *18 Rare Classics* .... (CCB)
I Left My Heart In San Francisco
Tony Bennett; *All-Time Greatest Hits* .... (COL)
I Left My Heart In San Francisco .... (COL)
Pop Classics/'60s .... (COL)
In San Francisco
Dinah Washington; *Echoes Of An Era* .... (RLL)
Earl "Fatha" Hines; *Another Monday Date* ...... (PRS)
Leavin' Memphis, Frisco Bound
Jesse Fuller; *Frisco Bound* .... (ARH)
Lone Cat .... (GTJ)
Lights
Journey; *Captured* .... (COL)
Infinity .... (COL)
Mean Old Frisco
Eric Clapton; *Slow Hand* .... (RSO)
Jimmy Witherspoon; *Best Of* .... (PRS)
Mean Old Frisco .... (PRS)
New Frisco Train
Washington White; *Mississippi*
Moaners-1927-1942 .... (YAZ)
Road To Santa Rosa
Frank Chacksfield; *Mirrors* .... (STA)
San Carlos
Don Grusin; *No Borders* .... (GRP)
San Franciscan Nights
Eric Burdon/Animals; *Greatest Hits* .... (MGM)
History Of British Rock-#8 .... (RHI)
San Francisco
Judy Garland; *America's Treasure* .... (DHL)
At Carnegie Hall .... (CAP)
One & Only .... (CAP)
Vikki Carr; *Best Of* .... (UA)
Village People; *Live & Sleazy* .... (CAS)
Village People .... (CAS)
San Francisco Bay Blues
Eric Clapton; *Unplugged* .... (RPR)
Janis Joplin; *ST/Janis* .... (COL)
Jesse Fuller; *Brother Low Down* .... (FAN)
Great Blues Men .... (VAN)
San Francisco Bay Blues .... (GTJ)
Paul McCartney; *Unplugged-Official Bootleg* ... (CAP)
Ramblin' Jack Elliott; *Bread & Roses Festival-Acoustic*
Music-#1 .... (FAN)
Essential .... (VAN)
Hard Travelin' .... (FAN)
Troubadours Of The Folk Era-#1 .... (RHI)
San Francisco Blues
Quincy Jones; *P's & Q's* .... (CAP)
San Francisco Days
Chris Isaak; *San Francisco Days* .... (RPR)
San Francisco Fan
Cab Calloway; *Hi De Ho Man* .... (COL)
Joe Jackson; *Jumpin' Jive* .... (A&M)
San Francisco Girls
Fever Tree; *Best Of* .... (BCT)
Nuggets-#11 .... (RHI)
Sixties Rule-#1 .... (OW)
San Francisco Holiday (Worry Later)
Thelonius Monk; *In Person* .... (MS)
San Francisco Is A Lonely Town
Orion; *Sunrise* .... (SUN)

San Francisco Mabel Joy
Joan Baez; *Country Music Album* .... (VAN)
John Denver; *Some Days Are Diamonds* ....(RCA)
Kenny Rogers; *The Gambler* .... (EMI)
Mickey Newbury; *Bread & Roses Festival-Acoustic*
Music-#1 ....(FAN)
   Heaven Help The Child .... (ELE)
   Live At Montezuma Hall .... (ELE)
San Francisco (Be Sure To Wear Some...)
Scott McKenzie; *Nuggets-#10-Folk Rock* .... (RHI)
   Rock Artifacts-#3 ....(COL)
   ST/Forrest Gump ....(EPX)
   Summer Of Love .... (RHI)
San Francisco (You've Got Me)
Village People; *Billboard Top Dance Hits-1977* .. (RHI)
   Greatest Hits .... (RHI)
San Jose
Blind Snooks Eaglin; *Down Yonder (Snooks Eaglin*
Today) .... (CRS)
Santa Rosa
Gino Vannelli; *Nightwalker* .... (ARI)
Sausalito
Ashra; *Belle Alliance* ....(BP)
Grover Washington, Jr.; *Live At The Bijou* ...... (MOT)
Mark Murphy; *Bridging A Gap* .... (MUS)
   September Ballads .... (MS)
SOS All-Stars; *Greetings From New York* .... (CMG)
Sausalito Summernight
Diesel; *Watts In A Tank* ....(REG)
(Sittin' On) The Dock Of The Bay
Michael Bolton; *The Hunger* ....(COL)
Otis Redding; *Best Of* ....(ATC)
   Golden Age Of Black Music 1960-1970 .... (ATL)
   Golden Soul .... (ATL)
   Soul Years .... (ATL)
   Story .... (ATL)
   (Sittin' On) The Dock Of The Bay ....(ATC)
Snow In San Anselmo
Van Morrison; *Hard Nose The Highway* ....(WB)
Song For Frisco
Quicksilver Messenger Service; *Quicksilver* ...... (CAP)
Streets Of San Francisco
Statler Brothers; *Carry Me Back* .... (MER)
"Streets Of San Francisco" Theme
Original Music; *Television's Greatest Hits-#3* .... (TVT)
Summer In San Francisco
Hendrik Meurkens; *Sambahia* .... (CP)
Union Square
Cal Tjader; *San Francisco Moods* .... (FAN)
We Built This City
Starship; *Greatest Hits-Ten Years &*
Change-1979-91 ....(RCA)
   Knee Deep In The Hoopla .... (GRU)
   Nipper's Greatest Hits-'80s ....(RCA)

CITIES: SANTA FE
See Also: STATES: NEW MEXICO

Along The Santa Fe Trail
Glenn Miller; *Original Live Recordings* .... (PRR)
Sons Of The Pioneers; *Sunset On The Range* ..... (PRR)
Back To Santa Fe
Cee Cee Chapman; *Twist Of Fate* ....(CCB)
Lee Hunter; *Texas Blues-Gold Star Sessions* ..... (ARH)
Girls Of Santa Fe
Bill Morrissey; *Standing Eight* ....(PHO)
Memories Of Old Santa Fe
Randy Travis; *Wind In The Wire* ....(WB)
Over The Santa Fe Trail
Sons Of The Pioneers; *Empty Saddles* ....(MCA)
   Tumbling Tumbleweeds ....(MSP)
Santa Fe
Bellamy Brothers; *Crazy From The Heart* .... (MCA)
   Greatest Hits-#3 ....(MCA)
Bob Dylan; *Bootleg Series-#1-3-1961-1989* ..... (COL)
Bon Jovi; *Blaze Of Glory* .... (MER)
Little Brother Montgomery; *Tasty Blues* .... (PRS)
   Urban Blues ....(FAN)
Roosevelt Sykes & L. Brother Montgomery; *Urban*
Blues ....(FAN)
Santa Fe Blues
Lightnin' Hopkins; *Nothin' But The Blues-Golden*
Classics-#4 ....(COL)

Pee Wee Hughes; *Sugar Mama Blues (1949)* .....(BIO)
Sam Ambrose; *Zydeco-#2* .... (ARH)
Santa Fe/Beautiful Obsession
Van Morrison; *Wavelength* ....(WB)

CITIES: SAVANNAH
See Also: STATES: GEORGIA

Savannah
Eternal Wind; *Eternal Wind* ....(FF)
Gary Brooker; *No More Fear Of Flying* .... (CHR)
Kurt Riemann; *Gaia* ....(NW)
Tommy Wiggins; *Cool Saturdays* .... (NUV)
Savannah Awakes
Barbra Streisand; *ST/Prince Of Tides* ....(COL)
Savannah Blues
Thomas "Fats" Waller; *Fats & His*
Buddies-1927-1929 .... (BLU)
Savannah Dance
Michael Pluznick; *Where The Rain Is Born* ...... (SOG)
Savannah Mama
Blind Willie McTell; *Early Years 1927-1932* ....(YAZ)
   Three Shades Of Blues ....(BIO)
Blind Willie McTell & Memphis Minnie; *Love Changin'*
Blues ....(BIO)
Paul Geremia; *My Kinda Place* ....(FF)
Savannah Nights
Tom Johnston; *Everything You've Heard Is True* ... (WB)
Savannah Russet/Jete The Dancing Cat
Jeanne Newhall; *Novice* .... (MAR)
Savannah The Serene
Billy Cobham; *Crosswinds* .... (ATL)
Savannah Woman
Brother Noland; *Pacific Bad Boy* .... (MAC)
Tommy Bolin; *Teaser* .... (NEM)
Sweet Savannah Sue
Fats Waller; *Turn On The Heat-Fats Waller Piano*
Solos .... (BLU)
Louis Armstrong; *#5-In New York* ....(COL)

CITIES: ST. LOUIS
See Also: STATES: MISSOURI

Dancing In St. Louis
Li'l Wally; *Here Comes* ....(JJ)
East St. Louis Toodle oo
Duke Ellington; *Bethlehem Years-#1* .... (BET)
   Brunswick Era-#1 ....(MCA)
   Era ....(COL)
   Jazz Heritage-Beginning 1926-1928 ....(MCA)
Steely Dan; *Greatest Hits* ....(MCA)
   Pretzel Logic ....(MCA)
Going To St. Louis
Yank Rachell/Others; *Chicago Style* .... (DEL)
Meet Me In St. Louis, Louis
Judy Garland; *Best Of* ....(MCA)
New East St. Louis Toodle-oo
Duke Ellington; *Reminiscing In Tempo* ....(COL)
New St. Louis Blues
Johnny Dodds; *South Side Chicago Jazz* .... (MCA)
Shim, Sham Shimmy On The St. Louis Blues
Dizzy Gillespie; *Best Of* .... (PAB)
Spirits Of St. Louis
Johnny Paycheck; *Take This Job & Shove It* ...... (EPI)
Stranded In St. Louis
Omar Sharif; *The Raven* .... (ARH)
St. Louis Blues
Bessie Smith; *Beauty Of The Blues* ....(COL)
   Collection ....(COL)
Big Joe Turner; *Boss Of The Blues* ....(ATL)
Billie Holiday; *Quintessential-#9-1940-1942* .....(COL)
   Story-#3 ....(COL)
Bob Wills/Texas Playboys; *24 Great Hits* ...... (POL)
Cleo Laine; *Jazz* ....(RCA)
Dave Brubeck Quartet; *25th Anniversary*
Reunion ....(A&M)
   At Carnegie Hall ....(COL)
   Paper Moon ....(CCJ)
Duke Ellington; *1953 Pasadena Concert* .... (CRS)
Ella Fitzgerald; *These Are The Blues* ....(VRV)

Louis Armstrong; *At The Crescendo* .... (MCA)
  Legendary Performer ....(RCA)
  Nipper's Greatest Hits-'30s-#2 ....(RCA)
  #6-St. Louis Blues ....(COL)
Original Broadway Cast; *Black & Blue* .... (DRG)
Pete Fountain; *Best Of* .... (MCA)
Preservation Hall Jazz Band; *New Orleans-#2* ..(COL)
You Came A Long Way From St. Louis
  Peggy Lee & George Shearing; *Beauty & The
  Beat* .... (BLN)
Perry Como; *This Is-#2* ....(RCA)

CITIES: T

See Also: CITIES: TOKYO, TULSA

Battle Of Trenton
  Jim Burroughs; *Songs Of Rebellion* ....(AUF)
Going Back To Tampa
  Roy Bookbinder; *Going Back To Tampa* ...... (FF)
Goin' Down To Tampa
  Jeff Warner & Jeff Davis; *Wilder Joy-Trad. American
  Folk Songs* ....(FF)
Old Tucson
  Youssou N'Dour; *The Lion* .... (VIA)
Send Me Down To Tucson
  Mel Tillis; *Very Best Of* .... (MCA)
Tacoma Trailer
  Leonard Cohen; *The Future* ....(COL)
Tallahassee
  Country Gazette; *Hello Operator...This Is* ....(FF)
Tallahassee Lassie
  Freddy Cannon; *14 Booming Hits* .... (RHI)
  His Latest & Greatest .... (CRI)
  Partytime '50s ....(PRY)
Tampico
  Stan Kenton & June Christy; *Birth Of A Dream-Capitol's
  Early Hits* ....(CAP)
Tampico Trauma
  Jimmy Buffett; *Boats Beaches Bars & Ballads* ... (MGR)
  Changes In Latitudes, Changes In... .... (MCA)
  You Had To Be There-In Concert .... (MCA)
Taos
  Oregon; *Oregon* .... (ECM)
Taos To Tennessee
  Tish Hinojosa; *Taos To Tennessee* .... (WAT)
Ten O'Clock In Toronto
  Christine Lavin; *Compass* ....(PHO)
Texarkana
  R.E.M.; *Out Of Time* ....(WB)
Texarkana Baby
  Billy Hardwick, Jr.; *Too Country* ....(JRS)
  Kenny Wayne; *Borned With The Blues & Raised On
  Rock* .... (CAN)
Thomasville
  Stanley Turrentine; *More Than A Mood* .... (MM)
Tiburon
  Stan Kenton/Orchestra; *Kenton '76* ....(CW)
Tijuana
  Memphis Slim; *Memphis Slim* ....(CSS)
  Real Folk Blues ....(CSS)
Tijuana Jail
  Gilby Clarke; *Pawnshop Guitars* ....(VIA)
  Kingston Trio; *25 Years Non-stop* ....(XER)
  Best Of ....(CAP)
  Capitol Collectors Series ....(CAP)
  Greatest Hits ....(CCB)
Tijuana Moon
  Tim Buckley; *Look At The Fool* .... (BIZ)
Tijuana Sauerkraut
  Herb Alpert/Tijuana Brass; *Lonely Bull* ....(A&M)
Tijuana Taxi
  Herb Alpert/Tijuana Brass; *Classics-#1* ....(A&M)
  Four Sider ....(A&M)
  Greatest Hits ....(A&M)
Tipperary Far Away
  Clancy Brothers/Tommy Makem; *Irish Songs Of
  Drinking & Rebellion* .... (BSL)
Tipperary Town
  Larry Cunningham; *Golden Irish Favorites* ....(GAT)
Toledo
  John Denver; *Evening With* ....(RCA)
Toronto
  Lenny Breau; *Five O'Clock Bells* .... (ADE)

Toytown
  Walking Wounded; *New West* ....(CHS)
Toytown People
  Fabulous Poodles; *Mirror Stars* .... (EPI)
Trenchtown Rock
  Bob Marley/Wailers; *Confrontation* .... (TUF)
  Live ....(TUF)
  More Of The Mighty .... (TUF)
  Songs Of Freedom .... (TUF)
Tucson, Arizona (Gazette)
  Dan Fogelberg; *Windows & Walls* .... (FM)
Tupelo
  John Lee Hooker; *Best Of* .... (CRS)
  Great Bluesmen At Newport .... (VAN)
  Steve Cropper/Albert King/Pops Staples; *Stax Blues
  Brothers* ....(STX)
  Subdudes; *Subdudes* ....(ATL)
Tupelo County Jail
  Mel Tillis; *American Originals* ....(COL)
  Webb Pierce; *Golden Hits* .... (PLN)
Tupelo Honey
  Van Morrison; *Van Morrison* ....(WB)
Tupelo Mississippi Flash
  Jerry Reed; *Beset Of* ....(RCA)
Wild Goose Grasses In Tarrytown
  Weavers; *Classics* .... (VAN)
  Greatest Hits .... (VAN)

CITIES: TOKYO

See Also: COUNTRIES: JAPAN

All Right Tokyo!!
  Adrenalin O.D.; *Ishtar* .... (RES)
Calling From Tokyo
  Ryuichi Sakamoto; *Beauty* .... (VIA)
Love From Tokyo
  Rita Coolidge; *Classics-#5* ....(A&M)
Midnight In Tokyo
  Y & T; *Best Of '81 To '85* ....(A&M)
  Mean Streak ....(A&M)
  Yesterday & Today Live .... (MET)
Rainy Night In Tokyo
  Michael Franks; *Passionfruit* ....(WB)
Storm Over Tokyo Bay
  Jessie Allen Cooper; *Soft Wave* ....(SOG)
Tokyo
  10 CC; *Bloody Tourists* ....(POL)
  Brothers Johnson; *Classics-#11* ....(A&M)
  Bruce Cockburn; *Humans* ....(COL)
  Donna Summer; *She Works Hard For The Money* (MER)
Tokyo Joe
  Bryan Ferry; *In Your Mind* .... (RPR)
Tokyo Nights
  Bee Gees; *One* ....(WB)
  Rob Mullins; *Tokyo Nights* .... (NVA)
Tokyo Road
  Bon Jovi; *7800 Degrees Fahrenheit* .... (JBC)
Tokyo Rose
  Shok Paris; *Steel & Starlight* ....(IRS)
  Van Dyke Parks; *Tokyo Rose* ....(WB)
Tokyo Storm Warning
  Elvis Costello; *Girls Girls Girls* ....(COL)
  Elvis Costello/Attractions; *Blood & Chocolate* ...(COL)
Tokyo, Oklahoma
  John Anderson; *Greatest Hits-#2* ....(WB)
Vacation In Tokyo
  Urge Overkill; *Supersonic Storybook* .... (T&G)
When It's Cherry Time In Tokio
  James P. Johnson; *Rare Piano Roll Solos-#2-1917* (BIO)
Woman From Tokyo
  Deep Purple; *Deepest Purple-Very Best Of* ....(WB)
  Nobody's Perfect .... (MER)
  When We Rock We Rock-When We Roll... .... (WB)
  Who Do You Think We Are .... (WB)

CITIES: TULSA

See Also: STATES: OKLAHOMA

24 Hours From Tulsa
  Gene Pitney; *45* .... (MCR)
  Double Gold .... (MCR)

Ian & Sylvia; *Best Of* .... (VAN)
   Greatest Hits .... (VAN)
   Play One More .... (VAN)
Almost Of Tulsa
  Red Rhodes; *Steel Guitar Favorites* .... (ALS)
Big Tulsa Tillie
  Donnie Rohrs; *Country Music USA* .... (PC)
Last Trip To Tulsa
  Neil Young; *Neil Young* .... (RPR)
Take Me Back To Tulsa
  Asleep At The Wheel; *Route 66* .... (LIB)
  Bob Wills/Texas Playboys; *Bob Wills Anthology* ..(SSP)
   Columbia Country Classics-#1-Golden Age .....(COL)
   Tiffany Transcriptions-#2-Best Of Tiff. ....(KAL)
Tulsa County
  Byrds; *Byrds (collection)* ....(COL)
Tulsa Queen
  Emmylou Harris; *Luxury Liner* .... (WB)
Tulsa Time
  Don Williams; *Best Of-#2* .... (MCA)
   Country's Greatest Hits-#6 .... (PRY)
   Expressions .... (MCA)
   Legends .... (MCA)
  Eric Clapton; *Backless* .... (RSO)
   Just One Night .... (POL)
Tulsa Turnaround
  Kenny Rogers/First Edition; *All-Time Greatest*
   Hits-#2 .... (MSP)
   Country Songs .... (MSP)
Tulsa (Don't Let The Sun Set On You)
  Waylon Jennings; *Taker/Tulsa & Honky Tonk*
   Heroes .... (MOB)
Twenty-Four Hours From Tulsa
  Burt Bacharach; *Walk On By* .... (MSP)
  Gene Pitney; *Best Of* .... (KT)
T-U-L-S-A Straight Ahead
  Asleep At The Wheel; *10* .... (EPI)
   Swinging Best Of .... (EPI)
  Texas Playboys; *Today* .... (CAP)

CITIES: U

Ukiah
  Doobie Brothers; *Captain & Me* .... (WB)

CITIES: V

See Also: CITIES: VIENNA

Bobby's In Vicksburg
  Sylvia; *Snapshot* ....(RCA)
Carnival Of Venice
  Carmen Cavallaro; *Best Of* .... (MCA)
  Mantovani; *Mantovani's Italia* ....(BAI)
Moon Over Venice
  Thom Rotella; *Home Again* .... (DIG)
Send Me Down To Vicksburg
  John Mayall/Bluesbreakers; *Sense Of Place* .... (ISL)
Valdosta Blues
  Larry Willis; *Steal Away* .... (AQ)
Van Nuys Jam
  Alex Acuna/Unknowns; *Alex Acuna/Unknowns* .. (JVC)
Vancouver
  Andrew Calhoun; *Gates Of Love* .... (FF)
Vancouver Shakedown
  Nazareth; *Close Enough For Rock & Roll* .... (A&M)
   Hot Tracks .... (A&M)
Venice
  Love Tractor; *Themes From Venus* .... (DB)
  Modern Jazz Quartet; *One Never Knows* .... (ATL)
Venice Blue
  Bobby Darin; *Capitol Collectors Series* ....(CAP)
Venice Drowning
  Duran Duran; *Liberty* ....(CAP)
Venice U.S.A.
  Van Morrison; *Wavelength* .... (WB)
Vera Cruz
  Warren Zevon; *Excitable Boy* .... (ASY)
Vicksburg Blues
  Little Brother Montgomery; *Atlantic Blues-Piano* . (ATL)
   Tasty Blues .... (PRS)

We Open In Venice
  Original Cast; *Kiss Me Kate* .... (MCA)

CITIES: VIENNA

See Also: COUNTRIES: A

Do You Ever Dream Of Vienna
  Original Cast; *Little Mary Sunshine* ....(OOP)
Goodnight Vienna
  Ringo Starr; *Goodnight Vienna* ....(CAP)
Non-Viennese Waltz Blues
  Joe Gordon; *Lookin' Good!* .... (CTM)
One Night In Vienna
  Schoenerz & Scott; *One Night In Vienna* ....(WH)
Summer In Vienna
  Mantovani; *Golden Hits* ....(LON)
Tales From The Vienna Woods
  101 Strings Orchestra; *Best Of Johann Strauss Jr.* (ALS)
  Lawrence Welk; *22 Great Waltzes* .... (RAN)
Vienna
  Billy Joel; *The Stranger* ....(COL)
  Rippingtons; *Weekend in Monaco* .... (GRP)
  Ultravox; *Collection* .... (CHR)
   If I Was-Very Best Of Midge Ure & .... (CHR)
   Vienna .... (CHR)
Vienna Calling
  Falco; *Remix Hit Collection* .... (SIR)
   #3 .... (A&M)
Vienna Echoes
  Lawrence Welk; *Celebrates 50 Years In Music* .. (RAN)
Vienna Life
  Lawrence Welk; *22 All-Time Favorite Waltzes* .. (RAN)

CITIES: W

As Falls Wichita, So Falls Wichita Falls
  Pat Metheny & Lyle Mays; *As Falls Wichita, So Falls*
   Wichita Falls .... (ECM)
Big Noise From Winnetka
  Bette Midler; *Divine Madness* .... (ATL)
   Thighs & Whispers .... (ATL)
  Bob Crosby Orchestra; *Play 22 Original Big Band*
   Hits .... (HIN)
  Bob Crosby/Bob Cats; *Best Of* .... (MCA)
Cross The Brazos At Waco
  Billy Walker; *Columbia Country*
   Classics-#3-Americana ....(COL)
   Super Hits Country-1960s .... (IGR)
Goin' To D.C.
  Sonny Stitt; *Soul Classics* .... (PRS)
Hail Wichita
  Wichita State University Marching Band; *Wichita State*
   University Marching Band ....(FID)
Jack Straw (Wichita)
  Bruce Hornsby/Range; *Deadicated* .... (ARI)
  Grateful Dead; *Europe '72* .... (WB)
   What A Long Strange Trip It's Been .... (WB)
Not Being In Warsaw
  Colin Newman; *It Seems* .... (RES)
Pearl From Warsaw
  Klezmer Conservatory Band; *Jumpin' Night In The*
   Garden Of Eden .... (ROU)
Warsaw
  Joy Division; *Substance* .... (QUE)
Warsaw 1943 (I Never Betrayed The...)
  Johnny Clegg/Savuka; *Cruel, Crazy, Beautiful*
   World ....(CAP)
Warsaw Concerto
  Roger Williams; *Moments To Remember* .... (MSP)
Washington Bullets
  Clash; *On Broadway* .... (EPI)
   Sandinista .... (EPI)
Washington March/Waiting For Nancy
  Bertram Levy; *That Old Gut Feeling* ....(FF)
Washington We're Watching You
  Staple Singers; *45* .... (STX)
Washington, D.C. Hospital Center Blues
  Skip James; *Greatest Of The Delta Blues Singers* ...(BIO)
   Today .... (VAN)
Waterloo
  Abba; *Greatest Hits* .... (ATL)
   Waterloo .... (ATL)

Stonewall Jackson; *American Originals* ....(COL)
   Billboard Top Country Hits-1959 ....(RHI)
   Columbia Country Classics-#3-Americana ......(COL)
   Country Music Classics-#1-1950s ....(KT)
Waterloo Sunset
Kinks; *Kink Kronikles* ....(RPR)
   Something Else ....(RPR)
"Way" Cross Georgia
David Sanborn; *Takin' Off* ....(WB)
Wichita
Jayhawks; *Hollywood Town Hall* ....(DEF)
Peter Buffett; *Yonnondio* ....(NAR)
Wichita Cross Winds
John Stewart; *Centennial* ....(HOM)
Wichita Jail
Charlie Daniels Band; *Banded Together* ....(EPI)
   Saddle Tramp ....(EPI)
Wichita Lineman
Glen Campbell; *Best Of* ....(LIB)
   Classics Collection ....(LIB)
   Country Music Classics-#3-1965-1970 ....(KT)
   Greatest Hits ....(LIB)
   Jimmy Webb Collection ....(COL)
   Live ....(CAP)
Winnipeg
Tom Russell; *Hurricane Season* ....(PHO)
Winter In Winnipeg
Rob McConnell/Boss Brass; *Brass Is Back* .... (CCJ)
Woodstock
Crosby, Stills & Nash; *Crosby, Stills & Nash*
   (collection) ....(ATL)
Crosby, Stills, Nash & Young; *Deja Vu* ....(ATL)
   So Far ....(ATL)
Joni Mitchell; *Ladies Of The Canyon* ....(RPR)
   Miles Of Aisles ....(ASY)
   Shadows & Light ....(ASY)

CLOTHES, Fashion, Glasses, Laundry
  See Also: HATS, SHOES

Alice Blue Gown
Edith Day; *Nipper's Greatest Hits-'20s* ....(RCA)
All Dressed Up & Lonely
Jim Reeves; *Touch Of Velvet* ....(RCA)
All Night Laundromat Blues
Joe Walsh; *So What* ....(MCA)
Ants In My Pants
Bo Carter; *Rare Blues Of The Twenties-1927-1930* (HIS)
Baby Don't You Tear My Clothes
Lightnin' Hopkins; *Lost Texas Tapes-#4* ....(CLT)
Baby Makes Her Blue Jeans Talk
Dr. Hook; *Players In The Dark* ....(CAS)
Baby's Got Her Blue Jeans On
Mel McDaniel; *All-Time Country Classics-#2* ....(CAP)
   Greatest Hits ....(CAP)
   Let It Roll ....(CAP)
Bandit In A Bathing Suit
David Bromberg; *Bandit In A Bathing Suit* ......(FAN)
Beggar In Blue Jeans
Rowans; *Rowans* ....(ASY)
Bell Bottom Blues
Derek/Dominos; *Layla* ....(RSO)
Eric Clapton; *24 Nights* ....(RPR)
Bell Bottom Plants
Loudon Wainwright III; *45* ....(COL)
Between Blue Eyes And Jeans
Conway Twitty; *Don't Call Him A Cowboy* ....(WB)
Bikini Girls With Machine Guns
Cramps; *Stay Sick!* ....(ENC)
Birthday Suit
Johnny Kemp; *ST/Sing* ....(COL)
Black Slacks
Joe Bennett; *Vintage Music-Orig. Classic*
   1950s-60s-16 ....(MCA)
Robert Gordon; *Rock Billy Boogie* ....(RCA)
Sparkletones; *Black Slacks* ....(MCA)
Blue Collar
Bachman-Turner Overdrive; *Best Of* ....(MER)
Blue Collar Man
Styx; *Caught In The Act* ....(A&M)
   Classics-#15 ....(A&M)
   Pieces Of Eight ....(A&M)

Blue Jean Blues
Hank Williams, Jr.; *Strong Stuff* ....(WB)
ZZ Top; *Best Of* ....(WB)
   Fandango ....(WB)
   Six Pack ....(WB)
Blue Jean Bop
Gene Vincent; *Bop That Just Won't Stop* ....(CAP)
   Greatest ....(CAP)
   Greatest ....(IRS)
Blue Jean Boy
Michael Stanley Band; *Ladies' Choice* ....(EPI)
Blue Jeans
Chocolate Milk; *45* ....(RCA)
Blue Skirt Waltz
Frankie Yankovic/Yanks; *Greatest Hits* ....(COL)
Mom & Dads; *Best Of* ....(CRS)
   Blue Canadian Rockies ....(CRS)
Blue Velvet
Bobby Vinton; *16 Most Requested* ....(EPI)
   All-Time Greatest Hits ....(EPI)
   Greatest Hits ....(EPI)
Bobby Sox To Stockings
Frankie Avalon; *Best Of* ....(MCA)
   Collectables Presents History Of Rock-#3 ......(CLT)
   Greatest Hits ....(EVR)
   Greatest Of Fabian and Frankie Avalon ....(MCA)
   Pick Of ....(FFT)
   Super Oldies/'50s-#7 ....(AUF)
Bring Me A Shawl From Galway
Mary O'Hara; *At The Royal Festival Hall* ....(SHA)
   Song For Ireland ....(SHA)
Button Off My Shirt
Ronnie Milsap; *Greatest Hits-#3* ....(RCA)
   Heart & Soul ....(RCA)
Button Up Your Overcoat
Rose Murphy; *Sings Again* ....(MCA)
Sarah Vaughan; *Sarah Vaughan* ....(EVR)
Buttons And Bows
Dinah Shore; *16 Most Requested Songs-1940s-#1* (COL)
   Golden Hits/'40s ....(COL)
Chantilly Lace
Big Bopper; *45s On CD-#1 (1958-1959)* .... (MER)
   Cruisin' 1958 ....(INC)
   Oldies But Goodies-#4 ....(OSR)
   ST/American Graffiti ....(MCA)
Jerry Lee Lewis; *Best Of-#2* ....(MER)
   "Killer" Rocks On ....(MER)
Cheap Sunglasses
ZZ Top; *Deguello* ....(WB)
   ST/Teachers ....(WB)
Clothesline Saga
Bob Dylan/Band; *Basement Tapes* ....(COL)
Cowboy In The Continental Suit
Chris LeDoux; *Rodeo & Living Free* ....(LIB)
Marty Robbins; *American Originals* ....(COL)
Dance Naked
John Mellencamp; *Dance Naked* ....(MER)
Dance With A Dolly (Hole In...Stocking)
Bill Haley; *Rockin' & Rollin'* ....(ACC)
   /Comets: King Of Rock & Roll ....(ALS)
Dedicated Follower Of Fashion
Kinks; *Greatest Hits-#1* ....(RHI)
   Kinkdom ....(RHI)
   Kinks-Size Kinkdom ....(RHI)
Devil With A Blue Dress On
Bruce Springsteen; *ST/No Nukes-Muse Concerts* .. (ASY)
Mitch Ryder/Detroit Wheels; *Frat Rock-#4* ......(RHI)
   Rev Up-Best Of ....(RHI)
   Son Of Frat Rock ....(RHI)
   Toga Rock ....(DHL)
Dirty Laundry
Don Henley; *I Can't Stand Still* ....(ASY)
Dress Me Up As A Robber
Paul McCartney; *Tug Of War* ....(COL)
Dress You Up
Madonna; *Like A Virgin* ....(SIR)
Dressed For Success
Roxette; *Look Sharp!* ....(EMI)
Dressed In Black
Depeche Mode; *Black Celebration* ....(SIR)
Hoodoo Gurus; *Kinky* ....(RCA)
Dressed To Kill
Lita Ford; *Dancin' On The Edge* ....(MER)

Nazareth; *Classics-#16* .... (A&M)
  Fool Circle .... (A&M)
  'Snaz .... (A&M)
Dresses Too Short
Syl Johnson; *45* .... (OOP)
Drinkin' In My Sunday Dress
Maria McKee; *Maria McKee* .... (GEF)
Dry Cleaner From Des Moines
Joni Mitchell; *Mingus* .... (ASY)
  Shadows & Light .... (ASY)
Easter Parade
Andy Russell; *Puttin' On The Ritz-Capitol Sings
Berlin* .... (CAP)
Bing Crosby; *All Time Best Of* .... (CCB)
Judy Garland & Fred Astaire; *ST/Easter Parade* .. (SSP)
Sarah Vaughan; *Complete On Mercury-#2-American
Songs* .... (MER)
Eat My Shorts
Rick Dees; *45* .... (ATL)
Emperor's New Clothes
Sinead O'Connor; *I Do Not Want What I Haven't
Got* .... (ENS)
Fashion
David Bowie; *Changesbowie* ....(RYK)
  Changestwobowie .... (RCA)
  Scary Monsters .... (RYK)
  The Singles-1969-1993 .... (RYK)
Fashion For Me
Brooklyn Dreams; *Sleepness Nights* .... (CAS)
Fool For Your Stockings
ZZ Top; *Deguello* .... (WB)
Forever In Blue Jeans
Neil Diamond; *12 Greatest Hits-#2* .... (COL)
  Hot August Night II .... (COL)
  You Don't Bring Me Flowers .... (COL)
Future's So Bright I Gotta Wear Shades
Timbuk 3; *Greetings From* .... (IRS)
German Overalls
Peter Hammill; *Chameleon In The Shadow Of The
Night* .... (BP)
Girl In A T-Shirt
ZZ Top; *Antenna* .... (RCA)
Got A Bran' New Suit
Louis Armstrong; *Jazz Heritage-Back In New
York* .... (MCA)
Green Shirt
Elvis Costello; *Girls Girls Girls* .... (COL)
Elvis Costello/Attractions; *Armed Forces* .... (COL)
Harper Valley P.T.A.
Jeannie C. Riley; *Greatest Hits* .... (PLN)
  Harper Valley P.T.A. .... (PLN)
  Oldies But Goodies-#4 .... (OSR)
  Souvenirs Of Music City USA .... (PLN)
High Fashion Queen
Flying Burrito Brothers; *Last Of The Red Hot
Burritos* .... (A&M)
Honey, Can I Put On Your Clothes
Barbra Streisand; *Songbird* .... (COL)
Hot Pants
James Brown; *In The Jungle Groove* .... (POL)
  Revolution Of The Mind .... (POL)
Hot Pants In The Summertime
Dramatics; *Whatcha See Is Whatcha Get* .... (STX)
I Can't Dance
Genesis; *We Can't Dance* .... (ATL)
I Left My Hat In Haiti
Fred Astaire; *ST/Royal Wedding* .... (SSP)
If The Love Fits Wear It
Leslie Pearl; *Words & Music* .... (RCA)
In The Raw
Whispers; *Love Is Where You Find It* .... (SLR)
Itsy Bitsy Teenie Weenie Yellow Polka...
Brian Hyland; *Dr. Demento's Greatest-#3* .... (RHI)
  Greatest Hits .... (RHI)
  Vintage Music-Classics-'50s/'60s-#5 .... (MCA)
Jeans On
David Dundas; *David Dundas* .... (CHR)
King Is Half-Undressed
Jellyfish; *Bellybutton* .... (CHS)
Laundromat Blues
Albert King; *Masterworks* .... (ATL)
Laundromat Monday
Joe Jackson; *ST/Mike's Murder* .... (A&M)

Laundry Man
Fenton Robinson; *Genuine Houserockin' Music* ...(ALG)
  Nightflight .... (ALG)
Leader Of The Laundromat
Detergents; *45* .... (RLL)
Leather Britches
John Hartford; *Aereo-Plain* .... (WB)
Pete Sutherland; *Poor Man's Dream* .... (FF)
Leather Jacket
Mick Taylor; *Mick Taylor* ....(COL)
Leather & Lace
Stevie Nicks & Don Henley; *Bella Donna* .... (MOD)
Leopard Skin Pillbox Hat
Bob Dylan; *Blonde On Blonde* ....(COL)
London Leatherboys
Accept; *Balls To The Wall* .... (POR)
  Compilation .... (POR)
Long Cool Woman In A Black Dress
Hollies; *Best Of* .... (EMI)
  Best Of-#2 .... (EMI)
  Billboard Top Rock 'N' Roll Hits-1972 .... (RHI)
  Distant Light .... (EPI)
  Epic Anthology-From The Original Masters ..... (EPI)
  Greatest Hits .... (EPI)
Low Spark Of High Heeled Boys
Traffic; *Low Spark Of High Heeled Boys* .... (ISL)
  On The Road .... (ISL)
Makeup & Faded Blue Jeans
Merle Haggard; *Back To The Barrooms* .... (MCA)
  Country Classics_#4-1984-1985 .... (MCA)
  His Best .... (MCA)
Mama Don't You Tear My Clothes
Blind Snooks Eaglin; *Rural Blues* .... (FAN)
Mini Dress
Luther Johnson & Muddy Waters; *Chicken Shack* (MUS)
Miniskirt Minnie
Wilson Pickett; *45* .... (OOP)
One Shirt, Soulless Shoes
Latimore; *I'll Do Anything For You* .... (MAL)
Orange Was The Color Of Her Dress
Charles Mingus; *Changes Two* .... (ATL)
  In Europe-#2 .... (ENJ)
Gil Evans; *Live At Sweet Basil-#1* .... (EVD)
  /Laurent Cugny Big Band-Golden Hair .... (EMA)
Out Of The Wardrobe
Kinks; *Misfits* .... (ARI)
Overcoats
John Hiatt; *Overcoats* .... (EPI)
Paddy McGinty's Coat
Pat Harrington; *St. Patrick's Day Celebration* ....(COL)
Penny Loafers & Bobby Socks
Joe Bennett/Sparkletones; *Rock This Town-Rockabilly
Hits-#2* .... (RHI)
"Petticoat Junction" Theme
Flatt & Scruggs; *20 All-Time Great Recordings* ...(COL)
Original Music; *TV Theme Sing-Along Album* .... (RHI)
Pink Cashmere
Prince; *Hits 1* .... (PAI)
  Hits/B-Sides ....(PAI)
Pink Pedal Pushers
Carl Perkins; *Best Of-Jive After 5-1958-1978* .... (RHI)
  Restless-Columbia Recordings ....(COL)
Jerry Lee Lewis; *Monsters* .... (SUN)
Pink Petticoats
Big Bopper; *Chantilly Lace/Big Bopper* .... (MER)
  Hellooo Baby! Best Of-1954-1959 .... (RHI)
Pizza In My Shorts
Da Yoopers; *Yoopy Do Wah* .... (YOU)
Pseudo Silk Kimono
Marillion; *Misplaced Childhood* .... (CAP)
Put On Your Old Grey Bonnet
Jimmy Dean; *Greatest Hits* ....(COL)
Pete Fountain; *Best Of* .... (MCA)
  Mr. New Orleans .... (MCA)
Put On Your Sunday Clothes
Original Cast; *Hello Dolly* .... (RCA)
Put Your Cat Clothes On
Carl Perkins; *Legends Of Rock Guitar-'50s* ...... (RHI)
  Original Sun Greatest Hits .... (RHI)
Put Your Clothes Back On
Joe Stampley; *Biggest Hits* .... (EPI)
  Encore .... (EPI)
Puttin' On My Sunday Best
Dick & Mel Tunney; *Let The Dreamers Dream* ....(WB)

Puttin' On The Ritz
Ella Fitzgerald; *Silver Collection-Songbooks* ......(VRV)
Fred Astaire; *Irving Berlin Always* ....(VRV)
   Irving Berlin Songbook ....(VRV)
Judy Garland; *One & Only* ....(CAP)
Mandy Patinkin; *Mandy Patinkin* ....(COL)
Taco; *After Eight* ....(RCA)
   Nipper's Greatest Hits-'80s ....(RCA)
Red Bandana
Merle Haggard; *Greatest Hits* ....(MCA)
   More Of The Best .... (RHI)
   Serving 190 Proof ....(MCA)
Red Sex Dress
Alfonia Tims/Flying Tigers; *Future Funk/Uncut!* . (ROI)
Rednecks, White Socks & Blue Ribbon Beer
Johnny Russell; *Beer Redneck Mothers* ....(RCA)
   Rednecks, White Socks & Blue Ribbon Beer ..(RCA)
Rose Colored Glasses
John Conlee; *Backstage At The Grand Ole Opry* .(RCA)
   Greatest Hits ....(MCA)
   Legends ....(MCA)
   MCA 30 Years Of Hits-1958-1988 ....(MCA)
   Rose Colored Glasses ....(MCA)
Sam, You Made The Pants Too Long
Barbra Streisand; *Color Me Barbra* ....(COL)
   Greatest Hits ....(COL)
Saturday Clothes
Gordon Lightfoot; *If You Could Read My Mind* .. (RPR)
Saturday Suit
Art Garfunkel; *Watermark* ....(COL)
Save That Dress
T. Graham Brown; *Brilliant Conversationalist* ....(CAP)
Second Hand Rose
Barbra Streisand; *Greatest Hits* ....(COL)
   Happening In Central Park ....(COL)
   Just For The Record ....(COL)
   My Name Is Barbra Two ....(COL)
   & Other Musical Instruments ....(COL)
Shake Your Pants
Cameo; *Cameosis* ....(CAS)
Sharp Dressed Man
ZZ Top; *Eliminator* ....(WB)
   Greatest Hits ....(WB)
She Got Me (When She Got Her Dress On)
Masters Of Reality; *Sunrise On The Sufferbus* ... (CHR)
Shiny Stockings
Count Basie; *April In Paris* ....(VRV)
   Basie In London ....(VRV)
   Dedication-#11 ....(MCA)
   The Deacon .... (INT)
Jon Hendricks; *Compact Jazz-Best Of The Jazz*
   Vocalists ....(VRV)
   Recorded In Person At The Trident .... (SMA)
Shirt
Bonzo Dog Band; *Best Of* ....(RHI)
   Tadpoles ....(LIB)
Shopping For Clothes
Coasters; *Their Greatest Recordings-Early Years* ..(ATL)
Short Shorts
Royal Teens; *Cruisin'-1958* ....(INC)
   Goofy Greats .... (KT)
   Short Shorts ....(MCA)
Silver Threads Among The Gold
Mike Auldridge; *Dobro/Blues & Bluegrass* ......(TAK)
Silver Threads & Golden Needles
Honky Tonk Angels; *Honky Tonk Angels* ....(COL)
Linda Ronstadt; *Don't Cry Now* ....(ASY)
   Greatest Hits ....(ASY)
   Hand Sown ....(CAP)
   Retrospective ....(CAP)
Slit Skirts
Pete Townshend; *All The Best Cowboys Have Chinese*
   Eyes ....(ATC)
Something In Red
Lorrie Morgan; *Something In Red* ....(RCA)
Streak, The
Ray Stevens; *All-Time Greatest Comic Hits* ....(CCB)
   Greatest Hits ....(MCA)
   Greatest Hits ....(RCA)
   Super Hits/'70s-Have A Nice Day-#12 .... (RHI)
Strip Polka
Andrews Sisters; *Best Of* .... (MCA)
Bobby Vinton; *Greatest Polka Hits Of All-Time* ...(CCB)

Stripper
David Rose; *Dick Bartley-One-Hit*
   Wonders-'60s-#1 .... (RHI)
Style Kills
Robert Palmer; *Addictions-#1* .... (ISL)
Sucker In A 3-Piece Suit
Van Halen; *OU812* ....(WB)
Suedehead
Morrissey; *Bona Drag* ....(SIR)
   Viva Hate ....(SIR)
Suit Of Lights
Costello Show (Featuring Elvis Costello); *King Of*
   America ....(COL)
Sunglasses At Night
Corey Hart; *First Offense* .... (EMI)
   The Singles .... (EMI)
Take Off That Dress
Ray Charles; *Love & Peace* ....(ATL)
Take Off Your Uniform
John Hiatt; *Slug Line* .... (MCA)
Take Your Clothes Off When You Dance
Frank Zappa; *We're Only In It For The.../Lumpy*
   Gravy ....(RYK)
   You Can't Do That On Stage Anymore-#6 ......(RYK)
Terrorist Trousers
Jim Carroll; *Praying Mantis* .... (GIA)
Tiger In A Dress
Dan Reed Network; *Slam* ....(MEr)
Tight Fittin' Jeans
Conway Twitty; *Classic Conway* ....(MCA)
   Legends ....(MCA)
   Mister T. ....(MCA)
Top Hat Bar & Grille
Jim Croce; *50th Anniversary Collection* ....(SAJ)
Top Hat, White Tie & Tails
Fred Astaire; *Irving Berlin Songbook* ....(VRV)
Louis Armstrong; *Irving Berlin Songbook* ....(VRV)
Totally Nude
Talking Heads; *Naked* ....(FLY)
Wallets; *Take It* .... (TT)
Trouser Press
Bonzo Dog Band; *Best Of* .... (RHI)
Tuxedo Junction
Boston Pops Orchestra/Arthur Fiedler; *Greatest*
   Hits/'40s-#2 ....(RCA)
Ella Fitzgerald; *Things Ain't What They Used To*
   Be ....(BAI)
Glenn Miller; *Best Of* ....(RCA)
   Legendary Performer ....(BLU)
   Memorial 1944-1969 ....(BLU)
   Pure Gold ....(BLU)
   ST/Story ....(MCA)
Glenn Miller/Orchestra; *Unforgettable* ....(RCA)
Harry James/Sextet; *1940s-Small Groups* ....(COL)
Joe Jackson; *Jumpin' Jive* ....(A&M)
Manhattan Transfer; *Anthology-Down In Birdland* (RHI)
   Best Of ....(ATL)
   Manhattan Transfer ....(ATL)
New York City Gay Men's Chorus; *Love Lives On* (VIA)
Undone-The Sweater
Weezer; *Weezer* ....(DGC)
Velcro Fly
ZZ Top; *Afterburner* ....(WB)
Venus In Blue Jeans
Jimmy Clanton; *All-Star Chartbusters* .... (INT)
   Golden Years-1962 ....(DOM)
Vicar In A Tutu
Smiths; *Rank* ....(SIR)
   The Queen Is Dead ....(SIR)
Violets For Your Furs
Frank Sinatra; *Concepts* ....(CAP)
   Gift Set ....(CAP)
   Songs For Young Lovers & Swing Easy ....(CAP)
Jesse Davis; *Horn Of Passion* ....(CCJ)
John Coltrane; *Prestige Recordings* .... (PRS)
Tommy Dorsey & Frank Sinatra; *Sessions-#1-Feb. 1*
   1940-July 17 1940 ....(RCA)
Vogue
Madonna; *Immaculate Collection* ....(SIR)
   I'm Breathless ....(SIR)
   Royal Box ....(SIR)
Watching The Clothes
Pretenders; *Learning To Crawl* ....(SIR)

We Don't Have To Take Our Clothes Off
Jermaine Stewart; *Frantic Romantic* .... (ARI)
Wear Your Love Like Heaven
Donovan; *Gift From A Flower To A Garden* ...... (EPI)
   Greatest Hits .... (EPI)
   Summer Of Love .... (RHI)
   Troubadour-Definitive Collection .... (EPI)
Sarah McLachlan; *Solace* .... (ARI)
West Nashville Grand Ballroom Gown
Jimmy Buffett; *Living & Dying In 3/4 Time* ..... (MCA)
Where Do My Socks Go?
Ray Stevens; *Lend Me Your Ears* .... (CCB)
White Sport Coat & A Pink Carnation
Marty Robbins; *16 Most Requested Songs/'50s-#2* (COL)
   Greatest Hits .... (COL)
   Lifetime Of Song-1951-1982 .... (COL)
Who Threw The Overalls In Mrs....
Bing Crosby; *Shillelaghs & Shamrocks* .... (MCA)
Words By Heart
Billy Ray Cyrus; *It Won't Be The Last* .... (MER)
Yellow Roses On Her Gown
Johnny Mathis; *I Only Have Eyes For You* .... (COL)
You Make My Pants Want To Get Up & Dance
Dr. Hook; *Pleasure & Pain* .... (CAP)
You Wear It Well
DeBarge; *Greatest Hits* .... (MOT)
   Rhythm Of The Night .... (MOT)
Rod Stewart; *Best Of* .... (MER)
   Sing It Again Rod .... (MER)
   Storyteller-Complete Anthology-1964-1990 ...... (WB)
You're Never Fully Dressed Without A...
Original Broadway Cast; *Annie* .... (COL)

COFFEE, Tea
See Also: FOOD, RESTAURANTS

Afternoon Tea
Kinks; *Something Else* .... (RPR)
All The Tea In China
Buck Owens; *Kickin'* .... (CCB)
Another Cup Of Coffee & A Cigarette
Robbin Thompson; *Robbin Thompson* .... (NEM)
Another Cup Of Coffee (Then I'll Go)
Brook Benton; *Anthology* .... (RHI)
Black Coffee
Black Flag; *Slip It In* .... (SST)
Humble Pie; *Best* ....(A&M)
   Eat It ....(A&M)
k.d. lang; *Just Say Yo-#2 Of Just Say Yes* .... (SIR)
   Shadowland .... (SIR)
Lacy J. Dalton; *Lacy J.* .... (CAP)
Peggy Lee; *Best Of* .... (MCA)
Black Coffee In Bed
Squeeze; *Sweets From A Stranger* ....(A&M)
Cigarettes & Coffee
Otis Redding; *Best Of* .... (ATC)
   Best Of .... (ATL)
   Story .... (ATL)
Coffee
Billy Falcon; *Letters From A Paper Ship* .... (MER)
Flowerhead; *Ka-Bloom* .... (ZOO)
Coffee At Midnite
Bluegrass Parlor Band; *Two Colors* .... (PIN)
Coffee Beans
Moondog; *Moondog* .... (COL)
Coffee Blues
Lightnin' Hopkins; *Mojo Hand-Anthology* .... (RHI)
Mississippi John Hurt; *Best Of* .... (VAN)
   Today! .... (VAN)
Coffee Break
Billy McLaughlin; *Inhale Pink* .... (AML)
Will T. Massey; *Will T. Massey* .... (MCA)
Coffee Grindin' Blues
Jaybird Coleman; *Alabama Blues-1927-1931* .... (YAZ)
Coffee Homeground
Kate Bush; *Lionheart* .... (EMI)
Coffee House Blues
Lightnin' Hopkins; *Best Of The Blues* .... (TRD)
Coffee In A Cardboard Cup
Original Broadway Cast; *70 Girls 70* .... (SMC)
Coffee Shoppe
Margaret Whiting; *Then & Now* .... (DRG)

Coffee Song (Brazil)
Frank Sinatra; *Greatest Hits-Early Years* .... (COL)
   In The Beginning-1943-1951 .... (COL)
Frank Sinatra & Johnny Mandel; *Ring-A-Ding*
   Ding .... (RPR)
Coffee Time
Li'l Wally; *My Polish Girlfriend & Others* .... (JJ)
Coffee Train
David Thomas; *Monster Walks The Winter Lake* ... (TT)
Coffee & Kisses
Duke Ellington/Orchestra; *Happy Birthday*
   Duke-Birthday Sessions-#4 .... (LAS)
Coffee, Donuts & Death
Paris; *Sleeping With The Enemy* .... (SCA)
Cup Of Coffee, A Sandwich And You
Enoch Light/Charleston City All-Stars; *Music Of The*
   1920s .... (MCA)
Cup Of Tea
Kinks; *Muswell Hillbillies* .... (RHI)
Don't Forget The Coffee Billy Joe
Tom T. Hall; *Essential-Twentieth Anniversary*
   Collect. .... (MER)
Espresso Logic
Chris Rea; *espresso logic* .... (EW)
Hot Coffee
Carl Anderson; *Pieces Of A Heart* .... (GRP)
I'll Just Have A Cup Of Coffee
Claude Gray; *Super Hits: Country-1960s* .... (GUS)
Java Jive
Ink Spots; *Best Of* .... (MCA)
Manhattan Transfer; *Best Of* .... (ATL)
   Manhattan Transfer .... (ATL)
Let's Have Another Cup Of Coffee
Glenn Miller; *Complete-#8-1941-1942* .... (RCA)
Michael Feinstein; *Rememeber-Sings Irving Berlin* (ELE)
Morning Coffee
Joe King Carrasco/Crowns; *Tales From The*
   Crypt-Basement Tapes-1979 .... (ROI)
One Cup Of Coffee
Bob Marley/Wailers; *Songs Of Freedom* .... (TUF)
One More Cup Of Coffee
Bob Dylan; *At Budokan* .... (COL)
   Desire .... (COL)
Over A Cup Of Coffee
Castelles; *Sweet Sounds Of The* .... (CLT)
Pot Of Coffee
Pinchers; *Reggae Jamdown-The Ras Tapes* .... (RYK)
Smoking Cigarettes & Drinking Coffee...
Marty Robbins; *Essential-1951-1982* .... (COL)
Sunday For Tea
Peter & Gordon; *Best Of* .... (RHI)
Tea For One
Led Zeppelin; *Presence* .... (SS)
Tea For The Tillerman
Cat Stevens; *Tea For The Tillerman* .... (A&M)
Tea For Two
Fred Waring/Pennsylvanians; *Nipper's Greatest*
   Hits-'30s-#2 .... (RCA)
Julie Andrews; *Love Julie* .... (USA)
Leigh Kaplan & Lincoln Mayorga; *Dizzy Fingers* (CMB)
Original Cast/Ruby Keeler; *No No Nanette* ......(COL)
Tommy Dorsey/Orchestra; *Best Of* .... (CCB)
Tea In The Sahara
Police; *Message In A Box-Complete Recordings* .. (A&M)
   Synchronicity ....(A&M)
Sting; *Bring On The Night* .... (A&M)
Texas Tea Party
Benny Goodman; *Early Years* .... (BIO)
That's What I Like-No Cream In My Coffee
Cooly Live; *Livewire* .... (RCA)
Wake Up & Smell The Coffee
Killbilly; *Stranger In This Place* .... (FF)
You're The Cream In My Coffee
Lawrence Welk; *16 Most Requested Songs* .... (COL)
Les Brown; *Best Of* .... (MCA)

COLD, Freezing
See Also: COOL, SNOW

August Freeze
Grace Pool; *Where We Live* .... (RPR)
Autumn's Not That Cold
Lorrie Morgan; *Something In Red* .... (RCA)

Skip Ewing; *Coast Of Colorado* .... (MCA)
Baby Ice Dog
Blue Oyster Cult; *Tyranny & Mutation* ....(COL)
Baby, It's Cold Outside
Pearl Bailey; *16 Most Requested Songs* ....(COL)
Ray Charles; *His Greatest Hits-#2* ....(DHL)
Chill Of An Early Fall
George Strait; *Chill Of An Early Fall* ....(MCA)
Cold Blooded
Rick James; *Cold Blooded* ....(MOT)
Greatest Hits ....(MOT)
Cold Blue Steel & Sweet Fire
Joni Mitchell; *For The Roses* ....(ASY)
Miles Of Aisles ....(ASY)
Cold Cold Heart
Hank Williams; *24 Greatest Hits* ....(MGM)
40 Greatest Hits ....(POL)
Hank Williams ....(MGM)
Live At Opry ....(MGM)
Long Gone Lonesome Blues ....(POL)
Jerry Lee Lewis; *Duets* ....(SUN)
Golden Cream Of ....(SUN)
& Friends: Duets ....(SUN)
Cold Cold World
Teddy Pendergrass; *Life Is A Song Worth Singing* .. (PI)
Cold Day In December
George Jones; *You Oughta Be Here With Me* ......(EPI)
Cold Day In Hell
Gary Moore; *After Hours* ....(CHS)
Cold Day In July
Joy White; *Between Midnight & Hindsight* ....(COL)
Ray Price; *For The Good Times/I Won't Mention
It..* ....(COL)
Suzy Bogguss; *Voices In The Wind* ....(LIB)
Cold Day In Tennessee
Rob Crosby; *Another Time & Place* .... (ARI)
Cold December
Mike Auldridge; *& Old Dog* .... (FF)
Cold Fever
Models; *Out Of Mind Out Of Sight* ....(GEF)
Cold Fire
Rush; *Counterparts* ....(ATL)
Cold Hands From New York
Gordon Lightfoot; *United Artists Collection* ...... (EMI)
Cold Hard Cash
Greg Kihn; *Next Of Kihn* .... (BES)
Cold Hard Truth
Jamie O'Hara; *Rise Above It* ....(RCA)
Cold Hearted
Paula Abdul; *Forever Your Girl* .... (VIA)
Get Up & Dance-Dance Mixes .... (VIA)
Cold Love
Donna Summer; *The Wanderer* ....(GEF)
Cold November
John O'Connor; *Songs For Our Times* ....(FF)
Cold On The Shoulder
Gordon Lightfoot; *Cold On The Shoulder* ....(RPR)
Gord's Gold ....(RPR)
Cold Rain
Crosby, Stills & Nash; *CSN* ....(ATL)
Cold Rain And Snow
Grateful Dead; *Grateful Dead* ....(WB)
Steal Your Face! ....(GRD)
Cold Rain In Kansas
Don Lange; *Natural Born Heathen* ....(FF)
Cold Shot
Johnny Otis; *Cold Shot* ....(KNT)
Stevie Ray Vaughan; *Couldn't Stand The Weather* .(EPI)
Live Alive ....(EPI)
Cold Sky
Cyndi Lauper; *Music Speaks Louder Than Words* . (EPI)
Cold Summer Day In Georgia
Gene Watson; *Memories To Burn* ....(EPI)
Cold Sweat
James Brown; *Billboard Top R&B Hits-1967* ..... (RHI)
Can Your Heart Stand It ....(SSM)
Greatest Hits ....(RHI)
Live At The Apollo-Vol. 2-#1 ....(RHI)
Warrant; *Dirty Rotten Filthy Stinking Rich* ....(COL)
Cold Wind In August
Van Morrison; *Period Of Transition* ....(WB)
Cold Windy City Of Chicago
Boxcar Willie; *Best Of-#1* ....(MAI)

Cold Winter Day
Blind Willie McTell; *Doing That Atlanta
Strut-1927-1935* ....(YAZ)
Cold Winter's Day
BoDeans; *Go Slow Down* ....(SLS)
Colder Are My Nights
Isley Brothers; *45* ....(WB)
Colder Than Winter
Vince Gill; *Things That Matter* ....(RCA)
Cold, Cold, Cold
Little Feat; *Feats Don't Fail Me Now* ....(WB)
Sailin' Shoes ....(WB)
Cool Daddy In A Cadillac
Elvis Hitler; *Disgraceland* .... (RES)
Deep Freeze
Judas Priest; *Hero Hero* ....(RCA)
Rocka-Rolla ....(RCA)
Electron Cold
Sea Level; *On The Edge* ....(OOP)
Funky Cold Medina
Tone Loc; *Loc-ed After Dark* .... (DV)
Hot Corn, Cold Corn
Flatt & Scruggs; *At Carnegie Hall* ....(COL)
Hot Love Cold World
Bob Welch; *French Kiss* ....(CAP)
Ice Ice Baby
Vanilla Ice; *To The Extreme* .... (SBK)
Is It Cold In Here
Joe Diffie; *Regular Joe* ....(EPI)
Let's Chill
Guy; *Future* .... (UT)
Long Cold Winter
Pure Prairie League; *If The Shoe Fits* ....(RCA)
Out In The Cold
George Howard; *When Summer Comes* ....(GRP)
Judas Priest; *Priest...Live!* ....(COL)
Turbo ....(COL)
Tom Petty/Heartbreakers; *Into The Great Wide
Open* ....(MCA)
She's Coming Back Some Cold Rainy Day
Georgia Cotton Pickers; *Greatest Country
Blues-1929-1956-#3* ....(SB)
She's So Cold
Rolling Stones; *Emotional Rescue* .... (RS)
Stone Cold
Rainbow; *Finyl Vinyl* ....(MER)
Straight Between The Eyes ....(MER)
Stone Cold Country
Gibson/Miller Band; *Where There's Smoke* ....(EPI)
Stone Cold Crazy
Queen; *Classic* ....(HOL)
Sheer Heart Attack ....(HOL)
ST/Encino Man ....(HOL)
Stone Cold Dead In The Market
Ella Fitzgerald; *Best Of-#2* ....(MCA)
Stone Cold Drag
James Brown; *People* .... (POL)
Stone Cold Fever
Humble Pie; *Best Of* ....(A&M)
Classics-#14 ....(A&M)
Performance ....(A&M)
Rock On ....(A&M)
Stone Cold Gentleman
Ralph Tresvant; *Ralph Tresvant* ....(MCA)
Stone Cold Sober
Rod Stewart; *Atlantic Crossing* ....(WB)
Storyteller-Complete Anthology-1964-1990 ......(WB)
Summer Chill
Grover Washington, Jr.; *Next Exit* ....(COL)
Summer In Dixie
Confederate Railroad; *Notorious* ....(ATL)
Sure Got Cold After The Rain
ZZ Top; *Rio Grande Mud* ....(WB)
Six Pack ....(WB)
Ten Degrees & Gettin' Colder
Nanci Griffith; *Other Voices Other Rooms* .... (ELE)
This Cold War With You
Floyd Tillman; *Columbia Country Classics-#2* ...(COL)
John Prine; *Pink Cadillac* ....(ASY)
Merle Haggard; *Friend In California* ....(EPI)
Ray Price; *Greatest Hits-#4-By Request* ....(SO)
Willie Nelson; *San Antonio Rose* ....(COL)
Too Cold At Home
Mark Chesnutt; *S* ....(MCA)

Too Cold In The Winter
Cry Of Love; *Brother* .... (\OL)
Warm Beer & Cold Women
Tom Waits; *Nighthawks At The Diner* .... (ASY)
When It's Springtime In Alaska
Johnny Horton; *American Originals* ....(COL)
Greatest Hits ....(COL)

COLORS: BLACK

Baby's In Black
Beatles; *Box Set* .... (CAP)
For Sale ....(CAP)
'65 ....(CAP)
Back In Black
AC/DC; *Back In Black* .... (ATL)
Classic Rock 1966-1988 .... (ATL)
Be Real Black For Me
Roberta Flack & Donny Hathaway; *Roberta Flack &*
Donny Hathaway .... (ATL)
Beautiful Black Girl
Quincy Jones; *Mellow Madness* .... (A&M)
Beyond The Black
Metal Church; *Metal Church* .... (ELE)
Big Black Cadillac Blues
Lightnin' Hopkins; *Drinkin' In The Blues-Golden*
Classics-#1 ....(CLT)
Lightnin' Hopkins ....(EVR)
Big Black Smoke
Kinks; *Kink Kronikles* .... (RPR)
Black
Pearl Jam; *Ten* .... (EPA)
Black Africa
Devonsquare; *Walking On Ice* .... (ATL)
Black And Blue
Van Halen; *OU812* .... (WB)
Black And White Television
Ian Anderson; *Walk Into Light* .... (CHR)
Black Autumn
Charlie Daniels Band; *Te John Grease & Wolfman* (EPI)
Black Bayou
Charlie Daniels Band; *Midnight Wind* .... (EPI)
Black Bear Road
C.W. McCall; *Greatest Hits* .... (POL)
Black Blade
Blue Oyster Cult; *Career Of Evil* ....(COL)
Cultasaurus Erectus ....(COL)
Extraterrestrial Live ....(COL)
Black Bottom
Eddie Condon; *Best Of* .... (MCA)
Johnny Hamp's Kentucky Serenaders; *Nipper's Greatest*
Hits-'20s ....(RCA)
Black Boys On The Corner
Thin Lizzy; *London Collector-Rocker* ....(LON)
Black Boys, White Boys
Original Broadway Cast; *Hair* ....(RCA)
Black Butterfly
Deniece Williams; *Let's Hear It For The Boy* .....(COL)
Duke Ellington; *Best Of* .... (PAB)
Black Cadillac
Catfish Hodge Band; *Eyewitness Blues* .... (ADE)
Lightnin' Hopkins; *How Many More Years I Got* . (FAN)
Black Cat
Chris Daniels/Kings; *In Your Face* ....(FF)
Janet Jackson; *Rhythm Nation-1814* .... (A&M)
Black Cat Blues
John Lee Hooker; *...Alone* .... (SPE)
Memphis Minnie; *Hoodoo Lady-1933-1937* .....(COL)
Black Cat Bone
Albert Collins & Johnny Copeland; *Alligator Records*
20th Anniversary Coll. ....(ALG)
Johnny Winter; *Progressive Blues Experiment* ..... (OW)
Lightnin' Hopkins; *Dark Muddy Bottom Blues* ... (SPE)
Mojo Hand-Anthologoy ....(RHI)
Lonesome Sundown; *Been Gone Too Long* .... (HT)
Roy Rogers; *Blues On The Range* ....(BLI)
Black Cat Moan
Beck, Bogert & Appice; *Beckology* .... (EPI)
Beck, Bogert & Appice ....(EPI)
Black Cat Shuffle
Al DiMeola; *Electric Rendezvous* ....(COL)
Black Coffee
Black Flag; *Slip It In* ....(SST)

**Humble Pie; *Best* .... (A&M)
Eat It .... (A&M)
k.d. lang; *Just Say Yo-#2 Of Just Say Yes* .... (SIR)
Shadowland .... (SIR)
Lacy J. Dalton; *Lacy J.* ....(CAP)
Peggy Lee; *Best Of* ....(MCA)
Black Coffee In Bed
Squeeze; *Sweets From A Stranger* .... (A&M)
Black Country Rock
David Bowie; *Man Who Sold The World* ....(RYK)
Sound + Vision ....(RYK)
Black Country Woman
Led Zeppelin; *Physical Graffiti* .... (SS)
Black Cow
Steely Dan; *Aja* .... (MCA)
Gold ....(MCA)
Black Crow
Joni Mitchell; *Hejira* .... (ASY)
Shadows & Light .... (ASY)
Black Crow Blues
Bob Dylan; *Another Side Of* ....(COL)
Black Day In July
Gordon Lightfoot; *Best Of* .... (EMI)
Did She Mention My Name .... (UA)
Lightfoot .... (UA)
Black Denim Trousers & Motorcycle Boots
Cheers; *Monster Summer Hits-Drag City* ....(CAP)
Black Diamond
Kiss; *Alive* .... (CAS)
Double Platinum .... (CAS)
Kiss .... (CAS)
Originals ....(CAS)
Black Diamond Bay
Bob Dylan; *Desire* ....(COL)
Black Dog
Led Zeppelin; *IV* .... (ATL)
Led Zeppelin .... (ATL)
Black Eyed Blues
Esther Phillips; *Best Of* ....(CBA)
Joe Cocker; *Greatest Hits* .... (A&M)
Joe Cocker .... (A&M)
Black Flag
King's X; *King's X* .... (ATL)
Black Friday
Splinter; *Two Man Band* .... (MCA)
Steely Dan; *Greatest Hits* .... (MCA)
Katy Lied .... (MCA)
Black Gold
Soul Asylum; *Grace Dancers Union* ....(COL)
Black Hearted Woman
Allman Brothers Band; *Allman Brothers Band* ... (POL)
Beginnings ....(POL)
Road Goes On Forever .... (POL)
Black Hole Sun
Soundgarden; *Superunknown* .... (A&M)
Black Honey
Graham Parker; *Heart Treatment* ....(MER)
Live! Alone In America ....(RCA)
Black Is Black
Los Bravos; *History Of British Rock-#7* .... (RHI)
London Collector-Rock Invasion ....(LON)
Black Is The Color
Joan Baez; *Ballad Book* .... (VAN)
In Concert .... (VAN)
Black Is The Night
Sandy Posey; *45* .... (WB)
Black Jack Blues
Fleetwood Mac; *In Chicago* .... (SIR)
Gabriel Brown; *Country Blues Classics-#4* ...... (BCL)
Black Jack David
Alice Stuart; *All The Good Times* .... (ARH)
Steeleye Span; *All Around My Hat* .... (CHR)
Story .... (CHR)
Warren Smith; *45* .... (SUN)
Black Land Farmer
Frankie Miller; *45* .... (GUS)
Sleepy LaBeef; *Bull's Night Out* .... (SUN)
Souvenirs Of Music City U.S.A. .... (PLN)
Black Licorice
Grand Funk Railroad; *Caught In The Act* ....(CAP)
We're An American Band ....(CAP)
Black Limousine
Rolling Stones; *Tattoo You* .... (RS)

Black Magic Woman
Fleetwood Mac; *25 Years-The Chain* ....(WB)
 Vintage Years ....(SIR)
Santana; *Abraxas* ....(COL)
 Greatest Hits ....(COL)
 Moonflower ....(COL)
 Rock Classics/'70s ....(COL)
 Viva Santana ....(COL)
Black Man
Alberta Hunter; *Look For The Silver Lining* ......(COL)
Stevie Wonder; *Songs In The Key Of Life* ....(MOT)
Black Man Can't Get A Cab
U.T.F.O.; *Bag It & Bone It* ....(JVA)
Black Maria
Todd Rundgren; *Back To The Bars* ....(RHI)
 Something/Anything ....(RHI)
Black Messiah
Kinks; *Misfits* ....(ARI)
Black Money
Vinnie James; *All-American Boy* ....(RCA)
Black Moonlight
Bing Crosby; *In Hollywood* ....(OOP)
Black Mountain Blues
Bessie Smith; *Collection* ....(COL)
Janis Joplin; *ST/Janis* ....(COL)
Black Mountain Breakdown
Youngbloods; *Youngbloods* ....(RCA)
Black Mountain Rag
Doc Watson; *Doc Watson* ....(VAN)
 Essential-#2 ....(VAN)
 Newport Country Music & Blues ....(VAN)
Doc Watson/Hot Rize/Dan Crary/P. Rowan;
 Tellulive ....(FF)
Nitty Gritty Dirt Band; *Will The Circle Be
 Unbroken* ....(EMI)
Black Mountain Side
Led Zeppelin; *Led Zeppelin* ....(ATL)
Black Night
Bob Seger; *Beautiful Loser* ....(CAP)
Deep Purple; *Deepest Purple-Very Best Of* ....(WB)
 Nobody's Perfect ....(MER)
Dr. John; *In A Sentimental Mood* ....(WB)
Muddy Waters; *Chess Box* ....(CSS)
Black Nights
Bobby Bland; *Ain't Nothing You Can Do* ....(MCA)
 Introspective Of The Early Years ....(MCA)
Charles Brown; *45* ....(UA)
Black Notes
David Crosby & Graham Nash; *David Crosby &
 Graham Nash* ....(ATL)
Black Or White
Michael Jackson; *Dangerous* ....(EPI)
Black Orpheus
Roger Williams; *Best Of* ....(MCA)
Vince Guaraldi & Bola Sete; *Live At El Matador* .(FAN)
Black Pearl
Sonny Charles; *Soul Shots-#2:* "
 In" Crowd-Sweet Soul ....(RHI)
Sonny Charles/Checkmates; *Soul Shots-'60s Soul
 Classics-Best Of* ....(RHI)
Black Peter
Grateful Dead; *History Of-#1-Bear's Choice* ......(WB)
 What A Long Strange Trip It's Been ....(WB)
 Workingman's Dead ....(WB)
Black Polished Chrome
Doors; *An American Prayer* ....(ELE)
Black Queen
Crosby, Stills & Nash; *Crosby, Stills & Nash* .....(ATL)
Jimmy Cliff; *Unlimited* ....(RPR)
Stephen Stills; *Stephen Stills* ....(ATL)
Black Rose
Eric Clapton; *Another Ticket* ....(RSO)
John David Souther; *Black Rose* ....(ASY)
Sad Cafe; *Misplaced Ideals* ....(A&M)
Waylon Jennings; *Honky Tonk Heroes* ....(RCA)
Willie Nelson; *Me & Paul* ....(COL)
Black Sabbath
Black Sabbath; *Black Sabbath* ....(WB)
 Live Evil ....(WB)
 We Sold Our Soul For Rock 'N' Roll ....(WB)
Ozzy Osbourne; *Speak Of The Devil* ....(JET)
Black Satin Dancer
Jethro Tull; *Minstrel In The Gallery* ....(CHR)

Black Sheep
John Anderson; *All The People Are Talkin'* ....(WB)
 Greatest Hits ....(WB)
Sam The Sham/Pharaohs; *Pharaohization! (Best
 Of)* ....(RHI)
Black Sheep Boy
Tim Hardin; *Memorial Album* ....(POL)
Black Sheep Of The Family
Ritchie Blackmore; *Rainbow* ....(POL)
Black Skies
Rex Allen, Jr.; *Today's Generation* ....(SSS)
Black Sky
Ozark Mountain Daredevils; *It's Alive* ....(A&M)
 Ozark Mountain Daredevils ....(A&M)
Black Slacks
Joe Bennett; *Vintage Music-Orig. Classic
 1950s-60s-16* ....(MCA)
Robert Gordon; *Rock Billy Boogie* ....(RCA)
Sparkletones; *Black Slacks* ....(MCA)
Black Snake
John Lee Hooker; *Country Blues Of* ....(RVR)
Ramblin' Jack Elliott; *Essential* ....(VAN)
Black Snake Blues
Clifton Chenier; *Sixty Minutes With The King Of
 Zydeco* ....(ARH)
Black Snake Dream Blues
Blind Lemon Jefferson; *Master Of The
 Blues-#2-1926-1929* ....(BIO)
Black Snake Moan
Blind Lemon Jefferson; *Great Blues Guitarists-String
 Dazzlers* ....(COL)
Leadbelly; *Leadbelly* ....(COL)
Black Soul
Burning Spear; *Live* ....(ISL)
 Man In The Hills ....(ISL)
Black Summer Rain
Eric Clapton; *No Reason To Cry* ....(RSO)
Black Sunday
Jethro Tull; *A* ....(CHR)
Skatalites; *Ska Bonanza-Studio One Ska Years* ...(HRT)
Black Sunshine
White Zombie; *La Sexorcisto-Devil Music-#1* ....(GEF)
Black Throated Wind
Bob Weir; *Ace* ....(GRD)
Grateful Dead; *Steal Your Face* ....(GRD)
Black Train
Gun Club; *Fire Of Love* ....(SLS)
Montrose; *Montrose* ....(WB)
Black Uncle Remus
Loudon Wainwright III; *Loudon Wainwright III* ..(ATL)
Black Velvet
Alannah Myles; *Alannah Myles* ....(ATL)
Robin Lee; *Black Velvet* ....(ATL)
Black Water
Doobie Brothers; *Best Of* ....(WB)
 What Were Once Vices Are Now Habits ....(WB)
Black Widow
Alice Cooper; *Alice Cooper Show* ....(WB)
 Welcome To My Nightmare ....(ATL)
Jefferson Starship; *Winds Of Change* ....(GRU)
Lita Ford; *Dangerous Curves* ....(RCA)
Black & Blue
Louis Armstrong; *Greatest Hits* ....(COL)
 Satchmo At Symphony Hall ....(COL)
 & The Big Bands ....(DSQ)
 #5: Louis In New York ....(COL)
Original Cast; *Ain't Misbehavin'* ....(RCA)
Black & Tan Fantasy
Duke Ellington; *Echoes Of An Era;
 Ellington/Armstrong* ....(RLL)
 Beginning ....(MCA)
 Carnegie Hall ....(PRS)
 Carnegie Hall Concert 12-11-43 ....(EVR)
 Continuum ....(FAN)
 Greatest Hits ....(RPR)
 Pure Gold ....(RCA)
 /M. Ellington ....(FAN)
Black & White
INXS; *Dekadance* ....(ATC)
 Shabooh Shoobah ....(ATC)
Jackson Browne; *Lives In The Balance* ....(ASY)
Rosanne Cash; *Hits 1979-1989* ....(COL)

Three Dog Night; *Best Of* .... (MCA)
  Billboard Top Rock 'N' Roll Hits-1972 .... (RHI)
  Joy To The World-Greatest Hits .... (MCA)
  Todd Rundgren; *Anthology 1968-1985* .... (RHI)
  Back To The Bars .... (RHI)
  Faithful .... (RHI)
Blackbird
  Beatles; *Box Set* ....(CAP)
  White Album ....(CAP)
  Crosby, Stills & Nash; *Crosby, Stills & Nash* .. (ATL)
  Paul McCartney; *Unplugged-The Official Bootleg* (CAP)
  Paul McCartney/Wings; *Over America-#1* ......(CAP)
Blackleg Miner
  Steeleye Span; *Hark The Village Wait* .... (CHR)
  Story .... (CHR)
Blackmail
  10 CC; *Original Soundtrack* .... (MER)
  Robert Palmer; *Sneakin' Sally Through The Alley* . (ISL)
Blackout
  David Bowie; *Heroes* ....(RYK)
  Stage ....(RYK)
  Scorpions; *Blackout* .... (MER)
  World Wide Live .... (MER)
Blacks Are Giving Me The Blues
  Martin Mull; *No Hits Four Errors* ....(CPC)
  Normal ....(CPC)
Blondes In Black Cars
  Autograph; *That's The Stuff* ....(RCA)
Bye Bye Blackbird
  Dean Martin; *Swingin' Down Yonder* ....(CAP)
  Joe Cocker; *With A Little Help From My Friends* (A&M)
  Liza Minnelli; *ST/Liza With A Z* ....(COL)
  Miles Davis; *Ballads* ....(COL)
  Quintet/Jazz Sampler #2 ....(COL)
  'Round About Midnight ....(COL)
Collard Greens & Black-Eyed Peas
  Bud Powell; *Best Of* .... (BLN)
Creature From The Black Lagoon
  Dave Edmunds; *Best Of* .... (SS)
  Elvira Presents Haunted Hits .... (RHI)
  Repeat When Necessary .... (SS)
Dressed In Black
  Depeche Mode; *Black Celebration* .... (SIR)
  Hoodoo Gurus; *Kinky* ....(RCA)
Ebony Affair
  Timmy Thomas; *You're The Song I've Always Wanted
  To...* ....(GLA)
Ebony Eyes
  Bob Welch; *French Kiss* ....(CAP)
  Everly Brothers; *Golden Hits* ....(WB)
  Very Best Of ....(WB)
  Rick James & Smokey Robinson; *Greatest Hits* . (MOT)
  Stevie Wonder; *Songs In The Key Of Life* .... (MOT)
Ebony & Ivory
  Paul McCartney; *Tripping The Live Fantastic* ....(CAP)
  Paul McCartney & Stevie Wonder; *All The Best* .(CAP)
  Tug Of War ....(CAP)
Endless Black Ribbon
  Red Simpson; *Trucks Trains & Airplanes* .... (IGR)
  Red Sovine/Willis Bros./Reno & Smiley; *Heavy
  Haulers* .... (PP)
Fear Of A Black Planet
  Public Enemy; *Fear Of A Black Planet* ....(DFC)
Fell On Black Days
  Soundgarden; *Superunknown* ....(A&M)
Let's Make The Water Turn Black
  Mothers Of Invention; *Lumpy Gravy/Only In It For The
  Money* ....(RYK)
Light In The Black
  Blackmore's Rainbow; *Rainbow Rising* .... (OYS)
Little Black Book
  Jimmy Dean; *American Originals* ....(COL)
  Greatest Hits ....(COL)
Long Black Limousine
  Bobby Bare; *This Is* ....(RCA)
  Elvis Presley; *From Elvis In Memphis* ....(RCA)
  Memphis Record ....(RCA)
Long Black Veil
  Band; *Music From Big Pink* ....(CAP)
  To Kingdom Come-Definitive Collection ...... (CAP)
  Joan Baez; *Contemporary Ballad Book* .... (VAN)
  In Concert .... (VAN)
  One Day At A Time .... (VAN)

Johnny Cash; *At Folsom Prison & San Quentin* ...(COL)
  Classic Cash-Hall Of Fame Series .... (MER)
  Lefty Frizzell; *American Originals* ....(COL)
  Columbia Country Classics-#3-Americana ......(COL)
Long Cool Woman In A Black Dress
  Hollies; *Best Of* .... (EMI)
  Best Of-#2 .... (EMI)
  Billboard Top Rock 'N' Roll Hits-1972 .... (RHI)
  Distant Light .... (EPI)
  Epic Anthology-From The Original Masters ...... (EPI)
  Greatest Hits .... (EPI)
Man In Black
  Johnny Cash; *Essential* ....(COL)
  Patriot ....(COL)
Mexican Blackbird
  ZZ Top; *Fandango* .... (WB)
  Six Pack ....(WB)
My Black Cadillac
  Lightnin' Hopkins; *Complete Prestige/Bluesville
  Recordings* .... (BV)
My TV Went Black & White On Me
  Young Black Teenagers; *Young Black Teenagers* . (SOL)
Old Black Choo Choo
  Rose Maddox; *Rose Of The West Coast Country* (ARH)
Paint It Black
  Eric Burdon/Animals; *Greatest Hits* .... (ALL)
  Rolling Stones; *Aftermath* ....(AKO)
  Flashpoint ....(RS)
  Hot Rocks-1964-1971 ....(AKO)
  Singles Collection-London Years ....(AKO)
  Through The Past Darkly-Big Hits-#2 .... (AKO)
Pink And Black
  Robert Plant; *Shaken 'N Stirred* .... (EPR)
Proud To Be Black
  Run-D.M.C.; *Raising Hell* ....(PRO)
  Young Black Teenagers; *Young Black Teenagers* . (SOL)
Red And The Black
  Blue Oyster Cult; *Career Of Evil* ....(COL)
  Extraterrestrial Live ....(COL)
  On Your Feet Or On Your Knees ....(COL)
  Tyranny & Mutation ....(COL)
Red & Black
  Original Broadway Cast; *Les Miserables* ....(GEF)
Reverend Mr. Black
  Johnny Cash; *Biggest Hits* ....(COL)
  Kingston Trio; *Capitol Collectors Series* ....(CAP)
Say It Loud I'm Black & I'm Proud
  Afrika Bambaataa; *Decade Of Darkness* .... (EMI)
  James Brown; *Billboard Top R&B
  Hits-1965-1969* .... (RHI)
Slick Black Cadillac
  Quiet Riot; *Heavy Metal Memories* .... (RHI)
  Metal Health ....(EPA)
Sweet Black Angel
  Rolling Stones; *Exile On Main Street* .... (RS)
Sweet Black Girl
  Buddy Guy & Junior Wells; *Alone & Acoustic* ...(ALG)
That Black Snake Moan
  Blind Lemon Jefferson; *Blind Lemon Jefferson* .... (MS)
That Old Black Magic
  Ella Fitzgerald; *Best Of* .... (MCA)
  Big Bands Of The Swinging Years ...(EVR)
  In Rome-Birthday Concert ....(VRV)
  Frank Sinatra; *Come Swing With Me* ....(CAP)
  Glenn Miller/Orchestra; *Chattanooga Choo-Choo-#1
  Hits* .... (BLU)
  Judy Garland; *Best Of* .... (MCA)
  Louis Prima & Keely Smith; *Memories Are Made Of
  This* .... (CAP)
  Marcels; *Best Of* .... (RHI)
  Sammy Davis, Jr.; *Hey There-At His Dynamite
  Greatest* .... (MCA)
  Spike Jones; *Best Of-#2* ....(RCA)
This Black Cat Has 9 Lives
  Louis Armstrong; *What A Wonderful World* ..... (BLU)
Under The Big Black Sun
  X; *Under The Big Black Sun* ....(ELE)
We Work The Black Seam
  Sting; *Bring On The Night* ....(A&M)
  Dream Of The Blue Turtles ....(A&M)
White Man/Black Man
  James Gang; *Thirds* ....(OW)
  James Gary; *16 Greatest Hits* .... (MCA)

COLORS: BLUE

Afro Blue
Cal Tjader; *Concert By The Sea* .... (FAN)
    Greatest Hits-#1 .... (FAN)
    Monterey Concerts .... (PRS)
John Coltrane; *Afro Blue Impressions* .... (PAB)
    Best Of .... (PAB)
    Best Of-His Greatest Years .... (MCA)
Mongo Santamaria; *Afro-Roots* .... (PRS)
    Greatest Hits .... (FAN)
Alice Blue Gown
Edith Day; *Nipper's Greatest Hits-'20s* .... (RCA)
Am I Blue
Barbra Streisand; *ST/Funny Lady* .... (ARI)
Billie Holiday; *God Bless The Child* .... (COL)
George Strait; *Country Classics-#11-1987-1988* (MCA)
    Greatest Hits-#2 .... (MCA)
    MCA #1 Hits Of The '80s-#3 .... (MCA)
    Ocean Front Property .... (MCA)
Ray Charles; *Genius Of* .... (ATL)
Angel In Blue
J. Geils Band; *Freeze-Frame* .... (EMI)
Atlanta Blue
Statler Brothers; *14 Country Favorites* .... (MER)
    Atlanta Blue .... (MER)
    Greatest Hits .... (MER)
Baby Blue
Beach Boys; *L.A.-The Light Album* .... (CAR)
Echoes; *Super Oldies!'60s-#5* .... (AUF)
Gene Vincent; *Capitol Collectors Series* .... (CAP)
George Strait; *If You Ain't Lovin' (You Ain't*
    Livin') .... (MCA)
Paul Butterfield; *North South* .... (RHI)
Baby's Got Her Blue Jeans On
Mel McDaniel; *All-Time Country Classics-#2* .... (CAP)
    Greatest Hits .... (CAP)
    Let It Roll .... (CAP)
Barstow Blue Eyes
Jo Jo Gunne; *Jo Jo Gunne* .... (ASY)
Behind Blue Eyes
Who; *Hooligans* .... (MCA)
    Join Together .... (MCA)
    Who's Last .... (MCA)
    Who's Next .... (MCA)
Between Blue Eyes And Jeans
Conway Twitty; *Don't Call Him A Cowboy* .... (WB)
Between The Devil And The Deep Blue Sea
Chris Rea; *espresso logic* .... (EW)
Between The Devil & The Deep Blue Sea
Cab Calloway; *Jazz Heritage: Mr. Hi-De-Ho* ... (MCA)
Ella Fitzgerald; *Harold Arlen Songbook-#1* ... (VRV)
Black And Blue
Van Halen; *OU812* .... (WB)
Black & Blue
Louis Armstrong; *Greatest Hits* .... (COL)
    Satchmo At Symphony Hall .... (COL)
    & The Big Bands .... (DSQ)
    #5: Louis In New York .... (COL)
Original Cast; *Ain't Misbehavin'* .... (RCA)
Blue
Emotional Fish; *Emotional Fish* .... (ATL)
Fine Young Cannibals; *Fine Young Cannibals* ..... (IRS)
Joni Mitchell; *Blue* .... (RPR)
    Miles Of Aisles .... (ASY)
Peter, Paul & Mary; *In Concert* .... (WB)
Blue Angel
Roy Orbison; *All-Time Greatest Hits* .... (MON)
    For The Lonely-18 Greatest Hits .... (RHI)
    Greatest Hits .... (MON)
    In Dreams-Greatest Hits .... (VIA)
    Very Best Of .... (MON)
Blue Angel Suite
Strawbs; *Best Of* .... (A&M)
Blue Autumn
Bobby Goldsboro; *10th Anniversary Album* .... (UA)
    Greatest Hits .... (UA)
    Honey-Best Of .... (EMI)
Blue Avenue
Elton John; *Sleeping With The Past* .... (MCA)

Blue Bayou
Linda Ronstadt; *Greatest Hits-#2* .... (ASY)
    Simple Dreams .... (ASY)
Roy Orbison; *All-Time Greatest Hits-#2* .... (MON)
    For The Lonely: Anthology 1956-1965 .... (RHI)
    In Dreams-Greatest Hits .... (VIA)
    More Greatest Hits .... (MON)
Roy Orbison & Friends; *Black & White Night-Live* (VIA)
Blue Boy
Jim Reeves; *Best Of* .... (RCA)
    Live At The Opry .... (CMF)
Joni Mitchell; *Ladies Of The Canyon* .... (RPR)
Blue Canadian Rockies
Byrds; *Sweetheart Of The Rodeo* .... (COL)
Gene Autry; *50th Anniversary* .... (REP)
    Live From Madison Square Garden .... (REP)
Jimmy C. Newman; *Cajun Cowboy* .... (PLN)
Blue Champagne
Manhattan Transfer; *Manhattan Transfer* .... (ATL)
Blue Christmas
Anne Wilson & Nancy Wilson; *Very Special*
    Christmas-#2 .... (A&M)
Beach Boys; *Christmas Album* .... (CAP)
Booker T./M.G.s; *In The Christmas Spirit* ...... (ATL)
Earl Thomas Conley; *Best Of Christmas* .... (RCA)
Eddy Raven; *Warner Bros. Christmas Tradition* ... (WB)
Elvis Presley; *Blue Christmas* .... (RCA)
    Christmas Album .... (RCA)
    Memories Of Christmas .... (RCA)
Ernest Tubb; *Billboard's Greatest Christmas Hits* . (RHI)
Freddy Fender; *Christmas Time In The Valley* ... (MSP)
Highway 101; *Warner Bros. Christmas*
    Tradition-#2 .... (WB)
Jim Reeves; *12 Songs Of Christmas* .... (RCA)
Sawyer Brown; *Christmas Country Classics-#1* ... (CCB)
    Christmas For The '90s-#1 .... (LIB)
Blue Collar
Bachman-Turner Overdrive; *Best Of* .... (MER)
Blue Collar Man
Styx; *Caught In The Act* .... (A&M)
    Classics-#15 .... (A&M)
    Pieces Of Eight .... (A&M)
Blue Darlin'
Jimmy C. Newman; *Greatest Hits* .... (PLN)
Blue Eden
Neil Young/Crazy Horse; *Sleeps With Angels* ..... (RPR)
Blue Eyes
Elton John; *Greatest Hits-1976-1986* .... (MCA)
    Jump Up! .... (MCA)
Blue Eyes Crying In The Rain
Roy Acuff; *Greatest Hits-#1* .... (ELE)
Roy Acuff/Smokey Mountain Boys; *Columbia Country*
    Classics-#1-Golden Age .... (COL)
Willie Nelson; *Columbia Country Classics-#5-New*
    Trad. .... (COL)
    Greatest Hits & Some That Will Be .... (COL)
    Red Headed Stranger .... (COL)
    ST/Honeysuckle Rose .... (COL)
Blue Gardenia
Nat King Cole; *Story* .... (CAP)
Blue Hawaii
Billy Vaughn; *16 Great Performances* .... (MCA)
    Best Of .... (MCA)
    Golden Hits .... (MCA)
    & Orchestra: Play 22 Greatest Hits .... (RAN)
Elvis Presley; *Legendary Performer-#2* .... (RCA)
    ST/Blue Hawaii .... (RCA)
Blue Jay Way
Beatles; *Box Set* .... (CAP)
    Magical Mystery Tour .... (CAP)
Blue Jean
David Bowie; *Changesbowie* .... (RYK)
    The Singles-1969-1993 .... (RYK)
    Tonight .... (EMI)
Blue Jean Blues
Hank Williams, Jr.; *Strong Stuff* .... (WB)
ZZ Top; *Best Of* .... (WB)
    Fandango .... (WB)
    Six Pack .... (WB)
Blue Jean Bop
Gene Vincent; *Bop That Just Won't Stop* .... (CAP)
    Greatest .... (CAP)
    Greatest .... (IRS)

Blue Jean Boy
Michael Stanley Band; *Ladies' Choice* .... (EPI)
Blue Jeans
Chocolate Milk; *45* ....(RCA)
Blue Kentucky Girl
Emmylou Harris; *Blue Kentucky Girl* .... (WB)
   Profile 2-Best Of .... (WB)
Loretta Lynn; *Greatest Hits* .... (MCA)
Blue Kiss
Jane Wiedlin; *Jane Wiedlin* .... (IRS)
Blue Lamp
Stevie Nicks; *ST/Heavy Metal* .... (FA)
Blue Letter
Fleetwood Mac; *Fleetwood Mac* .... (RPR)
Blue Lou
Benny Carter; *1933* .... (PRS)
Ella Fitzgerald; *Best Of-#2* .... (MCA)
   Ella Sings-Chic Swings ....(OLR)
Blue Memories
Patty Loveless; *On Down The Line* .... (MCA)
Blue Monday
Bobby Darin; *Darin 1963-73* .... (MOT)
Fats Domino; *At Montreux* .... (ATL)
   Fats Domino ....(AUF)
   Greatest Hits ....(EVR)
   Greatest Hits ....(MCA)
   Super Oldies/'50s-#5 ....(AUF)
Huey Lewis/News; *Four Chords & Several Years
Ago* .... (ELE)
Kingsnakes; *19 Lucky Strikes* .... (BWV)
   Hardlife Boogie .... (BWV)
Blue Monday At Kansas City Red's
Cary Bell; *Blues Harp* ....(DEL)
Blue Monday People
Curtis Mayfield; *America Today* .... (CUR)
Blue Money
Van Morrison; *His Band & Street Choir* .... (WB)
Blue Monk
Bill Evans; *Conversations With Myself* ....(VRV)
Thelonius Monk; *Alone In San Francisco* ....(RVR)
   Composer ....(COL)
Blue Moon
Billie Holiday; *Billie's Blues* .... (BLN)
   First Verve Sessions ....(VRV)
   History Of ....(VRV)
Elvis Presley; *Complete Sun Sessions* ....(RCA)
   Elvis Presley ....(RCA)
Marcels; *Best Of* .... (RHI)
   Billboard Top Rock 'N' Roll Hits-1961 .... (RHI)
Blue Moon Of Kentucky
Bill Monroe; *American Originals* ....(COL)
   Bean Blossom/Lester Flatt .... (MCA)
   Best Of .... (MCA)
Elvis Presley; *Date With* ....(RCA)
   Golden Celebration ....(RCA)
   Sun Sessions ....(RCA)
Blue Moon With Heartache
Rosanne Cash; *19 Hot Country Requests-#2* ...... (EPI)
   Hits 1979-1989 ....(COL)
   Seven Year Ache ....(COL)
Blue Morning Blue Day
Foreigner; *Double Vision* .... (ATL)
Blue Motel Room
Joni Mitchell; *Hejira* .... (ASY)
Blue Motorcycle Eyes
Havana 3 A.M.; *Havana 3 A.M.* .... (IRS)
Blue Must Be The Color Of The Blues
Willie Nelson; *There'll Be No Teardrops Tonight* .. (UA)
Blue On Blue
Bobby Vinton; *16 Most Requested* .... (EPI)
   All-Time Greatest Hits .... (EPI)
   Autumn Memories .... (EPI)
Blue Oyster Cult
Blue Oyster Cult; *Imaginos* ....(COL)
Blue Railroad Train
Doc Watson; *Essential* .... (VAN)
   Lonesome Road .... (UA)
   & Merl Watson: Southbound .... (VAN)
Blue Red & Grey
Who; *By Numbers* .... (MCA)
Blue Ridge Mountain Blues
Doc Watson; *Essential* .... (VAN)
John Fogerty; *Blue Ridge Rangers* .... (FAN)
Norman Blake; *Directions* ....(TAK)

Blue Ridge Mountain Sky
Marshall Tucker Band; *New Life* .... (AJK)
Blue Ridge Mountains Turnin' Green
Charley Pride; *Amazing Love* ....(RCA)
Blue River
Elvis Presley; *Lost Album* ....(RCA)
   ST/Double Trouble ....(RCA)
Blue Rock Montana
Willie Nelson; *Red Headed Stranger* ....(COL)
Blue Room
Diana Ross/Supremes; *25th Anniversary* .... (MOT)
Ella Fitzgerald; *Rodgers & Hart Songbook* ....(VRV)
Blue Rose Is
Pam Tillis; *Put Yourself In My Place* .... (ARI)
Blue Rose Of Texas
Holly Dunn; *Blue Rose Of Texas* .... (WB)
Blue Shadows
Blasters; *ST/Streets Of Fire* .... (MCA)
B.B. King; *From The Beginning* ....(KNT)
   Greatest Hits ....(KNT)
   The Jungle ....(KNT)
Blue Shadows On The Trail
Sons Of The Pioneers; *Cool Water* ....(RCA)
Blue Side
Crystal Gayle; *Greatest Hits* ....(CAP)
   Miss The Mississippi ....(CAP)
Blue Side Of Lonesome
George Jones; *Sings The Great Songs Of Leon
Payne* ....(GUS)
Jim Reeves; *45* ....(RCA)
   Best Of-#4 ....(RCA)
Blue Side Of Town
Patty Loveless; *Greatest Hits* .... (MCA)
   Honky Tonk Angel .... (MCA)
Blue Skies
Benny Goodman; *Carnegie Hall Jazz Concert* ....(COL)
   Complete Goodman ....(RCA)
   This Is ....(RCA)
   Today ....(LON)
Bing Crosby; *Greatest Hits* .... (MCA)
Duke Ellington; *Carnegie Hall* .... (PRS)
   Golden Duke .... (PRS)
Willie Nelson; *Stardust* ....(COL)
Blue Skirt Waltz
Frankie Yankovic/Yanks; *Greatest Hits* ....(COL)
Mom & Dads; *Best Of* ....(CRS)
   Blue Canadian Rockies ....(CRS)
Blue Sky
Allman Brothers Band; *An Evening With-First Set* (POL)
   Best Of .... (POL)
   Decade Of Hits-1969-1979 .... (POL)
   Dreams .... (POL)
   Eat A Peach .... (POL)
   Road Goes On Forever .... (POL)
A-Ha; *Hunting High & Low* .... (WB)
Sweethearts Of The Rodeo; *Buffalo Zone* ....(COL)
Blue Sky Mine
Midnight Oil; *Blue Sky Mining* ....(COL)
Blue Sky Shinin'
Marie Osmond; *There's No Stopping Your Heart* . (CAP)
Mickey Newbury; *Sailor* .... (MCA)
Blue Spruce Woman
Foghat; *Rock & Roll Outlaws* .... (RHI)
Blue Star
Blue Notes; *Early Years* ....(CLT)
Charlie Daniels Band; *Million Mile Reflections* ... (EPI)
Mystics; *16 Golden Classics* ....(CLT)
Blue Street
Blood, Sweat & Tears; *45* .... (MCA)
Blue Suede Shoes
Carl Perkins; *Blue Suede Shoes* ....(SUN)
   Cruisin'-1956-1957 ....(DHL)
   Oldies But Goodies-#4 ....(OSR)
   Original Sun Greatest Hits .... (RHI)
Elvis Presley; *Elvis Presley* ....(RCA)
   Elvis-Aloha From Hawaii ....(RCA)
   In Person ....(RCA)
   Legendary Performers-#2 ....(RCA)
   ST/G.I. Blues ....(RCA)
Blue Sunday
Doors; *Morrison Hotel/Hard Rock Cafe* .... (ELE)
Blue Tail Fly
Burl Ives; *Best Of* .... (MCA)
Pete Seeger; *20 Golden Pieces Of* ....(BLD)

Blue Tango
Billy Vaughn; *String Of Pearls-Greatest Hits* ...... (POE)
Leroy Anderson; *45* .... (MCA)
Blue Thursday
Franz Jackson Original All-Stars; *Featuring Bob
Shoffner* .... (RVR)
Blue Train
John Coltrane; *Best Of Blue Note-#1* .... (BLN)
Blue Train .... (BLN)
Johnny Cash; *Classic Cash-Hall Of Fame Series* . (MER)
Man-The World-His Music .... (SUN)
Original Johnny Cash .... (SUN)
Story Songs Of The Trains & Rivers .... (SUN)
Blue Turning Grey Over You
Billie Holiday; *Billie's Blues* .... (BLN)
Louis Armstrong/Luis Russell & Orchestra; *Satchmo
Style* .... (DSQ)
Ringo Starr; *Sentimental Journey* .... (CAP)
Blue Turns To Grey
Rolling Stones; *December's Children* .... (AKO)
Blue Umbrella
Ed Bruce; *Ed Bruce* .... (MCA)
John Prine; *Sweet Revenge* .... (ATL)
Blue Valentine
Tom Waits; *Blue Valentine* .... (ASY)
Blue Velvet
Bobby Vinton; *16 Most Requested* .... (EPI)
All-Time Greatest Hits .... (EPI)
Greatest Hits .... (EPI)
Blue Water
Poco; *Crazy Eyes* .... (EPI)
Ride The Country .... (EPI)
Blue Yodel #1
Bob Wills; *Anthology* .... (SSP)
Lynyrd Skynyrd; *Best Of The Rest* .... (MCA)
One More From The Road .... (MCA)
Blue Yodel #4 (California Blues)
Bill Monroe; *Columbia Historic Edition* .... (COL)
Jimmie Rodgers; *Early Years 1928-1929* .... (ROU)
Never No Mo' Blues .... (RCA)
This Is .... (RCA)
Blueberry Hill
Elvis Presley; *Loving You* .... (RCA)
Recorded Live On Stage .... (RCA)
Fats Domino; *Greatest Hits* .... (EVR)
Greatest Hits .... (MCA)
My Blue Heaven-Best Of-#1 .... (EMI)
Little Richard; *Big Hits* .... (CRS)
Louis Armstrong; *Best Of* .... (MCA)
Essential .... (VAN)
I Like Jazz: Essence Of .... (COL)
Bluebird
Buffalo Springfield; *Again* .... (ATC)
Classic Rock 1966-1988 .... (ATL)
Retrospective .... (ATC)
Electric Light Orchestra; *Secret Messages* .... (JET)
Helen Reddy; *Live In London* .... (CAP)
No Way To Treat A Lady .... (CAP)
Leon Russell; *Best Of* .... (SHE)
Will O' The Wisp .... (SHE)
Paul McCartney/Wings; *Band On The Run* ...... (CAP)
Over America .... (CAP)
Robin Trower; *In City Dreams* .... (CHR)
Bluebird Is Dead
Electric Light Orchestra; *Afterglow* .... (EPI)
On The Third Day .... (JET)
Bluebird Of Happiness
Lee Andrews/Hearts; *Biggest Hits* .... (CLT)
Gotham Recording Sessions .... (CLT)
Bluebirds Over the Mountain
Beach Boys; *Absolute Best-#2* .... (CAP)
Friends/20/20 .... (CAP)
Sunshine Dream .... (CAP)
'69 .... (CAP)
Ritchie Valens; *Best Of* .... (RHI)
History Of .... (RHI)
Ritchie Valens .... (RHI)
Bluer Than Blue
Michael Johnson; *Album* .... (EMI)
Bluest Eyes In Texas
Restless Heart; *Big Dreams In A Small Town* ....(RCA)
Born To Be Blue
George Shearing & Mel Torme; *Evening With* ... (CCJ)

Judds; *Greatest Hits-#2* .... (RCA)
Love Can Build A Bridge .... (RCC)
Steve Miller; *Born 2 B Blue* .... (CAP)
Boy Blue
Cyndi Lauper; *True Colors* .... (POR)
Electric Light Orchestra; *Afterglow* .... (EPI)
Eldorado .... (JET)
Ole ELO .... (JET)
Brown To Blue
Elvis Costello/Attractions; *Almost Blue* .... (COL)
Bullet The Blue Sky
U2; *Joshua Tree* .... (ISL)
ST/Rattle & Hum .... (ISL)
California Blue
Herb Alpert; *Fandango* .... (A&M)
Roy Orbison; *Mystery Girl* .... (VIA)
Carolina Blue
Annie McGowan; *Rattlesnakes & Rusty Water* ....(RAT)
Chicken Cordon Blues
Steve Goodman; *Somebody Else's Troubles* .... (OOP)
Child Of The Wild Blue Yonder
John Hiatt; *Stolen Moments* .... (A&M)
Clear Blue Skies
Crosby, Stills, Nash & Young; *American Dream* .. (ATL)
Cold Blue Steel & Sweet Fire
Joni Mitchell; *For The Roses* .... (ASY)
Miles Of Aisles .... (ASY)
Computer Blue
Prince/Revolution; *ST/Purple Rain* .... (WB)
Corpus Christi Blue
Dewayne Blackwell & Jill Hollier; *45* .... (WB)
Crystal Blue Persuasion
Tommy James/Shondells; *Anthology* .... (RHI)
Best Of .... (RLL)
Deacon Blues
Steely Dan; *Aja* .... (MCA)
Gold .... (MCA)
Devil With A Blue Dress On
Bruce Springsteen; *ST/No Nukes-Muse Concerts* .. (ASY)
Mitch Ryder/Detroit Wheels; *Frat Rock-#4* ...... (RHI)
Rev Up-Best Of .... (RHI)
Son Of Frat Rock .... (RHI)
Toga Rock .... (DHL)
Dog Blue
Mimi & Richard Farina; *Best Of* .... (VAN)
Don't It Make My Brown Eyes Blue
Crystal Gayle; *Classic Crystal* .... (EMI)
Heartbreak Hotel .... (EMI)
ST/Convoy .... (UA)
We Must Believe In Magic .... (UA)
Dream Of The Blue Turtles
Sting; *Dream Of The Blue Turtles* .... (A&M)
Drunken Blue Rooster
Todd Rundgren; *Todd* .... (RHI)
Electric Blue
Icehouse; *Man Of Colours* .... (CHR)
Eskimo Blue Day
Jefferson Airplane; *2400 Fulton Street-Anthology* (RCA)
Volunteers .... (RCA)
Woodstock Two .... (ATL)
Five Foot Two, Eyes Of Blue
Mom & Dads; *Very Best Of* .... (CRS)
For You Blue
Beatles; *Box Set* .... (CAP)
Let It Be .... (CAP)
George Harrison; *Best Of* .... (CAP)
Forever In Blue Jeans
Neil Diamond; *12 Greatest Hits-#2* .... (COL)
Hot August Night II .... (COL)
You Don't Bring Me Flowers .... (COL)
Goodbye Blue Monday
City Boy; *Dinner At The Ritz* .... (MER)
Goodbye Blue Sky
Daryl Braithwaite; *Higher Than Hope* .... (EPA)
Rise .... (EPA)
Pink Floyd; *The Wall* .... (COL)
Roger Waters; *The Wall Live In Berlin* .... (MER)
Hot, Blue & Righteous
ZZ Top; *Six Pack* .... (WB)
Tres Hombres .... (WB)
House Of Blue Lights
Andrews Sisters; *Best Of-#2* .... (MCA)

Asleep At The Wheel; *10* ....(EPI)
  Greatest Country Hits!'80s-1987 ....(COL)
  More Hot Country Requests-#2 ....(EPI)
  Trucker's Jukebox-#2 ....(COL)
Canned Heat; *Human Conditions* ....(TAK)
  & John Lee Hooker: Live At Fox Venice .... (RHI)
Chuck Berry; *Chess Box* ....(CSS)
  More Rock 'N' Roll Rarities-Golden Era ....(CSS)
House Of Blue Lovers
James O'Gwynn; *Greatest Hits* ....(PLN)
  Souvenirs Of Music City U.S.A. ....(PLN)
How Blue
Reba McEntire; *Greatest Hits* ....(MCA)
  MCA #1 Hits!'80s-#1 ....(MCA)
  My Kind Of Country ....(MCA)
How Blue Can You Get
B.B. King; *Best Of* ....(MCA)
  Live At The Regal ....(MCA)
  Live In Cook County Jail ....(MCA)
It's All Over Now Baby Blue
Bob Dylan; *Biograph* ....(COL)
  Bringing It All Home ....(COL)
  Greatest Hits-#2 ....(COL)
Byrds; *Ballad Of Easy Rider* ....(COL)
  Byrds ....(COL)
I'm In Love With A Big Blue Frog
Peter, Paul & Mary; *Album 1700* .... (WB)
Jackie Blue
Ozark Mountain Daredevils; *Billboard Top
  Hits-1975* .... (RHI)
  It'll Shine When It Shines ....(A&M)
  It's Alive ....(A&M)
  Super Hits!'70s-Have A Nice Day-#14 .... (RHI)
  The Best ....(A&M)
Lady Blue
George Benson; *Weekend In L.A.* .... (WB)
Leon Russell; *Best Of* ....(MCA)
  Will O' The Wisp ....(MCA)
Little Blue Man
Betty Johnson; *45* ....(ATL)
Little Blue Whale
Country Joe McDonald; *Goodbye Blues* ....(FAN)
Little Boy Blue
Elegants; *45* ....(RLL)
Little Girl Blue
Ella Fitzgerald; *Rodgers & Hart Songbook* ....(VRV)
Lonely Blue Boy
Conway Twitty; *Greatest Hits* ....(CCB)
  Very Best Of ....(MCA)
Love Is Blue
Andre Kostelanetz; *16 Most Requested Songs* ....(COL)
Paul Mauriat; *Love Is Blue* ....(MER)
Sandpipers; *Softly* ....(A&M)
Midnight Blue
Electric Light Orchestra; *Afterglow* ....(EPI)
  Discovery ....(JET)
Johnny Mathis; *Feelings* ....(COL)
King Curtis; *Enjoy...Best Of* ....(CLT)
  Soul Twist & Other Golden Classics ....(CLT)
Lou Gramm; *Ready Or Not* ....(ATL)
Louise Tucker; *Midnight Blue* ....(ARI)
Melissa Manchester; *Greatest Hits* ....(ARI)
  Melissa ....(ARI)
Seals & Crofts; *Takin' It Easy* ....(WB)
Misty Blue
Dorothy Moore; *Blues Is Alright* ....(MAL)
  Misty Blue ....(MAL)
Eddy Arnold; *Best Of-#2* ....(RCA)
  Country Gold ....(RCA)
  This Is ....(RCA)
Mr. Blue
Fleetwoods; *Best Of* ....(RHI)
Garth Brooks; *No Fences* ....(CAP)
Michael Franks; *Art Of Tea* ....(RPR)
Timmy/Tulips; *ST/American Hot Wax* ....(A&M)
Mr. Blue Sky
Electric Light Orchestra; *Afterglow* ....(EPI)
  Greatest Hits ....(JET)
  Out Of The Blue ....(JET)
My Blue Angel
Aaron Tippin; *Read Between The Lines* ....(RCA)
My Blue Heaven
Artie Shaw; *Complete-#4* ....(RCA)
  This Is ....(RCA)

Fats Domino; *Greatest Hits* ....(EVR)
  Legendary Masters ....(UA)
  My Blue Heaven-Best Of-#1 ....(EMI)
  Oldies But Goodies-#10 ....(OSR)
Frank Sinatra; *Gift Set* ....(CAP)
  Swingin' Session ....(CAP)
New Blue Moon
Traveling Wilburys; *#3* .... (WIL)
New Shade Of Blue
Bobby Fuller Four; *Best Of* ....(RHI)
  Tapes-#1 ....(RHI)
Southern Pacific; *Country Love Songs* ....(WB)
  Greatest Hits ....(WB)
  Zuma ....(WB)
Ode To Big Blue
Gordon Lightfoot; *Don Quixote* ....(RPR)
Old Blue
Byrds; *Byrds* ....(COL)
Furry Lewis; *Back On My Feet Again* ....(PRS)
  Shake 'Em On Down ....(FAN)
Joan Baez; *Ballad Book* ....(VAN)
  Joan Baez-#2 ....(VAN)
Old Blue Car
Peter Case; *Peter Case* ....(GEF)
Once In A Blue Moon
Earl Thomas Conley; *Greatest Hits* ....(RCA)
  Hits Of '86 ....(RCA)
Once In A Very Blue Moon
Nanci Griffith; *One Fair Summer Evening* .... (MCA)
  Steal This Disc ....(RYK)
Pat Alger; *True Love & Other Short Stories* ....(SH)
Orange Was The Color Of Her Dress
Charles Mingus; *Changes Two* ....(ATL)
  In Europe-#2 ....(ENJ)
Gil Evans; *Live At Sweet Basil-#1* ....(EVD)
  /Laurent Cugny Big Band-Golden Hair .... (EMA)
Out Of The Blue
Band; *Last Waltz* .... (WB)
Debbie Gibson; *Out Of The Blue* ....(ATL)
Didier Lockwood; *Out Of The Blue* ....(GRM)
Elton John; *Blue Moves* ....(MCA)
Foreigner; *Inside Information* ....(ATL)
George Harrison; *All Things Must Pass* ....(CAP)
John Lennon; *Lennon* ....(CAP)
  Mind Games ....(CAP)
Reba McEntire; *Unlimited* ....(MER)
Roxy Music; *Country Life* ....(RPR)
  Greatest Hits ....(ATC)
  Heart Still Beating ....(RPR)
  Viva!-Live Album ....(RPR)
Tommy James/Shondells; *Anthology* .... (RHI)
Perfect Blue Buildings
Counting Crows; *August And Everything After* .. (DGC)
Pink Cocktail For A Blue Lady
Glenn Miller/Orchestra; *Complete* ....(BLU)
  Complete-#9 ....(RCA)
Pink Turns To Blue
Husker Du; *Zen Arcade* ....(SST)
Powder Blue Mercedes Queen
Paul Revere/Raiders; *Legend Of* ....(COL)
Red Roses For A Blue Lady
Al Martino; *Best Of* ....(CAP)
  Capitol Collectors Series ....(CAP)
Andy Williams; *16 Most Requested Songs* ....(COL)
  Mom & Dads; Best Of ....(CRS)
Roger Whittaker; *All-Time Heart-Touching
  Favorites* ....(CAP)
  Classics Collection-#1 ....(CAP)
Vaughn Monroe; *Best Of* ....(RCA)
Red Wine & Blue Memories
Joe Stampley; *Biggest Hits* ....(EPI)
Rednecks, White Socks & Blue Ribbon Beer
Johnny Russell; *Beer Redneck Mothers* ....(RCA)
  Rednecks, White Socks & Blue Ribbon Beer .....(RCA)
Rhapsody In Blue
Boston Pops Orchestra/Arthur Fiedler;
  Gershwin-Greatest Hits ....(RCA
Columbia Jazz Band/Michael Tilson Thomas; *Classic
  Gershwin* ....(COL
Freddy Martin/Orchestra; *Fascinatin' Rhythm-Cap. Sing
  Gershwin* ....(CAP
George Gershwin; *Rhapsody In Blue* ....(BIO)
George Gershwin & Paul Whiteman/Orch.; *Nipper's
  Greatest Hits-'20s* ....(RCA

Larry Adler & George Martin; *Glory Of Gershwin*
Featuring Larry Adler .... (MER)
Rio De Janeiro Blue
Nicolette Larson; *In The Nick Of Time* ....(WB)
Randy Crawford; *Secret Combination* ....(WB)
Runnin' Blue
Doors; *Soft Parade* .... (ELE)
Weird Scenes Inside The Gold Mine ....(ELE)
September Blue
Chris Rea; *Dancing With The Strangers* ....(MOT)
Serenade In Blue
Glenn Miller; *Best Of-#2* ....(RCA)
Legendary Performer-#2 ....(RCA)
Memorial: 1944-1969 ....(RCA)
Glenn Miller/Orchestra; *Complete-#8* ....(RCA)
Unforgettable ....(RCA)
Gloria Lynne; *Golden Classics* ....(CLT)
Tonight Show Band/Doc Severinsen; *Tonight Show*
Band/Doc Severinsen-#2 ....(AMH)
Shades Of Blue
Desert Rose Band; *True Love* .... (MCC)
Silver Blue
Linda Ronstadt; *Prisoner In Disguise* ....(ASY)
Silver Stars, Purple Sage, Eyes Of Blue
Roy Rogers/Sons Of The Pioneers; *Roy Rogers/Sons Of*
The Pioneers ....(VS)
Silver, Blue & Gold
Bad Company; *Run With The Pack* .... (SS)
Soldier Blue
Buffy Sainte-Marie; *Native North American Child* (VAN)
She Used To Wanna Be A Ballerina ....(VAN)
Cult; *Sonic Temple* .... (SIR)
Julian Cope; *Peggy Suicide* ....(ISL)
Song Sung Blue
Neil Diamond; *Glory Road-1968-1972* ....(MCA)
His 12 Greatest Hits ....(MCA)
Hot August Night ....(MCA)
Love At The Greek ....(COL)
Moods ....(MCA)
Soulful Shade Of Blue
Buffy Sainte-Marie; *Best Of* ....(VAN)
I'm Gonna Be A Country Girl Again ....(VAN)
Stella Blue
Grateful Dead; *Steal Your Face* .... (GRD)
Wake Of The Flood ....(GRD)
Robert Hunter; *Box Of Rain* ....(RYK)
Stone Blue
Foghat; *Best Of* .... (RHI)
Stone Blue .... (RHI)
Suite Madame Blue
Styx; *Caught In The Act* .... (A&M)
Classics-#15 ....(A&M)
Equinox ....(A&M)
Suite: Judy Blue Eyes
Crosby, Stills & Nash; *Crosby, Stills & Nash* ..... (ATL)
Crosby, Stills & Nash (collection) ....(ATL)
ST/Woodstock ....(ATL)
Crosby, Stills, Nash & Young; *So Far* ....(ATL)
Sweet Little Bullet From A Pretty...
Tom Waits; *Blue Valentine* ....(ASY)
Sweet Summer Blue & Gold
Linda Ronstadt; *Stone Poneys* ....(CAP)
Tangled Up In Blue
Bob Dylan; *Biograph* ....(COL)
Blood On The Tracks ....(COL)
Bootleg Series-#1-3-Rare & Unreleased ....(COL)
Real Live ....(COL)
There's A Blue Sky Way Out Yonder
Riders In The Sky; *Riders Go Commercial* ...... (MCA)
Saturday Morning With ....(MCA)
Tired Of Midnight Blue
George Harrison; *Extra Texture* ....(CAP)
True Blue
Madonna; *True Blue* .... (SIR)
Rod Stewart; *Best Of-#2* ....(MER)
Storyteller-Complete Anthology-1964-1990 ......(WB)
Under Blue Canadian Skies
Glenn Miller/Orchestra; *Complete* ....(BLU)
Used To Blue
Sawyer Brown; *Greatest Hits* ....(CCB)
Sawyer Brown ....(CCB)
Venice Blue
Bobby Darin; *Capitol Collectors Series* ....(CAP)

Venus In Blue Jeans
Jimmy Clanton; *All-Star Chartbusters* .... (INT)
Golden Years-1962 ....(DOM)
Visions In Blue
Ultravox; *Collection* .... (CHR)
When My Blue Moon Turns To Gold Again
Elvis Presley; *50 Worldwide Gold Award Hits-#2* (RCA)
Elvis ....(RCA)
Golden Celebration ....(RCA)
Merle Haggard; *His Best* ....(MCA)
Ramblin' Fever ....(MCA)
When Sunny Gets Blue
Barbra Streisand; *Simply Streisand* ....(COL)
Johnny Mathis; *All-Time Greatest Hits* ....(COL)
First 25 Years-Silver Anniversary Album ....(COL)
Greatest Hits ....(COL)
Love Songs ....(COL)
Kenny Rankin; *Album* ....(LD)
Steve Miller; *Born 2 B Blue* ....(CAP)
When Sunny Gets Blue Lady
Vaughn Monroe; *Best Of* ....(RCA)
This Is ....(RCA)
Where The Blue Of The Night Meets The...
Bing Crosby; *All-Time Best Of* ....(CCB)
Best Of ....(MCA)
Where The Blue Of The Night Meets The... ....(BIO)
Wild & Blue
Hank Williams, Jr.; *Major Moves* ....(W/C)
John Anderson; *Greatest Hits* ....(WB)
Wild & Blue ....(WB)
You Put The Blue In Me
Whites; *Greatest Hits* ....(CCB)
Old Familiar Feeling .... (E/C)

COLORS: BROWN

Black & Tan Fantasy
Duke Ellington; *Echoes Of An Era;*
Ellington/Armstrong .... (RLL)
Beginning ....(MCA)
Carnegie Hall ....(PRS)
Carnegie Hall Concert 12-11-43 ....(EVR)
Continuum ....(FAN)
Greatest Hits ....(RPR)
Pure Gold ....(RCA)
/M. Ellington ....(FAN)
Blonde Hair, Brown Nose
Dweezil Zappa; *Havin' A Bad Day* ....(RYK)
Brown Earth
Laura Nyro; *Christmas & The Beads Of Sweat* ...(COL)
Brown Eyed Girl
Isley Brothers; *Live It Up* .... (TN)
Jimmy Buffett; *One Particular Harbour* .... (MCA)
Van Morrison; *Bang Masters* ....(EPI)
Best Of ....(MER)
ST/Born On The Fourth Of July ....(MCA)
ST/Sleeping With The Enemy ....(COL)
Wonder Years-Music From Emmy Shows/Era ...(ATL)
Brown Eyed Handsome Man
Buddy Holly; *For The First Time Anywhere* ..... (MCA)
Rock & Roll Collection ....(MCA)
& Crickets: 20 Golden Greats ....(MCA)
Chuck Berry; *Best Of The Best Of* ....(GUS)
Chess Box ....(CSS)
Roll Over Beethoven ....(ALL)
Brown Eyed Woman
Grateful Dead; *Europe '72* ....(WB)
What A Long Strange Trip It's Been ....(WB)
Brown Eyes
Fleetwood Mac; *25 Years-The Chain* ....(WB)
Tusk ....(WB)
Jimmy Cliff; *Cliff Hanger* ....(COL)
Brown Girl In The Ring
Boney M; *Nightflight To Venus* .... (SIR)
Brown Man Do
Small Faces; *78 In The Shade* ....(ATL)
Brown Skin Gal
Bob Wills; *Best Of* ....(MCA)
Brown Skin Girl
Jesse Fuller; *Brother Lowdown* ....(FAN)
San Franciso Bay Blues ....(GTJ)

Brown Sugar
Rolling Stones; *Classic Rock 1966-1988* .... (ATL)
Flashpoint + Collectibles .... (RS)
Hot Rocks-1964-1971 .... (AKO)
Made In The Shade .... (RS)
Sticky Fingers .... (RS)
ZZ Top; *First Album* .... (WB)
Six Pack .... (WB)
Brown To Blue
Elvis Costello/Attractions; *Almost Blue* .... (COL)
California Dreamin'
Beach Boys; *Made In The U.S.A.* .... (CAP)
Mamas & The Papas; *20 Golden Hits* .... (MCA)
At The Hop .... (MCA)
Good Feeling Music-Big Chill-#1 .... (MOT)
ST/Air America .... (MCA)
ST/American Pop .... (RLL)
ST/Forrest Gump .... (EPX)
Capt. Fantastic & The Brown Dirt Cowboy
Elton John; *Capt. Fantastic & The Brown Dirt
Cowboy* .... (POL)
Don't It Make My Brown Eyes Blue
Crystal Gayle; *Classic Crystal* .... (EMI)
Heartbreak Hotel .... (EMI)
ST/Convoy .... (UA)
We Must Believe In Magic .... (UA)
Hazy Shade Of Winter
Bangles; *Greatest Hits* .... (COL)
ST/Less Than Zero .... (DFC)
Simon & Garfunkel; *Bookends* .... (COL)
Collected Works .... (COL)
I Dream Of Jeanie With Light Brown Hair
Al Jolson; *Story-#5* .... (MCA)
Joan Baez; *Diamonds & Rust* .... (A&M)
Mormon Tabernacle Choir; *Beautiful Dreamer* ...(COL)
Greatest Hits-#3 .... (COL)
Old Beloved Songs .... (COL)
Little Brown Bird
Elvin Bishop; *Raisin' Hell* .... (CPC)
Little Brown Dog
Judy Collins; *Golden Apples Of The Sun* .... (ELE)
Little Brown Jug
Glenn Miller; *Best Of* .... (RCA)
Legendary Performer .... (RCA)
Pure Gold .... (RCA)
Story .... (RCA)
Glenn Miller/Orchestra; *Unforgettable* .... (RCA)
Mrs. Brown You've Got A Lovely Daughter
Herman's Hermits; *Something Good Again* ...... (AKO)
XX-Their Greatest Hits .... (AKO)
My Brown Eyed Texas Rose
Tex Ritter; *Arizona Days* .... (MSP)
Country Music Hall Of Fame .... (MCA)
My Little Brown Book
Duke Ellington; *& John Coltrane* .... (MCI)
John Coltrane; *Gentle Side Of* .... (GRP)
Old Brown Shoe
Beatles; *Box Set* .... (CAP)
Hey Jude .... (CAP)
Past Masters-#2 .... (CAP)
One Brown Mouse
Jethro Tull; *Bursting Out* .... (CHR)
Heavy Horses .... (CHR)
Orange, Brown & Green
Herb Ellis & Freddie Green; *Rhythm Willie* ...... (CCJ)
Plain Brown Wrapper
Count Basie/Orchestra; *I Told You So* .... (PAB)
Gary Morris; *Greatest Hits-#2* .... (WB)
Plain Brown Wrapper .... (WB)
Pound For A Brown On The Bus
Frank Zappa; *Electric Aunt Jemima* .... (RHI)
Uncle Meat .... (BAR)
Sweet Georgia Brown
Anita O'Day; *Compact Jazz-Best Of The Jazz
Vocalists* .... (VRV)
Beatles; *In The Beginning-Circa 1960* .... (POL)
Coasters; *Greatest Hits* .... (ATC)
Django Reinhardt; *Djangologie USA-#1* .... (DSQ)
Quintet Of The Hot Club Of France .... (PRS)
Ella Fitzgerald; *In London* .... (PAB)
Whisper Not .... (VRV)
Ella Fitzgerald & Count Basie; *Perfect Match* .... (PAB)
Original Cast; *Bubbling Brown Sugar* .... (AMH)
Stephane Grappelli; *Live In London* .... (BL)

Tito Puente; *Out Of This World* .... (CP)
Sweet Marijuana Brown
Paula Lockheart; *It Ain't The End Of The World* ...(FF)
Two Hits & The Joint Turned Brown
Pfaff Family Dog; *Marijuana's Greatest Hits
Revisited* .... (RHA)
Rodney & Doug Dillard/John Hartford; *Glitter Grass
From The Nashwood...* .... (FF)

A Tisket, A Tasket
Ella Fitzgerald; *Best Of* .... (MCA)
Ella Fitzgerald .... (LAS)
Glenn Miller/Army Air Force Band; *Glenn Miller/Army
Air Force Band* .... (LAS)
Tommy Dorsey; *Complete-#7* .... (RCA)
All In Green Went My Love Riding
Joan Baez; *Love Song Album* .... (VAN)
Almost Green
John Bergamo; *On The Edge* .... (CMU)
Another Green World
Brian Eno; *Another Green World* .... (EDI)
Avocado Green
Johnny Winter; *About Blues* .... (OOP)
Before The Storm .... (OOP)
Ballad Of The Green Berets
Barry Sadler; *Cruisin'-1966* .... (INC)
Hits Of The '60s .... (IMC)
More American Graffiti-#4 .... (MCA)
Nipper's Greatest Hits-'60s-#2 .... (RCA)
Super Hits-#3 .... (GUS)
Bein' Green
Frank Sinatra; *Greatest Hits-#1 & 2* .... (RPR)
Frank Sinatra & Antonio Carlos Jobim; *Sinatra &
Company* .... (RPR)
Muppets/Kermit The Frog; *Muppet Show* .... (ARI)
Van Morrison; *Hard Nose The Highway* .... (VAN)
Big Bright Green Pleasure Machine
Simon & Garfunkel; *Collected Works* .... (COL)
Parsley Sage Rosemary & Thyme .... (COL)
ST/The Graduate .... (COL)
Blue Ridge Mountains Turnin' Green
Charley Pride; *Amazing Love* .... (RCA)
Cabbage Greens
Champion Jack Dupree; *New Orleans Barrelhouse
Boogie-Complete* .... (COL)
Collard Greens & Black-Eyed Peas
Bud Powell; *Best Of* .... (BLN)
Evergreen (Theme From "A Star Is Born")
Barbra Streisand; *Greatest Hits* .... (COL)
Greatest Hits-#2 .... (COL)
Memories .... (COL)
ST/A Star Is Born .... (COL)
Luther Vandross; *Songs* .... (EPI)
Paul Williams; *Classics* .... (A&M)
Green Christmas
Stan Freberg; *Capitol Collectors Series* .... (CAP)
Christmas Comedy Classics .... (PRY)
Dr. Demento Greatest Christmas CD .... (RHI)
Dr. Demento's Greatest Novelty-#6 .... (RHI)
Green Door
Jim Lowe; *Billboard Top Rock 'N' Roll Hits-1956* (RHI)
Super Hits-#4 .... (GUS)
Green Earrings
Steely Dan; *Gold* .... (MCA)
Royal Scam .... (MCA)
Green Eyed Lady
Sugarloaf; *45* .... (UA)
Green Eyes
Husker Du; *Flip Your Wig* .... (SST)
Jimmy Dorsey; *Best Of* .... (MCA)
Greatest Hits .... (MCA)
Green Fields Of America
Paddy Tunney; *Stone Fiddle* .... (GRE)
Green Fields Of Canada
Eric Schoenberg; *Acoustic Guitar* .... (ROU)
Green Fields Of France
Phil Coulter; *Forgotten Dreams* .... (SHA)
Green Finch & Linnet Bird
Original Cast/Angela Lansbury/Len Cariou; *Sweeney
Todd* .... (RCA)

Green Gorilla
Spirit; *Time Circle* .... (EPI)
Green Grass & High Tides
Outlaws; *Bring It Back Alive* .... (ARI)
Outlaws .... (ARI)
Green Green Grass Of Home
Burl Ives; *Best Of-#2* .... (MCA)
Elvis Presley; *Our Memories Of-#2* ....(RCA)
Today ....(RCA)
George Jones; *20 Golden Pieces Of* .... (BLD)
Tom Jones; *Country Side Of* ....(LON)
London Collector ....(LON)
Things That Matter Most To Me ....(MER)
Green Grow The Lilacs
Tex Ritter; *An American Legend* ....(CAP)
Best Of ....(CAP)
Best Of Town & Country-#3 ....(GUS)
Hillbilly Heaven ....(CAP)
Green Grow The Rushes, Ho
Chieftains; *Bonaparte's Retreat* ....(SHA)
"Green Hornet" Theme
Original Music; *Television's Greatest Hits-#2* .....(TVT)
Green Kentucky Eyes
Pal Rakes; *Midnight Rain* .... (AA)
Green Leaves Of Summer
Brothers Four; *Greatest Hits* ....(COL)
Greenfields & Other Gold .... (FIR)
Hollywood Magic-1960s ....(COL)
Green Light
Cliff Richard; *Green Light* .... (ROC)
Sonic Youth; *Evol* ....(SST)
Green Lights
Bonnie Raitt; *Green Light* .... (WB)
NRBQ; *At Yankee Stadium* .... (MER)
Peek-A-Boo-Best Of-1969-1989 .... (RHI)
Green Manalishi
Fleetwood Mac; *25 Years-The Chain* ....(WB)
Judas Priest; *Hell Bent For Leather* ....(COL)
Unleashed In The East ....(COL)
Green Onions
Booker T./M.G.s; *Best Of* .... (ATL)
Billboard Top R&B Hits-1962 .... (RHI)
Green Onions .... (ATL)
ST/American Graffiti ....(MCA)
ST/Quadrophenia ....(POL)
Green River
Alabama; *Mountain Music* ....(RCA)
Creedence Clearwater Revival; *1969* ....(FAN)
Chronicle ....(FAN)
Green River ....(FAN)
Live In Europe ....(FAN)
Royal Albert Hall Concert ....(FAN)
ST/1969 ....(POL)
Green Rocky Road
Dave Van Ronk; *In The Tradition* .... (PRS)
Tim Hardin; *Memorial Album* ....(POL)
Green Shirt
Elvis Costello; *Girls Girls Girls* ....(COL)
Elvis Costello/Attractions; *Armed Forces* ....(COL)
Green Tambourine
Lemon Pipers; *Best Of Ohio Express/Other
Bubblegum-#1* .... (RHI)
Best Of/Ohio Express-#1 .... (RHI)
Billboard Top Rock 'N' Roll Hits-1968 .... (RHI)
Bubble Gum Greatest Hits-#3 .... (ACC)
Fabulous Bubblegum Years .... (FFT)
Greenback Dollar
Kingston Trio; *Best Of The Best Of* .... (POE)
Capitol Collectors Series ....(CAP)
Very Best Of ....(CAP)
Greensleeves
Jeff Beck; *Truth* .... (EPI)
Olivia Newton-John; *Come On Over* ....(MCA)
Ray Conniff Singers; *Christmas* ....(COL)
Vienna Boys Choir; *Christmas Festival* ....(RCA)
Greenwood Creek
Doobie Brothers; *Doobie Brothers* ....(WB)
Green, Green
New Christy Minstrels; *Greatest Hits* ....(COL)
Grey To Green
Stephen Stills; *Right By You* .... (ATL)
His Green Eyes
Barbara Fairchild; *Standing In Your Line* ....(COL)

John Deere Green
Joe Diffie; *Thousand Winding...* .... (EPI)
Leaves That Are Green
Country Gentlemen; *Country Gentlemen* .... (VAN)
Simon & Garfunkel; *Collected Works* ....(COL)
Sounds Of Silence ....(COL)
Little Bit Of Green
Elvis Presley; *Back In Memphis* ....(RCA)
From Memphis To Vegas ....(RCA)
Little Green Apples
O.C. Smith; *Pop Classics/'60s* ....(COL)
Long Green
Kingsmen; *Best Of* .... (RHI)
Mountain Greenery
Ella Fitzgerald; *Rodgers & Hart Songbook* ......(VRV)
Tony Bennett; *Rodgers & Hart Songbook* .... (DRG)
Sings More Great Rodgers & Hart ....(IPV)
New Greenback Dollar
Roy Acuff; *Columbia Historic Edition* ....(COL)
Off To Dublin In The Green
Dubliners; *Best Of-Irish Favorites* ....(TRD)
On Green Dolphin Street
Anita O'Day; *Anita O'Day* ....(GLN)
Carmen McRae; *At The Great American Music
Hall* .... (BLN)
Miles Davis; *Basic Miles* ....(COL)
Red Garland; *Saying Something* .... (PRS)
On The Greener Side
Michelle Shocked; *Captain Swing* .... (MER)
Orange And The Green
Irish Rovers; *Greatest Hits* .... (MCA)
The Unicorn .... (MCA)
Northeast Winds; *Folk Era's Live Sampler* .... (FOL)
Irleand By Sail .... (FOL)
Orange, Brown & Green
Herb Ellis & Freddie Green; *Rhythm Willie* ...... (CCJ)
Paddy's Green Shamrock Shore
Chieftains; *Another Country* ....(RCA)
Pretty Green Island
George Tucker; *George Tucker* .... (ROU)
Redwood Evergreen
Lorraine Duisit; *Hawks & Herons* .... (FF)
Shades Of Green (Pt. II)
Mission U.K.; *Masque* .... (MER)
Six O'Clock Train & A Girl With Green...
John Hartford; *All In The Name Of Love* ....(FF)
Sure The Boy Was Green
Horslips; *Aliens* .... (DJM)
Theme From "Green Acres"
Eddie Albert & Eva Gabor; *ST/Son In Law* ......(HOL)
Velvet Green Whistler
Jethro Tull; *Songs From The Wood* .... (CHR)
Village Green
Kinks; *Are The Village Green Preservation...* ......(RPR)
Village Green Preservation Society
Kinks; *Kink Kronikles* .... (RPR)
Village Green Preservation Society ....(RPR)
When The Wind Was Green
Frank Sinatra; *September Of My Years* ....(RPR)

COLORS: GREY

Another Grey Morning
James Taylor; *JT* ....(COL)
As The Seasons Grey
Testament; *The Ritual* .... (ATL)
Blue Red & Grey
Who; *By Numbers* ....(MCA)
Blue Turning Grey Over You
Billie Holiday; *Billie's Blues* ....(BLN)
Louis Armstrong/Luis Russell & Orchestra; *Satchmo
Style* ....(DSQ)
Ringo Starr; *Sentimental Journey* ....(CAP)
Blue Turns To Grey
Rolling Stones; *December's Children* .... (AKO)
California Dreamin'
Beach Boys; *Made In The U.S.A.* ....(CAP)
Mamas & The Papas; *20 Golden Hits* ....(MCA)
At The Hop ....(MCA)
Good Feeling Music-Big Chill-#1 ....(MOT)
ST/Air America ....(MCA)
ST/American Pop ....(RLL)
ST/Forrest Gump ....(EPX)

Celebration For A Grey Day
Mimi & Richard Farina; *Best Of* .... (VAN)
  Celebration For A Grey Day .... (VAN)
  Memories .... (VAN)
Daddy's Gone Grey
Lonesome Strangers; *Lonesome Strangers* .... (HT)
Everything Turns Grey
Agent Orange; *Living In Darkness* .... (PBO)
  Real Live Sound .... (RES)
Gray Eagle
Taylor's Kentucky Boys; *Traditional Country Classics 1927-1929* .... (HIS)
Gray Haired Young Man
Don Potter; *Over The Rainbow* .... (MRR)
Grey Cloud Over New York
Philip Glass; *1000 Airplanes On The Roof* .... (VIA)
Grey Cloudy Lies
George Harrison; *Extra Texture* ....(OOP)
Grey Day
Madness; *Madness* .... (GEF)
Grey Ghost
Henry Paul Band; *Grey Ghost* .... (ATL)
Grey Goose/Sixpenny Money
Joe Burke; *Traditional Music Of Ireland* ....(GRE)
Grey Lagoons
Roxy Music; *For Your Pleasure...Second Album* .. (RPR)
Grey Matter
An Emotional Fish; *An Emotional Fish* .... (ATL)
Oingo Boingo; *Boingo Alive* .... (MCA)
  Nothing To Fear .... (A&M)
  Skeletons In The Closet-Best Of .... (A&M)
Grey October Clouds
Tommy Makem & Liam Clancy; *Two For The Early Dew* .... (SHA)
Grey Seal
Elton John; *Goodbye Yellow Brick Road* .... (POL)
Grey Talk
Francis X/Bushmen; *Scream-The Compilation* ... (GEF)
Grey To Green
Stephen Stills; *Right By You* .... (ATL)
Grey Victory
10,000 Maniacs; *Hope Chest-Fredonia Recordings 1982-1983* .... (ELE)
  Wishing Chair .... (ELE)
Greystoke
Soundtrack; *Greystoke-Legend Of Tarzan* .... (WB)
It's Gray
T.S.O.L.; *Change Today* .... (ENI)
Morse Moose & The Grey Goose
Wings; *London Town* ....(CAP)
New Grey Bonnet
Johnny Gimble; *Still Fiddlin' Around* .... (MSP)
Pearl Grey
Adam Makowicz; *The Name Is Makowicz* .... (SHF)
Put On Your Old Grey Bonnet
Jimmy Dean; *Greatest Hits* ....(COL)
Pete Fountain; *Best Of* .... (MCA)
  Mr. New Orleans .... (MCA)
Saddle Up The Grey
New Lost City Ramblers; *20 Years Of Concert Performances* .... (FF)
Shade Of Grey
Bob Weir; *Heaven Help The Fool* .... (ARI)
Shades Of Gray
Billy Barber; *Shades Of Gray* .... (DIG)
Monkees; *Greatest Hits* .... (ARI)
  Listen To The Bank .... (RHI)
Shades Of Grey
Al B. Sure!; *Private Times & The Whole 9* .... (WB)
Monkees; *10th Anniversary Tour-1986* .... (RHI)
  Greatest Hits .... (ARI)
Thoughts On A Grey Day
Fleetwood Mac; *Bare Trees* .... (RPR)
Touch Of Grey
Grateful Dead; *Heart Of Rock* ....(COL)
  In The Dark .... (ARI)

COLORS: ORANGE

See Also: FRUIT

Apples & Oranges
Pink Floyd; *Shine On* ....(COL)

Bright Orange Spot
Dharma Bums; *Welcome* ....(FRN)
Orange
10,000 Maniacs; *Hope Chest-Fredonia Recordings-1982-1983* .... (ELE)
Frank Sinatra; *Conducts Tone Poems Of Color* ...(CAP)
Miles Davis; *Aura* ....(COL)
Romeo Void; *Benefactor* ....(COL)
Orange And The Green
Irish Rovers; *Greatest Hits* .... (MCA)
  The Unicorn .... (MCA)
Northeast Winds; *Folk Era's Live Sampler* .... (FOL)
  Irleand By Sail .... (FOL)
Orange Blossom Lane
Glenn Miller/Orchestra; *Complete* .... (BLU)
  Complete-#7 ....(RCA)
Orange Blossom Mandolin
Northeast Winds; *In Concert* .... (FOL)
Orange Blossom Special
Bill Monroe; *Bean Blossom* .... (MCA)
  Stars Of The Grand Ole Opry 1926-1974 ......(RCA)
  & Bluegrass Boys-60 Years Of Country ......(RCA)
Charlie Daniels Band; *Fire On The Mountain* ..... (EPI)
  Urban Cowboy-#2 .... (EPI)
Flatt & Scruggs; *Hear The Whistles Blow* .... (GUS)
Gordon Terry; *20 Golden Souvenirs* .... (PLN)
  Disco Country .... (PLN)
Johnny Cash; *Columbia Records 1958-1986* .....(COL)
  Essential ....(COL)
  Greatest Hits ....(COL)
Nitty Gritty Dirt Band; *Will The Circle Be Unbroken* .... (EMI)
Orange Blossom Time
Bing Crosby; *Crooner-Columbia Years-1928-1934* ....(COL)
Orange City
Laszlo Gardony; *Legend Of Tsumi* .... (AND)
Orange Claw Hammer
Captain Beefheart/Magic Band; *Trout Mask Replica* .... (RPR)
Orange Colored Sky
Johnny Mathis; *Live* ....(COL)
Nat King Cole; *Story* ....(CAP)
  Unforgettable Nat King Cole ....(CAP)
Natalie Cole; *Unforgettable With Love* .... (ELE)
Orange Crush
R.E.M.; *Best Of MTV's 120 Minutes-#2* .... (RHI)
  Green ....(WB)
Orange Express
Miami Sound Machine; *Eyes Of Innocence* .... (EPI)
Orange Guitars
Jimmy Haslip; *Arc* ....(GRP)
Orange Juice Blues
Bob Dylan/Band; *Basement Tapes* ....(COL)
Orange King
Cafe Noir; *Window To The Sea* .... (CD)
Orange Lady
Weather Report; *Weather Report* ....(COL)
Orange Sherbert
Count Basie; *Basie Big Band* .... (PAB)
Orange Skies
Love; *Best Of* .... (RHI)
Orange Was The Color Of Her Dress
Charles Mingus; *Changes Two* .... (ATL)
  In Europe-#2 .... (ENJ)
Gil Evans; *Live At Sweet Basil-#1* ....(EVD)
  /Laurent Cugny Big Band-Golden Hair ....(EMA)
Orange, Brown & Green
Herb Ellis & Freddie Green; *Rhythm Willie* ...... (CCJ)
Why Is A Carrot More Orange Than An...
Amboy Dukes; *Journey To The Center Of The Mind* ....(MST)

COLORS: PINK

Cherry Pink And Apple Blossom White
Fabulous Thunderbirds; *Butt Rockin'* .... (CHR)
Perez Prado; *This Is-Decade Of The '50s* ....(RCA)
Freeway Of Love
Aretha Franklin; *Who's Zoomin' Who?* .... (ARI)
Hot Pink
Eddy Raven; *Right For The Flight* .... (LIB)
Meat Puppets; *Up On The Sun* .... (SST)

Pink And Black
Robert Plant; *Shaken 'N Stirred* .... (EPR)
Pink And Velvet
Berlin; *Count Three & Pray* .... (GEF)
Pink Bedroom
John Hiatt; *Y'All Caught? Ones That Got*
Away-1975-85 .... (GEF)
Rosanne Cash; *Rhythm & Romance* .... (COL)
Pink Cadillac
Bruce Springsteen; *45* .... (COL)
Natalie Cole; *Everlasting* .... (ELE)
Gotta Have House-Best Of House Music-#2 .... (PRO)
Southern Pacific; *Greatest Hits* .... (WB)
Killbilly Hill .... (WB)
Rockin' Country .... (WB)
Pink Cashmere
Prince; *Hits 1* .... (PAI)
Hits/B-Sides .... (PAI)
Pink Christmas
Leo Kottke; *Regards From Chuck Pink* .... (PRV)
Pink Cocktail For A Blue Lady
Glenn Miller/Orchestra; *Complete* .... (BLU)
Complete-#9 .... (RCA)
Pink Elephants
Eddie Lang Blue Five/Joe Venuti; *Jazz In The*
Thirties .... (DSQ)
Pink Elephants On Parade
Barbara Cook; *Disney Album* .... (MCA)
Pink Flamingos
Rickie Lee Jones; *Traffic From Paradise* .... (GEF)
Pink Houses
John Cougar Mellencamp; *Rock For Amnesty* ... (MER)
Uh-Huh .... (RIV)
Pink Pedal Pushers
Carl Perkins; *Best Of-Jive After 5-1958-1978* .... (RHI)
Restless-Collection Recordings .... (COL)
Jerry Lee Lewis; *Monsters* .... (SUN)
Pink Petticoats
Big Bopper; *Chantilly Lace/Big Bopper* .... (MER)
Helloo Baby! Best Of-1954-1959 .... (RHI)
Pink Pussycat
Devo; *Duty Now For The Future* .... (WB)
Rest Of-Greatest Misses .... (WB)
Pink Shoe Laces
Dodie Stevens; *Original '50s & '60s Classics-#18* (MCA)
Pink Thunderbird
Jeff Beck; *Crazy Legs* .... (EPI)
Pink Turns To Blue
Husker Du; *Zen Arcade* .... (SST)
Pinky
Elton John; *Caribou* .... (POL)
Pink-Eyed Pussycat
Bill Haley/Comets; *Rock Around The Country* ... (CRS)
Rockin' & Rollin' .... (ACC)
Pretty In Pink
Psychedelic Furs; *All Of This & Nothing* .... (COL)
ST/Pretty In Pink .... (A&M)
Talk Talk Talk .... (COL)
Pretty Little Pink
Doc Watson; *Old Timey Concert* .... (VAN)
Pretty Pink Rose
Adrian Belew; *Young Lions* .... (ATL)
Theme From "The Pink Panther"
Henry Mancini; *All-Time Greatest Hits-#1* .... (RCA)
Legendary Performer .... (RCA)
Pure Gold .... (RCA)
ST/Revenge Of The Pink Panther .... (EMI)
Television's Greatest Hits-#2 .... (TVT)
White Sport Coat & A Pink Carnation
Marty Robbins; *16 Most Requested Songs!/'50s-#2* (COL)
Greatest Hits .... (COL)
Lifetime Of Song-1951-1982 .... (COL)

COLORS: PURPLE

Approaching Lavender
Gordon Lightfoot; *If You Could Read My Mind* .. (RPR)
Deep Purple
Art Tatum; *Group Masterpieces-#2* .... (PAB)
Masterpieces .... (MCA)
Solo Masterpieces-#3 .... (PAB)
Johnny Mathis; *First 25 Years* .... (COL)

Nino Tempo & April Stevens; *Hit Singles*
1958-1977 .... (ATL)
Sarah Vaughan; *After Hours* .... (SSP)
Divine Sarah Vaughan-Columbia Years .... (COL)
Mood Indigo
Duke Ellington; *1954 Los Angeles Concert* ...... (CRS)
Black Brown & Beige .... (BLU)
Carnegie Hall Concert-Jan. 23 1943 .... (PRS)
Ellington Indigos .... (COL)
Sophisticated Ellington .... (RCA)
Ella Fitzgerald; *Ella A Nice* .... (PAB)
Sings-#2 .... (VRV)
Frank Sinatra; *In The Wee Small Hours* .... (CAP)
What Is This Thing Called Love .... (CAP)
Preservation Hall Jazz Band; *Best Of* .... (COL)
New Orleans-#4 .... (COL)
Pilots Of Purple Twilight
Tangerine Dream; *Exit* .... (ELE)
Purple Avenue
Holly Cole Trio; *Blame It On My Youth* .... (BLN)
Purple Haze
Cure; *Stone Free-Tribute To Jimi Hendrix* .... (RPR)
Jimi Hendrix Experience; *Are You Experienced* ... (RPR)
Essential .... (RPR)
Kiss The Sky .... (RPR)
Radio One .... (RYK)
Smash Hits .... (RPR)
ST/Jimi Hendrix .... (RPR)
Winger; *Winger* .... (ATL)
Purple Heart
David Allan Coe; *Invictus Means Unconquered* ..(COL)
T-Bone Burnett; *Talking Animals* .... (COL)
Purple Heather
Van Morrison; *Hard Nose The Highway* .... (WB)
Purple Mountain
Scott Cossu; *Wind Dance* .... (WH)
Windham Hill Retrospective .... (WH)
Purple People Eater
Sheb Wooley; *45s On CD-#1 (1956-1959)* ..... (MER)
Dr. Demento 20th Anniversary Collection ..... (RHI)
Halloween Hits .... (RHI)
Horror Rock Classics-#2 .... (RHI)
Super Hits-#4 .... (GUS)
Purple People Eater Meets The Witch Doc.
Big Bopper; *Helloo Baby! Best Of-1954-1959* .. (RHI)
Purple Rain
Prince/Revolution; *ST/Purple Rain* .... (WB)
Purple Rivers
Swimming Pool Q's; *Swimming Pool Q's* .... (A&M)
Purple Rose Of Cairo
New Orleans Ragtime Orchestra; *New Orleans*
Jazz .... (ARH)
Purple Shades
Troggs; *Archeology-1966-1976* .... (FON)
Purple Sky
Gillan; *Magic* .... (MET)
Purples
Chicago; *Toronto Rock & Roll Revival 1969-#1* . (ACC)
Silver Stars, Purple Sage, Eyes Of Blue
Roy Rogers/Sons Of The Pioneers; *Roy Rogers/Sons Of*
The Pioneers .... (VS)
Southern California Purples
Chicago; *At Carnegie Hall* .... (COL)
Chicago Transit Authority .... (COL)
Two Purple Shadows
Jerry Vale; *17 Most Requested Songs* .... (COL)
All-Time Greatest Hits .... (COL)
Violet
Seal; *Seal* .... (SIR)

COLORS: RED

99 Luftballons (99 Red Balloons)
Nena; *99 Luftballons* .... (EPI)
Blue Monday At Kansas City Red's
Cary Bell; *Blues Harp* .... (DEL)
Blue Red & Grey
Who; *By Numbers* .... (MCA)
Bongo Red
Gladiators; *Best Of Reggae Sunsplash* .... (GEN)
& Israel Vibration Live! .... (GEN)
Bottle Of Red Wine
Eric Clapton; *Eric Clapton* .... (RSO)

Cadillac Red
Judds; *Collection-1983-1990* ....(RCA)
  River Of Time ....(RCA)
  This Country's Rockin' ....(RCA)
Cherry Red
Big Joe Turner; *Atlantic Blues-Piano* ....(ATL)
  Boss Of The Blues ....(ATL)
Count Basie & Big Joe Turner; *Bosses* ....(PAB)
Ella Fitzgerald; *These Are The Blues* ....(VRV)
Esther Phillips; *Confessin' The Blues-Jazzlore-#41* (RHI)
Lime Spiders; *Beethoven's Fist* ....(CRL)
Little Richard; *Big Hits* ....(CRS)
Country Ham & Red Gravy
Hotmud Family; *Live As We Know It* ....(FF)
Crimson & Clover
Joan Jett/Blackhearts; *I Love Rock 'N' Roll* ....(BW)
Tommy James/Shondells; *Anthology* ....(RHI)
  Best Of ....(RLL)
  Billboard Top Rock 'N' Roll Hits-1969 ....(RHI)
  Jewels-#1 ....(SSS)
East Texas Red
Arlo Guthrie; *Tribute To Woody Guthrie And
Leadbelly* ....(COL)
Flowers Are Red
Harry Chapin; *Legends Of The Lost & Found* .... (ELE)
  Living Room Suite ....(ELE)
I Saw Red
Warrant; *Cherry Pie* ....(COL)
In The Court Of The Crimson King
King Crimson; *The Court Of The Crimson King* .. (ATL)
Indian Red
Wild Tchoupitoulas; *Wild Tchoupitoulas* .... (ISL)
I'm In Love With My Little Red Tricycle
Napoleon XIV; *They're Coming To Take Me
Away...Ha-Ha* .... (RHI)
Lady In Red
Charlie Daniels Band; *Windows* .... (EPI)
Chris DeBurgh; *Into The Light* .... (A&M)
Joan Jett/Blackhearts; *I Love Rock 'N' Roll* ....(BW)
Stan Getz; *Greatest Hits* .... (PRS)
Little Red Corvette
Prince; *1999* ....(WB)
Little Red Hen
Johnny Otis; *Original Johnny Otis Show* .... (SAV)
Little Red Lights
Todd Rundgren; *Something/Anything?* .... (RHI)
Little Red Rooster
Big Mama Thornton; *Jail* .... (VAN)
B.B. King/Muddy Waters/Big Mama Thornton; *Live At
Newport* .... (INT)
Rolling Stones; *Love You Live* ....(RS)
  Now! ....(AKO)
Sam Cooke; *Having A Party* ....(RCA)
  This Is ....(RCA)
Li'l Red Riding Hood
Sam The Sham/Pharaohs; *Best Of* ....(POL)
  Cruisin'-1966 ....(INC)
  Pharaohization-Best Of ....(RHI)
My Little Red Book
Love; *Best Of* ....(RHI)
  Elektrock- '60s ....(ELE)
  Nuggets-#2-Punk ....(RHI)
One Color Red
G.G.F.H.; *Eclipse/Reality* ....(DRT)
One Red Rose
John Prine; *Anthology-Great Days* .... (RHI)
  Storm Windows ....(ASY)
(Only Angels Wanna Wear My) Red Shoes
Elvis Costello; *Girls Girls Girls* ....(COL)
  My Aim Is True ....(COL)
Elvis Costell/Attractions; *Best Of* ....(COL)
Panama Red
New Riders Of The Purple Sage; *Adventures Of Panama
Red* ....(COL)
  Best Of ....(COL)
  Rock Classics Of The '70s ....(COL)
Poor Red Georgia Dirt
Robin & Linda Williams; *Close As We Can Get* ....(FF)
Red
Bette Midler; *Broken Blossom* ....(ATL)
Chris Rea; *espresso logic* ....(EW)
King Crimson; *Red* ....(EDI)
Sammy Hagar; *Live* ....(CAP)
  Sammy Hagar ....(CAP)

XTC; *Go 2* ....(GEF)
Red Alert
Quiet Riot; *Condition Critical* ....(PSH)
Red Garland; *Red Alert* ....(GAL)
Saxon; *Destiny* ....(ENI)
Red And Rio Grande
Doug Supernaw; *Red And Rio Grande* ....(BNA)
Red And The Black
Blue Oyster Cult; *Career Of Evil* ....(COL)
  Extraterrestrial Live ....(COL)
  On Your Feet Or On Your Knees ....(COL)
  Tyranny & Mutation ....(COL)
Red Army Blues
Waterboys; *Pagan Place* .... (CHR)
Red Bandana
Merle Haggard; *Greatest Hits* ....(MCA)
  More Of The Best ....(RHI)
  Serving 190 Proof ....(MCA)
Red Barchetta
Rush; *Chronicles* ....(MER)
  Exit...Stage Left ....(MER)
  Moving Pictures ....(MER)
Red Beans
Coleman Hawkins & Red Garland Trio; *Coleman
Hawkins & Red Garland Trio* .... (PRS)
Kingsnakes; *19 Lucky Strikes* ....(BWV)
Professor Longhair; *Crawfish Fiesta* ....(ALG)
Red Beans And Rice
Booker T./M.G.s; *Back To Back/Mar-Keys & Booker
T./M.G.s* ....(ATL)
  Best Of ....(ATL)
  Legends Of Rock Guitar-'60s-#1 ....(RHI)
Red Bird Tennessee Waltz
Clark Kessinger & Gene Meade; *Clark Kessinger & Gene
Meade* ....(ROU)
Red Cab To Manhattan
Stephen Bishop; *Best Of Bish* .... (RHI)
Red Cadillac
Colin Winski; *Rock Therapy* ....(TAK)
Red Chevrolet
Jimmie Dale Gilmore; *Jimmie Dale Gilmore* ...... (HT)
  Points West-New Horizons In Country .... (HT)
Red Eye
Devo; *Duty Now For The Future* ....(WB)
Joe Beck; *Beck & Sanborn* ....(CBA)
  Fire Into Music-#2 ....(CBA)
Nicky Thomas & Dolares; *Explosive Rock
Steady-Amalgamated Label* ....(HRT)
Red Headed Irishman
J.P. Fraley & Annadeene; *Wild Rose Of The
Mountain* .... (ROU)
Red Headed Stranger
Willie Nelson; *Red Headed Stranger* ....(COL)
Red Hot
Robert Gordon; *Rock This Town-Rockabilly
Hits-#2* .... (RHI)
Robert Gordon & Link Wray; *Robert Gordon & Link
Wray* ....(RCA)
Red Hot Chicken
Wet Willie; *Drippin' Wet Live* ....(CPC)
  Greatest Hits ....(POL)
Red Hot Poker
Rufus; *Rufus* ....(MCA)
Red House
David Byrne; *Catherine Wheel* ....(SIR)
Great White; *Recovery-Live!* ....(ENC)
Jimi Hendrix; *Concerts* ....(RPR)
  Kiss The Sky ....(RPR)
  Lifelines/Jimi Hendrix Story ....(RPR)
  Live At Winterland ....(RYK)
  Smash Hits ....(RPR)
  ST/Jimi Hendrix ....(RPR)
Red Light Mama Red Hot
Humble Pie; *Humble Pie* .... (A&M)
Red Money
David Bowie; *Lodger* ....(RYK)
Red Moon Over Boston
Romanovsky & Phillips; *Be Political Not Polite* ... (FRE)
Red Neck Friend
Jackson Browne; *For Everyman* .... (ASY)

Red Neckin' Love Makin' Night
Conway Twitty; *Classic Conway* .... (MCA)
  Legends .... (MCA)
  Mr. T .... (MCA)
  Night With .... (MCA)
Red Plains
Bruce Hornsby/Range; *The Way It Is* ....(RCA)
Red Rain
Peter Gabriel; *Greenpeace-Rainbow Warriors* ....(GEF)
  Secret World Live ....(GEF)
  Shaking The Tree-16 Golden Greats ....(GEF)
  So ....(GEF)
Red Red Rose
Dave Mallett; *Vital Signs* ....(FF)
Emmylou Harris; *Brand New Dance* ....(RPR)
Red Red Sun
INXS; *Listen Like Thieves* ....(ATL)
Red Red Wine
Neil Diamond; *Hot August Night* .... (MCA)
  Classics (Early Years) ....(COL)
  Double Gold ....(BNG)
  Greatest Hits ....(BNG)
Replacements; *Pleased To Meet Me* .... (SIR)
UB40; *Labour Of Love* .... (A&M)
Red River
Alabama; *Closer You Get* ....(RCA)
  Live ....(RCA)
BoDeans; *Home* ....(SLS)
Leadbelly; *Leadbelly* ....(COL)
  Midnight Special ....(ROU)
Red River Blues
Jesse Fuller; *Jesse Fuller's Favorites* .... (PRS)
Sonny Terry; *Sonny Terry* ....(EVR)
  With Brownie McGhee; Midnight Special ......(FAN)
Red River Rock
Johnny/Hurricanes; *Echoes Of A Rock Era-Middle
Years* .... (RLL)
  History Of Rock Instrumentals-#1 .... (RHI)
Red River Valley
Gene Autry; *Country Music Hall Of Fame* ......(COL)
  Cowboy Hall Of Fame .... (REP)
  Western Classics ....(COL)
Pete Seeger; *American Favorite Ballads-#5* ..... (FLW)
Red Rocking Chair
Jody Stecher & Kate Brislin; *Song That Will
Linger* .... (ROU)
Red Rooster
Howlin' Wolf; *Chess Box* .... (CSS)
Paula Lockheart; *It Ain't The End Of The World* ...(FF)
Red Rose
Alphaville; *Afternoons In Utopia* .... (ATL)
  Singles Collection .... (ATL)
Red Roses
Midnight Star; *Work It Out* .... (SLR)
Red Roses For A Blue Lady
Al Martino; *Best Of* .... (CAP)
  Capitol Collectors Series .... (CAP)
Andy Williams; *16 Most Requested Songs* ....(COL)
Mom & Dads; *Best Of* .... (CRS)
Roger Whittaker; *All-Time Heart-Touching
Favorites* .... (CAP)
  Classics Collection-#1 .... (CAP)
Vaughn Monroe; *Best Of* ....(RCA)
Red Roses (Won't Work Now)
Reba McEntire; *Have I Got A Deal For You* .... (MCA)
Red Rubber Ball
Cyrkle; *Even More Nuggets* .... (RHI)
  Pop Classics Of The '60s ....(COL)
  Red Rubber Ball (collection) ....(COL)
Red Sails
David Bowie; *Lodger* ....(RYK)
  Sound + Vision ....(RYK)
Red Sails In The Sunset
Big Joe Turner; *Nobody In Mind* .... (PAB)
Dinah Washington; *Echoes Of An Era* .... (RLL)
Jarmels; *Golden Classics* ....(CLT)
Nat King Cole; *Unforgettable* .... (CAP)
Platters; *Greatest Hits* ....(EVR)
Red Sector A
Rush; *Chronicles* .... (MER)
  Grace Under Pressure .... (MER)
  Show Of Hands .... (MER)
Red Sex Dress
Alfonia Tims/Flying Tigers; *Future Funk/Uncut!* . (ROI)

Red Sharks
Crimson Glory; *Transcendance* .... (MCA)
Red Shoes
Chris Rea; *Auberge* ....(ATC)
Tom Waits; *Big Time* .... (ISL)
Red Shoes By The Drugstore
Tom Waits; *Blue Valentine* ....(ASY)
Red Skies
Fixx; *One Thing Leads To Another-Greatest Hits* (MCA)
  React .... (MCA)
  Shuttered Room .... (MCA)
Red Skies Over Georgia
Charlie Walker; *45* .... (PLN)
Red Sky
Michael Schenker; *Built To Destroy* .... (CHR)
Status Quo; *Status Quo* .... (MER)
Red Streamliner
Little Feat; *Hoy-Hoy!* ....(WB)
  Time Loves A Hero ....(WB)
Red Telephone
Love; *Forever Changes* ....(ELE)
Red Tide
Rush; *Presto* ....(ATL)
Red Wine & Blue Memories
Joe Stampley; *Biggest Hits* ....(EPI)
Red & Black
Original Broadway Cast; *Les Miserables* ....(GEF)
Redneck Fiddlin' Man
Charlie Daniels Band; *Greatest Fiddlin' Licks* .....(EPI)
  Midnight Wind ....(EPI)
Redneck Girl
Bellamy Brothers; *Greatest Hits* .... (MCA)
Redneck In A Rock & Roll Bar
Jerry Reed; *Redneck Mothers* ....(RCA)
Redneck Is The Backbone Of America
John Schneider; *You Ain't Seen The Last Of Me* . (MCA)
Redneck Rock N' Roll
Pirates Of The Mississippi; *Pirates Of The
Mississippi* ....(CAP)
Redneck School Of Technology
Flaming Lips; *Telepathic Surgery* .... (RES)
Rednecks
Randy Newman; *Good Old Boys* .... (RPR)
Rednecks, White Socks & Blue Ribbon Beer
Johnny Russell; *Beer Redneck Mothers* ....(RCA)
  Rednecks, White Socks & Blue Ribbon Beer .....(RCA)
Redwood Evergreen
Lorraine Duisit; *Hawks & Herons* ....(FF)
Redwood Tree
Van Morrison; *St. Dominic's Preview* ....(WB)
Rev On The Red Line
Foreigner; *Head Games* ....(ATL)
Rhode Island Red
Brew Moore; *Brew Moore* ....(FAN)
Rhythm From A Red Car
Hardline; *Double Eclipse* .... (MCA)
River Runs Red
Midnight Oil; *Blue Sky Mining* ....(COL)
Rose Colored Glasses
John Conlee; *Backstage At The Grand Ole Opry* .(RCA)
  Greatest Hits .... (MCA)
  Legends .... (MCA)
  MCA 30 Years Of Hits-1958-1988 .... (MCA)
  Rose Colored Glasses .... (MCA)
Roses Ain't Red
Diane Pfeifer; *Diane Pfeifer* .... (CAP)
Roses Are Red
Bobby Vinton; *16 Most Requested* ....(EPI)
  All-Time Greatest Hits ....(EPI)
  Spring Sensations ....(EPI)
Ruby Red
Kingston Trio; *Hidden Treasures* .... (FOL)
  Treasure Chest .... (FOL)
Run, Red Run
Coasters; *45* ....(ATL)
Sad Old Red
Simply Red; *Picture Book* ....(ELE)
Scarlet Begonias
Grateful Dead; *From The Mars Hotel* .... (GRD)
Scarlet Fever
Kenny Rogers; *We've Got Tonight* .... (EMI)

Scarlet Ribbons
Harry Belafonte; *All-Time Greatest Hits-#1* ......(RCA)
 Legendary Performer ....(RCA)
 This Is ....(RCA)
Kingston Trio; *At Large/Here We Go Again!* .....(CAP)
 Capitol Collectors Series ....(CAP)
Lennon Sisters; *Best Of* .... (RAN)
Les Paul; *Legend & The Legacy-#1-4* ....(CAP)
NRBQ; *Diggin' Uncle Q* ....(ROU)
Patti Page; *16 Most Requested Songs* ....(COL)
Roger Whittaker; *Classics Collections-#2* ....(LIB)
Scarlet Water
Johnny Duncan; *Best Of* ....(COL)
 Greatest Hits ....(COL)
Snoopy Vs. The Red Baron
Royal Guardsmen; *Best Of-#1* .... (RHI)
 Collectables Presents History Of Rock-#9 ....(CLT)
 Cruisin'-1967 .... (INC)
 Million-Dollar Memories #1 ....(RCA)
 Super Oldies!'60s-#6 ....(AUF)
Something In Red
Lorrie Morgan; *Something In Red* ....(RCA)
Sweet Rhode Island Red
Ike & Tina Turner; *Proud Mary-Best Of* .... (EMI)
Take A Red
New Riders Of The Purple Sage; *Alive & Kicking* (MSP)
 Marin County Line ....(MCA)
Texas Red
Strength In Numbers; *Telluride Sessions* .... (MCA)
They're Red Hot
Red Hot Chili Peppers; *Blood Sugar Sex Magik* ...(WB)
Robert Johnson; *Complete Recordings* ....(COL)
Thin Red Line
Cretones; *Cretones* .... (PNT)
Under The Red Sky
Bob Dylan; *Under The Red Sky* ....(COL)
When The Red, Red Robin
Al Jolson; *Best Of* ....(MCA)
 Story-#3 .... (MCA)
Louis Armstrong; *I Like Jazz-Essence Of* ....(COL)
Mitch Miller; *16 Most Requested Songs* ....(COL)
White Heat, Red Hot
Judas Priest; *Stained Class* ....(COL)
Yes It Is
Beatles; *Box Set* ....(CAP)
 Love Songs ....(CAP)
 Past Masters-#1 ....(CAP)
 VI .... (CAP)

COLORS: WHITE

Big White Cloud
John Cale; *Vintage Violence* ....(COL)
Black And White Television
Ian Anderson; *Walk Into Light* .... (CHR)
Black Boys, White Boys
Original Broadway Cast; *Hair* ....(RCA)
Black Or White
Michael Jackson; *Dangerous* .... (EPI)
Black & White
INXS; *Dekadance* ....(ATC)
 Shabooh Shoobah ....(ATC)
Jackson Browne; *Lives In The Balance* ....(ASY)
Rosanne Cash; *Hits 1979-1989* ....(COL)
Three Dog Night; *Best Of* .... (MCA)
 Billboard Top Rock 'N' Roll Hits-1972 .... (RHI)
 Joy To The World-Greatest Hits ....(MCA)
Todd Rundgren; *Anthology 1968-1985* .... (RHI)
 Back To The Bars .... (RHI)
 Faithful .... (RHI)
Blanca Navidad (White Christmas)
Freddy Fender; *Tejano Country Christmas* ....(ART)
Cherry Pink And Apple Blossom White
Fabulous Thunderbirds; *Butt Rockin'* .... (CHR)
Perez Prado; *This Is-Decade Of The '50s* ....(RCA)
China White
Little Feat; *Hoy-Hoy!* ....(WB)
Scorpions; *Blackout* ....(MER)
Dirty White Boy
Foreigner; *Head Games* ....(ATL)
 Records ....(ATL)
Ebony & Ivory
Paul McCartney; *Tripping The Live Fantastic* ....(CAP)

Paul McCartney & Stevie Wonder; *All The Best* .(CAP)
 Tug Of War ....(CAP)
Great White Buffalo
Ted Nugent; *Double Live Gonzo* .... (EPI)
Great White Hope
Styx; *Pieces Of Eight* .... (A&M)
Great White Horse
Guy & Ralna; *22 Golden Country Classics* ...... (RAN)
 Country .... (RAN)
Great White Line
Point Blank; *On A Roll* .... (MCA)
Little White Cloud That Cried
Johnnie Ray; *Best Of* ....(COL)
 Greatest Hits ....(SSP)
Johnny Ray; *Best Of* ....(EXA)
Little White Lies
Romantics; *Romantics* .... (NEM)
Tommy Dorsey; *Best Of* ....(RCA)
 Complete-#6-1937-1938 ....(RCA)
Long White Cadillac
Blasters; *Collection* ....(SLS)
Dave Alvin; *Romeo's Escape* .... (EPI)
Dwight Yoakam; *Just Lookin' For A Hit* ....(RPR)
Long White Car
Hipsway; *Hipsway* ....(COL)
My TV Went Black & White On Me
Young Black Teenagers; *Young Black Teenagers* . (SOL)
My White Bicycle
Nazareth; *Classics-#16* .... (A&M)
 Hot Tracks .... (A&M)
My White Devil
Echo/Bunnymen; *Porcupine* .... (SIR)
My White Knight
Original Broadway Cast; *Music Man* .... (ANG)
Original Cast; *Music Man* ....(CAP)
Nights In White Satin
Moody Blues; *Billboard Top Rock 'N' Roll
 Hits-1972* .... (RHI)
 Caught Live Plus Five ....(POL)
 Days Of Future Passed ....(POL)
 History Of British Rock-#8 .... (RHI)
 This Is The .... (POL)
Poor White Hound Dog
Merry Clayton; *ST/Performance* ....(WB)
Po' White Trash
White Trash; *White Trash* .... (ELE)
Rednecks, White Socks & Blue Ribbon Beer
Johnny Russell; *Beer Redneck Mothers* ....(RCA)
 Rednecks, White Socks & Blue Ribbon Beer .....(RCA)
Sail On White Moon
Boz Scaggs; *Slow Dancer* ....(COL)
Some Folks Is Even Whiter Than Me
Todd Rundgren; *Something/Anything?* .... (RHI)
There'll Be Bluebirds Over The White...
Kay Kyser; *Best Of The Big Bands* ....(COL)
Top Hat, White Tie & Tails
Fred Astaire; *Irving Berlin Songbook* ....(VRV)
Louis Armstrong; *Irving Berlin Songbook* ....(VRV)
Trapped In The Body Of A White Girl
Julie Brown; *Trapped In The Body Of A White Girl* (SIR)
Two White Horses
John Lee Hooker; *That's Where It's At* .... (STX)
When The White Lilacs Bloom Again
Billy Vaughn; *Best Of* .... (MCA)
 Greatest Hits ....(CCB)
White Bird
It's A Beautiful Day; *Bill Graham Presents-Fillmore-Last
 Days* ....(EPA)
 It's A Beautiful Day ....(COL)
White Boys
Original Cast; *ST/Hair* ....(RCA)
White Car In Germany
Associates; *Popera-Singles Collection* .... (SIR)
White Cliffs Of Dover
Kay Kyser/Orchestra; *16 Most Requested
 Songs!'40s-#1* ....(COL)
Lee Andrews/Hearts; *Biggest Hits* ....(CLT)
Mystics; *16 Golden Classics* ....(CLT)
Righteous Brothers; *Anthology-1962-1974* .... (RHI)
 Greatest Hits ....(VRV)
Rosemary Clooney; *For The Duration* ....(CCJ)
White Dove
Lynyrd Skynyrd; *First & Last* .... (MCA)

White Fishes
John Renbourn; *Sir Jon Alot Of Merrie Englanders* (RPR)
White Freightliner Blues
Jimmie Dale Gilmore; *Fair & Square* .... (HT)
New Grass Revival; *When The Storm Is Over* ...... (FF)
Townes Van Zandt; *Live & Obscure* .... (SH)
White Heat, Red Hot
Judas Priest; *Stained Class* .... (COL)
White Honey
Graham Parker/Rumour; *Howlin' Wind* .... (MER)
White Horse
Laid Back; *Castles In The Sand* .... (SIR)
  For The Record .... (SIR)
  Greatest Hits Of The Street .... (PRY)
  Keep Smiling .... (SIR)
White Horses
Outlaws; *Ghost Riders* .... (ARI)
White Hot
Black Flag; *In My Head* .... (SST)
Red Rider; *Don't Fight It* .... (CAP)
White House Blues
Doc Watson; *Essential* .... (VAN)
Doc Watson & Family; *Treasures Untold* .... (VAN)
Stanley Brothers; *Shadows Of The Past* .... (COP)
White Houses
Eric Burdon/Animals; *Greatest Hits* .... (MGM)
White Knuckles
Elvis Costello/Attractions; *Trust* .... (RYK)
White Lies
Grin; *Rock Artifacts-#1-From The Vaults* .... (COL)
Nils Lofgren; *Grin* .... (EPA)
White Light
Gene Clark; *White Light* .... (A&M)
White Lightning
Angel; *Live Without A Net* .... (CAS)
  On Earth As It Is In Heaven .... (CAS)
Babys; *Head First* .... (CHR)
Big Bopper; *Helloo Baby!-Best Of* .... (RHI)
Def Leppard; *Adrenalize* .... (MER)
Furry Lewis; *Back On My Feet Again* .... (PRS)
  Shake 'Em Down On .... (FAN)
George Jones; *All-Time Greatest Hits-#1* .... (EPI)
  Best Of-1955-1967 .... (RHI)
  Billboard Top Country Hits-1959 .... (RHI)
Hank Williams, Jr.; *Whiskey Bent & Hell Bound* .. (W/C)
White Lightning & Wine
Heart; *Dreamboat Annie* .... (CAP)
White Light/White Heat
David Bowie; *Sound + Vision* .... (RYK)
  ST/Ziggy Stardust-The Motion Picture .... (RCA)
Lou Reed; *1969 Live* .... (MER)
  Live-#1 .... (JCI)
  Rock 'N' Roll Animal .... (RCA)
  Walk On The Wild Side-Best Of .... (RCA)
Velvet Underground; *White Light/White Heat* ..... (VRV)
White Line
Emmylou Harris; *Ballad Of Sally Rose* .... (WB)
Neil Young/Crazy Horse; *Ragged Glory* .... (RPR)
White Line Fever
Flying Burrito Brothers; *Close Encounters To The West
Coast* .... (RLX)
Merle Haggard; *More Of The Best* .... (RHI)
Merle Haggard/Strangers; *Okie From Muskogee* .. (CAP)
White Man
Queen; *Day At The Races* .... (HOL)
White Man In Hammersmith Palais
Clash; *Clash* .... (EPI)
  On Broadway .... (EPI)
  Story Of-#1 .... (EPI)
White Man/Black Man
James Gang; *Thirds* .... (OW)
James Gary; *16 Greatest Hits* .... (MCA)
White Minority
Black Flag; *First Four Years* .... (SST)
  ST/Decline Of Western Civilization .... (SLS)
White Mountain
Genesis; *Trespass* .... (MCA)
White Nigger
Big Boys; *The Fat Elvis* .... (T&G)
White Noise
Jay Ferguson; *White Noise* .... (CAP)
White Palace
Clay Walker; *Clay Walker* .... (GIA)

White Punks On Dope
Tubes; *Tubes* .... (A&M)
  T.R.A.S.H.-Tubes Rarities & Smash Hits .... (A&M)
  What Do You Want From-Live .... (A&M)
White Queen
Queen; *#2* .... (HOL)
White Rabbit
Damned; *Best Of* .... (ROA)
  Machine Gun Etiquette .... (ROA)
George Benson; *Collection* .... (WB)
  White Rabbit .... (CBA)
Jefferson Airplane; *2400 Fulton Street-An
Anthology* .... (RCA)
  Flight Log 1966-1976 .... (GRU)
  Loves You .... (RCA)
  ST/Platoon-& Songs From The Era .... (ATL)
  Surrealistic Pillow .... (RCA)
  Worst Of .... (RCA)
White Rhythm & Blues
J.D. Souther; *You're Only Lonely* .... (COL)
Linda Ronstadt; *Living In The U.S.A.* .... (ASY)
White Riot
Clash; *Clash* .... (EPI)
  On Broadway .... (EPI)
  Story Of-#1 .... (EPI)
White Room
Cream; *History Of British Rock-#9* .... (RHI)
  Live-#2 .... (POL)
  Strange Brew-Very Best Of .... (POL)
  Wheels Of Fire .... (POL)
Eric Clapton; *24 Nights* .... (RPR)
  Crossroads .... (POL)
White Russia
Dirt Band; *Dirt Band* .... (UA)
White Shadow
Peter Gabriel; *Peter Gabriel* .... (ATL)
White Ship
H.P. Lovecraft; *H.P. Lovecraft* .... (OOP)
White Silver Sands
Ace Cannon; *Golden Classics* .... (GUS)
Ray Anthony; *Great Golden Hits* .... (RAN)
Sonny James; *45* .... (COL)
White Sport Coat & A Pink Carnation
Marty Robbins; *16 Most Requested Songs/'50s-#2* (COL)
  Greatest Hits .... (COL)
  Lifetime Of Song-1951-1982 .... (COL)
White Sugar
Frampton's Camel; *Frampton's Camel* .... (A&M)
White Sun
Doobie Brothers; *Toulouse Street* .... (WB)
White Tornado
R.E.M.; *Dead Letter Office* .... (IRS)
White Trash
Bad Religion; *How Could Hell Be Any Worse* .... (EPT)
Bellamy Brothers; *Crazy From The Heart* .... (MCA)
Orchestral Manoeuvres In The Dark; *Junk
Culture* .... (A&M)
Red Kross; *Born Innocent* .... (FRN)
Steve Cash; *White Mansions* .... (A&M)
White Trash Song
Steve Young; *Honky-Tonk Man* .... (ROU)
  Solo/Live .... (WAT)
White Trash Wife
Exene Cervenka; *Old Wives' Tales* .... (RHI)
White Trash With Cash
Southgang; *Group Therapy* .... (CHS)
White Wall
Bob Seger System; *Ramblin' Gamblin' Man* ...... (CAP)
White Wedding
Billy Idol; *Billy Idol* .... (CHR)
  Vital Idol .... (CHR)
Whitelines (Don't Don't Do It)
Grandmaster Flash/Melle Mel/Furious Five; *Message
From Beat Street-Best Of* .... (RHI)
Whiter Shade Of Pale
Procol Harum; *Best Of* .... (A&M)
  Classics-#17 .... (A&M)
  History Of British Rock-#8 .... (RHI)
  ST/Big Chill .... (MOT)
Winterwhite
Nitty Gritty Dirt Band; *Dream* .... (UA)

COLORS: YELLOW

A Tisket, A Tasket
Ella Fitzgerald; *Best Of* .... (MCA)
  Ella Fitzgerald .... (LAS)
Glenn Miller/Army Air Force Band; *Glenn Miller/Army*
  Air Force Band .... (LAS)
Tommy Dorsey; *Complete-#7* .... (RCA)
Big Yellow Taxi
Amy Grant; *House Of Love* .... (A&M)
Joni Mitchell; *Ladies Of The Canyon* .... (RPR)
  Miles Of Aisles .... (ASY)
Don't Eat The Yellow Snow
Frank Zappa; *Apostrophe/Overnite Sensation* .... (RYK)
Goodbye Yellow Brick Road
Elton John; *Billboard Top Rock 'N' Roll Hits-1973* (RHI)
  Goodbye Yellow Brick Road .... (POL)
  Greatest Hits .... (POL)
Itsy Bitsy Teenie Weenie Yellow Polka...
Brian Hyland; *Dr. Demento's Greatest-#3* .... (RHI)
  Greatest Hits .... (RHI)
  Vintage Music-Classics-'50s/'60s-#5 .... (MCA)
Mellow Yellow
Donovan; *Greatest Hits* .... (EPI)
  Seems Like Yesterday-#5-Mid '60s .... (KT)
Moon Was Yellow
Frank Sinatra; *Greatest Hits-#2* .... (COL)
  Moonlight Sinatra .... (RPR)
Mother's Little Helper
Rolling Stones; *Flowers* .... (AKO)
  Hot Rocks-1964-1971 .... (AKO)
  Through The Past Darkly-Big Hits-#2 .... (AKO)
Tesla; *Five Man Acoustical Jam* .... (GEF)
My Canary Is Yellow
Chesterfield Kings; *Stop* .... (MRR)
My Old Yellow Car
Dan Seals; *Best Of* .... (CAP)
  Classics Collection-#1 .... (CAP)
  Early Dan Seals .... (CAP)
  San Antone .... (EMI)
Lacy J. Dalton; *Blue Eyed Blues* .... (COL)
  Dream Baby .... (COL)
Tie A Yellow Ribbon 'Round The Old...
Frank Sinatra; *Some Nice Things I've Missed* ..... (RPR)
Lawrence Welk; *Best Of-20 Great Hits* .... (RAN)
Sonny James & Karla Taylor; *Classic Country*
  Duets .... (CCB)
Tony Orlando/Dawn; *45* .... (FSB)
Yellow Beach Umbrella
Bette Midler; *Broken Blossom* .... (ATL)
Yellow Bird
Brothers Four; *Greatest Hits* .... (COL)
Lawrence Welk; *Best Of-20 Great Hits* .... (RAN)
Mills Brothers; *16 Great Performances* .... (MCA)
  22 Great Hits .... (RAN)
  Cab Driver .... (RAN)
Roger Whittaker; *Greatest Hits* .... (RCA)
Yellow Cat
John Denver; *Rhymes & Reasons* .... (RCA)
Yellow Days
Frank Sinatra & Duke Ellington; *Francis A. Sinatra &*
  Edward K. Ellington .... (RPR)
Yellow Dog Blues
Bessie Smith; *Complete Recordings-#2* .... (COL)
Eddie Condon; *Best Of* .... (MCA)
Yellow Gal
Leadbelly; *Leadbelly* .... (FAN)
  Legend Of .... (TRD)
  Memorial-#2 .... (STO)
  Take This Hammer .... (FLW)
Yellow Magic
Yellow Magic Orchestra; *Yellow Magic*
  Orchestra .... (A&M)
Yellow Man
Randy Newman; *12 Songs* .... (RPR)
  Randy Newman .... (RPR)
Yellow Raven
Scorpions; *Best Of The Ballads Hot & Slow* ..... (RCA)
  Virgin Killer .... (RCA)
Yellow River
Christie; *Rock Artifacts-#1-From The Vaults* ....(COL)
  Super Hits/'70s-Have A Nice Day-#4 .... (RHI)

Compton Brothers; *45* .... (MCA)
Yellow Rose
Johnny Lee & Lane Brody; *You & I-Classic Country*
  Duets .... (WB)
  'Til The Bars Burns Down .... (FW)
Yellow Rose Of Texas
Hoyt Axton; *Songs Of The Civil War* ....(COL)
Michael Martin Murphey; *Cowboy Songs* .... (WB)
Mitch Miller; *16 Most Requested Songs* ....(COL)
Roy Rogers; *Great American Singing Cowboys* ... (REP)
Yellow Roses
Dolly Parton; *Greatest Country Hits/'80s-1989* ...(COL)
  White Limozeen .... (COL)
Ry Cooder; *Chicken Skin Music* .... (RPR)
Yellow Roses On Her Gown
Johnny Mathis; *I Only Have Eyes For You* ....(COL)
Yellow Star
Donovan; *Essence To Essence* .... (EPI)
Yellow Submarine
Beatles; *1962-1966* .... (CAP)
  Box Set .... (CAP)
  Reel Music .... (CAP)
  Revolver .... (CAP)
  Yellow Submarine .... (CAP)
Yellow Woman's Door Bells
Leadbelly; *Leadbelly* .... (EVR)
  Leadbelly .... (FAN)

COMMUNICATION: CONVERSATION, Voices

Computer Voice
Robert Schroeder; *Computer Voice* .... (RAC)
Conversation
Hank Williams, Jr.; *Live* ....(W/C)
  Whiskey Bent & Hell Bound ....(W/C)
Joan Armatrading; *Whatever's For Us* .... (A&M)
Joni Mitchell; *Ladies Of The Canyon* .... (RPR)
Waylon Jennings; *Greatest Hits-#2* ....(RCA)
  Waylon/Company ....(RCA)
  You & I-Classic Country Duets .... (WB)
Conversations
Journey; *Journey* ....(COL)
Saga; *Worlds Apart* .... (POR)
Language Of Love
Dan Fogelberg; *Windows & Walls* .... (FM)
Heart; *Passionworks* .... (EPI)
Intrigues; *Golden Classics* .... (CLT)
Orleans; *Grown-Up Children* .... (MCA)
Steve Wariner; *I Got Dreams* .... (MCA)
New York Telephone Conversation
Lou Reed; *Transformer* ....(RCA)
  Walk On The Wild Side-Best Of ....(RCA)
Sound Of Your Voice
38 Special; *Bone Against Steel* .... (CHS)
Voice Of America
Asia; *Astra* .... (GEF)
  Then & Now .... (GEF)
Little Steven; *Voice Of America* .... (R&T)
Voice Of America's Son
John Cafferty/Beaver Brown Band; *ST/Cobra* .... (SCO)
  Tough All Over .... (SCO)
Voice Of Harold
R.E.M.; *Dead Letter Office* .... (IRS)
Voice Of The Eagle
Robbie Basho; *Voice Of The Eagle* .... (VAN)
Voice On Tape
Laurie Anderson; *United States Live* .... (WB)
Voice On The Radio
Andre Cymone; *Livin' In The New Wave* ....(COL)
Sheena Easton; *Sheena Easton* .... (EMI)
Voices
Cheap Trick; *Dream Police* .... (EPI)
  Greatest Hits .... (EPI)
Russ Ballard; *Russ Ballard* .... (EMI)
Voices Carry
'Til Tuesday; *Voices Carry* .... (EPI)
Voices In My Head
Naked Eyes; *Best Of* .... (EMI)
Voices In The Rain
Joe Sample; *Voices In The Rain* .... (MCA)
Voices In The Sky
Moody Blues; *In Search Of The Lost Chord* ...... (POL)

Voices In The Wind
Little Feat; *Let It Roll* .... (WB)
Voices Inside My Head
Police; *Zenyatta Mondatta* .... (A&M)
Voices Of Babylon
Outfield; *Voices Of Babylon* .... (COL)
Voices Of Freedom
J. Browne/P. Gabriel/Y. N'Dour/L. Reed; *Secret
Policeman's Third Ball-The Music* .... (VIA)
Lou Reed; *Between Thought &
Expression-Anthology* .... (RCA)
Voices Of Old People
Simon & Garfunkel; *Bookends* .... (COL)
Collected Works .... (COL)
Voices That Care
Voices That Care; *Voices That Care* .... (GIA)
Voice, The
Alan Parsons Project; *I Robot* .... (ARI)
Moody Blues; *Long Distance Voyager* .... (POL)
Ultravox; *Collection* .... (CHR)
Rage In Eden .... (CHR)
Vox Humana
Kenny Loggins; *Vox Humana* .... (COL)

COMMUNICATION: GENERAL

See Also: Other Communication Categories

Language Of The Kiss
Indigo Girls; *Swamp Ophelia* .... (EPI)
Misunderstanding
Genesis; *Duke* .... (ATL)
Three Sides Live .... (ATL)
James "D Train" Williams; *45* .... (COL)
Misunderstood
Motley Crue; *Motley Crue* .... (ELE)
Sign, The
Ace Of Base; *The Sign* .... (ARI)
Understanding
Xscape; *Hummin' Comin' At 'Cha* .... (COL)

COMMUNICATION: SAY

All The Things She Said
Simple Minds; *Once Upon A Time* .... (A&M)
As You Said
Cream; *Wheels Of Fire* .... (RSO)
Betcha Say That
Gloria Estefan/Miami Sound Machine; *Let It
Loose* .... (EPI)
Can'tcha Say (You Believe In Me)
Boston; *Third Stage* .... (MCA)
Do I Have To Come Right Out & Say It
Buffalo Springfield; *Buffalo Springfield* .... (ATC)
Do I Have To Say The Words?
Bryan Adams; *Waking Up The Neighbours* ...... (A&M)
Don't Say Goodnight
Valentines; *Original Rock 'N' Roll Hits Of The
'50s* .... (RLL)
Don't Say No Tonight
Eugene Wilde; *45* .... (PHL)
Don't Say Nothing Bad About My Baby
Cookies; *Golden Girl Groups* .... (KT)
Original Rock 'N' Roll Hits Of The '60s .... (RLL)
Don't Say Things You Don't Mean
Lynn Anderson; *Greatest Hits* .... (COL)
Don't Say You Love Me
Billy Squier; *Hear & Now* .... (CAP)
Crickets; *Liberty Years* .... (EMI)
Freddie Jackson; *Do Me Again* .... (CAP)
Easier Said Than Done
Essex; *Billboard Top Rock 'N' Roll Hits-1963* .... (RHI)
Original Rock 'N' Roll Hits Of The '60s .... (RLL)
Radney Foster; *Del Rio TX 1959* .... (ARI)
Easy For You To Say
Emmylou Harris; *Brand NEW Dance* .... (RPR)
Linda Ronstadt; *Get Closer* .... (ASY)
Goodbye Says It All
BlackHawk; *BlackHawk* .... (ARI)
Goodnight Tonight (Don't Say It)
Paul McCartney/Wings; *All The Best* .... (CAP)

Hard To Say
Dan Fogelberg; *Greatest Hits* .... (FM)
Innocent Age .... (FM)
Sawyer Brown; *Outskirts Of Town* .... (CRB)
Hard To Say Goodbye, My Love
Original Cast; *Dreamgirls* .... (GEF)
Hard To Say I'm Sorry
Chicago; *16* .... (FM)
Hear Say
Soul Children; *15 Original Big Hits-#3* .... (STX)
Chronicle .... (STX)
Hello Goodbye
Beatles; *1967-1970* .... (CAP)
20 Greatest Hits .... (CAP)
Box Set .... (CAP)
Magical Mystery Tour .... (CAP)
Hope You Love Me Like You Say You Do
Huey Lewis/News; *Picture This* .... (CHR)
How Can I Help You Say Goodbye
Patty Loveless; *Only What I Feel* .... (EPI)
How Do You Say Auf Wiedersehen
George Shearing & Mel Torme; *Top Drawer* .... (CCJ)
I Am...I Said
Neil Diamond; *12 Greatest Hits* .... (MCA)
Hot August Night .... (MCA)
Hot August Night II .... (MCA)
Stones .... (MCA)
I Cain't Say No
Original Broadway Cast; *Oklahoma* ....(RCA)
Original Cast; *Oklahoma* .... (MCA)
I Can't Say It On The Radio
Girls Next Door; *Girls Next Door* .... (MTM)
Susie Allanson; *45* .... (ENI)
I Can't Say No
Natalie Cole; *Collection* .... (CAP)
Inseparable .... (CAP)
Reaching For The Sky-Towering Soul/'70s ...... (CAP)
I Just Called To Say I Love You
Aretha Franklin; *Best Of* .... (ATL)
Gold .... (ATL)
Greatest Hits .... (ATL)
Stevie Wonder; *ST/Lady In Red* .... (MOT)
I Meant Every Word He Said
Ricky Van Shelton; *Greatest Country Hits/'90s-#2* (COL)
RVS III .... (COL)
I Only Want To Say (Gethsemane)
Original London Cast; *Jesus Christ Superstar* .... (MCA)
Soundtrack; *Jesus Christ Superstar* .... (MCA)
I Say A Little Prayer
Aretha Franklin; *Best Of* .... (ATL)
Gold .... (ATL)
Greatest Hits .... (ATL)
Burt Bacharach; *Classics-#23* .... (A&M)
Greatest Hits .... (A&M)
Reach Out .... (A&M)
Dionne Warwick; *Anthology* .... (RHI)
Dionne Warwick .... (EVR)
Greatest Hits .... (EVR)
Original Rock 'N' Roll Hits Of The '60s .... (RLL)
I Wanna Say Yes
Louise Mandrell; *Maybe My Baby* ....(RCA)
If I Say Yes
Five Star; *Silk & Steel* ....(RCA)
It's Hard To Say Goodbye To Yesterday
Boyz II Men; *Cooleyhighharmony* .... (MOT)
It's Not For Me To Say
Johnny Mathis; *16 Most Requested Songs* ....(COL)
All-Time Greatest Hits .... (COL)
First 25 Years .... (COL)
Greatest Hits .... (COL)
I'd Still Say Yes
Klymaxx; *Klymaxx* .... (CON)
I'll Never Say No
Harve Presnell; *Unsinkable Molly Brown* .... (MCA)
Jackie Wilson Said (I'm In Heaven...)
Van Morrison; *Best Of* .... (MER)
St. Dominic's Preview .... (WB)
ST/Queen's Logic .... (EPI)

Maggie May
Rod Stewart; *Absolutely Live* .... (WB)
  Best Of .... (MER)
  Billboard Top Rock 'N' Roll Hits-1971 .... (RHI)
  Every Picture Tells A Story .... (MER)
  Greatest Hits .... (WB)
  Sing It Again Rod .... (MER)
  Storyteller/Complete Anthology-1964-1990 ...... (WB)
Mama Said
Shirelles; *Anthology-1959-1964* .... (RHI)
  Classics .... (BCT)
  Greatest Hits .... (EVR)
  Original Rock 'N' Roll Hits Of The '60s .... (RLL)
  Super Oldies/'60s-#3 .... (AUF)
Mama Say
Heptones; *Night Food* .... (ISL)
Mama Used To Say
Junior; *Jr.* .... (MER)
  Sophisticated Street .... (LON)
Man Of My Word
Collin Raye; *Extremes* .... (EPI)
Martha Say
John Cougar Mellencamp; *Big Daddy* .... (MER)
More Than I Can Say
Bobby Vee; *Golden Greats* .... (LIB)
  Legendary Masters .... (EMI)
Dolly Parton; *Rainbow* ....(COL)
Leo Sayer; *Have You Ever Been In Love* .... (WB)
More Than Words Can Say
Alias; *Alias* .... (EMI)
Mother Says
Joe Walsh; *Barnstorm* .... (MOB)
  Best Of .... (MCA)
"Murder", He Says
Roy Eldridge/Gene Krupa Or./Anita O'Day;
Uptown ....(COL)
Neither One Of Us (Wants To Be First...)
Gladys Knight/Pips; *All The Great Hits* .... (MOT)
  Anthology .... (MOT)
  Motown Grammy R&B Performances/'60s&'70s ... (MOT)
  Neither One Of Us .... (MOT)
  Superstars Series-#13 .... (MOT)
Never Did Say Goodbye
Lisa Brokop; *Every Little Girl's Dream* .... (PAT)
Never Say Never
Christopher Plummer/Phillip Glasser; *ST/American
Tail* ....(MCA)
Deniece Williams; *Water Under The Bridge* ......(COL)
Mr. Big; *Lean Into It* .... (ATL)
Romeo Void; *Benefactor* ....(COL)
  Never Say Never ....(COL)
  Warm In Your Coat ....(COL)
Styx; *Cornerstone* .... (A&M)
Third World; *Serious Business* .... (MER)
Triumph; *Surveillance* .... (MCA)
T. Graham Brown; *Best Of* .... (LIB)
  Come As You Were .... (CAP)
Never Say No
Original Cast; *Fantasticks* .... (POL)
Paul Butterfield; *East-West* .... (ELE)
Steve Miller Band; *Abracadabra* .... (CAP)
  CD Gift Set .... (CAP)
Nothing To Say
Jethro Tull; *Benefit* .... (CHR)
People Say
Dixie Cups; *Girl Groups* .... (RHI)
  Orig. Golden Hits Of The Great Groups-#1 ...... (SSS)
  Wonder Women-History Of Girl Group Sound .. (RHI)
People Will Say We're In Love
Frank Sinatra; *Greatest Hits-#2* ....(COL)
Original Broadway Cast; *Oklahoma* ....(RCA)
Spaniels; *45* .... (CLT)
Said I Loved You...But I Lied
Michael Bolton; *The One Thing* ....(COL)
Say Goodbye To Hollywood
Bette Midler; *Broken Blossom* .... (ATL)
Billy Joel; *Greatest Hits-#1 & 2* ....(COL)
  Songs In The Attic ....(COL)
  Turnstiles ....(COL)
Say Hello
April Wine; *Harder...Faster* .... (CAP)
Breathe; *Peace Of Mind* .... (A&M)
Heart; *Little Queen* .... (POR)

Say Hello To Heaven
Temple Of The Dog; *Temple Of The Dog* .... (A&M)
Say Hey (The Willie Mays Song)
Treniers; *Baseball's Greatest Hits* .... (RHI)
Say I Am
Tommy James/Shondells; *Anthology* .... (RHI)
Say It Again
Don Williams; *Best Of-#2* .... (MCA)
Santana; *Beyond Appearances* ....(COL)
Say It Isn't So
Daryl Hall & John Oates; *MTV's Rock 'N' Roll To
Go* .... (ELE)
  Rock & Soul Part 1-Greatest Hits ....(RCA)
Dinah Washington; *Irving Berlin Always* ....(VRV)
Michael Feinstein; *Remember-Sings Irving Berlin* . (ELE)
Outfield; *Play Deep* ....(COL)
Say It Isn't So Joe
Roger Daltrey; *Best Bits* .... (MCA)
  One Of The Boys .... (MCA)
Say It Loud I'm Black & I'm Proud
Afrika Bambaataa; *Decade Of Darkness* .... (EMI)
James Brown; *Billboard Top R&B
Hits-1965-1969* .... (RHI)
Say It With A Kiss
Billie Holiday; *Golden Hits-#2* ....(COL)
  Quintessential-$6-1938 ....(COL)
  Story-#3 ....(COL)
Say It With Trumpets
Maynard Ferguson; *Birdland Dreamband* .... (BLU)
Say It's Alright Joe
Genesis; *And Then There Were Three* .... (ATL)
Say I'm Your #1
Princess; *45* .... (PHL)
Say Say Say
Paul McCartney & Michael Jackson; *All the Best* (CAP)
  Pipes Of Peace .... (CAP)
Say What
Erasure; *Wonderland* .... (SIR)
Jesse Winchester; *Best Of* .... (RHI)
Stevie Ray Vaughan/Double Trouble; *Live Alive* .. (EPI)
  Soul To Soul .... (EPI)
Say What U Got To Say (Mix It Up)
Dan Reed Network; *Say What U Want-Rock The
Vote* .... (MER)
Say Yeah
Commodores; *All The Great Love Songs* .... (MOT)
  Natural High .... (MOT)
Say You Love Me
Ce Ce Rogers; *Never Give Up* .... (ATL)
Fleetwood Mac; *25 Years-The Chain* .... (WB)
  Fleetwood Mac .... (RPR)
  Greatest Hits .... (WB)
  Live .... (WB)
Jo-el Sonnier; *Come On Joe* ....(RCA)
Say You Love Me Or Say Goodbye
R.E.O. Speedwagon; *Decade Of Rock &
Roll-1970-1980* .... (EPI)
  You Can Tune A Piano But You Can't.. .... (EPI)
Say You Will
Al Hudson/One Way; *New Beginning* .... (CAP)
BoDeans; *Love & Hope & Sex & Dreams* .... (SLS)
Bridge 2 Far; *Bridge 2 Far* ....(WTG)
Dan Siegel; *Late One Night* .... (EPA)
Foreigner; *Inside Information* .... (ATL)
Gregory Abbott; *Shake You Down* ....(COL)
Isley Brothers; *Go All The Way* .... (TN)
Mick Jagger; *Primitive Cool* ....(COL)
Robert Palmer; *Pride* .... (ISL)
Say You, Say Me
Lionel Richie; *Back To Front* .... (MOT)
  Dancing On The Ceiling .... (MOT)
Say You'll Be Mine
Amy Grant; *House Of Love* .... (A&M)
Christopher Cross; *Christopher Cross* .... (WB)
Say You're Wrong
Julian Lennon; *Valotte* .... (ATL)
Saying Hello, Saying I Love You...
Jim Ed Brown & Helen Cornelius; *Greatest Hits* .(RCA)
She Can't Say I Didn't Cry
Rick Trevino; *Rick Trevino* ....(COL)
She Can't Say That Anymore
John Conlee; *Friday Night Blues* .... (MCA)
  Greatest Hits .... (MCA)

She Said She Said
Beatles; *Box Set* ....(CAP)
  Revolver ....(CAP)
She Said The Same Things To Me
John Hiatt; *Warming Up To The Ice Age* ....(GEF)
  Y'All Caught? Ones That Got Away-1975-85 ..(GEF)
She Said Yeah
Rolling Stones; *December's Children* ....(AKO)
Wilson Pickett; *A Man & A Half-Best Of* ....(RHI)
She Say (Oom Dooby Doom)
Diamonds; *Best Of* ....(RHI)
Smells Like Teen Spirit
Nirvana; *Nevermind* ....(DGC)
So Much To Say So Much To Give
Chicago; *2* ....(COL)
  At Carnegie Hall ....(COL)
  Group Portrait ....(COL)
Some Things Are Better Left Unsaid
Daryl Hall & John Oates; *Bigbamboom* ....(RCA)
Somebody's Always Saying Goodbye
Anne Murray; *Anne Murray's Country Hits* ....(LIB)
  Hottest Night Of The Year ....(CAP)
Somethin' Stupid
Frank & Nancy Sinatra; *Frank Sinatra's Greatest Hits* ....(RPR)
  World We Knew ....(RPR)
Nancy Sinatra & Frank Sinatra; *Boots-Nancy Sinatra's Greatest Hits* ....(RHI)
That's What He Said
Reba McEntire; *My Kind Of Country* ....(MCA)
That's What I Said
M.C. Hammer; *Let's Get It Started* ....(CAP)
  ST/Rocky V ....(BUS)
There! I've Said It Again
Bobby Vinton; *All-Time Greatest Hits* ....(EPI)
  Greatest Hits ....(EPI)
Johnny Mathis; *First 25 Years* ....(COL)
Vaughn Monroe; *Best Of* ....(MCA)
  Nipper's Greatest Hits-'40s-#1 ....(RCA)
These Lips Don't Know How To Say Goodbye
Doug Stone; *Doug Stone* ....(EPI)
  Greatest Country Hits!'90s-1991 ....(COL)
Forester Sisters; *Sincerely* ....(WB)
They Say It's Spring
Bobby Short; *Swing That Music* ....(TLR)
They Say It's Wonderful
Frank Sinatra; *The Voice-Columbia Years-1943-1952* ....(COL)
Johnny Mathis; *Heavenly* ....(COL)
Original Cast; *Annie Get Your Gun* ....(RCA)
Sarah Vaughan; *Irving Berlin Always* ....(VRV)
Things I Should Have Said
Grass Roots; *Anthology-1965-1975* ....(RHI)
  Greatest Hits-#2 ....(MCA)
  Their 16 Greatest Hits ....(MCA)
Things We Said Today
Beatles; *At The Hollywood Bowl* ....(CAP)
  Box Set ....(CAP)
  Hard Day's Night ....(CAP)
  Something New ....(CAP)
Paul McCartney; *Tripping The Live Fantastic* ....(CAP)
  Tripping The Live Fantastic-Highlights! ....(CAP)
To Make You Love Me (What Can I Say)
Alexander O'Neal; *All Mixed Up* ....(TAB)
  Hearsay ....(TAB)
Too Shy To Say
Stevie Wonder; *Fulfillingness' First Finale* ....(MOT)
Voice Your Choice
Radiants; *Best Of Chess Rhythm & Blues-#2* .....(CSS)
We Don't Have To Do It
Tanya Tucker; *Soon* ....(LIB)
What She Said
Smiths; *Meat Is Murder* ....(SIR)
  Rank ....(SIR)
What The President Meant To Say
Leaving Trains; *Fuck* ....(SST)
What Will My Mary Say
Jay/Americans; *Come A Little Bit Closer-Best Of* .(EMI)
Johnny Mathis; *16 Most Requested Songs* ....(COL)
  All-Time Greatest Hits ....(COL)

What'd I Say
Elvis Presley; *Collector's Gold* ....(RCA)
  Golden Records-#4 ....(RCA)
  Greatest Hits-#1 ....(RCA)
  In Concert ....(RCA)
Jerry Lee Lewis; *Milestones* ....(RHI)
  Original ....(SUN)
  Original Golden Hits-#2 ....(SUN)
  Rocket 88 ....(TOM)
  Rockin' My Life Away ....(TOM)
John Mayall/Bluesbreakers; *Bluesbreakers* ....(DER)
Ray Charles; *Anthology* ....(RHI)
  Atlantic R&B 1947-1974-#4-(1958-1962) .....(ATL)
  Atlantic Soul Classics ....(WSP)
  Frat Rock-#3 ....(RHI)
  Life In Music ....(ATL)
When All Is Said And Done
Abba; *45* ....(ATL)
(Who Says) You Can't Have It All
Alan Jackson; *A Lot About Livin' (And A Little...)* (ARI)
Whore Said It's Yours
Threat; *Sickinnahead* ....(MER)
You Don't Have To Say You Love Me
Dusty Springfield; *Golden Hits* ....(MER)
  History Of British Rock-#7 ....(RHI)
Elvis Presley; *50 Worldwide Gold Award Hits-#2* (RCA)
  As Recorded Live At Madison Sq. Garden ......(RCA)
  That's The Way It Is ....(RCA)
Vikki Carr; *Best Of* ....(EMI)
You Get The Best From Me (Say, Say, Say)
Alicia Myers; *I Appreciate* ....(MCA)
You Make It So Hard (To Say No)
Boz Scaggs; *Hits!* ....(COL)
  Slow Dancer ....(COL)
You Say Yes
Judas Priest; *Point Of Entry* ....(COL)
You Say You Will
Trisha Yearwood; *Hearts In Armor* ....(MCA)

COMMUNICATION: SCREAM

7 Screaming Diz Busters
Blue Oyster Cult; *On Your Feet Or On Your Knees* ....(COL)
  Tyranny & Mutation ....(COL)
And Even The Vegetables Screamed
Legendary Pink Dots; *Golden Age* ....(PIA)
Baby, Let Me Scream At You
Adam Ant; *Strip* ....(EPI)
From A Whisper To A Scream
Allen Toussaint; *Toussaint* ....(OOP)
Elvis Costello/Attractions; *Trust* ....(RYK)
Esther Phillips; *Best Of* ....(CBA)
  From A Whisper To A Scream ....(CBA)
Robert Palmer; *Sneakin' Sally Through The Alley* .(ISL)
I Shall Scream
Original Broadway Cast; *Oliver* ....(RCA)
Primal Scream
Maynard Ferguson; *Essence Of* ....(COL)
Motley Crue; *Decade Of Decadence* ....(ELE)
Scream
Collective Soul; *Hints Allegations And Things Left Unsaid* ....(ATL)
Scream Like A Baby
David Bowie; *Scary Monsters* ....(RYK)
Scream & Shout
Quiet Riot; *Condition Critical* ....(PSH)
  Winners Take All ....(SSP)
Screaming
Bronski Beat; *Age Of Consent* ....(MCA)
Payolas; *No Stranger To Danger* ....(A&M)
Screaming For A Lovebite
Accept; *Metal Heart* ....(POR)
  Staying A Life ....(EPI)
Screaming For Vengeance
Judas Priest; *Metal Giants* ....(COL)
  Screaming For Vengeance ....(COL)
Screaming In The Night
Krokus; *Headhunter* ....(ARI)
  Stayed Awake All Night-Best Of ....(ARI)
Screaming Skull
Fleshtones; *Living Legends* ....(IRS)

Screamin' Night Hog
Steppenwolf; *16 Greatest Hits* .... (MCA)
Screams
Blue Oyster Cult; *Blue Oyster Cult* .... (COL)
Screams Of Passion
Family; *Family* .... (WB)
Whisper To A Scream (Birds Fly)
Icicle Works; *Icicle Works* .... (ARI)

COMMUNICATION: SHOUT

Carolina Shout
Fats Waller; *Piano Solos* .... (RCA)
Holler & Shout
Elvin Bishop; *Rock My Soul* .... (OOP)
   Struttin' My Stuff .... (OOP)
It's All Over But The Shouting
Joe Cocker; *Jamaica* .... (OOP)
Rebel Yell
Billy Idol; *MTV's Rock 'N' Roll To Go* .... (ELE)
   Rebel Yell .... (CHR)
Roar Of The Masses Could Be Farts
Minutemen; *Double Nickels On The Dime* .... (SST)
San Antonio Shout
Bob Crosby Orchestra; *Play 22 Original Big Band Hits* .... (HIN)
Shout
Isley Brothers; *Nipper's Greatest Hits-'50s-#2* ....(RCA)
   Shout .... (CLT)
   ST/The Wanderers .... (WB)
Joey Dee/Starliters; *Echoes Of A Rock Era-Later Years* .... (RLL)
   Hey Let's Twist-Best Of .... (RHI)
   Live At The Peppermint Lounge .... (ACC)
   Original Rock 'N' Roll Hits Of The '60s .... (RLL)
   Sock Hoppin' Sixties .... (JCI)
Otis Day/Knights; *Shout* .... (MCA)
   ST/Animal House .... (MCA)
Tears For Fears; *Dance! Dance! Dance!-#2* .....(RCA)
   Songs From The Big Chair .... (MER)
   Tears Roll Down-Greatest Hits-1982-1992 ....(FON)
Tom Petty/Heartbreakers; *Pack Up The Plantation-Live* .... (MCA)
Shout And Shimmy
Who; *Who's Missing* .... (MCA)
Shout At The Devil
Motley Crue; *Decade Of Decadence* .... (ELE)
   Shout At The Devil .... (ELE)
Shout Bamalama
Mickey Murray; *Jewels-#2* .... (SSS)
   Soul Gold-#1 .... (SSS)
Wet Willie; *Greatest Hits* .... (POL)
   Southern Rock .... (KT)
Shout It Out
Burning Spear; *Dry & Heavy* .... (MGO)
Kingdom Come; *Kingdom Come* .... (POL)
Patrice Rushen; *Let There Be Funk* .... (PRS)
Slaughter; *ST/Bill & Ted's Bogus Journey* ...... (ISC)
Shout It Out Loud
Kiss; *Alive 2* .... (CAS)
   Destroyer .... (CAS)
   Smashes Thrashes & Hits .... (CAS)
Shout Shout
Ernie Maresca; *22 Leaders Of The Pack-#1* ......(LAU)
   Classic Old & Gold .... (LAU)
   Collectables-History Of Rock-#10 .... (CLT)
   Million Dollar Memories-#2 .... (RCA)
   Son Of Frat Rock .... (RHI)
Shout To The Devil
Alarm; *Declaration* .... (IRS)
Shout To The Top
Style Council; *Internationalists* .... (GEF)
   ST/Vision Quest .... (GEF)
Shouting Out Love
Emotions; *15 Original Big Hits-#2* .... (STX)
   Chronicle .... (STX)
   Sunshine .... (STX)
Stand Up & Shout
Dio; *Holy Diver* .... (WB)
Tubes; *What Do You Want From-Live* .... (A&M)
   Young & Rich .... (A&M)

Twist & Shout
Beatles; *At The Hollywood Bowl* .... (CAP)
   Box Set .... (CAP)
   Early .... (CAP)
   Please Please Me .... (CAP)
   Rock 'N' Roll Music-#1 .... (CAP)
   ST/Imagine-The Motion Picture .... (CAP)
Buck Owens/Buckaroos; *Live At Carnegie Hall* .. (CCB)
Isley Brothers; *Best Of* .... (CMF)
   Cruisin'-1963 .... (INC)
   Frat Rock .... (RHI)
   Oldies But Goodies-#10 .... (OSR)
   Solid Gold Music WCBS FM 101-'60s-#1 ... (CLT)
   Toga Rock .... (DHL)
Mamas & The Papas; *Best Of* .... (MCA)
Who; *Who's Last* .... (MCA)
You Cried Wolf
Todd Rundgren; *Anthology-1968-1985* .... (RHI)
   Hermit Of Mink Hollow .... (RHI)

COMMUNICATION: TALK

Ain't Talkin' 'Bout Love
Van Halen; *Van Halen* .... (WB)
Animal Speaks
Golden Palominos; *Visions Of Excess* .... (CEL)
Baby Makes Her Blue Jeans Talk
Dr. Hook; *Players In The Dark* .... (CAS)
Baby Talk
Billy Idol; *Don't Stop* .... (CHR)
Jan & Dean; *Best Of* .... (EMI)
   Collectables History Of Rock-#9 .... (CLT)
   One Summer Night/Live .... (RHI)
Baby Talks Dirty
Knack; *But The Little Girls Understand* .... (CAP)
Back Chat
Queen; *Hot Space* .... (HOL)
Big Boss Man
B.B. King; *Six Silver Strings* .... (MCA)
Elvis Presley; *Elvis* .... (RCA)
   ST/Clambake .... (RCA)
Grateful Dead; *Grateful Dead* .... (WB)
Jimmy Reed; *Best Of* .... (CRS)
   Oldies But Goodies-#1 .... (OSR)
John Hammond; *Best Of* .... (VAN)
   So Many Roads .... (VAN)
Body Talk
Deele; *Body Talk* .... (SLR)
   Street Beat .... (SLR)
Kix; *Cool Kids* .... (ATL)
Ratt; *Dancing Undercover* .... (ATL)
   Ratt & Roll 8191 .... (ATL)
   ST/Golden Child .... (CAP)
Wallets; *Body Talk* .... (TT)
Broken English
Marianne Faithfull; *Broken English* .... (ISL)
   Island Story (1962-1987)-25th Anniv. .... (ISL)
Can We Talk
Tevin Campbell; *I'm Ready* .... (QUE)
Can't We Talk It Over?
Bing Crosby; *16 Most Requested Songs* .... (COL)
Helen O'Connell; *Great Girl Singers Sing 22 Originals* .... (HIN)
Dialogue
Chicago; *5* .... (COL)
   Greatest Hits-#2 .... (COL)
Dirty Cash (Money Talks)
Adventures Of Stevie V; *Best Of '90s Dance Music-#1-Hip House* .... (PWL)
   Dirty Cash (Money Talks) .... (MER)
Don't Start Me To Talking
Doobie Brothers; *Farewell* .... (WB)
   Toulouse Street .... (WB)
Sonny Boy Williamson; *Blues-#1* .... (CSS)
   Down & Out Blues .... (CSS)
Don't Start Me To Talkin'
Doobie Brothers; *Toulouse Street* .... (WB)
New York Dolls; *In Too Much Too Soon* .... (MER)
Sonny Boy Williamson; *Down & Out Blues* ...... (CSS)
   Superblues-#2-All Time Classic Blues .... (STX)
Don't Talk To Strangers
Beau Brummels; *Best Of* .... (RHI)
   Just A Little & Other Hits .... (ACC)

Dio; *Holy Diver* ....(WB)
Rick Springfield; *Greatest Hits* ....(RCA)
   Success Hasn't Spoiled Me Yet ....(RCA)
Roger Daltrey; *Under A Raging Moon* ....(ATL)
Don't Tell Me No
   Cars; *Panorama* ....(ELE)
Don't Tell Me You Love Me
   Night Ranger; *Dawn Patrol* ....(CAM)
   Greatest Hits ....(CAM)
Elephant Talk
   King Crimson; *Abbreviated* ....(EDI)
   Compact ....(EDI)
   Discipline ....(EDI)
Everybody's Talkin'
   Nilsson; *ST/Forrest Gump* ....(EPX)
   ST/Midnight Cowboy ....(EMI)
   TT & Other Hits ....(RCA)
   Willie Nelson; *Best Of Willie* ....(RCA)
   Sweet Memories ....(RCA)
Girl Talk
   Betty Carter; *Finally* ....(RLL)
   Ella Fitzgerald & Joe Pass; *Speak Love* ....(PAB)
Girls Talk
   Dave Edmunds; *Best Of* ....(SS)
   I Hear You Rockin' ....(COL)
   Repeat When Necessary ....(SS)
   Elvis Costello; *Girls Girls Girls* ....(COL)
   Taking Liberties ....(COL)
   Linda Ronstadt; *Mad Love* ....(ASY)
Grey Talk
   Francis X/Bushmen; *Scream-The Compilation* ...(GEF)
Happy Talk
   Original Cast; *South Pacific* ....(COL)
Have A Talk With God
   Stevie Wonder; *Songs In The Key Of Life* ....(MOT)
He Talks To Me
   Lorrie Morgan; *Leave The Light On* ....(RCA)
Hey Bulldog
   Beatles; *Rock 'N' Roll Music-#2* ....(CAP)
   Yellow Submarine ....(CAP)
How Do You Speak To An Angel
   Popular Standard; *Out Of Print Recording* ....(OOP)
How Do You Talk To An Angel
   Heights; *ST/Heights* ....(CAP)
How Do You Talk To Girls
   Rick Springfield; *Success Hasn't Spoiled Me Yet* ..(RCA)
I Don't Want To Discuss It
   Delaney & Bonnie; *Best Of* ....(RHI)
   Delaney & Bonnie & Friends; *On Tour* ....(ATC)
I Don't Want To Talk About It
   Rita Coolidge; *Anytime...Anywhere* ....(A&M)
   Greatest Hits ....(A&M)
   Rod Stewart; *Absolutely Live* ....(WB)
   Atlantic Crossing ....(WB)
   Downtown Train-Storyteller Selections ....(WB)
   Greatest Hits ....(WB)
   Storyteller: Anthology 1964-1990 ....(WB)
I Heard It Through The Grapevine
   Creedence Clearwater Revival; *Chooglin'* ....(FAN)
   Chronicle ....(FAN)
   Cosmo's Factory ....(FAN)
   Gold ....(FAN)
   Movie Album ....(FAN)
   Gladys Knight/Pips; *16 #1 Hits From The Late*
   '60s ....(MOT)
   Command Compact Performances ....(MOT)
   Every Great Motown Song-First 25 Years ......(MOT)
   Motown Grammy R & B Performances ....(MOT)
   Motown Superstars Series-#13 ....(MOT)
   Top 10 With A Bullet-Motown Girl Groups ....(MOT)
   Marvin Gaye; *25 #1 Hits From 25 Years* ......(MOT)
   Anthology ....(MOT)
   Every Great Motown Hit Of Marvin Gaye .....(MOT)
   Live At London Palladium ....(MOT)
   Most Played Oldies On America's Jukebox .....(MOT)
   Motown Story ....(MOT)
   Motown Story-First 25 Years ....(MOT)
I Never Talk To Strangers
   Bette Midler; *Broken Blossom* ....(ATL)
   Tom Waits; *Anthology* ....(ELE)
   Foreign Affairs ....(ASY)
I Talk To The Trees
   Al Hirt; *Al Hirt* ....(DHL)
   Showtime ....(ALL)

I Talk To The Wind
   King Crimson; *In The Court Of The Crimson*
   King ....(ATL)
If These Old Walls Could Speak
   Nanci Griffith & Jimmy Webb; *Red Hot +*
   Country ....(MER)
If Walls Could Talk
   Ry Cooder; *Paradise & Lunch* ....(RPR)
It's The Talk Of The Town
   Art Tatum; *Complete Capitol Recordings-#2* .....(CAP)
   Hank Jones; *Live At Maybeck Recital Hall-#16* ...(CCJ)
   Ray Conniff Singers; *It's The Talk Of The Town* .(COL)
Jive Talkin'
   Bee Gees; *Greatest* ....(RSO)
   Main Course ....(RSO)
   ST/Saturday Night Fever ....(RSO)
Just A Little Talk With Jesus
   Elvis Presley; *Million-Dollar Quartet* ....(RCA)
Keep Talking
   Pink Floyd; *The Division Bell* ....(COL)
Lay Down Sally
   Eric Clapton; *Crossroads* ....(POL)
   Just One Night ....(RSO)
   Slow Hand ....(RSO)
   Time Pieces-Best Of ....(RSO)
Let Me Talk
   Earth, Wind & Fire; *Faces* ....(COL)
Let's Not Talk About It
   Original Broadway Cast; *Romance/Romance* ....(MCA)
Let's Stop Talkin' About It
   Janie Fricke; *17 Greatest Hits* ....(COL)
   Love Lies ....(COL)
   Very Best Of ....(COL)
Let's Talk About Me
   Alan Parsons Project; *Best Of-#2* ....(ARI)
   Vulture Culture ....(ARI)
Let's Talk About Sex
   Salt-N-Pepa; *Blacks' Magic* ....(LON)
   Blitz Of Salt-N-Pepa Hits ....(LON)
   MTV Party To Go-#2 ....(TMB)
Let's Talk About Us
   Jerry Lee Lewis; *Golden Hits-#3* ....(SUN)
   Jerry Lee's Greatest ....(RHI)
   Milestones ....(RHI)
Let's Talk It Over
   Vaneese Thomas; *Vaneese Thomas* ....(GEF)
Let's Talk It Over In The Ladies Room
   Curtie/Boom Box; *Black Kisses* ....(RCA)
Lip Service
   Elvis Costello; *This Year's Model* ....(COL)
   Jimmy Buffett; *Somewhere Over China* ....(MCA)
   John Astley; *Everyone Loves The Pilot Except The*
   Crew ....(ATL)
   Michael Franks; *Camera Never Lies* ....(WB)
Little Less Talk And A Lot More Action
   Toby Keith; *Toby Keith* ....(MER)
Loose Talk
   Carl Smith; *Very Special Love Song* ....(FFT)
   Patsy Cline; *Live At The Opry* ....(MCA)
Love Talks
   Ronnie McDowell; *In A New York Minute* ......(EPI)
   Older Women & Other Greatest Hits ....(EPI)
Money Talks
   Bar-Kays; *Money Talks* ....(STX)
   Gang Of Four; *Mall* ....(POL)
   J.J. Cale; *Number 8* ....(MER)
   Special Edition ....(MER)
   Living Colour; *Biscuits* ....(EPI)
   Rick James; *Street Songs/Throwin' Down* ....(MOT)
Moneytalks
   AC/DC; *Razor's Edge* ....(ATC)
Mothers Talk
   Tears For Fears; *Songs From The Big Chair* .....(MER)
   Tears Roll Down-Greatest Hits-1982-1992 .....(FON)
No Time For Talk
   Christopher Cross; *Another Page* ....(WB)
Nobody's Talking
   Exile; *Country's Greatest Hits-#3-Ten Gallon...* ...(PRY)
   Still Standing ....(ARI)
Now You're Talkin'
   Dixiana; *Now You're Talkin'* ....(EPI)
Our Lips Are Sealed
   Go-Go's; *Beauty & The Beat* ....(IRS)
   Greatest ....(IRS)

Pick-A-Little, Talk-A-Little
Hermione Gingold/Biddys; *ST/Music Man* .... (WB)
Original Cast; *Music Man* .... (CAP)
Pillow Talk
Sylvia; *All Platinum Gold* .... (ALP)
Super Bad Is Back .... (KT)
Please Don't Talk About Me When I'm Gone
Arlo Guthrie & Pete Seeger; *Precious Friend* ..... (WB)
Billie Holiday; *Compact Jazz* .... (VRV)
Ella Fitzgerald & Count Baise; *Perfect Match* .... (PAB)
Leon Redbone; *Champagne Charlie* .... (WB)
Ray Price; *Portrait Of A Singer* .... (SO)
Practice What I Preach
Hank Williams, Jr.; *America (The Way I See It)* ..(W/C)
Born To Boogie .... (W/C)
Practice What You Preach
Alex Taylor; *Dancing With The Devil* .... (ICH)
American Girls; *American Girls* .... (IRS)
Proven Innocent; *And Then There Were 2* .... (FP)
Santana; *Borboletta* .... (COL)
Testament; *Practice What You Preach* .... (MEG)
Psychobabble
Alan Parsons Project; *Best Of* .... (ARI)
Eye In The Sky .... (ARI)
Rastaman Chant
Bob Marley/Wailers; *Burnin'* .... (TUF)
Ronnie, Talk To Russia
Prince; *Controversy* .... (WB)
Sex Me, Talk Me
Berlin; *Count Three & Pray* .... (GEF)
Shaddup You Face
Joe Dolce; *45* .... (MCA)
She Don't Talk Like Us No More
K.T. Oslin; *This Woman* .... (RCA)
She Talks To Angels
Black Crowes; *Shake Your Money Maker* .... (DEF)
Shut Up And Kiss Me
Mary Chapin Carpenter; *Stones In The Road* ....(COL)
Sidewalk Talk
Jellybean; *Dance Mix* .... (EMI)
Wotupski .... (EMI)
Sleep Talk
Alyson Williams; *Raw* .... (OBR)
Small Talk
Doris Day; *ST/Pajama Game* .... (SSP)
Original Cast; *Pajama Game* .... (COL)
Something To Talk About
Bonnie Raitt; *Luck Of The Draw* .... (CAP)
Speak Softly-You're Talking To My Heart
Gene Watson; *Greatest Hits* .... (MCA)
Old Loves Never Die .... (MCA)
Stereo Chickens
Jerry Jeff Walker; *Man Must Carry On* .... (MCA)
Street Corner Talking
Savoy Brown; *Collection* .... (DER)
Street Corner Talking .... (DER)
Sweet Talker
Richard Thompson; *ST/Sweet Talker* .... (CAP)
Sweet Talking Woman
Electric Light Orchestra; *Afterglow* .... (EPI)
Box Of Their Best .... (JET)
Greatest Hits .... (JET)
Out Of The Blue .... (JET)
Sweet Talkin' Guy
Chiffons; *Best Of* .... (LAU)
Collectables Presents History Of Rock-#1 .... (CLT)
Everything You Always Wanted .... (LAU)
Golden Classics .... (CLT)
Talk About Suffering
Doc Watson; *Doc Watson* .... (VAN)
Ricky Skaggs; *Family & Friends* .... (ROU)
Live In London .... (EPI)
Talk About The Good Times
Elvis Presley; *Good Times* .... (RCA)
Talk Back Trembling Lips
Johnny Tillotson; *Cruisin'-1964* .... (INC)
Talk Dirty To Me
Poison; *Look What The Cat Dragged In* .... (CAP)
Swallow This Live .... (CAP)
Talk It Over
Grayson Hugh; *Blind To Reason* .... (RCA)
Pretty Girls Everywhere-Beach Classics-1 ....(RCA)

Talk Of The Town
Lightnin' Hopkins; *Nothin' But The Blues-Golden
Classics-#4* .... (CLT)
Pretenders; 2 .... (SIR)
The Singles .... (SIR)
Talk Talk
Music Machine; *Battle Of The Bands* .... (KT)
Nuggets-#1 or 2 .... (RHI)
Talk Talk; *History Revisited* .... (EMI)
Party's Over .... (EMI)
Spinning Pups .... (EMI)
ST/Night Shift .... (WB)
Very Best Of-Natural History .... (EMI)
Talk To Me
Anita Baker; *Compositions* .... (ELE)
Bonnie Raitt; *Green Light* .... (WB)
Chico DeBarge; *Chico DeBarge* .... (MOT)
Chris Isaak; *Silvertone* .... (WB)
Europe; *Prisoners In Paradise* .... (EPI)
Fiona; *Fiona* .... (ATL)
Joni Mitchell; *Don Juan's Reckless Daughter* ..... (ASY)
Mickey Gilley; *19 Hot Country Requests* .... (EPI)
Put Your Dreams Away .... (EPI)
Ten Years Of Hits .... (EPI)
NRBQ; *At Yankee Stadium* .... (MER)
Southside Johnny/Asbury Jukes; *Best Of* ...... (EPI)
Havin' A Party With .... (EPI)
Stevie Nicks; *Rock A Little* .... (MOD)
Timespace-Best Of .... (MOD)
Talk To Me Baby
Elmore James; *Golden Classics* .... (CLT)
Frank Sinatra; *Softly As I Leave You* .... (RPR)
Toni Tennille; *Never Let Me Go* ....(BAY)
Talk To Me Daddy
Thelma Cooper/Boyfriends; *Collectables Blues
Collection-#3* .... (CLT)
Talk To Me Like The Sea
Everything But The Girl; *Worldwide* .... (ATL)
Talk To Me Lonesome Heart
James O'Gwynn; *Greatest Hits* .... (PLN)
Talk To Me Texas
Keith Whitley; *Greatest Hits* .... (RCA)
Tracy Byrd; *Tracy Byrd* .... (MCA)
Talk To The Animals
Sammy Davis, Jr.; *Greatest Songs* .... (CCB)
Talk To The Lawyer
David Lindley & El Rayo-X; *Win This Record* ... (ELE)
Talk To Ya Later
Tubes; *Best Of* .... (CAP)
Completion Backward Principle .... (CAP)
Rock The First-#4 .... (SAN)
Talking About My Baby
Curtis Mayfield/Impressions; *Anthology* .... (MCA)
Impressions; *Greatest Hits* .... (MCA)
Talking Airplane Disaster
Phil Ochs; *Original New Folks* .... (VAN)
Talking Back To The Night
Steve Winwood; *Chronicles* .... (ISL)
Talking Back To The Night .... (ISL)
Talking Blues
Bob Marley/Wailers; *Natty Dread* .... (TUF)
Talking Cancer Blues
Dave Van Ronk; *Inside* .... (FAN)
Van Ronk .... (FAN)
Talking Casey
Mississippi John Hurt; *Best Of* .... (VAN)
Candy Man .... (INT)
Today .... (VAN)
Talking In The Dark
Elvis Costello; *2 1/2 Years* .... (RYK)
Elvis Costello/Attractions; *Armed Forces* ....(COL)
Linda Ronstadt; *Mad Love* .... (ASY)
Talking In Your Sleep
Crystal Gayle; *All-Time Greatest Hits* .... (CCB)
Classic Crystal .... (EMI)
Country Gold .... (PRY)
When I Dream .... (LIB)
Romantics; *Billboard Top Hits-1984* .... (RHI)
In Heat .... (EPA)
Rock Of The '80s-#3 .... (PRY)
Talking Old Soldiers
Elton John; *Tumbleweed Connection* .... (POL)
Talking Pay T.V.
Phil Ochs; *Broadside Tapes-#1* .... (FLW)

Talking To A Tennessee Moon
Candace Anderson; *Talking To A Tennessee Moon* .... (ADO)
Talking To My Angel
Melissa Etheridge; *Yes I Am* .... (ISL)
Talking To The Moon
Don Henley; *I Can't Stand Still* .... (GEF)
Talking To Yourself
Original Broadway Cast; *Hallelujah Baby!* ...... (SMC)
Talking Union
Pete Seeger; *Greatest Hits* ....(COL)
Pete Seeger/Others; *Songs Of America's Working People* ....(FF)
Talking Vietnam Pot Luck Blues
Tom Paxton; *Morning After* .... (ELE)
Talking Watergate
Tom Paxton; *New Songs From The Briarpatch* .. (VAN)
Talking World War III Blues
Bob Dylan; *Freewheelin'* ....(COL)
Talkin' About You
Animals; *Best Of* .... (AKO)
Talkin' At The Texaco
James McMurtry; *Too Long In The Wasteland* ...(COL)
Talkin' Fishin'
Ramblin' Jack Elliott; *Greatest Songs Of Woody Guthrie* .... (VAN)
Talkin' New York
Bob Dylan; *Bob Dylan* .... (COL)
Talkin' To The Moon
Charlie Daniels Band; *Me & The Boys* .... (EPI)
Gatlin Brothers; *Biggest Hits* ....(COL)
Live At 8:00 .... (CAP)
More Hot Country Requests-#2 .... (EPI)
Partners ....(COL)
Talkin' Trash
Chico Freeman; *Tradition In Transition* ...... (ELE)
Tom Principato; *Smokin'* .... (POW)
Talkin' 'Bout Love
Nazareth; *Malice In Wonderland* .... (A&M)
Talkin' 'Bout Women Obviously
Buddy Guy/Junior Mance/Junior Wells; *Buddy & The Juniors* .... (MCA)
Thank You For Talking To Me, Africa
Miki Howard; *Femme Fatale* .... (GIA)
Sly/Family Stone; *Anthology* .... (EPI)
There's A Riot Goin' On .... (EPI)
Thinkin' Out Loud
Band; *Cahoots* ....(CAP)
This Heart Speaks For Itself
Bobbie Cryner; *Bobbie Cryner* .... (EPI)
This Is Me
Randy Travis; *This Is Me* .... (WB)
Trash Talkin'
Albert Collins; *Complete Imperial Recordings* .... (EMI)
T.V. Talkin' Song
Bob Dylan; *Under The Red Sky* ....(COL)
Walkin', Talkin'...Beatin' Broken Heart
Highway 101; *Country's Greatest Hits-#4* .... (PRY)
Paint The Town .... (WB)
We Better Talk This Over
Bob Dylan; *Street Legal* ....(COL)
We Can Talk
Band; *Music From Big Pink* ....(CAP)
We Don't Have To Talk (About Love)
Peabo Bryson; *Collection* ....(CAP)
Don't Play With Fire ....(CAP)
We Don't Talk Anymore
Cliff Richard; *We Don't Talk Anymore* .... (EMI)
What They're Talkin' About
Rhett Akins; *A Thousand Memories* .... (DEC)
When I Get Home
Beatles; *Box Set* ....(CAP)
Hard Day's Night ....(CAP)
Something New ....(CAP)
When The Generals Talk
Midnight Oil; *Red Sails In The Sunset* ....(COL)
Wond'ring Aloud
Jethro Tull; *20 Years Of-Radio Archives & Rare Tracks* .... (CHR)
Aqualung .... (CHR)

Wouldn't It Be Nice
Beach Boys; *Absolutely Best-#2* .... (CAP)
Made In The U.S.A. ....(CAP)
Pet Sounds ....(CAP)
Still Cruisin' ....(CAP)
Yakety Yak
2 Live Crew; *ST/Twins* ....(WTG)
Coasters; *Atlantic*
R&B-1947-1974-#3-(1955-1958) .... (ATL)
Billboard Top Rock 'N' Roll Hits-1958 .... (RHI)
Cruisin'-1958 .... (INC)
Greatest Hits ....(ATC)
ST/Stand By Me .... (ATL)
You Should Hear How She Talks About You
Melissa Manchester; *Greatest Hits* .... (ARI)
Hey Ricky .... (ARI)
You Talk Too Much
Cheap Trick; *Next Position Please* .... (EPI)
George Thorogood/Destroyers; *Born To Be Bad* . (EMI)
Joe Jones; *American Graffiti-#3* .... (MCA)
Carnival Time-Best Of Ric Records-#1 .... (ROU)
Echoes Of A Rock Era-Middle Years .... (RLL)
Original Rock 'N' Roll Hits Of The '60s .... (RLL)
Run-D.M.C.; *King Of Rock* .... (PRO)

COMMUNICATION: TELL

Achy Breaky Heart
Billy Ray Cyrus; *Some Gave All* .... (MER)
And I Am Telling You I'm Not Going
Jennifer Holliday/Original Cast; *Dreamgirls* ...... (GEF)
Any Major Dude Will Tell You
Steely Dan; *Greatest Hits* .... (MCA)
Pretzel Logic .... (MCA)
Baby Won't You Tell Me
Johnny Hammond; *Big City Blues* .... (VAN)
Can You Dance (Baby Tell Me)
Shanice Wilson; *Discovery* ....(A&M)
Don't Tell Me Lies
Breathe; *All That Jazz* ....(A&M)
Don't Tell Me No
Cars; *Panorama* .... (ELE)
Don't Tell Me What To Do
Pam Tillis; *Put Yourself In My Place* .... (ARI)
Don't Tell Me You Love Me
Night Ranger; *Dawn Patrol* ....(CAM)
Greatest Hits ....(CAM)
Don't Tell Your Mama
Eddie Floyd; *Chronicle* .... (STX)
Don'tcha Tell Henry
Bob Dylan/Band; *Basement Tapes* ....(COL)
Girl Don't Tell Me
Beach Boys; *California Girls* ....(CAP)
Endless Summer ....(CAP)
Gift Set ....(CAP)
Go Tell It On The Mountain
Bobby Darin; *25th Day Of December* ....(ATC)
Dolly Parton; *Home For Christmas* ....(COL)
Garth Brooks; *Beyond The Season* ....(LIB)
Simon & Garfunkel; *Collected Works* ....(COL)
Wednesday Morning 3 A.M. ....(COL)
Weavers; *On Tour* .... (VAN)
Grandpa (Tell Me About The Good Old...)
Judds; *Greatest Hits* ....(RCA)
Rockin' With The Rhythm ....(RCA)
Super 10-#2 ....(RCA)
Have I Told You Lately
Original Broadway Cast; *I Can Get It For You Wholesale* ....(SMP)
Rod Stewart; *Unplugged...And Seated* .... (WB)
Vagabond Heart .... (WB)
Van Morrison; *Best Of* .... (MER)
I Can't Tell You Why
Eagles; *Greatest Hits-#2* .... (ASY)
Live .... (ASY)
The Long Run .... (ASY)
Vince Gill; *Common Thread-Songs Of The Eagles* (GIA)
I Want To Hold Your Hand
Beatles; *1962-1966* ....(CAP)
20 Greatest Hits ....(CAP)
Meet The Beatles ....(CAP)
Past Masters-#1 & 2 ....(CAP)
Lakeside; *Your Wish Is My Command* .... (SLR)

I Want To Tell You
Beatles; *Revolver* .... (CAP)
Informer
Snow; *12 Inches Of Snow* .... (EW)
I'm Telling You Now
Freddie/Dreamers; *History Of British Rock-#1* ... (RHI)
I've Told Ev'ry Little Star
David Allyn; *Sings Jerome Kern* .... (DCO)
Linda Scott; *45* .... (ERI)
Just Tell Her Jim Said Hello
Elvis Presley; *Collector's Gold* .... (RCA)
Gold Award Hits-#2 .... (RCA)
Golden Records-#4 .... (RCA)
Let Me Tell You About Love
Judds; *River Of Time* .... (RCA)
Mama Done Told Me
Miracles; *Greatest Hits-From The Beginning* ..... (MOT)
Mama Told Me Not To Come
Randy Newman; *12 Songs* .... (RPR)
Live .... (RPR)
Randy Newman .... (RPR)
Three Dog Night; *Best Of* .... (MCA)
Billboard Top Rock 'N' Roll Hits-1970 .... (RHI)
Wilson Pickett; *Greatest Hits* .... (ATL)
My Heart Can't Tell Me No
Rod Stewart; *Downtown Train-Storyteller*
Selections .... (WB)
Out Of Order .... (WB)
Storyteller-Complete Anthology-1964-1990 ...... (WB)
My Heart Tells Me
Etta Jones; *Something Nice* .... (PRS)
Nat King Cole; *Very Thought Of You* .... (CAP)
No Tell Lover
Chicago; *Greatest Hits-#2* .... (COL)
Group Portrait .... (COL)
Hot Streets .... (COL)
If You Leave Me Now .... (COL)
Nobody Told Me
John Lennon; *Lennon* .... (CAP)
John Lennon & Yoko Ono; *Milk & Honey* .... (POL)
Shop Around
Captain & Tennille; *Greatest Hits* .... (A&M)
Miracles; *Hi-We're The Miracles* .... (MOT)
Smokey Robinson/Miracles; *16 #1 Hits From The Early*
'60s .... (MOT)
Anthology .... (MOT)
Every Great Motown Song-First 25 Years ...... (MOT)
Show Don't Tell
Rush; *Chronicles* .... (MER)
Presto .... (ATL)
Stories I Tell
Toad The Wet Sprocket; *Fear* .... (COL)
Stories We Could Tell
Jimmy Buffett; *A-1-A* .... (MCA)
John Sebastian; *Best Of* .... (RHI)
Tom Petty/Heartbreakers; *Pack Up The*
Plantation-Live .... (MCA)
Tell All The People
Doors; *Soft Parade* .... (ELE)
Tell Her About It
Billy Joel; *An Innocent Man* .... (COL)
Greatest Hits-#1 & 2-1973-1985 .... (COL)
Tell Her No
Juice Newton; *Dirty Looks* .... (CAP)
Greatest Hits & More .... (LIB)
Zombies; *Best Of The Rest Of* .... (BCT)
History Of British Rock-#2 .... (RHI)
Live On The BBC .... (RHI)
Time Of The .... (EPI)
Tell It Like It Is
Aaron Neville; *Classic* .... (ROU)
Soul Shots-#5 .... (RHI)
Super Oldies Of The '60s-#7 .... (AUF)
Tell It Like It Is .... (CCB)
Treacherous: History Of The Neville Br. .... (RHI)
Billy Joe Royal; *Greatest Hits* .... (ATL)
Tell It Like It Is .... (AA)
George Benson; *Best Of* .... (A&M)
UB40; *Live In Moscow* .... (A&M)
Rat In The Kitchen .... (A&M)
Tell It Like It Used To Be
T. Graham Brown; *45* .... (CAP)

Tell It To Carrie
Romantics; *Romantics* .... (EPA)
What I Like About You & Other Hits .... (NEM)
Tell It To My Heart
Taylor Dayne; *Rock The First-#6* .... (SAN)
Tell It To My Heart .... (ARI)
Tell It To The Judge
Monotones; *Best Of Chess Vocal Groups* .... (CSS)
Tell It To The Judge On Sunday
Long Ryders; *Native Sons* .... (FRN)
Tell It To The Rain
Frankie Valli/Four Seasons; *Anthology* .... (RHI)
Greatest Hits-#2 .... (RHI)
Tell Laura I Love Her
Ray Peterson; *Nipper's Greatest Hits-'60s-#1* .....(RCA)
Teenage Tragedies .... (RHI)
Tell Mama
Etta James; *Essential* .... (CSS)
Soul Hits-#1 .... (RHI)
Tell Mama .... (CSS)
Janis Joplin; *Janis* .... (COL)
Savoy Brown; *Anthology* .... (DER)
Street Corner Talking .... (DER)
Tell Me
Al Jarreau; *High Crime* .... (WB)
Bangles; *All Over The Place* .... (COL)
Bob Dylan; *Bootleg Series-#1-3-Rare &*
Unreleased .... (COL)
Fabulous Thunderbirds; *Tuff Enuff* .... (EPA)
Howlin' Wolf; *Chess Box* .... (CSS)
Kenny G; *Kenny G* .... (ARI)
Lionel Richie; *Lionel Richie* .... (MOT)
Rolling Stones; *Big Hits-High Tide & Green Grass* (AKO)
England's Newest Hit Makers .... (AKO)
More Hot Rocks-Big Hits & Fazed Cookies ..... (AKO)
Singles Collection-London Years .... (AKO)
Stevie Ray Vaughan/Double Trouble; *In The*
Beginning .... (EPA)
Texas Flood .... (EPI)
White Lion; *Best Of* .... (ATL)
Pride .... (ATL)
Tell Me A Bedtime Story
Norman Connors; *Remember Who You Are* ...... (MOJ)
Quincy Jones; *Sounds...& Stuff Like That* .... (A&M)
Tell Me A Lie
Janie Fricke; *17 Greatest Hits* .... (COL)
19 Hot Country Requests .... (EPI)
Greatest Country Hits!'80s-1983 .... (COL)
It Ain't Easy .... (COL)
Love Lies .... (COL)
Very Best Of .... (COL)
Tell Me About It
Tanya Tucker & Delbert McClinton; *Can't Run From*
Yourself .... (LIB)
Tell Me All The Things You Do
Fleetwood Mac; *Kiln House* .... (RPR)
Tell Me If You Still Care
S.O.S. Band; *On The Rise* .... (TAB)
Tell Me I'm Crazy
Shelby Lynne; *Temptation* .... (MC)
Tell Me I'm Not Dreaming
Robert Palmer; *Heavy Nova* .... (EMI)
Tell Me I'm Not Dreamin'
Jermaine Jackson; *Jermaine Jackson* .... (ARI)
Tell Me I'm October
Porn Orchard; *Urges & Angers* .... (C/Z)
Tell Me I'm Only Dreaming
Lorrie Morgan; *Classics* .... (CCB)
Tell Me Love
Michael Wycoff; *45* .... (RCA)
Tell Me On A Sunday
Marti Webb; *Premiere Collection-Best Of A.L.*
Webber .... (MCA)
Michael Crawford; *Performs Andrew Lloyd*
Webber .... (ATL)
Tell Me Something Good
Rufus & Chaka Khan; *Classic Soul* .... (MCA)
Rags To Rufus .... (MCA)
Stompin' At The Savoy .... (WB)
Tell Me That It Isn't True
Bob Dylan; *Nashville Skyline* .... (COL)
Tell Me That You Love Me
Eric Clapton; *Backless* .... (RSO)

The Green Book Of Songs By Subject — Page 139

Tell Me The Truth
Billy Stewart; *One More Time/Chess Years* .... (CSS)
Midnight Oil; *Alternative NRG* ....(HOL)
    Earth & Sun & Moon ....(COL)
Timothy B. Schmit; *Tell Me The Truth* .... (MCA)
Tell Me This Is A Dream
Delfonics; *Best Of* .... (ARI)
Tell Me To My Face
Dan Fogelberg & Tim Weisberg; *Twin Sons Of Different Mothers* .... (FM)
Tell Me Tomorrow
Angela Bofill; *Angela Bofill* .... (ARI)
    Best Of .... (ARI)
Karyn White; *Karyn White* ....(WB)
Smokey Robinson; *Blame It On Love & All The Great Hits* .... (MOT)
Tell Me What The Papers Say
Elton John; *Ice On Fire* .... (MCA)
Tell Me What You See
Beatles; *Box Set* ....(CAP)
    Help! ....(CAP)
    Love Songs ....(CAP)
    VI ....(CAP)
Tell Me What You Want
Doobie Brothers; *What Were Once Vices Are Now Habits* ....(WB)
Tell Me What You Want Me To Do
Tevin Campbell; *T.E.V.I.N.* .... (QUE)
Tell Me When The Whistle Blows
Elton John; *Captain Fantastic & Brown Dirt Cowboy* .... (POL)
Tell Me Why
Beatles; *Box Set* ....(CAP)
    Something New ....(CAP)
    ST/Hard Day's Night ....(CAP)
Belmonts; *Classic Old & Gold* ....(LAU)
Berlin; *Pleasure Victim* ....(GEF)
Bobby Vinton; *16 Most Requested* .... (EPI)
    Greatest Hits .... (EPI)
Elvis Presley; *Valentine Gift For You* ....(RCA)
Genesis; *We Can't Dance* .... (ATL)
Jann Browne; *Tell Me Why* ....(CCB)
Neil Young; *After The Gold Rush* ....(RPR)
Sunbeams; *Harlem Holiday-New York R&B-#5* ..(CLT)
Wynonna; *Tell Me Why* ....(MCC)
Tell Me (How It Feels)
52nd St.; *Children Of The Night* .... (MCA)
Tell The Truth
David Lee Roth; *A Little Ain't Enough* ....(WB)
Derek/Dominos; *Crossroads* .... (POL)
    In Concert .... (POL)
    Layla .... (POL)
Otis Redding; *Best Of* ....(ATC)
    Story ....(ATL)
    Tell The Truth ....(RHI)
Ray Charles; *Birth Of Soul/Comp. Atlantic R&B 1952-59* ....(ATL)
Tell The World
Dells; *Harlem New York-Ballad Era* ....(CLT)
Ratt; *Ratt & Roll 8191* ....(ATL)
Tell The World How I Feel About 'Cha...
Harold Melvin/Blue Notes; *Wake Up Everybody* ... (PI)
Tell 'Em I'm Surfing
Fantastic Baggies; *Monster Summer Hits-Wild Surf* ....(CAP)
Telling Me Lies
D. Parton/E. Harris/L. Ronstadt; *Trio* .... (WB)
Tulip Or Turnip (Tell Me Dream Face)
Duke Ellington & Teresa Brewer; *It Don't Mean A Thing If It Ain't Got...* ....(COL)
We Tell Ourselves
Clint Black; *The Hard Way* ....(RCA)
(We've Been Told) Jesus Is Coming Soon
Eric Clapton; *One In In Every Crowd* ....(RSO)
You Can Tell The World
Simon & Garfunkel; *Collected Works* ....(COL)
    Wednesday Morning 3 A.M. ....(COL)
You Tell Me
Johnny Cash; *Original* ....(SUN)
Tom Petty/Heartbreakers; *Damn The Torpedoes* (MCA)
You Tell The World
Simon & Garfunkel; *Wednesday Morning 3 A.M.* .(COL)

COMMUNICATION: WHISPER

Careless Whisper
Wham!; *Make It Big* ....(COL)
    Music For The Miracle ....(CBA)
From A Whisper To A Scream
Allen Toussaint; *Toussaint* ....(OOP)
Elvis Costello/Attractions; *Trust* ....(RYK)
Esther Phillips; *Best Of* ....(CBA)
    From A Whisper To A Scream ....(CBA)
Robert Palmer; *Sneakin' Sally Through The Alley* . (ISL)
(I Could Only) Whisper Your Name
Harry Connick, Jr.; *She* ....(COL)
Shhh
Tevin Campbell; *I'm Ready* .... (QUE)
Speak Softly-You're Talking To My Heart
Gene Watson; *Greatest Hits* .... (MCA)
    Old Loves Never Die .... (MCA)
Whisper In The Dark
Dionne Warwick; *Friends* .... (ARI)
Whisper My Name
Randy Travis; *This Is Me* ....(WB)
Whisper To A Scream (Birds Fly)
Icicle Works; *Icicle Works* .... (ARI)
Whispering
Jan Garber; *& Orchestra Play 22 Orig. Big Band Faves* ....(HIN)
Les Paul & Mary Ford; *Selections From "Legend & The Legacy"* ....(CAP)
Miles Davis; *Chronicle-Complete Prestige Recordings* ....(PRS)
    Dig ....(PRS)
    Early Miles ....(PRS)
    & Horns ....(PRS)
Paul Whiteman/Orchestra; *Nipper's Greatest Hits-'20s* ....(RCA)
Wayne King; *Best Of* .... (MCA)
Whispering Grass
Hank Crawford; *Great Moments In Jazz* ....(ATL)
Ink Spots; *Best Of* .... (MCA)
    Greatest Hits .... (MCA)
    If I Didn't Care ....(FFT)
Ink Spots In London ....(EVR)
Sandy Denny; *Who Knows Where The Time Goes?* (HBL)
Whispering Pines
Band; *Band* ....(CAP)
Johnny Horton; *Greatest Hits* ....(COL)

COMMUNICATION: WORDS

Don't Believe A Word
Thin Lizzy; *Live & Dangerous* ....(WB)
    Lizzy Lives! ....(GS)
    'Live' Live-Double Album ....(WB)
Fill In The Words
Robert Klein/Original Cast; *They're Playing Our Song* ....(CAS)
From The Word Go
Michael Martin Murphey; *River Of Time* ....(WB)
Las Palabras De Amor
Queen; *Hot Space* ....(HOL)
Last Word, The
Mary Chapin Carpenter; *Stones In The Road* ....(COL)
Lost For Words
Pink Floyd; *The Division Bell* ....(COL)
Man Of My Word
Collin Raye; *Extremes* .... (EPI)
More Than Words
Extreme; *Pornograffitti* ....(A&M)
More Than Words Can Say
Alias; *Alias* .... (EMI)
Picasso's Last Words
Paul McCartney/Wings; *Band On The Run* ....(CAP)
    Wings Over America ....(CAP)
Pretty Words
Vince Gill; *I Still Believe In You* ....(MCA)
Revolutionary Words
Mutabaruka; *Mystery Unfolds* ....(SHA)
Simple Little Words
Cristy Lane; *At Her Best* .... (EMI)

Sorry Seems To Be The Hardest Word
Elton John; *Blue Moves* .... (MCA)
   Greatest Hits-#2 ....(POL)
   Live In Australia w/Melbourne Symphony ..... (MCA)
Joe Cocker; *Two Rooms-Songs Of E. John &*
   Taupin ....(POL)
Too Marvelous For Words
Billie Holiday; *Lady Sings The Blues* .... (VRV)
Frank Sinatra; *Capitol Years* ....(CAP)
   Gift Set ....(CAP)
Nat King Cole; *Nat King Cole* ....(CAP)
Wasted Words
Allman Brothers Band; *Brothers & Sisters* .... (POL)
   Decade Of Hits-1969-1979 ....(POL)
   Dreams ....(POL)
Gregg Allman; *Laid Back* ....(CPC)
Word Up
Cameo; *Word Up* .... (CAS)
Words
Bee Gees; *Gold-#1* ....(POL)
   Here At Last ....(RSO)
   History Of British Rock-#9 ....(RHI)
Elvis Presley; *From Memphis To Vegas* ....(RCA)
   In Person ....(RCA)
F.R. David; *Words* ....(CRR)
Joan Armatrading; *Shouting Stage* ....(A&M)
Missing Persons; *Best Of* ....(CAP)
Monkees; *Missing Links-#2* ....(RHI)
   More Greatest Hits Of .... (ARI)
Rita Coolidge; *Anytime...Anyway* ....(A&M)
   Classics-#5 ....(A&M)
   Greatest Hits ....(A&M)
Solomon Burke; *Best Of* .... (ATL)
   Home In Your Heart-Best Of ....(RHI)
Words By Heart
Billy Ray Cyrus; *It Won't Be The Last* .... (MER)
Words Get In The Way
Miami Sound Machine; *Primitive Love* ....(EPI)
Words Of Love
Beatles; *Box Set* ....(CAP)
   For Sale ....(CAP)
   Love Songs ....(CAP)
   VI ....(CAP)
Buddy Holly; *Buddy Holly* ....(MCA)
   Legend ....(MCA)
   Rock & Roll Collection ....(MCA)
Buddy Holly/Crickets; *20 Golden Greats* .... (MCA)
Mamas & The Papas; *16 Of Their Greatest Hits* . (MCA)
   Best Of ....(MCA)
   Farewell To The First Golden Era ....(MCA)
   Mama's Big Ones-Her Greatest Hits ....(MCA)
Words Of Wisdom
Christopher Cross; *Another Page* ....(WB)
Word, The
Beatles; *Box Set* ....(CAP)
   Rubber Soul ....(CAP)
You Took The Words Right Out Of My Mouth
Meatloaf; *Bat Out Of Hell* .... (EPI)
You're A Man Of Words, I'm A Woman
Betty LaVette; *Lost Soul-#1* ....(EPI)

COMPUTERS, Information

See Also: MACHINES, TELEPHONE

Access To Data
Brand X; *Masques* ....(BP)
Age Of Information
Bill Bruford; *Gradually Going Tornado* .... (EDI)
Age Of The Micro Man
Hawklords; *25 Years On* ....(OOP)
Byte-By-Byte
Software; *Chip Meditation* ....(INN)
Cheap Computer
Three Johns; *10 Roir Years-Anthology* .... (ROI)
   Deathrocker Scrapbook ....(ROI)
Computer
Bob Mintzer Big Band; *Incredible Journey* .... (DIG)
Circuitry/Sam Bostic; *Circuitry/Sam Bostic* ....(ATL)
Computer Age
Neil Young; *Trans* ....(GEF)
Newcleus; *Jam On Revenge* ....(SNY)
   Street Jams-Electric Funk-#2 ....(RHI)
Sonic Youth; *Bridge-Tribute To Neil Young* ......(CRL)

Computer Blue
Prince/Revolution; *ST/Purple Rain* ....(WB)
Computer Boogie
Valentine Brothers; *Have A Good Time* .... (A&M)
Computer Cowboy
Neil Young; *Trans* ....(GEF)
Computer Dub
Greater Than One; *London* ....(WAX)
Computer Eyes
Carole King; *Speeding Time* ....(ATL)
Computer Games
George Clinton; *Computer Games* ....(CAP)
Yellow Magic Orchestra; *Kyoretsu Na*
   Rhythm-Characters .... (RES)
Computer God
Black Sabbath; *Dehumanizer* ....(RPR)
Computer In Love
Perrey & Kingsley; *Essential* .... (VAN)
Computer Incantations For World Peace
Jean-Luc Ponty; *Individual Choice* ....(ATL)
Computer Love
Kraftwerk; *Computer World* ....(WB)
   The Mix ....(ELE)
NKRU; *Freaky To You* ....(RCA)
Techmaster P.E.B.; *Bass Computer* ....(NTN)
Zapp; *All The Greatest Hits* ....(RPR)
   New Zapp IV U ....(WB)
Computer Minds
Leroy Jenkins; *Live!* ....(BSA)
Computer One
Dear Enemy; *Ransom Notes* ....(CAP)
Computer Took My Job
Maurice John Vaughn; *Generic Blues Album* .....(ALG)
Computer Voice
Robert Schroeder; *Computer Voice* ....(RAC)
Computer World
Kraftwerk; *Computer World* ....(WB)
Computer "G"
Kenny Garrett; *Black Hope* ....(WB)
Computerize
Yellowman; *Rambo* ....(MOV)
Data Bank
Time; *Pandemonium* ....(PAI)
Data Control
Husker Du; *Land Speed Record* ....(SST)
Digital Display
Ready For The World; *Ready For The World* ... (MCA)
Electrical Language
Be Bop Deluxe; *Best Of-Raiding The Divine*
   Archive ....(CAP)
   Drastic Plastic .... (HAR)
Higher & Higher
Moody Blues; *To Our Children's Children's*
   Children ....(POL)
Homecomputer
Kraftwerk; *The Mix* ....(ELE)
Information
Dave Edmunds; *Information* ....(COL)
Eric Martin; *Eric Martin* ....(CAP)
Potatoland; *Spirit* ....(RHI)
Rainmakers; *Rainmakers* ....(MER)
Pocket Calculator
Kraftwerk; *Computer World* ....(WB)
   The Mix ....(ELE)
Silicon Valley
Peter Seiler; *Flying Frames* ....(INN)
Someone's Computer
Tom Paxton; *One Million Lawyers & Other*
   Disasters ....(FF)
User Friendly
Ian Anderson; *Walk Into Light* .... (CHR)

COOL

See Also: COLD

Be Cool
Joni Mitchell; *Wild Things Run Fast* ....(GEF)
Cool
Original Cast; *West Side Story* ....(COL)
Time; *Time* ....(WB)
Cool Breeze
Jeremy Spencer Band; *Flee* ....(ATL)

Cool Cat
Queen; *Hot Space* ....(HOL)
Cool Change
Little River Band; *First Under The Wire* ....(CAP)
Greatest Hits ....(CAP)
Cool Cool Water
Beach Boys; *10 Years Of Harmony* ....(CAR)
Sunflower ....(CAR)
Cool Down
Triumph; *Thunder Seven* ....(MCA)
Cool For Cats
Squeeze; *Classics-#25* ....(A&M)
Cool For Cats ....(A&M)
Single-45s & Under ....(A&M)
Cool It Down
Velvet Underground; *Loaded* ....(WSP)
Cool It Now
New Edition; *Greatest Hits-#1* ....(MCA)
New Edition ....(MCA)
Cool Jerk
Capitols; *Atlantic R&B 1947-1974-#5*
(1962-1966) ....(ATL)
Billboard Top R&B Hits-1966 ....(RHI)
Collectables History Of Rock-#5 ....(CLT)
Son Of Frat Rock ....(RHI)
Super Oldies/'60s-#5 ....(AUF)
Their Greatest Recordings ....(SSM)
Cool Love
Pablo Cruise; *Reflector* ....(A&M)
Sheena Easton; *Lover In Me* ....(MCA)
Wanda Jackson; *Rockin' In The Country-Best Of* . (RHI)
Cool Magic
Steve Miller Band; *Abracadabra* ....(CAP)
Cool Night
Paul Davis; *Cool Night* ....(ARI)
Cool Pearl
Capitols; *Golden Classics* ....(CLT)
Cool The Engines
Boston; *Third Stage* ....(MCA)
Cool Water
Bob Nolan; *Sound Of A Pioneer* ....(ELE)
Frankie Laine; *16 Most Requested Songs* ....(COL)
Jack Scott; *Capitol Collectors Series* ....(CAP)
Joni Mitchell; *Chalk Mark In A Rain Storm* ......(GEF)
Sons Of The Pioneers; *Best Of* ....(RCA)
60 Years Of Country Music ....(RCA)
Cool Water ....(RCA)
Western Country ....(GRA)
Talking Heads; *Naked* ....(FLY)
Cool, Calm, Collected
Atlantic Starr; *As The Band Turns* ....(A&M)
Cool, Clear Water
Bonnie Raitt; *Longing In Their Hearts* ....(CAP)
Daddy Cool
Boney M; *Love For Sale* ....(ATL)
Take The Heat Off Me ....(ATC)
Diamonds; *Best Of* ....(RHI)
I Was Country When Country Wasn't Cool
Barbara Mandrell; *Greatest Hits* ....(MCA)
Live ....(MCA)
In The Cool Cool Cool Of The Evening
Bing Crosby; *Best Of* ....(MCA)
Frank Sinatra; *Days Of Wine & Roses-Academy A.*
Winners ....(RPR)
It Ain't Cool To Be Crazy About You
George Strait; *Country Classics-#7: 1986-87* ... (MCA)
Greatest Hits-#2 ....(MCA)
MCA #1 Hits/'80s-#2 ....(MCA)
#7 ....(MCA)
I'm The Coolest
Alice Cooper; *Goes To Hell* ....(WB)
Just Coolin'
Levert; *Just Coolin'* ....(ATL)
King Cool
Donnie Iris; *King Cool* ....(MCA)
Long Cool Woman In A Black Dress
Hollies; *Best Of* ....(EMI)
Best Of-#2 ....(EMI)
Billboard Top Rock 'N' Roll Hits-1972 ....(RHI)
Distant Light ....(EPI)
Epic Anthology-From The Original Masters ......(EPI)
Greatest Hits ....(EPI)

Tall Cool One
Robert Plant; *Knebworth-The Album* ....(POL)
Now And Zen ....(EPR)
That's Cool, That's Trash
Kingsmen; *Best Of* ....(RHI)

COUNTRIES: A

See Also: Cities: A-Z, Specific Countries,
Countries: B-Z

Air Algiers
Country Joe McDonald; *Hold On It's Coming* ... (VAN)
Angola
Ambrosia; *Live Beyond L.A.* ....(WB)
Rolling Stones; *Goats Head Soup* ....(RS)
Ry Cooder; *ST/Johnny Handsome* ....(WB)
Arabia
Art Blakey/Jazz Messengers; *History Of* ....(BLN)
Mosaic ....(BLN)
Jerry Garcia & David Grisman; *Jerry Garcia & David*
Grisman ....(GRD)
Arabian Knights
Siouxsie/Banshees; *Juju* ....(GEF)
Once Upon A Time-The Singles ....(GEF)
Arabian Love Call
Art Neville; *That Old Time Rock 'N' Roll* ....(SPE)
Arabian Lover
Duke Ellington; *Jungle Nights In Harlem* ....(BLU)
Arabian Nights
Bruce Adler; *ST/Aladdin* ....(DIS)
Arabs With Knives & West German Skies
Roger Waters; *Pros & Cons Of Hitchhiking* ......(COL)
Armenia City In The Sky
Who; *Sell Out* ....(MCA)
Aruba
Jim Hall; *Circles* ....(CCJ)
Kenny Barron & Ted Dunbar; *In Tandem* ....(MUS)
Tim Weisberg; *Outrageous Temptations* ....(CYP)
Aruba!
Rippingtons; *Tourist In Paradise* ....(GRP)
Arubian Nights
Larry Coryell & Emily Remler; *Together* ....(CCJ)
At An Arabian House Party
Raymond Scott; *Reckless Nights & Turkish*
Twilights ....(COL)
Australia
Kinks; *Arthur Or Decline/Fall Of British Empire* .. (RPR)
Steve Howe; *Beginnings* ....(ATC)
Austrian Anthill
Brian Ritchie; *The Blend* ....(SST)
Bermuda Triangle Blues (Flight 45)
Blondie; *Plastic Letters* ....(CHR)
Buenos Dias Argentina
Marty Robbins; *All Around Cowboy* ....(COL)
Encore ....(COL)
Do The Boomerang
Junior Walker/All-Stars; *Anthology* ....(MOT)
Shotgun ....(MOT)
Don't Cry For Me Argentina
Original New York Cast; *Evita* ....(MCA)
Down Under (Australia)
Men At Work; *Business As Usual* ....(COL)
Far Away In Australia
De Danann; *Ballroom* ....(GRE)
Killing An Arab
Cure; *Boys Don't Cry* ....(ELE)
Standing On A Beach-The Singles ....(ELE)
New Argentina
Original New York Cast; *Evita* ....(MCA)
Sail To Australia
New Grass Revival; *When The Storm Is Over* ......(FF)
Secret Life Of Arabia
David Bowie; *Heroes* ....(RYK)
Sheik Of Araby
Benny Goodman; *Sextet feat. Charles*
Christian-1939-1941 ....(COL)
Django Reinhardt; *Djangologie/USA-#1* ....(DSQ)
Fred Astaire/Others; *Three Evenings With* ....(DRG)
Leon Redbone; *Double Time* ....(WB)
South Australia
Northeast Winds; *In Concert* ....(FOL)
Pogues; *If I Should Fall From Grace With God* .... (ISL)

Theme From "Lawrence Of Arabia"
BBC Concert Orchestra; *Golden Cinema Classics-Adventure Film* ....(BAI)
Cincinnati Pops Orchestra/Erich Kunzel; *Hollywood's Greatest Hits-#1* ....(TLR)
Waltzing Matilda
Burl Ives; *Best Of* ....(MCA)
Fred Astaire; *Three Evenings With* ....(DRG)
James Galway; *Pachebel Canon & Other Favorites* ....(RCA)
Waltzing Matilda (Australian Folk Song)
Burl Ives; *Best Of* ....(MCA)
Fred Astaire; *Three Evenings With* ....(DRG)
James Galway; *Pachebel Canon & Other Favorites* ....(RCA)
Winter In Austria
L. Subramaniam; *Spanish Wave* ....(MS)

COUNTRIES: AMERICA

See Also: MONTHS & DATES: JULY,
POLITICAL CLASSICS

4th Of July
U2; *Unforgettable Fire* ....(ISL)
Abraham, Martin & John
Dion; *24 Original Classics* ....(ARI)
Collectables Presents History Of Rock-#3 ....(CLT)
WCBS FM-History Of Rock-'60s-#2 ....(CLT)
Harry Belafonte; *All Time Greatest Hits-#1* ......(RCA)
Smokey Robinson/Miracles; *Anthology* ....(MOT)
Time Out For/Special Occasion ....(MOT)
All American
Original Cast/Sammy Davis, Jr.; *Stop The World I Want To Get Off* ....(WB)
Sammy Hagar; *Nine On A Ten Scale* ....(CAP)
All American Boy
Bill Parsons; *History Of Rock-#10* ....(CLT)
Statler Brothers; *Son Of The Motherland* ....(MER)
All American Girl
Daryl Hall & John Oates; *Bigbamboom* ....(RCA)
Melissa Etheridge; *Yes I Am* ....(ISL)
All American Girls
Sister Sledge; *45* ....(COT)
All American Man
Kiss; *Alive 2* ....(CAS)
All American Redneck
Geezinslaw Brothers; *If You Think I'm Crazy Now* ....(LNS)
All The Way From America
Joan Armatrading; *Classics-#21* ....(A&M)
Me Myself I ....(A&M)
America
Heart; *Private Audition* ....(EPI)
KBC Band; *KBC Band* ....(ARI)
Kurtis Blow; *America* ....(MER)
Neil Diamond; *12 Greatest Hits-#2* ....(COL)
Hot August Night II ....(COL)
ST/Jazz Singer ....(CAP)
Original Cast; *ST/West Side Story* ....(COL)
Pat Boone; *Star-Spangled Banner* ....(WOR)
Prince/Revolution; *Around The World In A Day* ..(WB)
Simon & Garfunkel; *Bookends* ....(COL)
Collected Works ....(COL)
Concert In Central Park ....(COL)
Greatest Hits ....(COL)
Live Rhymin' ....(WB)
Waylon Jennings; *Greatest Hits-#2* ....(RCA)
America Is My Home
James Brown; *45* ....(OOP)
America The Beautiful
Elvis Presley; *Elvis Aron Presley* ....(RCA)
Lee Greenwood; *American Patriot* ....(LIB)
Mormon Tabernacle Choir; *God Bless America* ..(COL)
This Is My Country ....(COL)
Ray Charles; *Greatest Hits-#2* ....(RHI)
His Greatest Hits-#2 ....(DHL)
America The Beautiful, 1976
Charlie Rich; *Greatest Hits* ....(EPI)
"American Bandstand" Theme
Original Music; *Television's Greatest Hits-#3* .....(TVT)
American Beat '84
Fleshtones; *Living Legends* ....(IRS)

American Beauty Rose
Frank Sinatra; *Come Swing With Me* ....(CAP)
Sentimental Journey ....(CAP)
American Boy
Eddie Rabbitt; *American Music Greatest Hits* .....(CCB)
Greatest Country Hits ....(CCB)
Jersey Boy ....(LIB)
American Boys
Deborah Galli; *Radio Active* ....(MER)
American City Suite
Cashman & West; *Super Hits/'70s-Have A Nice Day-#9* .... (RHI)
American Dream
Chicago; *XIV* ....(COL)
Crosby, Stills, Nash & Young; *American Dream* ..(ATL)
John Cougar Mellencamp; *Chestnut Street Incident* (RHI)
Early Years ....(RHI)
Nitty Gritty Dirt Band; *20 Years Of Dirt-Best Of* ..(WB)
Oak Ridge Boys; *American Dreams* ....(MCA)
Original London Cast; *Miss Saigon* ....(GEF)
American Girl
Tom Petty/Heartbreakers; *Pack Up The Plantation-Live* ....(MCA)
Tom Petty/Heartbreakers ....(MCA)
You're Gonna Get It ....(MCA)
American Girls
Rick Springfield; *Success Hasn't Spoiled Me Yet* ..(RCA)
American Heartbeat
Survivor; *Eye Of The Tiger* ....(SCO)
American Hearts
Air Supply; *Lost In Love* .... (ARI)
American Honky-Tonk Bar Association
Garth Brooks; *In Pieces* ....(LIB)
American Made
Oak Ridge Boys; *American Made* ....(MCA)
Greatest Hits-#2 ....(MCA)
American Music
Blasters; *Blasters* ....(SLS)
Collection ....(SLS)
Pointer Sisters; *So Excited* ....(PNT)
Violent Femmes; *Why Do Birds Sing?* ....(SLS)
American Patrol
Glenn Miller; *Moonlight Serenade* ....(RAN)
Pure Gold ....(BLU)
Glenn Miller/Orchestra; *Unforgettable* ....(RCA)
American Pie
Don McLean; *American Pie* .... (UA)
Best Of ....(EMI)
Greatest Hits Then & Now ....(EMI)
ST/Born On The Fourth Of July ....(MCA)
American Popular Song
Neil Diamond; *You Don't Bring Me Flowers* .....(COL)
American Prayer
Doors; *American Prayer* ....(ELE)
American Roulette
Robbie Robertson; *Robbie Robertson* ....(GEF)
American Squirm
Nick Lowe; *Basher: Best Of* ....(COL)
Labour Of Lust ....(COL)
American Storm
Bob Seger/Silver Bullet Band; *Like A Rock* ......(CAP)
American Trilogy
Elvis Presley; *Aloha From Hawaii* ....(RCA)
Elvis Aron ....(RCA)
Live On Stage ....(RCA)
Madison Square Garden ....(RCA)
ST/This Is ....(RCA)
Mickey Newbury; *45* ....(ELE)
American Tune
Paul Simon; *Live Rhymin'* ....(WB)
There Goes Rhymin' Simon ....(WB)
Simon & Garfunkel; *Concert In Central Park* ....(WB)
American Woman
Guess Who; *American Woman* ....(RCA)
Best Of ....(RCA)
Greatest Of ....(RCA)
Nipper's Greatest Hits-'70s ....(RCA)
Rock Classics ....(KT)
Americana
Moe Bandy; *Best Of Branson U.S.A.-#1* ....(CCB)
Country's Greatest Hits-American Pride ....(PRY)
Greatest Hits ....(CCB)
Americans
Tex Ritter; *An American Legend* ....(CAP)

America, I Believe In You
Charlie Daniels Band; *America, I Believe In You* ..(LIB)
Amerikka's Most Wanted
Ice Cube; *Amerikka's Most Wanted* ....(PRY)
Among The Americans
10,000 Maniacs; *Wishing Chair* ....(ELE)
Back In The U.S.A.
Chuck Berry; *Chess Box* ....(CSS)
Golden Hits ....(MER)
Greatest Hits ....(EVR)
Roll Over Beethoven ....(ALL)
Linda Ronstadt; *Greatest Hits-#2* ....(ELE)
Living In The U.S.A. ....(ASY)
Bad America
Gun Club; *Las Vegas Story* ....(ANI)
Banned In The U.S.A.
Luke Skyywalker; *Banned In The U.S.A.* ....(LUK)
Battle Hymn Of The Republic
Charlie Sexton; *Charlie Sexton* ....(MCA)
Judy Collins; *Songs Of The Civil War* ....(COL)
Mormon Tabernacle Choir; *God Bless America* ..(COL)
Stars & Stripes Forever ....(COL)
Pat Boone; *Star-Spangled Banner* ....(WOR)
Better In The USA
Glenn Frey; *The Allnighter* ....(MCA)
Bicentennial
London Wainwright III; *T-Shirt* ....(ARI)
Bicentennial Blues
Gil Scott-Heron; *It's Your World* ....(ARI)
Mind Of ....(ARI)
Big In America
Stranglers; *Dreamtime* ....(EPI)
Greatest Hits-1977-1990 ....(EPI)
Born In America
Riot; *Born In America* ....(QUA)
Born In The U.S.A.
Bruce Springsteen; *Born In The U.S.A.* ....(COL)
Bruce Springsteen/E Street Band;
Live-1975-1985 ....(COL)
Brand New Amerika
Poorboys; *Pardon Me* ....(HOL)
Breakfast In America
Supertramp; *Breakfast In America* ....(A&M)
Classics-#9 ....(A&M)
Paris ....(A&M)
Buy American
Tex Payer; *Work's Many Voices-#1 & 2* .... (ARH)
Buy, Buy This American Car
Charlie King; *Food Phone Gas Lodging* ....(FF)
Caissons Go Rolling Along
Leon Berry; *Best Of Theater Organ* ....(AUF)
Giant Wurlitzer Pipe Organ-#3 ....(AUF)
R. Merrill/Mormon Tabernacle Choir; *Yankee Doodle Dandies* ....(COL)
Calling America
Electric Light Orchestra; *Balance Of Power* ......(CBA)
Cheap Seats, The
Alabama; *Cheap Seats* ....(RCA)
City Of New Orleans
Arlo Guthrie; *Best Of* ....(WB)
Hobo's Lullaby ....(RPR)
Together In Concert w/Pete Seeger ....(RPR)
HARP; *HARP* ....(RWD)
Willie Nelson; *19 Hot Country Requests-#2* ....(EPI)
City Of New Orleans ....(COL)
Greatest Country Hits/'80s-#4 ....(COL)
Compared To What
Les McCann; *Atlantic Jazz-Soul* ....(ATL)
Les McCann & Eddie Harris; *Great Moments In Jazz* ....(ATL)
Jazz Years ....(ATL)
Swiss Movement ....(ATL)
Country's In The Best Of Hands
Original Cast; *Li'l Abner* ....(COL)
Cowboy, You're America
Dave Dudley; *King Of The Road* ....(SUN)
Crawling To The U.S.A.
Elvis Costello; *ST/Americathon* ....(COL)
Taking Liberties ....(COL)
Day We Lost The America's Cup
Tom Paxton; *One Million Lawyers & Other Disasters* ....(FF)
Deadline U.S.A.
Shalamar; *ST/D.C. Cab* ....(MCA)

Don't Give Us A Reason
Hank Williams, Jr.; *America (The Way I See It)* ..(W/C)
Dreams In America
Luka Bloom; *Riverside* ....(RPR)
Edge Of America
Duran Duran; *Big Thing* ....(CAP)
Fightin' Side Of Me
Merle Haggard; *All American* ....(CAP)
Capitol Collectors Series ....(CAP)
Merle Haggard/Strangers; *Songs I'll Always Sing* .(CAP)
For America
Jackson Browne; *Lives In The Balance* ....(ASY)
Forty Hour Week (For A Livin')
Alabama; *Forty Hour Week (For A Livin')* ....(RCA)
Greatest Hits ....(RCA)
Fourth Of July
Dave Alvin; *Romeo's Escape* ....(EPI)
Linda Waterfall; *Body English* ....(FF)
Rosalie Sorrels; *Lonesome Roving Wolves-Songs Of The West* ....(GRE)
X; *See How We Are* ....(ELE)
Fourth Of July At A County Fair
Red Clay Ramblers; *Chuckin' The Frizz* ....(FF)
Fourth Of July, Asbury Park (Sandy)
Bruce Springsteen; *Wild The Innocent & The E Street Shuffle* ....(COL)
Bruce Springsteen/E Street Band;
Live-1975-1985 ....(COL)
Geek U.S.A.
Smashing Pumpkins; *Siamese Dream* ....(VIA)
God Bless America
Frank Zappa; *Uncle Meat* ....(BIZ)
Kate Smith; *Best Of* ....(RCA)
God Bless America ....(PIC)
Legendary Performer ....(RCA)
Nipper's Greatest Hits-'30s-#1 ....(RCA)
Mormon Tabernacle Choir; *God Bless America* ..(COL)
God Bless America Again
Loretta Lynn & Conway Twitty; *From Seven Till Ten* ....(MSP)
United Talent ....(MCA)
Very Best Of ....(MCA)
God Bless The USA
Lee Greenwood; *Greatest Hits* ....(MCA)
Greatest Hits-#2 ....(MCA)
Inside Out/You've Got A Good Love Comin' ... (MCA)
Today's Country Classics-#1 ....(MCA)
God Must Have Blessed America
Lee Dorsey; *45* ....(MCA)
Goin' By The Book
Johnny Cash; *Mystery Of Life* ....(MER)
Good Old American Guest
Merle Haggard; *Big City* ....(EPI)
Green Fields Of America
Paddy Tunney; *Stone Fiddle* ....(GRE)
Happiest Girl In The Whole U.S.A.
Donna Fargo; *45* ....(MCA)
Jeanne Pruett; *Stand By Your Man* ....(ALL)
Happy Birthday, America
Li'l Wally; *Happy Birthday, America* ....(JJ)
Hello America
Def Leppard; *On Through The Night* ....(MER)
Here Comes The Freedom Train
Merle Haggard; *Capitol Collectors Series* ....(CAP)
House I Live In (That's America To Me)
Frank Sinatra; *A Man & His Music* ....(RPR)
Greatest Hits-Early Years ....(COL)
In The Beginning-1943-1951 ....(COL)
Main Event ....(SIN)
House Un-American Blues Activity Dream
Mimi & Richard Farina; *Best Of* ....(VAN)
Memories ....(VAN)
Reflections In A Crystal Wind ....(VAN)
I Am A Patriot
Jackson Browne; *World In motion* ....(ELE)
Little Steven; *Voice Of America* ....(EMI)
I Found My Girl In The Good Old U.S.A.
Jimmie Skinner; *45* ....(GUS)
I Like America
Noel Coward; *Album-Live From Las Vegas & New York* ....(COL)

In America
Charlie Daniels Band; *Decade Of Hits* .... (EPI)
   Full Moon .... (EPI)
   Me & The Boys .... (EPI)
Independence Day
Bruce Springsteen; *The River* ....(COL)
Bruce Springsteen/E Street Band;
Live-1975-1985 ....(COL)
It's Alright
Loggins & Messina; *Native Sons* ....(COL)
I'm A Yankee Doodle Dandy
Robert Merrill; *Yankee Doodle Dandies* ....(COL)
I'm So Bored With The U.S.A.
Clash; *Clash* .... (EPI)
Jammin' In America
Gap Band; *V-Jammin'* .... (POL)
Jesus Children Of America
Stevie Wonder; *Innervisions* .... (MOT)
June 25 At The Fourth Of July
Shel Silverstein; *Great Conch Train Robbery* .... (FF)
Kid's American
Matthew Wilder; *I Don't Speak The Language* .... (PRI)
King & Queen Of America
Eurythmics; *Greatest Hits* .... (ARI)
   We Too Are One .... (ARI)
Last Great American Whale
Lou Reed; *Greenpeace/Rainbow Warriors* .... (GEF)
   New York .... (SIR)
Letter From America
Proclaimers; *This Is The Story* .... (CHR)
Letter To Americans
Albert Brooks; *Star Is Bought* .... (ASY)
Little America
R.E.M.; *Reckoning* .... (IRS)
Living In America
Aztec Two-Step; *See It Was Like This-Acoustic*
Retrosp. .... (FF)
Donna Summer; *Donna Summer* .... (GEF)
Hiroshima; *East* .... (EPI)
James Brown; *Gravity* .... (SCO)
   Rocky Story .... (SCO)
   ST/Rocky IV .... (SCO)
Living In The Promiseland
Willie Nelson; *30 Years Of #1 Hits-#18* ....(COL)
   Greatest Country Hits/'80s-1986 ....(COL)
   More Hot Country Requests .... (EPI)
   The Promiseland ....(COL)
Living In The U.S.A.
Steve Miller Band; *Anthology* ....(CAP)
   Best Of-1968-1973 ....(CAP)
   Live ....(CAP)
   On The Road Again-Rock's New Frontiers ......(CAP)
   Sailor ....(CAP)
Lost In America
Crack The Sky; *From The Greenhouse* .... (GDG)
"Love, American Style" Theme
Original Music; *Television's Greatest Hits-#2* ..... (TVT)
Me & Crippled Soldiers
Merle Haggard; *American Music Greatest Hits* ...(CCB)
   Blue Jungle ....(CCB)
Meet Me In America
Lauren Christy; *Lauren Christy* .... (MER)
Memphis Slim U.S.A.
Memphis Slim; *Blue This Evening* ....(BL)
Miss America
Big Dish; *Satellites* .... (EW)
Mark Lindsay; *45* ....(COL)
Styx; *Caught In The Act* .... (A&M)
   Classics-#15 .... (A&M)
   Grand Illusion .... (A&M)
Mister Touchdown U.S.A.
University Of Michigan Band; *Greatest College Football*
Marches .... (VAN)
More Than A Name On The Wall
Statler Brothers; *Greatest Hits* .... (MER)
My America
Blow Monkeys; *Forbidden Fruit* ....(RCA)
Red Steagall/Coleman County Cowboys; *For All Our*
Cowboy Friends .... (MCA)
My Country 'Tis Of Thee
David Crosby; *Oh Yes I Can* .... (A&M)
Mormon Tabernacle Choir; *God Bless America* . (SMC)
My Little Miss America
Gary U.S. Bonds; *45* .... (LEG)

My Love Is In America
Chieftains; *10-Cotton-Eyed Joe* .... (SHA)
National Emotion
Tommy Tutone; *National Emotion* ....(COL)
New Age In America
Larry Coryell; *American Odyssey* .... (DRG)
New America
Flim/BB's; *Big Notes* .... (DIG)
Okie From Muskogee
Merle Haggard/Strangers; *Best of* ....(CAP)
   Capitol Collectors Series ....(CAP)
   Country Music Classics-#3-1965-1970 .... (KT)
   Friend In California .... (EPI)
   Songs I'll Always Sing ....(CAP)
   ST/Platoon (& Songs From The Era) .... (ATL)
Oklahoma USA
Kinks; *Muswell Hillbillies* .... (RHI)
Once Upon A Time In America
Dennio Morricone; *Film Music-#2* .... (VIA)
One Time, One Night
Los Lobos; *By The Light Of The Moon* ....(SLS)
Only For Americans
Andrews Sisters; *Beat Me Daddy Eight To The*
Bar ....(MSP)
Original Broadway Cast; *Miss Liberty* .... (SMC)
Only In America
Jay/Americans; *All-Time Greatest Hits* .... (RHI)
   Come A Little Bit Closer-Best Of .... (EMI)
Party Time U.S.A.
Oscar Peterson; *Silent Partner* .... (PAB)
Patriot's Dream
Gordon Lightfoot; *Don Quixote* .... (RPR)
Pink Houses
John Cougar Mellencamp; *Rock For Amnesty* ... (MER)
   Uh-Huh ....(RIV)
Pledge Of Allegiance
Lee Greenwood; *American Patriot* .... (LIB)
Mormon Tabernacle Choir; *American Tribute* ....(COL)
Proud To Be An American
Li'l Wally; *Happy Birthday America* .... (JJ)
Tubes; *Young & Rich* .... (A&M)
Queen Of The U.S.A.
Thompson Twins; *Big Trash* .... (RE)
Ragged Old Flag
Johnny Cash; *Patriot* ....(COL)
   We The People ....(FOL)
Rally 'Round The Flag
Pico Payne; *ST/Long Riders* .... (WB)
Ry Cooder; *Boomer's Story* .... (RPR)
White Mountain Singers; *Round The Bend* ....(FOL)
   We The People ....(FOL)
Real American
Derringer; *Wrestling Album* .... (EPI)
Real American Folk Song (Is A Rag)
Marni Nixon & Lincoln Mayorga; *Marni Nixon Sings*
Gershwin ....(REF)
Red White & Blue Medley
Chet Atkins; *My Country America* ....(RCA)
Redneck Is The Backbone Of America
John Schneider; *You Ain't Seen The Last Of Me* . (MCA)
Rednecks, White Socks & Blue Ribbon Beer
Johnny Russell; *Beer Redneck Mothers* ....(RCA)
   Rednecks, White Socks & Blue Ribbon Beer .....(RCA)
Reggae In The U.S.A.
Bunny Wailer; *Rule Dance Hall* .... (SHA)
Revolution Will Not Be Televised
Gil Scott-Heron; *Gil ScoRevolution Will Not Be*
Televised-Heron .... (BLU)
   Pieces Of A Man ....(OOP)
Rhythm Nation
Janet Jackson; *Janet Jackson's Rhythm Nation*
1814 .... (A&M)
Rock America
Afrika & Family Bambaataa; *Beware (The Funk Is*
Everywhere) .... (TMB)
Danger Danger; *Danger Danger* .... (IMI)
Rock In America
Night Ranger; *Greatest Hits* .... (CAM)
   Midnight Madness .... (CAM)
Rock Of America
Bad Company; *Dangerous Age* .... (ATL)
Rock The Nation
Montrose; *Montrose* .... (WB)

Rockin' In The U.S.A.
Kiss; *Alive 2* .... (CAS)
Royal Scam
Steely Dan; *Royal Scam* .... (MCA)
R.O.C.K. In The U.S.A.
John Cougar Mellencamp; *Scarecrow* ....(RIV)
Sail Away
Linda Ronstadt; *Don't Cry Now* .... (ASY)
Randy Newman; *Sail Away* .... (RPR)
Sailing To America
Saxon; *Crusader* ....(CRR)
Saturday In The Park
Chicago; *Greatest Hits* ....(COL)
If You Leave Me Now ....(COL)
ST/My Girl ....(EPI)
V ....(COL)
Saturday Night U.S.A.
Charlie Daniels Band; *Powder Keg* .... (EPI)
Save The Country
5th Dimension; *Anthology-1967-1973* .... (RHI)
Greatest Hits On Earth .... (ARI)
Bobby Darin; *Live At The Desert Inn* .... (MOT)
Laura Nyro; *New York Tendaberry* ....(COL)
Skateboard Surfin' U.S.A.
Jan Berry; *45* ....(A&M)
Skatetown U.S.A.
Dave Mason; *Skatetown U.S.A.* ....(COL)
Song For America
Kansas; *Best Of* ....(EPA)
Song For America ....(KIR)
Two For The Show ....(KIR)
Song Of The Patriot
Johnny Cash; *Patriot* ....(COL)
Star Spangled Banner
Duke Ellington; *Carnegie Hall Concerts-January 23
1943* .... (PRS)
Houston Symphony Orchestra; *Celebrate America* (POE)
Jimi Hendrix; *Essential-#2* ....(RPR)
Lifelines/Jimi Hendrix Story ....(RPR)
ST/Jimi Hendrix ....(RPR)
ST/Woodstock ....(ATL)
Lee Greenwood; *American Patriot* ....(LIB)
Marvin Gaye; *Musical Testament-1964-1984* ... (MOT)
Mormon Tabernacle Choir; *God Bless America* ..(COL)
This Is My Country ....(COL)
Vinnie Vincent Invasion; *Head Banging Metal* ... (PRY)
Stars & Stripes Forever
Boston Pops Orchestra/Arthur Fiedler; *Forever
Fiedler* ....(RCA)
Greatest Hits ....(POL)
Legendary Performer ....(RCA)
Mister Music U.S.A. ....(DGG)
Yankee Doodle Dandy ....(RCA)
Mormon Tabernacle Choir; *God Bless America* . (SMC)
Stars & Stripes Forever ....(COL)
Strictly U.S.A.
Tom Hooper; *Sings-Great Songs From Movie
Musicals* .... (HIN)
Surfin' U.S.A.
Beach Boys; *Absolute Best-#1* ....(CAP)
Best Of ....(CAP)
Billboard Top Rock 'N' Roll Hits-1963 .... (RHI)
Endless Summer ....(CAP)
Made In The U.S.A. ....(CAP)
Jesus & Mary Chain; *Barbed Wire Kisses* ....(DEF)
Sweet Young America
Roger Whittaker; *Wind Beneath My Wings* ......(RCA)
Take Pride In America
Oak Ridge Boys; *Greatest Hits 3* .... (MCA)
That's America
Johnnie Taylor; *This Is Your Night* .... (MAL)
There Are No Cats In America
Nehemiah Persoff/J. Guarnieri/W. Hays; *ST/An
American Tail* .... (MCA)
There's A Star-Spangled Banner
Ray Stevens; *American Music Greatest Hits* ....(CCB)
Greatest Hits ....(CCB)
This Is My Country
Mormon Tabernacle Choir; *God Bless America* . (SMC)
Greatest Hits ....(COL)
This Is My Country ....(COL)
This Is Not America
David Bowie & Pat Metheny Group; *ST/Falcon & The
Snowman* .... (EMI)

This Land Is Your Land
Bruce Springsteen/E Street Band;
Live-1975-1985 ....(COL)
Glen Campbell; *All American* ....(LIB)
Lee Greenwood; *American Patriot* ....(LIB)
Pete Seeger; *Complete Carnegie Hall
Concert-1963* ....(COL)
Sings Woody Guthrie ....(FLW)
Weavers; *Greatest Hits* .... (VAN)
Woody Guthrie; *Greatest Songs Of* .... (VAN)
Troubadours Of The Folk Era-#1 ....(RHI)
Woody Guthrie ....(VAN)
Together In America
King Errisson; *Global Music* .... (ICH)
Trader
Beach Boys; *10 Years Of Harmony* ....(CAR)
Holland ....(CAR)
U.S. Air Force
Mormon Tabernacle Choir; *Stars & Stripes
Together* ....(COL)
U.S. Blues
Grateful Dead; *From The Mars Hotel* .... (GRD)
One From The Vault .... (GRD)
Steal Your Face .... (GRD)
U.S. Male
Jerry Reed; *Best Of* ....(RCA)
U.S. Of A.
Donna Fargo; *Best Of* .... (MCA)
Country's Greatest Hits-American Pride ....(PRY)
U.S.A.
Beat; *Beat* ....(COL)
U.S.A. Today
George Jones; *Too Wild Too Long* .... (EPI)
Hank Williams, Jr.; *America (The Way I See It)* ..(W/C)
Lone Wolf ....(W/C)
Venice U.S.A.
Van Morrison; *Wavelength* ....(WB)
Vietnamerica
Stranglers; *IV* .... (IRS)
Voice Of America
Asia; *Astra* ....(GEF)
Then & Now ....(GEF)
Little Steven; *Voice Of America* ....(R&T)
Voice Of America's Son
John Cafferty/Beaver Brown Band; *ST/Cobra* ....(SCO)
Tough All Over ....(SCO)
Volunteers
Jefferson Airplane; *2400 Fulton Street-Anthology* (RCA)
Flight Log 1966-1976 .... (GRU)
ST/Forrest Gump ....(EPX)
ST/Woodstock ....(ATL)
Volunteers ....(RCA)
Worst Of ....(RCA)
"White Rabbit" & Other Hits ....(RCA)
We Love U.S.A.
Li'l Wally; *Happy Birthday America* ....(JJ)
We're An American Band
Grand Funk Railroad; *Capitol Collectors Series* ...(CAP)
Caught In The Act ....(CAP)
ST/Spirit Of '76 ....(RHI)
We're An American Band ....(CAP)
When AM Was King ....(CAP)
When It Rains In America
Sarah Brightman; *Dive* ....(A&M)
Which Way To America
Living Colour; *Vivid* ....(EPI)
Wild America
Tora Tora; *Wild America* ....(A&M)
Winter In America
Gil Scott-Heron; *Best Of* .... (ARI)
First Minute Of a New Day .... (ARI)
Margret Roadknight; *Living In The Land Of Oz* . (RWD)
With God On Our Side
Bob Dylan; *Times They Are A-Changin'* ....(COL)
Joan Baez; *First 10 Years* .... (VAN)
Neville Brothers; *Yellow Moon* ....(A&M)
XXX's And OOO's
Trisha Yearwood; *S* .... (MCA)
Yankee Doodle
Boston Pops Orchestra/Arthur Fiedler; *Fiedler's Favorite
Marches* ....(RCA)
Music For All Occasions .... (RCA)
Yankee Doodle Dandy
"C" Company/Terry Nelson; *Wake Up America* . (PLN)

Houston Symphony; *Top Of The Pops* .... (POE)
Yankee Rose
   David Lee Roth; *Eat 'Em & Smile* .... (WB)
(You Can Still) Rock In America
   Night Ranger; *Midnight Madness* .... (CAM)
Young Americans
   David Bowie; *Changesbowie* ....(RYK)
   Sound + Vision ....(RYK)
   The Singles-1969-1993 ....(RYK)
   Young Americans ....(RYK)
Your Flag Decal Won't Get You Into...
   John Prine; *John Prine* .... (ATL)
You're A Grand Old Flag
   Marilyn Horne; *Beautiful Dreamer-American*
   Songbook ....(LON)
   Mormon Tabernacle Choir; *God Bless America* . (SMC)
   Yankee Doodle Dandies ....(COL)

COUNTRIES: B

   See Also: COUNTRIES: BRAZIL

Bangladesh
   George Harrison; *Best Of* ....(CAP)
   Concert For Bangla Desh ....(CAP)
Barbados
   Charlie Parker; *Bird At The Roost* .... (SAV)
   Bird/Savoy Recordings ....(SAV)
   Charlie Parker ....(SAV)
   Encores-#2 ....(SAV)
   Jesse Colin Young; *Light Shine* ....(WB)
   Poco; *Legend* ....(MCA)
Belgian Ballad
   Connie Crothers & Lenny Popkin Quartet; *In*
   Motion .... (NA)
Belgian Team
   Hal Michael Ketchum; *Threadbare Alibis* .... (WAT)
Belgian Tom's Hat Trick
   Whitesnake; *Trouble* ....(GEF)
Belgium Stomp
   American Jazz Orchestra/John Lewis; *Music Of Jimmie*
   Lunceford .... (MM)
Bermuda
   Rocky Erickson; *Don't Slander Me* .... (RST)
   You're Gonna Miss Me-Best Of .... (RST)
Bermuda Triangle
   Fleetwood Mac; *Heroes Are Hard To Find* .... (RPR)
Down In Bermuda
   Del Vikings; *Del Vikings* ....(CLT)
Just Like Belgium
   Elton John; *The Fox* ....(MCA)
Mountains Of Burma
   Midnight Oil; *Blue Sky Mining* ....(COL)
Song Of Bangladesh
   Joan Baez; *Come From The Shadows* .... (A&M)

COUNTRIES: BRAZIL

Bird Of Brazil
   Joyce; *Music Inside* .... (VF)
Brazil
   Antonio Carlos Jobim; *Stone Flower* ....(CBA)
   Chris DeBurgh; *The End Of A Perfect Name* .... (A&M)
   Gato Barbieri; *Third World Revisited* ....(BLU)
   Jimmy Dorsey; *Best Of* ....(MCA)
Brazilian Memories
   Grover Washington, Jr.; *Best Is Yet To Come* .... (ELE)
Brazilian Stomp
   George Benson & Earl Klugh; *Collaboration* ...... (WB)
Brazilian Ukelele
   Buddy Merrill; *Best Of* ....(ACC)
   Latin Festival ....(ACC)
Coffee Song (Brazil)
   Frank Sinatra; *Greatest Hits-Early Years* ....(COL)
   In The Beginning-1943-1951 ....(COL)
   Frank Sinatra & Johnny Mandel; *Ring-A-Ding*
   Ding ....(RPR)
Down In Brazil
   Michael Franks; *Sleeping Gypsy* ....(WB)
Going To Brazil
   Motorhead; *1916* ....(WTG)
One Summer Night In Brazil
   Rippingtons; *Tourist In Paradise* ....(GRP)

Take Me To Brazil
   Dave MacKay/Lori Bell Sextet; *Take Me To*
   Brazil ....(DCO)
Wild Sewerage Tickles Brazil
   Squeeze; *Classics-#25* ....(A&M)

COUNTRIES: C

   See Also: COUNTRIES: CUBA

Czechoslovakia
   Michael McClure & Ray Manzarek; *Love Lion* .. (SHA)
Holiday In Cambodia
   Overlords; *Organic?* ....(AS)

COUNTRIES: CANADA

Acadian Driftwood
   Band; *Northern Lights Southern Cross* ....(CAP)
   To Kingdom Come (Definitive Collection) ....(CAP)
Alberta
   Blind Snooks Eaglin; *Rural Blues* ....(FAN)
   Doc Watson; *Essential* .... (VAN)
   Southbound .... (VAN)
   John Lee Hooker; *Alone* ....(SPE)
   Leadbelly; *Leadbelly* ....(COL)
   Maxwell Street Jimmy; *Rare Blues* ....(TAK)
Alberta Bound
   Curly Chaker; *Nashville Sundown* .... (CRS)
   Gordon Lightfoot; *Don Quixote* ....(RPR)
   Gord's Gold-#2 ....(WB)
Alberta, My Alberta
   Ray Griff; *Maple Leaf* .... (BOO)
Alone In Manitoba
   Humphrey/Dumptrucks; *Six Days Of Paper*
   Ladies .... (BOO)
Blue Canadian Rockies
   Byrds; *Sweetheart Of The Rodeo* ....(COL)
   Gene Autry; *50th Anniversary* .... (REP)
   Live From Madison Square Garden .... (REP)
   Jimmy C. Newman; *Cajun Cowboy* ....(PLN)
Canada
   Ray Griff; *Canada* ....(BOO)
   Greatest Hits ....(BOO)
Canadian Capers
   Tommy Dorsey; *Complete-#5* ....(RCA)
Canadian Errant
   Ian & Sylvia; *Best Of* .... (VAN)
   Greatest Hits ....(VAN)
   Ian & Sylvia ....(VAN)
   Newport Folk Festival '63 ....(VAN)
Canadian Lumber Jack
   Stompin' Tom Connors; *Bud The Spud* .... (BOO)
Canadian Pacific
   Ray Griff; *Canada* ....(BOO)
Canadian Railroad Trilogy
   Gordon Lightfoot; *Best Of* ....(EMI)
   Gord's Gold ....(RPR)
   Sunday Concert ....(UA)
   United Artists Collection ....(EMI)
   Way I Feel ....(UA)
Canadian Sunset
   Andy Williams; *16 Most Requested Songs* ....(COL)
   Etta Jones; *Greatest Hits* .... (PRS)
   Something Nice ....(PRS)
Case Of You
   Joni Mitchell; *Blue* ....(RPR)
   Miles Of Aisles ....(RPR)
Cross Canada
   Stompin' Tom Connors; *My Stompin' Concerts* .. (BOO)
Green Fields Of Canada
   Eric Schoenberg; *Acoustic Guitar* .... (ROU)
Justice In Ontario
   Steve Earle/Dukes; *Hard Way* .... (MCA)
O Canada
   Alan Mills; *Sings History Of Canada* .... (FLW)
Song For Canada
   Ian & Sylvia; *Greatest Hits* .... (VAN)
   Ian & Sylvia ....(VAN)
Thank You Canada
   Frank Snow; *45* ....(SND)
This Is My Country, Thank You Canada
   Shelley Looney; *45* ....(MER)

Under Blue Canadian Skies
Glenn Miller/Orchestra; *Complete* .... (BLU)
With Love From Alberta
Jim Post; *Shipshape* .... (FF)

COUNTRIES: CHINA

7 Chinese Bros.
R.E.M.; *Reckoning* .... (IRS)
All The Tea In China
Buck Owens; *Kickin'* .... (CCB)
Anita Goes To China
David Hayes; *Logos Through A Sideman* .... (GC)
Apolitical Blues
Little Feat; *Last Record Album* .... (WB)
   Sailing Shoes .... (WB)
   Waiting For Columbus .... (WB)
Van Halen; *OU812* .... (WB)
China
Bob Welch; *Three Hearts* .... (CAP)
Bobby Caldwell; *Heart Of Mine* .... (SD)
Grace Slick & Paul Kantner; *Sunfighter* .... (GRU)
Red Rockers; *Good As Gold* .... (COL)
Sammy Hagar; *Nine On A Ten Scale* .... (CAP)
China Boy
Benny Goodman; *Carnegie Hall Jazz Concert* ....(COL)
   Complete-#2 .... (RCA)
   ST/Story .... (MCA)
   Downbeats; 45 .... (RLL)
China Cat Sunflower
Grateful Dead; *Aoxomoxoa* .... (WB)
   Europe '72 .... (WB)
   Without A Net .... (ARI)
China Doll
Grateful Dead; *From The Mars Hotel* .... (MOB)
   Reckoning .... (ARI)
Slim Whitman; *15th Anniversary* .... (IMP)
   Best Of .... (EMI)
   Paloma Blanca-Best-Legendary Masters .... (EMI)
Suzanne Vega; *Deadicated* .... (ARI)
China Girl
David Bowie; *Changesbowie* .... (RYK)
   Let's Dance .... (EMI)
   The Singles-1969-1993 .... (RYK)
John Cougar Mellencamp; *American Fool* .... (RIV)
China Grove
Doobie Brothers; *Best Of* .... (WB)
   Captain & Me .... (WB)
   Farewell Tour .... (WB)
China Lady
Accept; *Accept* .... (PAS)
   Midnight Highway .... (PVC)
China White
Little Feat; *Hoy-Hoy!* .... (WB)
Scorpions; *Blackout* .... (MER)
Chinatown
Chaka Khan; *I Feel For You* .... (WB)
Doobie Brothers; *Livin' On The Fault Line* ...... (WB)
Greg Kihn; *Next Of Kihn* .... (BES)
Joe Jackson; *Night & Day* .... (A&M)
Chinatown My Chinatown
Al Jolson; *Story-#1* .... (MCA)
Louis Armstrong; *Armstrong #2* .... (EVR)
   Stardust .... (POR)
Chinese Arithmetic
Faith No More; *Introduce Yourself* .... (SLS)
Chinese Cafe
Joni Mitchell; *Wild Things Run Fast* .... (GEF)
Chinese Checkers
Booker T./M.G.s; *45* .... (ATL)
Chinese Kitchen
Fleshtones; *Fleshtones* .... (IRS)
   Roman Gods .... (IRS)
Chinese Mule Train
Spike Jones; *Best Of-#2* .... (RCA)
Everybody Works In China
Judy Collins; *Home Again* .... (ELE)
Going Down The China Road
Peter Lang; *Back To The Wall* .... (WTR)
Great Wall Of China
Christmas; *Ultraphrophets Of Thee Psykick Revol...* (IRS)
Kitaro; *Silk Road 1* .... (GRM)

I Can Sail To China
John Conlee; *American Faces* .... (COL)
In China Or A Woman's Heart
Kate Wolf; *Poet's Heart* .... (KAL)
Irishman In Chinatown
Luka Bloom; *Riverside* .... (RPR)
Living In China
Men Without Hats; *45* .... (BKS)
Many Chinas
Mark Isham; *Vapor Drawings* .... (WH)
Not In A Chinese Restaurant
Country Joe McDonald; *Child's Play* .... (RBB)
On A Chinese Honeymoon
Mills Brothers; *Story* .... (RAN)
On A Slow Boat To China
Jimmy Buffett; *Somewhere Over China* .... (MCA)
Kay Kyser; *16 Most Requested Songs/'40s-#2* ....(COL)
   Sentimental Favorites .... (COL)
Sonny Rollins; *First Recordings* .... (PRS)
   Vintage .... (PRS)
One Child China
Ecoteur; *Decorated Life* .... (DAL)
Overtones Of China
Sun Ra; *Visits Planet Earth/Intersteller...* ...... (EVD)
Rockin' Over China
Commander Cody; *Let's Rock* .... (BLI)
Sketches Of China
Grace Slick & Paul Kantner; *Baron Von Tollbooth &
The Chrome Nun* .... (RCA)
Jefferson Airplane; *Flight Log 1966-76* .... (GRU)
Slow Boat To China
Spike Robinson/Harry "Sweets" Edison; *Jusa Bit O'
Blues-#1* .... (CPI)
Take Me Back To My Love In China
Durell Coleman; *Durell Coleman* .... (ISL)
Tiananmen Square
Blazing Redheads; *Crazed Women* .... (REF)
Two Chinese Songs
Pete Seeger; *Banks Of Marble* .... (FLW)
Upstairs By A Chinese Lamp
Laura Nyro; *Christmas & The Beads Of Sweat* ...(COL)
Visions Of China
Japan; *Oil On Canvas* .... (BP)
   Tin Drum .... (BP)

COUNTRIES: CUBA

Another Cuba
U.K. Subs; *Japan Today* .... (RES)
Cuba
Gibson Brothers; *Island Story-1962-1987-25th
Anniversary* .... (ISL)
Cuban Connections
Outback; *Putumayo Presents Best Of World
Music-#2* .... (RHI)
Cuban Crime Of Passion
Jimmy Buffett; *Boats Beaches Bars & Ballads* ...(MGR)
   White Sport Coat & A Pink Crustacean .... (MCA)
Cuban Crisis
Phil Manzanera; *K-Scope* .... (EDI)
Cuban Fantasy
Cal Tjader; *Good Vibes* .... (CP)
Cuban Getaway
Sue Foley; *Young Girl Blues* .... (ANT)
Cuban Lullaby
Mario Bauza/Afro-Cuban Jazz Orchestra; *Tanga* (MES)
Cuban Nightingale
Joe Holiday; *Mambo Jazz* .... (PRS)
Cuban Slide
Pretenders; *Extended Play* .... (SIR)
Cubano Chant
Cal Tjader; *Greatest Hits-#1* .... (FAN)
   Latin Concert .... (FAN)
   Live At The Funky Quarters .... (FAN)
   Ritmos Calientes .... (FAN)
Moon Over Cuba
Duke Ellington; *Duke Ellington/Blanton-Webster
Band* .... (BLU)
Running Down To Cuba
John Townley/Press Gang; *Chesapeake Sailor's
Companion* .... (ADE)

COUNTRIES: D

Denmark Blues
Sleepy John Estes; *In Europe* .... (DEL)
Denmark Street
Kinks; *Lola Vs. Powerman & The Moneygoround* (RPR)
On Danish Shore
Oscar Peterson Four; *If You Could See Me Now* . (PAB)

COUNTRIES: E

See Also: COUNTRIES: EGYPT

Ecuador
Carlos Santana; *Havana Moon* .... (COL)
Stan Kenton; *Encores* ....(CW)
Ecuadorean Memories
Butch Thompson; *New Orleans Joys* .... (DAR)
Ethiopia
Joni Mitchell; *Dog Eat Dog* .... (GEF)
Ethiopia Rag
William Bolcom; *Heliotrope Bouquet Piano Rags-1900-1970* .... (NON)
Ethiopia Salaam
Judy Mowatt; *Working Wonders* .... (SHA)
Ethiopian National Anthem
Ethiopians; *Slave Call* ....(HRT)
Radio Ethiopia
Patti Smith Group; *Radio Ethiopia* .... (ARI)
Straight To Ethiopia
Augustus Pablo; *Rockers All-Star Explosion* ......(ALG)

COUNTRIES: EGYPT

Cleopatra, Queen Of Denial
Pam Tillis; *Homeward Looking Angel* .... (ARI)
Cleopatra's Cat
Spin Doctors; *Turn It Upside Down* .... (EPI)
Egypt
Kate Bush; *Never For Ever* .... (EMI)
Egypt Texas
Shadowy Men On A Shadowy Planet; *Savvy Show Stoppers* .... (CGO)
Egypt (The Chains Are On)
Dio; *Last In Line* .... (WB)
Egyptian
Litter; *Distortions* .... (KT)
Egyptian Cream
Robyn Hitchcock; *Fegmania* .... (SLS)
Egyptian Danza
Al DiMeola; *Casino* ....(COL)
Tour De Force-Live ....(COL)
Egyptian Gardens
Kaleidoscope; *Egyptian Candy-Collection* .... (EPI)
Side Trips .... (EPI)
Egyptian Song
Rufus & Chaka Khan; *Ask Rufus* .... (MCA)
Egypt, Egypt
Egyptian Lover; *Hip Hop Greats* .... (RHI)
West Coast Rap-First Dynasty-#1 .... (RHI)
Egypt's Revenge
Egyptian Lover; *West Coast Rap-Renegades* ...... (RHI)
Go Down, Moses
Paul Robeson; *The Power & The Glory* ....(COL)
Simon Estes; *Spirituals* ....(PHI)
Little Egypt
Coasters; *Atlantic R&B 1947-1974-#4-(1958-1962)* ....(ATL)
Their Greatest Recordings-Early Years ....(ATC)
Elvis Presley; *Sings Leiber & Stoller* ....(RCA)
Man Come Into Egypt
Peter, Paul & Mary; *Moving* .... (WB)
Nights Over Egypt
Jones Girls; *Get As Much Love As You Can* ...... (PI)
Rastine; *Afrodisiac* .... (ZOO)
Spirits Of Ancient Egypt
Paul McCartney/Wings; *Wings Over America* ....(CAP)
Wings; *Venus & Mars* .... (CAP)
Sue Egypt
Captain Beefheart; *Doc At The Radar Station* ...... (BP)

Walk Like An Egyptian
Bangles; *Different Light* ....(COL)
Greatest Hits ....(COL)
Modern A Cappella .... (RHI)
Walking Across Egypt
Tarwater Band; *Walking Across Egypt* .... (FF)

COUNTRIES: ENGLAND

See Also: CITIES: LONDON, COUNTRIES: SCOTLAND

Adventures In A Yorkshire Landscape
Be Bop Deluxe; *Best Of-Raiding The Divine Archive* .... (CAP)
Live In The Air Age .... (HAR)
An English Gentleman
Original Broadway Cast; *Me & My Girl* .... (MCA)
Anarchy In The U.K.
Megadeth; *So Far So Good So What* ....(CAP)
Sex Pistols; *Never Mind The Bollocks* ....(WB)
'A' Bomb In Waldour Street
Jam; *All Mad Cons* .... (POL)
Ballad Of Mad Dogs & Englishmen
Ivan "Boogaloo Joe" Jones; *Black Whip* .... (PRS)
Leon Russell; */Shelter People* .... (MCA)
Berkshire
Wha-Koo; *Berkshire* .... (MCA)
Berkshire Blues
Randy Weston; *Berkshire Blues* .... (ARI)
Self Portraits ....(VRV)
Berkshire Poppies
Traffic; *Mr. Fantasy* .... (ISL)
British Grenadiers
Cambridge Singers; *The Lark In THe Clear Air* ..(CLG)
British Pharmaceuticals
Miss World; *Miss World* .... (ATL)
British Summertime
Everything But The Girl; *Worldwide* .... (ATL)
England
Roger Whittaker; *Wind Beneath My Wings* ....(RCA)
England Rocks
Ian Hunter/Mott The Hoople; *Shades Of Ian Hunter* ....(COL)
England Swings
Roger Miller; *Best Of-#2-King Of The Road* .... (MER)
Golden Hits .... (SMA)
England's Carol
Modern Jazz Quartet; *Art Of The* .... (ATL)
Jazzlore-At Music Inn .... (ATL)
More From The Last Concert .... (ATL)
English Boys
Blondie; *The Hunter* .... (CHR)
English Boys (With Guns)
Deaf School; *English Boys/Working Girls* .... (WB)
English Civil War
Clash; *Give 'Em Enough Rope* .... (EPI)
Story Of-#1 .... (EPI)
English Dream
Generation X; *Valley Of The Dolls* .... (CHR)
English Eyes
Toto; *Turn Back* ....(COL)
English Rose
Jam; *All Mad Cons* .... (POL)
Snap .... (POL)
English Roses
Pretenders; *2* .... (SIR)
English Roundabout
XTC; *English Settlement* .... (GEF)
English Summer
Eurythmics; *In The Garden* ....(RCA)
Englishman In New York
Sting; *Nothing Like The Sun* .... (A&M)
Garden Of England
Gerry Rafferty; *Right Down The Line-Best Of* .... (EMI)
God Save The King
Popular Standard; *Out-Of-Print Recording* ....(OOP)
In Britain
Red Alert; *Punk & Disorderly* .... (PBO)
King & Queen Of England
Sandy Denny; *Circle Dance-Hokey Pokey Charity Comp.* ....(GRE)

Last God Of England
Pete Morton; *Frivolous Love* .... (PHO)
Little Old Church In England
Glenn Miller/Orchestra; *Complete* .... (BLU)
Long Haired Guys From England
Too Much Joy; *Cereal Killers* .... (GIA)
Mad Dogs & Englishmen
Noel Coward; *Album-Live From Las Vegas & New York* .... (COL)
Made In England
Ian Anderson; *Walk Into Light* .... (CHR)
Old England
Waterboys; *This Is The Sea* .... (CHR)
Picture Of England
Sun & The Moon; *Sun & The Moon* .... (GEF)
Rose Of England
Nick Lowe; *Basher-Best Of* .... (COL)
Something About England
Clash; *Sandinista* .... (EPI)
Summertime In England
Van Morrison; *Common One* .... (WB)
There'll Be Bluebirds Over The White...
Kay Kyser; *Best Of The Big Bands* .... (COL)
Why Can't The English
Rex Harrison; *ST/My Fair Lady* .... (COL)
Rex Harrison/Original Cast; *My Fair Lady* ......(COL)

COUNTRIES: FRANCE
See Also: CITIES: PARIS

1812 Overture
New York Philharmonic/Leonard Bernstein; *Conducts Tchaikovsky* ....(COL)
Great Tchaikovsky ....(COL)
Overtures and Tone Poems ....(COL)
Tchaikovsky's Greatest Hits-#1 ....(COL)
Various Overtures ....(COL)
Fields Of France
Al Stewart; *Last Days Of The Century* ....(ENC)
France
Grateful Dead; *Shakedown Street* .... (ARI)
France Chance
Ry Cooder; *Ry Cooder* .... (RPR)
French Kiss
Lil Louis/World; *This Beat Is Hot...Compilation* ... (EPI)
French Song
Monkees; *Present* .... (RHI)
French Waltz
Art Garfunkel; *Scissors Cut* ....(COL)
Green Fields Of France
Phil Coulter; *Forgotten Dreams* .... (SHA)
House In France
Doris Day & Andre Previn; *Duete* .... (DRG)
Sacha Distel; *Amour Tout Court* .... (DRG)
In France They Kiss On Main Street
Joni Mitchell; *Hissing Of Summer Lawns* .... (ASY)
Shadows & Light .... (ASY)
La Marseillaise
Mormon Tabernacle Choir; *THis Is My Country* .(COL)
Made In France
Bireli Lagrene; *Acoustic Moments* .... (BLU)
Place In France
Death Squad; *Split You At The Seams* .... (ER)
When He Takes You To France
Kevin Roth; *Voyages* .... (FF)

COUNTRIES: G

Almost Made It To Guam
Michael Gulezian; *Distant Memories & Dreams* .. (TIM)
Appointment In Ghana
Christopher Hollyday; *Christopher Hollyday* .... (NOV)
Jackie McLean; *Jackie's Bag* .... (BLN)
Girl From Greenland
Chet Baker; *Compact Jazz* .... (EMA)
Greece
George Harrison; *Gone Troppo* .... (DKH)
Greeks Don't Want No Freaks
Eagles; *The Long Run* .... (ASY)

Greenland Fisheries
Pete Seeger; *20 Golden Pieces Of* .... (BLD)
Pete Seeger ....(EVR)
Sings Folk Music Of The World .... (TRD)
Greenland Whale Fisheries
Judy Collins & Theodore Bikel; *Greatest Folksingers Of The '60s* .... (VAN)
Guatemala
Life Sex & Death; *Silent Majority* .... (RPR)
Pete Sears/Others; *Watchfire* .... (RWD)
Guatemala Connection
Hubert Laws; *Romeo & Juliet* ....(COL)
Payed Vacation: Greece
Camper Van Beethoven; *Telephone Free Landslide Victory* .... (IRS)
Shaft In Greenland
Dead Milkmen; *Soul Rotation* .... (HOL)
Stranded In Greenland
For Against; *December* .... (CHS)
"Zorba The Greek" Theme
Cincinnati Pops Orchestra/Erich Kunzel; *Hollywood's Greatest Hits-#2* .... (TLR)

COUNTRIES: GERMANY
See Also: CITIES: BERLIN

Arabs With Knives & West German Skies
Roger Waters; *Pros & Cons Of Hitchhiking* ......(COL)
Bavarian In New York
Triumvirat; *A LaCarte* .... (CAP)
Different Germany
Ian Anderson; *Walk Into Light* .... (CHR)
Fraulein
Bobby Helms; *Pop-A-Dilly* .... (MCA)
Super Hits Country/'50s .... (GUS)
Mickey Gilley; *Greatest Hits-#1* .... (EPI)
German Kid
Dee Dee King; *Standing In The Spotlight* .... (RE)
German Lunch
Frank Zappa; *You Can't Do That On Stage Anymore-#5* ....(RYK)
German Nun
Sex Gang Children; *Ecstasy & Vendetta Over New York* .... (ROI)
German Overalls
Peter Hammill; *Chameleon In The Shadow Of The Night* ....(BP)
German Special
Li'l Wally; *All Around The World* .... (JJ)
German Waltz Medley
Lawrence Welk; *Come Waltz With Me* .... (RAN)
Germans At The Spa
Original London Cast; *Nine* ....(RCA)
Germany
Sloppy Seconds; *Fist Seven Inches...& Then Some!* (TNG)
Stains; *Stains* ....(SST)
Girl From Germany
Sparks; *Profile: Ultimate Sparks Collection* .... (RHI)
How Do You Say Auf Wiedersehen
George Shearing & Mel Torme; *Top Drawer* .... (CCJ)
In Germany Before The War
Randy Newman; *Little Criminals* ....(WB)
Lili Marlene
Marlene Dietrich; *Best Of* ....(COL)
Essential ....(CAP)
Live At The Cafe De Paris ....(COL)
This Is Art Deco ....(COL)
Lost In Germany
King's X; *King's X* .... (ATL)
Snoopy Vs. The Red Baron
Royal Guardsmen; *Best Of-#1* .... (RHI)
Collectables Presents History Of Rock-#9 .... (CLT)
Cruisin'-1967 .... (INC)
Million-Dollar Memories #1 ....(RCA)
Super Oldies/'60s-#6 ....(AUF)
Springtime For Hitler
Mel Brooks; *ST/High Anxiety* .... (ASY)
To Germany With Love
Alphaville; *Forever Young* ....(ATL)
Wars Of Germany
Clancy Brothers/Tommy Makem; *Luck Of The Irish* ....(COL)

West Germany
Minutemen; *Double Nickels On The Dime* ....(SST)
White Car In Germany
Associates; *Popera-Singles Collection* ....(SIR)

COUNTRIES: H

Cowboys In Hong Kong (As Far As Siam)
Red Rider; *As Far As Siam* ....(CAP)
Dutch Morning
Phil Woods & Jim McNeely; *Flowers For Hodges* (CCJ)
Dutch Treat
Rex Stewart; *Capitol Jazz 50th Anniversary
Collection* ....(BLN)
Dutchman
Jerry Jeff Walker; *Hill Country Rain* ....(RYK)
Tommy Makem & Liam Clancy; *Collection* .....(SHA)
Dutchmen Bohemian Polka
Michigan Dutchmen; *Beer & Dutchmen Polkas* ......(JJ)
Haitian Divorce
Steely Dan; *Greatest Hits* ....(MCA)
Royal Scam ....(MCA)
Holland Park
John Williams; *Echoes Of London* ....(COL)
Hong Kong
Quinns; *Harlem Holiday-New York R&B-#4* .....(CLT)
Screamin' Jay Hawkins; *At Home With* ....(COL)
Cow Fingers & Mosquito Pie ....(EPI)
Hong Kong Bar
Tim Buckley; *Greetings From L.A.* ....(BIZ)
Hong Kong Blues
George Harrison; *Somewhere In England* ....(DKH)
Hoagy Carmichael; *Stardust Road* ....(MCA)
Hong Kong Fireworks
Henry Mancini; *ST/Revenge Of The Pink Panther* . (EMI)
Hong Kong Garden
Siouxsie/Banshees; *Once Upon A Time-The
Singles* ....(GEF)
I Left My Hat In Haiti
Fred Astaire; *ST/Royal Wedding* ....(SSP)
Little Dutch Girl
George Morgan; *American Originals* ....(COL)
Little Dutch Mill
Bing Crosby; *Crooner-Columbia
Years-1928-1934* ....(COL)
Little Dutch Town
Mac Davis; *Volume XC* ....(ALL)
With Love ....(ACC)
Road To Hong Kong
Billy May; *I Believe In You* ....(BAI)
Sail On Flying Dutchman
Nick Seeger; *Sail On Flying Dutchman* ....(BIO)

COUNTRIES: I

Beautiful Hills Of Galilee
Hazel Dickens; *Old-Timey Gospel Music* .... (ROU)
Funiculi, Funicula
Mario Lanza; *Legendary Tenor* ....(RCA)
Hatikvah
Barbra Streisand & Golda Meir; *Barbra Streisand...Just
For The Record* ....(COL)
Mormon Tabernacle Choir; *This Is My Country* ..(COL)
Hunting Tigers Out In India
Bonzo Dog Band; *Best Of* ....(RHI)
Tadpoles ....(LIB)
I Left My Heart In Iran
Forgotten Rebels; *Surfin' On Heroin* ....(RES)
India
John Coltrane; *Best Of-#2* ....(MCA)
John McLaughlin/Shakti; *Handful Of Beauty* ....(COL)
Roxy Music; *Avalon* ....(WB)
Heart Still Beating ....(RPR)
Israel
Bill Evans; *Complete Riverside Recordings* ....(RVR)
Miles Davis; *Birth Of The Cool* ....(CAP)
Siouxsie/Banshees; *Nocturne* ....(GEF)
Once Upon A Time-Singles ....(GEF)
Israel In Our House
Al Jolson; *Story-#5* ....(MCA)

Israelites (The)
Desmond Dekker; *Island Story-1962-1987-25th
Anniversary* .... (ISL)
ST/Drugstore Cowboy ....(NOV)
Italian From New York
Chicago; #7 ....(COL)
Italian Girls
Daryl Hall & John Oates; *H2O* ....(RCA)
Soulful Sounds ....(RCA)
Rod Stewart; *Best Of-#2* ....(MER)
Italian Plastic
Crowded House; *Woodface* ....(CAP)
Italian Shoes
Dynatones; *Shameless* ....(WB)
Man From Galilee
Billy Parker; *Average Man* ....(SNC)
New Electric India
Shadowfax; *Shadow Dance* ....(WH)
What Goes Around-Best Of ....(WH)
Postcard From India
Rosalie Sorrels; *Travelin' Lady Rides Again* ......(GRE)
Return From India
Jerry Holland; *Jerry Holland* .... (ROU)
Scenes From An Italian Restaurant
Billy Joel; *The Stranger* ....(COL)
Song Of India
101 Strings; *Big Band Hits-#1* .... (ALS)
BBC Big Band; *Age Of Swing-#1* ....(BAI)
Tommy Dorsey; *Best Of* ....(RCA)
This Is The Big Band Era ....(RCA)
Tommy Dorsey & Frank Sinatra; *Dorsey/Sinatra Radio
Years-1940-1942* ....(RCA)
Tommy Dorsey/Orchestra; *& The David Rose String
Orchestra* .... (LAS)
Sweet Song Of India
McGuire Sisters; *Best Of* ....(MCA)
Theme From "Exodus"
101 Strings Orchestra; *Golden Movie Themes* .... (ALS)
Boston Pops Orchestra/Arthur Fiedler; *Motion Picture
Classics-#1* ....(RCA)
Ferrante & Teicher; *Grand Pianos* ....(PRR)

COUNTRIES: IRELAND
See Also: CITIES: DUBLIN

Beautiful Ireland
Anne & Francie Brolly; *Ireland My Home* .... (RGO)
Come Back To Erin
Billy Shepherd Singers; *Irish Sing-Along* .... (MCA)
Did Your Mother Come From Ireland
Bing Crosby; *Shillelaghs & Shamrocks* .... (MCA)
Drink A Round To Ireland
Judy Collins; *Times Of Our Lives* .... (ELE)
Farewell To Ireland
Phil Cunningham; *Airs & Graces* ....(GRE)
Galway Bay
Bing Crosby; *Best Of* ....(MCA)
When Irish Eyes Are Smiling ....(MCA)
Ireland
Flim/BB's; *Further Adventures* .... (DIG)
Marianne Faithfull; *Child's Adventure* .... (ISL)
Maura O'Connell; *Real Life Story* ....(WB)
Ireland Mother Ireland
John McCormack; *Irish Minstrel* ....(RCA)
Louis Browne; *Evening In Ireland* .... (RGO)
Ireland My Home
Ann & Francie Brolly; *Ireland My Home* .... (RGO)
Barley Bree; *Speak Up For Old Ireland* ....(SHA)
Ireland We Know
Ed Reavy; *Ed Reavy* .... (ROU)
Ireland's 32
Paddy Noonan Band; *Happy Hours* .... (RGO)
Irish
Buddy Merrill; *Holiday For Guitars* ....(ACT)
Irish Boy
Mark Knopfler; *CT/Cal* .... (MER)
Irish Heartbeat
Van Morrison; *Inarticulate Speech Of The Heart* ..(WB)
Van Morrison/Chieftains; *Irish Heartbeat* .... (MER)
Irish Jig (The Ball)
Original Broadway Cast; *Meet Me In St. Louis* .. (DRG)
Irish Jubilee
Pat Harrington; *St. Patrick's Day Celebration* ....(COL)

Irish Love Song
Mormon Tabernacle Choir; *Old Beloved Songs* ...(COL)
Irish Lullabye
Paddy Noonan; *Irish Party* .... (RGO)
Irish March: March Of The Mayomen
Chieftains/RTE Concert Orchestra; *Year Of The French* .... (SHA)
Irish Rover
Clancy Brothers; *With Lou* .... (VAN)
Irish Rovers; *First Of* .... (MCA)
Irish Spring
Country Gentlemen; *With Ricky Skaggs* .... (VAN)
Irish Suite: Irish Washerwoman
Boston Pops Orchestra/Arthur Fiedler; *Irish Night At The Pops* ....(RCA)
Irishman In Chinatown
Luka Bloom; *Riverside* .... (RPR)
Luck Of The Irish
Elephants Memory/Invisible Strings; *Sometime In New York City/Live Jam* ....(CAP)
Memories Of Ireland
Paddy Noonan; *Memories Of Ireland* .... (RGO)
Minstrel Boy
Boston Pops Orchestra/Arthur Fiedler; *Irish Album* ....(RCA)
Irish Night At The Pops ....(RCA)
John McDermott; *Battlefields Of Green-Songs Of Love/Loss* .... (ANG)
My Irish Molly-O
De Danann; *Best Of* .... (SHA)
My Wild Irish Rose
Magic Organ; *22 Great Organ Favorites* ...... (RAN)
Mom & Dads; *One Dozen Roses* .... (CRS)
Paddy Doyle's Boots
Clancy Brothers/Tommy Makem; *Best Of* ....(TRD)
Paddy Goes To Nashville
Adrian Legg; *Mrs. Crowe's Blue Waltz* .... (REL)
Paddy Kelly's Brew
Tommy Makem; *Evening With* .... (SHA)
Paddy McGinty's Coat
Pat Harrington; *St. Patrick's Day Celebration* ....(COL)
Paddy On The Railway
Barley Bree; *Castles In The Air* .... (SHA)
Paddy Ryan's Dream
Matt Molloy; *Stony Steps* .... (GRE)
Paddy Won't You Drink Some Cider
Red Clay Ramblers; *Chuckin' The Frizz* .... (FF)
Paddy's Green Shamrock Shore
Chieftains; *Another Country* ....(RCA)
Rambling Irishman
De Danann; *Best Of* .... (SHA)
Red Headed Irishman
J.P. Fraley & Annadeene; *Wild Rose Of The Mountain* .... (ROU)
Rockin' Rockin' Leprechauns
Jonathan Richman/Modern Lovers; *Rock 'N' Roll With* .... (RHI)
Rose Of Tralee
Bing Crosby; *When Irish Eyes Are Smiling* .... (MCA)
Patrick O'Hagan; *22 Golden Shamrocks* .... (RGO)
Shall My Soul Pass Through Old Ireland
Pat Daly & Frank Fitzpatrick Band; *One Of The Old Brigade* .... (RGO)
Small Hills Of Offaly
Irish Tradition; *Times We've Had* ....(GRE)
There's A Little Bit Of Irish
Patrick O'Hagan; *22 Golden Shamrocks* .... (RGO)
They Wounded Old Ireland
Andy M. Stewart; *By The Hush* ....(GRE)
Too Ra Loo Ra Loo Ral
Band; *Last Waltz* ....(WB)
Bing Crosby; *Best Of Bing* .... (MCA)
When Irish Eyes Are Smiling .... (MCA)
When Irish Eyes Are Smiling
Billy Shepherd Singers; *Irish Sing-Along* .... (MCA)
Bing Crosby; *When Irish Eyes Are Smiling* .... (MCA)
Dennis Day; *Irish Album* ....(RCA)

COUNTRIES: JAMAICA

Boogie On Reggae Woman
Stevie Wonder; *Fulfillingness' First Finale* .... (MOT)
Motown Time Capsule-#2-'70s .... (MOT)
Original Musiquarium .... (MOT)
Come Back To Jamaica
Yellowman; *Going To The Chapel* .... (SHA)
Coming Back, Jamaica
Lester Bowie's Brass Fantasy; *I Only Have Eyes For You* .... (ECM)
Jamaica
Bobby Caldwell; *Carry On* ....(SD)
Caron Wheeler; *Uk Blak* .... (EMI)
George Benson & Earl Klugh; *Collaboration* ..... (WB)
Lacy J. Dalton; *16th Avenue* ....(COL)
Scott Cossu; *Wind Dance* ....(WH)
Jamaica Farewell
Harry Belafonte; *All-Time Greatest Hits-#1* ....(RCA)
Calypso ....(RCA)
Legendary Performer ....(RCA)
Pure Gold ....(RCA)
This Is ....(RCA)
Jamaica In My Mind
McGuffey Lane; *Day By Day* .... (AA)
Jamaica Jerkoff
Elton John; *Goodbye Yellow Brick Road* .... (POL)
Jamaica Lady
Nitty Gritty Dirt Band; *Dirt Silver & Gold* .... (UA)
Jamaica Say You Will
Jackson Browne; *Saturate Before Using* .... (ASY)
Jamaica Ska
Annette Funicello; *Best Of* .... (RHI)
Jamaica Sunday Morning
Kim Carnes; *St. Vincent's Court* ....(OOP)
My Jamaican Guy
Grace Jones; *Island Life* .... (ISL)
On Jamaica
Country Joe McDonald; *Paradise With An Ocean View* .... (FAN)
On & On
Stephen Bishop; *Best Of Bish* .... (RHI)
Rastafari Is
Peter Tosh; *Captured Live* .... (EMI)
Wanted Dread & Alive .... (EMI)
Rastafari Liveth
Peter Broggs; *Rastafari Liveth* .... (RAS)
Real Authentic Sampler .... (RAS)
Rastaman
Bunny Wailer; *Blackheart Man* ....(MGO)
Rastaman Chant
Bob Marley/Wailers; *Burnin'* ....(TUF)
Rastaman Live Up
Bob Marley/Wailers; *Confrontation* ....(TUF)
Reggae On Broadway
Bob Marley; *Chances Are* .... (COT)
Reggae Radio Station
Third World; *Hold On To Love* ....(COL)
Reggae Revolution
Ziggy Marley/Melody Makers; *Hey World!* ...... (EMI)
Time Has Come...Best Of .... (EMI)
Roots Woman
Jimmy Cliff; *Power & The Glory* ....(COL)
Rootsman Skanking
Bunny Wailer; *Rootsman Skanking* .... (SHA)
Roots, Rock, Reggae
Bob Marley/Wailers; *Rastaman Vibration* ....(TUF)
Sweet Jamaica
Cat Stevens; *Izitso* .... (A&M)
Temple Jamaica
Peter Manning Robinson; *Phoenix Rising* .... (CMG)
Vahevala
Loggins & Messina; *Best Of-Friends* ....(COL)
On Stage ....(COL)
Sittin' In ....(COL)
You're My Jamaica
Charley Pride; *Greatest Hits* ....(RCA)
Live ....(RCA)

COUNTRIES: JAPAN
See Also: CITIES: TOKYO

Big In Japan
Alphaville; *Forever Young* .... (ATL)
   Singles Collection .... (ATL)
Bird Of Japan
Joyce; *Music Inside* .... (VF)
Discovering Japan
Graham Parker; *Squeezing Out Sparks* .... (ARI)
Geisha Girl
Hank Locklin; *Golden Hits* .... (PLN)
Japan
Be Bop Deluxe; *Best Of-Raiding The Divine*
  Archive ....(CAP)
Oregon; *Our First Record* .... (VAN)
Japanese Drums
Kitaro; *Asia* .... (GEF)
Japanese Sandman
Benny Goodman; *Complete-#1-1935* ....(RCA)
Japanese Tears
Denny Laine; *Japanese Tears* ....(TAK)
Living In Japan
Fun Fun; *33* .... (TSR)
Made In Japan
Buck Owens; *All-Time Greatest-#1* ....(CCB)
  Collection-1959-1990 .... (RHI)
Kat; *Beethoven On Speed* .... (RR)
Silent Eyes
Paul Simon; *Still Crazy After All These Years* ....(COL)
Sukiyaki
Kyu Sakamoto; *When AM Was King* ....(CAP)
Taste Of Honey; *Golden Honey* ....(CAP)
  Twice As Sweet ....(CAP)
Turning Japanese
Vapors; *New Clear Days* .... (LIB)
  Rock Of The '80s-#3 ....(PRY)
Working For The Japanese
Loverboy; *Get Lucky* ....(COL)
Ray Stevens; *Top Ten Records* ....(CCB)
  #1 With A Bullet ....(CCB)
You're Still Not Safe In A Japanese Car
Jumpin' John Goldsmith; *45* .... (ATL)

COUNTRIES: K

Kenya
J.J. Johnson; *Lt's Hang Out* ....(VRV)
Rippingtons; *Welcome To The St. James' Club* ...(GRP)
Sad News From Korea
Lightnin' Hopkins; *Houston's King of the*
  Blues-1952-1953 .... (BCL)

COUNTRIES: M

Club Morocco
Azymuth; *Cascades* .... (MS)
Dawn In Malaysia
Kitaro; *Asia* .... (GEF)
El Morocco
Santana; *Moonflower* ....(COL)
Midnight In Morocco
Michael Powers; *Perpetual Motion* .... (NSY)
Moroccan Nights
John Tropea; *NY Cats Direct* .... (DIG)
Morocco
Rippingtons; *Kilimanjaro* ....(GRP)
Mozambique
Bob Dylan; *Desire* ....(COL)
Emily Remler; *Retrospective-#2-Compositions* .... (CCJ)
She Drives Me Madagascar
Chi; *Jet Stream* ....(SA)
Something Fine (Morocco)
Jackson Browne; *Jackson Browne* ....(ASY)

COUNTRIES: MEXICO
See Also: COUNTRIES: S, SPANISH

Acapulco
Neil Diamond; *Jazz Singer* ....(CAP)
Acapulco 1922
Herb Alpert/Tijuana Brass; *Lonely Bull* .... (A&M)
  Solid Brass ....(A&M)
Acapulco Gold
Rainy Daze; *Acapulco Gold* ....(OOP)
Ain't No God In Mexico
Waylon Jennings; *Honky Tonk Heroes* ....(RCA)
Bay Of Mexico
Kingston Trio; *Folk Era Sampler-Digitally* ....(FOL)
  Stereo Concert Plus ....(FOL)
  Tom Dooley ....(CAP)
Big Mexican Dinner
Kentucky HeadHunters; *Electric Barnyard* ...... (MER)
Blame It On Mexico
George Strait; *Strait Country* .... (MCA)
Border, The
America; *America In Concert* ....(CAP)
  Encore-More Greatest Hits .... (RHI)
  Your Move ....(CAP)
Brownsville Turnaround On The Tex-Mex...
KLF; *Chill Out* .... (WAX)
Down In Mexico
Coasters; *Greatest Hits* ....(ATC)
  Atlantic R&B 1947-1974-#3 (1955-1958) .... (ATL)
  Greatest Recordings ....(ATC)
Down To Mexico
Angie Meyer; *Texas Folk & Outlaw Music* ...... (ADE)
Dreams Of Mexico
Arlen Roth; *Guitarist* .... (ROU)
El Paso
Grateful Dead; *Steal Your Face* .... (GRD)
Marty Robbins; *Biggest Hits* ....(COL)
  Billboard Top Country Hits-1960 .... (RHI)
  Gunfighter Ballads & Trail Songs ....(COL)
  Radio Classics!'50s ....(COL)
Escape To Mexico
William Orbit; *Orbit* .... (IRS)
From Maine To Mexico
Leon Russell; *Americana* ....(OOP)
Going Down To Mexico
ZZ Top; *First Album* .... (WB)
  Six Pack .... (WB)
Going To Mexico
Steve Miller Band; *Anthology* ....(CAP)
  Best Of-1968-1973 ....(CAP)
  #5 ....(CAP)
Henry
New Riders Of The Purple Sage; *Best Of* ....(COL)
  Bill Graham Presents Fillmore-Last Days ...... (EPA)
  Home Home On The Road ....(COL)
  New Riders Of The Purple Sage ....(COL)
He'll Have To Go
Jim Reeves; *60 Years Of Country Music* ....(RCA)
  Best Of ....(RCA)
  Billboard Top Country Hits-1960 .... (RHI)
  Great Moments At The Grand Ole Opry ....(RCA)
  Nipper's Greatest Hits!'50s-#1 ....(RCA)
Jim Reeves & Patsy Cline; *Jim Reeves-Greatest*
  Hits ....(RCA)
Ry Cooder; *Chicken Skin Music* ....(RPR)
I Got Mexico
Eddy Raven; *14 #1 Country Hits* ....(RCA)
  Best Of ....(RCA)
  I Could Use Another You ....(RCA)
In Mexico
Moe Bandy; *45* ....(COL)
Late Winter, Early Spring
John Denver; *Rocky Mountain High* ....(RCA)
Lonely Rose Of Mexico
Sons Of The Pioneers; *Tumbleweed Trails* ...... (MCA)
Lost In Mexico
Billy Joe Walker, Jr.; *Treehouse* .... (MCA)
Lost John Boogied His Way Into Mexico
Maddox Brothers & Rose; *On The Air-#1 & 2* .. (ARH)
Maybe Mexico
Jerry Jeff Walker; *Mr. Bojangles* ....(BAI)

Mexican Blackbird
ZZ Top; *Fandango* .... (WB)
Six Pack .... (WB)
Mexican Connection
Billy Joel; *Streetlife Serenade* .... (COL)
Mexican Divorce
Drifters; *1959-1965-All-Time Greatest Hits &
More* .... (ATL)
Nicolette Larson; *Nicolette* .... (WB)
Ry Cooder; *Paradise & Lunch* .... (RPR)
Mexican Hat Dance
Percy Faith; *All-Time Greatest Hits* .... (COL)
Mexican Minutes
Brooks & Dunn; *Hard Workin' Man* .... (ARI)
Mexican Radio
Wall Of Voodoo; *Call Of The West* .... (IRS)
Ugly Americans In Australia .... (IRS)
Wall Of Voodoo .... (IRS)
Mexican Shuffle
Herb Alpert/Tijuana Brass; *Classics-#1* .... (A&M)
Greatest Hits .... (A&M)
Tijuana Brass; *South Of The Border* .... (A&M)
Mexican, The
Jellybean; *Rocks The House* .... (CHR)
Wotupski .... (EMI)
Mexico
Bob Moore; *45* .... (OOP)
Firefall; *Best Of* .... (ATL)
Firefall .... (ATL)
Herb Alpert/Tijuana Brass; *Lonely Bull* .... (A&M)
James Taylor; *Gorilla* .... (WB)
Greatest Hits .... (WB)
Jefferson Airplane; *2400 Fulton Street-An
Anthology* .... (RCA)
Katrina/Waves; *Katrina/Waves* .... (CAP)
Lee Dorsey; *Golden Classics* .... (CLT)
Nazareth; *2XS* .... (A&M)
Mexico Rain
Johnny Rodriguez; *Biggest Hits* .... (EPI)
Old Mexico
Bad Company; *Rough Diamonds* .... (SS)
Orion; *Fresh* .... (SUN)
Ride Like The Wind
Christopher Cross; *Christopher Cross* .... (WB)
Riding My Thumb To Mexico
Johnny Rodriguez; *40 Years Of Country
Music-#3-1970-1979* .... (MER)
All I Ever Meant To Do .... (MER)
Desperado .... (MER)
Greatest Hits .... (MER)
Romance In Durango
Bob Dylan; *Biograph* .... (COL)
Desire .... (COL)
Run To Mexico
Babys; *Head First* .... (CHR)
San Miguel
Beach Boys; *10 Years Of Harmony* .... (CAR)
Seashores Of Old Mexico
Merle Haggard & Willie Nelson; *Seashores Of Old
Mexico* .... (EPI)
Sexy Mexican Maid
Red Hot Chili Peppers; *Mother's Milkl* .... (EMI)
South Of The Border (Down Mexico Way)
Bob Wills; *Best Of* .... (MCA)
Greatest Hits .... (CCB)
Frank Sinatra; *Capitol Collectors Series* .... (CAP)
Come Fly With Me .... (CAP)
Gene Autry; *Country Music Hall Of Fame* ...... (COL)
Patsy Cline; *Always* .... (MCA)
Story .... (MCA)
Willie Nelson; *What A Wonderful World* .... (COL)
Sunrise In Mexico
Clifford Jordan; *Starting Time* .... (JZL)
Theme From "The Magnificent Seven"
BBC Concert Orchestra; *Golden Cinema
Classics-Adventure Film* .... (BAI)
They All Went To Mexico
Carlos Santana; *Havana Moon* .... (COL)
Willie Nelson & Carlos Santana; *Half Nelson* ....(COL)
Thief In Mexico
Don Michael Sampson; *Coyote* .... (RVL)
This Is My Year For Mexico
Crystal Gayle; *Crystal Gayle* .... (UA)

Till It Snows In Mexico
Reba McEntire; *What Am I Gonna Do About
You* .... (MCA)
Trail To Mexico
Peter La Farge; *Cowboy Songs On Folkways* .... (FLW)

COUNTRIES: N

Dream Home In New Zealand
English Beat; *Wha'ppen* .... (IRS)
Nicaragua
Bruce Cockburn; *Stealing Fire* .... (COL)
Nicaragua Blues
Gil Evans; *Bud & Bird* .... (EVD)
Nicaragua Nicaraguita
Billy Bragg; *Internationale* .... (ELE)
Nicaragua Night
Holly Near; *All-Ears Review-#7-Still Amazing...* . (ROM)
Nigerian Juju Hilife
Pharoah Sanders; *Rejoice* .... (EVD)
Nigerian Marketplace
Oscar Peterson Trio; *Nigerian Marketplace* .... (PAB)
Norwegian Aire
Magical Strings; *Crossing To Skellig* .... (FF)
Norwegian Dance
Stephane Grappelli; *Stephanova* .... (CCJ)
Norwegian Dance No. 2
Django Reinhardt & Stephane Grappelli; *Django
Reinhardt & Stephane Grappelli* .... (CRS)
Norwegian Girl
Vernon Castle; *Polka Update* .... (TAG)
Norwegian Waltz/Liza Lynn
Jackie Daly/Seamus & Manus McGuire; *Buttons &
Bows* .... (GRE)
Norwegian Wood
Beatles; *1962-1966* .... (CAP)
Box Set .... (CAP)
Love Songs .... (CAP)
Rubber Soul .... (CAP)
Shipyards Of New Zealand
Midnight Oil; *Red Sails In The Sunset* .... (COL)
Surf Nicaragua
Sacred Reich; *Mega Metal* .... (KT)

COUNTRIES: P
See Also: COUNTRIES: POLAND

Abril En Portugal
Julio Iglesias; *Libra* .... (COL)
April In Portugal
Eartha Kitt; *Best Of* .... (MCA)
In A Persian Market
Wilbur DeParis; *ST/New York Stories* .... (ELE)
Lost Paraguayos
Rod Stewart; *Best Of-#2* .... (MER)
Sing It Again Rod .... (MER)
Man From Pakistan
Flaming Lips; *Hear It Is* .... (RES)
Midnight 'N Peru
Ken Tamplin; *Soul Survivor* .... (INS)
My Paraguayan Song
Roberto Perera; *Erotica* .... (EPI)
Panama
Crosby, Stills & Nash; *After The Storm* .... (ATL)
Kid Ory's Creole Jazz Band; *Favorites!* .... (GTJ)
Louis Armstrong; *Best Of* .... (AUF)
Of New Orleans .... (MCA)
& His All-Stars .... (LAS)
#2 .... (EVR)
Preservation Hall Jazz Band; *New Orleans-#1* ...(COL)
Van Halen; *1984* .... (WB)
Panama Red
New Riders Of The Purple Sage; *Adventures Of Panama
Red* .... (COL)
Best Of .... (COL)
Rock Classics Of The '70s .... (COL)
Panama Tones/Nuevo Boogaloo
Iguanas; *Nuevo Boogaloo* .... (MGR)
Peru
Eric Tingstad & Nancy Rumbel; *Homeland* ..... (NAR)
Marcos Loya; *Love Is The Reason* .... (SPT)

Portuguese Love
Teena Marie; *Greatest Hits* .... (MOT)
It Must Be Magic .... (MOT)
Portuguese Washerwoman
Astrud Gilberto; *Look To The Rainbow* .... (VRV)
Buddy Merrill; *Holiday For Guitars* .... (ACT)
Puerto Rican Children
Hilton Ruiz; *Something Grand* .... (NOV)
Puerto Rican Rhythms
Last Poets; *Right On!* .... (CLT)
Puerto Rico
Charles Sepulveda/Turnaround; *Algo Nuestro* ... (AND)
Marisela/Others; *ST/Salsa* .... (MCA)
Two Gentlemen Of Peru
Simon & Bard Group; *Enormous Radio* .... (FF)
Villa In Portugal
Pursuit Of Happiness; *Downward Road* .... (MER)

COUNTRIES: POLAND

Children Of Poland
Si Kahn; *Unfinished Portraits* .... (FF)
My Polish Girlfriend
Li'l Wally; *My Polish Girlfriend & Others* .... (JJ)
Poland Whole/Madam I'm Adam
Tubes; *Young & Rich* .... (A&M)
Polish Feelings
Li'l Wally; *Polish Feelings* .... (JJ)
Polish Folk Song Medley
101 Strings Orchestra; *Greatest Hits Of* .... (ALS)
Polish Hop Polka
Cavaliers; *Have Polka Will Travel* .... (ACT)
Polish Lullaby
Marvin Hamlisch; *ST/Sophie's Choice* .... (SOU)
Polish Memories Waltz
New Yorkers; *Polka Smile* .... (JJ)
Polish National Anthem
101 Strings Orchestra; *Soul Of Poland* .... (ALS)
Polish Sausage Polka
Li'l Wally; *#1* .... (JJ)
Polish Song
Jimmy Sturr/Orchestra; *Sturr-It-Up* .... (RAN)
Road To Poland
Mike Figgis; *ST/Stormy Monday* .... (VMM)
Santa Must Be Polish
Bobby Vinton; *Great Songs Of Christmas* .... (CCB)

COUNTRIES: RUSSIA
See Also: CITIES: MOSCOW

1812 Overture
New York Philharmonic/Leonard Bernstein; *Conducts Tchaikovsky* .... (COL)
Great Tchaikovsky .... (COL)
Overtures and Tone Poems .... (COL)
Tchaikovsky's Greatest Hits-#1 .... (COL)
Various Overtures .... (COL)
Back In The U.S.S.R.
Beatles; *1967-1970* .... (CAP)
Box Set .... (CAP)
Rock 'N' Roll Music-#2 .... (CAP)
White Album .... (CAP)
Billy Joel; *KOHUEPT* .... (COL)
Paul McCartney; *Tripping The Live Fantastic* .... (CAP)
Bomb The Russians
Fear; *More Beer* .... (ENI)
Dressed To Kill
Lita Ford; *Dancin' On The Edge* .... (MER)
Nazareth; *Classics-#16* .... (A&M)
Fool Circle .... (A&M)
'Snaz .... (A&M)
From Russia With Love
Matt Monro; *13 Original James Bond Themes* .... (EMI)
Glorious Russian
Original Broadway Cast; *Stop The World I Want To Get Off* .... (POL)
Original Cast/Sammy Davis, Jr.; *Stop The World I Want To Get Off* .... (WB)
Hymn To The Russian Earth
Paul Winter Consort; *Concert For The Earth-Live At The U.N.* .... (LIV)

In America
Charlie Daniels Band; *Decade Of Hits* .... (EPI)
Full Moon .... (EPI)
Me & The Boys .... (EPI)
Lawyers, Guns & Money
Warren Zevon; *Excitable Boy* .... (ASY)
Quiet Normal Life-Best Of .... (ASY)
Stand In The Fire .... (ASY)
Meadowlands
101 Strings Orchestra; *Soul Of Russia* .... (ALS)
Jefferson Airplane; *Volunteers* ....(RCA)
Morrisey & The Russian Sailor
Tom Dahill; *Irish Music From St. Paul To Donegal* (FF)
Mother Russia
Iron Maiden; *No Prayer For The Dying* .... (EPI)
Renaissance; *Live At Carnegie Hall* .... (SIR)
Tales Of 1001 Nights-#1 .... (SIR)
Turn Of The Cards .... (SIR)
My Russia, You Are Beautiful
Ivan Rebroff; *Memories Of Russia* ....(COL)
Nikita
Elton John; *Greatest Hits-1976-1986* .... (MCA)
Ice On Fire .... (MCA)
Return To Russia
Kitaro; *Asia* .... (GEF)
Silver Cloud .... (GEF)
Rocking Over Russia
Elvis Hitler; *Disgraceland* .... (RES)
Ronnie, Talk To Russia
Prince; *Controversy* .... (WB)
Russian Bandstand
Spencer & Spencer; *Dr. Demento's Greatest-#2* .. (RHI)
Russian Imperial Anthem
Royal Scots Dragoon Guard; *Amazing Grace* ....(RCA)
Russian Lady
Karen Alexander; *Isn't It Always Love* .... (ASY)
Russian Lullaby
Al Cohn; *Standards Of Excellence* .... (CCJ)
Jerry Garcia; *Compliments* .... (GRD)
Jerry Garcia & David Grisman; *Jerry Garcia & David Grisman* .... (GRD)
John Coltrane; *Soultrane* .... (PRS)
Russian Radio
Red Flag; *Naive Art* ....(ENC)
Russian Reggae
Nina Hagen; *In Ekstasy* ....(COL)
Russian Roulette
Accept; *Russian Roulette* ....(POR)
Hollies; *Hollies* .... (EPI)
Joan Armatrading; *Sleight Of Hand* ....(A&M)
Lords Of The New Church; *Killer Lords* .... (IRS)
Lords Of The New Church .... (IRS)
Michelle Shocked; *Captain Swing* .... (MER)
Taxxi; *Expose* .... (MCA)
Russian Winter
Krokus; *Headhunter* .... (ARI)
Russians
Sting; *Dream Of The Blue Turtles* .... (A&M)
Russians & Americans
Al Stewart; *Russians & Americans* .... (PAS)
Siberian Khatru
Yes; *Close To The Edge* .... (ATL)
Yessongs .... (ATL)
Song Of Russia
Red Army Ensemble; *Red Army Ensemble* ...... (ANG)
Surfin' U.S.S.R.
Ray Stevens; *Collection* .... (MCA)
Everything Is Beautiful ....(MSP)
I Never Made A Record I Didn't Like .... (MCA)
Visitors
Abba; *Visitors* .... (ATL)
Waiting For The Russians
Trees; *Forrest Fires* .... (ADE)
White Russia
Dirt Band; *Dirt Band* .... (UA)
Young 'N' Russian
Korgis; *Korgis* .... (WB)

COUNTRIES: S

See Also: COUNTRIES: SCOTLAND, SWEDEN, SWITZERLAND

March Of The Siamese Children
Original Broadway Cast; King & I ....(RCA)
Original Cast; King & I .... (MCA)
On A Little Street In Singapore
Glenn Miller; Original Recordings-#4 .... (PRR)
Harry James; Two O'Clock Jump .... (POE)
Manhattan Transfer; Anthology-Down In Birdland (RHI)
Party In Senegal
Wallets; Take It .... (TT)
Queen Of Siam
Holy Moses; Queen Of Siam ....(GWR)
Senegal
Bireli LaGrene; Foreign Affairs .... (BLN)
Senegal Market Place
Sly Dunbar; Sly Wicked & Slick .... (FL)
Summer In Siam
Pogues; Essential Pogues .... (ISL)
Hell's Ditch .... (ISL)
Syria
Psychefunkapus; Skin ....(ATL)

COUNTRIES: SCOTLAND

See Also: COUNTRIES: ENGLAND

Back To Scotland
Chris Proctor; Delicate Dance .... (FF)
Misty Isles Of Scotland
Anne Brolly & Francie; Ireland My Home .... (RGO)
Roxanna Waltz & Scotland Calling Jesse
Jay Ungar/Others; Fiddle Fever .... (FF)
Scotland
Bill Monroe; MCA Records 30 Years Of
Hits-1958-1988 .... (MCA)
Emmylou Harris/Nash Ramblers; At The Ryman . (RPR)
King Missile; The Way To Salvation .... (ATL)
Scotland I
Larry Coryell; Essential .... (VAN)
Scotland The Brave
Original Cast; Forever Plaid ....(RCA)
Scotland/Big Mon
Richard Greene Band; Blue Rondo .... (SIE)
Scotsman
Bryan Bowers; Dr. Demento 20th Anniversary
Collection .... (RHI)
Dr. Demento's Greatest-#5-1980s .... (RHI)
Home Home On The Road .... (FF)
Scotsman Over The Border
Eugene O'Donnell & Mickey Moloney; Slow Airs & Set
Dances ....(GRE)
Scottish Air
Carl MacKenzie; Welcome To Your Feet Again . (ROU)
Scottish Medley
Pat Roper; From The Shannon To The Clyde .... (RGO)
Scottish Rain
Silencers; Blues For Buddha ....(RCA)
Greenpeace/Rainbow Warriors .... (GEF)
Scottish Settler's Lament
Tannahill Weavers; Land Of Light ....(GRE)
Scottish Tea
Ted Nugent/Amboy Dukes; Greatest Collection
Ever ....(DHL)
Skye Boat Song
King's Singers; Annie Laurie-Folksongs Of British
Isles .... (ANG)
Paul Robeson; American Balladeer-Golden
Classics-#1 .... (CLT)
Roger Whittaker; Live In Concert ....(RCA)

COUNTRIES: SPAIN

See Also: COUNTRIES: MEXICO; SPANISH

Echoes Of Spain
Django Reinhardt; Djangologie/USA-#2 .... (DSQ)
In A Little Spanish Town
Ray Charles; Live .... (ATL)

Lady Of Spain
Bing Crosby; Radio Years .... (CRS)
Les Paul; Legend & The Legacy ....(CAP)
Muppets/Amazing Marvin Suggs/Muppaphone; Muppet
Hits .... (JH)
Letter From Spain
Electric Light Orchestra; Secret Messages ......(JET)
Little Spain
Lee Morgan Quintet; Take Twelve .... (JZL)
Malaguena
Percy Faith; All Time Greatest Hits ....(COL)
Placido Domingo; Love Until The End Of
Time-Greatest ....(COL)
Ritchie Valens; Best Of .... (RHI)
History Of .... (RHI)
Roy Clark; Best Of .... (MCA)
Never Been To Spain
Elvis Presley; As Recorded Live At Madison Sq.
Garden ....(RCA)
Hoyt Axton; Never Been To Spain ....(MSP)
Three Dog Night; Best Of .... (MCA)
Joy To The World-Their Greatest Hits ... (MCA)
News From Spain
Al Stewart; Early Years .... (JNS)
Rain In Spain
Original Cast; Forbidden Broadway-#2 .... (DRG)
My Fair Lady ....(COL)
Rex Harrison & Audrey Hepburn; ST/My Fair
Lady ....(COL)
Spanish Castle Magic
Jimi Hendrix; Axis: Bold As Love .... (RPR)
Lifelines/Story .... (RPR)
Live At Winterland .... (RYK)
Radio One .... (RYK)
Spanish Town
Garland Jeffreys; Ghost Writer .... (A&M)
Matador & More .... (A&M)

COUNTRIES: SWEDEN

Serenade To Sweden
Duke Ellington; #4-Studio Sessions-New
York-1963 .... (SAJ)
Swedish Carol
Paul Winter; Wintersong .... (LIV)
Swedish Dance
Danny Thompson; Instruments-Collection .... (HBL)
Swedish Folk Song
Yvonne Roome & Toots Thielemans; Something
Cool .... (DRG)
Swedish Jig
John Renbourn & Stefan Grossman; Music Of
Ireland .... (SHA)
Swedish March
Pat Kilbride; Rock & More Roses .... (TEM)
Swedish Meatball
Steve Lyon; There's No Place Like Mars .... (FF)
Swedish Melody
Barry Hall; Virtuoso 5-String Banjo .... (FLW)
Swedish Pastry
Bill Evans; Time Remembered .... (MS)
Bill Evans Trio; At Shelly's Manne-Hole .... (RVR)
Bud Powell; Time Was .... (BLU)
Swedish Rhapsody (Midsummer Vigil)
Chet Atkins; RCA Years ....(RCA)
Percy Faith/Orchestra; Greatest Hits ....(COL)
Swedish Schnapps
Charlie Parker; Swedish Schnapps ....(VRV)
Verve Years-1950-1951 ....(VRV)
Swedish Suite
Dizzy Gillespie; Dizziest .... (BLU)

COUNTRIES: SWITZERLAND

Dancing In Sunrise, Switzerland
Muffins; Open City .... (CUN)
My Swiss Mountain Lullaby
Montana Slim; 60 Years Of Country Music ......(RCA)
Swiss Army Girl
Scatterbrain; Scamboogery .... (ELE)
Swiss Boy
Michigan Dutchmen; German Polka Favorites .... (JJ)

Swiss Boy Waltz
Michigan Dutchmen; *German Polka Favorites* .... (JJ)
Swiss Celebration
David Friedman; *Of The Wind's Eye* .... (ENJ)
Swiss Lullaby
Roy Eldridge/Gene Krupa Or./Anita O'Day;
Uptown ....(COL)
Swiss Maid
Del Shannon; *Greatest Hits* .... (RHI)
Legends ....(LAU)
Swiss Miss
Fred Astaire; *Crazy Feet!* .... (ALE)
Swiss Retreat
Nat King Cole; *L-O-V-E* .... (CAP)
Swiss Waltz
Ampol Aires; *Greatest Jay Jay Hits* ....(JJ)

COUNTRIES: T

Another Night In Tunisia
Bobby McFerrin; *Spontaneous Inventions* .... (BLN)
Manhattan Transfer; *Vocalese* .... (ATL)
In A Turkish Town
Ritchie Valens; *Best Of* .... (RHI)
History Of .... (RHI)
Ritchie Valens .... (RHI)
Night In Tunisia
Charlie Parker; *Bird On 52nd St.* .... (FAN)
Charlie Parker .... (PRS)
One Night In Birdland .... (COL)
Very Best Of Bird .... (WB)
Dizzy Gillespie; *Electrifying Evening* ....(VRV)
Jazz At Massey Hall .... (FAN)
Musician Composer Raconteur .... (PAB)
Nipper's Greatest Hits-'40s-#2 ....(RCA)
Tuxedo Junction; *Take The "A" Train* .... (BTF)
One Night In Trinidad
Earl Fatha Hines; *Lionel Hampton Presents* .....(WHO)
Return Of The Tasmanian Tiger
John Fahey; *Live In Tasmania* ....(TAK)
Tahiti
Milt Jackson; *Milt Jackson* .... (BLN)
Tahiti Condo
Michael Nesmith; *Newer Stuff* .... (RHI)
Tahitian Moon
Michael Franks; *Objects Of Desire* .... (WB)
Tahitian Skies
Chet Atkins & Mark Knopfler; *Neck & Neck* ....(COL)
Tibetan Side Of Town
Bruce Cockburn; *Big Circumstances* ....(COL)
Trinidad
Eddie Money; *Playing For Keeps* ....(COL)
Unplug It In ....(COL)
Tunnels Of Tunisia
Malaysian Pale; *Nature's Fantasies* ....(FOR)
Turkish March
Boston Pops Orchestra/Arthur Fiedler; *Fiedler's Favorite
Marches* ....(RCA)
Turkish Song Of The Damned
Pogues; *Essential* .... (ISL)
If I Should Fall From Grace With God .... (ISL)
Twilight In Turkey
Raymond Scott; *Reckless Nights & Turkish
Twilights* ....(COL)
Young Turks
Rod Stewart; *Absolutely Live* .... (WB)
Downtown Train-Storyteller Selections ....(WB)
Storyteller/Complete Anthology-1964-1990 ......(WB)
Tonight I'm Yours .... (WB)

COUNTRIES: U

Girl From Uganda
Les Baxter/Orchestra; *African Blue-Brazil Now* .. (CRS)

COUNTRIES: V

See Also: COUNTRIES: VIETNAM

Sweetheart From Venezuela
Harry Belafonte; *Pure Gold* ....(RCA)

Venezuela
Richard Dyer-Bennett; *Art Of* .... (VC)

COUNTRIES: VIETNAM

See Also: POLITICAL CLASSICS, WAR

Hello Vietnam
Johnny Wright; *ST/Full Metal Jacket* .... (WB)
I Feel Like I'm Fixing To Die Rag
Country Joe/Fish; *Greatest Hits* .... (VAN)
Greatest '60s Folksingers .... (VAN)
I Feel Like I'm Fixing To Die Rag .... (VAN)
Life & Times Of .... (VAN)
More American Graffiti-#4 .... (MCA)
ST/Woodstock .... (ATL)
Talking Vietnam Pot Luck Blues
Tom Paxton; *Morning After* .... (ELE)
Viet Cong Blues
Junior Wells; *Best Of The Chicago Blues* .... (VAN)
Chicago/The Blues/Today .... (VAN)
Junior Wells/Chicago Blues Band; *Legends Of Electric
Blues Guitar-#2* .... (RHI)
Viet Cong Live Next Door
Left; *Last Train To Hagerstown* .... (GRN)
Vietnam
Jimmy Cliff; *In Concert-Best Of* ....(RPR)
Reggae Spectacular .... (A&M)
Wonderful World Beautiful People .... (A&M)
Vietnam Blues
Champion Jack Dupree; *Legacy Of The Blues-#3* (CRS)
Vietnam Never Again
Country Joe McDonald; *Child's Play* .... (RGB)
Vietnam Veteran Still Alive
Country Joe McDonald; *Into The Fray* .... (RBB)
Vietnamerica
Stranglers; *IV* ....(IRS)

COUNTRY, Country Music, Countryside

See Also: FARMS, MUSIC

Barroom Country Singer
Roger Whittaker; *Greatest Hits* ....(RCA)
Black Country Rock
David Bowie; *Man Who Sold The World* ....(RYK)
Sound + Vision ....(RYK)
Black Country Woman
Led Zeppelin; *Physical Graffiti* .... (SS)
Born Country
Alabama; *Greatest Hits-#2* ....(RCA)
Brand New Country Star
Jimmy Buffett; *Living & Dying In 3/4 Time* ..... (MCA)
Bright Lights & Country Music
Bill Anderson; *Greatest Hits-#1* .... (MCA)
Bury Me Not On The Lone Prairie
Jimmy C. Newman; *Cajun Cowboy* .... (PLN)
Carefree Country Day
Buffalo Springfield; *Last The Around* ....(ATC)
City Put The Country Back In Me
Neal McCoy; *No Doubt About It* ....(ATL)
Country Air
Beach Boys; *Smiley Smile/Wild Honey* ....(CAP)
Country Boy
Johnny Cash; *Man-The World-His Music* .... (SUN)
Original Golden Hits-#3 ....(SUN)
Superbilly ....(SUN)
Little Jimmy Dickens; *Columbia Country
Classics-#2* ....(COL)
Ricky Skaggs; *19 Hot Country Requests-#3* .... (EPI)
Country Boy ....(EPI)
Greatest Country Hits/'80s-1985 ....(COL)
Live In London ....(EPI)
Country Boy Can Survive
Hank Williams, Jr.; *America (The Way I See It)* ..(W/C)
Greatest Hits .... (WB)
Live ....(W/C)
ST/Pressure Is On ....(W/C)
Country Boy (You Got Your Feet In L.A.)
Glen Campbell; *Best Of* .... (LIB)
Classics Collection .... (LIB)
Greatest Hits ....(CCB)
Country Club
Travis Tritt; *Country Club* .... (WB)

Country Comfort
Elton John; *Tumbleweed Connection* .... (POL)
Country Comforts
Rod Stewart; *Best Of-#2* .... (MER)
  Gasoline Alley .... (MER)
  Sing It Again Rod .... (MER)
Country Girl
Barbara Mandrell; *Live* .... (MCA)
Faron Young; *Billboard Top Country Hits-1959* . (RHI)
  Greatest Hits-#2 ....(SO)
Jeannie C. Riley; *Country Girl* .... (PLN)
  Greatest Hits .... (PLN)
Ozark Mountain Daredevils; *Best* .... (A&M)
  Ozark Mountain Daredevils .... (A&M)
Steve Earle/Dukes; *Hard Way* .... (MCA)
Country Girls
John Schneider; *Greatest Hits* .... (MCA)
  MCA #1 Hits/'80s-#1 .... (MCA)
  Today's Country Classics .... (MCA)
  Too Good To Stop Now .... (MCA)
Country Ham & Red Gravy
Hotmud Family; *Live As We Know It* ....(FF)
Country Honk
Rolling Stones; *Let It Bleed* .... (AKO)
Country Jail
Volumes; *I Love You-Golden Classics* .... (CLT)
Country Jail Blues
Eric Clapton; *No Reason To Cry* .... (RSO)
John T. Smith; *Original Howling Wolf* ....(YAZ)
Country Pie
Bob Dylan; *Nashville Skyline* ....(COL)
Country Road
Dolly Parton; *Eagle When She Flies* ....(COL)
James Taylor; *Greatest Hits* ....(WB)
  Sweet Baby James ....(WB)
Country State Of Mind
Hank Williams, Jr.; *Greatest Hits III* ....(W/C)
  Montana Cafe ....(W/C)
Country Sunshine
Dottie West; *Collector's* ....(RCA)
  Great Moments At The Grand Ole Opry ....(RCA)
Rita Remington; *Country Girl Gold* .... (PLN)
Don't Rock The Jukebox
Alan Jackson; *Don't Rock The Jukebox* .... (ARI)
Fast Lanes & Country Roads
Barbara Mandrell; *Country Classics-#2* .... (MCA)
  Country Classics-#6-1985-1986 .... (MCA)
  Get To The Heart .... (MCA)
Fields Of France
Al Stewart; *Last Days Of The Century* ....(ENC)
Fields Of Illinois
Don Lange; *Natural Born Heathen* .... (FF)
Girl From The North Country
Bob Dylan; *Freewheelin'* ....(COL)
  Nashville Skyline ....(COL)
  Real Live ....(COL)
Joe Cocker; *Mad Dogs & Englishmen* ....(A&M)
Going To The Country
Bruce Cockburn; *Waiting For A Miracle-Singles*
1970-1987 .... (GC)
Elvis Presley; *50 Worldwide Gold Award Hits-#2* (RCA)
Steve Miller Band; *Anthology* ....(CAP)
  Best Of-1968-1973 ....(CAP)
  Number 5 ....(CAP)
Going Up The Country
Canned Heat; *Best Of* ....(EMI)
  ST/1969 ....(POL)
  ST/Woodstock ....(ATL)
  Summer Of Love ....(RHI)
Golden Country
R.E.O. Speedwagon; *Decade Of Rock & Roll*
(1970-1980) .... (EPI)
  Live ....(EPI)
  T.W.O. ....(EPI)
Gone Country
Alan Jackson; *Who I Am* .... (ARI)
Green Fields Of America
Paddy Tunney; *Stone Fiddle* ....(GRE)
Green Fields Of Canada
Eric Schoenberg; *Acoustic Guitar* .... (ROU)
Green Fields Of France
Phil Coulter; *Forgotten Dreams* .... (SHA)
Heartland
George Strait; *ST/Pure Country* .... (MCA)

Sawyer Brown; *Boys Are Back* ....(CCB)
Steve Wariner; *Life's Highway* .... (MCA)
U2; *ST/Rattle & Hum* .... (ISL)
Home On The Range
Bing Crosby; *Crooner-Columbia*
Years-1928-1934 ....(COL)
Boston Pops Orchestra; *Yankee Doodle Dandy* ...(RCA)
Gene Autry; *50th Anniversary* .... (REP)
  Country Music Hall Of Fame ....(COL)
Neil Young; *ST/Where The Buffalo Roam* .... (BKS)
House In The Country
Blood, Sweat & Tears; *Child Is Father To The*
Man ....(COL)
How To Be A Country Star
Statler Brothers; *Best Of-Rides Again-#2* .... (MER)
I Dreamed Of A Hillbilly Heaven
Tex Ritter; *An American Legend* ....(CAP)
  Best Of ....(CAP)
  Hillbilly Heaven ....(CAP)
  Opry Legends ....(CAP)
In God's Country
U2; *Joshua Tree* .... (ISL)
In The Country
Chicago; *2* ....(COL)
  At Carnegie Hall ....(COL)
I'm Just A Country Boy
Don Williams; *Best Of-#2* .... (MCA)
  Country Boy .... (MCA)
Jukebox With A Country Song
Doug Stone; *I Thought It Was You* .... (EPI)
Just A Country Dream
Eric Andersen; *Best Of* .... (VAN)
  Country Dream .... (VAN)
Listen To A Country Song
Loggins & Messina; *On Stage* ....(COL)
  Sittin' In ....(COL)
Lynn Anderson; *Country Chartbusters-#2* ....(COL)
  Greatest Hits ....(COL)
"Little House On The Prairie" Theme
Original Music; *Television's Greatest Hits-#3* .....(TVT)
Long Haired Country Boy
Charlie Daniels Band; *Decade Of Hits* .... (EPI)
  Fire On The Mountain .... (EPI)
  Me & The Boys .... (EPI)
  South's Greatest Hits-#2 ....(CPC)
  Truckers' Jukebox-#2 ....(COL)
  Volunteer Jam-#3 & 4 .... (EPI)
Lord Have Mercy On A Country Boy
Don Williams; *True Love* ....(RCA)
Montana Plains
Moonshine Kate/Others; *Banjo Pickin' Girls* .... (ROU)
Now That's Country
Marty Stuart; *This One's Gonna Hurt You* ...... (MCA)
October Country
October Country; *Nuggets #3-Pop* .... (RHI)
Oklahoma Country Girl
Elvin Bishop; *Big Fun* ....(ALG)
Old Country Church
Hank Williams; *I Ain't Got Nothin' But Time* ....(POL)
Old Virginia Lowlands
John Townley/Press Gang; *Chesapeake Sailor's*
Companion .... (ADE)
Ol' Country
Mark Chesnutt; *Longnecks & Short Stories* ...... (MCA)
One Room Country Shack
Buddy Guy; *Man & The Blues* .... (VAN)
  My Time After Awhile .... (VAN)
Mercy Dee Walton; *Mercy's Troubles* .... (ARH)
  One Room Country Shack ....(SPE)
  Pity & A Shame ....(PRS)
Mose Allison; *Greatest Hits* ....(PRS)
Out In The Country
Three Dog Night; *Best Of* .... (MCA)
Out On The Texas Plains
Mom & Dads; *Golden Country* ....(CRS)
Outskirts Of Town
Sawyer Brown; *Outskirts Of Town* ....(CRB)
Place In The Country
Adam Ant; *Antics In The Forbidden Zone* .... (EPI)
  Friend Or Foe .... (EPI)
George Jones; *One Woman Man* .... (EPI)
Prairie Rose
Roxy Music; *Country Life* ....(ATC)

Red And Rio Grande
Doug Supernaw; *Red And Rio Grande* ....(BNA)
Red Plains
Bruce Hornsby/Range; *The Way It Is* ....(RCA)
Rock My World (Little Country Girl)
Brooks & Dunn; *Hard Workin' Man* .... (ARI)
Silver Stars, Purple Sage, Eyes Of Blue
Roy Rogers/Sons Of The Pioneers; *Roy Rogers/Sons Of The Pioneers* ....(VS)
Stone Cold Country
Gibson/Miller Band; *Where There's Smoke* ... (EPI)
Sweet Country Music
Atlanta; *Pictures* .... (MCA)
Today's Country Classics .... (MCA)
Sweet Country Woman
Johnny Duncan; *Country Music Classics-#11-Early '70s* .... (KT)
Greatest Hits ....(COL)
Winnin' Country .... (FFT)
Take Me Home, Country Roads
John Denver; *Evening With* ....(RCA)
Greatest Hits ....(RCA)
Poems Prayers & Promises ....(RCA)
Take Me Home, Country Roads-& Other Hits ...(RCA)
Toots/Maytals; *Brand New Second-Hand* ....(RYK)
Take Me To The Country
Mel McDaniel; *Take Me To The Country* ....(CAP)
Texas Plains
Riders In The Sky; *Cowboy Way* .... (MCA)
Saturday Morning With .... (MCA)
Stuart Hamblen; *A Man & His Music* ....(L&L)
Thank God I'm A Country Boy
John Denver; *Back Home Again* ....(RCA)
Evening With ....(RCA)
Greatest Hits-#2 ....(RCA)
Thanks For The Beautiful Land On The...
Duke Ellington; *New Orleans Suite* ....(ATL)
There Ain't No Country Music On This...
Tom T. Hall; *Out-of-print recording* ....(OOP)
There Won't Be No Country Music...
C.W. McCall; *Greatest Hits* .... (POL)
Warning Labels
Doug Stone; *From The Heart* .... (EPI)
Weekend In The Country
Original Cast; *A Little Night Music* ....(COL)
Original London Cast; *A Little Night Music* ......(RCA)
West Texas Plains
Rosie Flores; *After The Farm* .... (HT)
Wild Frontier
Bruce Hornsby/Range; *The Way It Is* ....(RCA)
Gary Moore; *Wild Frontier* .... (VIA)
Wild In The Country
Elvis Presley; *50 Worldwide Gold Award Hits-#2* (RCA)
You Can't Take The Country Out Of Me
Alabama; *American Pride* ....(RCA)

COWBOYS, Cowgirls

See Also: HORSES, REBELS, RODEO

All Around Cowboy
Marty Robbins; *All Around Cowboy* ....(COL)
Encore ....(COL)
All Lonesome Cowboys
Pure Prairie League; *Takin' The Stage* ....(RCA)
Along The Santa Fe Trail
Glenn Miller; *Original Live Recordings* ....(PRR)
Sons Of The Pioneers; *Sunset On The Range* ..... (PRR)
Are There Any Cowboys Left...
Lacy J. Dalton; *Lacy J. Dalton* ....(COL)
Are There Any More Real Cowboys
Willie Nelson & Neil Young; *Half Nelson* ....(COL)
Asphalt Cowboy
Sleepy LaBeef; *Bull's Night Out* .... (SUN)
Back In The Saddle
Aerosmith; *Classics Live 2* ....(COL)
Greatest Hits ....(COL)
Live Bootleg ....(COL)
Pandora's Box ....(COL)
Rocks ....(COL)

Back In The Saddle Again
Gene Autry; *50th Anniversary* .... (REP)
Columbia Country Classics-#1 ....(COL)
Cowboy Hall Of Fame .... (REP)
Great American Singing Cowboys ....(REP)
South Of The Border .... (REP)
Ballad Of A Well Known Gun
Elton John; *Tumbleweed Connection* ....(POL)
Ballad Of Paladin
Duane Eddy; *Pure Gold* ....(RCA)
Johnny Western; *Columbia Country Classics-#3* ..(COL)
Belfast Cowboys
Pretty Things; *Silk Torpedo* .... (SS)
Big Iron
Marty Robbins; *All-Time Greatest Hits* ....(COL)
Columbia Country Classics-#3-Americana ......(COL)
More Greatest Hits ....(COL)
Blazing Saddles
Mel Brooks; *ST/High Anxiety* .... (ASY)
Blue Shadows On The Trail
Sons Of The Pioneers; *Cool Water* ....(RCA)
"Bonanza" Theme
Cincinnati Pops Orchestra/Erich Kunzel; *Round-Up* .... (TLR)
Capt. Fantastic & The Brown Dirt Cowboy
Elton John; *Capt. Fantastic & The Brown Dirt Cowboy* .... (POL)
Coca-Cola Cowboy
Mel Tillis; *Greatest Hits* ....(CCB)
Very Best Of .... (MCA)
Computer Cowboy
Neil Young; *Trans* .... (GEF)
Cosmic Cowboy
Michael Murphey; *Cosmic Cowboy Souvenir* .... (A&M)
Nitty Gritty Dirt Band; *Dirt Silver & Gold* .... (UA)
Stars & Stripes Forever .... (UA)
Cowboy
Bow Wow Wow; *I Want Candy* ....(RCA)
C.W. McCall; *I/Company* .... (POL)
Harry Nilsson; *All-Time Greatest Hits* ....(RCA)
Johnny Rodriguez; *Rodriguez Was Here* ....(MER)
Randy Newman; *Live* .... (RPR)
Randy Newman .... (RPR)
Cowboy Band
Billy Dean; *Men'll Be Boys* .... (LIB)
Cowboy Bill
Garth Brooks; *Garth Brooks* .... (LIB)
Cowboy Blues
Gene Autry; *His Greatest Hits* ....(TRD)
South Of The Border .... (REP)
Cowboy Boogie
Randy Travis; *Wind In The Wire* ....(WB)
Cowboy Boots
Dave Dudley; *Red Simpson/Red Sovine/Dave Dudley* .... (GUS)
Cowboy Christmas Ball
Michael Martin Murphey; *Cowboy Christmas* .....(WB)
Cowboy From Wyoming
Sammi Smith; *Better Than Ever* .... (STE)
Cowboy Hat In Dallas
Charlie Daniels Band; *Homesick Heroes* ....(EPI)
Cowboy In The Continental Suit
Chris LeDoux; *Rodeo & Living Free* .... (LIB)
Marty Robbins; *American Originals* ....(COL)
Cowboy In The Jungle
Jimmy Buffett; *Son Of A Son Of A Sailor* .... (MCA)
Cowboy Man
Lyle Lovett; *Country Classics-#9 (1984-1987)* .. (MCA)
Lyle Lovett .... (MCA)
ST/Always .... (MCA)
Cowboy Movie
David Crosby; *If I Could Only Remember My Name* .... (ATL)
Cowboy Of Dreams
David Crosby & Graham Nash; *Wind On The Water* .... (MCA)
Cowboy Rides Away
George Strait; *Country Classics-#1* .... (MCA)
Does Fort Worth Ever Cross Your Mind .... (MCA)
Greatest Hits-#2 .... (MCA)
Cowboy Serenade (While I'm Rollin'...)
Glenn Miller/Orchestra; *Complete* .... (BLU)

Cowboy Singer
Sonny Curtis; *Love Is All Around* .... (ELE)
   Sonny Curtis .... (ELE)
Cowboy Song
Thin Lizzy; *Jailbreak* .... (MER)
   Lived Dangerous .... (WB)
   Lizzy Lives! (1976-1984) .... (GS)
Cowboy & The Hippie
Chris LeDoux; *Gold Buckle Dreams* .... (LIB)
   He Rides The Wild Horses .... (LIB)
Cowboy & The Lady
John Denver; *Some Days Are Diamonds* .... (RCA)
Johnny Duncan; *Come A Little Bit Closer* .... (COL)
Cowboys Ain't Supposed To Cry
Moe Brandy; *Cowboys Ain't Supposed To Cry* ...(COL)
Cowboys Don't Cry
Daron Norwood; *Daron Norwood* .... (GIA)
Dude Mowrey; *Honky Tonk* ....(CAP)
Ian Tyson; *All-Ears Review-#7-Still Amazing...* .. (ROM)
   I Outgrew The Wagon .... (VAN)
Cowboys Don't Get Lucky All The Time
Gene Watson;
   Beautiful Country ....(CAP)
   ST/Convoy .... (UA)
Cowboys Don't Shoot Straight
Tammy Wynette; *Biggest Hits* .... (EPI)
   Tears Of Fire-25th Anniversary Collect. .... (EPI)
Cowboys From Hollywood
Camper Van Beethoven; *II & III* .... (IRS)
Cowboys In Africa
Bush Tetras; *Better Late Than Never* .... (ROI)
Cowboys In Hong Kong (As Far As Siam)
Red Rider; *As Far As Siam* ....(CAP)
Cowboys To Girls
Intruders; *Soul Shots-Sixties Soul Classics* .... (RHI)
   Super Hits .... (PI)
Cowboys Trademarks
Gene Autry; *Cowboy Hall Of Fame* .... (REP)
Cowboys & Clowns
Billy Strange; *Great Western Themes* .... (CRS)
Ronnie Milsap; *ST/Bronco Billy* .... (ELE)
Cowboys & Playboys
Moe Brandy; *Best Of-#1* ....(COL)
Cowboy, You're America
Dave Dudley; *King Of The Road* .... (SUN)
Cowboy's Dream
Eddy Arnold; *Cattle Call* ....(RCA)
Jimmy C. Newman; *Cajun Cowboy* .... (PLN)
Cowboy's Dream No. 19
Dan Hicks/Hot Licks; *Last Train To Hicksville* .. (MCA)
Cowboy's Lament
Sons Of The Pioneers; *Country-Western*
   Songbook ....(RCA)
   Western Country .... (GRA)
Cowboy's Prayer
Goebel Reeves; *Songs Of The Old West* ....(GLN)
   Texas Drifter ....(GLN)
Cowgirl In The Sand
Crosby, Stills, Nash & Young; *Four-Way Street* .. (ATL)
Neil Young; *Decade* .... (RPR)
   Everybody Knows This Is Nowhere .... (RPR)
Cowgirl & The Dandy
Brenda Lee; *Even Better* .... (MCA)
   Greatest Country Hits .... (MCA)
Dolly Parton; *Here You Come Again* ....(RCA)
Dallas Cowboys
Charley Pride; *45* ....(RCA)
Damn Good Cowboy
Charlie Daniels Band; *Night Rider* .... (EPI)
Dancin' Cowboys
Bellamy Brothers; *Greatest Hits* .... (MCA)
   You Can Get Crazy ....(W/C)
Don't Call Him A Cowboy
Conway Twitty; *Don't Call Him A Cowboy* .... (WB)
   Number One's: Warner Bros. Years ....(WB)
Drug Store Cowboy
Humble Pie; *Eat It* .... (A&M)
El Paso
Grateful Dead; *Steal Your Face* .... (GRD)
Marty Robbins; *Biggest Hits* ....(COL)
   Billboard Top Country Hits-1960 .... (RHI)
   Gunfighter Ballads & Trail Songs ....(COL)
   Radio Classics/'50s ....(COL)

Even Cowgirls Get The Blues
Emmylou Harris; *Blue Kentucky Girl* ....(WB)
Johnny Cash & Waylon Jennings; *Heroes* ....(COL)
For All Our Cowboy Friends
Red Steagall/Coleman County Cowboys; *For All Our*
   Cowboy Friends .... (MCA)
God Must Be A Cowboy
Dan Seals; *Best Of* ....(CAP)
   Classics Collection-#1 ....(CAP)
   Rebel Heart .... (LIB)
Gunsmoke
Billy Strange; *Great Western Themes* .... (CRS)
Molly Hatchet; *Flirtin' With Disaster* .... (EPI)
Outlaws; *Hurry Sundown* .... (ARI)
Happy Trails
Michael Martin Murphey; *Cowboy Songs* ....(WB)
Quicksilver Messenger Service; *Sons Of Mercury* (RHI)
Randy Travis & Roy Rogers; *Heroes & Friends* ...(WB)
Riders In The Sky; *Cowboy Way* .... (MCA)
Roy Rogers/Dale Evans/Dusty Rogers; *Tribute* ..(RCA)
Van Halen; *Diver Down* ....(WB)
"Have Gun Will Travel" Theme
Johnny Western; *Television's Greatest Hits-#2* .... (TVT)
Home On The Range
Bing Crosby; *Crooner-Columbia*
   Years-1928-1934 ....(COL)
Boston Pops Orchestra; *Yankee Doodle Dandy* ...(RCA)
Gene Autry; *50th Anniversary* .... (REP)
   Country Music Hall Of Fame ....(COL)
Neil Young; *ST/Where The Buffalo Roam* .... (BKS)
I Ride An Old Paint/Whoopee Ti-Yi-Yo...
Michael Martin Murphey; *Cowboy Songs* ....(WB)
I Wanna Be A Cowboy
Boys Don't Cry; *Boys Don't Cry* ....(PRO)
Isis
Bob Dylan; *Biograph* ....(COL)
   Desire ....(COL)
I'm An Old Cowhand
Bing Crosby; *Best Of* .... (MCA)
Sons Of The Pioneers; *Empty Saddles* .... (MCA)
Jingle Jangle Jingle (I've Got Spurs...)
Kay Kyser; *Best Of The Big Bands* ....(COL)
   Golden Hits Of The '40s .... (CSP)
   Sentimental Favorites ....(COL)
Tex Ritter; *Opry Legends* ....(CAP)
   Out West ....(CAP)
Just Like Gene Autry
Moby Grape; *Very Best Of-Vintage* ....(COL)
Just Like Jesse James
Cher; *Heart Of Stone* .... (GEF)
King Of The Cowboys
Amazing Rhythm Aces; *Stacked Deck* .... (MCA)
Roy Rogers & Dusty Rogers; *Tribute* ....(RCA)
Lady Takes The Cowboy Every Time
Gatlin Brothers; *Biggest Hits* ....(COL)
Larry Gatlin/Gatlin Brothers; *Houston To Denver* (COL)
Lasso The Moon
Gary Morris; *Hits* ....(WB)
Last Cowboy Song
Ed Bruce; *16 Top Country Hits-#2* .... (MCA)
   Greatest Hits .... (MCA)
W. Jennings/W. Nelson/J. Cash/K. Krist.;
   Highwayman ....(COL)
Last Of The Singing Cowboys
Marshall Tucker Band; *Running Like The Wind* . (MCA)
Little Joe The Wrangler
Goebel Reeves; *Songs Of Old West* ....(GLN)
   Texas Drifter ....(GLN)
Littlest Cowboy Rides Again
Chris LeDoux; *Songbook Of The American West* ..(LIB)
   Sounds Of The Western Country .... (LIB)
Lone Star Trail
Dave Frederickson; *Cowboy Songs On Folkways* (FLW)
Lonesome Cowboy
Elvis Presley; *Essential-First Movies* ....(RCA)
   Loving You ....(RCA)
Lonesome L.A. Cowboy
New Riders Of The Purple Sage; *Adventures Of Panama*
   Red ....(COL)
   Midnight Moonlight .... (RLX)
Lonesome Rodeo Cowboy
George Strait; *Livin' It Up* .... (MCA)

Long Tall Texan
Beach Boys; *Best Of-#2* ....(CAP)
Concert ....(CAP)
Murry Kellum; *20 Golden Souvenirs Of Music City*
U.S.A. ....(PLN)
Country Comedy-20 Country Comedy Hits .....(PLN)
Mammas Don't Let Your Babies Grow Up...
Gibson Miller Band; *ST/The Cowboy Way* ....(EPI)
Waylon Jennings & Willie Nelson; *Greatest Hits* .(RCA)
Waylon & Willie ....(RCA)
Willie Nelson; *Greatest Hits & Some That Will Be* (COL)
ST/Electric Horseman ....(COL)
& Family Live ....(COL)
"Maverick" Theme
Original Music; *Television's Greatest Hits-#2* .....(TVT)
Modern Day Cowboy
Tesla; *Five Man Acoustical Jam* ....(GEF)
Mechanical Resonance ....(GEF)
Montana Cowboy
Emmylou Harris/Nash Ramblers; *At The Ryman* . (RPR)
Hot Rize; *Traditional Ties* ....(SH)
My Cowboy's Getting Old
Tanya Tucker; *Lovin' & Learnin'* .... (MCA)
My Cowboy's Last Ride
Jessi Colter; *That's The Way A Cowboy Rocks &*
Rolls ....(CAP)
Johnny Cash; *Rambler* ....(COL)
My Heroes Have Always Been Cowboys
Willie Nelson; *Greatest Country Hits/'80s-1980* ..(COL)
Greatest Hits & Some That Will Be ....(COL)
ST/Electric Horseman ....(COL)
ST/My Heroes Have Always Been Cowboys .....(RCA)
Night Rider's Lament
Chris LeDoux; *Old Cowboy Classics* ....(LIB)
Paint Me Back Home In Wyoming ....(LIB)
& The Saddle Boogie Band ....(LIB)
Garth Brooks; *The Chase* ....(LIB)
Jerry Jeff Walker; *Ridin' High* ....(MCA)
Nanci Griffith; *Other Voices Other Rooms* ....(ELE)
Suzy Bogguss; *Somewhere Between* ....(CAP)
Old Chisholm Trail
Michael Martin Murphey; *Cowboy Songs* ....(WB)
Randy Travis; *Wind In The Wire* ....(WB)
Old Nashville Cowboys
Hank Williams, Jr.; *Whiskey Bent & Hell Bound* ..(W/C)
Old Paint
Chris LeDoux; *Old Cowboy Classics* ....(LIB)
Western Tunesmith ....(LIB)
Linda Ronstadt; *Simple Dreams* ....(ELE)
Oregon Trail
Sons Of The Pioneers; *Sunset On The Range* ..... (PRR)
Over The Santa Fe Trail
Sons Of The Pioneers; *Empty Saddles* ....(MCA)
Tumbling Tumbleweeds ....(MSP)
Palo Alto Cowboy
Reilly & Maloney; *Profiles* ....(FRK)
Plastic Saddle
Danny O'Keefe; *American Roulette* ....(WB)
Queen Of The Cowboy Cafe
Si Kahn; *Home* ....(FF)
Ragtime Cowboy Joe
Jo Stafford; *Capitol Collectors Series* ....(CAP)
Spike Jones/City Slickers; *King Of Corn* ....(GLN)
Rhinestone Cowboy
Glen Campbell; *Classics Collection* ....(CAP)
Country's Greatest Hits-#6-Superstars ....(PRY)
Live ....(CAP)
Rhinestone Cowboy ....(CAP)
Very Best Of ....(CAP)
Ride Concrete Cowboy, Ride
Roy Rogers/Sons Of The Pioneers; *ST/Smokey & The*
Bandit .... (MCA)
Ride On Cowboy
Alvin Lee/Ten Years Later; *Ride On* .... (RSO)
Ride 'Em Cowboy
Paul Davis; *Ride 'Em Cowboy* ....(BNG)
Roy Rogers/Sons Of The Pioneers; *Roy Rogers/Sons Of*
The Pioneers ....(VS)
Ridin' Down The Canyon
Gene Autry; *Columbia Historic Edition* ....(COL)
Western Classics ....(COL)
Riders In The Sky; *Cowboy Way* ....(MCA)
Willie Nelson & Leon Russell; *One For The*
Road ....(COL)

Ro Deo Deo Cowboy
Jerry Jeff Walker; *A Man Must Carry On* .... (MCA)
Rodeo Cowboys
Lynn Anderson; *Greatest Hits-#2* ....(COL)
Rope The Moon
John Michael Montgomery; *Kickin' It Up* ....(ATL)
Roy Rogers
Elton John; *Goodbye Yellow Brick Road* ....(POL)
Saddle The Cow
Dr. John; *Brightest Smile In Town* ....(CLE)
Saddle Tramp
Marty Robbins; *More Greatest Hits* ....(COL)
Should've Been A Cowboy
Toby Keith; *Toby Keith* .... (MER)
Slim Carter
Nitty Gritty Dirt Band; *All The Good Times* .... (UA)
So You Think You're A Cowboy
Emmylou Harris; *ST/Electric Horseman* ....(COL)
ST/Honeysuckle Rose ....(COL)
So You Want To Be A Cowboy
Chris LeDoux; *Gold Buckle Dreams* ....(LIB)
He Rides The Wild Horses ....(LIB)
Radio & Rodeo Hits ....(LIB)
Someday Soon
Chris LeDoux; *Rodeo Songs Old & New* ....(LIB)
Ian & Sylvia; *Greatest Hits* ....(VAN)
Northern Journey ....(VAN)
Journey; *Departure* ....(COL)
Judy Collins; *Colors Of The Day-Best Of* ....(ELE)
Who Knows Where The Time Goes ....(ELE)
Moe Bandy; *Greatest Hits* ....(COL)
Rodeo Romeo ....(COL)
Suzy Bogguss; *Aces* ....(CAP)
Space Cowboy
Steve Miller Band; *Anthology* ....(CAP)
Best Of-1968-1973 ....(CAP)
Still They Ride
Journey; *Escape* ....(COL)
Streets Of Laredo
Buck Owens/Buckaroos; *Live At Carnegie Hall* .. (CMF)
Marty Robbins; *All-Time Greatest Hits* ....(COL)
More Greatest Hits ....(COL)
More Gunfighter Ballads & Trail Songs ....(COL)
Rex Allen; *Great American Singing Cowboys* .....(REP)
Sweet Baby James
Highway 101; *Paint The Town* ....(WB)
James Taylor; *Greatest Hits* ....(WB)
Sweet Baby James ....(WB)
Take Me Back To My Boots & Saddle
Gene Autry; *Essential* ....(COL)
Texas Cowboy
Luther Johnson/Magic Rockers; *I Want To Groove With*
You ....(BUL)
"The Rifleman" Theme
Cincinnati Pops Orchestra/Erich Kunzel;
Round-Up ....(TLR)
"The Virginian" Theme
101 Strings Orchestra; *Western Themes-#1* .... (ALS)
Original Music; *Television's Greatest Hits-#3* .....(TVT)
Theme From "Midnight Cowboy"
Cincinnati Pops Orchestra/Erich Kunzel; *Hollywood's*
Greatest Hits-#2 ....(TLR)
Theme From "Rawhide"
Blues Brothers; *Original Soundtrack* ....(ATL)
Frankie Laine; *Television's Greatest Hits-#2* ......(TVT)
This Ol' Cowboy
Marshall Tucker Band; *Greatest Hits* ....(CPC)
Where We All Belong ....(AJK)
True Western Movie
Chris LeDoux; *Songs Of Rodeo & Country* ....(LIB)
Tumbling Tumbleweeds
Billy Vaughn; *Greatest Hits* ....(CCB)
Gene Autry; *Essential* ....(COL)
Meat Puppets; *Meat Puppets* ....(SST)
Michael Martin Murphey; *Cowboy Songs* ....(WB)
Roy Rogers/K.T. Oslin/Restless Heart; *Tribute* ...(RCA)
Sons Of The Pioneers; *Country Music Hall Of*
Fame ....(MCA)
Twilight On The Trail
Michael Nesmith; *Tropical Campfires* .... (PA)
"Wagon Train" Theme
Original Music; *Television's Greatest Hits-#2* .....(TVT)
What The Cowgirls Do
Vince Gill; *When Love Finds You* ....(MCA)

Whatcha Gonna Do With A Cowboy
Chris LeDoux & Garth Brooks; *Whatcha Gonna Do With A Cowboy* .... (LIB)
Whoopee Ti Yi Yo
Burl Ives; *Best Of* .... (MCA)
David Bromberg; *How Late'll Ya Play 'Til?* ...... (FAN)
Roy Rogers/Sons Of The Pioneers; *Roy Rogers/Sons Of The Pioneers* .... (VS)
Woody Guthrie & Cisco Houston; *Cowboy Songs On Folkways* .... (FLW)
William Tell Overture (Lone Ranger)
Boston Pops Orchestra/Arthur Fiedler; *Fiedler-Greatest Hits* .... (RCA)
 TV Classics .... (RCA)
Spike Jones/City Slickers; *Best Of* .... (RCA)
Wind In The Wire
Randy Travis; *Wind In The Wire* .... (WB)

CRAZY, Confused, Dizzy, Nervous, Psychiatry, Spaced Out

Absent-Minded Me
Barbra Streisand; *People* .... (COL)
Acute Schizophrenia Paranoia Blues
Kinks; *Everybody's In Showbiz* .... (RHI)
 Muswell Hillbillies .... (RHI)
Ain't It Crazy
Lightnin' Hopkins; *Hootin' The Blues* .... (PRS)
 Lightnin' .... (ARH)
Aladdin Sane
David Bowie; *Aladdin Sane* .... (RYK)
 Changestwobowie .... (RCA)
 Live .... (RYK)
All Lovers Are Deranged
David Gilmour; *About Face* .... (COL)
All Mixed Up
Cars; *Cars* .... (ELE)
Tom Petty/Heartbreakers; *Let Me Up (I've Had Enough)* .... (MCA)
All Shook Up
Elvis Presley; *Elvis Aron* .... (RCA)
 Elvis In Person .... (RCA)
 From Memphis To Vegas .... (RCA)
 Golden Records .... (RCA)
 Madison Square Garden .... (RCA)
 Pure Gold .... (RCA)
All The Madmen
David Bowie; *Man Who Sold The World* .... (RYK)
Are You Crazy
Freddie McGregor; *Come On Over* .... (RAS)
Armed & Crazy
Johnny Paycheck; *Armed & Crazy* .... (EPI)
Baby Drives Me Crazy
Thin Lizzy; *Live & Dangerous* .... (WB)
Back At The Funny Farm
Motorhead; *Another Perfect Day* .... (MER)
Ball Of Confusion
Temptations; *All The Million-Sellers* .... (MOT)
 Anthology .... (MOT)
 Compact Command Performances .... (MOT)
 Greatest Hits-#2 .... (MOT)
 Top 10 With A Bullet-Motown Male Groups ... (MOT)
Basket Case
Green Day; *Dookie* .... (RPR)
Beep A Freak
Gap Band; *VI* .... (TE)
Blame It On Texas
Mark Chesnutt; *Too Cold At Home* .... (MCA)
Blow Top Blues
Esther Phillips; *Confessin' The Blues* .... (ATL)
Etta James & Huston Person; *Sugar* .... (MUS)
Koko Taylor; *From The Heart Of A Woman* .... (ALG)
Borderline
Madonna; *Immaculate Collection* .... (SIR)
 Madonna .... (SIR)
 Royal Box .... (SIR)
Boy Crazy
Tubes; *Tubes* .... (A&M)
 What Do You Want From-Live .... (A&M)

Brain Damage
Pink Floyd; *Dark Side Of The Moon* .... (CAP)
 Gift Set .... (CAP)
 Works .... (CAP)
Burnout
Green Day; *Dookie* .... (RPR)
Chantilly Lace
Big Bopper; *45s On CD-#1 (1958-1959)* .... (MER)
 Cruisin' 1958 .... (INC)
 Oldies But Goodies-#4 .... (OSR)
 ST/American Graffiti .... (MCA)
Jerry Lee Lewis; *Best Of-#2* .... (MER)
 "Killer" Rocks On .... (MER)
Church Of The Poison Mind
Culture Club; *At Worst-Best Of Boy George & C. Club* .... (SBK)
 Colour By Numbers .... (VIA)
Cockeyed Optimist
Mary Martin/Original Cast; *South Pacific* .... (COL)
Mitzi Gaynor; *ST/South Pacific* .... (RCA)
Come Undone
Duran Duran; *Duran Duran* .... (CAP)
Confusion
Electric Light Orchestra; *Discovery* .... (JET)
New Order; *Substance* .... (QUE)
Cracking Up
Nick Lowe; *Basher: Best Of* .... (COL)
 Labour Of Lust .... (COL)
Paul McCartney; *Tripping The Live Fantastic* .... (CAP)
Rolling Stones; *Love You Live* .... (RS)
Crazay
Jesse Johnson/Sly Stone; *Shockadelica* .... (A&M)
Crazed Weasel
Ricky Peterson; *Night Watch* .... (WB)
Crazy
Aerosmith; *Get A Grip* .... (GEF)
Boyz; *Boyz* .... (MOT)
Georgia Satellites; *In The Land Of Salvation & Sin* .... (ELE)
Icehouse; *Man Of Colours* .... (CHR)
Jimmy Dale Gilmore & Willie Nelson; *Red Hot + Country* .... (MER)
Kay Starr; *Capitol Collectors Series* .... (CAP)
Kenny Rogers; *Greatest Hits* .... (RCA)
 What About Me? .... (RCA)
Linda Ronstadt; *Hasten Down The Wind* .... (ASY)
Manhattans; *Forever By Your Side* .... (COL)
Meat Puppets; *Huevos* .... (SST)
Miki Howard; *Love Confessions* .... (ATL)
Neil Diamond; *Primitive* .... (COL)
Patsy Cline; *12 Greatest Hits* .... (MCA)
 Songwriter's Tribute .... (MCA)
 Story .... (MCA)
 ST/Sweet Dreams .... (MCA)
Ray Price; *Greatest Hits-#2* .... (STE)
R.E.M.; *Dead Letter Office* .... (IRS)
Seal; *Seal* .... (SIR)
Supertramp; *Famous Last Words* .... (A&M)
Willie Nelson; *Best Of* .... (EMI)
 Healing Hands Of Time .... (LIB)
 Nite Life-Greatest Hits & Rare Tracks .... (RHI)
 & Family Live .... (COL)
Crazy About Her
Rod Stewart; *Out Of Order* .... (WB)
 Storyteller/Complete Anthology-1964-1990 ...... (WB)
Crazy Arms
Chuck Berry; *Chess Box* .... (CSS)
Jerry Lee Lewis; *18 Original Sun Greatest Hits* ... (RHI)
 Golden Rock Hits .... (SMA)
 Jerry Lee Lewis .... (RHI)
Linda Ronstadt; *Retrospective* .... (CAP)
Patsy Cline; *Last Sessions* .... (MCA)
 Portrait Of .... (MCA)
Ray Price; *Columbia Country Classics-#2* .... (COL)
 Greatest Hits .... (COL)
 Greatest Hits-#1 .... (STE)
Willie Nelson; *San Antonio Rose* .... (COL)
Crazy Baby
Doug Sahm; *Juke Box Music* .... (ANT)
Rodney Crowell; *Diamonds & Dirt* .... (COL)
Crazy Baldhead
Bob Marley/Wailers; *Rastaman Vibration* .... (TUF)
 Rebel Music .... (TUF)
 Songs Of Freedom .... (TUF)

Crazy Bells
Marcels; *Best Of* .... (RHI)
Crazy Circles
Bad Company; *Desolation Angels* .... (SS)
Crazy Eyes
Daryl Hall & John Oates; *Bigger Than Both Of
Us* ....(RCA)
Crazy Feelin'
Jefferson Starship; *Earth* .... (GRU)
Crazy For You
Heartbeats; *Best Of* .... (RHI)
Madonna; *Immaculate Collection* .... (SIR)
Royal Box .... (SIR)
ST/Vision Quest .... (GEF)
Crazy For Your Love
Bee Gees; *E.S.P.* .... (WB)
Exile; *Greatest Country Hits/'80s-1985* ....(COL)
Greatest Hits .... (EPI)
Kentucky Hearts .... (EPI)
Crazy From The Heart
Bellamy Brothers; *Crazy From The Heart* ...... (MCA)
Greatest Hits-III .... (MCA)
Crazy Heart
Forester Sisters; *Forester Sisters* .... (WB)
Hank Williams; *24 Greatest Hits-#2* .... (POL)
40 Greatest Hits .... (POL)
Hey Good Lookin' (Dec. 1950-July 1951) ...... (POL)
Rare Takes & Radio Cuts .... (POL)
Crazy In Love
Joe Cocker; *Civilized Man* .... (CAP)
Kenny Rogers; *Love Is Strange* .... (RPR)
Crazy Little Mama
Eldorados; *Greatest Groups/'50s-#2* .... (CLT)
Sock Hop .... (DHL)
Crazy Little Thing Called Love
Queen; *Greatest Hits* .... (HOL)
The Game .... (HOL)
Crazy Love
Allman Brothers Band; *Decade Of
Hits-1969-1979* .... (POL)
Bryan Ferry; *ST/She's Having A Baby* .... (IRS)
Buddy Guy; *Left My Blues In San Francisco* ...... (CSS)
Joey Dee/Starliters; *Hey Let's Twist-Best Of* ...... (RHI)
Paul Anka; *21 Golden Hits* ....(RCA)
Best Of .... (RHI)
Vintage Years '57-'61 .... (SIR)
Poco; *Backtracks* .... (MCA)
Legend .... (MCA)
Rita Coolidge; *Classics-#5* .... (A&M)
Van Morrison; *Moondance* .... (WB)
Crazy Mama
J.J. Cale; *Naturally* .... (MCA)
Rolling Stones; *Black & Blue* .... (RS)
Sucking In The Seventies .... (RS)
Crazy Man Michael
Fairport Convention; *Chronicles* .... (A&M)
In Real Time-Live '87 .... (ISL)
Liege & Lief .... (A&M)
Crazy On You
Heart; *Dreamboat Annie* .... (CAP)
Greatest Hits/Live .... (EPI)
Crazy Over You
Foster & Lloyd; *Crazy Over You* ....(RCA)
Foster & Lloyd ....(RCA)
Maureen Gray; *45* .... (CLT)
Ricky Van Shelton; *Wild-Eyed Dream* ....(COL)
Crazy She Calls Me
Abbey Lincoln; *Blue Series-Female Vocals* .... (BLN)
Aretha Franklin; *Aretha's Jazz* .... (ATL)
Billie Holiday; *From The Original Decca Masters* (MCA)
Joe Mooney; *Ertegun's New York N.Y. Cabaret
Music* .... (ATL)
Linda Ronstadt; *What's New* .... (ASY)
Lurlean Hunter; *Atlantic Jazz-Singers* .... (ATL)
Crazy Train
Ozzy Osbourne; *Blizzard Of Ozz* ....(JET)
Tribute ....(CBA)
Crazy Water
Elton John; *Blue Moves* .... (MCA)
Crazy 'Bout That Married Woman
Rockin' Dopsie; *Saturday Night Zydeco* .... (MSO)
Dazed And Confused
Jake Holmes; *Nuggets-#10-Folk Rock* .... (RHI)

Led Zeppelin; *Classic Rock 1966-1988* .... (ATL)
Led Zeppelin .... (ATL)
Led Zeppelin (collection) .... (ATL)
ST/Song Remains The Same .... (SS)
Delirious
Prince; *1999* .... (WB)
ZZ Top; *Afterburner* .... (WB)
Diamonds On The Soles Of Her Shoes
Paul Simon; *Concert In The Park-August 15 1991* (WB)
Graceland .... (WB)
Negotiations & Love Songs-1971-1986 .... (WB)
Diary Of A Madman
Ozzy Osbourne; *Diary Of A Madman* ....(JET)
Dizzy
Tommy Roe; *Greatest Hits* .... (MCA)
Orig. Classic Oldies/'60s-#10 .... (MCA)
Super Hits-#1 .... (GUS)
Dizzy Atmosphere
Dizzy Gillespie; *Dizzy's Diamonds-Best Of Verve
Years* ....(VRV)
Oscar Peterson & Dizzy Gillespie; *Oscar Peterson &
Dizzy Gillespie* .... (PAB)
Dizzy Miss Lizzy
Beatles; *At The Hollywood Bowl* .... (CAP)
Help! .... (CAP)
Rock 'N' Roll Music-#2 .... (CAP)
VI .... (CAP)
Ronnie Hawkins/Hawks; *Best Of* .... (RHI)
East Tennessee Blues/Goin' Crazy
Stepping Stones; *Fresh Old Time String Band
Music* .... (ROU)
Excitable Boy
Warren Zevon; *Excitable Boy* .... (ASY)
Quiet Normal Life-Best Of .... (ASY)
Stand In The Fire .... (ASY)
Foggy Mental Breakdown
Steppenwolf; *7* .... (MCA)
Freak a Ristic
Atlantic Starr; *As The Band Turns* .... (A&M)
Classics-#10 .... (A&M)
Secret Lovers...Best Of .... (A&M)
Freak A Zoid
Midnight Star; *Greatest Hits* .... (SLR)
No Parking On The Dance Floor .... (SLR)
Freak Me
Silk; *Lose Control* .... (ELE)
Freak Out
Chic; *LeFreak* .... (ATL)
Go Insane
Lindsey Buckingham; *Go Insane* .... (WB)
Going Out Of My Mind
McBride & The Ride; *Sacred Ground* .... (MCA)
Goin' Crazy
David Lee Roth; *Eat 'Em & Smile* .... (WB)
Goin' Down
Greg Guidry; *Over The Line* .... (B/C)
Goin' Out Of My Head
Lettermen; *All-Time Greatest Hits* .... (CAP)
Best Of-#2 .... (CAP)
Little Anthony/Imperials; *Best Of* .... (RHI)
EMI Legends Or Rock 'N' Roll-24 Greatest ..... (EMI)
Helter Skelter
Aerosmith; *Pandora's Box* ....(COL)
Beatles; *Box Set* .... (CAP)
Rarities .... (CAP)
Rock 'n' Roll Music-#2 .... (CAP)
White Album .... (CAP)
Husker Du; *12"* .... (WB)
Motley Crue; *Shout At The Devil* .... (ELE)
Pat Benatar; *Precious Time* .... (CHR)
Siouxsie/Banshees; *Nocturne* .... (GEF)
The Scream .... (GEF)
U2; *ST/Rattle & Hum* .... (ISL)
Honky-Tonk Crazy
Gene Watson; *Honky-Tonk Crazy* .... (EPI)
George Strait; *Strait From The Heart* .... (MCA)
Hot! Wild! Unrestricted! Crazy Love
Millie Jackson; *Imitation Of Love* .... (JVA)
Hypnotized
Fleetwood Mac; *25 Years-The Chain* .... (WB)
I Almost Lost My Mind
Eddy Arnold; *World Of Hits* ....(MGM)
Fats Domino; *Greatest Hits* .... (MCA)
Ivory Joe Hunter; *Since I Met You Baby* .... (MER)

I Fall To Pieces
Aaron Neville & Trisha Yearwood; *Rhythm Country &*
    Blues .... (MCA)
Patsy Cline; *12 Greatest Hits* .... (MCA)
    Always .... (MCA)
    Story .... (MCA)
    ST/Sweet Dreams .... (MCA)
I Go Crazy
Paul Davis; *Best Of* .... (BNG)
    Billboard Top Hits-1978 .... (RHI)
    Singer Of Songs-Teller Of Tales .... (BNG)
I Go To Pieces
Del Shannon; *Rock On!* .... (GG)
Peter & Gordon; *Best Of* .... (RHI)
    History Of British Rock-#3 .... (RHI)
Southern Pacific; *County Line* .... (WB)
    Greatest Hits .... (WB)
I Had The Craziest Dream
Frank Sinatra; *Trilogy* .... (RPR)
I Need A Lover Who Won't Drive Me Crazy
John Cougar Mellencamp; *John Cougar*
    Mellencamp .... (RIV)
Pat Benatar; *In The Heat Of The Night* .... (CHR)
I Try To Think About Elvis
Patty Loveless; *When Fallen Angels Fly* .... (EPI)
Impulsive
Wilson Phillips; *Wilson Phillips* .... (SBK)
Infatuation
Rod Stewart; *Camouflage* .... (WB)
    Downtown Train (Selections-Storyteller) .... (WB)
    Storyteller-Complete Anthology-1964-1990 ...... (WB)
It Ain't Cool To Be Crazy About You
George Strait; *Country Classics-#7: 1986-87* ... (MCA)
    Greatest Hits-#2 .... (MCA)
    MCA #1 Hits/'80s-#2 .... (MCA)
    #7 .... (MCA)
It Hit Me Like A Hammer
Huey Lewis/News; *Hard At Play* .... (EMI)
I'm Freaky
O'Bryan; *You And I* .... (CAP)
Jungle Love
Steve Miller Band; *Book Of Dreams* .... (CAP)
    Gift Set .... (CAP)
    Greatest Hits-1964-1978 .... (CAP)
    Live .... (CAP)
Just Another Nervous Wreck
Supertramp; *Breakfast In America* .... (A&M)
Just Crazy Love
Fleetwood Mac; *Mystery To Me* .... (RPR)
Land Of Confusion
Genesis; *Invisible Touch* .... (ATL)
Le Freak
Chic; *45* .... (ATL)
Let's Go Crazy
Prince; *ST/Purple Rain* .... (WB)
Sly Fox; *Let's Go Crazy* .... (CAP)
Life In The Fast Lane
Eagles; *Hotel California* .... (ASY)
    Live .... (ASY)
    ST/FM .... (MCA)
Little Crazy
Fight; *War Of Words* .... (EPI)
Loco
Iguanas; *Nuevo Boogaloo* .... (MGR)
Losing My Mind
Bobby Short; *50 By* .... (ATL)
Cleo Laine; *Sings Sondheim* .... (RCA)
Liza Minnelli; *Results* .... (EPI)
Original Broadway Cast; *Follies* .... (ANG)
    Follies .... (CAP)
Losin' Your Mind
Pride & Glory; *Pride & Glory* .... (GEF)
Love Bizarre
Sheila E.; *Romance 1600* .... (PAI)
Love Her Madly
Doors; *Best Of* .... (ELE)
    Classics .... (ELE)
    L.A. Woman .... (ELE)
    Weird Scenes From Inside The Gold Mine .... (ELE)
Lunatic Fringe
Red Rider; *As Far As Siam* .... (CAP)
    Neruda + 3 .... (CAP)
    ST/Vision Quest .... (GEF)

Mad About The Boy
Dinah Shore; *Love Songs* .... (COL)
Dinah Washington; *Golden Hits* .... (MER)
Mad About You
Belinda Carlisle; *Belinda* .... (IRS)
Sting; *Soul Cages* .... (A&M)
Mad House
Robin Trower; *Victims Of The Fury* .... (CHR)
Mad Love
Linda Ronstadt; *Mad Love* .... (ASY)
Madman Across The Water
Elton John; *Live In Australia w/Melbourne*
    Orchestra .... (MCA)
    Madman Across The Water .... (POL)
Madness
Elton John; *Single Man* .... (MCA)
Madness; *One Step Beyond* .... (SIR)
Make Me Lose Control
Eric Carmen; *Best Of* .... (ARI)
    Dirty Dancing Live In Concert .... (RCA)
Mama He's Crazy
Judds; *Greatest Hits* .... (RCA)
    Judds .... (RCA)
    Why Not Me .... (RCA)
Mama Weer All Crazee Now
Quiet Riot; *Condition Critical* .... (PSH)
Maniac
D.C. 3; *Porgram: Annihilator* .... (SST)
Michael Sembello; *Bossa Nova Hotel* .... (WB)
    ST/Flashdance .... (CAS)
Manic Depression
Jeff Beck & Seal; *Stone Free: A Tribute To Jimi*
    Hendrix .... (RPR)
Manic Monday
Bangles; *Different Light* .... (COL)
    Greatest Hits .... (COL)
Mental Illness Can Be Beautiful
John Trubee; *Naked Teenage Girls In Outer Space* (ENI)
Mi Vida Loca
Pam Tillis; *Sweetheart's Dance* .... (ARI)
Midnight Madness
Clockwork; *Made In The U.S. Of Japan* .... (MER)
Foghat; *Stone Blue* .... (RHI)
Midnight Maniac
Krokus; *Blitz* .... (ARI)
Military Madness
Graham Nash; *Bread & Roses Festival-#2* .... (FAN)
    Songs For Beginners .... (ATL)
Mind Blowin'
D.O.C.; *No One Can Do It Better* .... (RUT)
Mind Disaster
Initial Shock; *Nuggets-#8* .... (RHI)
Miss You Like Crazy
Natalie Cole; *Good To Be Back* .... (ELE)
Mixed Up, Shook Up Girl
Mink De Ville; *Mink De Ville* .... (CAP)
Motor City Madhouse
Ted Nugent; *Double Live Gonzo* .... (EPI)
    Ted Nugent .... (EPI)
My Mother Is A Space Cadet
Dweezil Zappa; *45* .... (BAR)
Nineteenth Nervous Breakdown
Rolling Stones; *Big Hits-High Tide & Green Grass* (AKO)
    Got Live If You Want It .... (AKO)
    Hot Rocks-1964-1971 .... (AKO)
    Singles Collection-London Years .... (AKO)
No Control
Eddie Money; *Greatest Hits-Sound Of Money* ....(COL)
    No Control .... (COL)
Nobody In His Right Mind Would've...
George Strait; *Country Classics-#6-1985-1986* ..(MSP)
    Greatest Hits-#2 .... (MCA)
    #7 .... (MCA)
Obsession
Fem 2 Fem; *Woman To Woman* .... (CRI)
Oh You Crazy Moon
Frank Sinatra; *Moonlight Sinatra* .... (RPR)
    Sings The Songs Of Van Heusen & Cahn .... (RPR)
Mark Murphy; *Sings Nat's Choice-Cole*
    Songbook-#1 .... (MUS)
Out Of Control
Eagles; *Desperado* .... (ASY)
George Jones; *Very Best Of* .... (EPI)
Jefferson Starship; *Winds Of Change* .... (GRU)

Judy Collins; *Bread & Roses* .... (ELE)
Saxon; *Denim & Leather* .... (CAP)
Squeeze; *U.K. Squeeze* .... (A&M)
Ted Nugent; *Cat Scratch Fever* .... (EPI)
Todd Rundgren; *Hermit Of Mink Hollow* .... (RHI)
Tribe After Tribe; *Tribe After Tribe* .... (MEG)
U2; *Boy* .... (ISL)
Out Of My Mind
Buffalo Springfield; *Buffalo Springfield* .... (ATC)
Over My Head
Fleetwood Mac; *25 Years-The Chain* .... (WB)
  Fleetwood Mac .... (RPR)
  Greatest Hits .... (WB)
  Live .... (WB)
O'Sanity
John Lennon & Yoko Ono; *Milk & Honey* .... (POL)
Poisoned Heart & A Twisted Memory
Richard Thompson; *Hand Of Kindness* .... (HBL)
Pop Pop Pop Goes My Mind
Levert; *Bloodline* .... (ATL)
  Golden Age Of Black Music 1977-1988 .... (ATL)
Possession Obsession
Daryl Hall & John Oates; *Bigbamboom* .... (RCA)
  /Others-Live At The Apollo .... (RCA)
Pretty Vacant
Joan Jett; *Hit List* .... (EPA)
Sex Pistols; *Live At Chelmsford Top Security*
  Prison .... (RES)
  Never Mind The Bollocks .... (WB)
Psycho Dyke
Dead Serios; *Possessed By Polka* .... (LGS)
Psycho Killer
Talking Heads; *Name Of This Band Is Talking*
  Heads .... (SIR)
  ST/Stop Making Sense .... (SIR)
  '77 .... (SIR)
Psychotic Reaction
Count Five; *Collectables Presents History Of*
  Rock-#6 .... (CLT)
  Cruisin' 1966 .... (INC)
  Nuggets-Classic Collection/'60s .... (RHI)
  Nuggets-#1 .... (RHI)
  Rockin' 60s .... (PRY)
Questioning My Sanity
L7; *Hungry For Stink* .... (SLS)
Radio Spot/Nervous Breakdown
Bobby Fuller; *Tapes-#1* .... (RHI)
Rave On
Buddy Holly; *20 Golden Greats* .... (MCA)
  Buddy Holly .... (MCA)
  Legend .... (MCA)
  Rock & Roll Collection .... (MCA)
  ST/American Graffiti .... (MCA)
Gary Busey; *ST/Buddy Holly Story* .... (EPI)
John Mellencamp; *ST/Cocktail* .... (ELE)
Rhymes Fo Da Funny Farm
The Jaz; *Ya Don't Stop* .... (EMI)
Roads To Madness
Queensryche; *The Warning* .... (EMI)
Rock That Boogie
Commander Cody/Lost Planet Airmen; *Country*
  Casanova .... (MCA)
  Too Much Fun-Best Of .... (MCA)
  We've Got A Live One Here .... (WB)
Rock & Roll Crazies
Stephen Stills; *Manassas* .... (ATL)
  Still Stills .... (ATL)
Scatterbrain
Erroll Garner; *Best Of Garner* .... (MER)
Jeff Beck; *Blow By Blow* .... (EPI)
Schizophrenia
Descendants; *All* .... (SST)
Sonic Youth; *Sister* .... (SST)
Sea Of Madness
Crosby, Stills, Nash & Young; *ST/Woodstock* .... (ATL)
Self Control
Laura Branigan; *Hit Singles-1980-1988* .... (ATL)
  Self Control .... (ATL)
Sex Fiend
Awesome Dre/Hardcore Committee; *Explicit Rap* (PRY)
  You Can't Hold Me Back .... (PRY)
Sex Maniac
Bobby Nunn; *Private Party* .... (MOT)

Shape I'm In
Band; *Anthology* .... (CAP)
  Best Of .... (CAP)
  Last Waltz .... (WB)
  Rock Of Ages-#1 & 2 .... (CAP)
  Stage Fright .... (CAP)
  To Kingdom Come-Definitive Collection .... (CAP)
Bob Dylan/Band; *Before The Flood* .... (COL)
Marty Stuart; *Marty Stuart* .... (COL)
She Don't Have A License To Drive Me...
Porter Wagoner; *45* .... (WB)
She Drives Me Crazy
Fine Young Cannibals; *Raw & The Cooked* .... (IRS)
  Raw & The Remix .... (MCA)
  Rock The First-#1 .... (SAN)
She's Crazy For Leavin'
Rodney Crowell; *30 Years Of #1 Hits-#19* ......(COL)
  Diamonds & Dirt .... (COL)
  Greatest Country Hits!'80s-1989 .... (COL)
Steve Wariner; *Life's Highway* .... (MCA)
She's Funny That Way (I Got A Woman...)
Art Tatum; *Solo Masterpieces-#8* .... (PAB)
Count Basie Jam; *Montreux '77* .... (PAB)
Frank Sinatra; *At The Movies* .... (CAP)
  Nice 'N' Easy .... (CAP)
Jackie Gleason; *Lush Moods* .... (PRR)
Nat King Cole; *Big Band Cole* .... (BLN)
Shine On You Crazy Diamond
Pink Floyd; *Collection Of Great Dance Songs* ....(COL)
  Delicate Sound Of Thunder .... (COL)
  Wish You Were Here .... (COL)
Silly
Deniece Williams; *My Melody* .... (COL)
Someday, Someway
Marshall Crenshaw; *Marshall Crenshaw* .... (WB)
  ST/Nightshift .... (WB)
State Of Shock
Jacksons; *Victory* .... (EPI)
Ted Nugent; *State Of Shock* .... (EPI)
Still Crazy After All These Years
Paul Simon; *Greatest Hits* .... (COL)
  Negotiations & Love Songs-1971-1986 .... (WB)
  Still Crazy After All These Years .... (COL)
Simon & Garfunkel; *Concert In Central Park* ..... (WB)
Stone Cold Crazy
Queen; *Classic* .... (HOL)
  Sheer Heart Attack .... (HOL)
  ST/Encino Man .... (HOL)
Stress In Marriage
Negativeland; *Escape From Noise* .... (SST)
Suicidal Mania
Suicidal Tendencies; *How Will I Laugh Tomorrow When*
  I... .... (EPI)
Suicidal Maniac
Suicidal Tendencies; *Join The Army* .... (CRL)
Suicide Madness
Germs; *Germicide-Live At The Whisky-1977* ..... (ROI)
Super Freak
Rick James; *Greatest Hits* .... (MOT)
  Mega Hits Dance Classics-#7 .... (PRY)
Sweet Daddy (Your Mama's Done Gone Mad)
Little Brother Montgomery; *Chicago-Living*
  Legends-South Side Blues .... (RVR)
Sweet Little Girl
Stevie Wonder; *Music Of My Mind* .... (MOT)
Teenage Lobotomy
Ramones; *All The Stuff & More-#2* .... (SIR)
  Ramones Mania .... (SIR)
  Rocket To Russia .... (SIR)
Teenage Nervous Breakdown
Little Feat; *Hoy-Hoy!* .... (WB)
  Sailin' Shoes .... (WB)
Tell Me I'm Crazy
Shelby Lynne; *Temptation* .... (MC)
That Song Is Driving Me Crazy
Tom T. Hall; *Greatest Hits-#2* .... (MER)
They're Coming To Take Me Away, Ha Ha
Napoleon XIV; *Dr. Demento's Greatest Novelty-#3* (RHI)
  Silly Songs .... (KT)
  They're Coming To Take Me Away, Ha Ha ..... (RHI)

This Crazy Love
Oak Ridge Boys; *Country Classics-#10-1987* .... (MSP)
   Greatest Hits-#3 .... (MCA)
   This Crazy Love .... (MSP)
   Where The Fast Lane Ends .... (MCA)
Those Lazy Hazy Crazy Days Of Summer
Nat King Cole; *Best Of* .... (CAP)
   Capitol Collectors Series .... (CAP)
'Til I Gain Control Again
Crystal Gayle; *45* .... (ELE)
   45 ....(WB)
   Best Of ....(WB)
   True Love .... (ELE)
   True Love ....(WB)
Emmylou Harris; *Elite Hotel* .... (RPR)
Rodney Crowell; *Collection* .... (WB)
   Rodney Crowell ....(WB)
Willie Nelson; *Greatest Hits & Some That Will Be* (COL)
Willie Nelson & Waylon Jennings; *45* ....(COL)
   Greatest Hits ....(COL)
   Take It To The Limit ....(COL)
   Willie & Family Live ....(COL)
Tonight I Climbed The Wall
Alan Jackson; *Lot About Livin' (& A Little 'Bout
Love)* .... (ARI)
Touch Of Madness
Night Ranger; *Midnight Madness* .... (CAM)
Touch & Go Crazy
Lee Greenwood; *Country
Classics-#12-1987-1988* .... (MSP)
   Greatest Hits-#2 .... (MCA)
Twenty-First Century Schizoid Man
King Crimson; *Abbreviated* .... (EDI)
   Compact .... (EDI)
   In The Court Of The Crimson King .... (EDI)
Twisted
Bette Midler; *Bette Midler* .... (ATL)
Joni Mitchell; *Court & Spark* .... (ASY)
Lambert, Hendricks & Ross; *Twisted-Best Of* .... (RHI)
U Bring The Freak Out
Rick James; *Cold Blooded* .... (MOT)
Untanglin' My Mind
Clint Black; *One Emotion* ....(RCA)
Upside Down
Diana Ross; *All The Great Hits* .... (MOT)
   Anthology .... (MOT)
   Billboard Top Dance Hits-1980 .... (RHI)
   Billboard Top Hits-1980 .... (RHI)
   Diana .... (MOT)
Victim Of The Insane
Trouble; *Psalm 9* .... (MET)
Walk Right In
Rooftop Singers; *Best Of* .... (VAN)
   Cruisin'-1963 .... (INC)
   Greatest Folksingers Of The '80s .... (VAN)
   ST/Forrest Gump .... (EPX)
   Troubadours Of The Folk Era-#3 .... (RHI)
We Must Have Been Out Of Our Minds
George Jones; *Greatest Country Hits* ....(CCB)
George Jones & Melba Montgomery; *Best Of George
Jones-1955-1967* .... (RHI)
   Party Pickin' .... (IGR)
Whammer Jammer
J. Geils Band; *Best Of* .... (ATL)
   Full House .... (ATL)
When A Man Loves A Woman
Barbara Mandrell; *Best Of* .... (LIB)
   Key's In The Mailbox .... (LIB)
Bette Midler; *ST/The Rose* .... (ATL)
Michael Bolton; *Time Love & Tenderness* ....(COL)
Percy Sledge; *Atlantic
R&B-1947-1974-#5-(1962-1966)* .... (ATL)
   Atlantic Soul Classics ....(WSP)
   Best Of .... (ATL)
   Golden Age Of Black Music-1960-1970 .... (ATL)
   ST/Platoon & Songs Of The Era .... (ATL)
Whenever You Come Around
Vince Gill; *When Love Finds You* .... (MCA)
Where Was I
Ricky Van Shelton; *Bridge I Didn't Burn* ....(COL)

White Room
Cream; *History Of British Rock-#9* .... (RHI)
   Live-#2 .... (POL)
   Strange Brew-Very Best Of .... (POL)
   Wheels Of Fire .... (POL)
Eric Clapton; *24 Nights* .... (RPR)
   Crossroads .... (POL)
Wild Nights, Hot & Crazy Days
Judas Priest; *Metal Works-1973-1993* ....(COL)
   Turbo ....(COL)
Wild & Crazy Love
Mary Jane Girls; *Only Four You* .... (MOT)
You Could Drive A Person Crazy
Original Cast; *Company* ....(COL)
You Go To My Head
Billie Holiday; *At Storyville* ....(BL)
   First Verve Sessions ....(VRV)
Bing Crosby; *Radio Years* .... (CRS)
Frank Sinatra; *Nice 'N' Easy* .... (CAP)
   Round #1 .... (CAP)
   Voice-The Columbia Years-1943-1952 ....(COL)
Linda Ronstadt; *For Sentimental Reasons* .... (ASY)
You Make Me Crazy
Sammy Hagar; *Musical Chairs* .... (CAP)
   Three Decades Of Rock-'60s-'70s-'80s .... (PRY)
Utopia; *Adventures In Utopia* .... (RHI)
   Anthology-1974-1985 .... (RHI)
You May Be Right
Billy Joel; *Glass Houses* ....(COL)
   Greatest Hits-#1&2-1973-1985 ....(COL)
You Might Think
Cars; *Greatest Hits* .... (ELE)
   Heartbreak City .... (ELE)
You Nearly Lose Your Mind
E. Tubb/Willie Nelson/Waylon Jennings; *Ernest Tubb
Collection* ....(SO)
Merle Haggard & Janie Fricke; *It's All In The
Game* .... (EPI)
You Really Got Me
Kinks; *Come Dancing With-Best Of-1977-1986* .. (ARI)
   Greatest Hits-#1 .... (RHI)
   History Of British Rock-#1 .... (RHI)
   Live .... (RPR)
Van Halen; *ST/Over The Edge* ....(WB)
   Van Halen ....(WB)
You're Driving Me Crazy
Art Pepper; *Return Of-Complete Aladdin
Recordings-#1* .... (BLN)
Big Joe Turner; *Boss Of The Blues* .... (ATL)
Dinah Shore; *Love & Kisses Dinah* ....(RCA)
Frank Sinatra; *Strangers In The Night* .... (RPR)
Louis Armstrong; *#7-You're Driving Me Crazy* ...(COL)
You're Insane
Rod Stewart; *Footloose & Fancy Free* .... (WB)
Zombie
Cranberries; *No Need To Argue* .... (ISL)
Zombie Jamboree
Kingston Trio; *25 Years Non-Stop* ....(XER)
   From The Hungry i .... (CAP)

CRIME, Rape, Steal

*See Also: FIGHT, LAW & ORDER, POLICE,
PRISON, REBELS*

Ain't No Crime
Billy Joel; *Piano Man* ....(COL)
Almost Illegal
Rod Stewart; *Out Of Order* .... (WB)
Arrested For Driving While Blind
ZZ Top; *Six Pack* .... (WB)
   Tejas .... (WB)
Assault & Battery
Howard Jones; *Animal Liberation* .... (WAX)
   Dream Into Action .... (ELE)
Bandit
Jerry Reed; *ST/Smokey And The Bandit* .... (MCA)
Bandit In A Bathing Suit
David Bromberg; *Bandit In A Bathing Suit* .... (FAN)
Bankrobber
Clash; *On Broadway* .... (EPI)
   Story Of-#1 .... (EPI)

Bankrobber/Robber Dub
Clash; *Black Market Clash* .... (EPI)
Rhythm Come Forward-#3 ....(COL)
Before You Accuse Me
Bo Diddley; *Bo Diddley* .... (CSS)
Creedence Clearwater Revival; *1970* ....(FAN)
Chronicle-#2 ....(FAN)
Cosmo's Factory ....(FAN)
Creedence Country ....(FAN)
Eric Clapton; *Journeyman* ....(DUC)
Unplugged ....(RPR)
Black Money
Vinnie James; *All-American Boy* ....(RCA)
Blackmail
10 CC; *Original Soundtrack* .... (MER)
Robert Palmer; *Sneakin' Sally Through The Alley* . (ISL)
Bubba Shot The Jukebox
Mark Chesnutt; *Longnecks & Short Stories* ...... (MCA)
Burnin' & Lootin'
Bob Marley/Wailers; *Burnin'* .... (ISL)
Burnin' Love ....(ISL)
Live ....(ISL)
Commit A Crime
Howlin' Wolf; *Chess Box* .... (CSS)
Conspiracy
Black Browes; *Amorica* ....(AME)
Coward Of The County
Kenny Rogers; *20 Greatest Hits* ....(LIB)
Greatest Hits ....(EMI)
Kenny ....(LIB)
Crime Don't Pay
Joe Jackson Band; *Beat Crazy* .... (A&M)
Crime In The City
Neil Young/Crazy Horse; *Arc Weld* ....(RPR)
Crime Of Passion
Bonnie Raitt; *Nine Lives* ....(WB)
Diana Ross; *Eaten Alive* ....(RCA)
Loudon Wainwright III; *Unrequited* ....(COL)
Ricky Van Shelton; *More Hot Country Requests-#2* (EPI)
Wild-Eyed Dream ....(COL)
Rita Coolidge; *Satisfied* ....(A&M)
Crime Of The Century
Supertramp; *Classics-#9* ....(A&M)
Crime Of The Century ....(A&M)
Paris ....(A&M)
Crime Wave
Prism; *See Forever Eyes* ....(ARL)
Crime & Punishment
Agony Column; *Brave Words & Bloody Knuckles* (BCH)
Crimes Of Paris
Elvis Costello; *Girls Girls Girls* ....(COL)
Elvis Costello/Attractions; *Blood & Chocolate* ...(COL)
Criminal Kind
Tom Petty/Heartbreakers; *Hard Promises* .... (MCA)
Criminal World
David Bowie; *Let's Dance* .... (EMI)
Cuban Crime Of Passion
Jimmy Buffett; *Boats Beaches Bars & Ballads* ... (MGR)
White Sport Coat & A Pink Crustacean .... (MCA)
Date Rape
Tribe Called Quest; *Low End Theory* .... (JVA)
Desperados Waiting For The Train
Guy Clark; *Old No. 1* ....(SH)
Jerry Jeff Walker; *Best Of* ....(MCA)
Great Gonzos ....(MCA)
Viva Terlingua ....(MCA)
W. Jennings/W. Nelson/J. Cash/K. Krist.;
Highwayman ....(COL)
Did You Steal My Money
Who; *Face Dances* ....(MCA)
Dirty Deeds Done Dirt Cheap
AC/DC; *Dirty Deeds Done Dirt Cheap* ....(ATL)
Don't Rob Another Man's Castle
Ernest Tubb; *Story* ....(MCA)
Don't Take The Girl
Tim McGraw; *Not A Moment Too Soon* ....(CRB)
Dress Me Up As A Robber
Paul McCartney; *Tug Of War* ....(COL)
Fingerprint File
Rolling Stones; *It's Only Rock 'N' Roll* ....(RS)
Love You Live ....(RS)
Forbidden Fruit
Band; *Northern Lights-Southern Cross* ....(CAP)

Framed
Cheech & Chong; *ST/Up In Smoke* ....(WB)
Little Feat; *Hoy! Hoy!* ....(WB)
Los Lobos; *ST/La Bamba* ....(SLS)
Ritchie Valens; *History Of* ....(RHI)
Ritchie Valens ....(RHI)
Fugitive
Indigo Girls; *Swamp Ophelia* ....(EPI)
Glendale Train
New Riders Of The Purple Sage; *Best Of* ....(COL)
New Riders Of The Purple Sage ....(COL)
Great Filling Station Holdup
Jimmy Buffett; *White Sport Coat & A Pink*
Crustacean .... (MCA)
Have Mercy On The Criminal
Elton John; *Don't Shoot Me I'm Only The Piano*
Player ....(POL)
Live In Australia w/Melbourne Symphony ...... (MCA)
Highway Robbery
Tanya Tucker; *Strong Enough To Bend* ....(CAP)
House Arrest
Bryan Adams; *Waking Up The Neighbours* ...... (A&M)
Husband Stealer
Barbara Mandrell; *This Is* .... (MCA)
I Love Robbing Banks
Greg Austin Band; *Midnight Driver* ....(XER)
Illegal Smile
John Prine; *John Prine* ....(ATL)
Prime Prine ....(ATL)
Is It A Crime
Judy Holliday/Original Cast; *Bells Are Ringing* ...(COL)
Sade; *Promise* ....(POR)
It's Not A Crime
Nils Lofgren; *Best Of* ....(A&M)
Classics-#13 ....(A&M)
Cry Tough ....(A&M)
Joe Hill
Arlo Guthrie & Pete Seeger; *Together In Concert* (RPR)
Joan Baez; *Carry It On* ....(VAN)
From Every Stage ....(A&M)
One Day At A Time ....(VAN)
ST/Woodstock ....(ATL)
Soundtrack; *Carry It On* ....(VAN)
Johnny 99
Bruce Springsteen; *Nebraska* ....(COL)
Bruce Springsteen/E Street Band;
Live-1975-1985 ....(COL)
Johnny Cash; *Cover Me* .... (RHI)
Johnny Porter
Persuasions; *Chirpin'* .... (ELE)
Ry Cooder; *Borderline* ....(WB)
Jungleland
Bruce Springsteen; *Born To Run* ....(COL)
Lee Harvey Oswald
Skatalites; *Stretching Out* .... (ROI)
Listen Like Thieves
INXS; *Listen Like Thieves* ....(ATL)
Little Criminals
Randy Newman; *Little Criminals* ....(WB)
Love In The First Degree
Alabama; *Feels So Right* ....(RCA)
Greatest Hits ....(RCA)
Live ....(RCA)
Nipper's Greatest Hits/'80s ....(RCA)
Love Is So Good When You're Stealing It
Z.Z. Hill; *Lost Soul-#3* .... (EPI)
Machine Gun Kelly
James Taylor; *Mud Slide Slim* ....(WB)
Maggie Mae
Beatles; *Let It Be* ....(CAP)
Manslaughter
EPMD; *Business As Usual* ....(DFC)
Me & A Gun
Tori Amos; *Little Earthquakes* ....(ATL)
Movin' Violation
Skyy; *Skyyjammer* ....(SSL)
Murder Gonna Be My Crime
Sippie Wallace; *Women Be Wise* ....(ALG)
No Sense Of Crime
Iggy Pop & James Williamson; *Kill City* ....(BMP)
Perfect Crime
Guns N' Roses; *Use Your Illusion I* ....(GEF)
Pittsburgh Stealers
Kendalls; *20 Favorites* ....(EPI)

Police & Thiefs
Clash; *Clash* .... (EPI)
  On Broadway .... (EPI)
  Story Of-#1 .... (EPI)
Junior Murvin; *Jammin'* .... (MGO)
  Police & Thiefs .... (MGO)
  ST/Rockers .... (MGO)
  This Is Reggae Music #3 .... (ISL)

Pretty Boy Floyd
Arlo Guthrie & Pete Seeger; *Precious Friend* ...... (WB)
Bob Dylan; *Folkways-Tribute To W.*
  Guthrie/Leadbelly ....(COL)
Byrds; *Byrds (collection)* ....(COL)
  Sweetheart of The Rodeo ....(COL)
Joan Baez; *Greatest Songs Of Woody Guthrie* ... (VAN)
Woody Guthrie; *Dust Bowl Ballads* .... (ROU)
  Legendary ....(TRD)
  Struggle .... (FLW)
  Woody Guthrie ....(EVR)
  Worried Man Blues-Golden Classics-#1 ...... (CLT)

Punishment Fits The Crime
Ramones; *Brain Drain* .... (SIR)

Ragin' Cajun
Charlie Daniels Band; *Windows* .... (EPI)

Raised On Robbery
Joni Mitchell; *Court & Spark* .... (ASY)

Robber
Bram Tchaikovsky; *Strange Man Changed Man* .. (POL)

Robbery Assault & Battery
Genesis; *Seconds Out* .... (ATL)
  Trick Of The Tail ....(ATC)

Robbery With Violins
Steeleye Span; *Parcel Of Rogues* .... (CHR)

Rock & Roll Crook
Nils Lofgren; *Best Of* .... (A&M)
  Classics-#13 .... (A&M)
  Night After Night .... (A&M)
  Nils Lofgren ....(RYK)

Run Like A Thief
Bonnie Raitt; *Home Plate* .... (WB)
J.D. Souther; *J.D. Souther* .... (ASY)

Runaway Train
Soul Asylum; *Grave Dancers Union* ....(COL)

Scene Of A Perfect Crime
Concrete Blonde; *Free* .... (IRS)

Scene Of The Crime
Lime Spiders; *Beethoven's Fist* .... (CRL)

Seven Eleven
Commander Cody; *Midnight Man* ....(OOP)

Sex Crime
Eurythmics; *Greatest Hits* .... (ARI)

Sexual Harassment In The Workplace
Frank Zappa; *Guitar* ....(RYK)

Shakespeare Stole My Baby
Eye To Eye; *Shakespeare Stole My Baby* .... (WB)

Silent Fury
Gary Wright; *Light Of Smiles* .... (WB)

Sing You Sinners
Sammy Davis, Jr./Original Cast; *Mr. Wonderful* (MCA)
Tony Bennett; *All-Time Greatest Hits* ....(COL)
  At Carnegie Hall ....(SSP)
  Forty Years-Artistry Of ....(COL)

Smuggler's Blues
Glenn Frey; *Allnighter* .... (MCA)
  Rock The First-#2 ....(SAN)
  ST/Miami Vice .... (MCA)

Sneaky Private Lee
Paice/Ashton/Lord; *Malice In Wonderland* .... (WB)

So You Want To Be A Gangster
Too $hort; *Shorty The Player* .... (JVA)

Somebody Stole My Gal
Benny Goodman; *Best Of The Big Bands* ....(COL)
  B.G. In Hi-Fi .... (BLN)

Steal Away
Billy Joe Royal; *Greatest Hits* ....(COL)
Johnnie Taylor; *Chronicle* .... (STX)
  Super Hits .... (STX)
Joy; *Joy* .... (FAN)
Nils Lofgren; *Classics-#13* .... (A&M)
  Nils .... (A&M)
Poco; *Rose Of Cimarron* .... (MCA)
Robbie Dupree; *Robbie Dupree* .... (ELE)
Whitesnake; *Snakebite* ....(GEF)

Steal Your Heart Away
Bonnie Raitt; *Longing In Their Hearts* ....(CAP)

Stealer
Free; *Best Of* .... (A&M)
  Highway .... (A&M)

Stealing Love
Emotions; *Chronicle* .... (STX)

Stealin'
David Bromberg; *Reckless Abandon* ....(FAN)
Jacky Ward; *Best Of* .... (MER)
  Lover's Question ....(MER)
Janis Joplin; *ST/Janis* ....(COL)
Max Romeo; *War In Babylon* .... (ISL)
Uriah Heep; *Sweet Freedom* .... (CHR)

Stealin' Con
Merle Haggard/Strangers; *Fightin' Side Of Me* ...(CAP)

Stealin' Each Other Blind
Chip Taylor; *45* ....(CAP)

Stealin' Feelin'
Mike Lunsford; *Mike Lunsford* .... (GUS)
  Super Country Hits-1970s .... (GUS)

Stealin' Watermelons
Elvin Bishop; *Best Of* .... (EPI)
  Let It Flow ....(CPC)
  Raisin' Hell ....(CPC)

Stole & Sold From Africa
John McCutcheon; *Live At Wolf Trap* .... (ROU)

Stolen Car
Bruce Springsteen; *The River* ....(COL)

Stop Thief
Carla Thomas; *Queen Alone* .... (RHI)
Fabian; *Best Of* .... (MCA)

Sweetest Taboo
Sade; *Promise* ....(POR)

Take The Money & Run
Steve Miller Band; *CD Gift Set* ....(CAP)
  Fly Like An Eagle ....(CAP)
  Greatest Hits-1974-1978 ....(CAP)
  Live .... (CAP)

Talking Watergate
Tom Paxton; *New Songs From The Briarpatch* .. (VAN)

Taxman Mr. Thief
Cheap Trick; *Cheap Trick* .... (EPI)

Terrorist Trousers
Jim Carroll; *Praying Mantis* .... (GIA)

Terrorist's Life
D.I.; *What Good Is Grief To A God* .... (XXX)

That's A Crime
Original Broadway Cast; *Irma La Douce* .... (SMC)

Theme From "Raiders Of The Lost Ark"
Neil Norman; *Greatest Science Fiction Hits-#3* ... (CRS)

Theme From "The Godfather"
Henry Mancini/Mancini Pops Orchestra; *Cinema
  Italiano* ....(RCA)

Thief In Mexico
Don Michael Sampson; *Coyote* .... (RVL)

Thief Of Hearts
Madonna; *Erotica* .... (MAV)
Melissa Manchester; *ST/Thief Of Hearts* .... (CAS)

Thieves
Ministry; *In Case You Didn't Feel Like Showing Up* (SIR)
  Mind Is A Terrible Thing To Taste .... (SIR)

Thieves In The Temple
Prince; *ST/Graffiti Bridge* ....(PAI)

Time Off For Bad Behaviour
Confederate Railroad; *Confederate Railroad* ..... (ATL)

Too Much Fun
Commander Cody/Lost Planet Airmen; *Live From Deep
  In The Heart Of Texas* .... (MCA)
  Too Much Fun-Best Of .... (MCA)
  We've Got A Live One Here ....(WB)

Too Much Monkey Business
Chuck Berry; *Classic Oldies From The '50s &
  '60s-#16* .... (MCA)
  Roll Over Beethoven .... (ALL)
  ST/Hail! Hail! Rock 'N' Roll .... (MCA)
  Toronto Rock 'N' Roll Revival-#2 .... (ACC)
Elvis Presley; *Guitar Man* ....(RCA)
  Million-Dollar Quartet ....(RCA)
  ST/This Is ....(RCA)
Yardbirds; *Five Live Yardbirds* .... (RHI)
  For Your Love .... (ACC)
  Greatest Hits-#1-1964-1966 .... (RHI)

Untouchables
Ennio Morricone; *ST/Untouchables* .... (A&M)
Victim Or The Crime
Grateful Dead; *Built To Last* .... (ARI)
Without A Net .... (ARI)
Violent Crimes
Riot; *Restless Breed* .... (ELE)
Walkaway Joe
Trisha Yearwood; *Hearts In Armor* .... (MCA)
Waltzing Matilda
Burl Ives; *Best Of* .... (MCA)
Fred Astaire; *Three Evenings With* .... (DRG)
James Galway; *Pachebel Canon & Other*
Favorites ....(RCA)
Who But A Fool (Thief In Paradise)
Bonnie Raitt; *Nine Lives* .... (WB)
Who Stole The Jukebox (From Lucy's...)
Johnny Bond; *Johnny Gimble's Texas Honky-Tonk*
Hits .... (CMH)
Who's The Thief?
Original Cast; *Joseph/Amazing Technicolor*
Dreamcoat .... (MCA)
Joseph/Amazing Technicolor Dreamcoat .... (POL)
Working On The Highway
Bruce Springsteen; *Born In The U.S.A.* ....(COL)
Bruce Springsteen/E Street Band;
Live-1975-1985 .... (COL)

CRYING, Tears
See Also: RAIN

After My Laughter Came Tears
Big Joe Turner; *Midnight Special* .... (PAB)
Ain't Nobody Cryin' But Me
Tasty Licks; *Anchored To The Shore* .... (ROU)
Ain't That A Shame
Cheap Trick; *At Budokan* .... (EPI)
Fats Domino; *Best Of* .... (EMI)
Greatest Hits .... (EVR)
Greatest Hits .... (MCA)
ST/American Graffiti .... (MCA)
Hank Williams, Jr.; *14 Greatest Hits* .... (POL)
Standing In The Shadows .... (POL)
John Lennon; *Lennon* .... (CAP)
Rock 'N' Roll .... (CAP)
Tanya Tucker; *Lovin' & Learnin'* .... (MCA)
All Choked Up
Original Broadway Cast; *Grease* .... (POL)
All Cried Out
Alison Moyet; *Alf* ....(COL)
Dusty Springfield; *Golden Greats* .... (PHI)
Golden Hits .... (MER)
Lisa Lisa & Cult Jam With Full Force; *Lisa Lisa & Cult*
Jam With Full Force ....(COL)
All I Can Do Is Cry
Arthur Prysock; *Here's To Good Friends* .... (MCA)
All Out Of Tears/Lovin' Tears Suite
French Kiss; *Panic* ....(POL)
All The Cryin' In The World
Jeris Ross; *45* .... (MCA)
And Her Tears Flowed Like Wine
Stan Kenton; *Greatest Hits* .... (CAP)
Lighter Side ....(CW)
Stan Kenton & Anita O'Day; *Comprehensive*
Kenton .... (CAP)
And The Baby Never Cries
Harry Chapin; *Sniper & Other Love Songs* .... (ELE)
And The Heavens Cried
Anthony Newley; *Genuis Of* ....(LON)
Angels Don't Cry
Psychedelic Furs; *Midnight To Midnight* ....(COL)
Are You Weepin'
Gary Wright; *Light Of Smiles* .... (WB)
As Tears Go By
Marianne Faithfull; *Greatest Hits* .... (AKO)
Strange Weather .... (ISL)
Rolling Stones; *Big Hits-High Tide & Green Grass* (AKO)
December's Children .... (AKO)
Hot Rocks 1964-1971 .... (AKO)
Singles Collection-London Years .... (AKO)
Baby Don't You Cry
Alvin Lee; *Rocket Fuel* .... (RSO)
Ray Charles; *His Greatest Hits-#1* ....(DHL)

Baby Stop Crying
Bob Dylan; *Street Legal* ....(COL)
Baby, Baby, Don't Cry
Miracles; *Motown Story: First 25 Years* .... (MOT)
Time Out For/Special Occasion .... (MOT)
Smokey Robinson; *Top 10 With A Bullet-Motown Male*
Groups .... (MOT)
Smokey Robinson/Miracles; *Anthology* .... (MOT)
Compact Command Performances .... (MOT)
Baby, I Don't Cry Over You
Billie Holiday; *& Ella Fitzgerald* .... (MCA)
Back Doors Crying
Peter Allen; *Taught By Experts* ....(A&M)
Battle Of Glass Tears
King Crimson; *Lizard* .... (EDI)
Before The Next Teardrop Falls
Freddie Fender; *Before The Next Teardrop Falls* (MCA)
Best Of .... (MCA)
Oldies But Goodies-#2 .... (OSR)
Ray Anthony; *Great Golden Hits* .... (RAN)
Beggin' & Cryin'
Sonny Terry & Brownie McGhee; *Midnight*
Special .... (FAN)
Betcha Can't Cry Just One
David Frizzell & Shelly West; *In Session* ....(VVA)
Big Boys Don't Cry
Extreme; *Extreme* ....(A&M)
Big Girls Don't Cry
Frankie Valli/Four Seasons; *Anthology* .... (RHI)
Billboard Top Rock 'N' Roll Hits-1962 .... (RHI)
Greatest Hits-#1 .... (RHI)
More Dirty Dancing ....(RCA)
Bitter Tears
INXS; *X* .... (ATL)
Blue Eyes Crying In The Rain
Roy Acuff; *Greatest Hits-#1* .... (ELE)
Roy Acuff/Smokey Mountain Boys; *Columbia Country*
Classics-#1-Golden Age ....(COL)
Willie Nelson; *Columbia Country Classics-#5-New*
Trad. ....(COL)
Greatest Hits & Some That Will Be ....(COL)
Red Headed Stranger ....(COL)
ST/Honeysuckle Rose ....(COL)
Boo-Hoo-Hoo-Hoo
Little Richard; *Grooviest 17 Original Hits* .... (SPE)
His Biggest Hits .... (SPE)
Born To Cry
Dion/Belmonts; *20 Golden Classics* ....(CLT)
24 Original Classics .... (ARI)
Everything You've Always Wanted ....(LAU)
More Great Hits ....(LAU)
Boys Cry Tough
Bad Company; *Holy Water* ....(ATC)
Brush Those Tears From Your Eyes
Li'l Wally; *Unforgettable Hits* ....(JJ)
Bubba Shot The Jukebox
Mark Chesnutt; *Longnecks & Short Stories* ...... (MCA)
Can't Cry Hard Enough
Williams Brothers; *Williams Brothers* .... (WB)
Check Your Tears At The Door
Drivin' N' Cryin'; *Whisper Tames The Lion* ..... (ISL)
Cloudy, With A Chance Of Tears
Manhattans; *After Midnight* ....(COL)
Cowboys Ain't Supposed To Cry
Moe Brandy; *Cowboys Ain't Supposed To Cry* ...(COL)
Cowboys Don't Cry
Daron Norwood; *Daron Norwood* .... (GIA)
Dude Mowrey; *Honky Tonk* .... (CAP)
Ian Tyson; *All-Ears Review-#7-Still Amazing...* .. (ROM)
I Outgrew The Wagon .... (VAN)
Cry
Crystal Gayle; *Best Of* .... (WB)
Janie Fricke; *Celebration* ....(COL)
I'll Need To Hold Someone When I Cry ....(COL)
Johnnie Ray; *Best Of* ....(COL)
Radio Classics Of The '50s ....(COL)
Lynn Anderson; *Greatest Hits* ....(COL)
Ray Charles; *Anthology* .... (RHI)
Greatest Hits-#2 .... (RHI)
Roxette; *Look Sharp!* .... (EMI)
Cry Baby
Enchanters; *Billboard Top R&B Hits-1963* .... (RHI)
Soul Shots-#5-Soul Ballads .... (RHI)

Janis Joplin; *Greatest Hits* ....(COL)
  Pearl ....(COL)
  ST/Janis ....(COL)
Johnny Otis; *Original Johnny Otis Show* ....(SAV)
Kix; *Midnite Dynamite* ....(ATL)
Mad Lads; *Best Of* ....(STX)
Madonna; *I'm Breathless* ....(SIR)
Percy Mayfield; *Best Of* ....(SPE)
Quincy Jones; *Mellow Madness* ....(A&M)
Scarlets; *Golden Classics* ....(CLT)
Sheila E.; *Sex Cymbal* ....(WB)
Cry Baby Cry
  Aldo Nova; *Subject...Aldo Nova* ....(POR)
Angels; *My Boyfriend's Back* ....(CLT)
  Super Oldies/'60s-#4 ....(AUF)
  WCBS FM101-History Of Rock-'60s-#5 ....(CLT)
Beatles; *Beatles* ....(CAP)
Judy Garland; *Collector's Items 1936-1945* .... (MCA)
Cry Cry
  Cheap Trick; *Cheap Trick* ....(EPI)
Cry Cry Darlin'
  Jimmie C. Newman; *Greatest Hits* ....(PLN)
Cry For A Shadow
  Beatles; *Beatles* ....(AUF)
  In The Beginning (Circa 1960) ....(POL)
Cry For Freedom
  White Lion; *Big Game* ....(ATL)
Cry For Help
  Rick Astley; *Free* ....(RCA)
Cry For Home
  Van Morrison; *Inarticulate Speech Of The Heart* .. (WB)
Cry For Love
  Iggy Pop; *Blah Blah Blah* ....(A&M)
Cry For Me
  Blasters; *Collection* ....(SLS)
Cry For Me Baby
  Elmore James/Jimmy Reed/Eddie Taylor; *Street
  Talkin'* ....(MUS)
Cry For Mercy
  Raindogs; *Lost Souls* ....(ATC)
Cry For The Bad Man
  Lynyrd Skynyrd; *Best Of* ....(MSP)
  Gimme Back My Bullets ....(MCA)
Cry For The Nations
  Michael Schenker Group; *Michael Schenker
  Group* ....(CHR)
  One Night At Budokan ....(CHR)
Cry For You
  Jodeci; *Diary Of A Mad Band* .... (UT)
Cry If You Want
  Who; *It's Hard* ....(MCA)
Cry Just A Little
  Marie Osmond; *I Only Wanted You* ....(CAP)
Cry Just A Little Bit
  Sylvia; *Greatest Hits* ....(RCA)
Cry Like A Baby
  Bourgeois Tagg; *Yoyo* ....(ISL)
  Box Tops; *Billboard Top Rock 'N' Roll Hits-1968* (RHI)
  Greatest Hits ....(RHI)
  Super Hits-#5 ....(GUS)
  WCBS FM101-History Of Rock-'60s-#4 ....(CLT)
Flock Of Seagulls; *Dream Come True* ....(JVA)
Cry Like A Rainstorm
  Bonnie Raitt; *Takin' My Time* ....(WB)
Linda Ronstadt; *Cry Like A Rainstorm-Howl Like The
  Wind* ....(ELE)
Cry Me A River
  Aerosmith; *Rock In A Hard Place* ....(COL)
Barbra Streisand; *Barbra Streisand Album* ..(COL)
  Happening In Central Park ....(COL)
Crystal Gayle; *When I Dream* .... (UA)
Joe Cocker; *Classics-#4* ....(A&M)
  Greatest Hits ....(A&M)
  Mad Dogs & Englishmen ....(A&M)
Cry Myself To Sleep
  Del Shannon; *Runaway Hits!* .... (RHI)
Frankie Valli/Four Seasons; *Rarities-#1* ....(RHI)
Judds; *Collector's Series* ....(RCA)
  Greatest Hits ....(RCA)
  Hits Of '87 ....(RCA)
  Rockin' With The Rhythm ....(RCA)
Cry No More
  L.A. Guns; *L.A. Guns* ....(VTG)
Outlaws; *Outlaws* ....(ARI)

Cry Not For Me
  Patsy Cline; *Hungry For Love: Her First
  Recordings-#2* .... (RHI)
  Patsy Cline ....(AUF)
Cry Of The Gypsy
  Dokken; *Back For The Attack* .... (ELE)
Cry Of The Wild Goose
  Frankie Laine; *Golden Hits* .... (MER)
Cry On
  Irma Thomas; *New Orleans Jazz/Heritage 1976* .. (RHI)
Cry On My Shoulder
  Bonnie Raitt; *Nick Of Time* ....(CAP)
Cry On Your Own Shoulder
  General Public; *Hand To Mouth* .... (IRS)
Cry One More Time
  Gram Parsons; *GP/Grievous Angel* ....(RPR)
  Gram Parsons/Fallen Angels Live 1973 ....(SIE)
J. Geils Band; *Best Of* ....(ATL)
Cry So Easy
  Erasure; *Wonderland* .... (SIR)
Cry Softly Lonely One
  Roy Orbison; *Classic (1965-1968)* .... (RHI)
Cry To Me
  Betty Harris; *Soul Shots-#11: More Ballads* ...... (RHI)
  Super Oldies-#3 ....(AUF)
Bob Marley/Wailers; *Rastaman Vibration* ....(TUF)
Contours; *Dirty Dancing Live In Concert* ....(RCA)
Heart; *Little Queen* ....(POR)
Professor Longhair; *Crawfish Fiesta* ....(ALL)
  Last Mardi Gras ....(ATL)
Rolling Stones; *Out Of Our Heads* ....(AKO)
Solomon Burke; *Atlantic R&B
  1947-1974-#4-1958-1962* ....(ATL)
  Best Of ....(ATL)
  More Dirty Dancing ....(RCA)
Cry Tough
  Nils Lofgren; *Best Of* ....(A&M)
  Classics-#13 ....(A&M)
Poison; *Look What The Cat Dragged In* ....(CAP)
Cry Wolf
  Laura Branigan; *Touch* ....(ATL)
Stevie Nicks; *Other Side Of The Mirror* ....(MOD)
Victoria Shaw; *In Full View* ....(RPR)
Crybaby
  Utopia; *Anthology-1974-1985* .... (RHI)
Crying
  Don McLean; *Best Of* ....(EMI)
  Greatest Hits Then & Now ....(EMI)
Roy Orbison; *All-Time Greatest Hits-#1* ....(MON)
  For The Lonely: 18 Greatest Hits .... (RHI)
  For The Lonely: Anthology 1956-1965 ....(RHI)
  In Dreams-Greatest Hits ....(VIA)
Crying Again
  Oak Ridge Boys; *Greatest Hits* .... (MCA)
  Room Service ....(MCA)
Crying Days
  Scorpions; *Best Of-#2* ....(RCA)
  Virgin Killer ....(RCA)
Crying Game
  Boy George; *At Worst-Best Of Boy George/Culture
  Club* ....(SBK)
Crying In The Chapel
  Elvis Presley; *How Great Thou Art* ....(RCA)
  Legendary Performer-#3 ....(RCA)
  Top Ten Hits ....(RCA)
  Worldwide 50 Gold Award Hits-#1 ....(RCA)
June Valli; *Nipper's Greatest Hits-'50s-#2* ....(RCA)
Little Richard; *Shut Up-Rare Tracks-1951-1964* . (RHI)
Orioles; *Super Oldies/'50s-#1* ....(AUF)
Sonny Til/Orioles; *Echoes Of A Rock Era-Early
  Years* ....(RLL)
  Greatest Hits ....(CLT)
  ST/American Graffiti ....(MCA)
Crying In The Morning
  Billy Tate; *Southern Blues* ....(SAV)
  *Crying In The Morning-Anthology Of Postwar
  Blues* ....(MUS)
Crying In The Night
  Melba Moore; *Soul Exposed* ....(CAP)
Crying In The Rain
  Art Garfunkel & James Taylor; *Up 'Til Now* .....(COL)
A-Ha; *East Of The Sun West Of The Moon* ....(WB)
Dave Edmunds & Nick Lowe; *Dave Edmunds
  Anthology-1968-1990* .... (RHI)

Everly Brothers; *All-Time Greatest Hits* ....(CCB)
  Golden Hits Of ....(WB)
  Very Best Of ....(WB)
Londonbeat; *In The Blood* ....(RAD)
Rockpile; *Seconds Of Pleasure* ....(COL)
Tammy Wynette; *Biggest Hits* ....(EPI)
  Tears Of Fire-25th Anniversary Collect. ....(EPI)
Whitesnake; *Saints & Sinners* ....(GEF)
  Whitesnake ....(GEF)
Crying In The Shadows
Gary Moore; *Wild Frontier* ....(VIA)
Crying My Heart Out For You
Diana Ross; *All The Great Love Songs* .... (MOT)
  Anthology ....(MOT)
Doris Day; *Sings 22 Great Songs* ....(HIN)
  Uncollected w/Page Cavanaugh Trio-#2 ....(HIN)
Crying My Heart Out Over You
Ricky Skaggs; *Greatest Country Hits/'80s-1981* ..(COL)
  Waiting For the Sun To Shine ....(EPI)
Crying On Your Shoulder Again
Doug Stone; *Doug Stone* ....(EPI)
Crying Overtime
Alexander O'Neal; *Hearsay* ....(TAB)
Crying Scene
Aztec Camera; *Stray* ....(SIR)
Crying Shame
Kate Wolf; *Evening In Austin* ....(KAL)
  Poet's Heart ....(KAL)
Michael Johnson; *Best Of* ....(RCA)
  That's That ....(RCA)
Crying Song
Pink Floyd; *ST/More* ....(CAP)
Crying Steel
Chuck Berry; *Chess Box* ....(CSS)
Crying Time
Buck Owens & Emmylou Harris; *Act Naturally* ..(CAP)
Ray Charles; *Anthology* ....(RHI)
  Greatest Hits-#1 ....(RHI)
  His Greatest Hits-#1 ....(DHL)
Crying & Laughing
Chris DeBurgh; *The Getaway* .... (A&M)
Crying, Waiting, Hoping
Marshall Crenshaw; *ST/La Bamba* ....(SLS)
Cryin'
Aerosmith; *Get A Grip* ....(GEF)
Cryin' Eyes
Don Williams; *One Good Well* ....(RCA)
Cryin' In The Streets
Lou Christie; *Enlightnin'ment: Best Of* .... (RHI)
Cryin' Shame
Faster Pussycat; *Wake Me When It's Over* ....(ELE)
Lyle Lovett/Large Band; *Lyle Lovett/Large Band* (MCA)
Cryin' Through The Night
Stevie Wonder; *Characters* ....(MOT)
Cryin' Time
Barbra Streisand; *Butterfly* ....(COL)
Julio Iglesias; *Starry Night* ....(COL)
Kendalls; *20 Favorites* ....(EPI)
Cryin' To Be Heard
Traffic; *Traffic* ....(ISL)
Cry, Cry, Cry
Bobby Bland; *Best Of* ....(MCA)
  Two Steps From The Blues ....(MCA)
Highway 101; *Greatest Hits* ....(WB)
  Highway 101 ....(WB)
Jack Scott; *Capitol Collectors Series* ....(CAP)
Johnny Cash; *Classic Cash-Hall Of Fame Series* .(MER)
  Legend ....(SUN)
  Original Golden Hits-#1 ....(SUN)
  Show Time ....(SUN)
  Superbilly ....(SUN)
Pere Ubu; *Worlds In Collision* ....(FON)
Ritchie Valens; *History Of* ....(RHI)
  Ritchie ....(RHI)
Roxy Music; *Manifesto* ....(RPR)
Do You Really Want To Hurt Me
Culture Club; *Billboard Top Hits-1983* .... (RHI)
  Kissing To Be Clever ....(VIA)
Don't Cry
Asia; *Alpha* ....(GEF)
  Then & Now ....(GEF)
Edith Piaf; *Vie En Rose* ....(COL)
  Vie En Rose ....(SSP)
Guns N' Roses; *Use Your Illusion I* ....(GEF)

Neil Young; *Freedom* ....(RPR)
Seal; *Seal* ....(ZTT)
Don't Cry Baby
Aretha Franklin; *Aretha After Hours* ....(COL)
Bob Wills/Texas Playboys; *Tiffany*
  Transcriptions-#5-Fun Dancing To ....(KAL)
Don't Cry Cherie
Glenn Miller; *Complete-#6-1940-1941* ....(RCA)
Don't Cry Daddy
Elvis Presley; *Always On My Mind* ....(RCA)
  Memphis Record ....(RCA)
  Top Ten Hits ....(RCA)
  Worldwide 50 Gold Award Hits-#1 ....(RCA)
Don't Cry For Me Argentina
Original New York Cast; *Evita* .... (MCA)
Don't Cry Joe (Let Her Go, Let Her Go)
Frank Sinatra; *Sinatra Swings* .... (RPR)
Don't Cry Joni
Conway Twitty; *Greatest Hits-#1* .... (MCA)
  Very Best Of .... (MCA)
  #1s-#1 ....(CAP)
Don't Cry No More
Bobby Bland; *Two Steps From The Blues* .... (MCA)
  Vintage Music-'50s/'60s-#13 ....(MCA)
Bobby Bland & B.B. King; *Together For The First*
  Time ....(MCA)
Don't Cry No Tears
Neil Young & Crazy Horse; *Zuma* ....(RPR)
Don't Cry Now
Linda Ronstadt; *Don't Cry Now* ....(ASY)
Don't Cry Out Loud
Melissa Manchester; *Greatest Hits* .... (ARI)
Peter Allen; *It Is Time For* ....(A&M)
  The Best ....(A&M)
Don't Cry, I'll Be Back Before You...
Ted Nugent; *Scream Dream* ....(EPI)
Don't Cry, My Lady Love
Quicksilver Messenger Service; *Anthology* ......(CAP)
Don't Let The Sun Catch You Cryin'
Gerry/Pacemakers; *Best Of* ....(EMI)
  Greatest Hits ....(LAU)
  History Of British Rock-#1 ....(RHI)
  Super Oldies/'60s-#5 ....(AUF)
Louis Jordan; *Best Of* ....(MCA)
Paul McCartney; *Tripping The Live Fantastic* ...(CAP)
Ray Charles; *Genius Of* ....(ATL)
Rickie Lee Jones; *Flying Cowboys* ....(GEF)
Don't You Hear Jerusalem Moan
Nitty Gritty Dirt Band; *Will The Circle Be*
  Unbroken-#2 .... (UNI)
Down To My Last Teardrop
Tanya Tucker; *What Do I Do With Me* ....(CAP)
Drive All Night
Bruce Springsteen; *The River* ....(COL)
Driven To Tears
Police; *ST/Urgh! A Music War* ....(A&M)
  Zenyatta Mondatta ....(A&M)
Sting; *Bring On The Night* ....(A&M)
Drivin' & Cryin'
Steve Wariner; *Drive* .... (ARI)
Dublin In My Tears
Fureys/Dave Arthur; *Dublin Songs* .... (AJK)
Even The Man In The Moon Is Crying
Mark Collie; *Mark Collie* ....(MCA)
Every Day I Have To Cry
Steve Alaimo; *Vintage Music-Orig. Classic*
  Oldies-#8 ....(MCA)
Every Night When The Sun Goes In
Jo Stafford; *Jo Plus Blues* ....(CRN)
Finders Keepers, Losers Weepers
Elvis Presley; *For Everyone* ....(RCA)
Folsom Prison Blues
Brooks & Dunn & Johnny Cash; *Red Hot +*
  Country ....(MER)
Johnny Cash; *At Folsom Prison & San Quentin* ..(COL)
  Billboard Top Country Hits-1968 ....(RHI)
  Classic Cash-Hall Of Fame Series ....(MER)
  Greatest Hits #2 ....(COL)
  Original Golden Hits #1 ....(SUN)
  Superbilly ....(SUN)
Fool To Cry
Rolling Stones; *Black & Blue* ....(RS)
  Rewind (1971-1984) ....(RS)
  Sucking In The Seventies ....(RS)

For Crying Out Loud
Davis Daniel; *Fighting Fire With Fire* .... (MER)
Golden Memories & Silver Tears
Jim Reeves; *Best Of* ....(RCA)
  Great Moments With ....(RCA)
  w/Patsy Cline: Greatest Hits ....(RCA)
Gonna Cry 'Til My Tears Run Dry
Irma Thomas; *Louisiana Scrapbook* ....(RYK)
Guess I'll Hang My Tears Out To Dry
Diane Schuur; *In Tribute* ....(GRP)
Frank Sinatra; *Capitol Years* ....(CAP)
Frank Sinatra & Carly Simon; *Frank Sinatra*
Duets ....(CAP)
Linda Ronstadt; *What's New* .... (ASY)
Hey, Baby
Marty Stuart; *This One's Gonna Hurt You* ..... (MCA)
How Can I Help You Say Goodbye
Patty Loveless; *Only What I Feel* .... (EPI)
I Ain't Gonna Cry
Little Angels; *Young Gods* .... (POL)
I Ain't Gonna Cry No More
Penguins; *Golden Classics* ....(CLT)
Ronnie Milsap; *Back To The Grindstone* ....(RCA)
I Ain't Gonna Cry Tonight
Barbra Streisand; *Wet* ....(COL)
I Can't Stop Crying
Ronnie Milsap; *16 Greatest Hits-#2* .... (TRP)
I Couldn't Keep From Crying
Marty Robbins; *Columbia Country Classics-#2* ...(COL)
  Essential-1951-1982 ....(COL)
I Cried A Tear
La Vern Baker; *Atlantic R&B 1947-1974-#4*
(1958-1962) .... (ATL)
  Billboard Top R&B Hits-1959 .... (RHI)
I Cried All The Way To The Altar
Patsy Cline; *20 Golden Pieces Of* .... (BLD)
  Patsy Cline ....(AUF)
  Walkin' Dreams: Her First Recordings-#1 ...... (RHI)
I Cried For You
Billie Holiday; *Essential-Carnegie Hall Concert* ...(VRV)
Ella Fitzgerald; *Intimate Ella* ....(VRV)
I Cried For You (Now It's Your Turn...)
Billie Holiday; *First Verve Sessions* ....(VRV)
  Quintessential-#2-1936 ....(COL)
  Songbook ....(VRV)
Sarah Vaughan; *Complete-On Mercury-#2* ...... (MER)
  Divine: Columbia Years 1949-1953 ....(COL)
  Roulette Years ....(RLL)
I Cried Last Night
Charles Brown; *One More For The Road* .... (ALL)
I Cry
Smokey Robinson/Miracles; *Miracles Greatest*
Hits .... (MOT)
I Cry For You
Willie Dixon; *Hidden Charms* ....(BUG)
I Cry Just A Little Bit
Shakin' Stevens; *45* .... (EPI)
I Do My Bawling In The Bathroom
David Peel/Lower East Side; *Have A Marijuana* . (ELE)
I Don't Wanna Cry
Larry Gatlin/Gatlin Brothers; *17 Greatest Hits* ...(COL)
  Greatest Hits ....(COL)
  Greatest Hits Encore ....(CAP)
Mariah Carey; *Mariah Carey* ....(COL)
I Go To Pieces
Del Shannon; *Rock On!* .... (GG)
Peter & Gordon; *Best Of* .... (RHI)
  History Of British Rock-#3 ....(RHI)
Southern Pacific; *County Line* ....(WB)
  Greatest Hits ....(WB)
If I Was To Start Crying
Oak Ridge Boys; *American Dreams* .... (MCA)
If The Jukebox Took Teardrops
Billy Joe Royal; *Out Of The Shadows* .... (ATL)
Mike Henderson; *Country Music Made Me Do It* .(RCA)
It Only Hurts When I Cry
Dwight Yoakam; *If There Was A Way* .... (RPR)
It Takes A Lot To Laugh, It Takes A...
Bob Dylan; *Bootleg Series-#1-3* ....(COL)
  Highway 61 Revisited ....(COL)
M. Bloomfield/A. Kooper/S. Stills; *Super Session* .(COL)
It's All Over But The Crying
Hank Williams, Jr.; *14 Greatest Hits* .... (POL)

It's My Party
Lesley Gore; *Anthology* .... (RHI)
  Billboard Top Rock 'N' Roll Hits-1963 .... (RHI)
  Golden Hits Of .... (MER)
  Good Time Rock 'N' Roll .... (MCA)
  Oldies But Goodies-#3 .... (OSR)
I'll Cry Instead
Beatles; *Box Set* .... (CAP)
  Hard Day's Night .... (CAP)
  Something New .... (CAP)
  ST/Hard Day's Night .... (CAP)
I'm Not In Love
10 CC; *Greatest Hits 1972-78* .... (POL)
  Super Hits/'70s-Have A Nice Day-#14 .... (RHI)
Will To Power; *Journey Home* .... (EPI)
I'm So Lonesome I Could Cry
B.J. Thomas; *Greatest Hits* .... (RHI)
Cowboy Junkies; *Trinity Session* ....(RCA)
Hank Williams; *24 Greatest Hits* .... (POL)
  40 Greatest Hits .... (POL)
  I'm So Lonesome I Could Cry .... (POL)
Hank Williams, Jr.; *Very Best Of* .... (POL)
Jim Rooney; *One Day At A Time* .... (ROU)
Johnny Cash; *Hank Williams Songbook* ....(COL)
I've Cried My Last Tear For You
Ricky Van Shelton; *Greatest Country*
Hits-'90s-1990 ....(COL)
  RVS III ....(COL)
Japanese Tears
Denny Laine; *Japanese Tears* ....(TAK)
Joy Inside My Tears
Stevie Wonder; *Songs In The Key Of Life* ...... (MOT)
Judy's Turn To Cry
Lesley Gore; *Anthology* .... (RHI)
  Golden Hits .... (MER)
  '60s Dance Party-#2 ....(DOM)
Just Like A Woman
Bob Dylan; *At Budokan* ....(COL)
  Before The Flood ....(COL)
  Biograph ....(COL)
  Blonde On Blonde ....(COL)
  Greatest Hits ....(COL)
Byrds; *Byrds (collection)* ....(COL)
Keep Me Cryin'
Al Green; *Greatest Hits-#2* .... (MOT)
Letter Full Of Tears
Gladys Knight/Pips; *Anthology* .... (MOT)
  Echoes Down The Hall-16 Orig. Doo-Wop ..... (ARI)
  Greatest Hits ....(CCB)
Little Bitty Tear
Burl Ives; *Best Of-#2* .... (MCA)
  Live .... (MCA)
  MCA Records 30 Years Of Hits (1958-1988) .. (MCA)
Little White Cloud That Cried
Johnnie Ray; *Best Of* .... (COL)
  Greatest Hits ....(SSP)
Johnny Ray; *Best Of* .... (EXA)
Lonely Teardrops
Jackie Wilson; *Billboard Top R&B Hits-1958* .... (RHI)
  Reet Petite-Best Of ....(COL)
  Story .... (EPI)
  Story-#2 .... (EPI)
Lonesome Road
Anita O'Day; *Rules Of The Road* .... (PAB)
Frank Sinatra; *Capitol Years* ....(CAP)
Frankie Valli/Four Seasons; *25th Anniversary*
Collection .... (RHI)
Preservation Hall Jazz Band; *New Orleans-#4* ...(COL)
Tommy Dorsey; *Sentimental Memories* ....(PRR)
Van Morrison; *Too Long In Exile* .... (POL)
Man Who Couldn't Cry
Johnny Cash; *American Recordings* .... (AME)
Misty
Erroll Garner; *Other Voices* ....(COL)
Johnny Mathis; *All-Time Greatest Hits* ....(COL)
  First 25 Years ....(COL)
  Heavenly ....(COL)
  Live ....(COL)
Sarah Vaughan; *Golden Hits* ....(MER)

Monday Monday
Mamas & The Papas; *Best Of* .... (MCA)
  Billboard Top Rock 'N' Roll Hits-1966 .... (RHI)
  Farewell To The First Golden Era .... (ARI)
  Gathering Of The Flowers ....(DHL)
  ST/Stardust ....(DHL)
  Vintage Music-Orig. Classics/'60s-#9 .... (MCA)
Neil Diamond; *Double Gold* ....(BNG)
  Feel Of ....(BNG)
  Gang At Bang ....(BNG)
  Shilo ....(BNG)
Moon Tears
Nils Lofgren; *Best Of Grin* .... (EPI)
  Classics-#13 .... (A&M)
  Grin ....(EPA)
  Night After Night .... (A&M)
My Heart Cries For You
Charlie Rich; *20 Golden Hits* .... (SUN)
  Time For Tears ....(SUN)
Dinah Shore; *Nipper's Greatest Hits-'50s-#1* ......(RCA)
Guy Mitchell; *16 Most Requested Songs* ....(COL)
Night Time Is Cry Time
Jimmy C. Newman; *Greatest Hits* .... (PLN)
No More Tears
Ozzy Osbourne; *No More Tears* .... (EPA)
No More Tears (Enough Is Enough)
Barbra Streisand & Donna Summer; *Memories* ...(COL)
  Wet ....(COL)
Donna Summer; *Dance Collection* .... (CAS)
  On The Radio-Greatest Hits-#1&2 .... (CAS)
No One Has To Cry
Fixx; *Ink* ....(IPA)
No Woman, No Cry
Bob Marley; *Live* ....(TUF)
Bob Marley/Wailers; *Legend* ....(TUF)
  Natty Dread ....(TUF)
  Songs Of Freedom ....(TUF)
Londonbeat; *In The Blood* .... (RAD)
Ocean I'll Cry
Jackie Wilson; *Soul Time* ....(BRU)
Oh Mary Don't You Weep
Pete Seeger; *Live At Newport* .... (VAN)
Oh, Susanna
James Taylor; *Sweet Baby James* .... (WB)
Myron Floren; *Best Of The Wurstfest* .... (RAN)
  Myron Floren .... (RAN)
One Last Cry
Brian McKnight; *Brian McKnight* .... (MER)
Out Of Tears
Rolling Stones; *Voodoo Lounge* .... (VIA)
Piano In The Dark
Brenda Russell; *Get Here* .... (A&M)
  Greatest Hits .... (A&M)
  Making Love ....(PRY)
  Slow Dancin' ....(KT)
Piece Of My Heart
Big Brother/Holding Company; *Cheap Thrills* ....(COL)
  Rock Classics Of The '60s ....(COL)
  Seems Like Yesterday-#6-Late '60s .... (KT)
Bryan Ferry; *These Foolish Things* ....(RPR)
Delaney & Bonnie; *Best Of* .... (RHI)
Faith Hill; *Take Me As I Am* .... (WB)
Janis Joplin; *Greatest Hits* ....(COL)
  In Concert ....(COL)
  ST/Janis ....(COL)
Sammy Hagar; *Standing Hampton* .... (GEF)
Tara Kemp; *Tara Kemp* .... (GIA)
Pretty Girls Don't Cry
Chris Isaak; *Silvertone* .... (WB)
Puke & Cry
Dinosaur Jr.; *Green Mind* .... (SIR)
  Just Say Anything-#5 Of Just Say Yes .... (SIR)
Queen Of Tears
Gladys Knight/Pips; *Every Beat Of My Heart/Greatest
Hits* .... (CML)
Read 'Em & Weep
Barry Manilow; *Greatest Hits-#3* .... (ARI)
Richard Cory Cries
Midnight Reign; *Mountain Of Metal* .... (MNT)
River Of Tears
Bonnie Raitt; *Green Light* .... (WB)
Highway 101; *Bing Bang Boom* .... (WB)
York Brothers; *Super Hits Country-1940s* .... (GUS)

Run From Tears
Crosby, Stills & Nash; *CSN* .... (ATL)
Sad Movies (Make Me Cry)
Sue Thompson; *Collectables History Of Rock-#10* (CLT)
  Greatest Hits ....(CCB)
Sailing Down The Tears
Hanoi Rocks; *Back To Mystery City* .... (GEF)
She Can't Say I Didn't Cry
Rick Trevino; *Rick Trevino* ....(COL)
She Cried
Jay/Americans; *All-Time Greatest Hits* .... (RHI)
  Come A Little Bit Closer-Best Of .... (EMI)
Toad The Wet Sprocket; *Pale* ....(COL)
She Doesn't Cry Anymore
Shenandoah; *Road Not Taken* ....(COL)
  Shenandoah ....(COL)
She Needs Someone To Hold Her...
Conway Twitty; *Best Of-#2* ....(MSP)
  Greatest Hits-#2 ....(MCA)
She's Crying For Me
New Orleans Rhythm Kings; *RCA Victor Jazz-First
Half-Century* ....(RCA)
She's Long, She's Tall, She Weeps...
John Lee Hooker; *Black Snake* ....(FAN)
  Country Blues Of ....(RVR)
She's Not Cryin' Anymore
Billy Ray Cyrus; *Some Gave All* .... (MER)
Sister Don't Cry
Collective Soul; *Hints Allegations And Things Left
Unsaid* .... (ATL)
Sky Is Crying
Albert King; *I'm In A Phone Booth Baby* .... (STX)
  Years Gone By ....(STX)
Elmore James; *Complete Fire & Enjoy
Sessions-#1* ....(CLT)
  Red Hot Blues ....(INT)
Eric Clapton; *Crossroads* ....(POL)
George Thorogood/Destroyers; *Live* .... (EMI)
  Move It On Over ....(ROU)
Stevie Ray Vaughan/Double Trouble; *Sky Is
Crying* .... (EPI)
Smoke Gets In Your Eyes
Bryan Ferry; *Another Time Another Place* .... (RPR)
  Street Life-20 Great Hits ....(RPR)
Dinah Washington; *Golden Classics* ....(CLT)
Lawrence Welk; *Musical Memories With* .... (RAN)
Patti Austin; *Real Me* ....(QUE)
Platters; *Encore Of Golden Hits* .... (MER)
  Greatest Hits ....(EVR)
  Oldies But Goodies-#14 ....(OSR)
  ST/Always ....(MCA)
  ST/American Graffiti ....(MCA)
  Super Oldies/'50s-#5 ....(AUF)
Spilled Perfume
Pam Tillis; *Sweetheart's Dance* .... (ARI)
Standin' Round Crying
Eric Clapton; *From The Cradle* .... (DUC)
Stop Your Sobbing
Kinks; *Greatest Hits-#1* ....(RHI)
  One For The Road .... (ARI)
  You Really Got Me ....(RHI)
Pretenders; *Pretenders* .... (SIR)
  Singles .... (SIR)
Summer Kisses, Winter Tears
Elvis Presley; *Collector's Gold* ....(RCA)
Summertime
Billy Stewart; *Best Of Chess Rhythm & Blues* ..... (CSS)
  Summer & Sun ....(RHI)
Booker T./M.G.s; *Best Of* .... (ATL)
Carmen McRae; *Greatest Of* ....(MCA)
Chet Baker; *My Favourite Songs-#1-Last Great
Concert* .... (ENJ)
Courtney Pine; *Glory Of Gershwin Featuring Larry
Adler* .... (MER)
D.J. Jazzy Jeff & The Fresh Prince; *Homebase* ... (JVA)
Ella Fitzgerald & Louis Armstrong; *Porgy & Bess* (VRV)
George Benson; *Best Of Benson* ....(CBA)
Janis Joplin; *Greatest Hits* ....(COL)
  ST/Janis ....(COL)
Lambert, Hendricks & Ross; *Best Of* ....(COL)
Miles Davis/Orchestra; *Porgy & Bess* ....(COL)
Original Cast; *Porgy & Bess* ....(MCA)
Peter Gabriel; *Glory Of Gershwin-Featuring Larry
Adler* .... (MER)

Rick Nelson; *Best Of-#2* .... (EMI)
Sam Cooke; *Best Of* ....(RCA)
Sarah Vaughan; *1940s-The Singers* ....(COL)
  Divine-Columbia Years-1949-1953 ....(COL)
Stan Getz; *Compact Jazz* ....(VRV)
Willie Nelson; *One For The Road* ....(COL)
Tear Drops
Elton John & k.d. lang; *Duets* ....(MCA)
Jonathan Butler; *Deliverance* ....(JVA)
Tear Fell, A
Teresa Brewer; *Best Of* ....(MCA)
Tear For Tear
Walter Jackson; *Greatest Hits* ....(EPI)
Tear For The Girl
Martha Reeves/Vandellas; *Live
Wire!-Singles-1962-1972* ....(MOT)
Tear In Your Hand
Tori Amos; *Little Earthquakes* ....(ATL)
Tear Stained Letter
Jo-el Sonnier; *Best Of Country Rock* ....(KT)
  Come On Joe ....(RCA)
Richard Thompson; *Hand Of Kindness* ....(HBL)
Teardrop Collector
Love & Rockets; *Love & Rockets* ....(BEG)
Teardrop On A Rose
Hank Williams; *Let's Turn Back The
Years-1951-1952* ....(POL)
Teardrops
George Ducas; *George Ducas* ....(LIB)
George Harrison; *Somewhere In England* ....(DKH)
Lee Andrews/Hearts; *Best Of Chess Rock 'N' Roll* (CSS)
  Biggest Hits ....(CLT)
  WCBS FM101-History Of Rock-For Lovers-#1 .(CLT)
  WOGL Oldies 98-History Of Rock-#2 ....(CLT)
Rick James; *Street Songs/Throwin' Down* ....(MOT)
Teardrops From My Eyes
Ruth Brown; *Miss Rhythm-Greatest Hits & More* . (RHI)
Teardrops In My Eyes
David Grisman; *Home Is Where The Heart Is* ... (ROU)
New Riders Of The Purple Sage; *Adventures Of Panama
Red* ....(COL)
Teardrops In My Heart
Marty Robbins; *Biggest Hits* ....(COL)
Sons Of The Pioneers; *Cool Water* ....(RCA)
Teardrops Will Fall
Ry Cooder; *Into The Purple Valley* ....(RPR)
Wilson Pickett; *In The Midnight Hour* .... (RHI)
Tears
Bobby Vinton; *More Of Bobby's Greatest Hits* ..... (EPI)
Chet Atkins & Mark Knopfler; *Neck & Neck* ...(COL)
Chris Isaak; *Silvertone* ....(WB)
Django Reinhardt & Stephane Grappelli; *Django
Reinhardt & Stephane Grappelli* .... (CRS)
Missing Persons; *Best Of* ....(CAP)
  Spring Session M ....(CAP)
Persuaders; *Harlem Holiday-New York R&B-#4* ...(CLT)
  Harlem Holiday-N.Y. Rhythm & Blues-#4 ......(CLT)
Rush; *2112* .... (MER)
Tears Are Just For Fools
Starlites; *Harlem Holiday-N.Y. Rhythm &
Blues-#7* ....(CLT)
Tears Before Bedtime
Elvis Costello/Attractions; *Imperial Bedroom* ....(COL)
Tears Came Rollin' Down
John Mayall/Bluesbreakers; *Chicago Line* .... (ISL)
Tears Don't Care Who Cries Them
k.d. lang; *Shadowland* ....(SIR)
Tears For You
Judds; *Collection-1983-1990* ....(RCA)
  Collector's Series ....(RCA)
  Rockin' With The Rhythm ....(RCA)
Tears In Heaven
Eric Clapton; *ST/Rush* ....(RPR)
  Unplugged ....(RPR)
Tears In My Eyes
Baltineers; *For Collectors Only-Rarities-#1* ....(CLT)
  Great Groups/'50s-II ....(CLT)
Dreamers; *Harlem New York-Ballad Era* ....(CLT)
Joan Baez; *Very Early Joan Baez* ....(VAN)
Tears In The Morning
Beach Boys; *Sunflower* ....(CAR)
Tears In The Rain
Triumph; *Classics* ....(MCA)
  Sport Of Kings ....(MCA)

Tears Keep On Falling
Jerry Vale; *17 Most Requested Songs* ....(COL)
  All-Time Greatest Hits ....(COL)
Tears Of A Clown
English Beat; *I Just Can't Stop It* .... (IRS)
  What Is Beat .... (IRS)
Smokey Robinson/Miracles; *25 #1 Hits From 25
Years* .... (MOT)
  Anthology .... (MOT)
  Billboard Top Rock 'N' Roll Hits-1970 .... (RHI)
  Compact Command Performances .... (MOT)
  Endless Love-Mot. Greatest Love Songs .... (MOT)
  Tears Of A Clown .... (MOT)
Tears Of Rage
Band; *Best Of* ....(CAP)
  Music From Big Pink ....(CAP)
  To Kingdom Come-Definitive Collection ....(CAP)
Bob Dylan/Band; *Basement Tapes* ....(COL)
Tears Of Sahara
Tony MacAlpine; *Maximum Security* .... (MER)
Tears Of The Dragon
Bruce Dickinson; *Balls To Picasso* .... (MER)
Tears Of The Lonely
Mickey Gilley; *Biggest Hits* .... (EPI)
  Ten Years Of Love .... (EPI)
Tears On My Pillow
Chimes; *Golden Groups* .... (SPE)
  Original Rock Oldies-Golden Hits-#2 ....(SPE)
Kylie Minogue; *Enjoy Yourself* ....(GEF)
Little Anthony/Imperials; *Best Of* .... (EMI)
  Best Of .... (RHI)
  Billboard Top R&B Hits-1958 .... (RHI)
  Good Time Rock 'N' Roll .... (MCA)
Lorrie Morgan; *Something In Red* ....(RCA)
New Edition/Little Anthony; *Under The Blue
Moon* .... (MCA)
Reba McEntire; *Feel The Fire* .... (MER)
Sha-Na-Na; *ST/Grease* ....(POL)
Tears Will Be The Chaser For Your Wine
Wanda Jackson; *Greatest Hits* ....(GUS)
  Rockin' In The Country-Best Of .... (RHI)
Tell Me Why
Beatles; *Box Set* ....(CAP)
  Something New ....(CAP)
  ST/Hard Day's Night ....(CAP)
That's Why I'm Crying
Ivy League; *History Of British Rock-#2* .... (RHI)
Koko Taylor; *I Got What It Takes* ....(ALG)
There'll Be No Teardrops Tonight
Anita Carter; *Hank Williams Songbook* ....(COL)
Hank Williams; *24 Greatest Hits* .... (MER)
  Greatest Hits ....(POL)
There'll Be Sad Songs (To Make You Cry)
Billy Ocean; *Greatest Hits* ....(JVA)
  Love Zone ....(JVA)
Thirty Years Of Tears
John Hiatt; *Stolen Moments* ....(A&M)
'Til A Tear Becomes A Rose
Kieth Whitley; *Greatest Hits* ....(RCA)
Time To Cry
Paul Anka; *Paul Anka's 21 Golden Hits* ....(RCA)
To Cry You A Song
Jethro Tull; *Benefit* ....(CHR)
  Repeat-Best Of-#2 ....(CHR)
To See An Angel Cry
Conway Twitty; *Greatest Hits-#1* .... (MCA)
  #1's-#1 ....(CAP)
Today's Teardrops
Rick Nelson; *Best Of-#2* .... (EMI)
Roy Orbison; *Rare Orbison* .... (MON)
Too Beautiful To Cry
Roger Whittaker; *Greatest Hits* ....(RCA)
  Wind Beneath My Wings ....(RCA)
Tracks Of My Tears
Bryan Ferry; *These Foolish Things* ....(RPR)
Gladys Knight/Pips; *Anthology* .... (MOT)
Johnny Rivers; *Best Of* .... (EMI)
Linda Ronstadt; *Greatest Hits* ....(ASY)
  Prisoner In Disguise ....(ASY)
Smokey Robinson/Miracles; *Anthology* .... (MOT)
  Billboard Top R&B Hits-1965-1969 .... (RHI)
  Greatest Hits-#2 .... (MOT)
  ST/Big Chill .... (MOT)
  ST/Sound Of "Murphy Brown" .... (MCA)

Trail Of Tears
Guadalcanal Diary; *Walking In The Shadow Of The Big Man* .... (ELE)
John Denver; *Dreamland Express* ....(RCA)
Southern Pacific; *Greatest Hits* ....(WB)
Zuma ....(WB)
Tanya Tucker; *What Do I Do With Me* ....(LIB)
True Love, True Love (If You Can Cry)
Drifters; *1959-1965-All-Time Greatest Hits & More* ....(ATL)
Golden Hits ....(ATL)
Two Kinds Of Teardrops
Del Shannon; *Greatest Hits* ....(RHI)
Valley Of Tears
Buddy Holly; *Buddy Holly* ....(MCA)
Fats Domino; *Antoine "Fats" Domino* ....(RHI)
My Blue Heaven-Best Of-#1 ....(EMI)
Walkin', Talkin'...Beatin' Broken Heart
Highway 101; *Country's Greatest Hits-#4* ....(PRY)
Paint The Town ....(WB)
Wall Of Tears
K.T. Oslin; *80's Ladies* ....(RCA)
New Faces Of Country ....(KT)
Whales Weep Not (Overture)
Paul Winter Consort; *Whales Alive* ....(LIV)
Paul Winter Consort/Paul Halley; *Living Music Collection II* ....(LIV)
What A Crying Shame
Mavericks; *What A Crying Shame* ....(MCA)
When Doves Cry
Prince; *ST/Purple Rain* ....(WB)
When She Cries
Restless Heart; *Big Iron Horses* ....(RCA)
When The Children Cry
White Lion; *Best Of* ....(ATL)
Pride ....(ATL)
When You See The Tears From My Eyes
Buddy Guy; *Very Best Of* ....(RHI)
Buddy Guy & Junior Wells; *Drinkin' TNT 'N' Smokin' Dynamite* ....(BLI)
While My Guitar Gently Weeps
Beatles; *1967-1970* ....(CAP)
Box Set ....(CAP)
White Album ....(CAP)
George Harrison; *Best Of* ....(CAP)
Concert For Bangladesh ....(CAP)
George Harrison & Eric Clapton & Band; *Live In Japan* ....(DKH)
Whose Shoulder Will You Cry On
Kitty Wells; *Greatest Hits-#1* ....(SO)
Willow Weep For Me
Art Tatum; *Best Of* ....(PAB)
Solo Masterpieces-#1 ....(PAB)
Billie Holiday; *Billie's Blues* ....(BLD)
Lady Sings The Blues ....(VRV)
Live ....(VRV)
Stormy Blues ....(VRV)
Chad & Jeremy; *Best Of* ....(CAP)
History Of British Rock-#3 ....(RHI)
Super Oldies!'60s-#11 ....(AUF)
Dinah Shore; *16 Most Requested Songs* ....(COL)
Lou Rawls; *Legendary* ....(BLN)
Roy Eldridge; *Best Of* ....(PAB)
Steve Miller; *Born 2 B Blue* ....(CAP)
You Don't Have To Be A Baby To Cry
Ann J. Morton; *45* ....(PRA)
You Won't See Me Cry
Wilson Phillips; *Shadows & Light* ....(SBK)

DANCE, Boogie, Dance Styles, Shaking, Shuffle
See Also: MUSIC, PARTY, ROCK

African Dance
Soul II Soul; *Keep On Movin'* ....(VIA)
After The Ball
Barbara Cook; *Show Boat* ....(COL)
After The Dance
Marvin Gaye; *Greatest Hits* ....(MOT)
I Heard It Through The.../I Want You ....(MOT)
I Want You ....(MOT)
Musical Testament 1964-1984 ....(MOT)
Air Dance
Black Sabbath; *Never Say Die* ....(WB)

All Night Long (All Night)
Lionel Richie; *Can't Slow Down* ....(MOT)
Motown Story-First 25 Years ....(MOT)
All She Wants To Do Is Dance
Don Henley; *Building The Perfect Beast* ....(GEF)
And We Danced
Hooters; *Nervous Night* ....(COL)
Apache Dance
Woody Herman/Orchestra; *Uncollected* ....(HIN)
Apeman Hop
Ramones; *Animal Boy* ....(SIR)
April Waltz
Critton Hollow; *Great Dreams* ....(FF)
At The Ballet
Original Cast; *Chorus Line* ....(COL)
At The Hop
Danny/Juniors; *Billboard Top Rock 'N' Roll Hits-1958* ....(RHI)
Cruisin' 1958 ....(INC)
Oldies/Goodies-#2 ....(OSR)
Rockin' With ....(MCA)
Super Oldies!'50s-#6 ....(AUF)
Sha-Na-Na; *ST/Woodstock* ....(ATL)
At The Mambo Inn
George Benson; *Tenderly* ....(WB)
Baby Do The Philly Dog
Olympics; *Official Record Album Of* ....(RHI)
Bad Luck Streak In Dancing School
Warren Zevon; *Bad Luck Streak In Dancing School* ....(ASY)
Ballerina Girl
Lionel Richie; *Dancing On The Ceiling* ....(MOT)
Ballroom Dancing
Paul McCartney; *Give My Regards To Broad Street* ....(CAP)
Tug Of War ....(COL)
Batdance
Prince; *ST/Batman* ....(WB)
Begin The Beguine
Art Tatum; *Solos (1940)* ....(MCA)
Ella Fitzgerald; *Cole Porter Songbook* ....(VRV)
Johnny Mathis; *Best Days Of My Life* ....(COL)
First 25 Years ....(COL)
Live ....(COL)
Tony Bennett; *Forty Years: Artistry Of* ....(COL)
Black Cat Shuffle
Al DiMeola; *Electric Rendezvous* ....(COL)
Black Satin Dancer
Jethro Tull; *Minstrel In The Gallery* ....(CHR)
Blame It On The Bossa Nova
Eydie Gorme; *45* ....(COL)
Blue Jean Bop
Gene Vincent; *Bop That Just Won't Stop* ....(CAP)
Greatest ....(CAP)
Greatest ....(IRS)
Blue Tango
Billy Vaughn; *String Of Pearls-Greatest Hits* ......(POE)
Leroy Anderson; *45* ....(MCA)
Boogie Ala Georgia
Peggy Gilbert; *Dixieland Jazz* ....(CMB)
Boogie Child
Bee Gees; *Boogie Child* ....(RSO)
Child Of The World ....(RSO)
Here At Last ....(RSO)
Boogie Chillun
John Lee Hooker; *Best Of* ....(CRS)
Best Of ....(VJ)
Boogie Chillun ....(FAN)
Hooked On The Blues ....(EVR)
Boogie In Your Butt
Eddie Murphy; *45* ....(COL)
Boogie Nights
Heatwave; *Greatest Hits* ....(EPI)
Skatetown U.S.A. ....(COL)
Too Hot To Handle ....(EPI)
Boogie On Reggae Woman
Stevie Wonder; *Fulfillingness' First Finale* ....(MOT)
Motown Time Capsule-#2-'70s ....(MOT)
Original Musiquarium ....(MOT)
Boogie Wonderland
Earth, Wind & Fire; *Best Of-#2* ....(COL)
I Am ....(COL)
Roller Boogie ....(CAS)
Skatetown U.S.A. ....(COL)

Boot Scootin' Boogie
Brooks & Dunn; *Brand New Man* .... (ARI)
Bop
Dan Seals; *Best Of* ....(CAP)
Greatest Hits ....(CAP)
Won't Be Blue Anymore .... (EMI)
Bop 'Til You Drop
Ramones; *Halfway To Sanity* .... (SIR)
Mania .... (SIR)
Rick Springfield; *Greatest Hits* ....(RCA)
ST/Hard To Hold ....(RCA)
Born To Boogie
Hank Williams, Jr.; *Born To Boogie* ....(W/C)
Greatest Hits III ....(W/C)
T. Rex; *T. Rextasy: Best Of T. Rex 1970-1973* ....(WB)
Brand New Dance
Emmylou Harris; *Brand New Dance* .... (RPR)
Brand New Tennessee Waltz
Jesse Winchester; *Best Of* .... (RHI)
Jesse Winchester .... (RHI)
Joan Baez; *Country Music Album* .... (VAN)
Brazilian Stomp
George Benson & Earl Klugh; *Collaboration* ...... (WB)
Breakdance
Irene Cara; *What A Feelin'* .... (GEF)
Breakin' (There's No Stoppin' Us)
Ollie & Jerry; *ST/Breakin'* .... (POL)
Bring On The Dancing Horses
Echo/Bunnymen; *Songs To Learn & Sing* .... (SIR)
ST/Pretty In Pink ....(A&M)
Bumble Bee Stomp
Benny Goodman; *On The Air-1937-1938* ....(COL)
Bump & Grind
R. Kelly; *12 Play* .... (JVA)
Burn This Disco Out
Michael Jackson; *Off The Wall* .... (EPI)
Burning The Ballroom Down
Amazing Rhythm Aces; *Burning The Ballroom
Down* .... (MCA)
Buttermilk Biscuits (Keep On Square...)
Sir Mix-A-Lot; *Swass* .... (NSY)
Can You Dance (Baby Tell Me)
Shanice Wilson; *Discovery* ....(A&M)
Can't Stop Dancing
Sylvester; *Greatest Hits* .... (FAN)
Living Proof .... (FAN)
Can't Stop Dancin'
Captain & Tennille; *Greatest Hits* ....(A&M)
Carioca
Artie Shaw; *Begin The Beguine* .... (BLU)
Complete ....(RCA)
Plays 22 Original Big Band Recordings .... (HIN)
This Is-#2 ....(RCA)
Carol
Chuck Berry; *Berry Is On Top* .... (CSS)
Golden Hits .... (MER)
Greatest Hits .... (EVR)
Roll Over Beethoven .... (ALL)
Rolling Stones; *Get Yer Ya-Ya's Out* .... (AKO)
Rolling Stones .... (AKO)
Cheap Sunglasses
ZZ Top; *Deguello* .... (WB)
ST/Teachers .... (WB)
Cheek To Cheek
Ella Fitzgerald; *Silver Collection-Songbooks* ......(VRV)
Frank Sinatra; *Come Dance With Me* ....(CAP)
Fred Astaire; *Cheek To Cheek* .... (POE)
Irving Berlin Songbook ....(VRV)
Mundell Lowe; *Quartet* ....(RVR)
Pete Fountain; *Cheek To Cheek* .... (RAN)
Tommy Dorsey; *Irving Berlin 100th Anniversary
Collect.* .... (MCA)
Tony Bennett; *Bennett/Berlin* ....(COL)
Choo Choo Ch'Boogie
Asleep At The Wheel; *Asleep At The Wheel* .... (EPI)
Served Live ....(CAP)
Beach Boys; *Ten Years Of Harmony* ....(CAR)
Clifton Chenier; *Alligator Stomp-#2* .... (RHI)
Louis Jordan; *Best Of* .... (MCA)
Quincy Jones; *Birth Of A Band-#2* .... (MER)
Cincinnati Stomp
Big Joe Duskin; *Cincinnati Stomp* .... (ARH)
Circle Dance
Bonnie Raitt; *Longing In Their Hearts* ....(CAP)

Cloud Dancing
Roches; *Speak* ....(MCA)
Come Dancing
Kinks; *Come Dancing-Best Of* .... (ARI)
Live-The Road .... (MCA)
State Of Confusion .... (ARI)
Come On, Do The Jerk
Smokey Robinson/Miracles; *Anthology* .... (MOT)
Greatest Hits-#2 .... (MOT)
Conga
Leonard Bernstein; *Songbook* ....(COL)
Miami Sound Machine; *Primitive Love* .... (EPI)
Cool Jerk
Capitols; *Atlantic R&B 1947-1974-#5
(1962-1966)* .... (ATL)
Billboard Top R&B Hits-1966 .... (RHI)
Collectables History Of Rock-#5 ....(CLT)
Son Of Frat Rock .... (RHI)
Super Oldies/'60s-#5 ....(AUF)
Their Greatest Recordings .... (SSM)
Copacabana (At The Copa)
Barry Manilow; *Even Now* .... (ARI)
Greatest Hits-#2 .... (ARI)
ST/Foul Play .... (ARI)
Columbia Ballroom Orchestra; *Let's Dance-#6* .. (DEN)
Could I Have This Dance?
Ann Murray; *Greatest Hits* ....(CAP)
ST/Urban Cowboy ....(ASY)
Cowboy Boogie
Randy Travis; *Wind In The Wire* .... (WB)
Cow-Cow Boogie
Ella Fitzgerald; *Best Of-#2* .... (MCA)
Freddie Slack/Ella Mae Morse; *Jukebox Saturday
Night* ....(CAP)
Judds; *Heartland* ....(RCA)
Cuban Slide
Pretenders; *Extended Play* .... (SIR)
Curly Shuffle
Jump 'N The Saddle Band; *Dr. Demento's Greatest
Novelty-#5* .... (RHI)
Dance Dance Dance
Beach Boys; *Absolute Best-#1* ....(CAP)
Dance Dance Dance ....(CAP)
Greatest Hits .... (BVM)
Made In The U.S.A. ....(CAP)
Spirit Of America ....(CAP)
Clarence Clemons; *Night With Mr. C* ....(COL)
Steve Miller Band; *Fly Like An Eagle* ....(CAP)
Greatest Hits ....(CAP)
Dance Electric
Andre Cymone; *A.C.* ....(COL)
Pointer Sisters; *Break Out* ....(PNT)
Dance Floor
Zapp; *II* .... (WB)
Dance Hall Days
Wang Chung; *Points On The Curve* .... (GEF)
Dance Little Jean
Nitty Gritty Dirt Band; *Let's Go* .... (WB)
Twenty Years Of Dirt-Best Of .... (WB)
Dance Naked
John Mellencamp; *Dance Naked* .... (MER)
Dance Of Electricity
Laurie Anderson; *United States Live* .... (WB)
Dance Of The Imbeciles
D.C. 3; *This Is The Dream* ....(SST)
Dance Of The Sugar Plum Fairy
Boston Pops Orchestra; *Encores* .... (DGG)
Sleigh Ride!-Classic Christmas Favorites ....(RCA)
Dance On A Volcano
Genesis; *Seconds Out* .... (ATL)
Trick Of The Tail ....(ATC)
Dance On Little Girl
Paul Anka; *21 Golden Hits* ....(RCA)
Best Of .... (RHI)
She's A Lady ....(RCA)
Vintage Years '57-'61 .... (SIR)
Dance Only With Me
Blossom Dearie; *Blossoms On Broadway* .... (DRG)
Maxine Sullivan/Keith Ingham Sextet; *Together (Maxine
Sings Jules Styne)* ....(ATL)
Dance The Night Away
Cream; *Disraeli Gears* .... (RSO)
Europe; *Wings Of Tomorrow* .... (EPI)
Van Halen; *2* .... (WB)

Dance Time In Texas
George Strait; *Something Special* .... (MCA)
Dance To The Music
Sly/Family Stone; *Anthology* .... (EPI)
  Frat Rock! .... (RHI)
  Frat Rock-#2 .... (RHI)
  Greatest Hits .... (EPI)
Dance With A Dolly (Hole In...Stocking)
Bill Haley; *Rockin' & Rollin'* .... (ACC)
  /Comets: King Of Rock & Roll .... (ALS)
Dance With Me
Rufus & Chaka Khan; *Rufus* .... (MCA)
  Stompin' At The Savoy-Live .... (WB)
Dance With The Dragon
Jefferson Starship; *Spitfire* .... (RCA)
Dance With The One That Brought You
Shania Twain; *Shania Twain* .... (MER)
Dance Wit' Me
Rick James; *Reflections: Greatest Hits* .... (MOT)
  Street Songs/Throwin' Down .... (MOT)
Dance Your Ass Off
Bohannon; *Dance Your Ass Off* .... (DAK)
Dance: Ten; Looks: Three
Original Cast; *Chorus Line* .... (COL)
Dance, The
Garth Brooks; *Garth Brooks* .... (CAP)
Dancing Bumble Bee
Neil Diamond; *You Don't Bring Me Flowers* .....(COL)
Dancing In Berlin
Berlin; *Love Life* .... (GEF)
Dancing In Rackville, Maryland
Fred Frith; *Gravity* .... (RAL)
Dancing In St. Louis
Li'l Wally; *Here Comes* .... (JJ)
Dancing In Sunrise, Switzerland
Muffins; *Open City* .... (CUN)
Dancing In The Bathtub
John Hartford; *All In The Name Of Love* .... (FF)
Dancing In The Dark
Bruce Springsteen; *Born In The U.S.A.* ....(COL)
Tony Bennett; *Forty Years-Artistry Of* ....(COL)
  Jazz .... (COL)
Dancing In The Key Of Life
Steve Arrington; *Dance Traxx* .... (ATL)
  Dancing In The Key Of Life .... (ATL)
Dancing In The Moonlight
Be Bop Deluxe; *Modern Music* .... (HAR)
Liza Minnelli; *Singer* ....(COL)
Thin Lizzy; *Bad Reputation* .... (MER)
  Live & Dangerous .... (WB)
  Lizzy Lives! (1976-1984) .... (WB)
Dancing In The Sheets
Shalamar; *Greatest Hits* .... (SLR)
  ST/Footloose ....(COL)
Dancing In The Street
David Bowie & Mick Jagger; *Bowie-The
Singles-1969-1993* ....(RYK)
Grateful Dead; *Terrapin Station* .... (ARI)
Martha Reeves/Vandellas; *20 Greatest Songs In Motown
History* .... (MOT)
  Compact Command Performances .... (MOT)
  Motown Story .... (MOT)
  Oldies But Goodies-#14 .... (OSR)
Van Halen; *Diver Down* .... (WB)
Dancing Machine
Jackson 5; *14 Greatest Hits* .... (MOT)
  Anthology .... (MOT)
  Billboard Top Rock 'N' Roll Hits-1974 .... (MOT)
  Get It Together .... (MOT)
  Motown Dance Party-#2 .... (MOT)
  Motown Story-First 25 Years .... (MOT)
  Motown Superstar Series-#12 .... (MOT)
  Top 10 With A Bullet-Motown Dance Songs ... (MOT)
Dancing On Ground Zero
Carol Nethen; *Narada Mystique Sampler One* ... (NAR)
  View From The Bridge .... (NAR)
Dancing On The Ceiling
Chet Baker; *Sings It Could Happen To You* ......(RVR)
Ella Fitzgerald; *Rodgers & Hart Songbook* ....(VRV)
Frank Sinatra; *In The Wee Small Hours* ....(CAP)
Lionel Richie; *Dancing On The Ceiling* .... (MOT)

Dancing Queen
Abba; *Arrival* .... (ATL)
  Greatest Hits-#2 .... (ATL)
  Live .... (ATL)
  Singles (First Ten Years) .... (ATL)
Dancing Shoes
Bob Marley/Wailers; *Birth Of A Legend* .... (EPA)
  Early Music .... (CAL)
Dan Fogelberg; *Nether Lands* .... (FM)
Side Effect; *Greatest Hits* .... (FAN)
Dancing With Mr. D
Rolling Stones; *Goat's Head Soup* .... (RS)
Dancing Your Memory Away
Charly McClain; *Biggest Hits* .... (EPI)
  Ten Year Anniversary .... (EPI)
  Too Good To Hurry .... (EPI)
Dancin' Cowboys
Bellamy Brothers; *Greatest Hits* .... (MCA)
  You Can Get Crazy ....(W/C)
Dancin' Feet
Montrose; *Montrose* .... (WB)
Dancin' Fool
Frank Zappa; *Sheik Yerbouti* .... (ZAP)
Guess Who; *Greatest Of* ....(RCA)
Dancin' In The Ruins
Blue Oyster Cult; *Club Ninja* ....(COL)
Death Disco
Public Image, Ltd.; *Greatest Hits So Far* .... (VIA)
Death Of A Disco Dancer
Smiths; *Strangeways Here We Come* .... (SIR)
Disco Apocalypse
Jackson Browne; *Hold Out* .... (ASY)
Disco Doctor
Robert Parker; *Golden Classics-Barefootin'* .... (CLT)
Disco Duck
Rick Dees/Cast Of Idiots; *Original Disco Duck* .. (RSO)
Disco Inferno
Trammps; *Best Of* .... (ATL)
  Disco Inferno .... (ATL)
  Disco Years-#1 .... (RHI)
  ST/Saturday Night Fever .... (RSO)
Disco Strangler
Eagles; *Long Run* .... (ASY)
Disco's Out, Murder's In
Suicidal Tendencies; *Lights...Camera...Revolution* .. (EPI)
Do I Hear A Waltz?
Elizabeth Allen; *Broadway Magic-1960s* ....(COL)
Original Broadway Cast; *Do I Hear A Waltz?* ... (SMC)
Do It (Let Me See You Shake)
Bar-Kays; *Propositions* .... (MER)
Do The Bartman
Bart Simpson; *Simpsons Sing The Blues* .... (GEF)
Do The Bird
Dee Dee Sharp; *Let's Dance* .... (GUS)
  Rock-O-Rama-#2 .... (AKO)
Do The Boomerang
Junior Walker/All-Stars; *Anthology* .... (MOT)
  Shotgun .... (MOT)
Do The Freddy
Chubby Checker; *Greatest Hits* .... (AKO)
Do The Funky Chicken
Rufus Thomas; *15 Original Big Hits-III* .... (STX)
  Chronicle .... (STX)
  Let's Dance .... (GUS)
Do The Funky Penguin
Rufus Thomas; *15 Original Big Hits-III* .... (STX)
  Chronicle .... (STX)
  Rufus Thomas .... (GUS)
Do The Strand
Roxy Music; *Atlantic Years: 1973-1980* .... (ATC)
  For Your Pleasure...(Second Album) .... (RPR)
  Street Life-20 Great Hits .... (RPR)
  Viva! Roxy Music (Live Album) .... (RPR)
Do You Love Me (Now That I Can Dance?)
Contours; *Frat Rock* .... (RHI)
  Greatest Movie Rock Hits .... (RHI)
  Oldies But Goodies-#12 .... (MOT)
  ST/More Dirty Dancing ....(RCA)
  ST/Wanderers .... (WB)
Do You Wanna Dance?
Beach Boys; *Absolute Best-#1* .... (CAP)
  Spirit Of America .... (CAP)
Bette Midler; *Divine Miss M* .... (ATL)
  Live At Last .... (ATL)

Bobby Freeman; *ST/American Graffiti* .... (MCA)
Doctor Dance
  Frankie Valli; *45* .... (MCA)
Doin' The Do
  Betty Boo; *Boomania* .... (RK)
Dolphin Dance
  Herbie Hancock; *Best Of-Blue Note Years* .... (BLN)
    Maiden Voyage .... (BLN)
Domino Dancing
  Pet Shop Boys; *Introspective* .... (EMI)
Don't Stop Dancing
  Bar-Kays; *Gotta Groove* .... (STX)
Don't Stop The Dance
  Bryan Ferry; *Boys & Girls* .... (WB)
    Greenpeace/Rainbow Warriors .... (GEF)
Down At The Twist And Shout
  Mary Chapin Carpenter; *Greatest Country
  Hits/'90s-1992* ....(COL)
    Hitchhiker Exemplar 2 ....(COL)
    Shooting Straight In The Dark ....(COL)
    Today's Hot Country .... (KT)
Down To The Night Club
  Tower Of Power; *Bump City* ....(WB)
    Live & In Living Color ....(WB)
Dracula's Dance
  Flip Phillips; *Flipenstein* ....(PRG)
Dream Dancing
  Ella Fitzgerald; *Dream Dancing* ....(PAB)
Eighth Avenue Shuffle
  Doobie Brothers; *Takin' It To The Streets* ....(WB)
Euthanasia Waltz
  Brand X; *Livestock* ....(BP)
    Unorthodox Behaviour ....(BP)
Everybody Dance
  Ta Mara/Seen; *Ta Mara/Seen* ....(A&M)
"E" Street Shuffle
  Bruce Springsteen; *Wild The Innocent & The E Street
  Shuffle* ....(COL)
Face Dances, Part 2
  Pete Townshend; *All The Best Cowboys Have Chinese
  Eyes* ....(ATC)
Fancy Dancer
  Bread; *Anthology* .... (ELE)
    Best Of-#2 .... (ELE)
  Commodores; *Compact Command Performances* (MOT)
    Greatest Hits ....(MOT)
    Hot On The Tracks ....(MOT)
    Live ....(MOT)
Flashdance...What A Feeling
  Irene Cara; *ST/Flashdance* .... (CAS)
Footloose
  Kenny Loggins; *ST/Footloose* ....(COL)
Freak Show On The Dance Floor
  Bar-Kays; *Dangerous* .... (MER)
    ST/Breakin' .... (MER)
Freaky Dancin'
  Cameo; *Knights Of The Sound Table* .... (CHC)
Freight Train Boogie
  Delmore Brothers; *45* .... (STR)
  Johnny Otis; *Original Johnny Otis Show-#2* ...... (SAV)
German Waltz Medley
  Lawrence Welk; *Come Waltz With Me* .... (RAN)
Get Down On It
  Kool/Gang; *Something Special* .... (DL)
Get Down Tonight
  K.C./Sunshine Band; *Best Of* .... (RHI)
    Billboard Top Hits-1975 .... (RHI)
    Get Down Tonight-Best Of T.K. .... (RHI)
Get Off Your Ass & Jam
  George Clinton/Parliament/Funkadelic; *Mothership
  Connection* ....(CAP)
Get Up! (Before The Night Is Over)
  Technotronic; *Pump Up The Jam-The Album* .... (SBK)
Getto Jam
  Domino; *Domino* ....(OUT)
Ghost Dance
  Patti Smith; *Easter* ....(ARI)
God Blessed Texas
  Little Texas; *Big Time* ....(WB)
Going To A Go Go
  Miracles; *Billboard Top R&B Hits-1966* .... (MOT)
  Rolling Stones; *Still Life* ....(RS)

Smokey Robinson/Miracles; *Anthology* .... (MOT)
    Compact Command Performances ....(MOT)
    Greatest Hits-#2 ....(MOT)
Gonna Make You Sweat (Everybody...)
  C & C Music Factory; *Gonna Make You Sweat* ..(COL)
    Hot #1 Hits ....(FTN)
Harlem Shuffle
  Bill Deal/Rhondels; *Best Of* ....(RHI)
  Bob & Earl; *Cruisin' 1964* ....(INC)
    Soul Shots-#1-We Got More Soul ....(RHI)
  Johnny & Edgar Winter; *Together* ....(BS)
  Rolling Stones; *Dirty Work* ....(RS)
    Flashpoint & Collectibles ....(RS)
Hokey Pokey
  Ray Anthony; *Capitol Collector Series* ....(CAP)
Holdin' Heaven
  Tracy Byrd; *Tracy Byrd* .... (MCA)
Hollywood Waltz
  Eagles; *One Of These Nights* .... (ASY)
How To Dance
  Bingoboys; *Best Of* ....(ATL)
Humpin' Around
  Bobby Brown; *Bobby* .... (MCA)
Humpty Dance
  Digital Underground; *Sex Packets* .... (TMB)
Hustle
  Van McCoy/Soul City Symphony; *21 Oldies But
  Goodies* ....(OSR)
    21 #1 Hits ....(OSR)
    Disco Years-#1-Turn The Beat Around .... (RHI)
I Came To Dance
  Nils Lofgren; *Best* ....(A&M)
    Classics-#13 ....(A&M)
    Cry Tough ....(A&M)
I Can Make You Dance
  Zapp; *3* ....(WB)
I Can Tell By The Way You Dance
  Vern Gosdin; *10 Years Of Greatest Hits Newly
  Recorded* ....(COL)
    There Is A Season ....(CMP)
I Can't Dance
  Genesis; *We Can't Dance* ....(ATL)
I Can't Stop Dancing
  Archie Bell; *45* ....(ATL)
I Could Have Danced All Night
  Julie Andrews/Original Cast; *My Fair Lady* ......(COL)
I Just Came Here To Dance
  David Frizzell & Shelly West; *Album* ....(VVA)
    Golden Duets ....(VVA)
  Peabo Bryson & Roberta Flack; *Born To Love* ...(CAP)
    Peabo Bryson Collection ....(CAP)
I Love Rock 'N Roll
  Joan Jett/Blackhearts; *I Love Rock 'N Roll* .... (BLK)
    ST/Wayne's World 2 ....(RPR)
I Saw Her (Him) Standing There
  Beatles; *Meet The* ....(CAP)
    Please Please Me ....(EMI)
    Rock 'n' Roll Music-#1 ....(CAP)
  Paul McCartney; *Tripping The Live Fantastic* ....(CAP)
    Tripping The Live Fantastic-Highlights! ....(CAP)
  Tiffany; *Tiffany* .... (MCA)
I Still Believe In Waltzes
  Conway Twitty & Loretta Lynn; *45* .... (MCA)
I Wanna Dance With Somebody (Who...)
  Whitney Houston; *Whitney* .... (ARI)
I Won't Dance
  Frank Sinatra; *Sinatra-Basie* ....(RPR)
  Original Cast; *Roberta* ....(SSP)
If Bubba Can Dance (I Can Too)
  Shenandoah; *Under The Kudzu* ....(RCA)
If I Could Only Dance With You
  Jim Glaser; *Man In The Mirror* ....(NBL)
If The Devil Danced (In Empty Pockets)
  Joe Diffie; *A Thousand Winding Roads* ....(EPI)
Irish Jig (The Ball)
  Original Broadway Cast; *Meet Me In St. Louis* .. (DRG)
It's 3 O'Clock In The Morning
  Mom & Dads; *Blue Hawaii* ....(CRS)
I'm Gonna Charleston Back To Charleston
  Firehouse Five Plus Two; *Goes South* ....(GTJ)
I'm Happy Just To Dance With You
  Anne Murray; *Somebody's Waiting* ....(CAP)
  Beatles; *Something New* ....(CAP)
    ST/Hard Day's Night ....(CAP)

Jazzie's Groove
Soul II Soul; *Keep On Movin'* .... (VIA)
Jerk Out
Time; *Pandemonium* ....(PAI)
Jersey Bounce
Benny Goodman; *Hits Of* ....(CAP)
Live At Carnegie Hall ....(LON)
John I'm Only Dancing
David Bowie; *Changesbowie* ....(RYK)
Sound + Vision ....(RYK)
The Singles-1969-1993 ....(RYK)
Juke Joint Jump
Elvin Bishop; *Juke Joint Jump* ....(CPC)
Raisin' Hell ....(CPC)
Jungle Boogie
Kool/Gang; *Everything Is-Greatest Hits* ....(MER)
Soul Hits/'70s-#12 ....(RHI)
Spin Their Top Hits ....(DL)
Jungle Hop
Cramps; *Psychedelic Jungle/Gravest Hits* ....(IRS)
Just Like Gene Autry
Moby Grape; *Very Best Of-Vintage* ....(COL)
Kansas City Stomp
Jelly Roll Morton; *1923-1924* ....(MS)
Jelly Roll Morton ....(BLU)
La Bamba
Jose Feliciano; *Greatest '60s Folksingers* ....(VAN)
Newport Folk Musical Festival-1964 ....(VAN)
Los Lobos; *ST/La Bamba* ....(WB)
Ritchie Valens; *American Graffiti-#3* ....(MCA)
Oldies But Goodies-#8 ....(OSR)
Xavier Cugat; *Best Of* ....(MCA)
Pure Gold ....(RCA)
Lambada
Kaoma; *World Beat* ....(EPI)
Lambeth Walk
Original Broadway Cast; *Me & My Girl* ....(MCA)
Original Cast; *Me & My Girl* ....(EMI)
Land Of 1000 Dances
Cannibal/Headhunters; *History Of Latino Rock-#1* (RHI)
Super Oldies/'60s-#8 ....(AUF)
Toga Rock ....(DHL)
Wilson Pickett; *Atlantic R&B
1947-1974-#6-(1966-1969)* ....(ATL)
Best Of ....(ATL)
Greatest Hits ....(ATL)
ST/Forrest Gump ....(EPX)
Last Cheater's Waltz
Emmylou Harris; *Cimarron* ....(WB)
T.G. Sheppard; *All-Time Greatest Hits* ....(WB)
Greatest Hits ....(WB)
Last Dance
Donna Summer; *Dance Collection* ....(CAS)
Greatest Hits ....(CAS)
Live & More ....(CAS)
On The Radio-Greatest Hits-#1 & 2 ....(CAS)
Studio 54 ....(CAS)
Summer Collection ....(MER)
Walk Away-Best Of 1977-1980 ....(CAS)
Frank Sinatra; *Come Dance With Me* ....(CAP)
Reprise Collection ....(RPR)
Sinatra Reprise-The Very Good Years ....(RPR)
George Clinton; *Best Of* ....(CAP)
Last Tango In Paris
Herb Alpert/Tijuana Brass; *Four Sider* ....(A&M)
Greatest Hits-#2 ....(A&M)
Le Freak
Chic; *45* ....(ATL)
Let's Dance
Beatles; *In The Beginning-Circa 1960* ....(POL)
Benny Goodman; *All-Time Greatest Hits* ....(COL)
Big Bands Of The Swinging Years-#1 ....(CLT)
Big Band-Let's Dance ....(COL)
Live At Carnegie Hall ....(LON)
Swing's The Thing ....(CAP)
David Bowie; *Changesbowie* ....(RYK)
Let's Dance ....(EMI)
The Singles-1969-1993 ....(RYK)
Let's Face The Music And Dance
Ella Fitzgerald; *Irving Berlin Always* ....(VRV)
Tony Bennett; *Bennett/Berlin* ....(COL)
Jazz ....(COL)
Let's Go Dancin'
Kool/Gang; *As One* ....(DL)

Let's Twist Again
Chubby Checker; *Good Time Rock 'N' Roll* .....(MCA)
Greatest Hits ....(AKO)
Greatest Hits ....(EVR)
Hits Of The Sixties ....(IMC)
Life's A Dance
John Michael Montgomery; *Life's A Dance* ......(ATL)
Limbo Rock
Chubby Checker; *Greatest Hits* ....(EVR)
Moonlighting ....(MCA)
Rock-O-Rama #2 ....(AKO)
Limousine Boogie (Hey Hey Mama)
Savoy Brown; *Make Me Sweat* ....(CRS)
Little Night Dancin'
John Cougar Mellencamp; *John Cougar
Mellencamp* ....(RIV)
Locomotion
Grand Funk Railroad; *Billboard Top Rock 'N' Roll
Hits-1974* ....(RHI)
Caught In The Act ....(CAP)
Hits ....(CAP)
Kylie Minogue; *Kylie* ....(GEF)
Little Eva; *Billboard Top Rock 'N' Roll Hits-1962* (RHI)
Groove 'N' Grind/'50s-'60s Dance Hits ....(RHI)
More American Graffiti ....(MCA)
Orchestral Manoeuvres In The Dark; *Best Of* ...(A&M)
Junk Culture ....(A&M)
Los Angeles Boogie
Lightnin' Hopkins; *Los Angeles Blues* ....(RHI)
Louisiana Stomp
Clifton Chenier; *Zydeco-Early Years* ....(ARH)
Louisiana Two-Step
Clifton Chenier; *King Of Zydeco Live At
Montreux* ....(ARH)
Out West ....(ARH)
Lynda
Steve Wariner; *Country Classics-#11-1987-1988* (MCA)
Greatest Hits ....(MCA)
It's A Crazy World ....(MCA)
MCA #1 Hits/'80s-#3 ....(MCA)
Make Believe Ballroom Time
Glenn Miller; *Complete-#5 & #9* ....(RCA)
Legendary Performer-#2 ....(RCA)
Malaguena
Percy Faith; *All Time Greatest Hits* ....(COL)
Placido Domingo; *Love Until The End Of
Time-Greatest* ....(COL)
Ritchie Valens; *Best Of* ....(RHI)
History Of ....(RHI)
Roy Clark; *Best Of* ....(MCA)
Mambo In Miami
Peggy Lee & George Shearing; *Beauty & The
Beat!* ....(BLN)
Mambo Las Vegas
Howard Rumsey's Lighthouse All-Stars; *Music For
Lighthousekeeping* ....(CTM)
Mardi Gras Mambo
Hawketts; *Treacherous: History Of Neville Bros.* .. (RHI)
Martian Boogie
Brownsville Station; *Brownsville Station* ....(PVS)
Martian Hop
Ran-Dells; *Dr. Demento Greatest Novelty
Records-#3* ....(RHI)
Elvira Presents Haunted Hits ....(RHI)
Halloween Hits ....(RHI)
Mary Jane's Last Dance
Tom Petty/Heartbreakers; *Greatest Hits* ....(MCA)
Mashed Potato Time
Dee Dee Sharp; *21 Oldies But Goodies* ....(OSR)
Big Bad Bossa Beat ....(OSR)
Oldies But Goodies-#6 ....(OSR)
Masochism Tango
Tom Lehrer; *Dr. Demento's Greatest
Novelty-#2-1950s* ....(RHI)
Evening Wasted With ....(RPR)
Memphis Boogie
Dr. Isaiah Ross; *Boogie Disease* ....(ARH)
Memphis Hip Shake
Cult; *Electric* ....(SIR)
Mexican Hat Dance
Percy Faith; *All-Time Greatest Hits* ....(COL)
Mexican Shuffle
Herb Alpert/Tijuana Brass; *Classics-#1* ....(A&M)
Greatest Hits ....(A&M)

Tijuana Brass; *South Of The Border* .... (A&M)
Milk Cow Blues Boogie
Elvis Presley; *Complete Sun Sessions* ....(RCA)
   Date With ....(RCA)
   Sun Sessions ....(RCA)
Ricky Nelson; *Live In '85* .... (RHI)
Milwaukee Waltz
Michigan Dutchmen; *W.J.R.T. TV All-Time Polkas* .. (JJ)
Milwaukee's Favorite Waltz
Li'l Wally; *America's Favorite* ....(JJ)
Mobile Boogie
Hank Williams, Jr.; *Early Years* ....(W/C)
   One Night Stands ....(WB)
Monday's Dance
Ira Sullivan; *Ira Sullivan* ....(FF)
Red Rodney & Ira Sullivan; *Alive In New York* . (MUS)
Monster Mash
Beach Boys; *Concert/'69-Live In London* ....(CAP)
Big O; *ST/Return Of The Living Dead-Pt. 2* .... (ISL)
Bobby Boris Pickett; *Dr. Demento 20th Anniversary*
   Collection .... (RHI)
   Dr. Demento's Greatest Novelty-#3 ....(RHI)
   Halloween Hits ....(RHI)
   Horror Rock Classics-#2 ....(LON)
Moondance
Van Morrison; *Best Of* .... (MER)
   Moondance ....(WB)
Morning Dance
Spyro Gyra; *Access All Areas* .... (MCA)
   Collection ....(GRP)
   Morning Dance ....(MCA)
Moscow Diskow
Telex; *12"* .... (SIR)
Mr. Bojangles
David Bromberg; *Out Of The Blues-Best Of* ......(COL)
Jerry Jeff Walker; *Best Of* .... (MCA)
   Gypsy Songman ....(RYK)
   Man Must Carry On ....(MCA)
   Mr. Bojangles ....(BAI)
Nitty Gritty Dirt Band; *Best Of* .... (EMI)
   On The Road Again ....(CAP)
   Super Hits/'70s-Have A Nice Day-#4 .... (RHI)
   Twenty Years Of Dirt-Best Of ....(WB)
Music That Makes Me Dance
Barbra Streisand/Original Cast; *Funny Girl* ......(CAP)
Michael Feinstein & Jule Styne; *M. Feinstein Sings Jule*
   Styne Songbook ....(ELE)
Mystery Dance
Elvis Costello; *Girls Girls Girls* ....(COL)
   My Aim Is True ....(COL)
Neal's Fandango
Doobie Brothers; *Stampede* .... (WB)
Neutron Dance
Pointer Sisters; *Break Out* .... (PNT)
   Greatest Hits ....(RCA)
   ST/Beverly Hills Cop ....(MCA)
Never Felt Like Dancing
Teddy Pendergrass; *Workin' It Back* .... (ASY)
New Hawaiian Boogie
George Thorogood/Destroyers; *Move It On Over* (ROU)
New Jack Swing
Wreckx-N-Effect; *Rap: On The Lighter Tip* .... (KT)
   Wreckx-N-Effect ....(MOT)
New Orleans Bump
Jelly Roll Morton; *Jazz Classics In Digital Stereo* .(ABC)
New Orleans Shuffle
Johnny Otis; *Original Johnny Otis Show* .... (SAV)
New Orleans Waltz
Nathan Abshire; *French Blues* .... (ARH)
New Spanish Two-Step
Bob Wills/Texas Playboys; *Country Music*
   Classics-#14-1940s .... (KT)
   Essential ....(COL)
New York Shuffle
Graham Parker/Rumour; *Parkerilla* .... (MER)
   Stick To Me .... (MER)
Night Fever
Bee Gees; *Greatest* .... (POL)
   ST/Saturday Night Fever .... (POL)
Non-Viennese Waltz Blues
Joe Gordon; *Lookin' Good!* .... (CTM)
North Gulfport Boogie
Roosevelt Sykes; *Hard Drivin' Blues* ....(DEL)

Norwegian Dance
Stephane Grappelli; *Stephanova* .... (CCJ)
Norwegian Dance No. 2
Django Reinhardt & Stephane Grappelli; *Django*
   Reinhardt & Stephane Grappelli .... (CRS)
Norwegian Waltz/Liza Lynn
Jackie Daly/Seamus & Manus McGuire; *Buttons &*
   Bows ....(GRE)
Oh What A Night For Dancing
Barry White; *Greatest Hits-#2* .... (CAS)
   Sings For Someone You Love .... (20)
Oklahoma Dancer
Monkees; *Monkees Present* .... (RHI)
Oklahoma Stomp
Duke Ellington; *Hot In Harlem* .... (MCA)
   Jazz Heritage-Vocalion Rarities .... (MCA)
Spade Cooley; *Columbia Historic Edition* ....(COL)
Spade Cooley/Orchestra; *Legends Of Country*
   Guitar-#1 .... (RHI)
Oklahoma Swing
Vince Gill & Reba McEntire; *When I Call Your*
   Name ....(MCA)
Oklahoma Waltz
Cavaliers; *Have Polka Will Travel* ....(ACT)
Old Folks Boogie
Little Feat; *Time Loves A Hero* .... (WB)
   Waiting For Columbus .... (WB)
Old Maid Boogie
Eddie "Cleanhead" Vinson; *Late Show* ....(FAN)
Our Waltz
David Rose/Orchestra; *Tommy Dorsey & The* .... (LAS)
Sarah Vaughan; *Complete On*
   Mercury-#3-1954-1956 .... (MER)
Palm Springs Jump
Flat Foot Floogie Boys & Slim Gaillard; *1940s-The*
   Singers ....(COL)
Papa Loves Mambo
Perry Como; *All-Time Greatest Hits-#1* ....(RCA)
   Golden Records ....(RCA)
   Pure Gold ....(RCA)
   This Is ....(RCA)
Peach Tree Shuffle
Panama Francis; *All-Stars 1949* .... (CLT)
Philadelphia Boogie
Len McCall; *Philadelphia Boogie* .... (CLT)
Philadelphia Hop
Li'l Wally; *Here Comes* .... (JJ)
Philadelphia Mambo
Cal Tjader; *Black Orchid* .... (FAN)
Philly Dog
Mar-Keys; *Back To Back/Mar-Keys & Booker*
   T/MGs ....(ATL)
   Great Memphis Sound ....(ATL)
   Stax/Volt Revue-#1-Live In London ....(ATL)
   Super Hits-#1 ....(ATL)
Philly Freeze
Alvin Cash/Registers; *45* ....(ERI)
Polish Memories Waltz
New Yorkers; *Polka Smile* .... (JJ)
Poor Boy Shuffle
Creedence Clearwater Revival; *1969* ....(FAN)
   Willy & The Poor Boys ....(FAN)
Popcorn, Pretzels & Beer Waltz
Michigan Dutchmen; *Beer & Dutchmen Polkas* ......(JJ)
Port Arthur Waltz
Harry Choates; *Fiddle King Of Cajun Swing* ..... (ARH)
Pretty Ballerina
Left Banke; *History Of* .... (RHI)
   Nuggets-#11-Pop-#4 .... (RHI)
Private Dancer
Tina Turner; *Live In Europe* ....(CAP)
   Private Dancer ....(CAP)
   Simply The Best ....(CAP)
Pump Up The Jam
Technotronic; *Pump Up The Jam* .... (SBK)
   Rock The First-#3 ....(SAN)
Puppets' Dance
Jean-Luc Ponty; *Cosmic Messenger* .... (RHI)
Queen Of The Hop
Bobby Darin; *Story* ....(ATC)
Dave Edmunds; *ST/Porky's Revenge* ....(COL)
Dion; *Sings The Hits Of The '50s & '60s* ....(LAU)
Ragtime Dance
Jean-Pierre Rampal; *Plays Scott Joplin* ....(COL)

Richard Zimmerman; *His Greatest Hits-Scott
Joplin* .... (EVR)
Scott Joplin; *The Entertainer* .... (BIO)
Rhumba Girl
Nicolette Larson; *Nicolette* .... (WB)
Riverboat Shuffle
Hoagy Carmichael; *Stardust Road* .... (MCA)
Rock A Beatin' Boogie
Bill Haley/Comets; *Golden Hits* .... (MCA)
Greatest Hits .... (EVR)
Legends Of Rock Guitar-'50s-#2 .... (RHI)
Rock And Roll Music
Beach Boys; *15 Big Ones* .... (CAR)
Gift Set .... (CAP)
Made In The U.S.A. .... (CAP)
Ten Years Of Harmony .... (CAR)
Beatles; *Box Set* .... (CAP)
For Sale .... (CAP)
Rock And Roll Music-#1 .... (CAP)
'65 .... (CAP)
Chuck Berry; *Chess Box* .... (CSS)
Cruisin'-1958 .... (INC)
Golden Hits .... (MER)
Greatest Hits .... (EVR)
R.E.O. Speedwagon; *Nine Lives* .... (EPI)
Rock Billy Boogie
Robert Gordon; *Rock Billy Boogie* .... (RCA)
Rock That Boogie
Commander Cody/Lost Planet Airmen; *Country
Casanova* .... (MCA)
Too Much Fun-Best Of .... (MCA)
We've Got A Live One Here .... (WB)
Rock With You
Jacksons; *Live* .... (EPI)
Michael Jackson; *Off The Wall* .... (EPI)
Rock & Roll Waltz
Kay Starr; *Capitol Collectors Series* .... (CAP)
Nipper's Greatest Hits-'50s-#1 .... (RCA)
Rockin' Boogie
Fleetwood Mac; *In Chicago* .... (SIR)
Roxanna Waltz & Scotland Calling Jesse
Jay Ungar/Others; *Fiddle Fever* .... (FF)
Rump Shaker
Wreckx-N-Effect; *Hard Or Smooth* .... (MCA)
Sad Pig Dance
Chris Proctor; *Delicate Dance* .... (FF)
Safety Dance
Men Without Hats; *Rhythm Of Youth* .... (MCA)
Sally Can't Dance
Lou Reed; *Sally Can't Dance* .... (RCA)
Walk On The Wild Side & Other Hits .... (RCA)
Walk On The Wild Side-Best Of .... (RCA)
Salsa Smurf
Special Request; *Tommy Boy Greatest Beats* .... (TMB)
Same Old Song & Dance
Aerosmith; *Classics Live 2* .... (COL)
Get Your Wings .... (COL)
Greatest Hits .... (COL)
Pandora's Box .... (COL)
San Antonio Stroll
Tanya Tucker; *Collection* .... (MCA)
Greatest Hits .... (MCA)
Greatest Hits Encore .... (LIB)
MCA Records 30 Years Of Hits-1958-1988 ... (MCA)
Tanya Tucker .... (MCA)
Saturday Dance
Bob Cooper; *Coop! Music Of* .... (CTM)
Saturday Night Boogie
Harry Crafton; *Harry Crafton* .... (CLT)
Saturday Night Stomp
Eddie "Blues Man" Kirkland; *It's The Blues Man!* .. (TS)
Savannah Dance
Michael Pluznick; *Where The Rain Is Born* .... (SOG)
Savannah Russet/Jete The Dancing Cat
Jeanne Newhall; *Novice* .... (MAR)
Save The Last Dance For Me
Buck Owens; *Collection-1959-1990* .... (RHI)
Dolly Parton; *Best Of-#3* .... (RCA)
Great Pretender .... (RCA)
Drifters; *20 Top 10 Hits/'50s & '60s* .... (LAU)
Atlantic Rhythm & Blues 1947-74-#4 .... (ATL)
Billboard Top Rock 'N' Roll Hits-1960 .... (RHI)
Cruisin'-1960 .... (INC)
Golden Hits .... (ATL)

Emmylou Harris; *Blue Kentucky Girl* .... (WB)
Profile 2: Best Of .... (WB)
Jerry Lee Lewis; *20 Classic Jerry Lee Lewis Hits* . (OSR)
Duets .... (SUN)
Monsters .... (SUN)
Original Golden Hits-#2 .... (SUN)
Sexy Dancer
Prince; *Prince* .... (WB)
Shadow Dancing
Andy Gibb; *Collection Of His Greatest Hits* ...... (POL)
Greatest Hits .... (RSO)
Shadow Dancing .... (RSO)
Shake
Ike & Tina Turner; *Greatest Hits-#1* .... (SAJ)
Otis Redding; *Best Of* .... (ATC)
History Of .... (ATC)
Live In Europe .... (ATC)
Story .... (ATL)
Rod Stewart/Brian Auger & The Trinity;
Storyteller-Complete Anthology-1964-1990 .... (WB)
Sam Cooke; *Man & His Music* .... (RCA)
Supremes; *We Remember Sam Cooke* .... (MOT)
Shake And Fingerpop
Junior Walker/All-Stars; *All The Great Hits* ..... (MOT)
Anthology .... (MOT)
Greatest Hits .... (MOT)
Shotgun .... (MOT)
Shake Down
Evelyn "Champagne" King; *Face To Face* .... (RCA)
Shake It
Ian Matthews; *Stealin' Home* .... (MSH)
Shake It And Break It
Charley Patton; *Founder Of The Delta Blues* .... (YAZ)
Joe Turner; *Things That I Used To Do* .... (PAB)
Shake It Like A White Girl
E.U.; *Livin' Large* .... (VIA)
Shake It Up
Bad Company; *Dangerous Age* .... (ATL)
Cars; *Greatest Hits* .... (ELE)
Shake It Up .... (ELE)
Shake It Up Tonight
Cheryl Lynn; *Club Columbia* .... (COL)
In The Night .... (COL)
Shake It Up!
Jamaica Boys; *J Boys* .... (RPR)
Shake Me I Rattle
Cristy Lane; *At Her Best* .... (EMI)
Cristy Lane Is The Name .... (LS)
Shake Rattle & Roll
Big Joe Turner; *Every Day I Have The Blues* ..... (PAB)
Greatest Hits .... (ATL)
Oldies But Goodies-#2 .... (OSR)
Soul Years .... (ATL)
Bill Haley/Comets; *Golden Hits* .... (MCA)
Greatest Hits .... (MCA)
Elvis Presley; *For LP Fans Only* .... (RCA)
Rocker .... (RCA)
ST/This Is Elvis .... (RCA)
Fats Domino; *Greatest Hits* .... (MCA)
Huey Lewis/News; *Four Chords & Several Years
Ago* .... (ELE)
NRBQ; *At Yankee Stadium* .... (MER)
Vern Gosdin; *Best Of* .... (WB)
Shake Shake Shake
Jackie Wilson; *Baby Workout* .... (BRU)
Greatest Hits .... (BRU)
Mr. Excitement .... (RHI)
My Golden Favorites .... (BRU)
Shake That Fat
Jo Jo Gunne; *Jo Jo Gunne* .... (ASY)
Shake Your Ass!
Blowfly; *Twisted World Of* .... (OPS)
Shake Your Body (Down To The Ground)
Jacksons; *Destiny* .... (EPI)
Live .... (EPI)
ST/Skatetown USA .... (COL)
Shake Your Booty
K.C./Sunshine Band; *Best Of* .... (RHI)
Greatest Hits .... (TK)
Mega Hits Dance Classics-#4 .... (PRY)
Part 3 .... (TK)

Shake Your Groove Thing
Peaches & Herb; *2 Hot* .... (POL)
  Billboard Top Dance Hits-1978 .... (RHI)
  Disco Years-#1-1974-1978 .... (RHI)
  Mega Hits Dance Classics-#2 .... (PRY)
  Night At Studio 54 .... (POL)
  Polydor Dance Classics .... (POL)
Shake Your Hips
Love Sculpture; *Blues Helping* .... (AMR)
Rolling Stones; *Exile On Main Street* .... (RS)
Slim Harpo; *Best Of* .... (RHI)
Shake Your Love
Climax Blues Band; *FM/Live* .... (SIR)
Debbie Gibson; *Out Of The Blue* .... (ATL)
Shake Your Money Maker
Elmore James; *King Of The Slide Guitar* .... (CPC)
Fleetwood Mac; *Vintage Years* .... (SIR)
George Thorogood; *Born To Be Bad* .... (EMI)
Paul Butterfield; *Golden Butter* .... (ELE)
  Paul Butterfield Blues Band .... (ELE)
Shake Your Pants
Cameo; *Cameosis* .... (CAS)
Shake Your Tailfeather
Blues Brothers & Ray Charles; *ST/Blues Brothers* (ATL)
Shakin'
Eddie Money; *Greatest Hits-Sound Of Money* ....(COL)
  No Control ....(COL)
Sawyer Brown; *Greatest Hits* .... (LIB)
  Shakin' .... (LIB)
Shakin' All Over
Guess Who; *Grandson Of Frat Rock-#3* .... (RHI)
  Greatest Of ....(RCA)
Pirates; *Out Of Their Skulls* .... (WB)
  Skull Wars ....(WB)
Who; *Live At Leeds* .... (MCA)
Shakin' Shakin' Shakes
Los Lobos; *By The Light Of The Moon* ....(SLS)
Shall We Dance
Ella Fitzgerald; *George & Ira Gershwin Songbook* (VRV)
Original Broadway Cast; *King & I* ....(RCA)
Original Cast; *King & I* .... (MCA)
Shanghai Shuffle
Bunny Berigan Orchestra; *Bunny Berigan*
  Orchestra-1937-1938 .... (HIN)
Fletcher Henderson Orchestra; *1924-1941* ....(BIO)
She Wants To Dance With Me
Rick Astley; *Hold Me In Your Arms* ....(RCA)
She's Got The Rhythm (& I Got The Blues)
Alan Jackson; *Lot About Livin' (& A Little 'Bout*
  Love .... (ARI)
She's Only Happy When She's Dancin'
Bryan Adams; *Reckless* ....(A&M)
Shim Sham Shimmy
Dorsey Brothers; *Best Of The Big Bands* ....(COL)
  I'm Getting Sentimental Over You ....(POE)
Shimmy Like Kate
Olympics; *Official Record Album Of* .... (RHI)
Shimmy Shake
Beatles; *45* ....(CLT)
Shimmy Shakin' Daddy
Maddox Brothers & Rose; *1946-1951-#2* ...... (ARH)
  America's Most Colorful Hillbilly Band .... (ARH)
Shimmy Shimmy
Bobby Freeman; *Let's Dance* ....(GUS)
Shim, Sham Shimmy On The St. Louis Blues
Dizzy Gillespie; *Best Of* .... (PAB)
Shit House Shuffle
Aerosmith; *Pandora's Box* ....(COL)
Shout And Shimmy
Who; *Who's Missing* .... (MCA)
Shut Up And Dance
Pointer Sisters; *Serious Slammin'* ....(RCA)
Simon Smith & His Amazing Dancing Bear
Randy Newman; *Sail Away* ....(RPR)
Skip To My Lou
Cathy Fink; *When The Rain Comes Down* ....(ROU)
Leadbelly; *Defense Blues-Golden Classics-#2* ....(CLT)
Pete Seeger; *American Favorite Ballads-#1* ...... (FLW)
Skip To My Lu
Lisa Lisa; *Lisa Lisa 77* ....(PEN)
Sleeping Beauty Waltz
101 Strings; *Million Seller Themes From*
  Tchaikovsky .... (ALS)

Slow Dance
R. Kelly & Public Announcement; *Born Into The*
  '90s .... (JVA)
Slow Dancer
Boz Scaggs; *Hits* ....(COL)
  Slow Dancer ....(COL)
Robert Plant; *Pictures At Eleven* .... (SS)
Spanish Dancer
Steve Winwood; *Arc Of A Diver* .... (ISL)
  Chronicles .... (ISL)
Spanish Fandango
Bob Wills/Texas Playboys; *24 Great Hits* ......(MGM)
Chet Atkins; *Pickin' My Way-In Hollywood*
  Alone .... (MOB)
Mississippi John Hurt; *Best Of* .... (VAN)
Spanish Two Step
Bob Wills; *Anthology* ....(SSP)
Step That Step
Sawyer Brown; *Greatest Hits* .... (LIB)
  New Faces Of Country .... (KT)
  Sawyer Brown .... (LIB)
Stockholm Stomp
California Ramblers; *Miss Annabelle Lee-#1* ......(BIO)
Stomp
Brothers Johnson; *Billboard Top Dance Hits-1980* (RHI)
  Classics-#11 ....(A&M)
  Light Up The Night ....(A&M)
Stompin' At The Savoy
Benny Goodman; *All-Time Greatest Hits* ....(COL)
  Carnegie Hall Jazz Concert ....(COL)
  Pure Gold ....(RCA)
  Stompin' At The Savoy .... (BLU)
Doc Severinsen; *Facets* ....(AMH)
Ella Fitzgerald & Louis Armstrong; *Ella & Louis* (VRV)
Louis Armstrong; *Essential* .... (VAN)
Stompin' In The '90s
Yo-Yo; *Make Way For The Motherlode* ....(EW)
Stop, Stop, Stop
Hollies; *Best Of* .... (EMI)
  Greatest .... (CAP)
  Greatest Hits .... (EPI)
Stray Cat Strut
Stray Cats; *Best Of-Rock This Town* .... (EMI)
  Built For Speed .... (EMI)
  Rock The First-#4 .... (SAN)
Strike It Up
Black Box; *Dreamland* ....(RCA)
  Mixedup! ....(RCA)
Stroll, The
Diamonds; *Groove 'N' Grind-'50s/'60s Dance Hits* (RHI)
  Partytime '50s ....(PRY)
  ST/American Graffiti .... (MCA)
Sundance
Danny Joe Brown Band; *Danny Joe Brown Band* . (EPI)
Kitaro; *Light Of The Spirit* ....(GEF)
Sundancing (For The Hopi/Navajo Energy)
Jon Anderson; *In The City Of Angels* ....(COL)
Super Bowl Shuffle
Chicago Bears Shufflin' Crew; *45* ....(RED)
Swayin' To The Music
Johnny Rivers; *Anthology-1964-1977* .... (RHI)
Swedish Dance
Danny Thompson; *Instruments-Collection* ....(HBL)
Swedish Jig
John Renbourn & Stefan Grossman; *Music Of*
  Ireland ....(SHA)
Take Your Clothes Off When You Dance
Frank Zappa; *We're Only In It For The.../Lumpy*
  Gravy ....(RYK)
  You Can't Do That On Stage Anymore-#6 ......(RYK)
Tango In Paris
Regina Belle; *Passion* ....(COL)
Taxi Dancer
John Mellencamp; *John Cougar Mellencamp* ....(RIV)
Taxi War Dance
Count Basie; *Essential-#1* ....(COL)
  I Like Jazz-Essence Of ....(COL)
Teach Me How To Shimmy
Calamities; *Calamities* ....(PBO)
Teach Me (The "Philly" Dog)
Manhattans; *Dedicated To You-Golden*
  Classics-#1 ....(CLT)
Ten Cents A Dance
Eileen Farrell; *I Gotta Right To Sing The Blues* .. (SMC)

Ella Fitzgerald; *Rodgers & Hart Songbook* ....(VRV)
Tennessee Two Step
Charlie Daniels; *America I Believe In You* ....(LIB)
Tennessee Waltz
Emmylou Harris; *Cimarron* ....(WB)
  Country's Greatest Hits-#5 ....(WB)
  New Tradition Sings The Old Tradition ....(WB)
Guy Lombardo; *Best Of* ....(CCB)
Hank Williams, Jr.; *Living Proof-MGM
Recordings-1963-1975* .... (MER)
Lacy J. Dalton; *Greatest Hits* ....(COL)
Les Paul & Mary Ford; *Les Paul-Selections From Legend
& Legacy* ....(CAP)
Patti Page; *Golden Hits* ....(MER)
  Greatest Hits ....(COL)
Roy Acuff; *Essential* ....(COL)
  Greatest Hits ....(COL)
Roy Rogers; *Best Of* ....(CCB)
Sammy Kaye; *Best Of The Big Bands* ....(COL)
Spike Jones; *Best Of* ....(RCA)
Terrific Band & A Real Nice Crowd
Original Broadway Cast; *Ballroom* .... (SMC)
Texas Jump
Ozzie Nelson/Orchestra; *Uncollected-1940-1942* (HIN)
Texas Shuffle
Count Basie; *Basie Reunions* .... (PRS)
  Best Of ....(MCA)
Houston Person; *Heavy Juice* ....(MUS)
Texas Sidestep
Deanna Cox; *Country Jukebox Greatest Hits-#2* ...(WB)
Texas Two Step
Bob Wills; *Country Music Hall Of Fame* .... (MCA)
That Boy Could Dance
Weird Al Yankovic; *In 3-D* ....(SCO)
That Girl Wants To Dance With Me
Gregory Hines; *Gregory Hines* ....(EPI)
That Ol' Texas Two-Step
Charlie Walker; *Charlie Walker* ....(DOT)
Theme From "Dances With Wolves"
John Barry; *Moviola* ....(EPI)
They Don't Dance Like Carmen No More
Jimmy Buffett; *Boats Beaches Bars & Ballads* ... (MGR)
  White Sport Coat & A Pink Crustacean .... (MCA)
Thorazine Shuffle
Savatage; *Gutter Ballet* ....(ATL)
Time Of My Life (I've Had The)
Bill Medley; *Best Of* ....(CCB)
Bill Medley & Jennifer Warnes; *Dirty Dancing Live In
Concert* ....(RCA)
  ST/Dirty Dancing ....(RCA)
Tiny Dancer
Elton John; *Live In Australia w/Melbourne
Symphony* ....(MCA)
  Madman Across The Water ....(POL)
Toucan's Dance
Sergio Mendes; *Arara* ....(A&M)
Touch Me When We're Dancing
Alabama; *The Touch* ....(RCA)
Carpenters; *Classics-#2* ....(A&M)
  Made In America ....(A&M)
  Yesterday Once More ....(A&M)
Trance Dance
D-Mob; *Little Bit Of This Little Bit Of That* ......(LON)
Tripe Face Boogie
Little Feat; *Feats Don't Fail Me Now* .... (WB)
  Sailin' Shoes ....(WB)
  Waiting For Columbus ....(WB)
Trumpet Boogie
Ray Anthony Orchestra; *Young Man With A
Horn-1952-1954* .... (HIN)
Tubesnake Boogie
ZZ Top; *El Loco* ....(WB)
  Greatest Hits ....(WB)
  Six Pack ....(WB)
Twist Twist Senora
Gary U.S. Bonds; *School Rock 'N' Roll-Best Of* ... (RHI)
Twist & Shout
Beatles; *At The Hollywood Bowl* ....(CAP)
  Box Set ....(CAP)
  Early ....(CAP)
  Please Please Me ....(CAP)
  Rock 'N' Roll Music-#1 ....(CAP)
  ST/Imagine-The Motion Picture ....(CAP)
Buck Owens/Buckaroos; *Live At Carnegie Hall* .. (CMF)

Isley Brothers; *Best Of* ....(CCB)
  Cruisin'-1963 ....(INC)
  Frat Rock ....(RHI)
  Oldies But Goodies-#10 ....(OSR)
  Solid Gold Music WCBS FM 101-'60s-#1 ......(CLT)
  Toga Rock ....(DHL)
Mamas & The Papas; *Best Of* ....(MCA)
  Who; Who's Last ....(MCA)
Twistin' Postman
Marvelettes; *Anthology* ....(MOT)
  Compact Command Performances ....(MOT)
  Greatest Hits ....(MOT)
Twistin' The Night Away
Rod Stewart; *Best Of-#2* ....(MER)
  Never A Dull Moment ....(MER)
  Sing It Again Rod ....(MER)
  Storyteller-Complete Anthology-1964-1990 ......(WB)
Sam Cooke; *At The Copa* ....(RCA)
  Best Of ....(RCA)
  Dance Music ....(RCA)
  Man & His Music ....(RCA)
  Nipper's Greatest Hits-'60s-#2 ....(RCA)
  ST/Animal House ....(MCA)
Twistin' With Linda
Isley Brothers; *Scepter Records Story* ....(CPC)
  Story-#1-Rockin' Soul-1959-1968 .... (RHI)
Twist, The
Chubby Checker; *Billboard Top Rock 'N' Roll
Hits-1960* ....(RHI)
  Greatest Hits ....(AKO)
  Let's Dance ....(GUS)
Two O'Clock Jump
Harry James; *All-Time Favorites By* ....(SSP)
  Greatest Hits ....(COL)
  Two O'Clock Jump ....(POE)
Two To Tango
Bing Crosby; *Radio Years* ....(CRS)
Unskinny Bop
Poison; *Flesh & Blood* ....(CAP)
  Swallow This Live ....(CAP)
Varsity Drag
Jonathan & Darlene Edwards; *Songs For Shieks &
Flappers* ....(CRN)
Les Elgart; *Best Of The Big Bands-#2* ....(COL)
Wah Watusi
Orlons; *Rock-O-Rama-#1* ....(AKO)
Wall Street Shuffle
10 CC; *Greatest Hits '72-'78* ....(POL)
  Live & Let Live ....(MER)
Waltz Across Texas
Ernest Tubb & Willie Nelson; *Ernest Tubb
Collection* ....(SO)
Waltz Me To Heaven
Waylon Jennings; *Greatest Hits-#2* ....(RCA)
Waltz Of The Flowers
Lawrence Welk; *22 All-Time Favorite Waltzes* .. (RAN)
Waltz Of The Wind
Hank Williams; *I'm So Lonesome I Could
Cry-1949* ....(POL)
Roy Acuff; *Best Of* ....(CCB)
  Essential ....(COL)
Waltz You Saved For Me
Bob Wills; *Anthology* ....(SSP)
Lawrence Welk; *22 All-Time Big Band Favorites* (RAN)
Mom & Dads; *20 Favorite Waltzes* ....(CRS)
Wayne King; *Best Of* ....(MCA)
Waltzing Back
Cranberries; *Everybody Else Is Doing It So Why...* . (ISL)
Waltzing Matilda
Burl Ives; *Best Of* ....(MCA)
Fred Astaire; *Three Evenings With* ....(DRG)
James Galway; *Pachebel Canon & Other
Favorites* ....(RCA)
Wango Tango
Ted Nugent; *Scream Dream* ....(EPI)
Watusi
Vibrations; *Best Of Chess Rhythm & Blues-#1* .... (CSS)
West Nashville Boogie
Steve Earle/Dukes; *Shut Up & Die Like An
Aviator* ....(MCA)
  The Hard Way ....(MCA)
West Nashville Grand Ballroom Gown
Jimmy Buffett; *Living & Dying In 3/4 Time* .....(MCA)

West Oakland Strut
Ed Kelly & Pharoah Sanders; *Ed Kelly & Pharoah
Sanders* ....(EVD)
West Texas Waltz
Butch Hancock; *Own & Own* ....(SH)
When You Dance I Can Really Love
Neil Young; *After The Gold Rush* ....(RPR)
Neil Young/Crazy Horse; *Live Rust* ....(RPR)
(When You Fall In Love) Everything's...
Ed Bruce; *45* ....(MCA)
One To One ....(MCA)
Whole Lotta Shakin' Goin' On
Elvis Presley; *Recorded Live On Stage In
Memphis* ....(RCA)
Jerry Lee Lewis; *Cruisin'-1957* .... (INC)
Golden Hits Of ....(SMA)
Oldies But Goodies-#4 ....(OSR)
Original Memphis Rock & Roll-#1 ....(SUN)
Sun Story ....(RHI)
Sun's Greatest Hits ....(RCA)
Wiggle It
2 In A Room; *S* ....(CUT)
You Make Me Feel Like Dancing
Leo Sayer; *Billboard Top Rock 'N' Roll Hits-1977* (RHI)
Endless Flight ....(CHR)
Mega Hits Dance Classics-#3 ....(PRY)
You Make My Pants Want To Get Up & Dance
Dr. Hook; *Pleasure & Pain* ....(CAP)
You Should Be Dancing
Bee Gees; *Billboard Top Dance Hits-1976* .... (RHI)
Children Of The World ....(RSO)
Greatest ....(POL)
Here At Last ....(RSO)
ST/Saturday Night Fever ....(POL)
Your Mama Don't Dance
Loggins & Messina; *Best Of-Friends* ....(COL)
Loggins & Messina ....(COL)
On Stage ....(COL)
Pop Classics Of The '70s ....(COL)
Poison; *Open Up And Say Ahhhh* ....(CAP)
Swallow This Live ....(CAP)

DAYS OF THE WEEK: FRIDAY

Bad Friday
Eek-A-Mouse; *Assassinator* ....(RAS)
Black Friday
Splinter; *Two Man Band* ....(MCA)
Steely Dan; *Greatest Hits* ....(MCA)
Katy Lied ....(MCA)
Born On A Friday
Cleo Laine; *Born On A Friday* ....(RCA)
Return To Carnegie ....(RCA)
Linda Hopkins; *How Blue Can You Get* ....(QKS)
Chattahoochee
Alan Jackson; *Lot About Livin' (& A Little 'Bout
Love)* .... (ARI)
Friday
Joe Jackson; *I'm The Man* ....(A&M)
J.J. Cale; *5* .... (SHE)
Friday I'm In Love
Cure; *Wish* .... (ELE)
Friday Night
Loverboy; *Lovin' Every Minute Of It* ....(COL)
Roy Orbison; *Laminar Flow* ....(ASY)
Friday Night Blues
John Conlee; *Friday Night Blues* ....(MCA)
Greatest Hits ....(MCA)
Sonny Throckmorton; *45* ....(MER)
Friday On My Mind
David Bowie; *Pin-Ups* ....(RYK)
Easybeats; *Best Of* ....(RHI)
Nuggets-Classic Collection/'60s .... (RHI)
Friday The 13th
Alvin Lee; *Rocket Fuel* ....(RSO)
Friday The 13th Child
David Clayton-Thomas; *Clayton* ....(MCA)
Friday's Angels
Generation X; *Valley Of The Dolls* ....(CHR)
Get 'Em Out By Friday
Genesis; *Foxtrot* ....(CHS)
Good Friday
Crust; *Crust* ....(TNC)

Livin' For The Weekend
O'Jays; *Collector's Items* .... (PI)
Family Reunion .... (PI)
Livin' It Up (Friday Night)
Bell & James; *Bell & James* ....(A&M)
Monday Thru' Friday
Cliff Richard; *We Don't Talk Anymore* .... (EMI)
Never On Friday
Willie Smith; *Best Of* ....(CRS)
Quiet Friday
Stan Kenton Orchestra; *Fire Fury & Fun* ....(CW)
Thank God It's Friday
Love & Kisses; *12"* ....(CAS)
Thank Goodness It's Friday
Moe Bandy & Joe Stampley; *Greatest Hits* ....(COL)
Just Good Ol' Boys ....(COL)

DAYS OF THE WEEK: MONDAY

48 Hours Till Monday
Sawyer Brown; *Buick* ....(CCB)
Another Monday
John Renbourn; *John Renbourn* ....(RPR)
Atlantic Monday
Nick Heyward; *North Of A Miracle* .... (ARI)
Blue Monday
Bobby Darin; *Darin 1963-73* ....(MOT)
Fats Domino; *At Montreux* ....(ATL)
Fats Domino ....(AUF)
Greatest Hits ....(EVR)
Greatest Hits ....(MCA)
Super Oldies/'50s-#5 ....(AUF)
Huey Lewis/News; *Four Chords & Several Years
Ago* .... (ELE)
Kingsnakes; *19 Lucky Strikes* ....(BWV)
Hardlife Boogie ....(BWV)
Blue Monday At Kansas City Red's
Cary Bell; *Blues Harp* ....(DEL)
Blue Monday People
Curtis Mayfield; *America Today* .... (CUR)
Born On A Monday
Michael Quatro; *Bottom Line* .... (SPC)
Chelsea Monday
Marillion; *Script For A Jester's Tear* ....(CAP)
Thieving Magpie ....(CAP)
Come Monday
Jimmy Buffett; *Living & Dying In 3/4 Time* ..... (MCA)
Songs You Know By Heart ....(MCA)
You Had To Be There ....(MCA)
Except For Monday
Lorrie Morgan; *Something In Red* ....(RCA)
Gloomy Monday
Jimi Hendrix & Curtis Knight; *Get That Feeling* .. (FFT)
Go To Work On Monday
Si Kahn; *Doing My Job* ....(FF)
Gonna Go To Work On Monday One More Time
Fiction Brothers; *Things Are Coming My Way* ......(FF)
Goodbye Blue Monday
City Boy; *Dinner At The Ritz* .... (MER)
Goodbye Monday Blues
Si Kahn; *Home* ....(FF)
I Don't Like Mondays
Bob Geldof/Johnny Fingers; *Secret Policeman's Other
Ball* .... (ISL)
Boomtown Rats; *Fine Art Of Surfacing* ....(COL)
If We're Not Back In Love By Monday
Merle Haggard; *Greatest Hits* ....(MCA)
Legends ....(MCA)
MCA Records 30 Years Of Hits-1958-1988 ... (MCA)
More Of The Best ....(MCA)
Ramblin' Fever ....(MCA)
It Sure Is Monday
Mark Chesnutt; *Almost Goodbye* ....(MCA)
Jam On Monday Morning
Buddy Guy; *Man & The Blues* .... (VAN)
Laundromat Monday
Joe Jackson; *ST/Mike's Murder* ....(A&M)
Manic Monday
Bangles; *Different Light* ....(COL)
Greatest Hits ....(COL)
Monday
Sonny & Cher; *Two Of Us* ....(ATL)

Monday Date
Earl "Fatha" Hines; *Hot Hazz 1928-30* .... (NIM)
  Monday Date .... (RVR)
  Piano Giants .... (PRS)
Louis Armstrong; *Hot Fives & Hot Sevens-#3* ....(COL)
Satchmo-Musical Autobiography .... (MCA)
Monday Love
Tara Kemp; *Tara Kemp* .... (GIA)
Monday Monday
Mamas & The Papas; *Best Of* .... (MCA)
  Billboard Top Rock 'N' Roll Hits-1966 .... (RHI)
  Farewell To The First Golden Era .... (ARI)
  Gathering Of The Flowers ....(DHL)
  ST/Stardust ....(DHL)
  Vintage Music-Orig. Classics/'60s-#9 ......(MCA)
Neil Diamond; *Double Gold* ....(BNG)
  Feel Of ....(BNG)
  Gang At Bang ....(BNG)
  Shilo ....(BNG)
Monday Morning
Church; *Gold Afternoon Fix* .... (ARI)
Fleetwood Mac; *25 Years-The Chain* .... (WB)
  Fleetwood Mac ....(RPR)
  Live ....(WB)
Peter, Paul & Mary; *Song Will Rise* .... (WB)
Monday Morning Blues
Breathe; *All That Jazz* .... (A&M)
Mississippi John Hurt; *Best Of* .... (VAN)
  Candy Man .... (INT)
Monday Morning In Paradise
Tom Paxton; *One Million Lawyers & Other
Disasters* .... (FF)
Monday Morning Quarterback
Frank Sinatra; *She Shot Me Down* .... (RPR)
Monday Morning Rock
Marshall Crenshaw; *Field Day* .... (WB)
Monday Morning Secretary
Statler Brothers; *Statler Brothers* .... (MER)
Monday Mornin' Keep A Hurtin' Blues
Sonny James; *Little Bit Of Saskatoon* ....(COL)
Monday Night
Golden Palominos; *Golden Palominos* .... (CEL)
  History-1982-1985 ....(MTR)
Pere Ubu; *Cloudland* .... (FON)
Monday Night Football & Me
Turner Rice; *45* ....(BNG)
Monday Struggle
Albert Ammons; *King Of Boogie
Woogie-1939-1949* ....(BCL)
Monday Through Sunday
Gigi Gryce; *Rat Race Blues* .... (NJ)
Monday Thru' Friday
Cliff Richard; *We Don't Talk Anymore* .... (EMI)
Monday We'll Be Together
Nikki D; *Daddy's Little Girl* ....(DFC)
Monday Will Never Be The Same
Husker Du; *Zen Arcade* ....(SST)
Monday's Child
Cambridge Singers; *Fancies* ....(CLG)
Monday's Dance
Ira Sullivan; *Ira Sullivan* .... (FF)
Red Rodney & Ira Sullivan; *Alive In New York* . (MUS)
Month Of Mondays
Jermaine Stewart; *Word Is Out* .... (ARI)
Moody Monday
Mustard's Retreat; *All-Ears Review-#4-More Hot New
Sounds* .... (ROM)
My Monday Date
Earl Hines; *Way Down Yonder In New Orleans* ...(BIO)
Louis Armstrong; *Jazz Masters-27 Classic
Performances* ....(COL)
Never On Monday
Diving For Pearls; *Diving For Pearls* .... (EPI)
New Moon On Monday
Duran Duran; *After The Hurricane* .... (CHR)
  Seven And The Ragged Tiger ....(CAP)
On A Monday
Arlo Guthrie & Pete Seeger; *Together In Concert* (RPR)
Arlo Guthrie/Others; *Tribute To Leadbelly* ...... (TOM)
Leadbelly; *Defense Blues-Golden Classics-#2* .....(CLT)
Ry Cooder; *Into The Purple Valley* ....(RPR)
Our Monday Date
Earl "Fatha" Hines/Band; *Our Monday Date* ....(RVR)
Louis Armstrong; *Hot Fives & Hot Sevens-#3* ....(COL)

Payday/Mine 'Til Monday
Original Broadway Cast; *Tree Grows In Brooklyn* (SMC)
Rainy Days & Mondays
Carpenters; *Carpenters* .... (A&M)
  Classics-#2 ....(A&M)
  Singles 1969-1973 ....(A&M)
  Yesterday Once More ....(A&M)
Paul Williams; *Classics-Here Comes Inspiration* . (A&M)
Stormy Monday (They Call It)
Allman Brothers Band; *At The Fillmore East* .....(POL)
  Road Goes On Forever ....(POL)
Big Joe Turner; *Stormy Monday (They Call It)* ... (PAB)
Bobby Bland; *Best Of* ....(MCA)
  Here's The Man ....(MCA)
  Legends Of Electric Blues Guitar-#1 .... (RHI)
  Tuesday's Just As Bad .... (KT)
Buddy Guy; *My Time After Awhile* .... (VAN)
Jethro Tull; *20 Years Of-Radio Archives & Rare
Tracks* .... (CHR)
Little Milton; *Best Of Chess Blues* .... (CSS)
Lou Rawls; *Legendary* .... (BLN)
T-Bone Walker; *Best Of Blues-#2* .... (MSP)
  Jazz Heritage-Dirty Mistreater .... (MCA)
Sunday Monday Or Always
Frank Sinatra; *Hello Young Lovers* ....(COL)
  In The Beginning ....(COL)
Sunday Mondays
Vanessa Paradis; *Vanessa Paradis* .... (POL)
Sunny Monday
Booker T./M.G.s; *Melting Pot* .... (STX)
Thank God It's Monday
Dene Anton; *Texas Soul* .... (JRS)

xxxxxxxxxxxxxxxxxxxxxxxxxxxxxxxxxxxxxxxxxxxxxxxxxxxxxxxxx

DAYS OF THE WEEK: SATURDAY, Sat. Night

10:15 Saturday Night
Cure; *Boys Don't Cry* .... (ELE)
  Standing On The Beach: Singles .... (ELE)
Almost Saturday Night
Dave Edmunds; *Anthology-1968-1990* .... (RHI)
  Best Of .... (SS)
  Twangin' .... (SS)
Gene Clark & Carla Olson; *So Rebellious A Lover* (RHI)
Georgia Satellites; *Let It Rock-Best Of* .... (ELE)
Rick Nelson; *Stay Young-Epic Recordings* .... (EPI)
Always Saturday
Guadalcanal Diary; *Flip-Flop* .... (ELE)
Another Lonely Saturday Night
Greg Kihn Band; *With The Naked Eye* .... (BES)
Another Saturday Night
Cat Stevens; *Greatest Hits* ....(A&M)
Sam Cooke; *Man & His Music* ....(RCA)
  This Is ....(RCA)
Book Of Saturday
King Crimson; *Lark's Tongues In Aspic* .... (EDI)
Clock Strikes Ten
Cheap Trick; *At Budokan* .... (EPI)
  In Color .... (EPI)
Come Dancing
Kinks; *Come Dancing-Best Of* .... (ARI)
  Live-The Road .... (MCA)
  State Of Confusion .... (ARI)
Come Saturday Morning
Sandpipers; *Four Sider* .... (A&M)
  Super Hits/'70s-Have A Nice Day-#1 .... (RHI)
Donald & Lydia
John Prine; *John Prine* ....(ATL)
  Prime Prine ....(ATL)
Down To The Night Club
Tower Of Power; *Bump City* .... (WB)
  Live & In Living Color .... (WB)
Drive In Saturday
David Bowie; *Aladdin Sane* ....(RYK)
  Sound + Vision ....(RYK)
  The Singles-1969-1993 ....(RYK)
Every Saturday Night
Young's Creole Band; *Chicago Jazz (1923-1929)* .(BIO)
Everybody Loves Saturday Night
New Christy Minstrels; *Greatest Hits* ....(COL)
Everyday/Saturday
Greg Kihn Band; *Kihntinued* .... (BES)

Heart Of Saturday Night (Looking For...)
Shawn Colvin; *Cover Girl* ....(COL)
Tom Waits; *Anthology* ....(ASY)
   Heart Of Saturday Night (Looking For...) ....(ASY)
Homegrown Western Saturday Night
Chris LeDoux; *Powder River* ....(LIB)
It Always Rains On Saturday
Reba McEntire; *Sweet Sixteen* ....(MCA)
It's Going On Saturday
Aztec Two-Step; *See It Was Like This...Acoustic
Retrosp.* ....(FF)
I've Got Five Dollars & It's Saturday...
Gene Pitney; *Anthology* ....(RHI)
Livingston Saturday Night
Jimmy Buffett; *Son Of A Son Of A Sailor* ...... (MCA)
   ST/FM ....(MCA)
Louisiana Saturday Night
Don Williams; *Best Of Cajun Country* ....(ERA)
   Best Of-#4 ....(MCA)
   Country Boy ....(MCA)
Jimmy C. Newman; *Progressive CC* ....(PLN)
Mel McDaniel; *Greatest Hits* ....(CAP)
On A Saturday Night
Journey; *In The Beginning* ....(COL)
   Look Into The Future ....(COL)
Queen Ida/Bon Temps Zydeco Band; *On A Saturday
Night* .... (CRS)
On Saturday Afternoons In 1963
Rickie Lee Jones; *Rickie Lee Jones* .... (WB)
One More Saturday Night
Bob Weir; *Ace* .... (GRD)
Grateful Dead; *Europe '72* .... (WB)
   Skeletons From The Closet-Best Of ....(WB)
   Without A Net .... (ARI)
Painless Saturday
Broken Homes; *Broken Homes* ....(MCA)
Piano Man
Billy Joel; *Greatest Hits-#1 & 2* ....(COL)
   Piano Man ....(COL)
   Rock Classics Of The '70s ....(COL)
Thelma Houston; *Motown Superstar Series-#20* . (MOT)
Ready For Saturday Night
Joanna Dean; *Misbehavin'* .... (POL)
Rockin' On A Saturday Night
Jason D. Williams; *Tore Up* ....(RCA)
Sabbath Prayer
Herschel Bernardi; *ST/Fiddler On The Roof* ....(COL)
Original Cast; *Fiddler On The Roof* ....(RCA)
Same Old Saturday Night
Frank Sinatra; *Capitol Collectors Series* ....(CAP)
Saturday
Andre Previn Trio; *Like Previn* .... (CTM)
Carpenters; *Carpenters* ....(A&M)
Deltones; *Oddball Boy* .... (ROI)
Judybeats; *Down In The Shacks Where The
Satellite.* ....(SIR)
Mose Allison; *Back Country Suite* ....(PRS)
Original Sins; *Move* .... (PSO)
Sarah Vaughan; *Complete On Mercury-#1-Great Jazz
Years* .... (MER)
Saturday Afternoon
Cassell Webb; *Thief Of Sadness* ....(VEN)
Jefferson Airplane; *After Bathing At Baxters* ......(RCA)
   Flight Log 1966-1976 .... (GRU)
   ST/Woodstock Two ....(ATL)
Thelonius Monsters; *Next Saturday Afternoon* .... (REL)
Saturday Asylum
Rain Parade; *Best Of The Radio Tokyo Tapes* ....(CHS)
Saturday At Midnight
Cheap Trick; *One On One* .... (EPI)
Saturday Blues
Ishman Bracey; *Canned Heat Blues-Masters Of Delta
Blues* ....(BLU)
Saturday Boy
Billy Bragg; *Back To Basics* ....(ELE)
Saturday Clothes
Gordon Lightfoot; *If You Could Read My Mind* .. (RPR)
Saturday Dance
Bob Cooper; *Coop! Music Of* .... (CTM)
Saturday Evening
Ronnie Laws; *Best Of* ....(BLN)
Saturday Evening Blues
Larry Johnson; *Country Blues* ....(BIO)

Saturday Freedom
Blue Cheer; *Good Times Are So Hard To Find* .. (MER)
Saturday Gigs
Ian Hunter/Mott The Hoople; *Shades Of Ian
Hunter* ....(COL)
Mott The Hoople; *Ballad Of MoSaturday
Gigs-Retrospective* ....(COL)
   Greatest Hits ....(COL)
Saturday In The Park
Chicago; *Greatest Hits* ....(COL)
   If You Leave Me Now ....(COL)
   ST/My Girl ....(EPI)
   V ....(COL)
Saturday Love
Cherrelle & Alexander O'Neal; *Club Epic* ....(EPI)
   High Priority ....(TAB)
Saturday Matinee
Gordon Brisker; *About Charlie* .... (DCO)
Saturday Miles
Miles Davis; *At Fillmore* ....(COL)
Saturday Morning
Harry Chapin; *Greatest Stories-Live* ....(ELE)
Joe Higgs; *Black Man Know Yourself* ....(SHA)
Meat Puppets; *Meat Puppets* ....(SST)
Tom Chapin; *In The City Of Mercy* ....(SPC)
Van Morrison; *Best Of* ....(BNG)
Saturday Morning Cartoons
Sergio Salvatore; *Sergio Salvatore* ....(GRP)
Saturday Morning Confusion
Bobby Russell; *Super Hits/'70s-Have A Nice
Day-#6* .... (RHI)
Saturday Morning Fever
Loudon Wainwright III; *Fame & Wealth* .... (ROU)
Saturday Morning Movies
Bonnie Koloc; *At Her Best* ....(OVA)
   Bonnie Koloc ....(OVA)
Saturday Night
Bay City Rollers; *Bay City Rollers* .... (ARI)
   Billboard Top Rock 'N' Roll Hits-1976 ....(RHI)
   Greatest Hits .... (ARI)
   Super Hits/'70s-Have A Nice Day-#15 ....(RHI)
Blue Nile; *Hats* ....(A&M)
Bobby Fuller Four; *Best Of* ....(RHI)
Bobby King & Terry Evans; *Live & Let Live* .... (ROU)
Buddy Blue; *Guttersnipes 'N' Zealots* ....(RHI)
Bunny Wailer; *Rule Dance Hall* ....(SHA)
Commodores; *In The Pocket* ....(MOT)
Count Basie; *Comnpact Jazz-Standards* ....(VRV)
Eagles; *Desperado* ....(ASY)
   Live ....(ASY)
Herman Brood/Wild Romance; *Herman Brood/Wild
Romance* ....(ARL)
John Waite; *No Brakes* ....(EMI)
Kay Starr; *Country* ....(CRS)
Maynard Ferguson; *Maynard '61* ....(RLL)
Original Cast; *Marry Me A Little* ....(RCA)
Red Norvo Quintet; *Forward Look* ....(REF)
Schoolly-D; *Adventures Of* ....(RYK)
Ten Years After; *About Time* ....(CHR)
Saturday Night At Sea
John Townley/Press Gang; *Chesapeake Sailor's
Companion* .... (ADE)
Saturday Night At The General Store
Margo Smith; *Happiness* ....(WB)
Saturday Night At The Movies
Drifters; *16 Greatest Hits* ....(TRP)
   All-Time Greatest Hits & More-1959-1965 .....(ATL)
   Golden Hits ....(ATL)
   Save The Last Dance For Me ....(FFT)
Saturday Night At The World
Mason Williams; *Music-1968-1971* ....(VAN)
Mason Williams/Mannheim Steamroller; *Classical
Gas* ....(AG)
Saturday Night Blues
Kenny Burrell; *Midnight Blue* ....(BLN)
Saturday Night Boogie
Harry Crafton; *Harry Crafton* ....(CLT)
Saturday Night Down South
Charlie Daniels Band; *Simple Man* ....(EPI)
Saturday Night Fish Fry
Louis Jordan; *Best Of* ....(MCA)
   No Moe! Greatest Hits ....(VRV)
Pearl Bailey; *16 Most Requested Songs* ....(COL)

Saturday Night Fish Fry Drag
Joe Robichaux/New Orleans Boys; *Joe Robichaux/New Orleans Boys-1933* .... (FLK)
Saturday Night Function
Duke Ellington; *Okeh Ellington* ....(COL)
Saturday Night In Dallas
Kenny Seratt; *45* ....(MDJ)
Saturday Night In Dublin
Michael "Jesse" Owens; *Across The Sea To Ireland* .... (RGO)
Saturday Night Is The Loneliest Night...
Frank Sinatra; *Come Dance With Me* ....(CAP)
  Greatest Hits-Early Years ....(COL)
  In The Beginning ....(COL)
Saturday Night Jag
Clarence Williams/Orchestra; *Clarence Williams/Orchestra-#1 (1927-1929)* ....(BIO)
"Saturday Night Live" Theme
Original Music; *Television's Greatest Hits-#3* .....(TVT)
Saturday Night Live Band; *Jazz...The Digital Age* ... (PJ)
Saturday Night Rub
Big Bill Broonzy; *Young Big Bill Broonzy-1928-1935* ....(YAZ)
Saturday Night Special
Lynyrd Skynyrd; *Gold & Platinum* ....(MCA)
  Nuthin' Fancy ....(MCA)
  One More From The Road ....(MCA)
  Skynyrd's Innyrds ....(MCA)
Terry McBride/Ride; *Skynyrd Frynds* ....(MCA)
Saturday Night Stomp
Eddie "Blues Man" Kirkland; *It's The Blues Man!* .. (TS)
Saturday Night U.S.A.
Charlie Daniels Band; *Powder Keg* ....(EPI)
Saturday Night & Sunday Morning
Phil Collins; *...But Seriously* ....(ATL)
Saturday Night (I Get All My Lovin')
Billy Strange; *Best Of* ....(CRS)
Saturday Night, Sunday Morning
Thelma Houston; *Motown Superstars Series-#20* (MOT)
  Ride To The Rainbow ....(MOT)
Saturday Night's Alright For Fighting
Elton John; *Goodbye Yellow Brick Road* ....(POL)
  Greatest Hits ....(POL)
  Knebworth-The Album ....(POL)
  Rock Classics .... (KT)
Who; *Two Rooms-Songs Of E. John & B. Taupin* (POL)
Saturday Nite
Earth, Wind & Fire; *Best Of-#2* ....(COL)
  Eternal Dance ....(COL)
  Spirit ....(COL)
Saturday Nite Is Dead
Graham Parker/Rumour; *Squeezing Out Sparks* .. (ARI)
Saturday Nite Live
Masta Ace; *Slaughtahouse* .... (DV)
Saturday Sailing
James Morrison; *Postcards From Down Under* ...(ATL)
Saturday Suit
Art Garfunkel; *Watermark* ....(COL)
Saturday Sun
Nick Drake; *Five Leaves Left* ....(HBL)
Saturday & Sunday
Jackie McLean; *One Step Beyond* ....(BLN)
Saturdays
David Benoit; *Every Step Of The Way* ....(GRP)
Saturday's Child
Monkees; *Listen To The Band* .... (RHI)
  More Greatest Hits Of .... (ARI)
Saturday's Father
Frankie Valli/Four Seasons; *25th Anniversrary Collection* .... (RHI)
Saturday's Heroes
Business; *Business-1979-1989* ....(BLA)
Saturday's Kids
Jam; *Setting Sons* ....(POL)
She's My Saturday Night Special
Ronnie McDowell; *Unchained Melody* ....(CCB)
Wayne Newton; *Best Of-Now* ....(CCB)
Small Town Saturday Night
Hal Ketchum; *Past The Point Of Rescue* ....(CRB)
Soul Meeting Saturday Night
Priscilla Bowman; *45* ....(OOP)
Standing On The Corner
Broadway Cast; *Most Happy Fella* ....(RCA)
Four Lads; *16 Most Requested Songs* ....(COL)

Original Broadway Cast; *Most Happy Fella* ..... (SMC)
Sugar Hill Saturday Night
Charlie Daniels Band; *Midnight Wind* ....(EPI)
Sunless Saturday
Fishbone; *Reality Of My Surroundings* ....(COL)
Sunshine Saturday Morning
Jim Aikin; *Light's Broken Speech Revived* ....(LIN)
Tennessee Saturday Night
Ella Mae Morse; *Capitol Collectors Series* ....(CAP)
Tennessee Saturday Nite
Commander Cody/Lost Planet Airmen; *Aces High* ....(RLX)
Texas On A Saturday Night
Willie Nelson & Mel Tillis; *Half Nelson* ....(COL)
Whatever Happened To Saturday Night
Tim Curry; *ST/Rocky Horror Picture Show* .... (RHI)
Tim Curry/Original Roxy Cast; *Rocky Horror Show* .... (RHI)
Where Did Robinson Crusoe Go With Friday
Ian Whitcomb; *45* ....(OSR)

DAYS OF THE WEEK: SUNDAY

Always On A Sunday
Frank Anderson & Tommy McCook; *Ska Bonanza-Studio One Ska Years* ....(HRT)
Angel's Sunday
Jim Ed Brown; *Best Of* ....(RCA)
Another Kind Of Sunday
Gerry Mulligan; *Little Big Horn* ....(GRP)
Another Park, Another Sunday
Doobie Brothers; *What Were Once Vices...* ....(WB)
As Long As There's A Sunday
Sammi Smith; *As Long As There's A Sunday* .. (ELE)
Beautiful Sunday
Daniel Boone; *Back To The Seventies-#2* ....(DOM)
  Super Hits/'70s-Have A Nice Day-#9 ....(RHI)
Roy Drusky; *English Gold* ....(PLN)
Birmingham Sunday
Joan Baez; *Contemporary Ballad Book* ....(VAN)
  Joan Baez ....(VAN)
Black Sabbath
Black Sabbath; *Black Sabbath* ....(WB)
  Live Evil ....(WB)
  We Sold Our Soul For Rock 'N' Roll ....(WB)
Ozzy Osbourne; *Speak Of The Devil* ....(JET)
Black Sunday
Jethro Tull; *A* ....(CHR)
Skatalites; *Ska Bonanza-Studio One Ska Years* ....(HRT)
Blue Sunday
Doors; *Morrison Hotel/Hard Rock Cafe* .... (ELE)
Come Sunday
Jennifer Holliday; *Say You Love Me* ....(GEF)
Johnny Mathis; *In A Sentimental Mood-Sings Ellington* ....(COL)
Dayton Ohio 1903
Randy Newman; *Sail Away* ....(RPR)
Don't Take My Sunday Paper
Holly Near & Jeff Langley; *You Can Know All I Am* ....(RWD)
Drinkin' In My Sunday Dress
Maria McKee; *Maria McKee* ....(GEF)
Eastern Sundays
Moraz & Bruford; *Music For Piano & Drums* .... (EDI)
Easy
Commodores; *20 Greatest Songs In Motown History* ....(MOT)
  All The Great Love Songs ....(MOT)
  Commodores ....(MOT)
  Compact Command Performances ....(MOT)
  Composer-Great Love Songs By L. Richie ......(MOT)
  Greatest Hits ....(MOT)
Every Day Is Like Sunday
Morrissey; *Best Of MTV's 120 Minutes-#2* ....(RHI)
  Bona Drag ....(SIR)
  Viva Hate ....(SIR)
Every Day Seems Like Sunday
Buddy Moss; *Rediscovery* ....(BIO)
Every Sunday Afternoon
Bobby Short; *Celebrates Rodgers & Hart* ....(ATL)
Food (Till Sunday) (No)
Click Click; *Wet Skin & Curious Eye* ....(PIA)

Girl With Faraway Eyes
Rolling Stones; *Some Girls* ....(RS)
Gloomy Sunday
Billie Holiday; *Greatest Hits* ....(COL)
Legacy Box 1933-1958 ....(COL)
Hymn For A Sunday Evening
Original Cast; *Bye Bye Birdie* ....(COL)
I Met Him On A Sunday
Shirelles; *16 Greatest Hits* ....(TRP)
Anthology 1959-1967 ....(RHI)
Classics ....(BCT)
Greatest Hits ....(EVR)
It Always Rains On Sundays
Box; *Pleasure & The Pain* ....(CAP)
It Must Be Sunday
Phoebe Snow; *Phoebe Snow* .... (MCA)
It's A Shame To Ship Your Wife On Sunday
Fiddlin' John Carson; *Old Hen Cackled (& The
Rooster's...)* .... (ROU)
It's Sunday
Frank Sinatra; *Reprise Collection* ....(RPR)
I'll Be Back A Sunday
Little Jimmy Dickens; *Columbia Historic Edition* .(COL)
Jamaica Sunday Morning
Kim Carnes; *St. Vincent's Court* ....(OOP)
Just Another Sunday
Blasters; *Hard Line* ....(SLS)
George Benson & Jack McDuff; *George Benson & Jack
McDuff* ....(PRS)
Lazy Day
Moody Blues; *On The Threshold Of A Dream* .... (POL)
Lazy Sunday
Small Faces; *Immediate Singles Collection-#2* .....(SSP)
Ogden's Nut Gone-Flake ....(AKO)
Like A Sunday In Salem
Gene Cotton; *No Strings Attached* ....(ARL)
Save The Dancer ....(ARL)
Louisiana Sunday Afternoon
Diane Schuur; *Collection* ....(GRP)
Talkin' 'Bout You ....(GRP)
Loving You Sunday Morning
Scorpions; *Lovedrive* ....(MER)
World Wide Live ....(MER)
Monday Through Sunday
Gigi Gryce; *Rat Race Blues* .... (NJ)
Month Of Sundays
Church; *Remote Luxury* ....(ARI)
Ernest Tubb; *45* ....(FSG)
Saigon Kick; *Saigon Kick* ....(THI)
Vern Gosdin; *Out Of My Heart* ....(COL)
Mr. Sunday
Simon Townshend; *Sweet Sound* .... (21)
My Sunday Feeling
Jethro Tull; *This Was* .... (CHR)
My Sunday Gal
Duke Ellington; *Great Ellington Units* .... (BLU)
Naked Sunday
Stone Temple Pilots; *Core* ....(ATL)
Never On Sunday
Andy Williams; *Moon River & Other Great Movie
Themes* ....(COL)
Boston Pops Orchestra/Arthur Fiedler; *Greatest Hits Of
The '60s* ....(RCA)
Motion Pictures Classics ....(RCA)
Boston Pops Orchestra/John Williams; *Digital
Jukebox* ....(PHI)
Chordettes; *Greatest Hits* ....(EVR)
No Plane On Sunday
Jimmy Buffett; *Floridays* .... (MCA)
On A Sunday Afternoon
Lighter Shade Of Brown & Huggy Boy; *Brown &
Proud* ....(PMP)
On A Sunday By The Sea
Original Broadway Cast; *Jerome Robbins'
Broadway* ....(RCA)
On Sunday
'Til Tuesday; *Welcome Home* ....(EPI)
On Sunday Afternoon
Harptones; *Echoes Of A Rock Era* ....(RLL)
One Million Billionth Of A...
Flaming Lips; *Oh My Gawd The Flaming Lips* ... (RES)
Our Sunday Morning
Yoshio "Chin" Suzuki; *Morning Picture* .... (JVC)

Palm Sunday
Jerry Garcia; *Cats Under The Stars* .... (ARI)
Pleasant Valley Sunday
Monkees; *Greatest Hits* .... (ARI)
Listen To The Band .... (RHI)
Nuggets-Classic Collection/Psyched. '60s .... (RHI)
Put On Your Sunday Clothes
Original Cast; *Hello Dolly* ....(RCA)
Puttin' On My Sunday Best
Dick & Mel Tunney; *Let The Dreamers Dream* .... (WB)
Rockport Sunday
Tom Rush; *Circle Game* .... (ELE)
Sabbath, Bloody Sabbath
Anthrax; *I'm The Man* .... (ISL)
Black Sabbath; *Sabbath, Bloody Sabbath* .... (WB)
We Sold Our Soul For Rock 'N' Roll ....(WB)
Ozzy Osbourne; *Speak Of The Devil* ....(JET)
Sad Rush on Sunday
Dylans; *Dylans* ....(BEG)
Saturday Night & Sunday Morning
Phil Collins; *...But Seriously* ....(ATL)
Saturday Night, Sunday Morning
Thelma Houston; *Motown Superstars Series-#20* (MOT)
Ride To The Rainbow ....(MOT)
Saturday & Sunday
Jackie McLean; *One Step Beyond* .... (BLN)
Second Sunday In August
Weather Report; *I Sing The Body Electric* ....(COL)
Seven Days Come Sunday
Rodney Lay; *Silent Partners* ....(SUN)
Seven Sundays
Extreme; *III Sides To Every Story* .... (A&M)
Seventeen Come Sunday
John Wright & Catherine Perrier; *Traditional Music Of
France, Ireland...* ....(GRE)
She Used To Sing On Sunday
Larry Gatlin/Gatlin Brothers; *17 Greatest Hits* ...(COL)
Greatest Hits-#2 ....(COL)
Six-Thirty Sunday Morning
Peter Allen; *Taught By Experts* .... (A&M)
Sugar On Sunday
Tommy James/Shondells; *Anthology* .... (RHI)
Best Of .... (RLL)
Crimson & Clover/Cellophane Symphony .... (RHI)
Sunday
Andreas Vollenweider; *Trilogy (Behind The
Gardens)* ....(COL)
Carmen McRae; *Blue Note Meets The L. A.
Philharmonic* .... (BLN)
Great American Songbook ....(ATL)
In Person ....(MST)
Cranberries; *Everybody Else Is Doing It So Why...* . (ISL)
Frank Sinatra; *Songs For Young Lovers & Swing
Easy* ....(CAP)
Michael Feinstein; *Sings The Julie Styne Songbook* (ELE)
Original Cast; *ST/Flower Drum Song* ....(COL)
Sunday In The Park With George ....(RCA)
Sunday Afternoon
Candy Dulfer; *Sax-A-Go-Go* ....(RCA)
Sunday Afternoon In The Park
Van Halen; *Fair Warning* .... (WB)
Sunday Bloody Sunday
Elephants Memory/Invisible Strings; *Sometime In New
York City* ....(CAP)
U2; *Under A Blood Red Sky* .... (ISL)
War .... (ISL)
Sunday Driving
Jerry Lewis; *Capitol Collectors Series* ....(CAP)
Dr. Demento's Greatest-#2-1950s .... (RHI)
Sunday For Tea
Peter & Gordon; *Best Of* .... (RHI)
Sunday Girl
Blondie; *Best Of* .... (CHR)
Parallel Lines ....(CHR)
Sunday In Genoa
101 Strings Orchestra; *30th Anniversary* .... (ALS)
Sunday In New York
Mel Torme; *Songs Of New York* ....(ATL)
Sunday In The Park With George
Original Cast; *Sunday In The Park With George* ..(RCA)
Sunday In The South
Shenandoah; *30 Years Of #1 Hits-#19* ....(COL)
Greatest Hits ....(COL)
Road Not Taken ....(COL)

Sunday Kind Of Love
Ben Sidran; *That's Life I Guess* ....(BLU)
Ella Fitzgerald; *Best Of-#2* ....(MCA)
Harptones; *Collectables Presents History Of
Rock-#6* ....(CLT)
Kenny Rankin; *Inside* ....(LD)
Reba McEntire; *Reba* ....(MCA)
Sunday Kind Of Woman
Charlie Rich; *Behind Closed Doors* ....(EPI)
Sunday Monday Or Always
Frank Sinatra; *Hello Young Lovers* ....(COL)
In The Beginning ....(COL)
Sunday Mondays
Vanessa Paradis; *Vanessa Paradis* ....(POL)
Sunday Morning
Velvet Underground; *Live At Max's Kansas City* . (COT)
Sunday Morning Blues
Big Joe Turner; *Big Joe Is Here* ....(SAV)
Have No Fear ....(SAV)
Sunday Morning Coming Down
Johnny Cash; *Classic Cash-Hall Of Fame Series* . (MER)
Greatest Hits-#2 ....(COL)
Kris Kristofferson; *Me & Bobby McGee* ....(COL)
Songs Of ....(COL)
Vikki Carr; *Best Of* ....(EMI)
Willie Nelson; *Sings Kristofferson* ....(COL)
Willie ....(RCA)
Sunday Morning Fool
Michael Dinner; *Great Pretenders* ....(FAN)
Sunday Morning Movies
Bonnie Koloc; *At Her Best* ....(OVA)
Bonnie Koloc ....(OVA)
Sunday Morning Radio
Sha-Na-Na; *Sh-Boom* ....(ACC)
Sunday Morning Sunshine
Harry Chapin; *Anthology* ....(ELE)
Savoy Brown Collection ....(DER)
Sunday Night In San Fernando
Mel Torme/Mel-Tones; *California Suite* ....(DCO)
Sunday Papers
Joe Jackson; *Live-1980-1986* ....(A&M)
Look Sharp! ....(A&M)
No Wave ....(A&M)
Sunday Rider
David Gates; *First* ....(ELE)
Goodbye Girl ....(ELE)
Sunday School To Broadway
Sammi Smith; *45* ....(ELE)
Sunday Song
Courtney Pine; *Jorney To The Urge Within* ......(AND)
Sunday Sun
Neil Diamond; *Glory Road-1968-1972* ....(MCA)
Velvet Gloves & Spit ....(MCA)
Sunday Sunrise
Brenda Lee; *Greatest Country Hits* ....(MCA)
Sunday Will Never Be The Same
Spanky & Our Gang; *Flower Power* ....(KT)
Sunday & Me
Jay/Americans; *All-Time Greatest Hits* ....(RHI)
Come A Little Bit Closer-Best Of ....(EMI)
Teen Rock Singles-1956-1966 ....(EMI)
Sunday's Best
Elvis Costello; *Girls Girls Girls* ....(COL)
Taking Liberties ....(COL)
Sweet Sunday Kinda Love
Honeys; *Capitol Collectors Series* ....(CAP)
Tell It To The Judge On Sunday
Long Ryders; *Native Sons* ....(FRN)
Tell Me On A Sunday
Marti Webb; *Premiere Collection-Best Of A.L.
Webber* ....(MCA)
Michael Crawford; *Performs Andrew Lloyd
Webber* ....(ATL)
That Sunday That Summer
Betty Carter; *Compact Jazz-Best Of The Jazz
Vocalists* ....(VRV)
Nat King Cole; *Nat King Cole* ....(CAP)
Unforgettable Nat King Cole ....(CAP)
Natalie Cole; *Unforgettable* ....(ELE)
Theme For Sunday
Stan Kenton; *Jazz Compositions Of* ....(CW)
Retrospective-Capitol Years-#1 ....(BLN)
Tippin' Home From Sunday School
Oliver Jones; *Class Act* ....(JUS)

Ugly Sunday
Mark Lanegan; *Grunge Years* ....(SP)
Winding Sheet ....(SP)
Warm Sunday
Conrad Herwig Quintet; *The Amulet* ....(KNR)
Whiskey On A Sunday (Puppet Song)
Irish Rovers; *Greatest Hits* ....(MCA)

DAYS OF THE WEEK: THURSDAY

3:10 Smokey Thursday
Danny O'Keefe; *Seattle Tapes* ....(FIR)
Blue Thursday
Franz Jackson Original All-Stars; *Featuring Bob
Shoffner* ....(RVR)
He Met Me On A Thursday Morning
Johnie Lewis; *Alabama Slide Guitar* ....(ARH)
Holy Thursday
Greg Brown; *Songs Of Innocence & Experience* . (RDH)
Misty Thursday
Duke Jordan; *Misty Thursday* ....(IC)
Sweet Thursday
Helen Traubel/Original Cast; *Pipe Dream* ....(RCA)
Icicle Works; *If You Want To Defeat Your
Enemy...* ....(BEG)
Sweet Thursday; *Sweet Thursday* ....(OOP)
Thursday
Count Basie; *Good Morning Blues* ....(MCA)
Country Joe/Fish; *I Feel Like I'm Fixin' To Die* .. (VAN)
Cranes; *Wings Of Joy* ....(DED)
Jim Croce; *50th Anniversary Collection* ....(SAJ)
I Got A Name ....(LIF)
Time In A Bottle ....(21)
Mike Auldridge & Old Dog; *Mike Auldridge & Old
Dog* ....(FF)
Thursday Afternoon
Brian Eno; *Thursday Afternoon* ....(EDI)
Thursday Club
Truth; *Playground* ....(IRS)
Thursday Miles
Miles Davis; *At Fillmore* ....(COL)
Thursday Morning Garden Club
Buddy Winfield; *45* ....(NAT)
Thursday Night Fever
Legendary Pink Dots; *Legendary Pink Dots* ......(PIA)
Thursday's Child
Abbey Lincoln; *Abbey Is Blue* ....(RVR)
A. Davis/J. Newton/A. Wadud; *Trio 2* ....(GRM)
Barbara Lea; *Barbara Lea* ....(PRS)
Bev Kelly; *Love Locked Out* ....(RVR)
Chameleons UK; *Script Of The Bridge* ....(MCA)
Tanita Tikaram; *Sweet Keeper* ....(RPR)

DAYS OF THE WEEK: TUESDAY

Everything's Tuesday
Chairmen Of The Board; *Soul Hits/'70s-#3* ......(RHI)
Love You Til Tuesday
David Bowie; *London Collector-Starting Point* ....(LON)
Love You Til Tuesday ....(LON)
No More Booze (On Tuesdays)
Freewheelers; *Freewheelers* ....(DGC)
Ruby Tuesday
Rolling Stones; *Between The Buttons* ....(AKO)
Flashpoint ....(RS)
Flowers ....(AKO)
Hot Rocks-1964-1971 ....(AKO)
Singles Collection-London Years ....(AKO)
Through The Past Darkly-Big Hits-#2 ....(AKO)
Sun Comes Up, It's Tuesday
Cowboy Junkies; *Caution Horses* ....(RCA)
Sweet Tuesday Morning
Badfinger; *Straight Up* ....(CAP)
Tuesday Afternoon
Moody Blues; *Caught Live Plus Five* ....(POL)
Days Of Future Passed ....(POL)
ST/1969 ....(POL)
This Is The ....(POL)
Tuesday At Ten
Count Basie; *Essential-#3* ....(COL)
Tuesday Heartbreak
Stevie Wonder; *Talking Book* ....(MOT)

Tuesday Next
Stan Getz; *Billy Highstreet Samba* .... (EMA)
Tuesday Wednesday
Woodentops; *Wooden Foot Cops On The*
Highway ....(COL)
Tuesday's Child
Trouble; *Run To The Light* .... (MET)
Tuesday's Dead
Cat Stevens; *Classics-#24* .... (A&M)
Teaser & The Firecat .... (A&M)
Tuesday's Gone
Hank Williams, Jr.; *Skynyrd Frynds* .... (MCA)
Wild Streak ....(W/C)
Lynyrd Skynyrd; *Gold & Platinum* .... (MCA)
One More From The Road .... (MCA)
Pronounced Leh-nerd Skin-nerd .... (MCA)

DAYS OF THE WEEK: WEDNESDAY

Big Wednesday
Surf M.C.'s; *Surf Or Die* ....(PRO)
She's Leaving Home
Al Jarreau; *All Fly Home* .... (WB)
Beatles; *Box Set* ....(CAP)
Love Songs ....(CAP)
Sgt. Pepper's Lonely Hearts Club Band ....(CAP)
Tuesday Wednesday
Woodentops; *Wooden Foot Cops On The*
Highway ....(COL)
Wednesday
Detroit Emeralds; *Feel The Need* ....(WSB)
Wednesday Car
Johnny Cash; *Rambler* ....(COL)
Wednesday Evening Blues
John Lee Hooker; *Black Snake* ....(FAN)
John Lee Hooker ....(EVR)
That's My Story ....(RVR)
World's Greatest Blues Singer .... (VJ)
Wednesday Morning, 3 AM
Simon & Garfunkel; *Collected Works* ....(COL)
Wednesday Morning, 3 AM ....(COL)

DEATH

See Also: CAPITAL PUNISHMENT, HEAVEN,
HELL, KILL, LIFE

7 Deadly Sins
Mary's Danish; *Circa* ....(MC)
Traveling Wilburys; *#3* .... (WIL)
About To Die
Procol Harum; *Home* .... (A&M)
Ain't No Grave Can Hold My Body Down
Odetta; *Essential* .... (VAN)
One Grain Of Sand .... (VAN)
All Dead All Dead
Queen; *News Of The World* ....(HOL)
American Pie
Don McLean; *American Pie* .... (UA)
Best Of .... (EMI)
Greatest Hits Then & Now .... (EMI)
ST/Born On The Fourth Of July ....(MCA)
And When I Die
Blood, Sweat & Tears; *Blood, Sweat & Tears* ....(COL)
Greatest Hits ....(COL)
In Concert ....(COL)
Laura Nyro; *First Songs* ....(COL)
Live At The Bottom Line ....(CYP)
Another Man Done Gone
Jorma Kaukonen & Tom Hobson; *Quah* ....(RLX)
Pete Seeger/Memphis Slim/Willie Dixon; *Pete Seeger At*
The Village Gate ....(FLW)
Another One Bites The Dust
Queen; *Greatest Hits* ....(HOL)
The Game ....(HOL)
Art Of Dying
George Harrison; *All Things Must Pass* ....(CAP)
At My Funeral
Crash Test Dummies; *The Ghosts That Haunt Me* (ARI)
Axe Victim
Be Bop Deluxe; *Axe Victim* ....(CAP)
Best Of-And The Rest Of ....(CAP)

Baby's In Black
Beatles; *Box Set* ....(CAP)
For Sale ....(CAP)
'65 ....(CAP)
Bang, You're Dead
Bette Midler; *Live At Last* .... (ATL)
Barbara Allen
Joan Baez; *Ballad Book* .... (VAN)
Ballad Book-#2 .... (VAN)
Vol. 2 .... (VAN)
Tom Rush; *Blues Songs Ballads* .... (PRS)
Tom Rush ....(FAN)
Better Off Dead
Elton John; *Captain Fantastic & Brown Dirt*
Cowboy .... (POL)
Ice Cube; *Amerikkka's Most Wanted* ....(PRY)
Blue Tail Fly
Burl Ives; *Best Of* ....(MCA)
Pete Seeger; *20 Golden Pieces Of* ....(BLD)
Bluebird Is Dead
Electric Light Orchestra; *Afterglow* .... (EPI)
On The Third Day ....(JET)
Body Count
Ice-T; *Body Count* .... (WB)
Body To Dust
Joan Armatrading; *Back To The Night* .... (A&M)
Bury Me Beneath The Willow
Jimmy Davis; *Best Of* ....(MCA)
Wilma Lee Cooper; *Wilma Lee Cooper* .... (ROU)
Bury Me Not On The Lone Prairie
Jimmy C. Newman; *Cajun Cowboy* .... (PLN)
Bury My Body
Animals; *Best Of* .... (AKO)
But I Might Die Tonight
Cat Stevens; *Tea For The Tillerman* .... (A&M)
Cadillac Ranch
Bruce Springsteen; *The River* ....(COL)
Bruce Springsteen/E Street Band;
Live-1975-1985 ....(COL)
Nitty Gritty Dirt Band; *More Great Dirt-Best*
Of-#3 .... (WB)
Plain Dirt Fashion .... (WB)
Careful With That Axe Eugene
Pink Floyd; *Relics* ....(CAP)
Umma Gumma ....(CAP)
Casey Jones
Fred McDowell & Furry Lewis; *When I Lay My Burden*
Down ....(BIO)
Clementine
Bobby Darin; *At The Copa* ....(BAI)
Story ....(ATC)
Cockles & Mussels
Emily Mitchell; *The Irish Album* ....(RCA)
Coffee, Donuts & Death
Paris; *Sleeping With The Enemy* .... (SCA)
Dead Babies
Alice Cooper; *Killer* .... (WB)
Dead By X-Mas
Hanoi Rocks; *Self-Destruction Blues* ....(GEF)
Dead Cat
Shelleyan Orphan; *Humroot* ....(COL)
Dead Cat Alley
Dirty White Boy; *Bad Reputation* ....(POL)
Dead Cat On The Line
Lucky Peterson; *Lucky Strikes!* ....(ALG)
Dead Flowers
Rolling Stones; *Sticky Fingers* ....(RS)
Steve Earle/Dukes; *Shut Up & Die Like An*
Aviator ....(MCA)
Dead Girls Of London
Frank Zappa; *You Can't Do That On Stage*
Anymore-#5 ....(RYK)
Dead Is A Risin'
Loretta Lynn; *Out Of My Head & Back In My*
Bed ....(MCA)
Dead Man
Asleep At The Wheel; *Asleep At The Wheel* .... (EPI)
Dead Man's Curve
Jan & Dean; *21 Legendary Superstars* .... (OSR)
Best Of .... (EMI)
Dead Man's Curve .... (EMI)
Dead Man's Hill
Indigo Girls; *Swamp Ophelia* ....(EPI)

Dead Next Door
Billy Idol; *Rebel Yell* .... (CHR)
Dead Of The Night
Bad Company; *Holy Water* ....(ATC)
Shawn Colvin; *Steady On* ....(COL)
Dead On Arrival
Billy Idol; *Billy Idol* .... (CHR)
Trees; *Forrest Fires* .... (ADE)
Dead Or Alive
Deep Purple; *Nobody's Perfect* .... (MER)
Journey; *Escape* ....(COL)
Oingo Boingo; *Boingo Alive* .... (MCA)
Good For Your Soul ....(A&M)
Too $hort; *Short Dog's In The House* .... (JVA)
Dead Puppies
Ogden Edsl; *Dr. Demento's Greatest Novelty CD* . (RHI)
Dr. Demento's Greatest-#4 .... (RHI)
Dead Skunk
Loudon Wainwright III; *Dr. Demento's Greatest
Novelties-#4* .... (RHI)
Super Hits/'70s-Have A Nice Day-#10 .... (RHI)
Dead & Alive
Dead Boys; *We Have Come For Your Children* .... (SIR)
Dead & Bloated
Stone Temple Pilots; *Core* .... (ATL)
Death Alley Driver
Rainbow; *Straight Between The Eyes* .... (MER)
Death At One's Elbow
Smiths; *Strangeways Here We Come* .... (SIR)
Death By Misadventure
John Hiatt; *Riding With The King* ....(GEF)
Ted Nugent; *Cat Scratch Fever* .... (EPI)
Death Defying
Hoodoo Gurus; *Mars Needs Guitars* .... (ELE)
Death Disco
Public Image, Ltd.; *Greatest Hits So Far* .... (VIA)
Death Don't Have No Mercy
Grateful Dead; *Live/Dead* ....(WB)
Hot Tuna; *Hot Tuna* ....(RCA)
Rev. Gary Davis; *Great Bluesmen At Newport* .. (VAN)
Death From Your TV Screen
Voice Of Destruction; *Steamroller Tactics* ....(CPA)
Death In The Autumn Air
Michael McDermott; *620 W. Surf* .... (GIA)
Death Letter Blues
Leadbelly; *King Of The Twelve-String Guitar* .....(COL)
Leadbelly ....(COL)
Death March
Faith No More; *Introduce Yourself* ....(SLS)
Death Of A Clown
Kinks; *Kink Kronikles* .... (RPR)
Something Else .... (RPR)
Death Of A Disco Dancer
Smiths; *Strangeways Here We Come* .... (SIR)
Death Of A Ladies' Man
Leonard Cohen; *Death Of A Ladies' Man* ....(COL)
Death Of A Salesman
Steve Goodman; *Words We Can Dance To* .... (ASY)
Death Of An Unpopular Poet
Jimmy Buffett; *White Sport Coat & A Pink
Crustacean* .... (MCA)
Death Of Hank Williams
Jack Cardwell; *Super Country Hits Of The 50's* .. (GUS)
Death Of Harry Simms
Pete Seeger; *Essential* .... (VAN)
Death Of Louis
Champion Jack Dupree; *Happy To Be Free* ...... (CRS)
Death Of Mother Nature
Kansas; *Kansas* .... (KIR)
Death Of Queen Jane
Joan Baez; *Joan Baez* .... (VAN)
Love Song Album .... (VAN)
Death On Two Legs
Queen; *Live Killers* ....(HOL)
Night At The Opera ....(HOL)
Death or Glory
Clash; *London Calling* .... (EPI)
Death Sentence
Big Daddy Kane; *Prince Of Darkness* ....(CLD)
Capital Punishment; *Livin' On The Edge Of A
Razor* ....(W/I)
Death Sound Blues
Country Joe/Fish; *Life & Times Of* .... (VAN)

Death Train
Beat Farmers; *Glad 'N' Greasy* .... (RHI)
Deathwish
Police; *Regatta De Blanc* ....(A&M)
Die By The Sword
Slayer; *Live* ....(DEF)
Die Nigger Die
Schoolly D; *How A Black Man Feels* ....(CAP)
Die With Your Boots On
Iron Maiden; *Live After Death-World Slavery
Tour* ....(CAP)
Piece Of Mind ....(CAP)
Die Young, Stay Pretty
Blondie; *Eat To The Beat* .... (CHR)
Died For Love
Richard & Linda Thompson; *First Light* .... (CHR)
Diggin' Up Bones
Randy Travis; *Storms Of Life* ....(WB)
Ding Dong The Witch Is Dead
Fifth Estate; *Dick Bartley's One-Hit
Wonders-'60s-#2* .... (RHI)
Meco; *Wizard Of Oz* .... (MIL)
MGM Studio Orchestra; *ST/Wizard Of Oz* ....(SSP)
Do It Or Die
Atlanta Rhythm Section; *Underdog* .... (POL)
Do Or Die
Captain Beyond; *Dawn Explosion* ....(WB)
Grace Jones; *Fame* .... (ISL)
Island Life .... (ISL)
Human League; *Dare* ....(A&M)
Doin' It To Death
James Brown; *Doin' It To Death* .... (POL)
Philly Cream; *Philly Cream* .... (WMO)
(Don't Fear) The Reaper
Blue Oyster Cult; *Agents Of Fortune* ....(COL)
Extraterrestrial Live ....(COL)
Metalmania ....(COL)
Some Enchanted Evening ....(COL)
Don't Take Me Alive
Steely Dan; *Royal Scam* .... (MCA)
Don't Take The Girl
Tim McGraw; *Not A Moment Too Soon* .... (CRB)
Dreams Die Hard
Gary Morris; *Gary Morris* ....(WB)
Greatest Hits-II ....(WB)
Dying Cub Fan's Last Request
Steve Goodman; *Baseball's Greatest Hits* .... (RHI)
Dying Miner
Woody Guthrie; *Struggle* .... (FLW)
Dying Soldier
Christy Moore; *Christy Moore* .... (ATL)
Dying To Meet You
Judas Priest; *Best Of* ....(RCA)
Hero Hero ....(RCA)
Rocka-Rolla ....(RCA)
Dyin' Crapshooter's Blues
Blind Willie McTell; *Atlanta Twelve-String* ...... (ATL)
David Bromberg; *How Late'll Ya Play 'Til* ....(FAN)
Dyin' Gambler
Blind James Campbell; *& His Nashville Street
Band* .... (ARH)
Dyin' Gambler's Blues
Bessie Smith; *Complete Recordings-#2* ....(COL)
D.O.A.
Bloodrock; *Heavy Metal Memories* .... (RHI)
Loverboy; *Loverboy* ....(COL)
Van Halen; *2* ....(WB)
El Paso
Grateful Dead; *Steal Your Face* .... (GRD)
Marty Robbins; *Biggest Hits* ....(COL)
Billboard Top Country Hits-1960 .... (RHI)
Gunfighter Ballads & Trail Songs ....(COL)
Radio Classics/'50s ....(COL)
Elephant's Graveyard
Boomtown Rats; *Greatest Hits* ....(COL)
Mondo Bongo ....(COL)
End Of The Road
Boyz II Men; *Cooleyhighharmony* .... (MOT)
Endless Sleep
Babys; *Babys* .... (CHR)
Jody Reynolds; *American Graffiti #3* .... (MCA)
Teenage Tragedies .... (RHI)
Every Day A Little Death
Original Cast; *Little Night Music* ....(COL)

Original London Cast; *Little Night Music* ....(RCA)
Everybody Gotta Go
Atlanta Rhythm Section; *Rock & Roll Alternative* . (POL)
Flight Of Icarus
Iron Maiden; *Live After Death* ....(CAP)
Piece Of Mind ....(CAP)
Foggy, Foggy Dew
Burl Ives; *Best Of* .... (MCA)
Freddie's Dead
Curtis Mayfield; *45* ....(OOP)
Fishbone; *Truth & Soul* ....(COL)
Funeral For A Friend
Elton John; *Goodbye Yellow Brick Road* .... (MCA)
Here & There ....(MCA)
Genocide
Judas Priest; *Hero Hero* ....(RCA)
Sad Wings Of Destiny ....(RCA)
Unleashed In The East ....(COL)
Golden Vanity
Pete Seeger & Arlo Guthrie; *Together In Concert* (RPR)
Grave
Don McLean; *American Pie* .... (EMI)
Graveyard
Public Image, Ltd.; *Second Edition* .... (ISL)
Graveyard Blues
John Lee Hooker; *Alone* .... (SPE)
Graveyard People
Traffic; *When The Eagle Flies* ....(ASY)
Graveyard Shift
Bobby "Boris" Pickett; *Monster Mash* ....(OOP)
Sawyer Brown; *Out Goin' Cattin'* ....(CAP)
Graveyard Train
Creedence Clearwater Revival; *1968/1969* ......(FAN)
Bayou Country ....(FAN)
Grim Reaper
Detective; *Detective* .... (SS)
He Stopped Loving Her Today
George Jones; *Anniversary* ....(EPI)
First Time Love ....(EPI)
Greatest Country Hits/'80s-1980 ....(COL)
Greatest Hits From The Jukebox ....(EPI)
I Am What I Am ....(EPI)
Heroes Die Young
Sleeze Beez; *Screwed Blued & Tattooed* ....(ATL)
Waysted; *Save Your Prayers* ....(CAP)
How Can I Help You Say Goodbye
Patty Loveless; *Only What I Feel* ....(EPI)
Howard's Dead & Gone
Weavers; *Classics* .... (VAN)
I Ain't Livin' Long Like This
Emmylou Harris; *Quarter Moon In A Ten-Cent*
Town ....(WB)
Rodney Crowell; *Collection* ....(WB)
I Ain't Livin' Long Like This ....(WB)
Waylon Jennings; *Greatest Hits-#2* ....(RCA)
What Goes Around Comes Around ....(RCA)
I Feel Like I'm Fixing To Die Rag
Country Joe/Fish; *Greatest Hits* .... (VAN)
Greatest '60s Folksingers ....(VAN)
I Feel Like I'm Fixing To Die Rag ....(VAN)
Life & Times Of ....(VAN)
More American Graffiti-#4 ....(MCA)
ST/Woodstock ....(ATL)
I Got A Mind To Give Up Living
Paul Butterfield Blues Band; *East-West* .... (ELE)
(I Just) Died In Your Arms
Cutting Crew; *Broadcast* ....(VIA)
MTV-VH1 Powerplayers ....(AMR)
I Love The Dead
Alice Cooper; *Alice Cooper Show* ....(WB)
Billion Dollar Babies ....(WB)
I Want My Baby Back
Jimmy Cross; *Teenage Tragedies* ....(RHI)
World's Worst Records ....(RHI)
Tyrone Ashley/Funky Music Machine; *45* ....(PLL)
I Would Die 4 U
Prince/Revolution; *ST/Purple Rain* ....(WB)
If I Should Die Tonight
Marvin Gaye; *Let's Get It On* ....(MOT)
Musical Testament-1964-1984 ....(MOT)
If The Good Die Young
Tracy Lawrence; *Alibis* ....(ATL)
If Tomorrow Never Comes
Garth Brooks; *Garth Brooks* ....(CAP)

In My Time Of Dying
Led Zeppelin; *Led Zeppelin* ....(ATL)
Physical Graffiti ....(SS)
In My Time Of Dyin'
Bob Dylan; *Bob Dylan* ....(COL)
Islands Of The Dead
Be Bop Deluxe; *Drastic Plastic* ....(CAP)
I'd Be Better Off (In A Pine Box)
Doug Stone; *Doug Stone* .... (EPI)
Greatest Country Hits-'90s-1990 ....(COL)
I'd Die Without You
P.M. Dawn; *Bliss Album...?* ....(GEE)
I'd Rather Be Dead
Nilsson; *Son Of Schmilsson* ....(RCA)
I'll Be Glad When You're Dead...
Cab Calloway; *Jazz Heritage: Mr. Hi-De-Ho* ... (MCA)
I'm Too Old To Die Young
Moe Bandy; *45* .... (MCC)
Jack You're Dead
Joe Jackson; *Jumpin' Jive* ....(A&M)
Louis Jordan; *Jazz Heritage-Greatest*
Hits-#2-1941-1947 ....(MCA)
John Brown's Body
Pete Seeger; *American Favorite Ballads-#3* ...... (FLW)
John Doe No. 24
Mary Chapin Carpenter; *Stones In The Road* ....(COL)
John Henry
Harry Belafonte; *All-Time Greatest Hits* ....(RCA)
At Carnegie Hall ....(RCA)
Legendary Performer ....(RCA)
Little Jimmy Dickens; *Columbia Historic Edition* .(COL)
Odetta; *Essential* .... (VAN)
Greatest Folksingers Of The '60s .... (VAN)
Woody Guthrie; *Immortal-Golden Classics-#2* ....(CLT)
Legendary ....(TRD)
John Peel
Hermes Nye; *Anglo-American Songs* .... (FLW)
Johnny Bye Bye
Bruce Springsteen; *45* ....(COL)
Just Another Death In NYC
Judy Small; *One Voice In The Crowd* ....(RWD)
Keep It Between The Lines
Ricky Van Shelton; *Backroads* ....(COL)
King Must Die
Elton John; *Elton John* .... (POL)
Live In Australia w/Melbourne Symphony ...... (MCA)
Kiss Me Deadly
Lita Ford; *Best Of* ....(DRM)
Lita ....(DRM)
Kiss The World Goodbye
Kris Kristofferson; *Border Lord* ....(COL)
Last Kiss
Frank Wilson; *Collectables Presents History Of*
Rock-#2 ....(CLT)
J. Frank Wilson; *Billboard Top Rock 'N' Roll*
Hits-1964 ....(RHI)
Oldies But Goodies-#9 ....(OSR)
Teenage Tragedies ....(RHI)
Let The Mystery Be
10,000 Maniacs; *Few & Far Between* ....(ELE)
Iris DeMent; *Infamous Angel* ....(PHO)
Infamous Angel ....(WB)
Live Until I Die
Clay Walker; *Clay Walker* ....(GIA)
Live & Let Die
Paul McCartney; *13 Original James Bond Themes* (EMI)
Tripping The Live Fantastic ....(CAP)
Paul McCartney/Wings; *All The Best* ....(CAP)
Over America ....(CAP)
Wings Greatest ....(CAP)
Wings; *ST/Live & Let Die* ....(EMI)
Man Of My Word
Collin Raye; *Extremes* .... (EPI)
More Than A Name On The Wall
Statler Brothers; *Greatest Hits* .... (MER)
Mummy
Bob McFadden & Dor; *Dr. Demento's Greatest*
Novelty-#2-1950s ....(RHI)
Vintage Music-Orig. Oldies/'50s-'60s-#15 ..... (MCA)
My Dead Dog Rover
Hank, Stu, Dave, & Hank; *Dr. Demento's Greatest*
Novelty-#4-1970s ....(RHI)
My Mummy's Dead
John Lennon; *Lennon* ....(CAP)

John Lennon/Plastic Ono Band; *John Lennon/Plastic Ono Band* .... (CAP)
My Wife & My Dead Wife
Robyn Hitchcock/Egyptians; *Fegmania* .... (SLS)
Needle Of Death
Ian & Sylvia; *Best Of* .... (VAN)
Night Chicago Died
Paper Lace; *Back To The '70s-#3* .... (DOM)
Super Hits/'70s-Have A Nice Day-#13 .... (RHI)
Night Game
Paul Simon; *Still Crazy After All These Years* ...... (WB)
Nightshift
Commodores; *Nightshift* .... (MOT)
Nothing Short Of Dying
Travis Tritt; *It's All About To Change* .... (WB)
Nuclear Funeral
D.I.; *Team Goon* .... (XXX)
Oh Bury Me Not
Johnny Cash; *American Recordings* .... (AME)
Only Losers Take The Bus (Dump The Dead)
Fatima Mansions; *Viva Dead Ponies* .... (RAD)
Only The Good Die Young
Billy Joel; *Greatest Hits-#1&2-1973-1985* ...... (COL)
KOHUEPT .... (COL)
The Stranger .... (COL)
Open Casket
Death; *Best Of* .... (REL)
Order Of Death
Public Image, Ltd.; *ST/Hardware* .... (VS)
Party In The Graveyard
Haunted Garage; *Possession Park* .... (MET)
Passing Of The Graveyard
Eddie Money; *No Control* .... (COL)
Pimp Or Die
Father M.C.; *ST/Who's The Man?* .... (UT)
Please Don't Bury Me
John Prine; *Prime Prine-Best Of* .... (ATL)
Sweet Revenge .... (ATL)
Please Don't Talk About Me When I'm Gone
Arlo Guthrie & Pete Seeger; *Precious Friend* ...... (WB)
Billie Holiday; *Compact Jazz* .... (VRV)
Ella Fitzgerald & Count Baise; *Perfect Match* .... (PAB)
Leon Redbone; *Champagne Charlie* .... (WB)
Ray Price; *Portrait Of A Singer* .... (SO)
Poor Jud Is Dead
Original Broadway Cast; *Oklahoma* .... (RCA)
Original Cast; *Oklahoma* .... (MCA)
Postmortem
Slayer; *Live* .... (AME)
Reign In Blood .... (AME)
Prayer For The Dying
Seal; *Seal* .... (ZTT)
Pretty Girls Make Graves
Smiths; *Smiths* .... (SIR)
Pretty Wreath For Mother's Grave
Reno & Smiley; *1983 Collector's Edition-#9* ..... (IGR)
Prop Me Up Beside The Jukebox
Joe Diffie; *Honky Tonk Attitude* .... (EPI)
Punks Not Dead
Exploited; *Apocalypse '77* .... (REL)
Real Niggaz Don't Die
N.W.A.; *Efil4zaggin* .... (RUP)
Rest In Peace
Extreme; *III Sides To Every Story* .... (A&M)
Ride To A Funeral In A V-8
Dan Pickett; *1949 Country Blues* .... (CLT)
Rigor Mortis
Split-Second; *Split-Second* .... (WAX)
Rock Me 'Till I Die
Grim Reaper; *Rock You To Hell* .... (RCA)
Rock Will Never Die
Michael Schenker; *Built To Destroy* .... (CHR)
Rock Will Never Die .... (CHR)
Rock & Roll Widow
Wishbone Ash; *Live Dates* .... (MCA)
Wishbone Four .... (MCA)
Roll Over & Play Dead
Lizzy Borden; *Master Of Disguise* .... (MET)
Rosewood Casket
D. Parton/E. Harris/L. Ronstadt; *Trio* .... (WB)
R&B Skeletons (In The Closet)
George Clinton; *R&B Skeletons (In The Closet)* ... (CAP)

R.I.P.
Blood Feast; *Face Fate* .... (NEW)
Kill For Pleasure .... (NEW)
See That My Grave Is Kept Clean
Blind Lemon Jefferson; *#1-1926-1929* .... (BIO)
Bob Dylan; *Bob Dylan* .... (COL)
Service For A Vacant Coffin
Autopsy; *Severed Survival* .... (PV)
Seven Deadly Sins
Bryan Ferry; *Bete Noire* .... (RPR)
Seven Deadly Virtues
Original Cast; *Camelot* .... (COL)
Sex And Dying In High Society
X; *Los Angeles* .... (SLS)
She Thinks Her Name Was John
Reba McEntire; *Read My Mind* .... (MCA)
Sheer Heart Attack
Queen; *Live Killers* .... (HOL)
News Of The World .... (HOL)
She's Not Dead
Suede; *Suede* .... (COL)
Skeletons
Rickie Lee Jones; *Pirates* .... (WB)
Stevie Wonder; *Characters* .... (MOT)
MTV-VH1 Powerplayers .... (EMI)
Some Gave All
Billy Ray Cyrus; *Some Gave All* .... (MER)
Some Memories Just Won't Die
Marty Robbins; *American Originals* .... (COL)
Come Back To Me .... (COL)
Lifetime Of Song-1951-1982 .... (COL)
Some Memories Just Won't Die .... (COL)
Souls Of The Departed
Bruce Springsteen; *Lucky Town* .... (COL)
Stairway To Heaven
Led Zeppelin; *4* .... (ATL)
Remasters .... (ATL)
Led Zeppelin (collection) .... (ATL)
ST/Song Remains The Same .... (SS)
Neil Sedaka; *All-Time Greatest Hits* .... (RCA)
Sings-His Greatest Hits .... (RCA)
O'Jays; *Collector's Items* .... (PI)
Family Reunion .... (PI)
Greatest Hits .... (PI)
Stanley Jordan; *Flying Home* .... (EMI)
Standing Knee Deep In A River
Kathy Mattea; *Lonesome Standard Time* .... (MER)
Stone Cold Dead In The Market
Ella Fitzgerald; *Best Of-#2* .... (MCA)
Stop Dead
Cure; *Standing On A Beach-The Singles* .... (ELE)
Streets Of Laredo
Buck Owens/Buckaroos; *Live At Carnegie Hall* .. (CMF)
Marty Robbins; *All-Time Greatest Hits* .... (COL)
More Greatest Hits .... (COL)
More Gunfighter Ballads & Trail Songs .... (COL)
Rex Allen; *Great American Singing Cowboys* ..... (REP)
Streets Of Philadelphia
Bruce Springsteen; *ST/Philadelphia* .... (COL)
St. James Infirmary
Benny Goodman; *Yale Recordings-#5-Private Collection* .... (MM)
Cab Calloway; *Cab Calloway* .... (GLN)
Jack Teagarden; *Hundred Years From Today* ... (GDG)
Joe Cocker; *Joe Cocker* .... (A&M)
Lou Rawls; *Best From* .... (CAP)
Louis Armstrong; *Best Of-Story-#3* .... (AUF)
Essential .... (VAN)
Pops: 1940s Small Band Sides .... (BLU)
Young .... (RCA)
Louis Armstrong & Earl Hines; *#4* .... (COL)
Preservation Hall Jazz Band; *New Orleans-#4* ...(COL)
Surprise! You're Dead!
Faith No More; *The Real Thing* .... (SLS)
Survival Handbook Vs. Global Extinction
Sister Souljah; *360 Degrees Of Power* .... (EPI)
Tears In Heaven
Eric Clapton; *ST/Rush* .... (RPR)
Unplugged .... (RPR)
Texas Girl At The Funeral Of Her Father
Randy Newman; *Little Criminals* .... (WB)

Texas (When I Die)
Tanya Tucker; *Best Of* .... (MCA)
  Collection .... (MCA)
  Greatest Hits Encore .... (LIB)
  Live .... (MCA)
  ST/Hard Country .... (EPI)

That'll Be The Day
Buddy Holly; *ST/American Graffiti* .... (MCA)
Buddy Holly/Crickets; *20 Golden Greats* .... (MCA)
  Chirping Crickets .... (MCA)
Crickets; *Billboard Top Rock 'N' Roll Hits-1957* . (RHI)
Foghat; *Best Of-#2* .... (RHI)
  Energized .... (RHI)
Linda Ronstadt; *Greatest Hits* .... (ASY)
  Hasten Down The Wind .... (ASY)

They're Moving Father's Grave To...
Clancy Brothers/Tommy Makem; *Luck Of The Irish* .... (COL)

Things To Do In Denver When You're Dead
Warren Zevon; *Mr. Bad Example* .... (GIA)

This Jesus Must Die
Original London Cast; *Jesus Christ Superstar* .... (MCA)

Thought I'd Died & Gone To Heaven
Bryan Adams; *Waking Up The Neighbours* ...... (A&M)

'Til I Die
Beach Boys; *10 Years Of Harmony* .... (CAR)
  Surf's Up .... (CAR)

Till Death Do Us Part
Madonna; *Like A Prayer* .... (SIR)

Till I'm Too Old To Die Young
Moe Bandy; *Great Records Of The Decade-'80s Hits* .... (CCB)
  Greatest Hits .... (CCB)

To Live And Die In L.A.
Wang Chung; *ST/To Live And Die In L.A.* .... (GEF)

To Live Is To Die
Metallica; *...And Justice For All* .... (ELE)

Tomb Of The Unknown Love
Cassell Webb; *Songs Of A Stranger* .... (VEN)
Kenny Rogers; *Heart Of The Matter* .... (RCA)

Tombstone
Crowded House; *Crowded House* .... (CAP)
Pogues; *Peace & Love* .... (ISL)

Tombstone Blues
Bob Dylan; *Biograph* .... (COL)
  Highway 61 Revisited .... (COL)
  Real Live .... (COL)

Tombstone Every Mile
Dave Dudley; *Interstate Gold* .... (SUN)

Tombstone Shadow
Creedence Clearwater Revival; *1969* .... (FAN)
  Chronicle-#2 .... (FAN)
  Green River .... (FAN)
  The Concert .... (FAN)

Too Old To Rock 'N' Roll, Too Young...
Jethro Tull; *Bursting Out* .... (CHR)
  Classic Case w/London Symphony Orchestra ...(RCA)
  Original Masters .... (CHR)
  Repeat-Best Of-#2 .... (CHR)
  Too Old To Rock 'N' Roll, Too Young... ..... (CHR)

Tryin' To Get Over You
Vince Gill; *I Still Believe In You* .... (MCA)

Tuesday's Dead
Cat Stevens; *Classics-#24* .... (A&M)
  Teaser & The Firecat .... (A&M)

Victim To The Tomb
Country Gentlemen; *Folk Songs & Bluegrass* .... (FLW)

Waiting For The Worms
Pink Floyd; *The Wall* .... (COL)
Roger Waters; *The Wall Live In Berlin* .... (MER)

Wall Of Death
Richard Thompson; *Watching The Dark-History Of* .... (RYK)
Richard & Linda Thompson; *Shoot Out The Lights* .... (HBL)

Wanted Dead Or Alive
Bon Jovi; *Slippery When Wet* .... (JBC)

War Widow
Country Joe McDonald; *War War War* .... (VAN)

Washed Up & Left For Dead
Selecter; *Celebrate The Bullet* .... (CHR)
  Selected Selections .... (CHR)

We Are The Dead
David Bowie; *Diamond Dogs* .... (RYK)

We Die Young
Alice In Chains; *Facelift* .... (COL)

What A Way To Go
Ray Kennedy; *What A Way To Go* .... (ATL)

When I Die
Watson Family; *Watson Family* .... (FLW)

Will The Circle Be Unbroken
Charlie Daniels Band/Friends; *Volunteer Jam #3 & #4* .... (EPI)
Joan Baez; *Country Music Album* .... (VAN)
  First 10 Years .... (VAN)
Nitty Gritty Dirt Band; *Will The Circle Be Unbroken* .... (EMI)
Roy Acuff; *Best Of* .... (CCB)
Willie Nelson; *Willie & Family Live* .... (COL)

Work That Sucker To Death
Xavier; *Point Of Pleasure* .... (LIB)

DEVILS, Satan
See Also: HELL, MONSTERS, SPIRITS

Beat The Devil
Blow Up; *ST/Up The Academy* .... (CAP)

Between The Devil And The Deep Blue Sea
Chris Rea; *espresso logic* .... (EW)

Between The Devil & The Deep Blue Sea
Cab Calloway; *Jazz Heritage: Mr. Hi-De-Ho* ... (MCA)
Ella Fitzgerald; *Harold Arlen Songbook-#1* ...... (VRV)

Caballo Diablo
Charlie Daniels Band; *Fire On The Mountain* ..... (EPI)

Detour (Devil Took A)
Patti Page; *Golden Hits* .... (MER)

Devil
Hoyt Axton; *Bread & Roses Festival Of Music-#2* (FAN)
  Fearless .... (A&M)
Urban Dance Squad; *Mental Floss For The Globe* (ARI)

Devil Ain't A Lonely Woman's Friend
Red Steagall; *45* .... (MCA)

Devil Came From Kansas
Procol Harum; *A Salty Dog* .... (A&M)

Devil Comes Back To Georgia
Marc O'Connor; *Heroes* .... (WB)

Devil Delight
Heart; *Magazine* .... (CAP)

Devil In A Fast Car
Sheena Easton; *Best Kept Secret* .... (EMI)

Devil In Disguise
Elvis Presley; *Golden Records-#4* .... (RCA)
  Top Ten Hits .... (RCA)
J.J. Cale; *Grasshopper* .... (MER)
  Special Edition .... (MER)

Devil In Her Heart
Beatles; *Second Album* .... (CAP)
  With The .... (CAP)
Donays; *Beatles Originals* .... (RHI)

Devil In The Bottle
T.G. Sheppard; *Greatest Hits-#2* .... (W/C)

Devil In The Cane Field
Mose Allison; *Down Home Piano* .... (PRS)
  Ol' Devil Mose .... (PRS)

Devil Inside
INXS; *Kick* .... (ATL)
Pop Will Eat Itself; *Now For A Feast!* .... (RT)

Devil Is Dope
Dramatics; *Best Of* .... (STX)
  Dramatic Experience .... (STX)

Devil Jumped The Blackman
Lightnin' Hopkins; *Best Of* .... (PRS)
  How Many More Years I Got .... (FAN)

Devil Loose In Georgia
Orrin Star & Gary Mehalick; *Premium Blend* ......(FF)

Devil May Care
Frank Sinatra; *What'll I Do* .... (RCA)
Tommy Dorsey & Frank Sinatra; *Sessions-#1* ...(RCA)

Devil Or Angel
Bobby Vee; *Best Of* .... (EMI)
  Golden Hits .... (LIB)
  Legendary Masters .... (EMI)
Clovers; *Atlantic R&B*
  1947-1974-#3-(1955-1958) .... (ATL)
  Oldies But Goodies-#2 .... (OSR)

Devil Went Down To Georgia
Charlie Daniels Band; *Billboard Top Hits-1979* .. (RHI)
  Decade Of Hits .... (EPI)
  Me & The Boys .... (EPI)
  Million Mile Reflections .... (EPI)
  ST/Urban Cowboy .... (ASY)
Devil Wind
Bob Welch; *Three Hearts* .... (CAP)
Devil With A Blue Dress On
Bruce Springsteen; *ST/No Nukes-Muse Concerts* .. (ASY)
Mitch Ryder/Detroit Wheels; *Frat Rock-#4* ..... (RHI)
  Rev Up-Best Of .... (RHI)
  Son Of Frat Rock .... (RHI)
  Toga Rock .... (DHL)
Devil Woman
Buddy Knox; *Best Of* .... (RHI)
Hanoi Rocks; *Oriental Beat* .... (GEF)
Marty Robbins; *Billboard Top Country Hits-1962* (RHI)
  Columbia Country Classics-#4 .... (COL)
  Greatest Hits-#4 .... (COL)
  Lifetime Of Song .... (COL)
Devil's Food
Alice Cooper; *Show* .... (WB)
  Welcome To My Nightmare .... (ATL)
Devil's Radio
George Harrison; *Cloud Nine* .... (DKH)
George Harrison/Eric Clapton & Band; *Live In Japan* .... (DKH)
Devil's Right Hand
Steve Earle; *Essential* .... (MCA)
Steve Earle/Dukes; *Early Tracks* .... (EPI)
  Shut Up & Die Like An Aviator .... (MCA)
Waylon Jennings; *Will The Wolf Survive* .... (MCA)
Devil's Toy
Almighty; *Soul Destruction* .... (POL)
Devil's Train
Hank Williams; *Lovesick Blues* .... (POL)
Roy Acuff; *Greatest Hits* .... (COL)
Devil's Whorehouse
Misfits; *Walk Among Us* .... (RUB)
Friend Of The Devil
Grateful Dead; *American Beauty* .... (WB)
  Best Of-Skeletons From The Closet .... (WB)
  Dead Set .... (ARI)
Lyle Lovett; *Deadicated* .... (ARI)
If The Devil Danced (In Empty Pockets)
Joe Diffie; *A Thousand Winding Roads* .... (EPI)
I'm Living With The 3-Foot Anti-Christ
Mojo Nixon; *Frenzy* .... (RES)
Jesus & Mama
Confederate Railroad; *Confederate Railroad* ..... (ATL)
My White Devil
Echo/Bunnymen; *Porcupine* .... (SIR)
Old Devil Moon
Anita O'Day; *Sings The Most* .... (VRV)
Frank Sinatra & Nelson Riddle Orchestra; *Songs For Swingin' Lovers* .... (CAP)
John Raitt; *Highlights Of Broadway/Under Open Skies* .... (CAP)
Lena Horne; *The Lady* .... (DHL)
Michael Feinstein; *Sings The Burton Lane Songbook-#1* .... (NON)
Miles Davis; *Blue Haze* .... (PRS)
Original Cast; *Finian's Rainbow* .... (COL)
Tony Bennett; *Forty Years-Artistry Of* .... (COL)
Phone Call From The Devil
Jim Nesbitt; *Phone Call From The Devil* .... (SCO)
Preaching Blues (Up Jumped The Devil)
Robert Johnson; *Complete Recordings* .... (COL)
  King Of The Delta Blues Singers-#2 .... (COL)
Race With The Devil
Gene Vincent; *Capitol Collectors Series* .... (CAP)
Gene Vincent/Blue Caps; *Legends Of Rock Guitar-'50s-#1* .... (RHI)
Rainbow Demon
Uriah Heep; *Demons & Wizards* .... (MER)
Runnin' With The Devil
Van Halen; *Van Halen* .... (WB)
Satan Place
Jeannie C. Riley; *Harper Valley P.T.A.* .... (PLN)
Satan Takes A Holiday
Ozzie Nelson/Orchestra; *Uncollected Ozzie Nelson/Orch.-#2-1937* .... (HIN)

Tommy Dorsey/Orchestra; *Seventeen Number Ones* .... (RCA)
Tommy Vig/Orchestra; *Space Race* .... (DCO)
Satan's Choir
Red Clay Ramblers; *It Ain't Right* .... (FF)
Satan's Doll
Floyd Cramer; *Best Of* .... (RCA)
Satan's Jewel Crown
Emmylou Harris; *Elite Hotel* .... (RPR)
Satan's Kingdom
Jimmy Cliff; *I Am The Living* .... (MCA)
Shake The Devil
Tommy Bolin; *Metal Giants* .... (COL)
  Metalmania .... (COL)
  Private Eyes .... (OOP)
  The Ultimate .... (GEF)
Shout At The Devil
Motley Crue; *Decade Of Decadence* .... (ELE)
  Shout At The Devil .... (ELE)
Shout To The Devil
Alarm; *Declaration* .... (IRS)
Sympathy For The Devil
Bryan Ferry; *These Foolish Things* .... (RPR)
Jane's Addiction; *Jane's Addiction* .... (XXX)
Rolling Stones; *Beggars Banquet* .... (AKO)
  Flashpoint .... (RS)
  Get Yer Ya-Ya's Out .... (AKO)
  Hot Rocks-1964-1971 .... (AKO)
  Love You Live .... (RS)
Take The Devil
Eagles; *Eagles* .... (ASY)
That Old Devil Called Love
Chet Baker; *Baker's Holiday* .... (VRV)
  Compact Jazz .... (VRV)
Ella Fitzgerald; *All That Jazz* .... (PAB)
Tie A Knot In The Devil's Tail
Chris LeDoux; *Old Cowboy Classics* .... (LIB)
  Rodeo & Living Free .... (LIB)
To Hell With The Devil
Stryper; *Can't Stop The Rock-Collection-1984-1991* .... (HOL)
  To Hell With The Devil .... (HOL)
Tying Knots In The Devil's Tail
Michael Martin Murphey; *Cowboy Songs* .... (WW)
Watch What Happens (Lola's Theme)
Frank Sinatra; *My Way* .... (RPR)
Henry Mancini; *Mancini Magic* .... (PRR)
Sergio Mendes; *Four Sider* .... (A&M)
  Golden Records #4 .... (RCA)

DIVORCE, Broken Marriage
  See Also: MARRIAGE

5 Minutes
Lorrie Morgan; *Leave The Light On* .... (RCA)
Alimony
Ry Cooder; *Ry Cooder* .... (RPR)
  Show Time .... (WB)
Weird Al Yankovic; *Even Worse* .... (SCO)
Alimony Blues
T-Bone Walker; *T-Bone Walker* .... (BLN)
All My Ex's Live In Texas
George Strait; *Country Classics-#10-1987* ...... (MCA)
  Greatest Hits-#2 .... (MCA)
  Ocean Front Property .... (MCA)
All These Years
Sawyer Brown; *Cafe On The Corner* .... (CRB)
Boats Against The Current
Eric Carmen; *Best Of* .... (ARI)
  Boats Against The Current .... (ARI)
Olivia Newton-John; *Totally Hot* .... (MCA)
D I V O R C E
Tammy Wynette; *Anniversary: 20 Years Of Hits* .. (EPI)
  Biggest Hits .... (EPI)
  Greatest Hits .... (EPI)
  Greatest Hits-#1 .... (EPI)
Drivin' & Cryin'
Steve Wariner; *Drive* .... (ARI)
Easy From Now On
Emmylou Harris; *Profile-Best Of* .... (WB)
  Quarter Moon In A Ten-Cent Town .... (WB)
Everything You Did
Steely Dan; *Royal Scam* .... (MCA)

Fifty Ways To Leave Your Lover
Paul Simon; *Greatest Hits Etc.* ....(COL)
   Negotiations & Love Songs 1971-1986 ....(WB)
   Still Crazy After All These Years ....(COL)
Simon & Garfunkel; *Concert In Central Park* .....(WB)
Goin' Through The Big D
Mark Chesnutt; *What A Way To Live* .... (DEC)
Grandpa (Tell Me About The Good Old...)
Judds; *Greatest Hits* ....(RCA)
   Rockin' With The Rhythm ....(RCA)
   Super 10-#2 ....(RCA)
Haitian Divorce
Steely Dan; *Greatest Hits* .... (MCA)
   Royal Scam .... (MCA)
He Thinks He'll Keep Her
Mary Chapin Carpenter; *Come On Come On* ....(COL)
Her Town Too
James Taylor & J.D. Souther; *Dad Loves His*
Work ....(COL)
How Blue Can You Get
B.B. King; *Best Of* .... (MCA)
   Live At The Regal .... (MCA)
   Live In Cook County Jail .... (MCA)
How Can I Help You Say Goodbye
Patty Loveless; *Only What I Feel* .... (EPI)
Hungry Heart
Bruce Springsteen; *The River* ....(COL)
Bruce Springsteen/E Street Band;
Live-1975-1985 ....(COL)
Husband Stealer
Barbara Mandrell; *This Is* .... (MCA)
I Don't Call Him Daddy
Doug Supernaw; *Red & Rio Grande* ....(BNA)
I Just Came Home To Count The Memories
John Anderson; *Greatest Hits* ....(WB)
   Honky-Tonk Country-Tender Lovin' Country ...(PRY)
   I Just Came Home To Count The Memories ......(WB)
In A Small Moment
Carly Simon; *Boys In The Trees* .... (ELE)
Is It Over Yet
Wynonna; *Tell Me Why* ....(MCC)
Is It Still Over
Randy Travis; *Old 8 X 10* ....(WB)
It's A Little Too Late
Tanya Tucker; *Can't Run From Yourself* ....(LIB)
Let That Pony Run
Pam Tillis; *Homeward Looking Angel* .... (ARI)
Marriage
Ted Nugent/Amboy Dukes; *Marriage On The*
Rocks ....(POL)
   Rock Bottom .... (POL)
Marriage On Paper Only
Dramatics; *Anytime Anyplace* .... (MCA)
Married But Not To Each Other
Barbara Mandrell; *Best Of* .... (MCA)
   Lovers Friends & Strangers .... (MCA)
   Midnight Angel .... (MCA)
Married Man's A Fool
Blind Willie McTell; *Last Session* .... (PRS)
Ry Cooder; *Paradise & Lunch* .... (RPR)
Married Strangers
Johnny Russell; *Perspectives* .... (MER)
Mexican Divorce
Drifters; *1959-1965-All-Time Greatest Hits &*
More ....(ATL)
Nicolette Larson; *Nicolette* ....(WB)
Ry Cooder; *Paradise & Lunch* .... (RPR)
Mommy Where's Daddy
Red Hot Chili Peppers; *Red Hot Chili Peppers* ... (EMI)
My Husband's Got No Courage In Him
Maddy Prior & June Tabor; *Silly Sisters* .... (SHA)
My Next Ex-Wife
Little Charlie/Nightcats; *Night Vision* ....(ALG)
My Second Home
Tracy Lawrence; *Alibis* .... (ATL)
My Son Calls Another Man Daddy
Hank Williams; *16 Great Hits* .... (EVR)
   40 Greatest Hits .... (POL)
   Rare Takes & Radio Cuts .... (POL)
One More Last Chance
Vince Gill; *I Still Believe In You* .... (MCA)
Paradise By The Dashboard Light
Meatloaf; *Bat Out Of Hell* .... (EPI)

Pay Me Alimony
Maddox Brothers & Rose; *America's Most Colorful*
Hillbilly Band .... (ARH)
Please Don't Ask
Genesis; *Duke* ....(ATL)
Quittin' Time
Mary Chapin Carpenter; *Greatest Country*
Hits-'90s-1990 ....(COL)
   State Of The Heart ....(COL)
She Got The Goldmine (I Got The Shaft)
Jerry Reed; *14 #1 Country Hits* ....(RCA)
   Greatest Hits ....(RCA)
   Solid Country Gold ....(RCA)
She's Gone
Daryl Hall & John Oates; *Abandoned*
Luncheonette .... (ATL)
   Rock 'N Soul-#1-Greatest Hits ....(RCA)
She's Gone, Gone, Gone
Lefty Frizzell; *American Originals* ....(COL)
   Best Of .... (RHI)
She's Single Again
Janie Fricke; *17 Greatest Hits* ....(COL)
   19 Hot Country Requests-#3 .... (EPI)
   Greatest Country Hits/'80s-1985 ....(COL)
   Very Best Of ....(COL)
Reba McEntire; *Have I Got A Deal For You* .... (MCA)
Starting Over Again
Dolly Parton; *Dolly Dolly Dolly* ....(RCA)
Natalie Cole; *Good To Be Back* .... (ELE)
Steve Wariner; *Country Classics-#7-1986-1987* . (MCA)
   Greatest Hits .... (MCA)
   Life's Highway .... (MCA)
Take That
Lisa Brokop; *Every Little Girl's Dream* .... (PAT)
"The Brady Bunch" Theme
Brady Bunch Kids; *It's A Sunshine Day-Best Of* . (MCA)
   Television's Greatest Hits-#2 ....(TVT)
Truck Driver Divorce
Frank Zappa; *Them Or Us* ....(BAR)
   You Can't Do That On Stage Anymore-#4 ......(RYK)
Tryin' To Get Over You
Vince Gill; *I Still Believe In You* .... (MCA)
Watch Me
Lorrie Morgan; *Watch Me* ....(BNA)
Who's That Man
Toby Keith; *Boomtown* ....(PYN)
Yard Sale
Sammy Kershaw; *Don't Go Near The Water* .... (MER)
Yes Yes Yes
Bill Cosby; *Is Not Himself These Days* ....(CAP)
You Already Drove Me There
Lisa Brokop; *Every Little Girl's Dream* .... (PAT)
You Make It Easy
James Taylor; *Gorilla* ....(WB)

DOCTORS, Diseases, Healing, Hospitals, Hurting, Pain

   See Also: HEART

Achy Breaky Heart
Billy Ray Cyrus; *Some Gave All* .... (MER)
Adelaide's Lament
Original Cast; *Guys & Dolls* .... (MCA)
   Guys & Dolls ....(MOT)
Amnesia
Pousette-Dart Band; *Amnesia* ....(CAP)
And The Healing Has Begun
Van Morrison; *Into The Music* ....(WB)
Annalee The Healer
Beach Boys; *Friends/20/20* ....(CAP)
Appointment At The Fat Clinic
Digable Planets; *Reachin'-New Refutation Of Time &*
Space ....(PEN)
Arthritis Blues
Ramblin' Jack Elliott; *Country Style* .... (PRS)
Back On My Feet Again
Babys; *Anthology* ....(CHR)
   Union Jacks ....(CHR)
Furry Lewis; *Back On My Feet Again* ....(PRS)
   Shake 'Em Down ....(FAN)
Randy Newman; *Good Old Boys* ....(RPR)

Bad Case Of Lovin' You
Robert Palmer; *Addictions-#1* .... (ISL)
 Secrets .... (ISL)
Bad Habits & Infections
Daryl Hall & John Oates; *Beauty On A Back
Street* ....(RCA)
Bad Liver & A Broken Heart
Tom Waits; *Small Change* .... (ASY)
Bad Medicine
Bon Jovi; *New Jersey* .... (MER)
"Ben Casey" Theme
Original Music; *Television's Greatest Hits-#2* ..... (TVT)
Biggest Hurt, The
Barbara Fairchild; *The Biggest Hurt* .... (AUD)
Bingo Fever
Da Yoopers; *Camp Fever* .... (YOU)
Bush Doctor
Peter Tosh; *Bush Doctor* .... (RS)
 Captured Live .... (EMI)
 The Toughest ....(CAP)
Call The Doctor
J.J. Cale; *Naturally* .... (MCA)
Calling Dr. Love
Kiss; *Alive 2* .... (CAS)
 Double Platinum .... (CAS)
 Rock & Roll Over .... (CAS)
 Smashes Thrashes & Hits .... (MER)
Cat Fever
Little Feat; *Sailin' Shoes* .... (WB)
Cat Scratch Fever
Ted Nugent; *Cat Scratch Fever* .... (EPI)
 Double Live Gonzo .... (EPI)
Chest Fever
Band; *Anthology-#1* ....(CAP)
 Music From Big Pink ....(CAP)
 Rock Of Ages-#1 & 2 ....(CAP)
 To Kingdom Come (Definitive Collection) ....(CAP)
Chest Pains
Greg "Fingers" Taylor; *Chest Pains* .... (MCA)
Coconut
Nilsson; *All-Time Greatest Hits* ....(RCA)
 Schmilsson ....(RCA)
 Songwriter ....(RCA)
Cold Fever
Models; *Out Of Mind Out Of Sight* .... (GEF)
Come In Out Of The Pain
Doug Stone; *I Thought It Was You* .... (EPI)
Connection
Montrose; *Paper Money* .... (WB)
Contagious
Whispers; *So Good* .... (SLR)
Y & T; *Contagious* .... (GEF)
Convulsion
Skinny Puppy; *Too Dark Park* .... (CAP)
Crash Course In Brain Surgery
Metallica; *Garage Days Re-Revisited* .... (ELE)
Crippled Inside
John Lennon/Plastic Ono Band; *Imagine* ....(CAP)
Cure
Nitty Gritty Dirt Band; *Dirt Silver & Gold* .... (UA)
 Uncle Charlie ....(LIB)
Cure Me...Or Kill Me
Gilby Clarke; *Pawnshop Guitars* .... (VIA)
Daytime Nightime Suffering
Wings; *Back To The Egg* ....(CAP)
Dear Doctor
Rolling Stones; *Beggar's Banquet* .... (AKO)
Disco Doctor
Robert Parker; *Golden Classics-Barefootin'* ....(CLT)
Dizzy Spells
Benny Goodman; *Carnegie Hall Jazz Concert* ....(COL)
Do You Really Want To Hurt Me
Culture Club; *Billboard Top Hits-1983* .... (RHI)
 Kissing To Be Clever .... (VIA)
Doctor
Cheap Trick; *Doctor* .... (EPI)
Doobie Brothers; *Cycles* ....(CAP)
INXS; *INXS* ....(ATC)
Wishbone Ash; *Wishbone 4* .... (MCA)
Doctor Boogie
Don Downing; *Doctor Boogie* .... (RDS)
Doctor Brown
Buster Brown; *Collectables Blues Collection-#2* ...(CLT)
 New King Of The Blues .... (CLT)

Fleetwood Mac; *Vintage Years* .... (SIR)
Doctor Dance
Frankie Valli; *45* .... (MCA)
Doctor Do It Good
Vernon Burch; *Get Up* .... (CHC)
Doctor Doctor
Thompson Twins; *Greatest Mixes-Best Of* .... (ARI)
 Into The Gap .... (ARI)
UFO; *Phenomenon* ....(CHR)
 Strangers In The Night ....(CHR)
Who; *Magic Bus* .... (MCA)
Doctor Feelgood
Aretha Franklin; *30 Greatest Hits* ....(ATL)
 Aretha's Gold ....(ATL)
 Best Of ....(ATL)
 I Never Loved A Man ....(ATL)
 Live At Fillmore East ....(ATL)
Doctor Frankenstein
Parliament; *Clones Of* .... (CAS)
 Live .... (CAS)
Doctor Hip
Country Joe McDonald; *Country Joe* .... (VAN)
 Essential .... (VAN)
Doctor My Eyes
Jackson Browne; *Jackson Browne* .... (ASY)
Doctor Robert
Beatles; *Revolver (European Version)* ....(CAP)
 Yesterday & Today ....(CAP)
Doctor Time
Rick Trevino; *Rick Trevino* ....(COL)
Doctor Wu
Steely Dan; *Greatest Hits* .... (MCA)
 Katy Lied .... (MCA)
Doctor's Orders
Joe Stampley; *Memory Lane* .... (EPI)
Oak Ridge Boys; *Bobby Sue* .... (MCA)
Doc's Guitar
Doc Watson; *Doc Watson* .... (VAN)
 On Stage .... (VAN)
 Out In The Country .... (INT)
Doc's Tune
Pure Prairie League; *Pure Prairie League* ....(RCA)
Don't Call Me No Doctor
Pyramid; *Pyramid* ....(BNG)
Don't Tear Me Up
Mick Jagger; *Wandering Spirit* .... (ATL)
Don't You Ever Get Tired Of Hurtin' Me
Ray Price; *Greatest Hits-#2* .... (STE)
Ronnie Milsap; *Stranger Things Have Happened* ..(RCA)
Dose Of You
Nick Lowe; *Labour Of Lust* ....(COL)
Down With Disease
Phish; *Hoist* .... (ELE)
Drive The Pain
Soup Dragons; *Lovegod* ....(BIG)
Dr. Heckyll & Mr. Jive
Men At Work; *Cargo* ....(COL)
Dr. Jimmy
Who; *Quadrophenia* .... (MCA)
 ST/Quadrophenia .... (POL)
Dr. Love
Bananarama; *Deep Sea Skiving* ....(LON)
Whispers; *Excellence* ....(ALL)
 Shhhh ....(DOR)
Dr. Music
Blue Oyster Cult; *Extraterrestrial Live* ....(COL)
 Mirrors ....(COL)
Dyslexic Heart
Paul Westerberg; *ST/Singles* .... (EPI)
D.O.C. & The Doctor
D.O.C.; *No One Can Do It Better* ....(RUT)
Every Little Bit Hurts
Brenda Holloway; *Motown Legends-Love Songs* . (MOT)
 Motown Memories-#2-Where Were You... ...... (MOT)
 Motown Story-First 25 Years .... (MOT)
Gladys Knight/Pips; *Anthology* .... (MOT)
 Motown Legends .... (MOT)
Spencer Davis Group; *Best Of* .... (EMI)
 Best Of .... (RHI)
Everybody Hurts
R.E.M.; *Automatic For The People* .... (WB)
Feel A Whole Lot Better
Flamin' Groovies; *Now* .... (SIR)
Gene Clark; *Firebyrd* .... (TAK)

Feel The Pain
Dinosaur Jr.; *Without A Sound* .... (SIR)
Feelin' Alright
Dave Mason; *Best Of* ....(COL)
  Certified Love ....(COL)
  Greatest Hits ....(COL)
  Skatetown ....(COL)
  U.S.A. ....(MCA)
Joe Cocker; *Greatest Hits* .... (A&M)
  Mad Dogs & Englishmen .... (A&M)
  Rockin' '60s .... (PRY)
  With A Little Bit Of Help From My... .... (A&M)
Feelin' Stronger Every Day
Chicago; *Greatest Hits* ....(COL)
  Group Portrait ....(COL)
  If You Leave Me Now ....(COL)
  #6 ....(COL)
Fever
Aerosmith; *Get A Grip* ....(GEF)
Buddy Guy; *This Is* .... (VAN)
Doctor Ice; *Mic Stalker* .... (JVA)
Elvis Presley; *Aloha From Hawaii* ....(RCA)
  Pure Gold ....(RCA)
  Valentine Gift For You ....(RCA)
Peggy Lee; *Memories Are Made Of This* ....(CAP)
Rita Coolidge; *Classics-#5* ....(A&M)
  Greatest Hits ....(A&M)
Southside Johnny/Asbury Jukes; *Cover Me* .... (RHI)
  Havin' A Party ....(EPI)
  I Don't Want To Go Home ....(EPI)
For You
Bruce Springsteen; *Greetings From Asbury Park,*
N.J. ....(COL)
Greg Kihn; *Kihnsolidation* ....(RHI)
  Unkihntrollable-Live ....(RHI)
Manfred Mann's Earth Band; *Chance* ....(WB)
Girl, I've Been Hurt
Snow; *12 Inches Of Snow* ....(EW)
Good Lovin'
Grateful Dead; *Shakedown Street* .... (ARI)
Rascals; *Greatest Hits* ....(ATL)
  Hit Singles 1958-1977 ....(ATL)
  ST/Big Chill ....(MOT)
  Super Hits ....(ATL)
Haven't Got Time For The Pain
Carly Simon; *Best Of* ....(ELE)
  Hot Cakes ....(ELE)
Hay Fever
Kinks; *Misfits* .... (ARI)
Headache Tomorrow (Or A Heartache...)
Mickey Gilley; *Biggest Hits* ....(EPI)
  Ten Years Of Hits ....(EPI)
  That's All That Matters To Me ....(EPI)
Healing Hands Of Time
Willie Nelson; *Healing Hands Of Time* .... (LIB)
Healing.
Wynonna & Michael English; *ST/Silent Fall* .....(CRB)
Heart Attack
Olivia Newton-John; *Greatest Hits-#2* .... (MCA)
  Physical ....(MCA)
Heart Trouble
Martina McBride; *The Way That I Am* ....(RCA)
Steve Wariner; *Country Classics-#3-1984-1985* . (MCA)
  Greatest Hits ....(MCA)
  One Good Night Deserves Another ....(MCA)
High Blood Pressure
Huey "Piano" Smith/Clowns; *Serious Clownin'-History*
Of ....(RHI)
Paula Lockheart & Peter Ecklund; *Paula Lockheart &*
Peter Ecklund ....(FF)
Hope You're Feeling Better
Santana; *Abraxas* ....(COL)
  Greatest Hits ....(COL)
  Rock Classics-#2 .... (KT)
Hospital Lady
Loudon Wainwright III; *Loudon Wainwright III* .. (ATL)
Hotel Illness
Black Crowes; *Southern Harmony & Musical*
Companion ....(DEF)
House Of Pain
Faster Pussycat; *Wake Me When it's Over* ...... (ELE)
Van Halen; *1984* ....(WB)
How Can I Ease The Pain
Lisa Fischer; *So Intense* ....(ELE)

How Can I Help You Say Goodbye
Patty Loveless; *Only What I Feel* ....(EPI)
Hurt
Carly Simon; *Torch* ....(WB)
Elvis Presley; *Always On My Mind* ....(RCA)
  Golden Records-#5 ....(RCA)
Juice Newton; *Old Flame* ....(RCA)
Little Anthony/Imperials; *Best Of* ....(EMI)
Manhattans; *Greatest Hits* ....(COL)
Tom Petty/Heartbreakers; *You're Gonna Get It* . (MCA)
Hurt Me Bad (In A Real Good Way)
Patty Loveless; *Greatest Hits* ....(MCA)
  Up Against My Heart ....(MCA)
Hurt So Bad
Lettermen; *All-Time Greatest Hits* ....(CAP)
Linda Ronstadt; *Greatest Hits-#2* ....(ASY)
  Mad Love ....(ASY)
Little Anthony/Imperials; *Best Of* ....(EMI)
  Best Of ....(RHI)
Hurting Kind (I've Got My Eyes On You)
Robert Plant; *Manic Nirvana* .... (EPR)
Hurtin' Inside
Brook Benton; *Golden Hits* .... (MER)
Hurts So Good
John Cougar Mellencamp; *American Fool* ....(RIV)
Hurts To Be In Love
Gino Vannelli; *Black Cars* ....(CBA)
I Ain't Got The Fever No More
Southside Johnny/Asbury Jukes; *This Time It's For*
Real ....(EPI)
I Don't Hurt Anymore
Hank Snow; *Stars Of The Grand Ole Opry* ....(RCA)
I Don't Need No Doctor
Humble Pie; *Best* ....(A&M)
  Classics-#14 ....(A&M)
  Performance-Rockin' The Fillmore ....(A&M)
New Riders Of The Purple Sage; *Best Of* ....(COL)
Ray Charles; *Anthology* .... (RHI)
  Greatest Hits-#1 .... (RHI)
I Feel Like Homemade Shit
Fugs; *Greatest Hits-#1* ....(PVC)
I Feel So Bad
Elvis Presley; *Golden Records-#3* ....(RCA)
  Reconsider Baby ....(RCA)
  Top Ten Hits ....(RCA)
  Worldwide 50 Gold Award Hits-#1 ....(RCA)
I Get Weak
Belinda Carlisle; *Heaven On Earth* ....(MCA)
I Got It Bad & That Ain't Good
Duke Ellington; *All Star Road Band* ....(DOC)
  Intimate ....(PAB)
  This Is ....(RCA)
Johnny Mathis; *In A Sentimental Mood-Sings*
Ellington ....(COL)
I Guess It Never Hurts To Hurt Sometimes
Oak Ridge Boys; *Deliver* .... (MCA)
  Greatest Hits-#2 .... (MCA)
I Hurt For You
Deborah Allen; *45* ....(RCA)
I Just Cut Myself
Ronnie McDowell; *Love To Burn* .... (EPI)
I Think I Got It (V.D.)
Legs Diamond; *Diamond Is A Hard Rock* .... (MER)
Infekshun
Ron Wood; *Gimme Some Neck* ....(COL)
Influenza
Todd Rundgren; *Ever Popular Tortured Artist*
Effect .... (RHI)
It Doesn't Have To Hurt Everytime
Johnny Mathis; *First 25 Years-Silver Anniversary*
Album ....(COL)
It Hurt Me Too
Marvin Gaye; *Greatest Hits* ....(MOT)
  That Stubborn Kinda' Fellow ....(MOT)
It Hurts As Much In Texas (As It Did...
George Jones & Ricky Van Shelton; *Friends In High*
Places ....(EPI)
It Hurts Me Too
Bob Dylan; *Self Portrait* ....(COL)
Elmore James; *Golden Classics* ....(CLT)
Eric Clapton; *From The Cradle* ....(DUC)
It Hurts To Be In Love
Betty Everett; *Very Best Of* .... (VJ)

Gene Pitney; *Anthology* .... (RHI)
   Greatest Hits .... (EVR)
It Only Hurts When I Cry
   Dwight Yoakam; *If There Was A Way* .... (RPR)
I'm Not A Well Man
   Original Cast; *I Can Get It For You Wholesale* ....(SSP)
I'm Tore Down
   Eric Clapton; *From The Cradle* .... (DUC)
I've Been Hurt
   Bill Deal/Rhondels; *Best Of* .... (RHI)
   Oldies/Goodies-#7 .... (OSR)
   Soul Shots-#6 .... (RHI)
   Soul Shots/'60s Classics-#2 .... (RHI)
Jack (V.D.)
   AC/DC; *High Voltage* ....(ATC)
   If You Want Blood You've Got It .... (ATL)
Joy And Pain
   Donna Allen; *Heaven On Earth* .... (OCE)
   Maze featuring Frankie Beverly; *Live In Los*
   Angeles ....(CAP)
   Live In New Orleans ....(CAP)
   Maze/Kurtis Blow; *Lifelines-#1* ....(CAP)
   Rob Base & D.J. EZ-Rock; *It Takes Two* ....(PRO)
Jungle Fever
   Stevie Wonder; *ST/Jungle Fever* .... (MOT)
Just What The Doctor Ordered
   Ted Nugent; *Double Live Gonzo* .... (EPI)
   Ted Nugent .... (EPI)
King Of Pain
   Police; *Every Breath You Take-Singles* .... (A&M)
   MTV's Rock 'N' Roll To Go .... (ELE)
   Synchronicity .... (A&M)
Kiss Away The Pain
   Patti Labelle; *Winner In You* .... (MCA)
Lady Doctor
   Graham Parker/Rumour; *Howlin' Wind* .... (MER)
   Parkerilla .... (MER)
Like A Surgeon
   Weird Al Yankovic; *Dare To Be Stupid* .... (RAR)
   Greatest Hits .... (RAR)
Living With A Hernia
   Weird Al Yankovic; *Greatest Hits* .... (RAR)
   Polka Party .... (RAR)
Living With AIDS
   Romanovsky & Phillips; *Emotional Rollercoaster* . (FRE)
London Homesick Blues
   David Allan Coe; *Biggest Hits* ....(COL)
   Jerry Jeff Walker; *Great Gonzos* .... (MCA)
   Viva Terlingua .... (MCA)
Lookin' Good But Feelin' Bad
   Original Cast; *Ain't Misbehavin'* .... (RCA)
Love All The Hurt Away
   George Benson; *Collection* .... (WB)
Love Disease
   Butterfield Blues Band; *Live* .... (ELE)
Love Hangover
   Diana Ross; *20 Greatest Songs In Motown*
   History-CD .... (MOT)
   20/20 .... (MOT)
   All The Great Hits .... (MOT)
   Anthology .... (MOT)
   Greatest Hits .... (MOT)
Love Hurt Me Love Healed Me
   Lenny Williams; *Love Current* .... (MCA)
Love Hurts
   Emmylou Harris & Gram Parsons; *Duets* .... (RPR)
   Gram Parsons; *Grievous Angel* .... (RPR)
   Judy Collins; *Bread & Roses* .... (ELE)
   Nazareth; *Classics-#16* .... (A&M)
   Hair Of The Dog .... (A&M)
   Hot Tracks .... (A&M)
   'Snaz .... (A&M)
   Ralph Tresvant; *Ralph Tresvant* .... (MCA)
   Roy Orbison; *All-Time Greatest Hits-#1 & 2* ....(MON)
   Legendary ....(SSP)
Love Hurts Love Heals
   Daryl Hall & John Oates; *Beauty On A Back*
   Street .... (RCA)
Love Is A Hurtin' Thing
   Lou Rawls; *Best Of* ....(CAP)
   Live .... (PI)
   Soul Shots-#5-La-La Means I Love You .... (RHI)

Love Is The Healing
   Roberta Flack & Donny Hathaway; *Blue Lights In The*
   Basement .... (ATL)
Lovesick Blues
   Gary Morris; *Plain Brown Wrapper* .... (WB)
   Hank Williams; *24 Greatest Hits* .... (MER)
   Lovesick Blues .... (POL)
   Linda Ronstadt; *Retrospective* ....(CAP)
   Silk Purse ....(CAP)
   Patsy Cline; *Live At The Opry* .... (MCA)
Love-itis
   J. Geils Band; *Blow Your Face Out* .... (ATL)
   Hotline .... (ATL)
Love's Got A Hold On You
   Alan Jackson; *Don't Rock The Jukebox* .... (ARI)
"Marcus Welby, M.D." Theme
   Original Music; *Television's Greatest Hits-#3* ..... (TVT)
"Medical Center" Theme
   Original Music; *Television's Greatest Hits-#2* ..... (TVT)
Medicated Goo
   Traffic; *Best Of* .... (ISL)
   Last Exit .... (ISL)
   Welcome To The Canteen .... (ISL)
Medicine Jar
   Paul McCartney/Wings; *Over America* ....(CAP)
   Wings; *Venus & Mars* ....(CAP)
Medicine Song
   Stephanie Mills; *Greatest Hits In My Life* .... (CAS)
   I've Got The Cure .... (CAS)
Medicine Woman
   Paul Davis; *Southern Tracks & Fantasies* ....(BNG)
Miracle Cure
   Who; *Join Together* .... (MCA)
   ST/Tommy ....(POL)
   Tommy .... (MCA)
My Asthma Problem
   John Trubee; *Communists Are Coming To Kill Us* (ENI)
My Head Hurts, My Feet Stink...
   Jimmy Buffett; *Havana Daydreamin'* .... (MCA)
My Heart Is Failing Me
   Riff; *Riff* .... (SBK)
Needles & Pins
   Jackie DeShannon; *Very Best Of* .... (EMI)
   Searchers; *Greatest Hits* .... (RHI)
   History Of British Rock-#1 .... (RHI)
   Tom Petty/Heartbreakers-Stevie Nicks; *Pack Up The*
   Plantation-Live .... (MCA)
Night Fever
   Bee Gees; *Greatest* .... (POL)
   ST/Saturday Night Fever .... (POL)
Nothin' But A Heartache
   Doobie Brothers; *Livin' On The Fault Line* .... (WB)
Only Love Is Worth This Pain
   Country Joe McDonald; *Hold On It's Coming* ... (VAN)
Ooh! My Feet!
   Original Broadway Cast; *Most Happy Fella* ..... (SMC)
Ordinary Pain
   Stevie Wonder; *Songs In The Key Of Life* .... (MOT)
Pac Man Fever
   Buckner & Garcia; *Pac Man Fever* ....(COL)
Pain In My Heart
   David Johansen; *David Johansen* .... (BS)
   Otis Redding; *Best Of* ....(ATC)
   History Of ....(ATC)
   In Person At The Whisky A Go Go .... (RHI)
   Pain In My Heart ....(ATC)
   Story .... (ATL)
   Rolling Stones; *Now!* .... (AKO)
Paralysed
   Gang Of Four; *Brief History Of The Twentieth*
   Century .... (WB)
Paralyzed
   Black Flag; *In My Head* ....(SST)
   Dave Edmunds; *I Hear You Rockin' (Live)* ....(COL)
   Dave Mason; *Best Of* ....(COL)
   Elvis Presley; *Elvis* ....(RCA)
   Million Dollar Quartet ....(RCA)
   Fabulous Thunderbirds; *Walk That Walk Talk That*
   Talk .... (EPA)
   Kiss; *Revenge* .... (MER)
   Rosanne Cash; *Interiors* ....(COL)
   Ted Nugent; *State Of Shock* .... (EPI)
Pervert Nurse
   D.I.; *Horse Bites Dog Cries* .... (XXX)

Pins & Needles
Whites; *Forever You* .... (MCC)
   Greatest Hits .... (CCB)
Plastic Surgery
Adam/Ants; *Fun Filth & Fury* .... (BP)
Pneumonia Blues
Lightnin' Hopkins; *How Many More Years I Got* . (FAN)
Poison Ivy
Coasters; *Atlantic R&B 1947-74-#4-1958-1962* . (ATL)
   Billboard Top R&B Hits-1959 .... (RHI)
   Greatest Hits .... (ATC)
   More American Graffiti .... (MCA)
   Their Greatest Recordings-Early Years .... (ATC)
Nylons; *Rockapella* .... (WH)
   ST/Stealing Home .... (ATL)
Rolling Stones; *More Hot Rocks-Big Hits & Fazed*
Cookies .... (AKO)
Poison Was The Cure
Megadeth; *Rust In Peace* .... (CAP)
Postpone The Pain
Mark Chesnutt; *Longnecks & Short Stories* ...... (MCA)
Puke & Cry
Dinosaur Jr.; *Green Mind* .... (SIR)
   Just Say Anything-#5 Of Just Say Yes .... (SIR)
Purple People Eater Meets The Witch Doc.
Big Bopper; *Hellooo Baby! Best Of-1954-1959* .. (RHI)
P.M.S. Blues
Dolly Parton; *Heart Songs* .... (COL)
"Quincy" Theme
Original Music; *Television's Greatest Hits-#3* ..... (TVT)
Ramblin' Fever
Merle Haggard; *Greatest Hits* .... (MCA)
   More Of The Best .... (RHI)
   Ramblin' Fever .... (MCA)
Remedy
Black Crowes; *Southern Harmony & Musical*
Companion .... (DEF)
Return Of Dr. X
UB40; *PResent Arms In Dub* .... (VIA)
Road Fever
Blackfoot; *Strikes* .... (ATC)
Foghat; *Foghat* .... (RHI)
   Live .... (RHI)
Rock N Roll Disease
Green On Red; *Here Come The Snakes* .... (RES)
Rock & Roll Doctor
Black Sabbath; *Technical Ecstasy* .... (WB)
Little Feat; *Feats Don't Fail Me Now* .... (WB)
   Hoy-Hoy! .... (WB)
Travesty Ltd.; *Dr. Demento's Greatest-#5* .... (RHI)
Rockin' Pneumonia And The Boogie...
Aerosmith; *ST/Less Than Zero* .... (DFJ)
Huey "Piano" Smith; *All-Star Chartbusters* .... (INT)
Huey "Piano" Smith/Clowns; *Jimpin' Jive '50s* .. (PRY)
Johnny Rivers; *Anthology 1964-1977* .... (RHI)
   Best Of .... (EMI)
Professor Longhair; *Rock 'N' Roll Gumbo* ...... (DAN)
Rodney Lay; *Rockabilly Nuggets* .... (SUN)
Ross Memorial Hospital
Phil Cunningham; *Palomino Waltz* .... (GRE)
Ruby Don't Take Your Love To Town
Kenny Rogers; *20 Great Years* .... (RPR)
   Ten Years Of Gold .... (EMI)
   Twenty Greatest Hits .... (EMI)
Kenny Rogers/First Edition; *Greatest Hits* ...... (KT)
   Hits & Pieces .... (MCA)
Mel Tillis/Statesiders; *24 Great Hits* .... (MGM)
   Best Of .... (MCA)
   M-M-Mel Live .... (MCA)
Saturday Morning Fever
Loudon Wainwright III; *Fame & Wealth* .... (ROU)
Scarlet Fever
Kenny Rogers; *We've Got Tonight* .... (EMI)
Seasick, Yet Still Docked
Morrissey; *Your Arsenal* .... (SIR)
Seven Year Ache
Rosanne Cash; *Columbia Country Classics-#5* ..(COL)
   Greatest Country Hits/'80s-1981 ....(COL)
   Hits-1979-1989 ....(COL)
   Seven Year Ache ....(COL)

Sexual Healing
Marvin Gaye; *Last Concert Tour* .... (GIA)
   Midnight Love ....(COL)
   Seems Like Yesterday-#4-Early '80s ....(KT)
   Tribute To Black Entertainers ....(COL)
Shake The Disease
Depeche Mode; *101* .... (SIR)
   Catching Up With .... (SIR)
Shape I'm In
Band; *Anthology* .... (CAP)
   Best Of .... (CAP)
   Last Waltz .... (WB)
   Rock Of Ages-#1 & 2 .... (CAP)
   Stage Fright .... (CAP)
   To Kingdom Come-Definitive Collection .... (CAP)
Bob Dylan/Band; *Before The Flood* ....(COL)
Marty Stuart; *Marty Stuart* ....(COL)
She Thinks His Name Was John
Reba McEntire; *Read My Mind* .... (MCA)
Sick Again
Led Zeppelin; *Physical Graffiti* .... (SS)
Sick As A Dog
Aerosmith; *Live Bootleg* ....(COL)
   Rocks ....(COL)
Silver Threads & Golden Needles
Honky Tonk Angels; *Honky Tonk Angels* ....(COL)
Linda Ronstadt; *Don't Cry Now* .... (ASY)
   Greatest Hits .... (ASY)
   Hand Sown .... (CAP)
   Retrospective .... (CAP)
Sister Of Pain
Vince Neil; *Exposed* .... (WB)
Social Disease
Bon Jovi; *Slippery When Wet* .... (JBC)
Elton John; *Goodbye Yellow Brick Road* .... (POL)
Somebody Get Me A Doctor
Van Halen; *2* .... (WB)
Soul Doctor
Foreigner; *Very Best...And Beyond* .... (ATL)
Soul Vaccination
Tower Of Power; *Tower Of Power* .... (WB)
Souvenir Of London (V.D.)
Procol Harum; *Grand Hotel* .... (CHR)
Spring Fever
Elvis Presley; *ST/Girl Happy* ....(RCA)
Loretta Lynn; *Out Of My Head & Back In Bed* . (MCA)
Nantucket; *Nantucket* .... (EPI)
Stone Cold Fever
Humble Pie; *Best Of* .... (A&M)
   Classics-#14 .... (A&M)
   Performance .... (A&M)
   Rock On .... (A&M)
Streets Of Pain
Richard Marx; *Rush Street* .... (CAP)
Streets Of Philadelphia
Bruce Springsteen; *ST/Philadelphia* ....(COL)
"St. Elsewhere" Theme
Dave Grusin; *Night-Lines* .... (GRP)
Original Music; *Television's Greatest Hits-#3* ..... (TVT)
Subterranean Homesick Blues
Bob Dylan; *Biograph* ....(COL)
   Bootleg Series-#1-3-1961-1989 ....(COL)
   Bringing It All Back Home ....(COL)
   Greatest Hits ....(COL)
Red Hot Chili Peppers; *Uplift Mofo Party Plan* .. (EMI)
Suffer To Sing The Blues
David Bromberg; *Out Of The Blues-Best Of* ......(COL)
Take Me Down To The Hospital
Replacements; *Hootenanny* .... (CML)
Take Your Pain Away
Eurythmics; *Revenge* ....(RCA)
Talk About Suffering
Doc Watson; *Doc Watson* .... (VAN)
Ricky Skaggs; *Family & Friends* .... (ROU)
   Live In London .... (EPI)
Teenage Brain Surgeon
Spike Jones; *In Stereo* .... (WB)
Tennessee Homesick Blues
Dolly Parton; *Best Of-#3* ....(RCA)
   RCA Years-1967-1986 ....(RCA)
   Star-Spangled Country ....(RCA)
   ST/Rhinestone ....(RCA)
"The Bob Newhart Show" Theme
Original Music; *Television's Greatest Hits-#3* ..... (TVT)

Theme From "Doctor Zhivago"
101 Strings Orchestra; *Music From Doctor Zhivago &*
Others .... (ALS)
Theme From "Dr. Kildare"
Betty Carter; *'Round Midnight* .... (ATL)
There's A Doctor I've Found
Who; *Join Together* .... (MCA)
STITommy .... (POL)
Tommy .... (MCA)
Thinkin' Problem
David Ball; *Thinkin' Problem* .... (WB)
This One's Gonna Hurt You (For A...)
Marty Stuart & Travis Tritt; *This One's Gonna Hurt You*
(For A...) .... (MCA)
Thorn In My Side
Eurythmics; *Greatest Hits* .... (ARI)
Live-1983-1989 .... (ARI)
Revenge .... (RCA)
Thursday Night Fever
Legendary Pink Dots; *Legendary Pink Dots* ...... (PIA)
Tie You Up (The Pain Of Love)
Rolling Stones; *Undercover* .... (RS)
Till I Can't Take it Anymore
Billy Joe Royal; *Greatest Hits* .... (ATL)
Tell It Like It Is .... (ATA)
Charlie Rich; *Behind Closed Doors* .... (EPI)
Don Williams; *Traces* .... (CAP)
Time Heals
Todd Rundgren; *Anthology-1968-1985* .... (RHI)
Healing .... (RHI)
Try Not To Look So Pretty
Dwight Yoakam; *This Time* .... (RPR)
T.B. Is Whipping Me
Wilco & Syd Straw; *Red Hot + Country* .... (MER)
Ulcer
Michael Schenker; *Assault Attack* .... (CHR)
U.M.M.G. (Upper Manhattan Medical Group)
Art Farmer Quartet; *Warm Valley* .... (CCJ)
Branford Marsalis; *Trio Jeepy* .... (COL)
Duke Ellington & Dizzy Gillespie; *Jazz Party* ....(COL)
Vasectomy
Limeliters; *Singing For The Fun* .... (CRS)
Virus Called The Blues
Charles Brown & Dr. John; *All My Life* .... (BUL)
Voodoo Medicine Man
Aerosmith; *Pump* .... (GEF)
Washington, D.C. Hospital Center Blues
Skip James; *Greatest Of The Delta Blues Singers* ...(BIO)
Today .... (VAN)
Weak
SWV; *It's About Time* .... (RCA)
Where've You Been
Kathy Mattea; *Collection Of Hits* .... (MER)
Willow In The Wind .... (MER)
White Line Fever
Flying Burrito Brothers; *Close Encounters To The West*
Coast .... (RLX)
Merle Haggard; *More Of The Best* .... (RHI)
Merle Haggard/Strangers; *Okie From Muskogee* ..(CAP)
Witch Doctor
Chipmunks; *Rockin' Through The Decades* .... (EMI)
David Seville; *Dr. Demento 20th Anniversary*
Collection .... (RHI)
Wacky Weirdos .... (KT)
World Is A Little Bit Under The Weather
Meters; *Trick Bag* .... (RPR)
World Of Pain
Cream; *Disraeli Gears* .... (POL)
W.S. Walcott Medicine Show
Band; *Rock Of Ages-#1 & 2* .... (CAP)
Stage Fright .... (CAP)
To Kingdom Come-Definitive Collection .... (CAP)
You Always Hurt The One You Love
Brenda Lee; *Story-Her Greatest Hits* .... (MCA)
Clarence Henry; *Rich Roots* .... (ALL)
Mills Brothers; *16 Great Performances* .... (MCA)
Best Of .... (MCA)
Greatest Hits .... (MCA)
Spike Jones; *Best Of* .... (RCA)
You've Got A Cold
10 CC; *Deceptive Bends* .... (MER)
Live & Let Live .... (MER)

You've Got It Bad Girl
Quincy Jones; *Best Of-#2* .... (A&M)
Classics-#3 .... (A&M)
Stevie Wonder; *Talking Book* .... (MOT)

DOGS
See Also: ANIMALS: A-Z

Amsterdam Dog Shit Blues
Mojo Nixon & Skid Roper; *Enigma Variations 2* .(ENC)
Arkansas Dog
Pinkard & Bowden; *Writers In Disguise* .... (WB)
Atomic Dog
George Clinton; *Best Of* .... (CAP)
Computer Games .... (CAP)
Baby Do The Philly Dog
Olympics; *Official Record Album Of* .... (RHI)
Baby Ice Dog
Blue Oyster Cult; *Tyranny & Mutation* ....(COL)
Back In The Doghouse Again
Ray Stevens; *#1 With A Bullet* .... (CCB)
Ballad Of Mad Dogs & Englishmen
Ivan "Boogaloo Joe" Jones; *Black Whip* .... (PRS)
Leon Russell; */Shelter People* .... (MCA)
Bark At The Moon
Ozzy Osbourne; *Bark At The Moon* .... (CBA)
Bird Dog
Everly Brothers; *Best Of* .... (RHI)
Billboard Top Rock 'N' Roll Hits-1958 .... (RHI)
Cadence Classics-Their 20 Greatest Hits .... (RHI)
Fabulous Style .... (RHI)
Very Best Of .... (WB)
Black Dog
Led Zeppelin; *IV* .... (ATL)
Led Zeppelin .... (ATL)
Bride Of Rain Dog
Tom Waits; *Rain Dogs* .... (ISL)
By-Tor & The Snow Dog Suite
Rush; *All The World's A Stage* .... (MER)
Archives .... (MER)
Fly By Night .... (MER)
Damned Old Dog
k.d. lang; *Tame Yourself* .... (RHI)
Roches; *Roches* .... (WB)
Dawgs (Are A Man's Best Friend)
Original Cast; *Dawgs* .... (GLN)
Dead Puppies
Ogden Edsl; *Dr. Demento's Greatest Novelty CD* . (RHI)
Dr. Demento's Greatest-#4 .... (RHI)
Diamond Dogs
David Bowie; *Changesbowie* ....(RYK)
Diamond Dogs .... (RYK)
Live .... (RYK)
The Singles-1969-1993 .... (RYK)
Dirty Dawg
NKOTB; *Face The Music* .... (COL)
Dirty Old Egg-Sucking Dog
Johnny Cash; *At Folsom Prison & San Quentin* ...(COL)
Essential .... (COL)
Discount Dogs
Joe Perry Project; *Let The Music Do The Talking* .(COL)
Dog
Rufus Thomas; *Walking The Dog* .... (ATL)
Dog Blue
Mimi & Richard Farina; *Best Of* .... (VAN)
Dog Breath
Frank Zappa; *Uncle Meat* .... (BAR)
Mothers Of Invention; *Just Another Band From*
L.A. .... (BIZ)
Dog Days
Atlanta Rhythm Section; *Dog Days* .... (POL)
Dog Eat Dog
AC/DC; *Let There Be Rock* .... (ATC)
Adam Ant; *Antics In The Forbidden Zone* .... (EPI)
Kings Of The Wild Frontier .... (EPI)
Ted Nugent; *Free-For-All* .... (EPI)
Weird Al Yankovic; *Polka Party* .... (SCO)
Dog & Butterfly
Heart; *Dog & Butterfly* .... (POR)
Greatest Hits/Live .... (EPI)

Doggie In The Window
Patti Page; *16 Most Requested Songs* ....(COL)
  Golden Hits .... (MER)
  Greatest Hits ....(COL)
Doggin' Around
Jackie Wilson; *Great Soul Hits* ....(BRU)
  My Golden Favorites ....(BRU)
  Reet Petite-Best Of ....(COL)
  Story .... (EPI)
Doggin' The Dog
Big Joe Turner; *Big Joe* .... (MCA)
  Jazz Heritage-Blues & All That Jazz .... (MCA)
  Jazz Heritage-Early Big Joe .... (MCA)
Doggone Right
Smokey Robinson/Miracles; *Anthology* .... (MOT)
  Compact Command Performances .... (MOT)
Doggy Dogg World
Snoop Doggy Dogg; *Doggystyle* .... (DR)
Dogman
King's X; *Dogman* ....(ATL)
Dogs
Motorhead; *Mega Metal* .... (KT)
  No Sleep At All ....(GWR)
Pink Floyd; *Animals* ....(COL)
Stan Ridgway; *Mosquitos* ....(GEF)
Who; *Who's Missing* ....(MCA)
Dogs Among At Bushes
Chieftans; *8* ....(COL)
Dogs In The Yard
King Musker Band; *45* .... (EPI)
Paul McCrane; *ST/Fame* ....(RSO)
Dogs Part 2
Who; *Who's Missing* ....(MCA)
Dogs & Ferretts
Steeleye Span; *Commoner's Crown* .... (CHR)
Dogtown
Harry Chapin; *Heads & Tales* ....(ELE)
Dog's Life
Gentle Giant; *Octopus* ....(COL)
Don't Let The Same Dog Bite You Twice
Robin Lee; *Heart On A Chain* .... (ATL)
Every Dog Has His Day
Charlie Gonzales; *Charlie Gonzales* ....(CLT)
Every Dog Has Its Day
Eddie Bo; *Check Mr. Popeye* ....(ROU)
Gonna Buy Me A Dog
Monkees; *Monkee Flips* .... (RHI)
  Monkees .... (ARI)
Got No More Home Than A Dog
Ian & Sylvia; *Greatest Hits* .... (VAN)
  Ian & Sylvia ....(VAN)
Hair Of The Dog
Guns N' Roses; *The Spaghetti Incident?* ....(GEF)
Nazareth; *Classics-#16* ....(A&M)
  Hair Of The Dog ....(A&M)
  Heavy Metal Memories .... (RHI)
  Hot Tracks ....(A&M)
  'Snaz ....(A&M)
Hangdog Hotel Room
Gordon Lightfoot; *Gord's Gold-#2* .... (WB)
Hard Day's Night
Beatles; *1962-1966* ....(CAP)
  20 Greatest Hits ....(CAP)
  At The Hollywood Bowl ....(CAP)
  Hard Day's Night ....(CAP)
  Reel Music ....(CAP)
  ST/Hard Day's Night ....(CAP)
Hey Bulldog
Beatles; *Rock 'N' Roll Music-#2* ....(CAP)
  Yellow Submarine ....(CAP)
Hound Dog
Elvis Presley; *Aloha From Hawaii* ....(RCA)
  As Recorded In Madison Square Garden ....(RCA)
  Elvis Aron Presley ....(RCA)
  Elvis Presley ....(RCA)
  Golden Records ....(RCA)
  In Concert ....(RCA)
  In Person ....(RCA)
  Legendary Performer-#3 ....(RCA)
  Number One Hits ....(RCA)
  Recorded Live On Stage At Memphis ....(RCA)
  ST/Forrest Gump ....(EPX)
House The Dog Built
Jibri Wise One; *S* ....(EAR)

"Huckleberry Hound" Theme
Original Music; *Television's Greatest Hits-#2* .....(TVT)
I Buyed Me A Little Dog
Dave Van Ronk; *Van Ronk* ....(FAN)
I Wanna Be Your Dog
Joan Jett/Blackhearts; *Up Your Alley* ....(BLK)
Stooges; *Stooges* ....(ELE)
I Wanna Be Your Puppy, Baby
John Lee Hooker; *JAzz Heritage-Lonesome Mood* (MCA)
I Want A Dog
Pet Shop Boys; *Introspective* ....(EMI)
If Dogs Run Free
Bob Dylan; *New Morning* ....(COL)
I'm Walking The Dog
Webb Pierce; *Best Of* ....(MCA)
  Golden Hits ....(PLN)
Jealous Dogs
Pretenders; *II* ....(SIR)
John Peel
Hermes Nye; *Anglo-American Songs* ....(FLW)
King Of The Dogs
Spread Eagle; *Open To The Public* ....(MCA)
Let Me Play With Your Poodle
Lightnin' Hopkins; *Complete Aladdin Recordings* . (EMI)
Little Brown Dog
Judy Collins; *Golden Apples Of The Sun* ....(ELE)
Low Down Dog
Big Joe Turner; *Boss Of The Blues* ....(ATL)
  Have No Fear-Big Joe Is Here ....(SAV)
Mad Dogs & Englishmen
Noel Coward; *Album-Live From Las Vegas & New York* ....(COL)
Man Bites Dog
Plan 9; *Enigma Variations 2* ....(ENC)
Me & You & A Dog Named Boo
Lobo; *Best Of* ....(BT)
  Super Hits/'70s-Have A Nice Day-#5 .... (RHI)
My Dead Dog Rover
Hank, Stu, Dave, & Hank; *Dr. Demento's Greatest Novelty-#4-1970s* ....(RHI)
My Life As A Dog
Active Ingredient; *Extrastrength* ....(BAI)
Nasty Dogs & Funky Kings
ZZ Top; *Fandango* ....(WB)
  Six Pack ....(WB)
No Dogs Allowed
McSkat Kat/Stray Mob; *Adventures Of* ....(CPT)
  Original Cast; *Dawgs* ....(GLN)
Not Much Of A Dog
Michael Feinstein; *Pure Imagination* ....(ELE)
Old Dogs, Children & Watermelon Wine
Tom T. Hall; *Essential Twentieth Anniversary Collect.* ....(MER)
  Greatest Hits-#2 ....(MER)
Open Up The Doghouse
Nat King Cole; *Nat King Cole (collection)* ....(CAP)
Peace Dog
Cult; *Electric* ....(SIR)
Philly Dog
Mar-Keys; *Back To Back/Mar-Keys & Booker T/MGs* ....(ATL)
  Great Memphis Sound ....(ATL)
  Stax/Volt Revue-#1-Live In London ....(ATL)
  Super Hits-#1 ....(ATL)
Play With Your Poodle
B.B. King; *King Of The Blues* ....(MCA)
Please Throw This Poor Dog A Bone
Junior Wells; *Blues Hit Big Town* ....(DEL)
Police Dog Blues
Blind Blake; *Georgia Blues-1927-1930* ....(YAZ)
Hot Tuna; *Splashdown* ....(RLX)
Jorma Kaukonen & Tom Hobson; *Quah* ....(RLX)
Ry Cooder; *Ry Cooder* ....(RPR)
Poor White Hound Dog
Merry Clayton; *ST/Performance* ....(WB)
Puppet Dog
Thin White Rope; *Ruby Sea* ....(FRN)
Puppy Love
Donny Osmond; *Greatest Hits* ....(CCB)
Ike & Tina Turner; *Golden Classics* ....(CLT)
Little Jimmy Rivers/Tops; *45* ....(CLT)
Paul Anka; *21 Golden Hits* ....(RCA)
  30th Anniversary Collection .... (RHI)

Quarterdrawing Of The Dog
Siouxsie/Banshees; *Tinderbox* ....(GEF)
Rain Dogs
Tom Waits; *Big Time* ....(ISL)
Rain Dogs ....(ISL)
Rattling Dog
Irish Rovers; *First Of* ....(MCA)
Rockin' Rollin' Rover
Bill Haley/Comets; *Golden Hits* ....(MCA)
Rockin' The Dog
Hellecasters; *Town South Of Bakersfield-#3* ...... (RES)
Salty Dog
Procol Harum; *Best Of* ....(A&M)
Classics-#17 ....(A&M)
Live With The Edmonton Orchestra ....(A&M)
Salty Dog ....(A&M)
Salty Dog Blues
Flatt & Scruggs; *Golden Hits Of* ....(GUS)
Greatest Folksingers/'60s ....(VAN)
"Scooby Doo" Theme
Original Music; *Television's Greatest Hits-#3* ..... (TVT)
Shadow & Me
Leon Russell; *Americana* ....(PRD)
Shaggy Dog
Lightnin' Hopkins; *Nothin' But The Blues-Golden Classics-#4* ....(CLT)
Sick As A Dog
Aerosmith; *Live Bootleg* ....(COL)
Rocks ....(COL)
Snoopy Vs. The Red Baron
Royal Guardsmen; *Best Of-#1* ....(RHI)
Collectables Presents History Of Rock-#9 ....(CLT)
Cruisin'-1967 ....(INC)
Million-Dollar Memories #1 ....(RCA)
Super Oldies/'60s-#6 ....(AUF)
Snoopy's Christmas
Royal Guardsmen; *Snoopy & His Friends* ....(LAU)
Song Dog
Michael Murphey; *Lonewolf* ....(EPI)
Space Dog
Tori Amos; *Under The Pink* ....(ATL)
Stop Doggin' Me
Johnnie Taylor; *45* ....(STX)
Stop Kicking My Dog Around
Rufus Thomas; *Can't Get Away From This Dog* .. (STX)
Tennessee Hound Dog
Osborne Brothers; *Best Of* ....(MCA)
Thanks To The Cat House...
Johnny Paycheck; *Armed & Crazy* ....(EPI)
That Dog Won't Hunt
Waylon Jennings; *Will The Wolf Survive* .... (MCA)
That Hound Dog In The Window
Homer & Jethro; *Duets-Collector's* ....(RCA)
Trashy Dog
Steve Cropper/Albert King/Pops Staples; *Jammed Together* .... (STX)
Two Headed Dog (Red Temple Prayer)
Roky Erickson; *You're Gonna Miss Me-Best Of* .. (RES)
"Underdog Theme"
Original Music; *Television's Greatest Hits-#2* ..... (TVT)
Walk The Dog
Laurie Anderson; *United States Live* ....(WB)
Walking My Cat Named Dog
Norma Tanega; *45* ....(ERI)
Walkin' The Dog
Aerosmith; *Aerosmith* ....(COL)
Pandora's Box ....(COL)
Luther Allison; *Atlantic Blues-Chicago* ....(ATL)
Rolling Stones; *England's Newest Hitmakers* ... (AKO)
Rufus Thomas; *Can't Get Away From This Dog* .. (STX)
Rufus Thomas ....(GUS)
Super Hits-#2 ....(GUS)
Walkin' The Dog ....(ATL)
Watch Dog
Etta Jones; *Tell Mama* ....(CSS)
Muddy Waters Blues Band; *Mud In Your Ear* ... (MUS)
Watchdogs Of The Night
UB40; *Live In Moscow* ....(A&M)
Rat In The Kitchen ....(A&M)
Where Did That Little Dog Go
Original Cast; *Snoopy* ....(DRG)
Where Has My Little Dog Gone
Horace Heidt/Musical Knights; *Uncollected-1939* (HIN)

Wild Dog Moon
Drivin' N' Cryin'; *Mystery Road* .... (ISL)
Wild Dogs
Hank Williams, Jr.; *Bocephus*
Box-Collection-1979-1992 ....(CPC)
Tommy Bolin; *The Ultimate...* ....(GEF)
Wild West Show/Dog Act
Original Broadway Cast; *Will Rogers Follies* ......(COL)
Yellow Dog Blues
Bessie Smith; *Complete Recordings-#2* ....(COL)
Eddie Condon; *Best Of* ....(MCA)
You're In The Doghouse Now
Brenda Lee; *ST/Dick Tracy* .... (SIR)

DOORS
See Also: SECRETS

At My Front Door
Harry Nilsson; *Son Of Schmilsson* ....(RCA)
Baby, I Knocked On Your Door
Sonny Terry & Brownie McGhee; *At Sugar Hill* .. (FAN)
Back Door Angels
Jethro Tull; *War Child* .... (CHR)
Back Door Friend
Johnny Winter; *Johnny Winter* ....(COL)
Lightnin' Hopkins; *The Jewel/Paula Records Story* (CPC)
Back Door Love Affair
ZZ Top; *Best Of* ....(WB)
First Album ....(WB)
Six Pack ....(WB)
Back Door Man
Doors; *13* ....(ELE)
Doors ....(ELE)
Howlin' Wolf; *Best Of-Chess Blues* ....(CSS)
John Hammond; *Best Of* .... (VAN)
Willie Dixon; *I Am The Blues* ....(COL)
Back Door Santa
Bon Jovi; *Very Special Christmas* ....(A&M)
Clarence Carter; *Christmas Classics* ....(RHI)
Snatching It Back-Best Of ....(RHI)
Soul Christmas ....(ATL)
Back Doors Crying
Peter Allen; *Taught By Experts* ....(A&M)
Banging The Door
Public Image, Ltd.; *Flowers Of Romance* ....(WB)
Live In Tokyo ....(ELE)
Behind Closed Doors
Charlie Rich; *American Originals* ....(COL)
Behind Closed Doors ....(EPI)
Columbia Country Classics-#4 ....(COL)
Greatest Hits ....(EPI)
Behind That Locked Door
George Harrison; *All Things Must Pass* ....(CAP)
Can't You Hear Me Knockin'
Rolling Stones; *Sticky Fingers* ....(RS)
Check Your Tears At The Door
Drivin' N' Cryin'; *Whisper Tames The Lion* ...... (ISL)
Close The Door
Teddy Pendergrass; *Best Of-Philadelphia International* ....(PI)
Greatest Hits ....(PI)
Life Is A Song Worth Singing ....(PI)
Live ....(PI)
Philly Ballads-#2 ....(PI)
Ten Years Of #1 Hits ....(PI)
Crack In Your Door
Little Feat; *Little Feat* ....(WB)
Crazy Little Mama
Eldorados; *Greatest Groups/'50s-#2* ....(CLT)
Sock Hop ....(DHL)
Danger At My Door
Mark Chesnutt; *Too Cold At Home* .... (MCA)
Dead Next Door
Billy Idol; *Rebel Yell* .... (CHR)
Don't Answer The Door
B.B. King; *Back In The Alley* ....(MCA)
Blues 'N' Jazz/Electric ....(MCA)
Electric ....(MCA)
Live & Well ....(MCA)
Don't Bother To Knock
Barbara Mandrell; *Moods* ....(MCA)
Jim Ed Brown & Helen Cornelius; *Greatest Hits* .(RCA)

Don't Turn Me From Your Door
John Lee Hooker; *Don't Turn Me From Your
Door* .... (ATL)
Door
George Jones; *Anniversary* .... (EPI)
Best Of .... (EPI)
Skip Ewing; *Will To Love* .... (MCA)
Door Is Always Open
Dave & Sugar; *Greatest Hits* ....(RCA)
Door Peep
Burning Spear; *Man In The Hills* .... (ISL)
Door To Door
Cars; *Door To Door* .... (ELE)
Creedence Clearwater Revival; *Live In Europe* ... (FAN)
Mardi Gras .... (FAN)
Door To Door Blues
Champion Jack Dupree; *Blues Roots-#6* .... (STY)
Door You Closed To Me
Box Tops; *45* .... (FSB)
Door #3
Jimmy Buffett; *A 1 A* .... (MCA)
Doors Of Your Heart
English Beat; *What Is Beat* .... (IRS)
Wha'ppen .... (IRS)
Everybody's Key Fits My Baby's Door
Rockin' Tabby Thomas; *King Of Swamp Blues* .. (MDS)
Girl Next Door
Bobby Brown; *Dance!...Ya Know It!* .... (MCA)
King Of Stage .... (MCA)
Earl Lewis/Channels; *Harlem Holiday-New York
R&B-#2* .... (CLT)
New York's Finest .... (CLT)
Frank Sinatra; *Gift Set* .... (CAP)
Johnny Crawford; *Best Of* .... (RHI)
Green Door
Jim Lowe; *Billboard Top Rock 'N' Roll Hits-1956* (RHI)
Super Hits-#4 .... (GUS)
Happiness Lives Next Door
Willie Nelson; *Diamonds In The Night* .... (DEL)
Legend Begins/Wild & Willie .... (ALL)
Honey (Open That Door)
Ricky Skaggs; *Don't Cheat In Our Hometown* .... (EPI)
Greatest Country Hits!'80s-1984 .... (COL)
Live In London .... (EPI)
House Of Four Doors
Moody Blues; *In Search Of The Lost Chord* ...... (POL)
I Hear You Knockin'
Smiley Lewis; *Billboard Top R&B Hits-1955* ..... (RHI)
Non-Stop Party Rock .... (EMI)
I Left My Heart At The Stage Door...
Jo Stafford; *G.I. Jo* .... (CRN)
Keep A'Knocking
Wallace "Cheese" Read; *Cajun House Party "C'ez
Cheese"* .... (ARH)
Knocking At Your Back Door
Deep Purple; *Nobody's Perfect* .... (MER)
Perfect Strangers .... (MER)
Knockin' On Heaven's Door
Bob Dylan; *At Budokan* .... (COL)
Biograph .... (COL)
Rock Classics/'70s .... (COL)
ST/Pat Garrett & Billy The Kid .... (COL)
Bob Dylan/Band; *Before The Flood* .... (COL)
Bob Dylan/Grateful Dead; *Dylan & The Dead* ...(COL)
Eric Clapton; *Crossroads* .... (POL)
Time Pieces-Best Of .... (RSO)
Guns N' Roses; *ST/Days Of Thunder* .... (DGC)
Use Your Illusion II .... (GEF)
Jerry Garcia; *Run For The Roses* .... (ARI)
Randy Crawford; *Rich & Poor* .... (WB)
Let My Love Open The Door
Pete Townshend; *Empty Glass* .... (ATC)
Let 'Em In
Paul McCartney/Wings; *All The Best* .... (CAP)
Over America .... (CAP)
Wings Greatest .... (CAP)
Wings; *At The Speed Of Sound* .... (CAP)
Let's Lock The Door
Jay/Americans; *All-Time Greatest Hits* .... (RHI)
Looking At The Front Door
Main Source; *Breaking Atoms* .... (EMI)
Nasty Wax .... (KT)

Lookin' Out My Back Door
Creedence Clearwater Revival; *1970* .... (FAN)
Chronicle .... (FAN)
Cosmo's Factory .... (FAN)
Creedence Country .... (FAN)
More Creedence Gold .... (FAN)
Love Come Knocking
Staple Singers; *Hold Onto Your Dreams* ....(OOP)
My Baby Done Changed The Lock On The...
Sonny Terry & Brownie McGhee; *Great Bluesmen At
Newport* .... (VAN)
My Back Door
Melissa Etheridge; *Brave & Crazy* .... (ISL)
Next Door To An Angel
Neil Sedaka; *All-Time Greatest Hits* ....(RCA)
Sings His Greatest Hits ....(RCA)
One Less Bell To Answer
5th Dimension; *Anthology 1967-1973* .... (RHI)
Greatest Hits On Earth .... (ARI)
Barbra Streisand; *Barbra Joan* ....(COL)
Gladys Knight/Pips; *Anthology* .... (MOT)
If I Were Your Woman .... (MOT)
Open The Door
Betty Carter; *Now It's My Turn* .... (RLL)
Otis Redding; *Dock Of The Bay* ....(ATC)
Remember Me .... (STX)
Royal Teens; *Short Shorts* .... (CLT)
Open The Door To Your Heart
Little Milton; *Stax Blues Masters-Blue Monday* ... (STX)
Walking The Back Streets .... (STX)
Open The Door, Homer
Bob Dylan/Band; *Basement Tapes* ....(COL)
Thunderclap Newman; *Hollywood Dream* ...... (MCA)
Open The Door, Richard
Louis Jordan; *Jazz Heritage-Greatest Hits-#2* .... (MCA)
Open Up A New Door
John Mayall/Bluesbreakers; *Bare Wires* ....(LON)
Open Up Your Door
Romantics; *In Heat* .... (NEM)
What I Like About You (& Other Hits) .... (NEM)
Steve Earle/Dukes; *Early Tracks* .... (EPI)
Opened The Door
Journey; *Infinity* ....(COL)
Out That Door
Hoodoo Gurus; *Blow Your Cool* .... (ELE)
Please Take That Train From My Door
Wayne Horvitz; *This New Generation* .... (ELE)
Seven Doors Hotel
Europe; *Europe* .... (EPI)
Somebody Done Changed The Lock On My...
Louis Jordan; *Best Of* .... (MCA)
Jazz Heritage-Greaist Hits-#2-1941-1947 ...... (MSP)
Somebody Knockin'
Izzy Stradlin/Ju Ju Hounds; *Izzy Stradlin/Ju Ju
Hounds* .... (GEF)
Somebody's Knockin'
Terri Gibbs; *Best Of* .... (MCA)
Country Gold .... (PRY)
Country Music Classics-#6-1980-1985 .... (KT)
Stage Door
Justin Hayward; *Songwriter* ....(DER)
Stagedoor Johnny
Donnie Iris; *Fortune 410* .... (MCA)
Stone Outside Dan Murphy's Door
Anna McGoldrick; *Ireland On My Mind* .... (RGO)
Storming The Gates Of Hell
Riot; *Privilege Of Power* .... (EPA)
Swing Wide Your Gate Of Love
Hank Thompson; *Country Music Hall Of Fame* . (MCA)
Greatest Hits-#1 .... (SO)
Swinging Doors
George Jones; *20 Golden Pieces Of* .... (BLD)
Merle Haggard; *Capitol Collectors Series* .... (CAP)
Merle Haggard/Strangers; *Best Of* .... (CAP)
Okie From Muskogee .... (CAP)
Songs I'll Always Sing .... (CAP)
There He Is (At My Door)
Martha Reeves/Vandellas; *Anthology* .... (MOT)
Live Wire! Singles-1962-1972 .... (MOT)
This Side Of The Door
Mark Chesnutt; *What A Way To Live* .... (DEC)
To The Door Of The Sun
Al Martino; *Capitol Collectors Series* .... (CAP)
Greatest Hits ....(CCB)

Twenty-Nine Ways (To My Baby's Door)
Koko Taylor; *Koko Taylor* .... (CSS)
  South Side Lady ....(EVD)
Marc Cohn; *Marc Cohn* ....(ATL)
Willie Dixon; *Chess Box* .... (CSS)
Two Doors Down
Dolly Parton; *Collector's Series* ....(RCA)
  Greatest Hits ....(RCA)
  Here You Come Again ....(RCA)
What If I Came Knocking
John Mellencamp; *Human Wheels* .... (MER)
Who Can It Be Now
Men At Work; *Billboard Top Hits-1982* .... (RHI)
  Business As Usual ....(COL)
Who's Behind The Door
Zebra; *Live* ....(ATL)
  Zebra ....(ATL)
Who's That Knockin'
Genies; *WOGL Oldies 98-History Of Rock-#2* ....(CLT)
Yellow Woman's Door Bells
Leadbelly; *Leadbelly* ....(EVR)
  Leadbelly ....(FAN)

DRAFT
  See Also: POLITICAL CLASSICS, PROTEST, WAR

Alice's Restaurant Massacre
Arlo Guthrie; *Alice's Restaurant Massacre* .... (RPR)
  Best Of ....(WB)
Boogie Woogie Bugle Boy
Andrews Sisters; *16 Great Performances* .... (MCA)
  Best Of ....(MCA)
  Boogie Woogie Bugle Girls ....(MCA)
  Rarities ....(MCA)
Bette Midler; *Divine Miss M* ....(ATL)
  Live At Last ....(ATL)
  ST/Divine Madness ....(ATL)
Call Up
Clash; *Sandinista* .... (EPI)
Draft Dodger Rag
Phil Ochs; *Chords Of Fame* ....(A&M)
  I Ain't Marching Anymore ....(CTH)
  Newport Folk Music Festival '64 .... (VAN)
  There But For Fortune ....(ELE)
Draft Me If You Can
Joady Guthrie; *Spys On Wall Street* .... (RBB)
Draft Morning
Byrds; *Notorious Byrd Brothers* ....(COL)
  Byrds (collection) ....(COL)
Draft Resister
Steppenwolf; *Live* ....(MCA)
  Move Over ....(MSP)
Gone With The Draft
Benny Goodman; *Sextet Feat. Charles
Christian-1939-1941* ....(COL)
Hey Mr. Draft Board
David Peel; *American Revolution* ....(OOP)
I Don't Wanna Get Drafted
Frank Zappa; *45* .... (ZAP)
I Feel Like I'm Fixing To Die Rag
Country Joe/Fish; *Greatest Hits* ....(VAN)
  Greatest '60s Folksingers ....(VAN)
  I Feel Like I'm Fixing To Die Rag ....(VAN)
  Life & Times Of ....(VAN)
  More American Graffiti-#4 ....(MCA)
  ST/Woodstock ....(ATL)
I've Been Drafted
Chuck Foster & Jimmy Castle; *Uncollected Chuck
Foster/Orchestra-1940* .... (HIN)
No No No To Draft & War
Minutemen; *Ballot Result* ....(SST)

DREAMS
  See Also: PRETEND, SLEEP

35 Millimeter Dreams
Garland Jeffreys; *Ghost Rider* ....(A&M)
  Ghost Writer ....(A&M)
African Dream
Stewart Copeland; *Rhythmatist* ....(A&M)

All I Have To Do Is Dream
Everly Brothers;
  All They Had To Do Was Dream .... (RHI)
  Best Of ....(RHI)
  Fabulous Style Of ....(RHI)
  Heartaches 'N' Harmonies ....(RHI)
  Oldies But Goodies-#12 ....(OSR)
  ST/Stealing Home ....(ATL)
  Very Best Of ....(WB)
Nitty Gritty Dirt Band; *Best Of* .... (EMI)
  Heartbreak Hotel ....(EMI)
All My Dreams
Pretenders; *Last Of The Independents* .... (SIR)
All That You Dream
Linda Ronstadt; *Living In The U.S.A.* ....(ASY)
Little Feat; *Hoy-Hoy!* ....(WB)
  Last Record Album ....(WB)
  ST/Over The Edge ....(WB)
  Waiting For Columbus ....(WB)
American Dream
Chicago; *XIV* ....(COL)
Crosby, Stills, Nash & Young; *American Dream* .. (ATL)
John Cougar Mellencamp; *Chestnut Street Incident* (RHI)
  Early Years ....(RHI)
Nitty Gritty Dirt Band; *20 Years Of Dirt-Best Of* ..(WB)
Oak Ridge Boys; *American Dreams* ....(MCA)
Original London Cast; *Miss Saigon* ....(GEF)
And Dream Of Sheep
Kate Bush; *Hounds Of Love* .... (EMI)
Anita, You're Dreaming
Waylon Jennings; *Best Of* ....(RCA)
  Early Years ....(RCA)
Any Dream Will Do
Michael Crawford; *Performs Andrew Lloyd
Webber* ....(ATL)
Original Cast; *Joseph & The Amazing
Technicolor...* ....(MCA)
Are You Sitting Comfortably/The Dream
Moody Blues; *Caught Live Plus Five* ....(POL)
  On The Threshold Of A Dream ....(POL)
  This Is The ....(POL)
Army Dreamers
Kate Bush; *Never For Ever* .... (EMI)
  The Whole Story ....(EMI)
Beautiful Dreamer
Mormon Tabernacle Choir; *Album* ....(COL)
  Beautiful Dreamer ....(COL)
  Greatest Hits ....(COL)
  This Land Is Your Land ....(COL)
Big Dreams In A Small Town
Restless Heart; *Big Dreams In A Small Town* ....(RCA)
Black Snake Dream Blues
Blind Lemon Jefferson; *Master Of The
Blues-#2-1926-1929* ....(BIO)
Bob Dylan's 115th Dream
Bob Dylan; *Bringing It All Back Home* ....(COL)
Bob Dylan's Dream
Bob Dylan; *Freewheelin'* ....(COL)
Peter, Paul & Mary; *Album 1700* ....(WB)
Book Of Dreams
Bruce Springsteen; *Lucky Town* ....(COL)
Boulevard Of Broken Dreams
Tony Bennett; *16 Most Requested Songs* ....(COL)
  All-Time Greatest Hits ....(COL)
  Forty Years: Artistry Of ....(COL)
California Dreamin'
Beach Boys; *Made In The U.S.A.* ....(CAP)
Mamas & The Papas; *20 Golden Hits* ....(MCA)
  At The Hop ....(MCA)
  Good Feeling Music-Big Chill-#1 ....(MOT)
  ST/Air America ....(MCA)
  ST/American Pop ....(RLL)
  ST/Forrest Gump ....(EPX)
Carolina Dreams
Ronnie Milsap; *Inside* ....(RCA)
Castle Of Dreams
Dave Koz; *Dave Koz* ....(CAP)
Could've Been Me
Billy Ray Cyrus; *Some Gave All* .... (MER)
Cowboy Of Dreams
David Crosby & Graham Nash; *Wind On The
Water* ....(MCA)
Cowboy's Dream
Eddy Arnold; *Cattle Call* ....(RCA)

Jimmy C. Newman; *Cajun Cowboy* .... (PLN)
Cowboy's Dream No. 19
Dan Hicks/Hot Licks; *Last Train To Hicksville* .. (MCA)
Creepin'
Kenny Rankin; *Inside* .... (LD)
Luther Vandross; *Night I Fell In Love* .... (EPI)
Stevie Wonder; *Fulfillingness' First Finale* .... (MOT)
Daddy's Dream
Vikki Carr; *Live At The Greek Theatre* ....(COL)
Dancy's Dream
Restless Heart; *Fast Moving Train* ....(RCA)
Day Dream
Duke Ellington; *And His Mother Called Him Bill* . (BLU)
  Carnegie Hall Concert .... (PRS)
  Greatest Jazz Concert In The World .... (PAB)
  Jazz Violin Session ....(ATL)
Journey; *Evolution* ....(COL)
Robin Trower; *Live* .... (CHR)
  Twice Removed From Yesterday .... (CHR)
Daydream
Lovin' Spoonful; *Anthology* .... (RHI)
Daydream Believer
Anne Murray; *Greatest Hits* ....(CAP)
  I'll Always Love You ....(CAP)
Monkees; *Billboard Top Rock 'N' Roll Hits-1967* . (RHI)
  Greatest Hits .... (ARI)
  Mellow '60s .... (PRY)
Daydream Romance
Ray Stevens; *Feel The Music* .... (WB)
  Feeling's Not Right Again .... (WB)
Daydreaming
Aretha Franklin; *Ten Years Of Gold* .... (ATL)
  Young Gifted & Black .... (ATL)
Daydreams About Night Things
Ronnie Milsap; *Collectors' Series* ....(RCA)
  Greatest Hits ....(RCA)
  Live ....(RCA)
  Night Things ....(RCA)
Deep In A Dream
Artie Shaw; *This Is* ....(RCA)
Frank Sinatra; *In The Wee Small Hours* ....(CAP)
Detroit Snackbar Dreamer
Edgar Froese; *Stuntman* .... (BP)
Did You Ever See A Dream Walking
Bing Crosby; *Crosby Classics* ....(COL)
Hal Kemp/Skinnay Ennis; *Uncollected-#2 & #3* .. (HIN)
Dixie Dreamin'
Atlanta; *Pictures* .... (MCA)
Do You Ever Dream Of Vienna
Original Cast; *Little Mary Sunshine* ....(OOP)
Dolphin Dreams
Lee Ritenour; *Captain Fingers* .... (EPI)
  Collection .... (GRP)
  On The Line .... (GRP)
Don't Dream It's Over
Crowded House; *Crowded House* .... (CAP)
Don't Fall In Love With A Dreamer
Kenny Rogers; *20 Greatest Hits* .... (LIB)
Kenny Rogers & Kim Carnes; *Gideon* .... (UA)
  Greatest Hits .... (EMI)
Don't Make Me Dream About You
Chris Isaak; *Heart Shaped World* .... (RPR)
Down The River Of Golden Dreams
Mom & Dads; *Down The River Of Golden*
  Dreams .... (CRS)
Slim Whitman; *Home On The Range* .... (UA)
Dream
Frank Sinatra; *Greatest Hits-Early Years* ....(COL)
  Round #1 ....(CAP)
Dream A Little Dream Of Me
Ella Fitzgerald; *All That Jazz* .... (PAB)
Mama Cass; *Mama's Big Ones-Greatest Hits* .... (MCA)
Mamas & The Papas; *20 Golden Hits* .... (MCA)
  Best Of .... (MCA)
Dream All Day
Posies; *Frosting On The Beater* .... (DGC)
Dream Baby (How Long Must I Dream)
Lacy J. Dalton; *Dream Baby (How Long Must I*
  Dream) ....(COL)
  Greatest Country Hits/'80s-1983 ....(COL)
  Greatest Hits ....(COL)

Roy Orbison; *All-Time Greatest Hits-#1* .... (MON)
  For The Lonely: 18 Greatest Hits .... (RHI)
  For The Lonely: Anthology .... (RHI)
  In Dreams-Greatest Hits .... (VIA)
Dream Dancing
Ella Fitzgerald; *Dream Dancing* .... (PAB)
Dream Gerrard
Traffic; *When The Eagle Flies* .... (ASY)
Dream Girl
Stephen Bishop; *ST/Animal House* .... (MCA)
Dream Goes On Forever
Todd Rundgren; *Anthology 1968-1985* .... (RHI)
  Back To The Bars .... (RHI)
  Rock 'n' Roll High School .... (SIR)
  Todd .... (RHI)
Dream Home In New Zealand
English Beat; *Wha'ppen* .... (IRS)
Dream In June
Tom Harrell; *Sail Away* .... (CTM)
Dream Is A Wish Your Heart Makes
Barbara Cook; *Disney Album* .... (MCA)
Michael Bolton; *Simply Mad About The Mouse* ..(COL)
Dream Is Over
Van Halen; *For Unlawful Carnal Knowledge* ..... (WB)
Dream Is Still Alive
Wilson Phillips; *Wilson Phillips* .... (SBK)
Dream Lady
Bread; *Baby I'm A-Want You* .... (ELE)
  Best Of-#2 .... (ELE)
Dream Lover
Bobby Darin; *At The Copa* .... (BAI)
  Story ....(ATC)
Dion; *Runaround Sue* .... (CLT)
Marshall Tucker Band; *Best Of Country Rock* ..... (KT)
  Together Forever .... (AJK)
Regina Belle; *Stay With Me* ....(COL)
Tanya Tucker & Glen Campbell; *Best Of Tanya*
  Tucker .... (MCA)
Dream Maker
Rick James/Stone City Band; *Come Get It* ...... (MOT)
Dream Of Life
Billie Holiday; *Billie Holiday* ....(COL)
  Story-#1 ....(COL)
Carmen McRae; *Greatest Of* .... (MCA)
Patti Smith; *Dream Of Life* .... (ARI)
Dream Of Me
Vern Gosdin; *Today My World Slipped Away* .... (AMI)
Dream Of The Blue Turtles
Sting; *Dream Of The Blue Turtles* .... (A&M)
Dream On
Aerosmith; *Aerosmith* ....(COL)
  Classics Live ....(COL)
  Greatest Hits ....(COL)
  Live Bootleg ....(COL)
Mission U.K.; *Children* .... (MER)
Oak Ridge Boys; *Greatest Hits* .... (MCA)
  Oak Ridge Boys Have Arrived .... (MCA)
Southern Pacific; *Zuma* .... (WB)
Dream On Dreamer
Brand New Heavies; *Brother Sister* .... (DV)
Dream On Texas Ladies
John Michael Montgomery; *Life's A Dance* ...... (ATL)
  ST/Maverick .... (ATL)
Dream Police
Cheap Trick; *Dream Police* .... (EPI)
Dream That Can Last
Neil Young/Crazy Horse; *Sleeps With Angels* ..... (RPR)
Dream Weaver
Gary Wright; *Billboard Top Hits-1976* .... (RHI)
  Dream Weaver .... (WB)
Dream World
Jerry Butler; *Nothing Says I Love You Like I Love*
  You .... (PI)
Dreamboat Annie
Heart; *Dreamboat Annie* ....(CAP)
  Greatest Hits/Live .... (EPI)
Dreamer
Foghat; *Rock & Roll Outlaws* .... (RHI)
Supertramp; *Classics-#9* .... (A&M)
  Crime Of The Century .... (A&M)
  Paris .... (A&M)
Tommy Bolin; *Teaser* .... (NEM)
  The Ultimate... .... (GEF)
Toni Childs; *Union* .... (A&M)

Dreamer's Ball
Queen; *Jazz* .... (HOL)
   Live Killers .... (HOL)
Dreaming
Blondie; *Best Of* .... (CHR)
   Eat To The Beat .... (CHR)
Cliff Richard; *I'm No Hero* .... (EMI)
Kate Bush; *Dreaming* .... (EMI)
   Whole Story .... (EMI)
Orchestral Manoeuvres In The Dark; *Best Of*
OMD .... (A&M)
Dreaming A Dream
Crown Heights Affair; *Hustle Hits* .... (DL)
   Saturday Night Disco .... (DL)
Dreaming From The Waist
Who; *By Numbers* .... (MCA)
Dreaming In Metaphors
Seal; *Seal* .... (ZTT)
Dreaming My Dreams With You
Cowboy Junkies; *Trinity Session* ....(RCA)
Waylon Jennings; *Dreaming My Dreams* ....(RCA)
Dreaming While You Sleep
Genesis; *We Can't Dance* .... (ATL)
Dreaming With My Eyes Open
Clay Walker; *Clay Walker* .... (GIA)
Dreamin'
Vanessa Williams; *Right Stuff* .... (WIN)
Will To Power; *ST/Speedzone* .... (GDG)
   Will To Power .... (EPI)
Dreamin' Again
Jim Croce; *Life & Times* .... (LIF)
   Time In A Bottle .... (21)
Dreamland
Joni Mitchell; *Don Juan's Reckless Daughter* ..... (ASY)
   Shadows & Light .... (ASY)
Dreamland Express
John Denver; *Dreamland Express* .... (RCA)
Dreamline
Rush; *Roll The Bones* .... (ATL)
Dreamlover
Mariah Carey; *Music Box* .... (COL)
Dreams
BoDeans; *Outside Looking In* ....(SLS)
Cranberries; *Everybody Else Is Doing It So Why...* .. (ISL)
Fleetwood Mac; *25 Years-The Chain* .... (WB)
   Greatest Hits .... (WB)
   Live .... (WB)
   Rumours .... (WB)
Gabrielle; *S* .... (GO!)
Van Halen; *5150* .... (WB)
Dreams A Dream/Courtney Blows
Soul II Soul; *S* .... (VIA)
Dreams Die Hard
Gary Morris; *Gary Morris* .... (WB)
   Greatest Hits-II .... (WB)
Dreams Go By
Harry Chapin; *Greatest Stories-Live* .... (ELE)
   Portrait Gallery .... (ELE)
Dreams In America
Luka Bloom; *Riverside* .... (RPR)
Dreams Of Mexico
Arlen Roth; *Guitarist* .... (ROU)
Dreams Of The Everyday Housewife
Glen Campbell; *Classics Collection* .... (CAP)
   Greatest Hits .... (CAP)
   Live .... (CAP)
   Very Best Of .... (CAP)
Dreams (I'll Never See)
Allman Brothers Band; *Allman Brothers Band* .. (POL)
   An Evening With-First Set .... (EPI)
   Beginnings .... (POL)
   Best Of .... (POL)
   Decade Of Hits-1969-1979 .... (POL)
   Gregg Allman Tour .... (CPC)
   Road Goes On Forever .... (POL)
Molly Hatchet; *Molly Hatchet* .... (EPI)
Dreamsville
Henny Mancini; *Brass On Ivory* .... (RCA)
   Peter Gunn .... (RCA)
   This Is .... (RCA)
   With Doc Severinsen .... (RCA)
Dreamtime
Daryl Hall; *Three Hearts In The Happy Ending*
Machine .... (RCA)

Stranglers; *Dreamtime* .... (EPI)
Dreamy Georgiana Moon
Asa Martin; *Dr. Ginger Blue* .... (ROU)
Drift Off To Dream
Travis Tritt; *Country Club* .... (WB)
Drinkin' & Dreamin'
Waylon Jennings; *Best Of* ....(RCA)
   Greatest Greatest Hits ....(RCA)
   Turn The Page ....(RCA)
English Dream
Generation X; *Valley Of The Dolls* .... (CHR)
Every Little Girl's Dream
Lisa Brokop; *Every Little Girl's Dream* .... (PAT)
Fast Car
Tracy Chapman; *Tracy Chapman* .... (ELE)
Find A Dream
Crosby, Stills & Nash; *After The Storm* .... (ATL)
Gemini Dream
Moody Blues; *Long Distance Voyager* .... (POL)
   Voices In The Sky-Best Of ....(T/P)
Get Outta My Dreams, Get Into My Car
Billy Ocean; *Greatest Hits* .... (JVA)
   ST/License To Drive .... (MCA)
Girl Of My Dreams
Bram Tchaikovsky; *D.I.Y.-#4-UK Pop II-Starry*
Eyes-1978-79 .... (RHI)
   Strange Man Changed Man .... (POL)
Buddy Clark; *16 Most Requested Songs* ....(COL)
Dizzy Gillespie & Stan Getz; *Diz & Getz* ....(VRV)
Had A Dream (Sleeping With The Enemy)
Roger Hodgson; *In The Eye Of The Storm* ...... (A&M)
Havana Daydreamin'
Jimmy Buffett; *Havana Daydreamin'* .... (MCA)
   You Had To Be There .... (MCA)
Help You Dream
Blasters; *Collection* .... (SLS)
   Hard Line .... (SLS)
High Hopes And Empty Pockets
Terry McBride/Ride; *Terry McBride & The Ride* (MCA)
Hold On Tight
Electric Light Orchestra; *Exposition* .... (EPI)
   Time .... (JET)
Hollywood Dream
James Gang; *Jesse Come Home* ....(ATC)
Steve Miller Band; *Italian X-Rays* .... (CAP)
Thunderclap Newman; *Hollywood Dream* .... (MCA)
Hollywood Dreaming
Father's Children; *Father's Children* .... (MER)
House Un-American Blues Activity Dream
Mimi & Richard Farina; *Best Of* .... (VAN)
   Memories .... (VAN)
   Reflections In A Crystal Wind .... (VAN)
How Can We Hang Onto A Dream
Tim Hardin; *Memorial Album* .... (POL)
I Can Dream About You
Dan Hartman; *I Can Dream About You* .... (MCA)
   Soundtrack Smashes!'80s .... (MCA)
   ST/Streets Of Fire .... (MCA)
I Dream Of Jeanie With Light Brown Hair
Al Jolson; *Story-#5* .... (MCA)
Joan Baez; *Diamonds & Rust* .... (A&M)
Mormon Tabernacle Choir; *Beautiful Dreamer* ...(COL)
   Greatest Hits-#3 .... (COL)
   Old Beloved Songs .... (COL)
I Dream Of Women Like You
Ronnie McDowell; *Country Boy's Heart* .... (EPI)
   Older Women & Other Greatest Hits .... (EPI)
I Dreamed I Saw St. Augustine
Bob Dylan; *John Wesley Harding* ....(COL)
Joan Baez; *Any Day Now* .... (VAN)
I Dreamed Of A Hillbilly Heaven
Tex Ritter; *An American Legend* .... (CAP)
   Best Of .... (CAP)
   Hillbilly Heaven .... (CAP)
   Opry Legends .... (CAP)
I Found A Dream
Bob Wills; *Anthology* .... (SSP)
I Got Dreams
Steve Wariner; *I Got Dreams* .... (MCA)
I Guess I Was Dreaming
Kingsmen; *Nuggets-#8* .... (WB)
I Had A Dream
John Sebastian; *ST/Woodstock* .... (ATL)

I Had A Dream Last Night
Buddy Guy; *Best Of The Chicago Blues* .... (VAN)
   This Is .... (VAN)
I Had The Craziest Dream
Frank Sinatra; *Trilogy* .... (RPR)
I Had Too Much To Dream (Last Night)
Electric Prunes; *Even More Nuggets* .... (RHI)
   Nuggets-#1-The Hits .... (RHI)
   Summer Of Love .... (RHI)
I Have Dreamed
Barbra Streisand; *Broadway Album* .... (COL)
   Original Broadway Cast; *King & I* .... (RCA)
   Original Cast; *King & I* .... (MCA)
I Never Dreamed
Lynyrd Skynyrd; *Best Of The Rest* .... (MCA)
   Street Survivors .... (MCA)
I Touched A Dream
Dells; *Ear Candy-#2* .... (20)
   I Touched A Dream .... (20)
I Was Born A Dreamer
Mickey Gilley; *Live At Gilley's* .... (EPI)
   ST/Tough Enough .... (LIB)
I Wish I Was Still In Your Dreams
Conway Twitty; *Still In Your Dreams* .... (MCA)
If I Can Dream
Elvis Presley; *Golden Records-#5* .... (RCA)
   Great Performances .... (RCA)
   Legendary Performer-#2 .... (RCA)
   Worldwide 50 Gold Award Hits-#1 .... (RCA)
If There Were No Dreams
Neil Diamond; *Lovescape* .... (COL)
If You Are But A Dream
Frank Sinatra; *Greatest Hits-Early Years* .... (COL)
   Sarah Vaughan; *Slightly Classical* .... (RLL)
Impossible Dream
Andy Williams; *16 Most Requested Songs* .... (COL)
   Greatest Hits-#2 .... (COL)
   Impossible Dream .... (COL)
   Ed Ames; *Best Of* .... (RCA)
   Impossible Dream .... (RCA)
   Pure Gold .... (RCA)
   This Is .... (RCA)
   Jack Jones; *Best Of* .... (MCA)
   Kate Smith; *Best Of* .... (RCA)
   Legendary Performer .... (RCA)
   Luther Vandross; *Songs* .... (EPI)
   Original Cast; *Man Of La Mancha* .... (MCA)
   Original London Cast; *Man Of La Mancha* ..... (MCA)
   Robert Goulet; *Greatest Hits* .... (COL)
In A Daydream
Freddy Jones Band; *Waiting For The Night* .... (CPC)
In City Dreams
Robin Trower; *In City Dreams* .... (CHR)
In My Dreams
Big Audio Dynamite II; *The Globe* .... (COL)
   Crosby, Stills & Nash; *CSN* .... (ATL)
   Dokken; *Beast From The East* .... (ELE)
   Under Lock & Key .... (ELE)
   Emmylou Harris; *White Shoes* .... (WB)
   Judds; *Love Can Build A Bridge* .... (RCC)
   R.E.O. Speedwagon; *Hits* .... (EPI)
   Life As We Know It .... (EPI)
   Tracie Spencer; *Tracie Spencer* .... (CAP)
I'll See You In My Dreams
Doris Day; *At The Movies* .... (COL)
   Doris Day & Danny Thomas; *Calamity Jane/I'll See You*
   In My Dreams .... (SSP)
I'll Tennessee You In My Dreams
Tanya Tucker; *Love Me Like You Used To* .... (CAP)
I'm Dreamin'
Christopher Williams; *ST/New Jack City* .... (GIA)
I've Got Dreams To Remember
Delbert McClinton; *Live From Austin* .... (ALG)
   Etta James; *Sticking To My Guns* .... (ISL)
   Otis Redding; *Story* .... (ATL)
Just A Country Dream
Eric Andersen; *Best Of* .... (VAN)
   Country Dream .... (VAN)
Just A Dream
Jimmy Clanton; *Good Old Rock & Roll* .... (GUS)
   Lovin' '50s .... (PRY)
   Super Oldies/'50s-#1 .... (AUF)
Just Another Dream
Cathy Dennis; *Move To This* .... (POL)

Keep On Dreamin'
Alabama; *My Home's In Alabama* .... (RCA)
Kiss To Build A Dream On
Louis Armstrong; *Best Of* .... (MCA)
   Essential .... (VAN)
   Hello Dolly (& Other Hits) .... (MCA)
Last Night I Had A Dream
Randy Newman; *Sail Away* .... (RPR)
   "Live" .... (RPR)
Last Night I Had The Strangest Dream
Simon & Garfunkel; *Collected Works* .... (COL)
   Wednesday Morning 3 A.M. .... (COL)
Lazarus Heart
Sting; *...Nothing Like The Sun* .... (A&M)
Life Is But A Dream
Harptones; *Echoes Of A Rock Era* .... (RLL)
   ST/Goodfellas .... (ATL)
   Super Oldies/'50s-#4 .... (AUF)
Little Dreamer
Van Halen; *Van Halen* .... (WB)
Living In A Dream
Arc Angels; *Arc Angels* .... (DGC)
   Band; *Anthology-#2* .... (CAP)
   Islands .... (CAP)
   Sea Level; *On The Edge* .... (CPC)
Long Hard Road (Sharecropper's Dream)
Nitty Gritty Dirt Band; *Live Two Five* .... (CAP)
   Plain Dirt Fashion .... (WB)
   Tewenty Years Of Dirt-Best Of .... (WB)
Lost In A Dream
Buster Brown; *New King Of The Blues* .... (CLT)
   Johnny Otis; *Roots Of Rock & Roll* .... (SAV)
   R.E.O. Speedwagon; *Decade Of Rock &*
   Roll-1970-1980 .... (EPI)
   Lost In A Dream .... (EPI)
L.A. Dreams
Charlie; *Lines* .... (JNS)
Maggie's Dream
Don Williams; *Cafe Carolina* .... (MCA)
   Country Classics-#4-1984-1985 .... (MCA)
Midnight Dreamer
Journey; *Look Into The Future* .... (COL)
Mister Sandman
Chordettes; *Best Of* .... (RHI)
   Emmylou Harris; *Evangeline* .... (WB)
   Profile 2-Best Of .... (WB)
Moonage Daydream
David Bowie; *Live* .... (RYK)
   Man Who Sold The World .... (RYK)
   Rise & Fall Of Ziggy Stardust .... (RYK)
   Sound + Vision .... (RYK)
   ST/Ziggy Stardust-The Motion Picture .... (RCA)
Mothers Dream
Candlebox; *Candlebox* .... (MAV)
Music In Dreamland
Be Bop Deluxe; *Best Of & The Rest Of* .... (HAR)
   Best Of-Raiding The Divine Archive .... (CAP)
   Futurama .... (HAR)
My Exclusive Dreams
Bobby Vinton; *All-Time Greatest Hits* .... (EPI)
   Autumn Memories .... (EPI)
   Charlie Rich; *Greatest Hits* .... (EPI)
Neon Moon
Brooks & Dunn; *Brand New Man* .... (ARI)
Never Dreamed You'd Leave In Summer
Joan Baez; *Best Of* .... (A&M)
   Classics-#8 .... (A&M)
   Diamond & Rust .... (A&M)
   Stevie Wonder; *20 Classic Hits* .... (MOT)
   Greatest Hits-#2 .... (MOT)
   Looking Back .... (MOT)
   Where I'm Coming From .... (MOT)
Never Had A Dream Come True
Stevie Wonder; *Greatest Hits-#2* .... (MOT)
   Signed Sealed & Delivered .... (MOT)
New Gold Dream
Simple Minds; *In The City Of Light (Live)* .... (A&M)
   New Gold Dream .... (A&M)
   Utah Saints; *Utah Saints* .... (LON)
Nickel Dreams
Nanci Griffith; *Lone Star State Of Mind* .... (MCA)
Nightmare
Artie Shaw; *Begin The Beguine* .... (BLU)
   Best Of The Big Bands .... (COL)

Black Sabbath; *Eternal Idol* .... (WB)
Eddie Money; *Life For The Taking* ....(COL)
Slaughterhouse; *Face Reality* .... (MET)
Stevie Nicks; *Rock A Little* .... (MOD)
Nightmares
A Flock Of Seagulls; *Best Of* .... (JVA)
  Listen .... (JVA)
Dana Dane; *Rap Hall Of Fame* .... (KT)
  With Fame ....(PRO)
J. Geils Band; *Nightmares* ....(ATL)
Omen; *Nightmares* .... (MET)
Violent Femmes; *2* ....(SLS)
Number 9 Dream
John Lennon; *John Lennon Collection* ....(CAP)
  Lennon ....(CAP)
  Shaved Fish ....(CAP)
  Walls & Bridges ....(CAP)
Ocean Of Thoughts & Dreams
Dramatics; *Shake It Well* .... (MCA)
Oklahoma Heartaches & California Dreams
Kris Carpenter; *45* .... (DOO)
One Summer Dream
Electric Light Orchestra; *Afterglow* .... (EPI)
  Face The Music ....(JET)
Only A Dream In Rio
James Taylor; *That's Why I'm Here* ....(COL)
Only In My Dreams
Debbie Gibson; *Out Of The Blue* .... (ATL)
Out Of My Dreams
Original Broadway Cast; *Oklahoma* ....(RCA)
Original Cast; *Oklahoma* .... (MCA)
Paddy Ryan's Dream
Matt Molloy; *Stony Steps* ....(GRE)
Patriot's Dream
Gordon Lightfoot; *Don Quixote* .... (RPR)
Pilate's Dream
Original London Cast; *Jesus Christ Superstar* .... (MCA)
Pipe Dreams
Asleep At The Wheel; *Collision Course* ....(CAP)
Planet Of My Dreams
Frank Zappa; *Them Or Us* ....(BAR)
Psychobabble
Alan Parsons Project; *Best Of* .... (ARI)
  Eye In The Sky .... (ARI)
Put Your Dreams Away
Frank Sinatra; *16 Most Requested Songs* ....(COL)
  Capitol Years ....(CAP)
  Greatest Hits-Early Years ....(COL)
  Man & His Music ....(RPR)
Mickey Gilley; *Put Your Dreams Away* ....(EPI)
  Ten Years Of Hits ....(EPI)
Rachel's Dream
Benny Goodman; *I Like Jazz-Essence Of* ....(COL)
  Yale Recordings-#5 ....(MM)
Radio Dream Girl
Roger Voudouris; *Radio Dream Girl* .... (WB)
Rest Of The Dream
John Hiatt; *Stolen Moments* .... (A&M)
Nitty Gritty Dirt Band; *Rest Of The Dream* ..... (MCA)
River Of Dreams
Billy Joel; *River Of Dreams* ....(COL)
Rock And Roll Dreams Come...
Meat Loaf; *Bat Out Of Hell II-Back Into Hell* ... (MCA)
Runnin' Down A Dream
Tom Petty; *Full Moon Fever* .... (MCA)
Scene From A Night's Dream
Genesis; *And Then There Were Three* ....(ATL)
Send Me The Pillow You Dream On
Dwight Yoakam; *Buenas Noches From A Lonely*
Room .... (RPR)
Hank Locklin; *20 Golden Souvenirs* ....(RCA)
  Nipper's Greatest Hits-'50s-#1 ....(RCA)
  Stars Of The Grand Ole Opry 1926-1974 ......(RCA)
Willie Nelson & Hank Snow; *Brand On My*
Heart ....(COL)
Sewer Pipe Dream
Close Lobsters; *Foxheads Stalk This Land* .... (ENI)
Shadow Dream Song
Tom Rush; *Circle Game* ....(ELE)
  Classic Rush ....(ELE)
Shattered Dreams
Johnny Hates Jazz; *Turn Back The Clock* .... (VIA)
Lowell Fulson; *Blues Around Midnight* ....(FLA)

She Dreams
Mark Chesnutt; *What A Way To Live* .... (DEC)
Ship Of Dreams
Nazareth; *Malice In Wonderland* ....(A&M)
Sh-Boom
Chords; *Atlantic R&B 1947-1974-#2*
(1952-1955) ....(ATL)
Crew Cuts; *Partytime '50s* ....(PRY)
Stan Freberg; *Capitol Collectors Series* ....(CAP)
Silver Dreams
Babys; *Broken Heart* ....(CHR)
Simple Man Simple Dream
J.D. Souther; *Black Rose* .... (ASY)
Linda Ronstadt; *Simple Dreams* .... (ASY)
Smoke Dreams (Chesterfield Supper Club)
Benny Goodman; *Complete-#3* ....(RCA)
  This Is-#2 ....(RCA)
Mildred Bailey; *Her Greatest* ....(COL)
Spanish Pipedream
John Prine; *John Prine* .... (ATL)
Straight Back
Fleetwood Mac; *Mirage* .... (WB)
Street Of Dreams
Ella Fitzgerald; *Best Of* .... (PAB)
Frank Sinatra; *Reprise Collection* .... (RPR)
  Sinatra At The Sands-In Concert ....(RPR)
Ink Spots; *Best Of* .... (MCA)
  Greatest Hits ....(MCA)
Nia Peeples; *Nia Peeples* ....(CHS)
Rainbow; *Bent Out Of Shape* ....(MER)
  Finyl Vinyl ....(MER)
Ray Brown Trio; *Red Hot Ray Brown Trio* .... (CCJ)
Tommy Dorsey & Frank Sinatra; *All-Time Greatest*
Hits-#1 ....(RCA)
Tony Bennett; *Jazz* ....(COL)
Stuff That Dreams Are Made Of
Carly Simon; *Coming Around Again* .... (ARI)
Sugar Magnolia
Grateful Dead; *American Beauty* .... (WB)
  Europe '72 .... (WB)
  Live-#1 .... (JCI)
  Skeletons From The Closet-Best Of .... (WB)
Summertime Dream
Gordon Lightfoot; *Summertime Dream* .... (RPR)
Sunset Dream
Clannad; *Banba* .... (ATL)
Sweet Dream
Jethro Tull; *20 Years Of-Radio Archives & Rare*
Tracks .... (CHR)
  Bursting Out .... (CHR)
  Living In The Past .... (CHR)
  Original Masters .... (CHR)
Sweet Dreams
Air Supply; *Greatest Hits* .... (ARI)
  The One That You Love .... (ARI)
Chet Atkins & Mark Knopfler; *Neck & Neck* ....(COL)
Don Gibson; *18 Greatest Hits* ....(CCB)
  All-Time Greatest Hits ....(RCA)
Emmylou Harris; *Elite Hotel* .... (RPR)
  Profile-Best Of .... (WB)
Patsy Cline; *Greatest Hits* .... (MCA)
  ST/Sweet Dreams .... (MCA)
Reba McEntire; *Out Of A Dream* ....(MER)
Yes; *Time & A Word* ....(ATL)
  Yesterdays .... (ATL)
Sweet Dreams Of You
Emmylou Harris; *Brand New Dance* ....(RPR)
Jim Reeves & Patsy Cline; *Greatest Hits* ....(RCA)
Patsy Cline; *Story* .... (MCA)
Sweet Dreams (Are Made Of This)
Eurythmics; *Greatest Hits* .... (ARI)
  Sweet Dreams (Are Made Of This) ....(RCA)
Television Nightmare
Madrigal; *Madrigal* .... (SSS)
Tell Me I'm Not Dreaming
Robert Palmer; *Heavy Nova* .... (EMI)
Tell Me I'm Not Dreamin'
Jermaine Jackson; *Jermaine Jackson* .... (ARI)
Tell Me I'm Only Dreaming
Lorrie Morgan; *Classics* ....(CCB)
Tell Me This Is A Dream
Delfonics; *Best Of* .... (ARI)
These Dreams
Heart; *Heart* ....(CAP)

Jim Croce; *Photographs & Memories-Greatest Hits* . (21)
   Time In A Bottle .... (21)
These Dreams Of You
Van Morrison; *It's Too Late To Stop Now* ....(WB)
   Moondance ....(WB)
This Dream's On Me
Gene Watson; *Greatest Hits* .... (MCA)
   MCA Records 30 Years Of Hits-1958-1988 ... (MCA)
This Time The Dream's On Me
Annie Ross & Gerry Mulligan; *Annie Ross Sings A Song
With Mulligan* .... (EMI)
Anthony Newley; *Great American Songwriters-#2-J.
Mercer* .... (RHI)
Charlie Parker; *Bebop & Bird-#2* .... (RHI)
Ella Fitzgerald; *Harold Arlen Songbook-#1* .....(VRV)
Harry Connick, Jr.; *25* ....(COL)
Those Good Old Dreams
Carpenters; *Classics-#2* ....(A&M)
   Yesterday Once More ....(A&M)
To Dream The Dream
Frankie Miller; *Standing On The Edge* ....(CAP)
Tomorrow's Dreams
Black Sabbath; *We Sold Our Soul For Rock & Roll* (WB)
   #4 ....(WB)
Trucker's Nightmare
Lawrence Hammond; *Coyote's Dream* ....(TAK)
   Critic's Choice ....(TAK)
Tulip Or Turnip (Tell You Dream Face)
Duke Ellington & Teresa Brewer; *It Don't Mean A
Thing If It Ain't Got...* ....(COL)
TV Dreams
Charlie; *Fantasy Girls* ....(COL)
Wake Up Dreaming
Little Feat; *Down On The Farm* ....(WB)
Waking & Dreaming
Orleans; *Waking & Dreaming* ....(ASY)
Walking Dream
Patsy Cline; *Forever & Always* ....(EPI)
   Here's ....(MCA)
When I Dream
Barbra Streisand; *Emotion* ....(COL)
Crystal Gayle; *All-Time Greatest Hits* ....(CCB)
   Classic Crystal .... (EMI)
Willie Nelson; *Partners* ....(COL)
When I Grow Too Old To Dream
Benny Goodman/Orchestra; *Best Of* ....(CCB)
Linda Ronstadt; *Living In The U.S.A.* ....(ASY)
Louis Armstrong; *Essential* ....(VAN)
When My Ship Comes In
Clint Black; *Hard Way* ....(RCA)
Wide Awake In Dreamland
Pat Benatar; *Wide Awake In Dreamland* ....(CHR)
Wildest Dreams
Annie Haslam; *Annie Haslam* .... (EPI)
Asia; *Asia* ....(GEF)
   Then & Now ....(GEF)
Dolly Parton; *Eagle When She Flies* ....(COL)
Wild-Eyed Dream
Ricky Van Shelton; *Wild-Eyed Dream* ....(COL)
With My Eyes Wide Open I'm Dreaming
Patti Page; *Golden Hits* .... (MER)
   Greatest Hits ....(COL)
Yesterday's Dreams
Four Tops; *Anthology* ....(MOT)
You Can Dream Of Me
Steve Wariner; *Greatest Hits* .... (MCA)
   Life's Highway ....(MCA)
You Dream Flat Tires
Joni Mitchell; *Wild Things Run Fast* ....(GEF)
You Make My Dreams
Daryl Hall & John Oates; *Rock & Soul-Part 1-Greatest
Hits* ....(RCA)
   Voices ....(RCA)
You Stepped Out Of A Dream
Morgana King; *Higher Ground* ....(MUS)
Nat King Cole; *Gift Set* ....(CAP)
   Sings For Two In Love ....(CAP)
Oscar Peterson; *Live At The North Sea Jazz
Festival* ....(PAB)
Sarah Vaughan; *Roulette Years* ....(RLL)
Young Dreams
Elvis Presley; *50 Worldwide Gold Award Hits-#2* (RCA)
   ST/King Creole ....(RCA)

Young Thing, Wild Dreams (Rock Me)
Red Rider; *Breaking Curfew* ....(CAP)
Your Summer Dream
Beach Boys; *Surfer Girl/Shut Down-#2* ....(CAP)
   Surfer Girl/Surfin' U.S.A. ....(MOB)
Your Wildest Dreams
Moody Blues; *Other Side Of Life* ....(POL)

DRUGS, Addictions, Anti-drugs, High Consciousness, Natural High

> *See Also: ALCOHOL, DRUGS: COCAINE, MARIJUANA*

25th Floor
Patti Smith; *Easter* .... (ARI)
7 Things To Do On Speed
God's Acre; *Ten Gospel Greats* ....(WAX)
Addicted
Dan Seals; *Greatest Hits* ....(CAP)
   Rage On ....(CAP)
Le Roux; *Last Safe Place* ....(RCA)
Addicted To Love
Robert Palmer; *Addictions-#1* .... (ISL)
   Island Story (1962-1987)-25th Annivers. .... (ISL)
   Riptide .... (ISL)
Tina Turner; *Live In Europe* ....(CAP)
Addicted To Spuds
Weird Al Yankovic; *Food Album* ....(RAR)
   Greatest Hits ....(RAR)
Addictive Love
Be Be & Ce Ce Winans; *Different Lifestyles* ......(CAP)
Ain't It Strange
Patti Smith; *Radio Ethiopia* .... (ARI)
All Time High
Rita Coolidge; *13 Original James Bond Themes* .. (EMI)
   Classics-#5 ....(A&M)
   ST/Octopussy ....(A&M)
Am I High
Asleep At The Wheel; *Served Live* ....(CAP)
Amphetamine Annie
Canned Heat; *Best Of* .... (EMI)
   Boogie With ....(LIB)
And It Stoned Me
Van Morrison; *Best Of* .... (MER)
   Moondance ....(WB)
Angel Dust
Gil Scott-Heron & Brian Jackson; *Secrets* .... (ARI)
New Order; *Brotherhood* ....(QUE)
Aspirin Damage
Alice Cooper; *Flush The Fashion* ....(WB)
Been On A Train
Laura Nyro; *Christmas & The Beads Of Sweat* ...(COL)
Billy Dee
Kris Kristofferson; *Silver Tongued Devil & I* ......(COL)
Boys 'R A Drug
Julie Brown; *Trapped In The Body Of A White Girl* (SIR)
Break It Up
Patti Smith; *Horses* .... (ARI)
British Pharmaceuticals
Miss World; *Miss World* ....(ATL)
Candy Man
Fred Neil; *Little Bit Of Rain* .... (ELE)
Grateful Dead; *American Beauty* ....(WB)
Mississippi John Hurt; *Best Of* ....(VAN)
   Today ....(VAN)
Roy Orbison; *All-Time Greatest Hits* .... (MON)
   Greatest Hits .... (MON)
   In Dreams: Greatest Hits .... (VIA)
   Very Best Of .... (MON)
Carmelita
Linda Ronstadt; *Simple Dreams* ....(ASY)
Warren Zevon; *Warren Zevon* ....(ASY)
Cheap Shot
John Cougar Mellencamp; *Early Years* .... (RHI)
   Kid Inside .... (RHI)
   Nothin' Matters & What If It Did ....(RIV)
Cloud Nine
Temptations; *25 Years Of Grammy Greats* ...... (MOT)
   Cloud Nine .... (MOT)
   Greatest Hits-#2 .... (MOT)
   Motown Grammy R&B Performances-'60s/'70s (MOT)
   Motown Story .... (MOT)

Cold Blue Steel & Sweet Fire
Joni Mitchell; *For The Roses* .... (ASY)
   Miles Of Aisles .... (ASY)
Cold Turkey
John Lennon; *Live In New York City* ....(CAP)
   Shaved Fish ....(CAP)
   /Plastic Ono Band: Live Peace In Toronto ......(CAP)
Comfortably Numb
Pink Floyd; *Delicate Sound Of Thunder* ....(COL)
   Knebworth-The Album ....(POL)
   The Wall ....(COL)
Roger Waters; *The Wall Live In Berlin* .... (MER)
Coming Down (Drug Tongue)
Cult; *The Cult* .... (SIR)
Copenhagen Junkie
Chris LeDoux; *Melodies & Memories* .... (LIB)
Crystal Ship
Doors; *13* .... (ELE)
   Best Of .... (ELE)
   Classics .... (ELE)
   Doors .... (ELE)
Dangerous Drug
Electric Angels; *Electric Angels* .... (ATL)
Dealer
Deep Purple; *Come Taste The Band* .... (MET)
Santana; *Inner Secrets* ....(COL)
Traffic; *Mr. Fantasy* .... (ISL)
Devil Is Dope
Dramatics; *Best Of* .... (STX)
   Dramatic Experience .... (STX)
Dope Addict
Sly Dunbar; *Sly Wicked & Slick* .... (FL)
Dope Head Blues
Victoria Spivey; *News & The Blues-Telling It Like It
Is* ....(COL)
Doper Than Dope
Salt-N-Pepa; *Black's Magic* ....(LON)
Drug Dealer
Reggie Knighton; *Reggie Knighton* ....(COL)
Drug Squad
Steel Pulse; *Reggae Fever (Caught You)* ....(MGO)
Drug Store Cowboy
Humble Pie; *Eat It* .... (A&M)
Drug Store Truck Drivin' Man
Byrds; *Best Of-Greatest Hits-#2* ....(COL)
   Byrds ....(COL)
   Dr. Byrds & Mr. Hyde ....(COL)
Gram Parsons/Fallen Angels; *Live 1973* ....(SIE)
Joan Baez & Jeffrey Shurtleff; *ST/Woodstock* ....(ATL)
Drug Store Woman
John Lee Hooker; *Best Of* ....(CRS)
   Best Of .... (VJ)
Drug Train
Cramps; *Bad Music For Bad People* .... (IRS)
Social Distortion; *Social Distortion* .... (EPI)
Drug (It's Just A State Of Mind)
Duran Duran; *Big Thing* ....(CAP)
Drugland Weekend
Hounds; *Unleashed* ....(COL)
Drugs
Lazy Cowgirls; *Lazy Cowgirls* .... (RES)
   ST/Border Radio .... (ENI)
Talking Heads; *Fear Of Music* .... (SIR)
   Name Of This Band Is .... (SIR)
Drugs Suck
Steve Jones; *Mercy* ....(GLM)
Drug-Stabbing Time
Clash; *Give 'Em Enough Rope* .... (EPI)
Eclipse
Pink Floyd; *Dark Side Of The Moon* ....(CAP)
   Works ....(CAP)
Eight Miles High
Byrds; *Byrds* ....(COL)
   Fifth Dimension ....(COL)
   Greatest Hits ....(COL)
   Original Singles-#1-1965-1967 ....(COL)
   (Untitled) ....(COL)
Leo Kottke; *Best Of* ....(CAP)
   Mudlark ....(CAP)
Roxy Music; *Flesh & Blood* ....(RPR)
Euphoria
Youngbloods; *Best Of The* ....(RCA)
   This Is The ....(RCA)

Everyday Feels Like Another Drug
Bill Nelson; *Vistamix* .... (EPI)
Friendly Neighborhood Narco Agent
Jef Jaisun; *Dr. Demento's Delight* ....(WB)
Get My Rocks Off
Dr. Hook/Medicine Show; *Revisited* ....(COL)
   Sloppy Seconds ....(COL)
Getaway
Earth, Wind & Fire; *Best Of-#1* ....(COL)
   Spirit ....(COL)
Kiss; *Dressed To Kill* ....(CAS)
   Originals ....(CAS)
Rossington-Collins Band;
   Anytime-Anyplace-Anywhere ....(MCA)
Ghost Dance
Patti Smith; *Easter* .... (ARI)
Happiness Is A Warm Gun
Beatles; *White Album* ....(CAP)
Hard Habit To Break
Chicago; *17* ....(WB)
   Greatest Hits-1982-1989 .... (FM)
Hard Monkeys
Ten Years After; *A Space In Time* ....(COL)
Heroin
Lou Reed; *Rock 'n' Roll Animal* ....(RCA)
Velvet Underground; *1969 Live* .... (MER)
   ST/Doors .... (ELE)
   Velvet Underground & Nico ....(VRV)
Hi Hi Hi
Paul McCartney/Wings; *Greatest* ....(CAP)
   Over America ....(CAP)
High Enough
Damn Yankees; *Damn Yankees* .... (WB)
High On Drugs
Lou & Peter Berryman; *February March* .... (COR)
High On Emotion
Chris DeBurgh; *Man On The Line* ....(A&M)
High On Love
Foghat; *Stone Blue* .... (RHI)
High On Sunshine
Commodores; *Hot On The Tracks* ....(MOT)
High On You
Survivor; *Vital Signs* ....(SCO)
High On Your Love Suite/One Mo Hit
Rick James; *Bustin' Out Of L Seven* .... (GOR)
Higher Ground
Stevie Wonder; *Innervisions* ....(MOT)
   Original Musiquarium ....(MOT)
UB40; *Promises And Lies* .... (VIA)
Higher & Higher (Your Love Keeps...)
Bette Midler; *Bette Midler* ....(ATL)
Bonnie Bramlett; *It's Time* ....(CPC)
Jackie Wilson; *Billboard Top R&B Hits-1967* .... (RHI)
   Greatest Hits ....(BRU)
   Greatest Hits-#2 ....(BRU)
   Reet Petite-Best Of ....(COL)
   Soul Shots-#1 .... (RHI)
   Story .... (EPI)
Rita Coolidge; *Anytime...Anywhere* ....(A&M)
   Classics-#5 ....(A&M)
   Greatest Hits ....(A&M)
   Havana Jam ....(COL)
Home Is Where The Hatred Is
Esther Phillips; *Best Of* ....(CBA)
   From A Whisper To A Scream ....(CBA)
Gil Scott-Heron; *Gil ScoHome Is Where The Hatred
Is-Heron* ....(BLU)
   It's Your World .... (ARI)
   Pieces Of A Man ....(FLD)
Horse With No Name
America; *America* ....(WB)
   Billboard Top Rock 'N' Roll Hits-1972 .... (RHI)
   History-Greatest Hits ....(WB)
   In Concert ....(WB)
I Can Get Off On You
Waylon Jennings & Willie Nelson; *Waylon &
Willie* ....(RCA)
Willie Nelson; *Willie & Family Live* ....(RCA)
I Like Drugs
Simpletones; *Posh Hits-#1* ....(PBO)
I Wanna Be Sedated
Ramones; *Ramones Mania* .... (SIR)
   Road To Ruin .... (SIR)

I Want A New Drug
Huey Lewis/News; *Sports* .... (CHR)
I Want To Take You Higher
Ike & Tina Turner; *Proud Mary-Best Of* .... (EMI)
Sly/Family Stone; *Anthology* .... (EPI)
Greatest Hits .... (EPI)
Illegal Smile
John Prine; *John Prine* .... (ATL)
Prime Prine .... (ATL)
In Praise Of Drugs & Alcohol
San Francisco Mime Troupe; *Steel Town* .... (FF)
It Ain't Nobody's Business
Billie Holiday; *History Of-Real Billie Holiday* .... (VRV)
Mississippi John Hurt; *Best Of* .... (VAN)
I'm Waiting For The Man
Lou Reed; *Live* .... (RCA)
Velvet Underground; *Live* .... (COT)
Velvet Underground & Nico .... (VRV)
Johnny Bye Bye
Bruce Springsteen; *45* .... (COL)
Jukebox Junkie
Ken Mellons; *Ken Mellons* .... (EPI)
Jukebox Junky
Jerry Lee Lewis; *Out-of-print recording* .... (OOP)
Kenny Price; *Out-of-print recording* .... (OOP)
Julie's In The Drug Squad
Clash; *Give 'Em Enough Rope* .... (EPI)
Junker's Blues
King Curtis & Champion Jack Dupree; *Blues At Montreaux* .... (ATL)
Mike Bloomfield; *Best Of* .... (TAK)
Cruisin' For A Bruisin' .... (TAK)
Junkie
Dead Milkmen; *Big Lizard In My Backyard* ...... (RES)
Junkie For My Music
Lonnie Jordan; *Different Moods Of Me* .... (MCA)
Junkie For You
Ray Stevens; *Feel The Music* .... (WB)
Junkie For Your Love
Cash McCall; *Omega Man* .... (PLA)
Junkie's Lament
James Taylor; *In The Pocket* .... (WB)
Junkie's Prayer
Fishbone; *Reality Of My Surroundings* ....(COL)
Statler Brothers; *Bed Of Rose's* .... (MER)
Junkman
Danny O'Keefe; *Breezy Stories* .... (ATL)
Kicks
Paul Revere/Raiders; *Greatest Hits* ....(COL)
Legend Of .... (COL)
Midnight Ride .... (COL)
King Heroin
James Brown; *Soul Classics* .... (OOP)
James Chance/Contortions; *Live In New York* ... (ROI)
New York Rockers .... (ROI)
Soul Exorcism .... (ROI)
Jazzy Jeff; *On Fire* .... (JVA)
Land
Patti Smith; *Horses* .... (ARI)
Let It Bleed
Rolling Stones; *Let It Bleed* .... (AKO)
More Hot Rocks .... (AKO)
Life In The Fast Lane
Eagles; *Hotel California* .... (ASY)
Live .... (ASY)
ST/FM .... (MCA)
Lively Up Yourself
Bob Marley/Wailers; *Babylon By Bus* .... (TUF)
Live .... (TUF)
Natty Dread .... (TUF)
Love Is The Drug
Grace Jones; *Island Life* .... (ISL)
Warm Leatherette .... (ISL)
Roxy Music; *Atlantic Years 1973-1980* ....(ATC)
Greatest Hits .... (ATC)
Heart Still Beating .... (RPR)
Siren .... (RPR)
Street Life-20 Great Hits .... (RPR)
Love Potion #9
Clovers; *ST/American Graffiti* .... (MCA)
Super Oldies/'50s-#7 .... (AUF)
Herb Alpert/Tijuana Brass; *Classics-#1* .... (A&M)
Greatest Hits .... (A&M)

Searchers; *Greatest Hits* .... (RHI)
History Of British Rock-#3 .... (RHI)
Low Spark Of High Heeled Boys
Traffic; *Low Spark Of High Heeled Boys* .... (ISL)
On The Road .... (ISL)
LSD Fixation
Jerry Porter; *Don't Bother Me* .... (MRR)
Lucy In The Sky With Diamonds
Beatles; *1967-1970* .... (CAP)
Sgt. Pepper's Lonely Hearts Club Band .... (CAP)
Yellow Submarine .... (CAP)
Elton John; *All This & World War 2* .... (20)
Greatest Hits-#2 .... (POL)
John Lennon; *Lennon* .... (CAP)
Me & Baby Jane
Leon Russell; *Carney* .... (MCA)
Meditation
Astrud Gilberto; *Compact Jazz* .... (VRV)
Billy Stritch; *Billy Stritch* .... (DRG)
Frank Sinatra & Antonio Carlos Jobim; *Frank Sinatra & Antonio Carlos Jobim* .... (RPR)
Lena Horne; *Goes Latin & Sings Your Requests* .. (DRG)
Original Cast; *Shenandoah* ....(RCA)
Meditation #2
Laraaji; *Day Of Radiance* .... (EDI)
Meditation: Psalm 1-6
Paul Horn; *Inside The Great Pyramid* .... (KUC)
Monkey On Your Back
Aldo Nova; *Portrait Of* .... (EPI)
Subject...Aldo Nova .... (POR)
Mother's Little Helper
Rolling Stones; *Flowers* .... (AKO)
Hot Rocks-1964-1971 .... (AKO)
Through The Past Darkly-Big Hits-#2 .... (AKO)
Tesla; *Five Man Acoustical Jam* .... (GEF)
Mr. Pharmacist
Other Half; *Nuggets-#12-Punk-#3* .... (RHI)
Much Higher
Gary Wright; *Dream Weaver* ....(WB)
My Drug Buddy
Lemonheads; *It's A Shame About Ray* ....(ATL)
Natural High
Bloodstone; *Greatest Hits* .... (TN)
Soul Hits/'70s-#11 .... (RHI)
Needle Of Death
Ian & Sylvia; *Best Of* .... (VAN)
Needle & Spoon
Savoy Brown; *Best Of* .... (PRT)
London Collector ....(LON)
Raw Sienna .... (PRT)
Needle & The Damage Done
Neil Young; *Decade* .... (RPR)
Harvest .... (RPR)
Live Rust .... (RPR)
Needle & The Spoon
Lynyrd Skynyrd; *One More From The Road* ..... (MCA)
Second Helping .... (MCA)
New Amphetamine Shriek
Fugs; *Fugs 4 Rounders Score* .... (ESP)
Nickel Bags
Digable Planets; *Reachin'-New Refutation Of Time & Space* .... (PEN)
No No Song
Ringo Starr; *Blast From Your Past* ....(CAP)
Goodnight Vienna .... (CAP)
Now I Wanna Sniff Some Glue
Ramones; *All The Stuff (& More)-#1* .... (SIR)
Ramones .... (SIR)
Om
John Coltrane; *Fire Into Music-Best Of*
Impulse!-#3 .... (MCI)
Om .... (MCI)
Moody Blues; *In Search Of The Lost Chord* ...... (POL)
Opiate
Tool; *Opiate* .... (ZOO)
Opiate Of The Masses
Heathen; *Victims Of Deception* .... (ROA)
Opiated
Tragically Hip; *Up To Here* .... (MCA)
Opium Bride
Annabouboula; *Greek Fire* .... (SHA)
Opium Dentine
Brothers & Systems; *Transcontinental Weekend* ...(NET)

Overdose
AC/DC; *Let There Be Rock* ....(ATC)
Pass The Valium (With Knobs On)
Adrian Legg; *Guitars & Other Cathedrals* .... (REL)
Passage To Bangkok
Rush; *2112* .... (MER)
   Chronicles .... (MER)
   Exit...Stage Left .... (MER)
Penicillin Penny
Dr. Hook; *& The Medicine Show Revisited* ....(COL)
Pigs In Zen
Jane's Addiction; *Jane's Addiction* .... (XXX)
   Nothing's Shocking .... (WB)
Poppies
Buffy Sainte-Marie; *Best Of-#2* .... (VAN)
   Illuminations .... (VAN)
   Native North American Child .... (VAN)
Patti Smith Group; *Radio Ethiopia* .... (ARI)
Post Toastee
Tommy Bolin; *Private Eyes* ....(COL)
Poverty Train
Laura Nyro; *Eli & The 13th Confession* ....(COL)
Priests On Drugs
Paper Bag; *No Age-Compilation Of SST*
Instrumentals ....(SST)
Psychedelic Sex Reaction
Babylon A.D.; *Nothing Sacred* .... (ARI)
Purple Haze
Cure; *Stone Free-Tribute To Jimi Hendrix* .... (RPR)
Jimi Hendrix Experience; *Are You Experienced* ... (RPR)
   Essential .... (RPR)
   Kiss The Sky .... (RPR)
   Radio One ....(RYK)
   Smash Hits .... (RPR)
   ST/Jimi Hendrix .... (RPR)
Winger; *Winger* .... (ATL)
Pusherman
Curtis Mayfield; *Pimps Players & Private Eyes* .... (SIR)
Pusher, The
Steppenwolf; *16 Greatest Hits* .... (MCA)
   Classic Rock-#2 .... (MCA)
   Gold ....(MCA)
   Live .... (MCA)
   Steppenwolf .... (MCA)
Radio Ethiopia
Patti Smith Group; *Radio Ethiopia* .... (ARI)
Rock & Roll Junkie
Back Street Crawler; *Band Plays On* ....(ATC)
Herman Brood/Wild Romance; *Herman Brood/Wild*
Romance ....(ARL)
Rock 'N' Roll Junkie
Motley Crue; *Decade Of Decadence* .... (ELE)
Rolaids, Doan's Pills & Preparation H
Dave Dudley; *King Of The Road* .... (SUN)
Sailin' Shoes
Little Feat; *Sailin' Shoes* .... (WB)
   Waiting For Columbus .... (WB)
Sam Stone
John Prine; *John Prine* .... (ATL)
   Prime Prine .... (ATL)
Santa Doesn't Cop Out On Dope
Martin Mull; *45* ....(CPC)
Seeing Things
Black Crowes; *Shake Your Money Maker* .... (DEF)
Sex, Drugs & Rock & Roll
Ian Dury; *New Boots & Panties* .... (STF)
Mantronix; *This Should Move Ya* .... (CAP)
She Gets Too High
Rob Rule; *Rob Rule* .... (MER)
She's Like Heroin To Me
Gun Club; *Fire Of Love* .... (SLS)
She's So High
Marc Tanner Band; *No Escape* .... (ELE)
Shootin' On Narcs
Pat Gangsta; *#1 Suspect* .... (ATL)
Sister Morphine
Marianne Faithfull; *Blazing Away* .... (ISL)
   Greatest Hits .... (AKO)
Rolling Stones; *Sticky Fingers* .... (RS)
Smuggler's Blues
Glenn Frey; *Allnighter* .... (MCA)
   Rock The First-#2 .... (SAN)
   ST/Miami Vice .... (MCA)

Snowblind Friend
David Allan Coe; *Unchained* ....(COL)
Hoyt Axton; *Snowblind Friend* .... (MCA)
Steppenwolf; *16 Greatest Hits* .... (MCA)
   7 .... (MCA)
So High
Dave Mason; *Best Of* ....(COL)
   Let It Flow ....(COL)
Soft Hearted Hana
George Harrison; *George Harrison* .... (DKH)
Spanish Pipedream
John Prine; *John Prine* .... (ATL)
Speed Kills
Steve Gibbons Band; *Caught In The Act* .... (MCA)
Spiritual High
Moodswings; *Moodfood* .... (ARI)
Suicidal Heroin
Ratos De Porao; *Brasil* .... (ROA)
Superfly
Curtis Mayfield; *Super Bad* .... (KT)
   Superfly .... (OOP)
Surfin' On Heroin
Forgotten Rebels; *Surfin' On Heroin* .... (RES)
Take A Red
New Riders Of The Purple Sage; *Alive & Kicking* (MSP)
   Marin County Line .... (MCA)
Take A Whiff
Byrds; *Untitled* ....(COL)
Cisco Houston; *Cisco Houston* .... (EVR)
Leadbelly; *Midnight Special* .... (ROU)
Television, The Drug Of The Nation
Disposable Heroes Of Hiphoprisy; *Hypocrisy Is The*
Greatest Luxury .... (4TH)
That Cat Is High
Manhattan Transfer; *Anthology-Down In Birdland* (RHI)
   Manhattan Transfer .... (RHI)
Them Downers
Hoyt Axton; *Free Sailin'* .... (MCA)
Thorazine Shuffle
Savatage; *Gutter Ballet* .... (ATL)
Time Out Of Mind
Steely Dan; *Gaucho* .... (MCA)
Too Much Seconal
Johnny Winter; *Still Alive & Well* ....(COL)
T.M. Song
Beach Boys; *15 Big Ones* .... (RPR)
War On Drugs
2 Black 2 Strong MMG; *Doin' Hard Time On Planet*
Earth ....(CLA)
White Punks On Dope
Tubes; *Tubes* .... (A&M)
   T.R.A.S.H.-Tubes Rarities & Smash Hits .... (A&M)
   What Do You Want From-Live .... (A&M)
White Rabbit
Damned; *Best Of* .... (ROA)
   Machine Gun Etiquette .... (ROA)
George Benson; *Collection* .... (WB)
   White Rabbit ....(CBA)
Jefferson Airplane; *2400 Fulton Street-An*
Anthology ....(RCA)
   Flight Log 1966-1976 .... (GRU)
   Loves You ....(RCA)
   ST/Platoon-& Songs From The Era .... (ATL)
   Surrealistic Pillow .... (RCA)
   Worst Of .... (RCA)
White Ship
H.P. Lovecraft; *H.P. Lovecraft* .... (OOP)
Who Put The Benzedrine In Mrs....
Harry Gibson;
   Dr. Demento's Delights .... (WB)
Willin'
Byrds; *Byrds (collection)* ....(COL)
Linda Ronstadt; *Heart Like A Wheel* .... (CAP)
Little Feat; *Little Feat* .... (WB)
   Sailin' Shoes .... (WB)
   Waiting For Columbus .... (WB)
With A Little Help From My Friends
Beatles; *1967-1970* .... (CAP)
   Box Set .... (CAP)
   Rarities .... (CAP)
   Sgt. Pepper's Lonely Hearts Club Band .... (CAP)

Joe Cocker; *Classics-#4* .... (A&M)
  Greatest Hits .... (A&M)
  History Of British Rock-#9 .... (RHI)
  ST/Woodstock .... (ATL)
  With A Little Help From My Friends .... (A&M)
Ringo Starr/All-Star Band; *Nobody's Child-Romanian*
  Angel Appeal .... (WB)
Your Mind Has Left Your Body
Paul Kantner; *Baron Von Tollbooth & The Chrome*
  Nun .... (GRU)

DRUGS: COCAINE, Crack

Cabbies On Crack
Ramones; *Mondo Bizarro* .... (RDO)
Casey Jones
Grateful Dead; *Best Of-Skeletons From The Closet* (WB)
  Bill Graham Presents Last Fillmore Days .... (EPA)
  Workingman's Dead .... (WB)
Jerry Garcia Acoustic Band; *Almost Acoustic* ... (GRD)
China White
Little Feat; *Hoy-Hoy!* .... (WB)
Scorpions; *Blackout* .... (MER)
Cocaine
Beautiful; *Storybook* .... (GIA)
Eric Clapton; *Crossroads* .... (POL)
  Just One Night .... (RSO)
  Slow Hand .... (RSO)
  Time Pieces .... (RSO)
J.J. Cale; *Special Edition* .... (MER)
  Troubadour .... (MCA)
Tom Rush; *Blues Songs Ballads* .... (PRS)
  Tom Rush .... (FAN)
Cocaine Blues
Dave Van Ronk; *Folksinger* .... (PRS)
  Inside .... (FAN)
  Troubadours Of The Folk Era-#1 .... (RHI)
David Bromberg; *My own House* .... (FAN)
George Thorogood/Destroyers; *Move It On Over* (ROU)
Jackson Browne; *Running On Empty* .... (ASY)
Johnny Cash; *At Folsom Prison & San Quentin* ... (COL)
  Essential .... (COL)
  Silver .... (COL)
Lonnie Mack; *Road Houses & Dance Halls* .... (EPI)
Rev. Gary Davis; *From Blues To Gospel* .... (BIO)
Cocaine Charlie
Atlanta Rhythm Section; *Boys From Doraville* ... (POL)
Cocaine Cocaine
Sly Dunbar; *Sly Wicked & Slick* .... (FL)
Cocaine Done Killed My Baby
Mance Lipscomb; *Texas Songwriter-#2* .... (ARH)
Cocaine Drain
John Hall; *Power* .... (COL)
Cocaine Go Away
Warren Ceaser/Creole Zydeco Snap; *Zydeco Shootout*
  At El Sid O's .... (ROU)
Cocaine Habit
Roy Bookbinder; *Going Back To Tampa* .... (FF)
Cocaine in My Brain
Dillinger; *Classic Reggae-#1* .... (PRO)
  Planet Reggae-World Of Reggae Music .... (RHY)
Cocaine In The Back Of The Ride
UGK-Underground Kingz; *Too Hard To Swallow* (JVA)
Cocaine Lil
Mekons; *Rock 'N' Roll* .... (A&M)
Cocaine Or Me
Hamell On Trial; *Conviction* .... (BWV)
Cocaine Train
Johnny Paycheck; *Banded Together* .... (EPI)
  Everybody's Got A Family .... (EPI)
Cocaine (Rock)
Country Joe McDonald; *Superstitious Blues* ...... (RYK)
Cocaine (Snow White)
Chris Thomas; *The Beginning* .... (ARH)
Crack
Freddie Hubbard & Friends; *Solo Brothers & Professor*
  Jive .... (DRG)
Crack House Woman
George "Wild Child" Butler; *These Mean Old*
  Blues .... (BUL)
Crack In New York
Culture; *Nuff Crisis!* .... (SHA)

Crack Killed Applejack
General Kane; *In Full Chill* .... (MOT)
Crack Pipe (Burnin' My Hand)
Coolies; *Doug (A Rock Opera & Comic Book)* .... (DB)
Don't Sniff Coke
Pato Banton; *Never Give In* .... (PMR)
Gimme No Crack
Shinehead; *Unity* .... (ELE)
Ike's Rap
Isaac Hayes; *45* .... (COL)
  Live At The Sahara Tahoe .... (STX)
In The Arms Of Cocaine
Hank Williams, Jr.; *Strong Stuff* .... (WB)
Kid Charlemagne
Steely Dan; *Greatest Hits* .... (MCA)
  Royal Scam .... (MCA)
Let The Cocaine Be
Doc & Merle Watson; *Live & Pickin'* .... (UA)
Little Cocaine
Lee Clayton; *Naked City* .... (CAP)
Toy Soldiers
Martika; *Martika* .... (COL)
Whitelines (Don't Don't Do It)
Grandmaster Flash/Melle Mel/Furious Five; *Message*
  From Beat Street-Best Of .... (RHI)

DRUGS: MARIJUANA, Getting Stoned
See Also: DRUGS, DRUGS: COCAINE

Acapulco Gold
Rainy Daze; *Acapulco Gold* .... (OOP)
Bush Doctor
Peter Tosh; *Bush Doctor* .... (RS)
  Captured Live .... (EMI)
  The Toughest .... (CAP)
Coming Into Los Angeles
Arlo Guthrie; *Best Of* .... (WB)
  Running Down The Road .... (RPR)
  ST/Woodstock .... (ATL)
Don't Bogart That Joint
Little Feat; *Last Record Album* .... (WB)
  Waiting For Columbus .... (WB)
Don't Step On The Grass Sam
Steppenwolf; *Live* .... (MCA)
  The Second .... (MCA)
Dope Sucks
Herman Brood/Wild Romance; *Herman Brood/Wild*
  Romance .... (ARL)
Down To Seeds & Stems Again Blues
Commander Cody/Lost Planet Airmen; *Live From*
  Texas .... (MCA)
  Lost In The Ozone .... (MCA)
Funny Lookin' Eyes
Barefoot Jerry; *Watchin' TV* .... (MON)
Get High
Sons Of Champlin; *Loosen Up Naturally* .... (CAP)
Henry
New Riders Of The Purple Sage; *Best Of* .... (COL)
  Bill Graham Presents Fillmore-Last Days ...... (EPA)
  Home Home On The Road .... (COL)
  New Riders Of The Purple Sage .... (COL)
Hey Nineteen
Steely Dan; *Gaucho* .... (MCA)
  Gold .... (MCA)
I Got Stoned & I Missed It
Dr. Hook; *Bankrupt* .... (CAP)
I Like Marijuana
David Peel/Lower East Side; *Have A Marijuana* . (ELE)
I Need A Joint
Basehead; *Not In Kansas Anymore* .... (IMG)
Illegal Smile
John Prine; *John Prine* .... (ATL)
  Prime Prine .... (ATL)
I've Got Some Grass
David Peel/Lower East Side; *Have A Marijuana* . (ELE)
Late In The Evening
Paul Simon; *Negotiations & Love*
  Songs-1971-1986 .... (WB)
  One-Trick Pony .... (WB)
Simon & Garfunkel; *Concert In Central Park* ..... (WB)
Legalize It
Peter Tosh; *Legalize It* .... (COL)
  Reggae Come Forward-Anthology .... (COL)

Let's Go Get Stoned
Joe Cocker; *Mad Dogs & Englishmen* .... (A&M)
Ray Charles; *Anthology* .... (RHI)
   Greatest Hits .... (RHI)
   His Greatest Hits-#1 ....(DHL)
Magnolia Blues
Paul Davis; *Southern Tracks & Fantasies* ....(BNG)
Marahuana
Bette Midler; *Songs For The New Depression* ..... (ATL)
Marijuana
Country Joe/Fish; *Life & Times Of* .... (VAN)
Mariwana
Soul Syndicate; *Harvested* ....(OOP)
Old Dope Peddler
Tom Lehrer; *Songs By* .... (RPR)
On Jamaica
Country Joe McDonald; *Paradise With An Ocean View* ....(FAN)
One Toke Over The Line
Brewer & Shipley; *Super Hits/'70s-Have A Nice Day-#4* .... (RHI)
   '70s Greatest Rock Hits-#10 .... (PRY)
Opium Trail
Thin Lizzy; *Bad Reputation* .... (MER)
Panama Red
New Riders Of The Purple Sage; *Adventures Of Panama Red* .... (COL)
   Best Of ....(COL)
   Rock Classics Of The '70s ....(COL)
Pass It On
Bob Marley/Wailers; *Burnin'* .... (TUF)
Pass The Joint
BFM; *City O' Dope* ....(W/I)
Pipe Dreams
Asleep At The Wheel; *Collision Course* .... (CAP)
Pot Smoker's Song
Neil Diamond; *Velvet Gloves & Spit* .... (MSP)
Rainy Day Women #12 & 35
Bob Dylan; *Greatest Hits* ....(COL)
   Blonde On Blonde ....(COL)
   Rock Classics/'60s ....(COL)
   ST/Forrest Gump ....(EPX)
Bob Dylan/Band; *Before The Flood* ....(COL)
Reefer Head Woman
Aerosmith; *Night In The Ruts* ....(COL)
Reefer Song
Original Cast; *Ain't Misbehavin'* ....(RCA)
Show Me The Way To Get Stoned
David Peel/Lower East Side; *Have A Marijuana* . (ELE)
Sinsemilla
Black Uhuru; *Island Story-1962-1987-25th Anniversary* .... (ISL)
   Sinsemilla ....(MGO)
   Tear It Up ....(MGO)
Stoned
Orleans; *Before The Dance* .... (MCA)
Stoned Out Of My Mind
Chi-Lites; *Chi-Lites* .... (BRU)
   Greatest Hits .... (RHI)
   Soul Hits/'70s-#15 .... (RHI)
Sweet Marijuana Brown
Paula Lockheart; *It Ain't The End Of The World* ...(FF)
Sweet Sensimilla
Jimmy Riley; *Put The People First* .... (SHA)
Take One Toke
Atomic Rooster; *Atomic Rooster* .... (ELE)
That Acapulco Gold
Rainy Daze; *Summer Of Love-#2-Turn On* .... (RHI)
Tokin' Tickets
Barefoot Jerry; *Barefootin'* .... (MON)
Two Hits & The Joint Turned Brown
Pfaff Family Dog; *Marijuana's Greatest Hits Revisited* .... (RHA)
Rodney & Doug Dillard/John Hartford; *Glitter Grass From The Nashwood...* ....(FF)
Various Tracks
Various Artists; *Marijuana's Greatest Hits* .... (RHA)

EARTH

See Also: ECOLOGY, STARS

Back Down To Earth
Carly Simon; *Boys In The Trees* .... (ELE)

Children Of The Earth
Tower Of Power; *Bump City* .... (WB)
Down To Earth
Stevie Wonder; *Down To Earth* .... (MOT)
   Looking Back .... (MOT)
Earth Angel
Elvis Presley; *Golden Celebration* ....(RCA)
New Edition; *ST/Under The Blue Moon* .... (MCA)
Penguins; *Billboard Top Rock 'N' Roll Hits-1955* . (RHI)
   Golden Classics ....(CLT)
   Oldies But Goodies-#1 ....(OSR)
   ST/American Graffiti ....(MCA)
Earth Blues
Jimi Hendrix; *Rainbow Bridge* ....(OOP)
Earth Crisis
Steel Pulse; *Earth Crisis* .... (ELE)
Earth Girls Are Easy
Julie Brown; *Goddess In Progress* .... (RHI)
Earth Mother
Grace Slick & Paul Kantner; *Sunfighter* .... (GRU)
Eartheart
Kenny Rankin; *Like A Seed* .... (LD)
For The Beauty Of The Earth
Paul Winter Consort; *Missa Gaia (Earth Mass)* ....(LIV)
Give Me Love (Give Me Peace On Earth)
George Harrison; *Best Of* .... (CAP)
   Living In The Material World ....(CAP)
Greatest Love On Earth
Chicago; *Hot Streets* ....(COL)
Greatest Show On Earth
Michael Jackson; *2 Classic Albums: Got To Be There/Ben* .... (MOT)
   Ben .... (MOT)
Heaven Is A Place On Earth
Belinda Carlisle; *Greenpeace/Rainbow Warriors* ..(GEF)
   Heaven On Earth .... (MCA)
Heaven On Earth
Platters; *16 Greatest Hits* .... (TRP)
   Anthology .... (RHI)
   Encore Of Golden Hits .... (MER)
   Red Sails In The Sunset ....(ALL)
Hymn To The Russian Earth
Paul Winter Consort; *Concert For The Earth-Live At The U.N.* ....(LIV)
Letter From Earth
Black Sabbath; *Dehumanizer* .... (RPR)
Mother Earth
Memphis Slim; *Memphis Slim* .... (CSS)
   Real Folk Blues .... (CSS)
Merry-Go-Round; *Best Of* .... (RHI)
Nitty Gritty Dirt Band; *Dirt Silver & Gold* .... (UA)
Tom Rush; *Best Of* ....(COL)
No One Else On Earth
Wynonna; *Wynonna* .... (CRB)
Not To Touch The Earth
Doors; *Greatest Hits* .... (ELE)
   Waiting For The Sun .... (ELE)
Planet Earth
Duncan Browne; *Wild Places* .... (SIR)
Duran Duran; *Arena* .... (CAP)
   Decade .... (CAP)
   Duran Duran .... (CAP)
Roads Girdle The Globe
XTC; *Drums & Wires* .... (GEF)
Salt Of The Earth
Rolling Stones; *Beggar's Banquet* .... (AKO)
Savage Earth Heart
Waterboys; *Waterboys* .... (ENS)
Save Mother Earth
Merl Saunders; *Heavy Turbulence* .... (FAN)
   /Friends-Fire Up .... (FAN)
   /Rainforest Band-Save The Planet... .... (SUM)
Save The Planet
Edgar Winter; *Roadwork* .... (EPI)
   White Trash .... (EPI)
Scum Of The Earth
Kinks; *Preservation-A Play In Two Acts* .... (RHI)
Third Rock From The Sun
Joe Diffie; *Thousand Winding...* .... (EPI)
Third Stone From The Sun
Jimi Hendrix; *Essential* .... (RPR)
   Kiss The Sky .... (RPR)
Jimi Hendrix Experience; *Are You Experienced?* (MCA)

This Bitter Earth
Aretha Franklin; *Jazz To Soul* ....(COL)
   Sings The Blues ....(COL)
Dinah Washington; *Essential-The Great Songs* ....(VRV)
   Unforgettable .... (MER)
To The Ends Of The Earth
Nat King Cole; *Story* ....(CAP)
You Make Your Own Heaven & Hell Right...
Temptations; *Psychedelic Shack* .... (MOT)

EARTHQUAKE

See Also: DANCE (SHAKING)

California Earthquake
John Hartford; *Catalogue* .... (FF)
Rodney Crowell; *Ain't Living Long Like This* ......(WB)
Earth A Quake
Johnny Green/Greenmen; *Seven Over From Mars* (AVI)
Earthquake
Al Wilson; *Count The Days* .... (RDS)
Graham Central Station; *Now Do You U Wanta*
Dance ....(WB)
Mickey Newbury; *Live At The Montezuma Hall* .. (ELE)
Ronnie Milsap; *Heart & Soul* ....(RCA)
Triumvirat; *Pompeii* ....(CAP)
Earthquake & Hurricane
Tina Turner; *Rough* .... (UA)
Willie Dixon; *Mighty Earthquake & Hurricane* ...(PAU)
Fault
John Hall; *John Hall* ....(ASY)
Housequake
Prince; *Sign O' The Times* ....(PAI)
I Feel The Earth Move
Carole King; *Greatest Hits* ....(EOD)
   Tapestry .... (EOD)
Little Earthquakes
Tori Amos; *Little Earthquakes* ....(ATL)
Livin' On The Fault Line
Doobie Brothers; *Livin' On The Fault Line* ...... (WB)
Our Love Is On The Faultline
Crystal Gayle; *Best Of* ....(WB)
   True Love ....(WB)
Outhouse Quake
Bootsauce; *Bull* .... (ISL)
Shakey Ground
Phoebe Snow; *Best Of* ....(COL)
   It Looks Like Snow ....(COL)
Temptations; *Anthology* .... (MOT)
   Song For You ....(MOT)
T. Graham Brown; *You Can't Take It With You* ..(CAP)
Shaky Ground
Lacy J. Dalton & Glen Campbell; *Country Duets Two*
By Two ....(LIB)
   Lacy J. ....(CAP)
When The Earth Moves Again
Jefferson Airplane; *30 Seconds Over Winterland* ..(RCA)
   Loves You ....(RCA)

EASTER

See Also: GOD

Easter
Joe Henry; *Shuffletown* ....(A&M)
Love Battery; *Between The Eyes* ....(SP)
Marillion; *Seasons End* ....(CAP)
   Six Of One-Half Dozen Of The Other ....(IRS)
Patti Smith Group; *Easter* ....(ARI)
Easter Day
Robyn Archer; *Robyn Archer* .... (ANG)
Easter Dinner
Tribe; *Abort* ....(SLS)
Easter Everywhere
Julian Cope; *My Nation Underground* .... (ISL)
Easter Island
Russ Freeman; *Nocturnal Playground* ....(BRA)
Easter Parade
Andy Russell; *Puttin' On The Ritz-Capitol Sings*
Berlin ....(CAP)
Bing Crosby; *All Time Best Of* ....(CCB)
Judy Garland & Fred Astaire; *ST/Easter Parade* ..(SSP)
Sarah Vaughan; *Complete On Mercury-#2-American*
Songs ....(MER)

Easter Tree
June Tabor; *Ashes & Diamonds* ....(GRE)
Easter Woman
Residents; *Commercial Album* ....(RAL)
Easter '88
Urge Overkill; *Americruiser/Jesus Urge Superstar* (T&G)
Easter (Ballade)
Jasper Van't Hof/Others; *Eyeball* ....(CMU)
Hallelujah Chorus
Philadelphia Orchestra/Eugene Ormandy; *Ave*
Maria-Christmas Favorites ....(RCA)
Robert Shaw Chorale; *Christmas Treasures* ....(RCA)
North Easter
Cusco; *Cusco 2000* .... (HO)
Watermelon In Easter Hay
Frank Zappa; *Guitar* ....(RYK)
   Joe's Garage Acts I-III ....(RYK)

ECHOES

See Also: REFLECTIONS, SHADOWS

Echo Beach
Martha/Muffins; *Metro Music* .... (VIA)
Echo Valley 2-6809
Partridge Family; *Greatest Hits* .... (ARI)
Echoes
Gene Clark; *Nuggets-#11-Pop-#4* .... (RHI)
New Riders Of The Purple Sage; *Marin County*
Line ....(MCA)
Pink Floyd; *Meddle* ....(HAR)
Echoes Of Harlem
Clark Terry Five; *Memories Of Duke* ....(PAB)
Claude Bolling; *Plays Ellington-#1* ....(COL)
Cootie Williams; *Jazz Sampler-#3* ....(COL)
Duke Ellington; *Mood Indigo* ....(POE)
Echoes Of Love
Doobie Brothers; *Best Of-#2* ....(WB)
   Livin' On The Fault Line ....(WB)
Elvis Presley; *ST/Kissin' Cousins* ....(RCA)
Pointer Sisters; *Energy* ....(PNT)
Echoes Of Spain
Django Reinhardt; *Djangologie/USA-#2* ....(DSQ)
Echoes Of Spring
Willie "The Lion" Smith; *Echoes Of Spring* ..... (MLN)
Echoes Of The African Forest
Saka Acquaye Ensemble; *Voices Of Africa* ..... (NON)
Echoes Of The Last Stampede
Norton Buffalo; *Desert Horizon* ....(CAP)
Everybody's Talkin'
Nilsson; *ST/Forrest Gump* ....(EPX)
   ST/Midnight Cowboy ....(EMI)
   TT & Other Hits ....(RCA)
Willie Nelson; *Best Of Willie* ....(RCA)
   Sweet Memories ....(RCA)
Traces
Classics IV; *Very Best Of* .... (EMI)
Classics IV/Dennis Yost; *Oldies But Goodies-#11* (OSR)
Ronnie Milsap; *16 Greatest Hits-#2* ....(TRP)
Traces/Memories
Lettermen; *All-Time Greatest Hits* ....(CAP)
   Capitol Collectors Series ....(CAP)
Vienna Echoes
Lawrence Welk; *Celebrates 50 Years In Music* .. (RAN)

ECOLOGY, Environment, Nature, Pollution

See Also: NUCLEAR ENERGY, POLITICAL
CLASSICS

Acid Rain
John Martyn; *Sapphire* ....(ISL)
Saigon Kick; *Saigon Kick* ....(THI)
Balance Of Nature
Dionne Warwick; *Dionne* ....(WB)
Beauty Of Nature
Edmund Sylvers; *Have You Heard* ....(CAS)
Before The Deluge
Jackson Browne; *Late For The Sky* ....(ASY)
Joan Baez; *Honest Lullaby* ....(POR)
Big Yellow Taxi
Amy Grant; *House Of Love* ....(A&M)

Joni Mitchell; *Ladies Of The Canyon* .... (RPR)
   Miles Of Aisles .... (ASY)
Blue Sky Mine
   Midnight Oil; *Blue Sky Mining* .... (COL)
Blues From The Rainforest
   Merl Saunders; *Blues From The Rainforest-A Musical*
   Suite .... (GRD)
Burn On
   Randy Newman; *Sail Away* .... (RPR)
Death Of Mother Nature
   Kansas; *Kansas* .... (KIR)
Do You Want My Job
   Little Village; *Little Village* .... (RPR)
Don't Go Near The Water
   Beach Boys; *10 Years Of Harmony* .... (CAR)
   Surf's Up .... (CAR)
Ecology Poem
   Mutabaruka; *Blakk Wi Blak...k...k...* .... (SHA)
Ecology Song
   Stephen Stills; *2* .... (ATL)
Every Natural Think
   Aretha Franklin; *Let Me In Your Life* .... (OOP)
For The Beauty Of The Earth
   Paul Winter Consort; *Missa Gaia (Earth Mass)* .... (LIV)
Fresh Air
   Quicksilver Messenger Service; *Anthology* .... (CAP)
   Sons Of Mercury .... (RHI)
Garden Of Eden
   New Riders Of The Purple Sage; *New Riders Of The*
   Purple Sage .... (COL)
Hand Me Down World
   Guess Who; *Best Of* .... (RCA)
   Greatest Of .... (RCA)
Hiroshima Hole
   Barefoot Jerry; *Barefootin'* .... (MON)
Johnny's Garden
   Stephen Stills; *Manassas* .... (ATL)
Let's Make The Water Turn Black
   Mothers Of Invention; *Lumpy Gravy/Only In It For The*
   Money .... (RYK)
Love & Maple Syrup
   Gordon Lightfoot; *Summer Side Of Life* .... (RPR)
Mercy Mercy Me (The Ecology)
   Marvin Gaye; *Anthology* .... (MOT)
   Every Great Motown Hit Of .... (MOT)
   Greatest Hits .... (MOT)
   What's Going On .... (MOT)
   Robert Palmer; *Don't Explain* .... (EMI)
Mother Nature
   Temptations; *Anthology* .... (MOT)
Mother Nature's Son
   Beatles; *Box Set* .... (CAP)
   White Album .... (CAP)
   John Denver; *Evening With* .... (RCA)
   Rocky Mountain High .... (RCA)
Mr. Pollution
   P'Cock; *Burning Beach* .... (INN)
Nature Avenue
   John Lodge; *Nature Avenue* .... (LON)
Nature Boy
   George Benson; *Collection* .... (WB)
   Jose Feliciano; *Encore* .... (RCA)
   Nat King Cole; *Blossom Fell* .... (CAP)
   Story .... (CAP)
   Unforgettable .... (ELE)
Nature Lover
   Mass Production; *Massterpiece* .... (COT)
Nature Planned It
   Four Tops; *Anthology* .... (MOT)
   Nature Planned It .... (MOT)
Nature Trail To Hell
   Weird Al Yankovic; *In 3-D* .... (RAR)
Nature's Child
   Triumph; *Progressions Of Power* .... (MCA)
Nature's Creation
   Valentines; *45* .... (RLL)
Nature's Disappearing
   John Mayall; *Room To Move-1969-1974-Chronicles*
   Series .... (POL)
   Wake Up Call .... (SIL)
Nature's Way
   Spirit; *12 Dreams Of Dr. Sardonicus* .... (EPI)
   Best Of .... (EPI)
   Time Circle .... (EPI)

New Mother Nature
   Guess Who; *American Woman* .... (RCA)
   Best Of .... (RCA)
Nine Types Of Industrial Pollution
   Frank Zappa; *Uncle Meat* .... (BAR)
   Mothers Of Invention; *Legends Of Rock*
   Guitar-'60s-#1 .... (RHI)
On A Clear Day You Can See Forever
   Barbra Streisand; *Barbra Streisand* .... (COL)
   Just For The Record .... (COL)
   Live At The Forum .... (COL)
   ST/On A Clear Day You Can See Forever ..... (SMP)
   Frank Sinatra; *Strangers In The Night* .... (RPR)
   Hollies; *Greatest Hits* .... (EPI)
   Roger Williams; *Best Of* .... (MCA)
   Somewhere In Time .... (BAI)
Once A Forest
   Grace Pool; *Where We Live* .... (RPR)
Ozone Alert
   Special EFX; *Global Village* .... (GRP)
Ozone Layer
   Augustus Pablo; *Rockers International Showcase* . (RYK)
   Black Uhuru; *Mystical Truth* .... (MSA)
Pass It On Down
   Alabama; *Pass It On Down* .... (RCA)
Pollution
   Tom Lehrer; *That Was The Year That Was* ...... (RPR)
Power (Nuclear Energy)
   John Hall; *Power* .... (COL)
   John Hall/Doobie Brothers/James Taylor; *No*
   Nukes .... (ASY)
Red Rain
   Peter Gabriel; *Greenpeace-Rainbow Warriors* .... (GEF)
   Secret World Live .... (GEF)
   Shaking The Tree-16 Golden Greats .... (GEF)
   So .... (GEF)
River Song
   Beach Boys; *10 Years Of Harmony* .... (CAR)
Rockin' In The Free World
   Neil Young; *Freedom* .... (RPR)
   Neil Young/Crazy Horse; *Weld* .... (RPR)
Save Mother Earth
   Merl Saunders; *Heavy Turbulence* .... (FAN)
   /Friends-Fire Up .... (FAN)
   /Rainforest Band-Save The Planet... .... (SUM)
Save The Planet
   Edgar Winter; *Roadwork* .... (EPI)
   White Trash .... (EPI)
Seminole Wind
   John Anderson; *Seminole Wind* .... (BNA)
Sky Is A Poisonous Garden
   Concrete Blonde; *Bloodletting* .... (IRS)
Smog
   Miracles; *City Of Angels* .... (TAM)

EGO, Identity, Pride, Self-respect
See Also: HAPPINESS, JEALOUSY, LIFE

2 Legit 2 Quit
   Hammer; *2 Legit 2 Quit* .... (CAP)
Ain't Too Proud To Beg
   Rolling Stones; *It's Only Rock 'n' Roll* .... (RS)
   Temptations; *25th Anniversary* .... (MOT)
   Anthology .... (MOT)
   Greatest Hits .... (MOT)
   Motown Story .... (MOT)
   ST/Big Chill .... (MOT)
Ain't Your Memory Got No Pride?
   Merle Haggard; *Ramblin' Fever* .... (MCA)
All I Need Is Me
   Elaine/Ellen; *Elaine/Ellen* .... (MER)
Are We Ourselves
   Fixx; *One Thing Leads To Another-Greatest Hits* (MCA)
   React .... (MCA)
Are You Hung Up
   Mothers Of Invention; *We're Only In It For The*
   Money .... (RYK)
Baby You Ain't Nothin' Without Me
   Karen Young; *Hot Shot* .... (WE)
Bad
   Michael Jackson; *Bad* .... (EPI)
Be Good To Yourself
   Frankie Miller; *Full House* .... (CHR)

Journey; *Greatest Hits* ....(COL)
   Raised On Radio ....(COL)
Be Somebody
Melissa Manchester; *Help Is On The Way* .... (ARI)
Be Your Own Best Friend
Ray Stevens; *Be Your Own Best Friend* ....(WB)
   Feeling's Not Right Again ....(WB)
Be Yourself
Cameo; *Alligator Woman* .... (CHC)
Patti LaBelle; *Be Yourself* .... (MCA)
Believe In Yourself
Lena Horne; *ST/The Wiz* .... (MCA)
Bell Bottom Blues
Derek/Dominos; *Layla* .... (RSO)
Eric Clapton; *24 Nights* .... (RPR)
Big Boys Don't Cry
Extreme; *Extreme* .... (A&M)
Big Girls Don't Cry
Frankie Valli/Four Seasons; *Anthology* .... (RHI)
   Billboard Top Rock 'N' Roll Hits-1962 .... (RHI)
   Greatest Hits-#1 .... (RHI)
   More Dirty Dancing ....(RCA)
Big Man
Charlie Daniels Band; *Uneasy Rider* .... (EPI)
Big Shot
Billy Joel; *52nd Street* ....(COL)
   Greatest Hits-#1 & 2 ....(COL)
   KOHUEPT ....(COL)
Boys Are Back In Town
Bon Jovi; *ST/Navy Seals* .... (ATL)
Gap Band; *II* .... (MER)
Thin Lizzy; *Dedication-Very Best Of* .... (MER)
   Jailbreak .... (MER)
   Live & Dangerous ....(WB)
   '70s Greatest Rock Hits-#14-King Of Rock ...... (PRY)
Brass In Pocket (I'm Special)
Pretenders; *Pretenders* .... (SIR)
Break My Stride
Matthew Wilder; *I Don't Speak The Language* .... (PRI)
Cause I Can Do It Right
Big Daddy Kane; *Taste Of Chocolate* ....(CLD)
Confident Rat
Ignorance; *Confident Rat* .... (MET)
Cool
Original Cast; *West Side Story* ....(COL)
Time; *Time* ....(WB)
Dawning Is The Day
Moody Blues; *Question Of Balance* .... (POL)
Dedicated Follower Of Fashion
Kinks; *Greatest Hits-#1* ....(RHI)
   Kinkdom ....(RHI)
   Kinks-Size Kinkdom ....(RHI)
Do Anything You Wanna Do
Eddie/Hot Rods; *Island Story (1962-1987)-25th*
   Annivers. .... (ISL)
   Life On The Line .... (ISL)
Do Anything You Want To
Thin Lizzy; *Black Rose/A Rock Legend* ....(WB)
Do What You Feel
Deniece Williams; *I'm So Proud* ....(COL)
Doggy Dogg World
Snoop Doggy Dogg; *Doggystyle* .... (DR)
Donna The Prima Donna
Dion; *24 Original Classics* .... (ARI)
   Bronx Blues-Columbia Recordings ....(COL)
Don't Cry Out Loud
Melissa Manchester; *Greatest Hits* .... (ARI)
Peter Allen; *It Is Time For* ....(A&M)
   The Best ....(A&M)
Don't Give Up
Peter Gabriel; *Shaking The Tree-16 Golden*
   Greats ....(GEF)
   So ....(GEF)
Ego
Betty Carter; *Family* .... (RLL)
Elton John; *45* .... (MCA)
Ego Tripper
Danny Kortchmar; *Innuendo* .... (ASY)
Ego Tripping Out
Marvin Gaye; *45* .... (TAM)
Erotica
Madonna; *Erotica* .... (MAV)
Everybody Else
Greg Kihn; *Next Of Kihn* .... (BES)

Everybody Else Is Wrong
Utopia; *Deface The Music* .... (RHI)
Everybody's A Star
Kinks; *Soap Opera* .... (RHI)
Foolish Pride
Daryl Hall; *Three Hearts In The Happy Ending*
   Machine ....(RCA)
Joan Armatrading; *The Key* .... (A&M)
Travis Tritt; *Ten Feet Tall And Bulletproof* ....(WB)
Friends In Low Places
Garth Brooks; *No Fences* .... (LIB)
Glory Of Love
Bette Midler; *ST/Beaches* .... (ATL)
Peter Cetera; *Solitude/Solitaire* .... (FM)
   ST/Karate Kid-#2 .... (EMI)
Velvetones; *Doo Wop Ballads-#2* .... (RHI)
Go Your Own Way
Fleetwood Mac; *25 Years-The Chain* ....(WB)
   Greatest Hits ....(WB)
   Live ....(WB)
   Rumours ....(WB)
Greatest Love Of All
George Benson; *Collection* ....(WB)
   ST/The Greatest .... (ARI)
   Weekend In L.A. ....(WB)
Whitney Houston; *Whitney Houston* .... (ARI)
Half The Man
Clint Black; *No Time To Kill* ....(RCA)
Happy To Be Just Like I Am
Taj Mahal; *Happy To Be Just Like I Am* ....(COL)
High Horse
Evelyn "Champagne" King; *45* ....(RCA)
Nitty Gritty Dirt Band; *20 Years Of Dirt-Best Of* .. (WB)
   Plain Dirt Fashion ....(WB)
Hold Your Head Up
Argent; *Anthology* .... (EPI)
   Encore .... (EPI)
   Rock Artifacts-#1-From The Vaults ....(COL)
   ST/Queen's Logic .... (EPI)
Honor Bound
Earl Thomas Conley; *Treadin' Water* ....(RCA)
I Am A Simple Man
Ricky Van Shelton; *Backroads* ....(COL)
I Am The Light Of This World
Jorma Kaukonen & Tom Hobson; *Quah* .... (RLX)
I Am Woman
Helen Reddy; *Greatest Hits* .... (CAP)
   I Am Woman .... (CAP)
   I Don't Know How To Love Him .... (CAP)
I Am...I Said
Neil Diamond; *12 Greatest Hits* .... (MCA)
   Hot August Night .... (MCA)
   Hot August Night II .... (MCA)
   Stones .... (MCA)
I Don't Call Him Daddy
Doug Supernaw; *Red & Rio Grande* ....(BNA)
I Don't Have To Crawl
Rodney Crowell; *Collection* ....(WB)
Rosanne Cash; *Hitchhiker Exampler* ....(COL)
   King's Record Shop ....(COL)
I Don't Need You
Kenny Rogers; *Share Your Love* .... (LIB)
   Twenty Greatest Hits .... (LIB)
I Got To Be Myself
Rance Allen; *15 Original Big Hits-#3* ....(STX)
Rufus Thomas; *I Ain't Gettin' Older* ....(AVI)
   If There Were No Music .... (AVI)
I Surrender Dear
Bing Crosby; *Where The Blue Of The Night Meets*
   The... ....(BIO)
Count Basie; *Basie & Zoot* .... (PAB)
   For The Second Time .... (PAB)
   Jam-#3 .... (PAB)
   Loose Walk .... (PAB)
Mel Torme; *Smooth As Velvet* ....(PIC)
Rosemary Clooney; *Sings Bing* .... (CCJ)
I Take A Lot Of Pride In What I Am
Clint Black; *Mama's Hungry Eyes-Merle Haggard*
   Tribute .... (ARI)
Merle Haggard; *Capitol Collectors Series* ....(CAP)
   Greatest Hits-#1 ....(CCB)
I Was A Punk Before You Were A Punk
Tubes; *What Do You Want From-Live* .... (A&M)

I Was Country When Country Wasn't Cool
Barbara Mandrell; *Greatest Hits* .... (MCA)
   Live .... (MCA)
I Won't Back Down
Tom Petty; *Full Moon Fever* .... (MCA)
If I Had My Way
Willie Nelson; *Healing Hands Of Time* .... (LIB)
Impossible Dream
Andy Williams; *16 Most Requested Songs* ....(COL)
   Greatest Hits-#2 ....(COL)
   Impossible Dream ....(COL)
Ed Ames; *Best Of* ....(RCA)
   Impossible Dream ....(RCA)
   Pure Gold ....(RCA)
   This Is ....(RCA)
Jack Jones; *Best Of* .... (MCA)
Kate Smith; *Best Of* ....(RCA)
   Legendary Performer ....(RCA)
Luther Vandross; *Songs* .... (EPI)
Original Cast; *Man Of La Mancha* .... (MCA)
Original London Cast; *Man Of La Mancha* ..... (MCA)
Robert Goulet; *Greatest Hits* ....(COL)
It Won't Be Me
Tanya Tucker; *Tennessee Woman* ....(CAP)
(It's Just) The Way That You Love Me
Paula Abdul; *Forever Your Girl* .... (VIA)
   Shut Up & Dance (Mixes) .... (VIA)
It's My Turn
Diana Ross; *All The Great Hits* .... (MOT)
   All The Great Love Songs .... (MOT)
   Anthology .... (MOT)
   To Love Again .... (MOT)
I'll Be Your Everything
Tommy Page; *Paintings In My Mind* .... (SIR)
I'm A Real Man
John Hiatt; *Warming Up To The Ice Age* .... (GEF)
I'm Alright
Kenny Loggins; *Alive* ....(COL)
   ST/Caddyshack ....(COL)
Little Anthony/Imperials; *Best Of* .... (RHI)
   Forever Yours .... (RLL)
   Tears On My Pillow .... (ACC)
Rolling Stones; *Got Live If You Want It* .... (AKO)
   Out Of Our Heads .... (AKO)
I'm Bad, I'm Nationwide
ZZ Top; *Deguello* .... (WB)
I'm Coming Out
Diana Ross; *All The Great Hits* .... (MOT)
   Anthology .... (MOT)
   Diana .... (MOT)
I'm Every Woman
Whitney Houston; *ST/Bodyguard* .... (ARI)
I'm Gonna Be Somebody
Travis Tritt; *Country Club* .... (WB)
I'm Gonna Sit Right Down & Write...
Frank Sinatra; *Sinatra-Basie* .... (RPR)
   Songs For Young Lovers & Swing Easy ....(CAP)
Nat King Cole; *Gift Set* ....(CAP)
   Just One OF Those Things (& More) ....(CAP)
Original Cast; *Ain't Misbehavin'* ....(RCA)
I'm Holding My Own
Lee Roy Parnell; *On The Road* .... (ARI)
I'm Not In Love
10 CC; *Greatest Hits 1972-78* .... (POL)
   Super Hits/'70s-Have A Nice Day-#14 .... (RHI)
Will To Power; *Journey Home* .... (EPI)
I'm So Great I Don't Have To Brag
Shel Silverstein; *Crouchin'* ....(OOP)
I'm So Proud
Impressions; *Greatest Hits* .... (MCA)
   Soul Shots-#11-More Ballads .... (RHI)
Main Ingredient; *Golden Classics* .... (CLT)
Todd Rundgren; *A Wizard A True Star* .... (RHI)
   Back To The Bars .... (RHI)
I'm Still Standing
Elton John; *Greatest Hits-1976-1986* .... (MCA)
   Too Low For Zero .... (MCA)
I'm The Coolest
Alice Cooper; *Goes To Hell* .... (WB)
I'm The Greatest
Ringo Starr; *Blast From Your Past* ....(CAP)
   Ringo ....(CAP)
I'm The Greatest Star
Barbra Streisand; *ST/Funny Girl* ....(COL)

Diana Ross/Supremes; *Anthology* .... (MOT)
I'm The One
Roberta Flack; *I'm The One* .... (ATL)
I'm The Only One
Melissa Etheridge; *Yes I Am* .... (ISL)
I'm Too Sexy
Right Said Fred; *Up* .... (CHS)
I've Learned To Respect The Power Of...
Angela Winbush; *Real Thing* .... (MER)
Stephanie Mills; *45* .... (MCA)
I've Never Been To Me
Charlene; *Endless Love-Greatest Love Songs* ..... (MOT)
   Hard-To-Find Motown Classics-#2 .... (MOT)
   I've Never Been To Me .... (MOT)
   Motown Memories-#4 .... (MOT)
Just As I Am
Air Supply; *Air Supply* .... (ARI)
Willie Nelson; *Red Headed Stranger* ....(COL)
Just Be Yourself
Cameo; *45* .... (CHC)
Legend In My Time
Don Gibson; *All-Time Greatest Hits* ....(RCA)
Ronnie Milsap; *Greatest Hits* ....(RCA)
   Legend In My Time ....(RCA)
   Live ....(RCA)
Legend In Your Own Time
Carly Simon; *Anticipation* .... (ELE)
   Best Of .... (ELE)
Little Respect, A
Erasure; *Innocents* .... (SIR)
Living Years
Mike/Mechanics; *Living Years* .... (ATL)
London Pride
John Williams; *Echoes Of London* ....(COL)
Look At Me I'm Wonderful
Bonzo Dog Band; *Best Of* .... (RHI)
Looking Out For Number One
Travis Tritt; *T-R-O-U-B-L-E* .... (WB)
Lookin' After #1
Boomtown Rats; *Boomtown Rats* .... (MER)
Lookin' Out For #1
Bachman-Turner Overdrive; *Best Of B.T.O.* ..... (MER)
UFO; *Obsession* .... (CHR)
Man In The Mirror
Jim Glaser; *Man In The Mirror* .... (NBL)
Michael Jackson; *Bad* .... (EPI)
Man Of My Word
Collin Raye; *Extremes* .... (EPI)
"Mary Tyler Moore" Theme
Original Music-Sonny Curtis; *Television's Greatest*
   Hits-#2 .... (TVT)
Misfits
Kinks; *Come Dancing With-Best Of-1977-1986* .. (ARI)
   Misfits .... (ARI)
   One For The Road .... (ARI)
Mr. Vain
Culture Beat; *S* ....(550)
My Baby Loves Me
Martina McBride; *Way That I Am* ....(RCA)
My Lady Loves Me (Just As I Am)
Leon Everette; *45* ....(RCA)
My Prerogative
Bobby Brown; *Dance!...Ya Know It!* .... (MCA)
   Don't Be Cruel .... (MCA)
   Rock The First-#1 .... (SAN)
My Son Calls Another Man Daddy
Hank Williams; *16 Great Hits* .... (EVR)
   40 Greatest Hits .... (POL)
   Rare Takes & Radio Cuts .... (POL)
My Way
Elvis Presley; *Aloha From Hawaii* ....(RCA)
   Canadian Tribute ....(RCA)
   In Concert ....(RCA)
Frank Sinatra; *Greatest Hits-#2* .... (RPR)
   Main Event-Live From Madison Sq. Garden ..... (RPR)
   My Way .... (RPR)
   Reprise Collection .... (RPR)
   Sinatra Reprise-The Very Good Years .... (RPR)
Paul Anka; *Very Best Of* .... (RAN)
Narcissus
City Boy; *Dinner At The Ritz* .... (MER)

New Attitude
Patti Labelle; *Classic Soul* .... (MCA)
Soundtrack Smashes-'80s .... (MCA)
ST/Beverly Hills Cop .... (MCA)
No Surrender
Bruce Springsteen; *Born In The U.S.A.* ....(COL)
November Rain
Guns N' Roses; *Use Your Illusion I* .... (GEF)
Now I Know
Lari White; *Wishes* ....(RCA)
Oh, Look At Me Now
Frank Sinatra; *A Swingin' Affair* .... (CAP)
Nancy Wilson; *But Beautiful* .... (BLN)
Sammy Kaye/Orchestra; *Play 22 Original Big Band
Recordings* .... (HIN)
Tommy Dorsey; *Boogie Woogie* .... (POE)
Tommy Dorsey & Frank Sinatra; *All-Time Greatest
Hits-#1* .... (BLU)
On Our Own
Bobby Brown; *Dance!...Ya Know It!* .... (MCA)
ST/Ghostbusters II .... (MCA)
One I Am
Dan Baird; *Love Songs For The Hearing Impaired* (DEF)
One Less Bell To Answer
5th Dimension; *Anthology 1967-1973* .... (RHI)
Greatest Hits On Earth .... (ARI)
Barbra Streisand; *Barbra Joan* .... (COL)
Gladys Knight/Pips; *Anthology* .... (MOT)
If I Were Your Woman .... (MOT)
O.P.P.
Naughty By Nature; *MTV Party To Go-#2* ..... (TMB)
Pick Yourself Up
Frank Sinatra; *Sinatra & Swingin' Brass* .... (RPR)
Fred Astaire; *Starring Fred Astaire* ....(COL)
That's Dancing .... (EMI)
Power Trip
Defiance; *Beyond Recognition* .... (RR)
Pretty As You Feel
Jefferson Airplane; *2400 Fulton Street-Anthology* (RCA)
Loves You ....(RCA)
Pride
Earth, Wind & Fire; *Eternal Dance* ....(COL)
Faces ....(COL)
Echo/Bunnymen; *Crocodiles* .... (SIR)
Husker Du; *Zen Arcade* ....(SST)
Isley Brothers; *Go For Your Guns* .... (TN)
Story-#2-T-Neck Years-1969-1985 .... (RHI)
Living Colour; *Time's Up* .... (EPI)
Ray Price; *Essential-1951-1962* ....(COL)
Greatest Hits-#4 .... (SO)
Robert Palmer; *Addictions-#1* .... (ISL)
Pride .... (ISL)
Robin Trower; *Long Misty Days* .... (CHR)
Pride Goes Before A Fall
Jim Reeves; *Best Of* ....(RCA)
Pride Of Franklin County
Tanya Tucker; *Greatest Hits* .... (MCA)
Lovin' & Learnin' .... (MCA)
Pride Of Man
Quicksilver Messenger Service; *Anthology* .... (CAP)
Quicksilver Messenger Service .... (CAP)
San Francisco Nights .... (RHI)
Sons Of Mercury .... (RHI)
Pride & Joy
Coverdale/Page; *Coverdale/Page* .... (GEF)
Lil' Ed/Blues Imperials; *Genuine Houserockin' Music
II* ....(ALG)
Roughhousin' ....(ALG)
Marvin Gaye; *Anthology* .... (MOT)
Greatest Hits .... (MOT)
Live At The London Palladium .... (MOT)
Super Hits .... (MOT)
That Stubborn Kinda Fellow .... (MOT)
Pride (In The Name Of Love)
Clivilles & Cole; *Greatest Remixes-#1* ....(COL)
ST/Gladiator ....(COL)
U2; *Greenpeace-Rainbow Warriors* .... (GEF)
ST/Rattle & Hum .... (ISL)
Unforgettable Fire .... (ISL)
Pride's Not Hard To Swallow
Hank Williams, Jr.; *14 Greatest Hits* .... (POL)
Living Proof-MGM Recordings 1963-1975 .... (MER)

Prima Donna
Jerry Vale; *All-Time Greatest Hits* ....(COL)
Greatest Hits ....(COL)
Proud Mary
Creedence Clearwater Revival; *1968-1969* ...... (FAN)
Bayou Country .... (FAN)
Chronicle .... (FAN)
Gold .... (FAN)
Live In Europe .... (FAN)
George Jones & Johnny Paycheck; *My Very Special
Guests* .... (EPI)
Ike & Tina Turner; *Best Of* .... (EMI)
EMI Legends Of Rock 'N' Roll-24 Greatest ...... (RHI)
Greatest Hits .... (CCB)
Soul Hits/'70s-#4 .... (RHI)
Proud To Be An American
Li'l Wally; *Happy Birthday America* ....(JJ)
Tubes; *Young & Rich* ....(A&M)
Proud To Be Black
Run-D.M.C.; *Raising Hell* .... (PRO)
Young Black Teenagers; *Young Black Teenagers* . (SOL)
Proud To Fall
Ian McCulloch; *Candleland* .... (SIR)
Real Man
Bonnie Raitt; *Nick Of Time* ....(CAP)
Bruce Springsteen; *Human Touch* ....(COL)
Todd Rundgren; *Anthology-1968-1985* .... (RHI)
Back To The Bars .... (RHI)
Real Niggaz
N.W.A.; *100 Miles & Runnin'* .... (RUP)
Efil4zaggin .... (RUP)
Real Niggaz Don't Die
N.W.A.; *Efil4zaggin* .... (RUP)
Respect
Aretha Franklin; *30 Greatest Hits* .... (ATL)
Best Of .... (ATL)
I Never Loved A Man (The Way I Love You) ... (ATL)
Live At Fillmore West .... (ATL)
Soul Years .... (ATL)
ST/Forrest Gump .... (EPX)
Otis Redding; *History Of* .... (ATC)
Live In Europe .... (ATC)
Otis Blue-Sings Soul .... (ATC)
Story .... (ATL)
Reba McEntire; *Reba* .... (MCA)
Respect Yourself
Bruce Willis; *Heart Of Soul* ....(COL)
Return Of Bruno .... (MOT)
Kane Gang; *Bad Guys* .... (CAS)
Lowdown .... (LON)
Staple Singers; *15 Original Big Hits-#2* .... (STX)
Chronicle .... (STX)
Greatest Hits .... (FAN)
Top Of The Stax-20 Greatest Hits .... (STX)
Stevie Wonder; *Motown Legends* .... (MOT)
Respectable
Isley Brothers; *Shout* .... (CLT)
Story-#1-Rockin' Soul-1959-1968 .... (RHI)
Outsiders; *Best Of* .... (RHI)
Capitol Collectors Series ....(CAP)
Rolling Stones; *Some Girls* .... (RS)
Righteous
Eric Johnson; *Ah Via Musicom* ....(CAP)
Rock Bottom
Wynonna; *Tell Me Why* .... (MCC)
Sacrifice
Elton John; *Sleeping With The Past* .... (MCA)
Front 242; *Tyranny For You* .... (EPI)
Naked Eyes; *Best Of* .... (EMI)
Sinead O'Connor; *Two Rooms-Songs Of E. John & B.
Taupin* .... (POL)
Steve Miller Band; *Book Of Dreams* ....(CAP)
CD Gift Set ....(CAP)
Say It Loud I'm Black & I'm Proud
Afrika Bambaataa; *Decade Of Darkness* .... (EMI)
James Brown; *Billboard Top R&B
Hits-1965-1969* .... (RHI)
Self Esteem
Offspring; *Smash* .... (EPT)
She Don't Know She's Beautiful
Sammy Kershaw; *Haunted Heart* .... (MER)

She'd Rather Be With Me
Turtles; *Best Of* .... (RHI)
   Greatest Hits .... (RHI)
   Oldies But Goodies-#3 .... (OSR)
Since I Don't Have To
Guns N' Roses; *The Spaghetti Incident?* .... (GEF)
Smells Like Teen Spirit
Nirvana; *Nevermind* .... (DGC)
Some Girls Do
Sawyer Brown; *Dirt Road* .... (CRB)
Stand
R.E.M.; *45* .... (WB)
   Green .... (WB)
R.E.M.; *Green* .... (WB)
Stand Back
Fleetwood Mac; *25 Years-The Chain* .... (WB)
Stevie Nicks; *Dance Traxx* ....(ATL)
   Timespace-Best Of .... (MOD)
   Wild Heart .... (MOD)
Stand Tall
Burton Cummings; *Burton Cummings* .... (POR)
   Rock Artifacts-#2-From The Vaults .... (COL)
   Seems Like Yesterday-#2-Mid '70s .... (KT)
Stand Up
AC/DC; *Fly On The Wall* .... (ATL)
Atlantic Starr; *Classics-#10* .... (A&M)
   Secret Lovers-Best Of .... (A&M)
Mel McDaniel; *All-Time Country Classics-#2* ..... (LIB)
   Greatest Hits .... (CAP)
   Stand Up .... (CAP)
Stand Up On Your Own Feet
Third World; *Arise In Harmony* .... (ISL)
Standing Tall
Billie Jo Spears; *Love Ain't Gonna Wait For Us* ... (UA)
   Standing Tall .... (UA)
Brenda Lee; *Brenda Lee* .... (WB)
Struttin' My Stuff
Elvin Bishop; *Raisin' Hell* .... (CPC)
   Struttin' My Stuff .... (CPC)
   '70s Greatest Rock Hits-#2-South Rules .... (PRY)
Superstar (Remember How You Got...)
Temptations; *Anthology* .... (MOT)
Take It Like A Man
Michelle Wright; *Now & Then* .... (ARI)
   Today's Top Country .... (KT)
Take Me As I Am
Faith Hill; *Take Me As I Am* .... (WB)
Take Pride In America
Oak Ridge Boys; *Greatest Hits 3* .... (MCA)
Tennessee Pride
Chet Atkins; *Country Gems* .... (PRR)
Texas Strut
Gary Moore; *Still Got The Blues* .... (CHS)
Thank You Falletin Me Be Mice Elf Again
Sly/Family Stone; *Anthology* .... (EPI)
   Greatest Hits .... (EPI)
   In Yo' Face!-History Of Funk-#1 .... (RHI)
They Can't Take That Away From Me
Billie Holiday; *God Bless The Child* .... (POE)
   I Like Jazz-Essence Of ....(COL)
Ella Fitzgerald; *Ella & Louis Again* ....(VRV)
Frank Sinatra; *My Kind Of Broadway* .... (RPR)
Frank Sinatra & Natalie Cole; *Duets* .... (CAP)
Fred Astaire; *Starring* ....(COL)
Kate Smith; *Best Of* ....(CCB)
Lisa Stansfield; *Glory Of Gershwin Featuring Larry Adler* .... (MER)
Mary Lou Williams; *In London* .... (CRS)
Original Broadway Cast; *Crazy For You* .... (ANG)
Original London Cast; *Crazy For You* .... (RCA)
Patti Austin; *The Real Me* .... (QUE)
Sarah Vaughan; *George Gershwin Songbook-#1* . (EMA)
Stanley Turrentine; *Blue Gershwin* .... (BLN)
Think For Yourself
Beatles; *Box Set* .... (CAP)
   Rubber Soul .... (CAP)
George Harrison; *Best Of* .... (CAP)
This Is Me
Randy Travis; *This Is Me* .... (WB)
This Town Ain't Big Enough For The...
Siouxsie/Banshees; *Through The Looking Glass* .. (GEF)
Sparks; *Island Story-1962-1987-25th Anniversary* . (ISL)
   Profile-Ultimate Sparks Collection .... (RHI)

Thorn In My Pride
Black Crowes; *Southern Harmony & Musical Companion* ....(DEF)
'Til I Can Make It On My Own
Kenny Rogers & Dottie West; *Classics* .... (EMI)
   Twenty Greatest Hits .... (EMI)
Tammy Wynette; *Greatest Hits-#4* .... (EPI)
   Tears Of Fire-25th Anniversary Collect. .... (EPI)
   'Til I Can Make It On My Own .... (EPI)
Time Is On My Side
Irma Thomas; *Best Of New Orleans R&B-#1* ..... (RHI)
   Simply The Best-Live .... (ROU)
Keith Richards/X-Pensive Winos; *Live At Hollywood Palladium-Dec. 1988* .... (VIA)
Rolling Stones; *12 x 5* .... (AKO)
   Big Hits-High Tides & Green Grass .... (AKO)
   Got Live If You Want It .... (AKO)
   Hot Rocks-1964-1971 .... (AKO)
   Still Life-American Concert-1981 .... (RS)
To Each His Own
Eddy Howard; *Big Band Treasures-#2* ....(DHL)
Eddy Howard/Orchestra; *Uncollected-1946-1951* (HIN)
Ink Spots; *Best Of* .... (MCA)
   Greatest Hits .... (MCA)
Willie Nelson; *What A Wonderful World* ....(COL)
   Without A Song ....(COL)
Too Legit To Quit
Hammer; *Too Legit To Quit* .... (CAP)
Tuff Enuff
Fabulous Thunderbirds; *Hot Stuff-Greatest Hits* .. (EPA)
   Rock The First-#2 .... (SAN)
   Tuff Enuff ....(EPA)
Unselfish Lover
Full Force; *Full Force* ....(COL)
Walk Like A Man
Bruce Springsteen; *Tunnel Of Love* ....(COL)
Four Seasons; *Anthology* .... (RHI)
   Billboard Top Rock 'N' Roll Hits-1963 .... (RHI)
   ST/Wanderers .... (WB)
Frankie Valli/Four Seasons; *Greatest Hits-#1* .... (RHI)
Grand Funk Railroad; *We're An American Band* .(CAP)
Watch Me
Lorrie Morgan; *Watch Me* .... (BNA)
Way I Am
Merle Haggard; *Greatest Hits* .... (MCA)
   Legends .... (MCA)
Well Respected Man
Kinks; *Greatest Hits-#1* .... (RHI)
   History Of British Rock-#4 .... (RHI)
   Kinks-Size Kinkdom .... (RHI)
What About Me
Anne Murray; *Country* ....(CAP)
Kenny Rogers w/Kim Carnes & James Ingram; *What About Me* ....(RCA)
Quicksilver Messenger Service; *Anthology* ....(CAP)
   Sons Of Mercury .... (RHI)
What Have You Done For Me Lately
Janet Jackson; *Control* .... (A&M)
What I Am
Edie Brickell/New Bohemians; *Shooting Rubberbands At The Stars* ....(GEF)
What Makes You Think You're The One
Fleetwood Mac; *25 Years-The Chain* ....(WB)
When I Paint My Masterpiece
Band; *Bob Dylan 30th Anniversary Concert* ......(COL)
   To Kingdom Come-Definitive Collection ....(CAP)
Bob Dylan; *Greatest Hits-#2* ....(COL)
When You're Hot, You're Hot
Jerry Reed; *60 Years Of Country Music* ....(RCA)
   Best Of ....(RCA)
   Super Hits/'70s-Have A Nice Day-#5 .... (RHI)
   When You're Hot, You're Hot ....(RCA)
Who Am I (What's My Name)?
Snoop Doggy Dogg; *Doggystyle* .... (DR)
Whole Lotta Pride
Robert Cray; *I Was Warned* .... (MER)
Yessir, That's My Baby
Frank Sinatra; *Strangers In The Night* .... (RPR)
Milt Jackson; *Best Of* .... (PAB)
Mom & Dads; *Dance With The Mom & Dads* .... (CRS)
   Very Best Of .... (CRS)
You Just Watch Me
Tanya Tucker; *Soon* ....(LIB)

You Make Me Feel Like A Man
Ricky Skaggs; *Live In London* .... (EPI)
You're So Vain
Carly Simon; *Best Of* .... (ELE)
    Greatest Hits Live .... (ARI)
    No Secrets .... (ELE)
    '70s Greatest Rock Hits-#3-High Times .... (PRY)
You're The Power
Kathy Mattea; *New Faces Of Country* .... (KT)
    Walk The Way The Wind Blows .... (MER)
You've Got To Stand For Something
Aaron Tippin; *You've Got To Stand For
Something* ....(RCA)

ENERGY, Electricity, Power, Solar Energy
See Also: GAS STATIONS, NUCLEAR ENERGY

Are Friends Electric
Gary Numan/Tubeway Army; *Replicas* ....(ATC)
Arkansas Coal
Nancy Sinatra & Lee Hazlewood; *Fairy Tales &
Fantasies-Best Of* .... (RHI)
A.C.D.C.
Sweet; *Desolation Boulevard* .... (CAP)
Back When Gas Was Thirty Cents A Gallon
Tom T. Hall; *Soldier Of Fortune* ....(RCA)
Big Electric Cat
Adrian Belew; *Desire Of The Rhino King* .... (ISL)
Body Electric
Rush; *Grace Under Pressure* .... (MER)
Chasin' That Neon Rainbow
Alan Jackson; *Here In The Real World* .... (ARI)
Dance Electric
Andre Cymone; *A.C.* ....(COL)
Pointer Sisters; *Break Out* .... (PNT)
Dance Of Electricity
Laurie Anderson; *United States Live* .... (WB)
Electric
Church; *Seance* .... (ARI)
Olivia Newton-John; *45* .... (MCA)
Electric Aunt Jemima
Frank Zappa; *Uncle Meat* ....(BAR)
Electric Avenue
Eddy Grant; *Killer On The Rampage* ....(POR)
Electric Blue
Icehouse; *Man Of Colours* .... (CHR)
Electric Boogaloo
Ollie & Jerry; *Breakin' 2 Electric Boogaloo* .... (POL)
Electric Chair
Prince; *ST/Batman* .... (WB)
Sleepy John Estes/Tennessee Jug Busters; *Broke &
Hungry (Ragged & Dirty Too)* ....(DEL)
Electric Chair Blues
Guitar Welch; *Angola Prisoner's Blues* .... (ARH)
Electric Chair, The
SNFU; *Last Of The Big Time Suspenders* .... (CGO)
Electric Co.
U2; *Boy* .... (ISL)
    Under A Blood Red Sky .... (ISL)
Electric Eye
Judas Priest; *Priest...Live!* ....(COL)
    Screaming For Vengeance ....(COL)
Electric Kingdom
Twilight 22; *Twilight 22* .... (VAN)
Electric Lady
Con Funk Shun; *Electric Lady* .... (MER)
Electric Land
Bad Company; *10 From 6* .... (ATL)
    Rough Diamonds .... (SS)
Electric L.A. Sunset
Al Stewart; *Early Years* ....(OOP)
Electric Messengers
220 Volt; *Electric Messengers* .... (EPI)
Electric Youth
Debbie Gibson; *Electric Youth* .... (ATL)
Electrical Language
Be Bop Deluxe; *Best Of-Raiding The Divine
Archive* .... (CAP)
    Drastic Plastic .... (HAR)
Electricity
Joni Mitchell; *For The Roses* .... (ASY)
Midnight Star; *Greatest Hits* .... (SLR)
    No Parking On The Dance Floor .... (SLR)

OMD; *Best Of* .... (A&M)
    OMD .... (VIA)
Electron Cold
Sea Level; *On The Edge* ....(OOP)
Energy
Melissa Manchester; *Mathematics* .... (MCA)
Face The Fire
Dan Fogelberg; *Phoenix* .... (FM)
Gallon Of Gas
Kinks; *Low Budget* .... (ARI)
Gasoline Alley
Rod Stewart; *Absolutely Live* .... (WB)
    Best Of .... (MER)
    Gasoline Alley .... (MER)
    Sing It Again Rod .... (MER)
    Storyteller/Complete Anthology .... (WB)
Heavy Fuel
Dire Straits; *On Every Street* .... (WB)
High Voltage
AC/DC; *High Voltage* .... (ATC)
    If You Want Blood You've Got It .... (ATL)
In Neon
Elton John; *Breaking Hearts* .... (MCA)
I've Learned To Respect The Power Of...
Angela Winbush; *Real Thing* .... (MER)
Stephanie Mills; *45* .... (MCA)
Jump Start
Natalie Cole; *Everlasting* .... (ELE)
    MTV & VH1 Powerplayers .... (EMI)
Lithium
Nirvana; *Nevermind* ....(DGC)
Live Wire
AC/DC; *High Voltage* ....(ATC)
Martha Reeves/Vandellas; *Anthology* .... (MOT)
    Compact Command Performances .... (MOT)
    Greatest Hits .... (MOT)
Lost In The Neon World
Be Bop Deluxe; *Modern Music* .... (HAR)
Love Power
Dionne Warwick & Jeffrey Osborne; *Reservations For
Two* .... (ARI)
Luminous Energy
Yusef Lateef; *Nocturnes* ....(ATL)
Magic Power
Triumph; *Allied Forces* .... (MCA)
    Classics .... (MCA)
    Stages .... (MCA)
Magnet & Steel
Walter Egan; *Rock Artifacts-#2* ....(COL)
Magnetic
Earth, Wind & Fire; *Electric Universe* ....(COL)
Mining For Coal
Randy Travis; *No Holdin' Back* .... (WB)
Neon Moon
Brooks & Dunn; *Brand New Man* .... (ARI)
Neon Moonlight
Rosco Martinez; *S* .... (ZOO)
New Electric India
Shadowfax; *Shadow Dance* ....(WH)
    What Goes Around-Best Of ....(WH)
Power
Almighty; *Blood Fire & Love* ....(POL)
Earth, Wind & Fire; *Eternal Dance* ....(COL)
    Last Days & Time ....(COL)
Holly Near; *Speed Of Light* ....(RWD)
Ice-T; *Power* .... (SIR)
John Hall; *Power* ....(COL)
John Hall/Doobie Brothers/James Taylor; *No
Nukes* .... (ASY)
Rainbow; *Finyl Vinyl* .... (MER)
    Straight Between The Eyes .... (MER)
Temptations; *25th Anniversary* .... (MOT)
    Anthology .... (MOT)
Power Age
Triumph; *Allied Forces* ....(RCA)
Power In The Blood
Weary Hearts; *By Heart* .... (FF)
Power Of God
L.L. Cool J; *Mama Said Knock You Out* ....(DFC)
Power Of Gold
Dan Fogelberg; *Live-Greetings From The West* .... (FM)
Dan Fogelberg & Tim Weisberg; *Dan
Fogelberg-Greatest Hits* .... (FM)
    Twin Sons Of Different Mothers .... (FM)

Power Of Love
Air Supply; *Air Supply* .... (ARI)
Celine Dion; *The Colour Of My Love* .... (550)
Charley Pride; *Greatest Hits-#2* .... (RCA)
  Power Of Love .... (RCA)
Deee-Lite; *World Clique* .... (ELE)
Huey Lewis/News; *ST/Back To The Future* ..... (MCA)
Jennifer Rush; *Jennifer Rush* .... (EPI)
Laura Branigan; *Touch* .... (ATL)
Lee Roy Parnell; *On The Road* .... (ARI)
Luther Vandross; *Power Of Love* .... (EPI)
Nana Mouskouri; *Nana* .... (PHI)
  Only Love-Very Best Of .... (RHI)
Trixter; *Hear!* .... (MCA)
T. Graham Brown; *Brilliant Conversationalist* .... (CAP)
T-Bone Burnett; *Truth Decay* .... (TAK)
Power Of My Love
Elvis Presley; *From Elvis In Memphis* .... (RCA)
  Memphis Record .... (RCA)
Power Of Positive Drinkin'
Mickey Gilley; *Biggest Hits* .... (EPI)
  Ten Years Of Hits .... (EPI)
Power Of The Press
Angelic Upstarts; *Brighton Bomb* .... (CHS)
Power Of Two
Indigo Girls; *Swamp Ophelia* .... (EPI)
Power Trip
Defiance; *Beyond Recognition* .... (RR)
Power & The Passion
Midnight Oil; *10-9-8-7-6-5-4-3-2-1* .... (COL)
Powerman
Kinks; *Lola Vs. The Powerman & The*
  Moneygoround .... (RPR)
Power, The
Alias; *Alias* .... (EMI)
Amy Grant; *House Of Love* .... (A&M)
Chill Rob G; *Rap Attack* .... (KT)
Jeffrey Osborne; *Don't Stop* .... (A&M)
Power Jam featuring Chill Rob G; *Best Of '90s Dance
Music-#1-Hip House* .... (PWL)
Snap!; *ST/Hangin' With The Homeboys* .... (LUK)
  World Power .... (ARI)
Temptations; *25th Anniversary* .... (MOT)
  Anthology .... (MOT)
Warrant; *ST/Gladiator* .... (COL)
Sauerkraut 'N' Solar Energy
Norman Blake/Others; *Norman Blake/Others* ...... (FF)
She's Got a 60 Cycle Brain
Paul Buff Organization; *45* .... (OSR)
Shock The Monkey
Peter Gabriel; *Greenpeace* .... (A&M)
  Plays Live .... (GEF)
  Security .... (GEF)
  Shaking The Tree-16 Golden Greats .... (GEF)
Solar
Miles Davis; *Chronicle-Complete Prestige
Recordings* .... (PRS)
  Greatest Hits .... (COL)
  Walkin' .... (COL)
Solar Prestige A Gammon
Elton John; *Caribou* .... (POL)
Sparks Will Fly
Rolling Stones; *Voodoo Lounge* .... (VIA)
Steam
Peter Gabriel; *Us* .... (GEF)
Stereotomy
Alan Parsons Project; *Best Of-#2* .... (ARI)
  Stereotomy .... (ARI)
Strength Of A Woman
Carpenters; *Made In America* .... (A&M)
Strong Enough To Bend
Tanya Tucker; *Greatest Hits* .... (LIB)
  Strong Enough To Bend .... (LIB)
Suit Of Lights
Costello Show (Featuring Elvis Costello); *King Of
America* .... (COL)
Sundancing (For The Hopi/Navajo Energy)
Jon Anderson; *In The City Of Angels* .... (COL)
Tap Into The Power
Suicidal Tendencies; *Art Of Rebellion* .... (EPI)
Texas Tea
Dee Mullins; *20 Great Hits* .... (PLN)
  Dee Mullins .... (PLN)

Train Running Low On Soul Coal
XTC; *Big Express* .... (GEF)
Twelve Volt Man
Jimmy Buffett; *Boats Beaches Bars & Ballads* ... (MGR)
  One Particular Harbor .... (MCA)
T-U-R-T-L-E Power!
Partners In Kryme; *ST/Teenage Mutant Ninja
Turtles* .... (SBK)
Wavelength
Van Morrison; *Wavelength* .... (WB)
What's On Your Mind (Pure Energy)
Information Society; *Information Society* .... (TMB)
Wichita Lineman
Glen Campbell; *Best Of* .... (LIB)
  Classics Collection .... (LIB)
  Country Music Classics-#3-1965-1970 .... (KT)
  Greatest Hits .... (LIB)
  Jimmy Webb Collection .... (COL)
  Live .... (CAP)
Wired All Night
Mick Jagger; *Wandering Spirit* .... (ATL)
Working In The Coal Mine
Devo; *Best Of-Greatest Hits* .... (WB)
  Greatest Hits .... (WB)
  New Traditionalists .... (WB)
  Now It Can Be Told (Devo At The Palace) ..... (ENI)
  ST/Heavy Metal .... (ASY)
Judds; *Collection-1983-1990* .... (RCA)
  Rockin' With The Rhythm .... (RCA)
Lee Dorsey; *Best Of New Orleans R&B-#2* .... (RHI)
  Golden Classics .... (CLT)
  History Of New Orleans R&B-#3-1962-1970 ... (RHI)
  Holy Cow .... (ARI)
  New Orleans Jazz & Heritage Fest.-1976 ...... (RHI)
You Got The Power
Esquires; *Chi-Town Show Down* .... (SSM)
You're The Power
Kathy Mattea; *New Faces Of Country* .... (KT)
  Walk The Way The Wind Blows .... (MER)

EYES, Blind, Glasses
See Also: FINDING, SEARCHING, SEEING

20/20
George Benson; *20/20* .... (WB)
  45 .... (WB)
Amazing Grace
Judy Collins; *Colors Of The Day-Best Of* .... (ELE)
  Whales & Nightingales .... (ELE)
Maverick Choir; *ST/Maverick* .... (ATL)
Nitty Gritty Dirt Band; *Will The Circle Be
Unbroken-#2* .... (UNI)
Angel Eyes
Abba; *Greatest Hits-#2* .... (ATL)
  Voulez-Vous .... (ATL)
Ella Fitzgerald; *Best Of-#2* .... (MCA)
Frank Sinatra; *At The Sands* .... (RPR)
  Main Event .... (RPR)
  Round #1 .... (CAP)
  Sings For Only The Lonely .... (CAP)
Jeff Healey Band; *See The Light* .... (ARI)
Roxy Music; *Atlantic Years 1973-1980* .... (ACO)
  Manifesto .... (ATC)
Angry Eyes
Loggins & Messina; *Best Of Friends* .... (COL)
  Loggins & Messina .... (COL)
  On Stage .... (COL)
Apple Of Your Eye
Peter Frampton; *Frampton* .... (A&M)
Arrested For Driving While Blind
ZZ Top; *Six Pack* .... (WB)
  Tejas .... (WB)
Barstow Blue Eyes
Jo Jo Gunne; *Jo Jo Gunne* .... (ASY)
Beautiful In My Eyes
Joshua Kadison; *Painted Desert Serenade* .... (SBK)
Bedroom Eyes
Eddie Rabbitt; *Radio Romance* .... (CAP)
Evelyn "Champagne" King; *Sweet Delight* .... (RCA)

Behind Blue Eyes
Who; *Hooligans* .... (MCA)
  Join Together .... (MCA)
  Who's Last .... (MCA)
  Who's Next .... (MCA)
Bette Davis Eyes
Kim Carnes; *Mistaken Identity* .... (EMI)
Between Blue Eyes And Jeans
Conway Twitty; *Don't Call Him A Cowboy* ...... (WB)
Black Eyed Blues
Esther Phillips; *Best Of* .... (CBA)
Joe Cocker; *Greatest Hits* .... (A&M)
  Joe Cocker .... (A&M)
Blind In Texas
W.A.S.P.; *Last Command* .... (CAP)
Blind Love & Whiskey
Little Mike/Tornadoes; *Heart Attack* .... (BLI)
Blind Man
Aerosmith; *Big Ones* .... (GEF)
Bobby Bland; *Best Of* .... (MCA)
  Introspective Of Early Years .... (MCA)
Champion Jack Dupree; *Back Home In New
  Orleans* .... (BUL)
Blinded By Rainbows
Rolling Stones; *Voodoo Lounge* .... (VIA)
Blinded By The Light
Bruce Springsteen; *Greetings From Asbury Park,
  NJ* ....(COL)
Manfred Mann; *Roaring Silence* .... (WB)
Bloodshot Eyes
Asleep At The Wheel; *Bloodshot Eyes* .... (EPI)
Wynonie Harris; *Good Rockin' Blues* .... (GUS)
Blue Eyes
Elton John; *Greatest Hits-1976-1986* .... (MCA)
  Jump Up! .... (MCA)
Blue Eyes Crying In The Rain
Roy Acuff; *Greatest Hits-#1* .... (ELE)
Roy Acuff/Smokey Mountain Boys; *Columbia Country
  Classics-#1-Golden Age* ....(COL)
Willie Nelson; *Columbia Country Classics-#5-New
  Trad.* ....(COL)
  Greatest Hits & Some That Will Be ....(COL)
  Red Headed Stranger ....(COL)
  ST/Honeysuckle Rose ....(COL)
Blue Motorcycle Eyes
Havana 3 A.M.; *Havana 3 A.M.* .... (IRS)
Bluest Eyes In Texas
Restless Heart; *Big Dreams In A Small Town* ....(RCA)
Born Cross-Eyed
Grateful Dead; *Anthem Of The Sun* .... (WB)
  What A Long Strange Trip It's Been .... (WB)
Brown Eyed Girl
Isley Brothers; *Live It Up* .... (TN)
Jimmy Buffett; *One Particular Harbour* .... (MCA)
Van Morrison; *Bang Masters* .... (EPI)
  Best Of .... (MER)
  ST/Born On The Fourth Of July .... (MCA)
  ST/Sleeping With The Enemy ....(COL)
  Wonder Years-Music From Emmy Shows/Era ... (ATL)
Brown Eyed Handsome Man
Buddy Holly; *For The First Time Anywhere* ..... (MCA)
  Rock & Roll Collection .... (MCA)
  & Crickets: 20 Golden Greats .... (MCA)
Chuck Berry; *Best Of The Best Of* .... (GUS)
  Chess Box .... (CSS)
  Roll Over Beethoven .... (ALL)
Brown Eyed Woman
Grateful Dead; *Europe '72* .... (WB)
  What A Long Strange Trip It's Been .... (WB)
Brown Eyes
Fleetwood Mac; *25 Years-The Chain* .... (WB)
  Tusk .... (WB)
Jimmy Cliff; *Cliff Hanger* ....(COL)
Brush Those Tears From Your Eyes
Li'l Wally; *Unforgettable Hits* .... (JJ)
Camera Eye
Rush; *Moving Pictures* .... (MER)
Can't Take My Eyes Off Of You
Frankie Valli; *Anthology* .... (RHI)
  Very Best Of .... (MCA)
  /Four Seasons: 25th Anniversary .... (RHI)
Can't You See It In My Eyes
Le Roux; *45* ....(RCA)

Cheap Sunglasses
ZZ Top; *Deguello* .... (WB)
  ST/Teachers .... (WB)
Close My Eyes Forever
Lita Ford & Ozzy Osbourne; *Lita* .... (DRM)
Close Your Eyes
Ella Fitzgerald; *Like Someone In Love* ....(VRV)
Oscar Peterson & Dizzy Gillespie; *Oscar Peterson &
  Dizzy Gillespie* .... (PAB)
Tony Bennett; *Jazz* ....(COL)
Cockeyed Optimist
Mary Martin/Original Cast; *South Pacific* ....(COL)
Mitzi Gaynor; *ST/South Pacific* ....(RCA)
Computer Eyes
Carole King; *Speeding Time* .... (ATL)
Cotton Eyed Joe
Bob Wills; *Columbia Historic Edition* ....(COL)
Carlton Moody/Moody Brothers; *Carlton Moody/Moody
  Brothers* .... (LAM)
Crazy Eyes
Daryl Hall & John Oates; *Bigger Than Both Of
  Us* ....(RCA)
Cryin' Eyes
Don Williams; *One Good Well* ....(RCA)
Dark Eyes
Bob Dylan; *Empire Burlesque* ....(COL)
Dizzy Gillespie & Stan Getz; *Diz & Getz* ....(VRV)
Tommy Dorsey/Orchestra; *& The David Rose String
  Orchestra* .... (LAS)
Dirty Looks
Diana Ross; *Red Hot Rhythm & Blues* ....(RCA)
Juice Newton; *Greatest Hits & More* ....(CAP)
Doctor My Eyes
Jackson Browne; *Jackson Browne* .... (ASY)
Don't Close Your Eyes
Keith Whitley; *Don't Close Your Eyes* ....(RCA)
  Greatest Hits ....(RCA)
Don't It Make My Brown Eyes Blue
Crystal Gayle; *Classic Crystal* .... (EMI)
  Heartbreak Hotel .... (EMI)
  ST/Convoy .... (UA)
  We Must Believe In Magic .... (UA)
Don't Let The Stars Get In Your Eyes
Perry Como; *All-Time Greatest Hits-#1* ....(RCA)
  Golden Records ....(RCA)
  Pure Gold ....(RCA)
  This Is ....(RCA)
Don't Let Your Eyes Go Shopping
Mark Murphy; *Sing's Nat's Choice-N.K. Cole
  Songbook-2* .... (MUS)
Double Vision
Foreigner; *Double Vision* .... (ATL)
  Records .... (ATL)
Dreaming With My Eyes Open
Clay Walker; *Clay Walker* .... (GIA)
Drink To Me Only With Thine Eyes
Paul Robeson; *Essential* .... (VAN)
Roger Whittaker; *Folk Songs Of Our Time* ....(RCA)
Drivin' With Your Eyes Closed
Don Henley; *Building The Perfect Beast* .... (GEF)
Ebony Eyes
Bob Welch; *French Kiss* ....(CAP)
Everly Brothers; *Golden Hits* .... (WB)
  Very Best Of .... (WB)
Rick James & Smokey Robinson; *Greatest Hits* . (MOT)
Stevie Wonder; *Songs In The Key Of Life* .... (MOT)
Electric Eye
Judas Priest; *Priest...Live!* ....(COL)
  Screaming For Vengeance ....(COL)
Emerald Eyes
Eric Johnson; *Tones* .... (RPR)
Fleetwood Mac; *Mystery To Me* .... (RPR)
Jimmy Page; *Outrider* .... (GEF)
English Eyes
Toto; *Turn Back* ....(COL)
Eye In The Sky
Alan Parsons Project; *Eye In The Sky* .... (ARI)
  Turn Of A Friendly Card .... (ARI)
Eye Of The Dragonfly
Friedemann; *Indian Summer* .... (NAR)

Eye Of The Tiger
Survivor; *Eye Of The Tiger* .... (SCO)
   Frankenstein & Other Rock Monsters .... (CBA)
   Rocky Story .... (SCO)
   ST/Rocky III .... (EMI)
Eye Of The Zombie
John Fogerty; *Eye Of The Zombie* .... (WB)
Eyes As Big As Dallas
Randy Wagner; *45* .... (DOO)
Eyes Like A Cat
Little Charlie/Nightcats; *All The Way Crazy* .... (ALG)
   Captured Live .... (ALG)
Eyes Of A Child
Moody Blues; *This Is The* .... (POL)
   To Our Children's Children's Children .... (POL)
Naked Eyes; *Best Of* .... (EMI)
Eyes Of A New York Woman
B.J. Thomas; *16 Greatest Hits* .... (TRP)
   Greatest Hits .... (RHI)
Eyes Of A Painter
Kate Wolf; *Close To You* .... (KAL)
   Evening In Austin .... (KAL)
   Gold In California (Retrospective...) .... (KAL)
Eyes Of Silver
Doobie Brothers; *What Were Once Vices Are Now
Habits* .... (WB)
Eyes Of Texas
Bill Boyd; *Western Swing-#1 & 2* .... (ARH)
Masters Of Reality; *Masters Of Reality* .... (DV)
Michigan University Band; *Kick Off, U.S.A.* ..... (VAN)
Sharkey/Kings Of Dixieland; *Sharkey/Kings Of
Dixieland* .... (STH)
Eyes Of The World
Fleetwood Mac; *25 Years-The Chain* .... (WB)
   Mirage .... (WB)
Grateful Dead; *One From The Vault* .... (GRD)
   Wake Of The Flood .... (GRD)
   Without A Net .... (ARI)
Eyes That See In The Dark
Kenny Rogers & Dolly Parton; *Eyes That See In The
Dark* .... (RCA)
Eyes Without A Face
Billy Idol; *Rebel Yell* .... (CHR)
Flesheaters; *ST/Return Of The Living Dead* .... (ENI)
Eyesight To The Blind
Pete Townshend; *Deep End-Live* .... (ATC)
Who; *Join Together* .... (MCA)
   Tommy .... (MCA)
Faraway Eyes
Rolling Stones; *Some Girls* .... (RS)
Five Foot Two, Eyes Of Blue
Mom & Dads; *Very Best Of* .... (CRS)
For Your Eyes Only
Sheena Easton; *13 Original Themes-James Bond* . (EMI)
   ST/For Your Eyes Only .... (LIB)
Funny Lookin' Eyes
Barefoot Jerry; *Watchin' TV* .... (MON)
Future's So Bright I Gotta Wear Shades
Timbuk 3; *Greetings From* .... (IRS)
Girl I Got My Eyes On You
Today; *Today* .... (MOT)
Girl With April In Her Eyes
Chris DeBurgh; *Crusader* .... (A&M)
Girl With Faraway Eyes
Rolling Stones; *Some Girls* .... (RS)
Girl With The Hungry Eyes
Jefferson Starship; *At Point Zero* .... (GRU)
Gleam In Your Eyes
Earl Lewis/Channels; *New York's Finest* .... (CLT)
Green Eyed Lady
Sugarloaf; *45* .... (UA)
Green Eyes
Husker Du; *Flip Your Wig* .... (SST)
Jimmy Dorsey; *Best Of* .... (MCA)
   Greatest Hits .... (MCA)
Green Kentucky Eyes
Pal Rakes; *Midnight Rain* .... (AA)
Heaven In Your Eyes
Loverboy; *Big Ones* .... (COL)
   ST/Top Gun .... (COL)
His Eye Is On The Sparrow
Carmen McRae; *Greatest Of* .... (MCA)
Marvin Gaye; *Musical Testament 1964-1984* ... (MOT)
Soundtrack; *Streetcar Named Desire* .... (ALL)

His Green Eyes
Barbara Fairchild; *Standing In Your Line* .... (COL)
Hit Between The Eyes
Scorpions; *Crazy World* .... (MER)
   ST/Free Jack .... (MC)
Hungry Eyes
Eric Carmen; *Best Of* .... (ARI)
   Dirty Dancing Live In Concert .... (RCA)
   ST/Dirty Dancing .... (RCA)
Hurting Kind (I've Got My Eyes On You)
Robert Plant; *Manic Nirvana* .... (EPR)
I Can See Forever In Your Eyes
Reba McEntire; *Feel The Fire* .... (MER)
I Got My Eyes On You
Buddy Guy; *This Is* .... (VAN)
Peter Frampton; *Frampton's Camel* .... (A&M)
I Only Have Eyes For You
Art Garfunkel; *Breakaway* .... (COL)
   Garfunkel .... (COL)
Flamingos; *Doo-Wop Ballads-#2* .... (RHI)
   Echoes Of A Rock Era-Middle Years .... (RLL)
   ST/American Graffiti .... (MCA)
I See The Lovelight In Your Eyes
Conway Twitty; *Number Ones* .... (MCA)
I See The Want In Your Eyes
Conway Twitty; *I'm Not Through Loving You
Yet* .... (MCA)
   Night With .... (MCA)
   Number Ones .... (MCA)
I Wish I Were Blind
Bruce Springsteen; *Human Touch* .... (COL)
In Buddy's Eyes
Jane Harvey; *Other Side Of Sondheim* .... (ATL)
In My Eyes
John Conlee; *Greatest Hits-#2* .... (MCA)
   In My Eyes .... (MCA)
Lionel Cartwright; *Lionel Cartwright* .... (MCA)
In Your Eyes
Babys; *Union Jacks* .... (CHR)
Billy Squier; *Emotions In Motion* .... (CAP)
Boy Meets Girl; *Boy Meets Girl* .... (A&M)
Bucks Fizz; *45* .... (POL)
George Benson; *In Your Eyes* .... (WB)
James "D Train" Williams; *In Your Eyes* .... (COL)
Jeffrey Osborne; *Emotional* .... (A&M)
Peter Gabriel; *So* .... (GEF)
Reivers; *Saturday* .... (CAP)
Shirley Murdock; *Let There Be Love!* .... (ELE)
Isabella's Eyes
Kenny Loggins; *Back To Avalon* .... (COL)
Jeepers Creepers
Frank Sinatra; *Gift Set* .... (CAP)
Louis Armstrong; *20 Golden Pieces Of* .... (BLD)
   At The Crescendo .... (MCA)
   Hello Dolly (& Other Hits) .... (MCA)
Jewel Eyed Judy
Fleetwood Mac; *Kiln House* .... (RPR)
John Doe No. 24
Mary Chapin Carpenter; *Stones In The Road* ....(COL)
Judy In Disguise (With Glasses)
John Fred/Playboys; *Billboard Top Rock 'N' Roll
Hits-1968* .... (RHI)
   Cruisin'-1967 .... (INC)
   ST/Drugstore Cowboy .... (NOV)
   Super Oldies Of The '60s-#7 .... (AUF)
Keep Your Eye On Me
Herb Alpert; *Keep Your Eye On Me* .... (A&M)
Killer's Eyes
Kinks; *Give The People What They Want* .... (ARI)
Last Game Of The Season (A Blind Man...
David Geddes; *Super Hits/'70s-Have A Nice
Day-#20* .... (RHI)
Living Years
Mike/Mechanics; *Living Years* .... (ATL)
Looking Through Patient Eyes
PM Dawn; *Bliss Album...?* .... (GEE)
Look, The
Roxette; *Look Sharp!* .... (EMI)
Vanessa Williams; *45* .... (WIN)
Lost In Your Eyes
Debbie Gibson; *Electric Youth* .... (ATL)
Jeff Healey Band; *Feel This* .... (ARI)
Love In Your Eyes
Eddie Money; *Nothing To Lose* .... (COL)

Love Theme From "Eyes Of Laura Mars"
Barbra Streisand; *Greatest Hits* ....(COL)
   Love Theme From "Eyes Of Laura Mars" ....(COL)
Loving Blind
Clint Black; *Put Yourself In My Shoes* ....(RCA)
Loving You With My Eyes
Starland Vocal Band; *4 x 4* ....(WS)
Lyin' Eyes
Eagles; *Anthology* ....(ASY)
   One Of These Nights ....(ASY)
   ST/Urban Cowboy ....(ASY)
   Their Greatest Hits-1971-1975 ....(ASY)
Ma (She's) Making Eyes At Me
Eddie Cantor; *Memories* .... (MCA)
Mama's Hungry Eyes
Emmylou Harris; *Mama's Hungry Eyes-Merle Haggard
Tribute* .... (ARI)
Mama's Never Seen Those Eyes
Forester Sisters; *Forester Sisters* ....(WB)
Miss Me Blind
Culture Club; *Colour By Numbers* .... (VIA)
Moon-faced, Starry-Eyed
Popular Standard; *Out of print recording* ....(OOP)
Motel Eyes
Rick Springfield; *Living In Oz* ....(RCA)
Mother's Eyes
Matthews, Wright & King; *Power Of Love* ....(COL)
My Brown Eyed Texas Rose
Tex Ritter; *Arizona Days* ....(MSP)
   Country Music Hall Of Fame ....(MCA)
My Eyes Adored You
Frankie Valli; *Greatest Hits-#2* .... (RHI)
Frankie Valli/Four Seasons; *25th Anniversary
Collection* .... (RHI)
My Mother's Eyes
Bette Midler; *ST/Divine Madness* ....(ATL)
Clovers; *Love Potion No. 9* ....(EMI)
Forester Sisters; *You Again* ....(WB)
My Sweet Eyed Georgia Girl
Atlanta; *Atlanta* .... (MCA)
Mystic Eyes
Them; *Here Comes The Night* ....(OOP)
   History Of British Rock-#6 ....(RHI)
Night Has A Thousand Eyes
Anita O'Day; *Night Has A Thousand Eyes* ...... (EML)
Bobby Vee; *Best Of* ....(EMI)
   Golden Years-1962 ....(DOM)
   Legendary Masters ....(EMI)
One Eyed Jack
Garland Jeffreys; *Matador & More* .... (A&M)
   One Eyed Jack ....(OOP)
Open Our Eyes
Earth, Wind & Fire; *Open Our Eyes* ....(COL)
Open Your Eyes
Asia; *Alpha* .... (GEF)
   Live In Moscow .... (RHI)
Black Box; *Dreamland* ....(RCA)
Bobby Caldwell; *Cat In The Hat* ....(SD)
Chiffons; *22 Leaders Of The Pack-#2* ....(LAU)
   Best Of ....(LAU)
   Golden Classics ....(CLT)
Doobie Brothers; *Minute By Minute* ....(WB)
Julian Lennon; *Mr. Jordan* ....(ATL)
Lords Of The New Church; *Lords Of The New
Church* .... (IRS)
Organized Konfusion; *Basic Beats Sampler* .... (HB)
   Organized Konfusion .... (HB)
Pinball Wizard
Elton John; *Greatest Hits-#2* ....(POL)
Pete Townshend; *Another Scoop* ....(ATC)
   Pete Townshend's Deep End-Live ....(ATC)
Rod Stewart; *Best Of* ....(MER)
   Sing It Again Rod ....(MER)
   Storyteller-Complete Anthology-1964-1990 ......(WB)
Who; *Greatest Hits* ....(MCA)
   Meaty Beaty Big & Bouncy ....(MCA)
   ST/Kids Are Alright ....(MCA)
   Tommy ....(MCA)
   Who's Last ....(MCA)
Pink-Eyed Pussycat
Bill Haley/Comets; *Rock Around The Country* ... (CRS)
   Rockin' & Rollin' .... (ACC)
Prettiest Eyes In California
B.W. Stevenson; *Rainbow Down The Road* ...... (AMA)

Pretty Little Angel Eyes
Curtis Lee; *Back To Mono-1958-1969* .... (AKO)
   Million Dollar Memories-#2 ....(RCA
   Oldies But Goodies-#2 ....(OSR
   Phil Spector-The Early Years 1958-61 ....(RHI
   Rock & Roll USA-21 Favorites-#2 ....(LAU
Private Eyes
Daryl Hall & John Oates; *Private Eyes* ....(RCA
   Rock 'N' Soul Pt. 1-Greatest Hits ....(RCA
Rainbow Eyes
Rainbow; *Long Live Rock 'n' Roll* ....(POL)
Rainbow In Your Eyes
Al Jarreau; *Glow* ....(RPR)
   Look To The Rainbow-Live In Europe ....(WB)
Leon Russell; *Wedding Album* ....(PRD)
Rat's Eyes
Black Flag; *Slip It In* ....(SST)
Red Eye
Devo; *Duty Now For The Future* ....(WB)
Joe Beck; *Beck & Sanborn* ....(CBA)
   Fire Into Music-#2 ....(CBA)
Nicky Thomas & Dolares; *Explosive Rock
Steady-Amalgamated Label* ....(HRT)
Right Before Your Eyes
America; *Encore-More Greatest Hits* .... (RHI)
   View From The Ground ....(CAP)
Rosalinda's Eyes
Billy Joel; *52nd Street* ....(COL)
Rose Colored Glasses
John Conlee; *Backstage At The Grand Ole Opry* .(RC
   Greatest Hits .... (MC
   Legends .... (MC
   MCA 30 Years Of Hits-1958-1988 .... (MC
   Rose Colored Glasses ....(MC
Sad Eyed Lady Of The Lowlands
Bob Dylan; *Blonde On Blonde* ....(CO
Joan Baez; *Any Day Now-Songs Of Bob Dylan* . (VA
   Lovesong Album ....(VA
Sad Eyes
Gary Wright; *Critics Choice-#2* ....(CY
   Who I Am ....(CY
Robert John; *Billboard Top Rock 'N' Roll
Hits-1979* .... (RH
   Robert John .... (EM
Robin Lee; *Black Velvet* ....(AT
Searching With My Good Eye Closed
Soundgarden; *Badmotorfinger* ....(A&M
See Me In Your Eyes
38 Special; *Tour De Force* ....(A&M
See You In Hell, Blind Boy
Ry Cooder; *ST/Crossroads* ....(W
Sexy Eyes
Dr. Hook; *Greatest Hits (& More)* ....(CA
   Sometimes You Win ....(CA
She Blinded Me With Science
Thomas Dolby; *Golden Age Of Wireless* ....(CA
She Closed Her Eyes
Chris Rea; *espresso logic* ....(EW
She Has Eyes
L7; *Hungry For Stink* ....(SL
Shelter Of Your Eyes
Don Williams; *Greatest Hits* ....(MCA
Silent Eyes
Paul Simon; *Still Crazy After All These Years* ...(COL
Silver Stars, Purple Sage, Eyes Of Blue
Roy Rogers/Sons Of The Pioneers; *Roy Rogers/Sons Of
The Pioneers* .... (V
Six O'Clock Train & A Girl With Green...
John Hartford; *All In The Name Of Love* ....(FF
Smile Has Left Your Eyes
Asia; *Alpha* .... (GEF
   Live In Moscow .... (RHI
   Then & Now ....(GEF
Smoke Gets In Your Eyes
Bryan Ferry; *Another Time Another Place* ....(RPR
   Street Life-20 Great Hits ....(RPR
Dinah Washington; *Golden Classics* ....(CLT
Lawrence Welk; *Musical Memories With* ....(RAN
Patti Austin; *Real Me* ....(QUE

Platters; *Encore Of Golden Hits* .... (MER)
   Greatest Hits .... (EVR)
   Oldies But Goodies-#14 .... (OSR)
   ST/Always .... (MCA)
   ST/American Graffiti .... (MCA)
   Super Oldies/'50s-#5 .... (AUF)
Snake Eyes
   Alan Parsons Project; *Turn Of A Friendly Card* .. (ARI)
Snowblind
   Black Sabbath; *Volume 4* .... (WB)
   We Sold Our Soul For Rock 'N' Roll .... (WB)
   Ozzy Osbourne; *Speak Of The Devil* .... (JET)
   Styx; *Caught In The Act* .... (A&M)
   Paradise Theater .... (A&M)
Snowblind Friend
   David Allan Coe; *Unchained* .... (COL)
   Hoyt Axton; *Snowblind Friend* .... (MCA)
   Steppenwolf; *16 Greatest Hits* .... (MCA)
   7 .... (MCA)
Spanish Eyes
   Al Martino; *Best Of* .... (CAP)
   Capitol Collectors Series .... (CAP)
   Spanish Eyes .... (CAP)
   Buddy Merrill; *All-Time Hits* .... (ACT)
   Engelbert Humperdinck; *His Greatest Hits* ...... (MER)
   Live In Concert/All Of Me .... (EPI)
   Man Without Love .... (MER)
   U2; *Joshua Tree* .... (ISL)
Star Eyes
   Charlie Parker; *Bebop & Bird-#2* .... (RHI)
   Chet Baker; *RCA Victor Jazz-First*
   Half-Century-#5 .... (RCA)
   Sonny Rollins; *Complete Prestige Recordings* ...... (PRS)
   Rollins Plays For Bird .... (PRS)
   Saxophone Colossus & More .... (PRS)
   Stephane Grappelli; *Compact Jazz* .... (VRV)
Starry Eyes
   Motley Crue; *Too Fast For Love* .... (ELE)
Stealin' Each Other Blind
   Chip Taylor; *45* .... (CAP)
Story In Your Eyes
   Moody Blues; *Every Good Boy Deserves Favour* .. (POL)
   This Is The .... (POL)
Suite: Judy Blue Eyes
   Crosby, Stills & Nash; *Crosby, Stills & Nash* ... (ATL)
   Crosby, Stills & Nash (collection) .... (ATL)
   ST/Woodstock .... (ATL)
   Crosby, Stills, Nash & Young; *So Far* .... (ATL)
Sunglasses At Night
   Corey Hart; *First Offense* .... (EMI)
   The Singles .... (EMI)
Sunshine In Their Eyes
   Stevie Wonder; *Where I'm Coming From* .... (MOT)
Sweet Sexy Eyes
   Cristy Lane; *At Her Best* .... (EMI)
   Country Classics .... (ARR)
Teardrops From My Eyes
   Ruth Brown; *Miss Rhythm-Greatest Hits & More* . (RHI)
Teardrops In My Eyes
   David Grisman; *Home Is Where The Heart Is* ... (ROU)
   New Riders Of The Purple Sage; *Adventures Of Panama*
   Red .... (COL)
Tears In My Eyes
   Baltineers; *For Collectors Only-Rarities-#1* ...... (CLT)
   Great Groups/'50s-II .... (CLT)
   Dreamers; *Harlem New York-Ballad Era* .... (CLT)
   Joan Baez; *Very Early Joan Baez* .... (VAN)
Teenage Eyes
   Flash Cadillac/Continental Kids; *Rock & Roll*
   Forever .... (EPI)
Television Eye
   John Mayall; *Room To Move-1969-1974-Chronicles*
   Series .... (POL)
Temptation Eyes
   Grass Roots; *Anthology-1965-1975* .... (RHI)
   Their 16 Greatest Hits .... (MCA)
Them There Eyes
   Anita O'Day; *Anita Sings The Most* .... (VRV)
   Billie Holiday; *At Storyville* .... (BL)
   Billie's Blues .... (BLN)
   From The Original Decca Masters .... (MCA)
   Legacy Box-1933-1958 .... (COL)
   Story .... (MCA)
   Diane Schuur; *In Tribute* .... (GRP)

Gene Ammons; *Story-78 Era* .... (PRS)
Rosemary Clooney; *Tribute To Billie Holiday* .... (CCJ)
Sarah Vaughan; *Singles Sessions* .... (RLL)
These Eyes
   Guess Who; *Best Of* .... (RCA)
   Greatest Of .... (RCA)
   Nipper's Greatest Hits-'60s-#1 .... (RCA)
   Track Record-Collection .... (RCA)
   Junior Walker/All-Stars; *All The Great Hits* ..... (MOT)
   Anthology .... (MOT)
Three Blind Mice
   Van Alexander; *Small Fry-Capitol Sings Kids*
   Songs .... (CAP)
Through The Eyes Of Love
   Melissa Manchester; *Greatest Hits* .... (ARI)
   ST/Ice Castles .... (ARI)
Too Shy
   Kajagoogoo; *White Feathers* .... (EMI)
Turn A Blind Eye
   Call; *Modern Romans* .... (MER)
   Walls Came Down-Best Of Mercury Years ..... (MER)
TV Eye
   Iggy/Stooges; *Legends Of Rock Guitar'70s* ..... (RHI)
   Stooges; *Elektrock-'60s* .... (ELE)
   Fun House .... (ELE)
U Got The Look
   Prince; *Sign "O" The Times* .... (PAI)
Under The Eye
   Dennis Linde; *Under The Eye* .... (MON)
Up Above My Head/Blind Bartimus
   Marty Stuart & Jerry & Tammy Sullivan; *Red Hot +*
   Country .... (MER)
Vision Of Love
   Mariah Carey; *Mariah Carey* .... (COL)
   MTV Unplugged .... (COL)
Wandering Eyes
   Ronnie McDowell; *Older Women & Other Greatest*
   Hits .... (EPI)
When I Look In Your Eyes
   Gap Band; *III* .... (MER)
   Jennifer Rush; *Passion* .... (EPI)
   Romantics; *What I Like About You-& Other Hits* (NEM)
When I Look Into Your Eyes
   Firehouse; *Hold Your Fire* .... (EPI)
When Irish Eyes Are Smiling
   Billy Shepherd Singers; *Irish Sing-Along* .... (MCA)
   Bing Crosby; *When Irish Eyes Are Smiling* .... (MCA)
   Dennis Day; *Irish Album* .... (RCA)
When Sunny Gets Blue
   Barbra Streisand; *Simply Streisand* .... (COL)
   Johnny Mathis; *All-Time Greatest Hits* .... (COL)
   First 25 Years-Silver Anniversary Album .... (COL)
   Greatest Hits .... (COL)
   Love Songs .... (COL)
   Kenny Rankin; *Album* .... (LD)
   Steve Miller; *Born 2 B Blue* .... (CAP)
When The Love Light Starts Shining...
   Diana Ross/Supremes; *Anthology* .... (MOT)
   Greatest Hits-#1 .... (MOT)
   Motown Superstar Series-#1 .... (MOT)
   Where Did Our Love Go .... (MOT)
When You Close Your Eyes
   Carly Simon; *No Secrets* .... (ELE)
   Night Ranger; *Greatest Hits* .... (CAM)
   Midnight Madness .... (CAM)
When You See The Tears From My Eyes
   Buddy Guy; *Very Best Of* .... (RHI)
   Buddy Guy & Junior Wells; *Drinkin' TNT 'N' Smokin'*
   Dynamite .... (BLI)
Wild Eyed Boy From Freecloud
   David Bowie; *Sound + Vision* .... (RYK)
   Space Oddity .... (RYK)
   ST/Ziggy Stardust-The Motion Picture .... (RYK)
Wild-Eyed Dream
   Ricky Van Shelton; *Wild-Eyed Dream* .... (COL)
Wild-Eyed Gypsies
   John Hiatt; *Hangin' Around The Observatory* ...... (EPI)
Wild-Eyed Southern Boys
   38 Special; *Wild-Eyed Southern Boys* .... (A&M)
Wink
   Neal McCoy; *No Doubt About It* .... (ATL)

With Just One Look In Your Eyes
Charly McClain & Wayne Massey; *19 Hot Country Requests-#3* .... (EPI)
  Biggest Hits .... (EPI)
  Radio Heart .... (EPI)
  Ten-Year Anniversary .... (EPI)
With My Eyes Wide Open I'm Dreaming
Patti Page; *Golden Hits* .... (MER)
  Greatest Hits .... (COL)
World In My Eyes
Depeche Mode; *Violator* .... (SIR)
You Can Close Your Eyes
James Taylor; *Mud Slide Slim & The Blue Horizon* (WB)
Linda Ronstadt; *Heart Like A Wheel* .... (CAP)

FARMS, Farmers

  See Also: ANIMALS

Animal Farm
Kinks; *Village Green Preservation Society* .... (RPR)
Ant Farm
Night Soil Man; *Garden of Delights* .... (VYL)
Young Fresh Fellows; *Men Who Loved Music* .... (FRN)
Ask Any Farmer
John McCutcheon; *What It's Like* .... (ROU)
Black Land Farmer
Frankie Miller; *45* .... (GUS)
Sleepy LaBeef; *Bull's Night Out* .... (SUN)
  Souvenirs Of Music City U.S.A. .... (PLN)
Bushel And A Peck
Andrews Sisters; *Best Of-#2* .... (MCA)
Original Cast; *Guys & Dolls* .... (MCA)
Cafe On The Corner
Sawyer Brown; *Cafe On The Corner* .... (CRB)
California Cotton Fields
Gram Parsons/Fallen Angels; *Live 1973* .... (SIE)
Carry Me Back To Old Virginny
Jerry Lee Lewis; *Doin' Just Fine* .... (ACC)
  Ole Tyme Country Music .... (SUN)
  Sunday Down South .... (SUN)
Cotton Fields
Beach Boys; *Absolute Best-#2* .... (CAP)
  Friends-20/20 .... (CAP)
Creedence Clearwater Revival; *1969* .... (FAN)
  Willy & The Poor Boys .... (FAN)
Highwaymen; *"Michael Row The Boat Ashore"-Best Of* .... (EMI)
Pogues; *Peace & Love* .... (ISL)
Devil In The Cane Field
Mose Allison; *Down Home Piano* .... (PRS)
  Ol' Devil Mose .... (PRS)
Diggin' My Potatoes
James Cotton; *High Compression* .... (ALG)
  Two Sides Of The Blues .... (INT)
Down On The Farm
Charley Pride; *Greatest Hits-#2* .... (RCA)
Joe Walsh; *There Goes The Neighborhood* .... (ASY)
Little Feat; *Down On The Farm* .... (WB)
Tim McGraw; *Not A Moment Too Soon* .... (CRB)
Farm
Jefferson Airplane; *Volunteers* .... (RCA)
Farmer In Florida
Sally Rogers; *Love Will Guide Us* .... (FF)
Farmer John
Neil Young/Crazy Horse; *Ragged Glory* .... (RPR)
Premiers; *Frat Rock-#2* .... (RHI)
  History Of Latino Rock-#1 .... (RHI)
Farmer & The Cowman
Original Broadway Cast; *Oklahoma* .... (RCA)
Farmer's Daughter
Beach Boys; *Surfin' Safari/Surfin' U.S.A.* .... (CAP)
Fleetwood Mac; *Live* .... (WB)
Merle Haggard; *Amber Waves Of Grain* .... (EPI)
  Best Of The Best Of .... (CAP)
Vince Gill; *Mama's Hungry Eyes-Merle Haggard Tribute* .... (ARI)
Field Worker
David Crosby & Graham Nash; *Wind On The Water* .... (MCA)
Fields Of Gold
Sting; *Ten Summoner's Tales* .... (A&M)
Harvest Moon
Neil Young; *Harvest Moon* .... (RPR)

Heartland
George Strait; *ST/Pure Country* .... (MCA)
Sawyer Brown; *Boys Are Back* .... (CCB)
Steve Wariner; *Life's Highway* .... (MCA)
U2; *ST/Rattle & Hum* .... (ISL)
High Cotton
Alabama; *Southern Star* .... (RCA)
I Want To Go Back To Michigan
Judy Garland; *ST/Easter Parade* .... (SSP)
John Barleycorn
Traffic; *John Barleycorn Must Die* .... (ISL)
John Deere Green
Joe Diffie; *Thousand Winding...* .... (EPI)
Junior's Farm
Paul McCartney/Wings; *All The Best* .... (CAP)
  Wings Greatest .... (CAP)
Long Hard Road (Sharecropper's Dream)
Nitty Gritty Dirt Band; *Live Two Five* .... (CAP)
  Plain Dirt Fashion .... (WB)
  Twenty Years Of Dirt-Best Of .... (WB)
Maggie's Farm
Bob Dylan; *At Budokan* .... (COL)
  Bringing It All Back Home .... (COL)
  Greatest Hits-#2 .... (COL)
  Hard Rain .... (COL)
  Real Live .... (COL)
Most Happy Fella
Original Broadway Cast; *Most Happy Fella* ..... (SMC)
Original Cast; *Most Happy Fella* .... (RCA)
Old Farm 1939
Randy Newman; *ST/The Natural* .... (WB)
Old Man On The Farm
Randy Newman; *Little Criminals* .... (WB)
Onion Field
Dandelion; *I Think I'm Gonna Be Sick* .... (RUC)
Out Behind The Barn
Little Jimmy Dickens; *Columbia Historic Edition* . (COL)
Parchman Farm
John Mayall; *Bluesbreakers* .... (DER)
John Mayall/Bluesbreakers; *Behind The Iron Curtain* .... (CRS)
  Last Of The British Blues .... (MCA)
  London Collection/Bluesbreakers .... (LON)
Johnny Winter; *About Blues* .... (JNS)
  Before The Storm .... (JNS)
Mose Allison; *Greatest Hits* .... (PRS)
  Mose Allison .... (PRS)
Party At The Prune Farm
Lou & Peter Berryman; *Cupid's Trash Truck* .... (COR)
Plant A Radish
Original Cast; *Fantasticks* .... (POL)
Rabbit In The Pea Patch
Red Clay Ramblers; *Merchant's Lunch* .... (FF)
Rain On The Scarecrow
John Mellencamp; *Scarecrow* .... (RIV)
Rainmaker
Dillards; *There Is A Time-1963-1970* .... (VAN)
Traffic; *Low Spark Of High-Heeled Boys* .... (ISL)
Reap What You Sow
Otis Rush; *Atlantic Blues-Chicago* .... (ATL)
  Mourning In The Morning .... (ATL)
Rhythm In The Barnyard
Joe Liggins/Honeydrippers; *Joe Liggins/Honeydrippers* .... (SPE)
Scarecrow
Siouxsie/Banshees; *Peepshow* .... (GEF)
Sex Farm
Spinal Tap; *ST/Spinal Tap* .... (POL)
Shoot Out On The Plantation
Leon Russell; *Best Of* .... (MCA)
  Leon Russell .... (MCA)
Somewhere Other Than The Night
Garth Brooks; *The Chase* .... (LIB)
Sowin' Love
Paul Overstreet; *Sowin' Love* .... (RCA)
Taxes On The Farmer Feeds Us All
Ry Cooder; *Into The Purple Valley* .... (RPR)
Tennessee Farmer
Stringbean; *Salute To Uncle Dave Macon* .... (STR)
That Summer
Garth Brooks; *The Chase* .... (LIB)
Theme From "Green Acres"
Eddie Albert & Eva Gabor; *ST/Son In Law* ...... (HOL)

Theme From "The Magnificent Seven"
BBC Concert Orchestra; *Golden Cinema*
Classics-Adventure Film ....(BAI)
Trouble In The Fields
Nanci Griffith; *Lone Star State Of Mind* .... (MCA)
  One Fair Summer Evening ....(MCA)
Turkey In The Straw
Stanley Brothers; *Stanley Series-Vol.1-#3* ....(COP)
Vassar Clements; *Grass Routes* .... (ROU)
Vermont Farmer's Song
Margaret MacArthur; *Almanac Of New England Farm*
Songs ....(GRE)

FAT, Skinny, Thin
  See Also: FOOD

Appointment At The Fat Clinic
Digable Planets; *Reachin'-New Refutation Of Time &*
Space ....(PEN)
Baby Fat
Wet Willie; *Greatest Hits* ....(POL)
Bacon Fat
Frank Zappa; *Broadway The Hard Way* ....(RYK)
  Our Man In Nirvana ....(RHI)
Big Fat Daddy
Jeannie & Jimmy Cheatham; *Midnight Mama* .... (CCJ)
Big Fat Funky Booty
Spin Doctors; *Up For Grabs...Live* ....(EPA)
Big Fat Ham
Jelly Roll Morton; *Immortal* ....(MS)
Big Fat Lady
George Benson; *Cookbook* ....(COL)
Big Fat Mama
Big Joe Williams; *Legacy Of The Blues-#6* .... (CRS)
Fred McDowell; *Long Way From Home* .... (MS)
Fred McDowell & Furry Lewis; *When I Lay My Burden*
Down ....(BIO)
Big Fat Woman
Leadbelly; *Bourgeois Blues-Golden Classics-#1* ...(CLT)
Tom Rush; *Blues Songs & Ballads* ....(FAN)
Bloat On
Cheech & Chong; *Let's Make A New Dope Deal* ..(WB)
Cellulite City
Redd Kross; *Born Innocent* ....(FRN)
Davy The Fat Boy
Randy Newman; *Live* ....(RPR)
  Randy Newman ....(RPR)
Diet Song
Shel Silverstein; *Songs & Stories* ....(OOP)
Fat
Paul Kantner; *Baron Van Tollbooth & The Chrome*
Nun ....(GRU)
Violent Femmes; *3* ....(SLS)
Weird Al Yankovic; *Dr. Demento 20th Anniversary*
Collection ....(RHI)
  Even Worse ....(SCO)
  Greatest Hits ....(SCO)
Fat Angel
Jefferson Airplane; *2400 Fulton Street-An*
Anthology ....(RCA)
  Bless Its Pointed Little Head ....(RCA)
Fat Bottomed Girls
Queen; *Greatest Hits* ....(HOL)
  Jazz ....(HOL)
Fat Boy
Billy Stewart; *One More Time/Chess Years* .... (CSS)
Fat Jack
Steppenwolf; *7* ....(MCA)
Fat Lady That Bumped Me Down
Paul Kelly; *Stand On The Positive Side* ....(WB)
Fat Man
Fats Domino; *Best Of* ....(EMI)
  Greatest Hits ....(MCA)
  My Blue Heaven-Best Of-#1 .... (EMI)
Jethro Tull; *20 Years Of-Boxed Set* ....(CHR)
  M.U.-Best Of ....(CHR)
  Stand Up ....(CHR)
Nazareth; *Nazareth* ....(A&M)
Radio Program Theme; *Themes From Old Times* .(VVA)
Fat Man In The Bathtub
Little Feat; *Dixie Chicken* ....(WB)
  Waiting For Columbus ....(WB)

Fat & Greasy
Original Cast; *Ain't Misbehavin'* ....(RCA)
Fatso
Terri Gibbs; *Take It From Me* .... (MCA)
Fattening Frogs For Snakes
Sonny Boy Williamson; *The Blues-#3* .... (CSS)
Fatty, Fatty
Heptones; *Night Food* ....(ISL)
I Like 'Em Fat Like That
Louis Jordan; *Five Guys Named Moe-Orig.*
Decca-#2 ....(DEC)
Me & Fat Boy
Mac Davis; *Texas In My Rear View Mirror* .... (CAS)
Shake That Fat
Jo Jo Gunne; *Jo Jo Gunne* ....(ASY)
Short Fat Fannie
Larry Williams; *Original Rock Oldies-Golden*
Hits-#1 .... (SPE)
  This Is How It All Began-#2 .... (SPE)
  Ultimate '50s Party ....(ERA)
Skin & Bone
Kinks; *Celluloid Heroes* ....(RCA)
  Everybody's In Show Biz ....(RHI)
  Greatest ....(RCA)
  Muswell Hillbillies ....(RHI)
Skinny Boy
Chicago; *Group Portrait* ....(COL)
  VII ....(COL)
Skinny Legs & All
Joe Tex; *Billboard Top R&B Hits* .... (RHI)
  I Believe I'm Gonna Make It!-Best Of ....(RHI)
  Soul Years ....(ATL)
Skinny Minnie
Bill Haley/Comets; *Golden Hits* ....(MCA)
  Greatest Hits ....(MCA)
Three Hundred Pounds Of Heavenly Joy
Big Twist/Mellow Fellows; *Alligator Records 20th*
Anniversary Coll. ....(ALG)
Howlin' Wolf; *Chess Box-Willie Dixon* ....(CSS)
Too Fat Polka
Arthur Godfrey; *Dr. Demento's Greatest*
Novelty-#1-1940s .... (RHI)
Frankie Yankovic; *16 Most Requested Polkas* ....(COL)
  America's Favorites ....(SMA)
Frankie Yankovic/Yanks; *Greatest Hits* ....(COL)
  Li'l Wally; I Love To Polka ....(JJ)
Too Fat To Fuck
Blowfly; *Fresh Juice* ....(OPS)
Unskinny Bop
Poison; *Flesh & Blood* ....(CAP)
  Swallow This Live ....(CAP)
You Can't Fool The Fat Man
Randy Newman; *Little Criminals* ....(WB)

FATHERS, Daddy
  See Also: MEN: GENERAL, MEN'S NAMES

Beat Me Daddy Eight To The Bar
Andrews Sisters; *16 Great Performances* .... (MCA)
  Best Of ....(MCA)
  Boogie Woogie Bugle Girls ....(MCA)
  Capitol Collectors Series ....(CAP)
Commander Cody/Lost Planet Airmen; *Lost In The*
Ozone ....(MCA)
Big Fat Daddy
Jeannie & Jimmy Cheatham; *Midnight Mama* .... (CCJ)
Carey
Joni Mitchell; *Blue* ....(RPR)
  Miles Of Aisles ....(ASY)
Cat's In The Cradle
Harry Chapin; *Anthology* .... (ELE)
  Greatest Stories-Live ....(ELE)
  Verities & Balderdash ....(ELE)
Cincinnati Daddy
Duke Ellington; *Jazz Heritage-Rockin' In*
Rhythm-#3 ....(MSP)
  Jungle Band-Brunswick Era-#2 ....(DEC)
Color Him Father
Linda Martell; *20 Great Hits* ....(PLN)
  Color Me Country ....(PLN)
Come To Poppa
Bob Seger; *Night Moves* ....(CAP)

Cool Daddy In A Cadillac
Elvis Hitler; *Disgraceland* .... (RES)
"Courtship Of Eddie's Father" Theme
Nilsson; *Television's Greatest Hits-#2* .... (TVT)
Daddy
Andrews Sisters; *Best Of-#2* .... (MCA)
 Boogie Woogie Bugle Girl .... (MCA)
Kenny Rogers; *I Prefer The Moonlight* ....(RCA)
Nicolette Larson; *In The Nick Of Time* .... (WB)
Sammy Kaye; *Big Band Sampler* .... (COL)
 Nipper's Greatest Hits-'40s ....(RCA)
Sammy Kaye/Orchestra; *Play 22 Original Big Band
Recordings* .... (HIN)
Daddy And Home
Jimmie Rodgers; *Best Of-Legendary* ....(RCA)
 Early Years 1928-1929 .... (ROU)
 This Is ....(RCA)
Tanya Tucker; *Greatest Hits* .... (CAP)
 Strong Enough To Bend .... (CAP)
 Superstars Salute Jimmie Rodgers .... (STE)
Daddy Come & Get Me
Dolly Parton; *Best Of* ....RCA)
Daddy Cool
Boney M; *Love For Sale* .... (ATL)
 Take The Heat Off Me .... (ATC)
Diamonds; *Best Of* .... (RHI)
Daddy Could Swear, I Declare
Gladys Knight/Pips; *All The Great Hits* .... (MOT)
 Anthology .... (MOT)
 Motown Memories-#3 .... (MOT)
 Neither One Of Us .... (MOT)
Daddy Don't Go
Jennifer Warnes; *Jennifer Warnes* .... (ARI)
Daddy Don't Live In That New York...
Steely Dan;
 Katy Lied .... (MCA)
Daddy Frank
Merle Haggard; *Best Of* .... (CAP)
 Capitol Collectors Series .... (CAP)
 Songs I'll Always Sing .... (CAP)
Daddy Kalled Me Niga Cause I Likeded...
Young Black Teenagers; *Young Black Teenagers* . (SOL)
Daddy Never Was The Cadillac Kind
Confederate Railroad; *Notorious* .... (ATL)
Daddy Sang Bass
Johnny Cash; *Columbia Country Classics-#5* .....(COL)
 Greatest Hits-#2 ....(COL)
Daddy Should Have Stayed In High School
Cheap Trick; *Cheap Trick* .... (EPI)
Daddy Was An Old Time Preacher Man
Porter Wagoner & Dolly Parton; *Best Of* ....(RCA)
Daddy What If
Bobby Bare; *Bobby Bare* ....(RCA)
 Great Moments At The Grand Ole Opry ....(RCA)
Daddy You Been On My Mind
Joan Baez; *Farewell Angelina* .... (VAN)
Judy Collins; *5th Album* .... (ELE)
 Recollections .... (ELE)
Daddy, Daddy, Daddy
Janis Joplin; *ST/Janis* ....(COL)
Daddy's All Gone
James Taylor; *In The Pocket* .... (WB)
Daddy's Baby
James Taylor; *Walking Man* .... (WB)
Daddy's Back
Kenny Loggins; *Celebrate Me Home* ....(COL)
Daddy's Come Around
Paul Overstreet; *Heroes* ....(RCA)
Daddy's Dream
Vikki Carr; *Live At The Greek Theatre* ....(COL)
Daddy's Drinking Up Our Christmas
Commander Cody; *Hillbilly Holiday* .... (RHI)
Daddy's Gone Grey
Lonesome Strangers; *Lonesome Strangers* .... (HT)
Daddy's Gonna Save My Soul
Golden Earring; *Switch* .... (MCA)
Daddy's Gonna Treat You Right
Commander Cody/Lost Planet Airmen; *Lost In The
Ozone* .... (MCA)
Daddy's Hands
Holly Dunn; *Country Love Songs* .... (WB)
 Holly Dunn ....(MTM)
Daddy's Home
Cliff Richard; *Wired For Sound* .... (EMI)

Jackson 5; *Anthology* .... (MOT)
Jermaine Jackson; *Motown Superstar Series-#17* (MOT)
Shep/Limelites; *Cruisin' 1961* .... (INC)
 Doo Wop Ballads-#2 .... (RHI)
 Oldies But Goodies-#5 .... (OSR)
Shep/Limelites-Heartbeats; *Best Of The
Heartbeats* .... (RHI)
Daddy's Little Boy
Eddy Howard; *45* .... (MER)
Mills Brothers; *45* .... (MCA)
Daddy's Little Girl
Al Martino; *Best Of* .... (CAP)
Mills Brothers; *50th Anniversary* .... (RAN)
 All Occasions Album .... (GAT)
 Best Of .... (MCA)
 Story .... (RAN)
Nikki D; *S* .... (DFJ)
Daddy's Tune
Jackson Browne; *Pretender* .... (ASY)
Don't Cry Daddy
Elvis Presley; *Always On My Mind* ....(RCA)
 Memphis Record ....(RCA)
 Top Ten Hits ....(RCA)
 Worldwide 50 Gold Award Hits-#1 ....(RCA)
Don't Sell Daddy Any More Whiskey
Joe Val/New England Bluegrass Boys; *Not A Word
From Home* .... (ROU)
Down At Papa Joe's
Dixiebelles; *45* ....(OOP)
Down The Road
Mac McAnally; *Knots* .... (MCA)
Drop Down Mama, Let Your Papa See
John Hammond; *Best Of* .... (VAN)
Sleepy John Estes; *Legend Of* .... (DEL)
Tom Rush; *Best Of* .... (COL)
 Tom Rush .... (COL)
Father
Cat Stevens; *Back To Earth* .... (A&M)
Father Christmas
Kinks; *Come Dancing With-Best Of-1977-1986* .. (ARI)
Father Dear Father
Doucette; *Douce Is Loose* .... (MSH)
Father Figure
George Michael; *Faith* ....(COL)
Father Of A Boy Named Sue
Shel Silverstein; *Songs & Stories* .... (OOP)
Father Of Day, Father Of Night
Manfred Mann's Earth Band; *Solar Fire* .... (POL)
Father Of Girls
Perry Como; *Legendary Performer* ....(RCA)
Father Of Night
Bob Dylan; *New Morning* ....(COL)
Father O.S.A.
Styx; *Lady* ....(RCA)
Father Steps In
Earl "Fatha" Hines; *Father Jumps* ....(RCA)
 Grand Terrace Band .... (QUI)
Father Sun
Wynonna; *Tell Me Why* .... (MCC)
Father To Son
Alarm; *Strength* .... (IRS)
Phil Collins; *...But Seriously* .... (ATL)
Queen; *II* ....(HOL)
Father & Son
Cat Stevens; *Classics-#24* .... (A&M)
 Footsteps In The Dark-Greatest Hits-#2 .... (A&M)
 Greatest Hits .... (A&M)
 Tea For The Tillerman .... (A&M)
Foggy, Foggy Dew
Burl Ives; *Best Of* .... (MCA)
Fool To Cry
Rolling Stones; *Black & Blue* .... (RS)
 Rewind (1971-1984) .... (RS)
 Sucking In The Seventies .... (RS)
Fun Fun Fun
Beach Boys; *Best Of* .... (CAP)
 Endless Summer .... (CAP)
 Gift Set .... (CAP)
 In Concert .... (CAR)
 Made In The U.S.A. .... (CAP)
Games That Daddies Play
Conway Twitty; *Greatest Hits-#2* .... (MCA)
 #1s-#11 .... (CAP)

Grandpa (Tell Me About The Good Old...)
Judds; *Greatest Hits* ....(RCA)
Rockin' With The Rhythm ....(RCA)
Super 10-#2 ....(RCA)
Greatest Man I Never Knew
Reba McEntire; *For My Broken Heart* .... (MCA)
Greatest Hits-#2 .... (MCA)
He Walked On Water
Randy Travis; *No Holdin' Back* .... (WB)
Heavenly Father
Castelles; *Home Of Grand Records* ....(CLT)
Sweet Sounds Of ....(CLT)
Hello Muddah, Hello Fadduh
Allan Sherman; *Dr. Demento Greatest Novelty CD* (RHI)
Dr. Demento's Greatest-#3 ....(RHI)
Hot Rod Lincoln
Asleep At The Wheel; *Western Standard Time* .... (EPI)
Commander Cody/Lost Planet Airmen; *Lost In The
Ozone* ....(MCA)
Super Hits/'70s-Have A Nice Day-#8 ....(RHI)
We've Got A Live One Here ....(WB)
Johnny Bond; *Best Of* .... (STR)
I Don't Call Him Daddy
Doug Supernaw; *Red & Rio Grande* ....(BNA)
I Want A Girl (Just Like The Girl)
Al Jolson; *Story-#1* .... (MCA)
Spike Jones; *King Of Corn* ....(GLN)
Independence Day
Bruce Springsteen; *The River* ....(COL)
Bruce Springsteen/E Street Band;
Live-1975-1985 ....(COL)
I'm A Long Gone Daddy
George Jones; *Too Wild Too Long* .... (EPI)
Hank Williams; *24 Greatest Hits-#2* ....(POL)
Lovesick Blues ....(POL)
Kansas City Papa
Leadbelly; *King Of The Twelve-String Guitar* .....(COL)
Leadbelly ....(COL)
Keep It Between The Lines
Ricky Van Shelton; *Backroads* ....(COL)
Lawyers, Guns & Money
Warren Zevon; *Excitable Boy* .... (ASY)
Quiet Normal Life-Best Of .... (ASY)
Stand In The Fire .... (ASY)
Leader Of The Band
Dan Fogelberg; *Greatest Hits* .... (FM)
Innocent Age .... (FM)
Living Years
Mike/Mechanics; *Living Years* .... (ATL)
Love Without End, Amen
George Strait; *Livin' It Up* .... (MCA)
Ten Strait Hits .... (MCA)
Mama Hated Diesels
Commander Cody/Lost Planet Airmen; *We Got A Live
One Here* ....(WB)
Hot Licks Cold Steel & Trucker's Fav. .... (MCA)
Mommy Where's Daddy
Red Hot Chili Peppers; *Red Hot Chili Peppers* ... (EMI)
My Dad
Paul Peterson; *45* .... (ERI)
My Dad Sucks
Descendants; *Bonus Fat* ....(SST)
Liveage ....(SST)
Somery ....(SST)
My Daddy
Jess Pearson; *Woody Guthrie's "We Ain't Down
Yet"* ....(CRE)
My Daddy Knows Best
Marvelettes; *Anthology* .... (MOT)
Compact Command Performances .... (MOT)
My Daddy Rocks Me
Benny Goodman Sextet; *Slipped Disc-1945-1946* (COL)
Mae West; *Fabulous* .... (MCA)
My Daddy Was A Jockey
John Lee Hooker; *Detroit Blues-1950-1951* ......(CLT)
Gotham Golden Classics ....(CLT)
My Daddy Was A Milkman
Kentucky HeadHunters; *Pickin' On Nashville* .... (MER)
My Daddy Was A Travelin' Man
Brenda Kaye Perry; *45* ....(MRC)
My Father
Barbara Cook; *At Carnegie Hall* ....(COL)

Judy Collins; *Colors Of The Day-Best Of* .... (ELE)
So Early In The Spring-First 15 Years .... (ELE)
Who Knows Where The Time Goes .... (ELE)
My Father's Fiddle
David Loggins; *Apprentice* .... (EPI)
My Father's Gun
Elton John; *Tumbleweed Connection* .... (POL)
My Father's Mansions
Pete Seeger; *Essential* .... (VAN)
My Father's Shoes
Leon Russell; *Will O' The Wisp* .... (MCA)
Level 42; *Guaranteed* ....(RCA)
My Father's Song
Barbra Streisand; *Lazy Afternoon* ....(COL)
My Heart Belongs To Daddy
Ella Fitzgerald & Cole Porter; *Dream Dancing* .. (PAB)
Peggy Lee; *Best Of* .... (MCA)
Rosemary Clooney; *Sings The Music Of Cole
Porter* .... (CCJ)
My Old Man
Jerry Jeff Walker; *Gypsy Songman* ....(RYK)
Mr. Bojangles ....(BAI)
Walker's Collectibles ....(MCA)
John Denver; *Rhymes & Reasons* ....(RCA)
Steve Goodman; *Say It In Private* ....(ASY)
My Son Calls Another Man Daddy
Hank Williams; *16 Great Hits* ....(EVR)
40 Greatest Hits ....(POL)
Rare Takes & Radio Cuts ....(POL)
Night I Called The Old Man Out
Garth Brooks; *In Pieces* .... (LIB)
No Sir
Darryl & Don Ellis; *No Sir* .... (EPI)
No Son Of Mine
Genesis; *We Can't Dance* ....(ATL)
Oh, Daddy
Fleetwood Mac; *Rumours* ....(WB)
Only Daddy That'll Walk The Line
Hank Williams, Jr.; *Family Tradition* ....(W/C)
Kentucky HeadHunters; *Electric Barnyard* ...... (MER)
Ricky Skaggs; *My Father's Son* .... (EPI)
Waylon Jennings; *Best Of* ....(RCA)
Early Years ....(RCA)
Greatest Hits ....(RCA)
Willie Nelson; *& Family Live* ....(COL)
Papa
Bill Anderson; *Story* .... (MCA)
Paul Anka; *Anka* .... (UA)
Times Of Your Life .... (UA)
Prince; *Come* ....(WB)
Papa Don't Preach
Madonna; *Immaculate Collection* .... (SIR)
Royal Box .... (SIR)
True Blue .... (SIR)
Papa Hobo
Paul Simon; *Paul Simon* ....(COL)
Papa Loved Mama
Garth Brooks; *Ropin' The Wind* .... (LIB)
Papa Loves Mambo
Perry Como; *All-Time Greatest Hits-#1* ....(RCA)
Golden Records ....(RCA)
Pure Gold ....(RCA)
This Is ....(RCA)
Papa Rolled His Own
Tommy James/Shondells; *Crimson & Clover/Cellophane
Symphony* .... (RHI)
Papa Was A Rollin' Stone
Temptations; *20-20* .... (MOT)
25 #1 Hits From 25 Years .... (MOT)
All The Million-Sellers .... (MOT)
Anthology .... (MOT)
Billboard Top Rock 'N' Roll Hits-1972 .... (RHI)
Compact Command Performances .... (MOT)
Papa's Billy Goat
Sarah Ogan Gunning; *Silver Dagger* .... (ROU)
Papa's Got A Brand New Bag
James Brown; *21 Legendary Superstars* ....(OSR)
Everybody's Doin' The Hustle ....(OOP)
Greatest Hits .... (RHI)
Live-Hot On The One ....(POL)
Otis Redding; *Story* ....(ATL)
Unlimited! ....(RPR)

Parents Just Don't Understand
D.J. Jazzy Jeff & The Fresh Prince; *He's The D.J. I'm The Rapper* .... (JVA)
Pistol Packin' Papa
Hank Snow; *Superstars Salute Jimmie Rodgers* ......(SO)
Jimmie Rodgers; *Riding High 1929-1930* .... (ROU)
This Is ....(RCA)
Pop, Let Me Have The Car
Carl Perkins; *Restless-Columbia Recordings* ......(COL)
Whole Lotta Shakin' ....(SSP)
Ray's Dad Cadillac
Joni Mitchell; *Night Ride Home* .... (GEF)
Rockin' Daddy
Howlin' Wolf; *Chess Box* .... (CSS)
Rosalita
Bruce Springsteen; *Wild The Innocent & The E Street Shuffle* ....(COL)
Bruce Springsteen/E Street Band; *Live-1975-1985* ....(COL)
Salty Papa Blues
Dinah Washington; *Golden Hits* .... (MER)
Saturday's Father
Frankie Valli/Four Seasons; *25th Anniversrary Collection* .... (RHI)
Seein' My Father In Me
Paul Overstreet; *Sowin' Love* ....(RCA)
Shimmy Shakin' Daddy
Maddox Brothers & Rose; *1946-1951-#2* ...... (ARH)
America's Most Colorful Hillbilly Band .... (ARH)
Silver Haired Daddy Of Mine
Frank Yankovic; *I Wish I Was 18 Again* ...... (SMA)
So Much Like My Dad
George Strait; *Holding My Own* .... (MCA)
Willie Nelson; *Partners* ....(COL)
Sugar Daddy
Bellamy Brothers; *Greatest Hits* .... (MCA)
You Can Get Crazy ....(WB)
Fleetwood Mac; *Fleetwood Mac* .... (RPR)
Jackson 5; *Anthology* ....(MOT)
Greatest Hits ....(MOT)
Michigan & Smiley; *Sugar Daddy* .... (RAS)
Thompson Twins; *Big Trash* .... (RE)
Sweet Daddy (Your Mama's Done Gone Mad)
Little Brother Montgomery; *Chicago-Living Legends-South Side Blues* ....(RVR)
Sweet Little Papa
Louis Armstrong; *Hot Fives & Hot Sevens-#2* ....(COL)
Sweet Lovin' Daddy
Betty Wright; *Golden Classics* .... (CLT)
Fontella Bass; *Rescued-Best Of* .... (CSS)
Swingin' Daddy
Buddy Knox; *Best Of* .... (RHI)
Talk To Me Daddy
Thelma Cooper/Boyfriends; *Collectables Blues Collection-#3* ....(CLT)
Texas Girl At The Funeral Of Her Father
Randy Newman; *Little Criminals* ....(WB)
That Silver Haired Daddy Of Mine
Doc Watson; *My Dear Old Southern Home* ....(SH)
Gene Autry; *Country Music Hall Of Fame* ......(COL)
That's My Pa
Champion Jack Dupree; *Blues For Everybody* .... (IGR)
Theme From "The Godfather"
Henry Mancini/Mancini Pops Orchestra; *Cinema Italiano* ....(RCA)
They Don't Make 'Em Like That Anymore
Boy Howdy; *She'd Give Anything* ....(CRB)
They're Moving Father's Grave To...
Clancy Brothers/Tommy Makem; *Luck Of The Irish* ....(COL)
This Child Needs Its Father
Gladys Knight/Pips; *Neither One Of Us* .... (MOT)
To Daddy
Emmylou Harris; *Profile-Best Of* ....(WB)
Quarter Moon In A Ten Cent Town ....(WB)
Truckin' Dad
Dave Dudley; *Diesel Express* ....(FFT)
Unwed Fathers
Gail Davies; *Best Of* .... (LIB)
Tammy Wynette; *Best Loved Hits* .... (EPI)
Voodoo Daddy
Lonnie Brooks; *Bayou Lightning* ....(ALG)

When I Grow Up (To Be A Man)
Beach Boys; *Absolute Best-#1* ....(CAP)
Dance Dance Dance ....(CAP)
Gift Set ....(CAP)
Made In The U.S.A. ....(CAP)
Spirit Of America ....(CAP)
When My Daddy Rode The West
Clarence Reid; *45* .... (DSH)
Your Mama Don't Dance
Loggins & Messina; *Best Of-Friends* ....(COL)
Loggins & Messina ....(COL)
On Stage ....(COL)
Pop Classics Of The '70s ....(COL)
Poison; *Open Up And Say Ahhhh* ....(CAP)
Swallow This Live ....(CAP)

FEAR, Courage, Panic, Paranoia, Shy, Worry
See Also: CHAOS, EGO, HIDING

1984
David Bowie; *Changestwobowie* ....(RCA)
David Live ....(RYK)
Diamond Dogs ....(RYK)
Fame & Fashion ....(RCA)
Spirit; *Best Of* ....(EPI)
Spirit Of '84 ....(MER)
Tina Turner; *Private Dancer* ....(CAP)
Van Halen; *1984* ....(WB)
Afraid
Willie Nelson; *Moonlight Becomes You* .... (JST)
Afraid Of Love
Toto; *IV* ....(COL)
Are You Hung Up
Mothers Of Invention; *We're Only In It For The Money* ....(RYK)
Ballad Of The Green Berets
Barry Sadler; *Cruisin'-1966* .... (INC)
Hits Of The '60s ....(IMC)
More American Graffiti-#4 ....(MCA)
Nipper's Greatest Hits-'60s-#2 ....(RCA)
Super Hits-#3 ....(GUS)
Better Watch Your Back
Daryl Hall & John Oates; *War Babies* .... (ATL)
Beware Of Darkness
George Harrison; *All Things Must Pass* ....(CAP)
Concert For Bangladesh ....(CAP)
Big Brother
David Bowie; *Diamond Dogs* ....(RYK)
Live ....(RYK)
Sound + Vision ....(RYK)
ST/Breaking Glass ....(A&M)
Stevie Wonder; *Talking Book* .... (MOT)
Bold As Love
Jimi Hendrix; *Axis: Bold As Love* .... (RPR)
Essential-#1 & 2 ....(RPR)
Brahma Fear
Jimmy Buffett; *Living & Dying In 3/4 Time* ..... (MCA)
Bravado
Rush; *Roll The Bones* ....(ATL)
Brave New World
Choirboys; *Big Bad Noise* ....(WTG)
Public Image, Ltd.; *9* ....(VIA)
Steve Miller Band; *Brave New World* ....(CAP)
Brave Strangers
Bob Seger/Silver Bullet Band; *Stranger In Town* .(CAP)
Can't Stop Worrying
Dave Mason; *Alone Together* ....(MCA)
Cold Sweat
James Brown; *Billboard Top R&B Hits-1967* ..... (RHI)
Can Your Heart Stand It ....(SSM)
Greatest Hits ....(RHI)
Live At The Apollo-Vol. 2-#1 ....(RHI)
Warrant; *Dirty Rotten Filthy Stinking Rich* ....(COL)
Courage
Tragically Hip; *Fully Completely* .... (MCA)
Coward Of The County
Kenny Rogers; *20 Greatest Hits* ....(LIB)
Greatest Hits ....(EMI)
Kenny ....(LIB)
Cowards Over Pearl Harbor
Wilma Lee Cooper; *Wilma Lee Cooper* .... (ROU)

Dare Me
Pointer Sisters; *Contact* ....(RCA)
Nipper's Greatest Hits-'80s ....(RCA)
Dear Jean (I'm Nervous)
City Boys; *Young Men Gone West* .... (MER)
(Don't Fear) The Reaper
Blue Oyster Cult; *Agents Of Fortune* ....(COL)
Extraterrestrial Live ....(COL)
Metalmania ....(COL)
Some Enchanted Evening ....(COL)
Don't Give Up
Peter Gabriel; *Shaking The Tree-16 Golden*
Greats ....(GEF)
So ....(GEF)
Don't Worry About Me
Doris Day; *Sings 22 Great Songs* .... (HIN)
Ella Fitzgerald; *Classy Pair* ....(PAB)
EAsy Living ....(PAB)
Don't Worry, Baby
Beach Boys; *Absolute Best-#1* ....(CAP)
Endless Summer ....(CAP)
Fun Fun Fun ....(CAP)
Made In The U.S.A. ....(CAP)
Don't Worry, Be Happy
Bobby McFerrin; *Simple Pleasures* .... (EMI)
ST/Cocktail ....(ELE)
Don'tcha Worry 'Bout A Thing
Stevie Wonder; *Innervisions* .... (MOT)
Fear
Sarah McLachlan; *Fumbling Towards Ecstasy* .... (ARI)
Fear Of A Black Planet
Public Enemy; *Fear Of A Black Planet* ....(DFC)
Fear Of The Marketplace
Neil Diamond; *On The Way To The Sky* ....(COL)
Fearless
Pink Floyd; *Meddle* ....(HAR)
Works ....(CAP)
Fly Me Courageous
Drivin' N' Cryin'; *Fly Me Courageous* .... (ISL)
Fools Rush In
Brook Benton; *Super Oldies/'60s-#10* ....(AUF)
Frank Sinatra/Tommy Dorsey Orchestra;
Sessions-#1 ....(RCA)
For What It's Worth
Buffalo Springfield; *Buffalo Springfield* ....(ATC)
Double History ....(ATC)
Hit Singles 1958-1977 ....(ATL)
Retrospective ....(ATC)
ST/Forrest Gump ....(EPX)
God Fearing Man
Steppenwolf; *At Your Birthday Party* ....(OOP)
Gun Shy
10,000 Maniacs; *In My Tribe* ....(ELE)
Moon Martin; *Escape From Domination* ....(CAP)
He's So Shy
Pointer Sisters; *Special Things* ....(PNT)
Hold Your Head Up
Argent; *Anthology* .... (EPI)
Encore .... (EPI)
Rock Artifacts-#1-From The Vaults ....(COL)
ST/Queen's Logic .... (EPI)
I Ain't Down Yet
Debbie Reynolds; *Unsinkable Molly Brown* ..... (MCA)
I Scare Myself
Dan Hicks/Hot Licks; *Striking It Rich* ....(OOP)
Thomas Dolby; *Flat Earth* ....(CAP)
I Will Survive
Gloria Gaynor; *Billboard Top Hits-1979* .... (RHI)
Disco Years-#2-On The Beat-1978-1982 .... (RHI)
Love Tracks ....(POL)
Impossible Dream
Andy Williams; *16 Most Requested Songs* ....(COL)
Greatest Hits-#2 ....(COL)
Impossible Dream ....(COL)
Ed Ames; *Best Of* ....(RCA)
Impossible Dream ....(RCA)
Pure Gold ....(RCA)
This Is ....(RCA)
Jack Jones; *Best Of* ....(MCA)
Kate Smith; *Best Of* ....(RCA)
Legendary Performer ....(RCA)
Luther Vandross; *Songs* .... (EPI)
Original Cast; *Man Of La Mancha* ....(MCA)
Original London Cast; *Man Of La Mancha* ..... (MCA)

Robert Goulet; *Greatest Hits* ....(COL)
Independence Day
Martina McBride; *The Way That I Am* ....(RCA)
It's Only Me
Leon Russell; *Americana* ....(OOP)
I'm Afraid Of Me
Culture Club; *Kissing To Be Clever* .... (VIA)
I'm Afraid To Go Home
Brian Hyland; *Greatest Hits* .... (RHI)
Gene Pitney; *This Is* ....(OOP)
I'm Not Afraid
Frank Sinatra; *Greatest Hits-#2* ....(RPR)
I'm So Afraid
Fleetwood Mac; *25 Years-The Chain* .... (WB)
Fleetwood Mac .... (WB)
Live .... (WB)
I'm The Bravest Individual
Broadway Cast; *Sweet Charity* .... (EMI)
Original Cast; *Sweet Charity* ....(COL)
Learning To Live Again
Garth Brooks; *The Chase* .... (LIB)
Living Inside Myself
Gino Vannelli; *Nightwalker* .... (ARI)
Look Heart No Hands
Randy Travis; *Greatest Hits-#2* .... (WB)
My Brave Face
Paul McCartney; *Flowers In The Dirt* ....(CAP)
Tripping The Light Fantastic-Highlights! ....(CAP)
My Husband's Got No Courage In Him
Maddy Prior & June Tabor; *Silly Sisters* ....(SHA)
Never Surrender
Corey Hart; *Boy In The Box* .... (EMI)
Singles .... (EMI)
Triumph; *Never Surrender* .... (MCA)
Stages .... (MCA)
Once Bitten Twice Shy
Great White; *Rock The First-#2* ....(SAN)
...Twice Shy ....(CAP)
Vesta Williams; *Vesta* ....(A&M)
Panic
Anthrax; *Armed & Dangerous* .... (MEG)
Fistful Of Metal .... (MEG)
Smiths; *Best...1* .... (SIR)
Louder Than Bombs .... (SIR)
Rank .... (SIR)
Panic In Detroit
David Bowie; *Aladdin Sane* ....(RYK)
Scary Monsters ....(RYK)
Sound + Vision ....(RYK)
Panic In The World
Be Bop Deluxe; *Best Of & The Rest Of* ....(OOP)
Best Of-Raiding The Divine Archive ....(CAP)
Drastic Plastic ....(OOP)
Paranoid
Black Sabbath; *Live Evil* .... (WB)
Paranoid .... (WB)
We Sold Our Soul For Rock 'N' Roll .... (WB)
Grand Funk Railroad; *Grand Funk Railroad* .....(CAP)
Live ....(CAP)
Mark Don & Mel 1969-71 ....(CAP)
More Of The Best ....(CAP)
Ozzy Osbourne; *Speak Of The Devil* ....(JET)
Tribute ....(EPA)
Pressure
Billy Joel; *Greatest Hits-#1&2-1973-1985* ....(COL)
Nylon Curtain ....(COL)
Fishbone; *Reality Of My Surroundings* ....(COL)
Kinks; *One For The Road* .... (ARI)
Negative Approach; *Total Recall* .... (T&G)
Neil Young; *Landing On Water* ....(GEF)
Rude Boys; *Rude Awakening* ....(ATL)
Running Scared
Roy Orbison; *All-Time Greatest Hits-#1&2* ...... (MON)
For The Lonely-Anthology-1956-1965 .... (RHI)
In Dreams-Greatest Hits .... (VIA)
& Friends-Black & White Night .... (VIA)
San Francisco Holiday (Worry Later)
Thelonius Monk; *In Person* .... (MS)
Scarecrow
Siouxsie/Banshees; *Peepshow* ....(GEF)
Scared
John Lennon; *Lennon* ....(CAP)
Menlove Avenue ....(CAP)
Walls & Bridges ....(CAP)

The Green Book Of Songs By Subject — Page 233

Scarred & Scared
Rod Stewart; *Blondes Have More Fun* ....(WB)
Scary Monsters
David Bowie; *Golden Years* ....(RYK)
  Scary Monsters ....(RYK)
  The Singles-1969-1993 ....(RYK)
Scotland The Brave
Original Cast; *Forever Plaid* ....(RCA)
Shy
Carol Burnett/Original Cast; *Once Upon A Mattress* .... (MCA)
Somebody's Watching Me
Rockwell; *Somebody's Watching Me* ....(MOT)
Someone To Watch Over Me
Ella Fitzgerald; *Sings The George & Ira Gershwin Songbook* ....(VRV)
Elton John; *Glory Of Gershwin Featuring Larry Adler* .... (MER)
Frank Sinatra; *Nice 'N' Easy* ....(CAP)
  The Capitol Years ....(CAP)
Jack Jones; *Gershwin Album* ....(COL)
Original Broadway Cast; *Crazy For You* ....(ANG)
Oscar Peterson; *My Favorite Instrument* ....(VRV)
Sarah Vaughan; *George Gershwin Songbook-#2* .(EMA)
Willie Nelson; *Stardust* ....(COL)
Stage Fright
Band; *Best Of* ....(CAP)
  Last Waltz ....(WB)
  Rock Of Ages-#1&2 ....(CAP)
  Stage Fright ....(CAP)
  To Kingdom Come-Definitive Collection ....(CAP)
Bob Dylan/Band; *Before The Flood* ....(COL)
Standing Outside The Fire
Garth Brooks; *In Pieces* ....(LIB)
Stick It Out
Rush; *Counterparts* ....(ATL)
Tales Of Brave Ulysses
Cream; *Disraeli Gears* ....(POL)
  Eric Clapton-Crossroads ....(POL)
  Live Cream-#2 ....(POL)
Terrified
Anacrusis; *Speed Metal* ....(PRY)
Pursuit Of Happiness; *Downward Road* ....(MER)
Quiet Riot; *Terrified* ....(MOO)
Uncle Green; *You* ....(DB)
Terrifying
Rolling Stones; *Steel Wheels* ....(RS)
Terror On The Town
Lizzy Borden; *Menace To Society* ....(MET)
Terror Zone
Kreator; *Coma Of Souls* ....(EPI)
Terrorist Trousers
Jim Carroll; *Praying Mantis* .... (GIA)
Terrorist's Life
D.I.; *What Good Is Grief To A God* ....(XXX)
There Are No Cats In America
Nehemiah Persoff/J. Guarnieri/W. Hays; *ST/An American Tail* .... (MCA)
Too Much Paranoias
Devo; *Live-The Mongoloid Years* ....(RYK)
  Q: Are We Not Men? A: We Are Devo! ....(WB)
  Rest Of Devo-Greatest Misses ....(WB)
Too Shy
Kajagoogoo; *White Feathers* ....(EMI)
Too Shy To Say
Stevie Wonder; *Fulfillingness' First Finale* ....(MOT)
Touch Me
Doors; *13* ....(ELE)
  Best Of ....(ELE)
  Greatest Hits ....(ELE)
  Soft Parade ....(ELE)
Under Pressure
David Bowie & Queen; *Bowie-The Singles-1969-1993* ....(RYK)
Queen & David Bowie; *Classic Queen* ....(HOL)
  Hot Space ....(HOL)
  Queen Greatest Hits ....(HOL)
Wake Up, Little Susie
Everly Brothers; *All They Had To Do Was Dream* (RHI)
  All-Time Greatest Hits ....(CCB)
  American Graffiti-#3 ....(MCA)
  Everly Brothers ....(RHI)
  Oldies But Goodies-#7 ....(OSR)
  Very Best Of ....(WB)

Grateful Dead; *History Of-#1-Bear's Choice* ......(WB)
Simon & Garfunkel; *Concert In Central Park* .....(WB)
Walking The Floor Over You
Asleep At The Wheel; *Western Standard Time* ....(EPI)
Ernest Tubb; *Story* ....(MCA)
  Legend & The Legacy ....(FSG)
Ernest Tubb/M. Haggard/C. Daniels; *Ernest Tubb Collection* ....(SO)
Sandy Denny; *Who Knows Where The Time Goes?* (HBL)
Webb Pierce; *Golden Hits* ....(PLN)
White Knuckles
Elvis Costello/Attractions; *Trust* ....(RYK)
Whiter Shade Of Pale
Procol Harum; *Best Of* ....(A&M)
  Classics-#17 ....(A&M)
  History Of British Rock-#8 ....(RHI)
  ST/Big Chill ....(MOT)
Who Scared You
Doors; *Weird Scenes Inside The Gold Mine* ......(ELE)
Who's Afraid Of The Big Bad Wolf
Barbra Streisand; *Album* ....(COL)
  Just For The Record ....(COL)
L.L. Cool J; *Simply Mad About The Mouse* ......(COL)
Mormon Tabernacle Choir/Columbia Symph.; *When You Wish Upon A Star-Disney Tribute* ....(COL)
M. Moder/D. Compton/P. Colvig/Others; *Disney Collection-#1* ....(DIS)
Why Am I So Shy
Chiffons; *Everything You Always Wanted To Hear By* ....(LAU)
  Golden Classics ....(CLT)
Work Shy
Fabulous Poodles; *Mirror Stars* ....(EPI)
Worried Life Blues
B.B. King; *Turn On With* ....(KNT)
Eric Clapton; *24 Nights* ....(POL)
  Just One Night ....(POL)
John Lee Hooker; *Plays & Sings The Blues* ....(CSS)
Lightnin' Hopkins; *Best Of* ....(PRS)
  How Many More Years I Got ....(FAN)
You Can Call Me Al
Paul Simon; *Concert In The Park-August 15 1991* (WB)
  Graceland ....(WB)
  Negotiations & Love Songs-1971-1986 ....(WB)
You Don't Have To Worry
En Vogue; *Born To Sing* ....(ATL)
You'll Never Walk Alone
Andy Williams; *Greatest Songs* ....(CCB)
Jim Nabors; *16 Most Requested Songs* ....(COL)
Judy Garland; *Best Of The Capitol Masters* ....(CAP)
Mormon Tabernacle Choir; *Climb Every Mountain* ....(COL)
Original Broadway Cast; *Carousel* ....(ANG)
Original Cast; *Carousel* ....(MCA)
Pink Floyd; *Meddle* ....(CAP)

FEMINISM, Feminist Independence
See Also: EGO, WOMEN: GENERAL, WORK

80's Ladies
K.T. Oslin; *80's Ladies* ....(RCA)
  Greatest Hits ....(RCA)
  Nipper's Greatest Hits-'80s ....(RCA)
Company Time
Linda Davis; *Shoot For The Moon* ....(ARI)
Girls Just Want To Have Fun
Cyndi Lauper; *She's So Unusual* ....(POR)
Gym II
Meg Christian; *Turning It Over* ....(OLI)
Harry's House Centerpiece
Joni Mitchell; *Hissing Of Summer Lawns* ....(ASY)
He Thinks He'll Keep Her
Mary Chapin Carpenter; *Come On Come On* ....(COL)
I Am Woman
Helen Reddy; *Greatest Hits* ....(CAP)
  I Am Woman ....(CAP)
  I Don't Know How To Love Him ....(CAP)
I Will Survive
Gloria Gaynor; *Billboard Top Hits-1979* ....(RHI)
  Disco Years-#2-On The Beat-1978-1982 ....(RHI)
  Love Tracks ....(POL)
If Women Ruled The World
Joan Armatrading; *Square The Circle* ....(A&M)

Is There Life Out There
Reba McEntire; *For My Broken Heart* .... (MCA)
Greatest Hits-#2 .... (MCA)
I'm That Kind Of Girl
Patty Loveless; *Greatest Hits* .... (MCA)
On Down The Line .... (MCA)
Lady Is A Tramp
Ella Fitzgerald; *Rodgers & Hart Songbook* .... (VRV)
Frank Sinatra; *Capitol Years* .... (CAP)
Sinatra Reprise-Very Good Years .... (RPR)
Frank Sinatra & Luther Vandross; *Frank Sinatra
Duets* .... (CAP)
Man Smart, Woman Smarter
Harry Belafonte; *Pure Gold* .... (RCA)
Robert Palmer; *Some People Can Do What They
Like* .... (ISL)
Rosanne Cash; *Right Or Wrong* .... (COL)
"Mary Tyler Moore" Theme
Original Music-Sonny Curtis; *Television's Greatest
Hits-#2* .... (TVT)
"Maude" Theme
Original Music; *Television's Greatest Hits-#3* ..... (TVT)
Me & A Gun
Tori Amos; *Little Earthquakes* .... (ATL)
My Mom's A Feminist
Kristin Lems; *We Will Never Give Up* .... (CDP)
Nine To Five
Dolly Parton; *9 To 5 & Odd Jobs* .... (RCA)
Best There Is .... (RCA)
Greatest Hits .... (RCA)
Nipper's Greatest Hits-'80s .... (RCA)
P.M.S. Blues
Dolly Parton; *Heart Songs* .... (COL)
Respect
Aretha Franklin; *30 Greatest Hits* .... (ATL)
Best Of .... (ATL)
I Never Loved A Man (The Way I Love You) ... (ATL)
Live At Fillmore West .... (ATL)
Soul Years .... (ATL)
ST/Forrest Gump .... (EPX)
Otis Redding; *History Of* .... (ATC)
Live In Europe .... (ATC)
Otis Blue-Sings Soul .... (ATC)
Story .... (ATL)
Reba McEntire; *Reba* .... (MCA)
She Works Hard For The Money
Donna Summer; *She Works Hard For The Money* (MER)
Summer Collection .... (MER)
Think
Aretha Franklin; *Aretha's Gold* .... (ATL)
Best Of .... (ATL)
Greatest Hits .... (ATL)
ST/Blues Brothers .... (ATL)
What Part Of No
Lorrie Morgan; *Watch Me* .... (BNA)
Woman Is The Nigger Of The World
John Lennon; *Shaved Fish* .... (CAP)
Somewhere In New York City .... (CAP)
John Lennon/Plastic Ono Band; *Lennon* .... (CAP)
Woman Of Heart & Mind
Joni Mitchell; *For The Roses* .... (ASY)
Joni Mitchell/L.A. Express; *Miles Of Aisles* ...... (ASY)
Woman Of The Year
Original Cast; *Woman Of The Year* .... (BAY)
Woman Power
Yoko Ono; *Walking On Thin Ice Compilation* ....(RYK)
Woman To Woman
Beverley Craven; *Beverley Craven* .... (EPI)
Joe Cocker; *Classics-#4* .... (A&M)
Greatest Hits .... (A&M)
Shirley Brown; *Soul Hits!'70s-#15* .... (RHI)
Top Of The Stax-Twenty Great Hits .... (STX)
Woman To Woman .... (STX)
Tammy Wynette; *Anniversary-20 Years Of Hits* ... (EPI)
Greatest Hits-#3 .... (EPI)
Tears Of Fire-25th Anniversary Collect. .... (EPI)
Woman Walk The Line
Emmylou Harris; *Ballad Of Sally Rose* .... (WB)
Highway 101; *Featuring Paulette Carlson* .... (WB)
Trisha Yearwood; *Hearts In Armor* .... (MCA)
Woman's Got A Right To Change Her Mind
Rex Stewart/Ellingtonians; *Rex
Stewart/Ellingtonians* .... (RVR)

Woman's Point Of View
Shirley Murdock; *Woman's Point Of View* .... (ELE)
Woman's Prerogative
Pearl Bailey; *16 Most Requested Songs* ....(COL)
Woman's Smarter
Jolly Boys; *Sunshine 'N' Water* .... (RYK)
Women Walk More Determined
Kristin Lems; *Oh Mama!* .... (CDP)
Women Will Rule The World
Ry Cooder; *Get Rhythm* .... (WB)
Women's Love Rights
Laura Lee; *Greatest Hits* .... (HDH)
XXX's And OOO's
Trisha Yearwood; *S* .... (MCA)

FIGHT, Anger, Domestic Violence, Violence
*See Also: CRIME, DEATH, POLICE, PROTEST,
REBELS, WAR*

Angry
Eddy Arnold; *All Time Favorites* .... (RCA)
Paul McCartney; *Press To Play* .... (CAP)
Public Image, Ltd.; *Happy* .... (VIA)
Angry Eyes
Loggins & Messina; *Best Of Friends* .... (COL)
Loggins & Messina .... (COL)
On Stage .... (COL)
Angry Young Man
Billy Joel; *KOHUEPT (Live In Leningrad)* ....(COL)
Corey Hart; *Fields Of Fire* .... (EMI)
Steve Earle/Dukes; *Exit O* .... (MCA)
Attitude Adjustment
Hank Williams, Jr.; *Greatest Hits-#2* .... (W/C)
Major Moves .... (W/C)
Avenging Annie
Andy Pratt; *Andy Pratt* .... (COL)
Roger Daltrey; *Best Bits* .... (MCA)
One Of The Boys .... (MCA)
Back Stabbers
O'Jays; *Billboard Top Rock 'N' Roll Hits-1972* ... (RHI)
Collector's Items .... (PI)
Live In London .... (PI)
Bad Bad Leroy Brown
Jim Croce; *Billboard Top Rock 'N' Roll Hits-1973* (RHI)
Down The Highway .... (21)
Life & Times .... (OOP)
Photographs & Memories .... (21)
Ballad Of TV Violence
Cheap Trick; *Cheap Trick* .... (EPI)
Bangkok Cockfight
Martin Denny; *Exotica-Best Of* .... (RHI)
Beat It
Michael Jackson; *Thriller* .... (EPI)
Beat On The Brat
Ramones; *All The Stuff (& More)-#1* .... (SIR)
Mania .... (SIR)
Ramones .... (SIR)
Black Eyed Blues
Esther Phillips; *Best Of* .... (CBA)
Joe Cocker; *Greatest Hits* .... (A&M)
Joe Cocker .... (A&M)
Born Fighter
Nick Lowe; *Basher: Best Of* .... (COL)
Labour Of Lust .... (COL)
Boy Named Sue
Johnny Cash; *Biggest Hits* .... (COL)
Columbia Country Classics-#3 .... (COL)
Greatest Hits-#2 .... (COL)
Controlled By Hatred
Suicidal Tendencies; *TT/Feel Like Shit...Deja Vu* .. (EPI)
Coward Of The County
Kenny Rogers; *20 Greatest Hits* .... (LIB)
Greatest Hits .... (EMI)
Kenny .... (LIB)
Cruel To Be Kind
Nick Lowe; *Basher: Best Of* .... (COL)
Labour Of Lust .... (COL)
Cruising For Bruising
Basia; *London Warsaw New York* .... (EPI)
Don't Fight It
Flying Burrito Brothers; *Last Of The Red Hot
Burritos* .... (A&M)

Kenny Loggins & Steve Perry; *High Adventure* ...(COL)
Wilson Pickett; *Best Of* ....(ATL)
   Greatest Hits ....(ATL)
Don't You Get So Mad
Jeffrey Osborne; *Stay With Me Tonight* ....(A&M)
El Paso
Grateful Dead; *Steal Your Face* ....(GRD)
Marty Robbins; *Biggest Hits* ....(COL)
   Billboard Top Country Hits-1960 ....(RHI)
   Gunfighter Ballads & Trail Songs ....(COL)
   Radio Classics/'50s ....(COL)
Electric Avenue
Eddy Grant; *Killer On The Rampage* ....(POR)
Face To Face
Garth Brooks; *The Chase* ....(LIB)
Fight Apartheid
Peter Tosh; *No Nuclear War* ....(EMI)
Fight Dirty
Charlie; *Fight Dirty* ....(ARI)
Fight Fire With Fire
Kansas; *Best Of* ....(CBA)
   Drastic Measures ....(KIR)
Metallica; *Ride The Lightning* ....(ELE)
Fight For California
University Of California Marching Band; *University Of California Marching Band* ....(FID)
Fight For Your Right (To Party)
Beastie Boys; *Def Jam Classics-#1* ....(DFJ)
   Heart Of Soul ....(COL)
   Licensed To Kill ....(DFJ)
Fight From The Inside
Queen; *News Of The World* ....(HOL)
Fight On
Peter Tosh; *Mystic Man* ....(RS)
Fight On Christmas Fight On
John Fahey; *Essential* ....(VAN)
   John Fahey ....(VAN)
Fight On, U.S.C.
Michigan University Band; *Kick Off, U.S.A.* .....(VAN)
Fight Or Fall
Thin Lizzy; *Jailbreak* ....(MER)
Fight The Good Fight
Triumph; *Allied Forces* ....(MCA)
   Stages ....(MCA)
   Triumph Classics ....(MCA)
Fight The Power
Isley Brothers; *Forever Gold* ....(TN)
   Greatest Hits-#1 ....(TN)
   Heat Is On ....(TN)
   Story-#2 ....(RHI)
Public Enemy; *Def Jam Classics-#2* ....(DFJ)
   Fear Of A Black Planet ....(DFJ)
   ST/Do The Right Thing ....(MOT)
Fight The Team Across The Field
Ohio State University Marching Band; *Across The Field* ....(FID)
Fighting For Strangers
Steeleye Span; *Rocket Cottage; Story* ....(CHR)
Fighting Side Of Me
Merle Haggard; *Best Of* ....(CAP)
   Capitol Collector Series ....(CAP)
   Fighting Side Of Me ....(CAP)
   Songs I'll Always Sing ....(CAP)
Fightin' Side Of Me
Merle Haggard; *All American* ....(CAP)
   Capitol Collectors Series ....(CAP)
Merle Haggard/Strangers; *Songs I'll Always Sing* .(CAP)
Flying Colours
Jethro Tull; *Broadsword And The Beast* ....(CHR)
Gimme Three Steps
Lynyrd Skynyrd; *Gold & Platinum* ....(MCA)
   One More From The Road ....(MCA)
   Pronounced Leh-Nerd Skin-Nerd ....(MCA)
(I Can't Get No) Satisfaction
Devo; *45* ....(WB)
   Q: Are We Not Men ....(WB)
Otis Redding; *Best Of* ....(RPR)
   Otis Redding ....(ATL)
Rolling Stones; *Big Hits-High Tide & Green Grass* (AKO)
   Got Live If You Want It ....(AKO)
   Hot Rocks-1964-1971 ....(AKO)
   Out Of Our Heads ....(AKO)
I Can't Stay Mad At You
Skeeter Davis; *Nipper's Greatest Hits/'60s-#2* ....(RCA)

I Saw Red
Warrant; *Cherry Pie* ....(COL)
If You Don't Know Me By Now
Harold Melvin/Blue Notes; *Collector's Item* .... (PI)
   Philly Ballads-#1 ....(PI)
Simply Red; *New Flame* ....(ELE)
Incident On 57th Street
Bruce Springsteen; *Wild The Innocent & The E Street Shuffle* ....(COL)
Independence Day
Martina McBride; *The Way That I Am* ....(RCA)
Inner London Violence
Bad Manners; *ST/Dance Craze* .... (CHR)
Iowa Fight Song
University Of Iowa Band; *Go Hawkeyes Go* ......(FID)
University Of Michigan Band; *Greatest College Football Marches* ....(VAN)
Jukebox Argument
Mickey Gilley; *ST/Urban Cowboy 2* ....(EPI)
Keep On Fighting
Frankie/Knockouts; *Below The Belt* ....(MIL)
Kick A Little
Little Texas; *Kick A Little* ....(WB)
K.S.U. Fight Song
Kent State University Marching Band; *Kent State University Marching Band* ....(FID)
Land Of Nightmares
Rosanne Cash; *Interiors* ....(COL)
Little Fighter
White Lion; *Big Game* ....(ATL)
Living Years
Mike/Mechanics; *Living Years* ....(ATL)
Love Without End, Amen
George Strait; *Livin' It Up* ....(MCA)
   Ten Strait Hits ....(MCA)
Luka
Suzanne Vega; *Solitude Standing* ....(A&M)
Me & A Gun
Tori Amos; *Little Earthquakes* ....(ATL)
Mean Disposition
Rolling Stones; *Voodoo Lounge* ....(VIA)
Meanest Jukebox In Town
Johnny Paycheck; *Out-of-print recording* ....(OOP)
Mending Fences
Restless Heart; *Big Iron Horses* ....(RCA)
Midnight Rambler
Rolling Stones; *Get Yer Ya-Ya's Out* .... (AKO)
   Hot Rocks-1964-1971 ....(AKO)
   Let It Bleed ....(AKO)
Missouri Squabble
Alex Jackson Plantation; *Territory Bands-#2-1927-1931* ....(HIS)
M.S.U. Fight Song
Michigan State University Band; *Michigan State University Band* ....(FID)
Nevada Fighter
Michael Nesmith; *Older Stuff* .... (RHI)
Nigga Ya Love To Hate
Ice Cube; *Amerikkka's Most Wanted* ....(PRY)
Night I Called The Old Man Out
Garth Brooks; *In Pieces* ....(LIB)
No Son Of Mine
Genesis; *We Can't Dance* ....(ATL)
November Rain
Guns N' Roses; *Use Your Illusion I* ....(GEF)
One Of These Days-Pow
Jackie Gleason; *Dr. Demento Greatest Novelty Records-#2* ....(RHI)
O'Reilly At The Bar
Dan Hicks/Hot Licks; *Striking It Rich* ....(MCA)
Push Comes To Shove
Jackyl; *Push Comes To Shove* ....(GEF)
P.M.S. Blues
Dolly Parton; *Heart Songs* ....(COL)
Rage In The Cage
J. Geils Band; *Freeze-Frame* .... (EMI)
Red Roses (Won't Work Now)
Reba McEntire; *Have I Got A Deal For You* ....(MCA)
Rip Her To Shreds
Blondie; *Best Of* ....(CHR)
   Blondie ....(CHR)
River, The
Bruce Springsteen; *The River* ....(COL)

Bruce Springsteen/E Street Band;
Live-1975-1985 ....(COL)
Rosie Strikes Back
Eliza Gilkyson; *Texas-A Musical Celebration-150
Years* .... (TOM)
Rosanne Cash; *King's Record Shop* ....(COL)
Saturday Night's Alright For Fighting
Elton John; *Goodbye Yellow Brick Road* .... (POL)
Greatest Hits .... (POL)
Knebworth-The Album .... (POL)
Rock Classics .... (KT)
Who; *Two Rooms-Songs Of E. John & B. Taupin* (POL)
Shakin' The Blues
Screamin' Cheetah Wheelies; *Screamin' Cheetah
Wheelies* .... (ATL)
Silent Treatment
Earl Thomas Conley; *Fire & Smoke* ....(RCA)
Greatest Hits ....(RCA)
Small Town Saturday Night
Hal Ketchum; *Past The Point Of Rescue* ....(CRB)
Somebody To Shove
Soul Asylum; *Grave Dancers Union* ....(COL)
Stairs, The
Reba McEntire; *The Last One To Know* .... (MCA)
Stand Up & Fight Back
Jimmy Cliff; *Give Thanx* .... (WB)
Sticks & Stones
Tracy Lawrence; *Tracy Lawrence* .... (ATL)
Stop The Violence
Boogie Down Productions; *By All Means
Necessary* .... (JVA)
Live Hardcore Worldwide-Paris-London-NYC .. (JVA)
Straight Tequila Night
John Anderson; *Seminole Wind* ....(BNA)
Today's Hot Country .... (KT)
Street Fighting Man
Rod Stewart; *Best Of* ....(MER)
Sing It Again Rod ....(MER)
Storyteller-Complete Anthology-1964-1990 ..... (WB)
Rolling Stones; *Beggars Banquet* .... (AKO)
Get Yer Ya-Ya's Out .... (AKO)
Hot Rocks-1964-1971 .... (AKO)
Singles Collection-London Years .... (AKO)
Through The Past Darkly-Big Hits-#2 .... (AKO)
Suicidal Rage
Death Squad; *Split You At The Seams* .... (ER)
Tears Of Rage
Band; *Best Of* ....(CAP)
Music From Big Pink ....(CAP)
To Kingdom Come-Definitive Collection ....(CAP)
Bob Dylan/Band; *Basement Tapes* ....(COL)
Teen Angst (What The World Needs Now)
Cracker; *Cracker* .... (VIA)
Thunder Rolls, The
Garth Brooks; *No Fences* .... (LIB)
Time Is Running Out
Steve Winwood; *Steve Winwood* .... (ISL)
Too Weak To Fight
Clarence Carter; *Golden Age Of Black
Music-1960-1970* ....(ATL)
Snatching It Back-Best Of .... (RHI)
T.C.U. Fight Song
Southern Methodist Mustang Band; *Southwest
Conference Jazz* ....(FID)
Ultraviolence
New Order; *Power Corruption & Lies* .... (QUE)
U.N.M. Fight Song
University Of New Mexico Lobos Pep Band; *University
Of New Mexico Lobos Pep Band* ....(FID)
Video Violence
Lou Reed; *Between Thought &
Expression-Anthology* ....(RCA)
Vigilante Man
Bruce Springsteen; *Folkways-Tribute-W. Guthrie &
Leadbelly* ....(COL)
Ry Cooder; *Into The Purple Valley* ....(RPR)
Woody Guthrie; *Dust Bowl Ballads* .... (ROU)
Violence
Mott The Hoople; *Ballad Of Mott* ....(COL)
Live ....(COL)
Mott ....(COL)
Pet Shop Boys; *Please* .... (EMI)

Violence Of Truth
The The; *Mind Bomb* ....(EPI)
Shades Of Blue ....(EPI)
Violent Crimes
Riot; *Restless Breed* ....(ELE)
Violent Times
Call; *Walls Came Down-Best Of Mercury Years* . (MER)
We Can Work It Out
Beatles; *1962-1966* ....(CAP)
20 Greatest Hits ....(CAP)
Box Set ....(CAP)
Past Masters-#2 ....(CAP)
Yesterday...And Today ....(CAP)
Paul McCartney; *Unplugged-Official Bootleg* .... (CAP)
Stevie Wonder; *Beatles Songs By Greatest Stars* . (MOT)
Greatest Hits-#2 ....(MOT)
Signed Sealed & Delivered ....(MOT)
Top Ten With A Bullet-Motown Solo Stars ..... (MOT)
We Just Disagree
Billy Dean; *Fire In The Dark* .... (LIB)
Dave Mason; *Best Of* ....(COL)
Let It Flow ....(COL)
Rock Classics/'70s ....(COL)

FINDING
See Also: SEARCHING

Betcha'll Never Find
Chantay Savage; *Here We Go* ....(RCA)
Find A Dream
Crosby, Stills & Nash; *After The Storm* .... (ATL)
Find A Reason To Believe
Rod Stewart; *Best Of-#2* .... (MER)
Find A Way
Amy Grant; *Collection* .... (A&M)
Unguarded .... (A&M)
Find Another Fool
Quarterflash; *Quarterflash* .... (GEF)
Find Another Love
Tams; *45* ....(GUS)
Find Me A Girl
Jacksons; *Goin' Places* .... (EPI)
Philly Ballads-#2 .... (PI)
Find My Way
Cameo; *TGIF* ....(OOP)
Find Out What They Like
Original Cast; *Ain't Misbehavin'* ....(RCA)
Teresa Brewer; *Live At Carnegie Hall & Montreaux
Switz* .... (DOC)
Find The Cost Of Freedom
Crosby, Stills, Nash & Young; *Four-Way Street* .. (ATL)
So Far .... (ATL)
Find Your Way Back
Jefferson Starship; *Modern Times* .... (GRU)
Starship; *Greatest Hits-Ten Years & Change
1979-91* ....(RCA)
Find Yourself A Man
Original Cast; *Funny Girl* ....(CAP)
Finder Of Lost Loves
Dionne Warwick & Glenn Jones; *45* .... (ARI)
Finders Keepers
Beach Boys; *Surfin' Safari/Surfin' USA* ....(CAP)
Elvis Presley; *Elvis For Everyone* ....(RCA)
Soul Children; *Lost Soul-#1* ....(EPI)
Finders Keepers, Losers Weepers
Elvis Presley; *For Everyone* ....(RCA)
Finding My Way
Rush; *All The World's A Stage* .... (MER)
Archives .... (MER)
Rush .... (MER)
Finding You
Joe Stampley; *Backslidin'* .... (EPI)
Found Out About You
Gin Blossoms; *New Miserable Experience* .... (A&M)
Good Lovin's Hard To Find
Lynyrd Skynyrd; *Last Rebel* ....(ATL)
Heaven Can't Be Found
Hank Williams, Jr.; *Born To Boogie* ....(W/C)
Greatest Hits III ....(W/C)
Heroes Are Hard To Find
Fleetwood Mac; *25 Years-The Chain* .... (WB)
Heroes Are Hard To Find ....(RPR)

I Found A Dream
Bob Wills; *Anthology* .... (SSP)
I Found A Love
Eric Clapton; *Crossroads* .... (POL)
Falcons; *Atlantic Rhythm & Blues 1947-74-#4* ... (ATL)
Wilson Pickett; *Best Of* .... (ATL)
  Greatest Hits .... (ATL)
I Found A Million Dollar Baby
Barbra Streisand; *ST/Funny Girl* .... (ARI)
Nat King Cole; *Gift Set* .... (CAP)
I Found Love
Lone Justice; *Shelter* .... (GEF)
Paul Carrack; *Suburban Voodoo* .... (EPI)
Quicksilver Messenger Service; *Anthology* ...... (CAP)
  Sons Of Mercury .... (RHI)
I Found My Baby
Gap Band; *45* .... (TE)
I Found Somebody
Glenn Frey; *No Fun Aloud* .... (ASY)
I Found Someone
Cher; *Cher* .... (GEF)
Laura Branigan; *Hold Me* .... (ATL)
I Found The Brains Of Santa Claus
Jason/Straptones; *Demento's Mementos* .... (PVC)
I Have Found Me A Home
Jimmy Buffett; *White Sport Coat & A Pink
  Crustacean* .... (MCA)
I Still Haven't Found What I'm...
U2; *Joshua Tree* .... (ISL)
  ST/Rattle & Hum .... (ISL)
If You Want To Find Love
Kenny Rogers; *Back Home Again* .... (RPR)
I'll Never Find Another You
Seekers; *Best Of* .... (CAP)
  History Of British Rock-#3 .... (RHI)
Sonny James; *All-Time Country Classics-#2* ..... (CAP)
  Opry Legends .... (CAP)
I've Found A New Baby
Benny Goodman; *Complete-#2* .... (RCA)
  Live At Carnegie Hall .... (LON)
  On Stage .... (LON)
I've Found Someone Of My Own
Free Movement; *45* .... (MCA)
Lost & Found
Brooks & Dunn; *Brand New Man* .... (ARI)
Echo/Bunnymen; *Echo/Bunnymen* .... (SIR)
Original Broadway Cast; *City Of Angels* .... (COL)
Sparks; *Profile-The Ultimate Sparks Collection* ... (RHI)
Love Is Gonna Find You
Manhattans; *Forever By Your Side* .... (COL)
Love She Found In Me
Gary Morris; *Hits* .... (WB)
  Why Lady Why .... (WB)
Love Will Find A Way
George Howard; *Dancing In The Sun* .... (GRP)
Lionel Richie; *Can't Slow Down* .... (MOT)
Pablo Cruise; *Worlds Away* .... (A&M)
Sam Cooke; *Man & His Music* .... (RCA)
  This Is .... (RCA)
Yes; *Big Generator* .... (ATC)
Love Will Find Its Way To You
Reba McEntire; *Greatest Hits-#2* .... (MCA)
  Last One To Know .... (MCA)
(Love Will) Find A Way
Amy Grant; *Unguarded* .... (A&M)
Love's Found You & Me
Ed Bruce; *Greatest Hits* .... (MCA)
Now That We Found Love
Heavy D./Boyz; *Peaceful Journey* .... (UT)
Third World; *Island Story-1962-87-25th
  Anniversary* .... (ISL)
  Journey To Addis .... (ISL)
Oh Girl (You Know Where To Find Me)
Vince Gill; *When I Call Your Name* .... (MCA)
Rediscovery
Chicago; *VI* .... (COL)
Search Find
Bee Gees; *Spirits Having Flown* .... (RSO)
Search Is Over
Survivor; *Greatest Hits* .... (SCO)
  Vital Signs .... (SCO)
Someday I'll Find You
Bobby Short; *Mad About Noel Coward* .... (ATL)

Mary Martin & Noel Coward; *Together With
  Music* .... (DRG)
Somewhere They Can't Find Me
Simon & Garfunkel; *Collected Works* .... (COL)
  Sounds Of Silence .... (COL)
Sure Love
Hal Ketchum; *Sure Love* .... (CRB)
This Love That I've Found
Ella Fitzgerald; *Best Of* .... (PAB)
Till I Found You
Marty Stuart; *Tempted* .... (MCA)
To Find God
James Michaels; *Bouquet* .... (IS)
True Love Is Hard To Find
Bonnie Raitt; *Collection* .... (WB)
  Nine Lives .... (WB)
Try To Find Another Man
Righteous Brothers; *Anthology-1962-1974* .... (RHI)
We Tell Ourselves
Clint Black; *The Hard Way* .... (RCA)
When Love Finds You
Vince Gill; *When Love Finds You* .... (MCA)
While You See A Chance
Steve Winwood; *Arc Of A Diver* .... (ISL)
  Chronicles .... (ISL)
Who Found Who
Jellybean with Elisa Fiorillo; *12"* .... (CHR)
You'll Never Find Another Love Like Mine
Lou Rawls; *10 Years Of #1 Hits* .... (PI)
  Classics .... (PI)
  Live .... (PI)
  Mega Hits Dance Classics-#2 .... (PRY)
  Philly Ballads-#1 .... (PI)

FIRE, Ashes, Burning, Candles, Smoke
See Also: HOT

African Flame
Herb Alpert; *Wild Romance* .... (A&M)
After The Fire
Pete Townshend; *Deep End* .... (ATC)
Roger Daltrey; *Under A Raging Moon* .... (ATL)
After The Fire Is Gone
Conway Twitty & Loretta Lynn; *MCA Records 30 Years
  Of Hits-1958-1988* .... (MCA)
  Very Best Of .... (MCA)
Ain't No Smoke Without Fire
Eddie Kendricks; *Vintage '78* .... (ARI)
All Fired Up
Pat Benatar; *Best Shots* .... (CHR)
  Wide Awake In Dreamland .... (CHR)
Another Bridge To Burn
Mel Tillis; *Best Of* .... (MCA)
Ashes
Martina McBride; *The Way That I Am* .... (RCA)
Mary's Danish; *There Goes The Wondertruck* ..... (CML)
Poco; *Cowboys & Englishmen* .... (OW)
Ashes Are Burning
Renaissance; *Tales Of 1001 Nights-#2* .... (SIR)
Ashes By Now
Rodney Crowell; *Collection* .... (WB)
Ashes In The Wind
Moe Bandy; *No Regrets* .... (CCB)
Ashes Of Love
Chris Hillman; *Desert Rose* .... (SH)
Desert Rose Band; *Desert Rose Band* .... (CCB)
Rose Maddox; *Rose Of The West Coast Country* ... (ARH)
Ashes To Ashes
Darden Smith; *Trouble No More* .... (COL)
David Bowie; *Changesbowie* .... (RYK)
  Scary Monsters .... (RYK)
  Sound + Vision .... (RYK)
  The Singles-1969-1993 .... (RYK)
Gene Watson; *Honky Tonk Crazy* .... (EPI)
Ashes, The Rain & I
James Gang; *Best Of* .... (MCA)
  Greatest Hits .... (MCA)
  Rides Again .... (MCA)
Atlanta Burned Again Last Night
Atlanta; *Pictures* .... (MCA)
Atlanta's Burning Down
Dickey Betts/Great Southern; *Dickey Betts/Great
  Southern* .... (ARI)

Randy Howard; *All-American Redneck* .... (WB)
Attack Ships On Fire
Revolting Cocks; *Big Sexy Land* .... (WAX)
Baby I'm Burnin'
Dolly Parton; *Heartbreaker* .... (RCA)
Baby's On Fire
Great White; *...Twice Shy* .... (CAP)
Sammy Hagar; *Standing Hampton* .... (GEF)
Between Two Fires
Gary Morris; *Faded Blue* .... (WB)
Greatest Hits-#2 .... (WB)
Big Black Smoke
Kinks; *Kink Kronikles* .... (RPR)
Both Ends Burning
Roxy Music; *Heart Still Beating* .... (RPR)
Siren .... (RPR)
Viva .... (RPR)
Bridge That Just Won't Burn
Conway Twitty; *Number Ones* .... (MCA)
Bridges Burning
Mission U.K.; *God's Own Medicine* .... (MER)
Brush Fire In Hoboken
Chris Stamey; *It's A Wonderful Life* .... (DB)
Build A Fire
Drivin' N' Cryin'; *Fly Me Courageous* .... (ISL)
Burn
Bruce Cockburn; *Waiting For A Miracle-Singles*
1970-1987 .... (GC)
Deep Purple; *Burn* .... (WB)
Deepest Purple-Very Best Of .... (WB)
Made In Europe .... (WB)
When We Rock We Rock .... (WB)
Dream Syndicate; *Live At Raji's* .... (RES)
Medicine Show/This Is Not The New Album ... (A&M)
Burn Down The Bridges
Artch; *For The Sake Of Mankind* .... (MET)
Burn Down The Malls
Mojo Nixon & Skid Roper; *Enigma Variations 2* .(ENC)
Burn Down The Mission
Elton John; *11-17-70* .... (POL)
Live In Australia .... (MCA)
Tumbleweed Connection .... (POL)
Your Songs .... (MCA)
Phil Collins/Serious Band; *Two Rooms (Celebrating*
Songs Of...) .... (POL)
Burn Georgia Burn
Alabama; *Feels So Right* .... (RCA)
Burn Me Down
Marty Stuart; *Tempted* .... (MCA)
Burn Me Up
Kay Gees; *Burn Me Up* .... (DL)
Burn On
Randy Newman; *Sail Away* .... (RPR)
Burn One Down
Clint Black; *The Hard Way* .... (RCA)
Burn Rubber On Me
Gap Band; *12" Collection* .... (MER)
Gap Gold-Best Of .... (MER)
III .... (MER)
Burn That Bridge
Jimmy Buffett; *Riddles In The Sand* .... (MCA)
Burn That Candle
Bill Haley/Comets; *Golden Hits* .... (MCA)
Greatest Hits .... (MCA)
R-O-C-K .... (SUN)
Emmylou Harris; *Quarter Moon In A Ten Cent*
Town .... (WB)
Burn This Disco Out
Michael Jackson; *Off The Wall* .... (EPI)
Burn Your Money!
Mojo Nixon & Skid Roper; *Root Hog Or Die* ..... (IRS)
Burned
Buffalo Springfield; *Buffalo Springfield* .... (ATC)
Neil Young; *Decade* .... (RPR)
Burning Bridges
38 Special; *Bone Against Steel* .... (CHS)
Collective Soul; *Hints Allegations And Things Left*
Unsaid .... (ATL)
Garth Brooks; *Ropin' The Wind* .... (CAP)
George Jones; *Jones Country* .... (EPI)
One Woman Man .... (EPI)
Glen Campbell; *Greatest Hits* .... (CAP)
Jack Scott; *Capitol Collectors Series* .... (CAP)
Super Oldies/'60s-#6 .... (AUF)

Mike Curb Congregation; *Super Hits/'70s-Have A Nice*
Day-#5 .... (RHI)
Naked Eyes; *Best Of* .... (EMI)
Pink Floyd; *Gift Set* .... (CAP)
ST/Obscured By Clouds .... (CAP)
Roger Miller; *King Of The Road* .... (LAS)
Burning Down
R.E.M.; *Dead Letter Office* .... (IRS)
Suzy Bogguss; *Moment Of Truth* .... (LIB)
Burning Down One Side
Robert Plant; *Pictures At Eleven* .... (SS)
Burning Down The House
Talking Heads; *Speaking In Tongues* .... (SIR)
Stop Making Sense .... (SIR)
Burning Fingers
Shawn Phillips; *Collaboration* .... (A&M)
Burning Fire
Otis Spann; *Chicago/The Blues Today* .... (VAN)
Great Blues Men .... (VAN)
Burning For Me
Strawbs; *Burning For Me* .... (OYS)
Burning Heart
Survivor; *Rocky Story* .... (SCO)
ST/Rocky IV .... (SCO)
Vandenberg; *Best Of* .... (ATC)
Vandenberg .... (ATC)
Burning House Of Love
X; *Ain't Love Grand* .... (ELE)
Best Of MTV's 120 Minutes-#2 .... (RHI)
Live At The Whisky A Go-Go... .... (ELE)
Burning Love
Elvis Presley; *Aloha From Hawaii* .... (RCA)
Elvis Aron Presley .... (RCA)
Golden Records-#5 .... (RCA)
Top Ten Hits .... (RCA)
Burning Memories
Mel Tillis; *Best Of* .... (MCA)
Heart Healer .... (MCA)
Very Best Of .... (MCA)
Ray Price; *Greatest Hits-#1* .... (SO)
Greatest Hits-#1-3 .... (SO)
Burning My Rowboat
Maura O'Connell; *Real Life Story* .... (WB)
Burning Of Atlanta
Claude King; *American Originals* .... (COL)
Burning Of The Midnight Lamp
Jimi Hendrix; *Electric Ladyland* .... (RPR)
Essential-#1 & 2 .... (RPR)
Lifelines-Story .... (RPR)
Radio One .... (RYK)
Living Colour; *Biscuits* .... (EPI)
Burning Rope
Genesis; *And Then There Were Three* .... (ATL)
Burning The Ballroom Down
Amazing Rhythm Aces; *Burning The Ballroom*
Down .... (MCA)
Burning Up
Bad Company; *Fame & Fortune* .... (ATL)
Judas Priest; *Hell Bent For Leather* .... (COL)
Madonna; *Madonna* .... (SIR)
Burning Up Time
Stranglers; *No More Hereos* .... (A&M)
Burnin' A Hole In My Heart
Skip Ewing; *Class Of Country* .... (KT)
Coast Of Colorado .... (MCA)
Burnin' Bush
Earth, Wind & Fire; *Spirit* .... (COL)
Burnin' For You
Blue Oyster Cult; *Extraterrestrial Live* .... (COL)
Fire Of Unknown Origin .... (COL)
Burnin' In L.A.
Lightnin' Hopkins; *Lightnin' Sam Hopkins* ...... (ARH)
Burnin' Love
Con Funk Shun; *Burnin' Love* .... (MER)
Burnin' Sky
Bad Company; *Burnin' Sky* .... (SS)
Burnin' The Midnight Oil
Foghat; *Night Shift* .... (RHI)
Burnin' Thing
Mac Davis; *Burnin' Thing* .... (COL)
Greatest Hits .... (COL)

Burnin' & Lootin'
Bob Marley/Wailers; *Burnin'* .... (ISL)
 Burnin' Love .... (ISL)
 Live .... (ISL)
B-B-B-Burning Up With Love
Eddie Rabbitt; *Best Year Of My Life* .... (WB)
Candle In The Wind
Elton John; *Goodbye Yellow Brick Road* .... (POL)
 Live In Australia w/Melbourne Symphony .... (POL)
 Your Songs .... (POL)
Candle In The Window
Alabama; *Christmas* ....(RCA)
Candle Of Life
Moody Blues; *To Our Children's Children's*
Children .... (POL)
Candle On The Water
Helen Reddy; *Live In London* .... (CAP)
 ST/Pete's Dragon .... (CAP)
Candlelight
Janis Ian; *Miracle Row* ....(COL)
Wishbone Ash; *New England* .... (ATL)
Candles Of Our Lives
England Dan & John Ford Coley; *Fables* .... (A&M)
Cat People (Putting Out Fire)
David Bowie; *Let's Dance* .... (EMI)
 ST/Cat People .... (MCA)
 The Singles-1969-1993 ....(RYK)
Chariots Of Fire
Vangelis; *ST/Chariots Of Fire* .... (POL)
 Themes .... (POL)
Cheatin' Fire
Conway Twitty; *Mr. T* .... (MCA)
Cincinnati Fireball
Johnny Burnette; *Best Of-You're Sixteen* .... (EMI)
Cities On Flame With Rock & Roll
Blue Oyster Cult; *Blue Oyster Cult* ....(COL)
 Career Of Evil ....(COL)
 Extraterrestial Live ....(COL)
 On Your Feet Or On Your Knees ....(COL)
City's Burning
Heart; *Private Audition* .... (EPI)
Cold Blue Steel & Sweet Fire
Joni Mitchell; *For The Roses* .... (ASY)
 Miles Of Aisles .... (ASY)
Cold Fire
Rush; *Counterparts* .... (ATL)
Cook With Fire
Heart; *Dog & Butterfly* .... (POR)
Crack Pipe (Burnin' My Hand)
Coolies; *Doug (A Rock Opera & Comic Book)* .... (DB)
Crash & Burn
April Wine; *Nature Of The Beast* ....(CAP)
Bangles; *Everything* ....(COL)
Don Dokken; *Up From The Ashes* ....(GEF)
Pat Travers Band; *Crash & Burn* ....(POL)
'Til Tuesday; *Everything's Different Now* .... (EPI)
Disco Inferno
Trammps; *Best Of* .... (ATL)
 Disco Inferno .... (ATL)
 Disco Years-#1 .... (RHI)
 ST/Saturday Night Fever ....(RSO)
Don't Let It Bring You Down
Crosby, Stills, Nash & Young; *4-Way Street* ...... (ATL)
Neil Young; *After The Gold Rush* .... (RPR)
Down In Flames
Dead Boys; *Loud & Snotty* .... (SIR)
 Young .... (SIR)
Don Dokken; *Up From The Ashes* .... (GEF)
Eternal Flame
Bangles; *Everything* ....(COL)
 Greatest Hits ....(COL)
Everybody's Been Burned
Byrds; *Original Singles-#1-1965-1967* ....(COL)
 Byrds (collection) ....(COL)
 Younger Than Yesterday ....(COL)
Face The Fire
Dan Fogelberg; *Phoenix* .... (FM)
Feed The Fire
BoDeans; *Go Down Slow* .... (SLS)
Feel The Fire
Bob James; *Obsession* ....(TZ)
Claudja Berry; *Best Of* .... (HOT)
Overkill; *Feel The Fire* .... (MEG)
Peabo Bryson; *Collection* .... (CAP)

Roberta Flack & Peabo Bryson; *Live & More* .... (ATL)
Stephanie Mills; *Geratest Hits In My Life* .... (CAS)
Fight Fire With Fire
Kansas; *Best Of* .... (CBA)
 Drastic Measures .... (KIR)
Metallica; *Ride The Lightning* .... (ELE)
Fire
Bruce Springsteen/E Street Band;
Live-1975-1985 ....(COL)
Crazy World Of Arthur Brown; *History Of British*
Rock-#9 .... (RHI)
Jefferson Starship; *Earth* .... (GRU)
Jimi Hendrix; *Concerts* .... (RPR)
 Essential-#2 .... (RPR)
 Smash Hits ....(RPR)
Jimi Hendrix Experience; *Are You Experienced?* (MCA)
Mother's Finest; *Live* ....(EPI)
Ohio Players; *Gold* .... (MER)
 Soul Hits/'70s-#14 .... (RHI)
Pointer Sisters; *Cover Me* .... (RHI)
 Energy ....(PNT)
Red Hot Chili Peppers; *Mother's Milk* .... (EMI)
Robert Gordon & Link Wray; *Fresh Fish Special* .(RCA)
Television; *Adventure* ....(ELE)
U2; *October* .... (ISL)
Fire And Ice
Pat Benatar; *Best Shots* .... (CHR)
 Live From Earth .... (CHR)
 Precious Time .... (CHR)
Fire And Rain
James Taylor; *Greatest Hits* ....(WB)
 Sweet Baby James ....(WB)
Sammy Kershaw; *Red Hot + Country* .... (MER)
Fire At Midnight
Jethro Tull; *Songs From The Wood* .... (CHR)
Fire Ball Mail
John McEuen; *String Wizards* .... (VAN)
Roy Acuff; *Best Of* ....(CAP)
Fire Brothers
Quicksilver Messenger Service; *Anthology* .... (CAP)
 Quicksilver ....(CAP)
Fire Down Below
Bob Seger; *Night Moves* .... (CAP)
 Nine Tonight .... (CAP)
Fire Girl
Commodores; *Natural High* .... (MOT)
Fire I Can't Put Out
George Strait; *Greatest Hits* .... (MCA)
 Strait From The Heart .... (MCA)
Fire In Cairo
Cure; *Boys Don't Cry* .... (ELE)
Fire In The Engine Room
Richard Thompson; *Across A Crowded Room* .... (POL)
Fire In The Hole
Steely Dan; *Can't Buy A Thrill* .... (MCA)
Fire In The Mine
Stompin' Tom Connors; *Love & Laughter* ....(OOP)
 On Tragedy Trail ....(OOP)
Fire In The Morning
Melissa Manchester; *Melissa Manchester* .... (ARI)
Fire In The Sky
Nitty Gritty Dirt Band; *20 Years Of Dirt-Best Of* ..(WB)
Ozzy Osbourne; *No Rest For The Wickedd* ...... (CBA)
Saxon; *Denim & Leather* ....(CAP)
Fire Inside
Bob Seger/Silver Bullet Band; *Fire Inside* .... (CAP)
Fire Island
Village People; *Live & Sleazy* .... (CAS)
 Village People .... (CAS)
Woody Herman; *Blowin' Up A Storm* .... (PIC)
Fire Lake
Bob Seger/Silver Bullet Band; *Against The Wind* .(CAP)
 Nine Tonight .... (CAP)
Fire Of Two Old Flames
Roy Head; *In Our Room* .... (ELE)
Fire Of Unknown Origin
Blue Oyster Cult; *Fire Of Unknown Origin* ....(COL)
Fire On High
Electric Light Orchestra; *Face The Music* ....(JET)
Fire On The Mountain
Bill Monroe/Blue Grass Boys; *Kentucky*
Bluegrass .... (MCA)
Grateful Dead; *Dead Set* .... (ARI)
 Shakedown Street .... (ARI)

Marshall Tucker Band; *Greatest Hits* ....(CPC)
  Searchin' For A Rainbow ....(AJK)
  South's Greatest Hits ....(CPC)
Fire Woman
  Cult; *Sonic Temple* ....(SRR)
Fire & Desire
  Rick James; *All The Great Motown Love Duets* .. (MOT)
  Motown Memories-#4 ....(MOT)
  Reflections/Greatest Hits ....(MOT)
  Street Songs ....(MOT)
Fire & Smoke
  Earl Thomas Conley; *Fire & Smoke* ....(RCA)
  Greatest Hits ....(RCA)
  Jukebox Saturday Night ....(RCA)
Fire & Water
  Free; *Best Of* ....(A&M)
  Fire & Water ....(A&M)
  Live ....(A&M)
  Wilson Pickett; *45* ....(ATL)
Fireball
  Deep Purple; *Deepest Purple* ....(WB)
  Fireball ....(WB)
  Fireballs; *Legends Of Rock Guitar/'50s-#2* .... (RHI)
  Flatt & Scruggs; *Greatest Hits With The Foggy Mtn.*
  Boys ....(COL)
  Roy Acuff; *Greatest Hits-#1* ....(ELE)
Fireball Mail
  Roy Acuff; *Best Of* ....(CAP)
  Greatest Hits ....(COL)
  Opry Legends ....(CAP)
Firecracker
  Mass Production; *In The Purest Form* ....(COT)
Firehouse
  Kiss; *Alive* ....(CAS)
  Double Platinum ....(CAS)
  Kiss ....(CAS)
  Original ....(CAS)
Fireman
  George Strait; *Country Classics-#4* ....(MCA)
  Does Fort Worth Ever Cross Your Mind ....(MCA)
  Greatest Hits-#2 ....(MCA)
Fires
  Procol Harum; *Grand Hotel* ....(CHR)
Fireside Song
  Genesis; *London Collector-In The Beginning* ......(LON)
Firestarter
  38 Special; *Special Forces* ....(A&M)
  Tease; *Tease* ....(EPI)
Fireworks
  Alabama; *Live* ....(RCA)
  Blue Oyster Cult; *Spectres* ....(COL)
  Choirboys; *Big Bad Noise* ....(WTG)
  Jose Feliciano; *Fireworks* ....(RCA)
Flame
  Cheap Trick; *45* ....(EPI)
  Lap Of Luxury ....(EPI)
  Cheap Trick; *Lap Of Luxury* ....(EPI)
Flame Of Love
  Jean Carne; *Closer Than Close* ....(OMN)
Flame Thrower Love
  Dead Boys; *We Have Come For Your Children* .... (SIR)
Flaming
  Pink Floyd; *Nice Pair* ....(CAP)
Flaming Agnes
  Original Cast; *I Do! I Do!* ....(RCA)
Flaming Telepaths
  Blue Oyster Cult; *Career Of Evil* ....(COL)
  Secret Treaties ....(COL)
Flaming Youth
  Kiss; *Destroyer* .... (CAS)
Fuel My Fire
  L7; *Hungry For Stink* ....(SLS)
Gonna Burn Some Bridges
  Ray Price; *For The Good Times/I Won't Mention*
  It... ....(COL)

Great Balls Of Fire
  Jerry Lee Lewis; *Billboard Top Rock 'N' Roll*
  Hits-1958 .... (RHI)
  Jerry Lee's Greatest .... (RHI)
  Oldies But Goodies-#12 ....(OSR)
  Original ....(SUN)
  Original Golden Hits-#1 ....(SUN)
  Original Memphis Rock & Roll ....(SUN)
  Rock & Roll Show ....(GUS)
  Twenty Classic Jerry Lee Lewis Hits ....(OSR)
Hang Fire
  Rolling Stones; *Rewind 1971-1984* .... (RS)
  Tattoo You .... (RS)
Hearts On Fire
  Bryan Adams; *Into The Fire* .... (A&M)
  Eddie Rabbitt; *All-Time Greatest Hits* ....(WB)
  Best Of ....(ELE)
  Variations ....(ELE)
  Gram Parsons; *Grievous Angel* ....(RPR)
  Randy Meisner; *One More Song* ....(EPI)
  Steve Winwood; *Roll With It* .... (VIA)
Heart's On Fire
  38 Special; *Strength In Numbers* ....(A&M)
Heaven's On Fire
  Kiss; *Animalize* .... (MER)
  Hear 'N Aid .... (MER)
  Smashes Thrashes & Hits .... (MER)
His Latest Flame
  Elvis Presley; *50 Worldwide Gold Award Hits-#2* (RCA)
  Golden Records-#3 ....(RCA)
  Top Ten Hits ....(RCA)
  Residents; *King & Eye* .... (ENI)
Hong Kong Fireworks
  Henry Mancini; *ST/Revenge Of The Pink Panther* . (EMI)
House Burning Down
  Jimi Hendrix; *Electric Ladyland* .... (RPR)
  Essential ....(RPR)
House On Fire
  Boomtown Rats; *Greatest Hits* ....(COL)
  V Deep ....(COL)
I Can Feel The Fire
  Ron Wood; *Ron Wood* ....(OOP)
I Can't Stop The Fire
  Eric Martin; *ST/Teachers* ....(CAP)
I Don't Want To Set The World On Fire
  Ink Spots; *Best Of* .... (MCA)
If You Love Somebody, Set Them On Fire
  Dead Milkmen; *Metaphysical Graffiti* ....(ENC)
Into The Fire
  Bryan Adams; *Into The Fire* .... (A&M)
  Deep Purple; *Deep Purple In Rock* ....(WB)
  Dokken; *Beast From The East* ....(ELE)
  Tooth & Nail ....(ELE)
I'm On Fire
  Bruce Springsteen; *Born In The USA* ....(COL)
  Bruce Springsteen/E Street Band;
  Live-1975-1985 ....(COL)
  Dwight Twilley Band; *Super Hits/'70s-Have A Nice*
  Day-#15 .... (RHI)
Keep The Candle Burning
  Kenny Rankin; *Critics Choice II* ....(CYP)
  Rita Coolidge; *It's Only Love* ....(A&M)
Keep The Fire
  Kenny Loggins; *Alive* ....(COL)
  Keep The Fire ....(COL)
Keep The Fire Burning
  Louisiana's Le Roux; *Keep The Fire Burning* .....(CAP)
  R.E.O. Speedwagon; *Good Trouble* ....(EPI)
  Jane Fonda's New & Improved Workout ....(COL)
  Second Decade Of Rock & Roll-1981-1991 .....(EPI)
Keep The Home Fire Burning
  Latimore; *Get Down Tonight!-Best Of T.K. Records* (RHI)
  III ....(GLA)
  Millie Jackson; *Get It Out'cha System* ....(SPR)
  Live & Uncensored ....(SPR)
Keeper For Every Flame
  Mary Chapin Carpenter; *Stones In The Road* ....(COL)
Keepers Of the Flame
  Zamboni Brothers; *The Hockey Zone* ....(SPO)

Light My Fire
Doors; *13* .... (ELE)
  Best Of .... (ELE)
  Doors .... (ELE)
  Greatest Hits .... (ELE)
  ST/Doors .... (ELE)
Jose Feliciano; *All-Time Greatest Hits* ....(RCA)
  Encore ....(RCA)
Light The Sky On Fire
Jefferson Starship; *Gold* ....(RCA)
Lilacs & Fire
George Morgan; *Super Hits Country-'70s* .... (GUS)
Little Chicago Fire
Count Basie Orchestra; *Live At El Morocco* ..... (TLR)
London's Burning
Clash; *Clash* .... (EPI)
  On Broadway .... (EPI)
  Story Of-#1 .... (EPI)
Love That Burns
Fleetwood Mac; *25 Years-The Chain* .... (WB)
Match Box
Beatles; *Past Masters-#1* ....(CAP)
  Rock 'N' Roll Music-#1 ....(CAP)
  Something New ....(CAP)
Carl Perkins; *Original Golden Hits* .... (SUN)
  Original Sun Greatest Hits .... (RHI)
Paul McCartney; *Tripping The Live Fantastic* ....(CAP)
Matchbox
Carl Perkins, Duane Eddy & The Mavericks; *Red Hot +
Country* .... (MER)
Midnight Fire
Steve Wariner; *Best Of* ....(RCA)
  Greatest Hits ....(RCA)
Motel Matches
Elvis Costello; *Girls Girls Girls* ....(COL)
Elvis Costello/Attractions; *Get Happy!* ....(RYK)
Moth & The Flame
Sky Saxon Blues Band; *Full Spoon Of Seedy Blues* (CRS)
Moth & The Flame, Parts 1-5
Keith Jarrett; *Invocations-Moth & The Flame, Parts
1-5* ....(ECM)
My Ass Is On Fire
Mr. Bungle; *Mr. Bungle* .... (WB)
My Old Flame
Duke Ellington; *Nipper's Grea·est Hits-'30s-#1* ..(RCA)
J.J. Johnson; *Trombone Master* ....(COL)
Linda Ronstadt; *Lush Life* .... (ASY)
Rosemary Cloooney; *Great Girl Singers Sing 22 Original
Rec.* .... (HIN)
Stan Kenton/Orchestra; *Road Show* ....(CAP)
Tommy Smith; *Standards* ....(BLN)
Napalm For Breakfast
Rhythm Devils; *Apocalypse Now Sessions* ....(RYK)
New Way (To Light Up An Old Flame)
Joe Diffie; *A Thousand Winding Roads* .... (EPI)
Next Thing Smokin'
Joe Diffie; *Regular Joe* .... (EPI)
Night The Carousel Burned Down
Todd Rundgren; *Something/Anything?* .... (RHI)
No Smoke Without a Fire
Bad Company; *Dangerous Age* .... (ATL)
Nuclear Burn
Brand X; *Unorthodox Behaviour* ....(BP)
Old Flame
Alabama; *60 Years Of Country Music* ....(RCA)
  Feels So Right ....(RCA)
  Greatest Hits ....(RCA)
Church; *Priest-Aura* .... (ARI)
Juice Newton; *Old Flame* ....(RCA)
Old Flames Can't Hold A Candle To You
Dolly Parton; *Dolly Dolly Dolly* ....(RCA)
  Greatest Hits ....(RCA)
Joe Sun; *Old Flames Can't Hold A Candle To
You* .... (OVA)
Merle Haggard; *Kern River* .... (EPI)
Old Flames Have New Names
Mark Chesnutt; *Longnecks & Short Stories* ...... (MCA)
Out Of The Frying Pan (& Into The Fire)
Meatloaf; *Bat Out Of Hell II: Back Into Hell* .... (MCA)
Paper In Fire
John Cougar Mellencamp; *Lonesome Jubilee* .... (MER)
Paris Is Burning
Dokken; *Breaking The Chains* .... (ELE)

Phoenix
Cult; *Love* .... (SIR)
Dan Fogelberg; *Phoenix* ....(FM)
Wishbone Ash; *Live Dates* .... (MCA)
  Wishbone Ash .... (MCA)
Play With Fire
Rolling Stones; *Big Hits-High Tides & Green
Grass* .... (AKO)
  Hot Rocks-1964-1971 .... (AKO)
  Out Of Our Heads .... (AKO)
  Singles Collection-London Years .... (AKO)
Playing With Fire
David Foster; *David Foster* .... (ATL)
Lisa Lisa & Cult Jam; *Spanish Fly* ....(COL)
Richard Marx; *Rush Street* ....(CAP)
Sam Riney; *Playing With Fire* .... (SPT)
Playin' With Fire
Lita Ford; *Dangerous Curves* ....(RCA)
  Greatest Hits ....(RCA)
Vishugruv; *Vishugruv* .... (RL)
Porno For Pyros
Porno For Pyros; *Porno For Pyros* .... (WB)
Put Out The Fire
Queen; *Hot Space* ....(HOL)
Put This Fire Out
Toni Childs; *House Of Hope* .... (A&M)
Quest For Fire
Iron Maiden; *Piece Of Mind* ....(CAP)
Racin' Burnin' Bridges
Ranch Romance; *Blue Blazes* ....(SH)
Ring Of Fire
Country Joe McDonald; *Best Of-Vanguard
Years-1969-1975* .... (VAN)
  Tonight I'm Singing Just For You .... (VAN)
Dwight Yoakam; *Guitars Cadillacs Etc. Etc.* ..... (RPR)
Johnny Cash; *Billboard Top Country Hits-1963* .. (RHI)
  Classic Cash-Hall Of Fame Series .... (MER)
  Greatest Hits ....(COL)
Stan Ridgway/Wall Of Voodoo; *Best Of-Songs That
Made This Country...* .... (IRS)
Wall Of Voodoo; *Ugly Americans In Australia...* .. (IRS)
Rockin' With Fire
Isley Brothers; *Showdown* .... (TN)
Rooms On Fire
Stevie Nicks; *Other Side Of The Mirror* .... (MOD)
  Timespace-Best Of .... (MOD)
Saint Agnes & The Burning Train
Sting; *Soul Cages* .... (A&M)
Season In Hell (Fire Suite)
John Cafferty/Beaver Brown Band; *ST/Eddie & The
Cruisers* .... (SCO)
Serpentine Fire
Earth, Wind & Fire; *All 'n All* ....(COL)
  Best Of-#2 ....(COL)
  Eternal Dance ....(COL)
Settin' The Woods On Fire
Hank Williams; *24 Greatest Hits* .... (POL)
  40 Greatest Hits .... (POL)
She Keeps The Home Fires Burning
Ronnie Milsap; *Greatest Greatest Hits* ....(RCA)
Shot Down In Flames
AC/DC; *Highway To Hell* .... (ATL)
Silence Of A Candle
Oregon; *Essential* .... (VAN)
Paul Winter Consort; *Icarus* .... (EPI)
Sleep That Burns
Be Bop Deluxe; *Best Of & The Rest Of* .... (HAR)
  Best Of-Raiding The Divine Archives ....(CAP)
  Sunburst Finish .... (HAR)
Slow Burn
T.G. Sheppard; *All-Time Greatest Hits* .... (WB)
Slow Burning Memory
Vern Gosdin; *10 Years Of Greatest Hits Newly
Recorded* ....(COL)
  There Is A Season .... (CMP)
Smoke
Drivin' N' Cryin'; *Smoke* .... (ISL)
Smoke From A Distant Fire
Sanford/Townsend Band; *Smoke From A Distant
Fire* .... (WB)
Smoke Gets In Your Eyes
Bryan Ferry; *Another Time Another Place* .... (RPR)
  Street Life-20 Great Hits .... (RPR)
Dinah Washington; *Golden Classics* .... (CLT)

Lawrence Welk; *Musical Memories With* .... (RAN)
Patti Austin; *Real Me* .... (QUE)
Platters; *Encore Of Golden Hits* .... (MER)
   Greatest Hits .... (EVR)
   Oldies But Goodies-#14 .... (OSR)
   ST/Always .... (MCA)
   ST/American Graffiti .... (MCA)
   Super Oldies/'50s-#5 .... (AUF)
Smoke On The Water
Deep Purple; *Deepest Purple-Very Best Of* .... (WB)
   Machine Head .... (WB)
   Made In Japan .... (WB)
   Nobody's Perfect .... (MER)
   When We Rock We Rock .... (WB)
Smoke Signal
Band; *Cahoots* .... (CAP)
Smokescreen
Ted Nugent; *Weekend Warriors* .... (EPI)
Smokestack Lightning
George Thorogood/Destroyers; *Born To Be Bad* . (EMI)
Grateful Dead; *History Of-#1-Bear's Choice* ...... (WB)
Howlin' Wolf; *Best Of Chess Blues* .... (CSS)
   Blues-#1 .... (CSS)
   Moanin' In The Moonlight .... (CSS)
Lynyrd Skynyrd; *1991* .... (ATL)
Muddy Waters; *Chess Box* .... (CSS)
Soundgarden; *Ultramega OK* .... (SST)
Yardbirds; *Five Live Yardbirds* .... (RHI)
   For Your Love .... (ACC)
   Greatest Hits-#1 (1964-1966) .... (RHI)
Smokey Day
Zombies; *Time Of* .... (EPI)
Smokey Places
Billy Walker; *Greatest Hits* .... (MON)
Corsairs; *Best Of Chess Rhythm & Blues* .... (CSS)
   Collectables Presents History Of Rock-#5 .... (CLT)
Somebody Else's Fire
Janie Fricke; *Somebody Else's Fire* .... (COL)
Mollie O'Brien; *Every Night In The Week* .... (RSG)
Something's Burning
Kenny Rogers; *20 Great Years* .... (RPR)
   20 Greatest Hits .... (EMI)
   Ten Years Of Gold .... (EMI)
Mac Davis; *Greatest Hits* .... (COL)
Sparks Of The Tempest
Kansas; *Point Of Know Return* .... (KIR)
Standing Outside The Fire
Garth Brooks; *In Pieces* .... (LIB)
Still Burnin' For You
Rob Crosby; *Solid Ground* .... (ARI)
Streets Of Fire
Bruce Springsteen; *Darkness On The Edge Of*
   Town .... (COL)
Duncan Browne; *Streets Of Fire* .... (SIR)
Streets On Fire
Rhythm Corps; *Common Ground* .... (EPA)
U.K. Subs; *Japan Today* .... (RES)
St. Elmo's Fire
John Parr; *Hit Singles-1980-1988* .... (ATL)
   Romantic Hits/'80s .... (KT)
   ST/St. Elmo's Fire .... (ATL)
Summer's Cauldron
XTC; *Skylarking* .... (GEF)
Swamp Fire
Duke Ellington; *Best Of The Swing Bands* .... (HIN)
   Black Brown & Beige .... (BLU)
Sweet Fire Of Love
Robbie Robertson; *Robbie Robertson* .... (GEF)
Take Hold Of The Flame
Queensryche; *The Warning* .... (EMI)
(There's A) Fire In The Night
Alabama; *Roll On* .... (RCA)
This Wheel's On Fire
Band; *Anthology* .... (CAP)
   Music From Big Pink .... (CAP)
   Rock Of Ages-#1 & 2 .... (CAP)
Bob Dylan/Band; *Basement Tapes* .... (COL)
Byrds; *Byrds (collection)* .... (COL)
Ian & Sylvia; *Greatest Hits* .... (VAN)
Siouxsie/Banshees; *Through The Looking Glass* .. (GEF)
   Twice Upon A Time-The Singles .... (GEF)
Through The Fire
Chaka Khan; *I Feel For You* .... (WB)

To A Flame
Stephen Stills; *Stephen Stills* .... (ATL)
To The Fire
Bon Jovi; *7800 Degrees Fahrenheit* .... (JBC)
Trial By Fire
Jefferson Airplane; *30 Seconds Over Winterland* ..(RCA)
   Loves You ....(RCA)
Truck On Fire
White Zombie; *Soul-Crusher* .... (CRL)
Tryin' To Hide A Fire In The Dark
Billy Dean; *Fire In The Dark* .... (LIB)
Unforgettable Fire
U2; *Unforgettable Fire* .... (ISL)
Up In A Puff Of Smoke
Polly Brown; *Super Hits/'70s-Have A Nice*
   Day-#14 .... (RHI)
Vermont Is Afire In The Autumn
Lui Collins; *Made In New England* ....(GRE)
Walk Through Fire
Bad Company; *Holy Water* ....(ATC)
Walking Through Fire
Mary Chapin Carpenter; *Come On Come On* ....(COL)
We Didn't Start The Fire
Billy Joel; *Storm Front* ....(COL)
We'll Burn That Bridge
Brooks & Dunn; *Hard Workin' Man* .... (ARI)
We've Got A Good Fire Goin'
Don Williams; *Greatest Country Hits* ....(CCB)
   New Moves ....(CAP)
Where There's Smoke There's Fire
Blues Project; *No Time Like The Right Time-Best*
   Of .... (RHI)
Louise Mandrell & R.C. Bannon; *Me & My R.C.* ..(RCA)
Who By Fire
Leonard Cohen; *Best Of* ....(COL)
Wildfire
Michael Martin Murphey; *Best Of* .... (EMI)
   Super Hits/'70s-Have A Nice Day-#14 .... (RHI)
   '70s Greatest Rock Hits-#3-High Times .... (PRY)
Michael Murphey; *Blue Sky Night Thunder* .... (EPI)
Wildfire Woman
Bad Company; *Straight Shooter* .... (SS)
You're Gonna Get Your Fingers Burned
Alan Parsons Project; *Eye In The Sky* .... (ARI)

FISH, Fishing
   See Also: FOOD, WHALES

Any Little Fish
Bobby Short; *Bobby Noel & Cole* .... (ATL)
Bad Shark
Rick Dees/Cast Of Idiots; *Original Disco Duck* .. (RSO)
Barracuda
Heart; *Greatest Hits/Live* .... (EPI)
   Little Queen ....(POR)
Basket Of Oysters
Oscar Brand; *Bawdy Songs & Backroom Ballads* .(AUF)
Big Fish, Little Fish
Original Broadway Cast; *Purlie* ....(RCA)
Blue Oyster Cult
Blue Oyster Cult; *Imaginos* ....(COL)
Catchin' Crawfish
Leona Williams; *45* .... (MCA)
Catfish
Bob Dylan; *Bootleg Series-#1-3* ....(COL)
Danny O'Keefe; *Breezy Stories* ....(ATL)
Joe Cocker; *Stingray* ....(A&M)
John Lee Hooker; *Golden Classics* ....(CLT)
Catfish Blues
Ian & Sylvia; *Best Of* .... (VAN)
   Greatest Hits .... (VAN)
Jimi Hendrix; *Radio One* ....(RYK)
Catfish Sam'ich
Charles Williams; *Charles Williams* .... (MST)
Crab Man's Call
Original Cast; *Porgy & Bess* .... (MCA)
Crawfish
Elvis Presley; *Hits Like Never Before*
   (Essential-#3) ....(RCA)
   ST/King Creole ....(RCA)
Do You Want My Job
Little Village; *Little Village* .... (RPR)

Fins
Jimmy Buffett; *Songs You Know By Heart-Greatest Hits* .... (MCA)
Volcano .... (MCA)
Fish
Yes; *Fragile* .... (ATL)
Yessongs .... (ATL)
Fish Ain't Bitin'
David Lee Murphy; *Out With A Bang* .... (MCA)
Lamont Dozier; *45* .... (MCA)
Fish Aren't Bitin' Today
David Allan Coe; *Compass Point* .... (COL)
Fish Heads
Barnes & Barnes; *20th Anniversary Collection* .... (RHI)
Dr. Demento's Greatest-#4 .... (RHI)
Fish In The Sea
Karen Alexander; *Isn't It Always Love* .... (ASY)
Fish Song
Nitty Gritty Dirt Band; *All The Good Times* ...... (UA)
Dirt Silver & Gold .... (UA)
Fish & Chips
Eddie/Hot Rods; *Fish & Chips* .... (AMR)
Fish & Tits
Barefoot Jerry; *Barefoot Jerry's Grocery* .... (MON)
Fish & Whistle
John Prine; *Bruised Orange* .... (ASY)
Fisher's Hornpipe
Doc Watson; *Fresh Fish* .... (FF)
Fishes & Scorpions
Stephen Stills; *2* .... (ATL)
Fishin'
Elvin Bishop; *Let It Flow* .... (CPC)
Fishin' Blues
Jim Kweskin; *Best Of* .... (VAN)
/Jug Band .... (VAN)
Lovin' Spoonful; *Anthology* .... (RHI)
Taj Mahal; *Best Of-#1* .... (COL)
Real Thing .... (COL)
Going Fishing
Jimmy Reed; *History Of* .... (TRP)
Wailin' Blues .... (TRD)
Greenland Fisheries
Pete Seeger; *20 Golden Pieces Of* .... (BLD)
Pete Seeger .... (EVR)
Sings Folk Music Of The World .... (TRD)
Hold Tight, Hold Tight (Sea Food)
Andrews Sisters; *16 Great Performances* .... (MCA)
Best Of .... (MCA)
Boogie Woogie Bugle Girls .... (MCA)
I'm Gonna Go Fishing
Mel Torme; *Duke Ellington & Count Basie Songbook* .... (VRV)
Ray Charles; *My Kind Of Jazz-Part 3* .... (CRO)
"Jaws" Theme
John Williams; *ST/Jaws* .... (MCA)
Joy To The World
Three Dog Night; *Best Of* .... (MCA)
Good Feeling Music/Big Chill Gen.-#2 .... (MOT)
Good Feeling Music/Big Chill Gen.-#3 .... (MOT)
Joy To The World .... (MCA)
ST/Big Chill .... (MOT)
ST/Forrest Gump .... (EPX)
Just Like A Fish
Esther Phillips; *Atlantic Blues-Vocalists* .... (ATL)
Set Me Free .... (ATL)
Mistress Of The Salmon Salt
Blue Oyster Cult; *Tyranny & Mutation* .... (COL)
Mud Shark, The
Mothers Of Invention; *Fillmore East-June 1971* ... (BIZ)
Mudshark
Mothers Of Invention; *Live At The Fillmore East* . (RPR)
My Barracuda
Jimmy Buffett; *Hot Water* .... (MCA)
No Anchovies Please
J. Geils Band; *Love Stinks* .... (EMI)
Octopus's Garden
Beatles; *1967-1970* .... (CAP)
Abbey Road .... (CAP)
Box Set .... (CAP)
Pulling Mussels (From The Shell)
Squeeze; *Argybargy* .... (A&M)
Singles 45s & Under .... (A&M)
Rainbow Trout
Gordon Lightfoot; *Cold On The Shoulder* .... (RPR)

Reach, The
Dan Fogelberg; *Innocent Age* .... (FM)
Red Sharks
Crimson Glory; *Transcendance* .... (MCA)
Rock Lobster
B-52's; *B-52's* .... (WB)
Same Ol' Fishing Hole
Blues Boy Willie; *Be-Who* .... (ICH)
Saturday Night Fish Fry
Louis Jordan; *Best Of* .... (MCA)
No Moe! Greatest Hits .... (VRV)
Pearl Bailey; *16 Most Requested Songs* .... (COL)
Saturday Night Fish Fry Drag
Joe Robichaux/New Orleans Boys; *Joe Robichaux/New Orleans Boys-1933* .... (FLK)
Shark Attack
Split Enz; *True Colours* .... (A&M)
Wailing Souls; *All Over The World* .... (CHA)
Shark Walk
Shriekback; *Go Bang!* .... (ISL)
Shooting Shark
Blue Oyster Cult; *Revolutionary By Night* .... (COL)
Son Of A Fisherman
Tom Jones; *Memories Don't Leave Like People Do* (PRT)
Song Of The Shrimp
Elvis Presley; *ST/Girls Girls Girls* .... (RCA)
Sushi Girl
Tubes; *Best Of* .... (CAP)
Completion Backward Principle .... (CAP)
Swish Fish
Showmen; *It Will Stand-15 More Golden Classics* (CLT)
Talking Fishing Blues
Jack Elliot; *Greatest Songs Of Woody Guthrie* ... (VAN)
Talkin' Fishin'
Ramblin' Jack Elliott; *Greatest Songs Of Woody Guthrie* .... (VAN)
Tennessee Fish Fry
Helen O'Connell; *Uncollected With Irv Orton's Orchestra* .... (HIN)
Three Little Fishes
Andrews Sisters; *Boogie Woogie Bugle Girls* ..... (MCA)
Kay Kyser; *Dr. Demento Greatest-#1-'40s & Before* .... (RHI)
Sentimental Favorites .... (COL)
Throw Back The Little Ones
Steely Dan; *Katy Lied* .... (MCA)
Too Many Fish In The Sea
Marvelettes; *Anthology* .... (MOT)
Greatest Hits .... (MOT)
Mitch Ryder/Detroit Wheels; *Greatest Hits* ..... (VGO)
Rascals; *Anthology-1965-1972* .... (RHI)
Tremeloes; *Best Of* .... (RHI)
Trout
Neneh Cherry & Michael Stipe; *Homebrew* ...... (VIA)
Unidentified Flying Tuna Trot
R.E.O. Speedwagon; *You Can Tune A Piano But You Can't...* .... (EPI)
White Fishes
John Renbourn; *Sir Jon Alot Of Merrie Englanders* (RPR)
Wynkin', Blinkin' & Nod
Doobie Brothers; *In Harmony-Sesame Street* .....(COL)
Irish Rovers; *Greatest Hits* .... (MCA)
Simon Sisters; *Troubadours Of The Folk Era-#2* . (RHI)

FLOWERS, Gardens, Grass, Parks, Outdoors
See Also: ECOLOGY, ROSES, TREES

All The King's Gardens
Joan Armatrading; *Whatever's For Us* .... (A&M)
Artifical Rose
Jimmy C. Newman; *Greatest Hits* .... (PLN)
Artificial Flowers
Bobby Darin; *Story* .... (ATC)
Azalea
Louis Armstrong & Duke Ellington; *Complete Sessions* .... (RLL)
Bayou Girl
Bob Woodruff; *Dreams & Saturday Nights* .... (ASY)
Berkshire Poppies
Traffic; *Mr. Fantasy* .... (ISL)
Blossom
Candlebox; *Candlebox* .... (MAV)

Blossoms In The Snow
Skyliners; *Greatest Hits* .... (OSR)
Blue Gardenia
Nat King Cole; *Story* .... (CAP)
Central Park West
John Coltrane; *Art Of* .... (ATL)
Best Of .... (ATL)
Coltrane's Sound .... (ATL)
Cherry Blossom Time
Columbia Ballroom Orchestra; *Let's
Dance-#7-Competition Dance* .... (DEN)
China Cat Sunflower
Grateful Dead; *Aoxomoxoa* .... (WB)
Europe '72 .... (WB)
Without A Net .... (ARI)
Come Back As A Flower
Stevie Wonder; *Journey Through The Secret Life
Of...* .... (MOT)
Crimson & Clover
Joan Jett/Blackhearts; *I Love Rock 'N' Roll* .... (BW)
Tommy James/Shondells; *Anthology* .... (RHI)
Best Of .... (RLL)
Billboard Top Rock 'N' Roll Hits-1969 .... (RHI)
Jewels-#1 .... (SSS)
Daisy Jane
America; *America Live* .... (WB)
Hearts .... (WB)
History-Greatest Hits .... (WB)
In Concert .... (CAP)
Daisy Petal Pickin'
Jimmy Gilmer/Fireballs; *45* .... (MCA)
Daisys Up Your Butterfly
Cramps; *Stay Sick!* .... (ENC)
Dandelion
Rolling Stones; *More Hot Rocks-Big Hits & Fazed
Cookies* .... (AKO)
Through The Past Darkly-Big Hits-#2 .... (AKO)
Dead Flowers
Rolling Stones; *Sticky Fingers* .... (RS)
Steve Earle/Dukes; *Shut Up & Die Like An
Aviator* .... (MCA)
Delta Dawn
Bette Midler; *Divine Miss M* .... (ATL)
Live At Last .... (ATL)
Helen Reddy; *Greatest Hits* .... (CAP)
Tanya Tucker; *Greatest Hits* .... (COL)
Greatest Hits Encore .... (CAP)
Live .... (MCA)
Edelweiss
Mary Martin/Original Cast; *Sound Of Music* ..... (COL)
Egyptian Gardens
Kaleidoscope; *Egyptian Candy-Collection* .... (EPI)
Side Trips .... (EPI)
Elephants & Flowers
Prince; *ST/Graffiti Bridge* .... (PAI)
Empty Garden (Hey Hey Johnny)
Elton John; *Greatest Hits-1976-1986* .... (MCA)
Jump Up! .... (MCA)
Fading Like A Flower (Every Time You...)
Roxette; *Joyride* .... (EMI)
Flower Lady
Peter & Gordon; *Best Of* .... (RHI)
Phil Ochs; *Chords Of Fame* .... (A&M)
Pleasures Of The Harbor .... (A&M)
War Is Over-Best Of .... (A&M)
Flower & The Young Man
Strawbs; *Grave New World* .... (A&M)
Flowers
Emotions; *Flowers* .... (COL)
Flowers Are Red
Harry Chapin; *Legends Of The Lost & Found* .... (ELE)
Living Room Suite .... (ELE)
Flowers Mean Forgiveness
Frank Sinatra; *Forever Frank* .... (CAP)
Flowers Never Bend With The Rainfall
Simon & Garfunkel; *Collected Works* .... (COL)
Parsley Sage Rosemary & Thyme .... (COL)
Flowers Of The Night
Paul Kantner; *Baron Von Tollbooth & The Chrome
Nun* .... (GRU)

Flowers On The Wall
Statler Brothers; *Best Of The* .... (MER)
Billboard Top Country Hits-1966 .... (RHI)
Columbia Country Classics-#3 .... (COL)
Pop Classics/'60s .... (COL)
Forget Me Nots
Patrice Rushen; *Anthology* .... (ELE)
Disco Years-#2-On The Beat 1978-82 .... (RHI)
Straight From The Heart .... (ELE)
Garden City
Orchestral Manoeuvres In The Dark; *Junk
Culture* .... (A&M)
Garden Gate
James Gang; *Rides Again* .... (MCA)
Garden In The Rain
Four Aces; *20 Greatest Hits* .... (EVR)
Best Of .... (MCA)
Precious Memories .... (ACC)
Garden Of Eden
New Riders Of The Purple Sage; *New Riders Of The
Purple Sage* .... (COL)
Garden Of England
Gerry Rafferty; *Right Down The Line-Best Of* .... (EMI)
Garden Song
Arlo Guthrie & Pete Seeger; *Precious Friend* ...... (WB)
Gardening At Night
R.E.M.; *Chronic Town* .... (IRS)
Eponymous .... (IRS)
Garden, The
Magazine; *Magic Murder & The Weather* .... (IRS)
Green Green Grass Of Home
Burl Ives; *Best Of-#2* .... (MCA)
Elvis Presley; *Our Memories Of-#2* .... (RCA)
Today .... (RCA)
George Jones; *20 Golden Pieces Of* .... (BLD)
Tom Jones; *Country Side Of* .... (LON)
London Collector .... (LON)
Things That Matter Most To Me .... (MER)
Green Grow The Lilacs
Tex Ritter; *An American Legend* .... (CAP)
Best Of .... (CAP)
Best Of Town & Country-#3 .... (GUS)
Hillbilly Heaven .... (CAP)
Green Grow The Rushes, Ho
Chieftains; *Bonaparte's Retreat* .... (SHA)
Hawaiian Lei Song
Les Jansen; *45* .... (ACT)
Heather On The Hill
Gene Kelly; *ST/Brigadoon* .... (MCA)
Original Cast; *Brigadoon* .... (CSP)
Hissing Of Summer Lawns
Joni Mitchell; *Hissing Of Summer Lawns* .... (ASY)
Holland Park
John Williams; *Echoes Of London* .... (COL)
Honeysuckle Honey
Commander Cody/Lost Planet Airmen; *Country
Casanova* .... (MCA)
Hong Kong Garden
Siouxsie/Banshees; *Once Upon A Time-The
Singles* .... (GEF)
House Of Flowers
Barbra Streisand; *Just For The Record* .... (COL)
Harold Arlen & Barbra Streisand; *Harold Sings Arlen
(With Friend)* .... (SSP)
Original Cast; *House Of Flowers* .... (SSP)
Hyacinth House
Doors; *L.A. Woman* .... (ELE)
I Can Hear The Grass Grow
Blues Magoos; *Nuggets-#11-Pop-#4* .... (RHI)
Move; *Best Of* .... (A&M)
In Bloom
Nirvana; *Nevermind* .... (DGC)
Johnny's Garden
Stephen Stills; *Manassas* .... (ATL)
Kentucky Flower
King Edward IV/Knights; *45* .... (SND)
Let It Grow
Eric Clapton; *461 Ocean Boulevard* .... (RSO)
Crossroads .... (POL)
Lilacs & Fire
George Morgan; *Super Hits Country-'70s* .... (GUS)
Lily Of The Valley
Queen; *Sheer Heart Attack* .... (HOL)

FLOWERS — FLOWERS

Lily Of The West
Joan Baez; *Ballad Book* .... (VAN)
  Joan Baez .... (VAN)
Lotus
Tommy Bolin; *Teaser* ....(COL)
Lotus Blossom
David Frishberg; *Getting Some Fun Out Of Life* .. (CCJ)
Michael Franks; *One Bad Habit* ....(WB)
War; *Why Can't We Be Friends* .... (UA)
MacArthur Park
Andy Williams; *Greatest Hits-#2* ....(COL)
Donna Summer; *Live & More* .... (CAS)
  On The Radio-Greatest Hits-#1&2 .... (CAS)
  Summer Collection .... (CAS)
  Walk Away-Best Of 1977-1980 .... (CAS)
Richard Harris; *His Greatest Performances* ..... (MCA)
  Love Album ....(MCA)
  Tramp Shining ....(MCA)
  Vintage Music-Orig. Oldies/'50s-'60s-#13 ..... (MCA)
Waylon Jennings; *Are You Ready For The*
Country ....(RCA)
  Best Of ....(RCA)
Magnolia
J.J. Cale; *Naturally* .... (MCA)
Pat Travers; *Pat Travers* .... (POL)
Poco; *Crazy Eyes* .... (EPI)
Tom Petty/Heartbreakers; *You're Gonna Get It* . (MCA)
Magnolia Moon
Seals & Crofts; *Takin' It Easy* .... (WB)
Magnolia Triangle
Kansas; *Two For The Show* .... (KIR)
Mobile Bay (Magnolia Blossoms)
Cal Smith; *Stories Of Life By* ....(SO)
Johnny Cash; *Biggest Hits* ....(COL)
Merle Haggard & George Jones; *Taste Of Yesterday's*
Wine .... (EPI)
Moonflower
Santana; *Moonflower* ....(COL)
Moss Garden
David Bowie; *Heroes* ....(RYK)
Night Blooming Jasmine
Charles Lloyd Quartet; *Night In Copenhagen* ..... (BLN)
October Thorns
Flotsam & Jetsam; *When The Storm Comes*
Down .... (MCA)
Octopus's Garden
Beatles; *1967-1970* ....(CAP)
  Abbey Road ....(CAP)
  Box Set ....(CAP)
Orange Blossom Lane
Glenn Miller/Orchestra; *Complete* .... (BLU)
  Complete-#7 ....(RCA)
Orange Blossom Mandolin
Northeast Winds; *In Concert* .... (FOL)
Orange Blossom Special
Bill Monroe; *Bean Blossom* .... (MCA)
  Stars Of The Grand Ole Opry 1926-1974 ....(RCA)
  & Bluegrass Boys-60 Years Of Country ....(RCA)
Charlie Daniels Band; *Fire On The Mountain* ..... (EPI)
  Urban Cowboy-#2 .... (EPI)
Flatt & Scruggs; *Hear The Whistles Blow* .... (GUS)
Gordon Terry; *20 Golden Souvenirs* .... (PLN)
  Disco Country .... (PLN)
Johnny Cash; *Columbia Records 1958-1986* .....(COL)
  Essential ....(COL)
  Greatest Hits ....(COL)
Nitty Gritty Dirt Band; *Will The Circle Be*
Unbroken .... (EMI)
Orange Blossom Time
Bing Crosby; *Crooner-Columbia*
Years-1928-1934 ....(COL)
Paddy's Green Shamrock Shore
Chieftains; *Another Country* ....(RCA)
Passion Flower
Billy Strayhorn; *Lush Life* .... (RB)
Duke Ellington; *Big Band Hits CD Gift Set* ......(CAP)
  Piano Reflections ....(BLN)
Peach Blossom Spring
Yutaka; *Yutaka* ....(GRP)
Playing In God's Garden
Stevie Nicks; *Street Angel* ....(MOD)
Plum Blossom
Vangelis; *China* .... (POL)
Yusef Lateef/Others; *Eastern Sounds* .... (PRS)

Poisoning Pigeons In The Park
Tom Lehrer; *Dr. Demento 20th Anniversary*
Collection .... (RHI)
  Dr. Demento Presents Greatest Novelty CD ..... (RHI)
  Evening Wasted With ....(RPR)
Poppies
Buffy Sainte-Marie; *Best Of-#2* .... (VAN)
  Illuminations .... (VAN)
  Native North American Child .... (VAN)
Patti Smith Group; *Radio Ethiopia* .... (ARI)
Pretty Wreath For Mother's Grave
Reno & Smiley; *1983 Collector's Edition-#9* ..... (IGR)
Purple Heather
Van Morrison; *Hard Nose The Highway* ....(WB)
Pussy Willows Cat Tails
Gordon Lightfoot; *Best Of* .... (EMI)
  Lightfoot .... (EMI)
  Sunday Concert .... (EMI)
Roof Garden
Al Jarreau; *Breakin' Away* ....(WB)
  In London ....(WB)
Rose In The Heather
Nazareth; *Hair Of The Dog* .... (A&M)
Royal Garden Blues
Bix Beiderbecke; *At The Jazz Band Ball-#2* ......(COL)
Bix Beiderbecke/Wolverines; *History Of Classic*
Jazz ....(RVR)
Original Broadway Cast; *Black & Blue* .... (DRG)
Tommy Dorsey; *Best Of* ....(RCA)
  Complete-#2 ....(RCA)
Sagebrush Sports Report
Riders In The Sky; *Riders Radio Theater* .... (MCA)
San Francisco (Be Sure To Wear Some...)
Scott McKenzie; *Nuggets-#10-Folk Rock* .... (RHI)
  Rock Artifacts-#3 ....(COL)
  ST/Forrest Gump .... (EPX)
  Summer Of Love .... (RHI)
Sassafras Roots
Green Day; *Dookie* ....(RPR)
Saturday In The Park
Chicago; *Greatest Hits* ....(COL)
  If You Leave Me Now ....(COL)
  ST/My Girl ....(EPI)
  V ....(COL)
Scarlet Begonias
Grateful Dead; *From The Mars Hotel* .... (GRD)
Secret Garden
Alan Parsons Project; *Eve* .... (ARI)
Johnny Rivers; *Golden Hits* .... (IMP)
Quincy Jones; *Back On The Block* .... (QUE)
Secret Gardens
Judy Collins; *So Early In The Spring-First 15*
Years .... (ELE)
  True Stories & Other Dreams .... (ELE)
Send One Your Love
Stevie Wonder; *Journey...Secret Life Of Plants* ... (MOT)
  Original Musiquarium .... (MOT)
Silver Dew On The Bluegrass Tonight
Johnnie Lee Wills; *Tulsa Swing* .... (ROU)
Silver Stars, Purple Sage, Eyes Of Blue
Roy Rogers/Sons Of The Pioneers; *Roy Rogers/Sons Of*
The Pioneers ....(VS)
Sky Is A Poisonous Garden
Concrete Blonde; *Bloodletting* .... (IRS)
Sugar Magnolia
Grateful Dead; *American Beauty* ....(WB)
  Europe '72 ....(WB)
  Live-#1 .... (JCI)
  Skeletons From The Closet-Best Of ....(WB)
Sunday Afternoon In The Park
Van Halen; *Fair Warning* ....(WB)
Sunday In The Park With George
Original Cast; *Sunday In The Park With George* ..(RCA)
Sunflower
Beach Boys; *Sunflower* .... (CAR)
Glen Campbell; *Best Of* .... (LIB)
  Live ....(CAP)
  Southern Nights ....(CAP)
Mason Williams; *Music-1968-1971* .... (VAN)
Sunflower River Blues
John Fahey; *With Peter Lang & Leo Kottke* ....(TAK)
Sunflower Slow Drag
Dick Hyman; *Scott Joplin-Greatest Hits* ....(RCA)
Scott Joplin; *King Of Ragtime Writers* ....(BIO)

Sweet Little Flower
Sleepy John Estes; *Electric Sleep* .... (DEL)
Sweet Violets
Mitch Miller/Gang; *Sing Along With Mitch* ...... (COL)
Tend My Garden
James Gang; *16 Greatest Hits* .... (MCA)
Live In Concert .... (MOB)
Rides Again .... (MCA)
Thorn Tree In The Garden
Derek/Dominos; *Layla* .... (POL)
Three Flowers
McCoy Tyner; *Soliloquy* .... (BLN)
Today & Tomorrow .... (BLN)
Richard Hayward; *Ireland Of Treasures-Voices &
Melodies* .... (CAP)
Thursday Morning Garden Club
Buddy Winfield; *45* .... (NAT)
Tip-Toe Through The Tulips With Me
Tiny Tim; *Dr. Demento's Greatest Novelty-#3* .... (RHI)
Silly Songs .... (KT)
Touch A Four Leaf Clover
Atlantic Starr; *Classics-#10* .... (A&M)
Secret Lovers-Best Of .... (A&M)
Yours Forever .... (A&M)
Tulip Or Turnip (Tell Me Dream Face)
Duke Ellington & Teresa Brewer; *It Don't Mean A
Thing If It Ain't Got...* .... (COL)
Tulip Time
Andrews Sisters; *Capitol Collectors Series* .... (CAP)
Tumbling Tumbleweeds
Billy Vaughn; *Greatest Hits* .... (CCB)
Gene Autry; *Essential* .... (COL)
Meat Puppets; *Meat Puppets* .... (SST)
Michael Martin Murphey; *Cowboy Songs* .... (WB)
Roy Rogers/K.T. Oslin/Restless Heart; *Tribute* ...(RCA)
Sons Of The Pioneers; *Country Music Hall Of
Fame* .... (MCA)
Venus Flytrap & The Bug
Stevie Wonder; *Journey...Secret Life of Plants* ... (MOT)
Violets For Your Furs
Frank Sinatra; *Concepts* .... (CAP)
Gift Set .... (CAP)
Songs For Young Lovers & Swing Easy .... (CAP)
Jesse Davis; *Horn Of Passion* .... (CCJ)
John Coltrane; *Prestige Recordings* .... (PRS)
Tommy Dorsey & Frank Sinatra; *Sessions-#1-Feb. 1
1940-July 17 1940* .... (RCA)
Violets Of Dawn
Blues Project; *No Time Like The Right Time-Best
Of* .... (RHI)
Eric Andersen; *Best Of* .... (VAN)
Troubadours Of The Folk Era-#1 .... (RHI)
Violets & Silverbells
Original Cast; *Shenandoah* .... (RCA)
Waltz Of The Flowers
Lawrence Welk; *22 All-Time Favorite Waltzes* .. (RAN)
When The Cactus Is In Bloom
Jimmie Rodgers; *Down The Old
Road-1931-1932* .... (ROU)
When The White Lilacs Bloom Again
Billy Vaughn; *Best Of* .... (MCA)
Greatest Hits .... (CCB)
When You Wore A Tulip
Judy Garland; *Best Of* .... (MCA)
Where Have All The Flowers Gone
Johnny Rivers; *Anthology-1964-1977* .... (RHI)
Best Of .... (EMI)
Kingston Trio; *Capitol Collectors Series* .... (CAP)
Pete Seeger; *Essential* .... (VAN)
Greatest Hits .... (COL)
Peter, Paul & Mary; *Peter, Paul & Mary* .... (WB)
Wes Montgomery; *Classics-#22* .... (A&M)
White Sport Coat & A Pink Carnation
Marty Robbins; *16 Most Requested Songs/'50s-#2* (COL)
Greatest Hits .... (COL)
Lifetime Of Song-1951-1982 .... (COL)
Who's Gonna Mow Your Grass
Buck Owens; *All-Time Greatest-#1* .... (CCB)
Collection-1959-1990 .... (RHI)
Wicked Garden
Stone Temple Pilots; *Core* .... (ATL)
Wild Flowers
Jimmy Smith; *Best Of* .... (CCB)

Wild Goose Grasses In Tarrytown
Weavers; *Classics* .... (VAN)
Greatest Hits .... (VAN)
Wildflower
Carter Family; *60 years Of Country Music* ......(RCA)
O'Jays; *Collector's Items* .... (PI)
Live In London .... (PI)
Skylark; *Reaching For The Sky-Soul From The
'70s* .... (CAP)
Super Hits/'70s-#10 .... (RHI)
Wildflowers
D. Parton/E. Harris/L. Ronstadt; *Trio* .... (WB)
John Denver; *Some Days Are Diamonds* ....(RCA)
Wildwood Flower
Carter Family; *Legends Of Country Guitar-#2* ... (RHI)
Chet Atkins; *Tennessee Guitar Man* .... (PRR)
Hank Thompson & Merle Travis; *Great Records Of The
Decade-'50s Hits* .... (CCB)
Greatest Hits-#2 .... (CCB)
Kentucky Colonels; *Featuring Clarence White* ... (ROU)
You Are My Flower
Carter Family; *Country Music Hall Of Fame* .... (MCA)
Nitty Gritty Dirt Band; *Will The Circle Be
Unbroken* .... (EMI)
You Don't Bring Me Flowers
Barbra Streisand; *Songbird* ....(COL)
Barbra Streisand & Neil Diamond; *Greatest Hits
#2* .... (COL)
Just For The Record .... (COL)
Neil Diamond; *Hot August Night II* .... (COL)
Neil Diamond & Barbra Streisand; *12 Greatest
Hits-#2* .... (COL)
I'm Glad You're Here With Me Tonight .... (COL)
You Don't Bring Me Flowers .... (COL)

FLYING, Flight
See Also: AIRPLANES, BIRDS, DRUGS

20 Flight Rock
Commander Cody; *Lost In The Ozone* .... (MCA)
Eddie Cochran; *Great Hits* .... (LIB)
Montrose; *Montrose* .... (WB)
Above The Clouds
Electric Light Orchestra; *New World Record* .....(JET)
African Night Flight
David Bowie; *Lodger* ....(RYK)
Angel Flying Too Close To The Ground
Willie Nelson; *Greatest Hits & Some That Will Be* (COL)
ST/Honeysuckle Rose ....(COL)
Angel Spread Your Wings
Judy Collins; *Judith* .... (ELE)
Around The World (In 80 Days)
Boston Pops Orchestra/Arthur Fiedler; *Greatest
Hits/'50s-#2* .... (RCA)
Frank Sinatra; *Come Fly With Me* .... (CAP)
Roger Williams; *Greatest Hits* .... (MCA)
Bermuda Triangle
Fleetwood Mac; *Heroes Are Hard To Find* .... (RPR)
Bermuda Triangle Blues (Flight 45)
Blondie; *Plastic Letters* .... (CHR)
Bomber
James Gang; *Best Of* .... (MCA)
Rides Again .... (MCA)
Broken Wings
Chris DeBurgh; *At The End Of A Perfect Day* ..(A&M)
Mr. Mister; *Nipper's Greatest Hits-'80s* ....(RCA)
Welcome To The Real World ....(RCA)
Come Fly With Me
Frank Sinatra; *At The Sands* .... (RPR)
Capitol Years .... (CAP)
Come Fly With Me .... (CAP)
Man & His Music .... (CAP)
Coming Into Los Angeles
Arlo Guthrie; *Best Of* .... (WB)
Running Down The Road .... (RPR)
ST/Woodstock .... (ATL)
Danger Zone
Crystal Gayle; *Miss The Mississippi* .... (LIB)
Kenny Loggins; *ST/Top Gun* ....(COL)
Klymaxx; *Klymaxx* ....(CON)
L.A. Posse; *They Come In All Colors* .... (ATL)
Planet Patrol; *Planet Patrol* .... (TMB)
Tommy Boy Greatest Beats .... (TMB)

Ramones; *Too Tough To Die* .... (SIR)
Shirley Murdock; *Shirley Murdock* .... (ELE)
De Bat (Fly In Me Face)
Carly Simon; *Boys In The Trees* .... (ELE)
Down Here On The Ground
George Benson; *Weekend In L.A.* .... (WB)
Eight Miles High
Byrds; *Byrds* ....(COL)
  Fifth Dimension ....(COL)
  Greatest Hits ....(COL)
  Original Singles-#1-1965-1967 ....(COL)
  (Untitled) ....(COL)
Leo Kottke; *Best Of* ....(CAP)
  Mudlark ....(CAP)
Roxy Music; *Flesh & Blood* .... (RPR)
Expecting To Fly
Buffalo Springfield; *Again* ....(ATC)
  Buffalo Springfield ....(ATC)
  Retrospective ....(ATC)
Neil Young; *Decade* ....(RPR)
Flamingos Fly
Sammy Hagar; *Nine On A Ten Scale* ....(CAP)
Van Morrison; *Period Of Transition* .... (WB)
Flight 602
Chicago; *3* ....(COL)
  At Carnegie Hall ....(COL)
  Group Portrait ....(COL)
Flight Of Icarus
Iron Maiden; *Live After Death* ....(CAP)
  Piece Of Mind ....(CAP)
Flight Of The Fly
Dan Hicks/Hot Licks; *Striking It Rich* ....(OOP)
Flight (505)
Rolling Stones; *Aftermath* .... (AKO)
Flight (The Higher We Fly)
John Denver; *45* ....(RCA)
Fly
Al Jarreau; *All Fly Home* .... (WB)
Chubby Checker; *Echoes Of A Rock Era-Later
Years* ....(RLL)
  Greatest Hits ....(EVR)
Fly Away
Blackfoot; *Maurader* ....(ATC)
John Denver; *Greatest Hits-#2* ....(RCA)
  Windsong ....(RCA)
Patty Loveless; *If My Heart Had Windows* ...... (MCA)
Peter Allen; *Best* ....(A&M)
  Bi-Coastal ....(A&M)
Fly Away Home
Ozark Mountain Daredevils; *Best* ....(A&M)
Men From Earth ....(A&M)
Fly By Night
Rush; *All The World's A Stage* .... (MER)
  Archives ....(MER)
  Fly By Night .... (MER)
Fly Fly Fly
Brewer & Shipley; *On The Road Again* .... (ACC)
Fly Into Night
Charly McClain; *Biggest Hits* .... (EPI)
  Paradise ....(EPI)
Fly Into The Sun
Lou Reed; *New Sensations* ....(RCA)
Fly Into This Night
Gino Vannelli; *Best Of* .... (A&M)
  Classics-#7 ....(A&M)
  Gist Of The Gemini .... (A&M)
Fly Like An Eagle
Steve Miller Band; *Fly Like An Eagle* ....(CAP)
  Gift Set ....(CAP)
  Greatest Hits ....(CAP)
  Live ....(CAP)
  ST/FM ....(MCA)
Fly Me Courageous
Drivin' N' Cryin'; *Fly Me Courageous* .... (ISL)
Fly Me To The Moon
Frank Sinatra; *A Man & His Music* .... (RPR)
  At The Sands .... (RPR)
  It Might As Well Be Swing ....(RPR)
  Reprise Collection ....(RPR)
Fly Robin Fly
Silver Convention; *45* ....(OOP)
Flyer
Saga; *Heads Or Tales* ....(POR)

Flying
Beatles; *Box Set* ....(CAP)
  Magical Mystery Tour ....(CAP)
Flying Cloud
Doobie Brothers; *What Were Once Vices Are Now
Habits* ....(WB)
Flying Colours
Jethro Tull; *Broadsword And The Beast* .... (CHR)
Flying High
Commodores; *Natural High* .... (MOT)
Country Joe/Fish; *Collected 1965-1970* .... (VAN)
  Life & Times Of .... (VAN)
Karla Bonoff; *Karla Bonoff* ....(COL)
Flying High Again
Ozzy Osbourne; *Diary Of A Madman* ....(JET)
  Tribute ....(JET)
Flying High In The Friendly Sky
Marvin Gaye; *What's Goin' On* .... (MOT)
Flying Home
Benny Goodman; *Jazz Sampler-#6* ....(COL)
Ella Fitzgerald; *Best Of* .... (MCA)
Ella Fitzgerald & Count Basie; *Pablo Live* ...... (PAB)
Lionel Hampton; *Flying Home* ....(DHL)
Flying On The Ground Is Wrong
Buffalo Springfield; *Buffalo Springfield* ....(ATC)
Flying Turkey Trot
R.E.O. Speedwagon; *Decade Of Rock & Roll* ...... (EPI)
  Live ....(EPI)
  R.E.O. ....(EPI)
Free Fallin'
Tom Petty; *Full Moon Fever* .... (MCA)
Ghost Of Flight 401
Bob Welch; *Three Hearts* ....(OOP)
Ginny The Flying Girl
Janis Ian; *In Harmony II* ....(COL)
Give Me Wings
Michael Johnson; *Best Of* ....(RCA)
  Hits Of '87 ....(RCA)
  Wings ....(RCA)
Gonna Fly Now
Bill Conti; *ST/Rocky* .... (LIB)
  ST/Rocky II ....(EMI)
  ST/Rocky III .... (LIB)
Helicopter Sounds
Pink Floyd; *The Wall (Sound Effects)* ....(COL)
High Flying Bird
Elton John; *Don't Shoot Me I'm Only The Piano
Player* .... (POL)
High Flying, Adored
Original New York Cast; *Evita* .... (MCA)
Higher & Higher (Your Love Keeps...)
Bette Midler; *Bette Midler* ....(ATL)
Bonnie Bramlett; *It's Time* ....(CPC)
Jackie Wilson; *Billboard Top R&B Hits-1967* .... (RHI)
  Greatest Hits ....(BRU)
  Greatest Hits-#2 ....(BRU)
  Reet Petite-Best Of ....(COL)
  Soul Shots-#1 ....(RHI)
  Story ....(EPI)
Rita Coolidge; *Anytime...Anywhere* ....(A&M)
  Classics-#5 ....(A&M)
  Greatest Hits ....(A&M)
  Havana Jam ....(COL)
Icarus
Paul Winter Consort; *Common Ground* ....(A&M)
  Earthdance ....(A&M)
  Icarus ....(EPI)
  Pioneers Of The New Age ....(COL)
  Road ....(A&M)
I'm Flying
Mary Martin/Original Cast; *Peter Pan* ....(RCA)
I'm Mandy Fly Me
10 CC; *Greatest Hits 1972-1978* ....(POL)
  How Dare You ....(OOP)
  Live & Let Live ....(OOP)
Jet
Paul McCartney; *Tripping The Live Fantastic* ....(CAP)
Paul McCartney/Wings; *All The Best* ....(CAP)
  Band On The Run ....(CAP)
  Wings Greatest ....(CAP)
  Wings Over America ....(COL)

Jet Airliner
Steve Miller Band; *Book Of Dreams* ....(CAP)
Gift Set ....(CAP)
Greatest Hits-1974-1978 ....(CAP)
Live ....(CAP)
Jets At Dawn
Be Bop Deluxe; *Axe Victim* ....(OOP)
Las Vegas Turnaround
Daryl Hall & John Oates; *Abandoned*
Luncheonette ....(ATL)
No Goodbyes ....(ATL)
Learning To Fly
Pink Floyd; *Delicate Sound Of Thunder* ....(COL)
Momentary Lapse Of Reason ....(COL)
Tom Petty/Heartbreakers; *Into The Great Wide*
Open .... (MCA)
Letter, The
Box Tops; *Billboard Top Rock 'N' Roll Hits-1967* (RHI)
Cruisin'-1967 ....(INC)
Greatest Hits ....(RHI)
Oldies But Goodies-#12 ....(OSR)
Rockin' '60s ....(PRY)
Joe Cocker; *Classics-#4* ....(A&M)
Greatest Hits ....(A&M)
Live ....(CAP)
Mad Dogs & Englishmen ....(A&M)
Medallions; *Golden Classics* ....(CLT)
Oldies But Goodies-#1 ....(OSR)
Love Light In Flight
Stevie Wonder; *ST/Woman In Red* .... (MOT)
Magic Carpet Ride
Steppenwolf; *16 Greatest Hits* ....(MCA)
Gold ....(MCA)
Live ....(MCA)
Nuggets-#9-Acid Rock ....(RHI)
The Second ....(MCA)
"Monty Python's Flying Circus" Theme
Original Music; *Television's Greatest Hits-#2* .....(TVT)
Natural High
Bloodstone; *Greatest Hits* ....(TN)
Soul Hits/'70s-#11 ....(RHI)
Night Flight
Buddy Guy; *Complete Chess Studio Recordings* ... (CSS)
Led Zeppelin; *Physical Graffiti* .... (SS)
On The Wings Of Love
Jeffrey Osborne; *Jeffrey Osborne* ....(A&M)
Pegasus
Allman Brothers Band; *Enlightened Rogues* .... (POL)
Mahavishnu Orchestra; *Visions Of The Emerald*
Beyond ....(COL)
Pigs On The Wing
Pink Floyd; *Animals* ....(COL)
Shine On-Box Set ....(COL)
Pilot Error
Stephanie Mills; *Merciless* .... (CAS)
Rocky Mountain High
John Denver; *Evening With* ....(RCA)
Greatest Hits-#1 ....(RCA)
Rocky Mountain High ....(RCA)
Take Me Home Country Roads & Other Hits ....(RCA)
Sail On Flying Dutchman
Nick Seeger; *Sail On Flying Dutchman* ....(BIO)
Silver Wings
Merle Haggard; *More Of The Best* ....(RHI)
w/Willie Nelson: *Seashores Of Old Mexico* .... (EPI)
Merle Haggard/Strangers; *Okie From Muskogee* ..(CAP)
Songs I'll Always Sing ....(CAP)
Pam Tillis; *Mama's Hungry Eyes-Merle Haggard*
Tribute .... (ARI)
Spirits (Having Flown)
Bee Gees; *Greatest* ....(POL)
Spirits ....(POL)
Spread Your Wings
Queen; *Live Killers* ....(HOL)
News Of The World ....(HOL)
Straighten Up & Fly Right
Andrews Sisters; *Best Of-#2* .... (MCA)
Linda Ronstadt; *For Sentimental Reasons* ....(ASY)
Nat King Cole; *Best Of-#2* ....(CAP)
The Unforgettable ....(CAP)
Superman (I Wish I Could Fly Like)
Kinks; *Come Dancing With-Best Of-1977-1986* .. (ARI)
Low Budget ....(ARI)

Texas Bound & Flyin'
Jerry Reed; *ST/Smokey & The Bandit 2* .... (MCA)
Texas Bound & Flyin' ....(RCA)
Time For Me To Fly
R.E.O. Speedwagon; *Decade Of Rock &*
Roll-1970-1980 ....(EPI)
Hits ....(EPI)
You Can Tune A Piano But You Can't... .... (EPI)
Up, Up & Away
5th Dimension; *Anthology-1967-1973* .... (RHI)
Greatest Hits On Earth ....(ARI)
Waiting In The Wings
BBM; *Around The Next Dream* .... (VIA)
When I See An Elephant Fly
Barbara Cook; *Disney Album* .... (MCA)
C. Edwards/J. Carmichael/H. Johnson Ch.; *Disney*
Collection-#2 ....(DIS)
When The Eagle Flies
Traffic; *When The Eagle Flies* .... (ASY)
When The Fallen Angels Fly
Patty Loveless; *When Fallen Angels Fly* .... (EPI)
Why Walk When You Can Fly
Mary Chapin Carpenter; *Stones In The Road* ....(COL)
Wind Beneath My Wings
Bette Midler; *ST/Beaches* ....(ATL)
Gary Morris; *Country Love Songs* ....(WB)
Hits ....(WB)
Why Lady Why ....(WB)
James Galway; *Wind Beneath My Wings* ....(RCA)
Lee Greenwood; *Somebody's Gonna Love You* .. (MCA)
Lou Rawls; *When The Night Comes* .... (EPI)
Roger Whittaker; *Greatest Hits* .... (RCA)
Wind Beneath My Wings ....(RCA)
Willie Nelson; *City Of New Orleans* ....(COL)
Wingin' It Home To Texas
Jerry Jeff Walker; *Collectibles* .... (MCA)
Wings Of Your Love
Prism; *Small Change* ....(CAP)
Wings Wetted Down
Blue Oyster Cult; *Tyranny & Mutation* ....(COL)
You Got Me Floatin'
PM Dawn; *Stone Free: Tribute To Jimi Hendrix* ..(GEE)

FOOD, Cooking, Eating, Hungry, Kitchens, Meals

See Also: ALCOHOL, COFFEE, FISH, FRUIT,
RESTAURANTS, VEGETABLES

3 Martini Lunch
Graham Parker; *Best Of-1988-1991* ....(RCA)
Alan's Psychedelic Breakfast
Pink Floyd; *Atom Heart Mother* ....(CAP)
Alligator Milk
Carol Channing/Others; *& Her Country Friends* .. (PLN)
Alpine Milkman
Randy Erwin; *'Til The Cows Come Home/Cowboy*
Rhythm .... (ROM)
Amazing Bigfoot Diet
Mojo Nixon & Skid Roper; *Frenzy* .... (IRS)
Angel Food Cake
Siegel-Schwall Band; *Best Of* .... (VAN)
Animal Crackers
Anne Murray; *There's A Hippo In My Tub* ....(CAP)
Melanie; *Best Of* ....(BUD)
Another Piece Of Meat
Scorpions; *Lovedrive* ....(MER)
Worldwide Live ....(MER)
Ants In The Kitchen
Masters Of Reality; *Sunrise On The Sufferbus* .. (CHR)
Astronaut Food
Sopwith Camel; *Miraculous Hump Returns* .... (RPR)
Baby Lemonade
Syd Barrett; *Barrett* ....(CAP)
Baby Ruth
John Prine; *Storm Windows* ....(ASY)
Bacon Fat
Frank Zappa; *Broadway The Hard Way* ....(RYK)
Our Man In Nirvana ....(RHI)
Bar B Q
ZZ Top; *Rio Grande Mud* ....(WB)
Six Pack ....(WB)

Beef Jerky
John Lennon/Plastic Ono Band; *Walls & Bridges* ..(CAP)
Being Boiled
Human League; *Greatest Hits* ....(A&M)
Big Butter And Egg Man
Louis Armstrong; *Best Of* ....(AUF)
  Hot Fives And Hot Sevens-#2 ....(COL)
Merle Haggard; *Kern River* ....(EPI)
  Walking The Line ....(EPI)
Big Fat Ham
Jelly Roll Morton; *Immortal* .... (MS)
Big Mexican Dinner
Kentucky HeadHunters; *Electric Barnyard* ...... (MER)
Big Mouth Blues
Gram Parsons; *G.P./Grievous Angel* ....(RPR)
  Gram Parsons/Fallen Angels Live 1973 ....(SIE)
Binge & Purge
Clutch; *Transnational Speedway League* ....(EW)
Black Cow
Steely Dan; *Aja* ....(MCA)
  Gold ....(MCA)
Black Licorice
Grand Funk Railroad; *Caught In The Act* ....(CAP)
  We're An American Band ....(CAP)
Bloat On
Cheech & Chong; *Let's Make A New Dope Deal* ..(WB)
Blue Tail Fly
Burl Ives; *Best Of* ....(MCA)
Pete Seeger; *20 Golden Pieces Of* ....(BLD)
Blues For The Barbecue
Count Basie; *Farmers Market Barbecue* .... (PAB)
Bread & Blood
Air Supply; *The Earth Is...* .... (GIA)
Bread & Butter
Newbeats; *Billboard Top Rock 'N' Roll Hits-1964* (RHI)
  Collectables Presents History Of Rock-#9 ....(CLT)
  Oldies But Goodies-#2 ....(OSR)
Waitresses; *Best Of* ....(POL)
Bread & Roses
Judy Collins; *So Early In The Spring-First 15*
  Years .... (ELE)
Bread & Water
Gary Morris; *Stones* ....(LIB)
Breadline Blues
New Lost City Ramblers; *Depression Songs* ..... (FLW)
Breakfast For Dinosaurs
Fowler Brothers; *Breakfast For Dinosaurs* .... (FOS)
Breakfast In America
Supertramp; *Breakfast In America* ....(A&M)
  Classics-#9 ....(A&M)
  Paris ....(A&M)
Breakfast In Bed
Lorna Bennett; *This Is Reggae Music-#1* .... (ISL)
UB40; *UB40* ....(A&M)
Bring Home The Bacon
Drivin' N' Cryin'; *Scarred But Smarter* .... (ISL)
Bun & Cheese
Clement Irie & Robert French; *Dancehall Style-Best Of*
  Reggae Dancehall ....(PRO)
Burgers & Fries
Charley Pride; *Burgers & Fries* ....(RCA)
  Greatest Hits ....(RCA)
  When I Stop Leaving ....(RCA)
Buttermilk Biscuits (Keep On Square...)
Sir Mix-A-Lot; *Swass* ....(NSY)
Candy Store Rock
Led Zeppelin; *Led Zeppelin (collection)* ....(ATL)
  Presence .... (SS)
Catfish Sam'ich
Charles Williams; *Charles Williams* ....(MST)
Cheap Seats, The
Alabama; *Cheap Seats* ....(RCA)
Cheese & Onions
Rutles; *Rutles* .... (RHI)
Cheeseburger In Paradise
Jimmy Buffett; *Son Of A Son Of A Sailor* ....(MCA)
  Songs You Know By Heart ....(MCA)
Cherry Coke
Bob's Diner; *Bob's Diner* .... (DIG)
Chewing Gum
Carter Family; *Anchored In Love-Complete Victor*
  Rec. ....(ROU)
Elvis Costello; *Spike* ....(WB)
Uncle Dave Macon; *Laugh Your Blues Away* ... (ROU)

Chewin' Gum
Ella Fitzgerald; *Ella Fitzgerald* ....(LAS)
Chicken Cordon Blues
Steve Goodman; *Somebody Else's Troubles* ....(OOP)
Chicken Gumbo
Preston Love & Shuggie Otis; *Omaha BBQ* .....(KNT)
Chicken Heads
Jimmy Johnson; *Bar Room Preacher* ....(ALG)
Mighty Joe Young; *Chicken Heads* .... (OVA)
Chicken Soup
Angel; *Helluva Band* .... (MER)
Chicken Stew Part I
Geoff Muldaur & Amos Garrett; *Geoff Muldaur & Amos
Garrett* ....(FF)
Chinese Kitchen
Fleshtones; *Fleshtones* .... (IRS)
  Roman Gods .... (IRS)
Chocolate Cake
Crowded House; *Woodface* ....(CAP)
Chop Suey Louie
Jimmy Preston; *Rock The Joint-#2* ....(CLT)
Chopsticks
Liberace; *16 Most Requested Songs* ....(COL)
Church
Lyle Lovett; *Joshua Judges Ruth* ....(MCC)
Cinnamon
Derek; *Rock Artifacts-#3* ....(COL)
Cinnamon Girl
Neil Young; *Decade* ....(RPR)
Neil Young/Crazy Horse; *Arc Weld* ....(RPR)
  Everyone Knows This Is Nowhere ....(RPR)
  Live Rust ....(RPR)
Coca-Cola Cowboy
Mel Tillis; *Greatest Hits* ....(CCB)
  Very Best Of ....(MCA)
Cockles & Mussels
Emily Mitchell; *The Irish Album* ....(RCA)
Coffee, Donuts & Death
Paris; *Sleeping With The Enemy* ....(SCA)
Colorado Kool Aid
Johnny Paycheck; *Biggest Hits* .... (EPI)
  Greatest Hits-#2 ....(EPI)
  Take This Job & Shove It ....(EPI)
Come On In My Kitchen
Delaney & Bonnie; *Anthology-#2* ....(CPC)
  w/Duane Allman ....(CPC)
Robert Johnson; *Complete Recordings* ....(COL)
  King Of The Delta Blues Singers ....(COL)
Steve Miller Band; *Joker* ....(CAP)
Constant Craving
k.d. lang; *Ingenue* .... (SIR)
Cook Of The House
Wings; *At The Speed Of Sound* ....(CAP)
Cook With Fire
Heart; *Dog & Butterfly* ....(POR)
Cornflake Girl
Tori Amos; *Under The Pink* ....(ATL)
Country Ham & Red Gravy
Hotmud Family; *Live As We Know It* ....(FF)
Country Pie
Bob Dylan; *Nashville Skyline* ....(COL)
Cream
Prince/New Power Generation; *Diamonds &
Pearls* ....(PAI)
Custard Pie
Led Zeppelin; *Led Zeppelin* ....(ATL)
  Physical Graffiti .... (SS)
Days Of Pup & Taco
Lawndale; *Beyond Barbecue* ....(SST)
  No Age-Compilation Of SST Instrumentals ....(SST)
Devil's Food
Alice Cooper; *Show* ....(WB)
  Welcome To My Nightmare ....(ATL)
Dill Pickle Rag I
Mark O'Connor; *Championship Years* .... (CMF)
Dill Pickles Rag
Max Morath; *Ragtime Man* .... (OME)
Dinner For One Please James
Nat King Cole; *Blossom Fell* ....(CAP)
  Gift Set ....(CAP)
Dinner With Drac
Zacherle; *Rock-O-Rama-#2* .... (AKO)
Dinner With Gershwin
Brenda Russell; *Kiss Me With The Wind* ....(A&M)

Donna Summer; *All Systems Go* .... (GEF)
Dirty Old Egg-Sucking Dog
Johnny Cash; *At Folsom Prison & San Quentin* ...(COL)
  Essential ....(COL)
Does Your Chewing Gum Lose Its Flavor...
Lonnie Donegan; *Dr. Demento Presents Greatest Novelty
CD* .... (RHI)
  Dr. Demento Presents Greatest-#3-'60s .... (RHI)
Donut Man
Rita Coolidge; *The Lady's Not For Sale* .... (A&M)
Don't Eat Stuff Off The Sidewalk
Cramps; *Psychedelic Jungle/Gravest Hits* .... (IRS)
Don't Eat The Yellow Snow
Frank Zappa; *Apostrophe/Overnite Sensation* .....(RYK)
Easter Dinner
Tribe; *Abort* ....(SLS)
Eat A Little Something
Original Cast; *I Can Get It For You Wholesale* ....(SSP)
Eat At Home
Paul & Linda McCartney; *Ram* ....(CAP)
Eat It
Weird Al Yankovic; *Dr. Demento 20th Anniversary
Collection* .... (RHI)
  Dr. Demento Presents Greatest Novelty-#5 ...... (RHI)
  Greatest Hits ....(SCO)
  In 3-D ....(SCO)
Eat The Rich
Aerosmith; *Get A Grip* .... (GEF)
Eat To The Beat
Blondie; *Eat To The Beat* .... (CHR)
Eaten Alive
Diana Ross; *Eaten Alive* ....(RCA)
Eggplant Pizza
Jimmy Bruno Trio; *Sleight Of Hand* .... (CCJ)
Eggs & Sausage (In A Cadillac...)
Tom Waits; *Nighthawks At The Diner* .... (ASY)
Everybody Eats When They Come To My...
Cab Calloway; *Hi De Ho Man* ....(COL)
Fast Food
Stevens & Grdnic; *Dr. Demento's Greatest-#5* .... (RHI)
Feed Jake
Pirates Of The Mississippi; *Pirates Of The
Mississippi* ....(CAP)
Feed Me
Elton John; *Rock Of The Westies* .... (MCA)
Fish Heads
Barnes & Barnes; *20th Anniversary Collection* .... (RHI)
  Dr. Demento's Greatest-#4 .... (RHI)
Fish & Chips
Eddie/Hot Rods; *Fish & Chips* .... (AMR)
Follow The Drinking Gourd
Richie Havens; *Songs Of The Civil War* ....(COL)
Weavers; *Greatest Hits* .... (VAN)
Food Glorious Food
Original Broadway Cast; *Oliver* ....(RCA)
Food Phone Gas Lodging
Charlie King; *Food Phone Gas Lodging* .... (FF)
Food (Till Sunday) (No)
Click Click; *Wet Skin & Curious Eye* ....(PIA)
Fort Worth Hambone Blues
Johnny Gimble/Texas Swing Pioneers; *Johnny Gimble's
Texas Honky Tonk Hits* .... (CMH)
Fourteen Minutes Old
Doug Stone; *Doug Stone* ....(EPI)
Fried Chicken
Rufus Thomas; *45* .... (HIR)
Gator Tails And Monkey Ribs
Spats; *45* ....(OOP)
German Lunch
Frank Zappa; *You Can't Do That On Stage
Anymore-#5* ....(RYK)
Gimme A Pig Foot
Billie Holiday; *From The Original Decca Masters* (MCA)
  Story ....(MCA)
Gimme Some Water
Eddie Money; *Life For The Taking* ....(COL)
Go For Soda
Kim Mitchell; *Akimbo Alogo* .... (BRZ)
Guacamole
Texas Tornados; *Hangin' On By A Thread* .... (RPR)
Hey, Good Lookin'
Hank Williams; *24 Greatest Hits* .... (MER)
  40 Greatest Hits ....(POL)
  Hey, Good Lookin'-December 1950-July 1951 .. (POL)

Loretta Lynn & Conway Twitty; *Hey, Good
Lookin'* ....(MSP)
Hold Tight, Hold Tight (Sea Food)
Andrews Sisters; *16 Great Performances* .... (MCA)
  Best Of .... (MCA)
  Boogie Woogie Bugle Girls .... (MCA)
Home Cookin'
Junior Walker/All-Stars; *Anthology* .... (MOT)
  Greatest Hits .... (MOT)
Honey Bun
Original Cast; *South Pacific* ....(COL)
Hot Cakes
Carly Simon; *Hot Cakes* .... (ELE)
Hot Chili
Steve Miller Band; *Number 5* ....(CAP)
Hot Chili Mama
Beausoleil; *Hot Chili Mama* .... (ARH)
Hot Dog
Elvis Presley; *Essential Elvis-First Movies* ....(RCA)
  Loving You ....(RCA)
  Sings Lieber & Stoller ....(RCA)
Led Zeppelin; *In Through The Out Door* .... (SS)
Mongo Santamaria; *Greatest Hits* ....(COL)
Hot Dogs & Cabbage
Li'l Wally; *One Man Band* ....(JJ)
Hot Dogs & Hamburgers
John Mellencamp; *Lonesome Jubilee* .... (MER)
Hot Pastrami
Dartells; *Frat Rock! Box Set* .... (RHI)
  Frat Rock-#4 .... (RHI)
  History Of Rock Instrumentals-#1 .... (RHI)
  Son Of Frat Rock .... (RHI)
Hot Tamale
Jackie Mittoo; *Jackie Mittoo* .... (EMI)
  New & Old Songs .... (EMI)
Hot Tamale Baby
Buckwheat Zydeco; *Best Of Louisiana Music* .... (ROU)
Clifton Chenier; *Zydeco Dynamite-Anthology* .... (RHI)
  Zydeco Party .... (KT)
Hunger
Waylon Jennings; *Ramblin' Man* ....(RCA)
Hunger Strike
Temple Of The Dog; *Temple Of The Dog* .... (A&M)
Hungry
Coasters; *It Ain't Sanitary* .... (TRP)
Sammy Hagar; *Sammy Hagar* ....(CAP)
Winger; *Winger* ....(ATL)
Hungry Eyes
Eric Carmen; *Best Of* .... (ARI)
  Dirty Dancing Live In Concert ....(RCA)
  ST/Dirty Dancing ....(RCA)
Hungry For Love
Patsy Cline; *20 Golden Pieces Of* .... (BLD)
  Patsy Cline .... (MCA)
  Hungry For Love-Her First Recordings-#2 ...... (RHI)
Todd Rundgren; *A Wizard A True Star* .... (RHI)
Hungry For Your Love
Van Morrison; *ST/Officer & A Gentleman* .... (ISL)
  Wavelength .... (WB)
Hungry Heart
Bruce Springsteen; *The River* ....(COL)
Bruce Springsteen/E Street Band;
Live-1975-1985 ....(COL)
Hungry Like The Wolf
Duran Duran; *Arena* ....(CAP)
  Decade ....(CAP)
  Duran Duran ....(CAP)
  Rio ....(CAP)
Hungry (For Those Good Things)
Paul Revere/Raiders; *Best Of-#1* .... (BCT)
  Frat Rock! .... (RHI)
  Greatest Hits ....(COL)
  Legend Of ....(COL)
I Ain't Gonna Eat Out My Heart Anymore
Rascals; *Time Piece-Rascals Greatest Hits* .... (ATL)
  Young Rascals .... (RHI)
I Ain't Gonna Give Nobody None Of My...
Bobby Darin/Johnny Mercer/Billy May Orc.; *Two Of A
Kind* ....(ATC)
I Am A Pizza
Peter Alsop; *Wha' D' Ya Wanna Do* ....(FF)
I Left My Heart At The Stage Door...
Jo Stafford; *G.I. Jo* ....(CRN)

FOOD — FOOD

I Love Rocky Road
Weird Al Yankovic; *Weird Al Yankovic* .... (SCO)
I Need Lunch
Dead Boys; *Young Loud & Snotty* .... (SIR)
Ice Cream
Sarah McLachlan; *Fumbling Towards Ecstasy* .... (ARI)
Ice Cream Castles
Time; *Ice Cream Castles* .... (WB)
Incense & Peppermints
Strawberry Alarm Clock; *Billboard Top Rock 'N' Roll Hits-1967* .... (RHI)
   Cruisin'-1967 .... (INC)
   Even More Nuggets .... (RHI)
   Nuggets-#8-Acid Rock .... (RHI)
I'm Putting All My Eggs In One Basket
Carmen McRae; *Greatest Of* .... (MCA)
Fred Astaire; *Irving Berlin Songbook* .... (VRV)
I'm Throwing Rice
Jerry Lee Lewis; *Taste Of Country* .... (SUN)
Jambalaya
Blue Ridge Rangers; *Blue Ridge Rangers* .... (FAN)
Fats Domino; *Greatest Hits* .... (MCA)
Hank Williams; *16 Great Hits* .... (EVR)
   24 Of Hank Williams' Greatest Hits .... (POL)
   40 Greatest Hits .... (POL)
Hank Williams, Jr.; *ST/Your Cheatin' Heart* ...... (SSP)
Jerry Lee Lewis; *Golden Cream Of The Country* . (SUN)
   Twenty Classic Hits .... (SUN)
Nitty Gritty Dirt Band; *All The Good Times* .... (UA)
   Stars & Stripes Forever .... (UA)
Jumbo Malt
Skatalites; *African Roots* .... (LIB)
Junk Food Junkie
Larry Groce; *Dr. Demento's Greatest-#4* .... (RHI)
Lasagna
Weird Al Yankovic; *Even Worse* .... (RAR)
   Greatest Hits .... (RAR)
Leftovers
Millie Jackson; *Still Caught Up* .... (SPR)
Life In The Foodchain
Tonio K.; *Life In The Foodchain* .... (EPI)
Life Is A Minestrone
10 CC; *Original Soundtrack* .... (MER)
Lollipop
Chordettes; *Best Of* .... (RHI)
   Greatest Hits .... (EVR)
   Jukebox Classics-#2 .... (RHI)
   Little Bit Of Gold-3" CD Series .... (RHI)
   ST/Stand By Me .... (ATL)
Lost In The Supermarket
Clash; *London Calling* .... (EPI)
   On Broadway .... (EPI)
   Story Of-#1 .... (EPI)
Love Bites
Def Leppard; *Hysteria* .... (MER)
Judas Priest; *Defenders Of The Faith* .... (COL)
   Priest...Live! .... (COL)
Lumpy Gravy
Mothers Of Invention; *We're Only In It For The Money/Lumpy Gravy* .... (RYK)
Lunch Hour
Rupert Holmes; *Partners In Crime* .... (MCA)
MacArthur Park
Andy Williams; *Greatest Hits-#2* .... (COL)
Donna Summer; *Live & More* .... (CAS)
   On The Radio-Greatest Hits-#1&2 .... (CAS)
   Summer Collection .... (CAS)
   Walk Away-Best Of 1977-1980 .... (CAS)
Richard Harris; *His Greatest Performances* ...... (MCA)
   Love Album .... (MCA)
   Tramp Shining .... (MCA)
   Vintage Music-Orig. Oldies/'50s-'60s-#13 ..... (MCA)
Waylon Jennings; *Are You Ready For The Country* .... (RCA)
   Best Of .... (RCA)
Macon Hambone Blues
Wet Willie; *Drippin' Wet Live* .... (CPC)
Main Course
Freddie Jackson; *Do Me Again* .... (CAP)
Paul Laurence; *Underexposed* .... (CAP)
Mama's Hungry Eyes
Emmylou Harris; *Mama's Hungry Eyes-Merle Haggard Tribute* .... (ARI)

Maneater
Daryl Hall & John Oates; *H2O* .... (RCA)
   Nipper's Greatest Hits-'80s .... (RCA)
   Rock 'N' Soul Part 1-Greatest Hits .... (RCA)
Martika's Kitchen
Martika; *Martika's Kitchen* .... (COL)
Mashed Potatoes (Hot Pastrami With)
Joey Dee/Starliters; *Hey Let's Twist-Best Of* ...... (RHI)
Maximum Consumption
Kinks; *Everybody's In Show Biz* .... (RHI)
Mayonaise
Smashing Pumpkins; *Siamese Dream* .... (VIA)
Mean Mr. Mustard
Beatles; *Abbey Road* .... (CAP)
Melt In Your Mouth
Candyman; *Ain't No Shame In My Game* .... (EPI)
Memphis Jellyroll
Stefan Grossman; *Yazoo Basin Boogie* .... (SHA)
Memphis Soul Stew
King Curtis; *Atlantic Jazz-Soul* .... (ATL)
   Atlantic R&B 1947-1974-#6-(1966-1969) ..... (ATL)
   Best Of .... (ATL)
   Golden Soul .... (ATL)
   Live At The Fillmore West .... (ATL)
Mother Popcorn
Aerosmith; *Live Bootleg* .... (COL)
James Brown; *Sex Machine* .... (POL)
Muffin Man
Zappa/Beefheart; *Bongo Fury* .... (RYK)
My Big Iron Skillet
Wanda Jackson; *Rockin' In The Country-Best Of* . (RHI)
My Bologna
Weird Al Yankovic; *Dr. Demento's Dementia Royale* .... (RHI)
   Dr. Demento's Greatest Novelty-#4-1970s ...... (RHI)
   Weird Al Yankovic .... (SCO)
My Boy Lollipop
Millie Small; *Island Story-1962-1987-25th Anniversary* .... (ISL)
My Daddy Was A Milkman
Kentucky HeadHunters; *Pickin' On Nashville* .... (MER)
Napalm For Breakfast
Rhythm Devils; *Apocalypse Now Sessions* .... (RYK)
Need A Little Taste Of Love
Doobie Brothers; *Cycles* .... (WB)
No Milk Today
Herman's Hermits; *There's A Kind Of A Hush* ..(MGM)
   XX-Their Greatest Hits .... (AKO)
No Rice, No Peas, No Coconut Oil
Jolly Boys; *Beer Joint & Tailoring* .... (FLW)
Old Home Filler Up & Keep On A Truckin'
C.W. McCall; *Greatest Hits* .... (POL)
   Wolf Creek Pass ....(MGM)
Old Kidney Stew Is Fine
Eddie "Cleanhead" Vinson; *Old Kidney Stew Is Fine* .... (DLM)
On The Good Ship Lollipop
Firehouse Five Plus Two; *Goes To Sea* .... (GTJ)
Frankie Valli/Four Seasons; *Rarities-#1* .... (RHI)
On Top Of Spaghetti
Tom Glazer; *Silly Songs* .... (KT)
One Meat Ball
Ry Cooder; *Ry Cooder* .... (RPR)
One Meatball
Roy Bookbinder; *Hillbilly Blues Cats* .... (ROU)
Onion Roll
Herb Ellis & Ray Brown Sextet; *Hot Tracks* ..... (CCJ)
Orange Sherbert
Count Basie; *Basie Big Band* .... (PAB)
Oreo Cookie Blues
Lonnie Mack; *Strike Like Lightning* ....(ALG)
Out Of The Frying Pan (& Into The Fire)
Meatloaf; *Bat Out Of Hell II: Back Into Hell* .... (MCA)
Out To Lunch
Country Gazette; *Out To Lunch* .... (FF)
Eric Dolphy; *Out To Lunch* .... (BLN)
Paddy Won't You Drink Some Cider
Red Clay Ramblers; *Chuckin' The Frizz* .... (FF)
Pass The Pickle
Prime Minister Pete Nice & Daddy Rich; *Dust To Dust* .... (DFC)
Peak Hour (Lunch Break)
Moody Blues; *Caught Live Plus Five* .... (POL)
   Days Of Future Passed .... (POL)

FOOD — FOOD

Peanut Butter
Marathons; *Best Of Chess Vocal Groups* .... (CSS)
Cruisin'-1961 .... (INC)
Frat Rock-#2 .... (RHI)
Son Of Frat Rock .... (RHI)
Peanut Butter Conspiracy
Jimmy Buffett; *White Sport Coat & A Pink
Crustacean* .... (MCA)
Peanut Butter Time
Rolling Stones; *Made In The Shade* .... (RS)
Peanut Vendor
Judy Garland; *Star Is Born* ....(COL)
Stan Kenton; *Comprehensive* .... (CAP)
Greatest Hits .... (CAP)
Retrospective-Capitol Years-#1 .... (BLN)
Uncollected-#6-1962 .... (HIN)
Peanuts
Frankie Valli/Four Seasons; *25th Anniversary
Collection* .... (RHI)
Police; *Outlandos D'Amour* .... (A&M)
Peggy's Kitchen Wall
Bruce Cockburn; *Stealing Fire* ....(COL)
Picnic In The Jungle
Snakefinger; *Chewing Hides The Sound* .... (RAL)
Piece Of The Pie
Boom Crash Opera; *These here Are Crazy Times* . (GIA)
Jimmy Cliff; *Power & The Glory* ....(COL)
Kix; *Blow My Fuse* .... (ATL)
Pigmeat
Leadbelly; *King Of The Twelve-String Guitar* .....(COL)
Pigmeat Is What I Crave
Bo Carter; *Legends Of The Blues-#1* ....(COL)
Pizza Face
Barnes & Barnes; *Zabagabee-Best Of* .... (RHI)
Pizza In My Shorts
Da Yoopers; *Yoopy Do Wah* .... (YOU)
Pizza On The Ground
Austin Lounge Lizards; *Lizard Vision* ....(FF)
Polish Sausage Polka
Li'l Wally; *#1* .... (JJ)
Polk Salad Annie
Elvis Presley; *As Recorded Live At Madison Sq.
Garden* ....(RCA)
Tony Joe White; *Soul Shots-#6-Blue-Eyed Soul* .. (RHI)
Swingin' Country Favorites .... (WB)
Popcorn
Hot Butter; *Super Hits/'70s-Have A Nice Day-#9* . (RHI)
Popcorn Love
New Edition; *Club Classics-1982-1984-#1* .... (WL)
Greatest Hits-#1 .... (MCA)
Popcorn Pop Pop
Jessie Hill; *Golden Classics-Ooh Poo Pah Doo* ...(CLT)
Popcorn, Pretzels & Beer Waltz
Michigan Dutchmen; *Beer & Dutchmen Polkas* ......(JJ)
Popsicle
Jan & Dean; *Legendary Masters* .... (UA)
Surf City-Best Of .... (EMI)
New Kids On The Block; *New Kids On The
Block* ....(COL)
Talking Heads; *Popular Favorites-1984-1992* ..... (SIR)
Popsicle Toes
Manhattan Transfer; *Coming Out* .... (ATL)
Michael Franks; *Art Of Tea* .... (RPR)
Popsicles & Icicles
Murmaids; *Golden Girl Groups* .... (KT)
Oldies But Goodies-#2 .... (OSR)
Porcupine Pie
Neil Diamond; *Hot August Night* .... (MCA)
Moods .... (MCA)
Pork Chop Blues
Sam Collins; *Jailhouse Blues* ....(YAZ)
Pork Chop Stomp
Grady Martin/Winged Strings; *Legends Of Country
Guitar-#2* .... (RHI)
Pork Chops & Gravy
Ink Spots; *If I Didn't Care* ....(POE)
Pork & Beans
Willie "The Lion" Smith; *Pork & Beans* ....(BL)
Potatoe Chips
King Curtis; *Scepter Records Story* ....(CPC)
Poundcake
Van Halen; *For Unlawful Carnal Knowledge* ......(WB)

Pretty Girl Milking A Cow
Judy Garland; *Best Of* .... (MCA)
One & Only ....(CAP)
Pretzel Logic
Donald Fagen & Michael McDonald; *New York Rock &
Soul Revue-At The Beacon* .... (GIA)
Steely Dan; *Greatest Hits* .... (MCA)
Pretzel Logic .... (MCA)
Pretzel Man
Harry Chapin; *Legends Of The Lost & Found* .... (ELE)
Purple People Eater
Sheb Wooley; *45s On CD-#1 (1956-1959)* ..... (MER)
Dr. Demento 20th Anniversary Collection ...... (RHI)
Halloween Hits .... (RHI)
Horror Rock Classics-#2 .... (RHI)
Super Hits-#4 ....(GUS)
Quiche Lorraine
B-52's; *Tame Yourself* .... (RHI)
Wild Planet .... (WB)
Quiche Woman In A Barbecue Town
Tarwater Band; *Walking Across Egypt* ....(FF)
Rainbow Stew
Merle Haggard; *Greatest Hits* .... (MCA)
More Of The Best .... (RHI)
Rainbow Stew-Live At Anaheim Stadium ...... (MCA)
Rat In The Kitchen
UB40; *Live In Moscow* .... (A&M)
Rat In The Kitchen .... (A&M)
Rat Salad
Black Sabbath; *Paranoid* .... (WB)
Rats In My Kitchen
Sleepy John Estes; *Legend Of* ....(DEL)
Rats & Roaches In My Kitchen
Silas Hogan; *Louisiana Blues* .... (ARH)
Red Beans
Coleman Hawkins & Red Garland Trio; *Coleman
Hawkins & Red Garland Trio* .... (PRS)
Kingsnakes; *19 Lucky Strikes* .... (BWV)
Professor Longhair; *Crawfish Fiesta* ....(ALG)
Red Beans And Rice
Booker T./M.G.s; *Back To Back/Mar-Keys & Booker
T./M.G.s* .... (ATL)
Best Of .... (ATL)
Legends Of Rock Guitar-'60s-#1 .... (RHI)
Red Hot Chicken
Wet Willie; *Drippin' Wet Live* ....(CPC)
Greatest Hits ....(POL)
Reno Burrito
Tom Collier; *Pacific Aire* .... (NEB)
Rhapsody From Hunger
Spike Jones/City Slickers; *Spike Jones Is Murdering The
Classics* ....(RCA)
Rice Pudding
Jeff Beck; *Beck-ola* .... (EPI)
Rice & Peas
Wailers Band; *I.D.* .... (ATL)
Rock Candy
Bulletboys; *ST/Wayne's World* .... (RPR)
Montrose; *Montrose* .... (WB)
Rock & Roll Stew
Traffic; *Low Spark Of High-Heeled Boys* .... (ISL)
Root Beer Rag
Billy Joel; *Streetlife Serenade* ....(COL)
Rose & A Baby Ruth
George Hamilton IV; *At The Hop* .... (MCA)
Vintage Music-Orig. Classic Oldies-#12 .... (MCA)
Rubber Biscuit
Blues Brothers; *Best Of* .... (ATL)
Briefcase Full Of Blues .... (ATL)
Rum & Coca-Cola
Andrews Sisters; *16 Great Performances* .... (MCA)
Best Of .... (MCA)
Boogie Woogie Bugle Girls .... (MCA)
Capitol Collectors Series .... (CAP)
Professor Longhair; *Last Mardi Gras* .... (ATL)
Mardi Gras In Baton Rouge .... (RHI)
Salt Peanuts
Bud Powell; *Bluebird Sampler* .... (BLU)
Bud Powell Trio; *Time Was* .... (BLU)
Dizzy Gillespie; *Greatest Jazz Concert Ever* ...... (PRS)
In The Beginning .... (PRS)
Jazz At Massey Hall .... (FAN)
Jazz Trumpet-#2-Modern Time .... (PRS)
King Of Be-Bop ....(EVR)

The Green Book Of Songs By Subject — Page 253

Sam-The Hot Dog Man
Lil Johnson; *Raunchy Business-Hot Nuts &
Lollypops* ....(COL)
Sarah Cynthia Sylvia Stout
Shel Silverstein; *Dr. Demento 20th Anniversary
Collection* .... (RHI)
   Dr. Demento's Greatest Novelty-#4-1970s ...... (RHI)
   Where The Sidewalk Ends ....(COL)
Sashimi
101 North; *101 North* ....(CAP)
Sassafras Roots
Green Day; *Dookie* .... (RPR)
Saturday Night Fish Fry Drag
Joe Robichaux/New Orleans Boys; *Joe Robichaux/New
Orleans Boys-1933* .... (FLK)
Savoy Truffle
Beatles; *Box Set* ....(CAP)
   White Album ....(CAP)
Scarborough Fair
Simon & Garfunkel; *Collected Works* ....(COL)
   Concert In Central Park ....(WB)
   Greatest Hits ....(COL)
   Parsley Sage Rosemary & Thyme ....(COL)
   ST/The Graduate ....(COL)
Scottish Tea
Ted Nugent/Amboy Dukes; *Greatest Collection
Ever* ....(DHL)
Scrambled Eggs
Sandy Austin; *Cajun Music-Early '50s* .... (ARH)
Second Sitting For The Last Supper
10 CC; *Live & Let Live* .... (MER)
Shanghai Noodle Factory
Traffic; *Last Exit* .... (ISL)
She Kept Chewing Gum
Donald Jacob; *Zydeco Blues 'N' Boogie* ....(RYK)
Shortenin' Bread
Andrews Sisters; *50th Anniversary Collection-#2* (MCA)
Sam McNeil/Dent Wimmer/Others; *Old
Originals-#2* .... (ROU)
Sonny Terry; *Folkways Years-1944-1963* ...... (FLW)
Skin & Bone
Kinks; *Celluloid Heroes* ....(RCA)
   Everybody's In Show Biz .... (RHI)
   Greatest ....(RCA)
   Muswell Hillbillies .... (RHI)
Soup For One
Chic; *Dance Dance Dance-Best Of* .... (ATL)
Soup Of The Day
Chris Rea; *espresso logic* ....(EW)
Spider In My Stew
Buster Benton; *Spider In My Stew* .... (RON)
Standing Knee Deep In A River
Kathy Mattea; *Lonesome Standard Time* .... (MER)
Struttin' With Some Barbecue
Louis Armstrong; *Greatest Hits* ....(COL)
   Of New Orleans .... (MCA)
Newport Jazz Festival All-Stars; *Newport Jazz Festival
All-Stars* .... (CCJ)
Teddy Buckner; *Salute To Louis Armstrong* ...... (CRS)
St. Alphonzo's Pancake Breakfast
Frank Zappa; *Apostrophe/Overnite Sensation* .....(RYK)
Sukiyaki
Kyu Sakamoto; *When AM Was King* ....(CAP)
Taste Of Honey; *Golden Honey* ....(CAP)
   Twice As Sweet ....(CAP)
Sunnyside Up
Teresa Brewer/World's Greatest Jazz Band; *Good
News* .... (DOC)
Sunshine, Lollipops & Rainbows
Lesley Gore; *Anthology* ....(RHI)
   Golden Hits Of .... (MER)
Supper Time
Barbra Streisand; *People* ....(COL)
Ella Fitzgerald; *Irving Berlin Songbook-#2* ....(VRV)
Johnny Cash; *Classic Cash-Hall Of Fame Series* . (MER)
Nancy Wilson; *But Beautiful* .... (BLN)
Suppertime
Original Cast; *Little Shop Of Horrors* ....(GEF)
   You're A Good Man Charlie Brown ....(POL)
Supper's Ready
Genesis; *Seconds Out* .... (ATL)
Sushi Girl
Tubes; *Best Of* ....(CAP)
   Completion Backward Principle ....(CAP)

Swallow The Sun
Love Exchange; *Nuggets-#10-Folk Rock* .... (RHI)
Swamp Sauce
Albert Collins; *Complete Imperial Recordings* ..... (EMI)
Swedish Meatball
Steve Lyon; *There's No Place Like Mars* ....(FF)
Swedish Pastry
Bill Evans; *Time Remembered* ....(MS)
Bill Evans Trio; *At Shelly's Manne-Hole* ....(RVR)
Bud Powell; *Time Was* ....(BLU)
Sweet As Bear Meat
Johnny Hodges Orchestra; *Used To Be Duke* .....(VRV)
Sweet Gingerbread Man
Mike Curb Congregation; *Greatest Hits* ....(CCB)
Sweet Kentucky Ham
David Frishberg; *Can't Take You Nowhere* ....(FAN)
   Classics .... (CCJ)
Sweet Potato Pie
Al Jarreau; *We Got By* .... (RPR)
James Taylor; *Never Die Young* ....(COL)
Sweet Potatoe Pie
Domino; *Domino* .... (OUT)
Sweeter Than Chocolate
Burning Spear; *World Should Know* ....(HRT)
Sweets For My Sweet
Drifters; *1959-1965-All-Time Greatest Hits &
More* .... (ATL)
   Very Best Of .... (RHI)
Switchin' In The Kitchen
Big Joe Turner; *Rides Again-Jazzlore-#39* .... (ATL)
Taco Grande
Weird Al Yankovic; *Food Album* ....(RAR)
   Off The Deep End ....(SCO)
Taco Stand
Normaltown Flyers; *Normaltown Flyers* .... (MER)
Taco Wagon
Dale, Dick/Del-Tones; *King Of The Surf Guitar-Best
Of* .... (RHI)
Young Fresh Fellows; *This One's For The Ladies* . (FRN)
Tacos
Mongo Santamaria; *Skins* .... (MS)
Take Me Out To The Ball Game
Bruce Springstone; *Baseball's Greatest Hits* .... (RHI)
Doc & Merle Watson; *Baseball's Greatest Hits* ... (RHI)
Frank Zappa; *You Can't Do That On Stage
Anymore-#4* ....(RYK)
Tall Drink Of Water
Barbara Mandrell; *Best Of* ....(LIB)
Matraca Berg; *Speed Of Grace* ....(RCA)
Mel Tillis; *Best Of Branson U.S.A.-#2* ....(CCB)
   Greatest Hits ....(CCB)
Tapioca Tundra
Monkees; *Listen To The Band* .... (RHI)
Taste Of Bitter Love
Gladys Knight/Pips; *Best Of-Columbia Years* ....(COL)
Taste Of Chocolate
Big Daddy Kane; *Taste Of Chocolate* ....(CLD)
Tastes Just Like Chicken
Scatterbrain; *Scamboogery* ....(ELE)
Teddy Bears' Picnic
Anne Murray; *There's A Hippo In My Tub* ....(LIB)
Frank DeVol; *Small Fry-Capitol Sings Kids Songs* (CAP)
Tennessee Fish Fry
Helen O'Connell; *Uncollected With Irv Orton's
Orchestra* .... (HIN)
Texas Cookin'
Guy Clark; *Greatest Hits* ....(RCA)
G.Clark/R.Crowell/E.Harris/J.J. Walker; *Texas
Cookin'* ....(SH)
Texas Stew
Louis Jordan/Tympani Five; *Rock 'N Roll Call* ... (BLU)
Thanks For The Pepperoni
George Harrison; *All Things Must Pass* ....(CAP)
Them Belly Full
Bob Marley/Wailers; *Live* ....(TUF)
   Natty Dread ....(TUF)
   Rebel Music ....(TUF)
Theme From "Picnic"
Chet Atkins; *Pickin' My Way-In Hollywood
Alone* .... (MOB)
They Call Me The Popcorn Man
Luther Johnson; *Lonesome In My Bedroom* ....(EVD)

Thing That Only Eats Hippies
Dead Milkmen; *Eat Your Paisley* .... (RES)
Enigma Variations-#2 .... (ENC)
Tijuana Sauerkraut
Herb Alpert/Tijuana Brass; *Lonely Bull* .... (A&M)
Too Much Barbeque
Big Twist/Mellow Fellows; *Live From Chicago-Bigger Than Life* .... (ALG)
Top Hat Bar & Grille
Jim Croce; *50th Anniversary Collection* .... (SAJ)
Tortillas & Beans
Stan Kenton; *Lighter Side* .... (CW)
Trombone Butter
Dinah Washington; *Bessie Smith Songbook* ...... (EMA)
TV Dinners
ZZ Top; *Eliminator* .... (WB)
Two Minutes Till Lunch
Wall Of Voodoo; *Dark Continent* .... (A&M)
Two Triple Cheese, Side Order Of Fries
Commander Cody/Lost Planet Airmen; *Aces High* .... (RLX)
Veal Chop & Pork Chop
Blind Snooks Eaglin; *Country Boy In New Orleans* .... (ARH)
Venom Soup
Ted Nugent; *Weekend Warriors* .... (EPI)
Waldo's Discount Donuts
Red Knuckles/Trailblazers; *Hot Rize Presents* ...... (FF)
We Are Hungry Men
David Bowie; *London Collection* .... (LON)
Starting Point .... (DER)
Wedding Cake
Jeannie C. Riley; *Things Go Better With Love* .... (PLN)
When Bacon Was Scarce/Ryestraw
Red Clay Ramblers; *Twisted Laurel* .... (FF)
When Did We Have Sauerkraut?
Lou & Peter Berryman; *So Comfortable* .... (COR)
When The Cookie Jar Is Empty
Michael Franks; *Burchfield Nines* .... (WB)
Who Threw The Overalls In Mrs....
Bing Crosby; *Shillelaghs & Shamrocks* .... (MCA)
Wild Honey
Beach Boys; *Absolute Best-#2* .... (CAP)
Party!!/Stack-O-Tracks .... (CAP)
Smiley Smile/Wild Honey .... (CAP)
Wild Honey Pie
Beatles; *Box Set* .... (CAP)
White Album .... (CAP)
Wild Mountain Honey
Steve Miller Band; *Fly Like An Eagle* .... (CAP)
Greatest Hits-1974-1978 .... (CAP)
Wild Mountain Thyme
Armstrong Family; *Wheel Of The Year-Thirty Years With* .... (FF)
Byrds; *Fifth Dimension* .... (COL)
Joan Baez; *Farewell Angelina* .... (VAN)
Wild Rice
Lee Ritenour; *Best Of* .... (EPI)
First Course .... (EPI)
Worst Pies In London
Original Cast; *Sweeney Todd* .... (RCA)

FOOLS

See Also: INSULTS

Any Other Fool
Sadao Watanabe & Patti Austin; *Front Seat* ..... (ELE)
April Fool
Eric Dolphy; *Here & There* .... (PRS)
Pete Townshend & Ronnie Lane; *Rough Mix* .... (ATC)
Soul Asylum; *Grave Dancers Union* .... (COL)
April Fools
Aretha Franklin; *Young Gifted & Black* .... (MGM)
Dionne Warwick; *Anthology 1962-1971* .... (RHI)
Earl Klugh; *Living Inside Your Love* .... (EMI)
April Fool's Day Morn
Loudon Wainwright III; *Career Moves* .... (VIA)
Fame & Wealth .... (ROU)
April's Fool
Mark Chesnutt; *Almost Goodbye* .... (MCA)
Ray Price; *Greatest Hits-#4* .... (STE)
Tracy Lawrence; *Sticks & Stones* .... (ATL)

Arms Of A Fool
Mel Tillis; *Best Of* .... (MGM)
Brand New Mister Me .... (POL)
Be Young, Be Foolish, Be Happy
Tams; *45* .... (MCA)
45 .... (RLL)
Born A Fool
Freddie Hart; *Best Of* .... (MCA)
Broadway Fools
Branford Marsalis; *Random Abstract* .... (COL)
Card Carrying Fool
Randy Travis; *No Holdin' Back* .... (WB)
ST/Pink Cadillac .... (WB)
Certain Kind Of Fool
Eagles; *Desperado* .... (ASY)
Chain Of Fools
Aretha Franklin; *Aretha's Gold* .... (ATL)
Atlantic R&B 1947-1974-#6 .... (ATL)
Best Of .... (ATL)
Gold .... (ATL)
Greatest Hits .... (ATL)
Lady Of Soul .... (ATL)
Clint Black & Pointer Sisters; *Rhythm Country & Blues* .... (MCA)
Dancin' Fool
Frank Zappa; *Sheik Yerbouti* .... (ZAP)
Guess Who; *Greatest Of* .... (RCA)
Don't Be A Fool
Del Vikings; *Del Vikings* .... (CLT)
Loose Ends; *Look How Long* .... (MCA)
Don't Want To Be A Fool
Luther Vandross; *Power Of Love* .... (EPI)
Emperor's New Clothes
Sinead O'Connor; *I Do Not Want What I Haven't Got* .... (ENS)
Every Time Two Fools Collide
Kenny Rogers & Dottie West; *Every Time Two Fools Collide* .... (EMI)
Kenny Rogers' Greatest Hits .... (EMI)
Everybody Is Somebody's Fool
Heartbreakers; *45* .... (RLL)
Everybody Plays The Fool
Aaron Neville; *Warm Your Heart* .... (A&M)
Main Ingredient; *Golden Classics* .... (CLT)
Nipper's Greatest Hits-'70s .... (RCA)
Everybody's Somebody's Fool
Betty Carter; *'Round Midnight* .... (ATL)
Connie Francis; *Very Best Of* .... (POL)
Debby Boone; *Best Of* .... (CCB)
Find Another Fool
Quarterflash; *Quarterflash* .... (GEF)
Fool
38 Special; *Special Delivery* .... (A&M)
BoDeans; *Outside Looking In* .... (SLS)
Elvis Presley; *Golden Celebration* .... (RCA)
Quicksilver Messenger Service; *Anthology* .... (CAP)
Quicksilver Messenger Service .... (CAP)
Sons Of Mercury .... (RHI)
Sanford Clark; *Billboard Top Rock 'N' Roll Hits-1956* .... (RHI)
Original Classic Oldies/'50s-'60s-#17 .... (MCA)
Fool About A Cigarette
Tom Ball/Kenny Sultan; *Bloodshot Eyes* .... (FF)
Fool Button
Jimmy Buffett; *Son Of A Son Of A Sailor* .... (MCA)
Fool By Your Side
David Rowland & Sugar; *Pleasure* .... (ELE)
Fool For A Cigarette
Ry Cooder; *Paradise & Lunch* .... (RPR)
Fool For The City
Foghat; *Best Of* .... (RHI)
Best Of Hard Rock-#1 .... (MSP)
Fool For The City .... (RHI)
Live .... (RHI)
Fool For You
James Taylor; *One Man Dog* .... (WB)
Neil Diamond; *Heartlight* .... (COL)
Ray Charles; *Atlantic R&B 1947-1974-#2* .... (ATL)
Live .... (ATL)
Rod Stewart; *Night On The Town* .... (WB)
Rude Boys; *Rude Awakening* .... (ATL)
Fool For Your Love
Mickey Gilley; *19 Hot Country Requests* .... (EPI)
Fool For Your Love .... (EPI)

FOOLS — FOOLS

Fool For Your Loving
  Whitesnake; *Live...In The Heart Of The City* ..... (GEF)
  Slip Of The Tongue .... (GEF)
Fool For Your Stockings
  ZZ Top; *Deguello* .... (WB)
Fool Hearted Memory
  George Strait; *Greatest Hits* .... (MCA)
  Night Game .... (MCA)
  Strait From The Heart .... (MCA)
Fool In Love
  Etta James; *Sticking To My Guns* .... (ISL)
  Ike & Tina Turner; *Best Of* .... (EMI)
  Best Of Sue Records .... (CLT)
  Proud Mary-Best Of .... (EMI)
  Michael Smotherman; *ST/Always* .... (MCA)
  Robins; *Best Of* .... (CRS)
Fool In Love With You
  Jim Photoglo; *45* .... (20)
Fool In The Rain
  Led Zeppelin; *In Through The Out Door* .... (SS)
  Led Zeppelin (collection) .... (ATL)
Fool On The Hill
  Beatles; *1967-1970* .... (CAP)
  Box Set .... (CAP)
  Magical Mystery Tour .... (CAP)
Fool Such As I
  Baillie & The Boys; *Lights Of Home* ....(RCA)
  Elvis Presley; *Elvis Aron* ....(RCA)
  Legendary Performer-#1 ....(RCA)
  Worldwide 50 Gold Hits-#1 ....(RCA)
Fool To Cry
  Rolling Stones; *Black & Blue* .... (RS)
  Rewind (1971-1984) .... (RS)
  Sucking In The Seventies .... (RS)
Fool With My Money
  Special Forces; *Special Forces* .... (ERC)
Fool Yourself
  Bonnie Raitt; *Home Plate* .... (WB)
  Little Feat; *Dixie Chicken* .... (WB)
Fool & His Money
  Wang Chung; *Mosaic* .... (GEF)
Fool #1
  Brenda Lee; *Story-Greatest Hits* .... (MCA)
  Uniques; *Golden Hits* .... (PLA)
Fool (If You Think It's Over)
  Chris Rea; *New Light Through Old Windows* ..... (ATL)
  Whatever Happened To Benny Santini .... (UA)
Fooled Again
  Tom Petty/Heartbreakers; *Tom
  Petty/Heartbreakers* .... (MCA)
Fooled Around & Fell In Love
  Elvin Bishop; *Billboard Top Hits-1976* .... (RHI)
  South's Greatest Hits .... (CPC)
  Struttin' My Stuff .... (CPC)
Fooled By A Feeling
  Barbara Mandrell; *Just For The Record* .... (MCA)
Fooling Yourself
  Styx; *Caught In The Act* .... (A&M)
  Classics-#15 .... (A&M)
  Grand Illusion .... (A&M)
Foolin'
  Def Leppard; *Pyromania* .... (MER)
  Johnny Rodriguez; *19 Hot Country Requests-#2* ... (EPI)
Foolin' Around
  Patsy Cline; *Always* .... (MCA)
  Story .... (MCA)
  ST/Sweet Dreams .... (MCA)
Foolish Beat
  Debbie Gibson; *Hit Singles 1980-1988* .... (ATL)
  Out Of The Blue .... (ATL)
Foolish Heart
  Grateful Dead; *Built To Last* .... (ARI)
  Sharon Bryant; *Here I Am* .... (WIN)
  Steve Perry; *Street Talk* .... (COL)
Foolish Little Girl
  Shirelles; *16 Greatest Hits* .... (TRP)
  Anthology-1959-1964 .... (RHI)
  Greatest Hits .... (EVR)
Foolish Pride
  Daryl Hall; *Three Hearts In The Happy Ending
  Machine* ....(RCA)
  Joan Armatrading; *The Key* .... (A&M)
  Travis Tritt; *Ten Feet Tall And Bulletproof* .... (WB)

Fools
  Van Halen; *Women & Children First* .... (WB)
Fools Fall In Love
  Drifters; *Atlantic R&B 1947-1974-#3* .... (ATL)
  ST/Book Of Love .... (ATL)
  Their Greatest Recordings ....(ATC)
  Jacky Ward; *Best Of* .... (MER)
  Lover's Question .... (MER)
Fools Gold
  Stone Roses; *Stone Roses* .... (SIL)
Fools In Love
  Joe Jackson; *Live...1980-1986* .... (A&M)
  Look Sharp .... (A&M)
Fools Like Me
  Jerry Lee Lewis; *Golden Rock Hits Of* .... (SMA)
  Original .... (SUN)
  Original Golden Hits-#2 .... (SUN)
Fools Rush In
  Brook Benton; *Super Oldies/'60s-#10* ....(AUF)
  Frank Sinatra/Tommy Dorsey Orchestra;
  Sessions-#1 ....(RCA)
Fool's Gold
  Graham Parker; *Pourin' It All Out: Mercury
  Years* .... (MER)
  Graham Parker/Rumour; *Heat Treatment* .... (MER)
  Parkerilla .... (MER)
  Lee Greenwood; *Greatest Hits* .... (MCA)
  You've Got A Good Love Comin' .... (MCA)
  Poco; *Crazy Eyes* .... (EPI)
  Ride The Country .... (EPI)
  Very Best Of .... (EPI)
  Thin Lizzy; *Johnny The Fox* .... (WB)
Fool's Hall Of Fame
  Johnny Cash; *Man-The World-His Music* .... (SUN)
  Rough Cut King Of Country Music .... (SUN)
  Roy Orbison; *Sun Years* .... (RHI)
Fool's Overture
  Supertramp; *Even In The Quietest Moments* ..... (A&M)
  Paris .... (A&M)
Give This Fool Another Try
  Charlie Daniels Band; *Whisky* .... (EPI)
Heartaches Of A Fool
  Willie Nelson; *Greatest Hits & Some That Will Be* (COL)
Heaven Help The Fool
  Bob Weir; *Heaven Help The Fool* .... (ARI)
He's A Fool For You
  Boz Scaggs; *My Time* ....(COL)
Honky Tonky Fool
  Doug Supernaw; *Red & Rio Grande* ....(BNA)
How Do The Fools Survive
  Doobie Brothers; *Minute By Minute* .... (WB)
I Was A Fool To Care
  James Taylor; *Gorilla* .... (WB)
If You Gotta Make A Fool Of Somebody
  Aretha Franklin; *Soul '69* .... (RHI)
  Bonnie Raitt; *Give It Up* .... (WB)
  Eddie Floyd; *Knock On Wood* .... (ATL)
  Huey Lewis/News; *Four Chords & Several Years
  Ago* .... (ELE)
  James Ray; *Golden Classics* .... (CLT)
  Lou Rawls; *It's Supposed To Be Fun* .... (BLN)
  Maxine Brown; *Golden Classics* .... (CLT)
Kansas You Fooler
  Ozark Mountain Daredevils; *It'll Shine When It
  Shines* .... (A&M)
Kissing A Fool
  George Michael; *Faith* ....(COL)
Love's Made A Fool Of You
  Bobby Fuller Four; *Best Of* .... (RHI)
  Buddy Holly; *Rock & Roll Collection* .... (MCA)
  Greg Kihn; *Again* .... (BES)
Mama's Fool
  Tesla; *Bust A Nut* .... (GEF)
Married Man's A Fool
  Blind Willie McTell; *Last Session* .... (PRS)
  Ry Cooder; *Paradise & Lunch* .... (RPR)
Maybe I'm A Fool
  Aretha Franklin; *Sings The Blues* ....(COL)
  Eddie Money; *Life For The Taking* ....(COL)
My Foolish Heart
  Bill Evans; *Waltz For Debby* ....(RVR)
  Carmen McRae; *Live At Bubba's* ....(WHO)
  John McLaughlin; *Electric Guitarist* ....(COL)
  Liz Story; *My Foolish Heart* .... (WH)

Roberta Flack; *Set The Night To Music* .... (ATL)
Stephane Grappelli; *Stephanova* .... (CCJ)
Tony Bennett & Bill Evans; *Album* .... (FAN)
Never Gonna Be Your Fool Again
Lisa Brokop; *Every Little Girl's Dream* .... (PAT)
New Fool At An Old Game
Reba McEntire; *Country's Greatest Hits-#4-Sweet
Country* .... (PRY)
Live .... (MCA)
Reba .... (MCA)
Nobody But A Fool (Would Love You)
Connie Smith; *Best Of* .... (DOM)
Nobody Falls Like A Fool
Earl Thomas Conley; *Greatest Hits* .... (RCA)
Nobody Falls Like A Fool .... (RCA)
Nobody's Fool
Cinderella; *Night Songs* .... (MER)
Kenny Loggins; *Back To Avalon* .... (COL)
ST/Caddyshack II .... (COL)
Poco; *Pickin' Up The Pieces* .... (EPI)
October Fool
Charlie Shoemaker & Bill Holman; *Collaboration* (PAU)
Oh Me, Oh My (I'm A Fool For You Baby)
Aretha Franklin; *30 Greatest Hits* .... (ATL)
Buster Poindexter; *Buster Poindexter* ....(RCA)
Irma Thomas; *Simply The Best-Live* .... (ROU)
Lulu; *Super Hits/'70s-Have A Nice Day-#6* .... (RHI)
One Of A Kind Pair Of Fools
Barbara Mandrell; *Greatest Country Hits* ....(CCB)
Greatest Hits .... (MCA)
Spun Gold .... (MCA)
Poor Damned Fool
Harry Chapin; *Legends Of The Lost & Found* .... (ELE)
Living Room Suite .... (ELE)
Poor Fool
Ike & Tina Turner; *Golden Classics* ....(CLT)
Greatest Hits ....(CCB)
Proud Mary-Best Of .... (EMI)
Poor Little Fool
Rick Nelson; *Best Of* .... (EMI)
EMI Legends Of Rock 'N' Roll-24 Greatest ...... (EMI)
Legendary Masters .... (EMI)
Live In '85 .... (RHI)
Reckless
Alabama; *American Pride* ....(RCA)
Sentimental Fool
Roxy Music; *Siren* .... (RPR)
She's A Fool
Lesley Gore; *Anthology* .... (RHI)
Golden Hits Of .... (MER)
Ship Of Fools
Bob Seger; *Night Moves* .... (CAP)
Doors; *Morrison Hotel* .... (ELE)
Weird Scenes Inside The Goldmine .... (ELE)
Elvis Costello; *Deadicated* .... (ARI)
Garland Jeffreys; *American Boy & Girl* .... (A&M)
Grateful Dead; *From The Mars Hotel* .... (GRD)
Steal Your Face .... (GRD)
Robert Plant; *Now & Zen* .... (EPR)
World Party; *Greenpeace/Rainbow Warriors* ...... (GEF)
Private Revolution .... (ENS)
Silly Love Songs
Paul McCartney; *Give My Regards To Broad
Street* .... (CAP)
Paul McCartney/Wings; *All The Best* .... (CAP)
Wings Greatest .... (CAP)
Wings Over America .... (CAP)
Wings; *At The Speed Of Sound* .... (CAP)
Some Fools Never Learn
Steve Wariner; *Greatest Hits* .... (MCA)
One Good Night Deserves Another .... (MCA)
Statue Of A Fool
Jack Greene; *Country Hits* ....(EXA)
Greatest Hits .... (GUS)
MCA 30 Years Of Hits-1958-1988 .... (MCA)
Sings His Best .... (SO)
Ricky Van Shelton; *Greatest Hits Plus* ....(COL)
RVS III ....(COL)
Sunday Morning Fool
Michael Dinner; *Great Pretenders* .... (FAN)
Tears Are Just For Fools
Starlites; *Harlem Holiday-N.Y. Rhythm &
Blues-#7* ....(CLT)

Ten Feet Tall And Bulletproof
Travis Tritt; *Ten Feet Tall And Bulletproof* .... (WB)
"The Three Stooges" Theme
Original Music; *Television's Greatest Hits-#2* ..... (TVT)
These Foolish Things (Remind Me Of You)
Aaron Neville; *The Grand Tour* .... (A&M)
Art Pepper; *Today* ....(GAL)
Benny Goodman; *Stompin' At The Savoy* .... (BLU)
Billie Holiday; *16 Most Requested Songs* .... (COL)
Bobby Watson; *This Little Light Of Mine* .... (RDD)
Boston Pops Orchestra/Arthur Fiedler; *Popular Favorites
By* .... (PRR)
Bryan Ferry; *Street Life-20 Great Hits* .... (RPR)
These Foolish Things .... (RPR)
Chet Baker; *Baker's Holiday* .... (VRV)
Somewhere Over The Rainbow .... (BLU)
Count Basie Jam; *Montreux '77* .... (PAB)
Dave Brubeck; *Greatest Hits From The Fantasy
Years* .... (FAN)
Dinah Washington; *In Love* .... (RLL)
Frank Sinatra; *Point Of No Return* ....(CAP)
Nat King Cole; *Just One Of Those Things (&
More)* .... (CAP)
Ronnie Milsap; *True Believer* .... (LIB)
Ruby Braff; *Jazz-Club Mainstream-Trumpet* ...... (VRV)
Stan Getz; *Essential-Getz Songbook* .... (VRV)
Third Time Lucky
Foghat; *Best Of* .... (RHI)
Boogie Motel .... (RHI)
Thoughts Of A Fool
George Strait; *ST/Pure Country* .... (MCA)
Toast To The Fool
Dramatics; *Best Of* .... (STX)
Dramatically Yours .... (STX)
Live .... (STX)
Today's Lonely Fool
Tracy Lawrence; *Sticks & Stones* .... (ATL)
Trying To Make A Fool Of Me
Delfonics; *Best Of* .... (ARI)
Golden Classics ....(CLT)
Victim Or A Fool
Rodney Crowell; *Collection* .... (WB)
What A Fool Believes
Doobie Brothers; *Best Of-#2* .... (WB)
Minute By Minute .... (WB)
Kenny Loggins; *Alive* .... (COL)
Nightwatch ....(COL)
What Kind Of Fool
Barbra Streisand; *Collection-Greatest Hits & More* (COL)
One Voice ....(COL)
Barbra Streisand & Barry Gibb; *Guilty* ....(COL)
Lionel Cartwright; *Chasin' The Sun* .... (MCA)
What Kind Of Fool Am I
Bill Evans; *Solo Sessions-#1* .... (MS)
Marvin Gaye; *Hello Broadway* .... (MOT)
Original Broadway Cast; *Stop The World-I Want To Get
Off* .... (POL)
Rick Springfield; *Greatest Hits* ....(RCA)
Success Hasn't Spoiled Me Yet ....(RCA)
Robert Goulet; *16 Most Requested Songs* .... (COL)
Greatest Hits ....(COL)
Sammy Davis, Jr.; *Greatest Songs* ....(CCB)
What Kind Of Fool Do You Think I Am
Bill Deal/Rhondels; *Frat Rock-#2* .... (RHI)
Oldies But Goodies-#15 .... (OSR)
Lee Roy Parnell; *Love Without Mercy* .... (ARI)
Who But A Fool (Thief In Paradise)
Bonnie Raitt; *Nine Lives* .... (WB)
Why Am I A Fool For You
Jarmels; *14 Golden Classics* ....(CLT)
Why Do Fools Fall In Love
Beach Boys; *Spirit Of America* ....(CAP)
Diana Ross; *Why Do Fools Fall In Love* ....(RCA)
Frankie Lymon/Teenagers; *Best Of* .... (RHI)
Billboard Top Rock 'N' Roll Hits-1956 .... (RHI)
ST/American Graffiti .... (\CA)
Joni Mitchell; *Shadows & Light* .... (ASY)
Will Not Be Your Fool
David Bromberg Band; *How Late'll Ya Play Til* . (FAN)
Won't Get Fooled Again
Van Halen; *Live: Right Here Right Now* .... (WB)

Who; *Greatest Hits* .... (MCA)
ST/Kids Are Alright .... (MCA)
Who's Better Who's Best-Very Best Of .... (MCA)
Who's Last .... (MCA)
Who's Next .... (MCA)
You Can't Fool The Fat Man
Randy Newman; *Little Criminals* .... (WB)
You've Been In Love Too Long
Bonnie Raitt; *Takin' My Time* .... (WB)
Martha Reeves/Vandellas; *Anthology* .... (MOT)
Greatest Hits .... (MOT)

FOOTBALL

See Also: CITIES, FIGHT, SCHOOL, SPORTS,
STATES

Across The Field
Ohio State University Marching Band; *Pride Of The*
Buckeyes ....(FID)
All Alone In The End Zone
Jay Ferguson; *All Alone In The End Zone* .... (ASY)
Armchair Quarterback
Ray Stevens; *I Have Returned* .... (MCA)
Backfield In Motion
Mel & Tim; *Collectables Presents-History Of*
Rock-#4 ....(CLT)
Oldies/Goodies-#2 ....(OSR)
Soul Shots-#2 .... (RHI)
Super Oldies/'60s-#10 ....(AUF)
Bear Down, Chicago Bears
Chicago Symphony Orchestra & Chorus; *12"* ....(LON)
Dallas Cowboys
Charley Pride; *45* ....(RCA)
Down The Field
University Of Michigan Band; *Touchdown,*
U.S.A. .... (VAN)
Drop Kick Me Jesus (Through The Goal...)
Bobby Bare; *45* ....(OOP)
Fight The Team Across The Field
Ohio State University Marching Band; *Across The*
Field ....(FID)
Football Card
Glenn Sutton; *Close Encounters Of The Sutton*
Kind .... (MER)
Go U Northwestern
Northwestern University Marching Band; *Go U*
Northwestern ....(FID)
God's Footballer
Billy Bragg; *Don't Try This At Home* .... (ELE)
Hail Purdue
University Of Michigan Band; *Greatest College Football*
Marches .... (VAN)
Homecoming '63
Keith Whitley; *L.A. To Miami* ....(RCA)
Iowa Fight Song
University Of Iowa Band; *Go Hawkeyes Go* ......(FID)
University Of Michigan Band; *Greatest College Football*
Marches .... (VAN)
Minnesota Rouser
Ohio State University Marching Band; *Stadium Favorites*
In Brass ....(FID)
Mister Touchdown U.S.A.
University Of Michigan Band; *Greatest College Football*
Marches .... (VAN)
Monday Morning Quarterback
Frank Sinatra; *She Shot Me Down* ....(RPR)
Monday Night Football & Me
Turner Rice; *45* ....(BNG)
Moving The Goalposts
Billy Bragg; *Don't Try This At Home* .... (ELE)
M.S.U. Fight Song
Michigan State University Band; *Michigan State*
University Band ....(FID)
Notre Dame Victory March
University Of Notre Dame Band; *Songs Of The Fighting*
Irish ....(FID)
On Brave Old Army Team
All-Star Inter-Conference Band; *College Marches At*
Halftime .... (ALS)
Pass The Football
Original Broadway Cast; *Wonderful Town* ....(COL)
Wonderful Town ....(MCA)

Pride Of The Illini
University Of Michigan Band; *Greatest College Football*
Marches .... (VAN)
Princeton Cannon Song
University Of Michigan Band; *Greatest College Football*
Marches .... (VAN)
Roll On, Tulane
Michigan University Band; *Kick Off, U.S.A.* ..... (VAN)
Sing U.C.L.A.
University Of Michigan Band; *Greatest College Football*
Marches .... (VAN)
Super Bowl Shuffle
Chicago Bears Shufflin' Crew; *45* ....(RED)
Touchdown Raiders
Santana; *Beyond Appearances* ....(COL)
Wide Receiver
Michael Henderson; *45* ....(BUD)
Words By Heart
Billy Ray Cyrus; *It Won't Be The Last* .... (MER)
Yale Boola
All-Star Inter-Conference Band; *College Marches At*
Half-Time .... (ALS)
You've Got To Be A Football Hero
University Of Michigan Band; *Greatest College Football*
Marches .... (VAN)

FREEDOM

See Also: COUNTRIES: AMERICA, MONTHS:
JULY, PRISON, PROTEST, ROYALTY

2000 Blacks Got To Be Free
Fela Anikulapo Kuti & Roy Ayers; *Music Of Many*
Colours ....(CEL)
Abolitionist Hymn
Hermes Nye; *Ballads Of The Civil War-#1 & 2* . (FLW)
All I Want
Joni Mitchell; *Blue* ....(RPR)
Miles Of Aisles ....(ASY)
Almost Independence Day
Van Morrison; *St. Dominic's Preview* .... (WB)
Any Which Way...Freedom
Mutabaruka; *Any Which Way...Freedom* .... (SHA)
Anything Goes
Count Basie & Tony Bennett; *Basie Swings Bennett*
Sings ....(RLL)
Anything Goes-Capitol Sings Cole Porter ....(CAP)
Dionne Warwick; *Sings Cole Porter* ...... (ARI)
Ella Fitzgerald; *Night & Day-Cole Porter*
Songbook ....(VRV)
Frank Sinatra; *Sings The Select Cole Porter* ....(CAP)
Mary Martin; *16 Most Requested Songs* ....(COL)
Yo-Yo Ma; *Anything Goes-Music Of Cole Porter* .(COL)
Army Of The Free
Tennessee Ernie Ford; *Sings Songs Of The Civil*
War ....(CAP)
Asylum
Supertramp; *Crime Of The Century* .... (A&M)
Paris .... (A&M)
Battle Cry Of Freedom
Mormon Tabernacle Choir; *Album* ....(COL)
God Bless America ....(COL)
Greatest Hits ....(COL)
Songs Of The North & South 1861-1965 ....(COL)
Be Free
Loggins & Messina; *Best Of-Friends* ....(COL)
Finale ....(COL)
Mother Lode ....(COL)
Born Free
Andy Williams; *16 Most Requested Songs* ....(COL)
Greatest Hits ....(COL)
John Barry; *Film Music Of* ....(COL)
Matt Monro; *ST/Born Free* ....(MGM)
Roger Williams; *Best Of* ....(MCA)
Golden Hits ....(MCA)
Break Away
Art Garfunkel; *Break Away* ....(COL)
Garfunkel ....(COL)
Beach Boys; *Absolute Best-#2* ....(CAP)
Friends/20/20 ....(CAP)
Gift Set ....(CAP)
Spirit Of America ....(CAP)

Gail Davies; *ST/Sylvester* ....(RCA)
  Where Is A Woman To Go ....(RCA)
Neville Brothers; *Treacherous Too!-History Of-#2 1955-1987* .... (RHI)
Nick Lowe; *Basher: Best Of* ....(COL)
Break On Through (To The Other Side)
Doors; *Best Of* ....(ELE)
  Doors ....(ELE)
  Greatest Hits ....(ELE)
  Live ....(ELE)
  ST/Forrest Gump ....(EPX)
  ST/Doors ....(ELE)
  Weird Scenes Inside The Gold Mine ....(ELE)
Breakaway
ZZ Top; *Antenna* ....(RCA)
Butterfly (I'll Set You Free)
Perry Como; *Today* ....(RCA)
Cactus Tree
Joni Mitchell; *Joni Mitchell* ....(RPR)
  Miles Of Aisles ....(ASY)
Cage Of Freedom
Jon Anderson; *ST/Metropolis* ....(COL)
Chimes Of Freedom
Bob Dylan; *Another Side Of* ....(COL)
Bruce Springsteen; *Chimes Of Freedom* ....(COL)
Byrds; *Byrds* ....(COL)
  Greatest Hits ....(COL)
Closer To Free
Bodeans; *Go Down Slow* ....(SLS)
Cry For Freedom
White Lion; *Big Game* ....(ATL)
Cut Loose
Chrome Molly; *Angst* ....(IRS)
Paul Rodgers; *45* ....(ATL)
Do Anthing
Natural Selection; *S* ....(ATC)
Do Anything
Natural Selection; *Natural Selection* ....(EW)
Do What You Want, Be What You Are
Daryl Hall & John Oates; *Bigger Than Both Of Us* ....(RCA)
  Livetime ....(RCA)
Everybody's Talkin'
Nilsson; *ST/Forrest Gump* ....(EPX)
  ST/Midnight Cowboy ....(EMI)
  TT & Other Hits ....(RCA)
Willie Nelson; *Best Of Willie* ....(RCA)
  Sweet Memories ....(RCA)
Fancy Free
Oak Ridge Boys; *Fancy Free* ....(MCA)
  Greatest Hits-#2 ....(MCA)
Fifty Ways To Leave Your Lover
Paul Simon; *Greatest Hits Etc.* ....(COL)
  Negotiations & Love Songs 1971-1986 ....(WB)
  Still Crazy After All These Years ....(COL)
Simon & Garfunkel; *Concert In Central Park* ..(WB)
Find The Cost Of Freedom
Crosby, Stills, Nash & Young; *Four-Way Street* ..(ATL)
  So Far ....(ATL)
Free Bird
Lynyrd Skynyrd; *Gold & Platinum* ....(MCA)
  One More From The Road ....(MCA)
  Pronounced Leh-nerd Skin-nerd ....(MCA)
  Southern By The Grace Of God ....(MCA)
Wynonna; *Skynyrd Frynds* ....(MCA)
Free Fallin'
Tom Petty; *Full Moon Fever* ....(MCA)
Free Man In Paris
Joni Mitchell; *Court & Spark* ....(ASY)
  Shadows & Light ....(ASY)
Free Me
Roger Daltrey; *Best Bits* ....(MCA)
  ST/McVicar ....(POL)
Free Nelson Mandela
Special AKA; *In The Studio* ....(CHR)
Free South Africa
Kinsey Report; *Midnight Drive* ....(ALG)
Tackhead; *Friendly As A Hand Grenade* .....(TVT)
Free The People
Barbra Streisand; *Stoney End* ....(COL)
Delaney & Bonnie; *Best Of* ....(RHI)
Free Will
Rush; *Exit...Stage Left* ....(MER)

Free Your Mind
En Vogue; *Funky Divas* ....(EW)
Freeborn Man
Outlaws; *Bring It Back Alive* ....(ARI)
  Lady In Waiting ....(ARI)
  Legends Of Rock Guitar/'70s ....(RHI)
Freedom
Fleetwood Mac; *Behind The Mask* ....(WB)
George Michael; *Listen Without Prejudice* ..(COL)
Jefferson Airplane; *Jefferson Airplane* .....(EPI)
Jimi Hendrix; *Cry Of Love* ....(RPR)
  Essential-#1 & 2 ....(RPR)
Richie Havens; *ST/Woodstock* ....(ATL)
Wham!; *Make It Big* ....(COL)
Freedom Rider
Traffic; *John Barleycorn Must Die* ....(ISL)
  On The Road ....(ISL)
Freedom Song
Thin Lizzy; *Fighting* ....(MER)
Freedom '90
George Michael; *S* ....(COL)
Go Down, Moses
Paul Robeson; *The Power & The Glory* ......(COL)
Simon Estes; *Spirituals* ....(PHI)
Go Where You Wanna Go
Mamas & The Papas; *16 Of Their Greatest Hits* . (MCA)
  Best Of ....(MCA)
  Farewell To The First Golden Era ....(MCA)
  If You Can Believe Your Eyes & Ears ......(MCA)
Great Day For Freedom
Pink Floyd; *The Division Bell* ....(COL)
Here Comes The Freedom Train
Merle Haggard; *Capitol Collectors Series* ...(CAP)
Hungry Heart
Bruce Springsteen; *The River* ....(COL)
Bruce Springsteen/E Street Band; *Live-1975-1985* ....(COL)
I Shall Be Released
Band; *Anthology-#1* ....(CAP)
  Last Waltz ....(WB)
  Music From Big Pink ....(CAP)
  To Kingdom Come-Definitive Collection ....(CAP)
Bette Midler; *Bette Midler* ....(ATL)
  ST/Divine Madness ....(ATL)
Bob Dylan; *At Budokan* ....(COL)
  Biograph ....(COL)
  Bootleg Series-#1-3 ....(COL)
  Greatest Hits-#2 ....(COL)
Bob Dylan/Band; *Before The Flood* ....(ASY)
Box Tops; *Greatest Hits* ....(RHI)
Flying Burrito Brothers; *Farther Along-Best Of* .. (A&M)
Joan Baez; *Any Day Now* ....(VAN)
  Carry It On ....(VAN)
  From Every Stage ....(A&M)
Joe Cocker; *With A Little Help From My Friends* (A&M)
Nina Simone; *Best Of* ....(RCA)
Rick Nelson; *In Concert-Troubadour-1969* ...(MCA)
If Dogs Run Free
Bob Dylan; *New Morning* ....(COL)
If I Had A Hammer
Pete Seeger; *Sing-A-Long-Live At Sanders Theatre 1980* ....(FLW)
Peter, Paul & Mary; *In Concert* ....(WB)
  Peter, Paul & Mary ....(WB)
  Ten Years Together-Best Of ....(WB)
Trini Lopez; *Best Of* ....(EXA)
Weavers; *Greatest Hits* ....(VAN)
If You Love Somebody Set Them Free
Sting; *Dream Of The Blue Turtles* ....(A&M)
Independence Day
Bruce Springsteen; *The River* ....(COL)
Bruce Springsteen/E Street Band; *Live-1975-1985* ....(COL)
Martina McBride; *The Way That I Am* ......(RCA)
It's Your Thing
Isley Brothers; *Billboard Top R&B Hits-1969* ....(RHI)
  Story-#2-T-Neck Years-1969-1985 ....(RHI)
  Timeless ....(TN)
I.G.Y. (What A Beautiful World)
Donald Fagen; *The Nightfly* ....(WB)
I'm Free
Jon Secada; *Jon Secada* ....(SBK)
Rolling Stones; *December's Children* ....(AKO)
  More Hot Rocks-Big Hits & Fazed Cookies ....(AKO)

Soup Dragons; *Lovegod* ....(BL)
Who; *Join Together* .... (MCA)
 Tommy .... (MCA)
 Who's Better Who's Best-Very Best Of .... (MCA)
I'm Free (Heaven Help The Man)
Kenny Loggins; *ST/Footloose* ....(COL)
Justice & Independence '85
John Mellencamp; *Scarecrow* ....(RIV)
Letitgo
Prince; *Come* ....(WB)
Many A Mile To Freedom
Traffic; *Low Spark Of High-Heeled Boys* .... (ISL)
Many Thousan' Gone
Popular Standard; *Out-Of-Print Recording* ....(OOP)
Me & Bobby McGee
Grateful Dead; *Grateful Dead* ....(WB)
Janis Joplin; *Greatest Hits* ....(COL)
 Janis ....(COL)
 Pearl ....(COL)
 Rock Classics/'70s ....(COL)
Willie Nelson; *Sings Kristofferson* ....(COL)
Nigerian Marketplace
Oscar Peterson Trio; *Nigerian Marketplace* .... (PAB)
No More Tears (Enough Is Enough)
Barbra Streisand & Donna Summer; *Memories* ...(COL)
 Wet ....(COL)
Donna Summer; *Dance Collection* ....(CAS)
 On The Radio-Greatest Hits-#1&2 ....(CAS)
On The Loose
Europe; *Final Countdown* .... (EPI)
Saga; *Worlds Apart* ....(POR)
Outbound Plane
Nanci Griffith; *Little Love Affairs* .... (MCA)
Suzy Bogguss; *Aces* ....(LIB)
People Got To Be Free
Rascals; *Anthology 1965-1972* .... (RHI)
 Hit Singles 1958-1977 ....(ATL)
Philadelphia Freedom
Daryl Hall & John Oates; *Two Rooms-Songs Of E. John
 & B. Taupin* ....(POL)
Elton John; *Billboard Top Rock 'N' Roll Hits-1975* (RHI)
 Greatest Hits-#2 ....(POL)
Prayer For Everybody/To Be Free
Gil Scott-Heron & Brian Jackson; *Secrets* .... (ARI)
Queen Of Freedom
Joan Baez; *In Concert* .... (VAN)
Roads To Freedom
Robin Trower; *Victims Of The Fury* .... (CHR)
Rockin' In The Free World
Neil Young; *Freedom* ....(RPR)
Neil Young/Crazy Horse; *Weld* .... (RPR)
Running Free
Iron Maiden; *Iron Maiden* ....(CAP)
 Live After Death-World Slavery Tour ....(CAP)
 Maiden Japan ....(CAP)
Saturday Freedom
Blue Cheer; *Good Times Are So Hard To Find* .. (MER)
Set Me Free
Chris Rea; *Auberge* ....(ATC)
Gene Loves Jezebel; *House Of Dolls* .... (GEF)
Kinks; *Greatest Hits-#1* ....(RHI)
Merle Haggard; *Ramblin' Fever* ....(MCA)
Teddy Pendergrass; *Teddy* .... (PI)
Times 2; *Hi-Fi & Mighty* .... (EMI)
Utopia; *Adventures In Utopia* ....(RHI)
 Anthology-1974-1985 .... (RHI)
Set You Free This Time
Byrds; *Original Singles-#1-1965-1967* ....(COL)
 Turn! Turn! Turn! ....(COL)
Gene Clark; *Echoes* ....(COL)
Sleep Come Free Me
James Taylor; *Flag* ....(COL)
Some People Can Do What They Like
Robert Palmer; *Some People Can Do What They
 Like* .... (ISL)
Someday We'll All Be Free
Donny Hathaway; *Best Of* ....(ATC)
James Ingram; *It's Real* ....(WB)
Stone Free
Eric Clapton; *Unplugged* .... (RPR)
Struggle (Free South Africa)
Rochester/Easley Band; *One Minute Of Love* .... (GRM)

Sweet Freedom
Michael McDonald; *Soundtrack Smashes-'80s &
 More* .... (MCA)
 ST/Running Scared ....(MSP)
To Be Free
Chicago; *At Carnegie Hall* ....(COL)
 Group Portrait ....(COL)
 #II ....(COL)
Voices Of Freedom
J. Browne/P. Gabriel/Y. N'Dour/L. Reed; *Secret
 Policeman's Third Ball-The Music* .... (VIA)
Lou Reed; *Between Thought &
 Expression-Anthology* ....(RCA)
We Shall Be Free
Garth Brooks; *The Chase* .... (LIB)
You Keep Me Hangin' On
Diana Ross; *Evening With* .... (MOT)
Diana Ross/Supremes; *Anthology* .... (MOT)
 Motown Story .... (MOT)
Kim Wilde; *Another Step* .... (MCA)
Supremes; *Billboard Top R&B Hits-1965* .... (MOT)
 Greatest Hits-#2 .... (MOT)
Vanilla Fudge; *Best Of* ....(ATC)
 Vanilla Fudge ....(ATC)
Wilson Pickett; *Greatest Hits* ....(ATL)
 Man & A Half-Best Of .... (RHI)
Young Turks
Rod Stewart; *Absolutely Live* ....(WB)
 Downtown Train-Storyteller Selections ....(WB)
 Storyteller/Complete Anthology-1964-1990 ......(WB)
 Tonight I'm Yours ....(WB)
Your Saving Grace
Steve Miller Band; *Anthology* ....(CAP)
 Best Of-1968-1973 ....(CAP)
 Your Saving Grace ....(CAP)

FRIENDS

Adios Amigo
Jim Reeves; *Best Of* ....(RCA)
 Billboard Top Country Hits-1962 .... (RHI)
Marty Robbins; *Adios Amigo* ....(COL)
 American Originals ....(COL)
 Greatest Hits-#4 ....(COL)
African Friend
Jimmy Buffett; *Son Of A Son Of A Sailor* .... (MCA)
All I Really Want To Do
Bob Dylan; *Another Side Of* ....(COL)
 At Budokan ....(COL)
 Greatest Hits-#2 ....(COL)
Byrds; *Byrds* ....(COL)
 Greatest Hits ....(COL)
 Original Singles-#1-1965-1967 ....(COL)
 Play Dylan ....(COL)
Cher; *Best Of* ....(EMI)
All My Friends
Gregg Allman; *Laid Back* .... (CPC)
All My Friends Were There
Kinks; *Village Green Preservation Society* .... (RPR)
All My Rowdy Friends (Have Settled Down)
Hank Williams, Jr.; *Greatest Hits* ....(W/C)
 Live ....(W/C)
 Pressure Is On ....(W/C)
Anytime At All
Beatles; *Hard Day's Night* ....(CAP)
 Rock 'N' Roll Music-#2 ....(CAP)
 Something New ....(CAP)
Are Friends Electric
Gary Numan/Tubeway Army; *Replicas* ....(ATC)
Are We Making Love Or Making Friends
Moe Bandy; *Soft Lights & Hard Country Music* ..(COL)
Back Door Friend
Johnny Winter; *Johnny Winter* ....(COL)
Lightnin' Hopkins; *The Jewel/Paula Records Story* (CPC)
Bar Room Buddies
Merle Haggard & Clint Eastwood; *ST/Bronco
 Billy* .... (ELE)
Be My Friend
Free; *Highway* ....(A&M)
 Live ....(A&M)
Be One Now
Little Feat; *Down On The Farm* ....(WB)

Be Your Own Best Friend
Ray Stevens; *Be Your Own Best Friend* .... (WB)
Feeling's Not Right Again .... (WB)
Beautiful Friendship
Nat King Cole; *Sings/George Shearing Quintet
Plays* .... (CAP)
Beautiful Friendships
Loretta Lynn & Ernest Tubb; *Story* .... (MCA)
Lou Rawls; *Best From* .... (CAP)
Best Friend
English Beat; *I Just Can't Stop It* .... (IRS)
What Is Beat .... (IRS)
Best Friends
Basia; *London Warsaw New York* .... (EPI)
ET (Eddie Towns); *45* .... (TE)
Best Of Friends
Dangerous Toys; *Hellacious Acres* .... (COL)
Peter, Paul & Mary; *Reunion* .... (WB)
Best Old Friend
Bonnie Raitt; *The Glow* .... (WB)
Bobby Jean
Bruce Springsteen; *Born In The U.S.A.* .... (COL)
Bruce Springsteen/E Street Band;
Live-1975-1985 .... (COL)
Boys & Me
Sawyer Brown; *Outskirts Of Town* .... (CRB)
Bridge Over Troubled Water
Aretha Franklin; *30 Greatest Hits* .... (ATL)
Greatest Hits .... (ATL)
Live At Fillmore West .... (ATL)
Paul Simon; *Concert In The Park-August 15 1991* (WB)
Live Rhymin' .... (WB)
Simon & Garfunkel; *Bridge Over Troubled Water* (COL)
Collected Works .... (COL)
Concert In Central Park .... (WB)
Greatest Hits .... (COL)
Buddy
De La Soul; *3 Feet High & Rising* .... (TMB)
Call Me
Al Green; *Greatest Hits* .... (HIR)
Aretha Franklin; *Greatest Hits* .... (ATL)
Be Be & Ce Ce Winans; *Be Be & Ce Ce Winans* . (CAP)
Blondie; *Best Of* .... (CHR)
ST/American Gigolo .... (CHR)
Chambers Brothers; *Best Of* .... (FAN)
Dennis DeYoung; *Back To The World* .... (A&M)
Frank Sinatra; *Strangers In The Night* .... (RPR)
Phil Perry; *Heart Of The Man* .... (CAP)
Rick James; *Street Songs/Throwin' Down* .... (MOT)
Skyy; *Skyline* .... (CAL)
Can We Still Be Friends?
Robert Palmer; *Secrets* .... (ISL)
Rod Stewart; *Camouflage* .... (WB)
Todd Rundgren; *Anthology 1968-1985* .... (RHI)
Hermit Of Mink Hollow .... (RHI)
Can't We Be Friends
Art Tatum; *Standards* .... (BL)
Buck Clayton & Buddy Tate; *Buck & Buddy* ..... (PRS)
Ella Fitzgerald & Louis Armstrong; *Ella & Louis* (VRV)
Frank Sinatra; *In The Wee Small Hours* .... (CAP)
Linda Ronstadt; *Lush Life* .... (ASY)
Circle Of Friends
Ray Pillow; *20 Great Hits* .... (PLN)
People Music .... (PLN)
Cisco Kid
War; *All Day Music* .... (MCA)
Greatest Hits .... (UA)
Live .... (UA)
Consider Yourself
Original Broadway Cast; *Oliver* .... (RCA)
"Courtship Of Eddie's Father" Theme
Nilsson; *Television's Greatest Hits-#2* .... (TVT)
Dawgs (Are A Man's Best Friend)
Original Cast; *Dawgs* .... (GLN)
Daytime Friends
Kenny Rogers; *Daytime Friends* .... (LIB)
Ten Years Of Gold .... (EMI)
Twenty Greatest Hits .... (LIB)
Dear Friends
Queen; *Sheer Heart Attack* .... (HOL)
Wings; *Wings Wildlife* .... (CAP)
Devil Ain't A Lonely Woman's Friend
Red Steagall; *45* .... (MCA)

Diamonds Are A Girl's Best Friend
Carol Channing; *Broadway Magic-'50s* .... (COL)
Emmylou Harris; *White Shoes* .... (WB)
Marilyn Monroe; *Goodbye Primadonna* .... (ACC)
Pearl Bailey; *Back On Broadway* .... (RLL)
Echoes Of An Era .... (RLL)
Don't Give Up
Peter Gabriel; *Shaking The Tree-16 Golden
Greats* .... (GEF)
So .... (GEF)
Ebony & Ivory
Paul McCartney; *Tripping The Live Fantastic* .... (CAP)
Paul McCartney & Stevie Wonder; *All The Best* . (CAP)
Tug Of War .... (CAP)
Fairweather Friend
John Cale; *Vintage Violence* .... (COL)
Johnny Gill; *Johnny Gill* .... (MOT)
Fake Friends
Joan Jett/Blackhearts; *Joan Jett/Blackhearts* ..... (MCA)
For All Our Cowboy Friends
Red Steagall/Coleman County Cowboys; *For All Our
Cowboy Friends* .... (MCA)
Freight Train Be My Friend
John Lee Hooker; *At Newport* .... (VJ)
Friend
Roger McGuinn; *Born To Rock & Roll* .... (COL)
Cardiff Rose .... (COL)
Winans; *Return* .... (QUE)
Friend In California
Merle Haggard; *Friend In California* .... (EPI)
More Hot Country Requests .... (EPI)
Friend In Need
Supertramp; *Indelibly Stamped* .... (A&M)
Friend Is A Friend
Pete Townshend; *The Iron Man* .... (ATL)
Friend Of The Devil
Grateful Dead; *American Beauty* .... (WB)
Best Of-Skeletons From The Closet .... (WB)
Dead Set .... (ARI)
Lyle Lovett; *Deadicated* .... (ARI)
Friend To Friend
Diana Ross; *Diana* .... (MOT)
Friendly Beasts
Garth Brooks; *Beyond The Season* .... (LIB)
Peter, Paul & Mary/N.Y. Choral Society; *Holiday
Celebration* .... (WB)
Friendly Neighborhood Narco Agent
Jef Jaisun; *Dr. Demento's Delight* .... (WB)
Friendly Persuasion
Pat Boone; *16 Great Performances* .... (MCA)
Best Of .... (MCA)
Friends
Beach Boys; *Absolute Best-#2* .... (CAP)
TT/20/20 .... (CAP)
Bette Midler; *Divine Miss M* .... (ATL)
B.B. King; *Live & Well* .... (MCA)
Elton John; *Your Songs* .... (MCA)
Joan Armatrading; *Me Myself I* .... (A&M)
Jody Watley/Eric B. & Rakim; *You Wanna Dance With
Me?* .... (MCA)
Joe Satriani; *Extremist* .... (REL)
Led Zeppelin; *3* .... (ATL)
Led Zeppelin .... (ATL)
Razzy Bailey; *14 #1 Country Hits* .... (RCA)
Makin' Friends .... (RCA)
Friends In Love
Dionne Warwick; *Friends In Love* .... (ARI)
With Johnny Mathis .... (ARI)
Johnny Mathis & Dionne Warwick; *Friends In
Love* .... (COL)
Love Songs .... (COL)
Friends In Low Places
Garth Brooks; *No Fences* .... (LIB)
Friends & Lovers
Bread; *Best Of-#2* .... (ELE)
Bread .... (ELE)
Carl Anderson & Gloria Loring; *Gloria Loring* ... (ATL)
Friendship Train
Gladys Knight/Pips; *All The Great Hits* .... (MOT)
Anthology .... (MOT)
Compact Command Performances .... (MOT)
Motown Superstar Series-#13 .... (MOT)

Friend, Love, Woman, Life
Mac Davis; *Baby Don't Get Hooked On Me* ......(COL)
 Greatest Hits ....(COL)
Funeral For A Friend
Elton John; *Goodbye Yellow Brick Road* .... (MCA)
 Here & There .... (MCA)
Girlfriend
Beautiful South; *Welcome To The Beautiful South* (ELE)
Bobby Brown; *King Of Stage* .... (MCA)
Mary Jane Girls; *Only Four You* .... (MOT)
Matthew Sweet; *Girlfriend* .... (ZOO)
Michael Jackson; *Off The Wall* .... (EPI)
Pebbles; *Pebbles* .... (MCA)
Wings; *London Town* .... (CAP)
Girlfriend Is Better
Talking Heads; *Speaking In Tongues* .... (SIR)
 ST/Stop Making Sense .... (SIR)
Good Friend
Loggins & Messina; *Loggins & Messina* ....(COL)
Reba McEntire; *Reba Nell McEntire* .... (MER)
Violent Femmes; *Blind Leading The Naked* ....(SLS)
Good Friends & A Bottle Of Wine
Ted Nugent; *Weekend Warriors* .... (EPI)
Goodbye Old Buddies
Seals & Crofts; *Get Closer* .... (WB)
Hello Little Friend
Joe Cocker; *Joe Cocker* ....(A&M)
Hello Old Friend
Eric Clapton; *Crossroads* .... (POL)
 No Reason To Cry .... (RSO)
Heroes & Friends
Randy Travis; *Greatest Hits-#1* .... (WB)
 Heroes & Friends .... (WB)
Hold An Old Friend's Hand
Rita Coolidge; *Fall Into Spring* .... (A&M)
Tiffany; *Hold An Old Friend's Hand* .... (MCA)
Hold On
En Vogue; *Born To Sing* .... (ATL)
John Conlee; *Rose Colored Glasses* .... (MCA)
John Lennon; *Lennon* ....(CAP)
 Plastic Ono Band ....(CAP)
Steve Winwood; *Steve Winwood* .... (ISL)
Triumph; *Classics* .... (MCA)
 Just A Game .... (MCA)
 Stages .... (MCA)
Wilson Phillips; *Wilson Phillips* .... (SBK)
How Can We Be Lovers
Michael Bolton; *Soul Provider* ....(COL)
How Many Friends
Who; *By Numbers* .... (MCA)
I Think It's Gonna Rain Today
Bette Midler; *ST/Beaches* .... (ATL)
Judy Collins; *In My Life* .... (ELE)
Neil Diamond; *Rainbow* .... (MCA)
 Stones .... (MCA)
Randy Newman; *12 Songs* .... (RPR)
If I Were Your Girlfriend
Prince; *45* ....(PAI)
If You Really Want To Be My Friend
Rolling Stones; *It's Only Rock 'N' Roll* .... (RS)
I'll Be Around
Spinners; *Atlantic R&B
1947-1974-#6-1966-1969* .... (ATL)
 Best Of .... (ATL)
 Golden Age Of Black Music-1970-1975 .... (ATL)
 Golden Soul .... (ATL)
 Soul Years .... (ATL)
 Spinners .... (ATL)
I'll Be By Your Side
Stevie B; *Best Of* .... (LMR)
 Love & Emotion .... (LMR)
I'll Be Good To You
Brothers Johnson; *Classics-#11* .... (A&M)
 Look Out For No. 1 .... (A&M)
Najee; *Tokyo Blue* .... (EMI)
Quincy Jones w/Ray Charles & Chaka Khan; *Back On
The Block* .... (QUE)
I'll Be There
Escape Club; *Dollars & Sex* .... (ATL)
Gail Davies; *I'll Be There* .... (WB)
Gerry/Pacemakers; *Best Of* .... (EMI)
 History Of British Rock-#2 .... (RHI)

Jackson 5; *Anthology* .... (MOT)
 Compact Command Performances .... (MOT)
 Greatest Hits .... (MOT)
 Motown Superstar Series-#2 .... (MOT)
 Motown's Biggest Pop Hits .... (MOT)
Mariah Carey; *MTV Unplugged* ....(COL)
I'll Be There For You
Bon Jovi; *New Jersey* .... (MER)
I'll Do 4 U
Father M.C.; *Father's Day* .... (UT)
I'll Stand By You
Pretenders; *Last Of The Independents* .... (SIR)
Just A Friend
Biz Markie; *Bass Waves-#3* ....(LUK)
 Diabolical-The Biz Never Sleeps ....(CLD)
Just Friends
Charlie Parker; *Compact Jazz* ....(VRV)
Charlie Watts Quintet; *Tribute To Charlie Parker* (CUU)
Frank Sinatra; *No One Cares* ....(CAP)
Joe Pass; *I Remember Charlie Parker* .... (PAB)
L.A. Four; *Just Friends* .... (CCJ)
Sarah Vaughan; *Divine-Columbia
Years-1949-1953* ....(COL)
Tony Bennett; *Jazz* ....(COL)
Wynton Marsalis Quartet; *Live At Blues Alley* ....(COL)
Just Your Friends
Mink De Ville; *Return To Magenta* ....(CAP)
Lean On Me
Bill Withers; *Greatest Hits* ....(COL)
 Still Bill ....(COL)
Club Nouveau; *Life Love & Pain* .... (WB)
Grover Washington, Jr.; *Greatest Performances* .. (MOT)
Little Pal
Jimmy Roselli; *Daddy's Little Girl* .... (M&R)
 Rock-A-Bye Your Baby .... (M&R)
 Sold Out-Carnegie Hall Concert .... (M&R)
Long Lost Friend
Restless Heart; *Fast Moving Train* ....(RCA)
Meet On The Ledge
Fairport Convention; *Chronicles* .... (A&M)
 Fairport Convention .... (A&M)
 In Real Time-Live '87 .... (ISL)
More Than Friends
Jonathan Butler/Others; *More Than Friends* ...... (JVA)
My Best Friend
Air Supply; *Lost In Love* .... (ARI)
Jefferson Airplane; *2400 Fulton Street-An
Anthology* ....(RCA)
 Surrealistic Pillow ....(RCA)
Marshall Tucker Band; *Running Like The Wind* ...(WB)
My Best Friend Is A Buddha
Deuter; *Silence Is The Answer* .... (KUC)
My Best Friend's Girl
Cars; *Cars* .... (ELE)
 Greatest Hits .... (ELE)
My Buddy
Barbra Streisand; *The Way We Were* ....(COL)
Dr. John; *In A Sentimental Mood* .... (WB)
Rosemary Clooney & Woody Herman; *My Buddy* (CCJ)
My Friend
Jimi Hendrix; *Cry of Love* .... (RPR)
Take 6 (featuring Ray Charles); *Join The Band* .. (RPR)
My Friend The Jukebox
Mel Street; *45* .... (POL)
My Friends
Original Cast/Angela Lansbury/Len Cariou; *Sweeney
Todd* ....(RCA)
My Little Friend
Elvis Presley; *45* ....(RCA)
My Whiskey Head Buddies
Elvin Bishop; *Don't Let The Bossman Get You
Down* ....(ALG)
Newborn Friend
Seal; *Seal* .... (ZTT)
No Surrender
Bruce Springsteen; *Born In The U.S.A.* ....(COL)
Old Friends
Barry Manilow; *Showstoppers* .... (ARI)
Everything But The Girl; *Worldwide* .... (ATL)
Liza Minnelli; *At Carnegie Hall* .... (TLR)
Original Cast; *Merrily We Roll Along* ....(RCA)
Roger Miller & Willie Nelson; *Old Friends* ....(COL)

Simon & Garfunkel; *Bookends* ....(COL)
  Collected Works ....(COL)
  Concert In Central Park ....(WB)
Stephen Sondheim/Angela Lansbury & Co.; *Collector's*
Sondheim ....(RCA)
Willie Nelson & Waylon Jennings; *Take It To The*
Limit ....(COL)
One Too Many Girlfriends
R.E.O. Speedwagon; *Life As We Know It* ....(EPI)
  Second Decade Of Rock & Roll-1981-1991 .....(EPI)
Outside Of A Small Circle Of Friends
Phil Ochs; *There & Now-Live In Vancouver-1968* (RHI)
  War Is Over-Best Of ....(A&M)
Partners, Brothers, & Friends
Nitty Gritty Dirt Band; *Live Two Five* ....(CAP)
  Twenty Years Of Dirt-Best Of ....(WB)
Racist Friend
Special AKA; *In The Studio* ....(CHR)
Reach Out I'll Be There
Four Tops; *Anthology* ....(MOT)
  Compact Command Performances ....(MOT)
  Greatest Hits ....(MOT)
  Motown Dance Party-#2 ....(MOT)
  Reach Out I'll Be There ....(MOT)
Red Neck Friend
Jackson Browne; *For Everyman* ....(ASY)
Sally's Got A Friend In New York City
Larry McCray; *Ambition* ....(CHS)
Secret Friend
Paul McCartney; *CD Gift Set* ....(CAP)
  McCartney II ....(CAP)
Shilo
Neil Diamond; *Classics-Early Years* ....(COL)
  Glory Road-1968-1972 ....(MCA)
  His 12 Greatest Hits ....(MCA)
  Hot August Night ....(MCA)
Snowblind Friend
David Allan Coe; *Unchained* ....(COL)
Hoyt Axton; *Snowblind Friend* ....(MCA)
Steppenwolf; *16 Greatest Hits* ....(MCA)
  7 ....(MCA)
Some Kind Of Friend
Barry Manilow; *Greatest Hits-#1* ....(ARI)
Stand By Me
Ben E. King; *Atlantic Soul Classics* ....(WSP)
  Golden Age Of Black Music-1960-1970 ....(ATL)
  Greatest Hits ....(ATC)
  Stand By Me/Best Of ....(ATL)
  ST/Stand By Me ....(ATL)
Drifters; *Greatest Hits* ....(GUS)
John Lennon; *Rock 'N' Roll* ....(CAP)
  John Lennon (collection) ....(CAP)
  ST/Imagine-The Motion Picture ....(CAP)
Maurice White; *Maurice White* ....(COL)
Mickey Gilley; *Biggest Hits* ....(EPI)
  Greatest Country Hits From The Movies ....(EPI)
  ST/Urban Cowboy ....(ASY)
  Ten Years Of Hits ....(EPI)
Ry Cooder; *Chicken Skin Music* ....(RPR)
Streets Of Philadelphia
Bruce Springsteen; *ST/Philadelphia* ....(COL)
Thank You For Being A Friend
Andrew Gold; *All This & Heaven Too* ....(ASY)
That Old Gang Of Mine
Mitch Miller/Gang; *Sing Along With Mitch* ......(COL)
That's What Friends Are For
Barbara Mandrell; *Best Of* ....(MCA)
  This Is ....(MCA)
D. Warwick/E. John/G. Knight/S. Wonder; *Dionne*
Warwick Greatest Hits-1979-1990 ....(ARI)
  Friends ....(ARI)
Johnny Mathis & Deniece Williams; *That's What Friends*
Are For ....(COL)
There's A Place In Hell For Me & My...
Morrissey; *Kill Uncle* ....(SIR)
Touch A Hand, Make A Friend
Oak Ridge Boys; *Country's Greatest Hits-#4* .....(MSP)
  Greatest Hits-#3 ....(MCA)
  Step On Out ....(MSP)
Staple Singers; *15 Original Big Hits-#4* ....(STX)
  Chronicle ....(STX)
  Top Of The Stax-20 Greatest Hits-#2 ....(STX)
Treat You Right
Luther Vandross; *Best Of...Best Of Love* ....(EPI)

Truck Driving Buddy
Red Sovine/Willis Bros./Reno & Smiley; *Heavy*
Haulers ....(PP)
True Companion
Donald Fagen; *ST/Heavy Metal* ....(FA)
Marc Cohn; *Marc Cohn* ....(ATL)
Steely Dan/Donald Fagen; *Gold-Expanded*
Edition ....(MCA)
Turn Of A Friendly Card
Alan Parsons Project; *Best Of-#2* ....(ARI)
  Turn Of A Friendly Card ....(ARI)
User Friendly
Ian Anderson; *Walk Into Light* ....(CHR)
Vacant Chair
Steve Winwood; *Chronicles* ....(ISL)
  Steve Winwood ....(ISL)
Visiting An Old Friend
Nitty Gritty Dirt Band; *Dirt, Silver & Gold* ..... (UA)
Waiting On A Friend
Rolling Stones; *Rewind-1971-1984* ....(RS)
  Tattoo You ....(RS)
We Hate It When Our Friends Become...
Morrissey; *Your Arsenal* ....(SIR)
Weekend Friend
Con Hunley; *Con Hunley* ....(WB)
West Virginia Friend
Holly Near; *Watch Out* ....(RWD)
What A Friend We Have In Jesus
Nashville Superpickers; *Live From Austin City*
Limits ....(FF)
Sweet Honey In The Rock; *We All...Every One Of*
Us ....(FF)
What About Your Friends
TLC; *Oooooooohhh...On The TLC Tip* ....(LAF)
Whenever I Call You "Friend"
Kenny Loggins; *Alive* ....(COL)
Kenny Loggins & Stevie Nicks; *Nightwatch* ......(COL)
Melissa Manchester; *Greatest Hits* ....(ARI)
Why Can't We Be Friends
War; *Best Of & More* ....(RHI)
  Why Can't We Be Friends ....(AVE)
With A Little Help From My Friends
Beatles; *1967-1970* ....(CAP)
  Box Set ....(CAP)
  Rarities ....(CAP)
  Sgt. Pepper's Lonely Hearts Club Band ....(CAP)
Joe Cocker; *Classics-#4* ....(A&M)
  Greatest Hits ....(A&M)
  History Of British Rock-#9 ....(RHI)
  ST/Woodstock ....(ATL)
  With A Little Help From My Friends ....(A&M)
Ringo Starr/All-Star Band; *Nobody's Child-Romanian*
Angel Appeal ....(WB)
Woman, A Lover, A Friend
Jackie Wilson; *Greatest Hits #2* ....(BRU)
  Mr. Excitement ....(RHI)
Otis Redding; *Story* ....(ATL)
You Can Depend On Me
Brenda Lee; *Story-Her Greatest Hits* .... (MCA)
Count Basie; *Best Of* ....(MCA)
Louis Armstrong; *Stardust* ....(POR)
Manhattan Transfer; *Manhattan Transfer* ....(ATL)
Restless Heart; *Best Of* ....(RCA)
You're A Friend Of Mine
Clarence Clemons & Jackson Browne; *Hero* .....(COL)
You're Invited But Your Friends Can't...
Vince Neil; *ST/Encino Man* ....(HOL)
You're My Best Friend
Don Williams; *Best Of-#2* ....(MCA)
  Country Comes To Carnegie Hall ....(MCA)
  Country Music Classics-#4-1975-1980 .... (KT)
  Lovers & Best Friends ....(MCA)
  You're My Best Friend ....(MCA)
Queen; *A Night At The Opera* ....(HOL)
  Greatest Hits ....(HOL)
  Live Killers ....(HOL)
You're My Bestest Friend
Mac Davis; *Midnight Crazy* ....(CAS)
  Very Best & More... ....(CAS)
You've Got A Friend
Barbra Streisand; *Barbra Joan Streisand* ....(COL)
Carole King; *Tapestry* ....(EPI)
Donny Hathaway & Roberta Flack; *Best Of Donny*
Hathaway ....(ATL)

Jamaica Boys; *J Boys* .... (RPR)
James Taylor; *Greatest Hits* .... (WB)
  Mud Slide Slim & The Blue Horizon .... (WB)
Michael Jackson; *Got To Be There* .... (MOT)
  Original Soul Of .... (MOT)
Roberta Flack & Donny Hathaway; *Best Of Roberta
Flack* .... (ATL)
  Roberta Flack & Donny Hathaway .... (ATL)

FRUIT

See Also: *FOOD, VEGETABLES*

30,000 Pounds Of Bananas
Harry Chapin; *Anthology* .... (ELE)
  Greatest Stories-Live .... (ELE)
  Verities & Balderdash .... (ELE)
Apple Honey
Woody Herman; *Best Of Woody
Herman/Orchestra* ....(CCB)
  Big Band Treasures-#2 ....(DHL)
  Thundering Herds-1945-1947 ....(COL)
Apple Of Your Eye
Peter Frampton; *Frampton* ....(A&M)
Apple Orchard
Spirit; *Spirit* .... (EMI)
Apple Scruffs
George Harrison; *All Things Must Pass* ....(CAP)
Apple Suckling Tree
Bob Dylan/Band; *Basement Tapes* ....(COL)
Apples In Winter
Kim Robertson; *Angels In Disguise* .... (INV)
Apples Peaches Pumpkin Pie
Jay/Techniques; *Cruisin'-1967* .... (INC)
Apples & Oranges
Pink Floyd; *Shine On* ....(COL)
Apples, Peaches & Cherries
Peggy Lee; *Best Of* .... (MCA)
Apples, Peaches, Bananas & Pears
Monkees; *Missing Links* .... (RHI)
Apricot Love
Neil Norman; *Not Of This Earth* .... (CRS)
Attack Of The Killer Tomatoes
Lewis Lee; *Elvira Presents Haunted Hits* .... (RHI)
  Halloween Hits .... (RHI)
Avocado Green
Johnny Winter; *About Blues* ....(OOP)
  Before The Storm ....(OOP)
Baby Lemonade
Syd Barrett; *Barrett* ....(CAP)
Back To The Apple
Count Basie/Orchestra; *ST/Hannah & Her
Sisters* .... (MCA)
Banana Boat Song
Harry Belafonte; *Belafonte '89* .... (EMI)
  Nipper's Greatest Hits-'50s-#1 ....(RCA)
Kinks; *Everybody's In Show Biz* .... (RHI)
Banana Man
Clifton Chenier; *Louisiana Blues & Zydeco* ..... (ARH)
Banana Republic
Boomtown Rats; *Greatest Hits* ....(COL)
  Mondo Bongo ....(COL)
Banana Republics
Jimmy Buffett; *Changes In Latitudes/Changes In
Attitude* .... (MCA)
Bananas
Louis Jordan/Tympani Five; *Rock 'N Roll Call* ... (BLU)
Bananas By The Bunch
Lou & Peter Berryman; *So Comfortable* .... (COR)
Bananas & Cream
Kinky Friedman; *Lasso From El Paso* .... (EPI)
Big Apple
Tommy Dorsey/Clambake Seven; *Nipper's Greatest
Hits-'30s-#2* ....(RCA)
Tommy Dorsey/Orchestra; *Seventeen Number
Ones* ....(RCA)
Blueberry Hill
Elvis Presley; *Loving You* ....(RCA)
  Recorded Live On Stage ....(RCA)
Fats Domino; *Greatest Hits* ....(EVR)
  Greatest Hits .... (MCA)
  My Blue Heaven-Best Of-#1 .... (EMI)
Little Richard; *Big Hits* ....(CRS)

Louis Armstrong; *Best Of* .... (MCA)
  Essential .... (VAN)
  I Like Jazz: Essence Of ....(COL)
Bruised Orange
John Prine; *Bruised Orange* .... (ASY)
Cantaloop
US3; *Hand On The Torch* .... (CAP)
Cherry
Count Basie & Mills Brothers; *16 Great
Performances* .... (MCA)
Harry James/Orchestra; *Best Of* ....(CCB)
Oscar Peterson & Count Basie; *Satch & Josh
Again* .... (PAB)
Stanley Turrentine; *Best Of* ....(CBA)
UFO; *Obsession* .... (CHR)
Cherry Blossom Time
Columbia Ballroom Orchestra; *Let's
Dance-#7-Competition Dance* .... (DEN)
Cherry Bomb
John Cougar Mellencamp; *Check It Out* .... (MER)
  Lonesome Jubilee .... (MER)
Cherry Cherry
Neil Diamond; *Gold* .... (MCA)
  Bang & Shout ....(BNG)
  Classics-Early Years ....(COL)
  Gold .... (MCA)
  Greatest Hits ....(BNG)
  Hot August Night .... (MCA)
  Hot August Night II ....(COL)
  Shilo ....(BNG)
Cherry Coke
Bob's Diner; *Bob's Diner* .... (DIG)
Cherry Hill Park
Billy Joe Royal; *Greatest Hits* ....(COL)
  Super Hits/'70s-Have A Nice Day-#1 .... (RHI)
Cherry Oh Baby
Rolling Stones; *Black & Blue* ....(RS)
UB40; *Labour Of Love* ....(A&M)
  Live In Moscow ....(A&M)
Cherry Pie
Marvin & Johnny; *Collectables Presents History Of
Rock-#4* ....(CLT)
  Rock & Roll Festival-#1 ....(KNT)
Sade; *Diamond Life* ....(POR)
Warrant; *Cherry Pie* ....(COL)
Cherry Pink And Apple Blossom White
Fabulous Thunderbirds; *Butt Rockin'* .... (CHR)
Perez Prado; *This Is-Decade Of The '50s* ....(RCA)
Cherry Red
Big Joe Turner; *Atlantic Blues-Piano* .... (ATL)
  Boss Of The Blues .... (ATL)
Count Basie & Big Joe Turner; *Bosses* .... (PAB)
Ella Fitzgerald; *These Are The Blues* ....(VRV)
Esther Phillips; *Confessin' The Blues-Jazzlore-#41* (RHI)
Lime Spiders; *Beethoven's Fist* .... (CRL)
Little Richard; *Big Hits* .... (CRS)
Cherry, Cherry Coupe
Beach Boys; *Little Deuce Coupe/All Summer Long* (CAP)
Coconut
Nilsson; *All-Time Greatest Hits* ....(RCA)
  Schmilsson ....(RCA)
  Songwriter ....(RCA)
Coconut Grove
David Lee Roth; *Crazy From The Heat* .... (WB)
Lovin' Spoonful; *Anthology* .... (RHI)
Coconut Island
Junior Brown; *12 Shades Of Brown* ....(CCB)
Coconut Telegraph
Jimmy Buffett; *Boats Beaches Bars & Ballads* ... (MGR)
  Coconut Telegraph .... (MCA)
Don't Sit Under The Apple Tree
Andrews Sisters; *Capitol Collectors Series* .... (CAP)
  Greatest Hits ....(CCB)
Glenn Miller; *Memorial-1944-1969* ....(BLU)
Glenn Miller/Orchestra; *Unforgettable* ....(RCA)
Don't Your Peaches Look Mellow
Luke/Locomotives; *Luke/Locomotives* .... (AQ)
Elderberry Wine
Elton John; *Don't Shoot Me I'm Only The Piano
Player* .... (POL)
Fig Leaf Rag
Scott Joplin; *Ragtime-#2 (1900-1910)* ....(BIO)
Fig Tree
Bunny Wailer; *Blackheart Man* .... (ISL)

Fig Tree Bay
Peter Frampton; *Wind Of Change* .... (A&M)
Forbidden Fruit
Band; *Northern Lights-Southern Cross* .... (CAP)
Fruit Song
Martin Mull; *Never Perfect/Perfect* .... (ELE)
Funky Avocado
Michael Hedges; *Breakfast In The Field* .... (WH)
Live On The Double Planet .... (WH)
God's Great Banana Skin
Chris Rea; *espresso logic* .... (EW)
Golden Apples Of The Sun
Judy Collins; *Golden Apples Of The Sun* .... (ELE)
So Early In The Spring .... (ELE)
Grapefruit Juicy Fruit
Jimmy Buffett; *Songs You Know By Heart* ...... (MCA)
White Sport Coat & A Pink Crustacean .... (MCA)
You Had To Be There .... (MCA)
Grapes Of Wrath
Charlie Daniels Band; *Midnight Wind* .... (EPI)
Guacamole
Texas Tornados; *Hangin' On By A Thread* .... (RPR)
Guava Jelly
Barbra Streisand; *Butterfly* .... (COL)
Bob Marley/Wailers; *Songs Of Freedom* .... (TUF)
Owen Gray; *This Is Reggae Music-#1* .... (ISL)
I Like Bananas Because They Have No Bone
Hoosier Hot Shots; *Dr. Demento's Greatest*
Novelty-#1-1940s .... (RHI)
I Like Cherries
Audio Two; *What More Can I Say* .... (FP)
Last Mango In Paris
Jimmy Buffett; *Feeding Frenzy* .... (MCA)
Last Mango In Paris .... (MCA)
Lemon Pie
Strawbs; *Best* .... (A&M)
Ghosts .... (A&M)
Lemon Song
Led Zeppelin; *II* .... (ATL)
Lemon Tree
Kingston Trio; *Very Best Of* .... (CAP)
Peter, Paul & Mary; *10 Years Together-Best Of* ... (WB)
Peter, Paul & Mary .... (WB)
Trini Lopez; *Best Of* ....(EXA)
Life Is A Lemon And I Want My Money Back
Meat Loaf; *Bat Out Of Hell II-Back Into Hell* ... (MCA)
Life Is Just A Bowl Of Cherries
Rudy Vallee; *Heigh-Ho Everybody* .... (OLR)
Little Green Apples
O.C. Smith; *Pop Classics/'60s* .... (COL)
Old Dogs, Children & Watermelon Wine
Tom T. Hall; *Essential Twentieth Anniversary*
Collect. .... (MER)
Greatest Hits-#2 .... (MER)
One Bad Apple
Osmonds; *Billboard Top Rock 'N' Roll Hits-1971* (RHI)
Orange Blossom Lane
Glenn Miller/Orchestra; *Complete* .... (BLU)
Complete-#7 .... (RCA)
Orange Blossom Mandolin
Northeast Winds; *In Concert* .... (FOL)
Orange Blossom Special
Bill Monroe; *Bean Blossom* .... (MCA)
Stars Of The Grand Ole Opry 1926-1974 ..... (RCA)
& Bluegrass Boys-60 Years Of Country .... (RCA)
Charlie Daniels Band; *Fire On The Mountain* ..... (EPI)
Urban Cowboy-#2 .... (EPI)
Flatt & Scruggs; *Hear The Whistles Blow* .... (GUS)
Gordon Terry; *20 Golden Souvenirs* .... (PLN)
Disco Country .... (PLN)
Johnny Cash; *Columbia Records 1958-1986* ..... (COL)
Essential .... (COL)
Greatest Hits .... (COL)
Nitty Gritty Dirt Band; *Will The Circle Be*
Unbroken .... (EMI)
Orange Blossom Time
Bing Crosby; *Crooner-Columbia*
Years-1928-1934 .... (COL)
Orange Juice Blues
Bob Dylan/Band; *Basement Tapes* .... (COL)
Orange Sherbert
Count Basie; *Basie Big Band* .... (PAB)
Party At The Prune Farm
Lou & Peter Berryman; *Cupid's Trash Truck* .... (COR)

Peach
Prince; *Hits 2* .... (PAI)
Hits/B-Sides .... (PAI)
Peach Blossom Spring
Yutaka; *Yutaka* .... (GRP)
Peach Orchard Mamma
Big Joe Williams; *Piney Woods Blues* .... (DEL)
Peach Picking Time Down In Georgia
Jimmie Rodgers; *My Rough & Rowdy Days* ...... (RCA)
This Is .... (RCA)
Merle Travis; *Superstars Salute Jimmie Rodgers* ....(SO)
Peach Tree
Sonny Boy Williamson; *Real Folk Blues* .... (CSS)
Peach Tree Shuffle
Panama Francis; *All-Stars 1949* .... (CLT)
Peach Window
Julianna Raye; *Something Peculiar* .... (RPR)
Peacherine Rag
Scott Joplin; *King Of Ragtime Writers* .... (BIO)
Peaches
Captain Beefheart; *Unconditionally Guaranteed* ....(BP)
Junior Parker; *Best Of* .... (MCA)
Kristen Hall; *Fact & Fiction* .... (HIG)
Nat King Cole Trio; *Best Of* .... (BLN)
Stranglers; *Greatest Hits-1977-1990* .... (EPI)
Peaches En Regalia
Frank Zappa; *Hot Rats* .... (RYK)
Swiss Cheese/Fire .... (RHI)
Mothers Of Invention; *Fillmore East-June 1971* ...(BIZ)
Peaches & Cream
Wayne Shorter; *Wayne Shorter* .... (CRS)
Peaches & Diesel
Eric Clapton; *Slowhand* .... (POL)
Pineapple
Original Cast; *Cabaret* .... (COL)
Pisces Apple Lady
Leon Russell; *Leon Russell* .... (MCA)
Plum
George Benson; *Body Talk* .... (CBA)
Stanley Turrentine; *Best Of* .... (BLN)
Plum Blossom
Vangelis; *China* .... (POL)
Yusef Lateef/Others; *Eastern Sounds* .... (PRS)
Pomegranate
Ian McCulloch; *Mysterio* .... (SIR)
Raspberries, Strawberries
Kingston Trio; *Capitol Collectors Series* .... (CAP)
Sold Out/String Along .... (CAP)
Raspberry Beret
Prince/Revolution; *Around The World In A Day* .. (WB)
Raspberry Jam
Carole King; *Writer* .... (EPI)
Rotten Peaches
Elton John; *Madman Across The Water* .... (POL)
Stealin' Watermelons
Elvin Bishop; *Best Of* .... (EPI)
Let It Flow ....(CPC)
Raisin' Hell ....(CPC)
Strange Fruit
Billie Holiday; *History Of The Real Billie Holiday* (VRV)
Songbook .... (VRV)
Strange Fruit .... (ATL)
Nina Simone; *Nina Simone* .... (MER)
Strawberry Fields Forever
Beatles; *1967-1970* .... (CAP)
Box Set .... (CAP)
Magical Mystery Tour .... (CAP)
ST/Imagine-The Motion Picture .... (CAP)
Strawberry Flats
Little Feat; *Hoy-Hoy!* .... (WB)
Little Feat .... (WB)
Strawberry Letter #23
Brothers Johnson; *Classics-#11* .... (A&M)
Right On Time .... (A&M)
Tevin Campbell; *T.E.V.I.N.* .... (RPR)
Strawberry Wine
Band; *Stage Fright* .... (CAP)
Sweet Cherry Wine
Tommy James/Shondells; *Anthology* .... (RHI)
Very Best Of .... (PRR)
Sweet Guava Jelly
Lee "Scratch" Perry; *Soundzs From The Hot Line* (HRT)
Sweet Pear
Elvis Costello; *Mighty Like A Rose* .... (WB)

Tangerine
Benny Goodman; *Best Of The Big Bands* ....(COL)
Dave Brubeck Quartet; *Great*
 Concerts-Amsterdam-Copenhagen-etc. ....(COL)
Frank Sinatra; *& Swingin' Brass* ....(RPR)
Harry Connick, Jr.; *25* ....(COL)
Led Zeppelin; *III* ....(ATL)
 Led Zeppelin (collection) ....(ATL)
Nat King Cole; *At The Movies* ....(CAP)
Texas Lemon Flavor
Stefan Grossman; *Yazoo Basin Boogie* ....(SHA)
This Plum Is Too Ripe
Original Cast; *Fantasticks* ....(POL)
Tutti Frutti
Elvis Presley; *Elvis Presley* ....(RCA)
 Rocker ....(RCA)
Little Richard; *18 Greatest Hits* ....(RHI)
 Greatest Hits Recorded Live ....(EPI)
 Little Richard ....(SPE)
 More American Graffiti ....(MCA)
 This Is How It All Began-#2 ....(SPE)
 Tribute To Black Entertainers ....(COL)
Queen; *Live At Wembley '86* ....(HOL)
Two Scoops Of Raisins
Common Sense; *Can I Borrow A Dollar?* ....(REL)
Underneath The Apple Tree
Michael Franks; *Tiger In The Rain* ....(WB)
Watermelon
John McCutcheon; *Family Garden* .... (ROU)
Pops Cool Love; *A Man* ....(ELE)
Scorpio Rising; *Pig Symphony* ....(SIR)
 Zodiac Killers ....(SIR)
Watermelon Crawl
Tracy Byrd; *No Ordinary Man* ....(MCA)
Watermelon Hangin' On The Vine
Hodges Brothers; *Watermelon Hangin' On The
Vine* .... (ARH)
Watermelon In Easter Hay
Frank Zappa; *Guitar* ....(RYK)
 Joe's Garage Acts I-III ....(RYK)
Watermelon Man
Albert King; *Wednesday Night In San Francisco* .. (STX)
Buddy Guy; *Hold That Plane* ....(VAN)
Gun Club; *Miami* ....(IRS)
Herbie Hancock; *Best Of-Blue Note Years* .... (BLN)
 Head Hunters ....(COL)
 Takin' Off ....(BLN)
Johnny Taylor; *Wanted One Soul Singer* ....(ATL)
Mongo Santamaria; *Greatest Hits* ....(COL)
 Mongo's Greatest Hits ....(FAN)
New Grass Revival; *Too Late To Turn Back Now* ..(FF)
Watermelon On The Vine
Stanley Brothers; *Stanley Series-Vol.1-#2* ....(COP)
Watermelon Song
Hypnolovewheel; *Altered States* ....(ALI)
Watermelon Time In Georgia
Larry Boone; *Get In Line* ....(COL)
Watermelons
Johnny Shines; *Roots Of R&B-Tribute To Robert
Johnson* ....(COL)
When Banana Skins Are Falling
Slim Gaillard; *Cement Mixer Putti Putti* ....(FLK)
When It's Cherry Time In Tokio
James P. Johnson; *Rare Piano Roll Solos-#2-1917* (BIO)
When The Good Apples Fall
Seekers; *Capitol Collectors Series* ....(CAP)
When The World Was Young
Anita O'Day; *Mello'Day* ....(CRS)
Frank Sinatra; *Point Of No Return* ....(CAP)
White Port Lemon Juice
Mothers Of Invention; *Burnt Weeny Sandwich* .... (BIZ)
Why Is A Carrot More Orange Than An...
Amboy Dukes; *Journey To The Center Of The
Mind* ....(MST)
Wild Cherry
Foghat; *Best Of* ....(RHI)
 Energized ....(RHI)
Leroy Washington; *Sound Of The Swamp-Best Of
Excello-#1* ....(RHI)
Wild Strawberries
Gordon Lightfoot; *Waiting For You* ....(RPR)
Yes We Have No Bananas
Authentic Band Organ; *Catch The Brass Ring* ....(KLA)

Spike Jones; *Best Of-#2* ....(RCA)

FUN, Good Times
 See Also: DANCE, HAPPINESS, PARTY, SMILE

Ain't No Fun
Snoop Doggy Dogg; *Doggystyle* .... (ISC)
Ain't No Fun To Be Alone In San Antone
Gene Watson; *Mack In The Fire* ....(WB)
Ain't No Fun (If The Homies Can't...)
Snoop Doggy Dogg; *Doggystyle* ....(DR)
Ain't No Fun (Waiting 'Round To Be A...)
AC/DC; *Dirty Deeds Done Dirt Cheap* ....(ATL)
All I Wanna Do
Sheryl Crow; *Tuesday Night Music Club* ....(A&M)
Are The Good Times Really Over
Merle Haggard; *Big City* ....(EPI)
 Greatest Country Hits-'80s-1982 ....(COL)
 His Epic Hits-The First 11 ....(EPI)
Big Fun
Kool/Gang; *As One* ....(DL)
Scatterbrain; *Scamboogery* ....(ELE)
Blondes (Have More Fun)
Rod Stewart; *Blondes (Have More Fun)* ....(WB)
Dangerous Fun
Jesse Winchester; *Best Of* ....(RHI)
 Third Down 110 To Go ....(RHI)
Enjoy Yourself
Guy Lombardo; *Best Of* ....(MCA)
Jacksons; *Jacksons* ....(EPI)
Kylie Minogue; *Enjoy Yourself* ....(GEF)
Everybody Have Fun Tonight
Wang Chung; *Mosaic* ....(GEF)
Ffun
Con Funk Shun; *Secrets* ....(OOP)
Fun
Sly/Family Stone; *Anthology* ....(EPI)
 Greatest Hits ....(EPI)
Fun Day
Stevie Wonder; *ST/Jungle Fever* .... (MOT)
Fun Fun Fun
Beach Boys; *Best Of* ....(CAP)
 Endless Summer ....(CAP)
 Gift Set ....(CAP)
 In Concert ....(CAR)
 Made In The U.S.A. ....(CAP)
Fun In Texas
Britny Fox; *Britny Fox* ....(COL)
Fun Time
Bebe Buell; *Covers Girl* .... (RHI)
Fun & Games
Chuck Mangione; *Best Of* .... (A&M)
 Classics-#6 ....(A&M)
 Fun & Games ....(A&M)
Isley Brothers; *Showdown* .... (TN)
Funtime
Joe Cocker; *45* ....(OOP)
Get Up & Enjoy Yourself
Head East; *Live* ....(A&M)
Girls Just Want To Have Fun
Cyndi Lauper; *She's So Unusual* ....(POR)
Gonna Have A Good Time
Easybeats; *Best Of* .... (RHI)
Good Times
Chic; *Plus Grands Succes De Chic* ....(ATL)
 Risque ....(ATL)
Dan Seals; *Greatest Hits* ....(CAP)
 On Arrival ....(CAP)
Hoodoo Gurus; *Blow Your Cool* ....(ELE)
Jimi Hendrix; *Jimi Hendrix* ....(AUF)
Nat King Cole; *Ramblin' Rose* ....(CAP)
Persuasions; *Street Corner Symphony* ....(CAP)
Rita Coolidge; *Anytime...Anywhere* ....(A&M)
Rolling Stones; *12 X 5* ....(AKO)
 Big Hits (High Tide & Green Grass) ....(AKO)
 More Hot Rocks & Fazed Cookies ....(AKO)
 Out Of Our Heads ....(AKO)
Willie Nelson; *Best Of* ....(RCA)
 Minstrel Man ....(RCA)
 Music From "Songwriter" ....(COL)
Good Times Bad Times
Led Zeppelin; *Led Zeppelin* ....(ATL)

Good Times Roll
Cars; *Cars* .... (ELE)
Greatest Hits .... (ELE)
Have A Good Time
Elvin Bishop; *Struttin' My Stuff* .... (CPC)
Paul Simon; *Greatest Hits Etc.* .... (COL)
Negotiations & Love Songs-1971-1986 .... (WB)
Still Crazy After All These Years .... (COL)
Rufus & Chaka Khan; *Rufus* .... (MCA)
Having A Blast
Green Day; *Dookie* .... (RPR)
Hot Fun In The Summertime
Sly/Family Stone; *Anthology* .... (EPI)
Billboard Top R&B Hits-1969 .... (RHI)
Greatest Hits .... (EPI)
Summer & Sun .... (RHI)
I Wanna Have Some Fun
Samantha Fox; *I Wanna Have Some Fun* .... (JVA)
Jumpin' Jack Flash
Aretha Franklin; *Aretha* .... (ARI)
Johnny Winter; *Live* .... (COL)
Peter Frampton; *Frampton Comes Alive* .... (A&M)
Rolling Stones; *Flashpoint* .... (RS)
Flashpoint + Collectibles .... (RS)
Get Yer Ya-Ya's Out .... (AKO)
Hot Rocks 1964-1971 .... (AKO)
Love You Live .... (RS)
ST/Jumpin' Jack Flash .... (MER)
Through The Past Darkly-Big Hits-#2 .... (AKO)
Let The Good Times Roll
Barbra Streisand; *Butterfly* .... (COL)
Betty Everett & Jerry Butler; *Delicious Together* .... (VJ)
Starring Betty Everett .... (TRD)
Bobby Bland & B.B. King; *Together Again...* .... (MCA)
Harry Nilsson; *Nilsson Schmilsson* .... (RCA)
Jerry Lee Lewis; *Golden Rock & Roll* .... (SUN)
Louis Jordan; *Best Of* .... (MCA)
Molly Hatchet; *Flirtin' With Disaster* .... (EPI)
Phoebe Snow; *Phoebe Snow* .... (MCA)
Ray Charles; *Genius Of* .... (ATL)
Shirley & Lee; *Billboard Top R&B Hits-1956* .... (RHI)
History Of New Orleans R&B-#1-1950-1958 .. (RHI)
ST/Stand By Me .... (ATL)
Super Oldies/'50s-#4 .... (AUF)
Long Tall Sally
Beatles; *At The Hollywood Bowl* .... (CAP)
Past Masters-#1 .... (CAP)
Rock 'N' Roll Music-#1 .... (CAP)
Second Album .... (CAP)
Little Richard; *18 Greatest Hits* .... (RHI)
Billboard Top R&B Hits-1956 .... (RHI)
Greatest Hits .... (EVR)
Here's Little Richard .... (SPE)
Oldies But Goodies-#3 .... (OSR)
ST/Heaven Help Us .... (EMI)
Super Oldies/'50s-#3 .... (AUF)
Tutti Frutti .... (ACC)
Mama Told Me Not To Come
Randy Newman; *12 Songs* .... (RPR)
Live .... (RPR)
Randy Newman .... (RPR)
Three Dog Night; *Best Of* .... (MCA)
Billboard Top Rock 'N' Roll Hits-1970 .... (RHI)
Wilson Pickett; *Greatest Hits* .... (ATL)
No Fun
Iggy Pop; *Elektrock-Sixties* .... (ELE)
Stooges; *Stooges* .... (ELE)
On The One For Fun
Dazz Band; *Greatest Hits* .... (MOT)
Real Good Time Together
Lou Reed; *Between Thought &*
Expression-Anthology .... (RCA)
Street Hassle .... (OOP)
Really Good Time
Roxy Music; *Country Life* .... (RPR)
See The Funny Little Clown
Bobby Goldsboro; *10th Anniversary Album-#1* ... (EMI)
Greatest Hits .... (LIB)
Honey-Best Of .... (EMI)
Take It Easy
Crystal Gayle; *Greatest Hits* .... (COL)
These Days .... (LIB)
Duke Ellington; *Brunswick Era-#1-1926-1929* . (MCA)

Eagles; *Anthology* .... (ASY)
Eagles .... (ASY)
Hell Freezes Over .... (GEF)
Live .... (ASY)
Their Greatest Hits .... (ASY)
Jackson Browne; *For Everyman* .... (ASY)
Lacy J. Dalton; *Greatest Hits* .... (CAP)
Take It Easy .... (COL)
Travis Tritt; *Common Thread-Songs Of The*
Eagles .... (GIA)
Talk About The Good Times
Elvis Presley; *Good Times* .... (RCA)
Thanks For All The Good Times
White Mountain Singers; *Best* .... (FOL)
They're Coming To Take Me Away, Ha Ha
Napoleon XIV; *Dr. Demento's Greatest Novelty-#3* (RHI)
Silly Songs .... (KT)
They're Coming To Take Me Away, Ha Ha ..... (RHI)
Thrill Of It All
Roxy Music; *Country Life* .... (RPR)
Greatest Hits .... (ATC)
Tonight We're Gonna Tear Down The Walls
Randy Travis; *Always & Forever* .... (WB)
Too Much Fun
Commander Cody/Lost Planet Airmen; *Live From Deep*
In The Heart Of Texas .... (MCA)
Too Much Fun-Best Of .... (MCA)
We've Got A Live One Here .... (WB)
You Make Loving Fun
Fleetwood Mac; *25 Years-The Chain* .... (WB)
Greatest Hits .... (WB)
Rumours .... (WB)
You Ought To Be Havin' Fun
Tower Of Power; *Ain't Nothin' Stopping Us Now* (COL)

FUTURE, Predictions, Tomorrow
See Also: CHAOS, TIME: GENERAL

1999
Prince; *1999* .... (WB)
21st Century Schizoid Man
King Crimson; *In The Court Of The Crimson*
King .... (ATL)
"Back To The Future" Theme
Cincinnati Pops Orchestra/Erich Kunzel; *Star Tracks*
II .... (TLR)
Best Is Yet To Come
Frank Sinatra; *Sinatra Reprise-Very Good Years* .. (RPR)
Grover Washington, Jr.; *Anthology* .... (ELE)
Grover Washington, Jr. & Patti LaBelle; *Best Is Yet To*
Come .... (ELE)
Built For The Future
Fixx; *One Thing Leads To Another-Greatest Hits* (MCA)
React .... (MCA)
Walkabout .... (MCA)
Children Of The Future
Steve Miller Band; *Children Of The Future* ...... (CAP)
Don't Stop
Fleetwood Mac; *25 Years-The Chain* .... (WB)
Greatest Hits .... (WB)
Live .... (WB)
Rumours .... (WB)
Estimated Prophet
Burning Spear; *Deadicated* .... (ARI)
Grateful Dead; *Terrapin Station* .... (ARI)
Fly Like An Eagle
Steve Miller Band; *Fly Like An Eagle* .... (CAP)
Gift Set .... (CAP)
Greatest Hits .... (CAP)
Live .... (CAP)
ST/FM .... (MCA)
Fortune Teller
Benny Spellman; *Best Of New Orleans R&B-#1* .. (RHI)
History Of New Orleans R&B-#2 .... (RHI)
Rolling Stones; *Got Live If You Want It* .... (AKO)
More Hot Rocks .... (AKO)
Future
Little Johnny Taylor; *45* .... (RON)
Prince; *ST/Batman* .... (WB)
Future Games
Fleetwood Mac; *Future Games* .... (RPR)
Future Legend
David Bowie; *Diamond Dogs* .... (RYK)

Future Shock
Hello People; *45* ....(OOP)
Future's So Bright I Gotta Wear Shades
Timbuk 3; *Greetings From* .... (IRS)
Headache Tomorrow (Or A Heartache...)
Mickey Gilley; *Biggest Hits* .... (EPI)
  Ten Years Of Hits .... (EPI)
  That's All That Matters To Me .... (EPI)
Headed For The Future
Neil Diamond; *Headed For The Future* ....(COL)
  Hot August Night II ....(COL)
If Tomorrow Never Comes
Garth Brooks; *Garth Brooks* ....(CAP)
In The Year 2525
Zager & Evans; *Nipper's Greatest Hits-'60s-#2* ...(RCA)
It Won't Be Long Now
Barbeque Bob & Laughing Charley; *Story Of The
Blues* ....(COL)
I.G.Y. (What A Beautiful World)
Donald Fagen; *45* .... (WB)
  Nightfly ....(WB)
I'm Gonna Be A Wheel Someday
Fats Domino; *Best Of* .... (EMI)
  Fats Domino ....(AUF)
  Greatest Hits ....(EVR)
  Greatest Hits .... (MCA)
  My Blue Heaven-Best Of-#1 .... (EMI)
Los Lobos; *Fine Mess* .... (MOT)
I'm Gonna Leave You Tomorrow
John Schneider; *Country Classics-#6-1985-1986* (MCA)
  Greatest Hits .... (MCA)
  Tryin' To Outrun The Wind .... (MCA)
Living In The Future
John Prine; *Storm Windows* .... (ASY)
Living In The Future In A Plastic Dome
Country Joe McDonald; *Incredible Live* .... (VAN)
Living In The Plastic Age
Buggles; *Age Of Plastic* .... (ISL)
Lookin' At Tomorrow
Beach Boys; *Surf's Up* ....(CAR)
Love Is Gonna Come At Last
Badfinger; *Airwaves* ....(OOP)
  Best Of-#2 .... (RHI)
Love Me Tomorrow
Chicago; *Greatest Hits-1982-1989* .... (FM)
  XVI .... (FW)
Manana
Jimmy Buffett; *Son Of A Son Of A Sailor* .... (MCA)
Never Comes The Day
Moody Blues; *Caught Live Plus Five* .... (POL)
  On The Threshold Of A Dream .... (POL)
  This Is The ....(POL)
No Future In The Past
Vince Gill; *I Still Believe In You* .... (MCA)
No More Looking Back
Kinks; *Schoolboys In Disgrace* .... (RHI)
  Second Time Around ....(RCA)
One Fine Day
Carpenters; *From The Top* ....(A&M)
  Now & Then ....(A&M)
Chiffons; *Best Of* ....(LAU)
  Collectables Presents History Of Rock-#9 .... (CLT)
  Golden Classics ....(CLT)
  Oldies But Goodies-#12 ....(OSR)
One Of These Days
Camper Van Beethoven; *Our Beloved Revolutionary
Sweetheart* ....(VIA)
Emmylou Harris; *Elite Hotel* .... (RPR)
  Profile-Best Of ....(WB)
John Lee Hooker; *That's My Story* .... (RVR)
Marvin Gaye; *Greatest Hits* .... (MOT)
Matthews, Wright & King; *Dream Seekers* ....(COL)
Nanci Griffith; *Last Of The True Believers* ....(PHO)
Neil Young; *Harvest* .... (RPR)
Pink Floyd; *Collection Of Great Dance Songs* ....(COL)
  Delicate Sound Of Thunder ....(COL)
  Gift Set ....(COL)
  Meddle .... (CAP)
  Works .... (CAP)
Ronnie Hawkins/Hawks; *Best Of* .... (RHI)
Ten Years After; *Space In Time* .... (CHR)
Tom Grant; *Just The Right Moment* .... (VF)
Velvet Underground; *V.U.* ....(VRV)

Our Day Will Come
Ruby/Romantics; *21 Country Rock & Love
Songs/'50s&'60s-1* ....(LAU)
  Oldies But Goodies-#12 ....(OSR)
Our Time Is Coming
Brooks & Dunn; *Hard Workin' Man* .... (ARI)
Our Time Is Gonna Come (I Believe)
R.E.O. Speedwagon; *Decade Of Rock &
Roll-1970-1980* .... (EPI)
  Live-You Get What You Play For .... (EPI)
  R.E.O. .... (EPI)
See The Future
Front 242; *No Comment* .... (EPI)
Somebody's Gonna Love You
Lee Greenwood; *Greatest Hits* .... (MCA)
  Somebody's Gonna Love You .... (MCA)
Someday
Alan Jackson; *Don't Rock The Jukebox* .... (ARI)
Bobby Bland; *Best Of* .... (MCA)
  Introspective Of The Early Years .... (MCA)
BoDeans; *Outside Looking In* ....(SLS)
Concrete Blonde; *Walking In London* .... (IRS)
Flim/BB's; *Vintage* ....(DIG)
Greg Kihn; *Kihnsolidation-Best Of* .... (RHI)
Mariah Carey; *Mariah Carey* ....(COL)
  MTV Unplugged ....(COL)
Neil Young; *Freedom* .... (RPR)
Shawn Colvin; *Cover Girl* ....(COL)
Steve Earle/Dukes; *Guitar Town* .... (MCA)
  Shut Up & Die Like An Aviator .... (MCA)
Someday After A While
Eric Clapton; *From The Cradle* .... (DUC)
Someday I'll Find You
Bobby Short; *Mad About Noel Coward* .... (ATL)
Mary Martin & Noel Coward; *Together With
Music* ....(DRG)
Someday My Day Will Come
George Jones; *Anniversary-Ten Years Of Hits* ..... (EPI)
  Still The Same Ole Me ....(EPI)
Someday My Prince Will Come
Bill Evans Trio; *Portrait In Jazz* ....(RVR)
En Vogue; *Simply Mad About The Mouse* ....(COL)
Lena Horne; *A New Album* ....(RCA)
Lena Horne & Phil Woods; *I Have Dreamed* .... (NOV)
Miles Davis; *Greatest Hits* ....(COL)
  I Like Jazz-Essence Of ....(COL)
  Someday My Prince Will Come ....(COL)
Mormon Tabernacle Choir; *When You Wish Upon A
Star-Tribute-Disney* ....(COL)
Someday Never Comes
Creedence Clearwater Revival; *Chronicle* .... (FAN)
  Mardi Gras ....(FAN)
Someday Someday
Marvelettes; *Anthology* .... (MOT)
Someday Soon
Chris LeDoux; *Rodeo Songs Old & New* .... (LIB)
Ian & Sylvia; *Greatest Hits* .... (VAN)
  Northern Journey ....(VAN)
Journey; *Departure* ....(COL)
Judy Collins; *Colors Of The Day-Best Of* .... (ELE)
  Who Knows Where The Time Goes .... (ELE)
Moe Bandy; *Greatest Hits* ....(COL)
  Rodeo Romeo ....(COL)
Suzy Bogguss; *Aces* ....(CAP)
Someday Sweetheart
Bing Crosby; *Here Lies Love* .... (ALE)
Peggy Lee; *You Can Depend On Me* ....(GLN)
Zoot Sims; *Best Of* .... (PAB)
Someday We'll All Be Free
Donny Hathaway; *Best Of* ....(ATC)
James Ingram; *It's Real* .... (WB)
Someday We'll Be Together
Diana Ross/Supremes; *20-20* .... (MOT)
  Anthology .... (MOT)
  Evening With Diana Ross .... (MOT)
  Greatest Hits-#3 .... (MOT)
  Motown Story .... (MOT)
  Motown Superstar Series-#1 .... (MOT)
Someday We're Gonna Love Again
Barbara Lewis; *Golden Classics* ....(CLT)
Searchers; *Greatest Hits* .... (RHI)

Someday When Things Are Good
Merle Haggard; *His Epic Hits-First 11 To Be Continued* .... (EPI)
   That's The Way Love Goes .... (EPI)
Someday (You'll Want Me To Want You)
Gene Autry; *Country Music Hall Of Fame* ....(COL)
Mills Brothers; *Best Of* .... (MCA)
   Best Of The Decca Years .... (DEC)
Patsy Cline; *Last Sessions* .... (MCA)
   Portrait Of .... (MCA)
Vaughn Monroe; *Best Of* .... (MCA)
Someday (You're Gonna Want Me)
Bobby Vee; *Golden Greats* .... (LIB)
Someday, Someway
Marshall Crenshaw; *Marshall Crenshaw* .... (WB)
   ST/Nightshift .... (WB)
Something's Coming
Barbra Streisand; *Broadway Album* .... (COL)
   One Voice .... (COL)
Original Cast; *West Side Story* .... (COL)
Somewhere Down The Line
T.G. Sheppard; *All-Time Greatest Hits* .... (WB)
   Slow Burn .... (WB)
Soon
Ella Fitzgerald; *George & Ira Gershwin Songbook* (VRV)
Kiri Te Kanawa; *Kiri Sings Gershwin* .... (ANG)
Original Cast; *Little Night Music* .... (COL)
   My One & Only .... (ATL)
Tanya Tucker; *Soon* .... (LIB)
Sooner Or Later
Barbara Cook; *Disney Album* .... (MCA)
Eddy Raven; *Best Of* .... (LIB)
   Temporary Sanity .... (LIB)
Gary Morris; *Stones* .... (LIB)
Grass Roots; *Anthology-1965-1975* .... (RHI)
   Super Hits-#2 .... (GUS)
   Their 16 Greatest Hits .... (MCA)
Madonna; *I'm Breathless-Music From Dick Tracy* . (SIR)
Tell Me Tomorrow
Angela Bofill; *Angela Bofill* .... (ARI)
   Best Of .... (ARI)
Karyn White; *Karyn White* .... (WB)
Smokey Robinson; *Blame It On Love & All The Great Hits* .... (MOT)
That'll Be The Day
Buddy Holly; *ST/American Graffiti* .... (MCA)
Buddy Holly/Crickets; *20 Golden Greats* .... (MCA)
   Chirping Crickets .... (MCA)
Crickets; *Billboard Top Rock 'N' Roll Hits-1957* . (RHI)
Foghat; *Best Of-#2* .... (RHI)
   Energized .... (RHI)
Linda Ronstadt; *Greatest Hits* .... (ASY)
   Hasten Down The Wind .... (ASY)
Theme From "The Jetsons"
Stunners; *ST/Jetsons-The Movie* .... (MCA)
There Ain't No Future In This
Reba McEntire; *Best Of* .... (MER)
There's No Tomorrow
Squeeze; *East Side Story* .... (A&M)
Tony Martin; *Nipper's Greatest Hits-'40s-#2* .... (RCA)
Things We Said Today
Beatles; *At The Hollywood Bowl* .... (CAP)
   Box Set .... (CAP)
   Hard Day's Night .... (CAP)
   Something New .... (CAP)
Paul McCartney; *Tripping The Live Fantastic* .... (CAP)
   Tripping The Live Fantastic-Highlights! .... (CAP)
Time Is Running Out
Steve Winwood; *Steve Winwood* .... (ISL)
Tomorrow
Barbra Streisand; *Songbird* .... (COL)
Information Society; *Information Society* .... (TMB)
Jay/Americans; *Come A Little Bit Closer-Best Of* . (EMI)
Jimmy Somerville/Communards; *Singles Collection-1984-1990* .... (LON)
Joe Walsh; *But Seriously Folks* .... (ASY)
Morrissey; *Your Arsenal* .... (SIR)
Original Cast; *ST/Annie* .... (COL)
Poco; *Picking Up The Pieces* .... (EPI)
Strawberry Alarm Clock; *Best Of-#1* .... (BCT)
Three O'Clock; *Hoedown* .... (FON)
   Sixteen Tambourines .... (FON)
U2; *October* .... (ISL)
Wall Of Voodoo; *Call Of The West* .... (IRS)

Wings; *Wild Life* .... (CAP)
Tomorrow Belongs To Me
Liza Minnelli & Joel Grey; *ST/Cabaret* .... (MCA)
Original Cast; *Cabaret* .... (COL)
Tomorrow Doesn't Matter Tonight
Starship; *Knee Deep In The Hoopla* .... (GRU)
Tomorrow Is A Long Time
Bob Dylan; *Greatest Hits-#2* .... (COL)
Chris Hillman; *Morning Sky* .... (SH)
Elvis Presley; *Valentine Gift For You* .... (RCA)
Ian & Sylvia; *Four Strong Winds* .... (VAN)
   Greatest Hits .... (VAN)
   Troubadours Of The Folk Era-#1 .... (RHI)
Sandy Denny; *Who Knows Where The Time Goes* (HBL)
Tomorrow Is Such A Long Time
Rod Stewart; *Every Picture Tells A Story* ...... (MER)
   Greatest Hits-#2 .... (MER)
Tomorrow I'll Be Out Of Town
Ten Years After; *Classic Performances Of* ...... (COL)
   Universal .... (CHR)
Tomorrow Never Comes
Ernest Tubb; *Story* .... (MCA)
Ernest Tubb & B.J. Thomas; *Ernest Tubb Collection* (SO)
Slim Whitman; *Best Of-1952-1972* .... (RHI)
Tomorrow Never Knows
Beatles; *Box Set* .... (CAP)
   Revolver .... (CAP)
Phil Collins; *Face Value* .... (ATL)
Tomorrow Night
Barbra Streisand; *ST/Yentl* .... (COL)
Bob Dylan; *Good As I Been To You* .... (COL)
Elvis Presley; *Complete Sun Sessions* .... (RCA)
   For Everyone .... (RCA)
   Reconsider Baby .... (RCA)
   Sun's Greatest Hits .... (RCA)
La Vern Baker; *Atlantic R&B-1947-1974 (1952-1955)* .... (ATL)
   Soul On Fire .... (ATL)
Tomorrow Night In Baltimore
Roger Miller; *Best Of* .... (MER)
   More Golden Hits .... (SMA)
Tomorrow & Tonight
Kiss; *Alive 2* .... (CAS)
   Love Gun .... (CAS)
Tomorrow (A Better You, Better Me)
Quincy Jones & Tevin Campbell; *Back On The Block* .... (QUE)
Tomorrow's Dreams
Black Sabbath; *We Sold Our Soul For Rock & Roll* (WB)
   #4 .... (WB)
Tomorrow's Girls
Donald Fagen; *Kamakiriad* .... (RPR)
Tomorrow's Gonna Be Another Day
Charlie Daniels Band; *Night Rider* .... (EPI)
Te John-Grease & Wolfman .... (EPI)
Tomorrow's My Wedding Day
Country Gentlemen; *Country Songs Old & New* . (FLW)
Victims Of The Future
Gary Moore; *Early Years* .... (WTG)
   We Want Moore .... (VIA)
Vision Of The Future
Roachford; *Get Ready!* .... (EPI)
Wait Until Tomorrow
Jimi Hendrix; *Axis: Bold As Love* .... (RPR)
Jimi Hendrix Experience; *Radio One* .... (RYK)
Waiting For The Day
Gerry Rafferty; *City To City* .... (EMI)
We Shall Overcome
James Cleveland/Troubadors; *James Cleveland/Troubadors* .... (SAV)
Joan Baez; *Carry It On* .... (VAN)
   In Concert .... (VAN)
Pete Seeger; *Bitter & The Sweet* .... (MOB)
   Greatest Hits .... (COL)
When Tomorrow Comes
Eurythmics; *Greatest Hits* .... (ARI)
   Greenpeace/Rainbow Warriors .... (GEF)
   Revenge .... (RCA)
Who Knows What Tomorrow Will Bring
Traffic; *Traffic* .... (ISL)
Will You Still Love Me Tomorrow
Carole King; *Tapestry* .... (EPI)
Frankie Valli/Four Seasons; *Greatest Hits-#2* .... (RHI)
Linda Ronstadt; *Retrospective* .... (CAP)

Roberta Flack; *Best Of* .... (ATL)
  Quiet Fire .... (ATL)
Shirelles; *16 Greatest Hits* .... (TRP)
  Anthology-1959-1964 .... (RHI)
  Girl Groups .... (RHI)
  More Dirty Dancing ....(RCA)
  Oldies But Goodies-#14 .... (MCA)
  Wonder Women-#2 .... (MOT)
Year 2003 Minus 25
Waylon Jennings & Willie Nelson; *Waylon & Willie* ....(RCA)
Your Time Is Gonna Come
Led Zeppelin; *Led Zeppelin* .... (ATL)
  Led Zeppelin (collection) .... (ATL)
You've Got A Good Love Comin'
Lee Greenwood; *Inside Out/You've Got A Good Love Comin'* .... (MCA)

GAMBLING, Betting, Card Games, Casino Games, Chance, Dice

  See Also: CITIES: LAS VEGAS, LUCK, SPORTS, WINNING

100% Chance Of Rain
Gary Morris; *Anything Goes* .... (WB)
21
Eagles; *Desperado* .... (ASY)
50-50
Mothers Of Invention; *Apostrophe/Overnite Sensation* ....(RYK)
7-11 (A Winner)
Li'l Wally; *Polish Carnival* .... (JJ)
Ace In The Hole
George Feyer; *Cole Porter Songbook* .... (VAN)
George Strait; *Beyond The Blue Neon* ....(RCA)
Aces
Suzy Bogguss; *Aces* ....(CAP)
Against All Odds (Take A Look At Me Now)
Phil Collins; *Hit Singles 1980-1988* .... (ATL)
  Serious Hits...Live! .... (ATL)
  ST/Against All Odds .... (ATL)
All I Need (Is A Chance)
Take 6; *Join The Band* .... (RPR)
American Roulette
Robbie Robertson; *Robbie Robertson* ....(GEF)
Another Chance
Tammy Wynette; *45* .... (EPI)
Atlantic City Gambler
Grace Jones; *Muse* .... (ISL)
Bad Bad Leroy Brown
Jim Croce; *Billboard Top Rock 'N' Roll Hits-1973* (RHI)
  Down The Highway .... (21)
  Life & Times ....(OOP)
  Photographs & Memories .... (21)
Bangkok Cockfight
Martin Denny; *Exotica-Best Of* .... (RHI)
Beatin' The Odds
Molly Hatchet; *Beatin' The Odds* .... (EPI)
  Double Trouble-Live .... (EPI)
Bet Your Heart On Me
Johnny Lee; *Greatest Hits* .... (FA)
Betcha Can't Cry Just One
David Frizzell & Shelly West; *In Session* ....(VVA)
Betcha Gonna Need My Lovin'
LaToya Jackson; *Heart Don't Lie* .... (PRI)
Betcha Say That
Gloria Estefan/Miami Sound Machine; *Let It Loose* .... (EPI)
Betcha The Love Bug Bitcha
Dr. Buzzard's Band; *Original Savannah Band* ....(RCA)
Betcha' Wouldn't Hurt Me
Quincy Jones; *Classics-#3* .... (A&M)
  The Best .... (A&M)
  The Dude .... (A&M)
Caesar's Palace Blues
UK; *Danger Money* .... (EDI)
  Night After Night .... (EDI)
Call It A Loan
Jackson Browne; *Hold Out* .... (ASY)
Chance For Heaven
Christopher Cross; *Official Music Of The XXIIIrd Olympiad* ....(COL)

Chance Of Lovin' You
Earl Thomas Conley; *Greatest Hits-#2* ....(RCA)
  Treadin' Water ....(RCA)
Chances
Air Supply; *Greatest Hits* .... (ARI)
  Lost In Love .... (ARI)
Chances Are
Bob Marley; *Chances Are* .... (COT)
Johnny Mathis; *All-Time Greatest Hits* ....(COL)
  First 25 Years ....(COL)
  Greatest Hits ....(COL)
  Live ....(COL)
  Love Songs ....(COL)
Deal
Grateful Dead; *Dead Set* .... (ARI)
Jerry Garcia; *Garcia* ....(GRD)
Deck Of Cards
Bill Anderson; *American Music Greatest Hits* ....(CCB)
  Best Of ....(CCB)
Tex Ritter; *Capitol Collectors Series* ....(CAP)
  Greatest Hits ....(CCB)
"T" Texas Tyler; *45* ....(OOP)
Desperado
Alice Cooper; *Greatest Hits* .... (WB)
  Killer .... (WB)
Clint Black; *Common Thread-Songs Of The Eagles* ....(GIA)
Eagles; *Anthology* .... (ASY)
  Desperado .... (ASY)
  Hell Freezes Over ....(GEF)
  Live .... (ASY)
  Their Greatest Hits 1971-1975 .... (ASY)
Linda Ronstadt; *Don't Cry Now* .... (ASY)
  Greatest Hits .... (ASY)
Deuces Are Wild
Aerosmith; *Beavis & BuDeuces Are Wild-Head Experience* ....(GEF)
Devil Went Down To Georgia
Charlie Daniels Band; *Billboard Top Hits-1979* .. (RHI)
  Decade Of Hits .... (EPI)
  Me & The Boys .... (EPI)
  Million Mile Reflections .... (EPI)
  ST/Urban Cowboy .... (ASY)
Dime Queen Of Nevada
Tom Jones; *Darlin'* .... (MER)
Don't Bet Money
Whispers; *Best Of* .... (SLR)
  Don't Bet Money .... (SLR)
Don't Stand Another Chance
Janet Jackson; *Dream Street* ....(A&M)
Door #3
Jimmy Buffett; *A 1 A* .... (MCA)
Double Dealin' Four Flusher
Doobie Brothers; *Stampede* .... (WB)
Draw Of The Cards
Kim Carnes; *Mistaken Identity* .... (EMI)
Dyin' Crapshooter's Blues
Blind Willie McTell; *Atlanta Twelve-String* .... (ATL)
David Bromberg; *How Late'll Ya Play 'Til* ....(FAN)
Dyin' Gambler
Blind James Campbell; *& His Nashville Street Band* .... (ARH)
Dyin' Gambler's Blues
Bessie Smith; *Complete Recordings-#2* ....(COL)
Every Time I Roll The Dice
Delbert McClinton; *Never Been Rocked Enough* ..(CRB)
Fat Chance Hotel
Public Image, Ltd.; *Happy?* .... (VIA)
France Chance
Ry Cooder; *Ry Cooder* .... (RPR)
From A Jack To A King
Jim Reeves; *I Love You Because* ....(RCA)
  Pure Gold ....(RCA)
Ned Miller; *Billboard Top Country Hits-1963* .... (RHI)
Ricky Van Shelton; *Loving Proof* ....(COL)
Gambler
Emerson, Lake & Palmer; *Love Beach* ....(OOP)
Kenny Rogers; *20 Greatest Hits* .... (LIB)
  Gambler .... (EMI)
  Greatest Hits .... (EMI)
Madonna; *ST/Vision Quest* ....(GEF)
Whitesnake; *Slide It In* ....(GEF)

Gambler's Blues
B.B. King; *Back In The Alley* .... (MCA)
  Great Moments With .... (MCA)
Otis Rush; *Atlantic Blues-Chicago* .... (ATL)
Gambling Man
Bonnie Raitt; *Sweet Forgiveness* .... (WB)
Ghost Of A Chance
Rush; *Roll The Bones* .... (ATL)
Ghost Of A Chance With You
Billie Holiday; *Stormy Blues* .... (VRV)
  #2 .... (EVR)
Mel Torme; *Smooth As Velvet* .... (PIC)
Give Me One More Chance
Exile; *19 Hot Country Requests-#2* .... (EPI)
  Greatest Hits .... (EPI)
  Kentucky Hearts .... (EPI)
Go Down Gamblin'
Blood, Sweat & Tears; *Greatest Hits* .... (COL)
Good Run Of Bad Luck
Clint Black; *No Time To Kill* .... (RCA)
Hi Roller
Little Feat; *Time Loves A Hero* .... (WB)
Holdin' A Good Hand
Lee Greenwood; *Holdin' A Good Hand* .... (CAP)
House Of Cards
Elton John; *45* .... (MCA)
Mary Chapin Carpenter; *Stones In The Road* ....(COL)
I Feel Lucky
Mary Chapin Carpenter; *Come On Come On* ...(COL)
I Take My Chances
Mary Chapin Carpenter; *Come On Come On* ...(COL)
I'll Bet You A Kangaroo
Olivia Newton-John; *Don't Stop Believin'* .... (MCA)
I've Got The Horse Right Here
Original Cast; *Guys & Dolls* .... (MCA)
Jack Of Hearts
Bob Dylan; *Blood On The Tracks* ....(COL)
Jack O' Diamonds
Blind Snooks Eaglin; *Possum Up A Simmon Tree* (ARH)
Odetta; *Odetta* .... (EVR)
Kentucky Gambler
Merle Haggard/Strangers; *Songs I'll Always Sing* .(CAP)
Knock On Wood
Amii Stewart; *45* .... (ARL)
Buddy Guy; *This Is* .... (VAN)
Eddie Floyd; *15 Original Big Hits-#3* .... (STX)
  Atlantic R&B-1947-1974-#6-(1966-1969) .... (ATL)
  Best Of Wattstax .... (STX)
  Super Oldies/'60s-#11 .... (AUF)
Eric Clapton; *Behind The Sun* .... (DUC)
Ike & Tina Turner; *Greatest Hits-#3* .... (SAJ)
Las Vegas Turnaround
Daryl Hall & John Oates; *Abandoned
Luncheonette* .... (ATL)
  No Goodbyes .... (ATL)
Last Chance
Bryan Adams; *You Want It You Got It* .... (POL)
John Mellencamp; *Whenever We Wanted* .... (MER)
Level 42; *Pursuit Of Accidents* .... (POL)
Last Chance Texaco
Rickie Lee Jones; *Rickie Lee Jones* .... (WB)
Lido Shuffle
Boz Scaggs; *Hits!* ....(COL)
  Silk Degrees ....(COL)
  ST/FM .... (MCA)
Lottery Song
Nilsson; *Son Of Schmilsson* .... (RCA)
Louisiana Lou & Three-Card Monty John
Allman Brothers Band; *Win Lose Or Draw* .... (POL)
"Maverick" Theme
Original Music; *Television's Greatest Hits-#2* ..... (TVT)
No Chance Of Losing
Jerry Garcia; *Jerry Garcia* .... (WB)
One Eyed Jack
Garland Jeffreys; *Matador & More* .... (A&M)
  One Eyed Jack .... (OOP)
One Of A Kind Pair Of Fools
Barbara Mandrell; *Greatest Country Hits* .... (CCB)
  Greatest Hits .... (MCA)
  Spun Gold .... (MCA)
Ooh Las Vegas
Emmylou Harris; *Elite Hotel* .... (RPR)
Gram Parsons; *Grievous Angel* .... (RPR)

Queen Of Hearts
Dave Edmunds; *Best Of* .... (SS)
  Repeat When Necessary .... (SS)
Gregg Allman; *Laid Back* .... (POL)
Joan Baez; *Ballad Book* .... (VAN)
  In Concert .... (VAN)
Juice Newton; *All-Time Country Classics-#2* ..... (CAP)
  Greatest Hits .... (CAP)
  Greatest Hits & More .... (CAP)
  Juice .... (CAP)
Rodney Crowell; *Collection* .... (WB)
Whitesnake; *Snakebite* .... (GEF)
Queen Of Spades
Styx; *Pieces Of Eight* .... (A&M)
Rambler Gambler
Joan Baez; *Very Early* .... (VAN)
Rambling, Gambling Willie
Bob Dylan; *Bootleg Series-#1-3-1961-1989* .....(COL)
Ramblin' Gamblin' Man
Bob Seger; *Live Bullet* .... (CAP)
Read 'Em & Weep
Barry Manilow; *Greatest Hits-#3* .... (ARI)
Ready To Take A Chance Again
Barry Manilow; *Even Now* .... (ARI)
  Greatest Hits-#3 .... (ARI)
Reno
Doug Supernaw; *Red & Rio Grande* .... (BNA)
Riverboat Gambler
Chris LeDoux; *Songs Of Rodeo Life* .... (CAP)
Roll Of The Dice
Bruce Springsteen; *Human Touch* ....(COL)
Roll The Bones
Rush; *Roll The Bones* .... (ATL)
Roll The Dice
Ian Thomas; *Riders On Dark Horses* ....(RCA)
Ronnie Milsap; *Stranger Things Have Happened* ..(RCA)
Roving Gambler
Everly Brothers; *Songs Our Daddy Taught Us* .... (RHI)
Peter Rowan; *Walls Of Time* .... (SH)
Ramblin' Jack Elliott; *Essential* .... (VAN)
Russian Roulette
Accept; *Russian Roulette* .... (POR)
Hollies; *Hollies* .... (EPI)
Joan Armatrading; *Sleight Of Hand* .... (A&M)
Lords Of The New Church; *Killer Lords* .... (IRS)
  Lords Of The New Church .... (IRS)
Michelle Shocked; *Captain Swing* .... (MER)
Taxxi; *Expose* .... (MCA)
Save The Last Chance
Johnny Lee; *Keep Me Hangin' On* .... (FW)
Second Chance
38 Special; *Rock & Roll Strategy* .... (A&M)
Reivers; *Pop Beloved* .... (DB)
Seven Come Eleven
Benny Goodman; *Live At Carnegie Hall* ....(LON)
Charlie Christian; *Genius Of The Electric Guitar* .(COL)
Herb Ellis & Joe Pass; *Seven Come Eleven* .... (CCJ)
  Two For The Road .... (PAB)
Smoke! Smoke! Smoke!
Commander Cody/Lost Planet Airmen; *Country
Casanova* .... (MCA)
  Too Much Fun-Best Of .... (MCA)
  We Got A Live One .... (WB)
Doc Watson; *Red Rocking Chair* .... (FF)
Merle Travis; *Johnny Gimble's Texas Honky-Tonk
Hits* .... (CMH)
Tex Williams; *Birth Of A Dream-Capitol's Early
Hits* .... (CAP)
  Dr. Demento's Greatest-#1-1940s & Before .... (RHI)
Snake Eyes
Alan Parsons Project; *Turn Of A Friendly Card* .. (ARI)
Solitaire
Carpenters; *From The Top* .... (A&M)
  Horizon .... (A&M)
Elvis Presley; *Always On My Mind* ....(RCA)
  From Elvis Presley Blvd., Memphis, TN ....(RCA)
Erroll Garner; *Other Voices* ....(COL)
Jane Olivor; *Stay The Night* ....(COL)
Jerry Vale; *Greatest Hits* ....(COL)
Johnny Mathis; *Feelings* ....(COL)
Laura Branigan; *Branigan 2* .... (ATL)
Neil Sedaka; *I'm A Song* .... (FFT)
  Solitaire .... (FFT)

Public Image, Ltd.; *Live In Tokyo* .... (ELE)
   This Is What You Want...Is What You Get ...... (ELE)
Stan Kenton; *Artistry In Voices & Brass* ....(CW)
Son Of A Rotten Gambler
Anne Murray; *Anne Murray's Country Hits* .... (LIB)
   Country .... (CAP)
   Love Song .... (CAP)
Emmylou Harris; *Cimarron* .... (WB)
Still Taking Chances
Michael Murphey; *Best Of* .... (EMI)
   Michael Murphey .... (LIB)
Still The Same
Bob Seger; *Stranger In Town* ....(CAP)
Take A Chance
Bob Seger/Silver Bullet Band; *Fire Inside* ....(CAP)
Chicago; *Hot Streets* ....(COL)
Divinyls; *Desperate* ....(CHR)
Eric Clapton; *August* ....(DUC)
J; *We Are The Majority* ....(A&M)
Kingsnakes; *Take A Chance* ....(BWV)
Olivia Newton-John & John Travolta; *ST/Two Of A
Kind* .... (MCA)
Take A Chance On Me
Abba; *Billboard Top Rock 'N' Roll Hits-1978* .... (RHI)
   Greatest Hits-#2 .... (ATL)
   Singles .... (ATL)
   The Album .... (ATL)
Take A Chance On Me, Baby
Capitols; *Their Greatest Recordings* ....(OOP)
Taking A Chance On Love
Anita O'Day; *Anita Sings The Most* ....(VRV)
Barbra Streisand; *Third Album* ....(COL)
Benny Goodman; *I Like Jazz-Essence Of* ....(COL)
Ella Fitzgerald; *Early Years-#2* ....(GRP)
Frank Sinatra; *Songs For Young Lovers & Swing
Easy* ....(CAP)
Johnny Mathis & Henry Mancini; *Hollywood
Musicals* ....(COL)
Rosemary Clooney; *Show Tunes* ....(CCJ)
Tony Bennett; *I Left My Heart In San Francisco* .(COL)
There's A Place In The World For A...
Dan Fogelberg; *Live-Greetings From The West* .... (FM)
   Souvenirs .... (FM)
   ST/FM .... (MCA)
Tumbling Dice
Linda Ronstadt; *Greatest Hits-#2* ....(ASY)
   Simple Dreams ....(ASY)
   ST/FM .... (MCA)
Rolling Stones; *Exile On Main Street* .... (RS)
   Love You Live .... (RS)
   Made In The Shade .... (RS)
   Rewind (1971-1984) .... (RS)
Two Of A Kind, Workin' On A Full House
Garth Brooks; *No Fences* .... (LIB)
Wheel Of Fortune
Cardinals; *Atlantic R&B 1947-1974-collection* ... (ATL)
Kay Starr; *Capitol Collectors Series* ....(CAP)
Wheels Of Fortune
Doobie Brothers; *Takin' It To The Streets* .... (WB)
While You See A Chance
Steve Winwood; *Arc Of A Diver* .... (ISL)
   Chronicles .... (ISL)
Win Or Lose
Earth, Wind & Fire; *Faces* ....(COL)
Nitty Gritty Dirt Band; *Dirt Silver & Gold* ...... (UA)
Win Some, Lose Some
Bryan Adams; *Bryan Adams* ....(A&M)
Scandal; *Scandal* ....(COL)
Ya Got Trouble
Original Broadway Cast; *Music Man* .... (ANG)
Robert Preston/Original Cast; *Music Man* ....(CAP)

GAS STATIONS

*See Also: CARS, ENERGY, MOTORCYCLES,
TRAVELING, TRUCKS*

Diesel & Propane
Sandoz; *Unfamiliar Territory* ....(RLX)
Dollar's Worth Of Gasoline
Tom Russell; *Hurricane Season* ....(PHO)

Ethelene (The Truckstop Queen)
Ray Stevens; *I Never Made A Record I Didn't
Like* .... (MCA)
Food Phone Gas Lodging
Charlie King; *Food Phone Gas Lodging* ....(FF)
Gas Station Woman
Phil Ochs; *War Is Over-Best Of* ....(A&M)
Gasoline Alley
Rod Stewart; *Absolutely Live* .... (WB)
   Best Of .... (MER)
   Gasoline Alley .... (MER)
   Sing It Again Rod .... (MER)
   Storyteller/Complete Anthology .... (WB)
Gasoline Blues
Charley Jordan; *St. Louis Blues-1929-1935* ......(YAZ)
John Mayall; *Room To Move-1969-1974-Chronicle
Series* ....(POL)
Great Filling Station Holdup
Jimmy Buffett; *White Sport Coat & A Pink
Crustacean* .... (MCA)
Gulf And The Shell
Clinton Gregory; *Clinton Gregory* ....(PYN)
Heavy Fuel
Dire Straits; *On Every Street* .... (WB)
Last Chance Texaco
Rickie Lee Jones; *Rickie Lee Jones* .... (WB)
Master Mechanic
Johnny Winter; *Serious Business* ....(ALG)
Old Home Filler Up & Keep On A Truckin'
C.W. McCall; *Greatest Hits* ....(POL)
   Wolf Creek Pass ....(MGM)
Open All Night
Bruce Springsteen; *Nebraska* ....(COL)
Rock & Roll Gas Station
Adrenalin O.D.; *Wacky Hi-Jinks Of* ....(BOR)
Running On Empty
Jackson Browne; *Running On Empty* .... (ASY)
Talkin' At The Texaco
James McMurtry; *Too Long In The Wasteland* ...(COL)
Truck Stop
Lenny Dee; *Best Of-#2* .... (MCA)
Mills Brothers; *Cab Driver* .... (RAN)
Truck Stop At The End Of The World
Commander Cody; *Let's Rock* .... (BLI)
Truck Stop Girl
Byrds; *Byrds (collection)* ....(COL)
   (Untitled) ....(COL)
Little Feat; *Little Feat* .... (WB)
Truck Stop Rock
Commander Cody/Lost Planet Airmen; *Hot Licks, Cold
Steel & Trucker's Fav.* .... (MCA)
Under The Light Of The Texaco
Jeff Stevens/Bullets; *Jeff Stevens/Bullets* .... (ATL)
Lisa Stewart; *Lisa Stewart* ....(BNA)
Walkaway Joe
Trisha Yearwood; *Hearts In Armor* .... (MCA)

GOD, Church, Jesus Christ, Prayer, Religion

*See Also: ANGELS, CHRISTMAS, HEAVEN,
HELL, MARRIAGE*

Ain't No God In Mexico
Waylon Jennings; *Honky Tonk Heroes* ....(RCA)
All God's Chillun Got Rhythm
Judy Garland; *Collector's Items-1936-1945* ..... (MCA)
Amazing Grace
Judy Collins; *Colors Of The Day-Best Of* .... (ELE)
   Whales & Nightingales .... (ELE)
Maverick Choir; *ST/Maverick* ....(ATL)
Nitty Gritty Dirt Band; *Will The Circle Be
Unbroken-#2* .... (UNI)
American Prayer
Doors; *American Prayer* .... (ELE)
Any Dream Will Do
Michael Crawford; *Performs Andrew Lloyd
Webber* ....(ATL)
Original Cast; *Joseph & The Amazing
Technicolor...* .... (MCA)

Aqualung
Jethro Tull; *20 Years Of-Boxed Set* .... (CHR)
  Aqualung .... (CHR)
  Bursting Out .... (CHR)
  'M.U.'- Best Of .... (CHR)
Are You Building A Temple In Heaven
Hank Williams; *I'm So Lonesome I Could
Cry-1949* .... (POL)
Battle Hymn Of The Republic
Charlie Sexton; *Charlie Sexton* .... (MCA)
Judy Collins; *Songs Of The Civil War* ......(COL)
Mormon Tabernacle Choir; *God Bless America* ..(COL)
  Stars & Stripes Forever ....(COL)
Pat Boone; *Star-Spangled Banner* ....(WOR)
Big Jesus Trash Can
Birthday Party; *Best & Rarest* .... (MIS)
  Collection .... (MIS)
Black Messiah
Kinks; *Misfits* .... (ARI)
Bless The Lord
Original Cast; *Godspell* .... (ARI)
Soundtrack; *Godspell* .... (ARI)
Bless You
John Lennon; *Lennon* ....(CAP)
  Menlove Ave. ....(CAP)
  Walls & Bridges ....(CAP)
Martha Reeves/Vandellas; *Anthology* ....(MOT)
  Compact Command Performances ....(MOT)
  Motown Superstar Series-#11 ....(MOT)
Blessed
Al Green; *I Get Joy* ....(A&M)
Simon & Garfunkel; *Collected Works* ....(COL)
  Sounds Of Silence ....(COL)
Blessed Are
Joan Baez; *Blessed Are* ....(A&M)
  From Every Stage ....(A&M)
  Hits/Greatest & Others .... (VAN)
Blessed Are The Believers
Anne Murray; *Country Hits* ....(CAP)
  Greatest Hits-#2 ....(CAP)
Blue Eden
Neil Young/Crazy Horse; *Sleeps With Angels* ..... (RPR)
Bo Diddley Is Jesus
Jesus & Mary Chain; *Barbed Wire Kisses* ....(WB)
Born Again
Christians; *Christians* .... (ISL)
Brother Love's Traveling Salvation Show
Neil Diamond; *Hot August Night* .... (MCA)
  Gold .... (MCA)
  His 12 Greatest Hits .... (MCA)
  Love At The Greek ....(COL)
  Sweet Caroline .... (MCA)
Burn Down The Mission
Elton John; *11-17-70* .... (POL)
  Live In Australia .... (MCA)
  Tumbleweed Connection .... (POL)
  Your Songs .... (MCA)
Phil Collins/Serious Band; *Two Rooms (Celebrating
Songs Of...)* .... (POL)
Cathedral
Crosby, Stills & Nash; *CSN* .... (ATL)
  Replay .... (ATL)
Van Halen; *Diver Down* ....(WB)
Catholic Girls
Frank Zappa; *Joe's Garage* ....(RYK)
  You Can't Do That On Stage Anymore-#6 ......(RYK)
Catholic School Girls Rule
Red Hot Chili Peppers; *Abbey Road E.P.* .... (EMI)
  Freaky Styley .... (EMI)
  What Hits!? Best Of .... (EMI)
Chapel Of Love
Dixie Cups; *Girl Groups* .... (RHI)
  Girl Groups-Story of A Sound .... (MOT)
  Jewels #1 .... (SSS)
  Oldies But Goodies-#11 ....(OSR)
  Original New York Rock & Roll ....(OSR)
Chapel On The Hill
Mello-Kings; *Greatest Hits* .... (CLT)
Cheater's Prayer
Kendalls; *Stickin' Together* .... (MER)
  Thank God For The Radio (& All The Hits) ... (MER)
Children Go Where I Send Thee
Peter, Paul & Mary/N.Y. Choral Society; *Holiday
Celebration* ....(WB)

Weavers; *At Carnegie Hall* .... (VAN)
White Mountain Singers; *Best* ....(FOL)
Christ Child Lullaby
Judy Collins; *Golden Apples Of The Sun* .... (ELE)
Christian Life
Byrds; *Byrds (collection)* ....(COL)
  Sweetheart Of The Rodeo ....(COL)
Church
Lyle Lovett; *Joshua Judges Ruth* .... (MCC)
Church Bells May Ring
Diamonds; *Best Of* ....(RHI)
Willows; *Rockin' & Rollin' Wedding Songs* ....(RHI)
  ST/A Rage In Harlem ....(SIR)
  WCBS FM101-History Of Rock/'50s-#2 ....(CLT)
Church Of Logic, Sin & Love
Men; *The Men* ....(POL)
Church Of The Poison Mind
Culture Club; *At Worst-Best Of Boy George & C.
Club* .... (SBK)
  Colour By Numbers .... (VIA)
Church Of Your Heart
Roxette; *Joyride* .... (EMI)
City Of God
Rubber Rodeo; *Scenic Views* .... (MER)
Come Back...Barbara Lewis Hare Krisha...
John Prine; *Anthology-Great Days* .... (RHI)
  Common Sense .... (ATL)
  Prime Prine-Best Of .... (ATL)
Coming Out Of The Dark
Gloria Estefan; *Greatest Hits* .... (EPI)
  Hot #1 Hits ....(FTN)
  Into The Light .... (EPI)
Comin' In On A Wing & A Prayer
Ry Cooder; *Boomer's Story* .... (RPR)
Computer God
Black Sabbath; *Dehumanizer* .... (RPR)
Convict's Prayer
Li'l Wally; *One Man Band* ....(JJ)
Count Your Blessings
Ashford & Simpson; *Real Love* ....(CAP)
Eddie Fisher; *Best OF* .... (MCA)
Cowboy's Prayer
Goebel Reeves; *Songs Of The Old West* ....(GLN)
  Texas Drifter ....(GLN)
Creator Has A Master Plan
Pharoah Sanders; *Fire Into Music-Best Of
Impulse!-#3* .... (MCI)
  Karma .... (MCI)
Crucified
Agnostic Front; *Best Of* .... (REL)
  Last Warning .... (REL)
Army Of Lovers; *Massive Luxury Overdose* ...... (GIA)
Fixx; *Ink* .... (IPA)
Crying In The Chapel
Elvis Presley; *How Great Thou Art* .... (RCA)
  Legendary Performer-#3 ....(RCA)
  Top Ten Hits ....(RCA)
  Worldwide 50 Gold Award Hits-#1 ....(RCA)
June Valli; *Nipper's Greatest Hits-'50s-#2* ....(RCA)
Little Richard; *Shut Up-Rare Tracks-1951-1964* . (RHI)
Orioles; *Super Oldies/'50s-#1* ....(AUF)
Sonny Til/Orioles; *Echoes Of A Rock Era-Early
Years* .... (RLL)
  Greatest Hits .... (CLT)
  ST/American Graffiti .... (MCA)
Daddy Was An Old Time Preacher Man
Porter Wagoner & Dolly Parton; *Best Of* ....(RCA)
Daniel & The Sacred Harp
Band; *Anthology-#1* ....(CAP)
  Stage Fright ....(CAP)
  To Kingdom Come (Definitive Collection) ....(CAP)
Deacon Blues
Steely Dan; *Aja* .... (MCA)
  Gold .... (MCA)
Deal With The Preacher
Bad Company; *Straight Shooter* .... (SS)
Dear God
Elton John; *21 At 33* .... (MCA)
Patsy Cline; *Forever & Always* .... (EPI)
XTC; *Best Of MTV's 120 Minutes-#1* ....(RHI)
  Skylarking ....(GEF)
Dear Lord
Continentals; *Great Groups/'50s-#2* .... (CLT)
Thin Lizzy; *Bad Reputation* .... (MER)

Deck Of Cards
Bill Anderson; *American Music Greatest Hits* .....(CCB)
  Best Of ....(CCB)
Tex Ritter; *Capitol Collectors Series* ....(CAP)
  Greatest Hits ....(CCB)
"T" Texas Tyler; *45* ....(OOP)
Dedicated To The One I Love
Mamas & The Papas; *Best Of* .... (MCA)
  Farewell To The First Golden Era .... (MCA)
  Orig. Classic Oldies/'50s-'60s-#13 .... (MCA)
Shirelles; *Anthology: 1959-1964* .... (RHI)
  Greatest Hits ....(EVR)
  Oldies But Goodies-#10 ....(OSR)
  Super Oldies/'50s-#4 ....(AUF)
Dinosaur Jesus
Barbie Bones; *Brake For Nobody* .... (RES)
Do Right
Paul Davis; *Best Of* ....(BNG)
  Paul Davis ....(BNG)
Dominic Christ
Suicide; *Way Of Life* ....(WAX)
Don't Take The Girl
Tim McGraw; *Not A Moment Too Soon* ....(CRB)
Don't You Marry The Mormon Boys
Rosalie Sorrels; *Lonesome Roving Wolves-Songs Of The West* ....(GRE)
Drop Kick Me Jesus (Through The Goal...)
Bobby Bare; *45* ....(OOP)
Find A Way
Amy Grant; *Collection* ....(A&M)
  Unguarded ....(A&M)
Forever And Ever, Amen
Randy Travis; *Always & Forever* ....(WB)
Garden Of Eden
New Riders Of The Purple Sage; *New Riders Of The Purple Sage* ....(COL)
German Nun
Sex Gang Children; *Ecstasy & Vendetta Over New York* ....(ROI)
Get In Touch With Jesus
Joan Armatrading; *Back To The Night* ....(A&M)
Get Me To The Church On Time
Original Cast; *My Fair Lady* ....(COL)
Girl With Faraway Eyes
Rolling Stones; *Some Girls* ....(RS)
Give More Power To The People
Chi-Lites; *Greatest Hits* ....(EPI)
Go Down, Moses
Paul Robeson; *The Power & The Glory* ....(COL)
Simon Estes; *Spirituals* ....(PHI)
Go Tell It On The Mountain
Bobby Darin; *25th Day Of December* ....(ATC)
Dolly Parton; *Home For Christmas* ....(COL)
Garth Brooks; *Beyond The Season* ....(LIB)
Simon & Garfunkel; *Collected Works* ....(COL)
  Wednesday Morning 3 A.M. ....(COL)
Weavers; *On Tour* ....(VAN)
Go Up Moses
Roberta Flack; *Quiet Fire* ....(ATL)
God
Tori Amos; *Under The Pink* ....(ATL)
God Ain't No Stained Glass Window
Kathy Mattea; *Kathy Mattea* .... (MER)
God Bless America
Frank Zappa; *Uncle Meat* .... (BIZ)
Kate Smith; *Best Of* ....(RCA)
  God Bless America ....(PIC)
  Legendary Performer ....(RCA)
  Nipper's Greatest Hits-'30s-#1 ....(RCA)
Mormon Tabernacle Choir; *God Bless America* ..(COL)
God Bless America Again
Loretta Lynn & Conway Twitty; *From Seven Till Ten* ....(MSP)
  United Talent ....(MCA)
  Very Best Of ....(MCA)
God Bless The Child
Billie Holiday; *From The Original Decca Masters* (MCA)
  Greatest Hits ....(COL)
  Songbook ....(VRV)
  Story ....(MCA)
  Story-#2 ....(COL)
Blood, Sweat & Tears; *Blood, Sweat & Tears* ....(COL)
  Greatest Hits ....(COL)
Diana Ross; *ST/Lady Sings The Blues* ....(MOT)

Liza Minnelli; *4-Sider* ....(CYP)
  ST/Liza With A "Z" ....(COL)
Lou Rawls; *Best From* ....(CAP)
God Bless The Children
Loretta Lynn; *Out Of My Head & Back In My Bed* .... (MCA)
Motley Crue; *Shout At The Devil* .... (ELE)
God Bless The Grass
Pete Seeger; *Essential* .... (VAN)
God Bless The USA
Lee Greenwood; *Greatest Hits* .... (MCA)
  Greatest Hits-#2 .... (MCA)
  Inside Out/You've Got A Good Love Comin' ... (MCA)
  Today's Country Classics-#1 .... (MCA)
God Blessed Texas
Little Texas; *Big Time* ....(WB)
God Can
Paul Kelly; *Stand On The Positive Side* ....(WB)
Staples; *Unlock Your Mind* ....(WB)
God Don't Live In Nashville, Tennessee
Randy Howard; *All-American Redneck* ....(WB)
God Fearing Man
Steppenwolf; *At Your Birthday Party* ....(OOP)
God Gave Rock & Roll To You
Argent; *Anthology* ....(EPI)
  Encore ....(EPI)
Truth; *Jump* ....(IRS)
God Is Alive, Magic Is Afoot
Buffy Sainte-Marie; *Best Of* .... (VAN)
  Illuminations .... (VAN)
God Is Love
Marvin Gaye; *Live* ....(MOT)
  Pops We Love You ....(MOT)
  What's Going On ....(MOT)
God Knows
Bob Dylan; *Under The Red Sky* ....(COL)
Debby Boone; *Best Of* ....(CRB)
  Best Of ....(MCA)
  Midstream ....(WB)
God Knows I'm Good
David Bowie; *Space Oddity* ....(RYK)
God Loves A Drunk
Richard Thompson; *Rumor & Sigh* ....(CAP)
God Must Be A Boogie Man
Joni Mitchell; *Mingus* ....(ASY)
  Shadows & Light ....(ASY)
God Must Be A Cowboy
Dan Seals; *Best Of* ....(CAP)
  Classics Collection-#1 ....(CAP)
  Rebel Heart ....(LIB)
God Must Have Blessed America
Lee Dorsey; *45* ....(MCA)
God Of The Sun
America; *Harbor* ....(WB)
God Of Thunder
Kiss; *Alive 2* ....(CAS)
  Destroyer ....(CAS)
  Double Platinum ....(CAS)
God Only Knows
Beach Boys; *Best Of* ....(RPR)
  Greatest Hits ....(RPR)
  Made In The U.S.A. ....(CAP)
  Pet Sounds ....(CAP)
  Stack 'O' Tracks ....(CAP)
God Part II
U2; *ST/Rattle & Hum* .... (ISL)
God Rest Ye Merry Gentlemen
Bing Crosby; *Merry Christmas* ....(MSP)
  Sings Christmas Songs ....(MSP)
Bobby Vinton; *Christmas All-Time Greatest Records-#2* ....(CCB)
Ella Fitzgerald; *Best Of Christmas* ....(CAP)
Garth Brooks; *Beyond The Season* ....(LIB)
  Christmas For The '90s-#1 ....(LIB)
Jackie Wilson; *Merry Christmas From* ....(RHI)
Kenny Rogers; *Christmas In America* ....(RPR)
Leontyne Price; *Christmas Songs* ....(LON)
Mel Torme; *Christmas Songs* ....(TLR)
Nat King Cole; *Cole Christmas & Kids* ....(CAP)
Neil Diamond; *Christmas Album* ....(COL)
Randy Travis; *An Old Time Christmas* ....(WB)
Roger Whittaker; *Tidings Of Comfort & Joy* .....(LIB)
Smokey Robinson/Miracles; *Season For Miracles* (MOT)
Steve Wariner; *Christmas Memories* ....(MSP)

Take 6/Yellowjackets; *He Is Christmas* .... (RPR)
T-Bone Burnett; *Acoustic Christmas* ....(COL)
God Save The King
Popular Standard; *Out-Of-Print Recording* ....(OOP)
God Save The Queen
Anthrax; *Armed & Dangerous* .... (MEG)
Queen; *A Night At The Opera* ....(HOL)
Live Killers ....(HOL)
Sex Pistols; *Never Mind The Bollocks* ....(WB)
God Won't Get You
Dolly Parton; *ST/Rhinestones* ....(RCA)
God's A Gonna Cut You Down
Odetta; *Essential* .... (VAN)
God's Children
Kinks; *Kink Kronikles* .... (RPR)
God's Coloring Book
Dolly Parton; *Here You Come Again* ....(RCA)
God's Country
Al Jolson; *Story Pt. 4* .... (MCA)
Kool/Gang; *Forever* .... (MER)
God's Footballer
Billy Bragg; *Don't Try This At Home* .... (ELE)
God's Gonna Get'cha
George Jones & Tammy Wynette; *Greatest Hits* ... (EPI)
God's Great Banana Skin
Chris Rea; *espresso logic* ....(EW)
God's Own Drunk
Jimmy Buffett; *Living & Dying In 3/4 Time* ..... (MCA)
You Had To Be There .... (MCA)
God's Own Jukebox
Jesse Winchester; *Third Down 110 To Go* .... (RHI)
God's Own Singer
Flying Burrito Brothers; *Burrito Deluxe* .... (A&M)
Close Up The Honky Tonks .... (A&M)
Farther Along: Best Of .... (A&M)
God's Plan
Desert Rose Band; *Pages Of Life* ....(CCB)
God's Song (That's Why I Love Mankind)
Randy Newman; *Sail Away* .... (RPR)
Gospel According To Luke
Skip Ewing; *Coast Of Colorado* .... (MCA)
Gotta Serve Somebody
Bob Dylan; *Biograph* ....(COL)
Slow Train Coming ....(COL)
Bob Dylan/Grateful Dead; *Dylan & The Dead* ...(COL)
Green Grow The Rushes, Ho
Chieftains; *Bonaparte's Retreat* .... (SHA)
Hands To Heaven
Breathe; *All That Jazz* .... (A&M)
Hang On St. Christopher
Tom Waits; *Frank's Wild Years* .... (ISL)
Have A Talk With God
Stevie Wonder; *Songs In The Key Of Life* .... (MOT)
He Walked On Water
Randy Travis; *No Holdin' Back* ....(WB)
Hear Me Lord
George Harrison; *All Things Must Pass* ....(CAP)
Heaven Is 10 Zillion Light Years Away
Stevie Wonder; *Fulfillingness' First Finale* .... (MOT)
Heavenly Father
Castelles; *Home Of Grand Records* ....(CLT)
Sweet Sounds Of ....(CLT)
Here I Am, Oh Lord Send Me
Mississippi John Hurt; *Best Of* .... (VAN)
Hero Worship
B-52's; *B-52's* ....(WB)
Wild Planet ....(WB)
(Hey Lord) Don't Ask Me Questions
Graham Parker/Rumour; *Parkerilla* .... (MER)
He's Got The Whole World In His Hands
Laurie London; *45* .... (ERI)
Mormon Tabernacle Choir; *Greatest Hits-#2* .....(COL)
Odetta; *Essential* .... (VAN)
High On Jesus
Kinky Friedman; *Sold American* .... (VAN)
Hill Where The Lord Hides
Chuck Mangione; *Best Of* .... (A&M)
Best Of .... (MER)
Classics-#6 .... (A&M)
Evening Of Magic .... (A&M)
Friends & Love .... (MER)
Together .... (MER)
His Eye Is On The Sparrow
Carmen McRae; *Greatest Of* .... (MCA)

Marvin Gaye; *Musical Testament 1964-1984* ... (MOT)
Soundtrack; *Streetcar Named Desire* ....(ALL)
Holy Thursday
Greg Brown; *Songs Of Innocence & Experience* . (RDH)
Holy Water
Bad Company; *Holy Water* ....(ATC)
Houses Of The Holy
Led Zeppelin; *Led Zeppelin (collection)* .... (ATL)
Physical Graffiti .... (SS)
Hymn
James Taylor; *One Man Dog* ....(WB)
Patti Smith Group; *Wave* .... (ARI)
Peter, Paul & Mary; *Late Again* ....(WB)
Hymn 43
Jethro Tull; *Aqualung* .... (CHR)
Living In The Past .... (CHR)
Hymn For The Dudes
Mott The Hoople; *Greatest Hits* ....(COL)
Mott ....(COL)
Hymn To Him
Audrey Hepburn; *ST/My Fair Lady* ....(COL)
Julie Andrews/Original Cast; *My Fair Lady* ......(COL)
Hymn To Me
Brinsley Schwarz; *Brinsley Schwarz* ....(CAP)
I Am The Light Of This World
Jorma Kaukonen & Tom Hobson; *Quah* ....(RLX)
I Believe In The Man In The Sky
Elvis Presley; *Worldwide 50 Gold Award Hits-#2* (RCA)
I Guess The Lord Must Be In New York C.
Nilsson; *Greatest Hits* ....(RCA)
Harry ....(RCA)
I Knew Jesus (Before He Was A Star)
Glen Campbell; *Best Of* ....(CAP)
I Met Her In Church
Box Tops; *Greatest Hits* .... (RHI)
I Saw The Light
Hank Williams; *24 Greatest Hits-#2* ....(POL)
40 Greatest Hits ....(POL)
I Ain't Got Nothin' But Time ....(POL)
Legend In Song-With Hank Williams, Jr. ......(POL)
Rare Takes & Radio Cuts ....(POL)
I Say A Little Prayer
Aretha Franklin; *Best Of* .... (ATL)
Gold .... (ATL)
Greatest Hits .... (ATL)
Burt Bacharach; *Classics-#23* .... (A&M)
Greatest Hits .... (A&M)
Reach Out .... (A&M)
Dionne Warwick; *Anthology* .... (RHI)
Dionne Warwick .... (EVR)
Greatest Hits .... (EVR)
Original Rock 'N' Roll Hits Of The '60s .... (RLL)
If There's A God In Heaven
Elton John; *Blue Moves* .... (MCA)
In God We Trust
Barefoot Jerry; *Barefoot Jerry's Grocery* .... (MON)
In God's Country
U2; *Joshua Tree* .... (ISL)
In The Chapel In The Moonlight
Patti Page; *16 Most Requested Songs* ....(COL)
Inner Light
Beatles; *Past Masters-#2* ....(CAP)
Rarities ....(CAP)
Little River Band; *Diamantina Cocktail* ....(CAP)
It Ain't Necessarily So
Aretha Franklin; *The Great-First 12 Sides* ....(COL)
Cab Calloway; *Sullivan Years-Best Of Broadway* (TVT)
Cal Tjader; *Cal Tjader Plays/Mary Stallings Sings* (FAN)
Cher; *Glory Of Gershwin Featuring Larry Adler* . (MER)
Ella Fitzgerald & Louis Armstrong; *Porgy & Bess* (VRV)
Miles Davis/Orchestra; *Porgy & Bess* ....(COL)
It Wasn't God Who Made Honky Tonk Angels
Kitty Wells; *Greatest Hits-#1* ....(SO)
Story .... (MCA)
It's A Sin
George Thorogood/Destroyers; *Bad To The Bone* (EMI)
Marty Robbins; *All-Time Greatest Hits* ....(COL)
Pet Shop Boys; *Actually* .... (AMR)
I'm Living With The 3-Foot Anti-Christ
Mojo Nixon; *Frenzy* .... (RES)
Jesus Boy (You Only Look Like A Man)
Billy Paul; *45* .... (PI)
Jesus Children Of America
Stevie Wonder; *Innervisions* ....(MOT)

Jesus Christ
Cisco Houston; *Greatest Songs Of Woody Guthrie* (VAN)
U2; *Folkways-Tribute To W. Guthrie/Leadbelly* ...(COL)
Woody Guthrie; *Woody Guthrie* .... (WB)
Jesus Christ Superstar
Original Cast; *ST/Jesus Christ Superstar* .... (MCA)
Soundtrack; *Movie Greats* .... (MCA)
Jesus Gave Love Away For Free
Stephen Stills; *Manassas* .... (ATL)
Jesus Gonna Make It Alright
Sonny Terry & Brownie McGhee; *Sonny &*
Brownie .... (A&M)
Jesus He Knows Me
Genesis; *We Can't Dance* .... (ATL)
Jesus Is Just Alright
Byrds; *Ballad Of Easy Rider* .... (COL)
   Best Of-Greatest Hits-#2 .... (COL)
   Byrds .... (COL)
Doobie Brothers; *Best Of* .... (WB)
   Toulouse Street .... (WB)
Jesus Is Love
Commodores; *All The Great Love Songs* .... (MOT)
   Heroes .... (MOT)
Jesus Is My Kind Of People
Ray Price; *You're The Best Thing That...* .... (COL)
Jesus Is On The Mainline
Ry Cooder; *Paradise & Lunch* .... (RPR)
   Showtime .... (WB)
Jesus Is The Answer
Paul Simon; *Live Rhymin'* .... (COL)
Jesus Just Left Chicago
ZZ Top; *Best Of* .... (WB)
   Six-Pack .... (WB)
   Tres Hombres .... (WB)
Jesus Met The Woman At The Well
Peter, Paul & Mary; *In Concert* .... (WB)
Tracy Nelson; *Deep Are The Roots* .... (PRS)
Jesus On The Radio
Tom T. Hall; *Ol' T's In Town* .... (RCA)
Jesus Thinks You're A Jerk
Frank Zappa; *Broadway The Hard Way* .... (RYK)
Jesus Was a Capricorn
Kris Kristofferson; *Jesus Was a Capricorn* .... (COL)
Jesus & Mama
Confederate Railroad; *Confederate Railroad* ..... (ATL)
Journey From Eden
Steve Miller Band; *Anthology* .... (CAP)
   Recall The Beginning .... (CAP)
Just A Closer Walk With Thee
Jim Nabors; *16 Most Requested Songs* .... (COL)
Kid Thomas; *& His New Orleans Jazz Band* ..... (ARH)
Patsy Cline; *Best Of* .... (CCB)
   Here's .... (MCA)
Preservation Hall Jazz Band; *Best Of* .... (COL)
Tom Rush; *Blues Songs & Ballads* .... (FAN)
Just A Little Talk With Jesus
Elvis Presley; *Million-Dollar Quartet* .... (RCA)
Kathleen (Catholicism Made Easier)
Randy Newman; *Little Criminals* .... (WB)
Keep It Between The Lines
Ricky Van Shelton; *Backroads* .... (COL)
Kingdom Hall
Van Morrison; *Wavelength* .... (WB)
Last God Of England
Pete Morton; *Frivolous Love* .... (PHO)
Let It Be
Aretha Franklin; *Greatest Hits* .... (ATL)
Beatles; *1967-1970* .... (CAP)
   20 Greatest Hits .... (CAP)
   Let It Be .... (CAP)
   Past Masters-#2 .... (CAP)
   Reel Music .... (CAP)
Paul McCartney; *Tripping The Live Fantastic* ... (CAP)
   Tripping The Live Fantastic-Highlights! .... (CAP)
Rockestra; *Kampuchea* .... (ATL)
Light Of The World
Original Cast; *ST/Godspell* .... (ARI)
Like A Prayer
Madonna; *Like A Prayer* .... (SIR)
   Royal Box .... (SIR)
Little John Of God
Los Lobos; *The Neighborhood* .... (SLS)
Little Lady Preacher
Tom T. Hall; *Greatest Hits-#2* .... (MER)

Little Old Church In England
Glenn Miller/Orchestra; *Complete* .... (BLU)
Little Priest
Original Cast; *Sweeney Todd* ....(RCA)
Little Tin God
Don Henley; *End Of The Innocence* .... (GEF)
Livin' In The Light
Caron Wheeler; *UK Blak* .... (EMI)
Livin' On A Prayer
Bon Jovi; *Slippery When Wet* .... (MER)
Lord Have Mercy On A Country Boy
Don Williams; *True Love* ....(RCA)
Lord Have Mercy On My Soul
Black Oak Arkansas; *Best Of* ....(ATC)
   Black Oak Arkansas ....(ATC)
   Live Mutha ....(ATC)
Lord Have Mercy On The Working Man
Travis Tritt; *T-R-O-U-B-L-E* .... (WB)
Lord I Hope This Day Is Good
Don Williams; *Best Of-#3* .... (MCA)
   Especially For You .... (MCA)
Lord I Love Mashed Potatoes
Mayf Nutter; *Goin' Skinny Dippin'* .... (CRS)
Lord I Want To Go Back To California
Jim Post; *Magic: In Concert* .... (FF)
Lord Loves The One
George Harrison; *Living In The Material World* ..(CAP)
Lord Protect My Child
Bob Dylan; *Bootleg Series-#1-3-1961-1989* ......(COL)
Lord Take My Hand
Maddox Brothers & Rose; *On The Air-#1 & 2* .. (ARH)
Lord, Lord, Lord
Cyrus Chestnut; *Revelation* .... (ATL)
Lord, Lord, Lord, You Sure Been Good...
Preservation Hall Jazz Band; *When The Saints Go*
Marchin' In-#3 ....(COL)
Lord's Prayer
Original Broadway Cast; *Sarafina!* ....(RCA)
Randy Newman; *12 Songs* ....(OOP)
Sister Janet Mead; *Super Hits/'70s-Have A Nice*
Day-#12 .... (RHI)
Losing My Religion
R.E.M.; *Out Of Time* .... (WB)
(Love Will) Find A Way
Amy Grant; *Unguarded* ....(A&M)
Love Without End, Amen
George Strait; *Livin' It Up* .... (MCA)
   Ten Strait Hits .... (MCA)
Machine Messiah
Yes; *Drama* .... (ATL)
Mama Don't Forget To Pray For Me
Diamond Rio; *Diamond Rio* .... (ARI)
Mary's Prayer
Danny Wilson; *Meet Danny Wilson* .... (VIA)
Me & Jesus
Tom T. Hall; *Audiograph Alive* .... (AUD)
   Greatest Hits .... (MER)
Mercedes Benz
Janis Joplin; *Pearl* ....(COL)
   ST/Janis ....(COL)
Michael Row The Boat Ashore
Joe & Eddie; *Best Of* .... (CRS)
   Gospel Truth .... (CRS)
Weavers; *Greatest Hits* .... (VAN)
Mighty Fortress Is Our God
Leontyne Price; *God Bless America* ....(RCA)
Miner's Prayer
Dwight Yoakam; *Guitars Cadillacs Etc. Etc.* ..... (RPR)
Missionary Man
Eurythmics; *Greatest Hits* .... (ARI)
   Revenge ....(RCA)
Mississippi Squirrel Revival
Ray Stevens; *Country Classics-#1* .... (MCA)
   Greatest Hits .... (MCA)
   He Thinks He's Ray Stevens .... (MCA)
Mrs. Robinson
Simon & Garfunkel; *Bookends* ....(COL)
   Collected Works ....(COL)
   Concert In Central Park .... (WB)
   Greatest Hits ....(COL)
   Hollywood Magic-1960s ....(COL)
   ST/Forrest Gump .... (EPX)
   ST/The Graduate ....(COL)

My Best Friend Is A Buddha
Deuter; *Silence Is The Answer* .... (KUC)
My God
Alice Cooper; *Lace & Whiskey* .... (MET)
Jethro Tull; *Aqualung* .... (CHR)
My God Is A Powerful God
Sister Souljah; *360 Degrees Of Power* .... (EPI)
My God Is Real
Al Green; *Livin' For You* .... (MOT)
My God & I
Ray Charles; *Renaissance* .... (CRO)
My Head Hurts, My Feet Stink...
Jimmy Buffett; *Havana Daydreamin'* .... (MCA)
My Lover's Prayer
Otis Redding; *Story* .... (ATL)
 Very Best Of .... (RHI)
My Mother's Bible
Warrior River Boys; *New Beginnings* .... (ROU)
My Prayer
Ink Spots; *Best Of* .... (MCA)
Platters; *Anthology* .... (RHI)
 Encore Of Golden Hits .... (MER)
 Greatest Hits .... (EVR)
 Oldies But Goodies-#3 .... (OSR)
My Special Prayer
Percy Sledge; *Best Of* .... (ATL)
 Ultimate Collection-When A Man Loves... .... (ATL)
My Sweet Lord
George Harrison; *All Things Must Pass* .... (CAP)
 Best Of .... (CAP)
 Concert For Bangla Desh .... (CAP)
Nearer, My God, To Thee
Mississippi John Hurt; *Best Of* .... (VAN)
 Immortal .... (VAN)
New Gods
Meat Puppets; *II* .... (SST)
 No Strings Attached .... (SST)
Oh Thank You Great Spirit
Chicago; *VIII* .... (COL)
Old Country Church
Hank Williams; *I Ain't Got Nothin' But Time* .... (POL)
One Miner's Life-The Image Of God
Battlefield Band; *There's A Buzz* .... (FF)
One Toke Over The Line
Brewer & Shipley; *Super Hits/'70s-Have A Nice Day-#4* .... (RHI)
 '70s Greatest Rock Hits-#10 .... (PRY)
Only The Good Die Young
Billy Joel; *Greatest Hits-#1&2-1973-1985* .... (COL)
 KOHUEPT .... (COL)
 The Stranger .... (COL)
Outlaw's Prayer
Johnny Paycheck; *Armed & Crazy* .... (EPI)
 Biggest Hits .... (EPI)
Palm Sunday
Jerry Garcia; *Cats Under The Stars* .... (ARI)
People Get Ready
Aretha Franklin; *Aretha-Lady Soul* .... (ATL)
Impressions; *Greatest Hits* .... (MCA)
 Soul Shots-#5 .... (RHI)
Jeff Beck; *Flash* .... (EPI)
Rod Stewart; *Storyteller-Complete Anthology 1964-1990* .... (WB)
Personal Jesus
Depeche Mode; *Best Of MTV's 120 Minutes-#2* .. (RHI)
 Just Say Da-#4 Of Just Say Yes .... (SIR)
 Violator .... (SIR)
Phone Call From God
Ray Reeves; *45* .... (STR)
Pilate & Christ
Original London Cast; *Jesus Christ Superstar* .... (MCA)
Pilate's Dream
Original London Cast; *Jesus Christ Superstar* .... (MCA)
Place In This World
Michael W. Smith; *Go West Young Man* .... (REU)
Playing In God's Garden
Stevie Nicks; *Street Angel* .... (MOD)
Poems, Prayers & Promises
John Denver; *Evening With* .... (RCA)
 Greatest Hits-#1 .... (RCA)
 Poems, Prayers & Promises .... (RCA)
John Denver/Muppets; *Rocky Mountain Holiday* .(RCA)

Point Of Light
Randy Travis; *Heroes & Friends* .... (WB)
 High Lonesome .... (WB)
Poor Little Jesus
Weavers; *On Tour* .... (VAN)
Poor, Poor Joseph
Original Cast; *Joseph & The Amazing Technicolor...* .... (POL)
Pope Is A Potato
Mofungo; *Bugged* .... (SST)
Pope On A Rope (Cigarette Butt)
Squirrels; *What Gives?* .... (PL)
Power Of God
L.L. Cool J; *Mama Said Knock You Out* .... (DFC)
Praise The Lord & Pass The Ammunition
Kay Kyser; *Best Of The Big Bands* .... (COL)
 Sentimental Favorites .... (COL)
Pray For Me
John Cougar Mellencamp; *John Cougar Mellencamp* .... (RIV)
Prayer
Christian Death; *Only Theatre Of Pain* ....(FON)
Joe Walsh; *The Smoker You Drink The Player You Get* .... (MCA)
Stevie B; *Healing* .... (EPI)
Prayer For Everybody/To Be Free
Gil Scott-Heron & Brian Jackson; *Secrets* .... (ARI)
Prayer For The Dying
Seal; *Seal* .... (ZTT)
Prayer & A Juke Box
Little Anthony/Imperials; *Best Of* .... (RHI)
 Forever Yours .... (RLL)
Praying For Time
George Michael; *Listen Without Prejudice* .... (COL)
Praying Hands
Devo; *Live-Mongoloid Years* .... (RYK)
 Q: Are We Not Men? A: We are Devo! .... (WB)
Praying To The Aliens
Gary Numan/Tubeway Army; *Replicas* .... (ATC)
Preacher
Horace Silver; *Best Of-Blue Note Years* .... (BLN)
Louis Armstrong; *Greatest Hits* .... (CCB)
Preacher Man
Bananarama; *Pop Life* .... (LON)
Impressions; *45* .... (CUR)
Preacher & The Bear
Andy Griffith; *American Originals* .... (CAP)
Big Bopper; *Hellooo Baby! Best Of-1954-1959* .. (RHI)
Rufus Thomas & Carla Thomas; *Chronicle* ...... (STX)
Preacher's Daughter
Lynyrd Skynyrd; *First & Last* .... (MCA)
Preaching Blues (Up Jumped The Devil)
Robert Johnson; *Complete Recordings* .... (COL)
 King Of The Delta Blues Singers-#2 .... (COL)
Preaching, Praying, Singing
Bluegrass Album Band; *Bluegrass Class Of 1990* (ROU)
L. Flatt & E. Scruggs/Foggy Mtn. Boys; *Complete Mercury Sessions* .... (MER)
Preachin' The Blues
Bessie Smith; *Complete Recordings-#3* .... (COL)
 Nobody's Blues But Mine .... (COL)
Gun Club; *Fire Of Love* .... (SLS)
La Vern Baker; *Sings Bessie Smith* .... (ATL)
Linda Hopkins; *Me & Bessie* .... (COL)
Precious Lord, Take My Hand
Linda Hopkins; *How Blue Can You Get* .... (QKS)
Preservation Hall Jazz Band; *Best Of* .... (COL)
Presence Of The Lord
Blind Faith; *Blind Faith* .... (POL)
Derek/Dominos; *In Concert* .... (POL)
Eric Clapton; *Crossroads* .... (POL)
Priests On Drugs
Paper Bag; *No Age-Compilation Of SST Instrumentals* .... (SST)
Promised Land
Band; *Moondog Matinee* .... (CAP)
Bobby Caldwell; *Stuck On You* .... (SD)
Bruce Springsteen; *Darkness On The Edge Of Town* .... (COL)
 Live 1975-1985 .... (COL)
Chuck Berry; *Chess Box* .... (CSS)
 Rock 'N' Roll Rarities-20 Magic Tracks .... (CSS)
Elvis Presley; *Promised Land* .... (RCA)
 ST/This Is Elvis .... (RCA)

Freddy Weller; *Greatest Hits* ....(COL)
Gary Morris; *Full Moon Empty Heart* ....(LIB)
Grateful Dead; *Steal Your Face* ....(GRD)
Hollies; *Distant Light* ....(EPI)
James Taylor; *Walking Man* ....(WB)
Julian Cope; *Peggy Suicide* ....(ISL)
Kingfish; *Kingfish/Alive In Eighty Five-Double
Dose* ....(RLX)
Pure Religion
Rev. Gary Davis; *Pure Religion & Bad Company* (FLW)
Put Your Hand In The Hand
Anne Murray; *Country* ....(CAP)
Danny's Song ....(CAP)
Snowbird ....(CAP)
Elvis Presley; *Canadian Tribute* ....(RCA)
Now ....(RCA)
Ocean; *Super Hits/'70s-Have A Nice Day-#4* ..... (RHI)
Put Your Hands On The Screen
Martin Briley; *One Night With A Stranger* .... (MER)
Quicksand Jesus
Skid Row; *Slave To The Grind* ....(ATL)
Redemption
Johnny Cash; *American Recordings* ....(AME)
Rest My Mind On Jesus
Charles Ford Band; *Charles Ford Band* .... (ARH)
Reverend Jack & His Roamin' Cadillac...
Timbuk 3; *Eden Alley* ....(IRS)
Reverend Mr. Black
Johnny Cash; *Biggest Hits* ....(COL)
Kingston Trio; *Capitol Collectors Series* ....(CAP)
Rhythm Of The Saints
Paul Simon; *Rhythm Of The Saints* ....(WB)
Rich Man's Spiritual
Gordon Lightfoot; *Lightfoot* ....(UA)
Right Hand Of God
Move; *Yeah Whatever* ....(ATL)
River Of Jordan
Ricky Skaggs; *Family & Friends* ....(ROU)
Stained Glass Hour ....(ROU)
Rock Of Ages
Cristy Lane; *Amazing Grace* ....(EMI)
Johnny Cash; *Sings Precious Memories* ....(EPI)
Mormon Tabernacle Choir; *Rock Of Ages-30 Favorite
Hymns* ....(SMC)
Statler Brothers; *Todays' Gospel Favorites* .... (MER)
Tennessee Ernie Ford; *Country Gospel Classics-#1* (LIB)
Rocket To God
Daryl Hall & John Oates; *Ooh Yeah!* .... (ARI)
Sabbath Prayer
Herschel Bernardi; *ST/Fiddler On The Roof* ......(COL)
Original Cast; *Fiddler On The Roof* ....(RCA)
Sabbath, Bloody Sabbath
Anthrax; *I'm The Man* ....(ISL)
Black Sabbath; *Sabbath, Bloody Sabbath* ....(WB)
We Sold Our Soul For Rock 'N' Roll ....(WB)
Ozzy Osbourne; *Speak Of The Devil* ....(JET)
Sacred
Depeche Mode; *101* ....(SIR)
Music For The Masses ....(SIR)
Sacred Bird
Original Cast; *Miss Saigon* ....(GEF)
Sacred Emotion
Donny Osmond; *Donny Osmond* ....(CAP)
Sacred Ground
McBride & The Ride; *Sacred Ground* .... (MCA)
Sacred Heart
Dio; *Intermission* ....(WB)
Sacred Heart ....(WB)
Shakespear's Sister; *ST/Nuns On The Run* .... (MER)
Saint
Elton John; *Too Low For Zero* ....(MCA)
Thompson Twins; *Queer* ....(WB)
Saint Agnes & The Burning Train
Sting; *Soul Cages* ....(A&M)
Samson & Delilah
Blasters; *Collection* ....(SLS)
Blind Gary Davis; *Harlem Street Singer* .... (BV)
Grateful Dead; *Dead Set* ....(ARI)
Terrapin Station ....(ARI)
Rev. Gary Davis; *From Blues To Gospel* ....(BIO)
Sanctified Lady
Marvin Gaye; *Arena* ....(CAP)
Dream Of A Lifetime ....(COL)
Rio ....(CAP)

Sanctify Yourself
Simple Minds; *In The City Of Light* ....(A&M)
Once Upon A Time ....(A&M)
Save A Prayer
Duran Duran; *Arena* ....(CAP)
Decade ....(CAP)
Rio ....(CAP)
Secret Policeman's Third Ball-The Music .... (VIA)
"Saved" LP
Bob Dylan; *Various Tracks* ....(COL)
Say A Prayer
Breathe; *Peace Of Mind* ....(A&M)
Scratchings On The Bible Belt
Rain Tree Crow; *Rain Tree Crow* .... (VIA)
Second Sitting For The Last Supper
10 CC; *Live & Let Live* .... (MER)
Shall We Gather At The River?
Chuck Wagon Gang; *16 Country-Gospel
Favorites* .... (MCA)
Tennessee Ernie Ford; *All-Time Greatest Hymns* .(CCB)
Sings 22 Favorite Hymns ....(RAN)
She Gives Me Religion
Van Morrison; *Beautiful Vision* ....(WB)
Sinner's Prayer
Eric Clapton; *From The Cradle* .... (DUC)
Sister Christian
Night Ranger; *Greatest Hits* ....(CAM)
Midnight Madness ....(CAM)
Sit Down, You're Rockin' The Boat
Don Henley; *ST/Leap Of Faith* .... (MCA)
Original Cast; *Guys & Dolls* .... (MCA)
Slow Train
Bob Dylan; *Slow Train Coming* ....(COL)
Bob Dylan/Grateful Dead; *Dylan & The Dead* ...(COL)
Somebody Up There Likes Me
David Bowie; *Young Americans* ....(RYK)
Reba McEntire; *Sweet Sixteen* .... (MCA)
Sometimes Salvation
Black Crowes; *Southern Harmony & Musical
Companion* ....(DEF)
Son Of A Preacher Man
Dusty Springfield; *Dusty Springfield* .... (RHI)
Soul Searchin'
Glenn Frey; *Soul Searchin'* .... (MCA)
Leon Everette; *45* ....(RCA)
Spanish Pipedream
John Prine; *John Prine* ....(ATL)
Star Of Bethlehem
Emmylou Harris & Neil Young; *Duets* .... (RPR)
Neil Young; *Decade* .... (RPR)
Neil Young/Crazy Horse; *American Stars 'N'
Bars* ....(RPR)
Steal Away
Jackson Southernaires; *Presenting Joy Peace Happiness &
Love* ....(MSP)
Reverend James Cleveland; *Sings w/World's Greatest
Gospel Stars* ....(SAV)
St. Alphonzo's Pancake Breakfast
Frank Zappa; *Apostrophe/Overnite Sensation* .....(RYK)
Sun Goddess
Earth, Wind & Fire; *Eternal Dance* ....(COL)
Gratitude ....(COL)
Ramsey Lewis; *Best Of* ....(COL)
Sun Goddess ....(COL)
Swear To Your Heart
Russell Hitchcock; *S* ....(HOL)
Swearin' To God
Frankie Valli/Four Seasons; *25th Anniversary
Collection* .... (RHI)
Greatest Hits-#2 ....(RHI)
Sweet Jesus
Sugar Minott; *Ghetto Child* ....(HRT)
Sweet 'N' Sour Jesus
Supersuckers; *Smoke Of Hell* .... (SP)
Swing Down, Chariot
Rufus; *Rags To Rufus* .... (MCA)
Swing Low, Sweet Chariot
Eric Clapton; *Time Pieces-Best Of* .... (POL)
Glenn Miller/Orchestra; *Moonlight Serenade* .... (RAN)
Hi-Lo's; *Suddenly It's The Hi-Lo's* ....(COL)
Jerry Garcia Acoustic Band; *Almost Acoustic* ... (GRD)
Joan Baez; *From Every Stage* ....(A&M)
Peggy Lee; *Best Of* .... (MCA)

Take Your Burden To The Lord & Leave...
Blind Willie Johnson; *Complete* ....(COL)
Teach Them To Pray
Junior Walker/All-Stars; *Motown Superstar
Series-#5* ....(MOT)
Temple Jamaica
Peter Manning Robinson; *Phoenix Rising* ....(CMG)
Temple Of Love
Sisters Of Mercy; *Slight Case Of Overbombing-Greatest
Hits* ....(ELE)
Temple Of The Lord
Saints; *All Fools Day* ....(TVT)
Temple, The
20th Anniversary London Cast; *Jesus Christ
Superstar* ....(RCA)
Ten Commandments Of Love
Bob Marley/Wailers; *Birth Of A
Legend-1963-1966* ....(EPA)
Harvey/Moonglows; *Best Of Chess Rock 'N'
Roll-#2* ....(CSS)
  Collectables Presents History Of Rock-10 ....(CLT)
  Cruisin'-1958 ....(INC)
  Oldies But Goodies-#11 ....(OSR)
Testicle Of God (& It Was Good)
Gaye Bykers On Acid; *Stewed To The Gills* ......(CRL)
Thank God
Hank Williams; *Let's Turn Back The
Years-1951-1952* ....(POL)
Roy Acuff; *Greatest Hits-#2* ....(MCA)
Thank God For Kids
Oak Ridge Boys; *Christmas* ....(MSP)
  Christmas For The '90s-#1 ....(LIB)
  Collection ....(MCA)
  Greatest Hits-#2 ....(MCA)
Thank God For The Radio
Kendalls; *20 Favorites* ....(EPI)
  Movin' Train ....(MER)
Thank God For You
Sawyer Brown; *Outskirts Of Town* ....(CRB)
Thank God It's Monday
Dene Anton; *Texas Soul* ....(JRS)
Thank God I'm A Country Boy
John Denver; *Back Home Again* ....(RCA)
  Evening With ....(RCA)
  Greatest Hits-#2 ....(RCA)
Thank God & Greyhound
Roy Clark; *Best Of* ....(MCA)
  Greatest Hits-#1 ....(MCA)
  Live ....(MCA)
Thank The Lord For The Night Time
Neil Diamond; *Classics-Early Years* ....(COL)
  Glory Road-1968-1972 ....(MCA)
  Gold ....(MCA)
  Greatest Hits-1966-1992 ....(COL)
  Hot August Night-#2 ....(COL)
Thank You Lord
Bob Marley/Wailers; *Songs Of Freedom* ....(TUF)
Glenn Yarbrough/Limeliters; *Joy Across The
Land* ....(CRS)
Heptones; *Changing Times* ....(MOV)
Thanking The Good Lord
Merle Haggard; *Chill Factor* ....(EPI)
That's What God Looks Like To Me
Frank Sinatra; *Trilogy* ....(RPR)
That's Why God Made The Movies
Paul Simon; *ST/One-Trick Pony* ....(WB)
Theme From "Exodus"
101 Strings Orchestra; *Golden Movie Themes* ....(ALS)
Boston Pops Orchestra/Arthur Fiedler; *Motion Picture
Classics-#1* ....(RCA)
Ferrante & Teicher; *Grand Pianos* ....(PRR)
Theme From "Raiders Of The Lost Ark"
Neil Norman; *Greatest Science Fiction Hits-#3* ... (CRS)
Then God Made Malls
Uncle Bonsai; *Myn Ynd Wymyn* ....(YT)
There Goes God
Crowded House; *Woodface* ....(CAP)
There Will Never Be Any Peace
Chi-Lites; *Greatest Hits* ....(RHI)
There Will Never Be Any Peace (Until...)
Chi-Lites; *Greatest Hits* ....(RHI)
There's A Gold Mine In The Sky
Jimmy C. Newman; *Cajun Cowboy* ....(PLN)
Pat Boone; *Love Letters In The Sand* ....(MSP)

There's A Light
Doobie Brothers; *Livin' On The Fault Line* ....(WB)
Thieves In The Temple
Prince; *ST/Graffiti Bridge* ....(PAI)
This Is My Prayer
Engelbert Humperdinck; *Release Me* ....(MER)
Frank Sinatra; *World We Knew* ....(RPR)
Petula Clark; *20 Top 10 Hits!'50s & '60s* ....(LAU)
  Greatest Hits Of ....(CRS)
This Is The Way I Pray
Ella Jenkins; *African-American Folk Rhythms* ... (FLW)
This Jesus Must Die
Original London Cast; *Jesus Christ Superstar* .... (MCA)
Tiki Tiki Tiki Room
Original Music; *Disney Collection-#1* ....(DIS)
Time Of The Preacher
Willie Nelson; *Red Headed Stranger* ....(COL)
Tin Jesus
Wire Train; *Wire Train* ....(MCA)
Tippin' Home From Sunday School
Oliver Jones; *Class Act* ....(JUS)
To Find God
James Michaels; *Bouquet* ....(IS)
Transcendance
Santana; *Moonflower* ....(COL)
Travelin' Prayer
Billy Joel; *Piano Man* ....(COL)
Traveller's Prayer
George Jones/Sweethearts Of The Rodeo; *Friends In
High Places* ....(EPI)
Trial Before Pilate
Original London Cast; *Jesus Christ Superstar* .... (MCA)
Truck Driver's Prayer
Dave Dudley; *Diesel Express* ....(FFT)
Turn! Turn! Turn!
Byrds; *Billboard Top Rock 'N' Roll Hits-1965* .... (RHI)
  Greatest Hits ....(COL)
  Original Singles-#1-1965-1967 ....(COL)
  Byrds (collection) ....(COL)
  ST/Forrest Gump ....(EPX)
  Turn! Turn! Turn! ....(COL)
Pete Seeger; *Greatest Hits* ....(COL)
  Troubadours Of The Folk Era-#2 .... (RHI)
TV Preacher Man Blues
Glenn Sutton; *Close Encounters Of The Sutton
Kind* ....(MER)
Unanswered Prayers
Garth Brooks; *No Fences* ....(LIB)
Under God
Midge Ure; *Answers To Nothing* ....(CHR)
Under The God
Tin Machine; *Tin Machine* ....(EMI)
Vacation Bible School
Ray Stevens; *Everything Is Beautiful* ....(MSP)
  I Have Returned ....(MCA)
Vaya Con Dios
Bing Crosby; *Radio Years-#2* ....(CRS)
Freddy Fender; *Collection* ....(RPR)
Les Paul & Mary Ford; *Memories Are Made Of
This* ....(CAP)
Roger Whittaker; *All-Time Heart-Touching
Favorites-#1* ....(LIB)
Vicar In A Tutu
Smiths; *Rank* ....(SIR)
  The Queen Is Dead ....(SIR)
Watching Out For Jesus
Rave-Ups; *Chance* ....(EPI)
We Need A Lot More Jesus (& Less Rock..)
Linda Ronstadt; *Hand Sown Home Grown* ....(CAP)
What A Friend We Have In Jesus
Nashville Superpickers; *Live From Austin City
Limits* ....(FF)
Sweet Honey In The Rock; *We All...Every One Of
Us* ....(FF)
What God Wants (Part I)
Roger Waters; *Amused To Death* ....(COL)
When God Comes & Gathers His Jewels
Hank Williams; *Health & Happiness Shows* ..... (MER)
  I Saw The Light ....(MER)
Molly O'Day/Cumberland Mountain Folks; *Columbia
Country Classics-#1-Golden Age* ....(COL)
  Hank Williams Songbook ....(COL)

When Jesus Left Birmingham
John Mellencamp/Sounds Of Blackness; *Human Wheels* .... (MER)
When The Saints Go Marching In
Al Hirt; *Best Of* ....(RCA)
  Our Man-In New Orleans .... (NOV)
Jerry Lee Lewis; *Jerry Lee Lewis* .... (RHI)
Louis Armstrong; *At The Crescendo* .... (MCA)
  Big Bands Of The Swinging Years-#1 ....(CLT)
  C'Est Si Bon ....(RHI)
  Essential .... (VAN)
  Of New Orleans ....(MCA)
Pete Fountain; *Best Of* .... (MCA)
  Down On Rampart Street .... (INT)
  Pete Fountain's New Orleans .... (MCA)
Preservation Hall Jazz Band; *Best Of* ....(COL)
Wholy Holy
Aretha Franklin; *30 Greatest Hits* .....(ATL)
Marvin Gaye; *Musical Testament-1964-1984* ... (MOT)
  What's Going On ....(MOT)
Why Me Lord
Johnny Cash; *American Recordings* .... (AME)
Will Jesus Wash The Bloodstains From...
Exene Cervenka; *Running Sacred* .... (RHI)
Will The Circle Be Unbroken
Charlie Daniels Band/Friends; *Volunteer Jam #3 & #4* .... (EPI)
Joan Baez; *Country Music Album* .... (VAN)
  First 10 Years .... (VAN)
Nitty Gritty Dirt Band; *Will The Circle Be Unbroken* .... (EMI)
Roy Acuff; *Best Of* ....(CCB)
Willie Nelson; *Willie & Family Live* ....(COL)
Winchester Cathedral
New Vaudeville Band; *History Of British Rock-#7* (RHI)
Would Jesus Wear A Rolex
Ray Stevens; *All-Time Greatest Comic Hits* ....(CCB)
  Collection ....(MCA)
  Greatest Hits-#2 ....(MCA)
Yah Mo B There
James Ingram & Michael McDonald; *It's Your Night* .... (QUE)
  Power Of Great Music ....(WB)
Your Saving Grace
Steve Miller Band; *Anthology* ....(CAP)
  Best Of-1968-1973 ....(CAP)
  Your Saving Grace ....(CAP)
You're The Reason God Made Oklahoma
David Frizzell & Shelly West; *Carryin' On The Family Names* ....(WB)
  Country's Greatest Hits-#9-Country Duets ...... (PRY)
  Golden Duets ....(WB)

GOLD, Golden

3 Chains O' Gold
Prince/New Power Generation; *Love Symbol Album* ....(PAI)
After The Gold Rush
Neil Young; *After The Gold Rush* .... (RPR)
  Decade ....(RPR)
  Live Rust .... (RPR)
All That Glitters Ain't Gold
Spinners; *Pick Of The Litter* ....(ATL)
All The Gold In California
Larry Gatlin/Gatlin Brothers; *17 Greatest Hits* ...(COL)
  Greatest Hits-Encore ....(CAP)
  Greatest Hits-#2 ....(COL)
  Live At 8:00 ....(CAP)
  Straight Ahead ....(COL)
Almost Gold
Jesus & Mary Chain; *Honey's Dead* .... (DEF)
Band Of Gold
Freda Payne; *Beachbeat Draggin'* .... (DHL)
  Greatest Hits .... (HDH)
  Soul Hits/'70s-#2 .... (RHI)
Black Gold
Soul Asylum; *Grace Dancers Union* ....(COL)
California Gold
Rance Allen; *Straight From The Heart* .... (STX)
California Golden West Waltz
Golden West Singers/Cavaliers; *45* ....(ACT)

Chains Of Gold
Sweethearts Of The Rodeo; *More Hot Country Requests-#2* ....(EPI)
  Sweethearts Of The Rodeo ....(COL)
Days Of Autumn Gold
Hank Locklin; *There Never Was A Time* .... (PLN)
Devil Comes Back To Georgia
Marc O'Connor; *Heroes* ....(WB)
Devil Went Down To Georgia
Charlie Daniels Band; *Billboard Top Hits-1979* .. (RHI)
  Decade Of Hits ....(EPI)
  Me & The Boys ....(EPI)
  Million Mile Reflections ....(EPI)
  ST/Urban Cowboy ....(ASY)
Down The River Of Golden Dreams
Mom & Dads; *Down The River Of Golden Dreams* ....(CRS)
Slim Whitman; *Home On The Range* .... (UA)
Everything Is Turning To Gold
Rolling Stones; *Sucking In The Seventies* .... (RS)
Everything That Glitters (Is Not Gold)
Dan Seals; *Best Of* ....(LIB)
  Classics Collection-#2 .... (LIB)
  Greatest Hits .... (LIB)
  I Won't Be Blue Anymore ....(EMI)
Fields Of Gold
Sting; *Ten Summoner's Tales* ....(A&M)
Fools Gold
Stone Roses; *Stone Roses* .... (SIL)
Fool's Gold
Graham Parker; *Pourin' It All Out: Mercury Years* ....(MER)
Graham Parker/Rumour; *Heat Treatment* .... (MER)
  Parkerilla .... (MER)
Lee Greenwood; *Greatest Hits* ....(MCA)
  You've Got A Good Love Comin' .... (MCA)
Poco; *Crazy Eyes* ....(EPI)
  Ride The Country ....(EPI)
  Very Best Of ....(EPI)
Thin Lizzy; *Johnny The Fox* ....(WB)
Fourteen Karat Mind
Gene Watson; *Greatest Hits* .... (MCA)
  Old Loves Never Die ....(MCA)
Gold
John Stewart; *Bombs Away Dream Babies* ...... (RSO)
Spandau Ballet; *Singles Collection* .... (CHR)
  True ....(CHR)
Gold At The End Of My Rainbow
Be Bop Deluxe; *Modern Music* .... (HAR)
Gold Dust Woman
Fleetwood Mac; *25 Years-The Chain* ....(WB)
  Rumours ....(WB)
Gold In Africa
Tiger; *Where Was Butler?-Calypso Documentary* . (FLK)
Gold & Silver
Quicksilver Messenger Service; *Legends Of Rock Guitar-'60s-#1* ....(RHI)
  Quicksilver Messenger Service ....(CAP)
  Sons Of Mercury ....(RHI)
Golden Age
Ray Stevens; *Nashville* ....(BBY)
Golden Age Of Leather
Blue Oyster Cult; *Spectres* ....(COL)
Golden Age Of Rock & Roll
Mott The Hoople; *Ballad Of Mott* ....(COL)
  Greatest Hits ....(COL)
Golden Apples Of The Sun
Judy Collins; *Golden Apples Of The Sun* .... (ELE)
  So Early In The Spring .... (ELE)
Golden Arrow
Foghat; *Energized* .... (RHI)
Golden Boy
Tubes; *Now* ....(A&M)
Golden Coins
Elvis Presley; *ST/Harum Scarum* ....(RCA)
Golden Country
R.E.O. Speedwagon; *Decade Of Rock & Roll (1970-1980)* ....(EPI)
  Live ....(EPI)
  T.W.O. ....(EPI)
Golden Earrings
Peggy Lee; *Capitol Collectors Series-#1-Early Years* ....(CAP)
  Greatest Hits ....(CAP)

Golden Goose
Peter Frampton; *Somethin's Happening* .... (A&M)
Todd Rundgren; *Healing* .... (RHI)
Golden Guitar
Bill Anderson; *Greatest Hits-#1* .... (MCA)
Story .... (MCA)
Golden Helmet
Original Cast; *Man Of La Mancha* .... (MCA)
Golden Lady
Jose Feliciano; *And The Feeling's Good* .... (MOT)
Stevie Wonder; *Innervisions* .... (MOT)
Golden Lark
Styx; *Man Of Miracles* ....(WDN)
Golden Memories & Silver Tears
Jim Reeves; *Best Of* ....(RCA)
Great Moments With ....(RCA)
w/Patsy Cline: Greatest Hits ....(RCA)
Golden Mile
Babys; *Broken Heart* .... (CHR)
Golden Moments
James Taylor; *In The Pocket* .... (WB)
Golden Olden Days Of Rock & Roll
Johnny Winter; *J.D. Winter III* .... (BS)
Golden Rainbow
Looking Glass; *45* .... (EPI)
Seals & Crofts; *I'll Play For You* .... (WB)
Golden Ribbons
Loggins & Messina; *Loggins & Messina* ....(COL)
On Stage ....(COL)
Golden Ring
Eric Clapton; *Backless* .... (RSO)
Tammy Wynette & George Jones; *Anniversary-20 Years
Of Hits* .... (EPI)
Encore .... (EPI)
Greatest Hits .... (EPI)
Golden Road
Grateful Dead; *Best Of-Skeletons From The Closet* (WB)
Grateful Dead .... (WB)
Golden Rocket
Hank Snow; *All About Trains* ....(RCA)
Best Of ....(RCA)
Willie Nelson & Hank Snow; *Brand On My
Heart* ....(COL)
Golden Slumbers
Beatles; *Abbey Road* .... (CAP)
Box Set ....(CAP)
Golden Vanity
Pete Seeger & Arlo Guthrie; *Together In Concert* (RPR)
Golden Years
David Bowie; *Changesonebowie* ....(RCA)
Station To Station ....(RYK)
The Singles-1969-1993 ....(RYK)
Goldfinger
Shirley Bassey; *13 Original James Bond Themes* .. (EMI)
Best Of .... (EMI)
Great Performances .... (LIB)
Greatest Hits .... (EMI)
Live At Carnegie Hall .... (UA)
ST/Goldfinger .... (UA)
Heart Of Gold
Neil Young; *Decade* .... (RPR)
Harvest .... (RPR)
House Of Gold
Hank Williams; *I'm So Lonesome I Could Cry* ... (POL)
King Midas In Reverse
Hollies; *Best Of-#2* .... (EMI)
Epic Anthology From Orig. Master Tapes .... (EPI)
Greatest Hits .... (EPI)
Love Is A Golden Ring
Frankie Laine; *16 Most Requested Songs* ....(COL)
Love Over Gold
Dire Straits; *Live-Alchemy* .... (WB)
Love Over Gold .... (WB)
Man With The Golden Thumb
Jerry Reed; *Man With The Golden Thumb* ....(RCA)
Midas Touch
Midnight Star; *45* .... (SLR)
Original Cast; *Bells Are Ringing* ....(COL)
Mining For Gold
Cowboy Junkies; *Trinity Session* ....(RCA)
Molten Gold
Paul Kossoff; *Koss* ....(DJM)

New Gold Dream
Simple Minds; *In The City Of Light (Live)* ....(A&M)
New Gold Dream ....(A&M)
Utah Saints; *Utah Saints* ....(LON)
Ornaments Of Gold
Siouxsie/Banshees; *Peepshow* ....(GEF)
Pocket Full Of Gold
Vince Gill; *Pocket Full Of Gold* .... (MCA)
Poor Man's Roses (Or A Rich Man's Gold)
Patsy Cline; *Best Of* ....(CCB)
Forever & Always .... (EPI)
Stop, Look & Listen .... (MCA)
Story .... (MCA)
Reba McEntire; *Feel The Fire* ....(MER)
Power Of Gold
Dan Fogelberg; *Live-Greetings From The West* .... (FM)
Dan Fogelberg & Tim Weisberg; *Dan
Fogelberg-Greatest Hits* .... (FM)
Twin Sons Of Different Mothers .... (FM)
Rhythm In Gold
Jethro Tull; *20 Years Of-Radio Archives/Rare
Tracks* .... (CHR)
Ruby's Golden Wedding
Danny Wilson; *Meet Danny Wilson* .... (VIA)
Sailing Down This Golden River
Pete Seeger; *Bread & Roses Festival-Acoustic
Music-#1* ....(FAN)
Circles & Seasons .... (WB)
She Got The Goldmine (I Got The Shaft)
Jerry Reed; *14 #1 Country Hits* ....(RCA)
Greatest Hits ....(RCA)
Solid Country Gold ....(RCA)
Silence Is Golden
Frankie Valli/Four Seasons; *25th Anniversary
Collection* .... (RHI)
Anthology .... (RHI)
Tremeloes; *Best Of* .... (RHI)
History Of British Rock-#7 .... (RHI)
Rock Artifacts-#4-From The Vaults ....(COL)
Silver Threads Among The Gold
Mike Auldridge; *Dobro/Blues & Bluegrass* ....(TAK)
Silver Threads & Golden Needles
Honky Tonk Angels; *Honky Tonk Angels* ....(COL)
Linda Ronstadt; *Don't Cry Now* .... (ASY)
Greatest Hits .... (ASY)
Hand Sown ....(CAP)
Retrospective ....(CAP)
Silver Tongue & Gold Plated Lies
Hotmud Family; *Meat & Potatoes (& Stuff Like
That)* .... (FF)
Silver & Gold
Dolly Parton; *Eagle When She Flies* ....(COL)
U2; *ST/Rattle & Hum* .... (ISL)
Silver & Gold (Our Love Is Like)
Sweethearts Of The Rodeo; *Sisters* ....(COL)
Silver, Blue & Gold
Bad Company; *Run With The Pack* .... (SS)
Sister Golden Hair
America; *Billboard Top Rock 'N' Roll Hits-1975* . (RHI)
History-Greatest Hits .... (WB)
In Concert ....(CAP)
Solid Gold Cadillac
Mitch Woods/Rocket 88's; *Solid Gold Cadillac* ... (BLI)
Streets Of Gold
Fabulous Thunderbirds; *Hot Number* ....(EPA)
Ronnie Milsap; *Pure Love* ....(RCA)
Sweet Summer Blue & Gold
Linda Ronstadt; *Stone Poneys* ....(CAP)
That Acapulco Gold
Rainy Daze; *Summer Of Love-#2-Turn On* .... (RHI)
There's A Gold Mine In The Sky
Jimmy C. Newman; *Cajun Cowboy* ....(PLN)
Pat Boone; *Love Letters In The Sand* ....(MSP)
Train Of Gold
Electric Light Orchestra; *Secret Messages* ....(JET)
Trumpeter Blow Your Golden Horn
Michael Tilson Thomas; *Of Thee I Sing/Let 'Em Eat
Cake* ....(COL)
When My Blue Moon Turns To Gold Again
Elvis Presley; *50 Worldwide Gold Award Hits-#2* (RCA)
Elvis ....(RCA)
Golden Celebration ....(RCA)
Merle Haggard; *His Best* .... (MCA)
Ramblin' Fever .... (MCA)

When The Golden Leaves Begin To Fall
Joe Val/New England Bluegrass Boys; #2 ...... (ROU)
When The Golden Train Comes Down
Sons Of The Pioneers; *Columbia Historic Edition* (COL)
Where The Blue Of The Night Meets The...
Bing Crosby; *All-Time Best Of* ....(CCB)
   Best Of ....(MCA)
   Where The Blue Of The Night Meets The... ....(BIO)
White Bird
It's A Beautiful Day; *Bill Graham Presents-Fillmore-Last Days* ....(EPA)
   It's A Beautiful Day ....(COL)
Your Gold Teeth
Steely Dan; *Countdown To Ecstasy* ....(MCA)
Your Gold Teeth II
Steely Dan; *Katy Lied* ....(MCA)

GUNS, Arrows, Bullets, Hunting, Shooting

See Also: CRIME, DEATH, FIGHT, KILL,
POLICE, REBELS, WAR

.357-Break It On Down
L.L. Cool J; *Bigger & Deffer* ....(DFC)
38 Pistol Blues
Big Joe Williams; *Walking Blues* ....(FAN)
Arctic Whale Hunt
Mancini Pops Orchestra; *In Surround-Mostly Monsters Murders...* ....(RCA)
Armed
Shawn Phillips; *Collaboration* ....(A&M)
Armed & Crazy
Johnny Paycheck; *Armed & Crazy* ....(EPI)
Armed & Extremely Dangerous
Merry Clayton; *Emotion* ....(MCA)
Armed & Ready
Michael Schenker Group; *Essential* ....(CHR)
   Michael Schenker Group ....(CHR)
Arrow
Candlebox; *Candlebox* ....(MAV)
Cheryl Wheeler; *Cheryl Wheeler* ....(NS)
Arrow Through Me
Wings; *Back To The Egg* ....(CAP)
Arrow Thru Your Heart
Lou Gramm; *Ready or Not* ....(ATL)
Arrows
Crosby, Stills & Nash; *Live It Up* ....(ATL)
At The End Of A Pointed Gun
Tannahill Weavers; *Passage* ....(GRE)
Ballad Of A Well Known Gun
Elton John; *Tumbleweed Connection* ....(POL)
Bang Bang
Bar-Kays; *Too Hot To Stop* ....(MER)
Cher; *Cher* ....(GEF)
   EMI Legends Of Rock 'N' Roll-24 Greatest ...... (EMI)
Stevie Wonder; *Down To Earth* ....(MOT)
Vanilla Fudge; *Vanilla Fudge* ....(ATC)
Bang, You're Dead
Bette Midler; *Live At Last* ....(ATL)
Bayonet Rap
Tom Paxton; *Compleat* ....(ELE)
Big Gun
AC/DC; *ST/Last Action Hero* ....(COL)
Big Guns
Heatwave; *Greatest Hits* ....(EPI)
Skid Row; *Skid Row* ....(ATL)
Big Iron
Marty Robbins; *All-Time Greatest Hits* ....(COL)
   Columbia Country Classics-#3-Americana ......(COL)
   More Greatest Hits ....(COL)
Bikini Girls With Machine Guns
Cramps; *Stay Sick!* ....(ENC)
Blues From A Gun
Jesus & Mary Chain; *Automatic* ....(WB)
Boom Bye Bye
Buju Banton; *Voice Of Jamaica* ....(MER)
Bop Gun
Ice Cube & George Clinton; *S* ....(PRY)
British Grenadiers
Cambridge Singers; *The Lark In THe Clear Air* ..(CLG)
Broken Arrow
Buffalo Springfield; *Again* ....(ATC)
   Retrospective ....(ATC)

Chuck Berry; *Rockin' At The Hops* ....(CSS)
Neil Young; *Decade* ....(RPR)
Robbie Robertson; *Robbie Robertson* ....(GEF)
Rod Stewart; *Vagabond Heart* ....(WB)
Bubba Shot The Jukebox
Mark Chesnutt; *Longnecks & Short Stories* ...... (MCA)
Buffalo Gun
Michael Murphey; *Swans Against The Son* ....(EPI)
Bullet
Divinyls; *Divinyls* ....(VIA)
Bullet From A Gun
Derek B.; *Bullet From A Gun* ....(PRO)
Bullet In The Chamber
Loverboy; *Lovin' Every Minute Of It* ....(COL)
Bullet In The Head
Rage Against The Machine; *Rage Against The Machine* ....(EPA)
Bullet Proof
George Clinton; *Some Of My Best Jokes Are Friends* ....(CAP)
Sade; *Love Deluxe* ....(EPI)
Bullet The Blue Sky
U2; *Joshua Tree* ....(ISL)
   ST/Rattle & Hum ....(ISL)
Bullets To Spare
Dokken; *Tooth & Nail* ....(ELE)
Bullet-Ridden Bodies
Accused; *Grinning Like An Undertaker* ....(NSY)
Cannonball
Breeders; *Last Splash* ....(4AD)
Duane Eddy; *Compact Command Performances* . (MOT)
Supertramp; *Brother Where You Bound* ....(A&M)
   Classics-#9 ....(A&M)
Cowboys Don't Shoot Straight
Tammy Wynette; *Biggest Hits* ....(EPI)
   Tears Of Fire-25th Anniversary Collect. ....(EPI)
Crossfire
Jethro Tull; *"A"* ....(CHR)
Kansas; *Vinyl Confessions* ....(KIR)
Scorpions; *Love At First Sting* ....(MER)
Stevie Ray Vaughan/Double Trouble; *In Step* .....(EPI)
Cupid's Got A Brand New Gun
Michael Penn; *March* ....(RCA)
Day That Curly Bill Shot Down Crazy Sam
Hollies; *Hollies* ....(EPI)
Dirty Weapons
Killer Dwarfs; *Dirty Weapons* ....(EPI)
Don't Drop That Bomb On Me
Bryan Adams; *Waking Up The Neighbors* ....(A&M)
Don't Need A Gun
Billy Idol; *Whiplash Smile* ....(CHR)
Don't Take Your Guns To Town
Johnny Cash; *Billboard Top Country Hits-1959* ..(COL)
   Columbia Country Classics-#3 ....(COL)
   Greatest Hits ....(COL)
Down By The River
Neil Young; *Decade* ....(RPR)
   Everybody Knows This Is Nowhere ....(RPR)
Elephant Gun
David Lee Roth; *Eat 'Em & Smile* ....(WB)
English Boys (With Guns)
Deaf School; *English Boys/Working Girls* ....(WB)
Forty Thousand Headmen
Traffic; *Traffic* ....(ISL)
   Welcome To The Canteen ....(ISL)
Gimme A Bullet
AC/DC; *Powerage* ....(ATL)
Go For Your Guns
Isley Brothers; *Go For Your Guns* .... (TN)
Gone Shootin'
AC/DC; *Powerage* ....(ATL)
Gonna Go Huntin' Tonight
Hank Williams, Jr.; *Greatest Hits-#2* ....(W/C)
   Strong Stuff ....(WB)
Gun
John Cale; *Guts* ....(ISL)
Siouxsie/Banshees; *Through The Looking Glass* ..(GEF)
Gun Don't Mind
Winter Brothers Band; *Coast To Coast* ....(ATC)
Gun Love
ZZ Top; *Greatest Hits* ....(WB)
Gun Shy
10,000 Maniacs; *In My Tribe* ....(ELE)
Moon Martin; *Escape From Domination* ....(CAP)

Guns On The Roof
Clash; *Give 'Em Enough Rope* .... (EPI)
Gunslinger
Mink De Ville; *Mink De Ville* .... (CAP)
Gunsmoke
Billy Strange; *Great Western Themes* .... (CRS)
Molly Hatchet; *Flirtin' With Disaster* .... (EPI)
Outlaws; *Hurry Sundown* .... (ARI)
Guns, Guns, Guns
Burton Cummings; *Dream Of A Child* .... (POR)
Happiness Is A Warm Gun
Beatles; *White Album* .... (CAP)
"Have Gun Will Travel" Theme
Johnny Western; *Television's Greatest Hits-#2* .... (TVT)
Hey Joe
Jimi Hendrix; *Essential-#2* .... (RPR)
 Live At Winterland .... (RYK)
 Smash Hits .... (RPR)
Jimi Hendrix Experience; *Are You Experienced?* . (RPR)
Love; *Best Of* .... (RHI)
Hit Me With Your Best Shot
Pat Benatar; *Crimes Of Passion* .... (CHR)
 Live From Earth .... (CHR)
Homecoming Queen's Got A Gun
Julie Brown; *Dr. Demento Greatest Novelty
Records-#5* .... (RHI)
 Teenage Tragedies .... (RHI)
 Trapped In The Body Of A White Girl .... (SIR)
Hunter
Dokken; *Under Lock & Key* .... (ELE)
Free; *Best Of* .... (A&M)
 Live .... (A&M)
Paul Rodgers; *Muddy Water Blues-Tribute To M.
Waters* .... (VIC)
Hunter Gets Captured By The Game
Marvelettes; *Anthology* .... (MOT)
 Compact Command Performances .... (MOT)
Smokey Robinson/Miracles; *Motown Legends* ... (MOT)
Hunting The Wren
Steeleye Span; *Live At Last* .... (CHR)
Hunting Tigers Out In India
Bonzo Dog Band; *Best Of* .... (RHI)
 Tadpoles .... (LIB)
I Feel Like A Bullet
Elton John; *Rock Of The Westies* .... (POL)
I Fought The Law
Bobby Fuller; *Best Of* .... (RHI)
 Heart & Soul Of Rock & Roll-#1 .... (RHI)
Bobby Fuller Four; *Oldies But Goodies-#9* .... (OSR)
 Super Oldies/'60s-#7 .... (AUF)
Clash; *Clash* .... (EPI)
 Story Of-#1 .... (EPI)
I Shot The Sheriff
Bob Marley/Wailers; *Burnin'* .... (TUF)
 Legend .... (TUF)
 Live .... (TUF)
 This Is Reggae Music .... (ISL)
Eric Clapton; *461 Ocean Blvd.* .... (RSO)
 Crossroads .... (POL)
 Time Pieces-Best Of .... (RSO)
I Wanna Get Me A Gun
Bill Wyman; *Monkey Grip* .... (RS)
I'll Be Your .44
Dr. Blue; *Salt City Blues* .... (BWV)
Janie's Got A Gun
Aerosmith; *Pump* .... (GEF)
John Peel
Hermes Nye; *Anglo-American Songs* .... (FLW)
Johnny 99
Bruce Springsteen; *Nebraska* .... (COL)
Bruce Springsteen/E Street Band;
Live-1975-1985 .... (COL)
Johnny Cash; *Cover Me* .... (RHI)
Justice In The Barrel
Bon Jovi; *Blaze Of Glory* .... (MER)
Lawyers, Guns & Money
Warren Zevon; *Excitable Boy* .... (ASY)
 Quiet Normal Life-Best Of .... (ASY)
 Stand In The Fire .... (ASY)
Little Triggers
Elvis Costello; *This Year's Model* .... (COL)

Love Gun
Kiss; *Alive 2* .... (CAS)
 Double Platinum .... (CAS)
 Love Gun .... (CAS)
 Smashes Thrashes & Hits .... (MER)
Love Is In Control (Finger On The...)
Donna Summer; *Donna Summer* .... (GEF)
Love Is Like A Bullet
Shoes; *Best* .... (BLV)
 Stolen Wishes .... (BLV)
Machine Gun
Commodores; *All The Great Hits* .... (MOT)
 Greatest Hits .... (MOT)
 Machine Gun .... (MOT)
Jimi Hendrix; *Band Of Gypsys* .... (CAP)
 Essential-#2 .... (RPR)
 Midnight Lightning .... (RPR)
 ST/Jimi Hendrix .... (RPR)
Warrant; *Dog Eat Dog* .... (COL)
Machine Gun Kelly
James Taylor; *Mud Slide Slim* .... (WB)
Man Who Shot Himself
Tom T. Hall; *Places I've Done Time* .... (RCA)
Man Who Shot Liberty Valance
Gene Pitney; *Anthology* .... (RHI)
 Greatest Hits .... (EVR)
 Super Oldies/'60s-#9 .... (AUF)
Greg Kihn; *Glass House Rock* .... (BES)
Me & A Gun
Tori Amos; *Little Earthquakes* .... (ATL)
Me & My Arrow
Nilsson; *Greatest Hits* .... (RCA)
 The Point .... (RCA)
My Father's Gun
Elton John; *Tumbleweed Connection* .... (POL)
Nebraska
Bruce Springsteen; *Nebraska* .... (COL)
Bruce Springsteen/E Street Band;
Live-1975-1985 .... (COL)
Never Bit A Bullet Like This
George Jones; *High-Tech Redneck* .... (MCA)
Nigga Witta Gun
Dr. Dre; *The Chronic* .... (PRY)
Ohio
Crosby, Stills & Nash; *Crosby Stills & Nash
(collection)* .... (ATL)
Crosby, Stills, Nash & Young; *Four-Way Street* .. (ATL)
 So Far .... (ATL)
Neil Young; *Decade* .... (RPR)
 ST/Journey Through The Past .... (RPR)
Ohio/Machine Gun
Isley Brothers; *Timeless* .... (TN)
Our Shotgun Wedding Day
Howington Brothers/Tennessee Haymakers; *Long Gone
Daddy* .... (CLT)
Paradise Knife & Gun Club
Jerry Lansdowne; *Travel Light* .... (SO)
Roy Clark; *Live From Austin City Limits* .... (CHU)
Pass Me The Gun
House Of Freaks; *All My Friends* .... (RHI)
Pass The Ammo
C.E.B.; *Countin' Endless Bank* .... (RUC)
Pistol Packin' Mama
Al Dexter; *Columbia Country Classics-#1-Golden
Age* .... (COL)
 Great Records Of The Decade-'40s Hits .... (CCB)
Andrews Sisters; *16 Great Performances* .... (MCA)
 Boogie Woogie Bugle Girls .... (MCA)
Bing Crosby; *Greatest Hits* .... (MCA)
Glenn Miller/Army Air Force Band; *Nipper's Greatest
Hits-'40s-#1* .... (RCA)
Pistol Packin' Papa
Hank Snow; *Superstars Salute Jimmie Rodgers* ..... (SO)
Jimmie Rodgers; *Riding High 1929-1930* .... (ROU)
 This Is .... (RCA)
Point Blank
Bruce Springsteen; *The River* .... (COL)
Poison Arrow
ABC; *Absolutely ABC* .... (MER)
 Lexicon Of Love .... (MER)
Flesheaters; *Prehistoric Fits-#2* .... (SST)
Possum Hunt
Lightnin' Hopkins; *Lost Texas Tapes-#4* .... (CLT)

Praise The Lord & Pass The Ammunition
Kay Kyser; *Best Of The Big Bands* ....(COL)
   Sentimental Favorites ....(COL)
Put Down The Gun
Poison Dart; *Dancehall Roughneck* ....(HRT)
Put Out The Fire
Queen; *Hot Space* ....(HOL)
Rifle Range
Blondie; *Blondie* .... (CHR)
Riflemen Of Bennington
Jim Burroughs; *Songs Of Rebellion* .... (AUF)
Roland The Headless Thompson Gunner
Warren Zevon; *Excitable Boy* .... (ASY)
   Quiet Normal Life-Best Of .... (ASY)
Rubber Bullets
10 CC; *Greatest Hits 1972-78* .... (POL)
Running Gun Blues
David Bowie; *Man Who Sold The World* ....(RYK)
Russian Roulette
Accept; *Russian Roulette* .... (POR)
Hollies; *Hollies* .... (EPI)
Joan Armatrading; *Sleight Of Hand* .... (A&M)
Lords Of The New Church; *Killer Lords* .... (IRS)
   Lords Of The New Church .... (IRS)
Michelle Shocked; *Captain Swing* .... (MER)
Taxxi; *Expose* .... (MCA)
San Angelo
Marty Robbins; *All Around Cowboy* ....(COL)
   Essential Marty Robbins-1951-1982 ....(COL)
   More Gunfighter Ballads & Trail Songs ....(COL)
Sapphire Bullets Of Pure Love
They Might Be Giants; *Flood* .... (ELE)
Saturday Night Special
Lynyrd Skynyrd; *Gold & Platinum* .... (MCA)
   Nuthin' Fancy .... (MCA)
   One More From The Road .... (MCA)
   Skynyrd's Innyrds .... (MCA)
Terry McBride/Ride; *Skynyrd Frynds* .... (MCA)
"Sea Hunt" Theme
Original Music; *Greatest Hits-#2* .... (TVT)
Sex As A Weapon
Pat Benatar; *Seven The Hard Way* .... (CHR)
She Shot A Hole In My Soul
Clifford Curry; *Soul Shots-#2-"In" Crowd-Sweet*
Soul .... (RHI)
Huey Lewis/News; *Four Chords & Several Years*
Ago .... (ELE)
Shoot Down The Moon
Elton John; *Ice On Fire* .... (MCA)
Shoot Her If She Runs
Climax Blues Band; *Tightly Knit* .... (SIR)
Shoot High Aim Low
Yes; *Big Generator* ....(ATC)
Shoot Him
Sugarcubes; *Here Today Tomorrow Next Week!* .. (ELE)
Shoot Low Sheriff
Murry Kellum; *Country Comedy-20 Country Comedy*
Hits .... (PLN)
Shoot Me In The Dark
Brews Springstien; *Melting Plot* ....(SST)
Shoot Out At The Fantasy Factory
Traffic; *On The Road* .... (ISL)
   Shoot Out At The Fantasy Factory .... (ISL)
Shoot Out In Chinatown
Band; *Cahoots* ....(CAP)
Shoot Out On The Plantation
Leon Russell; *Best Of* .... (MCA)
   Leon Russell .... (MCA)
Shoot Out The Lights
Richard Thompson; *Watching The Dark-History*
Of ....(RYK)
Richard & Linda Thompson; *Shoot Out The*
Lights .... (HBL)
Shoot Shoot
Dio; *Sacred Heart* .... (WB)
Sons Of Freedom; *Sons Of Freedom* ....(SLS)
UFO; *Force It* .... (CHR)
   Strangers In The Night .... (CHR)
Shoot That Turkey
Holy Modal Rounders; *Alleged In Their Own*
Time .... (ROU)
Shoot To Thrill
AC/DC; *Back In Black* .... (ATL)

Shoot Your Shot
Junior Walker/All-Stars; *Anthology* .... (MOT)
   Greatest Hits .... (MOT)
   Shotgun .... (MOT)
J. Geils Band; *Blow Your Face Out* .... (ATL)
Shoot 'Em Down
Twisted Sister; *Big Hits & Nasty Cuts* .... (ATL)
Shoot 'Em Up
Cypress Hill; *ST/Juice* .... (SOL)
Shootin' On Narcs
Pat Gangsta; *#1 Suspect* .... (ATL)
Shot Down
Icehouse; *Sidewalk* .... (CHR)
Julian Cope; *Saint Julian* .... (ISL)
Neil Diamond; *Do It* ....(BNG)
   Double Gold ....(BNG)
Shot Down In Flames
AC/DC; *Highway To Hell* .... (ATL)
Shot Full Of Love
Chris LeDoux; *Western Underground* .... (LIB)
Don Williams; *New Moves* .... (CAP)
Juice Newton; *Greatest Hits & More* .... (LIB)
   Juice ....(CAP)
Shot In The Dark
Ozzy Osbourne; *Ultimate Sin* .... (CBA)
Utopia; *Adventures In Utopia* .... (RHI)
Shot In The Heart
Genya Ravan; *Urban Desire* .... (20)
Shot Me Down
Nazareth; *Expect No Mercy* .... (A&M)
Shot Through The Heart
Jennifer Warnes; *Best Of* .... (ARI)
   Shot Through The Heart .... (ARI)
Shotgun
Junior Walker/All-Stars; *Anthology* .... (MOT)
   Billboard Top R&B Hits-1965-1969 .... (RHI)
   Greatest Hits .... (MOT)
   Motown Superstar Series-#5 .... (MOT)
   Shotgun .... (MOT)
Los Lobos; *ST/American Me* .... (VIA)
Tanya Tucker; *Tennessee Woman* .... (LIB)
Vanilla Fudge; *Best Of* ....(ATC)
   Live .... (RHI)
Shotgun Blues
Blues Brothers; *Briefcase Full Of Blues* .... (ATL)
B.B. King; *From The Beginning* ....(KNT)
Guns N' Roses; *Use Your Illusion II* .... (GEF)
Shotgun Willie
Willie Nelson; *Shotgun Willie* .... (ATL)
Shoulder Holster
Elton John; *Blue Moves* .... (MCA)
Silver Bullet
Flo & Eddie; *History Of Flo & Eddie/Turtles* ..... (RHI)
Silver Gun
Robert Palmer; *Addictions-#2* .... (ISL)
   Pride .... (ISL)
Son Of A New York Gun
Gino Vannelli; *Powerful People* .... (A&M)
Sweet Little Bullet From A Pretty...
Tom Waits; *Blue Valentine* .... (ASY)
That Dog Won't Hunt
Waylon Jennings; *Will The Wolf Survive* .... (MCA)
"The Rifleman" Theme
Cincinnati Pops Orchestra/Erich Kunzel;
   Round-Up .... (TLR)
There Goes My Gun
Pixies; *Doolittle* .... (ELE)
Tragedy
Bee Gees; *Greatest* .... (POL)
   Mega Hits Dance Classics-#8 .... (PRY)
   Spirits Having Flown .... (POL)
Trigga Happy Nigga
Geto Boys; *Grip It! On That Other Level* .... (DEF)
Trigger Happy
Thrashpack; *Hard As hell-#2* .... (PRO)
Weird Al Yankovic; *Off The Deep End* .... (SCO)
Trigger Happy Kid
Kenny Rogers/First Edition; *All-Time Greatest*
Hits-#2 .... (MSP)
Two Bullets & A Gun
Stevie Salas Colorcode; *Stevie Salas Colorcode* .... (ISL)
Under The Gun
Aldo Nova; *Aldo Nova* .... (POR)
   Portrait Of .... (EPI)

Deep Purple; *Perfect Strangers* .... (MER)
Molly Hatchet; *No Guts No Glory* .... (EPI)
Poco; *Backtracks* .... (MCA)
  Under The Gun .... (MCA)
Robin Trower; *In The Line Of Fire* .... (ATL)
Suzy Bogguss; *Moment Of Truth* .... (CAP)
Willie Nelson & Kris Kristofferson; *Music From*
"Songwriter" ....(COL)

Vote With A Bullet
Corrosion Of Conformity; *Vote With A Bullet* .... (REL)

Washington Bullets
Clash; *On Broadway* .... (EPI)
  Sandinista .... (EPI)

Watch My .38
Commander Cody/Lost Planet Airmen; *Hot Licks Cold*
Steel & Trucker's Fav. .... (MCA)

With A Gun
Steely Dan; *Pretzel Logic* .... (MCA)

Young Guns
Wham!; *Fantastic* ....(COL)

※※※※※※※※※※※※※※※※※※※※※※※※※※※※※※※※※※※※※※

HAPPINESS, Feeling Good
See Also: DOCTORS, FUN, PARTY, SMILE

※※※※※※※※※※※※※※※※※※※※※※※※※※※※※※※※※※※※※※

59th St. Bridge Song (Feelin' Groovy)
Simon & Garfunkel; *Collected Works* ....(COL)
  Concert In Central Park .... (WB)
  Greatest Hits ....(COL)
  Parsley Sage Rosemary & Thyme ....(COL)

All Is Well
Chicago; *#5* ....(COL)

All Right Now
Free; *Best Of* .... (A&M)
  Fire & Water .... (A&M)
  Island Story (1962-1987)-25th Annivers. .... (ISL)
  Live .... (A&M)
  Rock Classics-#2 .... (KT)

Anticipation
Carly Simon; *Anticipation* .... (ELE)
  Best Of .... (ELE)

April Joy
Pat Metheny Group; *Pat Metheny Group* .... (ECM)

Are You Happy Baby?
Dottie West; *Best Of* .... (E/L)

Aren't You Glad?
Beach Boys; *Smiley Smile/Wild Honey* ....(CAP)
  Sunshine Dream ....(CAP)
  '69 ....(CAP)

Back In Stride
Maze featuring Frankie Beverly; *Can't Stop The*
Love ....(CAP)
  Lifelines-#1 ....(CAP)
  Live In Los Angeles ....(CAP)

Back In The High Life Again
Steve Winwood; *Back In The High Life* .... (ISL)

Back On My Feet Again
Babys; *Anthology* .... (CHR)
  Union Jacks .... (CHR)
Furry Lewis; *Back On My Feet Again* .... (PRS)
  Shake 'Em Down .... (FAN)
Randy Newman; *Good Old Boys* .... (RPR)

Back On The Streets Again
Tower Of Power; *Bill Graham Presents Fillmore-Last*
Days .... (EPA)
  East Bay Grease ....(OOP)

Be Young, Be Foolish, Be Happy
Tams; *45* .... (MCA)
  45 .... (RLL)

Best Days Of My Life
Johnny Mathis; *Best Days Of My Life* ....(COL)
  Best Of-1975-1980 ....(COL)
Rod Stewart; *Blondes Have More Fun* .... (WB)

Better Days
Bruce Springsteen; *Lucky Town* ....(COL)

Big Bright Green Pleasure Machine
Simon & Garfunkel; *Collected Works* ....(COL)
  Parsley Sage Rosemary & Thyme ....(COL)
  ST/The Graduate ....(COL)

Bluebird Of Happiness
Lee Andrews/Hearts; *Biggest Hits* .... (CLT)
  Gotham Recording Sessions .... (CLT)

Checkin' It Out
Van Morrison; *Wavelength* .... (WB)

Cheerful Little Earful
Ella Fitzgerald; *Swings Brightly With Nelson* .....(VRV)

Chessman's Delight
Randy Weston Trio/Cecil Payne; *Jazz A La*
Bohemia ....(RVR)

Comfort Zone
Vanessa Williams; *Comfort Zone* .... (WIN)

Comfortably Numb
Pink Floyd; *Delicate Sound Of Thunder* ....(COL)
  Knebworth-The Album .... (POL)
  The Wall ....(COL)
Roger Waters; *The Wall Live In Berlin* .... (MER)

Comforter
Shai; *If I Ever Fall In Love* .... (GAS)

Cool, Calm, Collected
Atlantic Starr; *As The Band Turns* .... (A&M)

Country Comfort
Elton John; *Tumbleweed Connection* .... (POL)

Country Comforts
Rod Stewart; *Best Of-#2* .... (MER)
  Gasoline Alley .... (MER)
  Sing It Again Rod .... (MER)

Daddy's Gonna Treat You Right
Commander Cody/Lost Planet Airmen; *Lost In The*
Ozone ....(MCA)

Days Of Wine And Roses
Andy Williams; *16 Most Requested Songs* ....(COL)
  Close Enough For Love ....(ATC)
  Greatest Hits ....(COL)
  TT/Moon River & Other Great Movie Themes ...(COL)
Dream Syndicate; *Days Of Wine & Roses* .... (SLS)
  Live At Raji's .... (RES)
Frank Sinatra; *Days Of Wine & Roses/Acad. Award*
Winners ....(RPR)
Henry Mancini; *All-Time Greatest Hits-#1* ......(RCA)
  Best Of ....(RCA)
  Pure Gold ....(RCA)

Digging Your Scene
Blow Monkeys; *Animal Magic* ....(RCA)

Do What You Do
Jermaine Jackson; *Jermaine Jackson* .... (ARI)

Doctor Feelgood
Aretha Franklin; *30 Greatest Hits* .... (ATL)
  Aretha's Gold ....(ATL)
  Best Of ....(ATL)
  I Never Loved A Man ....(ATL)
  Live At Fillmore East ....(ATL)

Don't Be So Serious
Starpoint; *It's So Delicious* .... (ELE)

Don't Worry, Baby
Beach Boys; *Absolute Best-#1* ....(CAP)
  Endless Summer ....(CAP)
  Fun Fun Fun ....(CAP)
  Made In The U.S.A. ....(CAP)

Don't Worry, Be Happy
Bobby McFerrin; *Simple Pleasures* .... (EMI)
  ST/Cocktail .... (ELE)

Ease My Mind
Arrested Development; *Zingalamaduni* .... (CHR)

Easy
Commodores; *20 Greatest Songs In Motown*
History .... (MOT)
  All The Great Love Songs .... (MOT)
  Commodores .... (MOT)
  Compact Command Performances .... (MOT)
  Composer-Great Love Songs By L. Richie ...... (MOT)
  Greatest Hits .... (MOT)

Easy Skanking
Bob Marley/Wailers; *Kaya* .... (ISL)

Encore
Cheryl Lynn; *Preppie* ....(COL)

Everybody's Gonna Be Happy
Kinks; *Greatest Hits-#1* .... (RHI)
  Kinks-Size .... (RHI)
  Kinks-Size Kinkdom .... (RHI)

Everything Is Going To Be All Right
Paul Butterfield Blues Band; *Live* .... (ELE)

Everything Is Kinda All Right
Charlie Daniels Band; *Night Rider* .... (EPI)

Everything's All Right
David Bowie; *Pinups* ....(RYK)

Feel Right
Tanya Tucker; *Changes* .... (ARI)

Feel So Good
Jefferson Airplane; *30 Seconds Over Winterland* ..(RCA)
Bark .... (GRU)
Flight Log 1966-76 .... (GRU)
Shirley & Lee; *Best Of New Orleans R&B-#1* .... (RHI)
Billboard Top R&B Hits-1955 .... (RHI)
History Of New Orleans R&B-#1-1950-1958 ... (RHI)
Feelin' Good About Feelin' Bad
Patty Loveless; *When Fallen Angels Fly* .... (EPI)
Feelin' Satisfied
Boston; *Don't Look Back* .... (EPI)
Feels Good
Tony! Toni! Tone!; *Revival* .... (WIN)
Feels So Good
Chuck Mangione; *70 Miles Young* .... (A&M)
Best Of .... (A&M)
Classics-#6 .... (A&M)
Evening With Magic .... (A&M)
Feels So Good .... (A&M)
Surface; *Surface* ....(COL)
Van Halen; *OU812* ....(WB)
Feels So Right
Alabama; *Feels So Right* ....(RCA)
Greatest Hits ....(RCA)
Fine Fine Day
Tony Carey; *Some Tough City* .... (MCA)
Fine & Dandy
Art Tatum; *Solo Masterpieces-#5* .... (PAB)
Barbra Streisand; *People* ....(COL)
Chet Baker; *Out Of Nowhere* .... (MS)
Milt Jackson & Sonny Stitt; *In The Beginning* ....(GAL)
Fine & Mellow
Billie Holiday; *Essential* ....(VRV)
Fine & Mellow ....(CLT)
History Of The Real Billie Holiday ....(VRV)
Flashdance...What A Feeling
Irene Cara; *ST/Flashdance* .... (CAS)
Fumbling Towards Ecstasy
Sarah McLachlan; *Fumbling Towards Ecstasy* .... (ARI)
Funiculi, Funicula
Mario Lanza; *Legendary Tenor* ....(RCA)
Future's So Bright I Gotta Wear Shades
Timbuk 3; *Greetings From* .... (IRS)
Get Off (You Fascinate Me)
Patrice Rushen; *Now* .... (ELE)
Gett Off
Prince/New Power Generation; *S* ....(PAI)
Glad
Traffic; *John Barleycorn Must Die* .... (ISL)
On The Road .... (ISL)
Glad All Over
Dave Clark Five; *45* ....(OOP)
Jeff Beck Group; *Jeff Beck Group* .... (EPI)
Glad Tidings
Van Morrison; *Moondance* ....(WB)
Glory Days
Bruce Springsteen; *Born In The U.S.A.* ....(COL)
Glory Of Love
Bette Midler; *ST/Beaches* .... (ATL)
Peter Cetera; *Solitude/Solitaire* .... (FM)
ST/Karate Kid-#2 .... (EMI)
Velvetones; *Doo Wop Ballads-#2* .... (RHI)
Good Clean Fun
Allman Brothers Band; *Seven Turns* .... (EPI)
Good Feelin' To Know
Poco; *Good Feelin' To Know* .... (EPI)
Ride The Country .... (EPI)
Songs Of Richie Furay .... (EPI)
Very Best Of .... (EPI)
Good Time Man Like Me...
Jim Croce; *Life & Times* ....(OOP)
Good Vibrations
Beach Boys; *Billboard Top Rock 'N' Roll
Hits-1966* .... (RHI)
Gift Set .... (CAP)
Good Vibrations .... (CAP)
Smiley Smile/Wild Honey .... (CAP)
Sunshine Dream .... (CAP)
Marky Mark/Funky Bunch; *Music For The People* (ISC)
Got The Feeling
Jeff Beck; *Rough & Ready* .... (EPI)
Groovin'
Aretha Franklin; *Lady Soul* .... (ATL)

Booker T./M.G.s; *Best Of* .... (ATL)
Soul Shots-#3 Soul Twist .... (RHI)
Rascals; *Greatest Hits* .... (ATL)
Groovin' .... (RHI)
Hit Singles-1958-1977 .... (ATL)
ST/Platoon .... (ATL)
Hang On To What You Got
Joe Tex; *45* ....(OOP)
Happier Than The Morning Sun
Stevie Wonder; *Music Of My Mind* .... (MOT)
Happiest Girl In The Whole U.S.A.
Donna Fargo; *45* .... (MCA)
Jeanne Pruett; *Stand By Your Man* .... (ALL)
Happiest Song On The Jukebox
Charley Pride; *Out-of-print recording* ....(OOP)
Happily Married Man
Duane Allman; *Anthology #2* ....(CPC)
Happiness
Billy Lawrence; *One Might Say* ....(EW)
Original Cast; *You're A Good Man Charlie
Brown* .... (POL)
Pointer Sisters; *Energy* ....(PNT)
Robert Palmer; *Don't Explain* .... (EMI)
Soul II Soul; *Keep On Movin'* .... (VIA)
Happiness Is A Warm Gun
Beatles; *White Album* ....(CAP)
Happiness Lives Next Door
Willie Nelson; *Diamonds In The Night* ....(DEL)
Legend Begins/Wild & Willie .... (ALL)
Happy
Boys; *Message From* .... (MOT)
Michael Jackson; *Best Of* .... (MOT)
Great Love Songs Of .... (MOT)
Music & Me .... (MOT)
Rolling Stones; *Exile On Main Street* .... (RS)
Love You Live ....(RS)
Made In The Shade ....(RS)
Sunshine Company; *Nuggets-#11-Pop-Part 4* .... (RHI)
Surface; *Surface* ....(COL)
Happy Anniversary
Little River Band; *Diamantina Cocktail* ....(CAP)
Greatest Hits ....(CAP)
Slim Whitman; *Best Of-Legendary Master Series* .. (EMI)
Happy Days
Pratt & McClean; *45* .... (RPR)
Talking Heads; *'77* .... (SIR)
Happy Days Are Here Again
Barbra Streisand; *Album* ....(COL)
Barbra Streisand ....(COL)
Greatest Hits ....(COL)
Happening In Central Park ....(COL)
One Voice ....(COL)
Happy Endings
Liza Minnelli & Larry Kert; *ST/New York New
York* .... (EMI)
Happy Feelin's
Maze featuring Frankie Beverly; *Lifelines-#1* ....(CAP)
Live In New Orleans ....(CAP)
Maze featuring Frankie Beverly ....(CAP)
Happy Go Lucky Local
Duke Ellington; *20 Golden Pieces Of* .... (BLD)
All Star Road Band-#2 .... (DOC)
Continuum .... (FAN)
Great Paris Concert .... (ATL)
Happy Heart
Andy Williams; *Greatest Hits* ....(COL)
Petula Clark; *Greatest Hits* .... (CRS)
Happy House
Siouxsie/Banshees; *Kaleidoscope* ....(GEF)
Nocturne ....(GEF)
Once Upon A Time-The Singles ....(GEF)
Happy Jack
Who; *Greatest Hits* .... (MCA)
Happy Jack .... (MCA)
Meaty Beaty Big & Bouncy .... (MCA)
ST/Kids Are Alright .... (MCA)
Who's Better Who's Best-Very Best Of .... (MCA)
Happy Loving Couples
Joe Jackson; *Look Sharp* .... (A&M)
Happy Man
Chicago; *Greatest Hits-#2* ....(COL)
VII ....(COL)
Greg Kihn Band; *Kihnsolidation-Best Of* .... (RHI)

Happy Organ
Dave "Baby" Cortez; *Billboard Top Rock 'N' Roll
Hits-1959* .... (RHI)
 History Of Rock Instrumentals-#1 .... (RHI)
 Super Oldies/'50s-#7 .... (AUF)
Happy Song
Box Tops; *Greatest Hits* .... (RHI)
Happy Talk
Original Cast; *South Pacific* .... (COL)
Happy To Be Just Like I Am
Taj Mahal; *Happy To Be Just Like I Am* .... (COL)
Happy Together
Flo & Eddie/Turtles; *History Of* .... (RHI)
Turtles; *Billboard Top Rock 'N' Roll Hits-1967* ... (RHI)
 Cruisin'-1967 .... (RHI)
 Greatest Hits .... (RHI)
 Happy Together .... (RHI)
 Turtlesized .... (RHI)
Happy Trails
Michael Martin Murphey; *Cowboy Songs* .... (WB)
Quicksilver Messenger Service; *Sons Of Mercury* (RHI)
Randy Travis & Roy Rogers; *Heroes & Friends* ... (WB)
Riders In The Sky; *Cowboy Way* .... (MCA)
Roy Rogers/Dale Evans/Dusty Rogers; *Tribute* .. (RCA)
Van Halen; *Diver Down* .... (WB)
Happy 'Cause I'm Going Home
Chicago; *At Carnegie Hall* .... (COL)
 III .... (COL)
(He's) Some Kind Of Wonderful
Carole King; *Music* .... (EPI)
High Cotton
Alabama; *Southern Star* .... (RCA)
Higher Love
Steve Winwood; *Back In The High Life* .... (ISL)
Hotel Happiness
Brook Benton; *Anthology* .... (RHI)
 It's Just A Mater Of Time-Greatest Hits .... (MER)
 Super Oldies/'60s-#11 .... (AUF)
Hungry (For Those Good Things)
Paul Revere/Raiders; *Best Of-#1* .... (BCT)
 Frat Rock! .... (RHI)
 Greatest Hits .... (COL)
 Legend Of .... (COL)
H.A.P.P.Y. Radio
Edwin Starr; *45* .... (OOP)
I Can't Be Satisfied
Bee Gees; *Spirits Having Flown* .... (LON)
Muddy Waters; *Best Of* .... (CSS)
 Chess Box .... (CSS)
 Hard Again .... (BS)
Rolling Stones; *More Hot Rocks-Big Hits & Fazed
Cookies* .... (AKO)
(I Can't Get No) Satisfaction
Devo; *45* .... (WB)
 Q: Are We Not Men .... (WB)
Otis Redding; *Best Of* .... (RPR)
 Otis Redding .... (ATL)
Rolling Stones; *Big Hits-High Tide & Green Grass* (AKO)
 Got Live If You Want It .... (AKO)
 Hot Rocks-1964-1971 .... (AKO)
 Out Of Our Heads .... (AKO)
I Enjoy Being A Girl
Original Cast; *Flower Drum Song* .... (COL)
I Feel Fine
Beatles; *1962-1966* .... (CAP)
 20 Greatest Hits .... (CAP)
 Past Masters-#1 .... (CAP)
 '65 .... (CAP)
Sweethearts Of The Rodeo; *One Time One Night* . (COL)
I Feel For You
Chaka Khan; *I Feel For You* .... (WB)
 Life Is A Dance/The Remix Project .... (WB)
Prince; *Prince* .... (WB)
I Had A Beautiful Time
Merle Haggard; *19 Hot Country Requests-#3* ..... (EPI)
 Friend In California .... (EPI)
 Greatest Country Hits/'80s-1986 .... (COL)
I Just Want to Satisfy You
O'Jays; *45* .... (PI)
I Like It
DeBarge; *All This Love* .... (MOT)
 Greatest Hits .... (MOT)
Gerry/Pacemakers; *Best Of* .... (EMI)
 History Of British Rock-#2 .... (RHI)

I Wouldn't Have It Any Other Way
Aaron Tippin; *Read Between The Lines* .... (RCA)
Pirates Of The Mississippi; *Walk The Plank* ...... (LIB)
If You Wanna Be Happy
Jimmy Soul; *Best Of* .... (RHI)
 Dick Bartley's One Hit Wonders/'60s-#1 .... (RHI)
 Son Of Frat Rock! .... (RHI)
 ST/Mermaids .... (GEF)
Rolling Stones; *Made In The Shade* .... (RS)
In The Mood
Andrews Sisters; *16 Greatest Performances* ...... (MCA)
Bette Midler; *Bette Midler* .... (ATL)
 Live At Last .... (ATL)
Glenn Miller; *Best Of* .... (RCA)
 Legendary Performer .... (RCA)
 Pure Gold .... (RCA)
 Story .... (RCA)
Glenn Miller/Orchestra; *Unforgettable Glenn
Miller/Orchestra* .... (RCA)
It's All Right
Impressions; *Billboard Top R&B Hits-1963* ...... (RHI)
 Cruisin'-1964 .... (INC)
 Greatest Hits .... (MCA)
 ST/Flamingo Kid .... (MOT)
Kinks; *Kinkdom* .... (RHI)
It's Getting Better
Beatles; *Sgt. Pepper's Lonely Hearts Club Band* .. (CAP)
It's Gonna Be Alright
Gerry/Pacemakers; *Best Of* .... (EMI)
 History Of British Rock-#3 .... (RHI)
Ruby Turner; *Paradise* .... (JVA)
It's Gonna Work Out Fine
Ike & Tina Turner; *Proud Mary-Best Of* .... (EMI)
 River Deep-Mountain High .... (A&M)
 Super Oldies/'60s-#3 .... (AUF)
It's Wonderful
Rascals; *Greatest Hits* .... (ATL)
 Nuggets-#8-Acid Rock .... (RHI)
 Once Upon A Time .... (RHI)
I'll Be Glad When You're Dead...
Cab Calloway; *Jazz Heritage: Mr. Hi-De-Ho* ... (MCA)
I'm Alright
Kenny Loggins; *Alive* .... (COL)
 ST/Caddyshack .... (COL)
Little Anthony/Imperials; *Best Of* .... (RHI)
 Forever Yours .... (RLL)
 Tears On My Pillow .... (ACC)
Rolling Stones; *Got Live If You Want It* .... (AKO)
 Out Of Our Heads .... (AKO)
I'm Feeling Fine
Head East; *Head East* .... (A&M)
 Live .... (A&M)
I'm Glad There Is You
Jimmy Dorsey Orchestra; *Then & Now-Fabulous New J.
Dorsey Orch.* .... (ATL)
Morgana King; *Stretchin' Out* .... (MUS)
Peggy Lee; *Best Of* .... (MCA)
I'm Happy Just To Dance With You
Anne Murray; *Somebody's Waiting* .... (CAP)
Beatles; *Something New* .... (CAP)
 ST/Hard Day's Night .... (CAP)
I'm Not Gonna Let It Bother Me Tonight
Atlanta Rhythm Section; *Are You Ready?* .... (POL)
 Champagne Jam .... (POL)
I'm Satisfied
Bee Gees; *Spirits Having Glown* .... (RSO)
Mississippi John Hurt; *Satisfied* .... (INT)
 Today .... (VAN)
I'm So Excited
Pointer Sisters; *Break Out* .... (PNT)
I'm So Glad
Cream; *Fresh Cream* .... (RSO)
 Goodbye .... (RSO)
Joy
Isaac Hayes; *Enterprise-His Greatest Hits* .... (STX)
 Greatest Hits Singles .... (STX)
 Joy .... (STX)
Marvin Gaye; *Midnight Love* .... (COL)
Mitch Ryder/Detroit Wheels; *Rev Up-Best Of* ... (RHI)
Joy And Pain
Donna Allen; *Heaven On Earth* .... (OCE)
Maze featuring Frankie Beverly; *Live In Los
Angeles* .... (CAP)
 Live In New Orleans .... (CAP)

Maze/Kurtis Blow; *Lifelines-#1* ....(CAP)
Rob Base & D.J. EZ-Rock; *It Takes Two* ....(PRO)
Joy Comes In The Morning
Oak Ridge Boys; *All Our Favorite Songs* ....(COL)
Joy Inside My Tears
Stevie Wonder; *Songs In The Key Of Life* ....(MOT)
Joy To The World
Three Dog Night; *Best Of* ....(MCA)
  Good Feeling Music/Big Chill Gen.-#2 ....(MOT)
  Good Feeling Music/Big Chill Gen.-#3 ....(MOT)
  Joy To The World ....(MCA)
  ST/Big Chill ....(MOT)
  ST/Forrest Gump ....(EPX)
Jubilation
Paul Anka; *Jubilation* ....(GRL)
  My Way ....(FFT)
  Very Best Of ....(RAN)
Just To Satisfy You
Hank Williams, Jr.; *Pure Hank* ....(W/C)
Waylon Jennings & Willie Nelson; *Best Of*
  Waylon ....(RCA)
  Collector's Duets ....(RCA)
  Waylon & Co. ....(RCA)
(Keep Feeling) Fascination
Human League; *Fascination* ....(A&M)
Keep The Customer Satisfied
Simon & Garfunkel; *Bridge Over Troubled Water* (COL)
  Collected Works ....(COL)
Keepin' My Lover Satisfied
Melba Moore; *Never Say Never* ....(CAP)
Lady (You Bring Me Up)
Commodores; *All The Great Hits* ....(MOT)
  All The Great Love Songs ....(MOT)
  Compact Command Performances ....(MOT)
Let Me Sing & I'm Happy
Al Jolson; *Best Of* ....(MCA)
  Story-#3 ....(MCA)
Let's Chill
Guy; *Future* .... (UT)
Life Is Happiness Indeed
Original Cast; *Candide* ....(COL)
Life's Been Good
Eagles; *Live* ....(ASY)
Joe Walsh; *But Seriously Folks* ....(ASY)
  ST/FM ....(MCA)
Lift Me Up
Yes; *Union* ....(ARI)
Light Up
Styx; *Equinox* ....(A&M)
Little Bit Of Happiness
New Christy Minstrels; *Greatest Hits* ....(COL)
Love Can Make You Happy
Mercy; *Super Oldies/'60s-#10* ....(AUF)
  WCBS FM101-History Of Rock/'60s-#2 ....(CLT)
Love Can Take Us All The Way
Jack Wagner & Valerie Carter; *Lighting Up The*
  Night .... (QUE)
Love Is A Wonderful Thing
Michael Bolton; *Time Love & Tenderness* ....(COL)
Love Is The Seventh Wave
Sting; *Dream Of The Blue Turtles* ....(A&M)
  Greenpeace/Rainbow Warriors ....(GEF)
Love & Happiness
Al Green; *I'm Still In Love With You* ....(MOT)
  Tokyo-Live ....(MOT)
John Mellencamp; *Whenever We Wanted* ....(MER)
Living Colour; *Biscuits* ....(EPI)
Lovin' What Your Lovin' Does To Me
Conway Twitty & Loretta Lynn; *45* ....(MCA)
Make Someone Happy
Stevie Wonder; *With A Song In My Heart* ....(MOT)
Tower Of Power; *Ain't Nothin' Stoppin' Us Now* .(COL)
Makin' Happy
Crystal Waters; *Surprise* ....(MER)
Mellow
Elton John; *Honky Chateau* ....(POL)
Mellow Down Easy
Paul Butterfield Blues Band; *Golden Butter* ......(ELE)
  Greatest Folksingers Of The '60s ....(VAN)
  Paul Butterfield Blues Band ....(ELE)
Most Happy Fella
Original Broadway Cast; *Most Happy Fella* ..... (SMC)
Original Cast; *Most Happy Fella* ....(RCA)

My Happiness
Andy Williams; *Greatest Songs* ....(CCB)
Connie Francis; *Very Best Of* ....(POL)
Elvis Presley; *Great Performances* ....(RCA)
Jim Reeves; *Pure Gold* ....(RCA)
Pied Pipers; *Capitol Collectors Series* ....(CAP)
New Orleans Joys
Butch Thompson; *New Orleans Joys* .... (DAR)
New Soldiers Joy
Kentucky Colonels feat. R. & C. White;
  1965-1967 .... (ROU)
Nice Work If You Can Get It
Billie Holiday; *Compact Jazz* ....(VRV)
Carmen McRae; *Greatest Of* .... (MCA)
Ella Fitzgerald; *George & Ira Gershwin Songbook* (VRV)
Frank Sinatra; *My Kind Of Broadway* ....(RPR)
Original Cast; *My One & Only* .... (ATL)
Sting; *Glory Of Gershwin-Featuring Larry Adler* . (MER)
O What A Thrill
Mavericks; *What A Crying Shame* .... (MCA)
Oh Happy Day
Edwin Hawkins Singers; *Soul Hits/'70s-#1* .... (RHI)
  Super Hits-#3 ....(GUS)
Five Satins; *Sing Their Greatest Hits* ....(CLT)
Oh, What A Beautiful Morning
Original Broadway Cast; *Oklahoma* ....(RCA)
Original Cast; *Oklahoma* .... (MCA)
One Fine Day
Carpenters; *From The Top* ....(A&M)
  Now & Then ....(A&M)
Chiffons; *Best Of* ....(LAU)
  Collectables Presents History Of Rock-#9 ......(CLT)
  Golden Classics ....(CLT)
  Oldies But Goodies-#12 ....(OSR)
One More Goodtime Band In Texas
Leon Rausch; *Rausch Touch* ....(STH)
Optimistic
Sounds Of Blackness; *Evolution Of Gospel* ....(PSP)
Our House
Crosby, Stills & Nash; *Crosby, Stills & Nash*
  (collection) .... (ATL)
Crosby, Stills, Nash & Young; *Deja Vu* ....(ATL)
  So Far .... (ATL)
  ST/Strawberry Statement ....(MCA)
Madness; *Madness* ....(GEF)
Outrageous
Lakeside; *Outrageous* ....(SLR)
Overjoyed
Stevie Wonder; *In Circle Square* .... (MOT)
Passionate Kisses
Mary Chapin Carpenter; *Come On Come On* ....(COL)
Pensacola Joy
Kellis Ethridge; *Tomorrow Sky* .... (IC)
Please Please Me
Beatles; *1962-1966* ....(CAP)
  Box Set ....(CAP)
  Early ....(CAP)
  Please Please Me ....(CAP)
Pleasure Seekers
System; *System* ....(MIR)
Positive Vibration
Bob Marley/Wailers; *Babylon By Bus* ....(TUF)
  Rastaman Vibration ....(TUF)
Pride & Joy
Coverdale/Page; *Coverdale/Page* ....(GEF)
Lil' Ed/Blues Imperials; *Genuine Houserockin' Music*
  II ....(ALG)
  Roughhousin' ....(ALG)
Marvin Gaye; *Anthology* .... (MOT)
  Greatest Hits ....(MOT)
  Live At The London Palladium ....(MOT)
  Super Hits ....(MOT)
  That Stubborn Kinda Fellow ....(MOT)
Put On A Happy Face
Dick Van Dyke; *Broadway Magic-1960s* ....(COL)
  ST/Bye Bye Birdie ....(RCA)
Dick Van Dyke/Original Cast; *Bye Bye Birdie* ...(COL)
Stevie Wonder; *WIth A Song In My Heart* ....(MOT)
Tony Bennett; *All-Time Greatest Hits* ....(COL)
  Forty Years-Artistry Of ....(COL)

Revival
Allman Brothers Band; *An Evening With-First Set* (POL)
  Beginnings .... (POL)
  Decade Of Hits-1969-1979 .... (POL)
  Dreams .... (POL)
  Idlewild South .... (POL)
Rise
Herb Alpert; *Classics-#20* .... (A&M)
  Rise .... (A&M)
Satisfaction Guaranteed
Firm; *Firm* .... (ATL)
Michael Franks; *Tiger In The Rain* .... (WB)
Rare Earth; *Ecology* .... (MOT)
Satisfaction (I Can't Get No)
Devo; *Best Of-Greatest Hits* .... (WB)
  Q: Are We Not Men? A: We Are Devo! .... (WB)
Otis Redding; *Best Of* .... (ATL)
  History Of .... (ATC)
  Story .... (ATL)
Rolling Stones; *Big Hits (High Tide & Green*
  Grass) .... (AKO)
  Flashpoint .... (RS)
  Got Live If You Want It .... (AKO)
  Hot Rocks-1964-1971 .... (AKO)
  Out Of Our Heads .... (AKO)
  Singles Collection-London Years .... (AKO)
Satisfied
Joe Cocker; *Unchain My Heart* .... (CAP)
Martha Carson; *Stars Of The Grand Ole*
  Opry-1926-1974 .... (RCA)
Richard Marx; *Repeat Offender* .... (CAP)
Squeeze; *Play* .... (RPR)
Ted Nugent; *State Of Shock* .... (EPI)
Van Morrison; *Common One* .... (WB)
Satisfied Man
Molly Hatchet; *Deed Is Done* .... (EPI)
  Double Trouble Live .... (EPI)
Satisfied Mind
Bob Dylan; *Saved* .... (COL)
Buckinghams; *Law & Order* .... (WB)
Byrds; *Turn! Turn! Turn!* .... (COL)
David Allan Coe; *Texas Moon* .... (PLN)
Ozark Mountain Daredevils; *It's Alive* .... (A&M)
  Ozark Mountain Daredevils .... (A&M)
Porter Wagoner; *Greatest* .... (TUD)
Satisfy My Soul
Bob Marley/Wailers; *Kaya* .... (TUF)
  Legend .... (TUF)
Winston Jarrett; *Heartbeat Reggae Roundup* ..... (HRT)
  Solid Foundation .... (HRT)
Satisfy Suzie
Lonnie Mack; *Attack Of The Killer V* .... (ALG)
  Strike Like Lightning .... (ALG)
Sea Of Joy
Blind Faith; *Blind Faith* .... (POL)
Eric Clapton; *History Of* .... (ATC)
Set Adrift On Memory Bliss
P.M. Dawn; *MTV Party To Go-#2* .... (TMB)
  Red Hot + Dance .... (COL)
Sha-La-La (Make Me Happy)
Al Green; *Explores Your Mind* .... (MOT)
  Greatest Hits-#2 .... (MOT)
  Tokyo...Live .... (MOT)
She Makes The Coming Home (Worth The....)
Shenandoah; *Extra Mile* .... (COL)
She's Only Happy When She's Dancin'
Bryan Adams; *Reckless* .... (A&M)
(She's) Some Kind Of Wonderful
Drifters; *16 Greatest Hits* .... (TRP)
  Golden Hits .... (ATL)
  ST/More Dirty Dancing .... (RCA)
  Very Best Of The .... (RHI)
Huey Lewis/News; *Four Chords & Several Years*
  Ago .... (ELE)
Jay/Americans; *Sands Of Time/Wax Museum* ... (EMI)
Marvin Gaye; *I Heard It Through The Grapevine* (MOT)
Shiny Happy People
R.E.M.; *Out Of Time* .... (WB)
Sing A Happy Song
O'Jays; *Identify Yourself* .... (PI)
Taj Mahal; *Evolution* .... (WB)

Singin' In The Rain
Gene Kelly; *ST/Clockwork Orange* .... (WB)
  ST/Singin' In The Rain .... (SSP)
  ST/Those Glorious MGM Musicals .... (MGM)
Soldier's Joy
Jimmy Driftwood; *Best Of* .... (MOT)
Marty Stuart; *Busy Bee Cafe* .... (SH)
Nitty Gritty Dirt Band; *Dirt Silver & Gold* .... (UA)
  Will The Circle Be Unbroken .... (EMI)
Tony Trischka; *Heartlands* .... (ROU)
Somebody's Doin' Me Right
Keith Whitley; *Kentucky Bluebird* .... (RCA)
Someday When Things Are Good
Merle Haggard; *His Epic Hits-First 11 To Be*
  Continued .... (EPI)
  That's The Way Love Goes .... (EPI)
Standing On The Top
Temptations featuring Rick James; *45* .... (MOT)
Still Alive & Well
Edgar Winter; *Roadwork* .... (EPI)
Johnny Winter; *Still Alive & Well* .... (COL)
Stuck In A Closet With Vanna White
Weird Al Yankovic; *Even Worse* .... (RAR)
Summer Of '69
Bryan Adams; *Reckless* .... (A&M)
Sunny Side To Every Situation
Original Cast; *42nd Street* .... (RCA)
Sunshine On My Shoulders
John Denver; *Greatest Hits-#1* .... (RCA)
  Take Me Home Country Roads & Other Hits ....(RCA)
Sweet Mama Goodtimes
Mickey Gilley; *Greatest Hits-#2* .... (EPI)
Take It Easy
Crystal Gayle; *Greatest Hits* .... (COL)
  These Days .... (LIB)
Duke Ellington; *Brunswick Era-#1-1926-1929* .. (MCA)
Eagles; *Anthology* .... (ASY)
  Eagles .... (ASY)
  Hell Freezes Over .... (GEF)
  Live .... (ASY)
  Their Greatest Hits .... (ASY)
Jackson Browne; *For Everyman* .... (ASY)
Lacy J. Dalton; *Greatest Hits* .... (CAP)
  Take It Easy .... (COL)
Travis Tritt; *Common Thread-Songs Of The*
  Eagles .... (GIA)
That Don't Satisfy Me
Brother Cane; *Brother Cane* .... (VIA)
That's Where The Happy People Go
Trammps; *Disco Hits-#1* .... (RHI)
  That's Where The Happy People Go .... (OOP)
They Say It's Wonderful
Frank Sinatra; *The Voice-Columbia*
  Years-1943-1952 .... (COL)
Johnny Mathis; *Heavenly* .... (COL)
Original Cast; *Annie Get Your Gun* .... (RCA)
Sarah Vaughan; *Irving Berlin Always* .... (VRV)
Things Can Only Get Better
Howard Jones; *Dream Into Action* .... (ELE)
Things Get Better
Delaney & Bonnie; *On Tour* .... (RHI)
Delaney & Bonnie & Friends; *On Tour* .... (ATC)
Three Hundred Pounds Of Heavenly Joy
Big Twist/Mellow Fellows; *Alligator Records 20th*
  Anniversary Coll. .... (ALG)
Howlin' Wolf; *Chess Box-Willie Dixon* .... (CSS)
Time Of My Life (I've Had The)
Bill Medley; *Best Of* .... (CCB)
Bill Medley & Jennifer Warnes; *Dirty Dancing Live In*
  Concert .... (RCA)
  ST/Dirty Dancing .... (RCA)
Too Good To Stop Now
Mickey Gilley; *Too Good To Stop Now* .... (EPI)
Tree Of Joy
Jeannie C. Riley; *Country Gold* .... (PLN)
T.M. Song
Beach Boys; *15 Big Ones* .... (RPR)
U Send Me
Mint Condition; *From The Mint Factory* .... (PSP)
Up On The Roof
Cover Girls; *We Can't Go Wrong* .... (CAP)
Cryan' Shames; *Scratch In The Sky* .... (COL)

Drifters; *16 Greatest Hits* .... (TRP)
  Cruisin'-1962 .... (INC)
  Golden Hits .... (ATL)
  Greatest Hits .... (GUS)
James Taylor; *Flag* ....(COL)
Nylons; *Four On The Floor* .... (SCO)
Uptight (Everything's Alright)
Stevie Wonder; *16 #1 Hits From The Early '60s* (MOT)
  Greatest Hits .... (MOT)
  Looking Back .... (MOT)
  Motown Dance Party-#1 .... (MOT)
  Motown Legends .... (MOT)
  Uptight (Everything's Alright) .... (MOT)
Way He Makes Me Feel
Barbra Streisand; *Collection-Greatest Hits & More* (COL)
  ST/Yentl ....(COL)
Way You Make Me Feel
Michael Jackson; *Bad* .... (EPI)
We Got A Groovy Thing Goin'
Simon & Garfunkel; *Sounds Of Silence* ....(COL)
What A Wonderful World
Louis Armstrong; *ST/Good Morning Vietnam* ... (A&M)
  Vocalists-Jazz Masters .... (BLU)
  What A Wonderful World .... (MCA)
Mormon Tabernacle Choir; *Songs From America's
Heartland* ....(LON)
Willie Nelson; *What A Wonderful World* ....(COL)
(What A) Wonderful World
Art Garfunkel; *Watermark* ....(COL)
Sam Cooke; *Best Of* ....(RCA)
  ST/Animal House .... (MCA)
  This Is ....(RCA)
When I'm Back On My Feet Again
Michael Bolton; *Soul Provider* ....(COL)
When The Feeling's Right
Con Funk Shun; *Loveshine* .... (OOP)
Wonderful Tonight
Eric Clapton; *24 Nights* .... (RPR)
  Crossroads .... (POL)
  Just One Night .... (POL)
  Slowhand .... (POL)
  Time Pieces-Best Of .... (POL)
Wonderful! Wonderful!
Johnny Mathis; *16 Most Requested Songs* ....(COL)
  All-Time Greatest Hits ....(COL)
  First 25 Years-Silver Anniversary Album ....(COL)
  Greatest Hits ....(COL)
Supremes; *I Hear A Symphony* .... (MOT)
Times; *Best Of* .... (AKO)
  Rock-O-Rama-#1 .... (AKO)
Wouldn't It Be Loverly
Original Cast; *My Fair Lady* ....(LON)
Wouldn't It Be Nice
Beach Boys; *Absolutely Best-#2* ....(CAP)
  Made In The U.S.A. ....(CAP)
  Pet Sounds ....(CAP)
  Still Cruisin' ....(CAP)
You Are The Sunshine Of My Life
Peter Nero; *Greatest Hits* ....(COL)
Stevie Wonder; *20/20* .... (MOT)
  Original Musiquarium .... (MOT)
  Talking Book .... (MOT)
You Can't Always Get What You Want
Rolling Stones; *Flashpoint* .... (RS)
  Hot Rocks-1964-1971 .... (AKO)
  Let It Bleed .... (AKO)
  Love You Live .... (RS)
  Singles Collection-London Years .... (AKO)
You Give Good Love
Whitney Houston; *Whitney Houston* .... (ARI)
You Light Up My Life
Debby Boone; *Best Of* .... (CCB)
  This Is Love-The Wedding Songs .... (SCO)
  You Light Up My Life .... (MCA)
You Send Me
Aretha Franklin; *Aretha's Gold* .... (ATL)
Manhattans; *Too Hot To Stop It* ....(COL)
Michael Bolton; *Timeless-Classics* ....(COL)
Sam Cooke; *Best Of* ....(RCA)
  Man & His Music ....(RCA)
  ST/American Pop .... (MCA)

Your Song
Elton John; *Elton John* ....(POL)
  Greatest Hits ....(POL)
  Live In Australia w/Melbourne Symphony ...... (MCA)
Rod Stewart; *Two Rooms-Songs Of E. John & B.
Taupin* ....(POL)
You're The Inspiration
Chicago; *Greatest Hits-1982-1989* .... (FM)
  #17 ....(WB)
You've Got A Good Love Comin'
Lee Greenwood; *Inside Out/You've Got A Good Love
Comin'* .... (MCA)
You've Made Me So Very Happy
Blood, Sweat & Tears; *Blood, Sweat & Tears* ....(COL)
  Greatest Hits ....(COL)
  Live & Improvised ....(COL)
  Pop Classics Of The '60s ....(COL)
Zip A Dee Doo Dah
Barbara Cook; *Disney Album* .... (DIS)
Bing Crosby; *Radio Years* .... (CRS)
Jackson 5; *Motown Legends* .... (MOT)
Johnny Mercer; *Capitol Collector Series* .... (CAP)
Kelly Stevens/Carnival; *When You Wish Upon A
Star* .... (AVI)
Mormon Tabernacle Choir/Columbia Symph.; *When
You Wish Upon A Star-Disney Tribute* ....(COL)
Ric Ocasek; *Simply Mad About The Mouse* ......(COL)
Steve Miller; *Born 2 B Blue* .... (CAP)

HATS, Berets, Veils
  See Also: CLOTHES

All Around My Hat
Steeleye Span; *All Around My Hat* .... (CHR)
  Story .... (CHR)
Any Place I Hang My Hat Is Home
Barbra Streisand; *Second Album* ....(COL)
Rosemary Clooney; *Sings The Lyrics Of Johnny
Mercer* .... (CCJ)
Ballad Of The Green Berets
Barry Sadler; *Cruisin'-1966* .... (INC)
  Hits Of The '60s .... (IMC)
  More American Graffiti-#4 .... (MCA)
  Nipper's Greatest Hits-'60s-#2 ....(RCA)
  Super Hits-#3 .... (GUS)
Cowboy Hat In Dallas
Charlie Daniels Band; *Homesick Heroes* .... (EPI)
Hats Off To Larry
Del Shannon; *Runaway Hits!* .... (RHI)
  Super Oldies/'60s-#2 .... (AUF)
  WCBS FM101-History Of Rock/'60s-#3 ...... (CLT)
Long Black Veil
Band; *Music From Big Pink* ....(CAP)
  To Kingdom Come-Definitive Collection ....(CAP)
Joan Baez; *Contemporary Ballad Book* .... (VAN)
  In Concert .... (VAN)
  One Day At A Time .... (VAN)
Johnny Cash; *At Folsom Prison & San Quentin* ...(COL)
  Classic Cash-Hall Of Fame Series .... (MER)
Lefty Frizzell; *American Originals* ....(COL)
  Columbia Country Classics-#3-Americana ......(COL)
Mexican Hat Dance
Percy Faith; *All-Time Greatest Hits* ....(COL)
New Grey Bonnet
Johnny Gimble; *Still Fiddlin' Around* .... (MSP)
Raspberry Beret
Prince/Revolution; *Around The World In A Day* .. (WB)
Top Hat, White Tie & Tails
Fred Astaire; *Irving Berlin Songbook* ....(VRV)
Louis Armstrong; *Irving Berlin Songbook* ....(VRV)
You Can Leave Your Hat On
Joe Cocker; *Cocker* ....(CAP)
  Live ....(CAP)
  ST/9 1/2 Weeks ....(CAP)
Randy Newman; *Sail Away* .... (RPR)
You Gotta Have A Hat
Ray Stevens; *#1 With A Bullet* ....(CCB)

HEAR, Listen, Silence
See Also: Various COMMUNICATION categories

Almost Hear You Sigh
Rolling Stones; *Steel Wheels* ....(RS)
Angels Listened In
Crests; *Greatest Hits* ....(CLT)
Super Oldies Of The '50s-#3 ....(AUF)
WCBS FM 101-History Of Rock-'50s-#2 ....(CLT)
Anybody Listening?
Queensryche; *Empire* ....(EMI)
Beautiful Noise
Neil Diamond; *12 Greatest Hits-#2* ....(COL)
Beautiful Noise ....(COL)
Love At The Greek ....(COL)
Big Noise From Winnetka
Bette Midler; *Divine Madness* ....(ATL)
Thighs & Whispers ....(ATL)
Bob Crosby Orchestra; *Play 22 Original Big Band Hits* ....(HIN)
Bob Crosby/Bob Cats; *Best Of* ....(MCA)
Can You Hear Me?
David Bowie; *Young Americans* ....(RYK)
Can You Hear The Music?
Rolling Stones; *Goats Head Soup* .... (RS)
Can't You Hear Me Callin'?
Ricky Skaggs; *Favorite Country Songs* .... (EPI)
Highway & Heartaches ....(EPI)
Can't You Hear Me Knockin'
Rolling Stones; *Sticky Fingers* ....(RS)
Can't You Hear My Heart Beat?
Herman's Hermits; *XX* ....(AKO)
Cheerful Little Earful
Ella Fitzgerald; *Swings Brightly With Nelson* .....(VRV)
Cryin' To Be Heard
Traffic; *Traffic* .... (ISL)
Cum On Feel The Noise
Quiet Riot; *Metal Health* .... (PSH)
Do I Hear A Waltz?
Elizabeth Allen; *Broadway Magic-1960s* ....(COL)
Original Broadway Cast; *Do I Hear A Waltz?* ... (SMC)
Do Nothin' Till You Hear From Me
Billie Holiday; *Compact Jazz* ....(VRV)
Stay With Me ....(VRV)
Cal Tjader & Carmen McRae; *Heat Wave* ....(CCJ)
Duke Ellington; *I Like Jazz-Essence Of Duke Ellington* ....(COL)
Duke Ellington/Orchestra; *ST/Fabulous Baker Boys* ....(GRP)
Johnny Mathis; *In A Sentimental Mood-Sings Ellington* ....(COL)
Mose Allison; *Greatest Hits* ....(PRS)
Do You Hear Wedding Bells
Jive Five; *Their Greatest Hits* ....(CLT)
Don't You Hear Jerusalem Moan
Nitty Gritty Dirt Band; *Will The Circle Be Unbroken-#2* ....(UNI)
Enjoy The Silence
Depeche Mode; *Violator* .... (SIR)
Even In The Quietest Moments
Supertramp; *Even In The Quietest Moments* ....(A&M)
Everybody's Talkin'
Nilsson; *ST/Forrest Gump* .... (EPX)
ST/Midnight Cowboy ....(EMI)
TT & Other Hits ....(RCA)
Willie Nelson; *Best Of Willie* ....(RCA)
Sweet Memories ....(RCA)
For What It's Worth
Buffalo Springfield; *Buffalo Springfield* ....(ATC)
Double History ....(ATC)
Hit Singles 1958-1977 ....(ATL)
Retrospective ....(ATC)
ST/Forrest Gump ....(EPX)
Have You Heard
Duprees; *Best Of* ....(CLT)
Best Of ....(RHI)
WCBS FM101 History Of Rock/'60s-#3 ....(CLT)
Moody Blues; *Caught Live Plus Five* ....(POL)
On The Threshold Of A Dream ....(POL)
This Is The ....(POL)
Have You Heard The News
Ben Sidran; *Puttin' In Time On Planet Earth* .... (MCA)

Vikki Carr; *Live At the Greek Theatre* ....(COL)
Haven't You Heard
George Strait; *Something Special* .... (MCA)
Patrice Rushen; *Anthology* .... (ELE)
Pizzazz .... (ELE)
Hear Me Lord
George Harrison; *All Things Must Pass* ....(CAP)
Hear My Train A'Comin'
Jimi Hendrix; *Band Of Gypsys 2* ....(CAP)
Concerts ....(RPR)
Radio One ....(RYK)
Hear Say
Soul Children; *15 Original Big Hits-#3* .... (STX)
Chronicle .... (STX)
Hear The Wind Howl
Leo Kottke; *Mudlark* ....(CAP)
My Feet Are Smiling ....(CAP)
Home On The Range
Bing Crosby; *Crooner-Columbia Years-1928-1934* ....(COL)
Boston Pops Orchestra; *Yankee Doodle Dandy* ...(RCA)
Gene Autry; *50th Anniversary* .... (REP)
Country Music Hall Of Fame ....(COL)
Neil Young; *ST/Where The Buffalo Roam* .... (BKS)
Hush
Deep Purple; *Nobody's Perfect* .... (MER)
Purple Passages .... (WB)
Super Oldies/'60s-#10 ....(AUF)
When We Rock We Rock .... (WB)
Hushabye
Mystics; *16 Golden Classics* ....(CLT)
Doo-Wop Uptempo-#2 .... (RHI)
Million Dollar Memories #1 ....(RCA)
I Can Hear Kentucky Calling Me
Chet Atkins; *Collector's* ....(RCA)
I Can Hear Music
Beach Boys; *Friends/20/20* ....(CAP)
Sunshine Dream ....(CAP)
I Can Hear The Grass Grow
Blues Magoos; *Nuggets-#11-Pop-#4* .... (RHI)
Move; *Best Of* ....(A&M)
I Hear A Rhapsody
John Coltrane; *Lush Life* .... (PRS)
More Lasting Than Bronze .... (PRS)
Prestige Twofer Giants-#2 .... (PRS)
I Hear A Symphony
Diana Ross/Supremes; *16 #1 Hits From The Early '60s* ....(MOT)
25th Anniversary ....(MOT)
Anthology ....(MOT)
Evening With Diana Ross ....(MOT)
Every Great #1 Hit ....(MOT)
Good Feeling Music/Big Chill Gen.-#2 ....(MOT)
Greatest Hits ....(MOT)
I Hear A Symphony ....(MOT)
Motown Story ....(MOT)
I Hear Music
Anita O'Day; *Big Band Session* ....(VRV)
Live At Mingos ....(EML)
I Hear The Music
Billie Holiday; *Golden Year-#2* ....(COL)
Story-#3 ....(COL)
I Hear Those Bells
Kings; *45* ....(CLT)
I Hear You Knockin'
Smiley Lewis; *Billboard Top R&B Hits-1955* ..... (RHI)
Non-Stop Party Rock ....(EMI)
I Hear You Now
Jon & Vangelis; *Best Of* .... (POL)
Short Stories ....(POL)
I Heard It Through The Grapevine
Creedence Clearwater Revival; *Chooglin'* ....(FAN)
Chronicle ....(FAN)
Cosmo's Factory ....(FAN)
Gold ....(FAN)
Movie Album ....(FAN)
Gladys Knight/Pips; *16 #1 Hits From The Late '60s* ....(MOT)
Command Compact Performances ....(MOT)
Every Great Motown Song-First 25 Years ......(MOT)
Motown Grammy R & B Performances ....(MOT)
Motown Superstars Series-#13 ....(MOT)
Top 10 With A Bullet-Motown Girl Groups ....(MOT)

Marvin Gaye; *25 #1 Hits From 25 Years* .... (MOT)
  Anthology .... (MOT)
  Every Great Motown Hit Of Marvin Gaye ..... (MOT)
  Live At London Palladium .... (MOT)
  Most Played Oldies On America's Jukebox ..... (MOT)
  Motown Story .... (MOT)
  Motown Story-First 25 Years .... (MOT)
I Heard The Jukebox Playing
  Faron Young; *Hi Tone Poppa* .... (CLT)
  Kitty Wells; *Story* .... (MCA)
(I Love The Sound Of) Breaking Glass
  Nick Lowe; *Pure Pop For Now People* ....(COL)
I Wanna Hear It From You
  Eddy Raven; *45* ....(RCA)
I Wanna Hear It From Your Lips
  Eric Carmen; *Eric Carmen* .... (GEF)
  Louise Mandrell; *Dreamin'* ....(RCA)
In A Silent Way
  Joe Zawinul; *Joe Zawinul* .... (ATL)
  Miles Davis; *In A Silent Way* ....(COL)
In My Own Quiet Way
  Pablo Cruise; *Pablo Cruise* .... (A&M)
In The Still Of The Night
  Dion; *Greatest Hits* ....(LAU)
  Sings The 15 Million Sellers ....(LAU)
  Dion/Belmonts; *Wish Upon A Star With* ....(CLT)
  Five Satins; *Billboard Top R&B Hits-1956* ... (RHI)
  Cruisin'-1956 ....(INC)
  In The Still Of The Night ....(CAP)
  Sing Their Greatest Hits ....(CLT)
  ST/Dirty Dancing ....(RCA)
  Johnny Mathis; *In The Still Of The Night* ......(COL)
I've Been Workin' On The Railroad
  Mitch Miller; *Sing Along With Mitch* ....(COL)
  Pete Seeger; *20 Golden Pieces Of* .... (BLD)
John Doe No. 24
  Mary Chapin Carpenter; *Stones In The Road* ...(COL)
Lisa, Listen To Me
  Blood, Sweat & Tears; *Greatest Hits* ....(COL)
Listen Here
  Brian Auger; *Best Of* ....(OOP)
Listen Like Thieves
  INXS; *Listen Like Thieves* .... (ATL)
Listen Listen
  Fairport Convention; *Chronicles* .... (A&M)
Listen People
  Herman's Hermits; *XX-Greatest Hits* .... (AKO)
Listen To A Country Song
  Loggins & Messina; *On Stage* ....(COL)
  Sittin' In ....(COL)
  Lynn Anderson; *Country Chartbusters-#2* ....(COL)
  Greatest Hits ....(COL)
Listen To Her Heart
  Tom Petty/Heartbreakers; *You're Gonna Get It* . (MCA)
Listen To Me
  Buddy Holly; *20 Golden Greats* ....(MCA)
  Buddy Holly ....(MCA)
  Rock & Roll Collection ....(MCA)
Listen To The Band
  Monkees; *Greatest Hits* .... (ARI)
  Present ....(RHI)
Listen To The Heartbeat
  Billy Squier; *Emotions In Motion* ....(CAP)
Listen To The Lion
  Van Morrison; *It's Too Late To Stop Now* ....(WB)
  St. Dominic's Preview ....(WB)
Listen To The Mocking Bird
  Lester Flatt; *Lester Raymond Flatt* ....(FF)
Listen To The Music
  Doobie Brothers; *Best Of* ....(WB)
  Farewell Tour ....(WB)
  Toulouse Street ....(WB)
Listen To The Radio
  Don Williams; *Best Of-#3* ....(MCA)
  Listen To The Radio ....(MCA)
  Kathy Mattea; *Lonesome Standard Time* ....(MER)
  Nanci Griffith; *Storms* ....(MCA)
Listen To What The Man Said
  Paul McCartney/Wings; *Over America* ....(CAP)
  Wings; *Venus & Mars* ....(CAP)
Listening To You
  Who; *Tommy* ....(MCA)

(Listen) Do You Want To Know A Secret?
  Beatles;
  Early 62-66 ....(CAP)
  Introducing ....(VJ)
Listen, The Snow Is Falling
  Yoko Ono Band; *45* ....(CAP)
Lonesome Whistle (I Heard That)
  Hank Williams; *24 Greatest Hits-#2* ....(POL)
  40 Greatest Hits ....(POL)
  Johnny Cash; *Story Songs Of The Trains & Rivers* (SUN)
  Little Feat; *Hoy-Hoy!* ....(WB)
My Silent Love
  Bing Crosby; *Where The Blue Of The Night Meets*
  The... ....(BIO)
One Day In March I Go Down To The Sea...
  Jan Garbarek Group; *It's OK To Listen To The Gray*
  Voice ....(ECM)
Quiet
  Smashing Pumpkins; *Siamese Dream* .... (VIA)
Quiet Afternoon
  Paul Rebhan; *Colors* ....(CRM)
  Stanley Clarke; *Live 1976-1977* ....(EPI)
  School Days ....(EPI)
Quiet Friday
  Stan Kenton Orchestra; *Fire Fury & Fun* ......(CW)
Quiet Nights Of Quiet Stars
  Antonio Carlos Jobim; *Terra Brasilis* ....(WB)
  Shirley Horn; *I Thought About You-Live At Vine*
  St. ....(VRV)
Radio Silence
  Boris Grebenshikov; *Radio Silence* ....(COL)
  Thomas Dolby; *Golden Age Of Wireless* ....(CAP)
Rhythm Of The Rain
  Cascades; *Collectables Presents History Of*
  Rock-#7 ....(CLT)
  Golden Years-1963 ....(DOM)
Right To Remain Silent
  Doug Stone; *I Thought It Was You* .... (EPI)
Rumor Has It
  Reba McEntire; *Greatest Hits-#2* .... (MCA)
  Rumor Has It ....(MCA)
Shhh
  Tevin Campbell; *I'm Ready* .... (QUE)
Shine Silently
  Nils Lofgren; *Classics-#13* ....(A&M)
  Nils ....(A&M)
  The Best ....(A&M)
Shit You Hear At Parties
  Minutemen; *Ballot Result* ....(SST)
Silence Is Broken
  Damn Yankees; *Don't Tread* ....(WB)
Silence Is Golden
  Frankie Valli/Four Seasons; *25th Anniversary*
  Collection ....(RHI)
  Anthology ....(RHI)
  Tremeloes; *Best Of* ....(RHI)
  History Of British Rock-#7 ....(RHI)
  Rock Artifacts-#4-From The Vaults ....(COL)
Silence Of A Candle
  Oregon; *Essential* ....(VAN)
  Paul Winter Consort; *Icarus* ....(EPI)
Silent Eyes
  Paul Simon; *Still Crazy After All These Years* .....(COL)
Silent Fury
  Gary Wright; *Light Of Smiles* ....(WB)
Silent Lucidity
  Queensryche; *Empire* ....(EMI)
Silent Movies
  Neil Sedaka; *Singer- Songwriter-Melody Maker* .. (ACC)
  Solitaire ....(FFT)
  Superbird ....(INT)
Silent Partners
  David Frizzell & Shelly West; *Golden Duets* .....(VVA)
  In Session ....(VVA)
  Laura Branigan; *Self Control* ....(ATL)
  Waylon Jennings; *Too Dumb For New York Too Ugly*
  For L.A. ....(EPI)
Silent Running
  Klaus Schulze; *Trancefer* ....(GRM)
  Mike/Mechanics; *Mike/Mechanics* ....(ATL)
Silent Treatment
  Earl Thomas Conley; *Fire & Smoke* ....(RCA)
  Greatest Hits ....(RCA)

Sleep's Dark & Silent Gate
Bonnie Raitt; *The Glow* .... (WB)
Jackson Browne; *Pretender* .... (ASY)
Sound Of Goodbye
Crystal Gayle; *Best Of* .... (WB)
Cage The Songbird .... (WB)
Sound Of Music
Mormon Tabernacle Choir; *Greatest Hits-22 Best-Loved*
Favorites .... (SMC)
Original Cast; *Sound Of Music* .... (COL)
Sound Of Your Voice
38 Special; *Bone Against Steel* .... (CHS)
Sound & Vision
David Bowie; *Changestwobowie* .... (RCA)
Low .... (RYK)
Sound + Vision .... (RYK)
The Singles-1969-1993 .... (RYK)
Sounds Like Love
Johnny Lee; *Greatest Hits* .... (FM)
Sounds Of Silence
Paul Simon; *Live Rhymin'* .... (COL)
Simon & Garfunkel; *Collected Works* .... (COL)
Concert In Central Park .... (WB)
Greatest Hits .... (COL)
More American Graffiti-#4 .... (MCA)
Sounds Of Silence .... (COL)
ST/The Graduate .... (COL)
Stillness Of The Night
R.E.O. Speedwagon; *Good Trouble* .... (EPI)
Stop, Look & Listen
Chiffons; *Best Of* .... (LAU)
Donna Summer; *She Works Hard For The Money* (MER)
Summer Collection .... (MER)
Dorsey Brothers; *1934-35 Decca Sessions* .... (MCA)
Complete Tommy Dorsey-#4 .... (RCA)
Elvis Presley; *Collector's Gold* .... (RCA)
Patsy Cline; *Loved & Lost Again* .... (FFT)
Rockin' Side-Her First Recordings-#3 .... (RHI)
Stop, Look & Listen .... (ALL)
Try Again .... (QKS)
That's The Way I've Always Heard It...
Carly Simon; *Best Of* .... (ELE)
Carly Simon .... (ELE)
There's A Kind Of Hush (All Over...)
Carpenters; *A Kind Of Hush* .... (A&M)
Classics-#2 .... (A&M)
Yesterday Once More .... (A&M)
Herman's Hermits; *XX-Their Greatest Hits* ...... (AKO)
Till There Was You
Beatles; *Box Set* .... (CAP)
Meet The Beatles .... (CAP)
With The Beatles .... (CAP)
Original Cast; *ST/Music Man* .... (CAP)
Tommy Can You Hear Me
Who; *Join Together* .... (MCA)
ST/Kids Are Alright .... (MCA)
ST/Tommy .... (POL)
Tommy .... (MCA)
Unheard Music
X; *Live At The Whisky A Go-Go* .... (ELE)
Los Angeles .... (SLS)
Whisper My Name
Randy Travis; *This Is Me* .... (WB)
White Noise
Jay Ferguson; *White Noise* .... (CAP)
Yesterday, I Heard The Rain
Bill Evans; *Tokyo Concert* .... (FAN)
Tony Bennett; *Essence Of* .... (COL)
You Could've Heard A Heart Break
Johnny Lee; *Workin' For A Livin'* .... (FW)
You Haven't Heard The Last Of Me
Moe Bandy; *You Haven't Heard The Last Of Me* (MCA)
Peter Allen; *Not The Boy Next Door* .... (ARI)
You Should Hear How She Talks About You
Melissa Manchester; *Greatest Hits* .... (ARI)
Hey Ricky .... (ARI)

HEART, Valentines

Achy Breaky Heart
Billy Ray Cyrus; *Some Gave All* .... (MER)

Affair Of The Heart
Rick Springfield; *Greatest Hits* .... (RCA)
Living In Oz .... (RCA)
Affairs Of The Heart
Fleetwood Mac; *25 Years-The Chain* .... (WB)
After All (Love Theme From Chances Are)
Cher; *Heart Of Stone* .... (GEF)
Always In My Heart
Bob Seger/Silver Bullet Band; *The Fire Inside* .... (CAP)
Tevin Campbell; *I'm Ready* .... (QUE)
American Heartbeat
Survivor; *Eye Of The Tiger* .... (SCO)
American Hearts
Air Supply; *Lost In Love* .... (ARI)
Anyone Who Had A Heart
Dionne Warwick; *Anthology 1962-1971* .... (RHI)
Greatest Hits .... (EVR)
Sultry Soul Sisters (Wonder Women-#3) .... (RHI)
April In My Heart
Billie Holiday; *Quintessential-#6-1938* .... (COL)
Arrow Thru Your Heart
Lou Gramm; *Ready or Not* .... (ATL)
Ashtray Heart
Captain Beefheart; *Doc At The Radar Station* ...... (BP)
Baby Don't Break Your Baby's Heart
Kashif; *Send Me Your Love* .... (ARI)
Baby Don't You Do It (Break My Heart)
Marvin Gaye; *Anthology* .... (MOT)
Musical Testament 1964-1984 .... (MOT)
Super Hits .... (MOT)
Bad Liver & A Broken Heart
Tom Waits; *Small Change* .... (ASY)
Bad Of The Heart
George LaMond; *S* .... (COL)
Be Careful, It's My Heart
Bing Crosby & Fred Astaire; *ST/Holiday Inn* ... (MCA)
Four Freshmen; *Puttin' On The Ritz-Irving Berlin* . (CAP)
Kate Smith; *16 Most Requested Songs* ....(COL)
Rosemary Clooney; *Sings The Music Of Irving*
Berlin .... (CCJ)
Tommy Dorsey & Frank Sinatra; *All-Time Greatest*
Hits-#1 .... (BLU)
Be Still My Beating Heart
Sting; *Nothing Like The Sun* .... (A&M)
Beat Of A Heart
Scandal featuring Patty Smyth; *Warrior* .... (COL)
Bet Your Heart On Me
Johnny Lee; *Greatest Hits* .... (FA)
Better Your Heart Than Mine
Trisha Yearwood; *The Song Remembers When* .. (MCA)
Black Hearted Woman
Allman Brothers Band; *Allman Brothers Band* ... (POL)
Beginnings .... (POL)
Road Goes On Forever .... (POL)
Blame It On Your Heart
Patty Loveless; *Only What I Feel* .... (EPI)
Blue Moon With Heartache
Rosanne Cash; *19 Hot Country Requests-#2* ...... (EPI)
Hits 1979-1989 .... (COL)
Seven Year Ache .... (COL)
Blue Valentine
Tom Waits; *Blue Valentine* .... (ASY)
Brand New Heartache
Everly Brothers; *Cadence Classics-Their Greatest*
Hits .... (RHI)
Everly Brothers .... (RHI)
Break My Heart
David Ruffin; *So Soon We Changed* .... (WB)
Shakespear's Sister; *Sacred Heart* .... (FFR)
Squeeze; *Cosi Fan Tutti Frutti* .... (A&M)
Broken Hearted Savior
Big Head Todd/Monsters; *Sister Sweetly* .... (GIA)
Broken Heartland
Don Williams; *One Good Well* .... (RCA)
Holly Dunn; *Heart Full Of Love* .... (WB)
Brokenhearted Me
Anne Murray; *15 Of The Best* .... (LIB)
Greatest Hits .... (LIB)
Burning Heart
Survivor; *Rocky Story* .... (SCO)
ST/Rocky IV .... (SCO)
Vandenberg; *Best Of* .... (ATC)
Vandenberg .... (ATC)

Burnin' A Hole In My Heart
Skip Ewing; *Class Of Country* .... (KT)
Coast Of Colorado .... (MCA)
Call To Your Heart
Giuffria; *Giuffria* .... (CAM)
Can I Trust You With My Heart
Travis Tritt; *T-R-O-U-B-L-E* .... (WB)
Can't Break It To My Heart
Tracy Lawrence; *Alibis* .... (ATL)
Can't Stop My Heart From Loving You
O'Kanes; *Greatest Country Hits/'80s-1987* .... (COL)
More Hot Country Requests-#2 .... (EPI)
O'Kanes .... (COL)
Can't You Hear My Heart Beat?
Herman's Hermits; *XX* .... (AKO)
Captain Of Her Heart
Double; *Blue* .... (A&M)
Romantic Hits Of The '80s .... (KT)
Chains Around My Heart
Richard Marx; *Rush Street* .... (CAP)
Change Of Heart
Cyndi Lauper; *True Colors* .... (POR)
Eric Carmen; *Best Of* .... (ARI)
Change Of Heart .... (ARI)
Judds; *Greatest Hits* .... (RCA)
Judds .... (RCA)
Stray Cats; *Rock Therapy* .... (EMI)
Tom Petty/Heartbreakers; *Long After Dark* ..... (MCA)
Toto; *Isolation* .... (COL)
Chrome Plated Heart
Melissa Etheridge; *Melissa Etheridge* .... (ISL)
Church Of Your Heart
Roxette; *Joyride* .... (EMI)
Closer To The Heart
Rush; *Chronicles* .... (MER)
Exit...Stage Left .... (MER)
Farewell To Kings .... (MER)
Show Of Hands .... (MER)
Clouds In My Heart
Muddy Waters; *Blues Deluxe* .... (ALL)
Cold Cold Heart
Hank Williams; *24 Greatest Hits* .... (MGM)
40 Greatest Hits .... (POL)
Hank Williams .... (MGM)
Live At Opry .... (MGM)
Long Gone Lonesome Blues .... (POL)
Jerry Lee Lewis; *Duets* .... (SUN)
Golden Cream Of .... (SUN)
& Friends: Duets .... (SUN)
Cold Hearted
Paula Abdul; *Forever Your Girl* .... (VIA)
Get Up & Dance-Dance Mixes .... (VIA)
Come From The Heart
Don Williams; *Traces* .... (CAP)
Kathy Mattea; *Willow In The Wind* .... (MER)
Conviction Of The Heart
Kenny Loggins; *Leap Of Faith* .... (COL)
Crazy From The Heart
Bellamy Brothers; *Crazy From The Heart* ...... (MCA)
Greatest Hits-III .... (MCA)
Crazy Heart
Forester Sisters; *Forester Sisters* .... (WB)
Hank Williams; *24 Greatest Hits-#2* .... (POL)
40 Greatest Hits .... (POL)
Hey Good Lookin' (Dec. 1950-July 1951) ..... (POL)
Rare Takes & Radio Cuts .... (POL)
Cross My Broken Heart
Jets; *Magic* .... (MCA)
Soundtrack Smashes-'80s .... (MCA)
ST/Beverly Hills Cop II .... (MCA)
Suzy Bogguss; *Somewhere Between* .... (CAP)
Cross My Heart
Billy Stewart; *Greatest Sides* .... (CSS)
Bruce Springsteen; *Human Touch* .... (COL)
Diana Ross; *Endless Love* .... (RCA)
Dolly Parton/Vince Gill/Ricky Skaggs; *Slow Dancing
With The Moon* .... (COL)
Eighth Wonder; *Fearless* .... (WTG)
Everything But The Girl; *Baby The Stars Shine
Bright* .... (SIR)
Johnny Ace; *Memorial Album* .... (MCA)
Johnny Lee; *Best Of* .... (CCB)
New Directions .... (CCB)
Martika; *Martika* .... (COL)

Tracie Spencer; *Tracie Spencer* .... (CAP)
Cross My Heart I Love You
Bob Wills/Texas Playboys; *24 Great Hits* .... (POL)
Cross My Heart & Hope To Try
Elvis Presley; *ST/Girl Happy* .... (RCA)
Cross Your Heart
Artie Shaw/Gramercy Five; *This Is* .... (BLU)
Brothers Figaro; *Gypsy Beat* .... (GEF)
Crying My Heart Out For You
Diana Ross; *All The Great Love Songs* .... (MOT)
Anthology .... (MOT)
Doris Day; *Sings 22 Great Songs* .... (HIN)
Uncollected w/Page Cavanaugh Trio-#2 .... (HIN)
Crying My Heart Out Over You
Ricky Skaggs; *Greatest Country Hits/'80s-1981* ..(COL)
Waiting For the Sun To Shine .... (EPI)
Cupid
Graham Parker; *Mona Lisa's Daughter* .... (RCA)
ST/True Love .... (RCA)
Sam Cooke; *Best Of* .... (RCA)
Man & His Music .... (RCA)
Spinners; *Love Trippin'* .... (ATL)
Danger Heartbreak Dead Ahead
Bonnie Raitt; *Bonnie Raitt* .... (WB)
Marvelettes; *Anthology* .... (MOT)
Greatest Hits .... (MOT)
ST/Good Morning Vietnam .... (A&M)
Dear Heart
Andy Williams; *16 Most Requested Songs* .... (COL)
Greatest Hits .... (COL)
Dear Lonely Hearts
Nat King Cole; *Capitol Collectors Series* .... (CAP)
Ramblin' Rose .... (CAP)
Deep In My Heart
Clubhouse; *S* .... (ATL)
Fleshtones; *Living Legends* .... (IRS)
Shells; *Golden Classics* .... (CLT)
Deep In The Heart Of Texas
Bing Crosby; *Greatest Hits* .... (MCA)
Bob Wills; *Best Of* .... (MCA)
Best Of-#2 .... (MCA)
Gene Autry; *Columbia Historic Edition* .... (COL)
Deserted Cities Of The Heart
Cream; *Live-#2* .... (POL)
Wheels Of Fire .... (POL)
Devil In Her Heart
Beatles; *Second Album* .... (CAP)
With The .... (CAP)
Donays; *Beatles Originals* .... (RHI)
Does Your Heart Beat For Me
Blue Barron; *Big Band Treasures-#2* .... (DHL)
Patsy Cline; *Always* .... (MCA)
Portrait Of .... (MCA)
Russ Morgan; *Best Of* .... (MCA)
Russ Morgan/Orchestra; *Play 22 Original Big Band
Recordings* .... (HIN)
Don't Be Cruel
Elvis Presley; *Billboard Top Rock 'N' Roll
Hits-1956* .... (RCA)
Great Performances .... (RCA)
Nipper's Greatest Hits-'50s-#2 .... (RCA)
Number One Hits .... (RCA)
Top Ten Hits .... (RCA)
Don't Believe My Heart Can Stand...
Tanya Tucker; *Collection* .... (MCA)
Greatest Hits .... (MCA)
Don't Go Breaking My Heart
Elton John; *Greatest Hits-#2* .... (POL)
Doo Doo Doo Doo Doo
Rolling Stones; *Goat's Head Soup* .... (RS)
Made In The Shade .... (RS)
Rewind (1971-1984) .... (RS)
Doors Of Your Heart
English Beat; *What Is Beat* .... (IRS)
Wha'ppen .... (IRS)
Down To My Last Broken Heart
Janie Fricke; *17 Greatest Hits* .... (COL)
Greatest Country Hits-'80s-1980 .... (COL)
Greatest Hits .... (COL)
Dream Is A Wish Your Heart Makes
Barbara Cook; *Disney Album* .... (MCA)
Michael Bolton; *Simply Mad About The Mouse* ..(COL)
Drunken Hearted Man
Robert Johnson; *Complete Recordings* .... (COL)

Dyslexic Heart
Paul Westerberg; *ST/Singles* .... (EPI)
Eartheart
Kenny Rankin; *Like A Seed* .... (LD)
Empty Heart
Rolling Stones; *12 X 5* .... (AKO)
Every Beat Of My Heart
Gladys Knight/Pips; *Anthology* .... (MOT)
   Hits From Legendary Vee-Jay Records .... (MOT)
   Oldies But Goodies-#6 .... (OSR)
   Sultry Soul Sisters-Wonder Women-#3 .... (RHI)
Rod Stewart; *Storyteller/Complete
Anthology-1964-1990* .... (WB)
Every Heartbeat
Amy Grant; *Heart In Motion* .... (A&M)
Everything Your Heart Desires
Daryl Hall & John Oates; *Oooh Yeah!* .... (ARI)
Ev'ry Heart Should Have One
Charley Pride; *Greatest Hits-#2* .... (RCA)
   Night Games .... (RCA)
Excuse Me (I Think I've Got A Heartache)
Buck Owens; *All-Time Greatest-#1* .... (CCB)
   Billboard Top Country Hits-1960 .... (RHI)
   Collection-1959-1990 .... (RHI)
Mavericks; *From Hell To Paradise* .... (MCA)
Expressway To Your Heart
Blues Brothers; *Best Of* .... (ATL)
Soul Survivors; *Dick Bartley's One-Hit
Wonders-'60s-#2* .... (RHI)
   Oldies But Goodies-#11 .... (OSR)
   Super Oldies/'60s-#6 .... (AUF)
   When The Whistle Blows Anything Goes .... (CLT)
February In My Heart
Osborne Brothers; *Some Things I Want To Sing
About* .... (SH)
Follow Your Heart
Joe Farrell; *Quartet* .... (CBA)
John McLaughlin; *CTI Masters Of The Guitar* .... (CBA)
   My Goals Beyond .... (ELE)
Manhattans; *Dedicated To You-Carnival
Classics-#1* .... (CLT)
Triumph; *Classics* .... (MCA)
   Stages .... (MCA)
   Thunder Seven .... (MCA)
Fool Hearted Memory
George Strait; *Greatest Hits* .... (MCA)
   Night Game .... (MCA)
   Strait From The Heart .... (MCA)
Foolish Heart
Grateful Dead; *Built To Last* .... (ARI)
Sharon Bryant; *Here I Am* .... (WIN)
Steve Perry; *Street Talk* .... (COL)
For My Broken Heart
Reba McEntire; *For My Broken Heart* .... (MCA)
   Greatest Hits-#2 .... (MCA)
Fortress Around Your Heart
Sting; *Dream Of The Blue Turtles* .... (A&M)
Give Back My Heart
Lyle Lovett; *Pontiac* .... (MCC)
Give One Heart
Linda Ronstadt; *Hasten Down The Wind* .... (ASY)
Good Hearted Woman
George Jones; *I Am What I Am* .... (EPI)
Waylon Jennings; *Good Hearted Woman* .... (RCA)
   Greatest Hits .... (RCA)
   The Outlaws .... (RCA)
Willie Nelson; *Greatest Hits & Some That Will Be* (COL)
   Willie .... (RCA)
Good Morning Heartache
Billie Holiday; *All Or Nothing At All* .... (VRV)
   From The Original Decca Masters .... (MCA)
   History Of .... (VRV)
   Story .... (MCA)
Diana Ross; *Anthology* .... (MOT)
   Greatest Hits .... (MOT)
   ST/Lady Sings The Blues .... (MOT)
Goodnight, Sweetheart
Flamingos; *Best Of* .... (RHI)
Spaniels; *Cruisin'-1957* .... (INC)
   Doo-Wop Ballads-#2 .... (RHI)
   Lovin' '50s .... (PRY)
Got My Heart Set On You
John Conlee; *Greatest Country hits/'80s-1986* .... (COL)
   More Hot Country Requests .... (EPI)

Groove Is In The Heart/What Is Love
Deee-Lite; *World Clique* .... (ELE)
Hang On To Your Heart
Exile; *Greatest Hits* .... (EPI)
   Hang On To Your Heart .... (EPI)
Hanging On A Heart Attack
Device; *45* .... (CHR)
Happy Birthday Dear Heartache
Barbara Mandrell; *Clean Cut* .... (MCA)
   Country Classics-#1 .... (MCA)
   Greatest Hits .... (MCA)
Happy Heart
Andy Williams; *Greatest Hits* .... (COL)
Petula Clark; *Greatest Hits* .... (CRS)
Hard Rock Bottom Of Your Heart
Randy Travis; *No Holdin' Back* .... (WB)
Harden My Heart
Quarterflash; *Quarterflash* .... (GEF)
Haunted Heart
Sammy Kershaw; *Haunted Heart* .... (MER)
Have A Heart
Bonnie Raitt; *Nick Of Time* .... (CAP)
Headache Tomorrow (Or A Heartache...)
Mickey Gilley; *Biggest Hits* .... (EPI)
   Ten Years Of Hits .... (EPI)
   That's All That Matters To Me .... (EPI)
Headed For A Heartache
Gary Morris; *Gary Morris* .... (WB)
   Hits .... (WB)
Headed For A Heartbreak
Winger; *Winger* .... (ATL)
Heart
Laura Branigan; *Self Control* .... (ATL)
Neneh Cherry; *Raw Like Sushi* .... (VIA)
Nick Lowe; *Basher-Best Of* .... (COL)
Original Broadway Cast; *Damn Yankees* .... (RCA)
Peggy Lee; *All-Time Greatest Hits-#1* .... (CCB)
Pet Shop Boys; *Actually* .... (EMI)
   Discography-Complete Singles Collection ..... (EMI)
Rockpile; *Seconds Of Pleasure* .... (COL)
Heart And Soul
Cleftones; *Echoes Of A Rock Era-Later Years* .... (RLL)
   ST/American Graffiti .... (MCA)
Four Aces; *20 Greatest Hits* .... (EVR)
Huey Lewis/News; *Sports* .... (CHR)
Jan & Dean; *Best Of* .... (EMI)
   Oldies/Goodies-#9 .... (OSR)
Heart Attack
Olivia Newton-John; *Greatest Hits-#2* .... (MCA)
   Physical .... (MCA)
Heart Don't Fall Now
Sawyer Brown; *Shakin'* .... (CAP)
Heart Full Of Love
Holly Dunn; *Heart Full Of Love* .... (WB)
Original Broadway Cast; *Les Miserables* .... (GEF)
Heart Full Of Soul
Chris Isaak; *Chris Isaak* .... (WB)
Yardbirds; *Greatest Hits-#1-1964-1966* .... (RHI)
   History Of British Rock-#2 .... (RHI)
Heart Hotels
Dan Fogelberg; *Greatest Hits* .... (FM)
   Phoenix .... (FM)
Heart In New York
Art Garfunkel; *Garfunkel* .... (COL)
   Scissors Cut .... (COL)
Simon & Garfunkel; *Concert In Central Park* ... (WB)
Heart Is In Africa
Rozalla; *Everybody's Free* .... (EPI)
Heart Like A Hurricane
Larry Stewart; *Heart Like A Hurricane* .... (COL)
Heart Like A Wheel
Linda Ronstadt; *Heart Like A Wheel* .... (CAP)
Steve Miller Band; *Circle Of Love* .... (CAP)
Heart Of Glass
Blondie; *Best Of* .... (CHR)
   Billboard Top Hits-1979 .... (RHI)
   Disco Years-#2-On The Beat-1978-1982 .... (RHI)
   Parallel Lines .... (CHR)
Heart Of Gold
Neil Young; *Decade* .... (RPR)
   Harvest .... (RPR)
Heart Of Mine
Oak Ridge Boys; *Greatest Hits* .... (MCA)
   Together .... (MCA)

The Green Book Of Songs By Subject — Page 295

Heart Of Rock & Roll
Huey Lewis/News; *Sports* .... (CHR)
Heart Of Saturday Night (Looking For...)
Shawn Colvin; *Cover Girl* ....(COL)
Tom Waits; *Anthology* .... (ASY)
  Heart Of Saturday Night (Looking For...) .... (ASY)
Heart Of Stone
Fleetwood Mac; *25 Years-The Chain* ....(WB)
Rolling Stones; *Big Hits-High Tide & Green Grass* (AKO)
  Hot Rocks-1964-1971 .... (AKO)
  Now .... (AKO)
Heart Of The Matter
Don Henley; *End Of The Innocence* .... (GEF)
Heart Of The Night
Juice Newton; *Greatest Hits* ....(CAP)
  Greatest Hits & More ....(CAP)
  Quiet Lies ....(CAP)
Poco; *Backtracks* .... (MCA)
  Legend .... (MCA)
Heart Over Mind
Lorrie Morgan; *War Paint* ....(BNA)
Heart That You Own
Dwight Yoakam; *If There Was A Way* .... (RPR)
  ST/White Sands .... (MC)
Heart To Heart
Kenny Loggins; *High Adventure* ....(COL)
Kenny Rogers; *What About Me* ....(RCA)
Heart Trouble
Martina McBride; *The Way That I Am* ....(RCA)
Steve Wariner; *Country Classics-#3-1984-1985* . (MCA)
  Greatest Hits ....(MCA)
  One Good Night Deserves Another .... (MCA)
Heart Won't Lie
Reba McEntire & Vince Gill; *It's Your Call* ..... (MCA)
Heartache Tonight
Conway Twitty; *Latest Greatest Hits-#1* ....(WB)
  Lost In The Feeling ....(WB)
Eagles; *Greatest Hits* ....(ASY)
  Live ....(ASY)
  Long Run ....(ASY)
John Anderson; *Common Thread-Songs Of The*
Eagles .... (GIA)
Heartaches By The Number
Ray Price; *Columbia Country Classics-#2* ....(COL)
  Greatest Hits ....(COL)
  Greatest Hits-#1 .... (SO)
Heartaches Of A Fool
Willie Nelson; *Greatest Hits & Some That Will Be* (COL)
Heartache, A Shadow, A Lifetime
Dave Mason; *At His Very Best* .... (MCA)
  Best Of .... (MCA)
Heartbeat
Buddy Holly; *Legend* .... (MCA)
Buddy Holly/Crickets; *20 Golden Greats* .... (MCA)
Dazz Band; *Jukebox* ....(MOT)
Dolly Parton; *Greatest Hits* ....(RCA)
Don Johnson; *Heartbeat* .... (EPI)
Gloria Jones; *Soul Shots-Sixties Soul Classics-#2* . (RHI)
  Soul Shots-#4-Tell Mama ....(RHI)
Midnight Star; *Midnight Star* ....(SLR)
Wham!; *Make It Big* ....(COL)
Heartbeat In The Darkness
Don Williams; *New Moves* ....(CAP)
  Prime Cuts ....(CAP)
Heartbeats
Yarbrough & Peoples; *45* .... (TE)
Heartbeat/Free Your Body
Seduction; *Nothing Matters Without Love* ....(VDT)
Heartbreak Express
Delia Bell/Bill Grant; *Cheer Of The Home Fires* . (ROU)
Dolly Parton; *Greatest Hits* ....(RCA)
  Heartbreak Express ....(RCA)
Heartbreak Hotel
Albert King; *Blues For Elvis* ....(STX)
Elvis Presley; *50 Worldwide Gold Award Hits-#1* (RCA)
  Elvis At Madison Square Garden ....(RCA)
  Golden Records-#1 ....(RCA)
  Golden Records-#2 ....(RCA)
  Legendary Performer-#1 ....(RCA)
  Nipper's Greatest Hits/'50s-#1 ....(RCA)
Jacksons; *Live* .... (EPI)
  Triumph .... (EPI)
Stan Freberg; *Capitol Collectors Series* ....(CAP)

Willie Nelson; *Greatest Hits & Some That Will Be* (COL)
  & Leon Russell: One For The Road ....(COL)
Heartbreak Station
Cinderella; *Heartbreak Station* ....(MER)
Heartbreaker
Dionne Warwick; *Heartbreaker* .... (ARI)
Grand Funk Railroad; *Capitol Collectors Series* ...(CAP)
Great White; *Hooked* ....(CAP)
Led Zeppelin; *II* ....(ATL)
  Led Zeppelin ....(ATL)
Pat Benatar; *Best Shots* .... (CHR)
  In The Heat Of The Night ....(CHR)
  Live From Earth ....(CHR)
Tanya Tucker; *Love Me Like You Used To* ....(CAP)
Heartbroke
George Strait; *Strait From The Heart* .... (MCA)
Ricky Skaggs; *Greatest Country Hits/'80s-#2* .....(COL)
  Highways & Heartaches .... (EPI)
  Live In London .... (EPI)
Rodney Crowell; *Collection* ....(WB)
Heartland
George Strait; *ST/Pure Country* .... (MCA)
Sawyer Brown; *Boys Are Back* ....(CCB)
Steve Wariner; *Life's Highway* ....(MCA)
U2; *ST/Rattle & Hum* .... (ISL)
Heartless
Heart; *Greatest Hits/Live* .... (EPI)
  Magazine ....(CAP)
Heartlight
Neil Diamond; *Heartlight* ....(COL)
  Hot August Night II ....(COL)
Hearts
Huey Lewis/News; *Huey Lewis/News* .... (CHR)
Marty Balin; *Balin* .... (EMI)
  Balince-Collection .... (RHI)
Hearts Are Gonna Roll
Hal Ketchum; *Sure Love* ....(CRB)
Hearts Aren't Made To Break
Lee Greenwood; *Country*
Classics-#5-1985-1986 .... (MCA)
  Greatest Hits-#2 .... (MCA)
  Streamline ....(MCA)
Hearts Don't Think (They Feel)
Natural Selection; *Natural Selection* ....(EW)
Hearts On Fire
Bryan Adams; *Into The Fire* ....(A&M)
Eddie Rabbitt; *All-Time Greatest Hits* ....(WB)
  Best Of .... (ELE)
  Variations .... (ELE)
Gram Parsons; *Grievous Angel* ....(RPR)
Randy Meisner; *One More Song* .... (EPI)
Steve Winwood; *Roll With It* .... (VIA)
Heart's On Fire
38 Special; *Strength In Numbers* ....(A&M)
Heart-Shaped Box
Nirvana; *In Utero* .... (DGC)
Heart-Shaped World
Chris Isaak; *Heart-Shaped World* .... (RPR)
Hello Mary Lou
Creedence Clearwater Revival; *Creedence*
Country .... (FAN)
Ricky Nelson; *Best Of* .... (EMI)
  Greatest Hits .... (RHI)
  In Concert-Troubadour-1969 .... (MCA)
  Souvenirs .... (EMI)
Statler Brothers; *14 Country Favorites* .... (MER)
  Pardners In Rhyme .... (MER)
Help Me Rhonda
Beach Boys; *Billboard Top Rock 'N' Roll*
Hits-1965 .... (RHI)
  California Girls ....(CAP)
  Dance Dance Dance ....(CAP)
  Endless Summer ....(CAP)
  Made In The U.S.A. ....(CAP)
He's A Heartache (Looking For A Place..)
Janie Fricke; *17 Greatest Hits* ....(COL)
  19 Hot Country Requests .... (EPI)
  It Ain't Easy ....(COL)
  Very Best Of ....(COL)
Hold On My Heart
Genesis; *We Can't Dance* .... (ATL)
Hole Hearted
Extreme; *Pornograffitti* ....(A&M)

Home Again In My Heart
Nitty Gritty Dirt Band; *More Great Dirt-Best
Of-#2* .... (WB)
  Partners Brothers & Friends .... (WB)
Home Is A Wounded Heart
Neil Diamond; *Beautiful Noise* ....(COL)
Home Is Where The Heart Is
Bobby Womack; *Home Is Where The Heart Is* ....(COL)
Gladys Knight/Pips; *Still Together* ....(BUD)
Kool/Gang; *In The Heart* .... (DL)
Homestead In My Heart
Amazing Rhythm Aces; *Amazing Rhythm Aces* ...(COL)
Honky Tonk Heart
Highway 101; *Greatest Hits* .... (WB)
  One-O-One .... (WB)
Jim Owen; *45* .... (SUN)
Keith Whitley; *Don't Close Your Eyes* ....(RCA)
Hot Rod Hearts
Robbie Dupree; *Robbie Dupree* .... (ELE)
Hotter Than Mojave In My Heart
Iris DeMent; *Infamous Angel* .... (WB)
How Can You Mend A Broken Heart
Al Green; *Compact Command Performances* .... (MOT)
  Greatest Hits-#1 .... (MOT)
  Let's Stay Together .... (MOT)
Bee Gees; *Gold-#1* .... (RSO)
  Here At Last .... (RSO)
  Nobody's Child-Romanian Angel Appeal .... (WB)
Hungry Heart
Bruce Springsteen; *The River* ....(COL)
Bruce Springsteen/E Street Band;
Live-1975-1985 ....(COL)
I Ain't Gonna Eat Out My Heart Anymore
Rascals; *Time Piece-Rascals Greatest Hits* .... (ATL)
  Young Rascals .... (RHI)
I Ain't Gonna Let You Break My Heart...
Bonnie Raitt; *Nick Of Time* ....(CAP)
I Can't Stand It
Eric Clapton; *Another Ticket* .... (RSO)
  Crossroads .... (POL)
I Cross My Heart
George Strait; *ST/Pure Country* .... (MCA)
I Don't Have The Heart
James Ingram; *It's Real* .... (WB)
I Know A Heartache When I See One
Jennifer Warnes; *Best Of* .... (ARI)
  Shot Through The Heart .... (ARI)
I Left My Heart At The Stage Door...
Jo Stafford; *G.I. Jo* .... (CRN)
I Left My Heart In Iran
Forgotten Rebels; *Livin' On Heroin* .... (RES)
I Left My Heart In San Francisco
Tony Bennett; *All-Time Greatest Hits* ....(COL)
  I Left My Heart In San Francisco ....(COL)
  Pop Classics/'60s ....(COL)
I Let A Song Go Out Of My Heart
Bill Jennings; *Stompin' With Bill* .... (CLT)
Duke Ellington; *Braggin' In Brass-Immortal 1938
Year* ....(POR)
Joe Pass; *Portraits Of Duke Ellington* .... (PAB)
Teresa Brewer; *Sophisticated Lady* ....(COL)
Tony Bennett; *Jazz* ....(COL)
I Love You By Heart
Sylvia & Michael Johnson; *Collector's Duets* .....(RCA)
I Sold My Heart To The Junkman
Carmen McRae; *Sound Of Silence* .... (ATL)
Patti LaBelle/Blue Belles; *Super Oldies/'60s-#3* ..(AUF)
I Wish You Could Have Turned My Head
Oak Ridge Boys; *Bobbie Sue* .... (MCA)
If I Only Had A Heart
Jack Haley; *ST/Wizard Of Oz* .... (SSP)
If My Heart Had Windows
Patty Loveless; *Country Classics-#12-1987-1988* (MCA)
  Greatest Hits .... (MCA)
  If My Heart Had Windows .... (MCA)
If Your Heart Ain't Busy Tonight
Tanya Tucker; *What Do I Do With Me* .... (LIB)
If Your Heart Isn't In It
Atlantic Starr; *As The Band Turns* .... (A&M)
  Classics-#10 .... (A&M)
  Secret Lovers-Best Of .... (A&M)
If You've Got Love
John Michael Montgomery; *Kickin' It Up* .... (ATL)

In China Or A Woman's Heart
Kate Wolf; *Poet's Heart* .... (KAL)
In Over My Heart
Bobby Womack; *Someday We'll All Be Free* ..... (BEV)
T.G. Sheppard; *Biggest Hits* ....(COL)
  Livin' On The Edge ....(COL)
In The Heart Of A Woman
Billy Ray Cyrus; *It Won't Be The Last* .... (MER)
In The Middle Of A Heartache
Wanda Jackson; *Greatest Hits* .... (GUS)
  Rockin' In The Country-Best Of .... (RHI)
In The Shape Of A Heart
Jackson Browne; *Lives In The Balance* .... (ASY)
Inside
Ronnie Milsap; *Greatest Hits-#2* ....(RCA)
  Inside Ronnie Milsap ....(RCA)
  Solid Country Gold ....(RCA)
Irish Heartbeat
Van Morrison; *Inarticulate Speech Of The Heart* ..(WB)
Van Morrison/Chieftains; *Irish Heartbeat* .... (MER)
It's A Heartache
Bonnie Tyler; *Billboard Top Hits-1978* ....(RCA)
  It's A Heartache ....(RCA)
Juice Newton; *Greatest Hits & More* ....(CAP)
Ronnie Spector; *Get Down Tonight!-Best Of T.K.
Records* .... (RHI)
It's Only A Heartache
Steve Wariner; *One Good Night Deserves
Another* .... (MCA)
I'll Follow My Secret Heart
Mary Martin & Noel Coward; *Together With
Music* .... (DRG)
I've Got A New Heartache
Ray Price; *Greatest Hits* ....(COL)
Ricky Skaggs; *Live In London* .... (EPI)
  More Hot Country Requests .... (EPI)
I've Got A Rock 'N' Roll Heart
Eric Clapton; *Money And Cigarettes* .... (DUC)
Janey, Don't Lose Heart
Bruce Springsteen; *45* ....(COL)
Jealous Heart
Tex Ritter; *An American Legend* ....(CAP)
  Best Of ....(CAP)
  Hillbilly Heaven ....(CAP)
Jealous Hearted Man
Muddy Waters; *Hard Again* .... (BS)
Jealous Hearted Me
Minnie Pearl; *Stars Of The Grand Ole
Opry-1926-1974* ....(RCA)
Just Take My Heart
Mr. Big; *Lean Into It* .... (ATL)
Keep My Heart In Line
Earl Thomas Conley; *Yours Truly* ....(RCA)
Keep This Heart In Mind
Bonnie Raitt; *Green Light* .... (WB)
King Of My Heart
Melba Moore; *Read My Lips* ....(CAP)
Lazarus Heart
Sting; *...Nothing Like The Sun* .... (A&M)
Let Me Call You Sweetheart
Bette Midler; *ST/The Rose* .... (ATL)
Billy Vaughn/Orchestra; *Play 22 Of His Greatest
Hits* .... (RAN)
Bob Ralston; *22 Great Organ Hits-#2* .... (RAN)
Let The Heartache Ride
Restless Heart; *Greatest Hits* ....(RCA)
  Restless Heart ....(RCA)
Like We Never Had A Broken Heart
Trisha Yearwood; *Trisha Yearwood* .... (MCA)
Listen To Her Heart
Tom Petty/Heartbreakers; *You're Gonna Get It* . (MCA)
Listen To The Heartbeat
Billy Squier; *Emotions In Motion* ....(CAP)
Longing In Their Hearts
Bonnie Raitt; *Longing In Their Hearts* ....(CAP)
Look Heart No Hands
Randy Travis; *Greatest Hits-#2* .... (WB)
Lose Your Heart
Bob Welch; *French Kiss* ....(CAP)
Love Bug Leave My Heart Alone
Martha Reeves/Vandellas; *Anthology* .... (MOT)
  Compact Command Performances .... (MOT)

HEART — HEART

Love Don't Care (Whose Heart It Breaks)
Earl Thomas Conley; *Greatest Greatest Hits* ......(RCA)
  Greatest Hits-#2 ....(RCA)
  Treadin' Water ....(RCA)
Miss You In A Heartbeat
Def Leppard; *Retro Active* .... (MER)
Mother The Queen Of My Heart
Pete Seeger & Arlo Guthrie; *Together In Concert* (RPR)
Murder In My Heart For The Judge
Lee Michaels; *Collection* .... (RHI)
Moby Grape; *Wow* ....(OOP)
My Beating Heart
Cathy Dennis; *Move To This* ....(POL)
My Bleeding Heart
Elmore James; *Complete Fire & Enjoy
Sessions-#2* ....(CLT)
My Foolish Heart
Bill Evans; *Waltz For Debby* ....(RVR)
Carmen McRae; *Live At Bubba's* ....(WHO)
John McLaughlin; *Electric Guitarist* ....(COL)
Liz Story; *My Foolish Heart* ....(WH)
Roberta Flack; *Set The Night To Music* ....(ATL)
Stephane Grappelli; *Stephanova* ....(CCJ)
Tony Bennett & Bill Evans; *Album* ....(FAN)
My Funny Valentine
Anita O'Day; *Anita O'Day* ....(GLN)
  Live At The City ....(EML)
  Sings The Winners ....(VRV)
Carly Simon; *My Romance* ....(ARI)
Ella Fitzgerald; *Rodgers & Hart Songbook* ....(VRV)
Mel Torme; *Easy To Remember* ....(GLN)
Miles Davis; *Columbia Years-1955-1985* ....(COL)
  Cookin' With The Miles Davis Quintet ....(PRS)
  Greatest Hits ....(COL)
  My Funny Valentine ....(COL)
Original Cast/Mary Martin; *Babes In Arms* ....(SSP)
Stan Getz; *Artistry Of-Best Of Verve Years-#1* ...(VRV)
My Heart
Neil Young/Crazy Horse; *Sleeps With Angels* .....(RPR)
Ronnie Milsap; *Collector's Series* ....(RCA)
  Milsap Magic ....(RCA)
My Heart Belongs To Daddy
Ella Fitzgerald & Cole Porter; *Dream Dancing* ..(PAB)
Peggy Lee; *Best Of* ....(MCA)
Rosemary Clooney; *Sings The Music Of Cole
Porter* ....(CCJ)
My Heart Belongs To Me
Barbra Streisand; *Greatest Hits-#2* ....(COL)
  Memories ....(COL)
  Streisand Superman ....(COL)
My Heart Belongs To Only You
Bobby Vinton; *16 Most Requested* ....(EPI)
  All-Time Greatest Hits ....(EPI)
  Greatest Hits ....(EPI)
My Heart Can't Tell Me No
Rod Stewart; *Downtown Train-Storyteller
Selections* ....(WB)
  Out Of Order ....(WB)
  Storyteller-Complete Anthology-1964-1990 ......(WB)
My Heart Cries For You
Charlie Rich; *20 Golden Hits* ....(SUN)
  Time For Tears ....(SUN)
Dinah Shore; *Nipper's Greatest Hits-'50s-#1* ......(RCA)
Guy Mitchell; *16 Most Requested Songs* ....(COL)
My Heart Has A Mind Of Its Own
Connie Francis; *Very Best Of* ....(MGM)
Debby Boone; *Best Of* ....(CRB)
My Heart Is A Hobo
Rosemary Clooney; *Sings The Music Of Jimmy Van
Heusen* ....(CCJ)
My Heart Is Failing Me
Riff; *Riff* ....(SBK)
My Heart Stood Still
Bud Powell; *Genius Of-#2* ....(VRV)
Frank Sinatra; *Concert Sinatra* ....(RPR)
Tony Bennett; *Rodgers & Hart Songbook* ....(DRG)
My Heart Tells Me
Etta Jones; *Something Nice* ....(PRS)
Nat King Cole; *Very Thought Of You* ....(CAP)
My Heart Would Know
Hank Williams; *24 Greatest Hits* ....(POL)
  Hey Good Lookin' (Dec. 1950-July 1951) ......(POL)
My Heart's Deep In The Heart Of Texas
Boxcar Willie; *King Of The Freight Train* ....(MSP)

My Next Broken Heart
Brooks & Dunn; *Brand New Man* .... (ARI)
My Sweetheart In Tennessee
Burnett & Rutherford; *Ramblin' Reckless Hobo* .. (ROU)
My Sweetheart Lives In San Antonio
Ray Duncan; *45* ....(OOP)
North Carolina Tune/Child Of My Heart
Liz Carroll; *Friend Indeed* ....(SHA)
Nothing Broken But My Heart
Celine Dion; *Celine Dion* ....(EPI)
Nothing But Heartaches
Diana Ross/Supremes; *Anthology* ....(MOT)
  Greatest Hits-#1 ....(MOT)
  Motown Story ....(MOT)
  Motown Superstar Series-#1 ....(MOT)
Nothin' But A Heartache
Doobie Brothers; *Livin' On The Fault Line* ....(WB)
Oklahoma Heartaches & California Dreams
Kris Carpenter; *45* ....(DOO)
Oklahoma Sweetheart
George Thorogood/Destroyers; *Boogie People* ... (EMI)
Oklahoma Sweetheart
Maddox Brothers; *America's Most Colorful Hillbilly
Band* .... (ARH)
Once You Lose Your Heart
Original Broadway Cast; *Me & My Girl* .... (MCA)
One Broken Heart For Sale
Elvis Presley; *50 Worldwide Gold Award Hits-#2* (RCA)
  Collector's Gold ....(RCA)
  World's Fair ....(RCA)
One Owner Heart
T.G. Sheppard; *Greatest Hits-#2* ....(W/C)
  One Owner Heart ....(W/C)
One Rose (That's Left In My Heart)
Bing Crosby; *Best Of* ....(MCA)
Leon Redbone; *Champagne Charlie* ....(WB)
Only A Lonely Heart Knows
Barbara Mandrell; *Clean Cut* ....(MCA)
Only A Lonely Heart Sees
Felix Cavaliere; *Castles In The Air* ....(OOP)
Only Love Can Break A Heart
Gene Pitney; *Anthology* .... (RHI)
  Gene Pitney ....(EVR)
  Love Sixties ....(JCI)
  Pick Of ....(FFT)
Open The Door To Your Heart
Little Milton; *Stax Blues Masters-Blue Monday* ... (STX)
  Walking The Back Streets ....(STX)
Open Up Your Heart
Buck Owens; *Collection-1959-1990* .... (RHI)
Open Your Heart
Europe; *Out Of This World* ....(EPI)
  Wings Of Tomorrow ....(EPI)
Human League; *Dare* ....(A&M)
  Greatest Hits ....(A&M)
Madonna; *Immaculate Collection* ....(SIR)
  Royal Box ....(SIR)
  True Blue ....(SIR)
Owner Of A Lonely Heart
Yes; *90125* ....(ATC)
Pain In My Heart
David Johansen; *David Johansen* .... (BS)
Otis Redding; *Best Of* ....(ATC)
  History Of ....(ATC)
  In Person At The Whisky A Go Go ....(RHI)
  Pain In My Heart ....(ATC)
  Story ....(ATL)
Rolling Stones; *Now!* ....(AKO)
Peace In My Heart
Carole Bayer Sager; *Too* .... (ELE)
Peg O' My Heart
Buddy Clark; *16 Most Requested Songs* ....(COL)
Three Suns; *Nipper's Greatest Hits-'40s-#2* ......(RCA)
Piece Of My Heart
Big Brother/Holding Company; *Cheap Thrills* ...(COL)
  Rock Classics Of The '60s ....(COL)
  Seems Like Yesterday-#6-Late '60s .... (KT)
Bryan Ferry; *These Foolish Things* ....(RPR)
Delaney & Bonnie; *Best Of* .... (RHI)
Faith Hill; *Take Me As I Am* ....(WB)
Janis Joplin; *Greatest Hits* ....(COL)
  In Concert ....(COL)
  ST/Janis ....(COL)
Sammy Hagar; *Standing Hampton* ....(GEF)

Tara Kemp; *Tara Kemp* .... (GIA)
Poet's Heart
  Kate Wolf; *Gold In*
  California-Retrospective-1975-85 ....(KAL)
  Poet's Heart ....(KAL)
Poison Heart
  Ramones; *Mondo Bizarro* .... (RAD)
Poisoned Heart & A Twisted Memory
  Richard Thompson; *Hand Of Kindness* .... (HBL)
Purple Heart
  David Allan Coe; *Invictus Means Unconquered* ...(COL)
  T-Bone Burnett; *Talking Animals* ....(COL)
Put A Little Love In Your Heart
  Annie Lennox & Al Green; *45* .... (A&M)
  Jackie DeShannon; *ST/Drugstore Cowboy* .... (NOV)
  Very Best Of .... (EMI)
Queen Of Hearts
  Dave Edmunds; *Best Of* .... (SS)
  Repeat When Necessary .... (SS)
  Gregg Allman; *Laid Back* .... (POL)
  Joan Baez; *Ballad Book* .... (VAN)
  In Concert .... (VAN)
  Juice Newton; *All-Time Country Classics-#2* .....(CAP)
  Greatest Hits ....(CAP)
  Greatest Hits & More ....(CAP)
  Juice ....(CAP)
  Rodney Crowell; *Collection* .... (WB)
  Whitesnake; *Snakebite* ....(GEF)
Queen Of My Heart
  DeBarge; *In A Special Way* .... (MOT)
  Hank Williams, Jr.; *Greatest Hits-#2* ....(W/C)
  Man Of Steel ....(W/C)
  Rene & Ray; *History Of Latino Rock-#1* .... (RHI)
Queen Of The Broken Hearts
  Loverboy; *Keep It Up* ....(COL)
Radio Heart
  Charly McClain; *19 Hot Country Requests-#3* .... (EPI)
  Biggest Hits .... (EPI)
  Greatest Country Hits/'80s-1985 ....(COL)
  Radio Heart .... (EPI)
Radio Sweetheart
  Elvis Costello; *Taking Liberties* ....(COL)
Rain In My Heart
  Frank Sinatra; *Cycles* .... (RPR)
Raining In My Heart
  Anne Murray; *New Kind Of Feeling* ....(CAP)
  Buddy Holly; *20 Golden Greats* ....(MCA)
  Vintage Music-Classic '50s/'60s-#6 ....(MCA)
  Jo-el Sonnier; *Come On Joe* ....(RCA)
  Leo Sayer; *Leo Sayer* .... (WB)
Rebel Heart
  Rod Stewart; *Vagabond Heart* .... (WB)
Rhythm Of My Heart
  Rod Stewart; *Vagabond Heart* .... (WB)
Road Of Broken Hearted Men
  Bobby Bland; *Introspective Of The Early Years* .. (MCA)
  Touch Of The Blues ....(MCA)
Road To Your Heart
  Barbara Mandrell; *Key's In The Mailbox* ....(CAP)
  Highway 101; *101 2* .... (WB)
Room In Your Heart
  Gladys Knight/Pips; *Every Beat Of My Heart-Greatest
  Hits* ....(CML)
  Letter Full Of Tears-Golden Classics ....(CLT)
Rough & Tumble Heart
  Highway 101; *Paint The Town* .... (WB)
Sacred Heart
  Dio; *Intermission* .... (WB)
  Sacred Heart .... (WB)
  Shakespear's Sister; *ST/Nuns On The Run* .... (MER)
Safe In My Heart
  Foreigner; *Unusual Heat* ....(ATL)
Savage Earth Heart
  Waterboys; *Waterboys* .... (ENS)
Savage Heart
  Pretty Maids; *Lethal Heroes* .... (EPI)
Save A Little Room In Your Heart For Me
  Eddie Money; *Eddie Money* ....(COL)
Saving My Heart
  Yes; *Union* .... (ARI)
Sea Of Heartbreak
  Don Gibson; *All-Time Greatest Hits* ....(RCA)
  Billboard Top Country Hits-1961 .... (RHI)

Seasons Of My Heart
  Buck Owens; *45* ....(WB)
  Jerry Lee Lewis; *Golden Cream Of* ....(SUN)
  Johnny Cash; *Columbia Records-1958-1968* .....(COL)
Seasons Of The Heart
  George Jones; *20 Golden Pieces Of* ....(BLD)
  John Denver; *Greatest Hits-#3* ....(RCA)
  Seasons Of The Heart ....(RCA)
Second Hand Heart
  Gary Morris; *Faded Blue* ....(WB)
Sgt. Pepper's Lonely Hearts Club Band
  Beatles; *1967-1970* ....(CAP)
  Box Set ....(CAP)
  Sgt. Pepper's Lonely Hearts Club Band ....(CAP)
  Jimi Hendrix; *Stages-Stockholm/Paris/San
  Diego/Atlanta* ....(RPR)
  Paul McCartney; *Tripping The Live Fantastic* ....(CAP)
Shape Of My Heart
  Sting; *Ten Summoner's Tales* .... (A&M)
She Gave Her Heart To A Soldier Boy
  Roy Rogers; *Country Music Hall Of Fame* ...... (MCA)
She Gave Her Heart To Jethro
  Tom T. Hall; *Essential-20th Anniversary
  Collection* .... (MER)
She Sure Got Away With My Heart
  John Anderson; *Eye Of A Hurricane* ....(WB)
  Greatest Hits-#2 ....(WB)
Sheer Heart Attack
  Queen; *Live Killers* ....(HOL)
  News Of The World ....(HOL)
She's A Heartbreaker
  Gene Pitney; *Anthology* ....(RHI)
  Best Of .... (KT)
  ZZ Top; *Six Pack* ....(WB)
  Tejas ....(WB)
She's Gonna Win Your Heart
  Eddy Raven; *I Could Use Another You* ....(RCA)
Shot In The Heart
  Genya Ravan; *Urban Desire* .... (20)
Shot Through The Heart
  Jennifer Warnes; *Best Of* .... (ARI)
  Shot Through The Heart .... (ARI)
Sign Your Name
  Terence Trent D'Arby; *Introducing The Hardline
  According To...* ....(COL)
  Slow Dancin' .... (KT)
Silver Threads & Golden Needles
  Honky Tonk Angels; *Honky Tonk Angels* ....(COL)
  Linda Ronstadt; *Don't Cry Now* ....(ASY)
  Greatest Hits ....(ASY)
  Hand Sown ....(CAP)
  Retrospective ....(CAP)
Sing My Heart Out
  O'Jays; *So Full Of Love* .... (PI)
Sleeping Heart
  Judds; *Talk About Love* ....(RCA)
  Why Not Me ....(RCA)
Soft Hearted Hana
  George Harrison; *George Harrison* .... (DKH)
Someday Sweetheart
  Bing Crosby; *Here Lies Love* ....(ALE)
  Peggy Lee; *You Can Depend On Me* ....(GLN)
  Zoot Sims; *Best Of* ....(PAB)
Someone Could Lose A Heart Tonight
  Eddie Rabbitt; *Best Of-Greatest Hits-#2* ....(WB)
  Number 1's ....(WB)
  Step By Step ....(LIB)
Something In My Heart
  Michel'le; *Michel'le* ....(RUT)
  Ricky Skaggs; *Country Boy* .... (EPI)
Somewhere In My Broken Heart
  Billy Dean; *Young Man* ....(CAP)
  Randy Travis; *No Holdin' Back* .... (WB)
Speak Softly-You're Talking To My Heart
  Gene Watson; *Greatest Hits* ....(MCA)
  Old Loves Never Die ....(MCA)
Steal Your Heart Away
  Bonnie Raitt; *Longing In Their Hearts* ....(CAP)
Still Right Here In My Heart
  Pure Prairie League; *45* ....(CAS)
Stop Draggin' My Heart Around
  Stevie Nicks & Tom Petty; *Bella Donna* .... (MOD)
  Timespace-Best Of Stevie Nicks ....(MOD)

Stop Steppin' On My Heart
Eddie Money; *Greatest Hits-Sound Of Money* ....(COL)
Stop, Look & Listen To Your Heart
Johnny Mathis; *I'm Coming Home* ....(COL)
Love Songs ....(COL)
Marvin Gaye & Diana Ross; *Diana & Marvin* .. (MOT)
Patti Austin; *Every Home Should Have One* ..... (QUE)
Stylistics; *45* ....(AMH)
Storm In The Heartland
Billy Ray Cyrus; *Storm In The Heartland* .... (MER)
Story Of A Broken Heart
Johnny Cash; *Original* ....(SUN)
Original Golden Hits #3 ....(SUN)
Rough Cut King Of Country Music ....(SUN)
The Man The World His Music ....(SUN)
Stout-Hearted Men
Barbra Streisand; *Simply Streisand* ....(COL)
Straight For The Heart
Toto; *Seventh One* ....(COL)
Whitesnake; *Whitesnake* ....(GEF)
Straight From My Heart
Sylvia; *Greatest Hits* ....(RCA)
Straight From The Heart
Bryan Adams; *Cuts Like A Knife* .... (A&M)
Coyote Sisters; *Coyote Sisters* .... (MOR)
Earth, Wind & Fire; *Powerlight* ....(COL)
Little Feat; *Down On The Farm* .... (WB)
Peabo Bryson; *Straight From The Heart* .... (ELE)
Straight To My Heart
Sting; *Nothing Like The Sun* .... (A&M)
Straight To The Heart
Crystal Gayle; *Best Of* ....(WB)
David Sanborn; *Straight To The Heart* ....(WB)
Straight To Your Heart
Bad English; *Backlash* ....(EPI)
Strangers Of The Heart
Heart; *Bad Animals* ....(CAP)
Strong Heart
T.G. Sheppard; *Biggest Hits* ....(COL)
Greatest Country Hits/'80s-1986 ....(COL)
More Hot Country Requests ....(EPI)
Subway Heart
Massacre; *Killing Time* ....(CEL)
Swear To Your Heart
Russell Hitchcock; *S* ....(HOL)
Sweetheart
Dan Hicks/Hot Licks; *Last Train To Hicksville* .. (MCA)
Frankie/Knockouts; *45* ....(MIL)
Thin Lizzy; *Chinatown* ....(WB)
Sweetheart From Venezuela
Harry Belafonte; *Pure Gold* ....(RCA)
Sweetheart Of The Rodeo
Emmylou Harris; *Ballad Of Sally Rose* ....(WB)
Sweetheart Of The Year
Ray Price; *Best Of* ....(COL)
Greatest Hits-#3 ....(SO)
Sweetheart You Done Me Wrong
Bill Monroe/Blue Grass Boys;
Essential-1945-1949 ....(COL)
Elvis Presley; *Million-Dollar Quartet* ....(RCA)
Sweethearts On Parade
Guy Lombardo; *Best Of* ....(CCB)
Best Of ....(MCA)
Louis Armstrong; *#7-You're Drivin' Me Crazy* ...(COL)
Pete Fountain; *Pete Fountain's New Orleans* ..... (MCA)
Roy Eldridge; *Happy Time* ....(PAB)
Take A Heart
Sorrows; *History Of British Rock-#4* .... (RHI)
Take Good Care Of My Heart
Whitney Houston & Jermaine Jackson; *Whitney*
Houston .... (ARI)
Take It Like A Man
Michelle Wright; *Now & Then* .... (ARI)
Today's Top Country ....(KT)
Take It To Heart
Michael McDonald; *Take It To Heart* ....(RPR)
Take Me To Heart
Neville Brothers; *Family Groove* ....(A&M)
Quarterflash; *Quarterflash/Take Another Picture* .. (GEF)
Take My Heart
Corey Hart; *Singles* ....(EMI)
Kool/Gang; *Something Special* .... (DL)
Neal McCoy; *At This Moment* ....(ATL)

Take These Chains From My Heart
Hank Williams; *24 Greatest Hits* ....(POL)
40 Greatest Hits ....(POL)
Ray Charles; *His Greatest Hits-#2* ....(DHL)
Take This Heart
Richard Marx; *Rush Street* ....(CAP)
Take This Heart Of Mine
Marvin Gaye; *Anthology* ....(MOT)
Motown Legends .... (MOT)
Talk To Me Lonesome Heart
James O'Gwynn; *Greatest Hits* ....(PLN)
Teardrops In My Heart
Marty Robbins; *Biggest Hits* ....(COL)
Sons Of The Pioneers; *Cool Water* ....(RCA)
Tell It To My Heart
Taylor Dayne; *Rock The First-#6* .... (SAN)
Tell It To My Heart .... (ARI)
Texas Heartache #1
Mickey Gilley; *Put Your Dreams Away* .... (EPI)
That Heart Belongs To Me
George Jones; *20 Golden Pieces Of* ....(BLD)
That's How A Heartache Begins
Patsy Cline; *Songwriter's Tribute* ....(MCA)
That's How Heartaches Are Made
Baby Washington; *Best Of* ....(CLT)
That's How Heartaches Are Made ....(CLT)
Marvelettes; *Anthology* ....(MOT)
Deliver-Singeles-1961-1971 ....(MOT)
That's What I Get (For Losin' You)
Hal Ketchum; *Every Little Word* ....(CRB)
That's What My Heart Needs
Otis Redding; *Pain In My Heart* ....(ATC)
Story ....(ATL)
That's When Your Heartaches Begin
Elvis Presley; *50 Worldwide Gold Award Hits-#1* (RCA)
Golden Records-#1 ....(RCA)
Million-Dollar Quartet ....(RCA)
Their Hearts Were Full Of Spring
Beach Boys; *Concert/'69-Live In London* ....(CAP)
Good Vibrations-Thirty Years Of ....(CAP)
Smiley Smile/Wild Honey ....(CAP)
There Goes My Heart
Mavericks; *What A Crying Shame* .... (MCA)
Nat King Cole; *Let's Fall In Love* ....(PAI)
Sings For Two In Love-& More ....(CAP)
There Goes My Heart Again
Holly Dunn; *Blue Rose Of Texas* ....(WB)
Greatest Country Dance Record Ever-#1 ....(WB)
Milestones-Greatest Hits ....(WB)
There Must Be An Angel Playing With...
Eurythmics; *Be Yourself Tonight* ....(RCA)
Greatest Hits .... (ARI)
Live-1983-1989 .... (ARI)
There's A Broken Heart For Every...
Mel Torme; *Songs Of New York* ....(ATL)
There's No Stopping Your Heart
Marie Osmond; *Best Of* ....(CCB)
Best Of Branson U.S.A.-#1 ....(CCB)
There's No Stopping Your Heart ....(CCB)
They Don't Make Hearts Like They Used To
Diamond Rio; *Diamond Rio* .... (ARI)
Thief Of Hearts
Madonna; *Erotica* ....(MAV)
Melissa Manchester; *ST/Thief Of Hearts* ....(CAS)
This Broken Heart
Mavericks; *From Hell To Paradise* ....(MCA)
This Heart
Aaron Tippin; *Read Between The Lines* ....(RCA)
Sweethearts Of The Rodeo; *Buffalo Zone* ....(COL)
This Heart Of Mine
Hi-Lo's; *Love Nest* ....(SSP)
Judy Garland & Victor Young/Orchestra; *Changing My*
Tune-Best Of Decca Years-#2 ....(DEC)
New Grass Revival; *Fly Through The Country* .....(FF)
This Heart Speaks For Itself
Bobbie Cryner; *Bobbie Cryner* ....(EPI)
This Missin' You Heart Of Mine
Sawyer Brown; *Somewhere In The Night* ....(LIB)

This Old Heart Of Mine
Isley Brothers; *25 Hard-To-Find Motown*
Classics-#3 .... (MOT)
Good Feeling Music/Big Chill Gen.-#1 .... (MOT)
Greatest By Holland/Dozier/Holland .... (MOT)
Motown Story: First 25 Years .... (MOT)
Motown Superstar Series-#6 .... (MOT)
This Old Heart Of Mine .... (MOT)
Rod Stewart; *Atlantic Crossing* .... (WB)
Rod Stewart & Ronald Isley; *Downtown*
Train/Selections-Storyteller .... (WB)
Storyteller-Complete Anthology-1964-1990 ...... (WB)
Thundering Hearts
John Mellencamp; *American Fool* .... (RIV)
Time (Clock Of The Heart)
Culture Club; *Kissing To Be Clever* .... (VIA)
To The Summer In Our Hearts
Curlew; *Bee* .... (CUN)
Live In Berlin .... (CUN)
Too Much On My Heart
Statler Brothers; *Partners In Rhyme* .... (MER)
Total Eclipse Of The Heart
Bonnie Tyler; *Billboard Top Hits-1983* .... (RHI)
Faster Than The Speed Of Night .... (COL)
Seems Like Yesterday-#4-Early '80s .... (KT)
Touch My Heart
Ray Price; *Greatest Hits-#2* .... (SO)
Toy Heart
Bill Monroe; *Columbia Historic Edition* .... (COL)
Bill Monroe/Blue Grass Boys;
Essential-1945-1949 .... (COL)
Bill Monroe/Flatt & Scruggs; *Bill Monroe/Flatt &*
Scruggs .... (ROU)
Ricky Skaggs; *Family & Friends* .... (ROU)
Trail Of Broken Hearts
k.d. lang/Reclines; *Absolute Torch & Twang* ..... (SIR)
Trolley Song
Judy Garland; *All-Time Greatest Hits* .... (CCB)
Best Of .... (MCA)
Original Broadway Cast; *Meet Me In St. Louis* .. (DRG)
True Heart
Oak Ridge Boys; *Country*
Classics-#11-1987-1988 .... (MSP)
Greatest Hits-#3 .... (MCA)
Heart Beat .... (MCA)
Tuesday Heartbreak
Stevie Wonder; *Talking Book* .... (MOT)
Two Hearts
Bruce Springsteen; *Live-1975-1985* .... (COL)
The River .... (COL)
Chris Isaak; *San Francisco Days* .... (RPR)
K.T. Oslin; *Love In A Small Town* .... (RCA)
Pebbles; *Pebbles* .... (MCA)
Phil Collins; *Serious Hits...Live!* .... (ATL)
Stephanie Mills; *Greatest Hits In My Life* ...... (CAS)
Two Hearts Beat As One
U2; *War* .... (ISL)
Two Of Hearts
Stacey Q; *Better Than Heaven* .... (ATL)
Dance Traxx-#2 .... (ATL)
Unborn Heart
Dan Hill; *Real Love* .... (COL)
Unbreakable Heart
Carlene Carter; *Little Love Letters* .... (GIA)
Unchain My Heart
Joe Cocker; *Live* .... (CAP)
Unchain My Heart .... (CAP)
Ray Charles; *Anthology* .... (RHI)
Greatest Hits-#1 .... (RHI)
His Greatest hits-#1 .... (DHL)
Valentine
Belinda Carlisle; *Runaway Horses* .... (MCA)
Bryan Ferry; *Boys & Girls* .... (WB)
Nils Lofgren & Bruce Springsteen; *Silver Lining* ..(RYK)
Psychedelic Furs; *World Outside* .... (COL)
Replacements; *Pleased To Meet Me* .... (SIR)
Toby Keith; *Toby Keith* .... (MER)
Willie Nelson; *Across The Borderline* .... (COL)
Valentine Day
Paul McCartney; *Gift Set* .... (CAP)
Paul McCartney .... (CAP)
Valentine's Day
ABC; *Lexicon Of Love* .... (MER)
Bruce Springsteen; *Tunnel Of Love* .... (COL)

James Taylor; *Never Die Young* .... (COL)
Victim Of A Broken Heart
Aldo Nova; *Portrait Of* .... (EPI)
Subject- .... (POR)
Victim Of The Modern Heart
Earth, Wind & Fire; *Touch Of The World* .... (COL)
Walk Softly On This Heart Of Mine
Bill Monroe; *Country Music Hall Of Fame* ...... (MCA)
Joey Welz; *Lovin' My Country* .... (CPC)
Kentucky HeadHunters; *Pickin' On Nashville* .... (MER)
Walkin' A Broken Heart
Don Williams; *Cafe Carolina* .... (MCA)
Greatest Hits .... (MSP)
Walkin', Talkin'...Beatin' Broken Heart
Highway 101; *Country's Greatest Hits-#4* .... (PRY)
Paint The Town .... (WB)
War Of The Hearts
Sade; *Promise* .... (POR)
Warm Your Heart
Aaron Neville; *Warm Your Heart* .... (A&M)
Drifters; *Let The Boogie Woogie Roll-Greatest Hits* (ATL)
Way We Make A Broken Heart
Rosanne Cash; *30 Years Of #1 Hits-#16* .... (COL)
Greatest Country Hits/'80s-1987 .... (COL)
Hits 1979-1989 .... (COL)
King's Record Shop .... (COL)
Love Gets Strange-Songs Of John Hiatt .... (RHI)
Ry Cooder; *Borderline* .... (WB)
Welcome To Heartlight
Kenny Loggins; *High Adventure* .... (COL)
Whaleheart
Marnie Jones; *Grace* .... (THR)
What Becomes Of The Brokenhearted
Jimmy Ruffin; *Motown Story* .... (MOT)
Jimmy & David Ruffin; *Motown Superstar*
Series-#8 .... (MOT)
Paul Young; *ST/Fried Green Tomatoes* .... (MCA)
When The Heart Rules The Mind
GTR; *GTR* .... (ARI)
Where Do Broken Hearts Go
Whitney Houston; *Whitney* .... (ARI)
Where Do You Keep Your Heart
Tommy Dorsey & Frank Sinatra; *All-Time Greatest*
Hits-#4 .... (RCA)
Dorsey/Sinatra Sessions-#1 .... (BLU)
Where Does My Heart Beat Now?
Celine Dion; *Unison* .... (EPI)
Wild Heart
Stevie Nicks; *Wild Heart* .... (MOD)
Wild Heart Of The Young
Karla Bonoff; *Wild Heart Of The Young* .... (COL)
Wild Hearted Son
Cult; *Ceremony* .... (SIR)
Wild Hearts
Roy Orbison; *Legendary* .... (SSP)
Wild Hearts Run Out Of Time
Roy Orbison; *King Of Hearts* .... (VIA)
With A Song In My Heart
Ella Fitzgerald; *Rodgers & Hart Songbook* ...... (VRV)
Jerry Vale; *Standing Ovation!-Carnegie Hall*
Concert .... (COL)
Jose Carreras; *The 3 Tenors In Concert 1994* .... (TEL)
Mario Lanza; *Be My Love* .... (RCA)
Stevie Wonder; *With A Song In My Heart* ...... (MOT)
With Each Beat Of My Heart
Stevie Wonder; *Characters* .... (MOT)
With Every Beat Of My Heart
Taylor Dayne; *Can't Fight Fate* .... (ARI)
Woman Of Heart & Mind
Joni Mitchell; *For The Roses* .... (ASY)
Joni Mitchell/L.A. Express; *Miles Of Aisles* ...... (ASY)
Wooden Heart
Elvis Presley; *50 Worldwide Gold Award*
Hits-#1&2 .... (RCA)
For Children .... (RCA)
ST/G.I. Blues .... (RCA)
Words By Heart
Billy Ray Cyrus; *It Won't Be The Last* .... (MER)
You Can't Run Away From Your Heart
Lacy J. Dalton; *You Can't Run Away From Your*
Heart .... (COL)
Patty Loveless; *On Down The Line* .... (MCA)
You Could've Heard A Heart Break
Johnny Lee; *Workin' For A Livin'* .... (FW)

You Let Your Heart Go Too Fast
Spin Doctors; *Turn It Upside Down* .... (EPI)
You Put The Beat In My Heart
Eddie Rabbitt; *Best Of/Greatest Hits-#2* .... (WB)
(You Sure Know Your Way) Around My Heart
Louise Mandrell & R.C. Bannon; *Me & My R.C.* .(RCA)
Young At Heart
Bing Crosby; *Radio Years* .... (CRS)
Frank Sinatra; *At The Movies* .... (CAP)
Sinatra's Sinatra .... (RPR)
Ray Price; *Portrait Of A Singer* .... (SO)
Rosemary Clooney; *Essence Of* .... (COL)
Young Turks
Rod Stewart; *Absolutely Live* .... (WB)
Downtown Train-Storyteller Selections .... (WB)
Storyteller/Complete Anthology-1964-1990 ...... (WB)
Tonight I'm Yours .... (WB)
Your Cheatin' Heart
Elvis Presley; *Elvis For Everyone* .... (RCA)
Welcome To My World .... (RCA)
Frankie Laine; *16 Greatest Hits* .... (TRP)
Greatest Hits .... (COL)
Hank Williams; *16 Great Hits* .... (EVR)
24 Greatest Hits .... (POL)
40 Greatest Hits .... (POL)
Hank Williams, Jr.; *Very Best Of* .... (POL)
Jerry Lee Lewis; *Golden Rock Hits Of* .... (SMA)
Live At The Star Club-Hamburg 1964 .... (RHI)
Patsy Cline; *Story* .... (MCA)
ST/Sweet Dreams .... (MCA)
Ray Charles; *Greatest Hits-#2* .... (RHI)
Your Heart's Not In It
Janie Fricke; *17 Greatest Hits* ....(COL)
First Word In Memory ....(COL)
Greatest Country Hits!'80s-1984 ....(COL)
Very Best Of ....(COL)
You'll Never Get To Heaven (If You...)
Dionne Warwick; *Anthology-1962-1971* .... (RHI)
Dionne Warwick ....(EVR)
Greatest Hits ....(EVR)
Hot! Live & Otherwise .... (ARI)
Say A Little Prayer .... (DHL)
Stylistics; *Best Of-#2* ....(AMH)
You're In My Heart
Rod Stewart; *Absolutely Live* .... (WB)
Footloose & Fancy Free .... (WB)
Greatest Hits .... (WB)
Storyteller/Complete Anthology-1964-1990 ...... (WB)
You're The Best Break This Old Heart...
Ed Bruce; *Greatest Hits* .... (MCA)
One To One .... (MCA)
You've Still Got A Place In My Heart
George Jones; *45* .... (EPI)
Zing Went The Strings Of My Heart
Coasters; *Greatest Hits* ....(ATC)
Rare Soul-Beach Music Classics-#1 .... (RHI)
Frank Sinatra; *Reprise Collection* ....(RPR)
Judy Garland; *At Carnegie Hall* .... (CAP)
Best Of .... (MCA)
Best Of The Decca Years-#1-Hits! .... (DEC)
The One & Only .... (CAP)

HEAVEN

See Also: ANGELS, DEATH, GOD, HAPPINESS,
HELL

All That Heaven Will Allow
Bruce Springsteen; *Tunnel Of Love* ....(COL)
All This And Heaven Too
Tommy Dorsey & Frank Sinatra; *All-Time Greatest*
Hits-#4 ....(RCA)
Dorsey/Sinatra Sessions-#1 ....(RCA)
All You Want Is Heaven
Daryl Hall & John Oates; *X-Static* ....(RCA)
Am I In Heaven
Del Reeves; *45* ....(OOP)
And The Heavens Cried
Anthony Newley; *Genuis Of* ....(LON)
Anywhere Like Heaven
James Taylor; *Sweet Baby James* ....(WB)
April 24, 1981
Rick Springfield; *Success Hasn't Spoiled Me Yet* ..(RCA)

Are You Building A Temple In Heaven
Hank Williams; *I'm So Lonesome I Could*
Cry-1949 ....(POL)
Body Heavenly
Full Force; *Get Busy 1 Time* ....(COL)
Breath Away From Heaven
George Harrison; *Cloud Nine* .... (DKH)
Buying My Way Into Heaven
Sammy Hagar; *Unboxed* .... (GEF)
Chance For Heaven
Christopher Cross; *Official Music Of The XXIIIrd*
Olympiad ....(COL)
Circus Of Heaven
Yes; *Tormato* .... (ATL)
Do You Wanna Go To Heaven
Original Broadway Cast; *Big River* .... (MCA)
T.G. Sheppard; *All-Time Greatest Hits* .... (WB)
Greatest Hits .... (WB)
Smooth Sailin' .... (WB)
Edge Of Heaven
Wham!; *Music From The Edge Of Heaven* ....(COL)
Fifty Miles Of Elbow Room
Iris DeMent; *Infamous Angel* ....(PHO)
Infamous Angel .... (WB)
Norman & Nancy Blake; *Blind Dog* .... (ROU)
Red Clay Ramblers; *Twisted Laurel* .... (FF)
Fish & Whistle
John Prine; *Bruised Orange* .... (ASY)
Ghetto Heaven
Family Stand; *Chain* .... (ATL)
Go To Heaven
Grateful Dead; *Go To Heaven* .... (ARI)
God Blessed Texas
Little Texas; *Big Time* .... (WB)
Good Girls Go To Heaven
Charlie Floyd; *Charlie Floyd* .... (LIB)
Great Gig In The Sky
Pink Floyd; *Dark Side Of The Moon* ....(CAP)
Gift Set ....(CAP)
Green Rolling Hills
Bottle Hill; *Rumor In Their Own Time-#1* ....(BIO)
Emmylou Harris; *Quarter Moon In A Ten Cent*
Town .... (WB)
Guitar Heaven
Neil Diamond; *On The Way To The Sky* ....(COL)
Hands To Heaven
Breathe; *All That Jazz* .... (A&M)
Heaven
Bryan Adams; *Reckless* .... (A&M)
Chris Rea; *Auberge* ....(ATC)
Joan Armatrading; *Track Record* .... (A&M)
Joe Cocker; *Cocker* ....(CAP)
Pere Ubu; *Terminal Tower-Archival Collection* .... (TT)
Psychedelic Furs; *All Of This & Nothing* ....(COL)
Mirror Moves ....(COL)
Robyn Hitchcock/Egyptians; *Fegmania* ....(SLS)
Rolling Stones; *Tattoo You* ....(RS)
Simply Red; *45* .... (A&M)
Talking Heads; *Fear Of Music* .... (SIR)
Heaven Above Me
Peabo Bryson & Roberta Flack; *Born To Love* ...(CAP)
Peabo Bryson Collection ....(CAP)
Heaven Can Be Anywhere
Charlie Daniels Band; *Midnight Wind* .... (EPI)
Heaven Can Wait
Iron Maiden; *Somewhere In Time* ....(CAP)
Meatloaf; *Bat Out Of Hell* .... (EPI)
Paul Young; *Other Voices* ....(COL)
Heaven Can't Be Found
Hank Williams, Jr.; *Born To Boogie* ....(W/C)
Greatest Hits III ....(W/C)
Heaven Every Day
Mel Tillis/Statesiders; *Best Of* ....(MGM)
Heaven Help
Lenny Kravitz; *Are You Gonna Go My Way* ..... (VIA)
Heaven Help Me
Deon Estus; *Spell* .... (MIK)
Heaven Help The Fool
Bob Weir; *Heaven Help The Fool* .... (ARI)
Heaven Help The Lonely
Willie Nile; *Places I Have Never Been* ....(COL)

Heaven Help Us All
Stevie Wonder; *Greatest Hits-#2* .... (MOT)
  Love Songs-20 Classic Hits .... (MOT)
  My Cherie Amour/Signed Sealed Delivered ..... (MOT)
  Signed Sealed & Delivered .... (MOT)
Heaven In The Back Seat
Eddie Money; *Right Here* .... (COL)
Heaven In Your Arms
R.J.'s Latest Arrival; *Hold On* .... (MAN)
Heaven In Your Eyes
Loverboy; *Big Ones* .... (COL)
  ST/Top Gun .... (COL)
Heaven Is 10 Zillion Light Years Away
Stevie Wonder; *Fulfillingness' First Finale* .... (MOT)
Heaven Is A Place On Earth
Belinda Carlisle; *Greenpeace/Rainbow Warriors* .. (GEF)
  Heaven On Earth .... (MCA)
Heaven Is Here
Anne Murray; *Country Collection* .... (CAP)
  New Kind Of Feeling .... (CAP)
Heaven Is In Your Mind
Three Dog Night; *Best Of* .... (MSP)
Traffic; *Mr. Fantasy* .... (ISL)
  Winwood .... (UA)
Heaven Knows
Commodores; *Heroes/Commodores* .... (MOT)
Donna Summer; *Live & More* .... (CAS)
  On The Radio .... (CAS)
  Summer Collection .... (MER)
Grass Roots; *Their 16 Greatest Hits* .... (MCA)
Lalah Hathaway; *Lalah Hathaway* .... (VIA)
Robert Plant; *Now And Zen* .... (EPR)
Heaven Must Be Missing An Angel
Tavares; *Best Of* .... (CAP)
  Sky High .... (CAP)
Heaven Must Have Sent You
Bonnie Pointer; *Greatest Songs By*
Holland-Dozier-Holland .... (MOT)
  Motown Memories-#4-Where Were You... ...... (MOT)
  Top 10 With A Bullet-Motown Dance .... (MOT)
Heaven On Earth
Platters; *16 Greatest Hits* .... (TRP)
  Anthology .... (RHI)
  Encore Of Golden Hits .... (MER)
  Red Sails In The Sunset .... (ALL)
Heaven On The 7th Floor
Paul Nicholas; *45* .... (OOP)
Heaven On Their Minds
Original London Cast; *ST/Jesus Christ Superstar* (MCA)
Heaven Only Knows
Emmylou Harris; *Bluebird* .... (RPR)
Richard Marx; *Richard Marx* .... (EMI)
Shangri-Las; *Best Of* .... (BCT)
  Golden Hits Of .... (MER)
  Remember The Shangri-Las At Their Best .... (CLT)
Heaven Or Las Vegas
Cocteau Twins; *Heaven Or Las Vegas* .... (CAP)
Heaven Sent
INXS; *Welcome To Wherever You Are* .... (ATL)
Heaven Sent You
Stanley Clarke; *Time Exposure* .... (EPI)
Heaven Tonight
Cheap Trick; *Heaven Tonight* .... (EPI)
Heaven & Hell
Assembled Multitude; *45* .... (ERI)
Black Sabbath; *Heaven & Hell* .... (WB)
  Live Evil .... (WB)
Easybeats; *Nuggets-Classic Collection/'60s* .... (RHI)
Who; *Who's Missing* .... (MCA)
Willie Nelson; *Phases & Stages* .... (ATL)
Heavenly Bodies
Earl Thomas Conley; *Somewhere Between Right And*
Wrong .... (RCA)
Heavenly Body
Chi-Lites; *Ear Candy-#2* .... (20)
  Heavenly Body .... (20)
Heavenly Father
Castelles; *Home Of Grand Records* .... (CLT)
  Sweet Sounds Of .... (CLT)
Heavenly Homes
Be Bop Deluxe; *Sunburst Finish* .... (CAP)
Heaven, Hell Or Houston
ZZ Top; *El Loco* .... (WB)
  Six Pack .... (WB)

Heaven's Already Here
Collective Soul; *Hints Allegations And Things Left*
Unsaid .... (ATL)
Heaven's On Fire
Kiss; *Animalize* .... (MER)
  Hear 'N Aid .... (MER)
  Smashes Thrashes & Hits .... (MER)
Heaven's Trail
Tesla; *Five Man Acoustical Jam* .... (GEF)
  Great Radio Controversy .... (GEF)
Hobo Heaven
Boxcar Willie; *Boxcar Willie* .... (DOT)
Holdin' Heaven
Tracy Byrd; *Tracy Byrd* .... (MCA)
I Dreamed Of A Hillbilly Heaven
Tex Ritter; *An American Legend* .... (CAP)
  Best Of .... (CAP)
  Hillbilly Heaven .... (CAP)
  Opry Legends .... (CAP)
If Heaven Could Find Me
Ambrosia; *Life Beyond L.A.* .... (WB)
If I Ever Lose This Heaven
Quincy Jones; *Best* .... (A&M)
  Body Heat .... (A&M)
  Classics-#3 .... (A&M)
  I Heard That! .... (A&M)
If There's A God In Heaven
Elton John; *Blue Moves* .... (MCA)
If You Wanna Get To Heaven
Hank Williams, Jr.; *High Notes* .... (W/C)
Ozark Mountain Daredevils; *Best* .... (A&M)
  It's Alive .... (A&M)
  Ozark Mountain Daredevils .... (A&M)
It's A Short Walk From Heaven To Hell
John Schneider; *Country Classics-#5-1985-1986* (MCA)
  Greatest Hits .... (MCA)
  Tryin' To Outrun The Wind .... (MCA)
I'm Free (Heaven Help The Man)
Kenny Loggins; *ST/Footloose* .... (COL)
Jackie Wilson Said (I'm In Heaven...)
Van Morrison; *Best Of* .... (MER)
  St. Dominic's Preview .... (WB)
  ST/Queen's Logic .... (EPI)
Knockin' On Heaven's Door
Bob Dylan; *At Budokan* .... (COL)
  Biograph .... (COL)
  Rock Classics/'70s .... (COL)
  ST/Pat Garrett & Billy The Kid .... (COL)
Bob Dylan/Band; *Before The Flood* .... (COL)
Bob Dylan/Grateful Dead; *Dylan & The Dead* ...(COL)
Eric Clapton; *Crossroads* .... (POL)
  Time Pieces-Best Of .... (RSO)
Guns N' Roses; *ST/Days Of Thunder* .... (DGC)
  Use Your Illusion II .... (GEF)
Jerry Garcia; *Run For The Roses* .... (ARI)
Randy Crawford; *Rich & Poor* .... (WB)
Let The Mystery Be
10,000 Maniacs; *Few & Far Between* .... (ELE)
Iris DeMent; *Infamous Angel* .... (PHO)
  Infamous Angel .... (WB)
Little Bit Of Heaven
Natalie Cole; *Dangerous* .... (MOD)
Ray Charles; *Seven Spanish Angels & Other Hits* .(COL)
Maid In Heaven
Be Bop Deluxe; *Best Of-Raiding The Divine*
Archive .... (CAP)
  Life In The Air Age .... (OOP)
Marriage Made In Heaven
Bob Crewe; *Motivation* .... (ELE)
My Blue Heaven
Artie Shaw; *Complete-#4* .... (RCA)
  This Is .... (RCA)
Fats Domino; *Greatest Hits* .... (EVR)
  Legendary Masters .... (UA)
  My Blue Heaven-Best Of-#1 .... (EMI)
  Oldies But Goodies-#10 .... (OSR)
Frank Sinatra; *Gift Set* .... (CAP)
  Swingin' Session .... (CAP)
No Telephone In Heaven
Doc Watson; *My Dear Old Southern Home* .... (SH)
Now You're In Heaven
Julian Lennon; *Mr. Jordan* .... (ATL)
Pennies From Heaven
Billie Holiday; *16 Most Requested Songs* .... (COL)

Bing Crosby; *Pennies From Heaven* ....(POE)
Frank Sinatra; *Songs For Swingin' Lovers* ....(CAP)
Lester Young; *Birdland All-Stars At Carnegie Hall* (RLL)
Louis Armstrong; *RCA Victor Jazz-First
Half-Century* ....(RCA)
Mandy Patinkin; *Mandy Patinkin* ....(COL)
Skyliners; *Greatest Hits* ....(OSR)
Stan Getz; *Essential-Getz Songbook* ....(VRV)
Stephane Grappelli; *Satin Doll-#1-Best Of* ...... (VAN)
Poor Wayfaring Stranger
Jim Hendricks; *Appalachian Memories-Front Porch
Favor.* ....(BEN)
Jo Stafford' *American Folk Songs* ....(CRN)
Rock & Roll Heaven
Righteous Brothers; *Anthology-1962-1974* .... (RHI)
Rockin' Heaven Down
Heart; *Bebe Le Strange* ....(EPI)
Say Hello To Heaven
Temple Of The Dog; *Temple Of The Dog* ....(A&M)
Seven Steps To Heaven
Miles Davis; *Greatest Hits* ....(COL)
Seven Steps To Heaven ....(COL)
Shall We Gather At The River?
Chuck Wagon Gang; *16 Country-Gospel
Favorites* ....(MCA)
Tennessee Ernie Ford; *All-Time Greatest Hymns* .(CCB)
Sings 22 Favorite Hymns ....(RAN)
She's Playing Hell Trying To Get Me...
George Strait; *Strait Country* ....(MCA)
Somebody Up There Likes Me
David Bowie; *Young Americans* ....(RYK)
Reba McEntire; *Sweet Sixteen* ....(MCA)
Somebody's Knockin'
Terri Gibbs; *Best Of* ....(MCA)
Country Gold ....(PRY)
Country Music Classics-#6-1980-1985 ... (KT)
Something Happened On The Way To Heaven
Phil Collins; *Serious Hits...Live!* ....(ATL)
...But Seriously ....(ATL)
Stairway To Heaven
Led Zeppelin; *4* ....(ATL)
Remasters ....(ATL)
Led Zeppelin (collection) ....(ATL)
ST/Song Remains The Same .... (SS)
Neil Sedaka; *All-Time Greatest Hits* ....(RCA)
Sings-His Greatest Hits ....(RCA)
O'Jays; *Collector's Items* .... (PI)
Family Reunion .... (PI)
Greatest Hits .... (PI)
Stanley Jordan; *Flying Home* .... (EMI)
Swing Low, Sweet Chariot
Eric Clapton; *Time Pieces-Best Of* .... (POL)
Glenn Miller/Orchestra; *Moonlight Serenade* .... (RAN)
Hi-Lo's; *Suddenly It's The Hi-Lo's* ....(COL)
Jerry Garcia Acoustic Band; *Almost Acoustic* ... (GRD)
Joan Baez; *From Every Stage* ....(A&M)
Peggy Lee; *Best Of* ....(MCA)
Take A Little Trip
Alabama; *American Pride* ....(RCA)
Taxi To Heaven
Pray For Rain; *ST/Sid & Nancy* ....(MCA)
Tears In Heaven
Eric Clapton; *ST/Rush* ....(RPR)
Unplugged ....(RPR)
Teenage Heaven
Eddie Cochran; *Greatest Hits* ....(CCB)
Legendary Masters ....(EMI)
Johnny Cymbal; *Teen Idols* ....(MSP)
Thank Heaven For Little Girls
Maurice Chevalier; *ST/Gigi* ....(SSP)
Merle Haggard & Janie Fricke; *It's All In The
Game* ....(EPI)
That Lucky Old Sun
Asleep At The Wheel; *Western Standard Time* ...(EPI)
Bing Crosby; *Radio Years* ....(CRS)
Frankie Laine; *16 Most Requested Songs* ....(COL)
Golden Hits ....(MER)
Greatest Hits ....(COL)
Jerry Garcia Band; *Jerry Garcia Band* ....(ARI)
Louis Armstrong; *Greatest Hits* ....(CCB)
Ray Charles; *Anthology* ....(RHI)
Willie Nelson; *Sound In Your Mind* ....(COL)
That's Heaven To Me
Sam Cooke; *Man & His Music* ....(RCA)

They Took The Stars Out Of Heaven
Floyd Tillman; *Country Music Hall Of Fame* ....(MCA)
This Is Heaven To Me
Billie Holiday; *From The Original Decca Masters* (MCA)
Story ....(MCA)
This Must Be Heaven
Rick Astley; *Free* ....(RCA)
Thought I'd Died & Gone To Heaven
Bryan Adams; *Waking Up The Neighbours* ......(A&M)
Three Hundred Pounds Of Heavenly Joy
Big Twist/Mellow Fellows; *Alligator Records 20th
Anniversary Coll.* ....(ALG)
Howlin' Wolf; *Chess Box-Willie Dixon* ....(CSS)
Three Steps To Heaven
Eddie Cochran; *Greatest Hits* ....(CCB)
Legendary Masters ....(EMI)
Ticket To Heaven
Dire Straits; *On Every Street* ....(WB)
Too Much Heaven
Bee Gees; *Greatest* ....(POL)
Up In Heaven
Clash; *Sandinista* ....(EPI)
Up To Heaven (You Lift Me)
Reba McEntire; *Best Of* ....(MER)
Feel The Fire ....(MER)
Waltz Me To Heaven
Waylon Jennings; *Greatest Hits-#2* ....(RCA)
We Have Heaven
Yes; *Fragile* ....(ATL)
Wear Your Love Like Heaven
Donovan; *Gift From A Flower To A Garden* ......(EPI)
Greatest Hits ....(EPI)
Summer Of Love ....(RHI)
Troubadour-Definitive Collection ....(EPI)
Sarah McLachlan; *Solace* ....(ARI)
When Did You Leave Heaven?
Bob Dylan; *Down In The Groove* ....(COL)
Hank Crawford; *After Hours* ....(ATL)
Will There Be A Shopping Mall In Heaven?
Reverend Billy C. Wirtz; *Deep Fried & Sanctified* . (HT)
You Are My Heaven
Roberta Flack & Donny Hathaway; *Featuring Donny
Hathaway* ....(ATL)
Roberta Flack & Peabo Bryson; *Best Of* ....(ATL)
Live & More ....(ATL)
Roberta Flack & Peabo Bryson ....(ATL)
You Make Your Own Heaven & Hell Right...
Temptations; *Psychedelic Shack* ....(MOT)
Your Flag Decal Won't Get You Into...
John Prine; *John Prine* ....(ATL)
You'll Never Get To Heaven (If You...)
Dionne Warwick; *Anthology-1962-1971* ....(RHI)
Dionne Warwick ....(EVR)
Greatest Hits ....(EVR)
Hot! Live & Otherwise ....(ARI)
Say A Little Prayer ....(DHL)
Stylistics; *Best Of-#2* ....(AMH)

HELL

See Also: DEATH, DEVILS, GOD, HEAVEN

Ain't Life Hell
Hank Cochran; *Hank Cochran* ....(CAP)
And All Hell Broke Loose
Billie Hutch; *In Tune* ....(WHI)
Aw, To Hell With Love
Jeri Fakter/Backporch Symphony; *Jeri Fakter/Backporch
Symphony* ....(AVI)
Bat Out Of Hell
Meatloaf; *Bat Out Of Hell* ....(EPI)
Beer Drinkers & Hell Raisers
ZZ Top; *Best Of* ....(WB)
Six Pack ....(WB)
Tres Hombres ....(WB)
Cold Day In Hell
Gary Moore; *After Hours* ....(CHS)
Devil Made Texas
Hermes Nye; *Cowboy Songs On Folkways* ......(FLW)
Texas Folk Songs ....(FLW)
Edge Of Heaven
Wham!; *Music From The Edge Of Heaven* ......(COL)
From Hell To Paradise
Mavericks; *From Hell To Paradise* ....(MCA)

Go To Hell
Alice Cooper; *Goes To Hell* .... (WB)
    Show .... (WB)
Megadeth; *ST/Bill & Ted's Bogus Journey* .... (ISC)
Good Day In Hell
Eagles; *On The Border* .... (ASY)
Heaven & Hell
Assembled Multitude; *45* .... (ERI)
Black Sabbath; *Heaven & Hell* .... (WB)
    Live Evil .... (WB)
Easybeats; *Nuggets-Classic Collection/'60s* .... (RHI)
Who; *Who's Missing* .... (MCA)
Willie Nelson; *Phases & Stages* .... (ATL)
Heaven, Hell Or Houston
ZZ Top; *El Loco* .... (WB)
    Six Pack .... (WB)
Hell
James Brown; *Hell* .... (OOP)
Hell Ain't A Bad Place To Be
AC/DC; *If You Want Blood You've Got It* .... (ATL)
    Let There Be Rock .... (ATC)
Hell Bent For Leather
Judas Priest; *Hell Bent For Leather* .... (COL)
Hell Cat
Scorpions; *Best Of* .... (RCA)
    Virgin Killer .... (RCA)
Hell Is For Children
Pat Benatar; *Best Shots* .... (CHR)
    Crimes Of Passion .... (CHR)
    Live From Earth .... (CHR)
    MTV's Rock & Roll To Go .... (ELE)
    ST/American Pop .... (MCA)
Hell To Pay
Bonnie Raitt; *Longing In Their Hearts* .... (CAP)
Hell & Half Of Georgia
Owen Brothers; *Audiograph Live* .... (AUD)
    Fool Of Fools .... (AUD)
Hellbound Train
Savoy Brown; *Greatest Hits-Live In Concert* ..... (TOW)
    Hellbound Train .... (PRT)
    London Collection-Best Of .... (LON)
Helldriver
Accept; *Accept* .... (PVC)
    Midnight Highway .... (PVC)
Hells Bells
AC/DC; *Back In Black* .... (ATL)
    Who Made Who .... (ATL)
Highway To Hell
AC/DC; *Back In Black* .... (ATL)
    Classic Rock-1966-1988 .... (ATL)
    Highway To Hell .... (ATL)
Hot Rails To Hell
Blue Oyster Cult; *Career Of Evil* .... (COL)
    Extraterrestrial Live .... (COL)
    Metal Giants .... (COL)
    On Your Feet Or On Your Knees .... (COL)
    Tyranny & Mutation .... (COL)
If Hell Had A Jukebox
Travis Tritt; *It's All About To Change* .... (WB)
If You Wanna Get To Heaven
Hank Williams, Jr.; *High Notes* .... (W/C)
Ozark Mountain Daredevils; *Best* .... (A&M)
    It's Alive .... (A&M)
    Ozark Mountain Daredevils .... (A&M)
It's A Short Walk From Heaven To Hell
John Schneider; *Country Classics-#5-1985-1986* (MCA)
    Greatest Hits .... (MCA)
    Tryin' To Outrun The Wind .... (MCA)
Nature Trail To Hell
Weird Al Yankovic; *In 3-D* .... (RAR)
One Hell Of A Woman
Mac Davis; *Greatest Hits* .... (COL)
Payback Is Hell
Candy Fresh; *Just The Way I Like It* .... (W/I)
Raisin' Hell
Elvin Bishop; *Raisin' Hell* .... (CPC)
Rock You To Hell
Grim Reaper; *Rock You To Hell* .... (RCA)
Run Like Hell
Pink Floyd; *Delicate Sound Of Thunder* .... (COL)
    Knebworth-The Album .... (POL)
    The Wall .... (COL)
Roger Waters; *The Wall Live In Berlin* .... (MER)

Season In Hell (Fire Suite)
John Cafferty/Beaver Brown Band; *ST/Eddie & The
    Cruisers* .... (SCO)
See You In Hell
Grim Reaper; *See You In Hell* .... (RCA)
See You In Hell (Don't Be Late)
Yngwie Malmsteen; *Eclipse* .... (POL)
See You In Hell, Blind Boy
Ry Cooder; *ST/Crossroads* .... (WB)
She's Playing Hell Trying To Get Me...
George Strait; *Strait Country* .... (MCA)
Storming The Gates Of Hell
Riot; *Privilege Of Power* .... (EPA)
Straight To Hell
Clash; *Combat Rock* .... (EPI)
    On Broadway .... (EPI)
    Story Of-#1 .... (EPI)
Drivin' N' Cryin'; *Mystery Road* .... (ISL)
Summer In Hell
Fred Schneider; *Fred Schneider* .... (RPR)
Sun Also Rises In Hell
XYZ; *Hungry* .... (CAP)
There's A Place In Hell For Me & My...
Morrissey; *Kill Uncle* .... (SIR)
To Hell With Poverty!
Gang Of Four; *Brief History Of The Twentieth
    Century* .... (WB)
To Hell With The Devil
Stryper; *Can't Stop The
    Rock-Collection-1984-1991* .... (HOL)
    To Hell With The Devil .... (HOL)
War Is Hell (On The Homefront Too)
T.G. Sheppard; *All-Time Greatest Hits* .... (WB)
    Greatest Hits .... (WB)
    Perfect Stranger .... (WB)
Whiskey Bent & Hell Bound
Hank Williams, Jr.; *Greatest Hits* .... (WB)
    Whiskey Bent & Hell Bound .... (W/C)
You Make Your Own Heaven & Hell Right...
Temptations; *Psychedelic Shack* .... (MOT)

HELP, Rescue, Save

911 Is A Joke
Public Enemy; *Fear Of A Black Planet* .... (DFJ)
    Yo! MTV Raps .... (JVA)
Both Sides Of The Story
Phil Collins; *Both Sides* .... (ATL)
Can You Help Me
Jesse Johnson's Revue; *Jesse Johnson's Revue* ... (A&M)
Can't Help Falling In Love
Elvis Presley; *From Memphis To Vegas* .... (RCA)
    In Person .... (RCA)
    Legendary Performer #1 .... (RCA)
    ST/Blue Hawaii .... (RCA)
    TV Special .... (RCA)
Julio Iglesias; *Starry Night* .... (COL)
UB40; *Promises & Lies* .... (VIA)
    ST/Sliver .... (VIA)
Can't Help Lovin' Dat Man
Lena Horne; *20 Golden Pieces Of* .... (BLD)
    Jazz Master .... (DRG)
    Jazzy Ladies .... (DHL)
    Live On Broadway .... (QUE)
Catch Me I'm Falling
Pretty Poison; *ST/Hiding Out* .... (VIA)
Cry For Help
Rick Astley; *Free* .... (RCA)
Cry For Mercy
Raindogs; *Lost Souls* .... (ATC)
Dreamlover
Mariah Carey; *Music Box* .... (COL)
Emotional Rescue
Rolling Stones; *Emotional Rescue* .... (RS)
    Rewind (1971-1984) .... (RS)
For You
Bruce Springsteen; *Greetings From Asbury Park,
    N.J.* .... (COL)
Greg Kihn; *Kihnsolidation* .... (RHI)
    Unkihntrollable-Live .... (RHI)
Manfred Mann's Earth Band; *Chance* .... (WB)

Girl Can't Help It
Journey; *Greatest Hits* ....(COL)
   Raised On Radio ....(COL)
Little Richard; *18 Greatest Hits* .... (RHI)
   Greatest Hits ....(EVR)
   Super Oldies!'50s-#3 ....(AUF)
   Well Alright! .... (SPE)
Heaven Help
Lenny Kravitz; *Are You Gonna Go My Way* ..... (VIA)
Heaven Help Me
Deon Estus; *Spell* .... (MIK)
Heaven Help The Fool
Bob Weir; *Heaven Help The Fool* .... (ARI)
Heaven Help The Lonely
Willie Nile; *Places I Have Never Been* ....(COL)
Heaven Help Us All
Stevie Wonder; *Greatest Hits-#2* .... (MOT)
   Love Songs-20 Classic Hits .... (MOT)
   My Cherie Amour/Signed Sealed Delivered ..... (MOT)
   Signed Sealed & Delivered .... (MOT)
Help Is On Its Way
Little River Band; *Diamantina Cocktail* ....(CAP)
   Greatest Hits ....(CAP)
Help Me
Elvis Presley; *Promised Land* .... (RCA)
Joni Mitchell; *Court & Spark* .... (ASY)
Larry Gatlin; *Rain-Rainbow* ....(COL)
Help Me Angel
Steve Winwood; *Talking Back To The Night* ...... (ISL)
Help Me Hold On
Travis Tritt; *Country Club* .... (WB)
Help Me Make It Through The Night
Bryan Ferry; *Another Time Another Place* .... (RPR)
Gladys Knight/Pips; *Anthology* .... (MOT)
   Compact Command Performance .... (MOT)
Joan Baez; *Blessed Are* .... (VAN)
   Hits/Greatest & Others .... (VAN)
Sammi Smith; *Super Hits/'70s-Have A Nice
   Day-#4* .... (RHI)
Willie Nelson; *Greatest Hits & Some That Will Be* (COL)
   Sings Kristofferson ....(COL)
   Sweet Memories ....(RCA)
Help Me Make It Through The Yard
Pinkard & Bowden; *Honky Tonk Country* .... (WB)
   Writers In Disguise .... (WB)
Help Me Make It (To My Rocking Chair)
B.J. Thomas; *45* .... (MCA)
Help Me Rhonda
Beach Boys; *Billboard Top Rock 'N' Roll
   Hits-1965* .... (RHI)
   California Girls ....(CAP)
   Dance Dance Dance ....(CAP)
   Endless Summer ....(CAP)
   Made In The U.S.A. ....(CAP)
Help Me Through The Day
Freddie King; *Best Of* .... (MCA)
Help Me Up
Eric Clapton; *ST/Rush* .... (RPR)
Help Stamp Out Loneliness
Stonewall Jackson; *45* ....(COL)
Help You Dream
Blasters; *Collection* ....(SLS)
   Hard Line ....(SLS)
Help Yourself
Tom Jones; *Live In Las Vegas* .... (PRT)
   London Collector-Greatest ....(LON)
Help Yourself To Each Other
Crystal Gayle; *These Days* ....(COL)
Don Williams; *Listen To The Radio* .... (MCA)
   You're My Best Friend .... (MCA)
Help Yourself To My Love
Kashif; *Kashif* .... (ARI)
Helpless
Band/Neil Young; *Last Waltz* .... (WB)
Crosby, Stills, Nash & Young; *Deja Vu* ....(ATL)
   So Far ....(ATL)
Four Tops; *Anthology* .... (MOT)
Johnny Otis; *Roots Of Rock 'N' Roll* ....(SAV)
Neil Young; *Decade* .... (RPR)
Platters; *Anthology* .... (RHI)
Sugar; *Copper Blue* ....(RYK)
Helplessly Hoping
Crosby, Stills & Nash; *Crosby, Stills & Nash* .....(ATL)
Crosby, Stills, Nash & Young; *So Far* ....(ATL)

Help!
Beatles; *1962-1966* ....(CAP)
   20 Greatest Hits ....(CAP)
   At The Hollywood Bowl ....(CAP)
   Help! ....(CAP)
   Rarities ....(CAP)
   Reel Music ....(CAP)
   ST/Help! ....(CAP)
Hey You
Pink Floyd; *The Wall* ....(COL)
Roger Waters; *The Wall Live In Berlin* .... (MER)
How Can I Help You Say Goodbye
Patty Loveless; *Only What I Feel* .... (EPI)
I Can Help
Billy Swan; *Billboard Top Rock 'N' Roll Hits-1974* (RHI)
   Rock This Town-Rockabilly Hits-#2 .... (RHI)
   Super Hits!'70s-Have A Nice Day-#13 .... (RHI)
I Can't Help It
Andy Gibb & Olivia Newton-John; *45* .... (RSO)
Michael Jackson; *Off The Wall* .... (EPI)
I Can't Help It (If I'm Still In Love..)
Hank Williams; *24 Of Hank Williams's Greatest
   Hits* ....(MGM)
   40 Greatest Hits .... (POL)
Hank Williams, Jr.; *ST/Your Cheatin' Heart* ...... (SSP)
Johnny Cash; *First Years* .... (ALL)
Johnny Cash & Jerry Lee Lewis; *Singing Story
   Teller* .... (SUN)
Linda Ronstadt; *Heart Like A Wheel* ....(CAP)
   Retrospective ....(CAP)
Ricky Nelson; *Legendary Masters* .... (UA)
   Sings Again .... (LIB)
I Can't Help Myself (Sugar Pie Honey...)
Four Tops; *16 #1 Hits From The Early '60s* ..... (MOT)
   Anthology .... (MOT)
   Billboard Top R&B Hits-1965 .... (RHI)
   Good Feeling Music/Big Chill Gen.-#1 .... (MOT)
   Greatest Hits .... (MOT)
   Motown Story .... (MOT)
   Motown Superstar Series #14 .... (MOT)
   ST/Forrest Gump .... (EPX)
   ST/Heaven Help Us .... (EMI)
   ST/Into The Night .... (MCA)
   ST/Where The Buffalo Roam ....(BKS)
I Can't Help Remembering You
Dean Martin; *Greatest Hits* .... (RPR)
I Couldn't Help Myself
Sara Hickman; *Shortstop* .... (ELE)
I'll Change Your Flat Tire, Merle
Pure Prairie League; *Two Lane Highway* ....(RCA)
I'll Take You There
General Public; *ST/Threesome* .... (EPX)
Staple Singers; *15 Original Big Hits #1* ....(STX)
   Chronicle ....(STX)
   Greatest Hits ....(FAN)
Last Night A D.J. Saved My Life
Indeep; *Disco Years-#2-On The Beat-1978-1982* (RHI)
   Last Night A D.J. Saved My Life ....(SON)
Lawyers, Guns & Money
Warren Zevon; *Excitable Boy* .... (ASY)
   Quiet Normal Life-Best Of .... (ASY)
   Stand In The Fire .... (ASY)
Lend A Helpin' Hand
Lynyrd Skynyrd; *Skynyrd's First & Last* .... (MCA)
Let Go Of The Stone
John Anderson; *Seminole Wind* ....(BNA)
Life Saver
Chicago; *VII* ....(COL)
Lifeline
10 CC; *Bloody Tourists* .... (POL)
Husker Du; *Metal Circus* ....(SST)
Spandau Ballet; *True* ....(CHR)
Love Rescue Me
U2; *ST/Rattle & Hum* .... (ISL)
Love Will Save The Day
Whitney Houston; *Whitney* .... (ARI)
Love You Save
Jackson 5; *14 Greatest Hits* .... (MOT)
   ABC .... (MOT)
   Anthology .... (MOT)
   Goin' Back To Indiana .... (MOT)
   Greatest Hits .... (MOT)
   Motown Superstar Series-#12 .... (MOT)
   TV ST/Diana .... (MOT)

Message In A Bottle
Police; *Every Breath You Take-The Singles* ...... (A&M)
   Reggatta De Blanc .... (A&M)
Sting; *Secret Policemen's Other Ball* .... (ISL)
Miner's Lifeguard
Almanac Singers/Peter Seeger/Chorus; *Talking Union & Other Union Songs* .... (FLW)
Mother's Little Helper
Rolling Stones; *Flowers* .... (AKO)
   Hot Rocks-1964-1971 .... (AKO)
   Through The Past Darkly-Big Hits-#2 .... (AKO)
Tesla; *Five Man Acoustical Jam* .... (GEF)
No Refuge
Eddie Schwartz; *No Refuge* .... (ATC)
Past The Point Of Rescue
Hal Ketchum; *Past The Point Of Rescue* .... (CRB)
Please Help
J.B. Hutto; *Chicago/The Blues/Today* .... (VAN)
   Great Bluesmen .... (VAN)
   Slideslinger .... (EVD)
Please Help Me, I'm Falling
Hank Locklin; *Billboard Top Country Hits-1960* . (RHI)
   Golden Hits .... (PLN)
   Nipper's Greatest Hits-'60s-#2 .... (RCA)
   Souvenirs Of Music City USA .... (PLN)
Janie Fricke; *Greatest Hits* .... (COL)
Reach Out I'll Be There
Four Tops; *Anthology* .... (MOT)
   Compact Command Performances .... (MOT)
   Greatest Hits .... (MOT)
   Motown Dance Party-#2 .... (MOT)
   Reach Out I'll Be There .... (MOT)
Rescue
Echo/Bunnymen; *Crocodiles* .... (SIR)
   Echo/Bunnymen .... (SIR)
   Songs To Learn & Sing .... (SIR)
Sam Harris; *Sam-I Am* .... (MOT)
Rescue Me
Al B. Sure!; *In Effect Mode* .... (WB)
Alarm; *Electric Folklore* .... (IRS)
   Eye Of The Hurricane .... (IRS)
   ST/21 Jump Street .... (IRS)
Diana Ross; *Swept Away* .... (RCA)
Fontella Bass; *Billboard Top R&B Hits-1965-1969* .... (RHI)
   Collectables Presents History Of Rock-#8 .... (CLT)
   Cruisin'-1965 .... (INC)
   Oldies But Goodies-#12 .... (OSR)
   ST/Air America .... (MCA)
Madonna; *Immaculate Collection* .... (SIR)
   Royal Box .... (SIR)
Red Hot & Blue Band; *Red Hot & Blue-All Time Great R&B Songs* .... (CRB)
Rhythm Saved The World
Bunny Berigan/Boys; *Take It Bunny* .... (SSP)
Rock 'N' Roll To The Rescue
Beach Boys; *Gift Set* .... (CAP)
   Made In The U.S.A. .... (CAP)
Save Me
Al Jarreau; *Jarreau* .... (WB)
Aretha Franklin; *Best Of* .... (ATL)
Bob & Marcia; *Reggae Spectacular* .... (A&M)
Crisis Party; *Rude Awakening* .... (MET)
Des'ree; *Mind Adventures* .... (EPI)
Fleetwood Mac; *25 Years-The Chain* .... (WB)
   Behind The Mask .... (RPR)
Joan Armatrading; *Joan Armatrading* .... (A&M)
k.d. lang; *Ingenue* .... (WB)
Lisa Fischer; *So Intense* .... (ELE)
Louise Mandrell; *Best Of The '80s-So Far* .... (RCA)
   Solid Country Gold .... (RCA)
Michael Bolton; *Time Love & Tenderness* .... (COL)
Neil Diamond; *On The Way To The Sky* .... (COL)
Public Image, Ltd.; *Happy?* .... (VIA)
Queen; *The Game* .... (HOL)
Rembrandts; *Rembrandts* .... (ATC)
Smokey Robinson/Miracles; *Anthology* .... (MOT)
   Away We Go-Go .... (MOT)
   Greatest Hits-#2 .... (MOT)
   Motown Legends .... (MOT)
Tanya Tucker; *Best Of* .... (MCA)
Vitamin Z; *Sharp Stone Rain* .... (GEF)

Save The Children
Diana Ross; *Anthology* .... (MOT)
   Touch Me In The Morning .... (MOT)
Gil Scott-Heron; *Gil Sco*Save The Children-Heron* (BLU)
   Revolution Will Not Be Televised .... (FLD)
Marvin Gaye; *Anthology* .... (MOT)
   Live At The London Palladium .... (MOT)
   Musical Testament 1964-1984 .... (MOT)
   What's Going On .... (MOT)
Save The Country
5th Dimension; *Anthology-1967-1973* .... (RHI)
   Greatest Hits On Earth .... (ARI)
Bobby Darin; *Live At The Desert Inn* .... (MOT)
Laura Nyro; *New York Tendaberry* .... (COL)
Save The Life Of My Child
Simon & Garfunkel; *Bookends* .... (COL)
   Collected Works .... (COL)
Save The People
Original Cast; *Godspell* .... (ARI)
Save The Whale
Nik Kershaw; *The Riddle* .... (MCA)
Save The Whales
Country Joe McDonald; *Bread & Roses Festival-Acoustic Music-#1* .... (FAN)
   Classics .... (FAN)
   Into The Fray .... (RBB)
   Paradise With An Ocean View .... (FAN)
Danny O'Keefe; *Global Blues* .... (WB)
Save The World
George Harrison; *Greenpeace* .... (A&M)
   Somewhere In England .... (DKH)
Saved
Band; *Moondog Matinee* .... (CAP)
Bob Dylan; *Saved* .... (COL)
Commitments; *ST/Commitments-#2* .... (MCA)
Elvis Presley; *Sings Leiber & Stoller* .... (RCA)
La Vern Baker; *Atlantic R&B 1947-1974-#4* .... (ATL)
   Rock Classics Of Leiber & Stoller .... (RHI)
   Soul On Fire .... (ATL)
   ST/Shag .... (SIR)
Saved By Love
Amy Grant; *Lead Me On* .... (A&M)
Rik Emmett; *Absolutely* .... (CHS)
Saved By Zero
Fixx; *One Thing Leads To Another-Greatest Hits* (MCA)
   Reach The Beach .... (MCA)
   React .... (MCA)
Saved My Life
Fee Waybill; *Read My Lips* .... (CAP)
   ST/St. Elmo's Fire .... (ATL)
Saving My Heart
Yes; *Union* .... (ARI)
Shelter From The Storm
Bob Dylan; *At Budokan* .... (COL)
   Blood On The Tracks .... (COL)
   Hard Rain .... (COL)
Shelter Me
Cinderella; *Heartbreak Station* .... (MER)
   Say What U Want-Rock The Vote .... (MER)
Joe Cocker; *Cocker* .... (CAP)
   Live .... (CAP)
Shelter Of Your Eyes
Don Williams; *Greatest Hits* .... (MCA)
Somebody Help Me
Iguanas; *Nuevo Boogaloo* .... (MGR)
Spencer Davis Group; *Best Of* .... (EMI)
   Winwood .... (UA)
Someone Saved My Life Tonight
Elton John; *Capt. Fantastic & The Brown Dirt Cowboy* .... (POL)
   Greatest Hits-#2 .... (POL)
Someone To Watch Over Me
Ella Fitzgerald; *Sings The George & Ira Gershwin Songbook* .... (VRV)
Elton John; *Glory Of Gershwin Featuring Larry Adler* .... (MER)
Frank Sinatra; *Nice 'N' Easy* .... (CAP)
   The Capitol Years .... (CAP)
Jack Jones; *Gershwin Album* .... (COL)
Original Broadway Cast; *Crazy For You* .... (ANG)
Oscar Peterson; *My Favorite Instrument* .... (VRV)
Sarah Vaughan; *George Gershwin Songbook-#2* . (EMA)
Willie Nelson; *Stardust* .... (COL)

Sometimes Salvation
Black Crowes; *Southern Harmony & Musical*
Companion .... (DEF)
Street To Lean On
Crosby, Stills & Nash; *After The Storm* .... (ATL)
S.O.S.
Abba; *Abba* .... (ATL)
Greatest Hits .... (ATL)
The Singles .... (ATL)
Aerosmith; *Get Your Wings* ....(COL)
Live Bootleg ....(COL)
Ex-Girlfriend; *X Marks The Spot* .... (RPR)
Manhattan Transfer; *Coming Out* .... (ATL)
S.O.S. Band; *45* .... (TAB)
Tim Curry; *Best Of* ....(A&M)
Urgent
Foreigner; *4* .... (ATL)
Records .... (ATL)
With A Little Help From My Friends
Beatles; *1967-1970* ....(CAP)
Box Set ....(CAP)
Rarities ....(CAP)
Sgt. Pepper's Lonely Hearts Club Band ....(CAP)
Joe Cocker; *Classics-#4* ....(A&M)
Greatest Hits ....(A&M)
History Of British Rock-#9 .... (RHI)
ST/Woodstock ....(ATL)
With A Little Help From My Friends ....(A&M)
Ringo Starr/All-Star Band; *Nobody's Child-Romanian*
Angel Appeal ....(WB)
You Cried Wolf
Todd Rundgren; *Anthology-1968-1985* .... (RHI)
Hermit Of Mink Hollow .... (RHI)

HERO

See Also: WAR, WINNING

Billy Don't Be A Hero
Bo Donaldson/Heywoods; *Super Hits/'70s-Have A Nice*
Day-#13 .... (RHI)
Broken Hearted Savior
Big Head Todd/Monsters; *Sister Sweetly* .... (GIA)
Celluloid Heroes
Joan Jett; *Hit List* ....(CBA)
Kinks; *Come Dancing-Best Of-1977-1986* .... (ARI)
Everybody's In Show Biz .... (RHI)
Greatest ....(RCA)
Childhood Hero
Bobby Bare; *Bare* ....(COL)
Die With Your Boots On
Iron Maiden; *Live After Death-World Slavery*
Tour .... (CAP)
Piece Of Mind .... (CAP)
Don Quixote
Gordon Lightfoot; *Gord's Gold* .... (RPR)
Nik Kershaw; *The Riddle* .... (MCA)
Eternal Idol
Black Sabbath; *Eternal Idol* .... (WB)
Everybody's Hero
Desert Rose Band; *Pages Of Life* .... (MCA)
Golden Vanity
Pete Seeger & Arlo Guthrie; *Together In Concert* (RPR)
Greatest Man I Never Knew
Reba McEntire; *For My Broken Heart* ...... (MCA)
Greatest Hits-#2 .... (MCA)
"Green Hornet" Theme
Original Music; *Television's Greatest Hits-#2* ..... (TVT)
He Walked On Water
Randy Travis; *No Holdin' Back* .... (WB)
Hero
Gladys Knight; *Visions* ....(COL)
Kris Kristofferson/Borderlords; *Third World*
Warrior .... (MER)
Mariah Carey; *Music Box* ....(COL)
Hero Takes A Fall
Bangles; *All Over The Place* ....(COL)
Greatest Hits ....(COL)
Hero Worship
B-52's; *B-52's* .... (WB)
Wild Planet .... (WB)
Hero #99
Gene Ryder; *Last Cigarette & A Blindfold* .... (MER)

Heroes
Commodores; *Heroes* .... (MOT)
Heroes/Commodores .... (MOT)
David Bowie; *Changesbowie* ....(RYK)
The Singles-1969-1993 ....(RYK)
David & David; *Boomtown* ....(A&M)
Johnny Cash & Waylon Jennings; *Heroes* ....(COL)
Paul Overstreet; *Heroes* ....(RCA)
Southern Pacific; *Southern Pacific* .... (WB)
Waylon Jennings & Willie Nelson; *WW2* ....(RCA)
Heroes Are Hard To Find
Fleetwood Mac; *25 Years-The Chain* .... (WB)
Heroes Are Hard To Find .... (RPR)
Heroes Die Young
Sleeze Beez; *Screwed Blued & Tattooed* .... (ATL)
Waysted; *Save Your Prayers* ....(CAP)
Heroes End
Judas Priest; *Stained Class* ....(COL)
Heroes & Friends
Randy Travis; *Greatest Hits-#1* .... (WB)
Heroes & Friends .... (WB)
Heroes & Heroines
Mary Chapin Carpenter; *Hometown Girl* ....(COL)
Heroes & Villains
Beach Boys; *Concert/'69* ....(CAP)
Made In The U.S.A. ....(CAP)
Smiley Smile ....(CAP)
Sunshine Dream ....(CAP)
"Hogan's Heroes" Theme
Original Music; *Television's Greatest Hits-#2* ..... (TVT)
Hometown Hero
Zamboni Brothers; *The Hockey Zone* .... (SPO)
Honky-Tonk Heroes
Billy Joe Shaver; *Rebels Renegades & Ramblers* ... (POL)
Waylon Jennings; *Greatest Hits* ....(RCA)
Outlaws ....(RCA)
I Would Die 4 U
Prince/Revolution; *ST/Purple Rain* .... (WB)
I'm Going To Be A Teenage Idol
Elton John; *Don't Shoot Me I'm Only The Piano*
Player .... (POL)
Jukebox Hero
Foreigner; *4* .... (ATL)
Classic Rock 1966-1988 .... (ATL)
Records .... (ATL)
Local Hero
Bruce Springsteen; *Lucky Town* ....(COL)
Meadowlands
101 Strings Orchestra; *Soul Of Russia* .... (ALS)
Jefferson Airplane; *Volunteers* ....(RCA)
My Hero
Blue Notes; *Early Years* ....(CLT)
Myron Floren; *Memory Waltzes* .... (RAN)
My Heroes Have Always Been Cowboys
Willie Nelson; *Greatest Country Hits/'80s-1980* ..(COL)
Greatest Hits & Some That Will Be ....(COL)
ST/Electric Horseman ....(COL)
ST/My Heroes Have Always Been Cowboys .....(RCA)
Nobody's Hero
Rush; *Counterparts* .... (ATL)
Nolan Ryan (He's A Hero To Us All)
Jerry Jeff Walker; *Navajo Rug* ....(RYK)
Remember The Heroes
Sammy Hagar; *Three Lock Box* .... (GEF)
Ride Of The Valkyries
Vienna Philharmonic Orchestra; *ST/Apocalypse*
Now .... (ELE)
Saturday's Heroes
Business; *Business-1979-1989* .... (BLA)
Some Gave All
Billy Ray Cyrus; *Some Gave All* .... (MER)
"Spiderman" Theme
Original Music; *Television's Greatest Hits-#2* ..... (TVT)
Super Heroes
Original London Cast; *Rocky Horror Show* ...... (RHI)
"The A-Team" Theme
Original Music; *Television's Greatest Hits-#3* ..... (TVT)
Theme From "Flash Gordon"
Neil Norman; *Greatest Science Fiction Hits-#3* ... (CRS)
Theme From "Lawrence Of Arabia"
BBC Concert Orchestra; *Golden Cinema*
Classics-Adventure Film ....(BAI)
Cincinnati Pops Orchestra/Erich Kunzel; *Hollywood's*
Greatest Hits-#1 ....(TLR)

Theme From "Superman"
London Symphony Orchestra/John Williams;
ST/Superman-The Movie .... (WB)
Neil Norman; Greatest Science Fiction Hits .... (CRS)
Theme From "The Magnificent Seven"
BBC Concert Orchestra; Golden Cinema
Classics-Adventure Film .... (BAI)
Thunder Road
Bruce Springsteen; Born To Run .... (COL)
Bruce Springsteen/E Street Band;
Live-1975-1985 .... (COL)
Time Loves A Hero
Little Feat; Time Loves A Hero .... (WB)
Waiting For Columbus .... (WB)
"Underdog Theme"
Original Music; Television's Greatest Hits-#2 ..... (TVT)
We Don't Need Another Hero (Thunderdome)
Tina Turner; Live In Europe .... (CAP)
Simply The Best .... (CAP)
Western Hero
Neil Young/Crazy Horse; Sleeps With Angels ..... (RPR)
When Heroes Go Down
Suzanne Vega; 99.9 Degrees F. .... (A&M)
Who Are Your Heroes
Bill Blue; Givin' Good Boys A Bad Name .... (ADE)
Wild West Hero
Electric Light Orchestra; Out Of The Blue .... (JET)
William Tell Overture (Lone Ranger)
Boston Pops Orchestra/Arthur Fiedler; Fiedler-Greatest
Hits .... (RCA)
TV Classics .... (RCA)
Spike Jones/City Slickers; Best Of .... (RCA)
"Wonder Woman" Theme
Original Music; Television's Greatest Hits-#3 ..... (TVT)
Working Class Hero
Alan Jackson; Don't Rock The Jukebox .... (ARI)
John Lennon; Lennon .... (CAP)
John Lennon/Plastic Ono Band; John Lennon/Plastic
Ono Band .... (CAP)
Johnny Holm; Work's Many Voices-#1 & 2 ..... (ARH)
Marianne Faithfull; Broken English .... (ISL)
You've Got To Be A Football Hero
University Of Michigan Band; Greatest College Football
Marches .... (VAN)
"Zorro" Theme
Original Music; Disney Collection-#2 .... (DIS)

HIDING

*See Also: CRIME, FEAR, FINDING, LAW &
ORDER, PRETEND, REBELS, SEARCHING*

Can't Hide Love
Earth, Wind & Fire; Best Of-#1 .... (COL)
Gratitude .... (COL)
Cover Me
Bruce Springsteen; Born In The U.S.A. .... (COL)
Music For The Miracle .... (CBA)
Bruce Springsteen/E Street Band;
Live-1975-1985 .... (COL)
Dead Giveaway
Molly Hatchet; Take No Prisoners .... (EPI)
Shalamar; The Look .... (SLR)
Desperado
Alice Cooper; Greatest Hits .... (WB)
Killer .... (WB)
Clint Black; Common Thread-Songs Of The
Eagles .... (GIA)
Eagles; Anthology .... (ASY)
Desperado .... (ASY)
Hell Freezes Over .... (GEF)
Live .... (ASY)
Their Greatest Hits 1971-1975 .... (ASY)
Linda Ronstadt; Don't Cry Now .... (ASY)
Greatest Hits .... (ASY)
Eli's Comin'
Laura Nyro; Eli & The Thirteenth Confession ..... (COL)
Three Dog Night; Best Of .... (MCA)
Best Of .... (MSP)
Rockin' '60s .... (PRY)
Everybody's Got Something To Hide...
Beatles; White Album .... (CAP)

Hide
Link Wray/Wraymen; 45 .... (EPI)
Hide In Your Shell
Supertramp; Classics-#9 .... (A&M)
Crime Of The Century .... (A&M)
Paris .... (A&M)
Hide Your Face
Spade Cooley; Columbia Historic Edition .... (COL)
Hide Your Love
Rolling Stones; Goat's Head Soup .... (RS)
Hide & Go Seek
Joe Turner; Rock This Joint .... (INT)
Hide & Seek
Bill Haley/Comets; Golden Hits .... (MCA)
Chuck Mangione; Evening Of Magic .... (A&M)
Feels So Good .... (A&M)
Howard Jones; Action Replay .... (ELE)
Human's Lib .... (ELE)
Spencer Davis Group; Greatest & Latest .... (PRY)
Hideaway
Beat Farmers; Poor & Famous .... (MCA)
Creedence Clearwater Revival; 1970 .... (FAN)
Chronicle-#2 .... (FAN)
Pendulum .... (FAN)
David Sanborn; Casino Lights-Live At Montreux ... (WB)
Hideaway .... (WB)
Straight To The Heart .... (WB)
Freddie King; Cruisin'-1961 .... (INC)
John Mayall/Bluesbreakers & Eric Clapton;
Bluesbreakers .... (LON)
Todd Rundgren; Anthology-1968-1985 .... (RHI)
Ever Popular Tortured Artist Effect .... (RHI)
Hidin' From Love
Bryan Adams; Bryan Adams .... (A&M)
Hidin' Out
Patsy Cline; Walkin' Dreams-Her First
Recordings-#1 .... (RHI)
Pete Townshend; White City .... (ATC)
Hidin' Places
Shylo; 45 .... (MER)
Hill Where The Lord Hides
Chuck Mangione; Best Of .... (A&M)
Best Of .... (MER)
Classics-#6 .... (A&M)
Evening Of Magic .... (A&M)
Friends & Love .... (MER)
Together .... (MER)
I Think We're Alone Now
Tiffany; Tiffany .... (MCA)
Tommy James/Shondells; Anthology .... (RHI)
Best Of .... (RLL)
Billboard Top Rock 'N' Roll Hits-1967 .... (RHI)
Love Hides
Doors; Absolutely Live .... (ELE)
Love Sneakin' Up On You
Bonnie Raitt; Longing In Their Hearts .... (CAP)
Love's Sneakin' Up On You
Bonnie Raitt; Longing In Their Hearts .... (CAP)
Married But Not To Each Other
Barbara Mandrell; Best Of .... (MCA)
Lovers Friends & Strangers .... (MCA)
Midnight Angel .... (MCA)
Nowhere To Run
Esther Phillips; A Way To Say Goodbye .... (MUS)
Isley Brothers; This Old Heart Of Mine .... (MOT)
J.J. Cale; Naturally .... (MCA)
Martha Reeves/Vandellas; Anthology .... (MOT)
Greatest Hits .... (MOT)
Motown Story-First 25 Years .... (MOT)
Motown Superstar Series-#11 .... (MOT)
ST/Sound Of "Murphy Brown" .... (MCA)
Pete Townshend & Ronnie Lane; Rough Mix ... (MCA)
Santana; Shango .... (COL)
Peek A Boo
Cadillacs; Best Of .... (RHI)
Devo; Best Of-Greatest Hits .... (WB)
EZ Listening Disc .... (RYK)
Oh No It's Devo .... (WB)
Siouxsie/Banshees; Peepshow .... (GEF)
Twice Upon A Time-The Singles .... (GEF)
Prisoner In Disguise
Linda Ronstadt; Prisoner In Disguise .... (ASY)

Refugee
Tom Petty/Heartbreakers; *Damn The Torpedoes* (MCA)
Pack Up The Plantation-Live .... (MCA)
U2; *War* .... (ISL)
R&B Skeletons (In The Closet)
George Clinton; *R&B Skeletons (In The Closet)* ...(CAP)
Secret Mountain Hideout
Michael Murphey; *Blue Sky Night Thunder* .... (EPI)
Smokescreen
Ted Nugent; *Weekend Warriors* .... (EPI)
Sneakin' Around
B.B. King; *16 Original Big Hits* .... (FAN)
Chet Atkins & Jerry Reed; *Sneakin' Around* .....(COL)
Dolly Parton & Burt Reynolds; *ST/Best Little Whorehouse In Texas* .... (MCA)
Little Milton; *Sings Big Blues* .... (CSS)
Sneakin' Sally Through The Alley
Robert Palmer; *Addictions-#2* .... (ISL)
Sneakin' Sally Through The Alley .... (ISL)
Somewhere They Can't Find Me
Simon & Garfunkel; *Collected Works* ....(COL)
Sounds Of Silence ....(COL)
There Ain't Nobody Here But Us Chickens
Original London Cast; *Five Guys Named Moe* .. (REL)
Time To Hide
Paul McCartney/Wings; *Wings Over America* ....(CAP)
Wings; *At The Speed Of Sound* .... (CAP)
Tryin' To Hide A Fire In The Dark
Billy Dean; *Fire In The Dark* .... (LIB)
We Hide & Seek
Jerry Douglas; *Slide Rule* .... (SH)
We Kiss In A Shadow
Barbra Streisand; *Broadway Album* .... (COL)
Original Broadway Cast; *King & I* .... (RCA)
Original Cast; *King & I* .... (MCA)
Yesterday
Beatles; *1962-1966* .... (CAP)
20 Greatest Hits ....(CAP)
Box Set .... (CAP)
Compact Disc E.P. Collection ....(CAP)
Love Songs ....(CAP)
Yesterday...And Today ....(CAP)
Elvis Presley/Imperial Quartet; *On Stage* ....(RCA)
En Vogue; *Funky Divas* ....(EW)
Frank Sinatra; *My Way* .... (RPR)
Paul McCartney; *Tripping The Live Fantastic* ....(CAP)
Placido Domingo; *Domingo Songbook* .... (SMC)
Ray Charles; *His Greatest Hits-#1* .... (DHL)
Supremes; *I Hear A Symphony* .... (MOT)
Wings; *Wings Over America* ....(CAP)
You Better Run
Pat Benatar; *Crimes Of Passion* .... (CHR)
ST/Roadie .... (WB)
You Can't Run Away From Your Heart
Lacy J. Dalton; *You Can't Run Away From Your Heart* ....(COL)
Patty Loveless; *On Down The Line* .... (MCA)
You Can't Run From Love
Eddie Rabbitt; *Best Of/Greatest Hits-#2* ....(WB)
Radio Romance ....(LIB)
#1's .... (WB)
You've Got To Hide Your Love Away
Beatles; *1962-1966* .... (CAP)
Box Set .... (CAP)
Help! .... (CAP)
Love Songs ....(CAP)
Reel Music ....(CAP)
ST/Help! ....(CAP)

HOLLYWOOD

See Also: CITIES: LOS ANGELES, MOVIES, SHOW BIZ

Celluloid Heroes
Joan Jett; *Hit List* ....(CBA)
Kinks; *Come Dancing-Best Of-1977-1986* .... (ARI)
Everybody's In Show Biz ....(RHI)
Greatest ....(RCA)
Cowboys From Hollywood
Camper Van Beethoven; *II & III* ....(IRS)
Down In Hollywood
Ry Cooder; *Bop Till You Drop* .... (WB)

Gone Hollywood
Supertramp; *Breakfast In America* .... (A&M)
Hollywood
999; *999* ....(POL)
Alabama; *Feels So Right* ....(RCA)
America; *Holiday* .... (WB)
Live .... (WB)
Billy Squier; *Creatures Of Habit* .... (CAP)
Boz Scaggs; *Down Two Then Left* ....(COL)
Chicago; *VI* ....(COL)
Connie Francis; *Rocksides 1957-1964* ....(POL)
Crystal Gayle; *Hollywood Tennessee* .... (CAP)
Freddie James; *Get Up & Boogie* .... (WB)
Jimmy Holiday; *How Can I Forget-Golden Classics* ....(CLT)
Lauren Wood; *Lauren Wood* .... (WB)
Rick James/Stone City Band; *Come Get It* ...... (GOR)
Rufus & Chaka Khan; *Ask Rufus* .... (MCA)
Shooting Star; *Hang On For Your Life* ....(VIA)
Statler Brothers; *Atlanta Blue* .... (MER)
Hollywood A Go Go
Hollywood Persuaders; *45* .... (OSR)
Hollywood Bed
Big Joe Turner; *Have No Fear Big Joe Is Here* ... (SAV)
...And The Blues'll Make You Happy Too! ...... (SAV)
Blasters; *Collection* .... (SLS)
Hollywood Blues
Boz Scaggs; *Moments* ....(COL)
Hollywood Dream
James Gang; *Jesse Come Home* .... (ATC)
Steve Miller Band; *Italian X-Rays* .... (CAP)
Thunderclap Newman; *Hollywood Dream* ...... (MCA)
Hollywood Dreaming
Father's Children; *Father's Children* .... (MER)
Hollywood Heckle & Jive
England Dan & John Ford Coley; *Dr. Heckle & Mr. Jive* ....(BT)
Hollywood Hopeful
Loudon Wainwright III; *Live One* .... (ROU)
T-Shirt .... (ARI)
Hollywood Lady
Burt Compton & Steve Mele; *Rock 'N' Roll Genius* ....(WIZ)
Hollywood Movie Girls
Dusty Springfield; *It Begins Again* .... (UA)
Hollywood Nights
Bob Seger/Silver Bullet Band; *Nine Tonight* ......(CAP)
Stranger In Town ....(CAP)
Hollywood Perfume
Pretenders; *Last Of The Independents* .... (SIR)
Hollywood Squares
Bootsy's Rubber Band; *Bootsy Player Of The Year* (WB)
George Strait; *Beyond The Blue Neon* .... (MCA)
Hollywood Swinging
Kool/Gang; *Everything Is* .... (MER)
Spin Their Top Hits .... (DL)
Hollywood Town
Manfred Mann's Earth Band; *Angel Station* .... (WB)
Hollywood Waltz
Eagles; *One Of These Nights* ....(ASY)
Hollywood (Down On Your Luck)
Thin Lizzy; *Lizzy Lives (1976-1984)* ....(GS)
Renegade .... (WB)
Hooray For Hollywood
Coney Island Chorus Girls; *Hot Disco Night* ..... (AVI)
Ella Fitzgerald; *Harold Arlen Songbook-#1* ......(VRV)
Rosemary Clooney; *Sings Lyrics Of Johnny Mercer* .... (CCJ)
If Hollywood Don't Need You
Don Williams; *Best Of-#3* .... (MCA)
Listen To The Radio .... (MCA)
Sings Bob McDill ....(MCA)
King Of Hollywood
Eagles; *The Long Run* .... (ASY)
Little Hollywood Girl
Crickets; *Liberty Years* .... (EMI)
Long Way To Hollywood
Hank Williams, Jr.; *Early Years* ....(W/C)
New South .... (WB)
Steve Young; *Seven Bridges Road* .... (ROU)
Lost In Hollywood
Neil Diamond; *Headed For The Future* ....(COL)
Rainbow; *Down To Earth* .... (POL)

Poor Little Hollywood Star
Virginia Martin; *Little Me* ....(RCA)
Queen Of Hollywood High
John Stewart; *Blondes* ....(ALL)
Say Goodbye To Hollywood
Bette Midler; *Broken Blossom* ....(ATL)
Billy Joel; *Greatest Hits-#1 & 2* ....(COL)
Songs In The Attic ....(COL)
Turnstiles ....(COL)
We're Going To Hollywood
Sicilian Vespers; *Sicilian Vespers* ....(PRO)

HOME
See Also: HOUSES, TRAVELING

2000 Light Years From Home
Rolling Stones; *45* ....(LON)
Big Hits-#2 ....(AKO)
More Hot Rocks ....(AKO)
Their Satanic Majesties Request ....(AKO)
About To Make Me Leave Home
Bonnie Raitt; *Collection* ....(WB)
Sweet Forgiveness ....(WB)
Ain't Got No Home
Band; *Moondog Matinee* ....(CAP)
Clarence "Frogman" Henry; *Best Of Chess Rock 'N'
Roll* ....(CSS)
History Of New Orleans R&B-#1-1950-1958 ... (RHI)
Vintage Music-Orig. Classics-1950s-#2 ....(MCA)
Ain't Nobody Home
Bonnie Raitt; *Streetlights* ....(WB)
B.B. King; *Best Of* ....(MCA)
Ain't Nobody Home (In California)
John Kay; *All In Good Time* ....(MER)
America Is My Home
James Brown; *45* ....(OOP)
Angel Come Home
Beach Boys; *L.A.-The Light Album* ....(CAR)
Any Place I Hang My Hat Is Home
Barbra Streisand; *Second Album* ....(COL)
Rosemary Clooney; *Sings The Lyrics Of Johnny
Mercer* .... (CCJ)
Avalon My Home Town
Mississippi John Hurt; *Best Of* ....(VAN)
Baby Come On Home
Led Zeppelin; *Boxed Set 2* ....(ATL)
Baby Please Come Home
Lloyd Price; *Original Rock Oldies-Golden-#2* ..... (SPE)
Baby Won't You Please Come Home
Billie Holiday; *Last Recordings* ....(VRV)
Dinah Washington; *Echoes Of An Era* ....(RLL)
Frank Sinatra; *Night We Called It A Day* ....(CAP)
Louis Armstrong; *Most Blues* ....(OLR)
Louis Armstrong/Friends; *20 Golden Pieces Of* ..(BLD)
Ray Charles; *20 Golden Pieces Of* ....(BLD)
Baby, Let Me Take You Home
Animals; *Best Of The* ....(AKO)
Back Home
Beach Boys; *15 Big Ones* ....(RPR)
Booker T. Jones; *Runaway* ....(MCA)
/M.G.s: Melting Pot ....(STX)
China Crisis; *Diary Of A Hollow Horse* ....(A&M)
Back Home Again
John Denver; *Back Home Again* ....(RCA)
Greatest Hits-#2 ....(RCA)
Back Home Again In Indiana
Les Paul; *Legend & The Legacy* ....(CAP)
Back Home In Derry
Christy Moore; *Ride On* ....(GRE)
Spirit Of Freedom ....(GRE)
Back Home In Huntsville Again
Bobby Bare; *20 Great Country Hits* ....(RCA)
20 Greatest Country Hits ....(RCA)
Back Home In Indiana
Peggy Gilbert/Dixie Bells; *Dixieland Jazz* .... (CMB)
Back In Your Own Back Yard
Billie Holiday; *Billie Holiday* ....(COL)
Quintessential-#5-1937-1938 ....(COL)
Story-#1 ....(COL)
Backyard
Pebbles w/Salt-N-Pepa; *Always* .... (MCA)

Banana Boat Song
Harry Belafonte; *Belafonte '89* ....(EMI)
Nipper's Greatest Hits-'50s-#1 ....(RCA)
Kinks; *Everybody's In Show Biz* .... (RHI)
Beautiful Homes
Chris Isaak; *San Francisco Days* ....(RPR)
Bill Bailey
Louis Armstrong; *Essential* ....(VAN)
Louis Armstrong ....(AUF)
Pearl Bailey; *Echoes Of An Era* ....(RLL)
Preservation Hall Jazz Band; *New Orleans-#1* ...(COL)
Bring Christmas Home
Lee Greenwood; *Christmas To Christmas* ....(MSP)
Bring Home The Bacon
Drivin' N' Cryin'; *Scarred But Smarter* .... (ISL)
Bring It On Home
Led Zeppelin; *II* ....(ATL)
Nighthawks; *Best Of* ....(GEN)
Best Of The Blues ....(ADE)
Side Pocket Shot ....(ADE)
Sonny Boy Williamson; *Best Of Chess Blues* ..... (CSS)
Chess Box-Willie Dixon ....(CSS)
Real Folk Blues ....(CSS)
Bring It On Home To Me
Animals; *Best Of* ....(AKO)
Bill Haley/Comets; *Rock & Roll* ....(CRS)
Dave Mason; *Certified Live* ....(COL)
Dave Mason ....(COL)
Eddie Floyd; *Chronicle* ....(STX)
John Lennon; *Rock 'N' Roll* ....(CAP)
Mickey Gilley; *Greatest Hits-#2* ....(PBY)
Ten Years Of Hits ....(EPI)
Paul McCartney; *CHOBA B CCCP-The Russian
Album* ....(CAP)
Sam Cooke; *Best Of* ....(RCA)
Man & His Music ....(RCA)
This Is ....(RCA)
Van Morrison; *It's Too Late To Stop Now* .... (WB)
Buffalo River Home
John Hiatt; *Perfectly Good Guitar* .... (A&M)
Bus Fare Home
Spaniels; *Heart & Soul-#2* .... (VJ)
Cabin Home On The Hill
Ricky Skaggs; *Sweet Temptation* ....(SH)
Can't Find My Way Home
Blind Faith; *Blind Faith* ....(RSO)
Crossroads ....(POL)
ST/1969 ....(POL)
Celebrate Me Home
Kenny Loggins; *Alive* ....(COL)
Celebrate Me Home ....(COL)
Chicago Send Her Home
Thelma Houston & Jerry Butler; *Two To One* ... (MOT)
Come To My Window
Melissa Etheridge; *Yes I Am* .... (ISL)
Coming Home
Cinderella; *Long Cold Winter* .... (MER)
Fleetwood Mac; *Heroes Are Hard To Find* .... (RPR)
Vintage Years .... (SIR)
Holly Near; *Speed Of Light* ....(RWD)
Scorpions; *Love At First Sting* .... (MER)
World Wide Live ....(MER)
Coming Home Soldier
Bobby Vinton; *All-Time Greatest Hits* .... (EPI)
Coming Home To See You
Supertramp; *Indelibly Stamped* .... (A&M)
Comin' Home
Bob Seger/Silver Bullet Band; *The Distance* ...... (CAP)
Delaney & Bonnie; *Best Of* .... (RHI)
Crossroads ....(POL)
Delaney & Bonnie & Friends/Eric Clapton; *On
Tour* ....(ATC)
Lynyrd Skynyrd; *First & Last* ....(MCA)
Golden & Platinum ....(MCA)
Southern By The Grace Of God-Tribute ....(MCA)
Nutmegs; *Greatest Hits* ....(CLT)
Harlem Holiday-New York R&B-#7 ....(CLT)
Crawlin' Home Puker
Da Yoopers; *Yoopanese* ....(YOU)
Cry For Home
Van Morrison; *Inarticulate Speech Of The Heart* .. (WB)
Daddy's Home
Cliff Richard; *Wired For Sound* ....(EMI)
Jackson 5; *Anthology* ....(MOT)

Jermaine Jackson; *Motown Superstar Series-#17* (MOT)
Shep/Limelites; *Cruisin' 1961* .... (INC)
   Doo Wop Ballads-#2 .... (RHI)
   Oldies But Goodies-#5 .... (OSR)
Shep/Limelites-Heartbeats; *Best Of The*
Heartbeats .... (RHI)
Darling Are You Ever Coming Home
Jeannie Seely; *Greatest Hits* .... (MON)
Darling Come Back Home
Eddie Kendricks; *45* .... (MOT)
Darlin' Be Home Soon
Joe Cocker; *Classics-#4* .... (A&M)
   Greatest Hits .... (A&M)
   Joe Cocker .... (A&M)
Lovin' Spoonful; *Anthology* .... (RHI)
   Best Of-#2 .... (RHI)
   Lovin' '60s .... (PRY)
Deep River Woman
Lionel Richie; *Dancing On The Ceiling* .... (MOT)
Diamonds On My Windshield
Tom Waits; *Anthology* .... (ASY)
   Heart Of Saturday Night .... (ASY)
Dirty Water
Standells; *Best Of* .... (RHI)
   Nuggets-Classics From Psychedelic Era .... (RHI)
   Super Oldies/'60s-#10 .... (AUF)
Dolphins & Whales (Come Home To The Sea)
Mannheim Steamroller; *Saving The Wildlife* .... (AG)
Domestic Life
John Conlee; *American Faces* ....(COL)
   Greatest Country Hits/'80s-1987 ....(COL)
   More Hot Country Requests-#2 .... (EPI)
Don't Cheat In Our Hometown
Ricky Skaggs; *Don't Cheat In Our Hometown* .... (EPI)
Don't Come Home A Drinkin' (With...
Loretta Lynn; *Greatest Hits* .... (MCA)
   Greatest Hits Live .... (KT)
   MCA Records 30 Years Of Hits-1958-1988 ... (MCA)
Don't Come Home A Lovin' With Venison...
Debby McClatchy; *Someday Cafe* ....(GRE)
Don't Go Home With Your Hard On
Leonard Cohen; *Death Of A Ladies' Man* ....(COL)
Down Home
Alabama; *Pass It On Down* ....(RCA)
John Hiatt; *Overcoats* ....(EPI)
Original Broadway Cast; *Purlie* .... (RCA)
Down Home Girl
Nazareth; *Play'n' The Game* .... (A&M)
Rolling Stones; *Now!* .... (AKO)
Down Home In Kentucky
Frankie Jaxon; *Frankie "*
Half-Pint" Jaxon-1927-1940 .... (SB)
Down Home In New Orleans
Magic Organ; *Traveling With* .... (RAN)
Down Home Town
Electric Light Orchestra; *Face The Music* ....(JET)
Dream Home In New Zealand
English Beat; *Wha'ppen* .... (IRS)
Drinkin' My Way Back Home
Gene Watson/Farewell Party Band; *Greatest Hits* (MCA)
   Little By Little .... (MCA)
   Texas Saturday Night .... (MCA)
Drive
Cars; *Greatest Hits* .... (ELE)
   Heartbeat City .... (ELE)
   MTV's Rock 'N Roll To Go .... (ELE)
Eat At Home
Paul & Linda McCartney; *Ram* .... (CAP)
Fly Away Home
Ozark Mountain Daredevils; *Best* .... (A&M)
   Men From Earth .... (A&M)
Flying Home
Benny Goodman; *Jazz Sampler-#6* ....(COL)
Ella Fitzgerald; *Best Of* .... (MCA)
Ella Fitzgerald & Count Basie; *Pablo Live* .... (PAB)
Lionel Hampton; *Flying Home* .... (DHL)
Get Back
Beatles; *1967-1970* .... (CAP)
   20 Greatest Hits .... (CAP)
   Box Set .... (CAP)
   Let It Be .... (CAP)
   Past Masters-#2 .... (CAP)
   Reel Music .... (CAP)
   Rock 'N' Roll Music-#2 .... (CAP)

Paul McCartney; *Tripping The Live Fantastic* ....(CAP)
Go Back Home
Andrew Gold; *What's Wrong With This Picture* ... (ASY)
Stephen Stills; *Stephen Stills* .... (ATL)
   Still Stills .... (ATL)
T-Connection; *Magic* .... (DSH)
Go Home
Stevie Wonder; *In Square Circle* .... (MOT)
Go Home Girl
Ry Cooder; *Bop Till You Drop* .... (WB)
Going Home
Buddy Guy; *Left My Blues In San Francisco* ..... (CSS)
Dire Straits; *Live-Alchemy* .... (WB)
Elvis Presley; *Collector's Gold* .... (RCA)
Fats Domino; *Legendary Masters* .... (UA)
Kenny G; *Live* .... (ARI)
Little Richard; *Greatest Hits* .... (TRP)
Osmonds; *Greatest Hits* .... (POL)
Rolling Stones; *Aftermath* .... (LON)
Santana; *Lotus* ....(COL)
Going Home To Louisiana
Chris Thomas; *The Beginning* .... (ARH)
Goin' Back
Byrds; *20 Essential Tracks From The Box Set* ....(COL)
   Byrds ....(COL)
Dusty Springfield; *Golden Hits* .... (PHI)
Neil Young; *Comes A Time* .... (RPR)
Nils Lofgren; *Best Of* .... (A&M)
   Night After Night .... (A&M)
   Nils Lofgren .... (RYK)
Goin' Home
Alvin Lee/Ten Years After; *ST/Woodstock* ....(OOP)
Alvin Lee/Ten Years Later; *Ride On* .... (RSO)
Golden Slumbers
Beatles; *Abbey Road* .... (CAP)
   Box Set .... (CAP)
Got No More Home Than A Dog
Ian & Sylvia; *Greatest Hits* .... (VAN)
   Ian & Sylvia .... (VAN)
Got No Reason Now For Goin' Home
Gene Watson; *Country Classics-#9-1984-1987* . (MCA)
   Heartaches Love & Stuff .... (MCC)
   Texas Saturday Night .... (MCC)
Gotta Get You Home Tonight
Eugene Wilde; *Eugene Wilde* .... (PHL)
Green Green Grass Of Home
Burl Ives; *Best Of-#2* .... (MCA)
Elvis Presley; *Our Memories Of-#2* .... (RCA)
   Today .... (RCA)
George Jones; *20 Golden Pieces Of* .... (BLD)
Tom Jones; *Country Side Of* .... (LON)
   London Collector .... (LON)
   Things That Matter Most To Me .... (MER)
Gypsy Woman (She's Homeless)
Crystal Waters; *Red Hot + Dance* ....(COL)
   Surprise .... (MER)
Happy 'Cause I'm Going Home
Chicago; *At Carnegie Hall* ....(COL)
   III ....(COL)
Harriet Tubman's Gonna Carry Me Home
Long Ryders; *Two-Fisted Tales* .... (ISL)
He Calls Home
Candlebox; *Candlebox* .... (MAV)
Heavenly Homes
Be Bop Deluxe; *Sunburst Finish* .... (CAP)
Home
Gary Puckett/Union Gap; *Greatest Hits* ....(COL)
Hothouse Flowers; *Home* .... (LON)
Ian Matthews; *Some Days You Eat The Bear* ..... (ELE)
Jamaica Boys; *Jamaica Boys* .... (WB)
Jerry Lee Lewis; *Golden Cream Of* .... (SUN)
Jethro Tull; *Stormwatch* .... (CHR)
Joe Walsh/Barnstorm; *Joe Walsh/Barnstorm* .... (MCA)
Lene Lovich; *Stateless* .... (STF)
Loretta Lynn; *Home* .... (MCA)
Original Cast/Stephanie Mills; *The Wiz* .... (ATL)
Public Image, Ltd.; *Greatest Hits So Far* .... (VIA)
Home Again
Al Green; *Livin' For You* .... (MOT)
Barry Manilow; *2* .... (ARI)
Carole King; *Tapestry* .... (EOD)
Judy Collins; *Home Again* .... (ELE)
Supertramp; *Supertramp* .... (A&M)

Home Again In My Heart
Nitty Gritty Dirt Band; *More Great Dirt-Best Of-#2* .... (WB)
Partners Brothers & Friends .... (WB)

Home At Last
Steely Dan; *Aja* .... (MCA)

Home Cookin'
Junior Walker/All-Stars; *Anthology* .... (MOT)
Greatest Hits .... (MOT)

Home Grown
Neil Young/Crazy Horse; *American Stars & Bars* (RPR)

Home In Indiana
Magic Organ; *Traveling With* .... (RAN)

Home In Louisiana
Country Gentlemen; *Home In Louisiana* .... (VAN)
Remembrances & Forecasts .... (VAN)

Home In My Hand
Dave Edmunds; *Repeat When Necessary* .... (SS)
Foghat; *Best Of* .... (RHI)
Energized .... (RHI)
Live .... (RHI)

Home In San Antone
Bob Wills/Texas Playboys; *Tiffany Transcriptions-#4* .... (KAL)
Texas Playboys/Leon McAuliffe; *Greatest Hits Of Texas* .... (RHI)
San Antonio Rose Story .... (DEL)

Home Is A Wounded Heart
Neil Diamond; *Beautiful Noise* .... (COL)

Home Is Where The Hatred Is
Esther Phillips; *Best Of* .... (CBA)
From A Whisper To A Scream .... (CBA)
Gil Scott-Heron; *Gil ScoHome Is Where The Hatred Is-Heron* .... (BLU)
It's Your World .... (ARI)
Pieces Of A Man .... (FLD)

Home Is Where The Heart Is
Bobby Womack; *Home Is Where The Heart Is* ....(COL)
Gladys Knight/Pips; *Still Together* .... (BUD)
Kool/Gang; *In The Heart* .... (DL)

Home Lovin' Man
Andy Williams; *Greatest Hits-#2* .... (COL)

Home Of The Blues
Dwight Yoakam; *Buenas Noches From A Lonely Room* .... (RPR)
Johnny Cash; *Classic Cash-Hall Of Fame Series* . (MER)
Legend .... (SUN)
Original .... (SUN)
Original Golden Hits #1 .... (SUN)
Superbilly .... (SUN)

Home On The Range
Bing Crosby; *Crooner-Columbia Years-1928-1934* .... (COL)
Boston Pops Orchestra; *Yankee Doodle Dandy* ..(RCA)
Gene Autry; *50th Anniversary* .... (REP)
Country Music Hall Of Fame .... (COL)
Neil Young; *ST/Where The Buffalo Roam* .... (BKS)

Home Sweet Home
Lawrence Welk; *200 Years Of American Music* . (RAN)
Motley Crue; *Theatre Of Pain* .... (ELE)
Peter Gabriel; *Peter Gabriel* .... (ATL)

Home To New Orleans
Queen Ida; *Caught In The Act* .... (CRS)

Home You're Tearing Down
Loretta Lynn; *Greatest Hits* .... (MCA)

Home & Dry
Gerry Rafferty; *City To City* .... (EMI)

Homebound
Ted Nugent; *Cat Scratch Fever* .... (EPI)

Homeboy
Michael McDonald; *Take It To Heart* .... (RPR)
Steve Arrington; *45* .... (ATL)

Homecoming
Floyd Cramer; *Forever Floyd Cramer* ....(SO)
Just Me & My Piano .... (SO)
Tom T. Hall; *Essential -20th Anniversary Collection* .... (MER)
Greatest Hits .... (MER)

Homecomputer
Kraftwerk; *The Mix* .... (ELE)

Homegrown Western Saturday Night
Chris LeDoux; *Powder River* .... (LIB)

Homemade Love
Kenny Rogers; *Love Lifted Me* .... (EMI)

Homemade Lovin'
Whispers; *Whisper In Your Ear* .... (SLR)

Homestead In My Heart
Amazing Rhythm Aces; *Amazing Rhythm Aces* ...(COL)

Hometown Blues
Rosanne Cash; *Seven Year Ache* .... (COL)
Tom Petty/Heartbreakers; *Tom Petty/Heartbreakers* .... (MCA)

Hometown Honeymoon
Alabama; *American Pride* .... (RCA)

Hometown New Orleans
Champion Jack Dupree; *Forever & Ever* .... (BUL)

Homeward Bound
Fleetwood Mac; *Bare Trees* .... (RPR)
Paul Simon; *Live Rhymin'* .... (WB)
Paul Simon & George Harrison; *Nobody's Child-Romanian Angel Appeal* .... (WB)
Simon & Garfunkel; *Collected Works* .... (COL)
Concert In Central Park .... (WB)
Greatest Hits .... (COL)
Parsley Sage Rosemary & Thyme .... (COL)
Willie Nelson & Waylon Jennings; *Take It To The Limit* .... (COL)

Home, Sweet Oklahoma
Tom Paxton; *It Ain't Easy* .... (FF)

House Is Not A Home
Burt Bacharach; *Classics-#23* .... (A&M)
Dionne Warwick; *Anthology* .... (RHI)
Greatest Hits .... (EVR)
Hot-Live & Otherwise .... (ARI)
Say A Little Prayer .... (DHL)
Luther Vandross; *Best Of-Best Of Love* .... (EPI)
Never Too Much .... (EPI)
Mavis Staples; *15 Original Big Hits-#3* .... (STX)
Mavis Staples .... (STX)

I Have Found Me A Home
Jimmy Buffett; *White Sport Coat & A Pink Crustacean* .... (MCA)

I Just Came Home To Count The Memories
John Anderson; *Greatest Hits* .... (WB)
Honky-Tonk Country-Tender Lovin' Country ...(PRY)
I Just Came Home To Count The Memories ......(WB)

I Want To Walk You Home
Fats Domino; *Billboard Top R&B Hits-1959* ..... (RHI)
Greatest Hits .... (MCA)
My Blue Heaven-Best Of-#1 .... (EMI)

I Wonder If I Take You Home
Lisa Lisa & Cult Jam With Full Force; *Breakdancing* .... (COL)
Lisa Lisa & Cult Jam With Full Force .... (COL)

I Won't Be Home No More
Hank Williams; *24 Of His Greatest Hits-#2* ...... (POL)
40 Greatest Hits .... (POL)

I Won't Be Home Tonight
Tony Carey; *Tony Carey* .... (ROC)

In My Own Backyard
Joe Diffie; *Thousand Winding...* .... (EPI)

Infamous Angel
Iris DeMent; *Infamous Angel* .... (PHO)
Infamous Angel .... (WB)

Ireland My Home
Ann & Francie Brolly; *Ireland My Home* .... (RGO)
Barley Bree; *Speak Up For Old Ireland* .... (SHA)

It Won't Be Long
Beatles; *Meet The Beatles* .... (CAP)
With The Beatles .... (CAP)

I'll Be Home
Barbra Streisand; *Stoney End* .... (COL)
Flamingos; *Alan Freed's Memory Lane* .... (RLL)
Best Of .... (RHI)
Super Oldies/'50s-#6 .... (AUF)
Randy Newman; *Little Criminals* .... (WB)
Live .... (RPR)

I'll Be Your Shelter
Taylor Dayne; *Can't Fight Fate* .... (ARI)

I'll Go Home With Bonnie Jean
Original Cast; *Brigadoon* .... (RCA)

I'll Take You Home Again Kathleen
Billy Shepherd Singers; *Irish Sing-Along* .... (MCA)
Bing Crosby; *When Irish Eyes Are Smiling* .... (MCA)
Slim Whitman; *Paloma Blanca-Best Of-Legendary Masters* .... (EMI)

I'm Afraid To Go Home
Brian Hyland; *Greatest Hits* .... (RHI)

Gene Pitney; *This Is* ....(OOP)
I'm Coming Home
  Carmen McRae; *Jazzy Ladies* ....(DHL)
  Elvis Presley; *Return Of The Rocker* ....(RCA)
  Johnny Mathis; *First 25 Years-Silver Anniversary* .(COL)
    I'm Coming Home ....(COL)
  Left Banke; *History Of* ....(RHI)
I'm Going Home
  Ten Years After; *ST/Woodstock* .... (ATL)
I'm Gonna Hire A Wino To Decorate...
  David Frizzell; *Family's Fine But This One's All*
  Mine .... (WB)
Jukebox Never Plays "Home Sweet Home"
  Jack Greene; *Out-of-print recording* ....(OOP)
Keep The Home Fire Burning
  Latimore; *Get Down Tonight!-Best Of T.K. Records* (RHI)
    III ....(GLA)
  Millie Jackson; *Get It Out'cha System* .... (SPR)
    Live & Uncensored .... (SPR)
Let Me Take You Home Tonight
  Boston; *Boston* .... (EPI)
Letter From Home
  Eddie Jefferson; *Letter From Home* .... (RVR)
Letter Home
  Elvis Costello/Brodsky Quartet; *Juliet Letters* ..... (WB)
  Forester Sisters; *Greatest Hits* .... (WB)
  Memphis Slim; *All Kinds Of Blues* .... (BV)
  Wendy Waldman; *Letters Home* .... (CYP)
Lida Rose
  Original Broadway Cast; *Music Man* .... (ANG)
  Robert Preston/Original Cast; *Music Man* ....(CAP)
Little Home In Tennessee
  Bill Harrell/Virginians; *Ballads & Bluegrass* ..... (ADE)
London Homesick Blues
  David Allan Coe; *Biggest Hits* ....(COL)
  Jerry Jeff Walker; *Great Gonzos* .... (MCA)
    Viva Terlingua .... (MCA)
Lonesome & A Long Way From Home
  Eric Clapton; *Eric Clapton* .... (RSO)
Long Long Way From Home
  Foreigner; *Foreigner* .... (ATL)
    Records .... (ATL)
Long Way From Home
  Neil Diamond; *Double Gold* ....(BNG)
    Just For You ....(BNG)
  Whitesnake; *Love Hunter* ....(GEF)
(Love Always) Letter To Home
  Glen Campbell; *(Love Always) Letter To Home* ... (AA)
Major Tom (Coming Home)
  Peter Schilling; *Different Story (World Of Lust &*
  Crime) .... (ELE)
    Error In The The System .... (ELE)
Make Me The Woman That You Go Home To
  Gladys Knight/Pips; *Anthology* ....(MOT)
    All The Great Hits ....(MOT)
    Compact Command Performances ....(MOT)
    Standing Ovation .... (SOL)
Mama, I'm Coming Home
  Ozzy Osbourne; *No More Tears* .... (EPA)
Martians Go Home
  Shorty Rogers; *Great Moments In Jazz* .... (ATL)
Meet Me Tonight By My Old Kentucky Home
  Joe Val/New England Bluegrass Boys; *#2* ...... (ROU)
My Adobe Hacienda
  Bob Wills; *Best Of* .... (MCA)
My Home Ain't In The Hall Of Fame
  Jonathan Edwards; *Lucky Day* ....(ATC)
  J.D. Crowe/New South; *My Home Ain't In The Hall Of*
  Fame .... (ROU)
My Home Is In The Delta
  Muddy Waters; *Chess Box* .... (CSS)
    Folk Singer .... (CSS)
My Hometown
  Bruce Springsteen; *Born In The U.S.A.* ....(COL)
My Home's In Alabama
  Alabama; *Gonna Have A Party...Live* ....(RCA)
    Greatest Hits ....(RCA)
    Live .... (RCA)
    My Home's In Alabama ....(RCA)
My Little Home Down In New Orleans
  Jimmie Rodgers; *Early Years-1928-1929* .... (ROU)
My North Dakota Home
  Lawrence Welk; *Reminiscing-#1* .... (RAN)

My Old Kentucky Home
  Al Jolson; *Story-#5* .... (MCA)
  Randy Newman; *Live* .... (RPR)
    Randy Newman .... (RPR)
  Ry Cooder; *Ry Cooder* .... (RPR)
  Salli Terri; *Songs Of The American Land* .... (ANG)
My Ol' Kentucky Rock & Roll Home
  Original New York Cast; *Oil City Symphony* ... (DRG)
My Second Home
  Tracy Lawrence; *Alibis* .... (ATL)
My Tennessee Mountain Home
  Dolly Parton; *Best Of* ....(RCA)
    Best Of A Great Year-#3 ....(RCA)
    My Tennessee Mountain Home ....(RCA)
  Rose Maddox; *Reckless Love & Bold Adventure* ..(TAK)
New Way Home
  K.T. Oslin; *Love In A Small Town* ....(RCA)
    Songs From An Aging Sex Bomb-Greatest ......(RCA)
Nobody Home
  Pink Floyd; *The Wall* ....(COL)
  Roger Waters; *The Wall Live In Berlin* .... (MER)
Nobody's Home
  Clint Black; *Killin' Time* ....(RCA)
Oklahoma Going Home
  Kate Wolf/Wildwood Flower; *Back Roads* ....(KAL)
Old Folks At Home
  Mormon Tabernacle Choir; *Songs Of The Civil War & S.*
  Foster Fav. .... (SMC)
  Paul Robeson; *A Man & His Beliefs-Golden*
  Classics-#2 .... (CLT)
Old Home Filler Up & Keep On A Truckin'
  C.W. McCall; *Greatest Hits* .... (POL)
    Wolf Creek Pass ....(MGM)
On The Way Home
  Buffalo Springfield; *Buffalo Springfield* ....(ATC)
    Last Time Around ....(ATC)
    Retrospective ....(ATC)
  Crosby, Stills, Nash & Young; *4-Way Street* ...... (ATL)
One Room Country Shack
  Buddy Guy; *Man & The Blues* .... (VAN)
    My Time After Awhile .... (VAN)
  Mercy Dee Walton; *Mercy's Troubles* .... (ARH)
    One Room Country Shack .... (SPE)
  Mose Allison; *Greatest Hits* .... (PRS)
    Pity & A Shame .... (PRS)
One Way Ticket Home
  Phil Ochs; *Greatest Hits* ....(A&M)
    The War Is Over-Best Of ....(A&M)
Our House
  Crosby, Stills & Nash; *Crosby, Stills & Nash*
  (collection) .... (ATL)
  Crosby, Stills, Nash & Young; *Deja Vu* .... (ATL)
    So Far ....(ATL)
    ST/Strawberry Statement .... (MCA)
  Madness; *Madness* .... (GEF)
Paint Me Back Home In Wyoming
  Chris LeDoux; *Paint Me Back Home In Wyoming* . (LIB)
    Sounds Of The Western Country ....(LIB)
Party Till The Cows Come Home
  Elvin Bishop Group; *Bill Graham-Fillmore-Last*
  Days .... (EPA)
Pictures Of Home
  Deep Purple; *Machine Head* .... (WB)
Please Call Home
  Allman Brothers Band; *Beginnings* ....(POL)
    Idlewild South .... (POL)
  Gregg Allman; *Laid Back* ....(CPC)
Please Come Home For Christmas
  Aaron Neville; *Soulful Christmas* .... (A&M)
  Bon Jovi; *Very Special Christmas-#2* .... (A&M)
  Charles Brown; *Billboard Greatest Christmas Hits* (RHI)
  Eagles; *45* ....(ELE)
  Freddy Fender; *Country Christmas* ....(MSP)
    Merry Christmas From ....(MSP)
    Tejano Country Christmas ....(ART)
  James Brown; *Santa's Got A Brand New Bag* ... (RHI)
  John Schneider; *Tennessee Christmas* ....(MSP)
  Leon Rausch; *Rausch Touch* .... (STH)
  Little Johnny Taylor; *It's Christmas Time Again* ... (STX)
  Sawyer Brown; *Christmas For The '90s-#2* .... (LIB)
    Family Christmas Treasury ....(LIB)
Queen Of My Double Wide Trailer
  Sammy Kershaw; *Haunted Heart* .... (MER)

Rollin' Home
Eric Andersen; *Best Of* .... (VAN)
Peter, Paul & Mary; *Album 1700* .... (WB)
Safe European Home
Clash; *Give 'Em Enough Rope* .... (EPI)
On Broadway .... (EPI)
Story Of-#1 .... (EPI)
Sailing Home For Christmas
Doug Stone; *First Christmas* .... (EPI)
Sailing Toward Home
Oak Ridge Boys; *All Our Favorite Songs* .... (COL)
Second Home By The Sea
Genesis; *Genesis* .... (ATL)
She Gonna Come Home Wit' Me
Original Broadway Cast; *Most Happy Fella* ..... (SMC)
She Keeps The Home Fires Burning
Ronnie Milsap; *Greatest Greatest Hits* .... (RCA)
She Makes The Coming Home (Worth The...)
Shenandoah; *Extra Mile* .... (COL)
She's Leaving Home
Al Jarreau; *All Fly Home* .... (WB)
Beatles; *Box Set* .... (CAP)
Love Songs .... (CAP)
Sgt. Pepper's Lonely Hearts Club Band .... (CAP)
Show Me The Way To Go Home
Artie Shaw; *Best Of* .... (MCA)
Randy Erwin; *Back Home* .... (ROM)
Sing Me Back Home
Alabama; *Mama's Hungry Eyes-Merle Haggard*
Tribute .... (ARI)
Flying Burrito Brothers; *Farther Along-Best Of* .. (A&M)
Merle Haggard/Strangers; *Best Of* .... (CAP)
Capitol Collectors Series .... (CAP)
Okie From Muskogee .... (CAP)
Songs I'll Always Sing .... (CAP)
Six Days On The Road
Dave Dudley; *Billboard Top Country Hits-1963* .. (RHI)
Country Music Classics-#2-1960-1965 .... (KT)
Legends Of Country Guitar-#2 .... (RHI)
Flying Burrito Brothers; *Cabin Fever* .... (RLX)
Farther Along-Best Of .... (A&M)
Last Of The Red Hot Burritos .... (A&M)
Taj Mahal; *Giant Step/De Ole Folks At Home* ....(COL)
Legends Of Rock Guitar-'60s-#2 .... (RHI)
Sloop John B
Beach Boys; *Absolute Best-#2* .... (CAP)
Best Of (Good Vibrations) .... (RPR)
Gift Set .... (CAP)
Made In The U.S.A. .... (CAP)
Pet Sounds .... (CAP)
ST/Forrest Gump .... (EPX)
Sort Of Homecoming
U2; *Unforgettable Fire* .... (ISL)
Wide Awake In America .... (ISL)
Subterranean Homesick Blues
Bob Dylan; *Biograph* .... (COL)
Bootleg Series-#1-3-1961-1989 .... (COL)
Bringing It All Back Home .... (COL)
Greatest Hits .... (COL)
Red Hot Chili Peppers; *Uplift Mofo Party Plan* .. (EMI)
Suburban Home
Descendants; *Liveage* .... (SST)
Milo Goes To College .... (SST)
Somery .... (SST)
Swamps Of Home
Original Cast; *Once Upon A Mattress* .... (MCA)
Sweet Chicago Home
David Bromberg; *How Late'll Ya Play 'Til* .... (FAN)
Sweet Home Alabama
Alabama; *Skynyrd Frynds* .... (MCA)
Charlie Daniels Band, Etc.; *Volunteer Jam 7* ...... (EPI)
Hank Williams, Jr.; *Hank Live* .... (W/C)
Lynyrd Skynyrd; *Billboard Top Rock 'N' Roll*
Hits-1974 .... (RHI)
Gold & Platinum .... (MCA)
One More For The Road .... (MCA)
Second Helping .... (MCA)
South's Greatest Hits .... (CPC)
ST/Forrest Gump .... (EPX)
Sweet Home Chicago
Blues Brothers; *ST/Blues Brothers* .... (ATL)
Foghat; *Best Of-#2* .... (RHI)
Stone Blue .... (RHI)
Junior Parker; *Best Of* .... (MCA)

Leon Russell & Marc Benno; *Asylum Choir-#2* . (MCA)
Magic Sam; *Live* .... (DEL)
Robert Johnson; *Complete Recordings* .... (COL)
King Of The Delta Blues Singers-#2 .... (COL)
Taj Mahal; *Recycling The Blues-Other Related*
Stuff .... (COL)
Sweet Mama Hurry Home Or I'll Be Gone
Leon Redbone; *On The Track* .... (WB)
Sweet Wyoming Home
Chris LeDoux; *& The Saddle Boogie Band* .... (LIB)
Swing Low, Sweet Chariot
Eric Clapton; *Time Pieces-Best Of* .... (POL)
Glenn Miller/Orchestra; *Moonlight Serenade* .... (RAN)
Hi-Lo's; *Suddenly It's The Hi-Lo's* .... (COL)
Jerry Garcia Acoustic Band; *Almost Acoustic* ... (GRD)
Joan Baez; *From Every Stage* .... (A&M)
Peggy Lee; *Best Of* .... (MCA)
Take Me Back To My Old Carolina Home
Uncle Dave Macon; *Laugh Your Blues Away* ... (ROU)
Take Me Home
Cher; *Night At Studio 54* .... (CAS)
Take Me Home .... (CAS)
Crystal Gayle; *ST/One From The Heart* .... (COL)
Phil Collins; *Miami Vice II* .... (MCA)
No Jacket Required .... (ATL)
Serious Hits...Live! .... (ATL)
Take Me Home Tonight
Eddie Money; *Can't Hold Back* .... (COL)
Greatest Hits/Sound Of Money .... (COL)
Take Me Home, Country Roads
John Denver; *Evening With* .... (RCA)
Greatest Hits .... (RCA)
Poems Prayers & Promises .... (RCA)
Take Me Home, Country Roads-& Other Hits ... (RCA)
Toots/Maytals; *Brand New Second-Hand* .... (RYK)
Take The Long Way Home
John Schneider; *Country Classics-#8-1986-1987* . (MSP)
Greatest Hits .... (MCA)
Supertramp; *Breakfast In America* .... (A&M)
Classics-#9 .... (A&M)
Paris .... (A&M)
Take The Short Way Home
Dionne Warwick; *Heartbreaker* .... (ARI)
Take Your Whiskey Home
Van Halen; *Women & Children First* .... (WB)
Tennessee Homesick Blues
Dolly Parton; *Best Of-#3* .... (RCA)
RCA Years-1967-1986 .... (RCA)
Star-Spangled Country .... (RCA)
ST/Rhinestone .... (RCA)
That I Get Back Home
NRBQ; *Honest Dollar* .... (RYK)
Thirty Days (To Come Back Home)
Chuck Berry; *Blues-#2* .... (CSS)
Golden Hits .... (MER)
Johnny Winter; *Rock N' Roll Collection* .... (COL)
'Til My Baby Comes Home
Luther Vandross; *Best Of...Best Of Love* .... (EPI)
Night I Fell In Love .... (EPI)
Tippin' Home From Sunday School
Oliver Jones; *Class Act* .... (JUS)
Tones Of Home
Blind Melon; *Blind Melon* .... (CAP)
Tonight My Baby's Coming Home
Barbara Mandrell; *Best Of* .... (COL)
Too Cold At Home
Mark Chesnutt; *S* .... (MCA)
Tuck Me To Sleep In My Old Kentucky Home
Firehouse Five Plus Two; *Goes South* .... (GTJ)
Turning For Home
Mike Reid; *Turning For Home* .... (COL)
Oak Ridge Boys; *American Dreams* .... (MCA)
Two Of Us
Beatles; *Box Set* .... (CAP)
Let It Be .... (CAP)
Two Thousand Light Years From Home
Rolling Stones; *More Hot Rocks-Big Hits & Fazed*
Cookies .... (AKO)
Singles Collection-London Years .... (AKO)
Their Satanic Majesties Request .... (AKO)
Through The Past Darkly-Big Hits #2 .... (AKO)

Vahevala
Loggins & Messina; *Best Of-Friends* ....(COL)
   On Stage ....(COL)
   Sittin' In ....(COL)
Wait
Beatles; *Box Set* ....(CAP)
   Rubber Soul ....(CAP)
Walkin' My Baby Back Home
Johnny Ray; *16 Most Requested Songs* ....(COL)
   Greatest Hits ....(SSP)
Nat King Cole; *Capitol Collectors Series* ....(CAP)
   Story ....(CAP)
   Walkin' My Baby Back Home ....(CAP)
War Is Hell (On The Homefront Too)
T.G. Sheppard; *All-Time Greatest Hits* ....(WB)
   Greatest Hits ....(WB)
   Perfect Stranger ....(WB)
West Virginia My Home
Hazel Dickens & Alice Gerrard; *Hazel Dickens & Alice
Gerrard* .... (ROU)
When I Could Come Home To You
Steve Wariner; *Greatest Hits-#2* .... (MCA)
   I Got Dreams .... (MCA)
When I Get Home
Beatles; *Box Set* ....(CAP)
   Hard Day's Night ....(CAP)
   Something New ....(CAP)
When Johnny Comes Marching Home
Marilyn Horne; *Beautiful Dreamer-Great Amer.
Songbook* ....(LON)
Mormon Tabernacle Choir; *Songs Of The Civil War & S.
Foster Faves* ....(SMC)
United States Military Academy Band; *Songs Of The
Civil War* ....(COL)
When My Dreamboat Comes Home
Kay Starr; *Capitol Collectors Series* ....(CAP)
Why Can't You Bring Me Home
Jay/Americans; *All-Time Greatest Hits* .... (RHI)
   Come A Little Big Closer-Best Of .... (EMI)
Why Can't You Come Home
Ex-Girlfriend; *X Marks The Spot* .... (RPR)
Wingin' It Home To Texas
Jerry Jeff Walker; *Collectibles* .... (MCA)
Yellow Submarine
Beatles; *1962-1966* ....(CAP)
   Box Set ....(CAP)
   Reel Music ....(CAP)
   Revolver ....(CAP)
   Yellow Submarine ....(CAP)
You Don't Have To Go Home Tonight
Triplets; *...Thicker Than Water* .... (MER)

HOMOSEXUALS, Sexual Variations

See Also: SEX

Ain't Nobody Straight In L.A.
Miracles; *City Of Angels* .... (TAM)
All The Girls Love Alice
Elton John; *Goodbye Yellow Brick Road* .... (POL)
Ballad Of Ben Gay
Ben Gay/Silly Savages; *Dr. Demento's Delights* ...(WB)
Boom Bye Bye
Buju Banton; *Voice Of Jamaica* .... (MER)
Dude (Looks Like A Lady)
Aerosmith; *Permanent Vacation* ....(GEF)
Flame
Metro; *Metro* .... (SIR)
Glad To Be Gay
Tom Robinson Band; *Power In The Darkness* ... (HAR)
He's So Gay
Frank Zappa; *Thing-Fish* ....(RYK)
Killing Of Georgie
Rod Stewart; *Greatest Hits* ....(WB)
   Night On The Town ....(WB)
Leaping Lesbians
Meg Christian; *Face The Music* ....(OLI)
Sue Fink; *Lesbian Concentrate* .....,............(OLI)

Lola
Kinks; *Come Dancing With-Best Of-1977-1986* .. (ARI)
   Everybody's In Show Biz .... (RHI)
   Kink Kronikles ....(RPR)
   Lola Vs. Powerman & The Moneygoround ..... (RPR)
   One For The Road .... (ARI)
   Second Time Around ....(RCA)
Long Hair Queer
Vandals; *Slippery When Ill* .... (RES)
Masculine Women, Feminine Men
Margaret Roadknight; *Living In The Land Of Oz* (RWD)
Out Of The Wardrobe
Kinks; *Misfits* .... (ARI)
Psycho Dyke
Dead Serios; *Possessed By Polka* .... (LGS)
Straight In A Gay World
Skyhooks; *Livin' In The 70s* ....(OOP)
Strange Night
Heart; *BeBe Le Strange* ....(EPI)
Sweet Transvestite
Original London Cast; *Rocky Horror Show* ...... (RHI)
Tim Curry; *ST/Rocky Horror Picture Show* ...... (RHI)
Tim Curry/Original Roxy Cast; *Rocky Horror
Show* .... (RHI)
Turned You Into A Lesbian
Mentors; *Rock Bible* .... (MEN)
Two Headed Sex Change
Cramps; *Look Mom No Head!* .... (RES)
Walk On The Wild Side
Edie Brickell/New Bohemians; *ST/Flashback* ...(WTG)
Lou Reed; *Between Thought &
Expression-Anthology* ....(RCA)
   Live ....(RCA)
   Transformer ....(RCA)
   Walk On The Wild Side-Best Of ....(RCA)
Y.M.C.A.
Village People; *Billboard Top Dance Hits-1978* .. (RHI)
   Billboard Top Rock 'N' Roll Hits-1979 .... (RHI)
   Cruisin' ....(CAS)
   Greatest Hits .... (RHI)
   Live & Sleazy ....(CAS)
   Night At Studio 54 ....(CAS)

HORSES, Riding

See Also: COWBOYS, REBELS, RODEO

All In Green Went My Love Riding
Joan Baez; *Love Song Album* .... (VAN)
All The King's Horses
Aretha Franklin; *Young Gifted & Black* ....(ATL)
Firm; *Mean Business* ....(ATL)
Lynn Anderson; *Greatest Hits-#2* ....(COL)
Nazareth; *Expect No Mercy* ....(A&M)
Triumph; *Surveillance* ....(MCA)
Appaloosa
Gino Vannelli; *Best Of* ....(A&M)
   Brother To Brother ....(A&M)
   Classics-#7 ....(A&M)
Back In The Saddle
Aerosmith; *Classics Live 2* ....(COL)
   Greatest Hits ....(COL)
   Live Bootleg ....(COL)
   Pandora's Box ....(COL)
   Rocks ....(COL)
Back In The Saddle Again
Gene Autry; *50th Anniversary* .... (REP)
   Columbia Country Classics-#1 ....(COL)
   Cowboy Hall Of Fame .... (REP)
   Great American Singing Cowboys .... (REP)
   South Of The Border .... (REP)
Bring On The Dancing Horses
Echo/Bunnymen; *Songs To Learn & Sing* .... (SIR)
   ST/Pretty In Pink ....(A&M)
Caballo Diablo
Charlie Daniels Band; *Fire On The Mountain* ..... (EPI)
Changing Horses
Dan Fogelberg; *Souvenirs* .... (FM)
Chariots Of Fire
Vangelis; *ST/Chariots Of Fire* ....(POL)
   Themes ....(POL)

Chestnut Mare
Byrds; *Best Of-Greatest Hits-#2* ....(COL)
  Byrds ....(COL)
  Rock Classics/'70s ....(COL)
  (Untitled) ....(COL)
Cowboy Rides Away
George Strait; *Country Classics-#1* ....(MCA)
  Does Fort Worth Ever Cross Your Mind ......(MCA)
  Greatest Hits-#2 ....(MCA)
Dark Horse
George Harrison; *Best Of* ....(CAP)
  Dark Horse ....(CAP)
Don't Change Horses
Tower Of Power; *Back To Oakland* ....(WB)
Don't Need No Horse
Little Walter; *Chess Blues* ....(CSS)
Freedom Rider
Traffic; *John Barleycorn Must Die* ....(ISL)
  On The Road ....(ISL)
(Ghost) Riders In The Sky
Gene Autry; *50th Anniversary* ....(REP)
  Cowboy Hall Of Fame ....(REP)
Outlaws; *Ghost Riders* ....(ARI)
Roy Clark; *Greatest Hits-#1* ....(MCA)
  In Concert ....(MCA)
  Superpicker ....(MCA)
Vaughn Monroe; *Best Of* ....(RCA)
  This Is ....(RCA)
  This Is/Decade Of The '40s ....(RCA)
Goin' To Dallas
Lightnin' Hopkins; *Drinkin' In The Blues-Golden
Classics-#1* ....(CLT)
  Lightnin' Hopkins ....(EVR)
Goin' To Dallas To See My Pony Run
Lightnin' Hopkins; *Blues In My Bottle* ....(BV)
  Drinkin' In The Blues-Golden Classics-#1 ....(CLT)
Great White Horse
Guy & Ralna; *22 Golden Country Classics* ......(RAN)
  Country ....(RAN)
Hi Ho Silver
Fleetwood Mac; *Kiln House* ....(RPR)
High Horse
Evelyn "Champagne" King; *45* ....(RCA)
Nitty Gritty Dirt Band; *20 Years Of Dirt-Best Of* ..(WB)
  Plain Dirt Fashion ....(WB)
Horse Latitudes
Doors; *Strange Days* ....(ELE)
Horse With No Name
America; *America* ....(WB)
  Billboard Top Rock 'N' Roll Hits-1972 ....(RHI)
  History-Greatest Hits ....(WB)
  In Concert ....(WB)
I Know You Rider
Big Brother/Holding Company; *Live* ....(RHI)
Grateful Dead; *Europe '72* ....(WB)
Hot Tuna; *Hot Tuna* ....(RCA)
I Ride An Old Paint/Whoopee Ti-Yi-Yo...
Michael Martin Murphey; *Cowboy Songs* ....(WB)
I've Got The Horse Right Here
Original Cast; *Guys & Dolls* ....(MCA)
Let That Pony Run
Pam Tillis; *Homeward Looking Angel* ....(ARI)
Littlest Cowboy Rides Again
Chris LeDoux; *Songbook Of The American West* ..(LIB)
  Sounds Of The Western Country ....(LIB)
Midnight Rider
Allman Brothers Band; *Anthology Of Duane
Allman-#2* ....(CPC)
  Beginnings ....(POL)
  Best Of ....(POL)
  Decade Of Hits-1969-1979 ....(POL)
  Idlewild South ....(POL)
  Road Goes On Forever ....(POL)
Gregg Allman; *Laid Back* ....(CPC)
  South's Greatest Hits ....(CPC)
Willie Nelson; *ST/Electric Horseman* ....(COL)
Montana
Frank Zappa; *You Can't Do That On Stage
Anymore* ....(RYK)
Mothers Of Invention; *Apostrophe/Overnite
Sensation* ....(RYK)
Mustang Sally
Rascals; *Greatest Hits* ....(ATL)

Wilson Pickett; *Atlantic R&B-1947-1974-#6* ....(ATL)
  Best Of ....(ATL)
  Greatest Hits ....(ATL)
  Man & A Half-Best Of ....(RHI)
  Super Hits ....(ATL)
Young Rascals; *Young Rascals* ....(RHI)
New Pony
Bob Dylan; *Street Legal* ....(COL)
Night Rider
Electric Light Orchestra; *Face The Music* ....(JET)
Elvis Presley; *Collector's Gold* ....(RCA)
  Live In Nashville ....(RCA)
  ST/Pot Luck ....(RCA)
Night Rider's Lament
Chris LeDoux; *Old Cowboy Classics* ....(LIB)
  Paint Me Back Home In Wyoming ....(LIB)
  & The Saddle Boogie Band ....(LIB)
Garth Brooks; *The Chase* ....(LIB)
Jerry Jeff Walker; *Ridin' High* ....(MCA)
Nanci Griffith; *Other Voices Other Rooms* ....(ELE)
Suzy Bogguss; *Somewhere Between* ....(CAP)
Old Paint
Chris LeDoux; *Old Cowboy Classics* ....(LIB)
  Western Tunesmith ....(LIB)
Linda Ronstadt; *Simple Dreams* ....(ELE)
Old Rockin' Horse
Slim Dusty; *Australia Is His Name* ....(PHO)
One Horse Town
Bobby Bland; *Introspective Of Early Years* ......(MCA)
  Touch Of The Blues ....(MCA)
David Frishberg; *Live At Vine Street* ....(FAN)
Elton John; *Blue Moves* ....(MCA)
Rembrandts; *Untitled* ....(ATC)
One-Trick Pony
Paul Simon; *ST/One-Trick Pony* ....(WB)
Pegasus
Allman Brothers Band; *Enlightened Rogues* ....(POL)
Mahavishnu Orchestra; *Visions Of The Emerald
Beyond* ....(COL)
Philadelphia Fillies
Del Reeves; *Super Country Hits Of The '70s* .....(GUS)
Pony Boy
Allman Brothers Band; *Brothers & Sisters* ....(POL)
Bruce Springsteen; *Human Touch* ....(COL)
Pony Express
Ted Nugent/Amboy Dukes; *Call Of The Wild* ....(BIZ)
Pony Man
Gordon Lightfoot; *Gord's Gold-#2* ....(WB)
  If You Could Read My Mind ....(RPR)
  Sit Down Young Stranger ....(RPR)
Pony Ride
Olivia Newton-John; *Come On Over* ....(MCA)
Pony Time
Chubby Checker; *Good Time Rock 'N' Roll* .....(MCA)
  Greatest Hits ....(AKO)
  Let's Dance ....(GUS)
Racehorse
Count Basie/Kansas City 3; *For The Second Time* (PAB)
Ride
David Allan Coe; *17 Greatest Hits* ....(COL)
  19 Hot Country Requests ....(EPI)
  Castles In The Sand ....(COL)
  For The Record-First 10 Years ....(COL)
  Trucker's Jukebox-#2 ....(COL)
Ride A Wild Horse
Kenny Nolan; *Night Miracles* ....(CAS)
Ride Like The Wind
Christopher Cross; *Christopher Cross* ....(WB)
Ride On Cowboy
Alvin Lee/Ten Years Later; *Ride On* ....(RSO)
Ride On Pony
Free; *Highway* ....(A&M)
  Live ....(A&M)
Ride Your Pony
Lee Dorsey; *Golden Classics* ....(CLT)
  History Of New Orleans R&B-#3-1962-1970 ...(RHI)
  '60s Soul Party ....(ERA)
Ride 'Em Cowboy
Paul Davis; *Ride 'Em Cowboy* ....(BNG)
Roy Rogers/Sons Of The Pioneers; *Roy Rogers/Sons Of
The Pioneers* ....(VS)
Rider In The Rain
Randy Newman; *Little Criminals* ....(WB)

Riders On The Storm
Doors; *Best Of* .... (ELE)
   Greatest Hits .... (ELE)
   L.A. Woman .... (ELE)
   ST/Doors .... (ELE)
   Weird Scenes Inside The Gold Mine .... (ELE)
Ride, Ride, Ride
Foghat; *Best Of* .... (RHI)
   Foghat .... (RHI)
Tex Ritter; *Country Music Hall Of Fame* .... (MCA)
Riding High In Texas
Peter Rowan; *Medicine Trail* .... (FF)
Ridin' Down The Canyon
Gene Autry; *Columbia Historic Edition* ....(COL)
   Western Classics ....(COL)
Riders In The Sky; *Cowboy Way* .... (MCA)
Willie Nelson & Leon Russell; *One For The
Road* ....(COL)
Rockin' Horse
Bad English; *Bad English* .... (EPI)
Run For The Roses
Dan Fogelberg; *Greatest Hits* .... (FM)
   Innocent Age .... (FM)
   Live-Greetings From The West .... (FM)
Saddle In The Rain
John Prine; *Common Sense* .... (ATL)
   Prime Prine-Best Of .... (ATL)
Saddle Up The Grey
New Lost City Ramblers; *20 Years Of Concert
Performances* ....(FF)
Saddle Up The Palomino
Neil Young/Crazy Horse; *American Stars N' Bars* (RPR)
She'll Be Coming 'Round The Mountain
Four Freshmen/Stan Kenton & Orchestra; *Live At Butler
University* ....(CW)
Mormon Tabernacle Choir; *This Land Is Your
Land* ....(COL)
Silver Stallion
W. Jennings/W. Nelson/J. Cash/K. Krist.; *Greatest
Country Hits/'90s-1990* ....(COL)
   Highwayman 2 ....(COL)
Sunday Rider
David Gates; *First* .... (ELE)
   Goodbye Girl .... (ELE)
Surrey With The Fringe On Top
Ellis Marsalis; *Heart Of Gold* ....(COL)
Original Broadway Cast; *Oklahoma* ....(RCA)
Original Cast; *Oklahoma* .... (MCA)
Swimming Horses
Siouxsie/Banshees; *Hyaena* .... (GEF)
   Twice Upon A Time/The Singles .... (GEF)
Trick Rider
McBride & The Ride; *Sacred Ground* .... (MCA)
Two White Horses
John Lee Hooker; *That's Where It's At* .... (STX)
When My Daddy Rode The West
Clarence Reid; *45* .... (DSH)
White Horse
Laid Back; *Castles In The Sand* .... (SIR)
   For The Record .... (SIR)
   Greatest Hits Of The Street .... (PRY)
   Keep Smiling .... (SIR)
White Horses
Outlaws; *Ghost Riders* .... (ARI)
Who's Gonna Ride Your Wild Horses
U2; *Achtung Baby* .... (ISL)
Wild Horses
Flying Burrito Brothers; *Farther Along-Best Of* .. (A&M)
Garth Brooks; *No Fences* .... (LIB)
Gino Vannelli; *Big Dreams Never Sleep* ......(EPA)
Prefab Sprout; *Jordan-The Comeback* .... (EPI)
   Life Of Surprises-Best Of .... (EPI)
Rolling Stones; *Hot Rocks-1964-1971* .... (AKO)
   Made In The Shade .... (RS)
   Singles Collection-London Years .... (AKO)
   Sticky Fingers .... (RS)
Sundays; *Blind* .... (DGC)
Suzy Bogguss; *Moment Of Truth* .... (CAP)
Wildfire
Michael Martin Murphey; *Best Of* .... (EMI)
   Super Hits!/'70s-Have A Nice Day-#14 .... (RHI)
   '70s Greatest Rock Hits-#3-High Times .... (PRY)
Michael Murphey; *Blue Sky Night Thunder* .... (EPI)

William Tell Overture (Lone Ranger)
Boston Pops Orchestra/Arthur Fiedler; *Fiedler-Greatest
Hits* ....(RCA)
   TV Classics ....(RCA)
Spike Jones/City Slickers; *Best Of* ....(RCA)
Yankee Doodle
Boston Pops Orchestra/Arthur Fiedler; *Fiedler's Favorite
Marches* ....(RCA)
   Music For All Occasions ....(RCA)

HOT, Heat, Warm
See Also: FIRE, HELL

99 In The Shade
Bon Jovi; *New Jersey* .... (JBC)
Don't Stop When You're Hot
Larry Graham; *45* .... (WB)
Gonna Make You Sweat (Everybody...)
C & C Music Factory; *Gonna Make You Sweat* ..(COL)
   Hot #1 Hits ....(FTN)
Heat Goes On
Asia; *Alpha* ....(GEF)
Heat In Harlem
Graham Parker; *Pourin' It All Out-Mercury Years* (MER)
Graham Parker/Rumour; *Parkerilla* .... (MER)
   Stick To Me .... (MER)
Heat In The Street
Pat Travers; *Go For What You Know* .... (POL)
   Heat In The Street .... (POL)
Heat Is On
Glenn Frey; *Soundtrack Smashes/'80s* .... (MCA)
   ST/Beverly Hills Cop .... (MCA)
Isley Brothers; *Heat Is On* .... (TN)
Heat Is On Is Saigon
Original London Cast; *Miss Saigon* ....(GEF)
Heat Of Heat
Patti Austin; *Gettin' Away With Murder* .... (QUE)
Heat Of The Moment
Asia; *Asia* ....(GEF)
   Then & Now ....(GEF)
Heat Of The Night
Bryan Adams; *Into The Fire* .... (A&M)
Jay Ferguson; *White Noise* ....(CAP)
Heat Treatment
Graham Parker; *Pourin' It All Out-Mercury Years* (MER)
Graham Parker/Rumour; *Heat Treatment* .... (MER)
   Parkerilla .... (MER)
Heat Wave
Linda Ronstadt; *Greatest Hits #1* .... (ASY)
   Prisoner In Disguise .... (ASY)
Martha Reeves/Vandellas; *Billboard Top R&B
Hits-1963* .... (RHI)
   Greatest Hits .... (MOT)
   More American Graffiti #4 .... (MCA)
   Motown Story .... (MOT)
Who; *Two's Missing* .... (MCA)
Hot
Carl Carlton; *Private Property* ....(CAS)
Roy Ayers; *You Might Be Surprised* ....(COL)
Hot As Sun
Paul McCartney; *Paul McCartney* ....(COL)
Hot Blooded
Foreigner; *Double Vision* .... (ATL)
   Records .... (ATL)
   ST/Vision Quest ....(GEF)
Hot Cakes
Carly Simon; *Hot Cakes* .... (ELE)
Hot Cherie
Hardline; *Double Eclipse* .... (MCA)
Hot Child In The City
Nick Gilder; *Billboard Top Hits-1978* .... (RHI)
   City Nights ....(CHR)
Hot Chili
Steve Miller Band; *Number 5* .... (CAP)
Hot Chili Mama
Beausoleil; *Hot Chili Mama* .... (ARH)
Hot Coffee
Carl Anderson; *Pieces Of A Heart* .... (GRP)
Hot Cop
Village People; *Cruisin'* ....(CAS)
   Greatest Hits .... (RHI)
   Live & Sleazy .... (CAS)

Hot Corn, Cold Corn
Flatt & Scruggs; *At Carnegie Hall* ....(COL)
Hot Diggity
Perry Como; *All-Time Greatest Hits-#1* ....(RCA)
  Golden Records ....(RCA)
  Pure Gold ....(RCA)
  This Is ....(RCA)
Hot Dog
Elvis Presley; *Essential Elvis-First Movies* ....(RCA)
  Loving You ....(RCA)
  Sings Lieber & Stoller ....(RCA)
Led Zeppelin; *In Through The Out Door* ....(SS)
Mongo Santamaria; *Greatest Hits* ....(COL)
Hot Dusty Roads
Buffalo Springfield; *Buffalo Springfield* ....(ATC)
Hot For Teacher
Van Halen; *1984* ....(WB)
Hot Fun In The Summertime
Sly/Family Stone; *Anthology* ....(EPI)
  Billboard Top R&B Hits-1969 ....(RHI)
  Greatest Hits ....(EPI)
  Summer & Sun ....(RHI)
Hot Girls In Love
Loverboy; *Big Ones* ....(COL)
  Keep It Up ....(COL)
Hot Legs
Rod Stewart; *Absolutely Live* ....(WB)
  Footloose & Fancy Free ....(WB)
  Greatest Hits ....(WB)
  Storyteller-Complete Anthology-1964-1990 ......(WB)
Hot Line
Black Sabbath; *Born Again* ....(WB)
Sylvers; *Best Of* ....(CAP)
Hot Love
Cheap Trick; *Cheap Trick* ....(EPI)
Five Star; *Five Star* ....(EPI)
Michael Bolton; *The Hunger* ....(COL)
Hot Love Cold World
Bob Welch; *French Kiss* ....(CAP)
Hot Night In New York City
Bonnie Koloc; *With You On My Side* ....(FF)
Hot Nite In Dallas
Moon Martin; *Shots From A Cold Nightmare* ....(CAP)
Hot Number
Fabulous Thunderbirds; *Hot Number* ....(CBA)
Foxy; *Get Down Tonight!-Best Of T.K. Records* ... (RHI)
  Hot Numbers ....(DSH)
Hot On A Thing Called Love
Chi-Lites; *Me And You* .... (20)
Hot Pants
James Brown; *In The Jungle Groove* ....(POL)
  Revolution Of The Mind ....(POL)
Hot Pants In The Summertime
Dramatics; *Whatcha See Is Whatcha Get* ....(STX)
Hot Pastrami
Dartells; *Frat Rock! Box Set* .... (RHI)
  Frat Rock-#4 ....(RHI)
  History Of Rock Instrumentals-#1 ....(RHI)
  Son Of Frat Rock ....(RHI)
Hot Pink
Eddy Raven; *Right For The Flight* ....(LIB)
Meat Puppets; *Up On The Sun* ....(SST)
Hot Potatoes
King Curtis; *Enjoy-Best Of* ....(CLT)
Kinks; *Everybody's In Show Biz* ....(RHI)
Hot Rails To Hell
Blue Oyster Cult; *Career Of Evil* ....(COL)
  Extraterrestrial Live ....(COL)
  Metal Giants ....(COL)
  On Your Feet Or On Your Knees ....(COL)
  Tyranny & Mutation ....(COL)
Hot Rockin'
Judas Priest; *Point Of Entry* ....(COL)
Hot Rod
Ray Charles; *Live* ....(ATL)
Hot Rod Baby
Ronny/Daytonas; *45* ....(FSB)
Hot Rod Hearts
Robbie Dupree; *Robbie Dupree* ....(ELE)
Hot Rod Lincoln
Asleep At The Wheel; *Western Standard Time* ....(EPI)

Commander Cody/Lost Planet Airmen; *Lost In The Ozone* ....(MCA)
  Super Hits/'70s-Have A Nice Day-#8 ....(RHI)
  We've Got A Live One Here ....(WB)
Johnny Bond; *Best Of* ....(STR)
Hot Spot
Dazz Band; *Hot Spot* ....(MOT)
Hot Streets
Chicago; *Hot Streets* ....(COL)
Hot Stuff
Donna Summer; *Bad Girls* ....(CAS)
  Dance Collection ....(CAS)
  On The Radio-Greatest Hits-#1 & 2 ....(CAS)
  Walk Away-Best Of-1977-1980 ....(CAS)
Rolling Stones; *Black & Blue* ....(RS)
  Love You Live ....(RS)
  Sucking In The Seventies ....(RS)
Whitesnake; *Come An' Get It* ....(GEF)
Hot Summer Day
David LaFlamme; *White Bird* ....(AMH)
It's A Beautiful Day; *It's A Beautiful Day* ....(COL)
Hot Summer Nights
Miami Sound Machine; *ST/Top Gun* ....(COL)
Rick James; *Wonderful* ....(RPR)
Walter Egan; *Not Shy* ....(COL)
Hot Tamale
Jackie Mittoo; *Jackie Mittoo* .... (EMI)
  New & Old Songs ....(EMI)
Hot Tamale Baby
Buckwheat Zydeco; *Best Of Louisiana Music* .... (ROU)
Clifton Chenier; *Zydeco Dynamite-Anthology* .... (RHI)
  Zydeco Party ....(KT)
Hot Texas Night
Mac Davis; *Texas In My Rear View Mirror* ....(CAS)
Hot To Trot
Hank Williams, Jr.; *Lone Wolf* ....(W/C)
Kings Of The Sun; *Kings Of The Sun* ....(RCA)
Wild Cherry; *Electrified Funk* ....(EPI)
Hot Water
Jefferson Starship; *Spitfire* ....(GRU)
Level 42; *Physical Presence-#2* ....(POL)
  True Colours ....(POL)
  World Machine ....(POL)
Hot Wire
Al Green; *45* ....(FSB)
Hot & Nasty
Black Oak Arkansas; *Best Of* ....(ATC)
  Black Oak Arkansas ....(ATC)
  Raunch 'N' Roll ....(ATC)
Humble Pie; *Best* ....(A&M)
  Classcs-#14 ....(A&M)
  Rockin' '60s ....(PRY)
  Smokin' ....(A&M)
Hot 'Lanta
38 Special; *Rock & Roll Strategy* ....(A&M)
Allman Brothers Band; *At The Fillmore East* .....(POL)
  Road Goes On Forever ....(POL)
Hot 'N' Ready
UFO; *Obsession* ....(CHR)
Hotter Than Mojave In My Heart
Iris DeMent; *Infamous Angel* ....(WB)
Hot, Blue & Righteous
ZZ Top; *Six Pack* ....(WB)
  Tres Hombres ....(WB)
Hot, Wet & Sticky
Galaxy; *Hot, Wet & Sticky* .... (ARI)
Hot! Wild! Unrestricted! Crazy Love
Millie Jackson; *Imitation Of Love* .... (JVA)
I Melt With You
Modern English; *After The Snow* ....(SIR)
  Pillow Lips ....(TVT)
In The Heat Of The Jungle
Chris Isaak; *Heart Shaped World* ....(RPR)
In The Heat Of The Night
Pat Benatar; *In The Heat Of The Night* ....(CHR)
Ray Charles; *His Greatest Hits-#2* ....(DHL)
  ST/In The Heat Of The Night ....(UA)
I've Got My Love To Keep Me Warm
Ella Fitzgerald; *Irving Berlin Songbook-#2* ....(VRV)
Les Brown; *Best Of The Big Bands* ....(COL)
Les Brown/Orchestra; *16 Most Requested Songs/'40s-#1* ....(COL)
Keep Each Other Warm
Barry Manilow; *Barry Manilow* ....(ARI)

Keep It Hot
Cameo; *45* .... (CHC)
Feel Me .... (CHC)
Keep It Warm
Flo & Eddie; *Best Of* .... (RHI)
Long Hot Summer
Aldo Nova; *Twitch* .... (POR)
Jimmie Rodgers; *Best Of* .... (RHI)
Style Council; *Introducing The* .... (MER)
Love In The Hot Afternoon
Gene Watson; *Best Of* .... (CAP)
Great Records Of The Decade-'70s-Country ....(CCB)
Greatest Hits ....(CCB)
Make You Sweat
Keith Sweat; *I'll Give All My Love To You* ....(VNT)
Melt In Your Mouth
Candyman; *Ain't No Shame In My Game* .... (EPI)
Memphis, Tennessee Hot Rock
Gordon Terry; *Tennessee Hot Rock* .... (PLN)
Pump It Hottie
Redhead Kingpin/F.B.I.; *Rap-On The Lighter Tip* .. (KT)
Red Hot
Robert Gordon; *Rock This Town-Rockabilly Hits-#2* .... (RHI)
Robert Gordon & Link Wray; *Robert Gordon & Link Wray* ....(RCA)
Red Hot Chicken
Wet Willie; *Drippin' Wet Live* ....(CPC)
Greatest Hits ....(POL)
Red Hot Poker
Rufus; *Rufus* .... (MCA)
Red Light Mama Red Hot
Humble Pie; *Humble Pie* ....(A&M)
Rhythm Of The Heat
Peter Gabriel; *Plays Live* ....(GEF)
Security ....(GEF)
Rock Is Hot
Crown Heights Affair; *Dance Lady Dance* .... (DL)
She Runs Hot
Little Village; *Little Village* ....(RPR)
She Was Hot
Rolling Stones; *Undercover* ....(RS)
She's Hot
Fabulous Thunderbirds; *Powerful Stuff* ....(EPA)
Some Like It Hot
Power Station; *Power Station* .... (CAP)
Robert Palmer; *Addictions-#1* .... (ISL)
Steam
Peter Gabriel; *Us* ....(GEF)
Steam Heat
Janis Paige/John Raitt/Original Cast; *Pajama Game* ....(COL)
Summer In The City
Lovin' Spoonful; *Anthology* .... (RHI)
Best Of ....(OOP)
Billboard Top Rock 'N' Roll Hits-1966 .... (RHI)
Rockin' '60s ....(PRY)
Sweat (A La La La Long)
Inner Circle; *Bad Boys* ....(BB)
There'll Be A Hot Time In The Old...
Bessie Smith; *Complete Recordings-#3* ....(COL)
Louis Armstrong; *Best Of* ....(AUF)
Turk Murphy's San Francisco Jazz Band; *#1* .... (GTJ)
There'll Be A Hot Time In...Berlin
Woody Herman; *Uncollected-& His First Herd* ... (HIN)
They're Red Hot
Red Hot Chili Peppers; *Blood Sugar Sex Magik* ... (WB)
Robert Johnson; *Complete Recordings* ....(COL)
This Beat Is Hot
B.G. The Prince Of Rap; *Power Of Rhythm* .... (EPI)
This Beat Is Hot-Compilation ....(EPI)
Too Darn Hot
Ella Fitzgerald; *Cole Porter Songbook* ....(VRV)
Erasure; *Red Hot+Blue* ....(CHR)
Mel Torme; *Swings Shubert Alley* ....(VRV)
Too Hot
Kool/Gang; *Everything's Kool/Gang-Greatest Hits* (MER)
Ladies Night ....(DL)
Loverboy; *Big Ones* ....(COL)
Specials; *Specials* ....(CHR)
Too Hot Ta Trot
Commodores; *Greatest Hits* .... (MOT)
Live ....(MOT)

Too Hot To Handle
Roosevelt Sykes; *Raining In My Heart* ....(DEL)
UFO; *Lights Out* ....(CHR)
Strangers In The Night ....(CHR)
Too Hot To Sleep
Louise Mandrell; *Too Hot To Sleep* ....(RCA)
Two Hot Girls (On A Hot Summer Night)
Carly Simon; *Coming Around Again* .... (ARI)
Greatest Hits Live ....(ARI)
Warm All Over
Barbra Streisand; *Highlights From "Just For The Record"* ....(COL)
...Just For The Record ....(COL)
Original Broadway Cast; *The Most Happy Fella* (SMC)
Warm It Up
Kris Kross; *Totally Krossed Out* ....(RUF)
Warm Love
Joan Armatrading; *Show Some Emotion* ....(A&M)
Van Morrison; *Best Of* ....(MER)
Hard Nose The Highway ....(WB)
It's Too Late To Stop Now ....(WB)
Warm Sunday
Conrad Herwig Quintet; *The Amulet* .... (KNR)
Warm Valley
Duke Ellington; *Money Jungle* ....(BLN)
Paul Desmond; *Pure Desmond* ....(CBA)
Warm Ways
Fleetwood Mac; *25 Years-The Chain* ....(WB)
Fleetwood Mac ....(RPR)
Warm Your Heart
Aaron Neville; *Warm Your Heart* ....(A&M)
Drifters; *Let The Boogie Woogie Roll-Greatest Hits* (ATL)
Warm & Beautiful
Wings; *At The Speed Of Sound* ....(CAP)
Warm & Tender
Johnny Mathis; *Greatest Hits* ....(COL)
Warm & Tender Love
Dave Mason; *Mariposa De Oro* ....(COL)
Percy Sledge; *Best Of* ....(ATL)
It Tears Me Up-Best Of ....(RHI)
Ultimate Collection-When A Man Loves... ....(ATL)
Warmth Of The Sun
Beach Boys; *Absolute Best-#1* ....(CAP)
Best Of ....(CAP)
Endless Summer ....(CAP)
Fun Fun Fun ....(CAP)
Gift Set ....(CAP)
ST/Good Morning Vietnam ....(A&M)
When You're Hot, You're Hot
Jerry Reed; *60 Years Of Country Music* ....(RCA)
Best Of ....(RCA)
Super Hits/'70s-Have A Nice Day-#5 .... (RHI)
When You're Hot, You're Hot ....(RCA)
White Heat, Red Hot
Judas Priest; *Stained Class* ....(COL)
White Hot
Black Flag; *In My Head* ....(SST)
Red Rider; *Don't Fight It* ....(CAP)
White Light/White Heat
David Bowie; *Sound + Vision* ....(RYK)
ST/Ziggy Stardust-The Motion Picture ....(RCA)
Lou Reed; *1969 Live* ....(MER)
Live-#1 ....(JCI)
Rock 'N' Roll Animal ....(RCA)
Walk On The Wild Side-Best Of ....(RCA)
Velvet Underground; *White Light/White Heat* .....(VRV)
Wild Nights, Hot & Crazy Days
Judas Priest; *Metal Works-1973-1993* ....(COL)
Turbo ....(COL)

HOTELS, Motels

At The Grand Hotel/Table With A View
Broadway Cast; *Grand Hotel* ....(RCA)
At The Mambo Inn
George Benson; *Tenderly* ....(WB)
Back To The Hotel
N2Deep; *Back To The Hotel* ....(PRO)
Big Hotel
Big Pig; *Bonk* ....(A&M)
Blue Motel Room
Joni Mitchell; *Hejira* ....(ASY)

Broadway Hotel
Al Stewart; *Year Of The Cat* .... (ARI)
Buenos Noches From A Lonely Room
Dwight Yoakam; *Buenos Noches From A Lonely
Room* .... (RPR)
Caesar's Palace Blues
UK; *Danger Money* .... (EDI)
Night After Night .... (EDI)
Cigarette Motel
Leaving Trains; *Kill Tunes* .... (SST)
Cold, Cold, Cold
Little Feat; *Feats Don't Fail Me Now* .... (WB)
Sailin' Shoes .... (WB)
Dinner At The Ritz
City Boy; *Dinner At The Ritz* .... (MER)
Evangeline Hotel
Katy Moffatt; *Greatest Show On Earth* .... (PHO)
Tom Russell; *Hurricane Season* .... (PHO)
Fat Chance Hotel
Public Image, Ltd.; *Happy?* .... (VIA)
Food Phone Gas Lodging
Charlie King; *Food Phone Gas Lodging* .... (FF)
Grand Hotel
Procol Harum; *Grand Hotel* .... (CHR)
Hangdog Hotel Room
Gordon Lightfoot; *Gord's Gold-#2* .... (WB)
Heart Hotels
Dan Fogelberg; *Greatest Hits* .... (FM)
Phoenix .... (FM)
Heartbreak Hotel
Albert King; *Blues For Elvis* .... (STX)
Elvis Presley; *50 Worldwide Gold Award Hits-#1* (RCA)
Elvis At Madison Square Garden .... (RCA)
Golden Records-#1 .... (RCA)
Golden Records-#2 .... (RCA)
Legendary Performer-#1 .... (RCA)
Nipper's Greatest Hits!'50s-#1 .... (RCA)
Jacksons; *Live* .... (EPI)
Triumph .... (EPI)
Stan Freberg; *Capitol Collectors Series* .... (CAP)
Willie Nelson; *Greatest Hits & Some That Will Be* (COL)
& Leon Russell: One For The Road .... (COL)
Holiday Hotel
Loggins & Messina; *Loggins & Messina* .... (COL)
On Stage .... (COL)
Holiday Inn
Elton John; *Madman Across The Water* .... (POL)
Holiday Inn Blues
Neil Diamond; *Velvet Gloves & Spit* .... (MCA)
Honeymoon Hotel
Alice Faye; *Hooray For Hollywood* .... (RCA)
Hotel 49
Chet Baker; *In New York* .... (RVR)
Hotel California
Al B. Sure!; *Private Times & The Whole 9* .... (WB)
Eagles; *Anthology* .... (ASY)
Greatest Hits-#2 .... (ASY)
Hell Freezes Over .... (GEF)
Hotel California .... (ASY)
Live .... (ASY)
Gipsy Kings; *Rubaiyat-Elektra's 40th Anniversary* (ELE)
Hotel For Women
Nails; *Hotel For Women* .... (PVC)
Hotel Happiness
Brook Benton; *Anthology* .... (RHI)
It's Just A Mater Of Time-Greatest Hits .... (MER)
Super Oldies/'60s-#11 .... (AUF)
Hotel Hobbies
Marillion; *Clutching At Straws* .... (CAP)
Hotel Illness
Black Crowes; *Southern Harmony & Musical
Companion* .... (DEF)
Hotel Indiscreet
Sagittarius; *Present Tense* .... (BCT)
Hotel Me
Gil Evans; *Individualism Of* .... (VRV)
Hotel Rats & Photostats
Jimmy Page; *ST/Death Wish 2* .... (SS)
Hotel Ritz
Hoyt Axton; *Rusty Old Halo* .... (JER)
Imperial Hotel
Stevie Nicks; *Rock A Little* .... (MOD)

Iron Bar Motel
Slave Raider; *What Do You Know About Rock &
Roll* .... (JVA)
King Of The Road
Roger Miller; *Billboard Top Country Hits-1965* .. (RHI)
Cruisin'-1965 .... (INC)
Golden Hits .... (SMA)
R.E.M.; *Dead Letter Office* .... (IRS)
Little Hotel Room
Merle Haggard; *Friendship* .... (COL)
It's All In The Game .... (EPI)
Loveless Motel
Eddie Moore; *Moore Country With* .... (COU)
L' Hotel
Yello; *45* .... (MER)
L-Ranko Motel
Bell & Shore; *L-Ranko Motel* .... (ROM)
Magic Hotel
Wild Swans; *Space Flower* .... (SIR)
Memory Hotel
Rolling Stones; *Black & Blue* .... (RS)
Moonlight Motel
Gun Club; *Las Vegas Story* .... (IRS)
Motel
Connells; *Fun & Games* .... (TVT)
Gang Of Four; *Mall* .... (POL)
Motel Blues
Big Star; *Live* .... (RYK)
Loudon Wainwright III; *Live One* .... (ROU)
Motel Eyes
Rick Springfield; *Living In Oz* .... (RCA)
Motel King
James Harman Band; *Do Not Disturb* .... (BTO)
Motel Lover
Marvin Sease; *Real Deal* .... (LON)
Motel Matches
Elvis Costello; *Girls Girls Girls* .... (COL)
Elvis Costello/Attractions; *Get Happy!* .... (RYK)
Motel Mourning
Sonny Wright; *45* .... (DOO)
Motel Party Baby
Dinosaurs; *Dinosaurs* .... (RLX)
Motel Room In My Bed
X; *Under The Big Black Sun* .... (ELE)
Motel Row
James & Michael Younger; *James & Michael
Younger* .... (MCA)
Motel Satellite
Wellsprings Of Hope; *Phonograph* .... (SAF)
Motel Time
Larry Coryell; *Bolero* .... (EVD)
Motels & Planes
Bill Morrissey; *Standing Eight* .... (PHO)
Mud Shark, The
Mothers Of Invention; *Fillmore East-June 1971* ... (BIZ)
Mudshark
Mothers Of Invention; *Live At The Fillmore East* . (RPR)
No Tell Motel
David Houston; *Best Of* .... (GUS)
Old Rose Motel
Great White; *Psycho City* .... (CAP)
One Night In The Hotel
Michel Petrucciani; *Promenade With Duke* .... (BLN)
Paper Thin Hotel
Leonard Cohen; *Death Of A Ladies Man* .... (COL)
Portmeirion
Fairport Convention; *Expletive Delighted* .... (VAR)
Rats Motel
Lord Tracy; *Deaf Gods Of Babylon* .... (UNI)
Roach Motel
Dead Youth; *Intense Brutality* .... (GCI)
Room 317
Original London Cast; *Miss Saigon* .... (GEF)
Room 608
Horace Silver; *Best Of-Blue Note Years* .... (BLN)
Room Service
Kiss; *Dressed To Kill* .... (CAS)
Po', Broke & Lonely?; *No Money No Honey* ..... (RUT)
Room With A View
Bobby Short; *Bobby Noel & Cole* .... (ATL)
Jeffrey Osborne; *Emotional* .... (A&M)
Johnny Adams; *Room With A View Of The Blues* (ROU)
Lou Rawls; *At Last* .... (BLN)
Legendary .... (BLN)

Noel Coward; *Live From Las Vegas & New York* .(COL)
Wall Of Voodoo; *Seven Days In Sammystown* .... (IRS)
Yellowjackets; *Four Corners* .... (MCA)
Room Without A View
Smithereens; *11* .... (CAP)
Seven Doors Hotel
Europe; *Europe* .... (EPI)
Sitting In My Hotel
Kinks; *Everybody's In Show Biz* .... (RHI)
Standin' At The Big Hotel
Joe Ely; *Down On The Drag* .... (MCA)
There's A Small Hotel
Benny Goodman; *Birth Of Swing* .... (BLU)
Complete-#2 .... (RCA)
Bobby Short; *Celebrates Rodgers & Hart* .... (ATL)
Ella Fitzgerald; *Rodgers & Hart Songbook* ...... (VRV)
Tony Bennett; *Rodgers & Hart Songbook* .... (DRG)
Third Rate Romance
Amazing Rhythm Aces; *45* .... (OOP)
Rosanne Cash; *Somewhere In The Stars* .... (COL)
Sammy Kershaw; *Feelin' Good Train* .... (MER)
This Hotel Room
Jimmy Buffett; *Havana Daydreamin'* .... (MCA)
Twilight Hotel
Quiet Riot; *QR III* .... (EPA)

HOUSES, Cabins, Roofs
See Also: HOME

At An Arabian House Party
Raymond Scott; *Reckless Nights & Turkish
Twilights* .... (COL)
Attics Of My Life
Grateful Dead; *American Beauty* .... (WB)
Baby Let's Play House
Elvis Presley; *Complete Sun Sessions* .... (RCA)
Date With Elvis .... (RCA)
Golden Celebration .... (RCA)
Sun Sessions .... (RCA)
Baby's House
Steve Miller Band; *Anthology* .... (CAP)
Your Saving Grace .... (CAP)
Barrel House Blues
Gertrude "Ma" Rainey; *Queen Of The Blues-#3* ...(BIO)
Barrelhouse Shakedown
Emerson, Lake & Palmer; *Works II* .... (ATL)
Blow The House Down
Living In A Box; *Gatecrashing* .... (CHR)
Siouxsie/Banshees; *Hyaena* .... (GEF)
Brick House
Commodores; *All The Great Hits* .... (MOT)
Commodores .... (MOT)
Compact Command Performances .... (MOT)
Greatest Hits .... (MOT)
Motown Dance Party-#2 .... (MOT)
Burning Down The House
Talking Heads; *Speaking In Tongues* .... (SIR)
Stop Making Sense .... (SIR)
Burning House Of Love
X; *Ain't Love Grand* .... (ELE)
Best Of MTV's 120 Minutes-#2 .... (RHI)
Live At The Whisky A Go-Go... .... (ELE)
Cabin Home On The Hill
Ricky Skaggs; *Sweet Temptation* ....(SH)
Cabin In The Sky
Andre Previn; *Plays Songs By Vernon Duke* ..... (CTM)
Mose Allison; *Creek Bank* .... (PRS)
Cabin On A Mountain
Country Gazette; *Bluegrass Tonight* .... (FF)
Cabin On The Hill
Flatt & Scruggs; *Columbia Historic Edition* ...... (COL)
Coffee House Blues
Lightnin' Hopkins; *Best Of The Blues* .... (TRD)
Cook Of The House
Wings; *At The Speed Of Sound* .... (CAP)
Crack House Woman
George "Wild Child" Butler; *These Mean Old
Blues* .... (BUL)
Everybody Eats When They Come To My...
Cab Calloway; *Hi De Ho Man* .... (COL)
Fiddler On The Roof
Original Cast; *Fiddler On The Roof* .... (RCA)

Get The Fuck Out Of My House
2 Live Crew; *As Nasty As They Wanna Be* ...... (LUK)
Ghost In This House
Shenandoah; *Extra Mile* .... (COL)
Glass House
Temptations; *25th Anniversary* .... (MOT)
Song For You .... (MOT)
Glass Houses
Tammy Wynette & Joe Diffie; *Without Walls* ..... (EPI)
Goin' Through The Big D
Mark Chesnutt; *What A Way To Live* .... (DEC)
Grand Tour
Aaron Neville; *Grand Tour* .... (A&M)
Guns On The Roof
Clash; *Give 'Em Enough Rope* .... (EPI)
Happy House
Siouxsie/Banshees; *Kaleidoscope* .... (GEF)
Nocturne .... (GEF)
Once Upon A Time-The Singles .... (GEF)
Harry's House Centerpiece
Joni Mitchell; *Hissing Of Summer Lawns* ...... (ASY)
House
Psychedelic Furs; *Theodore: An Alternative Music
Sampler* .... (COL)
House Arrest
Bryan Adams; *Waking Up The Neighbours* ...... (A&M)
House At Pooh Corner
Loggins & Messina; *Best Of-Friends* .... (COL)
On Stage .... (COL)
Sittin' In .... (COL)
Nitty Gritty Dirt Band; *Best Of* .... (EMI)
Dirt Silver & Gold .... (OOP)
House Behind A House
Bob Seger/Silver Bullet Band; *The Distance* ...... (CAP)
House Burning Down
Jimi Hendrix; *Electric Ladyland* .... (RPR)
Essential .... (RPR)
House Carpenter
Bob Dylan; *Bootleg Series-#1-3* .... (COL)
Joan Baez; *Ballad Book* .... (VAN)
Pete Seeger; *20 Golden Pieces Of* .... (BLD)
House Cleaning
Spaniels; *Goodnite It's Time To Go* .... (VJ)
House For Everyone
Traffic; *Mr. Fantasy* .... (ISL)
House I Live In (That's America To Me)
Frank Sinatra; *A Man & His Music* .... (RPR)
Greatest Hits-Early Years .... (COL)
In The Beginning-1943-1951 .... (COL)
Main Event .... (SIN)
House In France
Doris Day & Andre Previn; *Duete* .... (DRG)
Sacha Distel; *Amour Tout Court* .... (DRG)
House In The Country
Blood, Sweat & Tears; *Child Is Father To The
Man* .... (COL)
House Is Not A Home
Burt Bacharach; *Classics-#23* .... (A&M)
Dionne Warwick; *Anthology* .... (RHI)
Greatest Hits .... (EVR)
Hot-Live & Otherwise .... (ARI)
Say A Little Prayer .... (DHL)
Luther Vandross; *Best Of-Best Of Love* .... (EPI)
Never Too Much .... (EPI)
Mavis Staples; *15 Original Big Hits-#3* .... (STX)
Mavis Staples .... (STX)
House Is Rockin'
Cheap Trick; *Dream Police* .... (EPI)
Stevie Ray Vaughan/Double Trouble; *In Step* ..... (EPI)
House Of Blue Lights
Andrews Sisters; *Best Of-#2* .... (MCA)
Asleep At The Wheel; *10* .... (EPI)
Greatest Country Hits/'80s-1987 .... (COL)
More Hot Country Requests-#2 .... (EPI)
Trucker's Jukebox-#2 .... (COL)
Canned Heat; *Human Conditions* .... (TAK)
& John Lee Hooker: Live At Fox Venice .... (RHI)
Chuck Berry; *Chess Box* .... (CSS)
More Rock 'N' Roll Rarities-Golden Era .... (CSS)
House Of Blue Lovers
James O'Gwynn; *Greatest Hits* .... (PLN)
Souvenirs Of Music City U.S.A. .... (PLN)
House Of Cards
Elton John; *45* .... (MCA)

Mary Chapin Carpenter; *Stones In The Road* ....(COL)
House Of Flowers
  Barbra Streisand; *Just For The Record* ....(COL)
  Harold Arlen & Barbra Streisand; *Harold Sings Arlen*
   (With Friend) ....(SSP)
  Original Cast; *House Of Flowers* ....(SSP)
House Of Four Doors
  Moody Blues; *In Search Of The Lost Chord* ......(POL)
House Of Gold
  Hank Williams; *I'm So Lonesome I Could Cry* ...(POL)
House Of Love
  Amy Grant & Vince Gill; *House Of Love* ....(A&M)
House Of Marcus Lycus
  George Hearn/Bob Gunton & Women; *Collector's*
   Sondheim ....(RCA)
  Stephen Sondheim; *Collector's Sondheim* ....(RCA)
House Of Memories
  Merle Haggard/Strangers; *Best Of* ....(CAP)
House Of Pain
  Faster Pussycat; *Wake Me When it's Over* ..... (ELE)
  Van Halen; *1984* ....(WB)
House Of Rock
  James Brown; *45* ....(SCO)
House Of The Rising Sun
  Animals; *Best Of* ....(AKO)
   Greatest Hits ....(ALL)
   Rip It To Shreds-Greatest Hits Live ....(IRS)
  Hank Williams, Jr.; *Hank Live* ....(W/C)
  Ronnie Milsap; *16 Greatest Hits-#2* ....(TRP)
House On Fire
  Boomtown Rats; *Greatest Hits* ....(COL)
  V Deep ....(COL)
House On The Hill
  Stevie Wonder; *For Once In My Life* ....(MOT)
  Turtles; *Turtle Soup* ....(RHI)
   Turtle Wax-Best Of-#2 ....(RHI)
House Party
  J. Geils Band; *Best Of* ....(ATL)
   Bloodshot ....(ATL)
   Blow Your Face Out ....(ATL)
House Song
  Peter, Paul & Mary; *Album 1700* ....(WB)
House That Jack Built
  Aretha Franklin; *30 Greatest Hits* ....(ATL)
   Aretha's Gold ....(ATL)
House The Dog Built
  Jibri Wise One; *S* ....(EAR)
House Un-American Blues Activity Dream
  Mimi & Richard Farina; *Best Of* ....(VAN)
   Memories ....(VAN)
   Reflections In A Crystal Wind ....(VAN)
House Upon A Hill
  Paul Anka; *She's A Lady* ....(ACC)
   Very Best Of ....(RAN)
House Without Love
  Hank Williams; *24 Greatest Hits-#2* ....(POL)
   I'm So Lonesome I Could Cry ....(POL)
Housecall
  Shabba Ranks w/Maxi Priest; *As Raw As Ever* ....(EPI)
Housequake
  Prince; *Sign O' The Times* ....(PAI)
Houses
  Judy Collins; *Judith* ....(ELE)
   So Early In The Morning ....(ELE)
Houses Of The Holy
  Led Zeppelin; *Led Zeppelin (collection)* ....(ATL)
   Physical Graffiti ....(SS)
Housewife
  Leon Russell; *Americana* ....(PRD)
House-Cat
  Danielle Dax; *Dark Adapted Eye* .... (SIR)
Hyacinth House
  Doors; *L.A. Woman* ....(ELE)
I Don't Want To Play House
  Lynn Anderson; *Rose Garden* ....(COL)
Icehouse
  Icehouse; *Icehouse* ....(CHR)
In My House
  Mary Jane Girls; *Motown Story-First 25 Years* .. (MOT)
   Only For You ....(MOT)

Is It Raining At Your House
  Vern Gosdin; *10 Years Of Greatest Hits Newly*
   Recorded ....(COL)
   Chiseled In Stone ....(COL)
   Greatest Country Hits/'90s-1991 ....(COL)
Israel In Our House
  Al Jolson; *Story-#5* .... (MCA)
It's My House
  Diana Ross; *All The Great Hits* .... (MOT)
   Anthology ....(MOT)
   Composer-Greatest By Ashford & Simpson ... (MOT)
   The Boss ....(MOT)
I'm Gonna Tear Your Playhouse Down
  Ann Peebles; *Greatest Hits* ....(MCA)
  B.B. King; *Lucille Talks Back* ....(OOP)
  Graham Parker; *Pourin' It All Out-Mercury Years* (MER)
  Graham Parker/Rumour; *Parkerilla* ....(MER)
   Stick To Me ....(MER)
  Paul Young; *Secret Of Association* ....(COL)
Limehouse Blues
  Anita O'Day; *Mello'day* ....(CRS)
  Benny Goodman; *Small Groups-1941-1945* .....(COL)
  Dave McKenna; *Live At Maybeck Recital Hall-#2* ....(CCJ)
  Earl "Fatha" Hines/Orchestra; *Monday Date* ....(RVR)
  Glen Gray; *Big Band Sampler* ....(COL)
  Joe Pass; *Virtuoso-#2* ....(PAB)
  Kay Starr; *Back To The Roots* ....(CRS)
Little Boxes
  Malvina Reynolds; *Folk Classics-Roots Of American*
   Folk ....(COL)
  Pete Seeger; *Greatest Hits* ....(COL)
"Little House On The Prairie" Theme
  Original Music; *Television's Greatest Hits-#3* .....(TVT)
Little Houses
  Doug Stone; *Doug Stone G.H.* .... (EPI)
Little Pad
  Beach Boys; *Smiley Smile* ....(CAP)
Living In The Future In A Plastic Dome
  Country Joe McDonald; *Incredible Live* .... (VAN)
Log Cabin Home In The Sky
  Michael Martin Murphey; *Cowboy Christmas* .....(WB)
Love Don't Live Here Anymore
  Madonna; *Like A Virgin* .... (SIR)
  Rose Royce; *Greatest Hits* ....(WHI)
   Strikes Again ....(WHI)
Love Shack
  B-52's; *Cosmic Thing* ....(RPR)
  Friends Of Distinction; *Golden Classics* ....(CLT)
  X; *Ain't Love Grand* ....(ELE)
Mad House
  Robin Trower; *Victims Of The Fury* .... (CHR)
Mansion In The Slums
  Crowded House; *Temple Of Low Men* ....(CAP)
Mansion On The Hill
  Bruce Springsteen; *Nebraska* ....(COL)
  Emmylou Harris/Nash Ramblers; *At The Ryman* . (RPR)
  Hank Williams; *40 Greatest Hits* ....(POL)
   Lovesick Blues ....(POL)
  Neil Young/Crazy Horse; *Arc Weld* ....(RPR)
   Ragged Glory ....(RPR)
Mi Casa, Su Casa
  Perry Como; *Golden Records* ....(RCA)
My Baby's House
  Michael Cooper; *Just What I Like* ....(RPR)
My Cabin In Caroline
  Lester Flatt & Earl Scruggs; *Golden Hits Of* ..... (IGR)
  L. Flatt & E. Scruggs/Foggy Mtn. Boys; *Complete*
   Mercury Sessions ....(MER)
My Father's Mansions
  Pete Seeger; *Essential* .... (VAN)
My Little Grass Shack In Kealakekua, HI
  Mom & Dads; *Blue Hawaii* .... (CRS)
On The Roofs Of Paris
  Ennio Morricone; *ST/Frantic* .... (ELE)
Pink Houses
  John Cougar Mellencamp; *Rock For Amnesty* ... (MER)
   Uh-Huh ....(RIV)
Queen Of The House
  Diana Ross/Supremes; *At The Copa* ....(MOT)
  Jody Miller; *45* ....(CAP)
Rain On The Roof
  Lovin' Spoonful; *Anthology* ....(RHI)
   Best Of ....(RAG)
  Original Cast; *Follies In Concert* ....(RCA)

Rainy Night House
Joni Mitchell; *Ladies Of The Canyon* .... (RPR)
Joni Mitchell/L.A. Express; *Miles Of Aisles* .... (ASY)
Ramshackle Shack
Doc Watson; *Riding The Midnight Train* ....(SH)
Red House
David Byrne; *Catherine Wheel* .... (SIR)
Great White; *Recovery-Live!* ....(ENC)
Jimi Hendrix; *Concerts* .... (RPR)
   Kiss The Sky .... (RPR)
   Lifelines/Jimi Hendrix Story .... (RPR)
   Live At Winterland ....(RYK)
   Smash Hits .... (RPR)
   ST/Jimi Hendrix .... (RPR)
Rip This Joint
Rolling Stones; *Exile On Main Street* .... (RS)
   Made In The Shade .... (RS)
Roadhouse Blues
Doors; *13* .... (ELE)
   Best Of .... (ELE)
   Classics .... (ELE)
   Greatest Hits .... (ELE)
   Morrison Hotel .... (ELE)
   ST/Doors .... (ELE)
Rock The House
D.J. Jazzy Jeff & The Fresh Prince; *Rock The*
House .... (JVA)
Rockhouse
Ray Charles; *Best Of* .... (ATL)
Roy Orbison; *Original Sound* .... (SUN)
   Sun Years .... (RHI)
Roof Garden
Al Jarreau; *Breakin' Away* .... (WB)
   In London .... (WB)
Roof Is Leaking
Phil Collins; *Face Value* .... (ATL)
Seven Rooms Of Gloom
Four Tops; *Anthology* .... (MOT)
   Greatest Hits .... (MOT)
   Reach Out .... (MOT)
Shacks & Chalets
Critton Hollow; *Great Dreams* .... (FF)
Shit House Shuffle
Aerosmith; *Pandora's Box* ....(COL)
Stranger In My House
Ronnie Milsap; *Greatest Hits-#2* ....(RCA)
   Keyed Up ....(RCA)
Stranger In My Own House
Foreigner; *Agent Provocateur* .... (ATL)
Stranger In Our House Tonight
Gene Watson; *Memories To Burn* .... (EPI)
Stranger In The House
George Jones; */Elvis Costello-My Very Special*
Guests .... (EPI)
Sugar Shack
Jimmy Gilmer/Fireballs; *Billboard Top Rock 'N' Roll*
Hits-1963 .... (RHI)
   Golden Years-1963 .... (DOM)
   Good Old Rock & Roll .... (GUS)
Tear The Roof Off
Grandmaster Flash; *Ba-Dop-Boom-Bang* .... (ELE)
Triumph; *Progressions Of Power* .... (MCA)
Tear The Roof Off The Sucker
Parliament; *Son Of Super Bad* .... (KT)
There's A Cabin In The Pines
Bing Crosby; *Crooner-Columbia*
Years-1928-1934 ....(COL)
This House
Original Cast; *I Do! I Do!* ....(RCA)
Tracie Spencer; *Make The Difference* ....(CAP)
This Ole House
Rosemary Clooney; *16 Most Requested Songs* ....(COL)
Statler Brothers; *World Of* ....(COL)
Stuart Hamblen; *A Man & His Music* ....(L&L)
Tin Roof Blues
Dukes Of Dixieland; *Dixieland's Greatest Hits* ... (MCA)
George Lewis; *Jazz In The Classic New Orleans*
Trad. ....(RVR)
Harry Connick, Jr.; *Eleven* ....(COL)
Louis Armonstrong/All-Stars; *Evening With* ...... (CRS)
New Orleans Rhythm Kings; *New Orleans Rhythm*
Kings .... (MS)
Pete Fountain; *High Society* ....(BLU)

Two Of A Kind, Workin' On A Full House
Garth Brooks; *No Fences* .... (LIB)
Two-Story House
George Jones & Tammy Wynette; *20 Years Of Hits/First*
Lady Of Country .... (EPI)
   Encore .... (EPI)
   Greatest Hits-#2 .... (EPI)
   Tears Of Fire-25th Anniversary Collect. .... (EPI)
Under The House
Public Image, Ltd.; *Flowers Of Romance* .... (WB)
Up In My Treehouse
Chet Atkins; *Sails* ....(COL)
Up On The House Top
Michael Jackson/Jackson 5; *45* .... (MOT)
Up On The Roof
Cover Girls; *We Can't Go Wrong* ....(CAP)
Cryan' Shames; *Scratch In The Sky* ....(COL)
Drifters; *16 Greatest Hits* .... (TRP)
   Cruisin'-1962 .... (INC)
   Golden Hits .... (ATL)
   Greatest Hits .... (GUS)
James Taylor; *Flag* ....(COL)
Nylons; *Four On The Floor* .... (SCO)
Up The Ladder To The Roof
Bette Midler; *Live At Last* .... (ATL)
Nylons; *Best Of* ....(OPE)
   One Size Fits All ....(OPE)
Villa In Portugal
Pursuit Of Happiness; *Downward Road* .... (MER)
Villa Nueva
Victor Feldman/Generation Band; *Best Of* ...... (NVA)
Walk Across The Rooftops
Blue Nile; *Walk Across The Rooftops* ....(A&M)
We Can Have The Olympics...At Our House
Tom Paxton; *One Million Lawyers & Other*
Disasters .... (FF)
White House Blues
Doc Watson; *Essential* .... (VAN)
Doc Watson & Family; *Treasures Untold* .... (VAN)
Stanley Brothers; *Shadows Of The Past* ....(COP)
White Houses
Eric Burdon/Animals; *Greatest Hits* ....(MGM)

INSECTS, Bugs, Spiders

Ain't No Bugs On Me
New Lost City Ramblers; *20 Years Of Concert* ....(FF)
An Ant Alone
Bob Telson & Little Village; *An Ant Alone-Songs From*
The Warrior Ant .... (GRM)
Ant Farm
Night Soil Man; *Garden of Delights* .... (VYL)
Young Fresh Fellows; *Men Who Loved Music* ....(FRN)
Ant Man Bee
Captain Beefheart/Magic Band; *Trout Mask*
Replica .... (RPR)
Ant Rap
Adam Ant; *Antics In The Forbidden Zone* .... (EPI)
   Prince Charming .... (EPI)
Ant & The Elephant
Chick Corea Elektric Band II; *Paint The World* ..(GRP)
Ants
House Of Freaks; *Cakewalk* .... (GIA)
Ants Can Count
Bruce Fowler; *Ants Can Count* .... (TER)
Ants In My Pants
Bo Carter; *Rare Blues Of The Twenties-1927-1930* (HIS)
Ants In The Kitchen
Masters Of Reality; *Sunrise On The Sufferbus* ... (CHR)
Ants Invasion
Adam Ant; *Kings Of The Wild Frontier* .... (EPI)
Attack Of The Giant Ants
Blondie; *Blondie* .... (CHR)
Austrian Anthill
Brian Ritchie; *The Blend* ....(SST)
Betcha The Love Bug Bitcha
Dr. Buzzard's Band; *Original Savannah Band* ....(RCA)
Birds & The Bees
Jewel Akens; *American Graffiti-#3* .... (MCA)
   Collectables History Of Rock-#4 .... (CLT)
   Cruisin'-1965 .... (INC)
   Oldies But Goodies-#9 .... (OSR)
   Super Hits-#3 .... (GUS)

Black Butterfly
Deniece Williams; *Let's Hear It For The Boy* .....(COL)
Duke Ellington; *Best Of* ....(PAB)
Black Widow
Alice Cooper; *Alice Cooper Show* ....(WB)
   Welcome To My Nightmare ....(ATL)
Jefferson Starship; *Winds Of Change* ....(GRU)
Lita Ford; *Dangerous Curves* ....(RCA)
Blue Tail Fly
Burl Ives; *Best Of* .... (MCA)
Pete Seeger; *20 Golden Pieces Of* ....(BLD)
Boll Weevil
Brook Benton; *Anthology* .... (RHI)
   It's Just A Matter Of Time-His Greatest .... (MER)
   Pick Of ....(FFT)
Leadbelly; *Good Mornin' Blues 1936-1940* ......(BIO)
Boris The Spider
Who; *Meaty Beaty Big & Bouncy* .... (MCA)
   Quick One (Happy Jack)/Sell Out .... (MCA)
   Who's Last .... (MCA)
Bug, The
Dire Straits; *On Every Street* .... (WB)
Mary Chapin Carpenter; *Come On Come On* .....(WB)
Bumble Bee
Big Mama Thornton; *Ball N' Chain* .... (ARH)
La Vern Baker; *Live In Hollywood '91* .... (RHI)
Mance Lipscomb; *Texas Songster-#2* .... (ARH)
   You Got To Reap What You Sow .... (ARH)
Meryn Cadell; *Angel Food For Thought* .... (SIR)
Searchers; *Greatest Hits* .... (RHI)
Bumble Bee Blues
Brian Slawson & Stevie Ray Vaughan; *Distant*
Drums ....(COL)
Kansas Joe & Memphis Minnie; *Blues*
Masters-#12-Memphis Blues .... (RHI)
Memphis Minnie; *Country Blues Classics-#3* .....(BCL)
Bumble Bee Stomp
Benny Goodman; *On The Air-1937-1938* ....(COL)
Bumblebee
Eric Andersen; *Best Of* .... (VAN)
   Today Is The Highway .... (VAN)
Bumblebees
Christine Lavin; *Good Thing He Can't Read My*
Mind ....(PHO)
Butterflies/Everytime I See A Butterfly
Les McCann; *Hustle To Survive* .... (ATL)
Butterfly
Book Of Love; *Candy Carol* .... (SIR)
Charlie Gracie; *Rock-O-Rama-#1* ....(AKO)
Gladys Knight; *One & Only* ....(BUD)
Lenny Kravitz; *Mama Said* .... (VIA)
Terry Callier; *Fire On Ice* .... (ELE)
Butterfly For Bucky
Bobby Goldsboro; *Butterfly For Bucky* .... (UA)
Butterfly (I'll Set You Free)
Perry Como; *Today* ....(RCA)
Catch Another Butterfly
John Denver; *Rhymes & Reasons* ....(RCA)
Centipede
Rebbie Jackson; *Centipede* ....(COL)
Charlotte's Web
Statler Brothers; *10th Anniversary* ....(MER)
Cockroach
Albert King; *Years Gone By* ....(STX)
Sweet; *Give Us A Wink* ....(CAP)
Cockroach That Ate Cincinnati
Possum; *Dr. Demento's Delights* ....(WB)
Rose/Arrangement; *Dr. Demento's*
Greatest-#4-1970s ....(RHI)
Cricket Song
Donna Fargo; *Fargo Country* ....(WB)
Daisys Up Your Butterfly
Cramps; *Stay Sick!* ....(ENC)
Dancing Bumble Bee
Neil Diamond; *You Don't Bring Me Flowers* .....(COL)
Day Of The Locusts
Bob Dylan; *New Morning* ....(COL)
Dog & Butterfly
Heart; *Dog & Butterfly* ....(POR)
   Greatest Hits/Live ....(EPI)
Drunken Butterfly
Sonic Youth; *Dirty* ....(DGC)

Eagle Never Hunts The Fly
Music Machine; *Best Of* .... (RHI)
   Nuggets-#2-Punk ....(RHI)
Elusive Butterfly (Of Love)
Bob Lind; *Good Vibrations (Top 40: 1964-1967)* (CAP)
Eye Of The Dragonfly
Friedemann; *Indian Summer* .... (NAR)
Fireflies
Fleetwood Mac; *Live* ....(WB)
Gato Barbieri; *Caliente* ....(A&M)
Firefly
Emily Remler; *Firefly* ....(CCJ)
Levitation; *Coterie* ....(CAP)
Temptations; *Song For You* ....(MOT)
Tony Bennett; *All-Time Greatest Hits* ....(COL)
   At Carnegie Hall ....(SSP)
   Forty Years-Artistry Of ....(COL)
Firefly Serenade
Lawrence Welk; *22 Great Songs For Dancing* ... (RAN)
Fishes & Scorpions
Stephen Stills; *2* .... (ATL)
Flies Of Texas Are Upon You
Ray Stevens; *Crackin' Up* .... (MCA)
Flight Of The Fly
Dan Hicks/Hot Licks; *Striking It Rich* ....(OOP)
Glow Worm
Mills Brothers; *16 Great Performances* .... (MCA)
   Best Of ....(MCA)
   Cab Driver .... (RAN)
   Greatest Hits ....(MCA)
"Green Hornet" Theme
Original Music; *Television's Greatest Hits-#2* .... (TVT)
Honey For The Bees
Alison Moyet; *Alf* ....(COL)
Patti Austin; *Gettin' Away With Murder* ....(QUE)
I Got Stung
Elvis Presley; *Golden Records-#2* ....(RCA)
   Top Ten Hits ....(RCA)
   Worldwide 50 Gold Award Hits-#1 ....(RCA)
Insects
Altered Images; *Happy Birthday* .... (EPI)
Oingo Boingo; *Nothing To Fear* ....(A&M)
   Skeletons In The Closet-Best Of ....(A&M)
I'm A King Bee
Muddy Waters; *King Bee* .... (BS)
Rolling Stones; *Hitmakers* ....(LON)
   Hitmakers ....(OOP)
Slim Harpo; *Best Of* ....(RHI)
   Blues Classics .... (KT)
I'm Nature's Mosquito
Jonathan Richman/Modern Lovers; *Back In Your*
Life .... (RHI)
June Bug
Leo Kottke; *Did You Hear Me* ....(CAP)
   Mudlark ....(CAP)
   My Feet Are Smiling ....(CAP)
   The Best ....(CAP)
Lester Young; *Complete Savoy Recordings* ....(SAV)
   Master Takes ....(SAV)
King Cockroach
Chick Corea Elektric Band; *Chick Corea Elektric*
Band ....(GRP)
Lady Bug
Anne Murray; *Together* ....(CAP)
Bumblebee Unlimited; *Sting Like A Bee* ....(RCA)
Love Bug Leave My Heart Alone
Martha Reeves/Vandellas; *Anthology* .... (MOT)
   Compact Command Performances ....(MOT)
Love Is Like A Butterfly
Dolly Parton; *Best Of* ....(RCA)
   Collectors Series ....(RCA)
Lovebug
George Jones; *Pick Of* ....(FFT)
George Strait; *Easy Come Easy Go* ....(MCA)
Moth & The Flame
Sky Saxon Blues Band; *Full Spoon Of Seedy Blues* (CRS)
Moth & The Flame, Parts 1-5
Keith Jarrett; *Invocations-Moth & The Flame, Parts*
1-5 .... (ECM)
Moths
Jethro Tull; *20 Years Of-Radio Archives & Rare*
Tracks .... (CHR)
   Heavy Horses ....(CHR)

Moth, The
Hearing Voices; *Hearing Voices* .... (CMG)
My Cricket
Leon Russell; *Carney* .... (MCA)
Pestilence
Icepick Trotsky; *Ultraviolet Catastrophe* .... (SST)
Poor Butterfly
Sarah Vaughan; *Compact Jazz* .... (VRV)
   Golden Hits .... (MER)
   Live In Japan .... (MST)
Sonny Rollins; *Best Of* .... (BLN)
   #2 .... (BLN)
Queen Bee
Barbra Streisand; *ST/Star Is Born* .... (COL)
Grand Funk Railroad; *ST/Heavy Metal* .... (FM)
John Lee Hooker; *Greatest Hits Of* .... (KNT)
Koko Taylor; *Queen Of The Blues* .... (ALG)
Taj Mahal; *Evolution* .... (WB)
Rats & Roaches In My Kitchen
Silas Hogan; *Louisiana Blues* .... (ARH)
Return Of The Spiders
Alice Cooper; *Easy Action* .... (BIZ)
Roach Motel
Dead Youth; *Intense Brutality* .... (GCI)
Roaches
Bobby Jimmy/Critters; *Greatest Hits Of The Street* (PRY)
   Rap Beginnings-#1 .... (KT)
   Rapmasters 7-Best Of The Laughs .... (PRY)
   You A Fool-Best Of .... (KT)
Roger's Bumble Bee (Latter Day)
Roger Williams; *Best Of* .... (MCA)
   Golden Hits .... (MCA)
Salt On A Slug
Black Flag; *Family Man* .... (SST)
Salting Of The Slug
Riders In The Sky; *Cowboy Way* .... (MCA)
Several Species Of Small Furry Animals
Pink Floyd; *Umma Gumma* .... (CAP)
   Works .... (CAP)
Silver Mantis
Alpha Band; *II* .... (OOP)
Skunk, The Goose & The Fly
Tower Of Power; *East Bay Grease* .... (RHI)
Sleeping Bee
Al Jarreau; *1965* .... (BAI)
Barbra Streisand; *Barbra Streisand Album* ...... (COL)
   Just For The Record .... (COL)
Bill Evans; *Compact Jazz* .... (VRV)
Harold Arlen & Barbra Streisand; *Harold Sings Arlen*
   (With Friends) .... (SSP)
Kiri Te Kanawa & Andre Previn; *Kiri Side Tracks-Jazz*
   Album .... (PHI)
Mel Torme; *Swings Shubert Alley* .... (VRV)
Original Cast; *House Of Flowers* .... (SSP)
Tony Bennett; *Forty Years-Artistry Of* .... (COL)
Sleepin' Bee
Al Jarreau; *1965* .... (BAI)
Barbra Streisand; *Album* .... (COL)
   Highlights From "Just For The Record" .... (COL)
Bill Evans; *Compact Jazz* .... (VRV)
Carmen McRae; *Setting Standards* .... (PRR)
Harold Arlen & Barbra Streisand; *Harold Sings Arlen*
   (With Friend) .... (SSP)
Mel Torme; *Swings Shubert Alley* .... (VRV)
Tony Bennett; *Consummate Collection-Classics*
   Songs .... (COL)
Spanish Entomologist
Leo Kottke; *Best Of* .... (CAP)
   Greenhouse .... (CAP)
   Very Best Of .... (CAP)
Spanish Flea
Herb Alpert/Tijuana Brass; *Classics-#1* .... (A&M)
   Going Places .... (A&M)
   Greatest Hits .... (A&M)
Spanish Fly
Van Halen; *2* .... (WB)
Spider
Kansas; *Point Of Know Return* .... (KIR)
Spider Blues
John Koerner; *Spider Blues* .... (ELE)
Spider In My Stew
Buster Benton; *Spider In My Stew* .... (RON)

Spider & The Fly
Rolling Stones; *Out Of Our Heads* .... (AKO)
   Singles Collection-London Years .... (AKO)
"Spiderman" Theme
Original Music; *Television's Greatest Hits-#2* ..... (TVT)
Spiders & Snakes
Jim Stafford; *Jim Stafford* .... (POL)
   Super Hits/'70s-Have A Nice Day-#12 ...... (RHI)
Loretta Lynn & Conway Twitty; *Very Best Of* .. (MCA)
Sting Me
Black Crowes; *Southern Harmony & Musical*
   Companion .... (DEF)
Sugar Bee
Boozoo Chavis/Majic Sounds; *Stomp Down*
   Zydeco .... (ROU)
Jo-el Sonnier; *Complete Mercury Sessions* ...... (MER)
Rockin' Dopsie/Cajun Twisters; *Big Bad Zydeco* (CRS)
Sweet Honey Sucking Bees
Miranda Sex Garden; *Madra* .... (MUT)
Tangled In The Web
Lynch Mob; *Lynch Mob* .... (ELE)
There Ain't No Bugs On Me
Jerry Garcia & David Grisman; *Not For Kids Only* (AD)
Two Little Bees
Hollywood Flames; *Hollywood Flames* .... (SPE)
Two Thousand Pound Bee
Ventures; *Radical Guitars* .... (ILO)
   ST/Wired .... (VS)
Venus Flytrap & The Bug
Stevie Wonder; *Journey...Secret Life of Plants* ... (MOT)
Waiting For The Worms
Pink Floyd; *The Wall* .... (COL)
Roger Waters; *The Wall Live In Berlin* .... (MER)
Wasp (Texas Radio & The Big Beat)
Doors; *Alive She Cried* .... (ELE)
   Classics .... (ELE)
   L.A. Woman .... (ELE)
   Weird Scenes Inside The Goldmine .... (ELE)

INSULTS
See Also: FOOLS

Are You Teasing Me
Carl Smith; *Essential-1950-1956* .... (COL)
   Greatest Hits-#1 .... (GUS)
Asshole From El Paso
Kinky Friedman; *Lasso From El Paso* .... (EPI)
Kinky Friedman/Texas Jewboys; *Old Testaments & New*
   Revelations .... (FTT)
Assholes On Parade
Timbuk 3; *Best Of* .... (IRS)
Bird Brain Baby
Mercy Dee Walton; *Back Luck 'N' Trouble* ..... (ARH)
Birdbrain
Tom Buffalo; *Birdbrain* .... (BEG)
Bird-Brain Rag
Max Morath; *World Of Scott Joplin-#2* .... (VAN)
Bitch
Rolling Stones; *Made In The Shade* .... (RS)
   Sticky Fingers .... (RS)
Bitch Betta Have My Money
AMG; *Give A Dog A Bone* .... (SEL)
Blame It On Your Heart
Patty Loveless; *Only What I Feel* .... (EPI)
Brothers Ain't Shit
Roxanne Shante; *2 Nasty 4 Radio* .... (CLD)
Call Me Irresponsible
Frank Sinatra; *Man & His Music* .... (RPR)
   Sinatra's Sinatra .... (RPR)
Jackie Gleason; *Best Of Jackie Gleason & His*
   Orchestra .... (CCB)
Robert Goulet; *16 Most Requested Songs* .... (COL)
Rosemary Clooney; *Sings The Music Of Jimmy Van*
   Heusen .... (CCJ)
Charlie Brown
Coasters; *Billboard Top Rock 'N' Roll Hits-1957* . (RHI)
   Cruisin'-1959 .... (INC)
   Greatest Hits .... (ATC)
   Super Oldies/'50s-#7 .... (AUF)
   Their Greatest Recordings .... (ATC)
   Young Blood .... (ATL)

Christian Life
Byrds; *Byrds (collection)* ....(COL)
Sweetheart Of The Rodeo ....(COL)
Chump
Green Day; *Dookie* .... (RPR)
Cold Hearted
Paula Abdul; *Forever Your Girl* .... (VIA)
Get Up & Dance-Dance Mixes .... (VIA)
Crawlin' Home Puker
Da Yoopers; *Yoopanese* .... (YOU)
Daddy Could Swear, I Declare
Gladys Knight/Pips; *All The Great Hits* .... (MOT)
Anthology ....(MOT)
Motown Memories-#3 ....(MOT)
Neither One Of Us ....(MOT)
Daddy Kalled Me Niga Cause I Likeded...
Young Black Teenagers; *Young Black Teenagers* . (SOL)
Dammit Janet
Barry Bostwick; *ST/Rocky Horror Picture Show* .. (RHI)
Original London Cast; *Rocky Horror Show* ...... (RHI)
Dance Of The Imbeciles
D.C. 3; *This Is The Dream* ....(SST)
Dickie's Such An Asshole
Frank Zappa; *Broadway The Hard Way* ....(RYK)
You Can't Do That On Stage Anymore-#1 ......(RYK)
Die Nigger Die
Schoolly D; *How A Black Man Feels* ....(CAP)
Dirty Dawg
NKOTB; *Face The Music* ....(COL)
Dirty Old Egg-Sucking Dog
Johnny Cash; *At Folsom Prison & San Quentin* ..(COL)
Essential ....(COL)
Dog Breath
Frank Zappa; *Uncle Meat* ....(BAR)
Mothers Of Invention; *Just Another Band From*
L.A. .... (BIZ)
Donna The Prima Donna
Dion; *24 Original Classics* .... (ARI)
Bronx Blues-Columbia Recordings ....(COL)
Don't Be A Hog
Doctor Nerve; *Armed Observation* .... (CUN)
Don't Call Me Nigger, Whitey
Sly/Family Stone; *Anthology* .... (EPI)
Stand! .... (EPI)
Don't Come Home A Lovin' With Venison...
Debby McClatchy; *Someday Cafe* ....(GRE)
Don't Get Mad, Get Even
Aerosmith; *Pump* .... (GEF)
Don't Say Nothing Bad About My Baby
Cookies; *Golden Girl Groups* .... (KT)
Original Rock 'N' Roll Hits Of The '60s .... (RLL)
Don't Say Things You Don't Mean
Lynn Anderson; *Greatest Hits* ....(COL)
Don't Tell Me What To Do
Pam Tillis; *Put Yourself In My Place* .... (ARI)
Don't Think Twice, It's All Right
Bob Dylan; *Before The Flood* ....(COL)
Freewheelin' ....(COL)
Greatest Hits-#2 ....(COL)
Joan Baez; *First 10 Years* .... (VAN)
Don't Think You're Smart
Memphis Slim; *Raining The Blues* ....(FAN)
Don't Use Your Penis (For A Brain)
Romanovsky & Phillips; *Trouble In Paradise* ..... (FRE)
Eat My Shorts
Rick Dees; *45* .... (ATL)
Escape From The Island Of Living Puke
Zoogz Rift; *Island Of Living Puke* ....(SST)
Fool's Hall Of Fame
Johnny Cash; *Man-The World-His Music* .... (SUN)
Rough Cut King Of Country Music .... (SUN)
Roy Orbison; *Sun Years* ....(RHI)
For All My Niggaz & Bitches
Snoop Doggy Dogg; *Doggystyle* .... (DR)
For Those Who Dissed Me
2 Deep; *Honey That's Show Biz* ....(CLD)
Fuck Tha Police
N.W.A.; *Straight Outta Compton* ....(RUP)
Fuck You
D.O.A.; *War On 45/Bloodied But Unbowed* ...... (RES)
Fuck Your Attitude
War Zone; *Don't Forget The Struggle...* ....(CRL)
Fuck You, Man
Pussy Galore; *Right Now* ....(CRL)

F-ck Compton
Tim Dog; *S* ....(RUF)
Geek U.S.A.
Smashing Pumpkins; *Siamese Dream* .... (VIA)
Gentleman Is A Dope
Jo Stafford; *Greatest Hits* ....(CRN)
Morgana King; *Another Time Another Space* .... (MUS)
Get The Fuck Out
Skid Row; *Slave To The Grind* ....(ATL)
Get The Fuck Out Of My House
2 Live Crew; *As Nasty As They Wanna Be* ....(LUK)
Go To Hell
Alice Cooper; *Goes To Hell* ....(WB)
Show ....(WB)
Megadeth; *ST/Bill & Ted's Bogus Journey* ....(ISC)
He Thinks He'll Keep Her
Mary Chapin Carpenter; *Come On Come On* ...(COL)
Hey Stoopid
Alice Cooper; *Hey Stoopid* ....(EPI)
Hound Dog
Elvis Presley; *Aloha From Hawaii* ....(RCA)
As Recorded In Madison Square Garden ....(RCA)
Elvis Aron Presley ....(RCA)
Elvis Presley ....(RCA)
Golden Records ....(RCA)
In Concert ....(RCA)
In Person ....(RCA)
Legendary Performer-#3 ....(RCA)
Number One Hits ....(RCA)
Recorded Live On Stage At Memphis ....(RCA)
ST/Forrest Gump ....(EPX)
How Insensitive
Ella Fitzgerald; *Ella Abraca Jobim* .... (PAB)
Frank Sinatra & Antonio Carlos Jobim; *Frank Sinatra &*
Antonio Carlos Jobim .... (RPR)
Stan Getz; *Compact Jazz* ....(VRV)
I Feel Like Homemade Shit
Fugs; *Greatest Hits-#1* .... (PVC)
I Hate You
D.O.A.; *War On 45/Bloodied But Unbowed* ...... (RES)
Ronnie Milsap; *Greatest Hits* ....(RCA)
I Hate You, Baby
Count Basie Big Band; *Fun Time* ....(PAB)
Jimmy Soul; *Best Of* .... (RHI)
I Like 'Em Big & Stupid
Julie Brown; *Trapped In The Body Of A White Girl* (SIR)
I Love You (But You're Boring)
Beautiful South; *Welcome To The* .... (ELE)
Idiot Wind
Bob Dylan; *Blood On The Tracks* ....(COL)
Bootleg Series-#1-3 ....(COL)
Hard Rain ....(COL)
Ignoreland
R.E.M.; *Automatic For The People* .... (WB)
Indian Giver
1910 Fruitgum Company; *Best Of & Other Bubblegum*
Smashes-#2 .... (RHI)
I'll Be Glad When You're Dead...
Cab Calloway; *Jazz Heritage: Mr. Hi-De-Ho* ... (MCA)
I'm The Biggest Liar In Town
Reno & Smiley; *1983 Collector's Edition-#11* .... (GUS)
I'm The Laziest Gal In Town
Julie Wilson; *Cole Porter Songbook* .... (DRG)
I've Come To Expect It From You
George Strait; *Livin' It Up* .... (MCA)
Ten Strait Hits .... (MCA)
Jesus Thinks You're A Jerk
Frank Zappa; *Broadway The Hard Way* ....(RYK)
King Of Sleaze
Beat Farmers; *Loud & Plowed &...Live!* ....(CCB)
Poor & Famous ....(CCB)
Lady Is A Tramp
Ella Fitzgerald; *Rodgers & Hart Songbook* ....(VRV)
Frank Sinatra; *Capitol Years* ....(CAP)
Sinatra Reprise-Very Good Years ....(RPR)
Frank Sinatra & Luther Vandross; *Frank Sinatra*
Duets .... (CAP)
Liar Liar
Castaways; *Frat Rock-#3* .... (RHI)
Oldies But Goodies-#9 .... (OSR)
ST/Good Morning Vietnam .... (A&M)
Long Gone Geek
Procol Harum; *Best Of* .... (A&M)

Look At All Those Idiots
Simpsons; *Sing The Blues* .... (GEF)
Lyin' Ass Bitch
Fishbone; *Fishbone* ....(COL)
Man Smart, Woman Smarter
Harry Belafonte; *Pure Gold* ....(RCA)
Robert Palmer; *Some People Can Do What They Like* .... (ISL)
Rosanne Cash; *Right Or Wrong* ....(COL)
Man With The Lightbulb Head
Robyn Hitchcock/Egyptians; *Fegmania* ....(SLS)
Marry A Woman Uglier Than You
King's Singers; *10th Anniversary Concert-#2* ....(MMG)
May The Bird Of Paradise Fly Up Your...
Harlow Wilcox/Oakies; *Cripple Cricket* .... (PLN)
Little Jimmy Dickens; *Columbia Country Classics-#3-Americana* ....(COL)
More You Ignore
Morrissey; *Vauxhall And I* .... (SIR)
My Dad Sucks
Descendants; *Bonus Fat* ....(SST)
Liveage ....(SST)
Somery ....(SST)
My Little Bimbo
Clancy Hayes/Salt Dogs; *Oh By Jingo* ....(DEL)
Neanderthal Man
Hotlegs; *Rock Radio Vietnam* .... (KT)
Super Hits/'70s-Have A Nice Day-#3 .... (RHI)
Nigga Out The Projects
1-5ive Posse; *Lifestyles Of The Young & Crazy* .. (WEX)
Nigga Witta Gun
Dr. Dre; *The Chronic* ....(PRY)
Niggas Come In All Colors
L.A. Posse; *They Come In All Colors* ....(ATL)
Nigger Whitie
Sly Dunbar; *Sly Wicked & Slick* ....(FL)
No Son Of Mine
Genesis; *We Can't Dance* ....(ATL)
No Way To Treat A Lady
Bonnie Raitt; *Collection* ....(WB)
Nine Lives ....(WB)
Nobody But A Fool (Would Love You)
Connie Smith; *Best Of* ....(DOM)
Pencil Neck Geek
Fred Blassie; *Dr. Demento 20th Anniversary Collection* .... (RHI)
Dr. Demento's Dementia Royale .... (RHI)
Dr. Demento's Greatest-#4-1970s .... (RHI)
Piece Of Crap
Neil Young/Crazy Horse; *Sleeps With Angels* ..... (RPR)
Pizza Face
Barnes & Barnes; *Zabagabee-Best Of* .... (RHI)
Plastic People
Mothers Of Invention; *Absolutely Free* ....(RYK)
Potato Head Blues
Louis Armstrong; *Best Of The Decca Years-#2-The Composer* .... (MCA)
You Rascal You .... (POE)
Po' White Trash
White Trash; *White Trash* .... (ELE)
Pretty Vacant
Joan Jett; *Hit List* ....(EPA)
Sex Pistols; *Live At Chelmsford Top Security Prison* .... (RES)
Never Mind The Bollocks ....(WB)
Punk Bitch
Too $hort; *Short Dog's In The House* .... (JVA)
Punk & Belligerent
Warrior Soul; *Salutations From The Ghetto Nation* .... (DGC)
Real Niggaz
N.W.A.; *100 Miles & Runnin'* .... (RUP)
Efil4zaggin .... (RUP)
Real Niggaz Don't Die
N.W.A.; *Efil4zaggin* .... (RUP)
Red Hot
Robert Gordon; *Rock This Town-Rockabilly Hits-#2* .... (RHI)
Robert Gordon & Link Wray; *Robert Gordon & Link Wray* ....(RCA)
Rich Bitch
D.O.A.; *War On 45/Bloodied But Unbowed* ...... (RES)

Rich Girl
Daryl Hall & John Oates; *Bigger Than Both Of Us* ....(RCA)
Billboard Top Rock 'N' Roll Hits-1977 .... (RHI)
Livetime ....(RCA)
Nipper's Greatest Hits-'70s ....(RCA)
Rock 'N' Soul Part 1-Greatest Hits ....(RCA)
Soulful Sounds ....(RCA)
Rich Little Bitch
Dash Rip Rock; *Boiled Alive!* ....(MAM)
Not Of This World ....(MAM)
Roar Of The Masses Could Be Farts
Minutemen; *Double Nickels On The Dime* ....(SST)
Rock N Roll Nigger
Patti Smith Group; *Easter* .... (ARI)
Sassin' The Boss
Glen Gray; *Uncollected/Casa Loma Orch.-1939-1940* .... (HIN)
Scum Of The Earth
Kinks; *Preservation-A Play In Two Acts* .... (RHI)
See You In Hell (Don't Be Late)
Yngwie Malmsteen; *Eclipse* .... (POL)
See You In Hell, Blind Boy
Ry Cooder; *ST/Crossroads* ....(WB)
Shaddup You Face
Joe Dolce; *45* ....(MCA)
She Ain't Ugly (She Just Don't Look...)
Gary B.B. Coleman; *Romance Without Finance Is A Nuisance* .... (ICH)
She Ain't Worth It
Glenn Medeiros; *with Bobby Brown* .... (MCA)
She Loves The Jerk
John Hiatt; *Riding With The King* ....(GEF)
Y'all Caught? Ones That Got Away-1979-85 ..(GEF)
Rodney Crowell; *Street Language* ....(COL)
Short People
Randy Newman; *Dr. Demento-Greatest Novelty Records-#4* .... (RHI)
Little Criminals ....(WB)
Shut Up And Dance
Pointer Sisters; *Serious Slammin'* ....(RCA)
Shut Up And Kiss Me
Mary Chapin Carpenter; *Stones In The Road* ....(COL)
Silver Tongue & Gold Plated Lies
Hotmud Family; *Meat & Potatoes (& Stuff Like That)* ....(FF)
Sophisticated Bitch
Public Enemy; *Yo! Bum Rush The Show* ....(DFC)
Stop, Don't Tease Me
DeBarge; *All This Love* .... (MOT)
Greatest Hits .... (MOT)
Stupid Cupid
Connie Francis; *Very Best Of* .... (POL)
Neil Sedaka; *All-Time Greatest Hits-#2* ....(RCA)
Stupid Einstein
Three O'Clock; *Sixteen Tambourines* .... (FRN)
Stupid Girl
Neil Young; *Zuma* .... (RPR)
Rolling Stones; *Aftermath* .... (AKO)
Singles Collection-London Years ....(AKO)
Stupid Marriage
Specials; *Specials* .... (CHR)
Stupid War Movies
Paleface; *Paleface* ....(POL)
Sucker
Mott The Hoople; *All The Young Dudes* ....(COL)
Ballad Of MoSucker-Retrospective ....(COL)
Sucker In A 3-Piece Suit
Van Halen; *OU812* ....(WB)
Suicide Chump
Frank Zappa; *You Are What You Is* ....(RYK)
Surrounded By Idiots
Wrathchild America; *3-D* .... (ATL)
Take Back Your Mink
Original Cast; *Guys & Dolls* .... (MCA)
Take It Back
Cream; *Disraeli Gears* ....(POL)
Reba McEntire; *It's Your Call* .... (MCA)
Take This Job And Shove It Too
David Allan Coe; *I've Got Something To Say* ....(COL)
Take This Job & Shove It
David Allan Coe; *17 Greatest Hits* ....(COL)

Johnny Paycheck; *Biggest Hits* .... (EPI)
  Golden Hits .... (GUS)
  Greatest Hits-#2 .... (EPI)
  Take This Job & Shove It .... (EPI)
  Truckers' Jukebox-Top Radio Requests .... (EPI)
That Girl's A Slut
  Just-Ice; *Rapmasters 7-Best Of The Laughs* .... (PRY)
Then I'll Be Tired Of You
  Coleman Hawkins; *Real Thing* .... (PRS)
  Jonathan Schwartz; *Alone Together* .... (MUS)
  Paul Desmond; *Late Lament* .... (BLU)
There Is A Sucker Born Ev'ry Minute
  Cy Coleman; *Presents Barnum* ....(BAI)
These Boots Are Made For Walkin'
  Billy Ray Cyrus; *Some Gave All* .... (MER)
  Nancy Sinatra; *Billboard Top Rock 'N' Roll Hits-1966* .... (RHI)
  Boots-Greatest Hits .... (RHI)
They All Laughed
  Carmen McRae; *Setting Standards* .... (PRR)
  Fred Astaire; *Starring* ....(COL)
  Sarah Vaughan; *George Gershwin Songbook-#1* . (EMA)
  Tony Bennett; *Steppin' Out* ....(COL)
Too Dumb For New York City
  Waylon Jennings; *Too Dumb For N.Y. City-Too Ugly For L.A.* .... (EPI)
Too Fat Polka
  Arthur Godfrey; *Dr. Demento's Greatest Novelty-#1-1940s* .... (RHI)
  Frankie Yankovic; *16 Most Requested Polkas* ....(COL)
  America's Favorites .... (SMA)
  Frankie Yankovic/Yanks; *Greatest Hits* ....(COL)
  Li'l Wally; *I Love To Polka* ....(JJ)
Trapped In The Body Of A White Girl
  Julie Brown; *Trapped In The Body Of A White Girl* (SIR)
Trashy Lady
  Neon Judgement; *Horny As Hell* ....(PIA)
Trashy Women
  Confederate Railroad; *Confederate Railroad* ..... (ATL)
Treat Her Like A Prostitute
  Slick Rick; *Great Adventures Of* ....(DFC)
Ugliest Girl In The World
  Bob Dylan; *Down In The Groove* ....(COL)
Ugly
  Fishbone; *Fishbone* ....(COL)
  Rhythm Come Forward-#2 ....(COL)
  Saigon Kick; *Saigon Kick* ....(THI)
Ugly Duckling
  Danny Kaye; *45* ....(OOP)
Under My Thumb
  Rolling Stones; *12 X 5* .... (AKO)
  Aftermath .... (AKO)
  Got Live If You Want It .... (AKO)
  Hot Rocks 1964-1971 .... (AKO)
  Still Life-American Concert 1981 ....(RS)
  Who; *Who's Missing* .... (MCA)
Up Against The Wall Redneck Mother
  Jerry Jeff Walker; *A Man Must Carry On* .... (MCA)
  Best OF .... (MCA)
  Great Gonzos .... (MCA)
Vidiot
  Ken Nordine; *Best Of Word Jazz-#1* ...... (RHI)
Walk All Over You
  AC/DC; *Highway To Hell* .... (ATL)
Waylon Jennings
  Waylon Jennings; *Greatest Country Hits-'90s-1990* ....(COL)
What's The Ugliest Part Of Your Body
  Mothers Of Invention; *We're Only In It For The.../Lumpy Gravy* ....(RYK)
What's This Shit Called Love
  Meatmen; *We're The Meatmen...& You Still Suck!* .(CRL)
White Nigger
  Big Boys; *The Fat Elvis* ....(T&G)
White Trash Wife
  Exene Cervenka; *Old Wives' Tales* .... (RHI)
White Trash With Cash
  Southgang; *Group Therapy* ....(CHS)
Why Did You Waste My Time?
  Screamin' Jay Hawkins; *Collectables Blues Collection-#1* ....(CLT)
Yakety Yak
  2 Live Crew; *ST/Twins* ....(WTG)

Coasters; *Atlantic R&B-1947-1974-#3-(1955-1958)* .... (ATL)
  Billboard Top Rock 'N' Roll Hits-1958 .... (RHI)
  Cruisin'-1958 .... (INC)
  Greatest Hits .... (ATC)
  ST/Stand By Me .... (ATL)
You Get Ugly
  Contours; *Do You Love Me (Now That I Can Dance)* .... (MOT)
You Stupid Jerk
  Angry Samoans; *Back From Samoa* ....(PVC)
  Gimme Samoa-31 Garbage-Pit Hits ....(PVC)
You Talk Too Much
  Cheap Trick; *Next Position Please* ....(EPI)
  George Thorogood/Destroyers; *Born To Be Bad* . (EMI)
  Joe Jones; *American Graffiti-#3* .... (MCA)
  Carnival Time-Best Of Ric Records-#1 .... (ROU)
  Echoes Of A Rock Era-Middle Years .... (RLL)
  Original Rock 'N' Roll Hits Of The '60s .... (RLL)
  Run-D.M.C.; *King Of Rock* .... (PRO)
Your Feet's Too Big
  Beatles; *45* .... (CLT)
  Fats Waller; *20 Golden Pieces Of* ....(BLD)
  Ain't Misbehavin' ....(RCA)
  Joint Is Jumpin' .... (BLU)
  Legendary Performer ....(RCA)
  Original Cast; *Ain't Misbehavin'* ....(RCA)

ISLANDS
See Also: OCEAN, PARADISE

26 Miles
  Four Preps; *True* .... (CAP)
Back To The Island
  Leon Russell; *Best Of* .... (MCA)
  Rock Of The '70s ....(MSP)
  Will O' The Wisp .... (MCA)
Caribbean Queen
  Billy Ocean; *Greatest Hits* .... (JVA)
  Suddenly .... (JVA)
Coconut Island
  Junior Brown; *12 Shades Of Brown* ....(CCB)
Easter Island
  Russ Freeman; *Nocturnal Playground* ....(BRA)
Escape From The Island Of Living Puke
  Zoogz Rift; *Island Of Living Puke* ....(SST)
Fire Island
  Village People; *Live & Sleazy* .... (CAS)
  Village People .... (CAS)
  Woody Herman; *Blowin' Up A Storm* ....(PIC)
I Am A Rock
  Simon & Garfunkel; *Collected Works* ....(COL)
  Greatest Hits ....(COL)
  Sounds Of Silence ....(COL)
In The Middle Of An Island
  Tennessee Ernie Ford; *Capitol Collectors Series* ..(CAP)
Island
  Eddy Raven; *Temporary Sanity* ....(CAP)
  Gerry Rafferty; *City To City* .... (EMI)
  Greg Kihn; *Again* .... (ISL)
  Jimmy Buffett; *Coconut Telegraph* .... (MCA)
  Jimmy Messina; *One More Mile* ....(WB)
  Julia Fordham; *Porcelain* .... (VIA)
  Julie Andrews; *Julie Love* .... (USA)
  Patti Austin; *Every Home Should Have One* ..... (QUE)
  Sarah Vaughan; *Crazy & Mixed Up* ....(PAB)
Island Girl
  Beach Boys; *Still Cruisin'* ....(CAP)
  Elton John; *Billboard Top Hits-1975* .... (RHI)
  Greatest Hits-#2 ....(POL)
  Rock Of The Westies ....(POL)
Island Of Domination
  Judas Priest; *Best Of* ....(RCA)
  Sad Wings Of Destiny ....(RCA)
Island Of Love
  Elvis Presley; *ST/Blue Hawaii* ....(RCA)
  Rascals; *Freedom Suite* .... (RHI)
  Sheppards; *Golden Classics* .... (CLT)
Island Woman
  Pablo Cruise; *Pablo Cruise* ....(A&M)
Islands
  Band; *Islands* ....(CAP)
  John Denver; *Seasons Of The Heart* ....(RCA)

King Crimson; *Islands* .... (EDI)
Islands In The Stream
Kenny Rogers & Dolly Parton; *Eyes That See In The Dark* ....(RCA)
   Greatest Hits ....(RCA)
Islands Of The Dead
Be Bop Deluxe; *Drastic Plastic* ....(CAP)
Isle Of Capri
Billy Vaughn; *22 Of His Greatest Hits* ....(RAN)
Frank Sinatra; *Come Fly With Me* ....(CAP)
Isle Of You
Motels; *Little Robbers* ....(CAP)
Key Largo
Bertie Higgins; *Just Another Day In Paradise* .....(KAT)
Kokomo
Beach Boys; *Still Cruisin'* ....(CAP)
   ST/Cocktail ....(ELE)
La Isla Bonita
Madonna; *True Blue* ....(SIR)
Lady Of The Island
Crosby, Stills & Nash; *Crosby, Stills & Nash* .....(ATL)
Manhattan Island Serenade
Leon Russell; *Carney* ....(MCA)
Marooned
Pink Floyd; *The Division Bell* ....(COL)
Misty Isles Of Scotland
Anne Brolly & Francie; *Ireland My Home* ....(RGO)
Monkey Island
J. Geils Band; *Best Of* ....(ATL)
   Monkey Island ....(ATL)
Offshore Banking Business
Members; *At The 1980 Chelsea Night Club* ....(BP)
   ST/Urgh! A Music War ....(A&M)
On A Desert Island With You
Original Cast; *Sitting Pretty* ....(NW)
On Treasure Island
Louis Armstrong; *Louis Armstrong* ....(MSP)
Tommy Dorsey/Orchestra; *Seventeen Number Ones* ....(RCA)
One Night In Trinidad
Earl Fatha Hines; *Lionel Hampton Presents* .....(WHO)
Pretty Green Island
George Tucker; *George Tucker* ....(ROU)
Smiling Islands
Chris Proctor; *Delicate Dance* ....(FF)
Robbie Patton; *Orders From Headquarters* ....(ATL)
Tahiti
Milt Jackson; *Milt Jackson* ....(BLN)
Tahiti Condo
Michael Nesmith; *Newer Stuff* .... (RHI)
Tahitian Moon
Michael Franks; *Objects Of Desire* ....(WB)
Tahitian Skies
Chet Atkins & Mark Knopfler; *Neck & Neck* ....(COL)
Taking Islands In Africa
Japan; *Gentlemen Take Polaroids* ....(BP)
Three Mile Island
Pinkard & Bowden; *Writers In Disguise* ....(WB)
Three Mile Smile
Aerosmith; *Night In The Ruts* ....(COL)
   Pandora's Box ....(COL)
Thunder Island
Jay Ferguson; *Thunder Island* ....(OOP)
Tiki Tiki Tiki Room
Original Music; *Disney Collection-#1* ....(DIS)
Washed Ashore (On A Lonely Island In...)
Platters; *16 Greatest Hits* ....(TRP)
   Anthology ....(RHI)

JEALOUSY
See Also: EGO

Alright Already
Larry Stewart; *Down The Road* ....(RCA)
Bad Bad Leroy Brown
Jim Croce; *Billboard Top Rock 'N' Roll Hits-1973* (RHI)
   Down The Highway ....(21)
   Life & Times ....(OOP)
   Photographs & Memories ....(21)

Bird Dog
Everly Brothers; *Best Of* ....(RHI)
   Billboard Top Rock 'N' Roll Hits-1958 ....(RHI)
   Cadence Classics-Their 20 Greatest Hits ....(RHI)
   Fabulous Style ....(RHI)
   Very Best Of ....(WB)
Chain Lightning
38 Special; *Special Forces* ....(A&M)
Rush; *Presto* ....(ATL)
Steely Dan; *Gold* ....(MCA)
   Katy Lied ....(MCA)
Could've Been Me
Billy Ray Cyrus; *Some Gave All* ....(MER)
Damn I Wish I Was Your Lover
Sophie B. Hawkins; *Tongues & Tales* ....(COL)
Dance Only With Me
Blossom Dearie; *Blossoms On Broadway* ....(DRG)
Maxine Sullivan/Keith Ingham Sextet; *Together (Maxine Sings Jules Styne)* ....(ATL)
Does He Love You
Reba McEntire & Linda Davis; *Greatest Hits-#2* (MCA)
Don't Mess With Bill
Marvelettes; *Anthology* ....(MOT)
   Compact Command Performances ....(MOT)
   Greatest Hits ....(MOT)
   Top 10 With A Bullet-Motown Girl Groups ....(MOT)
Don't Mess With My Man
Irma Thomas; *We Got A Party-Best Of Ron Records-#1* ....(ROU)
Don't Sit Under The Apple Tree
Andrews Sisters; *Capitol Collectors Series* ....(CAP)
   Greatest Hits ....(CCB)
Glenn Miller; *Memorial-1944-1969* ....(BLU)
Glenn Miller/Orchestra; *Unforgettable* ....(RCA)
Everybody's Key Fits My Baby's Door
Rockin' Tabby Thomas; *King Of Swamp Blues* .. (MDS)
Everything You Did
Steely Dan; *Royal Scam* ....(MCA)
Get Off My Cloud
Rolling Stones; *Big Hits-High Tide & Green Grass* (AKO)
   December's Children ....(AKO)
   Got Live If You Want It ....(AKO)
   Hot Rocks-1964-1971 ....(AKO)
   Singles Collection-London Years ....(AKO)
Gettin' Mighty Crowded
Betty Everett; *Soul Shots-#8* ....(RHI)
   Very Best Of ....(VJ)
Elvis Costello; *Taking Liberties* ....(COL)
Girl Is Mine
Michael Jackson With Paul McCartney; *Thriller* .. (EPI)
He Ain't Worth Missing
Toby Keith; *Toby Keith* ....(MER)
Hey Jealousy
Gin Blossoms; *New Miserable Experience* ....(A&M)
He'll Have To Go
Jim Reeves; *60 Years Of Country Music* ....(RCA)
   Best Of ....(RCA)
   Billboard Top Country Hits-1960 ....(RHI)
   Great Moments At The Grand Ole Opry ....(RCA)
   Nipper's Greatest Hits/'50s-#1 ....(RCA)
Jim Reeves & Patsy Cline; *Jim Reeves-Greatest Hits* ....(RCA)
Ry Cooder; *Chicken Skin Music* ....(RPR)
He'll Never Love You (Like I Do)
Freddie Jackson; *Rock Me Tonight* ....(CAP)
Him
Rupert Holmes; *Partners In Crime* ....(MCA)
I Ain't Gonna Eat Out My Heart Anymore
Rascals; *Time Piece-Rascals Greatest Hits* ....(ATL)
   Young Rascals ....(RHI)
I Can't Stand It
Eric Clapton; *Another Ticket* ....(RSO)
   Crossroads ....(POL)
I Don't Call Him Daddy
Doug Supernaw; *Red & Rio Grande* ....(BNA)
I Heard It Through The Grapevine
Creedence Clearwater Revival; *Chooglin'* ....(FAN)
   Chronicle ....(FAN)
   Cosmo's Factory ....(FAN)
   Gold ....(FAN)
   Movie Album ....(FAN)

Gladys Knight/Pips; *16 #1 Hits From The Late '60s* .... (MOT)
  Command Compact Performances .... (MOT)
  Every Great Motown Song-First 25 Years ...... (MOT)
  Motown Grammy R & B Performances .... (MOT)
  Motown Superstars Series-#13 .... (MOT)
  Top 10 With A Bullet-Motown Girl Groups .... (MOT)
Marvin Gaye; *25 #1 Hits From 25 Years* ...... (MOT)
  Anthology .... (MOT)
  Every Great Motown Hit Of Marvin Gaye .... (MOT)
  Live At London Palladium .... (MOT)
  Most Played Oldies On America's Jukebox ..... (MOT)
  Motown Story .... (MOT)
  Motown Story-First 25 Years .... (MOT)
I Meant Every Word He Said
  Ricky Van Shelton; *Greatest Country Hits/'90s-#2* (COL)
  RVS III .... (COL)
I Wish I Had A Girl
  Henry Lee Summer; *Henry Lee Summer* .... (CBA)
I Wish I Were Blind
  Bruce Springsteen; *Human Touch* .... (COL)
I Wonder Who's Kissing Her Now
  Bobby Darin; *Capitol Collectors Series* .... (CAP)
  Ted Weems; *45* .... (MCA)
If It Weren't For Him
  Vince Gill & Rosanne Cash; *Collector's Duets* ...(RCA)
Is She Really Going Out With Him
  Joe Jackson; *Live-1980-1986* .... (A&M)
  Look Sharp .... (A&M)
It Could've Been Me
  Billy Ray Cyrus; *Some Gave All* .... (MER)
It's My Party
  Lesley Gore; *Anthology* .... (RHI)
  Billboard Top Rock 'N' Roll Hits-1963 .... (RHI)
  Golden Hits Of .... (MER)
  Good Time Rock 'N' Roll .... (MCA)
  Oldies But Goodies-#3 .... (OSR)
I'd Be Better Off (In A Pine Box)
  Doug Stone; *Doug Stone* .... (EPI)
  Greatest Country Hits-'90s-1990 .... (COL)
I'm Not Angry
  Elvis Costello; *My Aim Is True* .... (COL)
Jealous
  Gene Loves Jezebel; *Kiss Of Life* .... (GEF)
  Robert Palmer; *Secrets* .... (ISL)
  Rod Stewart; *Tonight I'm Yours* .... (WB)
Jealous Again
  Black Crowes; *Shake Your Money Maker* ...... (DEF)
  Black Flag; *First Four Years* .... (SST)
Jealous Bone
  Patty Loveless; *Greatest Hits* .... (MCA)
  Up Against My Heart .... (MCA)
Jealous Dogs
  Pretenders; *II* .... (SIR)
Jealous Girl
  New Edition; *Candy Girl* .... (STW)
Jealous Guy
  John Lennon; *Lennon* .... (CAP)
  John Lennon/Plastic Ono Band; *Collection* ...... (GEF)
  Imagine .... (CAP)
  ST/Imagine-The Motion Picture .... (CAP)
  Roxy Music; *Heart Still Beating* .... (RPR)
  High Road .... (WB)
  Street Life-20 Great Hits .... (RPR)
Jealous Heart
  Tex Ritter; *An American Legend* .... (CAP)
  Best Of .... (CAP)
  Hillbilly Heaven .... (CAP)
Jealous Hearted Man
  Muddy Waters; *Hard Again* .... (BS)
Jealous Hearted Me
  Minnie Pearl; *Stars Of The Grand Ole Opry-1926-1974* .... (RCA)
Jealous Kind
  Joe Cocker; *Classics-#4* .... (A&M)
  Greatest Hits .... (A&M)
Jealous Man
  Hoyt Axton; *Fearless* .... (A&M)
  Truth; *Jump* .... (IRS)
Jealousy
  Adventures Of Stevie V; *Adventures Of Stevie V* (MER)
  Call; *Let The Day Begin* .... (MCA)
  Escape Club; *Wild Wild West* .... (ATL)
  Frankie Miller; *Standing On The Edge* .... (CAP)

Heart; *Passionworks* .... (EPI)
Mary Jane Girls; *Mary Jane Girls* .... (GOR)
Pet Shop Boys; *Behavior* .... (EMI)
Queen; *Jazz* .... (HOL)
Ronnie McDowell; *Good Time Lovin' Man* ...... (EPI)
Tommy Shaw; *What If* .... (A&M)
Jump
  Loverboy; *Get Lucky* .... (COL)
Leave Him Out Of This
  Steve Wariner; *I Am Ready* .... (ARI)
Life #9
  Martina McBride; *The Way That I Am* .... (RCA)
Listen To Her Heart
  Tom Petty/Heartbreakers; *You're Gonna Get It* . (MCA)
Living In The Footsteps Of Another Man
  Chi-Lites; *Greatest Hits* .... (BRU)
  Half A Love .... (BRU)
Living Proof
  Ricky Van Shelton; *30 Years Of #1 Hits-#20* ....(COL)
  Greatest Country Hits/'80s-1989 .... (COL)
  Greatest Hits Plus .... (COL)
Matty Groves
  Fairport Convention; *Chronicles* .... (A&M)
  Liege & Lief .... (A&M)
My Best Friend's Girl
  Cars; *Cars* .... (ELE)
  Greatest Hits .... (ELE)
My Boyfriend's Back
  Angels; *Billboard Top Rock 'N' Roll Hits-1963* ... (RHI)
  Girl Groups-Story Of A Sound .... (RHI)
  My Boyfriend's Back .... (CLT)
  Oldies But Goodies-#11 .... (OSR)
  ST/Wanderers .... (WB)
  Wonder Women-#2-History Of Girl Group ...... (RHI)
My Son Calls Another Man Daddy
  Hank Williams; *16 Great Hits* .... (EVR)
  40 Greatest Hits .... (POL)
  Rare Takes & Radio Cuts .... (POL)
Next Time You See Her
  Eric Clapton; *Slow Hand* .... (RSO)
No Reply
  Beatles; *Box Set* .... (CAP)
  For Sale .... (CAP)
  '65 .... (CAP)
Nobody's Darlin' But Mine
  Chieftains & Emmylou Harris; *Another Country* .(RCA)
  Jimmie Davis; *Country Music Hall Of Fame* .... (MCA)
  Merle Haggard; *Going Where The Lonely Go* ..... (EPI)
Oh No
  Commodores; *All The Great Hits* .... (MOT)
  All The Great Love Songs .... (MOT)
  In The Pocket .... (MOT)
  Lionel Richie-Composer Series .... (MOT)
  Top 10 With A Bullet-Motown Love Songs ..... (MOT)
One I Love Belongs To Somebody Else
  Count Basie/Kansas City 3; *For The Second Time* (PAB)
  Etta Jones Featuring Houston Person; *Fine &
  Mellow/Save Your Love For Me* .... (MUS)
  Frank Sinatra; *I Remember Tommy* .... (RPR)
  Sheena Easton; *No Strings* .... (MCA)
Other Guy
  Little River Band; *Greatest Hits* .... (CAP)
Out Of Your Shoes
  Lorrie Morgan; *Leave The Light On* .... (RCA)
O.P.P.
  Naughty By Nature; *MTV Party To Go-#2* ...... (TMB)
Penis Envy
  Uncle Bonsai; *Lonely Grain Of Corn* .... (FRK)
Please Don't Squeeze My Sharmon
  Charlie Walker; *Country Music Classics-#10-Late '60s* .... (KT)
  Golden Hits .... (PLN)
Potential New Boyfriend
  Dolly Parton; *Best Of-#3* .... (RCA)
Put Out The Fire
  Queen; *Hot Space* .... (HOL)
Rumor Has It
  Reba McEntire; *Greatest Hits-#2* .... (MCA)
  Rumor Has It .... (MCA)
Run For Your Life
  Beatles; *Box Set* .... (CAP)
  Rubber Soul .... (CAP)
Sacred Ground
  McBride & The Ride; *Sacred Ground* .... (MCA)

She Used To Be Mine
Brooks & Dunn; *Hard Workin' Man* .... (ARI)
She's Got The Rhythm (& I Got The Blues)
Alan Jackson; *Lot About Livin' (& A Little 'Bout Love* .... (ARI)
She's Mine Tonight
Jay Ferguson; *White Noise* ....(CAP)
She's Not Cryin' Anymore
Billy Ray Cyrus; *Some Gave All* .... (MER)
Some Guys Have All The Love
Little Texas; *First Time For Everything* ....(WB)
Some Guys Have All The Luck
Maxi Priest; *Best Of Me* .... (CHS)
  Maxi .... (VIA)
Robert Palmer; *Addictions-#1* .... (ISL)
Rod Stewart; *Camouflage* ....(WB)
  Storyteller-Complete Anthology-1964-1990 ..... (WB)
Somebody Else's Guy
Jocelyn Brown; *Somebody Else's Guy* .... (VIN)
Somebody Else's Moon
Collin Raye; *In This Life* .... (EPI)
Somebody New
Billy Ray Cyrus; *It Won't Be The Last* .... (MER)
Somebody Stole My Gal
Benny Goodman; *Best Of The Big Bands* ....(COL)
  B.G. In Hi-Fi .... (BLN)
Surrey With The Fringe On Top
Ellis Marsalis; *Heart Of Gold* ....(COL)
Original Broadway Cast; *Oklahoma* ....(RCA)
Original Cast; *Oklahoma* ....(MCA)
Take Good Care Of My Baby
Bobby Vee; *Best Of* .... (EMI)
  Billboard Top Rock 'N' Roll Hits-1961 .... (RHI)
  'Til My Dreamin' Comes True ....(CAP)
Bobby Vinton; *16 Most Requested* ....(EPI)
Dion; *His Best* .... (EMI)
Tell Laura I Love Her
Ray Peterson; *Nipper's Greatest Hits-'60s-#1* .....(RCA)
  Teenage Tragedies .... (RHI)
Today's Lonely Fool
Tracy Lawrence; *Sticks & Stones* .... (ATL)
Two Princes
Spin Doctors; *Pocket Full Of Kryptonite* .... (EPI)
We Hate It When Our Friends Become...
Morrissey; *Your Arsenal* .... (SIR)
We'll Burn That Bridge
Brooks & Dunn; *Hard Workin' Man* .... (ARI)
Who's That Man
Toby Keith; *Boomtown* .... (PYN)
Will You Be Loving Another Man
Bill Monroe/Blue Grass Boys; *Essential Bill Monroe-1945-1949* ....(COL)
You Can't Do That
Beatles; *Box Set* ....(CAP)
  Hard Day's Night ....(CAP)
  Rock 'N' Roll Music-#1 ....(CAP)
  Second Album ....(CAP)
You, Me And He
Mtume; *You, Me And He* .... (EPI)
You're Gonna Lose That Girl
Beatles; *Help!* ....(CAP)
You're So Vain
Carly Simon; *Best Of* .... (ELE)
  Greatest Hits Live .... (ARI)
  No Secrets .... (ELE)
  '70s Greatest Rock Hits-#3-High Times .... (PRY)
You've Got A Lover
Ricky Skaggs; *19 Hot Country Requests-#2* .... (EPI)
  Highways & Heartaches .... (EPI)

JEWELRY, Diamonds, Gems, Precious Stones
See Also: GOLD, MONEY, ROYALTY

---

3 Chains O' Gold
Prince/New Power Generation; *Love Symbol Album* .... (PAI)
Baubles Bangles & Beads
Marlene Dietrich; *Live* ....(COL)
Original Cast; *Kismet* ....(COL)
Peggy Lee; *Best Of* ....(MCA)
Percy Faith; *All-Time Greaaatest Hits* ....(COL)
Bijou
Lambert, Hendricks & Ross; *Best Of* ....(COL)

Woody Herman; *20 Golden Pieces Of* .... (BLD)
  Thundering Herds-1945-1947 ....(COL)
Black Diamond
Kiss; *Alive* .... (CAS)
  Double Platinum .... (CAS)
  Kiss .... (CAS)
  Originals .... (CAS)
Black Diamond Bay
Bob Dylan; *Desire* ....(COL)
Black Pearl
Sonny Charles; *Soul Shots-#2: "In" Crowd-Sweet Soul* .... (RHI)
Sonny Charles/Checkmates; *Soul Shots-'60s Soul Classics-Best Of* ....(RHI)
Bo Diddley
Bo Diddley; *Good Time Rock 'N Roll* .... (MCA)
  History Of Rock-#5 ....(CLT)
  Oldies But Goodies-#10 .... (OSR)
  ST/Rage In Harlem .... (SIR)
Buddy Holly; *20 Golden Greats* .... (MCA)
  For The First Time Anywhere .... (MCA)
Buried Treasure
Flesheaters; *Prehistoric Fits-#2* ....(SST)
Kenny Rogers; *Eyes That See In The Dark* ......(RCA)
  Greatest Hits ....(RCA)
Chains Of Gold
Sweethearts Of The Rodeo; *More Hot Country Requests-#2* .... (EPI)
  Sweethearts Of The Rodeo ....(COL)
Cool Pearl
Capitols; *Golden Classics* ....(CLT)
Crystal Blue Persuasion
Tommy James/Shondells; *Anthology* .... (RHI)
  Best Of .... (RLL)
Cuff Link
Wings; *London Town* .... (CAP)
Diamond Dogs
David Bowie; *Changesbowie* ....(RYK)
  Diamond Dogs ....(RYK)
  Live ....(RYK)
  The Singles-1969-1993 ....(RYK)
Diamond Dust
Jeff Beck; *Blow By Blow* .... (EPI)
Diamond Girl
Seals & Crofts; *Diamond Girl* ....(WB)
  Greatest Hits ....(WB)
Diamond Head
Beach Boys; *Friends* ....(RPR)
Diamond In The Dust
Mark Gray; *This Ol' Piano* ....(COL)
Diamond Joe
Tom Rush; *Mind Ramblin'* .... (PRS)
  Tom Rush .... (FAN)
Diamond Mine
Blue Rodeo; *Diamond Mine* .... (ATL)
Hank Williams, Jr.; *Out Of Left Field* ....(CPC)
Diamond Smiles
Boomtown Rats; *Fine Art Of Surfacing* ....(COL)
Diamonds
Chris Rea; *Deltics* .... (UA)
Diamonds And Pearls
Prince/New Power Generation; *Diamonds And Pearls* ....(PAI)
Diamonds Are A Girl's Best Friend
Carol Channing; *Broadway Magic-'50s* ....(COL)
Emmylou Harris; *White Shoes* ....(WB)
Marilyn Monroe; *Goodbye Primadonna* ...... (ACC)
Pearl Bailey; *Back On Broadway* .... (RLL)
  Echoes Of An Era .... (RLL)
Diamonds Are Forever
Shirley Bassey; *13 Original James Bond Themes* .. (EMI)
  Best Of .... (EMI)
  Greatest Hits .... (EMI)
Diamonds In The Rough
John Prine; *Diamonds In The Rough* .... (ATL)
Diamonds In The Stars
Ray Price; *Greatest Hits-#3* ....(SO)
Diamonds On My Windshield
Tom Waits; *Anthology* .... (ASY)
  Heart Of Saturday Night .... (ASY)
Diamonds On The Soles Of Her Shoes
Paul Simon; *Concert In The Park-August 15 1991* (WB)
  Graceland ....(WB)
  Negotiations & Love Songs-1971-1986 ....(WB)

Diamonds & Pearls
Kansas; *Vinyl Confessions* .... (KIR)
Paradons; *Back Seat Jams* ....(DHL)
 Collectables Presents History Of Rock-#8 ....(CLT)
 Oldies But Goodies-#5 ....(OSR)
 Super Oldies/'60s-#3 ....(AUF)
Diamonds & Rust
Joan Baez; *Best Of* .... (A&M)
 Classics-#8 .... (A&M)
 Diamonds & Rust .... (A&M)
 From Every Single Stage ....(A&M)
Judas Priest; *Best Of* ....(COL)
 Sin After Sin ....(COL)
 Unleashed In The East ....(COL)
Don't Sell This Diamond Ring
Gary Lewis/Playboys; *Good Old Rock & Roll* .... (IGR)
Dupree's Diamond Blues
Grateful Dead; *Aoxomoxoa* .... (WB)
Emerald
Thin Lizzy; *Jailbreak* .... (MER)
 Live & Dangerous ....(WB)
Emerald Eyes
Eric Johnson; *Tones* .... (RPR)
Fleetwood Mac; *Mystery To Me* .... (RPR)
Jimmy Page; *Outrider* ....(GEF)
Georgia Keeps Pulling On My Ring
Conway Twitty; *Classic Conway* .... (MCA)
 Very Best Of .... (MCA)
Give Me A Ring Sometime
Lisa Brokop; *Every Little Girl's Dream* .... (PAT)
Golden Earrings
Peggy Lee; *Capitol Collectors Series-#1-Early
 Years* ....(CAP)
 Greatest Hits ....(CAP)
Green Earrings
Steely Dan; *Gold* .... (MCA)
 Royal Scam .... (MCA)
Hidden Treasure
Traffic; *Low Spark Of High Heeled Boys* .... (ISL)
I Need A Rolex
Toddy Tee; *Rhyme Syndicate Comin' Through* ....(WB)
In A Week Or Two
Diamond Rio; *Close To The Edge* .... (ARI)
Jewel
Eddie Rabbitt; *Eddie Rabbitt* .... (ELE)
Propaganda; *Secret Wish* .... (ISL)
Jewel Eyed Judy
Fleetwood Mac; *Kiln House* .... (RPR)
Little Rock
Reba McEntire; *Whoever's In New England* ..... (MCA)
 Woman To Woman-#2 .... (MCA)
Love Is A Golden Ring
Frankie Laine; *16 Most Requested Songs* ....(COL)
Lucy In The Sky With Diamonds
Beatles; *1967-1970* ....(CAP)
 Sgt. Pepper's Lonely Hearts Club Band ....(CAP)
 Yellow Submarine ....(CAP)
Elton John; *All This & World War 2* .... (20)
 Greatest Hits-#2 ....(POL)
John Lennon; *Lennon* ....(CAP)
Magic Jewelled Limousine
Nasa; *Insha-Allah!* .... (SIR)
 ST/Wild Orchid .... (SIR)
Mama's Pearl
Jackson 5; *3rd Album* .... (MOT)
 Anthology .... (MOT)
 Compact Command Performances .... (MOT)
 Greatest Hits .... (MOT)
Memphis Pearl
Lucinda Williams; *Sweet Old World* .... (CML)
Mother Of Pearl
Roxy Music; *Greatest Hits* ....(ATC)
 Stranded ....(RPR)
On The Other Hand
Randy Travis; *Greatest Hits-#1* .... (WB)
 Storms Of Life ....(WB)
On Treasure Island
Louis Armstrong; *Louis Armstrong* .... (MSP)
Tommy Dorsey/Orchestra; *Seventeen Number
 Ones* ....(RCA)
Pearl From Warsaw
Klezmer Conservatory Band; *Jumpin' Night In The
 Garden Of Eden* .... (ROU)

Pearl Necklace
ZZ Top; *El Loco* ....(WB)
 Greatest Hits ....(WB)
 Six Pack ....(WB)
Pearl Of The Quarter
Steely Dan; *Countdown To Ecstasy* .... (MCA)
Pearls
Sade; *Love Deluxe* ....(EPI)
Pearls In The Snow
Michael Martin Murphey; *Cowboy Christmas* ..... (WB)
Pearls, The
Canadian Brass; *Red Hot Jazz-Dixieland Album* ...(PHI)
Jelly Roll Morton; *Jelly Roll Morton* .... (BLU)
Pearly Queen
Dave Mason; *Certified Live* .... (COL)
 Very Best Of .... (MCA)
Traffic; *Traffic* .... (ISL)
Playing Marbles With Diamonds
Steve Camp; *Doing My Best-#2* ....(SPW)
Pledge Pin
Robert Plant; *Pictures At Eleven* .... (SS)
Pocket Full Of Gold
Vince Gill; *Pocket Full Of Gold* .... (MCA)
Put That Ring On My Finger
Andrews Sisters; *50th Anniversary Collection-#2* (MCA)
Woody Herman; *Best Of The Big Bands* ....(COL)
Reflections In A Crystal Wind
Mimi & Richard Farina; *Best Of* .... (VAN)
 Reflections In A Crystal Wind .... (VAN)
Rhinestone Cowboy
Glen Campbell; *Classics Collection* ....(CAP)
 Country's Greatest Hits-#6-Superstars ....(PRY)
 Live ....(CAP)
 Rhinestone Cowboy ....(CAP)
 Very Best Of ....(CAP)
Ring On Her Finger, Time On Her Hands
Lee Greenwood; *Greatest Hits* .... (MCA)
 Inside Out .... (MCA)
Ruby Red
Kingston Trio; *Hidden Treasures* .... (FOL)
 Treasure Chest .... (FOL)
Sapphire
Clash; *Sandinista* ....(EPI)
Royal Philharmonic Ensemble/John Keating; *Birthstone
 Suite* ....(USA)
TNT; *Tell No Tales* .... (MER)
Sapphire Bullets Of Pure Love
They Might Be Giants; *Flood* .... (ELE)
Satan's Jewel Crown
Emmylou Harris; *Elite Hotel* .... (RPR)
Serpentine Fire
Earth, Wind & Fire; *All 'n All* ....(COL)
 Best Of-#2 ....(COL)
 Eternal Dance ....(COL)
She Is A Diamond
Original New York Cast; *Evita* .... (MCA)
Shine On Ruby Mountain
Kenny Rogers/First Edition; *All-Time Greatest
 Hits-#2* .... (MSP)
 Best Of .... (KT)
Shine On You Crazy Diamond
Pink Floyd; *Collection Of Great Dance Songs* ....(COL)
 Delicate Sound Of Thunder ....(COL)
 Wish You Were Here ....(COL)
Some Days Are Diamonds
John Denver; *Greatest Hits-#3* ....(RCA)
 Some Days Are Diamonds ....(RCA)
Sparkling In The Sand
Tower Of Power; *East Bay Grease* ....(OOP)
 Live & In Living Color ....(WB)
String Of Pearls
Boston Pops Orchestra/Arthur Fiedler; *Greatest
 Hits/'40s-#2* ....(RCA)
Glenn Miller; *Best Of* ....(RCA)
 Legendary Performer ....(BLU)
 Memorial 1944-1969 ....(BLU)
 Moonlight Serenade ....(BLU)
 Pure Gold ....(RCA)
 Story ....(RCA)
Lawrence Welk; *22 All-Time Big Band Favorites* (RAN)
Les & Larry Elgart; *Best Of The Big Bands* ......(COL)
Take Back Your Mink
Original Cast; *Guys & Dolls* .... (MCA)

This Diamond Ring
Gary Lewis/Playboys; *Billboard Top Rock 'N' Roll Hits-1965* .... (RHI)
EMI Legends Of Rock 'N' Roll-24 Greatest ...... (EMI)
Golden Years-1965 .... (DOM)
Spring Break-#2-Cold Kegs & Tan Legs .... (CAP)

Topaz
B-52's; *Cosmic Thing* .... (RPR)
Journey; *In The Beginning* .... (COL)
Journey .... (COL)

Trouble With Diamonds
Mac McAnally; *Live & Learn* .... (MCA)

Turquoise Jewelry
Camper Van Beethoven; *Our Beloved Revolutionary Sweetheart* .... (VIA)

Wear My Ring Around Your Neck
Elvis Presley; *Golden Records-#2* ....(RCA)
Hits Like Never Before-Essential-#3 ....(RCA)
Top Ten Hits ....(RCA)
Worldwide 50 Gold Award Hits-#1&2 ....(RCA)
Ricky Van Shelton; *Greatest Hits Plus* ....(COL)

When God Comes & Gathers His Jewels
Hank Williams; *Health & Happiness Shows* ..... (MER)
I Saw The Light .... (MER)
Molly O'Day/Cumberland Mountain Folks; *Columbia Country Classics-#1-Golden Age* ....(COL)
Hank Williams Songbook .... (COL)

With This Ring
Platters; *Only Their Best For You* .... (PRR)
Rockin' & Rollin' Wedding Songs-#2 .... (RHI)
T. Graham Brown; *Best Of* .... (LIB)

Would Jesus Wear A Rolex
Ray Stevens; *All-Time Greatest Comic Hits* ...... (CCB)
Collection .... (MCA)
Greatest Hits-#2 .... (MCA)

JUKEBOX

See Also: MUSIC

All Night Juke
Lloyd Green; *Lloyd's Of Nashville* .... (BOO)

Anywhere There's A Jukebox
Razzy Bailey; *Makin' Friends* .... (RCA)

A-1 On The Jukebox
Dave Edmunds; *Best Of* .... (SS)
Tracks On Wax 4 .... (SS)

A-11
Buck Owens; *Collection-1959-1990* .... (RHI)
Johnny Paycheck; *Golden Hits* .... (IGR)

Brother Juke Box
Don Everly; *45* .... (MCA)
Paul Craft; *45* .... (RCA)

Brother
Mark Chesnutt; *Too Cold At Home* .... (MCA)

Bubba Shot The Jukebox
Mark Chesnutt; *Longnecks & Short Stories* ...... (MCA)

Canned Music
Dan Hicks/Hot Licks; *Striking It Rich* .... (MCA)

Danny's All-Star Joint
Rickie Lee Jones; *Rickie Lee Jones* .... (WB)

Don't Rock The Jukebox
Alan Jackson; *Don't Rock The Jukebox* .... (ARI)

God's Own Jukebox
Jesse Winchester; *Third Down 110 To Go* .... (RHI)

Happiest Song On The Jukebox
Charley Pride; *Out-of-print recording* ....(OOP)

Hey Mister, That's Me Up On The Jukebox
Linda Ronstadt; *Prisoner In Disguise* .... (ASY)

Honky Tonky Fool
Doug Supernaw; *Red & Rio Grande* ....(BNA)

Human
Scientists; *Absolute* .... (SP)

I Heard The Jukebox Playing
Faron Young; *Hi Tone Poppa* ....(CLT)
Kitty Wells; *Story* .... (MCA)

If Hell Had A Jukebox
Travis Tritt; *It's All About To Change* .... (WB)

If I Didn't Have A Dime (To Play The...)
Gene Pitney; *Anthology* .... (RHI)
Greatest Hits .... (EVR)

If The Jukebox Took Teardrops
Billy Joe Royal; *Out Of The Shadows* .... (ATC)
Mike Henderson; *Country Music Made Me Do It* .(RCA)

I'll Be Your Jukebox Tonight
Barbara Mandrell; *I'll Be Your Jukebox Tonight* ..(CAP)

Jerusalem On The Jukebox
Richard Thompson; *Amnesia* ....(CAP)

Jones On The Jukebox
Becky Hobbs; *All Keyed Up* ....(RCA)

Juke
Charlie Musselwhite; *Stone Blues* .... (VAN)
Little Walter; *Best Of* .... (CSS)

Juke Joint Blues
Joe Turner; *Best Of* .... (PAB)
Joe Turner/Others; *Nobody In Mind* .... (PAB)

Juke Joint Jump
Elvin Bishop; *Juke Joint Jump* ....(CPC)
Raisin' Hell .... (CPC)

Jukebox
Michael Martin Murphey; *Land Of Enchantment* ..(WB)

Jukebox Argument
Mickey Gilley; *ST/Urban Cowboy 2* .... (EPI)

Jukebox Charlie
Johnny Paycheck; *Out-of-print Recording* ....(OOP)

Jukebox Cinderella
Johnny Duncan; *Come A Little Bit Closer* ....(COL)

Jukebox Fury
Rickie Lee Jones; *The Magazine* ....(WB)

Jukebox Gypsy
Lindisfarne; *Back & Fourth* ....(ATC)

Jukebox Has A 45
Clinton Gregory; *Out-of-print recording* ....(OOP)

Jukebox Help Me Find My Baby
Rhythm Rockers; *Sun Rockabillies #1* .... (SUN)

Jukebox Hero
Foreigner; *4* .... (ATL)
Classic Rock 1966-1988 .... (ATL)
Records .... (ATL)

Jukebox In My Mind
Alabama; *Pass It On Down* ....(RCA)

Jukebox Junkie
Ken Mellons; *Ken Mellons* .... (EPI)

Jukebox Junky
Jerry Lee Lewis; *Out-of-print recording* ....(OOP)
Kenny Price; *Out-of-print recording* ....(OOP)

Jukebox Music
Kinks; *Come Dancing With-Best Of-1977-1986* .. (ARI)
Sleepwalker .... (ARI)

Jukebox Never Plays "Home Sweet Home"
Jack Greene; *Out-of-print recording* ....(OOP)

Jukebox Played Along
Gene Watson; *Back In The Fire* ....(WB)
Honky Tony Country .... (WB)

Jukebox Saturday Night
Glenn Miller; *Best Of* .... (RCA)
Legendary Performer .... (RCA)
Memorial 1944-1969 .... (RCA)
This Is .... (RCA)
Modernaires; *Big Bands' Greatest Hits-#1* ....(COL)
Roy Clark; *Out-of-print recording* ....(OOP)

Jukebox Serenade
David Frizell & Shelly West; *Out-of-print recording* .... (OOP)

Jukebox With A Country Song
Doug Stone; *I Thought It Was You* ....(EPI)

Jump Right Out Of This Jukebox
Dale Wheeler; *Memphis Country* .... (SUN)

Let The Jukebox Keep On Playing
Carl Perkins; *Blue Suede Shoes* .... (SUN)
Memphis Country .... (SUN)

Lyin' Jukebox
Hank Williams, Jr.; *Maverick* ....(CPC)

Me & The Jukebox
Leon Morris & Buzz Busby; *Honky Tonk Bluegrass* .... (ROU)

Meanest Jukebox In Town
Johnny Paycheck; *Out-of-print recording* ....(OOP)

My Friend The Jukebox
Mel Street; *45* .... (POL)

Nickelodeon
Sammi Smith; *Out-of-print recording* ....(OOP)

Old Rainbow Jukebox & You
John Schneider; *Memory Like You* .... (MCA)

Over At Herbie's Juke Joint
Donald Brown; *People Music* ....(MUS)

Play The Saddest Song On The Jukebox
Carmol Taylor; *Songwriter* ....(ELE)

Please Mr. Please
Olivia Newton-John; *Back To Basics-Essential Collection* .... (GEF)
Please Play The Jukebox
Jimmy Martin; *One Woman Man* .... (IGR)
Prayer & A Juke Box
Little Anthony/Imperials; *Best Of* .... (RHI)
Forever Yours .... (RLL)
Prop Me Up Beside The Jukebox
Joe Diffie; *Honky Tonk Attitude* .... (EPI)
Put A Nickel In The Jukebox...
Sharon McNight; *Another Side Of* .... (GLN)
Presenting Sharon McNight .... (GLN)
Put A Quarter In The Jukebox
Barry Manilow; *Greatest Hits #2* .... (ARI)
Buck Owens; *Out-of-print recording* .... (CAP)
School Days
Chuck Berry; *Best Of* .... (GUS)
Billboard Top Rock 'N' Roll Hits-1957 .... (RHI)
Golden Hits .... (MER)
ST/Rock 'N' Roll High School .... (SIR)
Set 'Em Up Joe (B24)
Vern Gosdin; *Chiseled In Stone* .... (COL)
Greatest Country Hits/'80s-1988 .... (COL)
Somethin' About A Jukebox
Johnny Rodriguez; *Out-of-print recording* .... (OOP)
Stoned At The Jukebox
Hank Williams, Jr.; *Best Of* .... (CCB)
Best Of-#1-Roots & Branches .... (MER)
Bocephus Box-Collection-1979-1992 .... (CPC)
Lone Wolf .... (W/C)
Straight Tequila Night
John Anderson; *Seminole Wind* .... (BNA)
Today's Hot Country .... (KT)
That's What Makes The Jukebox Play
Moe Bandy; *Out-of-print recording* .... (OOP)
There Ain't No Country Music On This...
Tom T. Hall; *Out-of-print recording* .... (OOP)
There's A Song On The Jukebox
David Wills; *Columbia Country Classics-#5-New Trad.* .... (COL)
Two Dollars In The Jukebox
Eddie Rabbitt; *All-Time Greatest Hits* .... (WB)
Best Of .... (WB)
Rocky Mountain Music .... (ELE)
Ten Years Of Greatest Hits .... (LIB)
Two Plays For A Quarter
Kathy Hart/Bluestars; *Tonight I Want It All* .... (BIO)
Warning Labels
Doug Stone; *From The Heart* .... (EPI)
We're The Kind Of People Who Make The...
Stonewall Jackson; *Out-of-print recording* .... (OOP)
Who Stole The Jukebox (From Lucy's...)
Johnny Bond; *Johnny Gimble's Texas Honky-Tonk Hits* .... (CMH)
Wurlitzer Prize
Waylon Jennings; *Out-of-print recording* .... (OOP)

JUNGLES

See Also: TREES

Animals In Jungles
China Crisis; *Working With Fire & Steel* .... (WB)
Back In Judy's Jungle
Brian Eno; *Desert Island Selection* .... (EDI)
Taking Tiger Mountain By Strategy .... (EDI)
Blues From The Rainforest
Merl Saunders; *Blues From The Rainforest-A Musical Suite* .... (GRD)
Bungle In The Jungle
Jethro Tull; *20 Years Of-Boxed Set* .... (CHR)
M.U.-Best Of .... (CHR)
Original Masters .... (CHR)
War Child .... (CHR)
Bush Doctor
Peter Tosh; *Bush Doctor* .... (RS)
Captured Live .... (EMI)
The Toughest .... (CAP)
Concrete Jungle
Anvil; *Best Of Metal Blade-#3* .... (MET)
Strength Of Steel .... (MET)

Bob Marley/Wailers; *Babylon By Bus* .... (ISL)
Catch A Fire .... (ISL)
Reggae Roots .... (GRL)
This Is Reggae Music-#1 .... (ISL)
Specials; *Specials* .... (CHR)
ST/Dance Craze .... (CHR)
Cowboy In The Jungle
Jimmy Buffett; *Son Of A Son Of A Sailor* ...... (MCA)
"George Of The Jungle" Theme
Original Music; *Television's Greatest Hits-#2* ..... (TVT)
Gitarzan
Ray Stevens; *Dr. Demento's Greatest Novelty-#3* . (RHI)
Greatest Hits .... (MCA)
Greatest Hits .... (RCA)
Greystoke
Soundtrack; *Greystoke-Legend Of Tarzan* .... (WB)
Hobo Jungle
Band; *Northern Lights-Southern Cross* .... (CAP)
In The Heat Of The Jungle
Chris Isaak; *Heart Shaped World* .... (RPR)
Jungle
Ashford & Simpson; *Ashford & Simpson* .... (CAP)
Solid Plus Seven .... (CAP)
ST/Body Rock .... (EMI)
Dwight Twilley Band; *Jungle* .... (EMI)
Electric Light Orchestra; *Box Of Their Best* ...... (JET)
Out Of The Blue .... (JET)
Jungle Boogie
Kool/Gang; *Everything Is-Greatest Hits* .... (MER)
Soul Hits/'70s-#12 .... (RHI)
Spin Their Top Hits .... (DL)
Jungle Boy
Bow Wow Wow; *I Want Candy* .... (RCA)
John Eddie; *John Eddie* .... (COL)
Jungle Comes Alive
Jamaica Boys; *J Boys* .... (RPR)
Jungle Drums
Artie Shaw; *Begin The Beguine* .... (POE)
This Is .... (RCA)
Jungle Fever
Stevie Wonder; *ST/Jungle Fever* .... (MOT)
Jungle Hop
Cramps; *Psychedelic Jungle/Gravest Hits* .... (IRS)
Jungle Line
Joni Mitchell; *Hissing Of Summer Lawns* .... (ASY)
Jungle Love
Gladys Knight/Pips; *Glad To Be* .... (ALL)
Letter Full Of Tears .... (ACC)
Steve Miller Band; *Book Of Dreams* .... (CAP)
Gift Set .... (CAP)
Greatest Hits-1974-1978 .... (CAP)
Live .... (CAP)
Time; *Ice Cream Castles* .... (WB)
Jungle Rock
Marshall Crenshaw; *45* .... (WB)
Jungle Strut
Gene Ammons; *Brother Jug* .... (PRS)
Greatest Hits .... (PRS)
Santana; *Santana* .... (COL)
Viva Santana! .... (COL)
Jungle Time
Neil Diamond; *Beautiful Noise* .... (COL)
Jungle Work
Warren Zevon; *Bad Luck Streak In Dancing School* .... (ASY)
Jungleland
Bruce Springsteen; *Born To Run* .... (COL)
King Of The Jungle
Lester Davenport; *When The Blues Hit You* ..... (EMC)
Life In The Jungle
John Mayall/Bluesbreakers; *Chicago Line* .... (ISL)
Livin' In The Jungle
Flo & Eddie/Turtles; *History Of* .... (RHI)
Oakland Jungle
Wild Boyz; *It Had To Be Done* .... (VOL)
Oh Jungleland
Simple Minds; *In The City Of Light (Live)* .... (A&M)
One Jungle
Fixx; *Ink* .... (IPA)
Picnic In The Jungle
Snakefinger; *Chewing Hides The Sound* .... (RAL)
Poor Tarzan
Little Charlie/Nightcats; *All The Way Crazy* ..... (ALG)

Queen Of The Jungle
Zarkons; *Riders In The Long Black Parade* ...... (ENI)
Rockin' In The Jungle
Eternals; *WCBS FM101 History Of
Rock-Doo-Wop-#2* ....(CLT)
Run Through The Jungle
Creedence Clearwater Revival; *1970* ....(FAN)
Chronicle ....(FAN)
Cosmo's Factory ....(FAN)
More Creedence Gold ....(FAN)
Space Safari
Nazareth; *Rampant* ....(A&M)
Stranded In The Jungle
Cadets; *Collectables Presents History Of Rock-#2* . (CLT)
Cruisin'-1956 ....(INC)
Oldies But Goodies-#1 ....(OSR)
Original Rock 'N' Roll Hits Of The '50s ....(RLL)
New York Dolls; *In Too Much Too Soon* ...... (MER)
Live In NYC '75 ....(RES)
Surfin' Safari
Beach Boys; *Absolute Best-#1* ....(CAP)
Endless Summer ....(CAP)
Made In The U.S.A. ....(CAP)
Monster Summer Hits-Wild Surf ....(CAP)
Swingin' Safari
Billy Vaughn; *Best Of* ....(MCA)
Greatest Hits ....(CCB)
Tarzan Boy
Baltimora; *Living In The Background* ....(MAN)
Tarzan Was A Bluesman
Timbuk 3; *Eden Alley* ....(IRS)
Tarzan & Jane
Sparks; *Angst In My Pants* ....(ATL)
Tarzan's Nuts
Madness; *One Step Beyond* ....(SIR)
Welcome To The Jungle
Guns N' Roses; *Appetite For Destruction* ......(GEF)
ST/Lean On Me ....(WB)
Wimoweh (Mbube)-The Lion Sleeps Tonight
Chet Atkins; *RCA Years* ....(RCA)
Kingston Trio; *Kingston Trio/From The Hungry i* . (CAP)
Nylons; *Seamless* ....(OPE)
Pete Seeger; *Greatest Hits* ....(COL)
Tokens; *Billboard Top Rock 'N' Roll Hits-1961* .. (RHI)
Nipper's Greatest Hits/'60s-#1 ....(RCA)
Weavers; *Greatest Hits* ....(VAN)

KILL, Murder

*See Also: CAPITAL PUNISHMENT, DEATH,
DRUGS, FIGHT, GUNS, REBELS, WAR*

1913 Massacre
Arlo Guthrie; *Hobo's Lullaby* ....(RPR)
Ramblin' Jack Elliott; *Greatest Songs Of Woody
Guthrie* ....(VAN)
Woody Guthrie; *Struggle* ....(FLW)
Annihilate This Week
Black Flag; *Loose Nut* ....(SST)
Ballad Of Danny Bailey
Elton John; *Goodbye Yellow Brick Road* ....(POL)
Before You Kill Us All
Randy Travis; *This Is Me* ....(WB)
Boom Bye Bye
Buju Banton; *Voice Of Jamaica* ....(MER)
Born To Kill
Damned; *Damned Damned Damned* ....(FRN)
Final Damnation ....(RES)
Gillan; *Double Trouble* ....(MET)
Breakfast In Mayfair
Fairport Convention; *Babbacombe Lee* ....(OOP)
Chronicles ....(A&M)
Bullet In The Head
Rage Against The Machine; *Rage Against The
Machine* ....(EPA)
Bullet-Ridden Bodies
Accused; *Grinning Like An Undertaker* ....(NSY)
Careful With That Axe Eugene
Pink Floyd; *Relics* ....(CAP)
Umma Gumma ....(CAP)
Cocaine Done Killed My Baby
Mance Lipscomb; *Texas Songwriter-#2* ....(ARH)

Cop Killer
Ice-T; *Body Count* ....(WB)
Cortez The Killer
Neil Young/Crazy Horse; *Decade* ....(RPR)
Live Rust ....(RPR)
Zuma ....(RPR)
Crush, Kill, Destroy
Elvis Hitler; *Hellbilly* ....(RES)
Cure Me...Or Kill Me
Gilby Clarke; *Pawnshop Guitars* ....(VIA)
Curiosity Killed The Cat
Curiosity Killed The Cat; *Keep Your Distance* .. (MER)
Cuts You Up
Peter Murphy; *Deep* ....(BEG)
Day That Curly Bill Shot Down Crazy Sam
Hollies; *Hollies* ....(EPI)
Dial A Hitman
Big Audio Dynamite; *No. 10 Upping St.* ....(COL)
Dire Wolf
Grateful Dead; *Reckoning* ....(ARI)
Workingman's Dead ....(WB)
Dirty Deeds Done Dirt Cheap
AC/DC; *Dirty Deeds Done Dirt Cheap* ....(ATL)
Disarm
Smashing Pumpkins; *Siamese Dream* ....(VIA)
Disco Strangler
Eagles; *Long Run* ....(ASY)
Disco's Out, Murder's In
Suicidal Tendencies; *Lights...Camera...Revolution* .. (EPI)
Divide & Conquer
Husker Du; *Flip Your Wig* ....(SST)
Don't Kill It Carol
Manfred Mann's Earth Band; *Angel Station* ....(WB)
Don't Kill Me
David Huff; *45* ....(UA)
Don't Kill The Animals
Lene Lovich; *Animal Liberation* ....(WAX)
Lene Lovich & Nina Hagen; *Tame Yourself* ...... (RHI)
Don't Kill The Whale
Yes; *Tormato* ....(ATL)
Yesshows ....(ATL)
Don't Slay That Potato
Tom Paxon; *One Million Lawyers & Other Disasters* (FF)
Down By The River
Neil Young; *Decade* ....(RPR)
Everybody Knows This Is Nowhere ....(RPR)
Dressed To Kill
Lita Ford; *Dancin' On The Edge* ....(MER)
Nazareth; *Classics-#16* ....(A&M)
Fool Circle ....(A&M)
'Snaz ....(A&M)
Euthanasia Waltz
Brand X; *Livestock* ....(BP)
Unorthodox Behaviour ....(BP)
Excitable Boy
Warren Zevon; *Excitable Boy* ....(ASY)
Quiet Normal Life-Best Of ....(ASY)
Stand In The Fire ....(ASY)
Folsom Prison Blues
Brooks & Dunn & Johnny Cash; *Red Hot +
Country* ....(MER)
Johnny Cash; *At Folsom Prison & San Quentin* ...(COL)
Billboard Top Country Hits-1968 ....(RHI)
Classic Cash-Hall Of Fame Series .... (MER)
Greatest Hits #2 ....(COL)
Original Golden Hits #1 ....(SUN)
Superbilly ....(SUN)
Genocide
Judas Priest; *Hero Hero* ....(RCA)
Sad Wings Of Destiny ....(RCA)
Unleashed In The East ....(COL)
Gettin' Away With Murder
Slaughter House; *Face Reality* ....(MET)
Ghostbusters
Ray Parker, Jr.; *Chartbusters* ....(ARI)
Elvira Presents Haunted Hits ....(RHI)
Greatest Movie Rock Hits ....(RHI)
ST/Ghostbusters ....(ARI)
Here Comes President Kill Again
XTC; *Oranges & Lemons* ....(GEF)
How To Kill A Radio Consultant
Public Enemy; *Apocalypse 91-Enemy Strikes
Black* ....(DFC)
Greatest Misses ....(CHA)

I Am A Predator
Ted Nugent; *Intensities In Ten Cities* .... (EPI)
I Don't Like Mondays
Bob Geldof/Johnny Fingers; *Secret Policeman's Other Ball* .... (ISL)
Boomtown Rats; *Fine Art Of Surfacing* .... (COL)
I Love A Murder Mystery
Jerry Lewis; *Capitol Collectors Series* .... (CAP)
I Shot The Sheriff
Bob Marley/Wailers; *Burnin'* .... (TUF)
Legend .... (TUF)
Live .... (TUF)
This Is Reggae Music .... (ISL)
Eric Clapton; *461 Ocean Blvd.* .... (RSO)
Crossroads .... (POL)
Time Pieces-Best Of .... (RSO)
If Drinkin' Don't Kill Me...
George Jones; *Anniversary-10 Years Of Hits* ...... (EPI)
I Am What I Am .... (EPI)
Jeannie Needs A Shooter
Warren Zevon; *Bad Luck Streak In Dancing School* .... (ASY)
Stand In The Fire .... (ASY)
Kill City
Iggy Pop & James Williamson; *Kill City* .... (BMP)
Kill For Peace
Fugs; *Fugs* .... (ESP)
Fugs 4 Rounders Score .... (ESP)
Kill Surf City
Jesus & Mary Chain; *Barbed Wire Kisses* .... (RPR)
Kill The King
Rainbow; *Long Live Rock 'n' Roll* .... (POL)
On Stage .... (OYS)
Killed A Cat
Kenny Rankin; *Silver Morning* .... (LD)
Killer
Adamski; *Liveandirect* .... (MCA)
Alice Cooper; *Alice Cooper* .... (WB)
Kiss; *Creatures Of The Night* .... (CAS)
Pat Travers; *Boom Boom...Best Of* .... (POL)
Seal; *Seal* .... (SIR)
Killer Cut
Charlie; *Fight Dirty* .... (ARI)
Killer Joe
Quincy Jones; *Classics-#3* .... (A&M)
I Heard That! .... (A&M)
ST/Listen Up-The Lives Of Quincy Jones ...... (QUE)
The Best .... (A&M)
Walking In Space .... (A&M)
Killer Queen
Queen; *Greatest Hits* .... (HOL)
Live Killers .... (HOL)
Sheer Heart Attack .... (HOL)
Killer Without A Cause
Thin Lizzy; *Bad Reputation* .... (MER)
Killer's Eyes
Kinks; *Give The People What They Want* .... (ARI)
Killer's Instinct
Pat Travers; *Heat In The Street* .... (POL)
Killing An Arab
Cure; *Boys Don't Cry* .... (ELE)
Standing On A Beach-The Singles .... (ELE)
Killing Machine
Judas Priest; *Hell Bent For Leather* .... (COL)
Killing Me Softly With His Song
Luther Vandross; *Songs* .... (EPI)
Roberta Flack; *Atlantic R&B 1947-1974-#6-(1966-1969)* .... (ATL)
Best Of .... (ATL)
Golden Age Of Black Music-1970-1975 .... (ATL)
Killing Me Softly With His Song .... (ATL)
Killing Moon
Echo/Bunnymen; *Ocean Rain* .... (SIR)
Songs To Learn And Sing .... (SIR)
Killing Of Georgie
Rod Stewart; *Greatest Hits* .... (WB)
Night On The Town .... (WB)
Killing The Blues
John Prine; *Pink Cadillac* .... (ASY)
Shawn Colvin; *Cover Girl* .... (COL)
Killin' Floor
Albert King; *Years Gone By* .... (STX)
Howlin' Wolf; *Real Folk Blues* .... (CSS)
Jimi Hendrix; *Kiss The Sky* .... (RPR)

Jimi Hendrix Experience; *Live At Winterland* ..... (RYK)
Radio One .... (RYK)
Killin' Time
Clint Black; *Killin' Time* .... (RCA)
RCA Award Winners .... (RCA)
Lady In Red
Charlie Daniels Band; *Windows* .... (EPI)
Chris DeBurgh; *Into The Light* .... (A&M)
Joan Jett/Blackhearts; *I Love Rock 'N' Roll* .... (BW)
Stan Getz; *Greatest Hits* .... (PRS)
Learning To Live Again
Garth Brooks; *The Chase* .... (LIB)
Life Takes A Life
Jon Butcher Axis; *Jon Butcher Axis* .... (POL)
Loser
Beck; *Mellow Gold* .... (DGC)
Lovin' You Is Killing Me
Alabama; *Mountain Music* .... (RCA)
Mack The Knife
Bobby Darin; *At The Copa* .... (BAI)
Hit Singles 1958-1977 .... (ATL)
Story .... (ATC)
Frank Sinatra; *Reprise Collection* .... (RPR)
Manslaughter
EPMD; *Business As Usual* .... (DFC)
Massacre
Thin Lizzy; *Johnny The Fox* .... (WB)
Live & Dangerous .... (WB)
Matty Groves
Fairport Convention; *Chronicles* .... (A&M)
Liege & Lief .... (A&M)
Maxwell's Silver Hammer
Beatles; *1967-1970* .... (CAP)
Abbey Road .... (CAP)
Mommy, Can I Go Out & Kill Tonight
Misfits; *Walk Among Us* .... (RUB)
Murder
Cavedogs; *Soul Martini* .... (CAP)
David Gilmour; *About Face* .... (COL)
General Public; *Hand To Mouth* .... (IRS)
New Order; *Substance* .... (QUE)
Selecter; *Selected Selections* .... (CHR)
Too Much Pressure .... (CHR)
Murder By Numbers
Police; *Synchronicity* .... (A&M)
Murder By Suicide
Gary Richrath; *Only The Strong Survive* .... (CRS)
Murder Gonna Be My Crime
Sippie Wallace; *Women Be Wise* .... (ALG)
Murder In High Heels
Kiss; *Animalize* .... (MER)
Murder In My Heart For The Judge
Lee Michaels; *Collection* .... (RHI)
Moby Grape; *Wow* .... (OOP)
Murder In The First Degree
Elvin Bishop; *Don't Let The Bossman Get You Down* .... (ALG)
Murder In The Skies
Gary Moore; *Early Years* .... (WTG)
We Want Moore .... (VIA)
Murder Inc.
Murder Inc.; *Murder Inc.* .... (RCA)
Murder Mystery
Velvet Underground; *Velvet Underground* .... (VRV)
Murder Of Love
Propaganda; *Secret Wish* .... (ISL)
Murder Of One
Counting Crows; *August And Everything After* .. (DGC)
Murder One
Awesome Dre/Hardcore Committee; *You Can't Hold Me Back* .... (PRY)
Murder Rap
Above The Law; *Livin' Like Hustlers* .... (RUT)
Murder Story
Simple Minds; *Life In A Day* .... (VIA)
Murder Style
Lords Of The New Church; *Method To Our Madness* .... (IRS)
Murder Was The Case
Snoop Doggy Dogg; *Doggystyle* .... (DR)
Murdered By Love
Gary Stewart; *Brand New* .... (HT)

Murderer's Confession
Original Broadway Cast; *Mystery Of Edwin
Drood* .... (POL)
Murder, Tonight, In The Trailer Park
Cowboy Junkies; *Black-Eyed Man* ....(RCA)
"Murder", He Says
Roy Eldridge/Gene Krupa Or./Anita O'Day;
Uptown ....(COL)
My Guitar Wants To Kill Your Mama
Frank Zappa; *You Can't Do That On Stage
Anymore-#4* ....(RYK)
Mothers Of Invention; *Weasels Ripped My Flesh* ... (BIZ)
Nebraska
Bruce Springsteen; *Nebraska* ....(COL)
Bruce Springsteen/E Street Band;
Live-1975-1985 ....(COL)
Never Kill Another Man
Steve Miller Band; *Anthology* ....(CAP)
#5 ....(CAP)
Night The Lights Went Out In Georgia
Lynn Anderson; *Top Of The World* ....(COL)
Reba McEntire; *For My Broken Heart* .... (MCA)
Vicki Lawrence; *Super Hits/'70s-Have A Nice
Day-#10* .... (RHI)
November 22, 1963
Original Cast; *Assassins* ....(RCA)
Overkill
Men At Work; *Cargo* ....(COL)
Motorhead; *No Remorse* ....(ROA)
No Sleep At All .... (ROA)
No Sleep 'Til Hammersmith ....(ROA)
Overkill .... (ROA)
Point Blank
Bruce Springsteen; *The River* ....(COL)
Poisoning Pigeons In The Park
Tom Lehrer; *Dr. Demento 20th Anniversary
Collection* .... (RHI)
Dr. Demento Presents Greatest Novelty CD ..... (RHI)
Evening Wasted With ....(RPR)
Psycho Killer
Talking Heads; *Name Of This Band Is Talking
Heads* .... (SIR)
ST/Stop Making Sense ....(SIR)
'77 ....(SIR)
Put Out The Fire
Queen; *Hot Space* ....(HOL)
Rock 'N' Roll Murder
Leaving Trains; *Loser Illusion-Pt. 0* ....(SST)
Salt On A Slug
Black Flag; *Family Man* ....(SST)
Salting Of The Slug
Riders In The Sky; *Cowboy Way* .... (MCA)
Search & Destroy
Deadly Blessing; *Ascend From The Cauldron* ... (NEW)
Dictators; *10 Roir Years-Anthology* .... (ROI)
Live-F..k 'Em If They Can't Take A Joke .... (ROD)
Manifest Destiny ....(ASY)
Iggy/Stooges; *Raw Power* ....(COL)
Overlords; *Organic?* ....(AS)
Serial Killa
Snoop Doggy Dogg; *Doggystyle* .... (DR)
Shoot Her If She Runs
Climax Blues Band; *Tightly Knit* ....(SIR)
Sky Is A Poisonous Garden
Concrete Blonde; *Bloodletting* ....(IRS)
Somebody Got Murdered
Clash; *On Broadway* ....(EPI)
Sandinista ....(EPI)
Story Of-#1 ....(EPI)
Somebody Killed Dewey Jones' Daughter
Lacy J. Dalton; *Takin' It Easy* ....(COL)
Speed Kills
Steve Gibbons Band; *Caught In The Act* .... (MCA)
Stranglehold
Paul McCartney; *Press To Play* ....(CAP)
Ted Nugent; *Double Live Gonzo* ....(EPI)
Heavy Metal Memories ....(RHI)
Ted Nugent ....(EPI)
Style Kills
Robert Palmer; *Addictions-#1* ....(ISL)
This Drinkin' Will Kill Me
Dwight Yoakam; *Hillbilly Deluxe* ....(RPR)
To Kill A Hooker
N.W.A.; *Efil4zaggin* ....(RUP)

Tom Dooley
Doc Watson; *Doc Watson* .... (VAN)
Essential .... (VAN)
Out In The Country ....(INT)
Kingston Trio; *Capitol Collectors Series* ....(CAP)
From The Hungry i ....(CAP)
Greatest Hits ....(CCB)
Tom Dooley ....(CAP)
Troubadours Of The Folk Era-#3 .... (RHI)
Video Killed The Radio Star
Bruce Woolly/Camera Club; *Bruce Woolly/Camera
Club* ....(COL)
Buggles; *Age Of Plastic* .... (ISL)
Island Story-1962-1987-25th Anniversary ...... (ISL)
Rock Of The '80s-#2 ....(PRY)
View To A Kill
Duran Duran; *Decade* .... (CAP)
ST/View To A Kill ....(CAP)
Virgin Killer
Scorpions; *Best Of* ....(RCA)
Virgin Killer ....(RCA)
Waitress, The
Tori Amos; *Under The Pink* .... (ATL)
Watch The Girl Destroy Me
Possum Dixon; *Possum Dixon* .... (ISC)
You Can't Kill Rock & Roll
Ozzy Osbourne; *Diary Of A Madman* ....(JET)

KINGS, Noblemen, Princes
See Also: QUEENS, ROYALTY

All The King's Castles
Shawn Phillips; *Bright White* .... (A&M)
All The King's Gardens
Joan Armatrading; *Whatever's For Us* .... (A&M)
All The King's Horses
Aretha Franklin; *Young Gifted & Black* .... (ATL)
Firm; *Mean Business* .... (ATL)
Lynn Anderson; *Greatest Hits-#2* ....(COL)
Nazareth; *Expect No Mercy* ....(A&M)
Triumph; *Surveillance* ....(MCA)
All The King's Weight
Andy Pratt; *Andy Pratt* ....(COL)
Camelot
Original 1982 London Cast; *Camelot* ....(VS)
Original Cast; *Camelot* ....(COL)
Richard Burton; *Broadway Magic-1960s* ....(COL)
Richard Harris; *ST/Camelot* ....(WB)
Capricorn Kings
Lee Wright; *45* ....(PRA)
Connecticut Yankee In The Court Of...
Robert Fripp/League Of Crafty Guitarists; *Show Of
Hands* .... (EDI)
Crawling King Snake
Doors; *L.A. Woman* ....(ELE)
John Lee Hooker; *Best Of* ....(CRS)
World's Greatest Blues Singer .... (VJ)
Muddy Waters; *They Call Me Muddy Waters* .... (CSS)
Davy Crockett
Hermes Nye; *Ballads Of The Civil War-#1 & 2* . (FLW)
Duke Of Earl
Gene Chandler; *21 Oldies But Goodies* .... (OSR)
Billboard Top Rock 'N' Roll Hits-1962 .... (RHI)
Cruisin'-1962 ....(INC)
Oldies But Goodies-#6 ....(OSR)
New Edition; *Under The Blue Moon* .... (MCA)
Emperor Of Wyoming
Neil Young; *Neil Young* ....(RPR)
Emperor's New Clothes
Sinead O'Connor; *I Do Not Want What I Haven't
Got* ....(ENS)
Every Man A King
Randy Newman; *Good Old Boys* .... (RPR)
Everybody Wants To Rule The World
Tears For Fears; *Knebworth: The Album* ....(POL)
Music For The Miracle ....(CBA)
Songs From The Big Chair ....(MER)
Farewell To Kings
Rush; *Farewell To Kings* ....(MER)
From A Jack To A King
Jim Reeves; *I Love You Because* ....(RCA)
Pure Gold ....(RCA)
Ned Miller; *Billboard Top Country Hits-1963* .... (RHI)

Ricky Van Shelton; *Loving Proof* ....(COL)
God Save The King
Popular Standard; *Out-Of-Print Recording* ....(OOP)
Great Pretender
Band; *Moondog Matinee* ....(CAP)
Platters; *Anthology* .... (RHI)
Billboard Top R&B Hits-1956 .... (RHI)
Cruisin'-1956 .... (INC)
Encore Of Golden Hits .... (MER)
ST/American Graffiti .... (MCA)
Super Oldies/'50s-#3 ....(AUF)
Roy Orbison; *Best-Loved Standards* .... (MON)
Stan Freberg; *Capitol Collectors Series* ....(CAP)
I Just Can't Wait To Be King
Elton John; *ST/The Lion King* ....(DIS)
I Used To Be A King
Graham Nash; *Songs For Beginners* .... (ATL)
I Wonder What The King Is Doing Tonight
Original Cast; *Camelot* ....(COL)
Richard Harris; *ST/Camelot* ....(WB)
If I Were King Of The Forest
Bert Lahr; *ST/Wizard Of Oz* ....(SSP)
In The Court Of The Crimson King
King Crimson; *The Court Of The Crimson King* .. (ATL)
In The Hall Of The Mountain King
Duke Ellington; *Three Suites* ....(COL)
Electric Light Orchestra; *On The Third Day* .....(JET)
Sounds Incorporated; *History Of British Rock-#3* . (RHI)
I'm A King Bee
Muddy Waters; *King Bee* .... (BS)
Rolling Stones; *Hitmakers* ....(LON)
Hitmakers ....(OOP)
Slim Harpo; *Best Of* .... (RHI)
Blues Classics .... (KT)
I'm Henry The VIII, I Am
Herman's Hermits; *Something Good Again* ......(OOP)
XX-Greatest Hits .... (AKO)
Kill The King
Rainbow; *Long Live Rock 'n' Roll* .... (POL)
On Stage .... (OYS)
King
Count Basie; *Basie's Best* .... (PAU)
UB40; *1980-83* .... (A&M)
King Cobra
Herbie Hancock; *Best Of-Blue Note Years* .... (BLN)
King Cobra; *Powerhouse Music* .... (AJK)
Tom Scott/L.A. Express; *Tom Scott/L.A. Express* .. (EPI)
King Cockroach
Chick Corea Elektric Band; *Chick Corea Elektric Band* ....(GRP)
King Cool
Donnie Iris; *King Cool* .... (MCA)
King Cotton
Mormon Tabernacle Choir; *Stars & Stripes Forever* ....(COL)
King Creole
Elvis Presley; *Great Performances* ....(RCA)
Hits Like Never Before-Essential-#3 ....(RCA)
ST/King Creole ....(RCA)
Worldwide 50 Gold Award Hits-#2 ....(RCA)
King David
Judy Collins; *Bread & Roses* .... (ELE)
King For A Day
Thompson Twins; *Here's To Future Days* .... (ARI)
XTC; *Oranges & Lemons* ....(GEF)
King Has Lost His Crown
Abba; *Voulez-Vous* .... (ATL)
King Herod's Song
Original London Cast; *Jesus Christ Superstar* .... (MCA)
King Heroin
James Brown; *Soul Classics* ....(OOP)
James Chance/Contortions; *Live In New York* ... (ROI)
New York Rockers .... (ROI)
Soul Exorcism .... (ROI)
Jazzy Jeff; *On Fire* ....(JVA)
King Holiday
King Dream Chorus/Holiday Crew; *45* .... (MER)
King Is Half-Undressed
Jellyfish; *Bellybutton* .... (CHS)
King Kong
Frank Zappa; *Uncle Meat* ....(BAR)
You Can't Do That On Stage Anymore ....(BAR)
Kinks; *Kink Kronikles* ....(RPR)

King Kong's Monkey
Gary U.S. Bonds; *45* ....(LEG)
King Midas In Reverse
Hollies; *Best Of-#2* .... (EMI)
Epic Anthology From Orig. Master Tapes .... (EPI)
Greatest Hits ....(EPI)
King Must Die
Elton John; *Elton John* ....(POL)
Live In Australia w/Melbourne Symphony ...... (MCA)
King Of All
Al Green; *Truth N' Time* ....(MOT)
King Of Hollywood
Eagles; *The Long Run* ....(ASY)
King Of Kansas
Skywalk; *Fall Into Winter Jazz Sampler '88* ..... (MCA)
King Of My Heart
Melba Moore; *Read My Lips* ....(CAP)
King Of New York
D Schoolly; *How A Black Man Feels* ....(CAP)
King Of Nothing
Seals & Crofts; *Greatest Hits* .... (WB)
King Of Oak Street
Kenny Rogers; *The Gambler* .... (EMI)
Kenny Rogers/First Edition; *Country Songs* ..... (MCA)
King Of Oklahoma
Michael Franks; *Previously Unavailable* .... (DRG)
King Of Pain
Police; *Every Breath You Take-Singles* .... (A&M)
MTV's Rock 'N' Roll To Go .... (ELE)
Synchronicity .... (A&M)
King Of Paris
Jo Stafford; *By Request* .... (CRN)
King Of Rats
Neighborhoods; *Neighborhoods* .... (THI)
King Of Rock
Run-D.M.C.; *King Of Rock* ....(PRO)
Mr. Magic's Rap Attack ....(PRO)
King Of Sleaze
Beat Farmers; *Loud & Plowed &...Live!* ....(CCB)
Poor & Famous ....(CCB)
King Of Soul
James Brown; *ST/Doctor Detroit* .... (BKS)
King Of Soul Medley
Soul Kings; *45* ....(GLM)
King Of The Castle
Soup Dragons; *This Is Our Art* .... (SIR)
King Of The Cowboys
Amazing Rhythm Aces; *Stacked Deck* .... (MCA)
Roy Rogers & Dusty Rogers; *Tribute* ....(RCA)
King Of The Dogs
Spread Eagle; *Open To The Public* .... (MCA)
King Of The Dollar
School Of Fish; *School Of Fish* ....(CAP)
King Of The Hill
Minutemen; *Ballot Result* ....(SST)
Project: Mersh ....(SST)
Quiet Riot; *Quiet Riot* ....(PSH)
Roger McGuinn; *Back From Rio* .... (ARI)
King Of The Jungle
Lester Davenport; *When The Blues Hit You* ..... (EMC)
King Of The Mountain
Bon Jovi; *7800 Degrees Fahrenheit* .... (MER)
King Of The New York Streets
Dion; *Yo Frankie* .... (ARI)
King Of The Night Time World
Kiss; *Alive 2* .... (CAS)
Destroyer .... (CAS)
King Of The Road
Roger Miller; *Billboard Top Country Hits-1965* .. (RHI)
Cruisin'-1965 .... (INC)
Golden Hits .... (SMA)
R.E.M.; *Dead Letter Office* .... (IRS)
King Of The Silver Screen
Alice Cooper; *Lace & Whisky* .... (MET)
King Of The Surf Guitar
Dick Dale/Del-Tones; *Beach Classics* ....(DHL)
Greatest Hits ....(CRS)
Tigers Loose .... (RHI)
King Of The Wheels
Bobby Fuller Four; *Best Of* .... (RHI)
King Of The World
Steely Dan; *Countdown To Ecstasy* .... (MCA)
Gold ....(MCA)

King Of Wishful Thinking
Go West; *ST/Pretty Woman* .... (EMI)
King Porter's Stomp
Benny Goodman; *Birth Of Swing* .... (BLU)
   Complete-#1-1935 ....(RCA)
   Live At Carnegie Hall ....(LON)
   This Is ....(RCA)
King Tut
Steve Martin/Toot Uncommons; *Dr. Demento Greatest*
   Novelty CD .... (RHI)
   Dr. Demento Greatest Novelty-#4-1970s .... (RHI)
King Without A Queen
Lefty Frizzell; *Columbia Historic Edition* ....(COL)
King & Queen
Moody Blues; *Caught Live Plus Five* .... (POL)
King & Queen Of America
Eurythmics; *Greatest Hits* .... (ARI)
   We Too Are One .... (ARI)
King & Queen Of England
Sandy Denny; *Circle Dance-Hokey Pokey Charity*
   Comp. ....(GRE)
Kingdom Come
David Bowie; *Scary Monsters* ....(RYK)
   Sound + Vision ....(RYK)
Kingdom Hall
Van Morrison; *Wavelength* .... (WB)
Kingdom Of Swing
Benny Goodman; *Complete-#7-1938-1939* ......(RCA)
   Complete-#8-1936-1939 ....(RCA)
Kingfish
Randy Newman; *Good Old Boys* .... (RPR)
Kings
Steely Dan; *Can't Buy A Thrill* ....(MCA)
Kings Road
Tom Petty/Heartbreakers; *Hard Promises* .... (BKS)
Kings & Queens
Aerosmith; *Classics Live* ....(COL)
   Draw The Line ....(COL)
   Greatest Hits ....(COL)
King's Chorale
Mountain; *Best Of* ....(COL)
King's Highway
Tom Petty/Heartbreakers; *Into The Great Wide*
   Open .... (MCA)
Lord Of The Highway
Joe Ely; *Lord Of The Highway* .... (HT)
Lord Of The Thighs
Aerosmith; *Classics Live* ....(COL)
   Gems ....(COL)
   Get Your Wings ....(COL)
   Live! Bootleg ....(COL)
   Pandora's Box ....(COL)
Midas Touch
Midnight Star; *45* .... (SLR)
Original Cast; *Bells Are Ringing* ....(COL)
Motel King
James Harman Band; *Do Not Disturb* .... (BTO)
My Kingdom
Echo/Bunnymen; *Ocean Rain* .... (SIR)
My Kingdom Come
Lords Of The New Church; *Method To Our*
   Madness .... (IRS)
My Kingdom For A Car
Gene Parsons; *Melodies* .... (SIE)
Jason/Scorchers; *Thunder & Fire* ....(A&M)
Phil Ochs; *Greatest Hits* ....(A&M)
My Lord & Master
Barbra Streisand; *People* ....(COL)
Original Broadway Cast; *King & I* ....(RCA)
Original Cast; *King & I* ....(MCA)
Nasty Dogs & Funky Kings
ZZ Top; *Fandango* .... (WB)
   Six Pack .... (WB)
Oh King Richard
Rodney Crowell; *Hot Country Rock-#2* .... (EPI)
   Street Language ....(COL)
Orange King
Cafe Noir; *Window To The Sea* .... (CD)
Out To Bomb Fresh Kings
Doctor Nerve; *Armed Observation* .... (CUN)
Palace Of The King
Freddie King; *Best Of* ....(MCA)
Pinball Wizard
Elton John; *Greatest Hits-#2* .... (POL)

Pete Townshend; *Another Scoop* ....(ATC)
   Pete Townshend's Deep End-Live ....(ATC)
Rod Stewart; *Best Of* ....(MER)
   Sing It Again Rod ....(MER)
   Storyteller-Complete Anthology-1964-1990 ..... (WB)
Who; *Greatest Hits* ....(MCA)
   Meaty Beaty Big & Bouncy ....(MCA)
   ST/Kids Are Alright ....(MCA)
   Tommy ....(MCA)
   Who's Last ....(MCA)
Prince Charming
Adam Ant; *Antics In The Forbidden Zone* .... (EPI)
   Prince Charming .... (EPI)
Prince Is Giving A Ball
Original Cast; *Cinderella-CBS Television*
   Production ....(COL)
Prince Of Darkness
Alice Cooper; *Raise Your Fist & Yell* ....(MCA)
Big Daddy Kane; *Prince Of Darkness* ....(CLD)
Indigo Girls; *Back On The Bus Y'All* .... (EPI)
   Indigo Girls .... (EPI)
Miles Davis; *Sorcerer* ....(COL)
Nylons; *Best Of* ....(OPE)
   One Size Fits All ....(OPE)
Prince Of The Punks
Kinks; *One For The Road* .... (ARI)
Prince Of Tides
Jimmy Buffett; *Hot Water* ....(MCA)
Prince Of Whales
Amy & Leslie; *Amy & Leslie* ....(ALC)
Joachim Kuhn; *Dynamics* ....(CMU)
Princes Of The Universe
Queen; *A Kind Of Magic* ....(HOL)
Rain King
Counting Crows; *August And Everything After* .. (DGC)
Riding With The King
John Hiatt; *Riding With The King* ....(GEF)
   Y'all Caught? Ones That Got Away-1979-85 ..(GEF)
Rock 'N' Roll Is King
Electric Light Orchestra; *Afterglow* .... (EPI)
   Secret Messages ....(JET)
Satan's Kingdom
Jimmy Cliff; *I Am The Living* ....(MCA)
Sheik Of Araby
Benny Goodman; *Sextet feat. Charles*
   Christian-1939-1941 ....(COL)
Django Reinhardt; *Djangologie/USA-#1* ....(DSQ)
Fred Astaire/Others; *Three Evenings With* ......(DRG)
Leon Redbone; *Double Time* .... (WB)
Someday My Prince Will Come
Bill Evans Trio; *Portrait In Jazz* ....(RVR)
En Vogue; *Simply Mad About The Mouse* ....(COL)
Lena Horne; *A New Album* ....(RCA)
Lena Horne & Phil Woods; *I Have Dreamed* ....(NOV)
Miles Davis; *Greatest Hits* ....(COL)
   I Like Jazz-Essence Of ....(COL)
   Someday My Prince Will Come ....(COL)
Mormon Tabernacle Choir; *When You Wish Upon A*
   Star-Tribute-Disney ....(COL)
Speed King
Deep Purple; *Deepest Purple* .... (WB)
   In Rock .... (WB)
Suburban King
Pat Benatar; *Tropico* .... (CHR)
Sun King
Beatles; *Abbey Road* ....(CAP)
   Box Set ....(CAP)
Cult; *Sonic Temple* .... (SIR)
Temple Of The King
Ritchie Blackmore; *Rainbow* .... (POL)
Trash Can King
Nick Seeger; *Sail On Flying Dutchman* ....(BIO)
TV Is King
Tubes; *Remote Control* ....(A&M)
Two Princes
Spin Doctors; *Pocket Full Of Kryptonite* .... (EPI)
Your Love Is King
Sade; *Diamond Life* ....(POR)

KISSING

See Also: SEX, various ANATOMY Categories

Always Late (With Your Kisses)
Dwight Yoakam; *Hillbilly Deluxe* .... (RPR)
Jo-El Sonnier; *Complete Mercury Sessions* .... (MER)
Lefty Frizzell; *American Originals* ....(COL)
  Best Of ....(RHI)
  Greatest Hits ....(COL)
Willie Nelson; *To Lefty From Willie* ....(COL)
As We Kiss Goodnight
Iguanas; *Nuevo Boogaloo* .... (MGR)
Baby's Smile Woman's Kiss
Johnny Duncan; *Best Of* ....(COL)
Blowing Kisses In The Wind
Paula Abdul; *Spellbound* ....(CPT)
Blue Kiss
Jane Wiedlin; *Jane Wiedlin* .... (IRS)
Coffee & Kisses
Duke Ellington/Orchestra; *Happy Birthday
Duke-Birthday Sessions-#4* .... (LAS)
Every Little Kiss
Bruce Hornsby/Range; *The Way It Is* ....(RCA)
French Kiss
Lil Louis/World; *This Beat Is Hot...Compilation* ... (EPI)
Give Him A Great Big Kiss
Shangri-Las; *Girl Groups* .... (RHI)
  Remember The Shangri-Las At Their Best ....(CLT)
I Was Born When You Kissed Me
Whispers; *Excellence* ....(ALL)
  Shhhh ....(DOR)
I Wonder Who's Kissing Her Now
Bobby Darin; *Capitol Collectors Series* ....(CAP)
Ted Weems; *45* .... (MCA)
In France They Kiss On Main Street
Joni Mitchell; *Hissing Of Summer Lawns* ....(ASY)
  Shadows & Light ....(ASY)
It's Been A Long, Long Time
Bing Crosby; *Best Of* .... (MCA)
Harry James & Kitty Kallen; *Best Of The Big
Bands* ....(COL)
Harry James/Orchestra; *Words & Music Of World War
II* ....(COL)
Jan Garber; *Best Of* ....(MCA)
Louis Armstrong; *Hello Dolly & Other Hits* ..... (MCA)
It's In His Kiss (Shoop Shoop Song)
Betty Everett; *Billboard Top R&B Hits-1964* ..... (RHI)
  Hits Of The Sixties ....(IMC)
  More American Graffiti ....(MCA)
  Oldies But Goodies-#3 ....(OSR)
  Very Best Of ....(VJ)
  Wonder Women (History Of Girl Groups) ....(RHI)
Cher; *ST/Mermaids* ....(GEF)
Kiss
Cure; *Kiss Me Kiss Me Kiss Me* .... (ELE)
Prince/Revolution; *Around The World In A Day* ..(WB)
  Parade-Music From "Under The Cherry..." ....(PAI)
Tom Jones; *Move Closer* .... (JVA)
Kiss Away The Pain
Patti Labelle; *Winner In You* .... (MCA)
Kiss For Cinderella
Michael Tilson Thomas; *Of Thee I Sing/Let 'Em Eat
Cake* ....(COL)
Kiss From A Rose
Seal; *Seal* .... (ZTT)
Kiss Him Goodbye
Nylons; *Happy Together* .... (OPE)
Kiss Me
El Cincos; *Taste Of Doo Wop-#1* .... (VJ)
Gutterboy; *Gutterboy* .... (MER)
Indecent Obsession; *Indio* .... (MCA)
Original Cast; *Sweeney Todd* ....(RCA)
Whycliffe; *Rough Side* ....(MCA)
Kiss Me Again
101 Strings Orchestra; *World's Greatest Standards* (ALS)
Victor Herbert; *Victor Herbert* .... (ALS)
Wayne King; *Best Of* .... (MCA)
Kiss Me Baby
Beach Boys; *Best Of* ....(CAP)
  Dance Dance Dance ....(CAP)
  Today/Summer Days (& Summer Nights) ....(CAP)

Kiss Me Deadly
Lita Ford; *Best Of* ....(DRM)
  Lita ....(DRM)
Kiss Me In The Car
John Berry; *John Berry* .... (LIB)
Kiss Me In The Rain
Barbra Streisand; *Wet* ....(COL)
Kiss Me On The Bus
Replacements; *Tim* .... (SIR)
Kiss Me, I'm Gone
Marty Stuart; *Love And Luck* .... (MCA)
Kiss On My List
Daryl Hall & John Oates; *Rock 'N Soul Part 1-Greatest
Hits* ....(RCA)
  Voices ....(RCA)
Kiss That Frog
Peter Gabriel; *Us* .... (GEF)
Kiss The Bride
Elton John; *Greatest Hits-1976-1986* .... (MCA)
  Too Low For Zero ....(MCA)
Kiss The World Goodbye
Kris Kristofferson; *Border Lord* ....(COL)
Kiss Them For Me
Siouxsie/Banshees; *Superstition* .... (GEF)
Kiss To Build A Dream On
Louis Armstrong; *Best Of* .... (MCA)
  Essential ....(VAN)
  Hello Dolly (& Other Hits) ....(MCA)
Kiss You All Over
Exile; *Best Of* ....(MCA)
  Greatest Hits ....(MCA)
  Mixed Emotions ....(MCA)
Kisses Sweeter Than Wine
Jimmie Rodgers; *Best Of* .... (RHI)
  Cruisin'-1958 ....(INC)
Weavers; *At Carnegie Hall* ....(VAN)
  Best Of ....(MCA)
  Greatest Hits ....(VAN)
  Reunion-At Carnegie Hall-1963 ....(VAN)
Kissing A Fool
George Michael; *Faith* ....(COL)
Kissing You
Keith Washington; *Make Time For Love* .... (QUE)
Knock Me A Kiss
Gene Krupa Orchestra & Roy Eldridge;
1940's-Singers ....(COL)
Louis Jordan; *Best Of* ....(MCA)
  No Moe! Greatest Hits ....(VRV)
Language Of The Kiss
Indigo Girls; *Swamp Ophelia* .... (EPI)
Last Kiss
Frank Wilson; *Collectables Presents History Of
Rock-#2* ....(CLT)
J. Frank Wilson; *Billboard Top Rock 'N' Roll
Hits-1964* .... (RHI)
  Oldies But Goodies-#9 ....(OSR)
  Teenage Tragedies ....(RHI)
Na Na Hey Hey Kiss Him Goodbye
Steam; *Billboard Top Rock 'N' Roll Hits-1969* ... (RHI)
  Super Hits/'70s-Have A Nice Day-#1 ....(RHI)
  Toga Rock ....(DHL)
One More Kiss
Original Broadway Cast; *Follies* .... (ANG)
  Follies ....(CAP)
Paul McCartney; *CD Gift Set* ....(CAP)
Passionate Kisses
Mary Chapin Carpenter; *Come On Come On* ....(COL)
Perfect Kiss
New Order; *Best Of MTV's 120 Minutes-#2* ...... (RHI)
  Low-Life ....(QUE)
  Substance ....(QUE)
Prelude To A Kiss
Bing Crosby/Others; *Tribute To Duke* ....(CCJ)
Carmen McRae; *Any Old Time* ....(DEN)
Diane Schuur; *Love Songs* ....(GRP)
Duke Ellington; *Ellington Indigos* ....(COL)
Duke Ellington/Orchestra; *Digital Duke* ....(GRP)
Nancy Wilson; *But Beautiful* ....(BLN)
Renee Fleming; *Salute To American Music* ....(RCA)
Sarah Vaughan; *Jazz 'Round Midnight* ....(VRV)
Put That Kiss Back Where You Found It
Benny Goodman; *All The Cats Join In* ....(COL)

Say It With A Kiss
Billie Holiday; *Golden Hits-#2* ....(COL)
   Quintessential-$6-1938 ....(COL)
   Story-#3 ....(COL)
Sealed With A Kiss
Bobby Vinton; *Greatest Hits* ....(CCB)
Brian Hyland; *Cruisin'-1962* ....(INC)
   Oldies But Goodies-#2 ....(OSR)
   Original Rock 'N' Roll Hits/'50s ....(RLL)
Lettermen; *Best Of-#2* ....(CAP)
   Capitol Collectors Series ....(CAP)
Shut Up And Kiss Me
Mary Chapin Carpenter; *Stones In The Road* ....(COL)
Suck My Kiss
Red Hot Chili Peppers; *Blood Sugar Sex Magik* ...(WB)
Summer Kisses, Winter Tears
Elvis Presley; *Collector's Gold* ....(RCA)
Television Kiss
Lave Love; *Aphrodisia* ....(SKY)
Tender Kisses
Tracie Spencer; *Make The Difference* ....(CAP)
Tenderest Kiss
Divine Horsemen; *Devil's River* ....(SST)
Then He Kissed Me
Crystals; *Back To Mono-1958-1969* ....(AKO)
   Best Of ....(AKO)
Then I Kissed Her
Beach Boys; *California Girls* ....(CAP)
   Sunshine Dream ....(CAP)
   Today/Summer Days (& Summer Nights) ....(CAP)
This Year's Kisses
Billie Holiday; *Quintessential-#3-1936-1937* .....(COL)
June Christy; *Misty June Christy* ....(BLN)
Lester Young & Roy Eldridge; *Jazz Giants* .....(VRV)
'Til I Kissed You
Everly Brothers; *Cadence Classics-Their 20 Greatest*
Hits ....(RHI)
   Fabulous Style Of ....(RHI)
   Very Best Of ....(WB)
Vision Of A Kiss
B-52's; *Good Stuff* ....(RPR)
Voodoo Kiss
Mr. Big; *Lean Into It* ....(ATL)
We Kiss In A Shadow
Barbra Streisand; *Broadway Album* ....(COL)
Original Broadway Cast; *King & I* ....(RCA)
Original Cast; *King & I* ....(MCA)
XXX's And OOO's
Trisha Yearwood; *S* ....(MCA)

LAW & ORDER, Justice, Lawyers

See Also: CAPITAL PUNISHMENT, CRIME,
POLICE, PRISON, REBELS

Against The Law
Warrant; *Dirty Rotten Filthy Stinking Rich* ....(COL)
Ain't Misbehavin'
Fats Waller; *20 Golden Pieces Of* ....(BLD)
   Ain't Misbehavin' ....(RCA)
   Legendary Performer ....(RCA)
   Live-#2 ....(GJ)
   Piano Solos ....(RCA)
Hank Williams, Jr.; *Five-0* ....(W/C)
   Greatest Hits III ....(W/C)
All Is Fair In Love And War
Ronnie Milsap; *Club* ....(RCA)
All Of The Law
Psychedelic Furs; *Midnight To Midnight* ....(COL)
Authority Song
John Cougar Mellencamp; *Uh-Huh* ....(RIV)
Bad Boys Get Spanked
Pretenders; *II* ....(SIR)
Bangkok Attorney
Doves; *Affinity* ....(ELE)
Book Of Rules, The
Heptones; *Night Food* ....(ISL)
   This Is Reggae Music-#1 ....(ISL)
Can I Get A Witness
Marvin Gaye; *Anthology* ....(MOT)
   Greatest Hits ....(MOT)
   Super Hits ....(MOT)

Rod Stewart; *Storyteller-Complete*
Anthology-1964-1990 ....(WB)
Rolling Stones; *England's Newest Hit Makers* .... (AKO)
Coming Into Los Angeles
Arlo Guthrie; *Best Of* ....(WB)
   Running Down The Road ....(RPR)
   ST/Woodstock ....(ATL)
Crime & Punishment
Agony Column; *Brave Words & Bloody Knuckles* (BCH)
Evidence
Steve Lacy & Don Cherry; *Evidence* .... (NJ)
Thelonius Monk; *Atlantic Jazz-Bebop* ....(ATL)
   Best Of ....(BLN)
   Evidence ....(MS)
Exhibit A
Art Blakey; *Ritual* ....(BLN)
Art Taylor; *Taylor's Wailers* ....(PRS)
Exhibit "A"
Shok Paris; *Steel & Starlight* ....(IRS)
F. Lee Bailey Blues
Sugar Ray/Bluetones; *Don't Stand In My Way* ...(BUL)
Goin' By The Book
Johnny Cash; *Mystery Of Life* ....(MER)
Good Morning Judge
10 CC; *Greatest Hits* ....(POL)
   Deceptive Bands ....(MER)
   Live & Let Live ....(MER)
(I Am A) Lonesome Fugitive
Roy Buchanan; *Roy Buchanan* ....(POL)
I Can't Drive 55
Sammy Hagar; *VOA* ....(GEF)
I Fought The Law
Bobby Fuller; *Best Of* ....(RHI)
   Heart & Soul Of Rock & Roll-#1 ....(RHI)
Bobby Fuller Four; *Oldies But Goodies-#9* ....(OSR)
   Super Oldies/'60s-#7 ....(AUF)
Clash; *Clash* ....(EPI)
   Story Of-#1 ....(EPI)
If I Had A Hammer
Pete Seeger; *Sing-A-Long-Live At Sanders Theatre*
1980 ....(FLW)
Peter, Paul & Mary; *In Concert* ....(WB)
   Peter, Paul & Mary ....(WB)
   Ten Years Together-Best Of ....(WB)
Trini Lopez; *Best Of* ....(EXA)
Weavers; *Greatest Hits* ....(VAN)
If There's Any Justice
Lee Greenwood; *Country*
Classics-#11-1987-1988 ....(MCA)
   Greatest Hits-#2 ....(MCA)
   If There's Any Justice ....(PAN)
Innocent
Alexander O'Neal; *Alexander O'Neal* ....(TAB)
   All Mixed Up ....(TAB)
Garland Jeffreys; *Escape Artist* ....(EPI)
Whispers; *More Of The Night* ....(CAP)
Judge Baby I'm Back
Cliff Nobles/Co.; *The Horse* ....(PLL)
Justice
Art Blakey/Jazz Messengers; *History Of* ....(BLN)
Bruce Cockburn; *Inner City Front* ....(COL)
Little Steven; *Voice Of America* ....(R&T)
Ziggy Marley/Melody Makers; *One Bright Day* .. (VIA)
Justice In Ontario
Steve Earle/Dukes; *Hard Way* .... (MCA)
Justice In The Barrel
Bon Jovi; *Blaze Of Glory* ....(MER)
Justice In Truth
Brenda Russell; *Greatest Hits* ....(A&M)
Justice Tonight/Rock It Over
Clash; *Black Market Clash* ....(EPI)
Justice & Independence '85
John Mellencamp; *Scarecrow* ....(RIV)
Keepin' Out Of Mischief Now
Barbra Streisand; *Album* ....(COL)
   ...Just For The Record ....(COL)
Bobby Henderson; *Handful Of Keys* ....(VAN)
Fats Waller; *Turn On The Heat-Fats Waller Piano*
Solos ....(BLU)
Louis Armstrong; *Satch Plays Fats* ....(COL)
Knife Feels Like Justice
Brian Setzer; *Knife Feels Like Justice* ....(EMI)
Knoxville Courthouse Blues
Hank Williams, Jr.; *Major Moves* ....(W/C)

Law Is For The Protection Of The People
Kris Kristofferson; *Me & Bobby McGee* ....(COL)
Laws Must Change
John Mayall; *Best Of* ....(POL)
   Turning Point ....(POL)
John Mayall/Bluesbreakers; *Behind The Iron*
   Curtain ....(CRS)
Lawyers
Billy Walker; *45* ....(CPE)
Lawyers In Love
Jackson Browne; *Lawyers In Love* ....(ASY)
Lawyers, Guns & Money
Warren Zevon; *Excitable Boy* ....(ASY)
   Quiet Normal Life-Best Of ....(ASY)
   Stand In The Fire ....(ASY)
Laying Down The Law
INXS & Jimmy Barnes; *ST/Lost Boys* ....(ATL)
Law; *Law* ....(ATL)
Legal Matter
Who; *Meaty Beaty Big & Bouncy* .... (MCA)
   Sings "My Generation" ....(MCA)
Living Proof
Ricky Van Shelton; *30 Years Of #1 Hits-#20* ....(COL)
   Greatest Country Hits!'80s-1989 ....(COL)
   Greatest Hits Plus ....(COL)
Long Arm Of The Law
Kenny Rogers; *Greatest Hits* .... (EMI)
Love In The First Degree
Alabama; *Feels So Right* ....(RCA)
   Greatest Hits ....(RCA)
   Live ....(RCA)
   Nipper's Greatest Hits!'80s ....(RCA)
Love Is Stronger Than Justice
Sting; *Ten Summoner's Tales* ....(A&M)
Love Is The Only Law
Ziggy Marley/Melody Makers; *One Bright Day* .. (VIA)
"L.A. Law" Theme
Original Music; *Television's Greatest Hits-#3* .....(TVT)
Man Who Shot Liberty Valance
Gene Pitney; *Anthology* .... (RHI)
   Greatest Hits ....(EVR)
   Super Oldies!'60s-#9 ....(AUF)
Greg Kihn; *Glass House Rock* ....(BES)
Maxwell's Silver Hammer
Beatles; *1967-1970* ....(CAP)
   Abbey Road ....(CAP)
Murder In My Heart For The Judge
Lee Michaels; *Collection* ....(RHI)
Moby Grape; *Wow* ....(OOP)
Murphy's Law
Al Jarreau; *High Crime* ....(WB)
Cheri; *45* ....(VEN)
Murphy's Law; *Murphy's Law* .... (RH)
My Attorney Bernie
David Frishberg; *Can't Take You Nowhere* .... (FAN)
   Classics .... (CCJ)
Night The Lights Went Out In Georgia
Lynn Anderson; *Top Of The World* ....(COL)
Reba McEntire; *For My Broken Heart* .... (MCA)
Vicki Lawrence; *Super Hits!'70s-Have A Nice*
   Day-#10 .... (RHI)
No Alibis
Eric Clapton; *Journeyman* ....(DUC)
No Law Or Order
Hanoi Rocks; *Oriental Beat* ....(GEF)
Old Judge Jones
Les Dudek; *Say No More* ....(COL)
One Million Lawyers
Tom Paxton; *One Million Lawyers & Other*
   Disasters .... (FF)
Oughta Be A Law
Lamont Cranston Band; *Up From The Alley* .. (WTR)
   Upper Mississippi Shakedown-Best Of .... (ERA)
Lee Roy Parnell; *Country's Greatest Hits-#8-Lonely*
   Hearts ....(PRY)
   Lee Roy Parnell ....(ARI)
"Perry Mason" Theme
Blues Brothers; *Made In America* .... (ATL)
Jerry Goodman; *It's Alive* .... (PRV)
Original Music; *TV Theme Sing-Along Album* .... (RHI)
Philadelphia Lawyer
Rose Maddox; *Rose Of The West Coast Country* (ARH)
   Super Hits Country-1940s ....(GUS)

Willie Nelson; *Tribute To Woody Guthrie &*
   Leadbelly ....(COL)
   Woody Guthrie; *Cowboy Songs On Folkways* ... (FLW)
Policy Of Truth
Depeche Mode; *Violator* .... (SIR)
Punishment Fits The Crime
Ramones; *Brain Drain* .... (SIR)
Read Me My Rights
Ann Peebles; *Fulltime Love* ....(BUL)
Dalton Reed; *Louisiana Soul Man* ....(BUL)
Regulate
Warren G. & Nate Dogg; *ST/Above The Rim* ..... (ISC)
Right And Wrong
Joe Jackson; *Big World* ....(A&M)
Right To Remain Silent
Doug Stone; *I Thought It Was You* ....(EPI)
Rock & Roll Lawyer
Austin Lounge Lizards; *Lizard Vision* ....(FF)
Rules & Regulations
Public Image, Ltd.; *Greatest Hits So Far* .... (VIA)
   Happy? ....(VIA)
Sue Me
Doctor Ice; *Mic Stalker* .... (JVA)
   Rap Wit' Cha 2 .... (KT)
Original Cast; *Guys & Dolls* ....(MCA)
   Guys & Dolls ....(MOT)
Sue Me, Sue You Blues
George Harrison; *Living In The Material World* ..(CAP)
Supreme Court Judges
Michael Tilson Thomas; *Of Thee I Sing/Let 'Em Eat*
   Cake ....(COL)
Sweetest Taboo
Sade; *Promise* ....(POR)
Talk To The Lawyer
David Lindley & El Rayo-X; *Win This Record* ... (ELE)
Tell It To The Judge
Monotones; *Best Of Chess Vocal Groups* .... (CSS)
Tell It To The Judge On Sunday
Long Ryders; *Native Sons* ....(FRN)
Ten Commandments Of Love
Bob Marley/Wailers; *Birth Of A*
   Legend-1963-1966 .... (EPA)
Harvey/Moonglows; *Best Of Chess Rock 'N'*
   Roll-#2 .... (CSS)
   Collectables Presents History Of Rock-10 .... (CLT)
   Cruisin'-1958 ....(INC)
   Oldies But Goodies-#11 ....(OSR)
Testify
David Bromberg; *Sideman Serenade* .... (ROU)
Greg Kihn Band; *Kihnsolidation-Best Of* .... (RHI)
Melissa Etheridge; *Brave & Crazy* ....(ISL)
Peter Tosh; *No Nuclear War* ....(EMI)
Testify (I Wanna)
Johnnie Taylor; *15 Original Big Hits-#4* ....(STX)
   Top Of The Stax-Twenty Greatest Hits-#2 ......(STX)
Parliament; *Soul Shots-#9-More Dance Party* .... (RHI)
Stevie Ray Vaughan/Double Trouble; *Texas Flood* (EPI)
Testimony
Robbie Robertson; *Robbie Robertson* ....(GEF)
Sweet Honey In The Rock; *We All...Everyone Of Us* (FF)
Texas Lawman
Regulators; *Regulators* ....(POL)
That's The Law
Point Blank; *Point Blank* .... (ARI)
There Ought To Be A Law
Five Keys; *Aladdin Years* ....(EMI)
There's No Justice
George Jones; *Sings The Great Songs Of Leon*
   Payne .... (IGR)
Trial
Pink Floyd; *Shine On-Box Set* ....(COL)
   The Wall ....(COL)
Roger Waters; *The Wall Live In Berlin* ....(MER)
Trial Before Pilate
Original London Cast; *Jesus Christ Superstar* ....(MCA)
Verdict
Professor Griff/Last Asiatic Disciples; *Pawns In The*
   Game ....(LUK)
You Made A Wanted Man Of Me
Ronnie McDowell; *19 Hot Country Requests-#2* ..(EPI)
   Country Boy's Heart ....(EPI)
   Older Women & Other Greatest Hits ....(EPI)

LIES, Cheating

See Also: HIDING, PRETEND

Alibi
Teena Marie; *Starchild* .... (EPI)
Alibis
Sergio Mendes; *Classics-#18* .... (A&M)
  Sergio Mendes .... (A&M)
Tracy Lawrence; *Alibis* .... (ATL)
All These Years
Sawyer Brown; *Cafe On The Corner* .... (CRB)
All Those Lies
Glenn Frey; *No Fun Aloud* .... (ASY)
Always True To You In My Fashion
Blossom Dearie; *Night & Day: Cole Porter Songbook* .... (VRV)
Broadway Cast; *Kiss Me Kate* .... (ANG)
Peggy Lee & George Shearing; *Anything Goes-Capitol Sings Cole Porter* .... (CAP)
Angels Don't Lie
Jim Reeves; *Best Of-#4* .... (RCA)
Avenging Annie
Andy Pratt; *Andy Pratt* .... (COL)
Roger Daltrey; *Best Bits* .... (MCA)
  One Of The Boys .... (MCA)
Baby I Lied
Deborah Allen; *Best Of The '80s So Far* .... (RCA)
  Cheat The Night .... (RCA)
Back Stabbers
O'Jays; *Billboard Top Rock 'N' Roll Hits-1972* ... (RHI)
  Collector's Items .... (PI)
  Live In London .... (PI)
Beautiful Lies
Kenny Rogers & Dottie West; *Every Time Two Fools Collide* .... (UA)
Blame It On Your Heart
Patty Loveless; *Only What I Feel* .... (EPI)
Broken Promise Land
Mark Chesnutt; *Too Cold At Home* .... (MCA)
Camera Never Lies
Elton John; *Reg Strikes Back* .... (MCA)
Michael Franks; *Camera Never Lies* .... (WB)
Cheat The Night
Deborah Allen; *Cheat The Night* .... (RCA)
Cheater
Gladiators; *Symbol Of Reality* .... (NH)
Judas Priest; *Hero Hero* .... (RCA)
  Rocka-Rolla .... (RCA)
Cheaters Never Win
Love Committee; *Beachbeat Shaggin'* .... (DHL)
Moe Bandy; *It's A Cheating Situation* .... (COL)
Cheater's Prayer
Kendalls; *Stickin' Together* .... (MER)
  Thank God For The Radio (& All The Hits) ... (MER)
Cheatin' Fire
Conway Twitty; *Mr. T* .... (MCA)
Cheatin' In School
Corey Hart; *First Offense* .... (EMI)
Cheatin' Is
Barbara Fairchild; *Biggest Hurt* .... (AUD)
  Country Stars Country Nights .... (FFT)
Glen Campbell; *Walkin' In The Sun* .... (CAP)
Cheatin' On A Cheater
Loretta Lynn; *Lookin' Good* .... (MCA)
Cheatin' Woman
Lynyrd Skynyrd; *Best Of* .... (MSP)
  Nuthin' Fancy .... (MCA)
Molly Hatchet; *Molly Hatchet* .... (EPI)
Cheatin's Only Cheatin'
Mel McDaniel/Oklahoma Wind; *Mel McDaniel/Oklahoma Wind* .... (CAP)
Cleopatra, Queen Of Denial
Pam Tillis; *Homeward Looking Angel* .... (ARI)
Day Tripper
Beatles; *1962-1966* .... (CAP)
  Box Set .... (CAP)
  Past Masters-#2 .... (CAP)
  Yesterday...And Today .... (CAP)
Jimi Hendrix Experience; *Radio One* .... (RYK)
Otis Redding; *Dictionary Of Soul* .... (ATC)
  Story .... (ATL)
Sergio Mendes & Brasil '66; *Greatest Hits* ...... (A&M)

Deceiver
Alarm; *Declaration* .... (IRS)
Beat Farmers; *Van Go* .... (CCB)
Judas Priest; *Best Of* .... (RCA)
  Sad Wings Of Destiny .... (RCA)
Digging In The Dirt
Peter Gabriel; *Us* .... (GEF)
Dirty Laundry
Don Henley; *I Can't Stand Still* .... (ASY)
Do You Know Where Your Man Is
Pam Tillis; *Homeward Looking Angel* .... (ARI)
Don't Believe The Hype
Public Enemy; *It Takes A Nation Of Millions To Hold...* .... (DFJ)
  Mr. Magic's Rap Attack-#4 .... (PRO)
Don't Cheat In Our Hometown
Ricky Skaggs; *Don't Cheat In Our Hometown* .... (EPI)
Don't Make Love To Mary (With Mabel...)
Merle Travis; *Johnny Gimble's Texas Honky-Tonk Hits* .... (CMH)
Don't Play That Song (You Lied)
Aretha Franklin; *30 Greatest Hits* .... (ATL)
  Golden Age Of Black Music-1970-1975 .... (ATL)
  Greatest Hits .... (ARL)
Don't Tell Me Lies
Breathe; *All That Jazz* .... (A&M)
Don't You Lie To Me
Chuck Berry; *New Jukebox Hits* .... (CSS)
Flamin' Groovies; *Groovies' Greatest Grooves* ..... (SIR)
End Of The Lyin'
Alabama; *Roll On* .... (RCA)
Fairweather Friend
John Cale; *Vintage Violence* .... (COL)
Johnny Gill; *Johnny Gill* .... (MOT)
Fake
Alexander O'Neal; *All Mixed Up* .... (TAB)
  Hearsay .... (TAB)
Golden Vanity
Pete Seeger & Arlo Guthrie; *Together In Concert* (RPR)
Great Deception
Van Morrison; *Hard Nose The Highway* .... (WB)
Grey Cloudy Lies
George Harrison; *Extra Texture* .... (OOP)
Harper Valley P.T.A.
Jeannie C. Riley; *Greatest Hits* .... (PLN)
  Harper Valley P.T.A. .... (PLN)
  Oldies But Goodies-#4 .... (OSR)
  Souvenirs Of Music City USA .... (PLN)
Heart Won't Lie
Reba McEntire & Vince Gill; *It's Your Call* ..... (MCA)
He's The Great Imposter
Fleetwoods; *ST/American Graffiti* .... (MCA)
I Don't Need You
Kenny Rogers; *Share Your Love* .... (LIB)
  Twenty Greatest Hits .... (LIB)
I Lie
Loretta Lynn; *I Lie* .... (MCA)
I Wouldn't Lie
Yarbrough & Peoples; *Guilty* .... (TE)
Imposter
Elvis Costello/Attractions; *Get Happy!* .... (RYK)
  Kampuchea .... (ATL)
Oingo Boingo; *Only A Lad* .... (A&M)
In A Small Moment
Carly Simon; *Boys In The Trees* .... (ELE)
In A Week Or Two
Diamond Rio; *Close To The Edge* .... (ARI)
Innuendo
Queen; *Innuendo* .... (HOL)
I'll Lie Myself To Sleep
Shelby Lynne; *Greatest Country Hits/'90s-1990* ..(COL)
  Tough All Over .... (EPI)
I'm A Little Liar
Kings; *45* .... (CLT)
I'm Not In Love
10 CC; *Greatest Hits 1972-78* .... (POL)
  Super Hits/'70s-Have A Nice Day-#14 .... (RHI)
Will To Power; *Journey Home* .... (EPI)
I'm The Biggest Liar In Town
Reno & Smiley; *1983 Collector's Edition-#11* .... (GUS)
I'm Tired Of Living This Lie
Bob Wills/Texas Playboys; *24 Greatest Hits* ..... (POL)
I've Seen That Movie Too
Elton John; *Goodbye Yellow Brick Road* .... (POL)

LIES — LIES

Last Cheater's Waltz
Emmylou Harris; *Cimarron* ....(WB)
T.G. Sheppard; *All-Time Greatest Hits* ....(WB)
  Greatest Hits ....(WB)
Liar
Argent; *Anthology* ....(EPI)
Bros; *Push* ....(EPI)
Buckinghams; *Matter Of Time* ....(RED)
Megadeth; *So Far So Good...So What* ....(CAP)
Pandoras; *Live Nymphomania* ....(RES)
Queen; *Queen* ....(HOL)
Sex Pistols; *Never Mind The Bollocks* ....(WB)
Three Dog Night; *Best Of* ....(MCA)
  Joy To The World-Greatest Hits ....(MCA)
Liar Liar
Castaways; *Frat Rock-#3* ....(RHI)
  Oldies But Goodies-#9 ....(OSR)
  ST/Good Morning Vietnam ....(A&M)
Liars A To E
Dexy's Midnight Runners; *Too-Rye-Ay* ....(MER)
Lie
Dream Theater; *Awake* ....(EW)
Lie Detector
Al Corley; *Square Rooms* ....(MER)
Lie For A Lie
Nick Mason & Rick Fenn; *Profiles* ....(COL)
Lie To You For Your Love
Bellamy Brothers; *Howard & David* .... (MCA)
Lies
EMF; *Schubert Dip* ....(CAP)
En Vogue; *Born To Sing* ....(ATL)
J.J. Cale; *Really* ....(MER)
  Special Edition ....(MER)
Knickerbockers; *Nuggets #3-Pop* ....(RHI)
  Oldies But Goodies-#9 ....(OSR)
  Super Oldies/'60s-#9 ....(AUF)
Linda Ronstadt; *Get Closer* ....(ASY)
Rolling Stones; *Some Girls* ....(RS)
Violent Femmes; *2* ....(SLS)
Life #9
Martina McBride; *The Way That I Am* ....(RCA)
Lipstick On Your Collar
Connie Francis; *Very Best Of* ....(POL)
Little Lies
Fleetwood Mac; *Greatest Hits* ....(WB)
  Tango In The Night ....(WB)
Little Rock
Reba McEntire; *Whoever's In New England* .....(MCA)
  Woman To Woman-#2 ....(MCA)
Little White Lies
Romantics; *Romantics* ....(NEM)
Tommy Dorsey; *Best Of* ....(RCA)
  Complete-#6-1937-1938 ....(RCA)
Lying
Baxter, Baxter & Baxter; *45* ....(SUN)
Peter Frampton; *Premonition* ....(ATL)
Lying Here Lying
Mac Davis; *Forty 82* ....(CAS)
Lying Time Again
Mel Tillis; *45* ....(ELE)
Lying To Yourself
Asia; *45* ....(GEF)
Lyin' Again
Kenny Rogers; *Daytime Friends* ....(LIB)
Mickey Gilley; *That's All That Matters To Me* .....(EPI)
Lyin' Ass Bitch
Fishbone; *Fishbone* ....(COL)
Lyin' Comes So Easy To Your Lips
David Allan Coe; *D.A.C.* ....(COL)
Lyin' Eyes
Eagles; *Anthology* ....(ASY)
  One Of These Nights ....(ASY)
  ST/Urban Cowboy ....(ASY)
  Their Greatest Hits-1971-1975 ....(ASY)
Lyin' Jukebox
Hank Williams, Jr.; *Maverick* ....(CPC)
Mama Didn't Lie
Jan Bradley; *Best Of Chess R&B* ....(CSS)
  ST/Hairspray ....(MCA)
Misled
Celine Dion; *The Colour Of My Love* ....(550)
Kool/Gang; *Emergency* ....(DL)
My Favorite Lies
George Jones; *All-Time Greatest Hits-#1* ....(EPI)

Never Gonna Be Your Fool Again
Lisa Brokop; *Every Little Girl's Dream* ....(PAT)
Never Lie
Immature; *Playtyme Is Over* ....(MCA)
New Kid In Town (Johnny Come Lately)
Eagles; *Greatest Hits-#2* ....(ASY)
  Hotel California ....(ASY)
  Live ....(ASY)
Trisha Yearwood; *Common Thread-Songs Of The
Eagles* ....(GIA)
Night The Lights Went Out In Georgia
Lynn Anderson; *Top Of The World* ....(COL)
Reba McEntire; *For My Broken Heart* ....(MCA)
Vicki Lawrence; *Super Hits/'70s-Have A Nice
Day-#10* ....(RHI)
No Lie
Buddy Guy; *Buddy Guy* ....(CSS)
  Complete Chess Studio Recordings ....(CSS)
  I Was Walkin' Through The Woods ....(CSS)
No Lies
Original Cast; *Best Little Whorehouse In Texas* .. (MCA)
No More Lies
Michel'le; *Michel'le* ....(RUT)
Moody Blues; *Sur La Mer* ....(POL)
Now I Lay Me Down To Cheat
David Allan Coe; *17 Greatest Hits* ....(COL)
  Biggest Hits ....(COL)
  For The Record-First 10 Years ....(COL)
  Rough Rider ....(COL)
Ocean Front Property
George Strait; *Country Classics-#8-1986-1987* . (MCA)
  Greatest Hits-#2 ....(MCA)
  MCA Records 30 Years Of Hits-1958-1988 ... (MCA)
  Ocean Front Property ....(MCA)
Pictures Don't Lie
Billy Ray Cyrus; *Red Hot + Country* ....(MER)
Pocket Full Of Gold
Vince Gill; *Pocket Full Of Gold* ....(MCA)
Propaganda Machine
1927; *...Ish* ....(ATL)
Said I Loved You...But I Lied
Michael Bolton; *The One Thing* ....(COL)
Sail Away
Linda Ronstadt; *Don't Cry Now* ....(ASY)
Randy Newman; *Sail Away* ....(RPR)
Say It Isn't So
Daryl Hall & John Oates; *MTV's Rock 'N' Roll To
Go* ....(ELE)
  Rock & Soul Part 1-Greatest Hits ....(RCA)
Dinah Washington; *Irving Berlin Always* ....(VRV)
Michael Feinstein; *Remember-Sings Irving Berlin* . (ELE)
Outfield; *Play Deep* ....(COL)
Say It Isn't So Joe
Roger Daltrey; *Best Bits* ....(MCA)
  One Of The Boys ....(MCA)
She Didn't Lie
Garland Jeffreys; *One-Eyed Jack* ....(OOP)
She Thinks I Still Care
Elvis Presley; *Moody Blue* ....(RCA)
George Jones; *All-Time Greatest Hits-#1* ....(EPI)
  Best Of-1955-1967 ....(RHI)
  Billboard Top Country Hits-1962 ....(RHI)
  Super Hits-#2 ....(EPI)
She's Lying
Lee Greenwood; *Greatest Hits* ....(MCA)
  Inside Out ....(MCA)
She's Not There
Santana; *Moonflower* ....(COL)
  Viva Santana! ....(COL)
Vanilla Fudge; *Vanilla Fudge* ....(ATC)
Zombies; *Best & The Rest Of* ....(EPI)
  Billboard Top Rock 'N' Roll Hits-1964 ....(RHI)
  History Of British Rock-#1 ....(RHI)
  Time Of The Zombies ....(BCT)
Shit You Hear At Parties
Minutemen; *Ballot Result* ....(SST)
Silver Tongue & Gold Plated Lies
Hotmud Family; *Meat & Potatoes (& Stuff Like
That)* ....(FF)
Smiling Faces Sometimes
Undisputed Truth; *Hard-To-Find Motown
Classics-#2* ....(MOT)
  Soul Hits/'70s-#5 ....(RHI)

The Green Book Of Songs By Subject — Page 345

Sorry I Lied
Cliff Thomas; *45* .... (SUN)
Substitute
Great White; *Great White* .... (EMI)
Sex Pistols; *Live At Chelmsford Top Security Prison* .... (RES)
Who; *Greatest Hits* .... (MCA)
   Live At Leeds .... (MCA)
   Meaty Beaty Big & Bouncy .... (MCA)
   Who's Better Who's Best-Very Best Of .... (MCA)
   Who's Last .... (MCA)
Take That
Lisa Brokop; *Every Little Girl's Dream* .... (PAT)
Tell Me A Lie
Janie Fricke; *17 Greatest Hits* ....(COL)
   19 Hot Country Requests .... (EPI)
   Greatest Country Hits/'80s-1983 ....(COL)
   It Ain't Easy ....(COL)
   Love Lies ....(COL)
   Very Best Of ....(COL)
Tell Me That It Isn't True
Bob Dylan; *Nashville Skyline* ....(COL)
Tell Me Why
Beatles; *Box Set* .... (CAP)
   Something New .... (CAP)
   ST/Hard Day's Night .... (CAP)
Tell The Truth
David Lee Roth; *A Little Ain't Enough* .... (WB)
Derek/Dominos; *Crossroads* .... (POL)
   In Concert .... (POL)
   Layla .... (POL)
Otis Redding; *Best Of* .... (ATC)
   Story .... (ATL)
   Tell The Truth .... (RHI)
Ray Charles; *Birth Of Soul/Comp. Atlantic R&B 1952-59* .... (ATL)
Telling Me Lies
D. Parton/E. Harris/L. Ronstadt; *Trio* .... (WB)
Tender Lie
Restless Heart; *Best Of* ....(RCA)
   Big Dreams In A Small Town ....(RCA)
That's My Story
Collin Raye; *Extremes* .... (EPI)
They Didn't Believe Me
Hal Mooney; *Heritage Of Broadway-Music Of J. Kern* .... (BAI)
Joe Williams; *Sings* .... (SJZ)
Johnny Mercer; *Song Is You-Capitol Sings Jerome Kern* .... (CAP)
Pearl Bailey; *16 Most Requested Songs* ....(COL)
Tommy Dorsey; *Best Of* .... (MCA)
Thunder Rolls, The
Garth Brooks; *No Fences* .... (LIB)
Tired Of Your Jive
B.B. King; *Electric-His Best* .... (MCA)
   Great Moments with .... (MCA)
Two-Timin' Me
Remingtons; *Blue Frontier* .... (BNA)
Ugly Hour
David Bromberg; *Bandit In A Bathing Suit* .... (FAN)
Unfaithful Servant
Band; *Band* .... (CAP)
   Gift Set .... (CAP)
   Rock Of Age-#1 & 2 .... (CAP)
   To Kingdom Come-Definitive Collection .... (CAP)
Unfaithfully Yours (One Love)
Stephen Bishop; *Best Of Bish* .... (RHI)
Use Me
Bill Withers; *Greatest Hits* ....(COL)
   Still Bill ....(COL)
Walkaway Joe
Trisha Yearwood; *Hearts In Armor* .... (MCA)
Wandering Eyes
Ronnie McDowell; *Older Women & Other Greatest Hits* .... (EPI)
We Tell Ourselves
Clint Black; *The Hard Way* ....(RCA)
White Lies
Grin; *Rock Artifacts-#1-From The Vaults* ....(COL)
Nils Lofgren; *Grin* .... (EPA)

Who's Cheatin' Who
Charly McClain; *Encore* ....(EPI)
   Greatest Country Hits/'80s-1980 ....(COL)
   Greatest Hits ....(EPI)
   Greatest Hits From The Jukebox ....(EPI)
   Ten Year Anniversary ....(EPI)
Who's Makin' Love
Blues Brothers; *Definitive Collection* .... (ATL)
   Made In America .... (ATL)
Johnnie Taylor; *Billboard Top R&B Hits-1965-1969* .... (RHI)
   Oldies But Goodies-#5 .... (OSR)
   Super Hits .... (STX)
   Top Of The Stax-Twenty Greatest Hits .... (STX)
Would I Lie To You
Charles & Eddie; *Duophonic* .... (CAP)
Eurythmics; *Be Yourself Tonight* ....(RCA)
   Greatest Hits .... (ARI)
Whitesnake; *Come An' Get It* ....(GEF)
You Lie
Reba McEntire; *Greatest Hits-#2* .... (MCA)
   Rumor Has It .... (MCA)
You Say You Will
Trisha Yearwood; *Hearts In Armor* .... (MCA)
Your Cheatin' Heart
Elvis Presley; *Elvis For Everyone* ....(RCA)
   Welcome To My World ....(RCA)
Frankie Laine; *16 Greatest Hits* .... (TRP)
   Greatest Hits ....(COL)
Hank Williams; *16 Great Hits* .... (EVR)
   24 Greatest Hits .... (POL)
   40 Greatest Hits .... (POL)
Hank Williams, Jr.; *Very Best Of* .... (POL)
Jerry Lee Lewis; *Golden Rock Hits Of* .... (SMA)
   Live At The Star Club-Hamburg 1964 .... (RHI)
Patsy Cline; *Story* .... (MCA)
   ST/Sweet Dreams .... (MCA)
Ray Charles; *Greatest Hits-#2* .... (RHI)

LIFE, Alive, Living, Philosophy, Survive
See Also: BABY, CIRCLES, DEATH, WORK

Ain't Got No (I Got Life)
Original Cast; *ST/Hair* ....(RCA)
Ain't Life Hell
Hank Cochran; *Hank Cochran* .... (CAP)
Ain't No Good Life
Lynyrd Skynyrd; *Street Survivors* .... (MCA)
Alive
Pearl Jam; *Ten* .... (EPA)
Alive Again
Chicago; *Greatest Hits-#2* ....(COL)
   Hot Streets ....(COL)
Alive & Kicking
Simple Minds; *In The City Of Light* .... (A&M)
   Once Upon A Time .... (VIA)
All My Life
Kenny Rogers; *We've Got Tonight* .... (LIB)
Linda Ronstadt; *Cry Like A Rainstorm Howl Like The Wind* .... (ELE)
And So It Goes
Billy Joel; *Storm Front* ....(COL)
And The Beat Goes On
Whispers; *Club Epic* .... (EPI)
Angel From Montgomery
Bonnie Raitt; *Streetlights* .... (WB)
Bonnie Raitt & John Prine; *Bonnie Raitt Collection* (WB)
John Prine; *John Prine* .... (ATL)
Army Life
Leadbelly; *Easy Rider* .... (FLW)
As Long As I Live
Count Basie; *Standards* ....(VRV)
Count Basie Trio; *For The First Time* .... (PAB)
Ella Fitzgerald; *Harold Arlen Songbook-#2* ......(VRV)
"As The World Turns" Theme
Rosemary Joyce & Bill Bartholomew; *Soap Opera Themes* .... (CRS)
Attics Of My Life
Grateful Dead; *American Beauty* .... (WB)
Autumn Of My Life
Bobby Goldsboro; *10th Anniversary Album* .... (UA)
   Greatest Hits .... (UA)

Back In The High Life Again
Steve Winwood; *Back In The High Life* .... (ISL)
Back Into My Life
UFO; *Best Of The Rest* .... (CHR)
   Mechanix .... (CHR)
Back Into My Life Again
Spencer Davis Group; *Best Of* .... (EMI)
Back To Life
Soul II Soul; *w/Caron Wheeler-Keep On Movin'* .. (VIA)
Be My Life's Companion
Mills Brothers; *Best Of* .... (MCA)
   Best Of The Decca Years .... (DEC)
Rosemary Clooney; *16 Most Requested Songs* ....(COL)
Beat Goes On
Sonny & Cher; *Beat Goes On* ....(ATC)
   Best Of ....(ATC)
   Hit Singles 1958-1977 .... (ATL)
   Live ....(MCA)
   Two Of Us ....(ATC)
Beautiful Noise
Neil Diamond; *12 Greatest Hits-#2* ....(COL)
   Beautiful Noise ....(COL)
   Love At The Greek ....(COL)
Being Alive
Barbra Streisand; *Broadway Album* ....(COL)
Mandy Patinkin; *Dress Casual* ....(COL)
Original Cast; *Company* ....(COL)
Best Days Of My Life
Johnny Mathis; *Best Days Of My Life* ....(COL)
   Best Of-1975-1980 ....(COL)
Rod Stewart; *Blondes Have More Fun* .... (WB)
Best Things In Life Are Free
June Allyson; *ST/Good News* .... (SSP)
Luther Vandross & Janet Jackson; *ST/Mo' Money* (BLU)
Mel Torme; *Easy To Remember* ....(GLN)
Sam Cooke; *At The Copa* ....(RCA)
Best Year Of My Life
Eddie Rabbitt; *Best Year Of My Life* .... (CAP)
   Number 1's .... (WB)
Born To Be Alive
Patrick Hernandez; *Let's Dance-DJ's Collection* ..(COL)
Both Sides Now
Joni Mitchell; *Clouds* .... (RPR)
Judy Collins; *Colors Of The Day-Best Of* .... (ELE)
   So Early In The Spring .... (ELE)
   Wildflowers .... (ELE)
Neil Diamond; *Gold* ....(MCA)
   Love Songs ....(MCA)
   Rainbow ....(MCA)
   Touching You Touching Me ....(MCA)
Breath Of Life
Brian Setzer; *Knife Feels Like Justice* .... (AMR)
Erasure; *Chorus* .... (SIR)
Bug, The
Dire Straits; *On Every Street* .... (WB)
Mary Chapin Carpenter; *Come On Come On* ..... (WB)
Ca Plane Por Moi (This Life's For Me)
Plastic Bertrand; *Ca Plane Por Moi (This Life's For Me)* .... (SIR)
Candle In The Wind
Elton John; *Goodbye Yellow Brick Road* .. (POL)
   Live In Australia w/Melbourne Symphony .... (POL)
   Your Songs .... (POL)
Candle Of Life
Moody Blues; *To Our Children's Children's Children* .... (POL)
(Can't Live Without...) Love & Affection
Nelson; *After The Rain* .... (DGC)
Cast Your Fate To The Wind
Sandpipers; *Guantanamera* ....(A&M)
Vince Guaraldi; *Greatest Hits* .... (FAN)
   Original Jazz Classics-#1 .... (FAN)
Chattahoochee
Alan Jackson; *Lot About Livin' (& A Little 'Bout Love)* .... (ARI)
Circle Of Life
Elton John; *ST/The Lion King* .... (DIS)
Coming Back To Life
Pink Floyd; *The Division Bell* ....(COL)
Comin' In And Out Of Your Life
Barbra Streisand; *Collection: Greatest Hits...& More* ....(COL)
   Memories ....(COL)

Country Boy Can Survive
Hank Williams, Jr.; *America (The Way I See It)* ..(W/C)
   Greatest Hits ....(WB)
   Live ....(W/C)
   ST/Pressure Is On ....(W/C)
C'est La Vie
Emerson, Lake & Palmer; *In Concert* .... (ATL)
   Works .... (ATL)
Emmylou Harris; *Luxury Liner* .... (WB)
   Profile-Best Of .... (WB)
Patti LaBelle/Blue Belles; *45* .... (CLT)
Queen Ida/Bon Temps Zydeco Band; *Queen Ida On Tour* .... (CRS)
   Zydeco A La Mode .... (CRS)
Robbie Nevil; *Heart Of Rock* ....(COL)
   Robbie Nevil .... (AMR)
Dancing In The Key Of Life
Steve Arrington; *Dance Traxx* .... (ATL)
   Dancing In The Key Of Life .... (ATL)
Day After Day
Alan Parsons Project; *I Robot* .... (ARI)
China Crisis; *Diary Of A Hollow Horse* ...... (A&M)
Pretenders; *II* .... (SIR)
   Singles .... (SIR)
Day By Day
Carmen McRae; *Great American Songbook* ...... (ATL)
Frank Sinatra; *Come Swing With Me!* ....(CAP)
   Greatest Hits-#2 ....(COL)
Generation X; *Generation X* ....(CHR)
Hooters; *Nervous Night* ....(COL)
Original Cast; *Godspell* .... (ARI)
Sarah Vaughan; *Complete-On Mercury-#3* ..... (MER)
   Misty .... (MER)
Day In The Life
Beatles; *1967-1970* ....(CAP)
   Sgt. Pepper's Lonely Hearts Club Band ....(CAP)
   ST/Imagine-The Motion Picture ....(CAP)
Dead Or Alive
Deep Purple; *Nobody's Perfect* .... (MER)
Journey; *Escape* ....(COL)
Oingo Boingo; *Boingo Alive* ....(MCA)
   Good For Your Soul .... (A&M)
Too $hort; *Short Dog's In The House* .... (JVA)
Dead & Alive
Dead Boys; *We Have Come For Your Children* .... (SIR)
Dog's Life
Gentle Giant; *Octopus* ....(COL)
Domestic Life
John Conlee; *American Faces* ....(COL)
   Greatest Country Hits/'80s-1987 ....(COL)
   More Hot Country Requests-#2 .... (EPI)
Don't Throw Your Life Away
Vickie Winans; *The Lady* .... (MCA)
Don't Wanna Live Without It
Pablo Cruise; *Worlds Away* .... (A&M)
Down The Road
Mac McAnally; *Knots* .... (MCA)
Dream Is Still Alive
Wilson Phillips; *Wilson Phillips* .... (SBK)
Dream Of Life
Billie Holiday; *Billie Holiday* ....(COL)
   Story-#1 ....(COL)
Carmen McRae; *Greatest Of* ....(MCA)
Patti Smith; *Dream Of Life* .... (ARI)
Drivin' My Life Away
Eddie Rabbitt; *All Time Greatest Hits* .... (WB)
   Greatest Hits-#2 .... (WB)
   Horizon .... (ELE)
   Number 1's .... (WB)
   Ten Years Of Greatest Hits ....(CAP)
Drop Kick Me Jesus (Through The Goal...)
Bobby Bare; *45* ....(OOP)
Easy Living
Billie Holiday; *Quintessential-#4-1937* ....(COL)
Ella Fitzgerald & Joe Pass; *Easy Living* .... (PAB)
Paul Desmond; *Easy Living* .... (BLU)
Every Day Of My Life
Open Skyz; *Open Skyz* .... (ZTO)
Everyday
Phil Collins; *Both Sides* .... (ATL)
Fast Car
Tracy Chapman; *Tracy Chapman* .... (ELE)
Fiddler On The Roof
Original Cast; *Fiddler On The Roof* ....(RCA)

For Once In My Life
Gladys Knight/Pips; *Anthology* .... (MOT)
  Motown Superstar Series #13 .... (MOT)
  Neither One Of Us .... (SOL)
Stevie Wonder; *Greatest Hits #2* .... (TAM)
  Love Songs-20 Classic Hits .... (MOT)
  Motown Story .... (MOT)
Tony Bennett; *All-Time Greatest Hits* ....(COL)
Vikki Carr; *Best Of* .... (EMI)
For Your Life
Led Zeppelin; *Led Zeppelin* .... (ATL)
  Presence .... (SS)
Friend, Love, Woman, Life
Mac Davis; *Baby Don't Get Hooked On Me* ......(COL)
  Greatest Hits ....(COL)
Game Of Life
Billy Paul; *First Class* .... (PI)
Get A Life
Julian Lennon; *Help Yourself* .... (ATL)
Soul II Soul; *Keep On Movin'* .... (VIA)
Get A Life/Fairplay
Soul II Soul; *Keep On Movin'* .... (VIA)
Get Out Of My Life, Woman
Lee Dorsey; *History Of New Orleans*
R&B-#3-1962-1970 .... (RHI)
Paul Butterfield Blues Band; *East-West* .... (ELE)
  Golden Butter .... (ELE)
Give Me Love (Give Me Peace On Earth)
George Harrison; *Best Of* .... (CAP)
  Living In The Material World .... (CAP)
Give To Live
Sammy Hagar; *I Never Said Goodbye* .... (GEF)
Glamorous Life
Original London Cast; *A Little Night Music* ......(RCA)
Sheila E.; *Glamorous Life* .... (WB)
God Is Alive, Magic Is Afoot
Buffy Sainte-Marie; *Best Of* .... (VAN)
  Illuminations .... (VAN)
Going To Live In L.A.
Roger Waters; *45* ....(COL)
Good Life
Betty Carter; *Atlantic Jazz-Singers* .... (ATL)
  'Round Midnight .... (ATL)
Ernie Maresca; *22 Leaders Of The pack-#1* ......(LAU)
Frank Sinatra & Count Basie; *It Might As Well Be*
Swing ....(RPR)
Tony Bennett; *16 Most Requested Songs* ....(COL)
  Sings His All-Time Hall Of Fame Hits ....(COL)
Got A Lot Of Livin' To Do
Elvis Presley; *50 Worldwide Gold Award Hits-#2* (RCA)
  Great Performances ....(RCA)
  Loving You ....(RCA)
Got To Get You Into My Life
Beatles; *Box Set* .... (CAP)
  Revolver .... (CAP)
  Rock 'N' Roll Music-#2 .... (CAP)
Earth, Wind & Fire; *Best Of-#1* ....(COL)
  ST/Sgt. Pepper ....(RSO)
Paul McCartney; *Tripping The Live Fantastic* .... (CAP)
Paul McCartney/Wings; *Kampuchea* .... (ATL)
Hand Of Fate
Rolling Stones; *Black & Blue* .... (RS)
Hangin' In
Tanya Tucker; *Soon* .... (LIB)
Hard Knock Life
Original Broadway Cast; *Annie* ....(COL)
Hard Life
Little River Band; *Backstage Pass* .... (CAP)
  First Under The Wire .... (CAP)
Roger Daltrey; *Daltrey* .... (MCA)
Heartache, A Shadow, A Lifetime
Dave Mason; *At His Very Best* .... (MCA)
  Best Of .... (MCA)
Here And Now
Luther Vandross; *Best Of: Best Of Love* .... (EPI)
Here We Are
Alabama; *Pass It On Down* ....(RCA)
Gloria Estefan; *Cuts Both Ways* .... (EPI)
Hey, Cinderella
Suzy Boggus; *Something Up My Sleeve* .... (LIB)
High Hopes And Empty Pockets
Terry McBride/Ride; *Terry McBride & The Ride* (MCA)
Hold On
En Vogue; *Born To Sing* .... (ATL)

John Conlee; *Rose Colored Glasses* .... (MCA)
John Lennon; *Lennon* ....(CAP)
  Plastic Ono Band ....(CAP)
Steve Winwood; *Steve Winwood* .... (ISL)
Triumph; *Classics* .... (MCA)
  Just A Game .... (MCA)
  Stages .... (MCA)
Wilson Phillips; *Wilson Phillips* .... (SBK)
House I Live In (That's America To Me)
Frank Sinatra; *A Man & His Music* .... (RPR)
  Greatest Hits-Early Years ....(COL)
  In The Beginning-1943-1951 ....(COL)
  Main Event .... (SIN)
How Am I Supposed To Live Without You
Laura Branigan; *Branigan 2* .... (ATL)
Michael Bolton; *Soul Provider* ....(COL)
How Can I Help You Say Goodbye
Patty Loveless; *Only What I Feel* .... (EPI)
How Do The Fools Survive
Doobie Brothers; *Minute By Minute* .... (WB)
How Much Is It Worth To Live In L.A.
Waylon Jennings; *New Classic Waylon* .... (MCA)
Human Nature
Michael Jackson; *Thriller* .... (EPI)
Miles Davis; *You're Under Arrest* ....(COL)
I Ain't Livin' Long Like This
Emmylou Harris; *Quarter Moon In A Ten-Cent*
Town .... (WB)
Rodney Crowell; *Collection* .... (WB)
  I Ain't Livin' Long Like This .... (WB)
Waylon Jennings; *Greatest Hits-#2* ....(RCA)
  What Goes Around Comes Around ....(RCA)
I Can't Live Without Your Love
Teddy Pendergrass; *45* .... (PI)
I Come Alive
Jay Ferguson; *White Noise* ....(CAP)
I Don't Live Today
Jimi Hendrix; *Concerts* .... (RPR)
  Essential-#2 .... (RPR)
  Kiss The Sky .... (RPR)
Jimi Hendrix Experience; *Are You Experienced?* (MCA)
I Don't Wanna Live Without Your Love
Chicago; *19* .... (FM)
  Greatest Hits 1982-1989 .... (FM)
I Don't Want To Live Without You
Foreigner; *Inside Information* .... (ATL)
I Get Up I Get Down
Yes; *Close To The Edge* .... (ATL)
I Got A Mind To Give Up Living
Paul Butterfield Blues Band; *East-West* .... (ELE)
I Live For Your Love
Natalie Cole; *Everlasting* .... (AMR)
I Love The Life I Live
Mose Allison; *Alive* .... (ATL)
  Best Of .... (ATL)
Muddy Waters; *Chess Box* .... (CSS)
I Never Thought I'd Live To Be A Hundred
Moody Blues; *To Our Children's Children's*
Children .... (POL)
I Never Thought I'd Live To Be A Million
Moody Blues; *To Our Children's Children's*
Children .... (POL)
I Want To Live In A Wigwam
Cat Stevens; *Footsteps In The Dark-Greatest*
Hits-#2 .... (A&M)
I Will Survive
Gloria Gaynor; *Billboard Top Hits-1979* .... (RHI)
  Disco Years-#2-On The Beat-1978-1982 .... (RHI)
  Love Tracks .... (POL)
If He Walked Into My Life
Original Cast; *Mame* ....(COL)
In My Life
Beatles; *1962-1966* ....(CAP)
  Love Songs ....(CAP)
  Rubber Soul ....(CAP)
  ST/Imagine-The Motion Picture ....(CAP)
Crosby, Stills & Nash; *After The Storm* .... (ATL)
Glen Campbell; *Still Within The Sound Of My*
Voice .... (MCA)
Judy Collins; *Colors Of The Day-Best Of* .... (ELE)
  In My Life .... (ELE)
Original Broadway Cast; *Les Miserables* .... (GEF)
Patti Austin; *Love Is Gonna Getcha* .... (GRP)

In This Life
Collin Raye; *In This Life* .... (EPI)
Inner Light
Beatles; *Past Masters-#2* .... (CAP)
   Rarities .... (CAP)
Little River Band; *Diamantina Cocktail* .... (CAP)
Is There Life Out There
Reba McEntire; *For My Broken Heart* .... (MCA)
   Greatest Hits-#2 .... (MCA)
Isn't Life Strange
Moody Blues; *Night At Red Rocks With Colorado
Symph.* .... (POL)
   Seventh Sojourn .... (POL)
   This Is The .... (POL)
   Voices In The Sky-Best Of .... (T/P)
It's My Life
Animals; *Best Of* .... (AKO)
   Greatest Hits .... (ALL)
Charlie Daniels Band; *Saddle Tramp* .... (EPI)
Talk Talk; *It's My Life* .... (EMI)
   Very Best Of-Natural History .... (EMI)
It's My Life Baby
Bobby Bland; *Barefoot Rock & You Got Me* .... (MCA)
   Best Of-#2 .... (MCA)
Johnny Winter; *Guitar Slinger* .... (ALG)
Junior Wells; *It's My Life Baby* .... (VAN)
I'm Alive
April Wine; *First Glance* .... (ELE)
Electric Light Orchestra; *ST/Xanadu* .... (MCA)
Gamma; *Gamma* .... (ELE)
Hollies; *Best Of-#1* .... (EMI)
   History Of British Rock-#2 .... (RHI)
Jackson Browne; *I'm Alive* .... (ELE)
Kiss; *Asylum* .... (MER)
Mose Allison; *Ever Since The World Ended* ..... (BLN)
Neil Diamond; *Heartlight* .... (COL)
Seal; *Seal* .... (ZTT)
Spooky Tooth; *Hell Or High Water* .... (ACC)
   Mirror .... (ISL)
Tarney/Spencer Band; *Run For Your Life* .... (A&M)
Tommy James/Shondells; *Crimson & Clover* ..... (RHI)
I'm In A Hurry (And Don't Know Why)
Alabama; *American Pride* .... (RCA)
I'm Tired Of Living This Lie
Bob Wills/Texas Playboys; *24 Greatest Hits* ..... (POL)
I've Got Life
Take 6; *Join The Band* .... (RPR)
Joe Knows How To Live
Eddy Raven; *Best Of* .... (RCA)
Nitty Gritty Dirt Band; *Hold On* .... (WB)
Just Seven Numbers
Four Tops; *Anthology* .... (MOT)
   Compact Command Performances .... (MOT)
Just The Way It Is, Baby
Rembrandts; *Rembrandts* .... (ATC)
Keep It Between The Lines
Ricky Van Shelton; *Backroads* .... (COL)
Keep On The Sunny Side
Randy Scruggs/Earl Scruggs/Doc Watson; *Red Hot +
Country* .... (MER)
Keep Yourself Alive
Queen; *Greatest Hits* .... (HOL)
   Live Killers .... (HOL)
   Queen .... (HOL)
Killing Yourself To Live
Black Sabbath; *Sabbath Bloody Sabbath* .... (WB)
Kodachrome
Paul Simon; *Greatest Hits* .... (COL)
   Negotiations & Love Songs 1971-1986 .... (WB)
   There Goes Rhymin' Simon .... (WB)
Simon & Garfunkel; *Concert In Central Park* .... (WB)
La Vie En Rose
Edith Piaf; *Voice Of The Sparrow-Very Best Of* .. (CAP)
Grace Jones; *Island Life* .... (ISL)
Louis Armstrong; *Best Of The Decca Years-#1-The
Singer* .... (DEC)
Marlene Dietrich; *The Cosmopolitan* .... (COL)
Melissa Manchester; *Tribute* .... (MIK)
Last Night A D.J. Saved My Life
Indeep; *Disco Years-#2-On The Beat-1978-1982* (RHI)
   Last Night A D.J. Saved My Life .... (SON)

Laughing At Life
Billie Holiday; *Billie Holiday* .... (COL)
   Quintessential-#8-1939-1940 .... (COL)
   Story-#2 .... (COL)
Learn How To Live
Billy Squier; *Emotions In Motion* .... (CAP)
Learning To Live Again
Garth Brooks; *The Chase* .... (LIB)
Lesson In Survival
Joni Mitchell; *For The Roses* .... (ASY)
Let Me Live Another Day
Lisa Brokop; *Every Little Girl's Dream* .... (PAT)
Let Me Make Something In Your Life
Steve Winwood; *Steve Winwood* .... (ISL)
Let's Live For Today
Grass Roots; *At The Hop* .... (MCA)
   Summer Of Love .... (RHI)
   Their 16 Greatest Hits .... (MCA)
   Vintage Music-Orig. Classics/'60s-#10 .... (MCA)
Life
Elvis Presley; *Love Letters From Elvis* .... (RCA)
Sly/Family Stone; *Anthology* .... (EPI)
   Greatest Hits .... (EPI)
Life After Death
Ian Hunter; *You're Never Alone With A
Schizophrenic* .... (CHR)
Life Ain't Easy
Dr. Hook/Medicine Show; *45* .... (COL)
Life As We Knew It
Kathy Mattea; *Class Of Country* .... (KT)
   Collection Of Hits .... (MER)
   Untasted Honey .... (MER)
Life Beyond L.A.
Ambrosia; *Life Beyond L.A.* .... (WB)
Life During Wartime
Talking Heads; *Fear Of Music* .... (SIR)
   Name Of This Band Is .... (SIR)
   ST/Stop Making Sense .... (SIR)
Life For The Taking
Eddie Money; *Life For The Taking* .... (COL)
Life Goes On
Big Mama Thornton; *With Muddy Waters' Blues
Band* .... (ARH)
Charlie Rich; *Fool Strikes Again* .... (UA)
   Nobody But You .... (UA)
Detergents; *45* .... (RLL)
Johnny Cash; *Man-The World-His Music* .... (SUN)
   Story Songs Of The Trains & Rivers .... (SUN)
Jones Girls; *Jones Girls* .... (MCA)
Kinks; *Sleepwalker* .... (ARI)
Leon Haywood; *Double My Pleasure* .... (MCA)
Peabo Bryson; *All My Love* .... (CAP)
Poison; *Flesh & Blood* .... (CAP)
Utopia; *Deface The Music* .... (RHI)
Life Has Its Little Ups & Down
Charlie Rich; *Best Of* .... (EPI)
   Greatest Hits .... (EPI)
Life Has Just Begun
Spirit; *12 Dreams Of Dr. Sardonicus* .... (EPI)
Life In A Northern Town
Dream Academy; *Dream Academy* .... (WB)
Life In A Song
Marshall Tucker Band; *Carolina Dreams* .... (CPC)
Life In London
Pat Travers; *Boom Boom...Best Of* .... (POL)
   Putting It Straight .... (POL)
Life In One Day
Howard Jones; *Dream Into Action* .... (ELE)
Life In Prison
Byrds; *Sweetheart Of The Rodeo* .... (COL)
Life In The Air Age
Be Bop Deluxe; *Live In The Air Age* .... (HAR)
   Sunburst Finish .... (HAR)
Life In The Bloodstream
Guess Who; *Best Of-#2* .... (RCA)
Life In The Fast Lane
Eagles; *Hotel California* .... (ASY)
   Live .... (ASY)
   ST/FM .... (MCA)
Life In The Foodchain
Tonio K.; *Life In The Foodchain* .... (EPI)
Life In The Jungle
John Mayall/Bluesbreakers; *Chicago Line* .... (ISL)

Life Is A Carnival
Band; *Anthology-#2* ....(CAP)
   Best Of ....(CAP)
   Cahoots ....(CAP)
   Last Waltz ....(WB)
   Rock Of Ages-#1 & 2 ....(CAP)
Life Is A Highway
Tom Cochrane; *Mad Mad World* ....(CAP)
Life Is A Lady
Santana; *Inner Secrets* ....(COL)
Life Is A Lemon And I Want My Money Back
Meat Loaf; *Bat Out Of Hell II-Back Into Hell* ... (MCA)
Life Is A Long Song
Jethro Tull; *Living In The Past* ....(CHR)
Life Is A Minestrone
10 CC; *Original Soundtrack* ....(MER)
Life Is A Rock (But The Radio Rolled Me)
Reunion; *Super Hits/'70s-Have A Nice Day-#13* .. (RHI)
Life Is A Song Worth Singing
Johnny Mathis; *I'm Coming Home* ....(COL)
Teddy Pendergrass; *Life Is A Song Worth Singing* .. (PI)
Life Is A Woman
Original Cast/Sammy Davis, Jr.; *Stop The World I Want
To Get Off* ....(WB)
Life Is But A Dream
Harptones; *Echoes Of A Rock Era* ....(RLL)
   ST/Goodfellas ....(ATL)
   Super Oldies/'50s-#4 ....(AUF)
Life Is Happiness Indeed
Original Cast; *Candide* ....(COL)
Life Is Just A Bowl Of Cherries
Rudy Vallee; *Heigh-Ho Everybody* ....(OLR)
Life Is Just A Tire Swing
Jimmy Buffett; *A-1-A* ....(MCA)
Life Of Illusion
Joe Walsh; *There Goes The Neighborhood* ....(ASY)
Life On Mars?
David Bowie; *Hunky Dory* ....(RYK)
   The Singles-1969-1993 ....(RYK)
Life On The Road
Kinks; *Sleepwalker* ....(ARI)
Life Saver
Chicago; *VII* ....(COL)
Life So Cruel
Charlie; *Lines* ....(JNS)
Life Takes A Life
Jon Butcher Axis; *Jon Butcher Axis* .... (POL)
Life To Win
Motorhead; *Ace Of Spades* ....(MER)
Life Turned Her That Way
Mel Tillis; *Best Of* ....(MCA)
Ricky Van Shelton; *Wild-Eyed Dream* ....(COL)
Life #9
Martina McBride; *The Way That I Am* ....(RCA)
Life (Everybody Needs Somebody)
Haddaway; *Haddaway* ....(ARI)
Lifeline
10 CC; *Bloody Tourists* ....(POL)
Husker Du; *Metal Circus* ....(SST)
Spandau Ballet; *True* ....(CHR)
Lifestyles Of The Not-So-Rich & Famous
Tracy Byrd; *No Ordinary Man* ....(MCA)
Life's A Dance
John Michael Montgomery; *Life's A Dance* ......(ATL)
Life's A Song
Kool/Gang; *Force* ....(DL)
Life's Been Good
Eagles; *Live* ....(ASY)
Joe Walsh; *But Seriously Folks* ....(ASY)
   ST/FM ....(MCA)
Life's Highway
Steve Wariner; *Country Classics-#2-Today's Country
Cl* ....(MCA)
   Life's Highway ....(MCA)
Life's In One Day
Howard Jones; *Dream Into Action* ....(ELE)
Life's Just A Ballgame
Womack & Womack; *Conscience* ....(ISL)
Life's Like Poetry
Lefty Frizzell; *Legendary* ....(MCA)
Life's Little Ups And Downs
Ricky Van Shelton; *RVS III* ....(COL)
Life's What You Make It
Talk Talk; *Colour Of Spring* ....(EMI)

Like A Prayer
Madonna; *Like A Prayer* ....(SIR)
   Royal Box ....(SIR)
Live Again
Tarney/Spencer Band; *Run For Your Life* ....(A&M)
Live For Loving You
Gloria Estefan; *Into The Light* ....(EPI)
Live For The Music
Bad Company; *10 From 6* ....(ATL)
   Run With The Pack .... (SS)
Live For Today
Jeffrey Osborne; *Don't Stop* ....(A&M)
Lords Of The New Church; *Is Nothing Sacred* ....(IRS)
   Killer Lords ....(IRS)
Sweet; *Off The Record* ....(CAP)
Toto; *Turn Back* ....(COL)
Live In Vain
Frankie Miller; *Full House* ....(CHR)
Live It Up
Crosby, Stills & Nash; *Live It Up* ....(ATL)
Isley Brothers; *Forever Gold* ....(TN)
   Greatest Hits-#1 ....(TN)
   Live It Up ....(TN)
Ted Nugent; *Cat Scratch Fever* ....(EPI)
Live Life
Kinks; *Misfits* ....(ARI)
Live Now Pay Later
Foghat; *Girls To Chat & Boys To Bounce* ......(RHI)
Live To Tell
Madonna; *Immaculate Collection* ....(SIR)
   Royal Box ....(SIR)
   True Blue ....(SIR)
Live Until I Die
Clay Walker; *Clay Walker* ....(GIA)
Live Wire
AC/DC; *High Voltage* ....(ATC)
Martha Reeves/Vandellas; *Anthology* ....(MOT)
   Compact Command Performances ....(MOT)
   Greatest Hits ....(MOT)
Live With Me
Rolling Stones; *Get Yer Ya-Ya's Out* ....(AKO)
   Let It Bleed ....(AKO)
Live & Learn
Joe Public; *Joe Public* ....(COL)
Live & Let Die
Paul McCartney; *13 Original James Bond Themes* (EMI)
   Tripping The Live Fantastic ....(CAP)
Paul McCartney/Wings; *All The Best* ....(CAP)
   Over America ....(CAP)
   Wings Greatest ....(CAP)
Wings; *ST/Live & Let Die* ....(EMI)
Lively Up Yourself
Bob Marley/Wailers; *Babylon By Bus* ....(TUF)
   Live ....(TUF)
   Natty Dread ....(TUF)
Living A Little, Laughing A Little
John Hiatt; *Warming Up To The Ice Age* ....(GEF)
Spinners; *Live* ....(ATL)
   New & Improved ....(ATL)
Living For The City
Stevie Wonder; *Innervisions* ....(MOT)
   Original Musiquarium ....(MOT)
Living Forever
Genesis; *We Can't Dance* ....(ATL)
Living In A Dream
Arc Angels; *Arc Angels* ....(DGC)
Band; *Anthology-#2* ....(CAP)
   Islands ....(CAP)
Sea Level; *On The Edge* ....(CPC)
Living In A Fantasy
Leo Sayer; *45* ....(WB)
Living In America
Aztec Two-Step; *See It Was Like This-Acoustic
Retrosp.* ....(FF)
Donna Summer; *Donna Summer* ....(GEF)
Hiroshima; *East* ....(EPI)
James Brown; *Gravity* ....(SCO)
   Rocky Story ....(SCO)
   ST/Rocky IV ....(SCO)
Living In China
Men Without Hats; *45* ....(BKS)
Living In Danger
Ace Of Base; *The Sign* ....(ARI)

Living In Europe
Thompson Twins; *In The Name Of Love* .... (ARI)
Living In Paradise
Elvis Costello; *This Year's Model* ....(COL)
Living In Shame
Supremes; *45* .... (MOT)
Living In The Blues
Johnny Winter; *About Blues* ....(JNS)
Before The Storm ....(JNS)
Living In The Footsteps Of Another Man
Chi-Lites; *Greatest Hits* ....(BRU)
Half A Love ....(BRU)
Living In The Future
John Prine; *Storm Windows* .... (ASY)
Living In The Future In A Plastic Dome
Country Joe McDonald; *Incredible Live* .... (VAN)
Living In The Ghetto
Toots/Maytals; *Reggae Got Soul* .... (ISL)
Living In The Material World
George Harrison; *Living In The Material World* ..(CAP)
Living In The Past
Jethro Tull; *20 Years Of-Boxed Set* .... (CHR)
Living In The Past .... (CHR)
Original Masters .... (CHR)
"M.U."-Best Of .... (CHR)
Living In The Plastic Age
Buggles; *Age Of Plastic* .... (ISL)
Living In The Promiseland
Willie Nelson; *30 Years Of #1 Hits-#18* ....(COL)
Greatest Country Hits/'80s-1986 ....(COL)
More Hot Country Requests .... (EPI)
The Promiseland ....(COL)
Living In The U.S.A.
Steve Miller Band; *Anthology* ....(CAP)
Best Of-1968-1973 ....(CAP)
Live ....(CAP)
On The Road Again-Rock's New Frontiers ......(CAP)
Sailor ....(CAP)
Living Inside Your Love
Earl Klugh; *Best Of* ....(BLN)
Living Inside Your Love .... (EMI)
George Benson; *Collection* .... (WB)
Living Inside Your Love .... (WB)
Living Is Easy
Cleo Laine; *Born On A Friday* ....(RCA)
Living It Down
Freddy Fender; *Best Of* .... (MCA)
Living Legend
Kris Kristofferson; *Easter Land* ....(COL)
Havana Jam ....(COL)
W. Jennings/W. Nelson/J. Cash/K. Krist.; *Highwayman*
2 ....(COL)
Living Loving Maid
Led Zeppelin; *II* .... (ATL)
Living Loving Voices
Jerry Lee Lewis; *45* .... (SUN)
Living Loving Wreck
Jerry Lee Lewis; *Golden Rock & Roll* .... (SUN)
Original .... (SUN)
Living My Life Just For You
Jerry Butler; *It All Comes Out In My Song* ...... (MOT)
Living Next Door To Alice
Johnny Carver; *Best Of* .... (MCA)
Living On My Own
Freddie Mercury; *The Great Pretender* ....(HOL)
Living On The Highway
Freddie King; *Best Of* .... (MCA)
Living On The Open Road
Delaney & Bonnie & Friends; *Duane Allman*
Anthology ....(CPC)
Living Proof
Ricky Van Shelton; *30 Years Of #1 Hits-#20* ....(COL)
Greatest Country Hits/'80s-1989 ....(COL)
Greatest Hits Plus ....(COL)
Living The Blues
Bob Dylan; *Self Portrait* ....(COL)
Living Together
Bee Gees; *Spirits Having Flown* ....(RSO)
Jacksons; *Jacksons* ....(EPI)
Whispers; *One For The Money* ....(STN)
Living Together, Growing Together
Burt Bacharach; *Classics-#23* ....(A&M)
Greatest Hits ....(A&M)
Living Together ....(A&M)

Living With A Hernia
Weird Al Yankovic; *Greatest Hits* ....(RAR)
Polka Party ....(RAR)
Living With AIDS
Romanovsky & Phillips; *Emotional Rollercoaster* . (FRE)
Living Without You
Nitty Gritty Dirt Band; *Best Of* .... (EMI)
Dirt Silver & Gold .... (EMI)
Uncle Charlie ....(LIB)
Workin' Band .... (WB)
Randy Newman; *Live* ....(RPR)
Randy Newman ....(RPR)
Living Without Your Love
Dusty Springfield; *Living Without Your Love* ..... (EMI)
Never Trust A Man In A Rented Tuxedo .... (EMI)
Joe Cocker; *Cocker* ....(CAP)
Living Years
Mike/Mechanics; *Living Years* .... (ATL)
Living & Learning
Mel Tillis/Statesiders; *24 Great Hits* ....(MGM)
Livin' Ain't Livin'
Firefall; *Firefall* .... (ATL)
Livin' Alone
Beck, Bogert & Appice; *Beck, Bogert & Appice* ...(EPI)
Livin' At The End Of The Rainbow
Dave & Sugar; *That's The Way Love Should Be* ..(RCA)
Livin' For Me
Garland Jeffreys; *American Boy & Girl* ....(A&M)
Livin' For The Weekend
O'Jays; *Collector's Items* .... (PI)
Family Reunion .... (PI)
Livin' For You
Al Green; *Compact Command Performances* .... (MOT)
Greatest Hits-#2 ....(HIR)
Livin' For You ....(MOT)
Sonny & Cher; *Best Of* ....(ATC)
Two Of Us ....(ATC)
Livin' For Your Love
Melba Moore; *Never Say Never* ....(CAP)
Livin' In South Central L.A.
South Central Posse; *We're All In The Same Gang* (WB)
Livin' In The Jungle
Flo & Eddie/Turtles; *History Of* .... (RHI)
Livin' In The Life
Isley Brothers; *Go For Your Guns* .... (TN)
Livin' In These Troubled Times
Crystal Gayle; *Greatest Hits* ....(COL)
Hollywood/Tennessee ....(COL)
Livin' On A Prayer
Bon Jovi; *Slippery When Wet* .... (MER)
Livin' On Love
Alan Jackson; *Who I Am* .... (ARI)
Livin' On The Edge
Aerosmith; *Get A Grip* ....(GEF)
Livin' On The Fault Line
Doobie Brothers; *Livin' On The Fault Line* .... (WB)
Livin' Thing
Electric Light Orchestra; *Exposition* .... (EPI)
Greatest Hits ....(JET)
New World Record ....(JET)
London Life
Ian & Sylvia; *Greatest Hits* .... (VAN)
Nashville .... (VAN)
Long Live Rock
Who; *Odds & Sods* ....(MCA)
ST/Kids Are Alright ....(MCA)
Who's Last ....(MCA)
Long Live Rock & Roll
Rainbow; *Finyl Vinyl* .... (MER)
Long Live Rock & Roll ....(POL)
Long Live Rock 'N' Roll
Elvis Presley; *Elvis Aron Presley* ....(RCA)
Long Promised Road
Beach Boys; *10 Years Of Harmony* ....(CAR)
Surf's Up ....(CAR)
Long & Winding Road
Beatles; *1967-1970* ....(CAP)
20 Greatest Hits ....(CAP)
Let It Be ....(CAP)
Love Songs ....(CAP)
Reel Music ....(CAP)
Paul McCartney; *Tripping The Live Fantastic* ....(CAP)
Tripping The Live Fantastic-Highlights! ....(CAP)
Paul McCartney/Wings; *Over America* ....(CAP)

Lot Of Living To Do
Original Broadway Cast; *Bye Bye Birdie* ....(COL)
Original Cast; *ST/Bye Bye Birdie* ....(RCA)
Love Alive
Heart; *California Jam 2* ....(COL)
Little Queen ....(POR)
Love Don't Live Here Anymore
Madonna; *Like A Virgin* ....(SIR)
Rose Royce; *Greatest Hits* ....(WHI)
Strikes Again ....(WHI)
Love Is Alive
Gary Wright; *Dream Weaver* ....(WB)
Joe Cocker; *Night Calls* ....(CAP)
Judds; *Collector's Series* ....(RCA)
Greatest Hits ....(RCA)
Why Not Me ....(RCA)
Love Of A Lifetime
Firehouse; *Firehouse* ....(EPI)
Larry Gatlin/Gatlin Brothers; *Alive & Well...Living In The Land Of...* ....(COL)
Biggest Hits ....(COL)
Country Love ....(KT)
Live At 8:00 ....(CAP)
Make My Life With You
Oak Ridge Boys; *Country Classics-#1* ..... (MCA)
Greatest Hits-#2 ....(MCA)
MCA #1 Hits/'80s-#1 ....(MCA)
Man In The Mirror
Jim Glaser; *Man In The Mirror* ....(NBL)
Michael Jackson; *Bad* ....(EPI)
Many Rivers To Cross
Jimmy Cliff; *In Concert* ....(RPR)
Reggae Spectacular ....(A&M)
ST/Harder They Come ....(MGO)
Wonderful World Beautiful People ....(A&M)
Linda Ronstadt; *Prisoner In Disguise* ....(ASY)
UB40; *Labour Of Love* ....(A&M)
Mi Vida Loca
Pam Tillis; *Sweetheart's Dance* ....(ARI)
Miner's Life
Tom Juravich; *Out Of Darkness (Mine Workers' Story)* ....(FF)
Weavers; *Reunion At Carnegie Hall-1963-#2* ... (VAN)
More You Live, The More You Love
A Flock Of Seagulls; *Best Of* ....(JVA)
Story Of A Young Heart ....(COL)
My Back Pages
Bob Dylan; *Another Side Of* ....(COL)
Greatest Hits-#2 ....(COL)
Byrds; *20 Essential Tracks From Box Set* ....(COL)
Byrds Play Dylan ....(COL)
Greatest Hits ....(COL)
Younger Than Yesterday ....(COL)
My Fate Is In Your Hands
Fats Waller; *Piano Solos (1929-1941)* ....(RCA)
Rare Piano Roll Solos-#3 ....(BIO)
Turn On The Heat-Fats Waller Piano Solos .....(BLU)
My Life
Billy Joel; *52nd Street* ....(COL)
Greatest Hits-#1&2-1973-1985 ....(COL)
My Life As A Dog
Active Ingredient; *Extrastrength* ....(BAI)
Never Been So Loved (In All My Life)
Charley Pride; *14 #1 Country Hits* ....(RCA)
Greatest Hits ....(RCA)
Never In My Life
Mountain; *Best Of* ....(COL)
Climbing! ....(COL)
Twin Peaks ....(COL)
Night Life
Charlie Daniels Band/Friends; *Volunteer Jam 3&4* (EPI)
Miracles; *Greatest Hits* ....(MOT)
Ray Price; *Greatest Hits-#2* ....(SO)
Thin Lizzy; *Night Life* ....(MER)
Willie Nelson; *Country Willie* ....(UA)
Healing Hands Of Time ....(LIB)
Souvenirs Of Music City U.S.A. ....(PLN)
Willie ....(RCA)
/Family Live ....(COL)
No Expectations
Rolling Stones; *Beggar's Banquet* ....(AKO)
More Hot Rocks-Big Hits & Fazed Cookies ..... (AKO)
Singles Collection-London Years ....(AKO)

No Time To Live
Traffic; *Traffic* ....(ISL)
Now I Know
Lari White; *Wishes* ....(RCA)
Ob La Di, Ob La Da
Beatles; *1967-1970* ....(CAP)
Box Set ....(CAP)
White Album ....(CAP)
Ocean Of Life
Gene Cotton; *No Strings Attached* ....(ARL)
Off The Wall
Jacksons; *Live* ....(EPI)
Michael Jackson; *Off The Wall* ....(EPI)
Once In A Lifetime
Aretha Franklin; *After Hours* ....(COL)
Chicago; *17* ....(FM)
Original Broadway Cast; *Stop The World I Want To Get Off* .....(POL)
Sammy Davis, Jr.; *Greatest Hits* ....(RPR)
Sammy Davis, Jr./Original Cast; *Stop The World I Want To Get Off* ....(WB)
Talking Heads; *Remain In Light* ....(SIR)
ST/Stop Making Sense ....(SIR)
Once Upon A Lifetime
Alabama; *American Pride* ....(RCA)
One Day At A Time
Cristy Lane; *At Her Best* ....(EMI)
John Lennon; *Lennon* ....(CAP)
Mind Games ....(CAP)
Willie Nelson; *Me & Paul* ....(COL)
Willie ....(RCA)
& Family Live ....(COL)
One Love In My Lifetime
Diana Ross; *Anthology* ....(MOT)
Diana Ross ....(MOT)
Greatest Hits ....(MOT)
One Miner's Life-The Image Of God
Battlefield Band; *There's A Buzz* ....(FF)
One Night A Day
Garth Brooks; *In Pieces* ....(LIB)
One Of The Living
Tina Turner; *ST/Beyond Thunderdome* ....(CAP)
One Of The Survivors
Kinks; *Greatest/Celluloid Heroes* ....(RCA)
Preservation (A Play In Two Acts) ....(RHI)
Only Living Boy In New York
Simon & Garfunkel; *Bridge Over Troubled Water* (COL)
Collected Works ....(COL)
Only The Strong Survive
Elvis Presley; *From Elvis In Memphis* ....(RCA)
Memphis Record ....(RCA)
Jerry Butler; *Best Of* ....(MER)
Best Of ....(RHI)
R.E.O. Speedwagon; *Decade Of Rock & Roll-1970-1980* .....(EPI)
Nine Lives ....(EPI)
Tubes; *Remote Control* ....(A&M)
T.R.A.S.H.-Tubes Rarities & Smash Hits ....(A&M)
Opposites
Eric Clapton; *There's One In Every Crowd* ....(RSO)
Other Side Of Life
Moody Blues; *Other Side Of Life* ....(POL)
Other Side Of This Life
Fred Neil; *Little Bit Of Rain* ....(ELE)
Troubadours Of The Folk Era-#2 ....(RHI)
Jefferson Airplane; *Bless Its Pointed Little Head* ..(RCA)
Loves You ....(RCA)
Peter, Paul & Mary; *Album* ....(WB)
O.D'd On Life Itself
Blue Oyster Cult; *Tyranny & Mutation* ....(COL)
Patience
Guns N' Roses; *G N' R Lies* ....(GEF)
Picture From Life's Other Side
George Jones; *Hallelujah Weekend* ....(EPI)
Goebel Reeves; *Texas Drifter* ....(GLN)
Hank Williams; *Beyond The Sunset* ....(POL)
Hey Good Lookin' (Dec. 1950-July 1951) ......(POL)
Pictured Life
Scorpions; *Best Of* ....(RCA)
Tokyo Tapes ....(RCA)
Virgin Killer ....(RCA)
Planets Of Life
Whispers; *I Can Remember* ....(ACC)
Vintage ....(SLR)

Poor Man Lives Longer Than The Rich
Freeman King; *45* ....(KNT)
Pop Life
Prince/Revolution; *Around The World In A Day* ..(PAI)
Prime Of Life
Neil Young/Crazy Horse; *Sleeps With Angels* ..... (RPR)
Private Life
Grace Jones; *Island Life* .... (ISL)
Warm Leatherette .... (ISL)
Pretenders; *Pretenders* .... (SIR)
Que Sera, Sera
Doris Day; *16 Most Requested Songs* ....(COL)
Greatest Hits ....(COL)
Radio Classics Of The '50s ....(COL)
Sly/Family Stone; *Anthology* .... (EPI)
Fresh .... (EPI)
Raise Your Hand
Bruce Springsteen/E Street Band;
Live-1975-1985 ....(COL)
Eddie Floyd; *Knock On Wood* ....(ATL)
Stax/Volt Revue-#2-Live In Paris ....(ATL)
J. Geils Band; *Blow Your Face Out* ....(ATL)
Rat Race
Bob Marley/Wailers; *Babylon By Bus* .... (TUF)
Rastaman Vibration ....(TUF)
Rebel Music ....(TUF)
Real Life
John Cougar Mellencamp; *Lonesome Jubilee* .... (MER)
Phil Woods/Little Big Band; *Real Life* ....(CHE)
Simple Minds; *Real Life* .... (A&M)
Real Life Love
Larry Stewart; *Heart Like A Hurricane* ....(COL)
Reap What You Sow
Otis Rush; *Atlantic Blues-Chicago* .... (ATL)
Mourning In The Morning ....(ATL)
Reflections Of My Life
Marmalade; *History Of British Rock* .... (RHI)
London Collector-Rock Invasion ....(LON)
Super Hits/'70s-Have A Nice Day-#2 ....(RHI)
Rhythm Of Life
Oleta Adams; *Circle Of One* ....(FON)
Original Cast; *Sweet Charity* ....(COL)
Richard Marx; *Richard Marx* ....(CAP)
Right Here/Human Nature
SWV; *It's About Time* ....(RCA)
Ripple
Grateful Dead; *American Beauty* .... (WB)
Reckoning ....(ARI)
What A Long Strange Trip It's Been ....(WB)
Jane's Addiction; *Deadicated* ....(ARI)
River Of Dreams
Billy Joel; *River Of Dreams* ....(COL)
River Of Life
Neville Brothers; *Brother's Keeper* .... (A&M)
R.E.O. Speedwagon; *This Time We Mean It* .... (EPI)
River, The
Bruce Springsteen; *The River* ....(COL)
Bruce Springsteen/E Street Band;
Live-1975-1985 ....(COL)
Dan Fogelberg; *Home Free* ....(COL)
Enya; *Watermark* ....(RPR)
Garth Brooks; *Ropin' The Wind* ....(LIB)
Joni Mitchell; *Blue* ....(RPR)
Roberta Flack; *Killing Me Softly* ....(ATL)
Santana; *Festival* ....(COL)
Roads Of Life
Bobby Womack; *Roads Of Life* .... (ARI)
Rock Is My Life And This Is My Song
Bachman-Turner Overdrive; *Not Fragile* .... (MER)
Rockin' My Life Away
Jerry Lee Lewis; *Rockin' My Life Away/Collection* (WB)
Survivors ....(COL)
Swingin' Country Favorites ....(WB)
Roll With It
Steve Winwood; *Rock The First-#2* ....(SAN)
Roll With It ....(VIA)
ST/Nuns On The Run ....(MER)
Run For Your Life
Beatles; *Box Set* ....(CAP)
Rubber Soul ....(CAP)
Sailor's Life
Fairport Convention; *Chronicles* ....(A&M)
Unhalfbricking ....(A&M)
Judy Collins; *Maid Of Constant Sorrow* ....(ELE)

Saturday Nite Live
Masta Ace; *Slaughtahouse* .... (DV)
Save The Life Of My Child
Simon & Garfunkel; *Bookends* ....(COL)
Collected Works ....(COL)
Saved My Life
Fee Waybill; *Read My Lips* ....(CAP)
ST/St. Elmo's Fire ....(ATL)
Secret Life Of Arabia
David Bowie; *Heroes* ....(RYK)
Secret O' Life
James Taylor; *JT* ....(COL)
Secret To A Long Life
Michelle Shocked; *Arkansas Traveler* .... (MER)
Texas Campfire Tapes .... (MER)
Separate Lives
Phil Collins; *Serious Hits...Live!* .... (ATL)
Phil Collins & Marilyn Martin; *ST/Two Of A
Kind* .... (ATL)
White Nights .... (ATL)
She's Out Of My Life
Jacksons; *Live* .... (EPI)
Michael Jackson; *Off The Wall* .... (EPI)
Showman's Life
Jesse Winchester; *Best Of* .... (RHI)
Touch On The Rainy Side .... (RHI)
Simple Life
Andy Childs; *Andy Childs* ....(RCA)
Elton John; *The One* ....(MCA)
Ricky Skaggs; *My Father's Son* .... (EPI)
Simple Twist Of Fate
Bob Dylan; *At Budokan* ....(COL)
Blood On The Tracks ....(COL)
Jerry Garcia Band; *Jerry Garcia Band* .... (ARI)
Joan Baez; *Best Of* .... (A&M)
Diamonds & Rust .... (A&M)
Tim Curry; *Best Of* .... (A&M)
Sing C'Est La Vie
Sonny & Cher; *Beat Goes On* .... (ATC)
Best Of .... (ATC)
Two Of Us .... (ATC)
Single Life
Cameo; *Single Life* .... (CAS)
So Alive
Love & Rockets; *Love & Rockets* .... (BEG)
Sole Survivor
Asia; *Asia* .... (GEF)
Live In Moscow .... (RHI)
Some Folks' Lives Roll Easy
Paul Simon; *Still Crazy After All These Years* ... (WB)
Someone Saved My Life Tonight
Elton John; *Capt. Fantastic & The Brown Dirt
Cowboy* .... (POL)
Greatest Hits-#2 .... (POL)
Song For The Life
Jerry Jeff Walker; *A Man Must Carry On* .... (MCA)
Kathy Mattea; *Walk The Way The Wind Blows* .. (MER)
Rodney Crowell; *Ain't Living Long Like This* ...... (WB)
Spice Of Life
Manhattan Transfer; *Bodies & Souls* .... (ATL)
Start A New Life
R.E.O. Speedwagon; *Ridin' The Storm Out* .... (EPI)
Starting A New Life
Van Morrison; *Tupelo Honey* .... (WB)
Stayin' Alive
Bee Gees; *Greatest* .... (RSO)
ST/Saturday Night Fever .... (POL)
ST/Stayin' Alive .... (POL)
Steamboat
Beach Boys; *Holland* ....(CAR)
Drifters; *Greatest Recordings* ....(ATC)
Let The Boogie Woogie Roll-Greatest Hits ...... (ATL)
Still Alive & Well
Edgar Winter; *Roadwork* .... (EPI)
Johnny Winter; *Still Alive & Well* ....(COL)
Storms Of Life
Randy Travis; *Storms Of Life* .... (WB)
Story Of My Life
Don Williams; *Lovers & Best Friends* .... (MCA)
Yellow Moon ....(MCA)
Guitar Slim; *Legends Of Electric Blues Guitar-#1* . (RHI)
Things That I Used To Do .... (SPE)

Marty Robbins; *Essential-1951-1982* ....(COL)
  Greatest Hits ....(COL)
  Lifetime Of Song-1951-1982 ....(COL)
Neil Diamond; *Headed For The Future* ....(COL)
Unrelated Segments; *Nuggets-#11* .... (RHI)
Street Life
Crusaders; *Mega Hits Dance Classics-#7* ... (PRY)
  Street Life ....(MCA)
Herb Alpert; *Classics-#20* ....(A&M)
  Rise ....(A&M)
Neil Diamond; *Beautiful Noise* ....(COL)
  Love At The Greek ....(COL)
Roxy Music; *Stranded* ....(RPR)
  Street Life-20 Great Hits ....(RPR)
Strenuous Life
Dick Hyman; *Scott Joplin-Greatest Hits* ....(RCA)
Scott Joplin; *King Of Ragtime Writers* ....(BIO)
Summer Side Of Life
Gordon Lightfoot; *Gord's Gold* ....(RPR)
  Summer Side Of Life ....(RPR)
Sun Don't Shine On The Same Folks...
Sawyer Brown; *Sawyer Brown* ....(LIB)
Survival
Bob Marley/Wailers; *Survival* .... (ISL)
Leonard Dillon The Ethiopian; *On The Road
Again* ....(HRT)
Moody Blues; *Octave* ....(POL)
O'Jays; *Collector's Items* ....(PI)
  Survival ....(PI)
Roachford; *Get Ready!* ....(EPI)
Yes; *Yes* ....(ATL)
  Yesterdays ....(ATL)
Survival Handbook Vs. Global Extinction
Sister Souljah; *360 Degrees Of Power* ....(EPI)
Survive
Jimmy Buffett; *Boats Beaches Bars & Ballads* ... (MGR)
  Volcano ....(MCA)
Surviving The Life
Neil Diamond; *Beautiful Noise* ....(COL)
  Love At The Greek ....(COL)
Susannah's Still Alive
Kinks; *Kink Kronikles* ....(RPR)
Sweet Life
Marie Osmond; */Paul Davis-All In Love* ....(CCB)
Paul Davis; *Best Of* ....(BNG)
  Singer Of Songs Teller Of Tales ....(BNG)
Taking My Life In Your Hands
Elvis Costello/Brodsky Quartet; *Juliet Letters* ..... (WB)
Terrorist's Life
D.I.; *What Good Is Grief To A God* .... (XXX)
That's Just The Way It Is
Phil Collins; *...But Seriously* .... (ATL)
That's Life
David Lee Roth; *Eat 'Em & Smile* ....(WB)
Frank Sinatra; *Collection* ....(RPR)
  Greatest Hits-#1&2 ....(RPR)
  Sinatra Reprise-Very Good Years ....(RPR)
  That's Life ....(RPR)
That's The Way It Goes
Benny Goodman & Peggy Lee; *Best Of The Big
Bands-#2* ....(COL)
  Featuring Peggy Lee ....(COL)
George Harrison; *Best Of Dark
Horse-1976-1989* ....(DKH)
  Gone Troppo ....(DKH)
Harptones; *WCBS FM101-History Of
Rock-Groups-#2* ....(CLT)
Theme From "One Life To Live"
Rosemary Joyce & Bill Bartholomew; *Soap Opera
Themes* ....(CRS)
There Are Many Stops Along The Way
Joe Sample; *Collection* ....(GRP)
  Rainbow Seeker ....(MCA)
There But For Fortune
Joan Baez; *First 10 Years* .... (VAN)
  Hits/Greatest & Others .... (VAN)
Phil Ochs; *Original New Folks* .... (VAN)
  There But For Fortune ....(ELE)
There's A Light
Doobie Brothers; *Livin' On The Fault Line* .... (WB)
There's A Lull In My Life
Ella Fitzgerald; *Essential-The Great Songs* ....(VRV)
  Like Someone In Love ....(VRV)

These Are The Days Of Our Lives
George Michael & Lisa Stansfield; *Five Live* .....(HOL)
Queen; *Classic Queen* ....(HOL)
  Innuendo ....(HOL)
Third Rock From The Sun
Joe Diffie; *Thousand Winding...* .... (EPI)
This Black Cat Has 9 Lives
Louis Armstrong; *What A Wonderful World* ...... (BLU)
Time Of My Life (I've Had The)
Bill Medley; *Best Of* ....(CCB)
Bill Medley & Jennifer Warnes; *Dirty Dancing Live In
Concert* ....(RCA)
  ST/Dirty Dancing ....(RCA)
Times Of Your Life
Paul Anka; *30th Anniversary Collection* .... (RHI)
  His Best .... (EMI)
To Give (The Reason I Live)
Frankie Valli/Four Seasons; *25th Anniversary
Collection* .... (RHI)
  Very Best Of ....(MCA)
To Keep My Love Alive
Ella Fitzgerald; *Rodgers & Hart Songbook* ....(VRV)
Mary Martin & Richard Rodgers; *Mary Martin Sings
Richard Rodgers Plays* ....(RCA)
To Life
Original Cast; *Fiddler On The Roof* ....(RCA)
To Live And Die In L.A.
Wang Chung; *ST/To Live And Die In L.A.* ....(GEF)
To Live Is To Die
Metallica; *...And Justice For All* ....(ELE)
Tomorrow Never Knows
Beatles; *Box Set* ....(CAP)
  Revolver ....(CAP)
Phil Collins; *Face Value* ....(ATL)
Touch Of Grey
Grateful Dead; *Heart Of Rock* ....(COL)
  In The Dark .... (ARI)
Treat Them Like They Want To Be Treated
Father M.C.; *Father's Day* .... (UT)
Treat 'Em Right
Chubb Rock; *Freddy's Dead-Final Nightmare* ... (MET)
  Nasty Wax .... (KT)
Tree Of Life
Les Baxter Orchestra & Chorus; *Brazil Now-African
Blue* ....(CRS)
Trying To Live My Life Without You
Bob Seger/Silver Bullet Band; *Nine Tonight* ......(CAP)
Turn! Turn! Turn!
Byrds; *Billboard Top Rock 'N' Roll Hits-1965* .... (RHI)
  Greatest Hits ....(COL)
  Original Singles-#1-1965-1967 ....(COL)
  Byrds (collection) ....(COL)
  ST/Forrest Gump ....(EPX)
  Turn! Turn! Turn! ....(COL)
Pete Seeger; *Greatest Hits* ....(COL)
  Troubadours Of The Folk Era-#2 .... (RHI)
Twist Of Fate
Olivia Newton-John; *Back To Basics-Essential
Collection* ....(GEF)
  ST/Two Of A Kind .... (MCA)
Two Lives
Bonnie Raitt; *Sweet Forgiveness* ....(WB)
Carpenters; *Voice Of The Heart* ....(A&M)
Randy Crawford; *Secret Combination* ....(WB)
Victim Of Life's Circumstances
Vince Gill; *Best Of* ....(RCA)
Vienna Life
Lawrence Welk; *22 All-Time Favorite Waltzes* .. (RAN)
Vietnam Veteran Still Alive
Country Joe McDonald; *Into The Fray* ....(RBB)
Wake Up & Live
Bob Marley/Wailers; *Survival* ....(TUF)
Cab Calloway; *Best Of The Big Bands* ....(COL)
Walk Of Life
Dire Straits; *Brothers In Arms* ....(WB)
  Money For Nothing ....(WB)
Way It Is
Bruce Hornsby/Range; *Heart Of Rock* ....(COL)
  Nipper's Greatest Hits-'80s ....(RCA)
  Way It Is ....(RCA)
We Gotta Live Together
Jimi Hendrix; *Band Of Gypsies* ....(CAP)
What Are You Doing In My Life
Tom Petty/Heartbreakers; *Damn The Torpedoes* (MCA)

What Are You Doing The Rest Of Your Life
Barbra Streisand; *Just For The Record* ....(COL)
   The Way We Were ....(COL)
Carmen McRae; *Great American Songbook* ......(ATL)
Joe Pass; *Best Of* ....(PAB)
What Do You Want From Life
Tubes; *Tubes* ....(A&M)
   T.R.A.S.H.-Tubes Rarities & Smash Hits ....(A&M)
   What Do You Want From-Live ....(A&M)
What Is Life
George Harrison; *All Things Must Pass* ....(CAP)
   Best Of ....(CAP)
George Harrison & Eric Clapton & Band; *Live In Japan* ....(DKH)
Wheel Of Life
Rance Allen; *Straight From The Heart* ....(STX)
Wheels Of Life
Gino Vannelli; *Best Of* ....(A&M)
   Brother To Brother ....(A&M)
   Classics-#7 ....(A&M)
Where Love Lives
Alison Limmerick; *S* ....(ARI)
Where'm I Gonna Live?
Billy Ray Cyrus; *Some Gave All* ....(MER)
Wild Life
INXS; *Kick* ....(ATL)
Wings; *Wild Life* ....(CAP)
Wild Side of Life
Freddie Fender; *Before The Next Teardrop Falls* (MCA)
   Best Of ....(MCA)
Hank Thompson; *All-Time Greatest Hits* ....(CCB)
   Best Of The Best Of ....(GUS)
   Capitol Collectors Series ....(CAP)
   Traditions In Country Music ....(CAP)
Rod Stewart; *Night On The Town* ....(WB)
Wild Wild Life
Talking Heads; *Popular Favorites-1984-1992* .....(SIR)
   True Stories ....(SIR)
Will The Wolf Survive
Los Lobos; *How Will The Wolf Survive* ....(SLS)
Waylon Jennings; *Country Classics-#6 (1985-1986)* ....(MSP)
   New Classic Waylon ....(MCA)
   Will The Wolf Survive ....(MCA)
Winter Of My Life
Freddy Fender; *Are You Ready For Freddy* .....(MCA)
Within You Without You
Beatles; *Box Set* ....(CAP)
   Sgt. Pepper's Lonely Hearts Club Band ....(CAP)
Worried Life Blues
B.B. King; *Turn On With* ....(KNT)
Eric Clapton; *24 Nights* ....(POL)
   Just One Night ....(POL)
John Lee Hooker; *Plays & Sings The Blues* .....(CSS)
Lightnin' Hopkins; *Best Of* ....(PRS)
   How Many More Years I Got ....(FAN)
Yellow Submarine
Beatles; *1962-1966* ....(CAP)
   Box Set ....(CAP)
   Reel Music ....(CAP)
   Revolver ....(CAP)
   Yellow Submarine ....(CAP)
You Are The Sunshine Of My Life
Peter Nero; *Greatest Hits* ....(COL)
Stevie Wonder; *20/20* ....(MOT)
   Original Musiquarium ....(MOT)
   Talking Book ....(MOT)
You Can't Always Get What You Want
Rolling Stones; *Flashpoint* ....(RS)
   Hot Rocks-1964-1971 ....(AKO)
   Let It Bleed ....(AKO)
   Love You Live ....(RS)
   Singles Collection-London Years ....(AKO)
You Decorated My Life
Kenny Rogers; *20 Great Years* ....(RPR)
   Greatest Hits ....(EMI)
   Twenty Greatest Hits ....(EMI)
You Light Up My Life
Debby Boone; *Best Of* ....(CCB)
   This Is Love-The Wedding Songs ....(SCO)
   You Light Up My Life ....(MCA)

You Stepped Into My Life
Bee Gees; *Children Of The World* ....(RSO)
   Greatest ....(POL)

LITTLE, Little In Amount
   See Also: SMALL for things of small size

Bring A Little Lovin'
Easybeats; *Best Of* ....(RHI)
Cheerful Little Earful
Ella Fitzgerald; *Swings Brightly With Nelson* .....(VRV)
Come A Little Bit Closer
Fleetwood Mac; *25 Years-The Chain* ....(WB)
   Heroes Are Hard To Find ....(RPR)
Jay/Americans; *All-Time Greatest Hits* ....(RHI)
   Good Vibrations (Sounds Of Top 40 Radio) ....(CAP)
   Greatest Hits ....(EMI)
Johnny Duncan & Janie Fricke; *Greatest Hits* ....(COL)
   Nice 'N' Easy ....(COL)
Cry Just A Little
Marie Osmond; *I Only Wanted You* ....(CAP)
Cry Just A Little Bit
Sylvia; *Greatest Hits* ....(RCA)
Eat A Little Something
Original Cast; *I Can Get It For You Wholesale* ....(SSP)
Every Day A Little Death
Original Cast; *Little Night Music* ....(COL)
Original London Cast; *Little Night Music* ....(RCA)
Every Little Bit Hurts
Brenda Holloway; *Motown Legends-Love Songs* . (MOT)
   Motown Memories-#2-Where Were You... ....(MOT)
   Motown Story-First 25 Years ....(MOT)
Gladys Knight/Pips; *Anthology* ....(MOT)
   Motown Legends ....(MOT)
Spencer Davis Group; *Best Of* ....(EMI)
   Best Of ....(RHI)
Give A Little
Nicolette Larson; *Nicolette* ....(WB)
Give A Little Bit
Supertramp; *Classics-#9* ....(A&M)
   Even In The Quietest Moments ....(A&M)
Give A Little Love
Judds; *Greatest Hits* ....(RCA)
Marvin Gaye & Tammi Terrell; *United* ....(MOT)
Stylistics; *45* ....(STW)
Ziggy Marley/Melody Makers; *Hey World!* ......(EMI)
   ST/Men At Work ....(MSA)
   ST/Tequila Sunrise ....(CAP)
   Time Has Come...Best Of ....(EMI)
Gotta Give A Little Love
Timmy Thomas; *Gotta Give A Little Love* ....(GLM)
Growin' A Little Each Day
Doobie Brothers; *Doobie Brothers* ....(WB)
I Cry Just A Little Bit
Shakin' Stevens; *45* ....(EPI)
In A Small Moment
Carly Simon; *Boys In The Trees* ....(ELE)
It's A Little Too Late
Tanya Tucker; *Can't Run From Yourself* ....(LIB)
I'm Gonna Love You Just A Little More
Barry White; *Greatest Hits* ....(20)
Just A Little
Beau Brummels; *Best Of* ....(RHI)
   Introducing The ....(RHI)
   Nuggets-#7-Early San Francisco ....(RHI)
   Super Oldies/'60s-#8 ....(AUF)
Just A Little Bit
Etta James; *Tell Mama* ....(CSS)
Jerry Butler; *Unavailable 16/Original Nitty Gritty* ...(VJ)
Mitch Ryder/Detroit Wheels; *Rev Up-Best Of* ....(RHI)
Steve Miller; *Born 2 B Blue* ....(CAP)
Just A Little Bit Better
Herman's Hermits; *XX-Greatest Hits* ....(AKO)
Just A Little Bit Of Rain
Fred Neil; *Just A Little Bit Of Rain* ....(ELE)
Linda Ronstadt; *Retrospective* ....(CAP)
Just A Little Bit Of You
Jackson 5; *Anthology* ....(MOT)
Michael Jackson; *Anthology* ....(MOT)
   Forever Michael ....(MOT)
   Motown Superstar Series-#7 ....(MOT)
Just A Little Bit South Of No. Carolina
Dean Martin; *Swingin' Down Yonder* ....(CAP)

Just A Little Closer
Pointer Sisters; *We Are The World* ....(COL)
Robbie Nevil; *Robbie Nevil* ....(EMI)
Just A Little Love
38 Special; *Strength In Numbers* ....(A&M)
B.B. King; *Live & Well* ....(MCA)
Reba McEntire; *45* ....(MCA)
 Greatest Hits ....(MCA)
 Just A Little Love ....(MCA)
Just A Little Lovin'
Barbra Streisand; *Stoney End* ....(COL)
Eddy Arnold; *Best Of* ....(RCA)
 Pure Gold ....(RCA)
Just A Little Too Much
Rick Nelson; *All My Best* ....(MCA)
 Souvenirs ....(LIB)
Kick A Little
Little Texas; *Kick A Little* ....(WB)
Lil' Ain't Enough
David Lee Roth; *Little Ain't Enough* ....(WB)
Little Bit Better
Herman's Hermits; *45* ....(AKO)
Little Bit Crazy
Eddy Raven; *Greatest Hits* ....(WB)
Little Bit In Love
Julie Andrews; *Little Bit Of Broadway* ....(COL)
Original Cast; *Wonderful Town* ....(MCA)
Patty Loveless; *16 Top Country Hits-#4* ....(MCA)
 If My Heart Had Windows ....(MCA)
Little Bit Independent
Fats Waller; *Complete-#3-1935-1936* ....(RCA)
Little Bit Me, A Little Bit You
Monkees; *Greatest Hits* ....(ARI)
Little Bit More
Dr. Hook; *Greatest Hits & More* ....(CAP)
 Rock Me Gently-Mellow Rock's Greatest ... (EMI)
Little Bit Of Emotion
Kinks; *Low Budget* ....(ARI)
Little Bit Of Green
Elvis Presley; *Back In Memphis* ....(RCA)
 From Memphis To Vegas ....(RCA)
Little Bit Of Happiness
New Christy Minstrels; *Greatest Hits* ....(COL)
Little Bit Of Heaven
Natalie Cole; *Dangerous* ....(MOD)
Ray Charles; *Seven Spanish Angels & Other Hits* .(COL)
Little Bit Of Love
Free; *Best Of* ....(A&M)
Little Bit Of Love (Is All It Takes)
New Edition; *All For Love* ....(MCA)
Little Bit Of Snow
Howard Jones; *One To One* ....(ELE)
Little Bit Of Soap
Jarmels; *Collectables Presents History Of Rock-#7* (CLT)
 Golden Classics ....(CLT)
 Laurie Golden Oldies ....(LAU)
 Million Dollar Memories-#1 ....(RCA)
 Pick Hits Of The Radio Good Guys ....(LAU)
Paul Davis; *Best Of* ....(BNG)
 Little Bit Of ....(BNG)
Little Bit Of Soul
Music Explosion; *Million Dollar Memories #1* ....(RCA)
 Best Of Ohio Express/Other Bubblegum-#1 ..... (RHI)
 Cruisin'-1967 ....(INC)
Little Bit Of Sympathy
Robin Trower; *Bridge Of Sighs* ....(CHR)
 Live ....(CHR)
Little Bit South Of North Carolina
Chuck Foster & Jimmy Castle; *Uncollected* ... (HIN)
Little Bit South Of Saskatoon
Sonny James; *American Originals* ....(COL)
Little Brains, A Little Talent
Original Cast; *Damn Yankees* ....(RCA)
Little By Little
Dusty Springfield; *Golden Hits* ....(MER)
James House; *Days Gone By* ....(EPI)
Nighthawks; *Open All Nite* ....(ADE)
Robert Plant; *Shaken 'N' Stirred* ....(EPR)
 Little By Little-Collector's Edition ....(EPR)
Rolling Stones; *Rolling Stones* ....(AKO)
Little Cocaine
Lee Clayton; *Naked City* ....(CAP)
Little Crazy
Fight; *War Of Words* ....(EPI)

Little Good News
Anne Murray; *Greatest Hits-#2* ....(CAP)
 Little Good News ....(CAP)
Little Gossip
Original Cast; *Man Of La Mancha* ....(MCA)
Little Less Talk And A Lot More Action
Toby Keith; *Toby Keith* ....(MER)
Little Love
Juice Newton; *Can't Wait All Night* ....(RCA)
 New Breed ....(RCA)
Little More Love
Janie Fricke; *It Ain't Easy* ....(COL)
Olivia Newton-John; *Greatest Hits-#2* .... (MCA)
 Totally Hot ....(MCA)
Little Night Dancin'
John Cougar Mellencamp; *John Cougar
 Mellencamp* ....(RIV)
Little Night Music
Original Cast; *Little Night Music* ....(COL)
Little Old Fashioned Karma
Willie Nelson; *Tougher Than Leather* ....(COL)
Little Rootie Tootie
Thelonius Monk; *High Priest* .... (PRS)
 In Person ....(MS)
 Memorial Album ....(MS)
 Piano Giants ....(PRS)
 Reflections #1 ....(PRS)
 Thelonius Monk ....(MS)
 Trio ....(PRS)
Little T & A
Rolling Stones; *Tattoo You* ....(RS)
Living A Little, Laughing A Little
John Hiatt; *Warming Up To The Ice Age* ....(GEF)
Spinners; *Live* ....(ATL)
 New & Improved ....(ATL)
Love A Little Stronger
Diamond Rio; *Love A Little Stronger* .... (ARI)
Love's Been A Little Bit Hard On Me
Juice Newton; *Greatest Hits* ....(CAP)
 Greatest Hits & More ....(CAP)
 Quiet Lies ....(CAP)
Minimum Love
Mac McAnally; *Nothin' But The Truth* ....(GEF)
Need A Little Taste Of Love
Doobie Brothers; *Cycles* ....(WB)
Only Here For A Little While
Billy Dean; *Young Man* ....(LIB)
Peking Theme (So Little Time)
Andy Williams; *ST/55 Days At Peking* ....(VS)
Put A Little Love Away
Emotions; *Chronicle* ....(STX)
 Sunshine ....(STX)
Put A Little Love In Your Heart
Annie Lennox & Al Green; *45* ....(A&M)
Jackie DeShannon; *ST/Drugstore Cowboy* ....(NOV)
 Very Best Of .... (EMI)
Save A Little Room In Your Heart For Me
Eddie Money; *Eddie Money* ....(COL)
Shine A Little Love
Electric Light Orchestra; *Afterglow* ....(EPI)
 Box Of Their Best ....(JET)
 Discovery ....(JET)
Spare Me A Little Of Your Love
Fleetwood Mac; *Bare Trees* ....(RPR)
Spend A Little Time
Joan Armatrading; *Whatever's For Us* ....(A&M)
Stand A Little Rain
Nitty Gritty Dirt Band; *20 Years Of Dirt-Best Of* .. (WB)
 Live Two Five ....(CAP)
Stay
Frankie Valli/Four Seasons; *Greatest Hits-#1* .... (RHI)
Jackson Browne; *Running On Empty* ....(ASY)
Maurice Williams/Zodiacs; *Best Of* ....(CLT)
 Billboard Top Rock 'N' Roll Hits-1960 ....(RHI)
 Cruisin'-1960 ....(INC)
 Rock & Roll Is Here To Stay ....(GUS)
 ST/Dirty Dancing ....(RCA)
Stay A Little Longer
Bob Wills; *Sounds Of Texas* ....(CAP)
Bob Wills/Texas Playboys; *Anthology-1935-1973* (RHI)
 Tiffany Transcriptions-#2 ....(KAL)
Willie Nelson; *Greatest Hits & Some That Will Be* (COL)
 Willie & Family Live ....(COL)

Take A Little Rhythm
Ali Thompson; *Take A Little Rhythm* .... (A&M)
Take Me For A Little While
Coverdale/Page; *Coverdale/Page* .... (GEF)
Try A Little Harder
Rolling Stones; *Singles Collection-London Years* . (AKO)
Try A Little Kindness
Glen Campbell; *Best Of* .... (LIB)
Best Of The Early Years .... (CCB)
Greatest Hits .... (LIB)
Try A Little Tenderness
Aretha Franklin; *Sweet Bitter Love* .... (COL)
Marty Robbins; *Don't Let Me Touch You* .... (COL)
Greatest Hits-#4 .... (COL)
Otis Redding; *Best Of* .... (ATC)
Best Of .... (ATL)
Live In Europe .... (ATC)
Story .... (ATC)
Very Best Of .... (RHI)
Three Dog Night; *Best Of* .... (MCA)
What A Little Moonlight Can Do
Billie Holiday; *Billie's Best* .... (VRV)
First Verve Sessions .... (VRV)
Greatest Hits .... (COL)
History Of The Real Billie Holiday .... (VRV)
Songbook .... (VRV)
Diana Ross; *ST/Lady Sings The Blues* .... (MOT)
Will He Wait A Little Longer
Stanley Brothers; *Stanley Series-Vol. 1-#3* ...... (COP)
With A Little Bit Of Luck
Julie Andrews/Original Cast; *My Fair Lady* ...... (COL)
Kiri Te Kanawa & Jeremy Irons/Orig. Cast; *My Fair
Lady* .... (LON)
Stanley Holloway; *ST/My Fair Lady* .... (COL)
With A Little Help From My Friends
Beatles; *1967-1970* .... (CAP)
Box Set .... (CAP)
Rarities .... (CAP)
Sgt. Pepper's Lonely Hearts Club Band .... (CAP)
Joe Cocker; *Classics-#4* .... (A&M)
Greatest Hits .... (A&M)
History Of British Rock-#9 .... (RHI)
ST/Woodstock .... (ATL)
With A Little Help From My Friends .... (A&M)
Ringo Starr/All-Star Band; *Nobody's Child-Romanian
Angel Appeal* .... (WB)
With A Little Luck
Paul McCartney/Wings; *All The Best* .... (CAP)
Wings Greatest .... (CAP)
Wings; *London Town* .... (CAP)
World Is A Little Bit Under The Weather
Meters; *Trick Bag* .... (RPR)

LUCK
See Also: CITIES: LAS VEGAS, GAMBLING

Bad Luck
B.B. King; *16 Original Big Hits* .... (FAN)
Harold Melvin/Blue Notes; *Collector's Item* .... (PI)
Philadelphia Classics .... (PI)
#12 .... (PI)
Bad Luck Streak In Dancing School
Warren Zevon; *Bad Luck Streak In Dancing
School* .... (ASY)
Better Luck Next Time
Judy Garland & Clinton Sundberg; *ST/Easter
Parade* .... (SSP)
Cowboys Don't Get Lucky All The Time
Gene Watson;
Beautiful Country .... (CAP)
ST/Convoy .... (UA)
Fortunate Son
Creedence Clearwater Revival; *1969* .... (FAN)
Chronicle .... (FAN)
Live In Europe .... (FAN)
More Gold .... (FAN)
ST/Forrest Gump .... (FAN)
Willy & The Poor Boys .... (FAN)
Friday The 13th
Alvin Lee; *Rocket Fuel* .... (RSO)
Friday The 13th Child
David Clayton-Thomas; *Clayton* .... (MCA)

Gone At Last
Paul Simon; *Still Crazy After All These Years* .....(COL)
Good Luck Charm
Elvis Presley; *50 Worldwide Gold Award Hits-#1* (RCA)
Golden Records-#3 ....(RCA)
Number One Hits ....(RCA)
Top Ten Hits ....(RCA)
Good Run Of Bad Luck
Clint Black; *No Time To Kill* ....(RCA)
Hard Luck Stories
Neil Young; *Landing On Water* ....(GEF)
Richard & Linda Thompson; *Pour Down Like
Silver* ....(CTH)
Hard Luck Story
Elton John; *Rock Of The Westies* ....(POL)
Hard Luck Woman
Garth Brooks; *Kiss My Ass* ....(MER)
Kiss; *Alive 2* ....(CAS)
Double Platinum ....(CAS)
Rock & Roll Over ....(CAS)
Hollywood (Down On Your Luck)
Thin Lizzy; *Lizzy Lives (1976-1984)* ....(GS)
Renegade ....(WB)
I Always Get Lucky With You
George Jones; *19 Hot Country Requests* ....(EPI)
By Request ....(EPI)
Shine On ....(EPI)
Merle Haggard; *Big City* ....(EPI)
I Feel Lucky
Mary Chapin Carpenter; *Come On Come On* ....(COL)
I'm Just A Lucky So & So
Duke Ellington; *Sophisticated Ellington* ....(RCA)
Ella Fitzgerald; *Fine & Mellow* ....(PAB)
I'm Looking Over A Four Leaf Clover
Al Jolson; *Story-#3-Rainbow 'Round My
Shoulder* ....(MCA)
Jerry Lee Lewis; *I Am What I Am* ....(MCA)
I'm Lucky
Joan Armatrading; *Classics-#21* ....(A&M)
Track Record ....(A&M)
Walk Under Ladders ....(A&M)
Just Lucky I Guess
Steve Goodman; *High & Outside* ....(ASY)
Just My Luck
Deele; *Street Beat* ....(SLR)
Knock On Wood
Amii Stewart; *45* ....(ARL)
Buddy Guy; *This Is* ....(VAN)
Eddie Floyd; *15 Original Big Hits-#3* ....(STX)
Atlantic R&B-1947-1974-#6-(1966-1969) .....(ATL)
Best Of Wattstax ....(STX)
Super Oldies/'60s-#11 ....(AUF)
Eric Clapton; *Behind The Sun* ....(DUC)
Ike & Tina Turner; *Greatest Hits-#3* ....(SAJ)
Lady Luck
David Lee Roth; *Little Ain't Enough* ....(WB)
Journey; *Captured* ....(COL)
Evolution ....(COL)
Kenny Loggins; *Celebrate Me Home* ....(COL)
Restless Heart; *Fast Moving Train* ....(RCA)
London Luck & Love
Daryl Hall & John Oates; *Bigger Than Both Of
Us* ....(RCA)
Love And Luck
Marty Stuart; *Love And Luck* ....(MCA)
Luck Be A Lady
Frank Sinatra; *Reprise Collection* ....(RPR)
Sinatra Reprise-The Very Good Years ....(RPR)
Original Cast; *Guys & Dolls* ....(MCA)
Luck Of The Irish
Elephants Memory/Invisible Strings; *Sometime In New
York City/Live Jam* ....(CAP)
Lucky Charm
Boys; *Messages From* ....(MOT)
Lucky For You
R.E.O. Speedwagon; *You Can Tune A Piano* ......(EPI)
Lucky Guy
Rickie Lee Jones; *Pirates* ....(WB)
Todd Rundgren; *Hermit Of Mink Hollow* ....(BRS)
Lucky In Love
Mick Jagger; *She's The Boss* ....(COL)
Sarah Vaughan; *Complete On
Mercury-#2-1956-1957* ....(MER)
Complete On Mercury-#3-1954-1956 ....(MER)

Lucky Man
Emerson, Lake & Palmer; *Best Of* .... (ATL)
  Emerson, Lake & Palmer .... (ATL)
Lucky Me
Anne Murray; *Country Hits* .... (CAP)
  Somebody's Waiting .... (CAP)
Lucky Moon
Oak Ridge Boys; *Unstoppable* .... (RCA)
Lucky Number
Artie Shaw; *Complete-#6-1942-1945* .... (RCA)
Lene Lovich; *Stateless* .... (STF)
Lucky One
Amy Grant; *House Of Love* .... (A&M)
Laura Branigan; *Self Control* .... (ATL)
Lucky Ones
Loverboy; *Big Ones* .... (COL)
  Get Lucky .... (COL)
Lucky Star
Madonna; *Immaculate Collection* .... (SIR)
  Madonna .... (SIR)
  MTV's Rock 'N' Roll To Go .... (ELE)
  Royal Box .... (SIR)
Lucky Town
Bruce Springsteen; *Lucky Town* .... (COL)
Luck's In
Steve Winwood; *Steve Winwood* .... (ISL)
Mr. Lucky
Henry Mancini; *All-Time Greatest Hits-#1* .... (RCA)
  Pure Gold .... (RCA)
John Lee Hooker; *Mr. Lucky* .... (POI)
  Urban Blues .... (MCA)
O Lucky Man
Alan Price; *ST/O Lucky Man* .... (WB)
Animals; *Greatest Hits Live! (Rip It To Shreds)* .... (IRS)
Only The Lucky
Walter Egan; *Fundamental Roll* .... (COL)
Running Out Of Luck
Mick Jagger; *She's The Boss* .... (COL)
She'd Rather Be With Me
Turtles; *Best Of* .... (RHI)
  Greatest Hits .... (RHI)
  Oldies But Goodies-#3 .... (OSR)
Some Guys Have All The Luck
Maxi Priest; *Best Of Me* .... (CHS)
  Maxi .... (VIA)
Robert Palmer; *Addictions-#1* .... (ISL)
Rod Stewart; *Camouflage* .... (WB)
  Storyteller-Complete Anthology-1964-1990 ..... (WB)
Sometimes I Get Lucky And Forget
Gene Watson; *Greatest Hits* .... (MCA)
Gene Watson/Farewell Party Band; *Sometimes I Get
Lucky* .... (MCA)
That Lucky Old Sun
Asleep At The Wheel; *Western Standard Time* .... (EPI)
Bing Crosby; *Radio Years* .... (CRS)
Frankie Laine; *16 Most Requested Songs* .... (COL)
  Golden Hits .... (MER)
  Greatest Hits .... (COL)
Jerry Garcia Band; *Jerry Garcia Band* .... (ARI)
Louis Armstrong; *Greatest Hits* .... (CCB)
Ray Charles; *Anthology* .... (RHI)
Willie Nelson; *Sound In Your Mind* .... (COL)
Third Time Lucky
Foghat; *Best Of* .... (RHI)
  Boogie Motel .... (RHI)
Three Coins In The Fountain
Andy Williams; *Moon River & Other Great Movie
Themes* .... (COL)
Doris Day & Frank De Vol Orchestra; *Hooray For
Hollywood-#2* .... (COL)
Frank Sinatra; *At The Movies* .... (CAP)
  Capitol Collectors Series .... (CAP)
Harry James; *Plays The Songs That Sold A
Million* .... (COL)
Till Good Luck Comes My Way
Original Cast; *Show Boat* .... (ANG)
Touch A Four Leaf Clover
Atlantic Starr; *Classics-#10* .... (A&M)
  Secret Lovers-Best Of .... (A&M)
  Yours Forever .... (A&M)
Try Your Luck
Four Coins; *20 Great Love Songs/'50s & '60s-#2* (LAU)
  22 LEaders Of The Pack-#1 .... (LAU)

Twinkle Twinkle Lucky Star
Merle Haggard; *Chill Factor* .... (EPI)
  Greatest Country Hits/'80s-1988 .... (COL)
Unlucky Girl
Big Mama Thornton; *Ball N' Chain* .... (ARH)
With A Little Bit Of Luck
Julie Andrews/Original Cast; *My Fair Lady* ...... (COL)
Kiri Te Kanawa & Jeremy Irons/Orig. Cast; *My Fair
Lady* .... (LON)
Stanley Holloway; *ST/My Fair Lady* .... (COL)
With A Little Luck
Paul McCartney/Wings; *All The Best* .... (CAP)
  Wings Greatest .... (CAP)
Wings; *London Town* .... (CAP)
You Got Lucky
Tom Petty/Heartbreakers; *Long After Dark* ..... (MCA)
  Pack Up The Plantation-Live .... (MCA)

MACHINES, Robots, Mind Control

Another Brick In The Wall, Part 2
Pink Floyd; *Collection Of Great Dance Songs* ....(COL)
  Delicate Sound Of Thunder .... (COL)
  The Wall .... (COL)
Roger Waters; *The Wall Live In Berlin* .... (MER)
Answering Machine
Kinsey Report; *Edge Of The City* .... (ALG)
Replacements; *Let It Be* .... (TT)
Rupert Holmes; *Partners In Crime* .... (INF)
Automatic
Go-Go's; *Beauty & The Beat* .... (IRS)
Jennifer Rush; *Jennifer Rush* .... (EPI)
Pointer Sisters; *Break Out* .... (PNT)
Prince; *1999* .... (WB)
Automatic Man
Michael Sembello; *Bossa Noval Hotel* .... (WB)
Automation
Howard Jones; *Dream Into Action* .... (ELE)
Big Bright Green Pleasure Machine
Simon & Garfunkel; *Collected Works* .... (COL)
  Parsley Sage Rosemary & Thyme .... (COL)
  ST/The Graduate .... (COL)
Brainwash
Rick Danko; *Rick Danko* .... (OOP)
Telex; *Sex* .... (PVC)
Brainwashed
Kinks; *Arthur Or Decline/Fall Of British Empire* .. (RPR)
  Everybody's In Show Biz .... (RHI)
Nuclear Assault; *Survive* .... (IRS)
Check My Machine
Paul McCartney; *CD Gift Set* .... (CAP)
  II .... (CAP)
Cool The Engines
Boston; *Third Stage* .... (MCA)
Custom Machine
Beach Boys; *Gift Set* .... (CAP)
  Little Deuce Coupe/All Summer Long .... (CAP)
  Spirit Of America .... (CAP)
Dancing Machine
Jackson 5; *14 Greatest Hits* .... (MOT)
  Anthology .... (MOT)
  Billboard Top Rock 'N' Roll Hits-1974 .... (MOT)
  Get It Together .... (MOT)
  Motown Dance Party-#2 .... (MOT)
  Motown Story-First 25 Years .... (MOT)
  Motown Superstar Series-#12 .... (MOT)
  Top 10 With A Bullet-Motown Dance Songs ... (MOT)
Feel Like A Number
Bob Seger/Silver Bullet Band; *Nine Tonight* ..... (CAP)
  Stranger In Town .... (CAP)
Fire In The Engine Room
Richard Thompson; *Across A Crowded Room* .... (POL)
Freak A Zoid
Midnight Star; *Greatest Hits* .... (SLR)
  No Parking On The Dance Floor .... (SLR)
Helpless Automation
Men At Work; *Business As Usual* .... (COL)
I Am A Machine
Guess Who; *No Strings Attached* .... (SST)
Meat Puppets; *Mirage* .... (SST)
I Am Not Mechanical
Judy Mowatt; *Only A Woman* .... (SHA)

I Am Your Robot
Elton John; *Jump Up!* .... (MCA)
I Love You (Miss Robot)
Buggles; *Age Of Plastic* .... (ISL)
I Robot
Alan Parsons Project; *Best Of-#2* .... (ARI)
   I Robot .... (ARI)
   Instrumental Voyages .... (ARI)
I'm Not A Robot
Newcleus; *Jam On Revenge* .... (SNV)
Jocko Homo (Q: Are We Not Men?)
Devo; *Best Of-Greatest Hits* .... (WB)
   Q: Are We Not Men? A: We Are Devo! .... (WB)
   Rest Of-Greatest Misses .... (WB)
John Henry
Harry Belafonte; *All-Time Greatest Hits* .... (RCA)
   At Carnegie Hall .... (RCA)
   Legendary Performer .... (RCA)
Little Jimmy Dickens; *Columbia Historic Edition* ..(COL)
Odetta; *Essential* .... (VAN)
   Greatest Folksingers Of The '60s .... (VAN)
Woody Guthrie; *Immortal-Golden Classics-#2* ... (CLT)
   Legendary .... (TRD)
Killing Machine
Judas Priest; *Hell Bent For Leather* ....(COL)
Lean, Mean, Lovin' Machine
Lee Greenwood; *You've Got A Good Love*
   Comin' .... (MCA)
Living In The Plastic Age
Buggles; *Age Of Plastic* .... (ISL)
Logical Song
Supertramp; *Breakfast In America* .... (A&M)
   Classics-#9 .... (A&M)
   Paris .... (A&M)
Lost My Drivin' Wheel
Tom Rush; *Best Of* ....(COL)
   Tom Rush ....(COL)
Love Has A Mind Of Its Own
Donna Summer; *She Works Hard For The Money* (MER)
Oak Ridge Boys; *Where The Fast Lane Ends* .... (MCA)
Love Machine
Country Joe/Fish; *C.J. Fish* .... (VAN)
   Life & Times Of .... (VAN)
Miracles; *12 #1 Hits From The '70s* .... (MOT)
   20-20 .... (MOT)
   Billboard Top Hits-1976 .... (RHI)
   Motown Story-First 25 Years .... (MOT)
   Top 10 With A Bullet-Motown Dance Songs ... (MOT)
Paul Butterfield Blues Band; *Keep On Movin'* ... (ELE)
Uriah Heep; *Live* .... (MER)
   Look At Yourself .... (MER)
Wham!; *Fantastic* ....(COL)
W.A.S.P.; *W.A.S.P.* .... (CAP)
Machine Messiah
Yes; *Drama* .... (ATL)
Machine Stops
Level 42; *Standing In The Light* .... (POL)
Machinery
Savage Republic; *Tragic Figures* .... (IP)
Sheena Easton; *Madness* .... (EMI)
   Money & Music .... (EMI)
Machines
Giorgio Moroder; *ST/Metropolis* ....(COL)
Modern English; *Ricochet Days* .... (SIR)
Queen; *Works* .... (HOL)
Master Mechanic
Johnny Winter; *Serious Business* ....(ALG)
Money Machine
James Taylor; *In The Pocket* .... (WB)
Mr. Roboto
Styx; *Caught In The Act* .... (A&M)
   Classics-#15 .... (A&M)
   Kilroy Was Here .... (A&M)
Muswell Hillbilly
Kinks; *Everybody's In Show Biz* .... (RHI)
   Muswell Hillbillies .... (RHI)
My Clone Sleeps Alone
Pat Benatar; *In The Heat Of The Night* .... (CHR)
M.A.C.H.I.N.E.
Stimulators; *Loud Fast Rules!* .... (ROI)
New Machine Pt. 1
Pink Floyd; *Momentary Lapse Of Reason* ....(COL)
   Shine On ....(COL)

New Machine Pt. 2
Pink Floyd; *Momentary Lapse Of Reason* ....(COL)
   Shine On ....(COL)
Propaganda Machine
1927; *...Ish* .... (ATL)
Radar For Love
Kiss; *Asylum* .... (MER)
Radar Love
Golden Earring; *Classic Rock-#1* .... (MCA)
   Live .... (MCA)
   Moontan .... (MCA)
   Super Hits/'70s-Have A Nice Day-#13 .... (RHI)
   '70s Greatest Rock Hits-#1-Hard N' Heavy .... (PRY)
Radar Rider
Riggs; *ST/Heavy Metal* .... (ASY)
Rhythm Machine
Bad Company; *Desolation Angels* .... (SS)
Robot
Robin Gibb; *Secret Agent* .... (MIR)
Robot Girl
Was (Not Was); *What Up Dog?* .... (CHR)
Robot Man
Connie Francis; *Rocksides-1957-1964* .... (POL)
Scorpions; *Best Of* ....(RCA)
   In Trance ....(RCA)
   Tokyo Tapes ....(RCA)
Robot Police
Baby Buddha; *Music For Teenage Sex* .... (PBO)
Robot Portrait
Quincy Jones/Orchestra; *Quintessence* .... (MCI)
Robots
Kraftwerk; *Man Machine* ....(CAP)
   The Mix .... (ELE)
Rock & Roll Machine
Triumph; *Classics* .... (MCA)
   Rock & Roll Machine .... (MCA)
   Stages .... (MCA)
Sex Machine
James Brown; *Revolution Of The Mind* .... (POL)
John Wagner Coalition; *Shades Of Brown-James
   Brown's Greatest* .... (KOA)
She Makes Me Shake Like A Soul Machine
Unrest; *Kustom Karnal Blackxploitation* ....(CRL)
She's My Machine
David Lee Roth; *Your Filthy Little Mouth* .... (RPR)
Situation
Heart; *Private Audition* .... (EPI)
Sixty Minute Man
Billy Ward/Dominoes; *Rock & Roll Show* .... (GUS)
Dominos; *Oldies But Goodies-#5* .... (OSR)
Rufus Thomas; */Carla Thomas-Chronicle* .... (STX)
Steel Monkey
Jethro Tull; *Crest Of A Knave* .... (CHR)
Street Machine
Super Stocks; *Monster Summer Hits-Drag City* ...(CAP)
Suicide Machine
Death; *Best Of* .... (REL)
Swell; *...Well?* .... (DEF)
Surfin' Sex Machine
Pajama Slave Dancers; *Blood Sweat & Beers* ..... (RES)
Time Machine
Barbra Streisand; *Emotion* ....(COL)
Black Sabbath; *Dehumanizer* .... (RPR)
   ST/Wayne's World .... (RPR)
Grand Funk Railroad; *Capitol Collectors Series* ..(CAP)
   Legends Of Rock Guitar-'70s .... (RHI)
   Mark Don & Mel: 1969-71 ....(CAP)
   On Time ....(CAP)
T. Graham Brown; *Come As You Were* ....(CAP)
Tin Man, The
Kenny Chesney; *In My Wildest Dreams* ....(CPC)
Turn On Your Radar
Prism; *Small Change* ....(CAP)
TVC 15
David Bowie; *Fame & Fashion* ....(RCA)
   Sound + Vision ....(RYK)
   Stage ....(RYK)
   Station To Station ....(RYK)
   ST/Christiane F ....(RCA)
   The Singles-1969-1993 ....(RYK)
War Machine
Kiss; *Creatures Of The Night* .... (CAS)
Way Back Machine
Heart; *Rock The House "Live"* ....(CAP)

Welcome To The Machine
Pink Floyd; *The Wall* ....(COL)
When The Machines Rock
Gary Numan/Tubeway Army; *Replicas* ....(ATC)
Zamboni
Martin Zellar; *The Hockey Zone* .... (SPO)

MAGIC, Miracles, Supernatural, Voodoo
See Also: MONSTERS, SPIRITS, UFO'S

Abracadabra
De Franco Family; *45* .... (20)
Steve Miller Band; *Abracadabra* ....(CAP)
Live ....(CAP)
Ain't No Trick (It Takes Magic)
Lee Greenwood; *Greatest Hits* ....(MCA)
Inside Out ....(MCA)
Inside Out/You've Got A Good Love Comin' ...(MCA)
All I Need Is A Miracle
Mike/Mechanics; *Classic Rock 1966-1988* ....(ATL)
Mike/Mechanics ....(ATL)
Amazing
Aerosmith; *Get A Grip* ....(GEF)
Animal Magic
Belouis Some; *Animal Magic* ....(CAP)
Blow Monkeys; *Animal Magic* ....(RCA)
Peter Gabriel; *Peter Gabriel* ....(ATL)
As If You Read My Mind
Stevie Wonder; *Hotter Than July* .... (MOT)
Astral Traveller
Yes; *Time & A Word* ....(ATL)
Yesterdays ....(ATL)
Astral Weeks
Van Morrison; *Astral Weeks* ....(WB)
Belgian Tom's Hat Trick
Whitesnake; *Trouble* ....(GEF)
Bermuda Triangle
Fleetwood Mac; *Heroes Are Hard To Find* ....(RPR)
Bermuda Triangle Blues (Flight 45)
Blondie; *Plastic Letters* ....(CHR)
Black Magic Woman
Fleetwood Mac; *25 Years-The Chain* ....(WB)
Vintage Years ....(SIR)
Santana; *Abraxas* ....(COL)
Greatest Hits ....(COL)
Moonflower ....(COL)
Rock Classics/'70s ....(COL)
Viva Santana ....(COL)
Book Of Miracles
Fleetwood Mac; *45* ....(WB)
Box Of Miracles
Barefoot Servants; *Barefoot Servants* ....(EPI)
Can You Read My Mind
Maureen McGovern; *Maureen McGovern* ....(WB)
Shirley Bassey; *ST/New York New York* .... (EMI)
Cool Magic
Steve Miller Band; *Abracadabra* ....(CAP)
Could It Be Magic
Barry Manilow; *Greatest Hits-#2* ....(ARI)
Live ....(ARI)
Donna Summer; *Love Trilogy* ....(CAS)
December Will Be Magic Again
Kate Bush; *12"* .... (EMI)
Deja Vu
Crosby, Stills, Nash & Young; *Deja Vu* ....(ATL)
So Far ....(ATL)
Dionne Warwick; *Dionne* ....(ARI)
Perfect 10 III ....(ARI)
Iron Maiden; *Somewhere In Time* ....(CAP)
Statler Brothers; *Maple Street Memories* ....(MER)
Teena Marie; *Compact Command Performances* (MOT)
Greatest Hits ....(MOT)
Wild & Peaceful ....(MOT)
Disappear
Church; *Seance* ....(ARI)
INXS; *X* ....(ATL)
Do You Believe In Magic?
Lovin' Spoonful; *Anthology* ....(RHI)
Best Of ....(ERI)
Even Better Than The Real Thing
U2; *Achtung Baby* .... (ISL)
Every Day Is Halloween
Ministry; *Twelve-Inch Singles-1981-1984* ....(WAX)

Every Little Thing He Does Is Magic
Shawn Colvin; *Cover Girl* ....(COL)
Every Little Thing She Does Is Magic
Police; *Every Breath You Take-Singles* .... (A&M)
Ghost In The Machine .... (A&M)
Eye In The Sky
Alan Parsons Project; *Eye In The Sky* .... (ARI)
Turn Of A Friendly Card .... (ARI)
E.S.P.
Bee Gees; *E.S.P.* ....(WB)
Deee-Lite; *World Clique* ....(ELE)
Duke Ellington; *In The Uncommon Market* ......(PAB)
#3-Studio Sessions-New York-1962 ....(SAJ)
Miles Davis; *E.S.P.* ....(COL)
Greatest Hits ....(COL)
Fortune Teller
Benny Spellman; *Best Of New Orleans R&B-#1* .. (RHI)
History Of New Orleans R&B-#2 .... (RHI)
Rolling Stones; *Got Live If You Want It* .... (AKO)
More Hot Rocks .... (AKO)
Friday The 13th
Alvin Lee; *Rocket Fuel* .... (RSO)
Friday The 13th Child
David Clayton-Thomas; *Clayton* .... (MCA)
Funky Cold Medina
Tone Loc; *Loc-ed After Dark* .... (DV)
God Is Alive, Magic Is Afoot
Buffy Sainte-Marie; *Best Of* .... (VAN)
Illuminations .... (VAN)
Grand Illusion
Eric Clapton; *August* ....(DUC)
Styx; *Classics-#15* ....(A&M)
Grand Illusion ....(A&M)
Happening
Diana Ross/Supremes; *Anthology* .... (MOT)
Greatest Hits-#1 & 2 .... (MOT)
Superstar Series-#1 .... (MOT)
Haunted Heart
Sammy Kershaw; *Haunted Heart* .... (MER)
He Walked On Water
Randy Travis; *No Holdin' Back* ....(WB)
Hocus Pocus
Gary Hoey; *Animal Instinct* ....(RPR)
Hypnotized
Fleetwood Mac; *25 Years-The Chain* ....(WB)
I Need A Miracle
Grateful Dead; *Shakedown Street* .... (ARI)
I Put A Spell On You
Creedence Clearwater Revival; *1968-1969* ......(FAN)
Chronicle ....(FAN)
Creedence Clearwater Revival ....(FAN)
More Creedence Gold .... (FAN)
Screamin' Jay Hawkins; *At Home With* ....(COL)
Elvira Presents Haunted Hits ....(RHI)
Rock & Roll Show ....(GUS)
If It's Magic
Stevie Wonder; *Songs In The Key Of Life* .... (MOT)
Tuck & Patti; *Love Warriors* ....(WH)
If You Could Read My Mind
Gordon Lightfoot; *Gord's Gold* ....(RPR)
If You Could Read My Mind ....(RPR)
Sit Down Young Stranger ....(RPR)
Into The Mystic
Van Morrison; *Moondance* ....(WB)
Too Late To Stop Now ....(WB)
Invisible Touch
Genesis; *Hit Singles 1980-1988* ....(ATL)
Invisible Touch ....(ATL)
It's A Miracle
Barry Manilow; *Greatest Hits-#1* .... (ARI)
II .... (ARI)
Live .... (ARI)
Culture Club; *Colour By Numbers* .... (VIA)
It's Gonna Take A Miracle
Deniece Williams; *Niecy* ....(COL)
Laura Nyro/LaBelle; *It's Gonna Take A Miracle* .(COL)
It's Magic
Dinah Washington; *What A Diff'rence A Day*
Makes .... (MER)
Doris Day; *Greatest Hits* ....(COL)
Michael Feinstein; *Sings The Jule Styne Songbook* (ELE)
Sarah Vaughan; *Complete On Mercury-#1-Great Jazz*
Years .... (MER)

Little Miss Magic
Jimmy Buffett; *Boats Beaches Bars & Ballads* ... (MGR)
   Coconut Telegraph .... (MCA)
Love Potion #9
Clovers; *ST/American Graffiti* .... (MCA)
   Super Oldies/'50s-#7 .... (AUF)
Herb Alpert/Tijuana Brass; *Classics-#1* .... (A&M)
   Greatest Hits .... (A&M)
Searchers; *Greatest Hits* .... (RHI)
   History Of British Rock-#3 .... (RHI)
Magic
Cars; *Greatest Hits* .... (ELE)
   Heartbeat City .... (ELE)
Eddie Money; *Nothing To Lose* .... (COL)
Electric Light Orchestra; *ST/Xanadu* .... (MCA)
Michael Nesmith; *Newer Stuff* .... (RHI)
Moody Blues; *Keys Of The Kingdom* .... (POL)
Olivia Newton-John; *Greatest Hits-#2* .... (MCA)
Pilot; *Super Hits/'70s-Have A Nice Day-#14* ..... (RHI)
Status Quo; *Status Quo* .... (MER)
Magic Bus
Who; *Greatest Hits* .... (MCA)
   Live At Leeds .... (MCA)
   Magic Bus .... (MCA)
   Meaty Beaty Big & Bouncy .... (MCA)
   ST/Kids Are Alright .... (MCA)
   Who's Last .... (MCA)
Magic Carpet Ride
Steppenwolf; *16 Greatest Hits* .... (MCA)
   Gold .... (MCA)
   Live .... (MCA)
   Nuggets-#9-Acid Rock .... (RHI)
   The Second .... (MCA)
Magic Fingers (25 Cents)
Birdsongs Of The Mesozoic; *Faultline* .... (CUN)
Magic Hotel
Wild Swans; *Space Flower* .... (SIR)
Magic In December
Tom Barabas; *Incredible Invincible Sampler* ...... (INV)
Magic Jewelled Limousine
Nasa; *Insha-Allah!* .... (SIR)
   ST/Wild Orchid .... (SIR)
Magic Man
Heart; *Dreamboat Annie* .... (CAP)
   Greatest Hits-Live .... (EPI)
Magic Mirror
Leon Russell; *Carney* .... (MCA)
Whirlers; *Harlem Holiday-New York R&B* .... (CLT)
Magic Moon
Peter Frampton; *Something's Happening* .... (A&M)
Magic Power
Triumph; *Allied Forces* .... (MCA)
   Classics .... (MCA)
   Stages .... (MCA)
Magical Mystery Tour
Beatles; *1967-1970* .... (CAP)
   Magical Mystery Tour .... (CAP)
   Reel Music .... (CAP)
Magic, Magic
Original Broadway Cast; *Carnival* .... (POL)
Make The Music Magic
Be Bop Deluxe; *Modern Music* .... (HAR)
Midnight Magic
38 Special; *Rock & Roll Strategy* .... (A&M)
Commodores; *Midnight Magic* .... (MOT)
Miracle
Bon Jovi; *Blaze Of Glory* .... (MER)
Moody Blues; *Sur La Mer* .... (POL)
Queen; *Classic Queen* .... (HOL)
   Miracle .... (HOL)
Stylistics; *Best Of-#2* .... (AMH)
Suicidal Tendencies; *How Will I Laugh Tomorrow When*
I... .... (EPI)
Whitney Houston; *I'm Your Baby Tonight* .... (ARI)
Miracle Cure
Who; *Join Together* .... (MCA)
   ST/Tommy .... (POL)
   Tommy .... (MCA)
Miracle Man
Elvis Costello; *My Aim Is True* .... (COL)
Ozzy Osbourne; *Just Say Ozzy* .... (EPA)
   No Rest For The Wicked .... (EPA)
Rain People; *Rain People* .... (EPI)

Miracles
Don Williams; *Best Of-#3* .... (MCA)
   Especially For You .... (MCA)
Jefferson Starship; *Balance-Collection* .... (RHI)
   Gold .... (GRU)
   Nipper's Greatest Hits-'70s .... (RCA)
   Red Octopus .... (GRU)
Motorcycle Mystics
Dave Stewart/Spiritual Cowboys; *Honest* ...... (ARI)
Music Trance
Ben E. King; *Music Trance* .... (ATL)
Mystic Eyes
Them; *Here Comes The Night* .... (OOP)
   History Of British Rock-#6 .... (RHI)
Mystic Rhythms
Rush; *Chronicles* .... (MER)
   Power Windows .... (MER)
   Show Of Hands .... (MER)
Mystic Traveler
Dave Mason; *Let It Flow* .... (COL)
Mystical Potato Head Groove Thing
Joe Satriani; *Flying In A Blue Dream* .... (REL)
Never Saw A Miracle
Curtis Stigers; *Curtis Stigers* .... (ARI)
Night Time Magic
Larry Gatlin/Gatlin Brothers; *17 Greatest Hits* ...(COL)
   Greatest Hits .... (COL)
   Live At 8:00 .... (CAP)
   Oh Brother .... (COL)
On A Clear Day You Can See Forever
Barbra Streisand; *Barbra Streisand* .... (COL)
   Just For The Record .... (COL)
   Live At The Forum .... (COL)
   ST/On A Clear Day You Can See Forever ..... (SMP)
Frank Sinatra; *Strangers In The Night* .... (RPR)
Hollies; *Greatest Hits* .... (EPI)
Roger Williams; *Best Of* .... (MCA)
   Somewhere In Time .... (BAI)
One-Trick Pony
Paul Simon; *ST/One-Trick Pony* .... (WB)
Open Sesame
Freddie Hubbard; *Best Of* .... (BLN)
   Open Sesame .... (BLN)
Kool/Gang; *Everything's Kool/Gang-Greatest Hits* (MER)
   Spin Their Top Hits .... (DL)
   ST/Saturday Night Fever .... (POL)
"Outer Limits" Theme
Original Music; *Television's Greatest Hits-#2* ..... (TVT)
Pinball Wizard
Elton John; *Greatest Hits-#2* .... (POL)
Pete Townshend; *Another Scoop* .... (ATC)
   Pete Townshend's Deep End-Live .... (ATC)
Rod Stewart; *Best Of* .... (MER)
   Sing It Again Rod .... (MER)
   Storyteller-Complete Anthology-1964-1990 ..... (WB)
Who; *Greatest Hits* .... (MCA)
   Meaty Beaty Big & Bouncy .... (MCA)
   ST/Kids Are Alright .... (MCA)
   Tommy .... (MCA)
   Who's Last .... (MCA)
Psychic Elephant
Shankar; *Vision* .... (ECM)
Puff (The Magic Dragon)
Peter, Paul & Mary; *In Concert* .... (WB)
   Moving .... (WB)
   Peter Paul & Mommy .... (WB)
   Ten Years Together-Best Of .... (WB)
Rainmaker
Dillards; *There Is A Time-1963-1970* .... (VAN)
Traffic; *Low Spark Of High-Heeled Boys* .... (ISL)
Rope The Moon
John Michael Montgomery; *Kickin' It Up* .... (ATL)
Rudy The Magic Crow
Swamp Zombies; *Chicken Vulture Crow* .... (DD)
Seven Wonders
Fleetwood Mac; *Tango In The Night* .... (WB)
Shaman's Blues
Doors; *Soft Parade* .... (ELE)
Shaman's Song
Shadowfax; *Dreams Of Children* .... (WH)
Shazam
Duane Eddy; *Twang Thang-Anthology* .... (RHI)

She's A Miracle
Exile; *19 Hot Country Requests-#3* .... (EPI)
   Greatest Hits .... (EPI)
   Kentucky Hearts .... (EPI)
Silver Springs
Fleetwood Mac; *25 Years-The Chain* .... (WB)
Snake Charmer
John Hiatt; *ST/White Nights* .... (ATL)
Ritchie Blackmore; *Rainbow* .... (POL)
Ted Nugent; *State Of Shock* .... (EPI)
Solsbury Hill
Peter Gabriel; *Peter Gabriel* .... (ATC)
   Plays Live .... (GEF)
   Shaking The Tree-16 Golden Greats .... (GEF)
Some Enchanted Evening
Jay/Americans; *All-Time Greatest Hits* .... (RHI)
   Come A Little Big Closer-Best Of .... (EMI)
Original Cast; *South Pacific* .... (COL)
Perry Como; *All-Time Greatest Hits-#1* ....(RCA)
Rosanno Brazzi; *ST/South Pacific* ....(RCA)
Willie Nelson; *What A Wonderful World* ....(COL)
Spanish Castle Magic
Jimi Hendrix; *Axis: Bold As Love* .... (RPR)
   Lifelines/Story .... (RPR)
   Live At Winterland ....(RYK)
   Radio One ....(RYK)
Spooky
Atlanta Rhythm Section; *Underdog* ....(COL)
Classics IV; *Good Vibrations* .... (CAP)
   Spooky .... (LIB)
   Spring Break-#1-Hot Rods & Hot Bods ...... (CAP)
   Very Best Of .... (EMI)
Springtime Magic
Lonnie Liston Smith; *Loveland* ....(COL)
Strange Brew
Cream; *Disraeli Gears* .... (POL)
   Strange Brew-Very Best Of .... (POL)
Eric Clapton; *Crossroads* .... (POL)
Strange Magic
Electric Light Orchestra; *Afterglow* .... (EPI)
   Face The Music .... (JET)
   Greatest Hits .... (JET)
   Ole E.L.O. .... (JET)
Supermen
David Bowie; *Hunky Dory* ....(RYK)
   Man Who Sold The World ....(RYK)
   Sound + Vision ....(RYK)
Supernatural
Army Of Lovers; *Army Of Lovers* .... (GIA)
John Mayall; *London Blues-1964-1969* ....(DER)
John Mayall/Bluesbreakers; *Legends Of Rock*
   Guitar-'60s-#2 .... (RHI)
Madonna; *Red Hot + Dance* ....(COL)
New Edition; *Soundtrack Smashes-'80s & More* . (MCA)
Supernatural Thing-Pt. 1
Ben E. King; *Soul Hits/'70s* .... (RHI)
   Stand By Me-Best Of .... (ATL)
Superstition
Stevie Wonder; *20/20* .... (MOT)
   Original Musiquarium .... (MOT)
   Talking Book .... (MOT)
That Old Black Magic
Ella Fitzgerald; *Best Of* .... (MCA)
   Big Bands Of The Swinging Years .... (EVR)
   In Rome-Birthday Concert .... (VRV)
Frank Sinatra; *Come Swing With Me* ....(CAP)
Glenn Miller/Orchestra; *Chattanooga Choo-Choo-#1*
   Hits .... (BLU)
Judy Garland; *Best Of* .... (MCA)
Louis Prima & Keely Smith; *Memories Are Made Of*
   This .... (CAP)
Marcels; *Best Of* .... (RHI)
Sammy Davis, Jr.; *Hey There-At His Dynamite*
   Greatest .... (MCA)
Spike Jones; *Best Of-#2* ....(RCA)
Theme From "Superman"
London Symphony Orchestra/John Williams;
   ST/Superman-The Movie .... (WB)
Neil Norman; *Greatest Science Fiction Hits* .... (CRS)
Theme From "The Addams Family"
Vic Mizzy; *Elvira Presents Haunted Hits* .... (RHI)
   Haunted Hits .... (RHI)
   Original Music From ....(RCA)

This Magic Moment
Drifters; *Golden Hits* .... (ATL)
   Greatest Hits ....(GUS)
Jay/Americans; *All-Time Greatest Hits* .... (RHI)
   Come A Little Bit Closer-Best Of .... (EMI)
Marvin Gaye; *M.P.G.* .... (MOT)
Thriller
Michael Jackson; *Thriller* .... (EPI)
Tiki Tiki Tiki Room
Original Music; *Disney Collection-#1* ....(DIS)
Trick Bag
Blues Brothers; *Red White & Blues* .... (TST)
Earl King; *Best Of New Orleans R&B-#1* .... (RHI)
Kevin Eubanks; *Face To Face* .... (GRP)
Robert Palmer; *Riptide* .... (ISL)
Trick Of The Light
Who; *Who Are You* .... (MCA)
Trick Of The Tail
Genesis; *Trick Of The Tail* .... (ATC)
Trick Rider
McBride & The Ride; *Sacred Ground* .... (MCA)
Twilight Zone
Golden Earring; *Cut* .... (21)
   Something Heavy Going Down .... (21)
Iron Maiden; *Killers* .... (CAP)
Manhattan Transfer; *Anthology-Down In Birdland* (RHI)
   Best Of .... (ATL)
   Extensions .... (ATL)
Neil Norman/Cosmic Orchestra; *Elvira Presents Haunted*
   Hits .... (RHI)
   Halloween Hits .... (RHI)
Under Your Spell
Atlantic Starr; *We're Movin' Up* .... (WB)
Bob Dylan; *Knocked Out Loaded* ....(COL)
Fire Town; *Good Life* .... (ATL)
Mason Ruffner; *Gypsy Blood* .... (EPA)
Phyllis Hyman; *Under Her Spell-Greatest Hits* .... (ARI)
Under Your Spell Again
Buck Owens; *All-Time Greatest Hits-#1* .... (CCB)
   Billboard Top Country Hits-1959 .... (RHI)
Veteran Of The Psychic Wars
Blue Oyster Cult; *Extraterrestrial-Live* ....(COL)
   Fire Of Unknown Origin ....(COL)
Voodoo
Black Sabbath; *Live Evil* .... (WB)
   Mob Rules .... (WB)
Body Count; *Body Count* .... (SIR)
Chris Isaak; *Silvertone* .... (WB)
Meters; *Good Old Funky Music* .... (ROU)
Neville Brothers; *Yellow Moon* .... (A&M)
Voodoo Child
Voodoo Child; *Best Of Techno-#1* .... (PRO)
Voodoo Chile
Jimi Hendrix; *Concerts* .... (RPR)
   Essential-#1 & 2 .... (RPR)
   Kiss The Sky .... (RPR)
   Lifelines/Story .... (RPR)
Jimi Hendrix Experience; *Electric Ladyland* ..... (RPR)
Stevie Ray Vaughan/Double Trouble; *Couldn't Stand*
   The Weather .... (EPI)
   Live Alive .... (EPI)
Voodoo Daddy
Lonnie Brooks; *Bayou Lightning* .... (ALG)
Voodoo Doll
Soul Asylum; *Say What You Will* .... (TT)
Voodoo Jammin'
Dancing Fantasy; *Moonlight Reflections* .... (INN)
Voodoo Kiss
Mr. Big; *Lean Into It* .... (ATL)
Voodoo Medicine Man
Aerosmith; *Pump* .... (GEF)
Voodoo Music
Tuck & Patti; *Dream* ....(WH)
Voodoo Sex Doll
Crisis Party; *Rude Awakening* .... (MET)
Voodoo Village
Bola Sete; *Incomparable* .... (FAN)
Voodoo Voodoo
La Vern Baker; *Elvira Presents Haunted Hits* ..... (RHI)
Voodoo Woman
Bobby Goldsboro; *Honey-The Best Of* .... (EMI)
Koko Taylor; *I Got What It Takes* .... (ALG)

Walk On The Water
Creedence Clearwater Revival; *1968-1969* ...... (FAN)
  Chronicle-#2 .... (FAN)
  Creedence Clearwater Revival .... (FAN)
Neil Diamond; *And The Singer Sings His Songs* . (MCA)
  Glory Road-1968-1972 .... (MCA)
  Moods .... (MCA)
Walk On Water
Dio; *Lock Up The Wolves* .... (RPR)
Eddie Money; *Greatest Hits-Sound Of Money* ....(COL)
  Nothing To Lose .... (COL)
Marc Cohn; *Marc Cohn* .... (ATL)
Marillion; *Six Of One-Half-Dozen Of The Other* .. (IRS)
T. Graham Brown; *Brilliant Conversationalist* ....(CAP)
When The Spell Is Broken
Richard Thompson; *Across A Crowded Room* .... (POL)
  Watching The Dark-History Of ....(RYK)
Which Way You Goin' Billy
Poppy Family; *Super Hits/'70s-Have A Nice
Day-#2* .... (RHI)
"Wonder Woman" Theme
Original Music; *Television's Greatest Hits-#3* ..... (TVT)
Wondrous Stories
Yes; *Classic Yes* .... (ATL)
  Going For The One .... (ATL)
  Yesshows .... (ATL)
Yellow Magic
Yellow Magic Orchestra; *Yellow Magic
Orchestra* .... (A&M)
You Can Do Magic
America; *Encore-More Greatest Hits* .... (RHI)
  In Concert .... (CAP)
  View From The Ground .... (CAP)
You Make Loving Fun
Fleetwood Mac; *25 Years-The Chain* .... (WB)
  Greatest Hits .... (WB)
  Rumours .... (WB)
Your Love Amazes Me
John Berry; *John Berry* .... (LIB)
Your Love Is A Miracle
Mark Chesnutt; *Too Cold At Home* .... (MCA)
You're Amazing
Robert Palmer; *Don't Explain* .... (EMI)

MAIL, Letters, Messages, Post Office

Air Mail Special
Ella Fitzgerald; *Billie Holiday & Ella* .... (MCA)
Lionel Hampton; *Best Of* .... (MCA)
  Hamp's Golden Favorites .... (MCA)
Quincy Jones; *Great Wide World Of Quincy Jones:
Live!* .... (MER)
All My Loving
Beatles; *At The Hollywood Bowl* .... (CAP)
  Beatles .... (CAP)
  Meet The Beatles .... (CAP)
  With The .... (CAP)
Another Day (Another Letter)
Boz Scaggs; *Boz Scaggs* .... (ATL)
Because I Love You (The Postman Song)
Stevie B; *Because I Love You (The Postman
Song)* .... (LMR)
  Best Of .... (LMR)
  Love & Emotion .... (LMR)
Blue Letter
Fleetwood Mac; *Fleetwood Mac* .... (RPR)
Bringing In The Georgia Mail
Norman Blake; *Back Home In Sulphur Springs* .. (ROU)
Calling, The
Yes; *Talk* .... (VCT)
Check's In The Mail
Victory; *Don't Get Mad-Get Even* .... (MRY)
C.O.D. (I'll Deliver)
Mtume; *You Me & He* .... (EPI)
Dear Jean (I'm Nervous)
City Boys; *Young Men Gone West* .... (MER)
Dear John Letter
Jean Shepard & Ferlin Husky; *45* .... (CAP)
Dear John Letter Lounge
Jerry Jeff Walker; *It's A Good Night For Singin'* . (MCA)
Dear John & Marsha Letter
Stan Freberg; *Capitol Collectors Series* .... (CAP)

Dear Me
Lorrie Morgan; *Leave The Light On* .... (BNA)
Death Letter Blues
Leadbelly; *King Of The Twelve-String Guitar* .....(COL)
  Leadbelly .... (COL)
Did You Get That Letter I Throwed In...
Arthur "Big Boy" Crudup; *Crudup's Mood* .... (DEL)
Down In The Valley
Elvis Presley; *Reconsider Baby* .... (RCA)
Leadbelly; *Defense Blues-Golden Classics-#2* ..... (CLT)
Pete Seeger; *American Favorite Ballads-#1* ...... (FLW)
Electric Messengers
220 Volt; *Electric Messengers* .... (EPI)
Faded Love
Bob Wills/Texas Playboys; *For The Last Time* .... (UA)
  24 Great Hits .... (POL)
  Tiffany Transcriptions-#2 .... (KAL)
Mickey Gilley; *Greatest Hits-#1* .... (EPI)
Patsy Cline; *12 Greatest Hits* .... (MCA)
Willie Nelson; *Greatest Hits & Some That Will Be* (COL)
Fan Mail
Blondie; *Plastic Letters* .... (CHR)
Dickies; *Dawn Of* .... (A&M)
  Great Dictations Of .... (A&M)
Fire Ball Mail
John McEuen; *String Wizards* .... (VAN)
Roy Acuff; *Best Of* .... (CAP)
Fireball Mail
Roy Acuff; *Best Of* .... (CAP)
  Greatest Hits .... (COL)
  Opry Legends .... (CAP)
Get The Message
Electronic; *Electronic* .... (WB)
Got A Letter From My Kid Today
Merle Haggard/Strangers; *Working Man Can't Get
Nowhere Today* .... (CAP)
Gotta Get A Message To You
Bee Gees; *Gold-#1* .... (OOP)
  Live .... (OOP)
Handle With Care
Traveling Wilburys; *Traveling Wilburys-#1* .... (WIL)
Hello Muddah, Hello Fadduh
Allan Sherman; *Dr. Demento Greatest Novelty CD* (RHI)
  Dr. Demento's Greatest-#3 .... (RHI)
Hey Western Union Man
Jerry Butler; *Best Of* .... (MER)
  Billboard Top R&B Hits-1968 .... (RHI)
I Got The Message
Big Jay McNeely; *Swingin'* .... (CLT)
Men Without Hats; *Rhythm Of Youth* .... (MCA)
ZZ Top; *Afterburner* .... (WB)
I Wrote A Letter
Starz; *Coliseum Rock* .... (CAP)
In A Letter To You
Eddy Raven; *Temporary Sanity* .... (CAP)
In Your Letter
R.E.O. Speedwagon; *Hi-Infidelity* .... (EPI)
  Jane Fonda's Workout .... (COL)
It Came In The Mail
Fuzztones; *In Heat* .... (BEG)
I'm Gonna Sit Right Down & Write...
Frank Sinatra; *Sinatra-Basie* .... (RPR)
  Songs For Young Lovers & Swing Easy .... (CAP)
Nat King Cole; *Gift Set* .... (CAP)
  Just One OF Those Things (& More) .... (CAP)
Original Cast; *Ain't Misbehavin'* .... (RCA)
Junk Mail
Circle Jerks; *Gig* .... (REL)
  Golden Shower Of Hits .... (AVE)
Keep In Touch
Robert Palmer; *Some People Can Do What They
Like* .... (ISL)
Last Letter
Jack Greene; *Sings His Best* .... (SO)
Ray Price; *Heart Of Country Music* .... (SO)
Last Love Letter
Alison Krauss & Union Station; *Every Time You Say
Goodbye* .... (ROU)
Letter
Karla Bonoff; *Restless Nights* .... (COL)

Loretta Lynn & Conway Twitty; *Best Of Conway &*
Loretta .... (MSP)
   Play Guitar Play .... (MCA)
   United Talent .... (MCA)
   Very Best Of .... (MCA)
Lowell Fulson; *Let's Go Get Stoned* .... (KNT)
   Now .... (KNT)
Letter From America
Proclaimers; *This Is The Story* .... (CHR)
Letter From Earth
Black Sabbath; *Dehumanizer* .... (RPR)
Letter From Home
Eddie Jefferson; *Letter From Home* .... (RVR)
Letter From Spain
Electric Light Orchestra; *Secret Messages* ...(JET)
Letter From Tina
Ike & Tina Turner; *Best Of* .... (EMI)
   Golden Classics .... (CLT)
Letter Full Of Tears
Gladys Knight/Pips; *Anthology* .... (MOT)
   Echoes Down The Hall-16 Orig. Doo-Wop ..... (ARI)
   Greatest Hits .... (CCB)
Letter Home
Elvis Costello/Brodsky Quartet; *Juliet Letters* ..... (WB)
Forester Sisters; *Greatest Hits* .... (WB)
Memphis Slim; *All Kinds Of Blues* .... (BV)
Wendy Waldman; *Letters Home* .... (CYP)
Letter In The Mail
James Taylor; *Never Die Young* .... (COL)
Letter Never Sent
R.E.M.; *Reckoning* .... (IRS)
Letter To Americans
Albert Brooks; *Star Is Bought* .... (ASY)
Letter To Elise
Cure; *Wish* .... (FIC)
Letter To Hermoine
David Bowie; *Space Oddity* .... (RYK)
Letter To L.A.
Joe Ely; *Live At Liberty Lunch* .... (MCA)
   Lord Of The Highway .... (HT)
Letters To The President
Sly & Robbie; *Silent Assassin* .... (ISL)
Letter, The
Box Tops; *Billboard Top Rock 'N' Roll Hits-1967* (RHI)
   Cruisin'-1967 .... (INC)
   Greatest Hits .... (RHI)
   Oldies But Goodies-#12 .... (OSR)
   Rockin' '60s .... (PRY)
Joe Cocker; *Classics-#4* .... (A&M)
   Greatest Hits .... (A&M)
   Live .... (CAP)
   Mad Dogs & Englishmen .... (A&M)
Medallions; *Golden Classics* .... (CLT)
   Oldies But Goodies-#1 .... (OSR)
Lettres D'Amour
Sweet; *Level-Headed* .... (CAP)
(Love Always) Letter To Home
Glen Campbell; *45* .... (AA)
   (Love Always) Letter To Home .... (AA)
Love Is The Message
MFSB; *Philadelphia Classics* .... (PI)
Love Letters
Elvis Presley; *Golden Records-#4* .... (RCA)
   Love Letters From Elvis .... (RCA)
   Valentine Gift For You .... (RCA)
Joe Walsh; *You Bought It You Name It* .... (WB)
Ketty Lester; *Sultry Soul Sisters-Wonder*
Women-#3 .... (RHI)
Peggy Lee; *Best Of* .... (MCA)
Ronnie Milsap; *Lost In the Fifties Tonight* .... (RCA)
Smokey Robinson; *Quiet Storm* .... (MOT)
Love Letters In The Sand
Pat Boone; *16 Great Performances* .... (MCA)
   Best Of .... (MCA)
   Vintage Music-Original Oldies/'50s-#2 .... (MCA)
Love, Me
Collin Raye; *All I Can Be* .... (EPI)
   Greatest Country Hits/'90s-1992 .... (COL)
Mail Order Annie
Harry Chapin; *Gold Medal Collection* .... (ELE)
   Short Stories .... (ELE)
Mail Order Woman
Champion Jack Dupree; *Blues For Everybody* .... (IGR)

Mailman Blues
Lloyd Price; *Greatest Hits* .... (CCB)
   Lloyd Price .... (SPE)
Mailman, Bring Me No More Blues
Buddy Holly; *Buddy Holly* .... (MCA)
Memphis Mail
Eli Owens; *Roosevelt Holts & His Friends* .... (ARH)
Message
Gene Loves Jezebel; *House Of Dolls* .... (GEF)
Grandmaster Flash/Furious Five; *Hip-Hop Greats* (RHI)
   Rap Hall Of Fame .... (KT)
Styx; *Pieces Of Eight* .... (A&M)
Message In A Bottle
Police; *Every Breath You Take-The Singles* ...... (A&M)
   Reggatta De Blanc .... (A&M)
Sting; *Secret Policemen's Other Ball* .... (ISL)
Message Of Love
Jimi Hendrix; *Band Of Gypsys* .... (CAP)
Pretenders; *Extended Play* .... (SIR)
   II .... (SIR)
   The Singles .... (SIR)
Message To Michael
Dionne Warwick; *Anthology-1962-1971* ...... (RHI)
   Dionne Warwick .... (EVR)
   Greatest Hits .... (EVR)
   Hot! Live & Otherwise .... (ARI)
   Original Rock 'N' Roll Hits Of The '60s .... (RLL)
Message To You Rudy
Specials; *Gangsters* .... (CHR)
No Letter Today
Bill Haley/Comets; *Rock Around The Country* ... (CRS)
No Reply
Beatles; *Box Set* .... (CAP)
   For Sale .... (CAP)
   '65 .... (CAP)
No Reply At All
Genesis; *Abacab* .... (ATL)
Note You Never Wrote
Wings; *At The Speeed Of Sound* .... (CAP)
One Sweet Letter From You
Benny Goodman; *Roll 'Em* .... (COL)
Open Letter To George Bush
Wayne Horvitz/The President; *Miracle Mile* ...... (ELE)
Open Letter (To A Landlord)
Living Colour; *Vivid* .... (EPI)
Personally
Karla Bonoff; *Wild Heart Of The Young* .... (COL)
Please Mr. Postman
Beatles; *Box Set* .... (CAP)
   Second Album .... (CAP)
   With The Beatles .... (CAP)
Carpenters; *Classics-#2* .... (A&M)
   Horizon .... (A&M)
   Yesterday Once More .... (A&M)
Marvelettes; *Anthology* .... (MOT)
   Billboard Top Rock 'N' Roll Hits-1961 .... (RHI)
   Greatest Hits .... (MOT)
   Motown Story .... (MOT)
Please Take A Letter Miss Brown
Ink Spots; *Best Of* .... (MCA)
Postcard From India
Rosalie Sorrels; *Travelin' Lady Rides Again* ...... (GRE)
Postcard From Paris
Jimmy Webb; *Suspending Disbelief* .... (ELE)
Postman Blues
Dinah Washington; *Complete On*
Mercury-#1-1946-1949 .... (MER)
Put The Message In The Box
World Party; *Best Of MTV's 120 Minutes-#1* .... (RHI)
   Goodbye Jumbo .... (ENS)
P.S. I Love You
Beatles; *Box Set* .... (CAP)
   Early Beatles .... (CAP)
   Love Songs .... (CAP)
   Please Please Me .... (CAP)
Bette Midler; *ST/For The Boys* .... (ATL)
Billie Holiday; *Lady Sings The Blues* .... (VRV)
Bing Crosby; *Radio Years* .... (CRS)
Dion; *His Best* .... (LAU)
Kay Starr; *Too Marvelous For Words-Sings J.*
Mercer .... (CAP)
Mel Torme; *That's All* .... (SSP)
Rosemary Clooney; *Sings Lyrics Of Johnny*
Mercer .... (CCJ)

Tom T. Hall; *Natural Dreams* .... (MER)
Woody Herman; *Best Of The Big Bands* ....(COL)
Return Mail Blues
Robert Nighthawk; *Drop Down Mama* .... (CSS)
Return To Sender
Elvis Presley; *Girls Girls Girls* ....(RCA)
   Great Performances ....(RCA)
   Top Ten Hits ....(RCA)
   Worldwide 50 Gold Award Hits-#1 ....(RCA)
Residents; *King & Eye* ....(ENC)
Rock & Roll Love Letter
Bay City Rollers; *Greatest Hits* .... (ARI)
   Rock & Roll Love Letter ....(ARI)
Sad Letter
Muddy Waters; *Can't Get No Grindin'* .... (CSS)
   More Real Folk Blues ....(CSS)
Sealed With A Kiss
Bobby Vinton; *Greatest Hits* ....(CCB)
Brian Hyland; *Cruisin'-1962* .... (INC)
   Oldies But Goodies-#2 ....(OSR)
   Original Rock 'N' Roll Hits/'50s ....(RLL)
Lettermen; *Best Of-#2* ....(CAP)
   Capitol Collectors Series ....(CAP)
Secret Messages
Electric Light Orchestra; *Secret Messages* ....(JET)
Send Her My Love
Journey; *Frontiers* ....(COL)
   Greatest Hits ....(COL)
Sensation Communication Together
Albert King; *Truckload Of Lovin'* .... (TOM)
Sex By Mail
Free Hot Lunch; *Penguin Love* .... (FF)
Signed Sealed Delivered
Stevie Wonder; *20/20* ....(MOT)
   Greatest Hits-#2 .... (MOT)
   Motown Grammy R&B Performances/'60s&'70s (MOT)
   Signed Sealed Delivered ....(MOT)
Soldier's Last Letter
Ernest Tubb; *Legend & The Legacy* .... (FSG)
   Living Legend .... (FSG)
Ernest Tubb & Johnny Cash; *Ernest Tubb*
   Collection ....(SO)
George Jones; *20 Golden Pieces Of* ....(BLD)
Merle Haggard; *Capitol Collectors Series* ....(CAP)
Strawberry Letter #23
Brothers Johnson; *Classics-#11* ....(A&M)
   Right On Time ....(A&M)
Tevin Campbell; *T.E.V.I.N.* ....(RPR)
Suicide Note
Pontiac Brothers; *Fuzzy Little Piece Of The World* (FRN)
Take A Letter Maria
R.B. Greaves; *Soul Hits/'70s-#1* .... (RHI)
Take A Message To Mary
Bob Dylan; *Self-Portrait* ....(COL)
Rockpile; *Seconds Of Pleasure* ....(COL)
Tear Stained Letter
Jo-el Sonnier; *Best Of Country Rock* .... (KT)
   Come On Joe ....(RCA)
Richard Thompson; *Hand Of Kindness* ....(HBL)
Teenage Letter
Big Joe Turner; *Rhythm & Blues Years* ....(ATL)
Jerry Lee Lewis; *Original Golden Hits-#1* ....(SUN)
Texas Chain Letter Massacre
Pajama Slave Dancers; *Blood Sweat & Beers* ..... (RES)
That's All She Wrote
Conway Twitty; *Hello Darlin'* ....(MSP)
Ghetto Girlz; *Ain't Takin' No S@#T* ....(HEA)
Marty Robbins; *Come Back To Me* ....(COL)
Reba McEntire; *Rumor Has It* ....(MCA)
Rick Nelson; *Garden Party* ....(MSP)
   Sings "For You" ....(MCA)
To Whom It May Concern
Nat King Cole; *At The Movies* ....(CAP)
Twistin' Postman
Marvelettes; *Anthology* ....(MOT)
   Compact Command Performances .... (MOT)
   Greatest Hits ....(MOT)
Wells Fargo Wagon
Original Broadway Cast; *Music Man* ....(ANG)
Robert Preston/Original Cast; *Music Man* ....(CAP)
Western Union
Five Americans; *Back To The '60s-Rock 'N' Roll* (DOM)
   Nuggets .... (RHI)

Whoever Finds This I Love You
Oak Ridge Boys; *All Our Favorite Songs* ....(COL)
Words By Heart
Billy Ray Cyrus; *It Won't Be The Last* .... (MER)
Write Me A Few Of Your Lines
Bonnie Raitt; *Takin' My Time* .... (WB)
XXX's And OOO's
Trisha Yearwood; *S* .... (MCA)
Your Old Love Letters
Ricky Skaggs; *Favorite Country Songs* ....(EPI)
   Waitin' For The Sun To Shine ....(EPI)

MARRIAGE, Weddings
   See Also: DIVORCE

A Mi Esposa Con Amor
Sonny James; *A Mi Esposa Con Amor* ....(COL)
   American Originals ....(COL)
Adelaide's Lament
Original Cast; *Guys & Dolls* .... (MCA)
   Guys & Dolls .... (MOT)
Arrangement
Joni Mitchell; *Ladies Of The Canyon* .... (RPR)
Babalu's Wedding Day
Eternals; *Doop-Wop Era-Harlem N.Y.-40 Hits* ...(CLT)
   Rockin' & Rollin' Wedding Songs .... (RHI)
Baby Please Set A Date
Elmore James; *Complete Fire & Enjoy*
   Sessions-#1 ....(CLT)
George Thorogood/Destroyers; *Move It On Over* (ROU)
Ballad Of John & Yoko
Beatles; *1967-70* .... (CAP)
   Box Set ....(CAP)
   Hey Jude ....(CAP)
   Past Masters-#2 ....(CAP)
   ST/Imagine-The Motion Picture ....(CAP)
Band Of Gold
Freda Payne; *Beachbeat Draggin'* ....(DHL)
   Greatest Hits ....(HDH)
   Soul Hits/'70s-#2 .... (RHI)
Barber & His Wife
Original Cast/Angela Lansbury; *Sweeney Todd* ..(RCA)
Be My Life's Companion
Mills Brothers; *Best Of* .... (MCA)
   Best Of The Decca Years ....(DEC)
Rosemary Clooney; *16 Most Requested Songs* ....(COL)
Be My Wife
David Bowie; *Low* ....(RYK)
   Sound + Vision ....(RYK)
   The Singles-1969-1993 ....(RYK)
Big Bad Bill Is Sweet William Now
Ry Cooder; *Jazz* .... (WB)
Big Bopper's Wedding
Big Bopper; *Chantilly Lace Starring The Big*
   Bopper .... (MER)
   Hellooo Baby! Best Of-1954-1959 .... (RHI)
   M. Dung's Idiot Classics .... (RHI)
Breaking In A Brand New Love
Seals & Crofts; *Takin' It Easy* .... (WB)
Bride Of Rain Dog
Tom Waits; *Rain Dogs* .... (ISL)
Bring Me My Bride
Original Broadway Cast; *Funny Thing Happened On The*
   Way To The.. .... (ANG)
Ceremony, The
George Jones & Tammy Wynette; *Greatest Hits* ... (EPI)
Chapel Of Love
Dixie Cups; *Girl Groups* .... (RHI)
   Girl Groups-Story of A Sound ....(MOT)
   Jewels #1 ....(SSS)
   Oldies But Goodies-#11 .... (OSR)
   Original New York Rock & Roll ....(OSR)
Chapel Of Love/I'm Gonna Get Married
Frankie Avalon; *You're My Life* .... (DL)
Chime Bells
Elton Britt; *S* ....(OOP)
Jody King; *Photographs & Memories* ....(CPC)
Church On Cumberland Road
Shenandoah; *Greatest Country Hits/'80s-1989* ....(COL)
   Road Not Taken ....(COL)
Could I Have This Dance?
Ann Murray; *Greatest Hits* ....(CAP)
   ST/Urban Cowboy ....(ASY)

Could've Been Me
Billy Ray Cyrus; *Some Gave All* .... (MER)
Crazy 'Bout That Married Woman
Rockin' Dopsie; *Saturday Night Zydeco* .... (MSO)
Dance Little Jean
Nitty Gritty Dirt Band; *Let's Go* .... (WB)
    Twenty Years Of Dirt-Best Of .... (WB)
Danny's Song
Anne Murray; *Country* .... (CAP)
    Danny's Song .... (CAP)
    Greatest Hits .... (CAP)
Loggins & Messina; *Best Of-Friends* .... (COL)
    On Stage .... (COL)
    Sittin' In .... (COL)
Darlin' Companion
Johnny Cash; *At Folsom Prison & San Quentin* ...(COL)
Lovin' Spoonful; *45* .... (OOP)
Diamond Girl
Seals & Crofts; *Diamond Girl* .... (WB)
    Greatest Hits .... (WB)
Do You Hear Wedding Bells
Jive Five; *Their Greatest Hits* .... (CLT)
Don't You Marry The Mormon Boys
Rosalie Sorrels; *Lonesome Roving Wolves-Songs Of The*
    West .... (GRE)
Down The Aisle Of Love
Quin-Tones; *Rockin' & Rollin' Wedding Songs-#2* (RHI)
Down The Road
Mac McAnally; *Knots* .... (MCA)
Eleanor Rigby
Beatles; *1962-1966* .... (CAP)
    Revolver .... (CAP)
Paul McCartney; *Tripping The Live Fantastic* .... (CAP)
Ray Charles; *Anthology* .... (RHI)
    Greatest Hits-#2 .... (RHI)
Follow Me
John Denver; *Greatest Hits-#1* .... (RCA)
    Take Me Home Country Roads & Other Hits ....(RCA)
For Me & My Gal
Bing Crosby; *Radio Years-#1* .... (CRS)
Harry Nilsson; *Little Touch Of Schmilsson In The*
    Night .... (RCA)
Judy Garland & Gene Kelly; *Best of The Decca*
    Years-#1-Hits! .... (DEC)
Forever's As Far As I'll Go
Alabama; *Pass It On Down* .... (RCA)
Froggie Went A Courtin'
Doc Watson; *Essential* .... (VAN)
    Home Again .... (VAN)
Get Me To The Church On Time
Original Cast; *My Fair Lady* .... (COL)
Girl That I Marry
Broadway Cast; *Annie Get Your Gun* .... (ANG)
Doris Day/Original Cast; *Annie Get Your Gun* ...(COL)
Ethel Merman/Original Cast; *Annie Get Your*
    Gun .... (RCA)
Frank Sinatra; *Greatest Hits-Early Years* .... (COL)
Give Me A Ring Sometime
Lisa Brokop; *Every Little Girl's Dream* .... (PAT)
Happily Married Man
Duane Allman; *Anthology #2* .... (CPC)
Happy Anniversary
Little River Band; *Diamantina Cocktail* .... (CAP)
    Greatest Hits .... (CAP)
Slim Whitman; *Best Of-Legendary Master Series* .. (EMI)
Harry, Let's Marry
Maxine Brown; *45* .... (CLT)
Harry's House Centerpiece
Joni Mitchell; *Hissing Of Summer Lawns* .... (ASY)
Hawaiian Wedding Song
Andy Williams; *16 Most Requested Songs* .... (COL)
    Greatest Hits .... (COL)
Jim Reeves; *Pure Gold* .... (RCA)
Hey Paula
Paul & Paula; *Cruisin'-1963* .... (INC)
    ST/Animal House .... (MCA)
    WCBS FM101-History Of Rock/'60s-#1 .... (CLT)
High Hopes And Empty Pockets
Terry McBride/Ride; *Terry McBride & The Ride* (MCA)
Hometown Honeymoon
Alabama; *American Pride* .... (RCA)
Honeymoon Hotel
Alice Faye; *Hooray For Hollywood* .... (RCA)

Honeymoon In Beirut
Rick Springfield; *Rock Of Life* .... (RCA)
Honeymoon On Mars
Be Bop Deluxe; *Modern Music* .... (CAP)
Honeymooners
City Boy; *Young Men Gone West* .... (MER)
Housewife
Leon Russell; *Americana* .... (PRD)
Husbands & Wives
Neil Diamond; *Love Songs* .... (MCA)
    Rainbow .... (MCA)
    Stones .... (MCA)
Roger Miller; *Best Of* .... (MER)
    More Golden Hits .... (SMA)
I Cried All The Way To The Altar
Patsy Cline; *20 Golden Pieces Of* .... (BLD)
    Patsy Cline .... (AUF)
    Walkin' Dreams: Her First Recordings-#1 .... (RHI)
I Do It For Your Love
Paul Simon; *Greatest Hits Etc.* .... (COL)
    Still Crazy After All These Years .... (COL)
I Knew The Bride
Dave Edmunds; *Best Of* .... (SS)
    Get It .... (SS)
Nick Lowe; *Basher-Best Of* .... (COL)
I Married An Angel
George Siravo; *Heritage Of Broadway-Rodgers &*
    Hart .... (BAI)
I Meant Every Word He Said
Ricky Van Shelton; *Greatest Country Hits/'90s-#2* (COL)
    RVS III .... (COL)
I Never Will Marry
Bailey Brothers; *Early Days Of Bluegrass-#6* .... (ROU)
Linda Ronstadt; *Simple Dreams* .... (ASY)
I Wanna Marry A Lighthouse Keeper
Erika Eigen; *ST/Clockwork Orange* .... (WB)
I Wanna Marry You
Bruce Springsteen; *The River* .... (COL)
I Want A Girl (Just Like The Girl)
Al Jolson; *Story-#1* .... (MCA)
Spike Jones; *King Of Corn* .... (GLN)
I Want To Marry You
Del Vikings; *Del Vikings* .... (CLT)
    Rockin' & Rollin' Wedding Songs-#1 .... (RHI)
I Wish That We Were Married
Ronnie/Hi-Lites; *Rockin' & Rollin' Wedding*
    Songs-#2 .... (RHI)
If I Were A Carpenter
Bobby Darin; *Live At The Desert Inn* .... (MOT)
Four Tops; *Anthology* .... (MOT)
    Compact Command Performances .... (MOT)
    Reach Out .... (MOT)
Tim Hardin; *Memorial Album* .... (POL)
In The Chapel In The Moonlight
Patti Page; *16 Most Requested Songs* .... (COL)
Indian Wedding
Roy Orbison; *Legendary* .... (SSP)
    More Greatest Hits .... (MON)
    Our Love Song .... (MON)
It Could've Been Me
Billy Ray Cyrus; *Some Gave All* .... (MER)
I'm Gonna Get Married
Lloyd Price; *Greatest Hits* .... (MCA)
    Super Oldies/'50s-#3 .... (AUF)
    Vintage Music-Classics/'50s-'60s-#15 .... (MCA)
I'm Throwing Rice
Jerry Lee Lewis; *Taste Of Country* .... (SUN)
Just Now It Feels So Right
Jesse Winchester; *Touch On The Rainy Side* ..... (RHI)
Kiss The Bride
Elton John; *Greatest Hits-1976-1986* .... (MCA)
    Too Low For Zero .... (MCA)
Let's Get Married
Al Green; *Compact Command Performances* .... (MOT)
    Greatest Hits-#1 .... (MOT)
Let's Get Married Again
John Conlee; *Friday Night Blues* .... (MCA)
Let's Pretend We're Married
Prince; *1999* .... (WB)
Tina Turner; *45* .... (CAP)
Lida Rose
Original Broadway Cast; *Music Man* .... (ANG)
Robert Preston/Original Cast; *Music Man* .... (CAP)

Little Band Of Gold
Sonny James; *American Originals* ....(COL)
  Greatest Hits ....(COL)
  Little Bit South Of Saskatoon ....(COL)
Long Honeymoon
Elvis Costello; *Girls Girls Girls* ....(COL)
Elvis Costello/Attractions; *Imperial Bedroom* ....(COL)
Longer
Dan Fogelberg; *Greatest Hits* .... (FM)
  Phoenix .... (FM)
Love Is A Golden Ring
Frankie Laine; *16 Most Requested Songs* ....(COL)
Love & Marriage
Frank Sinatra; *A Man & His Music* .... (RPR)
  Capitol Collector Series ....(CAP)
  Capitol Years ....(CAP)
  Reprise Collection ....(RPR)
Loving You
Elvis Presley; *Essential Elvis-The First Movies* ...(RCA)
  Golden Records-#1 ....(RCA)
  Pure Gold ....(RCA)
  Sings Leiber & Stoller ....(RCA)
  ST/Loving You ....(RCA)
Make Me The Woman That You Go Home To
Gladys Knight/Pips; *Anthology* .... (MOT)
  All The Great Hits ....(MOT)
  Compact Command Performances .... (MOT)
  Standing Ovation .... (SOL)
Make My Life With You
Oak Ridge Boys; *Country Classics-#1* .... (MCA)
  Greatest Hits-#2 ....(MCA)
  MCA #1 Hits/'80s-#1 ....(MCA)
Makin' Whoopie
Art Tatum; *Solo Masterpieces-#5* .... (PAB)
Eddie Cantor; *Nipper's Greatest Hits-'20s* ....(RCA)
Harry Nilsson; *Touch Of Schmilsson In The Night* (RCA)
Ray Charles; *His Greatest Hits-#2* ....(DHL)
Marriage
Ted Nugent/Amboy Dukes; *Marriage On The*
Rocks .... (POL)
  Rock Bottom .... (POL)
Marriage Bureau Rendezvous
10 CC; *Deceptive Bends* .... (MER)
  Live & Let Live .... (MER)
Marriage License
Chi-Lites; *Chi-Lites* ....(BRU)
Marriage Made In Heaven
Bob Crewe; *Motivation* .... (ELE)
Marriage On Paper Only
Dramatics; *Anytime Anyplace* .... (MCA)
Married
Liza Minnelli; *Liza With A 'Z'* ....(COL)
  Original Cast; *Cabaret* ....(COL)
Married But Not To Each Other
Barbara Mandrell; *Best Of* .... (MCA)
  Lovers Friends & Strangers .... (MCA)
  Midnight Angel .... (MCA)
Married Lady
Bill Anderson; *Ladies Choice* .... (MCA)
Married Men
Bette Midler; *Thighs & Whispers* .... (ATL)
Roches; *Bread & Roses Festival-#2* ....(FAN)
  Roches ....(WB)
Married Woman
Frankie Lee Sims; *Lucy Mae Blues* .... (SPE)
  This Is How It All Began-#1 .... (SPE)
Marry Me
Engelbert Humperdinck; *Engelbert* ....(PRT)
Original Cast; *The Rink* .... (POL)
Marry The Man Today
Original Cast; *Guys & Dolls* .... (MCA)
Marrying For Love
Original Cast/Dinah Shore; *Call Me Madam* ....(RCA)
Matchmaker, Matchmaker
Original Cast; *Fiddler On The Roof* ....(RCA)
Original London Cast; *Fiddler On The Roof* .....(COL)
My Baby's Coming With A Marriage License
Sunnyland Slim; *Blues Piano Orgy* .... (DEL)
My Mother's Wedding Day
Original Cast; *Brigadoon* ....(RCA)
My Only Love
Statler Brothers; *Atlanta Blue* .... (MER)
  Greatest Hits .... (MER)

My Wife
Who; *Greatest Hits* .... (MCA)
  ST/Kids Are Alright .... (MCA)
  Two's Missing .... (MCA)
  Who's Next .... (MCA)
Never Ending Song Of Love
Conway Twitty & Loretta Lynn; *Lead Me On* .. (MCA)
Delaney & Bonnie; *Best Of* .... (RHI)
Delaney & Bonnie/Friends; *Super Hits/'70s-Have A Nice*
Day-#16 .... (RHI)
Never My Love
Association; *Greatest Hits* .... (WB)
  Songs That Made Them Famous .... (PRR)
  There Is Still Love-Anniversary Songs .... (SCO)
Never Will I Marry
Barbra Streisand; *Third Album* .... (COL)
Not Too Young To Get Married
Bob B. Soxx/Blue Jeans; *Back To*
Mono-1958-1969 .... (AKO)
  Darlene Love; *Best Of* .... (AKO)
Now And Forever (You And Me)
Anne Murray; *Greatest Hits-#2* .... (LIB)
  Something To Talk About .... (CAP)
October Wedding
Montreux; *Let Them Say* .... (WH)
  Montreux-Windham Hill Retrospective .... (WH)
Old Fashioned Wedding
Ethel Merman/Bruce Yarnell/Original Cast; *Annie Get*
Your Gun .... (RCA)
On A Chinese Honeymoon
Mills Brothers; *Story* .... (RAN)
On A Wedding Anniversary
John Cale; *Fragments Of A Rainy Season* .... (HBL)
On The Other Hand
Randy Travis; *Greatest Hits-#1* .... (WB)
  Storms Of Life .... (WB)
One Boy
Ann-Margret; *ST/Bye Bye Birdie* ....(RCA)
One Thousand Dollar Wedding
Gram Parsons; *Grievous Angel* .... (RPR)
Opium Bride
Annabouboula; *Greek Fire* .... (SHA)
Our Shotgun Wedding Day
Howington Brothers/Tennessee Haymakers; *Long Gone*
Daddy ....(CLT)
Peggy Sue Got Married
Buddy Holly; *20 Golden Greats* .... (MCA)
  Rock & Roll Collection .... (MCA)
Pledging My Love
David Allan Coe; *17 Greatest Hits* ....(COL)
  Biggest Hits ....(COL)
  Elvis Presley; *Moody Blue* ....(RCA)
  Emmylou Harris; *Profile 2-Best Of* .... (WB)
  Freddie Fender; *Collection* ....(RPR)
  Johnny Ace; *Cruisin'-1955* ....(INC)
  Duke-Peacock Greatest Hits .... (MCA)
  Memorial Album .... (MCA)
  Oldies But Goodies-#10 .... (OSR)
  ST/A Rage In Harlem .... (MSP)
  Marvin Gaye & Diana Ross; *Diana & Marvin* .. (MOT)
  Teresa Brewer; *Best Of* .... (MCA)
Pocket Full Of Gold
Vince Gill; *Pocket Full Of Gold* .... (MCA)
Put That Ring On My Finger
Andrews Sisters; *50th Anniversary Collection-#2* (MCA)
Woody Herman; *Best Of The Big Bands* ....(COL)
Ready Or Not
Jackson Browne; *For Everyman* .... (ASY)
Ring On Her Finger, Time On Her Hands
Lee Greenwood; *Greatest Hits* .... (MCA)
  Inside Out .... (MCA)
Round And Round
Perry Como; *All-Time Greatest Hits-#1* ....(RCA)
  Golden Records ....(RCA)
  This Is ....(RCA)
Ruby's Golden Wedding
Danny Wilson; *Meet Danny Wilson* .... (VIA)
Sad Wedding
Marvin Gaye & Tammi Terrell; *United* .... (MOT)
Saigon Bride
Joan Baez; *Contemporary Ballad Book* .... (VAN)
Secret Marriage
Sting; *Nothing Like The Sun* ....(A&M)

She's No Lady
Lyle Lovett; *Great Records/Decade-'80s*
Hits-Country ....(CCB)
Pontiac ....(MCC)
Single Women
Dolly Parton; *Heartbreak Express* ....(RCA)
Stand By Your Man
Lyle Lovett/Large Band; *Lyle Lovett/Large Band* (MCC)
Tammy Wynette; *Biggest Hits* ....(EPI)
Columbia Country Classics-#3-1965-1970 ......(KT)
ST/Sleepless In Seattle ....(EPI)
Tears Of Fire-25th Anniversary Collect. ....(EPI)
Starting A New Life
Van Morrison; *Tupelo Honey* ....(WB)
Stop The Wedding
Etta James; *Sweetest Peaches-#1* ....(CSS)
Stress In Marriage
Negativeland; *Escape From Noise* ....(SST)
Stupid Marriage
Specials; *Specials* ....(CHR)
Sunrise, Sunset
Original Cast; *Fiddler On The Roof* ....(RCA)
Original London Cast; *Fiddler On The Roof* .....(COL)
Ten Commandments Of Love
Bob Marley/Wailers; *Birth Of A*
Legend-1963-1966 ....(EPA)
Harvey/Moonglows; *Best Of Chess Rock 'N'*
Roll-#2 ....(CSS)
Collectables Presents History Of Rock-10 ....(CLT)
Cruisin'-1958 ....(INC)
Oldies But Goodies-#11 ....(OSR)
That's The Way I've Always Heard It...
Carly Simon; *Best Of* ....(ELE)
Carly Simon ....(ELE)
"The Brady Bunch" Theme
Brady Bunch Kids; *It's A Sunshine Day-Best Of* . (MCA)
Television's Greatest Hits-#2 ....(TVT)
"The Honeymooners" Theme
Original Music; *Television's Greatest Hits-#2* .....(TVT)
Then He Kissed Me
Crystals; *Back To Mono-1958-1969* ....(AKO)
Best Of ....(AKO)
There Won't Be A Wedding
Jimmie Davis; *Golden Hits* ....(PLN)
They Just Got Married
Randy Newman; *Born Again* ....(WB)
This Diamond Ring
Gary Lewis/Playboys; *Billboard Top Rock 'N' Roll*
Hits-1965 ....(RHI)
EMI Legends Of Rock 'N' Roll-24 Greatest ......(EMI)
Golden Years-1965 ....(DOM)
Spring Break-#2-Cold Kegs & Tan Legs ....(CAP)
This Is The Day (A Wedding Song)
Scott Wesley Brown; *I Will Be Here-10 Contemp.*
Wedding Songs ....(SPW)
Three Steps From The Altar
Shep/Limelites; *Rockin' & Rollin' Wedding*
Songs-#2 ....(RHI)
To The Aisle
Five Satins; *Collectables Presents History Of*
Rock-#7 ....(CLT)
Cruisin'-1957 ....(INC)
Oldies But Goodies-#4 ....(OSR)
Rockin' & Rollin' Wedding Songs-#1 ....(RHI)
ST/American Graffiti ....(MCA)
(Today I Met) The Boy I'm Gonna Marry
Darlen Love; *Best Of* ....(AKO)
Darlene Love; *Back To Mono-1958-1969* .....(AKO)
Tomorrow's My Wedding Day
Country Gentlemen; *Country Songs Old & New* . (FLW)
Unwed Fathers
Gail Davies; *Best Of* ....(LIB)
Tammy Wynette; *Best Loved Hits* ....(EPI)
Vows Of Love
Paragons; *Best Of* ....(CLT)
Vow, The
Flamingos; *Best Of* ....(RHI)
Flamingos ....(CSS)
Wartime Wedding
Original Broadway Cast; *Over Here!* ....(SMC)
We Got Married
Paul McCartney; *Flowers In The Dirt* ....(CAP)
Tripping The Live Fantastic ....(CAP)

Wedding
Solitaires; *Rockin' & Rollin' Wedding Songs-#1* ... (RHI)
Wedding Bell Blues
5th Dimension; *Greatest Hits On Earth* ....(ARI)
Rockin' & Rollin' Wedding Songs-#1 ....(RHI)
ST/My Girl ....(EPI)
Wedding Bells
Hank Williams; *24 Greatest Hits* ....(POL)
40 Greatest Hits ....(POL)
Wedding Bells Are Breaking Up That...
Four Aces; *Best Of* ....(MCA)
Wedding Cake
Jeannie C. Riley; *Things Go Better With Love* ....(PLN)
Wedding Day
Paul Young; *Between Two Fires* ....(COL)
UB40; *Labour Of Love II* ....(VIA)
Wedding In Cherokee County
Randy Newman; *Good Old Boys* ....(RPR)
Wedding March
Jesse Crawford; *Wedding Music* ....(MCA)
Lawrence Welk; *Music For All Occasions* ....(KT)
Richard Ellsasser; *Wedding Album* ....(MGM)
Wedding Song
Arlo Guthrie/Shenandoah; *Outlasting The Blues* ...(WB)
Bob Dylan/Band; *Planet Waves* ....(ASY)
Captain & Tennille; *Greatest Hits* ....(A&M)
Rockin' & Rollin' Wedding Songs-#1 ....(RHI)
Judy Collins; *Running For My Life* ....(ELE)
Mary MacGregor; *45* ....(ARL)
Original Cast; *Threepenny Opera* ....(POL)
Paul Stookey; *45* ....(ERI)
Petula Clark; *There Is Love-Wedding Songs* ......(SCO)
Smokey Robinson; *Quiet Storm* ....(MOT)
Wedding's Over
Charlie Rich; *20 Golden Hits* ....(SUN)
Time For Tears ....(SUN)
We're All The Way
Don Williams; *Lovers & Best Friends* ....(MCA)
One Good Well ....(RCA)
Eric Clapton; *Slow Hand* ....(POL)
We've Only Just Begun
Barbra Streisand; *Just For The Record* ....(COL)
Carpenters; *Classics-#2* ....(A&M)
Close To You ....(A&M)
From The Top ....(A&M)
Singles-1969-1973 ....(A&M)
Yesterday Once More ....(A&M)
When I'm Sixty-Four
Beatles; *Box Set* ....(CAP)
Sgt. Pepper's Lonely Hearts Club Band ....(CAP)
When The Kids Get Married
Original Broadway Cast; *I Do! I Do!* ....(RCA)
When We Get Married
Dreamlovers; *Best Of-#1* ....(CLT)
Oldies But Goodies-#5 ....(OSR)
Rockin' & Rollin' Wedding Songs-#1 ....(RHI)
White Trash Wife
Exene Cervenka; *Old Wives' Tales* ....(RHI)
White Wedding
Billy Idol; *Billy Idol* ....(CHR)
Vital Idol ....(CHR)
Why Did I Choose You
Barbra Streisand; *Greatest Hits* ....(COL)
My Name Is Barbra ....(COL)
Marvin Gaye; *Romantically Yours* ....(COL)
Michael Crawford; *With Love* ....(ATL)
Wife & The Whore
Kristin Lems; *Born A Woman* ....(FF)
Will Never Marry
Morrissey; *Bona Drag* ....(SIR)
Just Say Yo-#2 Of Just Say Yes ....(SIR)
Will You Marry Me?
Original Cast; *Pipe Dream* ....(RCA)
Paula Abdul; *Spellbound* ....(CPT)
With This Ring
Platters; *Only Their Best For You* ....(PRR)
Rockin' & Rollin' Wedding Songs-#2 ....(RHI)
T. Graham Brown; *Best Of* ....(LIB)
Wives Are In Connecticut
Carly Simon; *Spoiled Girl* ....(EPI)

Wouldn't It Be Nice
Beach Boys; *Absolutely Best-#2* ....(CAP)
 Made In The U.S.A. ....(CAP)
 Pet Sounds ....(CAP)
 Still Cruisin' ....(CAP)
You Ain't Goin' Nowhere
Bob Dylan; *Greatest Hits-#2* ....(COL)
Bob Dylan/Band; *Basement Tapes* ....(COL)
Byrds; *Best Of-Greatest Hits-#2* ....(COL)
 Byrds Play Dylan ....(COL)
 Byrds (collection) ....(COL)
 Sweetheart Of The Rodeo ....(COL)
Chris Hillman & Roger McGuinn; *Will The Circle Be
Unbroken-#2* .... (UNI)
Joan Baez; *First 10 Years* .... (VAN)
You Don't Bring Me Flowers
Barbra Streisand; *Songbird* ....(COL)
Barbra Streisand & Neil Diamond; *Greatest Hits
#2* ....(COL)
 Just For The Record ....(COL)
Neil Diamond; *Hot August Night II* ....(COL)
Neil Diamond & Barbra Streisand; *12 Greatest
Hits-#2* ....(COL)
 I'm Glad You're Here With Me Tonight ....(COL)
 You Don't Bring Me Flowers ....(COL)
You Make It Easy
James Taylor; *Gorilla* .... (WB)
You Never Can Tell
Aaron Neville; *The Grand Tour* .... (A&M)
Chuck Berry; *Chess Box* .... (CSS)
 Rock 'N Roll Rarities-20 Magic Tracks .... (CSS)
You'll Accomp'ny Me
Bob Seger/Silver Bullet Band; *Against The Wind* .(CAP)
 Nine Tonight ....(CAP)

MEN: GENERAL, Boys

*See Also: FATHERS, MEN'S NAMES,
TEENAGERS*

20th Century Man
Beat Farmers; *Loud & Plowed &...Live!* ....(CCB)
Kinks; *Muswell Hillbillies* .... (RHI)
 One For The Road .... (ARI)
African Shadow Man
Johnny Clegg & Savuka; *Shadow Man* ....(CAP)
All American Boy
Bill Parsons; *History Of Rock-#10* .... (CLT)
Statler Brothers; *Son Of The Motherland* .... (MER)
All American Man
Kiss; *Alive 2* .... (CAS)
All The Man That I Need
Whitney Houston; *I'm Your Baby Tonight* .... (ARI)
All The Young Dudes
David Bowie; *Live* ....(RYK)
Ian Hunter; *Live/Welcome To The Club* .... (CHR)
 Shades Of .... (CHR)
Mott The Hoople; *All The Young Dudes* ....(COL)
 Greatest Hits ....(COL)
 Live ....(COL)
 ST/Queens Logic ....(EPI)
All True Man
Alexander O'Neal; *All True Man* .... (TAB)
Alligator Man
Jimmy C. Newman; *Greatest Hits* .... (PLN)
 Progressive CC .... (PLN)
 Souvenirs Of Music City USA .... (PLN)
Alpine Milkman
Randy Erwin; *'Til The Cows Come Home/Cowboy
Rhythm* .... (ROM)
American Boy
Eddie Rabbitt; *American Music Greatest Hits* .....(CCB)
 Greatest Country Hits ....(CCB)
 Jersey Boy .... (LIB)
American Boys
Deborah Galli; *Radio Active* .... (MER)
An English Gentleman
Original Broadway Cast; *Me & My Girl* ....(MCA)
Angels Love Bad Men
Barbara Mandrell; *Sure Feels Good* ....(EMI)
Barbara Mandrell & Waylon Jennings; *Country Duets
Two By Two* ....(CAP)

Angry Young Man
Billy Joel; *KOHUEPT (Live In Leningrad)* ....(COL)
Corey Hart; *Fields Of Fire* ....(EMI)
Steve Earle/Dukes; *Exit O* ....(MCA)
Animal Boy
Ramones; *Animal Boy* .... (SIR)
 Ramones Mania .... (SIR)
Another Man Done Gone
Jorma Kaukonen & Tom Hobson; *Quah* ....(RLX)
Pete Seeger/Memphis Slim/Willie Dixon; *Pete Seeger At
The Village Gate* ....(FLW)
Another Night With The Boys
Drifters; *All-Time Greatest Hits &
More-1959-1965* ....(ATL)
Persuasions; *Bread & Roses Festival-Acoustic
Music-#1* ....(FAN)
Ant Man Bee
Captain Beefheart/Magic Band; *Trout Mask
Replica* .... (RPR)
Armageddon Man
Black Flag; *Family Man* ....(SST)
Army Man In Vietnam
Big Joe Williams; *Shake Your Boogie* .... (ARH)
 Thinking Of What They Did To Me .... (ARH)
Astro Boy
Buggles; *Age Of Plastic* .... (ISL)
Astro Man
Jimi Hendrix; *Cry Of Love* .... (RPR)
Attack Of The Vegetable Men
Active Ingredient; *Extrastrength* ....(BAI)
Automatic Man
Michael Sembello; *Bossa Noval Hotel* ....(WB)
Baby You're A Rich Man
Beatles; *Box Set* ....(CAP)
 Magical Mystery Tour ....(CAP)
Back Door Man
Doors; *13* ....(ELE)
 Doors ....(ELE)
Howlin' Wolf; *Best Of-Chess Blues* ....(CSS)
John Hammond; *Best Of* .... (VAN)
Willie Dixon; *I Am The Blues* ....(COL)
Bad Boy
Beatles; *Box Set* ....(CAP)
 Past Masters-#1 ....(CAP)
 Rock 'N' Roll Music-#1 ....(CAP)
 VI ....(CAP)
Eddie Money; *Nothing To Lose* ....(COL)
Eddie Taylor; *Antone's Bringing You The Best In
Blues* ....(ANT)
Eric Clapton; *Eric Clapton* ....(POL)
Miami Sound Machine; *Primitive Love* .... (EPI)
Ray Parker, Jr.; *Greatest Hits* .... (ARI)
Ringo Starr; *Bad Boy* .... (EPI)
Bad Boys
Inner Circle; *Bad Boys* ....(BB)
Bad Boys Running Wild
Scorpions; *Love At First Sting* .... (MER)
 Wold Wide Live .... (MER)
Bad Boyz
Crosby, Stills & Nash; *After The Storm* .... (ATL)
Bad Boy/Having A Party
Luther Vandross; *Best Of...The Best Of Love* ...... (EPI)
 Forever For Always For Love ....(EPI)
Banana Man
Clifton Chenier; *Louisiana Blues & Zydeco* ..... (ARH)
Banjo Boy Chimes
White Brothers/New Kentucky Colonels; *Live In
Sweden* .... (ROU)
Belly Up To The Bar, Boys
Debbie Reynolds; *ST/Unsinkable Molly Brown* .. (MCA)
Original Cast; *Unsinkable Molly Brown* ....(CAP)
Better Man
Clint Black; *Killin' Time* ....(RCA)
Big Boss Man
B.B. King; *Six Silver Strings* .... (MCA)
Elvis Presley; *Elvis* ....(RCA)
 ST/Clambake ....(RCA)
Grateful Dead; *Grateful Dead* ....(WB)
Jimmy Reed; *Best Of* .... (CRS)
 Oldies But Goodies-#1 ....(OSR)
John Hammond; *Best Of* .... (VAN)
 So Many Roads .... (VAN)
Big Boys Don't Cry
Extreme; *Extreme* .... (A&M)

Big Butter And Egg Man
Louis Armstrong; *Best Of* ....(AUF)
  Hot Fives And Hot Sevens-#2 ....(COL)
Merle Haggard; *Kern River* ....(EPI)
  Walking The Line ....(EPI)
Big Man
Charlie Daniels Band; *Uneasy Rider* ....(EPI)
Big Man In Town
Frankie Valli/Four Seasons; *Anthology* ....(RHI)
  Greatest Hits-#1 ....(RHI)
Big Rig Rolling Man
Billy Larkin; *Blue Ribbon Country-#2* ....(ACC)
Big River, Big Man
Claude King; *American Originals* ....(COL)
  Best ....(GUS)
Birdman Of Alkatrash
Strawberry Alarm Clock; *45* .... (MCA)
Black Boys On The Corner
Thin Lizzy; *London Collector-Rocker* ....(LON)
Black Boys, White Boys
Original Broadway Cast; *Hair* ....(RCA)
Black Man
Alberta Hunter; *Look For The Silver Lining* ......(COL)
Stevie Wonder; *Songs In The Key Of Life* ....(MOT)
Black Man Can't Get A Cab
U.T.F.O.; *Bag It & Bone It* ....(JVA)
Black Sheep Boy
Tim Hardin; *Memorial Album* ....(POL)
Blind Man
Aerosmith; *Big Ones* ....(GEF)
Bobby Bland; *Best Of* .... (MCA)
  Introspective Of Early Years .... (MCA)
Champion Jack Dupree; *Back Home In New*
  Orleans ....(BUL)
Blow The Man Down
Paul Clayton; *Bay State Ballads* .... (FLW)
Blue Boy
Jim Reeves; *Best Of* ....(RCA)
  Live At The Opry .... (CMF)
Joni Mitchell; *Ladies Of The Canyon* ....(RPR)
Blue Collar Man
Styx; *Caught In The Act* .... (A&M)
  Classics-#15 .... (A&M)
  Pieces Of Eight .... (A&M)
Blue Jean Boy
Michael Stanley Band; *Ladies' Choice* .... (EPI)
Boogie Woogie Bugle Boy
Andrews Sisters; *16 Great Performances* .... (MCA)
  Best Of .... (MCA)
  Boogie Woogie Bugle Girls .... (MCA)
  Rarities .... (MCA)
Bette Midler; *Divine Miss M* .... (ATL)
  Live At Last .... (ATL)
  ST/Divine Madness .... (ATL)
Boy Blue
Cyndi Lauper; *True Colors* .... (POR)
Electric Light Orchestra; *Afterglow* .... (EPI)
  Eldorado ....(JET)
  Ole ELO ....(JET)
Boy Crazy
Tubes; *Tubes* .... (A&M)
  What Do You Want From-Live .... (A&M)
Boy From New York City
Ad-Libs; *Jewels-#1* .... (SSS)
  Oldies But Goodies-#6 .... (OSR)
  Original Golden Hits/Great Groups-#1 .... (SSS)
  Original New York Rock & Roll-#1 .... (SSS)
Manhattan Transfer; *Best Of* .... (ATL)
  Mecca For Moderns .... (ATL)
Boy In Ohio
Phil Ochs; *Greatest Hits* .... (A&M)
Boys
Beatles; *At The Hollywood Bowl* ....(CAP)
  Box Set ....(CAP)
  Early ....(CAP)
  Please Please Me ....(CAP)
  Rock 'N' Roll Music-#1 ....(CAP)
Shirelles; *Anthology-1959-1964* .... (RHI)
Boys And Me
Sawyer Brown; *Outskirts Of Town* .... (CRB)
Boys Are Back In Town
Bon Jovi; *ST/Navy Seals* .... (ATL)
Gap Band; *II* .... (MER)

Thin Lizzy; *Dedication-Very Best Of* .... (MER)
  Jailbreak .... (MER)
  Live & Dangerous ....(WB)
  '70s Greatest Rock Hits-#14-King Of Rock ...... (PRY)
Boys Cry Tough
Bad Company; *Holy Water* ....(ATC)
Boys In The Trees
Carly Simon; *Boys In The Trees* .... (ELE)
Boys Of Summer
Don Henley; *Building The Perfect Beast* .... (GEF)
Boys & Me
Sawyer Brown; *Outskirts Of Town* .... (CRB)
Boys 'R A Drug
Julie Brown; *Trapped In The Body Of A White Girl* (SIR)
Brand New Man
Brooks & Dunn; *Brand New Man* .... (ARI)
Brown Eyed Handsome Man
Buddy Holly; *For The First Time Anywhere* ..... (MCA)
  Rock & Roll Collection .... (MCA)
  & Crickets: 20 Golden Greats .... (MCA)
Chuck Berry; *Best Of The Best Of* .... (GUS)
  Chess Box .... (CSS)
  Roll Over Beethoven ....(ALL)
Brown Man Do
Small Faces; *78 In The Shade* .... (ATL)
California Kid
Beat Farmers; *Tales Of The New West* .... (RHI)
California Man
Cheap Trick; *Heaven Tonight* .... (EPI)
Can't Keep A Good Man Down
38 Special; *Special Delivery* .... (A&M)
Alabama; *Live* ....(RCA)
Carousel Man
Cher; *Greatest Hits* .... (MCA)
Cathy's Clown
Everly Brothers; *Billboard Top Rock 'N' Roll*
  Hits-1960 .... (RHI)
  Golden Hits ....(WB)
  Reunion Concert .... (MER)
  Very Best Of ....(WB)
Reba McEntire; *Sweet Sixteen* .... (MCA)
Chattanooga Shoe Shine Boy
Freddy Cannon; *14 Booming Hits* .... (RHI)
Cigarette Of A Single Man
Squeeze; *Babylon & On* .... (A&M)
Comfort Of A Man
Stephanie Mills; *Home* .... (MCA)
Common Man
Blasters; *Collection* ....(SLS)
John Conlee; *Busted* .... (MCA)
  Greatest Hits .... (MCA)
Company Man
James Taylor; *Flag* ....(COL)
Could You Love A Working Man
Stoker Brothers; *45* .... (CMS)
Country Boy
Johnny Cash; *Man-The World-His Music* .... (SUN)
  Original Golden Hits-#3 .... (SUN)
  Superbilly .... (SUN)
Little Jimmy Dickens; *Columbia Country*
  Classics-#2 ....(COL)
Ricky Skaggs; *19 Hot Country Requests-#3* ...... (EPI)
  Country Boy .... (EPI)
  Greatest Country Hits/'80s-1985 ....(COL)
  Live In London .... (EPI)
Country Boy Can Survive
Hank Williams, Jr.; *America (The Way I See It)* ..(W/C)
  Greatest Hits ....(WB)
  Live ....(W/C)
  ST/Pressure Is On ....(W/C)
Country Boy (You Got Your Feet In L.A.)
Glen Campbell; *Best Of* .... (LIB)
  Classics Collection .... (LIB)
  Greatest Hits ....(CCB)
Cowboy Man
Lyle Lovett; *Country Classics-#9 (1984-1987)* .. (MCA)
  Lyle Lovett .... (MCA)
  ST/Always .... (MCA)
Crab Man's Call
Original Cast; *Porgy & Bess* .... (MCA)
Cry For The Bad Man
Lynyrd Skynyrd; *Best Of* .... (MSP)
  Gimme Back My Bullets .... (MCA)

Danger Man
David Bromberg; *Wanted Dead Or Alive* ....(COL)
Dangerous Man
Dwight Yoakam; *If There Was A Way* ....(RPR)
Dawgs (Are A Man's Best Friend)
Original Cast; *Dawgs* ....(GLN)
Dead Man
Asleep At The Wheel; *Asleep At The Wheel* ....(EPI)
Dead Man's Hill
Indigo Girls; *Swamp Ophelia* ....(EPI)
Dear Mr. President
4 Non Blondes; *Bigger Better Faster More* ....(ISC)
Next Issue; *Next Issue* ....(EPI)
Dear Santa-Bring Me A Man This Christmas
Weather Girls; *Success* ....(COL)
Death Of A Ladies' Man
Leonard Cohen; *Death Of A Ladies' Man* ....(COL)
Detective Man
Detective; *Detective* .... (SS)
Diary Of A Madman
Ozzy Osbourne; *Diary Of A Madman* ....(JET)
Did You See His Name
Kinks; *Kink Kronikles* ....(RPR)
Dirty White Boy
Foreigner; *Head Games* ....(ATL)
Records ....(ATL)
Do You Know Where Your Man Is
Pam Tillis; *Homeward Looking Angel* .... (ARI)
Does She Love That Man?
Breathe; *Peace Of Mind* ....(A&M)
Donut Man
Rita Coolidge; *The Lady's Not For Sale* ....(A&M)
Don't Mess With My Man
Irma Thomas; *We Got A Party-Best Of Ron
Records-#1* .... (ROU)
Don't Pay The Ferryman
Chris DeBurgh; *Getaway* ....(A&M)
Don't You Marry The Mormon Boys
Rosalie Sorrels; *Lonesome Roving Wolves-Songs Of The
West* ....(GRE)
Down Boys
Cars; *Panorama* .... (ELE)
Warrant; *Dirty Rotten Stinking Filthy Rich* ....(COL)
Drug Store Truck Drivin' Man
Byrds; *Best Of-Greatest Hits-#2* ....(COL)
Byrds ....(COL)
Dr. Byrds & Mr. Hyde ....(COL)
Gram Parsons/Fallen Angels; *Live 1973* .... (SIE)
Joan Baez & Jeffrey Shurtleff; *ST/Woodstock* ....(ATL)
Drunken Hearted Boy
Allman Brothers Band; *Dreams* ....(POL)
Drunken Hearted Man
Robert Johnson; *Complete Recordings* ....(COL)
Dude (Looks Like A Lady)
Aerosmith; *Permanent Vacation* .... (GEF)
Dutchman
Jerry Jeff Walker; *Hill Country Rain* ....(RYK)
Tommy Makem & Liam Clancy; *Collection* .....(SHA)
El Matador
Kingston Trio; *Capitol Collectors Series* ....(CAP)
Sold Out/String Along ....(CAP)
English Boys
Blondie; *The Hunter* ....(CHR)
English Boys (With Guns)
Deaf School; *English Boys/Working Girls* ....(WB)
Englishman In New York
Sting; *Nothing Like The Sun* ....(A&M)
Enlisted Men's Mess
Glenn Miller; *Major Glenn Miller/Army Air Force
Band* ....(BLU)
Enter Sandman
Metallica; *Metallica* .... (ELE)
Even The Man In The Moon Is Crying
Mark Collie; *Mark Collie* ....(MCA)
Every Little Thing He Does Is Magic
Shawn Colvin; *Cover Girl* ....(COL)
Every Man A King
Randy Newman; *Good Old Boys* ....(RPR)
Excitable Boy
Warren Zevon; *Excitable Boy* ....(ASY)
Quiet Normal Life-Best Of ....(ASY)
Stand In The Fire ....(ASY)
Farmer & The Cowman
Original Broadway Cast; *Oklahoma* ....(RCA)

Fat Boy
Billy Stewart; *One More Time/Chess Years* ....(CSS)
Fat Man
Fats Domino; *Best Of* ....(EMI)
Greatest Hits ....(MCA)
My Blue Heaven-Best Of-#1 ....(EMI)
Jethro Tull; *20 Years Of-Boxed Set* ....(CHR)
M.U.-Best Of ....(CHR)
Stand Up ....(CHR)
Nazareth; *Nazareth* ....(A&M)
Radio Program Theme; *Themes From Old Times* .(VVA)
Fat Man In The Bathtub
Little Feat; *Dixie Chicken* ....(WB)
Waiting For Columbus ....(WB)
Find Yourself A Man
Original Cast; *Funny Girl* ....(CAP)
Five Guys Named Moe
Joe Jackson; *Jumpin' Jive* ....(A&M)
Louis Jordan; *Best Of* ....(MCA)
Original Decca Recordings-#2 .... (DEC)
Flower & The Young Man
Strawbs; *Grave New World* ....(A&M)
Fooling Yourself
Styx; *Caught In The Act* ....(A&M)
Classics-#15 ....(A&M)
Grand Illusion ....(A&M)
For He's A Jolly Good Fellow
Good Time Singers; *All Occasions Album* ....(GAT)
Free Man In Paris
Joni Mitchell; *Court & Spark* ....(ASY)
Shadows & Light ....(ASY)
Freeborn Man
Outlaws; *Bring It Back Alive* .... (ARI)
Lady In Waiting .... (ARI)
Legends Of Rock Guitar/'70s ....(RHI)
Fuck You, Man
Pussy Galore; *Right Now* ....(CRL)
Gambling Man
Bonnie Raitt; *Sweet Forgiveness* ....(WB)
Garbage Man
Cramps; *Bad Music For Bad People* .... (IRS)
Songs The Lord Taught Us .... (IRS)
Muddy Waters; *Can't Get No Grindin'* ....(CSS)
Gentleman Is A Dope
Jo Stafford; *Greatest Hits* ....(CRN)
Morgana King; *Another Time Another Space* ....(MUS)
Ghost Of A Texas Ladies' Man
Concrete Blonde; *Walking In London* .... (IRS)
Gimme Gimme Gimme (A Man After Midnight)
Erasure; *Two Ring Circus* .... (SIR)
Girl
Beatles; *1962-1966* ....(CAP)
Box Set ....(CAP)
Love Songs ....(CAP)
Rubber Soul ....(CAP)
Give Him A Great Big Kiss
Shangri-Las; *Girl Groups* .... (RHI)
Remember The Shangri-Las At Their Best ....(CLT)
Giving Him Something He Can Feel
En Vogue; *Funky Divas* ....(EW)
Go To The Mirror Boy
Who; *Tommy* ....(MCA)
God Fearing Man
Steppenwolf; *At Your Birthday Party* ....(OOP)
God Must Be A Boogie Man
Joni Mitchell; *Mingus* ....(ASY)
Shadows & Light ....(ASY)
God Rest Ye Merry Gentlemen
Bing Crosby; *Merry Christmas* ....(MSP)
Sings Christmas Songs ....(MSP)
Bobby Vinton; *Christmas All-Time Greatest
Records-#2* ....(CCB)
Ella Fitzgerald; *Best Of Christmas* ....(CAP)
Garth Brooks; *Beyond The Season* ....(LIB)
Christmas For The '90s-#1 ....(LIB)
Jackie Wilson; *Merry Christmas From* ....(RHI)
Kenny Rogers; *Christmas In America* ....(RPR)
Leontyne Price; *Christmas Songs* ....(LON)
Mel Torme; *Christmas Songs* ....(TLR)
Nat King Cole; *Cole Christmas & Kids* ....(CAP)
Neil Diamond; *Christmas Album* ....(COL)
Randy Travis; *An Old Time Christmas* ....(WB)
Roger Whittaker; *Tidings Of Comfort & Joy* ......(LIB)
Smokey Robinson/Miracles; *Season For Miracles* (MOT)

Steve Wariner; *Christmas Memories* .... (MSP)
Take 6/Yellowjackets; *He Is Christmas* .... (RPR)
T-Bone Burnett; *Acoustic Christmas* .... (COL)
Going Out With The Boys
Jimmie Mack; *Jimmie Mack* .... (BT)
Golden Boy
Tubes; *Now* .... (A&M)
Good Ole Boys From Louisiana
Jimmy C. Newman & Cajun Country; *Jimmy C.
Newman & Cajun Country* .... (DOT)
Good Time Boy
Buffalo Springfield; *Again* .... (ATC)
Good Time Man Like Me...
Jim Croce; *Life & Times* .... (OOP)
Goodnight, Good Guy
Collective Soul; *Hints Allegations And Things Left
Unsaid* .... (ATL)
Gray Haired Young Man
Don Potter; *Over The Rainbow* .... (MRR)
Greatest Man I Never Knew
Reba McEntire; *For My Broken Heart* .... (MCA)
Greatest Hits-#2 .... (MCA)
Guitar Man
Bread; *Anthology* .... (ELE)
Best Of-#2 .... (ELE)
Elvis Presley; *14 #1 Country Hits* .... (RCA)
Guitar Man .... (RCA)
Nipper's Greatest Hits-'80s .... (RCA)
TV Special .... (RCA)
Half The Man
Clint Black; *No Time To Kill* .... (RCA)
Hangman Jury
Aerosmith; *Permanent Vacation* .... (GEF)
Happily Married Man
Duane Allman; *Anthology #2* .... (CPC)
Happy Man
Chicago; *Greatest Hits-#2* .... (COL)
VII .... (COL)
Greg Kihn Band; *Kihnsolidation-Best Of* .... (RHI)
Hard Drivin' Man
J. Geils Band; *Full House* .... (ATL)
J. Geils Band .... (ATL)
Hard Lovin' Woman
Mark Collie; *Unleashed* .... (MCA)
Hard Workin' Man
Brooks & Dunn; *Hard Workin' Man* .... (ARI)
Jack Nitzsche; *ST/Blue Collar* .... (MCA)
He Ain't Worth Missing
Toby Keith; *Toby Keith* .... (MER)
He Calls Home
Candlebox; *Candlebox* .... (MAV)
He Feels Guilty
Bobbie Cryner; *Bobbie Cryner* .... (EPI)
He Stopped Loving Her Today
George Jones; *Anniversary* .... (EPI)
First Time Love .... (EPI)
Greatest Country Hits/'80s-1980 .... (COL)
Greatest Hits From The Jukebox .... (EPI)
I Am What I Am .... (EPI)
He Talks To Me
Lorrie Morgan; *Leave The Light On* .... (RCA)
He Thinks He'll Keep Her
Mary Chapin Carpenter; *Come On Come On* .... (COL)
He Went To Paris
Jimmy Buffett; *Songs You Know By Heart-Greatest
Hits* .... (MCA)
White Sport Coat & A Pink Crustacean .... (MCA)
You Had To Be There .... (MCA)
He Would Be Sixteen
Michelle Wright; *Now & Then* .... (ARI)
Here Comes A Man
Traffic; *Far From Home* .... (VIA)
Hey Harmonica Man
Stevie Wonder; *Greatest Hits* .... (MOT)
Hey Western Union Man
Jerry Butler; *Best Of* .... (MER)
Billboard Top R&B Hits-1968 .... (RHI)
He'll Have To Go
Jim Reeves; *60 Years Of Country Music* .... (RCA)
Best Of .... (RCA)
Billboard Top Country Hits-1960 .... (RHI)
Great Moments At The Grand Ole Opry .... (RCA)
Nipper's Greatest Hits/'50s-#1 .... (RCA)

Jim Reeves & Patsy Cline; *Jim Reeves-Greatest
Hits* .... (RCA)
Ry Cooder; *Chicken Skin Music* .... (RPR)
He'll Never Love You (Like I Do)
Freddie Jackson; *Rock Me Tonight* .... (CAP)
He's A Fool For You
Boz Scaggs; *My Time* .... (COL)
He's A Good Ole Boy
Chely Wright; *Woman In The Moon* .... (PYN)
He's A Heartache (Looking For A Place..)
Janie Fricke; *17 Greatest Hits* .... (COL)
19 Hot Country Requests .... (EPI)
It Ain't Easy .... (COL)
Very Best Of .... (COL)
He's A Rebel
Crystals; *Good Time Rock 'N' Roll* .... (MCA)
Phil Spector's Greatest Hits .... (SPC)
He's A Whore
Cheap Trick; *Cheap Trick* .... (EPI)
He's The Great Imposter
Fleetwoods; *ST/American Graffiti* .... (MCA)
(He's) Some Kind Of Wonderful
Carole King; *Music* .... (EPI)
High Tech Redneck
George Jones; *High Tech Redneck* .... (MCA)
Highwayman
Glen Campbell; *Highwayman* .... (CAP)
Willie Nelson; *Greatest Country Hits/'80s-1985* . (COL)
W. Jennings/W. Nelson/J. Cash/K. Krist.; *Columbia
Country Classics-#3* .... (COL)
Highwayman .... (COL)
Him
Rupert Holmes; *Partners In Crime* .... (MCA)
His Green Eyes
Barbara Fairchild; *Standing In Your Line* .... (COL)
Home Lovin' Man
Andy Williams; *Greatest Hits-#2* .... (COL)
Homeboy
Michael McDonald; *Take It To Heart* .... (RPR)
Steve Arrington; *45* .... (ATL)
Honky Tonk Night Time Man
Lynyrd Skynyrd; *Street Survivors* .... (MCA)
Merle Haggard/Strangers; *Presents His 30th
Album* .... (CAP)
Songs I'll Always Sing .... (CAP)
Hoochie Coochie Man
Eric Clapton; *From The Cradle* .... (DUC)
House Of The Rising Sun
Animals; *Best Of* .... (AKO)
Greatest Hits .... (ALL)
Rip It To Shreds-Greatest Hits Live .... (IRS)
Hank Williams, Jr.; *Hank Live* .... (W/C)
Ronnie Milsap; *16 Greatest Hits-#2* .... (TRP)
How Can A Poor Man Stand Such Times...
Blind Alfred Reed; *How Can A Poor Man Stand Such
Times...* .... (ROU)
Ry Cooder; *Ry Cooder* .... (RPR)
Show Time .... (WB)
Hurdy Gurdy Man
Donovan; *Greatest Hits* .... (EPI)
Hurdy Gurdy Man .... (EPI)
Hymn For The Dudes
Mott The Hoople; *Greatest Hits* .... (COL)
Mott .... (COL)
Hymn To Him
Audrey Hepburn; *ST/My Fair Lady* .... (COL)
Julie Andrews/Original Cast; *My Fair Lady* .... (COL)
I Am A Simple Man
Ricky Van Shelton; *Backroads* .... (COL)
I Don't Want Your Millions, Mister
Tom Rush; *Tom Rush* .... (FAN)
I Just Want To See His Face
Rolling Stones; *Exile On Main Street* .... (RS)
I Met Him On A Sunday
Shirelles; *16 Greatest Hits* .... (TRP)
Anthology 1959-1967 .... (RHI)
Classics .... (BCT)
Greatest Hits .... (EVR)
I Saw Her (Him) Standing There
Beatles; *Meet The* .... (CAP)
Please Please Me .... (EMI)
Rock 'n' Roll Music-#1 .... (CAP)
Paul McCartney; *Tripping The Live Fantastic* .... (CAP)
Tripping The Live Fantastic-Highlights! .... (CAP)

Tiffany; *Tiffany* .... (MCA)
I Want To Be Your Man
   Roger; *Unlimited!* .... (RPR)
If He Walked Into My Life
   Original Cast; *Mame* ....(COL)
If I Were A Rich Man
   Original Cast; *Fiddler On The Roof* ....(RCA)
   Original London Cast; *Fiddler On The Roof* .....(COL)
If It Weren't For Him
   Vince Gill & Rosanne Cash; *Collector's Duets* ...(RCA)
If You Were The Only Boy (In The World)
   Barbra Streisand; *My Name Is Barbra* ....(COL)
Indian Man
   Charlie Daniels Band; *Midnight Wind* .... (EPI)
Irish Boy
   Mark Knopfler; *CT/Cal* .... (MER)
Irishman In Chinatown
   Luka Bloom; *Riverside* .... (RPR)
Iron Man
   Black Sabbath; *Live Evil* ....(WB)
   Paranoid ....(WB)
   We Sold Our Soul For Rock 'N' Roll ....(WB)
   Ozzy Osbourne; *Tribute* ....(EPA)
   Sir Mix-A-Lot/Metal Church; *Swass* .... (NSY)
It's A Boy
   Who; *Tommy* .... (MCA)
It's A Man's Man's Man's World
   James Brown; *Billboard Top R&B Hits-1966* ..... (RHI)
   Greatest Hits .... (RHI)
It's In His Kiss (Shoop Shoop Song)
   Betty Everett; *Billboard Top R&B Hits-1964* ..... (RHI)
   Hits Of The Sixties .... (IMC)
   More American Graffiti .... (MCA)
   Oldies But Goodies-#3 .... (OSR)
   Very Best Of .... (VJ)
   Wonder Women (History Of Girl Groups) .... (RHI)
   Cher; *ST/Mermaids* ....(GEF)
I'm A One Woman Man
   George Jones; *I'm A One Woman Man* .... (EPI)
   Glen Campbell; *Still Within The Sound Of My*
   Voice .... (MCA)
   Johnny Horton; *American Originals* ....(COL)
I'm A Real Man
   John Hiatt; *Warming Up To The Ice Age* .... (GEF)
I'm A Steady Rollin' Man
   George Thorogood; *Baddest Of* .... (EMI)
I'm Free (Heaven Help The Man)
   Kenny Loggins; *ST/Footloose* ....(COL)
I'm Gonna Wash That Man Right Outta...
   Kiri Te Kanawa/Original Cast; *South Pacific* ....(COL)
   Mary Martin/Original Cast; *South Pacific* ....(COL)
   Mitzi Gaynor; *ST/South Pacific* ....(RCA)
   Weather Girls; *Success* ....(COL)
I'm Just A Country Boy
   Don Williams; *Best Of-#2* .... (MCA)
   Country Boy .... (MCA)
I'm Not A Well Man
   Original Cast; *I Can Get It For You Wholesale* .... (SSP)
I'm Not Your Man
   Tommy Conwell/Young Rumblers; *Rumble* ......(COL)
I'm Waiting For The Man
   Lou Reed; *Live* ....(RCA)
   Velvet Underground; *Live* ....(COT)
   Velvet Underground & Nico ....(VRV)
Japanese Sandman
   Benny Goodman; *Complete-#1-1935* ....(RCA)
Jealous Guy
   John Lennon; *Lennon* ....(CAP)
   John Lennon/Plastic Ono Band; *Collection* ....(GEF)
   Imagine ....(CAP)
   ST/Imagine-The Motion Picture ....(CAP)
   Roxy Music; *Heart Still Beating* ....(RPR)
   High Road ....(WB)
   Street Life-20 Great Hits ....(RPR)
Jealous Hearted Man
   Muddy Waters; *Hard Again* .... (BS)
Jealous Man
   Hoyt Axton; *Fearless* ....(A&M)
   Truth; *Jump* ....(IRS)
Journey Man
   Jethro Tull; *Heavy Horses* ....(CHR)
Jungle Boy
   Bow Wow Wow; *I Want Candy* ....(RCA)
   John Eddie; *John Eddie* ....(COL)

Junk Male
   Five Thirty; *Bed* ....(ATC)
Just Good Ol' Boys
   Moe Bandy & Joe Stampley; *Greatest Hits* ....(COL)
   Just Good Ol' Boys ....(COL)
   Truckers' Jukebox-#2 ....(COL)
Kentucky Man
   Elvis Presley; *Worldwide 50 Gold Award Hits-#1* (RCA)
Kiss Him Goodbye
   Nylons; *Happy Together* ....(OPE)
Last Game Of The Season (A Blind Man...
   David Geddes; *Super Hits/'70s-Have A Nice*
   Day-#20 .... (RHI)
Laughing Boy
   Mary Wells; *Compact Command Performances* . (MOT)
   Greatest Hits ....(MOT)
Laundry Man
   Fenton Robinson; *Genuine Houserockin' Music* ...(ALG)
   Nightflight ....(ALG)
Leave Him Out Of This
   Steve Wariner; *I Am Ready* .... (ARI)
Listen To What The Man Said
   Paul McCartney/Wings; *Over America* ....(CAP)
   Wings; *Venus & Mars* ....(CAP)
Little Beggar Man
   Ian & Sylvia; *Greatest Hits* .... (VAN)
   Northern Journey .... (VAN)
Little Blue Man
   Betty Johnson; *45* .... (ATL)
Little Boy Blue
   Elegants; *45* .... (RLL)
Little Boy Sad
   Johnny Burnette; *45* .... (UA)
Little London Boys
   Johnny Thunders; *Stations Of The Cross* .... (ROI)
Little Paper Boy
   Hank Williams; *Rare Takes & Radio Cuts* ...... (POL)
Littlest Cowboy Rides Again
   Chris LeDoux; *Songbook Of The American West* .. (LIB)
   Sounds Of The Western Country .... (LIB)
Living In The Footsteps Of Another Man
   Chi-Lites; *Greatest Hits* ....(BRU)
   Half A Love ....(BRU)
London Boys
   David Bowie; *London Collector-Starting Point* ....(LON)
   Love You Till Tuesday ....(LON)
London Leatherboys
   Accept; *Balls To The Wall* ....(POR)
   Compilation ....(POR)
Lonely Blue Boy
   Conway Twitty; *Greatest Hits* ....(CCB)
   Very Best Of .... (MCA)
Long Haired Country Boy
   Charlie Daniels Band; *Decade Of Hits* .... (EPI)
   Fire On The Mountain .... (EPI)
   Me & The Boys .... (EPI)
   South's Greatest Hits-#2 ....(CPC)
   Truckers' Jukebox-#2 ....(COL)
   Volunteer Jam-#3 & 4 .... (EPI)
Long Haired Guys From England
   Too Much Joy; *Cereal Killers* .... (GIA)
Long Legged Guitar Pickin' Man
   Johnny Cash & June Carter; *Greatest Hits-#2* ....(COL)
Looking For A Boy
   Eileen Farrell; *I Gotta Right To Sing The Blues* .. (SMC)
   Sarah Vaughan; *George Gershwin Songbook-#1* . (EMA)
Lord Have Mercy On A Country Boy
   Don Williams; *True Love* ....(RCA)
Lord Have Mercy On The Working Man
   Travis Tritt; *T-R-O-U-B-L-E* .... (WB)
Louisiana Man
   Dave Edmunds; *D.E. 7th* ....(COL)
   Doug Kershaw; *Alive & Pickin'* .... (WB)
   Best Of .... (WB)
   Louisiana Man .... (WB)
Louisiana Woman, Mississippi Man
   Loretta Lynn & Conway Twitty; *Louisiana Woman*
   Mississippi Man .... (MCA)
   Very Best Of .... (MCA)
Lover Boy
   Billy Ocean; *Greatest Hits* .... (JVA)
   Suddenly .... (JVA)
   Supertramp; *Even In The Quietest Moments* ..... (A&M)

Lover Man (Oh Where Can You Be)
Barbra Streisand; *Simply Streisand* ....(COL)
Billie Holiday; *Fine & Mellow* ....(CLT)
  History Of The Real ....(VRV)
Blossom Dearie; *Blossom Dearie* ....(VRV)
Lena Horne; *Goes Latin & Sings Your Requests* .. (DRG)
Sarah Vaughan; *Compact Jazz* ....(VRV)
  Jazz 'Round Midnight ....(VRV)
Sonny Stitt; *Soul Classics* .... (PRS)
Low Spark Of High Heeled Boys
Traffic; *Low Spark Of High Heeled Boys* .... (ISL)
  On The Road .... (ISL)
Lucky Guy
Rickie Lee Jones; *Pirates* .... (WB)
Todd Rundgren; *Hermit Of Mink Hollow* .... (BRS)
Lucky Man
Emerson, Lake & Palmer; *Best Of* .... (ATL)
  Emerson, Lake & Palmer .... (ATL)
Mad About The Boy
Dinah Shore; *Love Songs* ....(COL)
Dinah Washington; *Golden Hits* .... (MER)
Madman Across The Water
Elton John; *Live In Australia w/Melbourne
Orchestra* .... (MCA)
  Madman Across The Water .... (POL)
Magic Man
Heart; *Dreamboat Annie* ....(CAP)
  Greatest Hits-Live .... (EPI)
Make Love Like A Man
Def Leppard; *Adrenalize* .... (MER)
Mama He's Crazy
Judds; *Greatest Hits* ....(RCA)
  Judds ....(RCA)
  Why Not Me ....(RCA)
Mama Let Him Play
Doucette; *Mama Let Him Play* .... (MSH)
Mama's Never Seen Those Eyes
Forester Sisters; *Forester Sisters* .... (WB)
Man Bites Dog
Plan 9; *Enigma Variations 2* ....(ENC)
Man Come Into Egypt
Peter, Paul & Mary; *Moving* .... (WB)
Man For All Seasons
Al Stewart; *Time Passages* .... (ARI)
Billy Idol; *Whiplash Smile* .... (CHR)
Man From Bowling Green
Johnny Paycheck; *Take This Job & Shove It* ...... (EPI)
Man From Galilee
Billy Parker; *Average Man* .... (SNC)
Man From Harlem
Cab Calloway/Orchestra; *Tribute To Black
Entertainers* ....(COL)
Man From Pakistan
Flaming Lips; *Hear It Is* .... (RES)
Man From South Africa
Max Roach; *Percussion Bitter Sweet* .... (GRP)
Man I Love
Benny Goodman; *Carnegie Hall Jazz Concert* ....(COL)
Betty Carter; *'S Wonderful-Gershwin Songbook* .. (VRV)
Billie Holiday; *I Like Jazz-Essence Of* ....(COL)
Carmen McRae; *Blue Series-Female Vocals* ......(BLN)
Diana Ross; *ST/Lady Sings The Blues* ....(MOT)
Ella Fitzgerald; *Mack The Knife-In Berlin* ....(VRV)
Harry James; *Hollywood Magic-1950s* ....(COL)
Kate Bush; *Glory Of Gershwin Featuring Larry
Adler* .... (MER)
Mary Lou Williams; *Best Of* .... (PAB)
Nat King Cole Trio; *Best Of* ....(BLN)
Man In Black
Johnny Cash; *Essential* ....(COL)
  Patriot ....(COL)
Man In The Box
Alice In Chains; *Facelift* ....(COL)
Man In The Corner Shop
Jam; *Snap!* .... (POL)
Man In The Mirror
Jim Glaser; *Man In The Mirror* .... (NBL)
Michael Jackson; *Bad* ....(EPI)
Man Of My Word
Collin Raye; *Extremes* ....(EPI)
Man Of The World
Fleetwood Mac; *25 Years-The Chain* .... (WB)
Man On The Moon
R.E.M.; *Automatic For The People* .... (WB)

Man On The Silver Mountain
Ritchie Blackmore; *Rainbow* ....(POL)
Ritchie Blackmore/Rainbow; *Finyl Vinyl* .... (MER)
Man Out Of Time
Elvis Costello; *Girls Girls Girls* ....(COL)
Elvis Costello/Attractions; *Best Of* ....(COL)
  Imperial Bedroom ....(COL)
Man Overboard
Blondie; *Blondie* .... (CHR)
Eric Clapton; *Money & Cigarettes* .... (DUC)
Man Smart, Woman Smarter
Harry Belafonte; *Pure Gold* ....(RCA)
Robert Palmer; *Some People Can Do What They
Like* .... (ISL)
Rosanne Cash; *Right Or Wrong* ....(COL)
Man Who Couldn't Cry
Johnny Cash; *American Recordings* .... (AME)
Man Who Shot Himself
Tom T. Hall; *Places I've Done Time* ....(RCA)
Man Who Shot Liberty Valance
Gene Pitney; *Anthology* .... (RHI)
  Greatest Hits ....(EVR)
  Super Oldies!'60s-#9 ....(AUF)
Greg Kihn; *Glass House Rock* .... (BES)
Man Who Sold The World
David Bowie; *Man Who Sold The World* ....(RYK)
  Sound + Vision ....(RYK)
Man With The Golden Thumb
Jerry Reed; *Man With The Golden Thumb* ....(RCA)
Man With The Lightbulb Head
Robyn Hitchcock/Egyptians; *Fegmania* ....(SLS)
Man & The Donkey
Chuck Berry; *Missing Berries-Rarities-#3* ...... (CSS)
Married Man's A Fool
Blind Willie McTell; *Last Session* .... (PRS)
Ry Cooder; *Paradise & Lunch* .... (RPR)
Married Men
Bette Midler; *Thighs & Whispers* .... (ATL)
Roches; *Bread & Roses Festival-#2* ....(FAN)
  Roches .... (WB)
Marry The Man Today
Original Cast; *Guys & Dolls* .... (MCA)
Me & Fat Boy
Mac Davis; *Texas In My Rear View Mirror* ....(CAS)
Meet De Boys On The Battlefront
Wild Tchoupitoulas; *Treacherous-History Of The Neville
Bros.* .... (RHI)
  Wild Tchoupitoulas .... (ISL)
Men
Charly McClain; *Greatest Hits* ....(EPI)
Forester Sisters; *Talkin' 'Bout Men* .... (WB)
Gladys Knight; *Good Woman* .... (MCA)
Men Of Ohio
Ohio State University Marching Band; *Foot
Tappers* .... (FID)
Mercedes Boy
Pebbles; *Pebbles* .... (MCA)
Midnight Man
Allman Brothers Band; *Shades Of Two Worlds* ....(EPI)
James Gang; *16 Greatest Hits* .... (MCA)
  Best Of .... (MCA)
Rita Remington; *My Melody Of Love* .... (PLN)
Minstrel Boy
Boston Pops Orchestra/Arthur Fiedler; *Irish
Album* ....(RCA)
  Irish Night At The Pops ....(RCA)
John McDermott; *Battlefields Of Green-Songs Of
Love/Loss* .... (ANG)
Miracle Man
Elvis Costello; *My Aim Is True* ....(COL)
Ozzy Osbourne; *Just Say Ozzy* ....(EPA)
  No Rest For The Wicked ....(EPA)
Rain People; *Rain People* .... (EPI)
Mirror Man
Captain Beefheart/Magic Band; *Mirror Man* ..... (OW)
Human League; *Greatest Hits* ....(A&M)
Pere Ubu; *Worlds In Collision* ....(FON)
Prism; *Armageddon* ....(CAP)
Talk Talk; *Party's Over* ....(EMI)
Missionary Man
Eurythmics; *Greatest Hits* .... (ARI)
  Revenge ....(RCA)
Mister Please
Damn Yankees; *Don't Tread* .... (WB)

Monkey Man
Rolling Stones; *Let It Bleed* .... (AKO)
Toots/Maytals; *Live* .... (MGO)
Morning Man
Joy; *Joy* .... (FAN)
Most Happy Fella
Original Broadway Cast; *Most Happy Fella* ..... (SMC)
Original Cast; *Most Happy Fella* .... (RCA)
Most Peculiar Man
Simon & Garfunkel; *Sounds Of Silence* .... (COL)
Motorcycle Boys
Bill Molenhof; *All Pass By* .... (CEX)
Muffin Man
Zappa/Beefheart; *Bongo Fury* .... (RYK)
"Murder", He Says
Roy Eldridge/Gene Krupa Or./Anita O'Day;
Uptown .... (COL)
My Boyfriend's Back
Angels; *Billboard Top Rock 'N' Roll Hits-1963* ... (RHI)
Girl Groups-Story Of A Sound .... (RHI)
My Boyfriend's Back .... (CLT)
Oldies But Goodies-#11 .... (OSR)
ST/Wanderers .... (WB)
Wonder Women-#2-History Of Girl Group ..... (RHI)
My Daddy Was A Milkman
Kentucky HeadHunters; *Pickin' On Nashville* .... (MER)
My Guy
Mary Wells; *Greatest Hits* .... (MOT)
My Guy .... (MOT)
Oldies But Goodies-#11 .... (OSR)
My Jamaican Guy
Grace Jones; *Island Life* .... (ISL)
My Little Marine
Jamie Horton; *45* .... (ERI)
My Man
Barbra Streisand; *Greatest Hits* .... (COL)
Live At The Forum .... (COL)
My Name Is Barbra .... (COL)
ST/Funny Girl .... (COL)
Billie Holiday; *Essential Carnegie Hall Concert* ... (VRV)
Live .... (VRV)
Diana Ross; *Evening With* .... (MOT)
ST/Lady Sings The Blues .... (MOT)
Ella Fitzgerald & Tommy Flanagan Trio; *Montreux*
'77 .... (PAB)
Jeannie C. Riley; *Greatest Hits* .... (PLN)
Peggy Lee; *All-Time Greatest Hits* .... (CCB)
Regina Belle; *Passion* .... (COL)
Sarah Vaughan; *Jazz 'Round Midnight* .... (VRV)
My Man's Gone Now
Ella Fitzgerald & Louis Armstrong; *Porgy & Bess* (VRV)
Nina Simone; *Vocalists-Jazz Masters* .... (BLU)
Original Broadway Cast; *Porgy & Bess* ...... (MCA)
Sarah Vaughan/L.A. Philharmonic; *Gershwin*
Live .... (COL)
Sinead O'Connor; *Glory Of Gershwin Featuring Larry*
Adler .... (MER)
My Melancholy Baby
Barbra Streisand; *Third Album* .... (COL)
Coleman Hawkins; *Genius Of* .... (VRV)
Dorothy Loudon; *Saloon* .... (DRG)
Frank Sinatra; *Voice-Columbia Years-1943-1952* (COL)
Jan Garber Orchestra; *Play 22 Original Big Band*
Recordings .... (HIN)
Kate Smith; *16 Most Requested Songs* .... (COL)
Leon Redbone; *Double Time* .... (WB)
Marcels; *Best Of* .... (RHI)
My Rock & Roll Man
Rita Coolidge; *It's Only Love* .... (A&M)
Na Na Hey Hey Kiss Him Goodbye
Steam; *Billboard Top Rock 'N' Roll Hits-1969* ... (RHI)
Super Hits/'70s-Have A Nice Day-#1 .... (RHI)
Toga Rock .... (DHL)
Nature Boy
George Benson; *Collection* .... (WB)
Jose Feliciano; *Encore* .... (RCA)
Nat King Cole; *Blossom Fell* .... (CAP)
Story .... (CAP)
Unforgettable .... (ELE)
Neanderthal Man
Hotlegs; *Rock Radio Vietnam* .... (KT)
Super Hits/'70s-Have A Nice Day-#3 .... (RHI)

Never Kill Another Man
Steve Miller Band; *Anthology* .... (CAP)
#5 .... (CAP)
New World Man
Rush; *Chronicles* .... (MER)
Signals .... (MER)
Three Decades Of Rock ('60s, '70s, '80s) ...... (PRY)
New York Boy
Neil Diamond; *Glory Road-1968-1972* .... (MCA)
Touching You Touching Me .... (MCA)
No Man's Land
Billy Joel; *River Of Dreams* .... (COL)
Nowhere Man
Beatles; *1962-1966* .... (CAP)
Box Set .... (CAP)
Compact Disc E.P. Collection .... (CAP)
Rubber Soul .... (CAP)
Yesterday...And Today .... (CAP)
O Lucky Man
Alan Price; *ST/O Lucky Man* .... (WB)
Animals; *Greatest Hits Live! (Rip It To Shreds)* .... (IRS)
Oklahoma Boy
Dewayne Boyd/Silver Dollar Band; *45* .... (NAT)
Old Man
Alabama; *Just Us* .... (RCA)
Neil Young; *Decade* .... (RPR)
Harvest .... (RPR)
Randy Newman; *Sail Away* .... (RPR)
ZZ Top; *First Album* .... (WB)
Six Pack .... (WB)
Old Man Down The Road
John Fogerty; *Centerfield* .... (WB)
Old Man On The Farm
Randy Newman; *Little Criminals* .... (WB)
Ol' Man River
Al Jolson; *Best Of* .... (MCA)
Story-#6 .... (MCA)
Frank Sinatra; *Concert Sinatra* .... (RPR)
Greatest Hits-#2 .... (COL)
Voice-Columbia Years-1943-1952 .... (COL)
William Warfield; *ST/All Those Glorious MGM*
Musicals .... (MGM)
William Warfield/Original Cast; *Show Boat* .... (COL)
One And Only Man
Steve Winwood; *Refugees Of The Heart* .... (VIA)
One Boy
Ann-Margret; *ST/Bye Bye Birdie* .... (RCA)
One Good Man
Michelle Wright; *The Reasons Why* .... (ARI)
One Man Band
Moe Bandy; *Greatest Hits* .... (CCB)
You Haven't Heard The Last Of Me .... (MCA)
Roger Daltrey; *Daltrey* .... (MCA)
Three Dog Night; *Joy To The World-Greatest*
Hits .... (MCA)
One Man Woman
Judds; *Collection 1983-1990* .... (RCA)
River Of Time .... (RCA)
Only Living Boy In New York
Simon & Garfunkel; *Bridge Over Troubled Water* (COL)
Collected Works .... (COL)
Ordinary Average Guy
Joe Walsh; *Ordinary Average Guy* .... (EPA)
Other Guy
Little River Band; *Greatest Hits* .... (CAP)
Outlaw Man
Eagles; *Desperado* .... (ASY)
Phone Booth Man
Tuff Darts; *Tuff Darts* .... (SIR)
Piano Lesson & If You Don't Mind My...
Shirley Jones; *ST/Music Man* .... (WB)
Piano Man
Billy Joel; *Greatest Hits-#1 & 2* .... (COL)
Piano Man .... (COL)
Rock Classics Of The '70s .... (COL)
Thelma Houston; *Motown Superstar Series-#20* . (MOT)
Pickup Man
Joe Diffie; *Third Rock From The Sun* .... (EPI)
Pictures Of Matchstick Men
Camper Van Beethoven; *Edge Of Rock* .... (ERA)
Key Lime Pie .... (VIA)
Status Quo; *History Of British Rock-#8* .... (RHI)
Sixties Rule!-#1 .... (OW)

Please Mr. Jailer
Wynona Carr; *Jump Jack Jump!* .... (SPE)
Please Mr. Please
Olivia Newton-John; *Back To Basics-Essential*
Collection .... (GEF)
Poetry Man
Phoebe Snow; *Best Of* .... (COL)
Phoebe Snow .... (MCA)
Policeman
Chicago; *XI* .... (COL)
Pony Boy
Allman Brothers Band; *Brothers & Sisters* .... (POL)
Bruce Springsteen; *Human Touch* .... (COL)
Pony Man
Gordon Lightfoot; *Gord's Gold-#2* .... (WB)
If You Could Read My Mind .... (RPR)
Sit Down Young Stranger .... (RPR)
Poor Boy
Champion Jack Dupree; *Forever & Ever* .... (BUL)
Elvis Presley; *Essential Elvis-First Movies* ......(RCA)
For LP Fans Only .... (RCA)
Fabulous Thunderbirds; *T-Bird Rhythm* ....(CHR)
Howlin' Wolf; *Real Folk Blues* ....(CSS)
Nick Drake; *Bryter Layter* .... (HBL)
Fruit Tree .... (HBL)
Split Enz; *History Never Repeats-Best Of* .... (A&M)
True Colours .... (A&M)
Supertramp; *Crisis? What Crisis?* .... (A&M)
Woody Guthrie; *Legendary* .... (TRD)
Woody Guthrie .... (EVR)
Worried Man Blues-Golden Classics-#1 .....(CLT)
Poor Boy Shuffle
Creedence Clearwater Revival; *1969* .... (FAN)
Willy & The Poor Boys .... (FAN)
Poor Man
Tom Rush; *Tom Rush* .... (ELE)
Poor Man's Roses (Or A Rich Man's Gold)
Patsy Cline; *Best Of* ....(CCB)
Forever & Always .... (EPI)
Stop, Look & Listen .... (MCA)
Story .... (MCA)
Reba McEntire; *Feel The Fire* .... (MER)
Poor Man's Son
Rockin' Berries; *History Of British Rock-#2* ..... (RHI)
Postman Blues
Dinah Washington; *Complete On*
Mercury-#1-1946-1949 .... (MER)
Potential New Boyfriend
Dolly Parton; *Best Of-#3* ....(RCA)
Pow Wow The Indian Boy
Hot Rize; *Hot Rize* .... (FF)
Powerman
Kinks; *Lola Vs. The Powerman & The*
Moneygoround .... (RPR)
Preacher Man
Bananarama; *Pop Life* ....(LON)
Impressions; *45* ....(CUR)
Pretzel Man
Harry Chapin; *Legends Of The Lost & Found* .... (ELE)
Pride Of Man
Quicksilver Messenger Service; *Anthology* ....(CAP)
Quicksilver Messenger Service ....(CAP)
San Francisco Nights .... (RHI)
Sons Of Mercury .... (RHI)
Puppet Man
5th Dimension; *Greatest Hits On Earth* .... (ARI)
Pusherman
Curtis Mayfield; *Pimps Players & Private Eyes* .... (SIR)
Radio Man
World's Famous Supreme Team; *45* .... (ISL)
Radio M.U.S.I.C. Man
Womack & Womack; *Radio M.U.S.I.C. Man* ..... (ELE)
Railroad Boy
Joan Baez; *Ballad Book-#2* .... (VAN)
Joan Baez-#2 .... (VAN)
Very Best Of .... (VAN)
Rainy Day Man
Bonnie Raitt; *Streetlights* .... (WB)
James Taylor; *Flag* ....(COL)
James Taylor .... (CAP)
Tom Rush; *Tom Rush* .... (COL)
Rambling Irishman
De Danann; *Best Of* .... (SHA)

Ramblin' Boy
Tom Paxton; *Greatest Folksingers Of The 60's* ... (VAN)
Newport Folk Festival-1963 .... (VAN)
Ramblin' Boy .... (ELE)
Troubadours Of The Folk Era-#2 .... (RHI)
Ramblin' Gamblin' Man
Bob Seger; *Live Bullet* ....(CAP)
Ramblin' Man
Allman Brothers Band; *Best Of* .... (POL)
Billboard Top Rock 'N' Roll Hits-1973 .... (RHI)
Brothers & Sisters .... (POL)
Decade Of Hits-1969-1979 .... (POL)
Dreams .... (POL)
Road Goes On Forever .... (POL)
Rock Classics .... (KT)
South's Greatest Hits .... (CPC)
Wipe The Windows... .... (CPC)
Hank Williams; *16 Great Hits* .... (EVR)
24 Greatest Hits .... (POL)
40 Greatest Hits .... (POL)
Hank Williams, Jr.; *Rowdy* .... (W/C)
STI Your Cheatin' Heart .... (SSP)
Rastaman Chant
Bob Marley/Wailers; *Burnin'* .... (TUF)
Real Man
Bonnie Raitt; *Nick Of Time* ....(CAP)
Bruce Springsteen; *Human Touch* ....(COL)
Todd Rundgren; *Anthology-1968-1985* ...... (RHI)
Back To The Bars .... (RHI)
Red Headed Irishman
J.P. Fraley & Annadeene; *Wild Rose Of The*
Mountain .... (ROU)
Redneck Fiddlin' Man
Charlie Daniels Band; *Greatest Fiddlin' Licks* ..... (EPI)
Midnight Wind .... (EPI)
Rhumba Man
Jesse Winchester; *Best Of* .... (RHI)
Nothing But The Breeze .... (RHI)
Rich Man
Great Plains; *Great Plains* ....(COL)
Rich Man Poor Man
Peter, Paul & Mary; *Late Again* .... (WB)
Rich Man, Poor Boy
Joe Ely; *Dig All Night* .... (HT)
Rich Man's Frug
Original Cast; *Sweet Charity* ....(COL)
Rich Man's Spiritual
Gordon Lightfoot; *Lightfoot* .... (UA)
Richest Man In Bogota
Gil Melle; *Mindscape* .... (BLN)
Richest Man On Earth
Paul Overstreet; *Sowin' Love* ....(RCA)
Riflemen Of Bennington
Jim Burroughs; *Songs Of Rebellion* ....(AUF)
Right Hand Man
Eddy Raven; *Best Of* ....(RCA)
Right Hand Man ....(RCA)
River Boy
Willie Nelson; *There'll Be No Teardrops Tonight* .. (UA)
Road Of Broken Hearted Men
Bobby Bland; *Introspective Of The Early Years* .. (MCA)
Touch Of The Blues .... (MCA)
Robot Man
Connie Francis; *Rocksides-1957-1964* .... (POL)
Scorpions; *Best Of* ....(RCA)
In Trance ....(RCA)
Tokyo Tapes ....(RCA)
Rock & Roll Man
Kenny Rogers; *Daytime Friends* .... (EMI)
Savoy Brown; *Savage Return* ....(LON)
Rocket Man
Elton John; *Greatest Hits* .... (POL)
Here & There .... (POL)
Honky Chateau .... (POL)
Kate Bush; *Two Rooms-Songs Of E. John & B.*
Taupin .... (POL)
Rockit Man
J.T.; *Kick The Funk* .... (EW)
Rootsman Skanking
Bunny Wailer; *Rootsman Skanking* .... (SHA)
Rough Boy
ZZ Top; *Afterburner* .... (WB)
Greatest Hits .... (WB)

Rough Boys
Pete Townshend; *Classic Rock 1966-1988* .... (ATL)
  Empty Glass ....(ATC)
Who; *Join Together* .... (MCA)
Rubberband Man
Spinners; *Best Of* ....(ATL)
  Mega Hits Dance Classics-#9 .... (PRY)
  One Of A Kind Love Affair-Anthology ....(ATL)
Rude Boy Train
Desmond Dekker; *Rockin' Steady-Best Of* .... (RHI)
Sailor Boy
Chiffons; *Best Of* ....(LAU)
Satisfied Man
Molly Hatchet; *Deed Is Done* .... (EPI)
  Double Trouble Live .... (EPI)
Saturday Boy
Billy Bragg; *Back To Basics* .... (ELE)
School Boy Crush
Average White Band; *Cut The Cake* .... (ATL)
  Person To Person .... (ATL)
Scotsman
Bryan Bowers; *Dr. Demento 20th Anniversary*
  Collection .... (RHI)
  Dr. Demento's Greatest-#5-1980s .... (RHI)
  Home Home On The Road .... (FF)
Secret Agent Man
Devo; *Duty Now For The Future* .... (WB)
Johnny Rivers; *Anthology-1964-1977* .... (RHI)
  Best Of .... (EMI)
  Very Best Of .... (EMI)
See You In Hell, Blind Boy
Ry Cooder; *ST/Crossroads* .... (WB)
Sensitive New Age Guys
Christine Lavin; *Attainable Love* ....(PHO)
Shadow Of A Lonely Man
Alan Parsons Project; *Pyramid* .... (ARI)
Sharp Dressed Man
ZZ Top; *Eliminator* .... (WB)
  Greatest Hits .... (WB)
She's In Love With A Rodeo Man
Chris LeDoux; *Songs Of Rodeo & Country* .... (LIB)
Don Williams; *Greatest Hits* .... (MCA)
She's In Love With The Boy
Trisha Yearwood; *Trisha Yearwood* .... (MCA)
Shoe Salesman
Alice Cooper; *Easy Action* .... (BIZ)
Shoeshine Boy
Count Basie/Kansas City 7; *Count Basie/Kansas City
  7* .... (MCI)
Eddie Kendricks; *At His Best* .... (TAM)
  Motown Superstar Series-#19 .... (MOT)
Shoeshine Man
Tom T. Hall; *Greatest Hits* .... (MER)
Shoot Him
Sugarcubes; *Here Today Tomorrow Next Week!* .. (ELE)
Showman's Life
Jesse Winchester; *Best Of* .... (RHI)
  Touch On The Rainy Side .... (RHI)
Silver Girl
Survivor; *Eye Of The Tiger* .... (SCO)
Simple Man
Bad Company; *Run With The Pack* .... (SS)
Barbra Streisand; *Butterfly* ....(COL)
Charlie Daniels; *All-Time Greatest Hits* .... (EPI)
  Country Greatest Hits-#3 .... (PRY)
Charlie Daniels Band; *Simple Man* .... (EPI)
Confederate Railroad; *Skynyrd Frynds* .... (MCA)
Crosby, Stills & Nash; *Crosby, Stills & Nash* ..... (ATL)
Graham Nash; *Songs For Beginners* .... (ATL)
Hank Williams, Jr.; *Pure Hank* .... (W/C)
Junkyard; *Junkyard* .... (GEF)
Lynyrd Skynyrd; *Gold & Platinum* .... (MCA)
  Legend .... (MCA)
  Pronounced Leh-nerd Skin-nerd .... (MCA)
  What's Your Name .... (MSP)
Simple Man Simple Dream
J.D. Souther; *Black Rose* .... (ASY)
Linda Ronstadt; *Simple Dreams* .... (ASY)
Skinny Boy
Chicago; *Group Portrait* ....(COL)
  VII ....(COL)
Sleep Tight, Good Night Man
Kenny Rogers; *The Gambler* .... (EMI)

Smokin' In The Boys' Room
Brownsville Station; *Hit Singles-1958-1977* ..... (ATL)
  Legends Of Rock Guitar-'70s .... (RHI)
  ST/Rock & Roll High School .... (SIR)
Motley Crue; *Decade Of Decadence* .... (ELE)
  Theatre Of Pain .... (ELE)
Snake Man
Doobie Brothers; *Toulouse Street* .... (WB)
Soldier Boy
Elvis Presley; *Elvis Is Back* ....(RCA)
  Golden Celebration ....(RCA)
Shirelles; *Anthology-1959-1964* .... (RHI)
  Billboard Top Rock 'N' Roll Hits-1962 .... (RHI)
  Oldies But Goodies-#4 .... (OSR)
  ST/The Wanderers .... (WB)
Small Faces; *78 In The Shade* .... (ATL)
Solitary Man
Chris Isaak; *San Francisco Days* .... (RPR)
Neil Diamond; *Classics-Early Years* ....(COL)
  Glory Road-1968-1972 .... (MCA)
  Gold .... (MCA)
  Greatest Hits-1966-1992 ....(COL)
  Hot August Night .... (MCA)
Some Girls Do
Sawyer Brown; *Dirt Road* ....(CRB)
Some Guys Have All The Love
Little Texas; *First Time For Everything* .... (WB)
Some Guys Have All The Luck
Maxi Priest; *Best Of Me* ....(CHS)
  Maxi .... (VIA)
Robert Palmer; *Addictions-#1* .... (ISL)
Rod Stewart; *Camouflage* .... (WB)
  Storyteller-Complete Anthology-1964-1990 ..... (WB)
Somebody Else's Guy
Jocelyn Brown; *Somebody Else's Guy* .... (VIN)
Somebody's Knockin'
Terri Gibbs; *Best Of* .... (MCA)
  Country Gold ....(PRY)
  Country Music Classics-#6-1980-1985 .... (KT)
Someday Soon
Chris LeDoux; *Rodeo Songs Old & New* .... (LIB)
Ian & Sylvia; *Greatest Hits* .... (VAN)
  Northern Journey .... (VAN)
Journey; *Departure* ....(COL)
Judy Collins; *Colors Of The Day-Best Of* .... (ELE)
  Who Knows Where The Time Goes .... (ELE)
Moe Bandy; *Greatest Hits* ....(COL)
  Rodeo Romeo ....(COL)
Suzy Bogguss; *Aces* ....(CAP)
Son Of A Poor Man
R.E.O. Speedwagon; *Decade Of Rock &
  Roll-1970-1980* .... (EPI)
  Live-You Get What You Play For .... (EPI)
  Ridin' The Storm Out .... (EPI)
Son Of A Preacher Man
Dusty Springfield; *Dusty Springfield* .... (RHI)
Song Of The Volga Boatmen
Glenn Miller; *Best Of* ....(RCA)
  Chattanooga Choo Choo-#1 Hits .... (BLU)
  Legendary Performer .... (BLU)
  Memorial-1944-1969 .... (BLU)
  This Is ....(RCA)
Tuxedo Junction; *Tuxedo Junction* .... (BTF)
Soul Man
Blues Brothers; *Best Of* .... (ATL)
  Briefcase Full Of Blues .... (ATL)
  Definitive Collection .... (ATL)
Sam & Dave; *Best Of* .... (ATL)
  Golden Age Of Black Music-1960-1970 ...... (ATL)
  Soul Men .... (RHI)
Spaceboy
Smashing Pumpkins; *Siamese Dream* .... (VIA)
Spaceman
Harry Nilsson; *Songwriter* ....(RCA)
Journey; *In The Beginning* ....(COL)
  Next ....(COL)
Nilsson; *Son Of Schmilsson* ....(RCA)
Spilled Perfume
Pam Tillis; *Sweetheart's Dance* .... (ARI)
Stand By Your Man
Lyle Lovett/Large Band; *Lyle Lovett/Large Band* (MCC)

Tammy Wynette; *Biggest Hits* .... (EPI)
   Columbia Country Classics-#3-1965-1970 ...... (KT)
   ST/Sleepless In Seattle .... (EPI)
   Tears Of Fire-25th Anniversary Collect. .... (EPI)
Starman
   David Bowie; *Changestwobowie* ....(RCA)
   Fame & Fashion ....(RCA)
   Rise & Fall Of Ziggy Stardust ....(RYK)
   The Singles-1969-1993 ....(RYK)
Station Man
   Fleetwood Mac; *25 Years-The Chain* .... (WB)
   Kiln House .... (WB)
Stone Cold Gentleman
   Ralph Tresvant; *Ralph Tresvant* .... (MCA)
Stories For Boys
   U2; *Boy* .... (ISL)
Stout-Hearted Men
   Barbra Streisand; *Simply Streisand* ....(COL)
Street Fighting Man
   Rod Stewart; *Best Of* .... (MER)
   Sing It Again Rod .... (MER)
   Storyteller-Complete Anthology-1964-1990 ..... (WB)
   Rolling Stones; *Beggars Banquet* .... (AKO)
   Get Yer Ya-Ya's Out .... (AKO)
   Hot Rocks-1964-1971 .... (AKO)
   Singles Collection-London Years .... (AKO)
   Through The Past Darkly-Big Hits-#2 .... (AKO)
Struggling Man
   Jimmy Cliff; *In Concert-Best Of* .... (RPR)
   Struggling Man .... (ISL)
Stubborn Kind Of Fellow
   Marvin Gaye; *Anthology* .... (MOT)
   Greatest Hits .... (MOT)
   Superhits .... (MOT)
Suicidal Man
   Uriah Heep; *Wonderworld* .... (ROA)
Summer Boy
   Buffy Sainte-Marie; *Best Of* .... (VAN)
Sun Hasn't Set On This Boy Yet
   Nils Lofgren; *Classics-#13* ....(A&M)
   Nils Lofgren ....(RYK)
Supermen
   David Bowie; *Hunky Dory* ....(RYK)
   Man Who Sold The World ....(RYK)
   Sound + Vision ....(RYK)
Sure The Boy Was Green
   Horslips; *Aliens* .... (DJM)
Sweet Gingerbread Man
   Mike Curb Congregation; *Greatest Hits* ....(CCB)
Sweet Lover Man
   Pointer Sisters; *Best Of-1978-1981* ....(RCA)
   Sweet & Soulful ....(RCA)
Sweet Music Man
   Dolly Parton; *Here You Come Again* ....(RCA)
   Kenny Rogers; *Daytime Friends* .... (EMI)
   Millie Jackson; *Get It Out'cha System* .... (SPR)
   Live & Uncensored .... (SPR)
   Nana Mouskouri; *Song For Liberty* .... (MER)
Sweet Talkin' Guy
   Chiffons; *Best Of* ....(LAU)
   Collectables Presents History Of Rock-#1 ....(CLT)
   Everything You Always Wanted ....(LAU)
   Golden Classics ....(CLT)
Swiss Boy
   Michigan Dutchmen; *German Polka Favorites* .... (JJ)
Swiss Boy Waltz
   Michigan Dutchmen; *German Polka Favorites* .... (JJ)
Take Him Back, Rachel
   Basia; *London Warsaw New York* .... (EPI)
Take It Like A Man
   Michelle Wright; *Now & Then* .... (ARI)
   Today's Top Country .... (KT)
Taxman
   Beatles; *Box Set* ....(CAP)
   Revolver ....(CAP)
   Rock & Roll Music-#2 ....(CAP)
   George Harrison; *Best Of* ....(CAP)
   George Harrison & Eric Clapton; *Live In Japan* (DKH)
Taxman Mr. Thief
   Cheap Trick; *Cheap Trick* .... (EPI)
Telephone Man
   Meri Wilson; *First Take* .... (GRT)
   Super Hits/'70s-Have A Nice Day-#21 .... (RHI)

Television Man
   Talking Heads; *Little Creatures* .... (SIR)
Ten Dollar Man
   ZZ Top; *Six Pack* .... (WB)
   Tejas .... (WB)
Tennessee Flat Top Box
   Johnny Cash; *Classic Cash-Hall Of Fame Series* . (MER)
   Columbia Country Classics-#3-Americana ......(COL)
   Essential ....(COL)
   Rosanne Cash; *30 Years Of #1 Hits-#17* ....(COL)
   Hits-1979-1989 ....(COL)
   King's Record Shop ....(COL)
Texas Fiddle Man
   Asleep At The Wheel; *Keepin' Me Up Nights* .... (ARI)
Thank God I'm A Country Boy
   John Denver; *Back Home Again* ....(RCA)
   Evening With ....(RCA)
   Greatest Hits-#2 ....(RCA)
Thank You Boys
   Jane's Addiction; *Nothing's Shocking* .... (WB)
That Boy Could Dance
   Weird Al Yankovic; *In 3-D* .... (SCO)
That Man From New York City
   Lightnin' Hopkins; *Lost Texas Tapes-#1* .... (CLT)
That Mister Man Of Mine
   Original Off-Broadway Cast; *Dames At Sea* .... (SMC)
That Rhythm Man
   Louis Armstrong/Orchestra; *& The Big Bands* ...(DSQ)
That's A Man's Way
   Wilson Pickett; *In The Midnight Hour* .... (RHI)
   Man & A Half-Best Of .... (RHI)
That's My Baby
   Lari White; *Wishes* ....(RCA)
That's The Way Boys Are
   Lesley Gore; *Golden Hits Of* .... (MER)
That's What He Said
   Reba McEntire; *My Kind Of Country* .... (MCA)
That's What My Man Is For
   Delaney & Bonnie; *Best Of* .... (RHI)
   Delaney & Bonnie & Friends/Eric Clapton; *On*
   Tour ....(ATC)
"The Men" Theme
   Isaac Hayes; *Greatest Hit Singles* .... (STX)
Then He Kissed Me
   Crystals; *Back To Mono-1958-1969* .... (AKO)
   Best Of .... (AKO)
There He Is (At My Door)
   Martha Reeves/Vandellas; *Anthology* .... (MOT)
   Live Wire! Singles-1962-1972 .... (MOT)
There Once Was A Man
   Original Cast; *Pajama Game* ....(COL)
There's A Fella Waitin' In Poughkeepsie
   Pied Pipers; *Capitol Collectors Series* .... (CAP)
They Call Me The Popcorn Man
   Luther Johnson; *Lonesome In My Bedroom* ....(EVD)
Third Man Theme (Harry Lime Theme)
   Band; *Moondog Matinee* ....(CAP)
   Dukes Of Dixieland; *Greatest Hits* .... (MCA)
   Guy Lombardo; *Best Of* ....(CCB)
This Boy
   Beatles; *Box Set* ....(CAP)
   Love Songs ....(CAP)
   Meet The ....(CAP)
   Past Masters-#1 ....(CAP)
   ST/Hard Day's Night ....(CAP)
This Boy Needs To Rock
   Night Ranger; *7 Wishes* .... (CAM)
   ST/Explorers .... (VS)
This Guy's In Love With You
   Burt Bacharach; *Classics-#23* ....(A&M)
   Greatest Hits ....(A&M)
   Herb Alpert/Tijuana Brass; *Greatest Hits-#2* ....(A&M)
Thoroughly African Man
   Red Clay Ramblers; *Chuckin' The Frizz* .... (FF)
Tin Man, The
   Kenny Chesney; *In My Wildest Dreams* ....(CPC)
To Sir With Love
   Lulu; *History Of British Rock-#6* .... (RHI)
   Hollywood Magic-1960s ....(COL)
   Rock Artifacts-#3-From The Vaults ....(COL)
(Today I Met) The Boy I'm Gonna Marry
   Darlen Love; *Best Of* .... (AKO)
   Darlene Love; *Back To Mono-1958-1969* ...... (AKO)

Train Man
Bob Seger System; *Ramblin' Gamblin' Man* ......(CAP)
Trash Man
Jimi Hendrix; *Midnight Lightning* .... (RPR)
Trashmen
Phantom Opera; *Phantom Opera* ....(NAL)
Traveling Man
Dolly Parton; *Best Of* ....(RCA)
  Coat Of Many Colors ....(RCA)
Travelin' Man
Albert King; *I Wanna Get Funky* .... (STX)
Bob Seger; *Beautiful Loser* ....(CAP)
  Live Bullet ....(CAP)
Doobie Brothers; *Doobie Brothers* ....(WB)
Jacky Ward; *45* ....(ASY)
Lynyrd Skynyrd; *One More From The Road* ..... (MCA)
Rick Nelson; *Best Of* .... (EMI)
  Greatest Hits .... (RHI)
Stevie Wonder; *Greatest Hits-#2* .... (MOT)
Travelling Man
Simple Minds; *Real Life* .... (A&M)
Trouble Man
Grover Washington, Jr.; *Anthology* .... (MOT)
  Soul Box-#1 .... (MOT)
Marvin Gaye; *Anthology* .... (MOT)
  Every Great Motown Hit Of .... (MOT)
  Greatest Hits .... (MOT)
  Live At The London Palladium .... (MOT)
  ST/Trouble Man .... (MOT)
Truck Drivin' Man
Charlie Walker; *Trucker's Jukebox-#2* ....(COL)
Commander Cody/Lost Planet Airmen; *Hot Licks, Cold
Steel & Trucker's Fav.* .... (MCA)
  Too Much Fun-Best Of .... (MCA)
Flying Burrito Brothers; *Close Encounters To The West
Coast* ....(RLX)
Hank Wilson; *Hank Wilson's Back* .... (MCA)
J. Geils Band; *Blow Your Face Out* .... (ATL)
Larry Scott; *Keep On Truckin'* ....(EXA)
Lynyrd Skynyrd; *Legend* .... (MCA)
Truck Drivin' Son Of A Gun
Dave Dudley; *20 Golden Souvenirs Of Music City
U.S.A.* .... (PLN)
  Billboard Top Country Hits-1965 .... (RHI)
True Men Don't Kill Coyotes
Red Hot Chili Peppers; *Abbey Road E.P.* .... (EMI)
  Red Hot Chili Peppers .... (EMI)
  What Hits!? Best Of .... (EMI)
Try To Find Another Man
Righteous Brothers; *Anthology-1962-1974* .... (RHI)
TV Preacher Man Blues
Glenn Sutton; *Close Encounters Of The Sutton
Kind* .... (MER)
Tweeter & The Monkey Man
Traveling Wilburys; *#1* .... (WIL)
Twelve Volt Man
Jimmy Buffett; *Boats Beaches Bars & Ballads* ... (MGR)
  One Particular Harbor .... (MCA)
Twelve Year Old Boy
Elmore James; *Collectables Blues Collection-#1* .. (CLT)
  Golden Classics ....(CLT)
  Sky Is Crying-History Of .... (RHI)
Twentieth Century Man
Scorpions; *Animal Magnetism* .... (MER)
Twenty-First Century Schizoid Man
King Crimson; *Abbreviated* .... (EDI)
  Compact .... (EDI)
  In The Court Of The Crimson King .... (EDI)
Two Gentlemen Of Peru
Simon & Bard Group; *Enormous Radio* ....(FF)
Two Headed Man
Lonnie Brooks; *Genuine Houserockin' Music-#3* ..(ALG)
Two-Bit Man Child
Neil Diamond; *Glory Road-1968-1972* .... (MCA)
  Velvet Gloves & Spit ....(MSP)
Typical Male
Tina Turner; *Break Every Rule* .... (CAP)
  Hot Ladies Of The '80s .... (KT)
  Live In Europe ....(CAP)
  Simply The Best ....(CAP)
Umbrella Man
Kay Kyser; *Sentimental Favorites* ....(COL)

Undercover Man
Edgar Winter Group; *They Only Come Out At
Night* .... (EPI)
Understand Your Man
Johnny Cash; *Billboard Top Country Hits-1964* .. (RHI)
  Greatest Hits ....(COL)
U.S. Male
Jerry Reed; *Best Of* ....(RCA)
Vigilante Man
Bruce Springsteen; *Folkways-Tribute-W. Guthrie &
Leadbelly* ....(COL)
Ry Cooder; *Into The Purple Valley* ....(RPR)
Woody Guthrie; *Dust Bowl Ballads* .... (ROU)
Virginia Boys
Country Gazette; *Hello Operator-This Is* .... (FF)
  Strictly Instrumental ....(FF)
Voodoo Medicine Man
Aerosmith; *Pump* ....(GEF)
Walk Like A Man
Bruce Springsteen; *Tunnel Of Love* ....(COL)
Four Seasons; *Anthology* .... (RHI)
  Billboard Top Rock 'N' Roll Hits-1963 .... (RHI)
  ST/Wanderers ....(WB)
Frankie Valli/Four Seasons; *Greatest Hits-#1* .... (RHI)
Grand Funk Railroad; *We're An American Band* .(CAP)
Walking Dream
Patsy Cline; *Forever & Always* .... (EPI)
  Here's .... (MCA)
Walking Man
James Taylor; *Greatest Hits* ....(WB)
  Walking Man ....(WB)
Wanted Man
George Thorogood/Destroyers; *Bad To The Bone* (EMI)
Johnny Cash; *At Folsom Prison & San Quentin* ...(COL)
  Essential ....(COL)
Ratt; *Out Of The Cellar* ....(ATL)
  Ratt & roll 8191 ....(ATL)
War Of Man
Neil Young; *Harvest Moon* .... (RPR)
Water Boy
John Lee Hooker; *Country Blues Of* .... (RVR)
Paul Robeson; *Historic-Golden Classics-#3* ....(CLT)
Roger Whittaker; *Last Farewell & Other Hits* .....(RCA)
  New World In The Morning ....(RCA)
Watermelon Man
Albert King; *Wednesday Night In San Francisco* .. (STX)
Buddy Guy; *Hold That Plane* ....(VAN)
Gun Club; *Miami* .... (IRS)
Herbie Hancock; *Best Of-Blue Note Years* ....(BLN)
  Head Hunters ....(COL)
  Takin' Off ....(BLN)
Johnny Taylor; *Wanted One Soul Singer* ....(ATL)
Mongo Santamaria; *Greatest Hits* ....(COL)
  Mongo's Greatest Hits ....(FAN)
New Grass Revival; *Too Late To Turn Back Now* ..(FF)
Way He Makes Me Feel
Barbra Streisand; *Collection-Greatest Hits & More* (COL)
  ST/Yentl ....(COL)
We Are Hungry Men
David Bowie; *London Collection* ....(LON)
  Starting Point ....(DER)
Well Respected Man
Kinks; *Greatest Hits-#1* .... (RHI)
  History Of British Rock-#4 .... (RHI)
  Kinks-Size Kinkdom .... (RHI)
West Virginia Man
David Allan Coe; *20 Great Hits* .... (PLN)
Willie Nelson; *Longhorn Jamboree* .... (PLN)
  & His Friends .... (PLN)
What Kind Of Man Would I Be?
Chicago; *19* .... (FM)
  Greatest Hits 1982-1989 .... (FM)
Whatta Man
Salt-N-Pepa featuring En Vogue; *Very Necessary* . (NP)
When A Man Loves A Woman
Barbara Mandrell; *Best Of* .... (LIB)
  Key's In The Mailbox .... (LIB)
Bette Midler; *ST/The Rose* ....(ATL)
Michael Bolton; *Time Love & Tenderness* ....(COL)

Percy Sledge; *Atlantic*
R&B-1947-1974-#5-(1962-1966) .... (ATL)
  Atlantic Soul Classics .... (WSP)
  Best Of .... (ATL)
  Golden Age Of Black Music-1960-1970 .... (ATL)
  ST/Platoon & Songs Of The Era .... (ATL)
When I Grow Up (To Be A Man)
Beach Boys; *Absolute Best-#1* .... (CAP)
  Dance Dance Dance .... (CAP)
  Gift Set .... (CAP)
  Made In The U.S.A. .... (CAP)
  Spirit Of America .... (CAP)
When You Walk In The Room
Pam Tillis; *Sweetheart's Dance* .... (ARI)
White Boys
Original Cast; *ST/Hair* .... (RCA)
White Man
Queen; *Day At The Races* .... (HOL)
White Man In Hammersmith Palais
Clash; *Clash* .... (EPI)
  On Broadway .... (EPI)
  Story Of-#1 .... (EPI)
White Man/Black Man
James Gang; *Thirds* .... (OW)
James Gary; *16 Greatest Hits* .... (MCA)
Who's That Man
Toby Keith; *Boomtown* .... (PYN)
Wild Boys
Duran Duran; *Arena* .... (CAP)
  Decade .... (CAP)
Wild Eyed Boy From Freecloud
David Bowie; *Sound + Vision* .... (RYK)
  Space Oddity .... (RYK)
  ST/Ziggy Stardust-The Motion Picture .... (RYK)
Wild Man
J. Geils Band; *Flashback-Best Of* .... (EMI)
Ricky Van Shelton; *Greatest Hits Plus* .... (COL)
  Steppin' Country .... (COL)
Wild Man Blues
Jelly Roll Morton; *Jelly's Last Jam & Other Morton*
Classics .... (BLU)
Louis Armstrong; *Best Of Decca*
Years-#2-Composer .... (MCA)
Wild-Eyed Southern Boys
38 Special; *Wild-Eyed Southern Boys* .... (A&M)
Will You Be Loving Another Man
Bill Monroe/Blue Grass Boys; *Essential Bill*
Monroe-1945-1949 .... (COL)
Winter Boy
Buffy Sainte-Marie; *Best Of* .... (VAN)
  Little Wheel Spin & Spin .... (VAN)
Worker Man
PAtra; *Queen Of The Pack* .... (EPI)
Working Class Man
Lacy J. Dalton; *45* .... (COL)
Working For The Man
Roy Orbison; *All-Time Greatest Hits* .... (MON)
  For The Lonely-Anthology-1956-1965 .... (RHI)
  In Dreams-Greatest Hits .... (VIA)
  More Greatest Hits .... (MON)
Working Man
Glenn Frey; *Soul Searchin'* .... (MCA)
John Conlee; *Blue Highway* .... (MCA)
  Greatest Hits-#2 .... (MCA)
  Songs For The Working Man .... (MCA)
Otis Rush; *Mourning In The Morning* .... (ATL)
Rush; *All The World's A Stage* .... (MER)
  Archives .... (MER)
  Chronicles .... (MER)
  Rush .... (MER)
Working Man Can't Get Nowhere Today
Merle Haggard; *18 Rare Classics* .... (CCB)
Merle Haggard/Strangers; *Working Man Can't Get*
Nowhere Today .... (CAP)
Working Man's Ph.D.
Aaron Tippin; *Call Of The Wild* .... (RCA)
Workin' Man
Creedence Clearwater Revival; *1968-1969* ...... (FAN)
  Creedence Clearwater Revival .... (FAN)
Workin' Man Blues
Diamond Rio/Lee R. Parnell/Steve Wariner; *Mama's*
Hungry Eyes-Merle Haggard Tribute .... (ARI)
Gary Morris; *These Days* .... (LIB)

Merle Haggard/Strangers; *Best Of Country Blues* .(CCB)
  Capitol Collectors Series .... (CAP)
  Okie From Muskogee .... (CAP)
  Songs I'll Always Sing .... (CAP)
Ricky Van Shelton; *Wild-Eyed Dream* .... (COL)
Would They Love Him Down In Shreveport
George Jones; *Hallelujah Weekend* .... (EPI)
Oak Ridge Boys; *Bobbie Sue* .... (MCA)
Yellow Man
Randy Newman; *12 Songs* .... (RPR)
  Randy Newman .... (RPR)
Yo Mister
Patti Labelle; *Be Yourself* .... (MCA)
You Can't Fool The Fat Man
Randy Newman; *Little Criminals* .... (WB)
You Made A Wanted Man Of Me
Ronnie McDowell; *19 Hot Country Requests-#2* .. (EPI)
  Country Boy's Heart .... (EPI)
  Older Women & Other Greatest Hits .... (EPI)
You Make Me Feel Like A Man
Ricky Skaggs; *Live In London* .... (EPI)
Young Man Blues
Who; *Live At Leeds* .... (MCA)
  ST/Kids Are Alright .... (MCA)
You're A Man Of Words, I'm A Woman
Betty LaVette; *Lost Soul-#1* .... (EPI)
You're Still A Young Man
Tower Of Power; *Bump City* .... (WB)
  Live & In Living Color .... (WB)

MEN'S NAMES: A

   See Also: MEN: GENERAL

Abraham, Martin & John
Dion; *24 Original Classics* .... (ARI)
  Collectables Presents History Of Rock-#3 .... (CLT)
  WCBS FM-History Of Rock-'60s-#2 .... (CLT)
Harry Belafonte; *All Time Greatest Hits-#1* .....(RCA)
Smokey Robinson/Miracles; *Anthology* .... (MOT)
  Time Out For/Special Occasion .... (MOT)
Alan's Psychedelic Breakfast
Pink Floyd; *Atom Heart Mother* .... (CAP)
Alexander's Ragtime Band
Al Jolson/Bing Crosby; *Al Jolson Story-#1* ..... (MCA)
  Immortal Al Jolson .... (MCA)
Alfie
Barbra Streisand; *What About Today* .... (COL)
Dionne Warwick; *Anthology* .... (RHI)
  Greatest Hits .... (EVR)
Amos Moses
Jerry Reed; *Best Of* .... (RCA)
  Nipper's Greatest Hits-'70s .... (RCA)
  Super Hits Of '70s-Have A Nice Day-#3 .... (RHI)
Arnold Layne
Pink Floyd; *Relics* .... (CAP)
  Works .... (CAP)
Arthur
Badfinger; *Magic Christian Music By* .... (CAP)
Hoodoo Gurus; *Stoneage Romeos* .... (A&M)
Kinks; *Arthur Or Decline/Fall Of British Empire* .. (RPR)
Arthur In The Afternoon
Liza Minnelli/Original Cast; *The Act* .... (DRG)
Arthur's Theme
Christopher Cross; *ST/Arthur* .... (WB)
Connecticut Yankee In The Court Of...
Robert Fripp/League Of Crafty Guitarists; *Show Of*
Hands .... (EDI)
Man On The Moon (Andy)
R.E.M.; *Automatic For The People* .... (WB)
Me & Little Andy
Dolly Parton; *Collector's Series* .... (RCA)
  Greatest Hits .... (RCA)
  Here You Come Again .... (RCA)
Poland Whole/Madam I'm Adam
Tubes; *Young & Rich* .... (A&M)
Rock Me Amadeus
Falco; *3* .... (A&M)
  Remix Hit Collection .... (SIR)
Song For Adam
Jackson Browne; *Jackson Browne* .... (ASY)
St. Alphonzo's Pancake Breakfast
Frank Zappa; *Apostrophe/Overnite Sensation* .....(RYK)

"The Archies" Theme
Original Music; *Television's Greatest Hits-#3* ..... (TVT)
Trouble With Andre
Sheakespear's Sister; *Hormonally Yours* ....(LON)
Uncle Albert/Admiral Halsey
Paul McCartney; *Gift Set* ....(CAP)
Paul McCartney/Wings; *Wings Greatest* ....(CAP)
Paul & Linda McCartney; *All The Best* ....(CAP)
Ram ....(CAP)
You Can Call Me Al
Paul Simon; *Concert In The Park-August 15 1991* (WB)
Graceland ....(WB)
Negotiations & Love Songs-1971-1986 ....(WB)

MEN'S NAMES: B

Bach, Beethoven, Mozart & Me
Phil Ochs; *Greatest Hits* ....(A&M)
Ballad Of Ben Gay
Ben Gay/Silly Savages; *Dr. Demento's Delights* ..(WB)
Ballad Of Billy The Kid
Billy Joel; *Piano Man* ....(COL)
Songs In The Attic ....(COL)
Barney Google
Authentic Band Organ; *Catch The Brass
Ring-Merry-Go-Round* ....(KLA)
Firehouse Five Plus Two; *Twenty Years Later* .... (GTJ)
"Barney Miller" Theme
Original Music; *Television's Greatest Hits-#3* .....(TVT)
Ben
Jackson 5; *16 Greatest Hits* .... (MOT)
Anthology .... (MOT)
Jacksons; *Live* .... (EPI)
Michael Jackson; *Anthology* .... (MOT)
Best Of .... (MOT)
Motown Superstar Series-#7 .... (MOT)
Bennie & The Jets
Elton John; *Billboard Top Rock 'N' Roll Hits-1974* (RHI)
Classic Rock-#1 .... (MCA)
Goodbye Yellow Brick Road .... (POL)
Greatest Hits .... (POL)
Here & There .... (POL)
Big Bad Bill Is Sweet William Now
Ry Cooder; *Jazz* .... (WB)
Big Bopper's Wedding
Big Bopper; *Chantilly Lace Starring The Big
Bopper* .... (MER)
Hellooo Baby! Best Of-1954-1959 .... (RHI)
M. Dung's Idiot Classics .... (RHI)
Bill
Ava Gardner; *ST/Showboat* ....(SSP)
Original Cast; *Showboat* ....(RCA)
Bill Bailey
Louis Armstrong; *Essential* .... (VAN)
Louis Armstrong ....(AUF)
Pearl Bailey; *Echoes Of An Era* ....(RLL)
Preservation Hall Jazz Band; *New Orleans-#1* ...(COL)
Billy 1, 2 & 7
Bob Dylan; *ST/Pat Garrett & Billy The Kid* ....(COL)
Billy Dee
Kris Kristofferson; *Silver Tongued Devil & I* ......(COL)
Billy Don't Be A Hero
Bo Donaldson/Heywoods; *Super Hits/'70s-Have A Nice
Day-#13* .... (RHI)
Billy Get Me A Woman
Joe Stampley; *Biggest Hits* .... (EPI)
Billy Got Some Bad News Today
Tom Paxton; *It Ain't Easy* .... (FF)
Billy The Kid
Charlie Daniels Band; *High Lonesome* .... (EPI)
Marty Robbins; *Gunfighter Ballads & Trail Songs* (COL)
Ry Cooder; *Into The Purple Valley* .... (RPR)
Billy The Kid (I Miss...)
Billy Dean; *Billy Dean* .... (LIB)
Bo Diddley
Bo Diddley; *Good Time Rock 'N Roll* .... (MCA)
History Of Rock-#5 .... (CLT)
Oldies But Goodies-#10 .... (OSR)
ST/Rage In Harlem .... (SIR)
Buddy Holly; *20 Golden Greats* .... (MCA)
For The First Time Anywhere ... (MCA)
Bo Diddley Is Jesus
Jesus & Mary Chain; *Barbed Wire Kisses* .... (WB)

Bob Dylan's 115th Dream
Bob Dylan; *Bringing It All Back Home* ....(COL)
Bob Dylan's Dream
Bob Dylan; *Freewheelin'* ....(COL)
Peter, Paul & Mary; *Album 1700* ....(WB)
Bobby Orr Breakaway
Kirk Elliott; *No Fixed Address* .... (BOO)
Bobby's Girl
Marcie Blaine; *Collectables Presents History Of
Rock-#5* ....(CLT)
Million-Dollar Memories-#2 ....(RCA)
WCBS FM101-History Of Rock-'60s-#5 ....(CLT)
Bobby's In Vicksburg
Sylvia; *Snapshot* ....(RCA)
Bonaparte's Retreat
Chieftains; *Bonaparte's Retreat* ....(SHA)
Glen Campbell; *Classics Collection* .. (LIB)
Kay Starr; *Greatest Hits* ....(CCB)
Sons Of The Pioneers; *Country & Western
Memories* .... (PRR)
Boris The Spider
Who; *Meaty Beaty Big & Bouncy* .... (MCA)
Quick One (Happy Jack)/Sell Out .... (MCA)
Who's Last .... (MCA)
Brian's Song
Johnny Mathis; *First Time Ever I Saw Your Face* .(COL)
Michel LeGrand; *45* .... (FSB)
Bubba Shot The Jukebox
Mark Chesnutt; *Longnecks & Short Stories* ...... (MCA)
Buck Rogers In The 25th Century
Neil Norman/Cosmic Orchestra; *Greatest Science Fiction
Hits-#2* .... (CRS)
Candy Man
Fred Neil; *Little Bit Of Rain* .... (ELE)
Grateful Dead; *American Beauty* ....(WB)
Mississippi John Hurt; *Best Of* .... (VAN)
Today .... (VAN)
Roy Orbison; *All-Time Greatest Hits* .... (MON)
Greatest Hits .... (MON)
In Dreams: Greatest Hits .... (VIA)
Very Best Of .... (MON)
Cowboy Bill
Garth Brooks; *Garth Brooks* .... (LIB)
Did Beethoven Do The Dishes
Reilly & Maloney; *Profiles* .... (FRK)
Do The Bartman
Bart Simpson; *Simpsons Sing The Blues* .... (GEF)
Don't Forget The Coffee Billy Joe
Tom T. Hall; *Essential-Twentieth Anniversary
Collect.* .... (MER)
Don't Mess With Bill
Marvelettes; *Anthology* .... (MOT)
Compact Command Performances .... (MOT)
Greatest Hits .... (MOT)
Top 10 With A Bullet-Motown Girl Groups .... (MOT)
Hey Bobby
K.T. Oslin; *This Woman* .... (RCA)
Hobo Bill's Last Ride
Merle Haggard/Strangers; *Okie From Muskogee* ..(CAP)
Same Train Different Time .... (CAP)
If Bubba Can Dance (I Can Too)
Shenandoah; *Under The Kudzu* .... (RCA)
In Buddy's Eyes
Jane Harvey; *Other Side Of Sondheim* .... (ATL)
In Walked Bud
Art Blakey & Thelonius Monk; *Great Moments In
Jazz* .... (ATL)
Thelonius Monk; *Best Of* .... (BLN)
Genius Of Modern Music-#1 .... (BLN)
Lone Star Beer & Bob Wills Music
Red Steagall; *Lone Star Beer & Bob Wills Music* (MCA)
Texas Country .... (MCA)
Me & Bobby McGee
Grateful Dead; *Grateful Dead* .... (WB)
Janis Joplin; *Greatest Hits* .... (COL)
Janis .... (COL)
Pearl .... (COL)
Rock Classics/'70s .... (COL)
Willie Nelson; *Sings Kristofferson* .... (COL)
Mr. Blue
Fleetwoods; *Best Of* .... (RHI)
Garth Brooks; *No Fences* .... (CAP)
Michael Franks; *Art Of Tea* .... (RPR)
Timmy/Tulips; *ST/American Hot Wax* ....(A&M)

Mr. Blue Sky
Electric Light Orchestra; *Afterglow* .... (EPI)
   Greatest Hits .... (JET)
   Out Of The Blue .... (JET)
Mr. Bojangles
David Bromberg; *Out Of The Blues-Best Of* ......(COL)
Jerry Jeff Walker; *Best Of* .... (MCA)
   Gypsy Songman .... (RYK)
   Man Must Carry On .... (MCA)
   Mr. Bojangles .... (BAI)
Nitty Gritty Dirt Band; *Best Of* .... (EMI)
   On The Road Again .... (CAP)
   Super Hits/'70s-Have A Nice Day-#4 .... (RHI)
   Twenty Years Of Dirt-Best Of .... (WB)
My Attorney Bernie
David Frishberg; *Can't Take You Nowhere* ..... (FAN)
   Classics .... (CCJ)
My Name Is Bocephus
Hank Williams, Jr.; *Greatest Hits-#3* .... (W/C)
   Montana Cafe .... (W/C)
   "Live" .... (W/C)
November In The Snow/Lord Buckley
Mark Murphy; *Kerouac Then & Now* .... (MUS)
Ode To Billy Joe
Bobbi Gentry; *All-Time Country Classics-#1* ..... (CAP)
Railroad Bill
Etta Baker; *One-Dime Blues* .... (ROU)
Ramblin' Jack Elliott; *Hard Travelin'* .... (FAN)
   Ramblin' Jack Elliott .... (PRS)
Reverend Mr. Black
Johnny Cash; *Biggest Hits* ....(COL)
Kingston Trio; *Capitol Collectors Series* .... (CAP)
Roll Over Beethoven
Beatles; *At The Hollywood Bowl* .... (CAP)
   Box Set .... (CAP)
   Rock & Roll Music-#1 .... (CAP)
   Second Album .... (CAP)
   With The Beatles .... (CAP)
Byrds; *Byrds (collection)* .... (COL)
Chuck Berry; *Chess Box* .... (CSS)
   Cruisin'-1956 .... (INC)
   Golden Hits .... (MER)
   Greatest Hits .... (EVR)
   Oldies But Goodies-#10 .... (OSR)
Electric Light Orchestra; *Afterglow* .... (EPI)
   Ole ELO .... (JET)
Story Of Bo Diddley
Animals; *Best Of* .... (AKO)
Bo Diddley; *In The Spotlight* .... (CSS)
"The Bob Newhart Show" Theme
Original Music; *Television's Greatest Hits-#3* ..... (TVT)
Which Way You Goin' Billy
Poppy Family; *Super Hits/'70s-Have A Nice
Day-#2* .... (RHI)
Wild Bill Jones
Hot Rize; *Radio Boogie* ....(FF)
Kentucky Colonels; *Appalachian Swing!* .... (ROU)
Wild Billy's Circus Story
Bruce Springsteen; *Wild The Innocent & The E Street
Shuffle* ....(COL)
Wild Bill's Blues
Country Gazette; *Strictly Instrumental* ....(FF)

MEN'S NAMES: C

Bonnie & Clyde
Georgie Fame; *45* .... (EPI)
Casanova
Bryan Ferry; *Let's Stick Together* .... (RPR)
Levert; *Big Throwdown* .... (ATL)
   Golden Age Of Black Music-1977-1988 .... (ATL)
   ST/Fatal Beauty .... (ATL)
Roxy Music; *Country Life* .... (ATC)
Casey Jones
Fred McDowell & Furry Lewis; *When I Lay My Burden
Down* ....(BIO)
Casey's Last Ride
Johnny Cash; *Rainbow* .... (COL)

Charlie Brown
Coasters; *Billboard Top Rock 'N' Roll Hits-1957* . (RHI)
   Cruisin'-1959 .... (INC)
   Greatest Hits .... (ATC)
   Super Oldies/'50s-#7 .... (AUF)
   Their Greatest Recordings .... (ATC)
   Young Blood .... (ATL)
Charlie Don't Surf
Clash; *Sandinista* .... (EPI)
Charlie Dunn
Jerry Jeff Walker; *Gypsy Songman* .... (RYK)
   Jerry Jeff Walker .... (MCA)
Chubbster
Chubb Rock; *S* .... (SEL)
Chuck E.'s In Love
Rickie Lee Jones; *Rickie Lee Jones* .... (WB)
Cisco Kid
War; *All Day Music* .... (MCA)
   Greatest Hits .... (UA)
   Live .... (UA)
Clap Hands, Here Comes Charlie
Barbra Streisand; *ST/Funny Lady* .... (BC)
Charlie Barnet; *Big Band-1967* .... (MOB)
   Clap Hands, Here Comes Charlie .... (BLU)
   Complete-#6 .... (RCA)
Clyde
Waylon Jennings; *Music Man* .... (RCA)
Cocaine Charlie
Atlanta Rhythm Section; *Boys From Doraville* ...(POL)
Cortez The Killer
Neil Young/Crazy Horse; *Decade* .... (RPR)
   Live Rust .... (RPR)
   Zuma .... (RPR)
Cosmic Charlie
Grateful Dead; *Aoxomoxoa* .... (WB)
   What A Long Strange Trip It's Been .... (WB)
Curly Shuffle
Jump 'N The Saddle Band; *Dr. Demento's Greatest
Novelty-#5* .... (RHI)
C.C. Waterback
Merle Haggard & George Jones; *By Request* ...... (EPI)
   Greatest Country Duets .... (EPI)
   His Epic Hits-First 11 To Be Continued .... (EPI)
   Taste Of Yesterday's Wine .... (EPI)
Day That Curly Bill Shot Down Crazy Sam
Hollies; *Hollies* .... (EPI)
Diesel Cecil
Larry Scott; *Keep On Truckin'* .... (ALS)
General Custer
Tom Paxton; *How Come The Sun* ....(OOP)
Good Time Charlie's Got The Blues
Danny O'Keefe; *45* .... (ATL)
   Seattle Tapes .... (FIR)
Willie Nelson; *City Of New Orleans* ....(COL)
Hang On St. Christopher
Tom Waits; *Frank's Wild Years* .... (ISL)
I Remember Clifford
Lee Morgan; *Best Of* .... (BLN)
Pieces Of A Dream & Manhattan Transfer; *In
Performance At The Playboy Jazz Fest.* .... (ELE)
Jukebox Charlie
Johnny Paycheck; *Out-of-print Recording* ....(OOP)
Kid Charlemagne
Steely Dan; *Greatest Hits* .... (MCA)
   Royal Scam .... (MCA)
Mr. Custer
Larry Verne; *Collectables Presents History Of
Rock-10* .... (CLT)
   Dr. Demento Greatest Novelty CD-#3-'60s ..... (RHI)
   Wacky Weirdos .... (KT)
M.T.A. (Charlie)
Kingston Trio; *25 Years Non-Stop* .... (XER)
   Best Of .... (CAP)
   Capitol Collectors Series .... (CAP)
   Scarlet Ribbons .... (CAP)
   Very Best Of .... (CAP)
Nowadays Clancy Can't Even Sing
Buffalo Springfield; *Buffalo Springfield* .... (ATC)
   Retrospective .... (ATC)
Please Mr. Custer
Ray Stevens; *Gitarzan* .... (BBY)
Prince Charming
Adam Ant; *Antics In The Forbidden Zone* .... (EPI)
   Prince Charming .... (EPI)

Salute To Charlie Christian
Barney Kessel; *"Guitar Player" Presents Guitar
Classics* .... (PRS)
Trash Can Charlie
Billy Goat; *Bush Roaming Mammals* .... (TR)
TV Caesar
Procol Harum; *Grand Hotel* .... (CHR)
Uncle Clooney Played The Banjo
Country Gazette; *Hello Operator...This Is* .... (FF)
Out To Lunch .... (FF)
Utah Carl
Harry K. McClintock; *Cowboy Songs On
Folkways* .... (FLW)
You're A Good Man, Charlie Brown
Original Cast; *You're A Good Man, Charlie
Brown* .... (POL)

MEN'S NAMES: D

Ballad Of Danny Bailey
Elton John; *Goodbye Yellow Brick Road* .... (POL)
Ballad Of Davy Crockett
Bill Hayes; *45* .... (ERI)
Fess Parker; *16 Most Requested Songs/'50s-#1* ...(COL)
Columbia Country Classics-#3 ....(COL)
Hollywood Magic-'50s ....(COL)
Kentucky HeadHunters; *Electric Barnyard* ..... (MER)
Tennessee Ernie Ford; *Capitol Collectors Series* ..(CAP)
Black Jack David
Alice Stuart; *All The Good Times* .... (ARH)
Steeleye Span; *All Around My Hat* .... (CHR)
Story .... (CHR)
Warren Smith; *45* .... (SUN)
Dancing With Mr. D
Rolling Stones; *Goat's Head Soup* .... (RS)
Daniel
Elton John; *Don't Shoot Me I'm Only The Piano
Player* .... (POL)
Greatest Hits ....(POL)
Wilson Phillips; *Two Rooms-Songs Of E. John & B.
Taupin* .... (POL)
Daniel & The Sacred Harp
Band; *Anthology-#1* .... (CAP)
Stage Fright .... (CAP)
To Kingdom Come (Definitive Collection) .... (CAP)
Danny Boy
Bill Evans; *Complete Riverside Recordings* ....(RVR)
Bing Crosby; *When Irish Eyes Are Smiling* .... (MCA)
Conway Twitty; *Classics-#1* .... (WB)
Very Best Of ....(MCA)
Tony Bennett; *Jazz* ....(COL)
Danny's All-Star Joint
Rickie Lee Jones; *Rickie Lee Jones* .... (WB)
Danny's Song
Anne Murray; *Country* .... (CAP)
Danny's Song ....(CAP)
Greatest Hits ....(CAP)
Loggins & Messina; *Best Of-Friends* ....(COL)
On Stage ....(COL)
Sittin' In ....(COL)
David Watts
Kinks; *Kink Kronikles* .... (RPR)
Something Else .... (RPR)
David & Me
Jerry Jeff Walker; *Jerry Jeff Walker* .... (MCA)
Davy Crockett
Hermes Nye; *Ballads Of The Civil War-#1 & 2* . (FLW)
Davy The Fat Boy
Randy Newman; *Live* .... (RPR)
Randy Newman .... (RPR)
Davy's Dinghy
Ruth Wallis; *Dr. Demento's Dementia Royale* .... (RHI)
Dr. Demento's Greatest Novelties-#2 .... (RHI)
Dexter Digs In
Eddie Jefferson; *Come Along With Me* .... (PRS)
There I Go Again .... (PRS)
Dickie's Such An Asshole
Frank Zappa; *Broadway The Hard Way* ....(RYK)
You Can't Do That On Stage Anymore-#1 ......(RYK)
Dillon's Store
Lightnin' Hopkins; *Prison Blues-Golden
Classics-#2* .... (CLT)

Django
Chet Baker; *My Favourite Songs-#1-Last Great
Concert* .... (ENJ)
John Lewis; *Garden of Delight-Delaunay's
Dilemma* .... (EMA)
Midnight In Paris .... (EMA)
Modern Jazz Quartet; *Artistry Of* .... (PRS)
Django .... (PRS)
Modern Jazz Quartet .... (PRS)
Stephane Grappelli; *Feeling Plus Finesse Equals
Jazz* .... (ATL)
Vince Guaraldi Trio; *Vince Guaraldi Trio* ....(FAN)
Wynton Marsalis; *Hot House Flowers* ....(COL)
Dogman
King's X; *Dogman* .... (ATL)
Donald & Lydia
John Prine; *John Prine* .... (ATL)
Prime Prine .... (ATL)
Doolin Dalton
Eagles; *Desperado* .... (ASY)
Live .... (ASY)
"Dudley-Do-Right" Theme
Original Music; *Television's Greatest Hits-#3* ..... (TVT)
Duncan
Paul Simon; *Greatest Hits, Etc.* .... (COL)
Live Rhymin' ....(COL)
Paul Simon .... (WB)
Dupree's Diamond Blues
Grateful Dead; *Aoxomoxoa* .... (WB)
King David
Judy Collins; *Bread & Roses* .... (ELE)
Sir Duke
Stevie Wonder; *Original Musiquarium* .... (MOT)
Songs In The Key Of Life .... (MOT)
Somebody Killed Dewey Jones' Daughter
Lacy J. Dalton; *Takin' It Easy* ....(COL)
Stone Outside Dan Murphy's Door
Anna McGoldrick; *Ireland On My Mind* .... (RGO)
Street Man Named Desire
Pirates Of The Mississippi; *Street Man Named
Desire* .... (LIB)
Surfer Dan
Turtles; *Turtle Wax-Best Of-#2* .... (RHI)
Tom, Dick Or Harry
Original Cast; *Kiss Me Kate* ....(COL)
Trudy & Dave
John Hiatt; *Slow Turning* .... (A&M)
Uncle Dave's Travels-Misery In Arkansas
Uncle Dave Macon; *Country Music Hall Of
Fame* .... (MCA)

MEN'S NAMES: E

Ballad Of Fast Eddie
Rodney Crowell; *Street Language* ....(COL)
Calling Elvis
Dire Straits; *On Every Street* .... (WB)
Careful With That Axe Eugene
Pink Floyd; *Relics* .... (CAP)
Umma Gumma .... (CAP)
"Courtship Of Eddie's Father" Theme
Nilsson; *Television's Greatest Hits-#2* .... (TVT)
Einstein At The Pool Hall
Pat McDonald/Essentials; *Lowdown* .... (MOU)
Einstein On The Beach
Counting Crows; *August And Everything After* .. (DGC)
Eisenhower
John Scofield; *Meant To Be* .... (BLN)
Eisenhower Blues
Elvis Costello; *King Of America* .... (COL)
J.B. Lenoir; *Best Of Chess Blues* .... (CSS)
Natural Man ....(CSS)
Eli's Comin'
Laura Nyro; *Eli & The Thirteenth Confession* .....(COL)
Three Dog Night; *Best Of* .... (MCA)
Best Of ....(MSP)
Rockin' '60s ....(PRY)
Elmer's Tune
Glenn Miller; *Best Of* .... (RCA)
Best Of-#2 .... (RCA)
Complete-#7 ....(RCA)
Legendary Performer ....(RCA)
Memorial: 1944-1969 ....(RCA)

Peggy Lee; *Sings With Benny Goodman* ....(COL)
Peggy Lee/Benny Goodman Orchestra; *Miss Peggy Lee* ....(COL)
Elvis & Marilyn
Leon Russell; *Americana* ....(PRD)
Eugene You Genius
Bryan White; *Bryan White* .... (ASY)
I Try To Think About Elvis
Patty Loveless; *When Fallen Angels Fly* ....(EPI)
I Want Elvis For Christmas
Holly Twins & Eddie Cochran; *Legends Of Christmas Past-Rock & R&B* .... (EMI)
Spanish Eddie
Laura Branigan; *Hold Me* .... (ATL)
Stupid Einstein
Three O'Clock; *Sixteen Tambourines* .... (FRN)
Wreck Of The Edmund Fitzgerald
Gordon Lightfoot; *Gord's Gold-#2* .... (WB)
  Summertime Dream .... (RPR)

MEN'S NAMES: F

Ballad Of Frankie Lee & Judas Priest
Bob Dylan; *John Wesley Harding* ....(COL)
Capt. Fantastic & The Brown Dirt Cowboy
Elton John; *Capt. Fantastic & The Brown Dirt Cowboy* .... (POL)
Daddy Frank
Merle Haggard; *Best Of* ....(CAP)
  Capitol Collectors Series ....(CAP)
  Songs I'll Always Sing ....(CAP)
Dear Mr. Fantasy
Traffic; *Best Of* .... (ISL)
  Dear Mr. Fantasy .... (ISL)
  Welcome To The Canteen .... (ISL)
Do The Freddy
Chubby Checker; *Greatest Hits* .... (AKO)
Fernando
Abba; *Greatest Hits* .... (ATL)
  I Love Abba .... (ATL)
  Live .... (ATL)
  Singles .... (ATL)
Forrest Gump Suite
Alan Silvestri; *ST/Forrest Gump* .... (EPX)
Frankie
Connie Francis; *Very Best Of* .... (POL)
Sister Sledge; *When The Boys Meet The Girls* ..... (ATL)
Franklin D. Roosevelt's Back Again
New Lost City Ramblers; *Early Years-1958-1962* .... (FLW)
Freddie's Dead
Curtis Mayfield; *45* ....(OOP)
Fishbone; *Truth & Soul* ....(COL)
F. Lee Bailey Blues
Sugar Ray/Bluetones; *Don't Stand In My Way* ... (BUL)
Lord, Mr. Ford
Jerry Reed; *Best Of A Great Year-#3* ....(RCA)
  In Concert ....(RCA)
Pretty Boy Floyd
Arlo Guthrie & Pete Seeger; *Precious Friend* ...... (WB)
Bob Dylan; *Folkways-Tribute To W. Guthrie/Leadbelly* ....(COL)
Byrds; *Byrds (collection)* ....(COL)
  Sweetheart of The Rodeo ....(COL)
Joan Baez; *Greatest Songs Of Woody Guthrie* ... (VAN)
Woody Guthrie; *Dust Bowl Ballads* ....(ROU)
  Legendary ....(TRD)
  Struggle .... (FLW)
  Woody Guthrie .... (EVR)
  Worried Man Blues-Golden Classics-#1 ....(CLT)
Theme From "Flash Gordon"
Neil Norman; *Greatest Science Fiction Hits-#3* ... (CRS)
Where Did Robinson Crusoe Go With Friday
Ian Whitcomb; *45* ....(OSR)

MEN'S NAMES: G

Gabriel's Mother's Hiway Ballad 16 Blues
Arlo Guthrie; *Best Of* .... (WB)
"George Of The Jungle" Theme
Original Music; *Television's Greatest Hits-#2* ..... (TVT)

Georgy Porgy
Toto; *Past To Present-1977-1990* ....(COL)
  Toto ....(COL)
Gitarzan
Ray Stevens; *Dr. Demento's Greatest Novelty-#3* . (RHI)
  Greatest Hits ....(MCA)
  Greatest Hits ....(RCA)
"Gomer Pyle U.S.M.C." Theme
Original Music; *Television's Greatest Hits-#2* ..... (TVT)
Just Like Gene Autry
Moby Grape; *Very Best Of-Vintage* ....(COL)
Killing Of Georgie
Rod Stewart; *Greatest Hits* .... (WB)
  Night On The Town .... (WB)
Open Letter To George Bush
Wayne Horvitz/The President; *Miracle Mile* ...... (ELE)
President Garfield
Jerry Holland; *Jerry Holland* .... (ROU)
Shorty George
Count Basie; *Best Of* ....(MCA)
  Command Performances .... (ACC)
  Country Party .... (ACC)
  Sing Along With .... (RLL)
Leadbelly; *King Of The 12-String Guitar* ....(COL)
  Take This Hammer .... (FLW)
Sunday In The Park With George
Original Cast; *Sunday In The Park With George* ..(RCA)

MEN'S NAMES: H

Death Of Hank Williams
Jack Cardwell; *Super Country Hits Of The 50's* .. (GUS)
Death Of Harry Simms
Pete Seeger; *Essential* .... (VAN)
Der Fuehrer's Face
Spike Jones; *Best Of* ....(RCA)
Diary Of Horace Wimp
Electric Light Orchestra; *Discovery* .... (JET)
Don'tcha Tell Henry
Bob Dylan/Band; *Basement Tapes* ....(COL)
Dr. Heckyll & Mr. Jive
Men At Work; *Cargo* ....(COL)
Dr. Jeckyll & Mr. Hyde
Who; *Magic Bus* ....(MCA)
Harrigan
Mickey Finn; *Mickey Finn's Music* .... (CRS)
Harry
Big Brother/Holding Company; *Farewell Song* ...(COL)
  Live .... (RHI)
Harry The Hairy Ape
Ray Stevens; *Best Of* .... (MEr)
Harry The Hippie
Bobby Womack; *Greatest Hits* .... (LIB)
  Soul Survivor .... (EMI)
Harry, Let's Marry
Maxine Brown; *45* ....(CLT)
Harry's House Centerpiece
Joni Mitchell; *Hissing Of Summer Lawns* .... (ASY)
Henry
New Riders Of The Purple Sage; *Best Of* ....(COL)
  Bill Graham Presents Fillmore-Last Days ....(EPA)
  Home Home On The Road ....(COL)
  New Riders Of The Purple Sage ....(COL)
Henry Martin
Joan Baez; *Ballad Book* .... (VAN)
  Jack Orion .... (VAN)
  Joan Baez .... (VAN)
"Hogan's Heroes" Theme
Original Music; *Television's Greatest Hits-#2* ..... (TVT)
Howard's Dead & Gone
Weavers; *Classics* .... (VAN)
"Huckleberry Hound" Theme
Original Music; *Television's Greatest Hits-#2* ..... (TVT)
Hurricane (Carter)
Bob Dylan; *Desire* ....(COL)
I'm Henry The VIII, I Am
Herman's Hermits; *Something Good Again* ....(OOP)
  XX-Greatest Hits .... (AKO)
Little Hitler
Nick Lowe; *Pure Pop For Now People* ....(COL)
Open The Door, Homer
Bob Dylan/Band; *Basement Tapes* ....(COL)
Thunderclap Newman; *Hollywood Dream* ...... (MCA)

Over At Herbie's Juke Joint
Donald Brown; *People Music* .... (MUS)
Poor Howard
Leadbelly; *Gwine Dig A Hole To Put The Devil In* (ROU)
Leadbelly .... (EVR)
Leadbelly .... (FAN)
Memorial-#4 .... (STO)
President Hayes
Sonny Rollins; *Don't Stop The Carnival* .... (MS)
Save The Bones For Henry
Ray Charles; *Just Between Us* .... (COL)
Springtime For Hitler
Mel Brooks; *ST/High Anxiety* .... (ASY)
Tom, Dick Or Harry
Original Cast; *Kiss Me Kate* .... (COL)
Uncle Albert/Admiral Halsey
Paul McCartney; *Gift Set* .... (CAP)
Paul McCartney/Wings; *Wings Greatest* .... (CAP)
Paul & Linda McCartney; *All The Best* .... (CAP)
Ram .... (CAP)
Voice Of Harold
R.E.M.; *Dead Letter Office* .... (IRS)
We'd Like To Thank You Herbert Hoover
Original Broadway Cast; *Annie* .... (COL)

MEN'S NAMES: I

Uncle Isak Goes To Africa
Tom Wasinger; *Rock Music* .... (INV)

MEN'S NAMES: J

See Also: GOD (JESUS)

Abraham, Martin & John
Dion; *24 Original Classics* .... (ARI)
Collectables Presents History Of Rock-#3 .... (CLT)
WCBS FM-History Of Rock-'60s-#2 .... (CLT)
Harry Belafonte; *All Time Greatest Hits-#1* ...... (RCA)
Smokey Robinson/Miracles; *Anthology* .... (MOT)
Time Out For/Special Occasion .... (MOT)
Ballad Of Frankie Lee & Judas Priest
Bob Dylan; *John Wesley Harding* .... (COL)
Ballad Of Jed Clampett
Flatt & Scruggs; *Columbia Country Classics-#3* ..(COL)
On Foggy Mountain .... (FFT)
Ballad Of John & Yoko
Beatles; *1967-70* .... (CAP)
Box Set .... (CAP)
Hey Jude .... (CAP)
Past Masters-#2 .... (CAP)
ST/Imagine-The Motion Picture .... (CAP)
Be Good Johnny
Men At Work; *Business As Usual* .... (COL)
Big Bad John
Jimmy Dean; *American Originals* .... (COL)
Billboard Top Country Hits-1961 .... (RHI)
Columbia Country Classics-#3 .... (COL)
Greatest Hits .... (COL)
Big Joe & Phantom 309
Tom Waits; *Double Live* .... (ASY)
Nighthawks At The Diner .... (ASY)
Big John
Shirelles; *Anthology 1959-1964* .... (RHI)
Classics .... (BCT)
Greatest Hits .... (TRP)
Super Oldies/'60s-#10 .... (AUF)
Captain Jack
Billy Joel; *Greatest Hits-#1 & 2* .... (COL)
Piano Man .... (COL)
Songs In The Attic .... (COL)
Cotton Eyed Joe
Bob Wills; *Columbia Historic Edition* .... (COL)
Carlton Moody/Moody Brothers; *Carlton Moody/Moody Brothers* .... (LAM)
Dear John
Elton John; *Jump Up!* .... (MCA)
Hank Williams; *24 Greatest Hits-#2* .... (POL)
40 Greatest Hits .... (POL)
Hey Good Lookin' (Dec. 1950-July 1951) ...... (POL)
Joe Walsh; *Confessor* .... (FM)
Nazareth; *Nazareth* .... (A&M)

Dear John Letter
Jean Shepard & Ferlin Husky; *45* .... (CAP)
Dear John Letter Lounge
Jerry Jeff Walker; *It's A Good Night For Singin'* . (MCA)
Dear John & Marsha Letter
Stan Freberg; *Capitol Collectors Series* .... (CAP)
Devil Comes Back To Georgia (Johnny)
Marc O'Connor; *Heroes* .... (WB)
Devil Went Down To Georgia (Johnny)
Charlie Daniels Band; *Billboard Top Hits-1979* .. (RHI)
Decade Of Hits .... (EPI)
Me & The Boys .... (EPI)
Million Mile Reflections .... (EPI)
ST/Urban Cowboy .... (ASY)
Diamond Joe
Tom Rush; *Mind Ramblin'* .... (PRS)
Tom Rush .... (FAN)
Did You See Jackie Robinson Hit That...
Count Basie; *RCA Victor Blues & Rhythm Revue* .(RCA)
& Orchestra; Baseball's Greatest Hits .... (RHI)
Dinner For One Please James
Nat King Cole; *Blossom Fell* .... (CAP)
Gift Set .... (CAP)
Don't Cry Joe (Let Her Go, Let Her Go)
Frank Sinatra; *Sinatra Swings* .... (RPR)
Down At Papa Joe's
Dixiebelles; *45* .... (OOP)
Dr. Heckyll & Mr. Jive
Men At Work; *Cargo* .... (COL)
Dr. Jeckyll & Mr. Hyde
Who; *Magic Bus* .... (MCA)
Dr. Jimmy
Who; *Quadrophenia* .... (MCA)
ST/Quadrophenia .... (POL)
Empty Garden (Hey Hey Johnny)
Elton John; *Greatest Hits-1976-1986* .... (MCA)
Jump Up! .... (MCA)
Farmer John
Neil Young/Crazy Horse; *Ragged Glory* .... (RPR)
Premiers; *Frat Rock-#2* .... (RHI)
History Of Latino Rock-#1 .... (RHI)
Fat Jack
Steppenwolf; *7* .... (MCA)
Feed Jake
Pirates Of The Mississippi; *Pirates Of The Mississippi* .... (CAP)
Frankie & Johnny
Doc Watson; *Favorites* .... (LIB)
Jerry Lee Lewis; *Greatest* .... (RHI)
Frankie & Johnny Blues
Glenn Yarbrough; *Best Of* .... (RCA)
Kay Starr; *Country* .... (CRS)
Gentleman Jim
Joe Hackney; *Heavy Hitter* .... (HH)
Go Jimmy Go
Jimmy Clanton; *Super Oldies/'50s-#2* .... (AUF)
Goodbye Jimmy Goodbye
Kathy Linden; *45* .... (OOP)
Happy Jack
Who; *Greatest Hits* .... (MCA)
Happy Jack .... (MCA)
Meaty Beaty Big & Bouncy .... (MCA)
ST/Kids Are Alright .... (MCA)
Who's Better Who's Best-Very Best Of .... (MCA)
Haul Away, Joe
Burl Ives; *Best Of* .... (MCA)
Clancy Brothers; *Greatest Hits* .... (VAN)
Hey Joe
Jimi Hendrix; *Essential-#2* .... (RPR)
Live At Winterland .... (RYK)
Smash Hits .... (RPR)
Jimi Hendrix Experience; *Are You Experienced?* . (RPR)
Love; *Best Of* .... (RHI)
Hey Joe, Hey Moe
Moe Bandy & Joe Stampley; *Greatest Hits* .... (COL)
Hey Joe, Hey Moe .... (COL)
Live At Bad Bob's .... (COL)
Hey Jude
Beatles; *1967-1970* .... (CAP)
20 Greatest Hits .... (CAP)
Hey Jude .... (CAP)
Past Masters-#2 .... (CAP)
Paul McCartney; *Knebworth-The Album* .... (POL)
Tripping The Live Fantastic .... (CAP)

Wilson Pickett; *Greatest Hits* .... (ATL)
Hit The Road Jack
Ray Charles; *Anthology* .... (RHI)
   Greatest Hits-#1 .... (RHI)
   Greatest Hits-#2 ....(DHL)
House That Jack Built
Aretha Franklin; *30 Greatest Hits* .... (ATL)
   Aretha's Gold .... (ATL)
In Memoriam-John F. & Robert F. Kennedy
Clare Fischer; *'Twas Only Yesterday* .... (DCO)
I've Been Watching You (Jamie's Girl)
Randy Hall; *I Belong To You* .... (MCA)
Jack
AC/DC; *High Voltage* ....(ATC)
   If You Want Blood You've Got It .... (ATL)
Jack Straw
Bruce Hornsby/Range; *Deadicated* .... (ARI)
Grateful Dead; *Europe '72* .... (WB)
   What A Long Strange Trip It's Been .... (WB)
Jack You're Dead
Joe Jackson; *Jumpin' Jive* ....(A&M)
Louis Jordan; *Jazz Heritage-Greatest
Hits-#2-1941-1947* .... (MCA)
Jack & Diane
John Cougar Mellencamp; *American Fool* ....(RIV)
Jack & Jill
Ray Parker, Jr./Raydio; *Chartbusters* .... (ARI)
   Greatest Hits .... (ARI)
   Ray Parker, Jr.Raydio .... (ARI)
Jackie Brown
John Cougar Mellencamp; *Big Daddy* .... (MER)
Jackie Wilson Said (I'm In Heaven...)
Van Morrison; *Best Of* .... (MER)
   St. Dominic's Preview .... (WB)
   ST/Queen's Logic .... (EPI)
Jacob's Ladder
Bruce Hornsby/Range; *Scenes From The
Southside* ....(RCA)
Huey Lewis/News; *Fore!* .... (CHR)
Rush; *Exit...Stage Left* .... (MER)
   Permanent Waves .... (MER)
James Dean
Eagles; *On The Border* .... (ASY)
Jeremy
Pearl Jam; *Ten* ....(EPA)
Jesse
Carly Simon; *Come Upstairs* .... (WB)
Joan Armatrading; *Sleight Of Hand* ....(A&M)
Joan Baez; *Classics-#8* ....(A&M)
Roberta Flack; *Best Of* .... (ATL)
   Killing Me Softly .... (ATL)
Stephanie Mills; *If I Were Your Woman* .... (MCA)
Jesse James
Bob Seger; *Smokin' O.P.'s* ....(CAP)
Country Joe McDonald; *Country Joe* .... (VAN)
   Essential .... (VAN)
Sam McGee; *Granddad Of The Country Guitar
Pickers* .... (ARH)
Jessie's Girl
Rick Springfield; *Greatest Hits* ....(RCA)
   Nipper's Greatest Hits-'80s ....(RCA)
   Working Class Dog ....(RCA)
Jim
Big Maybelle; *Ladies Sing The Blues-#2* .... (SAV)
Jim Dandy
Black Oak Arkansas; *Best Of* ....(ATC)
   Super Hits/'70s-Have A Nice Day-#12 .... (RHI)
La Vern Baker; *Atlantic R&B
1947-1974-#3-1955-1958* .... (ATL)
Jim Dean Of Indiana
Phil Ochs; *Chords Of Fame* ....(A&M)
   Greatest Hits ....(A&M)
   War Is Over-Best Of ....(A&M)
Jimmy Jazz
Clash; *London Calling* .... (EPI)
Jimmy Lee
Aretha Franklin; *Aretha* .... (ARI)
Jimmy Mack
Martha Reeves/Vandellas; *Anthology* .... (MOT)
   Billboard Top R&B Hits-1967 .... (MOT)
   Compact Command Performances .... (MOT)
   Motown Story .... (MOT)
   Motown Superstar Series-#11 .... (MOT)
   Top 10 With A Bullet-Motown Girl Groups .... (MOT)

Jimmy Olsen's Blues
Spin Doctors; *Pocket Full Of Kryptonite* .... (EPI)
Jimmy, Jimmy
Madonna; *True Blue* .... (SIR)
Jim, What's Wrong With Him
Dramatics; *Dramatic Experience* .... (STX)
Jo Jo
Boz Scaggs; *Hits* ....(COL)
   Middle Man ....(COL)
Jody's Got Your Girl & Gone
Johnnie Taylor; *Super Hits* .... (STX)
Joe Hill
Arlo Guthrie & Pete Seeger; *Together In Concert* (RPR)
Joan Baez; *Carry It On* .... (VAN)
   From Every Stage ....(A&M)
   One Day At A Time .... (VAN)
   ST/Woodstock ....(ATL)
Soundtrack; *Carry It On* .... (VAN)
Joe Knows How To Live
Eddy Raven; *Best Of* ....(RCA)
Nitty Gritty Dirt Band; *Hold On* .... (WB)
Joe Slam And The Spaceship
Harry Connick, Jr.; *She* ....(COL)
Joey
Bob Dylan; *Desire* ....(COL)
Bob Dylan/Grateful Dead; *Bob Dylan/Grateful
Dead* ....(COL)
Concrete Blonde; *Bloodletting* .... (IRS)
Joey, Joey, Joey
Al Jarreau; *1965* ....(BAI)
Broadway Cast; *Most Happy Fella* ....(RCA)
Judy Garland; *Live* ....(CAP)
   One & Only ....(CAP)
Joey's On The Streets Again
Boomtown Rats; *Greatest Hits* ....(COL)
   Ratrospective ....(COL)
   Tonic For The Troops ....(COL)
John Barleycorn
Traffic; *John Barleycorn Must Die* .... (ISL)
John Brown's Body
Pete Seeger; *American Favorite Ballads-#3* ...... (FLW)
John Doe No. 24
Mary Chapin Carpenter; *Stones In The Road* ....(COL)
John Hardy
Leadbelly; *Bourgeois Blues-Golden Classics-#1* ... (CLT)
   Leadbelly .... (FAN)
   Legend Of ....(TRD)
Pete Seeger; *Essential* .... (VAN)
John Henry
Harry Belafonte; *All-Time Greatest Hits* ....(RCA)
   At Carnegie Hall ....(RCA)
   Legendary Performer ....(RCA)
Little Jimmy Dickens; *Columbia Historic Edition* .(COL)
Odetta; *Essential* .... (VAN)
   Greatest Folksingers Of The '60s .... (VAN)
Woody Guthrie; *Immortal-Golden Classics-#2* ....(CLT)
   Legendary ....(TRD)
John I'm Only Dancing
David Bowie; *Changesbowie* ....(RYK)
   Sound + Vision ....(RYK)
   The Singles-1969-1993 ....(RYK)
John Lee Hooker
Johnny Rivers; *Golden Hits* .... (IMP)
John Peel
Hermes Nye; *Anglo-American Songs* .... (FLW)
Johnny 99
Bruce Springsteen; *Nebraska* ....(COL)
Bruce Springsteen/E Street Band;
Live-1975-1985 ....(COL)
Johnny Cash; *Cover Me* .... (RHI)
Johnny Angel
Shelley Fabares; *Billboard Top Rock 'N' Roll
Hits-1962* .... (RHI)
   ST/Mermaids .... (GEF)
Johnny B
Hooters; *One Way Home* ....(COL)
Johnny Bye Bye
Bruce Springsteen; *45* ....(COL)
Johnny B. Goode
Chuck Berry; *Chess Box* .... (CSS)
   Classic Rock-#2 .... (MCA)
   Greatest Hits .... (EVR)
   Roll Over Beethoven .... (ALL)
   ST/American Graffiti .... (MCA)

Elvis Presley; *From Memphis To Vegas* ....(RCA)
  In Concert ....(RCA)
Grateful Dead; *Bill Graham Presents Fillmore-Last*
  Days ....(EPA)
Johnny Winter; *Live* ....(COL)
  Second Winter ....(COL)
Johnny Can't Read
  Don Henley; *I Can't Stand Still* ....(ASY)
Johnny Get Angry
  Joanie Sommers; *45* ....(AMP)
Johnny Has Gone For A Soldier
  Jo Stafford; *American Folk Songs* ....(CRN)
Johnny Have You Seen Her?
  Rembrandts; *United* ....(ATC)
Johnny I Love You
  Booker T./M.G.s; *Greatest Hits* ....(STX)
Johnny Needs A Fast Car
  Chris Rea; *espresso logic* ....(EW)
Johnny One Note
  Judy Garland; *Best Of-From MGM Classic Films* (MCA)
  Mary Martin/Original Cast; *Babes In Arms* ....(SSP)
Johnny Porter
  Persuasions; *Chirpin'* ....(ELE)
  Ry Cooder; *Borderline* ....(WB)
Johnny Strikes Up The Band
  Warren Zevon; *Excitable Boy* ....(ASY)
  Quiet Normal Life-Best Of ....(ASY)
Johnny The Fox Meets Jimmy The Weed
  Thin Lizzy; *Live & Dangerous* ....(WB)
Johnny Thunder
  Kinks; *Village Green Preservation Society* ....(RPR)
Johnny Too Bad
  John Martyn; *Foundations* ....(ISL)
  Lords Of The New Church; *Nothing's Sacred* .....(IRS)
  Slickers; *ST/The Harder They Come* ....(MGO)
  Taj Mahal; *Best Of-#1* ....(COL)
  Mo' Roots ....(COL)
  UB40; *Labour Of Love* ....(A&M)
  Live In Moscow ....(A&M)
Johnny's Garden
  Stephen Stills; *Manassas* ....(ATL)
John's Back In Town
  Gene Watson; *Best Of* ....(CAP)
John's Idea
  Count Basie; *Basie Reunions* ....(PRS)
  Best Of ....(MCA)
  One O'Clock Jump ....(MCA)
Joker James
  Brian Hyland; *Greatest Hits* ....(RHI)
Joltin' Joe DiMaggio
  Les Brown/Orchestra; *Baseball's Greatest Hits* ... (RHI)
  Words & Music Of World War II ....(COL)
Jones On The Jukebox
  Becky Hobbs; *All Keyed Up* ....(RCA)
Joshua Fought The Battle Of Jericho
  Elvis Presley; *His Hand In Mine* ....(RCA)
  Jordanaires; *Tribute To Elvis' Favorite Spirituals* ....(SO)
  New Messengers Of Happiness; *Swinging Gospel* . (ALS)
  Pete Seeger; *20 Golden Pieces Of* ....(BLD)
  Sister Rosetta Tharpe; *Live At The Hot Club De*
  France ....(MLN)
Jumpin' Jack Flash
  Aretha Franklin; *Aretha* ....(ARI)
  Johnny Winter; *Live* ....(COL)
  Peter Frampton; *Frampton Comes Alive* ....(A&M)
  Rolling Stones; *Flashpoint* ....(RS)
  Flashpoint + Collectibles ....(RS)
  Get Yer Ya-Ya's Out ....(AKO)
  Hot Rocks 1964-1971 ....(AKO)
  Love You Live ....(RS)
  ST/Jumpin' Jack Flash ....(MER)
  Through The Past Darkly-Big Hits-#2 ....(AKO)
Junior's Farm
  Paul McCartney/Wings; *All The Best* ....(CAP)
  Wings Greatest ....(CAP)
Just Like Jesse James
  Cher; *Heart Of Stone* ....(GEF)
Just Tell Her Jim Said Hello
  Elvis Presley; *Collector's Gold* ....(RCA)
  Gold Award Hits-#2 ....(RCA)
  Golden Records-#4 ....(RCA)

Killer Joe
  Quincy Jones; *Classics-#3* ....(A&M)
  I Heard That! ....(A&M)
  ST/Listen Up-The Lives Of Quincy Jones ......(QUE)
  The Best ....(A&M)
  Walking In Space ....(A&M)
Little Joe From Chicago
  Mary Lou Williams; *Best Of* ....(PAB)
  Nat King Cole; *Straighten Up & Fly Right* ....(POE)
Little Joe The Wrangler
  Goebel Reeves; *Songs Of Old West* ....(GLN)
  Texas Drifter ....(GLN)
Little John Of God
  Los Lobos; *The Neighborhood* ....(SLS)
Long Gone John From Bowling Green
  Red Knuckles/Trailblazers; *Red*
  Knuckles/Trailblazers ....(FF)
Lost John
  Doc Watson; *On Stage-featuring Merle Watson* .. (VAN)
  Rev. Gary Davis; *Legendary-#1* ....(BIO)
  Woody Guthrie; *Early Years* ....(TRD)
Lost John Boogied His Way Into Mexico
  Maddox Brothers & Rose; *On The Air-#1 & 2* .. (ARH)
Louisiana Joe
  Joe Douglas; *45* ....(BLR)
Louisiana Lou & Three-Card Monty John
  Allman Brothers Band; *Win Lose Or Draw* ....(POL)
Manny, Moe & Jack
  Dickies; *10 Roir Years-Anthology* ....(ROI)
  We Aren't The World! ....(ROI)
Master Jack
  Four Jacks & A Jill; *45* ....(OOP)
Me & Julio Down By The Schoolyard
  Paul Simon; *Greatest Hits Etc.* ....(COL)
  Live Rhymin' ....(WB)
  Negotiations & Love Songs-1971-1986 ....(WB)
  Paul Simon ....(WB)
  Simon & Garfunkel; *Concert In Central Park* .....(WB)
Mr. Jones
  Counting Crows; *August And Everything After* .. (DGC)
  Grass Roots; *Anthology-1965-1975* ....(RHI)
  Talking Heads; *Naked* ....(FLY)
New Kid In Town (Johnny Come Lately)
  Eagles; *Greatest Hits-#2* ....(ASY)
  Hotel California ....(ASY)
  Live ....(ASY)
  Trisha Yearwood; *Common Thread-Songs Of The*
  Eagles ....(GIA)
New York Mining Disaster 1941(Mr. Jones)
  Bee Gees; *Gold-#1* ....(POL)
  Here At Last ....(RSO)
  History Of British Rock-#8 ....(RHI)
Nightshift (Jackie)
  Commodores; *Nightshift* ....(MOT)
No Way Jose
  Ray Kennedy; *Guitar Man* ....(ATL)
Old Joe Clark
  Dillards; *Bluegrass Breakdown* ....(VAN)
  Eric Weissberg; *ST/Deliverance-Dueling Banjos* ...(WB)
Old Judge Jones
  Les Dudek; *Say No More* ....(COL)
Please Mr. Junkman
  Penguins; *Oldies* ....(DTN)
Poor Jud Is Dead
  Original Broadway Cast; *Oklahoma* ....(RCA)
  Original Cast; *Oklahoma* ....(MCA)
Poor Little Jimmie
  Burl Ives; *Best Of-#2* ....(MCA)
Poor, Poor Joseph
  Original Cast; *Joseph & The Amazing*
  Technicolor... ....(POL)
Ragtime Cowboy Joe
  Jo Stafford; *Capitol Collectors Series* ....(CAP)
  Spike Jones/City Slickers; *King Of Corn* ....(GLN)
Reverend Jack & His Roamin' Cadillac...
  Timbuk 3; *Eden Alley* ....(IRS)
Row Jimmy
  Grateful Dead; *Wake Of The Flood* ....(GRD)
Roxanna Waltz & Scotland Calling Jesse
  Jay Ungar/Others; *Fiddle Fever* ....(FF)
Run Joe
  Louis Jordan; *Best Of* ....(MCA)
  Neville Brothers; *Fiyo On The Bayou* ....(A&M)

Run Joey Run
David Geddes; *Super Hits/'70s-Have A Nice Day-#15* .... (RHI)
Say It Isn't So Joe
Roger Daltrey; *Best Bits* .... (MCA)
One Of The Boys .... (MCA)
Say It's Alright Joe
Genesis; *And Then There Were Three* .... (ATL)
Set Up Two Glasses, Joe
Ernest Tubb/Ferlin Husky/Simon Crum; *Ernest Tubb Collection* .... (SO)
Set 'Em Up Joe
Vern Gosdin; *Chiseled In Stone* .... (COL)
Greatest Country Hits/'80s-1988 .... (COL)
She Gave Her Heart To Jethro
Tom T. Hall; *Essential-20th Anniversary Collection* .... (MER)
She Thinks His Name Was John
Reba McEntire; *Read My Mind* .... (MCA)
Shoeless Joe From Hannibal, Mo.
Original Broadway Cast; *Damn Yankees* .... (RCA)
Skid Row Joe
Porter Wagoner; *Best Of-#1* .... (RCA)
Greatest .... (TUD)
Sloop John B
Beach Boys; *Absolute Best-#2* .... (CAP)
Best Of (Good Vibrations) .... (RPR)
Gift Set .... (CAP)
Made In The U.S.A. .... (CAP)
Pet Sounds .... (CAP)
ST/Forrest Gump .... (EPX)
Smackwater Jack
Carole King; *Greatest Hits* .... (EPI)
Tapestry .... (EPI)
Smokey Joe's Cafe
Coasters; *Their Greatest Recordings-Early Years* ..(ATC)
Young Blood .... (ATL)
Loudon Wainwright III; *Album III* .... (COL)
Stagedoor Johnny
Donnie Iris; *Fortune 410* .... (MCA)
Surabaya Johnny
Bette Midler; *Bette Midler* .... (ATL)
Dagmar Krause; *Lost In The Stars-Music Of Kurt Weill* .... (A&M)
Surfer Joe
Surfaris; *Surfin' Hits* .... (RHI)
Surfin' Sixties .... (JCI)
Sweet Baby James
Highway 101; *Paint The Town* .... (WB)
James Taylor; *Greatest Hits* .... (WB)
Sweet Baby James .... (WB)
Theme From Jack Johnson
Miles Davis; *Agharta* .... (COL)
Theme From "James Bond"
John Barry Orchestra; *Best Of James Bond-30th Anniversary* .... (EMI)
London Symphony Orchestra; *From London With Love-Music Of J. Bond* .... (POE)
Theme From "Tom & Jerry"
Henry Mancini; *ST/Tom & Jerry-The Movie* ..... (MCA)
This Is The Army, Mr. Jones
Mel Torme & George Shearing; *Mel & George Do World War II* .... (CCJ)
Mormon Tabernacle Choir; *God Bless America* . (SMC)
Tokyo Joe
Bryan Ferry; *In Your Mind* .... (RPR)
Top Jimmy
Van Halen; *1984* .... (WB)
Uncle Jack
Spirit; *Best Of* .... (EPI)
Spirit .... (EPI)
Spirit Of '84 .... (MER)
Time Circle .... (EPI)
Uncle John's Band
Grateful Dead; *Skeletons From The Closet-Best Of* (WB)
Workingman's Dead .... (WB)
Indigo Girls; *Deadicated* .... (ARI)
Walkaway Joe
Trisha Yearwood; *Hearts In Armor* .... (MCA)
When Johnny Comes Marching Home
Marilyn Horne; *Beautiful Dreamer-Great Amer. Songbook* .... (LON)
Mormon Tabernacle Choir; *Songs Of The Civil War & S. Foster Faves* .... (SMC)

United States Military Academy Band; *Songs Of The Civil War* .... (COL)
Who's Johnny
El DeBarge; *El DeBarge* .... (MOT)
You Don't Mess Around With Jim
Jim Croce; *Down The Highway* .... (21)
Photographs & Memories-His Greatest Hits .... (21)

Barbie & Ken
Weathermen; *Black Album According To The* .....(PIA)
Barbie & Ken Ferrari
John Hiatt; *Perfectly Good Guitar* .... (A&M)
Being For The Benefit Of Mr. Kite
Beatles; *Box Set* .... (CAP)
Sgt. Pepper's Lonely Hearts Club Band .... (CAP)
Cousin Kevin
Who; *Join Together* .... (MCA)
ST/Tommy .... (POL)
Tommy .... (MCA)
Gee, Officer Krupke
Original Cast; *ST/West Side Story* .... (COL)
Keith Don't Go
Nils Lofgren; *Best Of* .... (A&M)
Classics-#13 .... (A&M)
Night After Night .... (A&M)
Nils Lofgren .... (RYK)
King Holiday
King Dream Chorus/Holiday Crew; *45* .... (MER)
"Kojak" Theme
Original Music; *Television's Greatest Hits-#3* .....(TVT)
Kookie Kookie (Lend Me Your Comb)
Edd Byrnes; *45* .... (AMP)
Machine Gun Kelly
James Taylor; *Mud Slide Slim* .... (WB)
President Kennedy
Ry Cooder; *Boomer's Story* .... (RPR)
Son House; *Father Of The Delta Blues-1965 Sessions* .... (COL)
President Kennedy March
Lawrence Welk; *10th Anniversary Television Show* .... (RAN)
President Kennedy Stayed Away Too Long
Sleepy John Estes; *Electric Sleep* .... (DEL)
Kings Of Country Blues-#1 .... (ARH)
President Kennedy's Mile
Screaming Blue Messiahs; *Gun-Shy* .... (ELE)
Theme From "Dr. Kildare"
Betty Carter; *'Round Midnight* .... (ATL)
What's The Frequency, Kenneth?
R.E.M.; *Monster* .... (WB)

Bad Bad Leroy Brown
Jim Croce; *Billboard Top Rock 'N' Roll Hits-1973* (RHI)
Down The Highway .... (21)
Life & Times .... (OOP)
Photographs & Memories .... (21)
Blue Lou
Benny Carter; *1933* .... (PRS)
Ella Fitzgerald; *Best Of-#2* .... (MCA)
Ella Sings-Chic Swings .... (OLR)
Brother Louie
Stories; *Billboard Top Rock 'N' Roll Hits-1973* ... (RHI)
Brother Love's Traveling Salvation Show
Neil Diamond; *Hot August Night* .... (MCA)
Gold .... (MCA)
His 12 Greatest Hits .... (MCA)
Love At The Greek .... (COL)
Sweet Caroline .... (MCA)
Calling Dr. Love
Kiss; *Alive 2* .... (CAS)
Double Platinum .... (CAS)
Rock & Roll Over .... (CAS)
Smashes Thrashes & Hits .... (MER)
Chop Suey Louie
Jimmy Preston; *Rock The Joint-#2* .... (CLT)
Cincinnati Lou
Merle Travis; *Best Of* .... (RHI)

Death Of Louis
Champion Jack Dupree; *Happy To Be Free* ...... (CRS)
Hats Off To Larry
Del Shannon; *Runaway Hits!* .... (RHI)
Super Oldies/'60s-#2 .... (AUF)
WCBS FM101-History Of Rock/'60s-#3 .... (CLT)
Lee Harvey Oswald
Skatalites; *Stretching Out* .... (ROI)
Levon
Elton John; *Greatest Hits-#2* .... (POL)
Madman Across The Water .... (POL)
Lido Shuffle
Boz Scaggs; *Hits!* ....(COL)
Silk Degrees ....(COL)
ST/FM .... (MCA)
Lollipop
Chordettes; *Best Of* ....(RHI)
Greatest Hits ....(EVR)
Jukebox Classics-#2 ....(RHI)
Little Bit Of Gold-3" CD Series ....(RHI)
ST/Stand By Me ....(ATL)
Longfellow Serenade
Neil Diamond; *12 Greatest Hits-#2* ....(COL)
Love At The Greek ....(COL)
On The Way To The Sky ....(COL)
Serenade ....(COL)
Louisiana Lou & Three-Card Monty John
Allman Brothers Band; *Win Lose Or Draw* .... (POL)
Louisville Lou
Johnny Mercer; *Uncollected-1944* .... (HIN)
Man Who Shot Liberty Valance
Gene Pitney; *Anthology* .... (RHI)
Greatest Hits ....(EVR)
Super Oldies/'60s-#9 ....(AUF)
Greg Kihn; *Glass House Rock* ....(BES)
Meet Me In St. Louis, Louis
Judy Garland; *Best Of* .... (MCA)
Mr. Lee
Bobbettes; *Billboard Top R&B Hits-1957* .... (RHI)
ST/Stand By Me ....(ATL)
Pointer Sisters; *Rock Rhythm & Blues* .... (WB)
Mr. Lincoln
Hank Williams, Jr.; *America (The Way I See It)* ..(W/C)
Major Moves ....(W/C)
Mr. Lonely
Bobby Vinton; *16 Most Requested* .... (EPI)
All-Time Greatest Hits .... (EPI)
Mr. Lucky
Henry Mancini; *All-Time Greatest Hits-#1* ....(RCA)
Pure Gold ....(RCA)
John Lee Hooker; *Mr. Lucky* ....(POI)
Urban Blues ....(MCA)
My Boy Lollipop
Millie Small; *Island Story-1962-1987-25th
Anniversary* .... (ISL)
My Name Is Larry
Wild Man Fischer; *Dr. Demento's Dementia
Royale* .... (RHI)
Pancho & Lefty
Merle Haggard & Willie Nelson; *19 Hot Country
Requests* .... (EPI)
Columbia Country Classics-#3-Americana ......(COL)
His Epic Hits-First 11 To Be Continued ...... (EPI)
Pancho & Lefty .... (EPI)
Townes Van Zandt; *Live & Obscure* ....(SH)
Sneaky Private Lee
Paice/Ashton/Lord; *Malice In Wonderland* .... (WB)
Swap Meet Louie
Sir Mix-A-Lot; *Mack Daddy* .... (DEF)
Theme From "Lawrence Of Arabia"
BBC Concert Orchestra; *Golden Cinema
Classics-Adventure Film* ....(BAI)
Cincinnati Pops Orchestra/Erich Kunzel; *Hollywood's
Greatest Hits-#1* .... (TLR)

MEN'S NAMES: M

Abraham, Martin & John
Dion; *24 Original Classics* .... (ARI)
Collectables Presents History Of Rock-#3 ......(CLT)
WCBS FM-History Of Rock-'60s-#2 ....(CLT)
Harry Belafonte; *All Time Greatest Hits-#1* ......(RCA)

Smokey Robinson/Miracles; *Anthology* .... (MOT)
Time Out For/Special Occasion .... (MOT)
Bach, Beethoven, Mozart & Me
Phil Ochs; *Greatest Hits* .... (A&M)
Blue Monk
Bill Evans; *Conversations With Myself* ....(VRV)
Thelonius Monk; *Alone In San Francisco* ....(RVR)
Composer ....(COL)
Crazy Man Michael
Fairport Convention; *Chronicles* .... (A&M)
In Real Time-Live '87 .... (ISL)
Liege & Lief .... (A&M)
Dear Michael
Michael Jackson; *Anthology* .... (MOT)
One Day In Your Life .... (MOT)
Five Guys Named Moe
Joe Jackson; *Jumpin' Jive* .... (A&M)
Louis Jordan; *Best Of* .... (MCA)
Original Decca Recordings-#2 .... (DEC)
Go Down, Moses
Paul Robeson; *The Power & The Glory* ....(COL)
Simon Estes; *Spirituals* ....(PHI)
Hey Joe, Hey Moe
Moe Bandy & Joe Stampley; *Greatest Hits* ......(COL)
Hey Joe, Hey Moe ....(COL)
Live At Bad Bob's ....(COL)
House Of Marcus Lycus
George Hearn/Bob Gunton & Women; *Collector's
Sondheim* ....(RCA)
Stephen Sondheim; *Collector's Sondheim* ....(RCA)
I Love Mickey
Mickey Mantle & Teresa Brewer; *Baseball's Greatest
Hits* .... (RHI)
King Midas In Reverse
Hollies; *Best Of-#2* .... (EMI)
Epic Anthology From Orig. Master Tapes .... (EPI)
Greatest Hits .... (EPI)
Mack The Knife
Bobby Darin; *At The Copa* ....(BAI)
Hit Singles 1958-1977 .... (ATL)
Story ....(ATC)
Frank Sinatra; *Reprise Collection* ....(RPR)
Magic Johnson
Red Hot Chili Peppers; *Mother's Milk* ....(EMI)
"Magnum P.I." Theme
Original Music; *Television's Greatest Hits-#3* .....(TVT)
"Mannix" Theme
San Diego Symphony/Lalo Schifrin; *Hitchcock-Master
Of Mayhem* ....(POE)
Manny, Moe & Jack
Dickies; *10 Roir Years-Anthology* ....(ROI)
We Aren't The World! ....(ROI)
"Marcus Welby, M.D." Theme
Original Music; *Television's Greatest Hits-#3* .....(TVT)
Marvin I Love You
Marvin The Paranoid Android; *Dr. Demento's Greatest
Novelty-#5-1980s* .... (RHI)
Matty Groves
Fairport Convention; *Chronicles* .... (A&M)
Liege & Lief .... (A&M)
"Maverick" Theme
Original Music; *Television's Greatest Hits-#2* .....(TVT)
Maxwell's Silver Hammer
Beatles; *1967-1970* ....(CAP)
Abbey Road ....(CAP)
Mean Mr. Mustard
Beatles; *Abbey Road* ....(CAP)
Memphis Slim U.S.A.
Memphis Slim; *Blue This Evening* ....(BL)
Message To Michael
Dionne Warwick; *Anthology-1962-1971* .... (RHI)
Dionne Warwick ....(EVR)
Greatest Hits ....(EVR)
Hot! Live & Otherwise ....(ARI)
Original Rock 'N' Roll Hits Of The '60s ....(RLL)
Michael
Highwaymen; *45* ....(LIB)
Prefab Sprout; *Jordan-The Comeback* ....(EPI)
Michael Row The Boat Ashore
Joe & Eddie; *Best Of* ....(CRS)
Gospel Truth ....(CRS)
Weavers; *Greatest Hits* ....(VAN)
Mickey
Toni Basil; *Word Of Mouth* .... (CHR)

Mickey's Monkey
Smokey Robinson/Miracles; *Anthology* .... (MOT)
   Compact Command Performances .... (MOT)
   Greatest Hits .... (MOT)
   Motown Story-First 25 Years .... (MOT)
   Songs That Inspired 25th Anniv. Special ...... (MOT)

Mohammed's Radio
Linda Ronstadt; *Living In The U.S.A.* .... (ASY)
Warren Zevon; *Quiet Normal Life-Best Of* .... (ASY)
   Stand In The Fire .... (ASY)
   Warren Zevon .... (ASY)

"Monty Python's Flying Circus" Theme
Original Music; *Television's Greatest Hits-#2* ..... (TVT)

Morrisey & The Russian Sailor
Tom Dahill; *Irish Music From St. Paul To Donegal* (FF)

"Mr. Magoo" Theme
Original Music; *Television's Greatest Hits-#3* ..... (TVT)

Mr. Melody
Natalie Cole; *Collection* .... (CAP)
   Live .... (CAP)
   Natalie .... (CAP)

Mr. Mistofelees
Original Broadway Cast; *Cats* .... (GEF)
Original London Cast; *Cats* .... (GEF)

Mr. Moonlight
Beatles; *Box Set* .... (CAP)
   For Sale .... (CAP)
   '65 .... (CAP)

Murphy's Law
Al Jarreau; *High Crime* .... (WB)
Cheri; *45* .... (VEN)
Murphy's Law; *Murphy's Law* .... (RH)

Nightshift (Marvin)
Commodores; *Nightshift* .... (MOT)

Saturday Miles
Miles Davis; *At Fillmore* ....(COL)

Free Nelson Mandela
Special AKA; *In The Studio* .... (CHR)

Here's To The State Of Nixon
Phil Ochs; *Chords Of Fame* .... (A&M)

Nathan Jones
Bananarama; *ST/Rain Man* .... (CAP)
Supremes; *Top 10 With A Bullet-Motown Girl Groups* .... (MOT)

Neal's Fandango
Doobie Brothers; *Stampede* .... (WB)

Nolan Ryan (He's A Hero To Us All)
Jerry Jeff Walker; *Navajo Rug* .... (RYK)

Black Orpheus
Roger Williams; *Best Of* .... (MCA)
Vince Guaraldi & Bola Sete; *Live At El Matador* . (FAN)

Oklahoma Joe
Chris LeDoux; *Songs of Rodeo & Country* .... (LIB)

Oliver's Army
Elvis Costello; *Girls Girls Girls* .... (COL)
Elvis Costello/Attractions; *Armed Forces* .... (COL)
   Best Of .... (COL)

O'Reilly At The Bar
Dan Hicks/Hot Licks; *Striking It Rich* .... (MCA)

Rock Around With Ollie Vee
Buddy Holly; *Legend* .... (MCA)

Samba De Orfeu (Orpheus)
Pablo All-Stars Jam; *Montreux '77* .... (PAB)
Vince Guaraldi; *Greatest Hits* .... (FAN)
Vince Guaraldi Trio; *Jazz Impressions Of Black Orpheus* .... (FAN)

Ballad Of Paladin
Duane Eddy; *Pure Gold* ....(RCA)
Johnny Western; *Columbia Country Classics-#3* ..(COL)

Black Peter
Grateful Dead; *History Of-#1-Bear's Choice* ...... (WB)
   What A Long Strange Trip It's Been .... (WB)
   Workingman's Dead .... (WB)

Check Mr. Popeye
Eddie Bo; *Carnival Time-Best Of Ric Records-#1* (ROU)
   Check Mr. Popeye .... (ROU)
Southside Johnny/Asbury Jukes; *This Time It's For Real* .... (EPI)

I Loves You Porgy
Original Cast; *Porgy & Bess* .... (MCA)

I Loves You Porgy/Porgy, I's Your Woman
Barbra Streisand; *Broadway Album* ....(COL)

I'm Popeye The Sailor Man
Billy Costello; *Dr. Demento's Greatest-#1-'40s & Before* .... (RHI)

Me And Paul
Willie Nelson; *Best Of* ....(RCA)
   Me And Paul ....(COL)
   Nite Life-Greatest Hits & Rare Tracks .... (RHI)
   The Outlaws ....(RCA)
   Willie ....(RCA)

Mr. Pharmacist
Other Half; *Nuggets-#12-Punk-#3* .... (RHI)

Mr. Policeman
Rick James; *Street Songs* .... (MOT)

Mr. Pollution
P'Cock; *Burning Beach* .... (INN)

Mr. President (Have Pity On The...)
Randy Newman; *Good Old Boys* .... (RPR)
ST/*Forrest Gump* .... (EPX)

Oh Mr. Possum
Jimmy Preston; *Jimmy Preston* .... (CLT)

Paddy Doyle's Boots
Clancy Brothers/Tommy Makem; *Best Of* ....(TRD)

Paddy Goes To Nashville
Adrian Legg; *Mrs. Crowe's Blue Waltz* .... (REL)

Paddy Kelly's Brew
Tommy Makem; *Evening With* .... (SHA)

Paddy McGinty's Coat
Pat Harrington; *St. Patrick's Day Celebration* ....(COL)

Paddy On The Railway
Barley Bree; *Castles In The Air* .... (SHA)

Paddy Ryan's Dream
Matt Molloy; *Stony Steps* .... (GRE)

Paddy Won't You Drink Some Cider
Red Clay Ramblers; *Chuckin' The Frizz* .... (FF)

Paddy Works On The Erie
Popular Standard; *Out-Of-Print Recording* ....(OOP)

Paddy's Green Shamrock Shore
Chieftains; *Another Country* ....(RCA)

Pancho & Lefty
Merle Haggard & Willie Nelson; *19 Hot Country Requests* .... (EPI)
   Columbia Country Classics-#3-Americana ......(COL)
   His Epic Hits-First 11 To Be Continued .... (EPI)
   Pancho & Lefty .... (EPI)
Townes Van Zandt; *Live & Obscure* .... (SH)

Parker's Band
Steely Dan; *Pretzel Logic* .... (MCA)

Patches
Clarence Carter; *Atlantic R&B-1947-1974-#7* ... (ATL)
   Snatching It Back-Best Of .... (RHI)
   Super Hits-#1 .... (GUS)
Dickey Lee; *Teenage Tragedies* .... (RHI)
George Jones & B.B. King; *Rhythm Country & Blues* .... (MCA)

Paul Revere
Beastie Boys; *Licensed To Ill* .... (DFC)
   Rap Rap Rap .... (KT)
Johnny Cash; *Patriot* ....(COL)

Paul Wants A Pig
John Jarvis; *Whatever Works* .... (MCA)

Pepe
Duane Eddy; *16 Greatest Hits* .... (JAM)

Percy's Song
Arlo Guthrie; *Washington County* .... (RPR)
Bob Dylan; *Biograph* ....(COL)

"Perry Mason" Theme
Blues Brothers; *Made In America* .... (ATL)
Jerry Goodman; *It's Alive* .... (PRV)
Original Music; *TV Theme Sing-Along Album* .... (RHI)

Peter Gunn
Duane Eddy; *16 Greatest Hits* .... (JAM)

Henry Mancini; *All-Time Greatest Hits-#1* ....(RCA)
  Best Of ....(RCA)
  Legendary Performer ....(RCA)
  Pure Gold ....(RCA)
  Television's Greatest Hits-#2 ....(TVT)
Ray Anthony; *Capitol Collectors Series* ....(CAP)
Picasso's Last Words
Paul McCartney/Wings; *Band On The Run* .....(CAP)
  Wings Over America ....(CAP)
Pilate & Christ
Original London Cast; *Jesus Christ Superstar* .... (MCA)
Pilate's Dream
Original London Cast; *Jesus Christ Superstar* .... (MCA)
Please Mr. Postman
Beatles; *Box Set* ....(CAP)
  Second Album ....(CAP)
  With The Beatles ....(CAP)
Carpenters; *Classics-#2* .... (A&M)
  Horizon .... (A&M)
  Yesterday Once More .... (A&M)
Marvelettes; *Anthology* .... (MOT)
  Billboard Top Rock 'N' Roll Hits-1961 .... (RHI)
  Greatest Hits .... (MOT)
  Motown Story .... (MOT)
Pow Wow The Indian Boy
Hot Rize; *Hot Rize* .... (FF)
Remember Pat Boone
David Steinberg; *Booga! Booga!* ....(COL)
Roll 'Em Pete
Big Joe Turner; *Atlantic Blues-Piano* ....(ATL)
  Boss Of The Blues ....(ATL)
Count Basie & Big Joe Turner; *The Bosses* ....(PAB)
Sgt. Pepper's Lonely Hearts Club Band
Beatles; *1967-1970* ....(CAP)
  Box Set ....(CAP)
  Sgt. Pepper's Lonely Hearts Club Band ....(CAP)
Jimi Hendrix; *Stages-Stockholm/Paris/San*
  Diego/Atlanta ....(RPR)
Paul McCartney; *Tripping The Live Fantastic* ....(CAP)
Tall Paul
Annette Funicello; *Best Of* .... (RHI)
  Sherman Brothers ....(DIS)
Trial Before Pilate
Original London Cast; *Jesus Christ Superstar* .... (MCA)
Uncle Pen
Bill Monroe; *Bean Blossom* .... (MCA)
  Best Of .... (MCA)
Ricky Skaggs; *19 Hot Country Requests-#2* .... (EPI)
  Columbia Country Classics-#5-New Trad. ......(COL)
  Don't Cheat In Our Hometown .... (EPI)
  Live In London .... (EPI)

MEN'S NAMES: Q

Don Quixote
Gordon Lightfoot; *Gord's Gold* .... (RPR)
Nik Kershaw; *The Riddle* .... (MCA)
Man Of La Mancha
Original Cast; *Man Of La Mancha* .... (MCA)
Original London Cast; *Man Of La Mancha* ..... (MCA)

MEN'S NAMES: R

Ballad Of Richard Nixon
John Denver; *Rhymes & Reasons* ....(RCA)
Black Uncle Remus
Loudon Wainwright III; *Loudon Wainwright III* .. (ATL)
Blue Monday At Kansas City Red's
Cary Bell; *Blues Harp* ....(DEL)
Doctor Robert
Beatles; *Revolver (European Version)* ....(CAP)
  Yesterday & Today ....(CAP)
In Memoriam-John F. & Robert F. Kennedy
Clare Fischer; *'Twas Only Yesterday* .... (DCO)
Message To You Rudy
Specials; *Gangsters* .... (CHR)
Mr. Radio
Electric Light Orchestra; *Afterglow* .... (EPI)
  No Answer ....(JET)

Mr. Record Man
Willie Nelson; *Best Of* .... (EMI)
  Horse Called Music ....(COL)
  & Family Live ....(COL)
Mr. Roboto
Styx; *Caught In The Act* .... (A&M)
  Classics-#15 .... (A&M)
  Kilroy Was Here .... (A&M)
Oh King Richard
Rodney Crowell; *Hot Country Rock-#2* .... (EPI)
  Street Language ....(COL)
Open The Door, Richard
Louis Jordan; *Jazz Heritage-Greatest Hits-#2* .... (MCA)
President Roosevelt
Big Joe Williams; *Shake Your Boogie* .... (ARH)
  Tough Times .... (ARH)
Ray's Dad Cadillac
Joni Mitchell; *Night Ride Home* ....(GEF)
Reagonomics
D.R.I.; *Dealing With It!* .... (MET)
Johnnie Taylor; *Just Ain't Good Enough* .... (BEV)
Reuben James
Conway Twitty; *Hello Darlin'* .... (MCA)
Kenny Rogers; *20 Greatest Hits* .... (EMI)
  Greatest Hits .... (EMI)
  Ten Years Of Gold .... (EMI)
Kenny Rogers/First Edition; *Best Of* .... (KT)
White Mountain Singers; *Best* .... (FOL)
Reuben's Train
Doc Watson & Family; *Treasures Untold* .... (VAN)
Richard Cory
Paul McCartney/Wings; *Wings Over America* ....(CAP)
Simon & Garfunkel; *Collected Works* ....(COL)
  Sounds Of Silence ....(COL)
Richard Cory Cries
Midnight Reign; *Mountain Of Metal* .... (MNT)
Richard Hung Himself
D.I.; *Team Goon* .... (XXX)
Richard Nixon
Christmas; *Ultraprophets Of Thee Psykick*
  Revolution .... (IRS)
Robin Hood
38 Special; *Rockin' Into The Night* .... (A&M)
Robinson Crusoe
Art Of Noise; *Ambient Collection* .... (POL)
  Below The Waste .... (POL)
Cud; *Cub Band E.P.* .... (A&M)
Robinson Crusoe In New York
Silencers; *Dance To The Holy Man* ....(RCA)
Rodeo Romeo
Moe Bandy; *Greatest Hits* .... (COO)
Rodney On The ROQ
Target 13; *Rodney On The ROQ-#2* .... (PBO)
Roger's Bumble Bee (Latter Day)
Roger Williams; *Best Of* .... (MCA)
  Golden Hits .... (MCA)
Roland The Headless Thompson Gunner
Warren Zevon; *Excitable Boy* .... (ASY)
  Quiet Normal Life-Best Of .... (ASY)
Romeo
Cadillacs; *Best Of* .... (RHI)
Dino; *Swingin'* .... (POL)
Donna Summer; *ST/Flashdance* .... (CAS)
Jamaica Boys; *Jamaica Boys* .... (WB)
Times 2; *X 2* .... (RPR)
Romeo & Juliet
Andy Williams/Royal Philharmonic Orch.; *Greatest Love*
  Classics ....(CAP)
Chambers Brothers; *Time Has Come* ....(COL)
Dire Straits; *Live-Alchemy* .... (WB)
  Making Movies .... (WB)
  Money For Nothing .... (WB)
Honeys; *Capitol Collectors Series* ....(CAP)
Indigo Girls; *Rites Of Passage* .... (EPI)
Percy Faith; *16 Most Requested Songs* ....(COL)
Reflections; *45* .... (ERI)
Stacy Earl; *Stacy Earl* ....(RCA)
Romeo's Tune
Steve Forbert; *Jackrabbit Slim* .... (NEM)
Ronnie, Talk To Russia
Prince; *Controversy* .... (WB)
Ronny Zamora (My Friend Ron)
Deaf School; *English Boys/Working Girls* ....(WB)

Roy Rogers
Elton John; *Goodbye Yellow Brick Road* .... (POL)
Rudy
Supertramp; *Classics-#9* .... (A&M)
Crime Of The Century .... (A&M)
Paris .... (A&M)
Theme From "Romeo & Juliet"
101 Strings Orchestra; *World's Greatest Standards* (ALS)
Andre Kostelanetz; *16 Most Requested Songs* ....(COL)
This Romeo Ain't Got Julie Yet
Diamond Rio; *Close To The Edge* .... (ARI)
Tore Down A La Rimbaud
Van Morrison; *A Sense Of Wonder* .... (MER)
Waiting For The Robert E. Lee
Al Jolson; *My Mammy* .... (MSP)
Eddie Cantor; *Centennial Celebration* ....(RCA)
Where Did Robinson Crusoe Go With Friday
Ian Whitcomb; *45* .... (OSR)
Write Your Own Songs (Mr. Record Exec.)
Asleep At The Wheel; *Asleep At The Wheel* ..... (DOT)
Waylon Jennings & Willie Nelson; *WW2* ....(RCA)
Willie Nelson & Kris Kristofferson; *Music From
"Songwriter"* .... (COL)

MEN'S NAMES: S

Ballad Of Spiro Agnew
John Denver; *Rhymes & Reasons* ....(RCA)
Boogie With Stu
Led Zeppelin; *Physical Graffiti* .... (SS)
Boy Named Sue
Johnny Cash; *Biggest Hits* ....(COL)
Columbia Country Classics-#3 ....(COL)
Greatest Hits-#2 ....(COL)
Brush Up Your Shakespeare
Dick Hyman; *Cole Porter: All Through The Night* (MM)
Keenan Wynn & James Whitmore; *ST/Kiss Me
Kate* .... (MCA)
Original Cast; *Kiss Me Kate* ....(COL)
Cut Across Shorty
Eddie Cochran; *Legendary Masters* .... (EMI)
Rod Stewart; *Best Of* .... (MER)
Faces Live .... (MER)
Gasoline Alley .... (MER)
Storyteller/Complete Anthology-1964-1990 ..... (WB)
Unplugged...& Seated .... (WB)
Vintage .... (MER)
Day That Curly Bill Shot Down Crazy Sam
Hollies; *Hollies* .... (EPI)
Don't Step On The Grass Sam
Steppenwolf; *Live* .... (MCA)
The Second .... (MCA)
Father Of A Boy Named Sue
Shel Silverstein; *Songs & Stories* ....(OOP)
Hooray For Captain Spaulding
Groucho Marx; *Dr. Demento Greatest Novelty CD* (RHI)
Dr. Demento's Greatest-#1 .... (RHI)
Lord Stanley's Cup
Zamboni Brothers; *The Hockey Zone* .... (SPO)
Mister Sandman
Chordettes; *Best Of* .... (RHI)
Emmylou Harris; *Evangeline* .... (WB)
Profile 2-Best Of .... (WB)
Mr. Skin
Spirit; *12 Dreams Of Dr. Sardonicus* .... (EPI)
Best Of .... (EPI)
Spirit Of '84 .... (MER)
Time Circle .... (EPI)
Mr. Spaceman
Byrds; *Byrds* ....(COL)
Greatest Hits ....(COL)
Original Singles-#1-1965-1967 ....(COL)
(Untitled) ....(COL)
Mr. Sunday
Simon Townshend; *Sweet Sound* .... (21)
Nevada Smith
Mystic Moods Orchestra; *Nighttide* ....(BAI)
Please Mr. Sun
Johnnie Ray; *16 Most Requested Songs* ....(COL)
Back To The Early '50s .... (DOM)
Vogues; *Greatest Hits* .... (RHI)

Run, Samson, Run
Neil Sedaka; *All-Time Greatest Hits* ....(RCA)
Pure Gold ....(RCA)
Sings His Greatest Hits ....(RCA)
Sabu Visits The Twin Cities Alone
John Prine; *Bruised Orange* .... (ASY)
Sam
Meat Puppets; *Forbidden Places* ....(LON)
Olivia Newton-John; *Back To Basics-Essential
Coll-1971-1992* .... (GEF)
Don't Stop Believin' .... (MCA)
Sam Hall
Tex Ritter; *Country Music Hall Of Fame* .... (MCA)
Sam Stone
John Prine; *John Prine* .... (ATL)
Prime Prine .... (ATL)
Sam & Delilah
Original Cast; *Girl Crazy* .... (SSP)
Samson & Delilah
Blasters; *Collection* ....(SLS)
Blind Gary Davis; *Harlem Street Singer* .... (BV)
Grateful Dead; *Dead Set* .... (ARI)
Terrapin Station .... (ARI)
Rev. Gary Davis; *From Blues To Gospel* ....(BIO)
Sam, The Old Accordion Man
Doris Day & James Cagney; *ST/Love Me Or Leave
Me* .... (SSP)
Sam, You Made The Pants Too Long
Barbra Streisand; *Color Me Barbra* ....(COL)
Greatest Hits ....(COL)
Sam's Place
Buck Owens/Buckaroos; *Billboard Top Country
Hits-1967* .... (RHI)
Sam-The Hot Dog Man
Lil Johnson; *Raunchy Business-Hot Nuts &
Lollypops* ....(COL)
"Sanford & Son" Theme
Original Music; *Television's Greatest Hits-#3* ..... (TVT)
Shakespeare Stole My Baby
Eye To Eye; *Shakespeare Stole My Baby* .... (WB)
Shakespeare's Sister
Smiths; *Louder Than Bombs* .... (SIR)
Shorty Falls In Love
Dan Hicks/Hot Licks; *Where's The Money* ...... (MCA)
Simon Says
1910 Fruitgum Company; *Best Of-#2* .... (RHI)
Bubblegum's Greatest Hits #2 .... (ACC)
Fabulous Bubblegum Years .... (FFT)
Simon Smith & His Amazing Dancing Bear
Randy Newman; *Sail Away* .... (RPR)
Slim Carter
Nitty Gritty Dirt Band; *All The Good Times* ..... (UA)
Slim Jenkins' Place
Booker T./M.G.s; *Best Of* .... (ATL)
Hip Hug-Her .... (RHI)
Speedo
Cadillacs; *Best Of* .... (RHI)
Echoes Of A Rock Era-Early Times .... (RLL)
More American Graffiti .... (MCA)
Original Rock 'N' Roll Hits Of The '50s .... (RLL)
ST/Goodfellas .... (ATL)
Ry Cooder; *Borderline* .... (WB)
Speedy Gonzales
Pat Boone; *Best Of* .... (MCA)
Speedy's Coming
Scorpions; *Best Of* ....(RCA)
Fly To The Rainbow ....(RCA)
Tokyo Tapes ....(RCA)
"Spiderman" Theme
Original Music; *Television's Greatest Hits-#2* ..... (TVT)
Spoonman
Soundgarden; *Superunknown* .... (A&M)
Stagger Lee
Dion; *His Best* ....(LAU)
Huey Lewis/News; *Four Chords & Several Years
Ago* .... (ELE)
Ike & Tina Turner; *Best Of* .... (EMI)
Lloyd Price; *Billboard Top Rock 'N' Roll
Hits-1959* .... (RHI)
Collectables Presents History Of Rock-#5 .... (CLT)
Greatest Hits .... (MCA)
Oldies But Goodies-#1 .... (OSR)
Professor Longhair; *Rock 'N' Roll Gumbo* .... (DAN)
Wilson Pickett; *Man & A Half-Best Of* .... (RHI)

Streak, The
Ray Stevens; *All-Time Greatest Comic Hits* ......(CCB)
Greatest Hits ....(MCA)
Greatest Hits ....(RCA)
Super Hits/'70s-Have A Nice Day-#12 .... (RHI)
St. Stephen
Grateful Dead; *Aoxomoxoa* ....(WB)
Live Dead ....(WB)
Skeletons From The Closet ....(WB)
Two From The Vault ....(GRD)
What A Long Strange Trip It's Been ....(WB)
Theme From "Schindler's List"
John Williams/Itzhak Perlman; *ST/Schindler's
List* ....(MCA)
Theme From "Shaft"
Isaac Hayes; *Greatest Hit Singles* ....(STX)
Pimps Players & Private Eyes ....(STX)
Top Of The Stax-Twenty Greatest Hits ....(STX)
Theme From "Superman"
London Symphony Orchestra/John Williams;
ST/Superman-The Movie ....(WB)
Neil Norman; *Greatest Science Fiction Hits* ....(CRS)
Watching Scotty Grow
Bobby Goldsboro; *All-Time Greatest Hits* ....(CCB)
Honey-Best Of ....(EMI)

MEN'S NAMES: T

Belgian Tom's Hat Trick
Whitesnake; *Trouble* ....(GEF)
King Tut
Steve Martin/Toot Uncommons; *Dr. Demento Greatest
Novelty CD* ....(RHI)
Dr. Demento Greatest Novelty-#4-1970s .... (RHI)
Major Tom (Coming Home)
Peter Schilling; *Different Story (World Of Lust &
Crime)* ....(ELE)
Error In The The System ....(ELE)
Mister Touchdown U.S.A.
University Of Michigan Band; *Greatest College Football
Marches* ....(VAN)
Mr. Tambourine Man
Bob Dylan; *At Budokan* ....(COL)
Biograph ....(COL)
Bringin' It All Back Home ....(COL)
Greatest Hits ....(COL)
Byrds; *Billboard Top Rock 'N' Roll Hits-1965* .... (RHI)
Greatest Hits ....(COL)
Mr. Tambourine Man ....(COL)
Original Singles-#1-1965-1967 ....(COL)
Mr. Telephone Man
New Edition; *Greatest Hits-#1* .... (MCA)
New Edition ....(MCA)
Tar Top
Alabama; *Just Us* ....(RCA)
Tarzan Boy
Baltimora; *Living In The Background* .... (MAN)
Tarzan Was A Bluesman
Timbuk 3; *Eden Alley* ....(IRS)
Tarzan & Jane
Sparks; *Angst In My Pants* ....(ATL)
Tarzan's Nuts
Madness; *One Step Beyond* ....(SIR)
Ted, Just Admit It
Jane's Addiction; *Nothing's Shocking* ....(WB)
Tennessee Jed
Grateful Dead; *Europe '72* ....(WB)
What A Long Strange Trip It's Been ....(WB)
Terence's Farewell To Kathleen
John McCormack; *Ireland Of Treasures-Voices &
Melodies* ....(CAP)
Theme From "Tom & Jerry"
Henry Mancini; *ST/Tom & Jerry-The Movie* ..... (MCA)
Timothy
Buoys; *Scepter Records Story* ....(CPC)
Super Hits/'70s-Have A Nice Day-#6 .... (RHI)
Tom Dooley
Doc Watson; *Doc Watson* ....(VAN)
Essential ....(VAN)
Out In The Country ....(INT)

Kingston Trio; *Capitol Collectors Series* ....(CAP)
From The Hungry i ....(CAP)
Greatest Hits ....(CCB)
Tom Dooley ....(CAP)
Troubadours Of The Folk Era-#3 .... (RHI)
Tom Sawyer
Rush; *Chronicles* ....(MER)
Exit...Stage Left ....(MER)
Moving Pictures ....(MER)
Tom Thumb
Wayne Shorter; *Best Of-Blue Note Years* .... (BLN)
Tom & Jerry
Hot Rize; *Radio Boogie* ....(FF)
Mark O'Connor; *Championship Years* ....(CMF)
Tommy Can You Hear Me
Who; *Join Together* ....(MCA)
ST/Kids Are Alright ....(MCA)
ST/Tommy ....(POL)
Tommy ....(MCA)
Tom, Dick Or Harry
Original Cast; *Kiss Me Kate* ....(COL)
Tom's Diner
DNA/Suzanne Vega; *Solitude Standing* .... (A&M)
Tom's Album ....(A&M)

MEN'S NAMES: U

Tales Of Brave Ulysses
Cream; *Disraeli Gears* ....(POL)
Eric Clapton-Crossroads ....(POL)
Live Cream-#2 ....(POL)

MEN'S NAMES: V

Mr. Vain
Culture Beat; *S* ....(550)
Night Of Van Gogh
Boz Scaggs; *Other Roads* ....(COL)
Van Gogh's Left Ear
Kenny Garrett; *Black Hope* ....(WB)
Vincent
Don McLean; *American Pie* ....(EMI)
Best Of ....(EMI)
Greatest Hits Then & Now ....(EMI)

MEN'S NAMES: W

Big Bad Bill Is Sweet William Now
Ry Cooder; *Jazz* ....(WB)
Calling Mr. Welfare
Big Daddy Kane; *It's A Big Daddy Thing* ....(CLD)
Good Evening Mr. Waldheim
Lou Reed; *New York* ....(SIR)
Little Willie
Sweet; *Best Of-1910 Fruitgum Co.-#2* .... (RHI)
Mr. Wendal
Arrested Development; *3 Years 5 Months 2 Days In The
Life Of* ....(CHR)
Unplugged ....(CHR)
Poor Will & The Jolly Hangman
Richard Thompson; *Guitar Vocal* ....(HBL)
Rambling, Gambling Willie
Bob Dylan; *Bootleg Series-#1-3-1961-1989* ......(COL)
Say Hey (The Willie Mays Song)
Treniers; *Baseball's Greatest Hits* .... (RHI)
Shotgun Willie
Willie Nelson; *Shotgun Willie* .... (ATL)
Theme From "Wayne's World"
Mike Myers & Dana Carvey; *ST/Wayne's World* . (RPR)
Waldo P. Emerson Jones
Archies; *Grooviest Hits Of* ....(BCT)
Waldo's Discount Donuts
Red Knuckles/Trailblazers; *Hot Rize Presents* ......(FF)
Waltz Me Around Again Willie
Joan Morris & William Bolcom; *After The Ball* . (NON)
Warren Harding
Al Stewart; *Past Present & Future* .... (RHI)
Wild Little Willy
Ronnie Hawkins/Hawks; *Best Of* .... (RHI)

Willie Jones
Charlie Daniels Band; *Night Rider* .... (EPI)
Renegade .... (EPI)
Willie Short
Mary Chapin Carpenter; *Red Hot + Country* .... (MER)
Willie The Pimp
Frank Zappa; *Hot Rats* .... (RYK)
You Can't Do That On Stage Anymore-#4 ...... (RYK)
Mothers Of Invention; *Fillmore East-June 1971* .. (RPR)
Willie & The Hand Jive
Eric Clapton; *451 Ocean Boulevard* .... (POL)
Time Pieces-Best Of .... (POL)
George Thorogood/Destroyers; *Maverick* .... (EMI)
Johnny Otis; *All-Time Greatest Hits Of Rock &*
Roll .... (CCB)
Capitol Years .... (CAP)
Let The Good Times Roll .... (CAP)
W.S. Walcott Medicine Show
Band; *Rock Of Ages-#1 & 2* .... (CAP)
Stage Fright .... (CAP)
To Kingdom Come-Definitive Collection .... (CAP)

MEN'S NAMES: Z

Theme From "Doctor Zhivago"
101 Strings Orchestra; *Music From Doctor Zhivago &*
Others .... (ALS)
War Baby Son Of Zorro
Daryl Hall & John Oates; *War Babies* .... (ATL)
Ziggy Stardust
David Bowie; *Changesbowie* ....(RYK)
Rise & Fall Of Ziggy Stardust .... (RYK)
Sound + Vision .... (RYK)
Stage .... (RYK)
ST/Ziggy Stardust-The Motion Picture .... (RCA)
The Singles-1969-1993 .... (RYK)
"Zorba The Greek" Theme
Cincinnati Pops Orchestra/Erich Kunzel; *Hollywood's*
Greatest Hits-#2 .... (TLR)
"Zorro" Theme
Original Music; *Disney Collection-#2* .... (DIS)

MIDNIGHT

See Also: NIGHT

After Midnight
Eric Clapton; *Crossroads* .... (POL)
Eric Clapton .... (RSO)
Just One Night .... (RSO)
Time Pieces-Best Of .... (RSO)
J.J. Cale; *Naturally* .... (MCA)
At Midnight
Mighty Lemon Drops; *Laughter* .... (SIR)
Rufus & Chaka Khan; *Ask Rufus* .... (MCA)
Stompin' At The Savoy-Live .... (WB)
Burning Of The Midnight Lamp
Jimi Hendrix; *Electric Ladyland* .... (RPR)
Essential-#1 & 2 .... (RPR)
Lifelines-Story .... (RPR)
Radio One .... (RYK)
Living Colour; *Biscuits* .... (EPI)
Burnin' The Midnight Oil
Foghat; *Night Shift* .... (RHI)
Caravan To Midnight
Robin Trower; *Caravan To Midnight* .... (CHR)
Celery Stalks At Midnight
Will Bradley; *Swing Time! Fab. Big Band*
Era-1925-1955 ....(COL)
Coffee At Midnite
Bluegrass Parlor Band; *Two Colors* .... (PIN)
Confessin' Midnight
Robin Trower; *For Earth Below* .... (CHR)
Down In The Tube Station At Midnight
Jam; *Greatest Hits* .... (POL)
Snap! .... (POL)
Fire At Midnight
Jethro Tull; *Songs From The Wood* .... (CHR)
Gimme Gimme Gimme (A Man After Midnight)
Erasure; *Two Ring Circus* .... (SIR)

In The Midnight Hour
Rascals; *Classic Rock-1966-1988* ....(ATL)
ST/More Songs From "The Big Chill" .... (MOT)
Time Piece-Greatest Hits .... (ATL)
Roxy Music; *Flesh & Blood* .... (RPR)
Street Life-20 Great Hits .... (RPR)
Wilson Pickett; *Atlantic R&B*
1947-1974-#5-(1962-1966) .... (ATL)
Best Of .... (ATL)
Frat Rock-#4 .... (RHI)
Golden Soul .... (ATL)
Greatest Hits .... (ATL)
Soul Years .... (ATL)
Isn't It Midnight
Fleetwood Mac; *25 Years-The Chain* .... (WB)
London After Midnight
Wrathchild America; *Climbin' The Walls* .... (ATL)
Love In The Midnight
Styx; *Cornerstone* .... (A&M)
Midnight
Abby Marable; *45* .... (MCA)
Altered Images; *Happy Birthday* .... (EPI)
Ice-T; *O.G. Original Gangster* .... (SIR)
Maze; *Silky Soul* .... (WB)
Midnight Angel
Barbara Mandrell; *Best Of* .... (MCA)
Midnight Angel .... (MCA)
Highway 101; *Paint The Town* .... (WB)
Midnight At The Oasis
Maria Muldaur; *Maria Muldaur* .... (RPR)
Super Hits/'70s-Have A Nice Day-#13 .... (RHI)
Midnight Blue
Electric Light Orchestra; *Afterglow* .... (EPI)
Discovery .... (JET)
Johnny Mathis; *Feelings* ....(COL)
King Curtis; *Enjoy...Best Of* .... (CLT)
Soul Twist & Other Golden Classics .... (CLT)
Lou Gramm; *Ready Or Not* .... (ATL)
Louise Tucker; *Midnight Blue* .... (ARI)
Melissa Manchester; *Greatest Hits* .... (ARI)
Melissa .... (ARI)
Seals & Crofts; *Takin' It Easy* .... (WB)
Midnight Blues
Allman Brothers Band; *An Evening With-First Set* . (EPI)
Bessie Smith; *Complete Recordings* ....(COL)
Charlie Daniels Band; *Original* .... (SUN)
Time For Tears .... (SUN)
Gary Moore; *Still Got The Blues* .... (CHS)
Memphis Slim; *Traveling With The Blues* .... (STY)
Midnight Bus
Jesse Winchester; *Third Down 110 To Go* .... (RHI)
Midnight Carnival
Chris Mars; *Horseshoes & Hand Grenades* ...... (SMA)
Midnight Confessions
Grass Roots; *Anthology-1965-1975* .... (RHI)
Original Rock 'N' Roll Hits Of The '60s ...... (RLL)
Vintage Music-Orig. Classics/'60s-#9 .... (MCA)
Midnight Creeper
Elton John; *Don't Shoot Me I'm Only The Piano*
Player .... (POL)
Midnight Dreamer
Journey; *Look Into The Future* ....(COL)
Midnight Fire
Steve Wariner; *Best Of* .... (RCA)
Greatest Hits .... (RCA)
Midnight Flyer
Eagles; *On The Border* .... (ASY)
Midnight Hauler
Razzy Bailey; *Greatest Hits* ....(RCA)
Midnight In Memphis
Bette Midler; *ST/The Rose* .... (ATL)
Hoyt Axton; *Where Did The Money Go* ....(JER)
Meri Wilson; *First Take* ....(GRT)
Midnight In Montgomery
Alan Jackson; *Don't Rock The Jukebox* .... (ARI)
Midnight In Morocco
Michael Powers; *Perpetual Motion* .... (NSY)
Midnight In Moscow
Dukes Of Dixieland; *Dixieland's Greatest Hits* ... (MCA)
Kenny Ball; *45* .... (ERI)
Midnight In Old Amarillo
Buddy Emmons & Ray Pennington; *Swing & Other*
Things .... (SO)

Midnight In Paris
Michael Hurley/Unholy Modal Rounders; *Have Moicy* .... (ROU)
Stephen Stills; *Illegal Stills* ....(COL)
Midnight In San Juan
Earl Klugh; *Midnight In San Juan* .... (WB)
Midnight In Tokyo
Y & T; *Best Of '81 To '85* .... (A&M)
Mean Streak .... (A&M)
Yesterday & Today Live .... (MET)
Midnight Light
Le Blanc & Carr; *Midnight Light* ....(BT)
Midnight Lover
Leon Russell; *Americana* ....(PRD)
Midnight Madness
Clockwork; *Made In The U.S. Of Japan* .... (MER)
Foghat; *Stone Blue* .... (RHI)
Midnight Magic
38 Special; *Rock & Roll Strategy* .... (A&M)
Commodores; *Midnight Magic* ....(MOT)
Midnight Man
Allman Brothers Band; *Shades Of Two Worlds* .... (EPI)
James Gang; *16 Greatest Hits* ....(MCA)
Best Of ....(MCA)
Rita Remington; *My Melody Of Love* .... (PLN)
Midnight Maniac
Krokus; *Blitz* .... (ARI)
Midnight Mary
Joey Powers; *Dick Bartley's One-Hit Wonders/'60s-#1* .... (RHI)
Midnight Moodies
Joe Walsh; *The Smoker You Drink The Player You Get* ....(MCA)
Midnight On Mars
Ashra; *Blackouts* .... (BP)
Midnight On The Bay
Stills/Young Band; *Long May You Run* .... (RPR)
Midnight On The Radio
Mike Bloomfield; *Try It Before You Buy It* .... (OW)
Midnight Prowl
John David Souther; *Black Rose* .... (ASY)
Midnight Rambler
Rolling Stones; *Get Yer Ya-Ya's Out* .... (AKO)
Hot Rocks-1964-1971 .... (AKO)
Let It Bleed .... (AKO)
Midnight Ravers
Bob Marley/Wailers; *Catch A Fire* .... (TUF)
Midnight Rendezvous
Babys; *Anthology* .... (CHR)
Union Jacks .... (CHR)
Jacksons; *2300 Jackson Street* .... (EPI)
Midnight Rider
Allman Brothers Band; *Anthology Of Duane Allman-#2* .... (CPC)
Beginnings .... (POL)
Best Of .... (POL)
Decade Of Hits-1969-1979 .... (POL)
Idlewild South .... (POL)
Road Goes On Forever .... (POL)
Gregg Allman; *Laid Back* .... (CPC)
South's Greatest Hits .... (CPC)
Willie Nelson; *ST/Electric Horseman* ....(COL)
Midnight Rocks
Al Stewart; *24 Carrots* .... (ARI)
Midnight Rodeo
Leon Everette; *45* ....(RCA)
Midnight Shift
Commander Cody/Lost Planet Airmen; *Lost In The Ozone* ....(MCA)
Midnight Sky
Isley Brothers; *Live It Up* .... (TN)
Story-#2/T-Neck Years 1969-1985 .... (RHI)
Midnight Special
Creedence Clearwater Revival; *1969* ....(FAN)
Chronicle-#2 .... (FAN)
Gold .... (FAN)
Movie Album .... (FAN)
Willy & The Poor Boys .... (FAN)
Johnny Rivers; *Anthology 1964-1977* .... (RHI)
Very Best Of .... (EMI)
Paul Evans; *Super Oldies/'60s-#2* ....(AUF)

Midnight Special Train
Joe Turner; *Atlantic R&B 1947-1974-#3-(1955-1958)* ....(ATL)
Greatest Hits .... (ATL)
Midnight Sun
Ella Fitzgerald; *In Rome-Birthday Concert* .... (VRV)
Ella Fitzgerald & Oscar Peterson; *Ella & Oscar* .. (PAB)
Sarah Vaughan; *Best Of* .... (PAB)
How Long Has This Been Going On .... (PAB)
Midnight Tennessee Woman
Jack Greene; *Sings His Best* ....(SO)
Midnight Train To Georgia
Gladys Knight/Pips; *Billboard Top Rock 'N' Roll Hits-1973* .... (RHI)
Greatest Hits ....(BUD)
Imagination ....(BUD)
On & On .... (FFT)
Radio Active Hits ....(ACC)
Very Best Of ....(BUD)
Midnight Wind
Charlie Daniels Band; *Midnight Wind* .... (EPI)
John Stewart; *Bombs Away Dream Babies* .... (RSO)
Midnight 'N Peru
Ken Tamplin; *Soul Survivor* .... (INS)
Midnight, Me & The Blues
Mel Tillis/Statesiders; *24 Great Hits* ....(MGM)
Best Of ....(MGM)
Greatest Hits ....(MGM)
Midnite Cruiser
Steely Dan; *Can't Buy A Thrill* .... (MCA)
New York City Serenade
Bruce Springsteen; *Wild Innocent & The E Street Shuffle* ....(COL)
Private Life
Grace Jones; *Island Life* .... (ISL)
Warm Leatherette .... (ISL)
Pretenders; *Pretenders* .... (SIR)
Rainbow At Midnight
Ernest Tubb; *Collection* ....(SO)
Story ....(MCA)
Riding That Midnight Train
Doc Watson; *Riding That Midnight Train* ....(SH)
Rockin' After Midnight
Marvin Gaye; *Midnight Love* ....(COL)
Rockin' At Midnight
Honeydrippers; *Little By Little-Collectors Edition* . (EPR)
Volume 1 .... (EPR)
'Round Midnight
Carmen McRae; *Carmen Sings Monk* .... (NOV)
Ella Fitzgerald; *Fine & Mellow* .... (PAB)
Newport Jazz Festival ....(COL)
Ella Fitzgerald & Count Basie; *Perfect Match* .... (PAB)
John Lewis; *Midnight In Paris* .... (EMA)
Private Concert .... (EMA)
Miles Davis; *Collector's Items* .... (PRS)
Greatest Hits ....(COL)
Live At The Plugged Nickel ....(COL)
Miles Davis ....(PHI)
Miles Davis Quintet; *'Round Midnight* ....(COL)
Sarah Vaughan; *Roulette Years* .... (RLL)
Thelonius Monk; *At The It Club* ....(COL)
Best Of ....(BLN)
I Like Jazz-Essence Of ....(COL)
Thelonius Monk ....(CRS)
'Round Midnight .... (MS)
Wynton Marsalis; *All-American Hero* ....(WHO)
Saturday At Midnight
Cheap Trick; *One On One* .... (EPI)
South City Midnight Lady
Doobie Brothers; *Best Of* .... (WB)
Captain & Me .... (WB)
Theme From "Midnight Cowboy"
Cincinnati Pops Orchestra/Erich Kunzel; *Hollywood's Greatest Hits-#2* .... (TLR)
Tired Of Midnight Blue
George Harrison; *Extra Texture* .... (CAP)
Two Minutes To Midnight
Iron Maiden; *A Real Dead One* .... (CAP)
Live After Death-World Slavery Tour ....(CAP)
Powerslave ....(CAP)
Two More Bottles Of Wine
Delbert McClinton; *Honky Tonkin'-I Done Me Some* ....(ALG)

Emmylou Harris; *Honky Tonk Country* .... (WB)
   Profile-Best Of .... (WB)
   Quarter Moon In A Ten-Cent Town .... (WB)
Walkin' After Midnight
   Garth Brooks; *The Chase* .... (LIB)
   Loretta Lynn; *I Remember Patsy* .... (MCA)
   Oak Ridge Boys; *Unstoppable* .... (RCA)
   Patsy Cline; *20 Golden Pieces Of* .... (BLD)
   Greatest Hits .... (MCA)
   Let The Teardrops Fall .... (ACC)
   Live At The Opry .... (MCA)
   Patsy Cline .... (MCA)
   Story .... (MCA)
When The Midnight Choo Choo Leaves...
   Andrews Sisters; *Best Of-#2* .... (MCA)
   Judy Garland & Fred Astaire; *ST/Easter Parade* .. (SSP)
Young Blood
   Bad Company; *Run With The Pack* .... (SS)
   Coasters; *Greatest Hits* .... (ATC)
   Their Greatest Recordings-Early Years .... (ATC)

MINING

See Also: GOLD, MOUNTAINS, WORK

Blackleg Miner
   Steeleye Span; *Hark The Village Wait* .... (CHR)
   Story .... (CHR)
Blue Sky Mine
   Midnight Oil; *Blue Sky Mining* .... (COL)
Canary In A Coal Mine
   Police; *Zenyatta Mondatta* .... (A&M)
Clementine
   Bobby Darin; *At The Copa* .... (BAI)
   Story .... (ATC)
Diamond Mine
   Blue Rodeo; *Diamond Mine* .... (ATL)
   Hank Williams, Jr.; *Out Of Left Field* .... (CPC)
Don't Give Up
   Peter Gabriel; *Shaking The Tree-16 Golden*
   Greats .... (GEF)
   So .... (GEF)
Dying Miner
   Woody Guthrie; *Struggle* .... (FLW)
Explosion In The Fairmount Mines
   Blind Alfred Reed; *How Can A Poor Man Stand Such*
   Times... .... (ROU)
Miner's Blues
   Frank Hutchison; *Train That Carried My Girl From*
   Town .... (ROU)
Miner's Life
   Tom Juravich; *Out Of Darkness (Mine Workers'*
   Story) .... (FF)
   Weavers; *Reunion At Carnegie Hall-1963-#2* ... (VAN)
Miner's Lifeguard
   Almanac Singers/Peter Seeger/Chorus; *Talking Union &*
   Other Union Songs .... (FLW)
Miner's Prayer
   Dwight Yoakam; *Guitars Cadillacs Etc. Etc.* ..... (RPR)
Mining Camp Blues
   Fletcher Henderson & Trixie Smith; *Fletcher Henderson's*
   Orchestra-1923-1927 .... (BIO)
Mining For Coal
   Randy Travis; *No Holdin' Back* .... (WB)
Mining For Gold
   Cowboy Junkies; *Trinity Session* .... (RCA)
New York Mining Disaster 1941
   Bee Gees; *Gold-#1* .... (POL)
   Here At Last .... (RSO)
   History Of British Rock-#8 .... (RHI)
One Miner's Life-The Image Of God
   Battlefield Band; *There's A Buzz* .... (FF)
Open Pit Mine
   Nashville Bluegrass Band; *Waitin' For The Hard Times*
   To Go .... (SH)
Stripmining
   James; *Strip-Mine* .... (SIR)
There's A Gold Mine In The Sky
   Jimmy C. Newman; *Cajun Cowboy* .... (PLN)
   Pat Boone; *Love Letters In The Sand* .... (MSP)
We Work The Black Seam
   Sting; *Bring On The Night* .... (A&M)
   Dream Of The Blue Turtles .... (A&M)

Work In The Mines
   Bill Shute & Lisa Null; *American Primitive* .... (GRE)
Working In The Coal Mine
   Devo; *Best Of-Greatest Hits* .... (WB)
   Greatest Hits .... (WB)
   New Traditionalists .... (WB)
   Now It Can Be Told (Devo At The Palace) ..... (ENI)
   ST/Heavy Metal .... (ASY)
   Judds; *Collection-1983-1990* .... (RCA)
   Rockin' With The Rhythm .... (RCA)
   Lee Dorsey; *Best Of New Orleans R&B-#2* .... (RHI)
   Golden Classics .... (CLT)
   History Of New Orleans R&B-#3-1962-1970 ... (RHI)
   Holy Cow .... (ARI)
   New Orleans Jazz & Heritage Fest-1976 .... (RHI)

MONEY, Rich, Taxes, Wealth

See Also: GOLD, JEWELRY, POVERTY,
SHOPPING, WORK

1040 Blues
   Robert Cray; *Shame + Sin* .... (MER)
90 Days (Same As Cash)
   Midnight Star; *Midnight Star* .... (SLR)
Addicted To A Dollar
   Doug Stone; *More Love* .... (EPI)
Ain't Got No Money
   Bob Seger/Silver Bullet Band; *Stranger In Town* . (CAP)
Ain't No Fun (Waiting 'Round To Be A...)
   AC/DC; *Dirty Deeds Done Dirt Cheap* .... (ATL)
Ain't No Money
   Rosanne Cash; *Somewhere In The Stars* .... (COL)
Always True To You In My Fashion
   Blossom Dearie; *Night & Day: Cole Porter*
   Songbook .... (VRV)
   Broadway Cast; *Kiss Me Kate* .... (ANG)
   Peggy Lee & George Shearing; *Anything Goes-Capitol*
   Sings Cole Porter .... (CAP)
Another Day Another Dollar
   Alison Krauss & Union Station; *Every Time You Say*
   Goodbye .... (ROU)
Anything For Money
   DV8; *ST/Far Out Man* .... (CML)
   ST/Halloween V-Revenge Of Michael Myers .... (VS)
Baby You're A Rich Man
   Beatles; *Box Set* .... (CAP)
   Magical Mystery Tour .... (CAP)
Ballad Of Forty Dollars
   Johnny Cash & Waylon Jennings; *Heroes* .... (COL)
   Tom T. Hall; *Essential Anniversary Collection* ... (MER)
   Greatest Hits .... (MER)
Bankrobber
   Clash; *On Broadway* .... (EPI)
   Story Of-#1 .... (EPI)
Bankrobber/Robber Dub
   Clash; *Black Market Clash* .... (EPI)
   Rhythm Come Forward-#3 .... (COL)
Best Things In Life Are Free
   June Allyson; *ST/Good News* .... (SSP)
   Luther Vandross & Janet Jackson; *ST/Mo' Money* (BLU)
   Mel Torme; *Easy To Remember* .... (GLN)
   Sam Cooke; *At The Copa* .... (RCA)
Big Money
   Rush; *Power Windows* .... (MER)
   Show Of Hands .... (MER)
Billion Dollar Babies
   Alice Cooper; *Alice Cooper Show* .... (WB)
   Billion Dollar Babies .... (WB)
   Greatest Hits .... (WB)
Bitch Betta Have My Money
   AMG; *Give A Dog A Bone* .... (SEL)
Black Money
   Vinnie James; *All-American Boy* .... (RCA)
Blue Money
   Van Morrison; *His Band & Street Choir* .... (WB)
Brother, Can You Spare A Dime
   Bing Crosby; *16 Most Requested Songs* .... (COL)
   Odetta/Dr. John/John Campbell/Rufus Reid; *Strike A*
   Deep Chord-Blues For Homeless .... (JST)
   Peter, Paul & Mary; *See What Tomorrow Brings* .. (WB)
   Weavers; *Greatest Hits* .... (VAN)

Burn Your Money!
Mojo Nixon & Skid Roper; *Root Hog Or Die* ..... (IRS)
Bus Fare Home
Spaniels; *Heart & Soul-#2* .... (VJ)
Busted
John Conlee; *Greatest Hits* .... (MCA)
   Songs For The Working Man .... (MCA)
Ray Charles; *Greatest Hits-#1* .... (RHI)
   Greatest Hits-#2 ....(DHL)
Buy Me A Million Dollars
Love Tractor; *Love Tractor/'Til The Cows Come
Home* .... (DB)
Buying My Way Into Heaven
Sammy Hagar; *Unboxed* ....(GEF)
Can I Have My Money Back
Gerry Rafferty; *Can I Have My Money Back* .... (MCA)
Can't Buy Me Love
Beatles; *Hey Jude* ....(CAP)
   1962-1966 ....(CAP)
   At The Hollywood Bowl ....(CAP)
   Hard Day's Night ....(CAP)
   Reel Music ....(CAP)
Paul McCartney; *Tripping The Live Fantastic* ....(CAP)
Cash For Your Trash
Original Cast; *Ain't Misbehavin'* ....(RCA)
Check's In The Mail
Victory; *Don't Get Mad-Get Even* .... (MRY)
Cold Hard Cash
Greg Kihn; *Next Of Kihn* .... (BES)
Daddy Never Was The Cadillac Kind
Confederate Railroad; *Notorious* .... (ATL)
Diamonds On The Soles Of Her Shoes
Paul Simon; *Concert In The Park-August 15 1991* (WB)
   Graceland ....(WB)
   Negotiations & Love Songs-1971-1986 ....(WB)
Did You Steal My Money
Who; *Face Dances* .... (MCA)
Dime At A Time
Del Reeves; *Super Hits Country-1960s* .... (IGR)
Dime Store Mystery
Lou Reed; *New York* .... (SIR)
Dirty Cash (Money Talks)
Adventures Of Stevie V; *Best Of '90s Dance
Music-#1-Hip House* .... (PWL)
   Dirty Cash (Money Talks) .... (MER)
Dollar Bill
Screaming Trees; *Sweet Oblivion* .... (EPI)
Dollar's Worth Of Gasoline
Tom Russell; *Hurricane Season* ....(PHO)
Don't Bet Money
Whispers; *Best Of* .... (SLR)
   Don't Bet Money .... (SLR)
Don't Pay The Ferryman
Chris DeBurgh; *Getaway* ....(A&M)
Don't Put A Tax On The Beautiful Girls
Eddie Cantor; *Rare Early Recordings-1919-1921* .(BIO)
Don't Want Money
Jasmine Guy; *Jasmine Guy* .... (WB)
Easy Money
Benny Carter; *Over The Rainbow* .... (MM)
   The King ....(PAB)
Billy Joel; *Innocent Man* ....(COL)
James O'Gwynn; *Greatest Hits* .... (PLN)
Rickie Lee Jones; *Rickie Lee Jones* .... (WB)
R.E.O. Speedwagon; *Nine Lives* .... (EPI)
   You Can Tune A Piano... .... (EPI)
Eat The Rich
Aerosmith; *Get A Grip* ....(GEF)
Even It Up
Heart; *Be Be Le Strange* .... (EPI)
   Greatest Hits/Live .... (EPI)
Fancy
Bobbi Gentry; *All-Time Country Classics-#1* .....(CAP)
Reba McEntire; *Rumor Has It* .... (MCA)
Father Christmas
Kinks; *Come Dancing With-Best Of-1977-1986* .. (ARI)
First I Look At The Purse
Contours; *25 Hard To Find Motown Classics-#3* (MOT)
   Do You Love Me Now That I Can Dance ..... (MOT)
J. Geils Band; *Best Of* .... (ATL)
   Full House ....(ATL)
   J. Geils Band ....(ATL)
Fool With My Money
Special Forces; *Special Forces* ....(ERC)

Fool & His Money
Wang Chung; *Mosaic* ....(GEF)
For The Love Of Money
O'Jays; *Collector's Gems* .... (PI)
   Ship Ahoy .... (PI)
   Soul Hits/'70s-#14 .... (RHI)
Friends In Low Places
Garth Brooks; *No Fences* .... (LIB)
Gimme A Quarter, 25 Cents For The Bus
October Faction; *October Faction* ....(SST)
Golden Coins
Elvis Presley; *ST/Harum Scarum* ....(RCA)
Got To Get The Money
Levert; *45* .... (ATL)
Green Christmas
Stan Freberg; *Capitol Collectors Series* ....(CAP)
   Christmas Comedy Classics ....(PRY)
   Dr. Demento Greatest Christmas CD .... (RHI)
   Dr. Demento's Greatest Novelty-#6 .... (RHI)
Greenback Dollar
Kingston Trio; *Best Of The Best Of* ....(POE)
   Capitol Collectors Series ....(CAP)
   Very Best Of ....(CAP)
Grey Goose/Sixpenny Money
Joe Burke; *Traditional Music Of Ireland* ....(GRE)
Have A Cigar
Pink Floyd; *Wish You Were Here* ....(COL)
Here's A Quarter, Call Someone Who Cares
Travis Tritt; *It's All About To Change* .... (WB)
Hidden Treasure
Traffic; *Low Spark Of High Heeled Boys* .... (ISL)
Hissing Of Summer Lawns
Joni Mitchell; *Hissing Of Summer Lawns* ....(ASY)
I Don't Want Your Millions, Mister
Tom Rush; *Tom Rush* ....(FAN)
I Don't Want Your Money
Chicago; *3* ....(COL)
   At Carnegie Hall ....(COL)
I Found A Million Dollar Baby
Barbra Streisand; *ST/Funny Girl* .... (ARI)
Nat King Cole; *Gift Set* ....(CAP)
I Left My Wallet In El Segundo
Tribe Called Quest; *People's Instinctive Travels...* . (JVA)
   Rap: Most Valuable Players .... (KT)
I Love Robbing Banks
Greg Austin Band; *Midnight Driver* ....(XER)
I Wanna Be Rich
Calloway; *S* .... (SLR)
Original Broadway Cast; *Stop The World-I Want To Get
Off* ....(POL)
If Dirt Were Dollars
Don Henley; *End Of The Innocence* ....(GEF)
If I Didn't Have A Dime (To Play The...)
Gene Pitney; *Anthology* .... (RHI)
   Greatest Hits ....(EVR)
If I Had No Loot
Tony! Toni! Tone!; *Sons Of Soul* .... (WIN)
If I Were A Rich Man
Original Cast; *Fiddler On The Roof* ....(RCA)
Original London Cast; *Fiddler On The Roof* .....(COL)
If You've Got The Money I've Got The...
Lefty Frizzell; *American Originals* ....(COL)
   Columbia Country Classics-#2-Honky Tonk ....(COL)
   Greatest Hits ....(COL)
Willie Nelson; *Greatest Hits & Some That Will Be* (COL)
   Sound In Your Mind ....(COL)
   & Family Live ....(COL)
(It's Just) The Way That You Love Me
Paula Abdul; *Forever Your Girl* .... (VIA)
   Shut Up & Dance (Mixes) .... (VIA)
It's Money That Matters
Randy Newman; *Land Of Dreams* ....(RPR)
It's Your Money
James Brown; *I'm Real* ....(SCO)
I.O.U.
Lee Greenwood; *Greatest Hits* .... (MCA)
   MCA Records 30 Years Of Hits-1958-1988 ... (MCA)
   Somebody's Gonna Love You .... (MCA)
I've Got Five Dollars
Bobby Short; *50 By Bobby Short* .... (ATL)
Ella Fitzgerald; *Rodgers & Hart Songbook* ....(VRV)
Tony Bennett; *Rodgers & Hart Songbook* .... (DRG)
I've Got Five Dollars & It's Saturday...
Gene Pitney; *Anthology* .... (RHI)

Just Got Paid
ZZ Top; *Best Of* .... (WB)
  Rio Grande Mud .... (WB)
  Six Pack .... (WB)
King Of The Dollar
School Of Fish; *School Of Fish* .... (CAP)
Lawyers, Guns & Money
Warren Zevon; *Excitable Boy* .... (ASY)
  Quiet Normal Life-Best Of .... (ASY)
  Stand In The Fire .... (ASY)
Let's Go Spend Your Money Honey
Evangeline; *French Quarter Moon* .... (MGR)
Life Is A Lemon And I Want My Money Back
Meat Loaf; *Bat Out Of Hell II-Back Into Hell* ... (MCA)
Lifestyles Of The Not-So-Rich & Famous
Tracy Byrd; *No Ordinary Man* .... (MCA)
Life's Been Good
Eagles; *Live* .... (ASY)
Joe Walsh; *But Seriously Folks* .... (ASY)
  ST/FM .... (MCA)
Loan Me A Dime
Boz Scaggs; *Boz Scaggs* .... (ATC)
  Duane Allman Anthology .... (CPC)
Lookin' In The Same Direction
Ken Mellons; *Ken Mellons* .... (EPI)
Love At The Five & Dime
Kathy Mattea; *Collection of Hits* .... (MER)
  Fourteen Country Favorites .... (MER)
  Walk The Way The Wind Blows .... (MER)
Nanci Griffith; *Last Of The True Believers* ...... (PHO)
  One Fair Summer Evening .... (MCA)
Making Music For Money
Jimmy Buffett; *A-1-A* .... (MCA)
Kenny Rogers; *Gambler* .... (UA)
Mama Can't Buy You Love
Elton John; *Complete Thom Bell Sessions* ...... (MCA)
  Greatest Hits-1976-1986 .... (MCA)
Mansion In The Slums
Crowded House; *Temple Of Low Men* ...... (CAP)
Mansion On The Hill
Bruce Springsteen; *Nebraska* .... (COL)
Emmylou Harris/Nash Ramblers; *At The Ryman* . (RPR)
Hank Williams; *40 Greatest Hits* .... (POL)
  Lovesick Blues .... (POL)
Neil Young/Crazy Horse; *Arc Weld* .... (RPR)
  Ragged Glory .... (RPR)
Material Girl
Madonna; *Immaculate Collection* .... (SIR)
  Like A Virgin .... (SIR)
  Royal Box .... (SIR)
Material Thangz
Deele; *Material Thangz* .... (SLR)
Me & The I.R.S.
Johnny Paycheck; *Greatest Hits-#2* .... (EPI)
Million Dollar Bash
Bob Dylan; *Biograph* .... (COL)
Bob Dylan/Band; *Basement Tapes* .... (COL)
Millionaire
ABC; *How To Be A Zillionaire* .... (MER)
Minimum Wage
They Might Be Giants; *Flood* .... (ELE)
Money
Bros; *The Time* .... (EPI)
Cameo; *Emotional Violence* .... (RPR)
Charlie Daniels Band; *Full Moon* .... (EPI)
Clifton Chenier; *King Of Zydeco* .... (ARH)
  King Of Zydeco Live At Montreux .... (ARH)
K.T. Oslin; *This Woman* .... (RCA)
Laura Nyro; *Smile* .... (COL)
Peter Frampton; *Frampton* .... (A&M)
  Frampton Comes Alive .... (A&M)
Pink Floyd; *Collection Of Great Dance Songs* .... (COL)
  Dark Side Of The Moon .... (CAP)
  Delicate Sound Of Thunder .... (COL)
  Gift Set .... (CAP)
Yes; *Yesyears* .... (ATC)
Money Don't Matter 2 Night
Prince/New Power Generation; *Diamonds And Pearls* .... (PAI)
Money For Nothing
Dire Straits; *Brothers In Arms* .... (WB)
  Money For Nothing .... (WB)
Money Honey
38 Special; *Rockin' Into The Night* .... (A&M)

Bay City Rollers; *Greatest Hits* .... (ARI)
  Rock & Roll Love Letters .... (ARI)
Drifters; *Greatest Hits 1953-1958* .... (ATL)
  Greatest Recordings .... (ATC)
  Soul Years .... (ATC)
Elvis Presley; *Rocker* .... (RCA)
Little Richard; *Greatest Hits* .... (EVR)
Money In The Bank
John Anderson; *On Solid Ground* .... (BNA)
Money Machine
James Taylor; *In The Pocket* .... (WB)
Money Song
Original Cast; *Cabaret* .... (COL)
Money Tak
Pretenders; *Last Of The Independents* .... (SIR)
Money Talks
Bar-Kays; *Money Talks* .... (STX)
Gang Of Four; *Mall* .... (POL)
J.J. Cale; *Number 8* .... (MER)
  Special Edition .... (MER)
Living Colour; *Biscuits* .... (EPI)
Rick James; *Street Songs/Throwin' Down* .... (MOT)
Money (That's What I Want)
Barrett Strong; *Motown Story-First 25 Years* .... (MOT)
  Oldies But Goodies-#4 .... (OSR)
Beatles; *Box Set* .... (CAP)
  Rock & Roll Music-#1 .... (CAP)
  Second Album .... (CAP)
Buddy Guy; *Man & The Blues* .... (VAN)
Diana Ross/Supremes; *Sing Motown* .... (MOT)
Jerry Lee Lewis; *Jerry Lee's Greatest* ...... (RHI)
John Lennon; *Lennon* .... (CAP)
Junior Walker/All-Stars; *Anthology* .... (MOT)
  Greatest Hits .... (SOL)
Rolling Stones; *More Hot Rocks-Big Hits & Fazed Cookies* .... (AKO)
Ronnie Milsap; *Lost In The Fifties Tonight* ...... (RCA)
Todd Rundgren; *Something/Anything?* .... (RHI)
Moneytalks
AC/DC; *Razor's Edge* .... (ATC)
Money, Money, Money
Abba; *Arrival* .... (ATL)
  Greatest Hits-#2 .... (ATL)
  The Singles-First Ten Years .... (ATL)
More Than A Paycheck
Sweet Honey In The Rock; *We All...Every One Of Us* .... (FF)
Music For Money
Nick Lowe; *Pure Pop For Now People* ...... (COL)
New Greenback Dollar
Roy Acuff; *Columbia Historic Edition* ...... (COL)
Nickel Bags
Digable Planets; *Reachin'-New Refutation Of Time & Space* .... (PEN)
Nickel Dreams
Nanci Griffith; *Lone Star State Of Mind* ... (MCA)
Nickel For The Fiddler
Guy Clark; *Old No. 1* .... (SH)
Nickel In The Well
Shenandoah; *Under The Kudzu* .... (RCA)
Nickel Song
Melanie; *Best Of* .... (RHI)
Nickel & Dime
Journey; *Next* .... (COL)
  Time3 .... (COL)
Nickels & Dimes
Plimsouls; *...Plus* .... (RHI)
Nickels & Dimes & Love
John Michael Montgomery; *Live's A Dance* ...... (ATL)
Vern Gosdin; *Nickels & Dimes & Love* ...... (COL)
No Money Down
Chuck Berry; *Chess Box* .... (CSS)
John Hammond; *Best Of* .... (VAN)
  Blues Explosion .... (ATL)
Not Everyone's As Rich As Your Parents
Doctor Nerve; *Armed Observation* .... (CUN)
Offshore Banking Business
Members; *At The 1980 Chelsea Night Club* ...... (BP)
  ST/Urgh! A Music War .... (A&M)
One For The Money
Jesus Jones; *Liquidizer* .... (SBK)
T.G. Sheppard; *Biggest Hits* .... (COL)
  Greatest Country Hits/'80s-1987 .... (COL)

Whispers; *Best Of* .... (SLR)
  One For The Money .... (SLR)
One More Payment
  Clint Black; *Put Yourself In My Shoes* ....(RCA)
One Thousand Dollar Wedding
  Gram Parsons; *Grievous Angel* .... (RPR)
Opportunities (Let's Make Lots Of Money)
  Pet Shop Boys; *Disco* .... (EMI)
  Discography-Complete Singles Collection .... (EMI)
  Please .... (EMI)
Party 'Till The Money Runs Out
  Radiators; *Total Evaporation* .... (EPI)
Pay It Back
  Elvis Costello; *My Aim Is True* ....(COL)
Pay Me Alimony
  Maddox Brothers & Rose; *America's Most Colorful*
  Hillbilly Band .... (ARH)
Pay You Back With Interest
  Hollies; *Best Of* .... (EMI)
  Greatest Hits .... (EPI)
  History Of British Rock-#4 .... (RHI)
Payday/Mine 'Til Monday
  Original Broadway Cast; *Tree Grows In Brooklyn* (SMC)
Pennies From Heaven
  Billie Holiday; *16 Most Requested Songs* ....(COL)
  Bing Crosby; *Pennies From Heaven* .... (POE)
  Frank Sinatra; *Songs For Swingin' Lovers* .... (CAP)
  Lester Young; *Birdland All-Stars At Carnegie Hall* (RLL)
  Louis Armstrong; *RCA Victor Jazz-First*
  Half-Century ....(RCA)
  Mandy Patinkin; *Mandy Patinkin* ....(COL)
  Skyliners; *Greatest Hits* .... (OSR)
  Stan Getz; *Essential-Getz Songbook* ....(VRV)
  Stephane Grappelli; *Satin Doll-#1-Best Of* ...... (VAN)
Penny For Your Thoughts
  Peter Frampton; *Frampton Comes Alive* .... (A&M)
  Shine On-Collection .... (A&M)
  Tavares; *45* ....(OOP)
  Willie Nelson; *Sound In Your Mind* ....(COL)
Penny Lover
  Lionel Richie; *Back To Front* .... (MOT)
  Can't Slow Down .... (MOT)
Pocket Full Of Gold
  Vince Gill; *Pocket Full Of Gold* .... (MCA)
Poor Little Rich Girl
  Judy Garland; *Best Of* .... (MCA)
  Romantics; *National Breakout* .... (NEM)
  Tony Bennett & Count Basie; *Basie Swings Bennett*
  Sings .... (RLL)
  Uriah Heep; *Equator* ....(COL)
Poor Man Lives Longer Than The Rich
  Freeman King; *45* ....(KNT)
Poor Man's Roses (Or A Rich Man's Gold)
  Patsy Cline; *Best Of* ....(CCB)
  Forever & Always .... (EPI)
  Stop, Look & Listen .... (MCA)
  Story .... (MCA)
  Reba McEntire; *Feel The Fire* .... (MER)
Pound Is Sinking
  Paul McCartney; *Tug Of War* ....(COL)
Price I Pay
  Emmylou Harris; *Cimarron* ....(WB)
  Emmylou Harris & Desert Rose Band; *Classic Country*
  Duets ....(CCB)
Price Of Love
  Bad English; *Bad English* .... (EPI)
  Bon Jovi; *7800 Degrees Fahrenheit* .... (MER)
  Bryan Ferry; *Let's Stick Together* .... (RPR)
  Cactus Brothers; *Cactus Brothers* .... (LIB)
  Everly Brothers; *Reunion Concert-Live At Albert Hall*
  1983 .... (MER)
  Poco; *Cowboys & Englishmen* .... (OW)
  Crazy Loving-Best Of-1975-1982 .... (MCA)
  Roger Daltrey; *ST/Secret Of My Success* .... (MCA)
Price Of Paradise
  Minutemen; *3-Way Tie (For Last)* .... (SST)
  Ballot Result .... (SST)
Price To Pay
  Lucinda Williams; *Lucinda Williams* .... (CML)
Price You Pay
  Bruce Springsteen; *The River* ....(COL)

Private Dancer
  Tina Turner; *Live In Europe* ....(CAP)
  Private Dancer ....(CAP)
  Simply The Best ....(CAP)
Put A Nickel In The Jukebox...
  Sharon McNight; *Another Side Of* ....(GLN)
  Presenting Sharon McNight ....(GLN)
Put A Quarter In The Jukebox
  Barry Manilow; *Greatest Hits #2* .... (ARI)
  Buck Owens; *Out-of-print recording* ....(CAP)
Put The Money Down
  Who; *Odds & Sods* .... (MCA)
Puttin' On The Ritz
  Ella Fitzgerald; *Silver Collection-Songbooks* ......(VRV)
  Fred Astaire; *Irving Berlin Always* ....(VRV)
  Irving Berlin Songbook ....(VRV)
  Judy Garland; *One & Only* ....(CAP)
  Mandy Patinkin; *Mandy Patinkin* ....(COL)
  Taco; *After Eight* ....(RCA)
  Nipper's Greatest Hits-'80s ....(RCA)
Queen Of The Silver Dollar
  Dave & Sugar; *Greatest Hits* ....(RCA)
  Dr. Hook; *& The Medicine Show Revisited* ....(COL)
  Emmylou Harris; *Pieces Of The Sky* ....(RPR)
Rags To Riches
  Electric Boys; *Funk-O-Metal Carpet Ride* ....(ATC)
  John Scofield; *Shinola* .... (ENJ)
  Kool/Gang; *Everything Is-Greatest Hits* .... (MER)
  Tony Bennett; *16 Most Requested Songs* ....(COL)
  All-Time Greatest Hits ....(COL)
  Tony Bennett & Percy Faith/Orchestra; *Radio Classics*
  Of The '50s ....(COL)
Reagonomics
  D.R.I.; *Dealing With It!* .... (MET)
  Johnnie Taylor; *Just Ain't Good Enough* ....(BEV)
Red Money
  David Bowie; *Lodger* ....(RYK)
Rich Bitch
  D.O.A.; *War On 45/Bloodied But Unbowed* ...... (RES)
Rich Don't Rock
  Vamp; *Rich Don't Rock* .... (ATL)
Rich Get Richer
  O'Jays; *Survival* .... (PI)
Rich Girl
  Daryl Hall & John Oates; *Bigger Than Both Of*
  Us ....(RCA)
  Billboard Top Rock 'N' Roll Hits-1977 .... (RHI)
  Livetime ....(RCA)
  Nipper's Greatest Hits-'70s ....(RCA)
  Rock 'N' Soul Part 1-Greatest Hits ....(RCA)
  Soulful Sounds ....(RCA)
Rich Kind Of Poverty
  Sam & Dave; *Soul Men* .... (RHI)
Rich Little Bitch
  Dash Rip Rock; *Boiled Alive!* ....(MAM)
  Not Of This World ....(MAM)
Rich Man
  Great Plains; *Great Plains* ....(COL)
Rich Man Poor Man
  Peter, Paul & Mary; *Late Again* .... (WB)
Rich Man, Poor Boy
  Joe Ely; *Dig All Night* .... (HT)
Rich Man's Frug
  Original Cast; *Sweet Charity* ....(COL)
Rich Man's Spiritual
  Gordon Lightfoot; *Lightfoot* .... (UA)
Rich Woman
  Fabulous Thunderbirds; *Fabulous Thunderbirds* . (CHR)
Rich & Poor
  Randy Crawford; *Rich & Poor* .... (WB)
Richest Man In Bogota
  Gil Melle; *Mindscape* .... (BLN)
Richest Man On Earth
  Paul Overstreet; *Sowin' Love* ....(RCA)
Rich, The
  Original Broadway Cast; *Carnival* ....(POL)
Road To My Riches
  Vanilla Ice; *Extremely Live* ....(SBK)
Sales Tax On The Woman
  New Lost City Ramblers; *Early*
  Years-1958-1962 .... (FLW)
Send Me Your Money
  Suicidal Tendencies; *Lights...Camera...Revolution* .. (EPI)

Seven & A Half Cents
John Raitt; *ST/Pajama Game* ....(SSP)
Original Cast; *Pajama Game* ....(COL)
Shake Your Money Maker
Elmore James; *King Of The Slide Guitar* ....(CPC)
Fleetwood Mac; *Vintage Years* ....(SIR)
George Thorogood; *Born To Be Bad* .... (EMI)
Paul Butterfield; *Golden Butter* ....(ELE)
 Paul Butterfield Blues Band ....(ELE)
She Put Her Hand Where My Money Was
John Lee; *Down At The Depot* .... (ROU)
She Works Hard For The Money
Donna Summer; *She Works Hard For The Money* (MER)
 Summer Collection ....(MER)
Silver Dollar
April Wine; *First Glance* ....(CAP)
Lee Greenwood; *If There's Any Justice* ....(PAN)
Simply Irresistible
Robert Palmer; *Super Nova* .... (ISL)
Sold My Fortune
Sugartooth; *Sugartooth* ....(GEF)
Soldier Of Fortune
Alan O'Day; *Appetizers* ....(PAC)
Deep Purple; *Stormbringer* ....(WB)
Joe Perry Project; *I've Got The Rock 'N' Rolls
 Again* ....(COL)
Manhattan Transfer; *Bodies & Souls* ....(ATL)
Thin Lizzy; *Bad Reputation* ....(MER)
Some Girls
Rolling Stones; *Some Girls* ....(RS)
Stop On A Dime
Little Texas; *Big Time* ....(WB)
Straight To The Bank
Kid Frost; *Hispanic Causing Panic* .... (VIA)
Stranger To Himself
Sandy Denny; *Best Of* ....(HBL)
 Who Knows Where The Time Goes? ....(HBL)
Traffic; *John Barleycorn Must Die* .... (ISL)
Sugar Daddy
Bellamy Brothers; *Greatest Hits* ....(MCA)
 You Can Get Crazy ....(WB)
Fleetwood Mac; *Fleetwood Mac* ....(RPR)
Jackson 5; *Anthology* ....(MOT)
 Greatest Hits ....(MOT)
Michigan & Smiley; *Sugar Daddy* ....(RAS)
Thompson Twins; *Big Trash* .... (RE)
Take That To The Bank
Shalamar; *Greatest Hits* .... (SLR)
Take The Money & Run
Steve Miller Band; *CD Gift Set* ....(CAP)
 Fly Like An Eagle ....(CAP)
 Greatest Hits-1974-1978 ....(CAP)
 Live ....(CAP)
Taxes On The Farmer Feeds Us All
Ry Cooder; *Into The Purple Valley* ....(RPR)
Taxman
Beatles; *Box Set* ....(CAP)
 Revolver ....(CAP)
 Rock & Roll Music-#2 ....(CAP)
George Harrison; *Best Of* ....(CAP)
George Harrison & Eric Clapton; *Live In Japan* (DKH)
Taxman Mr. Thief
Cheap Trick; *Cheap Trick* .... (EPI)
Ten Cents A Chop
Phil Ochs; *Greatest Hits* ....(A&M)
Ten Cents A Dance
Eileen Farrell; *I Gotta Right To Sing The Blues* .. (SMC)
Ella Fitzgerald; *Rodgers & Hart Songbook* ....(VRV)
Ten Dollar Man
ZZ Top; *Six Pack* ....(WB)
 Tejas ....(WB)
That's The Way I Made My Millions
Charlie King; *Food Phone Gas Lodging* ....(FF)
That's Were My Money Goes
Loverboy; *Wildside* ....(COL)
That's Where My Money Goes
101 Strings Orchestra; *Beer Drinkin' Sing Alongs!!* (ALS)
"The Jeffersons" Theme
Original Music; *Television's Greatest Hits-#3* .....(TVT)
They Want Money
Kool Moe Dee; *Greatest Hits* ....(JVA)
 Knowledge Is King ....(JVA)
 Nasty Wax ....(KT)

This Money Is Yours
Original London Cast; *Miss Saigon* ....(GEF)
Three Coins In The Fountain
Andy Williams; *Moon River & Other Great Movie
 Themes* ....(COL)
Doris Day & Frank De Vol Orchestra; *Hooray For
 Hollywood-#2* ....(COL)
Frank Sinatra; *At The Movies* ....(CAP)
 Capitol Collectors Series ....(CAP)
Harry James; *Plays The Songs That Sold A
 Million* ....(COL)
Three Nickels & A Dime
Ricky Lynn Gregg; *Ricky Lynn Gregg* .... (LIB)
'Till The Money Runs Out
Tom Waits; *On Heartattack & Vine* ....(ASY)
Time Ain't Money
Huey Lewis/News; *Hard At Play* .... (EMI)
Too High A Price
Doobie Brothers; *Cycles* ....(CAP)
Too Much Candy For A Dime
Eddy Raven; *Best Of* ....(LIB)
 Right For The Flight ....(LIB)
Too Much Month At The End Of The Money
Billy Hill; *I Am Just A Rebel* ....(RPR)
Two Dollars In The Jukebox
Eddie Rabbitt; *All-Time Greatest Hits* ....(WB)
 Best Of ....(WB)
 Rocky Mountain Music ....(ELE)
 Ten Years Of Greatest Hits ....(LIB)
Two Plays For A Quarter
Kathy Hart/Bluestars; *Tonight I Want It All* ......(BIO)
Uptown Girl
Billy Joel; *An Innocent Man* ....(COL)
 Greatest Hits-#1 & 2-1973-1985 ....(COL)
 KOHUEPT ....(COL)
Wall Street Shuffle
10 CC; *Greatest Hits '72-'78* ....(POL)
 Live & Let Live ....(MER)
Wheel Of Fortune
Cardinals; *Atlantic R&B 1947-1974-collection* ... (ATL)
Kay Starr; *Capitol Collectors Series* ....(CAP)
Wheels Of Fortune
Doobie Brothers; *Takin' It To The Streets* ....(WB)
White Trash With Cash
Southgang; *Group Therapy* ....(CHS)
Why Don't You Do Right
Benny Goodman; *16 Most Requested Songs* ......(COL)
Ella Fitzgerald & Joe Pass; *Easy Living* ....(PAB)
Peggy Lee; *All-Time Greatest Hits-#1* ....(CCB)
 Capitol Collectors Series-#1-Early Years ....(CAP)
With Plenty Of Money & You
Ink Spots; *If I Didn't Care* ....(POE)
Tony Bennett & Count Basie; *Some Pair* ....(PRR)
You Don't Count The Cost
Billy Dean; *Billy Dean* ....(LIB)
Ricky Skaggs; *My Father's Son* ....(EPI)
You Got It
Roy Orbison; *Mystery Girl* .... (VIA)
You Never Give Me Your Money
Beatles; *Abbey Road* ....(CAP)
 Box Set ....(CAP)
George Benson; *The Best* ....(A&M)
Your Cash Ain't Nothin' But Trash
Clovers; *Down In The Alley* ....(ATL)
Huey Lewis/News; *Four Chords & Several Years
 Ago* ....(ELE)
Steve Miller Band; *The Joker* ....(CAP)

MONSTERS, Halloween, Vampires
 See Also: CHAOS, HELL, MAGIC, UFO'S

Amazing Bigfoot Diet
Mojo Nixon & Skid Roper; *Frenzy* .... (IRS)
Apeman
Kinks; *Kink Kronikles* ....(RPR)
 Live-The Road ....(MCA)
 Lola Vs. Powerman & The Moneygoround .....(RPR)
Attack Of The Fifty-Foot Woman
Tubes; *Best Of* ....(CAP)
 Completion Backward Principle ....(CAP)
 Elvira Presents Haunted Hits ....(RHI)
Attack Of The Killer Beers
Murphy's Law; *Back With A Bong!* ....(PRO)

Attack Of The Killer Tomatoes
Lewis Lee; *Elvira Presents Haunted Hits* .... (RHI)
   Halloween Hits .... (RHI)
Attack Of The Radioactive Hamsters
Weird Al Yankovic; *ST/UHF* .... (RAR)
Attack Of The Vegetable Men
Active Ingredient; *Extrastrength* .... (BAI)
Attacked By Monsters
Meat Puppets; *Monsters* .... (SST)
   No Strings Attached .... (SST)
Beast
Blondie; *The Hunter* .... (CHR)
Only Ones; *Special View* .... (EPI)
Twisted Sister; *Stay Hungry* .... (ATL)
Beast In Me
Bonnie Pointer; *ST/Heavenly Bodies* .... (PRI)
Johnny Cash; *American Recordings* .... (AME)
Beast Of Burden
Bette Midler; *No Frills* .... (ATL)
Rolling Stones; *Flashpoint + Collectibles* .... (RS)
   Rewind (1971-1984) .... (RS)
   Some Girls .... (RS)
   Sucking In The Seventies .... (RS)
Beast Within
Southside Johnny/Asbury Jukes; *Trash It Up* ..... (MIR)
Beastie
Jethro Tull; *Broadsword & The Beast* .... (CHR)
Beauty And The Beast
Celine Dion & Peabo Bryson; *Celine Dion & Peabo
Bryson* .... (EPI)
   ST/Beauty And The Beast .... (DIS)
Blob
Five Blobs; *Elvira Presents Haunted Hits* .... (RHI)
   Halloween Hits .... (RHI)
Little Stevie/McQueens; *Horror Rock Classics-#2* (RHI)
Cockroach That Ate Cincinnati
Possum; *Dr. Demento's Delights* .... (WB)
Rose/Arrangement; *Dr. Demento's
Greatest-#4-1970s* .... (RHI)
Creature Feature
Uptown Express; *45* .... (SUT)
Creature From The Black Lagoon
Dave Edmunds; *Best Of* .... (SS)
   Elvira Presents Haunted Hits .... (RHI)
   Repeat When Necessary .... (SS)
Creatures Of The Night
Kiss; *Creatures Of The Night* .... (CAS)
Dance With The Dragon
Jefferson Starship; *Spitfire* .... (RCA)
Dinner With Drac
Zacherle; *Rock-O-Rama-#2* .... (AKO)
Doctor Frankenstein
Parliament; *Clones Of* .... (CAS)
   Live .... (CAS)
Dracula's Dance
Flip Phillips; *Flipenstein* .... (PRG)
Dragon Lady
Blue Oyster Cult; *Revolution By Night* .... (COL)
Bob Dylan; *Infidels* .... (COL)
Germs; *Germs* .... (SLS)
Eggplant That Ate Chicago
Dr. West's Medicine Show & Junk Band; *Dr. Demento's
Greatest-#3* .... (RHI)
Eye Of The Zombie
John Fogerty; *Eye Of The Zombie* .... (WB)
Frankenstein
Edgar Winter Group; *Anthology* .... (BCT)
   Billboard Top Rock 'N' Roll Hits-1973 .... (RHI)
   Collection .... (RHI)
   They Only Come Out At Night .... (EPI)
New York Dolls; *Lipstick Killers* .... (ROI)
   New York Dolls .... (MER)
Godzilla
Blue Oyster Cult; *Career Of Evil* .... (COL)
   Extraterrestrial Live .... (COL)
   Some Enchanted Evening .... (COL)
   Spectres .... (COL)
Godzilla Stomp
Wedge; *Big Bad Boss Beat Of The Wedge* .... (RHI)
Goonies 'R' Good Enough
Cyndi Lauper; *ST/Goonies* .... (EPI)
I Was A Teenage Werewolf
Cramps; *Elvira Presents Haunted Hits* .... (RHI)
   Songs The Lord Taught Us .... (IRS)

King Kong
Frank Zappa; *Uncle Meat* .... (BAR)
   You Can't Do That On Stage Anymore .... (BAR)
Kinks; *Kink Kronikles* .... (RPR)
Loopzilla
George Clinton; *Computer Games* .... (CAP)
Maneater
Daryl Hall & John Oates; *H2O* .... (RCA)
   Nipper's Greatest Hits-'80s .... (RCA)
   Rock 'N' Soul Part 1-Greatest Hits .... (RCA)
March Of The Meanies
Beatles; *Yellow Submarine* .... (CAP)
Monster Mash
Beach Boys; *Concert/'69-Live In London* .... (CAP)
Big O; *ST/Return Of The Living Dead-Pt. 2* .... (ISL)
Bobby Boris Pickett; *Dr. Demento 20th Anniversary
Collection* .... (RHI)
   Dr. Demento's Greatest Novelty-#3 .... (RHI)
   Halloween Hits .... (RHI)
   Horror Rock Classics-#2 .... (LON)
Monster Surfing Time
Halibuts; *Halibut Beach* .... (WTR)
Mutants Of The Monster
Black Oak Arkansas; *Hot & Nasty-Best Of* ...... (RHI)
   Raunch 'N' Roll .... (ATC)
Night Creatures
Melissa Manchester; *Mathematics* .... (MCA)
Night Of The Vampire
Grim Reaper; *Rock You To Hell* .... (RCA)
Roky Erickson; *You're Gonna Miss Me-Best Of* .. (RES)
November Spawned A Monster
Morrissey; *Bona Drag* .... (SIR)
   Just Say Da-#4 Of Just Say Yes .... (SIR)
Over At The Frankenstein Place
Original London Cast; *Rocky Horror Show* ...... (RHI)
Original Roxy Cast; *Rocky Horror Show* .... (RHI)
Prelude To King Kong
Frank Zappa; *Uncle Meat* .... (BAR)
Pride Of Frankenstein
Too Much Joy; *Cereal Killers* .... (GIA)
Puff (The Magic Dragon)
Peter, Paul & Mary; *In Concert* .... (WB)
   Moving .... (WB)
   Peter Paul & Mommy .... (WB)
   Ten Years Together-Best Of .... (WB)
Purple People Eater
Sheb Wooley; *45s On CD-#1 (1956-1959)* ..... (MER)
   Dr. Demento 20th Anniversary Collection ...... (RHI)
   Halloween Hits .... (RHI)
   Horror Rock Classics-#2 .... (RHI)
   Super Hits-#4 .... (GUS)
Purple People Eater Meets The Witch Doc.
Big Bopper; *Hellooo Baby! Best Of-1954-1959* .. (RHI)
Return Of The Giant Hogweed
Genesis; *Live* .... (ATL)
   Nursery Cryme .... (ATL)
Road Mutants
Death Angel; *Frolic Through The Park* .... (ENC)
   Speed Metal .... (PRY)
Scary Monsters
David Bowie; *Golden Years* .... (RYK)
   Scary Monsters .... (RYK)
   The Singles-1969-1993 .... (RYK)
Sea Of Monsters
Beatles; *Box Set* .... (CAP)
   Yellow Submarine .... (CAP)
Suck On The Jugular
Rolling Stones; *Voodoo Lounge* .... (VIA)
Tattoo Vampire
Blue Oyster Cult; *Agents Of Fortune* .... (COL)
Tears Of The Dragon
Bruce Dickinson; *Balls To Picasso* .... (MER)
Teenage Frankenstein
Alice Cooper; *Constrictor* .... (MCA)
   Prince Of Darkness .... (MCA)
Theme From "Beetlejuice"
Alshire Hollywood Pops Orchestra; *20 Greatest Movie
Hits* .... (ALS)
Theme From "The Addams Family"
Vic Mizzy; *Elvira Presents Haunted Hits* .... (RHI)
   Haunted Hits .... (RHI)
   Original Music From .... (RCA)

Thing That Only Eats Hippies
Dead Milkmen; *Eat Your Paisley* .... (RES)
  Enigma Variations-#2 .... (ENC)
This Is Halloween
Danny Elfman/Citizens Of Halloween; *ST/Nightmare*
Before Christmas .... (DIS)
Thriller
Michael Jackson; *Thriller* .... (EPI)
Two Thousand Pound Bee
Ventures; *Radical Guitars* .... (ILO)
  ST/Wired .... (VS)
Vampire
Black Uhuru; *Sinsemilla* .... (MGO)
Blood Feast; *Face Fate* .... (NEW)
  Kill For Pleasure .... (NEW)
Buffy Sainte-Marie; *Best Of* .... (VAN)
Peter Tosh; *No Nuclear War* .... (EMI)
Vampire Bat
Twisters; *Twisters* .... (RHI)
Vampire Blues
Loudon Wainwright III; *More Love Songs* .... (ROU)
Neil Young; *On The Beach* .... (RPR)
Vampire Cows
Simon/Bard Group; *Enormous Radio* .... (FF)
Vampire Planet
Neil Norman/Cosmic Orchestra; *Greatest Science Fiction*
Hits-#2 .... (CRS)
Vlad The Impaler
Gwar; *Scumdogs Of The Universe* .... (MET)
Werewolves Of London
Warren Zevon; *Excitable Boy* .... (ASY)
  Quiet Normal Life-Best Of .... (ASY)
  Stand In The Fire .... (ASY)
  ST/Color Of Money .... (MCA)
Woke Up With A Monster
Cheap Trick; *Woke Up With A Monster* .... (WB)
Zomby Woof
Frank Zappa/Mothers Of Invention; *Apostrophe/Overnite*
Sensation .... (RYK)

MONTHS & DATES: APRIL
See Also: SEASONS: SPRING

Abril En Portugal
Julio Iglesias; *Libra* .... (COL)
April
Brand X; *Project* .... (PAS)
Dave Mallett; *Vital Signs* .... (FF)
Sarah Vaughan; *Singles Sessions* .... (RLL)
April 2031
Warrant; *Dog Eat Dog* .... (COL)
April 24, 1981
Rick Springfield; *Success Hasn't Spoiled Me Yet* .. (RCA)
April 5th
Talk Talk; *Colour Of Spring* .... (AMR)
April Afternoon
Joan Amalbert Latin Jazz Quintet; *Hot Sauce* .... (PRS)
April Avenue
Crickets; *Liberty Years* .... (EMI)
April Come She Will
Simon & Garfunkel; *Collected Works* .... (COL)
  Concert In Central Park .... (WB)
  Sounds Of Silence .... (COL)
  ST/The Graduate .... (COL)
April Fool
Eric Dolphy; *Here & There* .... (PRS)
Pete Townshend & Ronnie Lane; *Rough Mix* .... (ATC)
Soul Asylum; *Grave Dancers Union* .... (COL)
April Fools
Aretha Franklin; *Young Gifted & Black* .... (MGM)
Dionne Warwick; *Anthology 1962-1971* .... (RHI)
Earl Klugh; *Living Inside Your Love* .... (EMI)
April Fool's Day Morn
Loudon Wainwright III; *Career Moves* .... (VIA)
  Fame & Wealth .... (ROU)
April Give Me One More Day
Sarah Vaughan; *Complete On*
Mercury-#2-1956-1957 .... (MER)
April In Cambridge
Peter Walker; *Rainy Day Raga* .... (VAN)
April In My Heart
Billie Holiday; *Quintessential-#6-1938* .... (COL)

April In Paris
Charlie Parker; *Verve Years* .... (VRV)
  With Strings .... (VRV)
Ella Fitzgerald & Oscar Peterson; *Ella & Oscar* .. (PAB)
Frank Sinatra; *Come Fly With Me* .... (CAP)
Mel Torme; *Mel Torme* .... (GLN)
Sarah Vaughan; *Complete On Mercury-#1: Great Jazz*
Years .... (MER)
  Sarah Vaughan .... (EMA)
Wynton Marsalis; *Marsalis Standard Time-#1* ... (COL)
  Perspectives: Columbia Jazz Sampler .... (COL)
April In Portugal
Eartha Kitt; *Best Of* .... (MCA)
April Joy
Pat Metheny Group; *Pat Metheny Group* .... (ECM)
April Love
L.T.D.; *Classics-#27 (Feat. Jeffrey Osborne)* .... (A&M)
Pat Boone; *Best Of* .... (MCA)
  Greatest Hits .... (CCB)
April Mist
Tom Harrell; *Visions* .... (CTM)
April Seventh
Larry Coryell & John Scofield & Joe Beck;
Tributaries .... (NOV)
April Showers
Al Jolson; *Best Of* .... (MCA)
  Story-#2 .... (MCA)
Judy Garland; *Hits Of* .... (CAP)
  Judy .... (CAP)
April Skies
Jesus & Mary Chain; *Darklands* .... (WB)
Wardell Gray; *Memorial-#2* .... (PRS)
April Sky
Vinnie Moore; *Time Odyssey* .... (MER)
April Snow
Hi-Lo's; *Cherries & Other Delights* .... (HIN)
Northern Lights; *Take You To The Sky* .... (FF)
April Song
John Tesh; *Monterey Nights* .... (GTS)
  The Games .... (GTS)
April Waltz
Critton Hollow; *Great Dreams* .... (FF)
April Was The Month
Chris Farlowe; *Collection* .... (SSP)
Aprilling
Lee Konitz & Gil Evans; *Heroes* .... (VRV)
April's Fool
Mark Chesnutt; *Almost Goodbye* .... (MCA)
Ray Price; *Greatest Hits-#4* .... (STE)
Tracy Lawrence; *Sticks & Stones* .... (ATL)
Girl With April In Her Eyes
Chris DeBurgh; *Crusader* .... (A&M)
I'll Remember April
Cal Tjader; *Mambo With* .... (FAN)
Charlie Parker; *With Strings* .... (VRV)
Chet Baker; *Chet Baker* .... (EMA)
Cleo Laine; *Cleo's Choice* .... (CRS)
Doris Day/Frank DeVol Orchestra; *Hooray For*
Hollywood-#1 .... (COL)
Erroll Garner; *Concert By The Sea* .... (COL)
Frank Sinatra; *Point Of No Return* .... (CAP)
June Christy; *#2-1957* .... (HIN)
Modern Jazz Quartet; *Concorde* .... (PRS)
  Modern Jazz Quartet .... (PRS)
Stephane Grappelli & Martin Taylor; *Just One Of Those*
Things .... (ANG)
Wynton Marsalis; *Standard Time-#2-Intimacy*
Calling .... (COL)
Lost April
Nat King Cole; *Nat King Cole* .... (CAP)
  Unforgettable .... (CAP)
When April Comes Again
Paul Weston/Orchestra; *Music For Easy Listening* (CRN)

MONTHS & DATES: AUGUST
See Also: SEASONS: SUMMER

August
Anthony Phillips; *Private Parts & Pieces V-Twelve* (PVC)
Lyle Mays; *Street Dreams* .... (GEF)
August 19
Ralph Simon; *Time Being* .... (GRM)

August 1967
Holy Modal Rounders; *Last Round* .... (ADE)
August Afternoon
Mulgrew Miller; *The Countdown* ....(LAN)
August Blues
Dexter Gordon; *Tangerine* .... (PRS)
August Day
Daryl Hall & John Oates; *Along The Red Ledge* ..(RCA)
August Freeze
Grace Pool; *Where We Live* .... (RPR)
August In Forest City
Carol Montag; *Song For Carrie* .... (SLK)
August Moon
Ottmar Liebert & Luna Negra; *Borrasca* .... (HO)
August Rain
Murray Attaway; *In Thrall* .... (DGC)
August Was A Heavy Month
Bob Geldof; *Deep In The Heart Of Nowhere* ..... (ATL)
August & September
The The; *Mind Bomb* .... (EPI)
Bus Stop
Hollies; *Best Of-#1* .... (EMI)
Greatest Hits .... (EPI)
History Of British Rock-#3 .... (RHI)
Cold Wind In August
Van Morrison; *Period Of Transition* ....(WB)
Either End Of August
Bill Bruford; *Feels Good To Me* .... (EDI)
First Day In August
Carole King; *Rhymes & Reasons* .... (EOD)
Goin' Through The Big D
Mark Chesnutt; *What A Way To Live* .... (DEC)
Second Sunday In August
Weather Report; *I Sing The Body Electric* ....(COL)
Someday, August 29, 1968
Chicago; *Chicago Transit Authority* ....(COL)

MONTHS & DATES: DECEMBER

See Also: CHRISTMAS, COLD, SEASONS:
WINTER, SNOW

Anos Dourados (Looks Like December)
Antonio Carlos Jobim/New Band; *Passarim* ......(VRV)
Joanne Brackeen; *Breath Of Brazil* .... (CP)
Cold Day In December
George Jones; *You Oughta Be Here With Me* ...... (EPI)
Cold December
Mike Auldridge; *& Old Dog* .... (FF)
December
Anthony Phillips; *Private Parts & Pieces V Twelve* (PVC)
Expose; *Exposure* .... (ARI)
Robert Vaughan/Shadows; *Love & War* .... (EXI)
Waterboys; *Waterboys* .... (ISL)
December 1963 ('94)
Foure Seasons; *S* .... (CRB)
December African Rain
Juluka; *Best Of* ....(RHY)
December Days
Willie Nelson; *Love & Pain* .... (ARA)
Sweet Memories ....(RCA)
December Will Be Magic Again
Kate Bush; *12"* .... (EMI)
December '63
Frankie Valli/Four Seasons; *25th Anniversary*
Collection .... (RHI)
Anthology .... (RHI)
December's Boudoir
Laura Nyro; *Eli & The 13th Confession* ....(COL)
Gloomy December
Jean Redpath; *Songs Of Robert Burns-#6* ....(PHO)
I Am A Rock
Simon & Garfunkel; *Collected Works* ....(COL)
Greatest Hits ....(COL)
Sounds Of Silence ....(COL)
If We Make It Through December
Merle Haggard; *Christmas Gift* ....(CCB)
Eleven Winners .... (CAP)
Goin' Home For Christmas .... (EPI)
Very Best Of .... (CAP)
Magic In December
Tom Barabas; *Incredible Invincible Sampler* ...... (INV)

Same Old Lang Syne
Dan Fogelberg; *Greatest Hits* .... (FM)
Innocent Age .... (FM)
Live-Greetings From The West .... (FM)

MONTHS & DATES: FEBRUARY

See Also: SEASONS: WINTER

February
Anthony Phillips; *Private Parts & Pieces V-Twelve* (PVC)
Jennifer Hall; *Fortune & Men's Eyes* .... (WB)
February In My Heart
Osborne Brothers; *Some Things I Want To Sing*
About ....(SH)
February Ingenue
Don Dixon; *Romeo At Juilliard* .... (ENI)
February March
Lou & Peter Berryman; *February March* .... (COR)
February Moment
Herbie Hancock & Chick Corea; *Evening With* ..(COL)
February Sea
George Winston; *Winter Into Spring* ....(WH)
February Song
Barbi Benton & Jamii Szmadzinski; *Kinetic*
Voyage ....(TAK)
Blazing Redheads & Patricia Thumas; *Blazing*
Redheads .... (REF)
Two Days In February
Goo Goo Dolls; *Hold Me Up* .... (MET)
ST/Freddy's Dead-The Final Nightmare .... (MET)

MONTHS & DATES: JANUARY

See Also: SEASONS: WINTER

Back In January
Angst; *Mystery Spot* ....(SST)
Eighth Of January
Eric Weissberg; *ST/Dueling Banjos From*
Deliverance .... (WB)
Jan In January
Warren Bernhardt; *Hands On* .... (DIG)
January
Anthony Phillips; *Private Parts & Collectors* ......(PVC)
Mose Allison; *Back Country Suite* .... (PRS)
Painted Willie; *Mind Bowling* ....(SST)
January 23-30, 1978
Steve Forbert; *Jackrabbit Slim* .... (NEM)
January Rain
Hunters & Collectors; *Living Daylight* .... (IRS)
January Stars
George Winston; *Winter Into Spring* ....(WH)
June In January
Bing Crosby; *Best Of* .... (MCA)
Dean Martin; *Best Of* ....(CAP)
Month Of January
June Tabor; *Abyssinians* .... (SHA)
Sally Ann 28th Of January
Fuzzy Mountain String Band; *Fuzzy Mountain String*
Band .... (ROU)
Turnaround, January Thaw
Priscilla Herdmann; *Forgotten Dreams* ....(FF)

MONTHS & DATES: JULY

See Also: SEASONS: SUMMER

4th Of July
U2; *Unforgettable Fire* .... (ISL)
Black Day In July
Gordon Lightfoot; *Best Of* .... (EMI)
Did She Mention My Name .... (UA)
Lightfoot .... (UA)
Cold Day In July
Joy White; *Between Midnight & Hindsight* ....(COL)
Ray Price; *For The Good Times/I Won't Mention*
It... ....(COL)
Suzy Bogguss; *Voices In The Wind* ....(LIB)
Darlington County
Bruce Springsteen; *Born In The U.S.A.* ....(COL)
Fifth Of July
Terry Reid; *The Driver* ....(WB)

Fourth Of July
Dave Alvin; *Romeo's Escape* .... (EPI)
Linda Waterfall; *Body English* ....(FF)
Rosalie Sorrels; *Lonesome Roving Wolves-Songs Of The West* ....(GRE)
X; *See How We Are* .... (ELE)
Fourth Of July At A County Fair
Red Clay Ramblers; *Chuckin' The Frizz* .... (FF)
Fourth Of July, Asbury Park (Sandy)
Bruce Springsteen; *Wild The Innocent & The E Street Shuffle* ....(COL)
Bruce Springsteen/E Street Band; *Live-1975-1985* ....(COL)
Independence Day
Martina McBride; *The Way That I Am* ....(RCA)
July
Al Di Meola; *Soaring Through A Dream* .... (MAN)
Anthony Phillips; *Private Parts & Pieces-V Twelve* (PVC)
Vienna; *Guess What* ....(WB)
July Morning
Uriah Heep; *Best Of* ....(MER)
Live ....(MER)
June 25 At The Fourth Of July
Shel Silverstein; *Great Conch Train Robbery* .... (FF)
London In July
Corky Hale; *Plays George Gershwin & Vernon Duke* .... (CRS)
Nonstop July (Seemingly)
A-Ha; *East Of The Sun-West Of The Moon* .... (WB)
Saturday In The Park (July 4)
Chicago; *Greatest Hits* ....(COL)
Group Portrait ....(COL)
If You Leave Me Now ....(COL)
ST/My Girl ....(EPI)
V ....(COL)
See You In July
Jazzmasters; *Jazzmasters* .... (JVC)
Third Of July
Jody Grind; *Lefty's Deceiver* .... (DB)

MONTHS & DATES: JUNE
See Also: SEASONS: SUMMER

3rd Of June
Yello; *Flag* .... (MER)
Atlanta June
Pablo Cruise; *Place In The Sun* .... (A&M)
Desiree (June 3)
Neil Diamond; *12 Greatest Hits-#2* ....(COL)
I'm Glad You're Here With Me Tonight ....(COL)
Dream In June
Tom Harrell; *Sail Away* .... (CTM)
Goin' Through The Big D
Mark Chesnutt; *What A Way To Live* .... (DEC)
June 25 At The Fourth Of July
Shel Silverstein; *Great Conch Train Robbery* .... (FF)
June Bug
Leo Kottke; *Did You Hear Me* ....(CAP)
Mudlark ....(CAP)
My Feet Are Smiling ....(CAP)
The Best ....(CAP)
Lester Young; *Complete Savoy Recordings* .... (SAV)
Master Takes ....(SAV)
June In January
Bing Crosby; *Best Of* ....(MCA)
Dean Martin; *Best Of* ....(CAP)
June Is Bustin' Out All Over
Original Cast; *Carousel* ....(MCA)
June Night
Betty Everett; *Very Best Of* .... (VJ)
June Parade
Vic Shine; *Far & Distant Shore* ....(RCA)
June The 15, 1967
Gary Burton; *Artist's Choice* .... (BLU)
Juneteenth
Anthony Rivers/Others; *I've Known Rivers* ..... (GRM)
Memphis In June
Eddie Miller/Orchestra; *Uncollected-1944-1945* . (HIN)
Hoagy Carmichael; *Hoagy Sings Carmichael* ..... (EMI)
Hoagy Sings Carmichael ....(PAU)

MONTHS & DATES: MARCH
See Also: SEASONS: SPRING

23rd Of March
Gene Pitney; *Many Sides Of* ....(OOP)
March 19th Blues
Duke Ellington; *#1-Studio Sessions-Chicago-1956* (SAJ)
March 7th
Leaving Trains; *Well Down Blue Highway* .... (ENI)
March Sky
Alex DeGrassi; *Slow Circle* ....(WH)
One Day In March I Go Down To The Sea...
Jan Garbarek Group; *It's OK To Listen To The Gray Voice* .... (ECM)
Prague In March
Hendrik Meurkens; *Sambahia* .... (CP)
Waters Of March
Art Garfunkel; *Breakaway* ....(COL)
Winds Of March
Journey; *Infinity* ....(COL)

MONTHS & DATES: MAY
See Also: SEASONS: SPRING

Autumn To May
Peter, Paul & Mary; *Peter, Paul & Mary* ....(WB)
Blues For The Month Of May
Stan Getz/Others; *Tenors Anyone?* ....(BIO)
First Day Of May
James Taylor; *Never Die Young* ....(COL)
First Of May
Bee Gees; *Odessa* ....(RSO)
So; *Horseshoe In The Glove* ....(EMI)
In The Middle Of May
Pied Pipers; *Capitol Collectors Series* ....(CAP)
Lusty Month Of May
Julie Andrews; *Little Bit Of Broadway* ....(COL)
Original 1982 London Cast; *Camelot* ....(VS)
Original Cast; *Camelot* ....(COL)
May
Anthony Phillips; *Private Parts & Pieces-V Twelve* (PVC)
My Girl
Mamas & The Papas; *Best Of* .... (MCA)
Otis Redding; *Best Of* ....(ATC)
Rolling Stones; *Flowers* .... (AKO)
Temptations; *25th Anniversary* .... (MOT)
All The Million-Sellers .... (MOT)
Anthology .... (MOT)
Greatest Hits-#1 .... (MOT)
ST/Big Chill .... (MOT)
Night On The 4th Of May
Al Stewart; *Early Years* ....(OOP)
One Morning In May
Charlie Byrd Trio; *Isn't It Romantic?* .... (CCJ)
Jean Ritchie; *Love Is Teasin'* .... (ELE)
Seven Days Of May
Testament; *Souls Of Black* .... (MEG)
Then Came The Last Days Of May
Blue Oyster Cult; *Blue Oyster Cult* ....(COL)
On Your Feet Or On Your Knees ....(COL)

MONTHS & DATES: NOVEMBER
See Also: SEASONS: AUTUMN

Cold November
John O'Connor; *Songs For Our Times* ....(FF)
November
Anthony Phillips; *Private Parts & Pieces V Twelve* (PVC)
Chyld; *Chyld* ....(NEW)
Paul Greaver; *Joy* .... (GLO)
November 22, 1963
Original Cast; *Assassins* ....(RCA)
November 68th
Chick Corea; *CTI Masters Of The Keyboard* .....(CBA)
Joe Farrell; *Outback* ....(CTI)
November Afternoon
Dizzy Gillespie; *Composer's Concepts* .... (EMA)
James Moody; *Moving Forward* .... (NOV)
Paul Christopher; *Lavender* ....(ARY)

November Cotillion
Country Cooking; *Barrel Of Fun* .... (ROU)
November Day
Rob Mullins; *Nite Street* .... (RMC)
November Days
Origin; *Origin* .... (VIA)
November Girl
Carmen McRae; *November Girl* .... (JAZ)
November In The Snow/Lord Buckley
Mark Murphy; *Kerouac Then & Now* .... (MUS)
November Mood
Larry Coryell; *Toku Do* .... (MUS)
November Nights
Flim/BB's; *Tunnel* .... (DIG)
November Rain
Guns N' Roses; *Use Your Illusion I* .... (GEF)
November Song
Didier Lockwood; *Out Of The Blue* .... (GRM)
Norrie Paramor; *Autumn* .... (ANG)
November Spawned A Monster
Morrissey; *Bona Drag* .... (SIR)
Just Say Da-#4 Of Just Say Yes .... (SIR)
November Winds
Friedemann; *Indian Summer* .... (NAR)
Narada Equinox Sampler One .... (NAR)
Novembering
Claudia Schmidt; *Big Earful* .... (RDH)
November's Eve
Tim Story; *Untitled* .... (LLA)

MONTHS & DATES: OCTOBER
See Also: MONTHS & DATES: AUTUMN

Grey October Clouds
Tommy Makem & Liam Clancy; *Two For The Early Dew* .... (SHA)
Moondance
Van Morrison; *Best Of* .... (MER)
Moondance .... (WB)
My October Symphony
Pet Shop Boys; *Behavior* .... (EMI)
October
Anthony Phillips; *Private Parts & Pieces V-Twelve* (PVC)
A-Ha; *Scoundrel Days* .... (WB)
Borghesia; *Resistance* .... (PIA)
Danny Wright; *Phantasys* .... (MD)
Larry McNeely; *Power Play* .... (FF)
Leif Strand; *The Year* .... (INN)
Paul Desmond; *From The Hot Afternoon* .... (A&M)
Terry Garland; *Edge Of The Valley* .... (FIR)
U2; *October* .... (ISL)
Warren Bernhardt; *Hands On* .... (DIG)
October 17, 1988
Keith Jarrett; *Paris Concert* .... (ECM)
October 7
Mitch Watkins; *Strings With Wings* .... (ENJ)
October Anywhere
Giant Sand; *Valley Of Rain* .... (ENI)
October Ballad
Chick Corea; *Griffith Park-#2: The Concert* ..... (ELE)
October Country
October Country; *Nuggets #3-Pop* .... (RHI)
October Fool
Charlie Shoemaker & Bill Holman; *Collaboration* (PAU)
October Impressions (No. 38)
Mark O'Connor; *Elysian Forest* .... (WB)
October In September
John Nilsen; *October In September* .... (MW)
October Morning
Fourplay; *Fourplay* .... (WB)
October Night
Cliff Sarde; *Every Bit Better/Waiting* .... (MCA)
Waiting .... (MCA)
October Nights
Stone Soup; *October Nights* ....(WCH)
October Roses
Linda Allen; *October Roses* .... (NX)
October Sigh
Phil Sheeran; *Breaking Through* .... (SA)
October Song
Pat Kilbride; *Rock & More Roses* .... (TEM)

October Sunshine
First Brass; *First Brass* .... (MA)
Jazz Horizons-Best Of M-A Music-#1 ....(MA)
October Thorns
Flotsam & Jetsam; *When The Storm Comes Down* .... (MCA)
October Wedding
Montreux; *Let Them Say* ....(WH)
Montreux-Windham Hill Retrospective ....(WH)
October Winds
Bela Fleck; *Natural Bridge* .... (ROU)
October & The Frost Is Early
Dusing Singers; *Cool Of The Day-Music Of Jean Ritchie* .... (GHY)
October-Love Song
Chris & Cosey; *Funky Alternatives-18 Techno Remixes* .... (ROI)
October's Child
Elvin Jones; *Brother John* .... (PAJ)
Tell Me I'm October
Porn Orchard; *Urges & Angers* .... (C/Z)
When October Goes
Barry Manilow; *2 AM Paradise Cafe* .... (ARI)
Rosemary Clooney; *Sings The Lyrics Of Johnny Mercer* .... (CCJ)

MONTHS & DATES: SEPTEMBER
See Also: SEASONS: AUTUMN

And Then Comes September
Doris Day; *Duet* .... (DRG)
Sacha Distel; *Amour Tout Court* .... (DRG)
August & September
The The; *Mind Bomb* .... (EPI)
It Might As Well Rain Until September
Carole King; *More American Graffiti* .... (MCA)
Maybe September
Tony Bennett; *Forty Years-Artistry Of* ....(COL)
Movie Song Album ....(COL)
October In September
John Nilsen; *October In September* .... (MW)
Papa Was A Rollin' Stone (September 3)
Temptations; *20-20* .... (MOT)
25 #1 Hits From 25 Years .... (MOT)
All The Million-Sellers .... (MOT)
Anthology .... (MOT)
Billboard Top Rock 'N' Roll Hits-1972 .... (RHI)
Compact Command Performances .... (MOT)
Rocky Mountain September
C.W. McCall; *45* ....(OOP)
Sealed With A Kiss
Bobby Vinton; *Greatest Hits* ....(CCB)
Brian Hyland; *Cruisin'-1962* .... (INC)
Oldies But Goodies-#2 .... (OSR)
Original Rock 'N' Roll Hits/'50s .... (RLL)
Lettermen; *Best Of-#2* .... (CAP)
Capitol Collectors Series .... (CAP)
See You In September
Chiffons; *Best Of* ....(LAU)
Happenings; *ST/Purple People Eater* .... (AJK)
Tempos; *Cruisin'-1960* .... (INC)
ST/American Graffiti .... (MCA)
September
Anthony Phillips; *Private Parts & Pieces V Twelve* (PVC)
David Sylvian; *Secrets Of The Beehive* .... (VIA)
Earth, Wind & Fire; *Best Of-#1* ....(COL)
Eternal Dance ....(COL)
Mega Hits Dance Classics-#7 .... (PRY)
Michael Urbaniak; *Folk Songs-Children's Melodies-Jazz* .... (AND)
Nashville Rhythm Section; *Keep On Dancing* .... (KOA)
T Lavitz/Bad Habitz; *T Lavitz/Bad Habitz* .... (IMA)
Vladislav Sendecki; *Men From Wilnau* .... (AND)
September 13
Deodato; *Live At The Felt Forum-2001 Concert* ..(CBA)
Prelude ....(CBA)
September 1979
Bill Barron; *Variations In Blue* .... (MUS)
September Blue
Chris Rea; *Dancing With The Strangers* .... (MOT)
September Fifteenth
Mark Murphy; *September Ballads* .... (MS)

Pat Metheny & Lyle Mays; *As Falls Wichita So Falls Wichita Falls* ....(ECM)
September Girls
Bangles; *Different Light* ....(COL)
Big Star; *Live* ....(RYK)
September In The Rain
Chad & Jeremy; *Capitol Gold-Best Of* ....(CAP)
Soft Sound Of ....(KT)
Dinah Washington; *Golden Hits* ....(MER)
This Is My Story ....(MER)
Doris Day; *Sings 22 Great Songs On Orig. Big Band* ....(HIN)
Duprees; *Best Of* ....(RHI)
Frank Sinatra; *Round #1* ....(CAP)
Swingin' Session (& More) ....(CAP)
Joe Williams; *Swingin'...At Birdland* ....(RLL)
Marty Robbins; *Essential-1951-1982* ....(COL)
Peggy Lee; *You Can Depend On Me* ....(GLN)
September Love
Kool/Gang; *In The Heart* ....(DL)
September Morn
Mark Masters Jazz Composer Orchestra; *Early Start* ....(SEA)
Neil Diamond; *12 Greatest Hits-#2* ....(COL)
Hot August Night II ....(COL)
September Morn ....(COL)
September Night
Van Morrison; *Inarticulate Speech Of The Heart* ..(WB)
September Of My Years
Frank Sinatra; *A Man & His Music* ....(RPR)
At The Sands ....(RPR)
Greatest Hits-#2 ....(RPR)
September Of My Years ....(RPR)
Sings The Songs Of Van Heusen & Cahn ....(RPR)
September Rain
Full Swing; *Full Swing* ....(CYP)
George Howard; *Love Will Follow* ....(GRP)
September Snow
Danny Heines; *Aqua Touch* ....(SW)
September Song
Boston Pops Orchestra/Arthur Fiedler; *Greatest Hits Of The '30s* ....(RCA)
Mister Music U.S.A. ....(DGG)
Music For Every Mood-Yesterday ....(RCA)
Eddy Duchin & Stanley Worth; *Best Of The Big Bands* ....(COL)
Eydie Gorme; *Best Of* ....(CCB)
Flamingos/Moonglows; *On The Dusty Road Of Hits* (VJ)
Frank Sinatra; *Greatest Hits-#2* ....(COL)
Point Of No Return ....(CAP)
September Of My Years ....(RPR)
Jeff Lynne; *Armchair Theatre* ....(RPR)
Kate Wolf; *Safe At Anchor* ....(KAL)
Lindsey Buckingham; *Law & Order* ....(WB)
Lou Reed; *Lost In The Stars-Music Of Kurt Weill* (A&M)
Roger Williams; *Greatest Hits* ....(MCA)
Roy Clark; *Best Of* .... (MCA)
Sarah Vaughan & Clifford Brown; *Sarah Vaughan & Clifford Brown* ....(EMA)
Stan Kenton; *Comprehensive* ....(CAP)
Retrospective-Capitol Years ....(BLN)
Tony Bennett; *Forty Years-Artistry Of* ....(COL)
Willie Nelson; *Stardust* ....(COL)
Sweet September
Buddy Merrill; *Best Of* ....(ACT)
Holiday For Guitars ....(ACT)
Sweet September Morning
Buffy Sainte-Marie; *She Used To Wanna Be A Ballerina* ....(VAN)
Try To Remember
Original Cast; *Fantasticks* ....(POL)

MOON, Eclipse

Allegheny Moon
Patti Page; *Golden Hits* ....(MER)
Greatest Hits ....(COL)
Arizona Moon
Ranch Romance; *Blue Blazes* ....(SH)
Arthur's Theme
Christopher Cross; *ST/Arthur* ....(WB)
Au Clair De La Lune
Popular Standard; *Out-Of-Print Recording* ....(OOP)

August Moon
Ottmar Liebert & Luna Negra; *Borrasca* ....(HO)
Bad Moon Rising
Creedence Clearwater Revival; *1969* ....(FAN)
Chronicle ....(FAN)
Gold ....(FAN)
Green River ....(FAN)
Live In Europe ....(FAN)
Bad Side Of The Moon
Elton John; *11-17-70* ....(POL)
Banging My Head Against The Moon
John David Souther; *Black Rose* ....(ASY)
Bark At The Moon
Ozzy Osbourne; *Bark At The Moon* ....(CBA)
Bayou Girl
Bob Woodruff; *Dreams & Saturday Nights* .....(ASY)
Big Wheels In The Moonlight
Dan Seals; *Classics Collection-#2* ....(LIB)
Greatest Hits ....(LIB)
Rage On ....(LIB)
Black Moonlight
Bing Crosby; *In Hollywood* ....(OOP)
Black Water
Doobie Brothers; *Best Of* ....(WB)
What Were Once Vices Are Now Habits ....(WB)
Blow Out The Stars, Turn Off The Moon
Nitty Gritty Dirt Band; *Rest Of The Dream* .....(MCA)
Blue Moon
Billie Holiday; *Billie's Blues* ....(BLN)
First Verve Sessions ....(VRV)
History Of ....(VRV)
Elvis Presley; *Complete Sun Sessions* ....(RCA)
Elvis Presley ....(RCA)
Marcels; *Best Of* ....(RHI)
Billboard Top Rock 'N' Roll Hits-1961 ....(RHI)
Blue Moon Of Kentucky
Bill Monroe; *American Originals* ....(COL)
Bean Blossom/Lester Flatt ....(MCA)
Best Of ....(MCA)
Elvis Presley; *Date With* ....(RCA)
Golden Celebration ....(RCA)
Sun Sessions ....(RCA)
Blue Moon With Heartache
Rosanne Cash; *19 Hot Country Requests-#2* ......(EPI)
Hits 1979-1989 ....(COL)
Seven Year Ache ....(COL)
Born With The Moon In Virgo
Michael Franks; *Previously Unavailable* ....(DRG)
Brother Wolf, Sister Moon
Cult; *Love* ....(SIR)
By The Light Of The Silvery Moon
Al Jolson; *Story-#1* ....(MCA)
Doris Day; *Day At The Movies* ....(COL)
Julie Andrews; *Little Bit Of Broadway* ....(COL)
Mitch Miller; *34 All-Time Great Sing Along Selections* ....(COL)
Sing Along With ....(COL)
Cajun Moon
J.J. Cale; *Okie* ....(MCA)
Ricky Skaggs; *Greatest Country Hits/'80s-1986* ..(COL)
Live In London ....(EPI)
Rosanne Cash; *19 Hot Country Requests-#3* ......(EPI)
Carolina Moon
Slim Whitman; *Ghost Riders In The Sky* ....(LIB)
Thelonius Monk; *Genius Of Modern Music-#2* ...(BLN)
Chattahoochee
Alan Jackson; *Lot About Livin' (& A Little 'Bout Love)* ....(ARI)
Child Of The Moon
Rolling Stones; *More Hot Rocks-Big Hits & Fazed Cookies* ....(AKO)
Come To My Window
Melissa Etheridge; *Yes I Am* ....(ISL)
Dancing In The Moonlight
Be Bop Deluxe; *Modern Music* ....(HAR)
Liza Minnelli; *Singer* ....(COL)
Thin Lizzy; *Bad Reputation* ....(MER)
Live & Dangerous ....(WB)
Lizzy Lives! (1976-1984) ....(WB)
Desert Moon
Dennis DeYoung; *Desert Moon* ....(A&M)
Great White; *Hooked* ....(CAP)
Dreamy Georgiana Moon
Asa Martin; *Dr. Ginger Blue* ....(ROU)

Drunk On The Moon
Tom Waits; *Heart Of Saturday Night* .... (ASY)
East Of The Sun & West Of The Moon
Al Cohn & Zoot Sims; *RCA Victor Jazz-First
Half-Century* ....(RCA)
Billie Holiday; *Billie's Best* ....(VRV)
Tommy Dorsey & Frank Sinatra; *Stardust* ....(BLU)
Eclipse
Pink Floyd; *Dark Side Of The Moon* ....(CAP)
Works ....(CAP)
Eldorado To The Moon
Michael Nesmith; *Newer Stuff* .... (RHI)
Even The Man In The Moon Is Crying
Mark Collie; *Mark Collie* .... (MCA)
Fly Me To The Moon
Frank Sinatra; *A Man & His Music* ....(RPR)
At The Sands ....(RPR)
It Might As Well Be Swing ....(RPR)
Reprise Collection ....(RPR)
Full Moon
John Hiatt; *Hangin'Around The Observatory* .... (EPI)
Kinks; *Sleepwalker* ....(ARI)
Full Moon & Empty Arms
Frank Sinatra; *Greatest Hits-#2* ....(COL)
Sarah Vaughan; *Slightly Classical* ....(RLL)
Harvest Moon
Neil Young; *Harvest Moon* .... (RPR)
Havana Moon
Carlos Santana; *Havana Moon* ....(COL)
Chuck Berry; *After School Session* .... (CSS)
Chess Box .... (CSS)
Rockit ....(ATC)
Here Comes The Moon
George Harrison; *Best Of Dark Horse
1979-1989* .... (DKH)
George Harrison ....(DKH)
Honky Tonk Moon
Randy Travis; *Greatest Hits-#1* .... (WB)
Old 8 X 10 .... (WB)
Rosie Flores; *Once More With Feeling* .... (HT)
How Deep Is The Ocean (How High Is...)
Frank Sinatra; *Nice 'N' Easy* ....(CAP)
Liza Minnelli; *At Carnegie Hall* ....(TLR)
How High The Moon
Duke Ellington; *1954 Los Angeles Concert* .... (CRS)
Ella Fitzgerald; *Best Of* .... (MCA)
Les Paul & Mary Ford; *Memories Are Made Of
This* ....(CAP)
Nat King Cole Trio; *Best Of* .... (BLN)
Sarah Vaughan; *Compact Jazz-Best Of The Jazz
Vocalists* ....(VRV)
Complete On Mercury-#3-1954-1958 .... (MER)
Stephane Grappelli & Martin Taylor; *Just One Of Those
Things* .... (ANG)
Howlin' At The Moon
Hank Williams; *24 Greatest Hits-#2* .... (POL)
40 Greatest Hits .... (POL)
Hey Good Lookin' (Dec. 1950-July 1951) ....(POL)
I Got The Sun In The Morning
Doris Day/Original Cast; *Annie Get Your Gun* ......(COL)
Ethel Merman/Ray Middleton/Original Cast; *Annie Get
Your Gun* .... (MCA)
I Wished On The Moon
Billie Holiday; *Live* ....(VRV)
Stormy Blues ....(VRV)
Ella Fitzgerald; *Best Of* .... (MCA)
In The Chapel In The Moonlight
Patti Page; *16 Most Requested Songs* ....(COL)
It's Only A Paper Moon
Art Blakey/Jazz Messengers; *Big Beat* .... (BLN)
Bing Crosby; *Radio Years-#2* .... (CRS)
David Rose/Orchestra; *Music Of The 1930s* .... (MCA)
Ella Fitzgerald; *Harold Arlen Songbook-#2* ......(VRV)
Frank Sinatra; *Round #1* ....(CAP)
Mystics; *16 Golden Classics* ....(CLT)
Nat King Cole; *Story* ....(CAP)
Sammy Kaye/Orchestra; *Play 22 Original Big Band
Recordings* .... (HIN)
Killing Moon
Echo/Bunnymen; *Ocean Rain* .... (SIR)
Songs To Learn And Sing .... (SIR)
Lasso The Moon
Gary Morris; *Hits* ....(WB)

Lucky Moon
Oak Ridge Boys; *Unstoppable* ....(RCA)
Luna
Smashing Pumpkins; *Siamese Dream* .... (VIA)
Tom Petty/Heartbreakers; *Tom
Petty/Heartbreakers* .... (MCA)
Magic Moon
Peter Frampton; *Something's Happening* .... (A&M)
Magnolia Moon
Seals & Crofts; *Takin' It Easy* ....(WB)
Man On The Moon
R.E.M.; *Automatic For The People* ....(WB)
Mississippi Moon
Greg Brown; *One More Goodnight Kiss* .... (RDH)
Jerry Garcia; *Compliments* .... (GRD)
Jimmie Rodgers; *Down The Old
Road-1931-1932* .... (ROU)
Early Years-1928-1929 .... (ROU)
Seatrain; *Marblehead Messenger* .... (OW)
Moon At The Window
Joni Mitchell; *Wild Things Run Fast* ....(GEF)
Moon Is Still Over Her Shoulder
Michael Johnson; *Best Of* ....(RCA)
Country Love Songs ....(RCA)
That's That ....(RCA)
Wings ....(RCA)
Moon Is Up
Rolling Stones; *Voodoo Lounge* .... (VIA)
Moon Of Kentucky
Elvis Presley; *Golden Celebration* ....(RCA)
Moon Over Bourbon Street
Sting; *Bring On The Night* .... (A&M)
Dream Of The Blue Turtles .... (A&M)
Moon Over Brooklyn
Anne Murray; *Somebody's Waiting* ....(CAP)
Moon Over Cuba
Duke Ellington; *Duke Ellington/Blanton-Webster
Band* ....(BLU)
Moon Over Georgia
Shenandoah; *Extra Mile* ....(COL)
Greatest Hits ....(COL)
Moon Over Miami
Bourbon Street Stompers; *I Like Dixieland* ....(BAI)
Vaughn Monroe; *This Is* ....(RCA)
Moon Over Naples
Billy Vaughn; *Best Of* .... (MCA)
Moon Over Venice
Thom Rotella; *Home Again* .... (DIG)
Moon River
Andy Williams; *16 Most Requested Songs* ....(COL)
Greatest Hits ....(COL)
More American Graffiti-#4 .... (MCA)
Henry Mancini; *All-Time Greatest Hits-#1* ....(RCA)
Pure Gold ....(RCA)
Jerry Butler; *Best Of* .... (RHI)
Moon River .... (VJ)
Moon Shadow
Cat Stevens; *Classics-#24* .... (A&M)
Greatest Hits .... (A&M)
Teaser & The Firecat .... (A&M)
Moon Song (That Wasn't Meant For Me)
Art Tatum; *Solo Masterpieces-#7* .... (PAB)
Frank Sinatra; *Moonlight Sinatra* ....(RPR)
Moon Tears
Nils Lofgren; *Best Of Grin* .... (EPI)
Classics-#13 .... (A&M)
Grin ....(EPA)
Night After Night .... (A&M)
Moon Turn The Tide Gently Gently Away
Jimi Hendrix; *Electric Ladyland* .... (RPR)
Moon Was Yellow
Frank Sinatra; *Greatest Hits-#2* ....(COL)
Moonlight Sinatra ....(RPR)
Moonage Daydream
David Bowie; *Live* ....(RYK)
Man Who Sold The World ....(RYK)
Rise & Fall Of Ziggy Stardust ....(RYK)
Sound + Vision ....(RYK)
ST/Ziggy Stardust-The Motion Picture ....(RCA)
Moonchild
Iron Maiden; *Seventh Son Of A Seventh Son* .....(CAP)
King Crimson; *In The Court Of The Crimson
King* ....(ATL)
Shakespear's Sister; *Hormonally Yours* ....(LON)

Moondance
Van Morrison; *Best Of* .... (MER)
  Moondance .... (WB)
Moonflower
Santana; *Moonflower* ....(COL)
Moonglow
Art Tatum; *Solo Masterpieces-#1* .... (PAB)
Billie Holiday; *First Verve Sessions* ....(VRV)
Count Basie; *The Standards* ....(VRV)
Moonlight Becomes You
Frank Sinatra; *Moonlight Sinatra* .... (RPR)
  Sings The Songs Of Van Heusen & Cahn .... (RPR)
Moonlight Cocktail
Glenn Miller; *Best Of-#2* ....(RCA)
  Complete Glen Miller/Orchestra-#8 .... (BLU)
  Memorial 1944-1969 .... (BLU)
  Nipper's Greatest Hits- '40s-#1 ....(RCA)
Rivieras; *45* ....(CLT)
  45 ....(ERI)
Moonlight Drive
Doors; *13* .... (ELE)
  Alive She Cried .... (ELE)
  Strange Days .... (ELE)
Moonlight Feels Right
Starbuck; *45* ....(OOP)
Moonlight In Marrakesh
Otto Cesana; *#2* .... (TUD)
Moonlight In Vermont
Cal Tjader; *Latin Kick* .... (FAN)
Captain Beefheart/Magic Band; *Trout Mask*
  Replica ....(RPR)
Frank Sinatra; *Come Fly With Me* ....(CAP)
  Gift Set ....(CAP)
Nat King Cole Trio; *Best Of* ....(BLN)
Sarah Vaughan; *Complete On*
  Mercury-#3-1954-1956 .... (MER)
  Golden Hits .... (MER)
Moonlight Lady
Julio Iglesias; *1100 Bel Air Place* ....(COL)
Moonlight Mile
Rolling Stones; *Sticky Fingers* .... (RS)
Moonlight Montreal
Peter White; *Reveillez-Vous* .... (CMG)
Moonlight Motel
Gun Club; *Las Vegas Story* .... (IRS)
Moonlight On The Colorado
Sons Of The Pioneers; *Songs Of The Trail* .... (PRR)
Moonlight On The Ganges
Frank Sinatra; *Sinatra Swings* ....(RPR)
Glenn Miller; *Best Of The Big Bands* ....(COL)
Moonlight Savings Time (There Ought...)
Guy Lombardo; *Auld Lang Syne* .... (POE)
Moonlight Serenade
Frank Sinatra; *Moonlight Sinatra* ....(RPR)
  Reprise Collection ....(RPR)
Glenn Miller; *Best Of-#2* ....(RCA)
  Legendary Performer .... (BLU)
  Memorial 1944-1969 .... (BLU)
  Nipper's Greatest Hits-'30s-#1 ....(RCA)
  Pure Gold ....(RCA)
  Story ....(RCA)
Moonlight Sonata
Glenn Miller; *Legendary Performer-#2* ....(RCA)
Liberace; *Greatest Hits* ....(COL)
"Moonlighting" Theme
Al Jarreau; *ST/Moonlighting* .... (MCA)
"Moonraker" Theme
John Barry & Shirley Bassey; *ST/Moonraker* ..... (EMI)
Shirley Bassey; *Best Of James Bond-30th*
  Anniversary .... (EMI)
Moons Of Jupiter
Paul Halley; *Pianosong* ....(LIV)
Moonshadow Road
T. Graham Brown; *Best Of* ....(LIB)
Moon-faced, Starry-Eyed
Popular Standard; *Out of print recording* ....(OOP)
Mountains Of The Moon
Grateful Dead; *Aoxomoxoa* .... (WB)
Mr. Moonlight
Beatles; *Box Set* ....(CAP)
  For Sale ....(CAP)
  '65 ....(CAP)
Nashville Moon
Charlie Daniels Band; *Windows* .... (EPI)

Ronnie Milsap; *Lost In The Fifties Tonight* ....(RCA)
Neon Moon
Brooks & Dunn; *Brand New Man* .... (ARI)
Neon Moonlight
Rosco Martinez; *S* .... (ZOO)
New Blue Moon
Traveling Wilburys; *#3* ....(WIL)
New Moon On Monday
Duran Duran; *After The Hurricane* .... (CHR)
  Seven And The Ragged Tiger ....(CAP)
No Moon At All
Anita O'Day; *In A Mellow Tone* .... (DRG)
Billy Stritch; *Billy Stritch* .... (DRG)
Oh You Crazy Moon
Frank Sinatra; *Moonlight Sinatra* .... (RPR)
  Sings The Songs Of Van Heusen & Cahn .... (RPR)
Mark Murphy; *Sings Nat's Choice-Cole*
  Songbook-#1 .... (MUS)
Old Devil Moon
Anita O'Day; *Sings The Most* ....(VRV)
Frank Sinatra & Nelson Riddle Orchestra; *Songs For*
  Swingin' Lovers ....(CAP)
John Raitt; *Highlights Of Broadway/Under Open*
  Skies ....(CAP)
Lena Horne; *The Lady* ....(DHL)
Michael Feinstein; *Sings The Burton Lane*
  Songbook-#1 .... (NON)
Miles Davis; *Blue Haze* ....(PRS)
Original Cast; *Finian's Rainbow* ....(COL)
Tony Bennett; *Forty Years-Artistry Of* ....(COL)
Once In A Blue Moon
Earl Thomas Conley; *Greatest Hits* ....(RCA)
  Hits Of '86 ....(RCA)
Once In A Very Blue Moon
Nanci Griffith; *One Fair Summer Evening* .... (MCA)
  Steal This Disc ....(RYK)
Pat Alger; *True Love & Other Short Stories* ....(SH)
Pale Moon
Tommy Dorsey & Frank Sinatra; *All-Time Greatest*
  Hits-#4 ....(RCA)
Paper Moon
Ray McKinley; *Jiminy Crickets* .... (AER)
Phone Call From The Moon
Adrian Belew; *Young Lions* ....(ATL)
Polka Dots & Moonbeams
C. Parker/D. Gillespie/C. Mingus/others; *Greatest Jazz*
  Concert Ever .... (PRS)
Ella Fitzgerald; *Fine & Mellow* .... (PAB)
Frank Sinatra; *A Man & His Music* ....(RPR)
  I Remember Tommy .... (RPR)
  Sings The Songs Of Van Heusen & Cahn .... (RPR)
Quarter Moon
Cheryl Wheeler; *Cheryl Wheeler* ....(NS)
Kathy Mattea; *Time Passes By* .... (MER)
Rabbit In The Moon
Aztec Two-Step; *See It Was Like This...Acoustic*
  Retrosp. ....(FF)
Peter Erskine; *Transition* .... (DEN)
Racing With The Moon
Vaughn Monroe; *Best Of* .... (MCA)
  Best Of ....(RCA)
  Decade Of The '40s ....(RCA)
  This Is ....(RCA)
Reaching For The Moon
Ella Fitzgerald; *Irving Berlin Songbook-#2* ....(VRV)
Frank Sinatra; *Moonlight Sinatra* ....(RPR)
Red Moon Over Boston
Romanovsky & Phillips; *Be Political Not Polite* ... (FRE)
Rock On The Moon
Cramps; *Songs The Lord Taught Us* .... (IRS)
Rockin' Chair On The Moon
Bill Haley/Comets; *King Of Rock & Roll* .... (ALS)
Roll Along, Kentucky Moon
Jimmie Rodgers; *Down The Old*
  Road-1931-1932 .... (ROU)
Leon Redbone; *Sugar* ....(PRV)
Rope The Moon
John Michael Montgomery; *Kickin' It Up* .... (ATL)
Sail Along, Silv'ry Moon
Andy Williams; *Greatest Songs* ....(CCB)
Billy Vaughn; *Best Of* .... (MCA)
  Greatest Hits ....(CCB)
  & Orchestra Play 22 Of His Greatest Hits ...... (RAN)

Sail On White Moon
Boz Scaggs; *Slow Dancer* ....(COL)
Sailboat In The Moonlight
Billie Holiday; *Greatest Hits* ....(COL)
  Lady Day ....(COL)
  Legacy Box-1933-1958 ....(COL)
  Quintessential-#4-1937 ....(COL)
Same Moon
Maureen McGovern; *State Of The Heart* ....(COL)
Shadow On A Harvest Moon
Everything But The Girl; *Idlewild* .... (SIR)
Shadows In The Moonlight
Anne Murray; *15 Of The Best* ....(LIB)
  Greatest Hits ....(LIB)
  New Kind Of Feeling ....(CAP)
Shame On The Moon
Bob Seger/Silver Bullet Band; *The Distance* ......(CAP)
Mac Davis; *Very Best & More* ....(CAS)
Rodney Crowell; *Collection* ....(WB)
She Hung The Moon
George Jones; *Shine On* ....(EPI)
Shine On Harvest Moon
Dorsey Brothers; *I'm Getting Sentimental Over
You* .... (POE)
Jimmy Dorsey; *22 Original Big Band Recordings* . (HIN)
Leon Redbone; *Double Time* ....(WB)
Mitch Miller; *16 Most Requested Songs* ....(COL)
Shine On Moon
Lightnin' Hopkins; *Collectables Blues
Collection-#3* .... (CLT)
  Mojo Hand ....(CLT)
Shinin' Moon
Cowboy Junkies; *Whites Off Earth Now!* ....(RCA)
Lightnin' Hopkins; *Drinkin' The Blues-Golden
Classics-#1* .... (CLT)
  Gold Star Sessions-#2 ....(ARH)
Shoot Down The Moon
Elton John; *Ice On Fire* .... (MCA)
Shoot For The Moon
Poco; *45* ....(ATL)
Silver Moon
David Sylvian; *Gone To Earth* .... (VIA)
Kitaro; *In Person* ....(GRM)
  My Best ....(GRM)
  Silk Road II ....(GRM)
Lawrence Welk; *22 Great Waltzes* ....(RAN)
Michael Nesmith; *Older Stuff* ....(RHI)
Mom & Dads; *20 Favorite Waltzes* ....(CRS)
Sister Moonshine
Supertramp; *Crisis? What Crisis?* ....(A&M)
Sisters Of The Moon
Fleetwood Mac; *25 Years-The Chain* ....(WB)
  Tusk ....(WB)
Somebody Else's Moon
Collin Raye; *In This Life* ....(EPI)
Spanish Moon
Little Feat; *Feats Don't Fail Me Now* ....(WB)
  Waiting For Columbus ....(WB)
Robert Palmer; *Some People Can Do What They
Like* .... (ISL)
Standing On The Corner
Broadway Cast; *Most Happy Fella* ....(RCA)
Four Lads; *16 Most Requested Songs* ....(COL)
Original Broadway Cast; *Most Happy Fella* ..... (SMC)
Sugar Moon
Bob Wills/Texas Playboys; *Essential* ....(COL)
k.d. lang; *Shadowland* ....(SIR)
Pat Boone; *Best Of* ....(MCA)
Sun On The Moon
James Taylor; *Never Die Young* ....(COL)
Sun & Moon
Original London Cast; *Miss Saigon* .... (GEF)
Sun, Moon & Stars
Nanci Griffith; *Late Night Grande Hotel* .... (MCA)
Tahitian Moon
Michael Franks; *Objects Of Desire* .... (WB)
Talking To A Tennessee Moon
Candace Anderson; *Talking To A Tennessee
Moon* .... (ADO)
Talkin' To The Moon
Charlie Daniels Band; *Me & The Boys* ....(EPI)

Gatlin Brothers; *Biggest Hits* ....(COL)
  Live At 8:00 ....(CAP)
  More Hot Country Requests-#2 ....(EPI)
  Partners ....(COL)
There's A Moon Out Tonight
Capris; *20 Top 10 Hits/'50s & '60s* ....(LAU)
  22 Leaders Of The Pack-#2 ....(LAU)
  Collectables Presents History Of Rock-#3 ....(CLT)
  There's A Moon Out Tonight ....(CLT)
There's A New Moon Over My Shoulder
Gene Autry; *Columbia Historic Edition* ....(COL)
Jimmie Davis; *Best Of* ....(MCA)
  Country Music Hall Of Fame ....(MCA)
  Golden Hits ....(PLN)
Tex Ritter; *Greatest Hits* ....(CCB)
Tijuana Moon
Tim Buckley; *Look At The Fool* .... (BIZ)
Total Eclipse
Alan Parsons Project; *I Robot* .... (ARI)
Tropic Moon
Bruce Cockburn; *Trouble With Normal* ....(COL)
Tubas In The Moonlight
Bonzo Dog Band; *Tadpoles* .... (LIB)
Under A Raging Moon
Roger Daltrey; *Under A Raging Moon* ....(ATL)
Under The Harlem Moon
Fletcher Henderson/Orchestra; *Fletcher
Henderson/Orchestra* ....(ASV)
Under The Moon Of Love
Curtis Lee; *Back To Mono-1958-1969* .... (AKO)
Underneath The Harlem Moon
Randy Newman; *12 Songs* ....(RPR)
Waiting For The Moon
Bruce Cockburn; *The Trouble With Normal* .....(COL)
Was It Just The Moonlight
Timothy B. Schmit; *Tell Me The Truth* .... (MCA)
Watch The Moon Come Down
Graham Parker/Rumour; *Parkerilla* .... (MER)
  Stick To Me ....(MER)
Water From The Moon
Celine Dion; *Celine Dion* .... (EPI)
Lee Ritenour; *Earth Run* ....(GRP)
What A Little Moonlight Can Do
Billie Holiday; *Billie's Best* ....(VRV)
  First Verve Sessions ....(VRV)
  Greatest Hits ....(COL)
  History Of The Real Billie Holiday ....(VRV)
  Songbook ....(VRV)
Diana Ross; *ST/Lady Sings The Blues* ....(MOT)
When My Blue Moon Turns To Gold Again
Elvis Presley; *50 Worldwide Gold Award Hits-#2* (RCA)
  Elvis ....(RCA)
  Golden Celebration ....(RCA)
Merle Haggard; *His Best* ....(MCA)
  Ramblin' Fever ....(MCA)
When The Moon Comes Over The Mountain
Kate Smith; *16 Most Requested Songs* ....(COL)
  Best Of ....(RCA)
Whitey On The Moon
Gil Scott-Heron; *Whitey On The Moon* ....(BLU)
Whole Of The Moon
Jennifer Warnes; *The Hunter* ....(PRV)
Terry Reid; *The Driver* ....(WB)
Waterboys; *Greenpeace/Rainbow Warriors* ....(GEF)
  This Is The Sea ....(CHR)
Wild Dog Moon
Drivin' N' Cryin'; *Mystery Road* .... (ISL)
Wishing On The Moon
Dan Fogelberg; *Phoenix* .... (FM)
Wrong Side Of The Moon
Squeeze; *Argybargy* ....(A&M)

MORNING, Dawn
  See Also: SUN

59th St. Bridge Song (Feelin' Groovy)
Simon & Garfunkel; *Collected Works* ....(COL)
  Concert In Central Park ....(WB)
  Greatest Hits ....(COL)
  Parsley Sage Rosemary & Thyme ....(COL)
Ain't Going Down (Til The Sun Comes Up)
Garth Brooks; *In Pieces* ....(LIB)

Almost Dawn In Denver
Faron Young; *Greatest Hits-#3* ....(SO)
Amarillo By Morning
George Strait; *Greatest Hits* .... (MCA)
   Strait Country/Strait From The Heart .... (MCA)
   Strait From The Heart .... (MCA)
Angel Of The Morning
Juice Newton; *All-Time Country Classics-#2* ..... (CAP)
   Greatest Hits ....(CAP)
   Greatest Hits & More ....(CAP)
   Juice ....(CAP)
Merrilee Rush; *Dick Bartley's One-Hit*
   Wonders-'60s-#2 .... (RHI)
   Mellow '60s ....(PRY)
Another Dawn Breaking Over Georgia
David Frizzell & Shelly West; *Our Best To You* ... (WB)
Another Grey Morning
James Taylor; *JT* ....(COL)
April Fool's Day Morn
Loudon Wainwright III; *Career Moves* .... (VIA)
   Fame & Wealth .... (ROU)
As I Went Out One Morning
Bob Dylan; *John Wesley Harding* ....(COL)
At 4 A.M.
Tom Verlaine; *Flash Light* .... (IRS)
Bloody Mary Morning
Willie Nelson; *Best Of Willie* ....(RCA)
   Phases & Stages ....(ATL)
   ST/Honeysuckle Rose ....(COL)
   & Family Live ....(COL)
Blue Morning Blue Day
Foreigner; *Double Vision* ....(ATL)
Blues Before Sunrise
Eric Clapton; *From The Cradle* .... (DUC)
Brand New Day
Frankie Laine; *16 Greatest Hits* .... (TRP)
Van Morrison; *Moondance* ....(WB)
Can I See You In The Morning
Jackson 5; *Third Album* .... (MOT)
Carolina In The Morning
Al Jolson; *Best Of* ....(MCA)
   Story-#2 .... (MCA)
Chelsea Morning
Joni Mitchell; *Clouds* ....(RPR)
Neil Diamond; *Rainbow* ....(MCA)
   Stones ....(MCA)
City Of New Orleans
Arlo Guthrie; *Best Of* ....(WB)
   Hobo's Lullaby ....(RPR)
   Together In Concert w/Pete Seeger ....(RPR)
HARP; *HARP* ....(RWD)
Willie Nelson; *19 Hot Country Requests-#2* .... (EPI)
   City Of New Orleans ....(COL)
   Greatest Country Hits/'80s-#4 ....(COL)
Cloudy Morning
Carmen McRae & George Shearing; *Two For The*
   Road .... (CCJ)
Come Early Morning
Don Williams; *20 Greatest Hits* .... (MCA)
   Greatest Hits ....(MCA)
   Some Broken Hearts Never Mend ....(MSP)
Come Saturday Morning
Sandpipers; *Four Sider* ....(A&M)
   Super Hits/'70s-Have A Nice Day-#1 .... (RHI)
Crying In The Morning
Billy Tate; *Southern Blues* .... (SAV)
   Crying In The Morning-Anthology Of Postwar
   Blues .... (MUS)
Dawn In Malaysia
Kitaro; *Asia* ....(GEF)
Dawn Of Correction
Spokesmen; *Sixties Rule!-Chapter 1* .... (OW)
Dawning Is The Day
Moody Blues; *Question Of Balance* ....(POL)
Daybreak
Acoustic Alchemy; *Early Alchemy* ....(GRP)
Barry Manilow; *Greatest Hits-#1* .... (ARI)
   Live .... (ARI)
   This One's For You .... (ARI)
Chet Baker; *Let's Get Lost-Best Of Chet Baker*
   Sings ....(PJZ)
Pat Metheny; *New Chautauqua* ....(ECM)
Robin Trower; *Live* ....(CHR)

Special EFX; *Collection* ....(GRP)
   Global Village ....(GRP)
Steve Wariner; *Steve Wariner* ....(RCA)
Tommy Dorsey & Frank Sinatra; *All-Time Greatest*
   Hits-#4 ....(RCA)
Dolphin Morning
Paul Winter Consort; *Sun Singer* ....(LIV)
Draft Morning
Byrds; *Notorious Byrd Brothers* ....(COL)
   Byrds (collection) ....(COL)
Dutch Morning
Phil Woods & Jim McNeely; *Flowers For Hodges* (CCJ)
Early In The Morning
Bad Company; *Desolation Angels* .... (SS)
Gap Band; *12" Collection* ....(MER)
   Gap Gold (Best Of) ....(MER)
   IV ....(MER)
Peter Paul & Mary; *Peter Paul & Mary* ....(WB)
Robert Palmer; *Heavy Nova* ....(EMI)
Early Morning Blues
Jimmy Preston; *Jimmy Preston* ....(CLT)
Muddy Waters; *More Real Folk Blues* ....(CSS)
Early One Morning
Elmore James; *King Of The Slide Guitar* ....(CPC)
John Lee Hooker; *Jealous* ....(CMG)
Easy
Commodores; *20 Greatest Songs In Motown*
   History ....(MOT)
   All The Great Love Songs ....(MOT)
   Commodores ....(MOT)
   Compact Command Performances ....(MOT)
   Composer-Great Love Songs By L. Richie ......(MOT)
   Greatest Hits ....(MOT)
Fine Spring Morning
Blossom Dearie; *Blossom Dearie* ....(VRV)
Fire In The Morning
Melissa Manchester; *Melissa Manchester* .... (ARI)
For No One
Beatles; *Box Set* ....(CAP)
   Love Songs ....(CAP)
   Revolver ....(CAP)
Emmylou Harris; *Pieces Of The Sky* ....(RPR)
Four In The Morning
Faron Young; *Greatest Hits-#3* ....(SO)
Night Ranger; *7 Wishes* ....(CAM)
   Greatest Hits ....(CAM)
Good Day Sunshine
Beatles; *Box Set* ....(CAP)
   Revolver ....(CAP)
Good Morning Girl
Journey; *Departure* ....(COL)
Good Morning Good Morning
Beatles; *Box Set* ....(CAP)
   Sgt. Pepper's Lonely Heart Club Band ....(CAP)
Good Morning Heartache
Billie Holiday; *All Or Nothing At All* ....(VRV)
   From The Original Decca Masters ....(MCA)
   History Of ....(VRV)
   Story ....(MCA)
Diana Ross; *Anthology* ....(MOT)
   Greatest Hits ....(MOT)
   ST/Lady Sings The Blues ....(MOT)
Good Morning Judge
10 CC; *Greatest Hits* ....(POL)
   Deceptive Bends ....(MER)
   Live & Let Live ....(MER)
Good Morning Starshine
Oliver; *45* ....(UA)
Original Broadway Cast; *Hair* ....(RCA)
Good Morning To You
Steve Miller Band; *Number 5* ....(CAP)
Gotta Get Up
Nilsson; *Schmilsson* ....(RCA)
Happier Than The Morning Sun
Stevie Wonder; *Music Of My Mind* .... (MOT)
Here Comes The Sun
Beatles; *1967-1970* ....(CAP)
   Abbey Road ....(CAP)
George Benson; *Best* ....(A&M)
   Collection ....(WB)
George Harrison; *Bangladesh* ....(CAP)
   Best Of ....(CAP)
Here Comes Yet Another Day
Kinks; *Everybody's In Show Biz* ....(RHI)

Hold Me 'Til The Mornin' Comes
Paul Anka; *Live* ....(COL)
Walk A Fine Line ....(COL)
I Got The Sun In The Morning
Doris Day/Original Cast; *Annie Get Your Gun* ...(COL)
Ethel Merman/Ray Middleton/Original Cast; *Annie Get Your Gun* ....(MCA)
Illinois Dawn
Skyline; *Late To Work* ....(FF)
In The Morning Time
Tramaine; *45* ....(A&M)
In The Wee Small Hours Of The Morning
Frank Sinatra; *A Man & His Music* ....(RPR)
Capitol Years ....(CAP)
In The Wee Small Hours ....(CAP)
Sinatra's Sinatra ....(RPR)
What Is This Thing Called Love ....(CAP)
(It's A) Beautiful Morning
Rascals; *Greatest* ....(ATL)
I'm Gonna Miss You In The Morning
Quincy Jones; *Best* ....(A&M)
Classics-#3 ....(A&M)
Sounds... And Stuff Like That ....(A&M)
Jam On Monday Morning
Buddy Guy; *Man & The Blues* ....(VAN)
Jamaica Sunday Morning
Kim Carnes; *St. Vincent's Court* ....(OOP)
Jets At Dawn
Be Bop Deluxe; *Axe Victim* ....(OOP)
Joy Comes In The Morning
Oak Ridge Boys; *All Our Favorite Songs* ....(COL)
July Morning
Uriah Heep; *Best Of* ....(MER)
Live ....(MER)
Loving You Sunday Morning
Scorpions; *Lovedrive* ....(MER)
World Wide Live ....(MER)
Monday Morning
Church; *Gold Afternoon Fix* .... (ARI)
Fleetwood Mac; *25 Years-The Chain* ....(WB)
Fleetwood Mac ....(RPR)
Live ....(WB)
Peter, Paul & Mary; *Song Will Rise* ....(WB)
Monday Morning Blues
Breathe; *All That Jazz* .... (A&M)
Mississippi John Hurt; *Best Of* ....(VAN)
Candy Man ....(INT)
Monday Morning In Paradise
Tom Paxton; *One Million Lawyers & Other Disasters* ....(FF)
Monday Morning Quarterback
Frank Sinatra; *She Shot Me Down* ....(RPR)
Monday Morning Rock
Marshall Crenshaw; *Field Day* ....(WB)
Monday Morning Secretary
Statler Brothers; *Statler Brothers* ....(MER)
Monday Mornin' Keep A Hurtin' Blues
Sonny James; *Little Bit Of Saskatoon* ....(COL)
Morning
Call; *Reconciled* ....(ELE)
Jim Ed Brown; *Best Of* ....(RCA)
Stars Of The Grand Ole Opry 1926-74 ....(RCA)
Morning After
Alexander O'Neal; *All True Man* ....(TAB)
Barbra Streisand; *What About Today* ....(COL)
Faith No More; *Real Thing* ....(SLS)
Maureen McGovern; *Super Hits!/'70s-Have A Nice Day-#11* ....(RHI)
Ratt; *Out Of The Cellar* ....(ATL)
Morning Coffee
Joe King Carrasco/Crowns; *Tales From The Crypt-Basement Tapes-1979* .... (ROI)
Morning Comes Too Early
Jim Ed Brown & Helen Cornelius; *Greatest Hits* .(RCA)
Morning Dance
Spyro Gyra; *Access All Areas* ....(MCA)
Collection ....(GRP)
Morning Dance ....(MCA)
Morning Desire
Kenny Rogers; *Greatest Hits* ....(RCA)
Morning Dew
Blackfoot; *Vertical Smiles* ....(ATC)
Bonnie Dobson; *Troubadours Of The Folk Era-#1* (RHI)
Grateful Dead; *Europe '72* ....(WB)

Jeff Beck Group; *Truth* .... (EPI)
Lulu; *45* ....(EPI)
Nazareth; *Nazareth* ....(A&M)
Morning Has Broken
Cat Stevens; *Classics-#24* ....(A&M)
Greatest Hits ....(A&M)
Teaser & The Firecat ....(A&M)
Morning In Paris
John Lewis; *Private Concert* .... (EMA)
Morning Man
Joy; *Joy* ....(FAN)
Morning Morgantown
Joni Mitchell; *Ladies Of The Canyon* ....(RPR)
Morning Papers
Prince/New Power Generation; *Love Symbol Album* ....(PAI)
Morning Side
Neil Diamond; *Hot August Night* ....(MCA)
Moods ....(MCA)
Morning Sky
Dan Fogelberg; *Souvenirs* .... (FM)
Morning Sun
Bad Company; *Burnin' Sky* .... (SS)
Jesse Colin Young; *Best Of-Solo Years* ....(RHI)
Song For Juli ....(WB)
Morning Train (Nine To Five)
Sheena Easton; *Sheena Easton* .... (EMI)
Morning Will Come
Spirit; *12 Dreams Of Dr. Sardonicus* ....(EPI)
Best Of ....(EPI)
Time Circle ....(EPI)
Mornin'
Al Jarreau; *Jarreau* ....(WB)
New Day For You
Basia; *Time & Tide* ....(EPI)
New Morning
Bob Dylan; *New Morning* ....(COL)
New World In The Morning
Roger Whittaker;
Best Of ....(RCA)
Last Farewell & Other Hits ....(RCA)
Live In Concert ....(RCA)
New World In The Morning ....(RCA)
Nobody Knows The Way I Feel This Morning
Aretha Franklin; *Sings The Blues* ....(COL)
Ernest "Punch" Miller; *Atlantic Jazz-New Orleans* (ATL)
October Morning
Fourplay; *Fourplay* ....(WB)
Of A Summer Morn
Nightnoise; *At The End Of The Evening* ....(WH)
Oh, What A Beautiful Morning
Original Broadway Cast; *Oklahoma* ....(RCA)
Original Cast; *Oklahoma* ....(MCA)
One Morning In May
Charlie Byrd Trio; *Isn't It Romantic?* .... (CCJ)
Jean Ritchie; *Love Is Teasin'* .... (ELE)
One Too Many Mornings
Beau Brummels; *Best Of* .... (RHI)
Bob Dylan; *Hard Rain* ....(COL)
Times They Are A-Changin' ....(COL)
Johnny Cash & Waylon Jennings; *Heroes* ....(COL)
Kingston Trio; *American Troubadours* ....(PRR)
Our Sunday Morning
Yoshio "Chin" Suzuki; *Morning Picture* .... (JVC)
Princess Of The Dawn
Accept; *Compilation* ....(POR)
Restless & Wild ....(POR)
Staying A Life ....(EPI)
Promise Of A New Day
Paula Abdul; *Spellbound* ....(CPT)
Quite Early Morning
Pete Seeger; *Essential* ....(VAN)
Race You To The Top Of The Morning
Original Broadway Cast; *Secret Garden* ....(COL)
Rise 'N' Shine
Kool Moe Dee w/KRS-One & Chuck D; *Funke Funke Wisdom* ....(JVA)
Saturday Morning
Harry Chapin; *Greatest Stories-Live* .... (ELE)
Joe Higgs; *Black Man Know Yourself* ....(SHA)
Meat Puppets; *Meat Puppets* ....(SST)
Tom Chapin; *In The City Of Mercy* .... (SPC)
Van Morrison; *Best Of* ....(BNG)

Saturday Morning Cartoons
Sergio Salvatore; *Sergio Salvatore* .... (GRP)
Saturday Morning Confusion
Bobby Russell; *Super Hits!'70s-Have A Nice
Day-#6* .... (RHI)
Saturday Morning Fever
Loudon Wainwright III; *Fame & Wealth* .... (ROU)
Saturday Morning Movies
Bonnie Koloc; *At Her Best* .... (OVA)
Bonnie Koloc .... (OVA)
Saturday Night & Sunday Morning
Phil Collins; *...But Seriously* .... (ATL)
Save A Prayer
Duran Duran; *Arena* .... (CAP)
Decade .... (CAP)
Rio .... (CAP)
Secret Policeman's Third Ball-The Music .... (VIA)
Seattle Morning
David Benoit; *Urban Daydreams* .... (GRP)
September Morn
Mark Masters Jazz Composer Orchestra; *Early
Start* .... (SEA)
Neil Diamond; *12 Greatest Hits-#2* ....(COL)
Hot August Night II ....(COL)
September Morn ....(COL)
Shake Me Wake Me
Barbra Streisand; *Lazy Afternoon* .... (COL)
Four Tops; *Anthology* .... (MOT)
Greatest Hits .... (MOT)
Motown Superstar Series-#14 .... (MOT)
Shake Rattle & Roll
Big Joe Turner; *Every Day I Have The Blues* .... (PAB)
Greatest Hits .... (ATL)
Oldies But Goodies-#2 .... (OSR)
Soul Years .... (ATL)
Bill Haley/Comets; *Golden Hits* .... (MCA)
Greatest Hits .... (MCA)
Elvis Presley; *For LP Fans Only* .... (RCA)
Rocker .... (RCA)
ST/This Is Elvis .... (RCA)
Fats Domino; *Greatest Hits* .... (MCA)
Huey Lewis/News; *Four Chords & Several Years
Ago* .... (ELE)
NRBQ; *At Yankee Stadium* .... (MER)
Vern Gosdin; *Best Of* .... (WB)
She's Leaving Home
Al Jarreau; *All Fly Home* .... (WB)
Beatles; *Box Set* ....(CAP)
Love Songs ....(CAP)
Sgt. Pepper's Lonely Hearts Club Band ....(CAP)
Silver Morning
Kenny Rankin; *Silver Morning* .... (LD)
Six-Thirty Sunday Morning
Peter Allen; *Taught By Experts* .... (A&M)
Skating Away On The Thin Ice...
Jethro Tull; *Bursting Out* .... (CHR)
Original Masters .... (CHR)
War Child .... (CHR)
'M.U.'-Best Of .... (CHR)
Slow Train To Dawn
The The/Neneh Cherry; *Infected* .... (EPI)
Sun Comes Up, It's Tuesday
Cowboy Junkies; *Caution Horses* ....(RCA)
Sunday Morning
Velvet Underground; *Live At Max's Kansas City* . (COT)
Sunday Morning Blues
Big Joe Turner; *Big Joe Is Here* .... (SAV)
Have No Fear .... (SAV)
Sunday Morning Coming Down
Johnny Cash; *Classic Cash-Hall Of Fame Series* . (MER)
Greatest Hits-#2 .... (COL)
Kris Kristofferson; *Me & Bobby McGee* .... (COL)
Songs Of .... (COL)
Vikki Carr; *Best Of* .... (EMI)
Willie Nelson; *Sings Kristofferson* ....(COL)
Willie .... (RCA)
Sunday Morning Fool
Michael Dinner; *Great Pretenders* .... (FAN)
Sunday Morning Movies
Bonnie Koloc; *At Her Best* .... (OVA)
Bonnie Koloc .... (OVA)
Sunday Morning Radio
Sha-Na-Na; *Sh-Boom* .... (ACC)

Sunday Morning Sunshine
Harry Chapin; *Anthology* .... (ELE)
Savoy Brown Collection ....(DER)
Sunday Sunrise
Brenda Lee; *Greatest Country Hits* .... (MCA)
Sunrise
Chet Atkins & George Benson; *Stay Tuned* ......(COL)
Eric Carmen; *Eric Carmen* .... (ARI)
Grateful Dead; *Terrapin Station* .... (ARI)
Jefferson Starship/Paul Kantner; *Blows Against The
Empire* ....(RCA)
Jimmy Cliff; *Cliff Hanger* ....(COL)
Joe Sample; *Carmel* .... (MCA)
Collection ....(GRP)
New Order; *Low-Life* .... (QUE)
Originals; *Motown Superstar Series-#10* .... (MOT)
Seals & Crofts; *Takin' It Easy* .... (WB)
Triplets; *...Thicker Than Water* .... (MER)
Uriah Heep; *Best Of* .... (MER)
Magician's Birthday .... (MER)
White Mountain Singers; *Best* .... (FOL)
Memories-Live! .... (FOL)
Sunrise .... (TAK)
Sunrise In La Jolla
Kilauea; *Antigua Blue* .... (BRA)
Sunrise In Mexico
Clifford Jordan; *Starting Time* .... (JZL)
Sunrise Over Haleakala
Merl Saunders & Jerry Garcia; *Blues From The
Rainforest-Musical Suite* .... (SUM)
Sunrise Serenade
Frankie Carle/Orchestra; *Big Band Instrumentals-16
Most Requested* ....(COL)
Glenn Miller; *Best Of* .... (BLU)
Legendary Performer .... (BLU)
Pure Gold .... (BLU)
Sunrise, Sunset
Original Cast; *Fiddler On The Roof* ....(RCA)
Original London Cast; *Fiddler On The Roof* .....(COL)
Sunset To Sunrise
Duprees; *Best Of* .... (RHI)
Sunshine Saturday Morning
Jim Aikin; *Light's Broken Speech Revived* ....(LIN)
Sweet September Morning
Buffy Sainte-Marie; *She Used To Wanna Be A
Ballerina* .... (VAN)
Sweet Tuesday Morning
Badfinger; *Straight Up* ....(CAP)
Tears In The Morning
Beach Boys; *Sunflower* ....(CAR)
Texas Morning
Michael Nesmith/First National Band; *Complete* .. (PA)
Thursday Morning Garden Club
Buddy Winfield; *45* ....(NAT)
Till The Morning Comes
Grateful Dead; *American Beauty* .... (WB)
Neil Young; *After The Goldrush* .... (RPR)
To Raise The Morning Star
Bruce Cockburn; *Stealing Fire* ....(COL)
To The Morning
Dan Fogelberg; *Home Free* ....(COL)
Too Many Mornings
Original Broadway Cast; *Follies* ....(CAP)
Touch Me In The Morning
Diana Ross; *12 #1 Hits From The '70s* .... (MOT)
20 Greatest Songs In Motown History .... (MOT)
All The Great Hits .... (MOT)
Anthology .... (MOT)
Evening With .... (MOT)
Greatest Hits .... (MOT)
Touch Me In The Morning .... (MOT)
Touch The Morning
Don Gibson; *18 Greatest Hits* .... (CCB)
Best Of-#1 .... (CCB)
Train Leaves Here This Morning
Eagles; *Eagles* .... (ASY)
Two O'Clock In The Morning
Stuart Duncan; *Stuart Duncan* .... (ROU)
Violets Of Dawn
Blues Project; *No Time Like The Right Time-Best
Of* .... (RHI)
Eric Andersen; *Best Of* .... (VAN)
Troubadours Of The Folk Era-#1 .... (RHI)

Wake Up Morning
Rex Allen, Jr.; *Country Comfort* .... (PLN)
Today's Generation .... (SSS)
Wake Up Sunshine
Chicago; *II* ....(COL)
Wednesday Morning, 3 AM
Simon & Garfunkel; *Collected Works* ....(COL)
Wednesday Morning, 3 AM ....(COL)
When The Morning Comes
Bryan Adams; *Bryan Adams* .... (A&M)
Daryl Hall & John Oates; *Abandoned*
Luncheonette .... (ATL)
No Goodbyes .... (ATL)
Will It Be Love By Morning
Michael Martin Murphey; *Best Of* .... (EMI)
Heart Never Lies .... (LIB)
Will You Be There (In The Morning)
Heart; *Desire Walks On* ....(CAP)

MOTHERS, Mom, Mama

See Also: WOMEN: GENERAL, WOMEN'S
NAMES

And Her Mother Came Too
Bobby Short; *50 By* ....(ATL)
Big Fat Mama
Big Joe Williams; *Legacy Of The Blues-#6* .... (CRS)
Fred McDowell; *Long Way From Home* .... (MS)
Fred McDowell & Furry Lewis; *When I Lay My Burden*
Down ....(BIO)
Burn That Candle
Bill Haley/Comets; *Golden Hits* .... (MCA)
Greatest Hits .... (MCA)
R-O-C-K .... (SUN)
Emmylou Harris; *Quarter Moon In A Ten Cent*
Town ....(WB)
Choo Choo Mama
Ten Years After; *Recorded Live* .... (CHR)
Universal .... (CHR)
Come To Mama
Etta James; *Seven Year Itch* .... (ISL)
Koko Taylor; *Queen Of The Blues* ....(ALG)
Pete Townshend; *White City* ....(ATC)
Crazy Mama
J.J. Cale; *Naturally* .... (MCA)
Rolling Stones; *Black & Blue* ....(RS)
Sucking In The Seventies ....(RS)
Daddy's Come Around
Paul Overstreet; *Heroes* ....(RCA)
Did Your Mother Come From Ireland
Bing Crosby; *Shillelaghs & Shamrocks* ....(MCA)
Does Your Mother Know?
Abba; *Greatest Hits-#2* ....(ATL)
Live ....(ATL)
Singles (First 10 Years) ....(ATL)
Voulez-Vous ....(ATL)
Don't Tell Your Mama
Eddie Floyd; *Chronicle* ....(STX)
Down The Road
Mac McAnally; *Knots* .... (MCA)
Drop Down Mama, Let Your Papa See
John Hammond; *Best Of* ....(VAN)
Sleepy John Estes; *Legend Of* ....(DEL)
Tom Rush; *Best Of* ....(COL)
Tom Rush ....(COL)
Earth Mother
Grace Slick & Paul Kantner; *Sunfighter* .... (GRU)
Every Mother's Son
Traffic; *John Barleycorn Must Die* .... (UA)
Every Mother's Son
Pretenders; *Last Of The Independents* .... (SIR)
Fancy
Bobbi Gentry; *All-Time Country Classics-#1* .....(CAP)
Reba McEntire; *Rumor Has It* .... (MCA)
For A Thousand Mothers
Jethro Tull; *Stand Up* .... (CHR)
For Momma
Statler Brothers; *Christmas Present* .... (MER)
Gabriel's Mother's Hiway Ballad 16 Blues
Arlo Guthrie; *Best Of* ....(WB)

Grandma Got Run Over By A Reindeer
Elmo & Patsy; *Billboard's Greatest Christmas Hits* (RHI)
Dr. Demento Greatest Novelty CD .... (RHI)
Dr. Demento's Greatest-#6 .... (RHI)
Grandma Got Run Over By A Reindeer .... (EPI)
Greatest Children's Christmas Hits .... (EPI)
Grandmother Song
Steve Martin; *Let's Get Small* .... (WB)
Have You Seen Your Mother Baby...
Rolling Stones; *Flowers* .... (AKO)
Got Live If You Want It .... (AKO)
More Hot Rocks-Big Hits & Fazed Cookies ..... (AKO)
Through The Past Darkly-Big Hits-#2 .... (AKO)
He Thinks He'll Keep Her
Mary Chapin Carpenter; *Come On Come On* ....(COL)
He Would Be Sixteen
Michelle Wright; *Now & Then* .... (ARI)
Hello Muddah, Hello Fadduh
Allan Sherman; *Dr. Demento Greatest Novelty CD* (RHI)
Dr. Demento's Greatest-#3 .... (RHI)
Hobo & His Mother
Goebel Reeves; *Texas Drifter* ....(GLN)
Hot Chili Mama
Beausoleil; *Hot Chili Mama* .... (ARH)
How Can I Help You Say Goodbye
Patty Loveless; *Only What I Feel* .... (EPI)
I Want A Girl (Just Like The Girl)
Al Jolson; *Story-#1* .... (MCA)
Spike Jones; *King Of Corn* ....(GLN)
Is Your Mama Gonna Miss Ya?
Bryan Adams; *Waking Up The Neighbours* ...... (A&M)
I'm A Mother
Pretenders; *Last Of The Independents* .... (SIR)
I'm The One Mama Warned You About
Mickey Gilley; *Too Good To Stop Now* ....(EPI)
Jesus & Mama
Confederate Railroad; *Confederate Railroad* ..... (ATL)
Julia
Beatles; *Box Set* ....(CAP)
ST/Imagine-The Motion Picture ....(CAP)
White Album ....(CAP)
Lady Madonna
Beatles; *1967-1970* ....(CAP)
Hey Jude ....(CAP)
Past Masters-#2 ....(CAP)
Paul McCartney/Wings; *Over America* ....(CAP)
Letting Go
Suzy Bogguss; *Aces* ....(CAP)
Voices In The Wind ....(LIB)
Little Mama
Clovers; *45* .... (ATL)
L.A. Mama
Jim Stafford; *Jim Stafford* .... (POL)
Ma (She's) Making Eyes At Me
Eddie Cantor; *Memories* .... (MCA)
Mama
B.J. Thomas; *Greatest Hits* .... (RHI)
Electric Light Orchestra; *2* ....(JET)
Afterglow .... (EPI)
Genesis; *Genesis* ....(ATL)
Knebworth-The Album ....(POL)
Helen Reddy; *Live At London Palladium* ....(CAP)
Music Music ....(CAP)
Jerry Vale; *17 Most Requested Songs* ....(COL)
Original Broadway Cast; *Sarafina* ....(RCA)
Roy Orbison; *Greatest Hits* ....(MON)
Our Love Song ....(MON)
Rare Orbison II ....(MON)
Mama Can't Buy You Love
Elton John; *Complete Thom Bell Sessions* .... (MCA)
Greatest Hits-1976-1986 .... (MCA)
Mama Chicago
Bonnie Koloc; *With You On My Side* ....(FF)
Mama Didn't Lie
Jan Bradley; *Best Of Chess R&B* .... (CSS)
ST/Hairspray ....(MCA)
Mama Done Told Me
Miracles; *Greatest Hits-From The Beginning* ..... (MOT)
Mama Don't Forget To Pray For Me
Diamond Rio; *Diamond Rio* .... (ARI)
Mama Don't You Tear My Clothes
Blind Snooks Eaglin; *Rural Blues* ....(FAN)

Mama Hated Diesels
Commander Cody/Lost Planet Airmen; *We Got A Live*
One Here .... (WB)
Hot Licks Cold Steel & Trucker's Fav. .... (MCA)
Mama He's Crazy
Judds; *Greatest Hits* ....(RCA)
Judds ....(RCA)
Why Not Me ....(RCA)
Mama Kin
Aerosmith; *Aerosmith* ....(COL)
Classics Live ....(COL)
Gems ....(COL)
Live Bootleg ....(COL)
Guns N' Roses; *G N' R Lies* ....(GEF)
Mama Knows The Highway
Hal Ketchum; *Sure Love* ....(CRB)
Mama Let Him Play
Doucette; *Mama Let Him Play* .... (MSH)
Mama Lion
David Crosby & Graham Nash; *Wind On The*
Water .... (MCA)
Mama Said
Shirelles; *Anthology-1959-1964* .... (RHI)
Classics ....(BCT)
Greatest Hits ....(EVR)
Original Rock 'N' Roll Hits Of The '60s ....(RLL)
Super Oldies/'60s-#3 ....(AUF)
Mama Said Knock You Out
L.L. Cool J; *Mama Said Knock You Out* .... (DFJ)
Mama Say
Heptones; *Night Food* .... (ISL)
Mama Told Me Not To Come
Randy Newman; *12 Songs* ....(RPR)
Live ....(RPR)
Randy Newman ....(RPR)
Three Dog Night; *Best Of* .... (MCA)
Billboard Top Rock 'N' Roll Hits-1970 ....(RHI)
Wilson Pickett; *Greatest Hits* ....(ATL)
Mama Tried
Grateful Dead; *Grateful Dead* .... (WB)
John Anderson & Marty Stuart; *Mama's Hungry*
Eyes-Merle Haggard Tribute .... (ARI)
Merle Haggard/Strangers; *Best Of* ....(CAP)
Okie From Muskogee ....(CAP)
Songs I'll Always Sing ....(CAP)
Very Best Of Merle Haggard ....(CAP)
Mama Used To Say
Junior; *Jr.* .... (MER)
Sophisticated Street ....(LON)
Mama Weer All Crazee Now
Quiet Riot; *Condition Critical* .... (PSH)
Mama, I'm Coming Home
Ozzy Osbourne; *No More Tears* ....(EPA)
Mama's Always On Stage
Arrested Development; *3 Years 5 Months 2 Days In The*
Life Of ....(CHR)
Unplugged ....(CHR)
Mama's Fool
Tesla; *Bust A Nut* ....(GEF)
Mama's Hungry Eyes
Emmylou Harris; *Mama's Hungry Eyes-Merle Haggard*
Tribute .... (ARI)
Mama's Never Seen Those Eyes
Forester Sisters; *Forester Sisters* .... (WB)
Mama's Opry
Iris DeMent; *Infamous Angel* .... (WB)
Mama's Pearl
Jackson 5; *3rd Album* ....(MOT)
Anthology .... (MOT)
Compact Command Performances .... (MOT)
Greatest Hits ....(MOT)
Mammas Don't Let Your Babies Grow Up...
Gibson Miller Band; *ST/The Cowboy Way* ....(EPI)
Waylon Jennings & Willie Nelson; *Greatest Hits* .(RCA)
Waylon & Willie ....(RCA)
Willie Nelson; *Greatest Hits & Some That Will Be* (COL)
ST/Electric Horseman ....(COL)
& Family Live ....(COL)
Mindless Child Of Motherhood
Kinks; *Kink Kronikles* ....(RPR)
Momma
Bob Seger; *Beautiful Loser* ....(CAP)

Mommy For A Day
Kitty Wells; *Greatest Hits* .... (MCA)
It Wasn't God Who Made Honky Tonk Angels ..(MSP)
Mommy Where's Daddy
Red Hot Chili Peppers; *Red Hot Chili Peppers* ... (EMI)
Mommy, Can I Go Out & Kill Tonight
Misfits; *Walk Among Us* ....(RUB)
Mother
Barbra Streisand; *Barbra Joan Streisand* ....(COL)
Chicago; *At Carnegie Hall* ....(COL)
Group Portrait ....(COL)
III ....(COL)
Danzig; *Thrall Demonsweatlive* ....(AME)
John Lennon; *John Lennon* ....(CAP)
Live In New York City ....(CAP)
Shaved Fish ....(CAP)
ST/Imagine-The Motion Picture ....(CAP)
John Lennon/Plastic Ono Band; *John Lennon/Plastic*
Ono Band ....(CAP)
Pink Floyd; *The Wall* ....(COL)
Police; *Synchronicity* ....(A&M)
Roy Orbison; *Rare Orbison 2* ....(MON)
Mother Africa
Judy Mowatt; *Welcome* ....(SHA)
Santana; *Welcome* ....(COL)
Mother And Child Reunion
Paul Simon; *Live Rhymin'* .... (WB)
Negotiations & Love Songs 1971-1986 .... (WB)
Paul Simon .... (WB)
Mother Dear
Diana Ross/Supremes; *Motown Legends* .... (MOT)
Styx; *Equinox* ....(A&M)
Mother Earth
Memphis Slim; *Memphis Slim* .... (CSS)
Real Folk Blues .... (CSS)
Merry-Go-Round; *Best Of* .... (RHI)
Nitty Gritty Dirt Band; *Dirt Silver & Gold* ....(UA)
Tom Rush; *Best Of* ....(COL)
Mother Goose
Jethro Tull; *Aqualung* .... (CHR)
Mother In Law
Buddy Guy; *Left My Blues In San Francisco* .... (CSS)
Ernie K-Doe; *Best Of New Orleans R&B-#1* .... (RHI)
Collectables Presents History Of Rock-#7 ....(CLT)
New Orleans Jazz & Heritage Festival-'76 .... (RHI)
Huey Lewis/News; *Four Chords & Several Years*
Ago .... (ELE)
Mother In Law Blues
Junior Parker; *Best Of* ....(MCA)
Mother In Law Song
Martin Mull; *Sex & Violins* .... (MCA)
Mother Mary
Julian Lennon; *Mr. Jordan* ....(ATL)
Sheila E.; *Sex Cymbal* .... (WB)
UFO; *Force It* .... (CHR)
Strangers In The Night .... (CHR)
Mother Nature
Temptations; *Anthology* .... (MOT)
Mother Nature's Son
Beatles; *Box Set* .... (CAP)
White Album ....(CAP)
John Denver; *Evening With* ....(RCA)
Rocky Mountain High ....(RCA)
Mother Popcorn
Aerosmith; *Live Bootleg* ....(COL)
James Brown; *Sex Machine* .... (POL)
Mother Russia
Iron Maiden; *No Prayer For The Dying* .... (EPI)
Renaissance; *Live At Carnegie Hall* ....(SIR)
Tales Of 1001 Nights-#1 ....(SIR)
Turn Of The Cards ....(SIR)
Mother Says
Joe Walsh; *Barnstorm* ....(MOB)
Best Of ....(MCA)
Mother The Queen Of My Heart
Pete Seeger & Arlo Guthrie; *Together In Concert* (RPR)
Mother (You Make Me Want To Be A)
Tammy Wynette; *Greatest Hits-#3* ....(EPI)
Motherhood
Pearl Bailey/Broadway Cast; *Hello Dolly* ....(RCA)
Motherless Child
Eric Clapton; *From The Cradle* .... (DUC)
Steve Miller Band; *Anthology* ....(CAP)
Your Saving Grace ....(CAP)

Motherless Children
Eric Clapton; *461 Ocean Blvd.* .... (RSO)
Crossroads .... (POL)
Mothers Dream
Candlebox; *Candlebox* .... (MAV)
Mothers Of The Disappeared
U2; *The Joshua Tree* .... (ISL)
Mothers Talk
Tears For Fears; *Songs From The Big Chair* ..... (MER)
Tears Roll Down-Greatest Hits-1982-1992 .....(FON)
Mother's Day
7 Seconds; *Soulforce Revolution* .... (RES)
Rick Margitza; *Hope* .... (BLN)
Mother's Eyes
Matthews, Wright & King; *Power Of Love* ....(COL)
Mother's Lament
Cream; *Disraeli Gears* .... (POL)
Mother's Little Helper
Rolling Stones; *Flowers* .... (AKO)
Hot Rocks-1964-1971 .... (AKO)
Through The Past Darkly-Big Hits-#2 .... (AKO)
Tesla; *Five Man Acoustical Jam* .... (GEF)
Motorcycle Mama
Neil Young; *Comes A Time* .... (RPR)
Sailcat; *Back To The '70s-#2* .... (DOM)
Super Hits/'70s-Have A Nice Day-#8 .... (RHI)
Movies Are A Mother To Me
Loudon Wainwright III; *Loudon Wainwright III* .. (ATL)
Music Makin' Mama From Memphis
Hank Snow; *Best Of* ....(RCA)
My Guitar Wants To Kill Your Mama
Frank Zappa; *You Can't Do That On Stage Anymore-#4* ....(RYK)
Mothers Of Invention; *Weasels Ripped My Flesh* ... (BIZ)
My Mom's A Feminist
Kristin Lems; *We Will Never Give Up* ....(CDP)
My Mother Is A Space Cadet
Dweezil Zappa; *45* .... (BAR)
"My Mother The Car" Theme
Original Music; *Television's Greatest Hits-#2* ..... (TVT)
My Mother's Bible
Warrior River Boys; *New Beginnings* .... (ROU)
My Mother's Eyes
Bette Midler; *ST/Divine Madness* .... (ATL)
Clovers; *Love Potion No. 9* .... (EMI)
Forester Sisters; *You Again* ....(WB)
My Mother's Wedding Day
Original Cast; *Brigadoon* ....(RCA)
My Mummy's Dead
John Lennon; *Lennon* .... (CAP)
John Lennon/Plastic Ono Band; *John Lennon/Plastic Ono Band* ....(CAP)
New Mother Nature
Guess Who; *American Woman* .... (RCA)
Best Of ....(RCA)
Papa Loved Mama
Garth Brooks; *Ropin' The Wind* .... (LIB)
Parents Just Don't Understand
D.J. Jazzy Jeff & The Fresh Prince; *He's The D.J. I'm The Rapper* .... (JVA)
Peach Orchard Mamma
Big Joe Williams; *Piney Woods Blues* ....(DEL)
Pistol Packin' Mama
Al Dexter; *Columbia Country Classics-#1-Golden Age* ....(COL)
Great Records Of The Decade-'40s Hits ....(CCB)
Andrews Sisters; *16 Great Performances* .... (MCA)
Boogie Woogie Bugle Girls .... (MCA)
Bing Crosby; *Greatest Hits* .... (MCA)
Glenn Miller/Army Air Force Band; *Nipper's Greatest Hits-'40s-#1* ....(RCA)
Pretty Wreath For Mother's Grave
Reno & Smiley; *1983 Collector's Edition-#9* ..... (IGR)
Rag Mama Rag
Band; *Band* .... (CAP)
Gift Set .... (CAP)
Rock Of Ages-#1 & 2 .... (CAP)
To Kingdom Come-Definitive Collection .... (CAP)
RC's Mom
Dead Milkmen; *Beelzebubba* .... (FEV)
Remember Mother's Day
Al Jolson; *Story-#5* .... (MCA)

Rock Me Mama
Arthur Big Boy Crudup; *Mean Ole Frisco* ....(CLT)
That's All Right Mama ....(RCA)
Blind Snooks Eaglin; *Country Boy In New Orleans* ....(ARH)
Buddy Guy/Junior Mance/Junior Wells; *Buddy & The Juniors* .... (MCA)
Sonny Terry; *Chain Gang Blues* ....(CLT)
Rock Your Mama
Ten Years After; *Alvin Lee & Company* ....(DER)
London Collector ....(LON)
Roll On Big Mama
Joe Stampley; *Biggest Hits* .... (EPI)
Encore .... (EPI)
Greatest Hits .... (EPI)
Truckers' Jukebox-Top Radio Requests .... (EPI)
Roses For Mama
C.W. McCall; *Greatest Hits* .... (POL)
Savannah Mama
Blind Willie McTell; *Early Years 1927-1932* ....(YAZ)
Three Shades Of Blues ....(BIO)
Blind Willie McTell & Memphis Minnie; *Love Changin' Blues* ....(BIO)
Paul Geremia; *My Kinda Place* ....(FF)
Save It, Pretty Mama
Lionel Hampton; *Tempo & Swing* ....(BLU)
Louis Armstrong; *1940s Small Band Sides* ....(BLU)
Louis Armstrong-1928-1931 ....(NIM)
Louis Armstrong & Earl Hines; *#4-Louis Armstrong & Earl Hines* ....(COL)
Teddy Buckner; *Salute To Louis Armstrong* ..... (CRS)
Save Mother Earth
Merl Saunders; *Heavy Turbulence* .... (FAN)
/Friends-Fire Up .... (FAN)
/Rainforest Band-Save The Planet... .... (SUM)
Send A Picture Of Mother
Johnny Cash; *At Folsom Prison & San Quentin* ...(COL)
Shake My Mother's Hand
Bill Monroe/Blue Grass Boys; *Mule Skinner Blues* (RCA)
She's A Bad Mama Jama
Carl Carlton; *Carl Carlton* .... (20)
Shop Around
Captain & Tennille; *Greatest Hits* ....(A&M)
Miracles; *Hi-We're The Miracles* .... (MOT)
Smokey Robinson/Miracles; *16 #1 Hits From The Early '60s* .... (MOT)
Anthology ....(MOT)
Every Great Motown Song-First 25 Years ......(MOT)
Shortenin' Bread
Andrews Sisters; *50th Anniversary Collection-#2* (MCA)
Sam McNeil/Dent Wimmer/Others; *Old Originals-#2* ....(ROU)
Sonny Terry; *Folkways Years-1944-1963* .... (FLW)
Sometimes I Feel Like A Motherless Child
Dave Van Ronk; *Folksinger* .... (PRS)
Inside ....(FAN)
Grant Green; *Feelin' The Spirit* .... (BLN)
Iron City ....(MUS)
Jerry Butler; *Gold* .... (VJ)
Mormon Tabernacle Choir; *Songs Of The Civil War & Stephen Foster* ....(SMC)
Odetta; *Essential* ....(VAN)
O.V. Wright; *O.V. Wright* .... (MCA)
Peter, Paul & Mary; *The Song Will Rise* ....(WB)
Van Morrison; *Poetic Champions Compose* ...... (MER)
Squeezebox
Who; *By Numbers* .... (MCA)
Greatest Hits .... (MCA)
Hooligans .... (MCA)
Who's Better Who's Best-Very Best Of .... (MCA)
Stop Your Half Steppin' Mama
Ben Vereen; *Here I Am* .... (ACC)
Signed Sealed Delivered .... (FFT)
Sugar Mama
Bonnie Raitt; *Collection* ....(WB)
Home Plate ....(WB)
John Lee Hooker; *Blues-#2* .... (CSS)
House Of The Blues .... (CSS)
Sweet Daddy (Your Mama's Done Gone Mad)
Little Brother Montgomery; *Chicago-Living Legends-South Side Blues* ....(RVR)
Sweet Mama
Allman Brothers Band; *Win Lose Or Draw* ....(POL)

Sweet Mama Goodtimes
Mickey Gilley; *Greatest Hits-#2* .... (EPI)
Sweet Mama Hurry Home Or I'll Be Gone
Leon Redbone; *On The Track* .... (WB)
Sweet Mother Texas
Eddy Raven; *Greatest Hits* .... (WB)
Sylvia's Mother
Dr. Hook; *Dr. Hook & The Medicine Show*
Revisited .... (COL)
   Greatest Hits & More .... (CAP)
   Super Hits/'70s-Have A Nice Day-#8 .... (RHI)
Take Me Home, Country Roads
John Denver; *Evening With* .... (RCA)
   Greatest Hits .... (RCA)
   Poems Prayers & Promises .... (RCA)
   Take Me Home, Country Roads-& Other Hits ...(RCA)
Toots/Maytals; *Brand New Second-Hand* ....(RYK)
Tell Mama
Etta James; *Essential* .... (CSS)
   Soul Hits-#1 .... (RHI)
   Tell Mama .... (CSS)
Janis Joplin; *Janis* .... (COL)
Savoy Brown; *Anthology* .... (DER)
   Street Corner Talking ....(DER)
That's All Right (Mama)
Arthur "Big Boy" Crudup; *Best Of The Blues* .... (PRR)
   That's All Right (Mama) ....(RCA)
Carl Perkins; *Restless-Columbia Recordings* ......(COL)
Elvis Presley; *Complete Sun Sessions* .... (RCA)
   For LP Fans Only ....(RCA)
   Sun Story .... (RHI)
   Sun's Greatest Hits ....(RCA)
Marty Robbins; *Essential-1951-1982* ....(COL)
Merl Saunders/J. Garcia/B. Vitt/J. Kahn; *Live At*
Keystone .... (FAN)
Paul McCartney; *CHOBA B CCCP-Russian*
Album .... (CAP)
Rick Nelson; *Stay Young-Epic Recordings* .... (EPI)
Rod Stewart; *Every Picture Tells A Story* .... (MER)
   Vintage .... (MER)
Vince Gill; *ST/Honeymoon In Vegas* .... (EPI)
Thinkin' 'Bout Your Mother
Freewheelers; *Freewheelers* .... (DGC)
Three Times A Lady
Commodores; *All The Great Hits* .... (MOT)
   All The Great Love Songs .... (MOT)
   Endless Love-Motown Greatest Love Songs ..... (MOT)
   Greatest Hits .... (MOT)
   Natural High .... (MOT)
Tie Your Mother Down
Queen; *Classic Queen* .... (HOL)
   Live At Wembley '86 ....(HOL)
   Live Killers ....(HOL)
True Fine Mama
Little Richard; *Georgia Peach* .... (SPE)
   His Biggest Hits .... (SPE)
TV Mama
Big Joe Turner; *Atlantic Blues-Guitar* .... (ATL)
   Texas Style ....(EVD)
Dizzy Gillespie/Others; *Trumpet Kings Meet Joe*
Turner .... (PAB)
Freddie King; *Freddie King* ....(RSO)
Johnny Winter; *Nothin' But The Blues* ....(BS)
Leon Haywood; *It's Me Again* ....(CAS)
Vision Of Mother
Ricky Skaggs; *Don't Cheat In Our Hometown* .... (EPI)
R. Stanley/J. Marshall/A. Krauss; *Saturday Night &*
Sunday Morning ....(FRC)
Your Mama Don't Dance
Loggins & Messina; *Best Of-Friends* ....(COL)
   Loggins & Messina ....(COL)
   On Stage ....(COL)
   Pop Classics Of The '70s ....(COL)
Poison; *Open Up And Say Ahhhh* ....(CAP)
   Swallow This Live ....(CAP)
Your Mom's In My Business
K-Solo; *Tell The World My Name* .... (ATL)
Your Mother Should Know
Beatles; *Box Set* ....(CAP)
   Magical Mystery Tour ....(CAP)

MOTORCYCLES

Blue Motorcycle Eyes
Havana 3 A.M.; *Havana 3 A.M.* .... (IRS)
Leader Of The Pack
Bette Midler; *Divine Miss M* .... (ATL)
   ST/Divine Madness .... (ATL)
Original Cast; *Leader Of The Pack* .... (ELE)
Shangri-Las; *21 Number One Hits* .... (OSR)
   Billboard Top Rock 'N' Roll Hits-1964 .... (RHI)
   Girl Groups-Story Of A Sound .... (MOT)
   Golden Hits Of .... (MER)
   Oldies But Goodies-#15 .... (OSR)
   Radioactive Hits-#2 .... (ACC)
   Remember The Shangri-Las At Their Best ...... (CLT)
Little Honda
Beach Boys; *Absolute Best-#1* .... (CAP)
   All Summer Long .... (CAP)
   Best Of .... (CAP)
   Spirit Of America .... (CAP)
Hondells; *Beach Classics* .... (DHL)
   Cruisin'-1964 .... (INC)
Moter-bike In Afrika
Peter Hammill; *Future Now* .... (BP)
Motorcycle
Love & Rockets; *Love & Rockets* .... (BEG)
Motorcycle Boys
Bill Molenhof; *All Pass By* .... (CEX)
Motorcycle Driver
Joe Satriani; *The Extremist* .... (REL)
Motorcycle Emptiness
Manic Street Preachers; *Generation Terrorists* ....(COL)
Motorcycle Mama
Neil Young; *Comes A Time* .... (RPR)
Sailcat; *Back To The '70s-#2* .... (DOM)
   Super Hits/'70s-Have A Nice Day-#8 ...... (RHI)
Motorcycle Mystics
Dave Stewart/Spiritual Cowboys; *Honest* .... (ARI)
Motorcycle Song
Arlo Guthrie; *Alice's Restaurant* .... (RPR)
   Best Of .... (RPR)
Soul Brothers; *Three Hour Tour* .... (SI)
My White Bicycle
Nazareth; *Classics-#16* .... (A&M)
   Hot Tracks .... (A&M)

MOUNTAINS, Hills, Valleys, Volcanoes

Ain't No Mountain High Enough
Diana Ross; *20/20* .... (MOT)
   25 #1 Hits From 25 Years .... (MOT)
   Diana Ross .... (MOT)
   Every Great Motown Song-First 25 Years ...... (MOT)
   Greatest Hits .... (MOT)
   Greatest Songs By Ashford & Simpson .... (MOT)
   Motown Legends .... (MOT)
   Motown Story .... (MOT)
   Motown's Biggest Pop Hits .... (MOT)
   TV ST/Diana .... (MOT)
Marvin Gaye & Tammi Terrell; *20 Greatest Songs In*
Motown History .... (MOT)
   Classic Duets .... (MOT)
   Greatest Hits .... (MOT)
   Live At The London Palladium .... (MOT)
   Motown Grammy R & B .... (MOT)
   Performances Of The '60s & '70s .... (MOT)
   United .... (MOT)
Allegheny Moon
Patti Page; *Golden Hits* .... (MER)
   Greatest Hits .... (COL)
Alpine Milkman
Randy Erwin; *'Til The Cows Come Home/Cowboy*
Rhythm .... (ROM)
Away On The Mountain
Jimmie Rodgers; *Best Of-Legendary* .... (RCA)
   First Sessions-1927-28 .... (ROU)
   My Rough & Rowdy Ways .... (RCA)
   This Is ....(RCA)
Banjo In The Hills
Stanley Brothers/C. Story/Jim & Jesse; *Banjo In The*
Hills .... (STR)

Banjo On The Mountain
Doug Dillard Band; *Heartbreak Hotel* ....(FF)
Barstool Mountain
Moe Bandy; *Greatest Hits* ....(COL)
Wayne Carson; *45* .... (ELE)
Beautiful Hills Of Galilee
Hazel Dickens; *Old-Timey Gospel Music* .... (ROU)
Big Rock Candy Mountain
Pete Seeger; *20 Golden Pieces Of* ....(BLD)
Tex Ritter; *Capitol Collectors Series* ....(CAP)
Black Mountain Blues
Bessie Smith; *Collection* ....(COL)
Janis Joplin; *ST/Janis* ....(COL)
Black Mountain Breakdown
Youngbloods; *Youngbloods* ....(RCA)
Black Mountain Rag
Doc Watson; *Doc Watson* .... (VAN)
Essential-#2 .... (VAN)
Newport Country Music & Blues .... (VAN)
Doc Watson/Hot Rize/Dan Crary/P. Rowan;
Tellulive ....(FF)
Nitty Gritty Dirt Band; *Will The Circle Be
Unbroken* .... (EMI)
Black Mountain Side
Led Zeppelin; *Led Zeppelin* ....(ATL)
Blue Canadian Rockies
Byrds; *Sweetheart Of The Rodeo* ....(COL)
Gene Autry; *50th Anniversary* ....(REP)
Live From Madison Square Garden ....(REP)
Jimmy C. Newman; *Cajun Cowboy* ....(PLN)
Blue Ridge Mountain Blues
Doc Watson; *Essential* .... (VAN)
John Fogerty; *Blue Ridge Rangers* ....(FAN)
Norman Blake; *Directions* ....(TAK)
Blue Ridge Mountain Sky
Marshall Tucker Band; *New Life* .... (AJK)
Blue Ridge Mountains Turnin' Green
Charley Pride; *Amazing Love* ....(RCA)
Blueberry Hill
Elvis Presley; *Loving You* ....(RCA)
Recorded Live On Stage ....(RCA)
Fats Domino; *Greatest Hits* ....(EVR)
Greatest Hits ....(MCA)
My Blue Heaven-Best Of-#1 ....(EMI)
Little Richard; *Big Hits* ....(CRS)
Louis Armstrong; *Best Of* ....(MCA)
Essential .... (VAN)
I Like Jazz: Essence Of ....(COL)
Bluebirds Over the Mountain
Beach Boys; *Absolute Best-#2* ....(CAP)
Friends/20/20 ....(CAP)
Sunshine Dream ....(CAP)
'69 ....(CAP)
Ritchie Valens; *Best Of* ....(RHI)
History Of ....(RHI)
Ritchie Valens ....(RHI)
Cabin Home On The Hill
Ricky Skaggs; *Sweet Temptation* ....(SH)
Cabin On A Mountain
Country Gazette; *Bluegrass Tonight* ....(FF)
Cabin On The Hill
Flatt & Scruggs; *Columbia Historic Edition* ......(COL)
Car On A Hill
Joni Mitchell; *Court & Spark* ....(ASY)
Chapel On The Hill
Mello-Kings; *Greatest Hits* ....(CLT)
Child In These Hills
Jackson Browne; *Jackson Browne* ....(ASY)
Cliffs Of Dover
Eric Johnson; *Ah Via Musicom* ....(CAP)
Climb Ev'ry Mountain
Mary Martin/Original Cast; *Sound Of Music* .....(COL)
Mormon Tabernacle Choir; *Climb Ev'ry
Mountain* ....(COL)
Trapp Family Singers; *Sound Of Music* .... (WB)
Cumberland Blues
Grateful Dead; *Europe '72* .... (WB)
What A Long Strange Trip It's Been ....(WB)
Workingman's Dead ....(WB)
Cumberland Gap
Woody Guthrie; *Early Years* ....(TRD)
Woody Guthrie & Cisco Houston; *Folk Songs* .... (STO)

Cumberland Mountain #9
Charlie Daniels Band; *Saddletramp* ....(EPI)
Volunteer Jam 3 & 4 ....(EPI)
Dance On A Volcano
Genesis; *Seconds Out* .... (ATL)
Trick Of The Tail ....(ATC)
Dead Man's Hill
Indigo Girls; *Swamp Ophelia* .... (EPI)
Diamond Head
Beach Boys; *Friends* ....(RPR)
Down In The Valley
Elvis Presley; *Reconsider Baby* ....(RCA)
Leadbelly; *Defense Blues-Golden Classics-#2* ....(CLT)
Pete Seeger; *American Favorite Ballads-#1* ...... (FLW)
East Kentucky Mountains
Anne Hills; *Don't Panic (Panic Is On/Don't
Explain)* ....(HOG)
Eruption
Van Halen; *Van Halen* .... (WB)
Fire On The Mountain
Bill Monroe/Blue Grass Boys; *Kentucky
Bluegrass* ....(MCA)
Grateful Dead; *Dead Set* ....(ARI)
Shakedown Street ....(ARI)
Marshall Tucker Band; *Greatest Hits* ....(CPC)
Searchin' For A Rainbow ....(AJK)
South's Greatest Hits ....(CPC)
Flint Hill Special
Flatt & Scruggs; *Golden Era* .... (ROU)
Nitty Gritty Dirt Band; *Will The Circle Be
Unbroken* .... (EMI)
Foggy Mountain Breakdown
Flatt & Scruggs; *20 All-Time Great Recordings* ...(COL)
Truckers' Jukebox: Top Radio Requests ....(EPI)
Lester Flatt; *Foggy Mountain Breakdown* ....(RCA)
Live Bluegrass Festival ....(RCA)
Tony Trischka; *Banjoland* ....(ROU)
Fool On The Hill
Beatles; *1967-1970* ....(CAP)
Box Set ....(CAP)
Magical Mystery Tour ....(CAP)
Go Tell It On The Mountain
Bobby Darin; *25th Day Of December* ....(ATC)
Dolly Parton; *Home For Christmas* ....(COL)
Garth Brooks; *Beyond The Season* ....(LIB)
Simon & Garfunkel; *Collected Works* ....(COL)
Wednesday Morning 3 A.M. ....(COL)
Weavers; *On Tour* ....(VAN)
Gonna Build A Mountain
Monkees; *Live-1967* .... (RHI)
Original Broadway Cast; *Stop The World-I Want To Get
Off* ....(POL)
Sammy Davis, Jr.; *Greatest Songs* ....(CCB)
Green Rolling Hills
Bottle Hill; *Rumor In Their Own Time-#1* ....(BIO)
Emmylou Harris; *Quarter Moon In A Ten Cent
Town* .... (WB)
Heather On The Hill
Gene Kelly; *ST/Brigadoon* .... (MCA)
Original Cast; *Brigadoon* ....(CSP)
Henry
New Riders Of The Purple Sage; *Best Of* ....(COL)
Bill Graham Presents Fillmore-Last Days ....(EPA)
Home Home On The Road ....(COL)
New Riders Of The Purple Sage ....(COL)
High On A Hill Top
Merle Haggard/Strangers; *Best Of* ....(CAP)
High On A Hill Top ....(CAP)
High Sierra
Keith Carradine; *I'm Easy* ....(ASY)
Higher Ground
Stevie Wonder; *Innervisions* .... (MOT)
Original Musiquarium ....(MOT)
UB40; *Promises And Lies* ....(VIA)
Hill Where The Lord Hides
Chuck Mangione; *Best Of* ....(A&M)
Best Of ....(MER)
Classics-#6 ....(A&M)
Evening Of Magic ....(A&M)
Friends & Love ....(MER)
Together ....(MER)
Hills Of Alabam'
Kathy Mattea; *Willow In The Wind* .... (MER)

Hills Of Arkansas
Black Oak Arkansas; *Black Oak Arkansas* ......(ATC)
Hills Of Kentucky
Debby McClatchy/Red Clay Ramblers; *Debby McClatchy/Red Clay Ramblers* ....(GRE)
Kendalls; *Kendalls* ....(GUS)
Hills Of Old Wyomin'
Sons Of The Pioneers; *Country Music Hall Of Fame* .... (MCA)
Tex Ritter; *Country Music Hall Of Fame* .... (MCA)
House On The Hill
Stevie Wonder; *For Once In My Life* .... (MOT)
Turtles; *Turtle Soup* .... (RHI)
Turtle Wax-Best Of-#2 .... (RHI)
House Upon A Hill
Paul Anka; *She's A Lady* .... (ACC)
Very Best Of .... (RAN)
If You've Got Love
John Michael Montgomery; *Kickin' It Up* .... (ATL)
In The Hall Of The Mountain King
Duke Ellington; *Three Suites* ....(COL)
Electric Light Orchestra; *On The Third Day* .....(JET)
Sounds Incorporated; *History Of British Rock-#3* . (RHI)
Kentucky Hills Of Tennessee
Commander Cody/Lost Planet Airmen; *Hot Licks Cold Steel Trucker's Favorites* .... (MCA)
King Of The Hill
Minutemen; *Ballot Result* .... (SST)
Project: Mersh .... (SST)
Quiet Riot; *Quiet Riot* .... (PSH)
Roger McGuinn; *Back From Rio* .... (ARI)
King Of The Mountain
Bon Jovi; *7800 Degrees Fahrenheit* .... (MER)
Ladies Of The Canyon
Joni Mitchell; *Ladies Of The Canyon* .... (RPR)
Landslide
AC/DC; *Flick Of The Switch* .... (ATL)
Fleetwood Mac; *25 Years-The Chain* .... (WB)
Fleetwood Mac .... (RPR)
Live .... (WB)
Smashing Pumpkins; *Pisces Iscariot* .... (VIA)
Like A Rock
Bob Seger/Silver Bullet Band; *Like A Rock* ......(CAP)
Love Can Move Mountains
Celine Dion; *Celine Dion* .... (EPI)
Loves Me Like A Rock
Oak Ridge Boys; *Best Of* ....(COL)
Paul Simon; *Greatest Hits Etc.* ....(COL)
Live Rhymin' ....(COL)
Negotiations & Love Songs-1971-1986 ....(WB)
There Goes Rhymin' Simon ....(COL)
Man On The Silver Mountain
Ritchie Blackmore; *Rainbow* .... (POL)
Ritchie Blackmore/Rainbow; *Finyl Vinyl* .... (MER)
Mansion On The Hill
Bruce Springsteen; *Nebraska* ....(COL)
Emmylou Harris/Nash Ramblers; *At The Ryman* . (RPR)
Hank Williams; *40 Greatest Hits* .... (POL)
Lovesick Blues .... (POL)
Neil Young/Crazy Horse; *Arc Weld* .... (RPR)
Ragged Glory .... (RPR)
Mocking Bird Hill
Patti Page; *16 Most Requested Songs* ....(COL)
Golden Hits .... (MER)
Greatest Hits ....(COL)
Russ Morgan; *Best Of* .... (MCA)
Mountain Blues
Sonny Terry; *From Spirituals To Swing* .... (VAN)
Great Blues Men .... (VAN)
Mountain Dew
Charlie Daniels Band; *Volunteer Jam* ....(CPC)
Clancy Brothers; *Greatest Hits* .... (VAN)
Doc Watson; *Old Timey Concert* .... (VAN)
Eric Weissberg; ST/*Dueling Banjos From 'Deliverance'* ....(WB)
Stanley Brothers; *Stanley Series-Vol 1-#2* ....(COP)
Stanley Series-Vol 2-#2 ....(COP)
Mountain Greenery
Ella Fitzgerald; *Rodgers & Hart Songbook* ....(VRV)
Tony Bennett; *Rodgers & Hart Songbook* ....(DRG)
Sings More Great Rodgers & Hart ....(IPV)
Mountain Jam
Allman Brothers Band; *Eat A Peach* .... (POL)

Mountain Music
Alabama; *Greatest Hits* ....(RCA)
Mountain Music ....(RCA)
Mountain Of Love
Charley Pride; *Greatest Hits-#2* ....(RCA)
Solid Country Gold ....(RCA)
Harold Dorman; *Collectables Presents History Of Rock-10* ....(CLT)
Johnny Rivers; *Anthology-1964-1977* .... (RHI)
Best Of .... (EMI)
Mountains
Prince; *Parade-ST/Under The Cherry Moon* ...... (WB)
Rita Coolidge; *Rita Coolidge* ....(A&M)
Mountains Of Burma
Midnight Oil; *Blue Sky Mining* ....(COL)
Mountains Of The Moon
Grateful Dead; *Aoxomoxoa* .... (WB)
Mountain's High
Dick & Dee Dee; *'Til My Dreamin' Comes True* .(CAP)
My Swiss Mountain Lullaby
Montana Slim; *60 Years Of Country Music* ......(RCA)
My Tennessee Mountain Home
Dolly Parton; *Best Of* ....(RCA)
Best Of A Great Year-#3 ....(RCA)
My Tennessee Mountain Home ....(RCA)
Rose Maddox; *Reckless Love & Bold Adventure* ..(TAK)
No Matter How High
Oak Ridge Boys; *American Dreams* .... (MCA)
No Mountains In The State Of Kansas
Reilly & Maloney; *Everyday* .... (FRK)
Oklahoma Hills
Hank Thompson; *All-Time Greatest Hits* ....(CCB)
Jack Guthrie/Oklahomans; *Birth Of A Dream-Capitol's Early Hits* ....(CAP)
Great Records/Decade-'40s Hits-Country ....(CCB)
Kay Starr; *Country* ....(CRS)
On Squirrel Hill
Ian Matthews; *Legacy-Collection Of New Folk Music* .... (WH)
Walking A Changing Line .... (WH)
On Top Of Old Smokey
Bing Crosby; *Radio Years-#3* ....(CRS)
Weavers; *Best Of* .... (MCA)
Greatest Hits .... (VAN)
Reunion At Carnegie Hall-1963-#2 .... (VAN)
Oregon Hill
Cowboy Junkies; *Black Eyed Man* .... (RCA)
Oregon Hills
Martin Oberschelp; *Nightingale Lightdance* .... (HO)
Oregon Mountains
Woody Simmons; *Oregon Mountains* .... (DEP)
Ozark Mountain Jubilee
Oak Ridge Boys; *Deliver* .... (MCA)
Greatest Hits-#2 .... (MCA)
Ozark Mountain Jubilee .... (MSP)
Peace In The Valley
Carole King; *Rhymes & Reasons* .... (EPI)
Elvis Presley; *Golden Celebration* ....(RCA)
Legendary Performer #1 ....(RCA)
Million Dollar Quartet ....(RCA)
Johnny Cash; *At San Quentin* ....(COL)
Classic Cash-Hall Of Fame Series .... (MER)
J.L. Lewis/Carl Perkins-*The Survivors* ....(COL)
Purple Mountain
Scott Cossu; *Wind Dance* .... (WH)
Windham Hill Retrospective .... (WH)
Rattlesnake Mountain
Patrick Sky; *Patrick Sky* .... (VAN)
Red River Valley
Gene Autry; *Country Music Hall Of Fame* ....(COL)
Cowboy Hall Of Fame .... (REP)
Western Classics ....(COL)
Pete Seeger; *American Favorite Ballads-#5* ..... (FLW)
Redwood Hill
Vassar Clements; *Westport Drive* .... (MIN)
Ridgetop
Jesse Colin Young; *Best Of-Solo Years* .... (RHI)
On The Road .... (WB)
Song For Juli .... (WB)
Ridin' Down The Canyon
Gene Autry; *Columbia Historic Edition* ....(COL)
Western Classics ....(COL)
Riders In The Sky; *Cowboy Way* .... (MCA)

Willie Nelson & Leon Russell; *One For The Road* ....(COL)
River Deep Mountain High
  Erasure; *Innocents* .... (SIR)
  Four Tops; *Anthology* ....(MOT)
  Ike & Tina Turner; *Best Of* .... (EMI)
    Phil Spector's Greatest Hits .... (SPC)
    Proud Mary-Best Of .... (EMI)
  Tina Turner; *Simply The Best* .... (CAP)
Rocky Mountain Blues
  Billie Holiday; *Billie's Blues* .... (BLN)
  Duke Ellington; *Okeh Ellington* ....(COL)
  Lightnin' Hopkins; *Double Blues* .... (FAN)
    Soul Blues .... (PRS)
  Lightnin' Hopkins & Sonny Terry; *Gotta Move Your Baby* .... (PRS)
Rocky Mountain Breakdown
  Poco; *Forgotten Trail-1969-1974* .... (EPI)
    Ride The Country .... (EPI)
    Very Best Of .... (EPI)
Rocky Mountain High
  John Denver; *Evening With* ....(RCA)
    Greatest Hits-#1 ....(RCA)
    Rocky Mountain High ....(RCA)
    Take Me Home Country Roads & Other Hits ....(RCA)
Rocky Mountain Music
  Eddie Rabbitt; *All-Time Greatest Hits* .... (WB)
    Best Of .... (WB)
    Rocky Mountain Music ....(ELE)
    Ten Years Of Greatest Hits ....(CAP)
Rocky Mountain September
  C.W. McCall; *45* ....(OOP)
Rocky Mountain Suite
  John Denver; *Evening With* ....(RCA)
    Farewell To Andromeda ....(RCA)
Rocky Mountain Way
  Joe Walsh; *Best Of* ....(MCA)
    Classic Rock-#1 .... (MCA)
    Heavy Metal Memories .... (RHI)
    The Smoker You Drink The Player You Get .... (MCA)
    You Can't Argue With A Sick Mind ....(MCA)
Rocky Top
  Conway Twitty; *Hello Darlin'* .... (MCA)
  Flying Burrito Brothers; *Close Encounters To The West Coast* ....(RLX)
  Osborne Brothers; *Best Of* ....(MCA)
    Yesterday Today & The Osborne Brothers ..... (MCA)
  Roy Clark; *In Concert* ....(MCA)
  White Mountain Singers; *Best* .... (FOL)
'Round About The Mountain
  Kingston Trio; *At Large/Here We Go Again!* ..... (CAP)
Running Up That Hill
  Kate Bush; *Hounds Of Love* .... (EMI)
    The Whole Story .... (EMI)
  Kate Bush & David Gilmour; *Secret Policeman's Third Ball-The Music* .... (VIA)
Secret Mountain Hideout
  Michael Murphey; *Blue Sky Night Thunder* .... (EPI)
Secret Of The Andes
  Victor Feldman; *Secret Of The Andes* ....(PAJ)
  Victor Feldman/Generation Band; *Best Of* ...... (NVA)
She'll Be Coming 'Round The Mountain
  Four Freshmen/Stan Kenton & Orchestra; *Live At Butler University* ....(CW)
  Mormon Tabernacle Choir; *This Land Is Your Land* ....(COL)
She's My Rock
  George Jones; *19 Hot Country Requests-#2* .... (EPI)
    First Time Live .... (EPI)
    Ladies Choice .... (EPI)
Shine On Ruby Mountain
  Kenny Rogers/First Edition; *All-Time Greatest Hits-#2* .... (MSP)
    Best Of .... (KT)
Silverthorn Mountain
  Merle Haggard; *Friend In California* .... (EPI)
Singing Hills
  Gene Autry; *50th Anniversary* .... (REP)
  Slim Whitman; *Best Of-1952-1972* .... (RHI)
    Una Paloma Blanca-Best Of .... (EMI)
Small Hills Of Offaly
  Irish Tradition; *Times We've Had* ....(GRE)
Smokey Mountain Rain
  Ronnie Milsap; *Greatest Hits* ....(RCA)

Solid
  Ashford & Simpson; *Solid* ....(CAP)
    Solid Plus Seven ....(CAP)
Solsbury Hill
  Peter Gabriel; *Peter Gabriel* ....(ATC)
    Plays Live ....(GEF)
    Shaking The Tree-16 Golden Greats ....(GEF)
Song From Half Mountain
  Dan Fogelberg; *Souvenirs* .... (EPI)
Stony Mountain, West Virginia
  Jim & Jesse; *In The Tradition* .... (ROU)
Suddenly There's A Valley
  Reba McEntire; *Feel The Fire* .... (MER)
Sugar Hill Saturday Night
  Charlie Daniels Band; *Midnight Wind* .... (EPI)
Sugar Mountain
  Neil Young; *Decade* ....(RPR)
  Neil Young/Crazy Horse; *Live Rust* ....(RPR)
Sunny Hills
  Bobby Caldwell; *Carry On* ....(SD)
Sunny Side Of The Mountain
  Bill Monroe; *Bean Blossom* .... (MCA)
  Jimmy Martin/Sunny Mountain Boys; *Best Of Bluegrass* .... (KT)
  Nitty Gritty Dirt Band; *Will The Circle Be Unbroken* .... (EMI)
Sunrise Over Haleakala
  Merl Saunders & Jerry Garcia; *Blues From The Rainforest-Musical Suite* .... (SUM)
Swingtime In The Rockies
  Benny Goodman; *Birth Of Swing* .... (BLU)
    Carnegie Hall Jazz Concert ....(COL)
    ST/Swing Kids ....(HOL)
Take Me Home, Country Roads
  John Denver; *Evening With* ....(RCA)
    Greatest Hits ....(RCA)
    Poems Prayers & Promises ....(RCA)
    Take Me Home, Country Roads-& Other Hits ...(RCA)
  Toots/Maytals; *Brand New Second-Hand* ....(RYK)
Tales Of Kilimanjaro
  Carlos Santana; *Havana Moon* ....(COL)
  Santana; *Zebop* ....(COL)
Texas Hills
  Sons Of The Pioneers; *Western Country* .... (GRA)
That Ain't No Mountain
  Stacy Dean Campbell; *Lonesome Wins Again* ....(COL)
There Goes The Mountain
  Tom Paxton; *Heroes* .... (VAN)
    New Songs From The Briarpatch .... (VAN)
There Is A Mountain
  Donovan; *Greatest Hits* .... (EPI)
    Troubadour-Definitive Collection .... (EPI)
Twelve Thirty (Young Girls Are Coming..)
  Mamas & The Papas; *16 Of Their Greatest Hits* . (MCA)
    Best Of .... (MCA)
    Papas & The Mamas .... (MCA)
Up Where We Belong
  Joe Cocker; *Live* ....(CAP)
  Joe Cocker & Jennifer Warnes; *Island Story-1962-1987-25th Anniversary* .... (ISL)
    ST/Officer And A Gentleman .... (ISL)
Visionary Mountains
  Joan Armatrading; *Whatever's For Us* .... (A&M)
Volcano
  Band; *Cahoots* ....(CAP)
  Count Basie; *Essential-#2* ....(COL)
  Jimmy Buffett; *Boats Beaches Bars & Ballads* ... (MGR)
    Songs You Know By Heart-Greatest Hits ...... (MCA)
    Volcano .... (MCA)
  Rupture; *Hardness Of The World* .... (COT)
    Slave .... (COT)
Warm Valley
  Duke Ellington; *Money Jungle* .... (BLN)
  Paul Desmond; *Pure Desmond* ....(CBA)
When The Moon Comes Over The Mountain
  Kate Smith; *16 Most Requested Songs* ....(COL)
    Best Of ....(RCA)
White Cliffs Of Dover
  Kay Kyser/Orchestra; *16 Most Requested Songs/'40s-#1* ....(COL)
  Lee Andrews/Hearts; *Biggest Hits* .... (CLT)
  Mystics; *16 Golden Classics* .... (CLT)
  Righteous Brothers; *Anthology-1962-1974* .... (RHI)
    Greatest Hits ....(VRV)

MOUNTAINS — MOVIES

Rosemary Clooney; *For The Duration* .... (CCJ)
White Mountain
Genesis; *Trespass* .... (MCA)
Wild Mountain Honey
Steve Miller Band; *Fly Like An Eagle* .... (CAP)
Greatest Hits-1974-1978 .... (CAP)
Wild Mountain Thyme
Armstrong Family; *Wheel Of The Year-Thirty Years
With* .... (FF)
Byrds; *Fifth Dimension* .... (COL)
Joan Baez; *Farewell Angelina* .... (VAN)
Wolverton Mountain
Claude King; *American Originals* ....(COL)
Best .... (GUS)
Billboard Top Country Hits-1962 .... (RHI)
You Gave Me A Mountain
Elvis Presley; *Aloha From Hawaii* ....(RCA)
Always On My Mind ....(RCA)
In Concert ....(RCA)
Marty Robbins; *All-Time Greatest Hits* ....(COL)
Biggest Hits ....(COL)
Essential-1951-1982 ....(COL)
You Made A Rock Of A Rolling Stone
Oak Ridge Boys; *Seasons* .... (MCA)

MOVIES, Actors & Actresses

*See Also: HOLLYWOOD, SHOW BIZ,
TELEVISION*

35 Millimeter Dreams
Garland Jeffreys; *Ghost Rider* .... (A&M)
Ghost Writer .... (A&M)
Act Naturally
Beatles; *Help!* .... (CAP)
Yesterday & Today .... (CAP)
Buck Owens; *Beatle Originals* .... (RHI)
Buck Owens & Ringo Starr; *Act Naturally* ....(CAP)
Buck Owens/Buckaroos; *Live At Carnegie Hall* .. (CMF)
Charley Pride; *Country Pride* ....(RCA)
Johnny Russell; *20 Great Country Hits* ....(RCA)
Alone At A Drive In Movie
Olivia Newton-John & John Travolta; *ST/Grease* (RSO)
Original Broadway Cast; *Grease* .... (POL)
Another Cheap Western/Western Movies
Michael Murphey; *Peaks Valleys Honky Tonks &
Alleys* .... (EPI)
At The Movies
Bad Brains; *Rock For Light* ....(CRL)
Youth Are Getting Restless-Live .... (CRL)
B Movie
Delbert McClinton; *Second Wind* ....(CPC)
Elvis Costello/Attractions; *Get Happy!* ....(RYK)
B Movies
Fabulous Poodles; *Mirror Stars* .... (EPI)
Back It Up
Nils Lofgren; *Best Of* .... (A&M)
Classics-#13 .... (A&M)
Night After Night .... (A&M)
Nils Lofgren .... (A&M)
"B" Movie Box Car Blues
Blues Brothers; *Best Of* .... (ATL)
Briefcase Full Of Blues .... (ATL)
Delbert McClinton; *Live From Austin* ....(ALL)
Can I Have My Money Back
Gerry Rafferty; *Can I Have My Money Back* .... (MCA)
Celluloid Heroes
Joan Jett; *Hit List* ....(CBA)
Kinks; *Come Dancing-Best Of-1977-1986* .... (ARI)
Everybody's In Show Biz .... (RHI)
Greatest ....(RCA)
Cinema Show
Genesis; *Seconds Out* .... (ATL)
Cowboy Movie
David Crosby; *If I Could Only Remember My
Name* .... (ATL)
Creature Feature
Uptown Express; *45* .... (SUT)
Dirty Movies
Van Halen; *Fair Warning* .... (WB)
Drive-In Movies & Dashboard Lights
Nanci Griffith; *Storms* .... (MCA)

Elvis & Marilyn
Leon Russell; *Americana* ....(PRD)
Face On The Cutting Room Floor
Nitty Gritty Dirt Band; *Live Two Five* ....(CAP)
More Great Dirt-Best Of-#2 .... (WB)
Here In The Real World
Alan Jackson; *Here In The Real World* .... (ARI)
Hollywood Movie Girls
Dusty Springfield; *It Begins Again* .... (UA)
It's All In The Movies
Merle Haggard/Strangers; *Country's Greatest
Hits-#6-Superstars* ....(PRY)
I've Seen That Movie Too
Elton John; *Goodbye Yellow Brick Road* ....(POL)
James Dean
Eagles; *On The Border* ....(ASY)
Key Largo
Bertie Higgins; *Just Another Day In Paradise* .....(KAT)
King Of The Silver Screen
Alice Cooper; *Lace & Whisky* .... (MET)
Late Late Late Show
Stella Parton; *Stella Parton* .... (ELE)
Late Late Show
Dakota Station; *45* ....(CAP)
Nat King Cole; *Big Band Cole* .... (BLN)
Like A Movie
Climax Blues Band; *Shine On* .... (SIR)
Troy Shondell; *45* ....(COM)
Moonlight Drive-In
Turner Nichols; *Moonlight Drive-In* .... (BNA)
Motion Pictures
Neil Young; *On The Beach* ....(RPR)
Movie
Aerosmith; *Permanent Vacation* .... (GEF)
Doors; *American Prayer* .... (ELE)
Jim Morrison; *ST/The Doors* .... (ELE)
Movie Buff
Glenn Sutton; *Close Encounters Of The Sutton
Kind* .... (MER)
Movie In My Mind
Original London Cast; *Miss Saigon* .... (GEF)
Movie Magg
Carl Perkins; *Blue Suede Shoes* .... (SUN)
Original Sun Greatest Hits .... (RHI)
Movie Pictures
Kinks; *Low Budget* .... (ARI)
Movie Queen
Bill Anderson; *Scorpio* .... (MCA)
Prolifics; *45* .... (UA)
Movieola
Country Joe McDonald; *Paris Sessions* .... (VAN)
Movies
Hothouse Flowers; *Home* ....(LON)
Miami Sound Machine; *Primitive Love* ....(EPI)
Statler Brothers; *Best Of-Rides Again-#2* .... (MER)
Country American Loves .... (MER)
Steely Dan; *Katy Lied* .... (MCA)
Movies Are A Mother To Me
Loudon Wainwright III; *Loudon Wainwright III* .. (ATL)
Movie, The
Tom Waits; *Devout Catalyst* .... (GRD)
Optimistic Voices
Bette Midler; *Bette Midler* .... (ATL)
Pencil Thin Mustache
Jimmy Buffett; *Boats Beaches Bars & Ballads* ... (MGR)
Living & Dying In 3/4 Time .... (MCA)
Songs You Know By Heart .... (MCA)
You Had To Be There .... (MCA)
Put Me In The Movies
Daryle Ryce; *Carolina Blue* .... (ROU)
Riding With A Movie Star
L7; *Hungry For Stink* .... (SLS)
Road Movie To Berlin
They Might Be Giants; *Flood* .... (ELE)
Roy Rogers
Elton John; *Goodbye Yellow Brick Road* ....(POL)
Sad Movies (Make Me Cry)
Sue Thompson; *Collectables History Of Rock-#10* (CLT)
Greatest Hits ....(CCB)
Saturday Matinee
Gordon Brisker; *About Charlie* .... (DCO)
Saturday Morning Movies
Bonnie Koloc; *At Her Best* ....(OVA)
Bonnie Koloc ....(OVA)

Page 420 — The Green Book Of Songs By Subject

Saturday Night At The Movies
Drifters; *16 Greatest Hits* .... (TRP)
  All-Time Greatest Hits & More-1959-1965 ..... (ATL)
  Golden Hits .... (ATL)
  Save The Last Dance For Me .... (FFT)
Silent Movies
Neil Sedaka; *Singer- Songwriter-Melody Maker* .. (ACC)
  Solitaire .... (FFT)
  Superbird .... (INT)
Silver Screen
Little Feat; *Representing The Mambo* ....(WB)
Stupid War Movies
Paleface; *Paleface* .... (POL)
Sunday Morning Movies
Bonnie Koloc; *At Her Best* .... (OVA)
  Bonnie Koloc .... (OVA)
That's Why God Made The Movies
Paul Simon; *ST/One-Trick Pony* ....(WB)
Thriller
Michael Jackson; *Thriller* .... (EPI)
True Western Movie
Chris LeDoux; *Songs Of Rodeo & Country* .... (LIB)
Wake Up, Little Susie
Everly Brothers; *All They Had To Do Was Dream* (RHI)
  All-Time Greatest Hits .... (CCB)
  American Graffiti-#3 .... (MCA)
  Everly Brothers .... (RHI)
  Oldies But Goodies-#7 .... (OSR)
  Very Best Of ....(WB)
Grateful Dead; *History Of-#1-Bear's Choice* ......(WB)
Simon & Garfunkel; *Concert In Central Park* ....(WB)
Western Movies (My Baby Loves)
Olympics; *All-Time Greatest Hits Of Rock & Roll* .(CCB)
  American Graffiti-#3 .... (MCA)
  Best Of .... (VJ)
  Jumpin' Jive '50s .... (PRY)
Wide Screen
Barbra Streisand; *Lazy Afternoon* ....(COL)

MUSIC, Bands, Musicians, Singing, Songs

*See Also: DANCE, JUKEBOX, MUSICAL
INSTRUMENTS, PARTY, RADIO, RHYTHM*

33 R.P.M. Soul
Michelle Shocked; *Arkansas Traveler* .... (MER)
  Say What U Want-Rock The Vote .... (MER)
33, 45, 78 (Record Time)
Kathy Mattea; *Lonesome Standard Time* .... (MER)
Add Some Music To Your Day
Beach Boys; *Best Of (Good Vibrations)* .... (RPR)
  Sunflower ....(CAR)
  Ten Years Of Harmony .... (CAR)
Alexander's Ragtime Band
Al Jolson/Bing Crosby; *Al Jolson Story-#1* ...... (MCA)
  Immortal Al Jolson .... (MCA)
All Day Music
War; *All Day Music* .... (UA)
  Greatest Hits .... (UA)
  Live .... (UA)
All Our Favorite Songs
Oak Ridge Boys; *All Our Favorite Songs* ....(COL)
All The Children Sing
Todd Rundgren; *Anthology (1968-1985)* .... (RHI)
  Hermit Of Mink Hollow .... (RHI)
All Those Years Ago
George Harrison; *Best Of Dark Horse
1976-1989* .. (DKH)
  Somewhere In England .... (DKH)
"American Bandstand" Theme
Original Music; *Television's Greatest Hits-#3* ..... (TVT)
American Music
Blasters; *Blasters* .... (SLS)
  Collection .... (SLS)
Pointer Sisters; *So Excited* .... (PNT)
Violent Femmes; *Why Do Birds Sing?* ....(SLS)
And The Angels Sing
Ella Fitzgerald; *Lady Time* .... (PAB)
And Your Bird Can Sing
Beatles; *Revolver* .... (CAP)
  Yesterday & Today .... (CAP)
Another Sad Love Song
Toni Braxton; *Toni Braxton* .... (LAF)

Anyone Can Whistle
Cleo Laine; *Sings Sondheim* ....(RCA)
Original Broadway Cast; *Anyone Can Whistle* ...(COL)
Are You Sure Hank Done It This Way
Hank Williams, Jr.; *Rowdy* ....(W/C)
Waylon Jennings; *Greatest Hits* ....(RCA)
Bach, Beethoven, Mozart & Me
Phil Ochs; *Greatest Hits* .... (A&M)
Band From Chicago
Max Creek; *Windows* ....(RLX)
Band On The Run
Paul McCartney; *Tripping The Live Fantastic* ....(CAP)
Paul McCartney/Wings; *All The Best* ....(CAP)
  Band On The Run ....(CAP)
  Greatest ....(CAP)
  Over America ....(CAP)
Barroom Country Singer
Roger Whittaker; *Greatest Hits* ....(RCA)
Be Bop Baby
Rick Nelson; *Best Of* .... (EMI)
  Greatest Hits .... (RHI)
  Legendary Masters .... (UA)
Bebe Le Strange
Heart; *Bebe Le Strange* .... (EPI)
  Greatest Hits/Live .... (EPI)
Bennie & The Jets
Elton John; *Billboard Top Rock 'N' Roll Hits-1974* (RHI)
  Classic Rock-#1 .... (MCA)
  Goodbye Yellow Brick Road .... (POL)
  Greatest Hits .... (POL)
  Here & There .... (POL)
Big Music
Waterboys; *Pagan Place* .... (CHR)
Black Velvet
Alannah Myles; *Alannah Myles* .... (ATL)
Robin Lee; *Black Velvet* .... (ATL)
Blue Must Be The Color Of The Blues
Willie Nelson; *There'll Be No Teardrops Tonight* .. (UA)
Boomin' System
L.L. Cool J; *Mama Said Knock You Out* .... (DFJ)
Brand New Country Star
Jimmy Buffett; *Living & Dying In 3/4 Time* ..... (MCA)
Brass Band In African Chimes
Simple Minds; *45* .... (A&M)
Bright Lights & Country Music
Bill Anderson; *Greatest Hits-#1* .... (MCA)
Can You Hear The Music?
Rolling Stones; *Goats Head Soup* ....(RS)
Canned Music
Dan Hicks/Hot Licks; *Striking It Rich* .... (MCA)
Can't Stop The Music
Daryl Hall & John Oates; *No Goodbyes* .... (ATL)
  War Babies .... (ATL)
Village People; *Can't Stop The Music* .... (CAS)
  Greatest Hits .... (RHI)
Champagne Jam
Atlanta Rhythm Section; *Are You Ready* .... (POL)
  Champagne Jam .... (POL)
Cheap Shot
John Cougar Mellencamp; *Early Years* .... (RHI)
  Kid Inside .... (RHI)
  Nothin' Matters & What If It Did ....(RIV)
Chords Of Fame
Phil Ochs; *Chords Of Fame* .... (A&M)
  Greatest Hits .... (A&M)
  War Is Over: Best Of .... (A&M)
Chorus
Erasure; *Chorus* .... (SIR)
Club At The End Of The Street
Elton John; *Sleeping With The Past* .... (MCA)
Cowboy Band
Billy Dean; *Men'll Be Boys* .... (LIB)
Cowboy Singer
Sonny Curtis; *Love Is All Around* .... (ELE)
  Sonny Curtis .... (ELE)
Cum On Feel The Noise
Quiet Riot; *Metal Health* .... (PSH)
Dance To The Music
Sly/Family Stone; *Anthology* .... (EPI)
  Frat Rock! .... (RHI)
  Frat Rock-#2 .... (RHI)
  Greatest Hits .... (EPI)
Dazz
Brick; *Good High* ....(BNG)

Dear Mr. Fantasy
Traffic; *Best Of* .... (ISL)
  Dear Mr. Fantasy .... (ISL)
  Welcome To The Canteen .... (ISL)
Dedicated To The One I Love
Mamas & The Papas; *Best Of* .... (MCA)
  Farewell To The First Golden Era .... (MCA)
  Orig. Classic Oldies/'50s-'60s-#13 .... (MCA)
Shirelles; *Anthology: 1959-1964* .... (RHI)
  Greatest Hits .... (EVR)
  Oldies But Goodies-#10 .... (OSR)
  Super Oldies/'50s-#4 .... (AUF)
Devil Comes Back To Georgia
Marc O'Connor; *Heroes* .... (WB)
Devil Went Down To Georgia
Charlie Daniels Band; *Billboard Top Hits-1979* .. (RHI)
  Decade Of Hits .... (EPI)
  Me & The Boys .... (EPI)
  Million Mile Reflections .... (EPI)
  ST/Urban Cowboy .... (ASY)
Dim Lights Thick Smoke & Loud Loud Music
Flatt & Scruggs; *Golden Era* .... (ROU)
Flying Burrito Brothers; *Close Encounters Of The West*
Coast ....(RLX)
  Farther Along-Best Of ....(A&M)
Do I Hear A Waltz?
Elizabeth Allen; *Broadway Magic-1960s* ....(COL)
Original Broadway Cast; *Do I Hear A Waltz?* ... (SMC)
Do Re Mi
John Cougar Mellencamp; *Folkways: Tribute To*
Guthrie/Leadbelly ....(COL)
Julie Andrews; *ST/Sound Of Music* ....(RCA)
Original Cast; *Sound Of Music* ....(COL)
Ry Cooder; *Ry Cooder* .... (RPR)
  Showtime ....(WB)
Woody Guthrie; *Dust Bowl Ballads* ....(ROU)
Do Wa Diddy Diddy
Manfred Mann; *Best Of* .... (EMI)
  Billboard Top Rock 'N' Roll Hits-1964 .... (RHI)
  History Of British Rock-#2 .... (RHI)
Do You Like Good Music
Arthur Conley; *45* ....(OOP)
Don't Leave Your Records In The Sun
John Hartford; *Mark Twang* .... (FF)
Don't Play That Song
Aretha Franklin; *30 Greatest Hits* .... (ATL)
  Greatest Hits .... (ATL)
  Live At Fillmore West .... (ATL)
Ben E. King; *Atlantic R&B 1947-1974*
(1958-1962) .... (ATL)
  Greatest Hits .... (ATC)
  Stand By Me-Best Of .... (ATL)
Don't Play That Song (You Lied)
Aretha Franklin; *30 Greatest Hits* .... (ATL)
  Golden Age Of Black Music-1970-1975 .... (ATL)
  Greatest Hits .... (ARL)
Don't Rock The Jukebox
Alan Jackson; *Don't Rock The Jukebox* .... (ARI)
Don't Sing A Song About Texas
Charlie Walker; *Texas Gold* .... (PLN)
Don't Sing No Songs About Texas
David Hunter; *45* ....(NAT)
Don't Stop The Music
Yarbrough & Peoples; *Two Of Us* .... (MER)
Dr. Music
Blue Oyster Cult; *Extraterrestrial Live* ....(COL)
  Mirrors ....(COL)
Duchess
Genesis; *Duke* .... (ATL)
  Three Sides Live .... (ATL)
Stranglers; *Greatest Hits 1977-1990* .... (EPI)
  IV .... (IRS)
Dusic
Brick; *Brick* ....(BNG)
Edge Of Seventeen
Stevie Nicks; *Bella Donna* .... (MOD)
Empty Garden (Hey Hey Johnny)
Elton John; *Greatest Hits-1976-1986* .... (MCA)
  Jump Up! .... (MCA)
Euphonius Whale
Dan Hicks/Hot Licks; *Last Train To Hicksville* .. (MCA)
Every Long Song
Greg Kihn Band; *Kihntinued* .... (BES)

Face The Music
RTZ; *Return To Zero* .... (GIA)
Famous Groupies
Wings; *London Town* ....(CAP)
Follow The Music
Harry Connick, Jr.; *She* ....(COL)
Follow The Music Further
Harry Connick, Jr.; *She* ....(COL)
Free Man In Paris
Joni Mitchell; *Court & Spark* .... (ASY)
  Shadows & Light .... (ASY)
Funiculi, Funicula
Mario Lanza; *Legendary Tenor* ....(RCA)
Funky Music Sho Nuff Turns Me On
Temptations; *Anthology* .... (MOT)
Getting In Tune
Who; *Who's Next* .... (MCA)
God's Own Singer
Flying Burrito Brothers; *Burrito Deluxe* .... (A&M)
  Close Up The Honky Tonks ....(A&M)
  Farther Along: Best Of ....(A&M)
Harmony
Bar-Kays; *Coldblooded* .... (STX)
Elton John; *Goodbye Yellow Brick Road* .... (POL)
Happy Mondays; *Pills 'N' Thrills & Bellyaches* .... (ELE)
John Conlee; *45* ....(COL)
Limeliters; *Live In Concert* ....(CRS)
Take 6 (featuring Queen Latifah); *Join The Band* (RPR)
Havin' A Party
Norma Jean; *Norma Jean* .... (BRS)
Pointer Sisters; *Havin' A Party* .... (MCA)
Rod Stewart & Ronnie Wood; *MTV's Unplugged...And*
Seated ....(WB)
Sam Cooke; *Best Of* ....(RCA)
  Feel It ....(RCA)
  Live At The Harlem Square Club ....(RCA)
  This Is ....(RCA)
Southside Johnny/Asbury Jukes; *Havin' A Party*
With .... (EPI)
Homey Don't Play Dat
Terminator X; & *The Valley Of The Jeep Beets* .... (PD)
Honky Tonk Song
Webb Pierce; *Best Of* .... (MCA)
  Golden Hits #2 .... (PLN)
Hooked On Music
Mac Davis; *Best Of Country Rock* .... (KT)
  Very Best & More ....(CAS)
Pat Travers; *Go For What You Know* .... (POL)
  Makin' Magic .... (POL)
How Do You Keep The Music Playing
James Ingram & Patti Austin; *It's Your Night* ... (QUE)
  ST/Listen Up-Lives Of Quincy Jones .... (QUE)
How To Be A Country Star
Statler Brothers; *Best Of-Rides Again-#2* .... (MER)
Humming Song
Martin Mull; *I'm Everyone I Ever Loved* .... (MCA)
Hurdy Gurdy Man
Donovan; *Greatest Hits* .... (EPI)
  Hurdy Gurdy Man .... (EPI)
Hymn
James Taylor; *One Man Dog* ....(WB)
Patti Smith Group; *Wave* .... (ARI)
Peter, Paul & Mary; *Late Again* ....(WB)
Hymn 43
Jethro Tull; *Aqualung* .... (CHR)
  Living In The Past .... (CHR)
Hymn For The Dudes
Mott The Hoople; *Greatest Hits* ....(COL)
  Mott ....(COL)
Hymn To Him
Audrey Hepburn; *ST/My Fair Lady* ....(COL)
Julie Andrews/Original Cast; *My Fair Lady* ......(COL)
Hymn To Me
Brinsley Schwarz; *Brinsley Schwarz* ....(CAP)
I Can Hear Music
Beach Boys; *Friends/20/20* ....(CAP)
  Sunshine Dream ....(CAP)
I Feel Like Singing
Dan Hicks/Hot Licks; *Where's The Money?* ..... (MCA)
I Got Rhythm
Ella Fitzgerald; *George & Ira Gershwin Songbook* (VRV)
Happenings; *45* ....(VGO)
Judy Garland; *Collector's Items-1936-1945* ..... (MCA)

Robert Palmer; *Glory Of Gershwin Featuring Larry Adler* .... (MER)
I Gotta Have A Song
Stevie Wonder; *Looking Back* .... (MOT)
   Signed Sealed & Delivered .... (MOT)
I Guess That's Why...Call It The Blues
Elton John; *Greatest Hits-1976-1986* .... (MCA)
   Too Low For Zero .... (MCA)
I Hear A Rhapsody
John Coltrane; *Lush Life* .... (PRS)
   More Lasting Than Bronze .... (PRS)
   Prestige Twofer Giants-#2 .... (PRS)
I Hear A Symphony
Diana Ross/Supremes; *16 #1 Hits From The Early '60s* .... (MOT)
   25th Anniversary .... (MOT)
   Anthology .... (MOT)
   Evening With Diana Ross .... (MOT)
   Every Great #1 Hit .... (MOT)
   Good Feeling Music/Big Chill Gen.-#2 .... (MOT)
   Greatest Hits .... (MOT)
   I Hear A Symphony .... (MOT)
   Motown Story .... (MOT)
I Hear Music
Anita O'Day; *Big Band Session* .... (VRV)
   Live At Mingos .... (EML)
I Hear The Music
Billie Holiday; *Golden Year-#2* .... (COL)
   Story-#3 .... (COL)
I Let A Song Go Out Of My Heart
Bill Jennings; *Stompin' With Bill* .... (CLT)
Duke Ellington; *Braggin' In Brass-Immortal 1938 Year* .... (POR)
Joe Pass; *Portraits Of Duke Ellington* .... (PAB)
Teresa Brewer; *Sophisticated Lady* .... (COL)
Tony Bennett; *Jazz* .... (COL)
I Love Music
O'Jays; *Collector's Items* .... (PI)
   Family Reunion .... (PI)
   Philadelphia Classics .... (PI)
   Ten Years Of #1 Hits .... (PI)
Rozalla; *ST/Carlito's Way* .... (EPX)
I Love New Orleans Music
Ronnie Milsap; *Inside* .... (RCA)
I Sang Dixie
Dwight Yoakam; *Buenas Noches From A Lonely Room* .... (RPR)
   Just Lookin' For A Hit .... (RPR)
I Try To Think About Music
Patty Loveless; *When Fallen Angels Fly* .... (EPI)
I Was Country When Country Wasn't Cool
Barbara Mandrell; *Greatest Hits* .... (MCA)
   Live .... (MCA)
I Watched It All (On My Radio)
Lionel Cartwright; *I Watched It All On The Radio* .... (MCA)
I Write The Songs
Barry Manilow; *Greatest Hits-#2* .... (ARI)
   Live .... (ARI)
   Tryin' To Get The Feeling .... (ARI)
If I Could Sing Something In Spanish
Shelly West; *Don't Make Me Wait On The Moon* .(VVA)
If You're Gonna Play In Texas
Alabama; *Live* .... (RCA)
   Roll On .... (RCA)
   Stars Are Out In Texas .... (RCA)
It Don't Mean A Thing
Duke Ellington; *Carnegie Hall Concert* .... (PRS)
Duke Ellington & Teresa Brewer; *It Don't Mean A Thing* .... (COL)
Ella Fitzgerald; *In London* .... (PAB)
   /Duke At The Conte D'Azur .... (VRV)
It Was Almost Like A Song
Ronnie Milsap; *60 Years Of Country Music* ..... (RCA)
   Greatest Hits .... (RCA)
   It Was Almost Like A Song .... (RCA)
It's The Same Old Song
Four Tops; *Anthology* .... (MOT)
   Billboard Top R&B Hits-1965 .... (RHI)
   Compact Command Performances .... (MOT)
   Greatest Hits .... (MOT)
I'll Always Remember That Song
Charlie Daniels Band; *Whiskey* .... (EPI)

I'll Play For You
Seals & Crofts; *Greatest Hits* .... (WB)
   I'll Play For You .... (WB)
I'll Play The Blues For You
Albert King; *16 Original Big Hits-#2* .... (STX)
   Chronicle .... (STX)
   I'll Play The Blues For You .... (STX)
   Live .... (TOM)
   Superblues-#1-All-Time Classic Blues .... (STX)
I'll Write A Song For You
Earth, Wind & Fire; *All 'N All* .... (COL)
I'm Just A Singer In A Rock & Roll Band
Moody Blues; *Seventh Sojourn* .... (POL)
   This Is The .... (POL)
   Voices In The Sky-Best Of .... (T/P)
I'm My Own Walkman
Bobby McFerrin; *The Voice* .... (ELE)
I'm Playing For You
Ronnie Milsap; *True Believer* .... (LIB)
Jam
Michael Jackson; *Dangerous* .... (EPI)
Jamming
Bob Marley/Wailers; *Babylon By Bus* .... (TUF)
   Exodus .... (TUF)
   Legend .... (TUF)
Jody Like A Melody
David Allan Coe; *17 Greatest Hits* .... (COL)
   For The Record-First 10 Years .... (COL)
Johnny B. Goode
Chuck Berry; *Chess Box* .... (CSS)
   Classic Rock-#2 .... (MCA)
   Greatest Hits .... (EVR)
   Roll Over Beethoven .... (ALL)
   ST/American Graffiti .... (MCA)
Elvis Presley; *From Memphis To Vegas* .... (RCA)
   In Concert .... (RCA)
Grateful Dead; *Bill Graham Presents Fillmore-Last Days* .... (EPA)
Johnny Winter; *Live* .... (COL)
   Second Winter .... (COL)
Johnny One Note
Judy Garland; *Best Of-From MGM Classic Films* (MCA)
Mary Martin/Original Cast; *Babes In Arms* .... (SSP)
Johnny Strikes Up The Band
Warren Zevon; *Excitable Boy* .... (ASY)
   Quiet Normal Life-Best Of .... (ASY)
Jones On The Jukebox
Becky Hobbs; *All Keyed Up* .... (RCA)
Junkie For My Music
Lonnie Jordan; *Different Moods Of Me* .... (MCA)
Just A Song Before I Go
Crosby, Stills & Nash; *CSN* .... (ATL)
   Replay .... (ATL)
Keep On Singing
Helen Reddy; *Greatest Hits* .... (CAP)
   Love Song For Jeffrey .... (CAP)
Killing Me Softly With His Song
Luther Vandross; *Songs* .... (EPI)
Roberta Flack; *Atlantic R&B 1947-1974-#6-(1966-1969)* .... (ATL)
   Best Of .... (ATL)
   Golden Age Of Black Music-1970-1975 ...... (ATL)
   Killing Me Softly With His Song .... (ATL)
Lady Sings The Blues
Billie Holiday; *All Or Nothing At All* .... (VRV)
   Essential Carnegie Hall Concert .... (VRV)
   History Of The Real Billie Holiday .... (VRV)
   Lady Sings The Blues .... (VRV)
Large Time
Atlanta Rhythm Section; *Are You Ready* .... (POL)
   Champagne Jam .... (POL)
Last Love Song
Cat Stevens; *Back To Earth* .... (A&M)
Hank Williams, Jr.; *14 Greatest Hits* .... (POL)
   Standing In The Shadows .... (POL)
Last Of The Singing Cowboys
Marshall Tucker Band; *Running Like The Wind* . (MCA)
Last Song
Elton John; *The One* .... (MCA)
Late In The Evening
Paul Simon; *Negotiations & Love Songs-1971-1986* .... (WB)
   One-Trick Pony .... (WB)
Simon & Garfunkel; *Concert In Central Park* ..... (WB)

Leader Of The Band
Dan Fogelberg; *Greatest Hits* .... (FM)
Innocent Age .... (FM)
Let Me In
Bonnie Raitt; *Takin' My Time* .... (WB)
Sensations; *Billboard Top R&B Hits-1962* .... (RHI)
Chess Box .... (CSS)
Cruisin'-1962-1963 .... (DHL)
Vintage Music-Classics/'50s-'60s-#6 .... (MCA)
Let Me Sing For You
Kenny Rogers; *Daytime Friends* .... (LIB)
Let Me Sing Your Blues Away
Grateful Dead; *Wake Of The Flood* .... (GRD)
Let Me Sing & I'm Happy
Al Jolson; *Best Of* .... (MCA)
Story-#3 .... (MCA)
Let There Be Music
Orleans; *Before The Dance* .... (ELE)
Let There Be Music .... (ELE)
Let's Face The Music And Dance
Ella Fitzgerald; *Irving Berlin Always* .... (VRV)
Tony Bennett; *Bennett/Berlin* .... (COL)
Jazz ....(COL)
Life In A Song
Marshall Tucker Band; *Carolina Dreams* ....(CPC)
Life Is A Long Song
Jethro Tull; *Living In The Past* .... (CHR)
Life Is A Song Worth Singing
Johnny Mathis; *I'm Coming Home* ....(COL)
Teddy Pendergrass; *Life Is A Song Worth Singing* .. (PI)
Life's A Song
Kool/Gang; *Force* .... (DL)
Life's Been Good
Eagles; *Live* .... (ASY)
Joe Walsh; *But Seriously Folks* .... (ASY)
ST/FM .... (MCA)
Lights
Styx; *Cornerstone* .... (A&M)
Listen To A Country Song
Loggins & Messina; *On Stage* ....(COL)
Sittin' In ....(COL)
Lynn Anderson; *Country Chartbusters-#2* ....(COL)
Greatest Hits ....(COL)
Listen To The Band
Monkees; *Greatest Hits* .... (ARI)
Present .... (RHI)
Listen To The Music
Doobie Brothers; *Best Of* .... (WB)
Farewell Tour .... (WB)
Toulouse Street .... (WB)
Little Night Music
Original Cast; *Little Night Music* ....(COL)
Live For The Music
Bad Company; *10 From 6* .... (ATL)
Run With The Pack .... (SS)
Livingston Saturday Night
Jimmy Buffett; *Son Of A Son Of A Sailor* .... (MCA)
ST/FM .... (MCA)
Load Out/Stay
Jackson Browne; *Running On Empty* .... (ASY)
Lone Star Beer & Bob Wills Music
Red Steagall; *Lone Star Beer & Bob Wills Music* (MCA)
Texas Country .... (MCA)
Longfellow Serenade
Neil Diamond; *12 Greatest Hits-#2* ....(COL)
Love At The Greek ....(COL)
On The Way To The Sky ....(COL)
Serenade ....(COL)
Lost In The Fifties Tonight
Ronnie Milsap; *Greatest Hits-#2* ....(RCA)
Lost In The Fifties Tonight ....(RCA)
Louisiana Cajun Band
Jimmy C. Newman; *Backstage At The Grand Ole Opry* ....(RCA)
Cajun Country .... (DEL)
Louisiana Cajun Rock Band
Carol Channing & Jimmy C. Newman; */Others-& Her Country Friends* .... (PLN)
Love Song
Anne Murray; *Greatest Hits* ....(CAP)
Love Song ....(CAP)
Cure; *Disintegration* ....(ELE)
Mixed Up ....(ELE)

Damned; *Final Damnation* .... (RES)
Light At The End Of The Tunnel .... (MCA)
Elton John; *Here & There* .... (POL)
Tumbleweed Connection .... (POL)
Kenny Rogers; *20 Greatest Hits* .... (LIB)
Love Will Turn You Around .... (LIB)
Lee Greenwood; *Inside Out* .... (MCA)
Loggins & Messina; *Full Sail* .... (COL)
Madonna; *Like A Prayer* .... (SIR)
Oak Ridge Boys; *American Made* .... (MCA)
Greatest Hits-#2 .... (MCA)
Original Cast; *Pippin* .... (MOT)
Threepenny Opera .... (POL)
Tesla; *Five Man Acoustical Jam* .... (GEF)
Great Radio Controversy .... (GEF)
Make Love To The Music
Maria Muldaur; *Southern Winds* .... (WB)
Make The Music Magic
Be Bop Deluxe; *Modern Music* .... (HAR)
Making Music For Money
Jimmy Buffett; *A-1-A* .... (MCA)
Kenny Rogers; *Gambler* .... (UA)
Mama Let Him Play
Doucette; *Mama Let Him Play* .... (MSH)
Mama's Opry
Iris DeMent; *Infamous Angel* .... (WB)
Master Blaster
Stevie Wonder; *Hotter Than July* .... (MOT)
Original Musiquarium .... (MOT)
Melody
David Crosby; *Oh Yes I Can* .... (A&M)
Rolling Stones; *Black & Blue* .... (RS)
Melody Of Love
Frank Sinatra & Ray Anthony; *Capitol Collector Series* .... (CAP)
Memphis Soul Stew
King Curtis; *Atlantic Jazz-Soul* .... (ATL)
Atlantic R&B 1947-1974-#6-(1966-1969) ..... (ATL)
Best Of .... (ATL)
Golden Soul .... (ATL)
Live At The Fillmore West .... (ATL)
Mercury Poisoning
Graham Parker/Rumour; *Live Sparks* .... (ARI)
"Merrie Melodies" Theme
Original Music; *Television's Greatest Hits-#2* ... (TVT)
Minstrel Boy
Boston Pops Orchestra/Arthur Fiedler; *Irish Album* ....(RCA)
Irish Night At The Pops ....(RCA)
John McDermott; *Battlefields Of Green-Songs Of Love/Loss* .... (ANG)
Minstrel In The Gallery
Jethro Tull; *20 Years Of-Boxed Set* .... (CHR)
Bursting Out .... (CHR)
Minstrel In The Gallery .... (CHR)
Original Masters .... (CHR)
Repeat-Best Of-#2 .... (CHR)
Modern Music
Be Bop Deluxe; *Best Of-Raiding The Divine Archives* .... (CAP)
Modern Music .... (HAR)
Motown Song
Larry John McNally; *Fade To Black* ....(ATC)
Rod Stewart; *Vagabond Heart* .... (WB)
Motownphilly
Boyz II Men; *Cooleyhighharmony* .... (MOT)
Mountain Music
Alabama; *Greatest Hits* ....(RCA)
Mountain Music ....(RCA)
Mr. Melody
Natalie Cole; *Collection* ....(CAP)
Live ....(CAP)
Natalie ....(CAP)
Mr. Record Man
Willie Nelson; *Best Of* .... (EMI)
Horse Called Music ....(COL)
& Family Live ....(COL)
Music
Cat Stevens; *Buddha & The Chocolate Box* ..... (A&M)
Cleo Laine; *I Am A Song* ....(RCA)
Live At Carnegie Hall ....(RCA)
Exile; *Hang On To Your Heart* .... (EPI)
James Taylor; *Gorilla* .... (WB)

R.E.O. Speedwagon; *Decade Of Rock & Roll* ...... (EPI)
  Live .... (EPI)
  T.W.O. .... (EPI)
Music Band
  War; Music Band .... (MCA)
Music For Money
  Nick Lowe; *Pure Pop For Now People* ....(COL)
Music In Dreamland
  Be Bop Deluxe; *Best Of & The Rest Of* .... (HAR)
  Best Of-Raiding The Divine Archive ....(CAP)
  Futurama .... (HAR)
Music Is You
  John Denver; *Back Home Again* ....(RCA)
  Evening With ....(RCA)
Music Makin' Mama From Memphis
  Hank Snow; *Best Of* ....(RCA)
Music Must Change
  Who; *Who Are You* .... (MCA)
Music Never Stopped
  Grateful Dead; *Blues For Allah* .... (GRD)
  One From The Vault .... (GRD)
Music Of The Night
  Michael Crawford; *Premiere Collection-Best Of A.L.*
  Webber .... (MCA)
  Original London Cast; *Phantom Of The Opera* ... (POL)
Music That Makes Me Dance
  Barbra Streisand/Original Cast; *Funny Girl* ......(CAP)
  Michael Feinstein & Jule Styne; *M. Feinstein Sings Jule*
  Styne Songbook .... (ELE)
Music To Watch Girls By
  Andy Williams; *Greatest Hits-#2* ....(COL)
Music Trance
  Ben E. King; *Music Trance* .... (ATL)
Musical Box
  Genesis; *Genesis* ....(CHS)
  Live .... (ATL)
  Nursery Cryme .... (ATL)
  Seconds Out .... (ATL)
My Music
  Loggins & Messina; *Best Of Friends* ....(COL)
  Full Sail ....(COL)
Nashville Cats
  Lovin' Spoonful; *Anthology* .... (RHI)
  Hums Of ....(OOP)
Nashville Pickin'
  Doc Watson; *Southbound* .... (VAN)
Never Ending Song Of Love
  Conway Twitty & Loretta Lynn; *Lead Me On* .. (MCA)
  Delaney & Bonnie; *Best Of* .... (RHI)
  Delaney & Bonnie/Friends; *Super Hits/'70s-Have A Nice*
  Day-#16 .... (RHI)
Nickel For The Fiddler
  Guy Clark; *Old No. 1* ....(SH)
Nightclubbing
  Grace Jones; *Nightclubbing* .... (ISL)
  Iggy Pop; *Idiot* ....(RCA)
  TV Eye/1977 Live ....(RCA)
Nightshift
  Commodores; *Nightshift* .... (MOT)
No More Songs
  Phil Ochs; *Chords Of Fame* .... (A&M)
  Greatest Hits .... (A&M)
  No More Songs .... (A&M)
  The War Is Over-Best Of .... (A&M)
Now That's Country
  Marty Stuart; *This One's Gonna Hurt You* ...... (MCA)
Now They Call It Swing
  Billie Holiday; *Golden Years #1* ....(COL)
  Quintessential-#5-1937-1938 ....(COL)
  Story-#3 ....(COL)
Nowadays Clancy Can't Even Sing
  Buffalo Springfield; *Buffalo Springfield* ....(ATC)
  Retrospective .... (ATC)
Oh Yeah
  Roxy Music; *Flesh & Blood* .... (RPR)
  Street Life-20 Great Hits .... (RPR)
Old Songs
  Barry Manilow; *Greatest Hits-#3* .... (ARI)
  If I Should Love Again .... (ARI)
One Man Band
  Moe Bandy; *Greatest Hits* ....(CCB)
  You Haven't Heard The Last Of Me .... (MCA)
  Roger Daltrey; *Daltrey* .... (MCA)

Three Dog Night; *Joy To The World-Greatest*
Hits .... (MCA)
One More Goodtime Band In Texas
  Leon Rausch; *Rausch Touch* .... (STH)
Parker's Band
  Steely Dan; *Pretzel Logic* .... (MCA)
Phantom Of The Opera
  Iron Maiden; *Iron Maiden* ....(CAP)
  Live After Death (World Slavery Tour) ....(CAP)
  Original London Cast; *Phantom Of The Opera* ... (POL)
Piano Man
  Billy Joel; *Greatest Hits-#1 & 2* ....(COL)
  Piano Man ....(COL)
  Rock Classics Of The '70s ....(COL)
  Thelma Houston; *Motown Superstar Series-#20* . (MOT)
Play A Simple Melody
  Bing Crosby; *Best Of Bing* .... (MCA)
Play It All Night Long
  Warren Zevon; *Bad Luck Streak In Dancing*
  School .... (ASY)
  Quiet Normal Life-Best Of .... (ASY)
Play That Funky Music
  Vanilla Ice; *Extremely Live* .... (SBK)
  To The Extreme .... (SBK)
  Wild Cherry; *Billboard Top Rock 'N' Roll*
  Hits-1978 .... (RHI)
  ST/Queens Logic .... (EPI)
  Wild Cherry .... (EPI)
Play Those Oldies Mr. DJ
  Anthony/Sophomores; *WCBS-FM 101-History Of*
  Rock-Doo-Wop-#2 .... (CLT)
Polly-Wolly-Doodle
  Leon Redbone; *Live!* .... (PRR)
  On The Track ....(WB)
  Mance Lipscomb; *#3-Texas Songster In A Live*
  Performance .... (ARH)
  Pete Seeger/Woody Guthrie/Cisco Houston; *Lonesome*
  Valley .... (FLW)
Pop Goes The Weasel
  3rd Bass; *Derelicts Of Dialect* .... (DFJ)
  Bing Crosby; *Where The Blue Of The Night Meets*
  The... ....(BIO)
  Boston Pops Orchestra/Arthur Fiedler; *Forever*
  Fielder ....(RCA)
  Merry Macs; *Small Fry-Capitol Sings Kids Songs...* (CAP)
Pop Muzik
  M; *Just Say Yesterday-#6 Of Just Say Yes* .... (SIR)
  Mega Hits Dance Classics-#10 .... (PRY)
Pop Singer
  John Cougar Mellencamp; *12"* .... (MER)
Preaching, Praying, Singing
  Bluegrass Album Band; *Bluegrass Class Of 1990* (ROU)
  L. Flatt & E. Scruggs/Foggy Mtn. Boys; *Complete*
  Mercury Sessions .... (MER)
Pump Up The Bass
  D.J. Jazzy Jeff & The Fresh Prince; *He's The D.J. I'm*
  The Rapper .... (JVA)
Pump Up The Volume
  M/A/R/R/S; *ST/Bright Lights Big City* ....(WB)
Radio M.U.S.I.C. Man
  Womack & Womack; *Radio M.U.S.I.C. Man* ..... (ELE)
Ragtime Annie
  Byron Berline; *Dad's Favorites* .... (ROU)
  Mason Williams; *Fresh Fish* ....(FF)
Ragtime Cowboy Joe
  Jo Stafford; *Capitol Collectors Series* ....(CAP)
  Spike Jones/City Slickers; *King Of Corn* ....(GLN)
Ragtime Dance
  Jean-Pierre Rampal; *Plays Scott Joplin* ....(COL)
  Richard Zimmerman; *His Greatest Hits-Scott*
  Joplin .... (EVR)
  Scott Joplin; *The Entertainer* ....(BIO)
Ragtime Nightingale
  Max Morath; *Plays Best Of Scott Joplin & Other*
  Rags .... (VAN)
Ragtime Oriole
  Max Morath; *World Of Scott Joplin* .... (VAN)
Real American Folk Song (Is A Rag)
  Marni Nixon & Lincoln Mayorga; *Marni Nixon Sings*
  Gershwin .... (REF)
Rebel Music
  Bob Marley/Wailers; *Babylon By Bus* .... (TUF)
  Natty Dread .... (TUF)
  Rebel Music .... (TUF)

Rhumba Man
Jesse Winchester; *Best Of* .... (RHI)
  Nothing But The Breeze .... (RHI)
Ritmo Africano
Cal Tjader; *Greatest Hits-#2* .... (FAN)
  Ritmos Calientes .... (FAN)
Rock A Bye Your Baby With A Dixie Melody
Al Jolson; *Best Of* .... (MCA)
  Immortal .... (MCA)
  Jolson Sang 'Em .... (BIO)
  Story-#1 .... (MCA)
Judy Garland; *At Carnegie Hall* .... (CAP)
  Miss Show Business .... (CAP)
  One & Only .... (CAP)
Rock Is My Life And This Is My Song
Bachman-Turner Overdrive; *Not Fragile* .... (MER)
Rock Me Amadeus
Falco; *3* .... (A&M)
  Remix Hit Collection .... (SIR)
Rock & Soul Music
Country Joe/Fish; *ST/Woodstock* .... (ATL)
Rocky Mountain Music
Eddie Rabbitt; *All-Time Greatest Hits* .... (WB)
  Best Of .... (WB)
  Rocky Mountain Music .... (ELE)
  Ten Years Of Greatest Hits .... (CAP)
Rosalita
Bruce Springsteen; *Wild The Innocent & The E Street*
Shuffle .... (COL)
Bruce Springsteen/E Street Band;
Live-1975-1985 .... (COL)
Russian Bandstand
Spencer & Spencer; *Dr. Demento's Greatest-#2* .. (RHI)
R&B Skeletons (In The Closet)
George Clinton; *R&B Skeletons (In The Closet)* ... (CAP)
Sad Song
Joe Williams; *Live* .... (FAN)
Lou Reed; *Between Thought &*
Expression-Anthology .... (RCA)
  Live .... (RCA)
Rachel Sweet; *Fool Around* .... (RHI)
Sad Songs
Olivia Newton-John; *Making A Good Thing*
Better .... (MCA)
Sad Songs (Say So Much)
Elton John; *Breaking Hearts* .... (MCA)
  Greatest Hits-1976-1986 .... (MCA)
  Knebworth-The Album .... (POL)
Same Old Song & Dance
Aerosmith; *Classics Live 2* .... (COL)
  Get Your Wings .... (COL)
  Greatest Hits .... (COL)
  Pandora's Box .... (COL)
Satan's Choir
Red Clay Ramblers; *It Ain't Right* .... (FF)
Saturday Gigs
Ian Hunter/Mott The Hoople; *Shades Of Ian*
Hunter .... (COL)
Mott The Hoople; *Ballad Of MoSaturday*
Gigs-Retrospective .... (COL)
  Greatest Hits .... (COL)
Save Black Music
Steel Pulse; *Babylon The Bandit* .... (ELE)
Serenade
Liberace; *Best Of* .... (MCA)
Mario Lanza; *Best Of* .... (RCA)
Steve Miller Band; *CD Gift Set* .... (CAP)
  Fly Like An Eagle .... (CAP)
  Greatest Hits-1974-1978 .... (CAP)
Set The Night To Music
Roberta Flack & Maxi Priest; *Set The Night To*
Music .... (ATL)
Starship; *No Protection* .... (GRU)
Set 'Em Up Joe
Vern Gosdin; *Chiseled In Stone* .... (COL)
  Greatest Country Hits/'80s-1988 .... (COL)
Sexy Music
Meat Puppets; *Huevos* .... (SST)
Sgt. Pepper's Lonely Hearts Club Band
Beatles; *1967-1970* .... (CAP)
  Box Set .... (CAP)
  Sgt. Pepper's Lonely Hearts Club Band .... (CAP)
Jimi Hendrix; *Stages-Stockholm/Paris/San*
Diego/Atlanta .... (RPR)

Paul McCartney; *Tripping The Live Fantastic* .... (CAP)
She Put The Sad In All His Songs
Alabama; *Closer You Get* .... (RCA)
She's Got The Rhythm (& I Got The Blues)
Alan Jackson; *Lot About Livin' (& A Little 'Bout*
Love .... (ARI)
She's Just A Groupie
Bobby Nunn; *Second To Nunn* .... (MOT)
Side By Side
Kay Starr; *Greatest Hits* .... (CCB)
Mitch Miller; *16 Most Requested Songs* .... (COL)
Silly Love Songs
Paul McCartney; *Give My Regards To Broad*
Street .... (CAP)
Paul McCartney/Wings; *All The Best* .... (CAP)
  Wings Greatest .... (CAP)
  Wings Over America .... (CAP)
Wings; *At The Speed Of Sound* .... (CAP)
Sing
Barbra Streisand; *Live At The Forum* .... (COL)
Carpenters; *Classics-#2* .... (A&M)
  Now & Then .... (A&M)
  Singles 1969-1973 .... (A&M)
  Yesterday Once More .... (A&M)
Original Cast; *Chorus Line* .... (COL)
Sing A Happy Song
O'Jays; *Identify Yourself* .... (PI)
Taj Mahal; *Evolution* .... (WB)
Sing A Mean Tune Kid
Chicago; *At Carnegie Hall* .... (COL)
  III .... (COL)
Sing A Sad Song
Merle Haggard; *Epic Collection-Recorded Live* .... (EPI)
  More Of The Best .... (RHI)
  Sing A Sad Song .... (CAP)
  Songs I'll Always Sing .... (CAP)
Sing A Simple Song
Sly/Family Stone; *Anthology* .... (EPI)
  Greatest Hits .... (EPI)
Sing A Song
Earth, Wind & Fire; *Best Of-#1* .... (COL)
  Eternal Dance .... (COL)
  Gratitude .... (COL)
Sing About Love
Lynn Anderson; *Greatest Hits-#2* .... (COL)
  Top Of The World .... (COL)
Sing Baby Sing
Stylistics; *Best Of-#2* .... (AMH)
  Thank You Baby .... (H&L)
Sing Child
Heart; *Dreamboat Annie* .... (CAP)
Sing C'Est La Vie
Sonny & Cher; *Beat Goes On* .... (ATC)
  Best Of .... (ATC)
  Two Of Us .... (ATC)
Sing For The Day
Styx; *Pieces Of Eight* .... (A&M)
Sing Me Back Home
Alabama; *Mama's Hungry Eyes-Merle Haggard*
Tribute .... (ARI)
Flying Burrito Brothers; *Farther Along-Best Of* .. (A&M)
Merle Haggard/Strangers; *Best Of* .... (CAP)
  Capitol Collectors Series .... (CAP)
  Okie From Muskogee .... (CAP)
  Songs I'll Always Sing .... (CAP)
Sing My Heart Out
O'Jays; *So Full Of Love* .... (PI)
Sing My Song To Me
Jackson Browne; *For Everyman* .... (ASY)
Sing Sing Sing
Benny Goodman; *Carnegie Hall Jazz Concert* .... (COL)
  Complete-#4 .... (RCA)
  Greatest Hits .... (COL)
  Live At Carnegie Hall .... (LON)
  Nipper's Greatest Hits-'30s-#2 .... (RCA)
  Pure Gold .... (RCA)
  Stompin' At The Savoy .... (BLU)
  Today .... (LON)
Country Joe/Fish; *C.J. Fish* .... (VAN)
  Live & Times Of .... (VAN)
Sing This All Together
Rolling Stones; *Their Satanic Majesties Request* .. (AKO)

Sing To Me
R.E.O. Speedwagon; *You Can Tune A Piano But You Can't...* .... (EPI)
Sing You Sinners
Sammy Davis, Jr./Original Cast; *Mr. Wonderful* (MCA)
Tony Bennett; *All-Time Greatest Hits* ....(COL)
  At Carnegie Hall .... (SSP)
  Forty Years-Artistry Of ....(COL)
Singer Not The Song
Rolling Stones; *December's Children* .... (AKO)
  Singles Collection-London Years .... (AKO)
Singing All Day
Jethro Tull; *Living In The Past* .... (CHR)
Singing Bridge Of Memphis Tennessee
John Fahey; *Essential* .... (VAN)
Singing From My Soul
Melissa Manchester; *Don't Cry Out Loud* .... (ARI)
  Help Is On The Way .... (ARI)
Singing Hills
Gene Autry; *50th Anniversary* .... (REP)
Slim Whitman; *Best Of-1952-1972* .... (RHI)
  Una Paloma Blanca-Best Of .... (EMI)
Singing My Song
Guy & Ralna; *22 Golden Country Classics* ...... (RAN)
  Lovelight .... (RAN)
Tammy Wynette; *Anniversary-20 Years Of Hits-First Lady* .... (EPI)
  Greatest Hits-#1 .... (EPI)
Singing Rhymes
Marshall Tucker Band; *Together Forever* .... (AJK)
Singing Tree
Elvis Presley; *ST/Clambake* ....(RCA)
Singin' In The Rain
Gene Kelly; *ST/Clockwork Orange* .... (WB)
  ST/Singin' In The Rain ....(SSP)
  ST/Those Glorious MGM Musicals ....(MGM)
Sir Duke
Stevie Wonder; *Original Musiquarium* .... (MOT)
  Songs In The Key Of Life .... (MOT)
Someone's Final Song
Elton John; *Blue Moves* .... (MCA)
Song A Day In Nashville
John Sebastian; *Welcome Back* .... (RPR)
Song I Can Sing
Donna Fargo; *Best Of* .... (MCA)
Song I See You Three
Doobie Brothers; *What Were Once Vices Are Now Habits* .... (WB)
Song Is Over
Who; *Hooligans* .... (MCA)
  Who's Next .... (MCA)
Song Is You
Charlie Parker; *Compact Jazz* ....(VRV)
Chet Baker; *Once Upon A Summertime* ....(GAL)
Frank Sinatra; *Capitol Years* ....(CAP)
  Come Dance With Me ....(CAP)
  Reprise Collection ....(RPR)
Tommy Dorsey & Frank Sinatra; *Dorsey/Sinatra Radio Years-1940-1942* ....(RCA)
Song Of The South
Alabama; *Greatest Hits-#2* ....(RCA)
  Southern Star ....(RCA)
Song On The Radio
Al Stewart; *Best Of* .... (ARI)
  Time Passages .... (ARI)
Jane Gillman; *Jane Gillman* ....(GRE)
Song Remembers When
Trisha Yearwood; *Song Remembers When* .... (MCA)
Song Sung Blue
Neil Diamond; *Glory Road-1968-1972* .... (MCA)
  His 12 Greatest Hits .... (MCA)
  Hot August Night .... (MCA)
  Love At The Greek ....(COL)
  Moods .... (MCA)
Song & Emotion
Tesla; *Psychotic Supper* .... (GEF)
Songbird
Barbra Streisand; *Greatest Hits-#2* ....(COL)
  Songbird ....(COL)
Fleetwood Mac; *25 Years-The Chain* .... (WB)
  Rumours .... (WB)
Jesse Colin Young; *Songbird* .... (WB)
Kenny G; *Duotones* .... (ARI)
  Live .... (ARI)

Songs From The Wood
Jethro Tull; *20 Years Of-Radio Archives & Rare Tracks* .... (CHR)
  Bursting Out .... (CHR)
  Original Masters .... (CHR)
  Songs From The Wood .... (CHR)
Sound Of Music
Mormon Tabernacle Choir; *Greatest Hits-22 Best-Loved Favorites* .... (SMC)
Original Cast; *Sound Of Music* ....(COL)
Stone Cold Country
Gibson/Miller Band; *Where There's Smoke* .... (EPI)
Story Of Bo Diddley
Animals; *Best Of* .... (AKO)
Bo Diddley; *In The Spotlight* .... (CSS)
Strange Music
Dave Frishberg; *Let's Eat Home* .... (CCJ)
John Raitt; *Highlights Of Broadway-Under Open Skies* ....(CAP)
Strike Up The Band
Boston Pops Orchestra/Arthur Fiedler;
  Gershwin-Greatest Hits ....(RCA)
Count Basie Orchestra; *Fancy Pants* ....(PAB)
Ella Fitzgerald; *Sings The George & Ira Gershwin Songbook* ....(VRV)
Rosemary Clooney; *Sings The Lyrics Of Ira Gershwin* .... (CCJ)
Tony Bennett; *Fascinatin' Rhythm-Capitol Gershwin* ....(CAP)
Sultans Of Swing
Dire Straits; *Dire Straits* .... (WB)
  Live-Alchemy .... (WB)
  Money For Nothing .... (WB)
Sun Singer
Paul Winter; *Anthems* .... (LIV)
Paul Winter Consort; *Sun Singer* .... (LIV)
Swamp Music
Lynyrd Skynyrd; *Second Helping* .... (MCA)
  Skynyrd's Innyrds .... (MCA)
  Southern By The Grace Of God .... (MCA)
Swayin' To The Music
Johnny Rivers; *Anthology-1964-1977* .... (RHI)
Sweet Country Music
Atlanta; *Pictures* .... (MCA)
  Today's Country Classics .... (MCA)
Sweet Music Man
Dolly Parton; *Here You Come Again* ....(RCA)
Kenny Rogers; *Daytime Friends* .... (EMI)
Millie Jackson; *Get It Out'cha System* .... (SPR)
  Live & Uncensored .... (SPR)
Nana Mouskouri; *Song For Liberty* .... (MER)
Sweet Sixteen Bars
Earl Gray; *Best Of* .... (MCA)
Ray Charles; *Atlantic Jazz-Piano* .... (ATL)
  Best Of .... (ATL)
  Great Ray Charles .... (ATL)
Sweet Soul Music
Arthur Conley; *Atlantic Soul Classics* ....(WSP)
  Golden Age Of Black Music-1960-1970 .... (ATL)
Sweet Surf Music
Malibooz; *Malibooz Rule* .... (RHI)
Sweetest Sounds
Art Pepper; *Goin' Home* ....(GAL)
Barbra Streisand; *& Other Musical Instruments* ..(COL)
Original Broadway Cast; *No Strings* .... (ANG)
Rosemary Clooney; *Sings Rodgers Hart & Hammerstein* .... (CCJ)
Sarah Vaughan; *Compact Jazz* ....(VRV)
Swing That Music
Dukes Of Dixieland; *Tiger Rag* .... (PJ)
Louis Armstrong; *#2-1936-1938-Heart Full Of Rhythm* ....(GRP)
Swingin' On The Campus
Duke Ellington & Jimmy Hodges/Orchestra; *Duke's Men-Small Groups-#2* ....(COL)
Swingtime In Honolulu
Duke Ellington/Cootie Williams/R.Cutters; *Duke's Men-Small Groups-#2* ....(COL)
Swingtime In The Rockies
Benny Goodman; *Birth Of Swing* .... (BLU)
  Carnegie Hall Jazz Concert ....(COL)
  ST/Swing Kids .... (HOL)
Take It Away
Paul McCartney; *Tug Of War* ....(COL)

Tarzan Was A Bluesman
Timbuk 3; *Eden Alley* .... (IRS)
Terrific Band & A Real Nice Crowd
Original Broadway Cast; *Ballroom* .... (SMC)
Texas Playboy Rag
Bob Wills/Texas Playboys; *Essential* ....(COL)
Thank You For The Music
Abba; *Gold-Greatest Hits* .... (POL)
That Girl Could Sing
Jackson Browne; *Hold Out* .... (ASY)
That Old Song
Ray Parker, Jr.; *Greatest Hits* .... (ARI)
Ray Parker, Jr./Raydio; *A Woman Needs Love* ... (ARI)
That Song About The Midway
Bonnie Raitt; *Streetlights* .... (WB)
Joni Mitchell; *Clouds* .... (RPR)
That Song Is Driving Me Crazy
Tom T. Hall; *Greatest Hits-#2* .... (MER)
That's The Tune
Vogues; *Greatest Hits* .... (RHI)
"The Archies" Theme
Original Music; *Television's Greatest Hits-#3* ..... (TVT)
"The Bodyguard" Theme
Original Music; *ST/The Bodyguard* .... (ARI)
There Ain't No Country Music On This...
Tom T. Hall; *Out-of-print recording* ....(OOP)
There Goes Another Love Song
Outlaws; *Bring It Back Alive* .... (ARI)
Greatest Hits Of-High Tides Forever .... (ARI)
Southern Fried Rock .... (KT)
There Won't Be No Country Music...
C.W. McCall; *Greatest Hits* .... (POL)
There'll Be Sad Songs (To Make You Cry)
Billy Ocean; *Greatest Hits* .... (JVA)
Love Zone .... (JVA)
There's A Song On The Jukebox
David Wills; *Columbia Country Classics-#5-New Trad.* ....(COL)
They Pass By Singin'
Cleo Laine & Ray Charles; *Porgy & Bess* ....(RCA)
They're Playing Our Song
Original Cast; *They're Playing Our Song* .... (CAS)
This Song
George Harrison; *33 1/3* .... (DKH)
This Song Has No Title
Elton John; *Goodbye Yellow Brick Road* .... (POL)
This Song Will Last Forever
Lou Rawls; *All Things In Time* .... (PI)
Live .... (PI)
Those Good Old Sun Records
Sun Rhythm Section; *Old Time Rock 'N Roll* ....(FF)
Those Oldies But Goodies (Remind Me...)
John Cafferty/Beaver Brown Band; *ST/Eddie & The Cruisers* .... (SCO)
Little Caesar/Romans; *Best Love Songs* .... (OSR)
Collectables Presents-History Of Rock-#2 .... (CLT)
Cruisin'-1961 .... (INC)
Oldies But Goodies-#6 .... (OSR)
To Cry You A Song
Jethro Tull; *Benefit* .... (CHR)
Repeat-Best Of-#2 .... (CHR)
Today I Sing The Blues
Aretha Franklin; *Aretha Sings The Blues* ....(COL)
Aretha's Jazz .... (ATL)
Jazz To Soul .... (COL)
Top Of The Pops
Kinks; *Everybody's In Show Biz* .... (RHI)
Lola Vs. The Powerman & The Moneygoround . (RPR)
Smithereens; *Blow Up* .... (CAP)
Travelin' Band
Creedence Clearwater Revival; *1970* .... (FAN)
Chronicle .... (FAN)
Cosmo's Factory .... (FAN)
Live In Europe .... (FAN)
Royal Albert Hall Concert .... (FAN)
Trudy Sings The Blues
Trudy Lynn; *Trudy Sings The Blues* .... (ICH)
Tune Up
Miles Davis; *Blue Haze* .... (PRS)
Philly Joe Jones Sextet; *Blues For Dracula* ...... (RVR)
Sonny Stitt; *Tune Up* .... (MUS)
Wes Montgomery With Strings; *Fusion* .... (RVR)
Turn It Up Or Turn It Off
Drivin' N' Cryin'; *Smoke* .... (ISL)

Turn Up The Music
Sammy Hagar; *Best Of* ....(CAP)
Live ....(CAP)
Musical Chairs ....(CAP)
Unchained Melody
Elvis Presley; *Always On My Mind* ....(RCA)
Great Performances ....(RCA)
Moody Blue ....(RCA)
George Benson; *Livin' Inside Your Love* ....(WB)
Platters; *Greatest Hits* ....(EVR)
Red Sails In The Sunset ....(ALL)
Richard Clayderman; *Plays Love Songs Of The World* ....(COL)
Righteous Brothers; *Greatest Hits-#1* ....(VRV)
ST/Ghost ....(VS)
Willie Nelson; *Stardust* ....(COL)
Uncle John's Band
Grateful Dead; *Skeletons From The Closet-Best Of* (WB)
Workingman's Dead ....(WB)
Indigo Girls; *Deadicated* .... (ARI)
Uncle Pen
Bill Monroe; *Bean Blossom* ....(MCA)
Best Of ....(MCA)
Ricky Skaggs; *19 Hot Country Requests-#2* ......(EPI)
Columbia Country Classics-#5-New Trad. ......(COL)
Don't Cheat In Our Hometown ....(EPI)
Live In London ....(EPI)
Unheard Music
X; *Live At The Whisky A Go-Go* .... (ELE)
Los Angeles .... (SLS)
Voodoo Music
Tuck & Patti; *Dream* ....(WH)
Warning Labels
Doug Stone; *From The Heart* ....(EPI)
We'll Sing In The Sunshine
Gale Garnett; *21 Country Rock/Love Songs-'50s/'60s-#1* ....(LAU)
Nipper's Greatest Hits-'60s ....(RCA)
We're An American Band
Grand Funk Railroad; *Capitol Collectors Series* ...(CAP)
Caught In The Act ....(CAP)
ST/Spirit Of '76 ....(RHI)
We're An American Band ....(CAP)
When AM Was King ....(CAP)
When The Music Stops
Roger Daltrey; *Daltrey* ....(MCA)
When The Music's Over
Doors; *Absolutely Live* .... (ELE)
Best Of .... (ELE)
Strange Days .... (ELE)
ST/Doors .... (ELE)
Weird Scenes Inside The Goldmine .... (ELE)
When The Saints Go Marching In
Al Hirt; *Best Of* ....(RCA)
Our Man-In New Orleans .... (NOV)
Jerry Lee Lewis; *Jerry Lee Lewis* .... (RHI)
Louis Armstrong; *At The Crescendo* ....(MCA)
Big Bands Of The Swinging Years-#1 ....(CLT)
C'Est Si Bon .... (RHI)
Essential .... (VAN)
Of New Orleans ....(MCA)
Pete Fountain; *Best Of* ....(MCA)
Down On Rampart Street .... (INT)
Pete Fountain's New Orleans ....(MCA)
Preservation Hall Jazz Band; *Best Of* ....(COL)
Where The Blues Were Born In New Orleans
Louis Armstrong; *Pops: 1940s Small Band Sides* . (BLU)
Sings The Blues ....(BLU)
Whistle While You Work/Heigh Ho
Adriana Caselotti; *Disney Collection-#1* .... (DIS)
Mormon Tabernacle Choir; *When You Wish Upon A Star-Disney Tribute* ....(COL)
NRBQ; *Peek-A-Boo-Best Of-1969-1989* .... (RHI)
White Noise
Jay Ferguson; *White Noise* ....(CAP)
White Rhythm & Blues
J.D. Souther; *You're Only Lonely* ....(COL)
Linda Ronstadt; *Living In The U.S.A.* .... (ASY)
Who's Gonna Fill Their Shoes
George Jones; *Greatest Country Hits/'80s-1985* ...(COL)
Super Hits ....(EPI)
Who's Gonna Fill Their Shoes ....(EPI)

Why It Is I Sing The Blues
B.B. King; *Best Of* .... (MSP)
  Live & Well .... (MCA)
  Why It Is I Sing The Blues .... (MSP)
With A Little Help From My Friends
Beatles; *1967-1970* .... (CAP)
  Box Set .... (CAP)
  Rarities .... (CAP)
  Sgt. Pepper's Lonely Hearts Club Band .... (CAP)
Joe Cocker; *Classics-#4* .... (A&M)
  Greatest Hits .... (A&M)
  History Of British Rock-#9 .... (RHI)
  ST/Woodstock .... (ATL)
  With A Little Help From My Friends .... (A&M)
Ringo Starr/All-Star Band; *Nobody's Child-Romanian Angel Appeal* .... (WB)
With A Song In My Heart
Ella Fitzgerald; *Rodgers & Hart Songbook* .... (VRV)
Jerry Vale; *Standing Ovation!-Carnegie Hall Concert* .... (COL)
Jose Carreras; *The 3 Tenors In Concert 1994* .... (TEL)
Mario Lanza; *Be My Love* .... (RCA)
Stevie Wonder; *With A Song In My Heart* .... (MOT)
Without A Song
Duke Ellington; *Great Ellington Units* .... (BLU)
Frank Sinatra; *My Kind Of Broadway* .... (RPR)
James Ray; *Golden Classics* .... (CLT)
Supremes; *I Hear A Symphony* .... (MOT)
Tommy Dorsey & Frank Sinatra; *All-Time Greatest Hits-#1* .... (RCA)
Willie Nelson; *Without A Song* .... (COL)
Woodstock
Crosby, Stills & Nash; *Crosby, Stills & Nash (collection)* .... (ATL)
Crosby, Stills, Nash & Young; *Deja Vu* .... (ATL)
  So Far .... (ATL)
Joni Mitchell; *Ladies Of The Canyon* .... (RPR)
  Miles Of Aisles .... (ASY)
  Shadows & Light .... (ASY)
Working For MCA
Hank Williams, Jr.; *Hank "Live"* .... (W/C)
Lynyrd Skynyrd; *Best Of The Rest* .... (MCA)
  One More From The Road .... (MCA)
  Second Helping .... (MCA)
World Is A Concerto
Barbra Streisand; *& Other Musical Instruments* ...(COL)
World Needs A Melody
George Jones & Tammy Wynette; *Greatest Hits-#2* .... (EPI)
Kenny Rogers; *Love Lifted Me* .... (UA)
Wrote A Song For Everyone
Creedence Clearwater Revival; *1969* .... (FAN)
  Chronicle-#2 .... (FAN)
  Creedence Country .... (FAN)
  Green River .... (FAN)
Yesterday's Songs
Neil Diamond; *12 Greatest Hits-#2* ....(COL)
  On The Way To The Sky ....(COL)
You Are My Music, You Are My Song
Charly McClain & Wayne Massey; *Radio Heart* .. (EPI)
You Can All Join In
Traffic; *Best Of* .... (UA)
  Traffic .... (ISL)
You Spin Me Around (Like A Record)
Dead Or Alive; *Rip It Up* .... (EPI)
  Youthquake .... (EPI)
Your Song
Elton John; *Elton John* .... (POL)
  Greatest Hits .... (POL)
  Live In Australia w/Melbourne Symphony ...... (MCA)
Rod Stewart; *Two Rooms-Songs Of E. John & B. Taupin* .... (POL)

MUSICAL INSTRUMENTS
See Also: MUSIC

76 Trombones
Original Cast; *Music Man* .... (CAP)
Arkansas Traveler
Albert Lee; *Speechless* .... (MCA)
Floyd Cramer; *Country Gold* .... (STE)
Mark O'Connor; *Championship Years* .... (CMF)
Michelle Shocked; *Arkansas Traveler* .... (MER)

Sam Hinton; *Newport Folk Festival '63* .... (VAN)
At The Banjo Cafe
Pat Cloud; *Higher Power* .... (FF)
Baby Grand
Billy Joel; *KOHUEPT* ....(COL)
Bang A Gong
T. Rex; *Electric Warrior* .... (RPR)
Bang The Drum All Day
Todd Rundgren; *Anthology (1968-1985)* .... (RHI)
  Popular Tortured Artist Effect .... (RHI)
Banjo
Kaleidoscope; *Egyptian Candy-Collection* .... (EPI)
Banjo Bounce
Allen Shelton; *Rounder Bluegrass 1* .... (ROU)
Banjo Kings; *#1* .... (GTJ)
Banjo Boy Chimes
White Brothers/New Kentucky Colonels; *Live In Sweden* .... (ROU)
Banjo Breakdown
Stanley Brothers/C. Story/Jim & Jesse; *Banjo In The Hills* .... (STR)
Banjo In The Hills
Stanley Brothers/C. Story/Jim & Jesse; *Banjo In The Hills* .... (STR)
Banjo In The Hollow
Dillards; *Bluegrass Breakdown* .... (VAN)
Banjo On The Mountain
Doug Dillard Band; *Heartbreak Hotel* .... (FF)
Banjo Picking Girl
Lamar Grier; *Rounder Banjo* .... (ROU)
Banjo Signal
John Hickman; *Don't Mean Maybe* .... (ROU)
Banjo Story
Elizabeth Cotten; *Live* .... (ARH)
Banjos
Original Broadway Cast; *Meet Me In St. Louis* .. (DRG)
Belfast Hornpipe
James Galway; *Greatest Hits* ....(RCA)
Boogie Woogie Bugle Boy
Andrews Sisters; *16 Great Performances* .... (MCA)
  Best Of .... (MCA)
  Boogie Woogie Bugle Girls .... (MCA)
  Rarities .... (MCA)
Bette Midler; *Divine Miss M* .... (ATL)
  Live At Last .... (ATL)
  ST/Divine Madness .... (ATL)
Boss Guitar
Duane Eddy; *Vintage Years* ....(OOP)
Brazilian Ukelele
Buddy Merrill; *Best Of* .... (ACC)
  Latin Festival .... (ACC)
Bugle Call Rag
Benny Goodman; *Stompin' At The Savoy* .... (BLU)
Enoch Light/Light Brigade; *Big Band Hits/'30s-#2* . (P3)
New Orleans Rhythm Kings; *New Orleans Rhythm Kings* .... (MS)
Cello Solo
Laurie Anderson; *United States Live* .... (WB)
Cherokee Fiddle
Johnny Lee; *Greatest Hits* .... (FA)
  ST/Urban Cowboy .... (ASY)
Michael Martin Murphey; *Best Of* .... (EMI)
  Flowing Free Forever .... (EMI)
Conga
Leonard Bernstein; *Songbook* ....(COL)
Miami Sound Machine; *Primitive Love* .... (EPI)
Crowe On The Banjo
Jimmy Martin; *You Don't Know My Mind-1956-1966* .... (ROU)
Daddy Frank
Merle Haggard; *Best Of* .... (CAP)
  Capitol Collectors Series .... (CAP)
  Songs I'll Always Sing .... (CAP)
Daddy Sang Bass
Johnny Cash; *Columbia Country Classics-#5* .....(COL)
  Greatest Hits-#2 ....(COL)
Daniel & The Sacred Harp
Band; *Anthology-#1* .... (CAP)
  Stage Fright .... (CAP)
  To Kingdom Come (Definitive Collection) .... (CAP)
Devil Comes Back To Georgia
Marc O'Connor; *Heroes* .... (WB)

Devil Went Down To Georgia
Charlie Daniels Band; *Billboard Top Hits-1979* .. (RHI)
  Decade Of Hits .... (EPI)
  Me & The Boys .... (EPI)
  Million Mile Reflections .... (EPI)
  ST/Urban Cowboy .... (ASY)
Different Drum
Linda Ronstadt; *Different Drum* .... (ASY)
  Greatest Hits .... (CAP)
  Retrospective .... (CAP)
Stone Poneys/Linda Ronstadt; *In The Beginning* .. (EMI)
  On The Road Again (Rock's New Frontiers) ..... (CAP)
Doc's Guitar
Doc Watson; *Doc Watson* .... (VAN)
  On Stage .... (VAN)
  Out In The Country .... (INT)
Doo Wa Ditty (Blow That Thing)
Zapp; *II* .... (WB)
Drum Boogie
Gene Krupa; *Big Bands' Greatest Hits-#1* ....(COL)
Gene Krupa/Buddy Rich; *Original Drum Battle* ..(VRV)
Drum Song
Earth, Wind & Fire; *Open Our Eyes* ....(COL)
Drum Stomp
Sandy Nelson; *Collector's Gems #2* .... (LIB)
Drums
Tubes; *Outside/Inside* .... (CAP)
Dueling Banjos
Eric Weissberg; *ST/Deliverance* .... (WB)
Ebony & Ivory
Paul McCartney; *Tripping The Live Fantastic* ....(CAP)
Paul McCartney & Stevie Wonder; *All The Best* .(CAP)
  Tug Of War .... (CAP)
Fiddle About
Who; *Join Together* .... (MCA)
  ST/Tommy .... (MCA)
Fiddle & The Drum
Joni Mitchell; *Clouds* .... (RPR)
Fiddler On The Roof
Original Cast; *Fiddler On The Roof* .... (RCA)
Fiddlin' Around
Johnny Gimble; *Still Fiddlin' Around* .... (MCA)
  ST/Honeysuckle Rose .... (COL)
Free Form Guitar
Chicago; *Chicago Transit Authority* ....(COL)
Get It On (Bang A Gong)
Power Station; *Power Station* .... (CAP)
T. Rex; *Electric Warrior* .... (RPR)
Girls With Guitars
Wynonna; *Tell Me Why* .... (MCC)
Gitarzan
Ray Stevens; *Dr. Demento's Greatest Novelty-#3* . (RHI)
  Greatest Hits .... (MCA)
  Greatest Hits .... (RCA)
Golden Guitar
Bill Anderson; *Greatest Hits-#1* .... (MCA)
  Story .... (MCA)
Green Tambourine
Lemon Pipers; *Best Of Ohio Express/Other*
  Bubblegum-#1 .... (RHI)
  Best Of/Ohio Express-#1 .... (RHI)
  Billboard Top Rock 'N' Roll Hits-1968 .... (RHI)
  Bubble Gum Greatest Hits-#3 .... (ACC)
  Fabulous Bubblegum Years .... (FFT)
Guitar Boogie Shuffle
Virtues; *Legends Of Rock Guitar/'50s-#1* .... (RHI)
Guitar Heaven
Neil Diamond; *On The Way To The Sky* ....(COL)
Guitar Man
Bread; *Anthology* .... (ELE)
  Best Of-#2 .... (ELE)
Elvis Presley; *14 #1 Country Hits* ....(RCA)
  Guitar Man .... (RCA)
  Nipper's Greatest Hits-'80s .... (RCA)
  TV Special .... (RCA)
Guitar Picker From Rody, Wyoming
Joey Davis; *45* .... (MRC)
Guitar Town
Steve Earle/Dukes; *Country*
  Classics-#8-1986-1987 .... (MCA)
  Guitar Town .... (MCA)
Guitar & Pen
Who; *Who Are You* .... (MCA)

Guitars, Cadillacs
Dwight Yoakam; *Guitars Cadillacs Etc. Etc.* ..... (RPR)
  Just Lookin' For A Hit .... (RPR)
Happy Organ
Dave "Baby" Cortez; *Billboard Top Rock 'N' Roll*
  Hits-1959 .... (RHI)
  History Of Rock Instrumentals-#1 .... (RHI)
  Super Oldies/'50s-#7 .... (AUF)
Hey Harmonica Man
Stevie Wonder; *Greatest Hits* .... (MOT)
Holiday For Strings
Boston Pops Orchestra/Arthur Fiedler; *Greatest*
  Hits/'40s-#2 ....(RCA)
David Rose/Orchestra; *Nipper's Greatest*
  Hits-'40s-#1 ....(RCA)
Holiday For Trumpet
Al Hirt; *Best Of* ....(RCA)
I Love The Bass
Bardeux; *S* .... (ENI)
Japanese Drums
Kitaro; *Asia* .... (GEF)
Johnny B. Goode
Chuck Berry; *Chess Box* .... (CSS)
  Classic Rock-#2 .... (MCA)
  Greatest Hits .... (EVR)
  Roll Over Beethoven .... (ALL)
  ST/American Graffiti .... (MCA)
Elvis Presley; *From Memphis To Vegas* .... (RCA)
  In Concert ....(RCA)
Grateful Dead; *Bill Graham Presents Fillmore-Last*
  Days .... (EPA)
Johnny Winter; *Live* .... (COL)
  Second Winter .... (COL)
Jungle Drums
Artie Shaw; *Begin The Beguine* ....(POE)
  This Is ....(RCA)
Kentucky Mandolin
Bill Monroe/Blue Grass Boys; *Best Of* .... (MCA)
  Kentucky Bluegrass .... (MCA)
King Of The Surf Guitar
Dick Dale/Del-Tones; *Beach Classics* ....(DHL)
  Greatest Hits .... (CRS)
  Tigers Loose .... (RHI)
Kitten On The Keys
Claude Bolling; *Original Ragtime* ....(COL)
Dick Hyman; *Flip Side Of Red Seal* ....(RCA)
  Kitten On The Keys ....(RCA)
Liberace; *16 Most Requested Songs* ....(COL)
Let Me Bang Your Box
Toppers; *Risque Rhythm* .... (RHI)
Little Guitars
Van Halen; *Diver Down* .... (WB)
Long Legged Guitar Pickin' Man
Johnny Cash & June Carter; *Greatest Hits-#2* ....(COL)
Mandolin Rain
Bruce Hornsby/Range; *The Way It Is* ....(RCA)
Mandolin Wind
Rod Stewart; *Best Of-#2* .... (MER)
  Every Picture Tells A Story .... (MER)
  Sing It Again Rod .... (MER)
  Storyteller/Complete Anthology-1964-1990 ..... (WB)
Memphis Soul Stew
King Curtis; *Atlantic Jazz-Soul* .... (ATL)
  Atlantic R&B 1947-1974-#6-(1966-1969) .... (ATL)
  Best Of .... (ATL)
  Golden Soul .... (ATL)
  Live At The Fillmore West .... (ATL)
Mr. Tambourine Man
Bob Dylan; *At Budokan* ....(COL)
  Biograph ....(COL)
  Bringin' It All Back Home ....(COL)
  Greatest Hits ....(COL)
Byrds; *Billboard Top Rock 'N' Roll Hits-1965* ... (RHI)
  Greatest Hits ....(COL)
  Mr. Tambourine Man ....(COL)
  Original Singles-#1-1965-1967 ....(COL)
My Father's Fiddle
David Loggins; *Apprentice* .... (EPI)
My Guitar Sings The Blues
B.B. King; *Six Silver Strings* .... (MCA)
My Guitar Wants To Kill Your Mama
Frank Zappa; *You Can't Do That On Stage*
  Anymore-#4 ....(RYK)
Mothers Of Invention; *Weasels Ripped My Flesh* ... (BIZ)

My Old Piano
Diana Ross; *All The Great Hits* .... (MOT)
  Anthology .... (MOT)
  Diana .... (MOT)
Nickel For The Fiddler
Guy Clark; *Old No. 1* ....(SH)
Oh, Susanna
James Taylor; *Sweet Baby James* .... (WB)
Myron Floren; *Best Of The Wurstfest* .... (RAN)
  Myron Floren .... (RAN)
Old Kentucky Fiddle
Hoot Hester; *45* ....(NAT)
On Broadway
Drifters; *16 Greatest Hits* .... (TRP)
  Golden Hits ....(ATL)
George Benson; *Collection* .... (WB)
  ST/All That Jazz ....(CAS)
  Weekend In L.A. .... (WB)
Orange Blossom Mandolin
Northeast Winds; *In Concert* .... (FOL)
Orange Guitars
Jimmy Haslip; *Arc* ....(GRP)
Perfectly Good Guitar
John Hiatt; *Perfectly Good Guitar* .... (A&M)
Piano Has Been Drinking
Tom Waits; *Anthology* .... (ASY)
  Small Change .... (ASY)
Piano In The Dark
Brenda Russell; *Get Here* .... (A&M)
  Greatest Hits .... (A&M)
  Making Love .... (PRY)
  Slow Dancin' .... (KT)
Piano Man
Billy Joel; *Greatest Hits-#1 & 2* ....(COL)
  Piano Man ....(COL)
  Rock Classics Of The '70s ....(COL)
Thelma Houston; *Motown Superstar Series-#20* . (MOT)
Play Guitar
John Cougar Mellencamp; *Uh-Huh* ....(RIV)
Play The Bass
Stanley Clarke; *Let Me Know You* .... (EPI)
  Time Exposure .... (EPI)
Play, Guitar, Play
Conway Twitty; *Classic Conway* .... (MCA)
  Very Best Of .... (MCA)
Redneck Fiddlin' Man
Charlie Daniels Band; *Greatest Fiddlin' Licks* .... (EPI)
  Midnight Wind .... (EPI)
Rhythm Guitar
Emmylou Harris; *Ballad Of Sally Rose* .... (WB)
Johnny Paycheck; *Greatest Hits-#2* .... (EPI)
Oak Ridge Boys; *All Our Favorite Songs* ....(COL)
  Best Of ....(COL)
Robbery With Violins
Steeleye Span; *Parcel Of Rogues* .... (CHR)
Sad Banjo
Shrimp Boat; *Duende* .... (BN)
Sam, The Old Accordion Man
Doris Day & James Cagney; *ST/Love Me Or Leave*
Me ....(SSP)
Sax & Violins
Talking Heads; *ST/Until The End Of The World* .. (WB)
Saxafunk
Neville Brothers; *Family Groove* .... (A&M)
Saxophone Song
Kate Bush; *Kick Inside* .... (EMI)
Saxophones
Jimmy Buffett; *Living & Dying In 3/4 Time* ..... (MCA)
Say It With Trumpets
Maynard Ferguson; *Birdland Dreamband* .... (BLU)
Sex Cymbal
Sheila E.; *Sex Cymbal* ....(WB)
She Bangs The Drums
Stone Roses; *Stone Roses* .... (SIL)
Sloth (Drums)
Fairport Convention; *Chronicles* .... (A&M)
  Full House ....(CTH)
Something So Feminine About A Mandolin
Jimmy Buffett; *Havana Daydreamin'* .... (MCA)
Spanish Guitar
Squeeze; *45* .... (A&M)

Squeezebox
Who; *By Numbers* .... (MCA)
  Greatest Hits .... (MCA)
  Hooligans .... (MCA)
  Who's Better Who's Best-Very Best Of .... (MCA)
Tambourine
Book Of Love; *Lovebubble* .... (SIR)
Electric Boys; *Groovus Maximus* ....(ATC)
Prince/Revolution; *Around The World In A Day* .. (PAI)
Ten Guitars
Engelbert Humperdinck; *Release Me* .... (MER)
Tennessee Flat Top Box
Johnny Cash; *Classic Cash-Hall Of Fame Series* . (MER)
  Columbia Country Classics-#3-Americana .....(COL)
  Essential ....(COL)
Rosanne Cash; *30 Years Of #1 Hits-#17* ....(COL)
  Hits-1979-1989 ....(COL)
  King's Record Shop ....(COL)
Texas Fiddle Man
Asleep At The Wheel; *Keepin' Me Up Nights* ..... (ARI)
Texas Fiddle Song
Merle Haggard; *Big City* ....(EPI)
Texas Guitar Stomp
Maddox Brothers & Rose; *1946-1951-#2* ...... (ARH)
That Banjo Rag
Banjo Kings; *Banjo Kings-#1* .... (GTJ)
That Mellow Saxophone
Roy Montrell; *Best Of New Orleans Rhythm &*
Blues-#2 .... (RHI)
That Old Beat Up Guitar
Jerry Jeff Walker; *Jerry Jeff Walker* .... (MCA)
There Goes That Old Steel Guitar
Tammy Wynette; *Greatest Hits-#3* ....(EPI)
There Won't Be Trumpets
Barbra Streisand; *Just For The Record* ....(COL)
Original Broadway Cast; *Anyone Can Whistle* ...(COL)
Original Cast; *Marry Me A Little* ....(RCA)
This Old Guitar
John Denver; *Back Home Again* ....(RCA)
  Evening With ....(RCA)
  Greatest Hits-#2 ....(RCA)
This Old Piano
Mike Gray; *This Old Piano* .... (TT)
Three Guitar Special
Bob Wills/Texas Playboys; *Anthology-1935-1973* (RHI)
Tin Drum
Big Pig; *Bonk* .... (A&M)
Toni Childs; *Union* .... (A&M)
Trombone Butter
Dinah Washington; *Bessie Smith Songbook* ..... (EMA)
Trombone Cholly
Bessie Smith; *Complete Recordings-#3* ....(COL)
Teresa Brewer & Count Basie; *Songs Of Bessie*
Smith .... (DOC)
Trombone Dixie
Beach Boys; *Pet Sounds* ....(CAP)
Trombone Rag
Turk Murphy's San Francisco Jazz Band; *#1* .... (GTJ)
Trumpet
Chuck Mangione; *Children of Sanchez* .... (A&M)
Trumpet Blues & Cantabile
Harry James; *Best Of The Big Bands* ....(COL)
Trumpet Boogie
Ray Anthony Orchestra; *Young Man With A*
Horn-1952-1954 .... (HIN)
Trumpet Player's Lament
Louis Armstrong; *Jazz Heritage-Satchmo's*
Discoveries .... (MCA)
Trumpeter Blow Your Golden Horn
Michael Tilson Thomas; *Of Thee I Sing/Let 'Em Eat*
Cake ....(COL)
Trumpeter's Lullaby
Utah Symphony Orchestra/M. Abravanel; *Fiddle*
Faddle .... (VAN)
Trumpets
Waterboys; *This Is The Sea* .... (CHR)
Tubas In The Moonlight
Bonzo Dog Band; *Tadpoles* .... (LIB)
Two Bass Hit
Dizzy Gillespie; *Dizziest* .... (BLU)
Miles Davis; *Milestones* ....(COL)
Sonny Clark; *Blue Piano-#2* .... (BLN)

Uncle Clooney Played The Banjo
Country Gazette; *Hello Operator...This Is* ....(FF)
  Out To Lunch ....(FF)
Violin
Kate Bush; *Never For Ever* ....(EMI)
Violin Walk
Laurie Anderson; *United States Live* ....(WB)
While My Guitar Gently Weeps
Beatles; *1967-1970* ....(CAP)
  Box Set ....(CAP)
  White Album ....(CAP)
George Harrison; *Best Of* ....(CAP)
  Concert For Bangladesh ....(CAP)
George Harrison & Eric Clapton & Band; *Live In Japan* ....(DKH)
Whistle Song
Frankie Knuckles; *Beyond The Mix* ....(VIA)
Who's Gonna Play This Old Piano
Jerry Lee Lewis; *Best Of-#2* ....(MER)
  Milestones ....(RHI)
Wildwood Mandolin
Jack Tottle; *Rounder Bluegrass-#1* ....(ROU)

NATIVE AMERICANS, Indians

Alcatraz
Leon Russell; *& The Shelter People* ....(MCA)
Nazareth; *Razamanaz* ....(A&M)
Along The Navajo Trail
Riders In The Sky; *Riders Go Commercial* ......(MCA)
Roy Rogers; *Hooray For Hollywood* ....(RCA)
Apache
Shadows; *Legends Of Rock Guitar-'60s-#1* ....(RHI)
Sonny James; *Great Moments At The Grand Ole Opry* ....(RCA)
Apache Dance
Woody Herman/Orchestra; *Uncollected* ....(HIN)
Apache Woman
Rolling Stones; *Made In The Shade* ....(RS)
Arizona Indian Doll
Faster Pussycat; *Wake Me When It's Over* ....(ELE)
Big Chief
Dr. John; *Dr. John's Gumbo* ....(ALG)
Neville Brothers; *Live At Tipitina's-#1-Nevillization* ....(SPT)
Professor Longhair; *Crawfish Fiesta* ....(ALG)
  Mardi Gras Party ....(ROU)
  New Orleans Party Classics ....(RHI)
Big Chief From New Orleans
Mike Bloomfield; *Between The Hard Place & The Ground* ....(TAK)
Buffalo Gun
Michael Murphey; *Swans Against The Son* ....(EPI)
Chant: 13th Hour
Redbone; *Best Of* ....(OOP)
Cherokee
Charlie Barnet; *Big Bands Of The Swinging Years-#1* ....(CLT)
  Nipper's Greatest Hits/'30s-#2 ....(RCA)
  Swing's The Thing ....(CAP)
Europe; *Final Countdown* ....(EPI)
Sarah Vaughan; *Complete On Mercury-#1-Great Jazz Years* ....(MER)
  In The Land Of Hi-Fi ....(EMA)
Stephen Stills; *Stephen Stills* ....(ATL)
White Lion; *Fight To Survive* ....(GS)
Wynton Marsalis; *Marsalis Standard Time-#1* ....(COL)
  Quartet: Live At Blues Alley ....(COL)
Cherokee Fiddle
Johnny Lee; *Greatest Hits* ....(FA)
ST/*Urban Cowboy* ....(ASY)
Michael Martin Murphey; *Best Of* ....(EMI)
  Flowing Free Forever ....(EMI)
Cherokee Maiden
Merle Haggard; *All-Time Greatest Hits Of Country-#1* ....(CCB)
  Capitol Collectors Series ....(CAP)
Cherokee Mist
Jimi Hendrix; *Lifelines/Story* ....(RPR)
Cowboys & Indians
Billy Strange; *Great Western Themes* ....(CRS)
Rita Coolidge; *Fall Into Spring* ....(A&M)

Crow
Dan Fogelberg; *Captured Angel* ....(FM)
General Custer
Tom Paxton; *How Come The Sun* ....(OOP)
Give It Back To The Indians
Ella Fitzgerald; *Rodgers/Hart Songbook* ....(VRV)
Give It Back To The Indians (New York)
Ella Fitzgerald; *Rodgers & Hart Songbook* ....(VRV)
Half Breed
Cher; *Greatest Hits* ....(MCA)
I Want To Live In A Wigwam
Cat Stevens; *Footsteps In The Dark-Greatest Hits-#2* ....(A&M)
In God We Trust
Barefoot Jerry; *Barefoot Jerry's Grocery* ....(MON)
Indian Girl
Capris; *There's A Moon Out Tonight* ....(CLT)
Hollies; *Epic Anthology-Original Master Tapes* ....(EPI)
Rolling Stones; *Emotional Rescue* ....(RS)
Indian Giver
1910 Fruitgum Company; *Best Of & Other Bubblegum Smashes-#2* ....(RHI)
Indian Lady
Roger Whittaker; *Reflections Of Love* ....(RCA)
Indian Lake
Freddy Weller; *Greatest Hits* ....(COL)
Indian Love Call
Jeanette MacDonald/Nelson Eddy; *Legendary Performer* ....(RCA)
Ray Stevens; *Misty* ....(BBY)
  Very Best Of ....(BBY)
Slim Whitman; *Best Of-1952-1972* ....(RHI)
  Paloma Blanca-Best Of-Legendary Masters ....(EMI)
Indian Man
Charlie Daniels Band; *Midnight Wind* ....(EPI)
Indian Outlaw
Tim McGraw; *Not A Moment Too Soon* ....(CRB)
Indian Red
Wild Tchoupitoulas; *Wild Tchoupitoulas* ....(ISL)
Indian Reservation
Paul Revere/Raiders; *Legend Of* ....(COL)
  Pop Classics/'70s ....(COL)
Raiders; *Billboard Top Rock 'N' Roll Hits-1971* ..(RHI)
  Super Hits/'70s-Have A Nice Day-#5 ....(RHI)
Indian Summer
Doors; *Morrison Hotel* ....(ELE)
Ella Fitzgerald; *Newport Jazz Festival* ....(COL)
Frank Sinatra; *Reprise Collection* ....(RPR)
Glenn Miller; *Memorial 1944-1969* ....(RCA)
Joe Walsh; *But Seriously Folks* ....(ASY)
Poco; *Indian Summer* ....(MCA)
Roy Orbison/Gatlin Brothers; *Legendary Roy Orbison* ....(SSP)
Stan Getz; *Greatest Hits* ....(PRS)
Indian Summer Love
Con Funk Shun; *Secrets* ....(MER)
Indian Sunset
Elton John; *Madman Across The Water* ....(POL)
Indian Wedding
Roy Orbison; *Legendary* ....(SSP)
  More Greatest Hits ....(MON)
  Our Love Song ....(MON)
Indian Woman
Dan Hill; *Frozen In The Night* ....(20)
Sons Of The Pioneers; *Western Country* ....(GRA)
Indians
Anthrax; *Among The Living* ....(MEG)
Original Cast; *Peter Pan* ....(RCA)
Indians Here Dey Come
Wild Tchoupitoulas; *Wild Tchoupitoulas* .... (ISL)
I'm An Indian Too
Original Cast/Doris Day; *Annie Get Your Gun* ...(COL)
Original Cast/Ethel Merman/Bruce Yarnell; *Annie Get Your Gun* ....(RCA)
Original Cast/Ethel Merman/Ray Middleton; *Annie Get Your Gun* ....(MCA)
"Jumping Mouse" LP
Joyce Yarrow; *Various Tracks* ....(PA)
Land Of The Navajo
Peter Rowan; *New Grass Revival-Festival Tapes* ....(FF)
  Peter Rowan ....(FF)
Lonesome Indian
Country Gazette; *American & Clean* ....(FF)

Lost Indian
Clark Kessinger & Gene Meade; *Clark Kessinger & Gene Meade* .... (ROU)
Norman Blake & Tony Rice; *2* .... (ROU)
Massacre
Thin Lizzy; *Johnny The Fox* .... (WB)
Live & Dangerous .... (WB)
Native North American Child (Entire LP)
Buffy Sainte-Marie; *Native North American Child* (VAN)
Navajo Know
Pixies; *Trompe Le Monde* .... (ELE)
Navajo Land Blessing
Peter Kater & Carlos Nakai; *How The West Was Lost* .... (SW)
Navajo Rug
Ian Tyson; *Cowboyography* .... (SH)
Navajo Sky
James Asher; *Globalarium* .... (SW)
Navajo Trail
Michael Nesmith; *From A Radio Engine To The Photon Wing* .... (PA)
Navajo Wrangler
Chris LeDoux; *Western Tunesmith* .... (LIB)
Now That The Buffalo's Gone
Buffy Sainte-Marie; *American Child* .... (VAN)
Best Of .... (VAN)
Greatest Folksingers/'60s .... (VAN)
I'm Gonna Be A Country Child .... (VAN)
Please Mr. Custer
Ray Stevens; *Gitarzan* .... (BBY)
Pow Wow The Indian Boy
Hot Rize; *Hot Rize* .... (FF)
Pretty Little Indian
Dan Crary; *Lady's Fancy* .... (ROU)
Primitive People
Country Joe McDonald; *Goodbye Blues* .... (FAN)
Running Bear
Johnny Preston; *45s On CD-#1-1956-1959* ..... (MER)
Billboard Top Rock 'N' Roll Hits-1960 .... (RHI)
Cruisin'-1960 .... (INC)
Sonny James; *All-Time Country Classics-#1* ..... (CAP)
Seminole Wind
John Anderson; *Seminole Wind* .... (BNA)
Shenandoah
Bob Dylan; *Down In The Groove* .... (COL)
Harry Belafonte; *Legendary Performer* .... (RCA)
James Galway; *Greatest Hits* .... (RCA)
Leontyne Price; *God Bless America* .... (RCA)
Smoke Signal
Band; *Cahoots* .... (CAP)
Song Of Crazy Horse
J.D. Blackfoot; *Song Of Crazy Horse* .... (FAN)
Squaws Along The Yukon
Hank Thompson; *Capitol Collectors Series* ...... (CAP)
Greatest Hits-#2 .... (SO)
Straight Brother
Leon Russell & Marc Benno; *Asylum Choir-#2* . (MCA)
Sundancing (For The Hopi/Navajo Energy)
Jon Anderson; *In The City Of Angels* .... (COL)
Ten Little Indians
Beach Boys; *Surfin' Safari/Surfin' U.S.A.* .... (CAP)
Theme From "Dances With Wolves"
John Barry; *Moviola* .... (EPI)
Theme From "The Last Of The Mohicans"
Twentieth Century Fox Orchestra; *ST/The Last Of The Mohicans* .... (MC)
Trader
Beach Boys; *10 Years Of Harmony* .... (CAR)
Holland .... (CAR)
Voice Of The Eagle
Robbie Basho; *Voice Of The Eagle* .... (VAN)
Wedding In Cherokee County
Randy Newman; *Good Old Boys* .... (RPR)
Wigwam
Bob Dylan; *Self-Portrait* .... (COL)
Wild Injuns
Neville Brothers; *Yellow Moon* .... (A&M)
Wind In The Wire
Randy Travis; *Wind In The Wire* .... (WB)
Witchi Tai To
Jim Pepper; *Comin' & Goin'* .... (AND)
Pepper's Pow Pow .... (OOP)
Oregon; *Out Of The Woods* .... (ELE)
Winter Light .... (VAN)

With God On Our Side
Bob Dylan; *Times They Are A-Changin'* .... (COL)
Joan Baez; *First 10 Years* .... (VAN)
Neville Brothers; *Yellow Moon* .... (A&M)
Wooden Indian
John Denver; *Poems Prayers & Promises* .... (RCA)
Wounded Knee Soliloquy
Robbie Basho; *Voice Of The Eagle* .... (VAN)
Wreck Of The Edmund Fitzgerald
Gordon Lightfoot; *Gord's Gold-#2* .... (WB)
Summertime Dream .... (RPR)
Your Squaw Is On The Warpath
Loretta Lynn; *Greatest Hits-#2* .... (MCA)

NEWS, Magazines, Newspapers

Ain't That Good News
David "Fathead" Newman; *Bigger & Better-Many Facets Of* .... (RHI)
Attractive Female Wanted
Rod Stewart; *Blondes Have More Fun* .... (WB)
Bad News
Emmylou Harris; *Ballad Of Sally Rose* .... (WB)
Johnny Winter; *About Blues* .... (JNS)
Before The Storm .... (JNS)
Bad News Travels Fast
Bachman-Turner Overdrive; *Live Live Live* ...... (MCA)
Player; *Room With A View* .... (CAS)
Walter Egan; *Hi-Fi* .... (COL)
Billy Got Some Bad News Today
Tom Paxton; *It Ain't Easy* .... (FF)
Breakfast In Mayfair
Fairport Convention; *Babbacombe Lee* .... (OOP)
Chronicles .... (A&M)
Centerfold
J. Geils Band; *Flashback-Best Of* .... (EMI)
Freeze-Frame .... (EMI)
Showtime .... (EMI)
Cover Of Rolling Stone
Dr. Hook/Medicine Show; *Greatest Hits* .... (CAP)
Revisited .... (COL)
Day In The Life
Beatles; *1967-1970* .... (CAP)
Sgt. Pepper's Lonely Hearts Club Band .... (CAP)
ST/Imagine-The Motion Picture .... (CAP)
Digging In The Dirt
Peter Gabriel; *Us* .... (GEF)
Dirty Laundry
Don Henley; *I Can't Stand Still* .... (ASY)
Don't Give Me Bad News
Bobby Caldwell; *Stuck On You* .... (SD)
Don't Nobody Bring Me No Bad News
Mabel King; *ST/The Wiz* .... (ATL)
Don't Take My Sunday Paper
Holly Near & Jeff Langley; *You Can Know All I Am* .... (RWD)
Escape (Pina Colada Song)
Rupert Holmes; *Billboard Top Hits-1979* .... (RHI)
Partners In Crime .... (INF)
Front Page News
Angel City; *Two-Minute Warning* .... (MET)
Little Feat; *Down On The Farm* .... (WB)
Hoy-Hoy! .... (WB)
Front Page Story
Neil Diamond; *Heartlight* .... (COL)
Good News
Attitudes; *Good News* .... (DKH)
Kingston Trio; *Scarlet Ribbons* .... (CAP)
Mary Travers; *It's In Every One Of Us* .... (CHR)
Melissa Manchester; *Better Days & Happy Endings* .... (ARI)
Muddy Waters; *Chess Box* .... (CSS)
Red Rider; *Don't Fight It* .... (CAP)
Sweet Honey In The Rock; *Good News* .... (FF)
Good News Travels Fast
Jerry Lee Lewis; *When Two Worlds Collide* ..... (ELE)
Have You Heard The News
Ben Sidran; *Puttin' In Time On Planet Earth* .... (MCA)
Vikki Carr; *Live At the Greek Theatre* .... (COL)
Headlines
John Fogerty; *Eye Of The Zombie* .... (WB)
Midnight Star; *Headlines* .... (SLR)

I Got The News
Steely Dan; *Aja* .... (MCA)
In The Want Ads
Mickey Gilley; *Mickey Gilley* .... (PLA)
Little Good News
Anne Murray; *Greatest Hits-#2* .... (CAP)
   Little Good News ....(CAP)
Little Paper Boy
Hank Williams; *Rare Takes & Radio Cuts* .... (POL)
Magazine
Heart; *Magazine* ....(CAP)
Rickie Lee Jones; *The Magazine* .... (WB)
Magazine Lover
Pieces; *Pieces* .... (UA)
More News At 11
Public Enemy; *Apocalypse 91...The Enemy Strikes*
Black ....(DFC)
More Trouble Every Day
Frank Zappa/Mothers Of Invention; *Roxy &*
Elsewhere ....(OOP)
Morning Papers
Prince/New Power Generation; *Love Symbol*
Album ....(PAI)
News
Dire Straits; *Communique* .... (WB)
Jimmy Cliff; *Follow My Mind* .... (RPR)
News At Ten
Vapors; *New Clear Days* .... (LIB)
News For You Baby
Sonny Terry; *Sonny Terry* ....(CLT)
T-Bone Walker; *T-Bone Walker* .... (BLN)
News From Spain
Al Stewart; *Early Years* .... (JNS)
News From Up The Street
Dan Hicks/Hot Licks; *Where's The Money?* ......(OOP)
Newspapers
Automatic Man; *Automatic Man* .... (ISL)
Stan Ridgway; *Mosquitos* .... (GEF)
Newsreel Babies
INXS; *INXS* ....(ATC)
Nothing's News
Clint Black; *Killin' Time* ....(RCA)
   ST/My Heroes Have Always Been Cowboys ....(RCA)
One Reporter's Opinion
Minutemen; *Double Nickels On The Dime* ....(SST)
Power Of The Press
Angelic Upstarts; *Brighton Bomb* .... (CHS)
Pump It Up (Here's The News)
M.C. Hammer; *Let's Get It Started* ....(CAP)
Reader's Digest
Betty Comden & Adolph Green; *Party With* .... (DRG)
Richard Cory
Paul McCartney/Wings; *Wings Over America* ....(CAP)
Simon & Garfunkel; *Collected Works* ....(COL)
   Sounds Of Silence ....(COL)
Roll Over Beethoven
Beatles; *At The Hollywood Bowl* ....(CAP)
   Box Set ....(CAP)
   Rock & Roll Music-#1 ....(CAP)
   Second Album ....(CAP)
   With The Beatles ....(CAP)
Byrds; *Byrds (collection)* ....(COL)
Chuck Berry; *Chess Box* ....(CSS)
   Cruisin'-1956 ....(INC)
   Golden Hits ....(MER)
   Greatest Hits ....(EVR)
   Oldies But Goodies-#10 ....(OSR)
Electric Light Orchestra; *Afterglow* ....(EPI)
   Ole ELO ....(JET)
Sad News From Korea
Lightnin' Hopkins; *Houston's King of the*
Blues-1952-1953 ....(BCL)
Second Hand News
Fleetwood Mac; *25 Years-The Chain* .... (WB)
   Rumours .... (WB)
Seven O'Clock News
Simon & Garfunkel; *Collected Works* ....(COL)
   Parsley Sage Rosemary & Thyme ....(COL)
Six O'Clock News
John Prine; *John Prine* ....(ATL)
Sunday Papers
Joe Jackson; *Live-1980-1986* ....(A&M)
   Look Sharp! ....(A&M)
   No Wave ....(A&M)

Swimsuit Issue
Sonic Youth; *Dirty* ....(DGC)
Tell Me What The Papers Say
Elton John; *Ice On Fire* ....(MCA)
Tennessee Newsboy (Newsboy Blues)
Frank Sinatra; *Columbia Years-1943-1952-Complete*
Rec. ....(COL)
Tom's Diner
DNA/Suzanne Vega; *Solitude Standing* .... (A&M)
   Tom's Album .... (A&M)
Turn On The News
Husker Du; *Zen Arcade* ....(SST)
Vogue
Madonna; *Immaculate Collection* .... (SIR)
   I'm Breathless .... (SIR)
   Royal Box .... (SIR)
Want Ad Blues
John Lee Hooker; *Best Of* ....(CRS)
   John Lee Hooker ....(EVR)
   World's Greatest Blues Singer .... (VJ)
Want Ads
Honey Cone; *Greatest Hits* .... (HDH)
Your Picture In The Paper
Statler Brothers; *Best Of-Rides Again-#2* .... (MER)
   Harold Lew Phil & Don .... (MER)

NIGHT, Evening, Goodnight, Tonight
   See Also: SATURDAY, SATURDAY NIGHT;
   MIDNIGHT, MOON

African Night Flight
David Bowie; *Lodger* ....(RYK)
Again Tonight
John Mellencamp; *Whenever We Wanted* .... (MER)
Ain't Going Down (Til The Sun Comes Up)
Garth Brooks; *In Pieces* .... (LIB)
Alaskan Nights
David Schwartz; *ST/Music From "*
Northern Exposure" .... (MCA)
All Night
Entouch Featuring Keith Sweat; *All Nite* .... (VNT)
Keith Washington; *Make Time For Love* .... (QUE)
All Night Juke
Lloyd Green; *Lloyd's Of Nashville* .... (BOO)
All Night Laundromat Blues
Joe Walsh; *So What* .... (MCA)
All Night Long
Billy Squier; *Signs Of Life* ....(CAP)
Eagles; *Live* .... (ASY)
Jerry Lee Lewis; *18 Original Sun Greatest Hits* ... (RHI)
   Milestones .... (RHI)
Joe Houston; *20 Super Rhythm & Blues Hits* .....(KNT)
   Rock & Roll Festival-#1 ....(KNT)
Joe Walsh; *ST/Urban Cowboy* .... (ASY)
Little Richard; *Fabulous* .... (SPE)
   Well Alright .... (SPE)
All Night Long (All Night)
Lionel Richie; *Can't Slow Down* .... (MOT)
   Motown Story-First 25 Years .... (MOT)
All Night Television
3-D; *3-D* ....(POL)
All Quiet Along The Potomac Tonight
Hermes Nye; *Ballads Of The Civil War-#1 & 2* . (FLW)
All Through The Night
Cyndi Lauper; *She's So Unusual* ....(POR)
Original Broadway Cast; *Anything Goes* ....(RCA)
And We Bid You Goodnight
Grateful Dead; *Live Dead* .... (WB)
Angel Of The Night
Angela Bofill; *Angel Of The Night* .... (GRP)
   Best Of .... (ARI)
Another Honky Tonk Night On Broadway
David Frizzell & Shelly West; *Album* .... (WB)
   Golden Duets ....(VVA)
Another Night
Aretha Franklin; *Who's Zoomin' Who* .... (ARI)
Dionne Warwick; *Anthology 1962-1971* .... (RHI)
Hollies; *Best of-#2* .... (EMI)
   Epic Anthology From Original Masters .... (EPI)
Real McCoy; *S* .... (ARI)
Another Night In Tunisia
Bobby McFerrin; *Spontaneous Inventions* .... (BLN)

Manhattan Transfer; *Vocalese* .... (ATL)
Another Night With The Boys
  Drifters; *All-Time Greatest Hits &*
    More-1959-1965 .... (ATL)
  Persuasions; *Bread & Roses Festival-Acoustic*
    Music-#1 .... (FAN)
Another Rainy Night
  Queensryche; *Empire* .... (EMI)
Another Sleepless Night
  Anne Murray; *Country Hits* .... (CAP)
    Greatest Hits .... (CAP)
    Where Do You Go When You Dream .... (CAP)
  Shawn Christopher; *S* .... (ARI)
Arabian Nights
  Bruce Adler; *ST/Aladdin* .... (DIS)
Are You Lonesome Tonight
  Elvis Presley; *From Memphis To Vegas* .... (RCA)
    Golden Records-#3 .... (RCA)
    In Person .... (RCA)
    Valentine Gift For You .... (RCA)
    Worldwide 50 Gold Award Hits-#1 .... (RCA)
Arubian Nights
  Larry Coryell & Emily Remler; *Together* ...... (CCJ)
As Tears Go By
  Marianne Faithfull; *Greatest Hits* .... (AKO)
    Strange Weather .... (ISL)
  Rolling Stones; *Big Hits-High Tide & Green Grass* (AKO)
    December's Children .... (AKO)
    Hot Rocks 1964-1971 .... (AKO)
    Singles Collection-London Years .... (AKO)
As We Kiss Goodnight
  Iguanas; *Nuevo Boogaloo* .... (MGR)
At Night
  Cure; *Seventeen Seconds* .... (ELE)
  See No Evil; *See No Evil* .... (EPA)
At Night She Sleeps
  Night Ranger; *Dawn Patrol* .... (CAM)
Autumn Nocturne
  Sonny Rollins; *Don't Stop The Carnival* ...... (MS)
Baby, It's Tonight
  Jude Cole; *View From Third Street* .... (RPR)
Back To The Night
  Joan Armatrading; *Back To The Night* .... (A&M)
    Classics-#21 .... (A&M)
Be Mine Tonight
  Neil Diamond; *On The Way To The Sky* .... (COL)
Be Mine (Tonight)
  Grover Washington, Jr.; *Anthology* .... (ELE)
    Come Morning .... (ELE)
Because The Night
  10,000 Maniacs; *MTV's Unplugged* .... (ELE)
  Bruce Springsteen/E Street Band;
    Live-1975-1985 .... (COL)
  Patti Smith Group; *Cover Me* .... (RHI)
    Easter .... (ARI)
Berlin Tonight
  Bruce Cockburn; *World Of Wonders* .... (COL)
Betty Lou's Gettin' Out Tonight
  Bob Seger/Silver Bullet Band; *Against The Wind* (CAP)
    Nine Tonight .... (CAP)
Beware Of Darkness
  George Harrison; *All Things Must Pass* .... (CAP)
    Concert For Bangladesh .... (CAP)
Big City Nights
  Scorpions; *Best Of Rockers 'N' Ballads* ...... (MER)
    Love At First Sting .... (MER)
    World Wide Live .... (MER)
Black Is The Night
  Sandy Posey; *45* .... (WB)
Black Night
  Bob Seger; *Beautiful Loser* .... (CAP)
  Deep Purple; *Deepest Purple-Very Best Of* .... (WB)
    Nobody's Perfect .... (MER)
  Dr. John; *In A Sentimental Mood* .... (WB)
  Muddy Waters; *Chess Box* .... (CSS)
Black Nights
  Bobby Bland; *Ain't Nothing You Can Do* .... (MCA)
    Introspective Of The Early Years .... (MCA)
  Charles Brown; *45* .... (UA)
Black Water
  Doobie Brothers; *Best Of* .... (WB)
    What Were Once Vices Are Now Habits .... (WB)
Blues In The Night
  Bobby Bland; *Introspective Of The Early Years* (MCA)

Dinah Shore; *Nipper's Greatest Hits-'40s-#1* ... (RCA)
Doc Severinsen; *Best Of* .... (MCA)
Frank Sinatra; *Sings For Only The Lonely* ..... (CAP)
Mel Torme; *Torme* .... (VRV)
Robins; *Best Of* .... (CRS)
Rosemary Clooney; *16 Most Requested Songs* .... (COL)
Woody Herman; *Best Of The Decca Years* .... (DEC)
Bluest Eyes In Texas
  Restless Heart; *Big Dreams In A Small Town* ... (RCA)
Boogie Nights
  Heatwave; *Greatest Hits* .... (EPI)
    Skatetown U.S.A. .... (COL)
    Too Hot To Handle .... (EPI)
Bordello Night
  City Boy; *Young Men Gone West* .... (MER)
Buenos Noches From A Lonely Room
  Dwight Yoakam; *Buenos Noches From A Lonely*
    Room .... (RPR)
But I Might Die Tonight
  Cat Stevens; *Tea For The Tillerman* .... (A&M)
By The Time This Night Is Over
  Kenny G & Peabo Bryson; *Breathless* .... (ARI)
California Nights
  Lesley Gore; *Summer & Sun* .... (RHI)
  Sweet; *Level-Headed* .... (CAP)
Can I See You Tonight
  Tanya Tucker; *Best Of* .... (MCA)
    Live .... (MCA)
Can You Feel The Love Tonight
  Elton John; *ST/The Lion King* .... (DIS)
Cheat The Night
  Deborah Allen; *Cheat The Night* .... (RCA)
Children Of Darkness
  Joan Baez; *Contemporary Ballad Book* .... (VAN)
Children Of The Night
  Richard Marx; *Repeat Offender* .... (EMI)
Chug All Night
  Eagles; *Eagles* .... (ASY)
City Of Night
  Peter Schilling; *Different Story (World Of Lust &*
    Crime) .... (ELE)
Clock Strikes Ten
  Cheap Trick; *At Budokan* .... (EPI)
    In Color .... (EPI)
Colder Are My Nights
  Isley Brothers; *45* .... (WB)
Color Of The Night
  Lauren Christy; *ST/Color Of Night* .... (MER)
Coming Out Of The Dark
  Gloria Estefan; *Greatest Hits* .... (EPI)
    Hot #1 Hits .... (FTN)
    Into The Light .... (EPI)
Cool Night
  Paul Davis; *Cool Night* .... (ARI)
Creatures Of The Night
  Kiss; *Creatures Of The Night* .... (CAS)
Crying In The Night
  Melba Moore; *Soul Exposed* .... (CAP)
Cryin' Through The Night
  Stevie Wonder; *Characters* .... (MOT)
Dance The Night Away
  Cream; *Disraeli Gears* .... (RSO)
  Europe; *Wings Of Tomorrow* .... (EPI)
  Van Halen; *2* .... (WB)
Dancing In The Dark
  Bruce Springsteen; *Born In The U.S.A.* .... (COL)
  Tony Bennett; *Forty Years-Artistry Of* .... (COL)
    Jazz .... (COL)
Darkness On The Edge Of Town
  Bruce Springsteen; *Darkness On The Edge Of*
    Town .... (COL)
  Bruce Springsteen/E Street Band;
    Live-1975-1985 .... (COL)
Daydreams About Night Things
  Ronnie Milsap; *Collectors' Series* .... (RCA)
    Greatest Hits .... (RCA)
    Live .... (RCA)
    Night Things .... (RCA)
Daytime Nightime Suffering
  Wings; *Back To The Egg* .... (CAP)
Dead Of The Night
  Bad Company; *Holy Water* .... (ATC)
  Shawn Colvin; *Steady On* .... (COL)

December '63
Frankie Valli/Four Seasons; *25th Anniversary*
Collection .... (RHI)
Anthology .... (RHI)
Dedicated To The One I Love
Mamas & The Papas; *Best Of* .... (MCA)
Farewell To The First Golden Era .... (MCA)
Orig. Classic Oldies/'50s-'60s-#13 .... (MCA)
Shirelles; *Anthology: 1959-1964* .... (RHI)
Greatest Hits .... (EVR)
Oldies But Goodies-#10 .... (OSR)
Super Oldies/'50s-#4 .... (AUF)
Deeper Than The Night
Olivia Newton-John; *Totally Hot* .... (MCA)
Dim All The Lights
Donna Summer; *Bad Girls* .... (CAS)
Dance Collection .... (CAS)
Greatest Hits .... (CAS)
On The Radio-Greatest Hits-#1 & 2 .... (CAS)
Dimming Of The Day
Bonnie Raitt; *Longing In Their Hearts* .... (CAP)
Don't Crash The Car Tonight
Mary's Danish; *Experience (Live + Foxey Lady)* . (CML)
There Goes The Wondertruck... .... (CML)
Don't Let Me Be Lonely Tonight
James Taylor; *Greatest Hits* .... (WB)
One Man Dog .... (WB)
Don't Say Goodnight
Valentines; *Original Rock 'N' Roll Hits Of The*
'50s .... (RLL)
Don't Say No Tonight
Eugene Wilde; *45* .... (PHL)
Don't You Know What The Night Can Do
Steve Winwood; *Roll With It* .... (VIA)
Don't Your Mem'ry Ever Sleep At Night
Ronnie Milsap; *Keyed Up* .... (RCA)
Steve Wariner; *Best Of* .... (RCA)
Down That Road Tonight
Nitty Gritty Dirt Band; *More Great Dirt: Best*
Of-#2 .... (WB)
Workin' Band .... (WB)
Down The Road Tonight
Bruce Hornsby/Range; *The Way It Is* .... (RCA)
Drive
Cars; *Greatest Hits* .... (ELE)
Heartbeat City .... (ELE)
MTV's Rock 'N Roll To Go .... (ELE)
Drive All Night
Bruce Springsteen; *The River* .... (COL)
End Of The Night
Doors; *Doors* .... (ELE)
Weird Scenes Inside The Gold Mine .... (ELE)
Endless Night
Graham Parker/Rumour; *Up Escalator* .... (ARI)
Endless Summer Nights
Richard Marx; *Richard Marx* .... (EMI)
Even The Nights Are Better
Air Supply; *Greatest Hits* .... (ARI)
Now & Forever .... (ARI)
Evening In Casablanca
Art Farmer Quintet; *Art Farmer Quintet* .... (PRS)
Evening Rainbow
Sylvia St. James; *Echoes & Images* .... (ELE)
Evening Star
Gene Loves Jezebel; *Kiss Of Life* .... (GEF)
Judas Priest; *Hell Bent For Leather* .... (COL)
Kenny Rogers; *Eyes That See In The Dark* ...... (RCA)
Every Night
Chantels; *45* .... (RLL)
Joe Williams; *Every Night-Live At Vine St.* .... (VRV)
Paul McCartney; *Paul McCartney* .... (COL)
Unplugged .... (CAP)
Paul McCartney/Wings; *Kampuchea* .... (ATL)
Phoebe Snow; *Best Of* .... (COL)
Weavers; *Classics* .... (VAN)
Every Night When The Sun Goes In
Jo Stafford; *Jo Plus Blues* .... (CRN)
Everybody Have Fun Tonight
Wang Chung; *Mosaic* .... (GEF)
Father Of Night
Bob Dylan; *New Morning* .... (COL)
Flowers Of The Night
Paul Kantner; *Baron Von Tollbooth & The Chrome*
Nun .... (GRU)

Fly By Night
Rush; *All The World's A Stage* .... (MER)
Archives .... (MER)
Fly By Night .... (MER)
Fly Into Night
Charly McClain; *Biggest Hits* .... (EPI)
Paradise .... (EPI)
Fly Into This Night
Gino Vannelli; *Best Of* .... (A&M)
Classics-#7 .... (A&M)
Gist Of The Gemini .... (A&M)
Foggy Night In London Town
Fred Astaire; *45* .... (OOP)
Friday Night Blues
John Conlee; *Friday Night Blues* .... (MCA)
Greatest Hits .... (MCA)
Sonny Throckmorton; *45* .... (MER)
Gardening At Night
R.E.M.; *Chronic Town* .... (IRS)
Eponymous .... (IRS)
Get Down Tonight
K.C./Sunshine Band; *Best Of* .... (RHI)
Billboard Top Hits-1975 .... (RHI)
Get Down Tonight-Best Of T.K. .... (RHI)
Get Up! (Before The Night Is Over)
Technotronic; *Pump Up The Jam-The Album* .... (SBK)
Gettin' Into Tennessee Tonight
Gary Wolf; *45* .... (MER)
Girls Night Out
Judds; *Greatest Hits* .... (MCA)
Why Not Me .... (MCA)
Tyler Collins; *S* .... (RCA)
Give Me All Night
Carly Simon; *Coming Around Again* .... (ARI)
Give Me The Night
George Benson; *Collection* .... (WB)
Give Me The Night .... (WB)
Give Me Tonight
Shannon; *45* .... (MIR)
Go All Night
Pat Travers; *Boom Boom...Best Of* .... (POL)
Go For What You Know .... (POL)
Heat In The Street .... (POL)
Going Out Tonight
Mary Chapin Carpenter; *Shooting Straight In The*
Dark .... (COL)
Gonna Go Huntin' Tonight
Hank Williams, Jr.; *Greatest Hits-#2* .... (W/C)
Strong Stuff .... (WB)
Good Evening Mr. Waldheim
Lou Reed; *New York* .... (SIR)
Good Rockin' Tonight
Elvis Presley; *Date With Elvis* .... (SUN)
Sun Sessions .... (SUN)
Sun Story .... (RHI)
Jerry Lee Lewis; *20 Classic Jerry Lee Lewis Hits* . (OSR)
Trio Plus .... (SUN)
Jimmy Witherspoon; *Best Of* .... (PRS)
Spoon Concerts .... (FAN)
Goodnight
Beatles; *White Album* .... (CAP)
Original Broadway Cast; *I Do! I Do!* .... (RCA)
Rembrandts; *Rembrandts* .... (ATC)
Roy Orbison; *For The*
Lonely-Anthology-1958-1965 .... (RHI)
Legendary .... (SSP)
Our Love Song .... (MON)
Goodnight Dallas
Carlene Carter; *I Fell In Love* .... (RPR)
Goodnight Irene
Jim Reeves; *Pure Gold* .... (RCA)
Johnny Cash; *Man-The World-His Music* ...... (SUN)
Rough Cut King Of Country Music .... (SUN)
Ry Cooder; *Chicken Skin Music* .... (RPR)
Weavers; *At Carnegie Hall* .... (VAN)
Best Of .... (MCA)
Greatest Hits .... (VAN)
Goodnight My Love
Benny Goodman; *Best Of* .... (RCA)
Complete-#4 .... (RCA)
Pure Gold .... (RCA)
This Is .... (RCA)
Fleetwoods; *Best Of* .... (RHI)

Sarah Vaughan; *Divine-Columbia*
Years-1949-1953 ....(COL)
Goodnight My Someone
Original Cast; *ST/Music Man* ....(CAP)
Shirley Jones; *ST/Music Man* ....(WB)
Goodnight Now
Cheap Trick; *At Budokan* ....(EPI)
Goodnight Saigon
Billy Joel; *Greatest Hits #1 & 2-1978-85* ....(COL)
KOHUEPT ....(COL)
Nylon Curtain ....(COL)
Goodnight Tonight (Don't Say It)
Paul McCartney/Wings; *All The Best* ....(CAP)
Goodnight Vienna
Ringo Starr; *Goodnight Vienna* ....(CAP)
Goodnight Well It's Time To Go
Chuck Berry; *Greatest Hits* ....(EVR)
Spaniels; *Goodnight Well It's Time To Go* ....(VJ)
Hits From The Legendary Vee-Jay Records .....(MOT)
ST/American Graffiti ....(MCA)
Goodnight, Good Guy
Collective Soul; *Hints Allegations And Things Left
Unsaid* ....(ATL)
Goodnight, Sweetheart
Flamingos; *Best Of* ....(RHI)
Spaniels; *Cruisin'-1957* ....(INC)
Doo-Wop Ballads-#2 ....(RHI)
Lovin' '50s ....(PRY)
Gotta Get You Home Tonight
Eugene Wilde; *Eugene Wilde* ....(PHL)
Hard Day's Night
Beatles; *1962-1966* ....(CAP)
20 Greatest Hits ....(CAP)
At The Hollywood Bowl ....(CAP)
Hard Day's Night ....(CAP)
Reel Music ....(CAP)
ST/Hard Day's Night ....(CAP)
Harlem Nocturne
Mel Torme; *Gonna Get New York* ....(ATL)
Viscounts; *Soul Shots-#3-Soul Twist* ....(RHI)
Havana For A Night
Mae West; *Fabulous* ....(MCA)
Have You Seen The Stars Tonight
Jefferson Airplane; *Flight Log* .... (GRU)
Paul Kantner/Jefferson Starship; *Blows Against The
Empire* ....(RCA)
Hawaiian Nights
Kingston Trio; *Looking For The Sunrise* ....(XER)
Hazard (The River)
Richard Marx; *Rush Street* ....(CAP)
Headache Tomorrow (Or A Heartache...)
Mickey Gilley; *Biggest Hits* .... (EPI)
Ten Years Of Hits ....(EPI)
That's All That Matters To Me .... (EPI)
Heart Of The Night
Juice Newton; *Greatest Hits* ....(CAP)
Greatest Hits & More ....(CAP)
Quiet Lies ....(CAP)
Poco; *Backtracks* .... (MCA)
Legend .... (MCA)
Heartache Tonight
Conway Twitty; *Latest Greatest Hits-#1* ....(WB)
Lost In The Feeling ....(WB)
Eagles; *Greatest Hits* ....(ASY)
Live ....(ASY)
Long Run ....(ASY)
John Anderson; *Common Thread-Songs Of The
Eagles* ....(GIA)
Heartbeat In The Darkness
Don Williams; *New Moves* ....(CAP)
Prime Cuts ....(CAP)
Heat Of The Night
Bryan Adams; *Into The Fire* ....(A&M)
Jay Ferguson; *White Noise* ....(CAP)
Heaven Tonight
Cheap Trick; *Heaven Tonight* .... (EPI)
Help Me Make It Through The Night
Bryan Ferry; *Another Time Another Place* ....(RPR)
Gladys Knight/Pips; *Anthology* ....(MOT)
Compact Command Performance .... (MOT)
Joan Baez; *Blessed Are* ....(VAN)
Hits/Greatest & Others ....(VAN)
Sammi Smith; *Super Hits/'70s-Have A Nice
Day-#4* ....(RHI)

Willie Nelson; *Greatest Hits & Some That Will Be* (COL)
Sings Kristofferson ....(COL)
Sweet Memories ....(RCA)
Here Comes The Night
Beach Boys; *L.A.-Light Album* ....(CAR)
Smiley Smile/Wild Honey ....(CAP)
David Bowie; *Pinups* ....(RYK)
Van Morrison; *It's Too Late To Stop Now* ....(WB)
Van Morrison/Them; *Best Of* ....(MER)
Featuring Van Morrison ....(PRT)
High School Nights
Dave Edmunds; *Anthology-1968-1990* .... (RHI)
ST/Porky's Revenge ....(MOB)
Hold Back The Night
Graham Parker; *Pourin' It All Out-Mercury Years* (MER)
Trammps; *45* ....(ERI)
Hold On To The Nights
Richard Marx; *Richard Marx* .... (EMI)
Hollywood Nights
Bob Seger/Silver Bullet Band; *Nine Tonight* ......(CAP)
Stranger In Town ....(CAP)
Honky Tonk Night Time Man
Lynyrd Skynyrd; *Street Survivors* .... (MCA)
Merle Haggard/Strangers; *Presents His 30th
Album* ....(CAP)
Songs I'll Always Sing ....(CAP)
Hot Night In New York City
Bonnie Koloc; *With You On My Side* .... (FF)
Hot Nite In Dallas
Moon Martin; *Shots From A Cold Nightmare* ....(CAP)
Hot Summer Nights
Miami Sound Machine; *ST/Top Gun* ....(COL)
Rick James; *Wonderful* ....(RPR)
Walter Egan; *Not Shy* ....(COL)
Hot Texas Night
Mac Davis; *Texas In My Rear View Mirror* ....(CAS)
Hymn For A Sunday Evening
Original Cast; *Bye Bye Birdie* ....(COL)
I Ain't Gonna Cry Tonight
Barbra Streisand; *Wet* ....(COL)
I Could Have Danced All Night
Julie Andrews/Original Cast; *My Fair Lady* ......(COL)
I Couldn't Sleep A Wink Last Night
Frank Sinatra; *Greatest Hits-#2* ....(COL)
Voice-Columbia Years-1943-1952 ....(COL)
Mello Moods; *Great Groups/'50s-#3* ....(CLT)
I Cried Last Night
Charles Brown; *One More For The Road* .... (ALL)
I Drove All Night
Cyndi Lauper; *Night To Remember* .... (EPI)
I Fell In Love Again Last Night
Forester Sisters; *Country Love Songs* ....(WB)
Forester Sisters ....(WB)
Greatest Hits ....(WB)
I Got The Sun In The Morning
Doris Day/Original Cast; *Annie Get Your Gun* ...(COL)
Ethel Merman/Ray Middleton/Original Cast; *Annie Get
Your Gun* ....(MCA)
I Had A Dream
John Sebastian; *ST/Woodstock* ....(ATL)
I Love A Rainy Night
Eddie Rabbitt; *All-Time Greatest Hits* ....(WB)
Greatest Hits-#2 ....(WB)
Horizon ....(ELE)
Number 1's ....(WB)
Ten Years Of Greatest Hits ....(CAP)
I Love The Night
Blue Oyster Cult; *Spectres* ....(COL)
Joe Cocker; *Civilized Man* ....(CAP)
I Love The Night Life
Alicia Bridges; *Alicia Bridges* .... (POL)
Night At Studio 54 ....(CAS)
Oldies But Goodies-#14 ....(OSR)
Polydor Dance Classics ....(POL)
I Need Your Love Tonight
Elvis Presley; *Golden Records-#1* ....(RCA)
Top Ten Hits ....(RCA)
I Saw Her Again
Mamas & The Papas; *Best Of* .... (MCA)
Farewell To The First Golden Era .... (MCA)
Mamas & The Papas ....(MCA)
I Want You Tonight
Pablo Cruise; *45* ....(A&M)

I Watched It All (On My Radio)
Lionel Cartwright; *I Watched It All On The Radio* .... (MCA)
I Wish I Was In Texas Tonight
Patti Ford; *45* ....(NAT)
I Wish You Were Here Tonight
Ray Charles; *Greatest Hits Of Country Blues* .....(COL)
  I Wish You Were Here Tonight ....(COL)
I Wonder Where We'd Be Tonight
Vern Gosdin; *45* .... (CMP)
I Wonder Where You Are Tonight
Bill Monroe; *Bean Blossom* .... (MCA)
Jerry Lee Lewis; *Country Music Hall Of Fame Hits* .... (SMA)
Keith Whitley; *L.A. To Miami* ....(RCA)
I Wonder Who's Holding My Baby
Whites; *Greatest Hits* ....(W/C)
I Won't Be Home Tonight
Tony Carey; *Tony Carey* .... (ROC)
If I Could Be With You
Helen Humes; *Ladies Sing The Blues-#2* .... (SAV)
Louis Armstrong; *Satchmo-Musical Autobiography-#2* ....(MCA)
  Best Of ....(MCA)
  Story-#4 ....(COL)
If I Could Have Her Tonight
Neil Young; *Neil Young* ....(RPR)
If I Should Die Tonight
Marvin Gaye; *Let's Get It On* ....(MOT)
  Musical Testament-1964-1984 ....(MOT)
If Your Heart Ain't Busy Tonight
Tanya Tucker; *What Do I Do With Me* ....(LIB)
In The Air Tonight
Phil Collins; *Classic Rock 1966-1988* ....(ATL)
  Face Value ....(ATL)
  Miami Vice ....(MCA)
  Prince's Trust 10th Anniversary Party ....(A&M)
  Secret Policeman's Other Ball ....(ISL)
  Serious Hits...Live! ....(ATL)
In The Cool Cool Cool Of The Evening
Bing Crosby; *Best Of* .... (MCA)
Frank Sinatra; *Days Of Wine & Roses-Academy A. Winners* ....(RPR)
In The Dark
Billy Squier; *Don't Say No* ....(CAP)
Lonnie Brooks; *Bayou Lightning* ....(ALG)
Roy Ayers; *In The Dark* ....(COL)
In The Evening
Joe Turner; *In The Evening* ....(PAB)
Joe Williams; *Everyday I Have The Blues* .... (SAV)
Led Zeppelin; *In Through The Out Door* .... (SS)
  Led Zeppelin (collection) ....(ATL)
In The Evening When The Sun Goes Down
Ella Fitzgerald; *These Are The Blues* ....(VRV)
Mel Torme; *Duke Ellington & Count Basie Songbook* ....(VRV)
Pete Seeger; *20 Golden Pieces Of* ....(BLD)
  Sings Folk Music Of The World ....(TRD)
In The Heat Of The Night
Pat Benatar; *In The Heat Of The Night* .... (CHR)
Ray Charles; *His Greatest Hits-#2* ....(DHL)
  ST/In The Heat Of The Night .... (UA)
In The Still Of The Night
Dion; *Greatest Hits* ....(LAU)
  Sings The 15 Million Sellers ....(LAU)
Dion/Belmonts; *Wish Upon A Star With* ....(CLT)
Five Satins; *Billboard Top R&B Hits-1956* .... (RHI)
  Cruisin'-1956 ....(INC)
  In The Still Of The Night ....(CAP)
  Sing Their Greatest Hits ....(CLT)
  ST/Dirty Dancing ....(RCA)
Johnny Mathis; *In The Still Of The Night* ....(COL)
In The Still Of The Nite (I'll Remember)
Boyz II Men; *Cooleyhighharmony* ....(MOT)
Into The Night
Benny Mardones; *Benny Mardones* ....(CRB)
  Never Run Never Hide ....(POL)
B.B. King; *Six Silver Strings* ....(MCA)
  Soundtrack Smashes-The '80s & More ....(MCA)
  ST/Into The Night ....(MCA)
Julee Cruise; *Floating Into The Night* ....(WB)
  Twin Peaks ....(WB)
Sweet; *Desolation Boulevard* ....(CAP)

It's 3 O'Clock In The Morning
Mom & Dads; *Blue Hawaii* .... (CRS)
It's All Coming Down Tonight
Barbusters; *ST/Light Of Day* ....(CBA)
Frankie Miller; *Standing On The Edge* ....(CAP)
I'd Really Love To See You Tonight
England Dan & John Ford Coley; *Best Of* ....(BT)
  Hit Singles 1958-1977 ....(ATL)
  Nights Are Forever ....(BT)
I'll Be With You Tonight
Cheap Trick; *Dream Police* .... (EPI)
I'll Be Your Baby Tonight
Bob Dylan; *Biograph* ....(COL)
  Columbia Country Classics-#5-New Trad. ......(COL)
  Greatest Hits-#2 ....(COL)
  John Wesley Harding ....(COL)
Linda Ronstadt; *Different Drum* ....(CAP)
  Hand Sown ....(CAP)
  Retrospective ....(CAP)
I'll Be Your Jukebox Tonight
Barbara Mandrell; *I'll Be Your Jukebox Tonight* ..(CAP)
I'm Missing Texas Tonight
Kim Grayson; *45* ....(SND)
I'm Not Gonna Let It Bother Me Tonight
Atlanta Rhythm Section; *Are You Ready?* ....(POL)
  Champagne Jam ....(POL)
I'm Your Baby Tonight
Whitney Houston; *I'm Your Baby Tonight* ...... (ARI)
I'm Your Late Night Evening Prostitute
Tom Waits; *Early Years* ....(BIZ)
Jam Tonight
Freddie Jackson; *Just Like The First Time* ....(CAP)
June Night
Betty Everett; *Very Best Of* .... (VJ)
Just Another Night
Ian Hunter; *Shades Of* ....(CHR)
  You're Never Alone With A Schizophrenic ......(CHR)
Mick Jagger; *45* ....(COL)
  She's The Boss ....(COL)
Just For Tonight
Vanessa Williams; *Comfort Zone* ....(WIN)
Just One Night
McBride & The Ride; *Sacred Ground* ....(MCA)
Justice Tonight/Rock It Over
Clash; *Black Market Clash* .... (EPI)
Keep It Dark
Genesis; *Abacab* ....(ATL)
King Of The Night Time World
Kiss; *Alive 2* ....(CAS)
  Destroyer ....(CAS)
Ladies Night
Kool/Gang; *Ladies Night* .... (DL)
Ladies Night In Buffalo
David Lee Roth; *Eat 'Em & Smile* ....(WB)
Ladies Of The Night
Leon Russell; *Americana* ....(PRD)
Last Night
Buddy Holly/Crickets; *Chirping Crickets* .... (MCA)
Mar-Keys; *Atlantic R&B 1947-1974-#4-(1958-1962)* ....(ATL)
  Soul Shots-#3-Soul Twist ....(RHI)
Stephanie Mills; *Tantalizingly Hot* ....(CAS)
Traveling Wilburys; *Traveling Wilburys* ....(WIL)
Last Worthless Evening
Don Henley; *End Of The Innocence* ....(GEF)
Late In The Evening
Paul Simon; *Negotiations & Love Songs-1971-1986* ....(WB)
  One-Trick Pony ....(WB)
Simon & Garfunkel; *Concert In Central Park* .....(WB)
Late Night Radio
John Denver; *Windsong* ....(RCA)
Left In The Dark
Barbra Streisand; *Emotion* ....(COL)
Let It Roll
Little Feat; *Let It Roll* ....(WB)
Let Me Love You Tonight
Pure Prairie League; *Firin' Up* ....(CAS)
  TT & Other Hits ....(RCA)
Let Me Take You Home Tonight
Boston; *Boston* .... (EPI)
Let's Go
Cars; *Candy-O* ....(ELE)
  Greatest Hits ....(ELE)

Eurythmics; *Revenge* .... (RCA)
Nitty Gritty Dirt Band; *Let's Go* .... (LIB)
Wang Chung; *Mosaic* .... (GEF)
Let's Groove
Earth, Wind & Fire; *Best Of* .... (COL)
  Raise .... (COL)
Let's Spend The Night Together
David Bowie; *Aladdin Sane* .... (RYK)
  ST/Ziggy Stardust-The Motion Picture .... (RCA)
Rolling Stones; *Between The Buttons* .... (AKO)
  Flowers .... (AKO)
  Hot Rocks-1964-1971 .... (AKO)
  Still Life-American Concert-1981 .... (RS)
  Through The Past Darkly-Big Hits-#2 .... (AKO)
Let's Take All Night (To Say Goodbye)
Barry Manilow; *If I Should Love Again* .... (ARI)
Light My Fire
Doors; *13* .... (ELE)
  Best Of .... (ELE)
  Doors .... (ELE)
  Greatest Hits .... (ELE)
  ST/Doors .... (ELE)
Jose Feliciano; *All-Time Greatest Hits* .... (RCA)
  Encore .... (RCA)
Light Up The Night
Brothers Johnson; *Classics-#11* .... (A&M)
  Light Up The Night .... (A&M)
Like No Other Night
38 Special; *Flashback-Best Of* .... (A&M)
  Strength In Numbers .... (A&M)
Little Night Dancin'
John Cougar Mellencamp; *John Cougar*
  Mellencamp .... (RIV)
Little Night Music
Original Cast; *Little Night Music* .... (COL)
London By Night
Frank Sinatra; *Come Fly With Me* .... (CAP)
  Sinatra Rarities-Columbia Years .... (COL)
Lonely Is The Night
Billy Squier; *Don't Say No* .... (CAP)
Lonely Nights
Bryan Adams; *You Want It You Got It* .... (A&M)
Mickey Gilley; *Biggest Hits* .... (EPI)
  Greatest Country Hits/'80s-1982 .... (COL)
  Ten Years Of Hits .... (EPI)
  You Don't Know Me .... (EPI)
White Lion; *Pride* .... (ATL)
Lonely Ol' Night
John Cougar Mellencamp; *Scarecrow* .... (RIV)
Lost In The Fifties Tonight
Ronnie Milsap; *Greatest Hits-#2* .... (RCA)
  Lost In The Fifties Tonight .... (RCA)
Love Is Alright Tonight
Rick Springfield; *Greatest Hits* .... (RCA)
  Working Class Dog .... (RCA)
Love On My Mind Tonight
Temptations; *45* .... (GOR)
Lover Who Rocks You (All Night)
India; *Breaking Out* .... (JEL)
Lovers In The Night
Toto; *IV* .... (COL)
Love's Gonna Fall Here Tonight
Razzy Bailey; *45* .... (RCA)
Lovin' All Night
Rodney Crowell; *Greatest Country Hits/'90s-#2* ..(COL)
  Life Is Messy .... (COL)
Luck Be A Lady
Frank Sinatra; *Reprise Collection* .... (RPR)
  Sinatra Reprise-The Very Good Years .... (RPR)
Original Cast; *Guys & Dolls* .... (MCA)
Me Against The Night
Crystal Gayle; *Cage The Songbird* ....(WB)
Meet Me Tonight By My Old Kentucky Home
Joe Val/New England Bluegrass Boys; *#2* ...... (ROU)
Middle Of The Night
Divine Horsemen; *Devil's River* ....(SST)
  Middle Of The Night .... (SST)
Mel Tillis; *45* .... (MCA)
Mommy, Can I Go Out & Kill Tonight
Misfits; *Walk Among Us* .... (RUB)
Monday Night
Golden Palominos; *Golden Palominos* .... (CEL)
  History-1982-1985 .... (MTR)
Pere Ubu; *Cloudland* .... (FON)

Monday Night Football & Me
Turner Rice; *45* .... (BNG)
Money Don't Matter 2 Night
Prince/New Power Generation; *Diamonds And*
  Pearls .... (PAI)
Moroccan Nights
John Tropea; *NY Cats Direct* .... (DIG)
Moscow Nights
Feelies; *Crazy Rhythms* .... (A&M)
Murder, Tonight, In The Trailer Park
Cowboy Junkies; *Black-Eyed Man* .... (RCA)
Music Of The Night
Michael Crawford; *Premiere Collection-Best Of A.L.*
  Webber .... (MCA)
Original London Cast; *Phantom Of The Opera* ... (POL)
My First Night Alone Without You
Bonnie Raitt; *Collection* .... (WB)
  Home Plate .... (WB)
Jane Olivor; *First Night* ....(COL)
My First Night Without You
Cyndi Lauper; *Night To Remember* .... (EPI)
My Night To Howl
Lorrie Morgan; *War Paint* .... (BNA)
Nashville 1 A.M.
Harvey Mandel; *Cristo Redentor* .... (EDI)
Need You Tonight
INXS; *Hit Singles 1980-1988* .... (ATL)
  Kick .... (ATL)
  Live Baby Live .... (ATL)
Need Your Loving Tonight
Queen; *The Game* ....(HOL)
Nicaragua Night
Holly Near; *All-Ears Review-#7-Still Amazing...* . (ROM)
Night
Bruce Springsteen; *Born To Run* ....(COL)
Jackie Wilson; *Mr. Excitement* .... (RHI)
  My Golden Favorites ....(BRU)
Night And Day
Bette Midler; *Some People's Lives* .... (ATL)
Billie Holiday; *Legacy Box 1933-1958* ....(COL)
Ella Fitzgerald; *Cole Porter Songbook* ....(VRV)
Frank Sinatra; *& Strings* ....(RPR)
  Capitol Years ....(CAP)
  Man And His Music ....(RPR)
  Nipper's Greatest Hits-'40s-#1 ....(RCA)
  Reprise Collection ....(RPR)
  Sinatra Reprise-The Very Good Years ....(RPR)
U2; *Red Hot & Blue (Tribute To Cole Porter)* .... (CHR)
Night Bird Flying
Jimi Hendrix; *Cry Of Love* .... (RPR)
  Lifelines/Jimi Hendrix Story .... (RPR)
Night Blooming Jasmine
Charles Lloyd Quartet; *Night In Copenhagen* ..... (BLN)
Night Boat To Cairo
Madness; *One Step Beyond* .... (SIR)
  ST/Dance Craze .... (CHR)
Night By Night
Dokken; *Back For The Attack* .... (ELE)
Heather Mullen; *Heather Mullen* .... (EW)
Steely Dan; *Pretzel Logic* .... (MCA)
Night Chicago Died
Paper Lace; *Back To The '70s-#3* .... (DOM)
  Super Hits/'70s-Have A Nice Day-#13 .... (RHI)
Night Comes Down
Judas Priest; *Defenders Of The Faith* ....(COL)
Queen; *Queen* ....(HOL)
Night Creatures
Melissa Manchester; *Mathematics* .... (MCA)
Night Fever
Bee Gees; *Greatest* .... (POL)
  ST/Saturday Night Fever ....(POL)
Night Flight
Buddy Guy; *Complete Chess Studio Recordings* ... (CSS)
Led Zeppelin; *Physical Graffiti* .... (SS)
Night Game
Paul Simon; *Still Crazy After All These Years* ......(WB)
Night Games
Charley Pride; *Charley Pride* ....(RCA)
  Greatest Hits-#2 ....(RCA)
  Night Games ....(RCA)
Gregg Allman Band; *Just Before The Bullets Fly* ..(EPI)
Night Has A Thousand Eyes
Anita O'Day; *Night Has A Thousand Eyes* ...... (EML)

Bobby Vee; *Best Of* .... (EMI)
   Golden Years-1962 ....(DOM)
   Legendary Masters .... (EMI)
Night I Called The Old Man Out
Garth Brooks; *In Pieces* .... (LIB)
Night In Buenos Aires
101 Strings Orchestra; *Best Of Latin* .... (ALS)
Night In London
Poncho Sanchez; *Chile Con Soul* .... (CP)
Night In My Veins
Pretenders; *Last Of The Independents* .... (SIR)
Night In Oklahoma
Larry McNeely; *Power Play* .... (FF)
Night In The City
Joni Mitchell; *Joni Mitchell* .... (RPR)
Night In Tunisia
Charlie Parker; *Bird On 52nd St.* .... (FAN)
   Charlie Parker .... (PRS)
   One Night In Birdland ....(COL)
   Very Best Of Bird ....(WB)
Dizzy Gillespie; *Electrifying Evening* ....(VRV)
   Jazz At Massey Hall .... (FAN)
   Musician Composer Raconteur .... (PAB)
   Nipper's Greatest Hits-'40s-#2 ....(RCA)
Tuxedo Junction; *Take The "A" Train* .... (BTF)
Night Is Still Young
Billy Joel; *Greatest Hits-#1 & 2-1973-1985* ......(COL)
Night Life
Charlie Daniels Band/Friends; *Volunteer Jam 3&4* (EPI)
Miracles; *Greatest Hits* ....(MOT)
Ray Price; *Greatest Hits-#2* ....(SO)
Thin Lizzy; *Night Life* .... (MER)
Willie Nelson; *Country Willie* .... (UA)
   Healing Hands Of Time .... (LIB)
   Souvenirs Of Music City U.S.A. .... (PLN)
   Willie ....(RCA)
   /Family Live ....(COL)
Night Life In Pompeii
Earl Hines; *Earl Hines* .... (CRS)
Night Moves
Bob Seger; *Night Moves* ....(CAP)
   Nine Tonight ....(CAP)
   ST/FM ....(MCA)
Marilyn Martin; *Marilyn Martin* .... (ATL)
Night Of My Nights
Original Cast; *Kismet* ....(COL)
Vic Damone; *ST/Kismet* .... (SSP)
Night Of The Thumpasorus People
Parliament; *Live* .... (CAS)
   Mothership Connection .... (CAS)
Night Of The Vampire
Grim Reaper; *Rock You To Hell* ....(RCA)
Roky Erickson; *You're Gonna Miss Me-Best Of* .. (RES)
Night Of Van Gogh
Boz Scaggs; *Other Roads* ....(COL)
Night On The 4th Of May
Al Stewart; *Early Years* ....(OOP)
Night On The Town
Bruce Hornsby/Range; *Night On The Town* ....(RCA)
Night Owl
Carly Simon; *Best Of* .... (ELE)
   No Secrets .... (ELE)
Night Owls
Little River Band; *Greatest Hits* ....(CAP)
   Time Exposure ....(CAP)
Night Prowler
AC/DC; *Highway To Hell* .... (ATL)
Night Ride Out Of Phoenix
Gillan; *Future Shock* .... (MET)
Night Rider
Electric Light Orchestra; *Face The Music* ....(JET)
Elvis Presley; *Collector's Gold* ....(RCA)
   Live In Nashville ....(RCA)
   ST/Pot Luck ....(RCA)
Night Rider's Lament
Chris LeDoux; *Old Cowboy Classics* .... (LIB)
   Paint Me Back Home In Wyoming .... (LIB)
   & The Saddle Boogie Band .... (LIB)
Garth Brooks; *The Chase* .... (LIB)
Jerry Jeff Walker; *Ridin' High* .... (MCA)
Nanci Griffith; *Other Voices Other Rooms* .... (ELE)
Suzy Bogguss; *Somewhere Between* ....(CAP)
Night Shift
Bob Marley/Wailers; *Rastaman Vibrations* ....(TUF)

Foghat; *Best Of* .... (RHI)
   Night Shift .... (RHI)
Night The Carousel Burned Down
Todd Rundgren; *Somthing/Anything?* .... (RHI)
Night The Lights Went Out
Trammps; *Best Of* ....(ATL)
   III ....(ATL)
Night The Lights Went Out In Georgia
Lynn Anderson; *Top Of The World* ....(COL)
Reba McEntire; *For My Broken Heart* .... (MCA)
Vicki Lawrence; *Super Hits/'70s-Have A Nice
Day-#10* .... (RHI)
Night They Drove Old Dixie Down
Band; *Anthology* ....(CAP)
   Band ....(CAP)
   Best Of ....(CAP)
   Gift Set ....(CAP)
   Last Waltz ....(WB)
   Rock Of Ages-#1 & 2 ....(CAP)
Bob Dylan/Band; *Before The Flood* ....(COL)
Joan Baez; *Classics-#8* ....(A&M)
   Country Music Album ....(VAN)
   From Every Stage ....(A&M)
   Hits/Greatest & Others ....(VAN)
Night They Invented Champagne
Betty Wand/Louis Jordan/Others; *ST/Gigi* ....(SSP)
Original Cast; *Gigi* ....(RCA)
Night Time
J. Geils Band; *Love Stinks* .... (AMR)
Ted Nugent/Amboy Dukes; *Greatest Collection
Ever* ....(DHL)
Night Time In The Switching Yard
Warren Zevon; *Excitable Boy* .... (ASY)
Night Time Is Cry Time
Jimmy C. Newman; *Greatest Hits* .... (PLN)
Night Time Is The Right Time
Creedence Clearwater Revival; *1969* .... (FAN)
   Chronicle-#2 .... (FAN)
   Green River .... (FAN)
Ray Charles; *Complete Atlantic R&B
Recordings-1952-59* .... (ATL)
Night Time Magic
Larry Gatlin/Gatlin Brothers; *17 Greatest Hits* ...(COL)
   Greatest Hits ....(COL)
   Live At 8:00 ....(CAP)
   Oh Brother ....(COL)
Night To Remember
Cyndi Lauper; *Night To Remember* .... (EPI)
Foreigner; *Inside Information* .... (ATL)
Jody Watley; *Beginnings* .... (SLR)
Shalamar; *Friends* .... (SLR)
   Greatest Hits .... (SLR)
   Mega Hits Dance Classics-#5 ....(PRY)
Night Train
James Brown/Famous Flames; *Soul Shots-Collection Of
'60s Soul* .... (RHI)
   ST/Quadrophenia ....(POL)
Jimmy Forrest; *Heart Of The Forest* ....(PAJ)
   Night Train ....(DEL)
Lionel Richie; *Dancing On The Ceiling* ....(MOT)
Paul Revere/Raiders; *Legend Of* ....(COL)
Rickie Lee Jones; *Rickie Lee Jones* ....(WB)
Steve Winwood; *Arc Of A Diver* .... (ISL)
U2; *Island Story 1962-1987 25th Anniversary* .... (ISL)
Night Train To Madrid
Bertram Levy; *That Old Gut Feeling* .... (FF)
Night Train To Memphis
Jerry Lee Lewis; *Rare Tracks* .... (RHI)
   Taste Of Country ....(SUN)
Roy Acuff; *Best Of* ....(CAP)
   Greatest Hits ....(COL)
Night Watch
Fleetwood Mac; *Penguin* .... (RPR)
Night Watchman
Tom Petty/Heartbreakers; *Hard Promises* .... (MCA)
Night We Called It A Day
Frank Sinatra; *Night We Called It A Day* ....(CAP)
   Where Are You? ....(CAP)
Tommy Dorsey & Frank Sinatra; *Radio Years
1940-1942* ....(RCA)
Night (Feel Like Getting Down)
Billy Ocean; *Night (Feel Like Getting Down)* ...... (EPI)
Nightclubbing
Grace Jones; *Nightclubbing* .... (ISL)

Iggy Pop; *Idiot* .... (RCA)
  TV Eye/1977 Live .... (RCA)
Nightmare
Artie Shaw; *Begin The Beguine* .... (BLU)
  Best Of The Big Bands .... (COL)
Black Sabbath; *Eternal Idol* .... (WB)
Eddie Money; *Life For The Taking* .... (COL)
Slaughterhouse; *Face Reality* .... (MET)
Stevie Nicks; *Rock A Little* .... (MOD)
Nightmares
A Flock Of Seagulls; *Best Of* .... (JVA)
  Listen .... (JVA)
Dana Dane; *Rap Hall Of Fame* .... (KT)
  With Fame ....(PRO)
J. Geils Band; *Nightmares* .... (ATL)
Omen; *Nightmares* .... (MET)
Violent Femmes; *2* .... (SLS)
Nights
Ed Bruce; *Night Things* .... (RCA)
Nights Are Forever
Jennifer Warnes; *ST/Twilight Zone-The Movie* ... (WB)
Nights Are Forever Without You
England Dan & John Ford Coley; *Best Of* .... (BT)
  Nights Are Forever Without You .... (BT)
Nights In White Satin
Moody Blues; *Billboard Top Rock 'N' Roll
  Hits-1972* .... (RHI)
  Caught Live Plus Five .... (POL)
  Days Of Future Passed .... (POL)
  History Of British Rock-#8 .... (RHI)
  This Is The .... (POL)
Nights Like This
Stacey Q; *Nights Like This* .... (ATL)
Nights On Broadway
Bee Gees; *Greatest* .... (POL)
  Here At Last .... (RSO)
  Main Course .... (RSO)
Nights Over Egypt
Jones Girls; *Get As Much Love As You Can* .... (PI)
Rastine; *Afrodisiac* .... (ZOO)
Nighttrain
Guns N' Roses; *Appetite For Destruction* .... (GEF)
Public Enemy; *Apocalypse 91...The Enemy Strikes
  Black* .... (DFJ)
  Stanley Son Of Theodore-Music Sampler .... (EPI)
Nightwatch
Kenny Loggins; *Nightwatch* .... (COL)
Night's Too Long
Patty Loveless; *On Down The Line* .... (MCA)
Nine Tonight
Bob Seger/Silver Bullet Band; *Nine Tonight* ...... (CAP)
  ST/Urban Cowboy .... (ASY)
Nite And Day
Al B. Sure!; *In Effect Mode* .... (WB)
No More Lonely Nights
Paul McCartney; *All The Best* .... (CAP)
  ST/Give My Regards To Broad Street .... (CAP)
No Sugar Tonight
Guess Who; *American Woman* .... (RCA)
  Best Of .... (RCA)
  Track Record-Collection .... (RCA)
November Nights
Flim/BB's; *Tunnel* .... (DIG)
October Night
Cliff Sarde; *Every Bit Better/Waiting* .... (MCA)
  Waiting .... (MCA)
October Nights
Stone Soup; *October Nights* .... (WCH)
Oh What A Night For Dancing
Barry White; *Greatest Hits-#2* .... (CAS)
  Sings For Someone You Love .... (20)
Oh, What A Night
Dells; *Billboard Top R&B Hits-1965-1969* .... (RHI)
  Collectables History Of Rock-#9 .... (CLT)
  Cruisin' 1956 .... (INC)
  Oh, What A Night .... (VJ)
  Oldies But Goodies-#3 .... (OSR)
On A Night Like This
Bob Dylan; *Biograph* .... (COL)
  Planet Waves .... (COL)
On The Dark Side
John Cafferty/Beaver Brown Band; *ST/Eddie & The
  Cruisers* .... (SCO)

One Lonely Night
R.E.O. Speedwagon; *Hits* .... (EPI)
  Wheels Are Turnin' .... (EPI)
One More Night
Barbra Streisand; *Songbird* .... (COL)
Bob Dylan; *Nashville Skyline* .... (COL)
Bobby Brown; *Bobby* .... (MCA)
Corbin/Hanner; *Black & White Photograph* ..... (MER)
Fleetwood Mac; *Live* .... (WB)
Phil Collins; *No Jacket Required* .... (ATL)
  Serious Hits...Live! .... (ATL)
Stephen Bishop; *Best Of Bish* .... (RHI)
One Night
Albert King; *Blues For Elvis* .... (STX)
Elvis Presley; *50 Worldwide Gold Award Hits-#2* (RCA)
  Golden Records-#2 .... (RCA)
  Reconsider Baby .... (RCA)
  Top Ten Hits .... (RCA)
Ronnie Milsap; *Heart & Soul* .... (RCA)
One Night A Day
Garth Brooks; *In Pieces* .... (LIB)
One Night In Bangkok
Murray Head; *Chess Pieces* .... (RCA)
Original Broadway Cast; *Chess* .... (RCA)
One Night In Paris
John Boswell; *Count Me In* .... (HS)
One Night In The Hotel
Michel Petrucciani; *Promenade With Duke* .... (BLN)
One Night In Trinidad
Earl Fatha Hines; *Lionel Hampton Presents* .....(WHO)
One Night In Vienna
Schoenerz & Scott; *One Night In Vienna* .... (WH)
One Night Love Affair
Bryan Adams; *Reckless* .... (A&M)
One Night Stands
Hank Williams, Jr.; *Early Years* .... (W/C)
  One Night Stands .... (WB)
One Of These Nights
Eagles; *Anthology* .... (ASY)
  One Of These Nights .... (ASY)
  Their Greatest Hits 1971-1975 .... (ASY)
One Of Those Nights
Lisa Brokop; *Every Little Girl's Dream* .... (PAT)
One Sad Night In Kerrville
Tom Kell; *Sad Night* .... (WB)
One Summer Night
Danleers; *Mercury Vocal Group Collection* ...... (MER)
  More American Graffiti .... (MER)
  Remember When .... (GRL)
  Super Oldies/'50s-#1 .... (AUF)
  WCBS FM 101 History Of Rock-'50s-#1 .... (CLT)
One Summer Night In Brazil
Rippingtons; *Tourist In Paradise* .... (GRP)
One Time, One Night
Los Lobos; *By The Light Of The Moon* .... (SLS)
Open All Night
Bruce Springsteen; *Nebraska* .... (COL)
Daryl Hall & John Oates; *H20* .... (RCA)
Out Of Your Shoes
Lorrie Morgan; *Leave The Light On* .... (RCA)
Overnight Angels
Ian Hunter/Mott The Hoople; *Shades Of Ian
  Hunter* .... (COL)
Overnight Cafe
Chicago; *XIV* .... (COL)
Overnight Sensation
Mickey Gilley; *Greatest Hits-#2* .... (EPI)
Raspberries/Eric Carmen; *Best* .... (CAP)
Steve Wariner; *Best Of* .... (RCA)
Tina Turner; *Break Every Rule* .... (CAP)
  Live In Europe .... (CAP)
Overnight Success
George Strait; *Beyond The Blue Neon* .... (MCA)
  Ten Strait Hits .... (MCA)
Paradise Tonight
Charly McClain & Mickey Gilley; *19 Hot Country
  Requests* .... (EPI)
  Biggest Hits .... (EPI)
  It Takes Believers .... (EPI)
  Paradise .... (EPI)
  Ten Year Anniversary .... (EPI)
Party All Night
Quiet Riot; *Condition Critical* .... (EPA)
  Winners Take All .... (SSP)

Party Night
Curtis Mayfield; *Do It All Night* .... (CUR)
  Give Get Take & Have .... (CUR)
Isley Brothers; *Grand Slam* .... (TN)
Pilots Of Purple Twilight
Tangerine Dream; *Exit* .... (ELE)
Play It All Night Long
Warren Zevon; *Bad Luck Streak In Dancing
School* .... (ASY)
  Quiet Normal Life-Best Of .... (ASY)
Play The Game Tonight
Kansas; *Best Of* .... (EPA)
  Vinyl Confessions .... (KIR)
Neil Diamond; *On The Way To The Sky* ....(COL)
Prove It All Night
Bruce Springsteen; *Darkness On The Edge Of
Town* ....(COL)
Queen Of The Night
Whitney Houston; *ST/The Bodyguard* .... (ARI)
Quiet Nights Of Quiet Stars
Antonio Carlos Jobim; *Terra Brasilis* .... (WB)
Shirley Horn; *I Thought About You-Live At Vine
St.* ....(VRV)
Rainy Night House
Joni Mitchell; *Ladies Of The Canyon* .... (RPR)
Joni Mitchell/L.A. Express; *Miles Of Aisles* .... (ASY)
Rainy Night In Georgia
Brook Benton; *Anthology* .... (RHI)
  Atlantic R&B 1947-1974-#6-(1966-1969) ..... (ATL)
  Golden Age Of Black Music-1960-1970 .... (ATL)
  Pick Of .... (FFT)
  Soul Years .... (ATL)
  Today .... (COT)
Hank Williams, Jr.; *14 Greatest Hits* .... (POL)
Sam Moore & Conway Twitty; *Rhythm Country &
Blues* .... (MCA)
Rainy Night In Rio
Susannah McCorkle; *Thanks For The Memory* ...(PAU)
Rainy Night In Tokyo
Michael Franks; *Passionfruit* .... (WB)
Ramrod
Bruce Springsteen; *The River* ....(COL)
Reach Out Of The Darkness
Friend & Lover; *Flower Power* .... (KT)
Red Neckin' Love Makin' Night
Conway Twitty; *Classic Conway* .... (MCA)
  Legends .... (MCA)
  Mr. T .... (MCA)
  Night With .... (MCA)
Remember The Night
Johnny Law; *Johnny Law* .... (MET)
  ST/Freddy's Dead-Final Nightmare .... (MET)
Loungers; *Harlem Holiday-New York R&B-#6* ...(CLT)
Remember The Nights
Motels; *Best Of/No Vacancy* .... (CAP)
  Little Robbers .... (CAP)
Rest Of The Night
Natalie Cole; *Good To Be Back* .... (ELE)
Rhythm Of The Night
DeBarge; *Greatest Hits* .... (MOT)
  Motown Story-First 25 Years .... (MOT)
  Rhythm Of The Night .... (MOT)
Right Time Of The Night
Jennifer Warnes; *Best Of* .... (ARI)
  Jennifer Warnes .... (ARI)
River Of Dreams
Billy Joel; *River Of Dreams* ....(COL)
Rock Around The Clock
Bill Haley/Comets; *Billboard Top Rock 'N' Roll
Hits-1955* .... (RHI)
  Golden Hits .... (MCA)
  Greatest Hits .... (EVR)
  Greatest Hits .... (MCA)
  ST/American Graffiti .... (MCA)
Telex; *45* .... (SIR)
Rock Me Tonight (For Old Time's Sake)
Freddie Jackson; *Rock Me Tonight (For Old Time's
Sake)* ....(CAP)
Rock Me Tonite
Billy Squier; *Signs Of Life* .... (CAP)

Rock Steady
Aretha Franklin; *30 Greatest Hits* .... (ATL)
  Best Of ....(ATL)
  Ten Years Of Gold .... (ATL)
  Young Gifted & Black .... (ATL)
Whispers; *Just Gets Better With Time* .... (SLR)
Rock The Night
Europe; *Final Countdown* .... (EPI)
Rock With You
Jacksons; *Live* .... (EPI)
Michael Jackson; *Off The Wall* .... (EPI)
Rock & Roll Tonight
Grim Reaper; *Fear No Evil* ....(RCA)
Rock 'N' Roll Tonight
Cheap Trick; *Busted* .... (EPI)
Rockin' Every Night
Gary Moore; *Early Years* .... (WTG)
Rockin' Into The Night
38 Special; *Flashback-Best Of* .... (A&M)
  Rockin' Into The Night .... (A&M)
Running With The Night
Lionel Richie; *Back To Front-Greatest Hits* ...... (MOT)
  Can't Slow Down .... (MOT)
  Music For The Miracle .... (EPA)
Sable On Blond
Stevie Nicks; *Wild Heart* ....(MOD)
Sailing Nights
Bob Seger; *Beautiful Loser* .... (CAP)
Sambuca Nights
Special EFX; *Special EFX* .... (GRP)
San Antonio Nights
Eddy Raven; *Greatest Hits* .... (WB)
San Franciscan Nights
Eric Burdon/Animals; *Greatest Hits* ....(MGM)
  History Of British Rock-#8 .... (RHI)
San Francisco Days
Chris Isaak; *San Francisco Days* .... (RPR)
Saturday Night Jag
Clarence Williams/Orchestra; *Clarence
Williams/Orchestra-#1 (1927-1929)* ....(BIO)
Sausalito Summernight
Diesel; *Watts In A Tank* ....(REG)
Savannah Nights
Tom Johnston; *Everything You've Heard Is True* ... (WB)
Save Your Nights For Me
Placido Domingo; *Save Your Nights For Me* .....(COL)
Screaming In The Night
Krokus; *Headhunter* .... (ARI)
  Stayed Awake All Night-Best Of .... (ARI)
Screamin' Night Hog
Steppenwolf; *16 Greatest Hits* ....(MCA)
September Night
Van Morrison; *Inarticulate Speech Of The Heart* ..(WB)
Set The Night To Music
Roberta Flack & Maxi Priest; *Set The Night To
Music* ....(ATL)
Starship; *No Protection* .... (GRU)
Shadows Of The Night
Pat Benatar; *Best Shots* .... (CHR)
  Get Nervous .... (CHR)
Shake It Up Tonight
Cheryl Lynn; *Club Columbia* ....(COL)
  In The Night ....(COL)
Sharin' The Night Together
Dr. Hook; *Greatest Hits (& More)* .... (CAP)
  Pleasure & Pain .... (CAP)
Ships Don't Disappear In The Night
10 CC; *Live & Let Live* .... (MER)
Ships In The Night
Be Bop Deluxe; *Best Of-Raiding The Divine
Archive* ....(CAP)
  Live In The Air Age ....(OOP)
  Sunburst Finish .... (HAR)
Shot In The Dark
Ozzy Osbourne; *Ultimate Sin* ....(CBA)
Utopia; *Adventures In Utopia* .... (RHI)
Silver Bells (That Ring In The Night)
Bob Wills; *Anthology* .... (SSP)
  Best Of .... (MCA)
  Best Of-#2 .... (MCA)
Silver Dew On The Bluegrass Tonight
Johnnie Lee Wills; *Tulsa Swing* .... (ROU)

Six Days On The Road
Dave Dudley; *Billboard Top Country Hits-1963* .. (RHI)
  Country Music Classics-#2-1960-1965 .... (KT)
  Legends Of Country Guitar-#2 .... (RHI)
Flying Burrito Brothers; *Cabin Fever* .... (RLX)
  Farther Along-Best Of .... (A&M)
  Last Of The Red Hot Burritos .... (A&M)
Taj Mahal; *Giant Step/De Ole Folks At Home* ....(COL)
  Legends Of Rock Guitar-'60s-#2 .... (RHI)
Sleep Tight, Good Night Man
Kenny Rogers; *The Gambler* .... (EMI)
Sleepless Night
Dokken; *Back For The Attack* .... (ELE)
  Beast From The East .... (ELE)
John Lennon & Yoko Ono; *Milk & Honey* .... (POL)
Kinks; *Sleepwalker* .... (ARI)
Sleepless Nights
Emmylou Harris; *Pieces Of The Sky* .... (RPR)
Gram Parsons/Flying Burrito Brothers; *Sleepless
Nights* .... (A&M)
Judds; *Collector's Series* .... (RCA)
  River Of Time .... (RCA)
Slippin' Into Darkness
War; *All Day Music* .... (UA)
  Best Of...& More .... (RHI)
  ST/American Me .... (VIA)
  Super Bad .... (KT)
Snakes Crawl At Night
Charley Pride; *Best Of* ....(RCA)
Some Enchanted Evening
Jay/Americans; *All-Time Greatest Hits* .... (RHI)
  Come A Little Big Closer-Best Of .... (EMI)
Original Cast; *South Pacific* ....(COL)
Perry Como; *All-Time Greatest Hits-#1* .... (RCA)
Rosanno Brazzi; *ST/South Pacific* .... (RCA)
Willie Nelson; *What A Wonderful World* ....(COL)
Somebody Else's Night
Collin Raye; *In This Life* .... (EPI)
Someone Could Lose A Heart Tonight
Eddie Rabbitt; *Best Of-Greatest Hits-#2* .... (WB)
  Number 1's .... (WB)
  Step By Step .... (LIB)
Someone Saved My Life Tonight
Elton John; *Capt. Fantastic & The Brown Dirt
Cowboy* .... (POL)
  Greatest Hits-#2 .... (POL)
Somewhere In The Night
Barry Manilow; *Even Now* .... (ARI)
  Greatest Hits-#2 .... (ARI)
Somewhere Other Than The Night
Garth Brooks; *The Chase* .... (LIB)
Somewhere Tonight
Bob Seger/Silver Bullet Band; *Like A Rock* .... (CAP)
Highway 101; *Featuring Paulette Carlson* .... (WB)
  Greatest Hits .... (WB)
Toto; *Fahrenheit* ....(COL)
Song For A Winter's Night
Gordon Lightfoot; *Gord's Gold* .... (RPR)
  Way I Feel .... (UA)
Southern Nights
Chet Atkins & Allen Toussaint; *Rhythm Country &
Blues* .... (MCA)
Glen Campbell; *Best Of* .... (LIB)
  Classic Collection .... (LIB)
  Live .... (UA)
  Southern Nights .... (CAP)
  ST/Convoy .... (CAP)
Spend Another Night In Houston
Sonny James; *Sonny's Side Of The Street* .... (MON)
Spirit In The Dark
Aretha Franklin; *30 Greatest Hits* .... (ATL)
  Live At Fillmore West .... (ATL)
  Spirit In The Dark .... (ATL)
Spirit In The Night
Bruce Springsteen; *Greetings From Asbury Park* ..(COL)
Bruce Springsteen/E Street Band;
Live-1975-1985 ....(COL)
Manfred Mann's Earth Band; *Nightingales &
Bombers* .... (WB)
  Roaring Silence .... (WB)
Stay All Night
Backwoods Banjo; *Jes' Fine* .... (ROU)
Stay The Night
Benjamin Orr; *The Lace* .... (ELE)

Chicago; *Greatest Hits-1982-1989* .... (FM)
  #17 .... (FM)
Jane Olivor; *In Concert* ....(COL)
  Stay The Night ....(COL)
Stay With Me Tonight
Dave Edmunds; *Closer To The Flame* ....(CAP)
Jeffrey Osborne; *Stay With Me Tonight* .... (A&M)
Steal The Night Away
Stevie Woods; *Stevie Woods* .... (COT)
Stillness Of The Night
R.E.O. Speedwagon; *Good Trouble* .... (EPI)
Straight Tequila Night
John Anderson; *Seminole Wind* ....(BNA)
  Today's Hot Country .... (KT)
Strange Night
Heart; *BeBe Le Strange* .... (EPI)
Stranger In Our House Tonight
Gene Watson; *Memories To Burn* .... (EPI)
Strangered In The Night
Tom Petty/Heartbreakers; *Tom
Petty/Heartbreakers* .... (GG)
Strangers In The Night
Frank Sinatra; *Greatest Hits* .... (RPR)
  Sinatra Reprise-The Very Good Years .... (RPR)
  Strangers In The Night .... (RPR)
Such A Night
Band & Dr. John; *Last Waltz* .... (WB)
Dr. John & Chris Barber; *On A Mardi Gras Day* (GSR)
Elvis Presley; *From Nashville To Memphis-'60s
Masters* ....(RCA)
Summer Nights
Earl Klugh; *Whispers & Promises* .... (WB)
Marianne Faithfull; *Greatest Hits* .... (AKO)
Olivia Newton-John & John Travolta; *Back To
Basics-Essential-1971-1992* ....(GEF)
  ST/Grease .... (RSO)
Original Broadway Cast; *Grease* .... (POL)
Van Halen; *5150* .... (WB)
Sunday Night In San Fernando
Mel Torme/Mel-Tones; *California Suite* .... (DCO)
Sunglasses At Night
Corey Hart; *First Offense* .... (EMI)
  The Singles .... (EMI)
Sunrise, Sunset
Original Cast; *Fiddler On The Roof* ....(RCA)
Original London Cast; *Fiddler On The Roof* ....(COL)
Sweetwater Nights
Dave Grusin; *Out Of The Shadows* .... (GRP)
Sydney By Night
James Morrison; *Postcards From Down Under* ... (ATL)
Take Me Home Tonight
Eddie Money; *Can't Hold Back* ....(COL)
  Greatest Hits/Sound Of Money ....(COL)
Talking Back To The Night
Steve Winwood; *Chronicles* .... (ISL)
  Talking Back To The Night .... (ISL)
Teach Me Tonight
Al Jarreau; *Breakin' Away* .... (WB)
  Live In London .... (WB)
Diane Schuur; *Collection* .... (GRP)
Ella Fitzgerald; *Montreux '75* .... (PAB)
Phoebe Snow; *Best Of* ....(COL)
  It Looks Like Snow ....(COL)
Sarah Vaughan; *How Long Has This Been Going
On?* .... (PAB)
Teenage Good Night
Chordettes; *45* .... (BBY)
Tender Is The Night
Andy Williams; *Moon River & Other Great Movie
Themes* ....(COL)
Jackson Browne; *Lawyers In Love* .... (ASY)
Tony Bennett; *16 Most Requested Songs* ....(COL)
  I Left My Heart In San Francisco ....(COL)
Tennessee Nights
Pam Tillis; *Collection* .... (WB)
Thank The Lord For The Night Time
Neil Diamond; *Classics-Early Years* ....(COL)
  Glory Road-1968-1972 .... (MCA)
  Gold .... (MCA)
  Greatest Hits-1966-1992 ....(COL)
  Hot August Night-#2 ....(COL)
That Night In Las Vegas
Ennio Morricone; *ST/Bugsy* .... (EPI)

There Ain't No Santa Claus On The...
Captain Beefheart; *Spotlight Kid/Clear Spot* ...... (RPR)
There Ain't S... On T.V. Tonight
Minutemen; *Double Nickels On The Dime* ....(SST)
There Will Never Be Another Tonight
Bryan Adams; *Waking Up The Neighbours* ...... (A&M)
There'll Be A Hot Time In The Old...
Bessie Smith; *Complete Recordings-#3* ....(COL)
Louis Armstrong; *Best Of* ....(AUF)
Turk Murphy's San Francisco Jazz Band; *#1* .... (GTJ)
There'll Be No Teardrops Tonight
Anita Carter; *Hank Williams Songbook* ....(COL)
Hank Williams; *24 Greatest Hits* .... (MER)
Greatest Hits ....(POL)
There's A Kind Of Hush (All Over...)
Carpenters; *A Kind Of Hush* ....(A&M)
Classics-#2 ....(A&M)
Yesterday Once More ....(A&M)
Herman's Hermits; *XX-Their Greatest Hits* ...... (AKO)
There's A Moon Out Tonight
Capris; *20 Top 10 Hits/'50s & '60s* ....(LAU)
22 Leaders Of The Pack-#2 ....(LAU)
Collectables Presents History Of Rock-#3 ....(CLT)
There's A Moon Out Tonight ....(CLT)
(There's A) Fire In The Night
Alabama; *Roll On* ....(RCA)
They're Hanging Me Tonight
Marty Robbins; *Gunfighter Ballads & Trail Songs* (COL)
This Could Be The Night
Loverboy; *Big Ones* ....(COL)
Lovin' Every Minute Of It ....(COL)
This Flight Tonight
Joni Mitchell; *Blue* .... (RPR)
Nazareth; *Classics-#16* ....(A&M)
Hot Tracks ....(A&M)
This Is My Night
Chaka Khan; *I Feel For You* ....(WB)
Life Is A Dance/Remix Album ....(WB)
This Night Won't Last Forever
Bill La Bounty; *This Night Won't Last Forever* ..... (WB)
Michael Johnson; *Dialogue* .... (EMI)
Moe Bandy; *Many Mansions* ....(CCB)
Thursday Night Fever
Legendary Pink Dots; *Legendary Pink Dots* ....(PIA)
Tokyo Nights
Bee Gees; *One* ....(WB)
Rob Mullins; *Tokyo Nights* .... (NVA)
Tomorrow Doesn't Matter Tonight
Starship; *Knee Deep In The Hoopla* ....(GRU)
Tomorrow Night
Barbra Streisand; *ST/Yentl* ....(COL)
Bob Dylan; *Good As I Been To You* ....(COL)
Elvis Presley; *Complete Sun Sessions* ....(RCA)
For Everyone ....(RCA)
Reconsider Baby ....(RCA)
Sun's Greatest Hits ....(RCA)
La Vern Baker; *Atlantic R&B-1947-1974
(1952-1955)* ....(ATL)
Soul On Fire ....(ATL)
Tomorrow Night In Baltimore
Roger Miller; *Best Of* .... (MER)
More Golden Hits ....(SMA)
Tomorrow & Tonight
Kiss; *Alive 2* ....(CAS)
Love Gun ....(CAS)
Tonight
Barbara Mandrell; *Best Of* .... (MCA)
Love Ups & Downs .... (MCA)
Bryan Adams; *You Want It You Got It* ....(A&M)
Def Leppard; *Adrenalize* .... (MER)
Retro Active .... (MER)
Elton John; *Blue Moves* .... (MCA)
Live In Australia w/Melbourne Symphony ...... (MCA)
George Michael; *Two Rooms-Songs Of E. John & B.
Taupin* ....(POL)
Iggy Pop; *Lust For Life* .... (VIA)
John Mellencamp; *Nothin' Matters & What If It
Did* ....(RIV)
Kool/Gang; *In The Heart* .... (DL)
Larry Graham/Graham Central Station; *Star Walk* (WB)
New Kids On The Block; *Step By Step* ....(COL)
Nick Lowe; *Pure Pop For Now People* ....(COL)
Original Cast; *West Side Story* ....(COL)

Raspberries; *Best* ....(CAP)
Capitol Collectors Series ....(CAP)
Ready For The World; *Ready For The World* ... (MCA)
Rick Springfield; *Success Hasn't Spoiled Me Yet* ..(RCA)
Ringo Starr; *Bad Boy* ....(EPI)
Rude Boys; *Rude House* ....(ATL)
R.E.O. Speedwagon; *R.E.O.* ....(EPI)
Timothy B. Schmit; *Tell Me The Truth* .... (MCA)
Whispers; *Love For Love* ....(SLR)
Tonight Carmen
Marty Robbins; *All-Time Greatest Hits* ....(COL)
American Originals ....(COL)
Essential-1951-1982 ....(COL)
Tonight I Celebrate My Love
Peabo Bryson & Roberta Flack; *Born To Love* ...(CAP)
Collection ....(CAP)
Tonight I Climbed The Wall
Alan Jackson; *Lot About Livin' (& A Little 'Bout
Love)* ....(ARI)
Tonight I Give In
Angela Bofill; *Best Of* .... (ARI)
Too Tough .... (ARI)
Tonight I Shall Sleep With A Smile On...
Duke Ellington; *Black Brown & Beige* .... (BLU)
Sarah Vaughan; *Duke Ellington Songbook Two* ... (PAB)
Tonight Is So Right For Love
Elvis Presley; *ST/G.I. Blues* ....(RCA)
Tonight Is The Night
Betty Wright; *Best Of* .... (RHI)
Danger High Voltage ....(ATN)
Live .... (RHI)
Tonight It's You
Cheap Trick; *Greatest Hits* .... (EPI)
Standing On The Edge .... (EPI)
Tonight I'll Be Staying Here With You
Bob Dylan; *Greatest Hits-#2* ....(COL)
Nashville Skyline ....(COL)
Tonight I'm Yours
Rod Stewart; *Absolutely Live* ....(WB)
Storyteller-Complete Anthology-1964-1990 ......(WB)
Tonight I'm Yours ....(WB)
Tonight My Baby's Coming Home
Barbara Mandrell; *Best Of* ....(COL)
Tonight My Love Tonight
Paul Anka; *21 Golden Hits* ....(RCA)
30th Anniversary Collection .... (RHI)
Tonight She Comes
Cars; *Greatest Hits* ....(ELE)
Tonight Someone's Falling In Love
Johnny Carver; *Afternoon Delight* ....(MSP)
Best Of .... (MCA)
Tonight The Bottle Let Me Down
Brooks & Dunn; *Mama's Hungry Eyes-Merle Haggard
Tribute* ....(ARI)
Elvis Costello/Attractions; *Almost Blue* ....(COL)
Gram Parsons/Flying Burrito Brothers; *Sleepless
Night* ....(A&M)
Merle Haggard; *Swinging Doors* ....(OOP)
Tonight Tonight
Dion; *His Best* ....(LAU)
Mello-Kings; *Cruisin'-1956* .... (INC)
Greatest Hits ....(CLT)
Tonight We Just Might Fall In Love Again
Hal Ketchum; *Every Little Word* ....(CRB)
Tonight We're Gonna Tear Down The Walls
Randy Travis; *Always & Forever* ....(WB)
Tonight, Tonight, Tonight
Genesis; *Invisible Touch* ....(ATL)
Live-The Way We Walk-#1-The Shorts ....(ATL)
Tonight's All Right For Love
Elvis Presley; *Legendary Performer-#1* ....(RCA)
Tonight's The Night
Kool/Gang; *Ladies Night* .... (DL)
Neil Young; *Decade* .... (RPR)
Tonight's The Night .... (RPR)
Neil Young/Crazy Horse; *Live Rust* .... (RPR)
Shirelles; *16 Greatest Hits* ....(TRP)
Anthology-1959-1964 .... (RHI)
Tonight's The Night (Gonna Be All Right)
Rod Stewart; *Absolutely Live* ....(WB)
Downtown Train-Storyteller Selections ....(WB)
Greatest Hits ....(WB)
Night On The Town ....(WB)

Tonite
Boys; *Saga Continues* .... (MOT)
Tonite (Falling For Ya)
Jay Ferguson; *White Noise* .... (CAP)
Too Broke To Spend The Night
Buddy Guy; *Damn Right I've Got The Blues* .... (SIL)
Touch Me (All Night Long)
Cathy Dennis; *Move To This* .... (POL)
Touch The Night
Neil Young; *Landing On Water* .... (GEF)
Train Wreck On Prom Night
Pajama Slave Dancers; *Blood Sweat & Beers* ..... (RES)
Trying To Sleep Tonight
Clarence Carter; *Hooked On Love* .... (ICH)
   The Dr.'s Greatest Prescriptions-Best Of .... (ICH)
Twilight
Band; *Best Of* .... (CAP)
Electric Light Orchestra; *Time* .... (JET)
Neil Young; *This Note's For You* .... (RPR)
Paragons; *Best Of* .... (CLT)
Shawn Colvin; *Cover Girl* .... (COL)
Wynton Marsalis; *Wynton Marsalis* .... (COL)
Twilight Hotel
Quiet Riot; *QR III* .... (EPA)
Twilight In Boston
Jonathan Richman; *I Jonathan* .... (ROU)
Twilight In Turkey
Raymond Scott; *Reckless Nights & Turkish
   Twilights* .... (COL)
Twilight On The Trail
Michael Nesmith; *Tropical Campfires* .... (PA)
Twilight Time
Moody Blues; *Days Of Future Passed* .... (POL)
Platters; *Anthology* .... (RHI)
   Greatest Hits .... (TRP)
   Pick Of .... (FFT)
   Platters .... (EVR)
   Sold Out .... (FFT)
Willie Nelson; *What A Wonderful World* .... (COL)
Twistin' The Night Away
Rod Stewart; *Best Of-#2* .... (MER)
   Never A Dull Moment .... (MER)
   Sing It Again Rod .... (MER)
   Storyteller-Complete Anthology-1964-1990 ...... (WB)
Sam Cooke; *At The Copa* .... (RCA)
   Best Of .... (RCA)
   Dance Music .... (RCA)
   Man & His Music .... (RCA)
   Nipper's Greatest Hits-'60s-#2 .... (RCA)
   ST/Animal House .... (MCA)
Two Hot Girls (On A Hot Summer Night)
Carly Simon; *Coming Around Again* .... (ARI)
   Greatest Hits Live .... (ARI)
Undercover Of The Night
Rolling Stones; *Rewind (1971-1984)* .... (RS)
   Undercover .... (RS)
Until The Night
Billy Joel; *52nd Street* .... (COL)
Walk In The Night
Junior Walker/All-Stars; *All The Great Hits* ..... (MOT)
   Anthology .... (MOT)
   Motown Superstar Series-#5 .... (MOT)
Walkin' All Night
Little Feat; *Dixie Chicken* .... (WB)
Watchdogs Of The Night
UB40; *Live In Moscow* .... (A&M)
   Rat In The Kitchen .... (A&M)
Way You Look Tonight
Billie Holiday; *Quintessential-#2-1936* .... (COL)
Erroll Garner; *Body & Soul* .... (COL)
Frank Sinatra; *Days Of Wine & Roses* .... (RPR)
   Reprise Collection .... (RPR)
   Sinatra Reprise-Very Good Years .... (RPR)
Lettermen; *All-Time Greatest Hits* .... (CAP)
   Capitol Collectors Series .... (CAP)
We Belong
Pat Benatar; *Best Shots* .... (CHR)
   Tropico .... (CHR)
We Belong To The Night
UFO; *Mechanix* .... (CHR)

Wednesday Evening Blues
John Lee Hooker; *Black Snake* .... (FAN)
   John Lee Hooker .... (EVR)
   That's My Story .... (RVR)
   World's Greatest Blues Singer .... (VJ)
Well All Right (Tonight's The Night)
Andrews Sisters; *50th Anniversary Collection-#2* (MCA)
   Capitol Collectors Series .... (CAP)
We're Goin' Out Tonight
Cameo; *Cameosis* .... (CAS)
We've Got Tonite
Bob Seger/Silver Bullet Band; *Nine Tonight* ......(CAP)
   Stranger In Town .... (CAP)
Kenny Rogers & Sheena Easton; *20 Greatest Hits* (EMI)
   Greatest Country Hits .... (CCB)
   K. Rogers/K. Carnes/S. Easton/D. West .... (EMI)
   We've Got Tonite .... (EMI)
Whatever Gets You Thru The Night
John Lennon; *Collection* .... (CAP)
   Lennon .... (CAP)
   Shaved Fish .... (CAP)
   Walls & Bridges .... (CAP)
When Day Is Done
Coleman Hawkins; *Body & Soul* .... (BLU)
Helen Humes; *Swingin' With Humes* .... (CTM)
Mormon Tabernacle Choir/Columbia Orch.; *Songs
   America Loves Best-Memories* .... (COL)
When She Cries
Restless Heart; *Big Iron Horses* .... (RCA)
When The Night
Paul McCartney; *Gift Set* .... (CAP)
Wings; *Red Rose Speedway* .... (CAP)
When The Night Comes
Joe Cocker; *Best Of* .... (CAP)
   Live .... (CAP)
   One Night Of Sin .... (CAP)
When The Night Comes Falling From The...
Bob Dylan; *Bootleg Series-#1-3-1961-1989* ......(COL)
   Empire Burlesque .... (COL)
Jeff Healey Band; *ST/Road House* .... (ARI)
When The Night Falls
Eyes; *History Of British Rock-#6* .... (RHI)
When The Sun Goes Down
Count Basie & Joe Williams; *Count Basie Swings Joe
   Williams Sings* .... (VRV)
Fleetwood Mac; *Behind The Mask* .... (WB)
Mark Collie; *Born & Raised In Black & White* .. (MCA)
Marty Stuart; *Hillbilly Rock* .... (MCA)
T-Bone Walker; *Complete Imperial
   Recordings-1950-1954* .... (EMI)
When The Sun Goes Down In The South
Original Broadway Cast; *Big River-Adventures Of
   Huckleberry Finn* .... (MCA)
Where Do The Nights Go
Ronnie Milsap; *Greatest Hits-#3* .... (RCA)
   Heart & Soul .... (RCA)
Where The Blue Of The Night Meets The...
Bing Crosby; *All-Time Best Of* .... (CCB)
   Best Of .... (MCA)
   Where The Blue Of The Night Meets The... ....(BIO)
Whisper In The Dark
Dionne Warwick; *Friends* .... (ARI)
Why Don't You Spend The Night
Ronnie Milsap; *Milsap Music* .... (RCA)
Wild Night
John Mellencamp; *Dance Naked* .... (MER)
Martha Reeves; *ST/Thelma & Louise* .... (MCA)
Van Morrison; *Best Of* .... (MER)
   Tupelo Honey .... (WB)
Wild Night In Odessa
Klezmorim; *Metropolis* .... (FF)
Wild Nights, Hot & Crazy Days
Judas Priest; *Metal Works-1973-1993* .... (COL)
   Turbo .... (COL)
Wimoweh (Mbube)-The Lion Sleeps Tonight
Chet Atkins; *RCA Years* .... (RCA)
Kingston Trio; *Kingston Trio/From The Hungry i* (CAP)
Nylons; *Seamless* .... (OPE)
Pete Seeger; *Greatest Hits* .... (COL)
Tokens; *Billboard Top Rock 'N' Roll Hits-1961* .. (RHI)
   Nipper's Greatest Hits/'60s-#1 .... (RCA)
Weavers; *Greatest Hits* .... (VAN)
Wired All Night
Mick Jagger; *Wandering Spirit* .... (ATL)

Wishing On The Moon
Dan Fogelberg; *Phoenix* .... (FM)
With Me Tonight
Beach Boys; *Smiley Smile/Wild Honey* ....(CAP)
Without You (Not Another Lonely Night)
Frankie/Knockouts; *Below The Belt* .... (MIL)
Woman Tonight
America; *Hearts* ....(WB)
History-Greatest Hits ....(WB)
Wonderful Tonight
Eric Clapton; *24 Nights* .... (RPR)
Crossroads ....(POL)
Just One Night ....(POL)
Slowhand ....(POL)
Time Pieces-Best Of ....(POL)
Won'tcha Come Out Tonight
Beach Boys; *M.I.U. Album* ....(CAR)
Working Day & Night
Michael Jackson; *Off The Wall* .... (EPI)
You Belong To The City
Glenn Frey; *Soundtrack Smashes-'80s* .... (MCA)
ST/Miami Vice .... (MCA)
'80s Greatest Rock Hits-#1 .... (PRY)
You Don't Have To Go Home Tonight
Triplets; ...*Thicker Than Water* .... (MER)
You Need A Woman Tonight
Captain & Tennille; *Dreams* .... (A&M)
Young Turks
Rod Stewart; *Absolutely Live* .... (WB)
Downtown Train-Storyteller Selections ....(WB)
Storyteller/Complete Anthology-1964-1990 ...... (WB)
Tonight I'm Yours ....(WB)
Your Love
Boyz II Men; *Cooleyhighharmony* .... (MOT)
Dan Seals; *I Won't Be Blue Anymore* .... (EMI)
Outfield; *Play Deep* ....(COL)
Tammy Wynette; *Higher Ground* .... (EPI)
More Hot Country Requests-#2 .... (EPI)
You'll Be Back (Every Night...)
Statler Brothers; *45* .... (MER)
You're All I've Got Tonight
Cars; *Cars* .... (ELE)
You're Not Leaving Here Tonight
Ed Bruce; *Greatest Hits* .... (MCA)
You're Not Leaving Here Tonight .... (MCA)
You're Welcome To Tonight
Gary Morris & Lynn Anderson; *Greatest Hits-#2* .. (WB)
Lynn Anderson & Gary Morris; *Back* .... (PER)

NONSENSE WORDS

A Tisket, A Tasket
Ella Fitzgerald; *Best Of* .... (MCA)
Ella Fitzgerald .... (LAS)
Glenn Miller/Army Air Force Band; *Glenn Miller/Army Air Force Band* .... (LAS)
Tommy Dorsey; *Complete-#7* ....(RCA)
Abracadabra
De Franco Family; *45* .... (20)
Steve Miller Band; *Abracadabra* ....(CAP)
Live ....(CAP)
Alabambama
Willie Nelson & Roger Miller; *Old Friends* ....(COL)
Alley Oop
Hollywood Argyles; *American Graffiti-#3* ...(MCA)
Collectables History Of Rock-#5 .... (CLT)
M. Dung's Idiot Classics .... (RHI)
Ally Ally Oxen Free
Kingston Trio; *Capitol Collectors Series* ....(CAP)
Made In The U.S.A. .... (PRR)
Alphabet Song
Three Stooges; *ST/Violent Is The Word For Curlee* ....(OOP)
Assorted Glugs, Pbrts & Skks
Spike Jones; *Dinner Music-For People Who Aren't...* ....(RHI)
A-Ting A Ling
Stan Kenton; *Lighter Side* ....(CW)
Ba Doom
Nick Lowe; *Nick The Knife* ....(COL)
Be Bop A Lula
Everly Brothers; *Everly Brothers* .... (RHI)

Gene Vincent/Blue Caps; *Billboard Top Rock 'N' Roll Hits-1956* .... (RHI)
ST/Wild At Heart ....(POL)
Jerry Lee Lewis; *Monsters* .... (SUN)
Trio Plus .... (SUN)
John Lennon; *Rock 'N' Roll* ....(CAP)
Be Bop Baby
Rick Nelson; *Best Of* .... (EMI)
Greatest Hits .... (RHI)
Legendary Masters .... (UA)
Be Bop/Drop
Daryl Hall & John Oates; *X-Static* ....(RCA)
Beep Beep
Playmates; *Dr. Demento's 20th Anniversary Coll.* (RHI)
Beep Beep Beep
Bobby Day; *Best Of* .... (RHI)
Betcha By Golly Wow
Johnny Mathis; *First Time Ever I Saw Your Face* .(COL)
Stylistics; *Best Of* .... (AMH)
Bibbidi-Bobbidi-Boo
Mormon Tabernacle Choir/Columbia Symph.; *When You Wish Upon A Star-Disney Tribute* ....(COL)
Verna Felton/Ilene Woods/Disney Chorus; *Disney Collection-#1* .... (DIS)
Bing Bang Boom
Highway 101; *Bing Bang Boom* .... (WB)
Blue Moon
Billie Holiday; *Billie's Blues* .... (BLN)
First Verve Sessions ....(VRV)
History Of ....(VRV)
Elvis Presley; *Complete Sun Sessions* ....(RCA)
Elvis Presley ....(RCA)
Marcels; *Best Of* .... (RHI)
Billboard Top Rock 'N' Roll Hits-1961 .... (RHI)
Boogie Oogie Oogie
Taste Of Honey; *Disco Years-#1-Turn The Beat Around* .... (RHI)
Taste Of Honey ....(CAP)
Boom Boom Boom
Iguanas; *Nuevo Boogaloo* .... (MGR)
Boo-Hoo-Hoo-Hoo
Little Richard; *Grooviest 17 Original Hits* .... (SPE)
His Biggest Hits .... (SPE)
Bop
Dan Seals; *Best Of* ....(CAP)
Greatest Hits ....(CAP)
Won't Be Blue Anymore .... (EMI)
Chickery Chick
Sammy Kaye; *Dance To My Golden Favorites* ... (MCA)
Chim Chim Cheree
Julie Andrews & Dick Van Dyke; *ST/Mary Poppins* .... (DIS)
Ching-A-Ring-Ching-Chaw
Marilyn Horne; *Beautiful Dreamer-Great Amer. Songbook* ....(LON)
Chitty Chitty Bang Bang
Myron Floren; *22 Of The Greatest Polkas* .... (RAN)
Choo Choo Ch'Boogie
Asleep At The Wheel; *Asleep At The Wheel* ...... (EPI)
Served Live ....(CAP)
Beach Boys; *Ten Years Of Harmony* ....(CAR)
Clifton Chenier; *Alligator Stomp-#2* .... (RHI)
Louis Jordan; *Best Of* .... (MCA)
Quincy Jones; *Birth Of A Band-#2* .... (MER)
Come Go With Me
Del Vikings; *1956 Audition Tapes* .... (CLT)
Billboard Top R&B Hits-1957 .... (RHI)
Oldies But Goodies-#3 .... (OSR)
ST/American Graffiti .... (MCA)
ST/Stand By Me .... (ATL)
Da Doo Ron Ron
Crystals; *Good Time Rock 'N' Roll* .... (MCA)
Hits Of The Sixties .... (IMC)
Spector's Greatest Hits .... (SPC)
De Doo Doo Doo, De Da Da Da
Police; *Every Breath You Take-Singles* .... (A&M)
Zenyatta Mondatta .... (A&M)
Diga Diga Doo
Duke Ellington; *Okeh Ellington* ....(COL)
Ella Fitzgerald; *Ella Sings-Chick Swings* ....(OLR)
Diggy Diggy Lo
Commander Cody; *Deep In The Heart Of Texas* (MCA)
Hot Licks Cold Steel .... (MCA)

Doug Kershaw; *Best Of* .... (WB)
  Cajun Way .... (WB)
Guy & Ralna; *Best Of Cajun Country* .... (ERA)
  Lovelight .... (RAN)
Ditty Wa Ditty
Ry Cooder; *Paradise & Lunch* .... (RPR)
Do Wa Diddy Diddy
Manfred Mann; *Best Of* .... (EMI)
  Billboard Top Rock 'N' Roll Hits-1964 .... (RHI)
  History Of British Rock-#2 .... (RHI)
Don't You Just Know It
Huey "Piano" Smith; *New Orleans Party Classics* (RHI)
Huey "Piano" Smith/Clowns; *Oldies But*
  Goodies-#3 .... (OSR)
Doo Doo Doo Doo Doo
Rolling Stones; *Goat's Head Soup* .... (RS)
  Made In The Shade .... (RS)
  Rewind (1971-1984) .... (RS)
Doo Wa Ditty (Blow That Thing)
Zapp; *II* .... (WB)
Doobie Wah
Peter Frampton; *Classics-#12* .... (A&M)
  Frampton Comes Alive .... (A&M)
Dooby Dooby Wah
Ritchie Valens; *History Of* .... (RHI)
  Ritchie Valens .... (RHI)
Doodle De Doo Song
Maury Finney; *45* .... (SND)
Doodle Dee Doo
Sammy Kaye; *Best Of* .... (MCA)
Doo-Wah Days
Mickey Gilley; *Back To Basics* .... (EPI)
  More Hot Country Requests .... (EPI)
  One & Only .... (EPI)
Eeny Meeny Miney Mo
Benny Goodman; *Birth Of Swing* .... (BLU)
Billie Holiday; *Quintessential-#1-1933-1935* .... (COL)
Fa Fa Fa Fa Fa
Otis Redding; *Best Of* .... (ATL)
  History .... (ATC)
  Live In Europe .... (ATC)
  Story .... (ATL)
Fee Fi Fo Fum
Artie Shaw; *Best Of The Big Bands* .... (COL)
  Free For All .... (POR)
Fiddle Faddle
Boston Pops Orchestra/Arthur Fiedler; *Fiddle*
  Faddle .... (RCA)
Rochester Pops Orchestra; *Syncopated Clock* .... (POE)
Fi-Li-Mi-Oo-Re-Ay
Weavers; *On Tour* .... (VAN)
Fo Fi Fo
Pieces Of A Dream; *Imagine This* .... (ELE)
Funky Dunky
Harry Connick, Jr.; *She* .... (COL)
Gobbledygook
Wendys; *Gobbledygook* .... (EW)
Gypsy Woman (She's Homeless)
Crystal Waters; *Red Hot + Dance* .... (COL)
  Surprise .... (MER)
Hanky Panky
Chicago; *VII* .... (COL)
Lou Reed; *Transformer* .... (RCA)
Madonna; *I'm Breathless* .... (SIR)
Tommy James/Shondells; *Anthology* .... (RHI)
  Billboard Top Rock 'N' Roll Hits-1966 .... (RHI)
Hey Ba Ba Re Bop
Lionel Hampton; *Best Of* .... (MCA)
  Hamp's Big Band .... (AUF)
Hey Diddle Diddle
Marvin Gaye; *Moods Of/That's The Way Love Is* (MOT)
  Motown Legends .... (MOT)
Hey Pocky Way
Meters; *Uptown Rulers-Live On The Queen Mary* . (RHI)
Neville Brothers; *Fiyo On The Bayou* .... (A&M)
  New Orleans Party Classics .... (RHI)
  Treacherous-History Of-1955-1985 .... (RHI)
Hi De Hi, Hi De Ho
Kool/Gang; *As One* .... (DL)
Hi De Ho (That Old Sweet Roll)
Bobby Darin; *Live At The Desert Inn* .... (MOT)
Hi-De-Ho
Blood, Sweat & Tears; *Greatest Hits* .... (COL)

Hi-Diddle-Diddle
Fletcher Henderson/Dixie Stompers; *Fletcher*
  Henderson/Dixie Stompers-1925-1928 .... (DSQ)
Hi-Lili-Hi-Lo
Anne Murray; *THere's A Hippo In My Tub* ...... (CAP)
Soundtrack; *That's Entertainment-#2* .... (MCA)
Hokey Pokey
Ray Anthony; *Capitol Collector Series* .... (CAP)
Hold Tight, Hold Tight (Sea Food)
Andrews Sisters; *16 Great Performances* .... (MCA)
  Best Of .... (MCA)
  Boogie Woogie Bugle Girls .... (MCA)
Hoochie Coochie Man
Eric Clapton; *From The Cradle* .... (DUC)
Hot Diggity
Perry Como; *All-Time Greatest Hits-#1* .... (RCA)
  Golden Records .... (RCA)
  Pure Gold .... (RCA)
  This Is .... (RCA)
Hot Diggity (Dog Ziggity Boom)
Perry Como; *All-Time Greatest Hits-#1* .... (RCA)
  Nipper's Greatest Hits-'50s-#2 .... (RCA)
  Pure Gold .... (RCA)
I Ride An Old Paint/Whoopee Ti-Yi-Yo...
Michael Martin Murphey; *Cowboy Songs* .... (WB)
Iko Iko
Cyndi Lauper; *True Colors* .... (POR)
Dixie Cups; *Best Of* .... (BCT)
  Wonder Women-History Of Girl Group Sound .. (RHI)
Dr. John; *Dr. John's Gumbo* .... (ALG)
  New Orleans Party Classics .... (RHI)
Inka-Dinka Doo
Jimmy Durante; *Dr. Demento's Greatest-#1-1940s &*
  Before .... (RHI)
In-A-Gadda-Da-Vida
Iron Butterfly; *Atlantic Records-Classic*
  Rock-1966-1988 .... (ATL)
  In-A-Gadda-Da-Vida .... (ATC)
  Live .... (ATC)
  Nuggets-#9: Acid Rock .... (RHI)
  ST/Manhunter .... (MCA)
It's In His Kiss (Shoop Shoop Song)
Betty Everett; *Billboard Top R&B Hits-1964* ..... (RHI)
  Hits Of The Sixties .... (IMC)
  More American Graffiti .... (MCA)
  Oldies But Goodies-#3 .... (OSR)
  Very Best Of .... (VJ)
  Wonder Women (History Of Girl Groups) .... (RHI)
Cher; *ST/Mermaids* .... (GEF)
Jeepers Creepers
Frank Sinatra; *Gift Set* .... (CAP)
Louis Armstrong; *20 Golden Pieces Of* .... (BLD)
  At The Crescendo .... (MCA)
  Helly Dolly (& Other Hits) .... (MCA)
Jingle Jangle
Archies; *Grooviest Hits* .... (BCT)
Penguins; *Doo Wop Christmas* .... (RHI)
Jingle Jangle Jingle (I've Got Spurs...)
Kay Kyser; *Best Of The Big Bands* .... (COL)
  Golden Hits Of The '40s .... (CSP)
  Sentimental Favorites .... (COL)
Tex Ritter; *Opry Legends* .... (CAP)
  Out West .... (CAP)
Jocko Homo (Q: Are We Not Men?)
Devo; *Best Of-Greatest Hits* .... (WB)
  Q: Are We Not Men? A: We Are Devo! .... (WB)
  Rest Of-Greatest Misses .... (WB)
Jockomo Jockomo
James "Sugar Boy" Crawford; *History Of New Orleans*
  R&B-#1-1950-1958 .... (RHI)
La La La La
Blendells; *Frat Rock-#2* .... (RHI)
  History Of Latino Rock-#1 .... (RHI)
  Son Of Frat Rock .... (RHI)
  Toga Rock .... (DHL)
Stevie Wonder; *12-Year-Old Genius* .... (MOT)
La La Means I Love You
Delfonics; *Billboard Top R&B Hits-1968* .... (RHI)
  Lovin' '60s .... (PRY)
  Oldies But Goodies-#12 .... (OSR)
  Soul Shots-#5-La La Means I Love You .... (RHI)
Todd Rundgren; *A Wizard A True Star* .... (RHI)
  Back To The Bars .... (RHI)

Land Of 1000 Dances
Cannibal/Headhunters; *History Of Latino Rock-#1* (RHI)
   Super Oldies/'60s-#8 .... (AUF)
   Toga Rock ....(DHL)
Wilson Pickett; *Atlantic R&B*
1947-1974-#6-(1966-1969) .... (ATL)
   Best Of .... (ATL)
   Greatest Hits .... (ATL)
   ST/Forrest Gump .... (EPX)

Ling, Ting, Tong
Buddy Knox; *Best Of* .... (RHI)
Five Keys; *45* .... (CAP)

Little Rootie Tootie
Thelonius Monk; *High Priest* .... (PRS)
   In Person .... (MS)
   Memorial Album .... (MS)
   Piano Giants .... (PRS)
   Reflections #1 .... (PRS)
   Thelonius Monk .... (MS)
   Trio .... (PRS)

Lodi Dodi
Snoop Doggy Dogg; *Doggystyle* .... (DR)

Mairzy Doats
Merry Macs; *45* .... (OOP)

Makin' Whoopie
Art Tatum; *Solo Masterpieces-#5* .... (PAB)
Eddie Cantor; *Nipper's Greatest Hits-'20s* ....(RCA)
Harry Nilsson; *Touch Of Schmilsson In The Night* (RCA)
Ray Charles; *His Greatest Hits-#2* ....(DHL)

Minnie The Moocher
Cab Calloway; *Best Of The Big Bands* ....(COL)
   Cab Calloway ....(GLN)
   Dr. Demento's Greatest Novelty-#1 ....(RHI)
   Jazz Heritage: Mr. Hi-De-Ho .... (MCA)
   ST/Blues Brothers ....(ATL)

MMM MMM MMM MMM
Crash Test Dummies; *God Shuffled His Feet* .... (ARI)

Mumbo Jumbo
Original Broadway Cast; *Stop The World-I Want To Get
Off* ....(POL)
Squeeze; *East Side Story* ....(A&M)

My Ding-A-Ling
Chuck Berry; *Best Of The Best Of* ....(IGR)
   Billboard Top Rock 'N' Roll Hits-1972 ....(RHI)
   Chess Box ....(CSS)
   Roll Over Beethoven ....(ALL)
   Toronto Rock 'N' Roll Revival-#2 ....(ACC)

My My Hey Hey
Neil Young/Crazy Horse; *Live Rust* ....(RPR)
   Rust Never Sleeps ....(RPR)

My Toot Toot
Fats Domino; *Greatest Hits* ....(MCA)
Fats Domino & Doug Kershaw; *Alligator
Stomp-#2* ....(RHI)
Rockin' Sidney; *19 Hot Country Requests-#3* ...... (EPI)
   Alligator Stomp-#1 ....(RHI)

Na Na Hey Hey Kiss Him Goodbye
Steam; *Billboard Top Rock 'N' Roll Hits-1969* ... (RHI)
   Super Hits/'70s-Have A Nice Day-#1 ....(RHI)
   Toga Rock ....(DHL)

Name Game
Shirley Ellis; *Cruisin' 1965* .... (INC)

Ob La Di, Ob La Da
Beatles; *1967-1970* ....(CAP)
   Box Set ....(CAP)
   White Album ....(CAP)

Oh Gee, Oh Gosh
Kodaks; *Great Groups Of The Fifties-#1* ....(CLT)
   Lewis Lymon/Teen Chords Meet The Kodaks .....(CLT)

Oke-She-Moke-She-Pop
Big Joe Turner; *Atlantic Blues-Vocalists* ....(ATL)
   Greatest Hits ....(ATL)

Oo Poo Pah Doo
Paul Revere/Raiders; *Here They Come!* ....(COL)
   Legend Of Paul Revere ....(COL)

Oo Shoo Be Doo Be
Sammy Davis, Jr.; *Hey There-At His Dynamite
Greatest* .... (MCA)

Oo We
Ringo Starr; *45* ....(CAP)

Ooby Dooby
Creedence Clearwater Revival; *1970* ....(FAN)
   Cosmo's Factory ....(FAN)
   Creedence Country ....(FAN)

Roy Orbison; *Best Of* ....(CCB)
   In Dreams-Greatest Hits .... (VIA)
   Original Sound ....(SUN)
   Sun Years .... (RHI)
   Sun's Greatest Hits ....(RCA)

Oogum Boogum Song
Brenton Wood; *Collectables Presents-History Of
Rock-#9* ....(CLT)
   Oldies But Goodies-#7 ....(OSR)
   Soul Shots-Sixties Soul Classics-#2 .... (RHI)

Ooh La La
David Hallyday; *Rock 'N' Heart* ....(SCO)
Frankie Avalon; *45* ....(CLT)

Ooh La La La
Linear; *Caught In The Middle* .... (ATL)

Ooh Ooh Song
Pat Benatar; *Tropico* ....(CHR)

Ooh Poo Pah Doo
Etta James; *Rocks The House* .... (CSS)
Freddy Fender; *All-Star Chartbusters* .... (INT)
   Let The Good Times Roll ....(FFT)
Ike & Tina Turner; *Best Of* ....(EMI)
Jessie Hill; *Golden Classics-Ooh Poo Pah Doo* ...(CLT)
   History Of New Orleans R&B-#2-1959-1962 .. (RHI)
   ST/Everybody's All-American ....(CAP)
Rufus Thomas; *Walking The Dog* .... (ATL)

Ooh, Aah, Nah-Nah-Nah
Big Daddy Kane; *Prince Of Darkness* ....(CLD)

Ooh-Eee
Ric Cartey; *Get Hot Or Go Home-RCA Rockabilly-#1 &
2* ....(CMF)

Ooh-Wakka-Doo-Wakka-Day
Gilbert O'Sullivan; *Best Of* .... (RHI)

Ookey Ook
Penguins; *Golden Classics* ....(CLT)

Ool-Ya-Koo
Dizzy Gillespie; *Dizzy's Diamonds-Best Of The Verve
Years* ....(VRV)
Dizzy Gillespie & Sarah Vaughan; *Body & Soul* . (INT)

Oom Pah Pah
Original Broadway Cast; *Oliver!* ....(RCA)
Original London Cast; *Oliver!* ....(ANG)

Ooo Baba Leba
Helen Humes; *Let The Good Times Roll* .... (CJ)

Ooo La La La
Teena Marie; *Greatest Hits* .... (EPI)
   Naked To The World ....(EPI)

Ooo Wee
Louis Jordan; *One Guy Named Louis* .... (BLN)

Oooh-Whee Baby
Art Neville; *His Specialty Recordings-1956-1958* . (SPE)
   Tracherous Too!-Neville Brothers-#2 ....(RHI)

Oop Boopy Oop
Don Julian/Meadowlarks; *Golden Classics* ....(CLT)

Oop-Bop Sh-Bam
Charlie Parker; *#3* ....(EVR)
Kenny Clarke/52nd Street Boys; *Beat Generation* (RHI)

Oo-Shoo-Be-Doo-Be
Dizzy Gillespie; *Paris Concert* ....(CRS)
Sammy Davis, Jr.; *Hey There-At His Dynamite
Greatest* .... (MCA)

Oo-Wee
Sasm "The Man" Taylor; *Blues Masters-#13-New York
City Blues* .... (RHI)

Oo-Wee Baby
Ivy Tones; *Doo-Wop Era-Harlem N.Y.-40 Hits* ...(CLT)

Papa Oom Mow Mow
Rivingtons; *Cruisin'-1962* .... (INC)
   EMI Legends Of Rock 'N' Roll-24 Greatest ...... (EMI)
   In The Still Of The Night ....(CAP)
   Monster Summer Hits-Wild Surf ....(CAP)
   Spring Break-#1-Hot Rods & Hard Bods ....(CAP)

Polly-Wolly-Doodle
Leon Redbone; *Live!* ....(PRR)
   On The Track .... (WB)
Mance Lipscomb; *#3-Texas Songster In A Live
Performance* ....(ARH)
Pete Seeger/Woody Guthrie/Cisco Houston; *Lonesome
Valley* ....(FLW)

Razzamatazz
Quincy Jones; *Best Of-#2* ....(A&M)
   Classics-#3 ....(A&M)
   The Dude ....(A&M)

Razzle Dazzle
Bill Haley/Comets; *Bill Haley/Comets* .... (EVR)
   Golden Hits .... (MCA)
   Greatest Hits .... (EVR)
   Greatest Hits .... (MCA)
   Rockin' & Rollin' .... (ACC)
Re-Doo-Wopp-Little Star
Tokens; *Re-Doo-Wopp-Little Star* .... (RCA)
Riff Raff
AC/DC; *If You Want Blood You've Got It* .... (ATL)
   Powerage .... (ATL)
Rock & Roll Hoochie Koo
Edgar Winter; *Roadwork* .... (EPI)
Johnny Winter; *Johnny Winter And* ....(COL)
   Rock Classics .... (KT)
Johnny Winter/Rick Derringer; *Metal Age-Roots Of*
Metal .... (RHI)
Rick Derringer; *All American Boy* .... (BS)
   Legends Of Rock Guitar-'70s .... (RHI)
   Super Hits/'70s-Have A Nice Day-#12 .... (RHI)
Roly Poly
Asleep At The Wheel; *Western Standard Time* .... (EPI)
Bob Wills/Texas Playboys; *Anthology-1935-1973* (RHI)
Hank Williams; *I Ain't Got Nothin' But Time* ....(POL)
Joey Dee/Starliters; *Hey Let's Twist-Best Of* ..... (RHI)
Terence Trent D'Arby; *Neither Fish Nor Flesh* ...(COL)
Rootie Tootie
Hank Williams; *Lovesick Blues* .... (POL)
Rooty Toot Toot
Greg Brown; *All-Ears Review-#3-Songwriters For*
'90s .... (ROM)
John Mellencamp; *Lonesome Jubilee* .... (MER)
Rubber Biscuit
Blues Brothers; *Best Of* .... (ATL)
   Briefcase Full Of Blues .... (ATL)
Say La La
Pieces Of A Dream; *45* .... (MAN)
Scooba Doo
Moses Rascoe; *Blues* .... (FF)
Sha La La La Lee
Small Faces; *History Of British Rock-#6* .... (RHI)
Sha La La Means I Love You
Barry White; *Greatest Hits-#2* .... (CAS)
Sha Na Na (Get A Job)
Silhouettes; *ST/American Graffiti* .... (MCA)
Shama Lama Ding Dong
Otis Day/Knights; *Shout* .... (MCA)
   ST/Animal House .... (MCA)
Shang A Lang
Bay City Rollers; *Bay City Rollers* .... (ARI)
Shazam
Duane Eddy; *Twang Thang-Anthology* .... (RHI)
Sha-La-La
Manfred Mann; *History Of British Rock-#3* ..... (RHI)
Shirelles; *Anthology-1959-1964* .... (RHI)
   Scepter Records Story ....(CPC)
Sha-La-La (Make Me Happy)
Al Green; *Explores Your Mind* .... (MOT)
   Greatest Hits-#2 .... (MOT)
   Tokyo...Live .... (MOT)
She Bop
Cyndi Lauper; *Music For The Miracle* .... (EPA)
   She's So Unusual .... (POR)
She Say (Oom Dooby Doom)
Diamonds; *Best Of* .... (RHI)
Sheela-Na-Gig
PJ Harvey; *Dry* .... (IND)
Shim Sham Shimmy
Dorsey Brothers; *Best Of The Big Bands* ....(COL)
   I'm Getting Sentimental Over You ....(POE)
Shimmy Shimmy Ko Ko Bop
Little Anthony/Imperials; *American Graffiti-#2* . (MCA)
   Best Of .... (RHI)
   Forever Your .... (RLL)
Shim, Sham Shimmy On The St. Louis Blues
Dizzy Gillespie; *Best Of* .... (PAB)
Shipoopi
Original Broadway Cast; *Music Man* .... (ANG)
Robert Preston/Original Cast; *Music Man* ....(CAP)
Shoo Be Doo
Blue Riddim Band; *Restless Spirit* .... (FF)
Cars; *Candy-O* .... (ELE)
Shoo Be Doo Be Doo Da Day
Michael Jackson; *Ben* .... (MOT)

Stevie Wonder; *20 Classic Hits* .... (MOT)
   For Once In My Life .... (MOT)
   Good Feeling Music/Big Chill Generation ...... (MOT)
   Greatest Hits-#2 .... (MOT)
   Looking Back .... (MOT)
Shoo Shoo Baby
Andrews Sisters; *Capitol Collectors Series* ...... (CAP)
   Sentimental Journey-Great Ladies Of Song ......(CAP)
Shoo Shoo Boogiesboo
Big Joe Turner; *Blues Boss Live* .... (INT)
Shoo Shoo Wah
World; *Break The Silence* .... (ELE)
Shoop
Salt-N-Pepa; *Very Necessary* .... (NP)
Shoop Shoop, Diddy Wop, Cumma Cumma...
Monte Video/Cassettes; *Monte Video* .... (GEF)
Shoorah Shoorah
Allen Toussaint; *New Orleans Jazz & Heritage*
Fest.-1976 .... (RHI)
Betty Wright; *Get Down Tonight-Best Of T.K.*
Records .... (RHI)
Phoebe Snow; *Rock Away* .... (MIR)
Shout Bamalama
Mickey Murray; *Jewels-#2* .... (SSS)
   Soul Gold-#1 .... (SSS)
Wet Willie; *Greatest Hits* .... (POL)
   Southern Rock .... (KT)
Shu Ba Da Du Ma Ma Ma Ma
Steve Miller Band; *Best Of-1968-1973* ....(CAP)
   Joker ....(CAP)
Sh-Boom
Chords; *Atlantic R&B 1947-1974-#2*
(1952-1955) .... (ATL)
Crew Cuts; *Partytime '50s* .... (PRY)
Stan Freberg; *Capitol Collectors Series* ....(CAP)
Slick Titty Boom
Elvin Bishop; *Struttin' My Stuff* ....(CPC)
Snookeroo
Ringo Starr; *Goodnight Vienna* ....(CAP)
Solar Prestige A Gammon
Elton John; *Caribou* .... (POL)
Sookie Sookie
Steppenwolf; *16 Great Performances* .... (MCA)
   16 Greatest Hits .... (MCA)
   Gold .... (MCA)
   Live .... (MCA)
   Steppenwolf .... (MCA)
Supercalifragilisticexpialidocious
Julie Andrews; *ST/Mary Poppins* .... (DIS)
Ta-Ra-Ra-Boom-De-Ay
Walt Solek; *16 Most Requested Polkas* ....(COL)
Tenderoni
Leon Haywood; *45* .... (MOD)
Te-Ni-Nee-Ni-Nu
Slim Harpo; *Best Of* .... (RHI)
Te-Ta-Te-Ta-Ta
Ernie K. Doe; *Beachbeat Shaggin'* ....(DHL)
Tico Tico
Andrews Sisters; *Best Of* .... (MCA)
Desi Arnaz & Rene Touzet; *Best Of Desi Arnaz-The*
Mambo King ....(RCA)
Stan Kenton/Orchestra; *Live At Redlands*
University ....(CW)
Ting-A-Ling
Clovers; *Down In The Alley* .... (ATL)
Shabba Ranks; *X-Tra Naked* .... (EPI)
Tom's Diner
DNA/Suzanne Vega; *Solitude Standing* .... (A&M)
   Tom's Album .... (A&M)
Too Ra Loo Ra Loo Ral
Band; *Last Waltz* .... (WB)
Bing Crosby; *Best Of Bing* .... (MCA)
   When Irish Eyes Are Smiling .... (MCA)
Toot Toot Tootsie (Goo'Bye)
Al Jolson; *Best Of* .... (MCA)
   Best Of Decca Years .... (DEC)
Liza Minnelli; *At Carnegie Hall* .... (TLR)
Tra La La La La
Ike & Tina Turner; *Golden Classics* .... (CLT)
   Proud Mary-Best Of .... (EMI)
   Workin' It Out .... (PRR)
Tra La La La Suzy
Dean & Jean; *22 Leaders Of The Pack-#1* ....(LAU)
   Classic Old & Gold .... (LAU)

Tutti Frutti
Elvis Presley; *Elvis Presley* ....(RCA)
  Rocker ....(RCA)
Little Richard; *18 Greatest Hits* .... (RHI)
  Greatest Hits Recorded Live ....(EPI)
  Little Richard ....(SPE)
  More American Graffiti ....(MCA)
  This Is How It All Began-#2 ....(SPE)
  Tribute To Black Entertainers ....(COL)
Queen; *Live At Wembley '86* ....(HOL)
Tweedle Dee
Ike & Tina Turner; *Greatest Hits-#3* ....(SAJ)
La Vern Baker; *20 Million-Dollar Memories-#1* ..(LAU)
  Billboard Top Rock 'N' Roll Hits-1955 .... (RHI)
Uhh Ahh
Boyz II Men; *Cooleyhighharmony* ....(MOT)
Um, Um, Um, Um, Um, Um (Curious Mind)
Major Lance; *Seems Like Yesterday-#5-Mid-'60s* .. (KT)
Wah Diddy Wah
Little David/Harps; *Vocal Group Album* ....(SAV)
Wang Dang Doodle
Koko Taylor; *Atlantic Blues-Chicago* ....(ATL)
  Koko Taylor ....(CSS)
  Soul Shots-#4-Tell Mama .... (RHI)
  Superblues-#1-All-Time Classic Blues ....(STX)
Savoy Brown; *Best Of/London Collector* ....(LON)
  Live & Kickin' ....(CRS)
  Street Corner Talking ....(DER)
Willie Dixon; *Blues Deluxe* ....(ALG)
Wang Dang Sweet Poontang
Ted Nugent; *Cat Scratch Fever* ....(EPI)
  Double Live Gonzo ....(EPI)
Wang Wang Blues
Benny Goodman; *Small Groups-1941-1945* ....(COL)
Fletcher Henderson/Dixie Stompers; *1925-1928* .(DSQ)
Who Put The Bomp (In The Bomp Ba Bomp..)
Barry Mann; *Goofy Greats* .... (KT)
  Sixties Rule! Chapter 2 .... (OW)
Whoopee Ti Yi Yo
Burl Ives; *Best Of* ....(MCA)
David Bromberg; *How Late'll Ya Play 'Til?* ......(FAN)
Roy Rogers/Sons Of The Pioneers; *Roy Rogers/Sons Of*
The Pioneers ....(VS)
Woody Guthrie & Cisco Houston; *Cowboy Songs On*
Folkways ....(FLW)
Witch Doctor
Chipmunks; *Rockin' Through The Decades* .... (EMI)
David Seville; *Dr. Demento 20th Anniversary*
Collection .... (RHI)
  Wacky Weirdos .... (KT)
Wooly Booly
Sam The Sham/Pharaohs; *Best Of* ....(POL)
  Billboard Top Rock 'N' Roll Hits-1965 .... (RHI)
  Cruisin'-1965 ....(INC)
  Oldies But Goodies-#10 ....(OSR)
  ST/Full Metal Jacket ....(WB)
Smithereens; *ST/Encino Man* ....(HOL)
Wynkin', Blinkin' & Nod
Doobie Brothers; *In Harmony-Sesame Street* .....(COL)
Irish Rovers; *Greatest Hits* .... (MCA)
Simon Sisters; *Troubadours Of The Folk Era-#2* . (RHI)
Ya Ba Da Ba Do (So Are You)
George Jones; *One Woman Man* .... (EPI)
Ya Ya
Ike & Tina Turner; *Greatest Hits-#1* ....(SAJ)
John Lennon; *Rock 'N' Roll* ....(CAP)
  Walls & Bridges ....(CAP)
Lee Dorsey; *Cruisin'-1961* ....(INC)
  ST/American Graffiti ....(MCA)
  ST/Wanderers ....(WB)
Rufus Thomas; *Walking The Dog* ....(ATL)
Steve Miller; *Born 2 B Blue* ....(CAP)
Yale Boola
All-Star Inter-Conference Band; *College Marches At*
Half-Time .... (ALS)
You Should Be Mine (The Woo Woo Song)
Jeffrey Osborne; *Emotional* .... (A&M)
Yum, Ticky, Ticky, Tum, Tum
Original Broadway Cast; *Carnival* ....(POL)
Zing Zing Zing
Dells; *Oh What A Night* .... (VJ)
Zip A Dee Doo Dah
Barbara Cook; *Disney Album* ....(DIS)
Bing Crosby; *Radio Years* ....(CRS)

Jackson 5; *Motown Legends* ....(MOT)
Johnny Mercer; *Capitol Collector Series* ....(CAP)
Kelly Stevens/Carnival; *When You Wish Upon A*
Star .... (AVI)
Mormon Tabernacle Choir/Columbia Symph.; *When*
You Wish Upon A Star-Disney Tribute ....(COL)
Ric Ocasek; *Simply Mad About The Mouse* ......(COL)
Steve Miller; *Born 2 B Blue* ....(CAP)

NUCLEAR ENERGY, Nuclear War, Nuclear Weapons
See Also: PEACE, POLITICAL CLASSICS, WAR

Atom Tan
Clash; *Combat Rock* ....(EPI)
Atomic
Blondie; *Best Of* ....(CHR)
  Eat To The Beat ....(CHR)
Atomic Bombs
Kix; *Kix* ....(ATL)
Atomic Cafe
Motels; *Motels* ....(CAP)
Atomic Dog
George Clinton; *Best Of* ....(CAP)
  Computer Games ....(CAP)
Atomic Flash Deluxe
Nina Hagen; *In Ekstasy* ....(COL)
Atomic Funk
Nytro; *Nytro* ....(WHI)
Undisputed Truth; *Smokin'* ....(WHI)
Atomic Power
Uncle Tupelo; *March 16-20 1992* .... (RV)
Atomic Punk
Van Halen; *Van Halen* ....(WB)
Atomic Tests
John Trubee/Ugly Janitors Of America; *Communists Are*
Coming To Kill Us ....(ENI)
Atomic Waste
Peter Alsop; *Draw The Line* ....(FF)
Attack Of The Radioactive Hamsters
Weird Al Yankovic; *ST/UHF* ....(RAR)
Baby's Got A Neutron Bomb
Army Of Lovers; *Army Of Lovers* .... (GIA)
Crown Of Creation
Jefferson Airplane; *2400 Fulton Street-Anthology* (RCA)
  30 Seconds Over Winterland ....(RCA)
  Crown Of Creation ....(RCA)
  Worst Of ....(RCA)
Dancing On Ground Zero
Carol Nethen; *Narada Mystique Sampler One* ... (NAR)
  View From The Bridge ....(NAR)
Do You Want My Job
Little Village; *Little Village* ....(RPR)
Enola Gay
OMD; *Best Of* ....(A&M)
  Organization ....(VIA)
  ST/Urgh! A Music War ....(A&M)
Eve Of Destruction
Barry McGuire; *Billboard Top Rock 'N' Roll*
Hits-1965 .... (RHI)
  Cruisin'-1965 ....(INC)
  Good Feeling Music/Big Chill-#3 ....(MOT)
  Vintage Music-#9 & 10 ....(MCA)
Dickies; *Great Dictations (Definitive Collection)* . (A&M)
  Incredible Shrinking ....(A&M)
Turtles; *Turtle Wax-Best Of-#2* ....(RHI)
  Turtlesized ....(RHI)
Face The Fire
Dan Fogelberg; *Phoenix* .... (FM)
Ground Zero Brooklyn
Carnivore; *Retaliation* .... (RR)
Hard Rain's Gonna Fall
Bob Dylan; *Concert For Bangla Desh* ....(CAP)
  Freewheelin' ....(COL)
  Greatest Hits-#2 ....(COL)
Bryan Ferry; *Street Life-20 Great Hits* ....(RPR)
  These Foolish Things ....(RPR)
Edie Brickell/New Bohemians; *ST/Born On The Fourth*
Of July ....(MCA)
Joan Baez; *Farewell Angelina* ....(VAN)
  First 10 Years ....(VAN)

It's A Mistake
Men At Work; *Cargo* ....(COL)
Masters Of War
Bob Dylan; *Biograph* ....(COL)
Freewheelin' ....(COL)
Real Live ....(COL)
Morning Dew
Grateful Dead; *Europe '72* ....(WB)
Neutron Bomb
Arlo Guthrie & Pete Seeger; *Precious Friend* ......(WB)
Weirdos; *Weird World-#1* ....(FRN)
Neutron Dance
Pointer Sisters; *Break Out* ....(PNT)
Greatest Hits ....(RCA)
ST/Beverly Hills Cop ....(MCA)
New Frontier
Donald Fagen; *The Nightfly* ....(WB)
Nuclear Apathy
Crack The Sky; *Safety In Numbers* .... (LIF)
Nuclear Attack
Gary Moore; *Dirty Fingers* ....(ROA)
Rockin' Every Night-Live In Japan .... (VIA)
Greg Lake; *Greg Lake* .... (CHR)
Nuclear Burn
Brand X; *Unorthodox Behaviour* ....(BP)
Nuclear Device
Stranglers; *IV* .... (IRS)
Nuclear Funeral
D.I.; *Team Goon* .... (XXX)
Nuclear Hayride
Johnny J./Hitmen; *Nuclear Hayride* .... (GSR)
Nuclear Mishap
Lenny Hat; *Place In The Sun* ....(TF)
Nuclear War
Brian Ritchie; *The Blend* ....(SST)
Jimmy Cliff; *Cliff Hanger* ....(COL)
Nuclear Waste
Tuff Darts; *Tuff Darts* .... (SIR)
Oh Lord Don't Let Them Drop That...
Charles Mingus; *Oh Yeah-Jazzlore-#38* ....(ATL)
Party At Ground Zero
Fishbone; *Fishbone* ....(COL)
Richard Blade's Flashback Favorites ....(OGO)
Plutonium Is Forever
John Hall; *ST/No Nukes* ....(ASY)
Political Science
Randy Newman; *Sail Away* ....(RPR)
Power (Nuclear Energy)
John Hall; *Power* ....(COL)
John Hall/Doobie Brothers/James Taylor; *No Nukes* ....(ASY)
Radiation Day
Pandemonium; *Heavy Metal Soldiers* .... (MET)
Radiation Ranch
Brian Setzer; *Knife Feels Like Justice* .... (AMR)
Radioactive
Firm; *Firm* ....(ATL)
Gene Simmons; *Gene Simmons* ....(CAS)
Radium Rain
Bruce Cockburn; *Big Circumstance* ....(COL)
Russians
Sting; *Dream Of The Blue Turtles* ....(A&M)
Shades Of '45
Gary O'; *Strange Behavior* ....(RCA)
S.O.S. Fire In The Sky
Deodato; *Motion* ....(WB)
Thermonuclear War
Carnivore; *Carnivore* .... (RR)
Three Mile Island
Pinkard & Bowden; *Writers In Disguise* ....(WB)
Three Mile Smile
Aerosmith; *Night In The Ruts* ....(COL)
Pandora's Box ....(COL)
Uranium Rock
Cramps; *Bad Music For Bad People* ....(IRS)
We Got The Neutron Bombs
Weirdos; *D.I.Y.-#6-L.A. Scene-1976-1979* .... (RHI)
We Work The Black Seam
Sting; *Bring On The Night* ....(A&M)
Dream Of The Blue Turtles ....(A&M)
What Have They Done To The Rain
Malvina Reynolds; *ST/Dogfight* ....(NUV)
Searchers; *Greatest Hits* .... (RHI)

Wooden Ships
Crosby, Stills & Nash; *Crosby, Stills & Nash* ..... (ATL)
Crosby, Stills & Nash (collection) ....(ATL)
Crosby, Stills, Nash & Young; *So Far* ....(ATL)
ST/Woodstock ....(ATL)
Jefferson Airplane; *2400 Fulton Street-Anthology* (RCA)
Flight Log-1966-1976 ....(GRU)
Loves You ....(RCA)
Volunteers ....(RCA)

OCEAN, Bays, Beach, Coast, Harbor, Lake, Sea, Swamp

See Also: RIVERS, SAILING, SHIPS, SURFING, WATER

And The Tide Rushes In
Moody Blues; *Question Of A Balance* ....(POL)
This Is The ....(POL)
At The Seaside Cafe
Adrian Belew; *Desire Caught By The Tail* .... (ISL)
August Tides
Woody Simmons; *Woody Simmons* ....(DEP)
Autumn Sea
Robyn Hitchcock/Egyptians; *Queen Elvis* ....(A&M)
Backwater
Meat Puppets; *Too High To Die* ....(LON)
Bay Of Mexico
Kingston Trio; *Folk Era Sampler-Digitally* ......(FOL)
Stereo Concert Plus ....(FOL)
Tom Dooley ....(CAP)
Bayou Girl
Bob Woodruff; *Dreams & Saturday Nights* ....(ASY)
Between The Devil And The Deep Blue Sea
Chris Rea; *espresso logic* .... (EW)
Between The Devil & The Deep Blue Sea
Cab Calloway; *Jazz Heritage: Mr. Hi-De-Ho* ...(MCA)
Ella Fitzgerald; *Harold Arlen Songbook-#1* ...(VRV)
Black Diamond Bay
Bob Dylan; *Desire* ....(COL)
By The Waters Of Lake Minnetonka
Glenn Miller; *Best Of-#2* ....(RCA)
& Orchestra: Complete ....(BLU)
By The Waters Of Minnetonka
Glenn Miller; *Best Of* ....(RCA)
By-U, By-O (The Lou'siana Lullaby)
Woody Herman; *Best Of The Decca Years* ...... (DEC)
Captain Nemo
Michael Schenker; *Built To Destroy* .... (CHR)
Rock Will Never Die .... (CHR)
Carolina By The Sea
Super Grit Cowboy Band; *If You Can't Hang* ... (HOO)
Castles In The Sand
David Allan Coe; *Castles In The Sand* ....(COL)
Seals & Crofts; *Greatest Hits* ....(WB)
Stevie Wonder; *Greatest Hits* ....(MOT)
Castles Made Of Sand
Jimi Hendrix; *Axis Bold As Love* ....(RPR)
Essential-#1 & 2 ....(RPR)
Kiss The Sky ....(RPR)
Tuck & Patti; *Love Warriors* ....(WH)
Castles Of Sand
Jermaine Jackson; *Motown Superstar Series-#17* (MOT)
Circle In The Sand
Belinda Carlisle; *Heaven On Earth* ....(MCA)
Coast Of Colorado
Skip Ewing; *Coast Of Colorado* ....(MCA)
Coast Of Marseilles
Jimmy Buffett; *Son Of A Son Of A Sailor* ....(MCA)
Creature From The Black Lagoon
Dave Edmunds; *Best Of* .... (SS)
Elvira Presents Haunted Hits .... (RHI)
Repeat When Necessary .... (SS)
Dark & Rolling Sea
Al Stewart; *Modern Times* ....(JNS)
Daughters Of The Sea
Doobie Brothers; *What Were One Vices Are Now Habits* ....(WB)
Days Of Sand & Shovels
Bobby Vinton; *All-Time Greatest Hits* ....(EPI)
Waylon Jennings; *Best Of* ....(RCA)
Dolphins & Whales (Come Home To The Sea)
Mannheim Steamroller; *Saving The Wildlife* ....(AG)

Down By The Sea
Men At Work; *Business As Usual* ....(COL)
Strawbs; *Best Of* ....(A&M)
   Bursting At The Seam ....(A&M)
Down By The Seaside
Led Zeppelin; *Physical Graffiti* ....(SS)
Drifting
Jimi Hendrix; *Cry Of Love* ....(RPR)
   Essential ....(RPR)
Ebb Tide
Righteous Brothers; *Anthology 1962-1974* .... (RHI)
   Greatest Hits-#1 ....(VRV)
   Phil Spector's Greatest Hits ....(SPC)
Echo Beach
Martha/Muffins; *Metro Music* .... (VIA)
Einstein On The Beach
Counting Crows; *August And Everything After* .. (DGC)
Erie Canal
Burl Ives; *Best Of* .... (MCA)
Weavers; *Classics* .... (VAN)
   Greatest Folksingers/'60s .... (VAN)
   Greatest Hits .... (VAN)
February Sea
George Winston; *Winter Into Spring* ....(WH)
Fig Tree Bay
Peter Frampton; *Wind Of Change* ....(A&M)
Fire Lake
Bob Seger/Silver Bullet Band; *Against The Wind* .(CAP)
   Nine Tonight ....(CAP)
From Silver Lake
Jackson Browne; *Jackson Browne* .... (ASY)
Galway Bay
Bing Crosby; *Best Of* .... (MCA)
   When Irish Eyes Are Smiling .... (MCA)
Girls On The Beach
Beach Boys; *Absolute Best-#1* ....(CAP)
   Endless Summer ....(CAP)
   Little Deuce Coupe/All Summer Long ....(CAP)
Going Back To Big Sur
Johnny Rivers; *Anthology-1964-1977* .... (RHI)
   Touch Of Gold ....(IMP)
Going To Malibu
Malibooz; *Malibooz Rule* .... (RHI)
Green Grass & High Tides
Outlaws; *Bring It Back Alive* .... (ARI)
   Outlaws .... (ARI)
Grey Lagoons
Roxy Music; *For Your Pleasure...Second Album* .. (RPR)
Gulf And The Shell
Clinton Gregory; *Clinton Gregory* ....(PYN)
Harbor Lights
Boz Scaggs; *Silk Degrees* ....(COL)
Dinah Washington; *Complete On*
Mercury-#2-1950-1952 ....(MER)
   For Lonely Lovers ....(MER)
   Golden Hits ....(MER)
   This Is My Story ....(MER)
Platters; *Super Oldies/'60s-#9* ....(AUF)
How Deep Is The Ocean (How High Is...)
Frank Sinatra; *Nice 'N' Easy* ....(CAP)
Liza Minnelli; *At Carnegie Hall* ....(TLR)
I Can't Turn The Tide
Baillie & The Boys; *Turn The Tide* ....(RCA)
I Cover The Waterfront
Art Tatum; *Solo Masterpieces-#5* ....(PAB)
Billie Holiday; *Billie's Blues* ....(BLN)
   Songbook ....(VRV)
Eddie Jefferson; *Letter From Home* ....(RVR)
Errol Garner; *Long Ago & Far Away* ....(COL)
Frank Sinatra; *Where Are You?* ....(CAP)
John Lee Hooker; *Ultimate Collection-1948-1990* (RHI)
Woody Herman; *20 Golden Pieces Of* ....(BLD)
In A Restaurant By The Sea
Holly Near & Ronnie Gilbert; *Singing With You* . (RWD)
Indian Lake
Freddy Weller; *Greatest Hits* ....(COL)
Land Ho
Doors; *13* ....(ELE)
   Classics .... (ELE)
   Morrison Hotel/Hard Rock Cafe .... (ELE)
Legend Of Wooly Swamp
Charlie Daniels Band; *Decade Of Hits* ....(EPI)
   Full Moon ....(EPI)
   Me & The Boys ....(EPI)

Lighthouse
James Taylor; *Gorilla* ....(WB)
Lights
Journey; *Captured* ....(COL)
   Infinity ....(COL)
Like A River To The Sea
Steve Wariner; *I Am Ready* ....(ARI)
Love At The Pier
Blondie; *Plastic Letters* .... (CHR)
Love Letters In The Sand
Pat Boone; *16 Great Performances* ....(MCA)
   Best Of .... (MCA)
   Vintage Music-Original Oldies/'50s-#2 ....(MCA)
Midnight On The Bay
Stills/Young Band; *Long May You Run* .... (RPR)
Mobile Bay
Hank Crawford; *Night Beat* .... (MS)
Rex Stewart; *RCA Victor Jazz-First Half-Century* .(RCA)
Mobile Bay (Magnolia Blossoms)
Cal Smith; *Stories Of Life By* ....(SO)
Johnny Cash; *Biggest Hits* ....(COL)
Merle Haggard & George Jones; *Taste Of Yesterday's*
Wine ....(EPI)
Montego Bay
Amazulu; *Island Story-1962-1987-25th*
Anniversary .... (ISL)
Bobby Bloom; *Super Hits/'70s-Have A Nice*
Day-#3 .... (RHI)
Moon Turn The Tide Gently Gently Away
Jimi Hendrix; *Electric Ladyland* ....(RPR)
My Beach 2000
Surf Punks; *Oh No! Not Them Again!* ....(ENC)
My Bonnie Lies Over The Ocean
Ed McCurdy; *Best Of* ....(TRD)
Mitch Miller; *Favorite Irish Sing Alongs* ....(COL)
Tony Sheridan/Beatles; *History Of British Rock-#5* (RHI)
   In The Beginning-Circa 1960 ....(POL)
Ocean
John Hiatt; *Hangin' Around The Observatory* ......(EPI)
Led Zeppelin; *Houses Of The Holy* ....(ATL)
   Led Zeppelin ....(ATL)
U2; *Boy* .... (ISL)
Velvet Underground; *V.U.* ....(VRV)
Zebra; *Live* .... (ATL)
Ocean Breakup
Electric Light Orchestra; *On The Third Day* ......(JET)
Ocean Breeze
Pablo Cruise; *Pablo Cruise* ....(A&M)
Ocean Front Property
George Strait; *Country Classics-#8-1986-1987* . (MCA)
   Greatest Hits-#2 ....(MCA)
   MCA Records 30 Years Of Hits-1958-1988 ... (MCA)
   Ocean Front Property .... (MCA)
Ocean Gypsy
Renaissance; *Live At Carnegie Hall* ....(SIR)
   Scheherazade ....(SIR)
   Tales Of 1001 Nights-#1 ....(SIR)
Ocean I'll Cry
Jackie Wilson; *Soul Time* ....(BRU)
Ocean Of Life
Gene Cotton; *No Strings Attached* ....(ARL)
Ocean Of Thoughts & Dreams
Dramatics; *Shake It Well* ....(MCA)
Oceans Apart
Judy Garland; *Collector's Items-1936-1945* ..... (MCA)
Oceans Away
Phillip Goodhand-Tait; *Oceans Away* .... (CHR)
On A Sunday By The Sea
Original Broadway Cast; *Jerome Robbins'*
Broadway ....(RCA)
On Danish Shore
Oscar Peterson Four; *If You Could See Me Now* . (PAB)
On Jersey Shore
Paragon Ragtime Orchestra; *On The Boardwalk* .. (NC)
On Silver Waves
101 Strings Orchestra; *Romantic Songs Of The*
Sea .... (ALS)
On The Beach
Neil Young; *On The Beach* ....(RPR)
Sister Double Happiness; *Sister Double Happiness* .(SST)
Southside Johnny/Asbury Jukes; *Love Is A*
Sacrifice .... (MER)

On The Old Kentucky Shore
J.D. Crowe/Others; *Bluegrass Album-#5-Sweet Sunny South* .... (ROU)
One Day In March I Go Down To The Sea...
Jan Garbarek Group; *It's OK To Listen To The Gray Voice* .... (ECM)
Only Love
Wynonna; *Tell Me Why* .... (MCC)
Paddy's Green Shamrock Shore
Chieftains; *Another Country* ....(RCA)
Prince Of Tides
Jimmy Buffett; *Hot Water* .... (MCA)
Puff (The Magic Dragon)
Peter, Paul & Mary; *In Concert* .... (WB)
   Moving .... (WB)
   Peter Paul & Mommy .... (WB)
   Ten Years Together-Best Of .... (WB)
Puget Sound
Gillan; *Mr. Universe* .... (MET)
Reach The Beach
Fixx; *Reach The Beach* .... (MCA)
Reach, The
Dan Fogelberg; *Innocent Age* .... (FM)
Red Tide
Rush; *Presto* ....(ATL)
Redondo Beach
Patti Smith; *Horses* .... (ARI)
Remember (Walking In The Sand)
Aerosmith; *Greatest Hits* ....(COL)
   Night In The Ruts ....(COL)
Shangri-Las; *Girl Groups-Story Of A Sound* .... (MOT)
   Oldies But Goodies-#6 ....(OSR)
   Original Golden Hits Of The Great Groups ..... (SSS)
   ST/Goodfellas ....(ATL)
Ride The Tide
Screamin' Cheetah Wheelies; *Screamin' Cheetah Wheelies* .... (ATL)
Rock Coast Blues
Country Joe/Fish; *Collected-1965-1970* .... (VAN)
   I-Feel-Like-I'm-Fixin'-To-Die .... (VAN)
Rockaway Beach
Ramones; *Loco Live* .... (SIR)
   Ramones Mania .... (SIR)
   Rocket To Russia .... (SIR)
   Summer & Sun .... (RHI)
Safe Harbour
Fleetwood Mac; *Heroes Are Hard To Find* .... (RPR)
Sail Away
Linda Ronstadt; *Don't Cry Now* .... (ASY)
Randy Newman; *Sail Away* .... (RPR)
Sail Away To The Sea
Sandy Denny; *Who Knows Where The Time Goes?* (HBL)
Sailing Down The Chesapeake Bay
John Townley/Press Gang; *Chesapeake Sailor's Companion* .... (ADE)
San Francisco Bay Blues
Eric Clapton; *Unplugged* .... (RPR)
Janis Joplin; *ST/Janis* ....(COL)
Jesse Fuller; *Brother Low Down* ....(FAN)
   Great Blues Men .... (VAN)
   San Francisco Bay Blues .... (GTJ)
Paul McCartney; *Unplugged-Official Bootleg* .....(CAP)
Ramblin' Jack Elliott; *Bread & Roses Festival-Acoustic Music-#1* ....(FAN)
   Essential .... (VAN)
   Hard Travelin' ....(FAN)
   Troubadours Of The Folk Era-#1 .... (RHI)
Sand Castles In The Snow
Public Image, Ltd.; *9* .... (VIA)
Sand & The Sea
Nat King Cole; *Ballads Of The Day* ....(CAP)
   Story ....(CAP)
Santa Monica Pier
Christine Lavin; *Good Thing He Can't Read My Mind* ....(PHO)
Holly Near; *Live Album* ....(RWD)
Nitty Gritty Dirt Band; *Dream* .... (UA)
Satellite Beach
Peter Case; *Peter Case* .... (GEF)
Saturday Night At Sea
John Townley/Press Gang; *Chesapeake Sailor's Companion* .... (ADE)
Sea Breezes
Bryan Ferry; *Let's Stick Together* .... (RPR)

Roxy Music; *Roxy Music* .... (RPR)
Siouxsie/Banshees; *Through The Looking Glass* .. (GEF)
Sea Cruise
Billy "Crash" Craddock; *Changes* ....(CAP)
   Greatest Hits ....(CAP)
Frankie Ford; *American Hot Wax* .... (A&M)
   Best Of New Orleans R&B-#2 .... (RHI)
   Oldies But Goodies-#3 ....(OSR)
   Rock & Roll Show ....(GUS)
Glenn Frey; *No Fun Aloud* .... (ASY)
Johnny Rivers; *Anthology-1964-1977* .... (RHI)
Nighthawks; *Best Of* .... (GEN)
Robert Gordon & Link Wray; *Fresh Fish Special* .(RCA)
Sea Diver
Mott The Hoople; *All The Young Dudes* ....(COL)
   Ballad Of Mott ....(COL)
"Sea Hunt" Theme
Original Music; *Greatest Hits-#2* .... (TVT)
Sea Of Heartbreak
Don Gibson; *All-Time Greatest Hits* ....(RCA)
   Billboard Top Country Hits-1961 .... (RHI)
Sea Of Joy
Blind Faith; *Blind Faith* ....(POL)
Eric Clapton; *History Of* ....(ATC)
Sea Of Love
Honeydrippers; *Volume I* .... (EPR)
Phil Phillips/Twilights; *Cruisin' 1959* .... (INC)
   Remember When .... (GRL)
Sea Of Madness
Crosby, Stills, Nash & Young; *ST/Woodstock* ....(ATL)
Sea Of Monsters
Beatles; *Box Set* ....(CAP)
   Yellow Submarine ....(CAP)
Sea Of Time & Sea Of Holes
Beatles; *Box Set* ....(CAP)
   Yellow Submarine ....(CAP)
Sea Still Stings
Marc Almond; *Enchanted* ....(COL)
Sea & Sand
Who; *Quadrophenia* .... (MCA)
Seashores Of Old Mexico
Merle Haggard & Willie Nelson; *Seashores Of Old Mexico* ....(EPI)
Seasick, Yet Still Docked
Morrissey; *Your Arsenal* .... (SIR)
Second Home By The Sea
Genesis; *Genesis* .... (ATL)
Seminole Wind
John Anderson; *Seminole Wind* ....(BNA)
Ship To Shore
Chris DeBurgh; *The Getaway* .... (A&M)
Sinkin' In The Sea
Barefoot Jerry; *You Can't Get Off With Your Shoes On* ....(MON)
(Sittin' On) The Dock Of The Bay
Michael Bolton; *The Hunger* ....(COL)
Otis Redding; *Best Of* ....(ATC)
   Golden Age Of Black Music 1960-1970 .... (ATL)
   Golden Soul .... (ATL)
   Soul Years .... (ATL)
   Story .... (ATL)
   (Sittin' On) The Dock Of The Bay ....(ATC)
Sleeping On The Beach
Nitty Gritty Dirt Band; *Dream* .... (UA)
Sleepy Lagoon
Boston Pops Orchestra/Arthur Fiedler; *Boston Pops Orchestra/Arthur Fiedler* ....(RCA)
   Greatest Hits Of The '40s ....(RCA)
Boston Pops Orchestra/John Williams; *Swing Swing Swing* ....(PHI)
Harry James; *Best Of The Big Bands* ....(COL)
Harry James/Orchestra; *16 Most Requested Songs Of The '40s-#2* ....(COL)
Platters; *More Encore Of Golden Hits* ....(MER)
Sparkling In The Sand
Tower Of Power; *East Bay Grease* ....(OOP)
   Live & In Living Color .... (WB)
Storm Over Tokyo Bay
Jessie Allen Cooper; *Soft Wave* ....(SOG)
Storms Are On The Ocean
Carter Family; *Bristol Sessions-#1&2* ....(CMF)

Stranger On The Shore
Acker Bilk; *Best Of* .... (CRS)
   Collectables Presents History Of Rock-#8 ...... (CLT)
   Stranger On The Shore .... (ATC)
Roger Whittaker; *Classics Collection-#2* .... (LIB)

Swamp
Talking Heads; *Popular Favorites-1984-1992* ..... (SIR)
   Speaking In Tongues .... (SIR)
   ST/Stop Making Sense .... (SIR)

Swamp Fire
Duke Ellington; *Best Of The Swing Bands* .... (HIN)
   Black Brown & Beige .... (BLU)

Swamp Gas
Screamin' Jay Hawkins; *Black Music For White
People* .... (RHI)

Swamp Goo
Duke Ellington/Orchestra; *Yale Concert* .... (FAN)

Swamp Music
Lynyrd Skynyrd; *Second Helping* .... (MCA)
   Skynyrd's Innyrds .... (MCA)
   Southern By The Grace Of God .... (MCA)

Swamp Sauce
Albert Collins; *Complete Imperial Recordings* .... (EMI)

Swamp Thing
Malcolm McLaren; *Swamp Thing* .... (ISL)

Swampy River
Duke Ellington; *Okeh Ellington* .... (COL)

Swimming In The Ocean
David & David; *Boomtown* .... (A&M)

Talk To Me Like The Sea
Everything But The Girl; *Worldwide* .... (ATL)

That Was A River
Collin Raye; *In This Life* .... (EPI)

There's A Lovely Lake In London
Gracie Fields; *That Old Feeling* .... (ASV)

Thunder Bay
Sawyer Brown; *Buick* .... (LIB)

Tidal Wave
Sugarcubes; *Here Today Tomorrow Next Week!* .. (ELE)

Tide Is High
Blondie; *Autoamerican* .... (CHR)
   Best Of .... (CHR)
   Billboard Top Hits-1981 .... (RHI)

Time & Tide
Basia; *No Boundaries* .... (COL)
   Time & Tide .... (EPI)

Time (Keeps Flowing Like A River)
Alan Parsons Project; *Best Of* .... (ARI)
   Turn Of A Friendly Card .... (ARI)

Too Many Fish In The Sea
Marvelettes; *Anthology* .... (MOT)
   Greatest Hits .... (MOT)
Mitch Ryder/Detroit Wheels; *Greatest Hits* ...... (VGO)
Rascals; *Anthology-1965-1972* .... (RHI)
Tremeloes; *Best Of* .... (RHI)

Under The Boardwalk
Bette Midler; *ST/Beaches* .... (ATL)
Bruce Willis; *Return Of Bruno* .... (MOT)
Drifters; *16 Greatest Hits* .... (TRP)
   Atlantic R&B 1947-1974-#5 (1962-1966) ..... (ATL)
   Golden Hits .... (ATL)
   Super Oldies/'60s-#5 .... (AUF)
John Cougar Mellencamp; *45* .... (RIV)
Lynn Anderson; *What She Does Best* .... (MER)
Rickie Lee Jones; *Girl At Her Volcano* .... (WB)
Rolling Stones; *12 X 5* .... (AKO)
Untouchables; *Agent Double O Soul* .... (RES)

Undertow
Firefall; *Undertow* .... (ATL)
Genesis; *And Then There Were Three* .... (ATL)
Suzanne Vega; *Suzanne Vega* .... (A&M)

Up The Beach
Jane's Addiction; *Nothing's Shocking* .... (WB)

"Voyage To The Bottom Of The Sea" Theme
Original Music; *Television's Greatest Hits-#2* ..... (TVT)

Waiting For The Tide To Turn
Robert Cray Band; *Bad Influence* .... (HT)

Walk On The Ocean
Toad The Wet Sprocket; *Fear* .... (COL)

Washed Ashore (On A Lonely Island In...)
Platters; *16 Greatest Hits* .... (TRP)
   Anthology .... (RHI)

Waterfront
Simple Minds; *Greenpeace/Rainbow Warriors* .... (GEF)
   In The City Of Light-Live .... (A&M)
   Sparkle In The Rain .... (A&M)

Wave
Antonio Carlos Jobim; *Wave* .... (A&M)
Ella Fitzgerald; *Ella Abraca Jobim* .... (PAB)
Frank Sinatra & Antonio Carlos Jobim; *Sinatra &
Company* .... (RPR)
Tony Bennett; *Essence Of* .... (COL)

Waves Roll In On Oregon
Jim Post; *Magic-In Concert* .... (FF)

When The Coast Is Clear
Jimmy Buffett; *Boats Beaches Bars & Ballads* ... (MCA)
   Floridays .... (MCA)

White Silver Sands
Ace Cannon; *Golden Classics* .... (GUS)
Ray Anthony; *Great Golden Hits* .... (RAN)
Sonny James; *45* .... (COL)

Wishing You Were Here
Chicago; *Greatest Hits* .... (COL)
   Group Portrait .... (COL)
   If You Leave Me Now .... (COL)
   VII .... (COL)

Written In Sand
Santana; *Beyond Appearances* .... (COL)

Yellow Beach Umbrella
Bette Midler; *Broken Blossom* .... (ATL)

OPPOSITES

All Or Nothing
Milli Vanilli; *Girl You Know It's True* .... (ARI)
Original Broadway Cast; *Oklahoma* .... (RCA)
Original Cast; *Oklahoma* .... (MCA)
Shirley Jones; *ST/Oklahoma* .... (CAP)
X; *Ain't Love Grand* .... (ELE)

All Or Nothing At All
Al Jarreau; *Heart's Horizon* .... (RPR)
Frank Sinatra; *Man & His Music* .... (RPR)
   Reprise Collection .... (RPR)
   Sinatra-Reprise-The Very Good Years .... (RPR)
   Story In Music .... (SSP)
   Strangers In The Night .... (RPR)

All Or Nothin' At All
Bruce Springsteen; *Human Touch* .... (COL)

Back & Forth
Aaliyah; *S* .... (JVA)

Better Class Of Losers
Randy Travis; *High Lonesome* .... (WB)

Big Bad Bill Is Sweet William Now
Ry Cooder; *Jazz* .... (WB)

Big Fish, Little Fish
Original Broadway Cast; *Purlie* .... (RCA)

Binge & Purge
Clutch; *Transnational Speedway League* .... (EW)

Bittersweet
Big Head Todd/Monsters; *Sister Sweetly* .... (GIA)

Both Sides Now
Joni Mitchell; *Clouds* .... (RPR)
Judy Collins; *Colors Of The Day-Best Of* .... (ELE)
   So Early In The Spring .... (ELE)
   Wildflowers .... (ELE)
Neil Diamond; *Gold* .... (MCA)
   Love Songs .... (MCA)
   Rainbow .... (MCA)
   Touching You Touching Me .... (MCA)

Both Sides Of The Story
Phil Collins; *Both Sides* .... (ATL)

Come Rain Or Come Shine
Frank Sinatra & Gloria Estefan; *Frank Sinatra
Duets* .... (CAP)
Judy Garland; *America's Treasure* .... (DHL)
   At Carnegie Hall .... (CAP)
   Hits Of .... (CAP)
   Judy .... (CAP)

Cowboy & The Hippie
Chris LeDoux; *Gold Buckle Dreams* .... (LIB)
   He Rides The Wild Horses .... (LIB)

Cowgirl & The Dandy
Brenda Lee; *Even Better* .... (MCA)
   Greatest Country Hits .... (MCA)
Dolly Parton; *Here You Come Again* .... (RCA)

Cruel To Be Kind
Nick Lowe; *Basher: Best Of* ....(COL)
Labour Of Lust ....(COL)
Cure Me...Or Kill Me
Gilby Clarke; *Pawnshop Guitars* .... (VIA)
Cuts Both Ways
Gloria Estefan; *Cuts Both Ways* .... (EPI)
Dead Or Alive
Deep Purple; *Nobody's Perfect* .... (MER)
Journey; *Escape* ....(COL)
Oingo Boingo; *Boingo Alive* .... (MCA)
Good For Your Soul ....(A&M)
Too $hort; *Short Dog's In The House* .... (JVA)
Dead & Alive
Dead Boys; *We Have Come For Your Children* .... (SIR)
Death or Glory
Clash; *London Calling* ....(EPI)
Devil Or Angel
Bobby Vee; *Best Of* ....(EMI)
Golden Hits ....(LIB)
Legendary Masters ....(EMI)
Clovers; *Atlantic R&B*
1947-1974-#3-(1955-1958) .... (ATL)
Oldies But Goodies-#2 .... (OSR)
Different Drum
Linda Ronstadt; *Different Drum* .... (ASY)
Greatest Hits ....(CAP)
Retrospective ....(CAP)
Stone Poneys/Linda Ronstadt; *In The Beginning* .. (EMI)
On The Road Again (Rock's New Frontiers) .....(CAP)
Down In The Boondocks
Billy Joe Royal; *Greatest Hits* ....(COL)
Rock Classics/'60s ....(COL)
Easy Come Easy Go
George Strait; *Easy Come Easy Go* .... (MCA)
Ebony & Ivory
Paul McCartney; *Tripping The Live Fantastic* ...(CAP)
Paul McCartney & Stevie Wonder; *All The Best* .(CAP)
Tug Of War ....(CAP)
Every Rose Has Its Thorn
Poison; *Open Up & Say...Ahh!* ....(CAP)
Rock The First-#5 ....(SAN)
Swallow This Live ....(CAP)
Father Of Day, Father Of Night
Manfred Mann's Earth Band; *Solar Fire* .... (POL)
Feelin' Good About Feelin' Bad
Patty Loveless; *When Fallen Angels Fly* ....(EPI)
Fire And Ice
Pat Benatar; *Best Shots* ....(CHR)
Live From Earth ....(CHR)
Precious Time ....(CHR)
Fire And Rain
James Taylor; *Greatest Hits* .... (WB)
Sweet Baby James .... (WB)
Sammy Kershaw; *Red Hot + Country* .... (MER)
Follow You, Follow Me
Genesis; *And Then There Were Three* .... (ATL)
Three Sides Live ....(ATL)
From Cotton To Satin
Gene Watson; *This Dream's On Me* .... (MCA)
Johnny Paycheck; *Ake This Job & Shove It* .... (EPI)
From Hell To Paradise
Mavericks; *From Hell To Paradise* .... (MCA)
Head To Toe
Lisa Lisa & Cult Jam; *Spanish Fly* ....(COL)
Hello Goodbye
Beatles; *1967-1970* ....(CAP)
20 Greatest Hits ....(CAP)
Box Set ....(CAP)
Magical Mystery Tour ....(CAP)
Heroes & Villains
Beach Boys; *Concert/'69* ....(CAP)
Made In The U.S.A. ....(CAP)
Smiley Smile ....(CAP)
Sunshine Dream ....(CAP)
Hot Corn, Cold Corn
Flatt & Scruggs; *At Carnegie Hall* ....(COL)
Hot Love Cold World
Bob Welch; *French Kiss* ....(CAP)
Hunter Gets Captured By The Game
Marvelettes; *Anthology* ....(MOT)
Compact Command Performances .... (MOT)
Smokey Robinson/Miracles; *Motown Legends* ... (MOT)

I Cried For You (Now It's Your Turn...)
Billie Holiday; *First Verve Sessions* ....(VRV)
Quintessential-#2-1936 ....(COL)
Songbook ....(VRV)
Sarah Vaughan; *Complete-On Mercury-#2* ...... (MER)
Divine: Columbia Years 1949-1953 ....(COL)
Roulette Years ....(RLL)
I Go To Extremes
Billy Joel; *Storm Front* ....(COL)
I Want You Bad (And That Ain't Good)
Collin Raye; *In This Life* .... (EPI)
Joy And Pain
Donna Allen; *Heaven On Earth* .... (OCE)
Maze featuring Frankie Beverly; *Live In Los
Angeles* ....(CAP)
Live In New Orleans ....(CAP)
Maze/Kurtis Blow; *Lifelines-#1* ....(CAP)
Rob Base & D.J. EZ-Rock; *It Takes Two* ....(PRO)
Just Like A Woman
Bob Dylan; *At Budokan* ....(COL)
Before The Flood ....(COL)
Biograph ....(COL)
Blonde On Blonde ....(COL)
Greatest Hits ....(COL)
Byrds; *Byrds (collection)* ....(COL)
Leather & Lace
Stevie Nicks & Don Henley; *Bella Donna* ...... (MOD)
Life Has Its Little Ups & Down
Charlie Rich; *Best Of* .... (EPI)
Greatest Hits .... (EPI)
Life's Little Ups And Downs
Ricky Van Shelton; *RVS III* ....(COL)
Live & Let Die
Paul McCartney; *13 Original James Bond Themes* (EMI)
Tripping The Live Fantastic ....(CAP)
Paul McCartney/Wings; *All The Best* ....(CAP)
Over America ....(CAP)
Wings Greatest ....(CAP)
Wings; *ST/Live & Let Die* .... (EMI)
Lookin' Good But Feelin' Bad
Original Cast; *Ain't Misbehavin'* ....(RCA)
Lookin' In The Same Direction
Ken Mellons; *Ken Mellons* .... (EPI)
Lost & Found
Brooks & Dunn; *Brand New Man* .... (ARI)
Echo/Bunnymen; *Echo/Bunnymen* .... (SIR)
Original Broadway Cast; *City Of Angels* ....(COL)
Sparks; *Profile-The Ultimate Sparks Collection* ... (RHI)
Louisiana Woman, Mississippi Man
Loretta Lynn & Conway Twitty; *Louisiana Woman
Mississippi Man* ....(MCA)
Very Best Of .... (MCA)
Love Hurts Love Heals
Daryl Hall & John Oates; *Beauty On A Back
Street* ....(RCA)
Magnet & Steel
Walter Egan; *Rock Artifacts-#2* ....(COL)
Mansion In The Slums
Crowded House; *Temple Of Low Men* ....(CAP)
Most Likely You'll Go Your Way & I'll...
Bob Dylan; *Biograph* ....(COL)
Blonde On Blonde ....(COL)
Bob Dylan/Band; *Before The Flood* ....(COL)
My World Begins & Ends With You
Dave & Sugar; *Stay With Me/Golden Tears* ......(RCA)
Eddy Arnold; *Collector's Series* ....(RCA)
Night And Day
Bette Midler; *Some People's Lives* ....(ATL)
Billie Holiday; *Legacy Box 1933-1958* ....(COL)
Ella Fitzgerald; *Cole Porter Songbook* ....(VRV)
Frank Sinatra; *& Strings* ....(RPR)
Capitol Years ....(CAP)
Man And His Music ....(RPR)
Nipper's Greatest Hits-'40s-#1 ....(RCA)
Reprise Collection ....(RPR)
Sinatra Reprise-The Very Good Years ....(RPR)
U2; *Red Hot & Blue (Tribute To Cole Porter)* .... (CHR)
Nite And Day
Al B. Sure!; *In Effect Mode* .... (WB)
Nobody In His Right Mind Would've...
George Strait; *Country Classics-#6-1985-1986* .. (MSP)
Greatest Hits-#2 ....(MCA)
#7 ....(MCA)

Not Counting You
Garth Brooks; *Garth Brooks* .... (CAP)
On Again Off Again
Nashville Bluegrass Band; *Waitin' For The Hard Times To Go* .... (SH)
Opposites
Eric Clapton; *There's One In Every Crowd* .... (RSO)
Opposites Attract
Natalie Cole; *Dangerous* .... (MOD)
Paula Abdul; *Forever Your Girl* .... (VIA)
   Rock The First-#3 .... (SAN)
   Shut Up & Dance (Mixes) .... (VIA)
Other Side
Aerosmith; *Pump* .... (GEF)
Kevin Welch/Overtones; *Western Beat* .... (RPR)
Sweet Honey In The Rock; *Other Side* .... (FF)
Other Side Of Life
Moody Blues; *Other Side Of Life* .... (POL)
Other Side Of This Life
Fred Neil; *Little Bit Of Rain* .... (ELE)
   Troubadours Of The Folk Era-#2 .... (RHI)
Jefferson Airplane; *Bless Its Pointed Little Head* ..(RCA)
   Loves You .... (RCA)
Peter, Paul & Mary; *Album* .... (WB)
Part Of Me, Part Of You
Glenn Frey; *Strange Weather* .... (MCA)
   ST/Thelma & Louise .... (MCA)
Picture From Life's Other Side
George Jones; *Hallelujah Weekend* .... (EPI)
Goebel Reeves; *Texas Drifter* .... (GLN)
Hank Williams; *Beyond The Sunset* .... (POL)
   Hey Good Lookin' (Dec. 1950-July 1951) ...... (POL)
Poles Apart
Pink Floyd; *The Division Bell* .... (COL)
Police & Thiefs
Clash; *Clash* .... (EPI)
   On Broadway .... (EPI)
   Story Of-#1 .... (EPI)
Junior Murvin; *Jammin'* .... (MGO)
   Police & Thiefs .... (MGO)
   ST/Rockers .... (MGO)
   This Is Reggae Music #3 .... (ISL)
Poor Man Lives Longer Than The Rich
Freeman King; *45* .... (KNT)
Poor Man's Roses (Or A Rich Man's Gold)
Patsy Cline; *Best Of* .... (CCB)
   Forever & Always .... (EPI)
   Stop, Look & Listen .... (MCA)
   Story .... (MCA)
Reba McEntire; *Feel The Fire* .... (MER)
Quiche Woman In A Barbecue Town
Tarwater Band; *Walking Across Egypt* .... (FF)
Rags To Riches
Electric Boys; *Funk-O-Metal Carpet Ride* ...... (ATC)
John Scofield; *Shinola* .... (ENJ)
Kool/Gang; *Everything Is-Greatest Hits* .... (MER)
Tony Bennett; *16 Most Requested Songs* .... (COL)
   All-Time Greatest Hits .... (COL)
Tony Bennett & Percy Faith/Orchestra; *Radio Classics Of The '50s* .... (COL)
Rich Man Poor Man
Peter, Paul & Mary; *Late Again* .... (WB)
Rich Man, Poor Boy
Joe Ely; *Dig All Night* .... (HT)
Rich & Poor
Randy Crawford; *Rich & Poor* .... (WB)
Right And Wrong
Joe Jackson; *Big World* .... (A&M)
Right Left Hand
George Jones; *Greatest Country Hits/'80s-1987* ..(COL)
   More Hot Country Requests-#2 .... (EPI)
   Wine-Colored Glasses .... (EPI)
River Deep Mountain High
Erasure; *Innocents* .... (SIR)
Four Tops; *Anthology* .... (MOT)
Ike & Tina Turner; *Best Of* .... (EMI)
   Phil Spector's Greatest Hits .... (SPC)
   Proud Mary-Best Of .... (EMI)
Tina Turner; *Simply The Best* .... (CAP)
Say You, Say Me
Lionel Richie; *Back To Front* .... (MOT)
   Dancing On The Ceiling .... (MOT)
Shacks & Chalets
Critton Hollow; *Great Dreams* .... (FF)

Shadows & Light
Joni Mitchell; *Hissing Of Summer Lawns* .... (ASY)
   Shadows & Light .... (ASY)
She Got The Goldmine (I Got The Shaft)
Jerry Reed; *14 #1 Country Hits* .... (RCA)
   Greatest Hits .... (RCA)
   Solid Country Gold .... (RCA)
She's Playing Hell Trying To Get Me...
George Strait; *Strait Country* .... (MCA)
Silver & Gold
Dolly Parton; *Eagle When She Flies* .... (COL)
U2; *ST/Rattle & Hum* .... (ISL)
Silver & Gold (Our Love Is Like)
Sweethearts Of The Rodeo; *Sisters* .... (COL)
Simple Twist Of Fate
Bob Dylan; *At Budokan* .... (COL)
   Blood On The Tracks .... (COL)
Jerry Garcia Band; *Jerry Garcia Band* .... (ARI)
Joan Baez; *Best Of* .... (A&M)
   Diamonds & Rust .... (A&M)
Tim Curry; *Best Of* .... (A&M)
Sooner Or Later
Barbara Cook; *Disney Album* .... (MCA)
Eddy Raven; *Best Of* .... (LIB)
   Temporary Sanity .... (LIB)
Gary Morris; *Stones* .... (LIB)
Grass Roots; *Anthology-1965-1975* .... (RHI)
   Super Hits-#2 .... (GUS)
   Their 16 Greatest Hits .... (MCA)
Madonna; *I'm Breathless-Music From Dick Tracy* . (SIR)
Spider & The Fly
Rolling Stones; *Out Of Our Heads* .... (AKO)
   Singles Collection-London Years .... (AKO)
Stay (Faraway, So Close!)
U2; *Zooropa* .... (ISL)
Stupid Einstein
Three O'Clock; *Sixteen Tambourines* .... (FRN)
Summer Kisses, Winter Tears
Elvis Presley; *Collector's Gold* .... (RCA)
Summer Me, Winter Me
Barbra Streisand; *The Way We Were* .... (COL)
Sun & The Rainfall
Depeche Mode; *Broken Frame* .... (SIR)
Sunny Side To Every Situation
Original Cast; *42nd Street* .... (RCA)
Sunrise, Sunset
Original Cast; *Fiddler On The Roof* .... (RCA)
Original London Cast; *Fiddler On The Roof* ..... (COL)
Sweet 'N' Sour Jesus
Supersuckers; *Smoke Of Hell* .... (SP)
That's Cool, That's Trash
Kingsmen; *Best Of* .... (RHI)
To Live Is To Die
Metallica; *...And Justice For All* .... (ELE)
Toy Or Treasure
Kay Starr; *Capitol Collectors Series* .... (CAP)
Turn It Up Or Turn It Off
Drivin' N' Cryin'; *Smoke* .... (ISL)
Turn You Inside-Out
R.E.M.; *Green* .... (WB)
Ups & Downs
Paul Revere/Raiders; *Greatest Hits* .... (COL)
   Legend Of .... (COL)
Waking & Dreaming
Orleans; *Waking & Dreaming* .... (ASY)
Walk A Mile In My Shoes
Bryan Ferry; *Another Time Another Place* ...... (RPR)
Elvis Presley/Imperial Quartet; *On Stage* ...... (RCA)
Joe South; *Best Of* .... (RHI)
Warm Beer & Cold Women
Tom Waits; *Nighthawks At The Diner* .... (ASY)
Welfare Cadillac
Gary B.B. Coleman; *Too Much Weekend* .... (ICH)
Win Or Lose
Earth, Wind & Fire; *Faces* .... (COL)
Nitty Gritty Dirt Band; *Dirt Silver & Gold* .... (UA)
Win Some, Lose Some
Bryan Adams; *Bryan Adams* .... (A&M)
Scandal; *Scandal* .... (COL)
Winners & Losers
Rossington-Collins Band; *Anytime Anyplace Anywhere* .... (MCA)

Winner/Loser
Stomu Yamashta/Go; *Live From Paris* .... (ISL)
   Stomu Yamashta/Go .... (ISL)
Winter & The Summer
Strawbs; *Bursting At The Seams* .... (A&M)
You Make Your Own Heaven & Hell Right...
Temptations; *Psychedelic Shack* .... (MOT)

PARADISE, Utopia
See Also: ISLANDS

Afternoons In Utopia
Alphaville; *Afternoons In Utopia* .... (ATL)
Alice You've Made Dallas (Paradise...)
Lee Ferrell; *Hard Times* .... (TMS)
Almost Paradise
Eric Carmen & Merry Clayton; *Dirty Dancing Live In
Concert* .... (RCA)
Mike Reno & Ann Wilson; *ST/Footloose* .... (COL)
Roger Williams; *Best Of* .... (MCA)
   Golden Hits-#2 .... (MCA)
Another Day In Paradise
Phil Collins; *Serious Hits...Live!* .... (ATL)
   ...But Seriously .... (ATL)
Any Place In Paradise
Elvis Presley; *Elvis* ....(RCA)
Big Yellow Taxi
Amy Grant; *House Of Love* .... (A&M)
Joni Mitchell; *Ladies Of The Canyon* .... (RPR)
   Miles Of Aisles .... (ASY)
Birds Of Paradise
Ed Bruce; *Tell 'Em I've Gone Crazy* .... (MCA)
Pretenders; *II* .... (SIR)
California Paradise
Runaways; *Queens Of Noise* .... (MER)
Camelot
Original 1982 London Cast; *Camelot* .... (VS)
Original Cast; *Camelot* ....(COL)
Richard Burton; *Broadway Magic-1960s* ....(COL)
Richard Harris; *ST/Camelot* .... (WB)
Cheeseburger In Paradise
Jimmy Buffett; *Son Of A Son Of A Sailor* .... (MCA)
   Songs You Know By Heart .... (MCA)
Fall From Paradise
Little River Band; *Sleeper Catcher* .... (CAP)
From Hell To Paradise
Mavericks; *From Hell To Paradise* .... (MCA)
Halfway To Paradise
Bobby Vinton; *All-Time Greatest Hits* .... (EPI)
   Greatest Hits/Greatest Hits Of Love .... (EPI)
Hole In Paradise
Prism; *Small Change* .... (CAP)
In Paradise
Cookies; *Atlantic R&B 1947-74-#3-1955-1958* . (ATL)
I'll Build A Stairway To Paradise
George Gershwin; *Manhattan* .... (KLA)
Issy Van Randwyck; *Glory Of Gershwin Featuring Larry
Adler* .... (MER)
Liza Minnelli; *Fascinatin' Rhythm-Cap. Sings
Gershwin* .... (CAP)
Just Another Day In Paradise
Bertie Higgins; *Just Another Day In Paradise* .....(KAT)
Just Like Paradise
David Lee Roth; *Skyscraper* .... (WB)
Kentucky Means Paradise
Barbara Mandrell; *Vintage* .... (AUD)
Roger Bellow/Drifting Troubadours; *On The Road To
Prosperity* .... (FF)
Kokomo
Beach Boys; *Still Cruisin'* .... (CAP)
   ST/Cocktail .... (ELE)
Little Paradise
Pat Benatar; *Crimes Of Passion* .... (CHR)
Living In Paradise
Elvis Costello; *This Year's Model* ....(COL)
May The Bird Of Paradise Fly Up Your...
Harlow Wilcox/Oakies; *Cripple Cricket* .... (PLN)
Little Jimmy Dickens; *Columbia Country
Classics-#3-Americana* ....(COL)
Monday Morning In Paradise
Tom Paxton; *One Million Lawyers & Other
Disasters* .... (FF)

Paradise
Bette Midler; *ST/Divine Madness* ....(ATL)
Billy G. Smith; *45* ....(HAL)
BoDeans; *Black & White* .... (SLS)
Change; *45* .... (A/R)
Eugene Wilde; *How About Tonight* .... (MCA)
Everly Brothers; *Home Again* ....(RCA)
Grandmaster Flash; *They Said It Couldn't Be
Done* .... (ELE)
John Denver; *Rocky Mountain High* ....(RCA)
John Prine; *John Prine* .... (ATL)
Meat Puppets; *Huevos* ....(SST)
Michael Bolton; *Michael Bolton* ....(COL)
Nat King Cole; *Gift Set* .... (CAP)
   Story .... (CAP)
Ray Conniff; *'S Awful Nice* ....(COL)
Roger Whittaker; *Special Kind Of Man* .... (RCA)
Russ Colombo; *Nipper's Greatest Hits-'30s-#2* ..(RCA)
Temptations; *Meet The Temptations* .... (MOT)
Tesla; *Five Man Acoustical Jam* .... (GEF)
   Great Radio Controversy .... (GEF)
Paradise By The Dashboard Light
Meatloaf; *Bat Out Of Hell* .... (EPI)
Paradise Cafe
Arc Angels; *Arc Angels* .... (DGC)
Barry Manilow; *2:00 Paradise Cafe* .... (ARI)
Paradise City
Guns N' Roses; *Appetite For Destruction* .... (GEF)
Paradise Knife & Gun Club
Jerry Lansdowne; *Travel Light* ....(SO)
Roy Clark; *Live From Austin City Limits* .... (CHU)
Paradise Place
Siouxsie/Banshees; *Kaleidoscope* .... (GEF)
   Nocturne .... (GEF)
Paradise Tonight
Charly McClain & Mickey Gilley; *19 Hot Country
Requests* .... (EPI)
   Biggest Hits .... (EPI)
   It Takes Believers .... (EPI)
   Paradise .... (EPI)
   Ten Year Anniversary .... (EPI)
Price Of Paradise
Minutemen; *3-Way Tie (For Last)* .... (SST)
   Ballot Result .... (SST)
P'tit Fille O' Paradis
Queen Ida; *On Tour* .... (CRS)
Race To Paradise
Jeff Paris; *Race To Paradise* .... (MER)
Return To Paradise
Denny Martin; *From Maui With Love* .... (FIR)
Elton John; *Single Man* .... (MCA)
Rockin' The Paradise
Styx; *Caught In The Act* .... (A&M)
   Paradise Theatre .... (A&M)
Rose In Paradise
Waylon Jennings; *Country
Classics-#8-1986-1987* .... (MCA)
   MCA #1 Hits/'80s-#3 .... (MCA)
   New Classic Waylon .... (MCA)
Sailing
Christopher Cross; *Christopher Cross* .... (WB)
Rod Stewart; *Absolutely Live* .... (WB)
   Atlantic Crossing .... (WB)
   Greatest Hits .... (WB)
   Storyteller-Complete Anthology-1964-1990 ...... (WB)
Sailin' To Paradise
Pablo Cruise; *Worlds Away* .... (A&M)
Santa Lucia
Elvis Presley; *ST/Viva Las Vegas/Roustabout* .....(RCA)
Mario Lanza; *Legendary Tenor* ....(RCA)
See You In Paradise
Saints; *All Fools Day* .... (TVT)
Shangri La
Don Henley; *End Of The Innocence* .... (GEF)
Electric Light Orchestra; *Box Of Their Best* ......(JET)
   New World Record .... (JET)
Four Coins; *50's Vocal Groups* .... (KT)
Kim Wilde; *Teases & Dares* .... (MCA)
Kinks; *Kink Kronikles* .... (RPR)
Lettermen; *All-Time Greatest Hits* .... (CAP)
   Capitol Collectors Series .... (CAP)
Steve Miller Band; *Italian X-Rays* .... (CAP)

Small Paradise
John Cougar Mellencamp; *John Cougar
Mellencamp* ....(RIV)
Straight To Paradise
Koinonia; *Koinonia* .... (BM)
Stranger In Paradise
Arthur Lyman; *Pearly Shells* .... (CRS)
Bing Crosby; *Radio Years-#1* .... (CRS)
Original Cast; *Kismet* ....(COL)
Tony Bennett; *16 Most Requested Songs* ....(COL)
  All-Time Greatest Hits ....(COL)
Streets Of Paradise
Poco; *Blue & Gray* .... (OW)
Richard & Linda Thompson; *Pour Down Like
Silver* ....(HBL)
Surrender Paradise
Miami Sound Machine; *Primitive Love* .... (EPI)
Thanks For The Trip To Paradise
Jim & Jesse McReynolds; *Music Among Friends* . (ROU)
There Are No Cats In America
Nehemiah Persoff/J. Guarnieri/W. Hays; *ST/An
American Tail* .... (MCA)
To One In Paradise
Alan Parsons Project; *Tales Of Mystery &
Imagination* .... (MER)
Town Called Paradise
Van Morrison; *No Guru No Method No Teacher* (MER)
Trouble In Paradise
Al Jarreau; *Jarreau* .... (WB)
Crests; *Greatest Hits* ....(CLT)
Greg Kihn; *Rockihn'* ....(BES)
Huey Lewis/News; *Huey Lewis/News* .... (CHR)
  We Are The World ....(COL)
J.D. Souther; *You're Only Lonely* ....(COL)
Loretta Lynn; *Best Of-#2* ....(MSP)
Princess Pang; *Princess Pang* ....(MET)
Two Tickets To Paradise
Eddie Money; *Eddie Money* ....(COL)
  Greatest Hits-Sound Of Money ....(COL)
  Unplug It In ....(COL)
Visions Of Paradise
Moody Blues; *In Search Of The Lost Chord* ...... (POL)
Welcome To Paradise
Green Day; *Dookie* .... (RPR)
Who But A Fool (Thief In Paradise)
Bonnie Raitt; *Nine Lives* .... (WB)

PARTY, Celebrate

*See Also: CARNIVALS, DANCE, FUN,
HAPPINESS, MUSIC, NIGHT*

1999
Prince; *1999* .... (WB)
Ain't Going Down (Til The Sun Comes Up)
Garth Brooks; *In Pieces* .... (LIB)
All Night Long
Billy Squier; *Signs Of Life* ....(CAP)
Eagles; *Live* ....(ASY)
Jerry Lee Lewis; *18 Original Sun Greatest Hits* ... (RHI)
  Milestones ....(RHI)
Joe Houston; *20 Super Rhythm & Blues Hits* .....(KNT)
  Rock & Roll Festival-#1 ....(KNT)
Joe Walsh; *ST/Urban Cowboy* ....(ASY)
Little Richard; *Fabulous* ....(SPE)
  Well Alright ....(SPE)
All Night Long (All Night)
Lionel Richie; *Can't Slow Down* .... (MOT)
  Motown Story-First 25 Years ....(MOT)
Animal House
Stephen Bishop; *ST/Animal House* .... (MCA)
At An Arabian House Party
Raymond Scott; *Reckless Nights & Turkish
Twilights* ....(COL)
At The Christmas Ball
Bessie Smith; *Complete Recordings-#2* ....(COL)
  Nobody's Blues But Mine ....(COL)
At The President's Birthday Ball
Glenn Miller/Orchestra; *Complete* ....(BLU)
Bad Boy/Having A Party
Luther Vandross; *Best Of...The Best Of Love* ..... (EPI)
  Forever For Always For Love ....(EPI)

Boys & Me
Sawyer Brown; *Outskirts Of Town* ....(CRB)
Celebrate Me Home
Kenny Loggins; *Alive* ....(COL)
  Celebrate Me Home ....(COL)
Celebration
Kool/Gang; *Celebrate* .... (DL)
  Everything Is-Greatest Hits ....(MER)
Celebration Day
Led Zeppelin; *III* .... (ATL)
  Led Zeppelin .... (ATL)
  ST/Song Remains The Same .... (SS)
Celebration For A Grey Day
Mimi & Richard Farina; *Best Of* .... (VAN)
  Celebration For A Grey Day .... (VAN)
  Memories .... (VAN)
Celebration Of The Lizard
Doors; *Absolutely Live* .... (ELE)
Celebration Song
Steve Miller Band; *Anthology* ....(CAP)
  Brave New World ....(CAP)
Clock Strikes Ten
Cheap Trick; *At Budokan* .... (EPI)
  In Color .... (EPI)
Cowboys & Playboys
Moe Brandy; *Best Of-#1* ....(COL)
Down At The Twist And Shout
Mary Chapin Carpenter; *Greatest Country
Hits/'90s-1992* ....(COL)
  Hitchhiker Exemplar 2 ....(COL)
  Shooting Straight In The Dark ....(COL)
  Today's Hot Country .... (KT)
Enema Party
Buck Naked/Bare Bottom Boys; *Buck Naked/Bare
Bottom Boys* ....(HEY)
Enjoy Yourself
Guy Lombardo; *Best Of* .... (MCA)
Jacksons; *Jacksons* ....(EPI)
Kylie Minogue; *Enjoy Yourself* ....(GEF)
Escapade
Janet Jackson; *Rhythm Nation 1814* .... (A&M)
Everybody's Everything
Santana; *Greatest Hits* ....(COL)
  Santana ....(COL)
  Viva Santana! ....(COL)
Feelin' Single, Seein' Double
Emmylou Harris; *Elite Hotel* .... (RPR)
Fiesta In Rio
Bette Midler; *Live At Last* .... (ATL)
Fight For Your Right (To Party)
Beastie Boys; *Def Jam Classics-#1* .... (DFJ)
  Heart Of Soul ....(COL)
  Licensed To Kill .... (DFJ)
Give It Up, Turn It Loose
En Vogue; *Funky Divas* ....(EW)
Go To The Mardi Gras
Professor Longhair; *New Orleans Party Classics* .. (RHI)
Going Out With The Boys
Jimmie Mack; *Jimmie Mack* ....(BT)
Good Time Boy
Buffalo Springfield; *Again* ....(ATC)
Good Time Charlie's Got The Blues
Danny O'Keefe; *45* .... (ATL)
  Seattle Tapes ....(FIR)
Willie Nelson; *City Of New Orleans* ....(COL)
Good Time Girl
Lee Ferrell; *Hard Times* .... (TMS)
Good Times
Chic; *Plus Grands Succes De Chic* .... (ATL)
  Risque .... (ATL)
Dan Seals; *Greatest Hits* ....(CAP)
  On Arrival ....(CAP)
Hoodoo Gurus; *Blow Your Cool* .... (ELE)
Jimi Hendrix; *Jimi Hendrix* ....(AUF)
Nat King Cole; *Ramblin' Rose* ....(CAP)
Persuasions; *Street Corner Symphony* ....(CAP)
Rita Coolidge; *Anytime...Anywhere* .... (A&M)
Rolling Stones; *12 X 5* ....(AKO)
  Big Hits (High Tide & Green Grass) ....(AKO)
  More Hot Rocks & Fazed Cookies ....(AKO)
  Out Of Our Heads ....(AKO)
Willie Nelson; *Best Of* ....(RCA)
  Minstrel Man ....(RCA)
  Music From "Songwriter" ....(COL)

Green Door
Jim Lowe; *Billboard Top Rock 'N' Roll Hits-1956* (RHI)
    Super Hits-#4 .... (GUS)
Have A Good Time
Elvin Bishop; *Struttin' My Stuff* ....(CPC)
Paul Simon; *Greatest Hits Etc.* ....(COL)
    Negotiations & Love Songs-1971-1986 .... (WB)
    Still Crazy After All These Years ....(COL)
Rufus & Chaka Khan; *Rufus* .... (MCA)
Havin' A Party
Norma Jean; *Norma Jean* .... (BRS)
Pointer Sisters; *Havin' A Party* .... (MCA)
Rod Stewart & Ronnie Wood; *MTV's Unplugged...And
    Seated* ....(WB)
Sam Cooke; *Best Of* ....(RCA)
    Feel It ....(RCA)
    Live At The Harlem Square Club ....(RCA)
    This Is ....(RCA)
Southside Johnny/Asbury Jukes; *Havin' A Party
    With* .... (EPI)
House Party
J. Geils Band; *Best Of* .... (ATL)
    Bloodshot .... (ATL)
    Blow Your Face Out .... (ATL)
I Don't Want To Spoil The Party
Beatles; *For Sale* ....(CAP)
    VI ....(CAP)
Rosanne Cash; *Greatest Country Hits/'80s-1989* .(COL)
    Hits 19790-1989 ....(COL)
I Just Want To Celebrate
Rare Earth; *20 Hard To Find Motown
    Classics-#2* .... (MOT)
    In Concert ....(REH)
    Motown Superstar Series-#16 .... (MOT)
I Love The Night Life
Alicia Bridges; *Alicia Bridges* .... (POL)
    Night At Studio 54 .... (CAS)
    Oldies But Goodies-#14 ....(OSR)
    Polydor Dance Classics .... (POL)
I Need A Joint
Basehead; *Not In Kansas Anymore* .... (IMG)
It Sure Is Monday
Mark Chesnutt; *Almost Goodbye* .... (MCA)
It's My Party
Lesley Gore; *Anthology* .... (RHI)
    Billboard Top Rock 'N' Roll Hits-1963 .... (RHI)
    Golden Hits Of ....(MER)
    Good Time Rock 'N' Roll .... (MCA)
    Oldies But Goodies-#3 ....(OSR)
Jailhouse Rock
Blues Brothers; *ST/Blues Brothers* .... (ATL)
Elvis Presley; *Billboard Top Rock 'N' Roll
    Hits-1957* .... (RHI)
    Legendary Performer-#2 ....(RCA)
    Live On Stage ....(RCA)
    Number One Hits ....(RCA)
    Rocker ....(RCA)
    Worldwide 50 Gold Award Hits-#1 ....(RCA)
Jeff Beck; *Beck-Ola* .... (EPI)
Let The Good Times Roll
Barbra Streisand; *Butterfly* ....(COL)
Betty Everett & Jerry Butler; *Delicious Together* .... (VJ)
    Starring Betty Everett ....(TRD)
Bobby Bland & B.B. King; *Together Again...* .... (MCA)
Harry Nilsson; *Nilsson Schmilsson* ....(RCA)
Jerry Lee Lewis; *Golden Rock & Roll* .... (SUN)
Louis Jordan; *Best Of* .... (MCA)
Molly Hatchet; *Flirtin' With Disaster* .... (EPI)
Phoebe Snow; *Phoebe Snow* .... (MCA)
Ray Charles; *Genius Of* .... (ATL)
Shirley & Lee; *Billboard Top R&B Hits-1956* .... (RHI)
    History Of New Orleans R&B-#1-1950-1958 .... (RHI)
    ST/Stand By Me .... (ATL)
    Super Oldies/'50s-#4 ....(AUF)
Let's Celebrate
Midnight Star; *Planetary Invasion* .... (SLR)
Skyy; *45* .... (SSL)
Stranglers; *45* .... (EPI)
Let's Get Rocked
Def Leppard; *Adrenalize* .... (MER)
Let's Groove
Earth, Wind & Fire; *Best Of* ....(COL)
    Raise ....(COL)

Life In The Fast Lane
Eagles; *Hotel California* .... (ASY)
    Live .... (ASY)
    ST/FM ....(MCA)
Live It Up
Crosby, Stills & Nash; *Live It Up* .... (ATL)
Isley Brothers; *Forever Gold* .... (TN)
    Greatest Hits-#1 .... (TN)
    Live It Up .... (TN)
Ted Nugent; *Cat Scratch Fever* .... (EPI)
Lively Up Yourself
Bob Marley/Wailers; *Babylon By Bus* ....(TUF)
    Live ....(TUF)
    Natty Dread ....(TUF)
Livin' It Up (Friday Night)
Bell & James; *Bell & James* .... (A&M)
Louie Louie
Kingsmen; *Best Of* .... (RHI)
    Billboard Top Rock 'N' Roll Hits-1963 .... (RHI)
    Cruisin'-1963 ....(INC)
    Frat Rock! .... (RHI)
    Oldies But Goodies-#11 ....(OSR)
    Rock & Roll Is Here To Stay .... (GUS)
    ST/Quadrophenia .... (POL)
    WCBS FM101-History Of Rock/'60s-#1 .... (CLT)
Pretenders; *II* .... (SIR)
Mama Told Me Not To Come
Randy Newman; *12 Songs* .... (RPR)
    Live .... (RPR)
    Randy Newman ....(RPR)
Three Dog Night; *Best Of* .... (MCA)
    Billboard Top Rock 'N' Roll Hits-1970 .... (RHI)
Wilson Pickett; *Greatest Hits* .... (ATL)
Million Dollar Bash
Bob Dylan; *Biograph* ....(COL)
Bob Dylan/Band; *Basement Tapes* .... (COL)
Motel Party Baby
Dinosaurs; *Dinosaurs* ....(RLX)
New Orleans Ceremony
Dukes Of Dixieland; *Best Of* ....(COL)
Night (Feel Like Getting Down)
Billy Ocean; *Night (Feel Like Getting Down)* ...... (EPI)
Nothin' But A Good Time
Poison; *Open Up & Say...Ahh!* ....(CAP)
    Swallow This Live ....(CAP)
Omaha Celebration
Pat Metheny; *Bright Size Life* .... (ECM)
One More Last Chance
Vince Gill; *I Still Believe In You* .... (MCA)
Ozark Mountain Jubilee
Oak Ridge Boys; *Deliver* .... (MCA)
    Greatest Hits-#2 .... (MCA)
    Ozark Mountain Jubilee .... (MSP)
Party
Big Audio Dynamite; *This Is* ....(COL)
Boston; *Don't Look Back* .... (EPI)
Elvis Presley; *Essential Elvis-First Movies* ......(RCA)
    ST/Loving You ....(RCA)
En Vogue; *Born To Sing* .... (ATL)
Kris Kross; *Totally Krossed Out* ....(RUC)
Marillion; *Holidays In Eden* .... (IRS)
Ray Pillow; *45* .... (MCA)
Party All Night
Quiet Riot; *Condition Critical* .... (EPA)
    Winners Take All .... (SSP)
Party All The Time
Eddie Murphy; *How Could It Be* ....(COL)
Party At Ground Zero
Fishbone; *Fishbone* ....(COL)
    Richard Blade's Flashback Favorites ....(OGO)
Party At The Berlin Wall
Root Boy Slim/Sex Change Band; *Root 6* ...... (NL)
Party At The Prune Farm
Lou & Peter Berryman; *Cupid's Trash Truck* .... (COR)
Party Doll
Buddy Knox; *Best Of* .... (RHI)
    Billboard Top Rock 'N' Roll Hits-1957 ....(RHI)
    ST/American Graffiti .... (MCA)
Party Down
Willie Hutch; *45* .... (MOT)
Party Freak
Cashflow; *45* .... (MER)

Party Girl
Bernadette Carroll; *20 Million Dollar*
Memories-#2 .... (LAU)
  22 Leaders Of The Pack-#1 .... (LAU)
Elvis Costello; *Girls Girls Girls* .... (COL)
Elvis Costello/Attractions; *Armed Forces* .... (COL)
Linda Ronstadt; *Mad Love* .... (ASY)
T-Bone Walker; *Complete Imperial Recordings*
1950-1954 .... (EMI)
  T-Bone Walker .... (BLN)
U2; *Under A Blood Red Sky* .... (ISL)
Party Girls
Mink De Ville; *Mink De Ville* .... (CAP)
Rick James/Stone City Band; *In 'N' Out* .... (GOR)
Party In Senegal
Wallets; *Take It* .... (TT)
Party In The Graveyard
Haunted Garage; *Possession Park* .... (MET)
Party In The Parking Lot
Johnny Van Zant; *Brickyard Road* .... (ATL)
Party Lights
Claudine Clark; *Collectables Presents History Of*
Rock-#4 .... (CLT)
  Wonder Women-History Of Girl Group Sound .. (RHI)
Gap Band; *2* .... (MER)
Natalie Cole; *Collection* .... (CAP)
  Live .... (CAP)
  Unpredictable .... (CAP)
Party Night
Curtis Mayfield; *Do It All Night* .... (CUR)
  Give Get Take & Have .... (CUR)
Isley Brothers; *Grand Slam* .... (TN)
Party People
Joe South; *Best Of* .... (RHI)
Parliament; *Gloryhallastoopid* .... (CAS)
Solomon Burke; *Home In Your Heart-Best Of* .... (RHI)
Party Till The Cows Come Home
Elvin Bishop Group; *Bill Graham-Fillmore-Last*
Days .... (EPA)
Party Time
T.G. Sheppard; *All Time Greatest Hits* .... (WB)
  Greatest Hits .... (WB)
Party Time U.S.A.
Oscar Peterson; *Silent Partner* .... (PAB)
Party 'Till The Money Runs Out
Radiators; *Total Evaporation* .... (EPI)
Partyin' Gal
Charlie Daniels Band; *Windows* .... (EPI)
Partytown
Glenn Frey; *No Fun Aloud* .... (ASY)
Party's Over
Journey; *Captured* .... (COL)
Judy Garland; *One & Only* .... (CAP)
Judy Holliday; *Broadway Magic-'60s* .... (COL)
  Original Cast-Bells Are Ringing .... (COL)
Marvin Gaye; *Hello Broadway* .... (MOT)
Mel Torme; *Live At The Maisonette* .... (ATL)
Raspberries; *Capitol Collectors Series* .... (CAP)
Shirley Bassey; *Live At Carnegie Hall* .... (UA)
Tesla; *Great Radio Controversy* .... (GEF)
Willie Nelson; *Always On My Mind* .... (COL)
Prince Is Giving A Ball
Original Cast; *Cinderella-CBS Television*
Production .... (COL)
P.A.R.T.Y.
Denise LaSalle; *Under The Influence* .... (MCA)
Raisin' Cane In Texas
Gene Watson; *All-Time Country Classics-#1* ..... (CAP)
  Texas State Of Mind .... (CAP)
Raisin' Hell
Elvin Bishop; *Raisin' Hell* .... (CPC)
Really Good Time
Roxy Music; *Country Life* .... (RPR)
Rip It Up
Elvis Presley; *Elvis* .... (RCA)
  Rocker .... (RCA)
Little Richard; *18 Greatest Hits* .... (RHI)
  Big Hits .... (CRS)
  Greatest Hits .... (EVR)
  Grooviest 17 Original Hits .... (SPE)
Rip This Joint
Rolling Stones; *Exile On Main Street* .... (RS)
  Made In The Shade .... (RS)

Route 66
Asleep At The Wheel; *Served Live* .... (CAP)
  Wheelin' & Dealin' .... (CAP)
Depeche Mode; *ST/Earth Girls Are Easy* .... (SIR)
George Maharis; *45* .... (EPI)
Manhattan Transfer; *Bop Doo-Wopp* .... (ATL)
Nat King Cole; *Capitol Collectors Series* .... (CAP)
  Story .... (CAP)
  Unforgettable .... (CAP)
Natalie Cole; *Unforgettable* .... (ELE)
Rolling Stones; *December's Children* .... (AKO)
  Rolling Stones .... (AKO)
Shit You Hear At Parties
Minutemen; *Ballot Result* .... (SST)
Slow Bus Movin' (Howard's Beach Party)
Fishbone; *Truth & Soul* .... (COL)
Splish Splash
Barbra Streisand; *Wet* .... (COL)
Bobby Darin; *Greatest Hits* .... (CCB)
  Oldies But Goodies-#8 .... (OSR)
  Splish Splash-Best Of-#1 .... (ATL)
  Story .... (ATC)
Sha-Na-Na; *Having An Oldies Party With* .... (KT)
Stoned Soul Picnic
5th Dimension; *Greatest Hits On Earth* .... (ARI)
Laura Nyro; *Eli & The 13th Confession* .... (COL)
  Live At The Bottom Line .... (CYP)
Swingin'
John Anderson; *Greatest Hits* .... (WB)
  Swingin' Country Favorites .... (WB)
  Wild & Blue .... (WB)
Swiss Celebration
David Friedman; *Of The Wind's Eye* .... (ENJ)
Texas Party
Johnny Copeland; *Boom Boom* .... (ROU)
Texas Tea Party
Benny Goodman; *Early Years* .... (BIO)
That Party
Harry Connick, Jr.; *She* .... (COL)
Theme From "Wayne's World"
Mike Myers & Dana Carvey; *ST/Wayne's World* . (RPR)
There'll Be A Hot Time In The Old...
Bessie Smith; *Complete Recordings-#3* .... (COL)
Louis Armstrong; *Best Of* .... (AUF)
Turk Murphy's San Francisco Jazz Band; *#1* .... (GTJ)
They'll All Out Of Liquor, Let's Find...
Waitresses; *Best Of* .... (POL)
Tonight I Celebrate My Love
Peabo Bryson & Roberta Flack; *Born To Love* ... (CAP)
  Collection .... (CAP)
Too Much Fun
Commander Cody/Lost Planet Airmen; *Live From Deep*
In The Heart Of Texas .... (MCA)
  Too Much Fun-Best Of .... (MCA)
  We've Got A Live One Here .... (WB)
Too Pooped To Pop
Chuck Berry; *Chess Box* .... (CSS)
  Rockin' At The Hops .... (CSS)
Tupperware Party
Doughboys; *Happy Accidents* .... (RES)
TV Party
Black Flag; *7-Inch Wonders Of The World* .... (SST)
  Damaged .... (SST)
  ST/Repo Man .... (MCA)
Wasn't That A Party
Rovers; *Wasn't That A Party* .... (EPI)
Where Have All The Good Times Gone
David Bowie; *Pinups* .... (RYK)
Elton John; *Jump Up!* .... (MCA)
Kinks; *Greatest Hits-#1* .... (RHI)
  One For The Road .... (ARI)
Van Halen; *Diver Down* .... (WB)

PEACE
See Also: FRIENDS, HAPPINESS, POLITICAL
CLASSICS, WAR

All Quiet Along The Potomac Tonight
Hermes Nye; *Ballads Of The Civil War-#1 & 2* . (FLW)
Clasp
Jethro Tull; *20 Years Of-Boxed Set* .... (CHR)
  Broadsword & The Beast .... (CHR)

Computer Incantations For World Peace
Jean-Luc Ponty; *Individual Choice* .... (ATL)
Ebony & Ivory
Paul McCartney; *Tripping The Live Fantastic* .... (CAP)
Paul McCartney & Stevie Wonder; *All The Best* . (CAP)
 Tug Of War .... (CAP)
Get Together
Youngbloods; *Best Of* .... (RCA)
 Billboard Top Rock 'N' Roll Hits-1969 .... (RHI)
 Nipper's Greatest Hits-'60s-#2 .... (RCA)
 ST/Forrest Gump .... (EPX)
 Summer Of Love .... (RHI)
Give Me Love (Give Me Peace On Earth)
George Harrison; *Best Of* .... (CAP)
 Living In The Material World .... (CAP)
Give Peace A Chance
John Lennon; *Collection* .... (GEF)
 Lennon .... (CAP)
 Live In New York City .... (CAP)
 Shaved Fish .... (CAP)
Harmony
Bar-Kays; *Coldblooded* .... (STX)
Elton John; *Goodbye Yellow Brick Road* .... (POL)
Happy Mondays; *Pills 'N' Thrills & Bellyaches* .... (ELE)
John Conlee; *45* .... (COL)
Limeliters; *Live In Concert* .... (CRS)
Take 6 (featuring Queen Latifah); *Join The Band* (RPR)
I Wish You Peace
Eagles; *One Of These Nights* .... (ASY)
Imagine
Diana Ross; *Anthology* .... (MOT)
 Best Of The Beatles Songs .... (MOT)
 Touch Me In The Morning .... (MOT)
Joan Baez; *Best Of* .... (A&M)
 Come From The Shadows .... (A&M)
John Lennon; *Lennon* .... (CAP)
 Live In New York City .... (CAP)
 Shaved Fish .... (CAP)
John Lennon/Plastic Ono Band; *Collection* .... (GEF)
 Imagine .... (CAP)
 ST/Imagine-The Motion Picture .... (CAP)
Kill For Peace
Fugs; *Fugs* .... (ESP)
 Fugs 4 Rounders Score .... (ESP)
Live In Peace
Country Joe McDonald; *Peace On Earth* .... (RBB)
Firm; *Mean Business* .... (ATL)
Peace
Barry McGuire; *Seeds* .... (MYR)
Bobby McFerrin; *Bobby McFerrin* .... (ELE)
Branford Marsalis; *Trio Jeepy* .... (COL)
Greater Than One; *Funky Alternatives-18 Techno
 Remixes* .... (ROI)
 London .... (WAX)
Los Lobos; *Kiko* .... (SLS)
Peace Brother Peace
Bill Medley; *45* .... (MGM)
Peace Dog
Cult; *Electric* .... (SIR)
Peace For South Africa
Oscar Peterson Trio; *Live At The Blue Note* ...... (TLR)
Peace Frog
Doors; *Classics* .... (ELE)
 Morrison Hotel .... (ELE)
 Weird Scenes Inside The Gold Mine .... (ELE)
Peace In Liberia
Alpha Blondy; *Masada* .... (WP)
Peace In Mind
Joan Armatrading; *Show Some Emotion* .... (A&M)
Peace In Mississippi
Jimi Hendrix; *Crash Landing* .... (RPR)
Peace In My Heart
Carole Bayer Sager; *Too* .... (ELE)
Peace In Our Time
Eddie Money; *Greatest Hits-Sound Of Money* .... (COL)
Elvis Costello/Attractions; *Goodbye Cruel World* (COL)
Peace In The Valley
Carole King; *Rhymes & Reasons* .... (EPI)
Elvis Presley; *Golden Celebration* .... (RCA)
 Legendary Performer #1 .... (RCA)
 Million Dollar Quartet .... (RCA)
Johnny Cash; *At San Quentin* .... (COL)
 Classic Cash-Hall Of Fame Series .... (MER)
 J.L. Lewis/Carl Perkins-The Survivors .... (COL)

Peace Like A River
Paul Simon; *Paul Simon* .... (WB)
Peace Of Mind
Bad Company; *Burnin' Sky* .... (SS)
Blue Cheer; *Good Times Are So Hard To
 Find-History* .... (MER)
 Louder Than God-Best Of .... (RHI)
Boston; *Boston* .... (EPI)
Eddy Raven; *Greatest Hits* .... (WB)
Engelbert Humperdinck; *Miracles* .... (EPI)
Loggins & Messina; *Best Of-Friends* .... (COL)
 On Stage .... (COL)
 Sittin' In .... (COL)
Neil Young; *Comes A Time* .... (RPR)
Peace Officer
Jimmy Cliff; *Rhythm Come Forward-#3* .... (COL)
 Special .... (COL)
Peace On You
Charlie Rich; *Behind Closed Doors* .... (EPI)
Peace Pipe
Cry Of Love; *Brother* .... (COL)
Edgar Winter; *Entrance* .... (EPI)
Peace To New York
Doug E. Fresh/Get Fresh Crew; *Doin' What I Gotta
 Do* .... (BUS)
Peace Train
10,000 Maniacs; *In My Tribe* .... (ELE)
Cat Stevens; *Classics-#24* .... (A&M)
 Greatest Hits .... (A&M)
 Teaser & The Firecat .... (A&M)
Peace Will Come
Melanie; *Beautiful* .... (FFT)
 Best Of .... (RHI)
Peace & Understanding Is Hard To Find
Junior Walker/All-Stars; *Anthology* .... (MOT)
 Motown Superstar Series-#5 .... (MOT)
Peaceful
Helen Reddy; *Greatest Hits* .... (CAP)
Kenny Rankin; *Like A Seed* .... (LD)
Peaceful Easy Feeling
Eagles; *Anthology* .... (ASY)
 Eagles .... (ASY)
 Their Greatest Hits-1971-1975 .... (ASY)
Little Texas; *Common Thread-Songs Of The
 Eagles* .... (GIA)
Peaceful Journey
Fat Larry's Band; *Sweet Soul Music-Stax Groups* . (STX)
Heavy D./Boys; *Peaceful Journey* .... (UT)
Peaceful Waters
Gordon Lightfoot; *Lightfoot* .... (UA)
Peaceful World
Rascals; *Peaceful World* .... (OOP)
Peacemaker
Kool/Gang; *Everything's Kool & The
 Gang-Greatest* .... (MER)
Loggins & Messina; *Native Sons* .... (COL)
Peace, Love & Understanding
Curtis Stigers; *ST/Bodyguard* .... (ARI)
Elvis Costello/Attractions; *Armed Forces* .... (COL)
 Best Of .... (COL)
Reach Out And Touch
Diana Ross; *All The Great Hits* .... (MOT)
 Anthology .... (MOT)
 Live At Caesar's Palace .... (MOT)
 Most Played Songs On America's Jukeboxes .... (MOT)
 Motown Story .... (MOT)
Rest In Peace
Extreme; *III Sides To Every Story* .... (A&M)
Ripple
Grateful Dead; *American Beauty* .... (WB)
 Reckoning .... (ARI)
 What A Long Strange Trip It's Been .... (WB)
Jane's Addiction; *Deadicated* .... (ARI)
Santa Lucia
Elvis Presley; *ST/Viva Las Vegas/Roustabout* ..... (RCA)
Mario Lanza; *Legendary Tenor* .... (RCA)
Savannah The Serene
Billy Cobham; *Crosswinds* .... (ATL)
Sentimental Lady
Fleetwood Mac; *25 Years-The Chain* .... (WB)
 Bare Trees .... (WB)
Shhh/Peaceful
Miles Davis; *In A Silent Way* .... (COL)

Sunday In The South
Shenandoah; *30 Years Of #1 Hits-#19* ....(COL)
   Greatest Hits ....(COL)
   Road Not Taken ....(COL)
There Will Never Be Any Peace
Chi-Lites; *Greatest Hits* .... (RHI)
There Will Never Be Any Peace (Until...)
Chi-Lites; *Greatest Hits* .... (RHI)
Waitress, The
Tori Amos; *Under The Pink* .... (ATL)
War Is Over
Phil Ochs; *Chords Of Fame* .... (A&M)
   Tape From California .... (A&M)
   War Is Over-Best Of .... (A&M)
We're All In The Same Gang
West Coast Rap All-Stars; *We're All In The Same
Gang* .... (WB)
What's Goin' On
Cyndi Lauper; *True Colors* .... (POR)
Marvin Gaye; *20/20* .... (MOT)
   Anthology .... (MOT)
   Greatest Hits .... (MOT)
   Live At The London Palladium .... (MOT)
   More Songs From "Big Chill" Soundtrack ... (MOT)
   What's Goin' On .... (MOT)
Quincy Jones; *Best Of* .... (A&M)
Woodstock
Crosby, Stills & Nash; *Crosby, Stills & Nash
(collection)* .... (ATL)
Crosby, Stills, Nash & Young; *Deja Vu* .... (ATL)
   So Far .... (ATL)
Joni Mitchell; *Ladies Of The Canyon* .... (RPR)
   Miles Of Aisles .... (ASY)
   Shadows & Light .... (ASY)
You Gave Me Peace Of Mind
Spaniels; *16 Soulful Serenades* .... (SSM)
   Goodnite It's Time To Go .... (VJ)

PIGS

Gimme A Pig Foot
Billie Holiday; *From The Original Decca Masters* (MCA)
   Story .... (MCA)
I'm A Pig
Angry Samoans; *Gimme Samoa: 31 Garbage-Pit
Hits* .... (PVC)
Paul Wants A Pig
John Jarvis; *Whatever Works* .... (MCA)
Pig Feet
Fat Boys; *Coming Back Hard Again* .... (MER)
Piggies
Beatles; *Box Set* .... (CAP)
   White Album ....(CAP)
George Harrison & Eric Clapton & Band; *Live In
Japan* .... (DKH)
Piggy In the Mirror
Cure; *Top* .... (SIR)
Piggy Pig Pig
Procol Harum; *Home* .... (MOB)
   Procol Harum .... (A&M)
Pigmeat
Leadbelly; *King Of The Twelve-String Guitar* .....(COL)
Pigmeat Is What I Crave
Bo Carter; *Legends Of The Blues-#1* ....(COL)
Pigs
Pink Floyd; *Animals* ....(COL)
Pigs In Zen
Jane's Addiction; *Jane's Addiction* .... (XXX)
   Nothing's Shocking .... (WB)
Pigs On The Wing
Pink Floyd; *Animals* ....(COL)
   Shine On-Box Set ....(COL)
Pigs (Three Different Ones)
Pink Floyd; *Animals* ....(COL)
   Shine On-Box Set ....(COL)
Pig's Song
Jim Croce; *Faces I've Been* .... (LIF)
Sad Pig Dance
Chris Proctor; *Delicate Dance* .... (FF)
This Little Pig
Living Colour; *Stain* .... (EPI)
Three Little Pigs
Lloyd Price; *Greatest Hits* .... (MCA)

War Pigs
Black Sabbath; *Live Evil* ....(WB)
   Paranoid ....(WB)
   We Sold Our Soul For Rock & Roll ....(WB)
Faith No More; *Real Thing* ....(SLS)
Ozzy Osbourne; *Just Say Ozzy* ....(EPA)
   Speak Of The Devil ....(JET)

POLICE, Detectives, Secret Agents, Spies

*See Also: CRIME, GUNS, PRISONS, REBELS,
WAR*

10-4 (Calling All Cars)
Benny Spellman; *Fortune Teller* ....(CLT)
Alice's Restaurant Massacree
Arlo Guthrie; *Alice's Restaurant Massacree* .... (RPR)
   Best Of ....(WB)
All Along The Watchtower
Bob Dylan; *At Budokan* ....(COL)
   Before The Flood ....(COL)
   Biograph ....(COL)
   Greatest Hits-#2 ....(COL)
   John Wesley Harding ....(COL)
Jimi Hendrix; *Electric Ladyland* ....(RPR)
   Kiss The Sky ....(RPR)
   Lifelines/Jimi Hendrix Story ....(RPR)
Jimi Hendrix Experience; *Essential-#1 & 2* ......(RPR)
   Smash Hits ....(RPR)
U2; *ST/Rattle & Hum* .... (ISL)
And The Mouse Police Never Sleeps
Jethro Tull; *Heavy Horses* .... (CHR)
Arrest The President
Intelligent Hoodlum; *Intelligent Hoodlum* .... (A&M)
"Barney Miller" Theme
Original Music; *Television's Greatest Hits-#3* .....(TVT)
Big Brother
David Bowie; *Diamond Dogs* ....(RYK)
   Live ....(RYK)
   Sound + Vision ....(RYK)
   ST/Breaking Glass ....(A&M)
Stevie Wonder; *Talking Book* ....(MOT)
Body Count
Ice-T; *Body Count* ....(WB)
Bridge Of Spies
T'Pau; *Bridge Of Spies* .... (VIA)
Call The Police
Hot Chocolate; *Hot Chocolate* ....(BT)
Nat King Cole; *From The Very Beginning* .... (MCA)
"Car 54, Where Are You?" Theme
Original Music; *Television's Greatest Hits-#2* .....(TVT)
Cop Killer
Ice-T; *Body Count* ....(WB)
Cops
John Stewart; *Phoenix Concerts* ....(RCA)
Cops Of The World
Phil Ochs; *In Concert* .... (ELE)
   There But For Fortune .... (ELE)
Detective Man
Detective; *Detective* .... (SS)
Don't Let Nobody Turn You Around
Steve Miller Band; *Anthology* ....(CAP)
   Your Saving Grace ....(CAP)
Dream Police
Cheap Trick; *Dream Police* ....(EPI)
Every Breath You Take
Police; *Singles* ....(A&M)
   Synchronicity ....(A&M)
Tammy Wynette & Sting; *Without Walls* .... (EPI)
Fingerprint File
Rolling Stones; *It's Only Rock 'N' Roll* .... (RS)
   Love You Live .... (RS)
Friendly Neighborhood Narco Agent
Jef Jaisun; *Dr. Demento's Delight* ....(WB)
Fuck Tha Police
N.W.A.; *Straight Outta Compton* ....(RUP)
Gee, Officer Krupke
Original Cast; *ST/West Side Story* ....(COL)

Goldfinger
Shirley Bassey; *13 Original James Bond Themes* .. (EMI)
  Best Of .... (EMI)
  Great Performances ....(LIB)
  Greatest Hits .... (EMI)
  Live At Carnegie Hall .... (UA)
  ST/Goldfinger .... (UA)
"Green Hornet" Theme
Original Music; *Television's Greatest Hits-#2* .... (TVT)
Harder They Come
Jimmy Cliff; *Harder They Come* .... (ISL)
  In Concert-Best Of ....(RPR)
  Island Story-25th Anniversary .... (ISL)
Hawaii Five 0
Ventures; *45* .... (UA)
Highway Patrol
Reggie Knighton Band; *Reggie Knighton Band* ...(COL)
Highway Patrolman
Bruce Springsteen; *Nebraska* ....(COL)
"Hill Street Blues" Theme
Original Music; *Television's Greatest Hits-#3* ..... (TVT)
Hot Cop
Village People; *Cruisin'* .... (CAS)
  Greatest Hits .... (RHI)
  Live & Sleazy .... (CAS)
Hot Rod Lincoln
Asleep At The Wheel; *Western Standard Time* .... (EPI)
Commander Cody/Lost Planet Airmen; *Lost In The
  Ozone* .... (MCA)
  Super Hits/'70s-Have A Nice Day-#8 .... (RHI)
  We've Got A Live One Here .... (WB)
Johnny Bond; *Best Of* .... (STR)
I Ain't Livin' Long Like This
Emmylou Harris; *Quarter Moon In A Ten-Cent
  Town* .... (WB)
Rodney Crowell; *Collection* .... (WB)
  I Ain't Livin' Long Like This .... (WB)
Waylon Jennings; *Greatest Hits-#2* .... (RCA)
  What Goes Around Comes Around ....(RCA)
I Shot The Sheriff
Bob Marley/Wailers; *Burnin'* .... (TUF)
  Legend .... (TUF)
  Live .... (TUF)
  This Is Reggae Music .... (ISL)
Eric Clapton; *461 Ocean Blvd.* .... (RSO)
  Crossroads ....(POL)
  Time Pieces-Best Of .... (RSO)
"I Spy" Theme
Original Music; *Television's Greatest Hits-#2* ..... (TVT)
Indiana Wants Me
R. Dean Taylor; *Hard-To-Find Motown
  Classics-#2* .... (MOT)
  Super Hits-#5 .... (GUS)
  Super Hits/'70s-Have A Nice Day-#3 .... (RHI)
I'll Tell A Policeman On You
Jerry Lewis; *Capitol Collectors Series* ....(CAP)
I'm A Rocker
Bruce Springsteen; *The River* ....(COL)
Jeannie Needs A Shooter
Warren Zevon; *Bad Luck Streak In Dancing
  School* .... (ASY)
  Stand In The Fire .... (ASY)
Jolly Coppers On Parade
Randy Newman; *Little Criminals* .... (WB)
Kojak Theme
Henry Mancini; *Cop Show Themes* ....(RCA)
John Gregory; *TV's Greatest Detective Hits* ...... (MER)
"Kojak" Theme
Original Music; *Television's Greatest Hits-#3* ..... (TVT)
Lawyers, Guns & Money
Warren Zevon; *Excitable Boy* .... (ASY)
  Quiet Normal Life-Best Of .... (ASY)
  Stand In The Fire .... (ASY)
Lovely Rita
Beatles; *Sgt. Pepper's Lonely Hearts Club Band* ..(CAP)
"Magnum P.I." Theme
Original Music; *Television's Greatest Hits-#3* ..... (TVT)
"Man From U.N.C.L.E." Theme
Challengers; *25 Greatest Instrumental Hits* .... (CRS)
"Mannix" Theme
San Diego Symphony/Lalo Schifrin; *Hitchcock-Master
  Of Mayhem* .... (POE)

"Miami Vice" Theme
Jan Hammer; *Escape From Television* .... (MCA)
  Soundtrack Smashes-'80s .... (MCA)
  ST/"Miami Vice" Theme .... (MCA)
Original Music; *Television's Greatest Hits-#3* ... (TVT)
"Mission: Impossible" Theme
San Diego Symphony/Lalo Schifrin; *Hitchcock-Master
  Of Mayhem* .... (POE)
"Moonlighting" Theme
Al Jarreau; *ST/Moonlighting* .... (MCA)
"Moonraker" Theme
John Barry & Shirley Bassey; *ST/Moonraker* ..... (EMI)
Shirley Bassey; *Best Of James Bond-30th
  Anniversary* .... (EMI)
Mr. Policeman
Rick James; *Street Songs* .... (MOT)
New York State Police
UK Subs; *Left For Dead (Alive In Holland '86)* ... (ROI)
  Singles 1978-1982 ....(PGD)
Night Watchman
Tom Petty/Heartbreakers; *Hard Promises* .... (MCA)
Ninety Nine
Toto; *Hydra* ....(COL)
Nobody Does It Better
Carly Simon; *13 Original James Bond Themes* ... (EMI)
  Greatest Hits Live .... (ARI)
  ST/Spy Who Loved Me .... (EMI)
Nutbush City Limits
Bob Seger; *Beautiful Loser* ....(CAP)
  Live Bullet ....(CAP)
Ike & Tina Turner; *Best Of* .... (EMI)
  Proud Mary-Best Of .... (EMI)
  Simply The Best ....(CAP)
Tina Turner; *Live In Europe* ....(CAP)
One Way Mirror
Venus Beads; *Black Aspirin* .... (RR)
Passing Policeman
Johnson Brothers; *Bristol Sessions-#1 & 2* .... (CMF)
Peace Officer
Jimmy Cliff; *Rhythm Come Forward-#3* ....(COL)
  Special ....(COL)
Police Dog Blues
Blind Blake; *Georgia Blues-1927-1930* ....(YAZ)
Hot Tuna; *Splashdown* ....(RLX)
Jorma Kaukonen & Tom Hobson; *Quah* ....(RLX)
Ry Cooder; *Ry Cooder* .... (RPR)
Police On My Back
Clash; *On Broadway* .... (EPI)
  Sandinista .... (EPI)
Police Story
Black Flag; *Damaged* ....(SST)
Ventures; *TV Themes* .... (UA)
Police Woman
Henry Mancini; *Cop Show Themes* ....(RCA)
Police & Thiefs
Clash; *Clash* .... (EPI)
  On Broadway .... (EPI)
  Story Of-#1 .... (EPI)
Junior Murvin; *Jammin'* .... (MGO)
  Police & Thiefs .... (MGO)
  ST/Rockers .... (MGO)
  This Is Reggae Music #3 .... (ISL)
Policeman
Chicago; *XI* ....(COL)
Police, Police
Atlanta Rhythm Section; *Red Tape* .... (POL)
Private Eyes
Daryl Hall & John Oates; *Private Eyes* ....(RCA)
  Rock 'N' Soul Pt. 1-Greatest Hits ....(RCA)
Raid
Graham Parker/Rumour; *Stick To Me* .... (MER)
Robot Police
Baby Buddha; *Music For Teenage Sex* .... (PBO)
Secret Agent Man
Devo; *Duty Now For The Future* .... (WB)
Johnny Rivers; *Anthology-1964-1977* .... (RHI)
  Best Of .... (EMI)
  Very Best Of .... (EMI)
Secret Service
Original Cast; *Mr. President* .... (SMC)
Shakedown
Bob Seger; *ST/Beverly Hills Cop II* .... (MCA)
Sheriff
Emerson, Lake & Palmer; *Trilogy* .... (ATL)

Sheriff Of Hong Kong
Captain Beefheart; *Doc At The Radar Station* ......(BP)
Sheriff O.E. & Me
Big Mama Thornton; *Jail* .... (VAN)
Shoot Low Sheriff
Murry Kellum; *Country Comedy-20 Country Comedy Hits* .... (PLN)
Somebody's Watching Me
Rockwell; *Somebody's Watching Me* .... (MOT)
Space Patrol
Country Joe McDonald; *Classics* .... (FAN)
Rock & Roll From Planet Earth .... (FAN)
Spies
Randy Newman; *Born Again* .... (WB)
Spy
Carly Simon; *Spy* .... (ELE)
Doors; *Morrison Hotel* .... (ELE)
Weird Scenes Inside The Goldmine .... (ELE)
State Trooper
Bruce Springsteen; *Nebraska* ....(COL)
"Streets Of San Francisco" Theme
Original Music; *Television's Greatest Hits-#3* .....(TVT)
"S.W.A.T." Theme
Original Music; *Television's Greatest Hits-#3* .....(TVT)
Rhythm Heritage; *Billboard Top Rock 'N' Roll Hits-1976* .... (RHI)
Texas Lawman
Regulators; *Regulators* ....(POL)
Texas Rangers
Ian & Sylvia; *Greatest Hits* .... (VAN)
Northern Journey .... (VAN)
Michael Martin Murphey; *Cowboy Songs* ....(WB)
"The Avengers" Theme
Original Music; *Television's Greatest Hits-#2* ..... (TVT)
"The Bodyguard" Theme
Original Music; *ST/The Bodyguard* .... (ARI)
"The F.B.I." Theme
101 Strings Orchestra; *TV Themes* .... (ALS)
"The Rookies" Theme
Original Music; *Television's Greatest Hits-#3* ..... (TVT)
Theme From "James Bond"
John Barry Orchestra; *Best Of James Bond-30th Anniversary* .... (EMI)
London Symphony Orchestra; *From London With Love-Music Of J. Bond* .... (POE)
Theme From "Shaft"
Isaac Hayes; *Greatest Hit Singles* .... (STX)
Pimps Players & Private Eyes .... (STX)
Top Of The Stax-Twenty Greatest Hits .... (STX)
TV Private Eye
Now; *Now* .... (MDS)
Undercover Of The Night
Rolling Stones; *Rewind (1971-1984)* .... (RS)
Undercover .... (RS)
Watching The Detectives
Elvis Costello; *Girls Girls Girls* ....(COL)
My Aim Is True ....(COL)
Elvis Costello/Attractions; *Best Of* ....(COL)
Who Are The Brain Police
Frank Zappa; *Disconnected Synapses* .... (RHI)
Mothers Of Invention; *Freak Out* .... (BAR)
Whodunit
Tavares; *Love Storm* ....(CAP)
Window Up Above
George Jones; *All-Time Greatest Hits-#1* .... (EPI)
Super Hits .... (EPI)
Hank Wilson; *Hank Wilson's Back-#1* .... (MCA)
Mickey Gilley; *Greatest Hits-#1* .... (EPI)
Ten Years Of Hits .... (EPI)
Ricky Skaggs; *Country Boy* .... (EPI)

POLITICAL CLASSICS

See Also: ECOLOGY, NUCLEAR ENERGY,
PEACE, POVERTY, PROTEST, WAR, WORLD

911 Is A Joke
Public Enemy; *Fear Of A Black Planet* .... (DFJ)
Yo! MTV Raps .... (JVA)

Abraham, Martin & John
Dion; *24 Original Classics* .... (ARI)
Collectables Presents History Of Rock-#3 ....(CLT)
WCBS FM-History Of Rock-'60s-#2 ....(CLT)
Harry Belafonte; *All Time Greatest Hits-#1* ....(RCA)
Smokey Robinson/Miracles; *Anthology* .... (MOT)
Time Out For/Special Occasion .... (MOT)
Alabama
Neil Young; *Harvest* .... (RPR)
ST/Journey Through The Past .... (RPR)
Alice's Restaurant Massacree
Arlo Guthrie; *Alice's Restaurant Massacree* .... (RPR)
Best Of ....(WB)
All Along The Watchtower
Bob Dylan; *At Budokan* ....(COL)
Before The Flood ....(COL)
Biograph ....(COL)
Greatest Hits-#2 ....(COL)
John Wesley Harding ....(COL)
Jimi Hendrix; *Electric Ladyland* .... (RPR)
Kiss The Sky .... (RPR)
Lifelines/Jimi Hendrix Story .... (RPR)
Jimi Hendrix Experience; *Essential-#1 & 2* .... (RPR)
Smash Hits .... (RPR)
U2; *ST/Rattle & Hum* .... (ISL)
Almost Cut My Hair
Crosby, Stills, Nash & Young; *Deja Vu* .... (ATL)
Amerikkka's Most Wanted
Ice Cube; *Amerikka's Most Wanted* .... (PRY)
Ball Of Confusion
Temptations; *All The Million-Sellers* .... (MOT)
Anthology .... (MOT)
Compact Command Performances .... (MOT)
Greatest Hits-#2 .... (MOT)
Top 10 With A Bullet-Motown Male Groups ... (MOT)
Big Yellow Taxi
Amy Grant; *House Of Love* .... (A&M)
Joni Mitchell; *Ladies Of The Canyon* .... (RPR)
Miles Of Aisles .... (ASY)
Blowin' In The Wind
Bob Dylan; *At Budokan* ....(COL)
Before The Flood ....(COL)
Biograph ....(COL)
Freewheelin' ....(COL)
Greatest Folksingers Of The '60s .... (VAN)
Greatest Hits ....(COL)
Joan Baez; *ST/Forrest Gump* .... (EPX)
Peter, Paul & Mary; *Holiday Celebration* .... (GC)
In Concert ....(WB)
In The Wind ....(WB)
Peter, Paul & Mary ....(WB)
Ten Years Together ....(WB)
Chimes Of Freedom
Bob Dylan; *Another Side Of* ....(COL)
Bruce Springsteen; *Chimes Of Freedom* ....(COL)
Byrds; *Byrds* ....(COL)
Greatest Hits ....(COL)
Come Together
Beatles; *1967-1970* .... (CAP)
20 Greatest Hits .... (CAP)
Abbey Road .... (CAP)
Ike & Tina Turner; *Proud Mary-Best Of* .... (EMI)
Workin' Together .... (EMI)
John Lennon; *Live In New York City* .... (CAP)
Country's In The Best Of Hands
Original Cast; *Li'l Abner* ....(COL)
Don't Worry About The Government
Talking Heads; *Name Of This Band Is* .... (SIR)
Popular Favorites-1984-1992 .... (SIR)
'77 .... (SIR)
Eve Of Destruction
Barry McGuire; *Billboard Top Rock 'N' Roll Hits-1965* .... (RHI)
Cruisin'-1965 .... (INC)
Good Feeling Music/Big Chill-#3 .... (MOT)
Vintage Music-#9 & 10 .... (MCA)
Dickies; *Great Dictations (Definitive Collection)* . (A&M)
Incredible Shrinking .... (A&M)
Turtles; *Turtle Wax-Best Of-#2* .... (RHI)
Turtlesized .... (RHI)

Fight The Power
Isley Brothers; *Forever Gold* .... (TN)
   Greatest Hits-#1 .... (TN)
   Heat Is On .... (TN)
   Story-#2 .... (RHI)
Public Enemy; *Def Jam Classics-#2* .... (DFJ)
   Fear Of A Black Planet .... (DFJ)
   ST/Do The Right Thing .... (MOT)
For What It's Worth
Buffalo Springfield; *Buffalo Springfield* ....(ATC)
   Double History ....(ATC)
   Hit Singles 1958-1977 .... (ATL)
   Retrospective ....(ATC)
   ST/Forrest Gump .... (EPX)
Free Nelson Mandela
Special AKA; *In The Studio* .... (CHR)
Freedom
Fleetwood Mac; *Behind The Mask* .... (WB)
George Michael; *Listen Without Prejudice* ....(COL)
Jefferson Airplane; *Jefferson Airplane* .... (EPI)
Jimi Hendrix; *Cry Of Love* .... (RPR)
   Essential-#1 & 2 .... (RPR)
Richie Havens; *ST/Woodstock* .... (ATL)
Wham!; *Make It Big* ....(COL)
Get Together
Youngbloods; *Best Of* .... (RCA)
   Billboard Top Rock 'N' Roll Hits-1969 .... (RHI)
   Nipper's Greatest Hits-'60s-#2 .... (RCA)
   ST/Forrest Gump .... (EPX)
   Summer Of Love .... (RHI)
Give Me Love (Give Me Peace On Earth)
George Harrison; *Best Of* .... (CAP)
   Living In The Material World ....(CAP)
Give More Power To The People
Chi-Lites; *Greatest Hits* .... (EPI)
Give Peace A Chance
John Lennon; *Collection* .... (GEF)
   Lennon ....(CAP)
   Live In New York City ....(CAP)
   Shaved Fish ....(CAP)
He Ain't Heavy He's My Brother
Hollies; *Best Of* .... (EMI)
   Best Of-#2 .... (EMI)
   Epic Anthology-Original Master Tapes .... (EPI)
   Greatest Hits .... (EPI)
Highwire
Rolling Stones; *Flashpoint* ....(COL)
   Flashpoint & Collectibles ....(COL)
I Feel Like I'm Fixing To Die Rag
Country Joe/Fish; *Greatest Hits* .... (VAN)
   Greatest '60s Folksingers .... (VAN)
   I Feel Like I'm Fixing To Die Rag .... (VAN)
   Life & Times Of .... (VAN)
   More American Graffiti-#4 .... (MCA)
   ST/Woodstock .... (ATL)
If I Had A Hammer
Pete Seeger; *Sing-A-Long-Live At Sanders Theatre*
1980 .... (FLW)
Peter, Paul & Mary; *In Concert* .... (WB)
   Peter, Paul & Mary .... (WB)
   Ten Years Together-Best Of .... (WB)
Trini Lopez; *Best Of* .... (EXA)
Weavers; *Greatest Hits* .... (VAN)
Imagine
Diana Ross; *Anthology* .... (MOT)
   Best Of The Beatles Songs .... (MOT)
   Touch Me In The Morning .... (MOT)
Joan Baez; *Best Of* .... (A&M)
   Come From The Shadows .... (A&M)
John Lennon; *Lennon* ....(CAP)
   Live In New York City ....(CAP)
   Shaved Fish ....(CAP)
John Lennon/Plastic Ono Band; *Collection* .... (GEF)
   Imagine ....(CAP)
   ST/Imagine-The Motion Picture ....(CAP)
In The Ghetto
Elvis Presley; *From Elvis In Memphis* .... (RCA)
   From Memphis To Vegas .... (RCA)
   Golden Records-#5 .... (RCA)
   In Person .... (RCA)
   Pure Gold .... (RCA)
   Top Ten Hits .... (RCA)
Mac Davis; *Greatest Hits* ....(COL)

I'd Love To Change The World
Ten Years After; *A Space In Time* .... (CHR)
   Classic Performances Of ....(COL)
   Universal .... (CHR)
Joe Hill
Arlo Guthrie & Pete Seeger; *Together In Concert* (RPR)
Joan Baez; *Carry It On* .... (VAN)
   From Every Stage .... (A&M)
   One Day At A Time .... (VAN)
   ST/Woodstock .... (ATL)
Soundtrack; *Carry It On* .... (VAN)
Joy To The World
Three Dog Night; *Best Of* .... (MCA)
   Good Feeling Music/Big Chill Gen.-#2 .... (MOT)
   Good Feeling Music/Big Chill Gen.-#3 .... (MOT)
   Joy To The World .... (MCA)
   ST/Big Chill .... (MOT)
   ST/Forrest Gump .... (EPX)
Juneteenth
Anthony Rivers/Others; *I've Known Rivers* ...... (GRM)
Living For The City
Stevie Wonder; *Innervisions* .... (MOT)
   Original Musiquarium .... (MOT)
M.T.A.
Kingston Trio; *25 Years Non-Stop* ....(XER)
   Best Of ....(CAP)
   Capitol Collectors Series ....(CAP)
   Scarlet Ribbons ....(CAP)
   Very Best Of ....(CAP)
Ohio
Crosby, Stills & Nash; *Crosby Stills & Nash*
(collection) .... (ATL)
Crosby, Stills, Nash & Young; *Four-Way Street* .. (ATL)
   So Far .... (ATL)
Neil Young; *Decade* .... (RPR)
   ST/Journey Through The Past .... (RPR)
One Tin Soldier
Coven; *Super Hits/'70s-Have A Nice Day-#7* ..... (RHI)
Peace Train
10,000 Maniacs; *In My Tribe* .... (ELE)
Cat Stevens; *Classics-#24* .... (A&M)
   Greatest Hits .... (A&M)
   Teaser & The Firecat .... (A&M)
People Got To Be Free
Rascals; *Anthology 1965-1972* .... (RHI)
   Hit Singles 1958-1977 .... (ATL)
Power To The People
John Lennon; *Lennon* .... (CAP)
   Shaved Fish ....(CAP)
Reach Out And Touch
Diana Ross; *All The Great Hits* .... (MOT)
   Anthology .... (MOT)
   Live At Caesar's Palace .... (MOT)
   Most Played Songs On America's Jukeboxes .... (MOT)
   Motown Story .... (MOT)
Save The People
Original Cast; *Godspell* .... (ARI)
Share The Land
Guess Who; *American Woman, These Eyes & Other*
Hits ....(RCA)
   Best Of ....(RCA)
   Track Record-Collection ....(RCA)
Society's Child
Janis Ian; *45* .... (POL)
Lou Gramm; *Past Times Behind Rock & Roll* ..... (INT)
Something In The Air
Thunderclap Newman; *History Of British*
Rock-#9 .... (MCA)
   Hollywood Dream .... (MCA)
   ST/Strawberry Statement .... (MCA)
Sounds Of Silence
Paul Simon; *Live Rhymin'* ....(COL)
Simon & Garfunkel; *Collected Works* ....(COL)
   Concert In Central Park .... (WB)
   Greatest Hits ....(COL)
   More American Graffiti-#4 .... (MCA)
   Sounds Of Silence ....(COL)
   ST/The Graduate ....(COL)
Stand
Sly/Family Stone; *10 Years Too Soon* .... (EPI)
   Anthology .... (EPI)
   Greatest Hits .... (EPI)
State Of The World
Janet Jackson; *Rhythm Nation 1814* .... (A&M)

Sun City
  Artists United Against Apartheid; *Sun City* ..... (MAN)
Teach Your Children
  Crosby, Stills & Nash; *Crosby, Stills & Nash*
  (collection) .... (ATL)
  Crosby, Stills, Nash & Young; *Deja Vu* .... (ATL)
  Four-Way Street .... (ATL)
  So Far .... (ATL)
  ST/Wonder Years-Music From Show & Era ..... (ATL)
  Suzy Bogguss/Alison Krauss/Kathy Mattea; w/*Crosby
  Stills & Nash-Red Hot + Country* .... (MER)
This Land Is Your Land
  Bruce Springsteen/E Street Band;
  Live-1975-1985 ....(COL)
  Glen Campbell; *All American* .... (LIB)
  Lee Greenwood; *American Patriot* .... (LIB)
  Pete Seeger; *Complete Carnegie Hall
  Concert-1963* ....(COL)
  Sings Woody Guthrie .... (FLW)
  Weavers; *Greatest Hits* .... (VAN)
  Woody Guthrie; *Greatest Songs Of* .... (VAN)
  Troubadours Of The Folk Era-#1 ..... (RHI)
  Woody Guthrie .... (VAN)
Times They Are A-Changin'
  Billy Joel; *KOHUEPT* ....(COL)
  Bob Dylan; *At Budokan* .... (COL)
  Biograph ....(COL)
  Bootleg Series-#1-3-1961-1989 ....(COL)
  Greatest Hits ....(COL)
  Times They Are A-Changin' ....(COL)
  Byrds; *Byrds (collection)* ....(COL)
  Turn! Turn! Turn! ....(COL)
  Peter, Paul & Mary; *In Concert* .... (WB)
  Simon & Garfunkel; *Collected Works* ....(COL)
  Wednesday Morning 3 A.M. ....(COL)
Turn! Turn! Turn!
  Byrds; *Billboard Top Rock 'N' Roll Hits-1965* .... (RHI)
  Greatest Hits ....(COL)
  Original Singles-#1-1965-1967 ....(COL)
  Byrds (collection) ....(COL)
  ST/Forrest Gump .... (EPX)
  Turn! Turn! Turn! ....(COL)
  Pete Seeger; *Greatest Hits* ....(COL)
  Troubadours Of The Folk Era-#2 .... (RHI)
United We Stand
  Brotherhood Of Man; *Super Hits/'70s-Have A Nice
  Day-#2* .... (RHI)
  Mike Curb Congregation; *Greatest Hits* ....(CCB)
Universal Soldier
  Buffy Sainte-Marie; *Best Of* .... (VAN)
  Festival Of Acoustic Music-#1 .... (FAN)
  Troubadours Of The Folk Era-#1 .... (RHI)
  Donovan; *Catch The Wind* .... (GRL)
  History Of British Rock-#4 .... (RHI)
  Secret Policeman's Other Ball .... (ISL)
Voices That Care
  Voices That Care; *Voices That Care* .... (GIA)
Volunteers
  Jefferson Airplane; *2400 Fulton Street-Anthology* (RCA)
  Flight Log 1966-1976 .... (GRU)
  ST/Forrest Gump ....(EPX)
  ST/Woodstock ....(ATL)
  Volunteers ....(RCA)
  Worst Of ....(RCA)
  "White Rabbit" & Other Hits ....(RCA)
War
  Bruce Springsteen/E Street Band;
  Live-1975-1985 ....(COL)
  Edwin Starr; *Billboard Top Rock 'N' Roll
  Hits-1970* .... (RHI)
  Motown Superstar Series-#3 .... (MOT)
  Soul Hits/'70s-#3 .... (RHI)
  War & Peace .... (MOT)
We Are The World
  USA For Africa; *We Are The World* ....(COL)
We Didn't Start The Fire
  Billy Joel; *Storm Front* ....(COL)
We Shall Overcome
  James Cleveland/Troubadors; *James
  Cleveland/Troubadors* .... (SAV)
  Joan Baez; *Carry It On* .... (VAN)
  In Concert .... (VAN)
  Pete Seeger; *Bitter & The Sweet* .... (MOB)
  Greatest Hits ....(COL)

What The World Needs Now Is Love
  Burt Bacharach; *Greatest Hits* .... (A&M)
  Jackie DeShannon; *Flower Power* .... (KT)
  Good Vibrations ....(CAP)
  Oldies But Goodies-#14 .... (OSR)
  ST/Forrest Gump .... (EPX)
  Very Best Of .... (EMI)
  Luther Vandross; *Songs* .... (EPI)
  Tom Clay; *20 Hard-To-Find Motown
  Classics-#2* .... (MOT)
What's Goin' On
  Cyndi Lauper; *True Colors* .... (POR)
  Marvin Gaye; *20/20* .... (MOT)
  Anthology .... (MOT)
  Greatest Hits .... (MOT)
  Live At The London Palladium .... (MOT)
  More Songs From "Big Chill" Soundtrack ..... (MOT)
  What's Goin' On .... (MOT)
  Quincy Jones; *Best Of* .... (A&M)
Where Have All The Flowers Gone
  Johnny Rivers; *Anthology-1964-1977* .... (RHI)
  Best Of .... (EMI)
  Kingston Trio; *Capitol Collectors Series* .... (CAP)
  Pete Seeger; *Essential* .... (VAN)
  Greatest Hits ....(COL)
  Peter, Paul & Mary; *Peter, Paul & Mary* .... (WB)
  Wes Montgomery; *Classics-#22* .... (A&M)
Woman Is The Nigger Of The World
  John Lennon; *Shaved Fish* .... (CAP)
  Somewhere In New York City .... (CAP)
  John Lennon/Plastic Ono Band; *Lennon* .... (CAP)
Won't Get Fooled Again
  Van Halen; *Live: Right Here Right Now* ....(WB)
  Who; *Greatest Hits* .... (MCA)
  ST/Kids Are Alright .... (MCA)
  Who's Better Who's Best-Very Best Of .... (MCA)
  Who's Last .... (MCA)
  Who's Next .... (MCA)
Woodstock
  Crosby, Stills & Nash; *Crosby, Stills & Nash
  (collection)* .... (ATL)
  Crosby, Stills, Nash & Young; *Deja Vu* .... (ATL)
  So Far .... (ATL)
  Joni Mitchell; *Ladies Of The Canyon* .... (RPR)
  Miles Of Aisles .... (ASY)
  Shadows & Light .... (ASY)
World Is A Ghetto
  George Benson; *In Flight* ....(WB)
  War; *Greatest Hits* .... (MCA)
  Music Band .... (MCA)
  Music Band 2 .... (MCA)
  World Is A Ghetto .... (AVE)
You Don't Have To Be In The Army To...
  Mungo Jerry; *In The Summertime-Best Of* .... (RHI)

∞∞∞∞∞∞∞∞∞∞∞∞∞∞∞∞∞∞∞∞∞∞∞∞∞∞∞∞∞∞∞∞∞∞∞

POVERTY, Broke, Ghetto, Hard Times, Outcast, Poor

  *See Also: GAMBLING, LUCK, MONEY,
  ROYALTY, TRAINS*

∞∞∞∞∞∞∞∞∞∞∞∞∞∞∞∞∞∞∞∞∞∞∞∞∞∞∞∞∞∞∞∞∞∞∞

Ain't Got No Money
  Bob Seger/Silver Bullet Band; *Stranger In Town* . (CAP)
Angel From Montgomery
  Bonnie Raitt; *Streetlights* ....(WB)
  Bonnie Raitt & John Prine; *Bonnie Raitt Collection* (WB)
  John Prine; *John Prine* .... (ATL)
Another Day In Paradise
  Phil Collins; *Serious Hits...Live!* .... (ATL)
  ...But Seriously .... (ATL)
Bag Lady
  Todd Rundgren; *Hermit Of Mink Hollow* .... (RHI)
Bangladesh
  George Harrison; *Best Of* ....(CAP)
  Concert For Bangla Desh ....(CAP)
Banquet
  Joni Mitchell; *For The Roses* .... (ASY)
Beggar In Blue Jeans
  Rowans; *Rowans* .... (ASY)
Beggar's Day
  Nazareth; *Hair Of The Dog* .... (A&M)
  'Snaz .... (A&M)
  Nils Lofgren; *Classics-#13* .... (A&M)

Nils Lofgren/Grin; *Best Of Nils Lofgren* .... (A&M)
  Gone Crazy .... (A&M)
Skid Row; *Slave To The Grind* .... (ATL)
Beggar's Game
Dan Fogelberg; *Phoenix* .... (FM)
Bohemian Rhapsody
Queen; *Classic* ....(HOL)
  Live At Wembley '86 ....(HOL)
  Night At The Opera ....(HOL)
  ST/Wayne's World ....(RPR)
Both Sides Of The Story
Phil Collins; *Both Sides* .... (ATL)
Breadline Blues
New Lost City Ramblers; *Depression Songs* ..... (FLW)
Broke Again
Little River Band; *Diamantina Cocktail* .... (HAR)
Brother, Can You Spare A Dime
Bing Crosby; *16 Most Requested Songs* ....(COL)
Odetta/Dr. John/John Campbell/Rufus Reid; *Strike A Deep Chord-Blues For Homeless* .... (JST)
Peter, Paul & Mary; *See What Tomorrow Brings* ..(WB)
Weavers; *Greatest Hits* .... (VAN)
Cadillac Style
Sammy Kershaw; *Don't Go Near The Water* .... (MER)
Cafe On The Corner
Sawyer Brown; *Cafe On The Corner* ....(CRB)
Calling Mr. Welfare
Big Daddy Kane; *It's A Big Daddy Thing* ....(CLD)
Can't Afford No Shoes
Frank Zappa; *One Size Fits All* .... (DSC)
Child Of Poverty
Paul Martin; *Country Gold* .... (PLN)
  Great Country Gold .... (PLN)
Children Of The Ghetto
Courtney Pine; *Journey To The Urge Within* .... (AND)
Philip Bailey; *Chinese Wall* ....(COL)
Children Of The Night
Richard Marx; *Repeat Offender* .... (EMI)
Date With Poverty
Metal Church; *Human Factor* .... (EPI)
Dead End Street
Lou Rawls; *Best From* ....(CAP)
  Live .... (PI)
Do You Want My Job
Little Village; *Little Village* .... (RPR)
Double Trouble
Eric Clapton; *Crossroads* .... (POL)
  Just One Night ....(RSO)
  No Reason To Cry .... (RSO)
Down In The Boondocks
Billy Joe Royal; *Greatest Hits* ....(COL)
  Rock Classics/'60s ....(COL)
Drifter
Deep Purple; *Come Taste The Band* .... (MET)
Iron Maiden; *Killers* ....(CAP)
John Lee Hooker/Canned Heat; *Infinite Boogie* .. (RHI)
Neil Diamond; *On The Way To The Sky* ....(COL)
Neil Young; *Landing On Water* .... (GEF)
Sylvia; *Drifter* ....(RCA)
  Greatest Hits ....(RCA)
Textones; *Through The Canyon* .... (RHI)
Drifter's Escape
Bob Dylan; *John Wesley Harding* ....(COL)
Jimi Hendrix; *Lifelines/Story* ....(RPR)
Drifting Blues
Albert King; *Thursday Night In San Francisco* ... (STX)
Charles Brown; *Blues Masters-#3-Texas Blues* ... (RHI)
John Hammond; *Solo* .... (VAN)
Pete Townshend; *Another Scoop* ....(ATC)
Electric Avenue
Eddy Grant; *Killer On The Rampage* .... (POR)
Fallen On Hard Times
Jethro Tull; *20 Years Of-Boxed Set* .... (CHR)
  Broadsword & The Beast .... (CHR)
Fancy
Bobbi Gentry; *All-Time Country Classics-#1* .....(CAP)
Reba McEntire; *Rumor Has It* .... (MCA)
Follow The Drinking Gourd
Richie Havens; *Songs Of The Civil War* ....(COL)
Weavers; *Greatest Hits* .... (VAN)
Getto Jam
Domino; *Domino* .... (OUT)

Ghetto
Donny Hathaway; *Atlantic R&B 1947-1974-#7-(1969-1974)* .... (ATL)
  Best Of ....(ATC)
  Everything Is Everything .... (ATC)
  Live ....(ATC)
Joan Baez; *First 10 Years* .... (VAN)
  One Day At A Time .... (VAN)
Too Short; *Short Dog's In The House* .... (JVA)
Ghetto Child
Spinners; *Best Of* .... (ATL)
Ghetto Heaven
Family Stand; *Chain* .... (ATL)
Gonna Make It Somehow
Albert King; *Truckload Of Lovin'* .... (TOM)
Grapes Of Wrath
Charlie Daniels Band; *Midnight Wind* .... (EPI)
Gypsy Woman
Brian Hyland; *Greatest Hits* .... (RHI)
  Super Hits/'70s-Have A Nice Day-#3 .... (RHI)
Impressions; *Billboard Top R&B Hits-1961* ...... (RHI)
  Greatest Hits ....(MCA)
  Oldies But Goodies-#12 ....(OSR)
  Vintage/Classic Oldies From '50s-'60s-#6 ..... (MCA)
Muddy Waters; *Chess Box* ....(CSS)
  Real Folk Blues ....(CSS)
Ry Cooder; *Slide Area* ....(WB)
Gypsy Woman (She's Homeless)
Crystal Waters; *Red Hot + Dance* ....(COL)
  Surprise .... (MER)
Hallelujah, I'm A Bum
Al Jolson; *Mammy* ....(POE)
Bobby Short; *Celebrates Rodgers & Hart* .... (ATL)
Hard Candy Christmas
Dolly Parton; *Best Of Christmas* ....(RCA)
  Country Christmas-#2 ....(RCA)
  Greatest Hits ....(RCA)
  Season's Greetings ....(RCA)
  ST/Best Little Whorehouse In Texas ....(MCA)
Original Cast; *Best Little Whorehouse In Texas* .. (MCA)
Hard Times
Boz Scaggs; *Down Two Then Left* ....(COL)
  Hits! ....(COL)
Crusaders; *Best Of* .... (MCA)
  Scratch .... (MCA)
Desert Rose Band; *Desert Rose Band* .... (MCA)
Emmylou Harris/Nash Ramblers; *At The Ryman* . (RPR)
Eric Clapton; *24 Nights* .... (RPR)
  Journeyman .... (RPR)
Houston Person; *Goodness* ....(PRS)
James Taylor; *Dad Loves His Work* ....(COL)
Lacy J. Dalton; *Greatest Hits* ....(COL)
Ray Charles; *Best Of* .... (ATL)
Red Clay Ramblers; *Hard Times* ....(FF)
Run-D.M.C.; *Run-D.M.C.* ....(PRO)
Skip James; *Great Bluesmen At Newport* .... (VAN)
Hard Times Come Again No More
Jennifer Warnes; *Shot Through The Heart* .... (ARI)
Mustard's Retreat; *Home By The Morning* .... (RDH)
High Hopes And Empty Pockets
Terry McBride/Ride; *Terry McBride & The Ride* (MCA)
Home Sweet Home
Lawrence Welk; *200 Years Of American Music* . (RAN)
Motley Crue; *Theatre Of Pain* .... (ELE)
Peter Gabriel; *Peter Gabriel* .... (ATL)
How Can A Poor Man Stand Such Times...
Blind Alfred Reed; *How Can A Poor Man Stand Such Times...* .... (ROU)
Ry Cooder; *Ry Cooder* .... (RPR)
  Show Time ....(WB)
I Am A Rock
Simon & Garfunkel; *Collected Works* ....(COL)
  Greatest Hits ....(COL)
  Sounds Of Silence ....(COL)
I Got Plenty O'Nuttin'
Barbra Streisand; *My Name Is Barbra-Two* ......(COL)
Cleo Laine & Ray Charles; *Porgy & Bess* .... (RCA)
Ella Fitzgerald & Louis Armstrong; *Porgy & Bess* (VRV)
Original Cast; *Porgy & Bess* .... (MCA)
If I Didn't Have You
Randy Travis; *Greatest Hits-#1* .... (WB)
If I Had No Loot
Tony! Toni! Tone!; *Sons Of Soul* .... (WIN)

If I Were A Rich Man
Original Cast; *Fiddler On The Roof* ....(RCA)
Original London Cast; *Fiddler On The Roof* .....(COL)
If The Devil Danced (In Empty Pockets)
Joe Diffie; *A Thousand Winding Roads* ....(EPI)
In The Ghetto
Elvis Presley; *From Elvis In Memphis* ....(RCA)
  From Memphis To Vegas ....(RCA)
  Golden Records-#5 ....(RCA)
  In Person ....(RCA)
  Pure Gold ....(RCA)
  Top Ten Hits ....(RCA)
Mac Davis; *Greatest Hits* ....(COL)
I.O.U.
Lee Greenwood; *Greatest Hits* .... (MCA)
  MCA Records 30 Years Of Hits-1958-1988 ... (MCA)
  Somebody's Gonna Love You .... (MCA)
Johnny 99
Bruce Springsteen; *Nebraska* ....(COL)
Bruce Springsteen/E Street Band;
  Live-1975-1985 ....(COL)
Johnny Cash; *Cover Me* .... (RHI)
King Of The Road
Roger Miller; *Billboard Top Country Hits-1965* .. (RHI)
  Cruisin'-1965 ....(INC)
  Golden Hits ....(SMA)
R.E.M.; *Dead Letter Office* ....(IRS)
Life Ain't Easy
Dr. Hook/Medicine Show; *45* ....(COL)
Life So Cruel
Charlie; *Lines* ....(JNS)
Little Beggar Man
Ian & Sylvia; *Greatest Hits* .... (VAN)
  Northern Journey .... (VAN)
Living In The Ghetto
Toots/Maytals; *Reggae Got Soul* .... (ISL)
Livin' In These Troubled Times
Crystal Gayle; *Greatest Hits* ....(COL)
  Hollywood/Tennessee ....(COL)
Loan Me A Dime
Boz Scaggs; *Boz Scaggs* ....(ATC)
  Duane Allman Anthology ....(CPC)
Long Hard Road (Sharecropper's Dream)
Nitty Gritty Dirt Band; *Live Two Five* ....(CAP)
  Plain Dirt Fashion .... (WB)
  Twenty Years Of Dirt-Best Of .... (WB)
Lookin' At Tomorrow
Beach Boys; *Surf's Up* ....(CAR)
Lookin' In The Same Direction
Ken Mellons; *Ken Mellons* .... (EPI)
Love Child
Diana Ross/Supremes; *Anthology* .... (MOT)
  Billboard Top Rock 'N' Roll Hits-1968 .... (RHI)
  Every Great #1 Hit .... (MOT)
  Greatest Hits-#3 .... (MOT)
  Motown Story-1st 25 Years .... (MOT)
  Motown's Biggest Pop Hits .... (MOT)
Sweet Sensation; *Love Child* ....(ATC)
Mama's Hungry Eyes
Emmylou Harris; *Mama's Hungry Eyes-Merle Haggard*
  Tribute .... (ARI)
Mansion In The Slums
Crowded House; *Temple Of Low Men* ....(CAP)
Mr. Bojangles
David Bromberg; *Out Of The Blues-Best Of* ......(COL)
Jerry Jeff Walker; *Best Of* ....(MCA)
  Gypsy Songman ....(RYK)
  Man Must Carry On ....(MCA)
  Mr. Bojangles ....(BAI)
Nitty Gritty Dirt Band; *Best Of* ....(EMI)
  On The Road Again ....(CAP)
  Super Hits/'70s-Have A Nice Day-#4 ....(RHI)
  Twenty Years Of Dirt-Best Of ....(WB)
Nigga Out The Projects
1-5ive Posse; *Lifestyles Of The Young & Crazy* .. (WEX)
No Job Blues
Ramblin' Thomas; *Ramblin' Mind Blues* ....(BIO)
Nobody Knows You When You're Down & Out
Bessie Smith; *Collection* ....(COL)
  Complete Recordings-#4 ....(COL)
Derek/Dominos; *Layla* ....(POL)
Eric Clapton; *Unplugged* ....(DUC)
Otis Redding; *Soul Album* ....(ATC)
Rod Stewart; *Out Of Order* .... (WB)

Once Upon A Time In The Projects
Ice Cube; *Amerikka's Most Wanted* .... (PRY)
One Room Country Shack
Buddy Guy; *Man & The Blues* .... (VAN)
  My Time After Awhile .... (VAN)
Mercy Dee Walton; *Mercy's Troubles* .... (ARH)
  One Room Country Shack .... (SPE)
  Pity & A Shame .... (PRS)
Mose Allison; *Greatest Hits* .... (PRS)
Papa Was A Rollin' Stone
Temptations; *20-20* .... (MOT)
  25 #1 Hits From 25 Years .... (MOT)
  All The Million-Sellers .... (MOT)
  Anthology .... (MOT)
  Billboard Top Rock 'N' Roll Hits-1972 .... (RHI)
  Compact Command Performances .... (MOT)
Pits
Sammy Hagar; *Sammy Hagar* ....(CAP)
Poor Boy
Champion Jack Dupree; *Forever & Ever* .... (BUL)
Elvis Presley; *Essential Elvis-First Movies* ....(RCA)
  For LP Fans Only ....(RCA)
Fabulous Thunderbirds; *T-Bird Rhythm* .... (CHR)
Howlin' Wolf; *Real Folk Blues* .... (CSS)
Nick Drake; *Bryter Layter* .... (HBL)
  Fruit Tree .... (HBL)
Split Enz; *History Never Repeats-Best Of* .... (A&M)
  True Colours .... (A&M)
Supertramp; *Crisis? What Crisis?* .... (A&M)
Woody Guthrie; *Legendary* ....(TRD)
  Woody Guthrie ....(EVR)
  Worried Man Blues-Golden Classics-#1 .... (CLT)
Poor Boy Shuffle
Creedence Clearwater Revival; *1969* ....(FAN)
  Willy & The Poor Boys ....(FAN)
Poor Howard
Leadbelly; *Gwine Dig A Hole To Put The Devil In* (ROU)
  Leadbelly .... (EVR)
  Leadbelly .... (FAN)
  Memorial-#4 ....(STO)
Poor Immigrant
Judy Collins; *Who Knows Where The Time Goes* . (ELE)
Poor Jenny
Everly Brothers; *All They Had To Do Was Dream* (RHI)
  Everly Brothers .... (RHI)
  Fabulous Style Of .... (RHI)
Poor Little Fool
Rick Nelson; *Best Of* .... (EMI)
  EMI Legends Of Rock 'N' Roll-24 Greatest ...... (EMI)
  Legendary Masters .... (EMI)
  Live In '85 .... (RHI)
Poor Little Jimmie
Burl Ives; *Best Of-#2* .... (MCA)
Poor Little Rich Girl
Judy Garland; *Best Of* .... (MCA)
Romantics; *National Breakout* .... (NEM)
Tony Bennett & Count Basie; *Basie Swings Bennett*
  Sings .... (RLL)
Uriah Heep; *Equator* ....(COL)
Poor Man
Tom Rush; *Tom Rush* .... (ELE)
Poor Man Lives Longer Than The Rich
Freeman King; *45* ....(KNT)
Poor Man's Roses (Or A Rich Man's Gold)
Patsy Cline; *Best Of* ....(CCB)
  Forever & Always .... (EPI)
  Stop, Look & Listen .... (MCA)
  Story .... (MCA)
Reba McEntire; *Feel The Fire* .... (MER)
Poor Man's Son
Rockin' Berries; *History Of British Rock-#2* ...... (RHI)
Poor People
Alan Price; *ST/O Lucky Man* .... (WB)
Poor People Of Paris
Les Baxter; *Memories Are Made Of This* ....(CAP)
Poor Red Georgia Dirt
Robin & Linda Williams; *Close As We Can Get* ....(FF)
Poor Side Of Town
Johnny Rivers; *Anthology-1964-1977* .... (RHI)
  Best Of .... (EMI)
  Changes/Rewind .... (EMI)
  Very Best Of .... (EMI)

Poor Wayfaring Stranger
Jim Hendricks; *Appalachian Memories-Front Porch
Favor.* .... (BEN)
Jo Stafford; *American Folk Songs* .... (CRN)
Poverty
Bobby Bland; *Best Of* .... (MCA)
Poverty Train
Laura Nyro; *Eli & The 13th Confession* ....(COL)
Po' White Trash
White Trash; *White Trash* .... (ELE)
Rag Doll
Aerosmith; *Permanent Vacation* .... (GEF)
Frankie Valli/Four Seasons; *25th Anniversary
Collection* .... (RHI)
   Anthology .... (RHI)
   Billboard Top Rock 'N' Roll Hits-1964 .... (RHI)
   Greatest Hits-#2 .... (RHI)
Rags To Riches
Electric Boys; *Funk-O-Metal Carpet Ride* ....(ATC)
John Scofield; *Shinola* ....(ENJ)
Kool/Gang; *Everything Is-Greatest Hits* ....(MER)
Tony Bennett; *16 Most Requested Songs* ....(COL)
   All-Time Greatest Hits ....(COL)
Tony Bennett & Percy Faith/Orchestra; *Radio Classics
Of The '50s* ....(COL)
Ramblin' Hobo
Doc Watson; *Essential* .... (VAN)
   Old Time Music At Newport .... (VAN)
   & Family/Treasures Untold .... (VAN)
Watson Family; *Watson Family* .... (FLW)
Ramshackle Shack
Doc Watson; *Riding The Midnight Train* ....(SH)
Refugee
Tom Petty/Heartbreakers; *Damn The Torpedoes* (MCA)
   Pack Up The Plantation-Live .... (MCA)
U2; *War* .... (ISL)
Rich Kind Of Poverty
Sam & Dave; *Soul Men* .... (RHI)
Rich Man Poor Man
Peter, Paul & Mary; *Late Again* .... (WB)
Rich Man, Poor Boy
Joe Ely; *Dig All Night* .... (HT)
Rich & Poor
Randy Crawford; *Rich & Poor* .... (WB)
Royal Scam
Steely Dan; *Royal Scam* .... (MCA)
Sail Away
Linda Ronstadt; *Don't Cry Now* .... (ASY)
Randy Newman; *Sail Away* .... (RPR)
Second Hand Rose
Barbra Streisand; *Greatest Hits* ....(COL)
   Happening In Central Park ....(COL)
   Just For The Record ....(COL)
   My Name Is Barbra Two ....(COL)
   & Other Musical Instruments ....(COL)
She's Just A Drifter
Marty Robbins; *Biggest Hits* ....(COL)
   El Paso City ....(COL)
Sixteen Tons
Cactus Brothers; *Cactus Brothers* .... (LIB)
Stevie Wonder; *Down To Earth* .... (MOT)
Tennessee Ernie Ford; *16 Tons Of Boogie-Best Of* (RHI)
   Capitol Collectors Series .... (CAP)
   When AM Was King .... (CAP)
Weavers; *Greatest Hits* .... (VAN)
Skid Row
Herman Brood/Wild Romance; *Herman Brood/Wild
Romance* ....(ARL)
Original Cast; *Little Shop Of Corrors* .... (GEF)
Skid Row Joe
Porter Wagoner; *Best Of-#1* ....(RCA)
   Greatest .... (TUD)
Son Of A Poor Man
R.E.O. Speedwagon; *Decade Of Rock &
Roll-1970-1980* .... (EPI)
   Live-You Get What You Play For .... (EPI)
   Ridin' The Storm Out .... (EPI)
Spanish Harlem
Aretha Franklin; *30 Greatest Hits* .... (ATL)
   Best Of .... (ATL)
   Ten Years Of Gold .... (ATL)
Ben E. King; *Back To Mono-1958-1969* .... (AKO)
   Greatest Hits .... (ATC)
Crusaders; *At Their Best* .... (MOT)

Drifters; *Greatest Hits* .... (GUS)
Standing On The Corner
Broadway Cast; *Most Happy Fella* ....(RCA)
Four Lads; *16 Most Requested Songs* ....(COL)
Original Broadway Cast; *Most Happy Fella* ..... (SMC)
Stray Cat Strut
Stray Cats; *Best Of-Rock This Town* .... (EMI)
   Built For Speed .... (EMI)
   Rock The First-#4 ....(SAN)
Street Man Named Desire
Pirates Of The Mississippi; *Street Man Named
Desire* .... (LIB)
Struggling Man
Jimmy Cliff; *In Concert-Best Of* .... (RPR)
   Struggling Man .... (ISL)
Third World Child
Johnny Clegg & Savuka; *Sounds Of Soweto* .....(CAP)
   Third World Child ....(CAP)
To Hell With Poverty!
Gang Of Four; *Brief History Of The Twentieth
Century* .... (WB)
Too Broke To Spend The Night
Buddy Guy; *Damn Right I've Got The Blues* .... (SIL)
Too Much Month At The End Of The Money
Billy Hill; *I Am Just A Rebel* .... (RPR)
Town Without Pity
Gene Pitney; *Anthology* .... (RHI)
   ST/Hairspray ....(MSP)
   WCBS FM101-History Of Rock-'60s-#3 ....(CLT)
Tramp
Cisco Houston; *Don't Mourn-Organize-Songs Of Joe
Hill* .... (FLW)
Lowell Fulson; *Soul Shots-#7-Urban Blues* .... (RHI)
Otis Redding; *Bet Of* ....(ATC)
   Story ....(ATL)
Salt-N-Pepa; *Blitz Of Salt-N-Pepa Hits* ....(LON)
   Hot Cool & Vicious ....(LON)
Twentieth Century Drifter
Marty Robbins; *Best Of* ....(CCB)
Two Sparrows In A Hurricane
Tanya Tucker; *Can't Run From Yourself* ....(LIB)
   Greatest Hits-1990-1992 .... (LIB)
UFO Has Landed In The Ghetto
Ry Cooder; *The Slide Area* .... (WB)
Used Cars
Bruce Springsteen; *Nebraska* ....(COL)
Vagabond Virgin
Traffic; *Traffic* .... (ISL)
Victim Of The Ghetto
College Boyz; *Radio Fusion Radio* .... (VIA)
Village Ghetto Land
Stevie Wonder; *Songs In The Key Of Live* .... (MOT)
Waitin' In Your Welfare Line
Buck Owens/Buckaroos; *Billboard Top Country
Hits-1966* .... (RHI)
   Buck Owens Collection-1959-1990 .... (RHI)
   Live At Carnegie Hall ....(CMF)
Wanderer
Dion; *20 Million-Dollar Memories-#1* ....(LAU)
   Billboard Top Rock 'N' Roll Hits-1962 .... (RHI)
   Cruisin'-1962 .... (INC)
   Oldies But Goodies-#5 ....(OSR)
   ST/Wanderers .... (WB)
   Wanderer ....(LAU)
Donna Summer; *Wanderer* ....(GEF)
Wandering
James Taylor; *Gorilla* .... (WB)
Welfare Cadillac
Gary B.B. Coleman; *Too Much Weekend* .... (ICH)
Working Man Can't Get Nowhere Today
Merle Haggard; *18 Rare Classics* ....(CCB)
Merle Haggard/Strangers; *Working Man Can't Get
Nowhere Today* ....(CAP)
World Is A Ghetto
George Benson; *In Flight* .... (WB)
War; *Greatest Hits* ....(MCA)
   Music Band ....(MCA)
   Music Band 2 ....(MCA)
   World Is A Ghetto ....(AVE)

PREJUDICE

See Also: POLITICAL CLASSICS

Apartheid
C. Chris & Rich E. Rich/Rudy Pardee; *12"* ..... (MCA)
K-9 Posse; *On A Different Tip* .... (ARI)
Peter Tosh; *Equal Rights* ....(COL)
Aryanisms
Napalm Death; *Utopia Banished* ....(EAC)
Black Man Can't Get A Cab
U.T.F.O.; *Bag It & Bone It* .... (JVA)
Black Or White
Michael Jackson; *Dangerous* .... (EPI)
Black & White
INXS; *Dekadance* ....(ATC)
Shabooh Shoobah ....(ATC)
Jackson Browne; *Lives In The Balance* ....(ASY)
Rosanne Cash; *Hits 1979-1989* ....(COL)
Three Dog Night; *Best Of* ....(MCA)
Billboard Top Rock 'N' Roll Hits-1972 .... (RHI)
Joy To The World-Greatest Hits ....(MCA)
Todd Rundgren; *Anthology 1968-1985* ....(RHI)
Back To The Bars ....(RHI)
Faithful ....(RHI)
Blacks Are Giving Me The Blues
Martin Mull; *No Hits Four Errors* ....(CPC)
Normal ....(CPC)
Boom Bye Bye
Buju Banton; *Voice Of Jamaica* .... (MER)
Brother Louie
Stories; *Billboard Top Rock 'N' Roll Hits-1973* ... (RHI)
Company Time
Linda Davis; *Shoot For The Moon* ....(ARI)
Cop Killer
Ice-T; *Body Count* .... (WB)
Die Nigger Die
Schoolly D; *How A Black Man Feels* ....(CAP)
Don't Call Me Nigger, Whitey
Sly/Family Stone; *Anthology* .... (EPI)
Stand! .... (EPI)
Drug Store Truck Drivin' Man
Byrds; *Best Of-Greatest Hits-#2* ....(COL)
Byrds ....(COL)
Dr. Byrds & Mr. Hyde ....(COL)
Gram Parsons/Fallen Angels; *Live 1973* ....(SIE)
Joan Baez & Jeffrey Shurtleff; *ST/Woodstock* ....(ATL)
Ebony & Ivory
Paul McCartney; *Tripping The Live Fantastic* ....(CAP)
Paul McCartney & Stevie Wonder; *All The Best* .(CAP)
Tug Of War ....(CAP)
Equal Rights
Peter Tosh; *Equal Rights* ....(COL)
Every Kinda People
Robert Palmer; *Addictions-#1* .... (ISL)
Double Fun .... (ISL)
Maybe It's Live .... (ISL)
Fear Of A Black Planet
Public Enemy; *Fear Of A Black Planet* ....(DFC)
Fight Apartheid
Peter Tosh; *No Nuclear War* .... (EMI)
Fight The Power
Isley Brothers; *Forever Gold* .... (TN)
Greatest Hits-#1 .... (TN)
Heat Is On .... (TN)
Story-#2 .... (RHI)
Public Enemy; *Def Jam Classics-#2* ....(DFJ)
Fear Of A Black Planet ....(DFJ)
ST/Do The Right Thing ....(MOT)
Follow The Drinking Gourd
Richie Havens; *Songs Of The Civil War* ....(COL)
Weavers; *Greatest Hits* ....(VAN)
Free Your Mind
En Vogue; *Funky Divas* ....(EW)
He Thinks He'll Keep Her
Mary Chapin Carpenter; *Come On Come On* ....(COL)
Here's To The State Of Mississippi
Phil Ochs; *I Ain't Marching Anymore* ....(CTH)
There But For Fortune ....(ELE)

Hey Porter
Johnny Cash; *First Years* ....(ALL)
Greatest Hits-#2 ....(COL)
Legend ....(SUN)
Original Golden Hits-#1 ....(SUN)
Sun Years .... (RHI)
Vintage Years-1955-1963 .... (RHI)
Hurricane (Carter)
Bob Dylan; *Desire* ....(COL)
I'm Proud To Be A Redneck
Barefoot Jerry; *Barefoot Jerry's Grocery* .... (MON)
John Brown's Body
Pete Seeger; *American Favorite Ballads-#3* ...... (FLW)
Ku Klux Klan
Steel Pulse; *ST/Urgh! A Music War* .... (A&M)
Lady Is A Tramp
Ella Fitzgerald; *Rodgers & Hart Songbook* ....(VRV)
Frank Sinatra; *Capitol Years* ....(CAP)
Sinatra Reprise-Very Good Years ....(RPR)
Frank Sinatra & Luther Vandross; *Frank Sinatra Duets* ....(CAP)
Living For The City
Stevie Wonder; *Innervisions* ....(MOT)
Original Musiquarium ....(MOT)
Longhaired Redneck
David Allan Coe; *17 Greatest Hits* ....(COL)
For The Record-First 10 Years ....(COL)
Longhaired Redneck ....(COL)
Miami Beach
Garland Jeffreys; *Escape Artist* .... (EPI)
My Hometown
Bruce Springsteen; *Born In The U.S.A.* ....(COL)
Nigga Ya Love To Hate
Ice Cube; *Amerikkka's Most Wanted* ....(PRY)
Niggas Come In All Colors
L.A. Posse; *They Come In All Colors* ....(ATL)
Niggaz 4 Life
N.W.A.; *Efil4zaggin* ....(RUT)
Nigger Whitie
Sly Dunbar; *Sly Wicked & Slick* ....(FL)
Political Science
Randy Newman; *Sail Away* ....(RPR)
Power In The Darkness
Tom Robinson Band; *Power In The Darkness* ... (HAR)
Proud To Be Black
Run-D.M.C.; *Raising Hell* ....(PRO)
Young Black Teenagers; *Young Black Teenagers* . (SOL)
Racist
Boogie Down Productions; *Edutainment* .... (JVA)
Racist Friend
Special AKA; *In The Studio* ....(CHR)
Rednecks
Randy Newman; *Good Old Boys* ....(RPR)
Royal Scam
Steely Dan; *Royal Scam* ....(MCA)
Sail Away
Linda Ronstadt; *Don't Cry Now* ....(ASY)
Randy Newman; *Sail Away* ....(RPR)
Second Class Wait Here
Slim Dusty; *Australia Is His Name* ....(PHO)
Short People
Randy Newman; *Dr. Demento-Greatest Novelty Records-#4* ....(RHI)
Little Criminals .... (WB)
Society's Child
Janis Ian; *45* ....(POL)
Lou Gramm; *Past Times Behind Rock & Roll* ..... (INT)
Struggle (Free South Africa)
Rochester/Easley Band; *One Minute Of Love* ....(GRM)
Sun City
Artists United Against Apartheid; *Sun City* ..... (MAN)
Two Tribes
Frankie Goes To Hollywood; *Welcome To The Pleasuredome* .... (ISL)
Uneasy Rider
Charlie Daniels Band; *Decade Of Hits* .... (EPI)
Homesick Heroes .... (EPI)
Super Hits/'70s-Have A Nice Day-#11 ....(RHI)
Uneasy Rider .... (EPI)
We Shall Be Free
Garth Brooks; *The Chase* .... (LIB)
We Shall Overcome
James Cleveland/Troubadors; *James Cleveland/Troubadors* ....(SAV)

Joan Baez; *Carry It On* .... (VAN)
  In Concert .... (VAN)
Pete Seeger; *Bitter & The Sweet* .... (MOB)
  Greatest Hits ....(COL)
We're All In The Same Gang
West Coast Rap All-Stars; *We're All In The Same
Gang* ....(WB)
White Minority
Black Flag; *First Four Years* ....(SST)
  ST/Decline Of Western Civilization ....(SLS)
White Trash
Bad Religion; *How Could Hell Be Any Worse* .... (EPT)
Bellamy Brothers; *Crazy From The Heart* .... (MCA)
Orchestral Manoeuvres In The Dark; *Junk
Culture* .... (A&M)
Red Kross; *Born Innocent* .... (FRN)
Steve Cash; *White Mansions* .... (A&M)
White Trash Song
Steve Young; *Honky-Tonk Man* .... (ROU)
  Solo/Live .... (WAT)
Whitey On The Moon
Gil Scott-Heron; *Whitey On The Moon* .... (BLU)
Woman Is The Nigger Of The World
John Lennon; *Shaved Fish* ....(CAP)
  Somewhere In New York City ....(CAP)
John Lennon/Plastic Ono Band; *Lennon* ....(CAP)

PRESIDENTS

*See Also: KINGS, MEN'S NAMES, POLITICAL
CLASSICS, QUEENS, ROYALTY*

Abraham, Martin & John
Dion; *24 Original Classics* .... (ARI)
  Collectables Presents History Of Rock-#3 .... (CLT)
  WCBS FM-History Of Rock-'60s-#2 .... (CLT)
Harry Belafonte; *All Time Greatest Hits-#1* ......(RCA)
Smokey Robinson/Miracles; *Anthology* .... (MOT)
  Time Out For/Special Occasion .... (MOT)
Arrest The President
Intelligent Hoodlum; *Intelligent Hoodlum* .... (A&M)
At The President's Birthday Ball
Glenn Miller/Orchestra; *Complete* .... (BLU)
Ballad Of Richard Nixon
John Denver; *Rhymes & Reasons* ....(RCA)
Ballad Of Spiro Agnew
John Denver; *Rhymes & Reasons* ....(RCA)
Dear Mr. President
4 Non Blondes; *Bigger Better Faster More* .... (ISC)
Next Issue; *Next Issue* .... (EPI)
Eisenhower
John Scofield; *Meant To Be* .... (BLN)
Eisenhower Blues
Elvis Costello; *King Of America* ....(COL)
J.B. Lenoir; *Best Of Chess Blues* .... (CSS)
  Natural Man .... (CSS)
El Presidente
Swimming Pool Q's; *Firing Squad For God* .... (DB)
Franklin D. Roosevelt's Back Again
New Lost City Ramblers; *Early
Years-1958-1962* ....(FLW)
Good Evening Mr. Waldheim
Lou Reed; *New York* .... (SIR)
Here Comes President Kill Again
XTC; *Oranges & Lemons* ....(GEF)
Here's To The State Of Nixon
Phil Ochs; *Chords Of Fame* .... (A&M)
In Memoriam-John F. & Robert F. Kennedy
Clare Fischer; *'Twas Only Yesterday* .... (DCO)
Lee Harvey Oswald
Skatalites; *Stretching Out* .... (ROI)
Letters To The President
Sly & Robbie; *Silent Assassin* .... (ISL)
Mr. Lincoln
Hank Williams, Jr.; *America (The Way I See It)* ..(W/C)
  Major Moves ....(W/C)
Mr. President
Big Boy Henry; *Work's Many Voices-#1 & 2* .... (ARH)
Crack The Sky; *Dog City* .... (GDG)
Elliot Lawrence Band; *Plays Gerry Mulligan
Arrangements* ....(FAN)
George Fox; *With All My Might* .... (WB)
Meat Beat Manifesto; *Armed Audio Warfare* .... (WAX)

Mr. President (Have Pity On The...)
Randy Newman; *Good Old Boys* .... (RPR)
  ST/Forrest Gump .... (EPX)
November 22, 1963
Original Cast; *Assassins* ....(RCA)
Open Letter To George Bush
Wayne Horvitz/The President; *Miracle Mile* ...... (ELE)
President Garfield
Jerry Holland; *Jerry Holland* .... (ROU)
President Gas
Psychedelic Furs; *All Of This & Nothing* ....(COL)
  Forever Now ....(COL)
President Hayes
Sonny Rollins; *Don't Stop The Carnival* .... (MS)
President Kennedy
Ry Cooder; *Boomer's Story* .... (RPR)
Son House; *Father Of The Delta Blues-1965
Sessions* ....(COL)
President Kennedy March
Lawrence Welk; *10th Anniversary Television
Show* .... (RAN)
President Kennedy Stayed Away Too Long
Sleepy John Estes; *Electric Sleep* .... (DEL)
  Kings Of Country Blues-#1 .... (ARH)
President Kennedy's Mile
Screaming Blue Messiahs; *Gun-Shy* .... (ELE)
President Roosevelt
Big Joe Williams; *Shake Your Boogie* .... (ARH)
  Tough Times .... (ARH)
Presidente
Tijuana Brass; *South Of The Border* .... (A&M)
Presidential Rag
Arlo Guthrie & Pete Seeger; *Together In Concert* (RPR)
President's Nap
Power Tools; *Strange Meeting* .... (AND)
President's Share Of The Promised Land
Doves; *Affinity* .... (ELE)
Reagan Der Fuhrer
D.I.; *Team Goon* .... (XXX)
Reagonomics
D.R.I.; *Dealing With It!* .... (MET)
Johnnie Taylor; *Just Ain't Good Enough* .... (BEV)
Richard Nixon
Christmas; *Ultraprophets Of Thee Psykick
Revolution* .... (IRS)
Ronnie, Talk To Russia
Prince; *Controversy* .... (WB)
Secret Service
Original Cast; *Mr. President* .... (SMC)
Talking Watergate
Tom Paxton; *New Songs From The Briarpatch* .. (VAN)
Tweedledee For President
Michael Tilson Thomas; *Of Thee I Sing/Let 'Em Eat
Cake* ....(COL)
Warren Harding
Al Stewart; *Past Present & Future* .... (RHI)
We'd Like To Thank You Herbert Hoover
Original Broadway Cast; *Annie* ....(COL)
What The President Meant To Say
Leaving Trains; *Fuck* ....(SST)
When The Flintstones Meet The President
Dirty Dozen Brass Band; *Louisiana Scrapbook* ...(RYK)
White House Blues
Doc Watson; *Essential* .... (VAN)
Doc Watson & Family; *Treasures Untold* .... (VAN)
Stanley Brothers; *Shadows Of The Past* ....(COP)
Wintergreen For President
Michael Tilson Thomas; *Of Thee I Sing/Let 'Em Eat
Cake* ....(COL)

PRETEND, Disguise, Fantasy, Imagine, Wish, Wonder

See Also: DREAMS, HIDING, LIES

All In My Mind
Maxine Brown; *Golden Classics* .... (CLT)
  Sultry Soul Sisters .... (RHI)
  Super Oldies/'60s-#3 ....(AUF)
Almost Like Being In Love
Frank Sinatra; *Capitol Years* ....(CAP)
  Hello Young Lovers ....(COL)
Original Cast; *Brigadoon* ....(RCA)

Angel In Disguise
Earl Thomas Conley; *Don't Make It Easy For Me* (RCA)
   Greatest Hits ....(RCA)
Artifical Rose
Jimmy C. Newman; *Greatest Hits* ....(PLN)
Artificial Flowers
Bobby Darin; *Story* ....(ATC)
Artificial Rose
Jimmy C. Newman; *45* ....(SUN)
   Greatest Hits ....(PLN)
Billy The Kid (I Miss...)
Billy Dean; *Billy Dean* ....(LIB)
Black & Tan Fantasy
Duke Ellington; *Echoes Of An Era;*
Ellington/Armstrong ....(RLL)
   Beginning ....(MCA)
   Carnegie Hall ....(PRS)
   Carnegie Hall Concert 12-11-43 ....(EVR)
   Continuum ....(FAN)
   Greatest Hits ....(RPR)
   Pure Gold ....(RCA)
   /M. Ellington ....(FAN)
Button Off My Shirt
Ronnie Milsap; *Greatest Hits-#3* ....(RCA)
   Heart & Soul ....(RCA)
Cry Wolf
Laura Branigan; *Touch* ....(ATL)
Stevie Nicks; *Other Side Of The Mirror* ....(MOD)
Victoria Shaw; *In Full View* ....(RPR)
Cuban Fantasy
Cal Tjader; *Good Vibes* .... (CP)
Damn I Wish I Was Your Lover
Sophie B. Hawkins; *Tongues & Tales* ....(COL)
Dear Mr. Fantasy
Traffic; *Best Of* .... (ISL)
   Dear Mr. Fantasy .... (ISL)
   Welcome To The Canteen .... (ISL)
Devil In Disguise
Elvis Presley; *Golden Records-#4* ....(RCA)
   Top Ten Hits ....(RCA)
J.J. Cale; *Grasshopper* ....(MER)
   Special Edition ....(MER)
Don't Close Your Eyes
Keith Whitley; *Don't Close Your Eyes* ....(RCA)
   Greatest Hits ....(RCA)
Down Incognito
Winger; *Pull* ....(ATL)
Dream Is A Wish Your Heart Makes
Barbara Cook; *Disney Album* ....(MCA)
Michael Bolton; *Simply Mad About The Mouse* ..(COL)
Escape (Pina Colada Song)
Rupert Holmes; *Billboard Top Hits-1979* ....(RHI)
   Partners In Crime ....(INF)
Everything That Glitters (Is Not Gold)
Dan Seals; *Best Of* ....(LIB)
   Classics Collection-#2 ....(LIB)
   Greatest Hits ....(LIB)
   I Won't Be Blue Anymore ....(EMI)
Fake
Alexander O'Neal; *All Mixed Up* ....(TAB)
   Hearsay ....(TAB)
Fake Friends
Joan Jett/Blackhearts; *Joan Jett/Blackhearts* .....(MCA)
Fake Your Way To The Top
Original Broadway Cast; *Dreamgirls* ....(GEF)
Faking Love
T.G. Sheppard & Karen Brooks; *All-Time Greatest*
Hits ....(WB)
   Greatest Hits-#2 ....(WB)
   Perfect Stranger ....(WB)
   You & I-Classic Country Duets ....(WB)
Fakin' It
Simon & Garfunkel; *Bookends* ....(COL)
   Collected Works ....(COL)
Fantasy
Alabama; *Feels So Right* ....(RCA)
Aldo Nova; *Aldo Nova* ....(POR)
Black Box; *Decoded & Danced Up* ....(RCA)
   Dreamland ....(RCA)
Earth, Wind & Fire; *All 'N All* ....(COL)
   Best Of-#1 ....(COL)
   Best Of-#2 ....(COL)
   ST/Private Lessons ....(MCA)

Fantasy Girl
38 Special; *Flashback-Best Of* ....(A&M)
   Wild-Eyed Southern Boys ....(A&M)
Fantasy Serenade
Triumph; *Just A Game* ....(MCA)
Flesh For Fantasy
Billy Idol; *Rebel Yell* ....(CHR)
   Vital Idol ....(CHR)
Fools Gold
Stone Roses; *Stone Roses* .... (SIL)
Four Percent Pantomime
Band; *Cahoots* ....(CAP)
   To Kingdom Come-Definitive Collection ....(CAP)
Gold Digger
EPMD; *Business As Usual* .... (DFJ)
Grand Illusion
Eric Clapton; *August* ....(DUC)
Styx; *Classics-#15* ....(A&M)
   Grand Illusion ....(A&M)
Great Pretender
Band; *Moondog Matinee* ....(CAP)
Platters; *Anthology* ....(RHI)
   Billboard Top R&B Hits-1956 ....(RHI)
   Cruisin'-1956 .... (INC)
   Encore Of Golden Hits ....(MER)
   ST/American Graffiti ....(MCA)
   Super Oldies/'50s-#3 ....(AUF)
Roy Orbison; *Best-Loved Standards* ....(MON)
Stan Freberg; *Capitol Collectors Series* ....(CAP)
He Would Be Sixteen
Michelle Wright; *Now & Then* .... (ARI)
Hello
Luther Vandross; *Songs* .... (EPI)
Hey, Cinderella
Suzy Bogguss; *Something Up My Sleeve* ....(LIB)
High Hopes And Empty Pockets
Terry McBride/Ride; *Terry McBride & The Ride* (MCA)
Holding Her & Loving You
Earl Thomas Conley; *Don't Make It Easy For Me* (RCA)
   Greatest Hits ....(RCA)
House Of Cards
Elton John; *45* ....(MCA)
Mary Chapin Carpenter; *Stones In The Road* ....(COL)
I Pretend
Kim Carnes; *Cafe Racers* ....(EMI)
I Wish
Gabrielle; *Find Your Way* ....(GO!)
Stevie Wonder; *Original Musiquarium* ....(MOT)
   Songs In The Key Of Life ....(MOT)
I Wish He Didn't Trust Me So Much
Bobby Womack; *So Many Rivers* ....(MCA)
I Wish I Could Have Been There
John Anderson; *Solid Ground* ....(BNA)
I Wish I Had A Girl
Henry Lee Summer; *Henry Lee Summer* ....(CBA)
I Wish I Was In Chicago
Original Cast; *Charlie Sent Me* ....(GLN)
I Wish I Was In Nashville
Mel McDaniel; *Take Me To The Country* ....(CAP)
I Wish I Was In New Orleans
Tom Waits; *Small Change* ....(ASY)
I Wish I Was In Peoria
Max Morath; *& His Ragtime Stompers* .... (VAN)
I Wish I Was In Texas Tonight
Patti Ford; *45* ....(NAT)
I Wish I Was Still In Your Dreams
Conway Twitty; *Still In Your Dreams* ....(MCA)
I Wish I Were Blind
Bruce Springsteen; *Human Touch* ....(COL)
I Wish It Would Rain
Nanci Griffith; *Little Love Affairs* ....(MCA)
Temptations; *16 #1 Hits From The Late '60s* .... (MOT)
   All The Million-Sellers ....(MOT)
   Anthology ....(MOT)
   Billboard Top R&B Hits-1968 ....(MOT)
   Compact Command Performances ....(MOT)
   Motown Story ....(MOT)
I Wish It Would Rain Down
Phil Collins; *...But Seriously* ....(ATL)
I Wish That We Were Married
Ronnie/Hi-Lites; *Rockin' & Rollin' Wedding*
Songs-#2 ....(RHI)
I Wish You Could Have Turned My Head
Oak Ridge Boys; *Bobbie Sue* ....(MCA)

I Wish You Were Here Tonight
Ray Charles; *Greatest Hits Of Country Blues* .....(COL)
I Wish You Were Here Tonight ....(COL)
I Wished On The Moon
Billie Holiday; *Live* ....(VRV)
Stormy Blues ....(VRV)
Ella Fitzgerald; *Best Of* ....(MCA)
I Wonder
Abba; *Album* ....(ATL)
Greatest Hits-#2 ....(ATL)
I Love Abba ....(ATL)
Jimmy Witherspoon; *Best Of* ....(PRS)
Blue Spoon ....(PRS)
Rosanne Cash; *Hits 1979-1989* ....(COL)
Somewhere In The Stars ....(COL)
I Wonder As I Wander
Gary Morris; *Every Christmas* ....(LIB)
Mormon Tabernacle Choir; *This Land Is Your
Land* ....(COL)
Peter, Paul & Mary; *Holiday Celebration* ....(WB)
Philadelphia Orchestra/Eugene Ormandy; *Sleigh
Ride!-Classic Christmas Favorites* ....(RCA)
Sandi Patti; *Gift Goes On* ....(WOR)
I Wonder How It Is In Colorado
Gene Watson; *Reflections* ....(CAP)
I Wonder If I Care As Much
Everly Brothers; *All They Had To Do Was Dream* (RHI)
Cadence Classics-20 Greatest Hits ....(RHI)
Everly Brothers ....(RHI)
Ricky Skaggs; *Love's Gonna Get Ya* ....(EPI)
I Wonder If I Take You Home
Lisa Lisa & Cult Jam With Full Force;
Breakdancing ....(COL)
Lisa Lisa & Cult Jam With Full Force ....(COL)
I Wonder What The King Is Doing Tonight
Original Cast; *Camelot* ....(COL)
Richard Harris; *ST/Camelot* ....(WB)
I Wonder Where You Are Tonight
Bill Monroe; *Bean Blossom* .... (MCA)
Jerry Lee Lewis; *Country Music Hall Of Fame
Hits* .... (SMA)
Keith Whitley; *L.A. To Miami* ....(RCA)
I Wonder Who's Holding My Baby
Whites; *Greatest Hits* ....(W/C)
I Wonder Who's Kissing Her Now
Bobby Darin; *Capitol Collectors Series* ....(CAP)
Ted Weems; *45* ....(MCA)
I Wonder Why
Curtis Stigers; *Curtis Stigers* .... (ARI)
Dion/Belmonts; *Doo Wop Uptempo-#2* .... (RHI)
Everything You Always Wanted ....(LAU)
Million-Dollar Memories-#1 ....(RCA)
Oldies But Goodies-#12 ....(OSR)
Super Oldies!'50s-#7s ....(AUF)
You Found The Vocal Group Sound-#1 ....(SSM)
If
Bread; *Anthology* .... (ELE)
Best Of .... (ELE)
Manna .... (ELE)
Janet Jackson; *Janet.* .... (VIA)
If 6 Was 9
Jimi Hendrix; *Axis Bold As Love* .... (RPR)
Essential .... (RPR)
If He Walked Into My Life
Original Cast; *Mame* ....(COL)
If I Could Be With You
Helen Humes; *Ladies Sing The Blues-#2* .... (SAV)
Louis Armstrong; *Satchmo-Musical
Autobiography-#2* .... (MCA)
Best Of .... (MCA)
Story-#4 ....(COL)
If I Could Build My Whole World...
Marvin Gaye & Tammi Terrell; *Anthology* ...... (MOT)
Every Great Motown Hit Of Marvin Gaye ..... (MOT)
Greatest Hits .... (MOT)
Motown Superstar Series-#2 .... (MOT)
United .... (MOT)
If I Could Have Her Tonight
Neil Young; *Neil Young* .... (RPR)
If I Could Only Dance With You
Jim Glaser; *Man In The Mirror* .... (NBL)
If I Could Only Win Your Love
Emmylou Harris; *Pieces Of The Sky* .... (RPR)
Profile ....(WB)

If I Had You
Alabama; *Southern Star* ....(RCA)
Frank Sinatra; *Round #1* ....(CAP)
Voice-Columbia Years 1943-1952 ....(COL)
Judy Garland; *Collector's Items-1936-1945* ..... (MCA)
Platters; *Greatest Hits* ....(EVR)
If I Loved You
Barbra Streisand; *Broadway Album* ....(COL)
Original Cast; *Carousel* .... (MCA)
If I Needed You
Don Williams; *Especially For You* .... (MCA)
Emmylou Harris; *Cimarron* ....(WB)
Emmylou Harris & Don Williams; *Classic Country
Duets* .... (MCA)
Duets .... (RPR)
If I Only Had A Brain
Harry Connick, Jr.; *20* ....(COL)
Kay Kyser; *Best Of The Big Bands* ....(COL)
If I Only Had A Heart
Jack Haley; *ST/Wizard Of Oz* .... (SSP)
If I Were A Bell
Original Cast; *Guys & Dolls* .... (MCA)
Teena Marie; *Ivory* .... (EPI)
If I Were A Carpenter
Bobby Darin; *Live At The Desert Inn* .... (MOT)
Four Tops; *Anthology* .... (MOT)
Compact Command Performances .... (MOT)
Reach Out .... (MOT)
Tim Hardin; *Memorial Album* .... (POL)
If I Were A Rich Man
Original Cast; *Fiddler On The Roof* ....(RCA)
Original London Cast; *Fiddler On The Roof* .....(COL)
If I Were King Of The Forest
Bert Lahr; *ST/Wizard Of Oz* .... (SSP)
If I Were Your Girlfriend
Prince; *45* ....(PAI)
If I Were Your Woman
Gladys Knight/Pips; *All The Great Hits* .... (MOT)
Anthology .... (MOT)
Compact Command Performances .... (MOT)
Every Great Motown Song-First 25 Years ...... (MOT)
If I Were Your Woman .... (MOT)
Motown Superstar Series-#13 .... (MOT)
If I'd Been The One
38 Special; *Flashback (Best Of)* .... (A&M)
Tour De Force .... (A&M)
If The South Woulda Won
Hank Williams, Jr.; *Wild Streak* ....(W/C)
If There Hadn't Been You
Billy Dean; *Billy Dean* .... (LIB)
If This World Were Mine
Cheryl Lynn; *Instant Love* ....(COL)
Luther Vandross & Cheryl Lynn; *Best Of...Best Of
Love* .... (EPI)
Marvin Gaye & Tammi Terrell; *All The Great Motown
Love Song Duets* .... (MOT)
Anthology .... (MOT)
Classic Duets-Marvin Gaye & His Women ..... (MOT)
Greatest Hits .... (MOT)
Motown Superstar Series-#2 .... (MOT)
United .... (MOT)
If Wishes Came True
Sweet Sensation; *Love Child* ....(ATC)
If You Asked Me To
Celine Dion; *Celine Dion* .... (EPI)
Patti Labelle; *Be Yourself* .... (MCA)
Soundtrack Smashes-'80s & More .... (MCA)
If You Could Read My Mind
Gordon Lightfoot; *Gord's Gold* .... (RPR)
If You Could Read My Mind .... (RPR)
Sit Down Young Stranger .... (RPR)
If You Could See Me Now
Sarah Vaughan & Count Basie; *Pablo Today-Send In
The Clowns* .... (PAB)
If You Ever Change Your Mind
Crystal Gayle; *Greatest Hits* ....(COL)
These Days ....(COL)
If You Go Away
Neil Diamond; *Love Songs* .... (MCA)
Rainbow .... (MCA)
Stones .... (MCA)
If You Were The Only Boy (In The World)
Barbra Streisand; *My Name Is Barbra* ....(COL)

Imaginary Lover
Atlanta Rhythm Section; *Champagne Jam* .... (POL)
Imagination
B.B. & Q. Band; *B.B. & Q. Band* ....(CAP)
Cleo Laine; *That Old Feeling* ....(COL)
Frank Sinatra; *I Remember Tommy* .... (RPR)
Frank Sinatra & Tommy Dorsey; *Dorsey/Sinatra Sessions* ....(RCA)
Glenn Miller; *Complete-#4-1940* ....(RCA)
Harry Connick, Jr.; *Twenty* ....(COL)
Imagine
Diana Ross; *Anthology* .... (MOT)
Best Of The Beatles Songs ....(MOT)
Touch Me In The Morning ....(MOT)
Joan Baez; *Best Of* ....(A&M)
Come From The Shadows ....(A&M)
John Lennon; *Lennon* ....(CAP)
Live In New York City ....(CAP)
Shaved Fish ....(CAP)
John Lennon/Plastic Ono Band; *Collection* ......(GEF)
Imagine ....(CAP)
ST/Imagine-The Motion Picture ....(CAP)
It Should Have Been Me
Carly Simon; *Coming Around Again* .... (ARI)
Gladys Knight/Pips; *Anthology* ....(MOT)
Compact Command Performances ....(MOT)
Motown Superstar Series-#13 ....(MOT)
Neil Diamond; *Headed For The Future* ....(COL)
Ray Charles; *Birth Of Soul-Complete Atlantic R&B* .... (ATL)
It Should've Been Me
Commander Cody/Lost Planet Airmen; *Hot Licks Cold Steel & Trucker's Faves* .... (MCA)
It's Only A Paper Moon
Art Blakey/Jazz Messengers; *Big Beat* .... (BLN)
Bing Crosby; *Radio Years-#2* ....(CRS)
David Rose/Orchestra; *Music Of The 1930s* .... (MCA)
Ella Fitzgerald; *Harold Arlen Songbook-#2* ....(VRV)
Frank Sinatra; *Round #1* ....(CAP)
Mystics; *16 Golden Classics* ....(CLT)
Nat King Cole; *Story* ....(CAP)
Sammy Kaye/Orchestra; *Play 22 Original Big Band Recordings* .... (HIN)
It's Only Make Believe
Conway Twitty; *Conway's #1 Classics-#2* ....(WB)
Greatest Hits #2 ....(MCA)
Very Best Of ....(MCA)
#1s-#1 ....(MCA)
Glen Campbell; *Very Best Of* ....(CAP)
I'll Get You
Beatles; *Past Masters-#1* ....(CAP)
Second Album ....(CAP)
I've Got To Use My Imagination
Gladys Knight/Pips; *Best Of* ....(PRR)
Greatest Hits ....(CCB)
Soul Survivors-Best Of-1973-1988 ....(RHI)
ST/Forrest Gump ....(EPX)
Joe Cocker; *One Night Of Sin* ....(CAP)
Judy In Disguise (With Glasses)
John Fred/Playboys; *Billboard Top Rock 'N' Roll Hits-1968* .... (RHI)
Cruisin'-1967 ....(INC)
ST/Drugstore Cowboy ....(NOV)
Super Oldies Of The '60s-#7 ....(AUF)
Just My Imagination
Rolling Stones; *Some Girls* ....(RS)
Still Life-American Concert 1981 ....(RS)
Temptations; *12 #1 Hits From The '70s* .... (MOT)
20 Greatest Songs In Motown History ....(MOT)
25 #1 Hits From 25 Years ....(MOT)
25th Anniversary ....(MOT)
All The Million-Sellers ....(MOT)
Anthology ....(MOT)
Compact Command Performances ....(MOT)
Just One Night
McBride & The Ride; *Sacred Ground* .... (MCA)
King Of Wishful Thinking
Go West; *ST/Pretty Woman* .... (EMI)
Land Of Make Believe
Chuck Mangione; *Best Of* .... (MER)
Classics-#6 ....(A&M)
Encore ....(MER)
Evening Of Magic ....(A&M)
Land Of Make Believe ....(MER)

Moody Blues; *Seventh Sojourn* ....(POL)
Let's Pretend
Al Jarreau; *High Crime* ....(WB)
In London ....(WB)
Raspberries; *Best* ....(CAP)
Capitol Collectors Series ....(CAP)
Willie Nelson; *Broken Promises* ....(INT)
Diamonds In The Rough ....(DEL)
Let's Pretend We're Married
Prince; *1999* ....(WB)
Tina Turner; *45* ....(CAP)
Life Of Illusion
Joe Walsh; *There Goes The Neighborhood* ...... (ASY)
Living In A Fantasy
Leo Sayer; *45* ....(WB)
Longing In Their Hearts
Bonnie Raitt; *Longing In Their Hearts* ....(CAP)
Lyin' Eyes
Eagles; *Anthology* ....(ASY)
One Of These Nights ....(ASY)
ST/Urban Cowboy ....(ASY)
Their Greatest Hits-1971-1975 ....(ASY)
Make Believe
Barbara Cooke & John Raitt/Original Cast; *Showboat* ....(COL)
Barbra Streisand; *Third Album* ....(COL)
Kenny Rankin; *Album* .... (LD)
Toto; *IV* ....(COL)
Make Believe Ballroom Time
Glenn Miller; *Complete-#5 & #9* ....(RCA)
Legendary Performer-#2 ....(RCA)
Make Believe It's Your First Time
Bobby Vinton; *Encore* ....(TAP)
Carpenters; *Classics-#2* ....(A&M)
Voice Of The Heart ....(A&M)
Yesterday Once More ....(A&M)
Make Me A Mask
Fleetwood Mac; *25 Years-The Chain* ....(WB)
Marriage On Paper Only
Dramatics; *Anytime Anyplace* .... (MCA)
Masquerade
Basia; *Brave New Hope* ....(EPI)
Berlin; *Best Of-1979-1988* ....(GEF)
Pleasure Victim ....(GEF)
Dave Valentin; *Legends* ....(GRP)
Evelyn Thomas; *Best Of* .... (HOT)
First Call; *Human Song* ....(EPI)
Frames; *Another Love Song* .... (ISL)
Howard Hewett; *Allegiance* .... (ELE)
Original London Cast; *Phantom Of The Opera* ... (POL)
Swing Out Sister; *Kaleidoscope World* .... (FON)
Yes; *Union* ....(ARI)
Masquerade Is Over (I'm Afraid)
Al Jarreau; *1965* ....(BAI)
Carmen McRae; *Jazzy ladies* ....(DHL)
Ms. Magic ....(DHL)
Five Satins; *Sing Their Greatest Hits* ....(CLT)
Lodi Carr; *Lady Bird* ....(LAU)
Nancy Wilson & Cannonball Adderley; *Blue Series-Female Vocals* .... (BLN)
My Baby Thinks He's A Train
Rosanne Cash; *Hits 1979-1989* ....(COL)
Seven-Year Ache ....(COL)
Nickel In The Well
Shenandoah; *Under The Kudzu* ....(RCA)
No Imagination
Blondie; *Plastic Letters* ....(CHR)
No Myth
Michael Penn; *March* ....(RCA)
Nobody Knows You When You're Down & Out
Bessie Smith; *Collection* ....(COL)
Complete Recordings-#4 ....(COL)
Derek/Dominos; *Layla* ....(POL)
Eric Clapton; *Unplugged* ....(DUC)
Otis Redding; *Soul Album* ....(ATC)
Rod Stewart; *Out Of Order* ....(WB)
One Wish
Hiroshima; *Another Place* ....(EPI)
Plastic People
Mothers Of Invention; *Absolutely Free* ....(RYK)
Pretend
Nat King Cole; *Capitol Collectors Series* ....(CAP)
Story ....(CAP)
Unforgettable ....(CAP)

Pretend I Never Happened
Willie Nelson; *Me & Paul* ....(COL)
    Phases & Stages ....(ATL)
Pretend You Don't See Her
Jerry Vale; *17 Most Requested Songs* ....(COL)
    All-Time Greatest Hits ....(COL)
    Greatest Hits ....(COL)
Pretender
Hanoi Rocks; *Bangkok Shocks Saigon Shakes Hanoi
Rocks* ....(GEF)
Jackson Browne; *Pretender* ....(ASY)
Madonna; *Like A Virgin* ....(SIR)
Pretending
Eric Clapton; *24 Nights* ....(RPR)
    Journeyman ....(RPR)
Karen Brooks/Randy Sharp; *That's Another Story* (MER)
Pretending Love
Little Johnny & Ted Taylor; *Super Taylors* ...... (RON)
Pretending She's You
Jimmie Davis; *Golden Hits-#2* ....(PLN)
Pretending To Be Drunk
Sparks; *Pulling Rabbits Out Of A Hat* ....(ATL)
Pretending To Care
Daryl Braithwaite; *Edge* ....(EPA)
Jennifer Warnes; *The Hunter* ....(PRV)
Todd Rundgren; *A Cappella* ....(WB)
Pseudo Silk Kimono
Marillion; *Misplaced Childhood* ....(CAP)
Put Yourself In My Place
Pam Tillis; *Put Yourself In My Place* .... (ARI)
Rock & Roll Fantasy
Bad Company; *10 From 6* ....(ATL)
    Desolation Angels .... (SS)
Kinks; *15-Year History Of Rock* ....(ARI)
    Come Dancing With-Best Of-1977-1986 ....(ARI)
    Misfits ....(ARI)
    '70s Greatest Rock Hits-#14 ....(PRY)
She Dreams
Mark Chesnutt; *What A Way To Live* ....(DEC)
Should've Been A Cowboy
Toby Keith; *Toby Keith* ....(MER)
Sometimes A Fantasy
Billy Joel; *Glass Houses* ....(COL)
    KOHUEPT ....(COL)
Standing On The Corner
Broadway Cast; *Most Happy Fella* ....(RCA)
Four Lads; *16 Most Requested Songs* ....(COL)
Original Broadway Cast; *Most Happy Fella* ..... (SMC)
Substitute
Great White; *Great White* ....(EMI)
Sex Pistols; *Live At Chelmsford Top Security
Prison* .... (RES)
Who; *Greatest Hits* ....(MCA)
    Live At Leeds ....(MCA)
    Meaty Beaty Big & Bouncy ....(MCA)
    Who's Better Who's Best-Very Best Of ....(MCA)
    Who's Last ....(MCA)
Superman (I Wish I Could Fly Like)
Kinks; *Come Dancing With-Best Of-1977-1986* .. (ARI)
    Low Budget ....(ARI)
Swinging On A Star
Bing Crosby; *All-Time Best* ....(CCB)
    Best Of ....(MCA)
Dion/Belmonts; *Their Best* ....(LAU)
Frank Sinatra; *Sings The Songs Of Van Heusen &
Cahn* .... (RPR)
Ten Feet Tall And Bulletproof
Travis Tritt; *Ten Feet Tall And Bulletproof* ....(WB)
This Masquerade
Carpenters; *Classics-#2* ....(A&M)
    Now & Then ....(A&M)
    Yesterday Once More ....(A&M)
George Benson; *Breezin'* ....(WB)
    Collection ....(WB)
Leon Russell; *Best Of* ....(MCA)
    Carney ....(OOP)
Unbelievable
Bob Dylan; *Under The Red Sky* ....(COL)
EMF; *Schubert Dip* ....(CAP)
Was It Just The Moonlight
Timothy B. Schmit; *Tell Me The Truth* .... (MCA)
Was It Just The Wine
Vern Gosdin; *10 Years Of Greatest Hits Newly
Recorded* ....(COL)

West Virginia Fantasies
Chicago; *At Carnegie Hall* ....(COL)
    Group Portrait ....(COL)
    II ....(COL)
(What A) Wonderful World
Art Garfunkel; *Watermark* ....(COL)
Sam Cooke; *Best Of* ....(RCA)
    ST/Animal House ....(MCA)
    This Is ....(RCA)
What Might Have Been
Little Texas; *Big Time* ....(WB)
When You Wish Upon A Star
Barbara Cook; *Disney Album* ....(MCA)
Billy Joel; *Simply Mad About The Mouse* ....(COL)
Cliff Edwards; *ST/Pinocchio* ....(DIS)
Dion/Belmonts; *The Wanderer* ....(LAU)
Glenn Miller & Ray Eberle; *Chattanooga
Choo-Choo-#1 Hits* ....(BLU)
Linda Ronstadt; *For Sentimental Reasons* ....(ASY)
Little Anthony/Imperials; *We Are The Imperials* .. (RLL)
Rosemary Clooney; *16 Most Requested Songs* ...(COL)
Stevie Wonder; *With A Song In My Heart* ......(MOT)
Wynton Marsalis; *Hothouse Flowers* ....(COL)
Who's Holding Donna Now
DeBarge; *Greatest Hits* ....(MOT)
    Rhythm Of The Night ....(MOT)
Wish
Fixx; *Phantoms* ....(MCA)
Nine Inch Nails; *Broken* ....(ISC)
Wish I Had My Baby
Five Satins; *45* ....(CLT)
Wish Upon A Star
Steve Miller Band; *Book Of Dreams* ....(CAP)
    CD Gift Set ....(CAP)
Wish We Were Back In Missouri
Emmylou Harris; *Legend Of Jesse James* ....(A&M)
Wish You Were Here
Alice Cooper; *Alice Cooper Show* ....(WB)
    Goes To Hell ....(WB)
Barbara Mandrell; *Greatest Hits* ....(MCA)
    Live ....(MCA)
Bing Crosby; *Radio Years* ....(CRS)
Dead Or Alive; *Sophisticated Boom Boom* ....(EPI)
Eddie Fisher; *Best Of* ....(MCA)
Fleetwood Mac; *Mirage* ....(WB)
Nick Lowe; *Abominable Showman* ....(COL)
Pink Floyd; *Collection Of Great Dance Songs* ...(COL)
    Delicate Sound Of Thunder ....(COL)
    Wish You Were Here ....(COL)
Wish You Were Mine Again
Mickey Gilley; *Fool For Your Love* ....(EPI)
Wish You Were There
R.E.O. Speedwagon; *Hi-Infidelity* .... (EPI)
Wishful Thinking
China Crisis; *Working With Fire & Steel* ....(WB)
Dan Hill & Celine Dion; *Real Love* ....(COL)
Dolly Parton & Donna Fargo; *Queens Of Country* (INT)
Little Anthony/Imperials; *Best Of* ....(RHI)
Wishing
Asia; *Astra* ....(GEF)
Buddy Holly/Crickets; *20 Golden Greats* ....(MCA)
Electric Light Orchestra; *Box Of Their Best* ....(JET)
    Discovery ....(JET)
Joan Armatrading; *To The Limit* ....(A&M)
Wishing On A Star
Cover Girls; *Here It Is* ....(EPI)
Rose Royce; *Greatest Hits* ....(WHI)
Wishing On The Moon
Dan Fogelberg; *Phoenix* ....(FM)
Wishing Well
Black Sabbath; *Heaven & Hell* ....(WB)
Bobby Bland; *Call On Me* ....(MCA)
Gary Moore; *Early Years* ....(WTG)
INXS; *Welcome To Wherever You Are* ....(ATL)
Jackie Wilson; *Mr. Excitement* ....(RHI)
Mission U.K.; *First Chapeter* ....(MER)
Nitty Gritty Dirt Band; *Rest Of The Dream* ......(MCA)
Terence Trent D'Arby; *Introducing The Hardline
According To...* ....(COL)
Tyrone Davis; *Something's Mighty Wrong* ....(ICH)

Wishing You Were Here
Chicago; *Greatest Hits* ....(COL)
  Group Portrait ....(COL)
  If You Leave Me Now ....(COL)
  VII ....(COL)
Wishing (If I Had A Photograph Of You)
A Flock Of Seagulls; *Best Of* ....(JVA)
  Listen ....(JVA)
Wishin' & Hopin'
Dusty Springfield; *Golden Hits* .... (MER)
  History Of British Rock-#6 ....(RHI)
Wish, The
Eddie Money; *Playing For Keeps* ....(COL)
With Every Wish
Bruce Springsteen; *Human Touch* ....(COL)
Wond'ring Aloud
Jethro Tull; *20 Years Of-Radio Archives & Rare
Tracks* .... (CHR)
  Aqualung .... (CHR)
World's A Masquerade
Earth, Wind & Fire; *Head To The Sky* ....(COL)
Wouldn't It Be Nice
Beach Boys; *Absolutely Best-#2* ....(CAP)
  Made In The U.S.A. ....(CAP)
  Pet Sounds ....(CAP)
  Still Cruisin' ....(CAP)
You Could Be Mine
Guns N' Roses; *Use Your Illusion II* ....(GEF)
You Cried Wolf
Todd Rundgren; *Anthology-1968-1985* .... (RHI)
  Hermit Of Mink Hollow ....(RHI)
Your Imagination
Daryl Hall & John Oates; *Private Eyes* ....(RCA)

PRISON, Chains, Stymied

See Also: FREEDOM, LAW & ORDER, POLICE

21 Days In Jail
Magic Sam; *Chicago Boss Guitar* .... (PLA)
Alcatraz
Leon Russell; *& The Shelter People* .... (MCA)
Nazareth; *Razamanaz* ....(A&M)
All Tangled Up In Love
Gus Hardin & Earl Thomas Conley; *Collector's
Duets* ....(RCA)
  Wall Of Tears ....(RCA)
All Tied Up
Ronnie McDowell; *All Tied Up In Love* .... (MCC)
  Country Classics-#9-1984-1987 .... (MCA)
Allentown Jail
Jo Stafford; *International Hits* .... (CRN)
Kingston Trio; *Rediscover The* .... (FOL)
Another Brick In The Wall, Part 2
Pink Floyd; *Collection Of Great Dance Songs* ....(COL)
  Delicate Sound Of Thunder ....(COL)
  The Wall ....(COL)
Roger Waters; *The Wall Live In Berlin* .... (MER)
Attica State
John & Yoko Lennon; *Sometime In New York
City* ....(CAP)
Back On The Chain Gang
Pretenders; *Learning To Crawl* .... (SIR)
  Singles .... (SIR)
  ST/King Of Comedy .... (WB)
Back On The Street
Todd Rundgren/Utopia; *Jail* .... (VAN)
  Oops! Wrong Planet .... (RHI)
Ball And Chain
Paul Overstreet; *Heroes* ....(RCA)
Ball & Chain
Big Brother/Holding Company; *Cheap Thrills* ....(COL)
  Legends Of Rock Guitar-'60s-#1 .... (RHI)
  ST/Janis ....(COL)
Big Mama Thornton; *Ball & Chain* .... (ARH)
  Jail .... (VAN)
Dan Seals; *Greatest Hits* ....(CAP)
Elton John; *Jump Up* .... (GEF)
Janis Joplin; *Greatest Hits* ....(COL)
Behind These Prison Walls Of Love
Blue Sky Boys; *In Concert-1964* ....(ROU)
Country Gentlemen; *Folk Songs & Bluegrass* .... (FLW)
Peter Rowan; *All On A Rising Day* ....(SH)

Born In a Prison
John & Yoko Lennon/Others; *Sometime In New York
City* ....(CAP)
Break These Chains
Deborah Allen; *All That I Am* .... (GIA)
Broken Barricades
Procol Harum; *Procol Harum* .... (A&M)
Cage Of Freedom
Jon Anderson; *ST/Metropolis* ....(COL)
Cage The Songbird
Elton John; *Blue Moves* .... (MCA)
  Elton John ....(POL)
Can't Keep A Good Man Down
38 Special; *Special Delivery* .... (A&M)
Alabama; *Live* ....(RCA)
Caught Up In You
38 Special; *Flashback (The Best Of)* .... (A&M)
  Special Forces .... (A&M)
Chain Gang
Nylons; *Happy Together* ....(OPE)
Otis Redding; *Best Of* ....(ATC)
  Story ....(ATL)
Persuasions; *We Came To Play* ....(CAP)
Sam Cooke; *Best Of* ....(RCA)
  Man & His Music ....(RCA)
  Nipper's Greatest Hits-'60s-#1 ....(RCA)
Chain Of Fools
Aretha Franklin; *Aretha's Gold* .... (ATL)
  Atlantic R&B 1947-1974-#6 .... (ATL)
  Best Of .... (ATL)
  Gold .... (ATL)
  Greatest Hits .... (ATL)
  Lady Of Soul .... (ATL)
Clint Black & Pointer Sisters; *Rhythm Country &
Blues* .... (MCA)
Chained
Giant; *Time To Burn* .... (EPI)
Marvin Gaye; *Anthology* ....(MOT)
  I Heard It Through The Grapevine .... (MOT)
  Super Hits ....(MOT)
Chains
Beatles; *Early* ....(CAP)
  Please Please Me ....(CAP)
Carole King; *Pearls* ....(CAP)
Cookies; *45* .... (ERI)
Patty Loveless; *Greatest Hits* .... (MCA)
  Honky Tonk Angel .... (MCA)
Chains Around My Heart
Richard Marx; *Rush Street* ....(CAP)
Chains Of Gold
Sweethearts Of The Rodeo; *More Hot Country
Requests-#2* .... (EPI)
  Sweethearts Of The Rodeo ....(COL)
Chains Of Love
Big Joe Turner; *Greatest Hits* .... (ATL)
  In The Evening ....(PAB)
  Turns On The Blues ....(KNT)
Bobby Bland; *Introspective Of Early Years* .... (MCA)
  Spotlighting The Man .... (MCA)
Erasure; *Innocents* .... (SIR)
  Just So Yo-Volume 2 Of Just Say Yes .... (SIR)
Mickey Gilley; *Biggest Hits* .... (EPI)
  First Class ....(PBY)
Chain, The
Fleetwood Mac; *25 Years-The Chain* .... (WB)
  Rumours .... (WB)
Christmas In Prison
John Prine; *Sweet Revenge* .... (ATL)
Cincinnati Jail
Lonnie Mack; *Attack Of The Killer V* .... (ALG)
  Second Sight .... (ALG)
Columbus Stockade Blues
Doc Watson; *Memories* ....(UA)
Lenny Dee; *Best Of* .... (MCA)
Pete Fountain; *Best Of* .... (MCA)
Complete Control
Clash; *Clash* .... (EPI)
  Story Of-#1 .... (EPI)
Convict's Prayer
Li'l Wally; *One Man Band* ....(JJ)
Country Jail
Volumes; *I Love You-Golden Classics* .... (CLT)
Country Jail Blues
Eric Clapton; *No Reason To Cry* ....(RSO)

John T. Smith; *Original Howling Wolf* ....(YAZ)
Crumblin' Down
John Cougar Mellencamp; *Uh-Huh* ....(RIV)
Dark As A Dungeon
Johnny Cash; *At Folsom Prison & San Quentin* ...(COL)
  Essential ....(COL)
Maddox Brothers & Rose; *1946-1951-#1 & 2* .. (ARH)
Merle Travis; *Best Of* .... (RHI)
Nitty Gritty Dirt Band; *Will The Circle Be
Unbroken* .... (EMI)
Rose Maddox; *Rose Of The West Coast Country* (ARH)
Wall Of Voodoo; *Seven Days In Sammystown* ....(IRS)
Doin' Time
Justin Hayward; *Songwriter* ....(DER)
Meg Christian & Cris Williamson; *Meg-Cris At Carnegie
Hall* .... (SEC)
Spooner; *Every Corner Dance* ....(MOU)
  Wildest Dreams/Every Corner Dance ....(DAL)
Drifter's Escape
Bob Dylan; *John Wesley Harding* ....(COL)
Jimi Hendrix; *Lifelines/Story* ....(RPR)
Empty Cages
Dan Fogelberg; *Innocent Age* .... (FM)
Escape From The Island Of Living Puke
Zoogz Rift; *Island Of Living Puke* ....(SST)
Folsom Prison Blues
Brooks & Dunn & Johnny Cash; *Red Hot +
Country* .... (MER)
Johnny Cash; *At Folsom Prison & San Quentin* ...(COL)
  Billboard Top Country Hits-1968 ....(RHI)
  Classic Cash-Hall Of Fame Series ....(MER)
  Greatest Hits #2 ....(COL)
  Original Golden Hits #1 ....(SUN)
  Superbilly ....(SUN)
Fort Worth Jail
Tex Ritter; *Hillbilly Music...Thank God!-#1* ....(BUG)
Free Nelson Mandela
Special AKA; *In The Studio* .... (CHR)
Gimme Some Slack
Cars; *Panorama* .... (ELE)
Hurricane (Carter)
Bob Dylan; *Desire* ....(COL)
I Ain't Livin' Long Like This
Emmylou Harris; *Quarter Moon In A Ten-Cent
Town* .... (WB)
Rodney Crowell; *Collection* ....(WB)
  I Ain't Livin' Long Like This ....(WB)
Waylon Jennings; *Greatest Hits-#2* ....(RCA)
  What Goes Around Comes Around ....(RCA)
I Shall Be Released
Band; *Anthology-#1* ....(CAP)
  Last Waltz .... (WB)
  Music From Big Pink ....(CAP)
  To Kingdom Come-Definitive Collection ....(CAP)
Bette Midler; *Bette Midler* ....(ATL)
  ST/Divine Madness ....(ATL)
Bob Dylan; *At Budokan* ....(COL)
  Biograph ....(COL)
  Bootleg Series-#1-3 ....(COL)
  Greatest Hits-#2 ....(COL)
Bob Dylan/Band; *Before The Flood* ....(ASY)
Box Tops; *Greatest Hits* ....(RHI)
Flying Burrito Brothers; *Farther Along-Best Of* .. (A&M)
Joan Baez; *Any Day Now* .... (VAN)
  Carry It On .... (VAN)
  From Every Stage ....(A&M)
Joe Cocker; *With A Little Help From My Friends* (A&M)
Nina Simone; *Best Of* ....(RCA)
Rick Nelson; *In Concert-Troubadour-1969* ..... (MCA)
In The Jailhouse Now
Jimmie Rodgers; *First Sessions-1927-1928* ...... (ROU)
  Short But Brilliant Life ....(RCA)
  This Is ....(RCA)
Webb Pierce; *Best Of* ....(MCA)
  Golden Hits-#2 ....(PLN)
In The Jailhouse Now-#2
Jimmie Rodgers; *Legendary Performer* ....(RCA)
  My Rough & Rowdy Ways ....(RCA)
I'd Be Better Off (In A Pine Box)
Doug Stone; *Doug Stone* .... (EPI)
  Greatest Country Hits-'90s-1990 ....(COL)
I'll Kiss The World Goodbye
J.J. Cale; *Really* .... (MCA)

Jackson Cage
Bruce Springsteen; *The River* ....(COL)
Jailbait
Aerosmith; *Gems* ....(COL)
  Rock In A Hard Place ....(COL)
Nils Lofgren; *Cry Tough* ....(A&M)
Ted Nugent; *Intensities In 10 Cities* ....(EPI)
Jailbreak
Thin Lizzy; *Jailbreak* .... (MER)
  Live & Dangerous .... (WB)
  Lizzy Lives! 1976-1984 ....(GS)
Jailhouse Blues
Dinah Washington; *Bessie Smith Songbook* ...... (EMA)
Doc & Merle Watson; *Pickin' The Blues* .... (FF)
Sam Collins; *Jailhouse Blues* ....(YAZ)
Jailhouse Rock
Blues Brothers; *ST/Blues Brothers* .... (ATL)
Elvis Presley; *Billboard Top Rock 'N' Roll
Hits-1957* .... (RHI)
  Legendary Performer-#2 ....(RCA)
  Live On Stage ....(RCA)
  Number One Hits ....(RCA)
  Rocker ....(RCA)
  Worldwide 50 Gold Award Hits-#1 ....(RCA)
Jeff Beck; *Beck-Ola* ....(EPI)
Johnny 99
Bruce Springsteen; *Nebraska* ....(COL)
Bruce Springsteen/E Street Band;
Live-1975-1985 ....(COL)
Johnny Cash; *Cover Me* .... (RHI)
Laws Must Change
John Mayall; *Best Of* .... (POL)
  Turning Point .... (POL)
John Mayall/Bluesbreakers; *Behind The Iron
Curtain* .... (CRS)
Let Her Go
Mark Collie; *Hardin County Line* .... (MCA)
Life In Prison
Byrds; *Sweetheart Of The Rodeo* ....(COL)
Lonesome Jailhouse Blues
Aunt Molly Jackson; *Library Of Congress
Recordings* .... (ROU)
Mama Tried
Grateful Dead; *Grateful Dead* .... (WB)
John Anderson & Marty Stuart; *Mama's Hungry
Eyes-Merle Haggard Tribute* .... (ARI)
Merle Haggard/Strangers; *Best Of* ....(CAP)
  Okie From Muskogee ....(CAP)
  Songs I'll Always Sing ....(CAP)
  Very Best Of Merle Haggard ....(CAP)
Monterrey Pen
Marc Benno; *Lost In Austin* ....(A&M)
My Own Prison
Clarence "Gatemouth" Brown; *No Looking Back* (ALG)
My Song Bird
Emmylou Harris; *Quarter Moon In A Ten Cent
Town* .... (WB)
McCarters; *The Gift* .... (WB)
Never Gonna Give You Up
Rick Astley; *Whenever You Need Somebody* ......(RCA)
New Huntsville Jail
Joe Evans & John Dilleshaw; *Early Country Music* (HIS)
No Easy Way Out
Robert Tepper; *Rocky Story* ....(SCO)
  ST/Rocky IV ....(SCO)
No Way Out
Electric Light Orchestra; *Afterglow* .... (EPI)
Firefall; *Firefall* ....(ATL)
Jefferson Starship; *Nuclear Furniture* ....(GRU)
Oak Ridge Boys; *Monongahela* ....(MCA)
Restless Heart; *Big Dreams In A Small Town* ....(RCA)
Starship; *Greatest Hits (Ten Years & Change)* .....(RCA)
On Parole
Motorhead; *Motorhead* .... (ROA)
One Chain
Doobie Brothers; *Cycles* ....(CAP)
Santana; *Inner Secrets* ....(COL)
One Step Up
Bruce Springsteen; *Tunnel Of Love* ....(COL)
Padlock
Gwen Guthrie; *Island Story-1962-1987-25th
Anniversary* .... (ISL)
  Portrait .... (ISL)

Parchman Farm
John Mayall; *Bluesbreakers* ....(DER)
John Mayall/Bluesbreakers; *Behind The Iron*
Curtain) .... (CRS)
   Last Of The British Blues ....(MCA)
   London Collection/Bluesbreakers ....(LON)
Johnny Winter; *About Blues* ....(JNS)
   Before The Storm ....(JNS)
Mose Allison; *Greatest Hits* ....(PRS)
   Mose Allison ....(PRS)
Percy's Song
Arlo Guthrie; *Washington County* ....(RPR)
Bob Dylan; *Biograph* ....(COL)
Phone Call From Leavenworth
Chris Whitley; *Living With The Law* ....(COL)
Please Mr. Jailer
Wynona Carr; *Jump Jack Jump!* .... (SPE)
Please Take Me Out Of Jail
Fats Waller; *& His Buddies-1927-1929* ...... (BLU)
Prison Blues Come Down On Me
Lightnin' Hopkins; *Best Of* ....(TRD)
   Prison Blues-Golden Classics-#2 ....(CLT)
Prison Farm Blues
Lightnin' Hopkins; *Best Of* ....(PRS)
   Complete Prestige/Bluesville Recordings ....(BV)
   How Many More Years I Got ....(FAN)
Prison Sex
Tool; *Undertow* ....(ZOO)
Prison Song
Crosby, Stills & Nash; *Crosby, Stills & Nash*
(collection) .... (ATL)
Graham Nash; *Wild Tales* ....(ATL)
Prison Trilogy
Joan Baez; *Best Of* .... (A&M)
   Classics-#8 .... (A&M)
   Come From The Shadows ....(A&M)
Prisoner
Accept; *Eat The Heat* .... (EPI)
Dokken; *Back For The Attack* ....(ELE)
Howard Jones; *Cross That Line* ....(ELE)
Mariah Carey; *Mariah Carey* ....(COL)
Outlaws; *Bring It Back Alive* ....(ARI)
   Lady In Waiting ....(ARI)
Roger Daltrey; *One Of The Boys* ....(MCA)
Squeeze; *Classics-#25* ....(A&M)
Suicidal Tendencies; *Join The Army* ....(CRL)
Prisoner In Disguise
Linda Ronstadt; *Prisoner In Disguise* ....(ASY)
Prisoner Of Hope
Johnny Lee; *Greatest Hits* .... (FM)
Prisoner Of Love
Art Tatum; *Solo Masterpieces-#3* ....(PAB)
Bloodstone; *Greatest Hits* .... (TN)
Foreigner; *Very Best...And Beyond* ....(ATL)
Frank Sinatra; *Sinatra & Strings* ....(RPR)
James Brown; *Live At The Apollo-#2-Pt.2* ....(RHI)
Kiss; *Hot In The Shade* ....(MER)
Miami Sound Machine; *Eyes Of Innocence* ....(EPI)
Pat Benatar; *Crimes Of Passion* ....(CHR)
Perry Como; *Golden Records* ....(RCA)
   Nipper's Greatest Hits-'40s-#2 ....(RCA)
   Pure Gold ....(RCA)
   This Is ....(RCA)
Truth; *Jump* ....(IRS)
Prisoner Of The Highway
Ronnie Milsap; *Greatest Hits-#3* ....(RCA)
   One More Try For Love ....(RCA)
Prisoner Of Your Love
Player; *Danger Zone* ....(RSO)
Prisoner (Theme From Eyes Of Laura Mars)
Barbra Streisand; *Greatest Hits-#2* ....(COL)
   Prisoner (Theme From Eyes Of Laura Mars) ....(COL)
Prisoner's Song
Burl Ives; *Best Of* ....(MCA)
Vernon Dalhart; *Nipper's Greatest Hits-'20s* ......(RCA)
Put Me In That Dungeon
Charles Mingus; *Mingus Dynasty* ....(COL)
Rage In The Cage
J. Geils Band; *Freeze-Frame* .... (EMI)
Ragin' Cajun
Charlie Daniels Band; *Windows* ....(EPI)
Release Me
Dolly Parton; *Country & Western* ....(IMC)
Dolly Parton & Donna Fargo; *Queens Of Country* (INT)

Elvis Presley; *On Stage* ....(RCA)
   Welcome To My World ....(RCA)
Engelbert Humperdinck; *Greatest Hits* ....(PRT)
   Live In Concert/All Of Me ....(EPI)
   Release Me ....(PRT)
Esther Phillips; *Atlantic R&B*
1947-1974-#5-(1962-1966) ....(ATL)
   Billboard Top R&B Hits-1962 ....(RHI)
   Oldies But Goodies-#9 ....(OSR)
Kitty Wells; *Greatest Hits* ....(MCA)
   Story ....(MCA)
Lefty Frizzell; *Greatest Hits* ....(COL)
Meli'sa Morgan; *Still In Love With You* ....(PEN)
Ray Price; *Greatest Hits* ....(COL)
   Greatest Hits-#1 ....(SO)
Wilson Phillips; *Wilson Phillips* ....(SBK)
Riot In Cell Block #9
Blues Brothers; *Made In America* ....(ATL)
Coasters; *Greatest Recordings-Early Years* ....(ATC)
Commander Cody/Lost Planet Airmen; *Live From Deep*
In The Heart Of Texas ....(MCA)
   We've Got A Live One Here ....(WB)
Robins; *There's A Riot Goin' On! Rock Classics* .. (RHI)
Wanda Jackson; *Rockin' In The Country-Best Of* . (RHI)
Rock & A Hard Place
Rolling Stones; *Flashpoint* ....(RS)
   Steel Wheels ....(RS)
San Quentin
Johnny Cash; *At Folsom Prison & San Quentin* ...(COL)
   At San Quentin ....(COL)
   Columbia Records-1958-1986 ....(COL)
Serious Hold On Me
O'Jays; *Serious* .... (EMI)
Set Me Free (Rosa Lee)
Los Lobos; *By The Light Of The Moon* ....(SLS)
Shackles
R.J.'s Latest Arrival; *45* .... (QUA)
Shackles & Chains
Arlo Guthrie; *Hobo's Lullaby* ....(RPR)
Jimmie Davis; *Golden Hits* ....(PLN)
   Souvenirs Of Yesterday ....(PLN)
Shakin' The Cage
Zoo; *Shakin' The Cage* ....(CPC)
Slave
Elton John; *Honky Chateau* ....(POL)
Germs; *Germs* ....(SLS)
Rolling Stones; *Tattoo You* ....(RS)
Slave Driver
Bob Marley/Wailers; *Catch A Fire* ....(TUF)
   Rebel Music ....(TUF)
Taj Mahal; *Mo' Roots* ....(COL)
Slavery Days
Burning Spear; *24 Great Hits* ....(MGM)
   Live ....(COL)
   Marcus Garvey ....(ISL)
Slaves
Temptations; *Puzzle People* ....(MOT)
Snowbound
Genesis; *And Then There Were Three* ....(ATL)
Soul Cages
Sting; *Soul Cages* ....(A&M)
Starkville City Jail
Johnny Cash; *At Folsom Prison & San Quentin* ...(COL)
Still Doin' Time
George Jones; *Anniversary-Ten Years Of Hits* .....(EPI)
   By Request ....(EPI)
   Greatest Country Hits/'80s-1981 ....(COL)
Stuck Here Again
L7; *Hungry For Stink* ....(SLS)
Stuck In The Middle With You
Stealers Wheel; *Super Hits/'70s-Have A Nice*
Day-#10 .... (RHI)
Stuck Inside Of Mobile With The...
Bob Dylan; *Blonde On Blonde* ....(COL)
   Greatest Hits-#2 ....(COL)
   Hard Rain ....(COL)
Stuck On You
Elvis Presley; *Golden Records-#3* ....(RCA)
   Number One Hits ....(RCA)
   Return Of The Rocker ....(RCA)
   Worldwide 50 Gold Award Hits-#1 & 2 ....(RCA)
Lionel Richie; *Can't Slow Down* ....(MOT)
Stuck With You
Huey Lewis/News; *Fore!* ....(CHR)

Take These Chains
Lee Roy Parnell; *On The Road* .... (ARI)
Take These Chains From My Heart
Hank Williams; *24 Greatest Hits* .... (POL)
  40 Greatest Hits .... (POL)
Ray Charles; *His Greatest Hits-#2* ....(DHL)
Tangled In The Web
Lynch Mob; *Lynch Mob* .... (ELE)
Tangled Up In Blue
Bob Dylan; *Biograph* ....(COL)
  Blood On The Tracks ....(COL)
  Bootleg Series-#1-3-Rare & Unreleased ....(COL)
  Real Live ....(COL)
Teenage Jail
Eagles; *Long Run* .... (ASY)
Tender Trap (Love Is)
Frank Sinatra; *At The Movies* ....(CAP)
  Sings The Songs Of Van Heusen & Cahn ......(RPR)
Sammy Cahn; *Evening With* .... (DRG)
"The Prisoner" Theme
Neil Norman; *Greatest Science Fiction Hits* ...... (CRS)
There Ain't No Good Chain Gang
Johnny Cash & Waylon Jennings; *Country's Greatest-#15-Outlaw Country* .... (PRY)
  Hot Country Rock-#1 .... (EPI)
There's No Easy Way
James Ingram; *It's Your Night* .... (QUE)
  Power Of Great Music ....(WB)
Thirteen Years In Prison
Big Leon Brooks' Blues Harp Band; *Living Chicago Blues-#4* ....(ALG)
Thirty Days In The Hole
Humble Pie; *Best Of* ....(A&M)
  Classics-#14 ....(A&M)
  Smokin' ....(A&M)
Mr. Big; *Mr. Big* ....(ATL)
This Body Is A Prison
Spencer Bohren; *Live In New Orleans* .... (GSR)
Ties That Bind
Bruce Springsteen; *The River* ....(COL)
Tijuana Jail
Gilby Clarke; *Pawnshop Guitars* .... (VIA)
Kingston Trio; *25 Years Non-stop* ....(XER)
  Best Of ....(CAP)
  Capitol Collectors Series ....(CAP)
  Greatest Hits ....(CCB)
Too Many Walls
Cathy Dennis; *Move To This* .... (POL)
Tower Of London
ABC; *How To Be A Zillionaire* .... (MER)
Trapped
Bruce Springsteen/E Street Band; *We Are The World* ....(COL)
Trapped Again
Southside Johnny/Asbury Jukes; *Best Of* .... (EPI)
  Havin' A Party With ....(EPI)
  Hearts Of Stone ....(EPI)
Trapped In The Body Of A White Girl
Julie Brown; *Trapped In The Body Of A White Girl* (SIR)
Tupelo County Jail
Mel Tillis; *American Originals* ....(COL)
Webb Pierce; *Golden Hits* .... (PLN)
Turn Me Loose
Fabian; *Collectables Presents History Of Rock-#6* . (CLT)
  Good Time Rock 'N Roll .... (MCA)
  Teen Idols ....(RHI)
Loverboy; *Big Ones* ....(COL)
  Loverboy ....(COL)
Vince Gill; *Best Of* ....(RCA)
Unchain My Heart
Joe Cocker; *Live* ....(CAP)
  Unchain My Heart ....(CAP)
Ray Charles; *Anthology* .... (RHI)
  Greatest Hits-#1 ....(RHI)
  His Greatest hits-#1 ....(DHL)
Unchained
Van Halen; *Fair Warning* .... (WB)
Unchained Melody
Elvis Presley; *Always On My Mind* ....(RCA)
  Great Performances ....(RCA)
  Moody Blue ....(RCA)
George Benson; *Livin' Inside Your Love* .... (WB)
Platters; *Greatest Hits* ....(EVR)
  Red Sails In The Sunset ....(ALL)

Richard Clayderman; *Plays Love Songs Of The World* ....(COL)
Righteous Brothers; *Greatest Hits-#1* ....(VRV)
  ST/Ghost ....(VS)
Willie Nelson; *Stardust* ....(COL)
Velvet Chains
Gary Morris; *Hits* .... (WB)
  Swingin' Country Favorites .... (WB)
  Why Lady Why ....(WB)
Wall
Kansas; *Best Of* ....(EPA)
  Leftoverture .... (KIR)
  Two For The Show ....(KIR)
Walls Came Down
Call; *Modern Romans* ....(MER)
  Walls Came Down-Best Of Mercury Years .... (MER)
We Gotta Get Out Of This Place
Animals; *Best Of* ....(AKO)
  Greatest Hits Live! ....(IRS)
  Sullivan Years-British Invasion ....(TVT)
Fear; *The Record* ....(SLS)
White Bird
It's A Beautiful Day; *Bill Graham Presents-Fillmore-Last Days* ....(EPA)
  It's A Beautiful Day ....(COL)
Wichita Jail
Charlie Daniels Band; *Banded Together* .... (EPI)
  Saddle Tramp .... (EPI)
Willie Jones
Charlie Daniels Band; *Night Rider* ....(EPI)
  Renegade .... (EPI)
Working For The Clampdown
Clash; *London Calling* .... (EPI)
Wrapped Around Your Finger
Police; *Every Breath You Take-The Singles* ...... (A&M)
  Synchronicity ....(A&M)
You Keep Me Hangin' On
Diana Ross; *Evening With* .... (MOT)
Diana Ross/Supremes; *Anthology* .... (MOT)
  Motown Story ....(MOT)
Kim Wilde; *Another Step* ....(MCA)
Supremes; *Billboard Top R&B Hits-1965* .... (MOT)
  Greatest Hits-#2 ....(MOT)
Vanilla Fudge; *Best Of* ....(ATC)
  Vanilla Fudge ....(ATC)
Wilson Pickett; *Greatest Hits* ....(ATL)
  Man & A Half-Best Of ....(RHI)

PROSTITUTES, Pimps

See Also: Sex

Ain't No Free
NRBQ; *At Yankee Stadium* .... (MER)
Bad Girls
Donna Summer; *Bad Girls* ....(CAS)
  Dance Collection ....(CAS)
  On The Radio-Greatest Hits-#1 & 2 ....(CAS)
  Summer Collection ....(MER)
  Walk Away (Best Of 1977-1980) ....(CAS)
Bordello Night
City Boy; *Young Men Gone West* .... (MER)
Charlotte The Harlot
Iron Maiden; *Iron Maiden* ....(CAP)
Christmas Card From A Hooker...
Tom Waits; *Blue Valentine* .... (ASY)
Devil's Whorehouse
Misfits; *Walk Among Us* ....(RUB)
Edge
Danny O'Keefe; *Breezy Stories* .... (ATL)
Fancy Lady
Billy Preston; *It's My Pleasure* ....(OOP)
  The Best ....(A&M)
Gigolo
Damned; *Anything* ....(MCA)
O'Bryan; *Doin' Alright* ....(CAP)
Hey Negrita
Rolling Stones; *Black & Blue* .... (RS)
He's A Whore
Cheap Trick; *Cheap Trick* .... (EPI)
Honky Tonk Women
Elton John; *11-17-70* .... (POL)

Humble Pie; *Best* .... (A&M)
  Classics-#14 .... (A&M)
  Eat It .... (A&M)
Ike & Tina Turner; *Best Of* .... (EMI)
  Get Back .... (LIB)
Joe Cocker; *Mad Dogs & Englishmen* .... (A&M)
Rolling Stones; *Get Yer Ya-Ya's Out* .... (AKO)
  Hot Rocks-1964-1971 .... (AKO)
  Love You Live .... (RS)
  Through The Past Darkly-Big Hits-#2 .... (AKO)
Willie Nelson & Leon Russell; *Half Nelson* ...... (COL)
Hooker
Tom Paxton; *Morning After* .... (ELE)
Hotel California
Al B. Sure!; *Private Times & The Whole 9* ...... (WB)
Eagles; *Anthology* .... (ASY)
  Greatest Hits-#2 .... (ASY)
  Hell Freezes Over .... (GEF)
  Hotel California .... (ASY)
  Live .... (ASY)
Gipsy Kings; *Rubaiyat-Elektra's 40th Anniversary* (ELE)
House Of Flowers
Barbra Streisand; *Just For The Record* .... (COL)
Harold Arlen & Barbra Streisand; *Harold Sings Arlen*
  (With Friend) .... (SSP)
  Original Cast; *House Of Flowers* .... (SSP)
House Of The Rising Sun
Animals; *Best Of* .... (AKO)
  Greatest Hits .... (ALL)
  Rip It To Shreds-Greatest Hits Live .... (IRS)
Hank Williams, Jr.; *Hank Live* .... (W/C)
Ronnie Milsap; *16 Greatest Hits-#2* .... (TRP)
I'm Watching You
Daryl Hall & John Oates; *War Babies* .... (ATL)
I'm Your Late Night Evening Prostitute
Tom Waits; *Early Years* .... (BIZ)
Josie
Steely Dan; *Aja* .... (MCA)
  Greatest Hits .... (MCA)
Ladies Of The Night
Leon Russell; *Americana* .... (PRD)
Lady In Red
Charlie Daniels Band; *Windows* .... (EPI)
Chris DeBurgh; *Into The Light* .... (A&M)
Joan Jett/Blackhearts; *I Love Rock 'N' Roll* ...... (BW)
Stan Getz; *Greatest Hits* .... (PRS)
Lady Marmalade
Labelle; *Nightbirds* .... (EPI)
Patti Labelle; *Best Of* .... (EPI)
Sheila E.; *Sex Cymbal* .... (WB)
Lady's Not For Sale
Rita Coolidge; *Lady's Not For Sale* .... (A&M)
Little Sally, The Super Sex Star
Camille Yarborough; *Iron Pot Cooker* .... (VAN)
Louise
Bonnie Raitt; *Collection* .... (WB)
  Sweet Forgiveness .... (WB)
Leo Kottke; *Greenhouse* .... (CAP)
  My Feet Are Smiling .... (CAP)
  Very Best Of .... (CAP)
Linda Ronstadt; *Retrospective* .... (CAP)
  Silk Purse .... (CAP)
Paul Siebel; *Woodsmoke & Oranges* .... (ELE)
Naughty Lady Of Shady Lane
Ames Brothers; *Best Of The* .... (RCA)
  Nipper's Greatest Hits-'50s-#2 .... (RCA)
No Other Name
Peter, Paul & Mary; *Album 1700* .... (WB)
Nutbush City Limits
Bob Seger; *Beautiful Loser* .... (CAP)
  Live Bullet .... (CAP)
Ike & Tina Turner; *Best Of* .... (EMI)
  Proud Mary-Best Of .... (EMI)
  Simply The Best .... (CAP)
Tina Turner; *Live In Europe* .... (CAP)
One More Time Around Rosie
Manhattan Transfer; *Jukin'* .... (CAP)
Painted Ladies
Ian Thomas; *45* .... (JNS)
Pearl Of The Quarter
Steely Dan; *Countdown To Ecstasy* .... (MCA)
Pimp
Tubes; *Young & Rich* .... (A&M)

Pimp Behind The Wheels
Ice-T; *Home Invasion* .... (RHS)
Pimp Lane
Penthouse Players Clique; *Paid The Cost* .... (RUP)
Pimp Mentality
Who Am I; *Addictive Hip Hop Muzick* .... (RUT)
Pimp Of The Nation
Kid Rock; *Grits Sandwiches For Breakfast* ...... (JVA)
Pimp Of The Year
D-Nice; *Call Me D-Nice* .... (JVA)
Pimp Or Die
Father M.C.; *ST/Who's The Man?* .... (UT)
Pimp Posse
Cargo Cult; *Strange Men Bearing Gifts* .... (T&G)
Pimp The Ho
Too $hort; *Life Is...Too Short (Dirty Version)* ..... (JVA)
Pimpin' Ain't Easy
Big Daddy Kane; *It's A Big Daddy Thing* .... (CLD)
Pimpology
Too $hort; *Short Dog's In The House (Clean*
  Version) .... (JVA)
Red Light Mama Red Hot
Humble Pie; *Humble Pie* .... (A&M)
Roll 'Em Easy
Linda Ronstadt; *Prisoner In Disguise* .... (ASY)
Little Feat; *Dixie Chicken* .... (WB)
Roxanne
Police; *Every Breath You Take-Singles* .... (A&M)
  Outlandos D'Amour .... (A&M)
Sting; *Secret Policeman's Other Ball* .... (ISL)
She Sells
Roxy Music; *Siren* .... (RPR)
Spanish Moon
Little Feat; *Feats Don't Fail Me Now* .... (WB)
  Waiting For Columbus .... (WB)
Robert Palmer; *Some People Can Do What They*
  Like .... (ISL)
Star Spangled Bummer (Whores Die Hard)
Kris Kristofferson; *Spokey Lady's Sideshow* ...... (COL)
Star Whores
Christ Child; *Hard* .... (BUD)
Street Walker
Band; *Islands* .... (CAP)
Ian Akkerman; *Ian Akkerman* .... (ATL)
Sugar Shack
Jimmy Gilmer/Fireballs; *Billboard Top Rock 'N' Roll*
  Hits-1963 .... (RHD)
  Golden Years-1963 .... (DOM)
  Good Old Rock & Roll .... (GUS)
Sweet Painted Lady
Elton John; *Goodbye Yellow Brick Road* .... (POL)
Teenage Prostitute
Frank Zappa; *Ship Arriving Too Late To Save...* .. (BAR)
Teenage Whore
Hole; *Pretty On The Inside* .... (CRL)
Telephone Girl
Eddie/Hot Rods; *Life On The Line* .... (ISL)
Jade Warriors; *Jade Warriors* .... (VTG)
Texas Has A Whorehouse In It
Dom Deluise/Dogettes; *ST/Best Little Whorehouse In*
  Texas .... (MCA)
Original Cast; *Best Little Whorehouse In Texas* .. (MCA)
Thanks To The Cat House...
Johnny Paycheck; *Armed & Crazy* .... (EPI)
To Kill A Hooker
N.W.A.; *Efil4zaggin* .... (RUP)
Treat Her Like A Prostitute
Slick Rick; *Great Adventures Of* .... (DFC)
Whore
Bay Of Pigs; *Plastic Pig* .... (CML)
Whore Said It's Yours
Threat; *Sickinnahead* .... (MER)
Whores
Jane's Addiction; *Jane's Addiction* .... (XXX)
Whores Of Paris
Bernie Taupin; *He Who Rides The Tiger* .... (ASY)
Whore's Lament
Hedy West; *Welcome To Caffe Lena* .... (BIO)
Wife & The Whore
Kristin Lems; *Born A Woman* .... (FF)
Willie The Pimp
Frank Zappa; *Hot Rats* .... (RYK)
  You Can't Do That On Stage Anymore-#4 ...... (RYK)

Mothers Of Invention; *Fillmore East-June 1971* .. (RPR)

PROTEST, Revolution

See Also: CRIME, FIGHT, FREEDOM,
POLITICAL CLASSICS, PREJUDICE, WAR

Africa Unite
Bob Marley/Wailers; *Survival* .... (ISL)
Alice's Restaurant Massacree
Arlo Guthrie; *Alice's Restaurant Massacree* .... (RPR)
   Best Of .... (WB)
Anarchy In The U.K.
Megadeth; *So Far So Good So What* .... (CAP)
Sex Pistols; *Never Mind The Bollocks* .... (WB)
Another Brick In The Wall, Part 2
Pink Floyd; *Collection Of Great Dance Songs* ....(COL)
   Delicate Sound Of Thunder .... (COL)
   The Wall .... (COL)
Roger Waters; *The Wall Live In Berlin* .... (MER)
Banned In The U.S.A.
Luke Skyywalker; *Banned In The U.S.A.* .... (LUK)
Body Count
Ice-T; *Body Count* .... (WB)
Children Of The Revolution
Violent Femmes; *Blind Leading The Naked* .... (SLS)
Dissident
Pearl Jam; *Vs.* .... (EPA)
Don't Give Up
Peter Gabriel; *Shaking The Tree-16 Golden*
  Greats .... (GEF)
   So .... (GEF)
Don't Take No For An Answer
Tom Robinson; *Power In The Darkness* .... (HAR)
Equal Rights
Peter Tosh; *Equal Rights* ....(COL)
Fight The Power
Isley Brothers; *Forever Gold* .... (TN)
   Greatest Hits-#1 .... (TN)
   Heat Is On .... (TN)
   Story-#2 .... (RHI)
Public Enemy; *Def Jam Classics-#2* .... (DFJ)
   Fear Of A Black Planet .... (DFJ)
   ST/Do The Right Thing .... (MOT)
Free Nelson Mandela
Special AKA; *In The Studio* .... (CHR)
Free South Africa
Kinsey Report; *Midnight Drive* ....(ALG)
Tackhead; *Friendly As A Hand Grenade* .... (TVT)
Get Up
Kinks; *Misfits* .... (ARI)
Get Up, Stand Up
Bob Marley/Wailers; *Burnin'* .... (TUF)
   Legend .... (TUF)
   Live .... (TUF)
   Rebel Music .... (TUF)
   Songs Of Freedom .... (TUF)
Peter Tosh; *Captured Live* .... (EMI)
   Equal Rights ....(COL)
   Rhythm Come Forward ....(COL)
Grown Up Wrong
Rolling Stones; *12 x 5* .... (AKO)
Harder They Come
Jimmy Cliff; *Harder They Come* .... (ISL)
   In Concert-Best Of .... (RPR)
   Island Story-25th Anniversary .... (ISL)
Hey Joe
Jimi Hendrix; *Essential-#2* .... (RPR)
   Live At Winterland .... (RYK)
   Smash Hits .... (RPR)
Jimi Hendrix Experience; *Are You Experienced?* . (RPR)
Love; *Best Of* .... (RHI)
I Ain't Gonna Stand For It
Stevie Wonder; *Hotter Than July* .... (MOT)
I Ain't Marchin' Anymore
Phil Ochs; *Chords Of Fame* .... (A&M)
   War Is Over-Best Of .... (A&M)
I'd Love To Change The World
Ten Years After; *A Space In Time* .... (CHR)
   Classic Performances Of ....(COL)
   Universal .... (CHR)
Johnny Too Bad
John Martyn; *Foundations* .... (ISL)

Lords Of The New Church; *Nothing's Sacred* ..... (IRS)
Slickers; *ST/The Harder They Come* .... (MGO)
Taj Mahal; *Best Of-#1* ....(COL)
   Mo' Roots ....(COL)
UB40; *Labour Of Love* .... (A&M)
   Live In Moscow .... (A&M)
La Marseillaise
Mormon Tabernacle Choir; *THis Is My Country* .(COL)
My Generation
Who; *Greatest Hits* .... (MCA)
   Live At Leeds .... (MCA)
   Meaty Beaty Big & Bouncy .... (MCA)
   Sings My Generation .... (MCA)
   ST/Kids Are Alright .... (MCA)
No No No To Draft & War
Minutemen; *Ballot Result* ....(SST)
Ohio
Crosby, Stills & Nash; *Crosby Stills & Nash*
  (collection) .... (ATL)
Crosby, Stills, Nash & Young; *Four-Way Street* .. (ATL)
   So Far .... (ATL)
Neil Young; *Decade* .... (RPR)
   ST/Journey Through The Past .... (RPR)
Peace For South Africa
Oscar Peterson Trio; *Live At The Blue Note* ...... (TLR)
Power In The Darkness
Tom Robinson Band; *Power In The Darkness* ... (HAR)
Power To The People
John Lennon; *Lennon* .... (CAP)
   Shaved Fish .... (CAP)
Reggae Revolution
Ziggy Marley/Melody Makers; *Hey World!* ...... (EMI)
   Time Has Come...Best Of .... (EMI)
Revolution
Beatles; *1967-1970* .... (CAP)
   Box Set .... (CAP)
   Hey Jude .... (CAP)
   Past Masters-#2 .... (CAP)
   Rock & Roll Music-#2 .... (CAP)
   ST/Imagine-The Motion Picture .... (CAP)
Bob Marley/Wailers; *Natty Dread* .... (ISL)
Cult; *Love* .... (SIR)
Pretenders; *Last Of The Independents* .... (SIR)
Teena Marie; *It Must Be Magic* .... (MOT)
Revolution 1
Beatles; *Box Set* .... (CAP)
   White Album .... (CAP)
Revolution Blues
Neil Young; *On The Beach* .... (RPR)
Revolution Calling
Queensryche; *Operation: Mindcrime* .... (EMI)
Revolution Rock
Clash; *London Calling* .... (EPI)
Revolution Will Not Be Televised
Gil Scott-Heron; *Gil ScoRevolution Will Not Be*
  Televised-Heron .... (BLU)
   Pieces Of A Man ....(OOP)
Revolutionary Generation
Public Enemy; *Fear Of A Black Planet* .... (DFJ)
Revolutionary Words
Mutabaruka; *Mystery Unfolds* .... (SHA)
Ringing Of Revolution
Phil Ochs; *There But For Fortune* .... (ELE)
Riot Act
Elvis Costello; *Girls Girls Girls* ....(COL)
Elvis Costello/Attractions; *Get Happy!* ....(RYK)
Skid Row; *Slave To The Grind* .... (ATL)
Riot In Cell Block #9
Blues Brothers; *Made In America* .... (ATL)
Coasters; *Greatest Recordings-Early Years* .... (ATL)
Commander Cody/Lost Planet Airmen; *Live From Deep*
  In The Heart Of Texas .... (MCA)
   We've Got A Live One Here .... (WB)
Robins; *There's A Riot Goin' On! Rock Classics* .. (RHI)
Wanda Jackson; *Rockin' In The Country-Best Of* . (RHI)
Saturday Night Special
Lynyrd Skynyrd; *Gold & Platinum* .... (MCA)
   Nuthin' Fancy .... (MCA)
   One More From The Road .... (MCA)
   Skynyrd's Innyrds .... (MCA)
Terry McBride/Ride; *Skynyrd Frynds* .... (MCA)
Say It Loud I'm Black & I'm Proud
Afrika Bambaataa; *Decade Of Darkness* .... (EMI)

James Brown; *Billboard Top R&B
Hits-1965-1969* .... (RHI)
Something In The Air
Thunderclap Newman; *History Of British
Rock-#9* .... (MCA)
   Hollywood Dream .... (MCA)
   ST/Strawberry Statement .... (MCA)
Stand
Sly/Family Stone; *10 Years Too Soon* .... (EPI)
   Anthology .... (EPI)
   Greatest Hits .... (EPI)
Stand Up & Fight Back
Jimmy Cliff; *Give Thanx* .... (WB)
Street Fighting Man
Rod Stewart; *Best Of* .... (MER)
   Sing It Again Rod .... (MER)
   Storyteller-Complete Anthology-1964-1990 ...... (WB)
Rolling Stones; *Beggars Banquet* .... (AKO)
   Get Yer Ya-Ya's Out .... (AKO)
   Hot Rocks-1964-1971 .... (AKO)
   Singles Collection-London Years .... (AKO)
   Through The Past Darkly-Big Hits-#2 .... (AKO)
Student Demonstration Time
Beach Boys; *Surf's Up* ....(CAR)
Stupid, Stupid War
D.R.I.; *Dealing With It* .... (MET)
Tiananmen Square
Blazing Redheads; *Crazed Women* .... (REF)
United We Stand
Brotherhood Of Man; *Super Hits/'70s-Have A Nice
Day-#2* .... (RHI)
Mike Curb Congregation; *Greatest Hits* ....(CCB)
Untitled Protest
Country Joe/Fish; *Life & Times Of* .... (VAN)
   Together .... (VAN)
Volunteers
Jefferson Airplane; *2400 Fulton Street-Anthology* (RCA)
   Flight Log 1966-1976 .... (GRU)
   ST/Forrest Gump .... (EPX)
   ST/Woodstock .... (ATL)
   Volunteers .... (RCA)
   Worst Of .... (RCA)
   "White Rabbit" & Other Hits .... (RCA)
War
Bruce Springsteen/E Street Band;
Live-1975-1985 ....(COL)
Edwin Starr; *Billboard Top Rock 'N' Roll
Hits-1970* .... (RHI)
   Motown Superstar Series-#3 .... (MOT)
   Soul Hits/'70s-#3 .... (RHI)
   War & Peace .... (MOT)
Warsaw 1943 (I Never Betrayed The...)
Johnny Clegg/Savuka; *Cruel, Crazy, Beautiful
World* ....(CAP)
Wat About Di Workin' Class?
Linton Kwesi Johnson; *In Concert With The Dub
Band* .... (SHA)
We Shall Overcome
James Cleveland/Troubadors; *James
Cleveland/Troubadors* .... (SAV)
Joan Baez; *Carry It On* .... (VAN)
   In Concert .... (VAN)
Pete Seeger; *Bitter & The Sweet* .... (MOB)
   Greatest Hits ....(COL)
We're Not Gonna Take It
Twisted Sister; *Big Hits & Nasty Cuts* .... (ATL)
   Stay Hungry .... (ATL)
Who; *Join Together* .... (MCA)
   ST/Woodstock .... (ATL)
   Tommy .... (MCA)
Whitey On The Moon
Gil Scott-Heron; *Whitey On The Moon* .... (BLU)
Your Flag Decal Won't Get You Into...
John Prine; *John Prine* .... (ATL)
Your Generation
Generation X; *Generation X* .... (CHR)
   Perfect Hits-1975-1981 .... (CHR)

QUEENS, Princesses
See Also: KINGS, ROYALTY

Acid Queen
Ike & Tina Turner; *Best Of* .... (EMI)
   Proud Mary-Best Of .... (EMI)
Who; *Join Together* .... (MCA)
   Tommy .... (MCA)
African Queen
Ali Thompson; *Take A Little Rhythm* .... (A&M)
Alaskan Queen
Joe Hackney; *Heavy Hitter* .... (HH)
Arcade Queen
Rubinoos; *Back To The Drawing Board* .... (BES)
Backstage Queen
Scorpions; *Best Of* ....(RCA)
   Tokyo Tapes ....(RCA)
   Virgin Killer ....(RCA)
Ballad Of A Teenage Queen
Johnny Cash; *Johnny Cash* .... (SUN)
   Original Golden Hits-#2 .... (SUN)
   ST/Harper Valley PTA .... (SUN)
   Sun Years .... (RHI)
   The Legend .... (PLN)
Beauty Queen
Roxy Music; *For Your Pleasure-Second Album* ... (RPR)
Black Queen
Crosby, Stills & Nash; *Crosby, Stills & Nash* ..... (ATL)
Jimmy Cliff; *Unlimited* .... (RPR)
Stephen Stills; *Stephen Stills* .... (ATL)
Caribbean Queen
Billy Ocean; *Greatest Hits* .... (JVA)
   Suddenly .... (JVA)
Celestial The Queen
Blue Oyster Cult; *Spectres* ....(COL)
Cleopatra, Queen Of Denial
Pam Tillis; *Homeward Looking Angel* .... (ARI)
Cleopatra's Cat
Spin Doctors; *Turn It Upside Down* .... (EPI)
Colorado Queenie
Little David Wilkins; *20 Great Hits* .... (PLN)
Dancing Queen
Abba; *Arrival* ....(ATL)
   Greatest Hits-#2 .... (ATL)
   Live .... (ATL)
   Singles (First Ten Years) .... (ATL)
Death Of Queen Jane
Joan Baez; *Joan Baez* .... (VAN)
   Love Song Album .... (VAN)
Diana
Eugene Wilde; *Serenade* .... (PHL)
Paul Anka; *21 Golden Hits* ....(RCA)
   21 Legendary Superstars .... (OSR)
   Billboard Top Rock 'N' Roll Hits-1957 .... (RHI)
Dime Queen Of Nevada
Tom Jones; *Darlin'* .... (MER)
Ethelene (The Truckstop Queen)
Ray Stevens; *I Never Made A Record I Didn't
Like* .... (MCA)
God Save The Queen
Anthrax; *Armed & Dangerous* .... (MEG)
Queen; *A Night At The Opera* ....(HOL)
   Live Killers ....(HOL)
Sex Pistols; *Never Mind The Bollocks* .... (WB)
Gypsy Queen
Santana; *Abraxas* ....(COL)
   Lotus ....(COL)
   Moonflower ....(COL)
Van Morrison; *Van Morrison-His Band & Street
Choir* .... (WB)
Her Majesty
Beatles; *Abbey Road* ....(CAP)
Her Royal Majesty
James Darren; *45* ....(ERI)
High Fashion Queen
Flying Burrito Brothers; *Last Of The Red Hot
Burritos* ....(A&M)
Homecoming Queen's Got A Gun
Julie Brown; *Dr. Demento Greatest Novelty
Records-#5* .... (RHI)
   Teenage Tragedies .... (RHI)
   Trapped In The Body Of A White Girl .... (SIR)

Killer Queen
Queen; *Greatest Hits* ....(HOL)
  Live Killers ....(HOL)
  Sheer Heart Attack ....(HOL)
King & Queen
Moody Blues; *Caught Live Plus Five* .... (POL)
King & Queen Of America
Eurythmics; *Greatest Hits* .... (ARI)
  We Too Are One .... (ARI)
King & Queen Of England
Sandy Denny; *Circle Dance-Hokey Pokey Charity Comp.* ....(GRE)
Kings & Queens
Aerosmith; *Classics Live* ....(COL)
  Draw The Line ....(COL)
  Greatest Hits ....(COL)
Little Queen
Heart; *Little Queen* ....(POR)
Little Queenie
Chuck Berry; *Chess Box* .... (CSS)
  Rock & Roll Rarities .... (CSS)
Jerry Lee Lewis; *Original Golden Hits-#1* .... (SUN)
  Rockin' R&B ....(SUN)
Rolling Stones; *Get Yer Ya-Ya's Out* .... (AKO)
R.E.O. Speedwagon; *Live-You Get What You Play For* ....(EPI)
  R.E.O./Two ....(EPI)
Lost Queen
Shok Paris; *Steel & Starlight* .... (IRS)
Mary Queen Of Arkansas
Bruce Springsteen; *Greetings From Asbury Park, N.J.* ....(COL)
Memphis Queen
Southern Pacific; *County Line* ....(WB)
Mississippi Queen
Mountain; *Best Of* ....(COL)
  Heavy Metal Memories .... (RHI)
  Twin Peaks ....(COL)
Mother The Queen Of My Heart
Pete Seeger & Arlo Guthrie; *Together In Concert* (RPR)
Movie Queen
Bill Anderson; *Scorpio* .... (MCA)
Prolifics; *45* .... (UA)
Pearly Queen
Dave Mason; *Certified Live* ....(COL)
  Very Best Of .... (MCA)
Traffic; *Traffic* .... (ISL)
Planet Queen
T. Rex; *Electric Warrior* .... (RPR)
Powder Blue Mercedes Queen
Paul Revere/Raiders; *Legend Of* ....(COL)
Pretty Princess
Loggins & Messina; *Native Sons* ....(COL)
Princess
Elton John; *Jump Up!* .... (MCA)
Princess Leia's Theme
John Williams; *ST/Star Wars* .... (POL)
Princess Of The Dawn
Accept; *Compilation* ....(POR)
  Restless & Wild ....(POR)
  Staying A Life .... (EPI)
Queen Bee
Barbra Streisand; *ST/Star Is Born* ....(COL)
Grand Funk Railroad; *ST/Heavy Metal* .... (FM)
John Lee Hooker; *Greatest Hits Of* ....(KNT)
Koko Taylor; *Queen Of The Blues* ....(ALG)
Taj Mahal; *Evolution* ....(WB)
Queen Bitch
David Bowie; *Hunky Dory* ....(RYK)
Queen For A Day
Bobby Bland; *Best Of-#2* .... (MCA)
  Call On Me .... (MCA)
  Tell Mr. Bland .... (MCA)
Donna Summer; *Once Upon A Time* .... (CAS)
Queen Jane Approximately
Bob Dylan; *Highway 61 Revisited* ....(COL)
Bob Dylan/Grateful Dead; *Dylan & The Dead* ...(COL)
Frankie Valli/Four Seasons; *Sing Big Hits By Bacharach/David/Dylan* .... (RHI)
Queen Lucy
Original Cast; *You're A Good Man Charlie Brown* ....(POL)
Queen Of Freedom
Joan Baez; *In Concert* .... (VAN)

Queen Of Hearts
Dave Edmunds; *Best Of* .... (SS)
  Repeat When Necessary .... (SS)
Gregg Allman; *Laid Back* ....(POL)
Joan Baez; *Ballad Book* .... (VAN)
  In Concert .... (VAN)
Juice Newton; *All-Time Country Classics-#2* .....(CAP)
  Greatest Hits ....(CAP)
  Greatest Hits & More ....(CAP)
  Juice ....(CAP)
Rodney Crowell; *Collection* ....(WB)
Whitesnake; *Snakebite* ....(GEF)
Queen Of Hollywood High
John Stewart; *Blondes* .... (ALL)
Queen Of Las Vegas
B-52's; *Whammy* ....(WB)
Queen Of Memphis
Confederate Railroad; *Confederate Railroad* .....(ATL)
Queen Of My Double Wide Trailer
Sammy Kershaw; *Haunted Heart* .... (MER)
Queen Of My Heart
DeBarge; *In A Special Way* .... (MOT)
Hank Williams, Jr.; *Greatest Hits-#2* ....(W/C)
  Man Of Steel ....(W/C)
Rene & Ray; *History Of Latino Rock-#1* .... (RHI)
Queen Of Siam
Holy Moses; *Queen Of Siam* ....(GWR)
Queen Of Spades
Styx; *Pieces Of Eight* ....(A&M)
Queen Of Sydney
Oregon; *Crossing* .... (ECM)
Queen Of Tears
Gladys Knight/Pips; *Every Beat Of My Heart/Greatest Hits* .... (CML)
Queen Of The Broken Hearts
Loverboy; *Keep It Up* ....(COL)
Queen Of The Cowboy Cafe
Si Kahn; *Home* ....(FF)
Queen Of The Forest
Ted Nugent; *Ted Nugent* .... (EPI)
Queen Of The Highway
Doors; *Morrison Hotel* ....(ELE)
Queen Of The Hop
Bobby Darin; *Story* ....(ATC)
Dave Edmunds; *ST/Porky's Revenge* ....(COL)
Dion; *Sings The Hits Of The '50s & '60s* ....(LAU)
Queen Of The Hours
Electric Light Orchestra; *No Answer* ....(JET)
Queen Of The House
Diana Ross/Supremes; *At The Copa* .... (MOT)
Jody Miller; *45* ....(CAP)
Queen Of The Jungle
Zarkons; *Riders In The Long Black Parade* .... (ENI)
Queen Of The Night
Whitney Houston; *ST/The Bodyguard* .... (ARI)
Queen Of The Nile
Dangerous Toys; *Dangerous Toys* ....(COL)
Queen Of The Reich
Queensryche; *Queensryche* .... (EMI)
Queen Of The Senior Prom
Mills Brothers; *Best Of* .... (MCA)
Queen Of The Silver Dollar
Dave & Sugar; *Greatest Hits* ....(RCA)
Dr. Hook; *& The Medicine Show Revisited* ....(COL)
Emmylou Harris; *Pieces Of The Sky* ....(RPR)
Queen Of The Underground
Michael Franks; *Skin Dive* .... (WB)
Queen Of The U.S.A.
Thompson Twins; *Big Trash* .... (RE)
Queen & Country
Jethro Tull; *War Child* .... (CHR)
Queens Of Noise
Runaways; *Queens Of Noise* .... (MER)
Queen's Suite
Duke Ellington; *Best of* .... (PAB)
  Ellington Suites .... (PAB)
Queen's Tattoos
Aztec Camera; *High Land Hard Rain* .... (SIR)
Rock & Roll Queen
Mott The Hoople; *Ballad Of Mott* ....(COL)
  Mott The Hoople ....(ATL)
Roller Derby Queen
Jim Croce; *Life & Times* ....(OOP)
  Photographs & Memories-His Greatest Hits .... (21)

Teenage Queen
Rick Derringer; *All-American Boy* .... (BS)
Truck Driver's Queen
Willis Brothers; *45* .... (STR)
Tulsa Queen
Emmylou Harris; *Luxury Liner* .... (WB)
Victoria
Kinks; *Arthur Or The Decline & Fall...* .... (RPR)
Kink Kronikles .... (RPR)
White Queen
Queen; *#2* ....(HOL)

QUESTIONS

Ain't It Crazy
Lightnin' Hopkins; *Hootin' The Blues* .... (PRS)
Lightnin' .... (ARH)
Ain't It Heavy
Melissa Etheridge; *Never Enough* .... (ISL)
Ain't Life Hell
Hank Cochran; *Hank Cochran* .... (CAP)
Ain't That Good News
David "Fathead" Newman; *Bigger & Better-Many Facets
Of* .... (RHI)
Ain't Your Memory Got No Pride?
Merle Haggard; *Ramblin' Fever* .... (MCA)
Am I Blue
Barbara Streisand; *ST/Funny Lady* .... (ARI)
Billie Holiday; *God Bless The Child* ....(COL)
George Strait; *Country Classics-#11-1987-1988* . (MCA)
Greatest Hits-#2 .... (MCA)
MCA #1 Hits Of The '80s-#3 .... (MCA)
Ocean Front Property .... (MCA)
Ray Charles; *Genius Of* .... (ATL)
Am I Ever Going To Change
Extreme; *III Sides To Every Story* .... (A&M)
Am I High
Asleep At The Wheel; *Served Live* .... (CAP)
Am I In Heaven
Del Reeves; *45* ....(OOP)
Am I The Same Girl
Swing Out Sister; *Get In Touch With Yourself* ... (MER)
Anybody Listening?
Queensryche; *Empire* .... (EMI)
Anyone For Tennis
Cream; *Eric Clapton-Crossroads* .... (POL)
Strange Brew-Very Best Of Cream .... (POL)
Are The Good Times Really Over
Merle Haggard; *Big City* .... (EPI)
Greatest Country Hits-'80s-1982 ....(COL)
His Epic Hits-The First 11 .... (EPI)
Are The Roses Not Blooming
Judds; *Love Can Build A Bridge* ....(RCA)
Are There Any Cowboys Left...
Lacy J. Dalton; *Lacy J. Dalton* ....(COL)
Are There Any More Real Cowboys
Willie Nelson & Neil Young; *Half Nelson* ....(COL)
Are We Making Love Or Making Friends
Moe Bandy; *Soft Lights & Hard Country Music* ..(COL)
Are We Ourselves
Fixx; *One Thing Leads To Another-Greatest Hits* (MCA)
React .... (MCA)
Are You Building A Temple In Heaven
Hank Williams; *I'm So Lonesome I Could
Cry-1949* .... (POL)
Are You Crazy
Freddie McGregor; *Come On Over* .... (RAS)
Are You Experienced?
Jimi Hendrix; *Kiss The Sky* .... (RPR)
Jimi Hendrix Experience; *Are You Experienced?* . (RPR)
Essential .... (RPR)
Are You Gonna Go My Way
Lenny Kravitz; *Are You Gonna Go My Way* ..... (VIA)
Are You Happy Baby?
Dottie West; *Best Of* .... (E/L)
Are You Hung Up
Mothers Of Invention; *We're Only In It For The
Money* ....(RYK)
Are You Lonely For Me
Rude Boys; *Rude Awakening* .... (ATL)
Are You Lovin' Me Like I'm Lovin' You
Ronnie Milsap; *Back To The Grindstone* ....(RCA)

Are You On The Road To Lovin' Me Again
Debby Boone; *Best Of* ....(CRB)
Are You Ready For The Sex Girls
Gleaming Spires; *Best Of Rodney On The 'ROQ* .. (PBO)
Are You Ready To Rock
Michael Schenker; *One Night At Budokan* ...... (CHR)
Rock Will Never Die .... (CHR)
Are You Sitting Comfortably/The Dream
Moody Blues; *Caught Live Plus Five* .... (POL)
On The Threshold Of A Dream .... (POL)
This Is The .... (POL)
Are You Sleeping?
Nilsson; *The Point* ....(RCA)
Are You Sure Hank Done It This Way
Hank Williams, Jr.; *Rowdy* .... (W/C)
Waylon Jennings; *Greatest Hits* ....(RCA)
Are You Teasing Me
Carl Smith; *Essential-1950-1956* ....(COL)
Greatest Hits-#1 .... (GUS)
Are You Weepin'
Gary Wright; *Light Of Smiles* .... (WB)
Aren't You Glad?
Beach Boys; *Smiley Smile/Wild Honey* ....(CAP)
Sunshine Dream .... (CAP)
'69 .... (CAP)
Baby Won't You Let Me Rock & Roll You
Ten Years After; *A Space In Time* ....(COL)
Baby Won't You Please Come Home
Billie Holiday; *Last Recordings* .... (VRV)
Dinah Washington; *Echoes Of An Era* .... (RLL)
Frank Sinatra; *Night We Called It A Day* ....(CAP)
Louis Armstrong; *Most Blues* .... (OLR)
Louis Armstrong/Friends; *20 Golden Pieces Of* .. (BLD)
Ray Charles; *20 Golden Pieces Of* .... (BLD)
Baby Won't You Tell Me
Johnny Hammond; *Big City Blues* .... (VAN)
Bill Bailey
Louis Armstrong; *Essential* .... (VAN)
Louis Armstrong .... (AUF)
Pearl Bailey; *Echoes Of An Era* .... (RLL)
Preservation Hall Jazz Band; *New Orleans-#1* ...(COL)
Blowin' In The Wind
Bob Dylan; *At Budokan* ....(COL)
Before The Flood ....(COL)
Biograph ....(COL)
Freewheelin' ....(COL)
Greatest Folksingers Of The '60s .... (VAN)
Greatest Hits ....(COL)
Joan Baez; *ST/Forrest Gump* .... (EPX)
Peter, Paul & Mary; *Holiday Celebration* .... (GC)
In Concert .... (WB)
In The Wind .... (WB)
Peter, Paul & Mary .... (WB)
Ten Years Together .... (WB)
Brother, Can You Spare A Dime
Bing Crosby; *16 Most Requested Songs* ....(COL)
Odetta/Dr. John/John Campbell/Rufus Reid; *Strike A
Deep Chord-Blues For Homeless* .... (JST)
Peter, Paul & Mary; *See What Tomorrow Brings* ..(WB)
Weavers; *Greatest Hits* .... (VAN)
B.B.D. (I Thought It Was Me)?
Bell Biv Devoe; *Poison* .... (MCA)
Can I Count On You
McBride & The Ride; *Burnin' Up The Road* .... (MCA)
Can I Get A Witness
Marvin Gaye; *Anthology* .... (MOT)
Greatest Hits .... (MOT)
Super Hits .... (MOT)
Rod Stewart; *Storyteller-Complete
Anthology-1964-1990* .... (WB)
Rolling Stones; *England's Newest Hit Makers* .... (AKO)
Can I Get To Know You Better
Turtles; *Best Of-Golden Archive Series* .... (RHI)
Greatest Hits .... (RHI)
Can I Have A Smoke, Dude?
Mary's Danish; *Edge Of Rock* .... (ERA)
There Goes The Wondertruck... .... (CML)
Can I Have My Money Back
Gerry Rafferty; *Can I Have My Money Back* .... (MCA)
Can I Run
L7; *Hungry For Stink* .... (SLS)
Can I See You In The Morning
Jackson 5; *Third Album* .... (MOT)

QUESTIONS — QUESTIONS

Can I See You Tonight
Tanya Tucker; *Best Of* .... (MCA)
Live .... (MCA)
Can I Trust You With My Heart
Travis Tritt; *T-R-O-U-B-L-E* .... (WB)
Can We Spend Some Time
Surface; *2nd Wave* ....(COL)
Can We Still Be Friends?
Robert Palmer; *Secrets* .... (ISL)
Rod Stewart; *Camouflage* .... (WB)
Todd Rundgren; *Anthology 1968-1985* .... (RHI)
Hermit Of Mink Hollow .... (RHI)
Can We Talk
Tevin Campbell; *I'm Ready* .... (QUE)
Can You Dance (Baby Tell Me)
Shanice Wilson; *Discovery* .... (A&M)
Can You Feel The Love Tonight
Elton John; *ST/The Lion King* .... (DIS)
Can You Hear Me?
David Bowie; *Young Americans* .... (RYK)
Can You Hear The Music?
Rolling Stones; *Goats Head Soup* .... (RS)
Can You Help Me
Jesse Johnson's Revue; *Jesse Johnson's Revue* ... (A&M)
Can You Read My Mind
Maureen McGovern; *Maureen McGovern* .... (WB)
Shirley Bassey; *ST/New York New York* .... (EMI)
Can You See Me
Jimi Hendrix; *Smash Hits* .... (RPR)
ST/Jimi Plays Monterey .... (RPR)
Can You Stand The Rain
New Edition; *Heart Break* .... (MCA)
Can You Stop The Rain
Peabo Bryson; *Can You Stop The Rain* ....(COL)
Can't We Be Friends
Art Tatum; *Standards* ....(BL)
Buck Clayton & Buddy Tate; *Buck & Buddy* ..... (PRS)
Ella Fitzgerald & Louis Armstrong; *Ella & Louis* (VRV)
Frank Sinatra; *In The Wee Small Hours* ....(CAP)
Linda Ronstadt; *Lush Life* .... (ASY)
Can't We Talk It Over?
Bing Crosby; *16 Most Requested Songs* ....(COL)
Helen O'Connell; *Great Girl Singers Sing 22
Originals* .... (HIN)
Can't You Hear Me Callin'?
Ricky Skaggs; *Favorite Country Songs* .... (EPI)
Highway & Heartaches .... (EPI)
Can't You Hear Me Knockin'
Rolling Stones; *Sticky Fingers* .... (RS)
Can't You Hear My Heart Beat?
Herman's Hermits; *XX* .... (AKO)
Can't You See
Alabama; *Live* ....(RCA)
Charlie Daniels Band; *Volunteer Jam VII* .... (EPI)
Hank Williams, Jr.; *Rebels Renegades & Ramblers* (POL)
Standing In The Shadows .... (POL)
& Friends .... (POL)
Marshall Tucker Band; *Marshall Tucker Band* ... (AJK)
Searchin' For A Rainbow .... (AJK)
Peter Tosh; *Mystic Man* ....(RS)
Can't You See Darling
Ray Charles; *20 Golden Pieces Of* .... (BLD)
Can't You See It In My Eyes
Le Roux; *45* ....(RCA)
Can't You See What You're Doing To Me
Albert King; */Little Milton-Chronicle* .... (STX)
Can't You See (You Doin' Me Wrong)
Tower Of Power; *Back To Oakland* .... (WB)
Compared To What
Les McCann; *Atlantic Jazz-Soul* .... (ATL)
Les McCann & Eddie Harris; *Great Moments In
Jazz* ....(ATL)
Jazz Years .... (ATL)
Swiss Movement .... (ATL)
Could I Have This Dance?
Ann Murray; *Greatest Hits* ....(CAP)
ST/Urban Cowboy .... (ASY)
Could I Have Your Autograph
Dolly Parton; *Rainbow* ....(COL)
Could It Be Magic
Barry Manilow; *Greatest Hits-#2* .... (ARI)
Live .... (ARI)
Donna Summer; *Love Trilogy* .... (CAS)

Could You Love A Working Man
Stoker Brothers; *45* .... (CMS)
Daddy What If
Bobby Bare; *Bobby Bare* ....(RCA)
Great Moments At The Grand Ole Opry ....(RCA)
Darling Are You Ever Coming Home
Jeannie Seely; *Greatest Hits* .... (MON)
Did Beethoven Do The Dishes
Reilly & Maloney; *Profiles* .... (FRK)
Did You Ever See A Dream Walking
Bing Crosby; *Crosby Classics* ....(COL)
Hal Kemp/Skinnay Ennis; *Uncollected-#2 & #3* .. (HIN)
Did You Get That Letter I Throwed In...
Arthur "Big Boy" Crudup; *Crudup's Mood* ...... (DEL)
Did You See His Name
Kinks; *Kink Kronikles* .... (RPR)
Did You See Jackie Robinson Hit That...
Count Basie; *RCA Victor Blues & Rhythm Revue* .(RCA)
& Orchestra: Baseball's Greatest Hits .... (RHI)
Did You Steal My Money
Who; *Face Dances* .... (MCA)
Did Your Mother Come From Ireland
Bing Crosby; *Shillelaghs & Shamrocks* .... (MCA)
Do I Have To Come Right Out & Say It
Buffalo Springfield; *Buffalo Springfield* ....(ATC)
Do I Have To Say The Words?
Bryan Adams; *Waking Up The Neighbours* ...... (A&M)
Do I Hear A Waltz?
Elizabeth Allen; *Broadway Magic-1960s* ....(COL)
Original Broadway Cast; *Do I Hear A Waltz?* ... (SMC)
Do Ya Think I'm Sexy?
Rod Stewart; *Absolutely Live* .... (WB)
Blondes Have More Fun .... (WB)
Greatest Hits .... (WB)
Do You Believe In Magic?
Lovin' Spoonful; *Anthology* .... (RHI)
Best Of .... (ERI)
Do You Believe In Us?
Jon Secada; *Jon Secada* .... (SBK)
Do You Ever Dream Of Vienna
Original Cast; *Little Mary Sunshine* .... (OOP)
Do You Hear Wedding Bells
Jive Five; *Their Greatest Hits* .... (CLT)
Do You Hear What I Hear
Bing Crosby; *Best Of Christmas* ....(CAP)
Chet Atkins; *East Tennessee Christmas* ....(COL)
Nashville's Greatest Christmas Hits ....(COL)
Commodores; *Christmas* .... (CMO)
Connie Scott; *Christmas In Your Heart* .... (WOR)
Gladys Knight/Pips; *Bless The House* .... (MOT)
Mahalia Jackson; *Christmas With* ....(COL)
Sonny James; *It's Christmas Time* .... (LIB)
Steve Wariner; *Christmas Memories* .... (MSP)
Vince Gill; *Let There Be Peace On Earth* .... (MCA)
Whitney Houston; *Very Special Christmas* .... (A&M)
Do You Know The Way To San Jose
Dionne Warwick; *Anthology 1962-1971* .... (RHI)
Greatest Hits .... (EVR)
Hot! Live & Otherwise .... (ARI)
Do You Know What It Means To Miss New...
Billie Holiday; *Sing 2* .... (KNT)
Harry Connick, Jr.; *Twenty* ....(COL)
Louis Armstrong; *Chicago Concert 1956* .... (COL)
Mostly Blues .... (OLR)
Pops .... (BLU)
Pete Fountain; *Best Of* .... (MCA)
Do You Know Where Your Man Is
Pam Tillis; *Homeward Looking Angel* .... (ARI)
Do You Like Good Music
Arthur Conley; *45* .... (OOP)
Do You Love Me (Now That I Can Dance?)
Contours; *Frat Rock* .... (RHI)
Greatest Movie Rock Hits .... (RHI)
Oldies But Goodies-#12 .... (MOT)
ST/More Dirty Dancing ....(RCA)
ST/Wanderers .... (WB)
Do You Really Want To Hurt Me
Culture Club; *Billboard Top Hits-1983* .... (RHI)
Kissing To Be Clever .... (VIA)
Do You Remember Rock 'N' Roll Radio
Ramones; *End Of The Century* .... (SIR)
Mania .... (SIR)

Do You Remember?
Beach Boys; *Little Deuce Coupe/All Summer Long* (CAP)
   Spirit Of America ....(CAP)
Bob Marley/Wailers; *Birth Of A Legend*
   (1963-66) .... (EPA)
   Early Music ....(CAL)
Five Satins; *Sing Their Greatest Hits* .... (CLT)
Phil Collins; *Serious Hits...Live!* .... (ATL)
   ...But Seriously .... (ATL)
Do You Wanna Dance?
Beach Boys; *Absolute Best-#1* .... (CAP)
   Spirit Of America .... (CAP)
Bette Midler; *Divine Miss M* .... (ATL)
   Live At Last .... (ATL)
Bobby Freeman; *ST/American Graffiti* .... (MCA)
Do You Wanna Get Away
Shannon; *Do You Wanna Get Away* .... (MIR)
Do You Wanna Go To Heaven
Original Broadway Cast; *Big River* .... (MCA)
T.G. Sheppard; *All-Time Greatest Hits* .... (WB)
   Greatest Hits .... (WB)
   Smooth Sailin' .... (WB)
Do You Wanna Make Love?
Peter McCann; *Peter McCann* .... (20)
Do You Want Me
Salt-N-Pepa; *Blacks' Magic* .... (NP)
Do You Want My Job
Little Village; *Little Village* .... (RPR)
Do You Want To Know A Secret
Beatles; *Early Beatles* ....(CAP)
   Please Please Me ....(CAP)
Does Anybody Really Know What Time It Is
Chicago; *At Carnegie Hall* ....(COL)
   Chicago Transit Authority ....(COL)
   Greatest Hits ....(COL)
   If You Leave Me Now ....(COL)
Does Fort Worth Ever Cross Your Mind
George Strait; *Country Classics-#3* .... (MCA)
   Does Fort Worth Ever Cross Your Mind ...... (MCA)
   Greatest Hits-#2 .... (MCA)
   MCA #1 Hits/'80s-#1 .... (MCA)
Does He Love You
Reba McEntire & Linda Davis; *Greatest Hits-#2* (MCA)
Does She Love That Man?
Breathe; *Peace Of Mind* ....(A&M)
Does This Bus Stop At 82nd St.
Bruce Springsteen; *Greetings From Asbury Park
N.J.* ....(COL)
Does Your Chewing Gum Lose Its Flavor...
Lonnie Donegan; *Dr. Demento Presents Greatest Novelty
CD* .... (RHI)
   Dr. Demento Presents Greatest-#3-'60s .... (RHI)
Does Your Heart Beat For Me
Blue Barron; *Big Band Treasures-#2* ....(DHL)
Patsy Cline; *Always* .... (MCA)
   Portrait Of .... (MCA)
Russ Morgan; *Best Of* .... (MCA)
Russ Morgan/Orchestra; *Play 22 Original Big Band
Recordings* .... (HIN)
Does Your Mother Know?
Abba; *Greatest Hits-#2* .... (ATL)
   Live .... (ATL)
   Singles (First 10 Years) .... (ATL)
   Voulez-Vous .... (ATL)
Doggie In The Window
Patti Page; *16 Most Requested Songs* ....(COL)
   Golden Hits .... (MER)
   Greatest Hits ....(COL)
Donna
Los Lobos; *ST/La Bamba* .... (SLS)
Ritchie Valens; *American Graffiti-#3* .... (MCA)
   Best Of .... (RHI)
   Heart & Soul Of Rock 'N' Roll-#1 .... (RHI)
   History Of .... (RHI)
   History Of Latino Rock-#1 .... (RHI)
Don't You Ever Get Tired Of Hurtin' Me
Ray Price; *Greatest Hits-#2* .... (STE)
Ronnie Milsap; *Stranger Things Have Happened* ..(RCA)
Don't You Know What The Night Can Do
Steve Winwood; *Roll With It* .... (VIA)
Don't Your Mem'ry Ever Sleep At Night
Ronnie Milsap; *Keyed Up* ....(RCA)
Steve Wariner; *Best Of* ....(RCA)

Don't Your Peaches Look Mellow
Luke/Locomotives; *Luke/Locomotives* .... (AQ)
Down In The Valley
Elvis Presley; *Reconsider Baby* ....(RCA)
Leadbelly; *Defense Blues-Golden Classics-#2* ..(CLT)
Pete Seeger; *American Favorite Ballads-#1* ...... (FLW)
Dream Baby (How Long Must I Dream)
Lacy J. Dalton; *Dream Baby (How Long Must I
Dream)* ....(COL)
   Greatest Country Hits/'80s-1983 ....(COL)
   Greatest Hits ....(COL)
Roy Orbison; *All-Time Greatest Hits-#1* .... (MON)
   For The Lonely: 18 Greatest Hits .... (RHI)
   For The Lonely: Anthology .... (RHI)
   In Dreams-Greatest Hits .... (VIA)
Earth Angel
Elvis Presley; *Golden Celebration* ....(RCA)
New Edition; *ST/Under The Blue Moon* .... (MCA)
Penguins; *Billboard Top Rock 'N' Roll Hits-1955* . (RHI)
   Golden Classics ....(CLT)
   Oldies But Goodies-#1 ....(OSR)
   ST/American Graffiti .... (MCA)
Eternal Flame
Bangles; *Everything* ....(COL)
   Greatest Hits ....(COL)
Five Foot Two, Eyes Of Blue
Mom & Dads; *Very Best Of* .... (CRS)
Groove Is In The Heart/What Is Love
Deee-Lite; *World Clique* .... (ELE)
Has Anybody Seen Amy
John & Audrey Wiggins; *John & Audrey* .... (MER)
Have I Told You Lately
Original Broadway Cast; *I Can Get It For You
Wholesale* .... (SMP)
Rod Stewart; *Unplugged...And Seated* .... (WB)
   Vagabond Heart .... (WB)
Van Morrison; *Best Of* .... (MER)
Have You Ever Needed Someone So Bad
Def Leppard; *Adrenalize* .... (MER)
Have You Ever Seen The Rain
Creedence Clearwater Revival; *1970* .... (FAN)
   Chronicle .... (FAN)
   Pendulum .... (FAN)
Have You Heard
Duprees; *Best Of* ....(CLT)
   Best Of .... (RHI)
   WCBS FM101 History Of Rock/'60s-#3 ....(CLT)
Moody Blues; *Caught Live Plus Five* .... (POL)
   On The Threshold Of A Dream .... (POL)
   This Is The .... (POL)
Have You Heard The News
Ben Sidran; *Puttin' In Time On Planet Earth* .... (MCA)
Vikki Carr; *Live At the Greek Theatre* ....(COL)
Have You Seen Her
Chi-Lites; *Greatest Hits* .... (EPI)
Hammer; *Please Hammer Don't Hurt 'Em* ....(CAP)
Have You Seen The Saucers
Jefferson Airplane; *2400 Fulton Street-An
Anthology* ....(RCA)
   30 Seconds Over Winterland ....(RCA)
Have You Seen The Stars Tonight
Jefferson Airplane; *Flight Log* .... (GRU)
Paul Kantner/Jefferson Starship; *Blows Against The
Empire* ....(RCA)
Have You Seen Your Mother Baby...
Rolling Stones; *Flowers* .... (AKO)
   Got Live If You Want It .... (AKO)
   More Hot Rocks-Big Hits & Fazed Cookies ..... (AKO)
   Through The Past Darkly-Big Hits-#2 .... (AKO)
Haven't You Heard
George Strait; *Something Special* .... (MCA)
Patrice Rushen; *Anthology* .... (ELE)
   Pizzazz .... (ELE)
Honey, Can I Put On Your Clothes
Barbra Streisand; *Songbird* ....(COL)
How About That
Bad Company; *Here Comes Trouble* ....(ATC)
How Am I Supposed To Live Without You
Laura Branigan; *Branigan 2* .... (ATL)
Michael Bolton; *Soul Provider* ....(COL)
How Are Things In Glocca Mora
Julie Andrews; *Little Bit Of Broadway* ....(COL)
Original Cast; *Finian's Rainbow* ....(RCA)
Rosemary Clooney; *Show Tunes* .... (CCJ)

How Blue
Reba McEntire; *Greatest Hits* .... (MCA)
  MCA #1 Hits/'80s-#1 .... (MCA)
  My Kind Of Country .... (MCA)
How Blue Can You Get
B.B. King; *Best Of* .... (MCA)
  Live At The Regal .... (MCA)
  Live In Cook County Jail .... (MCA)
How Can A Poor Man Stand Such Times...
Blind Alfred Reed; *How Can A Poor Man Stand Such Times...* .... (ROU)
Ry Cooder; *Ry Cooder* .... (RPR)
  Show Time .... (WB)
How Can I Ease The Pain
Lisa Fischer; *So Intense* .... (ELE)
How Can I Fall
Breathe; *All That Jazz* .... (A&M)
How Can I Help You Say Goodbye
Patty Loveless; *Only What I Feel* .... (EPI)
How Can We Be Lovers
Michael Bolton; *Soul Provider* ....(COL)
How Can We Hang Onto A Dream
Tim Hardin; *Memorial Album* .... (POL)
How Can You Mend A Broken Heart
Al Green; *Compact Command Performances* .... (MOT)
  Greatest Hits-#1 .... (MOT)
  Let's Stay Together .... (MOT)
Bee Gees; *Gold-#1* .... (RSO)
  Here At Last .... (RSO)
  Nobody's Child-Romanian Angel Appeal .... (WB)
How Come U Don't Call Me Anymore
Stephanie Mills; *Merciless* .... (CAS)
How Deep Is The Ocean (How High Is...)
Frank Sinatra; *Nice 'N' Easy* .... (CAP)
Liza Minnelli; *At Carnegie Hall* .... (TLR)
How Do The Fools Survive
Doobie Brothers; *Minute By Minute* .... (WB)
How Do You Keep The Music Playing
James Ingram & Patti Austin; *It's Your Night* ... (QUE)
  ST/Listen Up-Lives Of Quincy Jones .... (QUE)
How Do You Say Auf Wiedersehen
George Shearing & Mel Torme; *Top Drawer* .... (CCJ)
How Do You Speak To An Angel
Popular Standard; *Out Of Print Recording* ....(OOP)
How Do You Talk To An Angel
Heights; *ST/Heights* .... (CAP)
How Do You Talk To Girls
Rick Springfield; *Success Hasn't Spoiled Me Yet* ..(RCA)
How Does It Feel
Ian Moore; *Ian Moore* .... (CPC)
How Far To Little Rock
Stanley Brothers; *Stanley Series-Vol. 1-#2* .... (COP)
How Long Blues
Eric Clapton; *From The Cradle* .... (DUC)
How Long Has This Been Going On?
Bon Jovi featuring Richie Sambora; *Glory Of Gershwin Featuring Larry Adler* .... (MER)
Ella Fitzgerald & Oscar Peterson; *Ella & Oscar* .. (PAB)
Judy Garland; *At Carnegie Hall* ....(CAP)
Louis Armstrong & Oscar Peterson; *Louis Armstrong Meets Oscar Peterson* ....(VRV)
Original Cast; *My One & Only* .... (ATL)
Patti Austin; *Real Me* .... (QUE)
Sarah Vaughan; *How Long Has This Been Going On?* .... (PAB)
How Long Must I Wait For You
Joe Jackson; *Jumpin' Jive* .... (A&M)
How Many Friends
Who; *By Numbers* .... (MCA)
How Many Ways
Toni Braxton; *Toni Braxton* .... (LAF)
How Much Is Enough
Fixx; *Ink* ....(IPA)
How You Gonna See Me Now
Alice Cooper; *From The Inside* .... (MET)
If You Wanna Leave Me (Can I Come Too?)
Bryan Adams; *Waking Up The Neighbours* ...... (A&M)
Is It A Crime
Judy Holliday/Original Cast; *Bells Are Ringing* ...(COL)
Sade; *Promise* .... (POR)
Is It A Star
Daryl Hall & John Oates; *War Babies* .... (ATL)
Is It Cold In Here
Joe Diffie; *Regular Joe* .... (EPI)

Is It Over Yet
Wynonna; *Tell Me Why* .... (MCC)
Is It Raining At Your House
Vern Gosdin; *10 Years Of Greatest Hits Newly Recorded* ....(COL)
  Chiseled In Stone ....(COL)
  Greatest Country Hits/'90s-1991 ....(COL)
Is It Still Over
Randy Travis; *Old 8 X 10* .... (WB)
Is It What You Wanted
Greta; *No Biting* .... (STD)
Is She Really Going Out With Him
Joe Jackson; *Live-1980-1986* .... (A&M)
  Look Sharp .... (A&M)
Is There Life Out There
Reba McEntire; *For My Broken Heart* .... (MCA)
  Greatest Hits-#2 .... (MCA)
Is This Love
Alison Moyet; *Raindancing* ....(COL)
Bob Marley/Wailers; *Babylon By Bus* ....(TUF)
  Kaya ....(TUF)
  Legend ....(TUF)
Carly Simon; *Hello Big Man* .... (WB)
Whitesnake; *Whitesnake* .... (GEF)
Is Your Mama Gonna Miss Ya?
Bryan Adams; *Waking Up The Neighbours* ..... (A&M)
Isn't It A Pity?
George Harrison; *All Things Must Pass* ....(CAP)
Mel Torme; *That's All* ....(SSP)
Michael Feinstein; *Pure Gershwin* .... (ELE)
Isn't It Midnight
Fleetwood Mac; *25 Years-The Chain* .... (WB)
Isn't It Romantic
Michael Feinstein; *Isn't It Romantic* .... (ELE)
Tony Bennett; *Rodgers & Hart Songbook* .... (DRG)
Isn't It Time
Babys; *Anthologoy* .... (CHR)
  Broken Heart .... (CHR)
Isn't Life Strange
Moody Blues; *Night At Red Rocks With Colorado Symph.* .... (POL)
  Seventh Sojourn .... (POL)
  This Is The .... (POL)
  Voices In The Sky-Best Of .... (T/P)
Isn't She Lovely
Lee Ritenour; *Best Of* .... (EPI)
Stevie Wonder; *Original Musiquarium* .... (MOT)
  Songs In The Key Of Life .... (MOT)
Isn't This A Lovely Day
Ella Fitzgerald; *Irving Berlin Songbook-#2* ....(VRV)
Fred Astaire; *Irving Berlin Songbook* ....(VRV)
  Sings .... (MCA)
  Starring ....(COL)
It's In His Kiss (Shoop Shoop Song)
Betty Everett; *Billboard Top R&B Hits-1964* ..... (RHI)
  Hits Of The Sixties .... (IMC)
  More American Graffiti .... (MCA)
  Oldies But Goodies-#3 .... (OSR)
  Very Best Of .... (VJ)
  Wonder Women (History Of Girl Groups) .... (RHI)
Cher; *ST/Mermaids* .... (GEF)
Jimmy Mack
Martha Reeves/Vandellas; *Anthology* .... (MOT)
  Billboard Top R&B Hits-1967 .... (MOT)
  Compact Command Performances .... (MOT)
  Motown Story .... (MOT)
  Motown Superstar Series-#11 .... (MOT)
  Top 10 With A Bullet-Motown Girl Groups .... (MOT)
Jim, What's Wrong With Him
Dramatics; *Dramatic Experience* .... (STX)
Jocko Homo (Q: Are We Not Men?)
Devo; *Best Of-Greatest Hits* .... (WB)
  Q: Are We Not Men? A: We Are Devo! .... (WB)
  Rest Of-Greatest Misses .... (WB)
Johnny Have You Seen Her?
Rembrandts; *United* ....(ATC)
Julie, Do Ya Love Me
Bobby Sherman; *Rock & Roll Is Here To Stay* .... (GUS)
  Super Hits/'70s-Have A Nice Day-#3 .... (RHI)
Kids
Original Broadway Cast; *Bye Bye Birdie* ....(COL)
Paul Lynde; *ST/Bye Bye Birdie* ....(RCA)

QUESTIONS — QUESTIONS

Life On Mars?
David Bowie; *Hunky Dory* ....(RYK)
  The Singles-1969-1993 ....(RYK)
Lover Man (Oh Where Can You Be)
Barbra Streisand; *Simply Streisand* ....(COL)
Billie Holiday; *Fine & Mellow* ....(CLT)
  History Of The Real ....(VRV)
Blossom Dearie; *Blossom Dearie* ....(VRV)
Lena Horne; *Goes Latin & Sings Your Requests* .. (DRG)
Sarah Vaughan; *Compact Jazz* ....(VRV)
  Jazz 'Round Midnight ....(VRV)
Sonny Stitt; *Soul Classics* .... (PRS)
"Mahogany" Theme (Do You Know Where...)
Diana Ross; *20/20* .... (MOT)
  Anthology ....(MOT)
  Diana Ross ....(MOT)
  Evening With ....(MOT)
  Greatest Hits ....(MOT)
Mommy Where's Daddy
Red Hot Chili Peppers; *Red Hot Chili Peppers* ... (EMI)
Mommy, Can I Go Out & Kill Tonight
Misfits; *Walk Among Us* ....(RUB)
New York Mining Disaster 1941
Bee Gees; *Gold-#1* ....(POL)
  Here At Last ....(RSO)
  History Of British Rock-#8 .... (RHI)
Not Too Much To Ask
Mary Chapin Carpenter & Joe Diffie; *Come On Come On* ....(COL)
Paddy Won't You Drink Some Cider
Red Clay Ramblers; *Chuckin' The Frizz* .... (FF)
People Asking Why
Seal; *Seal* .... (ZTT)
Question
Moody Blues; *Night At Red Rocks With Colorado Symph.* ....(POL)
  Question Of Balance ....(POL)
  This Is The ....(POL)
Question Of Time
Depeche Mode; *101* .... (SIR)
  Black Celebration ....(SIR)
Jack Bruce; *Question Of Time* .... (EPI)
Question This
Charlie Sexton; *Charlie Sexton* .... (MCA)
Questions
Buffalo Springfield; *Last Time Around* ....(ATC)
INXS; *Welcome To Wherever You Are* ....(ATL)
Questions 67 & 68
Chicago; *At Carnegie Hall* ....(COL)
  Chicago Transit Authority ....(COL)
  Greatest Hits-#2 ....(COL)
  Group Portrait ....(COL)
Riddle Song
Doc Watson; *Southbound* .... (VAN)
Joan Baez & Pete Seeger; *Very Early Joan Baez* (VAN)
Ruby Baby
Beatles; *In The Beginning* ....(POL)
Dion; *24 Original Classics* .... (ARI)
  Bronx Blues-Columbia Recordings-1962-65 ....(COL)
Donald Fagen; *The Nightfly* ....(WB)
Drifters; *Atlantic R&B 1947-1974-#3-(1955-1958)* ....(ATL)
  Let The Boogie Woogie Roll-Greatest Hits ....(ATL)
  Their Greatest Recordings-Early Years ....(ATC)
R. U. Ready To Rock
Blue Oyster Cult; *On Flame With Rock & Roll* ....(SSP)
  Some Enchanted Evening ....(COL)
  Spectres ....(COL)
Shall We Dance
Ella Fitzgerald; *George & Ira Gershwin Songbook* (VRV)
Original Broadway Cast; *King & I* ....(RCA)
Original Cast; *King & I* .... (MCA)
Shall We Gather At The River?
Chuck Wagon Gang; *16 Country-Gospel Favorites* .... (MCA)
Tennessee Ernie Ford; *All-Time Greatest Hymns* .(CCB)
  Sings 22 Favorite Hymns .... (RAN)
Tennis Anyone
Today; *New Formula* ....(MOT)
That Lady
Isley Brothers; *Greatest Hits-#1* .... (TN)
  Rock Artifacts-#1-From The Vaults ....(COL)
  Story-#2-T-Neck Years-1969-1985 .... (RHI)

Thing Called Love
Bonnie Raitt; *Nick Of Time* ....(CAP)
To Make You Love Me (What Can I Say)
Alexander O'Neal; *All Mixed Up* .... (TAB)
  Hearsay .... (TAB)
Tommy Can You Hear Me
Who; *Join Together* .... (MCA)
  ST/Kids Are Alright ....(MCA)
  ST/Tommy ....(POL)
  Tommy .... (MCA)
Was It Just The Moonlight
Timothy B. Schmit; *Tell Me The Truth* .... (MCA)
Was It Just The Wine
Vern Gosdin; *10 Years Of Greatest Hits Newly Recorded* ....(COL)
Was My Brother In The Battle
Kate & Anna McGarrigle; *Songs Of The Civil War* ....(COL)
Wasn't That A Mighty Storm
Eric Von Schmidt; *Troubadours Of The Folk Era-#1* .... (RHI)
Wasn't That A Party
Rovers; *Wasn't That A Party* .... (EPI)
Wat About Di Workin' Class?
Linton Kwesi Johnson; *In Concert With The Dub Band* .... (SHA)
What About Me
Anne Murray; *Country* ....(CAP)
Kenny Rogers w/Kim Carnes & James Ingram; *What About Me* ....(RCA)
Quicksilver Messenger Service; *Anthology* ......(CAP)
  Sons Of Mercury .... (RHI)
What About Your Friends
TLC; *Oooooooohhh...On The TLC Tip* ....(LAF)
What Are You Doing In My Life
Tom Petty/Heartbreakers; *Damn The Torpedoes* (MCA)
What Are You Doing The Rest Of Your Life
Barbra Streisand; *Just For The Record* ....(COL)
  The Way We Were ....(COL)
Carmen McRae; *Great American Songbook* ......(ATL)
Joe Pass; *Best Of* .... (PAB)
What Becomes Of The Brokenhearted
Jimmy Ruffin; *Motown Story* .... (MOT)
Jimmy & David Ruffin; *Motown Superstar Series-#8* .... (MOT)
Paul Young; *ST/Fried Green Tomatoes* ....(MCA)
What Do They Know
Tammy Wynette; *Without Walls* .... (EPI)
What Do You Want From Life
Tubes; *Tubes* .... (A&M)
  T.R.A.S.H.-Tubes Rarities & Smash Hits ....(A&M)
  What Do You Want From-Live ....(A&M)
What Do You Want From Me
Pink Floyd; *The Division Bell* ....(COL)
What Does It Take (To Win Your Love)
Junior Walker/All-Stars; *Anthology* ....(MOT)
  Billboard Top R&B Hits-1965-1969 .... (RHI)
  Greatest Hits .... (MOT)
  Oldies But Goodies-#13 .... (OSR)
What Have I Done To Deserve This
Pet Shop Boys & Dusty Springfield; *Actually* ..... (EMI)
  Discography-Complete Singles Collection ...... (EMI)
What Have They Done To The Rain
Malvina Reynolds; *ST/Dogfight* .... (NUV)
Searchers; *Greatest Hits* .... (RHI)
What Have You Done For Me Lately
Janet Jackson; *Control* .... (A&M)
What If I Came Knocking
John Mellencamp; *Human Wheels* .... (MER)
What Is Life
George Harrison; *All Things Must Pass* ....(CAP)
  Best Of ....(CAP)
George Harrison & Eric Clapton & Band; *Live In Japan* .... (DKH)
What Is Love
Deee-Lite; *World Clique* ....(ELE)
En Vogue; *Funky Divas* ....(EW)
Haddaway; *House Of Groove* ....(ARI)
Howard Jones; *Best Of-1983-1993* ....(ELE)
  Human's Lib ....(ELE)
Marc Almond; *Tenement Symphony* ....(SIR)
Shangri-Las; *Remember The Shangri-Las At Their Best* ....(CLT)
Shirelles; *16 Greatest Hits* ....(TRP)

What Is This Thing Called Love
Alexander O'Neal; *All True Man* .... (EPA)
  Greatest Hits Of .... (EPI)
Artie Shaw; *Begin The Beguine* .... (BLU)
Charlie Parker; *Cole Porter Songbook* .... (VRV)
Ella Fitzgerald; *Cole Porter Songbook* .... (VRV)
Frank Sinatra; *Sings The Select Cole Porter* ...... (CAP)
Julie London; *Sings Cole Porter* .... (EMI)
Kay Starr; *Back To The Roots* .... (CRS)
Mel Torme; *Night & Day-Cole Porter Songbook* .. (VRV)
What Kind Of Fool
Barbra Streisand; *Collection-Greatest Hits & More* (COL)
  One Voice .... (COL)
Barbra Streisand & Barry Gibb; *Guilty* .... (COL)
Lionel Cartwright; *Chasin' The Sun* .... (MCA)
What Kind Of Fool Am I
Bill Evans; *Solo Sessions-#1* .... (MS)
Marvin Gaye; *Hello Broadway* .... (MOT)
Original Broadway Cast; *Stop The World-I Want To Get Off* .... (POL)
Rick Springfield; *Greatest Hits* .... (RCA)
  Success Hasn't Spoiled Me Yet .... (RCA)
Robert Goulet; *16 Most Requested Songs* .... (COL)
  Greatest Hits .... (COL)
Sammy Davis, Jr.; *Greatest Songs* .... (CCB)
What Kind Of Fool Do You Think I Am
Bill Deal/Rhondels; *Frat Rock-#2* .... (RHI)
  Oldies But Goodies-#15 .... (OSR)
Lee Roy Parnell; *Love Without Mercy* .... (ARI)
What Kind Of Love
Rodney Crowell; *Life Is Messy* .... (COL)
What Kind Of Man Would I Be?
Chicago; *19* .... (FM)
  Greatest Hits 1982-1989 .... (FM)
What Makes You Think You're The One
Fleetwood Mac; *25 Years-The Chain* .... (WB)
What Now My Love
Barbra Streisand; *Je M'Appelle Barbra* .... (COL)
Elvis Presley; *Alternate Aloha* .... (RCA)
Frank Sinatra; *That's Life* .... (RPR)
Frank Sinatra & Aretha Franklin; *Frank Sinatra Duets* .... (CAP)
Herb Alpert/Tijuana Brass; *Classics-#1* .... (A&M)
  Greatest Hits-#2 .... (A&M)
Temptations; *In A Mellow Mood* .... (MOT)
What Part Of No
Lorrie Morgan; *Watch Me* .... (BNA)
What Time Is It?
Ken Nordine; *Best Of Word Jazz-#1* .... (RHI)
Spin Doctors; *Pocket Full Of Kryptonite* .... (EPA)
What Were You Thinkin'
Little Texas; *First Time For Everything* .... (WB)
What Will My Mary Say
Jay/Americans; *Come A Little Bit Closer-Best Of* . (EMI)
Johnny Mathis; *16 Most Requested Songs* .... (COL)
  All-Time Greatest Hits .... (COL)
Whatcha Gonna Do With A Cowboy
Chris LeDoux & Garth Brooks; *Whatcha Gonna Do With A Cowboy* .... (LIB)
Whatcha Gonna Do?
New Riders Of The Purple Sage; *New Riders Of The Purple Sage* .... (COL)
  Vintage NRPS .... (RLX)
Tyler Collins; *Girls Nite Out* .... (RCA)
Whatever Happened To Saturday Night
Tim Curry; *ST/Rocky Horror Picture Show* .... (RHI)
Tim Curry/Original Roxy Cast; *Rocky Horror Show* .... (RHI)
What'd I Say
Elvis Presley; *Collector's Gold* .... (RCA)
  Golden Records-#4 .... (RCA)
  Greatest Hits-#1 .... (RCA)
  In Concert .... (RCA)
Jerry Lee Lewis; *Milestones* .... (RHI)
  Original .... (SUN)
  Original Golden Hits-#2 .... (SUN)
  Rocket 88 .... (TOM)
  Rockin' My Life Away .... (TOM)
John Mayall/Bluesbreakers; *Bluesbreakers* .... (DER)
Ray Charles; *Anthology* .... (RHI)
  Atlantic R&B 1947-1974-#4-(1958-1962) ..... (ATL)
  Atlantic Soul Classics .... (WSP)
  Frat Rock-#3 .... (RHI)
  Life In Music .... (ATL)

What's A Telephone Bill
Bootsy's Rubber Band; *The Name Is Bootsy Baby* . (WB)
What's Going On In Your World
George Strait; *Beyond The Blue Neon* .... (MCA)
  Ten Strait Hits .... (MCA)
What's In It For Me
John Berry; *John Berry* .... (LIB)
What's It To You
Clay Walker; *Clay Walker* .... (GIA)
What's My Name?
Snoop Doggy Dogg; *Doggystyle* .... (DR)
What's New Pussycat
Tom Jones; *London Collector-Greatest Hits* ..... (LON)
What's On Your Mind (Pure Energy)
Information Society; *Information Society* .... (TMB)
What's The 411?
Mary J. Blige; *What's The 411?* .... (UT)
What's The Frequency, Kenneth?
R.E.M.; *Monster* .... (WB)
What's The Ugliest Part Of Your Body
Mothers Of Invention; *We're Only In It For The.../Lumpy Gravy* .... (RYK)
What's This Shit Called Love
Meatmen; *We're The Meatmen...& You Still Suck!* . (CRL)
What's Up
4 Non Blondes; *Bigger Better Faster More* .... (ISC)
DJ Miko; *S* .... (ZYX)
When Can I See You
Babyface; *For The Cool In You* .... (EPI)
When Can I See You Again
Babyface; *For The Cool In You* .... (EPI)
When Did We Have Sauerkraut?
Lou & Peter Berryman; *So Comfortable* .... (COR)
When Did You Leave Heaven?
Bob Dylan; *Down In The Groove* .... (COL)
Hank Crawford; *After Hours* .... (ATL)
When Did You Stop Loving Me
George Strait; *ST/Pure Country* .... (MCA)
When I'm Sixty-Four
Beatles; *Box Set* .... (CAP)
  Sgt. Pepper's Lonely Hearts Club Band .... (CAP)
When Will I Be Loved
Everly Brothers; *All-Time Greatest Hits* .... (CCB)
  Fabulous Style Of .... (RHI)
  Oldies But Goodies-#11 .... (OSR)
Linda Ronstadt; *Greatest Hits* .... (ASY)
  Heart Like A Wheel .... (CAP)
When Will I See You Again
Three Degrees; *Mega Hits Dance Classics-#2* .... (PRY)
  Soul Hits/'70s-#14 .... (RHI)
When Will I See You Smile Again?
Bell Biv Devoe; *Poison* .... (MCA)
  WBBD-Bootcity-Remix Album .... (MCA)
When Will It Rain
Jackyl; *Jackyl* .... (GEF)
Where Are You Now
Blue Rodeo; *Lost Together* .... (ATL)
Clint Black; *Put Yourself In My Shoes* .... (RCA)
Where Did I Go Wrong
Steve Wariner; *Country's Greatest Hits-#3* .... (PRY)
  Greatest Hits-#2 .... (MCA)
  I Got Dreams .... (MCA)
UB40; *UB40* .... (A&M)
Where Did Robinson Crusoe Go With Friday
Ian Whitcomb; *45* .... (OSR)
Where Did That Little Dog Go
Original Cast; *Snoopy* .... (DRG)
Where Do Broken Hearts Go
Whitney Houston; *Whitney* .... (ARI)
Where Do I Fit In
Clay Walker; *Clay Walker* .... (GIA)
Where Do My Socks Go?
Ray Stevens; *Lend Me Your Ears* .... (CCB)
Where Do The Children Play
Cat Stevens; *Classics-#24* .... (A&M)
  Footsteps In The Dark-#2 .... (A&M)
  Tea For The Tillerman .... (A&M)
Where Do The Nights Go
Ronnie Milsap; *Greatest Hits-#3* .... (RCA)
  Heart & Soul .... (RCA)
Where Do We Go From Here
Charles & Eddie; *Duophonic* .... (CAP)

Chicago; *At Carnegie Hall* ....(COL)
  Group Portrait ....(COL)
  #2 ....(COL)
Stacy Lattisaw & Johnny Gill; *What You Need* .. (MOT)
Waylon Jennings; *Man Called Hoss* .... (MCA)
Where Do You Go
Frank Sinatra; *No One Cares* ....(CAP)
Strawbs; *Best Of* ....(A&M)
  Ghosts ....(A&M)
Where Do You Keep Your Heart
Tommy Dorsey & Frank Sinatra; *All-Time Greatest
Hits-#4* ....(RCA)
  Dorsey/Sinatra Sessions-#1 .... (BLU)
Where Does My Heart Beat Now?
Celine Dion; *Unison* .... (EPI)
Where Has My Little Dog Gone
Horace Heidt/Musical Knights; *Uncollected-1939* (HIN)
Where Have All The Good Times Gone
David Bowie; *Pinups* ....(RYK)
Elton John; *Jump Up!* .... (MCA)
Kinks; *Greatest Hits-#1* ....(RHI)
  One For The Road ....(ARI)
Van Halen; *Diver Down* ....(WB)
Where Is My Love?
El DeBarge; *Heart Mind & Soul* ....(RPR)
Where Was I
Ricky Van Shelton; *Bridge I Didn't Burn* ....(COL)
Where Were You When I Was Falling In...
Lobo; *Greatest Hits* ....(CCB)
  Your Favorite Songs ....(CCB)
Where Were You (When I Needed You)
Bangles; *Greatest Hits* ....(COL)
Grass Roots; *Anthology-1965-1975* ...... (RHI)
  Greatest Hits-#1 .... (MCA)
  Their 16 Greatest Hits .... (MCA)
Where You Goin' Now
Damn Yankees; *Don't Tread* .... (WB)
Where'm I Gonna Live?
Billy Ray Cyrus; *Some Gave All* .... (MER)
Where's The Playground Susie
Glen Campbell; *Best Of* .... (LIB)
Where've You Been
Kathy Mattea; *Collection Of Hits* .... (MER)
  Willow In The Wind ....(MER)
Which Way To America
Living Colour; *Vivid* ....(EPI)
Which Way You Goin' Billy
Poppy Family; *Super Hits/'70s-Have A Nice
Day-#2* .... (RHI)
Who Am I (What's My Name)?
Snoop Doggy Dogg; *Doggystyle* .... (DR)
Who Am I?
Elvis Presley; *Memphis Record* ....(RCA)
Original Broadway Cast; *Les Miserables* ....(GEF)
Petula Clark; *Greatest Hits Of* ....(CRS)
Who Are The Brain Police
Frank Zappa; *Disconnected Synapses* .... (RHI)
Mothers Of Invention; *Freak Out* .... (BAR)
Who Are You
Who; *Greatest Hits* .... (MCA)
  Hooligans ....(MCA)
  Who Are You ....(MCA)
  Who's Better Who's Best-Best Of ....(MCA)
  Who's Last ....(MCA)
Who Are Your Heroes
Bill Blue; *Givin' Good Boys A Bad Name* .... (ADE)
Who But A Fool (Thief In Paradise)
Bonnie Raitt; *Nine Lives* ....(WB)
Who Can I Count On
Patsy Cline; *Portrait Of* .... (MCA)
Who Can It Be Now
Men At Work; *Billboard Top Hits-1982* .... (RHI)
  Business As Usual ....(COL)
Who Found Who
Jellybean with Elisa Fiorillo; *12"* ....(CHR)
Who Is It
Michael Jackson; *Dangerous* ....(EPI)
Who Knows Where The Time Goes
Fairport Convention; *Chronicles* ....(A&M)
  Circle Dance-Hokey Pokey Charity Compil. ..(GRE)
Judy Collins; *Colors Of The Day-Best Of* ....(ELE)
  Who Knows Where The Time Goes ....(ELE)
Sandy Denny; *Best Of* .... (HBL)
  Who Knows Where The Time Goes ....(HBL)

Who Needs You
Lisa Brokop; *Every Little Girl's Dream* ....(PAT)
Who Put The Benzedrine In Mrs....
Harry Gibson;
  Dr. Demento's Delights ....(WB)
Who Put The Bomp (In The Bomp Ba Bomp..)
Barry Mann; *Goofy Greats* ....(KT)
  Sixties Rule! Chapter 2 ....(OW)
(Who Says) You Can't Have It All
Alan Jackson; *A Lot About Livin' (And A Little...)* (ARI)
Who Scared You
Doors; *Weird Scenes Inside The Gold Mine* .... (ELE)
Who Stole The Jukebox (From Lucy's...)
Johnny Bond; *Johnny Gimble's Texas Honky-Tonk
Hits* ....(CMH)
Who Threw The Overalls In Mrs....
Bing Crosby; *Shillelaghs & Shamrocks* .... (MCA)
Who Wears These Shoes
Elton John; *Breaking Hearts* .... (MCA)
Whose Shoulder Will You Cry On
Kitty Wells; *Greatest Hits-#1* ....(SO)
Who'll Be The Next In Line
Kinks; *Greatest Hits-#1* ....(RHI)
  Kink-Size Kinkdom ....(RHI)
Who'll Stop The Rain
Creedence Clearwater Revival; *1970* ....(FAN)
  Chronicle ....(FAN)
  Cosmo's Factory ....(FAN)
  More Creedence Gold ....(FAN)
  Royal Albert Hall Concert ....(FAN)
Who's Afraid Of The Big Bad Wolf
Barbra Streisand; *Album* ....(COL)
  Just For The Record ....(COL)
L.L. Cool J; *Simply Mad About The Mouse* .....(COL)
Mormon Tabernacle Choir/Columbia Symph.; *When
You Wish Upon A Star-Disney Tribute* ....(COL)
M. Moder/D. Compton/P. Colvig/Others; *Disney
Collection-#1* .... (DIS)
Who's Been Sleeping Here
Rolling Stones; *Between The Buttons* .... (AKO)
Who's Been Sleeping In My Bed
Melanie; *Am I Real Or What* .... (AMH)
Who's Behind The Door
Zebra; *Live* .... (ATL)
  Zebra ....(ATL)
Who's Cheatin' Who
Charly McClain; *Encore* ....(EPI)
  Greatest Country Hits/'80s-1980 ....(COL)
  Greatest Hits ....(EPI)
  Greatest Hits From The Jukebox ....(EPI)
  Ten Year Anniversary ....(EPI)
Who's Driving Your Plane?
Rolling Stones; *Singles Collection-London Years* . (AKO)
Who's Gonna Fill Their Shoes
George Jones; *Greatest Country Hits/'80s-1985* ..(COL)
  Super Hits ....(EPI)
  Who's Gonna Fill Their Shoes ....(EPI)
Who's Gonna Mow Your Grass
Buck Owens; *All-Time Greatest-#1* ....(CCB)
  Collection-1959-1990 ....(RHI)
Who's Gonna Play This Old Piano
Jerry Lee Lewis; *Best Of-#2* .... (MER)
  Milestones ....(RHI)
Who's Gonna Ride Your Wild Horses
U2; *Achtung Baby* .... (ISL)
Who's Gonna Take Your Garbage Out
Ernest Tubb & Loretta Lynn; *Ernest Tubb & Loretta
Lynn* .... (MCA)
  More Great Country Duets ....(MSP)
  Story ....(MCA)
Who's Johnny
El DeBarge; *El DeBarge* .... (MOT)
Highway 101; *Country's Greatest Hits-#8-Lonely
Hearts* ....(PRY)
  Greatest Hits ....(WB)
  Paint The Town ....(WB)
Who's That Knockin'
Genies; *WOGL Oldies 98-History Of Rock-#2* ....(CLT)
Who's That Man
Toby Keith; *Boomtown* ....(PYN)
Who's The Thief?
Original Cast; *Joseph/Amazing Technicolor
Dreamcoat* .... (MCA)
  Joseph/Amazing Technicolor Dreamcoat ....(POL)

Who's Zoomin' Who
Aretha Franklin; *Who's Zoomin' Who* .... (ARI)
Why
Annie Lennox; *Diva* .... (ARI)
Byrds; *Original Singles-#1-1965-1967* ....(COL)
   Byrds (collection) ....(COL)
   Younger Than Yesterday ....(COL)
Cathy Dennis; *Into The Skyline* .... (POL)
Donny Osmond; *Greatest Hits* ....(CCB)
Fleetwood Mac; *25 Years-The Chain* .... (WB)
Robert Plant; *Now & Zen* .... (EPR)
Why Am I A Fool For You
Jarmels; *14 Golden Classics* .... (CLT)
Why Am I Drinkin'
Merle Haggard; *Going Where The Lonely Go* ..... (EPI)
   Super Hits .... (EPI)
Why Am I So Shy
Chiffons; *Everything You Always Wanted To Hear
By* ....(LAU)
   Golden Classics ....(CLT)
Why Baby Why
Charley Pride; *Greatest Hits-#2* ....(RCA)
George Jones; *All-Time Greatest Hits-#1* .... (EPI)
   Super Hits .... (EPI)
Red Sovine & Webb Pierce; *Greatest Country Duets Of
All Time* ....(MSP)
Webb Pierce; *Golden Hits-#2* .... (PLN)
Willie Nelson & Waylon Jennings; *Take It To The
Limit* ....(COL)
Why Can't The English
Rex Harrison; *ST/My Fair Lady* ....(COL)
Rex Harrison/Original Cast; *My Fair Lady* ......(COL)
Why Can't We Be Friends
War; *Best Of & More* .... (RHI)
   Why Can't We Be Friends ....(AVE)
Why Can't You Bring Me Home
Jay/Americans; *All-Time Greatest Hits* .... (RHI)
   Come A Little Big Closer-Best Of .... (EMI)
Why Can't You Come Home
Ex-Girlfriend; *X Marks The Spot* .... (RPR)
Why Did I Choose You
Barbra Streisand; *Greatest Hits* ....(COL)
   My Name Is Barbra ....(COL)
Marvin Gaye; *Romantically Yours* ....(COL)
Michael Crawford; *With Love* ....(ATL)
Why Did You Waste My Time?
Screamin' Jay Hawkins; *Collectables Blues
Collection-#1* ....(CLT)
Why Didn't I Think Of That
Doug Stone; *From The Heart* .... (EPI)
Why Do Fools Fall In Love
Beach Boys; *Spirit Of America* ....(CAP)
Diana Ross; *Why Do Fools Fall In Love* ....(RCA)
Frankie Lymon/Teenagers; *Best Of* .... (RHI)
   Billboard Top Rock 'N' Roll Hits-1956 .... (RHI)
   ST/American Graffiti .... (\CA)
Joni Mitchell; *Shadows & Light* .... (ASY)
Why Don't That Telephone Ring
Tracy Byrd; *Tracy Byrd* .... (MCA)
Why Don't We Get Drunk
Jimmy Buffett; *Boats Beaches Bars & Ballads* ... (MGR)
   Songs You Know By Heart-Greatest Hits .... (MCA)
   White Sport Coat & A Pink Crustacean ... (MCA)
   You Had To Be There-In Concert .... (MCA)
Why Don't You Do Right
Benny Goodman; *16 Most Requested Songs* ......(COL)
Ella Fitzgerald & Joe Pass; *Easy Living* ...... (PAB)
Peggy Lee; *All-Time Greatest Hits-#1* ....(CCB)
   Capitol Collectors Series-#1-Early Years ......(CAP)
Why Don't You Spend The Night
Ronnie Milsap; *Milsap Music* ....(RCA)
Why Haven't I Heard From You
Reba McEntire; *Read My Mind* .... (MCA)
Why Me Lord
Johnny Cash; *American Recordings* .... (AME)
Why Walk When You Can Fly
Mary Chapin Carpenter; *Stones In The Road* ....(COL)
Why Was I Born
Billie Holiday; *Quintessential-#3-1936-1937* ....(COL)
Elisabeth Welch; *Sings Jerome Kern* ....(RCA)
Frank Sinatra; *Voice: The Columbia
Years-1943-1952* ....(COL)
Lena Horne; *20 Golden Pieces Of* ....(BLD)
   The Lady ....(DHL)

Why You Get Funky On Me
Today; *New Formula* ....(MOT)
   ST/House Party ....(MOT)
Why'd You Come In Here Lookin' Like That
Dolly Parton; *White Limozeen* ....(COL)
Will He Wait A Little Longer
Stanley Brothers; *Stanley Series-Vol. 1-#3* ....(COP)
Will I Ever Understand You
Berlin; *Best Of-1979-1988* .... (GEF)
   Count Three & Pray .... (GEF)
Will I Start To Bleed
Marty Willson-Piper; *Spirit Level* ....(RYK)
Will It Be Love By Morning
Michael Martin Murphey; *Best Of* .... (EMI)
   Heart Never Lies .... (LIB)
Will It Go Round In Circles
Billy Preston; *Best Of* ....(A&M)
   Billboard Top Rock 'N' Roll Hits-1973 .... (RHI)
   Soul Hits/'70s-#11 .... (RHI)
Will The Circle Be Unbroken
Charlie Daniels Band/Friends; *Volunteer Jam #3 &
#4* .... (EPI)
Joan Baez; *Country Music Album* .... (VAN)
   First 10 Years .... (VAN)
Nitty Gritty Dirt Band; *Will The Circle Be
Unbroken* .... (EMI)
Roy Acuff; *Best Of* ....(CCB)
Willie Nelson; *Willie & Family Live* ....(COL)
Will There Be A Shopping Mall In Heaven?
Reverend Billy C. Wirtz; *Deep Fried & Sanctified* . (HT)
Will You Be Loving Another Man
Bill Monroe/Blue Grass Boys; *Essential Bill
Monroe-1945-1949* ....(COL)
Will You Be There
Michael Jackson; *Dangerous* .... (EPI)
   ST/Free Willy ....(MJJ)
Will You Be There (In The Morning)
Heart; *Desire Walks On* ....(CAP)
Will You Ever Save
Lisette Melendez; *True To Life* .... (FEV)
Will You Marry Me?
Original Cast; *Pipe Dream* ....(RCA)
Paula Abdul; *Spellbound* .... (CPT)
Will You Still Be Mine
Morgana King; *Simply Eloquent* ....(MUS)
Mundell Lowe; *Mundell Lowe Quartet* ....(RVR)
Red Garland Trio; *Groovy* ....(PRS)
Rosemary Clooney; *With Love* ....(CCJ)
Will You Still Love Me Tomorrow
Carole King; *Tapestry* .... (EPI)
Frankie Valli/Four Seasons; *Greatest Hits-#2* .... (RHI)
Linda Ronstadt; *Retrospective* ....(CAP)
Roberta Flack; *Best Of* ....(ATL)
   Quiet Fire ....(ATL)
Shirelles; *16 Greatest Hits* ....(TRP)
   Anthology-1959-1964 .... (RHI)
   Girl Groups .... (RHI)
   More Dirty Dancing ....(RCA)
   Oldies But Goodies-#14 .... (MCA)
   Wonder Women-#2 ....(MOT)
(Without You) What Do I Do With Me
Tanya Tucker; *What Do I Do With Me* .... (LIB)
Won'tcha Come Out Tonight
Beach Boys; *M.I.U. Album* ....(CAR)
Would I Lie To You
Charles & Eddie; *Duophonic* ....(CAP)
Eurythmics; *Be Yourself Tonight* ....(RCA)
   Greatest Hits .... (ARI)
Whitesnake; *Come An' Get It* .... (GEF)
Would Jesus Wear A Rolex
Ray Stevens; *All-Time Greatest Comic Hits* ....(CCB)
   Collection .... (MCA)
   Greatest Hits-#2 .... (MCA)
Would They Love Him Down In Shreveport
George Jones; *Hallelujah Weekend* .... (EPI)
Oak Ridge Boys; *Bobbie Sue* .... (MCA)
Would You Catch A Falling Star
John Anderson; *Greatest Hits* .... (WB)
   I Just Came Home To Count The Memories ...... (WB)
Wouldn't It Be Loverly
Original Cast; *My Fair Lady* ....(LON)

Wouldn't It Be Nice
Beach Boys; *Absolutely Best-#2* ....(CAP)
   Made In The U.S.A. ....(CAP)
   Pet Sounds ....(CAP)
   Still Cruisin' ....(CAP)
Would?
Alice In Chains; *Dirt* ....(COL)
   ST/Singles ....(EPI)

RADIO, DJs
See Also: MUSIC, ROCK

7 Dee Jays
Boogie Down Productions; *Edutainment (Education + Entertainment)* ....(JVA)
Airwaves
Thomas Dolby; *Blinded By Science* ....(CAP)
   Golden Age Of Wireless ....(CAP)
All The Love Is On The Radio
Tom Jones; *45* ....(MER)
Around The Dial
Kinks; *Give The People What They Want* ....(ARI)
   Live-The Road ....(MCA)
As The Radio Plays
Rick Hearst; *With Love From The Soaps* ....(QUA)
Atmospherics: Listen To The Radio
Tom Robinson; *Hope & Glory* ....(GEF)
Baby Won't You Let Me Rock & Roll You
Ten Years After; *A Space In Time* ....(COL)
Bad Boy/Having A Party
Luther Vandross; *Best Of...The Best Of Love* ......(EPI)
   Forever For Always For Love ....(EPI)
Beat Box
Art Of Noise; *Art Of Noise* ....(ISL)
   Best Of ....(CHI)
Bedside Radio
Krokus; *Alive & Screamin'* ....(ARI)
   Metal Rendez-vous ....(ARI)
Canned Music
Dan Hicks/Hot Licks; *Striking It Rich* ....(MCA)
Capital Radio One
Clash; *Story Of-#1* ....(EPI)
Caravan
Duke Ellington; *Best Of* ....(CAP)
   Money Jungle ....(BLN)
Ella Fitzgerald; *Montreux '75* ....(PAB)
Johnny Mathis; *In A Sentimental Mood-Sings Ellington* ....(COL)
Van Morrison; *Moondance* ....(WB)
Van Morrison/Band; *Last Waltz* ....(WB)
Wynton Marsalis; *Marsalis Standard Time-#1* ....(COL)
Dance Dance Dance
Beach Boys; *Absolute Best-#1* ....(CAP)
   Dance Dance Dance ....(CAP)
   Greatest Hits ....(BVM)
   Made In The U.S.A. ....(CAP)
   Spirit Of America ....(CAP)
Clarence Clemons; *Night With Mr. C* ....(COL)
Steve Miller Band; *Fly Like An Eagle* ....(CAP)
   Greatest Hits ....(CAP)
Devil's Radio
George Harrison; *Cloud Nine* ....(DKH)
George Harrison/Eric Clapton & Band; *Live In Japan* ....(DKH)
Disc Jockey Jump
Gene Krupa; *Be Bop Era* ....(COL)
Do You Remember Rock 'N' Roll Radio
Ramones; *End Of The Century* ....(SIR)
   Mania ....(SIR)
Don't Touch That Dial
Engelbert Humperdinck; *Live In Concert/All Of Me* ....(EPI)
   Love's Only Love ....(EPI)
D.J.
David Bowie; *Changestwobowie* ....(RCA)
   Lodger ....(RYK)
   The Singles-1969-1993 ....(RYK)
Every Little Thing
Beatles; *For Sale* ....(CAP)
   Love Songs ....(CAP)
   VI ....(CAP)
Carlene Carter; *Little Love Letters* ....(GIA)

Yes; *Yes* ....(ATL)
   Yesyears ....(ATC)
Fadin' In, Fadin' Out
Tommy Overstreet; *Audiograph Alive* ....(AUD)
FM
Steely Dan; *Gold* ....(MCA)
   ST/FM ....(MCA)
Havin' A Party
Norma Jean; *Norma Jean* ....(BRS)
Pointer Sisters; *Havin' A Party* ....(MCA)
Rod Stewart & Ronnie Wood; *MTV's Unplugged...And Seated* ....(WB)
Sam Cooke; *Best Of* ....(RCA)
   Feel It ....(RCA)
   Live At The Harlem Square Club ....(RCA)
   This Is ....(RCA)
Southside Johnny/Asbury Jukes; *Havin' A Party With* ....(EPI)
Hey D.J.
Bingoboys; *Best Of* ....(ATL)
Lighter Shade Of Brown; *ST/Mi Vida Loca* .....(MER)
World's Famous Supreme Team; *45* ....(ISL)
Hey Mr. DJ
Army Of Lovers; *Army Of Lovers* ....(GIA)
Zhane'; *S* ....(FLV)
How To Kill A Radio Consultant
Public Enemy; *Apocalypse 91-Enemy Strikes Black* ....(DFC)
   Greatest Misses ....(CHA)
H.A.P.P.Y. Radio
Edwin Starr; *45* ....(OOP)
I Can't Say It On The Radio
Girls Next Door; *Girls Next Door* ....(MTM)
Susie Allanson; *45* ....(ENI)
I Love The Radio
Joey Welz; *Return Of Haley's Comet* ....(CPR)
I Watched It All (On My Radio)
Lionel Cartwright; *I Watched It All On The Radio* ....(MCA)
I've Got A Radio
Coyote Sisters; *Coyote Sisters* ....(MOR)
Jesus On The Radio
Tom T. Hall; *Ol' T's In Town* ....(RCA)
KSOS
Emmylou Harris; *Ballad Of Sally Rose* ....(WB)
Last Night A D.J. Saved My Life
Indeep; *Disco Years-#2-On The Beat-1978-1982* (RHI)
   Last Night A D.J. Saved My Life ....(SON)
Late Night Radio
John Denver; *Windsong* ....(RCA)
Life Is A Rock (But The Radio Rolled Me)
Reunion; *Super Hits/'70s-Have A Nice Day-#13* .. (RHI)
Listen To The Radio
Don Williams; *Best Of-#3* ....(MCA)
   Listen To The Radio ....(MCA)
Kathy Mattea; *Lonesome Standard Time* ....(MER)
Nanci Griffith; *Storms* ....(MCA)
Mexican Radio
Wall Of Voodoo; *Call Of The West* ....(IRS)
   Ugly Americans In Australia ....(IRS)
   Wall Of Voodoo ....(IRS)
Midnight On The Radio
Mike Bloomfield; *Try It Before You Buy It* ....(OW)
Mohammed's Radio
Linda Ronstadt; *Living In The U.S.A.* ....(ASY)
Warren Zevon; *Quiet Normal Life-Best Of* ......(ASY)
   Stand In The Fire ....(ASY)
   Warren Zevon ....(ASY)
Morning Man
Joy; *Joy* ....(FAN)
Mr. D.J.
Charlie Daniels Band; *Simple Man* ....(EPI)
Joyce "Fenderella" Irby; *Maximum Thrust* ......(MOT)
Manhattans; *45* ....(COL)
Times 2; *X 2* ....(RPR)
Mr. Radio
Electric Light Orchestra; *Afterglow* ....(EPI)
   No Answer ....(JET)
My Radio Sure Sounds Good To Me
Larry Graham; *My Radio Sure Sounds Good To Me* ....(WB)
Oak Ridge Boys; *Oak Ridge Boys Have Arrived* .(MCA)
Nothing But The Radio On
Dave Koz & Joey Diggs; *Dave Koz* ....(CAP)

Oh Yeah
Roxy Music; *Flesh & Blood* .... (RPR)
Street Life-20 Great Hits .... (RPR)
On My Radio
Selecter; *Selected Selections* .... (CHR)
Too Much Pressure .... (CHR)
On The Radio
Cheap Trick; *Heaven Tonight* .... (EPI)
Donna Summer; *Greatest Hits* .... (CAS)
Summer Collection .... (MER)
On The Radio-Greatest Hits-#1&2 .... (CAS)
Walk Away-Best Of 1977-1980 .... (CAS)
Emmylou Harris; *White Shoes* .... (WB)
On Your Radio
Joe Jackson; *I'm The Man* .... (A&M)
Live..1980-1986 .... (A&M)
Overnight Sensation
Mickey Gilley; *Greatest Hits-#2* .... (EPI)
Raspberries/Eric Carmen; *Best* .... (CAP)
Steve Wariner; *Best Of* .... (RCA)
Tina Turner; *Break Every Rule* .... (CAP)
Live In Europe .... (CAP)
Pilot Of The Airwaves
Charlie Dore; *Where To Now* .... (ISL)
Play Those Oldies Mr. DJ
Anthony/Sophomores; *WCBS-FM 101-History Of
Rock-Doo-Wop-#2* .... (CLT)
Potato Radio
King & Moore; *Potato Radio* .... (JST)
Radio
Accelerators; *Accelerators* .... (PRO)
Dr. Hook; *Greatest Hits (& More)* .... (CAP)
Little Bit More .... (CAP)
Eazy-E; *Eazy Duz It* .... (RUP)
Nick Drake; *Fruit Tree* .... (HBL)
Pink Moon .... (HBL)
Roderick Falconer; *New Nation* .... (UA)
Steve Hillage; *Motivation Radio* .... (BP)
Steve Miller Band; *Italian X-Rays* .... (CAP)
Vince Gill; *Best Of* .... (RCA)
Radio 4
Public Image, Ltd.; *Second Edition* .... (WB)
Radio Active
Bryan Austin; *Bryan Austin* .... (PAT)
Radio Dream Girl
Roger Voudouris; *Radio Dream Girl* .... (WB)
Radio Ethiopia
Patti Smith Group; *Radio Ethiopia* .... (ARI)
Radio Free Europe
R.E.M.; *Eponymous* .... (IRS)
Murmur .... (IRS)
Radio Free Moscow
Jethro Tull; *Under Wraps* .... (CHR)
Radio Ga Fa
Queen; *Classic Queen* .... (HOL)
Works .... (HOL)
Radio Girl
John Hiatt; *Slug Line* .... (MCA)
Y'All Caught? Ones That Got Away-1975-85 .. (GEF)
Marshall Crenshaw; *Good Evening* .... (WB)
Radio Head
Talking Heads; *True Stories* .... (SIR)
Radio Heart
Charly McClain; *19 Hot Country Requests-#3* .... (EPI)
Biggest Hits .... (EPI)
Greatest Country Hits/'80s-1985 .... (COL)
Radio Heart .... (EPI)
Radio Is Broken
Frank Zappa; *Man From Utopia* .... (BAR)
Radio Kingdom
Beach Boys; *Holland* .... (CAR)
Radio Land
Michael Martin Murphey; *Best Of* .... (EMI)
Heart Never Lies .... (LIB)
Radio Lover
George Jones; *By Request* .... (EPI)
Jones Country .... (EPI)
One Woman Man .... (EPI)
Radio Man
World's Famous Supreme Team; *45* .... (ISL)
Radio M.U.S.I.C. Man
Womack & Womack; *Radio M.U.S.I.C. Man* ..... (ELE)
Radio People
Zapp; *New Zapp IV U* .... (WB)

Radio Radio
Elvis Costello; *Best Of Elvis Costello/Attractions* ..(COL)
This Year's Model .... (COL)
Radio Romance
Tiffany; *Hold An Old Friend's Hand* .... (MCA)
Tommy Roe; *45* .... (MCA)
Radio Silence
Boris Grebenshikov; *Radio Silence* .... (COL)
Thomas Dolby; *Golden Age Of Wireless* .... (CAP)
Radio Song
Dillard & Clark; *Fantastic Expedition/Through The
Morning* .... (MOB)
Joe Walsh; *Got Any Gum* .... (FM)
R.E.M.; *Out Of Time* .... (WB)
Radio Spot/Nervous Breakdown
Bobby Fuller; *Tapes-#1* .... (RHI)
Radio Station
Run-D.M.C.; *Tougher Than Leather* .... (PRO)
(Radio Station) EXP
Jimi Hendrix; *Axis Bold As Love* .... (RPR)
Radio Suckers
Ice-T; *Power* .... (SIR)
Radio Sweetheart
Elvis Costello; *Taking Liberties* .... (COL)
Radio Waves
Roger Waters; *Radio K.A.O.S.* .... (COL)
Radioland
Nicolette Larson; *Radioland* .... (MCA)
Radios In Motion
XTC; *White Music* .... (GEF)
Raised On Radio
Journey; *Raised On Radio* .... (COL)
Reggae Radio Station
Third World; *Hold On To Love* .... (COL)
Road Runner
Greg Kihn Band; *With The Naked Eye* .... (BES)
Joan Jett; *Hit List* .... (BLK)
Joan Jett/Blackhearts; *Good Music* .... (BLK)
Jonathan Richman/Modern Lovers; *Beserkley Years-Best
Of* .... (RHI)
Modern Lovers; *Modern Lovers* .... (RHI)
Pretty Things; *History Of British Rock-#5* .... (RHI)
Rock And Roll
Lou Reed; *Rock & Roll Animal* .... (RCA)
Velvet Underground; *Another View* .... (VRV)
Live 1969 .... (MER)
Live Rock & Roll Animal .... (MER)
Loaded .... (WSP)
Rock On The Radio
Firehouse; *Firehouse* .... (EPI)
Rock Radio Into The Nineties & Beyond
KLF; *Chill Out* .... (WAX)
Rock & Roll Radio
Ramones; *End Of The Century* .... (SIR)
Rockabilly On The Radio
Jack Smith/Rockabilly Planet; *Jack Smith/Rockabilly
Planet* .... (FF)
Rockin' Radio
Tom Browne; *45* .... (ARI)
Rodney On The ROQ
Target 13; *Rodney On The ROQ-#2* .... (PBO)
Roll Over Beethoven
Beatles; *At The Hollywood Bowl* .... (CAP)
Box Set .... (CAP)
Rock & Roll Music-#1 .... (CAP)
Second Album .... (CAP)
With The Beatles .... (CAP)
Byrds; *Byrds (collection)* .... (COL)
Chuck Berry; *Chess Box* .... (CSS)
Cruisin'-1956 .... (INC)
Golden Hits .... (MER)
Greatest Hits .... (EVR)
Oldies But Goodies-#10 .... (OSR)
Electric Light Orchestra; *Afterglow* .... (EPI)
Ole ELO .... (JET)
Russian Radio
Red Flag; *Naive Art* .... (ENC)
She Got The Radio
Cory Hart; *First Offense* .... (AMR)
Sleepin' With The Radio On
Charly McClain; *Greatest Hits* .... (EPI)
Surround Me With Love .... (EPI)
Ten Year Anniversary .... (EPI)

Song On The Radio
Al Stewart; *Best Of* .... (ARI)
   Time Passages .... (ARI)
Jane Gillman; *Jane Gillman* .... (GRE)
Spirit Of Radio
Rush; *Chronicles* .... (MER)
   Exit...Stage Left .... (MER)
   Permanent Waves .... (MER)
Stone Cold Country
Gibson/Miller Band; *Where There's Smoke* .... (EPI)
Sunday Morning Radio
Sha-Na-Na; *Sh-Boom* .... (ACC)
Surfin' U.S.A.
Beach Boys; *Absolute Best-#1* .... (CAP)
   Best Of .... (CAP)
   Billboard Top Rock 'N' Roll Hits-1963 .... (RHI)
   Endless Summer .... (CAP)
   Made In The U.S.A. .... (CAP)
Jesus & Mary Chain; *Barbed Wire Kisses* .... (DEF)
Texas Radio Horror
Strip Mind; *What's In Your Mouth* .... (SIR)
Thank God For The Radio
Kendalls; *20 Favorites* .... (EPI)
   Movin' Train .... (MER)
There Ain't Nothin' Wrong With The Radio
Aaron Tippin; *Read Between The Lines* .... (RCA)
   Today's Hit Country .... (KT)
This D.J.
Warren G.; *Regulate...G Funk Era* .... (VIO)
This Is Radio Clash
Clash; *On Broadway* .... (EPI)
   Story Of-#1 .... (EPI)
This Is Radio Etienne
Saint Etienne; *Foxbase Alpha* .... (WB)
This Is Something For The Radio
Biz Markie; *Goin' Off* .... (CLD)
Top 40 Radio (The History Of Rock)
Joel Welz; *Return Of Haley's Comet* .... (CPR)
Turn On The Radio
Rollers; *Elevator* .... (ARI)
Tommy Page; *Paintings In My Mind* .... (SIR)
Turn On Your Radio
Nilsson; *Son Of Schmilsson* .... (RCA)
Turn That Radio On
Ronnie Milsap; *Back To The Grindstone* .... (RCA)
   Club .... (RCA)
Turn The Radio On
Roy Acuff; *Best Of* .... (CCB)
Turn Up The Music
Sammy Hagar; *Best Of* .... (CAP)
   Live .... (CAP)
   Musical Chairs .... (CAP)
Turn Up The Radio
Autograph; *Sign In Please* .... (RCA)
Rockets; *Live Rockets* .... (CAP)
Turn Your Radio On
Chris Hillman; *Desert Rose* .... (SH)
John Hartford; *Aero Plain* .... (WB)
Ray Stevens; *Country Music*
Classics-#4-1970-1975 .... (KT)
   Greatest Hits .... (MCA)
Roy Acuff; *Best Of* .... (CCB)
   Greatest Hits-#1 .... (ELE)
Turn Your Radio On, Kentucky
Blue Sky Boys; *Sunny Side Of Life* .... (ROU)
Turn Yo' Radio On
Leadbelly; *Gwine Dig A Hole To Put The Devil In* (ROU)
Video Killed The Radio Star
Bruce Woolly/Camera Club; *Bruce Woolly/Camera*
Club .... (COL)
Buggles; *Age Of Plastic* .... (ISL)
   Island Story-1962-1987-25th Anniversary .... (ISL)
   Rock Of The '80s-#2 .... (PRY)
Voice On The Radio
Andre Cymone; *Livin' In The New Wave* .... (COL)
Sheena Easton; *Sheena Easton* .... (EMI)
Wasp (Texas Radio & The Big Beat)
Doors; *Alive She Cried* .... (ELE)
   Classics .... (ELE)
   L.A. Woman .... (ELE)
   Weird Scenes Inside The Goldmine .... (ELE)
We Want The Airwaves
Ramones; *Pleasant Dreams* .... (SIR)
   Ramones Mania .... (SIR)

"WKRP In Cincinnati" Theme
Steve Carlisle; *Sings WKRP* .... (MCA)
W.O.L.D.
Harry Chapin; *Anthology* .... (ELE)
   Gold Medal Collection .... (ELE)
   Greatest Stories-Live .... (ELE)
   Short Stories .... (ELE)
Yesterday Once More
Carpenters; *Classics-#2* .... (A&M)
   Now & Then .... (A&M)
   Singles 1969-1973 .... (A&M)
   Yesterday Once More .... (A&M)
You Turn Me On I'm A Radio
Ed Bruce; *Homecoming* .... (RCA)
Gail Davies; *45* .... (WB)
Joni Mitchell; *For The Roses* .... (ASY)
   Miles Of Aisles .... (ASY)

RAIN, Fog, Hurricanes, Lightning, Storms, Thunder

   See Also: CHAOS, SKY, SUN

100% Chance Of Rain
Gary Morris; *Anything Goes* .... (WB)
Acid Rain
John Martyn; *Sapphire* .... (ISL)
Saigon Kick; *Saigon Kick* .... (THI)
After The Rain
Bruce Cockburn; *Dancing In The Dragon's Jaws* .. (GC)
John Coltrane; *Best Of-His Greatest Years* .... (MCA)
   Gentle Side Of .... (MCA)
   Impressions .... (MCI)
Nelson; *After The Rain* .... (DGC)
After The Storm
Crosby, Stills & Nash; *After The Storm* .... (ATL)
Ain't No Sunshine
Bill Withers; *Greatest Hits* .... (OOP)
   Just As I Am .... (OOP)
Michael Jackson; *Original Soul Of* .... (MOT)
Alabama Rain
Jim Croce; *Down The Highway* .... (21)
   Time In A Bottle .... (21)
American Storm
Bob Seger/Silver Bullet Band; *Like A Rock* ...... (CAP)
And It Stoned Me
Van Morrison; *Best Of* .... (MER)
   Moondance .... (WB)
And The Heavens Cried
Anthony Newley; *Genuis Of* .... (LON)
Another Rainy Day In New York City
Chicago; *If You Leave Me Now* .... (COL)
   X .... (COL)
Another Rainy Night
Queensryche; *Empire* .... (EMI)
April Mist
Tom Harrell; *Visions* .... (CTM)
April Showers
Al Jolson; *Best Of* .... (MCA)
   Story-#2 .... (MCA)
Judy Garland; *Hits Of* .... (CAP)
   Judy .... (CAP)
Arkansas Traveler
Albert Lee; *Speechless* .... (MCA)
Floyd Cramer; *Country Gold* .... (STE)
Mark O'Connor; *Championship Years* .... (CMF)
Michelle Shocked; *Arkansas Traveler* .... (MER)
Sam Hinton; *Newport Folk Festival '63* .... (VAN)
Ashes, The Rain & I
James Gang; *Best Of* .... (MCA)
   Greatest Hits .... (MCA)
   Rides Again .... (MCA)
August Rain
Murray Attaway; *In Thrall* .... (DGC)
Baby The Rain Must Fall
Glenn Yarbrough; *Best Of* .... (RCA)
   Nipper's Greatest Hits-'60s-#1 .... (RCA)
Bangkok Rain
Cult; *Ceremony* .... (SIR)
Before The Deluge
Jackson Browne; *Late For The Sky* .... (ASY)
Joan Baez; *Honest Lullaby* .... (POR)

Before The Next Teardrop Falls
Freddie Fender; *Before The Next Teardrop Falls* (MCA)
  Best Of .... (MCA)
  Oldies But Goodies-#2 .... (OSR)
Ray Anthony; *Great Golden Hits* .... (RAN)
Black Summer Rain
Eric Clapton; *No Reason To Cry* .... (RSO)
Blame It On The Rain
Milli Vanilli; *Girl You Know It's True* .... (ARI)
Blue Eyes Crying In The Rain
Roy Acuff; *Greatest Hits-#1* .... (ELE)
Roy Acuff/Smokey Mountain Boys; *Columbia Country
Classics-#1-Golden Age* ....(COL)
Willie Nelson; *Columbia Country Classics-#5-New
Trad.* ....(COL)
  Greatest Hits & Some That Will Be ....(COL)
  Red Headed Stranger ....(COL)
  ST/Honeysuckle Rose ....(COL)
Blue Umbrella
Ed Bruce; *Ed Bruce* .... (MCA)
John Prine; *Sweet Revenge* .... (ATL)
Box Of Rain
Grateful Dead; *American Beauty* .... (WB)
Bride Of Rain Dog
Tom Waits; *Rain Dogs* .... (ISL)
Bus Stop
Hollies; *Best Of-#1* .... (EMI)
  Greatest Hits .... (EPI)
  History Of British Rock-#3 .... (RHI)
Can You Stand The Rain
New Edition; *Heart Break* .... (MCA)
Can You Stop The Rain
Peabo Bryson; *Can You Stop The Rain* ....(COL)
Chain Lightning
38 Special; *Special Forces* .... (A&M)
Rush; *Presto* .... (ATL)
Steely Dan; *Gold* .... (MCA)
  Katy Lied .... (MCA)
Cloudburst
Jon Hendricks; *Jon Hendricks* .... (ENJ)
Lambert, Hendricks & Bavan; *Swingin' Till The Girls
Come Home* .... (BLU)
Lambert, Hendricks & Ross; *Best Of* ....(COL)
  & Ike Isaacs Trio: Everybody's Boppin' ....(COL)
Pointer Sisters; *Retrospect* .... (MCA)
Cold Rain
Crosby, Stills & Nash; *CSN* .... (ATL)
Cold Rain And Snow
Grateful Dead; *Grateful Dead* .... (WB)
  Steal Your Face! .... (GRD)
Cold Rain In Kansas
Don Lange; *Natural Born Heathen* .... (FF)
Coloured Rain
Traffic; *Best Of* .... (UA)
  Mr. Fantasy .... (ISL)
Come Rain Or Come Shine
Frank Sinatra & Gloria Estefan; *Frank Sinatra
Duets* ....(CAP)
Judy Garland; *America's Treasure* ....(DHL)
  At Carnegie Hall ....(CAP)
  Hits Of ....(CAP)
  Judy ....(CAP)
Cry Like A Rainstorm
Bonnie Raitt; *Takin' My Time* .... (WB)
Linda Ronstadt; *Cry Like A Rainstorm-Howl Like The
Wind* .... (ELE)
Crying In The Rain
Art Garfunkel & James Taylor; *Up 'Til Now* .....(COL)
A-Ha; *East Of The Sun West Of The Moon* .... (WB)
Dave Edmunds & Nick Lowe; *Dave Edmunds
Anthology-1968-1990* .... (RHI)
Everly Brothers; *All-Time Greatest Hits* .... (CCB)
  Golden Hits Of .... (WB)
  Very Best Of .... (WB)
Londonbeat; *In The Blood* .... (RAD)
Rockpile; *Seconds Of Pleasure* ....(COL)
Tammy Wynette; *Biggest Hits* .... (EPI)
  Tears Of Fire-25th Anniversary Collect. ...... (EPI)
Whitesnake; *Saints & Sinners* .... (GEF)
  Whitesnake .... (GEF)
Dallas In The Rain
Clyde Crell; *45* ....(OOP)
December African Rain
Juluka; *Best Of* ....(RHY)

Diamonds On My Windshield
Tom Waits; *Anthology* .... (ASY)
  Heart Of Saturday Night .... (ASY)
Don't Count The Rainy Days
John Conlee; *In My Eyes* .... (MCA)
Michael Martin Murphey; *Best Of* .... (EMI)
  Heart Never Lies .... (LIB)
Don't Rain On My Parade
Barbra Streisand; *Greatest Hits* ....(COL)
  Live At The Forum ....(COL)
  Original Cast-Funny Girl ....(CAP)
  ST/Funny Girl ....(COL)
  & Other Musical Instruments ....(COL)
Don't Sleep In The Subway
Frank Sinatra; *Frank Sinatra* .... (RPR)
Petula Clark; *Greatest Hits* .... (CRS)
  Summer Of Love .... (RHI)
Earthquake & Hurricane
Tina Turner; *Rough* .... (UA)
Willie Dixon; *Mighty Earthquake & Hurricane* ...(PAU)
Fire And Rain
James Taylor; *Greatest Hits* .... (WB)
  Sweet Baby James .... (WB)
Sammy Kershaw; *Red Hot + Country* .... (MER)
Flowers Never Bend With The Rainfall
Simon & Garfunkel; *Collected Works* ....(COL)
  Parsley Sage Rosemary & Thyme ....(COL)
Fog In Monterey
Mary Black; *No Frontiers* .... (GFT)
Foggy Day
Ella Fitzgerald; *Ella In Rome-Birthday Concert* ..(VRV)
  George & Ira Gershwin Songbook ....(VRV)
Ella Fitzgerald & Joe Pass; *Take Love Easy* ...... (PAB)
Ella Fitzgerald & Louis Armstrong; *Ella & Louis* (VRV)
Frank Sinatra; *Songs For Young Lovers & Swing
Easy* ....(CAP)
Fred Astaire; *Sings* .... (MCA)
  Starring Fred Astaire ....(COL)
Judy Garland; *At Carnegie Hall* ....(CAP)
Wynton Marsalis; *Marsalis Standard Time-#1* ....(COL)
Foggy Day (In London Town)
Dick Hyman; *Music Of 1937-Maybeck Recital
Hall-#3* .... (CCJ)
Foggy Mountain Breakdown
Flatt & Scruggs; *20 All-Time Great Recordings* ...(COL)
  Truckers' Jukebox: Top Radio Requests .... (EPI)
Lester Flatt; *Foggy Mountain Breakdown* ....(RCA)
  Live Bluegrass Festival ....(RCA)
Tony Trischka; *Banjoland* .... (ROU)
Foggy Night In London Town
Fred Astaire; *45* ....(OOP)
Foggy Streets Of London
Special EFX; *Special EFX* .... (GRP)
Foggy Waterfall
Left Banke; *History Of* .... (RHI)
Foggy, Foggy Dew
Burl Ives; *Best Of* .... (MCA)
Fogtown
Michelle Shocked; *Texas Campfire Tapes* .... (MER)
Fog, The
Kate Bush; *Sensual World* ....(COL)
Fool In The Rain
Led Zeppelin; *In Through The Out Door* .... (SS)
  Led Zeppelin (collection) .... (ATL)
Garden In The Rain
Four Aces; *20 Greatest Hits* .... (EVR)
  Best Of .... (MCA)
  Precious Memories .... (ACC)
God Of Thunder
Kiss; *Alive 2* .... (CAS)
  Destroyer .... (CAS)
  Double Platinum .... (CAS)
Hard Rain's Gonna Fall
Bob Dylan; *Concert For Bangla Desh* ....(CAP)
  Freewheelin' ....(COL)
  Greatest Hits-#2 ....(COL)
Bryan Ferry; *Street Life-20 Great Hits* .... (RPR)
  These Foolish Things .... (RPR)
Edie Brickell/New Bohemians; *ST/Born On The Fourth
Of July* .... (MCA)
Joan Baez; *Farewell Angelina* .... (VAN)
  First 10 Years .... (VAN)

Have You Ever Seen The Rain
Creedence Clearwater Revival; *1970* ....(FAN)
   Chronicle ....(FAN)
   Pendulum ....(FAN)
Heart Like A Hurricane
Larry Stewart; *Heart Like A Hurricane* ....(COL)
Here's That Rainy Day
Frank Sinatra; *Capitol Years* ....(CAP)
Gene Ammons; *Boss Is Back* ....(PRS)
Kenny Rankin; *Kenny Rankin Album* ....(LD)
Rosemary Clooney; *Sings Ballads* ....(CCJ)
Hurricane
Bob Dylan; *Desire* ....(COL)
Joe Memphis & Larry Collins; *Rockabilly Stars-#3* (EPI)
Leon Everette; *45* ....(RCA)
Neil Diamond; *Heartlight* ....(COL)
I Love A Rainy Night
Eddie Rabbitt; *All-Time Greatest Hits* .... (WB)
   Greatest Hits-#2 ....(WB)
   Horizon ....(ELE)
   Number 1's ....(WB)
   Ten Years Of Greatest Hits ....(CAP)
I Made It Through The Rain
Barry Manilow; *Barry* ....(ARI)
   Greatest Hits-#3 ....(ARI)
I Sure Can Smell The Rain
BlackHawk; *BlackHawk* ....(ARI)
I Think It's Gonna Rain Today
Bette Midler; *ST/Beaches* ....(ATL)
Judy Collins; *In My Life* ....(ELE)
Neil Diamond; *Rainbow* ....(MCA)
   Stones ....(MCA)
Randy Newman; *12 Songs* ....(RPR)
I Wish It Would Rain
Nanci Griffith; *Little Love Affairs* ....(MCA)
Temptations; *16 #1 Hits From The Late '60s* .... (MOT)
   All The Million-Sellers ....(MOT)
   Anthology ....(MOT)
   Billboard Top R&B Hits-1968 ....(MOT)
   Compact Command Performances ....(MOT)
   Motown Story ....(MOT)
I Wish It Would Rain Down
Phil Collins; *...But Seriously* ....(ATL)
Is It Raining At Your House
Vern Gosdin; *10 Years Of Greatest Hits Newly*
   Recorded ....(COL)
   Chiseled In Stone ....(COL)
   Greatest Country Hits/'90s-1991 ....(COL)
It Always Rains On Saturday
Reba McEntire; *Sweet Sixteen* ....(MCA)
It Always Rains On Sundays
Box; *Pleasure & The Pain* ....(CAP)
It Might As Well Rain Until September
Carole King; *More American Graffiti* ....(MCA)
It Never Rains In Southern California
Albert Hammond; *Rock Artifacts-#2* ....(COL)
   Super Hits/'70s-Have A Nice Day-#10 ....(RHI)
Tony! Toni! Tone!; *Revival* ....(WIN)
It's Gonna Rain
Take 6; *Join The Band* ....(RPR)
It's Raining Again
Supertramp; *Classics-#9* ....(A&M)
   Famous Last Words ....(A&M)
I'm No Stranger To The Rain
Keith Whitley; *Don't Close Your Eyes* ....(RCA)
   Greatest Hits ....(RCA)
January Rain
Hunters & Collectors; *Living Daylight* ....(IRS)
Just A Little Bit Of Rain
Fred Neil; *Just A Little Bit Of Rain* ....(ELE)
Linda Ronstadt; *Retrospective* ....(CAP)
Just Like The Weather
Suzy Bogguss; *Something Up My Sleeve* ....(LIB)
Just Walkin' In The Rain
Johnny Ray; *16 Most Requested Songs/'50s-#1* ...(COL)
   Best Of ....(COL)
   Greatest Hits ....(SSP)
Kentucky Rain
Elvis Presley; *Golden Records-#5* ....(RCA)
   Memphis Record ....(RCA)
   Pure Gold ....(RCA)
Kiss Me In The Rain
Barbra Streisand; *Wet* ....(COL)

Laughter In The Rain
Johnny Mathis; *When Will Is See You Again* ......(COL)
Neil Sedaka; *My Friend* ....(POL)
Let A Smile Be Your Umbrella
Sammy Kaye; *Best Of* ....(MCA)
Let It Rain
Eric Clapton; *Crossroads* ....(POL)
   Derek/Dominos Live ....(RSO)
   Eric Clapton ....(RSO)
UFO; *Best Of The Rest* ....(CHR)
Lightning Strikes
Lou Christie; *Oldies But Goodies-#14* ....(OSR)
Like A Hurricane
Neil Young; *Decade* ....(RPR)
Neil Young/Crazy Horse; *American Stars & Bars* (RPR)
   Live Rust ....(RPR)
Little White Cloud That Cried
Johnnie Ray; *Best Of* ....(COL)
   Greatest Hits ....(SSP)
Johnny Ray; *Best Of* ....(EXA)
Louisiana Rain
Tom Petty/Heartbreakers; *Damn The Torpedoes* . (BKS)
MacArthur Park
Andy Williams; *Greatest Hits-#2* ....(COL)
Donna Summer; *Live & More* ....(CAS)
   On The Radio-Greatest Hits-#1&2 ....(CAS)
   Summer Collection ....(CAS)
   Walk Away-Best Of 1977-1980 ....(CAS)
Richard Harris; *His Greatest Performances* ......(MCA)
   Love Album ....(MCA)
   Tramp Shining ....(MCA)
   Vintage Music-Orig. Oldies/'50s-'60s-#13 ....(MCA)
Waylon Jennings; *Are You Ready For The*
   Country ....(RCA)
   Best Of ....(RCA)
Mandolin Rain
Bruce Hornsby/Range; *The Way It Is* ....(RCA)
Mexico Rain
Johnny Rodriguez; *Biggest Hits* ....(EPI)
Michigan Rain
Gregg Alexander; *Intoxifornication* ....(EPA)
Monterey Mist
Modern Jazz Quartet; *Blues At Carnegie Hall* ....(ATL)
Montgomery In The Rain
Hank Williams, Jr.; *Early Years* ....(W/C)
Steve Young; *No Place To Fall* ....(RCA)
   Seven Bridges Road ....(ROU)
Naked In The Rain
David Crosby & Graham Nash; *Wind On The*
   Water ....(MCA)
Dio; *Dream Evil* ....(WB)
Hank Ballard/Midnighters; *Naked In The Rain* ...(AH)
Loretta Lynn; *Best Of-#2* ....(MSP)
Red Hot Chili Peppers; *Blood Sugar Sex Magik* ...(WB)
Nashville In The Rain
Ginger Boatwright; *Fertile Ground* ....(FF)
No Rain
Blind Melon; *Blind Melon* ....(CAP)
Nobody's Gonna Rain On Our Parade
Kathy Mattea; *Walking Away A Winner* ....(MER)
November Rain
Guns N' Roses; *Use Your Illusion I* ....(GEF)
On Rainy Afternoons
Barbra Streisand; *Wet* ....(COL)
Oregon Rain Song
George Roessler; *Still Life & Old Dreams* ....(EAG)
Purple Rain
Prince/Revolution; *ST/Purple Rain* ....(WB)
Quicksilver Lightning
Roger Daltrey; *ST/Quicksilver* ....(ATL)
Quiet Storm
Smokey Robinson; *Compact Command*
   Performances ....(MOT)
   Motown Superstar Series-#18 ....(MOT)
   Quiet Storm ....(MOT)
   Smokin' ....(MOT)
Radium Rain
Bruce Cockburn; *Big Circumstance* ....(COL)
Rain
21 Guns; *Salute* ....(RCA)
Beatles; *Box Set* ....(CAP)
   Hey Jude ....(CAP)
   Past Masters-#2 ....(CAP)
Bette Midler; *Thighs & Whispers* ....(ATL)

Candlebox; *Candlebox* .... (MAV)
Cult; *Love* .... (SIR)
Ella Fitzgerald & Joe Pass; *Fitzgerald &*
Pass...Again .... (PAB)
Jerry Garcia; *Cats Under The Stars* .... (ARI)
Jive Five; *Greatest Hits* .... (CLT)
Johnny Winter; *Winter Of '88* .... (VOY)
Jose Feliciano; *All-Time Greatest Hits* .... (RCA)
Larry Gatlin/Gatlin Brothers; *Pure N' Simple* ....(CAP)
Lee Greenwood; *When You're In Love* .... (CAP)
Levert; *Rope A Dope Style* .... (ATL)
Little Charlie/Nightcats; *Alligator 20th Anniversary*
Collection ....(ALG)
Madonna; *Erotica* .... (MAV)
Marquees; *For Collectors Only-Rarities-#1* ...... (CLT)
Skinny Puppy; *Rabies* .... (CAP)
Terence Trent D'Arby; *Introducing The Hardline*
According To .... (COL)
Todd Rundgren; *Faithful* .... (RHI)
Uriah Heep; *Magician's Birthday* .... (MER)
Wally Badarou; *Echoes* .... (ISL)
Rain Dogs
Tom Waits; *Big Time* .... (ISL)
Rain Dogs .... (ISL)
Rain Fallin'
Reba McEntire; *Out Of A Dream* .... (MER)
Rain Forest
Cut To The Chase; *Cut To The Chase* .... (A&C)
David Lanz & Paul Speer; *Narada-Equinox Sampler*
One .... (NAR)
Natural States .... (NAR)
Jeremy Steig/Eddie Gomez; *Rain Forest* .... (CMU)
Jessica Williams; *Rivers Of Memory* .... (CLE)
Nelson Rangell; *Nelson Rangell* .... (GRP)
Paul Hardcastle; *Dance 2* .... (PRO)
Paul Hardcastle .... (CHR)
Rain Forest .... (PRO)
Rain In My Heart
Frank Sinatra; *Cycles* .... (RPR)
Rain In Spain
Original Cast; *Forbidden Broadway-#2* .... (DRG)
My Fair Lady .... (COL)
Rex Harrison & Audrey Hepburn; *ST/My Fair*
Lady .... (COL)
Rain In The Summertime
Alarm; *Eye Of The Hurricane* .... (IRS)
Rain King
Counting Crows; *August And Everything After* .. (DGC)
Rain On The Roof
Lovin' Spoonful; *Anthology* .... (RHI)
Best Of .... (RAG)
Original Cast; *Follies In Concert* .... (RCA)
Rain On The Scarecrow
John Mellencamp; *Scarecrow* ....(RIV)
Rain Rain Go Away
Bobby Vinton; *All-Time Greatest Hits* .... (EPI)
Gerry Mulligan; *Happy Anniversary Charlie*
Brown! .... (GRP)
Rain Song
Led Zeppelin; *Houses Of The Holy* .... (ATL)
Remasters .... (ATL)
Led Zeppelin (collection) .... (ATL)
ST/Song Remains The Same .... (SS)
Rain (Falling From The Skies)
Frank Sinatra; *Where Are You?* .... (CAP)
Raindrops
Dee Clark; *Best of* .... (VJ)
Collectables Presents History Of Rock-#7 .... (CLT)
Hits From The Legendary Vee-Jay Records ..... (MOT)
Oldies But Goodies-#6 .... (OSR)
Del Shannon; *Liberty Years* .... (EMI)
Honeys; *Capitol Collectors Series* .... (CAP)
Raindrops Keep Fallin' On My Head
B.J. Thomas; *16 Greatest Hits* .... (TRP)
Best Of .... (DOM)
Greatest Hits .... (RHI)
ST/Butch Cassidy & The Sundance Kid .... (A&M)
ST/Forrest Gump .... (EPX)
'70s Greatest Rock Hits-#9-#1 Hits .... (PRY)
Raining In Baltimore
Counting Crows; *August And Everything After* .. (DGC)
Raining In Dallas
Kelly Schoppa; *Amarillo By Morning* .... (BLR)

Raining In My Heart
Anne Murray; *New Kind Of Feeling* .... (CAP)
Buddy Holly; *20 Golden Greats* .... (MCA)
Vintage Music-Classic '50s/'60s-#6 .... (MCA)
Jo-el Sonnier; *Come On Joe* .... (RCA)
Leo Sayer; *Leo Sayer* .... (WB)
Rainmaker
Dillards; *There Is A Time-1963-1970* .... (VAN)
Traffic; *Low Spark Of High-Heeled Boys* .... (ISL)
Rains Came
Freddy Fender; *Best Of* .... (MCA)
Rainy Afternoon
Lee Konitz; *In Rio* ....(MA)
Rainy Day
America; *America* ....(WB)
Jimi Hendrix; *Electric Ladyland* .... (RPR)
Tony Bennett; *Art Of Excellence* ....(COL)
Rainy Day Blues
Lightnin' Hopkins; *Prison Blues-Golden*
Classics-#2 .... (CLT)
Willie Nelson; *Nite Life-Greatest Hits & Rare*
Tracks .... (RHI)
Rainy Day In London
Boulevard; *Into The Street* .... (MCA)
Rainy Day In Monterey
Joe Sample; *Carmel* .... (MCA)
Collection .... (GRP)
Rainy Day Man
Bonnie Raitt; *Streetlights* ....(WB)
James Taylor; *Flag* .... (COL)
James Taylor .... (CAP)
Tom Rush; *Tom Rush* .... (COL)
Rainy Day People
Gordon Lightfoot; *Gord's Gold* .... (RPR)
Cold On The Shoulder .... (RPR)
Rainy Day Woman
Waylon Jennings; *Live* .... (RCA)
Ramblin' Man .... (RCA)
Rainy Day Women #12 & 35
Bob Dylan; *Greatest Hits* .... (COL)
Blonde On Blonde .... (COL)
Rock Classics/'60s .... (COL)
ST/Forrest Gump .... (EPX)
Bob Dylan/Band; *Before The Flood* .... (COL)
Rainy Days & Mondays
Carpenters; *Carpenters* .... (A&M)
Classics-#2 .... (A&M)
Singles 1969-1973 .... (A&M)
Yesterday Once More .... (A&M)
Paul Williams; *Classics-Here Comes Inspiration* . (A&M)
Rainy Night House
Joni Mitchell; *Ladies Of The Canyon* .... (RPR)
Joni Mitchell/L.A. Express; *Miles Of Aisles* .... (ASY)
Rainy Night In Georgia
Brook Benton; *Anthology* .... (RHI)
Atlantic R&B 1947-1974-#6-(1966-1969) ....(ATL)
Golden Age Of Black Music-1960-1970 .... (ATL)
Pick Of .... (FFT)
Soul Years .... (ATL)
Today .... (COT)
Hank Williams, Jr.; *14 Greatest Hits* .... (POL)
Sam Moore & Conway Twitty; *Rhythm Country &*
Blues .... (MCA)
Rainy Night In Rio
Susannah McCorkle; *Thanks For The Memory* ...(PAU)
Rainy Night In Tokyo
Michael Franks; *Passionfruit* ....(WB)
Rain, The
Oran "Juice" Jones; *Rap's Greatest Hits-#3* ....(PRY)
Red Rain
Peter Gabriel; *Greenpeace-Rainbow Warriors* ....(GEF)
Secret World Live .... (GEF)
Shaking The Tree-16 Golden Greats .... (GEF)
So .... (GEF)
Rhythm Of The Rain
Cascades; *Collectables Presents History Of*
Rock-#7 .... (CLT)
Golden Years-1963 .... (DOM)
Rider In The Rain
Randy Newman; *Little Criminals* ....(WB)

Riders On The Storm
Doors; *Best Of* .... (ELE)
  Greatest Hits .... (ELE)
  L.A. Woman .... (ELE)
  ST/Doors .... (ELE)
  Weird Scenes Inside The Gold Mine .... (ELE)
Ridin' Around In The Rain
Bing Crosby; *The Crooner-Columbia*
Years-1928-1934 ....(COL)
River In The Rain
Original Broadway Cast; *Big River-Adventures Of*
Huckleberry Finn .... (MCA)
Rock Me Like A Hurricane
Scorpions; *Love At First Sting* .... (MER)
Rock You Like A Hurricane
Scorpions; *Best Of Rockers & Ballads* .... (MER)
  Love At First Sting .... (MER)
  Worldwide Live .... (MER)
Rockin' With The Rhythm Of The Rain
Judds; *Greatest Hits* ....(RCA)
  Rockin' With The Rhythm ....(RCA)
Rollin' Thunder
A-Ha; *East Of The Sun-West Of The Moon* .... (WB)
Bellamy Brothers; *Rollin' Thunder* .... (ATL)
Roof Is Leaking
Phil Collins; *Face Value* .... (ATL)
Saddle In The Rain
John Prine; *Common Sense* .... (ATL)
  Prime Prine-Best Of .... (ATL)
Same Old Rain
Kevin Welch/Overtones; *Western Beat* .... (RPR)
Scottish Rain
Silencers; *Blues For Buddha* ....(RCA)
  Greenpeace/Rainbow Warriors .... (GEF)
See The Sky About to Rain
Neil Young; *On The Beach* .... (RPR)
September In The Rain
Chad & Jeremy; *Capitol Gold-Best Of* .... (CAP)
  Soft Sound Of .... (KT)
Dinah Washington; *Golden Hits* .... (MER)
  This Is My Story .... (MER)
Doris Day; *Sings 22 Great Songs On Orig. Big*
Band .... (HIN)
Duprees; *Best Of* .... (RHI)
Frank Sinatra; *Round #1* .... (CAP)
  Swingin' Session (& More) .... (CAP)
Joe Williams; *Swingin'...At Birdland* .... (RLL)
Marty Robbins; *Essential-1951-1982* .... (COL)
Peggy Lee; *You Can Depend On Me* .... (GLN)
September Rain
Full Swing; *Full Swing* ....(CYP)
George Howard; *Love Will Follow* .... (GRP)
Shadows In The Rain
Police; *Zenyatta Mondatta* .... (A&M)
Sting; *Dream Of The Blue Turtles* .... (A&M)
Shelter From The Storm
Bob Dylan; *At Budokan* .... (COL)
  Blood On The Tracks .... (COL)
  Hard Rain .... (COL)
She's Coming Back Some Cold Rainy Day
Georgia Cotton Pickers; *Greatest Country*
Blues-1929-1956-#3 .... (SB)
Sign Of The Storm
Eric Gales Band; *Eric Gales Band* .... (ELE)
Silvery Rain
Olivia Newton-John; *Physical* .... (MCA)
Singin' In The Rain
Gene Kelly; *ST/Clockwork Orange* .... (WB)
  ST/Singin' In The Rain .... (SSP)
  ST/Those Glorious MGM Musicals ....(MGM)
Sky Is Crying
Albert King; *I'm In A Phone Booth Baby* .... (STX)
  Years Gone By .... (STX)
Elmore James; *Complete Fire & Enjoy*
Sessions-#1 .... (CLT)
  Red Hot Blues .... (INT)
Eric Clapton; *Crossroads* .... (POL)
George Thorogood/Destroyers; *Live* .... (EMI)
  Move It On Over .... (ROU)
Stevie Ray Vaughan/Double Trouble; *Sky Is*
Crying .... (EPI)
Smokestack Lightning
George Thorogood/Destroyers; *Born To Be Bad* . (EMI)
Grateful Dead; *History Of-#1-Bear's Choice* ..... (WB)

Howlin' Wolf; *Best Of Chess Blues* .... (CSS)
  Blues-#1 .... (CSS)
  Moanin' In The Moonlight .... (CSS)
Lynyrd Skynyrd; *1991* .... (ATL)
Muddy Waters; *Chess Box* .... (CSS)
Soundgarden; *Ultramega OK* .... (SST)
Yardbirds; *Five Live Yardbirds* .... (RHI)
  For Your Love .... (ACC)
  Greatest Hits-#1 (1964-1966) .... (RHI)
Smokey Mountain Rain
Ronnie Milsap; *Greatest Hits* ....(RCA)
Soldier In The Rain
England Dan & John Ford Coley; *Best Of* ....(BT)
  Dowdy Ferry Road .... (BT)
Soon It's Gonna Rain
Barbra Streisand; *Album* ....(COL)
Original Cast; *Fantasticks* .... (POL)
Southern Rains
Mel Tillis; *Greatest Hits* ....(CCB)
Stand A Little Rain
Nitty Gritty Dirt Band; *20 Years Of Dirt-Best Of* .. (WB)
  Live Two Five .... (CAP)
State Trooper
Bruce Springsteen; *Nebraska* ....(COL)
Stop The Rain
Shenandoah; *Shenandoah* ....(COL)
Storm
Bonham; *Mad Hatter* ....(WTG)
Original London Cast; *Moby Dick* ....(RCA)
Pirates Of The Mississippi; *Walk The Plank* ...... (LIB)
Ray Kennedy; *What A Way To Go* .... (ATL)
Ray Simpson; *Ray Simpson* .... (VIA)
Soul II Soul; *#3-Just Right* .... (VIA)
Storm Front
Billy Joel; *Storm Front* ....(COL)
Storm In The Heartland
Billy Ray Cyrus; *Storm In The Heartland* ...... (MER)
Storm Of Love
Highway 101; *Bing Bang Boom* .... (WB)
Storm Over Tokyo Bay
Jessie Allen Cooper; *Soft Wave* .... (SOG)
Storm Warning
Bonnie Raitt; *Longing In Their Hearts* ....(CAP)
Stormbringer
Deep Purple; *Deepest Purple-Very Best Of* .... (WB)
  Made In Europe .... (MET)
  Stormbringer .... (MET)
Storms
Fleetwood Mac; *25 Years-The Chain* .... (WB)
  Tusk .... (WB)
Nanci Griffith; *Storms* .... (MCA)
Storms Are On The Ocean
Carter Family; *Bristol Sessions-#1&2* .... (CMF)
Storms In Africa
Enya; *Watermark* .... (RPR)
Storms Never Last
Hank Williams, Jr.; *Early Years* ....(W/C)
Storms Of Life
Randy Travis; *Storms Of Life* .... (WB)
Stormy
Classics IV; *Back To The '60s-#4* ....(DOM)
  Spring Break-#2-Cold Kegs & Tan Legs ....(CAP)
  Very Best Of .... (EMI)
Santana; *Inner Secrets* .... (COL)
Stormy Blues
Billie Holiday; *Lady Sings The Blues* .... (VRV)
  Songbook .... (VRV)
  Stormy Blues .... (VRV)
Stormy Monday (They Call It)
Allman Brothers Band; *At The Fillmore East* ..... (POL)
  Road Goes On Forever .... (POL)
Big Joe Turner; *Stormy Monday (They Call It)* ... (PAB)
Bobby Bland; *Best Of* .... (MCA)
  Here's The Man .... (MCA)
  Legends Of Electric Blues Guitar-#1 .... (RHI)
  Tuesday's Just As Bad .... (KT)
Buddy Guy; *My Time After Awhile* .... (VAN)
Jethro Tull; *20 Years Of-Radio Archives & Rare*
Tracks .... (CHR)
Little Milton; *Best Of Chess Blues* .... (CSS)
Lou Rawls; *Legendary* .... (BLN)
T-Bone Walker; *Best Of Blues-#2* .... (MSP)
  Jazz Heritage-Dirty Mistreater .... (MCA)

Stormy Weather
Billie Holiday; *Fine & Mellow* .... (CLT)
   Jazz-Club Vocal .... (VRV)
Frank Sinatra; *No One Cares* .... (CAP)
Jackie Wilson; *Mr. Excitement* .... (RHI)
Judy Garland; *At Carnegie Hall* .... (CAP)
Lena Horne; *20 Golden Pieces Of* .... (BLD)
   Goes Latin & Sings Your Requests ...... (DRG)
   Live On Broadway .... (QUE)
   Nipper's Greatest Hits-'40s-#1 .... (RCA)
Pixies; *Bossanova* .... (ELE)
Willie Nelson; *One For The Road* .... (COL)
Such Sweet Thunder
Duke Ellington; *#6-Dance Dates-California-1958* .(SAJ)
Duke Ellington/Orchestra; *Such Sweet Thunder* ...(SSP)
Summer Rain
Alphaville; *Breathtaking Blue* .... (ATL)
Andreas Vollenweider; *Trilogy-Behind The*
  Gardens... ....(COL)
Belinda Carlisle; *Her Greatest Hits* .... (MCA)
   Runaway Horses .... (MCA)
Johnny Rivers; *Anthology-1964-1977* .... (RHI)
   Best Of .... (EMI)
Sun & The Rainfall
Depeche Mode; *Broken Frame* .... (SIR)
Sunshower
Chuck Mangione; *Best Of* .... (MER)
Sunshowers
Billie Holiday; *Golden Years-#2* ....(COL)
   Story-#3 ....(COL)
Sure Got Cold After The Rain
ZZ Top; *Rio Grande Mud* .... (WB)
   Six Pack .... (WB)
Sweet Rain
Stan Getz; *Artistry Of-Best Of Verve Years-#1* ...(VRV)
Stan Getz Quartet; *Sweet Rain* .... (VRV)
Tears In The Rain
Triumph; *Classics* .... (MCA)
   Sport Of Kings .... (MCA)
Tell It To The Rain
Frankie Valli/Four Seasons; *Anthology* .... (RHI)
   Greatest Hits-#2 .... (RHI)
Texas Flood
Fenton Robinson; *Somebody Loan Me A Dime* ...(ALG)
Larry Davis; *Best Of Duke-Peacock Blues* .... (MCA)
Stevie Ray Vaughan/Double Trouble; *Live Alive* ..(EPI)
   Texas Flood .... (EPI)
Texas Tornado
Doug Sahm; *Best Of-& Friends-Atlantic Sessions* . (RHI)
Texas Twister
Little Feat; *Representing The Mambo* .... (WB)
Through The Storm
Aretha Franklin & Elton John; *Through The*
  Storm .... (ARI)
Thunder
Prince/New Power Generation; *Diamonds &*
  Pearls ....(PAI)
Thunder Bay
Sawyer Brown; *Buick* .... (LIB)
Thunder Island
Jay Ferguson; *Thunder Island* .... (OOP)
Thunder Rising
Gary Moore; *Wild Frontier* .... (VIA)
Thunder Road
Bruce Springsteen; *Born To Run* ....(COL)
Bruce Springsteen/E Street Band;
  Live-1975-1985 ....(COL)
Thunder Rolls, The
Garth Brooks; *No Fences* .... (LIB)
Thunder & Lightning
Argent; *Anthology-Collection Of Greatest Hits* ..... (EPI)
Chi Coltrane; *Rock Artifacts-#1-From The Vaults* (COL)
   Super Hits/'70s-Have A Nice Day-#9 .... (RHI)
Chicago; *14* ....(COL)
   Group Portrait ....(COL)
   Take Me Back To Chicago ....(COL)
Phil Collins; *Face Value* .... (ATL)
Thunder & Lightnin'
Holly Dunn; *Blue Rose Of Texas* .... (WB)
Thunder & Rain
Graham Parker/Rumour; *Stick To Me* .... (MER)
Thunderer
Michigan University Band; *Hail Sousa* .... (VAN)

Tiger In The Rain
Michael Franks; *Tiger In The Rain* .... (WB)
Tokyo Storm Warning
Elvis Costello; *Girls Girls Girls* ....(COL)
Elvis Costello/Attractions; *Blood & Chocolate* ...(COL)
Tom's Diner
DNA/Suzanne Vega; *Solitude Standing* .... (A&M)
   Tom's Album .... (A&M)
Tryin' To Reason With Hurricane Season
Jimmy Buffett; *A-1-A* .... (MCA)
   Boats Beaches Bars & Ballads .... (MGR)
Two Sparrows In A Hurricane
Tanya Tucker; *Can't Run From Yourself* .... (LIB)
   Greatest Hits-1990-1992 .... (LIB)
Umbrella Man
Kay Kyser; *Sentimental Favorites* ....(COL)
Voices In The Rain
Joe Sample; *Voices In The Rain* .... (MCA)
Waiting For The Rain To Fall
Chris Isaak; *Chris Isaak* .... (WB)
Walk Out In The Rain
Eric Clapton; *Backless* .... (RSO)
   I Shall Be Unreleased-Songs Of Bob Dylan ..... (RHI)
Walkin' In The Rain
Grace Jones; *Island Life* .... (ISL)
   Nightclubbing .... (ISL)
Jay/Americans; *All-Time Greatest Hits* .... (RHI)
   Come A Little Big Closer-Best Of .... (EMI)
Marvin Gaye; *Romantically Yours* ....(COL)
Ronettes; *Back To Mono-1958-1969* .... (AKO)
Walkin' In The Rain With The One I Love
Love Unlimited; *Soul Hits/'70s-#11* .... (RHI)
Wasn't That A Mighty Storm
Eric Von Schmidt; *Troubadours Of The Folk*
  Era-#1 .... (RHI)
What Have They Done To The Rain
Malvina Reynolds; *ST/Dogfight* .... (NUV)
Searchers; *Greatest Hits* .... (RHI)
When It Rains
Steve Wariner; *It's A Crazy World* .... (MCA)
When It Rains In America
Sarah Brightman; *Dive* .... (A&M)
When It Rains, It Really Pours
Elvis Presley; *Complete Sun Sessions* ....(RCA)
   Reconsider Baby ....(RCA)
When The Rain Turns To Snow
Lee Greenwood; *Christmas To Christmas* .... (MSP)
When Will It Rain
Jackyl; *Jackyl* .... (GEF)
White Lightning
Angel; *Live Without A Net* .... (CAS)
   On Earth As It Is In Heaven .... (CAS)
Babys; *Head First* .... (CHR)
Big Bopper; *Hellooo Baby!-Best Of* .... (RHI)
Def Leppard; *Adrenalize* .... (MER)
Furry Lewis; *Back On My Feet Again* .... (PRS)
   Shake 'Em Down On .... (FAN)
George Jones; *All-Time Greatest Hits-#1* .... (EPI)
   Best Of-1955-1967 .... (RHI)
   Billboard Top Country Hits-1959 .... (RHI)
Hank Williams, Jr.; *Whiskey Bent & Hell Bound* ..(W/C)
White Lightning & Wine
Heart; *Dreamboat Annie* .... (CAP)
White Tornado
R.E.M.; *Dead Letter Office* .... (IRS)
Who'll Stop The Rain
Creedence Clearwater Revival; *1970* .... (FAN)
   Chronicle .... (FAN)
   Cosmo's Factory .... (FAN)
   More Creedence Gold .... (FAN)
   Royal Albert Hall Concert .... (FAN)
Wicked Rain
Los Lobos; *Just Another Band From East L.A.* ....(SLS)
   Kiko ....(SLS)
Yesterday, I Heard The Rain
Bill Evans; *Tokyo Concert* .... (FAN)
Tony Bennett; *Essence Of* ....(COL)
You Love The Thunder
Hank Williams, Jr.; *Early Years* ....(W/C)
Jackson Browne; *Runnin' On Empty* .... (ASY)

RAINBOWS, Colors: General

See Also: COLORS (Various), RAIN

Above The Rainbow
Flora Purim; *Encounter* .... (MS)
Any Color You Like
Pink Floyd; *Dark Side Of The Moon* .... (CAP)
At The End Of The Rainbow
Jerry Wallace; *45* .... (BMA)
Aurora Borealis
C.W. McCall; *Greatest Hits* .... (POL)
Meat Puppets; *2* .... (SST)
Blinded By Rainbows
Rolling Stones; *Voodoo Lounge* .... (VIA)
Catch The Rainbow
Rainbow; *On Stage* .... (OYS)
Richie Blackmore; *Rainbow* .... (POL)
Chasin' That Neon Rainbow
Alan Jackson; *Here In The Real World* .... (ARI)
Color Him Father
Linda Martell; *20 Great Hits* .... (PLN)
 Color Me Country .... (PLN)
Color Of The Mood
Dave Loggins; *One Way Ticket To Paradise* .... (EPI)
Color Of The Night
Lauren Christy; *ST/Color Of Night* .... (MER)
Colored Spade
Original Broadway Cast; *Hair* ....(RCA)
Colors
Angst; *Mystery Spot* ....(SST)
Ice-T; *ST/Colors* .... (WB)
Minutemen; *What Makes A Man Start Fires* ......(SST)
Ted Nugent/Amboy Dukes; *Ted Nugent/Amboy
 Dukes* ....(MST)
Colors Of The Sun
Bonnie Koloc; *At Her Best* .... (OVA)
 You're Gonna Love Yourself... .... (OVA)
Jackson Browne; *For Everyman* .... (ASY)
Colour My World
Chicago; *At Carnegie Hall* .... (COL)
 Greatest Hits .... (COL)
 II .... (COL)
Petula Clark; *Greatest Hits* .... (CRS)
Colour Of Love
Billy Ocean; *45* .... (JVA)
Coloured Rain
Traffic; *Best Of* .... (UA)
 Mr. Fantasy .... (ISL)
Colours
Donovan; *Catch The Wind* ....(GRL)
 Greatest Hits .... (EPI)
 History Of British Rock-#3 .... (RHI)
Phil Collins; *...But Seriously* .... (ELE)
Sisters Of Mercy; *Floodland* .... (ELE)
End Of The Rainbow
Judy Garland; *Collector's Items 1936-1945* ..... (MCA)
Evening Rainbow
Sylvia St. James; *Echoes & Images* .... (ELE)
Fancy Colours
Chicago; *At Carnegie Hall* .... (COL)
 Group Portrait .... (COL)
 II .... (COL)
Flying Colours
Jethro Tull; *Broadsword And The Beast* .... (CHR)
God's Coloring Book
Dolly Parton; *Here You Come Again* ....(RCA)
Gold At The End Of My Rainbow
Be Bop Deluxe; *Modern Music* .... (HAR)
Golden Rainbow
Looking Glass; *45* .... (EPI)
Seals & Crofts; *I'll Play For You* ....(WB)
Gone The Rainbow
Peter, Paul & Mary; *Moving* .... (WB)
 Peter, Paul & Mary .... (WB)
Here Comes The Rainbow
Crystal Gayle; *In Harmony 2* .... (COL)
I'm Always Chasing Rainbows
Judy Garland; *Best Of* .... (MCA)
 Judy Garland .... (AUF)
 Pick Of .... (FFT)
Livin' At The End Of The Rainbow
Dave & Sugar; *That's The Way Love Should Be* ..(RCA)

Look To The Rainbow
Al Jarreau; *Look To The Rainbow-Live In Europe* .(WB)
Aretha Franklin; *Aretha* .... (ARI)
Original Cast; *Finian's Rainbow* ....(COL)
Love Colours
Pretenders; *Last Of The Independents* .... (SIR)
Make Me Rainbows
Ella Fitzgerald & Count Basie; *Perfect Match* .... (PAB)
Sue Raney & Bob Florence; *Flight Of Fancy* .... (DCO)
Multi Colored Lady
Gregg Allman; *Laid Back* ....(CPC)
My Coloring Book
Barbra Streisand; *Greatest Hits* ....(COL)
 Second Album ....(COL)
Perry Como; *This Is-#2* ....(RCA)
Old Rainbow Jukebox & You
John Schneider; *Memory Like You* .... (MCA)
Over The Rainbow
Barbra Streisand; *Just For The Record* ....(COL)
Dave Brubeck; *Greatest Hits From The Fantasy
 Years* ....(FAN)
Ella Fitzgerald; *Silver Collection-Songbooks* ......(VRV)
Judy Garland; *At Carnegie Hall* ....(CAP)
 Best Of Capitol Masters-One & Only Box ....(CCB)
 Greatest Hits ....(CCB)
 Miss Show Business ....(CAP)
 One & Only ....(CAP)
 ST/Wizard Of Oz ....(SSP)
Quick As Rainbows
Kitchens Of Distinction; *Strange Free World* .... (ONE)
Rainbow
Candyland; *Suck It & See* .... (EW)
Marmalade; *45* ....(LON)
O'Jays; *Serious* .... (EMI)
Sandy Owen; *Soliloquy* .... (IVO)
Rainbow At Midnight
Ernest Tubb; *Collection* .... (SO)
 Story .... (MCA)
Rainbow Blues
Jethro Tull; *"M.U."-Best Of* .... (CHR)
Rainbow Connection
Muppets/Kermit The Frog; *45* .... (ATL)
Rainbow Demon
Uriah Heep; *Demons & Wizards* .... (MER)
Rainbow Doll
Jimmy Dell; *Get Hot Or Go Home-Vintage
 Rockabilly* .... (CMF)
Rainbow Eyes
Rainbow; *Long Live Rock 'n' Roll* .... (POL)
Rainbow High
Original Cast/Julie Covington; *Evita* .... (MCA)
Original New York Cast; *Evita* .... (MCA)
Rainbow In Your Eyes
Al Jarreau; *Glow* .... (RPR)
 Look To The Rainbow-Live In Europe .... (WB)
Leon Russell; *Wedding Album* ....(PRD)
Rainbow Ride
Charlie Daniels Band; *Million Mile Reflections* ....(EPI)
Jerry Reed; *East Bound & Down* ....(RCA)
Rainbow Song
America; *Hat Trick* .... (WB)
Rainbow Stew
Merle Haggard; *Greatest Hits* .... (MCA)
 More Of The Best .... (RHI)
 Rainbow Stew-Live At Anaheim Stadium ...... (MCA)
Rainbow Trout
Gordon Lightfoot; *Cold On The Shoulder* .... (RPR)
Rainbow '65
Gene Chandler; *Hits From Legendary Vee-Jay
 Records* ....(MOT)
Rainbow '80
Gene Chandler; *Ear Candy-#2* .... (20)
 '80 .... (20)
Rainbows All Over Your Blues
John Sebastian; *John B. Sebastian* .... (RPR)
 ST/Woodstock .... (ATL)
Rainbows Are Back In Style
Slim Whitman; *Best Of-1952-1972* .... (RHI)
 Paloma Blanca-Best Of-Legendary Masters ..... (EMI)
Rainbow's Cadillac
Bruce Hornsby; *Harbor Lights* ....(RCA)
Rainbow's End
Sergio Mendes; *Sergio Mendes* .... (A&M)

Ride On A Rainbow
Johnny Mathis; *Heavenly* .... (COL)
Searching For A Rainbow
Chris LeDoux; *& The Saddle Boogie Band* .... (LIB)
Searchin' For A Rainbow
Marshall Tucker Band; *Searchin' For A Rainbow* (AJK)
Seven Wonders
Fleetwood Mac; *Tango In The Night* .... (WB)
She Brakes For Rainbows
B-52's; *Bouncing Off The Satellites* .... (WB)
She Comes In Colors
Hooters; *Nervous Night* .... (COL)
Love; *Best Of* .... (RHI)
She's A Rainbow
Rolling Stones; *Get Yer Ya-Ya's Out* .... (AKO)
More Hot Rocks-Big Hits & Fazed Cookies ..... (AKO)
Singles Collection-London Years .... (AKO)
Their Satanic Majesties Request .... (AKO)
Through The Past Darkly-Big Hits-#2 .... (AKO)
Silver Rainbow
Genesis; *Genesis* .... (ATL)
Somewhere There's A Rainbow Over Texas
Ruby Falls; *45* .... (FIF)
Sunshine, Lollipops & Rainbows
Lesley Gore; *Anthology* .... (RHI)
Golden Hits Of .... (MER)
Swinging On A Rainbow
Frankie Avalon; *Best Of* .... (MCA)
That Terrific Rainbow
Original Broadway Cast; *Pal Joey* .... (ANG)
Original Cast; *Pal Joey* .... (COL)
There's A Rainbow 'Round My Shoulder
Al Jolson; *Jolson Sang 'Em* .... (BIO)
Mammy .... (POE)
Tie Dye On The Highway
Robert Plant; *Manic Nirvana* .... (EPR)
Too Many Rainbows
Dick Hammonds; *45* .... (SNC)
True Colors
Cyndi Lauper; *True Colors* .... (POR)
Under The Rainbow
Raindogs; *Lost Souls* .... (ATC)
Tommy Page; *From The Heart* .... (SIR)
When The Rainbow Comes
World Party; *Goodbye Jumbo* .... (ENS)
Wrong End Of The Rainbow
Anne Murray; *Yes I Do* .... (LIB)
You Will .... (LIB)
Tom Rush; *Wrong End Of The Rainbow* .... (COL)
Wrong Side Of The Rainbow
Jim Chestnut; *Show Me A Sign* .... (MCA)

REBELS, Outlaws, Rowdy, Runaways

See Also: COWBOYS, CRIME, LAW & ORDER,
POLICE, PRISON, TRAVELING

Against The Grain
Golden Earring; *Grab It For A Second* .... (MCA)
Against The Law
Warrant; *Dirty Rotten Filthy Stinking Rich* ....(COL)
Bad Boys Running Wild
Scorpions; *Love At First Sting* .... (MER)
Wold Wide Live .... (MER)
Ballad Of Billy The Kid
Billy Joel; *Piano Man* .... (COL)
Songs In The Attic .... (COL)
Billy 1, 2 & 7
Bob Dylan; *ST/Pat Garrett & Billy The Kid* ....(COL)
Billy The Kid
Charlie Daniels Band; *High Lonesome* .... (EPI)
Marty Robbins; *Gunfighter Ballads & Trail Songs* (COL)
Ry Cooder; *Into The Purple Valley* .... (RPR)
Billy The Kid (I Miss...)
Billy Dean; *Billy Dean* .... (LIB)
Black Sheep
John Anderson; *All The People Are Talkin'* .... (WB)
Greatest Hits .... (WB)
Sam The Sham/Pharaohs; *Pharaohization! (Best*
Of) .... (RHI)
Black Sheep Boy
Tim Hardin; *Memorial Album* .... (POL)

Black Sheep Of The Family
Ritchie Blackmore; *Rainbow* .... (POL)
Bonnie & Clyde
Georgie Fame; *45* .... (EPI)
Breaking All The Rules
Ozzy Osbourne; *No Rest For The Wicked* ....(CBA)
Peter Frampton; *Breaking All The Rules* .... (A&M)
Come Back...Barbara Lewis Hare Krisha...
John Prine; *Anthology-Great Days* .... (RHI)
Common Sense .... (ATL)
Prime Prine-Best Of .... (ATL)
Cry For The Bad Man
Lynyrd Skynyrd; *Best Of* .... (MSP)
Gimme Back My Bullets .... (MCA)
Desperado
Alice Cooper; *Greatest Hits* .... (WB)
Killer .... (WB)
Clint Black; *Common Thread-Songs Of The*
Eagles .... (GIA)
Eagles; *Anthology* .... (ASY)
Desperado .... (ASY)
Hell Freezes Over .... (GEF)
Live .... (ASY)
Their Greatest Hits 1971-1975 .... (ASY)
Linda Ronstadt; *Don't Cry Now* .... (ASY)
Greatest Hits .... (ASY)
Desperado Love
Conway Twitty; *Fallin' For You For Years* .... (WB)
Number One's: The Warner Brothers Years ...... (WB)
Desperados Waiting For The Train
Guy Clark; *Old No. 1* .... (SH)
Jerry Jeff Walker; *Best Of* .... (MCA)
Great Gonzos .... (MCA)
Viva Terlingua .... (MCA)
W. Jennings/W. Nelson/J. Cash/K. Krist.;
Highwayman .... (COL)
Don't Let Me Be Misunderstood
Animals; *Greatest Hits Live! (Rip It To Shreds)* .... (IRS)
Sullivan Years-British Invasion .... (TVT)
Joe Cocker; *With A Little Help From My Friends* (A&M)
Don't Take Me Alive
Steely Dan; *Royal Scam* .... (MCA)
El Paso
Grateful Dead; *Steal Your Face* .... (GRD)
Marty Robbins; *Biggest Hits* .... (COL)
Billboard Top Country Hits-1960 .... (RHI)
Gunfighter Ballads & Trail Songs .... (COL)
Radio Classics/'50s .... (COL)
Father Christmas
Kinks; *Come Dancing With-Best Of-1977-1986* .. (ARI)
Friend Of The Devil
Grateful Dead; *American Beauty* .... (WB)
Best Of-Skeletons From The Closet .... (WB)
Dead Set .... (ARI)
Lyle Lovett; *Deadicated* .... (ARI)
Fugitive
Indigo Girls; *Swamp Ophelia* .... (EPI)
Gee, Officer Krupke
Original Cast; *ST/West Side Story* .... (COL)
Gorilla, You're A Desperado
Warren Zevon; *Bad Luck Streak In Dancing*
School .... (ASY)
Hard To Handle
Black Crowes; *Shake Your Money Maker* .... (DEF)
Grateful Dead; *History Of-#1 (Bear's Choice)* ..... (WB)
Otis Redding; *Best Of* .... (ATL)
Story .... (ATL)
Heroes & Villains
Beach Boys; *Concert/'69* .... (CAP)
Made In The U.S.A. .... (CAP)
Smiley Smile .... (CAP)
Sunshine Dream .... (CAP)
He's A Rebel
Crystals; *Good Time Rock 'N' Roll* .... (MCA)
Phil Spector's Greatest Hits .... (SPC)
I Ain't Gonna Stand For It
Stevie Wonder; *Hotter Than July* .... (MOT)
I Ain't Livin' Long Like This
Emmylou Harris; *Quarter Moon In A Ten-Cent*
Town .... (WB)
Rodney Crowell; *Collection* .... (WB)
I Ain't Livin' Long Like This .... (WB)
Waylon Jennings; *Greatest Hits-#2* .... (RCA)
What Goes Around Comes Around .... (RCA)

(I Am A) Lonesome Fugitive
Roy Buchanan; *Roy Buchanan* .... (POL)
I Fought The Law
Bobby Fuller; *Best Of* .... (RHI)
   Heart & Soul Of Rock & Roll-#1 .... (RHI)
Bobby Fuller Four; *Oldies But Goodies-#9* ...... (OSR)
   Super Oldies/'60s-#7 .... (AUF)
Clash; *Clash* .... (EPI)
   Story Of-#1 .... (EPI)
I Will Not Go Quietly
Don Henley; *End Of The Innocence* .... (GEF)
I Won't Grow Up
Original Cast/Mary Martin; *Peter Pan* .... (RCA)
If The Good Die Young
Tracy Lawrence; *Alibis* .... (ATL)
Independence Day
Bruce Springsteen; *The River* .... (COL)
Bruce Springsteen/E Street Band;
Live-1975-1985 .... (COL)
Indian Outlaw
Tim McGraw; *Not A Moment Too Soon* .... (CRB)
Indiana Wants Me
R. Dean Taylor; *Hard-To-Find Motown
Classics-#2* .... (MOT)
   Super Hits-#5 .... (GUS)
   Super Hits/'70s-Have A Nice Day-#3 ...... (RHI)
Infamous Angel
Iris DeMent; *Infamous Angel* .... (PHO)
   Infamous Angel .... (WB)
I'm A Lonesome Fugitive
Merle Haggard/Strangers; *Best Of* .... (CAP)
   Capitol Collectors Series .... (CAP)
   Songs I'll Always Sing .... (CAP)
Roy Buchanan; *Roy Buchanan* .... (POL)
I'm Not A Juvenile Delinquent
Frankie Lymon/Teenagers; *Best Of* .... (RHI)
   Original Rock & Roll Hits Of The '50s .... (RLL)
James Dean
Eagles; *On The Border* .... (ASY)
Jesse James
Bob Seger; *Smokin' O.P.'s* .... (CAP)
Country Joe McDonald; *Country Joe* .... (VAN)
   Essential .... (VAN)
Sam McGee; *Granddad Of The Country Guitar
Pickers* .... (ARH)
Johnny Too Bad
John Martyn; *Foundations* .... (ISL)
Lords Of The New Church; *Nothing's Sacred* ..... (IRS)
Slickers; *ST/The Harder They Come* .... (MGO)
Taj Mahal; *Best Of-#1* .... (COL)
   Mo' Roots .... (COL)
UB40; *Labour Of Love* .... (A&M)
   Live In Moscow .... (A&M)
Just Like Jesse James
Cher; *Heart Of Stone* .... (GEF)
Kid Charlemagne
Steely Dan; *Greatest Hits* .... (MCA)
   Royal Scam .... (MCA)
Kids
Original Broadway Cast; *Bye Bye Birdie* .... (COL)
Paul Lynde; *ST/Bye Bye Birdie* .... (RCA)
Lookin' After #1
Boomtown Rats; *Boomtown Rats* .... (MER)
Love Child
Diana Ross/Supremes; *Anthology* .... (MOT)
   Billboard Top Rock 'N' Roll Hits-1968 .... (RHI)
   Every Great #1 Hit .... (MOT)
   Greatest Hits-#3 .... (MOT)
   Motown Story-1st 25 Years .... (MOT)
   Motown's Biggest Pop Hits .... (MOT)
Sweet Sensation; *Love Child* .... (ATC)
Mama Tried
Grateful Dead; *Grateful Dead* .... (WB)
John Anderson & Marty Stuart; *Mama's Hungry
Eyes-Merle Haggard Tribute* .... (ARI)
Merle Haggard/Strangers; *Best Of* .... (CAP)
   Okie From Muskogee .... (CAP)
   Songs I'll Always Sing .... (CAP)
   Very Best Of Merle Haggard .... (CAP)
Man Who Shot Liberty Valance
Gene Pitney; *Anthology* .... (RHI)
   Greatest Hits .... (EVR)
   Super Oldies/'60s-#9 .... (AUF)
Greg Kihn; *Glass House Rock* .... (BES)

Midnight Rider
Allman Brothers Band; *Anthology Of Duane
Allman-#2* ....(CPC)
   Beginnings .... (POL)
   Best Of .... (POL)
   Decade Of Hits-1969-1979 .... (POL)
   Idlewild South .... (POL)
   Road Goes On Forever .... (POL)
Gregg Allman; *Laid Back* .... (CPC)
   South's Greatest Hits .... (CPC)
Willie Nelson; *ST/Electric Horseman* .... (COL)
My Life
Billy Joel; *52nd Street* .... (COL)
   Greatest Hits-#1&2-1973-1985 .... (COL)
My Way
Elvis Presley; *Aloha From Hawaii* .... (RCA)
   Canadian Tribute .... (RCA)
   In Concert .... (RCA)
Frank Sinatra; *Greatest Hits-#2* .... (RPR)
   Main Event-Live From Madison Sq. Garden .... (RPR)
   My Way .... (RPR)
   Reprise Collection .... (RPR)
   Sinatra Reprise-The Very Good Years .... (RPR)
Paul Anka; *Very Best Of* .... (RAN)
Never Could Toe The Mark
Waylon Jennings; *Never Could Toe The Mark* ....(RCA)
New Delhi Freight Train
Little Feat; *Time Loves A Hero* .... (WB)
No Son Of Mine
Genesis; *We Can't Dance* .... (ATL)
Northfield, The Disaster
Charlie Daniels Band; *Legend Of Jesse James* ... (A&M)
Northfield, The Plan
Levon Helm; *Legend Of Jesse James* .... (A&M)
Nowhere Man
Beatles; *1962-1966* .... (CAP)
   Box Set .... (CAP)
   Compact Disc E.P. Collection .... (CAP)
   Rubber Soul .... (CAP)
   Yesterday...And Today .... (CAP)
Outlaw
Cult; *Electric* .... (SIR)
Dan Fogelberg; *High Country Snows* .... (FM)
Dangerous Toys; *Dangerous Toys* .... (COL)
Joan Jett/Blackhearts; *Good Music* .... (EPA)
Scream; *Let It Scream* .... (HOL)
Tom Johnston; *Everything You've Heard Is True* ... (WB)
War; *45* .... (RCA)
Whitesnake; *Love Hunter* .... (GEF)
Outlaw Blues
Bob Dylan; *Bringing It All Back Home* .... (COL)
Pat Benatar; *Best Shots* .... (CHR)
   Tropico .... (CHR)
Outlaw Man
Eagles; *Desperado* .... (ASY)
Outlaw Women
Hank Williams, Jr.; *Bocephus
Box-Collection-1979-1992* ....(CPC)
   Whiskey Bent & Hell Bound ....(W/C)
Outlaw & The Stranger
Ed Bruce; *Ed Bruce* .... (MCA)
Outlaws & Lone Star Beer
C.W. McCall; *& Co.* .... (POL)
Outlaw's Prayer
Johnny Paycheck; *Armed & Crazy* .... (EPI)
   Biggest Hits .... (EPI)
Outside The Law
Rundle Chowning Band; *Heart On Fire* .... (A&M)
Prince Of The Punks
Kinks; *One For The Road* .... (ARI)
Problem Child
3rd Bass; *Derelicts Of Dialect* .... (DFJ)
AC/DC; *Dirty Deeds Done Dirt Cheap* .... (ATL)
   If You Want Blood You've Got It .... (ATL)
   Let There Be Rock .... (ATC)
Damned; *Light At The End Of The Tunnel* ...... (MCA)
Graham Parker/Rumour; *Stick To Me* .... (MER)
Hanoi Rocks; *Self-Destruction Blues* .... (GEF)
Mitch Malloy; *Mitch Malloy* .... (RCA)
Royal Tramps; *Dangerous & Extremely Unhealthy* . (RL)
Punks Not Dead
Exploited; *Apocalypse '77* .... (REL)
Put Up Or Shut Up
Ted Nugent; *Intensities In 10 Cities* .... (EPI)

Rebel
Black Oak Arkansas; *Live Mutha* ....(ATC)
Bryan Adams; *Into the Fire* ....(A&M)
Quicksilver Messenger Service; *Quicksilver* ......(CAP)
Roger Daltrey; *Under A Raging Moon* ....(ATL)
Sly & Robbie; *Silent Assassin* ....(ISL)
Rebel Girl
Joe Glazer; *Songs Of Joe Hill* ....(FLW)
Outlaws; *Los Hombres Malo* ....(ARI)
Rebel Heart
Rod Stewart; *Vagabond Heart* .... (WB)
Rebel Music
Bob Marley/Wailers; *Babylon By Bus* ....(TUF)
Natty Dread ....(TUF)
Rebel Music ....(TUF)
Rebel Rebel
David Bowie; *Changesbowie* ....(RYK)
Diamond Dogs ....(RYK)
Live ....(RYK)
Sound + Vision ....(RYK)
The Singles-1969-1993 ....(RYK)
Rebel Rock Me
Pretenders; *Last Of The Independents* ....(SIR)
Rebel Rouser
Bob Welch; *Another One* ....(CAP)
Duane Eddy; *Pure Gold* ....(RCA)
16 Greatest Hits ....(JAM)
Cruisin'-1958 ....(INC)
Legends Of Rock Guitar-'50s-#1 ....(RHI)
Old 'N Golden ....(JAM)
ST/Forrest Gump ....(EPX)
Ventures; *Best Of* ....(EMI)
Rebel With A Cause
Indecent Obsession; *Indio* ....(MCA)
Silent Rage; *Shattered Hearts* ....(CML)
Rebel Without A Clue
Bonnie Tyler; *Secret Dreams & Forbidden Fire* ...(COL)
Rebel Without A Pause
Public Enemy; *Def Jam Classics-#1* ....(DFC)
It Takes A Nation Of Millions To Hold... ....(DFC)
Rap's Biggest Hits .... (KT)
Rebel Yell
Billy Idol; *MTV's Rock 'N' Roll To Go* ....(ELE)
Rebel Yell ....(CHR)
Rebels
Tom Petty/Heartbreakers; *Pack Up The
Plantation-Live* ....(MCA)
Southern Accents ....(MCA)
Rebels Are We
Chic; *Real People* ....(ATL)
Rebels Without A Clue
Bellamy Brothers; *Greatest Hits-#3* ....(MCA)
Rebels Without A Clue ....(MCA)
Refugee
Tom Petty/Heartbreakers; *Damn The Torpedoes* (MCA)
Pack Up The Plantation-Live ....(MCA)
U2; *War* .... (ISL)
Renegade
Styx; *Classics-#15* ....(A&M)
Pieces Of Eight ....(A&M)
Renegades, Rebels And Rogues
Tracy Lawrence; *ST/Maverick* .... (ATL)
Renegade, The
Ian & Sylvia; *Greatest Hits* ....(VAN)
Nashville ....(VAN)
Ride Like The Wind
Christopher Cross; *Christopher Cross* ....(WB)
Rock & Roll Outlaw
Foghat; *Rock & Roll Outlaws* .... (RHI)
Rock 'N' Roll Outlaw
Peter Wells; *Everything You Like Tries To Kill
You* .... (ZOO)
Rock 'N' Roll Rebel
Ozzy Osbourne; *Bark At The Moon* ....(EPA)
Rough Boy
ZZ Top; *Afterburner* ....(WB)
Greatest Hits ....(WB)
Rough Boys
Pete Townshend; *Classic Rock 1966-1988* ....(ATL)
Empty Glass ....(ATC)
Who; *Join Together* ....(MCA)
Run Away
Slade; *Keep Your Hands Off My Power Supply* ...(CBA)

Runaway
Bon Jovi; *Bon Jovi* ....(MER)
Bonnie Raitt; *Collection* ....(WB)
Sweet Forgiveness ....(WB)
Damn Yankees; *Damn Yankees* ....(WB)
Del Shannon; *Billboard Top Rock 'N' Roll
Hits-1961* .... (RHI)
Cruisin'-1961 ....(INC)
Greatest Hits ....(RHI)
Heart & Soul Of Rock 'N Roll-#1 ....(RHI)
Little Town Flirt ....(RHI)
ST/American Graffiti ....(MCA)
Elvis Presley; *Collector's Gold* ....(RCA)
Jefferson Starship; *Earth* ....(GRU)
Gold ....(GRU)
Melissa Manchester; *Greatest Hits* .... (ARI)
Runaway Child Running Wild
Temptations; *All The Million-Sellers* .... (MOT)
Anthology ....(MOT)
Cloud Nine ....(MOT)
Compact Command Performances ....(MOT)
Greatest Hits-#2 ....(MOT)
Runaway Girl
Dion; *Runaround Sue* ....(CLT)
Dion/Belmonts; *20 Golden Classics* ....(CLT)
Everything You Always Wanted To Hear ....(LAU)
Runaway Train
Soul Asylum; *Grave Dancers Union* ....(COL)
Sad Punk
Pixies; *Trompe Le Monde* .... (ELE)
She's Leaving Home
Al Jarreau; *All Fly Home* ....(WB)
Beatles; *Box Set* ....(CAP)
Love Songs ....(CAP)
Sgt. Pepper's Lonely Hearts Club Band ....(CAP)
Stop Running Away
Brenda Russell; *Greatest Hits* ....(A&M)
Take The Skinheads Bowling
Camper Van Beethoven; *Telephone Free Landslide
Victory* .... (IRS)
Theme From "The Magnificent Seven"
BBC Concert Orchestra; *Golden Cinema
Classics-Adventure Film* ....(BAI)
Ties That Bind
Bruce Springsteen; *The River* ....(COL)
Trouble Child
Joni Mitchell; *Court & Spark* .... (ASY)
Walkaway Joe
Trisha Yearwood; *Hearts In Armor* ....(MCA)
Wanderer
Dion; *20 Million-Dollar Memories-#1* ....(LAU)
Billboard Top Rock 'N' Roll Hits-1962 ....(RHI)
Cruisin'-1962 ....(INC)
Oldies But Goodies-#5 ....(OSR)
ST/Wanderers ....(WB)
Wanderer ....(LAU)
Donna Summer; *Wanderer* ....(GEF)
Wanted
Alan Jackson; *Country's Greatest Hits-#8-Lonely
Hearts* .... (PRY)
Here In The Real World ....(ARI)
Wanted Dead Or Alive
Bon Jovi; *Slippery When Wet* .... (JBC)
Wanted Man
George Thorogood/Destroyers; *Bad To The Bone* (EMI)
Johnny Cash; *At Folsom Prison & San Quentin* ...(COL)
Essential ....(COL)
Ratt; *Out Of The Cellar* ....(ATL)
Ratt & roll 8191 ....(ATL)
We're All In The Same Gang
West Coast Rap All-Stars; *We're All In The Same
Gang* ....(WB)
We're Not Gonna Take It
Twisted Sister; *Big Hits & Nasty Cuts* ....(ATL)
Stay Hungry ....(ATL)
Who; *Join Together* ....(MCA)
ST/Woodstock ....(ATL)
Tommy ....(MCA)
White Punks On Dope
Tubes; *Tubes* ....(A&M)
T.R.A.S.H.-Tubes Rarities & Smash Hits ....(A&M)
What Do You Want From-Live ....(A&M)

You Can't Run From Love
Eddie Rabbitt; *Best Of/Greatest Hits-#2* .... (WB)
   Radio Romance .... (LIB)
   #1's .... (WB)
You Keep Runnin' Away
38 Special; *Special Forces* .... (A&M)
Your Body Is An Outlaw
Mel Tillis; *Your Body Is An Outlaw* .... (ELE)

RECORD BUSINESS

See Also: MUSIC, SHOW BIZ

16th Avenue
Lacy J. Dalton; *19 Hot Country Requests-#2* ..... (EPI)
   Greatest Country Hits/'80s-1982 .... (COL)
   Greatest Hits .... (COL)
2120 So. Michigan Avenue
Rolling Stones; *12 x 5* .... (LON)
Fake Your Way To The Top
Original Broadway Cast; *Dreamgirls* .... (GEF)
Free Man In Paris
Joni Mitchell; *Court & Spark* .... (ASY)
   Shadows & Light .... (ASY)
Gimme Back My Bullets
Lynyrd Skynyrd; *Gimme Back My Bullets* .... (MCA)
   Gold & Platinum .... (MCA)
   Southern By The Grace Of God-Tribute .... (MCA)
Have A Cigar
Pink Floyd; *Wish You Were Here* .... (COL)
How To Kill A Radio Consultant
Public Enemy; *Apocalypse 91-Enemy Strikes
Black* ....(DFC)
   Greatest Misses .... (CHA)
I Wonder What It Takes To Make A Record
Kent Smith & Renda; *45* .... (FOU)
It's A Long Way To The Top
AC/DC; *High Voltage* .... (ATC)
Mercury Poisoning
Graham Parker/Rumour; *Live Sparks* .... (ARI)
Motown Song
Larry John McNally; *Fade To Black* .... (ATC)
Rod Stewart; *Vagabond Heart* .... (WB)
Mr. Record Man
Willie Nelson; *Best Of* .... (EMI)
   Horse Called Music .... (COL)
   & Family Live .... (COL)
Record Executive Blues
Catfish Hodge Band; *Eyewitness Blues* .... (ADE)
Rosalita
Bruce Springsteen; *Wild The Innocent & The E Street
Shuffle* ....(COL)
Bruce Springsteen/E Street Band;
Live-1975-1985 ....(COL)
So You Want To Be A Rock 'N' Roll Star
Byrds; *Greatest Hits* ....(COL)
   Original Singles-#1-1965-1967 ....(COL)
   Rock Classics/'60s ....(COL)
   Byrds (collection) ....(COL)
   (Untitled) ....(COL)
Patti Smith Group; *Wave* .... (ARI)
Tom Petty/Heartbreakers; *Pack Up The
Plantation-Live* .... (MCA)
   Ultimate Rock Album .... (FTN)
Suzi Wants To Be A Rock Star
Professor Griff/Last Asiatic Disciples; *Pawns In The
Game* ....(LUK)
They Call It Rock
Nick Lowe; *Pure Pop For Now People* ....(COL)
Under Assistant West Coast Promotion Man
Rolling Stones; *Out Of Our Heads* .... (AKO)
   Singles Collection-London Years .... (AKO)
Working For MCA
Hank Williams, Jr.; *Hank "Live"* ....(W/C)
Lynyrd Skynyrd; *Best Of The Rest* .... (MCA)
   One More From The Road .... (MCA)
   Second Helping .... (MCA)
Write Your Own Songs (Mr. Record Exec.)
Asleep At The Wheel; *Asleep At The Wheel* ..... (DOT)
Waylon Jennings & Willie Nelson; *WW2* ....(RCA)
Willie Nelson & Kris Kristofferson; *Music From
"Songwriter"* ....(COL)
Wrong Side Of Memphis
Matraca Berg; *Bittersweet Surrender* ....(RCA)

Trisha Yearwood; *Hearts In Armor* .... (MCA)

REFLECTIONS, Mirrors

See Also: ECHOES, SHADOWS

Go To The Mirror Boy
Who; *Tommy* .... (MCA)
Magic Mirror
Leon Russell; *Carney* .... (MCA)
Whirlers; *Harlem Holiday-New York R&B* ....(CLT)
Man In The Mirror
Jim Glaser; *Man In The Mirror* .... (NBL)
Michael Jackson; *Bad* .... (EPI)
Mirror
Graham Central Station; *Mirror* .... (WB)
King Swamp; *King Swamp* .... (VIA)
Spooky Tooth; *Mirror* .... (ISL)
Mirror Freak
Steve Harley & Cockney Rebel; *Closer Look* .... (HAR)
Mirror Image
Cher; *Prisoner* .... (CAS)
Rosanne Cash; *Interiors* .... (COL)
Mirror In The Bathroom
English Beat; *I Just Can't Stop It* .... (IRS)
   ST/Dance Craze .... (CHR)
   What Is Beat .... (IRS)
Mirror Man
Captain Beefheart/Magic Band; *Mirror Man* ..... (OW)
Human League; *Greatest Hits* .... (A&M)
Pere Ubu; *Worlds In Collision* .... (FON)
Prism; *Armageddon* .... (CAP)
Talk Talk; *Party's Over* .... (EMI)
Mirror Mirror
Barbara Mandrell; *I'll Be Your Jukebox Tonight* ..(CAP)
Diamond Rio; *Diamond Rio* .... (ARI)
Diana Ross; *Why Do Fools Fall In Love?* ....(RCA)
Mirror Star
Fabulous Poodles; *Mirror Stars* .... (EPI)
Mirrors
Blue Oyster Cult; *Mirrors* ....(COL)
King Crimson; *In The Court Of The Crimson
King* ....(ATL)
Objects In The Rear View Mirror...
Meat Loaf; *Bat Out Of Hell II-Back Into Hell* ... (MCA)
Piggy In the Mirror
Cure; *Top* .... (SIR)
Rearviewmirror
Pearl Jam; *Vs.* .... (EPA)
Reflection
Cure; *Seventeen Seconds* .... (ELE)
Tony Bennett; *Life Is Beautiful* .... (IPV)
Reflections
Charlie Daniels Band; *Million Mile Reflections* ....(EPI)
Diana Ross/Supremes; *25th Anniversary* .... (MOT)
   Anthology .... (MOT)
   Greatest Hits-#3 .... (MOT)
   Motown Story .... (MOT)
Four Tops; *Anthology* .... (MOT)
   Still Waters Run Deep .... (MOT)
Luther Vandross; *Songs* .... (EPI)
Steppenwolf; *The Second* .... (MCA)
Thelonius Monk; *Alone In San Francisco* .... (RVR)
   Composer ....(COL)
Reflections In A Crystal Wind
Mimi & Richard Farina; *Best Of* .... (VAN)
   Reflections In A Crystal Wind .... (VAN)
Reflections Of My Life
Marmalade; *History Of British Rock* .... (RHI)
   London Collector-Rock Invasion ....(LON)
   Super Hits/'70s-Have A Nice Day-#2 .... (RHI)
Room Full Of Mirrors
Jimi Hendrix; *Essential* .... (RPR)
   Lifelines/Story .... (RPR)
Pretenders; *Get Close* .... (SIR)
Smash The Mirror
Who; *Join Together* .... (MCA)
   Tommy .... (MCA)

REPTILES, Dinosaurs, Frogs, Snakes
See Also: ANIMALS: A-Z, FISH

Alligator
Charlie Daniels Band; *Homesick Heroes* .... (EPI)
Grateful Dead; *Anthem Of The Sun* .... (WB)
Alligator Boogaloo
Clarence "Gatemouth" Brown; *Alright Again* ... (ROU)
Alligator Crawl
Louis Armstrong; *Hot Fives & Hot Sevens-#2* ....(COL)
Alligator Man
Jimmy C. Newman; *Greatest Hits* .... (PLN)
   Progressive CC .... (PLN)
   Souvenirs Of Music City USA .... (PLN)
Alligator Milk
Carol Channing/Others; *& Her Country Friends* .. (PLN)
Alligator Woman
Cameo; *Alligator Woman* .... (CHC)
R.G./Bayou Zydeco; *Fire On The Bayou* .... (TAK)
Animal Trainer & The Toad
Mountain; *Best Of* ....(COL)
Baby Snakes
Frank Zappa; *Baby Snakes* .... (BAR)
   Sheik Yerbouti ....(OOP)
Black Snake
John Lee Hooker; *Country Blues Of* .... (RVR)
Ramblin' Jack Elliott; *Essential* .... (VAN)
Black Snake Blues
Clifton Chenier; *Sixty Minutes With The King Of
Zydeco* .... (ARH)
Black Snake Dream Blues
Blind Lemon Jefferson; *Master Of The
Blues-#2-1926-1929* ....(BIO)
Black Snake Moan
Blind Lemon Jefferson; *Great Blues Guitarists-String
Dazzlers* ....(COL)
Leadbelly; *Leadbelly* ....(COL)
Breakfast For Dinosaurs
Fowler Brothers; *Breakfast For Dinosaurs* .... (FOS)
Bull Frog Blues
Jenny Pope; *Pot Hound Blues-1923-1930* .... (HIS)
Bull Frog Bounce
Leo Parker & Sax Gill; *Back To Back Baritones* . (CLT)
Celebration Of The Lizard
Doors; *Absolutely Live* .... (ELE)
Chameleon
Creedence Clearwater Revival; *1970* .... (FAN)
   Pendulum ....(FAN)
Elton John; *Blue Moves* ....(MCA)
Herbie Hancock; *Best Of* ....(COL)
   Headhunters ....(COL)
Labelle; *Chameleon* .... (EPI)
Chameleon Day
Talk Talk; *Colour Of Spring* .... (EMI)
Cold Hearted
Paula Abdul; *Forever Your Girl* .... (VIA)
   Get Up & Dance-Dance Mixes .... (VIA)
Crawling King Snake
Doors; *L.A. Woman* .... (ELE)
John Lee Hooker; *Best Of* .... (CRS)
   World's Greatest Blues Singer .... (VJ)
Muddy Waters; *They Call Me Muddy Waters* ..... (CSS)
Crocodile Rock
Elton John; *Billboard Top Rock 'N' Roll Hits-1973* (RHI)
   Don't Shoot Me I'm Only The Piano Player .... (POL)
   Greatest Hits .... (POL)
   Here & There .... (POL)
Crocodiles
Echo/Bunnymen; *Crocodiles* .... (SIR)
Dinosaur
David Byrne; *The Catherine Wheel* .... (SIR)
Eyes Of The World; *Relix Bay Rock Sampler-#3* .(RLX)
Gabriel Bondage; *Angel Dust* .... (DHM)
Geezinslaws; *Geezinslaws* ....(SO)
Hank Williams, Jr.; *Habits Old & New* .... (WB)
Raw Youth; *Hot Diggity* .... (GIA)
Thin White Rope; *The Ruby Sea* .... (FRN)
Dinosaur Jesus
Barbie Bones; *Brake For Nobody* .... (RES)
Dinosaur Tracks
Different World; *ST/Roadside Prophets* .... (VAN)

Dinosaurs
King Missile; *The Way To Salvation* .... (ATL)
Doin' The Frog
Duke Ellington/Orchestra; *Brunswick
Era-#1-1926-1929* .... (MCA)
Dream Of The Blue Turtles
Sting; *Dream Of The Blue Turtles* .... (A&M)
Fattening Frogs For Snakes
Sonny Boy Williamson; *The Blues-#3* .... (CSS)
Frog Legs
Clifton Chenier; *Bon Ton Roulet & More* .... (ARH)
Froggie Went A Courtin'
Doc Watson; *Essential* .... (VAN)
   Home Again .... (VAN)
Frogs With Dirty Little Lips
Frank Zappa; *Them Or Us* ....(BAR)
Gator Tails And Monkey Ribs
Spats; *45* ....(OOP)
I'm A Little Dinosaur
Jonathan Richman/Modern Lovers; *Beserkley Years-Best
Of* .... (RHI)
I'm In Love With A Big Blue Frog
Peter, Paul & Mary; *Album 1700* .... (WB)
Karma Chameleon
Culture Club; *Colour By Numbers* .... (VIA)
King Cobra
Herbie Hancock; *Best Of-Blue Note Years* .... (BLN)
King Cobra; *Powerhouse Music* .... (AJK)
Tom Scott/L.A. Express; *Tom Scott/L.A. Express* .. (EPI)
Kiss That Frog
Peter Gabriel; *Us* ....(GEF)
Leap Frog
Les Brown; *Best Of The Swing Bands* .... (HIN)
   Big Band Sampler ....(COL)
   Greatest Hits ....(CCB)
Lizard Lady
Residents; *Duck Stab* .... (RAL)
Lizard Song
Max Demian Band; *Take It To The Max* ....(OOP)
Pass The Snakes
Hot Tuna; *Live At Sweetwater* .... (RLX)
Peace Frog
Doors; *Classics* .... (ELE)
   Morrison Hotel .... (ELE)
   Weird Scenes Inside The Gold Mine .... (ELE)
Rattle My Snake
Amboy Dukes; *Survival Of The Fittest* .... (POL)
Rattlesnake Mountain
Patrick Sky; *Patrick Sky* .... (VAN)
Rattlesnake Rock 'N' Roller
Blackfoot; *Marauder* ....(ATC)
Rattlesnake Shake
Aerosmith; *Pandora's Box* ....(COL)
Fleetwood Mac; *25 Years-The Chain* .... (WB)
   Then Play On ....(RPR)
Mick Fleetwood; *The Visitor* ....(RCA)
Motley Crue; *Dr. Feelgood* .... (ELE)
Omar/Howlers; *ST/Speed Zone* .... (GDG)
Skid Row; *Skid Row* .... (ATL)
Rattlesnakes
Lloyd Cole/Commotions; *1984-1989* ....(CAP)
   Rattlesnakes .... (GEF)
See You Later, Alligator
Bill Haley/Comets; *Bill Haley/Comets* .... (EVR)
   Billboard Top Rock 'N' Roll Hits-1956 .... (RHI)
   Golden Hits ....(MCA)
   Greatest Hits ....(MCA)
   Mr. Rock 'N' Roll .... (ACC)
   Rock & Roll Is Here To Stay .... (GUS)
   Rockin' & Rollin' .... (ACC)
Snake
Joe Satriani; *Not Of This Earth* .... (REL)
Luther Johnson & Muddy Waters; *Chicken Shack* .(MUS)
Muddy Waters Blues Band; *Mud In Your Ear* ... (MUS)
Snake Charmer
John Hiatt; *ST/White Nights* .... (ATL)
Ritchie Blackmore; *Rainbow* ....(POL)
Ted Nugent; *State Of Shock* ....(EPI)
Snake Drive
Eric Clapton; *Guitar Boogie* ....(RCA)
Snake Eyes
Alan Parsons Project; *Turn Of A Friendly Card* .. (ARI)
Snake Man
Doobie Brothers; *Toulouse Street* ....(WB)

REPTILES (cont.)

Snakes Alive
Dreadful Snakes; *Dreadful Snakes* .... (ROU)
Snakes And Ladders
Joni Mitchell; *Chalk Mark In A Rainstorm* .... (GEF)
Men At Work; *Two Hearts* ....(COL)
Snakes Crawl At Night
Charley Pride; *Best Of* ....(RCA)
Snakes On Everything
Little Feat; *Little Feat* .... (WB)
Spiders & Snakes
Jim Stafford; *Jim Stafford* .... (POL)
Super Hits/'70s-Have A Nice Day-#12 .... (RHI)
Loretta Lynn & Conway Twitty; *Very Best Of* .. (MCA)
Terrapin Station
Grateful Dead; *Terrapin Station* .... (ARI)
That Black Snake Moan
Blind Lemon Jefferson; *Blind Lemon Jefferson* .... (MS)
Theme From "Jurassic Park"
John Williams; *ST/Jurassic Park* .... (MCA)
Toad In The Hole
Ian Anderson; *Walk Into Light* .... (CHR)
Tree Frog
Count Basie; *Best Of* .... (PAB)
Count Basie/Orchestra; *I Told You So* .... (PAB)
Tubesnake Boogie
ZZ Top; *El Loco* .... (WB)
Greatest Hits .... (WB)
Six Pack .... (WB)
Turtle Blues
Big Brother/Holding Company; *Cheap Thrills* ....(COL)
Turtle Rock
Bela Fleck/Flecktones; *Flight Of The Cosmic
Hippo* .... (WB)
Turtle Shoes
Bobby McFerrin; *Spontaneous Inventions* .... (BLN)
Bobby McFerrin & Herbie Hancock; *ST/Twins* . (WTG)
T-U-R-T-L-E Power!
Partners In Kryme; *ST/Teenage Mutant Ninja
Turtles* .... (SBK)
Union Of The Snake
Duran Duran; *Arena* .... (CAP)
Decade .... (CAP)
Seven & The Ragged Tiger .... (CAP)
Venom Soup
Ted Nugent; *Weekend Warriors* .... (EPI)
Viper's Drag
Fats Waller; *Joint Is Jumpin'* .... (BLU)
Original Cast; *Ain't Misbehavin'* ....(RCA)
Walk The Dinosaur
George Clinton/Goombas; *ST/Super Mario
Brothers* .... (CAP)
Was (Not Was); *What Up Dog?* .... (CHR)
Yertle The Turtle
Red Hot Chili Peppers; *Freaky Styley* .... (EMI)

RESTAURANTS, Cafes

*See Also: BARS, COFFEE, FOOD, FRUIT,
VEGETABLES*

Abandoned Luncheonette
Daryl Hall & John Oates; *Abandoned
Luncheonette* .... (ATL)
Livetime ....(RCA)
Alice's Restaurant Massacree
Arlo Guthrie; *Alice's Restaurant Massacree* .... (RPR)
Best Of .... (WB)
Annie Mae's Cafe
Little Milton; *Annie Mae's Cafe* .... (MAL)
At A Dixie Roadside Diner
Duke Ellington; *Duke Ellington & Blanton-Webster
Band* .... (BLU)
At The Banjo Cafe
Pat Cloud; *Higher Power* .... (FF)
At The Grand Hotel/Table With A View
Broadway Cast; *Grand Hotel* ....(RCA)
At The Seaside Cafe
Adrian Belew; *Desire Caught By The Tail* .... (ISL)
Atomic Cafe
Motels; *Motels* .... (CAP)
Cafe On The Corner
Sawyer Brown; *Cafe On The Corner* ....(CRB)

Cafe On The Left Bank
Wings; *London Town* ....(CAP)
Chinese Cafe
Joni Mitchell; *Wild Things Run Fast* .... (GEF)
Coffee Shoppe
Margaret Whiting; *Then & Now* .... (DRG)
Danny's All-Star Joint
Rickie Lee Jones; *Rickie Lee Jones* .... (WB)
Days Of Pup & Taco
Lawndale; *Beyond Barbecue* ....(SST)
No Age-Compilation Of SST Instrumentals ....(SST)
Detroit Snackbar Dreamer
Edgar Froese; *Stuntman* .... (BP)
Diesel Cafe
Bellamy Brothers; *Restless* ....(MSP)
Dinner At The Ritz
City Boy; *Dinner At The Ritz* .... (MER)
Dinner For One Please James
Nat King Cole; *Blossom Fell* ....(CAP)
Gift Set ....(CAP)
Dixie Diner
Jimmy Buffett; *You Had To Be There (In
Concert)* ....(MCA)
Do Fries Go With That Shake
George Clinton; *Best Of* ....(CAP)
Drive-In
Beach Boys; *All Summer Long* ....(CAP)
Spirit Of America ....(CAP)
Empty Chairs At Empty Tables
Original Broadway Cast; *Les Miserables* ....(GEF)
Fast Food
Pete Townshend; *The Iron Man* ....(ATL)
Stevens & Grdnic; *Dr. Demento Greatest Novelty
Records-#5* .... (RHI)
Hard Rock Cafe
Carole King; *Simple Things* ....(CAP)
In A Restaurant By The Sea
Holly Near & Ronnie Gilbert; *Singing With You* . (RWD)
Ladies Who Lunch
Original Cast; *Company* ....(COL)
Learning To Live Again
Garth Brooks; *The Chase* .... (LIB)
Montana Cafe
Hank Williams, Jr.; *Montana Cafe* ....(W/C)
More Wine Waiter Please
Poor; *Who Cares* ....(550)
My Girlfriend Is A Waitress
Iguanas; *Nuevo Boogaloo* .... (MGR)
Nobody Eats At Linebaugh's Anymore
John Hartford; *Me Oh My How The Time Does
Fly-Anthology* ....(FF)
Not In A Chinese Restaurant
Country Joe McDonald; *Child's Play* .... (RBB)
Ooh! My Feet!
Original Broadway Cast; *Most Happy Fella* ..... (SMC)
Overnight Cafe
Chicago; *XIV* ....(COL)
Paradise Cafe
Arc Angels; *Arc Angels* .... (DGC)
Barry Manilow; *2:00 Paradise Cafe* .... (ARI)
Pretty Women/Ladies Who Lunch
Barbra Streisand; *Broadway Album* ....(COL)
Queen Of The Cowboy Cafe
Si Kahn; *Home* ....(FF)
River Diner
Jack Smith/Rockabilly Planet; *Jack Smith/Rockabilly
Planet* ....(FF)
Sad Cafe
Eagles; *Greatest Hits-#2* .... (ASY)
The Long Run .... (ASY)
Lorrie Morgan; *Common Thread-Songs Of The
Eagles* .... (GIA)
Scenes From An Italian Restaurant
Billy Joel; *The Stranger* ....(COL)
She's Not On The Menu
SNFU; *Last Of The Big Time Suspenders* .... (CGO)
Showdown At The Big Boy
Nazareth; *Malice In Wonderland* ....(A&M)
Smokey Joe's Cafe
Coasters; *Their Greatest Recordings-Early Years* ..(ATC)
Young Blood .... (ATL)
Loudon Wainwright III; *Album III* ....(COL)

Street Cafe
Icehouse; *Fresco* .... (CHR)
    Great Southern Land .... (CHR)
    Primitive Man .... (CHR)
Sunset Grill
Don Henley; *Building The Perfect Beast* .... (GEF)
Sweet Little Cafe In A Square
Lena Spencer/Others; *Welcome To Caffe Lena* ....(BIO)
Taco Stand
Normaltown Flyers; *Normaltown Flyers* .... (MER)
Taco Wagon
Dale, Dick/Del-Tones; *King Of The Surf Guitar-Best Of* .... (RHI)
Young Fresh Fellows; *This One's For The Ladies* . (FRN)
Texas Rose Cafe
Little Feat; *Sailin' Shoes* .... (WB)
That Girl Who Waits On Tables
Ronnie Milsap; *Collector's Series* ....(RCA)
Tom's Diner
DNA/Suzanne Vega; *Solitude Standing* .... (A&M)
    Tom's Album .... (A&M)
Two Triple Cheese, Side Order Of Fries
Commander Cody/Lost Planet Airmen; *Aces High* .... (RLX)
Waitress In A Donut Shop
Dan Hicks/Hot Licks; *Last Train To Hicksville* .. (MCA)
Waitress In The Sky
Replacements; *Tim* .... (SIR)
Waitress, The
Tori Amos; *Under The Pink* .... (ATL)
We Reserve The Right To Refuse...
Kinky Friedman; *Sold American* .... (VAN)

RHYTHM, Beat

See Also: DANCE, MUSIC

All God's Chillun Got Rhythm
Judy Garland; *Collector's Items-1936-1945* ..... (MCA)
And The Beat Goes On
Whispers; *Club Epic* .... (EPI)
Artistry In Rhythm
Stan Kenton; *Comprehensive* .... (CAP)
    Greatest Hits .... (CAP)
    Live In Europe .... (MER)
    Road Show .... (CAP)
    Summer Of '51 .... (GRL)
Beat
Elvis Costello; *This Year's Model* .... (COL)
Beat Goes On
Sonny & Cher; *Beat Goes On* .... (ATC)
    Best Of .... (ATC)
    Hit Singles 1958-1977 .... (ATL)
    Live .... (MCA)
    Two Of Us .... (ATC)
Beat Me Daddy Eight To The Bar
Andrews Sisters; *16 Great Performances* .... (MCA)
    Best Of .... (MCA)
    Boogie Woogie Bugle Girls .... (MCA)
    Capitol Collectors Series ....(CAP)
Commander Cody/Lost Planet Airmen; *Lost In The Ozone* .... (MCA)
Beat Street
Melle Mel; *Rap Hall Of Fame* .... (KT)
    ST/Beat Street .... (ATL)
Eat To The Beat
Blondie; *Eat To The Beat* .... (CHR)
Foolish Beat
Debbie Gibson; *Hit Singles 1980-1988* .... (ATL)
    Out Of The Blue .... (ATL)
Georgia Rhythm
Atlanta Rhythm Section; *Rock & Roll Alternative* . (POL)
Good Beat
Deee-Lite; *World Clique* .... (ELE)
Hit Me With Your Rhythm Stick
Ian Dury/Blockheads; *45* .... (STF)
I Got Rhythm
Ella Fitzgerald; *George & Ira Gershwin Songbook* (VRV)
Happenings; *45* .... (VGO)
Judy Garland; *Collector's Items-1936-1945* ..... (MCA)
Robert Palmer; *Glory Of Gershwin Featuring Larry Adler* .... (MER)

Let The Beat Hit 'Em
Lisa Lisa & Cult Jam; *Clivilles & Cole's Greatest Remixes-#1* ....(COL)
    Straight Outta Hell's Kitchen ....(COL)
Let The Rhythm Hit 'Em
Erik B. & Rakim; *Let The Rhythm Hit 'Em* ...... (MCA)
Let The Rhythm Pump
Doug Lazy; *Gettin' Crazy* .... (ATL)
Mystic Rhythms
Rush; *Chronicles* .... (MER)
    Power Windows .... (MER)
    Show Of Hands .... (MER)
On The Beat
B.B. & Q. Band; *B.B. & Q. Band* .... (CAP)
    Disco Years-#2-On The Beat-1978-1982 .... (RHI)
Painted Rhythm
Stan Kenton; *Comprehensive* .... (CAP)
    Greatest Hits .... (CAP)
    Kenton In Hi-Fi .... (BLN)
Play In Time
Jethro Tull; *Benefit* .... (CHR)
Puerto Rican Rhythms
Last Poets; *Right On!* .... (CLT)
Rhythm From A Red Car
Hardline; *Double Eclipse* .... (MCA)
Rhythm In Gold
Jethro Tull; *20 Years Of-Radio Archives/Rare Tracks* .... (CHR)
Rhythm In My Nursery Rhymes
Tommy Dorsey/Clambake Seven; *Music Goes Round & Round* .... (BLU)
Rhythm In The Barnyard
Joe Liggins/Honeydrippers; *Joe Liggins/Honeydrippers* .... (SPE)
Rhythm Is Gonna Get Ya
Gloria Estefan/Miami Sound Machine; *Heart Of Soul* ....(COL)
    Let It Loose .... (EPI)
Rhythm Machine
Bad Company; *Desolation Angels* .... (SS)
Rhythm Nation
Janet Jackson; *Janet Jackson's Rhythm Nation 1814* .... (A&M)
Rhythm Of Life
Oleta Adams; *Circle Of One* .... (FON)
Original Cast; *Sweet Charity* ....(COL)
Richard Marx; *Richard Marx* ....(CAP)
Rhythm Of Love
Scorpions; *Best Of Rockers 'N' Ballads* .... (MER)
    Savage Amusement .... (MER)
Screaming Iguanas Of Love; *Screaming Iguanas Of Love* .... (LGS)
Yes; *Big Generator* .... (ATC)
    Yesyears .... (ATC)
Rhythm Of My Heart
Rod Stewart; *Vagabond Heart* .... (WB)
Rhythm Of The Heat
Peter Gabriel; *Plays Live* .... (GEF)
    Security .... (GEF)
Rhythm Of The Night
DeBarge; *Greatest Hits* .... (MOT)
    Motown Story-First 25 Years .... (MOT)
    Rhythm Of The Night .... (MOT)
Rhythm Of The Rain
Cascades; *Collectables Presents History Of Rock-#7* ....(CLT)
    Golden Years-1963 .... (DOM)
Rhythm Of The Road
George Strait; *#7* .... (MCA)
Rhythm Of The Saints
Paul Simon; *Rhythm Of The Saints* .... (WB)
Rhythm Of Time
Front 242; *Tyranny For You* .... (EPI)
Rhythm Saved The World
Bunny Berigan/Boys; *Take It Bunny* .... (SSP)
Rhythm (Devoted To Art Of Moving Butts)
Tribe Called Quest; *People's Instinctive Travels...* . (JVA)
Rhythm-A-Ning
Art Blakey/Jazz Messengers; *With Thelonius Monk* .... (ATL)
Milt Jackson/Gold Medal Winners; *Brother Jim* .. (PAB)
Thelonius Monk; *In Italy* .... (RVR)
Thelonius Monk & Gerry Mulligan; *Mulligan Meets Monk* .... (RVR)

Ride On The Rhythm
Little Louie & Marc Anthony; *When The Night Is Over* .... (ATL)
Rock Me In The Rhythm Of Your Love
Eddy Raven; *Best Of* .... (LIB)
   Right For The Flight .... (CAP)
Rockin' In Rhythm
Duke Ellington; *Great Paris Concert* .... (ATL)
D. Ellington/E. Fitzgerald/O. Peterson; *Greatest Jazz Concert In The World* .... (PAB)
Hank Jones/Ray Brown/Jimmie Smith; *Rockin' In Rhythm* .... (CCJ)
Modern Jazz Quartet; *For Ellington* .... (EW)
Rockin' Over The Beat
Technotronic; *Pump Up The Jam-The Album* .... (SBK)
R&B Skeletons (In The Closet)
George Clinton; *R&B Skeletons (In The Closet)* ...(CAP)
She's Got Rhythm
Beach Boys; *M.I.U.* ....(CAR)
She's Got The Rhythm (& I Got The Blues)
Alan Jackson; *Lot About Livin' (& A Little 'Bout Love* .... (ARI)
Skate To The Rhythm
High Inergy; *Frenzie* .... (GOR)
Surf Beat
Dick Dale/Del-Tones; *Greatest Hits* .... (CRS)
   King Of The Surf Guitar-Best Of .... (RHI)
Take A Little Rhythm
Ali Thompson; *Take A Little Rhythm* .... (A&M)
Teen Beat
Fleetwood Mac; *25 Years-The Chain* .... (WB)
That Rhythm Man
Louis Armstrong/Orchestra; *& The Big Bands* ...(DSQ)
This Beat Is Hot
B.G. The Prince Of Rap; *Power Of Rhythm* .... (EPI)
   This Beat Is Hot-Compilation .... (EPI)
Throw That Beat In The Garbage Can
B-52's; *Mesopotamia* .... (WB)
Turn On (The Beat Box)
Earth, Wind & Fire; *Best Of-#2* .... (COL)
Turn The Beat Around
Vicki Sue Robinson; *Dance! Dance! Dance!-RCA's Greatest* ....(RCA)
   Never Gonna Let You Go ....(RCA)
   Nipper's Greatest Hits-'70s ....(RCA)
We Got The Beat
Go-Go's; *Beauty & The Beat* .... (IRS)
   Greatest .... (IRS)
   ST/Brimstone & Treacle .... (A&M)
   ST/Urgh! A Music War .... (A&M)

~~~~~~

RIVERS, Bayou, Creeks, Delta, Streams
See Also: OCEAN, SAILING, SHIPS, WATER

~~~~~~

Across The Great Divide
Band; *Band* ....(CAP)
   Rock Of Ages-#1 & 2 ....(CAP)
Across The River
Bruce Hornsby/Range; *Night On The Town* ......(RCA)
Original Cast; *Starting Here Starting Now* ....(RCA)
All Quiet Along The Potomac Tonight
Hermes Nye; *Ballads Of The Civil War-#1 & 2* . (FLW)
American Pie
Don McLean; *American Pie* .... (UA)
   Best Of .... (EMI)
   Greatest Hits Then & Now .... (EMI)
   ST/Born On The Fourth Of July .... (MCA)
Banks Of The Ohio
Doc Watson; *On Stage* .... (VAN)
Joan Baez; *Joan Baez* .... (VAN)
   Vol. 2 .... (VAN)
Bayou Jubilee
Nitty Gritty Dirt Band; *Dirt Silver & Gold* .... (UA)
   Dream .... (UA)
   Will The Circle Be Unbroken-#2 .... (UNI)
Bayou Lullaby
Penny De Haven; *ST/Bronco Billy* .... (ELE)
Big River
Beat Farmers; *Pursuit Of Happiness* .... (MCA)
Bob Seger System; *Mongrel* ....(CAP)
Grateful Dead; *One From The Vault* .... (GRD)
   Steal Your Face .... (GRD)

Johnny Cash; *Greatest Hits-#2* .... (COL)
   Legend .... (SUN)
   Sun Years .... (RHI)
   Superbilly .... (SUN)
Rosanne Cash; *Right Or Wrong* .... (COL)
Big River, Big Man
Claude King; *American Originals* .... (COL)
   Best .... (GUS)
Bitter Creek
Eagles; *Desperado* .... (ASY)
Black Bayou
Charlie Daniels Band; *Midnight Wind* .... (EPI)
Black Water
Doobie Brothers; *Best Of* .... (WB)
   What Were Once Vices Are Now Habits .... (WB)
Blue Bayou
Linda Ronstadt; *Greatest Hits-#2* .... (ASY)
   Simple Dreams .... (ASY)
Roy Orbison; *All-Time Greatest Hits-#2* .... (MON)
   For The Lonely: Anthology 1956-1965 .... (RHI)
   In Dreams-Greatest Hits .... (VIA)
   More Greatest Hits .... (MON)
Roy Orbison & Friends; *Black & White Night-Live* (VIA)
Blue River
Elvis Presley; *Lost Album* ....(RCA)
   ST/Double Trouble ....(RCA)
Boat On The River
Styx; *Cornerstone* .... (A&M)
Born On The Bayou
Creedence Clearwater Revival; *Bayou Country* ..(FAN)
   Chooglin' ....(FAN)
   Gold ....(FAN)
   Live In Europe ....(FAN)
   The Concert ....(FAN)
   '68-'69 ....(FAN)
Bridge On The River Kwai
Magic Organ; *Plays Movie Themes* .... (RAN)
Bridge Washed Out
Warner Mack; *Country's Greatest Hits-#3* .... (MCA)
   MCA 30 Years Of Hits 1958-1988 .... (MCA)
Buffalo River Home
John Hiatt; *Perfectly Good Guitar* .... (A&M)
Burn On
Randy Newman; *Sail Away* .... (RPR)
Chattahoochee
Alan Jackson; *Lot About Livin' (& A Little 'Bout Love)* .... (ARI)
Cripple Creek
Leo Kottke; *Best* ....(CAP)
   Did You Hear Me ....(CAP)
   Mudlark ....(CAP)
   Peter Lang/John Fahey .... (TAK)
Leon Kottke; *Very Best* ....(CAP)
Cripple Creek Ferry
Neil Young; *After The Goldrush* .... (RPR)
Cross The Brazos At Waco
Billy Walker; *Columbia Country Classics-#3-Americana* .... (COL)
   Super Hits Country-1960s .... (IGR)
Cry Me A River
Aerosmith; *Rock In A Hard Place* ....(COL)
Barbra Streisand; *Barbra Streisand Album* ....(COL)
   Happening In Central Park ....(COL)
Crystal Gayle; *When I Dream* .... (UA)
Joe Cocker; *Classics-#4* .... (A&M)
   Greatest Hits .... (A&M)
   Mad Dogs & Englishmen .... (A&M)
Cumberland Blues
Grateful Dead; *Europe '72* .... (WB)
   What A Long Strange Trip It's Been .... (WB)
   Workingman's Dead .... (WB)
Cuyahoga
R.E.M.; *Life's Rich Pageant* .... (IRS)
Deep Creek
Butch Thompson; *New Orleans Joys* .... (DAR)
Jelly Roll Morton; *Jelly Roll Morton* .... (BLU)
Deep River
Fats Waller; *In London* ....(DSQ)
Mormon Tabernacle Choir; *Songs From America's Heartland* ....(LON)
Paul Robeson; *Historic-Golden Classics-#3* .... (CLT)
Deep River Blues
Doc Watson; *Doc Watson* .... (VAN)

Deep River Woman
Lionel Richie; *Dancing On The Ceiling* .... (MOT)
Delta Lady
Joe Cocker; *Classics-#4* .... (A&M)
   Greatest Hits .... (A&M)
   Joe Cocker .... (A&M)
   Mad Dogs & Englishmen .... (A&M)
Leon Russell; *Best Of* .... (MCA)
   Leon Russell .... (MCA)
Don't Change Horses
Tower Of Power; *Back To Oakland* .... (WB)
Don't Cross The River
America; *History-Greatest Hits* .... (WB)
   Homecoming .... (WB)
Down By The Ohio
Andrews Sisters; *Best Of-#2* .... (MCA)
Down By The Old Mill Stream
Sammy Kaye; *Best Of* .... (MCA)
Down By The River
Neil Young; *Decade* .... (RPR)
   Everybody Knows This Is Nowhere .... (RPR)
Down By The Riverside
Elvis Presley; *Million-Dollar Quartet* ....(RCA)
Mormon Tabernacle Choir; *Songs From America's Heartland* ....(LON)
Sonny Terry & Brownie McGhee; *Blowin' The Fuses-Golden Classics* .... (CLT)
   Coffee House Blues .... (VJ)
   Giants Of The Blues .... (BSL)
Down On Deep River
Leon Russell; *Will O' The Wisp* .... (MCA)
Down On The Rio Grande
Brian Sharp; *Rio Grande Valley* .... (WWI)
Johnny Rodriguez; *Rodriguez* .... (EPI)
Down The River Of Golden Dreams
Mom & Dads; *Down The River Of Golden Dreams* .... (CRS)
Slim Whitman; *Home On The Range* .... (UA)
Downstream
Rainmakers; *Rainmakers* .... (MER)
Supertramp; *Even In The Quietest Moments* ..... (A&M)
Ferry Across The Mersey
Gerry/Pacemakers; *Ferry Across The Mersey-Best Of* .... (EMI)
   History Of British Rock-#4 .... (RHI)
Flow Gently, Sweet Afton
Mormon Tabernacle Choir; *Old Beloved Songs* ...(COL)
Green River
Alabama; *Mountain Music* ....(RCA)
Creedence Clearwater Revival; *1969* .... (FAN)
   Chronicle .... (FAN)
   Green River .... (FAN)
   Live In Europe .... (FAN)
   Royal Albert Hall Concert .... (FAN)
   ST/1969 .... (POL)
Greenwood Creek
Doobie Brothers; *Doobie Brothers* .... (WB)
Hazard (The River)
Richard Marx; *Rush Street* .... (CAP)
If The River Was Whiskey
Mississippi Fred McDowell; *Great Bluesmen At Newport* .... (VAN)
Islands In The Stream
Kenny Rogers & Dolly Parton; *Eyes That See In The Dark* ....(RCA)
   Greatest Hits ....(RCA)
Jambalaya
Blue Ridge Rangers; *Blue Ridge Rangers* .... (FAN)
Fats Domino; *Greatest Hits* .... (MCA)
Hank Williams; *16 Great Hits* .... (EVR)
   24 Of Hank Williams' Greatest Hits .... (POL)
   40 Greatest Hits .... (POL)
Hank Williams, Jr.; *ST/Your Cheatin' Heart* ...... (SSP)
Jerry Lee Lewis; *Golden Cream Of The Country* . (SUN)
   Twenty Classic Hits .... (SUN)
Nitty Gritty Dirt Band; *All The Good Times* .... (UA)
   Stars & Stripes Forever .... (UA)
Keep Me Turning
Pete Townshend & Ronnie Lane; *Rough Mix* ....(ATC)
Kern River
Merle Haggard; *Kern River* .... (EPI)
Lazy River
Bing Crosby; *All-Time Best Of* ....(CCB)
Bobby Darin; *Mack The Knife-Best Of-#2* .... (ATL)

Chet Atkins & Les Paul; *Masters Of The Guitar-Together* ....(PRR)
Harry Connick, Jr.; *Eleven* ....(COL)
Kay Starr; *Greatest Hits* ....(CCB)
Leon Redbone; *Up A Lazy River* ....(PRV)
Louis Armstrong; *Best Of The Decca Years-#1-The Singer* .... (DEC)
Mills Brothers; *Best Of The Decca Years* .... (DEC)
   Greatest Hits .... (MCA)
Let The River Run
Carly Simon; *Coming Around Again* .... (ARI)
   ST/Working Girl .... (ARI)
Let's All Go Down To The River
Johnny Paycheck; *Greatest Hits* .... (EPI)
Like A River To The Sea
Steve Wariner; *I Am Ready* .... (ARI)
Many Rivers To Cross
Jimmy Cliff; *In Concert* .... (RPR)
   Reggae Spectacular .... (A&M)
   ST/Harder They Come .... (MGO)
   Wonderful World Beautiful People .... (A&M)
Linda Ronstadt; *Prisoner In Disguise* .... (ASY)
UB40; *Labour Of Love* .... (A&M)
Mississippi Delta Blues
Bob Wills; *Anthology* .... (SSP)
Jimmie Rodgers; *Train Whistle Blues* ....(RCA)
Leon Redbone; *Double Time* .... (WB)
Mississippi Delta City Blues
Chicago; *Group Portrait* ....(COL)
   XI ....(COL)
Mississippi Mud
Bob Crosby Orchestra; *1952-1953* .... (HIN)
   Play 22 Original Big Band Hits .... (HIN)
Mississippi River
J.J. Cale; *Grasshopper* .... (MER)
Paul Davis; *Little Bit Of* ....(BNG)
Mississippi River Blues
Leon Redbone; *Double Time* .... (WB)
Moon River
Andy Williams; *16 Most Requested Songs* ....(COL)
   Greatest Hits ....(COL)
   More American Graffiti-#4 .... (MCA)
Henry Mancini; *All-Time Greatest Hits-#1* ....(RCA)
   Pure Gold ....(RCA)
Jerry Butler; *Best Of* .... (RHI)
   Moon River .... (VJ)
Moonlight On The Colorado
Sons Of The Pioneers; *Songs Of The Trail* .... (PRR)
Moonlight On The Ganges
Frank Sinatra; *Sinatra Swings* .... (RPR)
Glenn Miller; *Best Of The Big Bands* ....(COL)
My Home Is In The Delta
Muddy Waters; *Chess Box* .... (CSS)
   Folk Singer .... (CSS)
New River Train
Doc & Merle Watson; *Remembering Merle* ....(SH)
White Brothers & New Kentucky Colonels; *Live In Sweden* .... (ROU)
Ode To Billy Joe
Bobbi Gentry; *All-Time Country Classics-#1* .....(CAP)
Old Folks At Home
Mormon Tabernacle Choir; *Songs Of The Civil War & S. Foster Fav.* .... (SMC)
Paul Robeson; *A Man & His Beliefs-Golden Classics-#2* .... (CLT)
Ol' Man River
Al Jolson; *Best Of* .... (MCA)
   Story-#6 .... (MCA)
Frank Sinatra; *Concert Sinatra* .... (RPR)
   Greatest Hits-#2 ....(COL)
   Voice-Columbia Years-1943-1952 ....(COL)
William Warfield; *ST/All Those Glorious MGM Musicals* ....(MGM)
William Warfield/Original Cast; *Show Boat* .....(COL)
On The Amazon
Mabel Mercer & Bobby Short; *At Town Hall* ....(ATL)
On The Banks Of The Ohio
Carter Family & Johnny Cash; *Folk Classics-Roots Of American Folk* ....(COL)
Hodges Brothers; *Watermelon Hangin' On The Vine* .... (ARH)
Joan Baez; *Country Music Album* .... (VAN)
On The Banks Of The Old Tennessee
Doc Watson; *Old Timey Concert* .... (VAN)

On The Banks Of The Wabash
Mills Brothers; *22 Great Hits* .... (RAN)
  Story .... (RAN)
On The Mississippi
Claude Bolling; *Original Ragtime* ....(COL)
One More River
Alan Parsons Project; *Pyramid* .... (ARI)
Peace Like A River
Paul Simon; *Paul Simon* .... (WB)
Pond & The Stream
Sandy Denny; *Best Of* .... (HBL)
  Who Knows Where The Time Goes? .... (HBL)
Powder River/Carrie's Gone To Kansas C.
Bill Shute & Lisa Null; *American Primitive* ......(GRE)
Proud Mary
Creedence Clearwater Revival; *1968-1969* ......(FAN)
  Bayou Country ....(FAN)
  Chronicle ....(FAN)
  Gold ....(FAN)
  Live In Europe ....(FAN)
George Jones & Johnny Paycheck; *My Very Special*
  Guests ....(EPI)
Ike & Tina Turner; *Best Of* .... (EMI)
  EMI Legends Of Rock 'N' Roll-24 Greatest ..... (RHI)
  Greatest Hits ....(CCB)
  Soul Hits'70s-#4 .... (RHI)
Purple Rivers
Swimming Pool Q's; *Swimming Pool Q's* .... (A&M)
Queen Of The Nile
Dangerous Toys; *Dangerous Toys* ....(COL)
Red And Rio Grande
Doug Supernaw; *Red And Rio Grande* ....(BNA)
Red River
Alabama; *Closer You Get* .... (RCA)
  Live ....(RCA)
BoDeans; *Home* ....(SLS)
Leadbelly; *Leadbelly* ....(COL)
  Midnight Special ....(ROU)
Red River Blues
Jesse Fuller; *Jesse Fuller's Favorites* .... (PRS)
Sonny Terry; *Sonny Terry* ....(EVR)
  With Brownie McGhee; Midnight Special ....(FAN)
Red River Rock
Johnny/Hurricanes; *Echoes Of A Rock Era-Middle*
  Years ....(RLL)
  History Of Rock Instrumentals-#1 .... (RHI)
Red River Valley
Gene Autry; *Country Music Hall Of Fame* ......(COL)
  Cowboy Hall Of Fame ....(REP)
  Western Classics ....(COL)
Pete Seeger; *American Favorite Ballads-#5* ...... (FLW)
Ride Across The River
Dire Straits; *Brothers In Arms* .... (WB)
Rio Grande
Floyd Tillman; *Country Music Hall Of Fame* .... (MCA)
Sam Eskin; *Shanty Men-Songs Of*
  Sailormen/Lumbermen .... (FLW)
River Blood
Walkabouts; *Scavenger* .... (SP)
River Boy
Willie Nelson; *There'll Be No Teardrops Tonight* .. (UA)
River Deep Mountain High
Erasure; *Innocents* .... (SIR)
Four Tops; *Anthology* .... (MOT)
Ike & Tina Turner; *Best Of* .... (EMI)
  Phil Spector's Greatest Hits ....(SPC)
  Proud Mary-Best Of ....(EMI)
Tina Turner; *Simply The Best* ....(CAP)
River Diner
Jack Smith/Rockabilly Planet; *Jack Smith/Rockabilly*
  Planet ....(FF)
River Hymn
Band; *Cahoots* ....(CAP)
  To Kingdom Come-Definitive Collection ....(CAP)
River In The Pines
Joan Baez; *Farewell Angelina* .... (VAN)
  Love Song Album ....(VAN)
River In The Rain
Original Broadway Cast; *Big River-Adventures Of*
  Huckleberry Finn ....(MCA)
River Is Wide
Grass Roots; *16 Greatest Hits* .... (MCA)
  Anthology-1965-1975 ....(RHI)

River Jordan
Clancy Eddle/Others; *Ska Bonanza-Studio One Ska*
  Years ....(HRT)
River Must Flow
Gino Vannelli; *Brother To Brother* ....(A&M)
  Greatest Hits ....(A&M)
River Of Dreams
Billy Joel; *River Of Dreams* ....(COL)
River Of Jordan
Ricky Skaggs; *Family & Friends* .... (ROU)
  Stained Glass Hour ....(ROU)
River Of Life
Neville Brothers; *Brother's Keeper* ....(A&M)
R.E.O. Speedwagon; *This Time We Mean It* ....(EPI)
River Of Love
Angels; *My Boyfriend's Back* ....(CLT)
David Foster; *River Of Love* ....(ATL)
John Denver; *Farewell Andromeda* ....(RCA)
Lynch Mob; *Wicked Sensation* .... (ELE)
Richie Sambora; *Stranger In This Town* .... (MER)
T-Bone Burnett; *T-Bone Burnett* .... (DOT)
River Of Stone
Restless; *Fast Moving Train* ....(RCA)
River Of Tears
Bonnie Raitt; *Green Light* .... (WB)
Highway 101; *Bing Bang Boom* ....(WB)
York Brothers; *Super Hits Country-1940s* ....(GUS)
River Path
Little Anthony/Imperials; *Forever Yours* .... (RLL)
River Road
Crystal Gayle; *Favorites* .... (UA)
  We Must Believe In Magic ....(UA)
River Roll On
Judds; *Rockin' With The Rhythm* ....(RCA)
River Runs Deep
J.J. Cale; *Naturally* .... (MCA)
River Runs Low
Bruce Hornsby/Range; *The Way It Is* ....(RCA)
River Runs Red
Midnight Oil; *Blue Sky Mining* ....(COL)
River Song
Beach Boys; *10 Years Of Harmony* ....(CAR)
Riverboat
Robert Palmer; *Pressure Drop* .... (ISL)
Riverboat Gambler
Chris LeDoux; *Songs Of Rodeo Life* ....(CAP)
Riverboat Shuffle
Hoagy Carmichael; *Stardust Road* .... (MCA)
Rivers Of Babylon
Boney M; *Nightflow To Venus* .... (SIR)
Linda Ronstadt; *Hasten Down The Wind* ....(ASY)
Melodians; *ST/Harder They Come* ....(MGO)
River, The
Bruce Springsteen; *The River* ....(COL)
Bruce Springsteen/E Street Band;
  Live-1975-1985 ....(COL)
Dan Fogelberg; *Home Free* ....(COL)
Enya; *Watermark* ....(RPR)
Garth Brooks; *Ropin' The Wind* ....(LIB)
Joni Mitchell; *Blue* ....(RPR)
Roberta Flack; *Killing Me Softly* ....(ATL)
Santana; *Festival* ....(COL)
River's Invitation
Freddie Robinson; *Stax Blues Masters-Blue*
  Monday ....(STX)
Percy Mayfield; *Best Of* ....(SPE)
Stanley Turrentine; *Best Of* ....(BLN)
  Joyride ....(BLN)
Ted Taylor; *Atlantic Blues-Vocalists* ....(ATL)
Rockin' On The River
Jerry Jeff Walker; *Navajo Rug* ....(RYK)
Roll On Mississippi
Charley Pride; *Greatest Hits* ....(RCA)
Roll Tennessee River
Oak Ridge Boys; *Step On Out* .... (MCA)
Rose Of The Rio Grande
Bob Crosby Orchestra; *Play 22 Original Big Band*
  Hits ....(HIN)
Duke Ellington; *Great Paris Concert* ....(ATL)
Ella Fitzgerald & Duke Ellington; *At The Cote*
  D'Azur ....(VRV)

Sailing Down This Golden River
Pete Seeger; *Bread & Roses Festival-Acoustic Music-#1* ....(FAN)
   Circles & Seasons ....(WB)
Shady River Gal/Alabama Gals
Beverly Cotton; *Clogging Lessons* ....(FF)
Shall We Gather At The River?
Chuck Wagon Gang; *16 Country-Gospel Favorites* ....(MCA)
Tennessee Ernie Ford; *All-Time Greatest Hymns* .(CCB)
   Sings 22 Favorite Hymns ....(RAN)
Shenandoah
Bob Dylan; *Down In The Groove* ....(COL)
Harry Belafonte; *Legendary Performer* ....(RCA)
James Galway; *Greatest Hits* ....(RCA)
Leontyne Price; *God Bless America* ....(RCA)
Sitting By The Riverside
Kinks; *Are The Village Green Preservation...* ....(RPR)
Skunk Creek
Poco; *Forgotten Trail-1969-1974* ....(EPI)
Song Of The Volga Boatmen
Glenn Miller; *Best Of* ....(RCA)
   Chattanooga Choo Choo-#1 Hits ....(BLU)
   Legendary Performer ....(BLU)
   Memorial-1944-1969 ....(BLU)
   This Is ....(RCA)
Tuxedo Junction; *Tuxedo Junction* ....(BTF)
Squaws Along The Yukon
Hank Thompson; *Capitol Collectors Series* ....(CAP)
   Greatest Hits-#2 ....(SO)
Standing By A River
Climax Blues Band; *FM/Live* ....(SIR)
Standing Knee Deep In A River
Kathy Mattea; *Lonesome Standard Time* ....(MER)
Sunflower River Blues
John Fahey; *With Peter Lang & Leo Kottke* ....(TAK)
Surfin' Down The Swanee River
Honeys; *Capitol Collectors Series* ....(CAP)
Swampy River
Duke Ellington; *Okeh Ellington* ....(COL)
Swanee
Al Jolson; *Best Of* ....(MCA)
   Best Of The Decca Years ....(DEC)
   Jolson Sang 'Em ....(BIO)
George Gershwin; *Rhapsody In Blue* ....(BIO)
Judy Garland; *All-Time Greatest Hits* ....(CCB)
   At Carnegie Hall ....(CAP)
Swanee River
Dave Brubeck Quartet; *Gone With The Wind* ...(COL)
Firehouse Five Plus Two; *Goes South* ....(GTJ)
Swanee River Rock
Ray Charles; *Birth Of Soul-Complete Atlantic R&B* ....(ATL)
Sweet Thames Flow Softly
Alison Brown; *Twilight Motel* ....(VAN)
Swimming In The Delaware
Sam Hinton; *Wandering Folk Song* ....(FLW)
Swimming Upstream
Glen Campbell; *Somebody Like That* ....(LIB)
Ricky Van Shelton; *Loving Proof* ....(COL)
Take A Ride On A Riverboat
Louisiana's Le Roux; *Louisiana's Le Roux* ....(CAP)
Take Me To The River
Al Green; *Al Green Explores Your Mind* ....(MOT)
   Greatest Hits-#2 ....(HIR)
Bryan Ferry; *Bride Stripped Bare* ....(RPR)
Commitments; *ST/Commitments* ....(MCA)
Exile; *Exile* ....(EPI)
   Super Hits ....(EPI)
Foghat; *Best Of-#2* ....(RHI)
   Night Shift ....(RHI)
Talking Heads; *More Songs About Buildings & Food* ....(SIR)
   Popular Favorites-1984-1992 ....(SIR)
Tennessee River
Alabama; *Best Of The '80s...So Far* ....(RCA)
   Greatest Hits ....(RCA)
   Live ....(RCA)
   My Home's In Alabama ....(RCA)
Hank Williams, Jr.; *Rowdy* ....(W/C)
Thanks For The Beautiful Land On The...
Duke Ellington; *New Orleans Suite* ....(ATL)
That Song About The River
Don Williams; *Currents* ....(RCA)

That Was A River
Collin Raye; *In This Life* ....(EPI)
Till The Rivers All Run Dry
Don Williams; *Best Of-#2* ....(MCA)
   Country Comes To Carnegie Hall ....(MCA)
   Greatest Country Hits ....(CCB)
   Harmony ....(MCA)
   Till The Rivers All Run Dry ....(MSP)
Pete Townshend & Ronnie Lane; *Rough Mix* ...(MCA)
Time (Keeps Flowing Like A River)
Alan Parsons Project; *Best Of* ....(ARI)
   Turn Of A Friendly Card ....(ARI)
Too Many Rivers
Brenda Lee; *Story-Her Greatest Hits* ....(MCA)
Eddy Arnold; *Country Gold* ....(RCA)
Forester Sisters; *New Tradition Sings The Old Tradition* ....(WB)
Train & The River
Jimmy Giuffre; *Jimmy Giuffre Three* ....(ATL)
Traveling Riverside Blues
Hindu Love Gods; *Hindu Love Gods* ....(GIA)
John Hammond; *Best Of* ....(VAN)
Led Zeppelin; *Led Zeppelin (collection)* ....(ATL)
Robert Johnson; *King Of The Delta Blues Singers* .(COL)
   Slide Guitar-Bottles Knives & Steel ....(COL)
Two Rivers In Montana
Gove Scrivenor; *Coconut Gove* ....(FF)
Up On Cripple Creek
Band; *Band* ....(CAP)
   Best Of ....(CAP)
   Gift Set ....(CAP)
   Last Waltz ....(WB)
Band & Bob Dylan; *Before The Flood* ....(COL)
Wabash Cannonball
Nitty Gritty Dirt Band; *Will The Circle Be Unbroken* ....(EMI)
Roy Acuff; *Backstage At The Grand Ole Opry* ....(RCA)
   Best Of ....(CAP)
   Columbia Historic Edition ....(COL)
   Essential ....(COL)
   Greatest Hits ....(COL)
Walkin' By The River
Ella Fitzgerald; *Best Of* ....(MCA)
Watching The River Flow
Bob Dylan; *Greatest Hits-#2* ....(COL)
Joe Cocker; *Luxury You Can Afford* ....(ASY)
Watching The River Run
Loggins & Messina; *Best Of-Friends* ....(COL)
   Full Sail ....(COL)
Water Is Wide
Joan Baez; *Very Early Joan Baez* ....(VAN)
Karla Bonoff; *ST/Thirtysomething* ....(GEF)
Roger McGuinn; *Born To Rock & Roll* ....(COL)
Whiskey River
Willie Nelson; *Greatest Hits & Some That Will Be* (COL)
   Shotgun Willie ....(ATL)
   ST/Honeysuckle Rose ....(COL)
   & Family Live ....(COL)
Wide River
Steve Miller Band; *Wide River* ....(SAI)
Wild River
Golden Palominos; *Dead Horse* ....(CEL)
   Our World Of Music ....(CEL)
Yellow River
Christie; *Rock Artifacts-#1-From The Vaults* .....(COL)
   Super Hits/'70s-Have A Nice Day-#4 ....(RHI)
Compton Brothers; *45* ....(MCA)
Yes The River Knows
Doors; *Waiting For The Sun* ....(ELE)

ROAD, Highway
   See Also: CARS, TRAVELING, TRUCKS

Alabama Highway
Steve Young; *Honky-Tonk Man* ....(ROU)
Alaska Highway
Neon Judgement; *The Insult* ....(PIA)
All Roads Lead To Rome
Stranglers; *Feline* ....(EPI)

All Roads Lead To You
Steve Wariner; *14 #1 Country Hits* ....(RCA)
Best Of The '80s So Far ....(RCA)
Greatest Hits ....(RCA)
Steve Wariner ....(RCA)
Along The Road
Dan Fogelberg; *Phoenix* .... (FM)
Are You On The Road To Lovin' Me Again
Debby Boone; *Best Of* ....(CRB)
Arizona Highway
Tim Rex/Oklahoma; *45* ....(DJ)
Asphalt Cowboy
Sleepy LaBeef; *Bull's Night Out* .... (SUN)
At A Dixie Roadside Diner
Duke Ellington; *Duke Ellington & Blanton-Webster
Band* ....(BLU)
Backroads
Ricky Van Shelton; *Backroads* ....(COL)
Big Log
Robert Plant; *Principle Of Moments* .... (EPR)
Black Bear Road
C.W. McCall; *Greatest Hits* .... (POL)
Born Ready
Jesse Hunter; *A Man Like Me* ....(BNA)
Brickyard Road
Johnny Van Zant; *Brickyard Road* .... (ATL)
Bright Side Of The Road
Van Morrison; *Best Of* ....(MER)
Into The Music ....(WB)
Brooklyn Roads
Neil Diamond; *12 Greatest Hits* .... (MCA)
And The Singer Sings His Songs .... (MCA)
Velvet Gloves & Spit .... (MCA)
Brownsville Road
Peter Lang; *Prime Cuts* .... (WTR)
California Road
Mel Tillis; *45* ....(RCA)
Church On Cumberland Road
Shenandoah; *Greatest Country Hits/'80s-1989* ....(COL)
Road Not Taken ....(COL)
Country Road
Dolly Parton; *Eagle When She Flies* ....(COL)
James Taylor; *Greatest Hits* ....(WB)
Sweet Baby James ....(WB)
Crossroads
Cowboy Junkies; *Whites Off Earth Now!!* ....(RCA)
Cream; *Eric Clapton-Crossroads* ....(POL)
Strange Brew-Very Best Of ....(RSO)
Wheels Of Fire ....(RSO)
Derek/Dominos; *Eric Clapton-Crossroads* ....(POL)
Eric Clapton; *History Of* ....(ATC)
Secret Policeman's Other Ball .... (ISL)
& Jeff Beck .... (ISL)
Lynyrd Skynyrd; *One More From The Road* ...... (MCA)
Ry Cooder; *ST/Crossroads* ....(WB)
Darlington County
Bruce Springsteen; *Born In The U.S.A.* ....(COL)
Dirt Road
Sawyer Brown; *Dirt Road* ....(CCB)
Divided Highway
Doobie Brothers; *Brotherhood* ....(CAP)
Dixie Road
Lee Greenwood; *Country Classics-#3* ....(MCA)
Greatest Hits ....(MCA)
MCA #1 Hits/'80s-#2 .... (MCA)
Down That Road Tonight
Nitty Gritty Dirt Band; *More Great Dirt: Best
Of-#2* ....(WB)
Workin' Band ....(WB)
Down The Road
Cadillacs; *Best Of* .... (RHI)
Dan Fogelberg; *High Country Snows* .... (FM)
Doucette; *Mama Let Him Play* ....(MSH)
Kansas; *Song For America* .... (KIR)
Little Feat; *Feats Don't Fail Me Now* ....(WB)
Stephen Stills; *Down The Road* .... (ATL)
Steve Earle/Dukes; *Guitar Town* ....(MCA)
Down The Road A Piece
Chuck Berry; *Chess Box* .... (CSS)
More Rock 'N' Roll Rarities/Chess ....(CSS)
Rockin' At The Hops .... (CSS)
Rolling Stones; *Now!* ....(LON)
Down The Road I Go
Albert King; *Lost Session* ....(STX)

Don Williams; *#2* ....(MCA)
Down The Road Tonight
Bruce Hornsby/Range; *The Way It Is* ....(RCA)
Ease On Down The Road
Grateful Dead; *Go To Heaven* .... (ARI)
Original Cast; *ST/The Wiz* ....(ATL)
Eight Days On The Road
Foghat; *Best Of* .... (RHI)
Rock & Roll Outlaws .... (RHI)
End Of Our Road
Gladys Knight/Pips; *All The Great Hits* ....(MOT)
Anthology .... (MOT)
Compact Command Performances .... (MOT)
Jerry Lee Lewis; *Original* .... (SUN)
Original Golden Hits-#1 .... (SUN)
Marvin Gaye; *Anthology* .... (MOT)
Musical Testament 1964-1984 .... (MOT)
Super Hits .... (MOT)
End Of The Road
Boyz II Men; *Cooleyhighharmony* .... (MOT)
Endless Black Ribbon
Red Simpson; *Trucks Trains & Airplanes* ...... (IGR)
Red Sovine/Willis Bros./Reno & Smiley; *Heavy
Haulers* ....(PP)
Endless Highway
Band; *To Kingdom Come (Definitive Collection)* ..(CAP)
Bob Dylan/Band; *Before The Flood* ....(COL)
Eternity Road
Moody Blues; *To Our Children's Children's
Children* .... (POL)
Expressway To Your Heart
Blues Brothers; *Best Of* .... (ATL)
Soul Survivors; *Dick Bartley's One-Hit
Wonders-'60s-#2* .... (RHI)
Oldies But Goodies-#11 ....(OSR)
Super Oldies/'60s-#6 ....(AUF)
When The Whistle Blows Anything Goes ....(CLT)
Fast Lanes & Country Roads
Barbara Mandrell; *Country Classics-#2* .... (MCA)
Country Classics-#6-1985-1986 .... (MCA)
Get To The Heart .... (MCA)
Forty Miles Of Bad Road
Duane Eddy; *16 Greatest Hits* .... (JAM)
Compact Command Performances .... (MOT)
Roy Clark; *Hookin' It* .... (MCA)
My Music & Me .... (MCA)
Freeway Of Love
Aretha Franklin; *Who's Zoomin' Who?* .... (ARI)
Further Up The Road
Band; *Last Waltz* ....(WB)
Eric Clapton; *Crossroads* .... (POL)
Gabriel's Mother's Hiway Ballad 16 Blues
Arlo Guthrie; *Best Of* ....(WB)
Glory Road
Neil Diamond; *Love At The Greek* ....(COL)
Sweet Caroline ....(MCA)
Going Down The China Road
Peter Lang; *Back To The Wall* ....(WTR)
Going Down The Road Feeling Bad
Delaney & Bonnie; *Best Of* .... (RHI)
Doc Watson; *Elementary Doctor Watson* .... (POP)
Essential .... (VAN)
Grateful Dead; *One From The Vault* .... (GRD)
Skull & Roses Album ....(WB)
Golden Road
Grateful Dead; *Best Of-Skeletons From The Closet* (WB)
Grateful Dead ....(WB)
Goodbye Yellow Brick Road
Elton John; *Billboard Top Rock 'N' Roll Hits-1973* (RHI)
Goodbye Yellow Brick Road ....(POL)
Greatest Hits ....(POL)
Green Rocky Road
Dave Van Ronk; *In The Tradition* .... (PRS)
Tim Hardin; *Memorial Album* ....(POL)
Hard Nose The Highway
Van Morrison; *Hard Nose The Highway* .... (WB)
Hard Road
Black Sabbath; *Never Say Die* ....(WB)
Deep Purple; *Purple Passages* ....(WB)
When We Rock We Rock ....(WB)
John Mayall/Bluesbreakers; *Hard Road* ....(LON)
Joneses; *Hard* .... (ATL)
Rod Stewart; *Best Of-#2* ....(MER)
Triumph; *Progressions Of Power* ....(MCA)

Hard Road Down
Marilyn McCoo & Billy Davis, Jr.; *45* .... (MCA)
Hard Road To Travel
Jimmy Cliff; *Wonderful World Beautiful People* . (A&M)
Heading Down The Highway
Judas Priest; *Point Of Entry* ....(COL)
High Road Easy
Sass Jordan; *Rats* .... (IPA)
Highway 28
Paul Butterfield Blues Band; *Better Days* .... (RHI)
Highway 40 Blues
Ricky Skaggs; *19 Hot Country Requests* .... (EPI)
   Greatest Country Hits/'80s-1983 ....(COL)
   Highways & Heartaches .... (EPI)
   Live In London .... (EPI)
Highway 61 Revisited
Bob Dylan; *Highway 61 Revisited* ....(COL)
   Real Live ....(COL)
   /Band; Before The Flood ....(ASY)
James Taylor; *Mud Slide Slim & The Blue Horizon* (WB)
Johnny Winter; *Anthology* ....(BCT)
   Second Winter ....(COL)
Highway Blues
Champion Jack Dupree; *Collectables Blues*
Collection-#2 ....(CLT)
   Harlem Rock 'N' Blues-#3 ....(CLT)
Roy Harper; *Flashes From The Archives Of*
Oblivion .... (CHR)
   Lifemask .... (CHR)
Highway Child
Bob Seger System; *Mongrel* .... (CAP)
Highway Flyer
Doug Owen; *45* .... (MCA)
Highway Headin' South
Porter Wagoner; *Great Moments At The Grand Ole*
Opry ....(RCA)
Highway Lady
UFO; *No Heavy Petting* .... (CHR)
Highway Of Sorrow
Bill Monroe; *Best Of* .... (MCA)
Highway One
B.W. Stevenson; *B.W. Stevenson* ....(RCA)
Highway Patrol
Reggie Knighton Band; *Reggie Knighton Band* ...(COL)
Highway Patrolman
Bruce Springsteen; *Nebraska* ....(COL)
Highway Robbery
Tanya Tucker; *Strong Enough To Bend* .... (CAP)
Highway Song
Blackfoot; *Strikes* ....(ATC)
Free; *Best Of* .... (A&M)
   Highway .... (A&M)
James Taylor; *Mud Slide Slim & The Blue Horizon* (WB)
Highway Star
Deep Purple; *Deepest Purple* ....(WB)
   Machine Head ....(WB)
   Made In Japan ....(WB)
   When We Rock We Rock-When We Roll... ....(WB)
Highway To Hell
AC/DC; *Back In Black* ....(ATL)
   Classic Rock-1966-1988 ....(ATL)
   Highway To Hell ....(ATL)
Highwayman
Glen Campbell; *Highwayman* ....(CAP)
Willie Nelson; *Greatest Country Hits/'80s-1985* ..(COL)
W. Jennings/W. Nelson/J. Cash/K. Krist.; *Columbia*
Country Classics-#3 ....(COL)
   Highwayman ....(COL)
Highways
Jeff Beck Group; *Jeff Beck Group* .... (EPI)
Hit The Road Jack
Ray Charles; *Anthology* .... (RHI)
   Greatest Hits-#1 .... (RHI)
   Greatest Hits-#2 ....(DHL)
Hot Dusty Roads
Buffalo Springfield; *Buffalo Springfield* ....(ATC)
Human Highway
Neil Young; *Comes A Time* ....(RPR)
Interstate Love Song
Stone Temple Pilots; *Purple* ....(ATL)
Keep It In The Middle Of The Road
Exile; *Country's Greatest Hits-#1* ....(PRY)
   Still Standing ....(ARI)

Key To The Highway
David Bromberg; *You Should See The Rest Of The*
Band ....(FAN)
Derek/Dominos; *Eric Clapton-Crossroads* ....(POL)
   Layla (& Other Assorted Love Songs) ....(RSO)
John Hammond; *Best Of* .... (VAN)
Little Walter; *Best Of-#2* .... (CSS)
   Blues-#2 .... (CSS)
Sonny Terry & Brownie McGhee; *Great Blues*
Men .... (VAN)
King Of The Road
Roger Miller; *Billboard Top Country Hits-1965* .. (RHI)
   Cruisin'-1965 .... (INC)
   Golden Hits ....(SMA)
R.E.M.; *Dead Letter Office* .... (IRS)
Kings Road
Tom Petty/Heartbreakers; *Hard Promises* .... (BKS)
King's Highway
Tom Petty/Heartbreakers; *Into The Great Wide*
Open .... (MCA)
Life In The Fast Lane
Eagles; *Hotel California* .... (ASY)
   Live .... (ASY)
   ST/FM ....(MCA)
Life Is A Highway
Tom Cochrane; *Mad Mad World* .... (CAP)
Life On The Road
Kinks; *Sleepwalker* .... (ARI)
Life's Highway
Steve Wariner; *Country Classics-#2-Today's Country*
Cl. ....(MCA)
   Life's Highway ....(MCA)
Living On The Highway
Freddie King; *Best Of* .... (MCA)
Living On The Open Road
Delaney & Bonnie & Friends; *Duane Allman*
Anthology ....(CPC)
Lonesome Road
Anita O'Day; *Rules Of The Road* .... (PAB)
Frank Sinatra; *Capitol Years* ....(CAP)
Frankie Valli/Four Seasons; *25th Anniversary*
Collection .... (RHI)
Preservation Hall Jazz Band; *New Orleans-#4* ...(COL)
Tommy Dorsey; *Sentimental Memories* ....(PRR)
Van Morrison; *Too Long In Exile* ....(POL)
Lonesome Road Blues
Big Bill Broonzy; *Feelin' Low Down* ....(CRS)
   Lonesome Road Blues ....(CRS)
Kentucky Colonels/C. White/D. Watson; *Long Journey*
Home-Newport Folk Fest-1964 .... (VAN)
Muddy Waters; *Sings Big Bill Broonzy* ....(CSS)
Lonesome Roads
Dwight Yoakam; *This Time* .... (RPR)
Long Dark Road
Hollies; *Best Of-#2* .... (EMI)
   Epic Anthology-From The Original Masters ...... (EPI)
   Greatest Hits .... (EPI)
Long Hard Road (Sharecropper's Dream)
Nitty Gritty Dirt Band; *Live Two Five* ....(CAP)
   Plain Dirt Fashion ....(WB)
   Tewenty Years Of Dirt-Best Of ....(WB)
Long Lonely Highway
Elvis Presley; *ST/Kissin' Cousins* ....(RCA)
Long Long Texas Road
Roy Drusky; *Golden Hits* .... (PLN)
Long Promised Road
Beach Boys; *10 Years Of Harmony* ....(CAR)
   Surf's Up ....(CAR)
Long Road To Texas
Bill Wray; *ST/Tilt* .... (MCA)
Long & Winding Road
Beatles; *1967-1970* ....(CAP)
   20 Greatest Hits ....(CAP)
   Let It Be ....(CAP)
   Love Songs ....(CAP)
   Reel Music ....(CAP)
Paul McCartney; *Tripping The Live Fantastic* ....(CAP)
   Tripping The Live Fantastic-Highlights! ....(CAP)
Paul McCartney/Wings; *Over America* ....(CAP)
Lord Of The Highway
Joe Ely; *Lord Of The Highway* .... (HT)
Lost Highway
Hank Williams; *24 Greatest Hits-#2* ....(MGM)
   40 Greatest Hits ....(POL)

Nitty Gritty Dirt Band; *Will The Circle Be Unbroken* .... (EMI)

Louisiana Road Song
Tish Hinojosa; *Culture Swing* .... (ROU)

L.A. Freeway
Guy Clark; *Old No. 1* ....(SH)
Jerry Jeff Walker; *Best Of* .... (MCA)
  Great Gonzos .... (MCA)

Mama Knows The Highway
Hal Ketchum; *Sure Love* .... (CRB)

Many A Long & Lonesome Highway
Rodney Crowell; *Keys To The Highway* ....(COL)

Meet In The Middle
Diamond Rio; *Diamond Rio* .... (ARI)

Middle Of The Road
Pretenders; *Greenpeace/Rainbow Warriors* .... (GEF)
  Learning To Crawl .... (SIR)
  The Singles .... (SIR)

Miles And Miles Of Texas
Asleep At The Wheel; *Texas State Of Mind* ...... (CAP)

Moonlight Mile
Rolling Stones; *Sticky Fingers* .... (RS)

Moonshadow Road
T. Graham Brown; *Best Of* .... (LIB)

Navajo Trail
Michael Nesmith; *From A Radio Engine To The Photon Wing* .... (PA)

New Cut Road
Bobby Bare; *45* .... (COL)

New Jersey Roadbase
Johnboy; *Pistolswing* ....(TNC)

New Jersey Turnpike
Laurie Anderson; *United States Live* .... (WB)

New Lee Highway Blues
David Bromberg; *Out Of The Blues-Best Of* ......(COL)
  Wanted: Dead Or Alive .... (COL)

Old Dirt Road
John Lennon; *Lennon* ....(CAP)
  Menlove Avenue .... (CAP)
  Walls & Bridges .... (CAP)

Old Man Down The Road
John Fogerty; *Centerfield* .... (WB)

On Down The Line
Patty Loveless; *Greatest Hits* .... (MCA)
  On Down The Line .... (MCA)

On The Road
Lee Roy Parnell; *On The Road* .... (ARI)

On The Road Again
Aerosmith; *Pandora's Box* ....(COL)
Bob Dylan; *Bringing It All Back Home* ....(COL)
Grateful Dead; *Reckoning* .... (ARI)
Tom Rush; *Classic Rush* .... (ELE)
  Tom Rush .... (ELE)
Willie Nelson; *Greatest Country Hits/'80s-1980* ..(COL)
  Greatest Hits & Some That Will Be .... (COL)
  Hot Country Rock-#1 .... (EPI)
  ST/Forrest Gump .... (EPX)
  ST/Honeysuckle Rose .... (COL)

On The Road To Find Out
Cat Stevens; *Classics-#24* .... (A&M)
  Footsteps In The Dark-Greatest Hits-#2 .... (A&M)
  Tea For The Tillerman .... (A&M)

On The Road To Mandalay
Count Basie; *Compact Jazz-Standards* ....(VRV)
Frank Sinatra; *Come Fly With Me* ....(CAP)

Pacific Coast Highway
Bryan Savage; *Bryan Savage* ....(ELA)
Mamas & The Papas; *People Like Us* ....(MSP)

Passing Lane
Charlie Daniels Band; *Million Mile Reflections* ....(EPI)

Pathway To Glory
Loggins & Messina; *Full Sail* ....(COL)

Patty On The Turnpike
Don Stover; *Things In Life* .... (ROU)

Prisoner Of The Highway
Ronnie Milsap; *Greatest Hits-#3* ....(RCA)
  One More Try For Love ....(RCA)

Queen Of The Highway
Doors; *Morrison Hotel* .... (ELE)

Rhythm Of The Road
George Strait; *#7* .... (MCA)

Ribbon Of Darkness
Marty Robbins; *All-Time Greatest Hits* ....(COL)
  Greatest Hits ....(COL)
  Truckers' Jukebox-#2 ....(COL)

River Road
Crystal Gayle; *Favorites* .... (UA)
  We Must Believe In Magic .... (UA)

Road
Chicago; *II* ....(COL)
Doors; *13* .... (ELE)
Everything But The Girl; *Language Of Life* ......(ATL)
Jackson Browne; *Running On Empty* ....(ASY)
Kinks; *Live-Road* ....(MCA)

Road And The Sky
Jackson Browne; *Late For The Sky* .... (ASY)

Road Angel
Doobie Brothers; *What Were Once Vices Are Now Habits* .... (WB)

Road Beneath My Wheels
Dan Fogelberg; *Live-Greetings From The West* .... (FM)

Road Fever
Blackfoot; *Strikes* ....(ATC)
Foghat; *Foghat* .... (RHI)
  Live .... (RHI)

Road Less Travelled
Preston Reed; *Road Less Travelled* ....(FF)

Road Movie To Berlin
They Might Be Giants; *Flood* .... (ELE)

Road Mutants
Death Angel; *Frolic Through The Park* ....(ENC)
  Speed Metal ....(PRY)

Road Of Broken Hearted Men
Bobby Bland; *Introspective Of The Early Years* .. (MCA)
  Touch Of The Blues .... (MCA)

Road Rats
Alice Cooper; *Lace & Whiskey* .... (WB)

Road Runner
Greg Kihn Band; *With The Naked Eye* .... (BES)
Joan Jett; *Hit List* ....(BLK)
Joan Jett/Blackhearts; *Good Music* ....(BLK)
Jonathan Richman/Modern Lovers; *Beserkley Years-Best Of* .... (RHI)
Modern Lovers; *Modern Lovers* .... (RHI)
Pretty Things; *History Of British Rock-#5* .... (RHI)

Road Runner (I'm A)
Fleetwood Mac; *Penguin* .... (RPR)
Humble Pie; *Eat It* .... (A&M)
  Smokin' .... (A&M)
Junior Walker/All-Stars; *Anthology* ....(MOT)
  Greatest Hits ....(MOT)
  Motown Superstar Series-#5 ....(MOT)
  Shotgun ....(MOT)

Road To Bangor
Northeast Winds; *Songs Of Ireland & The Sea* ... (FOL)

Road To Columbus
Sally Van Meter; *All In Good Time* ....(SH)

Road To Hong Kong
Billy May; *I Believe In You* ....(BAI)

Road To Jakarta
Steve Hunter; *The Deacon* .... (IRN)

Road To My Riches
Vanilla Ice; *Extremely Live* .... (SBK)

Road To Nowhere
Ozzy Osbourne; *No More Tears* .... (EPA)

Road To Poland
Mike Figgis; *ST/Stormy Monday* ....(VMM)

Road To Rome
PFS; *279* .... (CUN)

Road To Santa Rosa
Frank Chacksfield; *Mirrors* .... (STA)

Road To Utopia
Utopia; *Adventures In Utopia* .... (RHI)

Road To Your Heart
Barbara Mandrell; *Key's In The Mailbox* ....(CAP)
Highway 101; *101 2* .... (WB)

Road You Didn't Take
Original Broadway Cast; *Follies* ....(CAP)
Original Cast; *Follies in Concert* ....(RCA)

Roadhouse Blues
Doors; *13* .... (ELE)
  Best Of .... (ELE)
  Classics .... (ELE)
  Greatest Hits .... (ELE)
  Morrison Hotel .... (ELE)
  ST/Doors .... (ELE)
Roads Girdle The Globe
XTC; *Drums & Wires* .... (GEF)
Roads Of Life
Bobby Womack; *Roads Of Life* .... (ARI)
Roads To Freedom
Robin Trower; *Victims Of The Fury* .... (CHR)
Roads To Madness
Queensryche; *The Warning* .... (EMI)
Roads To Moscow
Al Stewart; *Past Present Future* .... (JNS)
Road's My Middle Name
Bonnie Raitt; *Nick Of Time* .... (CAP)
Rockin' Down The Highway
Doobie Brothers; *Best Of* .... (WB)
  Toulouse Street .... (WB)
Rocky Road To Dublin
Dubliners; *Dublin Songs* .... (AJK)
Rocky Road To Kansas
Tony Ellis; *Dixie Banner* .... (FF)
Rodeo Road
Roy Rogers & Willie Nelson; *Tribute* ....(RCA)
Roll On Down The Highway
Bachman-Turner Overdrive; *Best Of B.T.O.-So Far* .... (MER)
  Not Fragile .... (MER)
  Rock Of The '70s .... (MSP)
Route 66
Asleep At The Wheel; *Served Live* ....(CAP)
  Wheelin' & Dealin' ....(CAP)
Depeche Mode; *ST/Earth Girls Are Easy* .... (SIR)
George Maharis; *45* .... (EPI)
Manhattan Transfer; *Bop Doo-Wopp* ....(ATL)
Nat King Cole; *Capitol Collectors Series* ....(CAP)
  Story ....(CAP)
  Unforgettable ....(CAP)
Natalie Cole; *Unforgettable* .... (ELE)
Rolling Stones; *December's Children* ....(AKO)
  Rolling Stones ....(AKO)
"Route 66" Theme
Nelson Riddle/Orchestra; *Beat Generation* .... (RHI)
  Television's Greatest Hits-#2 .... (TVT)
Serengeti Trail
Starr Parodi; *Change* .... (GFT)
Seven Bridges Road
Eagles; *Greatest Hits-#2* .... (ASY)
  Live .... (ASY)
Steve Young; *Seven Bridges Road* .... (ROU)
Shoulder Of The Road
Johnny/Distractions; *Let It Rock* ....(A&M)
  My Desire .... (BRN)
Six Days On The Road
Dave Dudley; *Billboard Top Country Hits-1963* .. (RHI)
  Country Music Classics-#2-1960-1965 .... (KT)
  Legends Of Country Guitar-#2 .... (RHI)
Flying Burrito Brothers; *Cabin Fever* ....(RLX)
  Farther Along-Best Of ....(A&M)
  Last Of The Red Hot Burritos ....(A&M)
Taj Mahal; *Giant Step/De Ole Folks At Home* ....(COL)
  Legends Of Rock Guitar-'60s-#2 .... (RHI)
Somewhere Down The Road
Barry Manilow; *If I Should Love Again* .... (ARI)
Kathy Mattea; *Kathy Mattea* .... (MER)
Stones In The Road
Mary Chapin Carpenter; *Stones In The Road* ....(COL)
Take Me Home, Country Roads
John Denver; *Evening With* ....(RCA)
  Greatest Hits ....(RCA)
  Poems Prayers & Promises ....(RCA)
  Take Me Home, Country Roads-& Other Hits ....(RCA)
Toots/Maytals; *Brand New Second-Hand* ....(RYK)
Tennessee Road
Anne Hills; *Woman Of A Calm Heart* .... (FF)
That Road Still Looks Real Good To Me
Lacy J. Dalton; *Lacy J.* ....(CAP)
There's A Rugged Road
Shawn Colvin; *Cover Girl* ....(COL)

Thunder Road
Bruce Springsteen; *Born To Run* ....(COL)
Bruce Springsteen/E Street Band;
  Live-1975-1985 ....(COL)
Tie Dye On The Highway
Robert Plant; *Manic Nirvana* .... (EPR)
Tobacco Road
Dan Seals; *I Won't Be Blue Anymore* .... (EMI)
David Lee Roth; *Eat 'Em & Smile* .... (WB)
Edgar Winter; *Collection* .... (RHI)
  Roadwork .... (EPI)
Eric Burdon/Animals; *Greatest Hits* ....(ALL)
Jefferson Airplane; *Loves You* ....(RCA)
  Takes Off ....(RCA)
John D. Loudermilk; *Rockabilly Stars-#3* .... (EPI)
Junior Wells; *Best Of The Chicago Blues* .... (VAN)
  Comin' At You .... (VAN)
Lou Rawls; *Best From* ....(CAP)
  Greatest Hits ....(CCB)
  Legendary .... (BLN)
  Live ....(CAP)
Nashville Teens; *London Collector-Rock Invasion* (LON)
Rare Earth; *Get Ready* .... (MOT)
Steve Young; *Redneck Mothers* ....(RCA)
  Solo/Live .... (WAT)
Tokyo Road
Bon Jovi; *7800 Degrees Fahrenheit* .... (JBC)
Tombstone Every Mile
Dave Dudley; *Interstate Gold* .... (SUN)
Trail To Mexico
Peter La Farge; *Cowboy Songs On Folkways* .... (FLW)
True Love Travels On A Gravel Road
Elvis Presley; *From Elvis In Memphis* ....(RCA)
  Memphis Record ....(RCA)
Percy Sledge; *It Tears Me Up-Best Of* .... (RHI)
Twenty-Five Miles
Edwin Starr; *Motown Superstar Series-#3* ...... (MOT)
Michael Jackson; *Original Soul Of* .... (MOT)
Two For The Road
Henry Mancini; *All-Time Greatest Hits-#1* ....(RCA)
  Legendary Performer ....(RCA)
James Galway; *Greatest Hits-#2* ....(RCA)
Two Lane Highway
Pure Prairie League; *Two Lane Highway* ....(RCA)
Valley Road
Bruce Hornsby/Nitty Gritty Dirt Band; *Will The Circle Be Unbroken-#2* .... (UNI)
Bruce Hornsby/Range; *Scenes From The Southside* ....(RCA)
Ventura Highway
America; *History-Greatest Hits* .... (WB)
  Homecoming .... (WB)
  Live .... (WB)
  '70s Greatest Rock Hits-#6-FM Hits .... (WB)
Walkin' Down The Road
Ozark Mountain Daredevils; *Best Of* ....(A&M)
  It'll Shine When It Shines ....(A&M)
  It's Alive ....(A&M)
West Texas Highway & Me
Gary Morris; *Faded Blue* .... (WB)
Western Highway
Maura O'Connell; *Helpless Heart* .... (WB)
White Line Fever
Flying Burrito Brothers; *Close Encounters To The West Coast* ....(RLX)
Merle Haggard; *More Of The Best* .... (RHI)
Merle Haggard/Strangers; *Okie From Muskogee* ..(CAP)
Why Don't We Do It In The Road
Beatles; *Box Set* ....(CAP)
  White Album ....(CAP)
Wicked Path
Bill Monore/Blue Grass Boys; *Essential Bill Monroe-1945-1949* ....(COL)
Jim & Jesse McReynolds; *Music Among Friends* . (ROU)
New Grass Revival; *Commonwealth* .... (FF)
Working On The Highway
Bruce Springsteen; *Born In The U.S.A.* ....(COL)
Bruce Springsteen/E Street Band;
  Live-1975-1985 ....(COL)
Working On The Road
Ten Years After; *Cricklewood Green* .... (CHR)

ROAD ACCIDENTS

See Also: CARS, DEATH, TRUCKS

Accidents
Thunderclap Newman; *Hollywood Dream* ...... (MCA)
Always Crashing In The Same Car
David Bowie; *Low* ....(RYK)
Auto Wreck
All; *Allroy Sez* ....(CRZ)
Barbie & Ken Ferrari
John Hiatt; *Perfectly Good Guitar* ....(A&M)
Big Joe & Phantom 309
Tom Waits; *Double Live* ....(ASY)
Nighthawks At The Diner ....(ASY)
Crawling From The Wreckage
Dave Edmunds; *Best Of* .... (SS)
Repeat When Necessary .... (SS)
Rockpile; *Kampuchea* ....(ATL)
Dead Man's Curve
Jan & Dean; *21 Legendary Superstars* ...... (OSR)
Best Of .... (EMI)
Dead Man's Curve .... (EMI)
Don't Crash The Car Tonight
Mary's Danish; *Experience (Live + Foxey Lady)* . (CML)
There Goes The Wondertruck... .... (CML)
Grandma Got Run Over By A Reindeer
Elmo & Patsy; *Billboard's Greatest Christmas Hits* (RHI)
Dr. Demento Greatest Novelty CD .... (RHI)
Dr. Demento's Greatest-#6 .... (RHI)
Grandma Got Run Over By A Reindeer .... (EPI)
Greatest Children's Christmas Hits .... (EPI)
Radar Love
Golden Earring; *Classic Rock-#1* .... (MCA)
Live .... (MCA)
Moontan .... (MCA)
Super Hits/'70s-Have A Nice Day-#13 .... (RHI)
'70s Greatest Rock Hits-#1-Hard N' Heavy ..... (PRY)
Teen Angel
Dion/Belmonts; *Everything You Always Wanted* ..(LAU)
Rock & Roll U.S.A.-21 R&R Favorites-#2 ......(LAU)
Mark Dinning; *45 On CD-#1-1956-1959* ...... (MER)
Golden Years-1959 ....(DOM)
Oldies But Goodies-#7 ....(OSR)
ST/American Graffiti ....(MCA)
Teenage Tragedies .... (RHI)
Teenage Queen
Rick Derringer; *All-American Boy* .... (BS)
Tell Laura I Love Her
Ray Peterson; *Nipper's Greatest Hits-'60s-#1* .....(RCA)
Teenage Tragedies .... (RHI)
Terror Of 101
Cheers; *45* ....(OOP)
Transfusion
Nervous Norvus; *Dr. Demento 20th Anniversary
Collection* .... (RHI)
Dr. Demento Greatest Novelty-#2-1950s .... (RHI)
Vintage Music-Original Classic Oldies-#3 ...... (MCA)
Wacky Weirdos .... (KT)
Wreck On The Highway
Bruce Springsteen; *The River* ....(COL)
Nitty Gritty Dirt Band; *Will The Circle Be
Unbroken* .... (EMI)
Roy Acuff; *Best Of* ....(CAP)
Essential ....(COL)
Greatest Hits ....(COL)

ROCK, Rock & Roll

*See Also: DANCE, MOUNTAINS, MUSIC,
PARTY, RADIO*

And The Cradle Will Rock
Van Halen; *Women & Children First* .... (WB)
Anything That's Rock 'N' Roll
Tom Petty/Heartbreakers; *ST/Voices* .... (PNT)
Tom Petty/Heartbreakers .... (MCA)
Are You Ready To Rock
Michael Schenker; *One Night At Budokan* ...... (CHR)
Rock Will Never Die .... (CHR)
Around & Around
38 Special; *38 Special* ....(A&M)
Animals; *Best Of* ....(AKO)

Chuck Berry; *Berry Is On Top* .... (CSS)
Chess Box .... (CSS)
ST/Hail! Hail! Rock 'N' Roll ....(MCA)
Grateful Dead; *One From The Vault* .... (GRD)
Steal Your Face .... (GRD)
Rolling Stones; *12 x 5* ....(AKO)
Love You Live .... (RS)
As Long As I'm Rockin' With You
John Conlee; *Greatest Hits-#2* .... (MCA)
In My Eyes .... (MCA)
Legends .... (MCA)
Baby Likes To Rock It
Tractors; *Tractors* .... (ARI)
Baby Won't You Let Me Rock & Roll You
Ten Years After; *A Space In Time* ....(COL)
Baby's A Rock 'N' Roller
Tom Petty/Heartbreakers; *You're Gonna Get It* . (MCA)
Black Country Rock
David Bowie; *Man Who Sold The World* ....(RYK)
Sound + Vision ....(RYK)
Blue Rock Montana
Willie Nelson; *Red Headed Stranger* ....(COL)
Born To Rock
Quiet Riot; *Condition Critical* .... (PSH)
Call It Rock N' Roll
Great White; *Hooked* ....(CAP)
Candy Store Rock
Led Zeppelin; *Led Zeppelin (collection)* ....(ATL)
Presence .... (SS)
Can't Stop Rockin'
ZZ Top; *Afterburner* ....(WB)
Champagne & Rock & Roll
Climax Blues Band; *Shine On* .... (SIR)
Cherub Rock
Smashing Pumpkins; *Siamese Dream* .... (VIA)
Cities On Flame With Rock & Roll
Blue Oyster Cult; *Blue Oyster Cult* ....(COL)
Career Of Evil ....(COL)
Extraterrestial Live ....(COL)
On Your Feet Or On Your Knees ....(COL)
Clash City Rockers
Clash; *Clash* .... (EPI)
Story Of-#1 .... (EPI)
Cleveland Rocks
Ian Hunter; *Shades Of* .... (CHR)
ST/Light Of Day ....(CBA)
You're Never Alone With A Schizophrenic ...... (CHR)
Crocodile Rock
Elton John; *Billboard Top Rock 'N' Roll Hits-1973* (RHI)
Don't Shoot Me I'm Only The Piano Player ..... (POL)
Greatest Hits .... (POL)
Here & There .... (POL)
Detroit Rock City
Kiss; *Alive II* .... (CAS)
Destroyer .... (CAS)
Double Platinum .... (CAS)
Smashes Thrashes & Hits .... (MER)
Dixieland Rock
Elvis Presley; *50 Gold Award Hits-#2* ....(RCA)
ST/King Creole ....(RCA)
Do You Remember Rock 'N' Roll Radio
Ramones; *End Of The Century* .... (SIR)
Mania .... (SIR)
Don't Rock The Jukebox
Alan Jackson; *Don't Rock The Jukebox* .... (ARI)
England Rocks
Ian Hunter/Mott The Hoople; *Shades Of Ian
Hunter* ....(COL)
Flying Saucers Rock 'N' Roll
Billy Lee Riley; *Legends Of Rock Guitar/'50s-#2* . (RHI)
Sun Story .... (RHI)
For A Rocker
Jackson Browne; *Lawyers In Love* .... (ASY)
For Those About To Rock
AC/DC; *For Those About To Rock* ....(ATL)
Who Made You ....(ATL)
God Gave Rock & Roll To You
Argent; *Anthology* .... (EPI)
Encore .... (EPI)
Truth; *Jump* .... (IRS)
Golden Age Of Rock & Roll
Mott The Hoople; *Ballad Of Mott* ....(COL)
Greatest Hits ....(COL)

Golden Olden Days Of Rock & Roll
Johnny Winter; *J.D. Winter III* .... (BS)
Good Rockin' Tonight
Elvis Presley; *Date With Elvis* .... (SUN)
  Sun Sessions .... (SUN)
  Sun Story .... (RHI)
Jerry Lee Lewis; *20 Classic Jerry Lee Lewis Hits* . (OSR)
  Trio Plus .... (SUN)
Jimmy Witherspoon; *Best Of* .... (PRS)
  Spoon Concerts .... (FAN)
Hang Up My Rock & Roll Shoes
Band; *Rock Of Ages-#1 & 2* .... (CAP)
Chuck Willis; *Atlantic R&B*
1947-1974-#3-(1955-1958) .... (ATL)
Hard Rock Bottom Of Your Heart
Randy Travis; *No Holdin' Back* .... (WB)
Hard Rock Cafe
Carole King; *Simple Things* .... (CAP)
Heart Of Rock & Roll
Huey Lewis/News; *Sports* .... (CHR)
Here We Go, Let's Rock And Roll
C & C Music Factory; *Gonna Make You Sweat* ..(COL)
Hot Rockin'
Judas Priest; *Point Of Entry* .... (COL)
House Is Rockin'
Cheap Trick; *Dream Police* .... (EPI)
Stevie Ray Vaughan/Double Trouble; *In Step* ..... (EPI)
I Dig Rock & Roll Music
Peter, Paul & Mary; *10 Years Together* .... (WB)
  1700 .... (WB)
I Knew The Bride
Dave Edmunds; *Best Of* .... (SS)
  Get It .... (SS)
Nick Lowe; *Basher-Best Of* .... (COL)
I Like To Rock
April Wine; *Harder Faster* .... (CAP)
I Love Rock 'N Roll
Joan Jett/Blackhearts; *I Love Rock 'N Roll* ...... (BLK)
  ST/Wayne's World 2 .... (RPR)
If You Can't Rock Me
Rick Nelson; *Legends Of Rock & Roll Series-Best*
Of-#2 .... (EMI)
Rolling Stones; *It's Only Rock 'N' Roll* .... (RS)
  Love You Live .... (RS)
If You Don't Like Rock 'N' Roll
Ritchie Blackmore; *Rainbow* .... (POL)
It's A Long Way To The Top
AC/DC; *High Voltage* .... (ATC)
It's Only Rock & Roll
Rolling Stones; *It's Only Rock & Roll* .... (RS)
  Love You Live .... (RS)
  Made In The Shade .... (RS)
  Rewind (1971-1984) .... (RS)
It's Still Rock & Roll To Me
Billy Joel; *Glass Houses* .... (COL)
  Greatest Hits-#1 & 2 .... (COL)
I'm A Rocker
Bruce Springsteen; *The River* .... (COL)
I'm Just A Singer In A Rock & Roll Band
Moody Blues; *Seventh Sojourn* .... (POL)
  This Is The .... (POL)
  Voices In The Sky-Best Of .... (T/P)
I've Got A Rock 'N' Roll Heart
Eric Clapton; *Money And Cigarettes* .... (DUC)
Jailhouse Rock
Blues Brothers; *ST/Blues Brothers* .... (ATL)
Elvis Presley; *Billboard Top Rock 'N' Roll*
Hits-1957 .... (RHI)
  Legendary Performer-#2 .... (RCA)
  Live On Stage .... (RCA)
  Number One Hits .... (RCA)
  Rocker .... (RCA)
  Worldwide 50 Gold Award Hits-#1 .... (RCA)
Jeff Beck; *Beck-Ola* .... (EPI)
Jungle Rock
Marshall Crenshaw; *45* .... (WB)
Just A-Sittin' & A-Rockin'
Cleo Laine; *Jazz* .... (RCA)
Duke Ellington; *Intimacy Of The Blues* .... (FAN)
Mel Torme; *Duke Ellington & Count Basie*
Songbook .... (VRV)
Justice Tonight/Rock It Over
Clash; *Black Market Clash* .... (EPI)

King Of Rock
Run-D.M.C.; *King Of Rock* .... (PRO)
  Mr. Magic's Rap Attack .... (PRO)
Let It Rock
Bob Seger; *Live Bullet* .... (CAP)
  Nine Tonight .... (CAP)
  Smokin' P.O.'s .... (CAP)
Bon Jovi; *Slippery When Wet* .... (MER)
Chuck Berry; *Chess Box* .... (CSS)
  Rockin' At The Hops .... (CSS)
Let It Roll (Let It Rock)
Mel McDaniel; *Greatest Hits* .... (CAP)
  Let It Roll (Let It Rock) .... (CAP)
Let There Be Rock
AC/DC; *If You Want Blood You've Got It* .... (ATL)
  Let There Be Rock .... (ATC)
Let's Get Rocked
Def Leppard; *Adrenalize* .... (MER)
Life Is A Rock (But The Radio Rolled Me)
Reunion; *Super Hits/'70s-Have A Nice Day-#13* .. (RHI)
Limbo Rock
Chubby Checker; *Greatest Hits* .... (EVR)
  Moonlighting .... (MCA)
  Rock-O-Rama #2 .... (AKO)
Long Live Rock
Who; *Odds & Sods* .... (MCA)
  ST/Kids Are Alright .... (MCA)
  Who's Last .... (MCA)
Long Live Rock & Roll
Rainbow; *Finyl Vinyl* .... (MER)
  Long Live Rock & Roll .... (POL)
Long Live Rock 'N' Roll
Elvis Presley; *Elvis Aron Presley* .... (RCA)
Louisiana Cajun Rock Band
Carol Channing & Jimmy C. Newman; */Others-& Her*
Country Friends .... (PLN)
Love Is Like A Rock
Donnie Iris; *King Cool* .... (MCA)
Memphis, Tennessee Hot Rock
Gordon Terry; *Tennessee Hot Rock* .... (PLN)
Midnight Rocks
Al Stewart; *24 Carrots* .... (ARI)
Modern Times Rock & Roll
Queen; *Queen* .... (HOL)
Monday Morning Rock
Marshall Crenshaw; *Field Day* .... (WB)
My Daddy Rocks Me
Benny Goodman Sextet; *Slipped Disc-1945-1946* (COL)
Mae West; *Fabulous* .... (MCA)
My Ol' Kentucky Rock & Roll Home
Original New York Cast; *Oil City Symphony* ... (DRG)
My Rock & Roll Man
Rita Coolidge; *It's Only Love* .... (A&M)
New Rock & Roll
Frank Marino & Mahogany Rush; *Live* .... (COL)
Old Time Rock & Roll
Bob Seger/Silver Bullet Band; *Nine Tonight* ...... (CAP)
  Stranger In Town .... (CAP)
One Of The Survivors
Kinks; *Greatest/Celluloid Heroes* .... (RCA)
  Preservation (A Play In Two Acts) .... (RHI)
One Rock & Roll Too Many
Marc Cohn; *ST/Starlight Express* .... (MCA)
Only One Way To Rock
Sammy Hagar; *Standing Hampton* .... (GEF)
Only You Can Rock Me
UFO; *Obsession* .... (CHR)
  Strangers In The Night .... (CHR)
Osaka Rocka
Jeff Watson; *Lone Ranger* .... (SHR)
Planet Rock
Afrika Bambaataa/Soulsonic Force; *Street Jams-Electric*
Funk-#1 .... (RHI)
  Tommy Boy Greatest Beats .... (TMB)
Raging Rock & Roll
Zeros; *4-3-2-1...The Zeroes* .... (RES)
Rattlesnake Rock 'N' Roller
Blackfoot; *Marauder* .... (ATC)
Ready Teddy
Buddy Holly; *Buddy Holly* .... (MCA)
  Rock & Roll Collection .... (MCA)
Elvis Presley; *Elvis* .... (RCA)
  Great Performances .... (RCA)
  Rocker .... (RCA)

Little Richard; *Georgia Peach* .... (SPE)
   Grooviest 17 Original Hits .... (SPE)
   More American Graffiti .... (MCA)
Rebel Rock Me
Pretenders; *Last Of The Independents* .... (SIR)
Redneck In A Rock & Roll Bar
Jerry Reed; *Redneck Mothers* ....(RCA)
Redneck Rock N' Roll
Pirates Of The Mississippi; *Pirates Of The*
Mississippi ....(CAP)
Reeling And Rocking
Chuck Berry; *Best Of The Best Of* .... (GUS)
   Chess Box ....(CSS)
   Frat Rock! ....(RHI)
   Greatest Hits ....(EVR)
   Rock & Roll Show .... (GUS)
Revolution Rock
Clash; *London Calling* .... (EPI)
Rich Don't Rock
Vamp; *Rich Don't Rock* .... (ATL)
Rock
Frankie Miller; *Rock* .... (CHR)
Garland Jeffreys; *Escape Artist* .... (EPI)
Otis Rush; *Chicago Blues Today* .... (VAN)
Who; *Quadrophenia* ....(MCA)
Rock A Beatin' Boogie
Bill Haley/Comets; *Golden Hits* .... (MCA)
   Greatest Hits ....(EVR)
   Legends Of Rock Guitar-'50s-#2 .... (RHI)
Rock A Bye Your Baby With A Dixie Melody
Al Jolson; *Best Of* .... (MCA)
   Immortal ....(MCA)
   Jolson Sang 'Em ....(BIO)
   Story-#1 ....(MCA)
Judy Garland; *At Carnegie Hall* ....(CAP)
   Miss Show Business ....(CAP)
   One & Only ....(CAP)
Rock America
Afrika & Family Bambaataa; *Beware (The Funk Is*
Everywhere) ....(TMB)
Danger Danger; *Danger Danger* .... (IMI)
Rock And Roll
Lou Reed; *Rock & Roll Animal* ....(RCA)
Velvet Underground; *Another View* ....(VRV)
   Live 1969 .... (MER)
   Live Rock & Roll Animal .... (MER)
   Loaded ....(WSP)
Rock And Roll Dreams Come...
Meat Loaf; *Bat Out Of Hell II-Back Into Hell* ... (MCA)
Rock And Roll Music
Beach Boys; *15 Big Ones* ....(CAR)
   Gift Set ....(CAP)
   Made In The U.S.A. ....(CAP)
   Ten Years Of Harmony ....(CAR)
Beatles; *Box Set* ....(CAP)
   For Sale ....(CAP)
   Rock And Roll Music-#1 ....(CAP)
   '65 ....(CAP)
Chuck Berry; *Chess Box* ....(CSS)
   Cruisin'-1958 .... (INC)
   Golden Hits .... (MER)
   Greatest Hits ....(EVR)
R.E.O. Speedwagon; *Nine Lives* .... (EPI)
Rock And Soul Music
Country Joe/Fish; *Collected-1965-1970* .... (VAN)
   Life & Times Of .... (VAN)
   Together .... (VAN)
Rock An' Roll Angels
Whitesnake; *Saints & Sinners* ....(GEF)
Rock Around The Clock
Bill Haley/Comets; *Billboard Top Rock 'N' Roll*
Hits-1955 .... (RHI)
   Golden Hits ....(MCA)
   Greatest Hits ....(EVR)
   Greatest Hits ....(MCA)
   ST/American Graffiti ....(MCA)
Telex; *45* .... (SIR)
Rock Around With Ollie Vee
Buddy Holly; *Legend* ....(MCA)
Rock Billy Boogie
Robert Gordon; *Rock Billy Boogie* ....(RCA)
Rock Box
Run-D.M.C.; *Rapmasters 3-Best Of The Cut* ...... (PRY)
   Run-D.M.C. ....(PRO)

Rock City
Damn Yankees; *Damn Yankees* .... (WB)
Rock Coast Blues
Country Joe/Fish; *Collected-1965-1970* .... (VAN)
   I-Feel-Like-I'm-Fixin'-To-Die .... (VAN)
Rock Dis Funky Joint
Poor Righteous Teachers; *Holy Intellect* ....(PRO)
Rock For The Forgotten
David & David; *Boomtown* .... (A&M)
Rock Forever
Judas Priest; *Hell Bent For Leather* ....(COL)
Rock In America
Night Ranger; *Greatest Hits* ....(CAM)
   Midnight Madness ....(CAM)
Rock Is Hot
Crown Heights Affair; *Dance Lady Dance* .... (DL)
Rock Is In My Blood
Sammy Hagar; *VOA* ....(GEF)
Rock Is My Life And This Is My Song
Bachman-Turner Overdrive; *Not Fragile* .... (MER)
Rock It
Queen; *Game* ....(HOL)
Steve Miller Band; *Box Set* ....(CAP)
Rock It Baby
Bob Marley/Wailers; *Catch A Fire* .... (ISL)
Rock Lobster
B-52's; *B-52's* .... (WB)
Rock Love
Steve Miller Band; *Rock Love* ....(CAP)
Utopia; *Adventures In Utopia* .... (RHI)
Rock Me
Abba; *Abba* .... (ATL)
   Greatest Hits-#2 .... (ATL)
Deborah Allen; *Delta Dreamland* .... (GIA)
Fresh Force Crew; *Rapmasters 2-Best Of The*
Rhyme .... (PRY)
Great White; *Once Bitten* ....(CAP)
Muddy Waters; *Chess Box* ....(CSS)
   I'm Ready ....(BS)
Nick Gilder; *Frequency* ....(CHR)
Nutmegs; *Greatest Hits* ....(CLT)
Steppenwolf; *16 Greatest Hits* ....(MCA)
   Gold ....(MCA)
Rock Me Amadeus
Falco; *3* ....(A&M)
   Remix Hit Collection .... (SIR)
Rock Me Baby
B.B. King; *Greatest Hits* ....(KNT)
   Now Appearing Live At Ole Miss ....(MCA)
   Rock Me Baby ....(KNT)
Etta James; *Red Hot 'N' Live* .... (INT)
Hot Tuna; *Historic* .... (RLX)
Jefferson Airplane; *Bless Its Pointed Little Head* ..(RCA)
Jimi Hendrix; *ST/Jimi Plays Monterey* ....(RPR)
   ST/Jimi Hendrix ....(RPR)
Otis Redding; *Best Of* ....(ATC)
Robin Trower; *Live* ....(CHR)
   Twice Removed From Yesterday ....(CHR)
Slim Harpo; *Best Of* .... (RHI)
Rock Me In The Rhythm Of Your Love
Eddy Raven; *Best Of* ....(LIB)
   Right For The Flight ....(CAP)
Rock Me Like A Hurricane
Scorpions; *Love At First Sting* .... (MER)
Rock Me Mama
Arthur Big Boy Crudup; *Mean Ole Frisco* ....(CLT)
   That's All Right Mama ....(RCA)
Blind Snooks Eaglin; *Country Boy In New*
Orleans .... (ARH)
Buddy Guy/Junior Mance/Junior Wells; *Buddy & The*
Juniors ....(MCA)
Sonny Terry; *Chain Gang Blues* ....(CLT)
Rock Me On The Water
Jackson Browne; *Jackson Browne* .... (ASY)
Kathy Mattea & Jackson Browne; *Red Hot +*
Country .... (MER)
Linda Ronstadt; *Different Drum* ....(CAP)
   Linda Ronstadt ....(CAP)
   Retrospective ....(CAP)
Rock Me Roll Me
Jerry Jeff Walker; *Collectibles* ....(MCA)
Rock Me Tonight (For Old Time's Sake)
Freddie Jackson; *Rock Me Tonight (For Old Time's*
Sake) ....(CAP)

Rock Me Tonite
Billy Squier; *Signs Of Life* .... (CAP)
Rock Me 'Till I Die
Grim Reaper; *Rock You To Hell* .... (RCA)
Rock Music
Jefferson Starship; *Freedom At Point Zero* .... (RCA)
Rock My Baby
Shenandoah; *S* .... (RCA)
Rock My Plimsoul
Jeff Beck Group; *Beckology* .... (EPI)
Truth .... (EPI)
Rock My Soul
Elvin Bishop; *Best Of* .... (EPI)
Raisin' Hell .... (EPI)
Rock My World (Little Country Girl)
Brooks & Dunn; *Hard Workin' Man* .... (ARI)
Rock N Roll Disease
Green On Red; *Here Come The Snakes* .... (RES)
Rock N Roll Nigger
Patti Smith Group; *Easter* .... (ARI)
Rock Of Ages
Bryan Ferry; *In Your Mind* .... (RPR)
Def Leppard; *Pyromania* .... (MER)
Rock Of America
Bad Company; *Dangerous Age* .... (ATL)
Rock Ola Jive
Hank Burnette; *Don't Mess With My Ducktail* .... (SUN)
Rock On
David Essex; *Billboard Top Rock 'N' Roll
Hits-1874* .... (RHI)
Pop Classics/'70s ....(COL)
Super Hits/'70s-Have A Nice Day-#12 .... (RHI)
Fastway; *Waiting For The Roar* ....(COL)
Gary Glitter; *Greatest Hits* .... (RHI)
Michael Damian; *Greatest Movie Rock Hits* ..... (RHI)
ST/Dream A Little Dream .... (CYP)
Vandenberg; *Best Of* .... (ATC)
Rock On The Moon
Cramps; *Songs The Lord Taught Us* .... (IRS)
Rock On The Radio
Firehouse; *Firehouse* .... (EPI)
Rock Radio Into The Nineties & Beyond
KLF; *Chill Out* .... (WAX)
Rock Soldiers
Ace Frehley; *Frehley's Comet* .... (MEG)
Metal Mania .... (PRY)
Rock Steady
Aretha Franklin; *30 Greatest Hits* .... (ATL)
Best Of .... (ATL)
Ten Years Of Gold .... (ATL)
Young Gifted & Black .... (ATL)
Whispers; *Just Gets Better With Time* .... (SLR)
Rock That
Earth, Wind & Fire; *I Am* ....(COL)
Rock That Boogie
Commander Cody/Lost Planet Airmen; *Country
Casanova* .... (MCA)
Too Much Fun-Best Of .... (MCA)
We've Got A Live One Here .... (WB)
Rock That Makes Me Roll
Stryper; *Head Banging Metal* .... (PRY)
Soldiers Under Command .... (HOL)
Rock The Casbah
Clash; *Combat Rock* .... (EPI)
On Broadway .... (EPI)
Seems Like Yesterday-#4-Early '80s .... (KT)
Story Of-#1 .... (EPI)
Rock The House
D.J. Jazzy Jeff & The Fresh Prince; *Rock The
House* .... (JVA)
Rock The Joint
Bill Haley/Comets; *Greatest Hits* ....(EVR)
Bill Haley/Saddlemen; *Rock This Town-Rockabilly
Hits-#1* .... (RHI)
Rock The Nation
Montrose; *Montrose* ....(WB)
Rock The Night
Europe; *Final Countdown* .... (EPI)
Rock The People
Stryper; *Against The Law* ....(HOL)
Rock The World
Third World; *Rock The World* ....(COL)
Rock This Boat
Thompson Twins; *Big Trash* .... (RE)

Rock This Joint
Alannah Myles; *Alannah Myles* .... (ATL)
Rock This Town
Stray Cats; *Best Of-Rock This Town* .... (EMI)
Built For Speed .... (EMI)
Reelin' In The Years-#1 .... (SAN)
Rock This Town-Rockabilly Hits-#2 .... (RHI)
Rock Will Never Die
Michael Schenker; *Built To Destroy* .... (CHR)
Rock Will Never Die .... (CHR)
Rock With You
Jacksons; *Live* .... (EPI)
Michael Jackson; *Off The Wall* .... (EPI)
Rock Wit'cha
Bobby Brown; *Dance!...Ya Know It!* .... (MCA)
Don't Be Cruel .... (MCA)
Rock You
Kool Moe Dee; *How Ya Like Me Now* .... (JVA)
Rock You All Around The World
Judas Priest; *Priest...Live!* ....(COL)
Turbo ....(COL)
Rock You Like A Hurricane
Scorpions; *Best Of Rockers & Ballads* .... (MER)
Love At First Sting .... (MER)
Worldwide Live .... (MER)
Rock You To Hell
Grim Reaper; *Rock You To Hell* .... (RCA)
Rock You Up
Romantics; *What I Like About You-Romantic
Hits* .... (NEM)
Rock Your Baby
George McCrae; *Get Down Tonight-Best Of T.K.
Records* .... (RHI)
Mega Hits Dance Classics-#2 .... (PRY)
Rock Your Baby .... (TK)
Soul Hits/'70s-#13 .... (RHI)
Rock Your Mama
Ten Years After; *Alvin Lee & Company* .... (DER)
London Collector .... (LON)
Rock & A Hard Place
Rolling Stones; *Flashpoint* .... (RS)
Steel Wheels .... (RS)
Rock & Roll
Dwight Twilley Band; *Twilley Don't Mind* ...... (ARI)
Gary Glitter; *Greatest Hits* .... (RHI)
Super Hits/'70s-Have A Nice Day-#9 .... (RHI)
Heart; *Greatest Hits/Live* .... (EPI)
Jane's Addiction; *Jane's Addiction* .... (XXX)
Jimmy Rushing; *Essential* ....(VAN)
Johnny Winter; *Still Alive & Well* ....(COL)
Led Zeppelin; *IV* .... (ATL)
Remasters .... (ATL)
Led Zeppelin (collection) .... (ATL)
ST/Song Remains The Same .... (SS)
Mitch Ryder/Detroit Wheels; *Detroit With* ...... (MCA)
Rev Up-Best Of .... (RHI)
R.B. Greaves; *Rock & Roll* .... (INT)
Velvet Underground; *Another View* ....(VRV)
Zapp; *New Zapp IV U* .... (WB)
Rock & Roll All Nite
Kiss; *Alive* .... (CAS)
Double Platinum .... (CAS)
Dressed To Kill .... (CAS)
Heavy Metal Memories .... (RHI)
The Originals .... (CAS)
Poison; *ST/Less Than Zero* .... (DFJ)
Rock & Roll Babylon
Love & Rockets; *Love & Rockets* .... (BEG)
Rock & Roll Band
Boston; *Boston* .... (EPI)
Mano Negra; *Puta's Fever* .... (VIA)
Wet Willie; *Wet Willie* ....(CPC)
Rock & Roll Boogie Woogie Blues
Edgar Winter Group; *They Only Come Out At
Night* .... (EPI)
Rock & Roll Crazies
Stephen Stills; *Manassas* .... (ATL)
Still Stills .... (ATL)
Rock & Roll Creation
Spinal Tap; *ST/Spinal Tap* .... (POL)

Rock & Roll Crook
Nils Lofgren; *Best Of* .... (A&M)
  Classics-#13 .... (A&M)
  Night After Night .... (A&M)
  Nils Lofgren ....(RYK)
Rock & Roll Doctor
Black Sabbath; *Technical Ecstasy* ....(WB)
Little Feat; *Feats Don't Fail Me Now* ....(WB)
  Hoy-Hoy! ....(WB)
Travesty Ltd.; *Dr. Demento's Greatest-#5* .... (RHI)
Rock & Roll Fantasy
Bad Company; *10 From 6* ....(ATL)
  Desolation Angels .... (SS)
Kinks; *15-Year History Of Rock* .... (ARI)
  Come Dancing With-Best Of-1977-1986 .... (ARI)
  Misfits .... (ARI)
  '70s Greatest Rock Hits-#14 ....(PRY)
Rock & Roll Feeling
Styx; *Miracles-Best Of* ....(RCA)
Rock & Roll Gas Station
Adrenalin O.D.; *Wacky Hi-Jinks Of* ....(BOR)
Rock & Roll Heart
Lou Reed; *Between Thought &*
Expression-Anthology ....(RCA)
  Rock & Roll Heart .... (ARI)
Rock & Roll Heaven
Righteous Brothers; *Anthology-1962-1974* .... (RHI)
Rock & Roll High School
Ramones; *End Of The Century* .... (SIR)
  Loco Live .... (SIR)
  Ramones Mania .... (SIR)
  ST/Rock & Roll High School .... (SIR)
Rock & Roll Hoochie Koo
Edgar Winter; *Roadwork* .... (EPI)
Johnny Winter; *Johnny Winter And* ....(COL)
  Rock Classics .... (KT)
Johnny Winter/Rick Derringer; *Metal Age-Roots Of*
Metal .... (RHI)
Rick Derringer; *All American Boy* .... (BS)
  Legends Of Rock Guitar-'70s .... (RHI)
  Super Hits/'70s-Have A Nice Day-#12 .... (RHI)
Rock & Roll Is Back Again
Village People; *Live & Sleazy* .... (CAS)
Rock & Roll Is Here To Stay
Danny/Juniors; *Rock & Roll Is Here To Stay* ..... (GUS)
  Rockin' With ....(MCA)
  '50s Dance Party-#2 .... (DOM)
Sha-Na-Na; *Sha Na Na Is Here To Stay* .... (BUD)
  ST/Grease .... (POL)
Rock & Roll Is Music
James Taylor; *Walking Man* .... (WB)
Rock & Roll Junkie
Back Street Crawler; *Band Plays On* ....(ATC)
Herman Brood/Wild Romance; *Herman Brood/Wild*
Romance ....(ARL)
Rock & Roll Lawyer
Austin Lounge Lizards; *Lizard Vision* .... (FF)
Rock & Roll Love Letter
Bay City Rollers; *Greatest Hits* .... (ARI)
  Rock & Roll Love Letter .... (ARI)
Rock & Roll Machine
Triumph; *Classics* ....(MCA)
  Rock & Roll Machine ....(MCA)
  Stages ....(MCA)
Rock & Roll Man
Kenny Rogers; *Daytime Friends* .... (EMI)
Savoy Brown; *Savage Return* ....(LON)
Rock & Roll Mood
Loggins & Messina; *Sittin' In* ....(COL)
Rock & Roll Music To The World
Ten Years After; *Classic Performances* ....(COL)
Rock & Roll Never Forgets
Bob Seger; *Night Moves* ....(CAP)
Bob Seger/Silver Bullet Band; *Nine Tonight* ......(CAP)
Rock & Roll Outlaw
Foghat; *Rock & Roll Outlaws* .... (RHI)
Rock & Roll Over
Mr. Big; *Mr. Big* ....(ATL)
Rock & Roll People
John Lennon; *Menlove Avenue* ....(CAP)
Johnny Winter; *Captured Live* .... (BS)
Rock & Roll Pussy
Todd Rundgren; *A Wizard A True Star* .... (RHI)

Rock & Roll Queen
Mott The Hoople; *Ballad Of Mott* ....(COL)
  Mott The Hoople ....(ATL)
Rock & Roll Radio
Ramones; *End Of The Century* .... (SIR)
Rock & Roll Records
J.J. Cale; *Okie* ....(MCA)
Rock & Roll Ruby
Warren Smith; *Memphis Country* ....(SUN)
  Original Memphis Rock & Roll-#1 .... (SUN)
Rock & Roll Shoes
Amos Garrett; *Go Cat Go* ....(FF)
Ray Charles & B.J. Thomas; *Friendship* ....(COL)
  Seven Spanish Angels & Other Hits ....(COL)
Rock & Roll Stew
Traffic; *Low Spark Of High-Heeled Boys* .... (ISL)
Rock & Roll Strategy
38 Special; *Rock & Roll Strategy* ....(A&M)
Rock & Roll Suicide
David Bowie; *Live* ....(RYK)
  Rise & Fall Of Ziggy Stardust ....(RYK)
  Sound + Vision ....(RYK)
  ST/Ziggy Stardust-The Motion Picture ....(RCA)
Rock & Roll The Place
Eddie Money; *Life For The Taking* ....(COL)
Rock & Roll The Weekend
Sammy Hagar; *Live* ....(CAP)
  Sammy Hagar ....(CAP)
Rock & Roll Time
Roger McGuinn; *Cardiff Rose* ....(COL)
Rock & Roll Tonight
Grim Reaper; *Fear No Evil* ....(RCA)
Rock & Roll Waltz
Kay Starr; *Capitol Collectors Series* ....(CAP)
  Nipper's Greatest Hits-'50s-#1 ....(RCA)
Rock & Roll Widow
Wishbone Ash; *Live Dates* ....(MCA)
  Wishbone Four ....(MCA)
Rock & Roll With Me
David Bowie; *Diamond Dogs* ....(RYK)
Rock & Roll Woman
Buffalo Springfield; *Again* ....(ATC)
  Buffalo Springfield ....(ATC)
  Retrospective ....(ATC)
Rock & Roll Women
Brinsley Schwarz; *Brinsley Schwarz* ....(CAP)
Whitesnake; *Love Hunter* ....(GEF)
Rock & Roller
Pablo Cruise; *Pablo Cruise* ....(A&M)
Rock & Soul Music
Country Joe/Fish; *ST/Woodstock* ....(ATL)
Rock 'N' Roll
Atlantic Starr; *Straight To The Point* ....(A&M)
Mac Davis; *All The Love In The World* ....(COL)
Rock 'N' Roll Angel
Kentucky HeadHunters; *Pickin' On Nashville* .... (MER)
Rock 'N' Roll Children
Dio; *Intermission* .... (WB)
  Sacred Heart .... (WB)
Rock 'N' Roll Damnation
AC/DC; *If You Want Blood You've Got It* ....(ATL)
  Powerage ....(ATL)
Rock 'N' Roll Ghost
Replacements; *Don't Tell A Soul* .... (SIR)
Rock 'N' Roll Hall Of Fame
Frank Marino & Mahogany Rush; *What's Next* ..(COL)
Rock 'N' Roll Is A Vicious Game
April Wine; *First Glance* ....(CAP)
Rock 'N' Roll Is King
Electric Light Orchestra; *Afterglow* .... (EPI)
  Secret Messages ....(JET)
Rock 'N' Roll Juggernaut
Meatmen; *Rock 'N' Roll Juggernaut* ....(CRL)
Rock 'N' Roll Junkie
Motley Crue; *Decade Of Decadence* ....(ELE)
Rock 'N' Roll Juvenile
Cliff Richard; *We Don't Talk Anymore* .... (EMI)
Rock 'N' Roll Lullaby
10 CC; *How Dare You* .... (MER)
B.J. Thomas; *16 Greatest Hits* ....(TRP)
  Back To The '70s-#2 .... (DOM)
  Greatest Hits .... (RHI)
  Super Hits-#2 ....(GUS)

Rock 'N' Roll Murder
Leaving Trains; *Loser Illusion-Pt. 0* ....(SST)
Rock 'N' Roll Outlaw
Peter Wells; *Everything You Like Tries To Kill You* .... (ZOO)
Rock 'N' Roll Over You
Moody Blues; *Other Side Of Life* ....(POL)
Rock 'N' Roll Rebel
Ozzy Osbourne; *Bark At The Moon* ....(EPA)
Rock 'N' Roll Susie
Pat Travers; *Makin' Music* ....(POL)
Rock 'N' Roll To The Rescue
Beach Boys; *Gift Set* ....(CAP)
Made In The U.S.A. ....(CAP)
Rock 'N' Roll Tonight
Cheap Trick; *Busted* ....(EPI)
Rock 'N' Rollers
Angel; *Angel* ....(CAS)
Live Without A Net ....(CAS)
Rock 'N' Soul
Grand Funk Railroad; *Caught In The Act* ....(CAP)
Phoenix ....(CAP)
Oaktown's 3.5.7.; *Wild & Loose* ....(CAP)
Rocka Rolla
Judas Priest; *Best Of* ....(RCA)
Hero Hero ....(RCA)
Rocka Rolla ....(RCA)
Rockabilly On The Radio
Jack Smith/Rockabilly Planet; *Jack Smith/Rockabilly Planet* ....(FF)
Rockaria
Electric Light Orchestra; *Afterglow* ....(EPI)
E.L.O. Classics ....(SSP)
Greatest Hits ....(JET)
New World Record ....(JET)
Rocker
AC/DC; *Dirty Deeds Done Dirt Cheap* ....(ATL)
If You Want Blood You've Got It ....(ATL)
Charlie Parker; *Bebop & Bird-#2* ....(RHI)
Verve Years-1950-1951 ....(VRV)
Thin Lizzy; *Live & Dangerous* ....(WB)
London Collector ....(LON)
Rockers 'N' Rollers
Brownsville Station; *Brownsville Station* ....(PVS)
Rockestra Theme
Wings; *Back To The Egg* ....(CAP)
Rockhouse
Ray Charles; *Best Of* ....(ATL)
Roy Orbison; *Original Sound* ....(SUN)
Sun Years ....(RHI)
Rocking Chair Blues
Bessie Smith; *Complete Recordings* ....(COL)
Ray Charles; *20 Golden Pieces Of* ....(BLD)
Rocking Over Russia
Elvis Hitler; *Disgraceland* ....(RES)
Rocking Steady
Bob Marley/Wailers; *One Love* ....(HRT)
Rocking Surfer
Beach Boys; *Surfer Girl/Shut Down-#2* ....(CAP)
Rockin' After Midnight
Marvin Gaye; *Midnight Love* ....(COL)
Rockin' Around In N.Y.C.
Marshall Crenshaw; *Marshall Crenshaw* ....(WB)
Rockin' Around (With You)
Tom Petty/Heartbreakers; *Pack Up The Plantation-Live* ....(MCA)
Tom Petty/Heartbreakers .... (GG)
Rockin' At Midnight
Honeydrippers; *Little By Little-Collectors Edition* . (EPR)
Volume 1 ....(EPR)
Rockin' Blues
Johnny Otis; *Original Johnny Otis Show* ....(SÁV)
Rockin' Boogie
Fleetwood Mac; *In Chicago* ....(SIR)
Rockin' Chair
Band; *Band* ....(CAP)
Gift Set ....(CAP)
Gwen McCrae; *Get Down Tonight!-Best Of T.K. Records* ....(RHI)
Soul Hits/'70s-#15 ....(RHI)
Hi-Lo's; *Swing-Best Of The Big Bands* ....(MCA)
Hoagy Carmichael; *Stardust Road* ....(MCA)
Jerry Garcia & David Grisman; *Jerry Garcia & David Grisman* ....(GRD)

Jerry Jeff Walker; *A Man Must Carry On* ....(MCA)
John Lee Hooker; *The Healer* ....(CML)
Louis Armstrong & Jack Teagarden; *Evening With-#2* ....(CRS)
Mildred Bailey; *Jazz Singers* ....(PRS)
Nipper's Greatest Hits-'30s-#2 ....(RCA)
Tom Waits; *Early Years* ....(BIZ)
Rockin' Chair On The Moon
Bill Haley/Comets; *King Of Rock & Roll* ....(ALS)
Rockin' Daddy
Howlin' Wolf; *Chess Box* ....(CSS)
Rockin' Down The Highway
Doobie Brothers; *Best Of* ....(WB)
Toulouse Street ....(WB)
Rockin' Every Night
Gary Moore; *Early Years* ....(WTG)
Rockin' Good Way (To Mess Around...)
Arthur Prysock; *Rockin' Good Way* ....(MS)
Brook Benton & Dinah Washington; *Anthology* .. (RHI)
Rockin' Goose
Johnny/Hurricanes; *45* ....(CLT)
Rockin' Heaven Down
Heart; *Bebe Le Strange* ....(EPI)
Rockin' Horse
Bad English; *Bad English* ....(EPI)
Rockin' In Rhythm
Duke Ellington; *Great Paris Concert* ....(ATL)
D. Ellington/E. Fitzgerald/O. Peterson; *Greatest Jazz Concert In The World* ....(PAB)
Hank Jones/Ray Brown/Jimmie Smith; *Rockin' In Rhythm* ....(CCJ)
Modern Jazz Quartet; *For Ellington* ....(EW)
Rockin' In The Congo
Hank Thompson; *Capitol Collectors Series* ....(CAP)
Rockin' In The Free World
Neil Young; *Freedom* ....(RPR)
Neil Young/Crazy Horse; *Weld* ....(RPR)
Rockin' In The Jungle
Eternals; *WCBS FM101 History Of Rock-Doo-Wop-#2* ....(CLT)
Rockin' In The Parkin' Lot
Razzy Bailey; *Country Classics-#6-1985-1986* .. (MCA)
Rockin' In The U.S.A.
Kiss; *Alive 2* ....(CAS)
Rockin' Into The Night
38 Special; *Flashback-Best Of* ....(A&M)
Rockin' Into The Night ....(A&M)
Rockin' It
Fearless Four; *Hip Hop Heritage-#1* ....(JVA)
Rockin' Little Tune
Bill Haley/Comets; *Golden Hits* ....(MCA)
Rockin' My Boogie
Big Walter Horton; *Chicago Blues Today* ....(VAN)
Memphis Charlie; *Best Of The Chicago Blues* ... (VAN)
Rockin' My Life Away
Jerry Lee Lewis; *Rockin' My Life Away/Collection* (WB)
Survivors ....(COL)
Swingin' Country Favorites ....(WB)
Rockin' On A Saturday Night
Jason D. Williams; *Tore Up* ....(RCA)
Rockin' On The River
Jerry Jeff Walker; *Navajo Rug* ....(RYK)
Rockin' Over China
Commander Cody; *Let's Rock* ....(BLI)
Rockin' Over The Beat
Technotronic; *Pump Up The Jam-The Album* .... (SBK)
Rockin' Pneumonia And The Boogie...
Aerosmith; *ST/Less Than Zero* ....(DFJ)
Huey "Piano" Smith; *All-Star Chartbusters* ......(INT)
Huey "Piano" Smith/Clowns; *Jimpin' Jive '50s* ..(PRY)
Johnny Rivers; *Anthology 1964-1977* ....(RHI)
Best Of ....(EMI)
Professor Longhair; *Rock 'N' Roll Gumbo* ....(DAN)
Rodney Lay; *Rockabilly Nuggets* ....(SUN)
Rockin' Radio
Tom Browne; *45* ....(ARI)
Rockin' Robin
Bobby Day; *Cruisin'-1958* ....(INC)
Oldies But Goodies-#5 ....(OSR)
Rockin' Robin ....(CLT)
Super Oldies/'50s-#2 ....(AUF)

Michael Jackson; *Anthology* .... (MOT)
  Best Of .... (MOT)
  Got To Be There .... (MOT)
  Original Soul Of .... (MOT)
Rockin' Rockin' Leprechauns
Jonathan Richman/Modern Lovers; *Rock 'N' Roll*
  With .... (RHI)
Rockin' Roll Baby
Stylistics; *Best Of* .... (AMH)
  Rockin' Roll Baby ....(H&L)
Rockin' Rollin' Rover
Bill Haley/Comets; *Golden Hits* .... (MCA)
Rockin' Shopping Center
Jonathan Richman/Modern Lovers; *Jonathan*
  Richman/Modern Lovers .... (RHI)
Rockin' The Boat
Ricky Skaggs; *Live In London* .... (EPI)
Wayland Patton; *Gulf Stream Dreamin'* .... (CAP)
Rockin' The Boat Of Love
Jerry Lee Lewis; *Golden Rock & Roll* .... (SUN)
Rockin' The Dog
Hellecasters; *Town South Of Bakersfield-#3* ...... (RES)
Rockin' The Mule
Barrence Whitfield/Savages; *Ow Ow Ow Ow* ... (ROU)
Rockin' The Paradise
Styx; *Caught In The Act* ....(A&M)
  Paradise Theatre ....(A&M)
Rockin' The Rock
Larry Stewart; *Heart Like A Hurricane* ....(COL)
Rockin' Time
Bunny Wailer; *Roots Radics Rockers Reggae* ...... (SHA)
Rockin' Train
Joe Perry Project; *Let The Music Do The Talking* .(COL)
Rockin' With Fes
Professor Longhair; *Mardi Gras In New*
  Orleans-1949-1957 .... (NH)
Rockin' With Fire
Isley Brothers; *Showdown* .... (TN)
Rockin' With The Rhythm Of The Rain
Judds; *Greatest Hits* ....(RCA)
  Rockin' With The Rhythm ....(RCA)
Rockin' Years
Dolly Parton & Ricky Van Shelton; *Eagle When She*
  Flies ....(COL)
Ricky Van Shelton & Dolly Parton; *Backroads* ..(COL)
Rocks
Primal Scream; *Give Out But Don't Give Up* ...... (SIR)
Rock-A-Hula Baby
Elvis Presley; *50 Worldwide Gold Award Hits-#1* (RCA)
  ST/Blue Hawaii ....(RCA)
Rock'n Me
Steve Miller Band; *Fly Like An Eagle* ....(CAP)
  Gift Set ....(CAP)
  Greatest Hits ....(CAP)
Rock-N-Roll Lady
Rick Nelson; *Best Of-1963-1975* .... (DEC)
Rock-N-Roll Weasel
Dead Serios; *Ralph Rules* .... (LGS)
Roots, Rock, Reggae
Bob Marley/Wailers; *Rastaman Vibration* .... (TUF)
R. U. Ready To Rock
Blue Oyster Cult; *On Flame With Rock & Roll* ....(SSP)
  Some Enchanted Evening ....(COL)
  Spectres ....(COL)
R-O-C-K
Bill Haley/Comets; *Golden Hits* .... (MCA)
  R-O-C-K ....(SUN)
R.O.C.K. In The U.S.A.
John Cougar Mellencamp; *Scarecrow* ....(RIV)
School Days
Chuck Berry; *Best Of* ....(GUS)
  Billboard Top Rock 'N' Roll Hits-1957 ....(RHI)
  Golden Hits ....(MER)
  ST/Rock 'N' Roll High School .... (SIR)
Sex, Drugs & Rock & Roll
Ian Dury; *New Boots & Panties* ....(STF)
Mantronix; *This Should Move Ya* ....(CAP)
Sheena Is A Punk Rocker
Ramones; *Leave Home* .... (SIR)
  Loco Live ....(SIR)
  Mania ....(SIR)
  Rocket To Russia ....(SIR)

Smack Dab In The Middle
Ry Cooder; *Chicken Skin Music* .... (RPR)
  Show Time ....(WB)
So High
Dave Mason; *Best Of* ....(COL)
  Let It Flow ....(COL)
So You Want To Be A Rock 'N' Roll Star
Byrds; *Greatest Hits* ....(COL)
  Original Singles-#1-1965-1967 ....(COL)
  Rock Classics/'60s ....(COL)
  Byrds (collection) ....(COL)
  (Untitled) ....(COL)
Patti Smith Group; *Wave* .... (ARI)
Tom Petty/Heartbreakers; *Pack Up The*
  Plantation-Live ....(MCA)
  Ultimate Rock Album ....(FTN)
Stick Around For Rock & Roll
Outlaws; *Bring It Back Alive* .... (ARI)
  Greatest Hits .... (ARI)
  Lady In Waiting .... (ARI)
Story Of Rock & Roll
Turtles; *Best Of* ....(RHI)
  Chalon Road ....(RHI)
  Greatest Hits ....(RHI)
Susy Is A Headbanger
Ramones; *All The Stuff & More-#1* .... (SIR)
  Leave Home .... (SIR)
Suzi Wants To Be A Rock Star
Professor Griff/Last Asiatic Disciples; *Pawns In The*
  Game ....(LUK)
Swanee River Rock
Ray Charles; *Birth Of Soul-Complete Atlantic*
  R&B ....(ATL)
Sweet Feelin'
Doobie Brothers; *Minute By Minute* .... (WB)
Sweet Little Rock & Roller
Chuck Berry; *Chess Box* .... (CSS)
  Chuck Berry Is On Top ....(CSS)
Richard Thompson; *Guitar Vocal* ....(CTH)
Rod Stewart; *Absolutely Live* ....(WB)
  Best Of ....(MER)
Take Me In Your Arms
Doobie Brothers; *Best Of* .... (WB)
  Stampede .... (WB)
Isley Brothers; *Motown Superstar Series-#6* ..... (MOT)
  Story-#1-Rockin' Soul-1959-1968 ..... (RHI)
Kim Weston; *25 Hard-To-Find Motown*
  Classics-#3 .... (MOT)
  Every Great Motown Song-First 25 Years ...... (MOT)
  Greatest By Holland/Dozier/Holland .... (MOT)
  Motown Dance Party-#1 .... (MOT)
That Is Rock & Roll
Chesterfields; *ST/American Hot Wax* .... (A&M)
Coasters; *Greatest Hits* .... (ATC)
  Greatest Recordings .... (ATC)
Coasters/Robins; *50 Coastin' Classics* .... (RHI)
That Rock Won't Roll
Restless Heart; *Best Of* ....(RCA)
  Country Music Classics-#22-1985-1990 .... (KT)
  Wheels ....(RCA)
That's Rock 'N' Roll
Eric Carmen; *Best Of* .... (ARI)
  Eric Carmen ....(RHI)
Shaun Cassidy; *Greatest Hits* ....(CCB)
  Yesterday's Heroes-'70s Teen Idols .... (RHI)
That's The Way I Wanna Rock N Roll
AC/DC; *Blow Up Your Video* ....(ATL)
  Live-Collector's Edition ....(ATC)
There Won't Be No Country Music...
C.W. McCall; *Greatest Hits* .... (POL)
There's Only One Way To Rock
Sammy Hagar; *Standing Hampton* .... (GEF)
  Ultimate Rock Album ....(FTN)
Van Halen; *Live: Right Here Right Now* .... (WB)
They Call It Rock
Nick Lowe; *Pure Pop For Now People* ....(COL)
This Boy Needs To Rock
Night Ranger; *7 Wishes* .... (CAM)
  ST/Explorers ....(VS)
This Is The Rock
Fleetwood Mac; *Kiln House* .... (RPR)

Too Old To Rock 'N' Roll, Too Young...
Jethro Tull; *Bursting Out* .... (CHR)
   Classic Case w/London Symphony Orchestra ...(RCA)
   Original Masters .... (CHR)
   Repeat-Best Of-#2 .... (CHR)
   Too Old To Rock 'N' Roll, Too Young... .... (CHR)
Top 40 Radio (The History Of Rock)
Joel Welz; *Return Of Haley's Comet* ....(CPR)
Trenchtown Rock
Bob Marley/Wailers; *Confrontation* .... (TUF)
   Live .... (TUF)
   More Of The Mighty .... (TUF)
   Songs Of Freedom .... (TUF)
Truck Stop Rock
Commander Cody/Lost Planet Airmen; *Hot Licks, Cold
Steel & Trucker's Fav.* .... (MCA)
Turtle Rock
Bela Fleck/Flecktones; *Flight Of The Cosmic
Hippo* .... (WB)
Twenty Flight Rock
Commander Cody/Lost Planet Airmen; *Lost In The
Ozone* .... (MCA)
   Too Much Fun-Best Of .... (MCA)
Eddie Cochran; *Greatest Hits* .... (CCB)
   Legendary Masters .... (EMI)
   On The Air .... (EMI)
Montrose; *Montrose* ....(WB)
Paul McCartney; *CHOBA B CCCP-Russian
Album* .... (CAP)
   Tripping The Live Fantastic .... (CAP)
Rolling Stones; *Still Life-American Concert 1981* ... (RS)
Uranium Rock
Cramps; *Bad Music For Bad People* .... (IRS)
Wanna Be A Rock 'N' Roll Star
Eddie Money; *Eddie Money* ....(COL)
We Built This City
Starship; *Greatest Hits-Ten Years &
Change-1979-91* ....(RCA)
   Knee Deep In The Hoopla .... (GRU)
   Nipper's Greatest Hits-'80s ....(RCA)
We Need A Lot More Jesus (& Less Rock..)
Linda Ronstadt; *Hand Sown Home Grown* .... (CAP)
We Will Rock You
Queen; *Greatest Hits* ....(HOL)
   Live At Wembley '86 ....(HOL)
   Live Killers ....(HOL)
   News Of The World ....(HOL)
   ST/FM .... (MCA)
When The Machines Rock
Gary Numan/Tubeway Army; *Replicas* ....(ATC)
When You Rock 'N' Roll With Me
David Bowie; *Live* ....(RYK)
Whiskey Rock A Roller
Lynyrd Skynyrd; *Gold & Platinum* .... (MCA)
   Nuthin' Fancy .... (MCA)
   One More From The Road .... (MCA)
White Noise
Jay Ferguson; *White Noise* ....(CAP)
(You Can Still) Rock In America
Night Ranger; *Midnight Madness* .... (CAM)
You Can't Kill Rock & Roll
Ozzy Osbourne; *Diary Of A Madman* ....(JET)
You Got Me Rocking
Rolling Stones; *Voodoo Lounge* .... (VIA)
Young Thing, Wild Dreams (Rock Me)
Red Rider; *Breaking Curfew* ....(CAP)
Your Mama Don't Dance
Loggins & Messina; *Best Of-Friends* ....(COL)
   Loggins & Messina ....(COL)
   On Stage ....(COL)
   Pop Classics Of The '70s ....(COL)
Poison; *Open Up And Say Ahhhh* .... (CAP)
   Swallow This Live .... (CAP)

RODEO

See Also: COWBOYS, HORSES

Lonesome Rodeo Cowboy
George Strait; *Livin' It Up* .... (MCA)
Midnight Rodeo
Leon Everette; *45* ....(RCA)
Montana Rodeo
Chris LeDoux; *Thirty-Dollar Cowboy* .... (LIB)

One More For The Rodeo
UFO; *Obsession* .... (CHR)
Ride 'Em Cowboy
Paul Davis; *Ride 'Em Cowboy* ....(BNG)
Roy Rogers/Sons Of The Pioneers; *Roy Rogers/Sons Of
The Pioneers* ....(VS)
Riding The Rodeo
Vince Gill; *When I Call Your Name* .... (MCA)
Ro Deo Deo Cowboy
Jerry Jeff Walker; *A Man Must Carry On* .... (MCA)
Rodeo
Garth Brooks; *Ropin' The Wind* .... (LIB)
Red Steagall/Coleman County Cowboys; *For All Our
Cowboy Friends* .... (MCA)
Rodeo Cowboys
Lynn Anderson; *Greatest Hits-#2* ....(COL)
Rodeo Girl
Rickie Lee Jones; *Flying Cowboys* .... (GEF)
Rodeo Girls
Tanya Tucker; *Best Of* .... (MCA)
Rodeo Road
Roy Rogers & Willie Nelson; *Tribute* ....(RCA)
Rodeo Romeo
Moe Bandy; *Greatest Hits* .... (COO)
Rodeo Song
Moe Bandy; *You Haven't Heard The Last Of Me* (MCA)
Rodeo Trails
Chris LeDoux; *Rodeo Songs Old & New* ....(CAP)
She's In Love With A Rodeo Man
Chris LeDoux; *Songs Of Rodeo & Country* ...... (LIB)
Don Williams; *Greatest Hits* .... (MCA)
Sweetheart Of The Rodeo
Emmylou Harris; *Ballad Of Sally Rose* ....(WB)
This Ain't My First Rodeo
Vern Gosdin; *10 Years Of Greatest Hits Newly
Recorded* ....(COL)
   Greatest Hits-#1 ....(COL)
   Super Hits ....(COL)
When The Rodeo Comes To Town
Chris LeDoux; *He Rides The Wild Horses* .... (LIB)

ROSES

See Also: FLOWERS

American Beauty Rose
Frank Sinatra; *Come Swing With Me* .... (CAP)
   Sentimental Journey .... (CAP)
Are The Roses Not Blooming
Judds; *Love Can Build A Bridge* ....(RCA)
Artificial Rose
Jimmy C. Newman; *45* .... (SUN)
   Greatest Hits .... (PLN)
Beanie G & The Rose Tattoo
Daryl Hall & John Oates; *No Goodbyes* .... (ATL)
   War Babies .... (ATL)
Bed Of Roses
Bon Jovi; *Keep The Faith* .... (MER)
Judy Clay; *Stax Soul Sisters* .... (STX)
Kenny Rogers; *Back Home Again* ....(RPR)
Oak Ridge Boys; *American Dreams* .... (MCA)
Screaming Trees; *Uncle Anesthesia* .... (EPI)
Warrant; *Cherry Pie* ....(COL)
Black Rose
Eric Clapton; *Another Ticket* ....(RSO)
John David Souther; *Black Rose* ....(ASY)
Sad Cafe; *Misplaced Ideals* ....(A&M)
Waylon Jennings; *Honky Tonk Heroes* ....(RCA)
Willie Nelson; *Me & Paul* ....(COL)
Blue Rose Is
Pam Tillis; *Put Yourself In My Place* .... (ARI)
Blue Rose Of Texas
Holly Dunn; *Blue Rose Of Texas* ....(WB)
Bread & Roses
Judy Collins; *So Early In The Spring-First 15
Years* .... (ELE)
Days Of Wine And Roses
Andy Williams; *16 Most Requested Songs* ....(COL)
   Close Enough For Love ....(ATC)
   Greatest Hits ....(COL)
   TT/Moon River & Other Great Movie Themes ...(COL)
Dream Syndicate; *Days Of Wine & Roses* ....(SLS)
   Live At Raji's ....(RES)

Frank Sinatra; *Days Of Wine & Roses/Acad. Award Winners* .... (RPR)
Henry Mancini; *All-Time Greatest Hits-#1* .... (RCA)
   Best Of .... (RCA)
   Pure Gold .... (RCA)
Desert Rose
Chris Hillman; *Desert Rose* .... (SH)
Desert Rose Band; *Pages Of Life* .... (CCB)
Eric Johnson; *Ah Via Musicom* .... (CAP)
Eighteen Wheels And A Dozen Roses
Kathy Mattea; *Collection Of Hits* .... (MER)
   Untasted Honey .... (MER)
Eleven Roses
Hank Williams, Jr.; *14 Greatest Hits* .... (POL)
   Eleven Roses .... (POL)
   Standing In The Shadows .... (POL)
English Rose
Jam; *All Mad Cons* .... (POL)
   Snap .... (POL)
English Roses
Pretenders; *2* .... (SIR)
Every Rose Has Its Thorn
Poison; *Open Up & Say...Ahh!* .... (CAP)
   Rock The First-#5 .... (SAN)
   Swallow This Live .... (CAP)
Everything's Coming Up Roses
Ethel Merman; *Broadway Magic: The '60s* .... (COL)
Original Cast; *Gypsy* .... (COL)
Original London Cast; *Gypsy* .... (RCA)
For The Roses
Joni Mitchell; *For The Roses* .... (ASY)
Forever Like The Rose
Seals & Crofts; *Takin' It Easy* .... (WB)
Give Her Thorns & She'll Find The Roses
Roger Whittaker; *Wind Beneath My Wings* .... (RCA)
Good Year For The Roses
George Jones & Alan Jackson; *The Bradley Barn Sessions* .... (MCA)
Honeysuckle Rose
Ella Fitzgerald & Count Basie; *Classy Pair* ..... (PAB)
   Perfect Match .... (PAB)
Fats; *Turn On The Heat-Fats Waller Piano Solos* . (BLU)
Fats Waller; *Ain't Misbehavin'* .... (EVR)
   Complete .... (RCA)
   Legendary Performer .... (RCA)
   Nipper's Greatest Hits!'30s-#1 .... (RCA)
   Piano Solos-1929-1941 .... (RCA)
I Don't Mind Thorns When You're The Rose
Lee Greenwood; *Country Classics-#6-1985-1986* .... (MCA)
   MCA #1 Hits!'80s-#2 .... (MCA)
   Streamline .... (MCA)
I Threw Away The Rose
George Jones; *20 Golden Pieces Of* .... (BLD)
Hank Williams, Jr.; *Living Proof-MGM Recordings-1963-1975* .... (MER)
Lorrie Morgan; *Mama's Hungry Eyes-Merle Haggard Tribute* .... (ARI)
Merle Haggard; *Best Of The Early Years* .... (CCB)
It Must Have Been The Roses
Grateful Dead; *Reckoning* .... (ARI)
   Steal Your Face .... (GRD)
Kiss From A Rose
Seal; *Seal* .... (ZTT)
La Vie En Rose
Edith Piaf; *Voice Of The Sparrow-Very Best Of* .. (CAP)
Grace Jones; *Island Life* .... (ISL)
Louis Armstrong; *Best Of The Decca Years-#1-The Singer* .... (DEC)
Marlene Dietrich; *The Cosmopolitan* .... (COL)
Melissa Manchester; *Tribute* .... (MIK)
Last Rose Of Summer
Boston Pops Orchestra/Arthur Fiedler; *Irish Album* .... (RCA)
James Galway/Chieftains; *Over The Sea To Skye-Celtic Connection* .... (RCA)
Judas Priest; *Sin After Sin* .... (COL)
Kiri Te Kanawa; *Come To The Fair* .... (ANG)
Phil Coulter; *Sea Of Tranquility* .... (SHA)
Lonely Rose Of Mexico
Sons Of The Pioneers; *Tumbleweed Trails* ...... (MCA)
Love Is A Rose
Linda Ronstadt; *Greatest Hits* .... (ASY)
   Prisoner In Disguise .... (ASY)

Lo, How A Rose E'er Blooming
Beane Family; *Christmas Classics From Around The World* .... (CRI)
John Fahey; *Christmas Guitar-#1* .... (VAR)
New York City Gay Men's Chorus; *Christmas Comes Anew* .... (VIA)
Pete Seeger; *Traditional Christmas Carols* .... (FLW)
Philadelphia Brass Ensemble/E. Ormandy; *Festival Of Carols In Brass* .... (COL)
Trapp Family Singers; *Christmas With* .... (MSP)
Vienna Boys Choir; *Christmas Festival* .... (RCA)
Vienna Boys Choir & Hermann Prey; *Christmas With* .... (RCA)
Mexicali Rose
Bing Crosby; *Best Of* .... (SSP)
Bob Wills; *Anthology* .... (COL)
Misty Roses
Johnny Mathis; *All-Time Greatest Hits* .... (COL)
Sandpipers; *Four Sider* .... (A&M)
   Greatest Hits .... (A&M)
Tim Hardin; *Memorial Album* .... (POL)
My Brown Eyed Texas Rose
Tex Ritter; *Arizona Days* .... (MSP)
   Country Music Hall Of Fame .... (MCA)
My Little Georgia Rose
David Grisman; *Home Is Where The Heart Is* ... (ROU)
Herb Pederson; *Son Of Rounder Banjo* .... (ROU)
My Rose Of Old Kentucky
Bill Monroe; *& Friends* .... (MCA)
Bill Monroe/Flatt & Scruggs; */Flatt & Scruggs* .. (ROU)
My San Antonio Rose
Freddy Powers; *45* .... (MCA)
My Wild Irish Rose
Magic Organ; *22 Great Organ Favorites* .... (RAN)
Mom & Dads; *One Dozen Roses* .... (CRS)
New Mexican Rose
Frankie Valli/Four Seasons; *25th Anniversary Collection* .... (RHI)
New San Antonio Rose
Bob Wills/Texas Playboys; *Columbia Country Classics-#1-Golden Age* .... (COL)
   Essential .... (COL)
   Greatest Hits .... (CCB)
October Roses
Linda Allen; *October Roses* .... (NX)
Old Rose Motel
Great White; *Psycho City* .... (CAP)
One Red Rose
John Prine; *Anthology-Great Days* .... (RHI)
   Storm Windows .... (ASY)
One Rose (That's Left In My Heart)
Bing Crosby; *Best Of* .... (MCA)
Leon Redbone; *Champagne Charlie* .... (WB)
Painted, Tainted Rose
Al Martino; *Best Of* .... (CAP)
   Capitol Collectors Series .... (CAP)
Poisoned Rose
Costello Show (Featuring Elvis Costello); *King Of America* .... (COL)
Elvis Costello; *Girls Girls Girls* .... (COL)
Poor Man's Roses (Or A Rich Man's Gold)
Patsy Cline; *Best Of* .... (CCB)
   Forever & Always .... (EPI)
   Stop, Look & Listen .... (MCA)
   Story .... (MCA)
Reba McEntire; *Feel The Fire* .... (MER)
Prairie Rose
Roxy Music; *Country Life* .... (ATC)
Pretty Pink Rose
Adrian Belew; *Young Lions* .... (ATL)
Purple Rose Of Cairo
New Orleans Ragtime Orchestra; *New Orleans Jazz* .... (ARH)
Ramblin' Rose
Chuck Berry; *Greatest Hits* .... (EVR)
Hank Snow; *Collector's Series-#2* .... (RCA)
Jerry Lee Lewis; *Golden Cream Of The Country* . (SUN)
Nat King Cole; *Best Of-#1* .... (CAP)
   Memories Are Made Of This .... (CAP)
   Ramblin' Rose .... (CAP)
Red Red Rose
Dave Mallett; *Vital Signs* .... (FF)
Emmylou Harris; *Brand New Dance* .... (RPR)

Red Rose
Alphaville; *Afternoons In Utopia* .... (ATL)
   Singles Collection .... (ATL)
Red Roses
Midnight Star; *Work It Out* .... (SLR)
Red Roses For A Blue Lady
Al Martino; *Best Of* .... (CAP)
   Capitol Collectors Series .... (CAP)
Andy Williams; *16 Most Requested Songs* .... (COL)
Mom & Dads; *Best Of* .... (CRS)
Roger Whittaker; *All-Time Heart-Touching*
Favorites .... (CAP)
   Classics Collection-#1 .... (CAP)
Vaughn Monroe; *Best Of* .... (RCA)
Red Roses (Won't Work Now)
Reba McEntire; *Have I Got A Deal For You* .... (MCA)
Room Full Of Roses
George Morgan; *Columbia Country Classics-#2* ..(COL)
Mickey Gilley; *Greatest Hits-#1* .... (EPI)
   Ten Years Of Hits .... (EPI)
Rosa De San Antonio
Santiago Jimenez, Jr.; *Mero Mero De San*
Antonio .... (ARH)
Rose By Any Other Name
Ronnie Milsap; *Rose By Any Other Name* .... (WB)
Rose Garden
k.d. lang; *Swingin' Country Favorites* .... (WB)
k.d. lang/Reclines; *Angel With A Lariat* .... (SIR)
Lynn Anderson; *Country music*
Classics-#4-1970-1975 .... (KT)
   Greatest Hits .... (COL)
   Rose Garden .... (COL)
   Super Hits/'70s-Have A Nice Day-#4 .... (RHI)
   Very Special Love Song .... (FFT)
Rose In Paradise
Waylon Jennings; *Country*
Classics-#8-1986-1987 .... (MCA)
   MCA #1 Hits/'80s-#3 .... (MCA)
   New Classic Waylon .... (MCA)
Rose In The Garden
Karla Bonoff; *Karla Bonoff* .... (COL)
Rose In The Heather
Nazareth; *Hair Of The Dog* .... (A&M)
Rose Of Cimarron
Emmylou Harris; *Cimarron* .... (WB)
Poco; *Backtracks* .... (MCA)
   Rose Of Cimarron .... (MCA)
Rose Of England
Nick Lowe; *Basher-Best Of* .... (COL)
Rose Of Old Monterey
Happy Polkateers; *Happy Polkateers* .... (CRS)
Rose Of San Antone
Bashful Brother Oswald; *Don't Say Aloha* ...... (ROU)
Rose Of The Rio Grande
Bob Crosby Orchestra; *Play 22 Original Big Band*
Hits .... (HIN)
Duke Ellington; *Great Paris Concert* .... (ATL)
Ella Fitzgerald & Duke Ellington; *At The Cote*
D'Azur .... (VRV)
Rose Of Tralee
Bing Crosby; *When Irish Eyes Are Smiling* ...... (MCA)
Patrick O'Hagan; *22 Golden Shamrocks* .... (RGO)
Rose Room
Benny Goodman; *I Like Jazz-Essence Of* .... (COL)
Charlie Christian; *Genius Of The Electric Guitar* .(COL)
Rose Tint In My World
Tim Curry/Original Roxy Cast; *Rocky Horror*
Show .... (RHI)
Rose & A Baby Ruth
George Hamilton IV; *At The Hop* .... (MCA)
   Vintage Music-Orig. Classic Oldies-#12 .... (MCA)
Roses
Janis Ian; *Aftertones* .... (COL)
Jim Reeves; *Jim Reeves* .... (RCA)
   Moonlight & Roses .... (RCA)
Roses Ain't Red
Diane Pfeifer; *Diane Pfeifer* .... (CAP)
Roses Are Red
Bobby Vinton; *16 Most Requested* .... (EPI)
   All-Time Greatest Hits .... (EPI)
   Spring Sensations .... (EPI)
Roses For Mama
C.W. McCall; *Greatest Hits* .... (POL)

Roses In The Snow
Emmylou Harris; *Roses In The Snow* .... (WB)
Roses In The Winter
Merle Haggard; *His Best* .... (MCA)
   Serving 190 Proof .... (MCA)
Roses & Thorns
Jeannie C. Riley; *Jeannie* .... (PLN)
Rose, The
Bette Midler; *Hit Singles 1980-1988* .... (ATL)
   ST/Rose, The .... (ATL)
Conway Twitty; *Dream Maker* .... (ELE)
   Latest Greatest Hits-#1 .... (WB)
   Number One's-Warner Bros. Years .... (WB)
Run For The Roses
Dan Fogelberg; *Greatest Hits* .... (FM)
   Innocent Age .... (FM)
   Live-Greetings From The West .... (FM)
Sally Go Round The Roses
Jaynettes; *Best Of Chess Rock 'N' Roll* .... (CSS)
   Cruisin'-1963 .... (INC)
   Girl Groups .... (RHI)
   Wonder Women .... (RHI)
Yvonne Elliman; *Night Flight* .... (RSO)
San Antonio Rose
Asleep At The Wheel; *Western Standard Time* .... (EPI)
Bob Wills; *Best Of-#2* .... (MCA)
   Sounds Of Texas .... (CAP)
   Texas State Of Mind .... (LIB)
Floyd Cramer; *Billboard Top Country Hits-1961* . (RHI)
   Country Love .... (SO)
Patsy Cline; *Story* .... (MCA)
Ricky Skaggs; *Comin' Home To Stay* .... (EPI)
Willie Nelson; *San Antonio Rose* .... (COL)
Spanish Harlem
Aretha Franklin; *30 Greatest Hits* .... (ATL)
   Best Of .... (ATL)
   Ten Years Of Gold .... (ATL)
Ben E. King; *Back To Mono-1958-1969* .... (AKO)
   Greatest Hits .... (ATC)
Crusaders; *At Their Best* .... (MOT)
Drifters; *Greatest Hits* .... (GUS)
Spanish Rose
Santana; *Inner Secrets* .... (COL)
Van Morrison; *Bang Masters* .... (EPI)
Stop & Smell The Roses
Mac Davis; *Greatest Hits* .... (COL)
   Stop & Smell The Roses .... (COL)
Summer Of Roses
Willie Nelson; *Tougher Than Leather* .... (COL)
Teardrop On A Rose
Hank Williams; *Let's Turn Back The*
Years-1951-1952 .... (POL)
Tennessee Rose
Emmylou Harris; *Cimarron* .... (WB)
Texas Rose Cafe
Little Feat; *Sailin' Shoes* .... (WB)
Thank You For The Roses
Kitty Wells; *Greatest Hits-#1* .... (SO)
Tiger Rose
Robert Hunter; *Tiger Rose* .... (RYK)
'Til A Tear Becomes A Rose
Kieth Whitley; *Greatest Hits* .... (RCA)
'Tis The Last Rose Of Summer
Lucy Shelton/Others; *Moore's Irish Melodies* ... (NON)
Two Dozen Roses
Shenandoah; *30 Years Of #1 Hits-#20* .... (COL)
   Greatest Hits .... (COL)
   Road Not Taken .... (COL)
When The Roses Bloom Again
Glenn Miller/Orchestra; *Complete* .... (BLU)
Johnny Cash; *Essential* .... (COL)
When The Snow Is On The Roses
Ed Ames; *Best Of* .... (RCA)
   Pure Gold .... (RCA)
Sonny James; *American Originals* .... (COL)
   Greatest Hits .... (COL)
Winter Rose Love Awake
Wings; *Back To The Egg* .... (CAP)
Yankee Rose
David Lee Roth; *Eat 'Em & Smile* .... (WB)
Yellow Rose
Johnny Lee & Lane Brody; *You & I-Classic Country*
Duets .... (WB)
   'Til The Bars Burns Down .... (FW)

Yellow Rose Of Texas
Hoyt Axton; *Songs Of The Civil War* ....(COL)
Michael Martin Murphey; *Cowboy Songs* ....(WB)
Mitch Miller; *16 Most Requested Songs* ....(COL)
Roy Rogers; *Great American Singing Cowboys* ... (REP)
Yellow Roses
Dolly Parton; *Greatest Country Hits/'80s-1989* ...(COL)
  White Limozeen ....(COL)
Ry Cooder; *Chicken Skin Music* ....(RPR)
Yellow Roses On Her Gown
Johnny Mathis; *I Only Have Eyes For You* ....(COL)

❖❖❖❖❖❖❖❖❖❖❖❖❖❖❖❖❖❖❖❖❖❖❖❖❖❖❖❖❖❖

ROYALTY, Bosses, Castles, Ruling Class, Slavery

See Also: KINGS, MONEY, POLITICAL SONGS,
PREJUDICE, QUEENS

❖❖❖❖❖❖❖❖❖❖❖❖❖❖❖❖❖❖❖❖❖❖❖❖❖❖❖❖❖❖

Abolitionist Hymn
Hermes Nye; *Ballads Of The Civil War-#1 & 2* . (FLW)
All The King's Castles
Shawn Phillips; *Bright White* ....(A&M)
Arabian Knights
Siouxsie/Banshees; *Juju* ....(GEF)
  Once Upon A Time-The Singles ....(GEF)
Big Boss Man
B.B. King; *Six Silver Strings* ....(MCA)
Elvis Presley; *Elvis* ....(RCA)
  ST/Clambake ....(RCA)
Grateful Dead; *Grateful Dead* ....(WB)
Jimmy Reed; *Best Of* ....(CRS)
  Oldies But Goodies-#1 ....(OSR)
John Hammond; *Best Of* ....(VAN)
  So Many Roads ....(VAN)
Blue Tail Fly
Burl Ives; *Best Of* ....(MCA)
Pete Seeger; *20 Golden Pieces Of* ....(BLD)
Boss
Diana Ross; *Anthology* ....(MOT)
  Boss ....(MOT)
  Composer-Greatest By Ashford & Simpson .... (MOT)
Camelot
Original 1982 London Cast; *Camelot* ....(VS)
Original Cast; *Camelot* ....(COL)
Richard Burton; *Broadway Magic-1960s* ....(COL)
Richard Harris; *ST/Camelot* ....(WB)
Castle Of Dreams
Dave Koz; *Dave Koz* ....(CAP)
Castle Walls
Styx; *Grand Illusion* ....(A&M)
Castles In The Air
Don McLean; *Best Of* ....(EMI)
  Greatest Hits-Then & Now ....(EMI)
  Tapestry ....(LIB)
Castles In The Sand
David Allan Coe; *Castles In The Sand* ....(COL)
Seals & Crofts; *Greatest Hits* ....(WB)
Stevie Wonder; *Greatest Hits* ....(MOT)
Castles Made Of Sand
Jimi Hendrix; *Axis Bold As Love* ....(RPR)
  Essential-#1 & 2 ....(RPR)
  Kiss The Sky ....(RPR)
Tuck & Patti; *Love Warriors* ....(WH)
Castles Of Sand
Jermaine Jackson; *Motown Superstar Series-#17* (MOT)
Don't Cry For Me Argentina
Original New York Cast; *Evita* ....(MCA)
Don't Let It Bring You Down
Crosby, Stills, Nash & Young; *4-Way Street* .....(ATL)
Neil Young; *After The Gold Rush* ....(RPR)
Don't Rob Another Man's Castle
Ernest Tubb; *Story* ....(MCA)
Duke Of Dubuque
Manhattan Transfer; *Bop Doo-Wopp* ....(ATL)
  Live ....(ATL)
Electric Kingdom
Twilight 22; *Twilight 22* ....(VAN)
Hay Una Mujer Desaparecida
Holly Near; *Imagine My Surprise* ....(RWD)
Holly Near & Ronnie Gilbert; *Lifeline* ....(RWD)
Head Of The Table
Joan Armatrading; *Whatever's For Us* ....(A&M)

High Society
Glen Gray; *Uncollected & The Casa Loma*
  Orchestra ....(HIN)
Louis Armstrong; *C'Est Si Bon* ....(RHI)
Pete Fountain; *Best Of* ....(MCA)
Teddy Buckner; *Salute To Louis Armstrong* ......(CRS)
I Wanna Be A Boss
10 CC; *How Dare You!* ....(OOP)
Ice Cream Castles
Time; *Ice Cream Castles* ....(WB)
If I Ruled The World
James Brown; *Sex Machine* ....(POL)
Sammy Davis, Jr.; *Greatest Hits* ....(RPR)
Stevie Wonder; *Looking Back* ....(MOT)
Supremes; *25th Anniversary* ....(MOT)
Tony Bennett; *Forty Years-Artistry Of* ....(COL)
If Women Ruled The World
Joan Armatrading; *Square The Circle* ....(A&M)
Invisible Touch
Genesis; *Hit Singles 1980-1988* ....(ATL)
  Invisible Touch ....(ATL)
Ivory Tower
Cathy Carr; *Jukebox Classics-#2* ....(RHI)
Long Ryders; *Native Sons* ....(FON)
Van Morrison; *No Guru No Method No Teacher* (MER)
I'm Sitting On Top Of The World
Al Jolson; *Jolson Sang 'Em* ....(BIO)
  Story-#3 ....(MCA)
Nitty Gritty Dirt Band; *Will The Circle Be*
  Unbroken-#2 ....(UNI)
Joker, The
Steve Miller Band; *Best Of-1968-1973* ....(CAP)
  Gift Set ....(CAP)
  Greatest Hits-1974-1978 ....(CAP)
  Live ....(CAP)
  The Joker ....(CAP)
King Of The Castle
Soup Dragons; *This Is Our Art* ....(SIR)
Kiss That Frog
Peter Gabriel; *Us* ....(GEF)
Leader Of The Band
Dan Fogelberg; *Greatest Hits* ....(FM)
  Innocent Age ....(FM)
Leader Of The Pack
Bette Midler; *Divine Miss M* ....(ATL)
  ST/Divine Madness ....(ATL)
Original Cast; *Leader Of The Pack* ....(ELE)
Shangri-Las; *21 Number One Hits* ....(OSR)
  Billboard Top Rock 'N' Roll Hits-1964 ....(RHI)
  Girl Groups-Story Of A Sound ....(MOT)
  Golden Hits Of ....(MER)
  Oldies But Goodies-#15 ....(OSR)
  Radioactive Hits-#2 ....(ACC)
  Remember The Shangri-Las At Their Best ....(CLT)
Leader, The
Burning Spear; *Mistress Music* ....(SLS)
Clash; *Sandinista* ....(EPI)
Mighty Fortress Is Our God
Leontyne Price; *God Bless America* ....(RCA)
Mob Rules
Black Sabbath; *Live Evil* ....(WB)
  Mob Rules ....(WB)
  ST/Heavy Metal ....(ASY)
Montana
Frank Zappa; *You Can't Do That On Stage*
  Anymore ....(RYK)
Mothers Of Invention; *Apostrophe/Overnite*
  Sensation ....(RYK)
My White Knight
Original Broadway Cast; *Music Man* ....(ANG)
Original Cast; *Music Man* ....(CAP)
Nobody Knows The Trouble I've Seen
Mahalia Jackson; *Gospels Spirituals & Hymns* ....(COL)
  Greatest Hits ....(COL)
Nat King Cole; *Every Time I Feel The Spirit* ......(CAP)
November In The Snow/Lord Buckley
Mark Murphy; *Kerouac Then & Now* ....(MUS)
Osaka Castle
Peter Erskine; *Transition* ....(DEN)
Paper Castles
Frankie Lymon/Teenagers; *Best Of* ....(RHI)
Power To The People
John Lennon; *Lennon* ....(CAP)
  Shaved Fish ....(CAP)

Power & The Glory
Jimmy Cliff; *Power & The Glory* ....(COL)
Limeliters; *Harmony!* ....(FOL)
  We The People ....(FOL)
Phil Ochs; *Chords Of Fame* ....(A&M)
  There But For Fortune ....(ELE)
Twisted Sister; *You Can't Stop Rock 'N' Roll* .....(ATL)
Wee Papa Girls; *Be Aware* ....(JVA)
Powerful People
Gino Vannelli; *Best Of* ....(A&M)
  Classics-#7 ....(A&M)
  Powerful People ....(A&M)
Radio Kingdom
Beach Boys; *Holland* ....(CAR)
Rock The Casbah
Clash; *Combat Rock* .... (EPI)
  On Broadway .... (EPI)
  Seems Like Yesterday-#4-Early '80s .... (KT)
  Story Of-#1 .... (EPI)
Royal Canal
Ian & Sylvia; *Four Strong Winds* .... (VAN)
  Greatest Hits .... (VAN)
Royal Garden Blues
Bix Beiderbecke; *At The Jazz Band Ball-#2* ......(COL)
Bix Beiderbecke/Wolverines; *History Of Classic
Jazz* ....(RVR)
Original Broadway Cast; *Black & Blue* .... (DRG)
Tommy Dorsey; *Best Of* ....(RCA)
  Complete-#2 ....(RCA)
Royal Nonesuch
Original Broadway Cast; *Big River-Adventures Of
Huckleberry Finn* .... (MCA)
Royal Orleans
Led Zeppelin; *Presence* .... (SS)
Royal Scam
Steely Dan; *Royal Scam* .... (MCA)
Royal Telephone
Burl Ives; *Best Of-#2* .... (MCA)
George Lewis/Eclipse Alley Five; *George Lewis Of New
Orleans* ....(RVR)
Shadow Captain
Crosby, Stills & Nash; *Allies* .... (ATL)
  CSN .... (ATL)
  Replay .... (ATL)
  Crosby, Stills & Nash (collection) .... (ATL)
Sheik Of Chicago
Joe Stampley; *Greatest Hits* .... (EPI)
Sir Duke
Stevie Wonder; *Original Musiquarium* .... (MOT)
  Songs In The Key Of Life .... (MOT)
Sitting On Top Of The World
Cream; *Goodbye* .... (POL)
  Wheels Of Fire .... (POL)
Howlin' Wolf; *Chess Box* .... (CSS)
  Real Folk Blues .... (CSS)
Sittin' On Top Of The World
Bob Wills/Texas Playboys; *24 Great Hits* .... (POL)
  Bob Wills Anthology .... (SSP)
  Tiffany Transcriptions-#8 .... (KAL)
Doc Watson; *Doc Watson* .... (VAN)
  Greatest Folksingers Of The '60s .... (VAN)
  Old Timey Concert .... (VAN)
Grateful Dead; *Grateful Dead* .... (WB)
Ray Charles; *20 Golden Pieces Of* .... (BLD)
Sweet Honey In The Rock; *Believe I'll Run On...* (RWD)
Skye Boat Song
King's Singters; *Annie Laurie-Folksongs Of British
Isles* .... (ANG)
Paul Robeson; *American Balladeer-Golden
Classics-#1* ....(CLT)
Roger Whittaker; *Live In Concert* ....(RCA)
Slave
Elton John; *Honky Chateau* .... (POL)
Germs; *Germs* .... (SLS)
Rolling Stones; *Tattoo You* .... (RS)
Slave Driver
Bob Marley/Wailers; *Catch A Fire* .... (TUF)
  Rebel Music ....(TUF)
Taj Mahal; *Mo' Roots* ....(COL)
Slavery Days
Burning Spear; *24 Great Hits* ....(MGM)
  Live ....(COL)
  Marcus Garvey ....(ISL)

Slaves
Temptations; *Puzzle People* .... (MOT)
Spanish Castle Magic
Jimi Hendrix; *Axis: Bold As Love* .... (RPR)
  Lifelines/Story .... (RPR)
  Live At Winterland ....(RYK)
  Radio One ....(RYK)
Steal Away
Jackson Southernaires; *Presenting Joy Peace Happiness &
Love* ....(MSP)
Reverend James Cleveland; *Sings w/World's Greatest
Gospel Stars* .... (SAV)
Sultan Of Sex
Neon Judgement; *Horny As Hell* ....(PIA)
Sultans Of Swing
Dire Straits; *Dire Straits* ....(WB)
  Live-Alchemy ....(WB)
  Money For Nothing ....(WB)
Tower Of London
ABC; *How To Be A Zillionaire* .... (MER)
Trader
Beach Boys; *10 Years Of Harmony* ....(CAR)
  Holland ....(CAR)
Under My Thumb
Rolling Stones; *12 X 5* .... (AKO)
  Aftermath ....(AKO)
  Got Live If You Want It .... (AKO)
  Hot Rocks 1964-1971 ....(AKO)
  Still Life-American Concert 1981 .... (RS)
Who; *Who's Missing* ....(MCA)
Unfaithful Servant
Band; *Band* ....(CAP)
  Gift Set ....(CAP)
  Rock Of Age-#1 & 2 ....(CAP)
  To Kingdom Come-Definitive Collection ....(CAP)
White Palace
Clay Walker; *Clay Walker* .... (GIA)
Women Will Rule The World
Ry Cooder; *Get Rhythm* ....(WB)
Working For The Man
Roy Orbison; *All-Time Greatest Hits* .... (MON)
  For The Lonely-Anthology-1956-1965 .... (RHI)
  In Dreams-Greatest Hits .... (VIA)
  More Greatest Hits ....(MON)

SAILING, Sailors
See Also: OCEAN, RIVERS, SHIPS, WATER

Anchors Aweigh
Firehouse Five Plus Two; *Goes To Sea* .... (GTJ)
Pat Boone; *Star Spangled Banner* .... (WOR)
Angels & Sailors
Doors; *American Prayer* .... (ELE)
Blow The Man Down
Paul Clayton; *Bay State Ballads* .... (FLW)
Clear Sailin'
Barbra Streisand; *Emotion* ....(COL)
Chris Hillman; *Clear Sailin'* ....(ASY)
Ian Thomas Band; *Still Here* ....(ATL)
Come On Down To My Boat
Every Mother's Son; *Battle Of The Bands-#3* ..... (KT)
Come Sail Away
Styx; *Caught In The Act* .... (A&M)
  Classics-#15 ....(A&M)
  Grand Illusion ....(A&M)
Davy's Dinghy
Ruth Wallis; *Dr. Demento's Dementia Royale* .... (RHI)
  Dr. Demento's Greatest Novelties-#2 .... (RHI)
Day We Lost The America's Cup
Tom Paxton; *One Million Lawyers & Other
Disasters* ....(FF)
I Can Sail To China
John Conlee; *American Faces* ....(COL)
I Go Sailing
Stevie Wonder; *ST/Jungle Fever* .... (MOT)
I'll Sail My Ship Aone
George Jones; *20 Golden Pieces Of* ....(BLD)
Mickey Gilley; *Greatest Hits-#1* .... (EPI)
Patsy Cline; *Always* ....(MCA)
  Portrait Of ....(MCA)
Ray Price; *Greatest Hits-#1* ....(SO)

I'm Popeye The Sailor Man
Billy Costello; *Dr. Demento's Greatest-#1-'40s & Before* .... (RHI)
Lee Shore
Crosby, Stills, Nash & Young; *4-Way Street* ...... (ATL)
David Crosby; *Bread & Roses Festival-Acoustic Music-#2* .... (FAN)
Morrisey & The Russian Sailor
Tom Dahill; *Irish Music From St. Paul To Donegal* (FF)
Nautical Wheelers
Jimmy Buffett; *A-1-A* .... (MCA)
Boats Beaches Bars & Ballads .... (MGR)
New York, New York/Sailors On The Town
Original Broadway Cast; *Jerome Robbins' Broadway* .... (RCA)
Only Love
Wynonna; *Tell Me Why* .... (MCC)
Orinoco Flow (Sail Away)
Enya; *Watermark* .... (RPR)
Red Sails
David Bowie; *Lodger* .... (RYK)
Sound + Vision .... (RYK)
Red Sails In The Sunset
Big Joe Turner; *Nobody In Mind* .... (PAB)
Dinah Washington; *Echoes Of An Era* .... (RLL)
Jarmels; *Golden Classics* .... (CLT)
Nat King Cole; *Unforgettable* .... (CAP)
Platters; *Greatest Hits* .... (EVR)
Ride Captain Ride
Blues Image; *Back To The '70s-#3* .... (DOM)
Hit Singles 1958-1977 .... (ATL)
Rime Of The Ancient Mariner
Iron Maiden; *Live After Death* .... (CAP)
Powerslave .... (CAP)
Rio Grande
Floyd Tillman; *Country Music Hall Of Fame* .... (MCA)
Sam Eskin; *Shanty Men-Songs Of Sailormen/Lumbermen* .... (FLW)
Sail Along, Silv'ry Moon
Andy Williams; *Greatest Songs* .... (CCB)
Billy Vaughn; *Best Of* .... (MCA)
Greatest Hits .... (CCB)
& Orchestra Play 22 Of His Greatest Hits ...... (RAN)
Sail Around The World
David Gates; *First* .... (ELE)
Sail Away
Allman Brothers Band; *Enlightened Rogues* .... (POL)
Bobby Darin; *Darin 1936-1973* .... (MOT)
Creedence Clearwater Revival; *Mardi Gras* ..... (FAN)
Great White; *Sail Away* .... (ZOO)
Judy Garland; *Live* .... (CAP)
Linda Ronstadt; *Don't Cry Now* .... (ASY)
Neil Young/Crazy Horse; *Rust Never Sleeps* ...... (RPR)
Noel Coward; *Live From Las Vegas & New York* ..(COL)
Oak Ridge Boys; *Greatest Hits* .... (MCA)
Have Arrived .... (MCA)
Peter Frampton; *Somethin's Happening* .... (A&M)
Randy Newman; *Sail Away* .... (RPR)
Roger Whittaker; *Voyager* .... (RCA)
Stylistics; *In Fashion* .... (MER)
Temptations; *Anthology* .... (MOT)
Sail Away Ladies
Kingston Trio; *Hidden Treasures* .... (FOL)
Odetta; *At The Gate Of Horn* .... (VAN)
Movin' It On .... (RQ)
One Grain Of Sand .... (VAN)
Sail Away Sweet Sister
Queen; *The Game* .... (HOL)
Sail Away To The Sea
Sandy Denny; *Who Knows Where The Time Goes?* (HBL)
Sail On
Commodores; *All The Great Hits* .... (MOT)
All The Great Love Songs .... (MOT)
Lionel Richie-Composer Series .... (MOT)
Midnight Magic .... (MOT)
Robin Trower; *Caravan To Midnight* .... (CHR)
Sail On Flying Dutchman
Nick Seeger; *Sail On Flying Dutchman* .... (BIO)
Sail On Sailor
Beach Boys; *10 Years Of Harmony* .... (CAR)
Best Of-Good Vibrations .... (RPR)
Holland .... (RPR)
In Concert .... (RPR)

Sail On White Moon
Boz Scaggs; *Slow Dancer* .... (COL)
Sail To Australia
New Grass Revival; *When The Storm Is Over* ...... (FF)
Sailboat In The Moonlight
Billie Holiday; *Greatest Hits* .... (COL)
Lady Day .... (COL)
Legacy Box-1933-1958 .... (COL)
Quintessential-#4-1937 .... (COL)
Sailing
Christopher Cross; *Christopher Cross* .... (WB)
Rod Stewart; *Absolutely Live* .... (WB)
Atlantic Crossing .... (WB)
Greatest Hits .... (WB)
Storyteller-Complete Anthology-1964-1990 ...... (WB)
Sailing Blues
John Lee Hooker; *Alone* .... (SPE)
Sailing Down The Chesapeake Bay
John Townley/Press Gang; *Chesapeake Sailor's Companion* .... (ADE)
Sailing Down The Tears
Hanoi Rocks; *Back To Mystery City* .... (GEF)
Sailing Down This Golden River
Pete Seeger; *Bread & Roses Festival-Acoustic Music-#2* .... (FAN)
Circles & Seasons .... (WB)
Sailing Home For Christmas
Doug Stone; *First Christmas* .... (EPI)
Sailing Nights
Bob Seger; *Beautiful Loser* .... (CAP)
Sailing Ships
Whitesnake; *Slip Of The Tongue* .... (GEF)
Sailing The Wind
Loggins & Messina; *Full Sail* .... (WB)
Sailing To America
Saxon; *Crusader* .... (CRR)
Sailing Toward Home
Oak Ridge Boys; *All Our Favorite Songs* ...... (COL)
Sailing Without A Sail
Michael Johnson; *Michael Johnson* .... (A&M)
Sailin'
Cecilio & Kapono; *Night Music* .... (COL)
New Riders Of The Purple Sage; *Gypsy Cowboy* (COL)
Sailin' On
Bad Brains; *Rock For Light* .... (CRL)
Youth Are Getting Restless-Paradiso-1987 ...... (CRL)
Sailin' On The Hawaii
Nitty Gritty Dirt Band; *Will The Circle Be Unbroken* .... (EMI)
Sailin' To Paradise
Pablo Cruise; *Worlds Away* .... (A&M)
Sailor
Derringer; *Derringer* .... (BS)
Live .... (BS)
Molly Hatchet; *Beatin' The Odds* .... (EPI)
Rod Stewart; *Best Of* .... (MER)
Sailor Boy
Chiffons; *Best Of* .... (LAU)
Sailor Song
Sister Double Happiness; *Heart & Soul* .... (RPR)
Sailor & The Mermaid
Libby Titus & Dr. John; *In Harmony-Sesame Street* .... (WB)
Sailor's Lament
Creedence Clearwater Revival; *1970* .... (FAN)
Pendulum .... (FAN)
Sailor's Life
Fairport Convention; *Chronicles* .... (A&M)
Unhalfbricking .... (A&M)
Judy Collins; *Maid Of Constant Sorrow* ...... (ELE)
Sailor's Misfortune
Dave Loggins; *Personal Belongings* .... (VAN)
Sails
Chet Atkins; *Sails* .... (COL)
Elton John; *Empty Sky* .... (POL)
Salty Dog
Procol Harum; *Best Of* .... (A&M)
Classics-#17 .... (A&M)
Live With The Edmonton Orchestra .... (A&M)
Salty Dog .... (A&M)
Salty Dog Blues
Flatt & Scruggs; *Golden Hits Of* .... (GUS)
Greatest Folksingers/'60s .... (VAN)

Saturday Sailing
James Morrison; *Postcards From Down Under* ... (ATL)
Sea Cruise
Billy "Crash" Craddock; *Changes* .... (CAP)
   Greatest Hits .... (CAP)
Frankie Ford; *American Hot Wax* .... (A&M)
   Best Of New Orleans R&B-#2 .... (RHI)
   Oldies But Goodies-#3 .... (OSR)
   Rock & Roll Show .... (GUS)
Glenn Frey; *No Fun Aloud* .... (ASY)
Johnny Rivers; *Anthology-1964-1977* .... (RHI)
Nighthawks; *Best Of* .... (GEN)
Robert Gordon & Link Wray; *Fresh Fish Special* .(RCA)
Shadow Captain
Crosby, Stills & Nash; *Allies* .... (ATL)
   CSN .... (ATL)
   Replay .... (ATL)
   Crosby, Stills & Nash (collection) .... (ATL)
Shakedown Cruise
Jay Ferguson; *Real Life Ain't This Way* .... (ASY)
Ship Without A Sail
Dave Frishberg; *Let's Eat Home* .... (CCJ)
Ella Fitzgerald; *Rodgers & Hart Songbook* ......(VRV)
Sarah Vaughan; *Rodgers & Hart Songbook* ...... (EMA)
Shiver Me Timbers
Bette Midler; *Live At Last* .... (ATL)
   Songs For The New Depression .... (ATL)
   ST/Divine Madness .... (ATL)
Tom Waits; *Heart Of Saturday Night* .... (ASY)
Skye Boat Song
King's Singers; *Annie Laurie-Folksongs Of British*
Isles .... (ANG)
Paul Robeson; *American Balladeer-Golden*
Classics-#1 .... (CLT)
Roger Whittaker; *Live In Concert* .... (RCA)
Sloop John B
Beach Boys; *Absolute Best-#2* .... (CAP)
   Best Of (Good Vibrations) .... (RPR)
   Gift Set .... (CAP)
   Made In The U.S.A. .... (CAP)
   Pet Sounds .... (CAP)
   ST/Forrest Gump .... (EPX)
Smooth Sailing
Arnett Cobb; *Giants Of The Blues Tenor Sax* ..... (PRS)
   Smooth Sailing .... (PRS)
Ella Fitzgerald; *Newport Jazz Festival* ....(COL)
   Best Of .... (MCA)
   Live In Tokyo .... (PAB)
Smooth Sailin'
T.G. Sheppard; *All-Time Greatest Hits* .... (WB)
Son Of A Son Of A Sailor
Jimmy Buffett; *Boats Beaches Bars & Ballads* ... (MGR)
   Son Of A Son Of A Sailor .... (MCA)
   Songs You Know By Heart-Greatest Hits .... (MCA)
   You Had To Be There .... (MCA)
Thousands Are Sailing
Pogues; *Essential* .... (ISL)
   If I Should Fall From Grace With God .... (ISL)
Through My Sails
Neil Young; *Zuma* .... (RPR)
Times Have Changed
Supertramp; *Indelibly Stamped* .... (A&M)
Uncle Albert/Admiral Halsey
Paul McCartney; *Gift Set* .... (CAP)
Paul McCartney/Wings; *Wings Greatest* .... (CAP)
Paul & Linda McCartney; *All The Best* .... (CAP)
   Ram .... (CAP)
Vahevala
Loggins & Messina; *Best Of-Friends* ....(COL)
   On Stage ....(COL)
   Sittin' In ....(COL)
Whaling And Sailing Songs
Paul Clayton; *Various Tracks* .... (TRD)
When My Ship Comes In
Clint Black; *Hard Way* .... (RCA)
Yo Heave Ho
Popular Standard; *Out-Of-Print Recording* ....(OOP)

SCHOOL, Instruction, Learning, Teachers
   See Also: TEENAGERS

3 O'Clock...School's Out!
Full Force; *Guess Who's Comin' To The Crib?* ...(COL)

ABC
Jackson 5; *ABC* .... (MOT)
   Anthology .... (MOT)
   Greatest Hits .... (MOT)
Abigail Beecher
Freddy Cannon; *14 Booming Hits* .... (RHI)
Adult Education
Daryl Hall & John Oates; *Live At The Apollo* ....(RCA)
   Rock 'N Soul Part 1 ....(RCA)
After School
Linda Allen; *Women's Work* .... (FF)
Randy Starr; *45* ....(OOP)
Young M.C.; *Brainstorm* .... (CAP)
All Hail Blue & Gold
University Of California Marching Band; *University Of*
California Marching Band ....(FID)
Alma Mater
Alice Cooper; *School's Out* .... (WB)
Chicago; *V* ....(COL)
Original Broadway Cast; *Grease* .... (POL)
Animal House
Stephen Bishop; *ST/Animal House* .... (MCA)
Another Brick In The Wall, Part 2
Pink Floyd; *Collection Of Great Dance Songs* ....(COL)
   Delicate Sound Of Thunder ....(COL)
   The Wall ....(COL)
Roger Waters; *The Wall Live In Berlin* .... (MER)
Back To School Days
Graham Parker; *Howlin' Wind* .... (MER)
   Live! Alone In America ....(RCA)
   Parkerilla .... (MER)
Bad Luck Streak In Dancing School
Warren Zevon; *Bad Luck Streak In Dancing*
School .... (ASY)
Be True To Your School
Beach Boys; *Absolute Best-#1* ....(CAP)
   Endless Summer ....(CAP)
   Gift Set ....(CAP)
   Little Deuce Coupe/All Summer Long ....(CAP)
   Made In The U.S.A. ....(CAP)
Beauty School Dropout
Original Broadway Cast; *Grease* .... (POL)
Bust The High School Students
Austin Lounge Lizards; *Lizard Vision* .... (FF)
Catholic School Girls Rule
Red Hot Chili Peppers; *Abbey Road E.P.* .... (EMI)
   Freaky Styley .... (EMI)
   What Hits!? Best Of .... (EMI)
Centerfold
J. Geils Band; *Flashback-Best Of* .... (EMI)
   Freeze-Frame .... (EMI)
   Showtime .... (EMI)
Charlie Brown
Coasters; *Billboard Top Rock 'N' Roll Hits-1957* . (RHI)
   Cruisin'-1959 .... (INC)
   Greatest Hits ....(ATC)
   Super Oldies/'50s-#7 ....(AUF)
   Their Greatest Recordings ....(ATC)
   Young Blood .... (ATL)
Chattahoochee
Alan Jackson; *Lot About Livin' (& A Little 'Bout*
Love) .... (ARI)
Cheatin' In School
Corey Hart; *First Offense* .... (EMI)
Chinese Arithmetic
Faith No More; *Introduce Yourself* ....(SLS)
Class Of '57
Statler Brothers; *Best Of* .... (MER)
Crash Course In Brain Surgery
Metallica; *Garage Days Re-Revisited* .... (ELE)
Daddy Should Have Stayed In High School
Cheap Trick; *Cheap Trick* .... (EPI)
Dear Old Nebraska U.
University Of Michigan Band; *Greatest College Football*
Marches .... (VAN)
Duke Blue & White
University Of Michigan Band; *Greatest College Football*
Marches .... (VAN)
Education
Kinks; *Schoolboys In Disgrace* .... (RHI)
Untouchables; *Agent Double O Soul* .... (RES)
Everybody's Got To Learn Sometime
Korgis; *Dumb Waiters* .... (ASY)

Fight For California
University Of California Marching Band; *University Of California Marching Band* ....(FID)
Fight On, Pennsylvania
All-Star Inter-Conference Band; *College Marches At Halftime U.S.A.* .... (ALS)
University Of Michigan Band; *Greatest College Football Marches* .... (VAN)
Fight On, U.S.C.
Michigan University Band; *Kick Off, U.S.A.* ..... (VAN)
Fight The Team Across The Field
Ohio State University Marching Band; *Across The Field* ....(FID)
Girls' School
Wings; *London Town* ....(CAP)
Glory Days
Bruce Springsteen; *Born In The U.S.A.* ....(COL)
Go U Northwestern
Northwestern University Marching Band; *Go U Northwestern* ....(FID)
Good Morning Little School Girl
Grateful Dead; *Grateful Dead* ....(WB)
Huey Lewis/News; *Four Chords & Several Years Ago* .... (ELE)
Johnny Winter; *Johnny Winter* ....(COL)
  Live ....(COL)
Ten Years After; *Classic Performances* ....(COL)
  Recorded Live ....(COL)
  Ssssh ....(CHR)
  Universal ....(CHR)
Yardbirds; *Crossroads* ....(POL)
  Five Live Yardbirds ....(RHI)
Gotta Learn To Love Without You
Michael Johnson; *Best Of* ....(RCA)
  Wings; ....(RCA)
Graduation Day
Beach Boys; *Gift Set* ....(CAP)
  Spirit Of America ....(CAP)
Rover Boys; *45* ....(OOP)
Graduation's Here
Fleetwoods; *Best Of* .... (RHI)
Hail Purdue
University Of Michigan Band; *Greatest College Football Marches* .... (VAN)
Hail To California
University Of California Marching Band; *Hail To California* ....(FID)
Hail Wichita
Wichita State University Marching Band; *Wichita State University Marching Band* ....(FID)
Harper Valley P.T.A.
Jeannie C. Riley; *Greatest Hits* .... (PLN)
  Harper Valley P.T.A. .... (PLN)
  Oldies But Goodies-#4 .... (OSR)
  Souvenirs Of Music City USA .... (PLN)
Here Comes Carolina
Ohio State University Marching Band; *Saturday Afternoon At Columbus* ....(FID)
High School Cadets
Band Of H.M. Royal Marines; *Stars & Stripes Forever* .... (ANG)
High School Confidential
Jerry Lee Lewis; *20 Classic Jerry Lee Lewis Hits* . (OSR)
  Original ....(SUN)
  Original Golden Hits-#2 ....(SUN)
  ST/Harper Valley PTA ....(PLN)
  Sun Story ....(RHI)
High School Nights
Dave Edmunds; *Anthology-1968-1990* .... (RHI)
  ST/Porky's Revenge .... (MOB)
Homecoming Queen's Got A Gun
Julie Brown; *Dr. Demento Greatest Novelty Records-#5* .... (RHI)
  Teenage Tragedies .... (RHI)
  Trapped In The Body Of A White Girl .... (SIR)
Hot For Teacher
Van Halen; *1984* ....(WB)
How To Dance
Bingoboys; *Best Of* ....(ATL)
I Deal With Mathematics
Movement Ex; *Movement Ex* ....(COL)
I Taught Her Everything She Knows
Billy Walker; *Greatest Hits* ....(MON)

It's Getting Better
Beatles; *Sgt. Pepper's Lonely Hearts Club Band* ..(CAP)
I've Got A Lot To Learn About Love
Storm; *Storm* ....(ISC)
K.S.U. Fight Song
Kent State University Marching Band; *Kent State University Marching Band* ....(FID)
Learn How To Live
Billy Squier; *Emotions In Motion* ....(CAP)
Learning How To Love You
George Harrison; *33 1/3* ....(DKH)
John Hiatt; *Bring The Family* ....(A&M)
Learning The Game
Andrew Gold; *What's Wrong With This Picture* ...(ASY)
Santa Esmeralda; *Beauty* ....(CAS)
Learning To Fly
Pink Floyd; *Delicate Sound Of Thunder* ....(COL)
  Momentary Lapse Of Reason ....(COL)
Tom Petty/Heartbreakers; *Into The Great Wide Open* .... (MCA)
Learning To Live Again
Garth Brooks; *The Chase* ....(LIB)
Learnin' The Blues
Frank Sinatra; *Capitol Collectors Series* ....(CAP)
  Capitol Years ....(CAP)
  Sinatra-Basie ....(RPR)
Lesson In Leaving
Dottie West; *Special Delivery* .... (EMI)
Lesson In Survival
Joni Mitchell; *For The Roses* ....(ASY)
Letting Go
Suzy Bogguss; *Aces* ....(CAP)
  Voices In The Wind ....(LIB)
Live & Learn
Joe Public; *Joe Public* ....(COL)
Living & Learning
Mel Tillis/Statesiders; *24 Great Hits* ....(MGM)
Love School
Divinyls; *Divinyls* .... (VIA)
Marquette University
Band Of H.M. Royal Marines; *Solid Men To The Front-Sousa Marches-#3* .... (ANG)
Maxwell's Silver Hammer
Beatles; *1967-1970* ....(CAP)
  Abbey Road ....(CAP)
Me & Julio Down By The Schoolyard
Paul Simon; *Greatest Hits Etc.* ....(COL)
  Live Rhymin' ....(WB)
  Negotiations & Love Songs-1971-1986 ....(WB)
  Paul Simon ....(WB)
Simon & Garfunkel; *Concert In Central Park* .....(WB)
Men Of Ohio
Ohio State University Marching Band; *Foot Tappers* ....(FID)
Michigan Victors
Ohio State University Marching Band; *Music For Cheerleaders & Song Girls* ....(FID)
  Saturday Afternoon At Columbus ....(FID)
Mighty Bears Of Baylor
Southern Methodist Mustang Band; *Southwest Conference Jazz* ....(FID)
Minnesota Rouser
Ohio State University Marching Band; *Stadium Favorites In Brass* ....(FID)
Moments To Remember
Four Lads; *16 Most Requested Songs* ....(COL)
  Radio Classics Of The '50s ....(COL)
  '50s Vocal Groups ....(KT)
Original Cast; *Forever Plaid* ....(RCA)
Ray Conniff/Orchestra; *Memories Are Made Of This* ....(COL)
Vogues; *Greatest Hits* ....(RHI)
My Old School
Steely Dan; *Countdown To Ecstasy* ....(MCA)
  Decade Of ....(MCA)
  Greatest Hits ....(MCA)
M.S.U. Fight Song
Michigan State University Band; *Michigan State University Band* ....(FID)
National Education Week
10,000 Maniacs; *Hope Chest-Fredonia Recordings-1982-1983* .... (ELE)

New Girl In School
Jan & Dean; *Legendary Masters* .... (EMI)
   Surf City-Best Of .... (EMI)
New Math
Tom Lehrer; *That Was The Week That Was* ..... (OOP)
No More Homework
Gary U.S. Bonds; *School Of Rock 'N' Roll-Best Of* (RHI)
Notre Dame Our Mother
University Of Notre Dame Band; *Songs Of The Fighting Irish* ....(FID)
Notre Dame Victory March
University Of Notre Dame Band; *Songs Of The Fighting Irish* ....(FID)
Ode To A Gym Teacher
Meg Christian; *I Know You Know* ....(OLI)
   Scrapbook ....(OLI)
Ohio
Crosby, Stills & Nash; *Crosby Stills & Nash (collection)* .... (ATL)
Crosby, Stills, Nash & Young; *Four-Way Street* .. (ATL)
   So Far .... (ATL)
Neil Young; *Decade* .... (RPR)
   ST/Journey Through The Past .... (RPR)
Old Schoolyard (Remember The Days Of...)
Cat Stevens; *Classics-#24* .... (A&M)
   Izitso .... (A&M)
Old School, The
John Conlee; *Country Classics-#6-1985-1986* ... (MSP)
   Greatest Hits-#2 .... (MCA)
   Old School, The .... (MSP)
On Brave Old Army Team
All-Star Inter-Conference Band; *College Marches At Halftime* .... (ALS)
On Iowa
University Of Iowa Marching Band; *Go Hawkeyes Go* ....(FID)
On Wisconsin
Magic Organ; *22 Great Organ Favorites* .... (RAN)
   Traveling With .... (RAN)
University Of Wisconsin Marching Band; *Fifth Quarter* ....(FID)
One More Try
George Michael; *Faith* ....(COL)
Pomp & Circumstance March #1 In D Op. 39
Boston Pops Orchestra/Arthur Fiedler; *Fiedler-Greatest Hits* ....(RCA)
   Fiedler's Favorite Marches .... (RCA)
Sir Edward Elgar; *ST/Clockwork Orange* .... (WB)
Pride Of The Illini
University Of Michigan Band; *Greatest College Football Marches* .... (VAN)
Pride Of The Wolverines
University Of Michigan Band; *Stars & Stripes Forever-Sousa Marches* .... (VAN)
Princeton Cannon Song
University Of Michigan Band; *Greatest College Football Marches* .... (VAN)
Principal's Office
Young M.C.; *Stone Cold Rhymin'* .... (DV)
Problems
Everly Brothers; *All-Time Greatest Hits* ....(CCB)
   Cadence Classics-Their 20 Greatest Hits .... (RHI)
   Fabulous Style Of .... (RHI)
Queen Of Hollywood High
John Stewart; *Blondes* .... (ALL)
Queen Of The Senior Prom
Mills Brothers; *Best Of* .... (MCA)
Red Raider Fanfare & Fight Song
Texas Tech University Band; *Grandioso* ....(FID)
Redneck School Of Technology
Flaming Lips; *Telepathic Surgery* .... (RES)
Rock & Roll High School
Ramones; *End Of The Century* .... (SIR)
   Loco Live .... (SIR)
   Ramones Mania .... (SIR)
   ST/Rock & Roll High School .... (SIR)
Roll On, Tulane
Michigan University Band; *Kick Off, U.S.A.* ..... (VAN)
Rose Goes To Yale
Jefferson Starship; *Nuclear Furniture* .... (GRU)
Roses Are Red
Bobby Vinton; *16 Most Requested* .... (EPI)
   All-Time Greatest Hits .... (EPI)
   Spring Sensations .... (EPI)

School
Lou & Peter Berryman; *Cupid's Trash Truck* .... (COR)
Nirvana; *Bleach* ....(SP)
Supertramp; *Crime Of The Century* .... (A&M)
   Live In Paris .... (A&M)
School Boy Crush
Average White Band; *Cut The Cake* .... (ATL)
   Person To Person .... (ATL)
School Boy Romance
Danny/Juniors; *Rockin' With* .... (MSP)
School Days
Chuck Berry; *Best Of* .... (GUS)
   Billboard Top Rock 'N' Roll Hits-1957 .... (RHI)
   Golden Hits .... (MER)
   ST/Rock 'N' Roll High School .... (SIR)
Louis Jordan; *Best Of* .... (MCA)
School Is In
Gary U.S. Bonds; *School Of Rock 'N' Roll-Best Of* (RHI)
School Is Out
Gary U.S. Bonds; *School Of Rock 'N' Roll-Best Of* (RHI)
School's Out
Alice Cooper; *Alice Cooper Show* .... (WB)
   Greatest Hits .... (WB)
   School's Out .... (WB)
   ST/Rock 'N' Roll High School .... (SIR)
Krokus; *First Degree Metal* .... (PRY)
   Stayed Awake All Night-Best Of .... (ARI)
See You In September
Chiffons; *Best Of* ....(LAU)
Happenings; *ST/Purple People Eater* .... (AJK)
Tempos; *Cruisin'-1960* ....(INC)
   ST/American Graffiti .... (MCA)
Sexy + 17
Stray Cats; *Best Of-Rock This Town* .... (EMI)
   Rant 'N' Rave With The Stray Cats .... (EMI)
Show Her
Ronnie Milsap; *Collector's Series* .... (RCA)
   Greatest Hits-#2 ....(RCA)
   Keyed Up ....(RCA)
Show Me
Cover Girls; *Dance Club Beat* .... (KT)
Del Shannon; *Greatest Hits* .... (RHI)
   Liberty Years .... (EMI)
Dells; *There Is* ....(CSS)
Howard Hewett; *Howard Hewett* .... (ELE)
Howard Jones; *In The Running* .... (ELE)
Joe Tex; *Best Of* .... (ATL)
   Commitments-Orig. Artists Recordings ....(ATC)
Original Cast; *My Fair Lady* ....(COL)
Percy Faith; *16 Most Requested Songs* ....(COL)
   All-Time Greatest hits ....(COL)
Pretenders; *Learning To Crawl* .... (SIR)
   Singles .... (SIR)
Seal; *Seal* .... (SIR)
Stacy Earl; *Stacy Earl* ....(RCA)
Show Me The Way
Peter Frampton; *Classics-#12* .... (A&M)
   Frampton Comes Alive .... (A&M)
   '70s Greatest Rock Hits-#8-Super Songs .... (PRY)
Regina Belle; *All By Myself* ....(COL)
Storm; *Storm* ....(ISC)
Styx; *Edge Of The Century* .... (A&M)
Sing U.C.L.A.
University Of Michigan Band; *Greatest College Football Marches* .... (VAN)
Some Fools Never Learn
Steve Wariner; *Greatest Hits* .... (MCA)
   One Good Night Deserves Another .... (MCA)
Sons Of California
University Of California Marching Band; *University Of California Marching Band* ....(FID)
Straight A's In Love
Johnny Cash; *King Of Country Music* .... (SUN)
   Original Golden Hits-#3 .... (SUN)
   Sun Story .... (RHI)
Student Demonstration Time
Beach Boys; *Surf's Up* ....(CAR)
Sunday School To Broadway
Sammi Smith; *45* .... (ELE)
Swingin' On The Campus
Duke Ellington & Jimmy Hodges/Orchestra; *Duke's Men-Small Groups-#2* ....(COL)
Take Care Of Your Homework
Johnnie Taylor; *Super Hits* .... (STX)

Teach Me How To Shimmy
Calamities; *Calamities* .... (PBO)
Teach Me Tonight
Al Jarreau; *Breakin' Away* .... (WB)
   Live In London .... (WB)
Diane Schuur; *Collection* .... (GRP)
Ella Fitzgerald; *Montreux '75* .... (PAB)
Phoebe Snow; *Best Of* .... (COL)
   It Looks Like Snow .... (COL)
Sarah Vaughan; *How Long Has This Been Going
On?* .... (PAB)
Teach Me (The "Philly" Dog)
Manhattans; *Dedicated To You-Golden
Classics-#1* .... (CLT)
Teach The Gifted Children
Lou Reed; *Between Thought &
Expression-Anthology* ....(RCA)
Teach Them To Pray
Junior Walker/All-Stars; *Motown Superstar
Series-#5* .... (MOT)
Teach Your Children
Crosby, Stills & Nash; *Crosby, Stills & Nash
(collection)* .... (ATL)
Crosby, Stills, Nash & Young; *Deja Vu* .... (ATL)
   Four-Way Street .... (ATL)
   So Far .... (ATL)
   ST/Wonder Years-Music From Show & Era ..... (ATL)
Suzy Bogguss/Alison Krauss/Kathy Mattea; *w/Crosby
Stills & Nash-Red Hot + Country* .... (MER)
Teacher
Jethro Tull; *20 Years Of-Radio Archives & Rare
Tracks* .... (CHR)
   Benefit .... (CHR)
   Living In The Past .... (CHR)
   "M.U."-Best Of .... (CHR)
Teacher I Need You
Elton John; *Don't Shoot Me I'm Only The Piano
Player* .... (POL)
Teacher Teacher
38 Special; *Flashback-Best Of* .... (A&M)
   ST/Teachers .... (CAP)
Johny Mathis; *More Greatest Hits* .... (COL)
Rockpile; *Seconds Of Pleasure* .... (COL)
Teacher (African Teacher)
Burning Spear; *Living Dub-#2* .... (HRT)
Teacher's Pet
Doris Day; *Greatest Hits* .... (COL)
Extreme; *Extreme* .... (A&M)
Teachin' The Blues
John Lee Hooker; *That's Where It's At* .... (STX)
   Ultimate Collection-1948-1990 .... (RHI)
Tippin' Home From Sunday School
Oliver Jones; *Class Act* .... (JUS)
To Sir With Love
Lulu; *History Of British Rock-#6* .... (RHI)
   Hollywood Magic-1960s .... (COL)
   Rock Artifacts-#3-From The Vaults .... (COL)
Train Wreck On Prom Night
Pajama Slave Dancers; *Blood Sweat & Beers* ..... (RES)
T.C.U. Fight Song
Southern Methodist Mustang Band; *Southwest
Conference Jazz* .... (FID)
U.N.M. Fight Song
University of New Mexico Lobos Pep Band; *University
Of New Mexico Lobos Pep Band* .... (FID)
Vacation Bible School
Ray Stevens; *Everything Is Beautiful* .... (MSP)
   I Have Returned .... (MCA)
Varsity Drag
Jonathan & Darlene Edwards; *Songs For Shieks &
Flappers* .... (CRN)
Les Elgart; *Best Of The Big Bands-#2* .... (COL)
Waitin' In School
Rick Nelson; *Legendary Masters* .... (EMI)
   Legends Of Rock Guitar-'50s-#2 .... (RHI)
Welcome Back
John Sebastian; *Best Of* .... (RHI)
Original Music; *Television's Greatest Hits-#3* ... (TVT)
(What A) Wonderful World
Art Garfunkel; *Watermark* .... (COL)
Sam Cooke; *Best Of* .... (RCA)
   ST/Animal House .... (MCA)
   This Is .... (RCA)

Whiffenpoof Song
Bing Crosby/Fred Waring & His Glee Club; *Bing
Crosby's Greatest Hits* .... (MCA)
Count Basie & Mills Brothers; *16 Great
Performances* .... (MCA)
Louis Armstrong; *Best Of* .... (MCA)
Mitch Miller; *34 All-Time Great Sing-Along
Selections* .... (COL)
Statler Brothers; *World Of The* .... (COL)
Words By Heart
Billy Ray Cyrus; *It Won't Be The Last* .... (MER)
Working Man's Ph.D.
Aaron Tippin; *Call Of The Wild* .... (RCA)
Yale Boola
All-Star Inter-Conference Band; *College Marches At
Half-Time* .... (ALS)
You've Got To Be Carefully Taught
Original Cast; *South Pacific* .... (SMC)

SEARCH, Looking For...
See Also: EYES, FINDING, SEEING

Around The World (In 80 Days)
Boston Pops Orchestra/Arthur Fiedler; *Greatest
Hits/'50s-#2* ....(RCA)
Frank Sinatra; *Come Fly With Me* ....(CAP)
Roger Williams; *Greatest Hits* .... (MCA)
Blue Sky Mine
Midnight Oil; *Blue Sky Mining* ....(COL)
Don't Look Any Further
Dennis Edwards & Siedah Garrett; *Don't Look Any
Further* .... (MOT)
Five Foot Two, Eyes Of Blue
Mom & Dads; *Very Best Of* .... (CRS)
Good Lovin's Hard To Find
Lynyrd Skynyrd; *Last Rebel* .... (ATL)
Heart Of Gold
Neil Young; *Decade* .... (RPR)
   Harvest .... (RPR)
Heart Of Saturday Night (Looking For...)
Shawn Colvin; *Cover Girl* .... (COL)
Tom Waits; *Anthology* .... (ASY)
   Heart Of Saturday Night (Looking For...) .... (ASY)
Hello
Luther Vandross; *Songs* .... (EPI)
Hey, Look Me Over
Jo Basile; *Hit Broadway Musicals* ....(AUF)
Judy Garland; *Live* ....(CAP)
He's A Heartache (Looking For A Place..)
Janie Fricke; *17 Greatest Hits* ....(COL)
   19 Hot Country Requests .... (EPI)
   It Ain't Easy ....(COL)
   Very Best Of ....(COL)
Hide & Go Seek
Joe Turner; *Rock This Joint* .... (INT)
Hide & Seek
Bill Haley/Comets; *Golden Hits* .... (MCA)
Chuck Mangione; *Evening Of Magic* .... (A&M)
   Feels So Good .... (A&M)
Howard Jones; *Action Replay* .... (ELE)
   Human's Lib .... (ELE)
Spencer Davis Group; *Greatest & Latest* .... (PRY)
I Still Haven't Found What I'm...
U2; *Joshua Tree* .... (ISL)
   ST/Rattle & Hum .... (ISL)
It Ain't Me Babe
Bob Dylan; *Another Side Of* ....(COL)
   Before The Flood ....(COL)
   Biograph ....(COL)
   Greatest Hits ....(COL)
   Real Live ....(COL)
Johnny Cash; *Greatest Hits* .... (COL)
Turtles; *Best Of* .... (RHI)
   Cruisin' 1965 .... (INC)
   Greatest Hits .... (RHI)
   Oldies But Goodies-#4 .... (OSR)
   Super Oldies/'60s-#4 ....(AUF)
I'm That Kind Of Girl
Patty Loveless; *Greatest Hits* .... (MCA)
   On Down The Line .... (MCA)

Just One Look
Doris Troy; *Atlantic Soul Classics* .... (WSP)
   Soul Sixties .... (JCI)
   ST/Mermaids .... (GEF)
Hollies; *All-Time Greatest Hits* .... (CCB)
   Best Of-#1 .... (EMI)
   Greatest Hits .... (EPI)
Linda Ronstadt; *Greatest Hits-#2* .... (ELE)
   Living In The U.S.A. .... (ASY)
Look At Us
Vince Gill; *Pocket Full Of Gold* .... (MCA)
Look For The Silver Lining
Alberta Hunter; *Look For The Silver Lining* .....(COL)
Chet Baker; *Let's Get Lost-Best Of Chet Baker*
Sings .... (PJZ)
Dave Brubeck Quartet; *Stardust* .... (FAN)
Look Into The Sun
Jethro Tull; *Stand Up* .... (CHR)
Look To The Rainbow
Al Jarreau; *Look To The Rainbow-Live In Europe* . (WB)
Aretha Franklin; *Aretha* .... (ARI)
Original Cast; *Finian's Rainbow* ....(COL)
Looking At The Front Door
Main Source; *Breaking Atoms* .... (EMI)
   Nasty Wax .... (KT)
Looking For A Boy
Eileen Farrell; *I Gotta Right To Sing The Blues* .. (SMC)
Sarah Vaughan; *George Gershwin Songbook-#1* . (EMA)
Looking For A Corner
Rosanne Cash; *Somewhere In The Stars* ....(COL)
Looking For A Feeling
Waylon Jennings & Willie Nelson; *Waylon &
Willie* .... (RCA)
Looking For A Good Sign
Daryl Hall & John Oates; *Private Eyes* ....(RCA)
Looking For A Love
Bobby Womack; *Greatest Hits* .... (LIB)
   Soul Survivor .... (EMI)
J. Geils Band; *Best Of* .... (ATL)
   Full House .... (ATL)
   Morning After .... (ATL)
Looking For A Lover
Neil Young; *Zuma* .... (RPR)
Looking For A New Love
Jody Watley; *Do You Wanna Dance With Me?* .. (MCA)
   Jody Watley .... (MCA)
Looking For A Reason
Creedence Clearwater Revival; *Chronicle-#2* .... (FAN)
   Creedence Country .... (FAN)
   Mardi Gras .... (FAN)
Looking For A Stranger
Pat Benatar; *Get Nervous* .... (CHR)
   Live From Earth .... (CHR)
Looking For A U.F.O.
Adrian Belew; *Young Lions* .... (ATL)
Looking For Another Pure Love
Stevie Wonder; *Talking Book* .... (MOT)
Looking For Mary Jane
Charlie Daniels Band; *Whiskey* .... (EPI)
Looking For Space
John Denver; *Greatest Hits-#2* .... (RCA)
   Windsong ....(RCA)
Looking For Suzanne
Waylon Jennings; *Greatest Hits-#2* .... (RCA)
Looking For The Right One
Art Garfunkel; *Breakaway* ....(COL)
Stephen Bishop; *Best Of Bish* .... (RHI)
   Bish .... (MCA)
Looking Through Patient Eyes
PM Dawn; *Bliss Album...?* .... (GEE)
Lookin' For Love
Babys; *Babys* .... (CHR)
Johnny Lee; *Country Love Songs* .... (WB)
   Greatest Hits .... (FM)
   ST/Urban Cowboy .... (ASY)
Lover Man (Oh Where Can You Be)
Barbra Streisand; *Simply Streisand* ....(COL)
Billie Holiday; *Fine & Mellow* .... (CLT)
   History Of The Real .... (VRV)
Blossom Dearie; *Blossom Dearie* ....(VRV)
Lena Horne; *Goes Latin & Sings Your Requests* .. (DRG)
Sarah Vaughan; *Compact Jazz* ....(VRV)
   Jazz 'Round Midnight ....(VRV)
Sonny Stitt; *Soul Classics* .... (PRS)

No More Looking Back
Kinks; *Schoolboys In Disgrace* .... (RHI)
   Second Time Around ....(RCA)
One Good Man
Michelle Wright; *The Reasons Why* .... (ARI)
One Of These Nights
Eagles; *Anthology* .... (ASY)
   One Of These Nights .... (ASY)
   Their Greatest Hits 1971-1975 .... (ASY)
Peace & Understanding Is Hard To Find
Junior Walker/All-Stars; *Anthology* .... (MOT)
   Motown Superstar Series-#5 .... (MOT)
Pleasure Seekers
System; *System* .... (MIR)
River Of Dreams
Billy Joel; *River Of Dreams* ....(COL)
Search Find
Bee Gees; *Spirits Having Flown* .... (RSO)
Search Is Over
Survivor; *Greatest Hits* ....(SCO)
   Vital Signs ....(SCO)
Search On
Aretha Franklin; *Love All The Hurt Away* .... (ARI)
Search & Destroy
Deadly Blessing; *Ascend From The Cauldron* ... (NEW)
Dictators; *10 Roir Years-Anthology* .... (ROI)
   Live-F..k 'Em If They Can't Take A Joke .... (ROI)
   Manifest Destiny .... (ASY)
Iggy/Stooges; *Raw Power* ....(COL)
Overlords; *Organic?* ....(AS)
Searching
Change/Luther Vandross; *Glow Of Love* ....(WB)
Hollies; *Greatest* ....(CAP)
Luther Vandross; *Best Of...Best Of Love* .... (EPI)
Lynyrd Skynyrd; *Gimme Back My Bullets* .... (MCA)
   One More From The Road .... (MCA)
Neil Sedaka; *Come See About Me* .... (MCA)
Searching For A Rainbow
Chris LeDoux; *& The Saddle Boogie Band* .... (LIB)
Searching For Lambs
June Tabor; *Aqaba* .... (SHA)
Peter Bellamy; *Peter Bellamy* ....(GRE)
Searching For Madge
Fleetwood Mac; *Then Play On* .... (RPR)
Searching For My Love
Bobby Moore/Rhythm Aces; *Best Of Chess Rhythm &
Blues* .... (CSS)
   Soul Shots-Collection Of '60s Soul-#2 .... (RHI)
   Soul Shots-#10-More Sweet Soul .... (RHI)
Huey Lewis/News; *Four Chords & Several Years
Ago* .... (ELE)
Searching For Someone Like You
Kitty Wells; *Greatest Hits* .... (MCA)
   Story .... (MCA)
Searching For You
Jamies; *45* .... (EPI)
Rhythm Tribe; *Sol Moderno* .... (ZOO)
Searching So Long
Chicago; *Greatest Hits* ....(COL)
   Group Portrait ....(COL)
   If You Leave Me Now ....(COL)
   VII ....(COL)
Searching With My Good Eye Closed
Soundgarden; *Badmotorfinger* .... (A&M)
Searchin'
Blackfoot; *Marauder* .... (ATC)
Coasters; *All-Star Chartbusters* .... (INT)
   Golden Years-1957 ....(DOM)
   Greatest Hits .... (ATC)
   Oldies But Goodies-#8 .... (OSR)
Santana; *Zebop* ....(COL)
Spencer Davis Group; *Best Of* .... (EMI)
   Best Of .... (RHI)
Will To Power; *Will To Power* .... (EPI)
Searchin' For A Rainbow
Marshall Tucker Band; *Searchin' For A Rainbow* (AJK)
Searchin' For Celine
Blue Oyster Cult; *Spectres* ....(COL)
Searchlight
John Fogerty; *Centerfield* .... (WB)
She Came From Fort Worth
Kathy Mattea; *Willow In The Wind* .... (MER)
Pat Alger & Kathy Mattea; *True Love & Other Short
Stories* .... (SH)

The Green Book Of Songs By Subject — Page 533

She Don't Look Back
Dan Fogelberg; *Exiles* .... (FM)
Something In Red
Lorrie Morgan; *Something In Red* ....(RCA)
Soul Searcher
Joe Lynn Turner; *Rescue You* .... (ELE)
Soul Searchin'
Glenn Frey; *Soul Searchin'* .... (MCA)
Leon Everette; *45* ....(RCA)
Stop, Look & Listen
Chiffons; *Best Of* ....(LAU)
Donna Summer; *She Works Hard For The Money* (MER)
Summer Collection .... (MER)
Dorsey Brothers; *1934-35 Decca Sessions* .... (MCA)
Complete Tommy Dorsey-#4 ....(RCA)
Elvis Presley; *Collector's Gold* ....(RCA)
Patsy Cline; *Loved & Lost Again* .... (FFT)
Rockin' Side-Her First Recordings-#3 .... (RHI)
Stop, Look & Listen ....(ALL)
Try Again ....(QKS)
Stop, Look & Listen To Your Heart
Johnny Mathis; *I'm Coming Home* ....(COL)
Love Songs ....(COL)
Marvin Gaye & Diana Ross; *Diana & Marvin* .. (MOT)
Patti Austin; *Every Home Should Have One* ..... (QUE)
Stylistics; *45* ....(AMH)
Take Me As I Am
Faith Hill; *Take Me As I Am* .... (WB)
They'll All Out Of Liquor, Let's Find...
Waitresses; *Best Of* ....(POL)
Want Ads
Honey Cone; *Greatest Hits* .... (HDH)
We Hide & Seek
Jerry Douglas; *Slide Rule* .... (SH)

SEASONS: AUTUMN

See Also: MONTHS & DATES: SEPTEMBER,
OCTOBER, NOVEMBER

And Then Comes September
Doris Day; *Duet* .... (DRG)
Sacha Distel; *Amour Tout Court* .... (DRG)
August & September
The The; *Mind Bomb* .... (EPI)
Autumn
Barbra Streisand; *People* ....(COL)
Edgar Winter; *They All Come Out At Night* .... (EPI)
Strawbs; *Hero & Heroine* .... (A&M)
Autumn Almanac
Kinks; *Kink Kronikles* .... (RPR)
Autumn Changes
Donna Summer; *Four Seasons Of Love* .... (CAS)
Autumn In London Town
Norrie Paramor; *Autumn* .... (ANG)
Autumn In New York
Frank Sinatra; *Capitol Years* .... (CAP)
Come Fly With Me .... (CAP)
Main Event .... (SIN)
Round #1 .... (CAP)
Sarah Vaughan; *Complete-On*
Mercury-#2-1956-1957 .... (MER)
Golden Hits .... (MER)
Autumn Leaves
Barbra Streisand; *Je M'Appele Barbra* ....(COL)
Frank Sinatra; *Night We Called It A Day* ....(CAP)
Grace Jones; *Fame* ....(ISL)
Nat King Cole; *Blossom Fell* ....(CAP)
Roger Miller; *Music Of The 1950s* .... (MCA)
Roger Williams; *Best Of* .... (MCA)
Golden Hits-#2 .... (MCA)
Autumn Nocturne
Sonny Rollins; *Don't Stop The Carnival* .... (MS)
Autumn Of My Life
Bobby Goldsboro; *10th Anniversary Album* .... (UA)
Greatest Hits .... (UA)
Autumn Sea
Robyn Hitchcock/Egyptians; *Queen Elvis* .... (A&M)
Autumn Song
Mose Allison; *Ol' Devil Mose* .... (PRS)
Van Morrison; *Hard Nose The Highway* .... (WB)
Autumn Suite
Strawbs; *Best Of* ....(A&M)

Autumn To May
Peter, Paul & Mary; *Peter, Paul & Mary* .... (WB)
Autumn's Not That Cold
Lorrie Morgan; *Something In Red* ....(RCA)
Skip Ewing; *Coast Of Colorado* .... (MCA)
Black Autumn
Charlie Daniels Band; *Te John Grease & Wolfman* (EPI)
Blue Autumn
Bobby Goldsboro; *10th Anniversary Album* .... (UA)
Greatest Hits .... (UA)
Honey-Best Of .... (EMI)
Bluegrass Autumn
Bottle Hill; *Light Our Way Along The Highway-#2* (BIO)
Cheyenne Autumn
Kansas; *Leftoverture* .... (KIR)
Chill Of An Early Fall
George Strait; *Chill Of An Early Fall* .... (MCA)
Cold November
John O'Connor; *Songs For Our Times* ....(FF)
Cool Change
Little River Band; *First Under The Wire* ....(CAP)
Greatest Hits .... (CAP)
Days Of Autumn Gold
Hank Locklin; *There Never Was A Time* .... (PLN)
Death In The Autumn Air
Michael McDermott; *620 W. Surf* .... (GIA)
Early Autumn
Cleo Laine & John Dankworth Orchestra; *Jazz*
Master .... (DRG)
Mel Torme; *Night At The Concord Pavilion* ...... (CCJ)
Stan Getz; *Essential-Getz Songbook* ....(VRV)
Woody Herman & Stan Getz; *Early Autumn* ..... (BLU)
Woody Herman/Orchestra; *Best Of* ....(CCB)
Evidence Of Autumn
Genesis; *Three Sides Live* .... (ATL)
Fall Breaks & Back To Winter
Beach Boys; *Smiley Smile/Wild Honey* ....(CAP)
Fall In Philadelphia
Daryl Hall & John Oates; *Whole Oats* .... (ATL)
Forever Autumn
Justin Hayward; *War Of The Worlds* ....(COL)
Grey October Clouds
Tommy Makem & Liam Clancy; *Two For The Early*
Dew ....(SHA)
In The Autumn
Bob Marsh; *The Forest* ....(DAL)
Indian Summer
Doors; *Morrison Hotel* .... (ELE)
Ella Fitzgerald; *Newport Jazz Fesitval* ....(COL)
Frank Sinatra; *Reprise Collection* .... (RPR)
Glenn Miller; *Memorial 1944-1969* ....(RCA)
Joe Walsh; *But Seriously Folks* ....(ASY)
Poco; *Indian Summer* .... (MCA)
Roy Orbison/Gatlin Brothers; *Legendary Roy*
Orbison ....(SSP)
Stan Getz; *Greatest Hits* .... (PRS)
Indian Summer Love
Con Funk Shun; *Secrets* .... (MER)
It Might As Well Rain Until September
Carole King; *More American Graffiti* .... (MCA)
Land Of A Thousand Autumns
Steve Hackett; *Please Don't Touch* .... (CHR)
Maybe September
Tony Bennett; *Forty Years-Artistry Of* ....(COL)
Movie Song Album ....(COL)
Moondance
Van Morrison; *Best Of* .... (MER)
Moondance .... (WB)
My Autumn Love
Frank Chacksfield; *Unmistakable* .... (RIM)
November
Anthony Phillips; *Private Parts & Pieces V Twelve* (PVC)
Chyld; *Chyld* ....(NEW)
Paul Greaver; *Joy* ....(GLO)
November 22, 1963
Original Cast; *Assassins* ....(RCA)
November 68th
Chick Corea; *CTI Masters Of The Keyboard* .....(CBA)
Joe Farrell; *Outback* ....(CTI)
November Afternoon
Dizzy Gillespie; *Composer's Concepts* .... (EMA)
James Moody; *Moving Forward* .... (NOV)
Paul Christopher; *Lavender* .... (ARY)

November Cotillion
Country Cooking; *Barrel Of Fun* .... (ROU)
November Day
Rob Mullins; *Nite Street* .... (RMC)
November Days
Origin; *Origin* .... (VIA)
November Girl
Carmen McRae; *November Girl* .... (JAZ)
November In The Snow/Lord Buckley
Mark Murphy; *Kerouac Then & Now* .... (MUS)
November Nights
Flim/BB's; *Tunnel* .... (DIG)
November Rain
Guns N' Roses; *Use Your Illusion I* .... (GEF)
November Song
Didier Lockwood; *Out Of The Blue* .... (GRM)
Norrie Paramor; *Autumn* .... (ANG)
November Spawned A Monster
Morrissey; *Bona Drag* .... (SIR)
  Just Say Da-#4 Of Just Say Yes .... (SIR)
November Winds
Friedemann; *Indian Summer* .... (NAR)
  Narada Equinox Sampler One .... (NAR)
Novembering
Claudia Schmidt; *Big Earful* .... (RDH)
November's Eve
Tim Story; *Untitled* .... (LLA)
October
Anthony Phillips; *Private Parts & Pieces V-Twelve* (PVC)
A-Ha; *Scoundrel Days* .... (WB)
Borghesia; *Resistance* .... (PIA)
Danny Wright; *Phantasys* ....(MD)
Larry McNeely; *Power Play* ....(FF)
Leif Strand; *The Year* .... (INN)
Paul Desmond; *From The Hot Afternoon* ...... (A&M)
Terry Garland; *Edge Of The Valley* .... (FIR)
U2; *October* .... (ISL)
Warren Bernhardt; *Hands On* .... (DIG)
October 17, 1988
Keith Jarrett; *Paris Concert* .... (ECM)
October 7
Mitch Watkins; *Strings With Wings* .... (ENJ)
October Anywhere
Giant Sand; *Valley Of Rain* .... (ENI)
October Ballad
Chick Corea; *Griffith Park-#2: The Concert* .... (ELE)
October Country
October Country; *Nuggets #3-Pop* .... (RHI)
October Fool
Charlie Shoemaker & Bill Holman; *Collaboration* (PAU)
October Impressions (No. 38)
Mark O'Connor; *Elysian Forest* .... (WB)
October In September
John Nilsen; *October In September* .... (MW)
October Morning
Fourplay; *Fourplay* .... (WB)
October Night
Cliff Sarde; *Every Bit Better/Waiting* .... (MCA)
  Waiting .... (MCA)
October Nights
Stone Soup; *October Nights* .... (WCH)
October Roses
Linda Allen; *October Roses* .... (NX)
October Sigh
Phil Sheeran; *Breaking Through* ....(SA)
October Song
Pat Kilbride; *Rock & More Roses* .... (TEM)
October Sunshine
First Brass; *First Brass* ....(MA)
  Jazz Horizons-Best Of M-A Music-#1 ....(MA)
October Thorns
Flotsam & Jetsam; *When The Storm Comes
Down* .... (MCA)
October Wedding
Montreux; *Let Them Say* ....(WH)
  Montreux-Windham Hill Retrospective ....(WH)
October Winds
Bela Fleck; *Natural Bridge* .... (ROU)
October & The Frost Is Early
Dusing Singers; *Cool Of The Day-Music Of Jean
Ritchie* .... (GHY)
October-Love Song
Chris & Cosey; *Funky Alternatives-18 Techno
Remixes* .... (ROI)

October's Child
Elvin Jones; *Brother John* .... (PAJ)
Reach, The
Dan Fogelberg; *Innocent Age* .... (FM)
Rocky Mountain September
C.W. McCall; *45* ....(OOP)
See You In September
Chiffons; *Best Of* ....(LAU)
Happenings; *ST/Purple People Eater* .... (AJK)
Tempos; *Cruisin'-1960* .... (INC)
  ST/American Graffiti .... (MCA)
September
Anthony Phillips; *Private Parts & Pieces V Twelve* (PVC)
David Sylvian; *Secrets Of The Beehive* ...... (VIA)
Earth, Wind & Fire; *Best Of-#1* ....(COL)
  Eternal Dance ....(COL)
  Mega Hits Dance Classics-#7 ....(PRY)
Michael Urbaniak; *Folk Songs-Children's
Melodies-Jazz...* .... (AND)
Nashville Rhythm Section; *Keep On Dancing* .... (KOA)
T Lavitz/Bad Habitz; *T Lavitz/Bad Habitz* .... (IMA)
Vladislav Sendecki; *Men From Wilnau* .... (AND)
September 13
Deodato; *Live At The Felt Forum-2001 Concert* ..(CBA)
  Prelude ....(CBA)
September 1979
Bill Barron; *Variations In Blue* .... (MUS)
September Blue
Chris Rea; *Dancing With The Strangers* .... (MOT)
September Fifteenth
Mark Murphy; *September Ballads* .... (MS)
Pat Metheny & Lyle Mays; *As Falls Wichita So Falls
Wichita Falls* .... (ECM)
September Girls
Bangles; *Different Light* ....(COL)
Big Star; *Live* .... (RYK)
September In The Rain
Chad & Jeremy; *Capitol Gold-Best Of* .... (CAP)
  Soft Sound Of .... (KT)
Dinah Washington; *Golden Hits* .... (MER)
  This Is My Story .... (MER)
Doris Day; *Sings 22 Great Songs On Orig. Big
Band* .... (HIN)
Duprees; *Best Of* .... (RHI)
Frank Sinatra; *Round #1* .... (CAP)
  Swingin' Session (& More) .... (CAP)
Joe Williams; *Swingin'...At Birdland* .... (RLL)
Marty Robbins; *Essential-1951-1982* ....(COL)
Peggy Lee; *You Can Depend On Me* .... (GLN)
September Love
Kool/Gang; *In The Heart* .... (DL)
September Morn
Mark Masters Jazz Composer Orchestra; *Early
Start* .... (SEA)
Neil Diamond; *12 Greatest Hits-#2* ....(COL)
  Hot August Night II ....(COL)
  September Morn ....(COL)
September Night
Van Morrison; *Inarticulate Speech Of The Heart* ..(WB)
September Of My Years
Frank Sinatra; *A Man & His Music* .... (RPR)
  At The Sands .... (RPR)
  Greatest Hits-#2 .... (RPR)
  September Of My Years .... (RPR)
  Sings The Songs Of Van Heusen & Cahn .... (RPR)
September Rain
Full Swing; *Full Swing* ....(CYP)
George Howard; *Love Will Follow* .... (GRP)
September Song
Boston Pops Orchestra/Arthur Fiedler; *Greatest Hits Of
The '30s* .... (RCA)
  Mister Music U.S.A. ....(DGG)
  Music For Every Mood-Yesterday .... (RCA)
Eddy Duchin & Stanley Worth; *Best Of The Big
Bands* .... (COL)
Eydie Gorme; *Best Of* .... (CCB)
Flamingos/Moonglows; *On The Dusty Road Of Hits* (VJ)
Frank Sinatra; *Greatest Hits-#2* ....(COL)
  Point Of No Return .... (CAP)
  September Of My Years .... (RPR)
Jeff Lynne; *Armchair Theatre* .... (RPR)
Kate Wolf; *Safe At Anchor* .... (KAL)
Lindsey Buckingham; *Law & Order* .... (WB)
Lou Reed; *Lost In The Stars-Music Of Kurt Weill* (A&M)

Roger Williams; *Greatest Hits* .... (MCA)
Roy Clark; *Best Of* .... (MCA)
Sarah Vaughan & Clifford Brown; *Sarah Vaughan &*
Clifford Brown .... (EMA)
Stan Kenton; *Comprehensive* .... (CAP)
Retrospective-Capitol Years .... (BLN)
Tony Bennett; *Forty Years-Artistry Of* .... (COL)
Willie Nelson; *Stardust* .... (COL)
Shine On Harvest Moon
Dorsey Brothers; *I'm Getting Sentimental Over*
You .... (POE)
Jimmy Dorsey; *22 Original Big Band Recordings* . (HIN)
Leon Redbone; *Double Time* .... (WB)
Mitch Miller; *16 Most Requested Songs* .... (COL)
Summer Song (In The Autumn)
Peter Hammill; *Fools Mate* .... (BP)
Time Passed Autumn
Claus Ogerman Orchestra; *Gate Of Dreams* ...... (WB)
'Tis Autumn
Ella Fitzgerald & Joe Pass; *Again* .... (PAB)
Two Shades Of Autumn
Stan Kenton; *Rendezvous With* .... (CW)
Vermont Is Afire In The Autumn
Lui Collins; *Made In New England* .... (GRE)
When Autumn Comes
Bill Evans; *Tokyo Concert* .... (FAN)
When October Goes
Barry Manilow; *2 AM Paradise Cafe* .... (ARI)
Rosemary Clooney; *Sings The Lyrics Of Johnny*
Mercer .... (CCJ)
When The Golden Leaves Begin To Fall
Joe Val/New England Bluegrass Boys; *#2* ...... (ROU)
When The Work's All Done This Fall
Doc Watson; *On Stage (Featuring Merle Watson)* (VAN)
Michael Martin Murphey; *Cowboy SOngs* .... (WW)
Wreck Of The Edmund Fitzgerald
Gordon Lightfoot; *Gord's Gold-#2* .... (WB)
Summertime Dream .... (RPR)

SEASONS: GENERAL

See Also: Other Seasons, MONTHS & DATES

All Season
LeVert; *Rope A Dope Style* .... (ATL)
As The Seasons Grey
Testament; *The Ritual* .... (ATL)
End Of The Seasons
Kinks; *Something Else* .... (RPR)
Man For All Seasons
Al Stewart; *Time Passages* .... (ARI)
Billy Idol; *Whiplash Smile* .... (CHR)
Pumpkin Season
Dave Maloney; *Harvest Is In* .... (FOL)
Rain Song
Led Zeppelin; *Houses Of The Holy* .... (ATL)
Remasters .... (ATL)
Led Zeppelin (collection) .... (ATL)
ST/Song Remains The Same .... (SS)
Season In Hell (Fire Suite)
John Cafferty/Beaver Brown Band; *ST/Eddie & The*
Cruisers .... (SCO)
Season Of Hollow Soul
k.d. lang; *Ingenue* .... (WB)
Season Of The Witch
Donovan; *American Graffiti-#4* .... (MCA)
Greatest Hits .... (EPI)
Sunshine Superman .... (EPI)
Troubadour-Definitive Collection .... (EPI)
Vanilla Fudge; *Best Of* .... (ATC)
Season Suite
John Denver; *Rocky Mountain High* .... (RCA)
Seasons
America; *Hearts* .... (WB)
Dave Mason; *Let It Flow* .... (COL)
Lynyrd Skynyrd; *First & Last* .... (MCA)
Oak Ridge Boys; *Seasons* .... (MCA)
Sarah Vaughan; *Crazy & Mixed Up* .... (PAB)
Steve Miller Band; *Anthology* .... (CAP)
Best Of-1968-1973 .... (CAP)
Brave New World .... (CAP)
Stevie Wonder; *Journey...Secret Life Of Plants* ... (MOT)
UB40; *Geffery Morgan* .... (A&M)

Seasons Change
Expose; *Exposure* .... (ARI)
Making Love .... (PRY)
Romantic Hits!'80s .... (KT)
Michael Murphey; *Swans Against The Son* .... (EPI)
Seasons End
Marillion; *Seasons End* .... (CAP)
Seasons For Girls
Trammps; *III* .... (ATL)
Seasons In The Abyss
Slayer; *Live-Decade Of Aggression* .... (DEF)
Seasons In The Sun
Kingston Trio; *Capitol Collectors Series* .... (CAP)
Terry Jacks; *Super Hits/'70s-Have A Nice*
Day-#12 .... (RHI)
'70s Greatest Rock Hits-#9-#1 Hits .... (PRY)
Seasons Of My Heart
Buck Owens; *45* .... (WB)
Jerry Lee Lewis; *Golden Cream Of* .... (SUN)
Johnny Cash; *Columbia Records-1958-1968* ..... (COL)
Seasons Of The Heart
George Jones; *20 Golden Pieces Of* .... (BLD)
John Denver; *Greatest Hits-#3* .... (RCA)
Seasons Of The Heart .... (RCA)
Seasons Of Wither
Aerosmith; *Get Your Wings* .... (COL)
Pandora's Box .... (COL)
Season's No Reason To Change
Gap Band; *Gap Gold-Best Of* .... (MER)
IV .... (MER)
Song For All Seasons
Jefferson Airplane; *Volunteers* .... (RCA)
Time Of The Season
Argent; *Anthology-Collection Of Greatest Hits* ..... (EPI)
Encore .... (EPI)
ST/Awakenings .... (RPR)
Zombies; *Billboard Top Rock 'N' Roll Hits-1969* . (RHI)
Odyssey & Oracle .... (RHI)
Rock Classics-#3 .... (KT)
ST/1969 .... (POL)
To The Morning
Dan Fogelberg; *Home Free* .... (COL)
Turn! Turn! Turn!
Byrds; *Billboard Top Rock 'N' Roll Hits-1965* .... (RHI)
Greatest Hits .... (COL)
Original Singles-#1-1965-1967 .... (COL)
Byrds (collection) .... (COL)
ST/Forrest Gump .... (EPX)
Turn! Turn! Turn! .... (COL)
Pete Seeger; *Greatest Hits* .... (COL)
Troubadours Of The Folk Era-#2 .... (RHI)

SEASONS: SPRING

See Also: MONTHS & DATES: MARCH, APRIL,
MAY

23rd Of March
Gene Pitney; *Many Sides Of* .... (OOP)
After All It's Spring
Original Cast; *Seventeen* .... (RCA)
April
Brand X; *Project* .... (PAS)
Dave Mallett; *Vital Signs* .... (FF)
Sarah Vaughan; *Singles Sessions* .... (RLL)
April 2031
Warrant; *Dog Eat Dog* .... (COL)
April 24, 1981
Rick Springfield; *Success Hasn't Spoiled Me Yet* ..(RCA)
April 5th
Talk Talk; *Colour Of Spring* .... (AMR)
April Afternoon
Joan Amalbert Latin Jazz Quintet; *Hot Sauce* .... (PRS)
April Come She Will
Simon & Garfunkel; *Collected Works* .... (COL)
Concert In Central Park .... (WB)
Sounds Of Silence .... (COL)
ST/The Graduate .... (COL)
April Fool
Eric Dolphy; *Here & There* .... (PRS)
Pete Townshend & Ronnie Lane; *Rough Mix* ....(ATC)
Soul Asylum; *Grave Dancers Union* .... (COL)

April Fools
Aretha Franklin; *Young Gifted & Black* ....(MGM)
Dionne Warwick; *Anthology 1962-1971* .... (RHI)
Earl Klugh; *Living Inside Your Love* .... (EMI)
April Fool's Day Morn
Loudon Wainwright III; *Career Moves* .... (VIA)
  Fame & Wealth .... (ROU)
April Give Me One More Day
Sarah Vaughan; *Complete On
Mercury-#2-1956-1957* .... (MER)
April In Cambridge
Peter Walker; *Rainy Day Raga* .... (VAN)
April In My Heart
Billie Holiday; *Quintessential-#6-1938* ....(COL)
April In Paris
Charlie Parker; *Verve Years* .... (VRV)
  With Strings .... (VRV)
Ella Fitzgerald & Oscar Peterson; *Ella & Oscar* .. (PAB)
Frank Sinatra; *Come Fly With Me* ....(CAP)
Mel Torme; *Mel Torme* ....(GLN)
Sarah Vaughan; *Complete On Mercury-#1: Great Jazz
Years* .... (MER)
  Sarah Vaughan .... (EMA)
Wynton Marsalis; *Marsalis Standard Time-#1* ....(COL)
  Perspectives: Columbia Jazz Sampler ....(COL)
April In Portugal
Eartha Kitt; *Best Of* .... (MCA)
April Joy
Pat Metheny Group; *Pat Metheny Group* .... (ECM)
April Love
L.T.D.; *Classics-#27 (Feat. Jeffrey Osborne)* .... (A&M)
Pat Boone; *Best Of* ....(MCA)
  Greatest Hits ....(CCB)
April Mist
Tom Harrell; *Visions* .... (CTM)
April Seventh
Larry Coryell & John Scofield & Joe Beck;
  Tributaries .... (NOV)
April Showers
Al Jolson; *Best Of* .... (MCA)
  Story-#2 .... (MCA)
Judy Garland; *Hits Of* ....(CAP)
  Judy ....(CAP)
April Skies
Jesus & Mary Chain; *Darklands* .... (WB)
Wardell Gray; *Memorial-#2* .... (PRS)
April Sky
Vinnie Moore; *Time Odyssey* .... (MER)
April Snow
Hi-Lo's; *Cherries & Other Delights* .... (HIN)
Northern Lights; *Take You To The Sky* ....(FF)
April Song
John Tesh; *Monterey Nights* .... (GTS)
  The Games .... (GTS)
April Waltz
Critton Hollow; *Great Dreams* .... (FF)
April Was The Month
Chris Farlowe; *Collection* .... (SSP)
Aprilling
Lee Konitz & Gil Evans; *Heroes* ....(VRV)
April's Fool
Mark Chesnutt; *Almost Goodbye* .... (MCA)
Ray Price; *Greatest Hits-#4* .... (STE)
Tracy Lawrence; *Sticks & Stones* .... (ATL)
Blue Ridge Mountains Turnin' Green
Charley Pride; *Amazing Love* ....(RCA)
Blues For The Month Of May
Stan Getz/Others; *Tenors Anyone?* ....(BIO)
Echoes Of Spring
Willie "The Lion" Smith; *Echoes Of Spring* ..... (MLN)
Fine Spring Morning
Blossom Dearie; *Blossom Dearie* ....(VRV)
First Day Of May
James Taylor; *Never Die Young* ....(COL)
First Of May
Bee Gees; *Odessa* .... (RSO)
So; *Horseshoe In The Glove* .... (EMI)
Here Comes The Sun
Beatles; *1967-1970* ....(CAP)
  Abbey Road ....(CAP)
George Benson; *Best* ....(A&M)
  Collection .... (WB)
George Harrison; *Bangladesh* ....(CAP)
  Best Of ....(CAP)

Irish Spring
Country Gentlemen; *With Ricky Skaggs* .... (VAN)
It Might As Well Be Spring
Bing Crosby; *Radio Years-#1* .... (CRS)
Frank Sinatra; *Days Of Wine & Roses/Academy
Winners* .... (RPR)
  & Strings .... (RPR)
Sarah Vaughan; *Divine-Columbia
Years-1949-1953* ....(COL)
I'll Remember April
Cal Tjader; *Mambo With* .... (FAN)
Charlie Parker; *With Strings* ....(VRV)
Chet Baker; *Chet Baker* .... (EMA)
Cleo Laine; *Cleo's Choice* .... (CRS)
Doris Day/Frank DeVol Orchestra; *Hooray For
Hollywood-#1* ....(COL)
Erroll Garner; *Concert By The Sea* ....(COL)
Frank Sinatra; *Point Of No Return* ....(CAP)
June Christy; *#2-1957* .... (HIN)
Modern Jazz Quartet; *Concorde* .... (PRS)
  Modern Jazz Quartet .... (PRS)
Stephane Grappelli & Martin Taylor; *Just One Of Those
Things* .... (ANG)
Wynton Marsalis; *Standard Time-#2-Intimacy
Calling* ....(COL)
Late Winter, Early Spring
John Denver; *Rocky Mountain High* ....(RCA)
Lusty Month Of May
Julie Andrews; *Little Bit Of Broadway* ....(COL)
Original 1982 London Cast; *Camelot* ....(VS)
Original Cast; *Camelot* ....(COL)
March 7th
Leaving Trains; *Well Down Blue Highway* .... (ENI)
March Sky
Alex DeGrassi; *Slow Circle* ....(WH)
Night On The 4th Of May
Al Stewart; *Early Years* ....(OOP)
One Day In March I Go Down To The Sea...
Jan Garbarek Group; *It's OK To Listen To The Gray
Voice* .... (ECM)
One Morning In May
Charlie Byrd Trio; *Isn't It Romantic?* .... (CCJ)
Jean Ritchie; *Love Is Teasin'* .... (ELE)
Paris In The Spring
Michel Legrand; *Legrand Piano* ....(COL)
Peach Blossom Spring
Yutaka; *Yutaka* ....(GRP)
Prague Spring
Legendary Pink Dots; *Shadow Weaver* ....(PIA)
Promises For Spring
Tom Browne; *Browne Sugar* ....(GRP)
Rambles Of Spring
Tommy Makem & Liam Clancy; *Concert* .... (SHA)
Rite Of Spring
Hubert Laws; *Best Of* ....(CBA)
  Rite Of Spring ....(CBA)
Willie Nile; *Places I Have Never Been* ....(COL)
Santa Claus Came In The Spring
Benny Goodman; *Birth Of Swing* ....(BLU)
So Early, Early In The Spring
Judy Collins; *5th Album* .... (ELE)
  So Early, Early In The Spring .... (ELE)
Some Other Spring
Billie Holiday; *Lady Sings The Blues* ....(VRV)
  All Or Nothing At All .... (VRV)
  Greatest Hits .... (COL)
Ella Fitzgerald & Count Basie; *Perfect Match* .... (PAB)
Spring
James Brown; *Take A Look At Those Cakes* ...... (POL)
John Denver; *Rocky Mountain High* ....(RCA)
Peter Walker; *Rainy Day Raga* .... (VAN)
Tanya Tucker; *You Are So Beautiful* ....(COL)
Spring Affair
Donna Summer; *Billboard Top Dance Hits-19076* (RHI)
  Four Seasons Of Love .... (CAS)
  Live & More .... (CAS)
Spring Again
Lou Rawls; *Unmistakably Lou* .... (PI)
Spring Can Really Hang You Up The Most
Barbra Streisand; *Just For The Record* ....(COL)
Bette Midler; *Some People's Lives* ....(ATL)
Betty Carter; *Compact Jazz* ....(VRV)
Carmen McRae; *Carmen McRae* ....(MST)
Ellis Marsalis; *Heart Of Gold* ....(COL)

Rickie Lee Jones; *Pop Pop* .... (GEF)
Toots Thielemans; *East Coast West Coast* .... (PRV)
Spring Fever
Elvis Presley; *ST/Girl Happy* .... (RCA)
Loretta Lynn; *Out Of My Head & Back In Bed* . (MCA)
Nantucket; *Nantucket* .... (EPI)
Spring Is Here
Carly Simon; *Torch* .... (WB)
Ella Fitzgerald; *Rodgers & Hart Songbook* .... (VRV)
Frank Sinatra; *Sings For Only The Lonely* .... (CAP)
John Coltrane; *Standard Coltrane* .... (PRS)
Shirley Bassey; *Shirley Bassey* .... (UA)
Tony Bennett; *Rodgers & Hart Songbook* .... (DRG)
Sings 10 Rodgers-Hart Songs .... (IPV)
Spring Manifestations
Santana; *Borboletta* .... (COL)
Spring Will Be A Little Late This Year
Sarah Vaughan; *Divine-Columbia*
Years-1949-1953 .... (COL)
In Hi-Fi .... (SSP)
Spring Wind
Shawn Phillips; *Collaboration* .... (A&M)
Springtime For Hitler
Mel Brooks; *ST/High Anxiety* .... (ASY)
Springtime Magic
Lonnie Liston Smith; *Loveland* .... (COL)
Spring, Spring, Spring
Bing Crosby & Fred Astaire; *Couple Of Song & Dance*
Men .... (UA)
Michael Feinstein; *M.G.M. Album* .... (ELE)
Suddenly It's Spring
Frank Sinatra; *Now Is The Hour* .... (INT)
Phil Woods; *Altology* .... (PRS)
Their Hearts Were Full Of Spring
Beach Boys; *Concert!'69-Live In London* .... (CAP)
Good Vibrations-Thirty Years Of .... (CAP)
Smiley Smile/Wild Honey .... (CAP)
Then Came The Last Days Of May
Blue Oyster Cult; *Blue Oyster Cult* .... (COL)
On Your Feet Or On Your Knees .... (COL)
There'll Be Another Spring
Peggy Lee & George Shearing; *Beauty & The*
Beat! .... (BLN)
They Say It's Spring
Bobby Short; *Swing That Music* .... (TLR)
When It's Springtime In Alaska
Johnny Horton; *American Originals* .... (COL)
Greatest Hits .... (COL)
Winds Of March
Journey; *Infinity* .... (COL)
Younger Than Springtime
Original Cast; *South Pacific* .... (COL)

SEASONS: SUMMER

See Also: HOT; MONTHS & DATES: JUNE,
JULY, AUGUST; SUN

4th Of July
U2; *Unforgettable Fire* .... (ISL)
African Summer
Herb Alpert & Hugh Masekela; *Herb Alpert & Hugh*
Masekela .... (A&M)
All Summer Long
Beach Boys; *Absolute Best-#1* .... (CAP)
All Summer Long .... (CAP)
Endless Summer .... (CAP)
ST/American Graffiti .... (MCA)
Summer & Sun .... (RHI)
Almost Summer
Celebration/Mike Love; *ST/Celebration* .... (MCA)
August
Anthony Phillips; *Private Parts & Pieces V-Twelve* (PVC)
Lyle Mays; *Street Dreams* .... (GEF)
August 19
Ralph Simon; *Time Being* .... (GRM)
August 1967
Holy Modal Rounders; *Last Round* .... (ADE)
August Afternoon
Mulgrew Miller; *The Countdown* .... (LAN)
August Blues
Dexter Gordon; *Tangerine* .... (PRS)

August Day
Daryl Hall & John Oates; *Along The Red Ledge* ..(RCA)
August Freeze
Grace Pool; *Where We Live* .... (RPR)
August In Forest City
Carol Montag; *Song For Carrie* .... (SLK)
August Moon
Ottmar Liebert & Luna Negra; *Borrasca* .... (HO)
August Rain
Murray Attaway; *In Thrall* .... (DGC)
August Tides
Woody Simmons; *Woody Simmons* .... (DEP)
August & September
The The; *Mind Bomb* .... (EPI)
Black Day In July
Gordon Lightfoot; *Best Of* .... (EMI)
Did She Mention My Name .... (UA)
Lightfoot .... (UA)
Black Summer Rain
Eric Clapton; *No Reason To Cry* .... (RSO)
Boys Of Summer
Don Henley; *Building The Perfect Beast* .... (GEF)
British Summertime
Everything But The Girl; *Worldwide* .... (ATL)
Bus Stop
Hollies; *Best Of-#1* .... (EMI)
Greatest Hits .... (EPI)
History Of British Rock-#3 .... (RHI)
California Girls
Beach Boys; *Best Of-#2* .... (CAP)
California Girls .... (CAP)
Endless Summer .... (CAP)
In Concert .... (CAR)
'69 .... (CAP)
David Lee Roth; *Crazy From The Heat* .... (MCA)
ST/Down & Out In Beverly Hills .... (WB)
Cold Day In July
Joy White; *Between Midnight & Hindsight* ....(COL)
Ray Price; *For The Good Times/I Won't Mention*
It.. .... (COL)
Suzy Bogguss; *Voices In The Wind* .... (LIB)
Cold Summer Day In Georgia
Gene Watson; *Memories To Burn* .... (EPI)
Cold Wind In August
Van Morrison; *Period Of Transition* .... (WB)
Cruel Summer
Bananarama; *Bananarama* .... (LON)
Dancing In The Street
David Bowie & Mick Jagger; *Bowie-The*
Singles-1969-1993 .... (RYK)
Grateful Dead; *Terrapin Station* .... (ARI)
Martha Reeves/Vandellas; *20 Greatest Songs In Motown*
History .... (MOT)
Compact Command Performances .... (MOT)
Motown Story .... (MOT)
Oldies But Goodies-#14 .... (OSR)
Van Halen; *Diver Down* .... (WB)
Dream In June
Tom Harrell; *Sail Away* .... (CTM)
El Verano
Pablo Cruise; *Place In The Sun* .... (A&M)
Endless Summer Nights
Richard Marx; *Richard Marx* .... (EMI)
"Endless Summer" Theme
Sandals; *Monster Summer Hits-Wild Surf* .... (CAP)
English Summer
Eurythmics; *In The Garden* .... (RCA)
First Day In August
Carole King; *Rhymes & Reasons* .... (EOD)
First Day Of Summer
Tony Carey; *Some Tough City* .... (MCA)
ST/Secret Admirer .... (MCA)
Fourth Of July
Dave Alvin; *Romeo's Escape* .... (EPI)
Linda Waterfall; *Body English* .... (FF)
Rosalie Sorrels; *Lonesome Roving Wolves-Songs Of The*
West .... (GRE)
X; *See How We Are* .... (ELE)
Fourth Of July, Asbury Park (Sandy)
Bruce Springsteen; *Wild The Innocent & The E Street*
Shuffle .... (COL)
Bruce Springsteen/E Street Band;
Live-1975-1985 .... (COL)

Girls Of Summer
Original Cast; *Marry Me A Little* ....(RCA)
Green Leaves Of Summer
Brothers Four; *Greatest Hits* ....(COL)
Greenfields & Other Gold ....(FIR)
Hollywood Magic-1960s ....(COL)
Has Anybody Seen Amy
John & Audrey Wiggins; *John & Audrey* .... (MER)
Hello Muddah, Hello Fadduh
Allan Sherman; *Dr. Demento Greatest Novelty CD* (RHI)
Dr. Demento's Greatest-#3 ....(RHI)
Here Comes Summer
Jerry Keller; *Vintage Music-Original Classics-#14* (MCA)
Here Comes The Summer
Undertones; *All Wraped Up* ....(CAP)
Hissing Of Summer Lawns
Joni Mitchell; *Hissing Of Summer Lawns* .... (ASY)
Hot Fun In The Summertime
Sly/Family Stone; *Anthology* ....(EPI)
Billboard Top R&B Hits-1969 ....(RHI)
Greatest Hits ....(EPI)
Summer & Sun ....(RHI)
Hot Pants In The Summertime
Dramatics; *Whatcha See Is Whatcha Get* .... (STX)
Hot Summer Day
David LaFlamme; *White Bird* ....(AMH)
It's A Beautiful Day; *It's A Beautiful Day* ....(COL)
Hot Summer Nights
Miami Sound Machine; *ST/Top Gun* ....(COL)
Rick James; *Wonderful* ....(RPR)
Walter Egan; *Not Shy* ....(COL)
In The Good Old Summertime
Andrews Sisters; *45* .... (MCA)
Mom & Dads; *In The Good Old Summertime* .... (CRS)
In The Summertime
Bob Dylan; *Shot Of Love* ....(COL)
Mungo Jerry; *Super Hits/'70s-Have A Nice Day-#3* .... (RHI)
In The Summertime-Best Of .... (RHI)
(In The Summertime) You Don't Want My...
Roger Miller; *Greatest Hits* .... (SMA)
Independence Day
Martina McBride; *The Way That I Am* ....(RCA)
Indian Summer
Doors; *Morrison Hotel* .... (ELE)
Ella Fitzgerald; *Newport Jazz Festival* ....(COL)
Frank Sinatra; *Reprise Collection* ....(RPR)
Glenn Miller; *Memorial 1944-1969* ....(RCA)
Joe Walsh; *But Seriously Folks* .... (ASY)
Poco; *Indian Summer* .... (MCA)
Roy Orbison/Gatlin Brothers; *Legendary Roy Orbison* .... (SSP)
Stan Getz; *Greatest Hits* .... (PRS)
Indian Summer Love
Con Funk Shun; *Secrets* .... (MER)
It Might As Well Rain Until September
Carole King; *More American Graffiti* ....(MCA)
It's OK
Beach Boys; *10 Years Of Harmony* ....(CAR)
15 Big Ones ....(CAR)
ST/Almost Summer ....(MCA)
It's Summer
Gladys Knight/Pips; *Motown Legends* ....(MOT)
July
Al Di Meola; *Soaring Through A Dream* .... (MAN)
Anthony Phillips; *Private Parts & Pieces-V Twelve* (PVC)
Vienna; *Guess What* ....(WB)
July Morning
Uriah Heep; *Best Of* ....(MER)
Live ....(MER)
June Bug
Leo Kottke; *Did You Hear Me* ....(CAP)
Mudlark ....(CAP)
My Feet Are Smiling ....(CAP)
The Best ....(CAP)
Lester Young; *Complete Savoy Recordings* ...... (SAV)
Master Takes ....(SAV)
June Is Bustin' Out All Over
Original Cast; *Carousel* ....(MCA)
June Night
Betty Everett; *Very Best Of* .... (VJ)
June The 15, 1967
Gary Burton; *Artist's Choice* .... (BLU)

June's Blues
Commandos; *Instrumentals (1959-1967)-Beat Is On* .... (EMI)
June Christy; *Uncollected w/Kentones-1946* ...... (HIN)
Last Rose Of Summer
Boston Pops Orchestra/Arthur Fiedler; *Irish Album* ....(RCA)
James Galway/Chieftains; *Over The Sea To Skye-Celtic Connection* ....(RCA)
Judas Priest; *Sin After Sin* ....(COL)
Kiri Te Kanawa; *Come To The Fair* .... (ANG)
Phil Coulter; *Sea Of Tranquility* ....(SHA)
Last Summer
Rod Stewart; *Blondes Have More Fun* ....(WB)
Lick Summer Love
Hanoi Rocks; *Back To Mystery City* ....(GEF)
Long Hot Summer
Aldo Nova; *Twitch* ....(POR)
Jimmie Rodgers; *Best Of* .... (RHI)
Style Council; *Introducing The* ....(MER)
Love Letters In The Sand
Pat Boone; *16 Great Performances* ....(MCA)
Best Of ....(MCA)
Vintage Music-Original Oldies/'50s-#2 .... (MCA)
Magic
Cars; *Greatest Hits* ....(ELE)
Heartbeat City ....(ELE)
Memphis In June
Eddie Miller/Orchestra; *Uncollected-1944-1945* . (HIN)
Hoagy Carmichael; *Hoagy Sings Carmichael* ..... (EMI)
Hoagy Sings Carmichael ....(PAU)
Mississippi Summer
Si Kahn; *Doing My Job* ....(FF)
My Summer Love
Malta; *High Pressure* .... (JVC)
My Summer Vacation
Ice Cube; *Death Certificate* ....(PRY)
My Summertime Thang
Time; *Pandemonium* ....(PAI)
Never Dreamed You'd Leave In Summer
Joan Baez; *Best Of* ....(A&M)
Classics-#8 ....(A&M)
Diamond & Rust ....(A&M)
Stevie Wonder; *20 Classic Hits* ....(MOT)
Greatest Hits-#2 ....(MOT)
Looking Back ....(MOT)
Where I'm Coming From ....(MOT)
Night Moves
Bob Seger; *Night Moves* ....(CAP)
Nine Tonight ....(CAP)
ST/FM ....(MCA)
Marilyn Martin; *Marilyn Martin* ....(ATL)
Of A Summer Morn
Nightnoise; *At The End Of The Evening* ....(WH)
Once Upon A Summertime
Barbra Streisand; *Je M'Appelle Barbra* ....(COL)
Dinah Shore; *Once Upon A Summertime* ....(BAI)
Miles Davis; *Jazz Sampler-#5* ....(COL)
One Summer Dream
Electric Light Orchestra; *Afterglow* .... (EPI)
Face The Music ....(JET)
One Summer Night
Danleers; *Mercury Vocal Group Collection* ...... (MER)
More American Graffiti ....(MER)
Remember When ....(GRL)
Super Oldies/'50s-#1 ....(AUF)
WCBS FM 101 History Of Rock-'50s-#1 ....(CLT)
One Summer Night In Brazil
Rippingtons; *Tourist In Paradise* ....(GRP)
Only A Summer Love
R.E.O. Speedwagon; *Live-You Get What You Play For* .... (EPI)
Other Side Of Summer
Elvis Costello; *Mighty Like A Rose* ....(WB)
Our Summer Love
Joey Welz; *Best Of-Decades* ....(CPR)
Blue Memories ....(CPR)
Over The Summer
Sparks; *Profile-Ultimate Collection* ....(RHI)
Palisades Park
Beach Boys; *15 Big Ones* ....(RPR)

Freddie "Boom Boom" Cannon; *14 Blooming Hits* (RHI)
  Billboard Top Rock 'N' Roll Hits-1962 .... (RHI)
  His Latest & Greatest .... (CRI)
  Memories Of The Cow Palace .... (RHI)
  Oldies But Goodies-#11-CD .... (OSR)
Ramones; *Brain Drain* .... (SIR)
Paris Summer
Nancy Sinatra & Lee Hazlewood; *Fairy Tales &*
  Fantasies-Best Of .... (RHI)
Poem Of Summer
J.D. Robb; *Triptyque/Other Electronic*
  Compositions .... (FLW)
Portraits Of Summer
Jim Bajor; *Gentle Images* .... (JBX)
Rain In The Summertime
Alarm; *Eye Of The Hurricane* .... (IRS)
Sausalito Summernight
Diesel; *Watts In A Tank* ....(REG)
School's Out
Alice Cooper; *Alice Cooper Show* .... (WB)
  Greatest Hits .... (WB)
  School's Out .... (WB)
  ST/Rock 'N' Roll High School .... (SIR)
Krokus; *First Degree Metal* .... (PRY)
  Stayed Awake All Night-Best Of .... (ARI)
Sealed With A Kiss
Bobby Vinton; *Greatest Hits* ....(CCB)
Brian Hyland; *Cruisin'-1962* .... (INC)
  Oldies But Goodies-#2 .... (OSR)
  Original Rock 'N' Roll Hits/'50s .... (RLL)
Lettermen; *Best Of-#2* ....(CAP)
  Capitol Collectors Series ....(CAP)
See You In September
Chiffons; *Best Of* ....(LAU)
Happenings; *ST/Purple People Eater* .... (AJK)
Tempos; *Cruisin'-1960* .... (INC)
  ST/American Graffiti ....(MCA)
She's My Summer Girl
Jan & Dean; *Surf City-Best Of* .... (EMI)
Someday, August 29, 1968
Chicago; *Chicago Transit Authority* ....(COL)
Suddenly Last Summer
Motels; *Best Of/No Vacancy* .... (CAP)
  Little Robbers ....(CAP)
  Rock The First-#5 ....(SAN)
Summer
David Sanborn; *Change Of Heart* .... (WB)
John Denver; *Evening With* ....(RCA)
  Rocky Mountain High ....(RCA)
Nuclear Valdez; *I Am I* .... (EPI)
War; *Best Of...& More* .... (RHI)
  Summer & Sun .... (RHI)
Summer Afternoon
Vogues; *Greatest Hits* .... (RHI)
Summer And Sandy
Lesley Gore; *45* ....(OOP)
Summer Boy
Buffy Sainte-Marie; *Best Of* .... (VAN)
Summer Breeze
Isley Brothers; *3+3* .... (TN)
  Forever Gold .... (TN)
  Story-#2-T-Neck Years-1969-1985 .... (RHI)
Seals & Crofts; *Greatest Hits* .... (WB)
  Summer Breeze .... (WB)
Summer Bunnies
R. Kelly; *12 Play* ....(JVA)
Summer Chill
Grover Washington, Jr.; *Next Exit* ....(COL)
Summer Days
Partridge Family; *Greatest Hits* .... (ARI)
Roger Whittaker; *Best Of* ....(RCA)
  Reflections Of Love ....(RCA)
Summer Days Alone
Brothers Four; *Greatest Hits* ....(COL)
Summer In Berlin
Alphaville; *Forever Young* ....(ATL)
Summer In Dixie
Confederate Railroad; *Notorious* ....(ATL)
Summer In Hell
Fred Schneider; *Fred Schneider* ....(RPR)
Summer In San Francisco
Hendrik Meurkens; *Sambahia* .... (CP)

Summer In Siam
Pogues; *Essential Pogues* .... (ISL)
  Hell's Ditch .... (ISL)
Summer In The City
Lovin' Spoonful; *Anthology* .... (RHI)
  Best Of ....(OOP)
  Billboard Top Rock 'N' Roll Hits-1966 .... (RHI)
  Rockin' '60s ....(PRY)
Summer Kisses, Winter Tears
Elvis Presley; *Collector's Gold* ....(RCA)
Summer Knows
Barbra Streisand; *Barbra Joan Streisand* ....(COL)
Frank Sinatra; *Some Nice Things I've Missed* .... (RPR)
Freddie Hubbard; *Best Of* ....(PAB)
  Live At The North Sea Jazz Festival ....(PAB)
Johnny Mathis; *First Time Ever I Saw Your Face* .(COL)
Summer Love
Chris Rea; *espresso logic* ....(EW)
R.E.O. Speedwagon; *R.E.O.* .... (EPI)
Summer Means New York
Beach Boys; *Today!/Summer Days & Summer*
  Nights! ....(CAP)
Summer Me, Winter Me
Barbra Streisand; *The Way We Were* ....(COL)
Summer Nights
Earl Klugh; *Whispers & Promises* .... (WB)
Marianne Faithfull; *Greatest Hits* .... (AKO)
Olivia Newton-John & John Travolta; *Back To*
  Basics-Essential-1971-1992 ....(GEF)
  ST/Grease ....(RSO)
Original Broadway Cast; *Grease* ....(POL)
Van Halen; *5150* .... (WB)
Summer Of Love
B-52's; *Bouncing Off The Satellites* .... (WB)
Jefferson Airplane; *Jefferson Airplane* .... (EPI)
Summer Of Roses
Willie Nelson; *Tougher Than Leather* ....(COL)
Summer Of The Silver Comet
Tracy Nelson; *Homemade Songs* .... (FF)
"Summer Of '42" Theme
George Benson; *Best Of* ....(CBA)
  White Rabbit ....(CBA)
Peter Nero; *Greatest Hits* ....(COL)
  "Summer Of '42" Theme ....(COL)
Summer Of '69
Bryan Adams; *Reckless* .... (A&M)
Summer Rain
Alphaville; *Breathtaking Blue* .... (ATL)
Andreas Vollenweider; *Trilogy-Behind The*
  Gardens... ....(COL)
Belinda Carlisle; *Her Greatest Hits* ....(MCA)
  Runaway Horses ....(MCA)
Johnny Rivers; *Anthology-1964-1977* .... (RHI)
  Best Of .... (EMI)
Summer Romance
Rolling Stones; *Emotional Rescue* .... (RS)
Summer Samba
Astrud Gilberto; *Compact Jazz* ....(VRV)
Summer Sequence
Woody Herman; *Greatest Hits* ....(COL)
Summer Side Of Life
Gordon Lightfoot; *Gord's Gold* .... (RPR)
  Summer Side Of Life ....(RPR)
Summer Snow
Blue Magic; *Magic Of The Blue-Greatest Hits* .... (CLT)
Lou Christie; *Enlightnin'ment-Best Of* .... (RHI)
Summer Soft
Stevie Wonder; *Songs In The Key Of Life* .... (MOT)
Summer Song
Chad & Jeremy; *Best Of* .... (KT)
  Capitol Gold-Best Of ....(CAP)
  History Of British Rock-#2 .... (RHI)
Dave Brubeck Quartet; *For Iola* ....(CCJ)
Grover Washington, Jr.; *Anthology* ....(MOT)
Joe Satriani; *The Extremist* ....(REL)
Kenny G; *Silhouette* .... (ARI)
Matt Bianco; *Matt Bianco* ....(ATL)
Tom Chapin; *Let Me Back Into Your Life* .... (FF)
Summer Song (In The Autumn)
Peter Hammill; *Fools Mate* .... (BP)
Summer Sounds
Robert Goulet; *Greatest Hits* ....(COL)
Summer Wind
Desert Rose Band; *Running* ....(MCA)

Frank Sinatra; *Greatest Hits* .... (RPR)
  Sinatra Reprise-The Very Good Years .... (RPR)
  Strangers In The Night .... (RPR)
Frank Sinatra & Julio Iglesias; *Frank Sinatra*
Duets .... (CAP)
Summer (Estate)
  Shirley Horn; *Here's To Life* .... (VRV)
Summer (The First Time)
  Bette Midler; *ST/Divine Madness* .... (ATL)
  Bobby Goldsboro; *Honey-Best Of* .... (EMI)
Summerlove
  Neil Diamond; *ST/Jazz Singer* .... (CAP)
Summersong
  Roy Orbison; *Legendary* .... (SSP)
Summertime
  Billy Stewart; *Best Of Chess Rhythm & Blues* .... (CSS)
    Summer & Sun .... (RHI)
  Booker T./M.G.s; *Best Of* .... (ATL)
  Carmen McRae; *Greatest Of* .... (MCA)
  Chet Baker; *My Favourite Songs-#1-Last Great*
Concert .... (ENJ)
  Courtney Pine; *Glory Of Gershwin Featuring Larry*
Adler .... (MER)
  D.J. Jazzy Jeff & The Fresh Prince; *Homebase* ... (JVA)
  Ella Fitzgerald & Louis Armstrong; *Porgy & Bess* (VRV)
  George Benson; *Best Of Benson* .... (CBA)
  Janis Joplin; *Greatest Hits* .... (COL)
    ST/Janis .... (COL)
  Lambert, Hendricks & Ross; *Best Of* .... (COL)
  Miles Davis/Orchestra; *Porgy & Bess* .... (COL)
  Original Cast; *Porgy & Bess* .... (MCA)
  Peter Gabriel; *Glory Of Gershwin-Featuring Larry*
Adler .... (MER)
  Rick Nelson; *Best Of-#2* .... (EMI)
  Sam Cooke; *Best Of* .... (RCA)
  Sarah Vaughan; *1940s-The Singers* .... (COL)
    Divine-Columbia Years-1949-1953 .... (COL)
  Stan Getz; *Compact Jazz* .... (VRV)
  Willie Nelson; *One For The Road* .... (COL)
Summertime Blues
  Alan Jackson; *Who I Am* .... (ARI)
  Blue Cheer; *Good Times Are Hard To Find-History*
Of .... (MER)
    Louder Than God-Best Of .... (RHI)
    San Francisco Nights .... (RHI)
  Brian Setzer; *ST/La Bamba* .... (SLS)
  Eddie Cochran; *EMI Legends Of Rock 'N' Roll-24*
Greatest .... (EMI)
    Greatest Hits .... (CCB)
    Legendary Masters .... (EMI)
  Joan Jett/Blackhearts; *I Love Rock & Roll* .... (BW)
  Who; *Hooligans* .... (MCA)
    Live At Leeds .... (MCA)
    Who's Last .... (MCA)
Summertime Dream
  Gordon Lightfoot; *Summertime Dream* .... (RPR)
Summertime In England
  Van Morrison; *Common One* .... (WB)
Summertime In The City
  Manhattans; *45* .... (COL)
Summertime Is Past & Gone
  Bill Monroe/Blue Grass Boys;
Essential-1945-1949 .... (COL)
  Elvis Presley; *Million-Dollar Quartet* .... (RCA)
Summertime Love
  Ta Mara/Seen; *Ta Mara/Seen* .... (A&M)
Summertime Rolls
  Jane's Addiction; *Nothing's Shocking* .... (WB)
Summertime, Summertime
  Jamies; *Summer & Sun* .... (RHI)
Summer, Highland Falls
  Billy Joel; *Songs In The Attic* .... (COL)
    Turnstiles .... (COL)
Summer's Almost Gone
  Doors; *Waiting For The Sun* .... (ELE)
Summer's Cauldron
  XTC; *Skylarking* .... (GEF)
Summer's Coming Around Again
  Carly Simon; *Anticipation* .... (ELE)
Summer's Day Song
  Paul McCartney; *CD Gift Set* .... (CAP)
    McCartney II .... (CAP)

Summer's Gone
  Paul Anka; *21 Golden Hits* .... (RCA)
    30th Anniversary Collection .... (RHI)
Summer's Here
  James Taylor; *Dad Loves His Work* .... (COL)
Swedish Rhapsody (Midsummer Vigil)
  Chet Atkins; *RCA Years* .... (RCA)
  Percy Faith/Orchestra; *Greatest Hits* .... (COL)
Sweet Summer Blue & Gold
  Linda Ronstadt; *Stone Poneys* .... (CAP)
Sweet Summer Day
  Freddy Fender; *Before The Next Teardrop Falls* . (MCA)
Sweet Summer Lovin'
  Dolly Parton; *45* .... (RCA)
That Summer
  Garth Brooks; *The Chase* .... (LIB)
That Sunday That Summer
  Betty Carter; *Compact Jazz-Best Of The Jazz*
Vocalists .... (VRV)
  Nat King Cole; *Nat King Cole* .... (CAP)
    Unforgettable Nat King Cole .... (CAP)
  Natalie Cole; *Unforgettable* .... (ELE)
Theme From "A Summer Place"
  Andy Williams; *Moon River & Other Great Movie*
Themes .... (COL)
  Percy Faith; *16 Most Requested Songs* .... (COL)
    All-Time Greatest Hits .... (COL)
    Best Love Songs .... (OSR)
  Percy Faith/Orchestra; *Greatest Hits* .... (COL)
Things We Did Last Summer
  Beach Boys; *Good Vibrations-Thirty Years Of* .... (CAP)
  Frank Sinatra; *Sinatra Rarities-Columbia Years* ...(COL)
  Michael Feinstein; *Sings The Jule Styne Songbook* (NON)
This Ain't The Summer Of Love
  Blue Oyster Cult; *Agents Of Fortune* .... (COL)
Those Lazy Hazy Crazy Days Of Summer
  Nat King Cole; *Best Of* .... (CAP)
    Capitol Collectors Series .... (CAP)
'Tis The Last Rose Of Summer
  Lucy Shelton/Others; *Moore's Irish Melodies* .... (NON)
To The Summer In Our Hearts
  Curlew; *Bee* .... (CUN)
    Live In Berlin .... (CUN)
Two Hot Girls (On A Hot Summer Night)
  Carly Simon; *Coming Around Again* .... (ARI)
    Greatest Hits Live .... (ARI)
Two Weeks Last Summer
  Sandy Denny; *Who Knows Where The Time Goes?* (HBL)
  Sandy Denny/Strawbs; *Sandy Denny/Strawbs* .... (HBL)
Under The Boardwalk
  Bette Midler; *ST/Beaches* .... (ATL)
  Bruce Willis; *Return Of Bruno* .... (MOT)
  Drifters; *16 Greatest Hits* .... (TRP)
    Atlantic R&B 1947-1974-#5 (1962-1966) ..... (ATL)
    Golden Hits .... (ATL)
    Super Oldies/'60s-#5 .... (AUF)
  John Cougar Mellencamp; *45* .... (RIV)
  Lynn Anderson; *What She Does Best* .... (MER)
  Rickie Lee Jones; *Girl At Her Volcano* .... (WB)
  Rolling Stones; *12 X 5* .... (AKO)
  Untouchables; *Agent Double O Soul* .... (RES)
Unimaginable Zero Summer
  Young Fresh Fellows; *The Men Who Loved Music* (FRN)
Up On The Roof
  Cover Girls; *We Can't Go Wrong* .... (CAP)
  Cryan' Shames; *Scratch In The Sky* .... (COL)
  Drifters; *16 Greatest Hits* .... (TRP)
    Cruisin'-1962 .... (INC)
    Golden Hits .... (ATL)
    Greatest Hits .... (GUS)
  James Taylor; *Flag* .... (COL)
  Nylons; *Four On The Floor* .... (SCO)
Winter & The Summer
  Strawbs; *Bursting At The Seams* .... (A&M)
Wonderful Summer
  Robin Ward; *Sixties Rule!-#2* .... (OW)
You Took The Words Right Out Of My Mouth
  Meatloaf; *Bat Out Of Hell* .... (EPI)
Your Summer Dream
  Beach Boys; *Surfer Girl/Shut Down-#2* .... (CAP)
    Surfer Girl/Surfin' U.S.A. .... (MOB)

SEASONS: WINTER

See Also: CHRISTMAS, MONTHS & DATES: DEC., JAN., FEB.; COLD, SNOW

Anos Dourados (Looks Like December)
Antonio Carlos Jobim/New Band; *Passarim* ...... (VRV)
Joanne Brackeen; *Breath Of Brazil* .... (CP)
Apples In Winter
Kim Robertson; *Angels In Disguise* .... (INV)
Back In January
Angst; *Mystery Spot* .... (SST)
Birds Of Winter
Zamfir; *Return To Romance* .... (PHI)
California Dreamin'
Beach Boys; *Made In The U.S.A.* .... (CAP)
Mamas & The Papas; *20 Golden Hits* .... (MCA)
At The Hop .... (MCA)
Good Feeling Music-Big Chill-#1 .... (MOT)
ST/Air America .... (MCA)
ST/American Pop .... (RLL)
ST/Forrest Gump .... (EPX)
Cold Winter Day
Blind Willie McTell; *Doing That Atlanta*
Strut-1927-1935 .... (YAZ)
Cold Winter's Day
BoDeans; *Go Slow Down* .... (SLS)
Colder Than Winter
Vince Gill; *Things That Matter* .... (RCA)
December
Anthony Phillips; *Private Parts & Pieces V Twelve* (PVC)
Expose; *Exposure* .... (ARI)
Robert Vaughan/Shadows; *Love & War* .... (EXI)
Waterboys; *Waterboys* .... (ISL)
December Days
Willie Nelson; *Love & Pain* .... (ARA)
Sweet Memories .... (RCA)
December Will Be Magic Again
Kate Bush; *12"* .... (EMI)
December '63
Frankie Valli/Four Seasons; *25th Anniversary*
Collection .... (RHI)
Anthology .... (RHI)
December's Boudoir
Laura Nyro; *Eli & The 13th Confession* .... (COL)
Don't Cut The Tree Down In Winter
Penny Little; *In A Light Garden* .... (GLO)
Fall Breaks & Back To Winter
Beach Boys; *Smiley Smile/Wild Honey* .... (CAP)
February
Anthony Phillips; *Private Parts & Pieces V-Twelve* (PVC)
Jennifer Hall; *Fortune & Men's Eyes* .... (WB)
February In My Heart
Osborne Brothers; *Some Things I Want To Sing*
About .... (SH)
February Ingenue
Don Dixon; *Romeo At Juilliard* .... (ENI)
February March
Lou & Peter Berryman; *February March* .... (COR)
February Moment
Herbie Hancock & Chick Corea; *Evening With* .. (COL)
February Sea
George Winston; *Winter Into Spring* .... (WH)
February Song
Barbi Benton & Jamii Szmadzinski; *Kinetic*
Voyage .... (TAK)
Blazing Redheads & Patricia Thumas; *Blazing*
Redheads .... (REF)
Hard, Hard Winter
Strawbs; *Deep Cuts* .... (OYS)
Hazy Shade Of Winter
Bangles; *Greatest Hits* .... (COL)
ST/Less Than Zero .... (DFC)
Simon & Garfunkel; *Bookends* .... (COL)
Collected Works .... (COL)
I Am A Rock
Simon & Garfunkel; *Collected Works* .... (COL)
Greatest Hits .... (COL)
Sounds Of Silence .... (COL)
In The Winter
Janis Ian; *Between The Lines* .... (COL)
January
Anthony Phillips; *Private Parts & Collectors* ...... (PVC)

Mose Allison; *Back Country Suite* .... (PRS)
Painted Willie; *Mind Bowling* .... (SST)
June In January
Bing Crosby; *Best Of* .... (MCA)
Dean Martin; *Best Of* .... (CAP)
Late Winter, Early Spring
John Denver; *Rocky Mountain High* .... (RCA)
Life In A Northern Town
Dream Academy; *Dream Academy* .... (WB)
Lion In The Winter
Hoyt Axton; *Road Songs* .... (A&M)
Southbound .... (A&M)
Long Cold Winter
Pure Prairie League; *If The Shoe Fits* .... (RCA)
Magic In December
Tom Barabas; *Incredible Invincible Sampler* .... (INV)
Monkey In Winter
Colourfield; *Deception* .... (CHR)
New England Winter
Shep Cooke; *Concert Tour Of Mars* .... (SIE)
Our Winter Love
Lettermen; *Capitol Collectors Series* .... (CAP)
Roses In The Winter
Merle Haggard; *His Best* .... (MCA)
Serving 190 Proof .... (MCA)
Russian Winter
Krokus; *Headhunter* .... (ARI)
Sometimes In Winter
Blood, Sweat & Tears; *Blood, Sweat & Tears* ....(COL)
Greatest Hits .... (COL)
Song For A Winter's Night
Gordon Lightfoot; *Gord's Gold* .... (RPR)
Way I Feel .... (UA)
Summer Kisses, Winter Tears
Elvis Presley; *Collector's Gold* .... (RCA)
Summer Me, Winter Me
Barbra Streisand; *The Way We Were* .... (COL)
Superwoman
Stevie Wonder; *Music Of My Mind* .... (MOT)
Original Musiquarium .... (MOT)
Three Seasons Of Winter
Joel Mabus; *Fairies & Fools* .... (FF)
Too Cold In The Winter
Cry Of Love; *Brother* .... (\OL)
Winter
John Denver; *Rocky Mountain High* .... (RCA)
Rolling Stones; *Goats Head Soup* .... (RS)
Tori Amos; *Crucify* .... (ATL)
Little Earthquakes .... (ATL)
Winter Boy
Buffy Sainte-Marie; *Best Of* .... (VAN)
Little Wheel Spin & Spin .... (VAN)
Winter In America
Gil Scott-Heron; *Best Of* .... (ARI)
First Minute Of a New Day .... (ARI)
Margret Roadknight; *Living In The Land Of Oz* . (RWD)
Winter In Austria
L. Subramaniam; *Spanish Wave* .... (MS)
Winter In Madrid
Stan Kenton & Ann Richards; *By*
Request-#5-1953-1960 .... (CW)
Winter In Maine
Bruce Fowler; *Ants Can Count* .... (TER)
Winter In Winnipeg
Rob McConnell/Boss Brass; *Brass Is Back* .... (CCJ)
Winter Long
Neil Young; *Decade* .... (RPR)
Winter Of My Life
Freddy Fender; *Are You Ready For Freddy* ..... (MCA)
Winter Rose Love Awake
Wings; *Back To The Egg* .... (CAP)
Winter Sky
Judy Collins; *Concert* .... (ELE)
Recollections .... (ELE)
Winter Song
Angel; *White Hot* .... (CAS)
Crash Test Dummies; *Ghosts That Haunt Me* ... (ARI)
Harry Chapin; *Gold Medal Collection* .... (ELE)
Sniper & Other Love Songs .... (ELE)
Screaming Trees; *Sweet Oblivion* .... (EPI)
Winter Time
Steve Miller Band; *Book Of Dreams* .... (CAP)
CD Gift Set .... (CAP)
Greatest Hits-1974-1978 .... (CAP)

Winter Wonderland
Alexander O'Neal; *My Gift To You* .... (TAB)
Amy Grant; *Home For Christmas* .... (A&M)
Andrews Sisters; *Christmas* .... (MSP)
Aretha Franklin; *Rock 'N' Roll Christmas Classics* (MFL)
Barbara Mandrell; *Christmas At Our House* ...... (MSP)
   Tennessee Christmas .... (MCA)
Bing Crosby; *Christmas Classics* .... (CAP)
Blue Notes; *Rhythm & Blues Christmas-#1* .... (CLT)
Brenda Lee; *Jingle Bell Rock* .... (MSP)
Carnie & Wendy Wilson; *Hey Santa!* .... (SBK)
Carpenters; *Christmas Portrait* .... (A&M)
Darlene Love; *Back To Mono-1958-1969* ...... (AKO)
   Christmas Gift For You From Phil Spector ..... (RHI)
   Phil Spector's Christmas Album .... (PAS)
Eddy Arnold; *Christmas With* ....(RCA)
Elvis Presley; *Sings The Wonderful World Of*
   Christmas ....(RCA)
Eurythmics; *Very Special Christmas* .... (A&M)
Faron Young; *Country Christmas* ....(SO)
George Strait; *Merry Christmas Strait To You* .... (MSP)
Hank Crawford; *We Got A Good Thing Going* .. (KDU)
Johnny Mercer/Pied Pipers; *Merry Christmas*
Baby-Romance & Reindeer .... (CAP)
Kathie Lee Gifford; *It's Christmas Time* .... (WB)
Kenny Rogers; *Christmas In America* .... (RPR)
London Symphony Orchestra; *Christmas*
   Traditions .... (SPM)
Merle Haggard; *Christmas Present* ....(CCB)
Randy Travis; *An Old Time Christmas* .... (WB)
Robert Goulet; *Essence Of Christmas* .... (A&M)
Roger Whittaker; *World's Most Beautiful Christmas*
   Songs .... (LIB)
Tanya Tucker; *Christmas For The '90s-#1* .... (LIB)
Travis Tritt; *Christmas-Loving Time Of The Year* .. (WB)
Winter World Of Love
Engelbert Humperdinck; *Engelbert Humperdinck* . (PRT)
   Greatest Hits .... (PRT)
Winter & My Soul
Grand Funk Railroad; *Grand Funk* .... (CAP)
Winter & The Summer
Strawbs; *Bursting At The Seams* .... (A&M)
Winterlude
Bob Dylan; *New Morning* ....(COL)
Winterness
Pousette-Dart Band; *Amnesia* .... (CAP)
Wintertime Love
Doors; *Waiting For The Sun* .... (ELE)
Winterwhite
Nitty Gritty Dirt Band; *Dream* .... (UA)
Wintry Feeling
Anne Murray; *Country Collection* .... (LIB)
   I'll Always Love You ....(CAP)
Jesse Winchester; *Touch On The Rainy Side* ..... (RHI)
Your Love Is Forever
George Harrison; *George Harrison* .... (DKH)

SECRETS

See Also: DOORS, HIDING, LIES, PRETEND

Achy Breaky Heart
Billy Ray Cyrus; *Some Gave All* .... (MER)
Ain't Nobody's Business
Billie Holiday; *From The Original Decca Masters* (MCA)
Bobby Bland; *Soul Of The Man* .... (MCA)
Jimmy Witherspoon; *Monterey Jazz Festival* ...... (EVR)
   Jazz Legacy ....(IC)
   Spoon Concerts .... (FAN)
Anonymous Love
Ray Charles; *True To Life* ....(ATC)
Baby Come Back To Me (Morse Code...)
Manhattan Transfer; *Bop Doo Wopp* .... (ATL)
Baby Won't You Tell Me
Johnny Hammond; *Big City Blues* .... (VAN)
Beauty Secrets
Be Bop Deluxe; *Sunburst Finish* ....(CAP)
Behind That Locked Door
George Harrison; *All Things Must Pass* .... (CAP)
Buried Treasure
Flesheaters; *Prehistoric Fits-#2* ....(SST)
Kenny Rogers; *Eyes That See In The Dark* ....(RCA)
   Greatest Hits ....(RCA)

Can't Break It To My Heart
Tracy Lawrence; *Alibis* .... (ATL)
Certain Girl
Warren Zevon; *Bad Luck Streak In Dancing*
   School .... (ASY)
Yardbirds; *Greatest Hits-#1-1964-1966* .... (RHI)
Confessing The Blues
B.B. King; *Completely Well* ...... / .... (MCA)
Jay McShann; *Atlantic Jazz-Kansas City* .... (ATL)
   Atlantic Jazz-Singers .... (ATL)
   Confessing The Blues .... (CJ)
Rolling Stones; *12 X 5* ....(LON)
Confessin' Midnight
Robin Trower; *For Earth Below* .... (CHR)
Confession
Laura Nyro; *Eli & The Thirteenth Confession* .....(COL)
Mabel Mercer & Bobby Short; *At Town Hall* ... (ATL)
Maureen McGovern; *Another Woman In Love* ...(COL)
Sammy Hagar; *Nine On A Ten Scale* ....(CAP)
Confessor, The
Joe Walsh; *Confessor, The* .... (FA)
Confidential
Fleetwoods; *Best Of* .... (RHI)
Radiators; *Zig-Zaggin' Through Ghostland* .... (EPI)
Sonny Knight; *Oldies But Goodies-#1* .... (OSR)
Daytime Friends
Kenny Rogers; *Daytime Friends* .... (LIB)
   Ten Years Of Gold .... (EMI)
   Twenty Greatest Hits .... (LIB)
Do I Have To Come Right Out & Say It
Buffalo Springfield; *Buffalo Springfield* ....(ATC)
Do You Want To Know A Secret
Beatles; *Early Beatles* ....(CAP)
   Please Please Me ....(CAP)
Don't Tell Your Mama
Eddie Floyd; *Chronicle* .... (STX)
Don'tcha Tell Henry
Bob Dylan/Band; *Basement Tapes* ....(COL)
Green Door
Jim Lowe; *Billboard Top Rock 'N' Roll Hits-1956* (RHI)
   Super Hits-#4 ....(GUS)
Hidden Treasure
Traffic; *Low Spark Of High Heeled Boys* .... (ISL)
High School Confidential
Jerry Lee Lewis; *20 Classic Jerry Lee Lewis Hits* . (OSR)
   Original ....(SUN)
   Original Golden Hits-#2 ....(SUN)
   ST/Harper Valley PTA .... (PLN)
   Sun Story .... (RHI)
I Heard It Through The Grapevine
Creedence Clearwater Revival; *Chooglin'* .... (FAN)
   Chronicle .... (FAN)
   Cosmo's Factory .... (FAN)
   Gold .... (FAN)
   Movie Album .... (FAN)
Gladys Knight/Pips; *16 #1 Hits From The Late*
   '60s .... (MOT)
   Command Compact Performances .... (MOT)
   Every Great Motown Song-First 25 Years ...... (MOT)
   Motown Grammy R & B Performances .... (MOT)
   Motown Superstars Series-#13 .... (MOT)
   Top 10 With A Bullet-Motown Girl Groups .... (MOT)
Marvin Gaye; *25 #1 Hits From 25 Years* .... (MOT)
   Anthology .... (MOT)
   Every Great Motown Hit Of Marvin Gaye ..... (MOT)
   Live At London Palladium .... (MOT)
   Most Played Oldies On America's Jukebox ..... (MOT)
   Motown Story .... (MOT)
   Motown Story-First 25 Years .... (MOT)
I Know There's Something Going On
Frida; *Something's Going On* .... (ATL)
If Walls Could Talk
Ry Cooder; *Paradise & Lunch* .... (RPR)
It Ain't Nobody's Business
Billie Holiday; *History Of-Real Billie Holiday* .....(VRV)
Mississippi John Hurt; *Best Of* .... (VAN)
It Is No Secret
Mark Collie; *Unleashed* .... (MCA)
I'll Follow My Secret Heart
Mary Martin & Noel Coward; *Together With*
   Music .... (DRG)
I'm Confessin' (That I Love You)
Ella Fitzgerald; *Ella Sings/Chick Swings* .... (OLR)
   Lady Time .... (PAB)

I've Got A Secret Miniature Camera
Peter Murphy; *ST/Pump Up The Volume* .... (MCA)
Keep It Confidential
Nona Hendryx; *45* .... (RCA)
Live To Tell
Madonna; *Immaculate Collection* .... (SIR)
   Royal Box .... (SIR)
   True Blue .... (SIR)
Midnight Confessions
Grass Roots; *Anthology-1965-1975* .... (RHI)
   Original Rock 'N' Roll Hits Of The '60s .... (RLL)
   Vintage Music-Orig. Classics!'60s-#9 .... (MCA)
Midnight Prowl
John David Souther; *Black Rose* .... (ASY)
Never Keeping Secrets
Babyface; *For The Cool In You* .... (EPI)
No Secrets
Carly Simon; *Best Of* .... (ELE)
   No Secrets .... (ELE)
Missing Persons; *Best Of* .... (CAP)
Van Stephenson; *ST/Secret Admirer* .... (MCA)
   Suspicious Heart .... (MCA)
No Tell Lover
Chicago; *Greatest Hits-#2* .... (COL)
   Group Portrait .... (COL)
   Hot Streets .... (COL)
   If You Leave Me Now .... (COL)
No Tell Motel
David Houston; *Best Of* .... (GUS)
Nobody Knows But Me
Billy Joel; *In Harmony 2* .... (COL)
Jimmie Rodgers; *Riding High-1929-1930* .... (ROU)
Merle Haggard/Strangers; *Same Train Different
Time* .... (CAP)
Nobody's Business
Billy Idol; *Billy Idol* .... (CHR)
Don Henley; *I Can't Stand Still* .... (ASY)
Frank Stokes; *Creator Of The Memphis Blues* .... (YAZ)
Oswald Brothers & Charlie Collins; *That's
Country* .... (ROU)
Out Behind The Barn
Little Jimmy Dickens; *Columbia Historic Edition* . (COL)
Password
Kitty Wells; *Country Music Hall Of Fame* .... (MCA)
   Greatest Hits .... (MCA)
   Greatest Hits-#1 .... (SO)
   MCA Records 30 Years Of Hits-1958-1988 ... (MCA)
Private Dancer
Tina Turner; *Live In Europe* .... (CAP)
   Private Dancer .... (CAP)
   Simply The Best .... (CAP)
Private Eyes
Daryl Hall & John Oates; *Private Eyes* .... (RCA)
   Rock 'N' Soul Pt. 1-Greatest Hits .... (RCA)
Private Number
Judy Clay & William Bell; *15 Original Big
Hits-#2* .... (STX)
   Private Numbers .... (STX)
   Top Of The Stax-Twenty Greatest Hits-#2 ..... (STX)
Saucerful Of Secrets
Pink Floyd; *Nice Pair* .... (CAP)
   Saucerful Of Secrets .... (CAP)
   Ummagumma .... (CAP)
Secret
Heart; *Brigade* .... (CAP)
Lynch Mob; *Lynch Mob* .... (ELE)
Madonna; *Bedtime Stories* .... (MAV)
Orchestral Manoeuvres In The Dark; *Best Of* ... (A&M)
   Crush .... (A&M)
Secret Agent Man
Devo; *Duty Now For The Future* .... (WB)
Johnny Rivers; *Anthology-1964-1977* .... (RHI)
   Best Of .... (EMI)
   Very Best Of .... (EMI)
Secret Combination
Randy Crawford; *Secret Combination* .... (WB)
Secret Friend
Paul McCartney; *CD Gift Set* .... (CAP)
   McCartney II .... (CAP)
Secret Garden
Alan Parsons Project; *Eve* .... (ARI)
Johnny Rivers; *Golden Hits* .... (IMP)
Quincy Jones; *Back On The Block* .... (QUE)

Secret Gardens
Judy Collins; *So Early In The Spring-First 15
Years* .... (ELE)
   True Stories & Other Dreams .... (ELE)
Secret Journey
Police; *Ghost In The Machine* .... (A&M)
Secret Life Of Arabia
David Bowie; *Heroes* .... (RYK)
Secret Love
Doris Day; *Greatest Hits* .... (COL)
   Hollywood Magic-1950s .... (COL)
Frank Sinatra; *Days Of Wine & Roses-Academy
Awards* .... (RPR)
Freddy Fender; *Collection* .... (RPR)
Guy Lombardo; *Golden Medleys* .... (MCA)
Moonglows; *Doo-Wop's Greatest Hits* .... (VJ)
Nancy Wilson; *Capitol Sings The Best Movie
Songs* .... (CAP)
Slim Whitman; *Best Of-1952-1972* .... (RHI)
   Greatest Hits .... (CCB)
Secret Lovers
Atlantic Starr; *As The Band Turns* .... (A&M)
   Classics-#10 .... (A&M)
   Secret Lovers-Best Of .... (A&M)
Secret Marriage
Sting; *Nothing Like The Sun* .... (A&M)
Secret Meetings
Greg Kihn; *Next Of Kihn* .... (BES)
Secret Messages
Electric Light Orchestra; *Secret Messages* .... (JET)
Secret Mountain Hideout
Michael Murphey; *Blue Sky Night Thunder* .... (EPI)
Secret Of The Andes
Victor Feldman; *Secret Of The Andes* .... (PAJ)
Victor Feldman/Generation Band; *Best Of* ..... (NVA)
Secret O' Life
James Taylor; *JT* .... (COL)
Secret Rendezvous
Karyn White; *Karyn White* .... (WB)
Secret Secrets
Joan Armatrading; *Secret Secrets* .... (A&M)
Secret Separation
Fixx; *One Thing Leads To Another-Greatest Hits* (MCA)
   Walkabout .... (MCA)
Secret To A Long Life
Michelle Shocked; *Arkansas Traveler* .... (MER)
   Texas Campfire Tapes .... (MER)
Secretly
Jimmie Rodgers; *Best Of* .... (RHI)
   Original Rock 'N' Roll Hits Of The '50s .... (RLL)
   Yours Truly .... (RLL)
Lettermen; *And I Love Her* .... (CAP)
   Best Of .... (CAP)
   Capitol Collectors Series .... (CAP)
Secrets
Bobby Womack; *The Poet* .... (BEV)
Bonham; *Mad Hatter* .... (WTG)
Cure; *Seventeen Seconds* .... (ELE)
Golden Earring; *Cut* .... (21)
Kidd Glove; *Kidd Glove* .... (MOR)
Mac Davis; *Very Best & More* .... (CAS)
Mick Jagger; *She's The Boss* .... (COL)
Natalie Cole; *Dangerous* .... (MOD)
Van Halen; *Diver Down* .... (WB)
Shhh, It's A Military Secret
Glenn Miller/Orchestra; *Complete* .... (BLU)
Six O'Clock News
John Prine; *John Prine* .... (ATL)
Stairs, The
Reba McEntire; *The Last One To Know* .... (MCA)
Suspicion
Bonzo Dog Band; *Best Of* .... (RHI)
Elvis Presley; *ST/Pot Luck* .... (RCA)
Terry Stafford; *Billboard Top Rock 'N' Roll
Hits-1964* .... (RHI)
   Cruisin'-1964 .... (INC)
   Oldies But Goodies-#8 .... (OSR)
Suspicions
Eddie Rabbitt; *All-Time Greatest Hits* .... (WB)
   Country's Greatest Hits-#6-Superstars .... (PRY)
   Number 1's .... (WB)
   Ten Years Of Greatest Hits .... (LIB)

Suspicious Minds
Elvis Presley; *Aloha From Hawaii* ....(RCA)
  In Person At The International Hotel ....(RCA)
  Memphis Record ....(RCA)
  Nipper's Greatest Hits-'60s-#2 ....(RCA)
  ST/This Is ....(RCA)
'Tain't Nobody's Business If I Do
Bessie Smith; *Collection* ....(COL)
Billie Holiday; *Story* ....(MCA)
Diana Ross; *ST/Lady Sings The Blues* .... (MOT)
Miki Howard; *Miki Sings Billie-Tribute To B.*
  Holiday .... (GIA)
Original Broadway Cast; *Black & Blue* .... (DRG)
They Don't Know
Tracey Ullman; *Best Of* .... (RHI)
  You Broke My Heart In 17 Places ....(MCA)
Time Will Reveal
DeBarge; *In A Special Way* .... (MOT)
Too Many Secrets
Patsy Cline; *20 Golden Pieces Of* ....(BLD)
  Patsy Cline ....(MCA)
Under Suspicion
Robert Palmer; *Secrets* ....(ISL)
Roy Orbison; *Legendary* ....(SSP)
Vanilla Fudge; *Mystery* ....(ATC)
Undercover Lover
38 Special; *Tour De Force* ....(A&M)
Dazz Band; *Jukebox* ....(MOT)
Undercover Man
Edgar Winter Group; *They Only Come Out At*
  Night .... (EPI)
Undercover Of The Night
Rolling Stones; *Rewind (1971-1984)* ....(RS)
  Undercover .... (RS)
What She Don't Know Won't Hurt Her
Gene Watson; *Greatest Hits* .... (MCA)
When She Cries
Restless Heart; *Big Iron Horses* ....(RCA)
Who's Behind The Door
Zebra; *Live* .... (ATL)
  Zebra .... (ATL)
Your Secret's Safe With Me
Michael Franks; *Skin Dive* .... (WB)
Robert Cray Band; *Don't Be Afraid Of The Dark* (MER)

SEEING, Looking At
See Also: EYES, FINDING, SEARCH

Ain't Seen Love Like That
Mr. Big; *Bump Ahead* .... (ATL)
As Tears Go By
Marianne Faithfull; *Greatest Hits* .... (AKO)
  Strange Weather .... (ISL)
Rolling Stones; *Big Hits-High Tide & Green Grass* (AKO)
  December's Children .... (AKO)
  Hot Rocks 1964-1971 .... (AKO)
  Singles Collection-London Years .... (AKO)
Can I See You In The Morning
Jackson 5; *Third Album* .... (MOT)
Can I See You Tonight
Tanya Tucker; *Best Of* .... (MCA)
  Live .... (MCA)
Can You See Me
Jimi Hendrix; *Smash Hits* .... (RPR)
  ST/Jimi Plays Monterey .... (RPR)
Can't You See
Alabama; *Live* ....(RCA)
Charlie Daniels Band; *Volunteer Jam VII* .... (EPI)
Hank Williams, Jr.; *Rebels Renegades & Ramblers* (POL)
  Standing In The Shadows .... (POL)
  & Friends .... (POL)
Marshall Tucker Band; *Marshall Tucker Band* ... (AJK)
  Searchin' For A Rainbow .... (AJK)
Peter Tosh; *Mystic Man* .... (RS)
Can't You See Darling
Ray Charles; *20 Golden Pieces Of* .... (BLD)
Can't You See It In My Eyes
Le Roux; *45* ....(RCA)
Can't You See What You're Doing To Me
Albert King; *ILittle Milton-Chronicle* .... (STX)
Can't You See (You Doin' Me Wrong)
Tower Of Power; *Back To Oakland* ....(WB)

Child Of Vision
Supertramp; *Breakfast In America* ....(A&M)
Come See About Me
Diana Ross/Supremes; *16 #1 Hits From The Early*
  '60s .... (MOT)
  Anthology .... (MOT)
  At The Copa .... (MOT)
  Every Great #1 Hit .... (MOT)
  Girl Groups-Story Of A Sound .... (MOT)
  Greatest Hits-#1 .... (MOT)
  Motown Story .... (MOT)
  Motown Superstar Series-#1 .... (MOT)
Coming Home To See You
Supertramp; *Indelibly Stamped* .... (A&M)
Did You Ever See A Dream Walking
Bing Crosby; *Crosby Classics* ....(COL)
Hal Kemp/Skinnay Ennis; *Uncollected-#2 & #3* .. (HIN)
Did You See His Name
Kinks; *Kink Kronikles* .... (RPR)
Did You See Jackie Robinson Hit That...
Count Basie; *RCA Victor Blues & Rhythm Revue* .(RCA)
  & Orchestra: Baseball's Greatest Hits .... (RHI)
Don't Turn Around
Ace Of Base; *The Sign* .... (ARI)
Dreams (I'll Never See)
Allman Brothers Band; *Allman Brothers Band* ...(POL)
  An Evening With-First Set .... (EPI)
  Beginnings ....(POL)
  Best Of ....(POL)
  Decade Of Hits-1969-1979 ....(POL)
  Gregg Allman Tour .... (CPC)
  Road Goes On Forever ....(POL)
Molly Hatchet; *Molly Hatchet* .... (EPI)
Drop Down Mama, Let Your Papa See
John Hammond; *Best Of* .... (VAN)
Sleepy John Estes; *Legend Of* .... (DEL)
Tom Rush; *Best Of* ....(COL)
  Tom Rush ....(COL)
Feelin' Single, Seein' Double
Emmylou Harris; *Elite Hotel* .... (RPR)
First Time Ever I Saw Your Face
Roberta Flack; *Atlantic R&B-#6-(1966-1969)* ... (ATL)
  Best Of .... (ATL)
  First Take .... (ATL)
From A Distance
Bette Midler; *Some People's Lives* .... (ATL)
Byrds; *20 Essential Tracks From The Box Set* .....(COL)
  Byrds (collection) ....(COL)
Judy Collins; *Fires Of Eden* ....(COL)
Kathy Mattea; *Time Passes By* .... (MER)
Nanci Griffith; *Lone Star State Of Mind* .... (MCA)
  One Fair Summer Evening .... (MCA)
Glass Onion
Beatles; *Box Set* ....(CAP)
  White Album ....(CAP)
Has Anybody Seen Amy
John & Audrey Wiggins; *John & Audrey* .... (MER)
Have You Ever Seen The Rain
Creedence Clearwater Revival; *1970* ....(FAN)
  Chronicle ....(FAN)
  Pendulum ....(FAN)
Have You Seen Her
Chi-Lites; *Greatest Hits* .... (EPI)
Hammer; *Please Hammer Don't Hurt 'Em* .... (CAP)
Have You Seen The Saucers
Jefferson Airplane; *2400 Fulton Street-An*
  Anthology ....(RCA)
  30 Seconds Over Winterland ....(RCA)
Have You Seen The Stars Tonight
Jefferson Airplane; *Flight Log* .... (GRU)
Paul Kantner/Jefferson Starship; *Blows Against The*
  Empire ....(RCA)
Have You Seen Your Mother Baby...
Rolling Stones; *Flowers* .... (AKO)
  Got Live If You Want It .... (AKO)
  More Hot Rocks-Big Hits & Fazed Cookies ..... (AKO)
  Through The Past Darkly-Big Hits-#2 .... (AKO)
How You Gonna See Me Now
Alice Cooper; *From The Inside* .... (MET)
I Can See An Angel
Patsy Cline; *20 Golden Pieces Of* ....(BLD)
  Hungry For Love-Her First Recordings-#2 ...... (RHI)
  Today Tomorrow & Forever .... (MCA)

I Can See Arkansas
Anne Murray; *Fifteen Of The Best* .... (LIB)
I Can See Clearly Now
Gladys Knight/Pips; *Greatest Hits* ....(BUD)
   Imagination ....(BUD)
   On & On .... (FFT)
Johnny Nash; *Billboard Top Rock 'N' Roll
Hits-1972* .... (RHI)
   Rock Artifacts-#2 ....(COL)
I Can See For Miles
Who; *Hooligans* .... (MCA)
   Join Together .... (MCA)
   Meaty Beaty Big & Bouncy .... (MCA)
   Sell Out .... (MCA)
   ST/Kids Are Alright .... (MCA)
   Who's Better Who's Best .... (MCA)
I Can See Forever In Your Eyes
Reba McEntire; *Feel The Fire* .... (MER)
I Can See It
Barbra Streisand; *Happening In Central Park* .....(COL)
   My Name Is Barbra .... (COL)
I Can't See Nobody
Bee Gees; *Gold-#1* .... (RSO)
   Here At Last .... (RSO)
I Can't See Texas From Here
George Strait; *Strait From The Heart* .... (MCA)
I Can't See You
Dokken; *Breaking The Chains* .... (ELE)
Tim Buckley; *Best Of* .... (RHI)
   Elektrock-Sixties .... (ELE)
I Can't See Your Face In My Mind
Doors; *Classics* .... (ELE)
   Strange Days .... (ELE)
I Couldn't See You Leavin'
Conway Twitty; *S* .... (MCA)
I Just Want To See His Face
Rolling Stones; *Exile On Main Street* .... (RS)
I Know A Heartache When I See One
Jennifer Warnes; *Best Of* .... (ARI)
   Shot Through The Heart .... (ARI)
I Saw Her Again
Mamas & The Papas; *Best Of* .... (MCA)
   Farewell To The First Golden Era .... (MCA)
   Mamas & The Papas .... (MCA)
I Saw Her (Him) Standing There
Beatles; *Meet The* .... (CAP)
   Please Please Me .... (EMI)
   Rock 'n' Roll Music-#1 .... (CAP)
Paul McCartney; *Tripping The Live Fantastic* ... (CAP)
   Tripping The Live Fantastic-Highlights! .... (CAP)
Tiffany; *Tiffany* .... (MCA)
I Saw It On TV
John Fogerty; *Centerfield* .... (WB)
I Saw Linda Yesterday
Dickey Lee; *45s On CD-#2-1960-1966* .... (MER)
I Saw The Light
Hank Williams; *24 Greatest Hits-#2* .... (POL)
   40 Greatest Hits .... (POL)
   I Ain't Got Nothin' But Time .... (POL)
   Legend In Song-With Hank Williams, Jr. .... (POL)
   Rare Takes & Radio Cuts .... (POL)
I Saw The Light (In The Window...)
Wynonna; *Wynonna* .... (MCC)
I See It Now
Tracy Lawrence; *I See It Now* .... (ATL)
I See The Lovelight In Your Eyes
Conway Twitty; *Number Ones* .... (MCA)
I See The Want In Your Eyes
Conway Twitty; *I'm Not Through Loving You
Yet* .... (MCA)
   Night With .... (MCA)
   Number Ones .... (MCA)
I See Your Face Before Me
Frank Sinatra; *In The Wee Small Hours* .... (CAP)
   What Is This Thing Called Love .... (CAP)
Miles Davis; *Chronicle* .... (PRS)
   Green Haze .... (PRS)
If Ever I See You Again
Roberta Flack; *Best Of* .... (ATL)
If You Could Only See Me Now
T. Graham Brown; *Bumper To Bumper* .... (CAP)
If You Could See Me Now
Sarah Vaughan & Count Basie; *Pablo Today-Send In
The Clowns* .... (PAB)

If You See Kay
Memphis Slim/Tampa Red/Lonnie Johnson; *Bawdy
Blues* .... (BV)
In A Different Light
Doug Stone; *Doug Stone* .... (EPI)
I'd Love Just Once To See You
Beach Boys; *Smiley Smile/Wild Honey* ....(CAP)
I'd Really Love To See You Tonight
England Dan & John Ford Coley; *Best Of* ....(BT)
   Hit Singles 1958-1977 .... (ATL)
   Nights Are Forever .... (BT)
I'll Be Seeing You
Judy Collins; *Judith* .... (ELE)
Skyliners; *Greatest Hits* .... (OSR)
I'll See You In My Dreams
Doris Day; *At The Movies* ....(COL)
Doris Day & Danny Thomas; *Calamity Jane/I'll See You
In My Dreams* .... (SSP)
I've Just Seen A Face
Beatles; *Help* .... (CAP)
   Rubber Soul .... (CAP)
Paul McCartney; *Unplugged-Official Bootleg* ..... (CAP)
Paul McCartney/Wings; *Over America* .... (CAP)
I've Never Seen The Likes Of You
Conway Twitty; *Heart & Soul* .... (MCA)
   Number Ones .... (MCA)
I've Seen All The Good People
Yes; *Classic Rock 1966-1988* .... (ATL)
   Yes Album .... (ATL)
   Yessongs .... (ATL)
I've Seen Better Days
Reba McEntire; *Whoever's In New England* ..... (MCA)
Tammy Wynette & George Jones; *Golden Ring* ...(EPI)
I've Seen That Face Before
Grace Jones; *Nightclubbing* .... (ISL)
   Island Life .... (ISL)
I've Seen That Look On Me
George Strait; *Something Special* .... (MCA)
Willie Nelson; *Don't You Ever Get Tired Of Hurting
Me* ....(RCA)
   Willie .... (RCA)
I've Seen That Movie Too
Elton John; *Goodbye Yellow Brick Road* .... (POL)
I've Seen The Saucers
Elton John; *Caribou* .... (POL)
Johnny Have You Seen Her?
Rembrandts; *United* ....(ATC)
Just To See Her
Smokey Robinson; *One Heartbeat* .... (MOT)
Last Time I Saw Paris
Jonathan & Darlene Edwards; *Greatest Hits* ..... (CRN)
   In Paris .... (CRN)
Soundtrack; *That's Entertainment-#2* .... (MCA)
Long As I Can See The Light
Creedence Clearwater Revival; *1970* ....(FAN)
   Chronicle ....(FAN)
   Cosmo's Factory ....(FAN)
Long Time No See
Chicago; *VIII* ....(COL)
Long Time No See, Baby
Glenn Miller; *Complete-#5-1940* ....(RCA)
   Complete-#9-1939-1942 ....(RCA)
Look At All Those Idiots
Simpsons; *Sing The Blues* .... (GEF)
Look At California
Maze featuring Frankie Beverly; *Live In New
Orleans* ....(CAP)
   Maze featuring Frankie Beverly ....(CAP)
Look At That Cadillac
Stray Cats; *Best Of-Rock This Town* .... (EMI)
Lookin' In The Same Direction
Ken Mellons; *Ken Mellons* .... (EPI)
Love At First Sight
Kylie Minogue; *Kylie* .... (GEF)
Mello-Kings; *Greatest Hits* .... (CLT)
Outlaws; *Playin' To Win* .... (ARI)
Styx; *End Of The Century* .... (A&M)
Love Saw It
Karyn White; *Karyn White* .... (WB)
Mama's Never Seen Those Eyes
Forester Sisters; *Forester Sisters* .... (WB)
More I See You
Boston Pops Orchestra/Arthur Fiedler; *Music For Every
Mood* .... (RCA)

Chet Baker; *Sings It Could Happen To You* ...... (RVR)
Dick Haymes; *Best Of* .... (CCB)
Nat King Cole; *Very Thought Of You* .... (CAP)
Never Saw A Miracle
Curtis Stigers; *Curtis Stigers* .... (ARI)
New York Mining Disaster 1941
Bee Gees; *Gold-#1* .... (POL)
  Here At Last .... (RSO)
  History Of British Rock-#8 .... (RHI)
Next Time You See Her
Eric Clapton; *Slow Hand* .... (RSO)
Next Time You See Me
Little Junior Parker; *Best Of* .... (MCA)
  Superblues-#2-All-Time Classic Blues .... (STX)
Nobody Knows The Trouble I've Seen
Mahalia Jackson; *Gospels Spirituals & Hymns* ...(COL)
  Greatest Hits ....(COL)
Nat King Cole; *Every Time I Feel The Spirit* ......(CAP)
Oh, Look At Me Now
Frank Sinatra; *A Swingin' Affair* ....(CAP)
Nancy Wilson; *But Beautiful* ....(BLN)
Sammy Kaye/Orchestra; *Play 22 Original Big Band
Recordings* .... (HIN)
Tommy Dorsey; *Boogie Woogie* ....(POE)
Tommy Dorsey & Frank Sinatra; *All-Time Greatest
Hits-#1* .... (BLU)
On A Clear Day You Can See Forever
Barbra Streisand; *Barbra Streisand* ....(COL)
  Just For The Record ....(COL)
  Live At The Forum ....(COL)
  ST/On A Clear Day You Can See Forever ......(SMP)
Frank Sinatra; *Strangers In The Night* ....(RPR)
Hollies; *Greatest Hits* .... (EPI)
Roger Williams; *Best Of* ....(MCA)
  Somewhere In Time ....(BAI)
One Vision
Queen; *A Kind Of Magic* ....(HOL)
  Classic ....(HOL)
  Live At Wembley '86 ....(HOL)
Only A Lonely Heart Sees
Felix Cavaliere; *Castles In The Air* ....(OOP)
Outside Looking In
Mary Chapin Carpenter; *Stones In The Road* ...(COL)
Pretend You Don't See Her
Jerry Vale; *17 Most Requested Songs* ....(COL)
  All-Time Greatest Hits ....(COL)
  Greatest Hits ....(COL)
Pretty Fuck Look
Pussy Galore; *Corpse Love-The First Year* ....(CRL)
Run, Come See Jerusalem
Arlo Guthrie & Pete Seeger; *Precious Friend* ......(WB)
See Emily Play
David Bowie; *Pinups* ....(RYK)
Pink Floyd; *Relics* ....(CAP)
  Works ....(CAP)
See Me In Your Eyes
38 Special; *Tour De Force* ....(A&M)
See Me, Feel Me
Who; *ST/Kids Are Alright* ....(MCA)
  Tommy ....(MCA)
  Who's Better Who's Best-Very Best Of ....(MCA)
  Who's Last ....(MCA)
See My Way
Blodwyn Pig; *Ahead Rings Out* ....(A&M)
Who; *Happy Jack/Who Sell Out* ....(MCA)
See Ruby Fall
Johnny Cash; *Essential* ....(COL)
See The Changes
Crosby, Stills & Nash; *CSN* ....(ATL)
  Crosby, Stills & Nash (collection) ....(ATL)
See The Funny Little Clown
Bobby Goldsboro; *10th Anniversary Album-#1* ... (EMI)
  Greatest Hits ....(LIB)
  Honey-Best Of ....(EMI)
See The Light
Aldo Nova; *Aldo Nova* ....(POR)
  Portrait Of ....(EPI)
Earth, Wind & Fire; *That's The Way Of The
World* ....(COL)
Five Americans; *Nuggets-Collection From Psychedelic
'60s* ....(RHI)
Jeff Healey Band; *See The Light* ....(ARI)
Marty Balin; *Better Generation* ....(GWE)

See The Lights
Simple Minds; *Real Life* ....(A&M)
See The Sky About to Rain
Neil Young; *On The Beach* ....(RPR)
See You
Depeche Mode; *Broken Frame* .... (SIR)
  Catching Up With .... (SIR)
See You In Hell
Grim Reaper; *See You In Hell* ....(RCA)
See You In Hell (Don't Be Late)
Yngwie Malmsteen; *Eclipse* ....(POL)
See You In Hell, Blind Boy
Ry Cooder; *ST/Crossroads* ....(WB)
See You In Paradise
Saints; *All Fools Day* ....(TVT)
See You In Rio
Joyce; *Music Inside* .... (VF)
See You In September
Chiffons; *Best Of* ....(LAU)
Happenings; *ST/Purple People Eater* .... (AJK)
Tempos; *Cruisin'-1960* .... (INC)
  ST/American Graffiti ....(MCA)
See You Later, Alligator
Bill Haley/Comets; *Bill Haley/Comets* ....(EVR)
  Billboard Top Rock 'N' Roll Hits-1956 .... (RHI)
  Golden Hits ....(MCA)
  Greatest Hits ....(MCA)
  Mr. Rock 'N' Roll ....(ACC)
  Rock & Roll Is Here To Stay ....(GUS)
  Rockin' & Rollin' ....(ACC)
See You Next Year
Cleftones; *Best Of* .... (RHI)
See You Sometime
Joni Mitchell; *For The Roses* ....(ASY)
See You When I Git There
Lou Rawls; *Classics* .... (PI)
  Live .... (PI)
  Unmistakably Lou .... (PI)
Seeing Is Believing
Bobby King & Terry Evans; *Live & Let Live* .... (ROU)
Mike/Mechanics; *Living Years* ....(ATL)
Three O'Clock; *Sixteen Tambourines* ....(FON)
Seeing The Elephant
Debby McClatchy/Red Clay Ramblers; *Debby
McClatchy/Red Clay Ramblers* ....(GRE)
Seeing Things
Black Crowes; *Shake Your Money Maker* ....(DEF)
Seein' My Father In Me
Paul Overstreet; *Sowin' Love* ....(RCA)
Seven Wonders
Fleetwood Mac; *Tango In The Night* ....(WB)
Sign, The
Ace Of Base; *The Sign* .... (ARI)
So You Like What You See
Samuelle; *Living In Black Paradise* ....(ATL)
Sound & Vision
David Bowie; *Changestwobowie* ....(RCA)
  Low ....(RYK)
  Sound + Vision ....(RYK)
  The Singles-1969-1993 ....(RYK)
Standing On The Corner
Broadway Cast; *Most Happy Fella* ....(RCA)
Four Lads; *16 Most Requested Songs* ....(COL)
Original Broadway Cast; *Most Happy Fella* ..... (SMC)
Take A Look At My Face
Michael Bolton; *The Hunger* ....(COL)
Tell Me What You See
Beatles; *Box Set* ....(CAP)
  Help! ....(CAP)
  Love Songs ....(CAP)
  VI ....(CAP)
Tennes-See Me
Jeannie C. Riley; *Here's* ....(PLY)
To See An Angel Cry
Conway Twitty; *Greatest Hits-#1* ....(MCA)
  #1's-#1 ....(CAP)
To See My Angel In Virginia
Livewire; *Wired* ....(ROU)
Turn Around, Look At Me
Vogues; *Greatest Hits* .... (RHI)
Vision Of A Child
Steve Young; *Honky Tonk Man* .... (ROU)
Vision Of A Kiss
B-52's; *Good Stuff* ....(RPR)

Vision Of Mother
 Ricky Skaggs; *Don't Cheat In Our Hometown* .... (EPI)
 R. Stanley/J. Marshall/A. Krauss; *Saturday Night &
 Sunday Morning* .... (FRC)
Vision Of The Future
 Roachford; *Get Ready!* .... (EPI)
Vision Of You
 Belinda Carlisle; *Her Greatest Hits* .... (MCA)
 Runaway Horses .... (MCA)
Visions
 Commodores; *Natural High* .... (MOT)
 Eagles; *One Of These Nights* .... (ASY)
 Stevie Wonder; *Innervisions* .... (MOT)
Visions In Blue
 Ultravox; *Collection* .... (CHR)
Visions Of Angels
 Genesis; *Trespass* .... (MCA)
Visions Of China
 Japan; *Oil On Canvas* .... (BP)
 Tin Drum .... (BP)
Visions Of Johanna
 Bob Dylan; *Biograph* .... (COL)
 Blonde On Blonde .... (COL)
Visions Of Paradise
 Moody Blues; *In Search Of The Lost Chord* ...... (POL)
Watch Me Bleed
 Tears For Fears; *The Hurting* .... (MER)
Watch My .38
 Commander Cody/Lost Planet Airmen; *Hot Licks Cold
 Steel & Trucker's Fav.* .... (MCA)
Watch The Moon Come Down
 Graham Parker/Rumour; *Parkerilla* .... (MER)
 Stick To Me .... (MER)
Watch The Sun Go Down
 X; *Ain't Love Grand* .... (ELE)
Watch What Happens (Lola's Theme)
 Frank Sinatra; *My Way* .... (RPR)
 Henry Mancini; *Mancini Magic* .... (PRR)
 Sergio Mendes; *Four Sider* .... (A&M)
Watcher Of The Skies
 Genesis; *Foxtrot* .... (ATL)
 Live .... (ATL)
Watching Me Watching You
 Jethro Tull; *Broadsword & The Beast* .... (CHR)
Watching Out For Jesus
 Rave-Ups; *Chance* .... (EPI)
Watching Scotty Grow
 Bobby Goldsboro; *All-Time Greatest Hits* .... (CCB)
 Honey-Best Of .... (EMI)
Watching The Clothes
 Pretenders; *Learning To Crawl* .... (SIR)
Watching The Detectives
 Elvis Costello; *Girls Girls Girls* .... (COL)
 My Aim Is True .... (COL)
 Elvis Costello/Attractions; *Best Of* .... (COL)
Watching The River Flow
 Bob Dylan; *Greatest Hits-#2* .... (COL)
 Joe Cocker; *Luxury You Can Afford* .... (ASY)
Watching The River Run
 Loggins & Messina; *Best Of-Friends* .... (COL)
 Full Sail .... (COL)
Watching The World Go By
 Gun; *Gallus* .... (A&M)
We Didn't See A Thing
 Ray Charles/George Jones/Chet Atkins;
 Friendship .... (COL)
When Can I See You
 Babyface; *For The Cool In You* .... (EPI)
When Can I See You Again
 Babyface; *For The Cool In You* .... (EPI)
When Will I See You Again
 Three Degrees; *Mega Hits Dance Classics-#2* .... (PRY)
 Soul Hits/'70s-#14 .... (RHI)
When Will I See You Smile Again?
 Bell Biv Devoe; *Poison* .... (MCA)
 WBBD-Bootcity-Remix Album .... (MCA)
While You See A Chance
 Steve Winwood; *Arc Of A Diver* .... (ISL)
 Chronicles .... (ISL)
You Ain't Seen Nothing Yet
 Bachman-Turner Overdrive; *Best Of B.T.O.-So
 Far* .... (MER)
 Metal Age-Roots Of Metal .... (RHI)
 Not Fragile .... (MER)

You Just Watch Me
 Tanya Tucker; *Soon* .... (LIB)
You Won't See Me
 Anne Murray; *Greatest Hits* .... (CAP)
 Love Song .... (CAP)
 Beatles; *Box Set* .... (CAP)
 Rubber Soul .... (CAP)
 Bryan Ferry; *These Foolish Things* .... (RPR)
You Won't See Me Cry
 Wilson Phillips; *Shadows & Light* .... (SBK)

SEX

See Also: KISSING, various ANATOMY categories

36-22-36
 Bobby Bland; *Best Of-#2* .... (MCA)
 Bobby Bland .... (MCA)
 Here's The Man .... (MCA)
Adultress
 Pretenders; *II* .... (SIR)
After Sex
 Curtis Mayfield; *ST/Let's Do It Again* .... (CUR)
Afternoon Delight
 Starland Vocal Band; *Starland Vocal Band* .... (WS)
All I Wanna Do Is Make Love To You
 Heart; *Brigade* .... (CAP)
All I Want To Do Is Make Love To You
 Impressions; *Come To My Party* .... (20)
All Of This Making Love
 Bee Gees; *Main Course* .... (RSO)
All The Way
 Whispers; *Headlights* .... (SLR)
All The Way Lover
 Millie Jackson; *Feelin' Bitchy* .... (SPR)
 Live & Uncensored .... (SPR)
Always Makin' Love
 Kentucky HeadHunters; *Electric Barnyard* ...... (MER)
Anti-Sex Backlash Of The '80s
 Roches; *Speak* .... (MCA)
Anytime You Wanna Make Love To Me
 Trini Lopez; *Transformed By Time* .... (RLL)
Arabian Lover
 Duke Ellington; *Jungle Nights In Harlem* .... (BLU)
Are We Making Love Or Making Friends
 Moe Bandy; *Soft Lights & Hard Country Music* ..(COL)
Are You Ready For The Sex Girls
 Gleaming Spires; *Best Of Rodney On The 'ROQ* .. (PBO)
Babies Makin' Babies
 Sly/Family Stone; *Anthology* .... (EPI)
 Fresh .... (EPI)
Baby Baby (Just A Little More Head)
 2 Live Crew; *Sports Weekend-As Clean As They Wanna
 Be* .... (LUK)
Baby Got Back
 Sir Mix-A-Lot; *Mack Daddy* .... (DEF)
Baby Talks Dirty
 Knack; *But The Little Girls Understand* .... (CAP)
Baby Workout
 Jackie Wilson; *Billboard Top R&B Hits-1963* .... (RHI)
 Reet Petite-Best Of .... (COL)
 Story .... (EPI)
Baby, Let Me Kiss You
 King Floyd; *Soul Hits/'70s-#5* .... (RHI)
Back Seat Of My Car
 Paul McCartney; *CD Gift Set* .... (CAP)
 Paul & Linda McCartney; *Ram* .... (CAP)
Bang A Gong
 T. Rex; *Electric Warrior* .... (RPR)
Bedroom
 Jim Ed Brown & Helen Cornelius; *One Man-One
 Woman* .... (RCA)
Bedroom Eyes
 Eddie Rabbitt; *Radio Romance* .... (CAP)
 Evelyn "Champagne" King; *Sweet Delight* ......(RCA)
Bedroom Reunion
 Barbara Mandrell; *Lovers Friends & Strangers* ... (MCA)
Bedroom Thang
 ZZ Top; *First Album* .... (WB)
 Six Pack .... (WB)
Bed's Too Big Without You
 Police; *Regatta De Blanc* .... (A&M)

Behind Closed Doors
  Charlie Rich; *American Originals* ....(COL)
    Behind Closed Doors .... (EPI)
    Columbia Country Classics-#4 ....(COL)
    Greatest Hits .... (EPI)
Big Balls
  AC/DC; *Dirty Deeds Done Dirt Cheap* ....(ATL)
Big Love
  Bellamy Brothers; *Greatest Hits-#3* .... (MCA)
    Rebels Without A Clue .... (MCA)
  Fleetwood Mac; *25 Years-The Chain* ....(WB)
    Greatest Hits ....(WB)
    Tango In The Night ....(WB)
Birds & The Bees
  Jewel Akens; *American Graffiti-#3* .... (MCA)
    Collectables History Of Rock-#4 ....(CLT)
    Cruisin'-1965 .... (INC)
    Oldies But Goodies-#9 ....(OSR)
    Super Hits-#3 ....(GUS)
Birthday Suit
  Johnny Kemp; *ST/Sing* ....(COL)
Blueberry Hill
  Elvis Presley; *Loving You* ....(RCA)
    Recorded Live On Stage ....(RCA)
  Fats Domino; *Greatest Hits* ....(EVR)
    Greatest Hits .... (MCA)
    My Blue Heaven-Best Of-#1 .... (EMI)
  Little Richard; *Big Hits* ....(CRS)
  Louis Armstrong; *Best Of* .... (MCA)
    Essential ....(VAN)
    I Like Jazz: Essence Of ....(COL)
Body Talk
  Deele; *Body Talk* .... (SLR)
    Street Beat .... (SLR)
  Kix; *Cool Kids* ....(ATL)
  Ratt; *Dancing Undercover* ....(ATL)
    Ratt & Roll 8191 ....(ATL)
    ST/Golden Child ....(CAP)
  Wallets; *Body Talk* .... (TT)
Boobs A Lot
  Fugs; *First Album* .... (ESP)
    Fugs 4 Rounders Score .... (ESP)
    Greatest Hits-#1 ....(PVC)
  Holy Modal Rounders; *Dr. Demento's Delights* ....(WB)
Bop Gun
  Ice Cube & George Clinton; *S* ....(PRY)
Butt Fuck
  Human Sexual Response; *Fig. 15* ....(EAT)
Californicatin'
  J. Geils Band; *You're Gettin' Even While I'm
  Gettin'*... .... (AMR)
Can't Get Enough Of Your Love
  Bad Company; *Bad Company* .... (SS)
  Taylor Dayne; *Soul Dancing* ....(ARI)
Careless Love
  Dinah Washington; *Bessie Smith Songbook* ......(EMA)
  Pete Fountain; *Mr. New Orleans* ....(MCA)
  Preservation Hall Jazz Band; *When The Saints Go
  Marchin' In-#3* ....(COL)
Casanova
  Bryan Ferry; *Let's Stick Together* ....(RPR)
  Levert; *Big Throwdown* ....(ATL)
    Golden Age Of Black Music-1977-1988 ....(ATL)
    ST/Fatal Beauty ....(ATL)
  Roxy Music; *Country Life* ....(ATC)
Centerfold
  J. Geils Band; *Flashback-Best Of* .... (EMI)
    Freeze-Frame .... (EMI)
    Showtime .... (EMI)
Cherry Hill Park
  Billy Joe Royal; *Greatest Hits* ....(COL)
    Super Hits/'70s-Have A Nice Day-#1 ....(RHI)
Closer
  Nine Inch Nails; *The Downward Spiral* ....(NOT)
Company Time
  Linda Davis; *Shoot For The Moon* ....(ARI)
Damn I Wish I Was Your Lover
  Sophie B. Hawkins; *Tongues & Tales* ....(COL)
Dancing In The Sheets
  Shalamar; *Greatest Hits* .... (SLR)
    ST/Footloose ....(COL)
Date Rape
  Tribe Called Quest; *Low End Theory* ....(JVA)

Davy's Dinghy
  Ruth Wallis; *Dr. Demento's Dementia Royale* .... (RHI)
    Dr. Demento's Greatest Novelties-#2 ....(RHI)
Daytime Friends
  Kenny Rogers; *Daytime Friends* ....(LIB)
    Ten Years Of Gold ....(EMI)
    Twenty Greatest Hits ....(LIB)
Delta Lady
  Joe Cocker; *Classics-#4* ....(A&M)
    Greatest Hits ....(A&M)
    Joe Cocker ....(A&M)
    Mad Dogs & Englishmen ....(A&M)
  Leon Russell; *Best Of* ....(MCA)
    Leon Russell ....(MCA)
Digital Display
  Ready For The World; *Ready For The World* ... (MCA)
Dim All The Lights
  Donna Summer; *Bad Girls* .... (CAS)
    Dance Collection .... (CAS)
    Greatest Hits .... (CAS)
    On The Radio-Greatest Hits-#1 & 2 .... (CAS)
Dirty Movies
  Van Halen; *Fair Warning* ....(WB)
Dirty White Boy
  Foreigner; *Head Games* ....(ATL)
    Records ....(ATL)
Do Me Again
  Freddie Jackson; *Do Me Again* ....(CAP)
Do Me Baby
  Meli'sa Morgan; *Do Me Baby* ....(CAP)
  Prince; *Controversy* ....(WB)
Do Me!
  Bell Biv Devoe; *Poison* .... (MCA)
Do That To Me One More Time
  Captain & Tennille; *Make Your Move* ....(CAS)
Do Ya Think I'm Sexy?
  Rod Stewart; *Absolutely Live* ....(WB)
    Blondes Have More Fun ....(WB)
    Greatest Hits ....(WB)
Do You Wanna Make Love?
  Peter McCann; *Peter McCann* .... (20)
Don't Come Home A Drinkin' (With...
  Loretta Lynn; *Greatest Hits* .... (MCA)
    Greatest Hits Live .... (KT)
    MCA Records 30 Years Of Hits-1958-1988 ... (MCA)
Don't Go Home With Your Hard On
  Leonard Cohen; *Death Of A Ladies' Man* ....(COL)
Don't Make Love To Mary (With Mabel...)
  Merle Travis; *Johnny Gimble's Texas Honky-Tonk
  Hits* .... (CMH)
Don't Stop Till You Get Enough
  Jacksons; *Jacksons Live* .... (EPI)
  Michael Jackson; *Off The Wall* .... (EPI)
Don't Touch Me There
  Tubes; *T.R.A.S.H.* ....(A&M)
    What Do You Want From-Live .... (A&M)
    Young & Rich ....(A&M)
Don't You Feel My Leg
  Maria Muldaur; *Maria Muldaur* .... (RPR)
Dreamlover
  Mariah Carey; *Music Box* ....(COL)
Dress You Up
  Madonna; *Like A Virgin* .... (SIR)
Dynamo Humm
  Mothers Of Invention; *Overnite Sensation* ....(RYK)
Earth Girls Are Easy
  Julie Brown; *Goddess In Progress* .... (RHI)
Easy Lover
  Phil Collins; *Serious Hits...Live!* ....(ATL)
  Philip Bailey & Phil Collins; *Chinese Walls* ......(COL)
Empty Bed Blues
  Bessie Smith; *Collection* ....(COL)
    Empty Bed Blues ....(COL)
  Bette Midler; *Broken Blossom* ....(ATL)
  La Vern Baker; *Atlantic Jazz-Singers* ....(ATL)
    Sings Bessie Smith ....(ATL)
Erotica
  Madonna; *Erotica* .... (MAV)
Everybody's Doin' It
  Commander Cody; *Country Casanova* .... (MCA)
Feel Like Makin' Love
  Bad Company; *10 From 6* ....(ATL)
    Straight Shooter .... (SS)

Roberta Flack; *Atlantic R&B*
1947-1974-#6-(1966-1969) .... (ATL)
  Best Of .... (ATL)
  Feel Like Makin' Love .... (ATL)
  Golden Age Of Black Music-1970-1975 .... (ATL)
  Golden Soul .... (ATL)
Feels Like The First Time
Foreigner; *Classic Rock-1966-1988* .... (ATL)
  Foreigner .... (ATL)
  Records .... (ATL)
Fez
Steely Dan; *Greatest Hits* .... (MCA)
  Royal Scam .... (MCA)
Flirt
Cameo; *Alligator Woman* .... (CHC)
Foxey Lady
Jimi Hendrix; *Essential-#2* .... (RPR)
  Smash Hits .... (RPR)
  ST/Jimi Plays Monterey .... (RPR)
  ST/Wayne's World .... (RPR)
Jimi Hendrix Experience; *Are You Experienced?* . (RPR)
Mary's Danish; *Circa* ....(MC)
Friends & Lovers
Bread; *Best Of-#2* .... (ELE)
  Bread .... (ELE)
Carl Anderson & Gloria Loring; *Gloria Loring* ... (ATL)
Funky Cold Medina
Tone Loc; *Loc-ed After Dark* .... (DV)
Get Down
War; *All Day Music* .... (UA)
  Live .... (UA)
Get Down Make Love
Queen; *Live Killers* ....(HOL)
  News Of The World ....(HOL)
Get Down Tonight
K.C./Sunshine Band; *Best Of* .... (RHI)
  Billboard Top Hits-1975 .... (RHI)
  Get Down Tonight-Best Of T.K. .... (RHI)
Get It On (Bang A Gong)
Power Station; *Power Station* .... (CAP)
T. Rex; *Electric Warrior* .... (RPR)
Get My Rocks Off
Dr. Hook/Medicine Show; *Revisited* ....(COL)
  Sloppy Seconds ....(COL)
Get Off
Foxy; *Get Down Tonight!-Best Of T.K.* .... (RHI)
  Get Off ....(DSH)
Gigolo
Damned; *Anything* .... (MCA)
O'Bryan; *Doin' Alright* ....(CAP)
Girl With The Hungry Eyes
Jefferson Starship; *At Point Zero* .... (GRU)
Girls Of Porn
Mr. Bungle; *Mr. Bungle* ....(WB)
Give It To Me Baby
Rick James; *25 No. 1 Hits From 25 Years* ...... (MOT)
  Greatest Hits .... (MOT)
  Street Songs .... (MOT)
Give Me A Ring Sometime
Lisa Brokop; *Every Little Girl's Dream* .... (PAT)
Giving Him Something He Can Feel
En Vogue; *Funky Divas* ....(EW)
Go All The Way
Raspberries; *Best Of* ....(CAP)
  Capitol Collectors Series ....(CAP)
Good Girls Don't
Knack; *Get The Knack* ....(CAP)
Good Girls Go To Heaven
Charlie Floyd; *Charlie Floyd* .... (LIB)
Hanky Panky
Chicago; *VII* ....(COL)
Lou Reed; *Transformer* ....(RCA)
Madonna; *I'm Breathless* ....(SIR)
Tommy James/Shondells; *Anthology* .... (RHI)
  Billboard Top Rock 'N' Roll Hits-1966 .... (RHI)
He Wants My Body
Starpoint; *Sensational* .... (ELE)
Heaven In The Back Seat
Eddie Money; *Right Here* ....(COL)
Help Me Make It Through The Night
Bryan Ferry; *Another Time Another Place* .... (RPR)
Gladys Knight/Pips; *Anthology* .... (MOT)
  Compact Command Performance .... (MOT)

Joan Baez; *Blessed Are* .... (VAN)
  Hits/Greatest & Others .... (VAN)
Sammi Smith; *Super Hits/'70s-Have A Nice
Day-#4* .... (RHI)
Willie Nelson; *Greatest Hits & Some That Will Be* (COL)
  Sings Kristofferson ....(COL)
  Sweet Memories ....(RCA)
Her Strut
Bob Seger/Silver Bullet Band; *Against The Wind* . (CAP)
  Nine Tonight .... (CAP)
Hit Me With Your Best Shot
Pat Benatar; *Crimes Of Passion* .... (CHR)
  Live From Earth .... (CHR)
Hot For Teacher
Van Halen; *1984* ....(WB)
Hot Legs
Rod Stewart; *Absolutely Live* ....(WB)
  Footloose & Fancy Free ....(WB)
  Greatest Hits ....(WB)
  Storyteller-Complete Anthology-1964-1990 .....(WB)
Hot Stuff
Donna Summer; *Bad Girls* .... (CAS)
  Dance Collection .... (CAS)
  On The Radio-Greatest Hits-#1 & 2 .... (CAS)
  Walk Away-Best Of-1977-1980 .... (CAS)
Rolling Stones; *Black & Blue* .... (RS)
  Love You Live .... (RS)
  Sucking In The Seventies .... (RS)
Whitesnake; *Come An' Get It* ....(GEF)
Hot, Wet & Sticky
Galaxy; *Hot, Wet & Sticky* .... (ARI)
House Of Blue Lights
Andrews Sisters; *Best Of-#2* .... (MCA)
Asleep At The Wheel; *10* .... (EPI)
  Greatest Country Hits/'80s-1987 ....(COL)
  More Hot Country Requests-#2 .... (EPI)
  Trucker's Jukebox-#2 ....(COL)
Canned Heat; *Human Conditions* .... (TAK)
  & John Lee Hooker: Live At Fox Venice .... (RHI)
Chuck Berry; *Chess Box* .... (CSS)
  More Rock 'N' Roll Rarities-Golden Era .... (CSS)
How Can We Be Lovers
Michael Bolton; *Soul Provider* ....(COL)
Humming Song
Martin Mull; *I'm Everyone I Ever Loved* .... (MCA)
Hungry Eyes
Eric Carmen; *Best Of* .... (ARI)
  Dirty Dancing Live In Concert ....(RCA)
  ST/Dirty Dancing ....(RCA)
Hungry For Love
Patsy Cline; *20 Golden Pieces Of* ....(BLD)
  Patsy Cline .... (MCA)
  Hungry For Love-Her First Recordings-#2 ...... (RHI)
Todd Rundgren; *A Wizard A True Star* .... (RHI)
Hungry For Your Love
Van Morrison; *ST/Officer & A Gentleman* .... (ISL)
  Wavelength ....(WB)
I Didn't Mean To Turn You On
Cherrelle; *Fragile* ....(TAB)
Robert Palmer; *Heart Of Rock* ....(COL)
  MTV-VH1 Powerplayers .... (EMI)
  Riptide .... (ISL)
I Don't Know
Blues Brothers; *Best Of* .... (ATL)
  Briefcase Full Of Blues .... (ATL)
I Don't Know If It's Right
Evelyn "Champagne" King; *Dance! Dance!
Dance!-#2* ....(RCA)
  Smooth Talk ....(RCA)
I Drove All Night
Cyndi Lauper; *Night To Remember* .... (EPI)
I Just Want To Make Love To You
Bill Medley; *Best Of* .... (MCA)
Cold Blood; *Bill Graham Presents-Fillmore-Last
Days* .... (EPA)
Etta James; *At Last* .... (CSS)
Foghat; *Best Of* .... (RHI)
  Foghat .... (RHI)
Muddy Waters; *Best Of* .... (CSS)
  Chess Box-Willie Dixon .... (CSS)
Righteous Brothers; *Anthology-1962-1974* .... (RHI)
Rolling Stones; *Rolling Stones* ....(AKO)
  Singles Collection-London Years ....(AKO)
Van Morrison; *It's Too Late To Stop Now* ....(WB)

I Like The Way (The Kissing Game)
Hi-Five; *Hi-Five* .... (JVA)
I Never Made Love 'Til I Made It With...
Mac Davis; *Country Classics-#5-1985-1986* .... (MCA)
   Till I Made It With You .... (MCA)
I Touch Myself
Divinyls; *Divinyls* .... (VIA)
I Wanna Be Your Lover
Bob Dylan; *Biograph* .... (COL)
Prince; *Prince* .... (WB)
I Wanna Sex You Up
Color Me Badd; *C.M.B.* .... (GIA)
   ST/New Jack City .... (GIA)
I Want It Now
Cameo; *Real Men Wear Black* .... (ATA)
I Want To Know You Before We Make Love
Conway Twitty; *Borderline* .... (MCA)
I Want Your Sex
George Michael; *Faith* .... (COL)
   ST/Beverly Hills Cop II .... (MCA)
I Wonder If I Take You Home
Lisa Lisa & Cult Jam With Full Force;
Breakdancing ....(COL)
   Lisa Lisa & Cult Jam With Full Force ....(COL)
If You Don't Wanna Get Pregnant
U.T.F.O.; *Bag It & Bone It* .... (JVA)
If You See Kay
Memphis Slim/Tampa Red/Lonnie Johnson; *Bawdy
Blues* .... (BV)
In Your Room
Bangles; *Everything* ....(COL)
   Greatest Hits ....(COL)
Insatiable Woman
Isley/Jasper/Isley; *Caravan Of Love* ....(CBA)
It's Ecstasy When You Lay Down Next...
Barry White; *Greatest Hits-#2* .... (20)
   Sings For Someone You Love .... (20)
I'd Love To Lay You Down
Conway Twitty; *45* .... (MCA)
I'll Make Love To You
Boyz II Men; *II* .... (MOT)
I'll Make Love To You Anytime
Eric Clapton; *Backless* .... (RSO)
I'm In You
Peter Frampton; *Classics-#12* .... (A&M)
   I'm In You .... (A&M)
I'm The One
Roberta Flack; *I'm The One* .... (ATL)
I'm Too Sexy
Right Said Fred; *Up* .... (CHS)
Joker, The
Steve Miller Band; *Best Of-1968-1973* .... (CAP)
   Gift Set .... (CAP)
   Greatest Hits-1974-1978 .... (CAP)
   Live .... (CAP)
   The Joker .... (CAP)
Joyride
Roxette; *Joyride* .... (EMI)
Joystick
Dazz Band; *Greatest Hits* .... (MOT)
   Joystick .... (MOT)
Just A Gigolo/I Ain't Got Nobody
David Lee Roth; *Crazy From The Heat* .... (WB)
Louis Prima; *Capitol Collectors Series* .... (CAP)
Thelonius Monk Quartet; *Monk's Dream* ....(COL)
Just The Way You Like It
S.O.S. Band; *Just The Way You Like It* .... (TAB)
Justify My Love
Madonna; *Immaculate Collection* .... (SIR)
   Royal Box .... (SIR)
Keepin' My Lover Satisfied
Melba Moore; *Never Say Never* ....(CAP)
King Of Sleaze
Beat Farmers; *Loud & Plowed &...Live!* ....(CCB)
   Poor & Famous ....(CCB)
Last Time I Made Love
Joyce Kennedy & Jeffrey Osborne; *Looking For
Trouble* .... (A&M)
Lay Lady Lay
Bob Dylan; *Biograph* ....(COL)
   Greatest Hits-#2 ....(COL)
   Hard Rain ....(COL)
   Nashville Skyline ....(COL)
Bob Dylan/Band; *Before The Flood* ....(COL)

Byrds; *Byrds* ....(COL)
Lemon Song
Led Zeppelin; *II* .... (ATL)
Let Me Bang Your Box
Toppers; *Risque Rhythm* .... (RHI)
Let Me Make Love To You
Charlie Gonzales; *Charlie Gonzales* .... (CLT)
O'Jays; *Collector's Items* .... (PI)
   Survival .... (PI)
Let's Get It On
By All Means; *Beyond A Dream* .... (ISL)
Marvin Gaye; *Billboard Top Rock 'N' Roll
Hits-1973* .... (RHI)
   Greatest Hits .... (MOT)
   Let's Get It On .... (MOT)
Let's Go All The Way
Sly Fox; *45* .... (CAP)
Let's Go Crazy
Prince; *ST/Purple Rain* .... (WB)
Sly Fox; *Let's Go Crazy* .... (CAP)
Let's Go To Bed
Cure; *Japanese Whispers-The Singles* .... (SIR)
   Standing On The Beach-The Singles .... (ELE)
   The Walk .... (SIR)
Let's Make Love Over The Telephone
Jose Feliciano; *45* .... (MOT)
Let's Put The X In Sex
Kiss; *Smashes Thrashes & Hits* .... (MER)
Let's Spend The Night Together
David Bowie; *Aladdin Sane* ....(RYK)
   ST/Ziggy Stardust-The Motion Picture ....(RCA)
Rolling Stones; *Between The Buttons* .... (AKO)
   Flowers .... (AKO)
   Hot Rocks-1964-1971 .... (AKO)
   Still Life-American Concert-1981 ....(RS)
   Through The Past Darkly-Big Hits-#2 .... (AKO)
Let's Take All Night (To Say Goodbye)
Barry Manilow; *If I Should Love Again* .... (ARI)
Let's Talk About Sex
Salt-N-Pepa; *Blacks' Magic* ....(LON)
   Blitz Of Salt-N-Pepa Hits ....(LON)
   MTV Party To Go-#2 .... (TMB)
Lick It Up
Kiss; *Lick It Up* .... (MER)
   MTV's Rock 'N Roll To Go .... (ELE)
   Smashes Thrashes & Hits .... (MER)
Light My Fire
Doors; *13* .... (ELE)
   Best Of .... (ELE)
   Doors .... (ELE)
   Greatest Hits .... (ELE)
   ST/Doors .... (ELE)
Jose Feliciano; *All-Time Greatest Hits* ....(RCA)
   Encore ....(RCA)
Like A Virgin
Madonna; *Immaculate Collection* .... (SIR)
   Like A Virgin .... (SIR)
   Royal Box .... (SIR)
Little Less Talk And A Lot More Action
Toby Keith; *Toby Keith* .... (MER)
Little Miss Lover
Jimi Hendrix; *Axis: Bold As Love* .... (RPR)
   Essential .... (RPR)
Little T & A
Rolling Stones; *Tattoo You* ....(RS)
Live With Me
Rolling Stones; *Get Yer Ya-Ya's Out* .... (AKO)
   Let It Bleed .... (AKO)
Lonely Women Make Good Lovers
Steve Wariner; *Best Of* ....(RCA)
   Greatest Hits ....(RCA)
   Midnight Fire ....(RCA)
Longview
Green Day; *Dookie* .... (RPR)
Louie Louie
Kingsmen; *Best Of* .... (RHI)
   Billboard Top Rock 'N' Roll Hits-1963 .... (RHI)
   Cruisin'-1963 .... (INC)
   Frat Rock! .... (RHI)
   Oldies But Goodies-#11 .... (OSR)
   Rock & Roll Is Here To Stay .... (GUS)
   ST/Quadrophenia .... (POL)
   WCBS FM101-History Of Rock/'60s-#1 .... (CLT)
Pretenders; *II* .... (SIR)

Love Come Down
Evelyn "Champagne" King; *45* ....(RCA)
James Ingram; *It's Real* ....(WB)
Love Machine
Country Joe/Fish; *C.J. Fish* ....(VAN)
    Life & Times Of ....(VAN)
Miracles; *12 #1 Hits From The '70s* ....(MOT)
    20-20 ....(MOT)
    Billboard Top Hits-1976 ....(RHI)
    Motown Story-First 25 Years ....(MOT)
    Top 10 With A Bullet-Motown Dance Songs ...(MOT)
Paul Butterfield Blues Band; *Keep On Movin'* ....(ELE)
Uriah Heep; *Live* ....(MER)
    Look At Yourself ....(MER)
Wham!; *Fantastic* ....(COL)
W.A.S.P.; *W.A.S.P.* ....(CAP)
Love On Top Of Love-Killer Kiss
Grace Jones; *Bulletproof Heart* ....(CAP)
Love Potion #9
Clovers; *ST/American Graffiti* ....(MCA)
    Super Oldies/'50s-#7 ....(AUF)
Herb Alpert/Tijuana Brass; *Classics-#1* ....(A&M)
    Greatest Hits ....(A&M)
Searchers; *Greatest Hits* ....(RHI)
    History Of British Rock-#3 ....(RHI)
Love To Love You Baby
Donna Summer; *Greatest Hits* ....(CAS)
    Live & More ....(CAS)
    Love To Love You Baby ....(CAS)
    On The Radio-Greatest Hits-#1&2 ....(CAS)
Love Won't Let Me Wait
Luther Vandross; *Any Love* ....(EPI)
    Best Of-Best Of Love ....(EPI)
Major Harris; *Atlantic R&B 1947-1974-#6* ......(ATL)
    Live ....(WMO)
    My Way ....(ATL)
Love You To
Beatles; *Revolver* ....(CAP)
Lover
Ella Fitzgerald; *Rodgers & Hart Songbook* ....(VRV)
John Coltrane; *Last Trane* ....(PRS)
Tony Bennett; *Rodgers & Hart Songbook* ....(DRG)
Lover Boy
Billy Ocean; *Greatest Hits* ....(JVA)
    Suddenly ....(JVA)
Supertramp; *Even In The Quietest Moments* ....(A&M)
Lover In Me
Sheena Easton; *Lover In Me* ....(MCA)
Lover Who Rocks You (All Night)
India; *Breaking Out* ....(JEL)
Lovergirl
Teena Marie; *Club Epic* ....(EPI)
    Starchild ....(EPI)
Lovin', Touchin', Squeezin'
Journey; *Captured* ....(COL)
    Evolution ....(COL)
    Greatest Hits ....(COL)
Lusty Month Of May
Julie Andrews; *Little Bit Of Broadway* ....(COL)
Original 1982 London Cast; *Camelot* ....(VS)
Original Cast; *Camelot* ....(COL)
Make A Move On Me
Olivia Newton-John; *Greatest Hits-#2* ....(MCA)
    Physical ....(MCA)
Make It With You
Bread; *Anthology* ....(ELE)
    Best Of ....(ELE)
    On The Waters ....(ELE)
Make Love Like A Man
Def Leppard; *Adrenalize* ....(MER)
Make Love To Me
Anne Murray; *Croonin'* ....(SBK)
Make Your Move On Me Baby
Charlie Singleton; *Modern Man* ....(ARI)
Making Love
Roberta Flack; *I'm The One* ....(ATL)
Making Love In A Subaru
Damaskas; *Dr. Demento's Dementia Royale* ......(RHI)
Making Love Out Of Nothing At All
Air Supply; *Greatest Hits* ....(ARI)
Makin' Love
Climax Blues Band; *Shine On* ....(SIR)
Floyd Robinson; *Nipper's Greatest Hits/'50s-#1* ..(RCA)

Kiss; *Alive 2* ....(CAS)
    Double Platinum ....(CAS)
    Rock & Roll Over ....(CAS)
Makin' Whoopie
Art Tatum; *Solo Masterpieces-#5* ....(PAB)
Eddie Cantor; *Nipper's Greatest Hits-'20s* ....(RCA)
Harry Nilsson; *Touch Of Schmilsson In The Night* (RCA)
Ray Charles; *His Greatest Hits-#2* ....(DHL)
Me So Horny
2 Live Crew; *As Clean As They Wanna Be* ......(LUK)
    As Nasty As They Wanna Be ....(LUK)
    Bass Waves-#3 ....(LUK)
Melt In Your Mouth
Candyman; *Ain't No Shame In My Game* ....(EPI)
Motel Lover
Marvin Sease; *Real Deal* ....(LON)
My Baby Gives It Away
Pete Townshend & Ronnie Lane; *Rough Mix* ...(MCA)
Need Your Love
Cheap Trick; *At Budokan* ....(EPI)
    Dream Police ....(EPI)
Need Your Loving Tonight
Queen; *The Game* ....(HOL)
Night Moves
Bob Seger; *Night Moves* ....(CAP)
    Nine Tonight ....(CAP)
    ST/FM ....(MCA)
Marilyn Martin; *Marilyn Martin* ....(ATL)
No Condom, No Sex
Cruise Control; *12"* ....(SIR)
Nobody Does It Better
Carly Simon; *13 Original James Bond Themes* ...(EMI)
    Greatest Hits Live ....(ARI)
    ST/Spy Who Loved Me ....(EMI)
Nothing But The Radio On
Dave Koz & Joey Diggs; *Dave Koz* ....(CAP)
Nothing Sure Looked Good On You
Gene Watson; *All-Time Country Classics-#2* .....(LIB)
    Country's Greatest Hits-#7 ....(PRY)
    Should I Come Home ....(CAP)
November Rain
Guns N' Roses; *Use Your Illusion I* ....(GEF)
Now You're Talkin'
Dixiana; *Now You're Talkin'* ....(EPI)
Nubian Nut
George Clinton; *You Shouldn't-Nuf Bit Fish* .....(CAP)
Obscene Phone Caller
Rockwell; *Somebody's Watching Me* ....(MOT)
One Night Love Affair
Bryan Adams; *Reckless* ....(A&M)
One Night Stands
Hank Williams, Jr.; *Early Years* ....(W/C)
    One Night Stands ....(WB)
Orgasm
Prince; *Come* ....(WB)
Out Of Your Shoes
Lorrie Morgan; *Leave The Light On* ....(RCA)
O.P.P.
Naughty By Nature; *MTV Party To Go-#2* ......(TMB)
Paradise By The Dashboard Light
Meatloaf; *Bat Out Of Hell* ....(EPI)
Part Time Lover
Stevie Wonder; *In Square Circle* ....(MOT)
People Are Still Having Sex
LaTour; *LaTour* ....(SMA)
Pervert Nurse
D.I.; *Horse Bites Dog Cries* ....(XXX)
Phone Sexxx
Jimmy Z; *Muzical Madness* ....(RUT)
Physical
Olivia Newton-John; *Back To Basics-Essential
    Collection* ....(GEF)
    Greatest Hits-#2 ....(MCA)
    Physical ....(MCA)
Pillow Talk
Sylvia; *All Platinum Gold* ....(ALP)
    Super Bad Is Back ....(KT)
Playboy Channel
Negativeland; *Escape From Noise* ....(SST)
Pocket Porn
Renegade Soundwave; *In Dub* ....(ELE)
Pop My Dick Song
Sloppy Seconds; *First Seven Inches...& Then
    Some!* ....(TNG)

Pop That Pussy
2 Live Crew; *Sports Weekend-As Nasty As They Wanna
Be* ....(LUK)
Porn Wars
Frank Zappa; *Meets The Mothers Of Prevention* ..(RYK)
Porno For Pyros
Porno For Pyros; *Porno For Pyros* ....(WB)
Porno Freak
Blowfly; *Twisted World Of* .... (OPS)
Pornograffitti
Extreme; *Pornograffitti* ....(A&M)
Pornography
Cure; *Cure* .... (ELE)
Pour Some Sugar On Me
Def Leppard; *Hysteria* ....(MER)
Pretty Fuck Look
Pussy Galore; *Corpse Love-The First Year* ....(CRL)
Prison Sex
Tool; *Undertow* ....(ZOO)
Prove It All Night
Bruce Springsteen; *Darkness On The Edge Of
Town* ....(COL)
Psychedelic Sex Reaction
Babylon A.D.; *Nothing Sacred* .... (ARI)
P.A.S.S.I.O.N.
Rythm Syndicate; *S* ....(IPA)
Queen Of Memphis
Confederate Railroad; *Confederate Railroad* .... (ATL)
Question Of Lust
Depeche Mode; *101* ....(SIR)
Black Celebration ....(SIR)
Rated X
Pat Benatar; *In The Heat Of The Night* ....(CHR)
Rated "X"
Loretta Lynn; *Best Of* ....(MSP)
Raunchy
Bill Justice; *Golden Years-1957* ....(DOM)
Raunchy ....(SMA)
Sun Story .... (RHI)
Bill Justice/Orchestra; *History Of Rock
Instrumentals-#2* .... (RHI)
Ernie Freeman; *Oldies But Goodies-#8* ....(OSR)
Really Suck
Pussy Galore; *Right Now!* ....(CRL)
Red Neckin' Love Makin' Night
Conway Twitty; *Classic Conway* ....(MCA)
Legends ....(MCA)
Mr. T ....(MCA)
Night With ....(MCA)
Red Sex Dress
Alfonia Tims/Flying Tigers; *Future Funk/Uncut!* . (ROI)
Reeling And Rocking
Chuck Berry; *Best Of The Best Of* ....(GUS)
Chess Box ....(CSS)
Frat Rock! ....(RHI)
Greatest Hits ....(EVR)
Rock & Roll Show ....(GUS)
Right Time Of The Night
Jennifer Warnes; *Best Of* .... (ARI)
Jennifer Warnes .... (ARI)
Ring My Bell
Anita Ward; *Billboard Top Dance Hits-1979* ..... (RHI)
Billboard Top Rock 'N' Roll Hits-1979 .... (RHI)
Get Down Tonight! Best Of T.K Records .... (RHI)
Mega Hits Dance Classics-#1 ....(PRY)
Songs Of Love ....(JUA)
Sweet Surrender ....(JUA)
Rock Me Baby
B.B. King; *Greatest Hits* ....(KNT)
Now Appearing Live At Ole Miss ....(MCA)
Rock Me Baby ....(KNT)
Etta James; *Red Hot 'N' Live* ....(INT)
Hot Tuna; *Historic* ....(RLX)
Jefferson Airplane; *Bless Its Pointed Little Head* ..(RCA)
Jimi Hendrix; *ST/Jimi Plays Monterey* ....(RPR)
ST/Jimi Hendrix ....(RPR)
Otis Redding; *Best Of* ....(ATC)
Robin Trower; *Live* ....(CHR)
Twice Removed From Yesterday ....(CHR)
Slim Harpo; *Best Of* .... (RHI)
Rock & Roll Pussy
Todd Rundgren; *A Wizard A True Star* ....(RHI)
Rocks Off
Def Leppard; *On Through The Night* ....(MER)

Rolling Stones; *Exile On Main Street* ....(RS)
Rump Shaker
Wreckx-N-Effect; *Hard Or Smooth* ....(MCA)
Save The Best For Last
Vanessa Williams; *Comfort Zone* ....(WIN)
Saving All My Love For You
Tom Waits; *On Heart Attack & Vine* .... (ASY)
Whitney Houston; *Whitney Houston* .... (ARI)
Set Adrift On Memory Bliss
P.M. Dawn; *MTV Party To Go-#2* ....(TMB)
Red Hot + Dance ....(COL)
Sex
Berlin; *Best Of-1979-1988* ....(GEF)
Pleasure Victim ....(GEF)
Ice-T; *Rhyme Pays* ....(SIR)
Kix; *Midnite Dynamite* ....(ATL)
Lee "Scratch" Perry; *Upsetter & The Beat* ....(HRT)
Paul Young; *No Parlez* ....(COL)
Sex And Dying In High Society
X; *Los Angeles* ....(SLS)
Sex As A Weapon
Pat Benatar; *Seven The Hard Way* .... (CHR)
Sex Beat
Gun Club; *Fire Of Love* ....(SLS)
Sex Bomb
Flipper; *Generic* ....(DEF)
Sex By Mail
Free Hot Lunch; *Penguin Love* ....(FF)
Sex Crime
Eurythmics; *Greatest Hits* .... (ARI)
Sex Cymbal
Sheila E.; *Sex Cymbal* ....(WB)
Sex Drive
Rolling Stones; *Flashpoint* ....(RS)
Sex Farm
Spinal Tap; *ST/Spinal Tap* ....(POL)
Sex Fiend
Awesome Dre/Hardcore Committee; *Explicit Rap* (PRY)
You Can't Hold Me Back ....(PRY)
Sex In A Pan
Bela Fleck/Flecktones; *UFO Tofu* ....(WB)
Sex In The '90s
Gloria Estefan; *Into The Light* .... (EPI)
Sex Machine
James Brown; *Revolution Of The Mind* ....(POL)
John Wagner Coalition; *Shades Of Brown-James
Brown's Greatest* .... (KOA)
Sex Maniac
Bobby Nunn; *Private Party* ....(MOT)
Sex Me, Talk Me
Berlin; *Count Three & Pray* ....(GEF)
Sex On Wheelz
My Life With The Thrill Kill Kult; *Sexplosion!* ..(WAX)
Sex Symbols
Ray Stevens; *Crackin' Up* ....(MCA)
Sex Wanderer
Freewheelers; *Freewheelers* ....(DGC)
Sex (I'm A...)
Berlin; *Best Of-1979-1988* ....(GEF)
Pleasure Victim ....(GEF)
Sexual Harassment In The Workplace
Frank Zappa; *Guitar* ....(RYK)
Sexual Healing
Marvin Gaye; *Last Concert Tour* ....(GIA)
Midnight Love ....(COL)
Seems Like Yesterday-#4-Early '80s .... (KT)
Tribute To Black Entertainers ....(COL)
Sexuality
Billy Bragg; *Don't Try This At Home* .... (ELE)
Erasure; *Chorus* .... (SIR)
Jamie Principle; *Midnite Hour* ....(SMA)
Prince; *Controversy* ....(WB)
Sexy Dancer
Prince; *Prince* ....(WB)
Sexy Eyes
Dr. Hook; *Greatest Hits (& More)* ....(CAP)
Sometimes You Win ....(CAP)
Sexy Girl
Glenn Frey; *Allnighter* ....(MCA)
Lillo Thomas; *Lillo Thomas* ....(CAP)
Sexy Ida
Ike & Tina Turner; *Proud Mary-Best Of* ....(EMI)

Sexy Lady
Carl Carlton; *Carl Carlton* .... (20)
  Ear Candy-#2 .... (20)
Commodores; *Midnight Magic* .... (MOT)
Rick James/Stone City Band; *Come Get It* ...... (MOT)
Sexy Mexican Maid
Red Hot Chili Peppers; *Mother's Milkl* .... (EMI)
Sexy Music
Meat Puppets; *Huevos* .... (SST)
Sexy M.F.
Prince/New Power Generation; *Love Symbol
Album* .... (PAI)
Sexy Rhino
Adrian Belew; *Desire Of The Rhino King* .... (ISL)
Sexy Sadie
Beatles; *Box Set* .... (CAP)
  White Album .... (CAP)
Sexy + 17
Stray Cats; *Best Of-Rock This Town* .... (EMI)
  Rant 'N' Rave With The Stray Cats .... (EMI)
Sex, Drugs & Rock & Roll
Ian Dury; *New Boots & Panties* .... (STF)
Mantronix; *This Should Move Ya* .... (CAP)
Shaking Your Tree (Somebody Else Been)
ZZ Top; *First Album* .... (WB)
  Six Pack .... (WB)
Sharin' The Night Together
Dr. Hook; *Greatest Hits (& More)* .... (CAP)
  Pleasure & Pain .... (CAP)
Shaving Cream
Benny Bell & Paul Wynn; *Dr. Demento's Dementia
Royale* .... (RHI)
  Dr. Demento's Greatest-#1-'40s & Before ...... (RHI)
She Bop
Cyndi Lauper; *Music For The Miracle* .... (EPA)
  She's So Unusual .... (POR)
She Thinks His Name Was John
Reba McEntire; *Read My Mind* .... (MCA)
She Was Hot
Rolling Stones; *Undercover* .... (RS)
She's Vibrator Dependent
Mojo Nixon & Skid Roper; *Root Hog Or Die* .... (IRS)
Silverfuck
Smashing Pumpkins; *Siamese Dream* .... (VIA)
Sixty Minute Man
Billy Ward/Dominoes; *Rock & Roll Show* ...... (GUS)
Dominos; *Oldies But Goodies-#5* .... (OSR)
Rufus Thomas; */Carla Thomas-Chronicle* .... (STX)
Slow Ride
Foghat; *Best Of* .... (RHI)
  Best Of King Biscuit Live-#1 .... (SAN)
  Fool For The City .... (RHI)
  Live .... (RHI)
Some Girls
Rolling Stones; *Some Girls* .... (RS)
Spanish Fly
Van Halen; *2* .... (WB)
Squeezebox
Who; *By Numbers* .... (MCA)
  Greatest Hits .... (MCA)
  Hooligans .... (MCA)
  Who's Better Who's Best-Very Best Of .... (MCA)
Stripper
David Rose; *Dick Bartley-One-Hit
Wonders-'60s-#1* .... (RHI)
Stuck In A Closet With Vanna White
Weird Al Yankovic; *Even Worse* .... (RAR)
Sugar Walls
Sheena Easton; *Dance Mix* .... (EMI)
  Private Heaven .... (EMI)
Sultan Of Sex
Neon Judgement; *Horny As Hell* .... (PIA)
"Summer Of '42" Theme
George Benson; *Best Of* .... (CBA)
  White Rabbit .... (CBA)
Peter Nero; *Greatest Hits* .... (COL)
  "Summer Of '42" Theme .... (COL)
Surfin' Sex Machine
Pajama Slave Dancers; *Blood Sweat & Beers* .... (RES)
Sweet Lover Man
Pointer Sisters; *Best Of-1978-1981* .... (RCA)
  Sweet & Soulful .... (RCA)

Sweet Sexy Eyes
Cristy Lane; *At Her Best* .... (EMI)
  Country Classics .... (ARR)
Sweet & Sexy Thing
Rick James; *Flag* .... (MOT)
Swimsuit Issue
Sonic Youth; *Dirty* .... (DGC)
Take A Little Trip
Alabama; *American Pride* .... (RCA)
Take Me Down
Alabama; *Greatest Hits-#2* .... (RCA)
  Live .... (RCA)
  Mountain Music .... (RCA)
Talk Dirty To Me
Poison; *Look What The Cat Dragged In* .... (CAP)
  Swallow This Live .... (CAP)
Teach Me Tonight
Al Jarreau; *Breakin' Away* .... (WB)
  Live In London .... (WB)
Diane Schuur; *Collection* .... (GRP)
Ella Fitzgerald; *Montreux '75* .... (PAB)
Phoebe Snow; *Best Of* .... (COL)
  It Looks Like Snow .... (COL)
Sarah Vaughan; *How Long Has This Been Going
On?* .... (PAB)
Teenage Lust
Jesus & Mary Chain; *Honey's Dead* .... (AME)
Tender Lover
Babyface; *Tender Lover* .... (SLR)
Tennessee Stud
Chris LeDoux; *Old Cowboy Classics* .... (LIB)
Eddy Arnold; *Best Of-#2* .... (RCA)
  Legendary Performer .... (RCA)
Hank Williams, Jr.; *The Pressure Is On* .... (W/C)
Johnny Cash; *American Recordings* .... (AME)
Nitty Gritty Dirt Band; *Will The Circle Be
Unbroken* .... (EMI)
That Summer
Garth Brooks; *The Chase* .... (LIB)
That's The Way (I Like It)
K.C./Sunshine Band; *Best Of* .... (RHI)
  Disco Hits-#1 .... (RHI)
  Mega Hits Dance Classics-#3 .... (PRY)
They Call It Making Love
Tammy Wynette; *Tears Of Fire-25th Anniversary
Collect.* .... (EPI)
Tammy Wynette & George Jones; *Encore* .... (EPI)
Thinking About Sex Again
Waitresses; *Best Of* .... (POL)
Third Rate Romance
Amazing Rhythm Aces; *45* .... (OOP)
Rosanne Cash; *Somewhere In The Stars* .... (COL)
Sammy Kershaw; *Feelin' Good Train* .... (MER)
To Be A Lover
Billy Idol; *Vital Idol* .... (CHR)
  Whiplash Smile .... (CHR)
Tonight's The Night (Gonna Be All Right)
Rod Stewart; *Absolutely Live* .... (WB)
  Downtown Train-Storyteller Selections .... (WB)
  Greatest Hits .... (WB)
  Night On The Town .... (WB)
Too Fat To Fuck
Blowfly; *Fresh Juice* .... (OPS)
Too Many Lovers
Crystal Gayle; *Greatest Country Hits/'80s-1981* ..(COL)
  Greatest Hits .... (CAP)
  These Days .... (LIB)
Touch Me (All Night Long)
Cathy Dennis; *Move To This* .... (POL)
Touch Me (I Want Your Body)
Samantha Fox; *Greatest Hits* .... (JVA)
  Touch Me (I Want Your Body) .... (JVA)
Tush
ZZ Top; *Best Of* .... (WB)
  Fandango .... (WB)
  Greatest Hits .... (WB)
  Six Pack .... (WB)
  ST/An Officer & A Gentleman .... (ISL)
Two Lovers
Mary Wells; *Greatest Hits* .... (MOT)
  Hitsville U.S.A.-Motown Singles-1959-71 ...... (MOT)
U Can't Touch This
Hammer; *Please Hammer Don't Hurt 'Em* .... (CAP)

Vagabond Virgin
Traffic; *Traffic* .... (ISL)
Voodoo Sex Doll
Crisis Party; *Rude Awakening* .... (MET)
Wake Up & Make Love To Me
Ian Dury; *New Boots & Panties* .... (STF)
  Stiff Live .... (STF)
We Don't Have To Take Our Clothes Off
Jermaine Stewart; *Frantic Romantic* .... (ARI)
We Don't Make Love Anymore
Anne Murray; *Country Collection* .... (LIB)
  Let's Keep It That Way .... (LIB)
We Should Be Making Love
Huey Lewis/News; *Hard At Play* .... (EMI)
Wet My Whistle
Midnight Star; *Greatest Hits* .... (SLR)
  No Parking On The Dance Floor .... (SLR)
When We Make Love
Alabama; *Roll On* .... (RCA)
Whole Lotta Love
Led Zeppelin; *II* .... (ATL)
  Remasters .... (ATL)
  Led Zeppelin (collection) .... (ATL)
  ST/Song Remains The Same .... (SS)
Who's Makin' Love
Blues Brothers; *Definitive Collection* .... (ATL)
  Made In America .... (ATL)
Johnnie Taylor; *Billboard Top R&B
Hits-1965-1969* .... (RHI)
  Oldies But Goodies-#5 .... (OSR)
  Super Hits .... (STX)
  Top Of The Stax-Twenty Greatest Hits ...... (STX)
Who's Zoomin' Who
Aretha Franklin; *Who's Zoomin' Who* .... (ARI)
Why Don't We Do It In The Road
Beatles; *Box Set* .... (CAP)
  White Album .... (CAP)
Why Don't We Get Drunk
Jimmy Buffett; *Boats Beaches Bars & Ballads* ... (MGR)
  Songs You Know By Heart-Greatest Hits .... (MCA)
  White Sport Coat & A Pink Crustacean .... (MCA)
  You Had To Be There-In Concert .... (MCA)
Wild Sex (In The Working Class)
Oingo Boingo; *Best O' Boingo* .... (MCA)
  Boingo Alive .... (MCA)
  Nothing To Fear .... (A&M)
Wild Thing
Jimi Hendrix; *Essential-#2* .... (RPR)
  ST/Jimi Plays Monterey .... (RPR)
Jimi Hendrix Experience; *Live At Winterland* .... (RYK)
Tone Loc; *Loc-ed After Dark* .... (DV)
  Rap's Biggest Hits .... (KT)
  Rock The First-#6 .... (SAN)
Troggs; *Billboard Top Rock 'N' Roll Hits-1966* ... (RHI)
  Frat Rock! .... (RHI)
  History Of British Rock-#3 .... (RHI)
Woman, A Lover, A Friend
Jackie Wilson; *Greatest Hits #2* .... (BRU)
  Mr. Excitement .... (RHI)
Otis Redding; *Story* .... (ATL)
Work With Me Annie
Hank Ballard/Midnighters; *45* .... (GUS)
Royals; *Risque Rhythm* .... (RHI)
World's Greatest Lover
Bellamy Brothers; *Greatest Hits-#2* .... (MCA)
  Restless .... (MCC)
Written In Sand
Santana; *Beyond Appearances* .... (COL)
Yank Me Crank Me
Ted Nugent; *Double Live Gonzo* .... (EPI)
  Twisted Metal .... (KT)
You Can Leave Your Hat On
Joe Cocker; *Cocker* .... (CAP)
  Live .... (CAP)
  ST/9 1/2 Weeks .... (CAP)
Randy Newman; *Sail Away* .... (RPR)
You Can't Play With My Yo-Yo
Yo-Yo & Ice Cube; *Make Way For The
Motherlode* .... (EW)
You Don't Have To Go Home Tonight
Triplets; *...Thicker Than Water* .... (MER)
You Need A Woman Tonight
Captain & Tennille; *Dreams* .... (A&M)

You Never Done It Like That
Captain & Tennille; *Dreams* .... (A&M)
You Sexy Thing
Hot Chocolate; *Hot Chocolate* .... (BT)
  Mega Hits Dance Classics-#8 .... (PRY)
  Super Hits/'70s-Have A Nice Day-#15 .... (RHI)
You Shook Me
Jeff Beck; *Truth* .... (EPI)
Led Zeppelin; *Led Zeppelin* .... (ATL)
Muddy Waters; *Chess Box* .... (CSS)
Willie Dixon; *I Am The Blues* .... (COL)
You Shook Me All Night Long
AC/DC; *Back In Black* .... (ATL)
  Who Made Who .... (ATL)
You Sure Love To Ball
Marvin Gaye; *Let's Get It On* .... (MOT)
Young Lust
Pink Floyd; *The Wall* .... (COL)
Roger Waters & Bryan Adams; *The Wall Live In
Berlin* .... (MER)
Your Body's Callin'
R. Kelly; *12 Play* .... (JVA)
(You're My) Aphrodisiac
Dennis Edwards; *Don't Look Any Further* .... (MOT)
You're Out Doing What I'm Here Doing...
Gene Watson; *Greatest Hits* .... (MCA)
Gene Watson/Farewell Party Band; *Sometimes I Get
Lucky* .... (MCA)

SHADOWS
See Also: ECHOES, REFLECTIONS

African Shadow Man
Johnny Clegg & Savuka; *Shadow Man* .... (CAP)
Blue Shadows
Blasters; *ST/Streets Of Fire* .... (MCA)
B.B. King; *From The Beginning* .... (KNT)
  Greatest Hits .... (KNT)
  The Jungle .... (KNT)
Blue Shadows On The Trail
Sons Of The Pioneers; *Cool Water* .... (RCA)
Chasing Shadows
Deep Purple; *Purple Passages* .... (WB)
Kansas; *Vinyl Confessions* .... (KIR)
Cry For A Shadow
Beatles; *Beatles* .... (AUF)
  In The Beginning (Circa 1960) .... (POL)
Crying In The Shadows
Gary Moore; *Wild Frontier* .... (VIA)
"Dark Shadows" Theme
Original Music; *Television's Greatest Hits-#2* ..... (TVT)
Got No Shadow
Little Feat; *Sailin' Shoes* .... (WB)
Have You Seen Your Mother Baby...
Rolling Stones; *Flowers* .... (AKO)
  Got Live If You Want It .... (AKO)
  More Hot Rocks-Big Hits & Fazed Cookies ..... (AKO)
  Through The Past Darkly-Big Hits-#2 .... (AKO)
Heartache, A Shadow, A Lifetime
Dave Mason; *At His Very Best* .... (MCA)
  Best Of .... (MCA)
In The Shadows
Stranglers; *Black & White* .... (A&M)
Moon Shadow
Cat Stevens; *Classics-#24* .... (A&M)
  Greatest Hits .... (A&M)
  Teaser & The Firecat .... (A&M)
Moonshadow Road
T. Graham Brown; *Best Of* .... (LIB)
"Sandpiper" Theme (Shadow Of Your Smile)
Barbra Streisand; *My Name Is Barbra-Two* ...... (COL)
Boston Pops Orchestra/Arthur Fiedler; *Greatest Hits Of
The '60s-#2* .... (RCA)
  Motion Picture Classics .... (RCA)
  Music For Every Mood .... (RCA)
Carmen McRae; *Alive* .... (MST)
  I Want You .... (MST)
Frank Sinatra; *Reprise Collection* .... (RPR)
James Morrison; *Snappy Doo* .... (ATL)
Marvin Gaye; *Romantically Yours* .... (COL)
Tony Bennett; *16 Most Requested Songs* .... (COL)
  All-Time Greatest Hits .... (COL)
  Movie Song Album .... (COL)

Shadow Boxer
Angel City; *Face To Face* .... (EPI)
Shadow Boxing
Giles Reaves & Jon Goin; *Letting Go* .... (MCA)
Teena Marie; *Robbery* .... (EPI)
Shadow Captain
Crosby, Stills & Nash; *Allies* .... (ATL)
CSN .... (ATL)
Replay .... (ATL)
Crosby, Stills & Nash (collection) .... (ATL)
Shadow Dancing
Andy Gibb; *Collection Of His Greatest Hits* ...... (POL)
Greatest Hits .... (RSO)
Shadow Dancing .... (RSO)
Shadow Dream Song
Tom Rush; *Circle Game* .... (ELE)
Classic Rush .... (ELE)
Shadow In The Street
Allan Clarke; *I Wasn't Born Yesterday* .... (ATL)
Shadow Knows
Coasters; *Greatest Hits* .... (ATC)
Shadow Of A Doubt
Earl Thomas Conley; *Yours Truly* .... (RCA)
Roxette; *Look Sharp!* .... (EMI)
Sonic Youth; *Evol* ....(SST)
Tom Petty/Heartbreakers; *Damn The Torpedoes* . (BKS)
Shadow Of A Lonely Man
Alan Parsons Project; *Pyramid* .... (ARI)
Shadow Of California
Blue Oyster Cult; *Revolution By Night* ....(COL)
Shadow Of Doubt
Bonnie Raitt; *Longing In Their Hearts* ....(CAP)
Shadow Of Love
Damned; *Light At The End Of The Tunnel* ...... (MCA)
Phantasmagoria .... (MCA)
Laura Branigan; *Touch* ....(ATL)
Shadow Of Your Love
Temptations; *Power* ....(MOT)
Shadow On A Harvest Moon
Everything But The Girl; *Idlewild* .... (SIR)
Shadow Puppets
Tor Dietrichson; *Global Village* .... (GLO)
Shadow Song
Supertramp; *Supertramp* .... (A&M)
Shadow Waltz
Bing Crosby; *Crooner-Columbia*
Years-1928-1934 ....(COL)
Original Broadway Cast; *42nd Street* ....(RCA)
Wayne King; *Best Of* .... (MCA)
Shadow & Me
Leon Russell; *Americana* .... (PRD)
Shadows Break
Jules/Polar Bears; *Got No Breeding* ....(COL)
Shadows In The Moonlight
Anne Murray; *15 Of The Best* .... (LIB)
Greatest Hits .... (LIB)
New Kind Of Feeling .... (CAP)
Shadows In The Rain
Police; *Zenyatta Mondatta* .... (A&M)
Sting; *Dream Of The Blue Turtles* .... (A&M)
Shadows Of Love
Bing Crosby; *Crooner-Columbia*
Years-1928-1934 ....(COL)
Glen Gray; *Best Of The Big Bands* ....(COL)
Rayburn Anthony; *45* ....(MER)
Shadows Of The Night
Pat Benatar; *Best Shots* ....(CHR)
Get Nervous ....(CHR)
Shadows On The Wall
Gene Watson; *Best Of* ....(CAP)
Moody Blues; *Keys Of The Kingdom* .... (POL)
Shadows & Light
Joni Mitchell; *Hissing Of Summer Lawns* ....(ASY)
Shadows & Light ....(ASY)
Shadows & The Wind
Uriah Heep; *Wonderworld* ....(WB)
Silhouettes
Diamonds; *Good Time Rock 'N' Roll* .... (MCA)
Herman's Hermits; *Their Greatest Hits* ....(AKO)
Nylons; *One Size Fits All* ....(OPE)
Rays; *Oldies But Goodies #4* ....(OSR)
Rock-O-Rama #1 ....(AKO)

Silver Shadow
Atlantic Starr; *As The Band Turns* .... (A&M)
Classics-#10 ....(A&M)
Secret Lovers...Best Of .... (A&M)
Standing In The Shadows Of Love
Barry White; *Greatest Hits* .... (CAS)
I've Got So Much To Give .... (20)
Four Tops; *Anthology* ....(MOT)
Greatest Hits ....(MOT)
Motown Story ....(MOT)
Motown Superstar Series-#14 ....(MOT)
Reach Out ....(MOT)
Rod Stewart; *Blondes Have More Fun* ....(WB)
Tombstone Shadow
Creedence Clearwater Revival; *1969* .... (FAN)
Chronicle-#2 .... (FAN)
Green River .... (FAN)
The Concert ....(FAN)
Two Purple Shadows
Jerry Vale; *17 Most Requested Songs* ....(COL)
All-Time Greatest Hits ....(COL)
Two Silhouettes
Dinah Shore; *16 Most Requested Songs* ....(COL)
Sha-Na-Na; *Best Of* .... (PRR)
Walking In The Shadow Of The Blues
Whitesnake; *Live In The Heart Of The City* ......(GEF)
Love Hunter ....(GEF)
We Kiss In A Shadow
Barbra Streisand; *Broadway Album* ....(COL)
Original Broadway Cast; *King & I* ....(RCA)
Original Cast; *King & I* .... (MCA)
White Shadow
Peter Gabriel; *Peter Gabriel* ....(ATL)

SHIPS, Boats, Shipwrecks
See Also: OCEAN, RIVERS, SAILING, WATER

Attack Ships On Fire
Revolting Cocks; *Big Sexy Land* ....(WAX)
Banana Boat Song
Harry Belafonte; *Belafonte '89* .... (EMI)
Nipper's Greatest Hits-'50s-#1 ....(RCA)
Kinks; *Everybody's In Show Biz* .... (RHI)
Blue Bayou
Linda Ronstadt; *Greatest Hits-#2* .... (ASY)
Simple Dreams ....(ASY)
Roy Orbison; *All-Time Greatest Hits-#2* .... (MON)
For The Lonely: Anthology 1956-1965 .... (RHI)
In Dreams-Greatest Hits .... (VIA)
More Greatest Hits .... (MON)
Roy Orbison & Friends; *Black & White Night-Live* (VIA)
Boat Drinks
Jimmy Buffett; *Songs You Know By Heart-Greatest
Hits* .... (MCA)
Volcano .... (MCA)
Boat On The River
Styx; *Cornerstone* .... (A&M)
Boat That I Row
Neil Diamond; *Classics (Early Years)* ....(COL)
Do It .... (BNG)
Double Gold .... (BNG)
Greatest Hits .... (BNG)
Just For You .... (BNG)
Boats Against The Current
Eric Carmen; *Best Of* .... (ARI)
Boats Against The Current .... (ARI)
Olivia Newton-John; *Totally Hot* .... (MCA)
Burning My Rowboat
Maura O'Connell; *Real Life Story* .... (WB)
Captain Nemo
Michael Schenker; *Built To Destroy* .... (CHR)
Rock Will Never Die .... (CHR)
Captain Of Her Heart
Double; *Blue* .... (A&M)
Romantic Hits Of The '80s .... (KT)
Carried Away
Television; *Adventure* .... (ELE)
Come On Down To My Boat
Every Mother's Son; *Battle Of The Bands-#3* ..... (KT)
Cripple Creek Ferry
Neil Young; *After The Goldrush* .... (RPR)

Crystal Ship
Doors; *13* .... (ELE)
  Best Of .... (ELE)
  Classics .... (ELE)
  Doors .... (ELE)
Dark Ship
Country Joe McDonald; *Rock & Roll Music From The
Planet Earth* ....(FAN)
Davy's Dinghy
Ruth Wallis; *Dr. Demento's Dementia Royale* .... (RHI)
  Dr. Demento's Greatest Novelties-#2 .... (RHI)
Do You Want My Job
Little Village; *Little Village* .... (RPR)
Don't Pay The Ferryman
Chris DeBurgh; *Getaway* .... (A&M)
Erie Canal
Burl Ives; *Best Of* .... (MCA)
Weavers; *Classics* .... (VAN)
  Greatest Folksingers/'60s .... (VAN)
  Greatest Hits .... (VAN)
Ferry Across The Mersey
Gerry/Pacemakers; *Ferry Across The Mersey-Best
Of* .... (EMI)
  History Of British Rock-#4 .... (RHI)
Golden Vanity
Pete Seeger & Arlo Guthrie; *Together In Concert* (RPR)
If I Had A Boat
Lyle Lovett; *Pontiac* .... (MCC)
I'll Sail My Ship Aone
George Jones; *20 Golden Pieces Of* .... (BLD)
Mickey Gilley; *Greatest Hits-#1* .... (EPI)
Patsy Cline; *Always* .... (MCA)
  Portrait Of .... (MCA)
Ray Price; *Greatest Hits-#1* ....(SO)
Longer Boats
Cat Stevens; *Tea For The Tillerman* .... (A&M)
Love Overboard
Gladys Knight/Pips; *All Our Love* .... (MCA)
  Soul Survivors-Best Of-1973-1988 .... (RHI)
Man Overboard
Blondie; *Blondie* .... (CHR)
Eric Clapton; *Money & Cigarettes* .... (DUC)
Michael Row The Boat Ashore
Joe & Eddie; *Best Of* .... (CRS)
  Gospel Truth .... (CRS)
Weavers; *Greatest Hits* .... (VAN)
Motorboat To Mars
Chicago; *At Carnegie Hall* ....(COL)
  III ....(COL)
My Ship
Lena Horne; *A New Album* ....(RCA)
Lena Horne & Phil Woods; *I Have Dreamed* .... (NOV)
Night Boat To Cairo
Madness; *One Step Beyond* .... (SIR)
  ST/Dance Craze .... (CHR)
Norfolk Ferry
Panama Francis; *& The Savoy Sultans* .... (CJ)
On A Slow Boat To China
Jimmy Buffett; *Somewhere Over China* .... (MCA)
Kay Kyser; *16 Most Requested Songs/'40s-#2* ....(COL)
  Sentimental Favorites ....(COL)
Sonny Rollins; *First Recordings* .... (PRS)
  Vintage .... (PRS)
On The Good Ship Lollipop
Firehouse Five Plus Two; *Goes To Sea* .... (GTJ)
Frankie Valli/Four Seasons; *Rarities-#1* .... (RHI)
One Of Our Submarines
Thomas Dolby; *Golden Age Of Wireless* .... (CAP)
One Small Boat
Altered State; *Altered State* .... (WB)
Only Love
Wynonna; *Tell Me Why* .... (MCC)
Proud Mary
Creedence Clearwater Revival; *1968-1969* ...... (FAN)
  Bayou Country .... (FAN)
  Chronicle .... (FAN)
  Gold .... (FAN)
  Live In Europe .... (FAN)
George Jones & Johnny Paycheck; *My Very Special
Guests* .... (EPI)
Ike & Tina Turner; *Best Of* .... (EMI)
  EMI Legends Of Rock 'N' Roll-24 Greatest ...... (RHI)
  Greatest Hits .... (CCB)
  Soul Hits/'70s-#4 .... (RHI)

Ride Captain Ride
Blues Image; *Back To The '70s-#3* .... (DOM)
  Hit Singles 1958-1977 ....(ATL)
Rio Grande
Floyd Tillman; *Country Music Hall Of Fame* .... (MCA)
Sam Eskin; *Shanty Men-Songs Of
Sailormen/Lumbermen* .... (FLW)
Riverboat
Robert Palmer; *Pressure Drop* .... (ISL)
Riverboat Gambler
Chris LeDoux; *Songs Of Rodeo Life* ....(CAP)
Riverboat Shuffle
Hoagy Carmichael; *Stardust Road* .... (MCA)
Rock The Boat
Hues Corporation; *Dance! Dance! Dance! Greatest
Dance* ....(RCA)
  Nipper's Greatest Hits-'70s ....(RCA)
  Soul Hits/'70s-#13 .... (RHI)
Rock This Boat
Thompson Twins; *Big Trash* .... (RE)
Rockin' In The Same Old Boat
Bobby Bland; *Spotlighting The Man* .... (MCA)
Rockin' The Boat
Ricky Skaggs; *Live In London* .... (EPI)
Wayland Patton; *Gulf Stream Dreamin'* ....(CAP)
Rockin' The Boat Of Love
Jerry Lee Lewis; *Golden Rock & Roll* .... (SUN)
Row Jimmy
Grateful Dead; *Wake Of The Flood* .... (GRD)
Row Row Row
Bobby Darin/Johnny Mercer/Billy May Orc.; *Two Of A
Kind* ....(ATC)
Spike Jones/City Slickers; *King Of Corn* .... (GLN)
Sail On Flying Dutchman
Nick Seeger; *Sail On Flying Dutchman* ....(BIO)
Sailboat
Jonathan Edwards; *Sailboat* .... (WB)
Sailboat In The Moonlight
Billie Holiday; *Greatest Hits* ....(COL)
  Lady Day ....(COL)
  Legacy Box-1933-1958 ....(COL)
  Quintessential-#4-1937 ....(COL)
Sailing Ships
Whitesnake; *Slip Of The Tongue* .... (GEF)
Salty Dog
Procol Harum; *Best Of* .... (A&M)
  Classics-#17 .... (A&M)
  Live With The Edmonton Orchestra .... (A&M)
  Salty Dog .... (A&M)
Santa Lucia
Elvis Presley; *ST/Viva Las Vegas/Roustabout* .....(RCA)
Mario Lanza; *Legendary Tenor* ....(RCA)
Ship Ahoy
O'Jays; *Ship Ahoy* .... (PI)
Ship In A Bottle
Dave Loggins; *One Way Ticket To Paradise* .... (EPI)
Ship Of Dreams
Nazareth; *Malice In Wonderland* .... (A&M)
Ship Of Fools
Bob Seger; *Night Moves* .... (CAP)
Doors; *Morrison Hotel* .... (ELE)
  Weird Scenes Inside The Goldmine .... (ELE)
Elvis Costello; *Deadicated* .... (ARI)
Garland Jeffreys; *American Boy & Girl* .... (A&M)
Grateful Dead; *From The Mars Hotel* .... (GRD)
  Steal Your Face .... (GRD)
Robert Plant; *Now & Zen* .... (EPR)
World Party; *Greenpeace/Rainbow Warriors* ..... (GEF)
  Private Revolution .... (ENS)
Ship Of Love
Nutmegs; *Echoes Down The Hall-16 Orig.
Doo-Wop* .... (ARI)
  Greatest Hits .... (CLT)
Ship Titanic
Pink Anderson; *Gospel Blues & Street Songs* .....(RVR)
Ship To Shore
Chris DeBurgh; *The Getaway* .... (A&M)
Ship Without A Sail
Dave Frishberg; *Let's Eat Home* .... (CCJ)
Ella Fitzgerald; *Rodgers & Hart Songbook* ...... (VRV)
Sarah Vaughan; *Rodgers & Hart Songbook* ...... (EMA)
Shipbuilding
Elvis Costello; *Girls Girls Girls* ....(COL)
Elvis Costello/Attractions; *Punch The Clock* .....(COL)

Shipmates In Cheyenne
Bobby Darin; *1936-1973* .... (MOT)
Ships
Barry Manilow; *Greatest Hits-#3* .... (ARI)
  One Voice .... (ARI)
Ian Hunter; *Shades Of* .... (CHR)
  You're Never Alone With A Schizophrenic ...... (CHR)
Patty Loveless; *When Fallen Angels Fly* .... (EPI)
Red Rider; *As Far As Siam* .... (CAP)
Ships Don't Disappear In The Night
10 CC; *Live & Let Live* .... (MER)
Ships In The Night
Be Bop Deluxe; *Best Of-Raiding The Divine*
Archive .... (CAP)
  Live In The Air Age .... (OOP)
  Sunburst Finish .... (HAR)
Ships That Don't Come In
Joe Diffie; *Regular Joe* .... (EPI)
Shipyards Of New Zealand
Midnight Oil; *Red Sails In The Sunset* .... (COL)
Sinkin' In The Sea
Barefoot Jerry; *You Can't Get Off With Your Shoes*
On .... (MON)
Sit Down, You're Rockin' The Boat
Don Henley; *ST/Leap Of Faith* .... (MCA)
Original Cast; *Guys & Dolls* .... (MCA)
Skye Boat Song
King's Singters; *Annie Laurie-Folksongs Of British*
Isles .... (ANG)
Paul Robeson; *American Balladeer-Golden*
Classics-#1 .... (CLT)
Roger Whittaker; *Live In Concert* ....(RCA)
Sloop John B
Beach Boys; *Absolute Best-#2* .... (CAP)
  Best Of (Good Vibrations) .... (RPR)
  Gift Set .... (CAP)
  Made In The U.S.A. .... (CAP)
  Pet Sounds .... (CAP)
  ST/Forrest Gump .... (EPX)
Slow Boat To China
Spike Robinson/Harry "Sweets" Edison; *Jusa Bit O'*
Blues-#1 .... (CPI)
Song Of The Volga Boatmen
Glenn Miller; *Best Of* ....(RCA)
  Chattanooga Choo Choo-#1 Hits .... (BLU)
  Legendary Performer .... (BLU)
  Memorial-1944-1969 .... (BLU)
  This Is ....(RCA)
Tuxedo Junction; *Tuxedo Junction* .... (BTF)
Steamboat
Beach Boys; *Holland* .... (CAR)
Drifters; *Greatest Recordings* .... (ATC)
  Let The Boogie Woogie Roll-Greatest Hits ...... (ATL)
Steamboat Whistle Blues
John Hartford; *Aereo-Plain* .... (WB)
Submarine Bells
Chills; *Submarine Bells* .... (SLS)
Submarine Song
Candy Skins; *Space I'm In* .... (DGC)
Submarine Soul
Barbie Bones; *Brake For Nobody* .... (RES)
Take A Ride On A Riverboat
Louisiana's Le Roux; *Louisiana's Le Roux* .... (CAP)
"The Love Boat" Theme
Original Music; *Television's Greatest Hits-#3* ..... (TVT)
There Is A Ship
Peter, Paul & Mary; *In Concert* .... (WB)
There's A Boat Dat's Leavin' Soon For NY
Ella Fitzgerald & Louis Armstrong; *Porgy & Bess* (VRV)
Original Cast; *Porgy & Bess* .... (MCA)
Titanic, The
John Townley/Press Gang; *Chesapeake Sailor's*
Companion .... (ADE)
Trains & Boats & Planes
Billy J. Kramer/Dakotas; *Definitive Collection* ... (EMI)
  History Of British Rock-#4 .... (RHI)
Dionne Warwick; *Anthology-1962-1971* .... (RHI)
  Dionne Warwick .... (EVR)
  Greatest Hits .... (EVR)
  Hot! Live & Otherwise .... (ARI)
Uncle Albert/Admiral Halsey
Paul McCartney; *Gift Set* .... (CAP)
Paul McCartney/Wings; *Wings Greatest* .... (CAP)

Paul & Linda McCartney; *All The Best* .... (CAP)
  Ram .... (CAP)
Volga Boatman
Les Elgart; *Greatest Dance Band In The Land* ....(SSP)
Waiting For The Robert E. Lee
Al Jolson; *My Mammy* .... (MSP)
Eddie Cantor; *Centennial Celebration* ....(RCA)
When My Ship Comes In
Clint Black; *Hard Way* ....(RCA)
When The Ship Comes In
Bob Dylan; *Bootleg Series-#1-3-1961-1969* ......(COL)
  Times They Are A-Changin' .... (COL)
Peter, Paul & Mary; *A Song Will Rise* .... (WB)
White Mountain Singers; *Best* .... (FOL)
White Ship
H.P. Lovecraft; *H.P. Lovecraft* .... (OOP)
Wooden Ships
Crosby, Stills & Nash; *Crosby, Stills & Nash* .... (ATL)
  Crosby, Stills & Nash (collection) .... (ATL)
Crosby, Stills, Nash & Young; *So Far* .... (ATL)
  ST/Woodstock .... (ATL)
Jefferson Airplane; *2400 Fulton Street-Anthology* (RCA)
  Flight Log-1966-1976 .... (GRU)
  Loves You ....(RCA)
  Volunteers ....(RCA)
Wreck Of The Edmund Fitzgerald
Gordon Lightfoot; *Gord's Gold-#2* .... (WB)
  Summertime Dream .... (RPR)
Yellow Submarine
Beatles; *1962-1966* .... (CAP)
  Box Set .... (CAP)
  Reel Music .... (CAP)
  Revolver .... (CAP)
  Yellow Submarine .... (CAP)

SHOES, Boots

See Also: CLOTHES

Baby Needs New Shoes
Restless Heart; *Matters Of The Heart* ....(RCA)
Bad Sneakers
Steely Dan; *Greatest Hits* .... (MCA)
  Katy Lied .... (MCA)
Black Denim Trousers & Motorcycle Boots
Cheers; *Monster Summer Hits-Drag City* .... (CAP)
Blue Suede Shoes
Carl Perkins; *Blue Suede Shoes* .... (SUN)
  Cruisin'-1956-1957 .... (DHL)
  Oldies But Goodies-#4 .... (OSR)
  Original Sun Greatest Hits .... (RHI)
Elvis Presley; *Elvis Presley* ....(RCA)
  Elvis-Aloha From Hawaii ....(RCA)
  In Person ....(RCA)
  Legendary Performers-#2 ....(RCA)
  ST/G.I. Blues ....(RCA)
Boot Scootin' Boogie
Brooks & Dunn; *Brand New Man* .... (ARI)
Boots Of Spanish Leather
Bob Dylan; *Times They Are A-Changin'* .... (COL)
Can't Afford No Shoes
Frank Zappa; *One Size Fits All* .... (DSC)
Chattanooga Shoe Shine Boy
Freddy Cannon; *14 Booming Hits* .... (RHI)
Cowboy Boots
Dave Dudley; *Red Simpson/Red Sovine/Dave*
Dudley .... (GUS)
Dancing Shoes
Bob Marley/Wailers; *Birth Of A Legend* .... (EPA)
  Early Music .... (CAL)
Dan Fogelberg; *Nether Lands* .... (FM)
Side Effect; *Greatest Hits* .... (FAN)
Diamonds On The Soles Of Her Shoes
Paul Simon; *Concert In The Park-August 15 1991* (WB)
  Graceland .... (WB)
  Negotiations & Love Songs-1971-1986 .... (WB)
Die With Your Boots On
Iron Maiden; *Live After Death-World Slavery*
Tour .... (CAP)
  Piece Of Mind .... (CAP)
Goody Two Shoes
Adam Ant; *Antics In The Forbidden Zone* .... (EPI)
  Friend Or Foe .... (EPI)

Hand Me Down My Jogging Shoes
Shaw Brothers; *Best Of* .... (FOL)
Collection .... (FOL)
Hang Up My Rock & Roll Shoes
Band; *Rock Of Ages-#1 & 2* .... (CAP)
Chuck Willis; *Atlantic R&B
1947-1974-#3-(1955-1958)* .... (ATL)
Hi Heel Sneakers
Tommy Tucker; *Soul Shots-#7-Urban Blues* .... (RHI)
Vintage Music-Original Classics-#7 .... (MCA)
High Heel Shoes
Bobby McClure; *45* ....(OOP)
Italian Shoes
Dynatones; *Shameless* ....(WB)
Just Walk In My Shoes
Gladys Knight/Pips; *Anthology* .... (MOT)
Motown Legends .... (MOT)
Knockin' Boots
Candyman; *Ain't No Shame In My Game* .... (EPI)
Knockin' Da Boots
H-Town; *Fever For Da Flavor* .... (LUK)
Leather Boots
Alice Cooper; *Flush The Fashion* .... (WB)
London Blues (Shoe Shiner's Drag)
Jelly Roll Morton; *1923-1924* .... (MS)
Murder In High Heels
Kiss; *Animalize* .... (MER)
My Adidas
Run-D.M.C.; *Raising Hell* .... (PRO)
Rap Hall Of Fame .... (KT)
Rapmasters 4-Best Of Hip Hop .... (PRY)
Rap's Greatest Hits-#3 .... (PRY)
My Father's Shoes
Leon Russell; *Will O' The Wisp* .... (MCA)
Level 42; *Guaranteed* ....(RCA)
My Shoes Keep Walking Back To You
Ray Price; *Essential-1951-1962* ....(COL)
Greatest Hits ....(COL)
Old Brown Shoe
Beatles; *Box Set* .... (CAP)
Hey Jude .... (CAP)
Past Masters-#2 .... (CAP)
Old Pair Of Shoes
Randy Travis; *Greatest Hits-#1* .... (WB)
Old Shoes
Eddie Jefferson; *Bebop Singers* .... (PRS)
Tom Waits; *Early Years-#2* .... (RHI)
One Shirt, Soulless Shoes
Latimore; *I'll Do Anything For You* .... (MAL)
One, Two, Button Your Shoe
Artie Shaw & Tony Pastor; *Best Of The Big
Bands* ....(COL)
Billie Holiday; *Quintessential-#2-1936* ....(COL)
(Only Angels Wanna Wear My) Red Shoes
Elvis Costello; *Girls Girls Girls* ....(COL)
My Aim Is True ....(COL)
Elvis Costell/Attractions; *Best Of* ....(COL)
Out Of Your Shoes
Lorrie Morgan; *Leave The Light On* ....(RCA)
Paddy Doyle's Boots
Clancy Brothers/Tommy Makem; *Best Of* ....(TRD)
Penny Loafers & Bobby Socks
Joe Bennett/Sparkletones; *Rock This Town-Rockabilly
Hits-#2* .... (RHI)
Pink Shoe Laces
Dodie Stevens; *Original '50s & '60s Classics-#18* (MCA)
Put My Little Shoes Away
Everly Brothers; *Songs Our Daddy Taught Us* .... (RHI)
Put Yourself In My Shoes
Clint Black; *Put Yourself In My Shoes* ....(RCA)
Ramblin' In My Shoes
Hank Williams, Jr.; *THe Pressure Is On* ....(W/C)
Red Shoes
Chris Rea; *Auberge* ....(ATC)
Tom Waits; *Big Time* .... (ISL)
Red Shoes By The Drugstore
Tom Waits; *Blue Valentine* .... (ASY)
Rock & Roll Shoes
Amos Garrett; *Go Cat Go* ....(FF)
Ray Charles & B.J. Thomas; *Friendship* ....(COL)
Seven Spanish Angels & Other Hits ....(COL)
Sailin' Shoes
Little Feat; *Sailin' Shoes* .... (WB)
Waiting For Columbus .... (WB)

Sensible Shoes
David Lee Roth; *A Little Ain't Enough* ....(WB)
She's Got Another Pair Of Shoes
Little Richard; *Grooviest 17 Original Hits* .... (SPE)
Shine On Your Shoes
Mel Torme; *Fujitsu-Concord Jazz Festival In
Japan* .... (CCJ)
Shoe Goes On The Other Foot Tonight
George Jones; *20 Golden Pieces Of* .... (BLD)
Shoe Salesman
Alice Cooper; *Easy Action* .... (BIZ)
Shoe Shoe Shine
Dynamic Superiors; *45* .... (MOT)
Shoe Soul
Smokey Robinson; *Love Breeze* .... (MOT)
Smokin' .... (MOT)
Shoeless Joe From Hannibal, Mo.
Original Broadway Cast; *Damn Yankees* ....(RCA)
Shoes
Bobby Bland; *Touch Of The Blues* .... (MCA)
Brook Benton; *Anthology* .... (RHI)
Shoeshine Boy
Count Basie/Kansas City 7; *Count Basie/Kansas City
7* ....(MCI)
Eddie Kendricks; *At His Best* .... (TAM)
Motown Superstar Series-#19 .... (MOT)
Shoeshine Man
Tom T. Hall; *Greatest Hits* .... (MER)
Silver Heels
Fleetwood Mac; *Heroes Are Hard To Find* .... (RPR)
Spanish Boots
Jeff Beck; *Beck-Ola* .... (EPI)
Take Off Them Shoes
Gene Watson; *Reflections* ....(CAP)
Take Your Shoes Off Baby
Artie Shaw/Orchestra; *Blues In The Night* .... (BLU)
Dinah Washington; *Echoes Of An Era* .... (RLL)
Tennis Shoes
Jimmy C. Newman; *Alligator Man* .... (ROU)
These Boots Are Made For Walkin'
Billy Ray Cyrus; *Some Gave All* .... (MER)
Nancy Sinatra; *Billboard Top Rock 'N' Roll
Hits-1966* .... (RHI)
Boots-Greatest Hits .... (RHI)
Those Shoes
Eagles; *Long Run* .... (ASY)
Turtle Shoes
Bobby McFerrin; *Spontaneous Inventions* .... (BLN)
Bobby McFerrin & Herbie Hancock; *ST/Twins* . (WTG)
Two Thousand Shoes
Big Audio Dynamite; *Tighten Up-#88* ....(COL)
Two-Tone Shoes
Homer & Jethro; *Get Hot Or Go Home-Vintage
Rockabilly* .... (CMF)
Walk A Mile In My Shoes
Bryan Ferry; *Another Time Another Place* .... (RPR)
Elvis Presley/Imperial Quartet; *On Stage* ....(RCA)
Joe South; *Best Of* .... (RHI)
Walking Shoes
Tanya Tucker; *Tennessee Woman* .... (LIB)
Who Wears These Shoes
Elton John; *Breaking Hearts* .... (MCA)
Who's Gonna Fill Their Shoes
George Jones; *Greatest Country Hits/'80s-1985* ..(COL)
Super Hits .... (EPI)
Who's Gonna Fill Their Shoes .... (EPI)

SHOPPING, Buying, Selling
See Also: MONEY

90 Days (Same As Cash)
Midnight Star; *Midnight Star* .... (SLR)
At The Mall
Patty Larkin; *Live In The Square* ....(PHO)
Burn Down The Malls
Mojo Nixon & Skid Roper; *Enigma Variations 2* .(ENC)
Buy American
Tex Payer; *Work's Many Voices-#1 & 2* .... (ARH)
Buying My Way Into Heaven
Sammy Hagar; *Unboxed* .... (GEF)
Buy, Buy This American Car
Charlie King; *Food Phone Gas Lodging* ....(FF)

Candy Store Rock
Led Zeppelin; *Led Zeppelin (collection)* .... (ATL)
   Presence .... (SS)
Can't Buy Me Love
Beatles; *Hey Jude* .... (CAP)
   1962-1966 .... (CAP)
   At The Hollywood Bowl .... (CAP)
   Hard Day's Night .... (CAP)
   Reel Music .... (CAP)
Paul McCartney; *Tripping The Live Fantastic* .... (CAP)
Checking Out The Checkout Girl
Wazmo Nariz; *10th Anniversary-These People Are*
Nuts .... (IRS)
Cockles & Mussels
Emily Mitchell; *The Irish Album* .... (RCA)
Come To The Supermarket (In Old Peking)
Barbra Streisand; *Album* .... (COL)
Come & Buy My Toys
David Bowie; *Starting Point* .... (DER)
Dillon's Store
Lightnin' Hopkins; *Prison Blues-Golden*
Classics-#2 .... (CLT)
Dime Store Mystery
Lou Reed; *New York* .... (SIR)
Discount Dogs
Joe Perry Project; *Let The Music Do The Talking* .(COL)
Doggie In The Window
Patti Page; *16 Most Requested Songs* .... (COL)
   Golden Hits .... (MER)
   Greatest Hits .... (COL)
Don't Let Your Eyes Go Shopping
Mark Murphy; *Sing's Nat's Choice-N.K. Cole*
Songbook-2 .... (MUS)
Don't Sell Daddy Any More Whiskey
Joe Val/New England Bluegrass Boys; *Not A Word*
From Home .... (ROU)
Don't Sell This Diamond Ring
Gary Lewis/Playboys; *Good Old Rock & Roll* .... (IGR)
Down In The Mall
Warren Zevon; *Transverse City* .... (VIA)
Fear Of The Marketplace
Neil Diamond; *On The Way To The Sky* .... (COL)
Funk Boutique
Cover Girls; *This Beat Is Hot-Compilation* .... (EPI)
Go To The Mall
Dead Serios; *Ralph Rules* .... (LGS)
I Don't Go Shopping
Peter Allen; *Best* .... (A&M)
I Found A Million Dollar Baby
Barbra Streisand; *ST/Funny Girl* .... (ARI)
Nat King Cole; *Gift Set* .... (CAP)
In A Persian Market
Wilbur DeParis; *ST/New York Stories* .... (ELE)
In The Market Place
Earth, Wind & Fire; *All 'N All* .... (COL)
I'm A Pleasure To Shop For
Ogden Nash; *Christmas With* .... (CAE)
Keep The Customer Satisfied
Simon & Garfunkel; *Bridge Over Troubled Water* (COL)
   Collected Works .... (COL)
Let's Go Spend Your Money Honey
Evangeline; *French Quarter Moon* .... (MGR)
Life Is A Lemon And I Want My Money Back
Meat Loaf; *Bat Out Of Hell II-Back Into Hell* ... (MCA)
Lost In The Supermarket
Clash; *London Calling* .... (EPI)
   On Broadway .... (EPI)
   Story Of-#1 .... (EPI)
Love At The Five & Dime
Kathy Mattea; *Collection of Hits* .... (MER)
   Fourteen Country Favorites .... (MER)
   Walk The Way The Wind Blows .... (MER)
Nanci Griffith; *Last Of The True Believers* .... (PHO)
   One Fair Summer Evening .... (MCA)
Love For Sale
Charlie Parker; *Cole Porter Songbook* .... (VRV)
Dexter Gordon; *Blue Porter* .... (BLN)
Dr. John; *In A Sentimental Mood* .... (WB)
Ella Fitzgerald; *Cole Porter Songbook* .... (VRV)
Fine Young Cannibals; *Red Hot + Blue-Tribute To*
Benefit AIDS .... (CHR)
Tony Bennett; *I Left My Heart In San Francisco* .(COL)
Love Under New Management
Miki Howard; *Miki Howard* .... (ATL)

Magic Fingers (25 Cents)
Birdsongs Of The Mesozoic; *Faultline* .... (CUN)
Mama Can't Buy You Love
Elton John; *Complete Thom Bell Sessions* .... (MCA)
   Greatest Hits-1976-1986 .... (MCA)
Man In The Corner Shop
Jam; *Snap!* .... (POL)
My Arms Stay Open All Night
Tanya Tucker; *Greatest Hits* .... (CAP)
Nigerian Marketplace
Oscar Peterson Trio; *Nigerian Marketplace* .... (PAB)
Peanut Vendor
Judy Garland; *Star Is Born* .... (COL)
Stan Kenton; *Comprehensive* .... (CAP)
   Greatest Hits .... (CAP)
   Retrospective-Capitol Years-#1 .... (BLN)
   Uncollected-#6-1962 .... (HIN)
Rockin' Shopping Center
Jonathan Richman/Modern Lovers; *Jonathan*
Richman/Modern Lovers .... (RHI)
Safeway Cart
Neil Young/Crazy Horse; *Sleeps With Angels* ..... (RPR)
Sales Tax On The Woman
New Lost City Ramblers; *Early*
Years-1958-1962 .... (FLW)
Salesgirl Blues
Rick Parker; *Wicked World* .... (GEF)
Saturday Night At The General Store
Margo Smith; *Happiness* .... (WB)
Sears-Roebuck Routine
Doc Watson; *Old Timey Concert* .... (VAN)
Second Hand Rose
Barbra Streisand; *Greatest Hits* .... (COL)
   Happening In Central Park .... (COL)
   Just For The Record .... (COL)
   My Name Is Barbra Two .... (COL)
   & Other Musical Instruments .... (COL)
Second Hand Store
Joe Walsh; *But Seriously Folks* .... (ASY)
Sell My Monkey
B.B. King; *Blues 'N' Jazz* .... (MCA)
   Blues 'N' Jazz/Electric B.B. King .... (MCA)
Selling The Drama
Live; *Throwing Copper* .... (RAD)
Senegal Market Place
Sly Dunbar; *Sly Wicked & Slick* .... (FL)
Shop Around
Captain & Tennille; *Greatest Hits* .... (A&M)
Miracles; *Hi-We're The Miracles* .... (MOT)
Smokey Robinson/Miracles; *16 #1 Hits From The Early*
'60s .... (MOT)
   Anthology .... (MOT)
   Every Great Motown Song-First 25 Years ...... (MOT)
Shopping For Clothes
Coasters; *Their Greatest Recordings-Early Years* ..(ATL)
Sixteen Tons
Cactus Brothers; *Cactus Brothers* .... (LIB)
Stevie Wonder; *Down To Earth* .... (MOT)
Tennessee Ernie Ford; *16 Tons Of Boogie-Best Of* (RHI)
   Capitol Collectors Series .... (CAP)
   When AM Was King .... (CAP)
Weavers; *Greatest Hits* .... (VAN)
Sold My Fortune
Sugartooth; *Sugartooth* .... (GEF)
Stone Cold Dead In The Market
Ella Fitzgerald; *Best Of-#2* .... (MCA)
Swap Meet
Nirvana; *Bleach* .... (SP)
Swap Meet Louie
Sir Mix-A-Lot; *Mack Daddy* .... (DEF)
That Ain't In Any Catalog
Mustard & Gravy; *Long Gone Daddy* .... (CLT)
That's Where My Money Goes
101 Strings Orchestra; *Beer Drinkin' Sing Alongs!!* (ALS)
Then God Made Malls
Uncle Bonsai; *Myn Ynd Wymyn* .... (YT)
Too High A Price
Doobie Brothers; *Cycles* .... (CAP)
Try It Before You Buy It
Mike Bloomfield; *Try It Before You Buy It* .... (OW)
Tupperware Party
Doughboys; *Happy Accidents* .... (RES)

Video Shop
Kinks; *Lost & Found-1986-1989* .... (MCA)
   Think Visual .... (MSP)
Waldo's Discount Donuts
Red Knuckles/Trailblazers; *Hot Rize Presents* ...... (FF)
Want Ads
Honey Cone; *Greatest Hits* .... (HDH)
Will There Be A Shopping Mall In Heaven?
Reverend Billy C. Wirtz; *Deep Fried & Sanctified* . (HT)
Window Shopping
Hank Williams; *24 Greatest Hits* .... (MER)
   40 Greatest Hits .... (POL)
Window Shoppin'
Hiram Bullock; *From All Sides* .... (ATL)
X-Mas Shopping Blues
Christmas Jug Band; *Mistletoe Jam* .... (RLX)
Yard Sale
Sammy Kershaw; *Don't Go Near The Water* .... (MER)
Yes We Have No Bananas
Authentic Band Organ; *Catch The Brass Ring* ....(KLA)
Spike Jones; *Best Of-#2* .... (RCA)

SHOW BIZ, Stardom

See Also: CITIES: NEW YORK (for Broadway),
HOLLYWOOD, MOVIES

42nd Street
Hal Kemp; *Best Of The Big Bands* ....(COL)
Academy Award
Jo Jo Gunne; *Jo Jo Gunne* .... (ASY)
Academy Award Performance
Sparks; *No. 1 In Heaven* .... (ELE)
Act Naturally
Beatles; *Help!* ....(CAP)
   Yesterday & Today ....(CAP)
Buck Owens; *Beatle Originals* .... (RHI)
Buck Owens & Ringo Starr; *Act Naturally* .....(CAP)
Buck Owens/Buckaroos; *Live At Carnegie Hall* .. (CMF)
Charley Pride; *Country Pride* ....(RCA)
Johnny Russell; *20 Great Country Hits* ....(RCA)
Actor
Moody Blues; *In Search Of The Lost Chord* ...... (POL)
   This Is The .... (POL)
Another Op'nin' Another Show
Original Cast; *Kiss Me Kate* ....(COL)
Artist Relations
Martin Mull; *I'm Everyone I Ever Loved* .... (MCA)
Baby I'm A Star
Helen Reddy; *Ear Candy* ....(CAP)
Prince; *ST/Purple Rain* ....(WB)
Backstage Queen
Scorpions; *Best Of* ....(RCA)
   Tokyo Tapes ....(RCA)
   Virgin Killer ....(RCA)
Ballroom Blitz
Sweet; *Desolation Boulevard* ....(CAP)
Bette Davis Eyes
Kim Carnes; *Mistaken Identity* .... (EMI)
Black Velvet
Alannah Myles; *Alannah Myles* .... (ATL)
Robin Lee; *Black Velvet* .... (ATL)
Blaze Of Glory
Alarm; *Declaration* .... (IRS)
   Electric Folklore .... (IRS)
Joe Jackson; *Blaze Of Glory* .... (A&M)
Jon Bon Jovi; *Blaze Of Glory* .... (MER)
Brand New Country Star
Jimmy Buffett; *Living & Dying In 3/4 Time* ..... (MCA)
Broadway
Clash; *On Broadway* .... (EPI)
   Sandinista .... (EPI)
Count Basie; *Essential-#3* ....(COL)
Count Basie/Orchestra; *Best Of-Roulette Years* ... (RLL)
Jack McDuff/Friends; *Color Me Blue* .... (CCJ)
Mel Torme; *Songs Of New York* .... (ATL)
Broadway Baby
Julia McKenzie; *Collector's Sondheim* ....(RCA)
Original Broadway Cast; *Follies* ....(CAP)
Broadway Ballet
Gene Kelly/Chorus; *ST/Singin' In The Rain* .... (SSP)
Broadway Fools
Branford Marsalis; *Random Abstract* ....(COL)

Broadway My Street
Original Broadway Cast; *70 Girls 70* .... (SMC)
Candle In The Wind
Elton John; *Goodbye Yellow Brick Road* .... (POL)
   Live In Australia w/Melbourne Symphony ... (POL)
   Your Songs .... (POL)
Celluloid Heroes
Joan Jett; *Hit List* ....(CBA)
Kinks; *Come Dancing-Best Of-1977-1986* .... (ARI)
   Everybody's In Show Biz .... (RHI)
   Greatest ....(RCA)
Child Star
Joan Armatrading; *Whatever's For Us* .... (A&M)
Chords Of Fame
Phil Ochs; *Chords Of Fame* .... (A&M)
   Greatest Hits .... (A&M)
   War Is Over: Best Of .... (A&M)
Could I Have Your Autograph
Dolly Parton; *Rainbow* ....(COL)
Cover Of Rolling Stone
Dr. Hook/Medicine Show; *Greatest Hits* ....(CAP)
   Revisited ....(COL)
Cracked Actor
David Bowie; *Aladdin Sane* ....(RYK)
   Live ....(RYK)
   Sound + Vision ....(RYK)
   ST/Ziggy Stardust-The Motion Picture ....(RCA)
Day After Day
Alan Parsons Project; *I Robot* .... (ARI)
China Crisis; *Diary Of A Hollow Horse* ... (A&M)
Pretenders; *II* .... (SIR)
   Singles .... (SIR)
Dirty Laundry
Don Henley; *I Can't Stand Still* .... (ASY)
Drive My Car
Beatles; *1962-1966* ....(CAP)
   Rock 'n' Roll Music-#2 ....(CAP)
   Rubber Soul ....(CAP)
   Yesterday...And Today ....(CAP)
Eminence Front
Who; *It's Hard* .... (MCA)
   Join Together .... (MCA)
Entertainer
Billy Joel; *Greatest Hits-#1 & 2* ....(COL)
   Streetlife Serenade ....(COL)
Graham Central Station; *Star Walk* ....(WB)
Marvin Hamlish; *Super Hits/'70s-Have A Nice*
Day-#12 .... (RHI)
Scott Joplin; *Entertainer-#4* ....(BIO)
Tony Clarke; *Best Of Chess R&B* ....(CSS)
   Soul Shots-#10-More Sweet Soul .... (RHI)
Evergreen (Theme From "A Star Is Born")
Barbra Streisand; *Greatest Hits* ....(COL)
   Greatest Hits-#2 ....(COL)
   Memories ....(COL)
   ST/A Star Is Born ....(COL)
Luther Vandross; *Songs* .... (EPI)
Paul Williams; *Classics* .... (A&M)
Everybody Is A Star
Gladys Knight/Pips; *Everybody Needs Love/If I Were*
Your... .... (MOT)
Sly/Family Stone; *Anthology* .... (EPI)
   Greatest Hits .... (EPI)
Everybody's A Star
Kinks; *Soap Opera* .... (RHI)
Everybody's In Shobizz
Shobizz; *Shobizz* ....(CAP)
Everybody's Making It Big But Me
Dr. Hook; *Bankrupt* ....(CAP)
Fake Your Way To The Top
Original Broadway Cast; *Dreamgirls* ....(GEF)
Fame
David Bowie; *Changesonebowie* ....(RCA)
   ST/Pretty Woman .... (EMI)
   The Singles-1969-1993 ....(RYK)
   Young Americans ....(RYK)
Irene Cara; *ST/Fame* .... (RSO)
Fame & Fortune
Bad Company; *Fame & Fortune* .... (ATL)
Elvis Presley; *Golden Records-#3* .... (RCA)
   Legendary Performer-#3 ....(RCA)
   Valentine Gift For You ....(RCA)
Famous Groupies
Wings; *London Town* ....(CAP)

Fan Mail
Blondie; *Plastic Letters* .... (CHR)
Dickies; *Dawn Of* .... (A&M)
   Great Dictations Of .... (A&M)
Fool's Hall Of Fame
Johnny Cash; *Man-The World-His Music* .... (SUN)
   Rough Cut King Of Country Music .... (SUN)
Roy Orbison; *Sun Years* .... (RHI)
Future Legend
David Bowie; *Diamond Dogs* .... (RYK)
Give My Regards To Broadway
Barry Manilow; *Showstoppers* .... (ARI)
Joel Grey; *Broadway Magic-1960s* .... (COL)
Original Cast; *George M.* .... (COL)
Glamorous Life
Original London Cast; *A Little Night Music* ...... (RCA)
Sheila E.; *Glamorous Life* .... (WB)
Glory
Television; *Adventure* .... (ELE)
Glory Road
Neil Diamond; *Love At The Greek* .... (COL)
   Sweet Caroline .... (MCA)
Greatest Show On Earth
Michael Jackson; *2 Classic Albums: Got To Be
There/Ben* .... (MOT)
   Ben .... (MOT)
Hard Act To Follow
Brother Cane; *Brother Cane* .... (VIA)
Have A Cigar
Pink Floyd; *Wish You Were Here* .... (COL)
Hello There
Cheap Trick; *At Budokan* .... (EPI)
   In Color .... (EPI)
   ST/Over The Edge .... (WB)
Hey Mister, That's Me Up On The Jukebox
Linda Ronstadt; *Prisoner In Disguise* .... (ASY)
How To Be A Country Star
Statler Brothers; *Best Of-Rides Again-#2* .... (MER)
I Knew Jesus (Before He Was A Star)
Glen Campbell; *Best Of* .... (CAP)
I Left My Heart At The Stage Door...
Jo Stafford; *G.I. Jo* .... (CRN)
I'll Be Your Audience
Shirley Bassey; *Good Bad But Beautiful* .... (EMI)
   Great Performances .... (LIB)
   Greatest Hits .... (EMI)
   Live In London .... (CAP)
I'm Going To Be A Teenage Idol
Elton John; *Don't Shoot Me I'm Only The Piano
Player* .... (POL)
I'm Gonna Be Somebody
Travis Tritt; *Country Club* .... (WB)
I'm Playing For You
Ronnie Milsap; *True Believer* .... (LIB)
I'm The Greatest Star
Barbra Streisand; *ST/Funny Girl* .... (COL)
Diana Ross/Supremes; *Anthology* .... (MOT)
King Of Hollywood
Eagles; *The Long Run* .... (ASY)
Legend In My Time
Don Gibson; *All-Time Greatest Hits* .... (RCA)
Ronnie Milsap; *Greatest Hits* .... (RCA)
   Legend In My Time .... (RCA)
   Live .... (RCA)
Legend In Your Own Time
Carly Simon; *Anticipation* .... (ELE)
   Best Of .... (ELE)
Let Me Entertain You
Original Cast; *Gypsy* .... (COL)
Original London Cast; *Gypsy* .... (RCA)
Pearl Bailey; *Back On Broadway* .... (RLL)
   Echoes Of An Era .... (RLL)
Queen; *Jazz* .... (HOL)
   Live Killers .... (HOL)
Lifestyles Of The Not-So-Rich & Famous
Tracy Byrd; *No Ordinary Man* .... (MCA)
Life's Been Good
Eagles; *Live* .... (ASY)
Joe Walsh; *But Seriously Folks* .... (ASY)
   ST/FM .... (MCA)
Little Sally, The Super Sex Star
Camille Yarborough; *Iron Pot Cooker* .... (VAN)

Lonely At The Top
Randy Newman; *Sail Away* .... (RPR)
   "Live" .... (RPR)
Lost In The Lights Of Broadway
Bernie Shanahan; *Bernie Shanahan* .... (ATL)
Lullaby Of Broadway
Andrews Sisters; *Best Of-#2* .... (MCA)
Bette Midler; *Bette Midler* .... (ATL)
   Live At Last .... (ATL)
Tony Bennett; *Jazz* .... (COL)
Mama's Always On Stage
Arrested Development; *3 Years 5 Months 2 Days In The
Life Of* .... (CHR)
   Unplugged .... (CHR)
Mirror Star
Fabulous Poodles; *Mirror Stars* .... (EPI)
Money For Nothing
Dire Straits; *Brothers In Arms* .... (WB)
   Money For Nothing .... (WB)
My Home Ain't In The Hall Of Fame
Jonathan Edwards; *Lucky Day* .... (ATC)
J.D. Crowe/New South; *My Home Ain't In The Hall Of
Fame* .... (ROU)
On Broadway
Drifters; *16 Greatest Hits* .... (TRP)
   Golden Hits .... (ATL)
George Benson; *Collection* .... (WB)
   ST/All That Jazz .... (CAS)
   Weekend In L.A. .... (WB)
On With The Show
Rolling Stones; *Their Satanic Majesty's Request* .. (AKO)
One Monkey Don't Stop No Show
Big Maybelline; *Okeh R&B Story-1949-1957* ..... (EPI)
Honey Cone; *Greatest Hits* .... (HDH)
Joe Tex; *Greatest Hits* .... (CCB)
   I Believe I'm Gonna Make It!-Best Of .... (RHI)
Overnight Sensation
Mickey Gilley; *Greatest Hits-#2* .... (EPI)
Raspberries/Eric Carmen; *Best* .... (CAP)
Steve Wariner; *Best Of* .... (RCA)
Tina Turner; *Break Every Rule* .... (CAP)
   Live In Europe .... (CAP)
Overnight Success
George Strait; *Beyond The Blue Neon* .... (MCA)
   Ten Strait Hits .... (MCA)
Pathway To Glory
Loggins & Messina; *Full Sail* .... (COL)
Performance
Esther Phillips; *Best Of* .... (CBA)
Joe Cocker; *I Can Stand A Little Rain* .... (A&M)
Neville Brothers; *Treacherous-History
Of-1955-1985* .... (RHI)
Performer
Marty Robbins; *Performer* .... (COL)
Poor Little Hollywood Star
Virginia Martin; *Little Me* .... (RCA)
Private Audition
Heart; *Private Audition* .... (EPI)
Riding With A Movie Star
L7; *Hungry For Stink* .... (SLS)
Rock 'N' Roll Hall Of Fame
Frank Marino & Mahogany Rush; *What's Next* .. (COL)
Sensation
Who; *Join Together* .... (MCA)
   Tommy .... (MCA)
Show
Doug E. Fresh/Get Fresh Crew; *Rapmasters 3-Best Of
The Cut* .... (PRY)
Show Biz
2 Deep; *Honey That's Show Biz* .... (CLD)
Dudley Moore; *Songs Without Words* .... (GRP)
Helen Reddy; *Free & Easy* .... (CAP)
Show Biz Blues
Fleetwood Mac; *Then Play On* .... (RPR)
Show Biz Kids
Steely Dan; *Countdown To Ecstasy* .... (MCA)
   Greatest Hits .... (MCA)
Show Bizness
Fred Koller; *Songs From The Night Before* .... (ALC)
Gil Scott-Heron & Brian Jackson; *Secrets* .... (ARI)
Show Must Go On
Carly Simon; *ST/This Is My Life* .... (QUE)
Dinah Washington; *Dinah '63* .... (RLL)
Four Tops; *45* .... (MCA)

Grim Reaper; *See You In Hell* ....(RCA)
Leo Sayer; *Silverbird* ....(WB)
Pink Floyd; *The Wall* ....(COL)
Queen; *Classic Queen* ....(HOL)
  Innuendo ....(HOL)
Shenandoah; *Shenandoah* ....(COL)
Three Dog Night; *Best Of* ....(MCA)
  Joy To The World-Their Greatest Hits ....(MCA)
Show Time
Sammy Davis, Jr.; *Live Performance* ....(WB)
Undisputed Truth; *Smokin'* ....(WHI)
Showman's Life
Jesse Winchester; *Best Of* ....(RHI)
  Touch On The Rainy Side ....(RHI)
Showtime
Gary's Gang; *Keep On Dancin'* ....(COL)
Simon Smith & His Amazing Dancing Bear
Randy Newman; *Sail Away* ....(RPR)
So You Are A Star
Hudson Brothers; *Super Hits/'70s-Have A Nice Day-#14* ....(RHI)
  Yesterday's Heroes-'70s Teen Idols ....(RHI)
So You Want To Be A Rock 'N' Roll Star
Byrds; *Greatest Hits* ....(COL)
  Original Singles-#1-1965-1967 ....(COL)
  Rock Classics/'60s ....(COL)
  Byrds (collection) ....(COL)
  (Untitled) ....(COL)
Patti Smith Group; *Wave* ....(ARI)
Tom Petty/Heartbreakers; *Pack Up The Plantation-Live* ....(MCA)
  Ultimate Rock Album ....(FTN)
Stage Door
Justin Hayward; *Songwriter* ....(DER)
Stage Fright
Band; *Best Of* ....(CAP)
  Last Waltz ....(WB)
  Rock Of Ages-#1&2 ....(CAP)
  Stage Fright ....(CAP)
  To Kingdom Come-Definitive Collection ....(CAP)
Bob Dylan/Band; *Before The Flood* ....(COL)
Star Star
Rolling Stones; *Goats Head Soup* ....(RS)
  Love You Live ....(RS)
Star Struck
Blackmore's Rainbow; *Rainbow Rising* ....(POL)
Kinks; *Are The Village Green Preservation...* ......(RPR)
Stardom In Action
Pete Townshend; *All The Best Cowboys Have Chinese Eyes* ....(ATC)
Starmaker
Kinks; *Celluloid Heroes* ....(RCA)
Statue Of A Fool
Jack Greene; *Country Hits* ....(EXA)
  Greatest Hits ....(GUS)
  MCA 30 Years Of Hits-1958-1988 ....(MCA)
  Sings His Best ....(SO)
Ricky Van Shelton; *Greatest Hits Plus* ....(COL)
  RVS III ....(COL)
Superstar
Bette Midler; *Divine Miss M* ....(ATL)
Carpenters; *Carpenters* ....(A&M)
  Singles-1969-1973 ....(A&M)
  Yesterday Once More ....(A&M)
Joe Cocker; *Mad Dogs & Englishmen* ....(A&M)
Murray Head; *Premiere Collection-Best Of A.L. Webber* ....(MCA)
  Super Hits/'70s-Have A Nice Day-#5 ....(RHI)
Original London Cast; *Jesus Christ Superstar* ....(MCA)
Paul Davis; *Southern Tracks & Fantasies* ....(BNG)
Richard Marx; *Rush Street* ....(CAP)
Superstar (Remember How You Got...)
Temptations; *Anthology* ....(MOT)
Superstars
Styx; *Grand Illusion* ....(A&M)
Suzi Wants To Be A Rock Star
Professor Griff/Last Asiatic Disciples; *Pawns In The Game* ....(LUK)
Teenage Idol
Blackfoot; *Blackfoot* ....(ATC)
Rick Nelson; *Best Of* ....(EMI)
  Greatest Hits ....(RHI)
  Legendary Masters ....(EMI)

There Ain't No Santa Claus On The...
Captain Beefheart; *Spotlight Kid/Clear Spot* ......(RPR)
There's No Business Like Show Business
Ethel Merman; *Irving Berlin 100th Anniv. Collection* ....(MCA)
  Merman Sings Merman ....(LON)
Original Cast; *Annie Get Your Gun* ....(MCA)
Video Killed The Radio Star
Bruce Woolly/Camera Club; *Bruce Woolly/Camera Club* ....(COL)
Buggles; *Age Of Plastic* ....(ISL)
  Island Story-1962-1987-25th Anniversary ....(ISL)
  Rock Of The '80s-#2 ....(PRY)
Wanna Be A Rock 'N' Roll Star
Eddie Money; *Eddie Money* ....(COL)
Watching The Wheels
John Lennon; *Lennon* ....(CAP)
John Lennon & Yoko Ono; *Double Fantasy* ......(CAP)
Wild West Show/Dog Act
Original Broadway Cast; *Will Rogers Follies* .....(COL)
You Are The Show
Outlaws; *Playin' To Win* ....(ARI)
You Are The Star Of My Show
Eugene Record; *Trying To Get To You* ....(WB)
You Don't Have To Be A Star
Marilyn McCoo & Billy Davis, Jr.; *45* ....(MCA)
Zap Zap
Frankie Miller; *Standing On The Edge* ....(CAP)

SILVER

By The Light Of The Silvery Moon
Al Jolson; *Story-#1* ....(MCA)
Doris Day; *Day At The Movies* ....(COL)
Julie Andrews; *Little Bit Of Broadway* ....(COL)
Mitch Miller; *34 All-Time Great Sing Along Selections* ....(COL)
  Sing Along With ....(COL)
Eyes Of Silver
Doobie Brothers; *What Were Once Vices Are Now Habits* ....(WB)
From Silver Lake
Jackson Browne; *Jackson Browne* ....(ASY)
Gold & Silver
Quicksilver Messenger Service; *Legends Of Rock Guitar-'60s-#1* ....(RHI)
  Quicksilver Messenger Service ....(CAP)
  Sons Of Mercury ....(RHI)
Golden Memories & Silver Tears
Jim Reeves; *Best Of* ....(RCA)
  Great Moments With ....(RCA)
  w/Patsy Cline: Greatest Hits ....(RCA)
Hi Ho Silver
Fleetwood Mac; *Kiln House* ....(RPR)
Jet Silver & The Dolls Of Venus
Be Bop Deluxe; *Ax Victim* ....(OOP)
  Best Of-Raiding The Divine Archive ....(CAP)
King Of The Silver Screen
Alice Cooper; *Lace & Whisky* ....(MET)
Look For The Silver Lining
Alberta Hunter; *Look For The Silver Lining* ......(COL)
Chet Baker; *Let's Get Lost-Best Of Chet Baker Sings* ....(PJZ)
Dave Brubeck Quartet; *Stardust* ....(FAN)
Man On The Silver Mountain
Ritchie Blackmore; *Rainbow* ....(POL)
Ritchie Blackmore/Rainbow; *Finyl Vinyl* ....(MER)
Maxwell's Silver Hammer
Beatles; *1967-1970* ....(CAP)
  Abbey Road ....(CAP)
On Silver Waves
101 Strings Orchestra; *Romantic Songs Of The Sea* ....(ALS)
Queen Of The Silver Dollar
Dave & Sugar; *Greatest Hits* ....(RCA)
Dr. Hook; *& The Medicine Show Revisited* ....(COL)
Emmylou Harris; *Pieces Of The Sky* ....(RPR)
Quicksilver
Horace Silver; *Trio* ....(BLN)
Pink Floyd; *ST/More* ....(CAP)

Quicksilver Girl
Steve Miller Band; *Best Of-1968-1973* ....(CAP)
   More Songs From "Big Chill" Soundtrack ......(MOT)
   Sailor ....(CAP)
Quicksilver Lightning
Roger Daltrey; *ST/Quicksilver* ....(ATL)
Sail Along, Silv'ry Moon
Andy Williams; *Greatest Songs* ....(CCB)
Billy Vaughn; *Best Of* ....(MCA)
   Greatest Hits ....(CCB)
   & Orchestra Play 22 Of His Greatest Hits ..(RAN)
Silver
Echo/Bunnymen; *Ocean Rain* ....(SIR)
   Songs To Learn & Sing ....(SIR)
Textones; *Through The Canyon* ....(RHI)
Silver Bells
Atlantic Starr; *ST/Home Alone 2-Lost In New
York* ....(FOX)
Bob Wills; *Fiddle* ....(CMF)
Booker T./M.G.s; *Soul Christmas* ....(ATL)
Brenda Lee; *Christmas* ....(WB)
Diana Ross/Supremes; *Merry Christmas* ....(MOT)
Earl Grant; *Winter Wonderland* ....(MSP)
Elvis Presley; *Memories Of Christmas* ....(RCA)
   Sings The Wonderful World Of Christmas .....(RCA)
Gary Morris; *Every Christmas* ....(LIB)
John Denver; *Rocky Mountain Christmas* ....(RCA)
Johnny Mathis/Percy Faith & Orchestra; *Merry
Christmas* ....(COL)
Judds; *Christmas Time With* ....(RCA)
Kenny Rogers; *Christmas In America* ....(RPR)
Kevin Eubanks; *GRP Christmas Collection* ......(GRP)
Lacy J. Dalton; *Christmas For The '90s-#1* ....(LIB)
Loretta Lynn; *Christmas Without Daddy* ....(MSP)
Margaret Whiting & Jimmy Wakely; *Christmas On The
Range-Cowboy Classics* ....(CAP)
Merle Haggard; *Christmas Gift* ....(CCB)
Miracles; *Christmas With* ....(MOT)
Mormon Tabernacle Choir; *White Christmas* .....(COL)
Oak Ridge Boys; *Christmas* ....(MSP)
Perry Como; *I Wish It Could Be Christmas
Forever* ....(RCA)
Ray Price; *Christmas Gift For You From* ....(SO)
Roches; *We Three Kings* ....(MSP)
Ronnie Milsap; *Christmas With* ....(RCA)
Stevie Wonder; *Someday At Christmas* ....(MOT)
Travis Tritt; *Christmas-Loving Time Of The Year* ..(WB)
Silver Bells (That Ring In The Night)
Bob Wills; *Anthology* ....(SSP)
   Best Of ....(MCA)
   Best Of-#2 ....(MCA)
Silver Bird
Mark Lindsay; *Super Hits/'70s-Have A Nice
Day-#4* .... (RHI)
Silver Blue
Linda Ronstadt; *Prisoner In Disguise* ....(ASY)
Silver Bullet
Flo & Eddie; *History Of Flo & Eddie/Turtles* .....(RHI)
Silver City
Joe Ely; *Lord Of The Highway* ....(HT)
Mance Lipscomb; *Texas Songster-#2* ....(ARH)
Silver Dagger
Dave Van Ronk; *Dave Van Ronk* ....(FAN)
   Inside ....(PRS)
Joan Baez; *Ballad Book* ....(VAN)
   Ballad Book-#2 ....(VAN)
   Joan Baez-#1 ....(VAN)
   Very Early ....(VAN)
Silver Dew On The Bluegrass Tonight
Johnnie Lee Wills; *Tulsa Swing* ....(ROU)
Silver Dollar
April Wine; *First Glance* ....(CAP)
Lee Greenwood; *If There's Any Justice* ....(PAN)
Silver Dreams
Babys; *Broken Heart* ....(CHR)
Silver Eagle
Merle Haggard & George Jones; *Taste Of Yesterday's
Wine* .... (EPI)
Reba McEntire; *Just A Little Love* ....(MCA)
Silver Girl
Survivor; *Eye Of The Tiger* ....(SCO)
Silver Gun
Robert Palmer; *Addictions-#2* ....(ISL)
   Pride ....(ISL)

Silver Haired Daddy Of Mine
Frank Yankovic; *I Wish I Was 18 Again* ....(SMA)
Silver Heels
Fleetwood Mac; *Heroes Are Hard To Find* ....(RPR)
Silver Lights
Sammy Hagar; *Nine On A Ten Scale* ....(CAP)
Silver Lining
Nils Lofgren & Levon Helm; *Silver Lining* ....(RYK)
Player; *Danger Zone* ....(OOP)
Silver Mantis
Alpha Band; *II* ....(OOP)
Silver Medals & Sweet Memories
Statler Brothers; *Best Of-Rides Again-#2* .... (MER)
   Short Stories ....(MER)
Silver Moon
David Sylvian; *Gone To Earth* .... (VIA)
Kitaro; *In Person* ....(GRM)
   My Best ....(GRM)
   Silk Road II ....(GRM)
Lawrence Welk; *22 Great Waltzes* ....(RAN)
Michael Nesmith; *Older Stuff* ....(RHI)
Mom & Dads; *20 Favorite Waltzes* ....(CRS)
Silver Morning
Kenny Rankin; *Silver Morning* .... (LD)
Silver Paper
Mountain; *Climbing* ....(COL)
   Twin Peaks ....(COL)
Silver Rainbow
Genesis; *Genesis* ....(ATL)
Silver Screen
Little Feat; *Representing The Mambo* ....(WB)
Silver Shadow
Atlantic Starr; *As The Band Turns* ....(A&M)
   Classics-#10 ....(A&M)
   Secret Lovers...Best Of ....(A&M)
Silver Springs
Fleetwood Mac; *25 Years-The Chain* ....(WB)
Silver Stallion
W. Jennings/W. Nelson/J. Cash/K. Krist.; *Greatest
Country Hits/'90s-1990* ....(COL)
   Highwayman 2 ....(COL)
Silver Stars, Purple Sage, Eyes Of Blue
Roy Rogers/Sons Of The Pioneers; *Roy Rogers/Sons Of
The Pioneers* ....(VS)
Silver Swan Rag
Scott Joplin; *Elite Syncopations* ....(BIO)
   Ragtime-#3 (early 1900s) ....(BIO)
Silver Sword
Flora Purim; *Stories To Tell* .... (MS)
Silver Threads Among The Gold
Mike Auldridge; *Dobro/Blues & Bluegrass* ....(TAK)
Silver Threads & Golden Needles
Honky Tonk Angels; *Honky Tonk Angels* ....(COL)
Linda Ronstadt; *Don't Cry Now* ....(ASY)
   Greatest Hits ....(ASY)
   Hand Sown ....(CAP)
   Retrospective ....(CAP)
Silver Thunderbird
Marc Cohn; *Marc Cohn* ....(ATL)
Silver Tongue & Gold Plated Lies
Hotmud Family; *Meat & Potatoes (& Stuff Like
That)* ....(FF)
Silver Train
Johnny Winter; *Still Alive & Well* ....(COL)
Rolling Stones; *Goats Head Soup* ....(RS)
Silver Waters
Ken Stover; *Cruisers 1.0* ....(HS)
   Sir Dancelot's Dream ....(HS)
Silver Wheels
Bruce Cockburn; *Waiting For A Miracle (Singles
1970-87)* ....(GC)
Heart; *Bebe Le Strange* ....(EPI)
   Greatest Hits/Live ....(EPI)
Silver Wings
Merle Haggard; *More Of The Best* ....(RHI)
   w/Willie Nelson: Seashores Of Old Mexico ......(EPI)
Merle Haggard/Strangers; *Okie From Muskogee* ..(CAP)
   Songs I'll Always Sing ....(CAP)
Pam Tillis; *Mama's Hungry Eyes-Merle Haggard
Tribute* ....(ARI)
Silver & Gold
Dolly Parton; *Eagle When She Flies* ....(COL)
U2; *ST/Rattle & Hum* ....(ISL)

Silver & Gold (Our Love Is Like)
  Sweethearts Of The Rodeo; *Sisters* ....(COL)
Silverfuck
  Smashing Pumpkins; *Siamese Dream* .... (VIA)
Silverthorn Mountain
  Merle Haggard; *Friend In California* ....(EPI)
Silverton
  C.W. McCall; *Greatest Hits* ....(POL)
Silvery Rain
  Olivia Newton-John; *Physical* ....(MCA)
Silver, Blue & Gold
  Bad Company; *Run With The Pack* .... (SS)
Summer Of The Silver Comet
  Tracy Nelson; *Homemade Songs* ....(FF)
That Silver Haired Daddy Of Mine
  Doc Watson; *My Dear Old Southern Home* ....(SH)
  Gene Autry; *Country Music Hall Of Fame* ....(COL)
White Silver Sands
  Ace Cannon; *Golden Classics* ....(GUS)
  Ray Anthony; *Great Golden Hits* ....(RAN)
  Sonny James; *45* ....(COL)

SKY, Clouds

See Also: RAIN, SUN

Above The Clouds
  Electric Light Orchestra; *New World Record* ......(JET)
Alabama Sky
  Alabama; *Closer You Get* ....(RCA)
Alaskan Suite: Northern Lights
  Lyle Mays; *Lyle Mays* .... (GEF)
Angel In The Sky
  Rose Royce; *Strikes Again* ....(WHI)
April Skies
  Jesus & Mary Chain; *Darklands* ....(WB)
  Wardell Gray; *Memorial-#2* ....(PRS)
April Sky
  Vinnie Moore; *Time Odyssey* ....(MER)
Arabs With Knives & West German Skies
  Roger Waters; *Pros & Cons Of Hitchhiking* ......(COL)
Arizona Skies
  Los Lobos; *Kiko* ....(SLS)
Arizona Sky
  China Crisis; *What Price Paradise* ....(A&M)
Armenia City In The Sky
  Who; *Sell Out* .... (MCA)
Aurora Borealis
  C.W. McCall; *Greatest Hits* ....(POL)
  Meat Puppets; *2* ....(SST)
Away From The Sky
  Rickie Lee Jones; *Flying Cowboys* ....(GEF)
Big Sky
  Kate Bush; *Hounds Of Love* .... (EMI)
Big White Cloud
  John Cale; *Vintage Violence* ....(COL)
Black Skies
  Rex Allen, Jr.; *Today's Generation* .... (SSS)
Black Sky
  Ozark Mountain Daredevils; *It's Alive* ....(A&M)
  Ozark Mountain Daredevils ....(A&M)
Blue Ridge Mountain Sky
  Marshall Tucker Band; *New Life* ....(AJK)
Blue Skies
  Benny Goodman; *Carnegie Hall Jazz Concert* ...(COL)
  Complete Goodman ....(RCA)
  This Is ....(RCA)
  Today ....(LON)
  Bing Crosby; *Greatest Hits* ....(MCA)
  Duke Ellington; *Carnegie Hall* ....(PRS)
  Golden Duke ....(PRS)
  Willie Nelson; *Stardust* ....(COL)
Blue Sky
  Allman Brothers Band; *An Evening With-First Set* (POL)
  Best Of ....(POL)
  Decade Of Hits-1969-1979 ....(POL)
  Dreams ....(POL)
  Eat A Peach ....(POL)
  Road Goes On Forever ....(POL)
  A-Ha; *Hunting High & Low* ....(WB)
  Sweethearts Of The Rodeo; *Buffalo Zone* ....(COL)
Blue Sky Mine
  Midnight Oil; *Blue Sky Mining* ....(COL)

Blue Sky Shinin'
  Marie Osmond; *There's No Stopping Your Heart* .(CAP)
  Mickey Newbury; *Sailor* ....(MCA)
Both Sides Now
  Joni Mitchell; *Clouds* ....(RPR)
  Judy Collins; *Colors Of The Day-Best Of* ....(ELE)
  So Early In The Spring ....(ELE)
  Wildflowers ....(ELE)
  Neil Diamond; *Gold* ....(MCA)
  Love Songs ....(MCA)
  Rainbow ....(MCA)
  Touching You Touching Me ....(MCA)
Bullet The Blue Sky
  U2; *Joshua Tree* .... (ISL)
  ST/Rattle & Hum .... (ISL)
Burnin' Sky
  Bad Company; *Burnin' Sky* .... (SS)
Cabin In The Sky
  Andre Previn; *Plays Songs By Vernon Duke* ..... (CTM)
  Mose Allison; *Creek Bank* .... (PRS)
Cadillac Of The Skies
  American Boy Choir; *Spielberg/Williams*
  Collaboration ....(COL)
California Dreamin'
  Beach Boys; *Made In The U.S.A.* ....(CAP)
  Mamas & The Papas; *20 Golden Hits* ....(MCA)
  At The Hop ....(MCA)
  Good Feeling Music-Big Chill-#1 ....(MOT)
  ST/Air America ....(MCA)
  ST/American Pop ....(RLL)
  ST/Forrest Gump ....(EPX)
Clear Blue Skies
  Crosby, Stills, Nash & Young; *American Dream* ..(ATL)
Cloud 9
  George Harrison; *Best Of* .... (DKH)
  Cloud 9 .... (DKH)
Cloud Busting
  Kate Bush; *Hounds Of Love* .... (EMI)
  Whole Story .... (EMI)
Cloud Dancing
  Roches; *Speak* ....(MCA)
Cloud Nine
  Temptations; *25 Years Of Grammy Greats* ...... (MOT)
  Cloud Nine ....(MOT)
  Greatest Hits-#2 ....(MOT)
  Motown Grammy R&B Performances-'60s/'70s (MOT)
  Motown Story ....(MOT)
Cloud On My Tongue
  Tori Amos; *Under The Pink* ....(ATL)
Cloudburst
  Jon Hendricks; *Jon Hendricks* .... (ENJ)
  Lambert, Hendricks & Bavan; *Swingin' Till The Girls*
  Come Home ....(BLU)
  Lambert, Hendricks & Ross; *Best Of* ....(COL)
  & Ike Isaacs Trio: Everybody's Boppin' ....(COL)
  Pointer Sisters; *Retrospect* ....(MCA)
Clouds
  Go-Betweens; *16 Lovers Lane* ....(CAP)
Clouds In My Heart
  Muddy Waters; *Blues Deluxe* ....(ALL)
Cloudscape
  Philip Glass; *Life Out Of Balance* .... (AND)
  ST/Koyaanisqatsi-Life Out Of Balance .... (AND)
Cloudy
  Average White Band; *Cut The Cake* ....(ATL)
  Simon & Garfunkel; *Collected Works* ....(COL)
  Parsley Sage Rosemary & Thyme ....(COL)
Cloudy Morning
  Carmen McRae & George Shearing; *Two For The*
  Road .... (CCJ)
Cloudy Skies
  Benny Carter; *Chocolate Dandies (1928-1933)* ..(DSQ)
Cloudy, With A Chance Of Tears
  Manhattans; *After Midnight* ....(COL)
Cold Sky
  Cyndi Lauper; *Music Speaks Louder Than Words* .(EPI)
Divided Sky
  Phish; *Junta* .... (ELE)
Eye In The Sky
  Alan Parsons Project; *Eye In The Sky* ....(ARI)
  Turn Of A Friendly Card ....(ARI)
Fire In The Sky
  Nitty Gritty Dirt Band; *20 Years Of Dirt-Best Of* ..(WB)
  Ozzy Osbourne; *No Rest For The Wickedd* ....(CBA)

Saxon; *Denim & Leather* ....(CAP)
Flying Cloud
  Doobie Brothers; *What Were Once Vices Are Now*
  Habits ....(WB)
Flying High In The Friendly Sky
  Marvin Gaye; *What's Goin' On* ....(MOT)
Foggy Waterfall
  Left Banke; *History Of* ....(RHI)
Get Off My Cloud
  Rolling Stones; *Big Hits-High Tide & Green Grass* (AKO)
    December's Children ....(AKO)
    Got Live If You Want It ....(AKO)
    Hot Rocks-1964-1971 ....(AKO)
    Singles Collection-London Years ....(AKO)
(Ghost) Riders In The Sky
  Gene Autry; *50th Anniversary* ....(REP)
    Cowboy Hall Of Fame ....(REP)
  Outlaws; *Ghost Riders* ....(ARI)
  Roy Clark; *Greatest Hits-#1* ....(MCA)
    In Concert ....(MCA)
    Superpicker ....(MCA)
  Vaughn Monroe; *Best Of* ....(RCA)
    This Is ....(RCA)
    This Is/Decade Of The '40s ....(RCA)
Goodbye Blue Sky
  Daryl Braithwaite; *Higher Than Hope* ....(EPA)
    Rise ....(EPA)
  Pink Floyd; *The Wall* ....(COL)
  Roger Waters; *The Wall Live In Berlin* .... (MER)
Great Gig In The Sky
  Pink Floyd; *Dark Side Of The Moon* ....(CAP)
    Gift Set ....(CAP)
Grey Cloud Over New York
  Philip Glass; *1000 Airplanes On The Roof* .... (VIA)
Grey Cloudy Lies
  George Harrison; *Extra Texture* ....(OOP)
Grey October Clouds
  Tommy Makem & Liam Clancy; *Two For The Early*
  Dew ....(SHA)
Hazy Shade Of Winter
  Bangles; *Greatest Hits* ....(COL)
    ST/Less Than Zero ....(DFC)
  Simon & Garfunkel; *Bookends* ....(COL)
    Collected Works ....(COL)
Home On The Range
  Bing Crosby; *Crooner-Columbia*
  Years-1928-1934 ....(COL)
  Boston Pops Orchestra; *Yankee Doodle Dandy* ...(RCA)
  Gene Autry; *50th Anniversary* ....(REP)
    Country Music Hall Of Fame ....(COL)
  Neil Young; *ST/Where The Buffalo Roam* ....(BKS)
I Believe In The Man In The Sky
  Elvis Presley; *Worldwide 50 Gold Award Hits-#2* (RCA)
I Sure Can Smell The Rain
  BlackHawk; *BlackHawk* ....(ARI)
It Came Out Of The Sky
  Creedence Clearwater Revival; *1969* ....(FAN)
    Chronicle-#2 ....(FAN)
    Live In Europe ....(FAN)
    Willie & The Poor Boys ....(FAN)
Light The Sky On Fire
  Jefferson Starship; *Gold* ....(RCA)
Little White Cloud That Cried
  Johnnie Ray; *Best Of* ....(COL)
    Greatest Hits ....(SSP)
  Johnny Ray; *Best Of* ....(EXA)
Log Cabin Home In The Sky
  Michael Martin Murphey; *Cowboy Christmas* .....(WB)
London Skyline
  Acoustic Alchemy; *New Edge* ....(GRP)
Lonely Looking Sky
  Neil Diamond; *Love At The Greek* ....(COL)
    ST/Jonathan Livingston Seagull ....(COL)
Lucy In The Sky With Diamonds
  Beatles; *1967-1970* ....(CAP)
    Sgt. Pepper's Lonely Hearts Club Band .....(CAP)
    Yellow Submarine ....(CAP)
  Elton John; *All This & World War 2* ....(20)
    Greatest Hits-#2 ....(POL)
  John Lennon; *Lennon* ....(CAP)
March Sky
  Alex DeGrassi; *Slow Circle* ....(WH)

Midnight Sky
  Isley Brothers; *Live It Up* ....(TN)
    Story-#2/T-Neck Years 1969-1985 ....(RHI)
Montana Skies
  James Galway; *Wayward Wind* ....(RCA)
Morning Sky
  Dan Fogelberg; *Souvenirs* ....(FM)
Mr. Blue Sky
  Electric Light Orchestra; *Afterglow* ....(EPI)
    Greatest Hits ....(JET)
    Out Of The Blue ....(JET)
Murder In The Skies
  Gary Moore; *Early Years* ....(WTG)
    We Want Moore ....(VIA)
Natural High
  Bloodstone; *Greatest Hits* ....(TN)
    Soul Hits/'70s-#11 ....(RHI)
Navajo Sky
  James Asher; *Globalarium* ....(SW)
Orange Colored Sky
  Johnny Mathis; *Live* ....(COL)
  Nat King Cole; *Story* ....(CAP)
    Unforgettable Nat King Cole ....(CAP)
  Natalie Cole; *Unforgettable With Love* ....(ELE)
Orange Skies
  Love; *Best Of* ....(RHI)
Orion In The Sky
  Shawn Colvin; *Fat City* ....(COL)
Piece Of Sky
  Barbra Streisand; *Just For The Record* ....(COL)
    ST/Yentl ....(COL)
Porcelain Sky
  Don Harriss; *Abacus Moon* ....(SA)
Purple Sky
  Gillan; *Magic* ....(MET)
Rain (Falling From The Skies)
  Frank Sinatra; *Where Are You?* ....(CAP)
Reach For The Sky
  No Man; *How The West Was Won* ....(SST)
Reaching For The Sky
  Peabo Bryson; *Collection* ....(CAP)
    Reaching For The Sky ....(CAP)
Red Skies
  Fixx; *One Thing Leads To Another-Greatest Hits* (MCA)
    React ....(MCA)
    Shuttered Room ....(MCA)
Red Skies Over Georgia
  Charlie Walker; *45* ....(PLN)
Red Sky
  Michael Schenker; *Built To Destroy* ....(CHR)
  Status Quo; *Status Quo* ....(MER)
Ribbon In The Sky
  Stevie Wonder; *Original Musiquarium* ....(MOT)
Road And The Sky
  Jackson Browne; *Late For The Sky* ....(ASY)
Rolling Sky
  Speedy West & Jimmy Bryant; *For The Last Time* .(SO)
Scandinavian Skies
  Billy Joel; *Nylon Curtain* ....(COL)
See The Sky About to Rain
  Neil Young; *On The Beach* ....(RPR)
Sky Blues
  R.E.O. Speedwagon; *Lost In A Dream* ....(EPI)
Sky Fell
  Judy Collins; *Wildflowers* ....(ELE)
Sky Fell Down
  Glenn Miller; *Complete-#3 (1939-1940)* ....(RCA)
  Tommy Dorsey & Frank Sinatra; *All-Time Greatest*
  Hits-#1 ....(RCA)
    Sessions-#1 ....(RCA)
Sky High
  Jigsaw; *Billboard Top Hits-1975* ....(RHI)
    Super Hits/'70s-Have A Nice Day-#15 ....(RHI)
Sky Is A Poisonous Garden
  Concrete Blonde; *Bloodletting* ....(IRS)
Sky Is Crying
  Albert King; *I'm In A Phone Booth Baby* ....(STX)
    Years Gone By ....(STX)
  Elmore James; *Complete Fire & Enjoy*
  Sessions-#1 ....(CLT)
    Red Hot Blues ....(INT)
  Eric Clapton; *Crossroads* ....(POL)
  George Thorogood/Destroyers; *Live* ....(EMI)
    Move It On Over ....(ROU)

Stevie Ray Vaughan/Double Trouble; *Sky Is Crying* .... (EPI)
Sky Over Michigan
Harmony Sisters; *Harmony Pie* .... (FF)
Sky Pilot
Eric Burdon/Animals; *Greatest Hits* ....(MGM)
History Of British Rock-#9 .... (RHI)
Sky Takes The Soul
Proclaimers; *This Is The Story* .... (CHR)
Skybird
Neil Diamond; *Love At The Greek* ....(COL)
ST/*Jonathan Livingston Seagull* ....(COL)
Skylark
Anita O'Day; *1940s-The Singers* ....(COL)
Bette Midler; *Bette Midler* .... (ATL)
Erroll Garner Trio; *Greatest Garner* ....(ATL)
Glenn Miller; *Best Of-#3* ....(RCA)
Hoagy Carmichael; *Hoagy Sings Carmichael* ..... (EMI)
Too Marvelous For Words ....(CAP)
Linda Ronstadt; *Lush Life* ....(ASY)
Tony Bennett; *Forty Years-Artistry Of* ....(COL)
Skyline Pigeon
Elton John; *Empty Sky* ....(POL)
Here & There .... (POL)
Skyscraper
David Lee Roth; *Skyscraper* ....(WB)
Skyway
Replacements; *Pleased To Meet Me* .... (SIR)
Skywriter
Jackson 5; *Anthology* ....(MOT)
Sky's Got The Blues
Aaron Tippin; *You've Got To Stand For Something* ....(RCA)
Sky's The Limit
Tony! Toni! Tone!; *Revival* ....(WIN)
Spirit In The Sky
Kentucky HeadHunters; *Electric Barnyard* ...... (MER)
Norman Greenbaum; *Billboard Top Rock 'N' Roll Hits-1970* .... (RHI)
Super Hits/'80s-Have A Nice Day-#2 ....(RHI)
Starry Sky In Oregon
Andrew White; *Conversations* ....(SOG)
Sunny Skies
James Taylor; *In Harmony 2* ....(COL)
Sweet Baby James ....(WB)
Jerry Douglas; *Fluxedo* ....(ROU)
Teena Marie; *Emerald City* .... (EPI)
Tahitian Skies
Chet Atkins & Mark Knopfler; *Neck & Neck* ....(COL)
There's A Blue Sky Way Out Yonder
Riders In The Sky; *Riders Go Commercial* ...... (MCA)
Saturday Morning With ....(MCA)
There's A Gold Mine In The Sky
Jimmy C. Newman; *Cajun Cowboy* .... (PLN)
Pat Boone; *Love Letters In The Sand* ....(MSP)
Thousand Stars In The Sky
Kathy Young/Innocents; *20 Great Love Songs/'50s & '60s-#2* ....(LAU)
Collectables-History Of Rock-#10 ....(CLT)
Oldies But Goodies-#5 ....(OSR)
Uncloudy Day
Don Henley; *I Can't Stand Still* .... (ASY)
Willie Nelson; *Greatest Hits & Some That Will Be* (COL)
Willie Nelson & Dyan Cannon; ST/*Honeysuckle Rose* ....(COL)
Under African Skies
Paul Simon; *Graceland* ....(WB)
Under Blue Canadian Skies
Glenn Miller/Orchestra; *Complete* ....(BLU)
Under Paris Skies
Arthur Murray/Orchestra; *Music For Dancing-Waltz* ....(RCA)
Gordon Jenkins; *France* ....(BAI)
Under The Falling Sky
Bonnie Raitt; *Collection* ....(WB)
Give It Up ....(WB)
Jackson Browne; *Jackson Browne* ....(ASY)
Under The Red Sky
Bob Dylan; *Under The Red Sky* ....(COL)
Under The Sky
Heart; *Brigade* ....(CAP)
Rock The House "Live" ....(CAP)
Voices In The Sky
Moody Blues; *In Search Of The Lost Chord* ......(POL)

Waitress In The Sky
Replacements; *Tim* .... (SIR)
War Clouds
New Orleans Ragtime Orchestra; *Nwe Orleans Jazz* .... (ARH)
Watcher Of The Skies
Genesis; *Foxtrot* ....(ATL)
Live ....(ATL)
We Almost Had Texas Skies Today
Hank Thompson; *Here's To Country Music* ....(SO)
Wheel In The Sky
Journey; *Captured* ....(COL)
Greatest Hits ....(COL)
Infinity ....(COL)
When The Night Comes Falling From The...
Bob Dylan; *Bootleg Series-#1-3-1961-1989* .....(COL)
Empire Burlesque ....(COL)
Jeff Healey Band; ST/*Road House* .... (ARI)
Wild Kentucky Skies
Marty Brown; *Wild Kentucky Skies* .... (MCA)
Wild Montana Skies
John Denver; *Greatest Hits-#3* ....(RCA)
It's About Time ....(RCA)
John Denver & Emmylou Harris; *Collector's-Duets* ....(RCA)
Will It Go Round In Circles
Billy Preston; *Best Of* ....(A&M)
Billboard Top Rock 'N' Roll Hits-1973 .... (RHI)
Soul Hits/'70s-#11 .... (RHI)
Winter Sky
Judy Collins; *Concert* ....(ELE)
Recollections ....(ELE)

SLEEP, Bed, Bored, Tired
See Also: DREAMS, SEX

And The Mouse Police Never Sleeps
Jethro Tull; *Heavy Horses* .... (CHR)
Another Sleepless Night
Anne Murray; *Country Hits* ....(CAP)
Greatest Hits ....(CAP)
Where Do You Go When You Dream ....(CAP)
Shawn Christopher; *S* .... (ARI)
Are You Sleeping?
Nilsson; *The Point* ....(RCA)
Asleep In The Desert
ZZ Top; *Six Pack* ....(WB)
Tejas ....(WB)
At Night She Sleeps
Night Ranger; *Dawn Patrol* .... (CAM)
Awake Ye Drowsy Sleepers
Ian & Sylvia; *Greatest Hits* .... (VAN)
Ian & Sylvia ....(VAN)
Awakening
Alice Cooper; *Welcome To My Nightmare* ....(ATL)
John Mahavishnu McLaughlin; *Inner Mounting Flame* ....(COL)
Be Bop/Drop
Daryl Hall & John Oates; *X-Static* ....(RCA)
Bedside Radio
Krokus; *Alive & Screamin'* .... (ARI)
Metal Rendez-vous .... (ARI)
Bedtime Story
Tammy Wynette; *Biggest Hits* .... (EPI)
First Lady Of Country Music .... (EPI)
Greatest Hits-#3 .... (EPI)
Behind The Wall Of Sleep
Black Sabbath; *Black Sabbath* ....(WB)
Smithereens; *Especially For You* ....(CAP)
Better Get Back In Bed
Beach Boys; *Holland* ....(CAR)
Big Sleep
Simple Minds; *In the City Of Light* ....(A&M)
New Gold Dream ....(A&M)
Black Coffee In Bed
Squeeze; *Sweets From A Stranger* ....(A&M)
Burnout
Green Day; *Dookie* ....(RPR)
Can't Sleep
Rockets; *Live* ....(CAP)
Rockets ....(RSO)
Cry Myself To Sleep
Del Shannon; *Runaway Hits!* .... (RHI)

Frankie Valli/Four Seasons; *Rarities-#1* .... (RHI)
Judds; *Collector's Series* .... (RCA)
  Greatest Hits .... (RCA)
  Hits Of '87 .... (RCA)
  Rockin' With The Rhythm .... (RCA)
Don't Sleep In The Subway
Frank Sinatra; *Frank Sinatra* .... (RPR)
Petula Clark; *Greatest Hits* .... (CRS)
  Summer Of Love .... (RHI)
Don't Smoke In Bed
Nina Simone; *Finest Of* .... (BET)
  In Concert/I Put A Spell On You .... (MER)
Peggy Lee; *Capitol Collectors Series-#1-Early
Years* .... (CAP)
  Greatest .... (CAP)
Don't You Ever Get Tired Of Hurtin' Me
Ray Price; *Greatest Hits-#2* .... (STE)
Ronnie Milsap; *Stranger Things Have Happened* .. (RCA)
Don't Your Mem'ry Ever Sleep At Night
Ronnie Milsap; *Keyed Up* .... (RCA)
Steve Wariner; *Best Of* .... (RCA)
Dreaming While You Sleep
Genesis; *We Can't Dance* .... (ATL)
Endless Sleep
Babys; *Babys* .... (CHR)
Jody Reynolds; *American Graffiti #3* .... (MCA)
  Teenage Tragedies .... (RHI)
Enter Sandman
Metallica; *Metallica* .... (ELE)
Exquisitely Bored
Pete Townshend; *All The Best Cowboys Have Chinese
Eyes* .... (ATC)
Flow Gently, Sweet Afton
Mormon Tabernacle Choir; *Old Beloved Songs* ...(COL)
Ft. Worth Featherbed
Donnie Rohrs; *Country Music USA* .... (PC)
Golden Slumbers
Beatles; *Abbey Road* .... (CAP)
  Box Set .... (CAP)
Green Door
Jim Lowe; *Billboard Top Rock 'N' Roll Hits-1956* (RHI)
  Super Hits-#4 .... (GUS)
Had A Dream (Sleeping With The Enemy)
Roger Hodgson; *In The Eye Of The Storm* ...... (A&M)
I Couldn't Sleep A Wink Last Night
Frank Sinatra; *Greatest Hits-#2* .... (COL)
  Voice-Columbia Years-1943-1952 .... (COL)
Mello Moods; *Great Groups/'50s-#3* .... (CLT)
I Go To Sleep
Pretenders; *II* .... (SIR)
  Singles .... (SIR)
I Love You (But You're Boring)
Beautiful South; *Welcome To The* .... (ELE)
If You Were To Wake Up
Tammy Wynette & Lyle Lovett; *Without Walls* ...(EPI)
It Sure Is Monday
Mark Chesnutt; *Almost Goodbye* .... (MCA)
I'll Lie Myself To Sleep
Shelby Lynne; *Greatest Country Hits/'90s-1990* ..(COL)
  Tough All Over .... (EPI)
I'll Never Get Tired Of You
Patty Loveless; *Honky Tonk Angel* .... (MCA)
I'm Only Sleeping
Beatles; *Rarities* .... (CAP)
  Revolver-Euro Version .... (CAP)
  Yesterday...And Today .... (CAP)
I'm So Bored With The U.S.A.
Clash; *Clash* .... (EPI)
I'm So Tired
Beatles; *White Album* .... (CAP)
I'm Tired
Mel Brooks; *ST/High Anxiety* .... (ASY)
Mel Tillis; *American Originals* .... (COL)
Phil Ochs; *Toast To Those Who Are Gone* .... (RHI)
Ricky Skaggs; *Comin' Home To Stay* .... (EPI)
Savoy Brown; *London Collector* .... (LON)
  Step Further .... (PRT)
Webb Pierce; *Best Of* .... (MCA)
  Golden Hits .... (PLN)
I'm Tired Of Living This Lie
Bob Wills/Texas Playboys; *24 Greatest Hits* ..... (POL)
I'm Tired Of Texas
Nancy Walker; *I Can Cook Too* .... (DRG)
  Sings Show Stoppers .... (ST)

Just Can't Go To Sleep
Kinks; *Kinks* .... (RPR)
  You Really Got Me .... (RHI)
Last Night I Didn't Get To Sleep At All
5th Dimension; *45* .... (BLG)
(Lay Your Head On My) Pillow
Tony Toni Tone; *Sons Of Soul* .... (WIN)
Lullaby
Book Of Love; *Lullaby* .... (SIR)
Cure; *Disintegration* .... (ELE)
  Mixed Up .... (ELE)
Take 6; *Join The Band* .... (RPR)
Tom Rush; *Tom Rush* .... (COL)
Lullaby For Myself
Barbra Streisand; *Streisand Superman* .... (COL)
Lullaby For Nancy Carol
Chuck Mangione; *Best Of* .... (MER)
  Land Of Make Believe .... (MER)
  Together .... (MER)
Lullaby Of Birdland
Ella Fitzgerald; *Best-#2* .... (MCA)
  With Billie Holiday .... (MCA)
Mel Torme; *Songs Of New York* .... (ATL)
Sarah Vaughan; *Golden Hits* .... (MER)
Tito Puente/Latin Ensemble; *Mambo Diablo* ..... (CCJ)
Lullaby Of Broadway
Andrews Sisters; *Best Of-#2* .... (MCA)
Bette Midler; *Bette Midler* .... (ATL)
  Live At Last .... (ATL)
Tony Bennett; *Jazz* .... (COL)
Magic Fingers (25 Cents)
Birdsongs Of The Mesozoic; *Faultline* .... (CUN)
Mister Sandman
Chordettes; *Best Of* .... (RHI)
Emmylou Harris; *Evangeline* .... (WB)
  Profile 2-Best Of .... (WB)
My Clone Sleeps Alone
Pat Benatar; *In The Heat Of The Night* .... (CHR)
No Sleep Till Brooklyn
Beastie Boys; *Licensed To Ill* .... (DFJ)
President's Nap
Power Tools; *Strange Meeting* .... (AND)
Rest My Mind On Jesus
Charles Ford Band; *Charles Ford Band* .... (ARH)
River Of Dreams
Billy Joel; *River Of Dreams* .... (COL)
Rock A Bye Your Baby With A Dixie Melody
Al Jolson; *Best Of* .... (MCA)
  Immortal .... (MCA)
  Jolson Sang 'Em .... (BIO)
  Story-#1 .... (MCA)
Judy Garland; *At Carnegie Hall* .... (CAP)
  Miss Show Business .... (CAP)
  One & Only .... (CAP)
Rock 'N' Roll Lullaby
10 CC; *How Dare You* .... (MER)
B.J. Thomas; *16 Greatest Hits* .... (TRP)
  Back To The '70s-#2 .... (DOM)
  Greatest Hits .... (RHI)
  Super Hits-#2 .... (GUS)
Rocks In My Bed
Duke Ellington; *Duke Ellington: Blanton-Webster
Band* .... (BLU)
Jimmy Witherspoon; *Baby Baby Baby* .... (PRS)
Ray Brown All-Stars; *Don't Forget The Blues* .... (CCJ)
Sarah Vaughan; *Duke Ellington Songbook Two* ... (PAB)
Rude Awakening No. 2
Creedence Clearwater Revival; *1970* .... (FAN)
  Pendulum .... (FAN)
Satin Sheets
Jeannie Pruett; *16 Top Country Hits-#1* .... (MCA)
  Country Chart-Toppers .... (DOM)
  MCA Recrods 30 Years Of Hits-(1958-1988) .. (MCA)
Shawn Colvin; *Cover Girl* .... (COL)
Savannah Awakes
Barbra Streisand; *ST/Prince Of Tides* .... (COL)
Send Me Your Pillow
John Lee Hooker; *Big Soul Of* .... (VJ)
John Lee Hooker/Canned Heat; *Hooker 'N Heat* . (EMI)
Set Adrift On Memory Bliss
P.M. Dawn; *MTV Party To Go-#2* .... (TMB)
  Red Hot + Dance .... (COL)
Shake Me Wake Me
Barbra Streisand; *Lazy Afternoon* .... (COL)

Four Tops; *Anthology* .... (MOT)
   Greatest Hits .... (MOT)
   Motown Superstar Series-#14 .... (MOT)
She Even Woke Me Up To Say Goodbye
Jerry Lee Lewis; *Best Of* .... (SMA)
   Heartbreak .... (TOM)
Kenny Rogers/First Edition; *Love Songs* ... (MSP)
Show Me The Way To Go Home
Artie Shaw; *Best Of* .... (MCA)
Randy Erwin; *Back Home* .... (ROM)
Sleep
Benny Goodman; *Yale Recordings-#5* .... (MM)
Les Paul; *Legend & The Legacy-#1-4* .... (CAP)
   London Collector ....(LON)
   Now ....(LON)
Midnight Oil; *Red Sails In The Sunset* ....(COL)
'Til Tuesday; *Voices Carry* .... (EPI)
Sleep Come Free Me
James Taylor; *Flag* ....(COL)
Sleep My Baby Sleep
Judy Garland; *Collector's Items* .... (MCA)
Sleep On It
Chaka Khan; *Chaka* .... (WB)
Sleep Song
Glenn Miller/Orchestra; *Complete* .... (BLU)
Graham Nash; *Songs For Beginners* .... (ATL)
Hot Tuna; *America's Choice* ....(RCA)
Sleep Talk
Alyson Williams; *Raw* .... (OBR)
Sleep That Burns
Be Bop Deluxe; *Best Of & The Rest Of* ...... (HAR)
   Best Of-Raiding The Divine Archives .... (CAP)
   Sunburst Finish .... (HAR)
Sleep Tight, Good Night Man
Kenny Rogers; *The Gambler* .... (EMI)
Sleeping
Band; *Stage Fright* ....(CAP)
Dwight Twilley Band; *Twilley Don't Mind* .... (ARI)
Sleeping Bag
ZZ Top; *Afterburner* .... (WB)
   Greatest Hits .... (WB)
Sleeping Beauty Waltz
101 Strings; *Million Seller Themes From
Tchaikovsky* .... (ALS)
Sleeping Bee
Al Jarreau; *1965* ....(BAI)
Barbra Streisand; *Barbra Streisand Album* ......(COL)
   Just For The Record ....(COL)
Bill Evans; *Compact Jazz* ....(VRV)
Harold Arlen & Barbra Streisand; *Harold Sings Arlen
(With Friends)* ....(SSP)
Kiri Te Kanawa & Andre Previn; *Kiri Side Tracks-Jazz
Album* ....(PHI)
Mel Torme; *Swings Shubert Alley* ....(VRV)
Original Cast; *House Of Flowers* ....(SSP)
Tony Bennett; *Forty Years-Artistry Of* ....(COL)
Sleeping Heart
Judds; *Talk About Love* ....(RCA)
   Why Not Me ....(RCA)
Sleeping In My Car
Roxette; *Crash! Boom! Bang!* .... (EMI)
Sleeping In Paris
Rosanne Cash; *The Wheel* ....(COL)
Sleeping Late
Dr. Hook; *Makin' Love & Music* ....(CAP)
Sleeping On The Beach
Nitty Gritty Dirt Band; *Dream* .... (UA)
Sleeping On The Sidewalk
Hank Crawford; *Night Beat* .... (MS)
Queen; *News Of The World* ....(HOL)
Sleeping Satellite
Tasmin Archer; *Great Expectations* .... (SBK)
Sleeping Single In A Double Bed
Barbara Mandrell; *Best Of* .... (MCA)
   Live ....(MCA)
   Moods ....(MCA)
Sleeping With The Television On
Billy Joel; *Glass Houses* ....(COL)
Sleeping With The TV On
Dictators; *Manifest Destiny* .... (ASY)
Sleepin'
Diana Ross; *Anthology* .... (MOT)
Sleepin' Bee
Al Jarreau; *1965* ....(BAI)

Barbra Streisand; *Album* ....(COL)
   Highlights From "Just For The Record" ....(COL)
Bill Evans; *Compact Jazz* ....(VRV)
Carmen McRae; *Setting Standards* .... (PRR)
Harold Arlen & Barbra Streisand; *Harold Sings Arlen
(With Friend)* ....(SSP)
Mel Torme; *Swings Shubert Alley* ....(VRV)
Tony Bennett; *Consummate Collection-Classics
Songs* ....(COL)
Sleepin' With The Radio On
Charly McClain; *Greatest Hits* .... (EPI)
   Surround Me With Love .... (EPI)
   Ten Year Anniversary .... (EPI)
Sleepless Night
Dokken; *Back For The Attack* .... (ELE)
   Beast From The East .... (ELE)
John Lennon & Yoko Ono; *Milk & Honey* .... (POL)
Kinks; *Sleepwalker* .... (ARI)
Sleepless Nights
Emmylou Harris; *Pieces Of The Sky* .... (RPR)
Gram Parsons/Flying Burrito Brothers; *Sleepless
Nights* .... (A&M)
Judds; *Collector's Series* ....(RCA)
   River Of Time ....(RCA)
Sleeps With Angels
Neil Young/Crazy Horse; *Sleeps With Angels* .... (RPR)
Sleepwalker
Kinks; *Come Dancing With-Best Of-1977-1986* .. (ARI)
   Sleepwalker .... (ARI)
Shawn Phillips; *Second Contribution* .... (A&M)
Sleepy Lagoon
Boston Pops Orchestra/Arthur Fiedler; *Boston Pops
Orchestra/Arthur Fiedler* ....(RCA)
   Greatest Hits Of The '40s ....(RCA)
Boston Pops Orchestra/John Williams; *Swing Swing
Swing* ....(PHI)
Harry James; *Best Of The Big Bands* ....(COL)
Harry James/Orchestra; *16 Most Requested Songs Of The
'40s-#2* ....(COL)
Platters; *More Encore Of Golden Hits* .... (MER)
Sleepy Serenade
Wayne King; *Best Of-#2* .... (MCA)
Sleepy Time Gal
Glenn Miller; *Best Of The Big Bands* ....(COL)
Harry James; *All-Time Favorites By* ....(SSP)
Liberace; *Encore* .... (AVI)
   Liberace .... (AVI)
   Piano Memories .... (AVI)
Mose Allison; *Creek Bank* .... (PRS)
Sleepy Time Time
Cream; *Fresh Cream* .... (POL)
   Live-#1 .... (POL)
Sleep's Dark & Silent Gate
Bonnie Raitt; *The Glow* .... (WB)
Jackson Browne; *Pretender* .... (ASY)
Small Town Saturday Night
Hal Ketchum; *Past The Point Of Rescue* .... (CRB)
Sweet Baby James
Highway 101; *Paint The Town* .... (WB)
James Taylor; *Greatest Hits* .... (WB)
   Sweet Baby James .... (WB)
Talking In Your Sleep
Crystal Gayle; *All-Time Greatest Hits* .... (CCB)
   Classic Crystal .... (EMI)
   Country Gold .... (PRY)
   When I Dream .... (LIB)
Romantics; *Billboard Top Hits-1984* .... (RHI)
   In Heat .... (EPA)
   Rock Of The '80s-#3 .... (PRY)
Tears Before Bedtime
Elvis Costello/Attractions; *Imperial Bedroom* ....(COL)
Tears On My Pillow
Chimes; *Golden Groups* .... (SPE)
   Original Rock Oldies-Golden Hits-#2 .... (SPE)
Kylie Minogue; *Enjoy Yourself* .... (GEF)
Little Anthony/Imperials; *Best Of* .... (EMI)
   Best Of .... (RHI)
   Billboard Top R&B Hits-1958 .... (RHI)
   Good Time Rock 'N' Roll .... (MCA)
Lorrie Morgan; *Something In Red* .... (RCA)
New Edition/Little Anthony; *Under The Blue
Moon* ....(MCA)
Reba McEntire; *Feel The Fire* .... (MER)
Sha-Na-Na; *ST/Grease* .... (POL)

Tell Me A Bedtime Story
Norman Connors; *Remember Who You Are* ...... (MOJ)
Quincy Jones; *Sounds...& Stuff Like That* .... (A&M)
Texas Lullaby
David Allan Coe; *Cowboys* .... (COL)
Longhaired Redneck ....(COL)
Doobie Brothers; *Stampede* .... (WB)
Then I'll Be Tired Of You
Coleman Hawkins; *Real Thing* .... (PRS)
Jonathan Schwartz; *Alone Together* .... (MUS)
Paul Desmond; *Late Lament* ....(BLU)
Tired Of Being Alone
Al Green; *Greatest Hits-#1* .... (MOT)
Tokyo...Live .... (MOT)
Tired Of Midnight Blue
George Harrison; *Extra Texture* ....(CAP)
Tired Of Waiting For You
Kinks; *Greatest Hits-#1* .... (RHI)
History Of British Rock-#3 .... (RHI)
Kinda Kinks .... (RHI)
Tired Of Your Jive
B.B. King; *Electric-His Best* .... (MCA)
Great Moments with .... (MCA)
Tired Wings
Four Horsemen; *Nobody Said It Was Easy* .... (DEF)
Tonight I Shall Sleep With A Smile On...
Duke Ellington; *Black Brown & Beige* .... (BLU)
Sarah Vaughan; *Duke Ellington Songbook Two* ... (PAB)
Too Hot To Sleep
Louise Mandrell; *Too Hot To Sleep* ....(RCA)
Too Pooped To Pop
Chuck Berry; *Chess Box* .... (CSS)
Rockin' At The Hops .... (CSS)
Too Tired
Gary Moore; *Still Got The Blues* ....(CHS)
Mary Chapin Carpenter; *State Of The Heart* .....(COL)
Tossin' & Turnin'
Bobby Lewis; *21 Oldies But Goodies* .... (OSR)
Billboard Top Rock 'N' Roll Hits-1961 ...... (RHI)
Collectables Presents History Of Rock-#6 .... (CLT)
Cruisin'-1961 .... (INC)
Try Counting Sheep
Black Sheep; *A Wolf In Sheep's Clothing* .... (MER)
Trying To Sleep Tonight
Clarence Carter; *Hooked On Love* ....(ICH)
The Dr.'s Greatest Prescriptions-Best Of ...... (ICH)
Tuck Me To Sleep In My Old Kentucky Home
Firehouse Five Plus Two; *Goes South* ....(GTJ)
TV Snooze
Nina Hagen; *Fearless* ....(COL)
Two Sleepy People
Art Garfunkel; *Up 'Til Now* ....(COL)
Jo Sullivan Loesser/Others; *Loesser By Loesser* .. (DRG)
Kay Kyser; *Best Of The Big Bands* ....(COL)
Wake Me Up Before You Go Go
Wham!; *Billboard Top Hits-1984* .... (RHI)
Make It Big ....(COL)
Wake Me When It's Over
Willie Nelson; *Best Of* .... (EMI)
Island In The Sea .... (COL)
Sweet Memories ....(RCA)
What Can You Do To Me Now ....(RCA)
Wake The World
Beach Boys; *Concert/'69-Live In London* .... (CAP)
Friends/20-20 ....(CAP)
Wake Up Dreaming
Little Feat; *Down On The Farm* .... (WB)
Wake Up Everybody
Harold Melvin/Blue Notes; *Collector's Item* ..... (PI)
Wake Up Everybody .... (PI)
Wake Up Morning
Rex Allen, Jr.; *Country Comfort* ....(PLN)
Today's Generation .... (SSS)
Wake Up Sunshine
Chicago; *II* ....(COL)
Wake Up Susan
Spinners; *Happiness Is Being With* .... (ATL)
One Of A Kind Love Affair-Anthology ....(ATL)
Wake Up & Live
Bob Marley/Wailers; *Survival* ....(TUF)
Cab Calloway; *Best Of The Big Bands* ....(COL)
Wake Up & Make Love To Me
Ian Dury; *New Boots & Panties* ....(STF)
Stiff Live ....(STF)

Wake Up & Smell The Coffee
Killbilly; *Stranger In This Place* ....(FF)
Wake Up, Little Susie
Everly Brothers; *All They Had To Do Was Dream* (RHI)
All-Time Greatest Hits ....(CCB)
American Graffiti-#3 .... (MCA)
Everly Brothers .... (RHI)
Oldies But Goodies-#7 .... (OSR)
Very Best Of ....(WB)
Grateful Dead; *History Of-#1-Bear's Choice* .... (WB)
Simon & Garfunkel; *Concert In Central Park* .....(WB)
We All Sleep Alone
Cher; *Cher* ....(GEF)
We Should Be Sleeping
Eddie Money; *Can't Hold Back* ....(COL)
Greatest Hits-Sound Of Money ....(COL)
When It's Sleepy Time Down South
Billie Holiday; *Last Recordings* ....(VRV)
Dizzy Gillespie; *20 Golden Pieces Of* ....(BLD)
Louis Armstrong; *At The Crescendo* .... (MCA)
Best Of .... (MCA)
Best Of Decca Years-#1-The Singer .... (DEC)
Essential ....(VAN)
Greatest Hits ....(COL)
I Like Jazz-Essence Of ....(COL)
Satchmo/Musical Autobiography .... (MCA)
Mel Torme; *Mel Torme* ....(GLN)
Wynton Marsalis; *Standard Time-#2-Intimacy*
Calling ....(COL)
When The Children Are Asleep
Original Broadway Cast; *Carousel* .... (ANG)
Original CAst; *Carousel* .... (MCA)
When You Awake
Band; *Band* ....(CAP)
Bob Dylan/Band; *Before The Flood* ....(COL)
Who's Been Sleeping Here
Rolling Stones; *Between The Buttons* .... (AKO)
Who's Been Sleeping In My Bed
Melanie; *Am I Real Or What* .... (AMH)
Wimoweh (Mbube)-The Lion Sleeps Tonight
Chet Atkins; *RCA Years* ....(RCA)
Kingston Trio; *Kingston Trio/From The Hungry i* .(CAP)
Nylons; *Seamless* ....(OPE)
Pete Seeger; *Greatest Hits* ....(COL)
Tokens; *Billboard Top Rock 'N' Roll Hits-1961* .. (RHI)
Nipper's Greatest Hits/'60s-#1 ....(RCA)
Weavers; *Greatest Hits* ....(VAN)
Woke Up In Love
Exile; *Exile* .... (EPI)
Greatest Hits .... (EPI)
Woke Up With A Monster
Cheap Trick; *Woke Up With A Monster* .... (WB)
You Can Close Your Eyes
James Taylor; *Mud Slide Slim & The Blue Horizon* (WB)
Linda Ronstadt; *Heart Like A Wheel* ....(CAP)

SMALL, Things Of Small Size
See Also: LITTLE for things of small amount

36 Inches High
Nick Lowe; *Pure Pop For Now People* ....(COL)
Any Little Fish
Bobby Short; *Bobby Noel & Cole* .... (ATL)
Big Dreams In A Small Town
Restless Heart; *Big Dreams In A Small Town* ....(RCA)
Big Fish, Little Fish
Original Broadway Cast; *Purlie* ....(RCA)
Bonnie Jean (Little Sister)
David Lynn Jones; *Best Of Country Rock* .... (KT)
Hard Times On Easy Street .... (MER)
Circle Is Small
Gordon Lightfoot; *Back Here On Earth* .... (UA)
Endless Wire .... (WB)
Crazy Little Mama
Eldorados; *Greatest Groups/'50s-#2* ....(CLT)
Sock Hop ....(DHL)
Crazy Little Thing Called Love
Queen; *Greatest Hits* ....(HOL)
The Game ....(HOL)
Cruel Little Number
Jeff Healey Band; *Feel This* .... (ARI)
Cut Across Shorty
Eddie Cochran; *Legendary Masters* ....(EMI)

Rod Stewart; *Best Of* .... (MER)
  Faces Live .... (MER)
  Gasoline Alley .... (MER)
  Storyteller/Complete Anthology-1964-1990 ...... (WB)
  Unplugged...& Seated .... (WB)
  Vintage .... (MER)
Daddy's Little Boy
  Eddy Howard; *45* .... (MER)
  Mills Brothers; *45* .... (MCA)
Daddy's Little Girl
  Al Martino; *Best Of* .... (CAP)
  Mills Brothers; *50th Anniversary* .... (RAN)
  All Occasions Album .... (GAT)
  Best Of .... (MCA)
  Story .... (RAN)
  Nikki D; *S* .... (DFJ)
Dance Little Jean
  Nitty Gritty Dirt Band; *Let's Go* .... (WB)
  Twenty Years Of Dirt-Best Of .... (WB)
Dance Little Sister
  Rolling Stones; *It's Only Rock 'N' Roll* .... (RS)
  Made In The Shade .... (RS)
  Terence Trent D'Arby; *Introducing The Hardline
  According To* .... (COL)
Dance On Little Girl
  Paul Anka; *21 Golden Hits* .... (RCA)
  Best Of .... (RHI)
  She's A Lady .... (RCA)
  Vintage Years '57-'61 .... (SIR)
Davy's Dinghy
  Ruth Wallis; *Dr. Demento's Dementia Royale* .... (RHI)
  Dr. Demento's Greatest Novelties-#2 .... (RHI)
Dirty Little Girl
  Elton John; *Goodbye Yellow Brick Road* .... (POL)
Dream A Little Dream Of Me
  Ella Fitzgerald; *All That Jazz* .... (PAB)
  Mama Cass; *Mama's Big Ones-Greatest Hits* .... (MCA)
  Mamas & The Papas; *20 Golden Hits* .... (MCA)
  Best Of .... (MCA)
Every Little Girl's Dream
  Lisa Brokop; *Every Little Girl's Dream* .... (PAT)
Every Little Kiss
  Bruce Hornsby/Range; *The Way It Is* .... (RCA)
Every Little Step
  Bobby Brown; *Dance!...Ya Know It!* .... (MCA)
  Don't Be Cruel .... (MCA)
Every Little Thing
  Beatles; *For Sale* .... (CAP)
  Love Songs .... (CAP)
  VI .... (CAP)
  Carlene Carter; *Little Love Letters* .... (GIA)
  Yes; *Yes* .... (ATL)
  Yesyears .... (ATC)
Every Little Thing He Does Is Magic
  Shawn Colvin; *Cover Girl* .... (COL)
Every Little Thing She Does Is Magic
  Police; *Every Breath You Take-Singles* .... (A&M)
  Ghost In The Machine .... (A&M)
Foolish Little Girl
  Shirelles; *16 Greatest Hits* .... (TRP)
  Anthology-1959-1964 .... (RHI)
  Greatest Hits .... (EVR)
Frogs With Dirty Little Lips
  Frank Zappa; *Them Or Us* .... (BAR)
Get A Little Closer
  Ricky Lynn Gregg; *Get A Little Closer* .... (LIB)
Go Away Little Girl
  Happenings; *45* .... (ERI)
  45 .... (VGO)
  Steve Lawrence; *Greatest Hits* .... (COL)
Good Morning Little School Girl
  Grateful Dead; *Grateful Dead* .... (WB)
  Huey Lewis/News; *Four Chords & Several Years
  Ago* .... (ELE)
  Johnny Winter; *Johnny Winter* .... (COL)
  Live .... (COL)
  Ten Years After; *Classic Performances* .... (COL)
  Recorded Live .... (COL)
  Ssssh .... (CHR)
  Universal .... (CHR)
  Yardbirds; *Crossroads* .... (POL)
  Five Live Yardbirds .... (RHI)
Hello Little Friend
  Joe Cocker; *Joe Cocker* .... (A&M)

Hey Little Bird
  Buffy Sainte-Marie; *Best Of-#2* .... (VAN)
  Fire & Fleet & Candlelight .... (VAN)
Hey Little Cobra
  Rip Chords; *Beach Classics* .... (DHL)
  Rock Classics/'60s .... (COL)
Hey Little Girl
  Dee Clark; *Jukebox Classics-#1* .... (RHI)
  Super Oldies/'50s-#2 .... (AUF)
  Icehouse; *Primitive Man* .... (CHR)
  Professor Longhair; *Atlantic R&B
  1947-1974-#1-(1947-1952)* .... (ATL)
  New Orleans Piano-Blues Originals-#2 .... (ATL)
Hey Little One
  Dorsey Burnette; *American Graffiti #3* .... (MCA)
  Glen Campbell; *Classics Collection* .... (CAP)
  Very Best Of .... (CAP)
I Buyed Me A Little Dog
  Dave Van Ronk; *Van Ronk* .... (FAN)
I Say A Little Prayer
  Aretha Franklin; *Best Of* .... (ATL)
  Gold .... (ATL)
  Greatest Hits .... (ATL)
  Burt Bacharach; *Classics-#23* .... (A&M)
  Greatest Hits .... (A&M)
  Reach Out .... (A&M)
  Dionne Warwick; *Anthology* .... (RHI)
  Dionne Warwick .... (EVR)
  Greatest Hits .... (EVR)
  Original Rock 'N' Roll Hits Of The '60s .... (RLL)
I Wanna Marry You
  Bruce Springsteen; *The River* .... (COL)
I Want A Little Girl
  Joe Turner; *Atlantic Jazz-Singers* .... (ATL)
  Ray Charles; *Life In Music* .... (ATL)
In A Little Spanish Town
  Ray Charles; *Live* .... (ATL)
In The Wee Small Hours Of The Morning
  Frank Sinatra; *A Man & His Music* .... (RPR)
  Capitol Years .... (CAP)
  In The Wee Small Hours .... (CAP)
  Sinatra's Sinatra .... (RPR)
  What Is This Thing Called Love .... (CAP)
Itsy Bitsy Teenie Weenie Yellow Polka...
  Brian Hyland; *Dr. Demento's Greatest-#3* .... (RHI)
  Greatest Hits .... (RHI)
  Vintage Music-Classics-'50s/'60s-#5 .... (MCA)
I'm A Little Dinosaur
  Jonathan Richman/Modern Lovers; *Beserkley Years-Best
  Of* .... (RHI)
I'm A Little Liar
  Kings; *45* .... (CLT)
I'm In Love With My Little Red Tricycle
  Napoleon XIV; *They're Coming To Take Me
  Away...Ha-Ha* .... (RHI)
I've Got A Secret Miniature Camera
  Peter Murphy; *ST/Pump Up The Volume* ... (MCA)
I've Told Ev'ry Little Star
  David Allyn; *Sings Jerome Kern* .... (DCO)
  Linda Scott; *45* .... (ERI)
Just A Little Talk With Jesus
  Elvis Presley; *Million-Dollar Quartet* .... (RCA)
Little America
  R.E.M.; *Reckoning* .... (IRS)
Little Band Of Gold
  Sonny James; *American Originals* .... (COL)
  Greatest Hits .... (COL)
  Little Bit South Of Saskatoon .... (COL)
Little Beggar Man
  Ian & Sylvia; *Greatest Hits* .... (VAN)
  Northern Journey .... (VAN)
Little Bird
  Beach Boys; *Friends/20/20* .... (CAP)
  Jerry Jeff Walker; *Mr. Bojangles* .... (BAI)
  Viva Terlingua .... (MCA)
Little Birdie
  Joe Williams; *Happy Anniversary Charie Brown* . (GRP)
  Stanley Brothers; *Stanley Brothers* .... (MEL)
  Stanley Series-#2, No. 1 .... (COP)
Little Bird, Little Bird
  Original Cast; *Man Of La Mancha* .... (MCA)
Little Bits & Pieces
  Jim Stafford; *45* .... (COL)

Little Bitty Pretty One
Huey Lewis/News; *Four Chords & Several Years*
Ago .... (ELE)
Jackson 5; *16 Greatest Hits* .... (MOT)
Anthology .... (MOT)
Lookin' Through The Windows .... (MOT)
Motown Legends .... (MOT)
Top 10 With A Bullet-Motown Male Groups ... (MOT)
Thurston Harris; *Billboard Top R&B Hits-1957* .. (RHI)

Little Bitty Tear
Burl Ives; *Best Of-#2* .... (MCA)
Live .... (MCA)
MCA Records 30 Years Of Hits (1958-1988) .. (MCA)

Little Black Book
Jimmy Dean; *American Originals* ....(COL)
Greatest Hits ....(COL)

Little Blue Man
Betty Johnson; *45* .... (ATL)

Little Blue Whale
Country Joe McDonald; *Goodbye Blues* .... (FAN)

Little Boxes
Malvina Reynolds; *Folk Classics-Roots Of American*
Folk ....(COL)
Pete Seeger; *Greatest Hits* ....(COL)

Little Boy Blue
Elegants; *45* .... (RLL)

Little Boy Sad
Johnny Burnette; *45* .... (UA)

Little Brown Bird
Elvin Bishop; *Raisin' Hell* ....(CPC)

Little Brown Dog
Judy Collins; *Golden Apples Of The Sun* .... (ELE)

Little Brown Jug
Glenn Miller; *Best Of* ....(RCA)
Legendary Performer ....(RCA)
Pure Gold ....(RCA)
Story ....(RCA)
Glenn Miller/Orchestra; *Unforgettable* ....(RCA)

Little Chicago Fire
Count Basie Orchestra; *Live At El Morocco* ...... (TLR)

Little Child
Beatles; *Meet The* ....(CAP)

Little Children
Billy J. Kramer; *History Of British Rock-#1* ...... (RHI)

Little Criminals
Randy Newman; *Little Criminals* .... (WB)

Little Darlin'
Diamonds; *Best Of* .... (RHI)
Billboard Top Rock 'N' Roll Hits-1957 .... (RHI)
Cruisin'-1957 .... (INC)
Good Time Rock 'N' Roll .... (MCA)
Oldies But Goodies-#11 .... (OSR)
ST/American Graffiti .... (MCA)

Little Darlin' (I Need You)
Doobie Brothers; *Livin' On The Fault Line* .... (WB)
Marvin Gaye; *Anthology* .... (MOT)
Live At The London Palladium .... (MOT)
Motown Legends .... (MOT)
Musical Testament 1964-1984 .... (MOT)

Little Deuce Coupe
Beach Boys; *Best Of* ....(CAP)
Concert ....(CAP)
Endless Summer ....(CAP)
Little Deuce Coupe ....(CAP)
Summer Means Fun-Calif. Surf Music ....(CAP)

Little Diane
Dion; *24 Original Classics* .... (ARI)
Dion/Belmonts; *Everything You Always Wanted To Hear*
By ....(LAU)
Reunion-Live At Madison Sq. Garden 1972 .... (RHI)

Little Dreamer
Van Halen; *Van Halen* ....(WB)

Little Dutch Girl
George Morgan; *American Originals* ....(COL)

Little Dutch Mill
Bing Crosby; *Crooner-Columbia*
Years-1928-1934 ....(COL)

Little Dutch Town
Mac Davis; *Volume XC* ....(ALL)
With Love ....(ACC)

Little Earthquakes
Tori Amos; *Little Earthquakes* .... (ATL)

Little Egypt
Coasters; *Atlantic R&B*
1947-1974-#4-(1958-1962) .... (ATL)
Their Greatest Recordings-Early Years ....(ATC)
Elvis Presley; *Sings Leiber & Stoller* ....(RCA)

Little Fighter
White Lion; *Big Game* .... (ATL)

Little Girl
Monkees; *Monkee Flips* .... (RHI)
Present .... (RHI)
Reba McEntire; *Sweet Sixteen* .... (MCA)
Ritchie Valens; *Best Of* .... (RHI)
History Of .... (RHI)
Steve Miller Band; *Anthology* ....(CAP)
Your Saving Grace ....(CAP)

Little Girl Blue
Ella Fitzgerald; *Rodgers & Hart Songbook* ....(VRV)

Little Girl From Little Rock
Original Cast; *Gentlemen Prefer Blondes* .. (SSP)

Little Girl Of Mine
Cleftones; *Original Rock 'N' Roll Hits Of The '50s* (RLL)
Dion; *Bronx Blues-Columbia Recordings* ....(COL)

Little Girls
Original Broadway Cast; *Annie* ....(COL)
Patti Labelle; *Best Of* .... (EPI)

Little Green Apples
O.C. Smith; *Pop Classics/'60s* ....(COL)

Little Ground In Texas
Capitols; *45* .... (RID)

Little Guitars
Van Halen; *Diver Down* ....'(WB)

Little Hitler
Nick Lowe; *Pure Pop For Now People* ....(COL)

Little Hollywood Girl
Crickets; *Liberty Years* .... (EMI)

Little Home In Tennessee
Bill Harrell/Virginians; *Ballads & Bluegrass* .... (ADE)

Little Honda
Beach Boys; *Absolute Best-#1* ....(CAP)
All Summer Long ....(CAP)
Best Of ....(CAP)
Spirit Of America ....(CAP)
Hondells; *Beach Classics* ....(DHL)
Cruisin'-1964 .... (INC)

Little Hotel Room
Merle Haggard; *Friendship* ....(COL)
It's All In The Game .... (EPI)

"Little House On The Prairie" Theme
Original Music; *Television's Greatest Hits-#3* ..... (TVT)

Little Houses
Doug Stone; *Doug Stone G.H.* .... (EPI)

Little Jeannie
Elton John; *21 At 33* ....(POL)
Greatest Hits-1976-1986 .... (MCA)

Little Joe From Chicago
Mary Lou Williams; *Best Of* ....(PAB)
Nat King Cole; *Straighten Up & Fly Right* .....(POE)

Little Joe The Wrangler
Goebel Reeves; *Songs Of Old West* ....(GLN)
Texas Drifter ....(GLN)

Little John Of God
Los Lobos; *The Neighborhood* .... (SLS)

Little Lady Preacher
Tom T. Hall; *Greatest Hits-#2* .... (MER)

Little Lamb
Original Cast; *Gypsy* ....(COL)

Little Latin Lupe Lu
Mitch Ryder/Detroit Wheels; *Greatest Hits* .... (RLL)
Rev Up-Best Of .... (RHI)
Righteous Brothers; *Anthology-1962-1974* .... (RHI)

Little Lies
Fleetwood Mac; *Greatest Hits* .... (WB)
Tango In The Night .... (WB)

Little London Boys
Johnny Thunders; *Stations Of The Cross* .... (ROI)

Little Maggie
Kingston Trio; *Tom Dooley* ....(CAP)

Little Mama
Clovers; *45* .... (ATL)

Little Marie
Chuck Berry; *Chess Box* .... (CSS)
Rock 'N' Roll Rarities .... (CSS)
St. Louis To Liverpool .... (CSS)

Little Martha
Allman Brothers Band; *Best Of* .... (POL)
  Decade Of Hits-1969-1979 .... (POL)
  Eat A Peach .... (POL)
Little Miss Can't Be Wrong
Spin Doctors; *Homebelly Groove* .... (EPA)
  Pocket Full Of Kryptonite .... (EPA)
  Up For Grabs...Live .... (EPA)
Little Miss Love
Eldorados; *45* .... (CLT)
Little Miss Lover
Jimi Hendrix; *Axis: Bold As Love* .... (RPR)
  Essential .... (RPR)
Little Miss Magic
Jimmy Buffett; *Boats Beaches Bars & Ballads* ... (MGR)
  Coconut Telegraph .... (MCA)
Little Old Church In England
Glenn Miller/Orchestra; *Complete* .... (BLU)
Little Old Lady From Pasadena
Beach Boys; *Concert* .... (CAP)
Jan & Dean; *Best Of* .... (EMI)
  Billboard Top Rock 'N' Roll Hits-1964 .... (RHI)
  Deadman's Curve .... (EMI)
  Surf City-Best Of .... (EMI)
Little Old Wine Drinker Me
Dean Martin; *Greatest Hits-#2* .... (RPR)
  Welcome To My World .... (RPR)
Mel Tillis; *Best Of* .... (MCA)
Little One
Chicago; *Take Me Back To Chicago* .... (COL)
  XI .... (COL)
Little Pad
Beach Boys; *Smiley Smile* .... (CAP)
Little Pal
Jimmy Roselli; *Daddy's Little Girl* .... (M&R)
  Rock-A-Bye Your Baby .... (M&R)
  Sold Out-Carnegie Hall Concert .... (M&R)
Little Paper Boy
Hank Williams; *Rare Takes & Radio Cuts* .... (POL)
Little Paradise
Pat Benatar; *Crimes Of Passion* .... (CHR)
Little Priest
Original Cast; *Sweeney Todd* .... (RCA)
Little Queen
Heart; *Little Queen* .... (POR)
Little Queenie
Chuck Berry; *Chess Box* .... (CSS)
  Rock & Roll Rarities .... (CSS)
Jerry Lee Lewis; *Original Golden Hits-#1* ...... (SUN)
  Rockin' R&B .... (SUN)
Rolling Stones; *Get Yer Ya-Ya's Out* .... (AKO)
R.E.O. Speedwagon; *Live-You Get What You Play*
  For .... (EPI)
  R.E.O./Two .... (EPI)
Little Rachel
Eric Clapton; *One In Every Crowd* .... (RSO)
Little Red Corvette
Prince; *1999* .... (WB)
Little Red Hen
Johnny Otis; *Original Johnny Otis Show* .... (SAV)
Little Red Lights
Todd Rundgren; *Something/Anything?* .... (RHI)
Little Red Rooster
Big Mama Thornton; *Jail* .... (VAN)
B.B. King/Muddy Waters/Big Mama Thornton; *Live At*
  Newport .... (INT)
Rolling Stones; *Love You Live* .... (RS)
  Now! .... (AKO)
Sam Cooke; *Having A Party* .... (RCA)
  This Is .... (RCA)
Little Rock
Reba McEntire; *Whoever's In New England* ..... (MCA)
  Woman To Woman-#2 .... (MCA)
Little Sadie
Bob Dylan; *Self-Portrait* .... (COL)
Little Sally Tease
Standells; *Best Of* .... (RHI)
Little Sally, The Super Sex Star
Camille Yarborough; *Iron Pot Cooker* .... (VAN)

Little Sister
Elvis Presley; *Golden Records-#3* .... (RCA)
  I Was The One .... (RCA)
  In Concert .... (RCA)
  Top Ten Hits .... (RCA)
  Worldwide 50 Gold Award Hits #1 .... (RCA)
Little Spain
Lee Morgan Quintet; *Take Twelve* .... (JZL)
Little Star
Elegants; *Billboard Top Rock 'N' Roll Hits-1958* . (RHI)
  Oldies But Goodies-#5 .... (OSR)
  Super Oldies/'50s-#7 .... (AUF)
Little Things
Bobby Goldsboro; *All-Time Greatest Hits* .... (CCB)
  Honey-Best Of .... (EMI)
  ST/Drugstore Cowboy .... (NOV)
Boyz II Men; *Cooleyhighharmony* .... (MOT)
Oak Ridge Boys; *Greatest Hits-#3* .... (MCA)
  Step On Out .... (MCA)
Willie Nelson; *Best Of Willie* .... (RCA)
Little Things Mean A Lot
McGuire Sisters; *Best Of* .... (MCA)
Little Things You Do Together
Original Cast; *Company* .... (COL)
Little Tin God
Don Henley; *End Of The Innocence* .... (GEF)
Little Triggers
Elvis Costello; *This Year's Model* .... (COL)
Little Turtle Dove
Bobby Day; *Best Of* .... (RHI)
Little Victories
Bob Seger/Silver Bullet Band; *The Distance* ...... (CAP)
Little Wheel
John Lee Hooker; *Best Of* .... (CRS)
  Best Of .... (VJ)
  John Lee Hooker .... (EVR)
Little Wheel Spin & Spin
Buffy Sainte-Marie; *Best Of* .... (VAN)
  Little Wheel Spin & Spin .... (VAN)
  Native North American Child .... (VAN)
Little White Lies
Romantics; *Romantics* .... (NEM)
Tommy Dorsey; *Best Of* .... (RCA)
  Complete-#6-1937-1938 .... (RCA)
Little Willie
Sweet; *Best Of-1910 Fruitgum Co.-#2* .... (RHI)
Little Wing
Derek/Dominos; *Layla* .... (RSO)
Jimi Hendrix; *Axis: Bold As Love* .... (RPR)
  Concerts .... (RPR)
  Essential-#1 & 2 .... (RPR)
  Lifelines/Jimi Hendrix Story .... (RPR)
Sting; *Nothing Like The Sun* .... (A&M)
Littlest Cowboy Rides Again
Chris LeDoux; *Songbook Of The American West* .. (LIB)
  Sounds Of The Western Country .... (LIB)
Li'l Red Riding Hood
Sam The Sham/Pharaohs; *Best Of* .... (POL)
  Cruisin'-1966 .... (INC)
  Pharaohization-Best Of .... (RHI)
Mary Had A Little Lamb
Stevie Ray Vaughan/Double Trouble; *Live Alive* .. (EPI)
  Texas Flood .... (EPI)
Wings; *Wings Wild Life* .... (CAP)
Me & Little Andy
Dolly Parton; *Collector's Series* .... (RCA)
  Greatest Hits .... (RCA)
  Here You Come Again .... (RCA)
Mother's Little Helper
Rolling Stones; *Flowers* .... (AKO)
  Hot Rocks-1964-1971 .... (AKO)
  Through The Past Darkly-Big Hits-#2 .... (AKO)
Tesla; *Five Man Acoustical Jam* .... (GEF)
My Little Bimbo
Clancy Hayes/Salt Dogs; *Oh By Jingo* .... (DEL)
My Little Brown Book
Duke Ellington; *& John Coltrane* .... (MCI)
John Coltrane; *Gentle Side Of* .... (GRP)
My Little Friend
Elvis Presley; *45* .... (RCA)
My Little Georgia Rose
David Grisman; *Home Is Where The Heart Is* ... (ROU)
Herb Pederson; *Son Of Rounder Banjo* .... (ROU)

My Little Girl
Crescendos; *45* .... (MCA)
Crickets; *EMI Legends Of Rock-24 Greatest Hits* . (EMI)
Liberty Years .... (EMI)
Roxy Music; *Manifesto* .... (RPR)
Spike Jones/City Slickers; *King Of Corn* ....(GLN)
My Little Girl In Tennessee
L. Flatt/E. Scruggs/Foggy Mountain Boys; *Complete
Mercury Sessions* .... (MER)
My Little Grass Shack In Kealakekua, HI
Mom & Dads; *Blue Hawaii* .... (CRS)
My Little Home Down In New Orleans
Jimmie Rodgers; *Early Years-1928-1929* .... (ROU)
My Little Lady
Jimmie Rodgers; *Early Years-1928-1929* ...... (ROU)
Roy Rogers; *Columbia Historic Edition* ....(COL)
My Little Marine
Jamie Horton; *45* .... (ERI)
My Little Miss America
Gary U.S. Bonds; *45* .... (LEG)
My Little Red Book
Love; *Best Of* .... (RHI)
Elektrock-'60s .... (ELE)
Nuggets-#2-Punk .... (RHI)
My Little Town
Paul Simon; *Still Crazy After All These Years* .....(COL)
On A Little Street In Singapore
Glenn Miller; *Original Recordings-#4* .... (PRR)
Harry James; *Two O'Clock Jump* .... (POE)
Manhattan Transfer; *Anthology-Down In Birdland* (RHI)
One Little Coyote
Riders In The Sky; *Harmony Ranch* ....(COL)
One Small Boat
Altered State; *Altered State* ....(WB)
Piggies
Beatles; *Box Set* .... (CAP)
White Album ....(CAP)
George Harrison & Eric Clapton & Band; *Live In
Japan* .... (DKH)
Pink Houses
John Cougar Mellencamp; *Rock For Amnesty* ... (MER)
Uh-Huh ....(RIV)
Poor Little Fool
Rick Nelson; *Best Of* .... (EMI)
EMI Legends Of Rock 'N' Roll-24 Greatest ...... (EMI)
Legendary Masters .... (EMI)
Live In '85 .... (RHI)
Poor Little Hollywood Star
Virginia Martin; *Little Me* ....(RCA)
Poor Little Jesus
Weavers; *On Tour* .... (VAN)
Poor Little Jimmie
Burl Ives; *Best Of-#2* .... (MCA)
Poor Little Rich Girl
Judy Garland; *Best Of* .... (MCA)
Romantics; *National Breakout* .... (NEM)
Tony Bennett & Count Basie; *Basie Swings Bennett
Sings* .... (RLL)
Uriah Heep; *Equator* ....(COL)
Pretty Litle Lady From Beaumont, Texas
George Jones; *One Woman Man* .... (EPI)
Pretty Little Angel
Crests; *Greatest Hits* ....(CLT)
Stevie Wonder; *Uptight* ....(MOT)
Pretty Little Angel Eyes
Curtis Lee; *Back To Mono-1958-1969* .... (AKO)
Million Dollar Memories-#2 ....(RCA)
Oldies But Goodies-#2 ....(OSR)
Phil Spector-The Early Years 1958-61 ...... (RHI)
Rock & Roll USA-21 Favorites-#2 ....(LAU)
Pretty Little Indian
Dan Crary; *Lady's Fancy* .... (ROU)
Pretty Little Picture
Original Cast; *Funny Thing Happened On The
Way...* ....(CAP)
Stephen Sondheim; *Collector's Sondheim* ....(RCA)
Pretty Little Pink
Doc Watson; *Old Timey Concert* .... (VAN)
Put My Little Shoes Away
Everly Brothers; *Songs Our Daddy Taught Us* .... (RHI)
Put Your Little Foot Right Out
Myron Floren; *22 Great Accordion Classics* ..... (RAN)
Russ Morgan; *Best Of* .... (MCA)

Re-Doo-Wopp-Little Star
Tokens; *Re-Doo-Wopp-Little Star* ....(RCA)
Rich Little Bitch
Dash Rip Rock; *Boiled Alive!* ....(MAM)
Not Of This World ....(MAM)
Rock My World (Little Country Girl)
Brooks & Dunn; *Hard Workin' Man* .... (ARI)
Rockin' Little Tune
Bill Haley/Comets; *Golden Hits* .... (MCA)
Run Little Rabbit
John & Jamie Hartford; *Hartford & Hartford* ......(FF)
See The Funny Little Clown
Bobby Goldsboro; *10th Anniversary Album-#1* ... (EMI)
Greatest Hits .... (LIB)
Honey-Best Of .... (EMI)
Short Fat Fannie
Larry Williams; *Original Rock Oldies-Golden
Hits-#1* .... (SPE)
This Is How It All Began-#2 .... (SPE)
Ultimate '50s Party ....(ERA)
Short People
Randy Newman; *Dr. Demento-Greatest Novelty
Records-#4* .... (RHI)
Little Criminals ....(WB)
Short Shorts
Royal Teens; *Cruisin'-1958* .... (INC)
Goofy Greats .... (KT)
Short Shorts .... (MCA)
Shorty Falls In Love
Dan Hicks/Hot Licks; *Where's The Money* ...... (MCA)
Shorty George
Count Basie; *Best Of* .... (MCA)
Command Performances .... (ACC)
Country Party .... (ACC)
Sing Along With .... (RLL)
Leadbelly; *King Of The 12-String Guitar* ....(COL)
Take This Hammer .... (FLW)
Simple Little Words
Cristy Lane; *At Her Best* .... (EMI)
Small Axe
Bob Marley/Wailers; *Burnin'* .... (ISL)
Gladiators; *Calling Rastafari* .... (NH)
Symbol Of Relaity .... (NH)
Small Fry
Georgie Fame/Annie Ross/Hoagy Carmichael; *In
Hoagland* ....(DRG)
June Christy; *Small Fry-Capitol Sings Kids Songs For
Grownups* ....(CAP)
Small Hills Of Offaly
Irish Tradition; *Times We've Had* ....(GRE)
Small Paradise
John Cougar Mellencamp; *John Cougar
Mellencamp* ....(RIV)
Small Town
John Cougar Mellencamp; *Scarecrow* ....(RIV)
Small Town Girl
John Cafferty/Beaver Brown Band; *Tough All
Over* ....(SCO)
Larry Carlton; *Collection* ....(GRP)
Steve Wariner; *Greatest Hits* .... (MCA)
It's A Crazy World .... (MCA)
Small Town Saturday Night
Hal Ketchum; *Past The Point Of Rescue* ....(CRB)
Small Victory
Faith No More; *Angel Dust* ....(SLS)
Small World
Adrian Belew; *Young Lions* ....(ATL)
Huey Lewis/News; *Greenpeace/Rainbow Warriors* (GEF)
Small World .... (CHR)
Johnny Mathis; *16 Most Requested Songs* ....(COL)
All-Time Greatest Hits ....(COL)
Original Cast; *Gypsy* ....(COL)
Original London Cast; *Gypsy* ....(RCA)
Sweet Little Angel
Buddy Guy; *Best Of The Chicago Blues* .... (VAN)
Man & The Blues .... (VAN)
B.B. King; *16 Original Big Hits* .... (FAN)
Back In The Alley .... (MCA)
Live At The Regal .... (MCA)
Live & Well .... (MCA)
Etta James; *Late Show* .... (FAN)
Rocks The House .... (CSS)
Sweet Little Bullet From A Pretty...
Tom Waits; *Blue Valentine* ....(ASY)

Sweet Little Cafe In A Square
Lena Spencer/Others; *Welcome To Caffe Lena* ....(BIO)
Sweet Little Country Girl
Charlie Daniels; *America I Believe In You* .... (LIB)
Sweet Little Flower
Sleepy John Estes; *Electric Sleep* ....(DEL)
Sweet Little Girl
Stevie Wonder; *Music Of My Mind* .... (MOT)
Sweet Little Missy
Lynyrd Skynyrd; *Legend* .... (MCA)
Sweet Little Papa
Louis Armstrong; *Hot Fives & Hot Sevens-#2* ....(COL)
Sweet Little Rock & Roller
Chuck Berry; *Chess Box* .... (CSS)
   Chuck Berry Is On Top .... (CSS)
Richard Thompson; *Guitar Vocal* ....(CTH)
Rod Stewart; *Absolutely Live* ....(WB)
   Best Of .... (MER)
Sweet Little Sixteen
Beatles; *45* ....(CLT)
Chuck Berry; *Best Of The Best Of* ....(GUS)
   Cruisin'-1965 .... (INC)
   Golden Hits .... (MER)
   Greatest Hits Live ....(QKS)
   Oldies But Goodies-#12 .... (OSR)
Jerry Lee Lewis; *Original Golden Hits #3* ....(SUN)
   /Friends-Duets ....(SUN)
John Lennon; *Lennon* ....(CAP)
   Rock 'N' Roll ....(CAP)
Sweet Little '66
Steve Earle/Dukes; *Exit 0* .... (MCA)
Ten Little Indians
Beach Boys; *Surfin' Safari/Surfin' U.S.A.* ....(CAP)
Thank Heaven For Little Girls
Maurice Chevalier; *ST/Gigi* ....(SSP)
Merle Haggard & Janie Fricke; *It's All In The*
Game .... (EPI)
That's My Little Suzie
Ritchie Valens; *Best Of* .... (RHI)
There's A Small Hotel
Benny Goodman; *Birth Of Swing* ....(BLU)
   Complete-#2 ....(RCA)
Bobby Short; *Celebrates Rodgers & Hart* ....(ATL)
Ella Fitzgerald; *Rodgers & Hart Songbook* .....(VRV)
Tony Bennett; *Rodgers & Hart Songbook* .... (DRG)
This Little Girl
Dion; *24 Original Classics* .... (ARI)
   Bronx Blues-Columbia Recordings-1962-65 ....(COL)
Gary U.S. Bonds; *Cover Me* .... (RHI)
Gary U.S. Bonds & Bruce Springsteen;
Dedication ....(R&T)
This Little Girl Of Mine
Everly Brothers; *Cadence Classics-Their 20 Greatest*
Hits .... (RHI)
Faron Young; *Greatest Hits-#3* ....(SO)
Herbie Mann; *Best Of* ....(ATL)
Ray Charles; *Atlantic R&B*
1947-1974-#2-(1952-1955) ....(ATL)
   Birth Of Soul-Atlantic R&B-1952-1959 ....(ATL)
   Life In Music ....(ATL)
This Little Pig
Living Colour; *Stain* .... (EPI)
This Town Ain't Big Enough For The...
Siouxsie/Banshees; *Through The Looking Glass* ..(GEF)
Sparks; *Island Story-1962-1987-25th Anniversary* . (ISL)
   Profile-Ultimate Sparks Collection .... (RHI)
Three Little Birds
Bob Marley/Wailers; *Exodus* ....(TUF)
   Legend ....(TUF)
   Songs Of Freedom ....(TUF)
Three Little Fishes
Andrews Sisters; *Boogie Woogie Bugle Girls* ..... (MCA)
Kay Kyser; *Dr. Demento Greatest-#1-'40s &*
Before .... (RHI)
   Sentimental Favorites ....(COL)
Three Little Pigs
Lloyd Price; *Greatest Hits* .... (MCA)
Three Little Words
Carmen McRae; *Great American Songbook* ...... (ATL)
Duke Ellington/Orchestra; *Nipper's Greatest*
Hits-'30s-#2 ....(RCA)
Nat King Cole; *L-O-V-E* ....(CAP)
Throw Back The Little Ones
Steely Dan; *Katy Lied* .... (MCA)

Tiny Bubbles (Hua Li'l)
Don Ho; *Greatest Hits* .... (RPR)
Lawrence Welk; *In Concert* ....(RAN)
Tiny Dancer
Elton John; *Live In Australia w/Melbourne*
Symphony .... (MCA)
   Madman Across The Water ....(POL)
Tiny Sparrow
Peter, Paul & Mary; *Moving* ....(WB)
Tiny Steps
Elvis Costello; *Girls Girls Girls* ....(COL)
Toys Are Made For Little Children
Uniques; *Golden Hits* .... (PLN)
Truckin' Little Baby
John Hammond; *Solo* .... (VAN)
Twinkle Twinkle Little Star
Bob Wills/Texas Playboys; *Tiffany*
Transcriptions-#8 ....(KAL)
Willie Nelson; *Somewhere Over The Rainbow* ....(COL)
Two Little Bees
Hollywood Flames; *Hollywood Flames* .... (SPE)
Wake Up, Little Susie
Everly Brothers; *All They Had To Do Was Dream* (RHI)
   All-Time Greatest Hits ....(CCB)
   American Graffiti-#3 ....(MCA)
   Everly Brothers .... (RHI)
   Oldies But Goodies-#7 ....(OSR)
   Very Best Of ....(WB)
Grateful Dead; *History Of-#1-Bear's Choice* .....(WB)
Simon & Garfunkel; *Concert In Central Park* .....(WB)
Where Did That Little Dog Go
Original Cast; *Snoopy* .... (DRG)
Where Has My Little Dog Gone
Horace Heidt/Musical Knights; *Uncollected-1939* (HIN)
Wild Little Willy
Ronnie Hawkins/Hawks; *Best Of* .... (RHI)
You're Lost, Little Girl
Doors; *13* ....(ELE)
   Strange Days ....(ELE)

SMILE, Funny, Laugh
See Also: FUN, HAPPINESS, PARTY

After My Laughter Came Tears
Big Joe Turner; *Midnight Special* ....(PAB)
Baby's Smile Woman's Kiss
Johnny Duncan; *Best Of* ....(COL)
Behind A Painted Smile
Isley Brothers; *Story-#1-Rockin' Soul-1959-1968* (RHI)
Can't Smile Without You
Barry Manilow; *Even Now* .... (ARI)
   Greatest Hits-#1 .... (ARI)
Certain Smile, A
Johnny Mathis; *16 Most Requested Songs* ....(COL)
   All-Time Greatest Hits ....(COL)
   Live ....(COL)
Crying & Laughing
Chris DeBurgh; *The Getaway* ....(A&M)
Diamond Smiles
Boomtown Rats; *Fine Art Of Surfacing* ....(COL)
Disarm
Smashing Pumpkins; *Siamese Dream* .... (VIA)
Dolphin's Smile
Byrds; *Notorious Byrd Brothers* ....(COL)
   Byrds (collection) ....(COL)
Funny
Boz Scaggs; *Other Roads* ....(COL)
Maxine Brown; *Golden Classics* ....(CLT)
Nat King Cole; *Blossom Fell* ....(CAP)
Ray Charles; *Life In Music* ....(ATL)
Funny Face
Donna Fargo; *Super Hits/'70s-#11* .... (RHI)
Original Cast; *My One & Only* ....(ATL)
Funny Girl
Barbra Streisand; *ST/Funny Girl* ....(COL)
Funny How Time Slips Away
Al Green & Lyle Lovett; *Rhythm Country &*
Blues .... (MCA)

Willie Nelson; *Best Of* .... (EMI)
  Collector's ....(RCA)
  Healing Hands Of Time .... (LIB)
  My Own Way ....(RCA)
  San Antonio Rose ....(COL)
  & Family Life ....(COL)
Willie Nelson & Faron Young; *Funny How Time Slips*
Away ....(COL)

Funny Way Of Laughin'
Burl Ives; *Best Of-#2* .... (MCA)
  Live ....(EVR)

Funny, Familiar, Forgotten Feelings
Tom Jones; *Country Side Of* ....(LON)
  London Collector-Greatest ....(LON)

I Go To Rio
Pablo Cruise; *Worlds Away* .... (A&M)
Peter Allen; *It Is Time For* .... (A&M)
  Taught By Experts .... (A&M)
  The Best ....(A&M)

I Love Your Smile
Shanice; *Inner Child* .... (MOT)

Illegal Smile
John Prine; *John Prine* .... (ATL)
  Prime Prine .... (ATL)

It Takes A Lot To Laugh, It Takes A...
Bob Dylan; *Bootleg Series-#1-3* ....(COL)
  Highway 61 Revisited ....(COL)
M. Bloomfield/A. Kooper/S. Stills; *Super Session* .(COL)

I'll Never Smile Again
Billie Holiday; *Last Recordings* ....(VRV)
Frank Sinatra; *A Man & His Music* .... (RPR)
Ink Spots; *Greatest Hits* ....(MCA)
Keely Smith; *Capitol's Great Ladies Of Song* ..... (CAP)
Sarah Vaughan; *In The Land Of Hi-Fi* ....(EMA)
Tommy Dorsey & Frank Sinatra; *All-Time Greatest*
Hits-#1 ....(RCA)
  Masters Of The Big Bands .... (BLU)

Jackie Wilson Said (I'm In Heaven...)
Van Morrison; *Best Of* .... (MER)
  St. Dominic's Preview ....(WB)
  ST/Queen's Logic .... (EPI)

Keep On Smilin'
Alfie; *45* ....(MOT)
Peaches & Herb; *45* ....(COL)
Wet Willie; *Greatest Hits* ....(POL)
  Super Hits/'70s-Have A Nice Day-#13 ....(RHI)

Keep Smiling At Trouble
Al Jolson; *Story-Rainbow 'Round My Shoulder* .. (MCA)
Tony Bennett; *Forty Years-Artistry Of* ....(COL)

Lady Grinning Soul
David Bowie; *Aladdin Sane* ....(RYK)

Laugh Laugh
Beau Brummels; *Best Of* .... (RHI)
  Heart & Soul Of Rock 'N' Roll .... (RHI)
  Introducing The .... (RHI)
  Nuggets-#7-Early San Francisco .... (RHI)

Laughing
Church; *Gold Afternoon Fix* .... (ARI)
Guess Who; *Best Of* ....(RCA)
  Greatest Of ....(RCA)
R.E.M.; *Murmur* ....(IRS)
Stranglers; *Aural Sculpture* .... (EPI)

Laughing At Life
Billie Holiday; *Billie Holiday* ....(COL)
  Quintessential-#8-1939-1940 ....(COL)
  Story-#2 ....(COL)

Laughing At The Blues
Jimmy Reed; *Best Of* ....(CRS)
  Now Appearing .... (VJ)

Laughing Blues
Bonzo Dog Band; *Tadpoles* ....(LIB)
Leon Redbone; *Sugar* ....(PRV)

Laughing Boy
Mary Wells; *Compact Command Performances* . (MOT)
  Greatest Hits ....(MOT)

Laughing Gnome
David Bowie; *London Collector-Starting Point* ....(LON)
  Love You Till Tuesday ....(LON)

Laughing On The Outside
Aretha Franklin; *Sings The Blues* ....(COL)

Laughing Song
Dan Hicks/Hot Licks; *Striking It Rich* .... (MCA)
Residents; *Duck Stab* ....(RAL)

Laughing Stock
Love; *Best Of* .... (RHI)

Laughter In The Rain
Johnny Mathis; *When Will Is See You Again* ......(COL)
Neil Sedaka; *My Friend* ....(POL)

Let A Smile Be Your Umbrella
Sammy Kaye; *Best Of* .... (MCA)

Light Of Smiles
Gary Wright; *Light Of Smiles* ....(OOP)

Living A Little, Laughing A Little
John Hiatt; *Warming Up To The Ice Age* ....(GEF)
Spinners; *Live* ....(ATL)
  New & Improved ....(ATL)

Make Me Smile
Chicago; *At Carnegie Hall* ....(COL)
  Greatest Hits ....(COL)
  II ....(COL)

Mona Lisa's Lost Her Smile
David Allan Coe; *17 Greatest Hits* ....(COL)
  19 Hot Country Requests-#2 .... (EPI)
  For The Record-First 10 Years ....(COL)
  Greatest Country Hits/'80s-1984 ....(COL)
  Just Divorced ....(COL)

My Funny Valentine
Anita O'Day; *Anita O'Day* ....(GLN)
  Live At The City .... (EML)
  Sings The Winners ....(VRV)
Carly Simon; *My Romance* ....(ARI)
Ella Fitzgerald; *Rodgers & Hart Songbook* ......(VRV)
Mel Torme; *Easy To Remember* ....(GLN)
Miles Davis; *Columbia Years-1955-1985* ....(COL)
  Cookin' With The Miles Davis Quintet .... (PRS)
  Greatest Hits ....(COL)
  My Funny Valentine ....(COL)
Original Cast/Mary Martin; *Babes In Arms* ....(SSP)
Stan Getz; *Artistry Of-Best Of Verve Years-#1* ...(VRV)

Nancy (With The Laughing Face)
Frank Sinatra; *Sinatra's Reprise-Very Good Years* (RPR)
  Sinatra's Sinatra ....(RPR)
John Coltrane; *Gentle Side Of* ....(GRP)
Tony Bennett; *Perfectly Frank* ....(COL)

Powder Your Face With Sunshine (Smile!)
Guy Lombardo; *Best Of* ....(CCB)
Sammy Kaye/Orchestra; *Play 22 Original Big Band*
Recordings .... (HIN)

"Sandpiper" Theme (Shadow Of Your Smile)
Barbra Streisand; *My Name Is Barbra-Two* ......(COL)
Boston Pops Orchestra/Arthur Fiedler; *Greatest Hits Of*
The '60s-#2 ....(RCA)
  Motion Picture Classics ....(RCA)
  Music For Every Mood ....(RCA)
Carmen McRae; *Alive* ....(MST)
  I Want You ....(MST)
Frank Sinatra; *Reprise Collection* ....(RPR)
James Morrison; *Snappy Doo* ....(ATL)
Marvin Gaye; *Romantically Yours* ....(COL)
Tony Bennett; *16 Most Requested Songs* ....(COL)
  All-Time Greatest Hits ....(COL)
  Movie Song Album ....(COL)

Sara Smile
Daryl Hall & John Oates; *Daryl Hall & John*
Oates ....(RCA)
  Livetime ....(RCA)
  Rock 'N' Soul-Part 1-Greatest Hits ....(RCA)
  Soulful Sounds ....(RCA)

She Smiled Sweetly
Rolling Stones; *Between The Buttons* .... (AKO)

She's Funny That Way (I Got A Woman...)
Art Tatum; *Solo Masterpieces-#8* .... (PAB)
Count Basie Jam; *Montreux '77* ....(PAB)
Frank Sinatra; *At The Movies* ....(CAP)
  Nice 'N' Easy ....(CAP)
Jackie Gleason; *Lush Moods* ....(PRR)
Nat King Cole; *Big Band Cole* .... (BLN)

Show Me A Smile
Fleetwood Mac; *Future Games* .... (RPR)

Smile
Betty Everett & Jerry Butler; *Very Best Of Betty*
Everett .... (VJ)
Dexter Gordon; *Best Of* .... (BLN)
Diana Ross; *Diana Ross* .... (MOT)
  Evening With .... (MOT)
Laura Nyro; *Smile* ....(COL)

Nat King Cole; *Story* .... (CAP)
The Unforgettable .... (CAP)
Natalie Cole; *Unforgettable* .... (ELE)
One Way; *Lady* .... (MCA)
Stevie Wonder; *With A Song In My Heart* ...... (MOT)
Tony Bennett; *All-Time Greatest Hits* .... (COL)
Movie Song Album ....(COL)
Was (Not Was); *Born To Laugh At Tornadoes* ...(GEF)
Smile Away
Paul McCartney; *Gift Set* .... (CAP)
Paul & Linda McCartney; *Ram* .... (CAP)
Smile Has Left Your Eyes
Asia; *Alpha* .... (GEF)
Live In Moscow .... (RHI)
Then & Now .... (GEF)
Smile Please
Stevie Wonder; *Fulfillingness' First Finale* .... (MOT)
Smiling
Kitchens Of Distinction; *Death of Cool* .... (A&M)
Smiling Faces Sometimes
Undisputed Truth; *Hard-To-Find Motown Classics-#2* .... (MOT)
Soul Hits/'70s-#5 .... (RHI)
Smiling Islands
Chris Proctor; *Delicate Dance* .... (FF)
Robbie Patton; *Orders From Headquarters* .... (ATL)
Smiling Phases
Blood, Sweat & Tears; *Blood, Sweat & Tears* ....(COL)
Traffic; *Best Of* .... (ISL)
Smilin'
Levert; *Just Cooolin'* .... (ATL)
Sly/Family Stone; *Anthology* .... (EPI)
Smilin' Through
Judy Garland; *Collector's Items* .... (MCA)
Judy Garland/Lyn Murray & Orchestra; *Changing My Tune-Best Of Decca Years-#2* .... (DEC)
Sunshine Of Your Smile
Tommy Dorsey & Frank Sinatra; *All-Time Greatest Hits-#4* ....(RCA)
Sweet, Sweet Smile
Carpenters; *Classics-#2* .... (A&M)
Passage .... (A&M)
Yesterday Once More .... (A&M)
That Joke Isn't Funny Anymore
Smiths; *Best 2* .... (SIR)
Meat Is Murder .... (SIR)
They All Laughed
Carmen McRae; *Setting Standards* .... (PRR)
Fred Astaire; *Starring* ....(COL)
Sarah Vaughan; *George Gershwin Songbook-#1* . (EMA)
Tony Bennett; *Steppin' Out* .... (COL)
Things Aren't Funny Anymore
Merle Haggard; *Capitol Collectors Series* .... (CAP)
Country Boy .... (PRR)
Epic Collection-Recorded Live .... (EPI)
This Funny World
Tony Bennett; *Rodgers & Hart Songbook* .... (DRG)
This Is No Laughing Matter
Sammy Kaye/Orchestra; *Play 22 Original Big Band Recordings* .... (HIN)
This Will Make You Laugh
Natalie Cole; *Take A Look* .... (ELE)
Three Mile Smile
Aerosmith; *Night In The Ruts* ....(COL)
Pandora's Box ....(COL)
Tonight I Shall Sleep With A Smile On...
Duke Ellington; *Black Brown & Beige* .... (BLU)
Sarah Vaughan; *Duke Ellington Songbook Two* ... (PAB)
When Irish Eyes Are Smiling
Billy Shepherd Singers; *Irish Sing-Along* .... (MCA)
Bing Crosby; *When Irish Eyes Are Smiling* .... (MCA)
Dennis Day; *Irish Album* ....(RCA)
When My Baby Smiles At Me
Pete Fountain; *Best Of* .... (MCA)
When Will I See You Smile Again?
Bell Biv Devoe; *Poison* .... (MCA)
WBBD-Bootcity-Remix Album .... (MCA)
When You Need A Laugh
Patsy Cline; *Portrait Of* .... (MCA)
Songwriter's Tribute .... (MCA)
When You're Smiling
Frank Sinatra; *Sinatra's Swinging Session-& More* (CAP)

Judy Garland; *At Carnegie Hall* .... (CAP)
Greatest Hits ....(CCB)
One & Only .... (CAP)
Louis Armstrong; *Best Of* .... (MCA)
Musical Autobiography-#2 .... (MCA)
#4-In New York .... (COL)
Your Smile
Rene & Angela; *Street Called Desire* .... (MER)
Your Smiling Face
James Taylor; *J.T.* ....(COL)
ST/FM .... (MCA)
You're Never Fully Dressed Without A...
Original Broadway Cast; *Annie* .... (COL)

SNOW, Ice

See Also: CHRISTMAS, COLD, MONTHS & DATES: DECEMBER, SEASONS: WINTER

April Snow
Hi-Lo's; *Cherries & Other Delights* .... (HIN)
Northern Lights; *Take You To The Sky* .... (FF)
At The First Fall Of Snow
Hank Williams; *Lovesick Blues* .... (POL)
Blizzard
Jim Reeves; *Best Of* ....(RCA)
Roy Rogers; *Out West* .... (CAP)
Blossoms In The Snow
Skyliners; *Greatest Hits* .... (OSR)
Clear As The Driven Snow
Doobie Brothers; *Captain & Me* .... (WB)
Cold As Ice
Foreigner; *Foreigner* .... (MCA)
Records ....(ATL)
ST/FM .... (MCA)
Cold Rain And Snow
Grateful Dead; *Grateful Dead* .... (WB)
Steal Your Face! .... (GRD)
Don't Eat The Yellow Snow
Frank Zappa; *Apostrophe/Overnite Sensation* .....(RYK)
Driven Like The Snow
Sisters Of Mercy; *Floodland* .... (ELE)
Fire And Ice
Pat Benatar; *Best Shots* .... (CHR)
Live From Earth .... (CHR)
Precious Time .... (CHR)
Footprints In The Snow
Bill Monroe; *Best Of* .... (MCA)
Clarence White; *Treasures Untold* .... (VAN)
Emerson, Lake & Palmer; *Black Moon* .... (VIC)
Isley Brothers; *Complete UA Sessions* .... (EMI)
Kentucky Colonels feat. Clarence White; *Kentucky Colonels feat. Clarence White* .... (ROU)
Ice
Sarah McLachlan; *Fumbling Towards Ecstasy* .... (ARI)
Icehouse
Icehouse; *Icehouse* .... (CHR)
Icicle
Tori Amos; *Under The Pink* .... (ATL)
Last Snow Leopard
Spencer Brewer; *Emerald* .... (NAR)
Listen, The Snow Is Falling
Yoko Ono Band; *45* .... (CAP)
Little Bit Of Snow
Howard Jones; *One To One* .... (ELE)
Love In The Ice Age
Pat Benatar; *Tropico* .... (CHR)
November In The Snow/Lord Buckley
Mark Murphy; *Kerouac Then & Now* .... (MUS)
October & The Frost Is Early
Dusing Singers; *Cool Of The Day-Music Of Jean Ritchie* .... (GHY)
On A Snowy Christmas Night
Elvis Presley; *Sings The Wonderful World Of Christmas* ....(RCA)
On Top Of Old Smokey
Bing Crosby; *Radio Years-#3* .... (CRS)
Weavers; *Best Of* .... (MCA)
Greatest Hits .... (VAN)
Reunion At Carnegie Hall-1963-#2 .... (VAN)
Out Of The Snow
Amazing Rhythm Aces; *Too Stuffed To Jump* .. (MCA)

Pearls In The Snow
Michael Martin Murphey; *Cowboy Christmas* ..... (WB)
Ring Of Ice
Jennifer Rush; *Jennifer Rush* .... (EPI)
Roses In The Snow
Emmylou Harris; *Roses In The Snow* .... (WB)
Running On Ice
Billy Joel; *The Bridge* ....(COL)
Sand Castles In The Snow
Public Image, Ltd.; *9* .... (VIA)
September Snow
Danny Heines; *Aqua Touch* .... (SW)
Six Feet Of Snow
Little Feat; *Down On The Farm* .... (WB)
Skating On Thin Ice
Tower Of Power; *Bump City* .... (WB)
Snow In San Anselmo
Van Morrison; *Hard Nose The Highway* .... (WB)
Snowbird
Anne Murray; *15 Of The Best* .... (LIB)
Country ....(CAP)
Greatest Hits ....(CAP)
Snowbird ....(CAP)
Elvis Presley; *Canadian Tribute* .... (RCA)
I'm 10,000 Years Old .... (RCA)
Loretta Lynn; *Coal Miner's Daughter* .... (MCA)
Snowblind
Black Sabbath; *Volume 4* .... (WB)
We Sold Our Soul For Rock 'N' Roll .... (WB)
Ozzy Osbourne; *Speak Of The Devil* ....(JET)
Styx; *Caught In The Act* ....(A&M)
Paradise Theater ....(A&M)
Snowblind Friend
David Allan Coe; *Unchained* ....(COL)
Hoyt Axton; *Snowblind Friend* .... (MCA)
Steppenwolf; *16 Greatest Hits* .... (MCA)
7 .... (MCA)
Snowbound
Genesis; *And Then There Were Three* .... (ATL)
Soul On Ice
Graham Parker/Rumour; *Stick To Me* .... (MER)
Summer Snow
Blue Magic; *Magic Of The Blue-Greatest Hits* .... (CLT)
Lou Christie; *Enlightnin'ment-Best Of* .... (RHI)
Thin Ice
Daryl Hall & John Oates; *H2O* .... (RCA)
Ozark Mountain Daredevils; *Car Over The Lake
Album* ....(A&M)
Pink Floyd; *Shine On-Box Set* ....(COL)
The Wall ....(COL)
Robin Trower & Jack Bruce; *Truce* .... (CHR)
Roger Waters; *The Wall-Live In Berlin* .... (MER)
Till It Snows In Mexico
Reba McEntire; *What Am I Gonna Do About
You* .... (MCA)
Under Ice
Kate Bush; *Hounds Of Love* .... (EMI)
Whales & Snow
Deep Jimi/Zep Creams; *Funky Dinosaur* ....(EW)
When The Rain Turns To Snow
Lee Greenwood; *Christmas To Christmas* .... (MSP)
When The Snow Is On The Roses
Ed Ames; *Best Of* .... (RCA)
Pure Gold ....(RCA)
Sonny James; *American Originals* .... (COL)
Greatest Hits ....(COL)

SPACE, Astronauts, Cosmos, Rockets, Satellites, Universe

*See Also: ASTROLOGY, EARTH, MOON, STARS,
SUN, UFO'S*

2001: A Space Odyssey Theme
Boston Pops Orchestra/John Williams; *Pops Out Of This
World* ....(PHI)
Neil Norman; *Greatest Science Fiction Hits* .... (CRS)
Original Soundtrack; *2001: A Space Odyssey
Theme* ....(MGM)

Across The Universe
Beatles; *1967-1970* ....(CAP)
Let It Be ....(CAP)
Past Masters-#2 ....(CAP)
Rarities ....(CAP)
David Bowie; *Young Americans* ....(RYK)
Alien Nation
Scorpions; *Face The Heat* .... (MER)
All The Love Of The Universe
Santana; *Caravanserai* ....(COL)
Another Satellite
XTC; *Rag & Bone Buffet* ....(GEF)
Skylarking ....(GEF)
Apollo 9
Adam Ant; *Antics In The Forbidden Zone* .... (EPI)
Apollo XI
Orchestral Manoeuvres In The Dark; *Sugar Tax* . (VIA)
Astral Traveller
Yes; *Time & A Word* ....(ATL)
Yesterdays ....(ATL)
Astral Weeks
Van Morrison; *Astral Weeks* .... (WB)
Astronomy
Blue Oyster Cult; *Imaginos* ....(COL)
Secret Treaties ....(COL)
Some Enchanted Evening ....(COL)
Astronomy Domine
Pink Floyd; *Nice Pair* ....(CAP)
Piper At The Gates Of Dawn ....(CAP)
Umma Gumma ....(CAP)
"Battlestar Galactica" Theme
Boston Pops Orchestra/John Williams; *Out Of This
World* ....(PHI)
Beyond The Universe
Rick Derringer; *Derringer* .... (BS)
Blues For Space Travellers
Victor Feldman; *Jazz Club Vibraphone* ....(VRV)
Buck Rogers In The 25th Century
Neil Norman/Cosmic Orchestra; *Greatest Science Fiction
Hits-#2* .... (CRS)
Cosmic Charlie
Grateful Dead; *Aoxomoxoa* ....(WB)
What A Long Strange Trip It's Been ....(WB)
Cosmic Cowboy
Michael Murphey; *Cosmic Cowboy Souvenir* .... (A&M)
Nitty Gritty Dirt Band; *Dirt Silver & Gold* .... (UA)
Stars & Stripes Forever ....(UA)
Defying Gravity
Emmylou Harris; *Quarter Moon In A Ten Cent
Town* ....(WB)
Jesse Winchester; *Best Of* ....(RHI)
Jimmy Buffett; *Havana Daydreamin'* ....(MCA)
Echoes
Gene Clark; *Nuggets-#11-Pop-#4* .... (RHI)
New Riders Of The Purple Sage; *Marin County
Line* .... (MCA)
Pink Floyd; *Meddle* .... (HAR)
Final Countdown
Europe; *Final Countdown* .... (EPI)
Heart Of Rock ....(COL)
Golden Rocket
Hank Snow; *All About Trains* ....(RCA)
Best Of ....(RCA)
Willie Nelson & Hank Snow; *Brand On My
Heart* ....(COL)
"Lost In Space" Theme
Neil Norman; *Greatest Science Fiction Hits-#3* ... (CRS)
Major Tom (Coming Home)
Peter Schilling; *Different Story (World Of Lust &
Crime)* ....(ELE)
Error In The The System ....(ELE)
Man On The Moon
R.E.M.; *Automatic For The People* .... (WB)
Motel Satellite
Wellsprings Of Hope; *Phonograph* ....(SAF)
Mr. Spaceman
Byrds; *Byrds* ....(COL)
Greatest Hits ....(COL)
Original Singles-#1-1965-1967 ....(COL)
(Untitled) ....(COL)
New Satellite Blues
Little Brother Montgomery; *South Side
Blues/Chicago-Living Legends* ....(RVR)

Princes Of The Universe
  Queen; *A Kind Of Magic* ....(HOL)
Ride My See Saw
  Moody Blues; *Caught Live Plus Five* ....(POL)
    In Search Of The Lost Chord ....(POL)
    This Is The ....(POL)
Rocket
  Def Leppard; *Hysteria* ....(MER)
  Smashing Pumpkins; *Siamese Dream* ....(VIA)
Rocket 2 U
  Jets; *Magic* ....(MCA)
Rocket Countdown (Blastoff)
  Brothers Johnson; *Blam!* ....(A&M)
Rocket Fuel
  Alvin Lee; *Rocket Fuel* ....(RSO)
Rocket In My Pocket
  Little Feat; *Hoy-Hoy!* ....(WB)
    Time Loves A Hero ....(WB)
    Waiting For Columbus ....(WB)
Rocket Man
  Elton John; *Greatest Hits* ....(POL)
    Here & There ....(POL)
    Honky Chateau ....(POL)
  Kate Bush; *Two Rooms-Songs Of E. John & B.
  Taupin* ....(POL)
Rocket O' Love
  Knack; *Serious Fun* ....(CHS)
Rocket Ride
  Kiss; *Alive II* ....(CAS)
Rocket To God
  Daryl Hall & John Oates; *Ooh Yeah!* .... (ARI)
Rockit Man
  J.T.; *Kick The Funk* ....(EW)
Santa And The Satellite
  Dickie Goodman; *Dr. Demento's Greatest-#6* .... (RHI)
Satellite
  Def Leppard; *On Through The Night* .... (MER)
  Depeche Mode; *Broken Frame* ....(SIR)
  Echo/Bunnymen; *Echo/Bunnymen* ....(SIR)
  Elton John; *Ice On Fire* ....(MCA)
  Elvis Costello; *Spike* ....(WB)
  Gang Of Four; *Mall* ....(POL)
  Hooters; *One Way Home* ....(COL)
  John Coltrane; *Coltrane's Sound* ....(ATL)
  Sex Pistols; *Live At Chelmsford Top Security
  Prison* .... (RES)
  War Babies; *War Babies* ....(COL)
Satellite Beach
  Peter Case; *Peter Case* ....(GEF)
Satellite Of Love
  Lou Reed; *Between Thought &
  Expression-Anthology* ....(RCA)
    City Lights .... (ARI)
    Live ....(RCA)
    Transformer ....(RCA)
    Walk On The Wild Side-Best Of ....(RCA)
Satellites
  Rhythm Corps; *Future's Not What It Used To Be* . (PSH)
Set The Controls For The Heart Of The...
  Pink Floyd; *Nice Pair* ....(CAP)
    Saucerful Of Secrets ....(CAP)
    Ummagumma ....(CAP)
    Works ....(CAP)
Sleeping Satellite
  Tasmin Archer; *Great Expectations* .... (SBK)
Space Baby
  Tubes; *Tubes* ....(A&M)
Space Captain
  Barbra Streisand; *Barbra Joan Streisand* ....(COL)
  Joe Cocker; *Mad Dogs & Englishmen* ....(A&M)
Space Child
  Spirit; *12 Dreams Of Dr. Sardonicus* ....(EPI)
  UFO; *Phenomenon* ....(CHR)
Space Cowboy
  Steve Miller Band; *Anthology* ....(CAP)
    Best Of-1968-1973 ....(CAP)
Space Dog
  Tori Amos; *Under The Pink* ....(ATL)
Space Invader
  Pretenders; *Pretenders* ....(SIR)
Space Junk
  Devo; *EZ Listening Disc* ....(RYK)
    Q: Are We Not Men? A: We Are Devo! ....(WB)

Space Monkey
  Patti Smith Group; *Easter* ....(ARI)
Space Oddity
  David Bowie; *Changesbowie* ....(RYK)
    Scary Monsters ....(RYK)
    Space Oddity ....(RYK)
    ST/Ziggy Stardust-The Motion Picture ....(RCA)
    The Singles-1969-1993 ....(RYK)
Space Patrol
  Country Joe McDonald; *Classics* ....(FAN)
    Rock & Roll From Planet Earth ....(FAN)
Space Race
  Billy Preston; *Best Of* ....(A&M)
Space Safari
  Nazareth; *Rampant* ....(A&M)
Space Song
  Stomu Yamashta/Go; *Live From Paris* .... (ISL)
    Stomu Yamashta/Go .... (ISL)
Space Station #5
  Montrose; *Montrose* ....(WB)
Space Truckin'
  Deep Purple; *Deepest Purple-Very Best Of* .... (WB)
    Machine Head ....(WB)
    Made In Japan ....(WB)
    When We Rock We Rock-When We Roll... .... (WB)
Spaceman
  Harry Nilsson; *Songwriter* ....(RCA)
  Journey; *In The Beginning* ....(COL)
    Next ....(COL)
  Nilsson; *Son Of Schmilsson* ....(RCA)
"Star Trek" Theme
  Cincinnati Pops Orchestra/Erich Kunzel; *Star Tracks
  II* .... (TLR)
Starship
  MC5; *Elektrock-'60s* .... (ELE)
  Paul Kantner/Jefferson Starship; *Blows Against The
  Empire* ....(RCA)
Starship Trooper
  Yes; *Classic Yes* ....(ATL)
    Yes Album ....(ATL)
    Yessongs ....(ATL)
Supersonic Rocket Ship
  Kinks; *Everybody's In Show Biz* .... (RHI)
Theme From "Flash Gordon"
  Neil Norman; *Greatest Science Fiction Hits-#3* ... (CRS)
Theme From "The Jetsons"
  Stunners; *ST/Jetsons-The Movie* .... (MCA)
Twilight Zone
  Golden Earring; *Cut* .... (21)
    Something Heavy Going Down .... (21)
  Iron Maiden; *Killers* ....(CAP)
  Manhattan Transfer; *Anthology-Down In Birdland* (RHI)
    Best Of ....(ATL)
    Extensions ....(ATL)
  Neil Norman/Cosmic Orchestra; *Elvira Presents Haunted
  Hits* .... (RHI)
    Halloween Hits .... (RHI)
Two Thousand Light Years From Home
  Rolling Stones; *More Hot Rocks-Big Hits & Fazed
  Cookies* .... (AKO)
    Singles Collection-London Years .... (AKO)
    Their Satanic Majesties Request .... (AKO)
    Through The Past Darkly-Big Hits #2 .... (AKO)
Walking In Space
  Original Cast; *ST/Hair* ....(RCA)
  Quincy Jones; *I Heard That!* ....(A&M)
    ST/Listen Up-Lives Of Quincy Jones .... (QUE)
    Walking In Space ....(A&M)

SPIRITS, Ghosts, Ghouls, Goblins, Witches
  See Also: ANGELS, DEVILS, MAGIC, UFO'S

Bewitched
  Anita O'Day; *Sings The Most* ....(VRV)
  Barbra Streisand; *Third Album* ....(COL)
  Original Cast; *Pal Joey* ....(COL)
"Bewitched" Theme
  Original Music; *Television's Greatest Hits-#2* ..... (TVT)
Big Joe & Phantom 309
  Tom Waits; *Double Live* ....(ASY)
    Nighthawks At The Diner ....(ASY)

Broomstick Cowboy
Bobby Goldsboro; *10th Anniversary Album-#1* .... (UA)
Honey-Best Of .... (EMI)
Ding Dong The Witch Is Dead
Fifth Estate; *Dick Bartley's One-Hit*
Wonders-'60s-#2 .... (RHI)
Meco; *Wizard Of Oz* .... (MIL)
MGM Studio Orchestra; *ST/Wizard Of Oz* .... (SSP)
Ghost
Fleetwood Mac; *Bare Trees* .... (RPR)
Ghost Dance
Patti Smith; *Easter* .... (ARI)
Ghost In This House
Shenandoah; *Extra Mile* .... (COL)
Ghost Lover
Ian & Sylvia; *Greatest Hits* .... (VAN)
Northern Journey .... (VAN)
Ghost Of A Chance
Rush; *Roll The Bones* .... (ATL)
Ghost Of A Chance With You
Billie Holiday; *Stormy Blues* .... (VRV)
#2 .... (EVR)
Mel Torme; *Smooth As Velvet* .... (PIC)
Ghost Of A Texas Ladies' Man
Concrete Blonde; *Walking In London* .... (IRS)
Ghost Of Flight 401
Bob Welch; *Three Hearts* .... (OOP)
Ghost Train
Counting Crows; *August And Everything After* .. (DGC)
Ghost Writer
Garland Jeffreys; *Ghost Writer* .... (A&M)
Ghostbusters
Ray Parker, Jr.; *Chartbusters* .... (ARI)
Elvira Presents Haunted Hits .... (RHI)
Greatest Movie Rock Hits .... (RHI)
ST/Ghostbusters .... (ARI)
Ghosts
Dan Fogelberg; *Innocent Age* .... (FM)
(Ghost) Riders In The Sky
Gene Autry; *50th Anniversary* .... (REP)
Cowboy Hall Of Fame .... (REP)
Outlaws; *Ghost Riders* .... (ARI)
Roy Clark; *Greatest Hits-#1* .... (MCA)
In Concert .... (MCA)
Superpicker .... (MCA)
Vaughn Monroe; *Best Of* .... (RCA)
This Is .... (RCA)
This Is/Decade Of The '40s .... (RCA)
Grey Ghost
Henry Paul Band; *Grey Ghost* .... (ATL)
Jean Genie
David Bowie; *Aladdin Sane* .... (RYK)
Changesbowie .... (RYK)
Live .... (RYK)
The Singles-1969-1993 .... (RYK)
Phantom Of The Opera
Iron Maiden; *Iron Maiden* .... (CAP)
Live After Death (World Slavery Tour) .... (CAP)
Original London Cast; *Phantom Of The Opera* ... (POL)
Purple People Eater Meets The Witch Doc.
Big Bopper; *Hellooo Baby! Best Of-1954-1959* .. (RHI)
Rhiannon
Fleetwood Mac; *25 Years-The Chain* .... (WB)
Fleetwood Mac .... (RPR)
Greatest Hits .... (WB)
Live .... (WB)
Waylon Jennings; *Best Of* .... (RCA)
Rock 'N' Roll Ghost
Replacements; *Don't Tell A Soul* .... (SIR)
Season Of The Witch
Donovan; *American Graffiti-#4* .... (MCA)
Greatest Hits .... (EPI)
Sunshine Superman .... (EPI)
Troubadour-Definitive Collection .... (EPI)
Vanilla Fudge; *Best Of* .... (ATC)
Spirit
Doobie Brothers; *What Were Once Vices Are Now*
Habits .... (WB)
Earth, Wind & Fire; *Eternal Dance* .... (COL)
Spirit .... (COL)
Moody Blues; *Other Side Of Life* .... (POL)
Spirit; *Introduce Yourself* .... (SLS)
Van Morrison; *Common One* .... (WB)

Spirit In The Dark
Aretha Franklin; *30 Greatest Hits* .... (ATL)
Live At Fillmore West .... (ATL)
Spirit In The Dark .... (ATL)
Spirit In The Night
Bruce Springsteen; *Greetings From Asbury Park* ..(COL)
Bruce Springsteen/E Street Band;
Live-1975-1985 .... (COL)
Manfred Mann's Earth Band; *Nightingales &*
Bombers .... (WB)
Roaring Silence .... (WB)
Spirit In The Sky
Kentucky HeadHunters; *Electric Barnyard* ...... (MER)
Norman Greenbaum; *Billboard Top Rock 'N' Roll*
Hits-1970 .... (RHI)
Super Hits/'80s-Have A Nice Day-#2 .... (RHI)
Spirit Of Radio
Rush; *Chronicles* .... (MER)
Exit...Stage Left .... (MER)
Permanent Waves .... (MER)
Spirit Slips Away
Thin Lizzy; *Fighting* .... (MER)
Spirits In The Material World
Police; *Every Breath You Take-The Singles* ...... (A&M)
Ghost In The Machine .... (A&M)
Spirits Of Ancient Egypt
Paul McCartney/Wings; *Wings Over America* .... (CAP)
Wings; *Venus & Mars* .... (CAP)
Spirits Of St. Louis
Johnny Paycheck; *Take This Job & Shove It* ...... (EPI)
Spirits (Having Flown)
Bee Gees; *Greatest* .... (POL)
Spirits .... (POL)
Superman's Ghost
Don McLean; *Greatest Hits Then & Now* .... (EMI)
Walking The Ghost
James; *Gold Mother* .... (FON)
James .... (FON)
Waltzing Matilda
Burl Ives; *Best Of* .... (MCA)
Fred Astaire; *Three Evenings With* .... (DRG)
James Galway; *Pachebel Canon & Other*
Favorites .... (RCA)
When The Spell Is Broken
Richard Thompson; *Across A Crowded Room* .... (POL)
Watching The Dark-History Of .... (RYK)
Witch Doctor
Chipmunks; *Rockin' Through The Decades* .... (EMI)
David Seville; *Dr. Demento 20th Anniversary*
Collection .... (RHI)
Wacky Weirdos .... (KT)
Witch Wolf
Styx; *Best Of* .... (RCA)
Serpent .... (RCA)
Witchcraft
Elvis Presley; *Collector's Gold* .... (RCA)
Golden Records-#4 .... (RCA)
Return Of The Rocker .... (RCA)
Frank Sinatra; *A Man & His Music* .... (RPR)
Capitol Years .... (CAP)
Man & His Music .... (RPR)
Sinatra's Sinatra .... (RPR)
Frank Sinatra & Anita Baker; *Frank Sinatra*
Duets .... (CAP)
Witches Promise
Jethro Tull; *Original Masters* .... (CHR)
Witches' Song
Marianne Faithfull; *Broken English* .... (ISL)
Witchy Woman
Eagles; *Eagles* .... (ASY)
Their Greatest Hits 1971-1975 .... (ASY)

SPORTS, Basketball, Boxing, Horse Racing, Olympics

See Also: BASEBALL, COWBOYS, FOOTBALL, RODEO, SURFING, SWIMMING, WINNING

"ABC's Wide World Of Sports" Theme
Original Music; *Television's Greatest Hits-#2* .....(TVT)
Anyone For Tennis
Cream; *Eric Clapton-Crossroads* .... (POL)
Strange Brew-Very Best Of Cream .... (POL)

Baron, The
Johnny Cash; *Biggest Hits* ....(COL)
  Columbia Records-1958-1986 ....(COL)
  Greatest Country Hits/'80s-1981 ....(COL)
Basketball
Greyson & Jasun; *Sweatin' Me Wet* .... (ATL)
Kurtis Blow; *Ego Trip* .... (MER)
Basketball Jones
Cheech & Chong; *Los Cochinos* ....(WB)
Bicycle Race
Queen; *Greatest Hits* .... (HOL)
  Jazz .... (HOL)
  Live Killers .... (HOL)
Bicyclettes De Belsize
Engelbert Humperdinck; *Engelbert* .... (PRT)
  Greatest Hits .... (PRT)
  Live In Concert/All Of Me .... (EPI)
Bobby Orr Breakaway
Kirk Elliott; *No Fixed Address* .... (BOO)
Boxer, The
Simon & Garfunkel; *Bridge Over Troubled Water* (COL)
  Collected Works ....(COL)
  Concert In Central Park .... (WB)
  Greatest Hits ....(COL)
Brand New Key
Melanie; *Best Of* .... (RHI)
  Super Hits/'70s-Have A Nice Day-#7 .... (RHI)
Brunswick Bowling Spot
Frankie Valli/Four Seasons; *Rarities-#1* .... (RHI)
Camptown Races
Marilyn Horne; *Beautiful Dreamer* ....(LON)
Mormon Tabernacle Choir; *Songs Of The Civil War & S.*
  Foster Fav. .... (SMC)
Pete Seeger; *American Favorite Ballads-#3* ...... (FLW)
Day We Lost The America's Cup
Tom Paxton; *One Million Lawyers & Other*
  Disasters .... (FF)
El Matador
Kingston Trio; *Capitol Collectors Series* .... (CAP)
  Sold Out/String Along ....(CAP)
Football Fugue
Pete Townshend; *Another Scoop* ....(ATC)
Game Seven
Chuck Brown/Soul Searchers; *12"* .... (SRC)
  Bustin' Loose .... (SRC)
Give It All You Got (1980 W. Olympics)
Chuck Mangione; *Best Of* .... (A&M)
  Classics-#6 .... (A&M)
  Fun & Games .... (A&M)
Going To The Racetrack
Etta Baker; *One-Dime Blues* .... (ROU)
Goin' To Dallas To See My Pony Run
Lightnin' Hopkins; *Blues In My Bottle* .... (BV)
  Drinkin' In The Blues-Golden Classics-#1 .... (CLT)
Golf Girl
Caravan; *Best Of* ....(LON)
  In The Land Of Grey & Pink ....(LON)
  London Collector ....(LON)
Golfin' Blues
Loudon Wainwright III; *Final Exam* .... (ARI)
Hand Me Down My Jogging Shoes
Shaw Brothers; *Best Of* .... (FOL)
  Collection .... (FOL)
Hit Me With Your Best Shot
Pat Benatar; *Crimes Of Passion* .... (CHR)
  Live From Earth .... (CHR)
Hockey
Jane Siberry; *Bound By The Beauty* .... (WB)
Hockey Song
Stompin' Tom Connors; *Hockey Song* .... (BOO)
Hockey Song, The
Tom Connors; *The Hockey Zone* .... (SPO)
Hometown Hero
Zamboni Brothers; *The Hockey Zone* .... (SPO)
Hurricane (Carter)
Bob Dylan; *Desire* ....(COL)
I Never Play Basketball Now
Prefab Sprout; *Swoon* .... (EPI)
I'll Tumble 4 Ya
Culture Club; *Kissing To Be Clever* .... (VIA)
I've Got The Horse Right Here
Original Cast; *Guys & Dolls* .... (MCA)
Joggers
Jerry Clower; *Starke Raving* ....(MCA)

Joggin'
Patsy; *Patsy* .... (RPR)
Ray Stevens; *He Thinks He's Ray Stevens* .... (MCA)
Joggin' Song
Barley Bree; *Castles In The Air* ....(THA)
Joystick
Dazz Band; *Greatest Hits* .... (MOT)
  Joystick .... (MOT)
Kansas Wildcats
Band Of H.M. Royal Marines; *Hands Across The*
  Sea-Sousa Marches .... (ANG)
Eastman Wind Ensemble; *Sousa On Review* .... (MER)
  Stars & Stripes Forever .... (MER)
Keepers Of the Flame
Zamboni Brothers; *The Hockey Zone* .... (SPO)
Lonely Bull
Herb Alpert/Tijuana Brass; *Classics-#1* .... (A&M)
  Four-Sider .... (A&M)
  Greatest Hits .... (A&M)
  Lonely Bull .... (A&M)
Lord Stanley's Cup
Zamboni Brothers; *The Hockey Zone* .... (SPO)
Love Is A Contact Sport
Whitney Houston; *Whitney* .... (ARI)
Love TKO
Teddy Pendergrass; *TP* .... (PI)
Main Event/Fight
Barbra Streisand; *Greatest Hits...& More* ....(COL)
  ST/Main Event/Fight ....(COL)
Mama Said Knock You Out
L.L. Cool J; *Mama Said Knock You Out* .... (DFJ)
Matador
Sylvia; *Drifter* ....(RCA)
Muscles
Diana Ross; *Endless Love* ....(RCA)
  Silk Electric ....(RCA)
  Why Do Fools Fall In Love ....(RCA)
My Daddy Was A Jockey
John Lee Hooker; *Detroit Blues-1950-1951* ......(CLT)
  Gotham Golden Classics ....(CLT)
Ode To A Gym Teacher
Meg Christian; *I Know You Know* ....(OLI)
  Scrapbook ....(OLI)
Olympia
Sergio Mendes; *Olympia* ....(A&M)
Olympian-Lighting Of The Torch
Philip Glass; *Official Music Of The XXIIIrd*
  Olympiad ....(COL)
Olympic Fanfare & Theme
Felix Slatkin Concert Band; *U.S.A.* .... (ANG)
John Williams; *Official Music Of The XXIIIrd*
  Olympiad ....(COL)
Olympic Joy
Kashif; *1988 Summer Olympics-One Moment In*
  Time .... (ARI)
Olympic Spirit
John Williams; *1988 Summer Olympics-One Moment In*
  Time .... (ARI)
Olympics
Mannheim Steamroller; *Fresh Aire VI* .... (AG)
One Hit (To The Body)
Rolling Stones; *Dirty Work* .... (RS)
One Moment In Time
Whitney Houston; *1984 Olympics Album* .... (ARI)
One On One
Daryl Hall & John Oates; *H20* ....(RCA)
  Live At The Apollo ....(RCA)
  Rock 'N Soul Pt. 1-Greatest Hits ....(RCA)
  Soulful Sounds ....(RCA)
Physical
Olivia Newton-John; *Back To Basics-Essential*
  Collection ....(GEF)
  Greatest Hits-#2 .... (MCA)
  Physical .... (MCA)
Possessed To Skate
Suicidal Tendencies; *Join The Army* ....(CRL)
Question Of Sport
Martin Carthy & Dave Swarbrick; *Life & Limb* ..(GRE)
Race Is On
Dave Edmunds; *Best Of* .... (SS)
  Twangin' .... (SS)
George Jones; *All-Time Greatest Hits-#1* .... (EPI)
  Best Of-1955-1967 .... (RHI)
  Billboard Top Country Hits-1964 .... (RHI)

Sawyer Brown; *Boys Are Back* .... (CCB)
   Greatest Hits .... (CCB)
Race The K-12
   Rupert Hine; *ST/Better Off Dead* .... (A&M)
Race To Win
   Blitzspeer; *Live* .... (EPI)
Race With The Devil
   Gene Vincent; *Capitol Collectors Series* .... (CAP)
   Gene Vincent/Blue Caps; *Legends Of Rock*
   Guitar-'50s-#1 .... (RHI)
Race You To The Top Of The Morning
   Original Broadway Cast; *Secret Garden* .... (COL)
Racehorse
   Count Basie/Kansas City 3; *For The Second Time* (PAB)
Racetrack
   Bad Company; *Rough Diamonds* .... (SS)
Racetrack Blues
   Lightnin' Hopkins; *Gold Star Sessions-#1* .... (ARH)
   Nashville Jug Band; *Nashville Jug Band* .... (ROU)
Roller Derby Queen
   Jim Croce; *Life & Times* ....(OOP)
   Photographs & Memories-His Greatest Hits .... (21)
Roller Skating Child
   Beach Boys; *Love You* ....(CAR)
   Ten Years In Harmony ....(CAR)
Roller Skatin' Mate
   Peaches & Herb; *Twice The Fire* .... (POL)
Run For The Roses
   Dan Fogelberg; *Greatest Hits* .... (FM)
   Innocent Age .... (FM)
   Live-Greetings From The West .... (FM)
Runner
   Manfred Mann's Earth Band; *Somewhere In*
   Afrika .... (ARI)
Sagebrush Sports Report
   Riders In The Sky; *Riders Radio Theater* .... (MCA)
Score, The
   Emerson, Lake & Powell; *Emerson, Lake &*
   Powell .... (POL)
Shadow Boxer
   Angel City; *Face To Face* .... (EPI)
Shadow Boxing
   Giles Reaves & Jon Goin; *Letting Go* .... (MCA)
   Teena Marie; *Robbery* .... (EPI)
Shake It Up
   Zamboni Brothers; *The Hockey Zone* .... (SPO)
Silver Medals & Sweet Memories
   Statler Brothers; *Best Of-Rides Again-#2* .... (MER)
   Short Stories .... (MER)
Skate To The Rhythm
   High Inergy; *Frenzie* .... (GOR)
Skateaway
   Dire Straits; *Making Movies* .... (WB)
Skateboard
   Jefferson Starship; *Earth* .... (GRU)
Skateboard Surfin' U.S.A.
   Jan Berry; *45* .... (A&M)
Skatetown U.S.A.
   Dave Mason; *Skatetown U.S.A.* .... (COL)
Skating Away On The Thin Ice...
   Jethro Tull; *Bursting Out* .... (CHR)
   Original Masters .... (CHR)
   War Child .... (CHR)
   "M.U."-Best Of .... (CHR)
Skating On Thin Ice
   Tower Of Power; *Bump City* .... (WB)
Spirit Of America (race car)
   Beach Boys; *Gift Set* .... (CAP)
   Little Deuce Coupe/All Summer Long ....(CAP)
   Spirit Of America ....(CAP)
Sports Fans
   Tubes; *45* .... (CAP)
Still In The Game
   Steve Winwood; *Talking Back To The Night* ...... (ISL)
Take The Skinheads Bowling
   Camper Van Beethoven; *Telephone Free Landslide*
   Victory .... (IRS)
Teen Archer
   Blue Oyster Cult; *Tyranny & Mutation* .... (COL)
Tennis Anyone
   Today; *New Formula* .... (MOT)
Tennis Shoes
   Jimmy C. Newman; *Alligator Man* .... (ROU)

Tennis Song
   Original Broadway Cast; *City of Angels* .... (COL)
   Original London Cast; *City Of Angels* .... (RCA)
Theme From Jack Johnson
   Miles Davis; *Agharta* .... (COL)
T.K.O. (Boxing Day)
   Elvis Costello/Attractions; *Punch The Clock* ..... (COL)
Up, Up & Away
   5th Dimension; *Anthology-1967-1973* .... (RHI)
   Greatest Hits On Earth .... (ARI)
We Can Have The Olympics...At Our House
   Tom Paxton; *One Million Lawyers & Other*
   Disasters .... (FF)
Wet My Whistle
   Midnight Star; *Greatest Hits* .... (SLR)
   No Parking On The Dance Floor .... (SLR)
Wide World Of Sports
   Instant Funk; *Instant Funk* .... (SSL)
Work That Body
   Diana Ross; *45* ....(RCA)
   Why Do Fools Fall In Love ....(RCA)
Ya Got Trouble
   Original Broadway Cast; *Music Man* .... (ANG)
   Robert Preston/Original Cast; *Music Man* ....(CAP)
You Can't Roller Skate In A Buffalo Herd
   Roger Miller; *Best Of-#2-King Of The Road* .... (MER)
   Golden Hits .... (SMA)
Y.M.C.A.
   Village People; *Billboard Top Dance Hits-1978* .. (RHI)
   Billboard Top Rock 'N' Roll Hits-1979 .... (RHI)
   Cruisin' .... (CAS)
   Greatest Hits .... (RHI)
   Live & Sleazy .... (CAS)
   Night At Studio 54 .... (CAS)
Zamboni
   Martin Zellar; *The Hockey Zone* .... (SPO)

STARS, Planets

   See Also: ASTROLOGY, EARTH, MOON,
   SPACE, SUN, UFO's

53 Miles West Of Venus
   B-52's; *Wild Planet* .... (WB)
Across The Universe
   Beatles; *1967-1970* ....(CAP)
   Let It Be ....(CAP)
   Past Masters-#2 ....(CAP)
   Rarities ....(CAP)
   David Bowie; *Young Americans* ....(RYK)
All The Love Of The Universe
   Santana; *Caravanserai* ....(COL)
Another Planet
   Alien Sex Fiend; *Another Planet* ....(CRL)
Another Star
   Stevie Wonder; *Songs In The Key Of Life* .... (MOT)
Astronomy
   Blue Oyster Cult; *Imaginos* ....(COL)
   Secret Treaties ....(COL)
   Some Enchanted Evening ....(COL)
Astronomy Domine
   Pink Floyd; *Nice Pair* ....(CAP)
   Piper At The Gates Of Dawn ....(CAP)
   Umma Gumma ....(CAP)
Attack Of The Radioactive Hamsters
   Weird Al Yankovic; *ST/UHF* ....(RAR)
Black Hole Sun
   Soundgarden; *Superunknown* .... (A&M)
Blow Out The Stars, Turn Off The Moon
   Nitty Gritty Dirt Band; *Rest Of The Dream* ..... (MCA)
Blue Star
   Blue Notes; *Early Years* .... (CLT)
   Charlie Daniels Band; *Million Mile Reflections* .... (EPI)
   Mystics; *16 Golden Classics* .... (CLT)
Carolina Star
   E. Scruggs & R. Dillard; *Top Of The World* ......(COL)
Catch A Falling Star
   Perry Como; *All-Time Greatest Hits-#1* ....(RCA)
   Golden Records ....(RCA)
   Nipper's Greatest Hits/'50s-#1 ....(RCA)
   Pure Gold ....(RCA)
   This Is ....(RCA)

Catch A Star
Men At Work; *Business As Usual* ....(COL)
Cats Under The Stars
Jerry Garcia; *Cats Under The Stars* .... (ARI)
Count Every Star
Grant Green; *Born To Be Blue* ....(BLN)
Counting The Stars
Ladders; *Doo-Wop Era-Harlem N.Y.-40 Hits* ..... (CLT)
   Harlem Holiday-New York R&B-#1 ....(CLT)
Dark Star
Crosby, Stills & Nash; *Allies* ....(ATL)
   CSN ....(ATL)
Grateful Dead; *Best Of/What A Long Strange Trip*
   It's... ....(WB)
   Live/Dead ....(WB)
Diamonds In The Stars
Ray Price; *Greatest Hits-#3* ....(SO)
Don't Let The Stars Get In Your Eyes
Perry Como; *All-Time Greatest Hits-#1* ....(RCA)
   Golden Records ....(RCA)
   Pure Gold ....(RCA)
   This Is ....(RCA)
Evening Star
Gene Loves Jezebel; *Kiss Of Life* ....(GEF)
Judas Priest; *Hell Bent For Leather* ....(COL)
Kenny Rogers; *Eyes That See In The Dark* ......(RCA)
Falling Star
Karla Bonoff; *Karla Bonoff* ....(COL)
Robin Trower; *In City Dreams* ....(CHR)
Fear Of A Black Planet
Public Enemy; *Fear Of A Black Planet* ....(DFC)
Five Planets In Leo
Brew Moore Quintet; *Brew Moore Quintet* ....(FAN)
Going To Mars
Little Ray Rapper; *Get That Future Funk* ....(FIR)
Good Morning Starshine
Oliver; *45* ....(UA)
Original Broadway Cast; *Hair* ....(RCA)
Have You Seen The Stars Tonight
Jefferson Airplane; *Flight Log* .... (GRU)
Paul Kantner/Jefferson Starship; *Blows Against The*
   Empire ....(RCA)
Highway Star
Deep Purple; *Deepest Purple* .... (WB)
   Machine Head .... (WB)
   Made In Japan .... (WB)
   When We Rock We Rock-When We Roll... ....(WB)
Honeymoon On Mars
Be Bop Deluxe; *Modern Music* ....(CAP)
Impossible Dream
Andy Williams; *16 Most Requested Songs* ....(COL)
   Greatest Hits-#2 ....(COL)
   Impossible Dream ....(COL)
Ed Ames; *Best Of* ....(RCA)
   Impossible Dream ....(RCA)
   Pure Gold ....(RCA)
   This Is ....(RCA)
Jack Jones; *Best Of* ....(MCA)
Kate Smith; *Best Of* ....(RCA)
   Legendary Performer ....(RCA)
Luther Vandross; *Songs* .... (EPI)
Original Cast; *Man Of La Mancha* ....(MCA)
Original London Cast; *Man Of La Mancha* .....(MCA)
Robert Goulet; *Greatest Hits* ....(COL)
Is It A Star
Daryl Hall & John Oates; *War Babies* .... (ATL)
It Was Written In The Stars
Ella Fitzgerald; *Harold Arlen Songbook-#2* ......(VRV)
I'm From Another Planet
Animotion; *Music Speaks Louder Than Words* ..... (EPI)
I've Told Ev'ry Little Star
David Allyn; *Sings Jerome Kern* ....(DCO)
Linda Scott; *45* ....(ERI)
January Stars
George Winston; *Winter Into Spring* ....(WH)
Jet Silver & The Dolls Of Venus
Be Bop Deluxe; *Ax Victim* ....(OOP)
   Best Of-Raiding The Divine Archive ....(CAP)
Journey To A Star
Judy Garland; *Collector's Items-1936-1945* .....(MCA)
Judgment Of The Moon & Stars
Joni Mitchell; *For The Roses* ....(ASY)
Jupiter
Earth, Wind & Fire; *All 'N All* ....(COL)

Jupiter Hollow
Band; *Northern Lights Southern Cross* ....(CAP)
Jupiter's Child
Steppenwolf; *16 Greatest Hits* .... (MCA)
Lady Stardust
David Bowie; *Rise & Fall Of Ziggy Stardust* ......(RYK)
Lady Starlight
Scorpions; *Animal Magnetism* .... (MER)
Life On Mars?
David Bowie; *Hunky Dory* ....(RYK)
   The Singles-1969-1993 ....(RYK)
Little Star
Elegants; *Billboard Top Rock 'N' Roll Hits-1958* . (RHI)
   Oldies But Goodies-#5 ....(OSR)
   Super Oldies!'50s-#7 ....(AUF)
Little Star/Eclipse
Sammy Hagar; *Sammy Hagar* ....(CAP)
Lost In The Stars
Frank Sinatra; *My Kind Of Broadway* .... (RPR)
Mormon Tabernacle Choir; *Climb Every*
   Mountain ....(COL)
Original Cast; *Lost In The Stars* .... (MCA)
Sarah Vaughan; *Complete On*
   Mercury-#2-1956-1957 ....(MER)
Sheila Jordan; *Lost & Found* ....(MUS)
Tony Bennett; *Forty Years-Artistry Of* ....(COL)
Lucky Star
Madonna; *Immaculate Collection* .... (SIR)
   Madonna ....(SIR)
   MTV's Rock 'N' Roll To Go .... (ELE)
   Royal Box ....(SIR)
Midnight On Mars
Ashra; *Blackouts* .... (BP)
Might As Well Be On Mars
Alice Cooper; *Hey Stoopid* .... (EPI)
Moons Of Jupiter
Paul Halley; *Pianosong* ....(LIV)
Moon-faced, Starry-Eyed
Popular Standard; *Out of print recording* ....(OOP)
Motorboat To Mars
Chicago; *At Carnegie Hall* ....(COL)
   III ....(COL)
One Way Ticket To Pluto
Dead Kennedys; *ST/Lovedolls To Superstar* ....(SST)
Orbit
Fred Schneider/Shake Society; *Fred Schneider/Shake*
   Society ....(RPR)
   Meteors; *Teenage Heart* ....(PVC)
Orbit Zero
Little River Band; *Time Exposure* ....(CAP)
Orion In The Sky
Shawn Colvin; *Fat City* ....(COL)
Passion Planet
Thompson Twins; *Into The Gap* .... (ARI)
Planet Caravan
Pantera; *Far Beyond Driven* ....(EW)
Planet Claire
B-52's; *B-52's* ....(WB)
Planet Of My Dreams
Frank Zappa; *Them Or Us* ....(BAR)
Planet Of New Orleans
Dire Straits; *On Every Street* ....(WB)
Planet Of The Clowns
Bruce Cockburn; *Trouble With Normal* ....(COL)
Planet Of Women
ZZ Top; *Afterburner* ....(WB)
   Greatest Hits ....(WB)
Planet Queen
T. Rex; *Electric Warrior* .... (RPR)
Planet Rock
Afrika Bambaataa/Soulsonic Force; *Street Jams-Electric*
   Funk-#1 .... (RHI)
   Tommy Boy Greatest Beats ....(TMB)
Planet Texas
John Andrew Parks; *John Andrew Parks* ....(CAP)
Kenny Rogers; *Something Inside So Strong* ....(RPR)
Planetary Invasion
Midnight Star; *Planetary Invasion* ....(SLR)
Planets Of Life
Whispers; *I Can Remember* ....(ACC)
   Vintage ....(SLR)
Prettiest Star
David Bowie; *Aladdin Sane* ....(RYK)
   Sound + Vision ....(RYK)

Quiet Nights Of Quiet Stars
Antonio Carlos Jobin; *Terra Brasilis* ....(WB)
Shirley Horn; *I Thought About You-Live At Vine
St.* ....(VRV)
Ranch On Mars Reprise
Galactic Cowboys; *Galactic Cowboys* ....(DGC)
Re-Doo-Wopp-Little Star
Tokens; *Re-Doo-Wopp-Little Star* ....(RCA)
Saturn
Alan Vega; *Saturn Strip* ....(ELE)
Stevie Wonder; *Songs In The Key Of Life* ....(MOT)
Second Star To The Right
Barbara Cook; *Disney Album* ....(MCA)
James Taylor; *Stay Awake-Music From Vintage
Disney* ....(A&M)
See The Constellation
They Might Be Giants; *Apollo 18* ....(ELE)
Shake Down The Stars
Benny Goodman; *Best Of The Big Bands* ....(COL)
Shining Star
Earth, Wind & Fire; *Best Of-#1* ....(COL)
   Eternal Dance ....(COL)
   Gratitude ....(COL)
   That's The Way Of The World ....(COL)
Manhattans; *After Midnight* ....(COL)
   Greatest Hits ....(COL)
   Seems Like Yesterday-#4-Early '80s .... (KT)
Shooting Star
Bad Company; *10 From 6* ....(ATL)
   Straight Shooter .... (SS)
Bob Dylan; *Oh Mercy* ....(COL)
Elton John; *Single Man* ....(MCA)
Harry Chapin; *Gold Medal Collection* ....(ELE)
   Verities & Balderdash ....(ELE)
Shooting Stars
Billy Idol; *Billy Idol* ....(CHR)
Silver Stars, Purple Sage, Eyes Of Blue
Roy Rogers/Sons Of The Pioneers; *Roy Rogers/Sons Of
The Pioneers* ....(VS)
Somebody Else's Moon
Collin Raye; *In This Life* ....(EPI)
South Saturn Delta
Jimi Hendrix; *Lifelines/Story* ....(RPR)
Southern Star
Alabama; *Southern Star* ....(RCA)
Stairway To The Stars
Blue Öyster Cult; *Blue Öyster Cult* ....(COL)
Ella Fitzgerald; *Best Of* ....(MCA)
   In Hollywood ....(VRV)
Glenn Miller & Ray Eberle; *Chattanooga Choo Choo-#1
Hits* ....(BLU)
   Memorial 1944-1969 ....(BLU)
Milt Jackson & Wes Montgomery; *Bags Meets
Wes!* ....(RVR)
Star
David Bowie; *Rise & Fall Of Ziggy Stardust* ......(RYK)
   Stage ....(RYK)
Erasure; *Just Say Da-#4 Of Just Say Yes* ....(SIR)
   Wild! ....(SIR)
Frank Sinatra; *Greatest Hits-#2* ....(RPR)
   Sings The Songs Of Van Heusen & Cahn ....(RPR)
Nazareth; *Classics-#6* ....(A&M)
Stealers Wheel; *Super Hits/'70s-Have A Nice
Day-#12* ....(RHI)
Star Eyes
Charlie Parker; *Bebop & Bird-#2* ....(RHI)
Chet Baker; *RCA Victor Jazz-First
Half-Century-#5* ....(RCA)
Sonny Rollins; *Complete Prestige Recordings* ......(PRS)
   Rollins Plays For Bird ....(PRS)
   Saxophone Colossus & More ....(PRS)
Stephane Grappelli; *Compact Jazz* ....(VRV)
Star Of Africa
Gerry Mulligan & Chet Baker; *Gerry Mulligan & Chet
Baker* ....(CRS)
Star Of Bethlehem
Emmylou Harris & Neil Young; *Duets* ....(RPR)
Neil Young; *Decade* ....(RPR)
Neil Young/Crazy Horse; *American Stars 'N'
Bars* ....(RPR)
Star Rider
Foreigner; *Foreigner* ....(ATL)

Star Spangled Banner
Duke Ellington; *Carnegie Hall Concerts-January 23
1943* ....(PRS)
Houston Symphony Orchestra; *Celebrate America* (POE)
Jimi Hendrix; *Essential-#2* ....(RPR)
   Lifelines/Jimi Hendrix Story ....(RPR)
   ST/Jimi Hendrix ....(RPR)
   ST/Woodstock ....(ATL)
Lee Greenwood; *American Patriot* ....(LIB)
Marvin Gaye; *Musical Testament-1964-1984* ...(MOT)
Mormon Tabernacle Choir; *God Bless America* ..(COL)
   This Is My Country ....(COL)
Vinnie Vincent Invasion; *Head Banging Metal* ....(PRY)
Star Track
Jefferson Airplane; *Crown Of Creation* ....(RCA)
"Star Trek" Theme
Cincinnati Pops Orchestra/Erich Kunzel; *Star Tracks
II* ....(TLR)
"Star Wars" Theme
John Williams; *ST/"Star Wars" Theme* ....(20)
Meco; *45* ....(CAS)
Neil Norman; *Greatest Science Fiction Hits* ......(CRS)
Star Whores
Christ Child; *Hard* ....(BUD)
Starchild
Teena Marie; *Starchild* ....(EPI)
Stardust
Artie Shaw; *Begin The Beguine* ....(BLU)
Artie Shaw/Orchestra; *22 Original Big Band
Recordings* ....(HIN)
   Nipper's Greatest Hits-'40s-#1 ....(RCA)
Benny Goodman; *Live At Carnegie Hall* ....(LON)
   Sextet feat. Charlie Christian-1939-1941 ......(COL)
Coleman Hawkins; *Hollywood Stampede* ....(CAP)
Dave Brubeck; *Art Of* ....(ATL)
   Greatest Hits From The Fantasy Years ....(FAN)
Dave Brubeck Quartet; *Jazz At Oberlin* ....(FAN)
   Stardust ....(FAN)
Frank Sinatra; *Sinatra & Strings* ....(RPR)
Hoagy Carmichael; *Nipper's Greatest
Hits-'30s-#1* ....(RCA)
   Stardust Road ....(MCA)
Johnny Mathis; *Feelings* ....(COL)
   First 25 Years-Silver Anniversary Album ....(COL)
Nat King Cole; *Story* ....(CAP)
Rob Wasserman/Aaron Neville; *Duets* ....(MCA)
Roger Williams; *Best Of* ....(MCA)
Tommy Dorsey; *Best Of* ....(RCA)
   This Is-#1 ....(RCA)
Tommy Dorsey & Frank Sinatra; *Stardust* ....(BLU)
Stargazer
Mark Knopfler; *Local Hero* ....(WB)
Neil Diamond; *Beautiful Noise* ....(COL)
   Love At The Greek ....(COL)
Starlight
Electric Light Orchestra; *Box Of Their Best* ......(JET)
   Out Of The Blue ....(JET)
Tom Rush; *Best Of* ....(COL)
Starlight, Starbright
Linda Scott; *45* ....(ERI)
Starman
David Bowie; *Changestwobowie* ....(RCA)
   Fame & Fashion ....(RCA)
   Rise & Fall Of Ziggy Stardust ....(RYK)
   The Singles-1969-1993 ....(RYK)
Starry Eyes
Motley Crue; *Too Fast For Love* ....(ELE)
Starry Sky In Oregon
Andrew White; *Conversations* ....(SOG)
Stars
Janis Ian; *Stars* ....(OW)
Original Broadway Cast; *Les Miserables* ....(GEF)
Simply Red; *Stars* ....(EW)
Stars Fell On Alabama
Art Tatum; *Group Masterpieces-#4* ....(PAB)
Frank Sinatra; *Capitol Years* ....(CAP)
Harry Connick, Jr.; *20* ....(COL)
Jimmy Buffett; *Boats Beaches Bars & Ballads* ...(MGR)
   Coconut Telegraph ....(MCA)
Stars On The Water
Jimmy Buffett; *Boats Beaches Bars & Ballads* ...(MGR)
   One Particular Harbour ....(MCA)
Rodney Crowell; *Collection* ....(WB)
   Rodney Crowell ....(WB)

Stella By Starlight
Bill Evans; *Jazzhouse* .... (MS)
Frank Sinatra; *Rarities-Columbia Years* ....(COL)
George Benson; *Tenderly* ....(WB)
Joe Pass; *Virtuoso* ....(PAB)
Keith Jarrett; *Standards Live* .... (ECM)
Miles Davis; *Cookin' At The Plugged Nickel* .....(COL)
Red Garland; *Red Alert* ....(GAL)
Stan Getz; *Plays* ....(VRV)
Tony Bennett; *Jazz* ....(COL)
Subway To Venus
Red Hot Chili Peppers; *Mother's Milk* .... (EMI)
Summer Of The Silver Comet
Tracy Nelson; *Homemade Songs* .... (FF)
Sun, Moon & Stars
Nanci Griffith; *Late Night Grande Hotel* .... (MCA)
Surfin' On Jupiter
Psychefunkapus; *Skin* ....(ATL)
Swinging On A Star
Bing Crosby; *All-Time Best* ....(CCB)
Best Of ....(MCA)
Dion/Belmonts; *Their Best* ....(LAU)
Frank Sinatra; *Sings The Songs Of Van Heusen &*
Cahn ....(RPR)
Telstar
Tornados; *History Of British Rock-#5* .... (RHI)
Ventures; *Play Telstar/In Space* .... (EMI)
They Took The Stars Out Of Heaven
Floyd Tillman; *Country Music Hall Of Fame* .... (MCA)
Thousand Stars In The Sky
Kathy Young/Innocents; *20 Great Love Songs/'50s &*
'60s-#2 ....(LAU)
Collectables-History Of Rock-#10 .... (CLT)
Oldies But Goodies-#5 .... (OSR)
To Raise The Morning Star
Bruce Cockburn; *Stealing Fire* ....(COL)
Trash Planet
Stewart/Gaskin; *Spin* ....(RYK)
Turn Out The Stars
Bill Evans Trio; *Since We Met* ....(FAN)
David Benoit; *Waiting For Spring* ....(GRP)
Gary Burton & Paul Bley; *Right Time Right Place* (CRS)
John McLaughlin; *Time Remembered-Plays Bill*
Evans ....(VRV)
Liz Story; *My Foolish Heart* ....(WH)
Twinkle Twinkle Little Star
Bob Wills/Texas Playboys; *Tiffany*
Transcriptions-#8 ....(KAL)
Willie Nelson; *Somewhere Over The Rainbow* ....(COL)
Twinkle Twinkle Lucky Star
Merle Haggard; *Chill Factor* .... (EPI)
Greatest Country Hits/'80s-1988 ....(COL)
Under The Milky Way
Church; *Best Of MTV's 120 Minutes-#1* .... (RHI)
Starfish ....(ARI)
Cinderella; *Long Cold Winter* ....(MER)
Vampire Planet
Neil Norman/Cosmic Orchestra; *Greatest Science Fiction*
Hits-#2 ....(CRS)
Venus & Mars
Paul McCartney/Wings; *Wings Over America* ....(CAP)
Wings; *Venus & Mars* ....(CAP)
Vincent
Don McLean; *American Pie* .... (EMI)
Best Of ....(EMI)
Greatest Hits Then & Now ....(EMI)
Waiting For A Star To Fall
Boy Meets Girl; *Nipper's Greatest Hits-'80s* ......(RCA)
Reel Life ....(RCA)
Wanderin' Star
Original Broadway Cast; *Paint Your Wagon* .....(RCA)
We Let The Stars Go
Prefab Sprout; *Jordan-The Comeback* .... (EPI)
Life Of Surprises-Best Of ....(EPI)
When You Wish Upon A Star
Barbara Cook; *Disney Album* ....(MCA)
Billy Joel; *Simply Mad About The Mouse* ....(COL)
Cliff Edwards; *ST/Pinocchio* ....(DIS)
Dion/Belmonts; *The Wanderer* ....(LAU)
Glenn Miller & Ray Eberle; *Chattanooga*
Choo-Choo-#1 Hits ....(BLU)
Linda Ronstadt; *For Sentimental Reasons* ......(ASY)
Little Anthony/Imperials; *We Are The Imperials* .. (RLL)
Rosemary Clooney; *16 Most Requested Songs* ....(COL)

Stevie Wonder; *With A Song In My Heart* .... (MOT)
Wynton Marsalis; *Hothouse Flowers* ....(COL)
Wish Upon A Star
Steve Miller Band; *Book Of Dreams* ....(CAP)
CD Gift Set ....(CAP)
Wishing On A Star
Cover Girls; *Here It Is* .... (EPI)
Rose Royce; *Greatest Hits* ....(WHI)
Workshop Of The Telescopes
Blue Oyster Cult; *Blue Oyster Cult* ....(COL)
Would You Catch A Falling Star
John Anderson; *Greatest Hits* ....(WB)
I Just Came Home To Count The Memories ......(WB)
Yellow Star
Donovan; *Essence To Essence* ....(EPI)
Ziggy Stardust
David Bowie; *Changesbowie* ....(RYK)
Rise & Fall Of Ziggy Stardust ....(RYK)
Sound + Vision ....(RYK)
Stage ....(RYK)
ST/Ziggy Stardust-The Motion Picture ....(RCA)
The Singles-1969-1993 ....(RYK)

STATES: ALABAMA

See Also: CITIES: BIRMINGHAM, MOBILE

Alabam
Minnie Pearl; *Trucks Trains & Airplanes* ....(GUS)
Alabama
Neil Young; *Harvest* ....(RPR)
ST/Journey Through The Past ....(RPR)
Alabama Bound
Doc & Merle Watson; *Ballads From Deep Gap* . (VAN)
Leadbelly/Woody Guthrie/Cisco Houston; *Leadbelly*
Sings Folk Songs ....(FLW)
Alabama Getaway
Grateful Dead; *Go To Heaven* ....(ARI)
Alabama Highway
Steve Young; *Honky-Tonk Man* ....(ROU)
Alabama Jubilee
Boston Pops Orchestra/Chet Atkins; *American*
Salute ....(RCA)
Leon Redbone; *Champagne Charlie* ....(WB)
Alabama Lady
Wright Brothers; *Easy Street* ....(MER)
Alabama Rain
Jim Croce; *Down The Highway* .... (21)
Time In A Bottle .... (21)
Alabama Shine
Ken Pollard; *45* ....(OOP)
Alabama Sky
Alabama; *Closer You Get* ....(RCA)
Alabama Song
Bette Midler; *Live At Last* ....(ATL)
Doors; *Doors* ....(ELE)
Alabama Woman Blues
John Hammond; *John Hammond* .... (VAN)
Alabambama
Willie Nelson & Roger Miller; *Old Friends* ....(COL)
Alabamy Bound
Tom Rush; *Blues Songs Ballads* .... (PRS)
Tom Rush ....(FAN)
Breeze From Alabama
Max Morath; *Plays Ragtime* .... (VAN)
World Of Scott Joplin .... (VAN)
Scott Joplin; *Entertainer-#4* ....(BIO)
Going Back To Alabama
Asa Martin; *Dr. Ginger Blue* .... (ROU)
Going Back To Alabam'
Alan Munde & Country Gazette; *Keep On Pushing* . (FF)
Going To Move To Alabama
Charley Patton; *Founder Of The Delta Blues* .....(YAZ)
Goin' Back To Alabama
Asa Martin; *Dr. Ginger Blue* ....(ROU)
Kenny Rogers; *Share Your Love* ....(LIB)
Hills Of Alabam'
Kathy Mattea; *Willow In The Wind* .... (MER)
I'm Alabammy Bound
Lonnie Donegan; *Golden Hits* ....(OOP)
I'm Going Back To Alabama
Jerry Douglas; *Fluxology* .... (ROU)

My Home's In Alabama
Alabama; *Gonna Have A Party...Live* .... (RCA)
   Greatest Hits .... (RCA)
   Live .... (RCA)
   My Home's In Alabama .... (RCA)
North Alabama
Cal Smith; *Stories Of Life By* .... (SO)
Oh, Susanna
James Taylor; *Sweet Baby James* .... (WB)
Myron Floren; *Best Of The Wurstfest* .... (RAN)
   Myron Floren .... (RAN)
Roll Alabama Roll
Northeast Winds; *Ireland By Sail* .... (FOL)
   We The People .... (FOL)
Shady River Gal/Alabama Gals
Beverly Cotton; *Clogging Lessons* .... (FF)
Stars Fell On Alabama
Art Tatum; *Group Masterpieces-#4* .... (PAB)
Frank Sinatra; *Capitol Years* .... (CAP)
Harry Connick, Jr.; *20* .... (COL)
Jimmy Buffett; *Boats Beaches Bars & Ballads* ... (MGR)
   Coconut Telegraph .... (MCA)
Sweet Home Alabama
Alabama; *Skynyrd Frynds* .... (MCA)
Charlie Daniels Band, Etc.; *Volunteer Jam 7* ...... (EPI)
Hank Williams, Jr.; *Hank Live* .... (W/C)
Lynyrd Skynyrd; *Billboard Top Rock 'N' Roll
Hits-1974* .... (RHI)
   Gold & Platinum .... (MCA)
   One More For The Road .... (MCA)
   Second Helping .... (MCA)
   South's Greatest Hits .... (CPC)
   ST/Forrest Gump .... (EPX)
When The Midnight Choo Choo Leaves...
Andrews Sisters; *Best Of-#2* .... (MCA)
Judy Garland & Fred Astaire; *ST/Easter Parade* .. (SSP)

STATES: ALASKA

Alaska
Bobby G. Rice; *Audiograph Alive* .... (AUD)
   Silk On Silk .... (AUD)
Danny Gottlieb; *Aquamarine* .... (ATL)
UK; *Night After Night* .... (EDI)
   UK .... (EDI)
Alaska Cats
Garrison Keillor & Frederica von Stade; *Songs Of The
Cat* .... (RCA)
Alaska Highway
Neon Judgement; *The Insult* .... (PIA)
Alaskan Nights
David Schwartz; *ST/Music From "
Northern Exposure"* .... (MCA)
Alaskan Queen
Joe Hackney; *Heavy Hitter* .... (HH)
Alaskan Suite: Northern Lights
Lyle Mays; *Lyle Mays* .... (GEF)
Alaskan Sunrise
Dick Pinney; *Devil Take My Shiny Coins* .... (MOU)
North To Alaska
Johnny Horton; *American Originals* .... (COL)
   Billboard Top Country Hits-1961 .... (RHI)
   Greatest Hits .... (COL)
"Northern Exposure" Theme
David Schwartz; *ST/Music From "Northern
Exposure"* .... (MCA)
When It's Springtime In Alaska
Johnny Horton; *American Originals* .... (COL)
   Greatest Hits .... (COL)

STATES: ARIZONA

Arizona
Mark Lindsay; *Super Hits/'70s-Have A Nice
Day-#1* .... (RHI)
Scorpions; *Blackout* .... (MER)
Arizona Days
Tex Ritter; *Arizona Days* .... (MSP)
Arizona Flash & Cloudy
Rod Hart; *45* .... (PLN)
Arizona Groovin'
Popular Local Standard; *45* .... (OOP)

Arizona Highway
Tim Rex/Oklahoma; *45* .... (DJ)
Arizona History
Popular Local Standard; *45* .... (OOP)
Arizona Indian Doll
Faster Pussycat; *Wake Me When It's Over* .... (ELE)
Arizona Moon
Ranch Romance; *Blue Blazes* .... (SH)
Arizona Skies
Los Lobos; *Kiko* .... (SLS)
Arizona Sky
China Crisis; *What Price Paradise* .... (A&M)
Arizona Waltz
Mom & Dads; *Souvenirs* .... (CRS)
Arizona Whiz
George Burns; *I Wish I Was 18 Again* .... (MER)
Arizona-Suite 3
Scott Moulton; *Four Corners Suite* .... (REV)
I Love You Arizona
Dolan Ellis; *45* .... (OOP)
It's Still Rock & Roll To Me
Billy Joel; *Glass Houses* .... (COL)
   Greatest Hits-#1 & 2 .... (COL)
Ocean Front Property
George Strait; *Country Classics-#8-1986-1987* . (MCA)
   Greatest Hits-#2 .... (MCA)
   MCA Records 30 Years Of Hits-1958-1988 ... (MCA)
   Ocean Front Property .... (MCA)
Rider In The Rain
Randy Newman; *Little Criminals* .... (WB)
Tucson, Arizona (Gazette)
Dan Fogelberg; *Windows & Walls* .... (FM)

STATES: ARKANSAS

Arkansas
Glen Campbell; *Still Within The Sound Of My
Voice* .... (MCA)
Ron Carter; *Spanish Blue* .... (CBA)
Whitstein Brothers; *Rose Of My Heart* .... (ROU)
Arkansas Blues
Eubie Blake; *Memories Of You* .... (BIO)
Marcus Roberts; *If I Could Be With You* .... (NOV)
Arkansas Coal
Nancy Sinatra & Lee Hazlewood; *Fairy Tales &
Fantasies-Best Of* .... (RHI)
Arkansas Dog
Pinkard & Bowden; *Writers In Disguise* .... (WB)
Arkansas Jane
Kong Cotton; *Bo Diddley Beats* .... (RHI)
Arkansas Road House Blues
Memphis Slim; *Traveling With The Blues* .... (STY)
Arkansas See Saw
Jerry Lee Lewis; *Keeps Rockin'* .... (MER)
Arkansas Time Traveler
Star-Spangled Washboard Band; *Collector's Item* ... (FF)
Arkansas Traveler
Albert Lee; *Speechless* .... (MCA)
Floyd Cramer; *Country Gold* .... (STE)
Mark O'Connor; *Championship Years* .... (CMF)
Michelle Shocked; *Arkansas Traveler* .... (MER)
Sam Hinton; *Newport Folk Festival '63* .... (VAN)
Arkansas/How Blest We Are
Original Broadway Cast; *Big River* .... (MCA)
Hills Of Arkansas
Black Oak Arkansas; *Black Oak Arkansas* .... (ATC)
Hot Springs, Arkansas
Bukka White; *Three Shades Of Blues* .... (BIO)
I Can See Arkansas
Anne Murray; *Fifteen Of The Best* .... (LIB)
Mary Queen Of Arkansas
Bruce Springsteen; *Greetings From Asbury Park,
N.J.* .... (COL)
State Of Arkansas
Rosalie Sorrels; *Lonesome Roving Wolves* .... (GRE)
Uncle Dave's Travels-Misery In Arkansas
Uncle Dave Macon; *Country Music Hall Of
Fame* .... (MCA)
What'd I Say
Elvis Presley; *Collector's Gold* .... (RCA)
   Golden Records-#4 .... (RCA)
   Greatest Hits-#1 .... (RCA)
   In Concert .... (RCA)

Jerry Lee Lewis; *Milestones* .... (RHI)
  Original .... (SUN)
  Original Golden Hits-#2 .... (SUN)
  Rocket 88 .... (TOM)
  Rockin' My Life Away .... (TOM)
John Mayall/Bluesbreakers; *Bluesbreakers* .... (DER)
Ray Charles; *Anthology* .... (RHI)
  Atlantic R&B 1947-1974-#4-(1958-1962) .. (ATL)
  Atlantic Soul Classics .... (WSP)
  Frat Rock-#3 .... (RHI)
  Life In Music .... (ATL)

STATES: CALIFORNIA

  See Also: CITIES: LOS ANGELES, SAN
  FRANCISCO; HOLLYWOOD

Ain't No California
Mel Tillis; *I Believe In You* .... (MCA)
  Very Best Of .... (MCA)
Ain't Nobody Home (In California)
John Kay; *All In Good Time* .... (MER)
Airwaves/Look Out California
Badfinger; *Airwaves* .... (OOP)
All Alone In California
Dan Hill; *Hold On* .... (20)
All The Gold In California
Larry Gatlin/Gatlin Brothers; *17 Greatest Hits* ..(COL)
  Greatest Hits-Encore .... (CAP)
  Greatest Hits-#2 .... (COL)
  Live At 8:00 .... (CAP)
  Straight Ahead .... (COL)
Back To California
Carole King; *Music* .... (EOD)
Blue Yodel #4 (California Blues)
Bill Monroe; *Columbia Historic Edition* .... (COL)
Jimmie Rodgers; *Early Years 1928-1929* .... (ROU)
  Never No Mo' Blues .... (RCA)
  This Is .... (RCA)
California
Babys; *Head First* .... (CHR)
Joni Mitchell; *Blue* .... (RPR)
Keith Stegall; *Keith Stegall* .... (EPI)
Kingston Trio; *Aspen Gold* .... (FFT)
  Best Of The Best .... (POE)
California Bloodlines
John Stewart; *American Originals* .... (CAP)
Shaw Brothers; *Greatest Hits-#1* .... (FOL)
California Blue
Herb Alpert; *Fandango* .... (A&M)
Roy Orbison; *Mystery Girl* .... (VIA)
California Blues
Sonny Terry & Brownie McGhee; *California*
Blues .... (FAN)
California Calling
Beach Boys; *Beach Boys* .... (CAR)
California Campground
John Mayall; *Best Of* .... (POL)
California Christmas
Hillary Kanter; *Country Christmas-#4* .... (RCA)
California Cotton Fields
Gram Parsons/Fallen Angels; *Live 1973* .... (SIE)
California Dreamin'
Beach Boys; *Made In The U.S.A.* .... (CAP)
Mamas & The Papas; *20 Golden Hits* .... (MCA)
  At The Hop .... (MCA)
  Good Feeling Music-Big Chill-#1 .... (MOT)
  ST/Air America .... (MCA)
  ST/American Pop .... (RLL)
  ST/Forrest Gump .... (EPX)
California Earthquake
John Hartford; *Catalogue* .... (FF)
Rodney Crowell; *Ain't Living Long Like This* ..... (WB)
California Girl
Eddie Floyd; *15 Original Big Hits-#4* .... (STX)
  Chronicle .... (STX)
California Girls
Beach Boys; *Best Of-#2* .... (CAP)
  California Girls .... (CAP)
  Endless Summer .... (CAP)
  In Concert .... (CAR)
  '69 .... (CAP)

David Lee Roth; *Crazy From The Heat* .... (MCA)
  ST/Down & Out In Beverly Hills .... (WB)
California Gold
Rance Allen; *Straight From The Heart* .... (STX)
California Golden West Waltz
Golden West Singers/Cavaliers; *45* .... (ACT)
California Here I Come
Al Jolson; *Best Of* .... (MCA)
California Kid
Beat Farmers; *Tales Of The New West* .... (RHI)
California Man
Cheap Trick; *Heaven Tonight* .... (EPI)
California Marching Song
UC Marching Band; *UC Marching Band* .... (FID)
California Mudslide
Lightnin' Hopkins; *Los Angeles Blues* .... (RHI)
California Nights
Lesley Gore; *Summer & Sun* .... (RHI)
Sweet; *Level-Headed* .... (CAP)
California Paradise
Runaways; *Queens Of Noise* .... (MER)
California PM
George Benson; *Weekend In L.A.* .... (WB)
California Promises
Jimmy Buffett; *One Particular Harbour* .... (MCA)
California Road
Mel Tillis; *45* .... (RCA)
California Saga
Beach Boys; *Holland* .... (CAR)
  Ten Years Of Harmony .... (CAR)
California Soul
5th Dimension; *Anthology 1967-1973* .... (RHI)
Marvin Gaye & Tammi Terrell; *Classic Duets: Marvin*
Gaye & His Women .... (MOT)
  Motown Superstars-#2 .... (MOT)
California Sun
Ramones; *All The Stuff (& More)* .... (SIR)
  Leave Home .... (SIR)
  ST/Rock & Roll High School .... (SIR)
Rivieras; *Beach Classics* .... (DHL)
  Frat Rock-#4 .... (RHI)
  Summer & Sun .... (RHI)
California Sunset
Neil Young; *Old Ways* .... (GEF)
California Surfer
Dee D. Hope; *History Of Surf Music-#2* .... (RHI)
California Turn Arounds
Jack Greene; *Greatest Hits* .... (GUS)
  Trucks Trains & Airplanes .... (GUS)
California Wine
Bobby Goldsboro; *10th Anniversary Album-#2* .... (UA)
Californicatin'
J. Geils Band; *You're Gettin' Even While I'm*
Gettin'... .... (AMR)
Estimated Prophet
Burning Spear; *Deadicated* .... (ARI)
Grateful Dead; *Terrapin Station* .... (ARI)
Everyone I Meet Is From California
America; *Encore-More Greatest Hits* .... (RHI)
Fight For California
University Of California Marching Band; *University Of*
California Marching Band .... (FID)
First Train To California
Cryan' Shames; *Best Of* .... (BCT)
Friend In California
Merle Haggard; *Friend In California* .... (EPI)
  More Hot Country Requests .... (EPI)
Going To California
John Lee Hooker; *Sings John Lee Hooker* .... (EVR)
Led Zeppelin; *Led Zeppelin (collection)* .... (ATL)
  #4 .... (ATL)
Hail To California
University Of California Marching Band; *Hail To*
California .... (FID)
Hanging Out In California
Cruzados; *Cruzados* .... (ARI)
Here In California
Kate Wolf; *Close To You* .... (KAL)
Hotel California
Al B. Sure!; *Private Times & The Whole 9* .... (WB)

Eagles; *Anthology* .... (ASY)
 Greatest Hits-#2 .... (ASY)
 Hell Freezes Over .... (GEF)
 Hotel California .... (ASY)
 Live .... (ASY)
Gipsy Kings; *Rubaiyat-Elektra's 40th Anniversary* (ELE)
I Got To Get To California
Marvin Gaye; *Trouble Man/M.P.G.* .... (MOT)
I Remember California
R.E.M.; *Green* .... (WB)
If We'd All Been Living In California
Frank Zappa/Mothers Of Invention; *Uncle Meat* . (BAR)
It Never Rains In Southern California
Albert Hammond; *Rock Artifacts-#2* ....(COL)
 Super Hits/'70s-Have A Nice Day-#10 .... (RHI)
Tony! Toni! Tone!; *Revival* .... (WIN)
Look At California
Maze featuring Frankie Beverly; *Live In New
 Orleans* ....(CAP)
 Maze featuring Frankie Beverly ....(CAP)
Lord I Want To Go Back To California
Jim Post; *Magic: In Concert* .... (FF)
My California
Lightnin' Hopkins; *Complete Aladdin Recordings* . (EMI)
Nevada, California
Jayhawks; *Hollywood Town Hall* .... (DEF)
Off To California
Russell Family; *Of Doolin, County Clare* ....(GRE)
Oklahoma Heartaches & California Dreams
Kris Carpenter; *45* .... (DOO)
Prettiest Eyes In California
B.W. Stevenson; *Rainbow Down The Road* ..... (AMA)
Shadow Of California
Blue Oyster Cult; *Revolution By Night* ....(COL)
Someday Soon
Chris LeDoux; *Rodeo Songs Old & New* ....(LIB)
Ian & Sylvia; *Greatest Hits* .... (VAN)
 Northern Journey .... (VAN)
Journey; *Departure* ....(COL)
Judy Collins; *Colors Of The Day-Best Of* ....(ELE)
 Who Knows Where The Time Goes ....(ELE)
Moe Bandy; *Greatest Hits* ....(COL)
 Rodeo Romeo ....(COL)
Suzy Bogguss; *Aces* ....(CAP)
Sons Of California
University Of California Marching Band; *University Of
 California Marching Band* ....(FID)
Southern California
Tammy Wynette & George Jones; *Encore* .... (EPI)
 Greatest Hits .... (EPI)
Southern California Purples
Chicago; *At Carnegie Hall* ....(COL)
 Chicago Transit Authority ....(COL)
Sweet Betsy From Pike
Cisco Houston; *Cowboy Ballads* .... (FLW)
Mormon Tabernacle Choir; *This Land Is Your
 Land* ....(COL)
Tape From California
Phil Ochs; *Gunfight At Carnegie Hall* .... (MOB)
 War Is Over-Best Of .... (A&M)
To Go To California Anymore (I Don't...)
Willie Nelson; *Born For Trouble* ....(COL)

STATES: CAROLINAS

Carolina
Charlie Daniels Band; *Full Moon* .... (EPI)
 High Lonesome .... (EPI)
Carolina Blue
Annie McGowan; *Rattlesnakes & Rusty Water* ....(RAT)
Carolina By The Sea
Super Grit Cowboy Band; *If You Can't Hang* ... (HOO)
Carolina Come On
Lacy J. Dalton; *Lacy J. Dalton* ....(COL)
Carolina Dreams
Ronnie Milsap; *Inside* ....(RCA)
Carolina In My Mind
James Taylor; *Greatest Hits* .... (WB)
Carolina In The Morning
Al Jolson; *Best Of* .... (MCA)
 Story-#2 .... (MCA)

Carolina In The Pines
Michael Martin Murphey; *Best Of* .... (EMI)
 Blue Sky Night Thunder .... (EPI)
Carolina Moon
Slim Whitman; *Ghost Riders In The Sky* .... (LIB)
Thelonius Monk; *Genius Of Modern Music-#2* ... (BLN)
Carolina Moonshiner
Porter Wagoner; *20 Great Country Hits* ....(RCA)
 Collector's ....(RCA)
Carolina On My Mind
Melanie; *What Have They Done To My Song Ma* (ACC)
Carolina Shout
Fats Waller; *Piano Solos* ....(RCA)
Carolina Star
E. Scruggs & R. Dillard; *Top Of The World* ......(COL)
Carolina Sun
Anne Murray; *Keeping In Touch* ....(CAP)
Carolina Sunshine Girl
Geoff Muldaur & Amos Garrett; *Geoff Muldaur & Amos
 Garrett* .... (FF)
Charlotte's In North Carolina
Ronnie McDowell; *Country Boy's Heart* ....(EPI)
Down A Carolina Lane
Duke Ellington/Famous Orchestra; *Ridin' In
 Rhythm* ....(DSQ)
Here Comes Carolina
Ohio State University Marching Band; *Saturday
 Afternoon At Columbus* ....(FID)
Just A Little Bit South Of No. Carolina
Dean Martin; *Swingin' Down Yonder* ....(CAP)
Kinfolks In Carolina
Merle Travis; *Best Of* .... (RHI)
Little Bit South Of North Carolina
Chuck Foster & Jimmy Castle; *Uncollected* ...... (HIN)
My Cabin In Caroline
Lester Flatt & Earl Scruggs; *Golden Hits Of* ..... (IGR)
L. Flatt & E. Scruggs/Foggy Mtn. Boys; *Complete
 Mercury Sessions* .... (MER)
My Carolina Sunshine Girl
Jimmie Rodgers; *Early Years-1928-1929* .... (ROU)
North Carolina
Anne Romaine; *Take A Stand* .... (FF)
North Carolina Bound
Connie & Babe/Backwoods Boys; *Backwoods
 Bluegrass* .... (ROU)
North Carolina Tune/Child Of My Heart
Liz Carroll; *Friend Indeed* .... (SHA)
Oh Carolina
Vince Gill; *Best Of* ....(RCA)
South Carolina Rag
John Jackson; *Step It Up & Go* .... (ROU)
Take Me Back To My Old Carolina Home
Uncle Dave Macon; *Laugh Your Blues Away* ... (ROU)
Way Down In North Carolina
Fields Ward/Buck Mountain Band; *Fields Ward/Buck
 Mountain Band* ....(HIS)

STATES: COLORADO
See Also: CITIES: DENVER

Along The Colorado Trail
Weavers; *Best Of* ....(MCA)
Coast Of Colorado
Skip Ewing; *Coast Of Colorado* .... (MCA)
Colorado
Linda Ronstadt; *Don't Cry Now* .... (ASY)
Stephen Stills; *Manassas* .... (ATL)
Colorado Kool Aid
Johnny Paycheck; *Biggest Hits* .... (EPI)
 Greatest Hits-#2 .... (EPI)
 Take This Job & Shove It .... (EPI)
Colorado Queenie
Little David Wilkins; *20 Great Hits* .... (PLN)
Colorado Song
Ozark Mountain Daredevils; *Ozark Mountain
 Daredevils* .... (A&M)
Colorado Trail
Ian Tyson; *Ian Tyson* ....(COL)
Salli Terri; *Songs Of The American Land* .... (ANG)
Come & Grow Old With Me In Colorado
Tom Paxton; *One Million Lawyers & Other
 Disasters* .... (FF)

Coors In Colorado
Ray Price; *Master Of The Art* .... (WB)
Don't Blame Me For Colorado
Gatlin Brothers; *Partners* .... (COL)
I Guess He'd Rather Be In Colorado
John Denver; *Poems Prayers & Promises* .... (RCA)
I Wonder How It Is In Colorado
Gene Watson; *Reflections* .... (CAP)
Long Afternoons
Jerry Jeff Walker; *Gypsy Songman* .... (RYK)
  Man Must Carry On .... (MCA)
Rocky Mountain High
John Denver; *Evening With* .... (RCA)
  Greatest Hits-#1 .... (RCA)
  Rocky Mountain High .... (RCA)
  Take Me Home Country Roads & Other Hits .... (RCA)
She Came From Fort Worth
Kathy Mattea; *Willow In The Wind* .... (MER)
Pat Alger & Kathy Mattea; *True Love & Other Short
Stories* .... (SH)
Someday Soon
Chris LeDoux; *Rodeo Songs Old & New* .... (LIB)
Ian & Sylvia; *Greatest Hits* .... (VAN)
  Northern Journey .... (VAN)
Journey; *Departure* .... (COL)
Judy Collins; *Colors Of The Day-Best Of* .... (ELE)
  Who Knows Where The Time Goes .... (ELE)
Moe Bandy; *Greatest Hits* .... (COL)
  Rodeo Romeo .... (COL)
Suzy Bogguss; *Aces* .... (CAP)
When My Ship Comes In
Clint Black; *Hard Way* .... (RCA)

STATES: CONNECTICUT

Connecticut
Judy Garland/Others; *Changing My Tune-Best Of Decca
Years-#2* .... (DEC)
Too Much Joy; *Son Of Sam I Am* .... (GIA)
Connecticut Yankee In The Court Of...
Robert Fripp/League Of Crafty Guitarists; *Show Of
Hands* .... (EDI)
Wives Are In Connecticut
Carly Simon; *Spoiled Girl* .... (EPI)

STATES: DELAWARE

Delaware
Drop Nineteens; *Delaware* .... (CRL)
Perry Como; *This Is* .... (RCA)
Delaware Slide
George Thorogood/Destroyers; *George
Thorogood/Destroyers* .... (ROU)

STATES: FLORIDA

See Also: CITIES: MIAMI

Deep Down In Florida
Muddy Waters; *Hard Again* .... (BS)
  Muddy "Mississippi" Waters Live .... (BS)
Deep Down In Florida #2
Muddy Waters; *King Bee* .... (BS)
Farmer In Florida
Sally Rogers; *Love Will Guide Us* .... (FF)
Florida Blues
Vassar Clements; *Crossing The Catskills* .... (ROU)
  Grass Routes .... (ROU)
Florida Greeting Song
Pat Metheny; *Watercolors* .... (ECM)
Going Back To Florida
Billie & De De Pierce; *New Orleans Jazz* .... (ARH)
Goin' Back To Florida
John Hammond; *Best Of* .... (VAN)
Lightnin' Hopkins; *Lightnin' Hopkins* .... (FLW)
  Roots Of .... (FLW)
Key Largo
Bertie Higgins; *Just Another Day In Paradise* ..... (KAT)
Mainline Florida
Eric Clapton; *461 Ocean Boulevard* .... (RSO)

Seminole Wind
John Anderson; *Seminole Wind* .... (BNA)

STATES: GEORGIA

See Also: CITIES: ATLANTA, SAVANNAH

Another Dawn Breaking Over Georgia
David Frizzell & Shelly West; *Our Best To You* ... (WB)
At A Georgia Camp Meeting
Kid Ory's Creole Jazz Band; *1956-The Legendary
Kid* .... (GTJ)
Back In Georgia
R.B. Greaves; *Rock & Roll* .... (INT)
Back To Georgia
Loggins & Messina; *On Stage* .... (COL)
  Sittin' In .... (COL)
Boogie Ala Georgia
Peggy Gilbert; *Dixieland Jazz* .... (CMB)
Born In Georgia
Tinsley Ellis; *Fanning The Flames* .... (ALG)
Bringing In The Georgia Mail
Norman Blake; *Back Home In Sulphur Springs* .. (ROU)
Burn Georgia Burn
Alabama; *Feels So Right* .... (RCA)
Caroline's Still In Georgia
Mac Davis; *Soft Talk* .... (CAS)
Cold Summer Day In Georgia
Gene Watson; *Memories To Burn* .... (EPI)
Devil Comes Back To Georgia
Marc O'Connor; *Heroes* .... (WB)
Devil Loose In Georgia
Orrin Star & Gary Mehalick; *Premium Blend* ...... (FF)
Devil Went Down To Georgia
Charlie Daniels Band; *Billboard Top Hits-1979* .. (RHI)
  Decade Of Hits .... (EPI)
  Me & The Boys .... (EPI)
  Million Mile Reflections .... (EPI)
  ST/Urban Cowboy .... (ASY)
Dreamy Georgiana Moon
Asa Martin; *Dr. Ginger Blue* .... (ROU)
Georgia In A Jug
Johnny Paycheck; *Greatest Hits #2* .... (EPI)
  I Don't Need To Know That Right Now .... (ALL)
  Take This Job & Shove It .... (EPI)
Georgia Keeps Pulling On My Ring
Conway Twitty; *Classic Conway* .... (MCA)
  Very Best Of .... (MCA)
Georgia On My Mind
Billie Holiday; *God Bless The Child* .... (COL)
  Story-#2 .... (COL)
Hoagy Carmichael; *Hoagy Sings Carmichael* ..... (EMI)
  Legendary Performer .... (RCA)
Ray Charles; *Anthology* .... (RHI)
  Greatest Hits-#2 .... (RHI)
Willie Nelson; *Greatest Hits & Some That Will Be* (COL)
  Stardust .... (COL)
  & Family Live .... (COL)
Georgia Pineywoods
Osborne Brothers; *Best Of The* .... (MCA)
Georgia Rhythm
Atlanta Rhythm Section; *Rock & Roll Alternative* . (POL)
Georgia Soul
Carmol Taylor; *I Think They Call It Homesick* .. (COU)
Georgia Sunshine
Jerry Reed; *Best Of* .... (RCA)
Going To Georgia
Johnson Mountain Boys; *At The Old Schoolhouse* (ROU)
Stanley Brothers; *Shadows Of The Past* .... (COP)
Hell & Half Of Georgia
Owen Brothers; *Audiograph Live* .... (AUD)
  Fool Of Fools .... (AUD)
I Been To Georgia On A Fast Train
Willie Nelson; *Me & Paul* .... (COL)
I'd Better Off (In A Pine Box)
Doug Stone; *Doug Stone* .... (EPI)
  Greatest Country Hits-'90s-1990 .... (COL)
Long Way Back To Georgia
John McCutcheon; *Gonna Rise Again* .... (ROU)
Macon Georgia Bad Girl
Jeannie C. Riley; *& Fancy Friends* .... (PLN)
Marching Through Georgia
American Music Consort; *Sentimental Songs Of The
Mid-19th Cent.* .... (TAK)

Midnight Train To Georgia
Gladys Knight/Pips; *Billboard Top Rock 'N' Roll
Hits-1973* .... (RHI)
   Greatest Hits ....(BUD)
   Imagination ....(BUD)
   On & On .... (FFT)
   Radio Active Hits .... (ACC)
   Very Best Of ....(BUD)
Moon Over Georgia
Shenandoah; *Extra Mile* ....(COL)
   Greatest Hits ....(COL)
My Little Georgia Rose
David Grisman; *Home Is Where The Heart Is* ... (ROU)
Herb Pederson; *Son Of Rounder Banjo* .... (ROU)
My Sweet Eyed Georgia Girl
Atlanta; *Atlanta* .... (MCA)
Night The Lights Went Out In Georgia
Lynn Anderson; *Top Of The World* ....(COL)
Reba McEntire; *For My Broken Heart* .... (MCA)
Vicki Lawrence; *Super Hits/'70s-Have A Nice
Day-#10* .... (RHI)
Peach Picking Time Down In Georgia
Jimmie Rodgers; *My Rough & Rowdy Days* ......(RCA)
   This Is ....(RCA)
Merle Travis; *Superstars Salute Jimmie Rodgers* ...(SO)
Poor Red Georgia Dirt
Robin & Linda Williams; *Close As We Can Get* .... (FF)
Rainy Night In Georgia
Brook Benton; *Anthology* .... (RHI)
   Atlantic R&B 1947-1974-#6-(1966-1969) .... (ATL)
   Golden Age Of Black Music-1960-1970 .... (ATL)
   Pick Of .... (FFT)
   Soul Years .... (ATL)
   Today .... (COT)
Hank Williams, Jr.; *14 Greatest Hits* .... (POL)
Sam Moore & Conway Twitty; *Rhythm Country &
Blues* .... (MCA)
Red Skies Over Georgia
Charlie Walker; *45* .... (PLN)
Send Me Back To Georgia
Si Kahn; *Unfinished Portraits* .... (FF)
Slow Train Through Georgia
Norman Blake; *Whiskey Before Breakfast* .... (ROU)
South Georgia Blues
Sonny Stitt & Sadik Hakim; *Sonny Stitt Meets Sadik
Hakim* .... (PRG)
Sweet Georgia Brown
Anita O'Day; *Compact Jazz-Best Of The Jazz
Vocalists* ....(VRV)
Beatles; *In The Beginning-Circa 1960* ....(POL)
Coasters; *Greatest Hits* ....(ATC)
Django Reinhardt; *Djangologie USA-#1* ....(DSQ)
   Quintet Of The Hot Club Of France ....(PRS)
Ella Fitzgerald; *In London* ....(PAB)
   Whisper Not ....(VRV)
Ella Fitzgerald & Count Basie; *Perfect Match* .... (PAB)
Original Cast; *Bubbling Brown Sugar* ....(AMH)
Stephane Grappelli; *Live In London* ....(BL)
Tito Puente; *Out Of This World* .... (CP)
Tall Trees In Georgia
Buffy Sainte-Marie; *Best Of-#2* .... (VAN)
   I'm Gonna Be A Country Girl Again .... (VAN)
Ticket Back To Georgia
Head East; *Flat As A Pancake* .... (A&M)
Walk All Over Georgia
Louisiana Red; *Midnight Rambler* .... (TOM)
Walkin' Back To Georgia
Jim Croce; *50th Anniversary Collection* .... (SAJ)
   Down The Highway .... (SAJ)
Watermelon Time In Georgia
Larry Boone; *Get In Line* ....(COL)
"Way" Cross Georgia
David Sanborn; *Takin' Off* .... (WB)

STATES: HAWAII

Aloha I Love You
Martin Denny; *From Maui With Love* ...... (FIR)
Aloha Oe
Elvis Presley; *ST/Blue Hawaii* ....(RCA)
Henry Mancini; *Music Of Hawaii* ....(RCA)
Marty Robbins; *All-Time Greatest Hits* ....(COL)
   Greatest Hits ....(COL)

Aloha Waltz
Walter Ostanek; *Little Bird Dance* .... (BOO)
Aloha (Also Means Goodbye)
Screamin' Scott Simon; *Transmissions From Space* (RHI)
Aux Iles Hawaii
Diana Ross; *Evening With* .... (MOT)
Beautiful Hawaii
Magic Organ; *Around The World* .... (RAN)
Blue Hawaii
Billy Vaughn; *16 Great Performances* .... (MCA)
   Best Of .... (MCA)
   Golden Hits .... (MCA)
   & Orchestra: Play 22 Greatest Hits .... (RAN)
Elvis Presley; *Legendary Performer-#2* ....(RCA)
   ST/Blue Hawaii ....(RCA)
Blues For Hawaiians
Chuck Berry; *Chuck Berry Is On Top* .... (CSS)
Everybody Does It In Hawaii
Jimmie Rodgers; *On The Way Up-1929* .... (ROU)
Hawaii
Beach Boys; *Concert* ....(CAP)
   Spirit Of America ....(CAP)
   Surfer Girl ....(CAP)
Henry Mancini; *Music Of Hawaii* ....(RCA)
Kingfish; *Hurricane* .... (ACC)
Hawaii Five 0
Ventures; *45* .... (UA)
Hawaiian Hospitality
Louis Armstrong; *Jazz Heritage-Satchmo's
Discoveries* .... (MCA)
Hawaiian Lei Song
Les Jansen; *45* ....(ACT)
Hawaiian Nights
Kingston Trio; *Looking For The Sunrise* ....(XER)
Hawaiian War Chant
Bette Midler; *Live At Last* .... (ATL)
Tommy Dorsey; *Complete-#8* ....(RCA)
   This Is ....(RCA)
Hawaiian Wedding Song
Andy Williams; *16 Most Requested Songs* ......(COL)
   Greatest Hits ....(COL)
Jim Reeves; *Pure Gold* ....(RCA)
It Happened In Hawaii
Glenn Miller; *Complete-#7-1941* ....(RCA)
Lovely Hula Hands
101 Strings; *Sound Of Magnificence* .... (ALS)
My Hawaii
Rascals; *Once Upon A Dream* .... (RHI)
My Little Grass Shack In Kealakekua, HI
Mom & Dads; *Blue Hawaii* .... (CRS)
New Hawaiian Boogie
George Thorogood/Destroyers; *Move It On Over* (ROU)
Sailin' On The Hawaii
Nitty Gritty Dirt Band; *Will The Circle Be
Unbroken* .... (EMI)
Sweet Hawaiian Sunshine
Jorma Kaukonen & Tom Hobson; *Quah* .... (RLX)
Sweet Leilani
Bing Crosby; *Best Of* .... (MCA)
King Sisters; *And The Winner Is-Best Movie Songs* (CAP)

STATES: IDAHO

Going To Idaho
Grandmothers; *Looking Up Granny's Dress* ...... (RHI)
Idaho
Benny Carter; *Gentleman & His Music* .... (CCJ)
Central Methodist College Band; *Circus Echoes* ...(FID)
   Mighty To Save ....(FID)
Count Basie; *Standards* ....(VRV)
Private Idaho
B-52's; *Party Mix/Mesopotamia* .... (WB)
   Wild Planet .... (WB)
Doughboys; *When Up Turns To Down* .... (RES)

STATES: ILLINOIS

   See Also: CITIES: CHICAGO

Fields Of Illinois
Don Lange; *Natural Born Heathen* .... (FF)
Illinois
Dan Fogelberg; *Souvenirs* .... (FM)

Illinois Blues
Skip James; *Devil Got My Woman* .... (VAN)
Great Bluesmen At Newport .... (VAN)
Tribute To-#1-1964 ....(BIO)
Illinois Dawn
Skyline; *Late To Work* ....(FF)
Illinois Loyalty
University Of Michigan Band; *Greatest College Football Marches* .... (VAN)
Illinois March
Eastman Wind Ensemble; *Marchtime* .... (MER)
Pride Of The Illini
University Of Michigan Band; *Greatest College Football Marches* .... (VAN)

STATES: INDIANA

Anna In Indiana
Eddie Cantor; *Rare Early Recordings-1919-1921* .(BIO)
Back Home Again In Indiana
Les Paul; *Legend & The Legacy* .... (CAP)
Back Home In Indiana
Peggy Gilbert/Dixie Bells; *Dixieland Jazz* .... (CMB)
Gary, Indiana
Original Cast; *ST/Music Man* .... (CAP)
Robert Preston; *ST/Music Man* .... (WB)
Going Back To Indiana
Sawyer Brown; *Sawyer Brown* .... (CAP)
Goin' Back To Indiana
Jackson 5; *Anthology* .... (MOT)
Goin' Back To Indiana .... (MOT)
Greatest Hits .... (MOT)
Third Album .... (MOT)
Home In Indiana
Magic Organ; *Traveling With* .... (RAN)
Indiana
Oscar Peterson; *Digital At Montreux* .... (PAB)
Oscar Peterson & Count Basie; *Grandmasters* .... (PAB)
Timekeepers .... (PAB)
Pete Fountain; *Best Of* .... (MCA)
Live In New Orleans .... (FIR)
Indiana Fight
Indiana University Marching 100; *Indiana Our Indiana* .... (FID)
Indiana University Marching 100 .... (FID)
Indiana Loyalty
Indiana University Marching 100; *Indiana Our Indiana* .... (FID)
Indiana My Indiana
Ohio State University Marching Band; *Saturday Afternoon At Columbus* .... (FID)
Indiana Our Indiana
Indiana University Marching 100; *Indiana Our Indiana* .... (FID)
Indiana University Marching 100 .... (FID)
Indiana Wants Me
R. Dean Taylor; *Hard-To-Find Motown Classics-#2* .... (MOT)
Super Hits-#5 .... (GUS)
Super Hits/'70s-Have A Nice Day-#3 .... (RHI)
Jim Dean Of Indiana
Phil Ochs; *Chords Of Fame* .... (A&M)
Greatest Hits .... (A&M)
War Is Over-Best Of .... (A&M)

STATES: IOWA

Iowa
Stone Soup; *October Nights* .... (WCH)
Iowa Fight Song
University Of Iowa Band; *Go Hawkeyes Go* ..... (FID)
University Of Michigan Band; *Greatest College Football Marches* .... (VAN)
Iowa Stubborn
Original Cast; *Music Man* .... (CAP)
Robert Preston; *ST/Music Man* .... (WB)
Iowa Waltz
Greg Brown; *Iowa Waltz* .... (RDH)
Iowa, Iowa-Out Where The Tall Corn Grows
Popular Standard; *Out of print recording* ....(OOP)
Jenny (Iowa Sunrise)
Janis Ian; *Night Trains* .... (COL)

Love Song For Iowa
Bonnie Koloc; *With You On My Side* .... (FF)
On Iowa
University Of Iowa Marching Band; *Go Hawkeyes Go* ....(FID)

STATES: KANSAS
See Also: CITIES: KANSAS CITY

Cold Rain In Kansas
Don Lange; *Natural Born Heathen* .... (FF)
Devil Came From Kansas
Procol Harum; *A Salty Dog* .... (A&M)
Kansas Polka
Michigan Dutchmen; *New Polka Compositions* ......(JJ)
Kansas Wildcats
Band Of H.M. Royal Marines; *Hands Across The Sea-Sousa Marches* .... (ANG)
Eastman Wind Ensemble; *Sousa On Review* .... (MER)
Stars & Stripes Forever .... (MER)
Kansas You Fooler
Ozark Mountain Daredevils; *It'll Shine When It Shines* .... (A&M)
King Of Kansas
Skywalk; *Fall Into Winter Jazz Sampler '88* ..... (MCA)
No Mountains In The State Of Kansas
Reilly & Maloney; *Everyday* .... (FRK)
Not In Kansas
Basehead; *Not In Kansas* .... (IMG)
Parsons, Kansas Blues
Bob Scobey's Frisco Band & Clancy Hayes; *Bob Scobey's Frisco Band & Clancy Hayes* .... (GTJ)
Rocky Road To Kansas
Tony Ellis; *Dixie Banner* ....(FF)

STATES: KENTUCKY

Blue Kentucky Girl
Emmylou Harris; *Blue Kentucky Girl* .... (WB)
Profile 2-Best Of .... (WB)
Loretta Lynn; *Greatest Hits* .... (MCA)
Blue Moon Of Kentucky
Bill Monroe; *American Originals* .... (COL)
Bean Blossom/Lester Flatt .... (MCA)
Best Of .... (MCA)
Elvis Presley; *Date With* .... (RCA)
Golden Celebration .... (RCA)
Sun Sessions .... (RCA)
Bus Fare To Kentucky
Skeeter Davis; *Best Of The Best Of* .... (GUS)
Cluckin' Hen, Going Back To Kentucky...
J.P. Fraley & Annadeene; *Wild Rose Of The Mountain* .... (ROU)
Down Home In Kentucky
Frankie Jaxon; *Frankie "Half-Pint" Jaxon-1927-1940* .... (SB)
East Kentucky Mountains
Anne Hills; *Don't Panic (Panic Is On/Don't Explain)* .... (HOG)
Goin' Back To Old Kentucky
New Grass Revival; *Festival Tapes* .... (FF)
Green Kentucky Eyes
Pal Rakes; *Midnight Rain* .... (AA)
Hills Of Kentucky
Debby McClatchy/Red Clay Ramblers; *Debby McClatchy/Red Clay Ramblers* .... (GRE)
Kendalls; *Kendalls* .... (GUS)
I Can Hear Kentucky Calling Me
Chet Atkins; *Collector's* .... (RCA)
I'm Going Back To Kentucky
Greg Austin Band; *Greg Austin Band* .... (XER)
I'm Going Back To Old Kentucky
Bill Monroe; *Best Of* .... (MCA)
Bill Monroe/Flatt & Scruggs .... (ROU)
Columbia Historic Edition .... (COL)
/Stars Of The Bluegrass-Hall Of Fame .... (MCA)
Kentuckian Song
Eddy Arnold; *Legendary Performer* .... (RCA)
Kentucky
Everly Brothers; *All They Had To Do Was Dream* (RHI)
Songs Our Daddy Taught Us .... (RHI)
Gail Davies; *I'll Be There* .... (WB)

Osborne Brothers; *Best Of* .... (MCA)
Whitstein Brothers; *Rose Of My Heart* .... (ROU)
Kentucky Avenue
Tom Waits; *Blue Valentine* .... (ASY)
Kentucky Avenue, A.C.
Duke Ellington; *Intimacy Of The Blues* ....(FAN)
Kentucky Bluebird
Keith Whitley; *Kentucky Bluebird* ....(RCA)
Kentucky Blues
Joy Ford; *45* ....(COU)
Roy Bookbinder; *Goin' Back To Tampa* ....(FF)
Kentucky Flower
King Edward IV/Knights; *45* ....(SND)
Kentucky Fried Blues
Nazareth; *Expect No Mercy* ....(A&M)
Kentucky Gambler
Merle Haggard/Strangers; *Songs I'll Always Sing* .(CAP)
Kentucky Hills Of Tennessee
Commander Cody/Lost Planet Airmen; *Hot Licks Cold
Steel Trucker's Favorites* .... (MCA)
Kentucky Man
Elvis Presley; *Worldwide 50 Gold Award Hits-#1* (RCA)
Kentucky Mandolin
Bill Monroe/Blue Grass Boys; *Best Of* .... (MCA)
Kentucky Bluegrass ....(MCA)
Kentucky Means Paradise
Barbara Mandrell; *Vintage* .... (AUD)
Roger Bellow/Drifting Troubadours; *On The Road To
Prosperity* .... (FF)
Kentucky Moonshine
Pure Prairie League; *Takin' The Stage* ....(RCA)
Two Lane Highway ....(RCA)
Kentucky Moonshiner
Dave Van Ronk; *Inside Dave Van Ronk* .... (FAN)
George Tucker; *George Tucker* .... (ROU)
Kentucky Pool
John Hartford; *Headin' Down Into The Mystery
Below* .... (FF)
Kentucky Rain
Elvis Presley; *Golden Records-#5* ....(RCA)
Memphis Record ....(RCA)
Pure Gold ....(RCA)
Kentucky Slop Song
NRBQ; *Best Of-Stay With Me* ....(COL)
Kentucky Song Bird
Roger Whittaker; *Mirrors Of My Mind* ....(RCA)
Kentucky Sunrise
Ringling Brothers B & B Band; *Circus Time* .... (MCA)
Kentucky Waltz
Bill Monroe; *Columbia Historic Edition* ....(COL)
/Emmylou Harris-& Friends .... (MCA)
Kentucky Woman
Billy Cole Reed; *Audiograph Alive* ....(AUD)
Deep Purple; *Purple Passages* .... (WB)
When We Rock We Rock .... (WB)
Gary Puckett/Union Gap; *Greatest Hits* ....(BCT)
Neil Diamond; *Classics* ....(COL)
Gold ....(MCA)
Love At The Greek ....(COL)
Ronnie Milsap; *16 Greatest Hits-#2* ....(TRP)
Meet Me Tonight By My Old Kentucky Home
Joe Val/New England Bluegrass Boys; *#2* ...... (ROU)
Moon Of Kentucky
Elvis Presley; *Golden Celebration* ....(RCA)
My Old Kentucky Home
Al Jolson; *Story-#5* .... (MCA)
Randy Newman; *Live* ....(RPR)
Randy Newman ....(RPR)
Ry Cooder; *Ry Cooder* ....(RPR)
Salli Terri; *Songs Of The American Land* ...... (ANG)
My Ol' Kentucky Rock & Roll Home
Original New York Cast; *Oil City Symphony* ... (DRG)
My Rose Of Old Kentucky
Bill Monroe; *& Friends* .... (MCA)
Bill Monroe/Flatt & Scruggs; */Flatt & Scruggs* .. (ROU)
No Christmas In Kentucky
Phil Ochs; *Toast To Those Who Are Gone* .... (RHI)
Old Kentucky Fiddle
Hoot Hester; *45* ....(NAT)
Old Kentucky Land
Kingston Trio; *Rediscovering* .... (FOL)
Tune Up! ....(FOL)
Old Kentucky Song
Oak Ridge Boys; *Bobbie Sue* .... (MCA)

On The Old Kentucky Shore
J.D. Crowe/Others; *Bluegrass Album-#5-Sweet Sunny
South* .... (ROU)
Roll Along, Kentucky Moon
Jimmie Rodgers; *Down The Old
Road-1931-1932* .... (ROU)
Leon Redbone; *Sugar* .... (PRV)
Somewhere In Kentucky
Charlie Bandy; *45* ....(SND)
Sweet Kentucky Ham
David Frishberg; *Can't Take You Nowhere* .... (FAN)
Classics ....(CCJ)
Take Me Back To Kentucky
Cross Country Grass; *Tribute To Bluegrass* ...... (BOO)
Tuck Me To Sleep In My Old Kentucky Home
Firehouse Five Plus Two; *Goes South* ....(GTJ)
Turn Your Radio On, Kentucky
Blue Sky Boys; *Sunny Side Of Life* ....(ROU)
Wild Kentucky Roan
Mike Auldridge; *& Old Dog* ....(FF)
Wild Kentucky Skies
Marty Brown; *Wild Kentucky Skies* ....(MCA)

STATES: LOUISIANA
See Also: CITIES: NEW ORLEANS

Blues From Louisiana
Illinois Jacquet/Big Band; *Jacquet's Got It* ...... (ATL)
Born In Louisiana
Clarence "Gatemouth" Brown; *Alligator Records 20th
Anniversary* ....(ALG)
Standing My Ground ....(ALG)
Troy Turner; *Handful Of Aces* .... (ICH)
By-U, By-O (The Lou'siana Lullaby)
Woody Herman; *Best Of The Decca Years* ...... (DEC)
Down At The Twist And Shout
Mary Chapin Carpenter; *Greatest Country
Hits/'90s-1992* ....(COL)
Hitchhiker Exemplar 2 ....(COL)
Shooting Straight In The Dark ....(COL)
Today's Hot Country .... (KT)
Down In Louisiana
Whites; *Whole New World* .... (MCA)
Going Back To Louisiana
Delbert McClinton; *Live From Austin* ....(ALG)
Joey Farr; *45* ....(FAI)
Going Home To Louisiana
Chris Thomas; *The Beginning* .... (ARH)
Going To Louisiana
John Lee Hooker; *Berkeley Blues Festival* ...... (ARH)
That's Where It's At ....(STX)
Goin' Down Louisiana
Blues Project; *No Time Like The Right Time-Best
Of* .... (RHI)
Good Ole Boys From Louisiana
Jimmy C. Newman & Cajun Country; *Jimmy C.
Newman & Cajun Country* .... (DOT)
Home In Louisiana
Country Gentlemen; *Home In Louisiana* .... (VAN)
Remembrances & Forecasts .... (VAN)
In A State Of Louisiana
Roddie Romero/Rockin' Cajuns; *Da Big Squeeze* (SWA)
It's Christmastime In Louisiana
Johnnie Allan; *Alligator Stomp-#4-Cajun
Christmas* .... (RHI)
La Louisianne
Queen Ida; *On Tour* ....(CRS)
Queen Ida/Bon Temps Zydeco Band; *In New
Orleans* .... (CRS)
Leaving Louisiana In The Broad Daylight
Emmylou Harris; *Quarter Moon In A Ten-Cent
Town* .... (WB)
Oak Ridge Boys; *Greatest Hits* .... (MCA)
Have Arrived ....(MCA)
Rodney Crowell; *Ain't Living Long Like This* ...... (WB)
Collection ....(WB)
Louisiana
Count Basie; *Essential-#2* ....(COL)
Jimmy C. Newman; *Cajun Country* ....(DEL)
John Wesley Ryles; *Reconsider Me* ....(PLN)
Louisiana 1927
Aaron Neville; *Warm Your Heart* ....(A&M)
Jo-el Sonnier; *Come On Joe* ....(RCA)

Randy Newman; *Good Old Boys* .... (RPR)
  ST/Blaze .... (A&M)
Louisiana Anna
  Maines Brothers Band; *High Rollin'* .... (MER)
Louisiana Blues
  Clifton Chenier; *Alligator Stomp-Cajun & Zydeco*
  Classics .... (RHI)
  Louisiana Blues & Zydeco .... (ARH)
  Jo-el Sonnier; *Louisiana Scrapbook* ....(RYK)
  Muddy Waters; *Best Of* .... (CSS)
  Chess Box .... (CSS)
  Savoy Brown; *London Collection-Best Of* ....(LON)
Louisiana Bound
  Big Joe Williams; *Shake Your Boogie* .... (ARH)
Louisiana Cajun Band
  Jimmy C. Newman; *Backstage At The Grand Ole*
  Opry ....(RCA)
  Cajun Country ....(DEL)
Louisiana Cajun Rock Band
  Carol Channing & Jimmy C. Newman; */Others-& Her*
  Country Friends .... (PLN)
Louisiana Christmas Day
  Aaron Neville; *Soulful Christmas* .... (A&M)
Louisiana Fais Dodo
  Charlie Daniels Band; *Me & The Boys* .... (EPI)
Louisiana Flood
  Paul Butterfield/Better Days; *It All Comes Back* .. (RHI)
Louisiana Hannah
  Webb Wilder; *Hybrid Vigor* .... (ISL)
Louisiana Joe
  Joe Douglas; *45* .... (BLR)
Louisiana Lady
  Bobby Penn; *45* .... (FIF)
  New Riders Of The Purple Sage; *Best Of* ....(COL)
  New Riders Of The Purple Sage ....(COL)
Louisiana Lonely
  Narvel Felts; *45* .... (GMC)
Louisiana Lou & Three-Card Monty John
  Allman Brothers Band; *Win Lose Or Draw* .... (POL)
Louisiana Man
  Dave Edmunds; *D.E. 7th* ....(COL)
  Doug Kershaw; *Alive & Pickin'* .... (WB)
  Best Of .... (WB)
  Louisiana Man .... (WB)
Louisiana Purchase
  Boyd Keith; *45* .... (DJ)
Louisiana Rain
  Tom Petty/Heartbreakers; *Damn The Torpedoes* . (BKS)
Louisiana Road Song
  Tish Hinojosa; *Culture Swing* .... (ROU)
Louisiana Saturday Night
  Don Williams; *Best Of Cajun Country* ....(ERA)
  Best Of-#4 .... (MCA)
  Country Boy .... (MCA)
  Jimmy C. Newman; *Progressive CC* .... (PLN)
  Mel McDaniel; *Greatest Hits* .... (CAP)
Louisiana Stomp
  Clifton Chenier; *Zydeco-Early Years* .... (ARH)
Louisiana Sun
  Doug Kershaw; *Louisiana Man* .... (WB)
  Wichita Wildcat .... (FFT)
Louisiana Sunday Afternoon
  Diane Schuur; *Collection* ....(GRP)
  Talkin' 'Bout You ....(GRP)
Louisiana Two-Step
  Clifton Chenier; *King Of Zydeco Live At*
  Montreux .... (ARH)
  Out West .... (ARH)
Louisiana Woman
  Catfish Hodge; *Bout With The Blues* .... (ADE)
  Rockin' Tabby Thomas; *King Of Swamp Blues* .. (MSO)
  R.G./Bayou Zydeco; *Fire On The Bayou* ....(TAK)
Louisiana Woman, Mississippi Man
  Loretta Lynn & Conway Twitty; *Louisiana Woman*
  Mississippi Man .... (MCA)
  Very Best Of .... (MCA)
Louisiana Women
  J.J. Cale; *Really* .... (MER)
  Wayne Stewart; *Aspen Skyline* .... (BRR)
Louisiana Zydeco
  Clarence "Gatemouth" Brown; *Standing My*
  Ground ....(ALG)
Louisiana, The Key To My Soul
  Jimmy C. Newman; *Jimmy C. Newman* .... (DOT)

My Louisiana Love
  Bill Monroe & Mel Tillis; *Bill Monroe & Friends* (MCA)
Oh Louisiana
  Pete Seeger; *Complete Carnegie Hall*
  Concert-1963 ....(COL)
Oh, Susanna
  James Taylor; *Sweet Baby James* .... (WB)
  Myron Floren; *Best Of The Wurstfest* .... (RAN)
  Myron Floren .... (RAN)
One More Time
  Seals & Crofts; *Takin' It Easy* .... (WB)
Polly-Wolly-Doodle
  Leon Redbone; *Live!* .... (PRR)
  On The Track .... (WB)
  Mance Lipscomb; *#3-Texas Songster In A Live*
  Performance .... (ARH)
  Pete Seeger/Woody Guthrie/Cisco Houston; *Lonesome*
  Valley .... (FLW)
Ragin' Cajun
  Charlie Daniels Band; *Windows* .... (EPI)
Sweet Louisiana
  Charlie Daniels Band; *Saddle Tramp* .... (EPI)
  Volunteer Jam-#3&4 .... (EPI)

STATES: MAINE

Back In Maine
  Neal Davis; *Warm Places* ....(CRT)
Farewell To Maine
  Paul Sullivan; *Sketches Of Maine* ....(RMS)
From Maine To Mexico
  Leon Russell; *Americana* ....(OOP)
Maine
  Original Cast; *No Strings* ....(OOP)
Maine Stein Song
  University Of Michigan Band; *Greatest College Football*
  Marches .... (VAN)
Reach, The
  Dan Fogelberg; *Innocent Age* .... (FM)
Sweet Woman (From Maine)
  Robert Lockwood, Jr.; *Blues Masters-#2-Post-War*
  Chicago Blues .... (RHI)
Winter In Maine
  Bruce Fowler; *Ants Can Count* .... (TER)

STATES: MARYLAND

See Also: CITIES: BALTIMORE

Dancing In Rackville, Maryland
  Fred Frith; *Gravity* ....(RAL)
Maryland, My Maryland
  Eastman Wind Ensemble; *Music Of The Civil*
  War .... (MER)
  Tennessee Ernie Ford; *Sings Songs Of The Civil*
  War ....(CAP)

STATES: MASSACHUSETTS

See Also: CITIES: BOSTON

Massachusetts
  Bee Gees; *Gold-#1* .... (RSO)
  Here At Last ....(RSO)
  Mystic Moods Orchestra; *English Muffins* ....(BAI)
  Stewart Brodian; *Self-Made Man* .... (MNT)

STATES: MICHIGAN

See Also: CITIES: DETROIT

I Want To Go Back To Michigan
  Judy Garland; *ST/Easter Parade* .... (SSP)
Michigan Blackhawk
  Monkees; *Missing Links-#2* .... (RHI)
Michigan Rain
  Gregg Alexander; *Intoxifornication* .... (EPA)
Michigan State Fight Song
  University Of Michigan Band; *Greatest College Football*
  Marches .... (VAN)
Michigan Stomps
  Willie Jones/Orchestra; *Territory*
  Bands-#2-1927-1931 ....(HIS)

Michigan Victors
Ohio State University Marching Band; *Music For
Cheerleaders & Song Girls* ....(FID)
Saturday Afternoon At Columbus ....(FID)
Michigan Water
Gregory Hines/Original Cast; *Jelly's Last Jam* .. (MER)
Michigan Water Blues
Little Brother Montgomery/Others; *Chicago
Breakdown* ....(TAK)
Michigander Blues
Jabbo Smith; *Jazz Heritage-Ace Of Rhythm* ...... (MCA)
Panther In Michigan
Michael Smith; *Michael Smith* ....(FF)
Saginaw, Michigan
Lefty Frizzell; *American Originals* ....(COL)
Billboard Top Country Hits-1964 ....(RHI)
Columbia Country Classics-#3-Americana ......(COL)
Greatest Hits ....(COL)
Sky Over Michigan
Harmony Sisters; *Harmony Pie* ....(FF)

STATES: MINNESOTA

Akapolka, Minnesota
Andy Badale/Beer Garden Band; *Nashville Beer
Garden* .... (RAN)
Biggest Ball Of Twine In Minnesota
Weird Al Yankovic; *ST/UHF* ....(RAR)
Minnesota
Detroit Concert Band; *Sousa American Bicentennial
Collection* ....(H&L)
George Russell; *Snake River* ....(GRE)
Minnesota Rouser
Ohio State University Marching Band; *Stadium Favorites
In Brass* ....(FID)
Minnesota Strip
Dictators; *Live-F... 'Em If They Can't Take A Joke* (ROI)
New York Rockers ....(ROI)
Fallen Angel; *Go For The Ride* ....(MCA)
Senator From Minnesota
Michael Tilson Thomas; *Of Thee I Sing/Let 'Em Eat
Cake* ....(COL)

STATES: MISSISSIPPI

Back In Mississippi
Elmore James; *King Of The Slide Guitar* ....(CPC)
Born In Mississippi
Chris LeDoux; *Wild & Wooly* ....(LIB)
Down In Mississippi
Pops Staples; *Peace In The Neighborhood* ....(POI)
Roy Rogers; *Slidewinder* ....(BLI)
Ry Cooder; *ST/Crossroads* ....(WB)
Far East Mississippi
Ohio Players; *Gold* .... (MER)
Going Down To Mississippi
Phil Ochs; *Toast To Those Who Are Gone* .... (RHI)
Here's To The State Of Mississippi
Phil Ochs; *I Ain't Marching Anymore* ....(CTH)
There But For Fortune ....(ELE)
I'm From Mississippi
Luther Johnson/Magic Rockers; *I Want To Groove With
You* ....(BUL)
Louisiana Woman, Mississippi Man
Loretta Lynn & Conway Twitty; *Louisiana Woman
Mississippi Man* .... (MCA)
Very Best Of .... (MCA)
Mississippi
Charlie Daniels Band; *Million-Mile Reflections* .... (EPI)
Duke Ellington; *Jubilee Stomp* ....(BLU)
Kay Starr; *Capitol Collectors Series* ....(CAP)
Mississippi Half-Step Uptown Toodeloo
Grateful Dead; *Steal Your Face* ....(GRD)
Wake Of The Flood ....(GRD)
Without A Net ....(GRD)
Mississippi Kid
Lynyrd Skynyrd; *Pronounced Leh-nerd Skin-nerd* (MCA)
Mississippi Lady
Jim Croce; *Down The Highway* .... (21)
Mississippi Moon
Greg Brown; *One More Goodnight Kiss* .... (RDH)
Jerry Garcia; *Compliments* ....(GRD)

Jimmie Rodgers; *Down The Old
Road-1931-1932* .... (ROU)
Early Years-1928-1929 .... (ROU)
Seatrain; *Marblehead Messenger* .... (OW)
Mississippi Mud
Bob Crosby Orchestra; *1952-1953* .... (HIN)
Play 22 Original Big Band Hits .... (HIN)
Mississippi Queen
Mountain; *Best Of* ....(COL)
Heavy Metal Memories ....(RHI)
Twin Peaks ....(COL)
Mississippi Squirrel Revival
Ray Stevens; *Country Classics-#1* .... (MCA)
Greatest Hits .... (MCA)
He Thinks He's Ray Stevens .... (MCA)
Mississippi Summer
Si Kahn; *Doing My Job* ....(FF)
Mississippi Woman
Willie Nelson; *Longhorn Jamboree* .... (PLN)
& His Friends .... (PLN)
Mississippi, You're On My Mind
Jerry Jeff Walker; *Ridin' High* .... (MCA)
Jesse Winchester; *Best Of* .... (RHI)
My Head's In Mississippi
ZZ Top; *Greatest Hits* ....(WB)
Recycler ....(WB)
Peace In Mississippi
Jimi Hendrix; *Crash Landing* .... (RPR)
Skippin' In The Mississippi Dew
John Hartford; *Anthology* ....(FF)
Mark Twang ....(FF)
New Grass Revival; *Fly Through The Country* .....(FF)
Tupelo Mississippi Flash
Jerry Reed; *Beset Of* ....(RCA)

STATES: MISSOURI

See Also: CITIES: KANSAS CITY, ST. LOUIS

Missouri
Paul Smith; *Mysterious Barricades* ....(FF)
Tirez Tirez; *Against All Flags* .... (PMR)
Missouri Loves Company
Art Essery; *45* .... (AMI)
Missouri Squabble
Alex Jackson Plantation; *Territory
Bands-#2-1927-1931* .... (HIS)
Missouri Uncompromised
Pat Metheny; *Bright Size Life* .... (ECM)
Missouri Waltz
Mom & Dads; *20 Favorite Waltzes* .... (CRS)
Again .... (CRS)
Wish We Were Back In Missouri
Emmylou Harris; *Legend Of Jesse James* .... (A&M)

STATES: MONTANA

Blue Rock Montana
Willie Nelson; *Red Headed Stranger* ....(COL)
Cut Bank Montana
Hank Williams, Jr.; *Maverick* ....(CPC)
Dynamics For Montana
Joachim Kuhn; *Dynamics* .... (CMU)
Goodbye Montana
George Winston; *Summer* ....(WH)
Long Legged Hannah (From Butte, Montana)
Jesse Hunter; *A Man Like Me* ....(BNA)
Meet Me In Montana
Dan Seals & Marie Osmond; *Best Of Dan Seals* . (CAP)
I Won't Be Blue Anymore .... (EMI)
Marie Osmond & Dan Seals; *Country Duets Two By
Two* .... (CAP)
There's No Stopping Your Heart ....(CAP)
Montana
Frank Zappa; *You Can't Do That On Stage
Anymore* ....(RYK)
Mothers Of Invention; *Apostrophe/Overnite
Sensation* ....(RYK)
Montana Cafe
Hank Williams, Jr.; *Montana Cafe* ....(W/C)
Montana Cowboy
Emmylou Harris/Nash Ramblers; *At The Ryman* . (RPR)
Hot Rize; *Traditional Ties* ....(SH)

Montana Crossing
John Stewart; *Centennial* .... (HOM)
Montana Half Light
Philip Aaberg; *High Plains* ....(WH)
Windham Hill-First Ten Years ....(WH)
Montana Plains
Moonshine Kate/Others; *Banjo Pickin' Girls* .... (ROU)
Montana Rodeo
Chris LeDoux; *Thirty-Dollar Cowboy* .... (LIB)
Montana Skies
James Galway; *Wayward Wind* ....(RCA)
Montana Song
Hank Williams, Jr.; *Living Proof-MGM Recordings
1963-1975* .... (MER)
& Friends .... (POL)
Montana Waltz
Ian Tyson; *Old Corrals & Sagebrush* ....(COL)
Two Rivers In Montana
Gove Scrivenor; *Coconut Gove* .... (FF)
Twodot Montana
Hank Williams, Jr.; *Strong Stuff* .... (WB)
View From Pony, Montana
Philip Aaberg; *Upright* ....(WH)
Wild Montana Skies
John Denver; *Greatest Hits-#3* ....(RCA)
It's About Time ....(RCA)
John Denver & Emmylou Harris;
Collector's-Duets ....(RCA)

STATES: NEBRASKA

Dear Old Nebraska U.
University Of Michigan Band; *Greatest College Football
Marches* .... (VAN)
Hazard (The River)
Richard Marx; *Rush Street* .... (CAP)
Nebraska
Bruce Springsteen; *Nebraska* ....(COL)
Bruce Springsteen/E Street Band;
Live-1975-1985 ....(COL)
Omaha, Nebraska
Doug Mathews; *Legacy II* .... (HIG)
Wildfire
Michael Martin Murphey; *Best Of* .... (EMI)
Super Hits/'70s-Have A Nice Day-#14 .... (RHI)
'70s Greatest Rock Hits-#3-High Times .... (PRY)
Michael Murphey; *Blue Sky Night Thunder* .... (EPI)

STATES: NEVADA

See Also: CITIES: LAS VEGAS

Dime Queen Of Nevada
Tom Jones; *Darlin'* .... (MER)
Nevada Fighter
Michael Nesmith; *Older Stuff* .... (RHI)
Nevada Smith
Mystic Moods Orchestra; *Nighttide* ....(BAI)
Nevada, California
Jayhawks; *Hollywood Town Hall* ....(DEF)
Reno, Nevada
Ian Matthews; *Circle Dance-Hokey Pokey Charity
Comp.* ....(GRE)
Mimi & Richard Farina; *Best Of* ....(VAN)
Celebrations For A Grey Day ....(VAN)
Troubadours Of The Folk Era-#1 ....(RHI)
Stop In Nevada
Billy Joel; *Piano Man* ....(COL)

STATES: NEW HAMPSHIRE

Aye, New Hampshire
White Mountain Singers; *We The People* .... (FOL)
It's Called New Hampshire
White Mountain Singers; *Best* ....(FOL)
Sunrise ....(TAK)
New Hampshire Hornpipe
Erich Kunzel/Cincinnati Pops Orchestra; *Sailing* . (TLR)
James Galway; *Beauty & The Beast-Galway At The
Movies* ....(RCA)
New Hampshire Naturally
Shaw Brothers; *Collection* .... (FOL)

Thing At The End Of New Hampshire Avenue
John Fahey; *Old Girlfriends-Other Horrible
Memories* ....(VAR)

STATES: NEW JERSEY

Jersey Bounce
Benny Goodman; *Hits Of* ....(CAP)
Live At Carnegie Hall ....(LON)
Jersey Girl
Bruce Springsteen/E Street Band;
Live-1975-1985 ....(COL)
Tom Waits; *Anthology Of* ....(ASY)
Heartattack & Vine ....(ASY)
New Jersey
Red House Painters; *Red House Painters* ....(4AD)
New Jersey Roadbase
Johnboy; *Pistolswing* ....(TNC)
New Jersey Turnpike
Laurie Anderson; *United States Live* ....(WB)
On Jersey Shore
Paragon Ragtime Orchestra; *On The Boardwalk* .. (NC)
Open All Night
Bruce Springsteen; *Nebraska* ....(COL)
Rosey From Jersey
Li'l Wally; *I Love To Polka* ....(JJ)
State Trooper
Bruce Springsteen; *Nebraska* ....(COL)

STATES: NEW MEXICO

See Also: CITIES: SANTA FE

New Mexican Rose
Frankie Valli/Four Seasons; *25th Anniversary
Collection* .... (RHI)
New Mexican Waltz
Frank Fischer; *Tales Of Mullumbimby* .... (INN)
New Mexico
Erich Avinger; *Si* ....(HMI)
Johnny Cash; *Get Rhythm* ....(SUN)
The Man-The World-His Music ....(SUN)
Rick Danko; *Rick Danko* ....(OOP)
New Mexico March
Eastman Wind Ensemble; *Sousa On Review* .... (MER)
Stars & Stripes Forever ....(MER)
New Mexico-Suite 2
Scott Moulton; *Four Corners Suite* ....(REV)

STATES: NEW YORK

See Also: CITIES: NEW YORK

New York Mining Disaster 1941
Bee Gees; *Gold-#1* ....(POL)
Here At Last ....(RSO)
History Of British Rock-#8 ....(RHI)
New York State Of Mind
Barbra Streisand; *Memories* ....(COL)
Streisand Superman ....(COL)
Billy Joel; *Greatest Hits-#1 & 2-1973-1985* ......(COL)
Turnstiles ....(COL)
Carmen McRae; *Ms. Magic* ....(DHL)
New York State Police
UK Subs; *Left For Dead (Alive In Holland '86)* ... (ROI)
Singles 1978-1982 ....(PGI)

STATES: NORTH DAKOTA

My North Dakota Girl
Dakota Harmony; *45* ....(ACT)
My North Dakota Home
Lawrence Welk; *Reminiscing-#1* .... (RAN)
North Dakota
Lyle Lovett; *Joshua Judges Ruth* ....(MCC)

STATES: OHIO

See Also: CITIES: CINCINNATI

Boy In Ohio
Phil Ochs; *Greatest Hits* ....(A&M)

Goodbye Ohio
Too Much Joy; *Cereal Killers* .... (GIA)
Men Of Ohio
Ohio State University Marching Band; *Foot Tappers* ....(FID)
My City Was Gone
Pretenders; *Learning To Crawl* .... (SIR)
Ohio
Crosby, Stills & Nash; *Crosby Stills & Nash (collection)* .... (ATL)
Crosby, Stills, Nash & Young; *Four-Way Street* .. (ATL)
So Far ....(ATL)
Leonard Bernstein; *Bernstein Songbook* ....(COL)
Neil Young; *Decade* .... (RPR)
ST/Journey Through The Past .... (RPR)
Original Broadway Cast; *Wonderful Town* ....(COL)
Wonderful Town .... (MCA)
Ohio Afternoon
Original New York Cast; *Oil City Symphony* ... (DRG)
Ohio Special March
Ohio State University Marching Band; *Pride Of The Buckeyes* ....(FID)
Ohio Starters' Round
Ohio State University Marching Band; *Buckeye Battle Cry* ....(FID)
Ohio/Machine Gun
Isley Brothers; *Timeless* .... (TN)
Ohio/Wrong Note Rage
Betty Comden & Adolph Green; *Party With* .... (DRG)
Polka Ohio
Li'l Wally; *Here Comes* .... (JJ)
That Old Beat Up Guitar
Jerry Jeff Walker; *Jerry Jeff Walker* .... (MCA)

STATES: OKLAHOMA

See Also: CITIES: TULSA

Home, Sweet Oklahoma
Tom Paxton; *It Ain't Easy* .... (FF)
If You're Ever In Oklahoma
J.J. Cale; *Really* .... (MER)
King Of Oklahoma
Michael Franks; *Previously Unavailable* .... (DRG)
My Oklahoma
Riders In The Sky; *Cowboy Way* .... (MCA)
Steve Young; *Seven Bridges Road* .... (ROU)
Night In Oklahoma
Larry McNeely; *Power Play* .... (FF)
Okie From Muskogee
Merle Haggard/Strangers; *Best of* .... (CAP)
Capitol Collectors Series .... (CAP)
Country Music Classics-#3-1965-1970 .... (KT)
Friend In California .... (EPI)
Songs I'll Always Sing .... (CAP)
ST/Platoon (& Songs From The Era) .... (ATL)
Oklahoma
Call; *Reconciled* .... (ELE)
Ohio State University Marching Band; *Brass Roots* (FID)
Original Broadway Cast; *Oklahoma* ....(RCA)
Original Cast; *Broadway Classics-#1* .... (MCA)
Oklahoma .... (MCA)
SWA; *Sex Doctor* .... (SST)
Oklahoma Blues
Patti Page; *Uncollected-1949* .... (HIN)
Oklahoma Borderline
Vince Gill; *Best Of* ....(RCA)
Oklahoma Boy
Dewayne Boyd/Silver Dollar Band; *45* .... (NAT)
Oklahoma City Times
Limeliters; *Harmony!* .... (FOL)
Oklahoma Country Girl
Elvin Bishop; *Big Fun* .... (ALG)
Oklahoma Dancer
Monkees; *Monkees Present* .... (RHI)
Oklahoma Going Home
Kate Wolf/Wildwood Flower; *Back Roads* .... (KAL)
Oklahoma Heartaches & California Dreams
Kris Carpenter; *45* .... (DOO)
Oklahoma Hills
Hank Thompson; *All-Time Greatest Hits* ....(CCB)
Jack Guthrie/Oklahomans; *Birth Of A Dream-Capitol's Early Hits* ....(CAP)
Great Records/Decade-'40s Hits-Country ....(CCB)

Kay Starr; *Country* .... (CRS)
Oklahoma Joe
Chris LeDoux; *Songs of Rodeo & Country* ....(LIB)
Oklahoma Kid
Goebel Reeves; *Texas Drifter* ....(GLN)
Oklahoma Rag
Bob Wills; *Fiddle* .... (CMF)
Oklahoma Rooster
Backwoods Banjo; *Jes' Fine* .... (ROU)
Oklahoma Stomp
Duke Ellington; *Hot In Harlem* .... (MCA)
Jazz Heritage-Vocalion Rarities .... (MCA)
Spade Cooley; *Columbia Historic Edition* ....(COL)
Spade Cooley/Orchestra; *Legends Of Country Guitar-#1* .... (RHI)
Oklahoma Stroke
Albert Lee; *Gagged But Not Bound* .... (MCA)
Oklahoma Sunshine
Mayf Nutter; *Goin' Skinny Dippin'* .... (CRS)
Oklahoma Sweetheart
George Thorogood/Destroyers; *Boogie People* ... (EMI)
Oklahoma Sweetheart Sally
Maddox Brothers; *America's Most Colorful Hillbilly Band* .... (ARH)
Oklahoma Swing
Vince Gill & Reba McEntire; *When I Call Your Name* .... (MCA)
Oklahoma USA
Kinks; *Muswell Hillbillies* .... (RHI)
Oklahoma Waltz
Cavaliers; *Have Polka Will Travel* ....(ACT)
Take Me Back To Oklahoma
Tim Rex/Oklahoma; *45* .... (DJ)
Tokyo, Oklahoma
John Anderson; *Greatest Hits-#2* .... (WB)
You're The Reason God Made Oklahoma
David Frizzell & Shelly West; *Carryin' On The Family Names* ....(WB)
Country's Greatest Hits-#9-Country Duets ...... (PRY)
Golden Duets .... (WB)

STATES: OREGON

Don't Take Me Alive
Steely Dan; *Royal Scam* .... (MCA)
Oregon
Dan Balmer; *Becoming Became* .... (CMG)
Oregon Hill
Cowboy Junkies; *Black Eyed Man* ....(RCA)
Oregon Hills
Martin Oberschelp; *Nightingale Lightdance* .... (HO)
Oregon Mountains
Woody Simmons; *Oregon Mountains* .... (DEP)
Oregon Rain Song
George Roessler; *Still Life & Old Dreams* .... (EAG)
Oregon Trail
Sons Of The Pioneers; *Sunset On The Range* ..... (PRR)
Starry Sky In Oregon
Andrew White; *Conversations* .... (SOG)
Waves Roll In On Oregon
Jim Post; *Magic-In Concert* .... (FF)

STATES: PENNSYLVANIA

See Also: CITIES: PHILADELPHIA

Fight On, Pennsylvania
All-Star Inter-Conference Band; *College Marches At Halftime U.S.A.* .... (ALS)
University Of Michigan Band; *Greatest College Football Marches* .... (VAN)
Pennsylvania 6-5000
Glenn Miller/Orchestra; *Complete-#4* ....(RCA)
Legendary Performer ....(RCA)
Memorial 1944-1969 ....(RCA)
Moonlight Serenade .... (RAN)
Pure Gold ....(RCA)
Story ....(RCA)
Unforgettable ....(RCA)
Pennsylvania Polka
Andrews Sisters; *16 Great Performances* .... (MCA)
Best Of .... (MCA)
Boogie Woogie Bugle Girls .... (MCA)

Frankie Yankovic/Yanks; *Greatest Hits* ....(COL)
Pittsburgh, Pennsylvania
101 Strings Orchestra; *Million Seller Hits From
Mexico* .... (ALS)
Guy Mitchell; *16 Most Requested Songs* ....(COL)

STATES: RHODE ISLAND

Rhode Island
Lucy Brown; *Lucy Brown* .... (MEG)
Rhode Island Is Famous For You
Blossom Dearie; *Blossoms On Broadway* .... (DRG)
Michael Feinstein; *Live At The Algonquin* .... (ELE)
Rhode Island Red
Brew Moore; *Brew Moore* .... (FAN)
Sweet Rhode Island Red
Ike & Tina Turner; *Proud Mary-Best Of* .... (EMI)

STATES: SOUTH DAKOTA

Deadwood, South Dakota
Nanci Griffith; *One Fair Summer Evening* .... (MCA)
South Dakota Lady
Buddy Red Bow; *Buddy Red Bow* .... (FIR)

STATES: TENNESSEE

See Also: CITIES: MEMPHIS, NASHVILLE

All My Ex's Live In Texas
George Strait; *Country Classics-#10-1987* ...... (MCA)
Greatest Hits-#2 .... (MCA)
Ocean Front Property .... (MCA)
Back To Tennessee
Commander Cody/Lost Planet Airmen; *Lost In The
Ozone* .... (MCA)
Brand New Tennessee Waltz
Jesse Winchester; *Best Of* .... (RHI)
Jesse Winchester .... (RHI)
Joan Baez; *Country Music Album* .... (VAN)
Cold Day In Tennessee
Rob Crosby; *Another Time & Place* .... (ARI)
C.L.I.T. (Cajuns Living In Tennessee)
Pinkard & Bowden; *Cousins Cattle & Other Love
Stories* .... (WB)
Davy Crockett
Hermes Nye; *Ballads Of The Civil War-#1 & 2* . (FLW)
Dixie Chicken
Little Feat; *Dixie Chicken* .... (WB)
Waiting For Columbus .... (WB)
Down In Nashville, Tennessee
Reno & Smiley; *1983 Collector's Edition-#2* ..... (GUS)
Down In Tennessee
John Anderson; *Greatest Hits-#2* .... (WB)
Tokyo Oklahoma .... (WB)
Mark Chesnutt; *What A Way To Live* .... (DEC)
Steve Wariner; *Best Of* ....(RCA)
Drink Muddy Water Leaving Tennessee
Rio Grande Band; *Rio Grande Band* .... (ROU)
Easin' Back To Tennessee
Sleepy John Estes; *In Europe* .... (DLM)
East Tennessee Blues/Goin' Crazy
Stepping Stones; *Fresh Old Time String Band
Music* .... (ROU)
Flight 309 To Tennessee
Shelly West; *West By West* ....(VVA)
From Tennessee To Texas
Johnny Bush/Bandoleros; *Live From Texas* .... (DEL)
Gettin' Into Tennessee Tonight
Gary Wolf; *45* .... (MER)
God Don't Live In Nashville, Tennessee
Randy Howard; *All-American Redneck* .... (WB)
Going Back To Tennessee
Tracy Nelson; *Doin' It My Way* .... (ADE)
Goodbye To Tennessee
Reilly & Maloney; *Alive* .... (FRK)
It Hurts As Much In Texas (As It Did...
George Jones & Ricky Van Shelton; *Friends In High
Places* .... (EPI)
I'll Tennessee You In My Dreams
Tanya Tucker; *Love Me Like You Used To* ....(CAP)

I've Never Lived In Tennessee
Leon MacAuliffe; *Columbia Historic Edition* .....(COL)
Kentucky Hills Of Tennessee
Commander Cody/Lost Planet Airmen; *Hot Licks Cold
Steel Trucker's Favorites* .... (MCA)
Little Home In Tennessee
Bill Harrell/Virginians; *Ballads & Bluegrass* ..... (ADE)
Memphis, Tennessee Hot Rock
Gordon Terry; *Tennessee Hot Rock* .... (PLN)
Midnight Tennessee Woman
Jack Greene; *Sings His Best* ....(SO)
My Little Girl In Tennessee
L. Flatt/E. Scruggs/Foggy Mountain Boys; *Complete
Mercury Sessions* .... (MER)
My Sweetheart In Tennessee
Burnett & Rutherford; *Ramblin' Reckless Hobo* .. (ROU)
My Tennessee Mountain Home
Dolly Parton; *Best Of* ....(RCA)
Best Of A Great Year-#3 ....(RCA)
My Tennessee Mountain Home ....(RCA)
Rose Maddox; *Reckless Love & Bold Adventure* ..(TAK)
Nashville, Tennessee
Troy Cory; *Real Country* ....(VRA)
Nashville, Tenn. Blues
Washboard Sam; *Blues Classics By* .... (BCL)
Old Tennessee
Dan Fogelberg; *Captured Angel* .... (FM)
Live-Greetings From The West .... (FM)
On The Banks Of The Old Tennessee
Doc Watson; *Old Timey Concert* .... (VAN)
Paris, Tennessee
Dennis Robbins; *Man With A Plan* .... (GIA)
Tracy Lawrence; *Sticks & Stones* ....(ATL)
Red Bird Tennessee Waltz
Clark Kessinger & Gene Meade; *Clark Kessinger & Gene
Meade* .... (ROU)
Right Now Tennessee Blues
Charlie Daniels Band; *High Lonesome* ....(EPI)
Rocky Top
Conway Twitty; *Hello Darlin'* .... (MCA)
Flying Burrito Brothers; *Close Encounters To The West
Coast* ....(RLX)
Osborne Brothers; *Best Of* .... (MCA)
Yesterday Today & The Osborne Brothers ..... (MCA)
Roy Clark; *In Concert* .... (MCA)
White Mountain Singers; *Best* .... (FOL)
Roll Tennessee River
Oak Ridge Boys; *Step On Out* .... (MCA)
Singing Bridge Of Memphis Tennessee
John Fahey; *Essential* .... (VAN)
Sunny Tennessee
Doc Watson; *Old Timey Concert* .... (VAN)
Talking To A Tennessee Moon
Candace Anderson; *Talking To A Tennessee
Moon* .... (ADO)
Taos To Tennessee
Tish Hinojosa; *Taos To Tennessee* .... (WAT)
Tennesee Jubilee
Uncle Dave Macon; *Country Music Hall Of
Fame* .... (MCA)
Tennessee
Arrested Development; *3 Years 5 Months 2 Days In The
Life Of* .... (CHR)
Carl Perkins; *Legends Of Country Guitar-#1* ..... (RHI)
Original Golden Hits .... (SUN)
Carol Channing & Webb Pierce; *C & W* .... (PLN)
Charlie Daniels Band; *High Lonesome* ....(EPI)
Crystal Gayle; *Hollywood/Tennessee* ....(CAP)
Glen Campbell; *Letter To Home* .... (AA)
Hank Williams, Jr.; *Early Years* ....(W/C)
New South .... (WB)
Jan & Dean; *Best Of* .... (EMI)
Manic Street Preachers; *Generation Terrorists* ....(COL)
Nitty Gritty Dirt Band; *Hold On* .... (WB)
NRBQ; *Honest Dollar* ....(RYK)
Shawn Colvin; *Fat City* ....(COL)
Tennessee Bird Walk
Blanchard & Morgan; *Super Hits-#2* .... (GUS)
Tennessee Guitars; *20 Great Hits* .... (PLN)
Golden Guitar Hits .... (SSS)
Tennessee Blues
J.D. Crowe/New South; *My Home Ain't In The Hall Of
Fame* .... (ROU)

Kris Kristofferson & Rita Coolidge; *Kris & Rita-Full Moon* .... (A&M)
Ted, Andy & Ricky Sage/Charlie Smithson; *Sagegrass* .... (FLW)
Tennessee Border
Hank Williams; *I Ain't Got Nothin' But Time-1946-1947* .... (POL)
Sonny Burgess & Dave Alvin; *Tennessee Border* ... (HT)
Tennessee Ernie Ford; *16 Tons Of Boogie-Best Of* (RHI)
  Capitol Collectors Series ....(CAP)
Tennessee Born & Bred
Eddie Rabbitt; *Jersey Boy* .... (LIB)
Tennessee Bottle
Kenny Rogers; *The Gambler* .... (EMI)
Tennessee Breakdown
Dillards; *Homecoming & Family Reunion* .... (FF)
Tennessee Choo Choo
Delmore Brothers; *Best Of* .... (STR)
Tennessee Christmas
Alabama; *Christmas* ....(RCA)
Amy Grant; *Christmas Album* .... (WOR)
Lee Greenwood; *Christmas To Christmas* .... (MSP)
Steve Wariner; *Country Christmas To Remember* . (MSP)
  Tennessee Christmas ....(MSP)
Tennessee Farmer
Stringbean; *Salute To Uncle Dave Macon* .... (STR)
Tennessee Fish Fry
Helen O'Connell; *Uncollected With Irv Orton's Orchestra* .... (HIN)
Tennessee Flat Top Box
Johnny Cash; *Classic Cash-Hall Of Fame Series* . (MER)
  Columbia Country Classics-#3-Americana ......(COL)
  Essential ....(COL)
Rosanne Cash; *30 Years Of #1 Hits-#17* ....(COL)
  Hits-1979-1989 ....(COL)
  King's Record Shop ....(COL)
Tennessee Fluxedo
Jerry Douglas; *Fluxedo* .... (ROU)
Tennessee Girl
Carl Jackson; *45* ....(COL)
Tennessee Homesick Blues
Dolly Parton; *Best Of-#3* ....(RCA)
  RCA Years-1967-1986 ....(RCA)
  Star-Spangled Country ....(RCA)
  ST/Rhinestone ....(RCA)
Tennessee Hound Dog
Osborne Brothers; *Best Of* .... (MCA)
Tennessee Jed
Grateful Dead; *Europe '72* .... (WB)
  What A Long Strange Trip It's Been .... (WB)
Tennessee Lonesome Blues
Jim & Jesse; *In The Tradition* .... (ROU)
Tennessee Newsboy (Newsboy Blues)
Frank Sinatra; *Columbia Years-1943-1952-Complete Rec.* ....(COL)
Tennessee Nights
Pam Tillis; *Collection* .... (WB)
Tennessee Plates
Charlie Sexton; *ST/Thelma & Louise* .... (MCA)
John Hiatt; *Slow Turning* .... (A&M)
Tennessee Polka
Mom & Dads; *Gratefully Yours* .... (CRS)
Tennessee Pride
Chet Atkins; *Country Gems* .... (PRR)
Tennessee River
Alabama; *Best Of The '80s...So Far* ....(RCA)
  Greatest Hits ....(RCA)
  Live ....(RCA)
  My Home's In Alabama ....(RCA)
Hank Williams, Jr.; *Rowdy* ....(W/C)
Tennessee Road
Anne Hills; *Woman Of A Calm Heart* .... (FF)
Tennessee Rose
Emmylou Harris; *Cimarron* .... (WB)
Tennessee Saturday Night
Ella Mae Morse; *Capitol Collectors Series* ....(CAP)
Tennessee Saturday Nite
Commander Cody/Lost Planet Airmen; *Aces High* ....(RLX)
Tennessee Stud
Chris LeDoux; *Old Cowboy Classics* .... (LIB)
Eddy Arnold; *Best Of-#2* ....(RCA)
  Legendary Performer ....(RCA)
Hank Williams, Jr.; *The Pressure Is On* ....(W/C)

Johnny Cash; *American Recordings* .... (AME)
Nitty Gritty Dirt Band; *Will The Circle Be Unbroken* .... (EMI)
Tennessee Toddy
Marty Robbins; *Essential-1951-1982* ....(COL)
Tennessee Traveler
Mike Auldridge; *Mike Auldridge* .... (FF)
Tennessee Two Step
Charlie Daniels; *America I Believe In You* .... (LIB)
Tennessee Wagoner
New Grass Revival; *When The Storm Is Over* ......(FF)
Tennessee Waltz
Emmylou Harris; *Cimarron* .... (WB)
  Country's Greatest Hits-#5 .... (WB)
  New Tradition Sings The Old Tradition .... (WB)
Guy Lombardo; *Best Of* ....(CCB)
Hank Williams, Jr.; *Living Proof-MGM Recordings-1963-1975* ....(MER)
Lacy J. Dalton; *Greatest Hits* ....(COL)
Les Paul & Mary Ford; *Les Paul-Selections From Legend & Legacy* ....(CAP)
Patti Page; *Golden Hits* ....(MER)
  Greatest Hits ....(COL)
Roy Acuff; *Essential* ....(COL)
  Greatest Hits ....(COL)
Roy Rogers; *Best Of* ....(CCB)
Sammy Kaye; *Best Of The Big Bands* ....(COL)
Spike Jones; *Best Of* ....(RCA)
Tennessee Whiskey
David Allan Coe; *17 Greatest Hits* ....(COL)
  Biggest Hits ....(COL)
  For The Record-First 10 Years ....(COL)
  Tennessee Whiskey ....(COL)
George Jones; *By Request* .... (EPI)
  First Time Live .... (EPI)
  Greatest Country Hits/'80s-1983 ....(COL)
  Shine On .... (EPI)
  Super Hits .... (EPI)
Merle Haggard; *19 Hot Country Requests-#2* ..... (EPI)
Tennessee Whiskey & Texas Women
Rayburn Anthony; *Audiograph Alive* .... (AUD)
  Dance Floor Crystal Ball .... (AUD)
Tennessee Wig Walk
Bonnie Lou; *Super Hits Country-1950s* ....(GUS)
Russ Morgan; *Best Of* .... (MCA)
Tennes-See Me
Jeannie C. Riley; *Here's* .... (PLY)
There Ain't No Beverly Hills In...
Shenandoah; *Long Time Comin'* ....(RCA)
There's A Tennessee Woman/Ben's Song
Tanya Tucker; *Tennessee Woman* .... (LIB)
There's No Love In Tennessee
Barbara Mandrell; *Country Classics-#3-1984-1985* .... (MCA)
  Greatest Hits .... (MCA)
This Ain't Tennessee & She Ain't You
Tom Jones; *Don't Let Our Dreams Die Young* ... (MER)
Tom Dooley
Doc Watson; *Doc Watson* .... (VAN)
  Essential .... (VAN)
  Out In The Country .... (INT)
Kingston Trio; *Capitol Collectors Series* ....(CAP)
  From The Hungry i ....(CAP)
  Greatest Hits ....(CCB)
  Tom Dooley ....(CAP)
  Troubadours Of The Folk Era-#3 ....(RHI)
Trains/Leavin' Tennessee
Tasty Licks; *Tasty Licks* .... (ROU)

STATES: TEXAS

  See Also: CITIES: DALLAS, HOUSTON, SAN ANTONIO

4 A.M. In Texas
7 Seconds; *Soulforce Revolution* .... (RES)
Alexis From Texas
Red Steagall; *Lone Star Beer & Bob Wills Music* (MCA)
All My Ex's Live In Texas
George Strait; *Country Classics-#10-1987* ...... (MCA)
  Greatest Hits-#2 .... (MCA)
  Ocean Front Property .... (MCA)

Another Texas Song
Eddy Raven; *45* .... (DIM)
Beautiful Texas
Leon Rausch; *Deep In The Heart Of Texas* .... (STH)
Big Texas
Jimmy C. Newman; *Happy Cajun* .... (PLN)
Blame It On Texas
Mark Chesnutt; *Too Cold At Home* .... (MCA)
Blind In Texas
W.A.S.P.; *Last Command* .... (CAP)
Blue Rose Of Texas
Holly Dunn; *Blue Rose Of Texas* .... (WB)
Blue Yodel #1
Bob Wills; *Anthology* .... (SSP)
Lynyrd Skynyrd; *Best Of The Rest* .... (MCA)
One More From The Road .... (MCA)
Bluest Eyes In Texas
Restless Heart; *Big Dreams In A Small Town* ...(RCA)
Boogie Back To Texas
Asleep At The Wheel; *10* .... (EPI)
Swinging Best Of .... (EPI)
Brownsville Turnaround On The Tex-Mex...
KLF; *Chill Out* .... (WAX)
Coming Back To Texas
Kenneth Threadgill; *ST/Honeysuckle Rose* ....(COL)
Dance Time In Texas
George Strait; *Something Special* .... (MCA)
Daughters Of Texas
Band Of H.M. Royal Marines; *Hands Across The
Sea-Sousa Marches* .... (ANG)
David & Me
Jerry Jeff Walker; *Jerry Jeff Walker* .... (MCA)
Deep In The Heart Of Texas
Bing Crosby; *Greatest Hits* .... (MCA)
Bob Wills; *Best Of* .... (MCA)
Best Of-#2 .... (MCA)
Gene Autry; *Columbia Historic Edition* ....(COL)
Devil Made Texas
Hermes Nye; *Cowboy Songs On Folkways* ...... (FLW)
Texas Folk Songs .... (FLW)
Don't Ask Me Why (I'm Going To Texas)
Asleep At The Wheel; *Asleep At The Wheel* .... (EPI)
Swinging Best Of .... (EPI)
Don't Sing A Song About Texas
Charlie Walker; *Texas Gold* .... (PLN)
Don't Sing No Songs About Texas
David Hunter; *45* ....(NAT)
Down In Texas
Allman Brothers Band; *Dreams* .... (POL)
Down In Texas Today
Curtis Potter; *Down In Texas Today* ....(SO)
Down In Texas Way
John Delafose/Eunice Playboys; *Pere Et Garcon
Zydeco* .... (ROU)
Dream On Texas Ladies
John Michael Montgomery; *Life's A Dance* ..... (ATL)
ST/Maverick .... (ATL)
East Texas Red
Arlo Guthrie; *Tribute To Woody Guthrie And
Leadbelly* ....(COL)
Egypt Texas
Shadowy Men On A Shadowy Planet; *Savvy Show
Stoppers* .... (CGO)
Eyes Of Texas
Bill Boyd; *Western Swing-#1 & 2* .... (ARH)
Masters Of Reality; *Masters Of Reality* .... (DV)
Michigan University Band; *Kick Off, U.S.A.* ..... (VAN)
Sharkey/Kings Of Dixieland; *Sharkey/Kings Of
Dixieland* .... (STH)
Five Miles To Texas
Stockton & Johnson; *Born By The River* ....(OOP)
Flies Of Texas Are Upon You
Ray Stevens; *Crackin' Up* .... (MCA)
From Tennessee To Texas
Johnny Bush/Bandoleros; *Live From Texas* .... (DEL)
Fun In Texas
Britny Fox; *Britny Fox* ....(COL)
Ghost Of A Texas Ladies' Man
Concrete Blonde; *Walking In London* .... (IRS)
God Blessed Texas
Little Texas; *Big Time* .... (WB)
Going Down To Texas
Shel Silverstein; *Great Conch Train Robbery* .... (FF)

Goin' Back To Texas
Bobby Bare; *Biggest Hits* ....(COL)
R.C. Smith; *I Have To Paint My Face* .... (ARH)
Hello Texas
Jimmy Buffett; *ST/Urban Cowboy* .... (ASY)
Hot Texas Night
Mac Davis; *Texas In My Rear View Mirror* .... (CAS)
I Can't See Texas From Here
George Strait; *Strait From The Heart* .... (MCA)
I Wish I Was In Texas Tonight
Patti Ford; *45* ....(NAT)
If This Was Texas
Curtis Potter; *Down In Texas Today* ....(SO)
If You're Gonna Play In Texas
Alabama; *Live* ....(RCA)
Roll On ....(RCA)
Stars Are Out In Texas ....(RCA)
It Hurts As Much In Texas (As It Did...
George Jones & Ricky Van Shelton; *Friends In High
Places* .... (EPI)
I'm A Texan
Eddie Moore; *Moore Country With* .... (COU)
I'm Missing Texas Tonight
Kim Grayson; *45* ....(SND)
I'm Tired Of Texas
Nancy Walker; *I Can Cook Too* .... (DRG)
Sings Show Stoppers .... (ST)
Leavin' Texas
Jerry Jeff Walker; *A Man Must Carry On* .... (MCA)
Best Of .... (MCA)
Little Ground In Texas
Capitols; *45* .... (RID)
Little Texas Shaker
Triumph; *Rock & Roll Machine* .... (MCA)
Livingston's Gone To Texas
Jimmy Buffett; *Living & Dying In 3/4 Time* ..... (MCA)
Lone Star Beer & Bob Wills Music
Red Steagall; *Lone Star Beer & Bob Wills Music* (MCA)
Texas Country .... (MCA)
Lone Star Christmas
Lee Greenwood; *Christmas To Christmas* .... (MCA)
Lone Star Rag
Bob Wills/Texas Playboys; *Tiffany
Transcriptions-#1* ....(KAL)
Lone Star State Of Mind
Don Williams; *Currents* ....(RCA)
Nanci Griffith; *Country Classics-#8-1986-1987* ..(MSP)
Lone Star State Of Mind .... (MCA)
Pat Alger/Nanci Griffith/Trisha Yearwood; *True Love &
Other Short Stories* ....(SH)
Lone Star Trail
Dave Frederickson; *Cowboy Songs On Folkways* (FLW)
Long Long Texas Road
Roy Drusky; *Golden Hits* .... (PLN)
Long Road To Texas
Bill Wray; *ST/Tilt* .... (MCA)
Long Tall Texan
Beach Boys; *Best Of-#2* .... (CAP)
Concert .... (CAP)
Murry Kellum; *20 Golden Souvenirs Of Music City
U.S.A.* .... (PLN)
Country Comedy-20 Country Comedy Hits ..... (PLN)
Memories Of East Texas
Michelle Shocked; *Short Sharp Shocked* .... (MER)
Merry Texas Christmas You All
Michael Martin Murphey; *Cowboy Christmas* ..... (WB)
Miles And Miles Of Texas
Asleep At The Wheel; *Texas State Of Mind* ....(CAP)
Miss Texas 1967
Colourfield; *Deception* .... (CHR)
Mobile/Texas Line
Tom Rush; *Blues Songs & Ballads* ....(FAN)
Mind Ramblin' .... (PRS)
Tom Rush ....(FAN)
My Brown Eyed Texas Rose
Tex Ritter; *Arizona Days* .... (MSP)
Country Music Hall Of Fame .... (MCA)
My First Taste Of Texas
Ed Bruce; *16 Top Country Hits-#4* .... (MCA)
Greatest Hits .... (MCA)
I Write It Down .... (MCA)
My Heart's Deep In The Heart Of Texas
Boxcar Willie; *King Of The Freight Train* .... (MSP)

My Train Rolled Up In Texas
Joe Turner; *Things That I Used To Do* .... (PAB)
Never Been To Texas
Power Of Dreams; *Immigrants Emigrants & Me* .. (POL)
No Place But Texas
Willie Nelson; *The Promiseland* ....(COL)
Northeast Texas Women
David Bromberg; *Bandit In A Bathing Suit* .... (FAN)
Willis Alan Ramsey; *Willis Alan Ramsey* .... (DHL)
One More Goodtime Band In Texas
Leon Rausch; *Rausch Touch* .... (STH)
Out On The Texas Plains
Mom & Dads; *Golden Country* .... (CRS)
Outlaws & Lone Star Beer
C.W. McCall; *& Co.* .... (POL)
People Up In Texas
Waylon Jennings; *Never Could Toe The Mark* ....(RCA)
Planet Texas
John Andrew Parks; *John Andrew Parks* .... (CAP)
Kenny Rogers; *Something Inside So Strong* .... (RPR)
Piano Texas Girl
Steve Wariner; *I Got Dreams* .... (MCA)
Pretty Litle Lady From Beaumont, Texas
George Jones; *One Woman Man* .... (EPI)
Put Me On A Train Back To Texas
Waylon Jennings & Willie Nelson; *Clean Shirt* .... (EPI)
Quand Je Suit Partis Pour Le Texas
Cleoma Breaux/Others; *Cajun-#1-Abbeville
Breakdown* ....(COL)
Raisin' Cane In Texas
Gene Watson; *All-Time Country Classics-#1* .....(CAP)
Texas State Of Mind ....(CAP)
Raywood Texas
Queen Ida; *Caught In The Act* .... (CRS)
Queen Ida/Zydeco Band; *In San Francisco* .... (CRS)
Riding High In Texas
Peter Rowan; *Medicine Trail* .... (FF)
Somewhere In Texas
Ray Price; *Greatest Hits-#4-By Request* ....(SO)
Willie Nelson; *Tougher Than Leather* ....(COL)
Somewhere There's A Rainbow Over Texas
Ruby Falls; *45* .... (FIF)
Sweet Girl In Texas
John Delafose/Eunice Playboys; *Joe Pete Got Two
Women* .... (ARH)
Sweet Mother Texas
Eddy Raven; *Greatest Hits* .... (WB)
Sweetwater, Texas
Charlie Daniels Band; *Saddle Tramp* .... (EPI)
T For Texas
Lynyrd Skynyrd; *Box Set* .... (MCA)
One More From The Road .... (MCA)
Waylon Jennings; *Only Daddy That'll Walk The
Line* ....(RCA)
Superstars Salute Jimmie Rodgers ....(SO)
Take Care Of Texas
Kris Carpenter; *45* .... (DOO)
Talk To Me Texas
Keith Whitley; *Greatest Hits* ....(RCA)
Tracy Byrd; *Tracy Byrd* .... (MCA)
Tangled Up In Texas
Billy Burnette; *Coming Home* .... (CPC)
Tennessee Flat Top Box
Johnny Cash; *Classic Cash-Hall Of Fame Series* . (MER)
Columbia Country Classics-#3-Americana .....(COL)
Essential ....(COL)
Rosanne Cash; *30 Years Of #1 Hits-#17* ......(COL)
Hits-1979-1989 ....(COL)
King's Record Shop ....(COL)
Tennessee Whiskey & Texas Women
Rayburn Anthony; *Audiograph Alive* .... (AUD)
Dance Floor Crystal Ball .... (AUD)
Texas
Beat Farmers; *Loud & Plowed-Live!* ....(CCB)
Pursuit Of Happiness ....(CCB)
Boiled In Lead; *Boiled In Lead* .... (OMU)
Charlie Daniels Band; *Greatest Fiddlin' Licks* .....(EPI)
Night Rider ....(EPI)
ST/Urban Cowboy-#2 ....(EPI)
Chris Rea; *Road To Hell* .... (ATL)
Electric Flag; *Legends Of Electric Blues Guitar-#2* (RHI)
Long Time Comin' ....(COL)
Junkyard; *Junkyard* .... (GEF)
Merle Haggard; *Friend In California* .... (EPI)

Underworld; *Change The Weather* .... (SIR)
W. Jennings/W. Nelson/J. Cash/K. Krist.; *Highwayman
2* ....(COL)
Texas Ann
Joe Beck; *Beck & Sanborn* .... (CBA)
Texas Blues
Foy Willing/Riders Of The Purple Sage; *Hillbilly
Music-Thank God-#1* ....(BUG)
Marshall Owens; *Alabama Blues-1927-1931* ....(YAZ)
Texas Playboys/Leon McAuliffe; *San Antonio Rose
Story* ....(DEL)
Vassar Clements; *Hillbilly Jazz Rides Again* .... (FF)
V. Clements/D. Bromberg/Doug Jernigan; *Hillbilly
Jazz* .... (FF)
Texas Bound
Gary Morris; *Full Moon Empty Heart* .... (LIB)
Texas Bound & Flyin'
Jerry Reed; *ST/Smokey & The Bandit 2* .... (MCA)
Texas Bound & Flyin' ....(RCA)
Texas Chain Letter Massacre
Pajama Slave Dancers; *Blood Sweat & Beers* ..... (RES)
Texas Cookin'
Guy Clark; *Greatest Hits* ....(RCA)
G.Clark/R.Crowell/E.Harris/J.J. Walker; *Texas
Cookin'* ....(SH)
Texas Cowboy
Luther Johnson/Magic Rockers; *I Want To Groove With
You* .... (BUL)
Texas Double Eagle
Bob Wills; *Best Of* .... (MCA)
Texas Fiddle Man
Asleep At The Wheel; *Keepin' Me Up Nights* ..... (ARI)
Texas Fiddle Song
Merle Haggard; *Big City* .... (EPI)
Texas Flood
Fenton Robinson; *Somebody Loan Me A Dime* ...(ALG)
Larry Davis; *Best Of Duke-Peacock Blues* .... (MCA)
Stevie Ray Vaughan/Double Trouble; *Live Alive* .. (EPI)
Texas Flood ....(EPI)
Texas Gales
Doc & Merle Watson; *Ballads From Deep Gap* . (VAN)
Texas Girl At The Funeral Of Her Father
Randy Newman; *Little Criminals* .... (WB)
Texas Guitar Stomp
Maddox Brothers & Rose; *1946-1951-#2* ...... (ARH)
Texas Has A Whorehouse In It
Dom Deluise/Dogettes; *ST/Best Little Whorehouse In
Texas* .... (MCA)
Original Cast; *Best Little Whorehouse In Texas* .. (MCA)
Texas Heartache #1
Mickey Gilley; *Put Your Dreams Away* .... (EPI)
Texas Hills
Sons Of The Pioneers; *Western Country* .... (GRA)
Texas Honky Tonk
David Houston; *Sings Texas Honky Tonk* .... (DEL)
Texas Country ....(DEL)
Texas Hop
Pee Wee Crayton; *Blues Masters-#3-Texas Blues* . (RHI)
Texas I Love You
Marty Robbins; *Lost & Found* ....(COL)
Texas In 1880
Foster & Lloyd; *Foster & Lloyd* ....(RCA)
Texas In My Rear View Mirror
Mac Davis; *Texas In My Rear View Mirror* .... (CAS)
Very Best & More ....(CAS)
Texas Is Bigger Than It Used To Be
Mark Chesnutt; *Almost Goodbye* .... (MCA)
ST/8 Seconds .... (MCA)
Texas Jalapenos
Texas Rubies; *Working Girl Blues* .... (MSD)
Texas Jump
Ozzie Nelson/Orchestra; *Uncollected-1940-1942* (HIN)
Texas Lawman
Regulators; *Regulators* .... (POL)
Texas Lemon Flavor
Stefan Grossman; *Yazoo Basin Boogie* .... (SHA)
Texas Love Song
Elton John; *Don't Shoot Me I'm Only The Piano
Player* .... (POL)
Texas Lullaby
David Allan Coe; *Cowboys* ....(COL)
Longhaired Redneck ....(COL)
Doobie Brothers; *Stampede* .... (WB)

Texas Me
Doug Sahm; *Best Of The Sir Douglas Quintet* ....(TAK)
Texas Moaner Blues
Louis Armstrong & King Oliver; *Louis Armstrong & King Oliver* .... (MS)
Texas Morning
Michael Nesmith/First National Band; *Complete* .. (PA)
Texas On A Saturday Night
Willie Nelson & Mel Tillis; *Half Nelson* ....(COL)
Texas Party
Johnny Copeland; *Boom Boom* .... (ROU)
Texas Plains
Riders In The Sky; *Cowboy Way* .... (MCA)
  Saturday Morning With .... (MCA)
Stuart Hamblen; *A Man & His Music* ....(L&L)
Texas Playboy Rag
Bob Wills/Texas Playboys; *Essential* ....(COL)
Texas Radio Horror
Strip Mind; *What's In Your Mouth* .... (SIR)
Texas Rangers
Ian & Sylvia; *Greatest Hits* .... (VAN)
  Northern Journey .... (VAN)
Michael Martin Murphey; *Cowboy Songs* ....(WB)
Texas Red
Strength In Numbers; *Telluride Sessions* .... (MCA)
Texas Ride Song
BoDeans; *Go Slow Down* ....(SLS)
Texas Rose Cafe
Little Feat; *Sailin' Shoes* .... (WB)
Texas Saturday Night
Moe Bandy; *Motel Matches* ....(COL)
Texas Serenade
Gun Club; *Miami* .... (IRS)
Texas Shuffle
Count Basie; *Basie Reunions* .... (PRS)
  Best Of .... (MCA)
Houston Person; *Heavy Juice* .... (MUS)
Texas Sidestep
Deanna Cox; *Country Jukebox Greatest Hits-#2* ... (WB)
Texas State Of Mind
David Frizzell & Shelly West; *Carryin' On The Family Names* ....(WB)
  Golden Duets ....(VVA)
Texas Stew
Louis Jordan/Tympani Five; *Rock 'N Roll Call* ... (BLU)
Texas Strut
Gary Moore; *Still Got The Blues* .... (CHS)
Texas Tattoo
Gibson/Miller Band; *Steppin' Country* ....(COL)
  Where There's Smoke ....(EPI)
Texas Tea
Dee Mullins; *20 Great Hits* ....(PLN)
  Dee Mullins ....(PLN)
Texas Tea Party
Benny Goodman; *Early Years* ....(BIO)
Texas Tornado
Doug Sahm; *Best Of-& Friends-Atlantic Sessions* . (RHI)
Texas Twister
Little Feat; *Representing The Mambo* ....(WB)
Texas Two Step
Bob Wills; *Country Music Hall Of Fame* .. (MCA)
Texas Woman Blues
Taj Mahal; *Recycling The Blues-Other Related Stuff* ....(COL)
Texas Women
Hank Williams, Jr.; *Greatest Hits* ....(WB)
  Rowdy ....(W/C)
Texas Women (Don't Stay Lonely Long)
Brooks & Dunn; *Hard Workin' Man* ....(ARI)
Texas & Pacific
Louis Jordan; *Five Guys Named Moe-Orig. Decca-#2* ....(DEC)
  Jazz Heritage-Greatest Hits #2 ....(MCA)
Texas (When I Die)
Tanya Tucker; *Best Of* ....(MCA)
  Collection ....(MCA)
  Greatest Hits Encore ....(LIB)
  Live ....(MCA)
  ST/Hard Country ....(EPI)
Texas, 1947
Guy Clark; *Greatest Hits* ....(RCA)
  Old No. 1 ....(SH)
Texas, Me & You
Asleep At The Wheel; *Route 66* ....(LIB)

That Ol' Texas Two-Step
Charlie Walker; *Charlie Walker* .... (DOT)
There Ain't A Cow In Texas
Vassar Clements & Buddy Emmons; *Sat. Night Shuffle-Merle Travis Celebr.* ....(SHA)
There'll Always Be Honky Tonks In Texas
Darrell McCall & Johnny Bush; *Hot Texas Country* (SO)
There's A Little Bit Of Everything...
Ernest Tubb; *Story* .... (MCA)
  Walking The Floor Over You ....(MSP)
Ernest Tubb & Roy Clark; *Ernest Tubb Collection* .(SO)
Waltz Across Texas
Ernest Tubb & Willie Nelson; *Ernest Tubb Collection* ....(SO)
Wasp (Texas Radio & The Big Beat)
Doors; *Alive She Cried* .... (ELE)
  Classics .... (ELE)
  L.A. Woman .... (ELE)
  Weird Scenes Inside The Goldmine .... (ELE)
Way Down Texas Way
Asleep At The Wheel; *10* .... (EPI)
  Swinging Best Of .... (EPI)
We Almost Had Texas Skies Today
Hank Thompson; *Here's To Country Music* ....(SO)
West Texas Highway & Me
Gary Morris; *Faded Blue* .... (WB)
West Texas Plains
Rosie Flores; *After The Farm* .... (HT)
West Texas Waltz
Butch Hancock; *Own & Own* ....(SH)
West Texas Wind
Joe Sun; *45* .... (AMI)
West Texas Women
Whistlin' Alex Moore; *I'm Wild About My Lovin'-1928-1930* .... (HIS)
When It's Christmas Time In Texas
Rick Orozco; *Tejano Country Christmas* ....(ART)
Wingin' It Home To Texas
Jerry Jeff Walker; *Collectibles* .... (MCA)
Woman In Texas
Jerry Jeff Walker; *Live At Gruene Hall* ....(RYK)
Yellow Rose Of Texas
Hoyt Axton; *Songs Of The Civil War* ....(COL)
Michael Martin Murphey; *Cowboy Songs* ....(WB)
Mitch Miller; *16 Most Requested Songs* ....(COL)
Roy Rogers; *Great American Singing Cowboys* ... (REP)
You Don't Have To Be From Texas
Leon Rausch; *Deep In The Heart Of Texas* .... (STH)

STATES: UTAH

Utah
Steve Lacy & Michael Smith; *Sidelines* .... (IAI)
X-Tal; *Everything Crash* ....(ALI)
Utah Carl
Harry K. McClintock; *Cowboy Songs On Folkways* .... (FLW)
Utah Carol
Marty Robbins; *Gunfighter Ballads & Trail Songs* (COL)
Utah Tribute
Chris LeDoux; *& The Saddle Boogie Band* ....(LIB)
Utah-Suite 4
Scott Moulton; *Four Corners Suite* .... (REV)

STATES: VERMONT

Moonlight In Vermont
Cal Tjader; *Latin Kick* ....(FAN)
Captain Beefheart/Magic Band; *Trout Mask Replica* .... (RPR)
Frank Sinatra; *Come Fly With Me* ....(CAP)
  Gift Set ....(CAP)
Nat King Cole Trio; *Best Of* ....(BLN)
Sarah Vaughan; *Complete On Mercury-#3-1954-1956* .... (MER)
  Golden Hits .... (MER)
Vermont Farmer's Song
Margaret MacArthur; *Almanac Of New England Farm Songs* ....(GRE)
Vermont Is Afire In The Autumn
Lui Collins; *Made In New England* ....(GRE)

STATES: VIRGINIA

Carry Me Back To Old Virginny
Jerry Lee Lewis; *Doin' Just Fine* .... (ACC)
  Ole Tyme Country Music .... (SUN)
  Sunday Down South .... (SUN)
Down In Virginia
Jimmy Reed; *Best Of* .... (CRS)
East Virginia
Joan Baez; *Ballad Book* .... (VAN)
  Greatest Folksingers Of The '60s .... (VAN)
  Joan Baez .... (VAN)
Pete Seeger; *Essential* .... (VAN)
  Folk Classics (Roots Of American Folk) .... (COL)
  Greatest Folksingers Of The '60s .... (VAN)
East Virginia Blues
Joan Baez; *Ballad Book* .... (VAN)
  Vol #1 .... (VAN)
Pete Seeger; *Essential* .... (VAN)
  Greatest Folksingers/'60s .... (VAN)
Going Back To Virginia
Jim & Jessie McReynolds; *Music Among Friends* (ROU)
Going To Virginia
Ralph Willis; *Southern Blues* .... (SAV)
I'm Coming Virginia
Bix Beiderbecke; *#1-Singin' The Blues* .... (COL)
Coleman Hawkins & Benny Carter; *Coleman Hawkins*
  & Benny Carter .... (DSQ)
Stephane Grappelli; *Compact Jazz* .... (VRV)
Lees Of Old Virginia
William Daniels/Original Cast; *1776* .... (SMC)
Missin' You
Little Feat; *Time Loves A Hero* .... (WB)
Old Virginia Lowlands
John Townley/Press Gang; *Chesapeake Sailor's*
  Companion .... (ADE)
Old Virginia March
Sam McNeil/Others; *Old Originals-#2* .... (ROU)
"The Virginian" Theme
101 Strings Orchestra; *Western Themes-#1* .... (ALS)
Original Music; *Television's Greatest Hits-#3* ..... (TVT)
To See My Angel In Virginia
Livewire; *Wired* .... (ROU)
Virginia
Marshall Tucker Band; *Searchin' For A Rainbow* (AJK)
Statler Brothers; *Harold Lew Phil & Don* .... (MER)
Virginia Boys
Country Gazette; *Hello Operator-This Is* .... (FF)
  Strictly Instrumental .... (FF)
Virginia Plain
Roxy Music; *Roxy Music* .... (RPR)
  Street Life-20 Great Hits .... (RPR)
Virginia's Bloody Soil
Tennessee Ernie Ford; *Sings Songs Of The Civil*
  War .... (CAP)
Virginia's Heritage
Reno & Smiley; *1983 Collector's Edition-#10* .... (IGR)

STATES: WASHINGTON

My Washington Woman
Kenny Rogers/First Edition; *All Time Greatest*
Hits-#1 .... (MSP)
  Featuring The Songs Of .... (MSP)

STATES: WEST VIRGINIA

Green Rolling Hills (West Virginia)
Bottle Hill; *Rumor In Their Own Time-#1* .... (BIO)
Emmylou Harris; *Quarter Moon In A Ten Cent*
Town .... (WB)
Leaving West Virginia
Kathy Mattea; *Walking The Way The Wind*
Blows .... (MER)
Muswell Hillbilly
Kinks; *Everybody's In Show Biz* .... (RHI)
  Muswell Hillbillies .... (RHI)
Salt Pork, West Virginia
Louis Jordan; *Jazz Heritage-Greatest Hits-#2* .... (MCA)
Stony Mountain, West Virginia
Jim & Jesse; *In The Tradition* .... (ROU)

Take Me Home, Country Roads
John Denver; *Evening With* .... (RCA)
  Greatest Hits .... (RCA)
  Poems Prayers & Promises .... (RCA)
  Take Me Home, Country Roads-& Other Hits ... (RCA)
Toots/Maytals; *Brand New Second-Hand* .... (RYK)
West Virginia
Maggie & Terre Roche; *Seductive Reasoning* ...... (SSP)
Tarwater Band; *Walking Across Egypt* .... (FF)
Trapezoid; *Three Forks Of Cheat* .... (ROU)
West Virginia Blues
Edward Thompson; *Alabama Blues-1927-1931* .. (YAZ)
West Virginia Fantasies
Chicago; *At Carnegie Hall* .... (COL)
  Group Portrait .... (COL)
  II .... (COL)
West Virginia Friend
Holly Near; *Watch Out* .... (RWD)
West Virginia Man
David Allan Coe; *20 Great Hits* .... (PLN)
Willie Nelson; *Longhorn Jamboree* .... (PLN)
  & His Friends .... (PLN)
West Virginia Mine Disaster
Betsy Rutherford; *Betsy Rutherford* .... (BIO)
Cindy Mangsen; *Long Time Traveling* .... (HOG)
West Virginia My Home
Hazel Dickens & Alice Gerrard; *Hazel Dickens & Alice*
Gerrard .... (ROU)

STATES: WISCONSIN

Back To Wisconsin Waltz
Michigan Dutchmen; *Umpa-Umpa-Umpapa* .... (JJ)
On Wisconsin
Magic Organ; *22 Great Organ Favorites* .... (RAN)
  Traveling With .... (RAN)
University Of Wisconsin Marching Band; *Fifth*
Quarter .... (FID)
On Wisconsin/If You Want To Be A Badger
University Of Wisconsin Marching Band; *Fifth*
Quarter .... (FID)
Up In Wisconsin
Peter & Lou Berryman; *No Relation* .... (COR)
Wisconsin Forward Forever
University Of Wisconsin Marching Band; *Fifth*
Quarter .... (FID)
Wisconsin's Pride
University Of Wisconsin Marching Band; *Fifth*
Quarter .... (FID)
Wreck Of The Edmund Fitzgerald
Gordon Lightfoot; *Gord's Gold-#2* .... (WB)
  Summertime Dream .... (RPR)

STATES: WYOMING

Cowboy From Wyoming
Sammi Smith; *Better Than Ever* .... (STE)
Emperor Of Wyoming
Neil Young; *Neil Young* .... (RPR)
Guitar Picker From Rody, Wyoming
Joey Davis; *45* .... (MRC)
Hills Of Old Wyomin'
Sons Of The Pioneers; *Country Music Hall Of*
Fame .... (MCA)
Tex Ritter; *Country Music Hall Of Fame* .... (MCA)
Paint Me Back Home In Wyoming
Chris LeDoux; *Paint Me Back Home In Wyoming* . (LIB)
  Sounds Of The Western Country .... (LIB)
Roamin' Wyomin'
Randy Travis; *Wind In The Wire* .... (WB)
Sweet Wyoming Home
Chris LeDoux; *& The Saddle Boogie Band* .... (LIB)
Take Me Back To Old Wyoming
Chris LeDoux; *Thirty Dollar Cowboy* .... (LIB)
Whoopee Ti Yi Yo
Burl Ives; *Best Of* .... (MCA)
David Bromberg; *How Late'll Ya Play 'Til?* ...... (FAN)
Roy Rogers/Sons Of The Pioneers; *Roy Rogers/Sons Of*
The Pioneers .... (VS)
Woody Guthrie & Cisco Houston; *Cowboy Songs On*
Folkways .... (FLW)

STOP

Ain't No Stoppin' Us Now
Luther Vandross; *Songs* .... (EPI)
McFadden & Whitehead; *Ten Years Of #1 Hits* .... (PI)
Baby Stop Crying
Bob Dylan; *Street Legal* .... (COL)
Can You Stop The Rain
Peabo Bryson; *Can You Stop The Rain* .... (COL)
Can't Do A Thing (To Stop Me)
Chris Isaak; *San Francisco Days* .... (RPR)
Can't Stop
After 7; *After 7* .... (VIA)
DeBarge; *All This Love* .... (MOT)
Madonna; *ST/Who's That Girl* .... (SIR)
Rick James; *Glow* .... (GOR)
Can't Stop Dancing
Sylvester; *Greatest Hits* .... (FAN)
Living Proof .... (FAN)
Can't Stop Dancin'
Captain & Tennille; *Greatest Hits* .... (A&M)
Can't Stop Lovin'
George Thorogood/Destroyers; *George
Thorogood/Destroyers* .... (ROU)
Can't Stop My Heart From Loving You
O'Kanes; *Greatest Country Hits/'80s-1987* ...... (COL)
More Hot Country Requests-#2 .... (EPI)
O'Kanes .... (COL)
Can't Stop Rockin'
ZZ Top; *Afterburner* .... (WB)
Can't Stop The Bum Rush
Kris Kross; *Totally Krossed Out* .... (RUF)
Can't Stop The Music
Daryl Hall & John Oates; *No Goodbyes* .... (ATL)
War Babies .... (ATL)
Village People; *Can't Stop The Music* .... (CAS)
Greatest Hits .... (RHI)
Can't Stop The Street (Krush Groove)
Chaka Khan; *45* .... (WB)
Can't Stop This Thing We Started
Bryan Adams; *Waking Up The Neighbours* ...... (A&M)
Can't Stop Worrying
Dave Mason; *Alone Together* .... (MCA)
Cool It Now
New Edition; *Greatest Hits-#1* .... (MCA)
New Edition .... (MCA)
Crazy Feelin'
Jefferson Starship; *Earth* .... (GRU)
Does This Bus Stop At 82nd St.
Bruce Springsteen; *Greetings From Asbury Park
N.J.* .... (COL)
Don't Disturb This Groove
System; *Don't Disturb This Groove* .... (ATL)
Golden Age Of Black Music-1977-1988 .... (ATL)
Don't Stop
Fleetwood Mac; *25 Years-The Chain* .... (WB)
Greatest Hits .... (WB)
Live .... (WB)
Rumours .... (WB)
Frankie Miller; *Standing On The Edge* .... (CAP)
Jeffrey Osborne; *Don't Stop* .... (A&M)
Lionel Richie; *Dancing On The Ceiling* .... (MOT)
Stone Roses; *Stone Roses* .... (SIL)
Don't Stop Believin'
Journey; *Escape* .... (COL)
Greatest Hits .... (COL)
Olivia Newton-John; *Don't Stop Believin'* .... (MCA)
Greatest Hits .... (MCA)
Don't Stop Dancing
Bar-Kays; *Gotta Groove* .... (STX)
Don't Stop Me Now
Queen; *Jazz* .... (HOL)
Live Killers .... (HOL)
Don't Stop The Dance
Bryan Ferry; *Boys & Girls* .... (WB)
Greenpeace/Rainbow Warriors .... (GEF)
Don't Stop The Music
Yarbrough & Peoples; *Two Of Us* .... (MER)
Don't Stop Till You Get Enough
Jacksons; *Jacksons Live* .... (EPI)
Michael Jackson; *Off The Wall* .... (EPI)

Don't Stop To Watch The Wheels
Doobie Brothers; *Minute By Minute* .... (WB)
Don't Stop When You're Hot
Larry Graham; *45* .... (WB)
He Stopped Loving Her Today
George Jones; *Anniversary* .... (EPI)
First Time Love .... (EPI)
Greatest Country Hits/'80s-1980 .... (COL)
Greatest Hits From The Jukebox .... (EPI)
I Am What I Am .... (EPI)
I Can't Stop
Alabama; *Just Us* .... (RCA)
Honeycombs; *45* .... (ERI)
I Can't Stop Crying
Ronnie Milsap; *16 Greatest Hits-#2* .... (TRP)
I Can't Stop Dancing
Archie Bell; *45* .... (ATL)
I Can't Stop Lovin' You
Don Gibson; *60 Years Of Country Music* .... (RCA)
Collector's .... (RCA)
Stars Of The Grand Ole Opry 1926-1974 ..... (RCA)
Elvis Presley; *Aloha From Hawaii* .... (RCA)
As Recorded At Madison Square Garden ...... (RCA)
From Memphis To Vegas .... (RCA)
In Person .... (RCA)
Recorded Live On Stage .... (RCA)
Ray Charles; *Anthology* .... (RHI)
Greatest Hits-#2 .... (RHI)
Roy Orbison; *Best-Loved Standards* .... (MON)
Legendary .... (SSP)
I Can't Stop Now
Wanda Jackson; *Greatest Hits* .... (GUS)
I Can't Stop The Fire
Eric Martin; *ST/Teachers* .... (CAP)
I Just Wanna Stop
Gino Vannelli; *Best Of* .... (A&M)
Brother To Brother .... (A&M)
Classics-#7 .... (A&M)
I'll Never Stop Loving You
Doris Day & James Cagney; *Love Me Or Leave
Me* .... (SMP)
Gary Morris; *Anything Goes* .... (WB)
Hits .... (WB)
Just Another Whistle Stop
Band; *Stage Fright* .... (CAP)
Just Can't Stop Me
J. Geils Band; *Sanctuary* .... (AMR)
Showtime .... (AMR)
Let's Stop Talkin' About It
Janie Fricke; *17 Greatest Hits* .... (COL)
Love Lies .... (COL)
Very Best Of .... (COL)
Machine Stops
Level 42; *Standing In The Light* .... (POL)
Music Never Stopped
Grateful Dead; *Blues For Allah* .... (GRD)
One From The Vault .... (GRD)
Never Stop
Brand New Heavies; *Brand New Heavies* .... (DV)
Echo/Bunnymen; *Songs To Learn & Sing* .... (SIR)
Front 242; *Front By Front* .... (EPI)
No Stoppin' Us Now
Doobie Brothers; *One Step Closer* .... (WB)
Other Way Of Stopping
Police; *Zenyatta Mondatta* .... (A&M)
Stop
James Gang; *16 Greatest Hits* .... (MCA)
Best Of .... (MCA)
Yer Album .... (OW)
Jane's Addiction; *Ritual De Lo Habitual* .... (WB)
Lonnie Mack; *Strike Like Lightning* .... (ALG)
Pink Floyd; *The Wall* .... (COL)
Stop And Think It Over
Dale & Grace; *45* .... (ERI)
Stop Breaking Down
Rolling Stones; *Exile On Main Street* .... (RS)
Stop Breakin' Down Blues
Robert Johnson; *Complete Recordings* .... (COL)
Legends Of The Blues-#1 .... (COL)
Stop Dead
Cure; *Standing On A Beach-The Singles* .... (ELE)
Stop Doggin' Me
Johnnie Taylor; *45* .... (STX)

Stop Draggin' My Heart Around
Stevie Nicks & Tom Petty; *Bella Donna* .... (MOD)
Timespace-Best Of Stevie Nicks .... (MOD)
Stop Hurting People
Pete Townshend; *All The Best Cowboys Have Chinese Eyes* .... (ATC)
Deep End-Live .... (ATC)
Stop In Nevada
Billy Joel; *Piano Man* .... (COL)
Stop In The Name Of Love
Diana Ross/Supremes; *16 No.1 Hits From The Early '60s* .... (MOT)
Anthology .... (MOT)
Evening With Diana Ross .... (MOT)
Girl Groups-Story Of A Sound .... (MOT)
Greatest Hits-#1 .... (MOT)
Motown Superstar Series-#1 .... (MOT)
Hollies; *45* .... (ATL)
Stop Making Sense
Talking Heads; *Stop Making Sense* .... (SIR)
Stop On A Dime
Little Texas; *Big Time* .... (WB)
Stop Running Away
Brenda Russell; *Greatest Hits* .... (A&M)
Stop Steppin' On My Heart
Eddie Money; *Greatest Hits-Sound Of Money* ....(COL)
Stop That Train
Bob Marley/Wailers; *Catch A Fire* .... (TUF)
Jerry Garcia Band; *Jerry Garcia Band* .... (ARI)
Peter Tosh; *Mama Africa* .... (EMI)
Stop The Rain
Shenandoah; *Shenandoah* ....(COL)
Stop The Violence
Boogie Down Productions; *By All Means Necessary* .... (JVA)
Live Hardcore Worldwide-Paris-London-NYC .. (JVA)
Stop The War Now
Edwin Starr; *45* .... (MOT)
Stop The Wedding
Etta James; *Sweetest Peaches-#1* .... (CSS)
Stop The World
Clash; *On Broadway* .... (EPI)
Extreme; *III Sides To Every Story* .... (A&M)
Teena Marie; *Robbery* .... (EPI)
Stop The World Right Here
Temptations; *Back To Basics* .... (MOT)
Stop The World (& Let Me Off)
Merle Haggard; *Big City* .... (EPI)
Patsy Cline; *20 Golden Pieces Of* .... (BLD)
Forever & Always .... (EPI)
Here's Patsy Cline .... (MCA)
Waylon Jennings; *Early Years* ....(RCA)
Stop Thief
Carla Thomas; *Queen Alone* .... (RHI)
Fabian; *Best Of* .... (MCA)
Stop This Game
Cheap Trick; *All Shook Up* .... (EPI)
Stop To Love
Luther Vandross; *Best Of-Best Of Love* .... (EPI)
Give Me The Reason .... (EPI)
Stop Your Half Steppin' Mama
Ben Vereen; *Here I Am* .... (ACC)
Signed Sealed Delivered .... (FFT)
Stop Your Sobbing
Kinks; *Greatest Hits-#1* .... (RHI)
One For The Road .... (ARI)
You Really Got Me .... (RHI)
Pretenders; *Pretenders* .... (SIR)
Singles .... (SIR)
Stop & Smell The Roses
Mac Davis; *Greatest Hits* ....(COL)
Stop & Smell The Roses ....(COL)
Stop, Don't Tease Me
DeBarge; *All This Love* .... (MOT)
Greatest Hits .... (MOT)
Stop, Look & Listen
Chiffons; *Best Of* ....(LAU)
Donna Summer; *She Works Hard For The Money* (MER)
Summer Collection .... (MER)
Dorsey Brothers; *1934-35 Decca Sessions* .... (MCA)
Complete Tommy Dorsey-#4 ....(RCA)
Elvis Presley; *Collector's Gold* ....(RCA)

Patsy Cline; *Loved & Lost Again* .... (FFT)
Rockin' Side-Her First Recordings-#3 .... (RHI)
Stop, Look & Listen ....(ALL)
Try Again .... (QKS)
Stop, Look & Listen To Your Heart
Johnny Mathis; *I'm Coming Home* ....(COL)
Love Songs ....(COL)
Marvin Gaye & Diana Ross; *Diana & Marvin* .. (MOT)
Patti Austin; *Every Home Should Have One* ..... (QUE)
Stylistics; *45* .... (AMH)
Stop, Stop, Stop
Hollies; *Best Of* .... (EMI)
Greatest ....(CAP)
Greatest Hits .... (EPI)
Sudden Stop
Colin James; *Sudden Stop* .... (VIA)
Percy Sledge; *Best Of* .... (ATL)
It Tears Me Up-Best Of .... (RHI)
That Train Don't Stop Here
Los Lobos; *Kiko* .... (SLS)
That Train Don't Stop Here Anymore
Mike Henderson; *Country Music Made Me Do It* .(RCA)
There Are Many Stops Along The Way
Joe Sample; *Collection* .... (GRP)
Rainbow Seeker .... (MCA)
There's No Stopping Us Now
Diana Ross/Supremes; *Greatest Hits-#2* .... (MOT)
There's No Stopping Your Heart
Marie Osmond; *Best Of* ....(CCB)
Best Of Branson U.S.A.-#1 ....(CCB)
There's No Stopping Your Heart ....(CCB)
They Just Can't Stop It (The Games...)
Spinners; *Best Of* .... (ATL)
Golden Age Of Black Music-1970-1975 .... (ATL)
Time Stands Still
Rush; *Chronicles* .... (MER)
Hold Your Fire .... (MER)
Show Of Hands .... (MER)
Time Stood Still
Vern Gosdin; *10 Years Of Hits Newly Recorded* ..(COL)
Too Good To Stop Now
Mickey Gilley; *Too Good To Stop Now* .... (EPI)
Truck Stop
Lenny Dee; *Best Of-#2* .... (MCA)
Mills Brothers; *Cab Driver* .... (RAN)
Truck Stop Girl
Byrds; *Byrds (collection)* ....(COL)
(Untitled) ....(COL)
Little Feat; *Little Feat* .... (WB)
Truck Stop Rock
Commander Cody/Lost Planet Airmen; *Hot Licks, Cold Steel & Trucker's Fav.* .... (MCA)
When Did You Stop Loving Me
George Strait; *ST/Pure Country* .... (MCA)
When The Music Stops
Roger Daltrey; *Daltrey* .... (MCA)
Where Time Stands Still
Mary Chapin Carpenter; *Stones In The Road* ....(COL)
Who'll Stop The Rain
Creedence Clearwater Revival; *1970* .... (FAN)
Chronicle .... (FAN)
Cosmo's Factory .... (FAN)
More Creedence Gold .... (FAN)
Royal Albert Hall Concert .... (FAN)
You Can't Stop Love
Schulyer, Knobloch & Overstreet; *45* ....(MTM)

STORYBOOK CHARACTERS

See Also: BOOKS, CARTOON CHARACTERS

After Robinson Crusoe
Ozzie Nelson/Orchestra; *Uncollected-#3-1938* ... (HIN)
Beauty And The Beast
Celine Dion & Peabo Bryson; *Celine Dion & Peabo Bryson* .... (EPI)
ST/Beauty And The Beast .... (DIS)
Black Orpheus
Roger Williams; *Best Of* .... (MCA)
Vince Guaraldi & Bola Sete; *Live At El Matador* . (FAN)
Black Uncle Remus
Loudon Wainwright III; *Loudon Wainwright III* .. (ATL)

Buck Rogers In The 25th Century
Neil Norman/Cosmic Orchestra; *Greatest Science Fiction Hits-#2* .... (CRS)
Captain Nemo
Michael Schenker; *Built To Destroy* .... (CHR)
   Rock Will Never Die .... (CHR)
Cupid
Graham Parker; *Mona Lisa's Daughter* ....(RCA)
   ST/True Love ....(RCA)
Sam Cooke; *Best Of* ....(RCA)
   Man & His Music ....(RCA)
Spinners; *Love Trippin'* ....(ATL)
Cupid's Got A Brand New Gun
Michael Penn; *March* ....(RCA)
Cupid's Toy
Squeeze; *Play* ....(RPR)
Cupid's Trash Truck
Lou & Peter Berryman; *Cupid's Trash Truck* .... (COR)
Dance Of The Sugar Plum Fairy
Boston Pops Orchestra; *Encores* .... (DGG)
   Sleigh Ride!-Classic Christmas Favorites ....(RCA)
Davy Crockett
Hermes Nye; *Ballads Of The Civil War-#1 & 2* . (FLW)
Daybreak (Storybook Children)
Cheryl Lynn; *Cheryl Lynn* ....(COL)
Ding Dong The Witch Is Dead
Fifth Estate; *Dick Bartley's One-Hit Wonders-'60s-#2* .... (RHI)
Meco; *Wizard Of Oz* .... (MIL)
MGM Studio Orchestra; *ST/Wizard Of Oz* ....(SSP)
Dinner With Drac
Zacherle; *Rock-O-Rama-#2* .... (AKO)
Doctor Frankenstein
Parliament; *Clones Of* .... (CAS)
   Live .... (CAS)
Dracula's Dance
Flip Phillips; *Flipenstein* .... (PRG)
Dr. Jeckyll & Mr. Hyde
Who; *Magic Bus* .... (MCA)
Fairy Tale
Elvis Presley; *In Concert* ....(RCA)
Pointer Sisters; *Retrospect* .... (MCA)
Rita Remington; *Country Girl Gold* .... (PLN)
Fairy Tale High
Donna Summer; *Live & More* .... (CAS)
   Once Upon A Time .... (CAS)
Fairy Tales
Anita Baker; *Compositions* .... (ELE)
Rivingtons; *Liberty Years-Legends Of Rock & Roll* (EMI)
Style Council; *Cost Of Loving* .... (POL)
Flight Of Icarus
Iron Maiden; *Live After Death* .... (CAP)
   Piece Of Mind ....(CAP)
"Fractured Fairy Tales" Theme
Original Music; *Television's Greatest Hits-#3* ..... (TVT)
Frankenstein
Edgar Winter Group; *Anthology* .... (BCT)
   Billboard Top Rock 'N' Roll Hits-1973 .... (RHI)
   Collection .... (RHI)
   They Only Come Out At Night .... (EPI)
New York Dolls; *Lipstick Killers* .... (ROI)
   New York Dolls .... (MER)
Georgy Porgy
Toto; *Past To Present-1977-1990* ....(COL)
   Toto ....(COL)
Hercules
Aaron Neville; *Classic* ....(ROU)
   Treacherous-History Of Neville Brothers ....(RHI)
Boz Scaggs; *Slow Dancer* ....(COL)
Elton John; *Honky Chateau* ....(POL)
Midnight Oil; *Scream in Blue Live* ....(COL)
   Species Deceases ....(COL)
Hey, Cinderella
Suzy Bogguss; *Something Up My Sleeve* .... (LIB)
House At Pooh Corner
Loggins & Messina; *Best Of-Friends* ....(COL)
   On Stage ....(COL)
   Sittin' In ....(COL)
Nitty Gritty Dirt Band; *Best Of* .... (EMI)
   Dirt Silver & Gold ....(OOP)

Icarus
Paul Winter Consort; *Common Ground* .... (A&M)
   Earthdance .... (A&M)
   Icarus ....(EPI)
   Pioneers Of The New Age ....(COL)
   Road .... (A&M)
Jack & Jill
Ray Parker, Jr./Raydio; *Chartbusters* .... (ARI)
   Greatest Hits .... (ARI)
   Ray Parker, Jr./Raydio .... (ARI)
Jukebox Cinderella
Johnny Duncan; *Come A Little Bit Closer* ....(COL)
King Kong
Frank Zappa; *Uncle Meat* .... (BAR)
   You Can't Do That On Stage Anymore .... (BAR)
Kinks; *Kink Kronikles* ....(RPR)
Kiss For Cinderella
Michael Tilson Thomas; *Of Thee I Sing/Let 'Em Eat Cake* ....(COL)
Li'l Red Riding Hood
Sam The Sham/Pharaohs; *Best Of* .... (POL)
   Cruisin'-1966 .... (INC)
   Pharaohization-Best Of .... (RHI)
Lonely Goatherd
Julie Andrews; *ST/Sound Of Music* ....(RCA)
Original Cast/Mary Martin; *Sound Of Music* .....(COL)
Mary Had A Little Lamb
Stevie Ray Vaughan/Double Trouble; *Live Alive* .. (EPI)
   Texas Flood ....(EPI)
Wings; *Wings Wild Life* .... (CAP)
Mona Lisas And Mad Hatters
Elton John; *Honky Chateau* .... (POL)
   Reg Strikes Back .... (MCA)
Mother Goose
Jethro Tull; *Aqualung* .... (CHR)
Narcissus
City Boy; *Dinner At The Ritz* .... (MER)
Over At The Frankenstein Place
Original London Cast; *Rocky Horror Show* ...... (RHI)
Original Roxy Cast; *Rocky Horror Show* .... (RHI)
Pegasus
Allman Brothers Band; *Enlightened Rogues* .... (POL)
Mahavishnu Orchestra; *Visions Of The Emerald Beyond* ....(COL)
Pride Of Frankenstein
Too Much Joy; *Cereal Killers* .... (GIA)
Puff (The Magic Dragon)
Peter, Paul & Mary; *In Concert* .... (WB)
   Moving .... (WB)
   Peter Paul & Mommy .... (WB)
   Ten Years Together-Best Of .... (WB)
Rhythm In My Nursery Rhymes
Tommy Dorsey/Clambake Seven; *Music Goes Round & Round* ....(BLU)
Rime Of The Ancient Mariner
Iron Maiden; *Live After Death* .... (CAP)
   Powerslave ....(CAP)
Robin Hood
38 Special; *Rockin' Into The Night* .... (A&M)
Robinson Crusoe
Art Of Noise; *Ambient Collection* .... (POL)
   Below The Waste .... (POL)
Cud; *Cub Band E.P.* .... (A&M)
Robinson Crusoe In New York
Silencers; *Dance To The Holy Man* ....(RCA)
Rockin' Rockin' Leprechauns
Jonathan Richman/Modern Lovers; *Rock 'N' Roll With* .... (RHI)
Romeo
Cadillacs; *Best Of* .... (RHI)
Dino; *Swingin'* ....(POL)
Donna Summer; *ST/Flashdance* .... (CAS)
Jamaica Boys; *Jamaica Boys* .... (WB)
Times 2; *X 2* ....(RPR)
Romeo & Juliet
Andy Williams/Royal Philharmonic Orch.; *Greatest Love Classics* ....(CAP)
Chambers Brothers; *Time Has Come* ....(COL)
Dire Straits; *Live-Alchemy* .... (WB)
   Making Movies .... (WB)
   Money For Nothing .... (WB)
Honeys; *Capitol Collectors Series* .... (CAP)
Indigo Girls; *Rites Of Passage* .... (EPI)
Percy Faith; *16 Most Requested Songs* ....(COL)

Reflections; *45* ....(ERI)
Stacy Earl; *Stacy Earl* ....(RCA)
Sailor & The Mermaid
Libby Titus & Dr. John; *In Harmony-Sesame Street* ....(WB)
"Sesame Street" Theme
Original Music; *Television's Greatest Hits-#3* .....(TVT)
Seven Dwarfs
Airto Moreira; *Struck By Lightning* ....(VEN)
Sleeping Beauty Waltz
101 Strings; *Million Seller Themes From Tchaikovsky* ....(ALS)
Snoopy Vs. The Red Baron
Royal Guardsmen; *Best Of-#1* ....(RHI)
Collectables Presents History Of Rock-#9 ....(CLT)
Cruisin'-1967 ....(INC)
Million-Dollar Memories #1 ....(RCA)
Super Oldies/'60s-#6 ....(AUF)
Snoopy's Christmas
Royal Guardsmen; *Snoopy & His Friends* ....(LAU)
"Spiderman" Theme
Original Music; *Television's Greatest Hits-#2* .....(TVT)
Stupid Cupid
Connie Francis; *Very Best Of* ....(POL)
Neil Sedaka; *All-Time Greatest Hits-#2* ....(RCA)
Super Heroes
Original London Cast; *Rocky Horror Show* ...... (RHI)
Tales Of Brave Ulysses
Cream; *Disraeli Gears* ....(POL)
Eric Clapton-*Crossroads* ....(POL)
Live Cream-#2 ....(POL)
Tarzan Boy
Baltimora; *Living In The Background* .... (MAN)
Tarzan Was A Bluesman
Timbuk 3; *Eden Alley* ....(IRS)
Tarzan & Jane
Sparks; *Angst In My Pants* ....(ATL)
Tarzan's Nuts
Madness; *One Step Beyond* ....(SIR)
"The Muppet Show" Theme
Muppets/Cast; *Muppet Hits* ....(JH)
Original Music; *Television's Greatest Hits-#3* .....(TVT)
Theme From "Beauty & The Beast"
Ron Perlman; *Theme From "Beauty & The Beast"* (CAP)
Theme From "Romeo & Juliet"
101 Strings Orchestra; *World's Greatest Standards* (ALS)
Andre Kostelanetz; *16 Most Requested Songs* ....(COL)
Three Little Pigs
Lloyd Price; *Greatest Hits* .... (MCA)
Tom Sawyer
Rush; *Chronicles* ....(MER)
Exit...Stage Left ....(MER)
Moving Pictures ....(MER)
Tom Thumb
Wayne Shorter; *Best Of-Blue Note Years* ....(BLN)
Tweedledee For President
Michael Tilson Thomas; *Of Thee I Sing/Let 'Em Eat Cake* ....(COL)
Venus
Frankie Avalon; *21 Oldies But Goodies* ....(OSR)
Billboard Top Rock 'N' Roll Hits-1959 ......(RHI)
Oldies But Goodies-#10 ....(OSR)
'50s Sock Hop ....(KT)
Shocking Blue; *Billboard Top Rock 'N' Roll Hits-1970* ....(RHI)
Oldies But Goodies-#15 ....(OSR)
Super Hits/'70s-Have A Nice Day-#1 ....(RHI)
'70s Smash Hits-#1 ....(RHI)
Venus In Blue Jeans
Jimmy Clanton; *All-Star Chartbusters* ....(INT)
Golden Years-1962 ....(DOM)
Where Did Robinson Crusoe Go With Friday
Ian Whitcomb; *45* ....(OSR)
Who's Afraid Of The Big Bad Wolf
Barbra Streisand; *Album* ....(COL)
Just For The Record ....(COL)
L.L. Cool J; *Simply Mad About The Mouse* ......(COL)
Mormon Tabernacle Choir/Columbia Symph.; *When You Wish Upon A Star-Disney Tribute* ....(COL)
M. Moder/D. Compton/P. Colvig/Others; *Disney Collection-#1* ....(DIS)

SUICIDE
See Also: DEATH, KILL

Auf Wiedersehen
Cheap Trick; *Heaven Tonight* ....(EPI)
Chrome Plated Suicide
Flaming Lips; *Telepathic Surgery* ....(RES)
Drown Yourself
Staple Singers; *Be What You Are* ....(STX)
I Think I'm Gonna Kill Myself
Buddy Knox; *Best Of* ....(RHI)
Elton John; *Honky Chateau* ....(POL)
Waylon Jennings; *Ol' Waylon* ....(RCA)
Jump Jump Jump
Rick Derringer; *All-American Boy* ....(BS)
Just Another Suicide
UFO; *Lights Out* ....(CHR)
Killing Yourself To Live
Black Sabbath; *Sabbath Bloody Sabbath* ....(WB)
Let Go Of The Stone
John Anderson; *Seminole Wind* ....(BNA)
Man Who Shot Himself
Tom T. Hall; *Places I've Done Time* ....(RCA)
Most Peculiar Man
Simon & Garfunkel; *Sounds Of Silence* ....(COL)
Murder By Suicide
Gary Richrath; *Only The Strong Survive* .... (CRS)
"M*A*S*H" Theme (Suicide Is Painless)
Ahmad Jamal; *Digital Works* ....(ATL)
ST/M-A-S-H ....(COL)
Percy Faith; *All-Time Greatest Hits* ....(COL)
On Suicide
Art Bears; *Hopes & Fears* ....(CUN)
Robyn Archer; *Robyn Archer* ....(ANG)
Peggy Suicide Is Missing
Julian Cope; *Jehovahkill* .... (ISL)
People Who Died
Jim Carroll Band; *Catholic Boy* ....(ATC)
ST/Tuff Turf ....(RHI)
Potential Suicide
Black Market Baby; *Faster & Louder-Hardcore Punk-#2* ....(RHI)
Richard Cory
Paul McCartney/Wings; *Wings Over America* ....(CAP)
Simon & Garfunkel; *Collected Works* ....(COL)
Sounds Of Silence ....(COL)
Richard Cory Cries
Midnight Reign; *Mountain Of Metal* .... (MNT)
Richard Hung Himself
D.I.; *Team Goon* ....(XXX)
Rock & Roll Suicide
David Bowie; *Live* ....(RYK)
Rise & Fall Of Ziggy Stardust ....(RYK)
Sound + Vision ....(RYK)
ST/Ziggy Stardust-The Motion Picture ......(RCA)
Save The Life Of My Child
Simon & Garfunkel; *Bookends* ....(COL)
Collected Works ....(COL)
Six O'Clock News
John Prine; *John Prine* ....(ATL)
Suicidal Failure
Suicidal Tendencies; *Still Cyco After All These Years* ....(EPI)
Suicidal Tendencies ....(FRN)
Suicidal Heroin
Ratos De Porao; *Brasil* ....(ROA)
Suicidal Man
Uriah Heep; *Wonderworld* ....(ROA)
Suicidal Mania
Suicidal Tendencies; *How Will I Laugh Tomorrow When I...* ....(EPI)
Suicidal Maniac
Suicidal Tendencies; *Join The Army* ....(CRL)
Suicidal Rage
Death Squad; *Split You At The Seams* .... (ER)
Suicide
Damned; *Machine Gun Etiquette* ....(ROA)
Dog; *Tom Troccoli's Dog* ....(SST)
Suzi Quatro; *If You Knew Suzi* ....(RSO)
Thin Lizzy; *Fighting* ....(MER)
Live & Dangerous ....(WB)

Suicide Blonde
INXS; *Live Baby Live* .... (ATL)
X .... (ATL)
Suicide Blues
Curtis Jones; *Trouble Blues* .... (BV)
Leroy Carr; *Singin' The Blues* ....(BIO)
Little Charlie/Nightcats; *All The Way Crazy* .....(ALG)
Suicide Child
Nuns; *Best Of Rodney On The ROQ* .... (PBO)
Posh Hits-#1 .... (PBO)
Suicide Chump
Frank Zappa; *You Are What You Is* ....(RYK)
Suicide Is Not The Way
Maurice John Vaughn; *In The Shadow Of The
City* ....(ALG)
Suicide Machine
Death; *Best Of* .... (REL)
Swell; *...Well?* .... (DEF)
Suicide Madness
Germs; *Germicide-Live At The Whisky-1977* ..... (ROI)
Suicide Note
Pontiac Brothers; *Fuzzy Little Piece Of The World* (FRN)
Suicide On Downing St.
Tim Finn; *Tim Finn* ....(CAP)
Suicide Solution
Ozzy Osbourne; *Blizzard Of Ozz* ....(JET)
Live & Loud .... (EPA)
Tribute .... (EPA)
Suicide Song
Loudon Wainwright III; *A Live One* .... (ROU)
Album 2 .... (ATL)
Suicide Won't Satisfy
Johnny Winter; *Birds Can't Row Boats* ....(RLX)
Suicide's An Alternative/You'll Be Sorry
Suicidal Tendencies; *Still Cyco After All These
Years* .... (EPI)
Suicidal Tendencies .... (FRN)
Suzy Suicide
Spread Eagle; *Spread Eagle* .... (MCA)
Teenage Suicide
Unrest; *Kustom Karnal Blackxploitation* ....(CRL)
Teenage Suicide (Don't Do It)
Don Dixon; *(If I'm A Ham We'll You're A
Sausage* .... (RES)
Waltzing Matilda
Burl Ives; *Best Of* .... (MCA)
Fred Astaire; *Three Evenings With* .... (DRG)
James Galway; *Pachebel Canon & Other
Favorites* ....(RCA)

SUN

*See Also: HOT, NIGHT, SEASONS: SUMMER,
SPACE*

African Sunrise
John Denver; *Dreamland Express* ....(RCA)
African Sunset
Tommy Page; *Tommy Page* .... (SIR)
Afternoon Sunshine
Edwin Starr; *Edwin Starr* .... (20)
Ain't Going Down (Til The Sun Comes Up)
Garth Brooks; *In Pieces* ....(LIB)
Ain't No Sunshine
Bill Withers; *Greatest Hits* ....(OOP)
Just As I Am ....(OOP)
Michael Jackson; *Original Soul Of* ....(MOT)
Alaskan Sunrise
Dick Pinney; *Devil Take My Shiny Coins* .... (MOU)
Always The Sun
Stranglers; *All Live & All Of The Night* .... (EPI)
Dreamtime .... (EPI)
Greatest Hits-1977-1990 .... (EPI)
Aquarius/Let The Sunshine In Medley
Fifth Dimension; *Billboard Top Rock & Roll
Hits-1969* .... (RHI)
Greatest Hits On Earth .... (ARI)
ST/1969 .... (POL)
ST/Forrest Gump .... (EPX)
At Sundown
Mom & Dads; *Blue Hawaii* .... (CRS)
Behind The Sun
Eric Clapton; *Behind The Sun* .... (DUC)

Red Hot Chili Peppers; *Uplift Mofo Party Plan* .. (EMI)
What Hits!? Best Of .... (EMI)
Black Hole Sun
Soundgarden; *Superunknown* .... (A&M)
Black Sunshine
White Zombie; *La Sexorcisto-Devil Music-#1* ....(GEF)
Blame It On The Sun
Stevie Wonder; *Talking Book* .... (MOT)
Blues Before Sunrise
Eric Clapton; *From The Cradle* .... (DUC)
California Sun
Ramones; *All The Stuff (& More)* .... (SIR)
Leave Home .... (SIR)
ST/Rock & Roll High School .... (SIR)
Rivieras; *Beach Classics* ....(DHL)
Frat Rock-#4 .... (RHI)
Summer & Sun .... (RHI)
California Sunset
Neil Young; *Old Ways* ....(GEF)
Carolina Sun
Anne Murray; *Keeping In Touch* ....(CAP)
Carolina Sunshine Girl
Geoff Muldaur & Amos Garrett; *Geoff Muldaur & Amos
Garrett* .... (FF)
Cheap Sunglasses
ZZ Top; *Deguello* .... (WB)
ST/Teachers .... (WB)
Colors Of The Sun
Bonnie Koloc; *At Her Best* .... (OVA)
You're Gonna Love Yourself... .... (OVA)
Jackson Browne; *For Everyman* .... (ASY)
Come Rain Or Come Shine
Frank Sinatra & Gloria Estefan; *Frank Sinatra
Duets* ....(CAP)
Judy Garland; *America's Treasure* ....(DHL)
At Carnegie Hall ....(CAP)
Hits Of ....(CAP)
Judy ....(CAP)
Country Sunshine
Dottie West; *Collector's* ....(RCA)
Great Moments At The Grand Ole Opry ....(RCA)
Rita Remington; *Country Girl Gold* .... (PLN)
Day In The Sun
Peter Frampton; *Peter Frampton* .... (REL)
Don't Leave Your Records In The Sun
John Hartford; *Mark Twang* .... (FF)
Don't Let The Sun Catch You Cryin'
Gerry/Pacemakers; *Best Of* .... (EMI)
Greatest Hits ....(LAU)
History Of British Rock-#1 .... (RHI)
Super Oldies/'60s-#5 ....(AUF)
Louis Jordan; *Best Of* .... (MCA)
Paul McCartney; *Tripping The Live Fantastic* ....(CAP)
Ray Charles; *Genius Of* .... (ATL)
Rickie Lee Jones; *Flying Cowboys* ....(GEF)
Don't Let The Sun Go Down On Me
Elton John; *Caribou* .... (POL)
Greatest Hits .... (POL)
Live In Australia w/Melbourne Symphony ...... (MCA)
Elton John & George Michael; *Duets* .... (MCA)
George Michael & Elton John; *Two Rooms Tribute To
E. John & B. Taupin* ....(COL)
East Of The Sun & West Of The Moon
Al Cohn & Zoot Sims; *RCA Victor Jazz-First
Half-Century* ....(RCA)
Billie Holiday; *Billie's Best* .... (VRV)
Tommy Dorsey & Frank Sinatra; *Stardust* ...... (BLU)
Electric L.A. Sunset
Al Stewart; *Early Years* ....(OOP)
Every Night When The Sun Goes In
Jo Stafford; *Jo Plus Blues* .... (CRN)
Father Sun
Wynonna; *Tell Me Why* .... (MCC)
Fly Into The Sun
Lou Reed; *New Sensations* ....(RCA)
Georgia Sunshine
Jerry Reed; *Best Of* ....(RCA)
God Of The Sun
America; *Harbor* .... (WB)
Golden Apples Of The Sun
Judy Collins; *Golden Apples Of The Sun* .... (ELE)
So Early In The Spring .... (ELE)

Good Day Sunshine
Beatles; *Box Set* .... (CAP)
   Revolver .... (CAP)
Groovin'
Aretha Franklin; *Lady Soul* .... (ATL)
Booker T./M.G.s; *Best Of* .... (ATL)
   Soul Shots-#3 Soul Twist .... (RHI)
Rascals; *Greatest Hits* .... (ATL)
   Groovin' .... (RHI)
   Hit Singles-1958-1977 .... (ATL)
   ST/Platoon .... (ATL)
Happier Than The Morning Sun
Stevie Wonder; *Music Of My Mind* .... (MOT)
Here Comes The Sun
Beatles; *1967-1970* .... (CAP)
   Abbey Road .... (CAP)
George Benson; *Best* .... (A&M)
   Collection .... (WB)
George Harrison; *Bangladesh* .... (CAP)
   Best Of .... (CAP)
High On Sunshine
Commodores; *Hot On The Tracks* .... (MOT)
Holidays In The Sun
Sex Pistols; *Never Mind The Bollocks* .... (WB)
Hot As Sun
Paul McCartney; *Paul McCartney* .... (COL)
House Of The Rising Sun
Animals; *Best Of* .... (AKO)
   Greatest Hits .... (ALL)
   Rip It To Shreds-Greatest Hits Live .... (IRS)
Hank Williams, Jr.; *Hank Live* .... (W/C)
Ronnie Milsap; *16 Greatest Hits-#2* .... (TRP)
Hurry Sundown
Outlaws; *Bring It Back Alive* .... (ARI)
   Hurry Sundown .... (ARI)
   South's Greatest Hits #2 .... (CPC)
I Can See Clearly Now
Gladys Knight/Pips; *Greatest Hits* .... (BUD)
   Imagination .... (BUD)
   On & On .... (FFT)
Johnny Nash; *Billboard Top Rock 'N' Roll*
Hits-1972 .... (RHI)
   Rock Artifacts-#2 .... (COL)
I Don't Care If The Sun Don't Shine
Elvis Presley; *Complete Sun Sessions* .... (RCA)
   Golden Celebration .... (RCA)
I Got The Sun In The Morning
Doris Day/Original Cast; *Annie Get Your Gun* .. (COL)
Ethel Merman/Ray Middleton/Original Cast; *Annie Get*
Your Gun .... (MCA)
If The Sun Doesn't Shine
Smithereens; *Green Thoughts* .... (CAP)
In The Evening When The Sun Goes Down
Ella Fitzgerald; *These Are The Blues* .... (VRV)
Mel Torme; *Duke Ellington & Count Basie*
Songbook .... (VRV)
Pete Seeger; *20 Golden Pieces Of* .... (BLD)
   Sings Folk Music Of The World .... (TRD)
Indian Sunset
Elton John; *Madman Across The Water* .... (POL)
I'll Follow The Sun
Beatles; *Box Set* .... (CAP)
   For Sale .... (CAP)
   Love Songs .... (CAP)
   '65 .... (CAP)
Jenny (Iowa Sunrise)
Janis Ian; *Night Trains* .... (COL)
Keep On The Sunny Side
Randy Scruggs/Earl Scruggs/Doc Watson; *Red Hot +*
Country .... (MER)
Kentucky Sunrise
Ringling Brothers B & B Band; *Circus Time* .... (MCA)
Lipstick Sunset
John Hiatt; *Bring The Family* .... (A&M)
Look Into The Sun
Jethro Tull; *Stand Up* .... (CHR)
Louisiana Sun
Doug Kershaw; *Louisiana Man* .... (WB)
   Wichita Wildcat .... (FFT)
L.A. Sunshine
War; *Platinim Jazz* .... (BLN)
Mad Dogs & Englishmen
Noel Coward; *Album-Live From Las Vegas & New*
York .... (COL)

Memphis Sun
Orion; *Rockabilly* .... (SUN)
Midnight Sun
Ella Fitzgerald; *In Rome-Birthday Concert* .... (VRV)
Ella Fitzgerald & Oscar Peterson; *Ella & Oscar* .. (PAB)
Sarah Vaughan; *Best Of* .... (PAB)
   How Long Has This Been Going On .... (PAB)
Miss Sun
Boz Scaggs; *Hits* .... (COL)
Toto; *Toto* .... (COL)
Morning Sun
Bad Company; *Burnin' Sky* .... (SS)
Jesse Colin Young; *Best Of-Solo Years* .... (RHI)
   Song For Juli .... (WB)
My Carolina Sunshine Girl
Jimmie Rodgers; *Early Years-1928-1929* ...... (ROU)
My Old Kentucky Home
Al Jolson; *Story-#5* .... (MCA)
Randy Newman; *Live* .... (RPR)
   Randy Newman .... (RPR)
Ry Cooder; *Ry Cooder* .... (RPR)
Salli Terri; *Songs Of The American Land* .... (ANG)
October Sunshine
First Brass; *First Brass* .... (MA)
   Jazz Horizons-Best Of M-A Music-#1 .... (MA)
Oklahoma Sunshine
Mayf Nutter; *Goin' Skinny Dippin'* .... (CRS)
On The Sunny Side Of The Street
Frank Sinatra; *Capitol Years* .... (CAP)
   Come Swing With Me! .... (CAP)
   One More For The Road .... (CAP)
   Sentimental Journey .... (CAP)
Judy Garland; *Best Of* .... (MCA)
Louis Armstrong; *Best Of* .... (MCA)
   Chicago Concert 1956 .... (COL)
   Jazz-Club Vocal .... (VRV)
   Music Autobiography .... (MCA)
One In The Sun
Lynyrd Skynyrd; *Legend* .... (MCA)
Steve Gaines; *Rockin' Southern Style* .... (MSP)
Place In The Sun
Pablo Cruise; *Place In The Sun* .... (A&M)
Stevie Wonder; *Greatest Hits-#1* .... (MOT)
   Looking Back .... (MOT)
Please Mr. Sun
Johnnie Ray; *16 Most Requested Songs* .... (COL)
   Back To The Early '50s .... (DOM)
Vogues; *Greatest Hits* .... (RHI)
Powder Your Face With Sunshine (Smile!)
Guy Lombardo; *Best Of* .... (CCB)
Sammy Kaye/Orchestra; *Play 22 Original Big Band*
Recordings .... (HIN)
Red Red Sun
INXS; *Listen Like Thieves* .... (ATL)
Red Rubber Ball
Cyrkle; *Even More Nuggets* .... (RHI)
   Pop Classics Of The '60s .... (COL)
   Red Rubber Ball (collection) .... (COL)
Red Sails In The Sunset
Big Joe Turner; *Nobody In Mind* .... (PAB)
Dinah Washington; *Echoes Of An Era* .... (RLL)
Jarmels; *Golden Classics* .... (CLT)
Nat King Cole; *Unforgettable* .... (CAP)
Platters; *Greatest Hits* .... (EVR)
Saturday Sun
Nick Drake; *Five Leaves Left* .... (HBL)
Sauerkraut 'N' Solar Energy
Norman Blake/Others; *Norman Blake/Others* ...... (FF)
Seasons In The Sun
Kingston Trio; *Capitol Collectors Series* .... (CAP)
Terry Jacks; *Super Hits/'70s-Have A Nice*
Day-#12 .... (RHI)
   '70s Greatest Rock Hits-#9-#1 Hits .... (PRY)
Set The Controls For The Heart Of The...
Pink Floyd; *Nice Pair* .... (CAP)
   Saucerful Of Secrets .... (CAP)
   Ummagumma .... (CAP)
   Works .... (CAP)
Slowdown, Sundown
Steve Winwood; *Arc Of A Diver* .... (ISL)

Sugar Magnolia
Grateful Dead; *American Beauty* .... (WB)
  Europe '72 .... (WB)
  Live-#1 .... (JCI)
  Skeletons From The Closet-Best Of .... (WB)
Sultry Sunset
Duke Ellington; *20 Golden Pieces Of* .... (BLD)
Duke Ellington/Orchestra; *Duke Ellington/Orchestra* .... (LAS)
Sun Ain't Gonna Shine Anymore
Walker Brothers; *History Of British Rock-#7* ..... (RHI)
  Love Sixties .... (JCI)
Sun Also Rises In Hell
XYZ; *Hungry* .... (CAP)
Sun Always Shines On T.V.
A-Ha; *Hunting High & Low* .... (WB)
Sun Comes Up, It's Tuesday
Cowboy Junkies; *Caution Horses* .... (RCA)
Sun Don't Shine
Inspiral Carpets; *Life* .... (ELE)
Sun Don't Shine On The Same Folks...
Sawyer Brown; *Sawyer Brown* .... (LIB)
Sun Goddess
Earth, Wind & Fire; *Eternal Dance* .... (COL)
  Gratitude .... (COL)
Ramsey Lewis; *Best Of* .... (COL)
  Sun Goddess .... (COL)
Sun Goes Down
Thin Lizzy; *Life Live* .... (WB)
  Thunder & Lightning .... (MET)
Sun Hasn't Set On This Boy Yet
Nils Lofgren; *Classics-#13* .... (A&M)
  Nils Lofgren .... (RYK)
Sun In My Hand
Scorpions; *Best Of-#2* .... (RCA)
  In Trance .... (RCA)
Sun Is Burning
Simon & Garfunkel; *Collected Works* .... (COL)
  Wednesday Morning 3 A.M. .... (COL)
Sun Is Gonna Shine Again
Graham Parker; *Best Of-1988-1991* .... (RCA)
Sun Is Out
Flora Purim & Airto Moriera; *Sun Is Out* .... (CRO)
Sun Is Shining
Bob Marley/Wailers; *Kaya* .... (TUF)
  Songs Of Freedom .... (TUF)
Elmore James; *Chess Blues* .... (CSS)
  Sky Is Crying-History Of .... (RHI)
Jeff Beck/Yardbirds; *Beckology* .... (EPI)
Jimmy Reed; *Speak The Lyrics To Me Mama Reed* . (VJ)
Sun Is Still Shining
Moody Blues; *To Our Children's Children's Children* .... (POL)
Sun King
Beatles; *Abbey Road* .... (CAP)
  Box Set .... (CAP)
Cult; *Sonic Temple* .... (SIR)
Sun Maid
Soul Asylum; *Grave Dancers Union* .... (COL)
Sun Of '79
Des'ree; *Mind Adventures* .... (EPI)
Sun On The Moon
James Taylor; *Never Die Young* .... (COL)
Sun Singer
Paul Winter; *Anthems* .... (LIV)
Paul Winter Consort; *Sun Singer* .... (LIV)
Sun Song
Dave Grusin; *Discovered Again* .... (SHF)
Lee Ritenour; *Best Of* .... (EPI)
  Captain Fingers .... (EPI)
Sun Won't Set
Original Cast; *A Little Night Music* .... (COL)
Original London Cast; *A Little Night Music* ...... (RCA)
Sun & Moon
Original London Cast; *Miss Saigon* .... (GEF)
Sun & The Rainfall
Depeche Mode; *Broken Frame* .... (SIR)
Sunburst
Bob Seger; *Night Moves* .... (CAP)
Sundance
Danny Joe Brown Band; *Danny Joe Brown Band* . (EPI)
Kitaro; *Light Of The Spirit* .... (GEF)
Sundancing (For The Hopi/Navajo Energy)
Jon Anderson; *In The City Of Angels* .... (COL)

Sunday Morning Sunshine
Harry Chapin; *Anthology* .... (ELE)
  Savoy Brown Collection .... (DER)
Sunday Sun
Neil Diamond; *Glory Road-1968-1972* .... (MCA)
  Velvet Gloves & Spit .... (MCA)
Sunday Sunrise
Brenda Lee; *Greatest Country Hits* .... (MCA)
Sundown
Gordon Lightfoot; *Gord's Gold* .... (RPR)
  Sundown .... (RPR)
Jesus & Mary Chain; *Honey's Dead* .... (DEF)
Sundown Blues
Riders In The Sky; *Riders Radio Theater* .... (MCA)
Sunface
Tanita Tikaram; *Everybody's Angel* .... (RPR)
Sunless Saturday
Fishbone; *Reality Of My Surroundings* .... (COL)
Sunlight
Jesse Colin Young; *Best Of-Solo Years* .... (RHI)
Youngbloods; *Best Of* .... (RCA)
  Elephant Mountain .... (MOB)
  Jesse Colin Young On The Road .... (WB)
  This Is The .... (RCA)
  Youngbloods .... (RCA)
Sunny
Bobby Hebb; *Billboard Top R&B Hits-1965-1969* (RHI)
  Oldies But Goodies-#11 .... (OSR)
Classics IV; *Very Best Of* .... (EMI)
Electric Flag; *Long Time Comin'* .... (COL)
Stevie Wonder; *For Once In My Life* .... (MOT)
Sunny Afternoon
Kinks; *Compleat Collection-20th Anniversary* ... (CMP)
  Greatest Hits-#1 .... (RHI)
  Kink Kronikles .... (RPR)
  Live .... (RPR)
Sunny Goodge Street
Donovan; *Catch The Wind* .... (GRL)
Judy Collins; *Colors Of The Day-Best Of* .... (ELE)
Sunny Hills
Bobby Caldwell; *Carry On* .... (SD)
Sunny Inside
Neil Young; *This Note's For You* .... (RPR)
Sunny Monday
Booker T./M.G.s; *Melting Pot* .... (STX)
Sunny Side Of The Mountain
Bill Monroe; *Bean Blossom* .... (MCA)
Jimmy Martin/Sunny Mountain Boys; *Best Of Bluegrass* .... (KT)
Nitty Gritty Dirt Band; *Will The Circle Be Unbroken* .... (EMI)
Sunny Side Of The Street
Pogues; *Essential* .... (ISL)
  Hell's Ditch .... (ISL)
Sunny Side To Every Situation
Original Cast; *42nd Street* .... (RCA)
Sunny Skies
James Taylor; *In Harmony 2* .... (COL)
  Sweet Baby James .... (WB)
Jerry Douglas; *Fluxedo* .... (ROU)
Teena Marie; *Emerald City* .... (EPI)
Sunny Tennessee
Doc Watson; *Old Timey Concert* .... (VAN)
Sunnyland
Elmore James; *Golden Classics* .... (CLT)
Sunrise
Chet Atkins & George Benson; *Stay Tuned* ...... (COL)
Eric Carmen; *Eric Carmen* .... (ARI)
Grateful Dead; *Terrapin Station* .... (ARI)
Jefferson Starship/Paul Kantner; *Blows Against The Empire* .... (RCA)
Jimmy Cliff; *Cliff Hanger* .... (COL)
Joe Sample; *Carmel* .... (MCA)
  Collection .... (GRP)
New Order; *Low-Life* .... (QUE)
Originals; *Motown Superstar Series-#10* .... (MOT)
Seals & Crofts; *Takin' It Easy* .... (WB)
Triplets; *...Thicker Than Water* .... (MER)
Uriah Heep; *Best Of* .... (MER)
  Magician's Birthday .... (MER)
White Mountain Singers; *Best* .... (FOL)
  Memories-Live! .... (FOL)
  Sunrise .... (TAK)

Sunrise In La Jolla
Kilauea; *Antigua Blue* .... (BRA)
Sunrise In Mexico
Clifford Jordan; *Starting Time* .... (JZL)
Sunrise Over Haleakala
Merl Saunders & Jerry Garcia; *Blues From The*
Rainforest-Musical Suite .... (SUM)
Sunrise Serenade
Frankie Carle/Orchestra; *Big Band Instrumentals-16*
Most Requested .... (COL)
Glenn Miller; *Best Of* .... (BLU)
Legendary Performer .... (BLU)
Pure Gold .... (BLU)
Sunrise, Sunset
Original Cast; *Fiddler On The Roof* .... (RCA)
Original London Cast; *Fiddler On The Roof* ..... (COL)
Sunset
Jackie Lomax; *Is This What You Want?* .... (CAP)
Jonathan Butler; *Jonathan Butler* .... (JVA)
Moody Blues; *Caught Live Plus Five* .... (POL)
Days Of Future Passed .... (POL)
Roxy Music; *Stranded* .... (RPR)
Sunset At Noon
Kenny G; *G-Force* .... (ARI)
Sunset Dreams
Clannad; *Banba* .... (ATL)
Sunset Grill
Don Henley; *Building The Perfect Beast* .... (GEF)
Sunset People
Donna Summer; *Bad Girls* .... (CAS)
Greatest Hits .... (CAS)
On The Radio-Greatest Hits-#1&2 .... (CAS)
Walk Away-Best Of 1977-1980 .... (CAS)
Sunset To Sunrise
Duprees; *Best Of* .... (RHI)
Sunshine
Alexander O'Neal; *Hearsay* .... (TAB)
Alice In Chains; *Facelift* .... (COL)
Babyface; *Tender Lover* .... (SLR)
Boys; *Messages From The Boys* .... (MOT)
Earth, Wind & Fire; *Gratitude* .... (COL)
The Eternal Dance .... (COL)
Jonathan Edwards; *Super Hits/'70s-Have A Nice*
Day-#7 .... (RHI)
Juice Newton; *Greatest Country Hits* .... (CCB)
Kenny Rogers; *Back Home Again* .... (RPR)
Kenny Rogers/First Edition; *Best Of* .... (KT)
Love Songs .... (MSP)
Original Cast; *Gentlemen Prefer Blondes* .... (SSP)
O'Jays; *Collector's Items* .... (PI)
Live In London .... (PI)
Timbuk 3; *Best Of* .... (IRS)
Sunshine In Their Eyes
Stevie Wonder; *Where I'm Coming From* .... (MOT)
Sunshine Of Your Love
Cream; *Disraeli Gears* .... (POL)
History Of British Rock-#8 .... (RHI)
Live-#2 .... (POL)
Strange Brew-Very best Of .... (POL)
Eric Clapton; *24 Nights* .... (RPR)
Crossroads .... (POL)
Knebworth-The Album .... (POL)
Sunshine Of Your Smile
Tommy Dorsey & Frank Sinatra; *All-Time Greatest*
Hits-#4 .... (RCA)
Sunshine On My Shoulders
John Denver; *Greatest Hits-#1* .... (RCA)
Take Me Home Country Roads & Other Hits .... (RCA)
Sunshine Saturday Morning
Jim Aikin; *Light's Broken Speech Revived* .... (LIN)
Sunshine Superman
Donovan; *Greatest Hits* .... (EPI)
History Of British Rock-#5 .... (RHI)
Sunshine Superman .... (EPI)
Troubadour-Definitive Collection .... (EPI)
Sunshine, Lollipops & Rainbows
Lesley Gore; *Anthology* .... (RHI)
Golden Hits Of .... (MER)
Sunshine, Sunshine
James Taylor; *James Taylor* .... (CAP)
Sunshower
Chuck Mangione; *Best Of* .... (MER)

Sunshowers
Billie Holiday; *Golden Years-#2* .... (COL)
Story-#3 .... (COL)
Sun, Moon & Stars
Nanci Griffith; *Late Night Grande Hotel* .... (MCA)
Sun's Gonna Shine Again
Ray Charles; *Birth Of Soul-Complete Atlantic*
R&B .... (ATL)
Swallow The Sun
Love Exchange; *Nuggets-#10-Folk Rock* .... (RHI)
Sweet Hawaiian Sunshine
Jorma Kaukonen & Tom Hobson; *Quah* .... (RLX)
Tequila Sunrise
Alan Jackson; *Common Thread-Songs Of The*
Eagles .... (GIA)
Eagles; *Anthology* .... (ASY)
Desperado .... (ASY)
Their Greatest Hits-1971-1975 .... (ASY)
Fagles; *Hell Freezes Over* .... (GEF)
That Lucky Old Sun
Asleep At The Wheel; *Western Standard Time* .... (EPI)
Bing Crosby; *Radio Years* .... (CRS)
Frankie Laine; *16 Most Requested Songs* .... (COL)
Golden Hits .... (MER)
Greatest Hits .... (COL)
Jerry Garcia Band; *Jerry Garcia Band* .... (ARI)
Louis Armstrong; *Greatest Hits* .... (CCB)
Ray Charles; *Anthology* .... (RHI)
Willie Nelson; *Sound In Your Mind* .... (COL)
Third Rock From The Sun
Joe Diffie; *Thousand Winding...* .... (EPI)
Three Sunrises
U2; *Unforgettable Fire* .... (ISL)
Wide Awake In America .... (ISL)
To The Door Of The Sun
Al Martino; *Capitol Collectors Series* .... (CAP)
Greatest Hits .... (CCB)
Tulsa (Don't Let The Sun Set On You)
Waylon Jennings; *Taker/Tulsa & Honky Tonk*
Heroes .... (MOB)
Under The Big Black Sun
X; *Under The Big Black Sun* .... (ELE)
Under The Same Sun
Scorpions; *Face The Heat* .... (MER)
Wait Till The Sun Shines Nellie
Joan Morris & William Bolcom; *After The Ball* . (NON)
Waiting For Sun
Jayhawks; *Hollywood Town Hall* .... (DEF)
Waiting For The Sun
Doors; *Best Of* .... (ELE)
Classics .... (ELE)
Morrison Hotel .... (ELE)
Waiting For The Sun To Shine
John Conlee; *In My Eyes* .... (MSP)
Lionel Cartwright; *Chasin' The Sun* .... (MCA)
Reba McEntire; *Reba Nell McEntire* .... (MER)
Ricky Skaggs; *Favorite Country Songs* .... (EPI)
Waiting For The Sun To Shine .... (EPI)
Wake Up Sunshine
Chicago; *II* .... (COL)
Walking In The Sun
Rufus; *Rags To Rufus* .... (MCA)
Zombies; *Time Of* .... (EPI)
Walking In The Sunshine
Frank Sinatra; *Hello Young Lovers* .... (COL)
Roger Miller; *Best Of* .... (MER)
King Of The Road .... (LAS)
More Golden Hits .... (SMA)
Statler Brothers; *Sing The Big Hits* .... (COL)
World Of .... (COL)
Walking Into Sunshine
Central Line; *45* .... (MER)
Walking On Sunshine
Eddy Grant; *Let's Dance-DJ's Collection* .... (COL)
Walking On Sunshine .... (EPI)
Katrina/Waves; *Katrina/Waves* .... (CAP)
Spring Break-#2-Cold Kegs & Tan Legs .... (CAP)
Warmth Of The Sun
Beach Boys; *Absolute Best-#1* .... (CAP)
Best Of .... (CAP)
Endless Summer .... (CAP)
Fun Fun Fun .... (CAP)
Gift Set .... (CAP)
ST/Good Morning Vietnam .... (A&M)

Was A Sunny Day
Paul Simon; *There Goes Rhymin' Simon* ....(COL)
Watch The Sun Go Down
X; *Ain't Love Grand* ....(ELE)
Waterloo Sunset
Kinks; *Kink Kronikles* ....(RPR)
Something Else ....(RPR)
Way Beyond The Sun
Byrds; *Byrds (collection)* ....(COL)
We'll Sing In The Sunshine
Gale Garnett; *21 Country Rock/Love
Songs-'50s/'60s-#1* ....(LAU)
Nipper's Greatest Hits-'60s ....(RCA)
What Sundown Does To You
Loretta Lynn; *Best OF-#2* .... (MSP)
Greatest Hits-#2 .... (MCA)
When The Sun Comes Out
Barbra Streisand; *Second Album* ....(COL)
...Just For The Record ....(COL)
Benny Goodman; *Clarinet A La King* ....(COL)
Ella Fitzgerald; *Harold Arlen Songbook* ....(VRV)
When The Sun Goes Down
Count Basie & Joe Williams; *Count Basie Swings Joe
Williams Sings* ....(VRV)
Fleetwood Mac; *Behind The Mask* ....(WB)
Mark Collie; *Born & Raised In Black & White* .. (MCA)
Marty Stuart; *Hillbilly Rock* ....(MCA)
T-Bone Walker; *Complete Imperial
Recordings-1950-1954* .... (EMI)
When The Sun Goes Down In The South
Original Broadway Cast; *Big River-Adventures Of
Huckleberry Finn* .... (MCA)
White Sun
Doobie Brothers; *Toulouse Street* .... (WB)
World Is Waiting For The Sunrise
Benny Goodman; *I Like Jazz-Essence Of* ....(COL)
Benny Goodman Orchestra & Quartet; *Let's
Dance* .... (LAS)
Les Paul & Mary Ford; *World Is Waiting For The
Sunrise* .... (LAS)
Roy Clark & Buck Trent; *Banjo Bandit* .... (MCA)
You Are My Sunshine
Bing Crosby; *Best Of* .... (MCA)
Greatest Hits .... (MCA)
Jimmie Davis; *20 Golden Souvenirs Of Music City
U.S.A.* .... (PLN)
Best Of .... (MCA)
Country Music Hall Of Fame .... (MCA)
Golden Hits .... (PLN)
Mississippi John Hurt; *Best Of* .... (VAN)
Mitch Miller; *16 Most Requested Songs* ....(COL)
Ray Charles; *Anthology* .... (RHI)
His Greatest Hits-#2 ....(DHL)
Willie Nelson & Leon Russell; *One For The
Road* ....(COL)
You Are The Sunshine Of My Life
Peter Nero; *Greatest Hits* ....(COL)
Stevie Wonder; *20/20* ....(MOT)
Original Musiquarium ....(MOT)
Talking Book ....(MOT)

SURFING
See Also: OCEAN, SPORTS

Body Surfing
Santana; *Shango* ....(COL)
California Surfer
Dee D. Hope; *History Of Surf Music-#2* .... (RHI)
Catch A Wave
Beach Boys; *Best Of* ....(CAP)
Endless Summer ....(CAP)
Party Stack-O-Tracks ....(CAP)
Charlie Don't Surf
Clash; *Sandinista* .... (EPI)
Kill Surf City
Jesus & Mary Chain; *Barbed Wire Kisses* .... (RPR)
King Of The Surf Guitar
Dick Dale/Del-Tones; *Beach Classics* ....(DHL)
Greatest Hits ....(CRS)
Tigers Loose .... (RHI)
Lonely Surfer
Jack Nitzsche; *Surfin' Hits* .... (RHI)
Surfin' Sixties .... (JCI)

Monster Surfing Time
Halibuts; *Halibut Beach* .... (WTR)
No Surfin' Today
Frankie Valli/Four Seasons; *Rarities-#1* .... (RHI)
Pipeline
Chantays; *Surfin' Hits* .... (RHI)
Surfin' U.S.A. ....(DOM)
Ride The Wild Surf
Jan & Dean; *Monmster Summer Hits-Wild Surf* ... (CAP)
Surf City-Best Of .... (EMI)
Surfin' Hits .... (RHI)
Rocking Surfer
Beach Boys; *Surfer Girl/Shut Down-#2* .... (CAP)
Skateboard Surfin' U.S.A.
Jan Berry; *45* ....(A&M)
Surf Beat
Dick Dale/Del-Tones; *Greatest Hits* .... (CRS)
King Of The Surf Guitar-Best Of .... (RHI)
Surf City
Jan & Dean; *Billboard Top Rock 'N' Roll
Hits-1963* .... (RHI)
Monster Summer Hits-Wild Surf ....(CAP)
Surf City-Best Of .... (EMI)
Surf Monkey
Freddie King; *Just Pickin'* .... (MBR)
Surf Nicaragua
Sacred Reich; *Mega Metal* .... (KT)
Surf Rider
Lively Ones; *Bustin' Surfboards* .... (CRS)
Legends Of Surf Guitar .... (RHI)
Surfer Dan
Turtles; *Turtle Wax-Best Of-#2* .... (RHI)
Surfer Girl
Beach Boys; *American Graffiti-#3* .... (MCA)
Best Of .... (CAP)
Endless Summer ....(CAP)
Made In The U.S.A. ....(CAP)
Oldies But Goodies-#2 ....(OSR)
Surfer Joe
Surfaris; *Surfin' Hits* .... (RHI)
Surfin' Sixties ....(JCI)
Surfin'
Beach Boys; *Monster Summer Hits-Wild Surf* .....(CAP)
Summer Hits .... (RHI)
Surfin' Bird
Pee-Wee Herman; *ST/Back To The Beach* ....(COL)
Ramones; *All The Stuff & More-#2* .... (SIR)
Rocket To Russia .... (SIR)
Trashmen; *Collectables Presents History Of
Rock-#1* .... (CLT)
History Of Surf Music-#2 .... (RHI)
Monster Summer Hits-Wild Surf ....(CAP)
ST/Full Metal Jacket .... (WB)
Super Oldies/'60s-#11 .... (AUF)
Surfin' Down The Swanee River
Honeys; *Capitol Collectors Series* .... (CAP)
Surfin' In Harlem
Swamp Dogg; *Surfin' In Harlem* .... (VOL)
Surfin' On Heroin
Forgotten Rebels; *Surfin' On Heroin* .... (RES)
Surfin' On Jupiter
Psychefunkapus; *Skin* ....(ATL)
Surfin' Safari
Beach Boys; *Absolute Best-#1* .... (CAP)
Endless Summer ....(CAP)
Made In The U.S.A. ....(CAP)
Monster Summer Hits-Wild Surf ....(CAP)
Surfin' Sex Machine
Pajama Slave Dancers; *Blood Sweat & Beers* ..... (RES)
Surfin' Tragedy
Bob Vaught/Renegaids; *Original Surfin' Hits* ..... (CRS)
Breakers; *World's Worst Records* .... (RHI)
Surfin' U.S.A.
Beach Boys; *Absolute Best-#1* .... (CAP)
Best Of .... (CAP)
Billboard Top Rock 'N' Roll Hits-1963 .... (RHI)
Endless Summer ....(CAP)
Made In The U.S.A. ....(CAP)
Jesus & Mary Chain; *Barbed Wire Kisses* .... (DEF)
Surfin' U.S.S.R.
Ray Stevens; *Collection* .... (MCA)
Everything Is Beautiful .... (MSP)
I Never Made A Record I Didn't Like ....(MCA)

Surf's Up
Beach Boys; *Surf's Up* ....(CAR)
Sweet Surf Music
Malibooz; *Malibooz Rule* .... (RHI)
Tell 'Em I'm Surfing
Fantastic Baggies; *Monster Summer Hits-Wild
Surf* ....(CAP)
Windsurfer
Roy Orbison; *Mystery Girl* ....(VIA)
Wipeout
Surfaris; *Billboard Top Rock 'N' Roll Hits-1963* .. (RHI)
Cruisin'-1966 ....(INC)
Frat Rock! ....(RHI)
Summer Hits ....(RHI)
Surfin' Hits ....(RHI)

SWIMMING

See Also: SPORTS

Arc Of A Diver
Steve Winwood; *Arc Of A Diver* .... (ISL)
Backstrokin'
Fatback Band; *Hot Box* .... (SPR)
I Go Swimming
Peter Gabriel; *Plays Live* ....(GEF)
Not Swimming Ground
Meat Puppets; *Out My Way* ....(SST)
Swim
Fishbone; *Give A Monkey A Brain & He'll
Swear...* ....(COL)
ST/Last Action Hero ....(COL)
Swimming Ground
Meat Puppets; *No Strings Attached* ....(SST)
Up On The Sun ....(SST)
Swimming Horses
Siouxsie/Banshees; *Hyaena* ....(GEF)
Twice Upon A Time/The Singles ....(GEF)
Swimming In The Delaware
Sam Hinton; *Wandering Folk Song* .... (FLW)
Swimming In The Ocean
David & David; *Boomtown* ....(A&M)
Swimming Song
Earl Scruggs Revue; *Live From Austin City Limits* (COL)
Kate & Anna McGarrigle; *Kate & Anna
McGarrigle* ....(HBL)
Swimming Upstream
Glen Campbell; *Somebody Like That* ....(LIB)
Ricky Van Shelton; *Loving Proof* ....(COL)
Swimmin' Hole
Cactus Brothers; *Cactus Brothers* ....(LIB)
Swimsuit Issue
Sonic Youth; *Dirty* ....(DGC)

TAXI

See Also: CARS, TRAVELING

Ashtray Taxi
Sam Chatmon; *Sam Chatmon's Advice* .... (ROU)
Big Yellow Taxi
Amy Grant; *House Of Love* ....(A&M)
Joni Mitchell; *Ladies Of The Canyon* ....(RPR)
Miles Of Aisles ....(ASY)
Black Man Can't Get A Cab
U.T.F.O.; *Bag It & Bone It* ....(JVA)
Cab Driver
Mills Brothers; *22 Great Hits* ....(RAN)
Cab Driver ....(RAN)
Close Harmony ....(RAN)
Cabbies On Crack
Ramones; *Mondo Bizarro* .... (RDO)
In The Back Of A Taxi
Penguin Cafe Orchestra; *Broadcasting From
Home* .... (EDI)
Lady Cab Driver
Prince; *1999* ....(WB)
Oriental Taxi
Sly Dunbar; *Sly Wicked & Slick* ....(FL)
Rainy Taxi
Jon St. James; *Enigma Variations-#2* ....(ENI)
Red Cab To Manhattan
Stephen Bishop; *Best Of Bish* ....(RHI)

Taxi
Bryan Ferry; *Taxi* ....(RPR)
Harry Chapin; *Anthology* .... (ELE)
Gold Medal Collection .... (ELE)
Greatest Stories-Live ....(ELE)
Heads & Tales ....(ELE)
Samples; *Last Drag* .... (WAR)
Steel Pulse; *Victims* ....(MCA)
Steps Ahead; *Yin-Yang* ....(NYC)
Taxi Blues
Bluzblasters; *Sooner Or Later* ....(FF)
Little Richard; *Shut Up-Collection Of Rare Tracks* (RHI)
Taxi Cab
Rhythm Pigs; *Choke On This* .... (C/Z)
Taxi Connection
Sly & Robbie; *Street Reggae* ....(KT)
Taxi Fare ....(HRT)
Taxi Dancer
John Mellencamp; *John Cougar Mellencamp* ......(RIV)
Taxi Driver
Hanoi Rocks; *All Those Wasted Years-Live* ....(GEF)
Self-Destruction Blues ....(GEF)
Joyce; *Language & Love* ....(VF)
Steel Pulse; *Rastafari Centennial-Live In Paris* ... (MCA)
Victims ....(MCA)
Taxi Driver Blues
Eddie "Cleanhead" Vinson; *"Clean" Machine* ... (MUS)
"Taxi Driver"-Night Piece For Orchestra
Royal Philharmonic Orchestra; *Bernard Herrmann Film
Scores* .... (MLN)
Taxi Grabb
Jethro Tull; *Too Old To Rock N' Roll-Too Young To
Die* .... (CHR)
Taxi Ride
Jane Siberry; *Speckless Sky* ....(OPE)
Taxi Suite
Rare Air; *Hard To Beat* ....(GRE)
Taxi To Heaven
Pray For Rain; *ST/Sid & Nancy* .... (MCA)
Taxi War Dance
Count Basie; *Essential-#1* ....(COL)
I Like Jazz-Essence Of ....(COL)
Tijuana Taxi
Herb Alpert/Tijuana Brass; *Classics-#1* .... (A&M)
Four Sider ....(A&M)
Greatest Hits ....(A&M)
You Already Drove Me There
Lisa Brokop; *Every Little Girl's Dream* ....(PAT)

TEENAGERS, Adolescence

See Also: BABY, CHILDREN, REBELS, SCHOOL

6 Teens
Sweet; *Desolation Boulevard* ....(CAP)
Adolescent Funk
Funkadelic; *Hardcore Jollies* ....(WB)
All The Young Dudes
David Bowie; *Live* ....(RYK)
Ian Hunter; *Live/Welcome To The Club* ....(CHR)
Shades Of .... (CHR)
Mott The Hoople; *All The Young Dudes* ....(COL)
Greatest Hits ....(COL)
Live ....(COL)
ST/Queens Logic ....(EPI)
All The Young Punks
Clash; *Give 'Em Enough Rope* ....(EPI)
Almost Eighteen
Roy Orbison; *Get Hot Or Go Home-Vintage
Rockabilly* ....(CMF)
Legendary .... (SSP)
Almost Grown
Chuck Berry; *Berry Is On Top* ....(CSS)
Chess Box ....(CSS)
Cruisin'-1959 ....(INC)
Roll Over Beethoven ....(ALL)
ST/American Graffiti ....(MCA)
At Seventeen
Janis Ian; *Between The Lines* ....(COL)
Super Hits/'70s-Have A Nice Day-#15 .... (RHI)

Baba O'Reilly (Teenage Wasteland)
Who; *Hooligans* .... (MCA)
  ST/Kids Are Alright .... (MCA)
  Who's Last .... (MCA)
  Who's Next .... (MCA)
Ballad Of A Teenage Queen
Johnny Cash; *Johnny Cash* .... (SUN)
  Original Golden Hits-#2 .... (SUN)
  ST/Harper Valley PTA .... (SUN)
  Sun Years .... (RHI)
  The Legend .... (PLN)
Be Young You
Jefferson Starship; *Dragon Fly* ....(RCA)
Be Young, Be Foolish, Be Happy
Tams; *45* .... (MCA)
  45 .... (RLL)
Beat On The Brat
Ramones; *All The Stuff (& More)-#1* .... (SIR)
  Mania .... (SIR)
  Ramones .... (SIR)
Because They're Young
Duane Eddy; *16 Greatest Hits* .... (JAM)
  Compact Command Performances .... (MOT)
  Cruisin' 1960 .... (INC)
  History Or Rock Instrumentals-#2 .... (RHI)
Chattahoochee
Alan Jackson; *Lot About Livin' (& A Little 'Bout
Love)* .... (ARI)
Christine 16
Kiss; *Alive 2* .... (CAS)
  Love Gun .... (CAS)
Come Back When You Grow Up
Bobby Vee; *Best Of* .... (EMI)
  Good Vibrations (Sounds Of Top 40 Radio) ....(CAP)
  Legendary Masters .... (EMI)
Coming Of Age
Damn Yankees; *Damn Yankees* .... (WB)
Davy The Fat Boy
Randy Newman; *Live* .... (RPR)
  Randy Newman .... (RPR)
Dirty White Boy
Foreigner; *Head Games* .... (ATL)
  Records .... (ATL)
Edge Of Seventeen
Stevie Nicks; *Bella Donna* .... (MOD)
Excitable Boy
Warren Zevon; *Excitable Boy* .... (ASY)
  Quiet Normal Life-Best Of .... (ASY)
  Stand In The Fire .... (ASY)
Fancy
Bobbi Gentry; *All-Time Country Classics-#1* .....(CAP)
Reba McEntire; *Rumor Has It* .... (MCA)
Girl, You'll Be A Woman Soon
Neil Diamond;
  Double Gold ....(BNG)
  Classics (Early Years) ....(COL)
  Greatest Hits ....(BNG)
  Hot August Night ....(MCA)
Growin' Up
Bruce Springsteen; *Greetings From Asbury Park,
N.J.* ....(COL)
Bruce Springsteen/E Street Band;
Live-1975-1985 ....(COL)
Growin' Up In The Hood
Compton's Most Wanted; *ST/Boyz N The Hood* (QUE)
He Would Be Sixteen
Michelle Wright; *Now & Then* .... (ARI)
Hey Nineteen
Steely Dan; *Gaucho* .... (MCA)
  Gold .... (MCA)
I Was A Teenage Werewolf
Cramps; *Elvira Presents Haunted Hits* .... (RHI)
  Songs The Lord Taught Us .... (IRS)
I'm Going To Be A Teenage Idol
Elton John; *Don't Shoot Me I'm Only The Piano
Player* .... (POL)
Jack & Diane
John Cougar Mellencamp; *American Fool* ....(RIV)
Kids
Original Broadway Cast; *Bye Bye Birdie* ....(COL)
Paul Lynde; *ST/Bye Bye Birdie* ....(RCA)
Kids Are Alright
Pete Townshend; *Another Scoop* ....(ATC)

Who; *Meaty Beaty Big & Bouncy* .... (MCA)
  Sings My Generation .... (MCA)
  Who's Better Who's Best-Very Best Of .... (MCA)
Letting Go
Suzy Bogguss; *Aces* .... (CAP)
  Voices In The Wind .... (LIB)
Lonely Teenager
Dion; *Everything You Always Wanted To Hear By* (LAU)
  His Best .... (LAU)
  The Wanderer ....(LAU)
My Back Pages
Bob Dylan; *Another Side Of* ....(COL)
  Greatest Hits-#2 ....(COL)
Byrds; *20 Essential Tracks From Box Set* ......(COL)
  Byrds Play Dylan ....(COL)
  Greatest Hits ....(COL)
  Younger Than Yesterday ....(COL)
My Generation
Who; *Greatest Hits* .... (MCA)
  Live At Leeds .... (MCA)
  Meaty Beaty Big & Bouncy .... (MCA)
  Sings My Generation .... (MCA)
  ST/Kids Are Alright .... (MCA)
My Little Town
Paul Simon; *Still Crazy After All These Years* .....(COL)
Only Sixteen
Dr. Hook; *Bankrupt* ....(CAP)
  Great Records Of The Decade-'70s Hits-#2 ....(CCB)
  Greatest Hits (& More) ....(CAP)
  Little Bit More ....(CAP)
Sam Cooke; *Best Of* ....(RCA)
  Man & His Music ....(RCA)
  This Is ....(RCA)
Our Teenage Love
Torquays; *45* .... (OSR)
Papa Don't Preach
Madonna; *Immaculate Collection* .... (SIR)
  Royal Box .... (SIR)
  True Blue .... (SIR)
Parents Just Don't Understand
D.J. Jazzy Jeff & The Fresh Prince; *He's The D.J. I'm
The Rapper* .... (JVA)
Raised On Robbery
Joni Mitchell; *Court & Spark* .... (ASY)
Restless Youth
Ian Hunter; *All American Alien Boy* ....(COL)
Swimming Poool Q's; *Deep End* .... (DB)
Rock 'N' Roll Juvenile
Cliff Richard; *We Don't Talk Anymore* .... (EMI)
Runaway Train
Soul Asylum; *Grave Dancers Union* ....(COL)
School Boy Romance
Danny/Juniors; *Rockin' With* .... (MSP)
Seventeen
Bobby Brown; *Dance! Ya Know It!* .... (MCA)
  King Of Stage .... (MCA)
Chambers Brothers; *Best Of* .... (FAN)
Chris LeDoux; *Radio & Rodeo Hits* .... (LIB)
Foreigner; *Head Games* .... (ATL)
Rusty Draper; *Greatest Hits* .... (MON)
Sex Pistols; *Never Mind The Bollocks* .... (WB)
Winger; *Winger* .... (ATL)
Seventeen Come Sunday
John Wright & Catherine Perrier; *Traditional Music Of
France, Ireland...* ....(GRE)
Seventeen Goin' On 21
Brian Elliot; *Brian Elliot* ....(WB)
Sexy + 17
Stray Cats; *Best Of-Rock This Town* .... (EMI)
  Rant 'N' Rave With The Stray Cats .... (EMI)
She Is Always Seventeen
Harry Chapin; *Anthology* .... (ELE)
  Greatest Stories-Live .... (ELE)
She Was Only Seventeen (He Was One...)
Marty Robbins; *American Originals* ....(COL)
  Greatest Hits ....(COL)
She's Leaving Home
Al Jarreau; *All Fly Home* .... (WB)
Beatles; *Box Set* ....(CAP)
  Love Songs ....(CAP)
  Sgt. Pepper's Lonely Hearts Club Band ....(CAP)
She's Nineteen Years Old
Muddy Waters; *Best Of Blues-#1* .... (MSP)
  Chess Box ....(CSS)

Show Biz Kids
Steely Dan; *Countdown To Ecstasy* .... (MCA)
 Greatest Hits .... (MCA)
Sixteen Candles
Crests; *Alan Freed's Memory Lane* .... (MCA)
 Billboard Top Rock 'N' Roll Hits-1959 .... (RHI)
 Cruisin'-1959 .... (INC)
 Greatest Hits .... (CLT)
 Oldies But Goodies-#14 .... (OSR)
 Rock & Roll U.S.A.-21 R&R Favorites-#2 ...... (LAU)
 ST/American Graffiti .... (MCA)
Sixteen Going On Seventeen
Original Cast; *Sound Of Music* .... (COL)
Smells Like Teen Spirit
Nirvana; *Nevermind* .... (DGC)
Story Of A Teenager
America; *Hearts* .... (WB)
Street Kids
Elton John; *Rock Of The Westies* .... (POL)
Sweet Little Sixteen
Beatles; *45* .... (CLT)
Chuck Berry; *Best Of The Best Of* .... (GUS)
 Cruisin'-1965 .... (INC)
 Golden Hits .... (MER)
 Greatest Hits Live .... (QKS)
 Oldies But Goodies-#12 .... (OSR)
Jerry Lee Lewis; *Original Golden Hits #3* ...... (SUN)
 /Friends-Duets .... (SUN)
John Lennon; *Lennon* .... (CAP)
 Rock 'N' Roll .... (CAP)
Sweet Sixteen
Big Joe Turner; *Greatest Hits* .... (ATL)
B.B. King; *Back In The Alley* .... (MCA)
 Best Of .... (MSP)
 Electric .... (MCA)
 Live In Cook County Jail .... (MCA)
Chuck Berry; *Greatest Hits* .... (EVR)
Judy Garland; *Best Of* .... (MCA)
Sweet Sixteen Bars
Earl Gray; *Best Of* .... (MCA)
Ray Charles; *Atlantic Jazz-Piano* .... (ATL)
 Best Of .... (ATL)
 Great Ray Charles .... (ATL)
Talking The Teenage Language
Lost Generation; *Chicago Soul* .... (EPI)
Teen Angel
Dion/Belmonts; *Everything You Always Wanted* .. (LAU)
 Rock & Roll U.S.A.-21 R&R Favorites-#2 ...... (LAU)
Mark Dinning; *45 On CD-#1-1956-1959* ...... (MER)
 Golden Years-1959 .... (DOM)
 Oldies But Goodies-#7 .... (OSR)
 ST/American Graffiti .... (MCA)
 Teenage Tragedies .... (RHI)
Teen Angst (What The World Needs Now)
Cracker; *Cracker* .... (VIA)
Teen Archer
Blue Oyster Cult; *Tyranny & Mutation* .... (COL)
Teen Beat
Fleetwood Mac; *25 Years-The Chain* .... (WB)
Teenage Abuse
Sicilian Vespers; *Sicilian Vespers* .... (PRO)
Teenage Brain Surgeon
Spike Jones; *In Stereo* .... (WB)
Teenage Clone
Germs; *Germicide-Live At The Whisky 1977* ..... (ROI)
Teenage Crush
Jerry Max Lane; *45* .... (MCA)
Teenage Cutie
Eddie Cochran; *Legendary Masters* .... (UA)
Teenage Darling
Fleetwood Mac; *Early Years* .... (PRR)
Teenage Depression
Eddie/Hot Rods; *D.I.Y.-#1-UK Punk-Anarchy In*
 UK-1976-77 .... (RHI)
 ST/Rock & Roll High School .... (SIR)
 Teenage Depression .... (ISL)
Teenage Eyes
Flash Cadillac/Continental Kids; *Rock & Roll*
 Forever .... (EPI)
Teenage Failure
Chad & Jeremy; *History Of British Rock-#7* ...... (RHI)
 Painted Dayglow Smile-Collection .... (COL)

Teenage Frankenstein
Alice Cooper; *Constrictor* .... (MCA)
 Prince Of Darkness .... (MCA)
Teenage Good Night
Chordettes; *45* .... (BBY)
Teenage Heaven
Eddie Cochran; *Greatest Hits* .... (CCB)
 Legendary Masters .... (EMI)
Johnny Cymbal; *Teen Idols* .... (MSP)
Teenage Idol
Blackfoot; *Blackfoot* .... (ATC)
Rick Nelson; *Best Of* .... (EMI)
 Greatest Hits .... (RHI)
 Legendary Masters .... (EMI)
Teenage Jail
Eagles; *Long Run* .... (ASY)
Teenage Lament '74
Alice Cooper; *Greatest Hits* .... (WB)
 Muscle Of Love .... (WB)
Teenage Letter
Big Joe Turner; *Rhythm & Blues Years* .... (ATL)
Jerry Lee Lewis; *Original Golden Hits-#1* ...... (SUN)
Teenage Lobotomy
Ramones; *All The Stuff & More-#2* .... (SIR)
 Ramones Mania .... (SIR)
 Rocket To Russia .... (SIR)
Teenage Love
Frankie Lymon/Teenagers; *Best Of* .... (RHI)
Teenage Love Affair
Rick Derringer; *All-American Boy* .... (BS)
 Live .... (BS)
Teenage Lust
Jesus & Mary Chain; *Honey's Dead* .... (AME)
Teenage Nervous Breakdown
Little Feat; *Hoy-Hoy!* .... (WB)
 Sailin' Shoes .... (WB)
Teenage Prostitute
Frank Zappa; *Ship Arriving Too Late To Save...* .. (BAR)
Teenage Queen
Rick Derringer; *All-American Boy* .... (BS)
Teenage Suicide
Unrest; *Kustom Karnal Blackxploitation* .... (CRL)
Teenage Suicide (Don't Do It)
Don Dixon; *(If I'm A Ham We'll You're A*
 Sausage .... (RES)
Teenage Vows Of Love
Dreamer; *45* .... (RLL)
Teenage Whore
Hole; *Pretty On The Inside* .... (CRL)
Teenager In Love
Dion/Belmonts; *Classic Gold & Old* .... (LAU)
 Collectables Presents History Of Rock-#6 ..... (CLT)
 Oldies But Goodies-#6 .... (OSR)
 Party Time Fifties .... (JCI)
 Their Best .... (LAU)
Teenarama
Records; *Records* .... (VIA)
Tenderness On The Block
Warren Zevon; *Excitable Boy* .... (ASY)
Treat The Youths Right
Jimmy Cliff; *Rhythm Come Forward-Reggae*
 Anthology .... (COL)
 Special .... (COL)
Two Sparrows In A Hurricane
Tanya Tucker; *Can't Run From Yourself* .... (LIB)
 Greatest Hits-1990-1992 .... (LIB)
Walkaway Joe
Trisha Yearwood; *Hearts In Armor* .... (MCA)
Watching Scotty Grow
Bobby Goldsboro; *All-Time Greatest Hits* .... (CCB)
 Honey-Best Of .... (EMI)
When I Was Young
Animals; *Best Of* .... (AKO)
 Greatest Hits Live!-Rip It To Shreds .... (IRS)
 History Of British Rock-#8 .... (RHI)
Wild One
Faith Hill; *Take Me As I Am* .... (WB)
Yakety Yak
2 Live Crew; *ST/Twins* .... (WTG)

Coasters; *Atlantic*
R&B-1947-1974-#3-(1955-1958) .... (ATL)
   Billboard Top Rock 'N' Roll Hits-1958 .... (RHI)
   Cruisin'-1958 .... (INC)
   Greatest Hits .... (ATC)
   ST/Stand By Me .... (ATL)
Young Americans
David Bowie; *Changesbowie* .... (RYK)
   Sound + Vision .... (RYK)
   The Singles-1969-1993 .... (RYK)
   Young Americans .... (RYK)
Young Blood
Bad Company; *Run With The Pack* .... (SS)
Coasters; *Greatest Hits* .... (ATC)
   Their Greatest Recordings-Early Years ....(ATC)
Young Girl Blues
Sammy Hagar; *9 On A 10-Scale* .... (CAP)
   Live .... (CAP)
Young Love
Sonny James; *Golden Jukebox Favorites* .... (CAP)
   Opry Legends .... (CAP)
   Stars Of The Grand Ole Opry 1926-1974 ......(RCA)
   Traditions In Country Music .... (CAP)
Young Man Blues
Who; *Live At Leeds* .... (MCA)
   ST/Kids Are Alright .... (MCA)
You're Sixteen
Johnny Burnette; *ST/American Graffiti* .... (MCA)
Ringo Starr; *Blast From Your Past* .... (CAP)
   Ringo .... (CAP)
You're Still A Young Man
Tower Of Power; *Bump City* .... (WB)
   Live & In Living Color .... (WB)

**TELEPHONE, Operator, Phone Numbers,
Telegraph**

   See Also: COMMUNICATION

1-900-2LONELY
David Grey; *Signature* .... (JRS)
1-900-2-COMPTON
N.W.A.; *Efil4zaggin* .... (RUP)
1-900-WORLD
Leaving Trains; *Lump In My Forehead* ....(SST)
606-0842
B-52's; *B-52's* .... (WB)
634-5789
Ry Cooder; *Borderline* .... (WB)
Wilson Pickett; *Greatest Hits* .... (ATL)
777-9311
Time; *45* .... (WB)
   What Time Is It .... (WB)
867-5309/Jenny
Tommy Tutone; *#2* .... (COL)
911 Is A Joke
Public Enemy; *Fear Of A Black Planet* .... (DFJ)
   Yo! MTV Raps .... (JVA)
Ain't That Lonely Yet
Dwight Yoakam; *This Time* .... (RPR)
All You Do Is Dial
Heatwave; *Too Hot To Handle* .... (EPI)
Answering Machine
Kinsey Report; *Edge Of The City* .... (ALG)
Replacements; *Let It Be* .... (TT)
Rupert Holmes; *Partners In Crime* .... (INF)
Apolitical Blues
Little Feat; *Last Record Album* .... (WB)
   Sailing Shoes .... (WB)
   Waiting For Columbus .... (WB)
Van Halen; *OU812* .... (WB)
As Soon As I Hang Up The Phone
Loretta Lynn; *Country Partners* .... (MCA)
Loretta Lynn & Conway Twitty; *Making Believe* (MCA)
   Very Best Of .... (MCA)
At The Sound Of The Tone
John Schneider; *Country Classics-#7-1986-1987* . (MSP)
   Greatest Hits .... (MCA)
   Take The Long Way Home .... (MSP)
Baby Don't Forget My Number
Milli Vanilli; *All Or Nothing* .... (ARI)
Baby Hang Up The Phone
Carl Graves; *45* .... (A&M)

Beechwood 4-5789
Carpenters; *Made In America* .... (A&M)
Marvelettes; *Anthology* .... (MOT)
   Compact Command Performances .... (MOT)
   Greatest Hits .... (MOT)
   More American Graffiti-#4 .... (MCA)
Beep A Freak
Gap Band; *VI* .... (TE)
Call Me
Al Green; *Greatest Hits* .... (HIR)
Aretha Franklin; *Greatest Hits* .... (ATL)
Be Be & Ce Ce Winans; *Be Be & Ce Ce Winans* .(CAP)
Blondie; *Best Of* .... (CHR)
   ST/American Gigolo .... (CHR)
Chambers Brothers; *Best Of* .... (FAN)
Dennis DeYoung; *Back To The World* .... (A&M)
Frank Sinatra; *Strangers In The Night* .... (RPR)
Phil Perry; *Heart Of The Man* .... (CAP)
Rick James; *Street Songs/Throwin' Down* ...... (MOT)
Skyy; *Skyline* .... (CAL)
Call My Job
Albert King; *King Albert* .... (TOM)
   Masterworks .... (ATL)
Call On Me
Bad Company; *Straight Shooter* .... (SS)
Bobby Bland; *Best Of* .... (MCA)
   Call On Me .... (MCA)
Chicago; *Greatest Hits* .... (COL)
   VII .... (COL)
Eddie Money; *Life For The Taking* .... (COL)
Michael Jackson; *Anthology* .... (MOT)
Tanya Tucker; *Strong Enough To Bend* .... (CAP)
Calling Elvis
Dire Straits; *On Every Street* .... (WB)
Callin' Baton Rouge
Garth Brooks; *In Pieces* .... (LIB)
New Grass Revival; *Anthology* .... (LIB)
Oak Ridge Boys; *Room Service* .... (MSP)
Chantilly Lace
Big Bopper; *45s On CD-#1 (1958-1959)* ...... (MER)
   Cruisin' 1958 .... (INC)
   Oldies But Goodies-#4 .... (OSR)
   ST/American Graffiti .... (MCA)
Jerry Lee Lewis; *Best Of-#2* .... (MER)
   "Killer" Rocks On .... (MER)
Coconut Telegraph
Jimmy Buffett; *Boats Beaches Bars & Ballads* ... (MGR)
   Coconut Telegraph .... (MCA)
Dial A Hitman
Big Audio Dynamite; *No. 10 Upping St.* ....(COL)
Dial Africa
John Coltrane & Wilbur Harden; *Africa-Savoy*
   Sessions .... (SAV)
   Dial Africa .... (SAV)
Dial That Telephone
Eddie Rabbitt; *Best Year Of My Life* .... (WB)
Disconnected Line
John Mayall; *Hard Core Passage* .... (MCA)
Don't Lose My Number
Phil Collins; *No Jacket Required* .... (ATL)
   Serious Hits...Live! .... (ATL)
Echo Valley 2-6809
Partridge Family; *Greatest Hits* .... (ARI)
Had To Phone Ya
Beach Boys; *15 Big Ones* .... (CAR)
Hanging On The Telephone
Blondie; *Best Of* .... (CHR)
   Parallel Lines .... (CHR)
He Calls Home
Candlebox; *Candlebox* .... (MAV)
Here's A Quarter, Call Someone Who Cares
Travis Tritt; *It's All About To Change* .... (WB)
He'll Have To Go
Jim Reeves; *60 Years Of Country Music* .... (RCA)
   Best Of .... (RCA)
   Billboard Top Country Hits-1960 .... (RHI)
   Great Moments At The Grand Ole Opry .... (RCA)
   Nipper's Greatest Hits/'50s-#1 .... (RCA)
Jim Reeves & Patsy Cline; *Jim Reeves-Greatest*
   Hits .... (RCA)
Ry Cooder; *Chicken Skin Music* .... (RPR)
Hot Line
Black Sabbath; *Born Again* .... (WB)
Sylvers; *Best Of* .... (CAP)

How Come U Don't Call Me Anymore
Stephanie Mills; *Merciless* .... (CAS)
I Can't Reach Her Anymore
Sammy Kershaw; *Haunted Heart* .... (MER)
I Got Your Number
Boz Scaggs; *Slow Dancer* ....(COL)
I Just Called To Say I Love You
Aretha Franklin; *Best Of* .... (ATL)
  Gold .... (ATL)
  Greatest Hits .... (ATL)
Stevie Wonder; *ST/Lady In Red* .... (MOT)
It's Me Again Margaret
Ray Stevens; *Country Classics-#3-1984-1985* ... (MCA)
  Greatest Hits .... (MCA)
  He Thinks He's Ray Stevens .... (MCA)
It's Your Call
Reba McEntire; *It's Your Call* .... (MCA)
Jesus Is On The Mainline
Ry Cooder; *Paradise & Lunch* .... (RPR)
  Showtime ....(WB)
Just Seven Numbers
Four Tops; *Anthology* .... (MOT)
  Compact Command Performances .... (MOT)
Let's Make Love Over The Telephone
Jose Feliciano; *45* .... (MOT)
Long Distance Call
Muddy Waters; *Best Of* .... (CSS)
  Chess Box .... (CSS)
  Mud In Your Ear .... (MUS)
Long Distance Love
Little Feat; *Last Record Album* ....(WB)
Long Distance Operator
Bob Dylan/Band; *Basement Tapes* ....(COL)
Long Distance Runaround
Yes; *Classic Yes* .... (ATL)
  Fragile .... (ATL)
  Yessongs .... (ATL)
Lost My Drivin' Wheel
Tom Rush; *Best Of* ....(COL)
  Tom Rush ....(COL)
Love On The Telephone
Foreigner; *Head Games* .... (ATL)
Memphis
Chuck Berry; *Chess Box* .... (CSS)
  Chuck Berry ....(AUF)
  Golden Hits .... (MER)
  Greatest Hits .... (EVR)
  St. Louis To Liverpool .... (CSS)
  ST/Hail! Hail! Rock 'N' Roll .... (MCA)
  Toronto Rock 'N' Roll Revival-#2 .... (ACC)
Joe Jackson; *ST/Mike's Murder* .... (A&M)
John Cale; *IRS Greatest Hits #2 & 3* .... (IRS)
Johnny Rivers; *Anthology-1964-1977* .... (RHI)
  Best Of .... (EMI)
Lonnie Mack; *Teen Beat-Instrumental*
Rock-1957-1965 .... (CAP)
Mr. Telephone Man
New Edition; *Greatest Hits-#1* .... (MCA)
  New Edition .... (MCA)
New York Telephone Conversation
Lou Reed; *Transformer* ....(RCA)
  Walk On The Wild Side-Best Of ....(RCA)
No Telephone In Heaven
Doc Watson; *My Dear Old Southern Home* ....(SH)
Nobody Home
Pink Floyd; *The Wall* ....(COL)
Roger Waters; *The Wall Live In Berlin* .... (MER)
Obscene Phone Caller
Rockwell; *Somebody's Watching Me* .... (MOT)
Off The Hook
Rolling Stones; *Now!* ....(LON)
On The Phone
Julian Lennon; *Valotte* .... (ATL)
Operator
Gladys Knight/Pips; *Letter Full Of Tears-Golden*
Classics .... (CLT)
Grateful Dead; *American Beauty* .... (WB)
Jim Croce; *Photographs & Memories* ....(LIF)
  Time In A Bottle ....(LIF)
  You Don't Mess Around With Jim ....(LIF)
Lloyd Price; *Walkin' The Track* ....(SPE)
Manhattan Transfer; *Best Of* .... (ATL)
  Manhattan Transfer .... (ATL)
Midnight Star; *Planetary Invasion* .... (SLR)

Operator, Long Distance Please
Barbara Mandrell; *In Black & White* .... (MCA)
Operator, Operator
Eddy Raven; *Best Of* ....(RCA)
Pennsylvania 6-5000
Glenn Miller/Orchestra; *Complete-#4* ....(RCA)
  Legendary Performer ....(RCA)
  Memorial 1944-1969 ....(RCA)
  Moonlight Serenade .... (RAN)
  Pure Gold ....(RCA)
  Story ....(RCA)
  Unforgettable ....(RCA)
Phone
House Of Love; *Spy In The House Of Love* ......(FON)
Records; *Records* .... (VIA)
Phone Booth
Albert King; *I'm In A Phone Booth Baby* .... (STX)
Robert Cray Band; *Bad Influence* .... (HT)
  Blues Masters-#9-Postmodern Blues .... (RHI)
Phone Booth Man
Tuff Darts; *Tuff Darts* .... (SIR)
Phone Call
Dan Hill; *Hold On* .... (20)
Joe Satriani; *Flying In A Blue Dream* .... (REL)
King Diamond; *Dark Sides* .... (ROA)
  Them .... (ROA)
Pretenders; *Pretenders* .... (SIR)
Phone Call From Chicago
Peter Himmelman; *From Strength To Strength* ..... (EPI)
Phone Call From God
Ray Reeves; *45* .... (STR)
Phone Call From Leavenworth
Chris Whitley; *Living With The Law* ....(COL)
Phone Call From The Devil
Jim Nesbitt; *Phone Call From The Devil* ....(SCO)
Phone Call From The Moon
Adrian Belew; *Young Lions* .... (ATL)
Phone Sexxx
Jimmy Z; *Muzical Madness* ....(RUT)
Pick Up The Phone
Aaron Hall; *The Truth* .... (SIA)
Jamaica Boys; *J Boys* ....(RPR)
Please Call Home
Allman Brothers Band; *Beginnings* ....(POL)
  Idlewild South .... (POL)
Gregg Allman; *Laid Back* ....(CPC)
Please Call Me, Baby
Tom Waits; *Heart Of Saturday Night* .... (ASY)
Private Number
Judy Clay & William Bell; *15 Original Big*
Hits-#2 .... (STX)
  Private Numbers .... (STX)
  Top Of The Stax-Twenty Greatest Hits-#2 .... (STX)
Red Telephone
Love; *Forever Changes* .... (ELE)
Rikki Don't Lose That Number
Steely Dan; *Classic Rock-#2* .... (MCA)
  Decade Of .... (MCA)
  Greatest Hits .... (MCA)
  Pretzel Logic .... (MCA)
Royal Telephone
Burl Ives; *Best Of-#2* .... (MCA)
George Lewis/Eclipse Alley Five; *George Lewis Of New*
Orleans ....(RVR)
Soon
Tanya Tucker; *Soon* ....(LIB)
Switchboard Susan
Nick Lowe; *Basher-Best Of* ....(COL)
  Labour Of Lust ....(COL)
Telefone (Long Distance Love Affair)
Sheena Easton; *Best Kept Secret* .... (EMI)
Telephone
Chaka Khan; *The Woman I Am* .... (WB)
Diana Ross; *Endless Love* ....(RCA)
  Swept Away ....(RCA)
Telephone Call From Istanbul
Tom Waits; *Big Time* .... (ISL)
  Frank's Wild Years-Un Operachi Romantico ..... (ISL)
Telephone Exchange
Angel; *Live Without A Net* .... (CAS)
Telephone Girl
Eddie/Hot Rods; *Life On The Line* .... (ISL)
Jade Warriors; *Jade Warriors* ....(VTG)

Telephone Girlie
Original Cast/Ruby Keeler; *No No Nanette* ......(RCA)
Telephone Hour
Original Cast; *Bye Bye Birdie* ....(COL)
Soundtrack; *Bye Bye Birdie* ....(RCA)
Telephone Line
Electric Light Orchestra; *Afterglow* ....(EPI)
E.L.O. Classics ....(SSP)
Greatest Hits ....(JET)
New World Record ....(JET)
Telephone Man
Meri Wilson; *First Take* ....(GRT)
Super Hits/'70s-Have A Nice Day-#21 ... (RHI)
Telephone Number
3-D; *3-D* ....(POL)
Telephone Song
Original Cast; *Cabaret* ....(COL)
Original London Cast; *Miss Saigon* ....(GEF)
Vaughan Brothers; *Family Style* ....(EPA)
Three Nickels & A Dime
Ricky Lynn Gregg; *Ricky Lynn Gregg* ....(LIB)
Trouble On The Line
Sawyer Brown; *Cafe On The Corner* ....(CRB)
Uncle Albert/Admiral Halsey
Paul McCartney; *Gift Set* ....(CAP)
Paul McCartney/Wings; *Wings Greatest* ....(CAP)
Paul & Linda McCartney; *All The Best* ....(CAP)
Ram ....(CAP)
Watin' For The Phone To Ring
Patty Loveless; *Up Against My Heart* .... (MCA)
Ronna Reeves; *What Comes Naturally* .... (MER)
What's A Telephone Bill
Bootsy's Rubber Band; *The Name Is Bootsy Baby* . (WB)
What's The 411?
Mary J. Blige; *What's The 411?* .... (UT)
Why Don't That Telephone Ring
Tracy Byrd; *Tracy Byrd* ....(MCA)
Why Haven't I Heard From You
Reba McEntire; *Read My Mind* ....(MCA)
You Can't Take The Telephone To Bed
Jill Hollier; *45* ....(WB)
You Know My Name, Look Up My Number
Beatles; *Box Set* ....(CAP)
Past Masters-#2 ....(CAP)
Rarities ....(CAP)
Your Phone's Off The Hook, But You're...
X; *Los Angeles* ....(SLS)

TELEVISION, Video

57 Channels (And Nothin' On)
Bruce Springsteen; *Human Touch* ....(COL)
'70s TV
Dramarama; *Stuck In Wonderamaland* .....(CHS)
"ABC's Wide World Of Sports" Theme
Original Music; *Television's Greatest Hits-#2* .....(TVT)
"All In The Family" Theme
Original Music; *Television's Greatest Hits-#3* .....(TVT)
All Night Television
3-D; *3-D* ....(POL)
"American Bandstand" Theme
Original Music; *Television's Greatest Hits-#3* .....(TVT)
Another Brick In The Wall, Part 3
Pink Floyd; *The Wall* ....(COL)
Ballad Of TV Violence
Cheap Trick; *Cheap Trick* ....(EPI)
"Barney Miller" Theme
Original Music; *Television's Greatest Hits-#3* .....(TVT)
"Battlestar Galactica" Theme
Boston Pops Orchestra/John Williams; *Out Of This World* ....(PHI)
"Ben Casey" Theme
Original Music; *Television's Greatest Hits-#2* .....(TVT)
"Beverly Hills, 90210" Theme
John Davis; *ST/"Beverly Hills, 90210" Theme* .... (GIA)
"Bewitched" Theme
Original Music; *Television's Greatest Hits-#2* .....(TVT)
Black And White Television
Ian Anderson; *Walk Into Light* .... (CHR)
Blow Up Your TV
John Denver; *Aerie* ....(RCA)

"Bonanza" Theme
Cincinnati Pops Orchestra/Erich Kunzel;
Round-Up ....(TLR)
Cable TV
Weird Al Yankovic; *Dare To Be Stupid* ....(RAR)
"Car 54, Where Are You?" Theme
Original Music; *Television's Greatest Hits-#2* .....(TVT)
"Cheers" Theme
Original Music; *Television's Greatest Hits-#3* .....(TVT)
Color TV Blues
Don McLean; *Prime Time* ....(ARI)
"Courageous Cat" Theme
Original Music; *Television's Greatest Hits-#2* .....(TVT)
"Dallas" Theme
Original Music; *Television's Greatest Hits-#3* .....(TVT)
"Dark Shadows" Theme
Original Music; *Television's Greatest Hits-#2* .....(TVT)
Death From Your TV Screen
Voice Of Destruction; *Steamroller Tactics* ....(CPA)
Dirty Laundry
Don Henley; *I Can't Stand Still* ....(ASY)
"Dudley-Do-Right" Theme
Original Music; *Television's Greatest Hits-#3* .....(TVT)
"Fractured Fairy Tales" Theme
Original Music; *Television's Greatest Hits-#3* .....(TVT)
"George Of The Jungle" Theme
Original Music; *Television's Greatest Hits-#2* .....(TVT)
"Gomer Pyle U.S.M.C." Theme
Original Music; *Television's Greatest Hits-#2* .....(TVT)
"Green Hornet" Theme
Original Music; *Television's Greatest Hits-#2* .....(TVT)
"Have Gun Will Travel" Theme
Johnny Western; *Television's Greatest Hits-#2* ....(TVT)
High Tech Redneck
George Jones; *High Tech Redneck* ....(MCA)
"Hill Street Blues" Theme
Original Music; *Television's Greatest Hits-#3* .....(TVT)
"Hogan's Heroes" Theme
Original Music; *Television's Greatest Hits-#2* .....(TVT)
"Huckleberry Hound" Theme
Original Music; *Television's Greatest Hits-#2* .....(TVT)
Human Video Game
D.J. Jazzy Jeff & The Fresh Prince; *He's The D.J. I'm The Rapper* ....(JVA)
I Lost On Jeopardy
Weird Al Yankovic; *Greatest Hits* ....(RAR)
In 3-D ....(RAR)
"I Love Lucy" Theme
Original Music; *TV Theme Sing-Along Album* .... (RHI)
I Saw It On TV
John Fogerty; *Centerfield* ....(WB)
"I Spy" Theme
Original Music; *Television's Greatest Hits-#2* .....(TVT)
I'm The Slime
Mothers Of Invention; *Apostrophe/Overnite Sensation* ....(RYK)
"Jeopardy" Theme (Think Music)
Original Music; *Television's Greatest Hits-#2* .....(TVT)
"Kojak" Theme
Original Music; *Television's Greatest Hits-#3* .....(TVT)
"Laverne & Shirley" Theme
Original Music; *Television's Greatest Hits-#3* .....(TVT)
Lazy Day
Moody Blues; *On The Threshold Of A Dream* .... (POL)
Lifestyles Of The Not-So-Rich & Famous
Tracy Byrd; *No Ordinary Man* .... (MCA)
"Little House On The Prairie" Theme
Original Music; *Television's Greatest Hits-#3* .....(TVT)
"Lost In Space" Theme
Neil Norman; *Greatest Science Fiction Hits-#3* ... (CRS)
"Love, American Style" Theme
Original Music; *Television's Greatest Hits-#2* .....(TVT)
"L.A. Law" Theme
Original Music; *Television's Greatest Hits-#3* .....(TVT)
"Magnum P.I." Theme
Original Music; *Television's Greatest Hits-#3* .... (TVT)
"Man From U.N.C.L.E." Theme
Challengers; *25 Greatest Instrumental Hits* ....(CRS)
Man In The Box
Alice In Chains; *Facelift* ....(COL)
"Mannix" Theme
San Diego Symphony/Lalo Schifrin; *Hitchcock-Master Of Mayhem* ....(POE)

"Marcus Welby, M.D." Theme
Original Music; *Television's Greatest Hits-#3* ..... (TVT)
"Mary Tyler Moore" Theme
Original Music-Sonny Curtis; *Television's Greatest Hits-#2* .... (TVT)
"Maude" Theme
Original Music; *Television's Greatest Hits-#3* ..... (TVT)
"Medical Center" Theme
Original Music; *Television's Greatest Hits-#2* ..... (TVT)
Mercedes Benz
Janis Joplin; *Pearl* .... (COL)
   ST/Janis .... (COL)
"Miami Vice" Theme
Jan Hammer; *Escape From Television* .... (MCA)
   Soundtrack Smashes-'80s .... (MCA)
   ST/"Miami Vice" Theme .... (MCA)
Original Music; *Television's Greatest Hits-#3* ..... (TVT)
"Mighty Mouse" Theme
Original Music; *Television's Greatest Hits-#2* ..... (TVT)
"Mission: Impossible" Theme
San Diego Symphony/Lalo Schifrin; *Hitchcock-Master Of Mayhem* .... (POE)
Money For Nothing
Dire Straits; *Brothers In Arms* .... (WB)
   Money For Nothing .... (WB)
"Monty Python's Flying Circus" Theme
Original Music; *Television's Greatest Hits-#2* ..... (TVT)
"Moonlighting" Theme
Al Jarreau; *ST/Moonlighting* .... (MCA)
More News At 11
Public Enemy; *Apocalypse 91...The Enemy Strikes Black* .... (DFC)
"Mr. Magoo" Theme
Original Music; *Television's Greatest Hits-#3* ..... (TVT)
My Color TV
Young Black Teenagers; *Young Black Teenagers* . (SOL)
"My Favorite Martian" Theme
Original Music; *Television's Greatest Hits-#2* ..... (TVT)
"My Mother The Car" Theme
Original Music; *Television's Greatest Hits-#2* ..... (TVT)
My TV Went Black & White On Me
Young Black Teenagers; *Young Black Teenagers* . (SOL)
"M*A*S*H" Theme (Suicide Is Painless)
Ahmad Jamal; *Digital Works* .... (ATL)
   ST/M-A-S-H .... (COL)
Percy Faith; *All-Time Greatest Hits* .... (COL)
News At Ten
Vapors; *New Clear Days* .... (LIB)
On TV
Renegade Soundwave; *Soundclash* .... (MUT)
"Outer Limits" Theme
Original Music; *Television's Greatest Hits-#2* ..... (TVT)
"Perry Mason" Theme
Blues Brothers; *Made In America* .... (ATL)
Jerry Goodman; *It's Alive* .... (PRV)
Original Music; *TV Theme Sing-Along Album* ... (RHI)
"Petticoat Junction" Theme
Flatt & Scruggs; *20 All-Time Great Recordings* ...(COL)
Original Music; *TV Theme Sing-Along Album* ... (RHI)
Playboy Channel
Negativeland; *Escape From Noise* .... (SST)
Prime Time
Alan Parsons Project; *Ammonia Avenue* .... (ARI)
   Best Of-#2 .... (ARI)
Tubes; *Remote Control* .... (A&M)
   Todd Rundgren-An Elpee's Worth Of Prod. .... (RHI)
   T.R.A.S.H.-Tubes Rarities & Smash Hits ...... (A&M)
Prime Time TV
Basia; *Time & Tide* .... (EPI)
Put Your Hands On The Screen
Martin Briley; *One Night With A Stranger* .... (MER)
"Quincy" Theme
Original Music; *Television's Greatest Hits-#3* ..... (TVT)
Revolution Will Not Be Televised
Gil Scott-Heron; *Gil ScoRevolution Will Not Be Televised-Heron* .... (BLU)
   Pieces Of A Man .... (OOP)
"Rocky & Bullwinkle" Theme
Original Music; *Television's Greatest Hits-#2* ..... (TVT)
Ronny Zamora (My Friend Ron)
Deaf School; *English Boys/Working Girls* .... (WB)
"Route 66" Theme
Nelson Riddle/Orchestra; *Beat Generation* .... (RHI)
   Television's Greatest Hits-#2 .... (TVT)

Roy Rogers
Elton John; *Goodbye Yellow Brick Road* .... (POL)
"Sanford & Son" Theme
Original Music; *Television's Greatest Hits-#3* ..... (TVT)
"Santa Barbara" Theme
Original Music; *Soap Opera's Greatest Love Themes* .... (SCO)
"Saturday Night Live" Theme
Original Music; *Television's Greatest Hits-#3* ..... (TVT)
Saturday Night Live Band; *Jazz...The Digital Age* ... (PJ)
"Scooby Doo" Theme
Original Music; *Television's Greatest Hits-#3* ..... (TVT)
"Sea Hunt" Theme
Original Music; *Greatest Hits-#2* .... (TVT)
"Sesame Street" Theme
Original Music; *Television's Greatest Hits-#3* ..... (TVT)
She Watch Channel Zero
Public Enemy; *It Takes A Nation Of Millions...* ... (DFJ)
Sleeping With The Television On
Billy Joel; *Glass Houses* .... (COL)
Sleeping With The TV On
Dictators; *Manifest Destiny* .... (ASY)
"Streets Of San Francisco" Theme
Original Music; *Television's Greatest Hits-#3* ..... (TVT)
"St. Elsewhere" Theme
Dave Grusin; *Night-Lines* .... (GRP)
Original Music; *Television's Greatest Hits-#3* ..... (TVT)
Sun Always Shines On T.V.
A-Ha; *Hunting High & Low* .... (WB)
"S.W.A.T." Theme
Original Music; *Television's Greatest Hits-#3* ..... (TVT)
Rhythm Heritage; *Billboard Top Rock 'N' Roll Hits-1976* .... (RHI)
Talking Pay T.V.
Phil Ochs; *Broadside Tapes-#1* .... (FLW)
Telecide
Tubes; *Remote Control* .... (A&M)
Television
Dave Edmunds; *Tracks On Wax 4* .... (SS)
Japan; *Adolescent Sex* .... (ARL)
Mind Over 4; *Out Here* .... (XXX)
Television Blues
Lowell Fulson; *San Francisco Blues* .... (BL)
Television Eye
John Mayall; *Room To Move-1969-1974-Chronicles Series* .... (POL)
Television Generation
Kursaal Flyers; *D.I.Y.-#3-UK Pop 1-Teenage Kicks-1976-79* .... (RHI)
   Permanent Wave .... (EPI)
Television Girl
Atlantics; *Big City Rock* .... (MCA)
Television Kiss
Lave Love; *Aphrodisia* .... (SKY)
Television Man
Talking Heads; *Little Creatures* .... (SIR)
Television Nightmare
Madrigal; *Madrigal* .... (SSS)
Television People
Psychefunkapus; *Skin* .... (ATL)
Television Station
Front 242; *Official Version* .... (EPI)
Televisions On My Leg
Squirrels; *What Gives?* .... (PL)
Television, The Drug Of The Nation
Disposable Heroes Of Hiphoprisy; *Hypocrisy Is The Greatest Luxury* .... (4TH)
Test Pattern
Lime Spiders; *Volatile* .... (CRL)
"That Girl" Theme
Original Music; *Television's Greatest Hits-#2* ..... (TVT)
"The Archies" Theme
Original Music; *Television's Greatest Hits-#3* ..... (TVT)
"The Avengers" Theme
Original Music; *Television's Greatest Hits-#2* ..... (TVT)
"The A-Team" Theme
Original Music; *Television's Greatest Hits-#3* ..... (TVT)
"The Bob Newhart Show" Theme
Original Music; *Television's Greatest Hits-#3* ..... (TVT)
"The Brady Bunch" Theme
Brady Bunch Kids; *It's A Sunshine Day-Best Of* . (MCA)
   Television's Greatest Hits-#2 .... (TVT)
"The Flintstones" Theme
Steve Hobbs; *Escape* .... (CEX)

"The F.B.I." Theme
  101 Strings Orchestra; *TV Themes* .... (ALS)
"The Honeymooners" Theme
  Original Music; *Television's Greatest Hits-#2* .... (TVT)
"The Jeffersons" Theme
  Original Music; *Television's Greatest Hits-#3* .... (TVT)
"The Love Boat" Theme
  Original Music; *Television's Greatest Hits-#3* .... (TVT)
"The Muppet Show" Theme
  Muppets/Cast; *Muppet Hits* .... (JH)
  Original Music; *Television's Greatest Hits-#3* .... (TVT)
"The Prisoner" Theme
  Neil Norman; *Greatest Science Fiction Hits* .... (CRS)
"The Rookies" Theme
  Original Music; *Television's Greatest Hits-#3* .... (TVT)
"The Smurfs" Theme
  Original Music; *Television's Greatest Hits-#3* .... (TVT)
"The Three Stooges" Theme
  Original Music; *Television's Greatest Hits-#2* . (TVT)
"The Virginian" Theme
  101 Strings Orchestra; *Western Themes-#1* .... (ALS)
  Original Music; *Television's Greatest Hits-#3* .... (TVT)
Theme From "Beauty & The Beast"
  Ron Perlman; *Theme From "Beauty & The Beast"* (CAP)
Theme From "Dr. Kildare"
  Betty Carter; *'Round Midnight* .... (ATL)
Theme From "Green Acres"
  Eddie Albert & Eva Gabor; *ST/Son In Law* ......(HOL)
Theme From "One Life To Live"
  Rosemary Joyce & Bill Bartholomew; *Soap Opera
  Themes* .... (CRS)
Theme From "Superman"
  London Symphony Orchestra/John Williams;
  ST/Superman-The Movie .... (WB)
  Neil Norman; *Greatest Science Fiction Hits* .... (CRS)
Theme From "The Addams Family"
  Vic Mizzy; *Elvira Presents Haunted Hits* .... (RHI)
  Haunted Hits .... (RHI)
  Original Music From ....(RCA)
Theme From "The Dukes Of Hazzard"
  Waylon Jennings; *Greatest Hits-#2* ....(RCA)
  Only Daddy That'll Walk The Line ....(RCA)
Theme From "The Guiding Light"
  Rosemary Joyce & Bill Bartholomew; *Soap Opera
  Themes* .... (CRS)
Theme From "The Jetsons"
  Stunners; *ST/Jetsons-The Movie* .... (MCA)
Theme From "Wayne's World"
  Mike Myers & Dana Carvey; *ST/Wayne's World* . (RPR)
There Ain't S... On T.V. Tonight
  Minutemen; *Double Nickels On The Dime* ....(SST)
This Ain't Dallas
  Hank Williams, Jr.; *Five-O* .... (W/C)
  Greatest Hits-#3 .... (W/C)
Top Of The Pops
  Kinks; *Everybody's In Show Biz* .... (RHI)
  Lola Vs. The Powerman & The Moneygoround . (RPR)
  Smithereens; *Blow Up* .... (CAP)
Turn It On Again
  Genesis; *Duke* .... (ATL)
  Three Sides Live .... (ATL)
Turn Me On
  Tubes; *Remote Control* .... (A&M)
  T.R.A.S.H.-Tubes Rarities And Smash Hits ..... (A&M)
TV
  Dwight Twilley Band; *Sincerely* .... (MCA)
  Flying Lizards; *Flying Lizards* .... (VIA)
TV Age
  Joe Jackson; *Night & Day* .... (A&M)
TV Blues
  Bob Mintzer Big Band; *Only In New York* .... (DIG)
  Country Joe McDonald; *Goodbye Blues* .... (FAN)
  Mick Clarke Band; *Steel & Fire* .... (BRN)
TV Caesar
  Procol Harum; *Grand Hotel* .... (CHR)
TV Dinners
  ZZ Top; *Eliminator* .... (WB)
TV Dreams
  Charlie; *Fantasy Girls* ....(COL)
TV Eye
  Iggy/Stooges; *Legends Of Rock Guitar'70s* .... (RHI)
  Stooges; *Elektrock-'60s* .... (ELE)
  Fun House .... (ELE)

TV Guide
  Graham Nash; *Earth & Sky* ....(CAP)
TV Is King
  Tubes; *Remote Control* .... (A&M)
TV Mama
  Big Joe Turner; *Atlantic Blues-Guitar* .... (ATL)
  Texas Style ....(EVD)
  Dizzy Gillespie/Others; *Trumpet Kings Meet Joe
  Turner* .... (PAB)
  Freddie King; *Freddie King* .... (RSO)
  Johnny Winter; *Nothin' But The Blues* .... (BS)
  Leon Haywood; *It's Me Again* .... (CAS)
TV Party
  Black Flag; *7-Inch Wonders Of The World* ....(SST)
  Damaged ....(SST)
  ST/Repo Man .... (MCA)
TV Preacher Man Blues
  Glenn Sutton; *Close Encounters Of The Sutton
  Kind* .... (MER)
TV Private Eye
  Now; *Now* .... (MDS)
TV Psychology
  Rockwell; *Captured* .... (MOT)
TV Savage
  Bow Wow Wow; *I Want Candy* .... (RCA)
TV Set
  Cramps; *Bad Music For Bad People* .... (IRS)
  Songs The Lord Taught Us .... (IRS)
TV Snooze
  Nina Hagen; *Fearless* ....(COL)
"Twelve O'Clock High" Theme
  Original Music; *Television's Greatest Hits-#2* . (TVT)
T.V. Mind
  Revolting Cocks; *Big Sexy Land* .... (WAX)
T.V. On
  Thompson Twins; *Big Trash* .... (RE)
T.V. Talkin' Song
  Bob Dylan; *Under The Red Sky* ....(COL)
T.V.O.D.
  Normal; *45* .... (SIR)
"Underdog Theme"
  Original Music; *Television's Greatest Hits-#2* ..... (TVT)
Video
  Jeff Lynne; *ST/Electric Dreams* .... (EPI)
Video Blues
  Hank Williams, Jr.; *Major Moves* ....(W/C)
Video Games
  Ronnie Jones; *Best Of Lollipop Records* .... (HOT)
Video Killed The Radio Star
  Bruce Woolly/Camera Club; *Bruce Woolly/Camera
  Club* ....(COL)
  Buggles; *Age Of Plastic* .... (ISL)
  Island Story-1962-1987-25th Anniversary .... (ISL)
  Rock Of The '80s-#2 .... (PRY)
Video Shop
  Kinks; *Lost & Found-1986-1989* .... (MCA)
  Think Visual .... (MSP)
Video Tape
  Steve Goodman; *Say It In Private* .... (ASY)
Video Violence
  Lou Reed; *Between Thought &
  Expression-Anthology* ....(RCA)
Vidiot
  Ken Nordine; *Best Of Word Jazz-#1* .... (RHI)
"Wagon Train" Theme
  Original Music; *Television's Greatest Hits-#2* ..... (TVT)
Watching TV
  Charlie; *Lines* .... (JNS)
Watching TV (With The Radio On)
  Barefoot Jerry; *Watching TV (With The Radio
  On)* .... (MON)
With The T.V. On
  Invaders; *Singles-Great New York Singles Scene* ... (ROI)
"WKRP In Cincinnati" Theme
  Steve Carlisle; *Sings WKRP* .... (MCA)
"Wonder Woman" Theme
  Original Music; *Television's Greatest Hits-#3* .....(TVT)
You Get A Little Extra When You Watch TV
  Peter Alsop; *Wha D'Ya Wanna Do* .... (FF)
"Zorro" Theme
  Original Music; *Disney Collection-#2* .... (DIS)

TIME: GENERAL

24 Hours From Tulsa
Gene Pitney; *45* .... (MCR)
  Double Gold .... (MCR)
Ian & Sylvia; *Best Of* .... (VAN)
  Greatest Hits .... (VAN)
  Play One More .... (VAN)
5-4-3-2 (Yo! Time Is Up)
Jade; *Mind Body & Soul* .... (GIA)
After All This Time
Rodney Crowell; *Diamonds & Dirt* .... (COL)
Ain't Wastin' Time No More
Allman Brothers Band; *Decade Of*
  Hits-1969-1979 .... (POL)
  Dreams .... (POL)
  Eat A Peach .... (POL)
All I Need
Forester Sisters; *All I Need* .... (WB)
Jack Wagner; *All I Need* .... (QUE)
All This Time
Sting; *Soul Cages* .... (A&M)
Any Time, Any Place
Janet Jackson; *Janet* .... (VIA)
Anytime
Eddie Fisher; *Best Of* .... (MCA)
Eddy Arnold/Tennessee Plowboys; *Nipper's Greatest
  Hits-'40s-#2* ....(RCA)
Journey; *Captured* ....(COL)
  Infinity ....(COL)
McAuley Schenker Group; *Save Yourself* .... (CAP)
Patsy Cline; *Best Of* .... (MSP)
Arkansas Time Traveler
Star-Spangled Washboard Band; *Collector's Item* ... (FF)
As Time Goes By
Andy Williams; *Moon River & Other Great Movie
  Themes* ....(COL)
Barbra Streisand; *Third Album* ....(COL)
Frank Sinatra; *Point Of No Return* .... (CAP)
Harry Nilsson; *All-Time Greatest Hits* ....(RCA)
  Little Touch Of Schmilsson In The Night ....(RCA)
Johnny Mathis; *Best Days Of My Life* ....(COL)
  First 25 Years ....(COL)
Natalie Cole; *Take A Look* .... (ELE)
Willie Nelson; *Without A Song* ....(COL)
Bidin' My Time
Original Cast; *Girl Crazy* .... (SSP)
Sarah Vaughan; *George Gershwin Songbook* .... (EMA)
Borrowed Time
John Lennon; *Lennon* .... (CAP)
John Lennon & Yoko Ono; *Milk & Honey* .... (POL)
Olivia Newton-John; *Totally Hot* .... (MCA)
Styx; *Cornerstone* .... (A&M)
Can We Spend Some Time
Surface; *2nd Wave* ....(COL)
Child In Time
Deep Purple; *Deepest Purple-Very Best Of* .... (WB)
  In Rock .... (WB)
  Made In Japan .... (WB)
City
Fleetwood Mac; *Mystery To Me* .... (RPR)
Coffee Time
Li'l Wally; *My Polish Girlfriend & Others* ....(JJ)
Crying Time
Buck Owens & Emmylou Harris; *Act Naturally* ..(CAP)
Ray Charles; *Anthology* .... (RHI)
  Greatest Hits-#1 .... (RHI)
  His Greatest Hits-#1 ....(DHL)
Cryin' Time
Barbra Streisand; *Butterfly* ....(COL)
Julio Iglesias; *Starry Night* ....(COL)
Kendalls; *20 Favorites* .... (EPI)
Dangerous Times
Cher; *Cher* ....(GEF)
Daughters Of Time
Judy Collins; *All-Ears Review-#7-Still Amazing...* (ROM)
Doctor Time
Rick Trevino; *Rick Trevino* ....(COL)

Does Anybody Really Know What Time It Is
Chicago; *At Carnegie Hall* ....(COL)
  Chicago Transit Authority ....(COL)
  Greatest Hits ....(COL)
  If You Leave Me Now ....(COL)
Doin' My Time
Flatt & Scruggs; *Golden Hits Of* .... (GUS)
Johnny Cash; *Get Rhythm* .... (SUN)
  Original Golden Hits-#3 .... (SUN)
  Strawberry Cake .... (SUN)
Doin' Time
Justin Hayward; *Songwriter* ....(DER)
Meg Christian & Cris Williamson; *Meg-Cris At Carnegie
  Hall* ....(SEC)
Spooner; *Every Corner Dance* .... (MOU)
  Wildest Dreams/Every Corner Dance ....(DAL)
Don't Waste Your Time
Five Stairsteps; *Greatest Hits* .... (CLT)
Yarbrough & Peoples; *45* .... (TE)
Drug-Stabbing Time
Clash; *Give 'Em Enough Rope* .... (EPI)
Endless Love
Diana Ross & Lionel Richie; *25 Years Of Grammy
  Greats* .... (MOT)
  All The Great Motown Love Song Duets .... (MOT)
  Motown Story: First 25 Years .... (MOT)
  ST/Endless Love .... (MER)
Luther Vandross & Mariah Carey; *Songs* .... (EPI)
Eternal Flame
Bangles; *Everything* ....(COL)
  Greatest Hits ....(COL)
Eternity
Chaka Khan; *C.K.* .... (WB)
Vikki Carr; *Best Of* .... (UA)
Eternity Road
Moody Blues; *To Our Children's Children's
  Children* .... (POL)
Every Once In Awhile
BlackHawk; *BlackHawk* .... (ARI)
Every Second
Collin Raye; *All I Can Be* .... (EPI)
Forever In Love
Kenny G; *Breathless* .... (ARI)
Forty-Five Minutes From Broadway
Mickey Finn; *Caught In The Act* .... (CRS)
Funny How Time Slips Away
Al Green & Lyle Lovett; *Rhythm Country &
  Blues* .... (MCA)
Willie Nelson; *Best Of* .... (EMI)
  Collector's ....(RCA)
  Healing Hands Of Time .... (LIB)
  My Own Way ....(RCA)
  San Antonio Rose ....(COL)
  & Family Life ....(COL)
Willie Nelson & Faron Young; *Funny How Time Slips
  Away* ....(COL)
Gimme Some Time
Natalie Cole; *Collection* .... (CAP)
  Reaching For The Sky-Towering Soul/'70s ..... (CAP)
  & Peabo Bryson: Best Of Friends .... (CAP)
Got The Time
Joe Jackson; *Live...1980-1986* .... (A&M)
  Look Sharp! .... (A&M)
  No Wave .... (A&M)
Haven't Got Time For The Pain
Carly Simon; *Best Of* .... (ELE)
  Hot Cakes .... (ELE)
Healing Hands Of Time
Willie Nelson; *Healing Hands Of Time* .... (LIB)
Hello Stranger
Barbara Lewis; *Atlantic R&B
  1947-1974-#5-1962-1966* .... (ATL)
  Billboard Top R&B Hits-1963 .... (RHI)
  Collectables Presents-History Of Rock-#5 .... (CLT)
I Believe My Time Ain't Long
Fleetwood Mac; *25 Years-The Chain* .... (WB)
I Can't Wait Another Minute
Hi-Five; *Hi-Five* .... (JVA)
I Didn't Know What Time It Was
Ella Fitzgerald; *Rodgers & Hart Songbook* .... (VRV)
Sarah Vaughan; *Crazy & Mixed Up* .... (PAB)
If I Could Turn Back Time
Cher; *Heart Of Stone* .... (GEF)

If You've Got The Money I've Got The...
Lefty Frizzell; *American Originals* ....(COL)
   Columbia Country Classics-#2-Honky Tonk ....(COL)
   Greatest Hits ....(COL)
Willie Nelson; *Greatest Hits & Some That Will Be* (COL)
   Sound In Your Mind ....(COL)
   & Family Live ....(COL)
In A New York Minute
Ronnie McDowell; *19 Hot Country Requests-#3* ..(EPI)
   In A New York Minute ....(EPI)
   Older Women & Other Greatest Hits ....(EPI)
In Times Like These
Barbara Mandrell; *Greatest Hits* .... (MCA)
   Spun Gold ....(MCA)
Isn't It Time
Babys; *Anthologoy* .... (CHR)
   Broken Heart .... (CHR)
It Takes Time
Louis Armstrong; *Pops* ....(BLU)
Marshall Tucker Band; *10th* ....(WB)
It Won't Be Long
Beatles; *Meet The Beatles* ....(CAP)
   With The Beatles ....(CAP)
It's Been A Long, Long Time
Bing Crosby; *Best Of* .... (MCA)
Harry James & Kitty Kallen; *Best Of The Big*
Bands ....(COL)
Harry James/Orchestra; *Words & Music Of World War*
II ....(COL)
Jan Garber; *Best Of* .... (MCA)
Louis Armstrong; *Hello Dolly & Other Hits* ..... (MCA)
It's Going To Take Some Time
Carpenters; *Singles 1963-73* .... (A&M)
   Song For You ....(A&M)
   Yesterday Once More ....(A&M)
It's High Time
Dottie West; *Best Of* ....(LIB)
It's Just A Matter Of Time
Beach Boys; *Beach Boys* ....(CAR)
Brook Benton; *45s On CD-#1-1956-1959* ...... (MER)
   Billboard Top R&B Hits-1959 ....(RHI)
Glen Campbell; *It's Just A Matter Of Time* .... (AA)
Randy Travis; *No Holdin' Back* ....(WB)
   Rock Rhythm & Blues ....(WB)
It's Time
Winans; *Return* .... (QUE)
It's Time For Love
Don Williams; *Best Of-#4* .... (MCA)
   Cafe Carolina ....(MCA)
   Don Williams Sings Bob McDill ....(MCA)
James Brown; *Love Overdue* ....(SCO)
I've Loved You For A Long Time
Spinners; *Love Trippin'* .... (ATL)
Just In Time
Barbra Streisand; *Third Album* ....(COL)
Frank Sinatra; *Come Dance With Me* ....(CAP)
Michael Feinstein; *Sings The Jule Styne Songbook* (ELE)
Tony Bennett; *16 Most Requested Songs* ....(COL)
Killin' Time
Clint Black; *Killin' Time* ....(RCA)
   RCA Award Winners ....(RCA)
Large Time
Atlanta Rhythm Section; *Are You Ready* .... (POL)
   Champagne Jam ....(POL)
Leave A Tender Moment Alone
Billy Joel; *Innocent Man* ....(COL)
Living Forever
Genesis; *We Can't Dance* ....(ATL)
Long Ago & Far Away
Jo Stafford; *International Hits* ....(CRN)
   Jukebox Saturday Night-Great Vocal Hits ....(CAP)
Joe Stafford; *Capitol Collector Series* ....(CAP)
Rosemary Clooney; *Sings Ira Gershwin Lyrics* ....(CCJ)
Long Long Time
Linda Ronstadt; *Different Drum* ....(CAP)
   Greatest Hits ....(ASY)
   Retrospective ....(CAP)
   Silk Purse ....(CAP)
Long Long While
Rolling Stones; *More Hot Rocks-Big Hits & Fazed*
Cookies .... (AKO)

Long Run
Eagles; *Greatest Hits-#2* .... (ASY)
   Live .... (ASY)
   Long Run ....(ASY)
Long Time
Boston; *Boston* ....(EPI)
Molly Hatchet; *Flirtin' With Disaster* ....(EPI)
Todd Rundgren; *Runt-Ballad Of* ....(RHI)
Long Time Ago
Remingtons; *Blue Frontier* ....(BNA)
Long Time Gone
38 Special; *38 Special* ....(A&M)
Crosby, Stills & Nash; *Crosby, Stills & Nash* ....(ATL)
Crosby, Stills, Nash & Young; *Four-Way Street* ..(ATL)
Triumph; *Surveillance* ....(MCA)
Long Time No See
Chicago; *VIII* ....(COL)
Long Time No See, Baby
Glenn Miller; *Complete-#5-1940* ....(RCA)
   Complete-#9-1939-1942 ....(RCA)
Longer
Dan Fogelberg; *Greatest Hits* .... (FM)
   Phoenix .... (FM)
Longest Time
Billy Joel; *An Innocent Man* ....(COL)
   Greatest Hits-#1 & 2 ....(COL)
Love Comes To Everyone
George Harrison; *Best Of Dark*
Horse-1976-1989 ....(DKH)
   George Harrison ....(DKH)
Love Takes Time
Mariah Carey; *Mariah Carey* ....(COL)
Orleans; *Forever* ....(INF)
Ralph Tresvant; *Ralph Tresvant* .... (MCA)
Lovin' Every Minute Of It
Loverboy; *Big Ones* ....(COL)
   Lovin' Every Minute Of It ....(COL)
Man Out Of Time
Elvis Costello; *Girls Girls Girls* ....(COL)
Elvis Costello/Attractions; *Best Of* ....(COL)
   Imperial Bedroom ....(COL)
Mexican Minutes
Brooks & Dunn; *Hard Workin' Man* .... (ARI)
Minute By Minute
Doobie Brothers; *Best Of-II* ....(WB)
   Minute By Minute ....(WB)
Minutes To Memories
John Cougar Mellencamp; *Scarecrow* ....(RIV)
Motel Time
Larry Coryell; *Bolero* ....(EVD)
My Baby's Got Good Timing
Dan Seals; *Best Of* ....(CAP)
   Classics Collection-#1 ....(CAP)
   Country Gold ....(PRY)
   Early Dan Seals ....(CAP)
   San Antone ....(EMI)
My Dark Hour
Steve Miller Band; *Anthology* ....(CAP)
   Best Of-1968-1973 ....(CAP)
My Time
Boz Scaggs; *My Time* ....(COL)
Gladys Knight/Pips; *Best Of-Columbia Years* ....(COL)
   Life ....(COL)
Jane's Addiction; *Jane's Addiction* ....(XXX)
Psychedelic Furs; *Mirror Moves* ....(COL)
My Time After Awhile
Buddy Guy; *Hold That Plane* .... (VAN)
   I Was Walkin' Through The Woods .... (CSS)
   My Time After Awhile .... (VAN)
Never A Time
Genesis; *We Can't Dance* ....(ATL)
Nick Of Time
AC/DC; *Blow Up Your Video* ....(ATL)
Bonnie Raitt; *Nick Of Time* ....(CAP)
Night Time
J. Geils Band; *Love Stinks* .... (AMR)
Ted Nugent/Amboy Dukes; *Greatest Collection*
Ever ....(DHL)
Night Time Is Cry Time
Jimmy C. Newman; *Greatest Hits* ....(PLN)
Night Time Is The Right Time
Creedence Clearwater Revival; *1969* ....(FAN)
   Chronicle-#2 ....(FAN)
   Green River ....(FAN)

Ray Charles; *Complete Atlantic R&B*
Recordings-1952-59 .... (ATL)
No Time
Guess Who; *American Woman* .... (RCA)
  Best Of .... (RCA)
  Greatest Of .... (RCA)
  Track Record-Collection .... (RCA)
No Time At All
Original Cast; *Pippin* .... (MOT)
No Time For Talk
Christopher Cross; *Another Page* .... (WB)
No Time To Kill
Clint Black; *No Time To Kill* .... (RCA)
No Time To Live
Traffic; *Traffic* .... (ISL)
No Time To Lose
Tarney/Spencer Band; *Run For Your Life* ... (A&M)
No Time To Think
Bob Dylan; *Street Legal* .... (COL)
Not Enough Time
INXS; *Welcome To Wherever You Are* .... (ATL)
Nothing But Time
Jackson Browne; *Running On Empty* .... (ASY)
Once Upon A Time
Dan Fogelberg; *Nether Lands* .... (FM)
Donna Summer; *Live & More* .... (CAS)
  Once Upon A Time .... (CAS)
Frank Sinatra; *September Of My Years* .... (RPR)
Marvin Gaye & Mary Wells; *Anthology* .... (MOT)
  Together .... (MOT)
Simple Minds; *In The City Of Light* .... (A&M)
  Once Upon A Time .... (A&M)
One Clear Moment
Little Feat; *Let It Roll* .... (WB)
One Million Billionth Of A...
Flaming Lips; *Oh My Gawd The Flaming Lips* ... (RES)
One Moment In Time
Whitney Houston; *1984 Olympics Album* .... (ARI)
Only Time Will Tell
Asia; *Asia* .... (GEF)
  Live In Moscow .... (RHI)
  Then & Now .... (GEF)
Blast; *It's In My Blood* .... (SST)
Out Of Time
Divinyls; *Temperamental* .... (CHR)
Rolling Stones; *Flowers* .... (AKO)
  More Hot Rocks-Big Hits & Fazed Cookies ..... (AKO)
  Singles Collection-London Years .... (AKO)
Sam Phillips; *Indescribable Wow* .... (VIA)
Party Time
T.G. Sheppard; *All Time Greatest Hits* .... (WB)
  Greatest Hits .... (WB)
Pass The Time
Cream; *Wheels Of Fire* .... (RSO)
Passing Time
Bad Company; *Burnin' Sky* .... (SS)
Peace In Our Time
Eddie Money; *Greatest Hits-Sound Of Money* ....(COL)
Elvis Costello/Attractions; *Goodbye Cruel World* (COL)
Peking Theme (So Little Time)
Andy Williams; *ST/55 Days At Peking* .... (VS)
Praying For Time
George Michael; *Listen Without Prejudice* ....(COL)
Precious Time
Journey; *Departure* ....(COL)
Pat Benatar; *Precious Time* .... (CHR)
Prime Time
Alan Parsons Project; *Ammonia Avenue* .... (ARI)
  Best Of-#2 .... (ARI)
Tubes; *Remote Control* .... (A&M)
  Todd Rundgren-An Elpee's Worth Of Prod. ...... (RHI)
  T.R.A.S.H.-Tubes Rarities & Smash Hits ... (A&M)
Queen Of The Hours
Electric Light Orchestra; *No Answer* .... (JET)
Question Of Time
Depeche Mode; *101* .... (SIR)
  Black Celebration .... (SIR)
Jack Bruce; *Question Of Time* .... (EPI)
Raging Winds Of Time
Walking Wounded; *Raging Winds Of Time* ...... (CML)
Remember The Time
Michael Jackson; *Dangerous* .... (EPI)
Rhythm Of Time
Front 242; *Tyranny For You* .... (EPI)

Ring On Her Finger, Time On Her Hands
Lee Greenwood; *Greatest Hits* .... (MCA)
  Inside Out .... (MCA)
Rock & Roll Time
Roger McGuinn; *Cardiff Rose* .... (COL)
Rocket Man
Elton John; *Greatest Hits* .... (POL)
  Here & There .... (POL)
  Honky Chateau .... (POL)
Kate Bush; *Two Rooms-Songs Of E. John & B.*
Taupin .... (POL)
Rockin' Time
Bunny Wailer; *Roots Radics Rockers Reggae* ..... (SHA)
'Round The Clock Lovin'
Gail Davies; *Best Of* .... (CAP)
K.T. Oslin; *This Woman* .... (RCA)
Sands Of Time
Fleetwood Mac; *Future Games* .... (RPR)
Howard Keel; *ST/Kismet* .... (SSP)
Original Cast; *Kismet* .... (COL)
Saving Forever For You
Shanice; *ST/Beverly Hills 90210* .... (GIA)
Sea Of Time & Sea Of Holes
Beatles; *Box Set* .... (CAP)
  Yellow Submarine .... (CAP)
Seems Like A Long Time
Rod Stewart; *Every Picture Tells A Story* .... (MER)
She Don't Care About Time
Byrds; *Original Singles-#1-1965-1967* ....(COL)
  Byrds (collection) .... (COL)
Sooner Or Later
Barbara Cook; *Disney Album* .... (MCA)
Eddy Raven; *Best Of* .... (LIB)
  Temporary Sanity .... (LIB)
Gary Morris; *Stones* .... (LIB)
Grass Roots; *Anthology-1965-1975* .... (RHI)
  Super Hits-#2 .... (GUS)
  Their 16 Greatest Hits .... (MCA)
Madonna; *I'm Breathless-Music From Dick Tracy* . (SIR)
Spend A Little Time
Joan Armatrading; *Whatever's For Us* .... (A&M)
Spending My Time
Roxette; *Joyride* .... (EMI)
Stay
Frankie Valli/Four Seasons; *Greatest Hits-#1* .... (RHI)
Jackson Browne; *Running On Empty* .... (ASY)
Maurice Williams/Zodiacs; *Best Of* .... (CLT)
  Billboard Top Rock 'N' Roll Hits-1960 ..... (RHI)
  Cruisin'-1960 .... (INC)
  Rock & Roll Is Here To Stay .... (GUS)
  ST/Dirty Dancing ....(RCA)
Stay A Little Longer
Bob Wills; *Sounds Of Texas* ....(CAP)
Bob Wills/Texas Playboys; *Anthology-1935-1973* (RHI)
  Tiffany Transcriptions-#2 ....(KAL)
Willie Nelson; *Greatest Hits & Some That Will Be* (COL)
  Willie & Family Live ....(COL)
Still Doin' Time
George Jones; *Anniversary-Ten Years Of Hits* ..... (EPI)
  By Request .... (EPI)
  Greatest Country Hits/'80s-1981 ....(COL)
Take The Time
Bad Company; *Desolation Angels* .... (SS)
Take Time
Chris Walker; *First Time* .... (PEN)
Take Time To Know Her
Percy Sledge; *Best Of* ....(ATL)
  It Tears Me Up-Best Of .... (RHI)
Take Your Time
Babyface; *Lovers* .... (SLR)
Jefferson Starship; *Earth* .... (GRU)
Judson Spence; *Judson Spence* ....(ATL)
Lynyrd Skynyrd; *Legend* .... (MCA)
Pebbles; *Pebbles* .... (MCA)
S.O.S. Band; *Billboard Top Hits-1980* .... (RHI)
  Club Epic .... (EPI)
  S.O.S. Band .... (TAB)
Takin' My Time
Bonnie Raitt; *Sweet Forgiveness* .... (WB)
Little Feat; *Little Feat* .... (WB)
Marvin Gaye; *Greatest Hits* .... (MOT)
  That Stubborn Kinda Fellow .... (MOT)
Telephone Hour
Original Cast; *Bye Bye Birdie* ....(COL)

Soundtrack; *Bye Bye Birdie* ....(RCA)
That Was Then, This Is Now
Monkees; *Listen To The Band* .... (RHI)
   Then & Now-Best Of .... (ARI)
Things Will Grow
Sweethearts Of The Rodeo; *Rodeo Waltz* ....(SH)
This Is The Right Time
Lisa Stansfield; *Affection* .... (ARI)
   Power Jams-Today's Hottest Hits .... (KT)
This Precious Time
Barry McGuire; *Anthology* .... (OW)
Grass Roots; *Greatest Hits-#1* .... (MCA)
P.F. Sloan; *Anthology* .... (OW)
Through The Test Of Time
Patti Austin; *GRP 10th Anniversary Collection* ...(GRP)
   Live ....(GRP)
   Love Is Gonna Getcha .... (GRP)
Tick Tock
Vaughan Brothers; *Family Style* .... (EPA)
'Til I Gain Control Again
Crystal Gayle; *Best Of* .... (WB)
   True Love .... (ELE)
Emmylou Harris; *Elite Hotel* .... (RPR)
Rodney Crowell; *Collection* .... (WB)
   Rodney Crowell .... (WB)
Willie Nelson; *Greatest Hits & Some That Will Be* (COL)
Willie Nelson & Waylon Jennings; *Take It To The*
   Limit ....(COL)
'Til I Kissed You
Everly Brothers; *Cadence Classics-Their 20 Greatest*
   Hits .... (RHI)
   Fabulous Style Of .... (RHI)
   Very Best Of .... (WB)
'Til Something Better Comes Along
Louise Mandrell & R.C. Bannon; *Me & My R.C.* ..(RCA)
Til The End
Vern Gosdin; *10 Years Of Greatest Hits Newly*
   Recorded ....(COL)
   Best Of .... (WB)
   Til The End .... (ELE)
Till
Roger Williams; *Best Of* .... (MCA)
Tony Bennett; *Forty Years-Artistry Of* ....(COL)
Vogues; *Greatest Hits* .... (RHI)
   Greatest Hits .... (RPR)
Till I Get It Right
Tammy Wynette; *Biggest Hits* .... (EPI)
   Greatest Hits-#3 .... (EPI)
   Tears Of Fire-25th Anniversary Collect. .... (EPI)
Till The End Of Time
Chicago; *XI* ....(COL)
Perry Como; *Golden Records* ....(RCA)
   Nipper's Greatest Hits-'40s-#2 ....(RCA)
   Pure Gold ....(RCA)
   There Is Love-Wedding Songs .... (SCO)
Till The Next Goodbye
Rolling Stones; *It's Only Rock 'N' Roll* .... (RS)
Till The Rivers All Run Dry
Don Williams; *Best Of-#2* .... (MCA)
   Country Comes To Carnegie Hall .... (MCA)
   Greatest Country Hits ....(CCB)
   Harmony .... (MCA)
   Till The Rivers All Run Dry .... (MSP)
Pete Townshend & Ronnie Lane; *Rough Mix* ... (MCA)
Till Then
Mills Brothers; *Best Of* .... (MCA)
   Cab Driver .... (RAN)
   Greatest Hits .... (MCA)
   Lazy River .... (MSP)
   Mills Brothers .... (EVR)
Till There Was You
Beatles; *Box Set* .... (CAP)
   Meet The Beatles .... (CAP)
   With The Beatles .... (CAP)
Original Cast; *ST/Music Man* .... (CAP)
Time
David Bowie; *Aladdin Sane* ....(RYK)
   ST/Ziggy Stardust-The Motion Picture .... (RCA)
Edwin Starr; *Motown Superstar Series-#3* .... (MOT)
   War & Peace .... (MOT)
Freddie Mercury; *Great Pretender* ....(HOL)
Morris Day; *45* .... (WB)

Pink Floyd; *Dark Side Of The Moon* .... (HAR)
   Delicate Sound Of Thunder ....(CAP)
   Gift Set ....(CAP)
Tesla; *Psychotic Supper* .... (GEF)
Tom Waits; *Big Time* .... (ISL)
   Rain Dogs .... (ISL)
Time After Time
Carly Simon; *My Romance* .... (ARI)
Cyndi Lauper; *She's So Unusual* ....(POR)
Frank Sinatra; *16 Most Requested Songs* ....(COL)
   Greatest Hits-#2 ....(COL)
Johnny Mathis; *Love Songs* ....(COL)
Miles Davis; *You're Under Arrest* ....(COL)
Ozzy Osbourne; *Live And Loud* .... (EPI)
   No More Tears ....(EPA)
Placido Domingo; *Domingo Songbook* ....(SMC)
Sarah Vaughan; *Jazzfest Masters* .... (JM)
Stephane Grappelli; *Afternoon In Paris* ....(VRV)
Tony Bennett; *Perfectly Frank* ....(COL)
Time Ain't Money
Huey Lewis/News; *Hard At Play* .... (EMI)
Time And Time Again
Counting Crows; *August And Everything After* .. (DGC)
Time Between
Byrds; *Byrds (collection)* ....(COL)
   Younger Than Yesterday ....(COL)
Desert Rose Band; *Desert Rose Band* ....(CCB)
Time Changes Everything
Bob Wills/Texas Playboys; *Anthology-1935-1973* (RHI)
   Columbia Country Classics-#1-Golden Age .....(COL)
   Essential ....(COL)
Roy Rogers; *Country Music Hall Of Fame* ...... (MCA)
Time Don't Run Out On Me
Anne Murray; *Country Hits* .... (LIB)
   Greatest Hits-#2 .... (LIB)
   Heart Over Mind ....(CAP)
Time For Everything
Jethro Tull; *Benefit* .... (CHR)
Time For Love
Kenny Rogers; *They Don't Make 'Em Like They Used*
   To ....(RCA)
Shirley Horn; *Here's To Life* ....(VRV)
Tony Bennett; *All-Time Greatest Hits* ....(COL)
   Forty Years-Artistry Of ....(COL)
Time For Me To Fly
R.E.O. Speedwagon; *Decade Of Rock &*
   Roll-1970-1980 .... (EPI)
   Hits .... (EPI)
   You Can Tune A Piano But You Can't.. .... (EPI)
Time Goes On
En Vogue; *Born To Sing* .... (ATL)
Time Has Come Today
Chambers Brothers; *Nuggets-#9-Acid Rock* ...... (RHI)
   Rock Classics/'60s ....(COL)
   Time Has Come ....(COL)
Time Heals
Todd Rundgren; *Anthology-1968-1985* .... (RHI)
   Healing .... (RHI)
Time In A Bottle
Jim Croce; *50th Anniversary Collection* ....(SAJ)
   Photographs & Memories-Greatest Hits .... (21)
   Time In A Bottle .... (21)
Time Is Here
Stomu Yamashta/Go; *Live From Paris* .... (ISL)
   Stomu Yamashta/Go .... (ISL)
Time Is On My Side
Irma Thomas; *Best Of New Orleans R&B-#1* ..... (RHI)
   Simply The Best-Live .... (ROU)
Keith Richards/X-Pensive Winos; *Live At Hollywood*
   Palladium-Dec. 1988 .... (VIA)
Rolling Stones; *12 x 5* ....(AKO)
   Big Hits-High Tides & Green Grass ....(AKO)
   Got Live If You Want It ....(AKO)
   Hot Rocks-1964-1971 ....(AKO)
   Still Life-American Concert-1981 .... (RS)
Time Is Running Out
Steve Winwood; *Steve Winwood* .... (ISL)
Time Is Tight
Booker T./M.G.s; *Greatest Hits* .... (STX)
   Soul Shots-#2 .... (RHI)
   Soul Shots-#3-Soul Twist .... (RHI)
Clash; *Black Market Clash* .... (EPI)

Time Is Wasting
Carlo; *20 Great Love Songs/'50s & '60s-#1* ......(LAU)
22 Leaders Of The Pack-#1 ....(LAU)
Time Isn't Kind
Fine Young Cannibals; *Fine Young Cannibals* ..... (IRS)
Time It's Time
Talk Talk; *Colour Of Spring* ....(EMI)
Time Loves A Hero
Little Feat; *Time Loves A Hero* ....(WB)
Waiting For Columbus ....(WB)
Time Machine
Barbra Streisand; *Emotion* ....(COL)
Black Sabbath; *Dehumanizer* ....(RPR)
ST/Wayne's World ....(RPR)
Grand Funk Railroad; *Capitol Collectors Series* ...(CAP)
Legends Of Rock Guitar-'70s ....(RHI)
Mark Don & Mel: *1969-71* ....(CAP)
On Time ....(CAP)
T. Graham Brown; *Come As You Were* ....(CAP)
Time Of My Life (I've Had The)
Bill Medley; *Best Of* ....(CCB)
Bill Medley & Jennifer Warnes; *Dirty Dancing Live In
Concert* ....(RCA)
ST/Dirty Dancing ....(RCA)
Time Of The Preacher
Willie Nelson; *Red Headed Stranger* ....(COL)
Time Of The Season
Argent; *Anthology-Collection Of Greatest Hits* ..... (EPI)
Encore .... (EPI)
ST/Awakenings ....(RPR)
Zombies; *Billboard Top Rock 'N' Roll Hits-1969* . (RHI)
Odyssey & Oracle ....(RHI)
Rock Classics-#3 ....(KT)
ST/1969 ....(POL)
Time Off For Bad Behaviour
Confederate Railroad; *Confederate Railroad* ..... (ATL)
Time On My Hands
Billie Holiday; *Billie Holiday* ....(COL)
Quintessential-#8-1939-1940 ....(COL)
Story-#2 ....(COL)
Duke Ellington; *Lullaby Of Birdland* .... (INT)
Glenn Miller; *Best Of The Big Bands* ....(COL)
Sweet Honey In The Rock; *Good News* .... (FF)
Time Out
Joe Walsh; *Best Of* .... (MCA)
Joe Walsh ....(MSP)
So What .... (MCA)
You Can't Argue With A Sick Mind ....(MCA)
Time Out Of Mind
Steely Dan; *Gaucho* .... (MCA)
Time Passages
Al Stewart; *Best Of* .... (ARI)
Live/Indian Summer .... (ARI)
Time Passages .... (ARI)
'70s Greatest Rock Hits-#6-FM Hits ....(PRY)
Time Passed Autumn
Claus Ogerman Orchestra; *Gate Of Dreams* ...... (WB)
Time Passes By
Kathy Mattea; *Time Passes By* .... (MER)
Time Passes Me By
Desert Rose Band; *Pages Of Life* ....(CCB)
Time Passes Slowly
Bob Dylan; *Biograph* ....(COL)
New Morning ....(COL)
Judy Collins; *Whales & Nightingales* .... (ELE)
Time Remembered
Bill Evans; *Loose Blues* .... (MS)
Time Remembered .... (MS)
Time Stands Still
Rush; *Chronicles* .... (MER)
Hold Your Fire .... (MER)
Show Of Hands .... (MER)
Time Stood Still
Vern Gosdin; *10 Years Of Hits Newly Recorded* ..(COL)
Time The Avenger
Pretenders; *Learning To Crawl* .... (SIR)
Time To Cry
Paul Anka; *Paul Anka's 21 Golden Hits* ....(RCA)
Time To Get Alone
Beach Boys; *Friends-20/20* ....(CAP)
Time To Hide
Paul McCartney/Wings; *Wings Over America* ....(CAP)
Wings; *At The Speed Of Sound* ....(CAP)

Time To Kill
Alice Cooper; *Raise Your Fist & Yell* .... (MCA)
Band; *Stage Fright* ....(CAP)
UK; *Night After Night* ....(EDI)
UK ....(EDI)
Time Waits For No One
Rolling Stones; *It's Only Rock 'N' Roll* .... (RS)
Sucking In The Seventies .... (RS)
Time Warp
Rocky Horror Picture Show Cast; *Dr. Demento Greatest
Novelty Records-#4* .... (RHI)
Tim Curry/Original Roxy Cast; *Rocky Horror
Show* .... (RHI)
Time Was
Kate Smith; *16 Most Requested Songs* ....(COL)
Time Will Reveal
DeBarge; *In A Special Way* .... (MOT)
Time Will Tell
Black Crowes; *Southern Harmony & Musical
Companion* .... (DEF)
Bob Marley/Wailers; *Kaya* .... (TUF)
Songs Of Freedom .... (TUF)
Gary Morris; *These Days* .... (LIB)
Jimmy Cliff; *Reggae Spectacular* .... (A&M)
Wonderful World Beautiful People .... (A&M)
Tower Of Power; *Back To Oakland* .... (WB)
Time Won't Let Me
Smithereens; *S* ....(RCA)
Time & A Word
Yes; *Time & A Word* .... (ATL)
Yesshows .... (ATL)
Yesterdays .... (ATL)
Time & Love
Barbra Streisand; *Stoney End* ....(COL)
Laura Nyro; *New York Tendaberry* ....(COL)
Sawyer Brown; *Dirt Road* .... (LIB)
Time & Tide
Basia; *No Boundaries* ....(COL)
Time & Tide .... (EPI)
Time (Clock Of The Heart)
Culture Club; *Kissing To Be Clever* .... (VIA)
Time (Keeps Flowing Like A River)
Alan Parsons Project; *Best Of* .... (ARI)
Turn Of A Friendly Card .... (ARI)
Timeless
Rick Derringer; *Guitars & Women* .... (BS)
Timeless & True Love
McCarters; *Country Love Songs* .... (WB)
The Gift .... (WB)
Times Have Changed
Supertramp; *Indelibly Stamped* .... (A&M)
Times Of Your Life
Paul Anka; *30th Anniversary Collection* .... (RHI)
His Best .... (EMI)
Times They Are A-Changin'
Billy Joel; *KOHUEPT* ....(COL)
Bob Dylan; *At Budokan* ....(COL)
Biograph ....(COL)
Bootleg Series-#1-3-1961-1989 ....(COL)
Greatest Hits ....(COL)
Times They Are A-Changin' ....(COL)
Byrds; *Byrds (collection)* ....(COL)
Turn! Turn! Turn! ....(COL)
Peter, Paul & Mary; *In Concert* .... (WB)
Simon & Garfunkel; *Collected Works* ....(COL)
Wednesday Morning 3 A.M. ....(COL)
Time, Love & Tenderness
Michael Bolton; *Time, Love & Tenderness* ....(COL)
Time, The
Baby Washington; *Best Of* ....(CLT)
Best Of Sue Records ....(CLT)
Five Satins; *Sing Their Greatest Hits* ....(CLT)
Inez Foxx; *Stax Soul Sisters* .... (STX)
Time, Time
Ed Ames; *Best Of* ....(RCA)
Pure Gold ....(RCA)
Time's Up
Southern Pacific/Carlene Carter; *County Line* ....(WB)
Favorite Country Duets .... (WB)
Greatest Hits .... (WB)
Tomorrow Is A Long Time
Bob Dylan; *Greatest Hits-#2* ....(COL)
Chris Hillman; *Morning Sky* .... (SH)
Elvis Presley; *Valentine Gift For You* ....(RCA)

Ian & Sylvia; *Four Strong Winds* .... (VAN)
  Greatest Hits .... (VAN)
  Troubadours Of The Folk Era-#1 .... (RHI)
Sandy Denny; *Who Knows Where The Time Goes* (HBL)
Tomorrow Is Such A Long Time
Rod Stewart; *Every Picture Tells A Story* .... (MER)
  Greatest Hits-#2 .... (MER)
Too Much Time On My Hands
Styx; *Caught In The Act* .... (A&M)
  Classics-#15 .... (A&M)
  Paradise Theatre .... (A&M)
Tulsa Time
Don Williams; *Best Of-#2* .... (MCA)
  Country's Greatest Hits-#6 .... (PRY)
  Expressions .... (MCA)
  Legends .... (MCA)
Eric Clapton; *Backless* .... (RSO)
  Just One Night .... (POL)
Turn Back The Hands Of Time
Tyrone Davis; *Atlantic Rhythm & Blues*
  1947-74-#7 .... (ATL)
  Greatest Hits .... (RHI)
  Sock Hop .... (DHL)
  Soul Hits/'70s-#2 .... (RHI)
Twenty-Five Minutes To Go
Johnny Cash; *At Folsom Prison & San Quentin* ...(COL)
  Essential .... (COL)
  True West .... (COL)
Ugly Hour
David Bromberg; *Bandit In A Bathing Suit* .... (FAN)
Until The End Of Time
Guy & Ralna; *22 Golden Country Classics* ...... (RAN)
Wasted Days & Wasted Nights
Freddy Fender; *Before The Next Teardrop Falls* . (MCA)
  Best Of .... (MCA)
  Collection .... (MCA)
  Country Comes To Carnegie Hall .... (MCA)
  Happy Trails .... (UA)
  Texas Country .... (UA)
Wasted On The Way
Crosby, Stills & Nash; *Daylight Again* .... (ATL)
  Crosby, Stills & Nash (collection) .... (ATL)
Wasting Time
Collective Soul; *Hints Allegations And Things Left*
  Unsaid .... (ATL)
What Time Is It?
Ken Nordine; *Best Of Word Jazz-#1* .... (RHI)
Spin Doctors; *Pocket Full Of Kryptonite* .... (EPA)
When It's Sleepy Time Down South
Billie Holiday; *Last Recordings* .... (VRV)
Dizzy Gillespie; *20 Golden Pieces Of* .... (BLD)
Louis Armstrong; *At The Crescendo* .... (MCA)
  Best Of .... (MCA)
  Best Of Decca Years-#1-The Singer .... (DEC)
  Essential .... (VAN)
  Greatest Hits .... (COL)
  I Like Jazz-Essence Of .... (COL)
  Satchmo/Musical Autobiography .... (MCA)
Mel Torme; *Mel Torme* .... (GLN)
Wynton Marsalis; *Standard Time-#2-Intimacy*
  Calling .... (COL)
Where Time Stands Still
Mary Chapin Carpenter; *Stones In The Road* ....(COL)
Who Knows Where The Time Goes
Fairport Convention; *Chronicles* .... (A&M)
  Circle Dance-Hokey Pokey Charity Compil. ..... (GRE)
Judy Collins; *Colors Of The Day-Best Of* .... (ELE)
  Who Knows Where The Time Goes .... (ELE)
Sandy Denny; *Best Of* .... (HBL)
  Who Knows Where The Time Goes .... (HBL)
Why Did You Waste My Time?
Screamin' Jay Hawkins; *Collectables Blues*
  Collection-#1 .... (CLT)
Wild Hearts Run Out Of Time
Roy Orbison; *King Of Hearts* .... (VIA)
Winter Time
Steve Miller Band; *Book Of Dreams* .... (CAP)
  CD Gift Set .... (CAP)
  Greatest Hits-1974-1978 .... (CAP)
Wintertime Love
Doors; *Waiting For The Sun* .... (ELE)

Young Turks
Rod Stewart; *Absolutely Live* .... (WB)
  Downtown Train-Storyteller Selections ...... (WB)
  Storyteller/Complete Anthology-1964-1990 ...... (WB)
  Tonight I'm Yours .... (WB)
Your Time Is Gonna Come
Led Zeppelin; *Led Zeppelin* .... (ATL)
  Led Zeppelin (collection) .... (ATL)

TOYS & GAMES, Puppets

See Also: CARTOON CHARACTERS,
CHILDREN, FUN, STORYBOOK CHARACTERS

8 Ball
N.W.A.; *Staight Outta Compton* .... (RUP)
"8" Ball
Herb Alpert; *Classics-#20* .... (A&M)
  Wild Romance .... (A&M)
Slammin' Watusis; *Kings Of Noise* .... (EPI)
99 Luftballons (99 Red Balloons)
Nena; *99 Luftballons* .... (EPI)
All Fall Down
Emmylou Harris & George Jones; *Duets* .... (EPI)
Five Star; *Luxury Of Life* .... (RCA)
Standells; *Best Of* .... (RHI)
Ally Ally Oxen Free
Kingston Trio; *Capitol Collectors Series* .... (CAP)
  Made In The U.S.A. .... (PRR)
Annie Get Your Yo Yo
Junior Parker; *Best Of* .... (MCA)
  Driving Wheel .... (MCA)
Arizona Indian Doll
Faster Pussycat; *Wake Me When It's Over* .... (ELE)
Arkansas See Saw
Jerry Lee Lewis; *Keeps Rockin'* .... (MER)
As The Toys Go Winding Down
Primus; *Frizzle Fry* .... (CRL)
Attack Of The Name Game
Stacy Lattisaw; *Sneakin' Out* .... (COT)
Baby Doll
Bessie Smith; *Complete Recordings-#3* ....(COL)
Carlo; *La Bamba & Other Original Hits* ....(LAU)
Devo; *Total Devo* ....(ENC)
Ella Fitzgerald; *Best Of* .... (MCA)
Farmers; *Rock Angel* .... (FF)
Marvin & Johnny; *Flipped Out* .... (SPE)
Memphis Slim; *Raining The Blues* .... (FAN)
Raindogs; *Border Drive-In Theatre* .... (ATC)
Rita Remington; *Girls Girls Girls* .... (PLN)
Tony! Toni! Tone!; *Who?* .... (WNG)
Baby Doll Polka
Frank Yankovic; *America's Favorites* .... (SMA)
  One More Time .... (CRS)
Baby Let's Play House
Elvis Presley; *Complete Sun Sessions* ....(RCA)
  Date With Elvis ....(RCA)
  Golden Celebration ....(RCA)
  Sun Sessions ....(RCA)
Barbi Doll
Barbara Weathers; *Barbara Weathers* .... (RPR)
Barbie Doll Look
Sky Saxon; *Best Of Rodney On The ROQ* .... (PBO)
Barbie & Ken
Weathermen; *Black Album According To The* ..... (PIA)
Barbie & Ken Ferrari
John Hiatt; *Perfectly Good Guitar* .... (A&M)
Baron, The
Johnny Cash; *Biggest Hits* ....(COL)
  Columbia Records-1958-1986 ....(COL)
  Greatest Country Hits/'80s-1981 ....(COL)
Beggar's Game
Dan Fogelberg; *Phoenix* .... (FM)
Billy The Kid (I Miss...)
Billy Dean; *Billy Dean* .... (LIB)
Bingo Fever
Da Yoopers; *Camp Fever* .... (YOU)
Brand New Key
Melanie; *Best Of* .... (RHI)
  Super Hits/'70s-Have A Nice Day-#7 .... (RHI)
Brand New Toy
Hot Tuna; *Pair A Dice Found* .... (EPI)

Broken Toys
B.J. Thomas; *Throwin' Rocks At The Moon* ......(COL)
Jerry Jeff Walker; *Mr. Bojangles* ....(BAI)
Broken Yo-Yo
Texas Alexander; *Story of The Blues* ....(COL)
Broomstick Cowboy
Bobby Goldsboro; *10th Anniversary Album-#1* .... (UA)
  Honey-Best Of ....(EMI)
Cat's In The Cradle
Harry Chapin; *Anthology* ....(ELE)
  Greatest Stories-Live ....(ELE)
  Verities & Balderdash ....(ELE)
Caught In The Game
Survivor; *Caught In The Game* ....(SCO)
Checkmate
Defiance; *Void Terra Firma* .... (RR)
Ernie Henry; *Presenting* ....(RVR)
Chess
Original Cast; *Chess* ....(RCA)
Chess Game
Jerry Jeff Walker; *Circus Maximus With* .... (VAN)
Original Cast; *March Of The Falsettos* ....(DRG)
Chess Players
Art Blakey/Jazz Messengers; *Big Beat* ....(BLN)
Chessman's Delight
Randy Weston Trio/Cecil Payne; *Jazz A La*
Bohemia ....(RVR)
China Doll
Grateful Dead; *From The Mars Hotel* .... (MOB)
  Reckoning .... (ARI)
Slim Whitman; *15th Anniversary* ....(IMP)
  Best Of ....(EMI)
  Paloma Blanca-Best-Legendary Masters ....(EMI)
Suzanne Vega; *Deadicated* .... (ARI)
Chinese Checkers
Booker T./M.G.s; *45* ....(ATL)
Circle Game
Buffy Sainte-Marie; *Best Of* .... (VAN)
  Fire & Fleet & Candlelight ....(VAN)
Ian & Sylvia; *Greatest Hits* ....(VAN)
Joni Mitchell; *Ladies Of The Canyon* ....(RPR)
  Miles Of Aisles ....(ASY)
Tom Rush; *Circle Game* ....(ELE)
  Classic Rush ....(ELE)
Come Out And Play
Offspring; *Smash* ....(EPT)
Come & Buy My Toys
David Bowie; *Starting Point* ....(DER)
Computer Games
George Clinton; *Computer Games* ....(CAP)
Yellow Magic Orchestra; *Kyoretsu Na*
Rhythm-Characters ....(RES)
Crossword Puzzle
Barbara Mandrell; *Clean Cut* .... (MCA)
  Country Classics-#4 (1984-1985) ....(MCA)
Crying Game
Boy George; *At Worst-Best Of Boy George/Culture*
Club ....(SBK)
Cuddly Toy (Feel For Me)
Roachford; *Roachford* .... (EPI)
Cupid's Toy
Squeeze; *Play* ....(RPR)
Darkness On The Playground
Desert Rose Band; *Pages Of Life* ....(CCB)
Dart Game
Shelly Manne/Men; *Swinging Sounds-#4* .... (CTM)
Days Of Sand & Shovels
Bobby Vinton; *All-Time Greatest Hits* .... (EPI)
Waylon Jennings; *Best Of* ....(RCA)
Devil's Toy
Almighty; *Soul Destruction* ....(POL)
Do The Boomerang
Junior Walker/All-Stars; *Anthology* ....(MOT)
  Shotgun ....(MOT)
Doll Parts
Hole; *Live Through This* ....(DGC)
Domino
Cramps; *Psychedelic Jungle/Gravest Hits* .... (IRS)
Genesis; *Invisible Touch* ....(ATL)
Masters Of Reality; *Masters Of Reality* ....(DEF)
Van Morrison; *Best Of* ....(MER)
  His Band & Street Choir ....(WB)
  It's Too Late To Stop Now ....(WB)

Domino Dancing
Pet Shop Boys; *Introspective* .... (EMI)
Dominoes
Flesheaters; *Destroyed By Fire-Greatest Hits* ......(SST)
Robbie Nevil; *Robbie Nevil* ....(EMI)
Syd Barrett; *Barrett* ....(CAP)
Einstein At The Pool Hall
Pat McDonald/Essentials; *Lowdown* ....(MOU)
End Game
Ian Anderson; *Walking Into Light* ....(CHR)
Robin Trower; *B.L.T.* ....(CHR)
  No Stopping Anytime ....(CHR)
Everybody Plays The Fool
Aaron Neville; *Warm Your Heart* ....(A&M)
Main Ingredient; *Golden Classics* ....(CLT)
  Nipper's Greatest Hits-'70s ....(RCA)
Everyone A Puzzle Lover
10,000 Maniacs; *Wishing Chair* .... (ELE)
Freeze Tag
Suzanne Vega; *Suzanne Vega* ....(A&M)
Fun & Games
Chuck Mangione; *Best Of* ....(A&M)
  Classics-#6 ....(A&M)
  Fun & Games ....(A&M)
Isley Brothers; *Showdown* .... (TN)
Future Games
Fleetwood Mac; *Future Games* ....(RPR)
Game Is Over
John Denver; *Whose Garden Was This* ....(RCA)
Game Number 9
Ray Charles; *True To Life* ....(ATL)
Game Of Life
Billy Paul; *First Class* .... (PI)
Game Of Love
Wayne Fontana/Mindbenders; *45s On CD-#2* .. (MER)
  ST/Good Morning Vietnam ....(A&M)
  Super Oldies/'60s-#10 ....(AUF)
Games
Ann Peebles; *If This Is Heaven* .... (HIR)
David Crosby & Graham Nash; *David Crosby &*
Graham Nash ....(ATL)
Husker Du; *Flip Your Wig* ....(SST)
New Kids On The Block; *No More Games/Remix*
Album ....(COL)
  Step By Step ....(COL)
Shalamar; *Circumstantial Evidence* ....(SLR)
  Greatest Hits ....(SLR)
Games People Play
Alan Parsons Project; *Best Of* .... (ARI)
  Turn Of A Friendly Card ....(ARI)
Joe South; *On The Road Again-Rock's New*
Frontiers ....(CAP)
Games That Daddies Play
Conway Twitty; *Greatest Hits-#2* ....(MCA)
  #1s-#11 ....(CAP)
Games Without Frontiers
Peter Gabriel; *Peter Gabriel* ....(GEF)
  Shaking The Tree-16 Golden Greats ....(GEF)
Games, Games
Tavares; *Madam Butterfly* ....(CAP)
Gamin' On A Swing
Parliament; *Clones Of Doctor Funkenstein* ....(CAS)
  Live ....(CAS)
Girl On A Swing
Gerry/Pacemakers; *History Of British Rock-#7* ... (RHI)
God's Coloring Book
Dolly Parton; *Here You Come Again* ....(RCA)
Guessing Games
Daryl Hall & John Oates; *H2O* ....(RCA)
Head Games
Foreigner; *Head Games* ....(ATL)
  Records ....(ATL)
Hide & Go Seek
Joe Turner; *Rock This Joint* .... (INT)
Hide & Seek
Bill Haley/Comets; *Golden Hits* ....(MCA)
Chuck Mangione; *Evening Of Magic* ....(A&M)
  Feels So Good ....(A&M)
Howard Jones; *Action Replay* ....(ELE)
  Human's Lib ....(ELE)
Spencer Davis Group; *Greatest & Latest* ....(PRY)
Honky Tonk Toys
John Conlee; *Friday Night Blues* ....(MCA)

Human Toy
Ready For The World; *Ready For The World* ... (MCA)
Human Video Game
D.J. Jazzy Jeff & The Fresh Prince; *He's The D.J. I'm
The Rapper* .... (JVA)
I Don't Want To Play House
Lynn Anderson; *Rose Garden* .... (COL)
I Don't Want To Play In Your Yard
Joan Morris & William Bolcom; *After The Ball* . (NON)
I Lost On Jeopardy
Weird Al Yankovic; *Greatest Hits* .... (RAR)
In 3-D .... (RAR)
I Wanna Be A Toy
Dead Or Alive; *Youthquake* .... (EPI)
Indoor Games
King Crimson; *Lizard* .... (ATL)
It's All In The Game
Four Tops; *Anthology* .... (MOT)
Compact Command Performances .... (MOT)
George Benson; *Weekend In L.A.* .... (WB)
Nat King Cole; *Gift Set* .... (CAP)
Tommy Edwards; *Oldies But Goodies-#7* .... (OSR)
I'm Forever Blowing Bubbles
Lawrence Welk; *I'm Forever Blowing Bubbles* ... (RAN)
Live At Lake Tahoe .... (RAN)
Reminiscing-#1 .... (RAN)
I'm Gonna Tear Your Playhouse Down
Ann Peebles; *Greatest Hits* .... (MCA)
B.B. King; *Lucille Talks Back* .... (OOP)
Graham Parker; *Pourin' It All Out-Mercury Years* (MER)
Graham Parker/Rumour; *Parkerilla* .... (MER)
Stick To Me .... (MER)
Paul Young; *Secret Of Association* .... (COL)
I'm In Love With My Little Red Tricycle
Napoleon XIV; *They're Coming To Take Me
Away...Ha-Ha* .... (RHI)
I'm On A Seesaw
Fats Waller; *Complete-#3-1935-1936* .... (RCA)
I'm Your Puppet
James & Bobby Purify; *Oldies But Goodies-#12* .. (OSR)
Soul Shots-#5 .... (RHI)
Sweet & Soulful '60s .... (KT)
I've Got The World On A String
Count Basie; *Standards* .... (VRV)
Ella Fitzgerald; *Harold Arlen Songbook-#1* ...... (VRV)
Frank Sinatra; *Capitol Collectors Series* .... (CAP)
Frank Sinatra & Liza Minnelli; *Frank Sinatra
Duets* .... (CAP)
Sarah Vaughan; *Best Of* .... (PAB)
Stephane Grappelli & Martin Taylor; *We've Got The
World On A String* .... (ANG)
"Jeopardy" Theme (Think Music)
Original Music; *Television's Greatest Hits-#2* ..... (TVT)
Jet Silver & The Dolls Of Venus
Be Bop Deluxe; *Ax Victim* .... (OOP)
Best Of-Raiding The Divine Archive .... (CAP)
Jigsaw Puzzle
Rolling Stones; *Beggar's Banquet* .... (AKO)
Just A Game
Triumph; *Just A Game* .... (MCA)
Kick The Can
Fred Frith; *Speechless* .... (RAL)
Kite
Nick Heyward; *From Monday To Sunday* .... (EPI)
Learning The Game
Andrew Gold; *What's Wrong With This Picture* ... (ASY)
Santa Esmeralda; *Beauty* .... (CAS)
Let Me Play With Your Yo-Yo
Moses Rascoe; *Blues* .... (FF)
Let The Children Play
Santana; *Festival* .... (COL)
Moonflower .... (COL)
Let's Chase Each Other Around The Room
Merle Haggard; *19 Hot Country Requests-#2* ..... (EPI)
It's All In The Game .... (EPI)
Life Is Just A Tire Swing
Jimmy Buffett; *A-1-A* .... (MCA)
Lincoln Logs
Mojo Nixon & Skid Roper; *Bo-Day-Shus!!!* .... (IRS)
Love Is A Dangerous Game
Millie Jackson; *45* .... (JVA)
Thelma Houston; *Qualifying Heat* .... (MCA)

Love Is Just A Game
Larry Gatlin/Gatlin Brothers; *17 Greatest Hits* ...(COL)
Live At 8:00 .... (CAP)
Larry Gatlin/Gatlin Brothers Band; *Greatest Hits* .(COL)
Mental Hopscotch
Missing Persons; *Best Of* .... (CAP)
Mind Playing Tricks On Me
Geto Boys; *S* .... (RAP)
Musical Box
Genesis; *Genesis* .... (CHS)
Live .... (ATL)
Nursery Cryme .... (ATL)
Seconds Out .... (ATL)
Mystical Potato Head Groove Thing
Joe Satriani; *Flying In A Blue Dream* .... (REL)
Name Game
Shirley Ellis; *Cruisin' 1965* .... (INC)
Name Of The Game
Abba; *Album* .... (ATL)
Greatest Hits-#2 .... (ATL)
New Fool At An Old Game
Reba McEntire; *Country's Greatest Hits-#4-Sweet
Country* .... (PRY)
Live .... (MCA)
Reba .... (MCA)
New York Broken Toy
Nazareth; *Expect No Mercy* .... (A&M)
Night Game
Paul Simon; *Still Crazy After All These Years* ...... (WB)
Night Games
Charley Pride; *Charley Pride* .... (RCA)
Greatest Hits-#2 .... (RCA)
Night Games .... (RCA)
Gregg Allman Band; *Just Before The Bullets Fly* .. (EPI)
Oh You Beautiful Doll
Guy Lombardo; *Dance To Songs Everybody
Knows* .... (MCA)
Old Playground
Bruce Hornsby/Range; *Scenes From The
Southside* .... (RCA)
Old Rockin' Horse
Slim Dusty; *Australia Is His Name* .... (PHO)
Old Toy Trains
Billy Strange; *Railroad Man* .... (CRS)
Glen Campbell; *All-Star Country Christmas* ...... (CAP)
That Christmas Feeling .... (CAP)
Statler Brothers; *Christmas Present* .... (MER)
Ollie Ollie Outs In Free
Carl Ravazza/Orchestra; *Uncollected-1941-1944* (HIN)
One Night In Bangkok (Chess)
Murray Head; *Chess Pieces* .... (RCA)
Original Broadway Cast; *Chess* .... (RCA)
Only A Pawn In Their Game
Bob Dylan; *The Times They Are A-Changin'* .....(COL)
Only Game In Town
Red Rider; *As Far As Siam* .... (CAP)
Pac Man Fever
Buckner & Garcia; *Pac Man Fever* .... (COL)
Paper Airplanes
Seals & Crofts; *Year Of Sunday* .... (WB)
Paper Doll
Bar-Kays; *Banging The Wall* .... (MER)
Fleetwood Mac; *25 Years-The Chain* .... (WB)
Mills Brothers; *22 Great Hits* .... (RAN)
Best Of .... (MCA)
Best Of The Decca Years .... (DEC)
Greatest Hits .... (MCA)
Paper Doll .... (MCA)
Patriot Game
Judy Collins; *Whales & Nightingales* .... (ELE)
Kingston Trio; *Capitol Collectors Series* .... (CAP)
Pat-A-Cake
Bill Haley/Comets; *King Of Rock & Roll* .... (ALS)
Pawns In The Game
Professor Griff/Last Asiatic Disciples; *Pawns In The
Game* .... (LUK)
Peek A Boo
Cadillacs; *Best Of* .... (RHI)
Devo; *Best Of-Greatest Hits* .... (WB)
EZ Listening Disc .... (RYK)
Oh No It's Devo .... (WB)
Siouxsie/Banshees; *Peepshow* .... (GEF)
Twice Upon A Time-The Singles .... (GEF)

(Peek-A-Boo) Game
Sir Mix-A-Lot; *Seminar* .... (NSY)
Peking Doll
Kazumi Watanabe/Resonance Vox; *Pandora* ... (GRM)
Picture Puzzle
Kate Wolf; *Evening In Austin* .... (KAL)
Give Yourself To Love .... (KAL)
Lines On The Paper .... (KAL)
Pinball Machine
Lonnie Irving; *Super Hits Country-1960s* .... (IGR)
Pinball Wizard
Elton John; *Greatest Hits-#2* .... (POL)
Pete Townshend; *Another Scoop* .... (ATC)
Pete Townshend's Deep End-Live ....(ATC)
Rod Stewart; *Best Of* .... (MER)
Sing It Again Rod .... (MER)
Storyteller-Complete Anthology-1964-1990 ..... (WB)
Who; *Greatest Hits* .... (MCA)
Meaty Beaty Big & Bouncy .... (MCA)
ST/Kids Are Alright .... (MCA)
Tommy .... (MCA)
Who's Last .... (MCA)
Play The Game
Joe Perry Project; *I've Got The Rock 'N' Rolls
Again* .... (COL)
Queen; *Greatest Hits* .... (HOL)
Play The Game .... (HOL)
Play The Game Tonight
Kansas; *Best Of* .... (EPA)
Vinyl Confessions .... (KIR)
Neil Diamond; *On The Way To The Sky* ....(COL)
Play To Win
Clash; *Cut The Crap* .... (EPI)
Heaven 17; *Best Of-Higher & Higher* .... (VIA)
Play With Fire
Rolling Stones; *Big Hits-High Tides & Green
Grass* .... (AKO)
Hot Rocks-1964-1971 .... (AKO)
Out Of Our Heads .... (AKO)
Singles Collection-London Years .... (AKO)
Play With Toys
Basehead; *Plays With Toys* .... (IMG)
Playground
Another Bad Creation; *Coolin' At The Playground Ya'
Know!* .... (MOT)
MTV Party To Go-#2 .... (TMB)
Playground In My Mind
Clint Holmes; *Rock Artifacts-#2* ....(COL)
Super Hits/'70s-Have A Nice Day-#11 .... (RHI)
Playing Games
Al B. Sure!; *Sexy Versus* .... (WB)
Playing Marbles With Diamonds
Steve Camp; *Doing My Best-#2* .... (SPW)
Playing With Fire
David Foster; *David Foster* .... (ATL)
Lisa Lisa & Cult Jam; *Spanish Fly* .... (COL)
Richard Marx; *Rush Street* .... (CAP)
Sam Riney; *Playing With Fire* .... (SPT)
Playin' With Fire
Lita Ford; *Dangerous Curves* .... (RCA)
Greatest Hits .... (RCA)
Vishugruv; *Vishugruv* .... (RL)
Pop Goes The Weasel
3rd Bass; *Derelicts Of Dialect* .... (DFJ)
Bing Crosby; *Where The Blue Of The Night Meets
The...* .... (BIO)
Boston Pops Orchestra/Arthur Fiedler; *Forever
Fielder* .... (RCA)
Merry Macs; *Small Fry-Capitol Sings Kids Songs...* (CAP)
Porcelain Doll
Tony MacAlpine; *Maximum Security* .... (MER)
Puppet
D.I.; *What Good Is Grief To A God* .... (XXX)
Echo/Bunnymen; *Songs To Learn & Sing* .... (SIR)
Lisa Germano; *Happiness* .... (CAP)
Puppet Dog
Thin White Rope; *Ruby Sea* .... (FRN)
Puppet Girl
Wendy James; *Now Ain't The Time For Your
Tears* .... (DGC)
Puppet Man
5th Dimension; *Greatest Hits On Earth* .... (ARI)
Puppet On A String
Elvis Presley; *ST/Girl Happy* ....(RCA)

Puppet Show
Danger Danger; *Screw It!* .... (EPA)
Puppet Song
Frankie Valli/Four Seasons; *Rarities-#2* .... (RHI)
Puppets
Depeche Mode; *Speak & Spell* .... (SIR)
Puppets' Dance
Jean-Luc Ponty; *Cosmic Messenger* .... (RHI)
Rag Doll
Aerosmith; *Permanent Vacation* ....(GEF)
Frankie Valli/Four Seasons; *25th Anniversary
Collection* .... (RHI)
Anthology .... (RHI)
Billboard Top Rock 'N' Roll Hits-1964 .... (RHI)
Greatest Hits-#2 .... (RHI)
Rainbow Doll
Jimmy Dell; *Get Hot Or Go Home-Vintage
Rockabilly* .... (CMF)
Real Toys
Altered Images; *Happy Birthday* ....(POR)
Red Rubber Ball
Cyrkle; *Even More Nuggets* .... (RHI)
Pop Classics Of The '60s ....(COL)
Red Rubber Ball (collection) ....(COL)
Ride My See Saw
Moody Blues; *Caught Live Plus Five* ....(POL)
In Search Of The Lost Chord ....(POL)
This Is The ....(POL)
Right String But The Wrong Yo-Yo
Carl Perkins; *Original Golden Hits* .... (SUN)
Elvin Bishop; *Big Fun* ....(ALG)
Ring-Around-A-Rosy Rag
Arlo Guthrie; *Alice's Restaurant* .... (RPR)
Rock 'N' Roll Is A Vicious Game
April Wine; *First Glance* ....(CAP)
Rockin' Horse
Bad English; *Bad English* .... (EPI)
Roll Over & Play Dead
Lizzy Borden; *Master Of Disguise* .... (MET)
'Round The World With The Rubber Duck
C.W. McCall; *Greatest Hits* ....(POL)
Row Of Dominoes
Joe Ely; *Lord Of The Highway* .... (HT)
Points West: New Horizons In Country .... (HT)
Sand Castles In The Snow
Public Image, Ltd.; *9* .... (VIA)
Sandbox
Too Much Joy; *Cereal Killers* .... (GIA)
Satan's Doll
Floyd Cramer; *Best Of* ....(RCA)
Satin Doll
Carmen McRae; *Great American Songbook* ...... (ATL)
Count Basie Orchestra; *Warm Breeze* .... (PAB)
Duke Ellington; *1954 Los Angeles Concert* .... (CRS)
Jazz Party ....(COL)
Harry James; *Golden Trumpet Of* ....(LON)
Stephane Grappelli & Jean-Luc Ponty; *Stephane
Grappelli & Jean-Luc Ponty* .... (ACC)
Stylistics; *All-Time Classics* .... (AMH)
See Emily Play
David Bowie; *Pinups* .... (RYK)
Pink Floyd; *Relics* .... (CAP)
Works ....(CAP)
See Saw
Aretha Franklin; *Aretha's Gold* .... (ATL)
Don Covay; *Memphis Soul* .... (WSP)
Pink Floyd; *Saucerful Of Secrets* .... (CAP)
Shabby Doll
Elvis Costello; *Girls Girls Girls* ....(COL)
Elvis Costello/Attractions; *Imperial Bedroom* ....(COL)
Shadow Puppets
Tor Dietrichson; *Global Village* .... (GLO)
Shake Me I Rattle
Cristy Lane; *At Her Best* .... (EMI)
Cristy Lane Is The Name ....(LS)
She's Playing Hard To Forget
Eddy Raven; *Greatest Country Hits* ....(CCB)
Greatest Hits .... (WB)
Shiny Toys
Joni Mitchell; *Dog Eat Dog* ....(GEF)
Show Don't Tell
Rush; *Chronicles* .... (MER)
Presto .... (ATL)

Simon Says
1910 Fruitgum Company; *Best Of-#2* .... (RHI)
Bubblegum's Greatest Hits #2 .... (ACC)
Fabulous Bubblegum Years .... (FFT)
Space Invader
Pretenders; *Pretenders* .... (SIR)
Stop This Game
Cheap Trick; *All Shook Up* .... (EPI)
Tangled Up Puppet
Harry Chapin; *Gold Medal Collection* .... (ELE)
Legends Of The Lost & Found .... (ELE)
Portrait Gallery .... (ELE)
Teddy Bear Song
Barbara Fairchild; *Back To The '70s-Country* ... (DOM)
Country Superstars .... (DOM)
Teddy Bear (Let Me Be Your)
Elvis Presley; *Golden Records-#1* .... (RCA)
In Concert .... (RCA)
Number One Hits .... (RCA)
ST/Loving You .... (RCA)
Top Ten Hits .... (RCA)
Teddy Bears
Barbra Streisand; *ST/Prince Of Tides* .... (COL)
Teddy Bears' Picnic
Anne Murray; *There's A Hippo In My Tub* .... (LIB)
Frank DeVol; *Small Fry-Capitol Sings Kids Songs* (CAP)
They Just Can't Stop It (The Games...)
Spinners; *Best Of* .... (ATL)
Golden Age Of Black Music-1970-1975 .... (ATL)
This Used To Be My Playground
Madonna; *Immaculate Collection* .... (SIR)
Tic-Tac-Toe
Booker T./M.G.s; *Best Of* .... (ATL)
Soul Dressing .... (ATL)
Kyper; *Tic-Tac-Toe* .... (ATL)
Tin Drum
Big Pig; *Bonk* .... (A&M)
Toni Childs; *Union* .... (A&M)
Too Many Games
Maze featuring Frankie Beverly; *Can't Stop The*
Love .... (CAP)
Live In Los Angeles .... (CAP)
Toy Heart
Bill Monroe; *Columbia Historic Edition* .... (COL)
Bill Monroe/Blue Grass Boys;
Essential-1945-1949 .... (COL)
Bill Monroe/Flatt & Scruggs; *Bill Monroe/Flatt &*
Scruggs .... (ROU)
Ricky Skaggs; *Family & Friends* .... (ROU)
Toy Or Treasure
Kay Starr; *Capitol Collectors Series* .... (CAP)
Toy Soldiers
Martika; *Martika* .... (COL)
Toys Are Made For Little Children
Uniques; *Golden Hits* .... (PLN)
Toys In The Attic
Aerosmith; *Classics Live 2* .... (COL)
Live Bootleg .... (COL)
Pandora's Box .... (COL)
Toys In The Attic .... (COL)
R.E.M.; *Dead Letter Office* .... (IRS)
Toytown
Walking Wounded; *New West* .... (CHS)
Toytown People
Fabulous Poodles; *Mirror Stars* .... (EPI)
Tug Of War
Paul McCartney; *Tug Of War* .... (CAP)
Two Can Play That Game
Bobby Brown; *Bobby* .... (MCA)
Remixes In The Key Of B .... (MCA)
Up In My Treehouse
Chet Atkins; *Sails* .... (COL)
Useless Toy
Doggy Style; *Don't Hit Me Up* .... (XXX)
Victim Of The Game
Garth Brooks; *No Fences* .... (LIB)
Restless Heart; *Wheels* .... (RCA)
Trisha Yearwood; *Trisha Yearwood* .... (MCA)
Video Games
Ronnie Jones; *Best Of Lollipop Records* .... (HOT)
Voodoo Doll
Soul Asylum; *Say What You Will* .... (TT)
Voodoo Sex Doll
Crisis Party; *Rude Awakening* .... (MET)

Waiting Game
Swing Out Sister; *Kaleidoscope World* .... (FON)
War Games
Crosby, Stills & Nash; *Allies* .... (ATL)
Paul Young; *Between Two Fires* .... (COL)
We Hide & Seek
Jerry Douglas; *Slide Rule* .... (SH)
Where Do The Children Play
Cat Stevens; *Classics-#24* .... (A&M)
Footsteps In The Dark-#2 .... (A&M)
Tea For The Tillerman .... (A&M)
Where's The Playground Susie
Glen Campbell; *Best Of* .... (LIB)
Whiskey On A Sunday (Puppet Song)
Irish Rovers; *Greatest Hits* .... (MCA)
Wicked Game
Chris Isaak; *Heart Shaped World* .... (RPR)
ST/Wild At Heart .... (POL)
Win, Lose Or Draw
Allman Brothers Band; *Best Of* .... (POL)
Win, Lose Or Draw .... (POL)
World On A String
Neil Young; *Tonight's The Night* .... (RPR)
Yesterday
Beatles; *1962-1966* .... (CAP)
20 Greatest Hits .... (CAP)
Box Set .... (CAP)
Compact Disc E.P. Collection .... (CAP)
Love Songs .... (CAP)
Yesterday...And Today .... (CAP)
Elvis Presley/Imperial Quartet; *On Stage* .... (RCA)
En Vogue; *Funky Divas* .... (EW)
Frank Sinatra; *My Way* .... (RPR)
Paul McCartney; *Tripping The Live Fantastic* .... (CAP)
Placido Domingo; *Domingo Songbook* .... (SMC)
Ray Charles; *His Greatest Hits-#1* .... (DHL)
Supremes; *I Hear A Symphony* .... (MOT)
Wings; *Wings Over America* .... (CAP)
Yo Yo
Billy Joe Royal; *Greatest Hits* .... (COL)
Kinks; *Give The People What They Want* .... (ARI)
You Can't Play With My Yo-Yo
Yo-Yo & Ice Cube; *Make Way For The*
Motherlode .... (EW)

※※※※※※※※※※※※※※※※※※※※※※※※※※※※※※

TRAINS, Hobos, Stations, Subways

2:10 Train
Linda Ronstadt; *Stone Poneys* .... (CAP)
Rising Sons; *Rising Sons* .... (COL)
Steve Gillette; *Steve Gillette* .... (VAN)
Another Journey By Train
Cure; *Standing On A Beach-The Singles* .... (ELE)
Another Train
Pete Morton; *One Big Joke* .... (GRE)
At The Station
Joe Walsh; *But Seriously Folks* .... (ASY)
Baby Likes To Rock It
Tractors; *Tractors* .... (ARI)
Been On A Train
Laura Nyro; *Christmas & The Beads Of Sweat* ...(COL)
Big Railroad Blues
Grateful Dead; *Grateful Dead* .... (WB)
Big Train From Memphis
John Fogerty; *Centerfield* .... (WB)
Black Train
Gun Club; *Fire Of Love* .... (SLS)
Montrose; *Montrose* .... (WB)
Blue Railroad Train
Doc Watson; *Essential* .... (VAN)
Lonesome Road .... (UA)
& Merl Watson: Southbound .... (VAN)
Blue Train
John Coltrane; *Best Of Blue Note-#1* .... (BLN)
Blue Train .... (BLN)
Johnny Cash; *Classic Cash-Hall Of Fame Series* . (MER)
Man-The World-His Music .... (SUN)
Original Johnny Cash .... (SUN)
Story Songs Of The Trains & Rivers .... (SUN)
Bus Stations & Train Yards
Gutterboy; *Gutterboy* .... (MER)

Canadian Railroad Trilogy
Gordon Lightfoot; *Best Of* .... (EMI)
   Gord's Gold .... (RPR)
   Sunday Concert .... (UA)
   United Artists Collection .... (EMI)
   Way I Feel .... (UA)
Casey Jones
Fred McDowell; *& Furry Lewis: When I Lay My Burden
Down* ....(BIO)
Fred McDowelll & Furry Lewis; *When I Lay My Burden
Down* ....(BIO)
Casey's Last Ride
Johnny Cash; *Rainbow* .... (COL)
Catch A Train
Free; *Best Of* .... (A&M)
Caution! (Do Not Stop On Tracks)
Grateful Dead; *Anthem Of The Sun* .... (WB)
Charleston Railroad Tavern
Bobby Bare; *This Is* .... (RCA)
Chattanooga Choo Choo
Billy Strange; *Railroad Man* .... (CRS)
Boston Pops Orchestra/Arthur Fiedler; *Boston Pops
Orchestra/Arthur Fiedler* ....(RCA)
   Greatest Hits Of The '40s ....(RCA)
Glenn Miller; *Best Of* ....(RCA)
   Decade Of The '40s ....(RCA)
   Legendary Performer ....(RCA)
   Memorial 1944-1969 ....(RCA)
   Nipper's Greatest Hits-'40s ....(RCA)
   Pure Gold ....(RCA)
Tuxedo Junction; *Best Of Butterfly Records* ...... (HOT)
   Tuxedo Junction .... (BTF)
Chinese Mule Train
Spike Jones; *Best Of-#2* ....(RCA)
Choo Choo Ch'Boogie
Asleep At The Wheel; *Asleep At The Wheel* .... (EPI)
   Served Live ....(CAP)
Beach Boys; *Ten Years Of Harmony* ....(CAR)
Clifton Chenier; *Alligator Stomp-#2* .... (RHI)
Louis Jordan; *Best Of* ....(MCA)
Quincy Jones; *Birth Of A Band-#2* .... (MER)
Choo Choo Mama
Ten Years After; *Recorded Live* .... (CHR)
   Universal .... (CHR)
Choo Choo Train
Box Tops; *Greatest Hits* .... (RHI)
City Of New Orleans
Arlo Guthrie; *Best Of* .... (WB)
   Hobo's Lullaby .... (RPR)
   Together In Concert w/Pete Seeger .... (RPR)
HARP; *HARP* .... (RWD)
Willie Nelson; *19 Hot Country Requests-#2* .... (EPI)
   City Of New Orleans ....(COL)
   Greatest Country Hits/'80s-#4 ....(COL)
Clack Clack/Oldest Living Son
John Stewart; *Last Campaign* .... (HOM)
Click Clack
Dicky Doo/Don'ts; *45* ....(CLT)
Cocaine Train
Johnny Paycheck; *Banded Together* .... (EPI)
   Everybody's Got A Family .... (EPI)
Coffee Train
David Thomas; *Monster Walks The Winter Lake* ... (TT)
Crazy Train
Ozzy Osbourne; *Blizzard Of Ozz* ....(JET)
   Tribute ....(CBA)
Crescent City Crawl On The St...
Wynton Marsalis; *ST/Tune In Tomorrow...* ....(COL)
Cross-Tie Walker
Creedence Clearwater Revival; *1969* .... (FAN)
   Creedence Country .... (FAN)
   Green River .... (FAN)
Death Train
Beat Farmers; *Glad 'N' Greasy* .... (RHI)
Desperados Waiting For The Train
Guy Clark; *Old No. 1* ....(SH)
Jerry Jeff Walker; *Best Of* ....(MCA)
   Great Gonzos ....(MCA)
   Viva Terlingua ....(MCA)
W. Jennings/W. Nelson/J. Cash/K. Krist.;
Highwayman ....(COL)
Devil's Train
Hank Williams; *Lovesick Blues* ....(POL)
Roy Acuff; *Greatest Hits* ....(COL)

Don't Forget The Trains
Asleep At The Wheel; *Route 66* ....(LIB)
Don't Sleep In The Subway
Frank Sinatra; *Frank Sinatra* .... (RPR)
Petula Clark; *Greatest Hits* ....(CRS)
   Summer Of Love .... (RHI)
Down In The Subway
Gene Pitney; *This Is* ....(OOP)
Down In The Tube Station At Midnight
Jam; *Greatest Hits* .... (POL)
   Snap! .... (POL)
Down There By The Train
Johnny Cash; *American Recordings* .... (AME)
Downtown Train
Mary Chapin Carpenter; *Hometown Girl* ....(COL)
Rod Stewart; *Storyteller/Complete Anthology:
1964-90* .... (WB)
   TT/Selections From Storyteller Anthology .... (WB)
Drill Ye Tarriers Drill
Weavers; *On Tour* .... (VAN)
Drug Train
Cramps; *Bad Music For Bad People* .... (IRS)
Social Distortion; *Social Distortion* ....(EPI)
East Bound Train
Lester Flatt & Earl Scruggs; *Hear The Whistles
Blow* .... (IGR)
End Of The Line
Allman Brothers Band; *Shades Of Two Worlds* .... (EPI)
Bob Wills/Texas Playboys; *24 Great Hits* .... (POL)
Buddy Emmons; *Sings Bob Wills* ....(FF)
J.J. Cale; *Travel-Log* ....(SIL)
Robin Lee; *Heart On A Chain* ....(ATL)
Roxy Music; *Siren* .... (RPR)
Traveling Wilburys; *#1* .... (WIL)
Engine 143
Joan Baez; *#2* .... (VAN)
Engine 999
Hooters; *One Way Home* ....(COL)
Engine #9
Midnight Star; *Headlines* .... (SLR)
Engineers Don't Wave From The Trains...
Earl Scruggs & Tom T. Hall; *Storyteller & The Banjo
Man* ....(COL)
Engine, Engine #9
Roger Miller; *Best Of-#2-King Of The Road* .... (MER)
   Golden Hits .... (SMA)
Every Night When The Sun Goes In
Jo Stafford; *Jo Plus Blues* .... (CRN)
Fast Moving Train
Restless Heart; *Best Of* ....(RCA)
   Fast Moving Train ....(RCA)
First Train To California
Cryan' Shames; *Best Of* ....(BCT)
Flint Hill Special
Flatt & Scruggs; *Golden Era* .... (ROU)
Nitty Gritty Dirt Band; *Will The Circle Be
Unbroken* .... (EMI)
Folsom Prison Blues
Brooks & Dunn & Johnny Cash; *Red Hot +
Country* .... (MER)
Johnny Cash; *At Folsom Prison & San Quentin* ..(COL)
   Billboard Top Country Hits-1968 .... (RHI)
   Classic Cash-Hall Of Fame Series .... (MER)
   Greatest Hits #2 ....(COL)
   Original Golden Hits #1 ....(SUN)
   Superbilly ....(SUN)
Freight Train
Sonny Terry & Brownie McGhee; *Back To New
Orleans* ....(FAN)
Freight Train Be My Friend
John Lee Hooker; *At Newport* ....(VJ)
Freight Train Blues
Bob Dylan; *Bob Dylan* ....(COL)
Roy Acuff; *Columbia Historic Edition* ....(COL)
   Greatest Hits ....(COL)
Freight Train Boogie
Delmore Brothers; *45* .... (STR)
Johnny Otis; *Original Johnny Otis Show-#2* ...... (SAV)
Friendship Train
Gladys Knight/Pips; *All The Great Hits* .... (MOT)
   Anthology .... (MOT)
   Compact Command Performances .... (MOT)
   Motown Superstar Series-#13 ....(MOT)

Funiculi, Funicula
Mario Lanza; *Legendary Tenor* ....(RCA)
Ghost Train
Counting Crows; *August And Everything After* .. (DGC)
Glendale Train
New Riders Of The Purple Sage; *Best Of* ....(COL)
New Riders Of The Purple Sage ....(COL)
Graveyard Train
Creedence Clearwater Revival; *1968/1969* ......(FAN)
Bayou Country ....(FAN)
Hear My Train A'Comin'
Jimi Hendrix; *Band Of Gypsys 2* ....(CAP)
Concerts ....(RPR)
Radio One ....(RYK)
Heartbreak Station
Cinderella; *Heartbreak Station* .... (MER)
Hellbound Train
Savoy Brown; *Greatest Hits-Live In Concert* ..... (TOW)
Hellbound Train ....(PRT)
London Collection-Best Of ....(LON)
Here Comes The Freedom Train
Merle Haggard; *Capitol Collectors Series* ....(CAP)
Hey Porter
Johnny Cash; *First Years* ....(ALL)
Greatest Hits-#2 ....(COL)
Legend ....(SUN)
Original Golden Hits-#1 ....(SUN)
Sun Years ....(RHI)
Vintage Years-1955-1963 ....(RHI)
Hitchcock Railway
Joe Cocker; *Joe Cocker* ....(A&M)
Live ....(CAP)
Jose Feliciano; *All-Time Greatest Hits* ....(RCA)
Hobo
Linda Ronstadt; *Different Drum* ....(CAP)
Retrospective ....(CAP)
Hobo Bill's Last Ride
Merle Haggard/Strangers; *Okie From Muskogee* ..(CAP)
Same Train Different Time ....(CAP)
Hobo Blues
John Lee Hooker; *Best Of* ....(CRS)
I'm John Lee Hooker .... (VJ)
Real Blues Brothers ....(DHL)
Hobo Heaven
Boxcar Willie; *Boxcar Willie* .... (DOT)
Hobo Jungle
Band; *Northern Lights-Southern Cross* ....(CAP)
Hobo Song
John Prine; *Bruised Orange* .... (ASY)
Johnny Cash; *Mystery Of Life* .... (MER)
Hobo & His Mother
Goebel Reeves; *Texas Drifter* ....(GLN)
Hobo, You Can't Ride This Train
Louis Armstrong; *Satchmo-The Musical* .... (MCA)
Hobo's Blues
Paul Simon; *Paul Simon* .... (WB)
Hobo's Lullaby
Arlo Guthrie; *Hobo's Lullaby* ....(RPR)
Goebel Reeves; *Texas Drifter* ....(GLN)
Hobo's Meditation
D. Parton/E. Harris/L. Ronstadt; *Trio* .... (WB)
Honky Tonk Train (Blues)
Emerson, Lake & Palmer; *Works 2* ....(ATL)
Meade Lux Lewis; *Atlantic Blues-Piano* ....(ATL)
Classic Jazz Piano ....(BLU)
Jazz Heritage-Kings & Queens Of Ivory-#1 .....(MCA)
Ridin' In Rhythm ....(DSQ)
Hot Rails To Hell
Blue Oyster Cult; *Career Of Evil* ....(COL)
Extraterrestrial Live ....(COL)
Metal Giants ....(COL)
On Your Feet Or On Your Knees ....(COL)
Tyranny & Mutation ....(COL)
I Been To Georgia On A Fast Train
Willie Nelson; *Me & Paul* ....(COL)

I Walk The Line
Johnny Cash; *At Folsom Prison & San Quentin* ...(COL)
Greatest Hits ....(COL)
Legends ....(DHL)
Memphis Country ....(SUN)
Original Golden Hits-#1 ....(SUN)
Show Time ....(SUN)
Souvenirs Of Music City U.S.A. ....(PLN)
Sun Story ....(RHI)
Sun Years ....(RHI)
Superbilly ....(SUN)
I Want To Work On The Railroad
Debby McClatchy; *Someday Cafe* ....(GRE)
In A Station
Band; *Music From Big Pink* ....(CAP)
It Takes A Lot To Laugh, It Takes A...
Bob Dylan; *Bootleg Series-#1-3* ....(COL)
Highway 61 Revisited ....(COL)
M. Bloomfield/A. Kooper/S. Stills; *Super Session* .(COL)
I'd Be Better Off (In A Pine Box)
Doug Stone; *Doug Stone* ....(EPI)
Greatest Country Hits-'90s-1990 ....(COL)
I'm Moving On
Elvis Presley; *Canadian Tribute* ....(RCA)
From Elvis In Memphis ....(RCA)
Guitar Man ....(RCA)
Memphis Record ....(RCA)
Emmylou Harris; *Last Date* ....(WB)
Profile 2-Best Of ....(WB)
George Thorogood/Destroyers; *Born To Be Bad* . (EMI)
Hank Snow; *60 Years Of Country Music* ....(RCA)
Best Of ....(RCA)
Great Moments At The Grand Ole Opry ....(RCA)
Nipper's Greatest Hits-'50s-#2 ....(RCA)
TT & Other Great Country Hits ....(RCA)
Rolling Stones; *December's Children* .... (AKO)
I've Been Workin' On The Railroad
Mitch Miller; *Sing Along With Mitch* ....(COL)
Pete Seeger; *20 Golden Pieces Of* ....(BLD)
John Henry
Harry Belafonte; *All-Time Greatest Hits* ....(RCA)
At Carnegie Hall ....(RCA)
Legendary Performer ....(RCA)
Little Jimmy Dickens; *Columbia Historic Edition* .(COL)
Odetta; *Essential* ....(VAN)
Greatest Folksingers Of The '60s ....(VAN)
Woody Guthrie; *Immortal-Golden Classics-#2* ....(CLT)
Legendary ....(TRD)
Just Another Whistle Stop
Band; *Stage Fright* ....(CAP)
Just Like This Train
Joni Mitchell; *Court & Spark* ....(ASY)
Kansas City Railroad Blues
Nashville Bluegrass Band; *Waitin' For The Hard Times
To Go* ....(SH)
Keep This Train A-Rollin'
Doobie Brothers; *One Step Closer* ....(WB)
Last Steam Engine Train
John Fahey; *Best Of: 1959-1977* ....(TAK)
Dance Of Death & Other Plantation Faves ......(TAK)
Leo Kottke; *Best* ....(CAP)
Greenhouse ....(CAP)
Very Best Of ....(CAP)
Last Train
Arlo Guthrie; *Best Of* ....(WB)
Robin Trower; & *Jack Bruce: Truce* ....(CHR)
Last Train Done Gone Down
Marty Stuart; *Let There Be Country* ....(COL)
Last Train To Clarksville
Monkees; *Greatest Hits* .... (ARI)
Live 1967 ....(RHI)
Monkees .... (ARI)
Then & Now...Best Of .... (ARI)
Last Train To London
Electric Light Orchestra; *Box Of Their Best* ....(JET)
Discovery ....(JET)
Last Train To Nuremberg
Pete Seeger; *Rainbow Race* ....(OOP)
Let The Train Blow The Whistle
Johnny Cash; *American Recordings* .... (AME)

Locomotion
Grand Funk Railroad; *Billboard Top Rock 'N' Roll Hits-1974* .... (RHI)
  Caught In The Act .... (CAP)
  Hits .... (CAP)
Kylie Minogue; *Kylie* .... (GEF)
Little Eva; *Billboard Top Rock 'N' Roll Hits-1962* (RHI)
  Groove 'N' Grind/'50s-'60s Dance Hits .... (RHI)
  More American Graffiti .... (MCA)
Orchestral Manoeuvres In The Dark; *Best Of* ... (A&M)
  Junk Culture .... (A&M)
Locomotive Breath
Jethro Tull; *20 Years Of-Boxed Set* .... (CHR)
  Aqualung .... (CHR)
  Bursting Out .... (CHR)
  Original Masters .... (CHR)
  Rock Classics .... (KT)
  "M.U."-Best Of .... (CHR)
Lonesome Whistle (I Heard That)
Hank Williams; *24 Greatest Hits-#2* .... (POL)
  40 Greatest Hits .... (POL)
Johnny Cash; *Story Songs Of The Trains & Rivers* (SUN)
Little Feat; *Hoy-Hoy!* .... (WB)
Long Train Runnin'
Doobie Brothers; *Best Of* .... (WB)
  Captain & Me .... (WB)
  Farewell Tour .... (WB)
Love In Vain
Rolling Stones; *Get Yer Ya-Ya's Out* .... (AKO)
  Let It Bleed .... (AKO)
Love Train
O'Jays; *Billboard Top Rock 'N' Roll Hits-1973* ... (RHI)
  Collector's Items .... (PI)
  Greatest Hits .... (PI)
  Philadelphia Classics .... (PI)
Marrakesh Express
Crosby, Stills & Nash; *Crosby, Stills & Nash* ..... (ATL)
  Replay .... (ATL)
  Woodstock Two .... (ATL)
Midnight Flyer
Eagles; *On The Border* .... (ASY)
Midnight Special Train
Joe Turner; *Atlantic R&B 1947-1974-#3-(1955-1958)* .... (ATL)
  Greatest Hits .... (ATL)
Midnight Train To Georgia
Gladys Knight/Pips; *Billboard Top Rock 'N' Roll Hits-1973* .... (RHI)
  Greatest Hits .... (BUD)
  Imagination .... (BUD)
  On & On .... (FFT)
  Radio Active Hits .... (ACC)
  Very Best Of .... (BUD)
Mobile Line
Jim Kweskin/Jug Band; *Greatest Hits* .... (VAN)
  Jim Kweskin/Jug Band .... (VAN)
  Troubadours Of The Folk Era-#3 .... (RHI)
Mobile & K.C. Line
Robert Shaw; *Ma Grinder* .... (ARH)
Mobile/Texas Line
Tom Rush; *Blues Songs & Ballads* .... (FAN)
  Mind Ramblin' .... (PRS)
  Tom Rush .... (FAN)
Morning Train (Nine To Five)
Sheena Easton; *Sheena Easton* .... (EMI)
My Baby Thinks He's A Train
Rosanne Cash; *Hits 1979-1989* .... (COL)
  Seven-Year Ache .... (COL)
My Heart Is A Hobo
Rosemary Clooney; *Sings The Music Of Jimmy Van Heusen* .... (CCJ)
My Train Rolled Up In Texas
Joe Turner; *Things That I Used To Do* .... (PAB)
Mystery Train
Band; *Anthology-#2* .... (CAP)
  Last Waltz .... (WB)
  Moondog Matinee .... (CAP)
  To Kingdom Come-Definitive Collection .... (CAP)
Elvis Presley; *Complete Sun Sessions* .... (RCA)
  For LP Fans Only .... (RCA)
  Sun Sessions .... (RCA)
Neil Young; *Neil & The Shocking Pinks* .... (GEF)
Neville Brothers; *Brother's Keeper* .... (A&M)

Paul Butterfield Blues Band; *Golden Butter* ...... (ELE)
  Paul Butterfield Blues Band .... (ELE)
Sam The Sham/Pharaohs; *Best Of* .... (POL)
M.T.A.
Kingston Trio; *25 Years Non-Stop* .... (XER)
  Best Of .... (CAP)
  Capitol Collectors Series .... (CAP)
  Scarlet Ribbons .... (CAP)
  Very Best Of .... (CAP)
New Delhi Freight Train
Little Feat; *Time Loves A Hero* .... (WB)
New Frisco Train
Washington White; *Mississippi Moaners-1927-1942* .... (YAZ)
New River Train
Doc & Merle Watson; *Remembering Merle* .... (SH)
White Brothers & New Kentucky Colonels; *Live In Sweden* .... (ROU)
Night Time In The Switching Yard
Warren Zevon; *Excitable Boy* .... (ASY)
Night Train
James Brown/Famous Flames; *Soul Shots-Collection Of '60s Soul* .... (RHI)
  ST/Quadrophenia .... (POL)
Jimmy Forrest; *Heart Of The Forest* .... (PAJ)
  Night Train .... (DEL)
Lionel Richie; *Dancing On The Ceiling* .... (MOT)
Paul Revere/Raiders; *Legend Of* .... (COL)
Rickie Lee Jones; *Rickie Lee Jones* .... (WB)
Steve Winwood; *Arc Of A Diver* .... (ISL)
U2; *Island Story 1962-1987 25th Anniversary* .... (ISL)
Night Train To Madrid
Bertram Levy; *That Old Gut Feeling* .... (FF)
Night Train To Memphis
Jerry Lee Lewis; *Rare Tracks* .... (RHI)
  Taste Of Country .... (SUN)
Roy Acuff; *Best Of* .... (CAP)
  Greatest Hits .... (COL)
Nighttrain
Guns N' Roses; *Appetite For Destruction* .... (GEF)
Public Enemy; *Apocalypse 91...The Enemy Strikes Black* .... (DFJ)
  Stanley Son Of Theodore-Music Sampler .... (EPI)
Nobody's Gonna Rain On Our Parade
Kathy Mattea; *Walking Away A Winner* .... (MER)
Oh My Old Train
Lonesome Strangers; *Lonesome Strangers* .... (HT)
Old Black Choo Choo
Rose Maddox; *Rose Of The West Coast Country* (ARH)
Old Toy Trains
Billy Strange; *Railroad Man* .... (CRS)
Glen Campbell; *All-Star Country Christmas* ...... (CAP)
  That Christmas Feeling .... (CAP)
Statler Brothers; *Christmas Present* .... (MER)
One Toke Over The Line
Brewer & Shipley; *Super Hits/'70s-Have A Nice Day-#4* .... (RHI)
  '70s Greatest Rock Hits-#10 .... (PRY)
Only A Hobo
Bob Dylan; *Bootleg Series-#1-3-1961-1989* ...... (COL)
Johnson Mountain Boys; *Blue Diamond* .... (ROU)
Rod Stewart; *Gasoline Alley* .... (MER)
  I Shall Be Released-Songs Of Bob Dylan ...... (RHI)
  Mercury Anthology .... (MER)
  Vintage .... (MER)
Orange Blossom Special
Bill Monroe; *Bean Blossom* .... (MCA)
  Stars Of The Grand Ole Opry 1926-1974 ...... (RCA)
  & Bluegrass Boys-60 Years Of Country .... (RCA)
Charlie Daniels Band; *Fire On The Mountain* ..... (EPI)
  Urban Cowboy-#2 .... (EPI)
Flatt & Scruggs; *Hear The Whistles Blow* .... (GUS)
Gordon Terry; *20 Golden Souvenirs* .... (PLN)
  Disco Country .... (PLN)
Johnny Cash; *Columbia Records 1958-1986* ..... (COL)
  Essential .... (COL)
  Greatest Hits .... (COL)
Nitty Gritty Dirt Band; *Will The Circle Be Unbroken* .... (EMI)
Outre Risque Locomotive
Neneh Cherry; *Raw Like Sushi* .... (VIA)
Paddy On The Railway
Barley Bree; *Castles In The Air* .... (SHA)

Paddy Works On The Erie
Popular Standard; *Out-Of-Print Recording* ....(OOP)
Papa Hobo
Paul Simon; *Paul Simon* ....(COL)
Passenger
Grateful Dead; *Dead Set* .... (ARI)
   Terrapin Station .... (ARI)
Passing Of The Train
Karen Tobin; *Carolina Smokey Moon* .... (ATL)
Passin' Train
Sawyer Brown; *The Boys Are Back* .... (LIB)
Peace Train
10,000 Maniacs; *In My Tribe* .... (ELE)
Cat Stevens; *Classics-#24* .... (A&M)
   Greatest Hits .... (A&M)
   Teaser & The Firecat .... (A&M)
People Get Ready
Aretha Franklin; *Aretha-Lady Soul* .... (ATL)
Impressions; *Greatest Hits* .... (MCA)
   Soul Shots-#5 .... (RHI)
Jeff Beck; *Flash* .... (EPI)
Rod Stewart; *Storyteller-Complete Anthology
1964-1990* .... (WB)
"Petticoat Junction" Theme
Flatt & Scruggs; *20 All-Time Great Recordings* ...(COL)
Original Music; *TV Theme Sing-Along Album* .... (RHI)
Please Take That Train From My Door
Wayne Horvitz; *This New Generation* .... (ELE)
Poverty Train
Laura Nyro; *Eli & The 13th Confession* ....(COL)
Put Me On A Train Back To Texas
Waylon Jennings & Willie Nelson; *Clean Shirt* ... (EPI)
Railroad
Grand Funk Railroad; *Caught In The Act* ....(CAP)
   We're An American Band .... (CAP)
Railroad Bill
Etta Baker; *One-Dime Blues* .... (ROU)
Ramblin' Jack Elliott; *Hard Travelin'* ....(FAN)
   Ramblin' Jack Elliott .... (PRS)
Railroad Blues
New Lost City Ramblers; *Early
Years-1958-1962* .... (FLW)
Norman Blake; *Blackberry Blossom* ....(FF)
Railroad Boy
Joan Baez; *Ballad Book-#2* .... (VAN)
   Joan Baez-#2 .... (VAN)
   Very Best Of .... (VAN)
Railroad Days
Poco; *From The Inside* .... (EPI)
   Very Best Of .... (EPI)
Railroad Lady
Jerry Jeff Walker; *A Man Must Carry On* .... (MCA)
   Gypsy Songman ....(RYK)
Jimmy Buffett; *White Sport Coat & A Pink
Crustacean* .... (MCA)
J.D. Crowe/New South; *My Home Ain't In The Hall Of
Fame* .... (ROU)
Willie Nelson; *Greatest Hits (& Some That Will
Be)* ....(COL)
   To Lefty From Willie ....(COL)
Railroad Song
Lynyrd Skynyrd; *Nuthin' Fancy* .... (MCA)
Railroad Steel
Georgia Satellites; *Georgia Satellites* .... (ELE)
Rainy Night In Georgia
Brook Benton; *Anthology* .... (RHI)
   Atlantic R&B 1947-1974-#6-(1966-1969) ..... (ATL)
   Golden Age Of Black Music-1960-1970 .... (ATL)
   Pick Of .... (FFT)
   Soul Years .... (ATL)
   Today .... (COT)
Hank Williams, Jr.; *14 Greatest Hits* .... (POL)
Sam Moore & Conway Twitty; *Rhythm Country &
Blues* .... (MCA)
Raised By The Railroad Line
Chris LeDoux; *Sounds Of The Western Country* ..(CAP)
Ramblin' Hobo
Doc Watson; *Essential* .... (VAN)
   Old Time Music At Newport .... (VAN)
   & Family/Treasures Untold .... (VAN)
Watson Family; *Watson Family* .... (FLW)
Red Streamliner
Little Feat; *Hoy-Hoy!* .... (WB)
   Time Loves A Hero .... (WB)

Reuben's Train
Doc Watson & Family; *Treasures Untold* .... (VAN)
Ride The Train
Alabama; *Feels So Right* ....(RCA)
Riding On A Railroad
James Taylor; *Mud Slide Slim & The Blue Horizon* (WB)
Riding That Midnight Train
Doc Watson; *Riding That Midnight Train* ....(SH)
Ridin' On The Gravy Train
Nat King Cole; *Jazz Encounters* .... (BLN)
Ridin' The L&N
Bluegrass Cardinals; *Welcome To Virginia* ...... (ROU)
Rock Island
Soundtrack; *Music Man* ....(WB)
Rock Island Line
Johnny Cash; *Story Songs Of The Trains & Rivers* (SUN)
   Sun Years .... (RHI)
   Vintage Years-1955-1963 .... (RHI)
Sonny Terry & Brownie McGhee; *Hootin'* ...... (MUS)
   Jazz Heritage .... (MCA)
Weavers; *At Carnegie Hall* .... (VAN)
   Best Of .... (MCA)
   Greatest Hits .... (VAN)
Rock Island Rocket
Tom Scott; *Best Of* ....(COL)
Tom Scott/L.A. Express; *Tom Cat* .... (EOD)
Rockin' Train
Joe Perry Project; *Let The Music Do The Talking* .(COL)
Rude Boy Train
Desmond Dekker; *Rockin' Steady-Best Of* .... (RHI)
Runaway Train
Dawn Sears; *S* .... (DEC)
Elton John featuring Eric Clapton; *The One* ..... (POL)
John Stewart; *Punch The Big Guy* .... (CYP)
Rosanne Cash; *Greatest Country Hits/'80s-1988* .(COL)
   King's Record Shop ....(COL)
Soul Asylum; *Grace Dancers Union* ....(COL)
Runaway Trains
Tom Petty/Heartbreakers; *Let Me Up (I've Had
Enough)* .... (MCA)
Saint Agnes & The Burning Train
Sting; *Soul Cages* .... (A&M)
Silver Train
Johnny Winter; *Still Alive & Well* ....(COL)
Rolling Stones; *Goats Head Soup* .... (RS)
Six O'Clock Train & A Girl With Green...
John Hartford; *All In The Name Of Love* ....(FF)
Slow Train
Bob Dylan; *Slow Train Coming* ....(COL)
Bob Dylan/Grateful Dead; *Dylan & The Dead* ...(COL)
Slow Train Through Georgia
Norman Blake; *Whiskey Before Breakfast* .... (ROU)
Slow Train To Dawn
The The/Neneh Cherry; *Infected* .... (EPI)
Slow Train To Memphis
Jim Horn; *Work It Out* ....(WB)
Station Man
Fleetwood Mac; *25 Years-The Chain* ....(WB)
   Kiln House ....(WB)
Stop That Train
Bob Marley/Wailers; *Catch A Fire* ....(TUF)
Jerry Garcia Band; *Jerry Garcia Band* .... (ARI)
Peter Tosh; *Mama Africa* ....(EMI)
Streamlined Cannonball
Limeliters; *Alive! In Concert-#1* .... (CRS)
Roy Acuff; *Columbia Historic Edition* ....(COL)
Subway
Alex DeGrassi; *Southern Exposure* ....(WH)
Quicksilver Messenger Service; *Sons Of Mercury* (RHI)
Vic Juris; *Bleecker Street* .... (MUS)
Subway Heart
Massacre; *Killing Time* .... (CEL)
Subway Love
Gary Windo; *Deep Water* .... (AND)
Subway Ride
P. Hofmann/D. Sasson/M.T. Thomas; *Bernstein On
Broadway* ....(COL)
Subway Rider
Pablo Moses; *In The Future* ....(ALG)
Subway Song
Cure; *Boys Don't Cry* .... (ELE)
Subway To Venus
Red Hot Chili Peppers; *Mother's Milk* ....(EMI)

Subway Train
New York Dolls; *New York Dolls* .... (MER)
Night Of The Living Dolls .... (MER)
Take The "A" Train
Bobby McFerrin; *The Voice* .... (ELE)
Dave Brubeck Quartet; *Jazz Goes To College* ...(COL)
Duke Ellington; *20 Golden Pieces Of* .... (BLD)
Greatest Jazz Concert In The World .... (PAB)
Sophisticated Lady .... (BLU)
Duke Ellington & Betty Roche; *Uptown* ....(COL)
Duke Ellington & Billy Strayhorn; *Great Times* .. (RVR)
Duke Ellington & Count Basie Orchestra; *First
Time!-Count Meets The Duke* .... (COL)
Glenn Miller; *Best Of-#2* .... (RCA)
Complete-#6 .... (RCA)
Legendary Performer .... (RCA)
Harry James; *Golden Trumpet Of* .... (LON)
Mel Torme; *Duke Ellington & Count Basie
Songbook* .... (VRV)
Sarah Vaughan; *Jazz-Club Vocal* .... (VRV)
Tamp 'Em Up Solid
Ry Cooder; *Paradise & Lunch* .... (RPR)
Tennessee Choo Choo
Delmore Brothers; *Best Of* .... (STR)
Terrapin Station
Grateful Dead; *Terrapin Station* .... (ARI)
That Same Old Train
Blind Snooks Eaglin; *Legacy Of The Blues-#2* .... (CRS)
That Train Don't Stop Here
Los Lobos; *Kiko* .... (SLS)
That Train Don't Stop Here Anymore
Mike Henderson; *Country Music Made Me Do It* .(RCA)
That Train That Carried My Girl From...
Watson Family; *Watson Family* .... (FLW)
This Train
Big Bill Broonzy; *Sings Folk Songs* .... (FLW)
Bob Marley/Wailers; *One Love* .... (HRT)
Bunny Wailer; *Blackheart Man* .... (MGO)
John Hammond; *John Hammond* .... (VAN)
Kingston Trio; *American Troubadours* .... (PRR)
Peter, Paul & Mary; *Peter, Paul & Mary* ...... (WB)
This Train Revised
Indigo Girls; *Swamp Ophelia* .... (EPI)
Took The Last Train
David Gates; *Goodbye Girl* ....(OOP)
Train
1910 Fruitgum Company; *Bubble Gum Greatest
Hits-#1* .... (ACC)
Bobby McFerrin; *Medicine Music* .... (EMI)
Graham Central Station; *Now Do You Wanna
Dance* ....(OOP)
Leo Sayer; *Just A Boy* ....(OOP)
Mose Allison; *Back Country Suite* .... (PRS)
Roches; *Roches* .... (WB)
Tommy Bolin; *Ultimate* .... (GEF)
Train 45
Bill Monroe; *Bean Blossom* .... (MCA)
Train 45 & A Half
Mike Auldridge; *Critic's Choice* .... (TAK)
Dobro ....(TAK)
Dobro/Blues & Bluegrass ....(TAK)
Train From Kansas City
Shangri-Las; *Golden Hits Of* .... (MER)
Train In The Distance
Paul Simon; *Concert In The Park-August 15 1991* (WB)
Hearts & Bones .... (WB)
Negotiations & Love Songs-1971-1986 .... (WB)
Train In Vain
Clash; *London Calling* .... (EPI)
On Broadway .... (EPI)
Story Of-#1 .... (EPI)
Train Kept A Rollin'
Aerosmith; *Classics Live* ....(COL)
Get Your Wings ....(COL)
Live Bootleg ....(COL)
Pandora's Box ....(COL)
Tiny Bradshaw; *Bles Masters-#5-Jump Blues
Classics* .... (RHI)
Yardbirds; *Greatest Hits-#1-1964-1966* .... (RHI)
Legends Of Rock Guitar-'60s-#1 .... (RHI)
Train Leaves Here This Morning
Eagles; *Eagles* .... (ASY)
Train Man
Bob Seger System; *Ramblin' Gamblin' Man* ...... (CAP)

Train Medley
Boxcar Willie; *45* ....(MAI)
Train No. 1262
Flatt & Scruggs; *Hear The Whistles Blow* ....(GUS)
Train Of Gold
Electric Light Orchestra; *Secret Messages* ....(JET)
Train Of Love
Johnny Cash; *Legend* .... (SUN)
Original Golden Hits-#1 .... (SUN)
Sun Years .... (RHI)
Superbilly .... (SUN)
Trucks Trains & Airplanes ....(GUS)
Neil Young/Crazy Horse; *Sleeps With Angels* .... (RPR)
Train Of Memories
Kathy Mattea; *14 Country Favorites* .... (MER)
Collection Of Hits .... (MER)
Walk The Way The Wind Blows .... (MER)
Train Running Low On Soul Coal
XTC; *Big Express* ....(GEF)
Train Song
Holly Near; *Watch Out* .... (RWD)
Tom Waits; *Big Time* .... (ISL)
Frank's Wild Years .... (ISL)
Train That Carried My Girl From Town
Doc Watson; *Essential* .... (VAN)
Train To Birmingham
Kevin Welch/Overtones; *Western Beat* .... (RPR)
Train To Bombay
Christopher Max; *More Than Physical* .... (EMI)
Train To Johannesburg
Original Cast; *Lost In The Stars* .... (MCA)
Train To Nowhere
Rare Earth; *Get Ready* .... (MOT)
Train To Rhodesia
Big Youth; *Dreadlocks Dread* ....(FL)
Train Wreck On Prom Night
Pajama Slave Dancers; *Blood Sweat & Beers* ..... (RES)
Train & The River
Jimmy Giuffre; *Jimmy Giuffre Three* ....(ATL)
Trains & Boats & Planes
Billy J. Kramer/Dakotas; *Definitive Collection* .... (EMI)
History Of British Rock-#4 .... (RHI)
Dionne Warwick; *Anthology-1962-1971* .... (RHI)
Dionne Warwick ....(EVR)
Greatest Hits ....(EVR)
Hot! Live & Otherwise .... (ARI)
Trains/Leavin' Tennessee
Tasty Licks; *Tasty Licks* .... (ROU)
Traintime
Cream; *Wheels Of Fire* .... (POL)
Trainwreck Of Emotion
Lorrie Morgan; *Leave The Light On* ....(BNA)
Train, Train
Blackfoot; *Legends Of Rock Guitar-'70s* .... (RHI)
Strikes ....(ATC)
Warrant; *Cherry Pie* ....(COL)
Trash Train
Band Of Susans; *Now* .... (RES)
Trolley Song
Judy Garland; *All-Time Greatest Hits* ....(CCB)
Best Of .... (MCA)
Original Broadway Cast; *Meet Me In St. Louis* .. (DRG)
Trouble's Comin' Like A Train
Mark Collie; *Mark Collie* .... (MCA)
Two Moose In A Caboose
Stan Kenton/Orchestra;
Uncollected-#5-1945-1947 .... (HIN)
Two Trains
Little Feat; *Dixie Chicken* .... (WB)
Hoy-Hoy! .... (WB)
Lowell George; *Thanks I'll Eat It Here* .... (WB)
Two Trains Running
Blues Project; *No Time Like The Right Time-Best
Of* .... (RHI)
Projections .... (POL)
Paul Butterfield Blues Band; *East-West* .... (ELE)
Under The Subway
No Face; *Wake Your Daughter Up* ....(RLC)
Wabash Cannonball
Nitty Gritty Dirt Band; *Will The Circle Be
Unbroken* .... (EMI)

Roy Acuff; *Backstage At The Grand Ole Opry* ....(RCA)
   Best Of ....(CAP)
   Columbia Historic Edition ....(COL)
   Essential ....(COL)
   Greatest Hits ....(COL)
Waiting For A Train
  Boz Scaggs; *Boz Scaggs* ....(ATL)
  Jimmie Rodgers; *Early Years-1928-1929* ....(ROU)
   This Is ....(RCA)
Walkin' Down The Road
  Ozark Mountain Daredevils; *Best Of* ....(A&M)
   It'll Shine When It Shines ....(A&M)
   It's Alive ....(A&M)
Watching Me Watching You
  Jethro Tull; *Broadsword & The Beast* ....(CHR)
When The Golden Train Comes Down
  Sons Of The Pioneers; *Columbia Historic Edition* (COL)
When The Midnight Choo Choo Leaves...
  Andrews Sisters; *Best Of-#2* ....(MCA)
  Judy Garland & Fred Astaire; *ST/Easter Parade* ..(SSP)
Whiskey Train
  Procol Harum; *Best Of* ....(A&M)
   Classics-#17 ....(A&M)
   Home ....(MOB)
Wreck Of The Old '97
  Johnny Cash; *At Folsom Prison & San Quentin* ...(COL)
   Man-The World-His Music ....(SUN)
   Original Golden Hits-#3 ....(SUN)
   Story Songs Of The Trains & Rivers ....(SUN)
   Superbilly ....(SUN)

TRASH, Garbage, Junk

Atomic Waste
  Peter Alsop; *Draw The Line* ....(FF)
Before The Trash Truck Comes
  Bob Frank; *Bob Frank* ....(VAN)
Big Jesus Trash Can
  Birthday Party; *Best & Rarest* ....(MIS)
   Collection ....(MIS)
Big Trash
  Thompson Twins; *Big Trash* ....(RE)
Birdman Of Alkatrash
  Strawberry Alarm Clock; *45* ....(MCA)
Cash For Your Trash
  Original Cast; *Ain't Misbehavin'* ....(RCA)
Cosmik Debris
  Frank Zappa; *Apostrophe/Overnight Sensation* ....(RYK)
   You Can't Do That On Stage Anymore ....(BAR)
Crotch Deep Trash
  Soup Dragons; *Lovegod* ....(BIG)
Cupid's Trash Truck
  Lou & Peter Berryman; *Cupid's Trash Truck* ......(COR)
Don't Throw Your Life Away
  Vickie Winans; *The Lady* ....(MCA)
Don't Throw Your Love Away
  Searchers; *Greatest Hits* ....(RHI)
   History Of British Rock-#2 ....(RHI)
Don't Toss Us Away
  Lone Justice; *Lone Justice* ....(GEF)
  Patty Loveless; *Greatest Hits* ....(MCA)
   Honky Tonk Angel ....(MCA)
Down In The Sewer
  Stranglers; *All Live & All Of The Night* ....(EPI)
Dust In The Wind
  Kansas; *Best Of* ....(KIR)
   Point Of Know Return ....(KIR)
   Two For The Show ....(KIR)
Euro-Trash Girl
  Cracker; *Kerosene Hat* ....(VIA)
Fresh Garbage
  Spirit; *Best Of* ....(EPI)
   Spirit ....(EPI)
   Time Circle ....(EPI)
Garbage
  Guy Carawan; *Songs Of Struggle & Celebration* ...(FF)
Garbage Man
  Cramps; *Bad Music For Bad People* ....(IRS)
   Songs The Lord Taught Us ....(IRS)
  Muddy Waters; *Can't Get No Grindin'* ....(CSS)
I Sold My Heart To The Junkman
  Carmen McRae; *Sound Of Silence* ....(ATL)
  Patti LaBelle/Blue Belles; *Super Oldies/'60s-#3* ..(AUF)

I Threw Away The Rose
  George Jones; *20 Golden Pieces Of* ....(BLD)
  Hank Williams, Jr.; *Living Proof-MGM*
   Recordings-1963-1975 ....(MER)
  Lorrie Morgan; *Mama's Hungry Eyes-Merle Haggard*
   Tribute ....(ARI)
  Merle Haggard; *Best Of The Early Years* ....(CCB)
Junk
  Chet Atkins; *Pickin' My Way-In Hollywood*
   Alone ....(MOB)
   RCA Years ....(RCA)
  Paul McCartney; *CD Gift Set* ....(CAP)
   McCartney ....(CAP)
Junk Cars
  Mac McAnally; *Live & Learn* ....(MCA)
Junk Culture
  O.M.D.; *Junk Culture* ....(A&M)
Junk Mail
  Circle Jerks; *Gig* ....(REL)
   Golden Shower Of Hits ....(AVE)
Junk Male
  Five Thirty; *Bed* ....(ATC)
Last Worthless Evening
  Don Henley; *End Of The Innocence* ....(GEF)
My Sweet Hunk O' Trash
  Louis Armstrong; *Jazz Heritage-Louis With Guest*
   Stars ....(MCA)
Nuclear Waste
  Tuff Darts; *Tuff Darts* ....(SIR)
One Man's Trash
  John McCutcheon; *What's It Like* ....(ROU)
(Our Love) Don't Throw It All Away
  Bee Gees; *Greatest* ....(RSO)
Piece Of Crap
  Neil Young/Crazy Horse; *Sleeps With Angels* .....(RPR)
Please Mr. Junkman
  Penguins; *Oldies* ....(DTN)
Po' White Trash
  White Trash; *White Trash* ....(ELE)
Put Me In The Trash
  Mick Jagger; *Wandering Spirit* ....(ATL)
Sarah Cynthia Sylvia Stout
  Shel Silverstein; *Dr. Demento 20th Anniversary*
   Collection ....(RHI)
   Dr. Demento's Greatest Novelty-#4-1970s ....(RHI)
   Where The Sidewalk Ends ....(COL)
Sewer Pipe Dream
  Close Lobsters; *Foxheads Stalk This Land* ....(ENI)
Singalong Junk
  Paul McCartney; *CD Gift Set* ....(CAP)
   McCartney ....(CAP)
Space Junk
  Devo; *EZ Listening Disc* ....(RYK)
   Q: Are We Not Men? A: We Are Devo! ....(WB)
Stray Cat Strut
  Stray Cats; *Best Of-Rock This Town* ....(EMI)
   Built For Speed ....(EMI)
   Rock The First-#4 ....(SAN)
Take It Back
  Cream; *Disraeli Gears* ....(POL)
  Reba McEntire; *It's Your Call* ....(MCA)
Take Out The Garbage
  Fowler Brothers; *Hunter* ....(FOS)
Talkin' Trash
  Chico Freeman; *Tradition In Transition* ....(ELE)
  Tom Principato; *Smokin'* ....(POW)
That's Cool, That's Trash
  Kingsmen; *Best Of* ....(RHI)
Throw It Away
  Joe Jackson; *Look Sharp* ....(A&M)
Throw That Beat In The Garbage Can
  B-52's; *Mesopotamia* ....(WB)
Throwaway
  Mick Jagger; *Primitive Cool* ....(COL)
Throwing It All Away
  Genesis; *Invisible Touch* ....(ATL)
   Live-The Way We Walk-#1-The Shorts ....(ATL)
Total Trash
  Sonic Youth; *Daydream Nation* ....(BF)
Trash
  Alice Cooper; *Trash* ....(EPI)
  Berlin; *Count Three & Pray* ....(GEF)
  Bobs; *Bobs* ....(KAL)
  Mondo Rock; *Mondo Rock Chemistry* ....(ATL)

New York Dolls; *Live In NYC-1975* .... (RES)
  New York Dolls .... (MER)
Roxy Music; *Manifesto* .... (RPR)
Trash Can Charlie
  Billy Goat; *Bush Roaming Mammals* .... (TR)
Trash Can City
  Bob Florence; *Jewels* .... (DCO)
Trash Can King
  Nick Seeger; *Sail On Flying Dutchman* ....(BIO)
Trash City
  Kik Tracee; *No Rules* ....(RCA)
  Transvision Vamp; *Pop Art* .... (UN)
Trash Man
  Jimi Hendrix; *Midnight Lightning* .... (RPR)
Trash Park
  T. Lavitz/Bad Habitz; *T. Lavitz/Bad Habitz* ...... (IMA)
Trash Planet
  Stewart/Gaskin; *Spin* ....(RYK)
Trash Talkin'
  Albert Collins; *Complete Imperial Recordings* .... (EMI)
Trash Train
  Band Of Susans; *Now* .... (RES)
Trash Truck
  Tad; *8-Way Santa* .... (SP)
Trashcan Oil Drum
  Pussy Galore; *Right Now* ....(CRL)
Trashed
  Black Sabbath; *Born Again* .... (WB)
Trashing All The Loves Of History
  Snakefinger; *Greener Postures* .... (RAL)
Trashmen
  Phantom Opera; *Phantom Opera* ....(NAL)
Trashpickin'
  Ben Vaughn; *Blows Your Mind* .... (RES)
Trashy Dog
  Steve Cropper/Albert King/Pops Staples; *Jammed*
  Together .... (STX)
Trashy Lady
  Neon Judgement; *Horny As Hell* .... (PIA)
Trashy Women
  Confederate Railroad; *Confederate Railroad* ..... (ATL)
White Trash
  Bad Religion; *How Could Hell Be Any Worse* .... (EPT)
  Bellamy Brothers; *Crazy From The Heart* .... (MCA)
  Orchestral Manoeuvres In The Dark; *Junk*
  Culture .... (A&M)
  Red Kross; *Born Innocent* .... (FRN)
  Steve Cash; *White Mansions* .... (A&M)
White Trash Song
  Steve Young; *Honky-Tonk Man* .... (ROU)
  Solo/Live .... (WAT)
White Trash Wife
  Exene Cervenka; *Old Wives' Tales* .... (RHI)
White Trash With Cash
  Southgang; *Group Therapy* ....(CHS)
Who's Gonna Take Your Garbage Out
  Ernest Tubb & Loretta Lynn; *Ernest Tubb & Loretta*
  Lynn ....(MCA)
  More Great Country Duets .... (MSP)
  Story ....(MCA)
Your Cash Ain't Nothin' But Trash
  Clovers; *Down In The Alley* .... (ATL)
  Huey Lewis/News; *Four Chords & Several Years*
  Ago .... (ELE)
  Steve Miller Band; *The Joker* ....(CAP)

TRAVELING, Movin' On, Running, Walking

See Also: BUS, CARS, JOME, PRISON, REBELS,
ROAD, TAXI, TRUCKS

---

4 Miles
  Take 6; *Join The Band* .... (RPR)
50 Ways To Leave Your Lover
  Paul Simon; *Greatest Hits Etc.* ....(COL)
  Still Crazy After All These Years ....(COL)
  & Garfunkel; *Concert In New York* .... (WB)
96 Miles To Birmingham
  Dick Silveras; *Negro Folk Songs & Ballads* .... (STO)
Across The Great Divide
  Band; *Band* ....(CAP)
  Rock Of Ages-#1 & 2 ....(CAP)

Alabama Bound
  Doc & Merle Watson; *Ballads From Deep Gap* . (VAN)
  Leadbelly/Woody Guthrie/Cisco Houston; *Leadbelly*
  Sings Folk Songs ....(FLW)
Alabama Getaway
  Grateful Dead; *Go To Heaven* .... (ARI)
Alabamy Bound
  Tom Rush; *Blues Songs Ballads* .... (PRS)
  Tom Rush ....(FAN)
All Revved Up With No Place To Go
  Meatloaf; *Bat Out Of Hell* .... (EPI)
Another Journey By Train
  Cure; *Standing On A Beach-The Singles* .... (ELE)
Are You Gonna Go My Way
  Lenny Kravitz; *Are You Gonna Go My Way* ..... (VIA)
Arkansas Time Traveler
  Star-Spangled Washboard Band; *Collector's Item* ... (FF)
Arkansas Traveler
  Albert Lee; *Speechless* .... (MCA)
  Floyd Cramer; *Country Gold* .... (STE)
  Mark O'Connor; *Championship Years* .... (CMF)
  Michelle Shocked; *Arkansas Traveler* .... (MER)
  Sam Hinton; *Newport Folk Festival '63* .... (VAN)
Around The World In A Day
  Prince/Revolution; *Around The World In A Day* ..(PAI)
Around The World (In 80 Days)
  Boston Pops Orchestra/Arthur Fiedler; *Greatest*
  Hits/'50s-#2 ....(RCA)
  Frank Sinatra; *Come Fly With Me* .... (CAP)
  Roger Williams; *Greatest Hits* .... (MCA)
Astral Traveller
  Yes; *Time & A Word* .... (ATL)
  Yesterdays .... (ATL)
Baby Elephant Walk
  Henry Mancini; *All-Time Greatest Hits-#1* ....(RCA)
  Pure Gold ....(RCA)
Baby Step Back
  Gordon Lightfoot; *Gord's Gold-#2* ....(WB)
"Back To The Future" Theme
  Cincinnati Pops Orchestra/Erich Kunzel; *Star Tracks*
  II .... (TLR)
Band On The Run
  Paul McCartney; *Tripping The Live Fantastic* ...(CAP)
  Paul McCartney/Wings; *All The Best* .... (CAP)
  Band On The Run ....(CAP)
  Greatest ....(CAP)
  Over America ....(CAP)
Beat It On Down The Line
  Grateful Dead; *Grateful Dead* .... (WB)
  Steal Your Face .... (GRD)
  Jesse Fuller; *Lone Cat* .... (GTJ)
Before They Make Me Run
  Rolling Stones; *Some Girls* ....(RS)
Big Log
  Robert Plant; *Principle Of Moments* .... (EPR)
Blazin' Your Own Trail Again
  R.E.O. Speedwagon; *You Can Tune A Piano...* .... (EPI)
Boogie Back To Texas
  Asleep At The Wheel; *10* .... (EPI)
  Swinging Best Of .... (EPI)
Born Ready
  Jesse Hunter; *A Man Like Me* ....(BNA)
Born To Be Wild
  Steppenwolf; *16 Greatest Hits* .... (MCA)
  Billboard Top Rock 'N' Roll Hits-1968 .... (RHI)
  Live ....(MCA)
  Steppenwolf ....(MCA)
  Vintage Music-Oldies-'60s-#9 & 10 ....(MCA)
Born To Move
  Creedence Clearwater Revival; *1970* ....(FAN)
  Chronicle-#2 ....(FAN)
  Pendulum ....(FAN)
Born To Run
  Bruce Springsteen; *Born To Run* ....(COL)
  Chimes Of Freedom ....(COL)
  Bruce Springsteen/E Street Band;
  Live-1975-1985 ....(COL)
  Emmylou Harris; *Cimarron* .... (WB)
  Profile 2-Best Of .... (WB)

Born To Wander
Rare Earth; *20 Hard-To-Find Motown*
Classics-#2 .... (MOT)
   Ecology .... (MOT)
   Hard-To-Find Motown Classics-#2 .... (MOT)
   Motown Superstar-#16 .... (MOT)
Break My Stride
Matthew Wilder; *I Don't Speak The Language* .... (PRI)
Cadillac Walk
Mink De Ville; *Mink De Ville* .... (CAP)
   Savoire Faire .... (CAP)
Can I Run
L7; *Hungry ~ or Stink* .... (SLS)
Caravan
Duke Ellington; *Best Of* .... (CAP)
   Money Jungle .... (BLN)
Ella Fitzgerald; *Montreux '75* .... (PAB)
Johnny Mathis; *In A Sentimental Mood-Sings*
Ellington ....(COL)
Van Morrison; *Moondance* .... (WB)
Van Morrison/Band; *Last Waltz* .... (WB)
Wynton Marsalis; *Marsalis Standard Time-#1* ....(COL)
Caravan Of Love
Isley/Jasper/Isley; *Caravan Of Love* .... (CBA)
Caravan To Midnight
Robin Trower; *Caravan To Midnight* .... (CHR)
Caribbean Queen
Billy Ocean; *Greatest Hits* .... (JVA)
   Suddenly .... (JVA)
Carry Me Back
Statler Brothers; *Best Of* .... (MER)
   Carry Me Back .... (MER)
Carry Me Back To Old Virginny
Jerry Lee Lewis; *Doin' Just Fine* .... (ACC)
   Ole Tyme Country Music .... (SUN)
   Sunday Down South .... (SUN)
Chariots Of Fire
Vangelis; *ST/Chariots Of Fire* .... (POL)
   Themes .... (POL)
Colorado Trail
Ian Tyson; *Ian Tyson* ....(COL)
Salli Terri; *Songs Of The American Land* ...... (ANG)
Come Go With Me
Del Vikings; *1956 Audition Tapes* ....(CLT)
   Billboard Top R&B Hits-1957 .... (RHI)
   Oldies But Goodies-#3 .... (OSR)
   ST/American Graffiti .... (MCA)
   ST/Stand By Me .... (ATL)
Come On Let's Go
Los Lobos; *And A Time To Dance* .... (SLS)
   Just Another Band From East L.A. .... (SLS)
   ST/La Bamba .... (SLS)
Ritchie Valens; *Best Of* .... (RHI)
   Oldies But Goodies-#4 .... (OSR)
   Story .... (DF)
Come Running
Van Morrison; *Moondance* .... (WB)
Come Running Back
Dean Martin; *Greatest Hits* .... (RPR)
Comin' Home
Bob Seger/Silver Bullet Band; *The Distance* ..... (CAP)
Delaney & Bonnie; *Best Of* .... (RHI)
   Crossroads .... (POL)
Delaney & Bonnie & Friends/Eric Clapton; *On*
Tour ....(ATC)
Lynyrd Skynyrd; *First & Last* .... (MCA)
   Golden & Platinum .... (MCA)
   Southern By The Grace Of God-Tribute .... (MCA)
Nutmegs; *Greatest Hits* ....(CLT)
   Harlem Holiday-New York R&B-#7 ....(CLT)
Crawling To The U.S.A.
Elvis Costello; *ST/Americathon* ....(COL)
   Taking Liberties ....(COL)
Cross-Tie Walker
Creedence Clearwater Revival; *1969* .... (FAN)
   Creedence Country .... (FAN)
   Green River .... (FAN)
Cruisin'
Alabama; *The Touch* .... (RCA)
Michael Nesmith; *Never Stuff* .... (RHI)

Smokey Robinson; *Compact Command*
Performances .... (MOT)
   Motown Love Songs .... (MOT)
   Motown Story: First 25 Years .... (MOT)
   Where There's Smoke .... (MOT)
Ted Nugent; *Weekend Warriors* .... (EPI)
Days Are Numbers (The Traveller)
Alan Parsons Project; *Best Of-#2* .... (ARI)
   Vulture Culture .... (ARI)
Destination Anywhere
Commitments; *ST/Commitments* .... (MCA)
Destination Unknown
Electric Light Orchestra; *Afterglow* .... (EPI)
Detour Ahead
Billie Holiday; *Billie's Blues* .... (BLN)
Herb Ellis; *Roll Call* .... (JST)
Herb Ellis/Others; *After You've Gone* .... (CCJ)
Sarah Vaughan; *Complete On Mercury-#3* ...... (MER)
Stan Getz; *Essential-Getz Songbook* .... (VRV)
Detour (Devil Took A)
Patti Page; *Golden Hits* .... (MER)
Did You Ever See A Dream Walking
Bing Crosby; *Crosby Classics* ....(COL)
Hal Kemp/Skinnay Ennis; *Uncollected-#2 & #3* .. (HIN)
Do You Wanna Get Away
Shannon; *Do You Wanna Get Away* .... (MIR)
Don't Get Around Much Anymore
Duke Ellington; *I Like Jazz-Essence Of* ....(COL)
Duke Ellington/Orchestra; *Nipper's Greatest*
Hits-'40s-#1 ....(RCA)
Etta James; *Second Time Around* .... (CSS)
Harry Connick, Jr.; *ST/When Harry Met Sally* ....(COL)
Johnny Mathis; *In A Sentimental Mood-Sings*
Ellington ....(COL)
Mel Torme; *Duke Ellington & Count Basie*
Songbook .... (VRV)
Mose Allison; *Greatest Hits* .... (PRS)
Nat King Cole; *Unforgettable* .... (CAP)
Natalie Cole; *Unforgettable* .... (ELE)
Shelby Lynne; *Tough All Over* .... (EPI)
Don't Run (Come Back To Me)
K.C./Sunshine Band; *45* .... (EPI)
Don't Turn Around
Ace Of Base; *The Sign* .... (ARI)
Don't Walk Away
Jade; *Jade To The Max* .... (GIA)
Down The Line
Buddy Holly; *Rock & Roll Collection* .... (MCA)
Jerry Lee Lewis; *Golden Hits* .... (SMA)
   Milestones .... (RHI)
   Original .... (SUN)
   Original Golden Hits-#1 .... (SUN)
Ease On Down The Road
Grateful Dead; *Go To Heaven* .... (ARI)
Original Cast; *ST/The Wiz* .... (ATL)
Eight More Miles To Louisville
Eric Weissberg; *Dueling Banjos From "Deliverance"* (WB)
Mike Auldridge; *Dobro/Blues & Bluegrass* ......(TAK)
Reno & Smiley; *1983 Collector's Edition-#3* .... (GUS)
   Best Of .... (STR)
Embryonic Journey
Hot Tuna; *Splashdown* .... (RLX)
Jefferson Airplane; *2400 Fulton Street-Anthology* (RCA)
   Surrealistic Pillow ....(RCA)
   Worst Of ....(RCA)
Every Little Step
Bobby Brown; *Dance!...Ya Know It!* .... (MCA)
   Don't Be Cruel .... (MCA)
Every Mother's Son
Traffic; *John Barleycorn Must Die* .... (UA)
Every Step Of The Way
John Waite; *Mask Of Smiles* .... (EMI)
Everybody's Talkin'
Nilsson; *ST/Forrest Gump* .... (EPX)
   ST/Midnight Cowboy .... (EMI)
   TT & Other Hits ....(RCA)
Willie Nelson; *Best Of Willie* ....(RCA)
   Sweet Memories ....(RCA)
Exodus
Bob Marley/Wailers; *Babylon By Bus* .... (TUF)
   Exodus .... (TUF)
   Legend .... (TUF)
Fantastic Voyage
Coolio; *S* .... (TMB)

Lakeside; *Club Epic* ....(EPI)
  Fantastic Voyage ....(SLR)
Farther Along
  Byrds; *Byrds (collection)* ....(COL)
  Elvis Presley; *Million-Dollar Quartet* ....(RCA)
  Flying Burrito Brothers; *Farther Along-Best Of* .. (A&M)
  Rose Maddox; *Rose Of The West Coast Country* (ARH)
Fearless
  Pink Floyd; *Meddle* ....(HAR)
  Works ....(CAP)
Fifteen Miles To Birmingham
  Happy & Artie Traum/Others; *Mud Acres* .....(ROU)
Find Your Way Back
  Jefferson Starship; *Modern Times* ....(GRU)
  Starship; *Greatest Hits-Ten Years & Change*
  1979-91 ....(RCA)
Five Miles To Texas
  Stockton & Johnson; *Born By The River* ....(OOP)
Follow You, Follow Me
  Genesis; *And Then There Were Three* ....(ATL)
  Three Sides Live ....(ATL)
Food Phone Gas Lodging
  Charlie King; *Food Phone Gas Lodging* ....(FF)
Get Away
  Bobby Brown; *Bobby* ....(MCA)
Get Back
  Beatles; *1967-1970* ....(CAP)
  20 Greatest Hits ....(CAP)
  Box Set ....(CAP)
  Let It Be ....(CAP)
  Past Masters-#2 ....(CAP)
  Reel Music ....(CAP)
  Rock 'N' Roll Music-#2 ....(CAP)
  Paul McCartney; *Tripping The Live Fantastic* ....(CAP)
Get Out Of Denver
  Bob Seger; *Live Bullet* ....(CAP)
  Seven ....(CAP)
  Dave Edmunds; *Get It* .... (SS)
Getaway
  Earth, Wind & Fire; *Best Of-#1* ....(COL)
  Spirit ....(COL)
  Kiss; *Dressed To Kill* ....(CAS)
  Originals ....(CAS)
  Rossington-Collins Band;
  Anytime-Anyplace-Anywhere ....(MCA)
Girl From Ipanema
  Antonio Carlos Jobim; *Antonio Carlos Jobim* .. (WB)
  Compact Jazz ....(VRV)
  Ella Fitzgerald; *Ella A Nice* ....(PAB)
  Montreux '75 ....(PAB)
  Pablo Today-Ella Embraces A.C. Jobim ....(PAB)
  Stan Getz & Astrud Gilberto; *Cruisin'-1964* .....(INC)
  Getz/Gilberto ....(VRV)
Go Now
  Moody Blues; *History Of British Rock-#5* ....(RHI)
  Moody Blues ....(LON)
  Wings; *Over America* ....(CAP)
Go Your Own Way
  Fleetwood Mac; *25 Years-The Chain* .... (WB)
  Greatest Hits .... (WB)
  Live .... (WB)
  Rumours .... (WB)
Going Back To Alabama
  Asa Martin; *Dr. Ginger Blue* ....(ROU)
Going Back To Alabam'
  Alan Munde & Country Gazette; *Keep On Pushing* . (FF)
Going Back To Big Sur
  Johnny Rivers; *Anthology-1964-1977* .... (RHI)
  Touch Of Gold ....(IMP)
Going Back To Birmingham
  Ten Years After; *Universal* ....(CHR)
Going Back To Detroit
  Platters; *Double Gold* ....(MCR)
Going Back To Dublin
  Eric Bogle; *Something Of Value* ....(PHO)
Going Back To Florida
  Billie & De De Pierce; *New Orleans Jazz* ..... (ARH)
Going Back To Indiana
  Sawyer Brown; *Sawyer Brown* ....(CAP)
Going Back To Iuka
  Albert King; *Lovejoy* ....(STX)
  Koko Taylor/Blues Machine; *Live From Chicago-With*
  The Queen ....(ALG)

Going Back To Liverpool
  Jackie Lomax; *Is This What You Want?* ....(CAP)
Going Back To Louisiana
  Delbert McClinton; *Live From Austin* ....(ALG)
  Joey Farr; *45* ....(FAI)
Going Back To Memphis
  Muddy Waters; *Muddy Brass & Blues* .... (CSS)
Going Back To Miami
  Blues Brothers; *Best Of* ....(ATL)
  Made In America ....(ATL)
  Wayne Cochran; *Soul Shots-#6* ....(RHI)
Going Back To New Orleans
  Dr. John; *Going Back To New Orleans* ....(WB)
Going Back To Okinawa
  Ry Cooder; *Get Rhythm* .... (WB)
Going Back To Tampa
  Roy Bookbinder; *Going Back To Tampa* ....(FF)
Going Back To Tennessee
  Tracy Nelson; *Doin' It My Way* .... (ADE)
Going Back To Virginia
  Jim & Jessie McReynolds; *Music Among Friends* (ROU)
Going Down To Liverpool
  Bangles; *All Over The Place* ....(COL)
  Greatest Hits ....(COL)
Going Down To Mexico
  ZZ Top; *First Album* .... (WB)
  Six Pack .... (WB)
Going Down To Mississippi
  Phil Ochs; *Toast To Those Who Are Gone* .... (RHI)
Going Down To Texas
  Shel Silverstein; *Great Conch Train Robbery* ....(FF)
Going Home
  Buddy Guy; *Left My Blues In San Francisco* ... (CSS)
  Dire Straits; *Live-Alchemy* .... (WB)
  Elvis Presley; *Collector's Gold* .... (RCA)
  Fats Domino; *Legendary Masters* .... (UA)
  Kenny G; *Live* ....(ARI)
  Little Richard; *Greatest Hits* ....(TRP)
  Osmonds; *Greatest Hits* ....(POL)
  Rolling Stones; *Aftermath* ....(LON)
  Santana; *Lotus* ....(COL)
Going Home To Louisiana
  Chris Thomas; *The Beginning* .... (ARH)
Going Mobile
  Who; *Who's Next* ....(MCA)
Going To Brazil
  Motorhead; *1916* ....(WTG)
Going To California
  John Lee Hooker; *Sings John Lee Hooker* ....(EVR)
  Led Zeppelin; *Led Zeppelin (collection)* ......(ATL)
  #4 ....(ATL)
Going To Chicago Blues
  Count Basie; *Essential-#1* ....(COL)
  Jimmy Rushing; *Essential* ....(VAN)
  Joe Williams; *Jazz Singers* ....(PRS)
  Lambert, Hendricks & Ross; *Twisted-Best Of* .... (RHI)
  Lowell Fulson; *Let's Go Get Stoned* ....(KNT)
Going To Georgia
  Johnson Mountain Boys; *At The Old Schoolhouse* (ROU)
  Stanley Brothers; *Shadows Of The Past* ....(COP)
Going To Louisiana
  John Lee Hooker; *Berkeley Blues Festival* .... (ARH)
  That's Where It's At ....(STX)
Going To Mexico
  Steve Miller Band; *Anthology* ....(CAP)
  Best Of-1968-1973 ....(CAP)
  #5 ....(CAP)
Going To New York
  Climax Blues Band; *FM/Live* .... (SIR)
  Jimmy Reed; *At Carnegie Hall* .... (VJ)
  Best Of ....(CRS)
  Greatest Hits-#2 ....(KNT)
  Legend-The Man .... (VJ)
  Siegel-Schwall Band; *Best Of* ....(VAN)
  Siegel-Schwall Band ....(VAN)
Going To Newport
  Frankie Laine; *16 Greatest Hits* ....(TRP)
Going To St. Louis
  Yank Rachell/Others; *Chicago Style* ....(DEL)
Going Up The Country
  Canned Heat; *Best Of* ....(EMI)
  ST/1969 ....(POL)
  ST/Woodstock ....(ATL)
  Summer Of Love ....(RHI)

Goin' Away Blues
Eric Clapton; *From The Cradle* .... (DUC)
Goin' Back
Byrds; *20 Essential Tracks From The Box Set* .....(COL)
Byrds ....(COL)
Dusty Springfield; *Golden Hits* ....(PHI)
Neil Young; *Comes A Time* ....(RPR)
Nils Lofgren; *Best Of* ....(A&M)
Night After Night ....(A&M)
Nils Lofgren ....(RYK)
Goin' Back To Alabama
Asa Martin; *Dr. Ginger Blue* ....(ROU)
Kenny Rogers; *Share Your Love* ....(LIB)
Goin' Back To Florida
John Hammond; *Best Of* ....(VAN)
Lightnin' Hopkins; *Lightnin' Hopkins* ....(FLW)
Roots Of ....(FLW)
Goin' Back To Indiana
Jackson 5; *Anthology* ....(MOT)
Goin' Back To Indiana ....(MOT)
Greatest Hits ....(MOT)
Third Album ....(MOT)
Goin' Back To Oakland
Isaac Scott; *S.F. Blues Festival-#2* .... (SSM)
Tom McFarland; *Travelin' With The Blues* ...... (ARH)
Goin' Back To Old Kentucky
New Grass Revival; *Festival Tapes* .... (FF)
Goin' Back To Paris
Bill Collins; *Charmin' Billy* ....(CHT)
Goin' Back To Texas
Bobby Bare; *Biggest Hits* ....(COL)
R.C. Smith; *I Have To Paint My Face* .... (ARH)
Goin' Down Louisiana
Blues Project; *No Time Like The Right Time-Best
Of* .... (RHI)
Goin' Down To Muskogee
Jim Pepper; *Comin' & Goin'* .... (AND)
Goin' Down To Tampa
Jeff Warner & Jeff Davis; *Wilder Joy-Trad. American
Folk Songs* .... (FF)
Goin' Home
Alvin Lee/Ten Years After; *ST/Woodstock* ......(OOP)
Alvin Lee/Ten Years Later; *Ride On* .... (RSO)
Goin' To Cairo
Joel Mabus; *Settin' The Woods On Fire* .... (FF)
Goin' To Chattanooga
Ralph Willis; *East Coast Blues* .... (CLT)
Goin' To Dallas To See My Pony Run
Lightnin' Hopkins; *Blues In My Bottle* .... (BV)
Drinkin' In The Blues-Golden Classics-#1 .... (CLT)
Goin' To Kansas City
Furry Lewis; *Shake 'Em On Down* .... (FAN)
Jimmy Witherspoon; *'Spoon Concerts* .... (FAN)
Goin' To Las Vegas
Suicide; *1/2 Alive* .... (ROI)
Goin' To Memphis
Carl Perkins; *Best Of-Jive After 5-1958-1978* .... (RHI)
Goin' To New Orleans
Rockin' Tabby Thomas; *Rockin' With The Blues* (MSO)
He Walked On Water
Randy Travis; *No Holdin' Back* .... (WB)
High Time We Went
Joe Cocker; *Classics-#4* .... (A&M)
Greatest Hits ....(A&M)
Joe Cocker ....(A&M)
Live ....(A&M)
(I Am A) Lonesome Fugitive
Roy Buchanan; *Roy Buchanan* .... (POL)
I Don't Wanna Walk Around With You
Ramones; *All The Stuff (& More)-#1* .... (SIR)
Ramones .... (SIR)
I Don't Want To Walk Without You
Barry Manilow; *One Voice* .... (ARI)
Harry James; *Best Of The Big Bands* ....(COL)
Rosemary Clooney; *For The Duration* .... (CCJ)
I Get Around
Beach Boys; *Best Of* ....(CAP)
Billboard Top Rock 'N' Roll Hits-1964 .... (RHI)
Endless Summer ....(CAP)
Made In The U.S.A. ....(CAP)
ST/Good Morning Vietnam .... (A&M)
I Gotta Move
Kinks; *Kinda Kinks* .... (RHI)
Kinks-Size .... (RHI)

Ted Nugent; *Scream Dream* .... (EPI)
I Ran (So Far Away)
A Flock Of Seagulls; *A Flock Of Seagulls* .... (JVA)
Best Of .... (JVA)
I Walk Alone
Los Lobos; *The Neighborhood* .... (SLS)
Marty Robbins; *All-Time Greatest Hits* ....(COL)
Greatest Hits-#3 ....(COL)
Lifetime Of Song-1951-1982 ....(COL)
I Want To Walk You Home
Fats Domino; *Billboard Top R&B Hits-1959* ..... (RHI)
Greatest Hits ....(MCA)
My Blue Heaven-Best Of-#1 .... (EMI)
I Wonder As I Wander
Gary Morris; *Every Christmas* .... (LIB)
Mormon Tabernacle Choir; *This Land Is Your
Land* ....(COL)
Peter, Paul & Mary; *Holiday Celebration* .... (WB)
Philadelphia Orchestra/Eugene Ormandy; *Sleigh
Ride!-Classic Christmas Favorites* ....(RCA)
Sandi Patti; *Gift Goes On* .... (WOR)
I Won't Let You Walk Away
Cleve Francis; *Walkin'* .... (LIB)
If You Go
Jon Secada; *Heart, Soul...* .... (SBK)
In Walked Bud
Art Blakey & Thelonius Monk; *Great Moments In
Jazz* ....(ATL)
Thelonius Monk; *Best Of* .... (BLN)
Genius Of Modern Music-#1 .... (BLN)
Into The Great Wide Open
Tom Petty/Heartbreakers; *Into The Great Wide
Open* .... (MCA)
It Keeps You Running
Carly Simon; *Another Passenger* .... (ELE)
Doobie Brothers; *Best Of* .... (WB)
ST/FM .... (MCA)
ST/Forrest Gump .... (EPX)
Takin' It To The Streets .... (WB)
It's A Long Way There
Little River Band; *Backstage Pass* .... (CAP)
Greatest Hits ....(CAP)
Little River Band ....(CAP)
It's A Short Walk From Heaven To Hell
John Schneider; *Country Classics-#5-1985-1986* (MCA)
Greatest Hits ....(MCA)
Tryin' To Outrun The Wind .... (MCA)
I'll Be Back
Beatles; *Hard Day's Night* .... (CAP)
Love Songs ....(CAP)
'65 ....(CAP)
I'll Follow The Sun
Beatles; *Box Set* ....(CAP)
For Sale ....(CAP)
Love Songs ....(CAP)
'65 ....(CAP)
I'm Alabammy Bound
Lonnie Donegan; *Golden Hits* ....(OOP)
I'm Going Back To Alabama
Jerry Douglas; *Fluxology* .... (ROU)
I'm Going Home
Ten Years After; *ST/Woodstock* .... (ATL)
I'm Gonna Be (500 Miles)
Proclaimers; *ST/Benny & Joon* .... (BMG)
Sunshine On Leith .... (CHR)
I'm Moving On
Elvis Presley; *Canadian Tribute* ....(RCA)
From Elvis In Memphis ....(RCA)
Guitar Man ....(RCA)
Memphis Record ....(RCA)
Emmylou Harris; *Last Date* .... (WB)
Profile 2-Best Of .... (WB)
George Thorogood/Destroyers; *Born To Be Bad* . (EMI)
Hank Snow; *60 Years Of Country Music* ....(RCA)
Best Of ....(RCA)
Great Moments At The Grand Ole Opry ....(RCA)
Nipper's Greatest Hits-'50s-#2 ....(RCA)
TT & Other Great Country Hits ....(RCA)
Rolling Stones; *December's Children* .... (AKO)
I'm Walking The Dog
Webb Pierce; *Best Of* .... (MCA)
Golden Hits .... (PLN)

I'm Walkin'
Fats Domino; *Billboard Top R&B Hits-1957* ..... (RHI)
  Greatest Hits .... (MCA)
  My Blue Heaven-Best Of-#1 .... (EMI)
Joey, Joey, Joey
Al Jarreau; *1965* ....(BAJ)
Broadway Cast; *Most Happy Fella* ....(RCA)
Judy Garland; *Live* ....(CAP)
  One & Only ....(CAP)
Journey
Boston; *Don't Look Back* ....(EPI)
Jimmy Cliff; *Power & The Glory* ....(COL)
Small Faces; *Ogdens' Nut Gone Flake* ....(SSP)
Journey From Eden
Steve Miller Band; *Anthology* ....(CAP)
  Recall The Beginning ....(CAP)
Journey From Mariabronn
Kansas; *Kansas* .... (KIR)
  Two For The Show .... (KIR)
Journey Man
Jethro Tull; *Heavy Horses* ....(CHR)
Journey Through The Past
Neil Young; *Time Fades Away* ....(RPR)
Journey To A Star
Judy Garland; *Collector's Items-1936-1945* ..... (MCA)
Journey To Capricorn
Stan Kenton; *Journey Into Capricorn* ....(CW)
Just A Closer Walk With Thee
Jim Nabors; *16 Most Requested Songs* ....(COL)
Kid Thomas; *& His New Orleans Jazz Band* ..... (ARH)
Patsy Cline; *Best Of* ....(CCB)
  Here's ....(MCA)
Preservation Hall Jazz Band; *Best Of* ....(COL)
Tom Rush; *Blues Songs & Ballads* ....(FAN)
Just Walk In My Shoes
Gladys Knight/Pips; *Anthology* ....(MOT)
  Motown Legends ....(MOT)
Just Walkin' In The Rain
Johnny Ray; *16 Most Requested Songs/'50s-#1* ...(COL)
  Best Of ....(COL)
  Greatest Hits ....(SSP)
Keep On Chooglin'
Creedence Clearwater Revival; *1968-1969* ..... (FAN)
  Bayou Country ....(FAN)
  Chooglin' ....(FAN)
  Live In Europe ....(FAN)
Keep On Movin'
Soul II Soul/Caron Wheeler; *Keep On Movin'* .... (VIA)
Keep On Running
Spencer Davis Group; *Best Of* .... (EMI)
  Best Of ....(RHI)
  History Of British Rock-#4 ....(RHI)
  Island Story-1962-1987-25th Anniversary .... (ISL)
Stevie Wonder; *Music Of My Mind* ....(MOT)
Keep On Truckin'
Eddie Kendricks; *12 #1 Hits From The '70s* .... (MOT)
  20/20 ....(MOT)
  At His Best ....(MOT)
  Motown Superstar Series-#19 ....(MOT)
  Motown's Biggest Pop Hits ....(MOT)
  Soul Hits/'70s-#11 ....(RHI)
Hot Tuna; *Burgers* ....(GRU)
  Final Vinyl ....(GRU)
  "Howling Blues" & Other Hits ....(RCA)
Keep On Walkin'
CeCe Peniston; *Finally* ....(A&M)
Kiss Me, I'm Gone
Marty Stuart; *Love And Luck* ....(MCA)
Leaving Kansas City
George Jackson; *Sweet Down Home Delta Blues* (AMB)
Leaving Las Vegas
Sheryl Crow; *Tuesday Night Music* ....(A&M)
Leaving Of Liverpool
Clancy Brothers; *Greatest Hits* .... (VAN)
Leaving On A Jet Plane
John Denver; *Greatest Hits-#1* ....(RCA)
  Rhymes & Reasons ....(RCA)
Kendalls; *Super Hits Country-1970s* ....(GUS)
Peter, Paul & Mary; *1700* ....(WB)
  Ten Years Together ....(WB)
Leaving This Town
Beach Boys; *Holland* ....(CAR)
  In Concert ....(RPR)

Leavin' Memphis, Frisco Bound
Jesse Fuller; *Frisco Bound* ....(ARH)
  Lone Cat ....(GTJ)
Let's Go
Cars; *Candy-O* ....(ELE)
  Greatest Hits ....(ELE)
Eurythmics; *Revenge* ....(RCA)
Nitty Gritty Dirt Band; *Let's Go* ....(LIB)
Wang Chung; *Mosaic* ....(GEF)
Let's Go Trippin'
Beach Boys; *Surfin' U.S.A.* ....(CAP)
Dick Dale/Del-Tones; *Beach Classics* ....(DHL)
  Greatest Hits ....(CRS)
  Tigers Loose ....(RHI)
Like A Rolling Stone
Bob Dylan; *At Budokan* ....(COL)
  Biograph ....(COL)
  Greatest Hits ....(COL)
  Highway 61 Revisited ....(COL)
  More American Graffiti-#4 ....(MCA)
  Self-Portrait ....(COL)
Bob Dylan/Band; *Before The Flood* ....(COL)
Jimi Hendrix Experience; *Jimi Hendrix Experience* (RPR)
  ST/Jimi Plays Monterey ....(RPO)
Long May You Run
Neil Young; *Decade* ....(RPR)
  Unplugged ....(RPR)
Stills/Young Band; *Long May You Run* ....(RPR)
Long Way
Dan Fogelberg; *Souvenirs* .... (FM)
Long Way Around
Chris Whitley; *Living With The Law* ....(COL)
Linda Ronstadt; *Hand Sown* ....(CAP)
  Retrospective ....(CAP)
Louisiana Bound
Big Joe Williams; *Shake Your Boogie* .... (ARH)
Love Can Run Faster
Robert Palmer; *Double Fun* .... (ISL)
Love Walked In
Chet Baker; *With Strings* ....(COL)
Frank Sinatra; *Reprise Collection* ....(RPR)
  Sinatra Swings ....(RPR)
Sarah Vaughan; *Complete On
  Mercury-#2-1956-1957* .... (MER)
Love Walks In
Van Halen; *5150* .... (WB)
"Mahogany" Theme (Do You Know Where...)
Diana Ross; *20/20* ....(MOT)
  Anthology ....(MOT)
  Diana Ross ....(MOT)
  Evening With ....(MOT)
  Greatest Hits ....(MOT)
Mama, I'm Coming Home
Ozzy Osbourne; *No More Tears* .... (EPA)
Many A Mile
Buffy Sainte-Marie; *Best Of* .... (VAN)
  Many A Mile ....(VAN)
Many A Mile To Freedom
Traffic; *Low Spark Of High-Heeled Boys* .... (ISL)
Many Rivers To Cross
Jimmy Cliff; *In Concert* ....(RPR)
  Reggae Spectacular ....(A&M)
  ST/Harder They Come ....(MGO)
  Wonderful World Beautiful People ....(A&M)
Linda Ronstadt; *Prisoner In Disguise* ....(ASY)
UB40; *Labour Of Love* ....(A&M)
Miles Away
Basia; *Greenpeace/Rainbow Warriors* ....(GEF)
  Time & Tide ....(EPI)
Fleetwood Mac; *Mystery To Me* ....(RPR)
Jackson Browne; *I'm Alive* ....(ELE)
Marc Cohn; *Marc Cohn* ....(ATL)
Winger; *In The Heart Of The Young* ....(ATL)
Most Likely You'll Go Your Way & I'll...
Bob Dylan; *Biograph* ....(COL)
  Blonde On Blonde ....(COL)
Bob Dylan/Band; *Before The Flood* ....(COL)
Move It
Chantays; *45* ....(MCA)
Move On
Abba; *Abba Album* ....(ATL)
An Emotional Fish; *An Emotional Fish* ....(ATL)
Bernadette Peters & Mandy Patinkin; *Collector's
Sondheim* ....(RCA)

Santana; *Inner Secrets* ....(COL)
Moving On
Dells; *Oh What A Night* ....(VJ)
Sweet Honey In The Rock; *Other Side* ....(FF)
Triumph; *Just A Game* ....(RCA)
Movin'
Brass Construction; *Brass Construction* ....(UA)
Psychefunkapus; *Psychefunkapus* ....(ATL)
R.E.O. Speedwagon; *Ridin' The Storm Out* ....(EPI)
Wes Montgomery; *Movin' Along* ....(RVR)
Movin' On
Bad Company; *10 From 6* ....(ATL)
Bad Company ....(SS)
Movin' Out
Aerosmith; *Aerosmith* ....(COL)
Classics Live 2 ....(COL)
Pandora's Box ....(COL)
Billy Joel; *Greatest Hits-#1&2-1973-1985* ....(COL)
Stranger ....(COL)
Sonny Rollins; *Movin' Out* ....(PRS)
Movin' & Groovin'
Duane Eddy; *16 Greatest Hits* ....(JAM)
Compact Command Performances ....(MOT)
My Daddy Was A Travelin' Man
Brenda Kaye Perry; *45* ....(MRC)
My Shoes Keep Walking Back To You
Ray Price; *Essential-1951-1962* ....(COL)
Greatest Hits ....(COL)
Mystic Traveler
Dave Mason; *Let It Flow* ....(COL)
Never Going Back Again
Fleetwood Mac; *25 Years-The Chain* ....(WB)
Live ....(WB)
Rumours ....(WB)
No One To Run With
Allman Brothers; *Where It All Begins* ....(EPI)
No Particular Place To Go
Chuck Berry; *Best Of The Best Of* ....(GUS)
Chess Box ....(CSS)
No Place To Go
Charlie Daniels Band; *Fire On The Mountain* .....(EPI)
Howlin' Wolf; *Moanin' In The Moonlight* ....(CSS)
No Place To Run
UFO; *No Place To Run* ....(CHR)
North Carolina Bound
Connie & Babe/Backwoods Boys; *Backwoods
Bluegrass* ....(ROU)
Nowhere Bound
Diamond Rio; *Diamond Rio* ....(ARI)
Nowhere To Run
Esther Phillips; *A Way To Say Goodbye* ....(MUS)
Isley Brothers; *This Old Heart Of Mine* ....(MOT)
J.J. Cale; *Naturally* ....(MCA)
Martha Reeves/Vandellas; *Anthology* ....(MOT)
Greatest Hits ....(MOT)
Motown Story-First 25 Years ....(MOT)
Motown Superstar Series-#11 ....(MOT)
ST/Sound Of "Murphy Brown" ...(MCA)
Pete Townshend & Ronnie Lane; *Rough Mix* ...(MCA)
Santana; *Shango* ....(COL)
Oh, Susanna
James Taylor; *Sweet Baby James* ....(WB)
Myron Floren; *Best Of The Wurstfest* ....(RAN)
Myron Floren ....(RAN)
Old Folks At Home
Mormon Tabernacle Choir; *Songs Of The Civil War & S.
Foster Fav.* ....(SMC)
Paul Robeson; *A Man & His Beliefs-Golden
Classics-#2* ....(CLT)
On The Road Again
Aerosmith; *Pandora's Box* ....(COL)
Bob Dylan; *Bringing It All Back Home* ....(COL)
Grateful Dead; *Reckoning* ....(ARI)
Tom Rush; *Classic Rush* ....(ELE)
Tom Rush ....(ELE)
Willie Nelson; *Greatest Country Hits/'80s-1980* ..(COL)
Greatest Hits & Some That Will Be ....(COL)
Hot Country Rock-#1 ....(EPI)
ST/Forrest Gump ....(EPX)
ST/Honeysuckle Rose ....(COL)
On The Run
Balaam & The Angel; *Live Free Or Die* ....(VIA)
Blackfoot; *Tomcattin'* ....(ATC)
Electric Light Orchestra; *Discovery* ....(JET)

Judas Priest; *Point Of Entry* ....(COL)
Marshall Crenshaw; *Good Evening* ....(WB)
Pink Floyd; *Dark Side Of The Moon* ....(CAP)
Gift Set ....(CAP)
Prophet; *Cycle Of The Moon* ....(MEG)
One More Mile
Clarence "Gatemouth" Brown; *One More Mile* ..(ROU)
Paul Butterfield Blues Band; *Golden Butter* ......(ELE)
One Step Closer
Doobie Brothers; *Best Of-#2* ....(WB)
One Step Closer ....(WB)
Highway 101; *Highway 101-featuring Paulette
Carlson* ....(WB)
One Step Closer To You
Gavin Christopher; *One Step Closer* ....(MAN)
One Step Up
Bruce Springsteen; *Tunnel Of Love* ....(COL)
One Way Ticket To Memphis
Bobby King & Terry Evans; *Rhythm Blues Soul &
Grooves* ....(ROU)
Ostrich Walk
Bob Crosby Orchestra; *Bob Crosby Orchestra* ....(HIN)
Bob Scobey's Frisco Band; *Direct From San
Francisco* ....(GTJ)
Pack It Up
Pretenders; *II* ....(SIR)
UFO; *Obsession* ....(CHR)
Papa Was A Rollin' Stone
Temptations; *20-20* ....(MOT)
25 #1 Hits From 25 Years ....(MOT)
All The Million-Sellers ....(MOT)
Anthology ....(MOT)
Billboard Top Rock 'N' Roll Hits-1972 ....(RHI)
Compact Command Performances ....(MOT)
Pascagoula Run
Jimmy Buffett; *Boats Beaches Bars & Ballads* ...(MGR)
Off To See The Lizard ....(MCA)
Peaceful Journey
Fat Larry's Band; *Sweet Soul Music-Stax Groups* .(STX)
Heavy D./Boys; *Peaceful Journey* ....(UT)
Planet Caravan
Pantera; *Far Beyond Driven* ....(EW)
Polly-Wolly-Doodle
Leon Redbone; *Live!* ....(PRR)
On The Track ....(WB)
Mance Lipscomb; *#3-Texas Songster In A Live
Performance* ....(ARH)
Pete Seeger/Woody Guthrie/Cisco Houston; *Lonesome
Valley* ....(FLW)
Poor Wayfaring Stranger
Jim Hendricks; *Appalachian Memories-Front Porch
Favor.* ....(BEN)
Jo Stafford; *American Folk Songs* ....(CRN)
Ramble On
Led Zeppelin; *II* ....(ATL)
Remasters ....(ATL)
Led Zeppelin (collection) ....(ATL)
Ramble On Rose
Grateful Dead; *Europe '72* ....(WB)
What A Long Strange Trip It's Been ....(WB)
Rambler
Molly Hatchet; *Beatin' The Odds* ....(EPI)
Rambling On My Mind
Eric Clapton; *Crossroads* ....(POL)
John Mayall/Bluesbreakers & Eric Clapton;
Bluesbreakers ....(LON)
Robert Johnson; *Complete Recordings* ....(COL)
King Of The Delta Blues Singers ....(COL)
Savoy Brown; *Slow Train* ....(RLX)
Ramblin'
Marshall Tucker Band; *Greatest Hits* ....(CPC)
Marshall Tucker Band ....(AJK)
Where We All Belong ....(AJK)
Ramblin' Boy
Tom Paxton; *Greatest Folksingers Of The 60's* ...(VAN)
Newport Folk Festival-1963 ....(VAN)
Ramblin' Boy ....(ELE)
Troubadours Of The Folk Era-#2 ....(RHI)
Ramblin' Fever
Merle Haggard; *Greatest Hits* ....(MCA)
More Of The Best ....(RHI)
Ramblin' Fever ....(MCA)
Ramblin' Gamblin' Man
Bob Seger; *Live Bullet* ....(CAP)

Ramblin' Hobo
Doc Watson; *Essential* .... (VAN)
  Old Time Music At Newport .... (VAN)
  & Family/Treasures Untold .... (VAN)
Watson Family; *Watson Family* .... (FLW)
Ramblin' In My Shoes
Hank Williams, Jr.; *THe Pressure Is On* .... (W/C)
Ramblin' Man
Allman Brothers Band; *Best Of* .... (POL)
  Billboard Top Rock 'N' Roll Hits-1973 .... (RHI)
  Brothers & Sisters .... (POL)
  Decade Of Hits-1969-1979 .... (POL)
  Dreams .... (POL)
  Road Goes On Forever .... (POL)
  Rock Classics .... (KT)
  South's Greatest Hits .... (CPC)
  Wipe The Windows .... (CPC)
Hank Williams; *16 Great Hits* .... (EVR)
  24 Greatest Hits .... (POL)
  40 Greatest Hits .... (POL)
Hank Williams, Jr.; *Rowdy* .... (W/C)
  ST/Your Cheatin' Heart .... (SSP)
Ramblin' Rose
Chuck Berry; *Greatest Hits* .... (EVR)
Hank Snow; *Collector's Series-#2* .... (RCA)
Jerry Lee Lewis; *Golden Cream Of The Country* . (SUN)
Nat King Cole; *Best Of-#1* .... (CAP)
  Memories Are Made Of This .... (CAP)
  Ramblin' Rose .... (CAP)
Ramblin' Round Your City
Linda Ronstadt; *Linda Ronstadt* .... (CAP)
  Retrospective .... (CAP)
Odetta; *Greatest Songs Of Woody Guthrie* .... (VAN)
Refugee
Tom Petty/Heartbreakers; *Damn The Torpedoes* (MCA)
  Pack Up The Plantation-Live .... (MCA)
U2; *War* .... (ISL)
Remember (Walking In The Sand)
Aerosmith; *Greatest Hits* ....(COL)
  Night In The Ruts ....(COL)
Shangri-Las; *Girl Groups-Story Of A Sound* .... (MOT)
  Oldies But Goodies-#6 .... (OSR)
  Original Golden Hits Of The Great Groups ..... (SSS)
  ST/Goodfellas .... (ATL)
Road Less Travelled
Preston Reed; *Road Less Travelled* .... (FF)
Road Runner (I'm A)
Fleetwood Mac; *Penguin* .... (RPR)
Humble Pie; *Eat It* .... (A&M)
  Smokin' .... (A&M)
Junior Walker/All-Stars; *Anthology* .... (MOT)
  Greatest Hits .... (MOT)
  Motown Superstar Series-#5 .... (MOT)
  Shotgun .... (MOT)
Roam
B-52's; *Cosmic Thing* .... (RPR)
Rollin' Home
Eric Andersen; *Best Of* .... (VAN)
Peter, Paul & Mary; *Album 1700* .... (WB)
Rollin' On
Doobie Brothers; *Brotherhood* .... (CAP)
Rollin' Stone
Humble Pie; *Rock On* .... (A&M)
  Rockin' The Fillmore .... (A&M)
Mose Allison; *Best Of* .... (ATL)
Muddy Waters; *Best Of* .... (CSS)
  Best Of Chess Blues .... (CSS)
Room To Move
John Mayall; *Best Of* .... (POL)
  Turning Point .... (POL)
'Round The World With The Rubber Duck
C.W. McCall; *Greatest Hits* .... (POL)
"Route 66" Theme
Nelson Riddle/Orchestra; *Beat Generation* ...... (RHI)
  Television's Greatest Hits-#2 .... (TVT)
Run Baby Run (Back Into My Arms)
Tremeloes; *Best Of* .... (RHI)
Run For Your Life
Beatles; *Box Set* .... (CAP)
  Rubber Soul .... (CAP)
Run From Tears
Crosby, Stills & Nash; *CSN* .... (ATL)
Run Joe
Louis Jordan; *Best Of* .... (MCA)

Neville Brothers; *Fiyo On The Bayou* .... (A&M)
Run Joey Run
David Geddes; *Super Hits/'70s-Have A Nice
Day-#15* .... (RHI)
Run Like A Deer
Beers Family Sings; *Seasons Of Peace* ....(BIO)
Run Like A Thief
Bonnie Raitt; *Home Plate* ....(WB)
J.D. Souther; *J.D. Souther* .... (ASY)
Run Like An Antelope
Phish; *Lawn Boy* .... (ELE)
Run Like Hell
Pink Floyd; *Delicate Sound Of Thunder* ....(COL)
  Knebworth-The Album ....(POL)
  The Wall ....(COL)
Roger Waters; *The Wall Live In Berlin* .... (MER)
Run Little Rabbit
John & Jamie Hartford; *Hartford & Hartford* .... (FF)
Run Possum Run!
Southern Rail; *Roadwork* .... (TUR)
Run Through The Jungle
Creedence Clearwater Revival; *1970* .... (FAN)
  Chronicle .... (FAN)
  Cosmo's Factory .... (FAN)
  More Creedence Gold .... (FAN)
Run To Me
Angela Winbush; *Sharp* .... (MER)
Animotion; *Animotion* .... (MER)
Bee Gees; *Gold-#1* .... (RSO)
  Here At Last .... (RSO)
Dionne Warwick & Barry Manilow; *Run To Me* . (ARI)
Run To Mexico
Babys; *Head First* .... (CHR)
Run To My Lovin' Arms
Jay/Americans; *Greatest Hits* .... (EMI)
Run To You
Bryan Adams; *Music For The Miracle* .... (EPA)
  Reckless .... (A&M)
Run With The Fox
Yes; *Yesyears* .... (ATC)
Run With The Wolf
Blackmore's Rainbow; *Rainbow Rising* .... (OYS)
Runaround
Fleetwoods; *Best Of* .... (RHI)
Van Halen; *For Unlawful Carnal Knowledge* ......(WB)
Runner
Manfred Mann's Earth Band; *Somewhere In
Afrika* .... (ARI)
Running Back
Eddie Money; *Playing For Keeps* ....(COL)
Emotions; *Chronicle* .... (STX)
  Sunshine .... (STX)
Freddy Fender; *Before The Next Teardrop Falls* . (MCA)
Thin Lizzy; *Jailbreak* .... (MER)
Running Back To You
Vanessa Williams; *Comfort Zone* .... (WIN)
Running Bear
Johnny Preston; *45s On CD-#1-1956-1959* ..... (MER)
  Billboard Top Rock 'N' Roll Hits-1960 .... (RHI)
  Cruisin'-1960 .... (INC)
Sonny James; *All-Time Country Classics-#1* ......(CAP)
Running Down To Cuba
John Townley/Press Gang; *Chesapeake Sailor's
Companion* .... (ADE)
Running Free
Iron Maiden; *Iron Maiden* ....(CAP)
  Live After Death-World Slavery Tour ....(CAP)
  Maiden Japan ....(CAP)
Running Like The Wind
Marshall Tucker Band; *Running Like The Wind* ...(WB)
Running On
Steve Winwood; *Refugees Of The Heart* .... (VIA)
Running On Empty
Jackson Browne; *Running On Empty* .... (ASY)
Running On Ice
Billy Joel; *The Bridge* ....(COL)
Running Scared
Roy Orbison; *All-Time Greatest Hits-#1&2* ...... (MON)
  For The Lonely-Anthology-1956-1965 .... (RHI)
  In Dreams-Greatest Hits .... (VIA)
  & Friends-Black & White Night .... (VIA)
Running Up That Hill
Kate Bush; *Hounds Of Love* .... (EMI)
  The Whole Story .... (EMI)

Kate Bush & David Gilmour; *Secret Policeman's Third Ball-The Music* .... (VIA)
Running Wild
Benny Goodman Quartet; *Bluebird Sampler* ..... (BLU)
Judas Priest; *Hell Bent For Leather* .... (COL)
  Unleashed In The East ....(COL)
Roxy Music; *Flesh & Blood* .... (RPR)
Sam Cooke; *Golden Sound* .... (TRP)
Soup Dragons; *Hotwired* .... (BL)
Running With The Night
Lionel Richie; *Back To Front-Greatest Hits* ...... (MOT)
  Can't Slow Down .... (MOT)
  Music For The Miracle .... (EPA)
Runnin'
Earth, Wind & Fire; *All 'N All* ....(COL)
Mason Ruffner; *Gypsy Blood* .... (EPA)
Santana; *Marathon* ....(COL)
Steve Wariner; *I Should Be With You* .... (MCA)
Runnin' Away
Sly/Family Stone; *Anthology* .... (EPI)
  There's A Riot Goin' On .... (EPI)
Runnin' Back To Saskatoon
Guess Who; *Track Record-Collection* ....(RCA)
Runnin' Blue
Doors; *Soft Parade* .... (ELE)
  Weird Scenes Inside The Gold Mine .... (ELE)
Runnin' For Your Lovin'
Brothers Johnson; *Classics-#11* .... (A&M)
  Right On Time .... (A&M)
Runnin' With The Devil
Van Halen; *Van Halen* .... (WB)
Runnin' With The Wind
Eddie Rabbitt; *Jersey Boy* ....(CAP)
  Ten Years Of Greatest Hits .... (CAP)
Run, Red Run
Coasters; *45* .... (ATL)
Run, Run, Run
Concrete Blonde; *Free* .... (IRS)
Diana Ross/Supremes; *Anthology* .... (MOT)
  Greatest Hits-#1&2 .... (MOT)
Jo Jo Gunne; *Super Hits/'70s-Have A Nice Day-#8* (RHI)
Supremes; *Greatest Hits-#1* .... (MOT)
Third Rail; *Even More Nuggets* .... (RHI)
  Rock Artifacts-#3-From The Vaults .... (COL)
Who; *Happy Jack* .... (MCA)
  Magic Bus .... (MCA)
Run, Samson, Run
Neil Sedaka; *All-Time Greatest Hits* .... (RCA)
  Pure Gold ....(RCA)
  Sings His Greatest Hits ....(RCA)
Run, Woman, Run
Tammy Wynette; *Anniversary-20 Years Of Hits* ... (EPI)
  Biggest Hits .... (EPI)
Secret Journey
Police; *Ghost In The Machine* .... (A&M)
Sentimental Journey
Dinah Shore; *Sentimental Journey-Capitol's Great Ladies Of Song* ....(CAP)
Doris Day; *Sings 22 Great Songs-Original Big Band* .... (HIN)
Hal McIntyre/Orchestra; *Nipper's Greatest Hits-'40s-#2* ....(RCA)
Les Brown; *Best Of The Big Bands* ....(COL)
Serengeti Long Walk
Stewart Copeland; *Rhythmatist* .... (A&M)
Serengeti Walk
Dave Grusin; *Collection* .... (GRP)
  Out Of The Shadows ....(GRP)
Dave Grusin & NY/LA Dream Band; *Dave Grusin & NY/LA Dream Band* .... (GRP)
Shuffle Off To Buffalo
Hal Kemp; *Best Of The Big Bands* .... (COL)
Original Broadway Cast; *42nd Street* ....(RCA)
Side By Side
Kay Starr; *Greatest Hits* .... (CCB)
Mitch Miller; *16 Most Requested Songs* ....(COL)
Silent Running
Klaus Schulze; *Trancefer* .... (GRM)
Mike/Mechanics; *Mike/Mechanics* .... (ATL)
Skippin' In The Mississippi Dew
John Hartford; *Anthology* .... (FF)
  Mark Twang .... (FF)
New Grass Revival; *Fly Through The Country* .....(FF)

So You Ran
Orion The Hunter; *Orion The Hunter* ....(POR)
Someday Soon
Chris LeDoux; *Rodeo Songs Old & New* .... (LIB)
Ian & Sylvia; *Greatest Hits* .... (VAN)
  Northern Journey .... (VAN)
Journey; *Departure* ....(COL)
Judy Collins; *Colors Of The Day-Best Of* .... (ELE)
  Who Knows Where The Time Goes .... (ELE)
Moe Bandy; *Greatest Hits* ....(COL)
  Rodeo Romeo ....(COL)
Suzy Bogguss; *Aces* ....(CAP)
Spanish Caravan
Doors; *Best Of* .... (ELE)
  Live At The Hollywood Bowl .... (ELE)
  Waiting For The Sun .... (ELE)
  Weird Scenes Inside The Goldmine .... (ELE)
"Star Trek" Theme
Cincinnati Pops Orchestra/Erich Kunzel; *Star Tracks II* .... (TLR)
State Of Mind
Clint Black; *No Time To Kill* ....(RCA)
Steal Away
Billy Joe Royal; *Greatest Hits* ....(COL)
Johnnie Taylor; *Chronicle* .... (STX)
  Super Hits .... (STX)
Joy; *Joy* ....(FAN)
Nils Lofgren; *Classics-#13* .... (A&M)
  Nils .... (A&M)
Poco; *Rose Of Cimarron* .... (MCA)
Robbie Dupree; *Robbie Dupree* .... (ELE)
Whitesnake; *Snakebite* .... (GEF)
Step By Step
Alan Parsons Project; *Eye In The Sky* .... (ARI)
Crests; *Doo Wop Uptempo-#2* .... (RHI)
  Greatest Hits .... (CLT)
  Oldies But Goodies-#9 .... (OSR)
  Super Oldies/'60s-#9 .... (AUF)
  WCBS FM 101-History Of Rock-'60s-#1 ...... (CLT)
Eddie Rabbitt; *Best Of/Greatest Hits-#2* .... (WB)
  #1s .... (WB)
New Kids On The Block; *No More Games/Remix Album* ....(COL)
  Step By Step ....(COL)
Sweet Honey In The Rock; *Other Side* .... (FF)
Steppin'
Gap Band; *2* .... (MER)
Steppin' In A Slide Zone
Moody Blues; *Octave* .... (POL)
Steppin' Out
Cream; *Crossroads* .... (POL)
  Live-#2 ....(POL)
Electric Light Orchestra; *Out Of The Blue* ....(JET)
Joan Armatrading; *Back To The Night* .... (A&M)
  Steppin' Out .... (A&M)
Joe Jackson; *Live-1980-1986* .... (A&M)
  Night & Day .... (A&M)
Mel Tillis; *Your Body Is An Outlaw* .... (ELE)
Michelle Shocked; *Texas Campfire Tapes* .... (MER)
Paul Revere/Raiders; *Greatest Hits* ....(COL)
  Legend Of ....(COL)
Strollin'
Gene Harris Quartet; *Like A Lover* .... (CCJ)
Horace Silver; *Horacescope* .... (BLN)
Jack Dupree; *Atlantic Blues-Piano* .... (ATL)
Strollin' Beale No. 1
Rufus Thomas; *Can't Get Away From This Dog* .. (STX)
Strollin' On
Maxi Priest; *Best Of Me* .... (CHS)
Strollin' (With My Moose)
Edgar Meyer; *Sampler '88-#2* .... (MCA)
Stroll, The
Diamonds; *Groove 'N' Grind-'50s/'60s Dance Hits* (RHI)
  Partytime '50s .... (PRY)
  ST/American Graffiti .... (MCA)
Strut
Sheena Easton; *Dance Mix* .... (EMI)
  Private Heaven .... (EMI)
Struttin' With Some Barbecue
Louis Armstrong; *Greatest Hits* ....(COL)
  Of New Orleans .... (MCA)
Newport Jazz Festival All-Stars; *Newport Jazz Festival All-Stars* .... (CCJ)
Teddy Buckner; *Salute To Louis Armstrong* ...... (CRS)

Sweet Betsy From Pike
Cisco Houston; *Cowboy Ballads* .... (FLW)
Mormon Tabernacle Choir; *This Land Is Your
Land* ....(COL)
Take A Giant Step
Taj Mahal; *Best Of-#1* ....(COL)
Giant Step/Ole Folks At Home ....(COL)
Troubadours Of The Folk Era-#2 ...... (RHI)
Take A Little Trip
Alabama; *American Pride* ....(RCA)
Take A Little Walk With Me
Big John Wrencher & Joe Carter; *Blues
Masters-#4-Harmonica Classics* .... (RHI)
Take It On The Run
R.E.O. Speedwagon; *High Infidelity* .... (EPI)
Second Decade Of Rock & Roll-1981-1991 .... (EPI)
The Hits .... (EPI)
Take Me Back To My Old Carolina Home
Uncle Dave Macon; *Laugh Your Blues Away* ... (ROU)
Take Me Back To New Orleans
Chris Barber & Dr. John; *Take Me Back To New
Orleans* .... (BL)
Gary U.S. Bonds; *School Of Rock 'N' Roll-Best Of* (RHI)
Take Me Back To New York City
Si Kahn; *Unfinished Portraits* ....(FF)
Take Me Back To Old Wyoming
Chris LeDoux; *Thirty Dollar Cowboy* ....(LIB)
Take Me Back To Tulsa
Asleep At The Wheel; *Route 66* ....(LIB)
Bob Wills/Texas Playboys; *Bob Wills Anthology* ..(SSP)
Columbia Country Classics-#1-Golden Age .....(COL)
Tiffany Transcriptions-#2-Best Of Tiff. ....(KAL)
Take Me To Los Angeles
Jimmy Soul; *Best Of* .... (RHI)
Take The Long Way Home
John Schneider; *Country Classics-#8-1986-1987* . (MSP)
Greatest Hits ....(MCA)
Supertramp; *Breakfast In America* .... (A&M)
Classics-#9 ....(A&M)
Paris ....(A&M)
Take The Money & Run
Steve Miller Band; *CD Gift Set* ....(CAP)
Fly Like An Eagle ....(CAP)
Greatest Hits-1974-1978 ....(CAP)
Live ....(CAP)
Take The Short Way Home
Dionne Warwick; *Heartbreaker* .... (ARI)
Tennessee Traveler
Mike Auldridge; *Mike Auldridge* ....(FF)
Texas Bound
Gary Morris; *Full Moon Empty Heart* ....(LIB)
Texas Bound & Flyin'
Jerry Reed; *ST/Smokey & The Bandit 2* ....(MCA)
Texas Bound & Flyin' ....(RCA)
There She Goes
Beat; *ST/Caddyshack* ....(COL)
Bob Marley/Wailers; *One Love* ....(HRT)
Chambers Brothers; *Best Of* ....(FAN)
Jerry Wallace; *Greatest Hits* ....(CCB)
La's; *La's* ....(LON)
These Boots Are Made For Walkin'
Billy Ray Cyrus; *Some Gave All* .... (MER)
Nancy Sinatra; *Billboard Top Rock 'N' Roll
Hits-1966* .... (RHI)
Boots-Greatest Hits .... (RHI)
Thirty Nine Miles To Mobile
Charlie Daniels Band; *Charlie Daniels Band* .....(CAP)
Ticket Back To Georgia
Head East; *Flat As A Pancake* .... (A&M)
Tickets To A Better Place
7 Seconds; *Soulforce Revolution* .... (RES)
Tiny Steps
Elvis Costello; *Girls Girls Girls* ....(COL)
Tip-Toe Through The Tulips With Me
Tiny Tim; *Dr. Demento's Greatest Novelty-#3* .... (RHI)
Silly Songs .... (KT)
Tomorrow I'll Be Out Of Town
Ten Years After; *Classic Performances Of* ....(COL)
Universal .... (CHR)
Trains & Boats & Planes
Billy J. Kramer/Dakotas; *Definitive Collection* .... (EMI)
History Of British Rock-#4 .... (RHI)

Dionne Warwick; *Anthology-1962-1971* .... (RHI)
Dionne Warwick ....(EVR)
Greatest Hits ....(EVR)
Hot! Live & Otherwise .... (ARI)
Trains/Leavin' Tennessee
Tasty Licks; *Tasty Licks* .... (ROU)
Tramp, Tramp, Tramp
Mormon Tabernacle Choir; *Songs Of The Civil War & S.
Foster Faves* .... (SMC)
Travel On My Way
Chambers Brothers; *Best Of* .... (FAN)
Traveling Blues
Loggins & Messina; *Finale* ....(COL)
Full Sail ....(COL)
Traveling Man
Dolly Parton; *Best Of* ....(RCA)
Coat Of Many Colors ....(RCA)
Traveling Riverside Blues
Hindu Love Gods; *Hindu Love Gods* ....(GIA)
John Hammond; *Best Of* .... (VAN)
Led Zeppelin; *Led Zeppelin (collection)* ....(ATL)
Robert Johnson; *King Of The Delta Blues Singers* .(COL)
Slide Guitar-Bottles Knives & Steel ....(COL)
Travelin' All Alone
Billie Holiday; *Billie Holiday* ....(COL)
Legacy Box-1933-1958 ....(COL)
Quintessential-#5-1937-1938 ....(COL)
Story-#1 ....(COL)
Travelin' At The Speed Of Thought
O'Jays; *Travelin' At The Speed Of Thought* .... (PI)
Travelin' Band
Creedence Clearwater Revival; *1970* ....(FAN)
Chronicle ....(FAN)
Cosmo's Factory ....(FAN)
Live In Europe ....(FAN)
Royal Albert Hall Concert ....(FAN)
Travelin' Blues
Blind Willie McTell; *Early Years-1927-1932* ....(YAZ)
Story Of The Blues ....(COL)
Jimmie Rodgers; *My Rough & Rowdy Ways* ......(RCA)
Travelin' Light
Billie Holiday; *All Or Nothing At All* ....(VRV)
History Of The Real ....(VRV)
Lady Sings The Blues ....(VRV)
Travelin' Man
Albert King; *I Wanna Get Funky* ....(STX)
Bob Seger; *Beautiful Loser* ....(CAP)
Live Bullet ....(CAP)
Doobie Brothers; *Doobie Brothers* ....(WB)
Jacky Ward; *45* ....(ASY)
Lynyrd Skynyrd; *One More From The Road* ..... (MCA)
Rick Nelson; *Best Of* ....(EMI)
Greatest Hits .... (RHI)
Stevie Wonder; *Greatest Hits-#2* ....(MOT)
Travelin' Prayer
Billy Joel; *Piano Man* ....(COL)
Traveller's Prayer
George Jones/Sweethearts Of The Rodeo; *Friends In
High Places* .... (EPI)
Travelling Man
Simple Minds; *Real Life* .... (A&M)
Travelin' Blues
Jimmie Rodgers; *America's Blue
Yodeler-1930-1931* ....(ROU)
Lefty Frizzell; *Best Of* .... (RHI)
Trip To Flagstaff
Kornos; *On Seven Winds* ....(GRE)
Truckin'
Bread; *Anthology* ....(ELE)
Best Of ....(ELE)
Manna ....(ELE)
Dwight Yoakam; *Deadicated* .... (ARI)
Grateful Dead; *American Beauty* ....(WB)
Europe '72 ....(WB)
Skeletons From The Closet-Best Of ....(WB)
What A Long Strange Trip It's Been ....(WB)
Mel Torme/Mel-Tones; *Back In Town* ....(VRV)
True Love Travels On A Gravel Road
Elvis Presley; *From Elvis In Memphis* ....(RCA)
Memphis Record ....(RCA)
Percy Sledge; *It Tears Me Up-Best Of* .... (RHI)
Twenty-Five Miles
Edwin Starr; *Motown Superstar Series-#3* .... (MOT)
Michael Jackson; *Original Soul Of* ....(MOT)

Two Tickets To Paradise
Eddie Money; *Eddie Money* ....(COL)
  Greatest Hits-Sound Of Money ....(COL)
  Unplug It In ....(COL)
Up Around The Bend
Creedence Clearwater Revival; *1970* ....(FAN)
  Chronicle ....(FAN)
  Cosmo's Factory ....(FAN)
  More Creedence Gold ....(FAN)
Hanoi Rocks; *Two Steps From The Move* ....(EPI)
Vacation
Go-Go's; *Greatest* ....(IRS)
  Vacation ....(IRS)
Vaya Con Dios
Bing Crosby; *Radio Years-#2* ....(CRS)
Freddy Fender; *Collection* ....(RPR)
Les Paul & Mary Ford; *Memories Are Made Of This* ....(CAP)
Roger Whittaker; *All-Time Heart-Touching Favorites-#1* ....(LIB)
Voyage
Christy Moore; *Voyage* ....(ATL)
Moody Blues; *Caught Live Plus Five* ....(POL)
  On The Threshold Of A Dream ....(POL)
  This Is The ....(POL)
"Voyage To The Bottom Of The Sea" Theme
Original Music; *Television's Greatest Hits-#2* ....(TVT)
Walk A Mile In My Shoes
Bryan Ferry; *Another Time Another Place* ....(RPR)
Elvis Presley/Imperial Quartet; *On Stage* ....(RCA)
Joe South; *Best Of* ....(RHI)
Walk A Thin Line
Fleetwood Mac; *25 Years-The Chain* ....(WB)
  Tusk ....(WB)
Walk Across The Rooftops
Blue Nile; *Walk Across The Rooftops* ....(A&M)
Walk All Over Georgia
Louisiana Red; *Midnight Rambler* ....(TOM)
Walk All Over You
AC/DC; *Highway To Hell* ....(ATL)
Walk Away
Cheap Trick; *Busted* ....(EPI)
Dionne Warwick; *Greatest Hits-1979-1990* ......(ARI)
Donna Summer; *Bad Girls* ....(CAS)
  Dance Collection ....(CAS)
  Walk Away-Best Of-1977-1980 ....(CAS)
Indigo Girls; *Strange Fire* ....(EPI)
James Gang; *16 Greatest Hits* ....(MCA)
  Best Of ....(MCA)
  Thirds ....(OW)
Joe Walsh; *Best Of* ....(MCA)
  You Can't Argue With A Sick Mind ....(MCA)
Michael Bolton; *The Hunger* ....(COL)
Sisters Of Mercy; *First & Last & Always* ....(ELE)
Tom Kell; *One Sad Night* ....(WB)
Walk Away From Love
David Ruffin; *At His Best* ....(MOT)
Jimmy & David Ruffin; *Motown Superstar Series-#8* ....(MOT)
Walk Away Renee
Four Tops; *Anthology* ....(MOT)
  Compact Command Performances ....(MOT)
  Reach Out ....(MOT)
Left Banke; *Cruisin'-1966* ....(INC)
  History Of ....(RHI)
Walk Awhile
Fairport Convention; *Full House* ....(CTH)
Walk Don't Run
Ventures; *Best Of* ....(EMI)
  EMI Legends Of Rock & Roll-24 Greatest ....(EMI)
Walk In My Mind
Siegel-Schwall Band; *Best Of* ....(VAN)
  '70 ....(VAN)
Walk In The Night
Junior Walker/All-Stars; *All The Great Hits* .....(MOT)
  Anthology ....(MOT)
  Motown Superstar Series-#5 ....(MOT)
Walk Like A Man
Bruce Springsteen; *Tunnel Of Love* ....(COL)
Four Seasons; *Anthology* ....(RHI)
  Billboard Top Rock 'N' Roll Hits-1963 ....(RHI)
  ST/Wanderers ....(WB)
Frankie Valli/Four Seasons; *Greatest Hits-#1* ....(RHI)
Grand Funk Railroad; *We're An American Band* .(CAP)

Walk Like An Egyptian
Bangles; *Different Light* ....(COL)
  Greatest Hits ....(COL)
  Modern A Cappella ....(RHI)
Walk My Way
Beth Nielsen Chapman; *Beth Nielsen Chapman* ..(RPR)
Walk Of Life
Dire Straits; *Brothers In Arms* ....(WB)
  Money For Nothing ....(WB)
Walk On
Neil Young; *Decade* ....(RPR)
  On The Beach ....(RPR)
Reba McEntire; *Greatest Hits-#2* ....(MCA)
  Sweet Sixteen ....(MCA)
Sonny Terry & Brownie McGhee; *Coffeehouse Blues* ....(VJ)
  Real Blues Brothers ....(DHL)
Walk On By
Dionne Warwick; *Anthology-1962-1971* ....(RHI)
  Hot! Live & Otherwise ....(ARI)
  Oldies But Goodies-#15 ....(OSR)
  scepter Records story ....(CPC)
Isaac Hayes; *Greatest Hit Singles* ....(STX)
Leroy Van Dyke; *Billboard Top Country Hits-1961* ....(RHI)
  Country Music Classics-#2-1960-1965 ....(KT)
  Souvenirs of Music City U.S.A. ....(PLN)
Melissa Manchester; *Romantic Hits Of The '80s* ...(KT)
  Tribute ....(MIK)
Sybil; *Sybil* ....(NP)
Walk On Faith
Mike Reid; *Greatest Country Hits/'90s-1991* .....(COL)
  Turning For Home ....(COL)
Walk On Out Of My Mind
Waylon Jennings; *Best Of* ....(RCA)
Walk On The Ocean
Toad The Wet Sprocket; *Fear* ....(COL)
Walk On The Water
Creedence Clearwater Revival; *1968-1969* ......(FAN)
  Chronicle-#2 ....(FAN)
  Creedence Clearwater Revival ....(FAN)
Neil Diamond; *And The Singer Sings His Songs* .(MCA)
  Glory Road-1968-1972 ....(MCA)
  Moods ....(MCA)
Walk On The Wild Side
Edie Brickell/New Bohemians; *ST/Flashback* ...(WTG)
Lou Reed; *Between Thought & Expression-Anthology* ....(RCA)
  Live ....(RCA)
  Transformer ....(RCA)
  Walk On The Wild Side-Best Of ....(RCA)
Walk On Water
Dio; *Lock Up The Wolves* ....(RPR)
Eddie Money; *Greatest Hits-Sound Of Money* ...(COL)
  Nothing To Lose ....(COL)
Marc Cohn; *Marc Cohn* ....(ATL)
Marillion; *Six Of One-Half-Dozen Of The Other* ..(IRS)
T. Graham Brown; *Brilliant Conversationalist* ....(CAP)
Walk Out In The Rain
Eric Clapton; *Backless* ....(RSO)
  I Shall Be Unreleased-Songs Of Bob Dylan .....(RHI)
Walk Right Back
Anne Murray; *Country Collection* ....(LIB)
  Country Hits ....(LIB)
  Let's Keep It That Way ....(LIB)
Everly Brothers; *Golden Hits Of* ....(WB)
  Very Best Of ....(WB)
Walk Right In
Rooftop Singers; *Best Of* ....(VAN)
  Cruisin'-1963 ....(INC)
  Greatest Folksingers Of The '80s ....(VAN)
  ST/Forrest Gump ....(EPX)
  Troubadours Of The Folk Era-#3 ....(RHI)
Walk Softly
Billy "Crash" Craddock; *Easy As Pie* ....(MCA)
  Live ....(MCA)
  Sings His Greatest Hits ....(MCA)
Walk Softly On The Bridge
Mel Street; *Greatest Hits* ....(GRT)
Walk Softly On This Heart Of Mine
Bill Monroe; *Country Music Hall Of Fame* ......(MCA)
Joey Welz; *Lovin' My Country* ....(CPC)
Kentucky HeadHunters; *Pickin' On Nashville* ....(MER)

Walk The Dinosaur
George Clinton/Goombas; *ST/Super Mario Brothers* .... (CAP)
Was (Not Was); *What Up Dog?* .... (CHR)
Walk The Dog
Laurie Anderson; *United States Live* .... (WB)
Walk The Way The Wind Blows
Hot Rize; *Traditional Ties* ....(SH)
Kathy Mattea; *Collection Of Hits* .... (MER)
Walk The Way The Wind Blows .... (MER)
Walk This Way
Aerosmith; *Classics Live 2* ....(COL)
Greatest Hits ....(COL)
Live Bootleg ....(COL)
Pandora's Box ....(COL)
Toys In The Attic ....(COL)
Run-D.M.C.; *Mr. Magic's Rap Attack* .... (PRO)
Raising Hell ....(PRO)
Rap's Biggest Hits ....(KT)
Walk Through This World With Me
George Jones; *All-Time Greatest Hits-#1* .... (EPI)
Best Of-1966-1967 .... (RHI)
Billboard Top Country Hits-1967 .... (RHI)
Double Gold ....(MCR)
Walkaway Joe
Trisha Yearwood; *Hearts In Armor* .... (MCA)
Walking Across Egypt
Tarwater Band; *Walking Across Egypt* .... (FF)
Walking Away
Information Society; *Information Society* .... (TMB)
Walking Back To Richmond
Dry Branch Fire Squad; *Fannin' The Flames* .... (ROU)
Walking Down Madison
Kirsty MacColl; *Electric Landlady* .... (CHS)
Walking Dream
Patsy Cline; *Forever & Always* .... (EPI)
Here's ....(MCA)
Walking In L.A.
Missing Persons; *Best Of* ....(CAP)
Walking In Memphis
Marc Cohn; *Marc Cohn* .... (ATL)
Walking In Space
Original Cast; *ST/Hair* ....(RCA)
Quincy Jones; *I Heard That!* .... (A&M)
ST/Listen Up-Lives Of Quincy Jones .... (QUE)
Walking In Space .... (A&M)
Walking In The Shadow Of The Blues
Whitesnake; *Live In The Heart Of The City* ...... (GEF)
Love Hunter ....(GEF)
Walking In The Sun
Rufus; *Rags To Rufus* .... (MCA)
Zombies; *Time Of* ....(EPI)
Walking In The Sunshine
Frank Sinatra; *Hello Young Lovers* ....(COL)
Roger Miller; *Best Of* .... (MER)
King Of The Road .... (LAS)
More Golden Hits .... (SMA)
Statler Brothers; *Sing The Big Hits* ....(COL)
World Of ....(COL)
Walking In The Wind
Traffic; *When The Eagle Flies* .... (ASY)
Walking Into Sunshine
Central Line; *45* .... (MER)
Walking Man
James Taylor; *Greatest Hits* .... (WB)
Walking Man ....(WB)
Walking On A Thin Line
Huey Lewis/News; *Sports* ....(CHR)
Walking On Broken Glass
Annie Lennox; *Diva* .... (ARI)
Walking On Sunshine
Eddy Grant; *Let's Dance-DJ's Collection* ....(COL)
Walking On Sunshine ....(EPI)
Katrina/Waves; *Katrina/Waves* ....(CAP)
Spring Break-#2-Cold Kegs & Tan Legs ....(CAP)
Walking Shoes
Tanya Tucker; *Tennessee Woman* .... (LIB)
Walking Slow
Jackson Browne; *Late For The Sky* .... (ASY)
Walking The Floor Over You
Asleep At The Wheel; *Western Standard Time* .... (EPI)
Ernest Tubb; *Story* .... (MCA)
Legend & The Legacy .... (FSG)

Ernest Tubb/M. Haggard/C. Daniels; *Ernest Tubb Collection* ....(SO)
Sandy Denny; *Who Knows Where The Time Goes?* (HBL)
Webb Pierce; *Golden Hits* .... (PLN)
Walking The Ghost
James; *Gold Mother* ....(FON)
James ....(FON)
Walking Through Fire
Mary Chapin Carpenter; *Come On Come On* ....(COL)
Walking To New Orleans
Fats Domino; *Fats Domino* .... (EVR)
Greatest Hits ....(MCA)
My Blue Heaven-Best Of-#1 .... (EMI)
They Call Me The Fat Man .... (EMI)
Walkin'
Bobby McFerrin; *Spontaneous Inventions* .... (BLN)
Cleve Francis; *Walkin'* .... (LIB)
Miles Davis; *Cookin' At The Plugged Nickel* ......(COL)
Greatest Hits ....(COL)
I Like Jazz-Essence Of ....(COL)
Willie Nelson; *Phases & Stages* .... (ATL)
Walkin' A Broken Heart
Don Williams; *Cafe Carolina* .... (MCA)
Greatest Hits ....(MSP)
Walkin' After Midnight
Garth Brooks; *The Chase* .... (LIB)
Loretta Lynn; *I Remember Patsy* .... (MCA)
Oak Ridge Boys; *Unstoppable* ....(RCA)
Patsy Cline; *20 Golden Pieces Of* .... (BLD)
Greatest Hits ....(MCA)
Let The Teardrops Fall ....(ACC)
Live At The Opry ....(MCA)
Patsy Cline ....(MCA)
Story ....(MCA)
Walkin' All Night
Little Feat; *Dixie Chicken* .... (WB)
Walkin' Away
Clint Black; *Killin' Time* ....(RCA)
Walkin' Back To Georgia
Jim Croce; *50th Anniversary Collection* ....(SAJ)
Down The Highway ....(SAJ)
Walkin' Back To San Antonio
Hank Thompson; *Here's To Country Music* ....(SO)
Walkin' Blues
Big Joe Williams; *Walkin' Blues* .... (FAN)
Bonnie Raitt; *Bonnie Raitt* .... (WB)
Grateful Dead; *Without A Net* .... (ARI)
Hindu Love Gods; *Hindu Love Gods* .... (GIA)
Paul Butterfield Blues Band; *East-West* .... (ELE)
Golden Butter .... (ELE)
Robert Johnson; *Complete Recordings* ....(COL)
Roy Rogers; *Prime Chops-Blind Pig Sampler* ...... (BLI)
Walkin' By Myself
Jimmy Rogers; *Best Of Chess Blues* .... (CSS)
Johnny Winter; *Hot & Blue* ....(BS)
Scorchin' Blues ....(EPA)
Walkin' By Myself ....(RLX)
White ....(BS)
Walkin' By The River
Ella Fitzgerald; *Best Of* .... (MCA)
Walkin' Down The Road
Ozark Mountain Daredevils; *Best Of* .... (A&M)
It'll Shine When It Shines ....(A&M)
It's Alive ....(A&M)
Walkin' In Jerusalem
Bill Monroe; *Country Music Hall Of Fame* ...... (MCA)
Doc Watson; *Old Timey Concert* .... (VAN)
Ricky Skaggs; *Love's Gonna Get Ya* ....(EPI)
Walkin' In The Rain
Grace Jones; *Island Life* .... (ISL)
Nightclubbing ....(ISL)
Jay/Americans; *All-Time Greatest Hits* .... (RHI)
Come A Little Big Closer-Best Of .... (EMI)
Marvin Gaye; *Romantically Yours* ....(COL)
Ronettes; *Back To Mono-1958-1969* ....(AKO)
Walkin' In The Rain With The One I Love
Love Unlimited; *Soul Hits/'70s-#1* .... (RHI)
Walkin' My Baby Back Home
Johnny Ray; *16 Most Requested Songs* ....(COL)
Greatest Hits ....(SSP)
Nat King Cole; *Capitol Collectors Series* ....(CAP)
Story ....(CAP)
Walkin' My Baby Back Home ....(CAP)

Walkin' One & Only
  Maria Muldaur; *Bread & Roses Festival/Acoustic
  Music-#1* .... (FAN)
    Maria Muldaur .... (RPR)
Walkin' The Dog
  Aerosmith; *Aerosmith* ....(COL)
    Pandora's Box ....(COL)
  Luther Allison; *Atlantic Blues-Chicago* ....(ATL)
  Rolling Stones; *England's Newest Hitmakers* .... (AKO)
  Rufus Thomas; *Can't Get Away From This Dog* .. (STX)
    Rufus Thomas ....(GUS)
    Super Hits-#2 ....(GUS)
    Walkin' The Dog ....(ATL)
Walkin', Talkin'...Beatin' Broken Heart
  Highway 101; *Country's Greatest Hits-#4* .... (PRY)
    Paint The Town ....(WB)
Walks Like A Lady
  Journey; *Captured* ....(COL)
    Departure ....(COL)
Walk, The
  Cure; *Japanese Whispers-The Singles* .... (SIR)
    Mixed Up ....(ELE)
    Standing On A Beach-The Singles .... (ELE)
    Walk, The ....(SIR)
  Eurythmics; *Sweet Dreams* ....(RCA)
  Jimmy McCracklin; *Best Of Chess Rhythm &
  Blues* .... (CSS)
    Groove 'N' Grind-'50s/'60s Dance Hits .... (RHI)
    Super Oldies/'50s-#7 ....(AUF)
  Rufus Thomas; *That Woman Is Poison!* ....(ALG)
  Sawyer Brown; *Buick* ....(LIB)
    Dirt Road ....(LIB)
  Time; *What Time Is It?* ....(WB)
Wanderer
  Dion; *20 Million-Dollar Memories-#1* ....(LAU)
    Billboard Top Rock 'N' Roll Hits-1962 .... (RHI)
    Cruisin'-1962 .... (INC)
    Oldies But Goodies-#5 ....(OSR)
    ST/Wanderers ....(WB)
    Wanderer ....(LAU)
  Donna Summer; *Wanderer* .... (GEF)
Wandering
  James Taylor; *Gorilla* ....(WB)
Wanderin' Star
  Original Broadway Cast; *Paint Your Wagon* .....(RCA)
Watermelon Crawl
  Tracy Byrd; *No Ordinary Man* .... (MCA)
Way I Walk
  Jack Scott; *Greatest Hits* ....(CCB)
    Rock This Town-Rockabilly Hits-#2 .... (RHI)
We Both Walk
  Lorrie Morgan; *Something In Red* ....(RCA)
We Gonna Move To Kansas City
  Walter Horton; *Fine Cuts* .... (BLI)
We May Never Pass This Way Again
  Seals & Crofts; *Diamond Girl* ....(WB)
    Greatest Hits ....(WB)
We're Gonna Move
  Elvis Presley; *Date With Elvis* ....(RCA)
    Essential Elvis-First Movies ....(RCA)
When I Reach The Place I'm Going
  Patty Loveless; *Red Hot + Country* .... (MER)
When The Saints Go Marching In
  Al Hirt; *Best Of* ....(RCA)
    Our Man-In New Orleans ....(NOV)
  Jerry Lee Lewis; *Jerry Lee Lewis* .... (RHI)
  Louis Armstrong; *At The Crescendo* .... (MCA)
    Big Bands Of The Swinging Years-#1 .... (CLT)
    C'Est Si Bon .... (RHI)
    Essential ....(VAN)
    Of New Orleans ....(MCA)
  Pete Fountain; *Best Of* .... (MCA)
    Down On Rampart Street .... (INT)
    Pete Fountain's New Orleans ....(MCA)
  Preservation Hall Jazz Band; *Best Of* ....(COL)
When You Walk In The Room
  Pam Tillis; *Sweetheart's Dance* .... (ARI)
Where Do You Go
  Frank Sinatra; *No One Cares* .... (CAP)
  Strawbs; *Best Of* ....(A&M)
    Ghosts ....(A&M)
Where You Goin' Now
  Damn Yankees; *Don't Tread* ....(WB)

Wherever I May Roam
  Metallica; *Metallica* .... (ELE)
Which Way You Goin' Billy
  Poppy Family; *Super Hits/'70s-Have A Nice
  Day-#2* .... (RHI)
Why Walk When You Can Fly
  Mary Chapin Carpenter; *Stones In The Road* ....(COL)
Wild Things Run Fast
  Joni Mitchell; *Wild Things Run Fast* ....(GEF)
Willin'
  Byrds; *Byrds (collection)* ....(COL)
  Linda Ronstadt; *Heart Like A Wheel* ....(CAP)
  Little Feat; *Little Feat* ....(WB)
    Sailin' Shoes ....(WB)
    Waiting For Columbus ....(WB)
Woman Walk The Line
  Emmylou Harris; *Ballad Of Sally Rose* ....(WB)
  Highway 101; *Featuring Paulette Carlson* ....(WB)
  Trisha Yearwood; *Hearts In Armor* .... (MCA)
Women Walk More Determined
  Kristin Lems; *Oh Mama!* ....(CDP)
Wrong Side Of Memphis
  Matraca Berg; *Bittersweet Surrender* ....(RCA)
  Trisha Yearwood; *Hearts In Armor* .... (MCA)
You Ain't Goin' Nowhere
  Bob Dylan; *Greatest Hits-#2* ....(COL)
  Bob Dylan/Band; *Basement Tapes* ....(COL)
  Byrds; *Best Of-Greatest Hits-#2* ....(COL)
    Byrds Play Dylan ....(COL)
    Byrds (collection) ....(COL)
    Sweetheart Of The Rodeo ....(COL)
  Chris Hillman & Roger McGuinn; *Will The Circle Be
  Unbroken-#2* .... (UNI)
  Joan Baez; *First 10 Years* ....(VAN)
You Better Move On
  Johnny Rivers; *Anthology-1964-1977* .... (RHI)
  Rolling Stones; *December's Children* .... (AKO)
You Better Run
  Pat Benatar; *Crimes Of Passion* .... (CHR)
    ST/Roadie ....(WB)
You Came A Long Way From St. Louis
  Peggy Lee & George Shearing; *Beauty & The
  Beat* .... (BLN)
  Perry Como; *This Is-#2* ....(RCA)
You Can't Run From Love
  Eddie Rabbitt; *Best Of/Greatest Hits-#2* ...... (WB)
    Radio Romance .... (LIB)
    #1's ....(WB)
You Gotta Move
  Rolling Stones; *Love You Live* .... (RS)
    Sticky Fingers .... (RS)
You Keep Running Away
  Four Tops; *Anthology* .... (MOT)
You'll Never Walk Alone
  Andy Williams; *Greatest Songs* ....(CCB)
  Jim Nabors; *16 Most Requested Songs* ....(COL)
  Judy Garland; *Best Of The Capitol Masters* ....(CAP)
  Mormon Tabernacle Choir; *Climb Every
  Mountain* ....(COL)
  Original Broadway Cast; *Carousel* .... (ANG)
  Original Cast; *Carousel* .... (MCA)
  Pink Floyd; *Meddle* ....(CAP)

TREES

See Also: ECOLOGY, FLOWERS, JUNGLES

29 Palms
  Robert Plant; *Fate Of NAtions* .... (EPR)
Alpine Milkman
  Randy Erwin; *'Til The Cows Come Home/Cowboy
  Rhythm* .... (ROM)
Apple Orchard
  Spirit; *Spirit* .... (EMI)
Apple Suckling Tree
  Bob Dylan/Band; *Basement Tapes* ....(COL)
Autumn Leaves
  Barbra Streisand; *Je M'Appele Barbra* ....(COL)
  Frank Sinatra; *Night We Called It A Day* ....(CAP)
  Grace Jones; *Fame* .... (ISL)
  Nat King Cole; *Blossom Fell* ....(CAP)
  Roger Miller; *Music Of The 1950s* .... (MCA)
  Roger Williams; *Best Of* .... (MCA)
    Golden Hits-#2 ....(MCA)

Babes In The Woods
Steve Miller Band; *Book Of Dreams* ....(CAP)
  CD Gift Set ....(CAP)
Baby Tree
Paul Kantner/Jefferson Starship; *Blows Against The
Empire* ....(RCA)
Bare Trees
Fleetwood Mac; *Bare Trees* .... (RPR)
Birds In My Tree
Strawberry Alarm Clock; *Best Of-#1* .... (BCT)
Blue Spruce Woman
Foghat; *Rock & Roll Outlaws* .... (RHI)
Boys In The Trees
Carly Simon; *Boys In The Trees* .... (ELE)
Bury Me Beneath The Willow
Jimmy Davis; *Best Of* .... (MCA)
Wilma Lee Cooper; *Wilma Lee Cooper* .... (ROU)
Cactus Tree
Joni Mitchell; *Joni Mitchell* .... (RPR)
  Miles Of Aisles .... (ASY)
Canadian Lumber Jack
Stompin' Tom Connors; *Bud The Spud* .... (BOO)
Carolina In The Pines
Michael Martin Murphey; *Best Of* .... (EMI)
  Blue Sky Night Thunder .... (EPI)
Cherry Blossom Time
Columbia Ballroom Orchestra; *Let's
Dance-#7-Competition Dance* .... (DEN)
Coconut Grove
David Lee Roth; *Crazy From The Heat* .... (WB)
Lovin' Spoonful; *Anthology* .... (RHI)
Cypress Avenue
Van Morrison; *Astral Weeks* .... (WB)
  It's Too Late To Stop Now .... (WB)
Cypress Grove Blues
Skip James; *Greatest Of The Delta Blues Singers* ...(BIO)
  Mississippi Blues-1927-1941 .... (YAZ)
  Tribute To .... (BIO)
Dallas Rag/Maple Leaf Rag
David Bromberg; *How Late'll Ya Play 'Til* .... (FAN)
Day In The Life Of A Tree
Beach Boys; *Surf's Up* ....(CAR)
Don't Cut The Tree Down In Winter
Penny Little; *In A Light Garden* .... (GLO)
Don't Sit Under The Apple Tree
Andrews Sisters; *Capitol Collectors Series* .... (CAP)
  Greatest Hits ....(CCB)
Glenn Miller; *Memorial-1944-1969* ....(BLU)
Glenn Miller/Orchestra; *Unforgettable* ....(RCA)
Down Among The Sheltering Pines
Barney Kessel; *Some Like It Hot* .... (CTM)
Lawrence Welk; *Champagne Music Of* .... (RAN)
East Of Ginger Trees
Seals & Crofts; *Greatest Hits* .... (WB)
Easter Tree
June Tabor; *Ashes & Diamonds* ....(GRE)
Echoes Of The African Forest
Saka Acquaye Ensemble; *Voices Of Africa* ..... (NON)
Evergreen (Theme From "A Star Is Born")
Barbra Streisand; *Greatest Hits* ....(COL)
  Greatest Hits-#2 ....(COL)
  Memories ....(COL)
  ST/A Star Is Born ....(COL)
Luther Vandross; *Songs* .... (EPI)
Paul Williams; *Classics* ....(A&M)
Fig Tree
Bunny Wailer; *Blackheart Man* .... (ISL)
Fig Tree Bay
Peter Frampton; *Wind Of Change* ....(A&M)
Georgia Pineywoods
Osborne Brothers; *Best Of The* .... (MCA)
Green Leaves Of Summer
Brothers Four; *Greatest Hits* ....(COL)
  Greenfields & Other Gold .... (FIR)
  Hollywood Magic-1960s ....(COL)
Hanging Tree
Marty Robbins; *All-Time Greatest Hits* ....(COL)
  Hollywood Magic-1950s ....(COL)
  Lifetime Of Song ....(COL)
Hickory Wind
Byrds; *Byrds* ....(COL)
  Columbia Country Classics-#5-New Trad. ......(COL)
  Sweetheart Of The Rodeo ....(COL)
Emmylou Harris; *Blue Kentucky Girl* .... (WB)

Gram Parsons; *Grievous Angel* .... (RPR)
I Talk To The Trees
Al Hirt; *Al Hirt* ....(DHL)
  Showtime .... (ALL)
If I Were King Of The Forest
Bert Lahr; *ST/Wizard Of Oz* ....(SSP)
In Chicago's Forest Preserve
Li'l Wally; *Polish Feelings* .... (JJ)
Leaves That Are Green
Country Gentlemen; *Country Gentlemen* .... (VAN)
Simon & Garfunkel; *Collected Works* ....(COL)
  Sounds Of Silence ....(COL)
Lemon Tree
Kingston Trio; *Very Best Of* ....(CAP)
Peter, Paul & Mary; *10 Years Together-Best Of* ...(WB)
  Peter, Paul & Mary .... (WB)
Trini Lopez; *Best Of* ....(EXA)
Lumberjack
Jackyl; *Jackyl* ....(GEF)
Magnolia
J.J. Cale; *Naturally* .... (MCA)
Pat Travers; *Pat Travers* .... (POL)
Poco; *Crazy Eyes* .... (EPI)
Tom Petty/Heartbreakers; *You're Gonna Get It* . (MCA)
Maple Leaf Rag
Joshua Rifkin; *Digital Ragtime* .... (ANG)
Scott Joplin; *Greatest Ragtime Of The Century* .....(BIO)
Oak Tree
Morris Day; *Color Of Success* .... (WB)
Once A Forest
Grace Pool; *Where We Live* .... (RPR)
Orange Blossom Lane
Glenn Miller/Orchestra; *Complete* ....(BLU)
  Complete-#7 ....(RCA)
Orange Blossom Mandolin
Northeast Winds; *In Concert* .... (FOL)
Orange Blossom Special
Bill Monroe; *Bean Blossom* .... (MCA)
  Stars Of The Grand Ole Opry 1926-1974 ......(RCA)
  & Bluegrass Boys-60 Years Of Country ....(RCA)
Charlie Daniels Band; *Fire On The Mountain* ..... (EPI)
  Urban Cowboy-#2 .... (EPI)
Flatt & Scruggs; *Hear The Whistles Blow* ....(GUS)
Gordon Terry; *20 Golden Souvenirs* ....(PLN)
  Disco Country ....(PLN)
Johnny Cash; *Columbia Records 1958-1986* .....(COL)
  Essential ....(COL)
  Greatest Hits ....(COL)
Nitty Gritty Dirt Band; *Will The Circle Be
Unbroken* .... (EMI)
Orange Blossom Time
Bing Crosby; *Crooner-Columbia
Years-1928-1934* ....(COL)
Out In The Woods
Leon Russell; *Best Of* .... (MCA)
  Carney .... (MCA)
Peach Blossom Spring
Yutaka; *Yutaka* ....(GRP)
Peach Orchard Mamma
Big Joe Williams; *Piney Woods Blues* ....(DEL)
Peach Tree
Sonny Boy Williamson; *Real Folk Blues* .... (CSS)
Peach Tree Shuffle
Panama Francis; *All-Stars 1949* ....(CLT)
People Tree
Sammy Davis, Jr.; *45* ....(MGM)
Pine Grove Blues
Nathan Abshire; *Alligator Stomp-#2* .... (RHI)
  French Blues .... (ARH)
Plum Blossom
Vangelis; *China* .... (POL)
Yusef Lateef/Others; *Eastern Sounds* ....(PRS)
Possum Up A Gum Stump
Dick Fegy; *Flatpicking Guitar Festival* ....(SHA)
Queen Of The Forest
Ted Nugent; *Ted Nugent* .... (EPI)
Rabbit In A Log
Stanley Brothers; *Stanley Series-Vol. 1 & 2* ......(COP)
Rain Forest
Cut To The Chase; *Cut To The Chase* ....(A&C)
David Lanz & Paul Speer; *Narada-Equinox Sampler
One* ....(NAR)
  Natural States ....(NAR)
Jeremy Steig/Eddie Gomez; *Rain Forest* ....(CMU)

Jessica Williams; *Rivers Of Memory* .... (CLE)
Nelson Rangell; *Nelson Rangell* .... (GRP)
Paul Hardcastle; *Dance 2* .... (PRO)
   Paul Hardcastle .... (CHR)
   Rain Forest .... (PRO)
Redwood Evergreen
   Lorraine Duisit; *Hawks & Herons* .... (FF)
Redwood Hill
   Vassar Clements; *Westport Drive* .... (MIN)
Redwood Tree
   Van Morrison; *St. Dominic's Preview* .... (WB)
River In The Pines
   Joan Baez; *Farewell Angelina* .... (VAN)
   Love Song Album .... (VAN)
Settin' The Woods On Fire
   Hank Williams; *24 Greatest Hits* .... (POL)
   40 Greatest Hits .... (POL)
Shade Tree Mechanic
   Joe Louis Walker; *The Gift* .... (HT)
   Z.Z. Hill; *Greatest Hits* .... (MAL)
   I'm A Blues Man .... (MAL)
Shady Grove
   Doc Watson; *Essential* .... (VAN)
   Memories .... (SH)
   Hot Rize; *In Concert* .... (FF)
   Kentucky Colonels; *Long JOurney Home* .... (VAN)
Shake My Tree
   Coverdale/Page; *Coverdale/Page* .... (GEF)
Shake The Sugar Tree
   Pam Tillis; *Homeward Looking Angel* .... (ARI)
Shaking The Tree
   Peter Gabriel; *Shaking The Tree-16 Golden
   Greats* .... (GEF)
Shaking Your Tree (Somebody Else Been)
   ZZ Top; *First Album* .... (WB)
   Six Pack .... (WB)
She's Long, She's Tall, She Weeps...
   John Lee Hooker; *Black Snake* .... (FAN)
   Country Blues Of .... (RVR)
Singing Tree
   Elvis Presley; *ST/Clambake* .... (RCA)
Song Of The Evergreens
   Chicago; *VII* .... (COL)
Songs From The Wood
   Jethro Tull; *20 Years Of-Radio Archives & Rare
   Tracks* .... (CHR)
   Bursting Out .... (CHR)
   Original Masters .... (CHR)
   Songs From The Wood .... (CHR)
Sycamore Leaves
   A-Ha; *East Of The Sun-West Of The Moon* .... (WB)
Sycamore Rag
   Dick Hyman; *Scott Joplin-Greatest Hits* .... (RCA)
   Scott Joplin; *Ragtime-#2-1900-1910* .... (BIO)
Tales From The Vienna Woods
   101 Strings Orchestra; *Best Of Johann Strauss Jr.* (ALS)
   Lawrence Welk; *22 Great Waltzes* .... (RAN)
Tall Trees In Georgia
   Buffy Sainte-Marie; *Best Of-#2* .... (VAN)
   I'm Gonna Be A Country Girl Again .... (VAN)
There Was A Tall Oak Tree
   Dorsey Burnette; *Super Hits-#1* .... (IGR)
There's A Cabin In The Pines
   Bing Crosby; *Crooner-Columbia
   Years-1928-1934* .... (COL)
Thorn Tree In The Garden
   Derek/Dominos; *Layla* .... (POL)
Tie A Yellow Ribbon 'Round The Old...
   Frank Sinatra; *Some Nice Things I've Missed* ..... (RPR)
   Lawrence Welk; *Best Of-20 Great Hits* .... (RAN)
   Sonny James & Karla Taylor; *Classic Country
   Duets* .... (CCB)
   Tony Orlando/Dawn; *45* .... (FSB)
Timber I'm Falling In Love
   Patty Loveless; *Country's Greatest Hits-#4* .... (PRY)
   Greatest Hits .... (MCA)
   Honky Tonk Angel .... (MCA)
Timberline
   Emmylou Harris; *Ballad Of Sally Rose* .... (WB)
Tree Frog
   Count Basie; *Best Of* .... (PAB)
   Count Basie/Orchestra; *I Told You So* .... (PAB)
Tree Grows In Burbank
   Harry James; *Uncollected-#5-1943-1953* .... (HIN)

Tree In The Meadow
   Lettermen; *Let It Be Me* .... (CAP)
   Margaret Whiting; *Capitol Collectors Series* ...... (CAP)
   Great Records Of The Decade-'40s-Pop-#1 .....(CCB)
Tree In The Park
   Sarah Vaughan; *Rodgers & Hart Songbook* ...... (EMA)
   William Bolcom & Joan Morris; *Rodgers & Hart
   Album* ....(RCA)
Tree Of Joy
   Jeannie C. Riley; *Country Gold* .... (PLN)
Tree Of Life
   Les Baxter Orchestra & Chorus; *Brazil Now-African
   Blue* .... (CRS)
Tree Too Weak To Stand
   Gordon Lightfoot; *Cold On The Shoulder* .... (RPR)
Trees
   Rush; *Chronicles* .... (MER)
   Exit...Stage Left .... (MER)
   Hemispheres .... (MER)
   Spaniels; *45* .... (CLT)
Trees In Philadelphia
   Patti Page; *Touch Of Country* .... (FFT)
Trees Of The Ages
   Laura Nyro; *Mother's Spiritual* ....(COL)
Trees They Do Grow High
   Joan Baez; *Ballad Book* .... (VAN)
   Joan Baez-#2 .... (VAN)
Under The Sycamore Tree
   Sara Hickman; *Equal Scary People* .... (ELE)
Under The Willow Tree
   Claude Thornhill/Orchestra/Buddy Hughes; *Best Of The
   Big Bands* ....(COL)
Underneath The Apple Tree
   Michael Franks; *Tiger In The Rain* .... (WB)
Up In My Treehouse
   Chet Atkins; *Sails* ....(COL)
Vermont Is Afire In The Autumn
   Lui Collins; *Made In New England* ....(GRE)
When The Golden Leaves Begin To Fall
   Joe Val/New England Bluegrass Boys; *#2* ...... (ROU)
When The World Was Young
   Anita O'Day; *Mello'Day* .... (CRS)
   Frank Sinatra; *Point Of No Return* .... (CAP)
Whispering Pines
   Band; *Band* .... (CAP)
   Johnny Horton; *Greatest Hits* ....(COL)
Wildwood Mandolin
   Jack Tottle; *Rounder Bluegrass-#1* .... (ROU)
Willow
   Joan Armatrading; *Classics-#21* .... (A&M)
   Show Some Emotion .... (A&M)
   Track Record .... (A&M)
Willow Weep For Me
   Art Tatum; *Best Of* .... (PAB)
   Solo Masterpieces-#1 .... (PAB)
   Billie Holiday; *Billie's Blues* .... (BLD)
   Lady Sings The Blues .... (VRV)
   Live .... (VRV)
   Stormy Blues .... (VRV)
   Chad & Jeremy; *Best Of* .... (CAP)
   History Of British Rock-#3 .... (RHI)
   Super Oldies-'60s-#11 .... (AUF)
   Dinah Shore; *16 Most Requested Songs* ....(COL)
   Lou Rawls; *Legendary* .... (BLN)
   Roy Eldridge; *Best Of* .... (PAB)
   Steve Miller; *Born 2 B Blue* .... (CAP)

TRUCKS, Truckin'

   *See Also: CARS, GAS STATIONS, ROAD,
   TRAVELING*

Before The Trash Truck Comes
   Bob Frank; *Bob Frank* .... (VAN)
Big Joe & Phantom 309
   Tom Waits; *Double Live* .... (ASY)
   Nighthawks At The Diner .... (ASY)
Big Rig
   Jimmy Buffett; *Havana Daydreamin'* .... (MCA)
Big Rig Rolling Man
   Billy Larkin; *Blue Ribbon Country-#2* .... (ACC)

Big Wheels In The Moonlight
Dan Seals; *Classics Collection-#2* .... (LIB)
   Greatest Hits .... (LIB)
   Rage On .... (LIB)
Bridge Washed Out
Warner Mack; *Country's Greatest Hits-#3* .... (MCA)
   MCA 30 Years Of Hits 1958-1988 .... (MCA)
Brother Trucker
James Taylor; *Flag* .... (COL)
Convoy
C.W. McCall; *Greatest Hits* .... (POL)
   ST/Convoy .... (POL)
   Super Hits/'70s-Have A Nice Day-#15 .... (RHI)
Cupid's Trash Truck
Lou & Peter Berryman; *Cupid's Trash Truck* .... (COR)
Detroit Diesel
Alvin Lee; *Detroit Diesel* .... (21)
Diesel Cecil
Larry Scott; *Keep On Truckin'* .... (ALS)
Diesel On My Tail
Jim & Jesse; *Truckers' Jukebox-Top Radio Requests* (EPI)
New Riders Of The Purple Sage; *Midnight
Moonlight* .... (RLX)
Diesel Only Theme
World Famous Blue Jays; *Rig Rock Jukebox* ...... (FIR)
Dime At A Time
Del Reeves; *Super Hits Country-1960s* .... (IGR)
Don't Come Home A Lovin' With Venison...
Debby McClatchy; *Someday Cafe* .... (GRE)
Drug Store Truck Drivin' Man
Byrds; *Best Of-Greatest Hits-#2* .... (COL)
   Byrds .... (COL)
   Dr. Byrds & Mr. Hyde .... (COL)
Gram Parsons/Fallen Angels; *Live 1973* .... (SIE)
Joan Baez & Jeffrey Shurtleff; *ST/Woodstock* .... (ATL)
Eighteen Wheels And A Dozen Roses
Kathy Mattea; *Collection Of Hits* .... (MER)
   Untasted Honey .... (MER)
Endless Black Ribbon
Red Simpson; *Trucks Trains & Airplanes* .... (IGR)
Red Sovine/Willis Bros./Reno & Smiley; *Heavy
Haulers* .... (PP)
Ethelene (The Truckstop Queen)
Ray Stevens; *I Never Made A Record I Didn't
Like* .... (MCA)
Giddy Up Go
Red Sovine; *Best Of* .... (STR)
Red Sovine/Willis Bros./Reno & Smiley; *Heavy
Haulers* .... (PP)
Henry
New Riders Of The Purple Sage; *Best Of* .... (COL)
   Bill Graham Presents Fillmore-Last Days .... (EPA)
   Home Home On The Road .... (COL)
   New Riders Of The Purple Sage .... (COL)
How Far To Little Rock
Stanley Brothers; *Stanley Series-Vol. 1-#2* ...... (COP)
I'm A Truck
Red Simpson; *Red Simpson/Red Sovine/Dave
Dudley* .... (GUS)
I'm Truckin'
Spirit; *Spirit* .... (EPI)
   Time Circle .... (EPI)
Just Good Ol' Boys
Moe Bandy & Joe Stampley; *Greatest Hits* .... (COL)
   Just Good Ol' Boys .... (COL)
   Truckers' Jukebox-#2 .... (COL)
Keep On Truckin'
Eddie Kendricks; *12 #1 Hits From The '70s* .... (MOT)
   20/20 .... (MOT)
   At His Best .... (MOT)
   Motown Superstar Series-#19 .... (MOT)
   Motown's Biggest Pop Hits .... (MOT)
   Soul Hits/'70s-#11 .... (RHI)
Hot Tuna; *Burgers* .... (GRU)
   Final Vinyl .... (GRU)
   "Howling Blues" & Other Hits .... (RCA)
Looking At The World Through A...
Commander Cody/Lost Planet Airmen; *Hot Licks Cold
Steel & Trucker's Fav.* .... (MCA)
Red Simpson; *Ramblin' Road* .... (FFT)
Red Sovine & Del Reeves; *Red Sovine & Del
Reeves* .... (EXA)

Mama Hated Diesels
Commander Cody/Lost Planet Airmen; *We Got A Live
One Here* .... (WB)
   Hot Licks Cold Steel & Trucker's Fav. .... (MCA)
Mama Knows The Highway
Hal Ketchum; *Sure Love* .... (CRB)
Midnight Hauler
Razzy Bailey; *Greatest Hits* .... (RCA)
Movin' On
Dave Dudley; *Interstate Gold* .... (SUN)
   Trucks Trains & Airplanes .... (IGR)
Merle Haggard; *Capitol Collectors Series* .... (CAP)
Merle Haggard/Strangers; *Winners* .... (CAP)
Mutton Trucker
Larry Scott; *Keep On Truckin'* .... (EXA)
Old Home Filler Up & Keep On A Truckin'
C.W. McCall; *Greatest Hits* .... (POL)
   Wolf Creek Pass .... (MGM)
Phantom 309
Red Sovine; *Best Of* .... (STR)
Pickup Man
Joe Diffie; *Third Rock From The Sun* .... (EPI)
Pinball Machine
Lonnie Irving; *Super Hits Country-1960s* .... (IGR)
Ribbon Of Darkness
Marty Robbins; *All-Time Greatest Hits* .... (COL)
   Greatest Hits .... (COL)
   Truckers' Jukebox-#2 .... (COL)
Ride
David Allan Coe; *17 Greatest Hits* .... (COL)
   19 Hot Country Requests .... (EPI)
   Castles In The Sand .... (COL)
   For The Record-First 10 Years .... (COL)
   Trucker's Jukebox-#2 .... (COL)
Rolaids, Doan's Pills & Preparation H
Dave Dudley; *King Of The Road* .... (SUN)
Roll On Big Mama
Joe Stampley; *Biggest Hits* .... (EPI)
   Encore .... (EPI)
   Greatest Hits .... (EPI)
   Truckers' Jukebox-Top Radio Requests .... (EPI)
Roll On Buddy
Ramblin' Jack Elliott; *Essential* .... (VAN)
Roll On Truckers
Juice Newton/Silver Spur; *Early Years* .... (RCA)
   Juice Newton/Silver Spur .... (RCA)
Roll On (Eighteen Wheeler)
Alabama; *Greatest Hits-#2* .... (RCA)
   Roll On (Eighteen Wheeler) .... (RCA)
Roll, Truck, Roll
Red Simpson; *Hillbilly Music-Thank God!-#1* .... (BUG)
Semi Diesel Blues
Super Grit Cowboy Band; *If You Can't Hang-Drag Your
Country Ass* .... (HOO)
Semi Suite
Tom Waits; *Heart Of Saturday Night* .... (ASY)
Semi-Truck
Commander Cody/Lost Planet Airmen; *Hot Licks Cold
Steel & Trucker's Fav.* .... (MCA)
Sitting In The Cab Of My Truck
Chip Dockery; *Country Folk Songs-Americans In
Vietnam* .... (FF)
Six Days On The Road
Dave Dudley; *Billboard Top Country Hits-1963* .. (RHI)
   Country Music Classics-#2-1960-1965 .... (KT)
   Legends Of Country Guitar-#2 .... (RHI)
Flying Burrito Brothers; *Cabin Fever* .... (RLX)
   Farther Along-Best Of .... (A&M)
   Last Of The Red Hot Burritos .... (A&M)
Taj Mahal; *Giant Step/De Ole Folks At Home* .... (COL)
   Legends Of Rock Guitar-'60s-#2 .... (RHI)
Space Truckin'
Deep Purple; *Deepest Purple-Very Best Of* .... (WB)
   Machine Head .... (WB)
   Made In Japan .... (WB)
   When We Rock We Rock-When We Roll... ...... (WB)
Speedball Tucker
Jim Croce; *Down The Highway* .... (SAJ)
   Life & Times .... (OOP)
Tombstone Every Mile
Dave Dudley; *Interstate Gold* .... (SUN)
Trash Truck
Tad; *8-Way Santa* .... (SP)

Truck
Larry Scott; *Keep On Truckin'* .... (ALS)
Truck Driver Divorce
Frank Zappa; *Them Or Us* .... (BAR)
   You Can't Do That On Stage Anymore-#4 ...... (RYK)
Truck Driver's Blues
Johnny Gimble/Texas Swing Pioneers; *Johnny Gimble's Texas Honky-Tonk Hits* .... (CMH)
Truck Driver's Lament
Johnny Dollar; *Blue Ribbon Country-#3* .... (ACC)
Truck Driver's Prayer
Dave Dudley; *Diesel Express* .... (FFT)
Truck Driver's Queen
Willis Brothers; *45* .... (STR)
Truck Driver's Sweetheart
Marcie Dickerson; *Country Gold* .... (PLN)
Truck Driving Buddy
Red Sovine/Willis Bros./Reno & Smiley; *Heavy Haulers* .... (PP)
Truck Drivin' Cat With Nine Wives
Charlie Walker; *Truckers' Jukebox-Top Radio Requests* .... (EPI)
Truck Drivin' Girl
Bonny Boekeker; *45* .... (ACT)
Truck Drivin' Man
Charlie Walker; *Trucker's Jukebox-#2* .... (COL)
Commander Cody/Lost Planet Airmen; *Hot Licks, Cold Steel & Trucker's Fav.* .... (MCA)
   Too Much Fun-Best Of .... (MCA)
Flying Burrito Brothers; *Close Encounters To The West Coast* .... (RLX)
Hank Wilson; *Hank Wilson's Back* .... (MCA)
J. Geils Band; *Blow Your Face Out* .... (ATL)
Larry Scott; *Keep On Truckin'* .... (EXA)
Lynyrd Skynyrd; *Legend* .... (MCA)
Truck Drivin' Son Of A Gun
Dave Dudley; *20 Golden Souvenirs Of Music City U.S.A.* .... (PLN)
   Billboard Top Country Hits-1965 .... (RHI)
Truck Load Of Lovin'
Albert King; *I'm In A Phone Booth Baby* .... (STX)
Truck Of Love
Blitzspeer; *Saves* .... (EPI)
Truck On Fire
White Zombie; *Soul-Crusher* .... (CRL)
Truck Stop
Lenny Dee; *Best Of-#2* .... (MCA)
Mills Brothers; *Cab Driver* .... (RAN)
Truck Stop At The End Of The World
Commander Cody; *Let's Rock* .... (BLI)
Truck Stop Girl
Byrds; *Byrds (collection)* .... (COL)
   (Untitled) .... (COL)
Little Feat; *Little Feat* .... (WB)
Truck Stop Rock
Commander Cody/Lost Planet Airmen; *Hot Licks, Cold Steel & Trucker's Fav.* .... (MCA)
Truck 'Em On Down
Stick "Horse" Hammond; *Alley Special* .... (CLT)
Trucker's Nightmare
Lawrence Hammond; *Coyote's Dream* .... (TAK)
   Critic's Choice .... (TAK)
Truckin'
Bread; *Anthology* .... (ELE)
   Best Of .... (ELE)
   Manna .... (ELE)
Dwight Yoakam; *Deadicated* .... (ARI)
Grateful Dead; *American Beauty* .... (WB)
   Europe '72 .... (WB)
   Skeletons From The Closet-Best Of .... (WB)
   What A Long Strange Trip It's Been .... (WB)
Mel Torme/Mel-Tones; *Back In Town* .... (VRV)
Truckin' Dad
Dave Dudley; *Diesel Express* .... (FFT)
Truckin' Down The Avenue
Sonny Burgess; *Sun Rockabillies-#1* .... (SUN)
Truckin' Little Baby
John Hammond; *Solo* .... (VAN)
Truckload Of Lovin'
Albert King; *I'm In A Phone Booth Baby* .... (FAN)
   Masterworks .... (ATL)
   Truckload Of Lovin' .... (TOM)
White Freightliner Blues
Jimmie Dale Gilmore; *Fair & Square* .... (HT)

New Grass Revival; *When The Storm Is Over* ...... (FF)
Townes Van Zandt; *Live & Obscure* .... (SH)
Willin'
Byrds; *Byrds (collection)* .... (COL)
Linda Ronstadt; *Heart Like A Wheel* .... (CAP)
Little Feat; *Little Feat* .... (WB)
   Sailin' Shoes .... (WB)
   Waiting For Columbus .... (WB)
Wolverton Mountain
Claude King; *American Originals* .... (COL)
   Best .... (GUS)
   Billboard Top Country Hits-1962 .... (RHI)

UFO'S, Alien Creatures, Space People
See Also: SPACE, STARS

Alien
Atlanta Rhythm Section; *Quinella* .... (COL)
Tanya Tucker; *Love Me Like You Used To* .... (CAP)
"Alien" Theme
Boston Pops Orchestra/John Williams; *Out Of This World* .... (PHI)
Arriving U.F.O.
Yes; *Tormato* .... (ATL)
Astro Boy
Buggles; *Age Of Plastic* .... (ISL)
Astro Man
Jimi Hendrix; *Cry Of Love* .... (RPR)
Astronaut Food
Sopwith Camel; *Miraculous Hump Returns* .... (RPR)
Attack Of The Radioactive Hamsters
Weird Al Yankovic; *ST/UHF* .... (RAR)
Bermuda Triangle
Fleetwood Mac; *Heroes Are Hard To Find* ...... (RPR)
Bermuda Triangle Blues (Flight 45)
Blondie; *Plastic Letters* .... (CHR)
Calling Occupants Of Interplanetary...
Carpenters; *Classics-#2* .... (A&M)
   Passages .... (A&M)
   Yesterday Once More .... (A&M)
Klaatu; *Klaatu* .... (CAP)
Ewok Celebration
Meco; *45* .... (ARI)
Extraterrestrial Intelligence
Blue Oyster Cult; *Agents Of Fortune* .... (COL)
   Career Of Evil .... (COL)
   Extraterrestrial Live .... (COL)
   Some Enchanted Evening .... (COL)
E.T.I. (Extra Terrestrial Intelligence)
Blue Oyster Cult; *Agents Of Fortune* .... (COL)
   Career Of Evil .... (COL)
   Extraterrestrial Live .... (COL)
   Some Enchanted Evening .... (COL)
"E.T." Theme
Boston Pops Orchestra/John Williams; *Out Of This World* .... (PHI)
Walter Murphy; *"E.T." Theme* .... (MCA)
Fly On U.F.O.
Chromium; *Star To Star* .... (INF)
Flying Saucers Rock 'N' Roll
Billy Lee Riley; *Legends Of Rock Guitar/'50s-#2* . (RHI)
   Sun Story .... (RHI)
Have You Seen The Saucers
Jefferson Airplane; *2400 Fulton Street-An Anthology* .... (RCA)
   30 Seconds Over Winterland .... (RCA)
Heartlight
Neil Diamond; *Heartlight* .... (COL)
   Hot August Night II .... (COL)
I've Seen The Saucers
Elton John; *Caribou* .... (POL)
Joe Slam And The Spaceship
Harry Connick, Jr.; *She* .... (COL)
Looking For A U.F.O.
Adrian Belew; *Young Lions* .... (ATL)
Loving The Alien
David Bowie; *The Singles-1969-1993* .... (RYK)
Martian Boogie
Brownsville Station; *Brownsville Station* .... (PVS)

Martian Hop
Ran-Dells; *Dr. Demento Greatest Novelty*
Records-#3 .... (RHI)
   Elvira Presents Haunted Hits .... (RHI)
   Halloween Hits .... (RHI)
Martian Love Song
Hypnolovewheel; *Angel Food* .... (ALI)
Martian Manhunter
Trotsky Icepick; *Ultraviolet Catastrophe* .... (SST)
Martians At The Window
Kaleidoscope; *Greetings From Kartoonistan* ...... (GFT)
Martians Go Home
Shorty Rogers; *Great Moments In Jazz* .... (ATL)
"My Favorite Martian" Theme
Original Music; *Television's Greatest Hits-#2* ..... (TVT)
Planetary Invasion
Midnight Star; *Planetary Invasion* .... (SLR)
Praying To The Aliens
Gary Numan/Tubeway Army; *Replicas* .... (ATC)
(Radio Station) EXP
Jimi Hendrix; *Axis Bold As Love* .... (RPR)
Rapture
Blondie; *Auto American* .... (CHR)
   Best Of .... (CHR)
   Once More Into The Bleach .... (CHR)
   Rock The First-#4 .... (SAN)
Saucerful Of Secrets
Pink Floyd; *Nice Pair* .... (CAP)
   Saucerful Of Secrets .... (CAP)
   Ummagumma .... (CAP)
Sure The Boy Was Green
Horslips; *Aliens* .... (DJM)
Theme From "Close Encounters Of The..."
John Williams; *ST/Close Encounters Of The Third*
Kind .... (VS)
Walter Murphy; *Themes From E.T.* .... (MCA)
Theme From "Return Of The Jedi"
Boston Pops Orchestra/John Williams; *Pops Out Of This*
World .... (PHI)
Neil Norman; *Greatest Science Fiction Hits-#3* ... (CRS)
Theme From "U.F.O."
Neil Norman; *Greatest Science Fiction Hits-#3* ... (CRS)
UFO Has Landed In The Ghetto
Ry Cooder; *The Slide Area* .... (WB)
UFO Over Cairo
NASA; *Insha-Allah* .... (SIR)
UFO's Are Real
Spot 1019; *Still...Again* .... (FRN)
Under The Eye
Dennis Linde; *Under The Eye* .... (MON)
Unidentified Flying Tuna Trot
R.E.O. Speedwagon; *You Can Tune A Piano But You*
Can't... .... (EPI)
U.F.O.
Country Joe McDonald; *Rock & Roll From The Planet*
Earth .... (FAN)
Nina Hagen; *Nunsexmonkrock* .... (COL)
Reggie Knighton Band; *Reggie Knighton Band* ...(COL)
Undisputed Truth; *45* .... (MOT)
U.F.O. Story
Flaming Lips; *Telepathic Surgery* .... (RES)
Waiting For The UFO's
Graham Parker/Rumour; *Squeezing Out Sparks* .. (ARI)
"War Of The Worlds" Theme
Neil Norman; *Greatest Science Fiction Hits-#3* ... (CRS)
We Are The Other People
Mothers Of Invention; *We're Only In It For The*
Money .... (VRV)
Ziggy Stardust
David Bowie; *Changesbowie* ....(RYK)
   Rise & Fall Of Ziggy Stardust .... (RYK)
   Sound + Vision .... (RYK)
   Stage .... (RYK)
   ST/Ziggy Stardust-The Motion Picture .... (RCA)
   The Singles-1969-1993 .... (RYK)

VEGETABLES

See Also: FOOD, FRUIT, RESTAURANTS

Addicted To Spuds
Weird Al Yankovic; *Food Album* .... (RAR)
   Greatest Hits .... (RAR)

And Even The Vegetables Screamed
Legendary Pink Dots; *Golden Age* .... (PIA)
Attack Of The Vegetable Men
Active Ingredient; *Extrastrength* .... (BAI)
Cabbage Greens
Champion Jack Dupree; *New Orleans Barrelhouse*
Boogie-Complete .... (COL)
Call Any Vegetable
Mothers Of Invention; *Just Another Band From*
L.A. .... (BIZ)
Celery Stalks At Midnight
Will Bradley; *Swing Time! Fab. Big Band*
Era-1925-1955 .... (COL)
Cheese & Onions
Rutles; *Rutles* .... (RHI)
Chop Suey Louie
Jimmy Preston; *Rock The Joint-#2* .... (CLT)
Collard Greens & Black-Eyed Peas
Bud Powell; *Best Of* .... (BLN)
Don't Slay That Potato
Tom Paxon; *One Million Lawyers & Other Disasters* (FF)
Eggplant Pizza
Jimmy Bruno Trio; *Sleight Of Hand* .... (CCJ)
Eggplant That Ate Chicago
Dr. West's Medicine Show & Junk Band; *Dr. Demento's*
Greatest-#3 .... (RHI)
Fish & Chips
Eddie/Hot Rods; *Fish & Chips* .... (AMR)
Glass Onion
Beatles; *Box Set* .... (CAP)
   White Album .... (CAP)
Goober Peas
Burl Ives; *Greatest Hits* .... (MCA)
Kingston Trio; *At Large/Here We Go Again!* ..... (CAP)
Good Old Cabbage Greens
Washboard Sam; *Rockin' My Blues Away* .... (RCA)
Green Onions
Booker T./M.G.s; *Best Of* .... (ATL)
   Billboard Top R&B Hits-1962 .... (RHI)
   Green Onions .... (ATL)
   ST/American Graffiti .... (MCA)
   ST/Quadrophenia .... (POL)
Hot Corn, Cold Corn
Flatt & Scruggs; *At Carnegie Hall* .... (COL)
Hot Dogs & Cabbage
Li'l Wally; *One Man Band* .... (JJ)
Hot Potatoes
King Curtis; *Enjoy-Best Of* .... (CLT)
Kinks; *Everybody's In Show Biz* .... (RHI)
Lord I Love Mashed Potatoes
Mayf Nutter; *Goin' Skinny Dippin'* .... (CRS)
Mashed Potato Time
Dee Dee Sharp; *21 Oldies But Goodies* .... (OSR)
   Big Bad Bossa Beat .... (OSR)
   Oldies But Goodies-#6 .... (OSR)
Mashed Potatoes (Hot Pastrami With)
Joey Dee/Starliters; *Hey Let's Twist-Best Of* ...... (RHI)
Motorcycle Song
Arlo Guthrie; *Alice's Restaurant* .... (RPR)
   Best Of .... (RPR)
Soul Brothers; *Three Hour Tour* .... (SI)
Mystical Potato Head Groove Thing
Joe Satriani; *Flying In A Blue Dream* .... (REL)
No Rice, No Peas, No Coconut Oil
Jolly Boys; *Beer Joint & Tailoring* .... (FLW)
Onion Field
Dandelion; *I Think I'm Gonna Be Sick* .... (RUC)
Onion In A Closet
Sergie Kuriokhin & Henry Kaiser; *Popular*
Science .... (RYK)
Onion Roll
Herb Ellis & Ray Brown Sextet; *Hot Tracks* ..... (CCJ)
Onion Skin
Boom Crash Opera; *These Here Are Crazy Times* (GIA)
Onion Song
Marvin Gaye & Tammi Terrell; *Easy* .... (MOT)
   Greatest Hits .... (MOT)
Onion Town
John Delafose/Eunice Playboys; *Stomp Down*
Zydeco .... (ROU)
Pass The Peas
Maceo Parker; *Life On Planet Groove* .... (VRV)
Pickin' Up The Cabbage
Cab Calloway; *Best Of The Big Bands* .... (COL)

Plant A Radish
Original Cast; *Fantasticks* .... (POL)
Polk Salad Annie
Elvis Presley; *As Recorded Live At Madison Sq.*
Garden ....(RCA)
Tony Joe White; *Soul Shots-#6-Blue-Eyed Soul* .. (RHI)
Swingin' Country Favorites .... (WB)
Pope Is A Potato
Mofungo; *Bugged* .... (SST)
Potato Head Blues
Louis Armstrong; *Best Of The Decca Years-#2-The*
Composer ....(MCA)
You Rascal You ....(POE)
Potato Pancake
Preston Reed; *Pointing Up* .... (FF)
Potato Picking
Mark Knopfler; *Screenplaying* .... (WB)
ST/Cal ....(MER)
Potato Radio
King & Moore; *Potato Radio* .... (JST)
Potato Salad
Jimmy Preston; *Jimmy Preston* .... (CLT)
Pumpkin
Andrew Hill; *Black Fire* .... (BLN)
Pumpkin Head
Dharma Bums; *Bliss* .... (FRN)
Pumpkin Time
Darol Anger & Barbara Higbie; *Live At Montreux* (WH)
Rabbit In The Pea Patch
Red Clay Ramblers; *Merchant's Lunch* .... (FF)
Rat Salad
Black Sabbath; *Paranoid* .... (WB)
Rice & Peas
Wailers Band; *I.D.* .... (ATL)
Rotten Lettuce
Jeffrey Frederick/Clamtones; *Spiders In The*
Moonlight .... (ROU)
Sauerkraut 'N' Solar Energy
Norman Blake/Others; *Norman Blake/Others* ...... (FF)
She Cooks Me Cabbage
Jack Dupree; *Blues For Everybody* .... (GUS)
Sweet Pea
Tommy Roe; *Best Of* ....(CCB)
Cruisin'-1966 .... (INC)
Greatest Hits ....(MCA)
Sweet Potato Pie
Al Jarreau; *We Got By* .... (RPR)
James Taylor; *Never Die Young* ....(COL)
Swee' Pea
Count Basie; *Best Of* .... (PAB)
Texas Jalapenos
Texas Rubies; *Working Girl Blues* .... (MSD)
Tomato Paste
Flop; *Flop & The Fall Of The Mopsqueezer* ...... (FRN)
Tulip Or Turnip (Tell Me Dream Face)
Duke Ellington & Teresa Brewer; *It Don't Mean A*
Thing If It Ain't Got.. ....(COL)
Vegetables
Beach Boys; *Smiley Smile/Wild Honey* ....(CAP)
Sunshine Dream ....(CAP)
Why Is A Carrot More Orange Than An...
Amboy Dukes; *Journey To The Center Of The*
Mind ....(MST)

WAITING

See Also: TIME: GENERAL

5-4-3-2 (Yo! Time Is Up)
Jade; *Mind Body & Soul* .... (GIA)
Ain't No Fun (Waiting 'Round To Be A...)
AC/DC; *Dirty Deeds Done Dirt Cheap* .... (ATL)
Anticipation
Carly Simon; *Anticipation* .... (ELE)
Best Of .... (ELE)
Crying, Waiting, Hoping
Marshall Crenshaw; *ST/La Bamba* ....(SLS)
Desperados Waiting For The Train
Guy Clark; *Old No. 1* ....(SH)
Jerry Jeff Walker; *Best Of* ....(MCA)
Great Gonzos ....(MCA)
Viva Terlingua ....(MCA)
W. Jennings/W. Nelson/J. Cash/K. Krist.;
Highwayman ....(COL)

Got Me Waiting
Heavy D/Boyz; *Nuttin' But Love* .... (UT)
Heaven Can Wait
Iron Maiden; *Somewhere In Time* ....(CAP)
Meatloaf; *Bat Out Of Hell* ....(EPI)
Paul Young; *Other Voices* ....(COL)
How Long Must I Wait For You
Joe Jackson; *Jumpin' Jive* .... (A&M)
I Can't Wait Another Minute
Hi-Five; *Hi-Five* .... (JVA)
I Just Can't Wait To Be King
Elton John; *ST/The Lion King* .... (DIS)
In The Air Tonight
Phil Collins; *Classic Rock 1966-1988* .... (ATL)
Face Value ....(ATL)
Miami Vice ....(MCA)
Prince's Trust 10th Anniversary Party .... (A&M)
Secret Policeman's Other Ball .... (ISL)
Serious Hits...Live! ....(ATL)
In The Midnight Hour
Rascals; *Classic Rock-1966-1988* ....(ATL)
ST/More Songs From "The Big Chill" .... (MOT)
Time Piece-Greatest Hits ....(ATL)
Roxy Music; *Flesh & Blood* ....(RPR)
Street Life-20 Great Hits ....(RPR)
Wilson Pickett; *Atlantic R&B*
1947-1974-#5-(1962-1966) .... (ATL)
Best Of ....(ATL)
Frat Rock-#4 ....(RHI)
Golden Soul ....(ATL)
Greatest Hits ....(ATL)
Soul Years ....(ATL)
Isn't It Time
Babys; *Anthologoy* ....(CHR)
Broken Heart ....(CHR)
I'm Waiting For The Man
Lou Reed; *Live* ....(RCA)
Velvet Underground; *Live* ....(COT)
Velvet Underground & Nico ....(VRV)
Linger
Cranberries; *Everybody Else Is Doing It So Why...* . (ISL)
Love Won't Let Me Wait
Luther Vandross; *Any Love* ....(EPI)
Best Of-Best Of Love ....(EPI)
Major Harris; *Atlantic R&B 1947-1974-#6* ......(ATL)
Live ....(WMO)
My Way ....(ATL)
Only Waiting For You
Crosby, Stills & Nash; *After The Storm* .... (ATL)
Push Push
Paula Abdul; *Spellbound* .... (VIA)
Right Here Waiting
Richard Marx; *Repeat Offender* ....(CAP)
Second Class Wait Here
Slim Dusty; *Australia Is His Name* ....(PHO)
Standing In The Shadows Of Love
Barry White; *Greatest Hits* ....(CAS)
I've Got So Much To Give .... (20)
Four Tops; *Anthology* .... (MOT)
Greatest Hits ....(MOT)
Motown Story ....(MOT)
Motown Superstar Series-#14 .... (MOT)
Reach Out ....(MOT)
Rod Stewart; *Blondes Have More Fun* .... (WB)
Take Your Time
Babyface; *Lovers* ....(SLR)
Jefferson Starship; *Earth* ....(GRU)
Judson Spence; *Judson Spence* ....(ATL)
Lynyrd Skynyrd; *Legend* ....(MCA)
Pebbles; *Pebbles* ....(MCA)
S.O.S. Band; *Billboard Top Hits-1980* ....(RHI)
Club Epic ....(EPI)
S.O.S. Band ....(TAB)
There's A Fella Waitin' In Poughkeepsie
Pied Pipers; *Capitol Collectors Series* ....(CAP)
Tie A Yellow Ribbon 'Round The Old...
Frank Sinatra; *Some Nice Things I've Missed* ..... (RPR)
Lawrence Welk; *Best Of-20 Great Hits* .... (RAN)
Sonny James & Karla Taylor; *Classic Country*
Duets ....(CCB)
Tony Orlando/Dawn; *45* ....(FSB)
Time Is Wasting
Carlo; *20 Great Love Songs/'50s & '60s-#1* ......(LAU)
22 Leaders Of The Pack-#1 ....(LAU)

Time Waits For No One
Rolling Stones; *It's Only Rock 'N' Roll* .... (RS)
  Sucking In The Seventies .... (RS)
Tired Of Waiting For You
Kinks; *Greatest Hits-#1* .... (RHI)
  History Of British Rock-#3 .... (RHI)
  Kinda Kinks .... (RHI)
Until She Comes
Psychedelic Furs; *World Outside* ....(COL)
Until You Come Back To Me
Aretha Franklin; *30 Greatest Hits* .... (ATL)
  Best Of .... (ATL)
  Golden Age Of Black Music 1970-1975 ...... (ATL)
Basia; *Brave New Hope* .... (EPI)
  London Warsaw New York .... (EPI)
Miki Howard; *Miki Howard* .... (ATL)
Stevie Wonder; *Love Songs-20 Classic Hits* ...... (MOT)
Wait
Beatles; *Box Set* .... (CAP)
  Rubber Soul .... (CAP)
Wait Till The Sun Shines Nellie
Joan Morris & William Bolcom; *After The Ball* . (NON)
Wait Until Tomorrow
Jimi Hendrix; *Axis: Bold As Love* .... (RPR)
Jimi Hendrix Experience; *Radio One* ....(RYK)
Waiting For A Star To Fall
Boy Meets Girl; *Nipper's Greatest Hits-'80s* ......(RCA)
  Reel Life .... (RCA)
Waiting For A Train
Boz Scaggs; *Boz Scaggs* .... (ATL)
Jimmie Rodgers; *Early Years-1928-1929* .... (ROU)
  This Is .... (RCA)
Waiting For Love
Alias; *Alias* .... (EMI)
Waiting For Sun
Jayhawks; *Hollywood Town Hall* .... (DEF)
Waiting For The Day
Gerry Rafferty; *City To City* .... (EMI)
Waiting For The End Of The World
Elvis Costello; *My Aim Is True* .... (COL)
Waiting For The Moon
Bruce Cockburn; *The Trouble With Normal* ..... (COL)
Waiting For The Rain To Fall
Chris Isaak; *Chris Isaak* .... (WB)
Waiting For The Robert E. Lee
Al Jolson; *My Mammy* .... (MSP)
Eddie Cantor; *Centennial Celebration* ....(RCA)
Waiting For The Russians
Trees; *Forrest Fires* .... (ADE)
Waiting For The Sun
Doors; *Best Of* .... (ELE)
  Classics .... (ELE)
  Morrison Hotel .... (ELE)
Waiting For The Sun To Shine
John Conlee; *In My Eyes* .... (MSP)
Lionel Cartwright; *Chasin' The Sun* .... (MCA)
Reba McEntire; *Reba Nell McEntire* .... (MER)
Ricky Skaggs; *Favorite Country Songs* .... (EPI)
  Waiting For The Sun To Shine .... (EPI)
Waiting For The Tide To Turn
Robert Cray Band; *Bad Influence* .... (HT)
Waiting For The UFO's
Graham Parker/Rumour; *Squeezing Out Sparks* .. (ARI)
Waiting For The Worms
Pink Floyd; *The Wall* ....(COL)
Roger Waters; *The Wall Live In Berlin* .... (MER)
Waiting Game
Swing Out Sister; *Kaleidoscope World* ....(FON)
Waiting In The Wings
BBM; *Around The Next Dream* .... (VIA)
Waiting On A Friend
Rolling Stones; *Rewind-1971-1984* .... (RS)
  Tattoo You .... (RS)
Waitin' For The Bus
ZZ Top; *Best Of* .... (WB)
  Six Pack .... (WB)
  Tres Hombres .... (WB)
Waitin' In School
Rick Nelson; *Legendary Masters* .... (EMI)
  Legends Of Rock Guitar-'50s-#2 .... (RHI)

Waitin' In Your Welfare Line
Buck Owens/Buckaroos; *Billboard Top Country
Hits-1966* .... (RHI)
  Buck Owens Collection-1959-1990 .... (RHI)
  Live At Carnegie Hall .... (CMF)
Wait
Sarah McLachlan; *Fumbling Towards Ecstasy* .... (ARI)
Watin' For The Phone To Ring
Patty Loveless; *Up Against My Heart* .... (MCA)
Ronna Reeves; *What Comes Naturally* .... (MER)
Will He Wait A Little Longer
Stanley Brothers; *Stanley Series-Vol. 1-#3* ......(COP)
World Is Waiting For The Sunrise
Benny Goodman; *I Like Jazz-Essence Of* ....(COL)
Benny Goodman Orchestra & Quartet; *Let's
Dance* .... (LAS)
Les Paul & Mary Ford; *World Is Waiting For The
Sunrise* .... (LAS)
Roy Clark & Buck Trent; *Banjo Bandit* .... (MCA)
You Better Wait
Steve Perry; *For The Love Of Strange Medicine* ..(COL)

≈≈≈≈≈≈≈≈≈≈≈≈≈≈≈≈≈≈≈≈≈≈≈≈≈≈≈≈≈≈≈≈≈≈≈≈≈≈

**WAR, Army, Battles, Bombs, Military, Soldiers,
Surrender**

*See Also: DEATH, DRAFT, GUNS, FIGHT,
POLITICAL SONGS*

≈≈≈≈≈≈≈≈≈≈≈≈≈≈≈≈≈≈≈≈≈≈≈≈≈≈≈≈≈≈≈≈≈≈≈≈≈≈

1812 Overture
New York Philharmonic/Leonard Bernstein; *Conducts
Tchaikovsky* ....(COL)
  Great Tchaikovsky ....(COL)
  Overtures and Tone Poems ....(COL)
  Tchaikovsky's Greatest Hits-#1 ....(COL)
  Various Overtures ....(COL)
19
Paul Hardcastle; *Paul Hardcastle* .... (CHR)
Abolitionist Hymn
Hermes Nye; *Ballads Of The Civil War-#1 & 2* . (FLW)
Ain't Gonna Study War No More
Nat King Cole; *Every Time I Feel The Spirit* ....(CAP)
Weavers; *Reunion* .... (VAN)
All Is Fair In Love And War
Ronnie Milsap; *Club* ....(RCA)
All Quiet Along The Potomac Tonight
Hermes Nye; *Ballads Of The Civil War-#1 & 2* . (FLW)
Anne Frank Story
Human Sexual Response; *Fig. 15* .... (EAT)
Another Old Soldier
Mark Collie; *Hardin County Line* .... (MCA)
Army Blues
Bobby Blue Bland; *I Pity The Fool/Duke
Recordings-#1* .... (MCA)
Army Dreamers
Kate Bush; *Never For Ever* .... (EMI)
  The Whole Story .... (EMI)
Army Life
Leadbelly; *Easy Rider* .... (FLW)
Army Man In Vietnam
Big Joe Williams; *Shake Your Boogie* .... (ARH)
  Thinking Of What They Did To Me .... (ARH)
Army Of The Free
Tennessee Ernie Ford; *Sings Songs Of The Civil
War* ....(CAP)
Army Song
Original Cast; *Threepenny Opera* .... (POL)
At War With The World
Foreigner; *4* .... (ATL)
Atlanta Burned Again Last Night
Atlanta; *Pictures* .... (MCA)
Atlanta's Burning Down
Dickey Betts/Great Southern; *Dickey Betts/Great
Southern* .... (ARI)
Randy Howard; *All-American Redneck* .... (WB)
Ballad For A Soldier
Leon Russell; *Asylum Choir 2* .... (MCA)
Ballad Of The Green Berets
Barry Sadler; *Cruisin'-1966* .... (INC)
  Hits Of The '60s ....(IMC)
  More American Graffiti-#4 .... (MCA)
  Nipper's Greatest Hits-'60s-#2 ....(RCA)
  Super Hits-#3 ....(GUS)

Battle Cry Of Freedom
Mormon Tabernacle Choir; *Album* ....(COL)
  God Bless America ....(COL)
  Greatest Hits ....(COL)
  Songs Of The North & South 1861-1965 ......(COL)
Battle Hymn Of The Republic
Charlie Sexton; *Charlie Sexton* .... (MCA)
Judy Collins; *Songs Of The Civil War* ....(COL)
Mormon Tabernacle Choir; *God Bless America* ..(COL)
  Stars & Stripes Forever ....(COL)
Pat Boone; *Star-Spangled Banner* ....(WOR)
Battle Of Atlanta
Reno & Smiley; *1983 Collector's Edition-#2* .....(GUS)
Battle Of Bunker Hill
Jim Burroughs; *Songs Of Rebellion* ....(AUF)
Battle Of Glass Tears
King Crimson; *Lizard* .... (EDI)
Battle Of New Orleans
Chet Atkins/Boston Pops; *Best Of* ....(RCA)
Johnny Horton; *American Originals* ....(COL)
  Greatest Hits ....(COL)
  Radio Classics/'50s ....(COL)
Nitty Gritty Dirt Band; *Dirt Silver & Gold* .... (UA)
  Dream .... (UA)
  Stars & Stripes Forever .... (UA)
Battle Of Trenton
Jim Burroughs; *Songs Of Rebellion* ....(AUF)
Being At War With Each Other
Barbra Streisand; *The Way We Were* ....(COL)
Carole King; *Fantasy* .... (EOD)
Bomb The Russians
Fear; *More Beer* .... (ENI)
Bomber
James Gang; *Best Of* .... (MCA)
  Rides Again .... (MCA)
Bombs Away
Bob Weir; *Heaven Help The Fool* .... (ARI)
Police; *Zenyatta Mondatta* .... (A&M)
Bomb, The
L7; *Hungry For Stink* ....(SLS)
Bonaparte's Retreat
Chieftains; *Bonaparte's Retreat* .... (SHA)
Glen Campbell; *Classics Collection* .... (LIB)
Kay Starr; *Greatest Hits* ....(CCB)
Sons Of The Pioneers; *Country & Western*
Memories .... (PRR)
Boogie Woogie Bugle Boy
Andrews Sisters; *16 Great Performances* .... (MCA)
  Best Of .... (MCA)
  Boogie Woogie Bugle Girls .... (MCA)
  Rarities .... (MCA)
Bette Midler; *Divine Miss M* .... (ATL)
  Live At Last .... (ATL)
  ST/Divine Madness .... (ATL)
Born In The U.S.A.
Bruce Springsteen; *Born In The U.S.A.* ....(COL)
Bruce Springsteen/E Street Band;
Live-1975-1985 ....(COL)
Bring Them Home
Pete Seeger; *Young Vs. Old* ....(OOP)
British Grenadiers
Cambridge Singers; *The Lark In THe Clear Air* ..(CLG)
Bugle Call Rag
Benny Goodman; *Stompin' At The Savoy* ....(BLU)
Enoch Light/Light Brigade; *Big Band Hits/'30s-#2* . (P3)
New Orleans Rhythm Kings; *New Orleans Rhythm*
Kings .... (MS)
Burning Of Atlanta
Claude King; *American Originals* ....(COL)
Business Goes On As Usual
Roberta Flack; *Chapter 2* .... (ATL)
Car Bomb
Negativeland; *Escape From Noise* ....(SST)
Cast The First Stone
Angel; *On Earth As It Is In Heaven* .... (CAS)
Coming Home Soldier
Bobby Vinton; *All-Time Greatest Hits* .... (EPI)
Comin' In On A Wing & A Prayer
Ry Cooder; *Boomer's Story* ....(RPR)
Conquistador
Procol Harum; *Best Of* .... (A&M)
  Classics-#17 .... (A&M)
  Live With The Edmonton Orchestra .... (A&M)

Cowards Over Pearl Harbor
Wilma Lee Cooper; *Wilma Lee Cooper* .... (ROU)
Cruel War
Peter, Paul & Mary; *Peter, Paul & Mary* ....(WB)
Davy's Dinghy
Ruth Wallis; *Dr. Demento's Dementia Royale* .... (RHI)
  Dr. Demento's Greatest Novelties-#2 .... (RHI)
Deck Of Cards
Bill Anderson; *American Music Greatest Hits* .....(CCB)
  Best Of ....(CCB)
Tex Ritter; *Capitol Collectors Series* ....(CAP)
  Greatest Hits ....(CCB)
"T" Texas Tyler; *45* ....(OOP)
Desaperecidos (Central America)
Little Steven; *Voice Of America* .... (EMI)
Dixie
Black Oak Arkansas; *Best Of* ....(ATC)
  Hot & Nasty-Best Of .... (RHI)
Boston Pops Orchestra/Arthur Fiedler; *American*
Salute ....(RCA)
Lee Greenwood; *American Patriot* .... (LIB)
Mormon Tabernacle Choir; *Greatest Hits-#2* .....(COL)
  Songs Of The Civil War & S. Foster Fav. ...... (SMC)
Tennessee Ernie Ford; *Sings Songs Of The Civil*
War ....(CAP)
Dying Soldier
Christy Moore; *Christy Moore* .... (ATL)
English Civil War
Clash; *Give 'Em Enough Rope* .... (EPI)
  Story Of-#1 .... (EPI)
Enlisted Men's Mess
Glenn Miller; *Major Glenn Miller/Army Air Force*
Band .... (BLU)
Eve Of Destruction
Barry McGuire; *Billboard Top Rock 'N' Roll*
Hits-1965 .... (RHI)
  Cruisin'-1965 .... (INC)
  Good Feeling Music/Big Chill-#3 .... (MOT)
  Vintage Music-#9 & 10 .... (MCA)
Dickies; *Great Dictations (Definitive Collection)* . (A&M)
  Incredible Shrinking .... (A&M)
Turtles; *Turtle Wax-Best Of-#2* .... (RHI)
  Turtlesized .... (RHI)
Fall Of Charleston
Tennessee Ernie Ford; *Sings Songs Of The Civil*
War ....(CAP)
Fall Of Saigon
Original London Cast; *Miss Saigon* .... (GEF)
Folk Song Army
Tom Lehrer; *That Was The Year That Was* ......(RPR)
Fortress Around Your Heart
Sting; *Dream Of The Blue Turtles* .... (A&M)
Forty Thousand Headmen
Traffic; *Traffic* .... (ISL)
  Welcome To The Canteen .... (ISL)
Foxhole
Television; *Adventure* .... (ELE)
Front Line
Stevie Wonder; *Original Musiquarium* .... (MOT)
General Custer
Tom Paxton; *How Come The Sun* .... (OOP)
"Gomer Pyle U.S.M.C." Theme
Original Music; *Television's Greatest Hits-#2* ..... (TVT)
Goodbye Blue Sky
Daryl Braithwaite; *Higher Than Hope* .... (EPA)
  Rise .... (EPA)
Pink Floyd; *The Wall* ....(COL)
Roger Waters; *The Wall Live In Berlin* .... (MER)
Hawaiian War Chant
Bette Midler; *Live At Last* .... (ATL)
Tommy Dorsey; *Complete-#8* ....(RCA)
  This Is ....(RCA)
Hay Una Mujer Desaparecida
Holly Near; *Imagine My Surprise* .... (RWD)
Holly Near & Ronnie Gilbert; *Lifeline* .... (RWD)
Hiroshima
Todd Rundgren/Utopia; *Ra* .... (RHI)
"Hogan's Heroes" Theme
Original Music; *Television's Greatest Hits-#2* ..... (TVT)
I Don't Want To Be A Soldier
John Lennon/Plastic Ono Band; *Imagine* ....(CAP)

I Feel Like I'm Fixing To Die Rag
Country Joe/Fish; *Greatest Hits* .... (VAN)
  Greatest '60s Folksingers .... (VAN)
  I Feel Like I'm Fixing To Die Rag .... (VAN)
  Life & Times Of .... (VAN)
  More American Graffiti-#4 .... (MCA)
  ST/Woodstock .... (ATL)
I Surrender Dear
Bing Crosby; *Where The Blue Of The Night Meets
The...* ....(BIO)
Count Basie; *Basie & Zoot* .... (PAB)
  For The Second Time .... (PAB)
  Jam-#3 .... (PAB)
  Loose Walk .... (PAB)
Mel Torme; *Smooth As Velvet* .... (PIC)
Rosemary Clooney; *Sings Bing* .... (CCJ)
If I Had A Rocket Launcher (C. America)
Bruce Cockburn; *Stealing Fire* .... (GLM)
  Waiting For A Miracle-Singles 1970-1987 ..... (GLM)
If The South Woulda Won
Hank Williams, Jr.; *Wild Streak* .... (W/C)
In Germany Before The War
Randy Newman; *Little Criminals* .... (WB)
In The Army Now
Big Bill Broonzy; *News & The Blues-Telling It Like It
Is* ....(COL)
Status Quo; *Status Quo* .... (MER)
I'd Surrender All
Randy Travis; *High Lonesome* .... (WB)
John Brown's Body
Pete Seeger; *American Favorite Ballads-#3* ...... (FLW)
Johnny Has Gone For A Soldier
Jo Stafford; *American Folk Songs* .... (CRN)
Join The Army
Suicidal Tendencies; *Join The Army* .... (CRL)
Joshua Fought The Battle Of Jericho
Elvis Presley; *His Hand In Mine* ....(RCA)
Jordanaires; *Tribute To Elvis' Favorite Spirituals* ....(SO)
New Messengers Of Happiness; *Swinging Gospel* . (ALS)
Pete Seeger; *20 Golden Pieces Of* .... (BLD)
Sister Rosetta Tharpe; *Live At The Hot Club De
France* .... (MLN)
Kansas City Bomber
Phil Ochs; *War Is Over-Best Of* .... (A&M)
Last Train To Nuremberg
Pete Seeger; *Rainbow Race* ....(OOP)
Life During Wartime
Talking Heads; *Fear Of Music* .... (SIR)
  Name Of This Band Is .... (SIR)
  ST/Stop Making Sense .... (SIR)
Like A Soldier
Johnny Cash; *American Recordings* .... (AME)
Lili Marlene
Marlene Dietrich; *Best Of* ....(COL)
  Essential ....(CAP)
  Live At The Cafe De Paris ....(COL)
  This Is Art Deco ....(COL)
Love Is A Battlefield
Pat Benatar; *Best Shots* .... (CHR)
  Live From Earth .... (CHR)
Lucky Man
Emerson, Lake & Palmer; *Best Of* .... (ATL)
  Emerson, Lake & Palmer .... (ATL)
Marines' Hymn
Mormon Tabernacle Choir; *God Bless America* . (SMC)
  Stars & Stripes Forever ....(COL)
Masters Of War
Bob Dylan; *Biograph* ....(COL)
  Freewheelin' ....(COL)
  Real Live ....(COL)
Me & Crippled Soldiers
Merle Haggard; *American Music Greatest Hits* ...(CCB)
  Blue Jungle ....(CCB)
Meadowlands
101 Strings Orchestra; *Soul Of Russia* .... (ALS)
Jefferson Airplane; *Volunteers* ....(RCA)
Meet De Boys On The Battlefront
Wild Tchoupitoulas; *Treacherous-History Of The Neville
Bros.* .... (RHI)
  Wild Tchoupitoulas .... (ISL)
Military Madness
Graham Nash; *Bread & Roses Festival-#2* .... (FAN)
  Songs For Beginners .... (ATL)

Minstrel Boy
Boston Pops Orchestra/Arthur Fiedler; *Irish
Album* ....(RCA)
  Irish Night At The Pops ....(RCA)
John McDermott; *Battlefields Of Green-Songs Of
Love/Loss* .... (ANG)
Moratorium
Buffy Sainte-Marie; *She Used To Wanna Be A
Ballerina* .... (VAN)
More Than A Name On The Wall
Statler Brothers; *Greatest Hits* .... (MER)
Mr. Custer
Larry Verne; *Collectables Presents History Of
Rock-10* ....(CLT)
  Dr. Demento Greatest Novelty CD-#3-'60s ... (RHI)
  Wacky Weirdos .... (KT)
My Little Marine
Jamie Horton; *45* ....(ERI)
"M*A*S*H" Theme (Suicide Is Painless)
Ahmad Jamal; *Digital Works* .... (ATL)
  ST/M-A-S-H ....(COL)
Percy Faith; *All-Time Greatest Hits* ....(COL)
Napalm For Breakfast
Rhythm Devils; *Apocalypse Now Sessions* ....(RYK)
New Orleans Wins The War
Randy Newman; *Land Of Dreams* .... (RPR)
New Soldiers Joy
Kentucky Colonels feat. R. & C. White;
1965-1967 .... (ROU)
Night They Drove Old Dixie Down
Band; *Anthology* ....(CAP)
  Band ....(CAP)
  Best Of ....(CAP)
  Gift Set ....(CAP)
  Last Waltz .... (WB)
  Rock Of Ages-#1 & 2 ....(CAP)
Bob Dylan/Band; *Before The Flood* ....(COL)
Joan Baez; *Classics-#8* ....(A&M)
  Country Music Album .... (VAN)
  From Every Stage ....(A&M)
  Hits/Greatest & Others .... (VAN)
No No No To Draft & War
Minutemen; *Ballot Result* ....(SST)
No Surrender
Bruce Springsteen; *Born In The U.S.A.* ....(COL)
Ohio
Crosby, Stills & Nash; *Crosby Stills & Nash
(collection)* .... (ATL)
Crosby, Stills, Nash & Young; *Four-Way Street* .. (ATL)
  So Far .... (ATL)
Neil Young; *Decade* .... (RPR)
  ST/Journey Through The Past .... (RPR)
Oliver's Army
Elvis Costello; *Girls Girls Girls* ....(COL)
Elvis Costello/Attractions; *Armed Forces* ....(COL)
  Best Of ....(COL)
On Brave Old Army Team
All-Star Inter-Conference Band; *College Marches At
Halftime* .... (ALS)
One Tin Soldier
Coven; *Super Hits/'70s-Have A Nice Day-#7* ..... (RHI)
Out To Bomb Fresh Kings
Doctor Nerve; *Armed Observation* .... (CUN)
Over There
Glenn Miller; *Original Recordings-#3-Army Air
Force* .... (PRR)
Glenn Miller/Army Air Force Band; *Legendary
Performer-#3* .... (BLU)
Mormon Tabernacle Choir; *God Bless America* . (SMC)
Pass The Hand Grenade
Eric B. & Rakim; *Don't Sweat The Technique* ... (MCA)
Patriot's Dream
Gordon Lightfoot; *Don Quixote* .... (RPR)
Planetary Invasion
Midnight Star; *Planetary Invasion* .... (SLR)
Played Around & Stayed Around Vietnam...
Chuck Rosenberg/Others; *Folk Songs Of Americans In
Vietnam War* ....(FF)
Please Mr. Custer
Ray Stevens; *Gitarzan* .... (BBY)
Political Science
Randy Newman; *Sail Away* .... (RPR)
Pop The Silo
Nazareth; *Fool Circle* ....(A&M)

Porn Wars
Frank Zappa; *Meets The Mothers Of Prevention* ..(RYK)
Post Cold War Politics
Fishbone; *In Your Face* ....(COL)
Readjustment Blues
John Denver; *Aerie* ....(RCA)
Red Army Blues
Waterboys; *Pagan Place* ....(CHR)
Remember Pearl Harbor
Sammy Kaye; *ST/Radio Days* .... (NOV)
Remember The Alamo
Johnny Cash; *We The People* ....(FOL)
Kingston Trio; *At Large/Here We Go Again* ......(CAP)
Renegade
Styx; *Classics-#15* ....(A&M)
Pieces Of Eight ....(A&M)
Renegade, The
Ian & Sylvia; *Greatest Hits* .... (VAN)
Nashville ....(VAN)
Rock Soldiers
Ace Frehley; *Frehley's Comet* ....(MEG)
Metal Mania .... (PRY)
Roland The Headless Thompson Gunner
Warren Zevon; *Excitable Boy* ....(ASY)
Quiet Normal Life-Best Of ....(ASY)
Ruby Don't Take Your Love To Town
Kenny Rogers; *20 Great Years* ....(RPR)
Ten Years Of Gold ....(EMI)
Twenty Greatest Hits ....(EMI)
Kenny Rogers/First Edition; *Greatest Hits* ....(KT)
Hits & Pieces ....(MCA)
Mel Tillis/Statesiders; *24 Great Hits* ....(MGM)
Best Of ....(MCA)
M-M-Mel Live ....(MCA)
Saigon Warrior
Saul Broudy & Robin Thomas; *In Country-Americans In
The Vietnam War* ....(FF)
Sailing Home For Christmas
Doug Stone; *First Christmas* ....(EPI)
Sam Stone
John Prine; *John Prine* ....(ATL)
Prime Prine ....(ATL)
Send The Marines
Tom Lehrer; *That Was The Year That Was* ......(RPR)
She Gave Her Heart To A Soldier Boy
Roy Rogers; *Country Music Hall Of Fame* ......(MCA)
Shhh, It's A Military Secret
Glenn Miller/Orchestra; *Complete* ....(BLU)
Skye Boat Song
King's Singers; *Annie Laurie-Folksongs Of British
Isles* ....(ANG)
Paul Robeson; *American Balladeer-Golden
Classics-#1* ....(CLT)
Roger Whittaker; *Live In Concert* ....(RCA)
Sloth (Drums)
Fairport Convention; *Chronicles* ....(A&M)
Full House ....(CTH)
Sneaky Private Lee
Paice/Ashton/Lord; *Malice In Wonderland* ....(WB)
Snoopy Vs. The Red Baron
Royal Guardsmen; *Best Of-#1* ....(RHI)
Collectables Presents History Of Rock-#9 ....(CLT)
Cruisin'-1967 .... (INC)
Million-Dollar Memories #1 ....(RCA)
Super Oldies/'60s-#6 ....(AUF)
Soldier
James Taylor; *Mud Slide Slim* ....(WB)
Neil Young; *Decade* ....(RPR)
ST/Journey Through The Past ....(RPR)
Spirit; *12 Dreams Of Dr. Sardonicus* ....(EPI)
Stephen Stills; *Illegal Stills* ....(COL)
Soldier Blue
Buffy Sainte-Marie; *Native North American Child* (VAN)
She Used To Wanna Be A Ballerina ....(VAN)
Cult; *Sonic Temple* .... (SIR)
Julian Cope; *Peggy Suicide* ....(ISL)
Soldier Boy
Elvis Presley; *Elvis Is Back* ....(RCA)
Golden Celebration ....(RCA)
Shirelles; *Anthology-1959-1964* ....(RHI)
Billboard Top Rock 'N' Roll Hits-1962 .... (RHI)
Oldies But Goodies-#4 ....(OSR)
ST/The Wanderers ....(WB)
Small Faces; *78 In The Shade* ....(ATL)

Soldier In The Rain
England Dan & John Ford Coley; *Best Of* ....(BT)
Dowdy Ferry Road ....(BT)
Soldier Of Fortune
Alan O'Day; *Appetizers* ....(PAC)
Deep Purple; *Stormbringer* ....(WB)
Joe Perry Project; *I've Got The Rock 'N' Rolls
Again* ....(COL)
Manhattan Transfer; *Bodies & Souls* ....(ATL)
Thin Lizzy; *Bad Reputation* ....(MER)
Soldier Of Love
Donny Osmond; *Donny Osmond* ....(CAP)
Kenny Rogers; *Love Is Strange* ....(RPR)
Lee Greenwood; *Love's On The Way* ....(LIB)
Marshall Crenshaw; *Marshall Crenshaw* ....(WB)
Nitty Gritty Dirt Band; *Workin' Band* ....(WB)
Soldier's Joy
Jimmy Driftwood; *Best Of* ....(MOT)
Marty Stuart; *Busy Bee Cafe* ....(SH)
Nitty Gritty Dirt Band; *Dirt Silver & Gold* ....(UA)
Will The Circle Be Unbroken ....(EMI)
Tony Trischka; *Heartlands* ....(ROU)
Soldier's Last Letter
Ernest Tubb; *Legend & The Legacy* ....(FSG)
Living Legend ....(FSG)
Ernest Tubb & Johnny Cash; *Ernest Tubb
Collection* ....(SO)
George Jones; *20 Golden Pieces Of* ....(BLD)
Merle Haggard; *Capitol Collectors Series* ....(CAP)
Some Gave All
Billy Ray Cyrus; *Some Gave All* .... (MER)
Spanish Bombs
Clash; *London Calling* .... (EPI)
On Broadway .... (EPI)
Story Of-#1 .... (EPI)
Star Spangled Banner
Duke Ellington; *Carnegie Hall Concerts-January 23
1943* ....(PRS)
Houston Symphony Orchestra; *Celebrate America* (POE)
Jimi Hendrix; *Essential-#2* ....(RPR)
Lifelines/Jimi Hendrix Story ....(RPR)
ST/Jimi Hendrix ....(RPR)
ST/Woodstock ....(ATL)
Lee Greenwood; *American Patriot* ....(LIB)
Marvin Gaye; *Musical Testament-1964-1984* ... (MOT)
Mormon Tabernacle Choir; *God Bless America* ..(COL)
This Is My Country ....(COL)
Vinnie Vincent Invasion; *Head Banging Metal* ....(PRY)
Still In Saigon
Charlie Daniels Band; *Decade Of Hits* ....(EPI)
Windows .... (EPI)
Stop The War Now
Edwin Starr; *45* ....(MOT)
Street Soldiers
Hammer; *Too Legit To Quit* ....(CAP)
Stupid War Movies
Paleface; *Paleface* ....(POL)
Stupid, Stupid War
D.R.I.; *Dealing With It* ....(MET)
Surrender
Cheap Trick; *At Budokan* .... (EPI)
Greatest Hits .... (EPI)
Heaven Tonight .... (EPI)
Elvis Presley; *Number One Hits* ....(RCA)
Top Ten Hits ....(RCA)
Gloria Estefan/Miami Sound Machine; *Let It
Loose* .... (EPI)
J. Geils Band; *Anthology* ....(RHI)
Monkey Island ....(ATL)
U2; *War* .... (ISL)
Surrender Paradise
Miami Sound Machine; *Primitive Love* ....(EPI)
Sweet Surrender
Bread; *Anthology* ....(ELE)
Best Of-#2 ....(ELE)
John Denver; *Back Home Again* ....(RCA)
Evening With ....(RCA)
Swiss Army Girl
Scatterbrain; *Scamboogery* ....(ELE)
Talking Old Soldiers
Elton John; *Tumbleweed Connection* ....(POL)
Talking Vietnam Pot Luck Blues
Tom Paxton; *Morning After* ....(ELE)

Talking World War III Blues
Bob Dylan; *Freewheelin'* ....(COL)
Taxi War Dance
Count Basie; *Essential-#1* ....(COL)
I Like Jazz-Essence Of ....(COL)
Terms Of Psychic Warfare
Husker Du; *New Day Rising* ....(SST)
Theme From "Exodus"
101 Strings Orchestra; *Golden Movie Themes* ....(ALS)
Boston Pops Orchestra/Arthur Fiedler; *Motion Picture Classics-#1* ....(RCA)
Ferrante & Teicher; *Grand Pianos* ....(PRR)
Theme From "Gone With The Wind"
Toronto Festival Pops Orchestra/B. Brott; *Hooray For Hollywood* ....(POE)
Theme From "Schindler's List"
John Williams/Itzhak Perlman; *ST/Schindler's List* ....(MCA)
There's Something About A War
Chris Groenendaal/Men; *Collector's Sondheim* ...(RCA)
Thermonuclear War
Carnivore; *Carnivore* .... (RR)
This Cold War With You
Floyd Tillman; *Columbia Country Classics-#2* ...(COL)
John Prine; *Pink Cadillac* ....(ASY)
Merle Haggard; *Friend In California* ....(EPI)
Ray Price; *Greatest Hits-#4-By Request* ....(SO)
Willie Nelson; *San Antonio Rose* ....(COL)
This Is The Army, Mr. Jones
Mel Torme & George Shearing; *Mel & George Do World War II* ....(CCJ)
Mormon Tabernacle Choir; *God Bless America* . (SMC)
This Means War
AC/DC; *Blow Up Your Video* ....(ATL)
Joan Jett/Blackhearts; *Good Music* ....(EPA)
Pariah; *To Mock A Killingbird* ....(GEF)
Throw Down The Sword
Wishbone Ash; *Argus* ....(MCA)
Live Dates ....(MCA)
Too Long A Soldier
Pat Benatar; *Wide Awake In Dreamland* .... (CHR)
Toy Soldiers
Martika; *Martika* ....(COL)
Tramp, Tramp, Tramp
Mormon Tabernacle Choir; *Songs Of The Civil War & S. Foster Faves* ....(SMC)
Tug Of War
Paul McCartney; *Tug Of War* ....(CAP)
"Twelve O'Clock High" Theme
Original Music; *Television's Greatest Hits-#2* .....(TVT)
Undercover Of The Night
Rolling Stones; *Rewind (1971-1984)* ....(RS)
Undercover ....(RS)
Universal Soldier
Buffy Sainte-Marie; *Best Of* ....(VAN)
Festival Of Acoustic Music-#1 ....(FAN)
Troubadours Of The Folk Era-#1 .... (RHI)
Donovan; *Catch The Wind* ....(GRL)
History Of British Rock-#4 ....(RHI)
Secret Policeman's Other Ball ....(ISL)
Unknown Soldier
Doors; *13* ....(ELE)
Best Of ....(ELE)
Classics ....(ELE)
Live At The Hollywood Bowl ....(ELE)
Waiting For The Sun ....(ELE)
Us & Them
Pink Floyd; *CD Gift Set* ....(CAP)
Dark Side Of The Moon ....(CAP)
Delicate Sound Of Thunder ....(COL)
Shine On-Box Set ....(COL)
U.S. Air Force
Mormon Tabernacle Choir; *Stars & Stripes Together* ....(COL)
Vera Cruz
Warren Zevon; *Excitable Boy* ....(ASY)
Veteran Of The Psychic Wars
Blue Oyster Cult; *Extraterrestrial-Live* ....(COL)
Fire Of Unknown Origin ....(COL)
Viet Cong Blues
Junior Wells; *Best Of The Chicago Blues* .... (VAN)
Chicago/The Blues/Today ....(VAN)
Junior Wells/Chicago Blues Band; *Legends Of Electric Blues Guitar-#2* ....(RHI)

Viet Cong Live Next Door
Left; *Last Train To Hagerstown* ....(GRN)
Vietnam
Jimmy Cliff; *In Concert-Best Of* ....(RPR)
Reggae Spectacular ....(A&M)
Wonderful World Beautiful People ....(A&M)
Vietnam Blues
Champion Jack Dupree; *Legacy Of The Blues-#3* (CRS)
Vietnam Never Again
Country Joe McDonald; *Child's Play* ....(RGB)
Vietnam Veteran Still Alive
Country Joe McDonald; *Into The Fray* .... (RBB)
Vietnamerica
Stranglers; *IV* ....(IRS)
Virginia's Bloody Soil
Tennessee Ernie Ford; *Sings Songs Of The Civil War* ....(CAP)
Walking On A Thin Line
Huey Lewis/News; *Sports* ....(CHR)
War
Bruce Springsteen/E Street Band; *Live-1975-1985* ....(COL)
Edwin Starr; *Billboard Top Rock 'N' Roll Hits-1970* ....(RHI)
Motown Superstar Series-#3 ....(MOT)
Soul Hits/'70s-#3 ....(RHI)
War & Peace ....(MOT)
War A Africa
Jimmy Cliff; *Breakout* ....(JRS)
War Baby
"C" Company/Terry Nelson; *Wake Up America* . (PLN)
War Baby Son Of Zorro
Daryl Hall & John Oates; *War Babies* ....(ATL)
War Child
Jethro Tull; *Repeat* ....(CHR)
War Child ....(CHR)
War Clouds
New Orleans Ragtime Orchestra; *Nwe Orleans Jazz* ....(ARH)
War Games
Crosby, Stills & Nash; *Allies* ....(ATL)
Paul Young; *Between Two Fires* ....(COL)
War In Babylon
Max Romeo/Upsetters; *This Is Reggae Music-#1* .. (ISL)
War In Babylon ....(ISL)
War Is Coming, War Is Coming
War; *Platinum Jazz* ....(BLN)
War Is Hell (On The Homefront Too)
T.G. Sheppard; *All-Time Greatest Hits* ....(WB)
Greatest Hits ....(WB)
Perfect Stranger ....(WB)
War Is Over
Phil Ochs; *Chords Of Fame* ....(A&M)
Tape From California ....(A&M)
War Is Over-Best Of ....(A&M)
War Machine
Kiss; *Creatures Of The Night* ....(CAS)
War Of Man
Neil Young; *Harvest Moon* ....(RPR)
War Of The Hearts
Sade; *Promise* ....(POR)
"War Of The Worlds" Theme
Neil Norman; *Greatest Science Fiction Hits-#3* ...(CRS)
War On Drugs
2 Black 2 Strong MMG; *Doin' Hard Time On Planet Earth* ....(CLA)
War Pigs
Black Sabbath; *Live Evil* ....(WB)
Paranoid ....(WB)
We Sold Our Soul For Rock & Roll ....(WB)
Faith No More; *Real Thing* ....(SLS)
Ozzy Osbourne; *Just Say Ozzy* ....(EPA)
Speak Of The Devil ....(JET)
War Song
Culture Club; *Waking Up With The House On Fire* (VIA)
War Widow
Country Joe McDonald; *War War War* .... (VAN)
Warrior
Public Image, Ltd.; *9* .... (VIA)
Greatest Hits So Far .... (VIA)
Warrior, The
Scandal; *Warrior* ....(COL)

Wars Of Germany
Clancy Brothers/Tommy Makem; *Luck Of The
Irish* ....(COL)
Wartime Wedding
Original Broadway Cast; *Over Here!* .... (SMC)
War/No More Trouble
Bob Marley/Wailers; *Babylon By Bus* .... (TUF)
Rebel Music .... (TUF)
Was My Brother In The Battle
Kate & Anna McGarrigle; *Songs Of The Civil
War* ....(COL)
Waterloo
Abba; *Greatest Hits* .... (ATL)
Waterloo .... (ATL)
Stonewall Jackson; *American Originals* ....(COL)
Billboard Top Country Hits-1959 .... (RHI)
Columbia Country Classics-#3-Americana ......(COL)
Country Music Classics-#1-1950s .... (KT)
We Didn't Start The Fire
Billy Joel; *Storm Front* ....(COL)
We Got The Neutron Bombs
Weirdos; *D.I.Y.-#6-L.A. Scene-1976-1979* .... (RHI)
Weekend Warriors
Ted Nugent; *Weekend Warriors* .... (EPI)
When Johnny Comes Marching Home
Marilyn Horne; *Beautiful Dreamer-Great Amer.
Songbook* ....(LON)
Mormon Tabernacle Choir; *Songs Of The Civil War & S.
Foster Faves* .... (SMC)
United States Military Academy Band; *Songs Of The
Civil War* ....(COL)
When The Generals Talk
Midnight Oil; *Red Sails In The Sunset* ....(COL)
Where Have All The Flowers Gone
Johnny Rivers; *Anthology-1964-1977* .... (RHI)
Best Of .... (EMI)
Kingston Trio; *Capitol Collectors Series* ....(CAP)
Pete Seeger; *Essential* .... (VAN)
Greatest Hits ....(COL)
Peter, Paul & Mary; *Peter, Paul & Mary* .... (WB)
Wes Montgomery; *Classics-#22* ....(A&M)
World War None
Frank Sinatra; *Trilogy (Past/Present/Future)* ...... (RPR)
You Don't Have To Be In The Army To...
Mungo Jerry; *In The Summertime-Best Of* .... (RHI)
You Dropped A Bomb On Me
Gap Band; *12" Collection* .... (MER)
4 .... (MER)
Gap Gold-Best Of .... (MER)
Your Squaw Is On The Warpath
Loretta Lynn; *Greatest Hits-#2* .... (MCA)

WATER, Waterfalls
See Also: OCEAN, RIVERS, SAILING, SHIPS

Aqua Boogie
Parliament; *Greatest Hits* .... (CAS)
Motor Booty Affair .... (CAS)
Beneath Still Waters
Emmylou Harris; *Blue Kentucky Girl* .... (WB)
Profile 2: Best Of .... (WB)
Black Water
Doobie Brothers; *Best Of* .... (WB)
What Were Once Vices Are Now Habits .... (WB)
Blue Water
Poco; *Crazy Eyes* .... (EPI)
Ride The Country .... (EPI)
Born In The Water
Tragically Hip; *Road Apples* .... (MCA)
Bread & Water
Gary Morris; *Stones* .... (LIB)
Bridge Over Troubled Water
Aretha Franklin; *30 Greatest Hits* .... (ATL)
Greatest Hits .... (ATL)
Live At Fillmore West .... (ATL)
Paul Simon; *Concert In The Park-August 15 1991* (WB)
Live Rhymin' .... (WB)
Simon & Garfunkel; *Bridge Over Troubled Water* (COL)
Collected Works ....(COL)
Concert In Central Park .... (WB)
Greatest Hits ....(COL)
Bring Me Some Water
Melissa Etheridge; *Melissa Etheridge* .... (ISL)

California Saga
Beach Boys; *Holland* ....(CAR)
Ten Years Of Harmony ....(CAR)
Candle On The Water
Helen Reddy; *Live In London* ....(CAP)
ST/Pete's Dragon ....(CAP)
Cool Cool Water
Beach Boys; *10 Years Of Harmony* ....(CAR)
Sunflower ....(CAR)
Cool Water
Bob Nolan; *Sound Of A Pioneer* .... (ELE)
Frankie Laine; *16 Most Requested Songs* ....(COL)
Jack Scott; *Capitol Collectors Series* ....(CAP)
Joni Mitchell; *Chalk Mark In A Rain Storm* ......(GEF)
Sons Of The Pioneers; *Best Of* ....(RCA)
60 Years Of Country Music ....(RCA)
Cool Water ....(RCA)
Western Country ....(GRA)
Talking Heads; *Naked* .... (FLY)
Cool, Clear Water
Bonnie Raitt; *Longing In Their Hearts* ....(CAP)
Crazy Water
Elton John; *Blue Moves* .... (MCA)
Danger Waters (Hold Me Tight)
Joan Baez; *In Concert* .... (VAN)
Lovesong Album .... (VAN)
Dirty Water
Standells; *Best Of* .... (RHI)
Nuggets-Classics From Psychedelic Era .... (RHI)
Super Oldies/'60s-#10 ....(AUF)
Don't Go Near The Water
Beach Boys; *10 Years Of Harmony* ....(CAR)
Surf's Up ....(CAR)
Down To The Water
America; *Harbor* .... (WB)
Down To The Waterline
Dire Straits; *Dire Straits* .... (WB)
Money For Nothing .... (WB)
Drift Away
Dobie Gray; *Classic Rock-#1* .... (MCA)
Oldies But Goodies-#10 ....(OSR)
Oldies But Goodies-#3 ....(OSR)
Super Hits/'70s-Have A Nice Day-#10 .... (RHI)
Michael Bolton; *Timeless-Classics* ....(COL)
Rod Stewart; *Atlantic Crossing* .... (WB)
Drink Muddy Water Leaving Tennessee
Rio Grande Band; *Rio Grande Band* .... (ROU)
Gimme Some Water
Eddie Money; *Life For The Taking* ....(COL)
Holy Water
Bad Company; *Holy Water* ....(ATC)
Hot Water
Jefferson Starship; *Spitfire* ....(GRU)
Level 42; *Physical Presence-#2* ....(POL)
True Colours ....(POL)
World Machine ....(POL)
I Fell In The Water
John Anderson; *On Solid Ground* ....(BNA)
Let's Make The Water Turn Black
Mothers Of Invention; *Lumpy Gravy/Only In It For The
Money* ....(RYK)
Like Water
Bad Company; *Burnin' Sky* .... (SS)
(Love Is) Thicker Than Water
Andy Gibb; *Flowing Rivers* ....(RSO)
Greatest Hits ....(RSO)
Madman Across The Water
Elton John; *Live In Australia w/Melbourne
Orchestra* .... (MCA)
Madman Across The Water ....(POL)
Michigan Water
Gregory Hines/Original Cast; *Jelly's Last Jam* .. (MER)
Michigan Water Blues
Little Brother Montgomery/Others; *Chicago
Breakdown* ....(TAK)
Muddy Water
Aretha Franklin; *Aretha Sings The Blues* ....(COL)
Clint Black; *Put Yourself In My Shoes* ....(RCA)
Johnny Rivers; *Anthology-1964-1977* .... (RHI)
Original Broadway Cast; *Big River* .... (MCA)
Sonny Terry & Brownie McGhee; *Best Of* .... (PRS)
Midnight Special ....(FAN)
One Good Well
Don Williams; *One Good Well* ....(RCA)

Our Lady Of The Well
Jackson Browne; *For Everyman* .... (ASY)
Over Rusty Water
XTC; *Rag & Bone Buffet* .... (GEF)
Peaceful Waters
Gordon Lightfoot; *Lightfoot* .... (UA)
Poison In The Well
10,000 Maniacs; *Blind Man's Zoo* .... (ELE)
Raging Waters
Al Jarreau; *High Crime* .... (WB)
   In London .... (WB)
Testament; *Legacy* .... (ATL)
Ripple
Grateful Dead; *American Beauty* .... (WB)
   Reckoning .... (ARI)
   What A Long Strange Trip It's Been .... (WB)
Jane's Addiction; *Deadicated* .... (ARI)
Rippin' Waters
Nitty Gritty Dirt Band; *Dirt Silver & Gold* .... (UA)
   Dream .... (UA)
   Live Two Five .... (CAP)
   Twenty Years Of Dirt-Best Of .... (WB)
Rock Me On The Water
Jackson Browne; *Jackson Browne* .... (ASY)
Kathy Mattea & Jackson Browne; *Red Hot +*
Country .... (MER)
Linda Ronstadt; *Different Drum* .... (CAP)
   Linda Ronstadt .... (CAP)
   Retrospective .... (CAP)
Scarlet Water
Johnny Duncan; *Best Of* .... (COL)
   Greatest Hits .... (COL)
Silver Springs
Fleetwood Mac; *25 Years-The Chain* .... (WB)
Silver Waters
Ken Stover; *Cruisers 1.0* .... (HS)
   Sir Dancelot's Dream .... (HS)
Smoke On The Water
Deep Purple; *Deepest Purple-Very Best Of* .... (WB)
   Machine Head .... (WB)
   Made In Japan .... (WB)
   Nobody's Perfect .... (MER)
   When We Rock We Rock .... (WB)
Stars On The Water
Jimmy Buffett; *Boats Beaches Bars & Ballads* ... (MGR)
   One Particular Harbour .... (MCA)
Rodney Crowell; *Collection* .... (WB)
   Rodney Crowell .... (WB)
Still Water
Four Tops; *Anthology* .... (MOT)
   Motown Superstar Series-#14 .... (MOT)
   Still Waters Run Deep .... (MOT)
Sawyer Brown; *Buick* .... (LIB)
Tall Drink Of Water
Barbara Mandrell; *Best Of* .... (LIB)
Matraca Berg; *Speed Of Grace* .... (RCA)
Mel Tillis; *Best Of Branson U.S.A.-#2* .... (CCB)
   Greatest Hits .... (CCB)
Walk On The Water
Creedence Clearwater Revival; *1968-1969* ..... (FAN)
   Chronicle-#2 .... (FAN)
   Creedence Clearwater Revival .... (FAN)
Neil Diamond; *And The Singer Sings His Songs* . (MCA)
   Glory Road-1968-1972 .... (MCA)
   Moods .... (MCA)
Walk On Water
Dio; *Lock Up The Wolves* .... (RPR)
Eddie Money; *Greatest Hits-Sound Of Money* ...(COL)
   Nothing To Lose .... (COL)
Marc Cohn; *Marc Cohn* .... (ATL)
Marillion; *Six Of One-Half-Dozen Of The Other* .. (IRS)
T. Graham Brown; *Brilliant Conversationalist* ....(CAP)
Water
Hothouse Flowers; *Home* .... (LON)
Rose Royce; *ST/Car Wash* .... (MCA)
Sugarcubes; *Here Today-Tomorrow Next Week* ... (ELE)
Who; *Two's Missing* .... (MCA)
Water Boy
John Lee Hooker; *Country Blues Of* .... (RVR)
Paul Robeson; *Historic-Golden Classics-#3* .... (CLT)
Roger Whittaker; *Last Farewell & Other Hits* ....(RCA)
   New World In The Morning .... (RCA)
Water From The Moon
Celine Dion; *Celine Dion* .... (EPI)

Lee Ritenour; *Earth Run* .... (GRP)
Water Into Wine
Bruce Cockburn; *In The Falling Dark* ....(TRN)
Water Is Wide
Joan Baez; *Very Early Joan Baez* .... (VAN)
Karla Bonoff; *ST/Thirtysomething* .... (GEF)
Roger McGuinn; *Born To Rock & Roll* ....(COL)
Water Of Love
Dire Straits; *Dire Straits* .... (WB)
Judds; *Collection-1983-1990* .... (RCA)
   River Of Time .... (RCA)
Water Sign
Gary Wright; *Light Of Smiles* .... (WB)
Parliament; *Motor-Booty Affair* .... (CAS)
Water Under The Bridge
Dan Seals; *Greatest Hits* .... (LIB)
   On Arrival .... (LIB)
Olivia Newton-John; *Have You Never Been*
Mellow .... (MCA)
Water With The Wine
Joan Armatrading; *Joan Armatrading* ....(A&M)
Waterfall
10 CC; *Live & Let Live* .... (MER)
Carly Simon; *Playing Possum* .... (ELE)
Electric Light Orchestra; *Afterglow* .... (EPI)
   Face The Music .... (JET)
Peter Frampton; *Somethin's Happening* ....(A&M)
Stone Roses; *Stone Roses* .... (SIL)
Waterhole
Outlaws; *Outlaws* .... (ARI)
Watermark
Art Garfunkel; *Watermark* .... (COL)
Enya; *Watermark* .... (RPR)
Waterwheel
Daryl Hall & John Oates; *Whole Oats* ....(ATL)
When The Levee Breaks
Led Zeppelin; *Led Zeppelin (collection)* ....(ATL)
   #4 .... (ATL)
Wind On The Water (To The Last Whale...)
Crosby, Stills & Nash; *Replay* .... (ATL)
   Crosby, Stills & Nash (collection) .... (ATL)
David Crosby & Graham Nash; *Best Of* .... (MCA)
   Wind On The Water .... (MCA)

WEEKEND

See Also: DAYS OF THE WEEK, WORK

48 Hours Till Monday
Sawyer Brown; *Buick* .... (CCB)
Drugland Weekend
Hounds; *Unleashed* .... (COL)
Friday Night Blues
John Conlee; *Friday Night Blues* .... (MCA)
   Greatest Hits .... (MCA)
Sonny Throckmorton; *45* .... (MER)
Friday On My Mind
David Bowie; *Pin-Ups* .... (RYK)
Easybeats; *Best Of* .... (RHI)
   Nuggets-Classic Collection/'60s .... (RHI)
Here Comes The Weekend
Dave Edmunds; *Best Of* .... (SS)
   Get It .... (SS)
It's All Coming Down Tonight
Barbusters; *ST/Light Of Day* .... (CBA)
Frankie Miller; *Standing On The Edge* ....(CAP)
Livin' For The Weekend
O'Jays; *Collector's Items* .... (PI)
   Family Reunion .... (PI)
Lonely Weekend
Yellowjackets; *Samurai Samba* .... (WB)
Lonely Weekends
Charlie Rich; *Complete Smash Sessions* ....(MER)
   Lonely Weekends .... (SUN)
   Sun's Greatest Hits .... (RCA)
Shelby Lynne; *Tough All Over* .... (EPI)
Long Weekend
Horslips; *Man Who Built America* .... (DJM)
Lost Weekend
Beat Farmers; *Tales Of The New West* ....(RHI)
Del Fuegos; *Smoking In The Fields* .... (RCA)
Lloyd Cole/Commotions; *Easy Pieces* ....(CAP)
Roy Lanham; *Legends Of Country Guitar-#1* ..... (RHI)

Sarah Vaughan/Lol Creme/Kevin Godley;
 Consequences .... (MER)
Wall Of Voodoo; *Call Of The West* .... (IRS)
Woody Herman/Woodchoppers; *1940s-Small
 Groups* ....(COL)
Payday/Mine 'Til Monday
 Original Broadway Cast; *Tree Grows In Brooklyn* (SMC)
Rock & Roll The Weekend
 Sammy Hagar; *Live* .... (CAP)
  Sammy Hagar .... (CAP)
Saturday Night & Sunday Morning
 Phil Collins; *...But Seriously* .... (ATL)
Vegas Weekend
 Thelonius Monster; *Beautiful Mess* .... (CAP)
Weekend
 Dictators; *Go Girl Crazy* .... (EPI)
 Eddie Cochran; *Legendary Masters* .... (EMI)
 Russ Ballard; *Winning* .... (EPI)
 Steve Wariner; *Country Classics-#10-1987* ...... (MSP)
  Greatest Hits .... (MCA)
  It's A Crazy World .... (MCA)
  '80s Biggest Country Hits-#3 .... (MSP)
 Wet Willie; *Which One's Willie* .... (EPI)
Weekend Friend
 Con Hunley; *Con Hunley* .... (WB)
Weekend In New England
 Barry Manilow; *Greatest Hits-#2* .... (ARI)
  Live .... (ARI)
  This One's For You .... (ARI)
Weekend In The Country
 Original Cast; *A Little Night Music* ....(COL)
 Original London Cast; *A Little Night Music* .....(RCA)
Weekend Love
 Golden Earring; *No Promises-No Debts* .... (POL)
 Queen Latifah; *Black Reign* .... (MOT)
Weekend Of A Private Secretary
 Eileen Farrell; *Sings Johnny Mercer* .... (REF)
 Mildred Bailey; *Her Greatest* ....(COL)
Weekend Song
 Billy Joel; *Streetlife Serenade* ....(COL)
Weekend Warriors
 Ted Nugent; *Weekend Warriors* .... (EPI)
Weekend With Feather
 Brook Benton; *This Is* .... (ALP)
Wild Weekend
 Bill Anderson; *MCA Records 30 Years Of
 Hits-1958-1988* .... (MCA)
  Still .... (MSP)
Working For The Weekend
 Loverboy; *Big Ones* ....(COL)
  Get Lucky ....(COL)

WHALES, Dolphins, Porpoises, Seals

 See Also: ANIMALS: A-Z, ECOLOGY, FISH

Arctic Whale Hunt
 Mancini Pops Orchestra; *In Surround-Mostly Monsters
 Murders...* ....(RCA)
Day Old Whale
 Uncle Bonsai; *Lonely Grain Of Corn* .... (FRK)
Digital Dolphins
 Dolphins; *Malayan Breeze* .... (DIG)
Dolphin
 Kenny Rankin; *Mindusters* ....(OOP)
 Stan Getz; *Dolphin* ....(CCJ)
Dolphin Dance
 Herbie Hancock; *Best Of-Blue Note Years* .... (BLN)
  Maiden Voyage .... (BLN)
Dolphin Dreams
 Lee Ritenour; *Captain Fingers* .... (EPI)
  Collection ....(GRP)
  On The Line .... (GRP)
Dolphin Field
 Meat Puppets; *7-Inch Wonders Of The World* .....(SST)
Dolphin Morning
 Paul Winter Consort; *Sun Singer* ....(LIV)
Dolphin Story
 Claudia Schmidt; *Midwestern Heart* ....(FF)
Dolphins
 Billy Bragg; *Don't Try This At Home* .... (ELE)
 Linda Ronstadt; *Hand Sown* ....(CAP)
 Mike Marshall & Darol Anger; *Chiaroscuro* ......(WH)
  Windham Hill-First Ten years ....(WH)

Shelleyan Orphan; *Humroot* ....(COL)
The The; *Shades Of Blue* .... (EPI)
Tim Buckley; *Best Of* .... (RHI)
 Sefronia .... (BIZ)
Dolphins & Whales (Come Home To The Sea)
 Mannheim Steamroller; *Saving The Wildlife* .... (AG)
Dolphin's Lullaby
 Firefall; *Firefall* .... (ATL)
 Lani Hall; *Sweet Bird* ....(A&M)
Dolphin's Smile
 Byrds; *Notorious Byrd Brothers* ....(COL)
  Byrds (collection) ....(COL)
Dolphin's Thoughts
 Jay B. Jay; *Dream Machine* .... (INN)
  Over Seas .... (INN)
Don't Kill The Whale
 Yes; *Tormato* .... (ATL)
  Yesshows .... (ATL)
D.O.L.F.I.N.
 Emiko Kai; *Alternatives* ....(COL)
Euphonius Whale
 Dan Hicks/Hot Licks; *Last Train To Hicksville* .. (MCA)
Farewell To Tarwaithie
 Judy Collins; *Colors Of The Day-Best Of* .... (ELE)
  So Early In The Spring .... (ELE)
  Whales & Nightingales .... (ELE)
Greenland Whale Fisheries
 Judy Collins & Theodore Bikel; *Greatest Folksingers Of
 The '60s* .... (VAN)
Grey Seal
 Elton John; *Goodbye Yellow Brick Road* .... (POL)
Last Great American Whale
 Lou Reed; *Greenpeace/Rainbow Warriors* .... (GEF)
  New York .... (SIR)
Little Blue Whale
 Country Joe McDonald; *Goodbye Blues* ....(FAN)
Luminous Dolphin
 Royal Trux; *End Of Music (As We Know It)* ...... (ROI)
Moby Book
 Stephen Goodman; *Jessie's Jig* .... (ASY)
Moby Dick
 Led Zeppelin; *II* .... (ATL)
  ST/Song Remains The Same .... (SS)
Ode To Big Blue
 Gordon Lightfoot; *Don Quixote* .... (RPR)
Odin
 John Stewart; *Dream Babies Go To Hollywood* ... (RSO)
On Green Dolphin Street
 Anita O'Day; *Anita O'Day* ....(GLN)
 Carmen McRae; *At The Great American Music
 Hall* .... (BLN)
 Miles Davis; *Basic Miles* ....(COL)
 Red Garland; *Saying Something* .... (PRS)
Other Songs Of The Whaling Era
 Ewan MacColl/A.L. Lloyd/Peggy Seeger; *Various
 Tracks* .... (FLW)
Porpoise Mouth
 Country Joe/Fish; *Collected (1965-1970)* .... (VAN)
  Electric Music For The Mind & Body .... (VAN)
  Life & Times Of .... (VAN)
Porpoise Song
 Monkees; *Head* .... (RHI)
  Listen To The Band .... (RHI)
  Monkee Business .... (RHI)
  Nuggets-#9-Acid Rock .... (RHI)
Prince Of Whales
 Amy & Leslie; *Amy & Leslie* ....(ALC)
 Joachim Kuhn; *Dynamics* ....(CMU)
Save The Whale
 Nik Kershaw; *The Riddle* ....(MCA)
Save The Whales
 Country Joe McDonald; *Bread & Roses Festival-Acoustic
 Music-#1* ....(FAN)
  Classics ....(FAN)
  Into The Fray .... (RBB)
  Paradise With An Ocean View ....(FAN)
 Danny O'Keefe; *Global Blues* .... (WB)
Songs Of The Humpback Whale
 Recorded Sounds; *Various Tracks* ....(CAP)
Sounds Of The Sea
 Dr. Coates; *Various Tracks* ....(FLW)
Sounds & Ultra-Sounds Of The Blue-Nose
 Dr. John C. Lilly; *Various Tracks* .... (FLW)

Theme From "The Great Whales"
Cincinnati Pops Orchestra/Erich Kunzel; *Sailing* . (TLR)
Whale
  Electric Light Orchestra; *Out Of The Blue* ....(JET)
  Wall Matthews; *Gathering The World* ....(CLE)
Whale Meat Again
  Jim Capaldi; *45* .... (ISL)
Whale Of A Tale
  Original London Cast; *Moby Dick* ....(RCA)
Whale Savers
  Melbourne Symphony Orchestra; *Film & TV Themes Of
  Bruce Rowland* ....(BAY)
Whale Song
  Chris Michell; *Dolphin Love* .... (WDM)
Whale Watch
  Peter Kater; *Moments Dreams & Visions* .... (SW)
Whalecatchers/Drunken Landlady
  John Faulkner; *Kind Providence* ....(GRE)
Whaleheart
  Marnie Jones; *Grace* ....(THR)
Whaler
  Montrose; *Montrose* .... (WB)
Whaler Out Of New Bedford
  Musical Film Score; *Whaler Out Of New Bedford* (FLW)
Whaler's Dues
  Jethro Tull; *Rock island* .... (CHR)
Whales Tails
  Cocteau Twins; *Victorialand* ....(CAP)
Whales Weep Not (Overture)
  Paul Winter Consort; *Whales Alive* ....(LIV)
  Paul Winter Consort/Paul Halley; *Living Music
  Collection II* ....(LIV)
Whales & Snow
  Deep Jimi/Zep Creams; *Funky Dinosaur* ....(EW)
Whalesong
  Michael Gettel; *San Juan Suite* .... (SNI)
Whale, The-Pt. 1 & 2
  John Tavener; *The WHale* ....(CAP)
Whale's Revenge
  Original London Cast; *Moby Dick* ....(RCA)
Whaling And Sailing Songs
  Paul Clayton; *Various Tracks* ....(TRD)
Whaling Songs And Ballads
  Paul Clayton; *Various Tracks* ....(STO)
Whaling Stories
  Procol Harum; *Classics-#17* ....(A&M)
  Home ....(MOB)
  Live In Concert With Edmonton Symphony .... (MOB)
Wind On The Water (To The Last Whale...)
  Crosby, Stills & Nash; *Replay* ....(ATL)
  Crosby, Stills & Nash (collection) ....(ATL)
  David Crosby & Graham Nash; *Best Of* ....(MCA)
  Wind On The Water ....(MCA)

WILD

See Also: CHAOS, REBELS

Bad Boys Running Wild
  Scorpions; *Love At First Sting* .... (MER)
  Wold Wide Live .... (MER)
Born To Be Wild
  Steppenwolf; *16 Greatest Hits* .... (MCA)
  Billboard Top Rock 'N' Roll Hits-1968 .... (RHI)
  Live ....(MCA)
  Steppenwolf ....(MCA)
  Vintage Music-Oldies-'60s-#9 & 10 ....(MCA)
Buck Wild
  E.U.; *Livin' Large* .... (VIA)
Call Of The Wild
  Aaron Tippin; *Call Of The Wild* ....(RCA)
Child Of The Wild Blue Yonder
  John Hiatt; *Stolen Moments* ....(A&M)
Cry Of The Wild Goose
  Frankie Laine; *Golden Hits* .... (MER)
Deuces Are Wild
  Aerosmith; *Beavis & BuDeuces Are Wild-Head
  Experience* ....(GEF)
Hot! Wild! Unrestricted! Crazy Love
  Millie Jackson; *Imitation Of Love* .... (JVA)
I Go Wild
  Rolling Stones; *Voodoo Lounge* .... (VIA)
My Wild Irish Rose
  Magic Organ; *22 Great Organ Favorites* .... (RAN)

Mom & Dads; *One Dozen Roses* .... (CRS)
Restless & Wild
  Accept; *Accept* ....(POR)
  Restless & Wild ....(POR)
Ride A Wild Horse
  Kenny Nolan; *Night Miracles* .... (CAS)
Ride The Wild Surf
  Jan & Dean; *Monmster Summer Hits-Wild Surf* ...(CAP)
  Surf City-Best Of .... (EMI)
  Surfin' Hits .... (RHI)
Runaway Child Running Wild
  Temptations; *All The Million-Sellers* ....(MOT)
  Anthology ....(MOT)
  Cloud Nine ....(MOT)
  Compact Command Performances ....(MOT)
  Greatest Hits-#2 ....(MOT)
Running Wild
  Benny Goodman Quartet; *Bluebird Sampler* ......(BLU)
  Judas Priest; *Hell Bent For Leather* ....(COL)
  Unleashed In The East ....(COL)
  Roxy Music; *Flesh & Blood* ....(RPR)
  Sam Cooke; *Golden Sound* ....(TRP)
  Soup Dragons; *Hotwired* ....(BL)
She Drives Me Wild
  Michael Jackson; *Dangerous* .... (EPI)
Some Girls Do
  Sawyer Brown; *Dirt Road* ....(CRB)
Something Wild
  John Hiatt; *Perfectly Good Guitar* ....(A&M)
Walk On The Wild Side
  Edie Brickell/New Bohemians; *ST/Flashback* ...(WTG)
  Lou Reed; *Between Thought &
  Expression-Anthology* ....(RCA)
  Live ....(RCA)
  Transformer ....(RCA)
  Walk On The Wild Side-Best Of ....(RCA)
Who's Gonna Ride Your Wild Horses
  U2; *Achtung Baby* .... (ISL)
Wild
  Seal; *Seal* ....(SIR)
  Thompson Twins; *Big Trash* ....(RE)
Wild About Me
  Prairie Oyster; *Prairie Oyster* ....(RCA)
Wild About My Loving
  Linda Ronstadt; *Stone Poneys* ....(CAP)
Wild About You Baby
  Elmore James; *Let's Cut It-Very Best Of* .... (FLA)
Wild America
  Tora Tora; *Wild America* ....(A&M)
Wild Angel
  John Mellencamp; *Nothin' Matters & What If It
  Did* ....(RIV)
Wild As A Wildcat
  Charlie Walker; *Golden Hits* ....(PLN)
Wild Bill Jones
  Hot Rize; *Radio Boogie* ....(FF)
  Kentucky Colonels; *Appalachian Swing!* .... (ROU)
Wild Billy's Circus Story
  Bruce Springsteen; *Wild The Innocent & The E Street
  Shuffle* ....(COL)
Wild Bill's Blues
  Country Gazette; *Strictly Instrumental* ....(FF)
Wild Boys
  Duran Duran; *Arena* ....(CAP)
  Decade ....(CAP)
Wild Cat
  UB40; *Present Arms* .... (VIA)
Wild Cherry
  Foghat; *Best Of* ....(RHI)
  Energized ....(RHI)
  Leroy Washington; *Sound Of The Swamp-Best Of
  Excello-#1* ....(RHI)
Wild Child
  Doors; *13* ....(ELE)
  Classics ....(ELE)
  Soft Parade ....(ELE)
  Heart; *Brigade* ....(CAP)
  Rock The House "Live" ....(CAP)
  Lou Reed; *Walk On The Wild Side-Best Of* ....(RCA)
  Untouchables; *Wild Child* ....(MCA)
  W.A.S.P.; *Head Banging Metal* ....(PRY)
  Last Command ....(CAP)
  Live...In The Raw ....(CAP)

Wild Children
Van Morrison; *Hard Nose The Highway* .... (WB)
It's Too Late To Stop Now .... (WB)
Wild Cow Moan
Big Joe Turner & Sonny Boy Williamson; *Story Of The Blues* .... (COL)
Wild Dog Moon
Drivin' N' Cryin'; *Mystery Road* .... (ISL)
Wild Dogs
Hank Williams, Jr.; *Bocephus Box-Collection-1979-1992* .... (CPC)
Tommy Bolin; *The Ultimate...* .... (GEF)
Wild Eyed Boy From Freecloud
David Bowie; *Sound + Vision* .... (RYK)
Space Oddity .... (RYK)
ST/Ziggy Stardust-The Motion Picture .... (RYK)
Wild Flowers
Jimmy Smith; *Best Of* .... (CCB)
Wild For You Baby (Goin')
Bonnie Raitt; *Collection* .... (WB)
The Glow .... (WB)
Wild Frontier
Bruce Hornsby/Range; *The Way It Is* .... (RCA)
Gary Moore; *Wild Frontier* .... (VIA)
Wild Goose Grasses In Tarrytown
Weavers; *Classics* .... (VAN)
Greatest Hits .... (VAN)
Wild Heart
Stevie Nicks; *Wild Heart* .... (MOD)
Wild Heart Of The Young
Karla Bonoff; *Wild Heart Of The Young* ...... (COL)
Wild Hearted Son
Cult; *Ceremony* .... (SIR)
Wild Hearts
Roy Orbison; *Legendary* .... (SSP)
Wild Hearts Run Out Of Time
Roy Orbison; *King Of Hearts* .... (VIA)
Wild Honey
Beach Boys; *Absolute Best-#2* .... (CAP)
Party!/Stack-O-Tracks .... (CAP)
Smiley Smile/Wild Honey .... (CAP)
Wild Honey Pie
Beatles; *Box Set* .... (CAP)
White Album .... (CAP)
Wild Horses
Flying Burrito Brothers; *Farther Along-Best Of* .. (A&M)
Garth Brooks; *No Fences* .... (LIB)
Gino Vannelli; *Big Dreams Never Sleep* ...... (EPA)
Prefab Sprout; *Jordan-The Comeback* .... (EPI)
Life Of Surprises-Best Of .... (EPI)
Rolling Stones; *Hot Rocks-1964-1971* .... (AKO)
Made In The Shade .... (RS)
Singles Collection-London Years .... (AKO)
Sticky Fingers .... (RS)
Sundays; *Blind* .... (DGC)
Suzy Bogguss; *Moment Of Truth* .... (CAP)
Wild In The Country
Elvis Presley; *50 Worldwide Gold Award Hits-#2* (RCA)
Wild In The Streets
Bon Jovi; *Slippery When Wet* .... (MER)
Circle Jerks; *Best Of Rodney On The ROQ* .... (PBO)
Group Sex/Wild In The Streets .... (FRN)
Wild Injuns
Neville Brothers; *Yellow Moon* .... (A&M)
Wild Is Love
Nat King Cole; *Nat King Cole* .... (CAP)
Story .... (CAP)
Wild Is The Wind
David Bowie; *Changestwobowie* .... (RCA)
Sound + Vision .... (RYK)
Station To Station .... (RYK)
Johnny Mathis; *16 Most Requested Songs* ...... (COL)
Greatest Hits .... (COL)
Wild Kentucky Roan
Mike Auldridge; *& Old Dog* .... (FF)
Wild Kentucky Skies
Marty Brown; *Wild Kentucky Skies* .... (MCA)
Wild Kids
David Benoit; *Urban Daydreams* .... (GRP)
Wild Life
INXS; *Kick* .... (ATL)
Wings; *Wild Life* .... (CAP)
Wild Little Willy
Ronnie Hawkins/Hawks; *Best Of* .... (RHI)

Wild Love
Chris Isaak; *Chris Isaak* .... (WB)
Wild Man
J. Geils Band; *Flashback-Best Of* .... (EMI)
Ricky Van Shelton; *Greatest Hits Plus* .... (COL)
Steppin' Country .... (COL)
Wild Man Blues
Jelly Roll Morton; *Jelly's Last Jam & Other Morton Classics* .... (BLU)
Louis Armstrong; *Best Of Decca Years-#2-Composer* .... (MCA)
Wild Montana Skies
John Denver; *Greatest Hits-#3* .... (RCA)
It's About Time .... (RCA)
John Denver & Emmylou Harris; *Collector's-Duets* .... (RCA)
Wild Mountain Honey
Steve Miller Band; *Fly Like An Eagle* .... (CAP)
Greatest Hits-1974-1978 .... (CAP)
Wild Mountain Thyme
Armstrong Family; *Wheel Of The Year-Thirty Years With* .... (FF)
Byrds; *Fifth Dimension* .... (COL)
Joan Baez; *Farewell Angelina* .... (VAN)
Wild Night
John Mellencamp; *Dance Naked* .... (MER)
Martha Reeves; *ST/Thelma & Louise* .... (MCA)
Van Morrison; *Best Of* .... (MER)
Tupelo Honey .... (WB)
Wild Night In Odessa
Klezmorim; *Metropolis* .... (FF)
Wild Nights, Hot & Crazy Days
Judas Priest; *Metal Works-1973-1993* .... (COL)
Turbo .... (COL)
Wild One
Faith Hill; *Take Me As I Am* .... (WB)
Wild One, Forever
Tom Petty/Heartbreakers; *Tom Petty/Heartbreakers* .... (GG)
Wild Places
Dan Fogelberg; *Live-Greetings From The West* .... (FM)
Wild Reaction
Gipsy Kings; *Prey* .... (SIM)
Wild Rice
Lee Ritenour; *Best Of* .... (EPI)
First Course .... (EPI)
Wild Ride
Dwight Yoakam; *This Time* .... (RPR)
Wild River
Golden Palominos; *Dead Horse* .... (CEL)
Our World Of Music .... (CEL)
Wild Rover
John Faulkner; *Kind Providence* .... (GRE)
Wild Sewerage Tickles Brazil
Squeeze; *Classics-#25* .... (A&M)
Wild Sex (In The Working Class)
Oingo Boingo; *Best O' Boingo* .... (MCA)
Boingo Alive .... (MCA)
Nothing To Fear .... (A&M)
Wild Side
Motley Crue; *Decade Of Decadence* .... (ELE)
Girls Girls Girls .... (ELE)
Wild Side of Life
Freddie Fender; *Before The Next Teardrop Falls* (MCA)
Best Of .... (MCA)
Hank Thompson; *All-Time Greatest Hits* ...... (CCB)
Best Of The Best Of .... (GUS)
Capitol Collectors Series .... (CAP)
Traditions In Country Music .... (CAP)
Rod Stewart; *Night On The Town* .... (WB)
Wild Strawberries
Gordon Lightfoot; *Waiting For You* .... (RPR)
Wild Streak
Hank Williams, Jr.; *Wild Streak* .... (W/C)
Wild Tales
Crosby, Stills & Nash; *Crosby, Stills & Nash* ..... (ATL)
Wild Thing
Jimi Hendrix; *Essential-#2* .... (RPR)
ST/Jimi Plays Monterey .... (RPR)
Jimi Hendrix Experience; *Live At Winterland* .....(RYK)
Tone Loc; *Loc-ed After Dark* .... (DV)
Rap's Biggest Hits .... (KT)
Rock The First-#6 .... (SAN)

Troggs; *Billboard Top Rock 'N' Roll Hits-1966* ... (RHI)
Frat Rock! .... (RHI)
History Of British Rock-#3 .... (RHI)
Wild Things Run Fast
Joni Mitchell; *Wild Things Run Fast* ....(GEF)
Wild Turkey
Lacy J. Dalton; *Hot Country Rock-#1* .... (EPI)
Wild Tyme
Jefferson Airplane; *2400 Fulton Street-Anthology* (RCA)
Best Of ....(RCA)
Wild Weekend
Bill Anderson; *MCA Records 30 Years Of*
Hits-1958-1988 .... (MCA)
Still .... (MSP)
Wild West End
Dire Straits; *Dire Straits* ....(WB)
Wild West Hero
Electric Light Orchestra; *Out Of The Blue* ....(JET)
Wild West Show
Darden Smith; *Native Soil* ....(WAT)
Wild West Show/Dog Act
Original Broadway Cast; *Will Rogers Follies* ......(COL)
Wild Wild Life
Talking Heads; *Popular Favorites-1984-1992* ..... (SIR)
True Stories .... (SIR)
Wild Women Do
Natalie Cole; *ST/Pretty Woman* .... (EMI)
Wild World
Cat Stevens; *Greatest Hits* ....(A&M)
Tea For The Tillerman ....(A&M)
Jimmy Cliff; *In Concert-Best Of* .... (RPR)
Reggae Spectacular ....(A&M)
Maxi Priest; *Best Of Me* .... (CHS)
Maxi .... (VIA)
Wild & Blue
Hank Williams, Jr.; *Major Moves* ....(W/C)
John Anderson; *Greatest Hits* ....(WB)
Wild & Blue ....(WB)
Wild & Crazy Love
Mary Jane Girls; *Only Four You* .... (MOT)
Wild & Loose
Time; *What Time Is It?* ....(WB)
Wild & Wooly
Chris LeDoux; *Radio & Rodeo Hits* .... (LIB)
Wild & Wooly .... (LIB)
Wilder Days
Baillie & The Boys; *Best Of* ....(RCA)
Wildest Dreams
Annie Haslam; *Annie Haslam* .... (EPI)
Asia; *Asia* ....(GEF)
Then & Now ....(GEF)
Dolly Parton; *Eagle When She Flies* ....(COL)
Wildfire
Michael Martin Murphey; *Best Of* .... (EMI)
Super Hits/'70s-Have A Nice Day-#14 .... (RHI)
'70s Greatest Rock Hits-#3-High Times .... (PRY)
Michael Murphey; *Blue Sky Night Thunder* ....(EPI)
Wildfire Woman
Bad Company; *Straight Shooter* .... (SS)
Wildflower
Carter Family; *60 years Of Country Music* ....(RCA)
O'Jays; *Collector's Items* ....(PI)
Live In London ....(PI)
Skylark; *Reaching For The Sky-Soul From The*
'70s ....(CAP)
Super Hits/'70s-#10 .... (RHI)
Wildflowers
D. Parton/E. Harris/L. Ronstadt; *Trio* ....(WB)
John Denver; *Some Days Are Diamonds* ....(RCA)
Wildlife
Yellowjackets; *Four Corners* .... (MCA)
Live Wires .... (GRP)
Wildside
Marky Mark/Funky Bunch; *Music For The People* (ISC)
Wildwood Flower
Carter Family; *Legends Of Country Guitar-#2* ... (RHI)
Chet Atkins; *Tennessee Guitar Man* ....(PRR)
Hank Thompson & Merle Travis; *Great Records Of The*
Decade-'50s Hits ....(CCB)
Greatest Hits-#2 ....(CCB)
Kentucky Colonels; *Featuring Clarence White* ... (ROU)
Wild, Wild West
Escape Club; *Rock The First-#3* .... (PRY)
Wild, Wild West ....(ATL)

Kool Moe Dee; *Greatest Hits* .... (JVA)
How Do Ya Like Me Now .... (JVA)
Jive Presents...Yo! MTV Raps .... (JVA)
Mr. Magic's Rap Attack-#4 ....(PRO)
Wild-Eyed Dream
Ricky Van Shelton; *Wild-Eyed Dream* ....(COL)
Wild-Eyed Gypsies
John Hiatt; *Hangin' Around The Observatory* ......(EPI)
Wild-Eyed Southern Boys
38 Special; *Wild-Eyed Southern Boys* ....(A&M)
Young Thing, Wild Dreams (Rock Me)
Red Rider; *Breaking Curfew* ....(CAP)
Your Wildest Dreams
Moody Blues; *Other Side Of Life* ....(POL)

WIND

See Also: CHAOS, LIFE, RAIN, SKY, SPIRITS

Against The Wind
Bob Seger/Silver Bullet Band; *Against The Wind* .(CAP)
Nine Tonight ....(CAP)
ST/Forrest Gump ....(EPX)
Any Way The Wind Blows
Frank Zappa; *Cruising With Ruben & The Jets* ...(BAR)
Freak Out ....(BAR)
Southern Pacific; *County Line* ....(WB)
ST/Pink Cadillac ....(WB)
Ashes In The Wind
Moe Bandy; *No Regrets* ....(CCB)
Black Throated Wind
Bob Weir; *Ace* .... (GRD)
Grateful Dead; *Steal Your Face* .... (GRD)
Blow Away
George Harrison; *Best Of Dark Horse*
1976-1989 ....(DKH)
George Harrison ....(DKH)
ST/Nuns On The Run ....(MER)
Grateful Dead; *Built To Last* .... (ARI)
Blowing Kisses In The Wind
Paula Abdul; *Spellbound* ....(CPT)
Blowin' In The Wind
Bob Dylan; *At Budokan* ....(COL)
Before The Flood ....(COL)
Biograph ....(COL)
Freewheelin' ....(COL)
Greatest Folksingers Of The '60s ....(VAN)
Greatest Hits ....(COL)
Joan Baez; *ST/Forrest Gump* ....(EPX)
Peter, Paul & Mary; *Holiday Celebration* ....(GC)
In Concert ....(WB)
In The Wind ....(WB)
Peter, Paul & Mary ....(WB)
Ten Years Together ....(WB)
Breeze From Alabama
Max Morath; *Plays Ragtime* ....(VAN)
World Of Scott Joplin ....(VAN)
Scott Joplin; *Entertainer-#4* ....(BIO)
Button Up Your Overcoat
Rose Murphy; *Sings Again* .... (MCA)
Sarah Vaughan; *Sarah Vaughan* ....(EVR)
Call Me The Breeze
J.J. Cale; *Naturally* .... (MCA)
Lynyrd Skynyrd; *Best Of The Rest* .... (MCA)
One More From The Road .... (MCA)
Second Helping .... (MCA)
Southern By The Grace Of God-Tribute '87 ... (MCA)
Mavericks; *Skynyrd Frynds* .... (MCA)
Calling In The Wind
Judds; *Collection-1983-1990* ....(RCA)
Love Can Build A Bridge ....(RCA)
Candle In The Wind
Elton John; *Goodbye Yellow Brick Road* ....(POL)
Live In Australia w/Melbourne Symphony ....(POL)
Your Songs ....(POL)
Cast Your Fate To The Wind
Sandpipers; *Guantanamera* ....(A&M)
Vince Guaraldi; *Greatest Hits* ....(FAN)
Original Jazz Classics-#1 ....(FAN)
Catch The Wind
Donovan; *Greatest Hits* .... (EPI)
History Of British Rock-#2 .... (RHI)
Hits .... (EPI)
Secret Policeman's Other Ball ....(ISL)

Chasin' The Wind
Chicago; *Twenty 1* .... (FM)
Cold Wind In August
Van Morrison; *Period Of Transition* .... (WB)
Cold Windy City Of Chicago
Boxcar Willie; *Best Of-#1* .... (MAI)
Devil Wind
Bob Welch; *Three Hearts* .... (CAP)
Down In The Valley
Elvis Presley; *Reconsider Baby* ....(RCA)
Leadbelly; *Defense Blues-Golden Classics-#2* .....(CLT)
Pete Seeger; *American Favorite Ballads-#1* ...... (FLW)
Dust In The Wind
Kansas; *Best Of* .... (KIR)
   Point Of Know Return .... (KIR)
   Two For The Show .... (KIR)
Evil Wind
Bad Company; *Desolation Angels* .... (SS)
Four Strong Winds
Ian & Sylvia; *Best Of* .... (VAN)
   Greatest Hits .... (VAN)
Neil Young; *Comes A Time* .... (RPR)
Gone With The Wind
Art Pepper; *Intensity* .... (CTM)
Art Tatum; *Solo Masterpieces-#2* .... (PAB)
Barney Kessel; *Music To Listen To Barney Kessel*
By .... (CTM)
Clifford Brown; *Clifford Brown* .... (EMI)
Dave Brubeck; *I Like Jazz-Essence Of* ....(COL)
Dave Brubeck Quartet; *Gone With The Wind* ....(COL)
Dick Jurgens; *Best Of The Sweet Bands* .... (HIN)
Duprees; *Best Of* .... (RHI)
Ella Fitzgerald & Joe Pass; *Speak Love* .... (PAB)
Sarah Vaughan; *Misty* .... (MER)
Gypsy Wind
Dan Fogelberg; *Phoenix* .... (FM)
Hasten Down The Wind
Linda Ronstadt; *Hasten Down The Wind* .... (ASY)
Warren Zevon; *Warren Zevon* .... (ASY)
Hear The Wind Howl
Leo Kottke; *Mudlark* .... (CAP)
   My Feet Are Smiling ....(CAP)
Hickory Wind
Byrds; *Byrds* ....(COL)
   Columbia Country Classics-#5-New Trad. ......(COL)
   Sweetheart Of The Rodeo ....(COL)
Emmylou Harris; *Blue Kentucky Girl* .... (WB)
Gram Parsons; *Grievous Angel* .... (RPR)
Howlin' Wind
Graham Parker; *Howlin' Wind* .... (MER)
   Pourin' It All Out-Mercury Years .... (MER)
I Talk To The Wind
King Crimson; *In The Court Of The Crimson*
King .... (ATL)
Idiot Wind
Bob Dylan; *Blood On The Tracks* ....(COL)
   Bootleg Series-#1-3 ....(COL)
   Hard Rain ....(COL)
Let It All Blow
Dazz Band; *Greatest Hits* .... (MOT)
   Jukebox .... (MOT)
Let The Four Winds Blow
Fats Domino; *Best Of* .... (EMI)
   Billboard Top R&B Hits-1961 .... (RHI)
Roy Brown; *Best Of New Orleans R&B-#1* .... (RHI)
Lonely Wind
Kansas; *Kansas* .... (KIR)
   Two For The Show .... (KIR)
Mandolin Wind
Rod Stewart; *Best Of-#2* .... (MER)
   Every Picture Tells A Story .... (MER)
   Sing It Again Rod .... (MER)
   Storyteller/Complete Anthology-1964-1990 ...... (WB)
Midnight Wind
Charlie Daniels Band; *Midnight Wind* .... (EPI)
John Stewart; *Bombs Away Dream Babies* .... (RSO)
November Winds
Friedemann; *Indian Summer* .... (NAR)
   Narada Equinox Sampler One .... (NAR)
Ocean Breeze
Pablo Cruise; *Pablo Cruise* ....(A&M)
October Winds
Bela Fleck; *Natural Bridge* .... (ROU)

Only The Wind
Billy Dean; *Billy Dean* ....(LIB)
Joey Welz; *Somewhere Elvis Is Smiling* ....(CPR)
Pet Shop Boys; *Behavior* .... (EMI)
People Of The Southwind
Kansas; *Monolith* .... (KIR)
Pillow Of Winds
Pink Floyd; *Gift Set* .... (CAP)
   Meddle ....(CAP)
Raging Winds Of Time
Walking Wounded; *Raging Winds Of Time* ...... (CML)
Reflections In A Crystal Wind
Mimi & Richard Farina; *Best Of* .... (VAN)
   Reflections In A Crystal Wind .... (VAN)
Ride Like The Wind
Christopher Cross; *Christopher Cross* ....(WB)
Riding On The Wind
Judas Priest; *Screaming For Vengeance* ....(COL)
Paul Horn; *China* .... (KUC)
   Sketches-Collection ....(LLA)
Running Like The Wind
Marshall Tucker Band; *Running Like The Wind* ...(WB)
Runnin' With The Wind
Eddie Rabbitt; *Jersey Boy* ....(CAP)
   Ten Years Of Greatest Hits ....(CAP)
Sailing The Wind
Loggins & Messina; *Full Sail* ....(WB)
Sea Breezes
Bryan Ferry; *Let's Stick Together* .... (RPR)
Roxy Music; *Roxy Music* .... (RPR)
Siouxsie/Banshees; *Through The Looking Glass* ..(GEF)
Seminole Wind
John Anderson; *Seminole Wind* ....(BNA)
Shadows & The Wind
Uriah Heep; *Wonderworld* ....(WB)
Shanghai Breezes
John Denver; *Greatest Hits-#3* ....(RCA)
   Seasons Of The Heart ....(RCA)
She's Like The Wind
Patrick Swayze; *ST/Dirty Dancing* ....(RCA)
Spring Wind
Shawn Phillips; *Collaboration* ....(A&M)
Summer Breeze
Isley Brothers; *3+3* .... (TN)
   Forever Gold .... (TN)
   Story-#2-T-Neck Years-1969-1985 .... (RHI)
Seals & Crofts; *Greatest Hits* ....(WB)
   Summer Breeze ....(WB)
Summer Wind
Desert Rose Band; *Running* ....(MCA)
Frank Sinatra; *Greatest Hits* .... (RPR)
   Sinatra Reprise-The Very Good Years ...... (RPR)
   Strangers In The Night .... (RPR)
Frank Sinatra & Julio Iglesias; *Frank Sinatra*
Duets .... (CAP)
Theme From "Gone With The Wind"
Toronto Festival Pops Orchestra/B. Brott; *Hooray For*
Hollywood .... (POE)
They Call The Wind Maria
Kingston Trio; *Early American Heroes* ....(PRR)
   Kingston Trio/From The Hungry i ....(CAP)
   Stereo Concert Plus ....(FOL)
Original Broadway Cast; *Paint Your Wagon* ....(RCA)
Tradewinds
Randy Crawford; *Secret Combination* ....(WB)
Rod Stewart; *A Night On The Town* ....(WB)
Tommy Dorsey & Frank Sinatra; *Sessions-#1* ...(RCA)
Walk The Way The Wind Blows
Hot Rize; *Traditional Ties* ....(SH)
Kathy Mattea; *Collection Of Hits* .... (MER)
   Walk The Way The Wind Blows .... (MER)
Walking In The Wind
Traffic; *When The Eagle Flies* ....(ASY)
Waltz Of The Wind
Hank Williams; *I'm So Lonesome I Could*
Cry-1949 .... (POL)
Roy Acuff; *Best Of* ....(CCB)
   Essential ....(COL)
Ways Of The Wind
PM Dawn; *Bliss Album...?* ....(GEE)
Wayward Wind
Gogi Grant; *Collectables Presents-History Of*
Rock-#7 .... (CLT)
   '50s Jukebox Favorites .... (KT)

Lynn Anderson & Emmylou Harris; *Cowboy's*
Sweetheart .... (LAS)
Patsy Cline; *Patsy Cline Story* .... (MCA)
West Texas Wind
Joe Sun; *45* .... (AMI)
When The Wind Was Green
Frank Sinatra; *September Of My Years* .... (RPR)
Wichita Cross Winds
John Stewart; *Centennial* .... (HOM)
Wild Is The Wind
David Bowie; *Changestwobowie* .... (RCA)
   Sound + Vision .... (RYK)
   Station To Station .... (RYK)
Johnny Mathis; *16 Most Requested Songs* .... (COL)
   Greatest Hits .... (COL)
Wind Beneath My Wings
Bette Midler; *ST/Beaches* .... (ATL)
Gary Morris; *Country Love Songs* .... (WB)
   Hits .... (WB)
   Why Lady Why .... (WB)
James Galway; *Wind Beneath My Wings* .... (RCA)
Lee Greenwood; *Somebody's Gonna Love You* .. (MCA)
Lou Rawls; *When The Night Comes* .... (EPI)
Roger Whittaker; *Greatest Hits* .... (RCA)
   Wind Beneath My Wings .... (RCA)
Willie Nelson; *City Of New Orleans* .... (COL)
Wind Blows Her Hair
Seeds; *Nuggets-#9-Acid Rock* .... (RHI)
Wind Cries Mary
Jimi Hendrix; *Essential-#2* .... (RPR)
   Smash Hits .... (RPR)
Jimi Hendrix Experience; *Are You Experienced?* . (RPR)
Wind In The Wire
Randy Travis; *Wind In The Wire* .... (WB)
Wind Of Change
Bee Gees; *Greatest* .... (POL)
   Main Course .... (RSO)
Peter Frampton; *Comes Alive* .... (A&M)
   Shine On-Collection .... (A&M)
   Wind Of Change .... (A&M)
Scorpions; *Crazy World* .... (MER)
Wind On The Water (To The Last Whale...)
Crosby, Stills & Nash; *Replay* .... (ATL)
   Crosby, Stills & Nash (collection) .... (ATL)
David Crosby & Graham Nash; *Best Of* .... (MCA)
   Wind On The Water .... (MCA)
Windmills Of Your Mind
Acker Bilk; *Best Of* .... (CRS)
Dusty Springfield; *Dusty In Memphis* .... (RHI)
Johnny Mathis; *How Do You Keep The Music*
Playing .... (COL)
Mel Torme; *Best Of* .... (CCB)
Philadelphia Orchestra/Eugene Ormandy; *Movie Love*
Songs .... (RCA)
Winds Of Change
Cinderella; *Heartbreak Station* .... (MER)
Guadalcanal Diary; *2 X 4* .... (ELE)
Jefferson Starship; *Winds Of Change* .... (GRU)
Winds Of March
Journey; *Infinity* .... (COL)
Windsurfer
Roy Orbison; *Mystery Girl* .... (VIA)
Windswept
Bryan Ferry; *Boys & Girls* .... (WB)
John Jarvis; *Whatever Works* .... (MCA)
Windy
Association; *Billboard Top Rock 'N' Roll*
Hits-1967 .... (RHI)
   Greatest Hits .... (WB)
   Summer Of Love-#1 .... (RHI)
   Vintage .... (FFT)
Wes Montgomery; *A Day In The Life* .... (A&M)
   Classics-#22 .... (A&M)
   Greatest Hits .... (A&M)
Written On The Wind
Four Aces; *20 Greatest Hits* .... (EVR)
   Best Of .... (MCA)
   Love Is A Many Splendored Thing .... (ACC)

WINNING

See Also: GAMBLING, LUCK, MONEY, SPORTS,
TOYS & GAMES

7-11 (A Winner)
Li'l Wally; *Polish Carnival* .... (JJ)
Alright Okay You Win
Marcels; *Best Of* .... (RHI)
Peggy Lee; *Greatest* .... (CAP)
Blaze Of Glory
Alarm; *Declaration* .... (IRS)
   Electric Folklore .... (IRS)
Joe Jackson; *Blaze Of Glory* .... (A&M)
Jon Bon Jovi; *Blaze Of Glory* .... (MER)
Cheaters Never Win
Love Committee; *Beachbeat Shaggin'* .... (DHL)
Moe Bandy; *It's A Cheating Situation* .... (COL)
Checkmate
Defiance; *Void Terra Firma* .... (RR)
Ernie Henry; *Presenting* .... (RVR)
Color Of Success
Morris Day; *Color Of Success* .... (WB)
Death or Glory
Clash; *London Calling* .... (EPI)
Dressed For Success
Roxette; *Look Sharp!* .... (EMI)
Easy Winners
Itzhak Perlman & Andre Previn; *Easy Winners* .. (ANG)
Joshua Rifkin; *Digital Ragtime-Music Of Scott*
Joplin .... (ANG)
Marvin Hamlisch; *ST/The Sting* .... (MCA)
Scott Joplin; *The Entertainer* .... (BIO)
Every 1's A Winner
Hot Chocolate; *Every 1's A Winner* .... (INF)
Everybody Loves A Winner
Linda Ronstadt; *Don't Cry Now* .... (ASY)
Rita Coolidge; *Lady's Not For Sale* .... (A&M)
William Bell; *Soul Of A Bell* .... (ATL)
Get A Leg Up
John Mellencamp; *Whenever We Wanted* .... (MER)
Grey Victory
10,000 Maniacs; *Hope Chest-Fredonia Recordings*
1982-1983 .... (ELE)
   Wishing Chair .... (ELE)
I Feel Lucky
Mary Chapin Carpenter; *Come On Come On* ....(COL)
If I Could Only Win Your Love
Emmylou Harris; *Pieces Of The Sky* .... (RPR)
   Profile .... (WB)
If The South Woulda Won
Hank Williams, Jr.; *Wild Streak* .... (W/C)
Impossible Dream
Andy Williams; *16 Most Requested Songs* .... (COL)
   Greatest Hits-#2 .... (COL)
   Impossible Dream .... (COL)
Ed Ames; *Best Of* .... (RCA)
   Impossible Dream .... (RCA)
   Pure Gold .... (RCA)
   This Is .... (RCA)
Jack Jones; *Best Of* .... (MCA)
Kate Smith; *Best Of* .... (RCA)
   Legendary Performer .... (RCA)
Luther Vandross; *Songs* .... (EPI)
Original Cast; *Man Of La Mancha* .... (MCA)
Original London Cast; *Man Of La Mancha* ..... (MCA)
Robert Goulet; *Greatest Hits* .... (COL)
Just Can't Win 'Em All
Stevie Woods; *Stevie Woods* .... (COT)
Just One Victory
Todd Rundgren; *A Wizard A True Star* .... (RHI)
   Anthology-1968-1985 .... (RHI)
Utopia; *Another Live* .... (RHI)
Life To Win
Motorhead; *Ace Of Spades* .... (MER)
Little Victories
Bob Seger/Silver Bullet Band; *The Distance* ...... (CAP)
Long Distance Winner
Buckingham/Nicks; *Buckingham/Nicks* .... (POL)
Michigan Victors
Ohio State University Marching Band; *Music For*
   Cheerleaders & Song Girls .... (FID)
   Saturday Afternoon At Columbus .... (FID)

New Orleans Wins The War
Randy Newman; *Land Of Dreams* .... (RPR)
Nobody Wins
Brenda Lee; *Greatest Country Hits* .... (MCA)
Elton John; *The Fox* .... (GEF)
Radney Foster; *Del Rio TX 1959* .... (ARI)
Notre Dame Victory March
University Of Notre Dame Band; *Songs Of The Fighting Irish* .... (FID)
Paths Of Victory
Bob Dylan; *Bootleg Series-#1-3-1961-1989* .....(COL)
Byrds; *20 Essential Tracks From The Box Set* ....(COL)
Pete Seeger; *I Shall Be Unreleased-Songs Of Bob Dylan* .... (RHI)
Picture Me In Victory
K-Yze; *Without Warning* ....(WB)
Place In The Sun
Pablo Cruise; *Place In The Sun* .... (A&M)
Stevie Wonder; *Greatest Hits-#1* .... (MOT)
 Looking Back .... (MOT)
Play To Win
Clash; *Cut The Crap* .... (EPI)
Heaven 17; *Best Of-Higher & Higher* .... (VIA)
Playing To Win
Bonham; *Disregard Of Timekeeping* ....(WTG)
Little River Band; *Playing To Win* ....(CAP)
Race To Win
Blitzspeer; *Live* .... (EPI)
Red Sox Are Winning
Earth Opera; *Elektrock-'60s* .... (ELE)
Right The First Time
Gamma; *3* .... (ELE)
 Best Of .... (CRS)
She's Gonna Win Your Heart
Eddy Raven; *I Could Use Another You* ....(RCA)
Small Victory
Faith No More; *Angel Dust* .... (SLS)
Success
Dan Hicks/Hot Licks; *Last Train To Hicksville* .. (MCA)
Iggy Pop; *Lust For Life* .... (VIA)
Loretta Lynn; *Country Music Hall Of Fame* ..... (MCA)
 Greatest Hits .... (MCA)
Success Has Made A Failure...
Sinead O'Connor; *Am I Not Your Girl?* .... (ENS)
Sweetest Victory
Touch; *ST/Rocky IV* .... (SCO)
Till Victory
Patti Smith Group; *Easter* .... (ARI)
Top Of The World
Carpenters; *Classics-#2* .... (A&M)
 Singles 1969-1973 .... (A&M)
 Song For You .... (A&M)
 Yesterday Once More .... (A&M)
Diana Ross; *Anthology* .... (MOT)
James; *James* .... (FON)
Lynn Anderson; *Country Superstars* ....(DOM)
 Greatest Hits-#2 .... (COL)
 Top Of The World .... (COL)
Van Halen; *For Unlawful Carnal Knowledge* ......(WB)
Triumph
Generation X; *Perfect Hits-1975-1981* .... (CHR)
Victor
Dick Dale/Del-Tones; *Greatest Hits* .... (CRS)
Victory
Eric Johnson; *Tones* .... (RPR)
No Means No; *Day Everything Became Isolated...* .. (AT)
Victory Day
Red Rider; *Victory Day* ....(RCA)
Victory Polka
Glenn Miller; *Major Glenn Miller/Army Air Force Band* .... (BLU)
Walking Away A Winner
Kathy Mattea; *Walking Away A Winner* .... (MER)
We Are The Champions
Queen; *Billboard Top Rock 'N' Roll Hits-1978* ... (RHI)
 Greatest Hits .... (HOL)
 Live At Wembley '86 .... (HOL)
 Live Killers .... (HOL)
 News Of The World .... (HOL)
We Can't Go Wrong
Cover Girls; *We Can't Go Wrong* .... (CAP)

We're A Winner
Impressions; *Billboard Top R&B Hits-1965-1969* (RHI)
 Classic Soul .... (MCA)
 Greatest Hits .... (MCA)
Rita Coolidge; *Greatest Hits* .... (A&M)
We're Going All The Way
Jeffrey Osborne; *Stay With Me Tonight* .... (A&M)
What Does It Take (To Win Your Love)
Junior Walker/All-Stars; *Anthology* .... (MOT)
 Billboard Top R&B Hits-1965-1969 .... (RHI)
 Greatest Hits .... (MOT)
 Oldies But Goodies-#13 .... (OSR)
What It Takes
Aerosmith; *Pump* .... (GEF)
When The Going Gets Tough, The Tough...
Billy Ocean; *Greatest Hits* .... (JVA)
 Love Zone .... (JVA)
Win
David Bowie; *Young Americans* .... (RYK)
Win Or Lose
Earth, Wind & Fire; *Faces* ....(COL)
Nitty Gritty Dirt Band; *Dirt Silver & Gold* .... (UA)
Win Some, Lose Some
Bryan Adams; *Bryan Adams* .... (A&M)
Scandal; *Scandal* ....(COL)
Winner
Chris LeDoux; *Rodeo & Living Free* .... (LIB)
Circle O' Fire; *Escape Hatch* .... (STX)
Dorothy Moore; *Winner* ....(VOL)
Winner Take All
Natalie Cole; *I Love You So* .... (CAP)
 I'm Ready .... (EPI)
Platters; *Anthology* .... (RHI)
Styx; *Best Of* .... (RCA)
 Serpent .... (A&M)
Winner Takes All
Holly Near; *Journeys* ....(RWD)
Isley Brothers; *Winner Takes All* .... (TN)
Winner Takes It All
Abba; *Super Trouper* .... (ATL)
Munich Philharmonic Orchestra/Leon Ives; *Plays Abba Classics* .... (ATL)
Sammy Hagar; *ST/Over The Top* ....(COL)
Winners
Frank Sinatra; *Ol' Blue Eyes Is Back* .... (RPR)
Kleeer; *Winners* .... (ATL)
Winners & Losers
Rossington-Collins Band; *Anytime Anyplace Anywhere* .... (MCA)
Winner/Loser
Stomu Yamashta/Go; *Live From Paris* .... (ISL)
 Stomu Yamashta/Go .... (ISL)
Winning
Santana; *Zebop* ....(COL)
Winning Streak
Rufus Thomas; *I Ain't Getting Older I'm Getting Better* ....(OOP)
Winning Ugly
Rolling Stones; *Dirty Work* .... (RS)
Win, Lose Or Draw
Allman Brothers Band; *Best Of* .... (POL)
 Win, Lose Or Draw .... (POL)
You Cannot Win If You Do Not Play
Steve Forbert; *Alive On Arrival* .... (NEM)
You Win Again
Hank Williams; *24 Greatest Hits* .... (POL)
 40 Greatest Hits .... (POL)
Jerry Lee Lewis; *Golden Rock Hits Of* .... (SMA)
 Heartbreak .... (TOM)
 Memphis Country .... (SUN)
 Rockin' My Life Away .... (TOM)
 Taste Of Country .... (SUN)
Johnny Cash; *Original Golden Hits-#3* .... (SUN)
Keith Whitley; *Kentucky Bluebird* ....(RCA)
Mary Chapin Carpenter; *Greatest Country Hits/'90s-#2* ....(COL)

WOMEN: GENERAL, Girls, Ladies
 See Also: MOTHERS, WOMEN'S NAMES

2nd Movement: African Lady
Randy Weston; *Uhuru Africa/Highlife* .... (RLL)

36-22-36
Bobby Bland; *Best Of-#2* .... (MCA)
   Bobby Bland ....(MCA)
   Here's The Man .... (MCA)
80's Ladies
K.T. Oslin; *80's Ladies* ....(RCA)
   Greatest Hits ....(RCA)
   Nipper's Greatest Hits-'80s ....(RCA)
About A Girl
Nirvana; *Unplugged In NY* .... (DGC)
African Woman
Third World; *Journey to Addis* .... (ISL)
Ah, Paree, Beautiful Girls
Millicent Martin; *Collector's Sondheim* ......(RCA)
Stephen Sondheim; *Collector's Sondheim* ....(RCA)
Alabama Lady
Wright Brothers; *Easy Street* .... (MER)
Alabama Woman Blues
John Hammond; *John Hammond* .... (VAN)
All American Girl
Daryl Hall & John Oates; *Bigbamboom* ....(RCA)
Melissa Etheridge; *Yes I Am* .... (ISL)
All American Girls
Sister Sledge; *45* .... (COT)
All She Wants To Do Is Dance
Don Henley; *Building The Perfect Beast* ....(GEF)
All That She Wants
Ace Of Base; *All That She Wants* .... (ARI)
All The Things She Said
Simple Minds; *Once Upon A Time* ....∴ (A&M)
All The Woman I Need
Luther Vandross; *Songs* ....(EPI)
Alligator Woman
Cameo; *Alligator Woman* .... (CHC)
R.G./Bayou Zydeco; *Fire On The Bayou* ....(TAK)
Am I The Same Girl
Swing Out Sister; *Get In Touch With Yourself* ... (MER)
American Girl
Tom Petty/Heartbreakers; *Pack Up The
   Plantation-Live* .... (MCA)
   Tom Petty/Heartbreakers .... (MCA)
   You're Gonna Get It .... (MCA)
American Girls
Rick Springfield; *Success Hasn't Spoiled Me Yet* ..(RCA)
American Pie
Don McLean; *American Pie* .... (UA)
   Best Of .... (EMI)
   Greatest Hits Then & Now .... (EMI)
   ST/Born On The Fourth Of July ....(MCA)
American Woman
Guess Who; *American Woman* ....(RCA)
   Best Of ....(RCA)
   Greatest Of ....(RCA)
   Nipper's Greatest Hits-'70s ....(RCA)
   Rock Classics .... (KT)
Angel Lady
Boz Scaggs; *Slow Dancer* ....(COL)
Angel Woman
Andrew Gold; *What's Wrong With This Picture* ... (ASY)
Another Girl
Beatles; *Box Set* .... (CAP)
   Help! ....(CAP)
   ST/Help! ....(CAP)
Apache Woman
Rolling Stones; *Made In The Shade* .... (RS)
April Come She Will
Simon & Garfunkel; *Collected Works* ....(COL)
   Concert In Central Park ....(WB)
   Sounds Of Silence ....(COL)
   ST/The Graduate ....(COL)
Are You Ready For The Sex Girls
Gleaming Spires; *Best Of Rodney On The 'ROQ* .. (PBO)
Around The Way Girl
L.L. Cool J; *Mama Said Knock You Out* .... (DFJ)
Ask Any Girl
Supremes; *Greatest Hits-#1* ....(MOT)
   Where Did Our Love Go ....(MOT)
At Night She Sleeps
Night Ranger; *Dawn Patrol* ....(CAM)
Atlanta Lady
Marty Balin; *Balin* ....(EMI)
   Balince-A Collection ....(RHI)

Attack Of The Fifty-Foot Woman
Tubes; *Best Of* ....(CAP)
   Completion Backward Principle ....(CAP)
   Elvira Presents Haunted Hits .... (RHI)
Attractive Female Wanted
Rod Stewart; *Blondes Have More Fun* ....(WB)
Baby Likes To Rock It
Tractors; *Tractors* .... (ARI)
Baby's Got Her Blue Jeans On
Mel McDaniel; *All-Time Country Classics-#2* ....(CAP)
   Greatest Hits ....(CAP)
   Let It Roll ....(CAP)
Baby's Smile Woman's Kiss
Johnny Duncan; *Best Of* ....(COL)
Bag Lady
Todd Rundgren; *Hermit Of Mink Hollow* .... (RHI)
Bald-Headed Woman
Kinks; *You Really Got Me* .... (RHI)
Lightnin' Hopkins; *Lightnin' Sam Hopkins* ...... (ARH)
Who; *Two's Missing* .... (MCA)
Ballerina Girl
Lionel Richie; *Dancing On The Ceiling* .... (MOT)
Banjo Picking Girl
Lamar Grier; *Rounder Banjo* .... (ROU)
Bayou Girl
Bob Woodruff; *Dreams & Saturday Nights* .... (ASY)
Beautiful Black Girl
Quincy Jones; *Mellow Madness* ....(A&M)
Beauty And The Beast
Celine Dion & Peabo Bryson; *Celine Dion & Peabo
   Bryson* ....(EPI)
   ST/Beauty And The Beast .... (DIS)
Beer Drinkin' Woman
Memphis Slim; *At The Gate Of Horn* .... (VJ)
   Raining The Blues ....(FAN)
Belles Of Paris
Beach Boys; *M.I.U. Album* ....(CAR)
Berkeley Woman
John Denver; *Farewell Andromeda* ....(RCA)
   John Denver ....(RCA)
Big Chested Girls
Prince Charles/City Beat Band; *Stone Killers!* .... (ROI)
Big Fat Lady
George Benson; *Cookbook* ....(COL)
Big Fat Woman
Leadbelly; *Bourgeois Blues-Golden Classics-#1* ...(CLT)
Tom Rush; *Blues Songs & Ballads* ....(FAN)
Big Girls Don't Cry
Frankie Valli/Four Seasons; *Anthology* .... (RHI)
   Billboard Top Rock 'N' Roll Hits-1962 .... (RHI)
   Greatest Hits-#1 .... (RHI)
   More Dirty Dancing ....(RCA)
Bikini Girls With Machine Guns
Cramps; *Stay Sick!* ....(ENC)
Billy Get Me A Woman
Joe Stampley; *Biggest Hits* .... (EPI)
Birdmad Girl
Cure; *The Top* .... (SIR)
Bitch
Rolling Stones; *Made In The Shade* .... (RS)
   Sticky Fingers .... (RS)
Bitch Betta Have My Money
AMG; *Give A Dog A Bone* .... (SEL)
Black Country Woman
Led Zeppelin; *Physical Graffiti* .... (SS)
Black Hearted Woman
Allman Brothers Band; *Allman Brothers Band* ...(POL)
   Beginnings ....(POL)
   Road Goes On Forever ....(POL)
Black Magic Woman
Fleetwood Mac; *25 Years-The Chain* ....(WB)
   Vintage Years ....(SIR)
Santana; *Abraxas* ....(COL)
   Greatest Hits ....(COL)
   Moonflower ....(COL)
   Rock Classics/'70s ....(COL)
   Viva Santana ....(COL)
Black Widow
Alice Cooper; *Alice Cooper Show* ....(WB)
   Welcome To My Nightmare ....(ATL)
Jefferson Starship; *Winds Of Change* ....(GRU)
Lita Ford; *Dangerous Curves* ....(RCA)

Blue Kentucky Girl
Emmylou Harris; *Blue Kentucky Girl* .... (WB)
   Profile 2-Best Of .... (WB)
Loretta Lynn; *Greatest Hits* .... (MCA)
Blue Spruce Woman
Foghat; *Rock & Roll Outlaws* .... (RHI)
Bobby Sox To Stockings
Frankie Avalon; *Best Of* .... (MCA)
   Collectables Presents History Of Rock-#3 ...... (CLT)
   Greatest Hits .... (EVR)
   Greatest Of Fabian and Frankie Avalon .... (MCA)
   Pick Of .... (FFT)
   Super Oldies/'50s-#7 .... (AUF)
Boogie On Reggae Woman
Stevie Wonder; *Fulfillingness' First Finale* ...... (MOT)
   Motown Time Capsule-#2-'70s .... (MOT)
   Original Musiquarium .... (MOT)
Born A Woman
Sandy Posey; *Best Of Town & Country-#3* .... (GUS)
   Cruisin'-1966 .... (INC)
   Sandy Posey/Skeeter Davis/Wanda Jackson ..... (GUS)
   Super Hits-#5 .... (GUS)
   With Skeeter Davis; Best Of .... (GUS)
Boston Lady
John Stewart; *Fire In The Wind* .... (RSO)
Breaking The Girl
Red Hot Chili Peppers; *Blood Sugar Sex Magik* ... (WB)
Bride Of Rain Dog
Tom Waits; *Rain Dogs* .... (ISL)
Bring Me My Bride
Original Broadway Cast; *Funny Thing Happened On The Way To The.* .... (ANG)
Brown Eyed Girl
Isley Brothers; *Live It Up* .... (TN)
Jimmy Buffett; *One Particular Harbour* .... (MCA)
Van Morrison; *Bang Masters* .... (EPI)
   Best Of .... (MER)
   ST/Born On The Fourth Of July .... (MCA)
   ST/Sleeping With The Enemy .... (COL)
   Wonder Years-Music From Emmy Shows/Era ... (ATL)
Brown Eyed Woman
Grateful Dead; *Europe '72* .... (WB)
   What A Long Strange Trip It's Been .... (WB)
Brown Girl In The Ring
Boney M; *Nightflight To Venus* .... (SIR)
Brown Skin Gal
Bob Wills; *Best Of* .... (MCA)
Brown Skin Girl
Jesse Fuller; *Brother Lowdown* .... (FAN)
   San Franciso Bay Blues .... (GTJ)
Brown Sugar
Rolling Stones; *Classic Rock 1966-1988* ...... (ATL)
   Flashpoint + Collectibles .... (RS)
   Hot Rocks-1964-1971 .... (AKO)
   Made In The Shade .... (RS)
   Sticky Fingers .... (RS)
ZZ Top; *First Album* .... (WB)
   Six Pack .... (WB)
Brownsville Blues (Girl I Love, She...)
Hammie Nixon; *Tappin' That Thing* .... (HW)
Brownsville Girl
Bob Dylan; *Knocked Out Loaded* .... (COL)
Bus Drivin' Woman
Chicago Bob; *Hit & Run Lover* .... (ICH)
Bus Stop
Hollies; *Best Of-#1* .... (EMI)
   Greatest Hits .... (EPI)
   History Of British Rock-#3 .... (RHI)
Cajun Girl
Little Feat; *Let It Roll* .... (WB)
Oak Ridge Boys; *American Dreams* .... (MCA)
California Girl
Eddie Floyd; *15 Original Big Hits-#4* .... (STX)
   Chronicle .... (STX)
California Girls
Beach Boys; *Best Of-#2* .... (CAP)
   California Girls .... (CAP)
   Endless Summer .... (CAP)
   In Concert .... (CAR)
   '69 .... (CAP)
David Lee Roth; *Crazy From The Heat* .... (MCA)
   ST/Down & Out In Beverly Hills .... (WB)
Callin' Baton Rouge
Garth Brooks; *In Pieces* .... (LIB)

New Grass Revival; *Anthology* .... (LIB)
Oak Ridge Boys; *Room Service* .... (MSP)
Carolina Sunshine Girl
Geoff Muldaur & Amos Garrett; *Geoff Muldaur & Amos Garrett* .... (FF)
Catholic Girls
Frank Zappa; *Joe's Garage* .... (RYK)
   You Can't Do That On Stage Anymore-#6 ..... (RYK)
Catholic School Girls Rule
Red Hot Chili Peppers; *Abbey Road E.P.* .... (EMI)
   Freaky Styley .... (EMI)
   What Hits!? Best Of .... (EMI)
Certain Girl
Warren Zevon; *Bad Luck Streak In Dancing School* .... (ASY)
Yardbirds; *Greatest Hits-#1-1964-1966* .... (RHI)
Cheatin' Woman
Lynyrd Skynyrd; *Best Of* .... (MSP)
   Nuthin' Fancy .... (MCA)
Molly Hatchet; *Molly Hatchet* .... (EPI)
Checking Out The Checkout Girl
Wazmo Nariz; *10th Anniversary-These People Are Nuts* .... (IRS)
Cherokee Maiden
Merle Haggard; *All-Time Greatest Hits Of Country-#1* .... (CCB)
   Capitol Collectors Series .... (CAP)
China Girl
David Bowie; *Changesbowie* .... (RYK)
   Let's Dance .... (EMI)
   The Singles-1969-1993 .... (RYK)
John Cougar Mellencamp; *American Fool* .... (RIV)
China Lady
Accept; *Accept* .... (PAS)
   Midnight Highway .... (PVC)
Cincinnati Underworld Woman
Bob Coleman/Cincinnati Jug Band; *Cincinnati Blues-1928-1936* .... (SB)
Cinnamon Girl
Neil Young; *Decade* .... (RPR)
Neil Young/Crazy Horse; *Arc Weld* .... (RPR)
   Everyone Knows This Is Nowhere .... (RPR)
   Live Rust .... (RPR)
Clean Up Woman
Betty Wright; *Atlantic R&B 1947-1974-#6-(1966-1969)* .... (ATL)
   Golden Classics .... (CLT)
   Live .... (ATL)
   Soul Years .... (ATL)
Clown Woman
Montrose; *Montrose* .... (WB)
Come Back When You Grow Up
Bobby Vee; *Best Of* .... (EMI)
   Good Vibrations (Sounds Of Top 40 Radio) .... (CAP)
   Legendary Masters .... (EMI)
Cornflake Girl
Tori Amos; *Under The Pink* .... (ATL)
Country Girl
Barbara Mandrell; *Live* .... (MCA)
Faron Young; *Billboard Top Country Hits-1959* (RHI)
   Greatest Hits-#2 .... (SO)
Jeannie C. Riley; *Country Girl* .... (PLN)
   Greatest Hits .... (PLN)
Ozark Mountain Daredevils; *Best* .... (A&M)
   Ozark Mountain Daredevils .... (A&M)
Steve Earle/Dukes; *Hard Way* .... (MCA)
Country Girls
John Schneider; *Greatest Hits* .... (MCA)
   MCA #1 Hits/'80s-#1 .... (MCA)
   Today's Country Classics .... (MCA)
   Too Good To Stop Now .... (MCA)
Cowboy & The Lady
John Denver; *Some Days Are Diamonds* .... (RCA)
Johnny Duncan; *Come A Little Bit Closer* .... (COL)
Cowboys To Girls
Intruders; *Soul Shots-Sixties Soul Classics* .... (RHI)
   Super Hits .... (PI)
Crack House Woman
George "Wild Child" Butler; *These Mean Old Blues* .... (BUL)
Crazy About Her
Rod Stewart; *Out Of Order* .... (WB)
   Storyteller/Complete Anthology-1964-1990 ..... (WB)

Crazy Little Mama
Eldorados; *Greatest Groups/'50s-#2* .... (CLT)
Sock Hop .... (DHL)
Crazy She Calls Me
Abbey Lincoln; *Blue Series-Female Vocals* ...... (BLN)
Aretha Franklin; *Aretha's Jazz* .... (ATL)
Billie Holiday; *From The Original Decca Masters* (MCA)
Joe Mooney; *Erteguns' New York N.Y. Cabaret*
Music .... (ATL)
Linda Ronstadt; *What's New* .... (ASY)
Lurlean Hunter; *Atlantic Jazz-Singers* .... (ATL)
Crazy 'Bout That Married Woman
Rockin' Dopsie; *Saturday Night Zydeco* .... (MSO)
Cruel Little Number
Jeff Healey Band; *Feel This* .... (ARI)
Dance On Little Girl
Paul Anka; *21 Golden Hits* .... (RCA)
Best Of .... (RHI)
She's A Lady .... (RCA)
Vintage Years '57-'61 .... (SIR)
Dangerous Woman
Mississippi Jook Band; *Good Time Blues* ....(COL)
Danger! She's A Stranger
Five Stairsteps; *Greatest Hits* .... (CLT)
Dark Lady
Cher; *Greatest Hits* .... (MCA)
Half Breed .... (MSP)
Scorpions; *Best Of* .... (RCA)
Hot & Heavy .... (RCA)
In Trance .... (RCA)
Tokyo Tapes .... (RCA)
Darlin'
Beach Boys; *Absolute Best-#2* .... (CAP)
Concert/'69 .... (CAP)
Smiley Smile/Wild Honey .... (CAP)
Sunshine Dream .... (CAP)
Darlin' Be Home Soon
Joe Cocker; *Classics-#4* .... (A&M)
Greatest Hits .... (A&M)
Joe Cocker .... (A&M)
Lovin' Spoonful; *Anthology* .... (RHI)
Best Of-#2 .... (RHI)
Lovin' '60s .... (PRY)
Daughter
Bread; *Baby I'm A-Want You* .... (ELE)
Best Of-#2 .... (ELE)
Pearl Jam; *Vs.* .... (EPA)
Day Tripper
Beatles; *1962-1966* .... (CAP)
Box Set .... (CAP)
Past Masters-#2 .... (CAP)
Yesterday...And Today .... (CAP)
Jimi Hendrix Experience; *Radio One* .... (RYK)
Otis Redding; *Dictionary Of Soul* .... (ATC)
Story .... (ATL)
Sergio Mendes & Brasil '66; *Greatest Hits* ...... (A&M)
Dead Girls Of London
Frank Zappa; *You Can't Do That On Stage*
Anymore-#5 .... (RYK)
Deep River Woman
Lionel Richie; *Dancing On The Ceiling* .... (MOT)
Delta Lady
Joe Cocker; *Classics-#4* .... (A&M)
Greatest Hits .... (A&M)
Joe Cocker .... (A&M)
Mad Dogs & Englishmen .... (A&M)
Leon Russell; *Best Of* .... (MCA)
Leon Russell .... (MCA)
Detroit Girls
Starz; *Live In Action* .... (MET)
Starz .... (MET)
Devil Ain't A Lonely Woman's Friend
Red Steagall; *45* .... (MCA)
Devil In Her Heart
Beatles; *Second Album* .... (CAP)
With The .... (CAP)
Donays; *Beatles Originals* .... (RHI)
Devil With A Blue Dress On
Bruce Springsteen; *ST/No Nukes-Muse Concerts* .. (ASY)
Mitch Ryder/Detroit Wheels; *Frat Rock-#4* ...... (RHI)
Rev Up-Best Of .... (RHI)
Son Of Frat Rock .... (RHI)
Toga Rock .... (DHL)

Devil Woman
Buddy Knox; *Best Of* .... (RHI)
Hanoi Rocks; *Oriental Beat* .... (GEF)
Marty Robbins; *Billboard Top Country Hits-1962* (RHI)
Columbia Country Classics-#4 .... (COL)
Greatest Hits-#4 .... (COL)
Lifetime Of Song .... (COL)
Diamonds Are A Girl's Best Friend
Carol Channing; *Broadway Magic-'50s* ....(COL)
Emmylou Harris; *White Shoes* .... (WB)
Marilyn Monroe; *Goodbye Primadonna* .... (ACC)
Pearl Bailey; *Back On Broadway* .... (RLL)
Echoes Of An Era .... (RLL)
Diamonds On The Soles Of Her Shoes
Paul Simon; *Concert In The Park-August 15 1991* (WB)
Graceland .... (WB)
Negotiations & Love Songs-1971-1986 .... (WB)
Did You Ever See A Dream Walking
Bing Crosby; *Crosby Classics* ....(COL)
Hal Kemp/Skinnay Ennis; *Uncollected-#2 & #3* .. (HIN)
Dime Queen Of Nevada
Tom Jones; *Darlin'* .... (MER)
Dirty Little Girl
Elton John; *Goodbye Yellow Brick Road* .... (POL)
Disney Girls
Art Garfunkel; *Breakaway* ....(COL)
Beach Boys; *Surf's Up* ....(CAR)
Captain & Tennille; *Greatest Hits* .... (A&M)
Do Wa Diddy Diddy
Manfred Mann; *Best Of* .... (EMI)
Billboard Top Rock 'N' Roll Hits-1964 .... (RHI)
History Of British Rock-#2 .... (RHI)
Does She Love That Man?
Breathe; *Peace Of Mind* .... (A&M)
Don't Kick Her In The Butt
Bobby Taylor & Carolyn Majors; *ST/Far Out*
Man .... (CML)
Don't Put A Tax On The Beautiful Girls
Eddie Cantor; *Rare Early Recordings-1919-1921* .(BIO)
Don't Take The Girl
Tim McGraw; *Not A Moment Too Soon* .... (CRB)
Down Home Girl
Nazareth; *Play'n' The Game* .... (A&M)
Rolling Stones; *Now!* .... (AKO)
Dragon Lady
Blue Oyster Cult; *Revolution By Night* ....(COL)
Bob Dylan; *Infidels* ....(COL)
Germs; *Germs* .... (SLS)
Dream Girl
Stephen Bishop; *ST/Animal House* .... (MCA)
Dream Lady
Bread; *Baby I'm A-Want You* .... (ELE)
Best Of-#2 .... (ELE)
Dream On Texas Ladies
John Michael Montgomery; *Life's A Dance* ..... (ATL)
ST/Maverick .... (ATL)
Dreams Of The Everyday Housewife
Glen Campbell; *Classics Collection* .... (CAP)
Greatest Hits .... (CAP)
Live .... (CAP)
Very Best Of .... (CAP)
Drug Store Woman
John Lee Hooker; *Best Of* .... (CRS)
Best Of .... (VJ)
Dublin Lady
Andy M. Stewart & Manus Lunny; *Dublin Lady* .(GRE)
Dude (Looks Like A Lady)
Aerosmith; *Permanent Vacation* .... (GEF)
Earth Girls Are Easy
Julie Brown; *Goddess In Progress* .... (RHI)
Easter Woman
Residents; *Commercial Album* .... (RAL)
Easy Lover
Phil Collins; *Serious Hits...Live!* .... (ATL)
Philip Bailey & Phil Collins; *Chinese Walls* ......(COL)
El Paso
Grateful Dead; *Steal Your Face* .... (GRD)
Marty Robbins; *Biggest Hits* ....(COL)
Billboard Top Country Hits-1960 .... (RHI)
Gunfighter Ballads & Trail Songs .... (COL)
Radio Classics/'50s .... (COL)
Electric Lady
Con Funk Shun; *Electric Lady* .... (MER)

European Female
Stranglers; *All Live & All Of The Night* .... (EPI)
  Feline .... (EPI)
  Greatest Hits-1977-1990 .... (EPI)
Euro-Trash Girl
Cracker; *Kerosene Hat* .... (VIA)
Every Little Girl's Dream
Lisa Brokop; *Every Little Girl's Dream* ...... (PAT)
Every Little Thing She Does Is Magic
Police; *Every Breath You Take-Singles* .... (A&M)
  Ghost In The Machine .... (A&M)
Every Woman
Dave Mason; *Best Of* ....(COL)
Every Woman In The World
Air Supply; *Greatest Hits* .... (ARI)
  Lost In Love .... (ARI)
Evil Woman
Doobie Brothers; *Captain & Me* ....(WB)
Electric Light Orchestra; *Afterglow* .... (EPI)
  Face The Music .... (JET)
  Greatest Hits .... (JET)
  Ole ELO .... (JET)
Fantasy Girl
38 Special; *Flashback-Best Of* .... (A&M)
  Wild-Eyed Southern Boys .... (A&M)
Fast Moving Train
Restless Heart; *Best Of* ....(RCA)
  Fast Moving Train ....(RCA)
Fat Bottomed Girls
Queen; *Greatest Hits* ....(HOL)
  Jazz ....(HOL)
Fat Lady That Bumped Me Down
Paul Kelly; *Stand On The Positive Side* ....(WB)
Father Of Girls
Perry Como; *Legendary Performer* ....(RCA)
Find Me A Girl
Jacksons; *Goin' Places* .... (EPI)
  Philly Ballads-#2 .... (PI)
Fire Girl
Commodores; *Natural High* .... (MOT)
Fire Woman
Cult; *Sonic Temple* .... (SRR)
Flower Lady
Peter & Gordon; *Best Of* .... (RHI)
Phil Ochs; *Chords Of Fame* .... (A&M)
  Pleasures Of The Harbor .... (A&M)
  War Is Over-Best Of .... (A&M)
Foolish Little Girl
Shirelles; *16 Greatest Hits* .... (TRP)
  Anthology-1959-1964 .... (RHI)
  Greatest Hits .... (EVR)
For Me & My Gal
Bing Crosby; *Radio Years-#1* .... (CRS)
Harry Nilsson; *Little Touch Of Schmilsson In The Night* ....(RCA)
Judy Garland & Gene Kelly; *Best of The Decca Years-#1-Hits!* .... (DEC)
Forever My Lady
Jodeci; *Forever My Lady* .... (UT)
Forever Your Girl
Paula Abdul; *Forever Your Girl* .... (VIA)
  Shut Up & Dance .... (VIA)
Foxey Lady
Jimi Hendrix; *Essential-#2* .... (RPR)
  Smash Hits .... (RPR)
  ST/Jimi Plays Monterey .... (RPR)
  ST/Wayne's World .... (RPR)
Jimi Hendrix Experience; *Are You Experienced?* .. (RPR)
Mary's Danish; *Circa* .... (MC)
Fraulein
Bobby Helms; *Pop-A-Dilly* .... (MCA)
  Super Hits Country/'50s .... (GUS)
Mickey Gilley; *Greatest Hits-#1* .... (EPI)
Fresno Beauties
Original Cast; *Most Happy Fella* ....(RCA)
Friend, Love, Woman, Life
Mac Davis; *Baby Don't Get Hooked On Me* ......(COL)
  Greatest Hits ....(COL)
Funky Cold Medina
Tone Loc; *Loc-ed After Dark* .... (DV)
Funny Girl
Barbra Streisand; *ST/Funny Girl* ....(COL)
Gas Station Woman
Phil Ochs; *War Is Over-Best Of* .... (A&M)

Geisha Girl
Hank Locklin; *Golden Hits* .... (PLN)
Gemini Girl
David Allan Coe; *Son Of The South* ....(COL)
German Nun
Sex Gang Children; *Ecstasy & Vendetta Over New York* .... (ROI)
Get Off My Back Woman
B.B. King; *Live & Well* .... (MCA)
Get Out Of My Life, Woman
Lee Dorsey; *History Of New Orleans R&B-#3-1962-1970* .... (RHI)
Paul Butterfield Blues Band; *East-West* .... (ELE)
  Golden Butter .... (ELE)
Ghost Of A Texas Ladies' Man
Concrete Blonde; *Walking In London* .... (IRS)
Girl
Beatles; *1962-1966* ....(CAP)
  Box Set ....(CAP)
  Love Songs ....(CAP)
  Rubber Soul ....(CAP)
Girl Can't Help It
Journey; *Greatest Hits* ....(COL)
  Raised On Radio ....(COL)
Little Richard; *18 Greatest Hits* .... (RHI)
  Greatest Hits .... (EVR)
  Super Oldies/'50s-#3 .... (AUF)
  Well Alright! .... (SPE)
Girl Don't Tell Me
Beach Boys; *California Girls* ....(CAP)
  Endless Summer ....(CAP)
  Gift Set ....(CAP)
Girl From Atlanta
Benny Carter All-Star Sax Ensemble; *Over The Rainbow* .... (MM)
Girl From Baltimore
Fleshtones; *Living Legends* .... (IRS)
Girl From Germany
Sparks; *Profile: Ultimate Sparks Collection* .... (RHI)
Girl From Greenland
Chet Baker; *Compact Jazz* .... (EMA)
Girl From Hiroshima
Third World; *Sense Of Purpose* ....(COL)
Girl From Ipanema
Antonio Carlos Jobim; *Antonio Carlos Jobim* .....(WB)
  Compact Jazz ....(VRV)
Ella Fitzgerald; *Ella A Nice* .... (PAB)
  Montreux '75 .... (PAB)
  Pablo Today-Ella Embraces A.C. Jobim ...... (PAB)
Stan Getz & Astrud Gilberto; *Cruisin'-1964* ..... (INC)
  Getz/Gilberto ....(VRV)
Girl From Key Biscayne
Diego Modena & Jean Philippe Audin; *Ocarina* . (PRV)
Girl From Knoxville
Dave Loggins; *Apprentice (In A Musical Workshop)* .... (EPI)
Girl From Mill Valley
Jeff Beck Group; *Beck-Ola* .... (EPI)
Girl From New York City
Beach Boys; *Today!/Summer Days (& Summer Nights!)* .... (CAP)
Girl From The North Country
Bob Dylan; *Freewheelin'* ....(COL)
  Nashville Skyline ....(COL)
  Real Live ....(COL)
Joe Cocker; *Mad Dogs & Englishmen* .... (A&M)
Girl From Uganda
Les Baxter/Orchestra; *African Blue-Brazil Now* .. (CRS)
Girl I Got My Eyes On You
Today; *Today* .... (MOT)
Girl In A T-Shirt
ZZ Top; *Antenna* ....(RCA)
Girl Is Mine
Michael Jackson With Paul McCartney; *Thriller* .. (EPI)
Girl Like You
Rascals; *Greatest Hits* .... (ATL)
  Groovin' .... (RHI)
Smithereens; *11* .... (ENI)
Girl Next Door
Bobby Brown; *Dance!...Ya Know It!* .... (MCA)
  King Of Stage .... (MCA)
Earl Lewis/Channels; *Harlem Holiday-New York R&B-#2* .... (CLT)
  New York's Finest .... (CLT)

Frank Sinatra; *Gift Set* .... (CAP)
Johnny Crawford; *Best Of* .... (RHI)
Girl Of My Dreams
Bram Tchaikovsky; *D.I.Y.-#4-UK Pop II-Starry Eyes-1978-79* .... (RHI)
   Strange Man Changed Man .... (POL)
Buddy Clark; *16 Most Requested Songs* .... (COL)
Dizzy Gillespie & Stan Getz; *Diz & Getz* .... (VRV)
Girl On A Swing
Gerry/Pacemakers; *History Of British Rock-#7* ... (RHI)
Girl Talk
Betty Carter; *Finally* .... (RLL)
Ella Fitzgerald & Joe Pass; *Speak Love* .... (PAB)
Girl Thang
Tammy Wynette & Wynonna; *Without Walls* ..... (EPI)
Girl That I Marry
Broadway Cast; *Annie Get Your Gun* ...... (ANG)
Doris Day/Original Cast; *Annie Get Your Gun* ..(COL)
Ethel Merman/Original Cast; *Annie Get Your Gun* .... (RCA)
Frank Sinatra; *Greatest Hits-Early Years* ....(COL)
Girl With April In Her Eyes
Chris DeBurgh; *Crusader* .... (A&M)
Girl With The Hungry Eyes
Jefferson Starship; *At Point Zero* .... (GRU)
Girl You Know It's True
Milli Vanilli; *All Or Nothing* .... (ARI)
   Girl You Know It's True .... (ARI)
Girlfriend
Beautiful South; *Welcome To The Beautiful South* (ELE)
Bobby Brown; *King Of Stage* .... (MCA)
Mary Jane Girls; *Only Four You* .... (MOT)
Matthew Sweet; *Girlfriend* .... (ZOO)
Michael Jackson; *Off The Wall* .... (EPI)
Pebbles; *Pebbles* .... (MCA)
Wings; *London Town* .... (CAP)
Girlfriend Is Better
Talking Heads; *Speaking In Tongues* .... (SIR)
   ST/Stop Making Sense .... (SIR)
Girls Just Want To Have Fun
Cyndi Lauper; *She's So Unusual* .... (POR)
Girls Night Out
Judds; *Greatest Hits* .... (MCA)
   Why Not Me .... (MCA)
Tyler Collins; *S* .... (RCA)
Girls Of Montreal
Artie Traum; *Life On Earth* .... (ROU)
Girls Of Porn
Mr. Bungle; *Mr. Bungle* .... (WB)
Girls Of Santa Fe
Bill Morrissey; *Standing Eight* .... (PHO)
Girls Of Summer
Original Cast; *Marry Me A Little* ....(RCA)
Girls On The Beach
Beach Boys; *Absolute Best-#1* .... (CAP)
   Endless Summer .... (CAP)
   Little Deuce Coupe/All Summer Long .... (CAP)
Girls Talk
Dave Edmunds; *Best Of* .... (SS)
   I Hear You Rockin' .... (COL)
   Repeat When Necessary .... (SS)
Elvis Costello; *Girls Girls Girls* .... (COL)
   Taking Liberties .... (COL)
Linda Ronstadt; *Mad Love* .... (ASY)
Girls With Guitars
Wynonna; *Tell Me Why* .... (MCC)
Girls' School
Wings; *London Town* .... (CAP)
Girl, I've Been Hurt
Snow; *12 Inches Of Snow* .... (EW)
Girl, You'll Be A Woman Soon
Neil Diamond;
   Double Gold .... (BNG)
   Classics (Early Years) .... (COL)
   Greatest Hits .... (BNG)
   Hot August Night .... (MCA)
Go Away Little Girl
Happenings; *45* .... (ERI)
   45 .... (VGO)
Steve Lawrence; *Greatest Hits* .... (COL)
Go Home Girl
Ry Cooder; *Bop Till You Drop* .... (WB)
God Blessed Texas
Little Texas; *Big Time* .... (WB)

Gold Digger
EPMD; *Business As Usual* .... (DFJ)
Gold Dust Woman
Fleetwood Mac; *25 Years-The Chain* .... (WB)
   Rumours .... (WB)
Golden Lady
Jose Feliciano; *And The Feeling's Good* .... (MOT)
Stevie Wonder; *Innervisions* .... (MOT)
Golf Girl
Caravan; *Best Of* .... (LON)
   In The Land Of Grey & Pink .... (LON)
   London Collector .... (LON)
Gone As A Girl Can Get
George Strait; *Holding My Own* .... (MCA)
Good Girls Don't
Knack; *Get The Knack* .... (CAP)
Good Girls Go To Heaven
Charlie Floyd; *Charlie Floyd* .... (LIB)
Good Hearted Woman
George Jones; *I Am What I Am* .... (EPI)
Waylon Jennings; *Good Hearted Woman* ....(RCA)
   Greatest Hits ....(RCA)
   The Outlaws ....(RCA)
Willie Nelson; *Greatest Hits & Some That Will Be* (COL)
   Willie ....(RCA)
Good Morning Girl
Journey; *Departure* ....(COL)
Good Morning Little School Girl
Grateful Dead; *Grateful Dead* .... (WB)
Huey Lewis/News; *Four Chords & Several Years Ago* .... (ELE)
Johnny Winter; *Johnny Winter* ....(COL)
   Live ....(COL)
Ten Years After; *Classic Performances* ....(COL)
   Recorded Live ....(COL)
   Ssssh ....(CHR)
   Universal ....(CHR)
Yardbirds; *Crossroads* ....(POL)
   Five Live Yardbirds .... (RHI)
Good Run Of Bad Luck
Clint Black; *No Time To Kill* ....(RCA)
Good Time Girl
Lee Ferrell; *Hard Times* .... (TMS)
Green Eyed Lady
Sugarloaf; *45* .... (UA)
Gulf And The Shell
Clinton Gregory; *Clinton Gregory* ....(PYN)
Gypsy Woman
Brian Hyland; *Greatest Hits* .... (RHI)
   Super Hits/'70s-Have A Nice Day-#3 .... (RHI)
Impressions; *Billboard Top R&B Hits-1961* ...... (RHI)
   Greatest Hits .... (MCA)
   Oldies But Goodies-#12 .... (OSR)
   Vintage/Classic Oldies From '50s-'60s-#6 ...... (MCA)
Muddy Waters; *Chess Box* .... (CSS)
   Real Folk Blues .... (CSS)
Ry Cooder; *Slide Area* .... (WB)
Gypsy Woman (She's Homeless)
Crystal Waters; *Red Hot + Dance* ....(COL)
   Surprise .... (MER)
Happiest Girl In The Whole U.S.A.
Donna Fargo; *45* .... (MCA)
Jeanne Pruett; *Stand By Your Man* .... (ALL)
Hard Headed Woman
Cat Stevens; *Greatest Hits* .... (A&M)
   Tea For The Tillerman .... (A&M)
Elvis Presley; *Billboard Top Rock 'N' Roll Hits-1958* ....(RCA)
   Number One Hits ....(RCA)
   ST/King Creole ....(RCA)
   Top Ten Hits ....(RCA)
   Worldwide 50 Gold Award Hits-#1 ....(RCA)
Hard Lovin' Woman
Mark Collie; *Unleashed* .... (MCA)
Hard Luck Woman
Garth Brooks; *Kiss My Ass* .... (MER)
Kiss; *Alive 2* .... (CAS)
   Double Platinum .... (CAS)
   Rock & Roll Over .... (CAS)
Harry's House Centerpiece
Joni Mitchell; *Hissing Of Summer Lawns* .... (ASY)
Have You Seen Her
Chi-Lites; *Greatest Hits* .... (EPI)
Hammer; *Please Hammer Don't Hurt 'Em* ....(CAP)

He Thinks He'll Keep Her
Mary Chapin Carpenter; *Come On Come On* ....(COL)
Hearts Are Gonna Roll
Hal Ketchum; *Sure Love* ....(CRB)
Her Strut
Bob Seger/Silver Bullet Band; *Against The Wind* .(CAP)
   Nine Tonight ....(CAP)
Her Town Too
James Taylor & J.D. Souther; *Dad Loves His Work* ....(COL)
Here, There & Everywhere
Beatles; *Box Set* ....(CAP)
   Love Songs ....(CAP)
   Revolver ....(CAP)
Kenny Loggins; *Alive* ....(COL)
Hey Girl (I Like Your Style)
Temptations; *Cloud Nine* ....(MOT)
   Masterpiece ....(MOT)
Hey Little Girl
Dee Clark; *Jukebox Classics-#1* ....(RHI)
   Super Oldies/'50s-#2 ....(AUF)
Icehouse; *Primitive Man* ....(CHR)
Professor Longhair; *Atlantic R&B 1947-1974-#1-(1947-1952)* ....(ATL)
   New Orleans Piano-Blues Originals-#2 ....(ATL)
Highway Lady
UFO; *No Heavy Petting* ....(CHR)
Hippychick
Soho; *Goddess* ....(ATC)
Holdin' Heaven
Tracy Byrd; *Tracy Byrd* ....(MCA)
Hollywood Lady
Burt Compton & Steve Mele; *Rock 'N' Roll Genius* .... (WIZ)
Hollywood Movie Girls
Dusty Springfield; *It Begins Again* ....(UA)
Honeysuckle Honey
Commander Cody/Lost Planet Airmen; *Country Casanova* .... (MCA)
Hospital Lady
Loudon Wainwright III; *Loudon Wainwright III* ..(ATL)
Hot Girls In Love
Loverboy; *Big Ones* ....(COL)
   Keep It Up ....(COL)
Hotel For Women
Nails; *Hotel For Women* ....(PVC)
Housewife
Leon Russell; *Americana* ....(PRD)
Houston, Treat My Lady Good
Joe Stampley; *Red Wine & Blue Memories* ....(EPI)
How Do You Talk To Girls
Rick Springfield; *Success Hasn't Spoiled Me Yet* ..(RCA)
How To Handle A Woman
Original Cast; *Camelot* ....(COL)
Richard Harris; *ST/Camelot* ....(WB)
I Am Woman
Helen Reddy; *Greatest Hits* ....(CAP)
   I Am Woman ....(CAP)
   I Don't Know How To Love Him ....(CAP)
I Can't Reach Her Anymore
Sammy Kershaw; *Haunted Heart* ....(MER)
I Dream Of Women Like You
Ronnie McDowell; *Country Boy's Heart* ....(EPI)
   Older Women & Other Greatest Hits ....(EPI)
I Enjoy Being A Girl
Original Cast; *Flower Drum Song* ....(COL)
I Found My Girl In The Good Old U.S.A.
Jimmie Skinner; *45* ....(GUS)
I Lost My Gal From Memphis
New Sunshine Jazz Band; *Too Much Mustard* .....(BIO)
I Love You (Miss Robot)
Buggles; *Age Of Plastic* ....(ISL)
I Met Her In Church
Box Tops; *Greatest Hits* ....(RHI)
I Saw Her Again
Mamas & The Papas; *Best Of* ....(MCA)
   Farewell To The First Golden Era ....(MCA)
   Mamas & The Papas ....(MCA)
I Saw Her (Him) Standing There
Beatles; *Meet The* ....(CAP)
   Please Please Me ....(EMI)
   Rock 'n' Roll Music-#1 ....(CAP)
Paul McCartney; *Tripping The Live Fantastic* ....(CAP)
   Tripping The Live Fantastic-Highlights! ....(CAP)

Tiffany; *Tiffany* .... (MCA)
I Taught Her Everything She Knows
Billy Walker; *Greatest Hits* ....(MON)
I Want A Girl (Just Like The Girl)
Al Jolson; *Story-#1* ....(MCA)
Spike Jones; *King Of Corn* ....(GLN)
I Want A Little Girl
Joe Turner; *Atlantic Jazz-Singers* ....(ATL)
Ray Charles; *Life In Music* ....(ATL)
I Wish I Had A Girl
Henry Lee Summer; *Henry Lee Summer* ....(CBA)
If Drinkin' Don't Kill Me...
George Jones; *Anniversary-10 Years Of Hits* ......(EPI)
   I Am What I Am ....(EPI)
If I Could Have Her Tonight
Neil Young; *Neil Young* ....(RPR)
If I Were Your Girlfriend
Prince; *45* ....(PAI)
If I Were Your Woman
Gladys Knight/Pips; *All The Great Hits* .... (MOT)
   Anthology ....(MOT)
   Compact Command Performances ....(MOT)
   Every Great Motown Song-First 25 Years ...... (MOT)
   If I Were Your Woman ....(MOT)
   Motown Superstar Series-#13 ....(MOT)
If She Knew What She Wants
Bangles; *Different Light* ....(COL)
   Greatest Hits ....(COL)
If Women Ruled The World
Joan Armatrading; *Square The Circle* ....(A&M)
In China Or A Woman's Heart
Kate Wolf; *Poet's Heart* ....(KAL)
In The Girls' Room
Rick James; *Wonderful* ....(RPR)
In The Heart Of A Woman
Billy Ray Cyrus; *It Won't Be The Last* ....(MER)
Indian Girl
Capris; *There's A Moon Out Tonight* ....(CLT)
Hollies; *Epic Anthology-Original Master Tapes* ....(EPI)
Rolling Stones; *Emotional Rescue* ....(RS)
Indian Lady
Roger Whittaker; *Reflections Of Love* ....(RCA)
Indian Woman
Dan Hill; *Frozen In The Night* .... (20)
Sons Of The Pioneers; *Western Country* .... (GRA)
Insatiable Woman
Isley/Jasper/Isley; *Caravan Of Love* ....(CBA)
Irish Suite: Irish Washerwoman
Boston Pops Orchestra/Arthur Fiedler; *Irish Night At The Pops* ....(RCA)
Is She Really Going Out With Him
Joe Jackson; *Live-1980-1986* ....(A&M)
   Look Sharp ....(A&M)
Is There Life Out There
Reba McEntire; *For My Broken Heart* .... (MCA)
   Greatest Hits-#2 ....(MCA)
Island Girl
Beach Boys; *Still Cruisin'* ....(CAP)
Elton John; *Billboard Top Hits-1975* ....(RHI)
   Greatest Hits-#2 ....(POL)
   Rock Of The Westies ....(POL)
Island Woman
Pablo Cruise; *Pablo Cruise* ....(A&M)
Isn't She Lovely
Lee Ritenour; *Best Of* ....(EPI)
Stevie Wonder; *Original Musiquarium* ....(MOT)
   Songs In The Key Of Life ....(MOT)
It Could've Been Me
Billy Ray Cyrus; *Some Gave All* .... (MER)
It Should've Been Me
Commander Cody/Lost Planet Airmen; *Hot Licks Cold Steel & Trucker's Faves* ....(MCA)
It Won't Be Over You
Steve Wariner; *Drive* .... (ARI)
Italian Girls
Daryl Hall & John Oates; *H2O* ....(RCA)
   Soulful Sounds ....(RCA)
Rod Stewart; *Best Of-#2* .... (MER)
It's A Shame To Ship Your Wife On Sunday
Fiddlin' John Carson; *Old Hen Cackled (& The Rooster's...)* .... (ROU)
I'll Come Back As Another Woman
Tanya Tucker; *Girls Like Me* ....(CAP)
   Greatest Hits ....(CAP)

I'm A One Woman Man
George Jones; *I'm A One Woman Man* ....(EPI)
Glen Campbell; *Still Within The Sound Of My
Voice* ....(MCA)
Johnny Horton; *American Originals* ....(COL)
I'm Every Woman
Whitney Houston; *ST/Bodyguard* ....(ARI)
I'm That Kind Of Girl
Patty Loveless; *Greatest Hits* ....(MCA)
On Down The Line ....(MCA)
I'm The Laziest Gal In Town
Julie Wilson; *Cole Porter Songbook* ....(DRG)
I've Got A Gal In Kalamazoo
Glenn Miller; *Best Of* ....(RCA)
Decade Of The '40s ....(RCA)
Legendary Performer-#1 & 2 ....(RCA)
Memorial 1944-1969 ....(RCA)
Pure Gold ....(RCA)
Story ....(RCA)
Unforgettable ....(RCA)
I've Got A Woman
Jimmy McGriff; *Best Of Sue Records* ....(CLT)
Toast To Jimmy McGriff's Golden Classics .....(CLT)
Jamaica Lady
Nitty Gritty Dirt Band; *Dirt Silver & Gold* ....(UA)
Jealous Girl
New Edition; *Candy Girl* .... (STW)
Jersey Girl
Bruce Springsteen/E Street Band;
Live-1975-1985 ....(COL)
Tom Waits; *Anthology Of* ....(ASY)
Heartattack & Vine ....(ASY)
Jessie's Girl
Rick Springfield; *Greatest Hits* ....(RCA)
Nipper's Greatest Hits-'80s ....(RCA)
Working Class Dog ....(RCA)
Jet City Woman
Queensryche; *Empire* .... (EMI)
Johannesburg Woman
David Rudder; *1990* .... (SIR)
Johnny Have You Seen Her?
Rembrandts; *United* ....(ATC)
Just Like A Woman
Bob Dylan; *At Budokan* ....(COL)
Before The Flood ....(COL)
Biograph ....(COL)
Blonde On Blonde ....(COL)
Greatest Hits ....(COL)
Byrds; *Byrds (collection)* ....(COL)
Just Tell Her Jim Said Hello
Elvis Presley; *Collector's Gold* ....(RCA)
Gold Award Hits-#2 ....(RCA)
Golden Records-#4 ....(RCA)
Just To See Her
Smokey Robinson; *One Heartbeat* ....(MOT)
Kansas City Woman
Little Charlie/Nightcats; *Big Break!* ....(ALG)
Keep In Touch
Robert Palmer; *Some People Can Do What They
Like* .... (ISL)
Kentucky Woman
Billy Cole Reed; *Audiograph Alive* ....(AUD)
Deep Purple; *Purple Passages* ....(WB)
When We Rock We Rock ....(WB)
Gary Puckett/Union Gap; *Greatest Hits* ....(BCT)
Neil Diamond; *Classics* ....(COL)
Gold ....(MCA)
Love At The Greek ....(COL)
Ronnie Milsap; *16 Greatest Hits-#2* ....(TRP)
Kicks
Paul Revere/Raiders; *Greatest Hits* ....(COL)
Legend Of ....(COL)
Midnight Ride ....(COL)
Knoxville Girl
Cathy Fink & Duck Donald; *Cathy Fink & Duck
Donald* ....(FF)
Jimmy Martin; *Me 'N Ole Pete* ....(IGR)
Stanley Brothers; *Stanley Series-Vol. 1-#1* ......(COP)
Ladies Night
Kool/Gang; *Ladies Night* .... (DL)
Ladies Night In Buffalo
David Lee Roth; *Eat 'Em & Smile* ....(WB)
Ladies Of The Canyon
Joni Mitchell; *Ladies Of The Canyon* ....(RPR)

Ladies Who Lunch
Original Cast; *Company* ....(COL)
Lady
George Benson; *Breezin'* ....(WB)
Jack Jones; *Best Of* ....(MCA)
Kenny Rogers; *20 Great Years* ....(RPR)
Greatest Hits ....(EMI)
Twenty Greatest Hits ....(EMI)
Little River Band; *Greatest Hits* ....(CAP)
Roger Williams; *Greatest Hits* ....(CCB)
Stryper; *Against The Law* ....(HOL)
Can't Stop The Rock-Collection-1984-1991 ....(HOL)
Styx; *Best Of* ....(RCA)
Lady ....(RCA)
Nipper's Greatest Hits-'70s ....(RCA)
Lady Blue
George Benson; *Weekend In L.A.* ....(WB)
Leon Russell; *Best Of* ....(MCA)
Will O' The Wisp ....(MCA)
Lady Bus Driver
Ultra Head; *Cement Truck* .... (IST)
Lady Cab Driver
Prince; *1999* ....(WB)
Lady Came From Baltimore
Joan Baez; *Contemporary Ballad Book* ....(VAN)
Joan ....(VAN)
John Stewart; *Neon Beach* ....(HOM)
Tim Hardin; *Hang On To A Dream-Verve
Recordings* ....(POL)
Lady Doctor
Graham Parker/Rumour; *Howlin' Wind* ....(MER)
Parkerilla ....(MER)
Lady Down On Love
Alabama; *Closer You Get* ....(RCA)
Greatest Hits-#2 ....(RCA)
Live ....(RCA)
Lady Grinning Soul
David Bowie; *Aladdin Sane* ....(RYK)
Lady Is A Tramp
Ella Fitzgerald; *Rodgers & Hart Songbook* ....(VRV)
Frank Sinatra; *Capitol Years* ....(CAP)
Sinatra Reprise-Very Good Years ....(RPR)
Frank Sinatra & Luther Vandross; *Frank Sinatra
Duets* ....(CAP)
Lady Luck
David Lee Roth; *Little Ain't Enough* ....(WB)
Journey; *Captured* ....(COL)
Evolution ....(COL)
Kenny Loggins; *Celebrate Me Home* ....(COL)
Restless Heart; *Fast Moving Train* ....(RCA)
Lady Of Spain
Bing Crosby; *Radio Years* ....(CRS)
Les Paul; *Legend & The Legacy* ....(CAP)
Muppets/Amazing Marvin Suggs/Muppaphone; *Muppet
Hits* .... (JH)
Lady Of The Island
Crosby, Stills & Nash; *Crosby, Stills & Nash* .....(ATL)
Lady Sings The Blues
Billie Holiday; *All Or Nothing At All* ....(VRV)
Essential Carnegie Hall Concert ....(VRV)
History Of The Real Billie Holiday ....(VRV)
Lady Sings The Blues ....(VRV)
Lady Stardust
David Bowie; *Rise & Fall Of Ziggy Stardust* ......(RYK)
Lady Starlight
Scorpions; *Animal Magnetism* .... (MER)
Lady Takes The Cowboy Every Time
Gatlin Brothers; *Biggest Hits* ....(COL)
Larry Gatlin/Gatlin Brothers; *Houston To Denver* (COL)
Lady Writer
Dire Straits; *Communique* ....(WB)
Lady (You Bring Me Up)
Commodores; *All The Great Hits* ....(MOT)
All The Great Love Songs ....(MOT)
Compact Command Performances ....(MOT)
Lady's In Love With You
Annie Ross & Gerry Mulligan; *Annie Ross Sings A Song
With G. Mulligan* .... (EMI)
Shirley Ross; *Thanks For The Memories* ....(DEC)
Las Vegas Girl
Leroy Van Dyke; *45* ....(MCA)

Lay Lady Lay
Bob Dylan; *Biograph* ....(COL)
  Greatest Hits-#2 ....(COL)
  Hard Rain ....(COL)
  Nashville Skyline ....(COL)
Bob Dylan/Band; *Before The Flood* ....(COL)
Byrds; *Byrds* ....(COL)
Let Her Down Easy
Terence Trent D'Arby; *Symphony Or Damn* .....(COL)
Life Is A Lady
Santana; *Inner Secrets* ....(COL)
Life Is A Woman
Original Cast/Sammy Davis, Jr.; *Stop The World I Want
To Get Off* ....(WB)
Little Dutch Girl
George Morgan; *American Originals* ....(COL)
Little Girl
Monkees; *Monkee Flips* .... (RHI)
  Present .... (RHI)
Reba McEntire; *Sweet Sixteen* ....(MCA)
Ritchie Valens; *Best Of* .... (RHI)
  History Of .... (RHI)
Steve Miller Band; *Anthology* ....(CAP)
  Your Saving Grace ....(CAP)
Little Girl Blue
Ella Fitzgerald; *Rodgers & Hart Songbook* ....(VRV)
Little Girl From Little Rock
Original Cast; *Gentlemen Prefer Blondes* ....(SSP)
Little Girl Of Mine
Cleftones; *Original Rock 'N' Roll Hits Of The '50s* (RLL)
Dion; *Bronx Blues-Columbia Recordings* ....(COL)
Little Girls
Original Broadway Cast; *Annie* ....(COL)
Patti Labelle; *Best Of* ....(EPI)
Little Hollywood Girl
Crickets; *Liberty Years* .... (EMI)
Little Lady Preacher
Tom T. Hall; *Greatest Hits-#2* .... (MER)
Little Miss Can't Be Wrong
Spin Doctors; *Homebelly Groove* ....(EPA)
  Pocket Full Of Kryptonite ....(EPA)
  Up For Grabs...Live ....(EPA)
Little Miss Love
Eldorados; *45* ....(CLT)
Little Miss Lover
Jimi Hendrix; *Axis: Bold As Love* ....(RPR)
  Essential ....(RPR)
Little Miss Magic
Jimmy Buffett; *Boats Beaches Bars & Ballads* ... (MGR)
  Coconut Telegraph ....(MCA)
Little Old Lady From Pasadena
Beach Boys; *Concert* ....(CAP)
Jan & Dean; *Best Of* .... (EMI)
  Billboard Top Rock 'N' Roll Hits-1964 .... (RHI)
  Deadman's Curve .... (EMI)
  Surf City-Best Of .... (EMI)
Little Wing
Derek/Dominos; *Layla* .... (RSO)
Jimi Hendrix; *Axis: Bold As Love* ....(RPR)
  Concerts ....(RPR)
  Essential-#1 & 2 ....(RPR)
  Lifelines/Jimi Hendrix Story ....(RPR)
Sting; *Nothing Like The Sun* ....(A&M)
Living Loving Maid
Led Zeppelin; *II* .... (ATL)
Lizard Lady
Residents; *Duck Stab* ....(RAL)
London Girl
Jam; *This Is The Modern World* ....(POL)
London Girls
Vibrators; *Pure Mania* ....(COL)
London Lady
Stranglers; *All Live & All Of The Night* .... (EPI)
  Rattus Norvegicus ....(A&M)
London You're A Lady
Pogues; *Peace & Love* ....(ISL)
Lonely Woman
Branford Marsalis; *Random Abstract* ....(COL)
Chris Connors; *Atlantic Jazz-Singers* ....(ATL)
Modern Jazz Quartet; *Lonely Woman* ....(ATL)
Sarah Vaughan; *Complete On Mercury-#1-Great Jazz
Years* .... (MER)
Sylvia Sims; *Atlantic Jazz-Singers* ....(ATL)

Lonely Women Make Good Lovers
Steve Wariner; *Best Of* ....(RCA)
  Greatest Hits ....(RCA)
  Midnight Fire ....(RCA)
Long Cool Woman In A Black Dress
Hollies; *Best Of* .... (EMI)
  Best Of-#2 .... (EMI)
  Billboard Top Rock 'N' Roll Hits-1972 .... (RHI)
  Distant Light .... (EPI)
  Epic Anthology-From The Original Masters ...... (EPI)
  Greatest Hits .... (EPI)
Lookin' In The Same Direction
Ken Mellons; *Ken Mellons* .... (EPI)
Louisiana Lady
Bobby Penn; *45* .... (FIF)
New Riders Of The Purple Sage; *Best Of* ....(COL)
  New Riders Of The Purple Sage ....(COL)
Louisiana Woman
Catfish Hodge; *Bout With The Blues* .... (ADE)
Rockin' Tabby Thomas; *King Of Swamp Blues* .. (MSO)
R.G./Bayou Zydeco; *Fire On The Bayou* ....(TAK)
Louisiana Woman, Mississippi Man
Loretta Lynn & Conway Twitty; *Louisiana Woman
Mississippi Man* ....(MCA)
  Very Best Of ....(MCA)
Louisiana Women
J.J. Cale; *Really* .... (MER)
Wayne Stewart; *Aspen Skyline* ....(BRR)
Love Will Bring Her Around
Rob Crosby; *Solid Ground* .... (ARI)
Lovergirl
Teena Marie; *Club Epic* .... (EPI)
  Starchild .... (EPI)
Luck Be A Lady
Frank Sinatra; *Reprise Collection* .... (RPR)
  Sinatra Reprise-The Very Good Years ....(RPR)
Original Cast; *Guys & Dolls* ....(MCA)
Lyin' Ass Bitch
Fishbone; *Fishbone* ....(COL)
Lyin' Eyes
Eagles; *Anthology* .... (ASY)
  One Of These Nights .... (ASY)
  ST/Urban Cowboy .... (ASY)
  Their Greatest Hits-1971-1975 .... (ASY)
L.A. Girls
Nazareth; *Play'n' The Game* .... (A&M)
L.A. Lady
New Riders Of The Purple Sage; *Adventures Of Panama
Red* ....(COL)
L.A. Woman
Billy Idol; *Charmed Life* .... (CHR)
Doors; *Best Of* .... (ELE)
  Greatest Hits .... (ELE)
  L.A. Woman .... (ELE)
  ST/Doors .... (ELE)
  Weird Scenes Inside The Gold Mine .... (ELE)
Macon Georgia Bad Girl
Jeannie C. Riley; *& Fancy Friends* .... (PLN)
Maid In Heaven
Be Bop Deluxe; *Best Of-Raiding The Divine
Archive* ....(CAP)
  Life In The Air Age ....(OOP)
Mail Order Woman
Champion Jack Dupree; *Blues For Everybody* .... (IGR)
Make Me The Woman That You Go Home To
Gladys Knight/Pips; *Anthology* ....(MOT)
  All The Great Hits ....(MOT)
  Compact Command Performances ....(MOT)
  Standing Ovation ....(SOL)
Man Smart, Woman Smarter
Harry Belafonte; *Pure Gold* ....(RCA)
Robert Palmer; *Some People Can Do What They
Like* .... (ISL)
Rosanne Cash; *Right Or Wrong* ....(COL)
Maneater
Daryl Hall & John Oates; *H2O* ....(RCA)
  Nipper's Greatest Hits-'80s ....(RCA)
  Rock 'N' Soul Part 1-Greatest Hits ....(RCA)
Married Lady
Bill Anderson; *Ladies Choice* ....(MCA)
Married Woman
Frankie Lee Sims; *Lucy Mae Blues* .... (SPE)
  This Is How It All Began-#1 .... (SPE)

Marry A Woman Uglier Than You
King's Singers; *10th Anniversary Concert-#2* ....(MMG)
Material Girl
Madonna; *Immaculate Collection* .... (SIR)
Like A Virgin .... (SIR)
Royal Box .... (SIR)
Medicine Woman
Paul Davis; *Southern Tracks & Fantasies* ....(BNG)
Meeting In The Ladies Room
Klymaxx; *Meeting In The Ladies Room* .... (CON)
ST/Secret Admirer .... (MCA)
Memphis Belle
Hank Williams, Jr.; *Pure Hank* ....(W/C)
Midnight Tennessee Woman
Jack Greene; *Sings His Best* ....(SO)
Miss Texas 1967
Colourfield; *Deception* .... (CHR)
Mississippi Lady
Jim Croce; *Down The Highway* .... (21)
Mississippi Woman
Willie Nelson; *Longhorn Jamboree* .... (PLN)
& His Friends .... (PLN)
Mistress Of The Salmon Salt
Blue Oyster Cult; *Tyranny & Mutation* ....(COL)
Mixed Up, Shook Up Girl
Mink De Ville; *Mink De Ville* ... . (CAP)
Money In The Bank
John Anderson; *On Solid Ground* .. ..(BNA)
Moon Over Georgia
Shenandoah; *Extra Mile* ....(COL)
Greatest Hits ....(COL)
Moonlight Lady
Julio Iglesias; *1100 Bel Air Place* ....(COL)
More Pretty Girls Than One
Tom Rush; *Blues Songs & Ballads* .... (FAN)
Woody Guthrie; *One Of A Kind* .... (PRR)
Most Beautiful Girl
Charlie Rich; *Behind Closed Doors* .... (EPI)
Columbia Country Classics-#4-Nashville ....(COL)
Greatest Hits .... (EPI)
Most Beautiful Girl In The World
Frank Sinatra; *Strangers In The Night* .... (RPR)
Prince; *S* .... (BLM)
Tony Bennett; *Rodgers & Hart Songbook* .... (DRG)
Sings More Great Rodgers & Hart ....(IPV)
Multi Colored Lady
Gregg Allman; *Laid Back* .... (CPC)
Murder In High Heels
Kiss; *Animalize* .... (MER)
Music To Watch Girls By
Andy Williams; *Greatest Hits-#2* ....(COL)
My Best Friend's Girl
Cars; *Cars* .... (ELE)
Greatest Hits .... (ELE)
My Carolina Sunshine Girl
Jimmie Rodgers; *Early Years-1928-1929* .... (ROU)
My Girl

Mamas & The Papas; *Best Of* .... (MCA)
Otis Redding; *Best Of* ....(ATC)
Rolling Stones; *Flowers* ....(AKO)
Temptations; *25th Anniversary* ....(MOT)
All The Million-Sellers .... (MOT)
Anthology .... (MOT)
Greatest Hits-#1 .... (MOT)
ST/Big Chill .... (MOT)
My Girlfriend Is A Waitress
Iguanas; *Nuevo Boogaloo* .... (MGR)
My Kinda Girl
Babyface; *Closer Look* .... (SLR)
Tender Lover .... (SLR)
My Little Girl
Crescendos; *45* .... (MCA)
Crickets; *EMI Legends Of Rock-24 Greatest Hits* . (EMI)
Liberty Years .... (EMI)
Roxy Music; *Manifesto* .... (RPR)
Spike Jones/City Slickers; *King Of Corn* ....(GLN)
My Little Girl In Tennessee
L. Flatt/E. Scruggs/Foggy Mountain Boys; *Complete Mercury Sessions* .... (MER)
My Little Lady
Jimmie Rodgers; *Early Years-1928-1929* .... (ROU)
Roy Rogers; *Columbia Historic Edition* ....(COL)

My Little Miss America
Gary U.S. Bonds; *45* .... (LEG)
My Melancholy Baby
Barbra Streisand; *Third Album* ....(COL)
Coleman Hawkins; *Genius Of* ....(VRV)
Dorothy Loudon; *Saloon* .... (DRG)
Frank Sinatra; *Voice-Columbia Years-1943-1952* (COL)
Jan Garber Orchestra; *Play 22 Original Big Band Recordings* .... (HIN)
Kate Smith; *16 Most Requested Songs* ....(COL)
Leon Redbone; *Double Time* ....(WB)
Marcels; *Best Of* .... (RHI)
My North Dakota Girl
Dakota Harmony; *45* .... (ACT)
My Polish Girlfriend
Li'l Wally; *My Polish Girlfriend & Others* ....(JJ)
My Sunday Gal
Duke Ellington; *Great Ellington Units* .... (BLU)
My Sweet Eyed Georgia Girl
Atlanta; *Atlanta* .... (MCA)
My Wife & My Dead Wife
Robyn Hitchcock/Egyptians; *Fegmania* ....(SLS)
My Wife, She Got Drunk
Li'l Wally; *All American Polkas* ....(JJ)
My Woman, My Woman, My Wife
Marty Robbins; *All-Time Greatest Hits* ....(COL)
Lifetime Of Song-1951-1952 ....(COL)
Nashville Women's Blues
Bessie Smith; *Complete Recordings-#2* ....(COL)
National Working Woman's Holiday
Sammy Kershaw; *Feelin' Good Train* .... (MER)
Naughty Girls Need Love Too
Samantha Fox; *Samantha Fox* .... (JVA)
New Girl In School
Jan & Dean; *Legendary Masters* .... (EMI)
Surf City-Best Of .... (EMI)
New Orleans Ladies
Louisiana's Le Roux; *Louisiana's Le Roux* .... (CAP)
'70s Greatest Rock Hits-#4 .... (PRY)
New York Girls
Kingston Trio; *Kingston Trio/From The Hungry i* . (CAP)
New York Lady
Burt Bacharach; *Classics-#23* .... (A&M)
Next Time You See Her
Eric Clapton; *Slow Hand* .... (RSO)
No Way To Treat A Lady
Bonnie Raitt; *Collection* ....(WB)
Nine Lives ....(WB)
No Woman, No Cry
Bob Marley; *Live* .... (TUF)
Bob Marley/Wailers; *Legend* .... (TUF)
Natty Dread .... (TUF)
Songs Of Freedom .... (TUF)
Londonbeat; *In The Blood* .... (RAD)
Norfolk Girls
John Townley/Press Gang; *Chesapeake Sailor's Companion* .... (ADE)
Northeast Texas Women
David Bromberg; *Bandit In A Bathing Suit* .... (FAN)
Willis Alan Ramsey; *Willis Alan Ramsey* ....(DHL)
Norwegian Girl
Vernon Castle; *Polka Update* .... (TAG)
Norwegian Wood
Beatles; *1962-1966* .... (CAP)
Box Set .... (CAP)
Love Songs .... (CAP)
Rubber Soul .... (CAP)
November Girl
Carmen McRae; *November Girl* .... (JAZ)
Oh Girl
Boy Meets Girl; *Boy Meets Girl* .... (A&M)
Chi-Lites; *Greatest Hits* .... (EPI)
Paul Young; *Other Voices* ....(COL)
Oh Girl (You Know Where To Find Me)
Vince Gill; *When I Call Your Name* .... (MCA)
Oh You Beautiful Doll
Guy Lombardo; *Dance To Songs Everybody Knows* .... (MCA)
Oh, Lady Be Good
Benny Goodman; *Live At Carnegie Hall* ....(LON)
Count Basie; *Essential-#1* ....(COL)
Count Basie Trio; *For The First Time* .... (PAB)
Ella Fitzgerald; *Compact Jazz-Live* ....(VRV)
Essential-Great Songs ....(VRV)

Erroll Garner; *Original Misty* .... (MER)
Lionel Hampton; *Jazz Club-Big Band* .... (VRV)
Pete Fountain; *Best Of* .... (MCA)
Supersax; *Plays Bird* .... (BLN)
Oh, Pretty Woman
2 Live Crew; *As Clean As They Wanna Be* ..... (LUK)
Al Green; *Greatest Hits-#2* .... (MOT)
   I'm Still In Love With You .... (MOT)
Albert King; *Blues Don't Change* .... (STX)
Gary Moore; *Blues Alive* .... (VIA)
   Still Got The Blues .... (CHS)
Ricky Van Shelton; *RVS III* .... (COL)
Roy Orbison; *All-Time Greatest Hits-#2* .... (MON)
   In Dreams-Greatest Hits .... (VIA)
   ST/Pretty Woman .... (EMI)
Van Halen; *Diver Down* .... (WB)
Oklahoma Country Girl
Elvin Bishop; *Big Fun* .... (ALG)
Old Flames Have New Names
Mark Chesnutt; *Longnecks & Short Stories* ..... (MCA)
Old Maid Boogie
Eddie "Cleanhead" Vinson; *Late Show* .... (FAN)
One Good Woman
Billy Squier; *Emotions In Motion* .... (CAP)
One Hell Of A Woman
Mac Davis; *Greatest Hits* .... (COL)
One Man Woman
Judds; *Collection 1983-1990* .... (RCA)
   River Of Time .... (RCA)
One Too Many Girlfriends
R.E.O. Speedwagon; *Life As We Know It* .... (EPI)
   Second Decade Of Rock & Roll-1981-1991 ..... (EPI)
Only Women Bleed
Alice Cooper; *Show* .... (WB)
   Welcome To My Nightmare .... (ATL)
Lita Ford; *Stiletto* .... (RCA)
Opium Bride
Annabouboula; *Greek Fire* .... (SHA)
Orange Lady
Weather Report; *Weather Report* .... (COL)
Other Woman
Loretta Lynn; *Greatest Hits* .... (MCA)
Ray Parker, Jr.; *Greatest Hits* .... (ARI)
Our Lady Of The Well
Jackson Browne; *For Everyman* .... (ASY)
Outlaw Women
Hank Williams, Jr.; *Bocephus*
Box-Collection-1979-1992 .... (CPC)
   Whiskey Bent & Hell Bound .... (W/C)
Party Girl
Bernadette Carroll; *20 Million Dollar*
Memories-#2 .... (LAU)
   22 Leaders Of The Pack-#1 .... (LAU)
Elvis Costello; *Girls Girls Girls* .... (COL)
Elvis Costello/Attractions; *Armed Forces* ..... (COL)
Linda Ronstadt; *Mad Love* .... (ASY)
T-Bone Walker; *Complete Imperial Recordings*
1950-1954 .... (EMI)
   T-Bone Walker .... (BLN)
U2; *Under A Blood Red Sky* .... (ISL)
Party Girls
Mink De Ville; *Mink De Ville* .... (CAP)
Rick James/Stone City Band; *In 'N' Out* .... (GOR)
Partyin' Gal
Charlie Daniels Band; *Windows* .... (EPI)
Pink Cocktail For A Blue Lady
Glenn Miller/Orchestra; *Complete* .... (BLU)
   Complete-#9 .... (RCA)
Pisces Apple Lady
Leon Russell; *Leon Russell* .... (MCA)
Planet Of Women
ZZ Top; *Afterburner* .... (WB)
   Greatest Hits .... (WB)
Plano Texas Girl
Steve Wariner; *I Got Dreams* .... (MCA)
Please Don't Go Girl
New Kids On The Block; *Hangin' Tough* .... (COL)
   No More Games/Remix Album .... (COL)
Police Woman
Henry Mancini; *Cop Show Themes* .... (RCA)
Poor Little Rich Girl
Judy Garland; *Best Of* .... (MCA)
Romantics; *National Breakout* .... (NEM)

Tony Bennett & Count Basie; *Basie Swings Bennett*
Sings .... (RLL)
Uriah Heep; *Equator* .... (COL)
Portland Woman
New Riders Of The Purple Sage; *New Riders Of The*
Purple Sage .... (COL)
   Vintage NRPS .... (RLX)
Portuguese Washerwoman
Astrud Gilberto; *Look To The Rainbow* .... (VRV)
Buddy Merrill; *Holiday For Guitars* .... (ACT)
Pretend You Don't See Her
Jerry Vale; *17 Most Requested Songs* .... (COL)
   All-Time Greatest Hits .... (COL)
   Greatest Hits .... (COL)
Pretending She's You
Jimmie Davis; *Golden Hits-#2* .... (PLN)
Pretty Girl Milking A Cow
Judy Garland; *Best Of* .... (MCA)
   One & Only .... (CAP)
Pretty Girls Don't Cry
Chris Isaak; *Silvertone* .... (WB)
Pretty Girls In Chicago Polka
Li'l Wally; *Brings Happiness To You* .... (JJ)
Pretty Girls Make Graves
Smiths; *Smiths* .... (SIR)
Pretty Lady
Original Broadway Cast; *Pacific Overtures* ..... (RCA)
Pretty Litle Lady From Beaumont, Texas
George Jones; *One Woman Man* .... (EPI)
Pretty Woman
Duke Ellington/Orchestra; *Play 22 Original Big Band*
Recordings .... (HIN)
Pretty Women
Original Cast; *Sweeney Todd* .... (RCA)
Pretty Women/Ladies Who Lunch
Barbra Streisand; *Broadway Album* .... (COL)
Punk Bitch
Too $hort; *Short Dog's In The House* .... (JVA)
Puppet Girl
Wendy James; *Now Ain't The Time For Your*
Tears .... (DGC)
Quiche Woman In A Barbecue Town
Tarwater Band; *Walking Across Egypt* .... (FF)
Quicksilver Girl
Steve Miller Band; *Best Of-1968-1973* .... (CAP)
   More Songs From "Big Chill" Soundtrack ..... (MOT)
   Sailor .... (CAP)
Radio Dream Girl
Roger Voudouris; *Radio Dream Girl* .... (WB)
Radio Girl
John Hiatt; *Slug Line* .... (MCA)
   Y'All Caught? Ones That Got Away-1975-85 .. (GEF)
Marshall Crenshaw; *Good Evening* .... (WB)
Railroad Lady
Jerry Jeff Walker; *A Man Must Carry On* .... (MCA)
   Gypsy Songman .... (RYK)
Jimmy Buffett; *White Sport Coat & A Pink*
Crustacean .... (MCA)
J.D. Crowe/New South; *My Home Ain't In The Hall Of*
Fame .... (ROU)
Willie Nelson; *Greatest Hits (& Some That Will*
Be) .... (COL)
   To Lefty From Willie .... (COL)
Rainy Day Woman
Waylon Jennings; *Live* .... (RCA)
   Ramblin' Man .... (RCA)
Rainy Day Women #12 & 35
Bob Dylan; *Greatest Hits* .... (COL)
   Blonde On Blonde .... (COL)
   Rock Classics/'60s .... (COL)
   ST/Forrest Gump .... (EPX)
Bob Dylan/Band; *Before The Flood* .... (COL)
Rebel Girl
Joe Glazer; *Songs Of Joe Hill* .... (FLW)
Outlaws; *Los Hombres Malo* .... (ARI)
Red Hot
Robert Gordon; *Rock This Town-Rockabilly*
Hits-#2 .... (RHI)
Robert Gordon & Link Wray; *Robert Gordon & Link*
Wray .... (RCA)
Red Roses For A Blue Lady
Al Martino; *Best Of* .... (CAP)
   Capitol Collectors Series .... (CAP)
Andy Williams; *16 Most Requested Songs* .... (COL)

Mom & Dads; *Best Of* .... (CRS)
Roger Whittaker; *All-Time Heart-Touching*
Favorites .... (CAP)
  Classics Collection-#1 .... (CAP)
Vaughn Monroe; *Best Of* .... (RCA)
Redneck Girl
  Bellamy Brothers; *Greatest Hits* .... (MCA)
Reefer Head Woman
  Aerosmith; *Night In The Ruts* .... (COL)
Reno
  Doug Supernaw; *Red & Rio Grande* .... (BNA)
Rhumba Girl
  Nicolette Larson; *Nicolette* .... (WB)
Rich Bitch
  D.O.A.; *War On 45/Bloodied But Unbowed* ...... (RES)
Rich Girl
  Daryl Hall & John Oates; *Bigger Than Both Of*
Us .... (RCA)
  Billboard Top Rock 'N' Roll Hits-1977 .... (RHI)
  Livetime .... (RCA)
  Nipper's Greatest Hits-'70s .... (RCA)
  Rock 'N' Soul Part 1-Greatest Hits .... (RCA)
  Soulful Sounds .... (RCA)
Rich Little Bitch
  Dash Rip Rock; *Boiled Alive!* .... (MAM)
  Not Of This World .... (MAM)
Rich Woman
  Fabulous Thunderbirds; *Fabulous Thunderbirds* . (CHR)
Richland Woman Blues
  Mississippi John Hurt; *Best Of* .... (VAN)
Rip Her To Shreds
  Blondie; *Best Of* .... (CHR)
  Blondie .... (CHR)
Robot Girl
  Was (Not Was); *What Up Dog?* .... (CHR)
Rock My World (Little Country Girl)
  Brooks & Dunn; *Hard Workin' Man* .... (ARI)
Rock & Roll Widow
  Wishbone Ash; *Live Dates* .... (MCA)
  Wishbone Four .... (MCA)
Rock & Roll Woman
  Buffalo Springfield; *Again* .... (ATC)
  Buffalo Springfield .... (ATC)
  Retrospective .... (ATC)
Rock-N-Roll Lady
  Rick Nelson; *Best Of-1963-1975* .... (DEC)
Rodeo Girl
  Rickie Lee Jones; *Flying Cowboys* .... (GEF)
Rodeo Girls
  Tanya Tucker; *Best Of* .... (MCA)
Roots Woman
  Jimmy Cliff; *Power & The Glory* .... (COL)
Rope The Moon
  John Michael Montgomery; *Kickin' It Up* .... (ATL)
Rumor Has It
  Reba McEntire; *Greatest Hits-#2* .... (MCA)
  Rumor Has It .... (MCA)
Runaway Girl
  Dion; *Runaround Sue* .... (CLT)
  Dion/Belmonts; *20 Golden Classics* .... (CLT)
  Everything You Always Wanted To Hear .... (LAU)
Run, Woman, Run
  Tammy Wynette; *Anniversary-20 Years Of Hits* ... (EPI)
  Biggest Hits .... (EPI)
Russian Lady
  Karen Alexander; *Isn't It Always Love* .... (ASY)
Sad Eyed Lady Of The Lowlands
  Bob Dylan; *Blonde On Blonde* .... (COL)
  Joan Baez; *Any Day Now-Songs Of Bob Dylan* . (VAN)
  Lovesong Album .... (VAN)
Sadder-But-Wiser Girl For Me
  Original Cast; *Music Man* .... (CAP)
  Robert Preston; *ST/Music Man* .... (WB)
Sail Away Ladies
  Kingston Trio; *Hidden Treasures* .... (FOL)
  Odetta; *At The Gate Of Horn* .... (VAN)
  Movin' It On .... (RQ)
  One Grain Of Sand .... (VAN)
Sales Tax On The Woman
  New Lost City Ramblers; *Early*
Years-1958-1962 .... (FLW)
Salesgirl Blues
  Rick Parker; *Wicked World* .... (GEF)

Same Old Fashioned Girl
  Gene Autry; *Columbia Historic Edition* .... (COL)
San Antonio Girl
  Steve Earle/Dukes; *Exit 0* .... (MCA)
San Francisco Girls
  Fever Tree; *Best Of* .... (BCT)
  Nuggets-#11 .... (RHI)
  Sixties Rule-#1 .... (OW)
Sanctified Lady
  Marvin Gaye; *Arena* .... (CAP)
  Dream Of A Lifetime .... (COL)
  Rio .... (CAP)
Santa Ana Woman
  Bobs; *Songs For Tomorrow Morning* .... (KAL)
Savannah Woman
  Brother Noland; *Pacific Bad Boy* .... (MAC)
  Tommy Bolin; *Teaser* .... (NEM)
Seasons For Girls
  Trammps; *III* .... (ATL)
Second-Hand Woman
  Steve Winwood; *Arc Of A Diver* .... (ISL)
Senorita
  Don Williams; *Greatest Country Hits* .... (CCB)
  New Moves .... (CAP)
Sentimental Lady
  Fleetwood Mac; *25 Years-The Chain* .... (WB)
  Bare Trees .... (WB)
Senza Una Donna (Without A Woman)
  Paul Young; *From Time To Time-Singles*
Collection .... (COL)
  Zucchero & Paul Young; *Zucchero & Paul*
Young .... (LON)
September Girls
  Bangles; *Different Light* .... (COL)
  Big Star; *Live* .... (RYK)
Sexy Girl
  Glenn Frey; *Allnighter* .... (MCA)
  Lillo Thomas; *Lillo Thomas* .... (CAP)
Sexy Lady
  Carl Carlton; *Carl Carlton* .... (20)
  Ear Candy-#2 .... (20)
  Commodores; *Midnight Magic* .... (MOT)
  Rick James/Stone City Band; *Come Get It* ...... (MOT)
Sexy Mexican Maid
  Red Hot Chili Peppers; *Mother's Milk!* .... (EMI)
Sexy + 17
  Stray Cats; *Best Of-Rock This Town* .... (EMI)
  Rant 'N' Rave With The Stray Cats .... (EMI)
Shady River Gal/Alabama Gals
  Beverly Cotton; *Clogging Lessons* .... (FF)
Shake It Like A White Girl
  E.U.; *Livin' Large* .... (VIA)
She
  Del Shannon; *Liberty Years (Runaway)* .... (EMI)
  Edie Brickell/New Bohemians; *Shooting Rubberbands At*
The Stars .... (GEF)
  Emmylou Harris; *Luxury Liner* .... (WB)
  Gram Parsons; *GP/Grievous Angel* .... (RPR)
  Green Day; *Dookie* .... (RPR)
  Harry Connick, Jr.; *She* .... (COL)
  Jacksons; *2300 Jackson Street* .... (EPI)
  Kiss; *Alive* .... (CAS)
  Double Platinum .... (CAS)
  Dressed To Kill .... (CAS)
  Monkees; *Greatest Hits* .... (ARI)
  Roy Orbison; *Classic-1965-1968* .... (RHI)
  Tommy James/Shondells; *Anthology* .... (RHI)
She Ain't Got No Hair
  Professor Longhair; *Mardi Gras In Baton Rouge* . (RHI)
She Ain't Ugly (She Just Don't Look...)
  Gary B.B. Coleman; *Romance Without Finance Is A*
Nuisance .... (ICH)
She Ain't Worth It
  Glenn Medeiros; *with Bobby Brown* .... (MCA)
She Bangs The Drums
  Stone Roses; *Stone Roses* .... (SIL)
She Blinded Me With Science
  Thomas Dolby; *Golden Age Of Wireless* .... (CAP)
She Brakes For Rainbows
  B-52's; *Bouncing Off The Satellites* .... (WB)
She Came In Through The Bathroom Window
  Beatles; *Abbey Road* .... (CAP)
  Box Set .... (CAP)

Joe Cocker; *Classics-#4* .... (A&M)
  Joe Cocker .... (A&M)
  Live .... (CAP)
  Mad Dogs & Englishmen .... (A&M)
She Can't Say I Didn't Cry
  Rick Trevino; *Rick Trevino* .... (COL)
She Can't Say That Anymore
  John Conlee; *Friday Night Blues* .... (MCA)
  Greatest Hits .... (MCA)
She Caught The Katy & Left Me A Mule...
  Blues Brothers; *Best Of* .... (ATL)
  ST/Blues Brothers .... (ATL)
  Taj Mahal; *Best Of-#1* .... (COL)
  Natch'l Blues .... (COL)
She Closed Her Eyes
  Chris Rea; *espresso logic* .... (EW)
She Comes In Colors
  Hooters; *Nervous Night* .... (COL)
  Love; *Best Of* .... (RHI)
She Cooks Me Cabbage
  Jack Dupree; *Blues For Everybody* .... (GUS)
She Cried
  Jay/Americans; *All-Time Greatest Hits* .... (RHI)
  Come A Little Bit Closer-Best Of .... (EMI)
  Toad The Wet Sprocket; *Pale* .... (COL)
She Deserves You
  Baillie & The Boys; *Best Of* .... (RCA)
  Turn The Tide .... (RCA)
She Didn't Lie
  Garland Jeffreys; *One-Eyed Jack* .... (OOP)
She Doesn't Cry Anymore
  Shenandoah; *Road Not Taken* .... (COL)
  Shenandoah .... (COL)
She Don't Care About Time
  Byrds; *Original Singles-#1-1965-1967* .... (COL)
  Byrds (collection) .... (COL)
She Don't Get The Blues
  Alan Jackson; *Here In The Real World* .... (ARI)
She Don't Have A License To Drive Me...
  Porter Wagoner; *45* .... (WB)
She Don't Know She's Beautiful
  Sammy Kershaw; *Haunted Heart* .... (MER)
She Don't Look Back
  Dan Fogelberg; *Exiles* .... (FM)
She Don't Love Nobody
  Desert Rose Band; *Running* .... (MCA)
  Nick Lowe; *Basher-Best Of* .... (COL)
She Don't Talk Like Us No More
  K.T. Oslin; *This Woman* .... (RCA)
She Dreams
  Mark Chesnutt; *What A Way To Live* .... (DEC)
She Drives Me Crazy
  Fine Young Cannibals; *Raw & The Cooked* ...... (IRS)
  Raw & The Remix .... (MCA)
  Rock The First-#1 .... (SAN)
She Drives Me Madagascar
  Chi; *Jet Stream* .... (SA)
She Drives Me Wild
  Michael Jackson; *Dangerous* .... (EPI)
She Even Woke Me Up To Say Goodbye
  Jerry Lee Lewis; *Best Of* .... (SMA)
  Heartbreak .... (TOM)
  Kenny Rogers/First Edition; *Love Songs* .... (MSP)
She Gave Her Heart To A Soldier Boy
  Roy Rogers; *Country Music Hall Of Fame* ..... (MCA)
She Gave Her Heart To Jethro
  Tom T. Hall; *Essential-20th Anniversary*
  Collection .... (MER)
She Gets Too High
  Rob Rule; *Rob Rule* .... (MER)
She Gives It All To Me (I Can't Believe)
  Conway Twitty; *Very Best Of* .... (MCA)
  #1s-#1 .... (CAP)
She Gives Me Religion
  Van Morrison; *Beautiful Vision* .... (WB)
She Goes Down
  Billy Squier; *Creatures Of Habit* .... (CAP)
  Motley Crue; *Dr. Feelgood* .... (ELE)
She Gonna Come Home Wit' Me
  Original Broadway Cast; *Most Happy Fella* ..... (SMC)
She Got A Mule Kick
  Harry Crafton; *Harry Crafton* .... (CLT)
She Got Me (When She Got Her Dress On)
  Masters Of Reality; *Sunrise On The Sufferbus* ... (CHR)

She Got The Goldmine (I Got The Shaft)
  Jerry Reed; *14 #1 Country Hits* .... (RCA)
  Greatest Hits .... (RCA)
  Solid Country Gold .... (RCA)
She Got The Radio
  Cory Hart; *First Offense* .... (AMR)
She Has Eyes
  L7; *Hungry For Stink* .... (SLS)
She Has Funny Cars
  Allman Brothers Band/Second Coming; *Dreams* . (POL)
  Jefferson Airplane; *2400 Fulton Street-Anthology* (RCA)
  Loves You .... (RCA)
  Surrealistic Pillow .... (RCA)
She Has No Memory Of Me
  Moe Bandy; *Greatest Hits* .... (CCB)
She Hung The Moon
  George Jones; *Shine On* .... (EPI)
She Is A Diamond
  Original New York Cast; *Evita* .... (MCA)
She Is Always Seventeen
  Harry Chapin; *Anthology* .... (ELE)
  Greatest Stories-Live .... (ELE)
She Is His Only Need
  Wynonna; *Wynonna* .... (MCC)
She Keeps The Home Fires Burning
  Ronnie Milsap; *Greatest Greatest Hits* .... (RCA)
She Kept Chewing Gum
  Donald Jacob; *Zydeco Blues 'N' Boogie* .... (RYK)
She Left Me A Mule To Ride
  Big Joe Williams; *Shake Your Boogie* .... (ARH)
She Loves Austin
  Johnny Rodriguez; *Gracias* .... (CAP)
She Loves My Automobile
  ZZ Top; *Deguello* .... (WB)
She Loves My Car
  Bobby Caldwell; *August Moon* .... (SD)
  Ronnie Milsap; *One More Try For Love* .... (RCA)
She Loves The Jerk
  John Hiatt; *Riding With The King* .... (GEF)
  Y'all Caught? Ones That Got Away-1979-85 .. (GEF)
  Rodney Crowell; *Street Language* .... (COL)
She Loves You
  Beatles; *1962-1966* .... (CAP)
  20 Greatest Hits .... (CAP)
  At The Hollywood Bowl .... (CAP)
  Box Set .... (CAP)
  Past Masters-#1 .... (CAP)
  Second Album .... (CAP)
She Makes Me Shake Like A Soul Machine
  Unrest; *Kustom Karnal Blackxploitation* .... (CRL)
She Makes The Coming Home (Worth The...)
  Shenandoah; *Extra Mile* .... (COL)
She Moved Through The Fair
  Art Garfunkel; *Watermark* .... (COL)
  James Galway/Chieftains; *In Ireland* .... (RCA)
She Moves Me
  Muddy Waters; *Best Of* .... (CSS)
  Rolling Stone .... (CSS)
She Needs Someone To Hold Her...
  Conway Twitty; *Best Of-#2* .... (MSP)
  Greatest Hits-#2 .... (MCA)
She Put Her Hand Where My Money Was
  John Lee; *Down At The Depot* .... (ROU)
She Put The Sad In All His Songs
  Alabama; *Closer You Get* .... (RCA)
She Runs Hot
  Little Village; *Little Village* .... (RPR)
She Said She Said
  Beatles; *Box Set* .... (CAP)
  Revolver .... (CAP)
She Said The Same Things To Me
  John Hiatt; *Warming Up To The Ice Age* .... (GEF)
  Y'All Caught? Ones That Got Away-1975-85 .. (GEF)
She Said Yeah
  Rolling Stones; *December's Children* .... (AKO)
  Wilson Pickett; *A Man & A Half-Best Of* .... (RHI)
She Say (Oom Dooby Doom)
  Diamonds; *Best Of* .... (RHI)
She Smiled Sweetly
  Rolling Stones; *Between The Buttons* .... (AKO)
She Suits Me To A Tee
  Buddy Guy; *Left My Blues In San Francisco* ..... (CSS)
  Very Best Of .... (RHI)

She Sure Got Away With My Heart
John Anderson; *Eye Of A Hurricane* .... (WB)
   Greatest Hits-#2 .... (WB)
She Takes My Breath Away
Eddie Money; *Right Here* .... (COL)
She Thinks His Name Was John
Reba McEntire; *Read My Mind* .... (MCA)
She Thinks I Still Care
Elvis Presley; *Moody Blue* .... (RCA)
George Jones; *All-Time Greatest Hits-#1* .... (EPI)
   Best Of-1955-1967 .... (RHI)
   Billboard Top Country Hits-1962 .... (RHI)
   Super Hits-#2 .... (EPI)
She Took It Like A Man
Confederate Railroad; *Confederate Railroad* ..... (ATL)
She Took You For A Ride
Aaron Neville; *Greatest Hits* .... (CCB)
   Tell it Like It Is-Golden Classics .... (CLT)
She Used To Be Mine
Brooks & Dunn; *Hard Workin' Man* .... (ARI)
She Used To Be Somebody's Baby
Gatlin Brothers; *Biggest Hits* .... (COL)
   Greatest Country Hits!'80s-1986 .... (COL)
She Used To Sing On Sunday
Larry Gatlin/Gatlin Brothers; *17 Greatest Hits* ...(COL)
   Greatest Hits-#2 .... (COL)
She Wants To Dance With Me
Rick Astley; *Hold Me In Your Arms* .... (RCA)
She Was Hot
Rolling Stones; *Undercover* .... (RS)
She Was Only Seventeen (He Was One...)
Marty Robbins; *American Originals* .... (COL)
   Greatest Hits .... (COL)
She Watch Channel Zero
Public Enemy; *It Takes A Nation Of Millions...* ... (DFJ)
She Works Hard For The Money
Donna Summer; *She Works Hard For The Money* (MER)
   Summer Collection .... (MER)
She'd Give Anything
Boy Howdy; *She'd Give Anything* .... (CRB)
She'd Rather Be With Me
Turtles; *Best Of* .... (RHI)
   Greatest Hits .... (RHI)
   Oldies But Goodies-#3 .... (OSR)
She'll Be Coming 'Round The Mountain
Four Freshmen/Stan Kenton & Orchestra; *Live At Butler
University* ....(CW)
Mormon Tabernacle Choir; *This Land Is Your
Land* .... (COL)
She's A Carnival
Siouxsie/Banshees; *Kiss In The Dream House* ....(GEF)
She's A Fool
Lesley Gore; *Anthology* .... (RHI)
   Golden Hits Of .... (MER)
She's A Heartbreaker
Gene Pitney; *Anthology* .... (RHI)
   Best Of .... (KT)
ZZ Top; *Six Pack* .... (WB)
   Tejas .... (WB)
She's A Latin From Manhattan
La Jolson; *Lullaby Of Broadway-Music Of H.
Warren* .... (PF)
She's A Little Past Forty
Ronnie McDowell; *Best Of* .... (CCB)
She's A Miracle
Exile; *19 Hot Country Requests-#3* .... (EPI)
   Greatest Hits .... (EPI)
   Kentucky Hearts .... (EPI)
She's A Mystery To Me
Roy Orbison; *Mystery Girl* .... (VIA)
She's A Natural
Rob Crosby; *Solid Ground* .... (ARI)
She's A Rainbow
Rolling Stones; *Get Yer Ya-Ya's Out* .... (AKO)
   More Hot Rocks-Big Hits & Fazed Cookies ..... (AKO)
   Singles Collection-London Years .... (AKO)
   Their Satanic Majesties Request .... (AKO)
   Through The Past Darkly-Big Hits-#2 .... (AKO)
She's A Woman
Beatles; *At The Hollywood Bowl* .... (CAP)
   Box Set .... (CAP)
   Compact Disc E.P. Collection .... (CAP)
   Past Masters-#1 .... (CAP)
   '65 .... (CAP)

Jeff Beck; *Blow By Blow* .... (EPI)
She's All I Got
Johnny Paycheck; *Biggest Hits* .... (EPI)
   Greatest Hits .... (EPI)
She's Already Made Up Her Mind
Lyle Lovett; *Joshua Judges Ruth* .... (MCC)
She's Always A Woman
Billy Joel; *Greatest Hits-#1&2-1973-1985* ....(COL)
   The Stranger .... (COL)
She's Coming Back Some Cold Rainy Day
Georgia Cotton Pickers; *Greatest Country
Blues-1929-1956-#3* .... (SB)
She's Crazy For Leavin'
Rodney Crowell; *30 Years Of #1 Hits-#19* ......(COL)
   Diamonds & Dirt .... (COL)
   Greatest Country Hits!'80s-1989 .... (COL)
Steve Wariner; *Life's Highway* .... (MCA)
She's Crying For Me
New Orleans Rhythm Kings; *RCA Victor Jazz-First
Half-Century* .... (RCA)
She's Funny That Way (I Got A Woman...)
Art Tatum; *Solo Masterpieces-#8* .... (PAB)
Count Basie Jam; *Montreux '77* .... (PAB)
Frank Sinatra; *At The Movies* .... (CAP)
   Nice 'N' Easy .... (CAP)
Jackie Gleason; *Lush Moods* .... (PRR)
Nat King Cole; *Big Band Cole* .... (BLN)
She's Gone
Daryl Hall & John Oates; *Abandoned
Luncheonette* .... (ATL)
   Rock 'N Soul-#1-Greatest Hits .... (RCA)
She's Gone To L.A. Again
Oak Ridge Boys; *Fancy Free* .... (MCA)
She's Gone, Gone, Gone
Lefty Frizzell; *American Originals* .... (COL)
   Best Of .... (RHI)
She's Gonna Win Your Heart
Eddy Raven; *I Could Use Another You* .... (RCA)
She's Got a 60 Cycle Brain
Paul Buff Organization; *45* .... (OSR)
She's Got A Cause
Ministry; *With Sympathy* .... (ARI)
She's Got A Way
Billy Joel; *Cold Spring Harbor* .... (COL)
   Greatest Hits-#1 & 2-1973-1985 .... (COL)
   Songs In The Attic .... (COL)
She's Got Another Pair Of Shoes
Little Richard; *Grooviest 17 Original Hits* .... (SPE)
She's Got It
Little Richard; *Here's* .... (SPE)
   His Best .... (DOM)
She's Got Rhythm
Beach Boys; *M.I.U.* ....(CAR)
She's Got The Rhythm (& I Got The Blues)
Alan Jackson; *Lot About Livin' (& A Little 'Bout
Love* .... (ARI)
She's Hot
Fabulous Thunderbirds; *Powerful Stuff* .... (EPA)
She's In Love With A Rodeo Man
Chris LeDoux; *Songs Of Rodeo & Country* .... (LIB)
Don Williams; *Greatest Hits* .... (MCA)
She's In Love With The Boy
Trisha Yearwood; *Trisha Yearwood* .... (MCA)
She's Just A Drifter
Marty Robbins; *Biggest Hits* .... (COL)
   El Paso City .... (COL)
She's Just A Groupie
Bobby Nunn; *Second To Nunn* .... (MOT)
She's Like Heroin To Me
Gun Club; *Fire Of Love* .... (SLS)
She's Like The Wind
Patrick Swayze; *ST/Dirty Dancing* .... (RCA)
She's Long, She's Tall, She Weeps...
John Lee Hooker; *Black Snake* .... (FAN)
   Country Blues Of .... (RVR)
She's Lookin' Good
Rodger Collins; *Soul Shots-#1-We Got More Soul* (RHI)
Wilson Pickett; *Greatest Hits* .... (ATL)
   Very Best Of .... (RHI)
She's Lying
Lee Greenwood; *Greatest Hits* .... (MCA)
   Inside Out .... (MCA)
She's Mine Tonight
Jay Ferguson; *White Noise* .... (CAP)

She's My Baby
Traveling Wilburys; *#3* .... (WIL)
Wings; *At The Speed Of Sound* ....(CAP)
She's My Cadillac
Santa Fe; *Santa Fe* .... (CIA)
She's My Girl
Turtles; *Greatest Hits* .... (RHI)
Nuggets-*#9* .... (RHI)
'60s Sound Explosion .... (KT)
She's My Machine
David Lee Roth; *Your Filthy Little Mouth* .... (RPR)
She's My Rock
George Jones; *19 Hot Country Requests-#2* .... (EPI)
First Time Live .... (EPI)
Ladies Choice .... (EPI)
She's My Saturday Night Special
Ronnie McDowell; *Unchained Melody* ....(CCB)
Wayne Newton; *Best Of-Now* .... (CCB)
She's My Summer Girl
Jan & Dean; *Surf City-Best Of* .... (EMI)
She's Nineteen Years Old
Muddy Waters; *Best Of Blues-#1* .... (MSP)
Chess Box .... (CSS)
She's No Lady
Lyle Lovett; *Great Records/Decade-'80s*
Hits-Country .... (CCB)
Pontiac .... (MCC)
She's Not Cryin' Anymore
Billy Ray Cyrus; *Some Gave All* .... (MER)
She's Not Just Another Woman
8th Day; *Soul Hits/'70s-#5* .... (RHI)
Biz Markie; *Diabolical-The Biz Never Sleeps* ....(CLD)
M.C. Peaches; *More Than Just A Pretty Face* ...... (EW)
She's Not On The Menu
SNFU; *Last Of The Big Time Suspenders* .... (CGO)
She's Not There
Santana; *Moonflower* ....(COL)
Viva Santana! ....(COL)
Vanilla Fudge; *Vanilla Fudge* ....(ATC)
Zombies; *Best & The Rest Of* ....(EPI)
Billboard Top Rock 'N' Roll Hits-1964 .... (RHI)
History Of British Rock-#1 .... (RHI)
Time Of The Zombies .... (BCT)
She's Not You
Elvis Presley; *Golden Records-#3* ....(RCA)
Top Ten Hits .... (RCA)
She's Only Happy When She's Dancin'
Bryan Adams; *Reckless* .... (A&M)
She's Out Of My Life
Jacksons; *Live* .... (EPI)
Michael Jackson; *Off The Wall* .... (EPI)
She's Playing Hard To Forget
Eddy Raven; *Greatest Country Hits* .... (CCB)
Greatest Hits .... (WB)
She's Playing Hell Trying To Get Me...
George Strait; *Strait Country* .... (MCA)
She's Pulling Me Back Again
Mickey Gilley; *Ten Years Of Hits* .... (EPI)
She's Ready For Someone To Love Her
Kenny Rogers; *Greatest Hits* ....(RCA)
I Prefer The Moonlight ....(RCA)
She's Single Again
Janie Fricke; *17 Greatest Hits* ....(COL)
19 Hot Country Requests-#3 .... (EPI)
Greatest Country Hits/'80s-1985 ....(COL)
Very Best Of ....(COL)
Reba McEntire; *Have I Got A Deal For You* .... (MCA)
She's So Cold
Rolling Stones; *Emotional Rescue* .... (RS)
She's So High
Marc Tanner Band; *No Escape* .... (ELE)
She's So Modern
Boomtown Rats; *Greatest Hits* ....(COL)
Tonic For The Troops ....(COL)
She's Still Here
Shenandoah; *Shenandoah* ....(COL)
She's Taken
Billy Dean; *Young Man* .... (LIB)
She's Vibrator Dependent
Mojo Nixon & Skid Roper; *Root Hog Or Die* ..... (IRS)

(She's) Some Kind Of Wonderful
Drifters; *16 Greatest Hits* .... (TRP)
Golden Hits .... (ATL)
ST/More Dirty Dancing ....(RCA)
Very Best Of The .... (RHI)
Huey Lewis/News; *Four Chords & Several Years*
Ago .... (ELE)
Jay/Americans; *Sands Of Time/Wax Museum* .... (EMI)
Marvin Gaye; *I Heard It Through The Grapevine* (MOT)
Shipoopi
Original Broadway Cast; *Music Man* .... (ANG)
Robert Preston/Original Cast; *Music Man* ......(CAP)
Shoot Her If She Runs
Climax Blues Band; *Tightly Knit* .... (SIR)
Show Her
Ronnie Milsap; *Collector's Series* ....(RCA)
Greatest Hits-#2 ....(RCA)
Keyed Up ....(RCA)
Simply Irresistible
Robert Palmer; *Super Nova* .... (ISL)
Single Women
Dolly Parton; *Heartbreak Express* ....(RCA)
Six O'Clock Train & A Girl With Green...
John Hartford; *All In The Name Of Love* .... (FF)
Sleepy Time Gal
Glenn Miller; *Best Of The Big Bands* ....(COL)
Harry James; *All-Time Favorites By* .... (SSP)
Liberace; *Encore* .... (AVI)
Liberace .... (AVI)
Piano Memories .... (AVI)
Mose Allison; *Creek Bank* .... (PRS)
Small Town Girl
John Cafferty/Beaver Brown Band; *Tough All*
Over .... (SCO)
Larry Carlton; *Collection* .... (GRP)
Steve Wariner; *Greatest Hits* .... (MCA)
It's A Crazy World .... (MCA)
Some Girls
Rolling Stones; *Some Girls* .... (RS)
Some Girls Do
Sawyer Brown; *Dirt Road* .... (CRB)
Some Kinda Woman
Traffic; *Far From Home* .... (VIA)
Somebody Stole My Gal
Benny Goodman; *Best Of The Big Bands* ....(COL)
B.G. In Hi-Fi .... (BLN)
Something So Feminine About A Mandolin
Jimmy Buffett; *Havana Daydreamin'* .... (MCA)
Sophisticated Bitch
Public Enemy; *Yo! Bum Rush The Show* ....(DFC)
Sophisticated Lady
Diane Schuur; *In Tribute* .... (GRP)
Duke Ellington; *Mood Indigo* .... (POE)
Reminiscing In Tempo ....(COL)
Linda Ronstadt; *Lush Life* .... (ASY)
Original Broadway Cast; *Bubbling Brown Sugar* (AMH)
Rosemary Clooney; *Essence Of* ....(COL)
Tito Puente/Latin Ensemble; *On Broadway* .... (CP)
South City Midnight Lady
Doobie Brothers; *Best Of* .... (WB)
Captain & Me .... (WB)
South Dakota Lady
Buddy Red Bow; *Buddy Red Bow* .... (FIR)
Spanish Lady
John Handy; *Monterey* ....(COL)
Spilled Perfume
Pam Tillis; *Sweetheart's Dance* .... (ARI)
Standing On The Corner
Broadway Cast; *Most Happy Fella* ....(RCA)
Four Lads; *16 Most Requested Songs* ....(COL)
Original Broadway Cast; *Most Happy Fella* ..... (SMC)
Straight Tequila Night
John Anderson; *Seminole Wind* ....(BNA)
Today's Hot Country .... (KT)
Strange Kind Of Woman
Deep Purple; *Deepest Purple-Very Best Of* .... (WB)
Fireball .... (WB)
Made In Japan .... (WB)
Nobody's Perfect .... (MER)
Streamline Woman
Muddy Waters; *Blues Sky* .... (EPA)
Chess Box .... (CSS)
Strength Of A Woman
Carpenters; *Made In America* .... (A&M)

Stupid Girl
Neil Young; *Zuma* .... (RPR)
Rolling Stones; *Aftermath* .... (AKO)
  Singles Collection-London Years .... (AKO)
Sugar Magnolia
Grateful Dead; *American Beauty* .... (WB)
  Europe '72 .... (WB)
  Live-#1 .... (JCI)
  Skeletons From The Closet-Best Of .... (WB)
Suicide Blonde
INXS; *Live Baby Live* .... (ATL)
  X .... (ATL)
Sun Maid
Soul Asylum; *Grave Dancers Union* ....(COL)
Sunday Girl
Blondie; *Best Of* .... (CHR)
  Parallel Lines .... (CHR)
Sunday Kind Of Woman
Charlie Rich; *Behind Closed Doors* .... (EPI)
Superwoman
Karyn White; *Karyn White* ....(WB)
Stevie Wonder; *Music Of My Mind* .... (MOT)
  Original Musiquarium .... (MOT)
Surfer Girl
Beach Boys; *American Graffiti-#3* .... (MCA)
  Best Of .... (CAP)
  Endless Summer .... (CAP)
  Made In The U.S.A. .... (CAP)
  Oldies But Goodies-#2 .... (OSR)
Sushi Girl
Tubes; *Best Of* .... (CAP)
  Completion Backward Principle .... (CAP)
Sweet Black Girl
Buddy Guy & Junior Wells; *Alone & Acoustic* ...(ALG)
Sweet City Woman
Stampeders; *Super Hits/'70s-Have A Nice Day-#6* (RHI)
  '70s Smash Hits-#5 .... (RHI)
Sweet Country Woman
Johnny Duncan; *Country Music Classics-#11-Early*
  '70s .... (KT)
  Greatest Hits ....(COL)
  Winnin' Country .... (FFT)
Sweet Girl In Texas
John Delafose/Eunice Playboys; *Joe Pete Got Two*
  Women .... (ARH)
Sweet Little Girl
Stevie Wonder; *Music Of My Mind* .... (MOT)
Sweet Little Rock & Roller
Chuck Berry; *Chess Box* .... (CSS)
  Chuck Berry Is On Top .... (CSS)
Richard Thompson; *Guitar Vocal* ....(CTH)
Rod Stewart; *Absolutely Live* .... (WB)
  Best Of .... (MER)
Sweet Little Sixteen
Beatles; *45* .... (CLT)
Chuck Berry; *Best Of The Best Of* .... (GUS)
  Cruisin'-1965 .... (INC)
  Golden Hits .... (MER)
  Greatest Hits Live .... (QKS)
  Oldies But Goodies-#12 .... (OSR)
Jerry Lee Lewis; *Original Golden Hits #3* .... (SUN)
  /Friends-Duets .... (SUN)
John Lennon; *Lennon* .... (CAP)
  Rock 'N' Roll .... (CAP)
Sweet Sixteen
Big Joe Turner; *Greatest Hits* .... (ATL)
B.B. King; *Back In The Alley* .... (MCA)
  Best Of .... (MSP)
  Electric .... (MCA)
  Live In Cook County Jail .... (MCA)
Chuck Berry; *Greatest Hits* .... (EVR)
Judy Garland; *Best Of* .... (MCA)
Sweet Talking Woman
Electric Light Orchestra; *Afterglow* .... (EPI)
  Box Of Their Best .... (JET)
  Greatest Hits .... (JET)
  Out Of The Blue .... (JET)
Sweet Woman Like You
Joe Tex; *Billboard Top R&B Hits-1965-1969* .... (RHI)
  Greatest Hits ....(CCB)
  I Believe I'm Gonna Make It!-Best Of .... (RHI)
Sweet Woman (From Maine)
Robert Lockwood, Jr.; *Blues Masters-#2-Post-War*
  Chicago Blues .... (RHI)

Swimsuit Issue
Sonic Youth; *Dirty* .... (DGC)
Swiss Army Girl
Scatterbrain; *Scamboogery* .... (ELE)
Swiss Maid
Del Shannon; *Greatest Hits* .... (RHI)
  Legends ....(LAU)
Swiss Miss
Fred Astaire; *Crazy Feet!* .... (ALE)
Take Back Your Mink
Original Cast; *Guys & Dolls* .... (MCA)
Take Time To Know Her
Percy Sledge; *Best Of* .... (ATL)
  It Tears Me Up-Best Of .... (RHI)
Talkin' 'Bout Women Obviously
Buddy Guy/Junior Mance/Junior Wells; *Buddy & The*
  Juniors .... (MCA)
Tallahassee Lassie
Freddy Cannon; *14 Booming Hits* .... (RHI)
  His Latest & Greatest .... (CRI)
  Partytime '50s .... (PRY)
Tarot Woman
Richie Blackmore's Rainbow; *Rainbow Rising* .... (POL)
Tear For The Girl
Martha Reeves/Vandellas; *Live*
  Wire!-Singles-1962-1972 .... (MOT)
Telephone Girlie
Original Cast/Ruby Keeler; *No No Nanette* ......(RCA)
Television Girl
Atlantics; *Big City Rock* .... (MCA)
Tell Her About It
Billy Joel; *An Innocent Man* ....(COL)
  Greatest Hits-#1 & 2-1973-1985 ....(COL)
Tell Her No
Juice Newton; *Dirty Looks* .... (CAP)
  Greatest Hits & More .... (LIB)
Zombies; *Best Of The Rest Of* .... (BCT)
  History Of British Rock-#2 .... (RHI)
  Live On The BBC .... (RHI)
  Time Of The .... (EPI)
Ten Girls Ago
Graham Parker; *Best Of-1988-1991* ....(RCA)
Tennessee Girl
Carl Jackson; *45* ....(COL)
Tennessee Whiskey & Texas Women
Rayburn Anthony; *Audiograph Alive* .... (AUD)
  Dance Floor Crystal Ball .... (AUD)
Texas Tattoo
Gibson/Miller Band; *Steppin' Country* ....(COL)
  Where There's Smoke .... (EPI)
Texas Twister
Little Feat; *Representing The Mambo* .... (WB)
Texas Woman Blues
Taj Mahal; *Recycling The Blues-Other Related*
  Stuff ....(COL)
Texas Women
Hank Williams, Jr.; *Greatest Hits* .... (WB)
  Rowdy ....(W/C)
Texas Women (Don't Stay Lonely Long)
Brooks & Dunn; *Hard Workin' Man* .... (ARI)
Thank Heaven For Little Girls
Maurice Chevalier; *ST/Gigi* .... (SSP)
Merle Haggard & Janie Fricke; *It's All In The*
  Game .... (EPI)
Thank You Girl
Beatles; *Box Set* .... (CAP)
  Past Masters-#1 .... (CAP)
  Second Album .... (CAP)
John Hiatt; *Bring The Family* .... (A&M)
Thank You Pretty Baby
Brook Benton; *At His Best* .... (PRR)
  It's Just A Matter Of Time-Greatest Hits .... (MER)
Professor Longhair; *'Fess-Anthology* .... (RHI)
That Girl
Bad Company; *Fame & Fortune* .... (ATL)
Crosby, Stills, Nash & Young; *American Dream* .. (ATL)
Glenn Frey; *No Fun Aloud* .... (ASY)
Stevie Wonder; *Original Musiquarium* .... (MOT)
That Girl Belongs To Yesterday
Gene Pitney; *Anthology* .... (RHI)
That Girl Could Sing
Jackson Browne; *Hold Out* .... (ASY)
That Girl Wants To Dance With Me
Gregory Hines; *Gregory Hines* .... (EPI)

That Girl Who Waits On Tables
Ronnie Milsap; *Collector's Series* ....(RCA)
"That Girl" Theme
Original Music; *Television's Greatest Hits-#2* ..... (TVT)
That Girl's A Slut
Just-Ice; *Rapmasters 7-Best Of The Laughs* .... (PRY)
That Kind Of Woman
Eric Clapton; *Nobody's Child-Romanian Angel
Appeal* .... (WB)
Gary Moore; *Still Got The Blues* .... (CHS)
That Lady
Isley Brothers; *Greatest Hits-#1* .... (TN)
Rock Artifacts-#1-From The Vaults ....(COL)
Story-#2-T-Neck Years-1969-1985 .... (RHI)
That Summer
Garth Brooks; *The Chase* .... (LIB)
That Train That Carried My Girl From...
Watson Family; *Watson Family* .... (FLW)
That's All She Wrote
Conway Twitty; *Hello Darlin'* .... (MSP)
Ghetto Girlz; *Ain't Takin' No S@#T* ....(HEA)
Marty Robbins; *Come Back To Me* ....(COL)
Reba McEntire; *Rumor Has It* .... (MCA)
Rick Nelson; *Garden Party* .... (MSP)
Sings "For You" .... (MCA)
That's Not Her Style
Billy Joel; *Storm Front* ....(COL)
That's What Girls Are Made For
Spinners; *One Of A Kind Love Affair-Anthology* .. (ATL)
Tammi Terrell; *Irresistible* .... (MOT)
That's Where My Money Goes
101 Strings Orchestra; *Beer Drinkin' Sing Alongs!!* (ALS)
Then I Kissed Her
Beach Boys; *California Girls* ....(CAP)
Sunshine Dream ....(CAP)
Today/Summer Days (& Summer Nights) ....(CAP)
There Is Nothing Like A Dame
Original Cast; *South Pacific* ....(COL)
There She Goes
Beat; *ST/Caddyshack* ....(COL)
Bob Marley/Wailers; *One Love* ....(HRT)
Chambers Brothers; *Best Of* ....(FAN)
Jerry Wallace; *Greatest Hits* ....(CCB)
La's; *La's* ....(LON)
There's A Girl
Original Broadway Cast; *Secret Garden* ....(COL)
There's A Tennessee Woman/Ben's Song
Tanya Tucker; *Tennessee Woman* .... (LIB)
There's The Girl
Heart; *Bad Animals* ....(CAP)
They Don't Make 'Em Like That Anymore
Boy Howdy; *She'd Give Anything* ....(CRB)
They'll Never Take Her Love From Me
Emmylou Harris; *Blue Kentucky Girl* ....(WB)
George Jones; *Sings The Great Songs Of Leon
Payne* .... (IGR)
Hank Williams; *24 Greatest Hits-#2* .... (MER)
40 Greatest Hits .... (POL)
This Ain't Tennessee & She Ain't You
Tom Jones; *Don't Let Our Dreams Die Young* ... (MER)
This Girl Is A Woman Now
Gary Puckett/Union Gap; *Best Of* ....(IGR)
Greatest Hits ....(COL)
Looking Glass-Collection ....(COL)
This Girl's In Love With You
Dionne Warwick; *At Her Very Best* ....(PRR)
Petula Clark; *Greatest Hits Of* ....(CRS)
This Little Girl
Dion; *24 Original Classics* ....(ARI)
Bronx Blues-Columbia Recordings-1962-65 ....(COL)
Gary U.S. Bonds; *Cover Me* ....(RHI)
Gary U.S. Bonds & Bruce Springsteen;
Dedication ....(R&T)
This Little Girl Of Mine
Everly Brothers; *Cadence Classics-Their 20 Greatest
Hits* .... (RHI)
Faron Young; *Greatest Hits-#3* .... (SO)
Herbie Mann; *Best Of* ....(ATL)
Ray Charles; *Atlantic R&B
1947-1974-#2-(1952-1955)* ....(ATL)
Birth Of Soul-Atlantic R&B-1952-1959 ....(ATL)
Life In Music ....(ATL)

This Woman
Kenny Rogers; *Eyes That See In The Dark* ......(RCA)
This Woman ....(RCA)
K.T. Oslin; *This Woman* ....(RCA)
This Woman's Work
Kate Bush; *Sensual World* ....(COL)
ST/She's Having A Baby .... (IRS)
This Year's Girl
Elvis Costello; *2 1/2 Years* ....(RYK)
Girls Girls Girls ....(COL)
This Year's Model ....(COL)
Thorn Tree In The Garden
Derek/Dominos; *Layla* .... (POL)
Three Drunken Maidens
Maddy Prior & Tim Hart; *Summer Solstice* ....(SHA)
Three Girls From Detroit
Will/Bushmen; *Will/Bushmen* .... (SBK)
Three Times A Lady
Commodores; *All The Great Hits* .... (MOT)
All The Great Love Songs .... (MOT)
Endless Love-Motown Greatest Love Songs ..... (MOT)
Greatest Hits .... (MOT)
Natural High .... (MOT)
Ticket To Ride
Beatles; *1962-1966* ....(CAP)
20 Greatest Hits ....(CAP)
At The Hollywood Bowl ....(CAP)
Box Set ....(CAP)
Help! ....(CAP)
Reel Music ....(CAP)
ST/Help! ....(CAP)
Carpenters; *Classics-#2* ....(A&M)
From The Top ....(A&M)
Singles-1969-1973 ....(A&M)
Ticket To Ride ....(A&M)
Yesterday Once More ....(A&M)
Vanilla Fudge; *Best Of* ....(ATC)
Vanilla Fudge ....(ATC)
Tiger In A Dress
Dan Reed Network; *Slam* .... (MEr)
Tiger Woman
Claude King; *American Originals* ....(COL)
Claude King's Best ....(GUS)
To All The Girls I've Loved Before
Julio Iglesias & Willie Nelson; *1100 Bel Air
Place* ....(COL)
Merle Haggard & Janie Fricke; *It's All In The
Game* .... (EPI)
Willie Nelson & Julio Iglesias; *Greatest Country
Hits/'80s-1984* ....(COL)
Half Nelson ....(COL)
Tomorrow's Girls
Donald Fagen; *Kamakiriad* .... (RPR)
Tonight Carmen
Marty Robbins; *All-Time Greatest Hits* ....(COL)
American Originals ....(COL)
Essential-1951-1982 ....(COL)
Trailer Park Woman
Pinkard & Bowden; *Cousins Cattle & Other Love
Songs* .... (WB)
Train That Carried My Girl From Town
Doc Watson; *Essential* .... (VAN)
Trapped In The Body Of A White Girl
Julie Brown; *Trapped In The Body Of A White Girl* (SIR)
Trashy Lady
Neon Judgement; *Horny As Hell* .... (PIA)
Trashy Women
Confederate Railroad; *Confederate Railroad* ..... (ATL)
Treat Her Like A Lady
Cornelius Brothers & Sister Rose; *Billboard Top Rock
'N' Roll Hits-1971* .... (RHI)
Soul Hits/'70s-#5 .... (RHI)
Jimmy Buffett; *Boats Beaches Bars & Ballads* ... (MGR)
Volcano .... (MCA)
Johnny Lee; *Best Of* ....(CCB)
Temptations; *Anthology* .... (MOT)
Truly For You .... (MOT)
Treat Her Right
Commitments; *ST/Commitments* .... (MCA)
George Thorogood/Destroyers; *Born To Be Bad* . (EMI)
Roy Head/Traits; *Billboard Top Rock 'N' Roll
Hits-1965* .... (RHI)
Truck Drivin' Girl
Bonny Boekeker; *45* ....(ACT)

Truck Stop Girl
Byrds; *Byrds (collection)* ....(COL)
  (Untitled) ....(COL)
Little Feat; *Little Feat* ....(WB)
Trying To Love Two Women
Oak Ridge Boys; *Collection* ....(MCA)
  Greatest Hits ....(MCA)
  Together ....(MCA)
Twelve Thirty (Young Girls Are Coming..)
Mamas & The Papas; *16 Of Their Greatest Hits* . (MCA)
  Best Of ....(MCA)
  Papas & The Mamas ....(MCA)
Twentieth Century Fox
Doors; *Doors* ....(ELE)
Twenty-Nine Ways (To My Baby's Door)
Koko Taylor; *Koko Taylor* ....(CSS)
  South Side Lady ....(EVD)
Marc Cohn; *Marc Cohn* ....(ATL)
Willie Dixon; *Chess Box* ....(CSS)
Twist Twist Senora
Gary U.S. Bonds; *School Rock 'N' Roll-Best Of* ... (RHI)
Two Hot Girls (On A Hot Summer Night)
Carly Simon; *Coming Around Again* ....(ARI)
  Greatest Hits Live ....(ARI)
Two Ladies
Original Cast; *Cabaret* ....(COL)
T-R-O-U-B-L-E
Travis Tritt; *T-R-O-U-B-L-E* ....(WB)
Ugliest Girl In The World
Bob Dylan; *Down In The Groove* ....(COL)
Under My Thumb
Rolling Stones; *12 X 5* ....(AKO)
  Aftermath ....(AKO)
  Got Live If You Want It ....(AKO)
  Hot Rocks 1964-1971 ....(AKO)
  Still Life-American Concert 1981 ....(RS)
Who; *Who's Missing* ....(MCA)
Unlucky Girl
Big Mama Thornton; *Ball N' Chain* ....(ARH)
Until She Comes
Psychedelic Furs; *World Outside* ....(COL)
Uptown Girl
Billy Joel; *An Innocent Man* ....(COL)
  Greatest Hits-#1 & 2-1973-1985 ....(COL)
  KOHUEPT ....(COL)
Vagabond Virgin
Traffic; *Traffic* ....(ISL)
Venus In Blue Jeans
Jimmy Clanton; *All-Star Chartbusters* ....(INT)
  Golden Years-1962 ....(DOM)
Voodoo Woman
Bobby Goldsboro; *Honey-The Best Of* ....(EMI)
Koko Taylor; *I Got What It Takes* ....(ALG)
Waitress In A Donut Shop
Dan Hicks/Hot Licks; *Last Train To Hicksville* .. (MCA)
Waitress In The Sky
Replacements; *Tim* ....(SIR)
Walk This Way
Aerosmith; *Classics Live 2* ....(COL)
  Greatest Hits ....(COL)
  Live Bootleg ....(COL)
  Pandora's Box ....(COL)
  Toys In The Attic ....(COL)
Run-D.M.C.; *Mr. Magic's Rap Attack* ....(PRO)
  Raising Hell ....(PRO)
  Rap's Biggest Hits ....(KT)
Walks Like A Lady
Journey; *Captured* ....(COL)
  Departure ....(COL)
Wannagirl
Jeremy Jordan; *Try My Love* ....(GIA)
War Widow
Country Joe McDonald; *War War War* ....(VAN)
Warm Beer & Cold Women
Tom Waits; *Nighthawks At The Diner* ....(ASY)
Watch The Girl Destroy Me
Possum Dixon; *Possum Dixon* ....(ISC)
Way She Loves Me
Richard Marx; *Paid Vacation* ....(CAP)
Ways Of A Woman In Love
Johnny Cash; *Best Of* ....(CCB)
  Essential ....(COL)
  Sun Years ....(RHI)

We Gotta Get You A Woman
Todd Rundgren; *Anthology-1968-1985* ....(RHI)
  Runt ....(RHI)
West End Girls
Pet Shop Boys; *Disco* ....(EMI)
  Discography-Complete Singles Collection ....(EMI)
  Please ....(EMI)
West Texas Women
Whistlin' Alex Moore; *I'm Wild About My
  Lovin'-1928-1930* ....(HIS)
Western Girls
Marty Stuart; *Hillbilly Rock* ....(MCA)
What A Way To Go
Ray Kennedy; *What A Way To Go* ....(ATL)
What She Don't Know Won't Hurt Her
Gene Watson; *Greatest Hits* ....(MCA)
What She Is (Is A Woman In Love)
Earl Thomas Conley; *Heart Of It All* ....(RCA)
What She Said
Smiths; *Meat Is Murder* ....(SIR)
  Rank ....(SIR)
What She's Doing Now
Garth Brooks; *Ropin' The Wind* ....(LIB)
What's New Pussycat
Tom Jones; *London Collector-Greatest Hits* ....(LON)
When A Man Loves A Woman
Barbara Mandrell; *Best Of* ....(LIB)
  Key's In The Mailbox ....(LIB)
Bette Midler; *ST/The Rose* ....(ATL)
Michael Bolton; *Time Love & Tenderness* ....(COL)
Percy Sledge; *Atlantic
  R&B-1947-1974-#5-(1962-1966)* ....(ATL)
  Atlantic Soul Classics ....(WSP)
  Best Of ....(ATL)
  Golden Age Of Black Music-1960-1970 ....(ATL)
  ST/Platoon & Songs Of The Era ....(ATL)
When A Woman Doesn't Want You
Elton John; *The One* ....(MCA)
When It Comes To You
Dire Straits; *On Every Street* ....(WB)
John Anderson; *Seminole Wind* ....(BNA)
When She Cries
Restless Heart; *Big Iron Horses* ....(RCA)
When Sunny Gets Blue Lady
Vaughn Monroe; *Best Of* ....(RCA)
  This Is ....(RCA)
Whenever You Come Around
Vince Gill; *When Love Finds You* ....(MCA)
Whiskey And Wimmen
John Lee Hooker; *Best Of* ....(CRS)
  Best Of ....(VJ)
  Infinite Boogie ....(RHI)
  Real Blues Brothers ....(DHL)
  World's Greatest Blues Singer ....(VJ)
Whiskey, If You Were A Woman
Highway 101; *Greatest Hits* ....(WB)
  Highway 101 ....(WB)
White Trash Wife
Exene Cervenka; *Old Wives' Tales* ....(RHI)
Wife & The Whore
Kristin Lems; *Born A Woman* ....(FF)
Wild One
Faith Hill; *Take Me As I Am* ....(WB)
Wild Thing
Jimi Hendrix; *Essential-#2* ....(RPR)
  ST/Jimi Plays Monterey ....(RPR)
Jimi Hendrix Experience; *Live At Winterland* ....(RYK)
Tone Loc; *Loc-ed After Dark* ....(DV)
  Rap's Biggest Hits ....(KT)
  Rock The First-#6 ....(SAN)
Troggs; *Billboard Top Rock 'N' Roll Hits-1966* ... (RHI)
  Frat Rock! ....(RHI)
  History Of British Rock-#3 ....(RHI)
Wild Women Do
Natalie Cole; *ST/Pretty Woman* ....(EMI)
Wildfire Woman
Bad Company; *Straight Shooter* ....(SS)
Wind Blows Her Hair
Seeds; *Nuggets-#9-Acid Rock* ....(RHI)
Wink
Neal McCoy; *No Doubt About It* ....(ATL)
Witchy Woman
Eagles; *Eagles* ....(ASY)
  Their Greatest Hits 1971-1975 ....(ASY)

Wives Are In Connecticut
Carly Simon; *Spoiled Girl* .... (EPI)
Woman
James Gang; *15 Greatest Hits* .... (MCA)
   Best Of .... (MCA)
   Rides Again .... (MCA)
John Lennon; *John Lennon (collection)* .... (CAP)
   ST/Imagine-The Motion Picture .... (CAP)
John Lennon & Yoko Ono; *Double Fantasy* ...... (CAP)
Peter & Gordon; *Best Of* .... (RHI)
   History Of British Rock-#4 .... (RHI)
Scorpions; *Face The Heat* .... (MER)
Simple Minds; *Real Life* .... (A&M)
Womack & Womack; *Love Wars* .... (ELE)
Woman Before Me
Trisha Yearwood; *Trisha Yearwood* .... (MCA)
Woman From Tokyo
Deep Purple; *Deepest Purple-Very Best Of* .... (WB)
   Nobody's Perfect .... (MER)
   When We Rock We Rock–When We Roll... ...... (WB)
   Who Do You Think We Are .... (WB)
Woman In Love
Frankie Laine; *Frankie's Gold-Greatest Hits-#2* .... (PB)
Ronnie Milsap; *Greatest Hits-#3* .... (RCA)
   Stranger Things Have Happened .... (RCA)
Woman In Texas
Jerry Jeff Walker; *Live At Gruene Hall* .... (RYK)
Woman Is The Nigger Of The World
John Lennon; *Shaved Fish* .... (CAP)
   Somewhere In New York City .... (CAP)
John Lennon/Plastic Ono Band; *Lennon* .... (CAP)
Woman Loves
Steve Wariner; *I Am Ready* .... (ARI)
Woman Of Heart & Mind
Joni Mitchell; *For The Roses* .... (ASY)
Joni Mitchell/L.A. Express; *Miles Of Aisles* .... (ASY)
Woman Of The Year
Original Cast; *Woman Of The Year* .... (BAY)
Woman Power
Yoko Ono; *Walking On Thin Ice Compilation* ....(RYK)
Woman To Woman
Beverley Craven; *Beverley Craven* .... (EPI)
Joe Cocker; *Classics-#4* .... (A&M)
   Greatest Hits .... (A&M)
Shirley Brown; *Soul Hits/'70s-#15* .... (RHI)
   Top Of The Stax-Twenty Great Hits .... (STX)
   Woman To Woman .... (STX)
Tammy Wynette; *Anniversary-20 Years Of Hits* ... (EPI)
   Greatest Hits-#3 .... (EPI)
   Tears Of Fire-25th Anniversary Collect. .... (EPI)
Woman Tonight
America; *Hearts* .... (WB)
   History-Greatest Hits .... (WB)
Woman Walk The Line
Emmylou Harris; *Ballad Of Sally Rose* .... (WB)
Highway 101; *Featuring Paulette Carlson* .... (WB)
Trisha Yearwood; *Hearts In Armor* .... (MCA)
Woman, A Lover, A Friend
Jackie Wilson; *Greatest Hits #2* .... (BRU)
   Mr. Excitement .... (RHI)
Otis Redding; *Story* .... (ATL)
Woman, Sensuous Woman
Mark Chesnutt; *Almost Goodbye* .... (MCA)
Woman, Woman
Gary Puckett/Union Gap; *Best Of* .... (IGR)
   Greatest Hits ....(COL)
Woman's Got A Right To Change Her Mind
Rex Stewart/Ellingtonians; *Rex*
Stewart/Ellingtonians .... (RVR)
Woman's Needs, A
Tammy Wynette & Elton John; *Without Walls* .... (EPI)
Woman's Point Of View
Shirley Murdock; *Woman's Point Of View* .... (ELE)
Woman's Prerogative
Pearl Bailey; *16 Most Requested Songs* ....(COL)
Woman's Smarter
Jolly Boys; *Sunshine 'N' Water* ....(RYK)
Women Walk More Determined
Kristin Lems; *Oh Mama!* .... (CDP)
Women Will Rule The World
Ry Cooder; *Get Rhythm* .... (WB)
Women's Love Rights
Laura Lee; *Greatest Hits* .... (HDH)

Words Of Love
Beatles; *Box Set* ....(CAP)
   For Sale ....(CAP)
   Love Songs ....(CAP)
   VI ....(CAP)
Buddy Holly; *Buddy Holly* .... (MCA)
   Legend .... (MCA)
   Rock & Roll Collection .... (MCA)
Buddy Holly/Crickets; *20 Golden Greats* ...... (MCA)
Mamas & The Papas; *16 Of Their Greatest Hits* . (MCA)
   Best Of .... (MCA)
   Farewell To The First Golden Era .... (MCA)
   Mama's Big Ones-Her Greatest Hits .... (MCA)
XXX's And OOO's
Trisha Yearwood; *S* .... (MCA)
Yankee Rose
David Lee Roth; *Eat 'Em & Smile* .... (WB)
Yellow Gal
Leadbelly; *Leadbelly* .... (FAN)
   Legend Of ....(TRD)
   Memorial-#2 ....(STO)
   Take This Hammer .... (FLW)
Yellow Woman's Door Bells
Leadbelly; *Leadbelly* ....(EVR)
   Leadbelly .... (FAN)
Yessir, That's My Baby
Frank Sinatra; *Strangers In The Night* .... (RPR)
Milt Jackson; *Best Of* ....(PAB)
Mom & Dads; *Dance With The Mom & Dads* .... (CRS)
   Very Best Of .... (CRS)
You Need A Woman Tonight
Captain & Tennille; *Dreams* .... (A&M)
You Should Hear How She Talks About You
Melissa Manchester; *Greatest Hits* .... (ARI)
   Hey Ricky .... (ARI)
Young Girl Blues
Sammy Hagar; *9 On A 10-Scale* ....(CAP)
   Live ....(CAP)
You're A Man Of Words, I'm A Woman
Betty LaVette; *Lost Soul-#1* .... (EPI)
You're Gonna Lose That Girl
Beatles; *Help!* .... (CAP)
You're Lost, Little Girl
Doors; *13* .... (ELE)
   Strange Days .... (ELE)
You've Got It Bad Girl
Quincy Jones; *Best Of-#2* .... (A&M)
   Classics-#3 .... (A&M)
Stevie Wonder; *Talking Book* .... (MOT)

WOMEN'S NAMES: A

Abigail Beecher
Freddy Cannon; *14 Booming Hits* .... (RHI)
Adelaide's Lament
Original Cast; *Guys & Dolls* .... (MCA)
   Guys & Dolls .... (MOT)
Alexis From Texas
Red Steagall; *Lone Star Beer & Bob Wills Music* (MCA)
Alice Blue Gown
Edith Day; *Nipper's Greatest Hits-'20s* .... (RCA)
Alice You've Made Dallas (Paradise...)
Lee Ferrell; *Hard Times* ....(TMS)
Alison
Elvis Costello; *Girls Girls Girls* ....(COL)
   My Aim Is True ....(COL)
Elvis Costello/Attractions; *Best Of* ....(COL)
All The Girls Love Alice
Elton John; *Goodbye Yellow Brick Road* .... (POL)
Allison Road
Gin Blossoms; *New Miserable Experience* .... (A&M)
Amanda
Boston; *Third Stage* .... (MCA)
Dionne Warwick; *Anthology* .... (RHI)
Don Williams; *Greatest Hits-#1* .... (MCA)
   Volume One .... (MCA)
Waylon Jennings; *Greatest Hits* .... (RCA)
Amelia Earhart
Bachman-Turner Overdrive; *Rock 'n' Roll Nights* (MER)

Amie
Pure Prairie League; *Bustin' Out* ....(RCA)
   Jukebox Saturday Night ....(RCA)
   Let Me Love You Tonight & Other Hits ....(RCA)
   Takin' The Stage ....(RCA)
Amoreena
Elton John; *Tumbleweed Connection* ....(POL)
Amphetamine Annie
Canned Heat; *Best Of* ....(EMI)
   Boogie With ....(LIB)
Angel Angelina
George Strait; *Beyond The Blue Neon* ....(MCA)
Angelia
Richard Marx; *Repeat Offender* ....(EMI)
Angie
Rolling Stones; *Goats Head Soup* ....(RS)
   Made In The Shade ....(RS)
   Rewind (1971-1984) ....(RS)
Angie Baby
Helen Reddy; *Greatest Hits* ....(CAP)
Angie Girl
Stevie Wonder; *Motown Legends* ....(MOT)
   My Cherie Amour ....(MOT)
Anita Goes To China
David Hayes; *Logos Through A Sideman* ....(GC)
Anita, You're Dreaming
Waylon Jennings; *Best Of* ....(RCA)
   Early Years ....(RCA)
Anna
Beatles; *Box Set* ....(CAP)
   Early Beatles ....(CAP)
   Please Please Me ....(CAP)
Toto; *Seventh One* ....(COL)
Anna Begins
Counting Crows; *August And Everything After* .. (DGC)
Anna In Indiana
Eddie Cantor; *Rare Early Recordings-1919-1921* .(BIO)
Annalee The Healer
Beach Boys; *Friends/20/20* ....(CAP)
Anne Frank Story
Human Sexual Response; *Fig. 15* ....(EAT)
Annie Get Your Yo Yo
Junior Parker; *Best Of* ....(MCA)
   Driving Wheel ....(MCA)
Annie Had A Baby
Hank Ballard/Midnighters; *Cruisin'-1955* ....(INC)
Annie Laurie
King's Singers; *Annie Laurie-Folk Songs Of British
Isles* ....(ANG)
Annie Mae's Cafe
Little Milton; *Annie Mae's Cafe* ....(MAL)
Annie's Song
John Denver; *Back Home Again* ....(RCA)
   Evening With ....(RCA)
   Greatest Hits-#2 ....(RCA)
Arizona
Mark Lindsay; *Super Hits/'70s-Have A Nice
Day-#1* ....(RHI)
Scorpions; *Blackout* ....(MER)
Aubrey
Bread; *Anthology* ....(ELE)
   Best Of-#2 ....(ELE)
Avenging Annie
Andy Pratt; *Andy Pratt* ....(COL)
Roger Daltrey; *Best Bits* ....(MCA)
   One Of The Boys ....(MCA)
Dallas Alice
Joe Stampley; *45* ....(MCA)
Dreamboat Annie
Heart; *Dreamboat Annie* ....(CAP)
   Greatest Hits/Live ....(EPI)
Flaming Agnes
Original Cast; *I Do! I Do!* ....(RCA)
Has Anybody Seen Amy
John & Audrey Wiggins; *John & Audrey* ....(MER)
Living Next Door To Alice
Johnny Carver; *Best Of* ....(MCA)
Louisiana Anna
Maines Brothers Band; *High Rollin'* ....(MER)
Mail Order Annie
Harry Chapin; *Gold Medal Collection* ....(ELE)
   Short Stories ....(ELE)

Miami, My Amy
Keith Whitley; *Greatest Hits* ....(RCA)
   L.A. To Miami ....(RCA)
   Star-Spangled Country ....(RCA)
Miss Amanda Jones
Rolling Stones; *Between The Buttons* ....(AKO)
Miss America
Big Dish; *Satellites* ....(EW)
Mark Lindsay; *45* ....(COL)
Styx; *Caught In The Act* ....(A&M)
   Classics-#15 ....(A&M)
   Grand Illusion ....(A&M)
My Angeline
Bing Crosby; *Crooner-Columbia
Years-1928-1934* ....(COL)
Once In Love With Amy
Barry Manilow; *Showstoppers* ....(ARI)
Lawrence Welk; *My Personal Favorites* ....(RAN)
Mel Torme; *Swings Shubert Alley* ....(VRV)
Polk Salad Annie
Elvis Presley; *As Recorded Live At Madison Sq.
Garden* ....(RCA)
Tony Joe White; *Soul Shots-#6-Blue-Eyed Soul* .. (RHI)
   Swingin' Country Favorites ....(WB)
Ragtime Annie
Byron Berline; *Dad's Favorites* ....(ROU)
Mason Williams; *Fresh Fish* ....(FF)
Saint Agnes & The Burning Train
Sting; *Soul Cages* ....(A&M)
Skin & Bone (Annie)
Kinks; *Celluloid Heroes* ....(RCA)
   Everybody's In Show Biz ....(RHI)
   Greatest ....(RCA)
   Muswell Hillbillies ....(RHI)
Sweet Adeline
Tommy Dorsey; *Best Of* ....(MCA)
Tommy Dorsey/Orchestra; *Big Bands-Greatest
Hits-#2* ....(MSP)
Sweet Angeline
David Allan Coe; *Just Divorced* ....(COL)
Mott The Hoople; *Ballad Of Mott* ....(COL)
   Live ....(COL)
Texas Ann
Joe Beck; *Beck & Sanborn* ....(CBA)
Work With Me Annie
Hank Ballard/Midnighters; *45* ....(GUS)
Royals; *Risque Rhythm* ....(RHI)
Yes, Anastasia
Tori Amos; *Under The Pink* ....(ATL)

WOMEN'S NAMES: B

Barbara Allen
Joan Baez; *Ballad Book* ....(VAN)
   Ballad Book-#2 ....(VAN)
   Vol. 2 ....(VAN)
Tom Rush; *Blues Songs Ballads* ....(PRS)
   Tom Rush ....(FAN)
Barbara Ann
Beach Boys; *Best Of-#2* ....(CAP)
   Frat Rock! ....(RHI)
   Gift Set ....(CAP)
   Spirit Of America ....(CAP)
   '69 ....(CAP)
Regents; *Cruisin'-1961* ....(INC)
   Original Rock 'N' Roll Hits Of The '60s ....(RLL)
   ST/American Graffiti ....(MCA)
Who; *Who's Missing* ....(MCA)
Barbi Doll
Barbara Weathers; *Barbara Weathers* ....(RPR)
Barbie Doll Look
Sky Saxon; *Best Of Rodney On The ROQ* ....(PBO)
Barbie & Ken
Weathermen; *Black Album According To The* .....(PIA)
Barbie & Ken Ferrari
John Hiatt; *Perfectly Good Guitar* ....(A&M)
Belle
Al Green; *Belle Album* ....(MOT)
   Tokyo...Live ....(MOT)

Bernadette
Four Tops; *Anthology* .... (MOT)
  Compact Command Performances .... (MOT)
  Greatest Hits .... (MOT)
  Motown Superstar Series-#14 .... (MOT)
  Reach Out .... (MOT)
Bess You Is My Woman Now
Miles Davis/Orchestra; *Porgy & Bess* ......(COL)
Original Cast; *Porgy & Bess* .... (MCA)
Beth
Kiss; *Alive 2* .... (CAS)
  Destroyer .... (CAS)
  Double Platinum .... (CAS)
  Smashes Trashes & Hits .... (MER)
Bette Davis Eyes
Kim Carnes; *Mistaken Identity* .... (EMI)
Betty Lou's Gettin' Out Tonight
Bob Seger/Silver Bullet Band; *Against The Wind* .(CAP)
  Nine Tonight ....(CAP)
Betty's Bein' Bad
Sawyer Brown; *Best Of Country Rock* .... (KT)
  Greatest Hits ....(CCB)
  Shakin' ....(CCB)
Billie Jean
Michael Jackson; *Thriller* .... (EPI)
Billie's Blues
Billie Holiday; *Billie's Blues* .... (BLN)
  Essential-Carnegie Hall Concert ....(VRV)
  I Like Jazz-Essence Of ....(COL)
  Songbook ....(VRV)
Billie's Bounce
Charlie Parker; *Story* .... (SJZ)
Count Baise; *Best Of* .... (PAB)
Shelly Manne; *The Tree & The Two* .... (CTM)
Stan Getz; *Artistry Of-#2* ....(VRV)
Bobby Jean
Bruce Springsteen; *Born In The U.S.A.* ....(COL)
Bruce Springsteen/E Street Band;
Live-1975-1985 ....(COL)
Bonnie Jean (Little Sister)
David Lynn Jones; *Best Of Country Rock* .... (KT)
  Hard Times On Easy Street .... (MER)
Bonnie & Clyde
Georgie Fame; *45* .... (EPI)
Brandy
Looking Glass; *Billboard Top Rock 'N' Roll
Hits-1972* .... (RHI)
  Rock Artifacts-#2 ....(COL)
Come Back...Barbara Lewis Hare Krisha...
John Prine; *Anthology-Great Days* .... (RHI)
  Common Sense .... (ATL)
  Prime Prine-Best Of .... (ATL)
I'll Go Home With Bonnie Jean
Original Cast; *Brigadoon* ....(RCA)
Mrs. Brown You've Got A Lovely Daughter
Herman's Hermits; *Something Good Again* ...... (AKO)
  XX-Their Greatest Hits .... (AKO)
My Bonnie Lies Over The Ocean
Ed McCurdy; *Best Of* ....(TRD)
Mitch Miller; *Favorite Irish Sing Alongs* ....(COL)
Tony Sheridan/Beatles; *History Of British Rock-#5* (RHI)
  In The Beginning-Circa 1960 ....(POL)
My Name Is Barbra
Barbra Streisand; *My Name Is Barbra* ....(COL)
Pictures Of Bernadette
Talk Talk; *45* .... (EMI)
Please Don't Ask About Barbara
Bobby Vee; *Best Of* .... (EMI)
  Golden Greats .... (LIB)
  Legendary Masters .... (EMI)
Please Take A Letter Miss Brown
Ink Spots; *Best Of* .... (MCA)
Suite Madame Blue
Styx; *Caught In The Act* .... (A&M)
  Classics-#15 .... (A&M)
  Equinox .... (A&M)
Sweet Becky Walker
Larry Gatlin/Gatlin Brothers; *17 Greatest Hits* ...(COL)
Larry Gatlin/Gatlin Brothers Band; *Greatest Hits* .(COL)
Sweet Betsy From Pike
Cisco Houston; *Cowboy Ballads* .... (FLW)
Mormon Tabernacle Choir; *This Land Is Your
Land* ....(COL)

Unfortunate Miss Bailey
Kingston Trio; *At Large/Here We Go Again!* .....(CAP)

WOMEN'S NAMES: C

Candida
Dawn; *45* .... (FSB)
Candy Girl
Four Seasons; *25th Anniversary Collection* .... (RHI)
  Lil' Bit Of Gold 3" CD Series .... (RHI)
Frankie Valli/Four Seasons; *Anthology* .... (RHI)
Candy O
Cars; *Candy O* .... (ELE)
Carmelita
Linda Ronstadt; *Simple Dreams* .... (ASY)
Warren Zevon; *Warren Zevon* .... (ASY)
Carol
Chuck Berry; *Berry Is On Top* .... (CSS)
  Golden Hits .... (MER)
  Greatest Hits ....(EVR)
  Roll Over Beethoven ....(ALL)
Rolling Stones; *Get Yer Ya-Ya's Out* .... (AKO)
  Rolling Stones .... (AKO)
Caroline's Still In Georgia
Mac Davis; *Soft Talk* .... (CAS)
Carrie
Europe; *Final Countdown* .... (EPI)
Michael Bolton; *Michael Bolton* ....(COL)
Carrie Anne
Hollies; *Best Of-#1* .... (EMI)
  Epic Anthology .... (EPI)
  Evolution .... (EPI)
  Greatest Hits .... (EPI)
Cathy's Clown
Everly Brothers; *Billboard Top Rock 'N' Roll
Hits-1960* .... (RHI)
  Golden Hits .... (WB)
  Reunion Concert .... (MER)
  Very Best Of .... (WB)
Reba McEntire; *Sweet Sixteen* .... (MCA)
Cecilia
Simon & Garfunkel; *Bridge Over Troubled Water* (COL)
  Collected Works ....(COL)
  Greatest Hits ....(COL)
Charlotte The Harlot
Iron Maiden; *Iron Maiden* ....(CAP)
Charlotte's Web
Statler Brothers; *10th Anniversary* .... (MER)
Cheryl
Charlie Parker; *Bird At The Hi-Hat* .... (BLN)
George Shearing & Don Thompson; *Live At The Cafe
Carlyle* ....(CCJ)
Chewy, Chewy
Ohio Express; *Best Of* .... (RHI)
  Best Of-& Other Bubblegum Smashes-#1 .... (RHI)
  Bubblegum Greatest Hits-#2 ....(ACC)
  Fabulous Bubblegum Years ....(FFT)
Christine 16
Kiss; *Alive 2* .... (CAS)
  Love Gun .... (CAS)
Cindy's Birthday
Johnny Crawford; *Best Of* .... (RHI)
  Super Oldies/'60s-#8 ....(AUF)
Cinnamon
Derek; *Rock Artifacts-#3* ....(COL)
Clair
Gilbert O'Sullivan; *Super Hits/'70s-Have A Nice
Day-#9* .... (RHI)
Clementine
Bobby Darin; *At The Copa* ....(BAI)
  Story ....(ATC)
Cleopatra, Queen Of Denial
Pam Tillis; *Homeward Looking Angel* .... (ARI)
Cleopatra's Cat
Spin Doctors; *Turn It Upside Down* .... (EPI)
Close To Cathy
Mike Clifford; *Cruisin' 1962* ....(INC)
  '60s Dance Party-#2 ....(DOM)
Corine, Corina
Asleep At The Wheel; *Tribute To Bob Wills* ...... (LIB)
Corrine, Corrina
Big Joe Turner; *Best Of* .... (PAB)
  Greatest Hits .... (ATL)

Bob Dylan; *Freewheelin'* ....(COL)
Ray Peterson; *Good Old Rock & Roll* ....(GUS)
  Super Hits-#1 ....(GUS)
Steppenwolf; *Live* ....(MCA)
Don't Cry Cherie
Glenn Miller; *Complete-#6-1940-1941* ....(RCA)
Don't Kill It Carol
Manfred Mann's Earth Band; *Angel Station* ....(WB)
Hey, Cinderella
Suzy Bogguss; *Something Up My Sleeve* ....(LIB)
Hot Cherie
Hardline; *Double Eclipse* ....(MCA)
Hush, Hush, Sweet Charlotte
Al Martino; *Best Of* ....(CAP)
Patti Page; *45* ....(OOP)
Kiss For Cinderella
Michael Tilson Thomas; *Of Thee I Sing/Let 'Em Eat
Cake* ....(COL)
Lawdy Miss Clawdy
Elvis Presley; *For LP Fans Only* ....(RCA)
  Golden Celebration ....(RCA)
  Live On Stage In Memphis ....(RCA)
  Rocker ....(RCA)
  TV Special ....(RCA)
Joe Cocker; *Joe Cocker* ....(A&M)
Lloyd Price; *Best Of New Orleans R&B-#2* ... (RHI)
  History Of New Orleans R&B-#1-1950-1958 ... (RHI)
Oh, Carol
Neil Sedaka; *All-Time Greatest Hits* ....(RCA)
  Nipper's Greatest Hits-'50s-#1 ....(RCA)
  Sings (His Greatest Hits) ....(RCA)
Planet Claire
B-52's; *B-52's* ....(WB)
Powder River/Carrie's Gone To Kansas C.
Bill Shute & Lisa Null; *American Primitive* ....(GRE)
Searchin' For Celine
Blue Oyster Cult; *Spectres* ....(COL)
Sweet Caroline
Neil Diamond; *Glory Road-1968-1972* ....(MCA)
  Gold ....(MCA)
  His 12 Greatest Hits ....(MCA)
  Hot August Night ....(MCA)
  Love At The Greek ....(COL)
Sweet Cleo Brown
Dave Brubeck; *Greatest Hits From The Fantasy
Years* ....(FAN)
Tell It To Carrie
Romantics; *Romantics* ....(EPA)
  What I Like About You & Other Hits ....(NEM)
They Don't Dance Like Carmen No More
Jimmy Buffett; *Boats Beaches Bars & Ballads* ... (MGR)
  White Sport Coat & A Pink Crustacean ....(MCA)
Utah Carol
Marty Robbins; *Gunfighter Ballads & Trail Songs* (COL)

WOMEN'S NAMES: D

Daisy Jane
America; *America Live* ....(WB)
  Hearts ....(WB)
  History-Greatest Hits ....(WB)
  In Concert ....(CAP)
Dancy's Dream
Restless Heart; *Fast Moving Train* ....(RCA)
Dandelion
Rolling Stones; *More Hot Rocks-Big Hits & Fazed
Cookies* ....(AKO)
  Through The Past Darkly-Big Hits-#2 ....(AKO)
Dandy
Herman's Hermits; *XX (Greatest Hits)* ....(AKO)
Darlene
Led Zeppelin; *Coda* ....(ATL)
T. Graham Brown; *Come As You Were* ....(CAP)
  Greatest Hits ....(CAP)
Dawn
Frankie Valli/Four Seasons; *25th Anniversary
Collection* ....(RHI)
  Anthology ....(RHI)
Deborah
Dave Edmunds; *Best Of* ....(SS)
  Tracks On Wax 4 ....(SS)

Dede Dinah
Frankie Avalon; *Greatest Hits* ....(EVR)
  Pick Of ....(FFT)
Delia's Gone
Johnny Cash; *American Recordings* ....(AME)
Delilah
Glenn Miller; *Best Of-#3* ....(RCA)
Platters; *16 Greatest Hits* ....(TRP)
Tom Jones; *Live In Las Vegas* ....(PRT)
  London Collector-Greatest Hits ....(LON)
Delta Dawn
Bette Midler; *Divine Miss M* ....(ATL)
  Live At Last ....(ATL)
Helen Reddy; *Greatest Hits* ....(CAP)
Tanya Tucker; *Greatest Hits* ....(COL)
  Greatest Hits Encore ....(CAP)
  Live ....(MCA)
Denise
Randy/Rainbows; *Doo Wop Uptempo-#2* .... (RHI)
  Super Oldies!'60s-#4 ....(AUF)
  WCBS FM101-History Of Rock!'60s-#1 ....(CLT)
Desiree (June 3)
Neil Diamond; *12 Greatest Hits-#2* ....(COL)
  I'm Glad You're Here With Me Tonight ....(COL)
Diana
Eugene Wilde; *Serenade* ....(PHL)
Paul Anka; *21 Golden Hits* ....(RCA)
  21 Legendary Superstars ....(OSR)
  Billboard Top Rock 'N' Roll Hits-1957 ....(RHI)
Diane
Bachelors; *45* ....(LON)
Kentucky HeadHunters; *Electric Barnyard* ..... (MER)
Dinah
Bing Crosby; *16 Most Requested Songs* ....(COL)
Cab Calloway; *Best Of The Big Bands* ....(COL)
Count Basie & Ethel Waters; *Tribute To Black
Entertainers* ....(COL)
Duke Ellington; *Jubilee Stomp* ....(BLU)
Lionel Hampton; *Tempo & Swing* ....(BLU)
Louis Armstrong; *#6-St. Louis Blues* ....(COL)
Mills Brothers; *50th Anniversary* ....(RAN)
Dinah Flo
Boz Scaggs; *Hits!* ....(COL)
  My Time ....(COL)
Dirty Diana
Michael Jackson; *Bad* ....(EPI)
Dominique
Singing Nun; *45* ....(OOP)
Donna
Los Lobos; *ST/La Bamba* ....(SLS)
Ritchie Valens; *American Graffiti-#3* ....(MCA)
  Best Of ....(RHI)
  Heart & Soul Of Rock 'N' Roll-#1 ....(RHI)
  History Of ....(RHI)
  History Of Latino Rock-#1 ....(RHI)
Donna Everywhere
Too Much Joy; *Mutiny* ....(GIA)
Donna From Mobile
Anne Hills; *Don't Panic (Panic Is On/Don't
Explain)* ....(HOG)
Donna Lee
Art Pepper; *Arthur's Blues* ....(GAL)
Charlie Parker; *Genius Of* ....(SJZ)
Claude Thornhill; *Be-Bop Era* ....(COL)
Donna The Prima Donna
Dion; *24 Original Classics* ....(ARI)
  Bronx Blues-Columbia Recordings ....(COL)
Dynamo Humm
Mothers Of Invention; *Overnite Sensation* ....(RYK)
Hello Dolly
Broadway Cast; *Hello Dolly* ....(RCA)
Carol Channing/Original Cast; *Hello Dolly* .....(RCA)
Louis Armstrong; *Essential* ....(VAN)
  Vintage Music-Original Classics-#16 ....(MCA)
Hey Donna
Rythm Syndicate; *Rythm Syndicate* ....(IPA)
I've Been Workin' On The Railroad(Dinah)
Mitch Miller; *Sing Along With Mitch* ....(COL)
Pete Seeger; *20 Golden Pieces Of* ....(BLD)
Jack & Diane
John Cougar Mellencamp; *American Fool* ....(RIV)
Little Diane
Dion; *24 Original Classics* ....(ARI)

Dion/Belmonts; *Everything You Always Wanted To Hear
By* ....(LAU)
  Reunion-Live At Madison Sq. Garden 1972 .... (RHI)
Oh Diane
Fleetwood Mac; *25 Years-The Chain* ....(WB)
Pretty Donna
Collective Soul; *Hints Allegations And Things Left
Unsaid* ....(ATL)
Sam & Delilah
Original Cast; *Girl Crazy* ....(SSP)
Samson & Delilah
Blasters; *Collection* ....(SLS)
Blind Gary Davis; *Harlem Street Singer* ....(BV)
Grateful Dead; *Dead Set* ....(ARI)
  Terrapin Station ....(ARI)
Rev. Gary Davis; *From Blues To Gospel* ....(BIO)
Waltz For Debby
Bill Evans; *Complete Riverside Recordings* ....(RVR)
  New Jazz Conceptions ....(RVR)
Bill Evans & Cannonball Adderley; *Know What I
Mean?* ....(RVR)
Tony Bennett; *Forty Years-Artistry Of* ....(COL)
Tony Bennett & Bill Evans; *Tony Bennett & Bill
Evans* ....(FAN)
Toots Thielemans; *East Coast West Coast* ....(PRV)
Who's Holding Donna Now
DeBarge; *Greatest Hits* ....(MOT)
  Rhythm Of The Night ....(MOT)

WOMEN'S NAMES: E

Come On Eileen
Dexy's Midnight Runners; *Too-Rye-Ay* ....(MER)
Edna
Vernon Green/Medallions; *Golden Classics* ......(CLT)
Eileen
Keith Richards; *Main Offender* ....(VIA)
Eleanor Rigby
Beatles; *1962-1966* ....(CAP)
  Revolver ....(CAP)
Paul McCartney; *Tripping The Live Fantastic* ....(CAP)
Ray Charles; *Anthology* ....(RHI)
  Greatest Hits-#2 ....(RHI)
Elena
Marc Tanner Band; *No Escape* ....(OOP)
Elenore
Turtles; *Best Of* ....(RHI)
  Greatest Hits ....(RHI)
  Oldies But Goodies-#7 ....(OSR)
  Super Oldies/'60s-#7 ....(AUF)
Elizabeth
Statler Brothers; *Greatest Hits* ....(MER)
  Today ....(MER)
Eloise
Damned; *Light At The End Of The Tunnel* ... (MCA)
David Frishberg; *Live At Vine Street* ....(FAN)
Kay Thompson; *Dr. Demento's Greatest-#2* ......(RHI)
Elsa
Bill Evans; *Compact Jazz* ....(VRV)
Bill Evans & Eddie Gomez; *Montreux III* ....(FAN)
Elvira
Murry Kellum; *Country Comedy (20 Country Comedy
Hits)* ....(PLN)
Oak Ridge Boys; *Fancy Free* ....(MCA)
  Greatest Hits-#2 ....(MCA)
  MCA 30 Years Of Hits (1958-1988) ....(MCA)
Emily
Beth Nielsen Chapman; *Beth Nielsen Chapman* .. (RPR)
Fear Of God; *Within The Veil* ....(WB)
Frank Sinatra; *Reprise Collection* ....(RPR)
  Softy As I Leave You ....(RPR)
Frankie Valli/Four Seasons; *Rarities-#2* ....(RHI)
Los Lobos; *Neighborhood* ....(SLS)
Emma
Hot Chocolate; *Super Hits/'70s-Have A Nice
Day-#14* .... (RHI)
Erica
Jesse Colin Young; *Highway is For Heroes* .....(CYP)
Ethelene (The Truckstop Queen)
Ray Stevens; *I Never Made A Record I Didn't
Like* ....(MCA)
Eva Braun (I Never Loved)
Boomtown Rats; *Tonic For The Troops* ....(COL)

Evangelina
Hoyt Axton; *Bread & Roses Festival-Acoustic
Music-#1* ....(FAN)
Evangeline
Band & Emmylou Harris; *The Last Waltz* ....(WB)
Emmylou Harris & The Band; *Duets* ....(RPR)
Jerry Garcia Band; *Jerry Garcia Band* ....(ARI)
Los Lobos; *How Will The Wolf Survive* ....(SLS)
Matthew Sweet; *Girlfriend* ....(ZOO)
For Emily, Wherever I May Find Her
Simon & Garfunkel; *Collected Works* ....(COL)
  Greatest Hits ....(COL)
  Parsley Sage Rosemary & Thyme ....(COL)
In Memory Of Elizabeth Reid
Allman Brothers Band; *Beginnings* ....(POL)
  Decade Of Hits-1969-1979 ....(POL)
  Live At The Fillmore East ....(POL)
Letter To Elise
Cure; *Wish* ....(FIC)
Miss Emily's Picture
John Conlee; *Country Gold* ....(PRY)
  Greatest Hits ....(MCA)
  With Love ....(MCA)
See Emily Play
David Bowie; *Pinups* ....(RYK)
Pink Floyd; *Relics* ....(CAP)
  Works ....(CAP)
Sweet Eloise
Glenn Miller; *Complete* ....(BLU)
Russ Morgan/Orchestra; *Play 22 Original Big Band
Recordings* ....(HIN)
Tex Beneke/Modernaires; *Reunion* ....(MCA)

WOMEN'S NAMES: F

Fancy
Bobbi Gentry; *All-Time Country Classics-#1* .....(CAP)
Reba McEntire; *Rumor Has It* ....(MCA)
Fanny
Bee Gees; *Greatest* ....(RSO)
  Main Course ....(RSO)
Fanny Mae
Buster Brown; *Billboard Top R&B Hits-1960* .... (RHI)
  Cruisin'-1960 ....(INC)
  New King Of The Blues ....(CLT)
  ST/American Graffiti ....(MCA)
Elvin Bishop; *Alligator Records 20th Anniversary
Coll.* ....(ALG)
  Don't Let The Bossman Get You Down ....(ALG)
Joey Dee/Starliters; *Hey Let's Twist-Best Of* ......(RHI)
Frankie & Johnny
Doc Watson; *Favorites* ....(LIB)
Jerry Lee Lewis; *Greatest* ....(RHI)
Frankie & Johnny Blues
Glenn Yarbrough; *Best Of* ....(RCA)
Kay Starr; *Country* ....(CRS)
Short Fat Fannie
Larry Williams; *Original Rock Oldies-Golden
Hits-#1* .... (SPE)
  This Is How It All Began-#2 ....(SPE)
  Ultimate '50s Party ....(ERA)
Weight, The
Band; *Best Of* ....(CAP)
  Last Waltz ....(WB)
  Music From Big Pink ....(CAP)
  Rock Of Ages-#1 & 2 ....(CAP)
Staple Singers; *Soul Folk In Action* ....(STX)
Staple Singers & Marty Stuart; *Rhythm Country &
Blues* ....(MCA)

WOMEN'S NAMES: G

Dinner With Gershwin
Brenda Russell; *Kiss Me With The Wind* ....(A&M)
Donna Summer; *All Systems Go* ....(GEF)
Georgia On My Mind
Billie Holiday; *God Bless The Child* ....(COL)
  Story-#2 ....(COL)
Hoagy Carmichael; *Hoagy Sings Carmichael* .....(EMI)
  Legendary Performer ....(RCA)
Ray Charles; *Anthology* ....(RHI)
  Greatest Hits-#2 ....(RHI)

Willie Nelson; *Greatest Hits & Some That Will Be* (COL)
  Stardust ....(COL)
  & Family Live ....(COL)
Georgy Girl
  Seekers; *History Of British Rock-#4* .... (RHI)
Gigi
  Charles Boyer; *Romantic Songs Of Love* ....(EVR)
  Louis Jordan; *ST/Gigi* ....(SSP)
Gina
  Johnny Mathis; *16 Most Requested Songs* ......(COL)
  All-Time Greatest Hits ....(COL)
  Michael Bolton; *Hunger* ....(COL)
  Stray Cats; *Blast Off* ....(EMI)
Ginny The Flying Girl
  Janis Ian; *In Harmony II* ....(COL)
Gloria
  Doors; *Alive She Cried* ....(ELE)
  Escorts; *Original Classic Oldies/'50s-'60s-#13* .. (MCA)
  Jimi Hendrix; *Essential-#1 & 2* ....(RPR)
  Laura Branigan; *Branigan* ....(ATL)
  Dance Traxx ....(ATL)
  Manhattan Transfer; *Best Of* ....(ATL)
  Live ....(ATL)
  Manhattan Transfer ....(ATL)
  Shadows Of Knight; *Nuggets-#2* ....(RHI)
  U2; *October* ....(ISL)
  Under A Blood Red Sky ....(ISL)
  Van Morrison; *It's Too Late To Stop Now* .....(WB)
  Van Morrison/Them; *Best Of* ....(MER)
Guinnevere
  Crosby, Stills & Nash; *Crosby, Stills & Nash* .... (ATL)
  Crosby, Stills, Nash & Young; *So Far* ....(ATL)
  Woodstock Two ....(ATL)
Lady Godiva
  Peter & Gordon; *History Of British Rock-#4* ..... (RHI)
Madame George
  Van Morrison; *Astral Weeks* ....(WB)
  Bang Masters ....(EPI)
Sweet Georgia Brown
  Anita O'Day; *Compact Jazz-Best Of The Jazz*
  Vocalists ....(VRV)
  Beatles; *In The Beginning-Circa 1960* ....(POL)
  Coasters; *Greatest Hits* ....(ATC)
  Django Reinhardt; *Djangologie USA-#1* ....(DSQ)
  Quintet Of The Hot Club Of France ....(PRS)
  Ella Fitzgerald; *In London* ....(PAB)
  Whisper Not ....(VRV)
  Ella Fitzgerald & Count Basie; *Perfect Match* ... (PAB)
  Original Cast; *Bubbling Brown Sugar* ....(AMH)
  Stephane Grappelli; *Live In London* ....(BL)
  Tito Puente; *Out Of This World* ....(CP)

WOMEN'S NAMES: H

Aunt Hagar's Blues
  Art Tatum; *Solo Masterpieces-#4* .... (PAB)
  Kid Ory's Creole Jazz Band; *This Kid's The*
  Greatest .... (GTJ)
Harriet Tubman
  Holly Near & Ronnie Gilbert; *Lifeline* ....(RWD)
  Redwood Collection ....(RWD)
Harriet Tubman's Gonna Carry Me Home
  Long Ryders; *Two-Fisted Tales* .... (ISL)
Heather Honey
  Tommy Roe; *Greatest Hits* ....(MCA)
  Sheila ....(ACC)
Helen Wheels
  Paul McCartney/Wings; *Band On The Run* ......(CAP)
Holly Holy
  Neil Diamond; *Gold* ....(MCA)
  His 12 Greatest Hits ....(MCA)
  Hot August Night ....(MCA)
  Hot August Night II ....(COL)
  Love At The Greek ....(COL)
  Touching You Touching Me ....(MCA)
Hooray For Hazel
  Tommy Roe; *Greatest Hits* ....(MCA)
  Original Rock 'N' Roll Hits Of The '60s .... (RLL)
  Sheila ....(ACC)
Long Legged Hannah (From Butte, Montana)
  Jesse Hunter; *A Man Like Me* ....(BNA)
Louisiana Hannah
  Webb Wilder; *Hybrid Vigor* .... (ISL)

Please, Mrs. Henry
  Bob Dylan/Band; *Basement Tapes* ....(COL)
Soft Hearted Hana
  George Harrison; *George Harrison* .... (DKH)

WOMEN'S NAMES: I

Goodnight Irene
  Jim Reeves; *Pure Gold* ....(RCA)
  Johnny Cash; *Man-The World-His Music* ....(SUN)
  Rough Cut King Of Country Music ....(SUN)
  Ry Cooder; *Chicken Skin Music* ....(RPR)
  Weavers; *At Carnegie Hall* ....(VAN)
  Best Of ....(MCA)
  Greatest Hits ....(VAN)
Iesha
  Another Bad Creation; *Coolin' At The Playground Ya'*
  Know! ....(MOT)
Irma La Douce
  Katherine Kovar; *Love Echoes* ....(ACT)
  Original Cast; *Irma La Douce* ....(SSP)
Isabella's Eyes
  Kenny Loggins; *Back To Avalon* ....(COL)
Isabelle
  Mary Lou Williams; *Jazz Pioneers* .... (PRS)
Oye Isabel
  Iguanas; *Nuevo Boogaloo* ....(MGR)
Sexy Ida
  Ike & Tina Turner; *Proud Mary-Best Of* .... (EMI)

WOMEN'S NAMES: J

867-5309/Jenny
  Tommy Tutone; *#2* ....(COL)
Arkansas Jane
  Kong Cotton; *Bo Diddley Beats* .... (RHI)
Baby Jane
  Rod Stewart; *Body Wishes* ....(WB)
  Storyteller/Complete Anthology-1964-1990 ......(WB)
Back In Judy's Jungle
  Brian Eno; *Desert Island Selection* .... (EDI)
  Taking Tiger Mountain By Strategy .... (EDI)
Blue Jean
  David Bowie; *Changesbowie* ....(RYK)
  The Singles-1969-1993 ....(RYK)
  Tonight ....(EMI)
Dammit Janet
  Barry Bostwick; *ST/Rocky Horror Picture Show* .. (RHI)
  Original London Cast; *Rocky Horror Show* .... (RHI)
Dance Little Jean
  Nitty Gritty Dirt Band; *Let's Go* ....(WB)
  Twenty Years Of Dirt-Best Of ....(WB)
Dear Jean (I'm Nervous)
  City Boys; *Young Men Gone West* ....(MER)
Death Of Queen Jane
  Joan Baez; *Joan Baez* ....(VAN)
  Love Song Album ....(VAN)
Don't Cry Joni
  Conway Twitty; *Greatest Hits-#1* ....(MCA)
  Very Best Of ....(MCA)
  #1s-#1 ....(CAP)
Electric Aunt Jemima
  Frank Zappa; *Uncle Meat* ....(BAR)
I Dream Of Jeanie With Light Brown Hair
  Al Jolson; *Story-#5* ....(MCA)
  Joan Baez; *Diamonds & Rust* ....(A&M)
  Mormon Tabernacle Choir; *Beautiful Dreamer* ..(COL)
  Greatest Hits-#3 ....(COL)
  Old Beloved Songs ....(COL)
Jack & Jill
  Ray Parker, Jr./Raydio; *Chartbusters* .... (ARI)
  Greatest Hits ....(ARI)
  Ray Parker, Jr./Raydio ....(ARI)
Jackie Blue
  Ozark Mountain Daredevils; *Billboard Top*
  Hits-1975 .... (RHI)
  It'll Shine When It Shines ....(A&M)
  It's Alive ....(A&M)
  Super Hits/'70s-Have A Nice Day-#14 .... (RHI)
  The Best ....(A&M)
Jamie
  Ray Parker, Jr.; *Chartbusters* .... (ARI)

Jane
Jefferson Starship; *Freedom At Point Zero* .... (GRU)
  Greatest Hits-Ten Years & Change ....(RCA)
Janet
Commodores; *Nightshift* .... (MOT)
Janey, Don't Lose Heart
Bruce Springsteen; *45* ....(COL)
Jane, Jane, Jane
Kingston Trio; *Capitol Collectors Series* ....(CAP)
  Hidden Treasures ....(FOL)
  Very Best Of ....(CAP)
Jane's Getting Serious
John Astley; *Everyone Loves The Pilot (Except The..)* .... (ATL)
Janie Baker
Shenandoah; *Under The Kudzu* ....(RCA)
Janie's Got A Gun
Aerosmith; *Pump* ....(GEF)
Jean
Jim Nabors; *16 Most Requested Songs* ....(COL)
Oliver; *45* ....(GUS)
Jean Genie
David Bowie; *Aladdin Sane* ....(RYK)
  Changesbowie ....(RYK)
  Live ....(RYK)
  The Singles-1969-1993 ....(RYK)
Jeannie Needs A Shooter
Warren Zevon; *Bad Luck Streak In Dancing School* .... (ASY)
  Stand In The Fire .... (ASY)
Jennie Lee
Jan & Dean; *Legendary Masters* .... (UA)
Jennifer
Eurythmics; *Sweet Dreams* ....(RCA)
Jennifer Eccles
Hollies; *Best Of-#2* .... (EMI)
  Epic Anthology-Original Master Tapes ....(EPI)
Jenny
Chicago; *VI* ....(COL)
Harry Chapin; *Living Room Suite* .... (ELE)
Marty Robbins; *Biggest Hits* ....(COL)
Jenny Take A Ride
Mitch Ryder/Detroit Wheels; *Greatest Hits* .... (RLL)
  Original Rock 'N' Roll Hits Of The '60s .... (RLL)
  Rev Up-Best Of .... (RHI)
  Toga Rock ....(DHL)
Jenny (Iowa Sunrise)
Janis Ian; *Night Trains* ....(COL)
Jenny, Jenny
Little Richard; *18 Greatest Hits* .... (RHI)
  Compact Command Performances ....(MOT)
  Grooviest ....(SPE)
  Little Richard ....(SPE)
  Tutti Frutti ....(ACC)
Jessica
Allman Brothers Band; *Best Of* ....(POL)
  Brothers & Sisters ....(POL)
  Decade Of Hits-1969-1979 ....(POL)
  Dreams ....(POL)
Jewel Eyed Judy
Fleetwood Mac; *Kiln House* ....(RPR)
Joan Crawford
Blue Oyster Cult; *Extraterrestrial Live* ....(COL)
  Fire Of Unknown Origin ....(COL)
Joanna
Kool/Gang; *Everything Is-Greatest Hits* .... (MER)
  In The Heart .... (DL)
Joanne
Michael Nesmith; *Compilation* ....(OOP)
Wall Of Voodoo; *Happy Planet* .... (IRS)
Jody Girl
Bob Seger; *Beautiful Loser* ....(CAP)
  Live Bullet ....(CAP)
Jody Like A Melody
David Allan Coe; *17 Greatest Hits* ....(COL)
  For The Record-First 10 Years ....(COL)
Johanna
Angela Lansbury & Len Cariou; *Sweeney Todd* ..(RCA)
Jolene
Dolly Parton; *Best Of* ....(RCA)
  Best There Is ....(RCA)
  Jolene ....(RCA)
  RCA Years-1967-1986 ....(RCA)

Joli Girl
Marty Robbins; *All-Time Greatest Hits* ....(COL)
Josephine
Wayne King; *Best Of* ....(MCA)
  Nipper's Greatest Hits-'30s-#1 ....(RCA)
Josie
Steely Dan; *Aja* ....(MCA)
  Greatest Hits ....(MCA)
Judy In Disguise (With Glasses)
John Fred/Playboys; *Billboard Top Rock 'N' Roll Hits-1968* .... (RHI)
  Cruisin'-1967 .... (INC)
  ST/Drugstore Cowboy ....(NOV)
  Super Oldies Of The '60s-#7 ....(AUF)
Judy's Turn To Cry
Lesley Gore; *Anthology* .... (RHI)
  Golden Hits ....(MER)
  '60s Dance Party-#2 ....(DOM)
Julia
Beatles; *Box Set* ....(CAP)
  ST/Imagine-The Motion Picture ....(CAP)
  White Album ....(CAP)
Juliet
Neil Diamond; *And The Singer Sings His Songs* . (MCA)
  Love Songs ....(MCA)
Oak Ridge Boys; *Country Classics-#2* ....(MCA)
  Country Classics-#6-1985-1986 ....(MCA)
  Seasons ....(MCA)
Stevie Nicks; *Other Side Of The Mirror* ....(MOD)
Julie, Do Ya Love Me
Bobby Sherman; *Rock & Roll Is Here To Stay* .... (GUS)
  Super Hits/'70s-Have A Nice Day-#3 ....(RHI)
Julie's In The Drug Squad
Clash; *Give 'Em Enough Rope* .... (EPI)
Lady Jane
Rolling Stones; *Aftermath* ....(AKO)
  Flowers ....(AKO)
  Got Live If You Want It ....(AKO)
  More Hot Rocks-Big Hits & Fazed Cookies .....(AKO)
Little Jeannie
Elton John; *21 At 33* ....(POL)
  Greatest Hits-1976-1986 ....(MCA)
Me & Baby Jane
Leon Russell; *Carney* ....(MCA)
Me & Mrs. Jones
Billy Paul; *Ten Years Of #1 Hits* .... (PI)
My Girl Josephine
Fats Domino; *Greatest Hits* ....(MCA)
  They Call Me The Fat Man .... (EMI)
Oh, Julie
Crescendos; *In The Still Of The Night* ....(CAP)
  Southern Rhythm 'N' Rock-Best Excello-#2 ..... (RHI)
Poor Jenny
Everly Brothers; *All They Had To Do Was Dream* (RHI)
  Everly Brothers .... (RHI)
  Fabulous Style Of .... (RHI)
Portrait Of Jenny
Nat King Cole; *Unforgettable* ....(CAP)
Red Garland & Ray Barretto; *Manteca* ....(PRS)
Queen Jane Approximately
Bob Dylan; *Highway 61 Revisited* ....(COL)
Bob Dylan/Grateful Dead; *Dylan & The Dead* ...(COL)
Frankie Valli/Four Seasons; *Sing Big Hits By Bacharach/David/Dylan* .... (RHI)
Ride On Josephine
George Thorogood/Destroyers; *George Thorogood/Destroyers* .... (ROU)
Romeo & Juliet
Andy Williams/Royal Philharmonic Orch.; *Greatest Love Classics* ....(CAP)
Chambers Brothers; *Time Has Come* ....(COL)
Dire Straits; *Live-Alchemy* ....(WB)
  Making Movies ....(WB)
  Money For Nothing ....(WB)
Honeys; *Capitol Collectors Series* ....(CAP)
Indigo Girls; *Rites Of Passage* ....(EPI)
Percy Faith; *16 Most Requested Songs* ....(COL)
  Reflections; 45 .... (ERI)
Stacy Earl; *Stacy Earl* ....(RCA)
Suite: Judy Blue Eyes
Crosby, Stills & Nash; *Crosby, Stills & Nash* .....(ATL)
  Crosby, Stills & Nash (collection) ....(ATL)
  ST/Woodstock ....(ATL)
Crosby, Stills, Nash & Young; *So Far* ....(ATL)

Sweet Jane
Cowboy Junkies; ST/Natural Born Killer .... (NOT)
   Trinity Session ....(RCA)
Lou Reed; Rock 'N' Roll Animal ....(RCA)
   Walk On The Wild Side-Best Of ....(RCA)
Mott The Hoople; All The Young Dudes ....(COL)
   Ballad Of Mott ....(COL)
Velvet Underground; Live At Max's Kansas City .. (CLT)
Tarzan & Jane
Sparks; Angst In My Pants .... (ATL)
Theme From "Romeo & Juliet"
101 Strings Orchestra; World's Greatest Standards (ALS)
Andre Kostelanetz; 16 Most Requested Songs ....(COL)
This Romeo Ain't Got Julie Yet
Diamond Rio; Close To The Edge .... (ARI)
Visions Of Johanna
Bob Dylan; Biograph ....(COL)
   Blonde On Blonde ....(COL)

WOMEN'S NAMES: K

If You See Kay
Memphis Slim/Tampa Red/Lonnie Johnson; Bawdy
   Blues .... (BV)
I'll Take You Home Again Kathleen
Billy Shepherd Singers; Irish Sing-Along .... (MCA)
Bing Crosby; When Irish Eyes Are Smiling .. (MCA)
Slim Whitman; Paloma Blanca-Best Of-Legendary
   Masters .... (EMI)
Kathleen
Blasters; Collection ....(SLS)
Roachford; Roachford ....(EPI)
Willie Nelson; Partners ....(COL)
Kathleen Mavourneen
Mormon Tabernacle Choir; Songs Of The Civil War & S.
   Foster Faves ....(SMC)
Kathleen (Catholicism Made Easier)
Randy Newman; Little Criminals .... (WB)
Kathy's Song
Simon & Garfunkel; Collected Works ....(COL)
   Greatest Hits ....(COL)
   Sounds Of Silence ....(COL)
Katie Left Memphis
Tangle Eye; Roots Of The Blues ....(NW)
Kitty's Back
Bruce Springsteen; The Wild The Innocent & E Street
   Shuffle ....(COL)
Kyrie
Mr. Mister; Welcome To The Real World ....(RCA)
Shimmy Like Kate
Olympics; Official Record Album Of .... (RHI)
Terence's Farewell To Kathleen
John McCormack; Ireland Of Treasures-Voices &
   Melodies ....(CAP)

WOMEN'S NAMES: L

Ah Leah
Donnie Iris; Back On The Streets .... (MCA)
Change In Louise
Joe Cocker; With A Little Help From My Friends (A&M)
Dizzy Miss Lizzy
Beatles; At The Hollywood Bowl ....(CAP)
   Help! ....(CAP)
   Rock 'N' Roll Music-#2 ....(CAP)
   VI ....(CAP)
Ronnie Hawkins/Hawks; Best Of .. (RHI)
Donald & Lydia
John Prine; John Prine ....(ATL)
   Prime Prine ....(ATL)
Honolulu Lulu
Jan & Dean; Deadman's Curve ....(EMI)
   Legendary Masters ....(EMI)
   Surf City-Best Of ....(EMI)
   /Bel-Air Bandits-One Summer Night ....(RHI)
"I Love Lucy" Theme
Original Music; TV Theme Sing-Along Album .... (RHI)
I Saw Linda Yesterday
Dickey Lee; 45s On CD-#2-1960-1966 .... (MER)
I'm Not Lisa
Jessi Colter; Heartbreak Hotel .... (EMI)
   Super Hits/'70s-Have A Nice Day-#15 .... (RHI)

Lara's Theme
Maurice Jarre Orchestra; Hollywood's Great
   Composers ....(SMP)
MGM Studio Orchestra; ST/Dr. Zhivago .... (MCA)
Laura
Frank Sinatra; Night We Called It A Day ....(CAP)
   Where Are You ....(CAP)
Sammy Davis, Jr.; Capitol Collectors Series ....(CAP)
Spike Jones; Best Of ....(RCA)
Laurie
Dickey Lee; 45 ....(ERI)
"Laverne & Shirley" Theme
Original Music; Television's Greatest Hits-#3 .....(TVT)
Layla
Derek/Dominos; Classic Rock-1966-1988 ....(ATL)
   Eric Clapton-Crossroads ....(POL)
   Eric Clapton-Time Pieces ....(POL)
   Layla ....(POL)
   ST/Goodfellas ....(ATL)
Eric Clapton; Unplugged ....(RPR)
Leah
Roy Orbison; All-Time Greatest Hits-#1 .... (MON)
   Anthology: 1956-1965 ....(RHI)
   In Dreams-Greatest Hits ....(VIA)
Lida Rose
Original Broadway Cast; Music Man .... (ANG)
Robert Preston/Original Cast; Music Man ......(CAP)
Lili Marlene
Marlene Dietrich; Best Of ....(COL)
   Essential ....(CAP)
   Live At The Cafe De Paris ....(COL)
   This Is Art Deco ....(COL)
Lily Was Here
Candy Dulfer & Dave Stewart; ST/Lily Was Here (ARI)
Linda On My Mind
Conway Twitty; Conway's #1 Classics-#2 ....(WB)
   Greatest Hits-#2 ....(MCA)
   Songwriter ....(MCA)
   Very Best Of ....(MCA)
Lisa
Cat Stevens; Tea For The Tillerman .... (A&M)
Lisa, Listen To Me
Blood, Sweat & Tears; Greatest Hits ....(COL)
Liza Jane
David Bowie; Love You Till Tuesday ..(LON)
Vince Gill; Pocket Full Of Gold ....(MCA)
Loddy Lo
Chubby Checker; Greatest Hits ....(EVR)
Lola
Kinks; Come Dancing With-Best Of-1977-1986 .. (ARI)
   Everybody's In Show Biz ....(RHI)
   Kink Kronikles ....(RPR)
   Lola Vs. Powerman & The Moneygoround .....(RPR)
   One For The Road ....(ARI)
   Second Time Around ....(RCA)
Louie Louie
Kingsmen; Best Of .... (RHI)
   Billboard Top Rock 'N' Roll Hits-1963 .... (RHI)
   Cruisin'-1963 ....(INC)
   Frat Rock! .... (RHI)
   Oldies But Goodies-#11 ....(OSR)
   Rock & Roll Is Here To Stay ....(GUS)
   ST/Quadrophenia ....(POL)
   WCBS FM101-History Of Rock/'60s-#1 ....(CLT)
Pretenders; II ....(SIR)
Louise
Bonnie Raitt; Collection .... (WB)
   Sweet Forgiveness ....(WB)
Leo Kottke; Greenhouse ....(CAP)
   My Feet Are Smiling ....(CAP)
   Very Best Of ....(CAP)
Linda Ronstadt; Retrospective ....(CAP)
   Silk Purse ....(CAP)
Paul Siebel; Woodsmoke & Oranges ....(ELE)
Love Theme From "Eyes Of Laura Mars"
Barbra Streisand; Greatest Hits ....(COL)
   Love Theme From "Eyes Of Laura Mars" ....(COL)
Lucille
Everly Brothers; Golden Hits ....(WB)
   Reunion Concert ....(MER)
   Very Best Of ....(WB)

Kenny Rogers; *Greatest Hits* .... (EMI)
  Kenny Rogers .... (UA)
  Ten Years Of Gold .... (EMI)
  Twenty Greatest Hits .... (LIB)
Little Richard; *American Graffiti-#3* .... (MCA)
  Big Hits .... (CRS)
  Greatest Hits .... (EVR)
  Oldies But Goodies-#12 .... (OSR)
Lucy In The Sky With Diamonds
Beatles; *1967-1970* .... (CAP)
  Sgt. Pepper's Lonely Hearts Club Band .... (CAP)
  Yellow Submarine .... (CAP)
Elton John; *All This & World War 2* .... (20)
  Greatest Hits-#2 .... (POL)
John Lennon; *Lennon* .... (CAP)
Luka
Suzanne Vega; *Solitude Standing* .... (A&M)
Lynda
Steve Wariner; *Country Classics-#11-1987-1988* (MCA)
  Greatest Hits .... (MCA)
  It's A Crazy World .... (MCA)
  MCA #1 Hits/'80s-#3 .... (MCA)
Norwegian Waltz/Liza Lynn
Jackie Daly/Seamus & Manus McGuire; *Buttons &*
  Bows .... (GRE)
Pearl Of The Quarter (Louise)
Steely Dan; *Countdown To Ecstasy* .... (MCA)
Pictures Of Lily
Pete Townshend; *Another Scoop* .... (ATC)
Who; *Magic Bus* .... (MCA)
  Meaty Beaty Big & Bouncy .... (MCA)
  Who's Better Who's Best-Very Best Of .... (MCA)
Princess Leia's Theme
John Williams; *ST/Star Wars* .... (POL)
Queen Lucy
Original Cast; *You're A Good Man Charlie*
  Brown .... (POL)
Quiche Lorraine
B-52's; *Tame Yourself* .... (RHI)
  Wild Planet .... (WB)
Shanghai Lil
Guy Lombardo; *16 Most Requested Songs* .... (COL)
Sweet Leilani
Bing Crosby; *Best Of* .... (MCA)
King Sisters; *And The Winner Is-Best Movie Songs* (CAP)
Sweet Lorraine
Art Tatum; *Solos-1940* .... (MCA)
  Standards .... (BL)
Carmen McRae; *You're Lookin' At Me* .... (CCJ)
Count Basie; *The Standards* .... (VRV)
Frank Sinatra; *Reprise Collection* .... (RPR)
Nat King Cole; *Complete-After Midnight Sessions* (CAP)
  Story .... (CAP)
Uriah Heep; *Best Of* .... (MER)
  Magician's Birthday .... (MER)
Woody Herman; *Big Band Treasures-#2* .... (DHL)
Tell Laura I Love Her
Ray Peterson; *Nipper's Greatest Hits-'60s-#1* ..... (RCA)
  Teenage Tragedies .... (RHI)
Thanks For Leaving, Lucille
Sherri Jerrico; *Best Of Town & Country-#3* ...... (IGR)
Think Of Laura
Christopher Cross; *Another Page* .... (WB)
  Soap Opera's Greatest Love Themes .... (SCO)
Twistin' With Linda
Isley Brothers; *Scepter Records Story* .... (CPC)
  Story-#1-Rockin' Soul-1959-1968 .... (RHI)
Watch Out For Lucy
Eric Clapton; *Backless* .... (RSO)
Watch What Happens (Lola's Theme)
Frank Sinatra; *My Way* .... (RPR)
Henry Mancini; *Mancini Magic* .... (PRR)
Sergio Mendes; *Four Sider* .... (A&M)
Who Stole The Jukebox (From Lucy's...)
Johnny Bond; *Johnny Gimble's Texas Honky-Tonk*
  Hits .... (CMH)

WOMEN'S NAMES: M

All The Way To Birmingham/Roaring Mary
Celtic Thunder; *Celtic Thunder* .... (GRE)

Along Comes Mary
Association; *Greatest Hits* .... (WB)
  Vintage .... (FFT)
Bloody Mary
Original Cast; *South Pacific* .... (COL)
Soundtrack; *South Pacific* .... (RCA)
Whitesnake; *Snakebite* .... (GEF)
Bony Moronie
John Lennon; *Rock 'N' Roll* .... (CAP)
Larry Williams; *Cruisin'-1957* .... (INC)
  Let The Good Times Roll .... (CAP)
  Original Rock Oldies-Golden Hits-#2 .... (SPE)
  ST/Christine .... (MOT)
  This Is-How It All Began-#2 .... (SPE)
Cockles & Mussels (Molly)
Emily Mitchell; *The Irish Album* .... (RCA)
C'mon Marianne
Frankie Valli/Four Seasons; *25th Anniversary*
  Collection .... (RHI)
  Anthology .... (RHI)
Dear John & Marsha Letter
Stan Freberg; *Capitol Collectors Series* .... (CAP)
Don't Make Love To Mary (With Mabel...)
Merle Travis; *Johnny Gimble's Texas Honky-Tonk*
  Hits .... (CMH)
Elvis & Marilyn
Leon Russell; *Americana* .... (PRD)
Good Golly Miss Molly
Creedence Clearwater Revival; *1968-1969* ...... (FAN)
  Bayou Country .... (FAN)
  Chronicle-#2 .... (FAN)
Little Richard; *18 Greatest Hits* .... (RHI)
  Big Hits .... (CRS)
  Cruisin'-1958 .... (INC)
  Greatest Hits Recorded Live .... (EPI)
  His Greatest Hits .... (VJ)
  ST/Flamingo Kid .... (MOT)
  Super Oldies/'50s-#2 .... (AUF)
Hello Mary Lou
Creedence Clearwater Revival; *Creedence*
  Country .... (FAN)
Ricky Nelson; *Best Of* .... (EMI)
  Greatest Hits .... (RHI)
  In Concert-Troubadour-1969 .... (MCA)
  Souvenirs .... (EMI)
Statler Brothers; *14 Country Favorites* .... (MER)
  Pardners In Rhyme .... (MER)
I Shall Call You Mary
Montage; *Nuggets-#11-Pop-#4* .... (RHI)
It's Me Again Margaret
Ray Stevens; *Country Classics-#3-1984-1985* ... (MCA)
  Greatest Hits .... (MCA)
  He Thinks He's Ray Stevens .... (MCA)
I'm Mandy Fly Me
10 CC; *Greatest Hits 1972-1978* .... (POL)
  How Dare You .... (OOP)
  Live & Let Live .... (OOP)
Lady Madonna
Beatles; *1967-1970* .... (CAP)
  Hey Jude .... (CAP)
  Past Masters-#2 .... (CAP)
Paul McCartney/Wings; *Over America* .... (CAP)
Lady Marmalade
Labelle; *Nightbirds* .... (EPI)
Patti Labelle; *Best Of* .... (EPI)
Sheila E.; *Sex Cymbal* .... (WB)
Little Maggie
Kingston Trio; *Tom Dooley* .... (CAP)
Little Marie
Chuck Berry; *Chess Box* .... (CSS)
  Rock 'N' Roll Rarities .... (CSS)
  St. Louis To Liverpool .... (CSS)
Little Martha
Allman Brothers Band; *Best Of* .... (POL)
  Decade Of Hits-1969-1979 .... (POL)
  Eat A Peach .... (POL)
Looking For Mary Jane
Charlie Daniels Band; *Whiskey* .... (EPI)
Maggie Mae
Beatles; *Let It Be* .... (CAP)

Maggie May
Rod Stewart; *Absolutely Live* .... (WB)
  Best Of .... (MER)
  Billboard Top Rock 'N' Roll Hits-1971 .... (RHI)
  Every Picture Tells A Story .... (MER)
  Greatest Hits .... (WB)
  Sing It Again Rod .... (MER)
  Storyteller/Complete Anthology-1964-1990 ..... (WB)
Maggie's Dream
Don Williams; *Cafe Carolina* .... (MCA)
  Country Classics-#4-1984-1985 .... (MCA)
Maggie's Farm
Bob Dylan; *At Budokan* .... (COL)
  Bringing It All Back Home .... (COL)
  Greatest Hits-#2 .... (COL)
  Hard Rain .... (COL)
  Real Live .... (COL)
Magnolia
J.J. Cale; *Naturally* .... (MCA)
Pat Travers; *Pat Travers* .... (POL)
Poco; *Crazy Eyes* .... (EPI)
Tom Petty/Heartbreakers; *You're Gonna Get It* . (MCA)
Mame
Louis Armstrong; *Mr. Music* .... (ACC)
Original Cast; *Mame* .... (COL)
Mandy
Barry Manilow; *Barry 2* .... (ARI)
  Greatest Hits-#1 .... (ARI)
  Live On Broadway .... (ARI)
Maria
Johnny Mathis; *All-Time Greatest Hits* .... (COL)
Marvin Gaye; *Romantically Yours* .... (COL)
Original Cast; *Sound Of Music* .... (COL)
Maria Elena
Indios Tabajaras; *Nipper's Greatest Hits-'60s-#1* . (RCA)
Jimmy Dorsey; *Greatest Hits* .... (MCA)
Smithereens; *11* .... (CAP)
Marian The Librarian
Original Broadway Cast; *Music Man* .... (ANG)
Robert Preston; *ST/Music Man* .... (WB)
Marie
Bachelors; *45* .... (LON)
Randy Newman; *Good Old Boys* .... (RPR)
Tommy Dorsey/Orchestra; *Seventeen Number
Ones* .... (RCA)
(Marie's The Name) His Latest Flame
Elvis Presley; *Golden Records-#3* .... (RCA)
  ST/This Is .... (RCA)
Marlena
Bobby Goldsboro; *10th Anniversary Album-#2* .... (UA)
Frankie Valli/Four Seasons; *25th Anniversary
Collection* .... (RHI)
  Anthology .... (RHI)
Marlene
Todd Rundgren; *Something Anything* .... (RHI)
Marlene On The Wall
Suzanne Vega; *Suzanne Vega* .... (A&M)
Martha My Dear
Beatles; *Box Set* .... (CAP)
  White Album .... (CAP)
Martha Say
John Cougar Mellencamp; *Big Daddy* .... (MER)
Mary
Sarah McLachlan; *Fumbling Towards Ecstasy* .... (ARI)
Mary Had A Little Lamb
Stevie Ray Vaughan/Double Trouble; *Live Alive* .. (EPI)
  Texas Flood .... (EPI)
Wings; *Wings Wild Life* .... (CAP)
Mary Jane's Last Dance
Tom Petty/Heartbreakers; *Greatest Hits* .... (MCA)
Mary Mary
Classics IV; *Spooky* .... (LIB)
  Very Best Of .... (EMI)
Monkees; *More Of The Monkees* .... (ARI)
Run-D.M.C.; *Tougher Than Leather* .... (PRO)
Mary Queen Of Arkansas
Bruce Springsteen; *Greetings From Asbury Park,
N.J.* .... (COL)
"Mary Tyler Moore" Theme
Original Music-Sonny Curtis; *Television's Greatest
Hits-#2* .... (TVT)
Mary's Prayer
Danny Wilson; *Meet Danny Wilson* .... (VIA)

Matilda Matilda
Harry Belafonte; *At Carnegie Hall* .... (RCA)
  Legendary Performer .... (RCA)
  Pure Gold .... (RCA)
  This Is .... (RCA)
"Maude" Theme
Original Music; *Television's Greatest Hits-#3* .. (TVT)
Maxine
Donald Fagen; *The Nightfly* .... (WB)
Maybelline
Chuck Berry; *Cruisin'-1955* .... (INC)
  Golden Hits .... (MER)
  Greatest Hits .... (EVR)
  Oldies But Goodies-#11 .... (OSR)
  Super Oldies/'50s-#5 .... (AUF)
Johnny Rivers; *Anthology-1964-1977* .... (RHI)
  Very Best Of .... (EMI)
Melissa
Allman Brothers Band; *An Evening With-First Set* . (EPI)
  Best Of .... (POL)
  Decade Of Hits-1969-1979 .... (POL)
  Eat A Peach .... (POL)
Memphis (Marie)
Chuck Berry; *Chess Box* .... (CSS)
  Chuck Berry .... (AUF)
  Golden Hits .... (MER)
  Greatest Hits .... (EVR)
  St. Louis To Liverpool .... (CSS)
  ST/Hail! Hail! Rock 'N' Roll .... (MCA)
  Toronto Rock 'N' Roll Revival-#2 .... (ACC)
Joe Jackson; *ST/Mike's Murder* .... (A&M)
John Cale; *IRS Greatest Hits-#2 & 3* .... (IRS)
Johnny Rivers; *Anthology-1964-1977* .... (RHI)
  Best Of .... (EMI)
Lonnie Mack; *Teen Beat-Instrumental
Rock-1957-1965* .... (CAP)
Michelle
Beatles; *1962-1966* .... (CAP)
  Love Songs .... (CAP)
  Rubber Soul .... (CAP)
Midnight Mary
Joey Powers; *Dick Bartley's One-Hit
Wonders/'60s-#1* .... (RHI)
Miniskirt Minnie
Wilson Pickett; *45* .... (OOP)
Minnie The Moocher
Cab Calloway; *Best Of The Big Bands* .... (COL)
  Cab Calloway .... (GLN)
  Dr. Demento's Greatest Novelty-#1 .... (RHI)
  Jazz Heritage: Mr. Hi-De-Ho .... (MCA)
  ST/Blues Brothers .... (ATL)
Mona
Bo Diddley; *Legends Of Rock Guitar-'50s-#1* .... (RHI)
  Vintage Music-Orig. Oldies-'50s/'60s-#6 .... (MCA)
James Taylor; *That's Why I'm Here* .... (COL)
Original Cast; *Pump Boys & Dinettes On
Broadway* .... (COL)
Quicksilver Messenger Service; *Anthology* .... (CAP)
  Happy Trails .... (CAP)
  Sons Of Mercury .... (RHI)
Rolling Stones; *Now* .... (AKO)
Wall Of Voodoo; *Seven Days In Sammystown* .... (IRS)
Monie In The Middle
Monie Love; *Down To Earth* .... (WB)
Mony Mony
Billy Idol; *Don't Stop* .... (CHR)
  Vital Idol .... (CHR)
  Whiplash Smile .... (CHR)
Tommy James/Shondells; *Anthology* .... (RHI)
  Billboard Top Rock 'N' Roll Hits-1968 .... (RHI)
  Frat Rock-#4 .... (RHI)
Mother Mary
Julian Lennon; *Mr. Jordan* .... (ATL)
Sheila E.; *Sex Cymbal* .... (WB)
UFO; *Force It* .... (CHR)
  Strangers In The Night .... (CHR)
My Irish Molly-O
De Danann; *Best Of* .... (SHA)
My Maria
B.W. Stevenson; *Nipper's Greatest Hits-'70s* ...... (RCA)
  Super Hits/'70s-Have A Nice Day-#11 .... (RHI)
Oh Mary Don't You Weep
Pete Seeger; *Live At Newport* .... (VAN)

Proud Mary
Creedence Clearwater Revival; *1968-1969* ...... (FAN)
  Bayou Country .... (FAN)
  Chronicle .... (FAN)
  Gold .... (FAN)
  Live In Europe .... (FAN)
George Jones & Johnny Paycheck; *My Very Special*
  Guests .... (EPI)
Ike & Tina Turner; *Best Of* .... (EMI)
  EMI Legends Of Rock 'N' Roll-24 Greatest ..... (RHI)
  Greatest Hits .... (CCB)
  Soul Hits/'70s-#4 .... (RHI)
Riding With Mary
X; *Live At The Whisky A Go-Go* .... (ELE)
  Under The Big Black Sun .... (ELE)
San Francisco Mabel Joy
Joan Baez; *Country Music Album* .... (VAN)
John Denver; *Some Days Are Diamonds* ....(RCA)
Kenny Rogers; *The Gambler* .... (EMI)
Mickey Newbury; *Bread & Roses Festival-Acoustic*
  Music-#1 .... (FAN)
  Heaven Help The Child .... (ELE)
  Live At Montezuma Hall .... (ELE)
Searching For Madge
Fleetwood Mac; *Then Play On* .... (RPR)
Skinny Minnie
Bill Haley/Comets; *Golden Hits* .... (MCA)
  Greatest Hits .... (MCA)
Suddenly Mary
Posies; *Dear 23* .... (DGC)
Superwoman (Mary)
Stevie Wonder; *Music Of My Mind* .... (MOT)
  Original Musiquarium .... (MOT)
Sweet Lady Mary
Rod Stewart/Faces; *Storyteller-Complete*
  Anthology-1964-1990 .... (WB)
Sweet Little Missy
Lynyrd Skynyrd; *Legend* .... (MCA)
Sweet Mary
Wadsworth Mansion; *Super Hits/'70s-Have A Nice*
  Day-#4 .... (RHI)
Sweet Maxine
Doobie Brothers; *Stampede* .... (WB)
Take A Letter Maria
R.B. Greaves; *Soul Hits/'70s-#1* .... (RHI)
Take A Message To Mary
Bob Dylan; *Self-Portrait* ....(COL)
Rockpile; *Seconds Of Pleasure* ....(COL)
They Call The Wind Maria
Kingston Trio; *Early American Heroes* .... (PRR)
  Kingston Trio/From The Hungry i .... (CAP)
  Stereo Concert Plus .... (FOL)
Original Broadway Cast; *Paint Your Wagon* .....(RCA)
Til Melinda Comes Around
Gene Watson; *Old Loves Never Die* .... (MCA)
To M.G. (Wherever She May Be)
John Mellencamp; *Nothin' Matters & What If It*
  Did ....(RIV)
Waltzing Matilda
Burl Ives; *Best Of* .... (MCA)
Fred Astaire; *Three Evenings With* .... (DRG)
James Galway; *Pachebel Canon & Other*
  Favorites ....(RCA)
What Will My Mary Say
Jay/Americans; *Come A Little Bit Closer-Best Of* . (EMI)
Johnny Mathis; *16 Most Requested Songs* ....(COL)
  All-Time Greatest Hits ....(COL)
Who Put The Benzedrine In Mrs....
Harry Gibson;
  Dr. Demento's Delights .... (WB)
Who Threw The Overalls In Mrs....
Bing Crosby; *Shillelaghs & Shamrocks* .... (MCA)
Wind Cries Mary
Jimi Hendrix; *Essential-#2* .... (RPR)
  Smash Hits .... (RPR)
Jimi Hendrix Experience; *Are You Experienced?* . (RPR)

WOMEN'S NAMES: N

99
Toto; *Hydra* ....(COL)

Candle In The Wind (Norma Jean)
Elton John; *Goodbye Yellow Brick Road* .... (POL)
  Live In Australia w/Melbourne Symphony ...... (POL)
  Your Songs .... (POL)
Lullaby For Nancy Carol
Chuck Mangione; *Best Of* .... (MER)
  Land Of Make Believe .... (MER)
  Together .... (MER)
Nancy Whiskey
Ian & Sylvia; *Greatest Hits* .... (VAN)
  Ian & Sylvia .... (VAN)
Irish Rovers; *Greatest Hits* .... (MCA)
Nancy (With The Laughing Face)
Frank Sinatra; *Sinatra's Reprise-Very Good Years* (RPR)
  Sinatra's Sinatra .... (RPR)
John Coltrane; *Gentle Side Of* ....(GRP)
Tony Bennett; *Perfectly Frank* ....(COL)
Nikita
Elton John; *Greatest Hits-1976-1986* .... (MCA)
  Ice On Fire .... (MCA)
Norma Jean Riley
Diamond Rio; *Diamond Rio* .... (ARI)
Wait Till The Sun Shines Nellie
Joan Morris & William Bolcom; *After The Ball* . (NON)

WOMEN'S NAMES: O

Ophelia
Band; *Best Of* ....(CAP)
  Last Waltz .... (WB)
  Northern Lights Southern Cross ....(CAP)
  To Kingdom Come-Definitive Collection ....(CAP)
Jesse Colin Young; *Best Of-Solo Years* .... (RHI)

WOMEN'S NAMES: P

Cool Pearl
Capitols; *Golden Classics* .... (CLT)
Dear Prudence
Beatles; *White Album* ....(CAP)
Siouxsie/Banshees; *Hyaena* ....(GEF)
  Nocturne ....(GEF)
Hey Paula
Paul & Paula; *Cruisin'-1963* .... (INC)
  ST/Animal House .... (MCA)
  WCBS FM101-History Of Rock/'60s-#1 ....(CLT)
My Name Is Petula
Petula Clark; *Petula Clark* .... (CRS)
Patricia
Perez Prado/Orchestra; *Nipper's Greatest*
  Hits-'50s-#2 ....(RCA)
Patty On The Turnpike
Don Stover; *Things In Life* .... (ROU)
Peg
Steely Dan; *Aja* .... (MCA)
  Decade Of .... (MCA)
  Greatest Hits .... (MCA)
Peggy Day
Bob Dylan; *Nashville Skyline* ....(COL)
Peggy Sue
Buddy Holly; *20 Golden Greats* .... (MCA)
  Billboard Top Rock 'N' Roll Hits-1957 .... (RHI)
  Buddy Holly .... (MCA)
  More American Graffiti .... (MCA)
  Oldies But Goodies-#4 .... (OSR)
  Rock & Roll Collection .... (MCA)
Peggy Sue Got Married
Buddy Holly; *20 Golden Greats* .... (MCA)
  Rock & Roll Collection .... (MCA)
Peggy Suicide Is Missing
Julian Cope; *Jehovahkill* .... (ISL)
Peggy's Kitchen Wall
Bruce Cockburn; *Stealing Fire* ....(COL)
Penny Lover
Lionel Richie; *Back To Front* .... (MOT)
  Can't Slow Down .... (MOT)
Polythene Pam
Beatles; *Abbey Road* ....(CAP)
  Box Set ....(CAP)

Sweet Pea
Tommy Roe; *Best Of* ....(CCB)
   Cruisin'-1966 ....(INC)
   Greatest Hits .... (MCA)
Sweet Peggy O'Neill
John McCormack; *Drop Of The Irish* ....(PF)
Swee' Pea
Count Basie; *Best Of* .... (PAB)

WOMEN'S NAMES: R

See Also: ROSES

Baby Ruth
John Prine; *Storm Windows* ....(ASY)
Big City Miss Ruth Ann
Gallery; *Super Hits!'70s-Have A Nice Day-#11* ... (RHI)
Company Time (Ruthie)
Linda Davis; *Shoot For The Moon* ....(ARI)
Cracklin' Rosie
Neil Diamond; *His 12 Greatest Hits* ....(MCA)
   Hot August Night ....(MCA)
   Hot August Night II ....(COL)
   Tap Root Manuscript ....(MCA)
Help Me Rhonda
Beach Boys; *Billboard Top Rock 'N' Roll Hits-1965* .... (RHI)
   California Girls ....(CAP)
   Dance Dance Dance ....(CAP)
   Endless Summer ....(CAP)
   Made In The U.S.A. ....(CAP)
It's The Truth Ruth
Big Bopper; *Hellooo Baby!-Best Of-1954-1959* .. (RHI)
Little Rachel
Eric Clapton; *One In Every Crowd* ....(RSO)
Li'l Red Riding Hood
Sam The Sham/Pharaohs; *Best Of* ....(POL)
   Cruisin'-1966 ....(INC)
   Pharaohization-Best Of ....(RHI)
Lovely Rita
Beatles; *Sgt. Pepper's Lonely Hearts Club Band* ..(CAP)
Mrs. Robinson
Simon & Garfunkel; *Bookends* ....(COL)
   Collected Works ....(COL)
   Concert In Central Park ....(WB)
   Greatest Hits ....(COL)
   Hollywood Magic-1960s ....(COL)
   ST/Forrest Gump ....(EPX)
   ST/The Graduate ....(COL)
My Brown Eyed Texas Rose
Tex Ritter; *Arizona Days* ....(MSP)
   Country Music Hall Of Fame .... (MCA)
One More Time Around Rosie
Manhattan Transfer; *Jukin'* ....(CAP)
Rachel
Al Martino; *Capitol Collectors Series* ....(CAP)
Jolly Boys; *Sunshine 'N' Water* ....(RYK)
Rachel's Dream
Benny Goodman; *I Like Jazz-Essence Of* ....(COL)
   Yale Recordings-#5 ....(MM)
Ramble On Rose
Grateful Dead; *Europe '72* ....(WB)
   What A Long Strange Trip It's Been ....(WB)
Ramblin' Rose
Chuck Berry; *Greatest Hits* ....(EVR)
Hank Snow; *Collector's Series-#2* ....(RCA)
Jerry Lee Lewis; *Golden Cream Of The Country* .(SUN)
Nat King Cole; *Best Of-#1* ....(CAP)
   Memories Are Made Of This ....(CAP)
   Ramblin' Rose ....(CAP)
Ramona
Ramones; *All The Stuff & More-#2* .... (SIR)
   Rocket To Russia .... (SIR)
Ramona From Daytona
Dave Holladay; *Ramona From Daytona* ....(SO)
Rhiannon
Fleetwood Mac; *25 Years-The Chain* ....(WB)
   Fleetwood Mac ....(RPR)
   Greatest Hits ....(WB)
   Live ....(WB)
Waylon Jennings; *Best Of* ....(RCA)

Rikki Don't Lose That Number
Steely Dan; *Classic Rock-#2* .... (MCA)
   Decade Of ....(MCA)
   Greatest Hits ....(MCA)
   Pretzel Logic ....(MCA)
Rock & Roll Ruby
Warren Smith; *Memphis Country* ....(SUN)
   Original Memphis Rock & Roll-#1 ....(SUN)
Rocky
Austin Roberts; *Super Hits/'70s-Have A Nice Day-#15* .... (RHI)
Roni
Bobby Brown; *Dance!...Ya Know It!* .... (MCA)
   Don't Be Cruel ....(MCA)
Ronnie
Frankie Valli/Four Seasons; *25th Anniversary Collection* .... (RHI)
   Anthology ....(RHI)
   Greatest Hits-#1 ....(RHI)
Rosa De San Antonio
Santiago Jimenez, Jr.; *Mero Mero De San Antonio* .... (ARH)
Rosalinda's Eyes
Billy Joel; *52nd Street* ....(COL)
Rosalita
Bruce Springsteen; *Wild The Innocent & The E Street Shuffle* ....(COL)
Bruce Springsteen/E Street Band; *Live-1975-1985* ....(COL)
Rosanna
Toto; *IV* ....(COL)
   Past To Present 1977-1990 ....(COL)
   '80s Greatest Rock Hits-#1 ....(PRY)
Rose Goes To Yale
Jefferson Starship; *Nuclear Furniture* .... (GRU)
Rose Of Old Monterey
Happy Polkateers; *Happy Polkateers* ....(CRS)
Rose Of San Antone
Bashful Brother Oswald; *Don't Say Aloha* ...... (ROU)
Rosemary
Grateful Dead; *Aoxomoxoa* ....(WB)
   Skeletons From The Closet-Best Of ....(WB)
Lenny Kravitz; *Let Love Rule* ....(VIA)
Rosey From Jersey
Li'l Wally; *I Love To Polka* ....(JJ)
Rose, Rose I Love You
Frankie Laine; *Greatest Hits* ....(COL)
Rose, The
Bette Midler; *Hit Singles 1980-1988* .... (ATL)
   ST/Rose, The .... (ATL)
Conway Twitty; *Dream Maker* .... (ELE)
   Latest Greatest Hits-#1 ....(WB)
   Number One's-Warner Bros. Years ....(WB)
Rose's Turn
Original Cast; *Gypsy* ....(COL)
Original London Cast; *Gypsy* ....(RCA)
Rosie
Beat Farmers; *Pursuit Of Happiness* .... (MCA)
Dick Van Dyke; *ST/Bye Bye Birdie* ....(RCA)
Jackson Browne; *Runnin' On Empty* ....(ASY)
Joan Armatrading; *Classics-#21* ....(A&M)
   Track Record ....(A&M)
Johnny/Distractions; *My Desire* ....(BRN)
Original Cast; *Bye Bye Birdie* ....(COL)
Richie Sambora; *Stranger In This Town* .... (MER)
Rosie Strikes Back
Eliza Gilkyson; *Texas-A Musical Celebration-150 Years* .... (TOM)
Rosanne Cash; *King's Record Shop* ....(COL)
Roxanne
Police; *Every Breath You Take-Singles* ....(A&M)
   Outlandos D'Amour ....(A&M)
Sting; *Secret Policeman's Other Ball* .... (ISL)
Ruby Ann
Marty Robbins; *American Originals* ....(COL)
   Billboard Top Country Hits-1963 ....(RHI)
   Essential-1951-1982 ....(COL)
Ruby Baby
Beatles; *In The Beginning* ....(POL)
Dion; *24 Original Classics* .... (ARI)
   Bronx Blues-Columbia Recordings-1962-65 ....(COL)
Donald Fagen; *The Nightfly* ....(WB)

Drifters; *Atlantic R&B*
1947-1974-#3-(1955-1958) .... (ATL)
  Let The Boogie Woogie Roll-Greatest Hits .... (ATL)
  Their Greatest Recordings-Early Years .... (ATC)
Ruby Don't Take Your Love To Town
Kenny Rogers; *20 Great Years* .... (RPR)
  Ten Years Of Gold .... (EMI)
  Twenty Greatest Hits .... (EMI)
Kenny Rogers/First Edition; *Greatest Hits* .... (KT)
  Hits & Pieces .... (MCA)
Mel Tillis/Statesiders; *24 Great Hits* ....(MGM)
  Best Of .... (MCA)
  M-M-Mel Live .... (MCA)
Ruby Tuesday
Rolling Stones; *Between The Buttons* .... (AKO)
  Flashpoint ....(RS)
  Flowers .... (AKO)
  Hot Rocks-1964-1971 .... (AKO)
  Singles Collection-London Years .... (AKO)
  Through The Past Darkly-Big Hits-#2 .... (AKO)
Ruby's Golden Wedding
Danny Wilson; *Meet Danny Wilson* .... (VIA)
San Antonio Rose
Asleep At The Wheel; *Western Standard Time* .... (EPI)
Bob Wills; *Best Of-#2* ....(MCA)
  Sounds Of Texas .... (CAP)
  Texas State Of Mind .... (LIB)
Floyd Cramer; *Billboard Top Country Hits-1961* . (RHI)
  Country Love ....(SO)
Patsy Cline; *Story* ....(MCA)
Ricky Skaggs; *Comin' Home To Stay* ....(EPI)
Willie Nelson; *San Antonio Rose* ....(COL)
Second Hand Rose
Barbra Streisand; *Greatest Hits* ....(COL)
  Happening In Central Park ....(COL)
  Just For The Record ....(COL)
  My Name Is Barbra Two ....(COL)
  & Other Musical Instruments ....(COL)
See Ruby Fall
Johnny Cash; *Essential* ....(COL)
Set Me Free (Rosa Lee)
Los Lobos; *By The Light Of The Moon* ....(SLS)
Sweet Milwaukee Rose
Andy Badale/Beer Garden Band; *Nashville Beer*
Garden .... (RAN)
Sweet Rosemary
Sandy Denny; *Who Knows Where The Time Goes?* (HBL)
Take Him Back, Rachel
Basia; *London Warsaw New York* .... (EPI)
To Ramona
Bob Dylan; *Another Side Of* ....(COL)
  Biograph ....(COL)
Flying Burrito Brothers; *Flying Burrito Brothers* . (MOB)
Texas Tornados; *Hangin' On By A Thread* .... (RPR)
Tokyo Rose
Shok Paris; *Steel & Starlight* ....(IRS)
Van Dyke Parks; *Tokyo Rose* ....(WB)
Walk Away Renee
Four Tops; *Anthology* ....(MOT)
  Compact Command Performances .... (MOT)
  Reach Out .... (MOT)
Left Banke; *Cruisin'-1966* ....(INC)
  History Of ....(RHI)

WOMEN'S NAMES: S

Dead Flowers (Susie)
Rolling Stones; *Sticky Fingers* .... (RS)
Steve Earle/Dukes; *Shut Up & Die Like An*
Aviator .... (MCA)
Eggs & Sausage (In A Cadillac...)(Susan)
Tom Waits; *Nighthawks At The Diner* .... (ASY)
Fourth Of July, Asbury Park (Sandy)
Bruce Springsteen; *Wild The Innocent & The E Street*
Shuffle ....(COL)
Bruce Springsteen/E Street Band;
Live-1975-1985 ....(COL)
Hang On Sloopy
McCoys; *21 Oldies But Goodies* .... (OSR)
  Billboard Top Rock 'N' Roll Hits-1965 .... (RHI)
  Frat Rock! .... (RHI)
  Oldies But Goodies-#14 .... (OSR)

Ramsey Lewis; *Greatest Hits Of* .... (CSS)
  Vintage Music-Cl. Oldies/'50s-'60s-#20 .... (MCA)
If You Knew Susie (Like I Know Susie)
Eddie Cantor; *Memories* .... (MCA)
Las Vegas Turnaround (Sarah)
Daryl Hall & John Oates; *Abandoned*
Luncheonette ....(ATL)
  No Goodbyes ....(ATL)
"Laverne & Shirley" Theme
Original Music; *Television's Greatest Hits-#3* .....(TVT)
Lay Down Sally
Eric Clapton; *Crossroads* .... (POL)
  Just One Night .... (RSO)
  Slow Hand .... (RSO)
  Time Pieces-Best Of .... (RSO)
Little Sadie
Bob Dylan; *Self-Portrait* ....(COL)
Little Sally Tease
Standells; *Best Of* .... (RHI)
Little Sally, The Super Sex Star
Camille Yarborough; *Iron Pot Cooker* .... (VAN)
Long Tall Sally
Beatles; *At The Hollywood Bowl* ....(CAP)
  Past Masters-#1 ....(CAP)
  Rock 'N' Roll Music-#1 ....(CAP)
  Second Album ....(CAP)
Little Richard; *18 Greatest Hits* .... (RHI)
  Billboard Top R&B Hits-1956 .... (RHI)
  Greatest Hits .... (EVR)
  Here's Little Richard .... (SPE)
  Oldies But Goodies-#3 .... (OSR)
  ST/Heaven Help Us .... (EMI)
  Super Oldies/'50s-#3 ....(AUF)
  Tutti Frutti .... (ACC)
Looking For Suzanne
Waylon Jennings; *Greatest Hits-#2* ....(RCA)
Me & Sarah Jane
Genesis; *Abacab* .... (ATL)
  Three Sides Live .... (ATL)
Miss Sun
Boz Scaggs; *Hits* ....(COL)
Toto; *Toto* ....(COL)
Mustang Sally
Rascals; *Greatest Hits* .... (ATL)
Wilson Pickett; *Atlantic R&B-1947-1974-#6* ....(ATL)
  Best Of .... (ATL)
  Greatest Hits .... (ATL)
  Man & A Half-Best Of .... (RHI)
  Super Hits .... (ATL)
Young Rascals; *Young Rascals* .... (RHI)
My Name Is Not Susan
Whitney Houston; *I'm Your Baby Tonight* .... (ARI)
My Sharona
Knack; *Billboard Top Hits-1979* .... (RHI)
  Get The Knack ....(CAP)
  Rock Of The '80s .... (PRY)
Oh, Sheila
Ready For The World; *Ready For The World* ... (MCA)
Oh, Sherrie
Steve Perry; *MTV's Rock 'N' Roll To Go* .... (ELE)
  Street Talk ....(COL)
Oh, Susanna
James Taylor; *Sweet Baby James* ....(WB)
Myron Floren; *Best Of The Wurstfest* .... (RAN)
  Myron Floren ....(RAN)
Oklahoma Sweetheart Sally
Maddox Brothers; *America's Most Colorful Hillbilly*
Band .... (ARH)
Please Don't Squeeze My Sharmon
Charlie Walker; *Country Music Classics-#10-Late*
'60s .... (KT)
  Golden Hits .... (PLN)
Rock 'N' Roll Susie
Pat Travers; *Makin' Music* .... (POL)
Runaround Sue
Dion; *Billboard Top Rock 'N' Roll Hits-1961* ..... (RHI)
  Everything You Always Wanted To Hear ....(LAU)
  Million-Dollar Memories #1 ....(RCA)
  Oldies But Goodies-#7 .... (OSR)
  ST/Flamingo Kid .... (MOT)
  ST/Wanderers ....(WB)
Sadie
Spinners; *Best Of* ....(ATL)
  One Of A Kind Love Affair-Anthology ....(ATL)

Sadie Was A Lady
Johnny Bond; *How I Love Them Old Songs* ...... (L&L)
Sadie, Sadie
Barbra Streisand; *ST/Funny Girl* .... (COL)
Sally
Stetsasonic; *Rapmasters 1-Best Of The Jam* ...... (PRY)
Sally Ann
Flatt & Scruggs; *20 All-Time Great Recordings* ...(COL)
Sally Ann 28th Of January
Fuzzy Mountain String Band; *Fuzzy Mountain String Band* .... (ROU)
Sally Can't Dance
Lou Reed; *Sally Can't Dance* .... (RCA)
Walk On The Wild Side & Other Hits .... (RCA)
Walk On The Wild Side-Best Of .... (RCA)
Sally Go Round The Roses
Jaynettes; *Best Of Chess Rock 'N' Roll* .... (CSS)
Cruisin'-1963 .... (INC)
Girl Groups .... (RHI)
Wonder Women .... (RHI)
Yvonne Elliman; *Night Flight* .... (RSO)
Sally Goodin
Bob Wills/Texas Playboys; *Tiffany Transcriptions-#6-Sally Goodin* .... (KAL)
Doc Watson; *Out In The Country* .... (INT)
Hot Rize; *In Concert* .... (FF)
John Hickman; *Don't Mean Maybe* .... (ROU)
Sally Johnson
Mark O'Connor; *Championship Years* ...... (CMF)
Mark O'Connor .... (ROU)
Sally (That Girl)
Gucci Crew II; *Super Bass-20 Boomin' All-Time Bass Hits* .... (REC)
Sally's Got A Friend In New York City
Larry McCray; *Ambition* .... (CHS)
Samantha
Count Basie/Orchestra; *Fancy Pants* .... (PAB)
Sandy
Dion; *His Best* .... (LAU)
Legends .... (LAU)
Dion/Belmonts; *20 Golden Classics* .... (CLT)
Larry Hall; *45* .... (CLT)
Sara
Bob Dylan; *Desire* .... (COL)
Fleetwood Mac; *25 Years-The Chain* .... (WB)
Greatest Hits .... (WB)
Live .... (WB)
Tusk .... (WB)
Starship; *Greatest Hits-Ten Years & Change-1979-91* .... (RCA)
Knee Deep In The Hoopla .... (GRU)
Sara Smile
Daryl Hall & John Oates; *Daryl Hall & John Oates* .... (RCA)
Livetime .... (RCA)
Rock 'N' Soul-Part 1-Greatest Hits .... (RCA)
Soulful Sounds .... (RCA)
Sarafina
Original Broadway Cast; *Sarafina! (The Music Of Liberation)* .... (RCA)
Sarah Cynthia Sylvia Stout
Shel Silverstein; *Dr. Demento 20th Anniversary Collection* .... (RHI)
Dr. Demento's Greatest Novelty-#4-1970s ...... (RHI)
Where The Sidewalk Ends .... (COL)
Sarah Jane
Bob Dylan; *Dylan* .... (COL)
Sarah, Sarah
Jonathan Butler; *45* .... (JVA)
Saro Jane
Country Gazette; *Hello Operator-This Is* .... (FF)
Kingston Trio; *From The Hungry i* .... (CAP)
Radio Flyer; *Old Strings New Strings* ..... (TUR)
Red Clay Ramblers; *Rambler* .... (SH)
Sassy Mae
Memphis Slim; *Legacy Of The Blues-#7* ...... (CRS)
Memphis Slim/House Rockers; *U.S.A.* .... (PEA)
Satisfy Suzie
Lonnie Mack; *Attack Of The Killer V* ...... (ALG)
Strike Like Lightning .... (ALG)
Scarlet Fever
Kenny Rogers; *We've Got Tonight* .... (EMI)

Sexy Sadie
Beatles; *Box Set* .... (CAP)
White Album .... (CAP)
Sheena Is A Punk Rocker
Ramones; *Leave Home* .... (SIR)
Loco Live .... (SIR)
Mania .... (SIR)
Rocket To Russia .... (SIR)
Sheila
Tommy Roe; *Billboard Top Rock 'N' Roll Hits-1962* .... (RHI)
Golden Years-1962 .... (DOM)
Greatest Hits .... (MCA)
Original Rock 'N' Roll Hits Of The '60s ...... (RLL)
Sheila .... (ACC)
Sherry
Bobby Caldwell; *August Moon* .... (SD)
Frankie Valli/Four Seasons; *Anthology* ...... (RHI)
Greatest Hits-#1 .... (RHI)
ST/The Wanderers .... (WB)
Sherry Darling
Bruce Springsteen; *The River* .... (COL)
Shirley
L7; *Hungry For Stink* .... (SLS)
Shirley Jean
Foghat; *Rock & Roll Outlaws* .... (RHI)
Shirley Lee
Rick Nelson; *Legendary Masters* .... (EMI)
Silicone Sally
Slammin' Gladys; *Slammin' Gladys* .... (PRY)
Silky Sam
Spirit; *Time Circle* .... (EPI)
Sioux City Sue
Bob Wills/Texas Playboys; *Tiffany Transcriptions-#8* .... (KAL)
Gene Autry; *Country Music Hall Of Fame* ...... (COL)
Jimmy C. Newman; *Cajun Cowboy* .... (PLN)
Mom & Dads; *In The Good Old Summertime* .... (CRS)
Willie Nelson & Leon Russell; *One For The Road* .... (COL)
Sneakin' Sally Through The Alley
Robert Palmer; *Addictions-#2* .... (ISL)
Sneakin' Sally Through The Alley .... (ISL)
Song For Sharon
Joni Mitchell; *Hejira* .... (ASY)
Spooky
Atlanta Rhythm Section; *Underdog* .... (COL)
Classics IV; *Good Vibrations* .... (CAP)
Spooky .... (LIB)
Spring Break-#1-Hot Rods & Hot Bods ...... (CAP)
Very Best Of .... (EMI)
Stella By Starlight
Bill Evans; *Jazzhouse* .... (MS)
Frank Sinatra; *Rarities-Columbia Years* ...... (COL)
George Benson; *Tenderly* .... (WB)
Joe Pass; *Virtuoso* .... (PAB)
Keith Jarrett; *Standards Live* .... (ECM)
Miles Davis; *Cookin' At The Plugged Nickel* ...... (COL)
Red Garland; *Red Alert* .... (GAL)
Stan Getz; *Plays* .... (VRV)
Tony Bennett; *Jazz* .... (COL)
Stormy
Classics IV; *Back To The '60s-#4* .... (DOM)
Spring Break-#2-Cold Kegs & Tan Legs .... (CAP)
Very Best Of .... (EMI)
Santana; *Inner Secrets* .... (COL)
Sue's Gotta Be Mine
Del Shannon; *Legends* .... (LAU)
Runaway .... (PRR)
Runaway Hits! .... (RHI)
Sunny
Bobby Hebb; *Billboard Top R&B Hits-1965-1969* (RHI)
Oldies But Goodies-#11 .... (OSR)
Classics IV; *Very Best Of* .... (EMI)
Electric Flag; *Long Time Comin'* .... (COL)
Stevie Wonder; *For Once In My Life* .... (MOT)
Susan
Buckinghams; *Greatest Hits* .... (COL)
Rock Artifacts-#3-From The Vaults .... (COL)
Statler Brothers; *Best Of* .... (MER)
Susannah
Lionel Cartwright; *Chasin' The Sun* ...... (MCA)
Susannah's Still Alive
Kinks; *Kink Kronikles* .... (RPR)

Susie
John Lee Hooker; *Mr. Lucky* ....(POI)
Susie Cincinnati
Beach Boys; *15 Big Ones* .... (RPR)
Susie Darlin'
Robin Luke; *Great Records Of The Decade-'50s-Pop-#1* ....(CCB)
More '50s Jukebox Favorites .... (KT)
Susie Q
Creedence Clearwater Revival; *1968-1969* ...... (FAN)
Chooglin' ....(FAN)
Chronicle ....(FAN)
Creedence Clearwater Revival ....(FAN)
Gold ....(FAN)
Live In Europe ....(FAN)
Dale Dawkins; *Collectables Presents History Of Rock-#3* ....(CLT)
Legends Of Rock Guitar-'50s-#1 .... (RHI)
Rockin' Rebels .... (KT)
Jose Feliciano; *All-Time Greatest Hits* ....(RCA)
Susy Is A Headbanger
Ramones; *All The Stuff & More-#1* .... (SIR)
Leave Home ....(SIR)
Suzanne
Journey; *Raised On Radio* ....(COL)
Judy Collins; *In My Life* ....(ELE)
Leonard Cohen; *Best Of* ....(COL)
Neil Diamond; *Love Songs* .... (MCA)
Stones .... (MCA)
Pearls Before Swine; *Best Of* .... (ADE)
Randy Newman; *12 Songs* ....(RPR)
Suzie-You Are
Maxi Priest; *Maxi Priest* .... (VIA)
Suzy Suicide
Spread Eagle; *Spread Eagle* .... (MCA)
Sweet Savannah Sue
Fats Waller; *Turn On The Heat-Fats Waller Piano Solos* ....(BLU)
Louis Armstrong; *#5-In New York* ....(COL)
Sweet Sue (Just You)
Benny Goodman; *Early Years* ....(BIO)
Big Joe Turner; *Rhythm & Blues Years* ....(ATL)
Bing Crosby; *Crooner-Columbia Years-1928-1934* ....(COL)
Leon Redbone; *Champagne Charlie* .... (WB)
Mom & Dads; *Goodnight Sweetheart* ....(CRS)
Sweet Suzanne
Mark O'Connor; *New Nashville Cats* .... (WB)
Sweet Suzie
Johnny Burnette; *Best Of-You're Sixteen* .... (EMI)
Switchboard Susan
Nick Lowe; *Basher-Best Of* ....(COL)
Labour Of Lust ....(COL)
Sylvia
Bo Deans; *Home* ....(SLS)
Elvis Presley; *Elvis Now* ....(RCA)
Eurythmics; *We Too Are One* .... (ARI)
Stevie Wonder; *Down To Earth* .... (MOT)
Sylvia's Mother
Dr. Hook; *Dr. Hook & The Medicine Show Revisited* ....(COL)
Greatest Hits & More ....(CAP)
Super Hits/'70s-Have A Nice Day-#8 .... (RHI)
Sylvie
Leadbelly & Anne Graham; *Folkways-Original Vision* .... (FLW)
Matthews' Southern Comfort; *Best Of* .... (MCA)
Weavers; *Best Of* .... (MCA)
Tequila Sheila
Bobby Bare; *Biggest Hits* ....(COL)
Encore ....(COL)
Mac Davis; *It's Hard To Be Humble* .... (CAS)
That's My Little Suzie
Ritchie Valens; *Best Of* .... (RHI)
Tra La La La Suzy
Dean & Jean; *22 Leaders Of The Pack-#1* .... (LAU)
Classic Old & Gold .... (LAU)
Wake Up Susan
Spinners; *Happiness Is Being With* .... (ATL)
One Of A Kind Love Affair-Anthology .... (ATL)

Wake Up, Little Susie
Everly Brothers; *All They Had To Do Was Dream* (RHI)
All-Time Greatest Hits ....(CCB)
American Graffiti-#3 .... (MCA)
Everly Brothers .... (RHI)
Oldies But Goodies-#7 ....(OSR)
Very Best Of .... (WB)
Grateful Dead; *History Of-#1-Bear's Choice* ..... (WB)
Simon & Garfunkel; *Concert In Central Park* .....(WB)
When Sunny Gets Blue
Barbra Streisand; *Simply Streisand* ....(COL)
Johnny Mathis; *All-Time Greatest Hits* ....(COL)
First 25 Years-Silver Anniversary Album ....(COL)
Greatest Hits ....(COL)
Love Songs ....(COL)
Kenny Rankin; *Album* ....(LD)
Steve Miller; *Born 2 B Blue* ....(CAP)
Where's The Playground Susie
Glen Campbell; *Best Of* .... (LIB)

WOMEN'S NAMES: T

Big Tulsa Tillie
Donnie Rohrs; *Country Music USA* .... (PC)
Letter From Tina
Ike & Tina Turner; *Best Of* .... (EMI)
Golden Classics ....(CLT)
Me & A Gun
Tori Amos; *Little Earthquakes* .... (ATL)
Sad Theresa
Warrant; *Dog Eat Dog* ....(COL)
Tammy
Columbia Ballroom Orchestra; *Let's Dance-#7* .. (DEN)
Debbie Reynolds; *Best Of* ....(CCB)
Tammy ....(MSP)
Roger Williams; *Greatest Hits* .... (MCA)
Tanya
Rockin' Dopsie/Cajun Twisters; *Hold On* .... (CRS)
Teresa
J. Geils Band; *Anthology-Houseparty* .... (RHI)
Tina
Frank Sinatra; *Reprise Collection* ....(RPR)
Weavers; *Classics* .... (VAN)
Toot Toot Tootsie (Goo'Bye)
Al Jolson; *Best Of* .... (MCA)
Best Of Decca Years .... (DEC)
Liza Minnelli; *At Carnegie Hall* .... (TLR)
Tracey's World
Smithereens; *Beauty & Sadness* ....(CAP)
Tracy
Cuff Links; *Super Hits/'70s-Have A Nice Day-#1* (RHI)
Tracy In The Bathroom Killing Thrills
Mary's Danish; *Circa* ....(MC)
Experience-Live + Foxey Lady .... (CML)
Trudy
Charlie Daniels Band; *Fire On The Mountain* ..... (EPI)
Trudy Sings The Blues
Trudy Lynn; *Trudy Sings The Blues* .... (ICH)
Trudy & Dave
John Hiatt; *Slow Turning* .... (A&M)

WOMEN'S NAMES: V

I'm Coming Virginia
Bix Beiderbecke; *#1-Singin' The Blues* ....(COL)
Coleman Hawkins & Benny Carter; *Coleman Hawkins & Benny Carter* ....(DSQ)
Stephane Grappelli; *Compact Jazz* .... (VRV)
Story Of Vanna White
Lawndale; *Beyond Barbecue* ....(SST)
Stuck In A Closet With Vanna White
Weird Al Yankovic; *Even Worse* .... (RAR)
Sweet Virginia
Rolling Stones; *Exile On Main Street* .... (RS)
Valerie
Bad Company; *Fame & Fortune* .... (ATL)
Marshall Crenshaw; *Good Evening* .... (WB)
Marty Balin; *Balince-Collection* .... (RHI)
Mello-Kings; *Greatest Hits* ....(CLT)
Quarterflash; *Quarterflash* ....(GEF)
Richard Thompson; *Daring Adventures* ....(POL)

Steve Winwood; *Chronicles* .... (ISL)
  Talking Back To The Night .... (ISL)
Valerie Loves Me
  Material Issue; *International Pop Overthrow* ..... (MER)
Valleri
  Monkees; *Birds Bees & The Monkees* .... (RHI)
  Missing Links .... (RHI)
  More Greatest Hits Of .... (ARI)
  Nuggets-Classic Collection From '60s .... (RHI)
Valotte
  Julian Lennon; *Valotte* .... (ATL)
Venus
  Frankie Avalon; *21 Oldies But Goodies* .... (OSR)
  Billboard Top Rock 'N' Roll Hits-1959 .... (RHI)
  Oldies But Goodies-#10 .... (OSR)
  '50s Sock Hop .... (KT)
  Shocking Blue; *Billboard Top Rock 'N' Roll
  Hits-1970* .... (RHI)
  Oldies But Goodies-#15 .... (OSR)
  Super Hits/'70s-Have A Nice Day-#1 .... (RHI)
  '70s Smash Hits-#1 .... (RHI)
Veronica
  Elvis Costello; *Spike* .... (WB)
Vicki
  Leaving Trains; *Kill Tunes* .... (SST)
Victoria
  Kinks; *Arthur Or The Decline & Fall...* .... (RPR)
  Kink Kronikles .... (RPR)
Virginia Woolf
  Indigo Girls; *Rites Of Passage* .... (EPI)

WOMEN'S NAMES: W

Wendy
  Beach Boys; *Absolute Best-#1* .... (CAP)
  All Summer Long .... (CAP)
  Best Of .... (CAP)
  Endless Summer .... (CAP)
  Gift Set .... (CAP)
Windy
  Association; *Billboard Top Rock 'N' Roll
  Hits-1967* .... (RHI)
  Greatest Hits .... (WB)
  Summer Of Love-#1 .... (RHI)
  Vintage .... (FFT)
  Wes Montgomery; *A Day In The Life* .... (A&M)
  Classics-#22 .... (A&M)
  Greatest Hits .... (A&M)
"Wonder Woman" Theme
  Original Music; *Television's Greatest Hits-#3* ..... (TVT)

WOMEN'S NAMES: Y

Ballad Of John & Yoko
  Beatles; *1967-70* .... (CAP)
  Box Set .... (CAP)
  Hey Jude .... (CAP)
  Past Masters-#2 .... (CAP)
  ST/Imagine-The Motion Picture .... (CAP)

WORK, Workingfolk

  See Also: POVERTY, WEEKEND

Addicted To A Dollar
  Doug Stone; *More Love* .... (EPI)
Against The Wind
  Bob Seger/Silver Bullet Band; *Against The Wind* . (CAP)
  Nine Tonight .... (CAP)
  ST/Forrest Gump .... (EPX)
Allentown
  Billy Joel; *Greatest Hits-#1 & 2* .... (COL)
  KOHUEPT Live In Leningrad .... (COL)
  Nylon Curtain .... (COL)
Another Day
  Paul McCartney/Wings; *All The Best* .... (CAP)
  Wings Greatest .... (CAP)
Another Day Another Dollar
  Alison Krauss & Union Station; *Every Time You Say
  Goodbye* .... (ROU)

Back On The Chain Gang
  Pretenders; *Learning To Crawl* .... (SIR)
  Singles .... (SIR)
  ST/King Of Comedy .... (WB)
Been A Long Day
  Original Cast; *How To Succeed In Business...* ...... (RCA)
Big Boss Man
  B.B. King; *Six Silver Strings* .... (MCA)
  Elvis Presley; *Elvis* .... (RCA)
  ST/Clambake .... (RCA)
  Grateful Dead; *Grateful Dead* .... (WB)
  Jimmy Reed; *Best Of* .... (CRS)
  Oldies But Goodies-#1 .... (OSR)
  John Hammond; *Best Of* .... (VAN)
  So Many Roads .... (VAN)
Blue Collar
  Bachman-Turner Overdrive; *Best Of* .... (MER)
Blue Collar Man
  Styx; *Caught In The Act* .... (A&M)
  Classics-#15 .... (A&M)
  Pieces Of Eight .... (A&M)
Bruised Orange
  John Prine; *Bruised Orange* .... (ASY)
Cadillac Assembly Line
  Albert King; *Masterworks* .... (ATL)
  Truckload Of Lovin' .... (TOM)
Cafe On The Corner
  Sawyer Brown; *Cafe On The Corner* .... (CRB)
Call My Job
  Albert King; *King Albert* .... (TOM)
  Masterworks .... (ATL)
Car Wash
  Rose Royce; *Best Of* .... (OMN)
  Billboard Top Hits-1977 .... (RHI)
  Disco Years-#1-1974-1978 .... (RHI)
  Greatest Hits .... (WHI)
Chain Gang
  Nylons; *Happy Together* .... (OPE)
  Otis Redding; *Best Of* .... (ATC)
  Story .... (ATL)
  Persuasions; *We Came To Play* .... (CAP)
  Sam Cooke; *Best Of* .... (RCA)
  Man & His Music .... (RCA)
  Nipper's Greatest Hits-'60s-#1 .... (RCA)
Clean Up Woman
  Betty Wright; *Atlantic R&B
  1947-1974-#6-(1966-1969)* .... (ATL)
  Golden Classics .... (CLT)
  Live .... (ATL)
  Soul Years .... (ATL)
Common Man
  Blasters; *Collection* .... (SLS)
  John Conlee; *Busted* .... (MCA)
  Greatest Hits .... (MCA)
Company Man
  James Taylor; *Flag* .... (COL)
Company Time
  Linda Davis; *Shoot For The Moon* .... (ARI)
Computer Took My Job
  Maurice John Vaughn; *Generic Blues Album* .....(ALG)
Could You Love A Working Man
  Stoker Brothers; *45* .... (CMS)
Darlington County
  Bruce Springsteen; *Born In The U.S.A.* ....(COL)
Did Beethoven Do The Dishes
  Reilly & Maloney; *Profiles* .... (FRK)
Dirty Business
  New Riders Of The Purple Sage; *New Riders Of The
  Purple Sage* .... (COL)
Dirty Work
  Fabulous Thunderbirds; *What's The Word* ...... (CHR)
  Rolling Stones; *Dirty Work* .... (RS)
  Steely Dan; *Can't Buy A Thrill* .... (MCA)
Do You Want My Job
  Little Village; *Little Village* .... (RPR)
Don't Give Up
  Peter Gabriel; *Shaking The Tree-16 Golden
  Greats* .... (GEF)
  So .... (GEF)
Don't Need No Job
  Lightnin' Hopkins; *Heard Recordings-#2* .... (CLT)
Drill Ye Tarriers Drill
  Weavers; *On Tour* .... (VAN)

Drinking On The Job
Rainmakers; *Rainmakers* .... (MER)
Erie Canal
Burl Ives; *Best Of* .... (MCA)
Weavers; *Classics* .... (VAN)
   Greatest Folksingers/'60s .... (VAN)
   Greatest Hits .... (VAN)
Everybody Works In China
Judy Collins; *Home Again* .... (ELE)
Fast Times
Heart; *Private Audition* .... (EPI)
Field Worker
David Crosby & Graham Nash; *Wind On The
Water* .... (MCA)
Five O'Clock World
Hal Ketchum; *Past The Point Of Rescue* .... (CRB)
Vogues; *Greatest Hits* .... (RHI)
   Greatest Hits .... (SSS)
   ST/Good Morning Vietnam .... (A&M)
Forty Hour Week (For A Livin')
Alabama; *Forty Hour Week (For A Livin')* ....(RCA)
   Greatest Hits ....(RCA)
Friends In Low Places
Garth Brooks; *No Fences* .... (LIB)
Get A Job
Sha-Na-Na; *Best Of* ....(BUD)
   Golden Age Of Rock & Roll ....(OOP)
Silhouettes; *Billboard Top Rock 'N' Roll Hits-1958* (RHI)
   ST/American Graffiti .... (MCA)
   ST/Stand By Me .... (ATL)
Go To Work On Monday
Si Kahn; *Doing My Job* .... (FF)
Gonna Go To Work On Monday One More Time
Fiction Brothers; *Things Are Coming My Way* ...... (FF)
Got A Job
Smokey Robinson/Miracles; *Anthology* .... (MOT)
   Greatest Hits-From The Beginning .... (MOT)
Government Center
Jonathan Richman/Modern Lovers; *Beserkley Years-Best
Of* .... (RHI)
   Chartbusters-Best Of Beserkley-1975-1978 ..... (RHI)
Grapes Of Wrath
Charlie Daniels Band; *Midnight Wind* .... (EPI)
Graveyard Shift
Bobby "Boris" Pickett; *Monster Mash* ....(OOP)
Sawyer Brown; *Out Goin' Cattin'* .... (CAP)
Hard Day's Night
Beatles; *1962-1966* .... (CAP)
   20 Greatest Hits .... (CAP)
   At The Hollywood Bowl .... (CAP)
   Hard Day's Night .... (CAP)
   Reel Music .... (CAP)
   ST/Hard Day's Night .... (CAP)
Hard Knock Life
Original Broadway Cast; *Annie* .... (COL)
Hard Life
Little River Band; *Backstage Pass* .... (CAP)
   First Under The Wire .... (CAP)
Roger Daltrey; *Daltrey* .... (MCA)
Hard Lovin' Woman
Mark Collie; *Unleashed* .... (MCA)
Hard Way
Mary Chapin Carpenter; *Come On Come On* ....(COL)
Hard Way, The
Clint Black; *Hard Way, The* ....(RCA)
Mary Chapin Carpenter; *Come On Come On* ....(COL)
Hard Work
John Handy; *45* .... (MCA)
Passion Fodder; *Fat Tuesday* .... (ISL)
Hard Work & No Play
Country Joe McDonald; *Leisure Suite* .... (FAN)
Hard Workin' Man
Brooks & Dunn; *Hard Workin' Man* .... (ARI)
Jack Nitzsche; *ST/Blue Collar* .... (MCA)
Harriet Tubman
Holly Near & Ronnie Gilbert; *Lifeline* .... (RWD)
   Redwood Collection .... (RWD)
Harriet Tubman's Gonna Carry Me Home
Long Ryders; *Two-Fisted Tales* .... (ISL)
Harry's House Centerpiece
Joni Mitchell; *Hissing Of Summer Lawns* .... (ASY)
He Thinks He'll Keep Her
Mary Chapin Carpenter; *Come On Come On* ....(COL)

Housewife
Leon Russell; *Americana* .... (PRD)
I Am A Simple Man
Ricky Van Shelton; *Backroads* .... (COL)
I Keep On Gettin' Paid The Same
Joe Ely; *Must Notta Gotta Lotta* .... (MCA)
I Want To Work On The Railroad
Debby McClatchy; *Someday Cafe* .... (GRE)
If I Were A Carpenter
Bobby Darin; *Live At The Desert Inn* .... (MOT)
Four Tops; *Anthology* .... (MOT)
   Compact Command Performances .... (MOT)
   Reach Out .... (MOT)
Tim Hardin; *Memorial Album* .... (POL)
It Sure Is Monday
Mark Chesnutt; *Almost Goodbye* .... (MCA)
It's My Job
Jimmy Buffett; *Coconut Telegraph* .... (MCA)
I'm In A Hurry (And Don't Know Why)
Alabama; *American Pride* ....(RCA)
I've Been Working
Bob Seger; *Live Bullet* .... (CAP)
Luther Vandross; *Never Too Much* .... (EPI)
Van Morrison; *It's Too Late To Stop Now* .... (WB)
   Van Morrison-His Band & Street Choir .... (WB)
I've Been Workin' On The Railroad
Mitch Miller; *Sing Along With Mitch* ....(COL)
Pete Seeger; *20 Golden Pieces Of* ....(BLD)
Jackson Cage
Bruce Springsteen; *The River* ....(COL)
Joe Hill
Arlo Guthrie & Pete Seeger; *Together In Concert* (RPR)
Joan Baez; *Carry It On* .... (VAN)
   From Every Stage .... (A&M)
   One Day At A Time .... (VAN)
   ST/Woodstock .... (ATL)
Soundtrack; *Carry It On* .... (VAN)
Johnny 99
Bruce Springsteen; *Nebraska* ....(COL)
Bruce Springsteen/E Street Band;
Live-1975-1985 ....(COL)
Johnny Cash; *Cover Me* .... (RHI)
Just A Job To Do
Genesis; *Genesis* .... (ATL)
Just Got Paid
ZZ Top; *Best Of* .... (WB)
   Rio Grande Mud .... (WB)
   Six Pack .... (WB)
Keep On Working
Pete Townshend; *Empty Glass* .... (ATC)
King Of The Road
Roger Miller; *Billboard Top Country Hits-1965* .. (RHI)
   Cruisin'-1965 .... (INC)
   Golden Hits .... (SMA)
R.E.M.; *Dead Letter Office* .... (IRS)
Labor Of Love
Radney Foster; *Labor Of Love* .... (ARI)
Let's Work
Mick Jagger; *Primitive Cool* .... (RS)
Prince; *Controversy* .... (WB)
Life Is A Lemon And I Want My Money Back
Meat Loaf; *Bat Out Of Hell II-Back Into Hell* ... (MCA)
Long Hard Road (Sharecropper's Dream)
Nitty Gritty Dirt Band; *Live Two Five* .... (CAP)
   Plain Dirt Fashion .... (WB)
   Tewenty Years Of Dirt-Best Of .... (WB)
Lord Have Mercy On The Working Man
Travis Tritt; *T-R-O-U-B-L-E* .... (WB)
Lunch Hour
Rupert Holmes; *Partners In Crime* .... (MCA)
Maggie's Farm
Bob Dylan; *At Budokan* ....(COL)
   Bringing It All Back Home ....(COL)
   Greatest Hits-#2 ....(COL)
   Hard Rain ....(COL)
   Real Live ....(COL)
Midnight Shift
Commander Cody/Lost Planet Airmen; *Lost In The
Ozone* .... (MCA)
Mill Worker
James Taylor; *Flag* ....(COL)
Minimum Wage
They Might Be Giants; *Flood* .... (ELE)

Monday Morning Secretary
Statler Brothers; *Statler Brothers* .... (MER)
Monday Thru' Friday
Cliff Richard; *We Don't Talk Anymore* .... (EMI)
"Moonlighting" Theme
Al Jarreau; *ST/Moonlighting* .... (MCA)
More Than A Paycheck
Sweet Honey In The Rock; *We All..Every One Of
Us* ....(FF)
Morning Train (Nine To Five)
Sheena Easton; *Sheena Easton* .... (EMI)
Mr. Businessman
Ray Stevens; *Greatest Hits* ....(RCA)
Greatest Hits-#2 .... (MCA)
Very Best Of ....(BBY)
Mr. President (Have Pity On The...)
Randy Newman; *Good Old Boys* .... (RPR)
ST/Forrest Gump ....(EPX)
National Working Woman's Holiday
Sammy Kershaw; *Feelin' Good Train* .... (MER)
New Career In A New Town
David Bowie; *Low* ....(RYK)
Nice Work If You Can Get It
Billie Holiday; *Compact Jazz* .... (VRV)
Carmen McRae; *Greatest Of* .... (MCA)
Ella Fitzgerald; *George & Ira Gershwin Songbook* (VRV)
Frank Sinatra; *My Kind Of Broadway* .... (RPR)
Original Cast; *My One & Only* .... (ATL)
Sting; *Glory Of Gershwin-Featuring Larry Adler* . (MER)
Night Shift
Bob Marley/Wailers; *Rastaman Vibrations* .... (TUF)
Foghat; *Best Of* .... (RHI)
Night Shift .... (RHI)
Nightshift
Commodores; *Nightshift* .... (MOT)
Nine To Five
Dolly Parton; *9 To 5 & Odd Jobs* .... (RCA)
Best There Is ....(RCA)
Greatest Hits ....(RCA)
Nipper's Greatest Hits-'80s ....(RCA)
No Job Blues
Ramblin' Thomas; *Ramblin' Mind Blues* ....(BIO)
Occupation
Sparks; *Introducing Sparks* ....(OOP)
One Bourbon One Scotch One Beer
George Thorogood/Destroyers; *George
Thorogood/Destroyers* .... (ROU)
Live .... (EMI)
John Lee Hooker; *Best Of Chess Blues* .... (CSS)
Real Folk Blues ....(CSS)
Ultimate Collection-1948-1990 .... (RHI)
Ooh! My Feet!
Original Broadway Cast; *Most Happy Fella* ..... (SMC)
Out Of Work
Gary U.S. Bonds; *On The Line* .... (EMI)
Paddy Works On The Erie
Popular Standard; *Out-Of-Print Recording* ....(OOP)
Payday/Mine 'Til Monday
Original Broadway Cast; *Tree Grows In Brooklyn* (SMC)
Peak Hour (Lunch Break)
Moody Blues; *Caught Live Plus Five* .... (POL)
Days Of Future Passed .... (POL)
Pittsburgh Town
Pete Seeger; *American Industrial Ballads* ...... (FLW)
Play It All Night Long
Warren Zevon; *Bad Luck Streak In Dancing
School* .... (ASY)
Quiet Normal Life-Best Of .... (ASY)
Quitting Time
Asleep At The Wheel; *Keepin' Me Up Nights* ..... (ARI)
John Anderson; *Blue Skies Again* .... (MCA)
Keith Whitley; *L.A. To Miami* .... (RCA)
Quittin' Time
Mary Chapin Carpenter; *Greatest Country
Hits-'90s-1990* ....(COL)
State Of The Heart ....(COL)
Roy Rogers
Elton John; *Goodbye Yellow Brick Road* .... (POL)
Runnin' Behind
Tracy Lawrence; *Sticks & Stones* .... (ATL)
Salt Of The Earth
Rolling Stones; *Beggar's Banquet* .... (AKO)

Sassin' The Boss
Glen Gray; *Uncollected/Casa Loma
Orch.-1939-1940* .... (HIN)
Saturday Boy
Billy Bragg; *Back To Basics* .... (ELE)
Save The Overtime (For Me)
Gladys Knight/Pips; *Best Of-Columbia Years* ....(COL)
Soul Survivors-Best Of-1973-1988 .... (RHI)
Visions ....(COL)
Sexual Harassment In The Workplace
Frank Zappa; *Guitar* ....(RYK)
Sha Na Na (Get A Job)
Silhouettes; *ST/American Graffiti* .... (MCA)
She Works Hard For The Money
Donna Summer; *She Works Hard For The Money* (MER)
Summer Collection .... (MER)
Sixteen Tons
Cactus Brothers; *Cactus Brothers* .... (LIB)
Stevie Wonder; *Down To Earth* ....(MOT)
Tennessee Ernie Ford; *16 Tons Of Boogie-Best Of* (RHI)
Capitol Collectors Series ....(CAP)
When AM Was King ....(CAP)
Weavers; *Greatest Hits* .... (VAN)
Sometimes It's A Bitch
Stevie Nicks; *Timespace-Best Of* .... (MOD)
Sweat (Til You Get Wet)
Brick; *Summer Heat* ....(BNG)
Oingo Boingo; *Best O' Boingo* ....(MCA)
System; *Sweat (Til You Get Wet)* .... (MIR)
Synchronicity II
Police; *Synchronicity* ....(A&M)
Take A Letter Maria
R.B. Greaves; *Soul Hits/'70s-#1* .... (RHI)
Take This Job And Shove It Too
David Allan Coe; *I've Got Something To Say* ....(COL)
Take This Job & Shove It
David Allan Coe; *17 Greatest Hits* ....(COL)
Johnny Paycheck; *Biggest Hits* ....(EPI)
Golden Hits ....(GUS)
Greatest Hits-#2 ....(EPI)
Take This Job & Shove It ....(EPI)
Truckers' Jukebox-Top Radio Requests ......(EPI)
Talking Union
Pete Seeger; *Greatest Hits* ....(COL)
Pete Seeger/Others; *Songs Of America's Working
People* ....(FF)
Tenth Avenue Freeze-Out
Bruce Springsteen; *Born To Run* ....(COL)
Bruce Springsteen/E Street Band;
Live-1975-1985 ....(COL)
That's My Job
Conway Twitty; *Borderline* .... (MCA)
Country Classics-#12-1987-1988 ....(MSP)
Silver Anniversary Collection .... (MCA)
Things Re Tough All Over
Shelby Lynne; *Greatest Country Hits/'90s-#2* .....(COL)
Tough All Over ....(EPI)
This Woman's Work
Kate Bush; *Sensual World* ....(COL)
ST/She's Having A Baby .... (IRS)
Try A Little Harder
Rolling Stones; *Singles Collection-London Years* . (AKO)
Typewriter, The
101 Strings Orchestra; *Strings Have Fun!* .... (ALS)
Rochester Pops Orchestra; *Leroy Anderson's Greatest
Hits* ....(POE)
Rochester Pops Orchestra/Erich Kunzel; *Syncopated
Clock* ....(POE)
Under Pressure
David Bowie & Queen; *Bowie-The
Singles-1969-1993* ....(RYK)
Queen & David Bowie; *Classic Queen* ....(HOL)
Hot Space ....(HOL)
Queen Greatest Hits ....(HOL)
Wat About Di Workin' Class?
Linton Kwesi Johnson; *In Concert With The Dub
Band* .... (SHA)
We Work The Black Seam
Sting; *Bring On The Night* ....(A&M)
Dream Of The Blue Turtles ....(A&M)

Weight, The
Band; *Best Of* .... (CAP)
   Last Waltz .... (WB)
   Music From Big Pink .... (CAP)
   Rock Of Ages-#1 & 2 .... (CAP)
Staple Singers; *Soul Folk In Action* .... (STX)
Staple Singers & Marty Stuart; *Rhythm Country &*
Blues .... (MCA)
Welcome To The Working Week
Elvis Costello; *My Aim Is True* ....(COL)
West Virginia Mine Disaster
Betsy Rutherford; *Betsy Rutherford* ....(BIO)
Cindy Mangsen; *Long Time Traveling* .... (HOG)
When I Lay My Burden Down
Fred McDowell & Furry Lewis; *When I Lay My Burden*
Down ....(BIO)
Roy Acuff; *Columbia Historic Edition* ....(COL)
When The Work's All Done This Fall
Doc Watson; *On Stage (Featuring Merle Watson)* (VAN)
Michael Martin Murphey; *Cowboy SOngs* .... (WW)
Whistle While You Work/Heigh Ho
Adriana Caselotti; *Disney Collection-#1* .... (DIS)
Mormon Tabernacle Choir; *When You Wish Upon A*
Star-Disney Tribute ....(COL)
NRBQ; *Peek-A-Boo-Best Of-1969-1989* .... (RHI)
Wild Sex (In The Working Class)
Oingo Boingo; *Best O' Boingo* .... (MCA)
   Boingo Alive .... (MCA)
   Nothing To Fear .... (A&M)
Work In The Mines
Bill Shute & Lisa Null; *American Primitive* ....(GRE)
Work Shy
Fabulous Poodles; *Mirror Stars* .... (EPI)
Work That Sucker To Death
Xavier; *Point Of Pleasure* .... (LIB)
Work To Do
Average White Band; *Average White Band* .... (ATL)
   Pick Up The Pieces-Best Of .... (RHI)
Isley Brothers; *Story-#2-T-Neck Years-1969-1985* (RHI)
Worker Man
PAtra; *Queen Of The Pack* .... (EPI)
Working Class Hero
Alan Jackson; *Don't Rock The Jukebox* .... (ARI)
John Lennon; *Lennon* ....(CAP)
John Lennon/Plastic Ono Band; *John Lennon/Plastic*
Ono Band ....(CAP)
Johnny Holm; *Work's Many Voices-#1 & 2* ..... (ARH)
Marianne Faithfull; *Broken English* .... (ISL)
Working Class Man
Lacy J. Dalton; *45* ....(COL)
Working Day & Night
Michael Jackson; *Off The Wall* .... (EPI)
Working For The Japanese
Loverboy; *Get Lucky* ....(COL)
Ray Stevens; *Top Ten Records* ....(CCB)
   #1 With A Bullet ....(CCB)
Working For The Man
Roy Orbison; *All-Time Greatest Hits* .... (MON)
   For The Lonely-Anthology-1956-1965 .... (RHI)
   In Dreams-Greatest Hits .... (VIA)
   More Greatest Hits .... (MON)
Working For The Weekend
Loverboy; *Big Ones* ....(COL)
   Get Lucky ....(COL)
Working In The Coal Mine
Devo; *Best Of-Greatest Hits* .... (WB)
   Greatest Hits .... (WB)
   New Traditionalists .... (WB)
   Now It Can Be Told (Devo At The Palace) ..... (ENI)
   ST/Heavy Metal .... (ASY)
Judds; *Collection-1983-1990* ....(RCA)
   Rockin' With The Rhythm ....(RCA)
Lee Dorsey; *Best Of New Orleans R&B-#2* .... (RHI)
   Golden Classics .... (CLT)
   History Of New Orleans R&B-#3-1962-1970 ... (RHI)
   Holy Cow .... (ARI)
   New Orleans Jazz & Heritage Fest-1976 .... (RHI)
Working Man
Glenn Frey; *Soul Searchin'* .... (MCA)
John Conlee; *Blue Highway* .... (MCA)
   Greatest Hits-#2 .... (MCA)
   Songs For The Working Man .... (MCA)
Otis Rush; *Mourning In The Morning* .... (ATL)

Rush; *All The World's A Stage* .... (MER)
   Archives .... (MER)
   Chronicles .... (MER)
   Rush .... (MER)
Working Man Can't Get Nowhere Today
Merle Haggard; *18 Rare Classics* ....(CCB)
Merle Haggard/Strangers; *Working Man Can't Get*
Nowhere Today ....(CAP)
Working Man's Ph.D.
Aaron Tippin; *Call Of The Wild* ....(RCA)
Working On A Building
Blue Ridge Rangers; *Blue Ridge Rangers* .... (FAN)
Kentucky Colonels feat. Clarence White; *Kentucky*
Colonels feat. Clarence White .... (ROU)
Working On It
Chris Rea; *New Light Through Old Windows* ..... (ATL)
Working On The Highway
Bruce Springsteen; *Born In The U.S.A.* ....(COL)
Bruce Springsteen/E Street Band;
Live-1975-1985 ....(COL)
Working On The Road
Ten Years After; *Cricklewood Green* .... (CHR)
Working Too Hard
Beat; *Beat* ....(COL)
Workin' At The Car Wash Blues
Jim Croce; *50th Anniversary Collection* .... (SAJ)
   Greatest Character Songs .... (LIF)
   I Got A Name .... (LIF)
   Photographs & Memories-His Greatest Hits ...... (21)
Workin' Man
Creedence Clearwater Revival; *1968-1969* ...... (FAN)
   Creedence Clearwater Revival .... (FAN)
Workin' Man Blues
Diamond Rio/Lee R. Parnell/Steve Wariner; *Mama's*
Hungry Eyes-Merle Haggard Tribute .... (ARI)
Gary Morris; *These Days* .... (LIB)
Merle Haggard/Strangers; *Best Of Country Blues* .(CCB)
   Capitol Collectors Series .... (CAP)
   Okie From Muskogee .... (CAP)
   Songs I'll Always Sing .... (CAP)
Ricky Van Shelton; *Wild-Eyed Dream* ....(COL)
Yakety Yak
2 Live Crew; *ST/Twins* .... (WTG)
Coasters; *Atlantic*
R&B-1947-1974-#3-(1955-1958) .... (ATL)
   Billboard Top Rock 'N' Roll Hits-1958 .... (RHI)
   Cruisin'-1958 .... (INC)
   Greatest Hits ....(ATC)
   ST/Stand By Me .... (ATL)

WORLD

See Also: LIFE, POLITICAL CLASSICS, SPACE,
STARS

1-900-WORLD
Leaving Trains; *Lump In My Forehead* ....(SST)
Ain't Nuthin' In The World
Miki Howard; *Miki Howard* .... (ATL)
All Around The World
Edwin Starr; *War & Peace* .... (MOT)
Lisa Stansfield; *Affection* .... (ARI)
Little Richard; *18 Greatest Hits* .... (RHI)
   Grooviest 17 Original Hits .... (SPE)
   Little Richard .... (SPE)
   Little Richard-His Biggest Hits .... (SPE)
All Over The World
Electric Light Orchestra; *ST/Xanadu* .... (MCA)
Nat King Cole; *Capitol Collectors Series* ....(CAP)
   Ramblin' Rose ....(CAP)
All The Cryin' In The World
Jeris Ross; *45* .... (MCA)
All The Love In The World
Dionne Warwick; *Heartbreaker* .... (ARI)
Outfield; *Play Deep* ....(COL)
Another Green World
Brian Eno; *Another Green World* .... (EDI)
Another World
Gary Morris & Crystal Gayle; *Favorite Country*
Duets .... (WB)
   Greatest Hits-#2 .... (WB)
Hoodoo Gurus; *Magnum Come Louder* ....(RCA)
Joe Jackson; *Night & Day* .... (A&M)

Richard Hell/Voidoids; *Blank Generation* .... (SIR)
Roches; *Another World* .... (WB)
Another World, Another Day
Soul Asylum; *Made To Be Broken* .... (TT)
Any World
Steely Dan; *Katy Lied* .... (MCA)
Around The World
Neil Young; *Lucky Thirteen* .... (GEF)
Weavers; *At Carnegie Hall* .... (VAN)
  Greatest Hits .... (VAN)
Around The World In A Day
Prince/Revolution; *Around The World In A Day* .. (PAI)
Around The World (In 80 Days)
Boston Pops Orchestra/Arthur Fiedler; *Greatest
Hits/'50s-#2* ....(RCA)
Frank Sinatra; *Come Fly With Me* .... (CAP)
Roger Williams; *Greatest Hits* .... (MCA)
As The World Falls Down
David Bowie; *ST/Labyrinth* .... (EMI)
"As The World Turns" Theme
Rosemary Joyce & Bill Bartholomew; *Soap Opera
Themes* .... (CRS)
At War With The World
Foreigner; *Foreigner* .... (ATL)
Ball Of Confusion
Temptations; *All The Million-Sellers* .... (MOT)
  Anthology .... (MOT)
  Compact Command Performances .... (MOT)
  Greatest Hits-#2 .... (MOT)
  Top 10 With A Bullet-Motown Male Groups ... (MOT)
Because
Beatles; *Abbey Road* .... (CAP)
  Box Set .... (CAP)
Best Of All Possible Worlds
Leonard Bernstein; *Bernstein Songbook* ....(COL)
Original Cast; *Candide* ....(COL)
Best Of Both Worlds
Midnight Oil; *Red Sails In The Sunset* ....(COL)
Robert Palmer; *Double Fun* .... (ISL)
Van Halen; *5150* .... (WB)
Biggest Airport In The World
Moe Bandy; *Best Of-#1* ....(COL)
Brave New World
Choirboys; *Big Bad Noise* .... (WTG)
Public Image, Ltd.; *9* .... (VIA)
Steve Miller Band; *Brave New World* .... (CAP)
Children Of The World
Amy Grant; *House Of Love* .... (A&M)
Bee Gees; *Children Of The World* .... (RSO)
  Greatest .... (RSO)
Third World; *Sense Of Purpose* ....(COL)
Wailers Band; *I.D.* .... (ATL)
Children Of The World Unite
Angela Bofill; *Angie* .... (GRP)
Cold Cold World
Teddy Pendergrass; *Life Is A Song Worth Singing* .. (PI)
Colour My World
Chicago; *At Carnegie Hall* ....(COL)
  Greatest Hits ....(COL)
  II ....(COL)
Petula Clark; *Greatest Hits* .... (CRS)
Computer Incantations For World Peace
Jean-Luc Ponty; *Individual Choice* .... (ATL)
Computer World
Kraftwerk; *Computer World* .... (WB)
Cops Of The World
Phil Ochs; *In Concert* .... (ELE)
  There But For Fortune .... (ELE)
Criminal World
David Bowie; *Let's Dance* .... (EMI)
Dark Side Of The World
Diana Ross; *Ain't No Mountain High Enough* ... (MOT)
Marvin Gaye; *Musical Testament-1964-1984* ... (MOT)
Different Worlds
Maureen McGovern; *Maureen McGovern* ...... (WB)
Vandenberg; *Best Of* ....(ATC)
Doggy Dogg World
Snoop Doggy Dogg; *Doggystyle* .... (DR)
Don't Wanna Change The World
Phyllis Hyman; *Prime Of My Life* .... (PIR)
Dream World
Jerry Butler; *Nothing Says I Love You Like I Love
You* .... (PI)

End Of The World
Skeeter Davis; *Best Of* .... (GUS)
  Billboard Top Country Hits-1963 .... (RHI)
  Nipper's Greatest Hits-'60s-#1 ....(RCA)
  Stars Of The Grand Ole Opry 1926-1974 .....(RCA)
  Super Country Hits-60s .... (GUS)
Every Woman In The World
Air Supply; *Greatest Hits* .... (ARI)
  Lost In Love .... (ARI)
Everybody Wants To Rule The World
Tears For Fears; *Knebworth: The Album* .... (POL)
  Music For The Miracle ....(CBA)
  Songs From The Big Chair ....(MER)
Eyes Of The World
Fleetwood Mac; *25 Years-The Chain* .... (WB)
  Mirage .... (WB)
Grateful Dead; *One From The Vault* .... (GRD)
  Wake Of The Flood .... (GRD)
  Without A Net .... (ARI)
Five O'Clock World
Hal Ketchum; *Past The Point Of Rescue* ....(CRB)
Vogues; *Greatest Hits* .... (RHI)
  Greatest Hits .... (SSS)
  ST/Good Morning Vietnam .... (A&M)
Hand Me Down World
Guess Who; *Best Of* ....(RCA)
  Greatest Of ....(RCA)
Heart-Shaped World
Chris Isaak; *Heart-Shaped World* .... (RPR)
Here At The Western World
Steely Dan; *Greatest Hits* .... (MCA)
Here In The Real World
Alan Jackson; *Here In The Real World* .... (ARI)
He's Got The Whole World In His Hands
Laurie London; *45* .... (ERI)
Mormon Tabernacle Choir; *Greatest Hits-#2* ....(COL)
Odetta; *Essential* .... (VAN)
Hot Love Cold World
Bob Welch; *French Kiss* .... (CAP)
I Am The Light Of This World
Jorma Kaukonen & Tom Hobson; *Quah* .... (RLX)
I Don't Want To Set The World On Fire
Ink Spots; *Best Of* .... (MCA)
I Want To Make The World Turn Around
Steve Miller Band; *Living In The 20th Century* ...(CAP)
I Watched It All (On My Radio)
Lionel Cartwright; *I Watched It All On The
Radio* .... (MCA)
I Wouldn't Have Missed It For The World
Ronnie Milsap; *There's No Gettin' Over Me* ......(RCA)
  Greatest Hits-#2 ....(RCA)
If I Could Build My Whole World...
Marvin Gaye & Tammi Terrell; *Anthology* ...... (MOT)
  Every Great Motown Hit Of Marvin Gaye ..... (MOT)
  Greatest Hits .... (MOT)
  Motown Superstar Series-#2 .... (MOT)
  United .... (MOT)
If I Ruled The World
James Brown; *Sex Machine* .... (POL)
Sammy Davis, Jr.; *Greatest Hits* .... (RPR)
Stevie Wonder; *Looking Back* .... (MOT)
Supremes; *25th Anniversary* .... (MOT)
Tony Bennett; *Forty Years-Artistry Of* ....(COL)
If This World Were Mine
Cheryl Lynn; *Instant Love* ....(COL)
Luther Vandross & Cheryl Lynn; *Best Of...Best Of
Love* .... (EPI)
Marvin Gaye & Tammi Terrell; *All The Great Motown
Love Song Duets* .... (MOT)
  Anthology .... (MOT)
  Classic Duets-Marvin Gaye & His Women ..... (MOT)
  Greatest Hits .... (MOT)
  Motown Superstar Series-#2 .... (MOT)
  United .... (MOT)
If Women Ruled The World
Joan Armatrading; *Square The Circle* .... (A&M)
If You Were The Only Boy (In The World)
Barbra Streisand; *My Name Is Barbra* ....(COL)
It's A Lovely Lovely World
Gail Davies; *45* .... (WB)
It's A Man's Man's Man's World
James Brown; *Billboard Top R&B Hits-1966* ..... (RHI)
  Greatest Hits .... (RHI)

I'd Love To Change The World
Ten Years After; *A Space In Time* .... (CHR)
  Classic Performances Of .... (COL)
  Universal .... (CHR)
I.G.Y. (What A Beautiful World)
Donald Fagen; *45* .... (WB)
  Nightfly .... (WB)
  The Nightfly .... (WB)
I'll Kiss The World Goodbye
J.J. Cale; *Really* .... (MCA)
I'm In A Different World
Four Tops; *Anthology* .... (MOT)
I'm Not Gonna Let It Bother Me Tonight
Atlanta Rhythm Section; *Are You Ready?* .... (POL)
  Champagne Jam .... (POL)
I'm Sitting On Top Of The World
Al Jolson; *Jolson Sang 'Em* .... (BIO)
  Story-#3 .... (MCA)
Nitty Gritty Dirt Band; *Will The Circle Be
Unbroken-#2* .... (UNI)
I've Got The World On A String
Count Basie; *Standards* ....(VRV)
Ella Fitzgerald; *Harold Arlen Songbook-#1* ......(VRV)
Frank Sinatra; *Capitol Collectors Series* .... (CAP)
Frank Sinatra & Liza Minnelli; *Frank Sinatra
Duets* ....(CAP)
Sarah Vaughan; *Best Of* .... (PAB)
Stephane Grappelli & Martin Taylor; *We've Got The
World On A String* .... (ANG)
Joy To The World
Three Dog Night; *Best Of* .... (MCA)
  Good Feeling Music/Big Chill Gen.-#2 .... (MOT)
  Good Feeling Music/Big Chill Gen.-#3 .... (MOT)
  Joy To The World .... (MCA)
  ST/Big Chill .... (MOT)
  ST/Forrest Gump .... (EPX)
King Of The Night Time World
Kiss; *Alive 2* .... (CAS)
  Destroyer .... (CAS)
King Of The World
Steely Dan; *Countdown To Ecstasy* .... (MCA)
  Gold .... (MCA)
Kiss The World Goodbye
Kris Kristofferson; *Border Lord* ....(COL)
Light Of The World
Original Cast; *ST/Godspell* .... (ARI)
Living In The Material World
George Harrison; *Living In The Material World* ..(CAP)
Looking At The World Through A...
Commander Cody/Lost Planet Airmen; *Hot Licks Cold
Steel & Trucker's Fav.* .... (MCA)
Red Simpson; *Ramblin' Road* .... (FFT)
Red Sovine & Del Reeves; *Red Sovine & Del
Reeves* ....(EXA)
Lost In A Lost World
Moody Blues; *Seventh Sojourn* .... (POL)
Lost In The Neon World
Be Bop Deluxe; *Modern Music* .... (HAR)
Love Makes The World Go Round
Deon Jackson; *Golden Classics* .... (CLT)
  Oldies But Goodies-#15 .... (OSR)
  Soul Shots-#2-The In Crowd .... (RHI)
  Super Oldies/'60s-#7 .... (AUF)
Jo Basile; *Hit Broadway Musicals* .... (AUF)
Madonna; *True Blue* .... (SIR)
Original Cast; *Me & My Girl* .... (EMI)
  Me & My Girl .... (MCA)
Love The World Away
Kenny Rogers; *Greatest Hits* .... (EMI)
  ST/Urban Cowboy .... (ASY)
  Twenty Greatest Hits .... (LIB)
Make The World Go Away
Eddy Arnold; *Best Of* ....(RCA)
  Billboard Top Country Hits-1965 .... (RHI)
  Nipper's Greatest Hits-'60s-#1 ....(RCA)
  Pure Gold ....(RCA)
  World Of Hits ....(MGM)
Man Of The World
Fleetwood Mac; *25 Years-The Chain* .... (WB)
Man Who Sold The World
David Bowie; *Man Who Sold The World* ....(RYK)
  Sound + Vision ....(RYK)
Mean Old World
Bobby Bland & B.B. King; *Together Again Live* . (MCA)

Climax Blues Band; *Climax Chicago Blues Band* .. (SIR)
Duane Allman; *Eric Clapton-Crossroads* ....(POL)
Duane Allman & Eric Clapton; *Duane Allman
Anthology* ....(CPC)
Robert Palmer; *Secrets* .... (ISL)
Money Song
Original Cast; *Cabaret* ....(COL)
Most Beautiful Girl In The World
Frank Sinatra; *Strangers In The Night* .... (RPR)
Prince; *S* .... (BLM)
Tony Bennett; *Rodgers & Hart Songbook* .... (DRG)
  Sings More Great Rodgers & Hart .... (IPV)
Most Beautiful World In The World
Nilsson; *Son Of Schmilsson* ....(RCA)
My World
Bee Gees; *Gold-#1* .... (RSO)
Descendants; *I Don't Wanna Grow Up* .... (SST)
Guns N' Roses; *Use Your Illusion II* .... (GEF)
My World Begins & Ends With You
Dave & Sugar; *Stay With Me/Golden Tears* ......(RCA)
Eddy Arnold; *Collector's Series* ....(RCA)
My World Is Empty Without You
Diana Ross/Supremes; *Anthology* .... (MOT)
  Evening With Diana Ross .... (MOT)
  Greatest Hits-#1 & 2 .... (MOT)
Stevie Wonder; *Down To Earth* .... (MOT)
New World
Boston; *Third Stage* .... (MCA)
Cause & Effect; *Another Minute* .... (ZOO)
Saigon Kick; *Saigon Kick* .... (THI)
Strawbs; *Grave New World* .... (A&M)
X; *Live At The Whisky A Go-Go* .... (ELE)
  More Fun In The New World .... (ELE)
New World In The Morning
Roger Whittaker;
  Best Of ....(RCA)
  Last Farewell & Other Hits ....(RCA)
  Live In Concert ....(RCA)
  New World In The Morning ....(RCA)
New World Man
Rush; *Chronicles* .... (MER)
  Signals .... (MER)
  Three Decades Of Rock ('60s, '70s, '80s) .... (PRY)
New World Rising
Electric Light Orchestra; *On The Third Day* ......(JET)
Not Enough Love In The World
Don Henley; *Building The Perfect Beast* ....(GEF)
Oldest Baby In The World
John Prine; *Aimless Love* .... (OB)
  Anthology-Great Days .... (RHI)
  Live .... (OB)
On Top Of The World
Cheap Trick; *Heaven Tonight* .... (EPI)
One World
Anthrax; *Among The Living* .... (ISL)
Dire Straits; *Brothers In Arms* .... (WB)
John Denver; *One World* ....(RCA)
Utopia; *Anthology-1974-1985* .... (RHI)
  Swing To The Right .... (RHI)
Ordinary World
Duran Duran; *Duran Duran* ....(CAP)
Out Of This World
Ella Fitzgerald; *Harold Harlen Songbook-#2* .....(VRV)
Rosemary Clooney; *Sings The Music Of Harold
Arlen* .... (CCJ)
Tito Puente; *Out Of This World* .... (CP)
Tony Bennett; *Jazz* ....(COL)
Outta The World
Ashford & Simpson; *Solid* ....(CAP)
  Solid Plus Seven ....(CAP)
Panic In The World
Be Bop Deluxe; *Best Of & The Rest Of* ....(OOP)
  Best Of-Raiding The Divine Archive ....(CAP)
  Drastic Plastic ....(OOP)
Peaceful World
Rascals; *Peaceful World* ....(OOP)
Perfect World
Huey Lewis/News; *Small World* .... (CHR)
Roger Daltrey; *Rocks In My Head* .... (ATL)
Talking Heads; *Little Creatures* .... (SIR)
Tevin Campbell; *T.E.V.I.N.* .... (RPR)
Place In This World
Michael W. Smith; *Go West Young Man* ....(REU)

Pretty World
Sergio Mendes & Brasil '66; *Classicss-#18* ..... (A&M)
Greatest Hits .... (A&M)
Rainy Night In Georgia
Brook Benton; *Anthology* .... (RHI)
Atlantic R&B 1947-1974-#6-(1966-1969) .... (ATL)
Golden Age Of Black Music-1960-1970 .... (ATL)
Pick Of .... (FFT)
Soul Years .... (ATL)
Today .... (COT)
Hank Williams, Jr.; *14 Greatest Hits* .... (POL)
Sam Moore & Conway Twitty; *Rhythm Country &*
Blues .... (MCA)
Reach Out And Touch
Diana Ross; *All The Great Hits* .... (MOT)
Anthology .... (MOT)
Live At Caesar's Palace .... (MOT)
Most Played Songs On America's Jukeboxes .... (MOT)
Motown Story .... (MOT)
Real World
Bangles; *Bangles* .... (IRS)
Bruce Springsteen; *Human Touch* ....(COL)
Jesus Jones; *Liquidizer* .... (SBK)
Mighty Lemon Drops; *Laughter* .... (SIR)
Richard Marx; *Repeat Offender* ....(CAP)
Rhythm Saved The World
Bunny Berigan/Boys; *Take It Bunny* .... (SSP)
Richest Man On Earth
Paul Overstreet; *Sowin' Love* ....(RCA)
Rock My World (Little Country Girl)
Brooks & Dunn; *Hard Workin' Man* .... (ARI)
Rock The World
Third World; *Rock The World* ....(COL)
Rock You All Around The World
Judas Priest; *Priest...Live!* ....(COL)
Turbo ....(COL)
Rock & Roll Music To The World
Ten Years After; *Classic Performances* ......(COL)
Rockin' In The Free World
Neil Young; *Freedom* .... (RPR)
Neil Young/Crazy Horse; *Weld* .... (RPR)
Rose Tint In My World
Tim Curry/Original Roxy Cast; *Rocky Horror*
Show .... (RHI)
'Round The World With The Rubber Duck
C.W. McCall; *Greatest Hits* .... (POL)
Sail Around The World
David Gates; *First* .... (ELE)
Saturday Night At The World
Mason Williams; *Music-1968-1971* .... (VAN)
Mason Williams/Mannheim Steamroller; *Classical*
Gas .... (AG)
Save The World
George Harrison; *Greenpeace* .... (A&M)
Somewhere In England .... (DKH)
Separate Ways (Worlds Apart)
Journey; *Frontiers* ....(COL)
Greatest Hits ....(COL)
Sitting On Top Of The World
Cream; *Goodbye* .... (POL)
Wheels Of Fire .... (POL)
Howlin' Wolf; *Chess Box* .... (CSS)
Real Folk Blues .... (CSS)
Sittin' On Top Of The World
Bob Wills/Texas Playboys; *24 Great Hits* .... (POL)
Bob Wills Anthology .... (SSP)
Tiffany Transcriptions-#8 .... (KAL)
Doc Watson; *Doc Watson* .... (VAN)
Greatest Folksingers Of The '60s .... (VAN)
Old Timey Concert .... (VAN)
Grateful Dead; *Grateful Dead* .... (WB)
Ray Charles; *20 Golden Pieces Of* .... (BLD)
Sweet Honey In The Rock; *Believe I'll Run On..* (RWD)
Small World
Adrian Belew; *Young Lions* .... (ATL)
Huey Lewis/News; *Greenpeace/Rainbow Warriors* (GEF)
Small World .... (CHR)
Johnny Mathis; *16 Most Requested Songs* ....(COL)
All-Time Greatest Hits ....(COL)
Original Cast; *Gypsy* ....(COL)
Original London Cast; *Gypsy* .... (RCA)
Spirits In The Material World
Police; *Every Breath You Take-The Singles* ...... (A&M)
Ghost In The Machine .... (A&M)

State Of The World
Janet Jackson; *Rhythm Nation 1814* ....(A&M)
Stop The World
Clash; *On Broadway* .... (EPI)
Extreme; *III Sides To Every Story* ....(A&M)
Teena Marie; *Robbery* .... (EPI)
Stop The World Right Here
Temptations; *Back To Basics* .... (MOT)
Stop The World (& Let Me Off)
Merle Haggard; *Big City* .... (EPI)
Patsy Cline; *20 Golden Pieces Of* .... (BLD)
Forever & Always .... (EPI)
Here's Patsy Cline .... (MCA)
Waylon Jennings; *Early Years* ....(RCA)
Teen Angst (What The World Needs Now)
Cracker; *Cracker* .... (VIA)
Tell The World
Dells; *Harlem New York-Ballad Era* .... (CLT)
Ratt; *Ratt & Roll 8191* .... (ATL)
Tell The World How I Feel About 'Cha...
Harold Melvin/Blue Notes; *Wake Up Everybody* ... (PI)
Thank You World
Statler Brothers; *Best Of* .... (MER)
That's The Way Of The World
Earth, Wind & Fire; *Best Of-#1* ....(COL)
Eternal Dance ....(COL)
Pop Classics/'70s ....(COL)
That's The Way Of The World ....(COL)
That's The Way That The World Goes...
John Prine; *Anthology-Great Days* .... (RHI)
Bruised Orange .... (ASY)
Theme From "Wayne's World"
Mike Myers & Dana Carvey; *ST/Wayne's World* . (RPR)
There Must Be A Better World Somewhere
B.B. King; *King Of The Blues* .... (MCA)
There Must Be A Better World Somewhere ..... (MCA)
There's A Kind Of Hush (All Over...)
Carpenters; *A Kind Of Hush* .... (A&M)
Classics-#2 .... (A&M)
Yesterday Once More .... (A&M)
Herman's Hermits; *XX-Their Greatest Hits* ... (AKO)
There's A Place In The World For A...
Dan Fogelberg; *Live-Greetings From The West* .... (FM)
Souvenirs .... (FM)
ST/FM .... (MCA)
This Funny World
Tony Bennett; *Rodgers & Hart Songbook* .... (DRG)
This Whole World
Beach Boys; *Sunflower* ....(CAR)
This World
Rosanne Cash; *Interiors* ....(COL)
Staple Singers; *Chronicle* .... (STX)
Greatest Hits .... (FAN)
This World Of Ours
Eddy Arnold; *World Of* ....(RCA)
Till The End Of The World Rolls 'Round
Flatt & Scruggs; *Columbia Historic Edition* ......(COL)
Golden Era .... (ROU)
Today My World Slipped Away
Vern Gosdin; *10 Years Of Greatest Hits Newly*
Recorded ....(COL)
Today My World Slipped Away .... (AMI)
Top Of The World
Carpenters; *Classics-#2* .... (A&M)
Singles 1969-1973 .... (A&M)
Song For You .... (A&M)
Yesterday Once More .... (A&M)
Diana Ross; *Anthology* .... (MOT)
James; *James* .... (FON)
Lynn Anderson; *Country Superstars* .... (DOM)
Greatest Hits-#2 ....(COL)
Top Of The World ....(COL)
Van Halen; *For Unlawful Carnal Knowledge* ...... (WB)
Tracey's World
Smithereens; *Beauty & Sadness* ....(CAP)
Truck Stop At The End Of The World
Commander Cody; *Let's Rock* .... (BLD)
Trying To Throw Your Arms Around The...
U2; *Achtung Baby* .... (ISL)
Two Less Lonely People In The World
Air Supply; *Now & Forever* .... (ARI)
Ugliest Girl In The World
Bob Dylan; *Down In The Groove* ....(COL)

Uno Mundo
Buffalo Springfield; *Buffalo Springfield* ....(ATC)
Until The End Of The World
U2; *Achtung Baby* ....(ISL)
ST/*Until The End Of The World* ....(WB)
Waiting For The End Of The World
Elvis Costello; *My Aim Is True* ....(COL)
Wake The World
Beach Boys; *Concert/'69-Live In London* ....(CAP)
Friends/20-20 ....(CAP)
Walk Through This World With Me
George Jones; *All-Time Greatest Hits-#1* ....(EPI)
Best Of-1966-1967 ....(RHI)
Billboard Top Country Hits-1967 ....(RHI)
Double Gold ....(MCR)
"War Of The Worlds" Theme
Neil Norman; *Greatest Science Fiction Hits-#3* ... (CRS)
Watching The World Go By
Gun; *Gallus* ....(A&M)
Way Of The World
Cheap Trick; *Dream Police* ....(EPI)
Genesis; *We Can't Dance* ....(ATL)
Roger Daltrey; *Daltrey* ....(MCA)
Tina Turner; *Simply The Best* ....(CAP)
We Are The World
USA For Africa; *We Are The World* ....(COL)
We Can Change The World
Graham Nash; *Songs For Beginners* ....(ATL)
Jacksons; *Victory* ....(EPI)
We Didn't Start The Fire
Billy Joel; *Storm Front* ....(COL)
We Don't Want The World
Jack Greene & Jeannie Seely; *Greatest Hits* ...... (IGR)
Jeannie Seely; *Best Of Town & Country -#3* ..... (IGR)
Weight Of The World
Ringo Starr; *Time Takes Time* ....(PRV)
Welcome To My World
Eddy Arnold; *Welcome To My World* ....(RCA)
World Of ....(RCA)
Elvis Presley; *Aloha From Hawaii* ....(RCA)
Welcome To My World ....(RCA)
Jim Reeves; *Am I That Easy To Forget* ....(RCA)
Best Of ....(RCA)
Legendary Performer ....(RCA)
Pure Gold-#1 ....(RCA)
Jim Reeves & Patsy Cline; *Greatest Hits* ....(RCA)
What A Wonderful World
Louis Armstrong; ST/*Good Morning Vietnam* ... (A&M)
Vocalists-Jazz Masters ....(BLU)
What A Wonderful World ....(MCA)
Mormon Tabernacle Choir; *Songs From America's
Heartland* ....(LON)
Willie Nelson; *What A Wonderful World* ....(COL)
(What A) Wonderful World
Art Garfunkel; *Watermark* ....(COL)
Sam Cooke; *Best Of* ....(RCA)
ST/*Animal House* ....(MCA)
This Is ....(RCA)
What The World Needs Now Is Love
Burt Bacharach; *Greatest Hits* ....(A&M)
Jackie DeShannon; *Flower Power* ....(KT)
Good Vibrations ....(CAP)
Oldies But Goodies-#14 ....(OSR)
ST/*Forrest Gump* ....(EPX)
Very Best Of ....(EMI)
Luther Vandross; *Songs* ....(EPI)
Tom Clay; *20 Hard-To-Find Motown
Classics-#2* .... (MOT)
What's Going On In Your World
George Strait; *Beyond The Blue Neon* ....(MCA)
Ten Strait Hits ....(MCA)
When The World Is Running Down...
Police; *Zenyatta Mondatta* ....(A&M)
When The World Was Young
Anita O'Day; *Mello'Day* ....(CRS)
Frank Sinatra; *Point Of No Return* ....(CAP)
When Two Worlds Collide
Rex Allen, Jr.; *20 Golden Souvenirs (Of Music City
USA)* ....(PLN)
Roger Miller; *Best Of-His Greatest Songs* ....(CCB)
When You're Smiling
Frank Sinatra; *Sinatra's Swinging Session-& More* (CAP)

Judy Garland; *At Carnegie Hall* ....(CAP)
Greatest Hits ....(CCB)
One & Only ....(CAP)
Louis Armstrong; *Best Of* ....(MCA)
Musical Autobiography-#2 ....(MCA)
#4-In New York ....(COL)
Whole New World (Aladdin's Theme)
Peabo Bryson & Regina Belle; ST/*Aladdin* ....(DIS)
Regina Belle & Peabo Bryson; *Passion* ....(COL)
Whole Wide World
A'me Lorain/Family Affair; *Starring In...Standing In A
Monkey Sea* ....(RCA)
Soup Dragons; *Hang Ten* ....(SIR)
Whole World's In Love When You're Lonely
B.J. Thomas; *45* .... (CI)
Wicked World
Black Sabbath; *Black Sabbath* ....(WB)
Jimmy Nail; *Growing Up In Public* ....(ATL)
Rick Parker; *Wicked World* ....(GEF)
Wide World Of Sports
Instant Funk; *Instant Funk* ....(SSL)
Wild World
Cat Stevens; *Greatest Hits* ....(A&M)
Tea For The Tillerman ....(A&M)
Jimmy Cliff; *In Concert-Best Of* ....(RPR)
Reggae Spectacular ....(A&M)
Maxi Priest; *Best Of Me* ....(CHS)
Maxi ....(VIA)
Window To The World
Shawn Colvin; *Cover Girl* ....(COL)
Winter World Of Love
Engelbert Humperdinck; *Engelbert Humperdinck* . (PRT)
Greatest Hits ....(PRT)
Woman Is The Nigger Of The World
John Lennon; *Shaved Fish* ....(CAP)
Somewhere In New York City ....(CAP)
John Lennon/Plastic Ono Band; *Lennon* ....(CAP)
Women Will Rule The World
Ry Cooder; *Get Rhythm* ....(WB)
Wonderful World, Beautiful People
Jimmy Cliff; *In Concert-Best Of* ....(RPR)
Reggae Spectacular ....(A&M)
Wonderful World, Beautiful People ....(A&M)
World
Bee Gees; *Here At Last* .... (RSO)
World Anthem
Frank Marino & Mahogany Rush; *Live* ....(COL)
World Anthem ....(COL)
World Full Of Strangers
B.B. King; *Midnight Believer* ....(MCA)
World I Used To Know
Glenn Yarbrough; *Best Of* ....(RCA)
World In Motion
Jackson Browne; *World In Motion* .... (ELE)
World In My Eyes
Depeche Mode; *Violator* .... (SIR)
World Is A Concerto
Barbra Streisand; *& Other Musical Instruments* ...(COL)
World Is A Ghetto
George Benson; *In Flight* ....(WB)
War; *Greatest Hits* ....(MCA)
Music Band ....(MCA)
Music Band 2 ....(MCA)
World Is A Ghetto ....(AVE)
World Is A Little Bit Under The Weather
Meters; *Trick Bag* ....(RPR)
World Is Africa
Black Uhuru; *Sinsemilla* ....(MGO)
World Is Changing Hands
Dave Davies; *Dave Davies* ....(RCA)
World Is Round
Rufus Thomas & Carla Thomas; *Chronicle* ...... (STX)
World Is Upside Down
Joe Higgs; *This Is Reggae Music-#1* .... (ISL)
World Is Waiting For The Sunrise
Benny Goodman; *I Like Jazz-Essence Of* ....(COL)
Benny Goodman Orchestra & Quartet; *Let's
Dance* .... (LAS)
Les Paul & Mary Ford; *World Is Waiting For The
Sunrise* .... (LAS)
Roy Clark & Buck Trent; *Banjo Bandit* ....(MCA)
World Needs A Melody
George Jones & Tammy Wynette; *Greatest
Hits-#2* ....(EPI)

Kenny Rogers; *Love Lifted Me* .... (UA)
World Of Our Own
Elvis Presley; *ST/It Happened At The World's
Fair* ....(RCA)
Mickey Gilley; *Mickey Gilley* .... (PLA)
Seekers; *Best Of Today* ....(CCB)
   Capitol Collectors Series ....(CAP)
Surface; *Best Of-A Nice Time 4 Lovin'* ....(COL)
World Of Pain
Cream; *Disraeli Gears* ....(POL)
World Of Stone
George Harrison; *Extra Texture* ....(CAP)
World Of Trouble
Lou Rawls; *Best From* ....(CAP)
   Legendary ....(BLN)
World On A String
Neil Young; *Tonight's The Night* ....(RPR)
World Turning
Fleetwood Mac; *Fleetwood Mac* ....(RPR)
World War None
Frank Sinatra; *Trilogy (Past/Present/Future)* ......(RPR)
World We Know
Frank Sinatra; *Greatest Hits* ....(RPR)
   World We Know ....(RPR)
Worlds Away
BoDeans; *Home* ....(SLS)
Pablo Cruise; *Worlds Away* ....(A&M)
Worlds In A Triangle
Fleetwood Mac; *In Chicago* .... (SIR)
World's A Masquerade
Earth, Wind & Fire; *Head To The Sky* ....(COL)
World's Greatest Lover
Bellamy Brothers; *Greatest Hits-#2* .... (MCA)
   Restless .... (MCC)
You Can Tell The World
Simon & Garfunkel; *Collected Works* ....(COL)
   Wednesday Morning 3 A.M. ....(COL)
You Mean The World To Me
Toni Braxton; *Toni Braxton* .... (LAF)
You Tell The World
Simon & Garfunkel; *Wednesday Morning 3 A.M.* .(COL)
Young World
Ricky Nelson; *All My Best* .... (MCA)
   Best Of-#2 .... (EMI)
   Greatest Hits .... (RHI)
   Teenage Idol .... (LIB)

20	Twentieth Century Fox	ATO	Atomic
21	21	AUD	Audiograph
40	40 Acres & A Mule Musicworks	AUF	Audio Fidelity
4AD	4AD	AVE	Avenue
4TH	4th & Broadway	AVI	American Variety
550	550 Music	AXI	Axiom
AA	Atlantic America	A&C	Art & Commerce
ABC	ABC	A&M	A & M
ACC	Accord	A/H	A&M/Hollywood
ACT	Accent	A/R	Atlantic/RFC
AD	Acoustic Disc	BAI	Bainbridge
ADE	Adelphi	BAR	Barking Pumpkin
ADO	Adobe	BAY	Bay Cities
AER	Aero Space	BB	Big Beat
AG	American Gramaphone	BBY	Barnaby
AH	After Hours	BCH	Big Chief
AJK	AJK Music	BCL	Blues Classics
AKO	Abkco	BCT	Bac-Trac
ALC	Alcazar	BEG	Beggar's Banquet
ALE	ASV Living Era	BEN	Benson
ALG	Alligator	BES	Beserkley
ALI	Alias	BET	Bethlehem
ALL	Allegiance	BEV	Beverly Glen
ALP	All Platinum	BF	Blast First
ALS	Alshire	BIG	Big Life
AMA	Amazing	BIO	Biograph
AMB	Amblin'	BIZ	Bizarre/Straight
AME	American Recordings	BKS	Backstreet
AMH	Amherst	BL	Black Lion
AMI	AMI	BLA	Blackout!
AML	A Major Label	BLD	Bulldog
AMP	American Pie	BLG	Bell Gold
AND	Antilles	BLI	Blind Pig
ANG	Angel	BLK	Blackheart
ANI	Animal	BLM	Bellmark
ANT	Antone's Records & Tapes	BLN	Blue Note
AP	August Productions	BLR	Bellaire
AQ	Audioquest	BLU	Bluebird
ARA	Aura	BLV	Black Vinyl
ARH	Arhoolie	BM	Blue Moon
ARI	Arista Texas	BMA	BMA
ARL	Ariola America	BMG	BMG
ARR	Arrival	BMP	Bomp
ART	Arista Texas	BN	Bar/None
ARY	Arylis	BNA	BNA Entertainment
AS	Antler Subway	BNG	Bang
ASV	ASV	BOO	Boot
ASY	Asylum	BOR	Buy Our Records
AT	Alternative Tentacles	BP	Blue Plate
ATA	Atlanta Artists	BPI	BPI
ATC	Atco	BRA	Brainchild
ATL	Atlantic	BRN	Burnside
ATN	Alston	BRR	Briar

BRS	Bearsville	CMG	Chase Music Group
BRU	Brunswick	CMH	CMH
BRZ	Bronze	CML	Chameleon
BS	Blue Sky	CMO	Commodores
BSA	Black Saint	CMP	Compleat
BSL	Bescol, Ltd.	CMS	Comstock
BSU	Black Sun	CMU	Creative Music Productions
BT	Big Tree	CNN	Canaan
BTF	Butterfly	CNQ	Conquest
BTO	Black Top	COL	Columbia
BTZ	Blitzz	COM	Commercial
BUD	Buddah	CON	Constellation
BUG	Bug	COP	Copper Creek
BUL	Bullseye Blues	COR	Cornbelt
BUS	Bust It	COT	Cotillion
BV	Bluesville	COU	Country International
BVM	Bovema	CP	Concord Picante Jazz
BW	Boardwalk	CPA	Cleopatra
BWV	Blue Wave	CPC	Capricorn
B/C	Badland	CPE	Caprice
CAE	Caedmon	CPI	Capri Ltd.
CAL	Calla	CPR	Caprice International
CAM	Camel	CPT	Captive
CAN	Candy	CRB	Curb
CAP	Capitol	CRE	Cream
CAR	Caribou	CRI	Critique
CAS	Casablanca	CRL	Caroline
CBA	CBS Associated	CRM	Carmel
CCB	Curb/Capitol	CRN	Corinthian
CCJ	Concord Jazz	CRO	Crossover
CD	Carpe Diem	CRR	Carrere
CDP	Carolsdatter Productions	CRS	Crescendo
CEL	Celluloid	CRT	Creative Energy Productions
CEX	Cexton	CRZ	Cruz
CGO	Cargo	CSP	Columbia Special Projects
CHA	Chaos	CSS	Chess
CHC	Chocolate City	CTH	Carthage
CHE	Chesky	CTI	CTI
CHI	China	CTM	Contemporary
CHR	Chrysalis	CUN	Cuneiform
CHS	Charisma	CUR	Curtom
CHT	Chestnut	CUT	Cutting
CHU	Churchill	CUU	Continuum
CIA	Creative Independent Artists	CW	Creative World
CJ	Classic Jazz	CYP	Cypress
CLA	Clappers	C/Z	C/Z
CLD	Cold Chillin'	DAK	Dakar
CLE	Clean Cuts	DAL	Dali
CLG	Collegium	DAN	Dancing Cat
CLS	Classified	DAR	Daring
CLT	Collectables	DB	DB
CMB	Cambria Records & Publishing	DCO	Discovery
CMF	Country Music Foundation	DD	Dr. Dream Music Group

DEC	Decca	EOD	Epic/Ode
DED	Dedicated	EPA	Epic Associated
DEF	Def American	EPI	Epic
DEL	Delmark	EPR	Es Paranza
DEN	Denon	EPT	Epitaph
DEP	Deep River	EPX	Epic Soundtrax
DER	Deram	ER	Ever Rat
DF	Del Fi	ERA	Era
DFC	Def Jam/Columbia	ERC	Empire Recording Communications
DFJ	Def Jam	ERI	Eric
DGC	DGC (David Geffen Co.)	ERT	Erato
DGG	Deutsche Grammophon Gesellschaft	ESP	ESP Disk
DHL	Dunhill Compact Classics	EVD	Evidence Music
DHM	Deutsche Harmonia Mundi	EVR	Everest
DIG	Digital Music Products	EW	East West
DIM	Dimension	EXA	Exact
DIS	Disney	EXI	Exit
DJ	Dee-Jay	E/C	Elektra/Curb
DJM	DJM	FA	Full Moon/Asylum
DKH	Dark Horse	FAI	Fairview
DL	De-Lite	FAN	Fantasy
DOC	Doctor Jazz	FEV	Fever
DOM	Dominion Entertainment	FF	Flying Fish
DOO	Door Knob	FFR	Full Frequency Range Recordings
DOR	Dore	FFT	Fifty One West
DOT	Dot	FIC	Fiction
DR	Death Row	FID	Fidelity Sound Recordings
DRG	DRG	FIF	Fifty States
DRM	Dreamland	FIR	First Warning
DRT	Dreamtime	FL	Front Line
DSC	Discreet	FLA	Flair
DSH	Dash	FLD	Flying Dutchman
DSQ	Disques Swing	FLK	Folklyric
DTA	Delta	FLV	Flavor Unit
DTN	Dooto	FLW	Smithsonian Folkways
DUC	Duck	FLY	Fly/Sire
DV	Delicious Vinyl	FM	Full Moon
EAC	Earache/Relativity	FOL	Folk Era
EAG	Eagle	FON	Fontana
EAR	Ear Candy	FOR	Fortuna
EAT	Eat	FOS	Fossil
ECM	ECM	FOU	Fountain
EDI	Editions E.G.	FOX	Fox/Arista
ELA	Elation	FP	First Priority
ELE	Elektra	FRE	Fresh Fruit
EMA	Emarcy	FRK	Freckle
EMC	Earwig Music Co.	FRN	Frontier
EMI	EMI	FSB	Flashback
EML	Emily	FSG	First Generation
ENC	Enigma Capitol	FTN	Foundation
ENI	Enigma	FTT	Fruit Of The Tune
ENJ	Enja	FW	Full Moon/Warner Bros.
ENS	Ensign	GAL	Galaxy

GAS	Gasoline Alley	HOM	Homecoming
GAT	Gateway	HOO	Hoodswamp
GC	Gold Castle	HOT	Hot Productions
GCI	Grind Core International	HRT	Heartbeat
GDG	Grudge	HS	Hearts Of Space
GEE	Gee Street	HT	Hightone
GEF	Geffen	HUR	Heads Up Records International
GEN	Genes Compact Disc Co.	HW	High Water Recording Co.
GFT	Gift Horse	H&L	H&L
GG	Gone Gator	IAI	Improvising Artists Inc.
GHY	Greenhays	IC	Inner City
GIA	Giant	ICH	Ichiban
GJ	Giants/Jazz	IGR	International Marketing Group
GLA	Glades	ILO	Iloki
GLB	Globo	IMA	Intima
GLM	Gold Mountain	IMC	Intercom Music Corp.
GLN	Glendale	IMG	Imago
GLO	Global Pacific	IMI	Imagine
GMC	GMC	IMP	Imperial
GOR	Gordy	INC	Increase
GO!	Go! Discs	IND	Indigo
GRA	Granite	INF	Infinity
GRD	Grateful Dead	INN	Innovative Communications
GRE	Green Linnet	INS	Intense
GRL	Garland	INT	Intermedia
GRM	Gramavision	INV	Invincible
GRN	Green World	IP	Independent Project
GRP	GRP	IPA	Impact
GRT	GRT	IPV	Improv
GRU	Grunt	IRN	I.R.S./No Speak
GS	Gland Slamm	IRS	I.R.S.
GSR	Great Southern	IS	Innersong
GTJ	Good Time Jazz	ISC	Interscope
GTS	GTS	ISL	Island
GUS	Gusto	IST	Imperial Stab Chamber
GWE	GWE	IVO	Ivory
GWR	GWR	JAM	Jamie
HAL	Halkat Country	JAZ	Jazz Man
HAR	Harvest	JBC	Jambco
HB	Hollywood Basic	JBX	JBX
HBL	Hannibal	JC	J.C.
HDH	HDH	JCI	JCI Music
HEA	Heat Wave	JEL	Jellybean Productions
HEY	Heyday	JER	Jeremiah
HH	Happy Hour Music	JET	Jet
HIG	High Street	JH	Jim Henson
HIN	Hindsight	JJ	Jay Jay
HIR	Hi	JM	Jazz Masters
HIS	Historical	JMT	Jazz Music Today
HMI	Heart Music Inc.	JNS	Janus
HO	Higher Octave	JRS	JRS
HOG	Hogeye	JST	Justice
HOL	Hollywood	JUA	Juana

JUS	Justin Time	MCP	MC
JVA	Jive	MCR	Mustcor
JVC	JVC Music	MD	Moulin D'Or Recordings
JZL	Jazz Land	MDJ	MDJ
KAL	Kaleidoscope	MEG	Megaforce
KAT	Kat Family	MEL	Melodeon
KDU	Kudo	MEN	Mentor/Mind Boggler
KEN	Kenwood	MER	Mercury
KIR	Kirshner	MES	Messidor
KLA	Klavier	MET	Metal Blade
KNR	Ken	MFL	Music For Little People
KNT	Kent	MG	Mardi Gras
KOA	Koala	MGM	MGM
KT	K-Tel	MGO	Mango
KUC	Kuckuck	MGR	Margaritaville
LAF	LaFace	MIK	Mika
LAM	Lamon	MIL	Millenium
LAN	Landmark	MIN	Mind Dust Music
LAS	Laser Light	MIR	Mirage
LAU	Laurie	MIS	Missing Link
LB	Luaka Bop	MJJ	MJJ
LCY	Lucy	MLN	Milan
LD	Little David	MM	Musicmasters
LDR	Little Darlin'	MNT	Mountain
LEC	Lection	MOB	Mobile Fidelity Sound Lab
LEG	LeGrand	MOD	Modern
LG	Little Giant	MOJ	Mojazz
LGS	Long Song	MON	Monument
LH	Los Hermanos	MOO	Moonstone
LIB	Liberty	MOR	Morocco
LIF	Lifesong	MOT	Motown
LIN	Linden	MOU	Mountain Railroad
LIV	Living Music	MOV	Moving Target
LLA	Lost Lake Arts	MPL	Metropolitan
LMR	LMR	MRC	MRC
LNS	Lone Star	MRR	Mirror
LON	London	MRY	Mercenary
LS	Laughing Stock	MS	Milestone
LUK	Luke	MSA	Mesa
L&L	Lamb & Lion	MSD	Monsterdisc
MA	M-A Music International	MSH	Mushroom
MAC	Mountain Apple Co.	MSO	Maison De Soul
MAI	Mainstreet	MSP	MCA Special Products
MAL	Malaco	MST	Mainstream
MAM	Mammoth	MTC	Manticore
MAN	Manhattan	MTM	MTM
MAR	Marzipan Music	MTO	Megatone
MAV	Maverick	MTR	Metrotone
MBR	Modern Blues Recordings	MUS	Muse
MC	Morgan Creek	MUT	Mute
MCA	MCA	MW	Magic Wind
MCC	Curb/MCA	MYR	Myrrh
MCI	MCA/Impulse	M&R	M&R

NA	New Artists	PAN	Panorama
NAL	New Allegiance	PAR	Parachute
NAR	Narada	PAS	Passport
NAT	Nationwide Sound Distributors	PAT	Patriot
NBL	Noble Vision	PAU	Pausa
NC	Newport Classic	PB	Playback
NEB	Nebula	PBO	Posh Boy
NEM	Nemperor	PBY	Playboy
NET	Nettwork	PC	Pacific Challenger
NEW	New Renaissance	PD	P.R.O. Division
NH	Nighthawk	PEA	Pearl
NIM	Nimbus	PEN	Pendulum
NJ	New Jazz	PER	Permian
NL	Naked Language	PF	Pearl Flapper
NON	Nonesuch	PFR	Performance
NOT	Nothing	PGI	Progressive International
NOV	Novus	PHI	Philips
NP	Next Plateau	PHL	Phil World
NS	North Star	PHO	Philo
NSY	Nastymix	PI	Philadelphia International
NTN	Newtown	PIA	Play It Again Sam
NTR	NuTrayl	PIC	Pickwick
NUV	Nouveau	PIN	Pinecastle
NVA	Nova	PIR	PIR
NW	Nightwork	PJ	Projazz
NYC	NYC	PJZ	Pacific Jazz
OB	Oh Boy	PL	Pop Llama Productions
OBR	OBR/Columbia	PLA	Paula
OCE	Oceana	PLL	Phil. LA
OGO	Oglio	PLN	Plantation
OLI	Olivia	PLY	Playback
OLR	Olympic	PMP	Pump
OME	Omega	PMR	PMRC
OMN	Omni	PNG	Pangaea
OMU	Omnium	PNT	Planet
ONE	One Little Indian	POE	Pro-Arte
OOP	out of print	POI	Pointblank
OPE	Open Air	POL	Polydor
OPS	Oops	POP	Poppy
OPT	Optimism	POR	Portrait
ORF	Orpheus	POW	Powerhouse
OSR	Original Sound	PP	Power Pak
OT	Old Timey	PRA	Prairie Dog
OUT	OutBurst	PRC	Parc
OVA	Ovation	PRD	Paradise
OW	One Way	PRG	Progressive
OYS	Oyster	PRI	Private I
P3	Project 3	PRO	Profile
PA	Pacific Arts Radio	PRR	Pair
PAB	Pablo	PRS	Prestige
PAC	Pacific	PRT	Parrot
PAI	Paisley Park	PRV	Private Music
PAJ	Palo Alto Jazz	PRY	Priority

PSH	Pasha	RLC	Ral/Columbia
PSO	Psonic	RLL	Roulette
PSP	Perspective	RLX	Relix
PVC	PVC	RMC	RMC
PVS	Private Stock	RMS	River Music
PWL	PWL America	ROA	Roadracer
PYN	Polydor Nashville	ROC	Rocket
PYR	Pyramid/Epic Associated	ROI	Roir
QKS	Quicksilver	ROM	Really Outstanding Music
QUA	Quality	RON	Ronn
QUE	Qwest	ROO	Rooster Blues
QUI	Quintessence	ROU	Rounder
RAC	Racket	RPR	Reprise
RAD	Radioactive	RQ	Rose Quartz
RAG	Radio Active Gold	RR	Roadrunner
RAL	Ralph	RS	Rolling Stones
RAN	Ranwood	RSG	Resounding
RAP	Rap-A-Lot	RSH	Rocshire
RAR	Rock 'N' Roll	RSO	RSO
RAS	Real Authentic Sound Recordings	RST	Rust
RAT	Rattlesnake	RT	Rough Trade
RB	Red Baron	RUB	Ruby
RBB	Rag Baby	RUC	Ruffhouse/Columbia
RCA	RCA	RUF	Ruffhouse
RCC	RCA/Curb	RUP	Ruthless/Priority
RDD	Red	RUT	Ruthless
RDH	Red House	RV	Rockville
RDS	Roadshow	RVL	Revolver
RE	Red Eye	RVR	Riverside
REA	Reality	RWD	Redwood
REC	Record Guys	RYK	Rykodisc
RED	Red Label	R&T	Razor & Tie
REF	Reference Recordings	SA	Sonic Atmospheres
REG	Regency/Atco	SAF	Safety Net
REH	Rare Earth	SAI	Sailor
REL	Relativity	SAJ	Saja
REP	Republic	SAN	Sandstone Music
RES	Restless	SAV	Savoy
REU	Reunion	SB	Story Of Blues
REV	Revere	SBK	SBK
RGB	Rag Baby	SCA	Scarface
RGO	Rego Irish Records & Tapes	SCO	Scotti Brothers
RH	Rock Hotel	SD	Sin-Drome
RHA	Rehash	SEA	Sea Breeze
RHI	Rhino	SEC	Second Wave
RHS	Rhyme Syndicate	SEL	Select
RHY	Rhythm Safari	SH	Sugar Hill
RID	Ridgetop	SHA	Shanachie
RIM	Rim	SHE	Sheher
RIT	Right Stuff	SHF	Sheffield Lab
RIV	Riva	SHO	Shoreline
RK	Rhythm King	SHR	Shrapnel
RL	Red Light	SI	Scheming Intelligentsia

SIA	Silas	STX	Stax
SIE	Sierra	STY	Storyville
SIL	Silvertone	SUM	Sumertone
SIN	Sinatra	SUN	Sun
SIR	Sire	SUR	Survival
SJZ	Savoy Jazz	SUT	Sutra
SKY	Sky	SW	Silver Wave
SLK	Salek	SWA	Swallow
SLM	Slamdek	TAB	Tabu
SLR	Solar	TAG	Taggart
SLS	Slash	TAJ	Taj
SMA	Smash	TAK	Takoma
SMC	Sony Classical	TAM	Tamla
SNC	Sunshine Country	TAP	Tapestry
SND	Soundwaves	TBA	TBA
SNI	Sounding	TE	Total Experience
SNV	Sunnyview	TEM	Temple
SNY	Sunnyview	TEN	Tenacious
SO	Step One	TER	Terra Nova
SOG	Sona Gaia	TF	Terra Firma
SOH	SOH Distributors Network	THI	Third Stone
SOL	S.O.U.L.	THR	Thriving Productions
SON	Sound Of New York	TIM	Timbreline
SOS	So So Def	TK	TK
SOU	Southern Cross	TLR	Telarc
SP	Sub Pop	TMB	Tommy Boy
SPC	Spector	TMS	TMS
SPE	Specialty	TN	T-Neck
SPI	Spindizzy	TNC	Trance Syndicate
SPM	Special Music Co.	TNG	Taang!
SPO	Sportsongs	TOM	Tomato
SPR	Spring	TOW	Townhouse
SPT	Spindletop	TR	Third Rail
SPW	Sparrow	TRD	Tradition
SRC	Source	TRI	Triloka
SRR	Sire/Reprise	TRN	True North
SS	Swan Song	TRP	Trip
SSL	Salsoul	TS	Tru-Sound
SSM	Solid Smoke	TSR	TSR
SSP	Sony Music Special Projects	TST	Turnstyle
SSS	SSS International	TT	Twin-Tone
SST	SST	TUD	Tudor
ST	Stet	TUF	Tuff Gong
STA	Starborn	TUR	Turquoise
STD	Stardog	TVT	TVT
STE	Step One	TZ	Tappan Zee
STF	Stiff	T&G	Touch & Go
STH	Southland	T/P	Threshold
STN	Soul Train	UA	United Artists
STO	Stinson	UG	Unlimited Gold
STR	Starday	UNI	Uni
STS	Statiras	USA	USA Music Group
STW	Streetwise	UT	Uptown

VAN	Vanguard		WWI	Westwind
VAR	Varrick		W/C	WB/Curb
VC	Vanguard Classics		W/I	Wrap/Ichiban
VCT	Victory		XER	Xeres
VDT	Vendetta		XXX	Triple X Entertainment
VEN	Venture		YAZ	Yazoo
VF	Verve/Forecast		YOU	You Guys
VGO	Virgo		YT	Yellow Tail
VIA	Virgin America		ZAP	Zappa
VIC	Victory Music		ZMB	Zombie
VIN	Vinyl Dreams		ZOO	Zoo Entertainment
VIO	Violator		ZTO	Zito
VIR	Virgin		ZTT	ZTT
VJ	Vee-Jay		ZYX	ZYX
VMM	Virgin Movie Music			
VNT	Vintertainment			
VOL	Volt			
VOS	Voss			
VOY	Voyager			
VRA	Video Record Albums			
VRV	Verve			
VS	Varese Sarabande			
VSO	V.S.O.P.			
VTG	Vertigo			
VVA	Viva			
VYL	Vinyl Communications			
WAR	Warfare			
WAT	Watermelon			
WAX	Wax Trax			
WB	Warner Bros.			
WBC	Warner Bros./Curb			
WC	Warner/Curb			
WCH	Windchime			
WDM	World Disc Music			
WDN	Wooden Nickel			
WE	West End			
WEX	World Export			
WH	Windham Hill			
WHI	Whitfield			
WHO	Who's Who In Jazz			
WIL	Wilbury/Warner Bros.			
WIN	Wing			
WIZ	Wizard			
WL	Warlock			
WMO	WMOT			
WOR	Word			
WP	World Pacific			
WS	Windsong			
WSB	Westbound			
WSP	Warner Special Projects			
WTG	WTG			
WTR	Waterhouse			
WW	Warner Western			

A

B

BOOTS *See* SHOES 558
BOOZE *See* ALCOHOL 13
BORED *See* SLEEP 567
BOSSES *See* ROYALTY 526
BOXING *See* SPORTS 580
BOYS *See* MEN: GENERAL 369
BREATHE *See* AIR 11
BRIDGES 49
 See also RIVERS, ROAD
BROKE *See* POVERTY 466
BROKEN MARRIAGE *See* DIVORCE 195
BRONX *See* CITIES: NEW YORK 98
BROOKLYN *See* CITIES: NEW YORK 98
BUGS *See* INSECTS 324
BULLETS *See* GUNS 282
BURNING *See* FIRE 238
BUS 50
 See also ROAD, TRAVELING
BUYING *See* SHOPPING 559

C

CABINS *See* HOUSES 322
CAFES *See* RESTAURANTS 506
CAMERAS *See* ART & PHOTOGRAPHY 35
CANDLES *See* FIRE 238
CAPITAL PUNISHMENT 50
 See also CRIME, DEATH, KILL, REBELS
CARD GAMES *See* GAMBLING 270
CARNIVALS 51
 See also FUN, HAPPINESS, CITIES: NEW
 ORLEANS
CARS 54
 See also CARS: CADILLAC, ROAD, ROAD
 ACCIDENTS, TAXI, TRAVELING,
 TRUCKS
CARS: CADILLAC 57
 See also CARS, ROAD, ROAD
 ACCIDENTS, TRAVELING, TRUCKS
CARTOON CHARACTERS 58
CASINO GAMES *See* GAMBLING 270
CASTLES *See* ROYALTY 526
CATS 59
 See also ANIMALS: A-Z
CELEBRATE *See* PARTY 458
CHAINS *See* PRISON 476
CHANCE *See* GAMBLING 270
CHAOS 60
 See also CRIME, LAW & ORDER, NU-
 CLEAR ENERGY, ROAD ACCIDENTS,
 SHIPS, WAR
CHEATING *See* LIES 344
CHILDREN 62
 See also BABY, REBELS, TEENAGERS,
 TOYS & GAMES
CHRISTMAS 66
 See also GOD
CHURCH *See* GOD 272

CIGARETTES 77
 See also FIRE
CIRCLES 78
 See also LIFE
CIRCUS *See* CARNIVALS 51
CITIES: A 81
 See also COUNTRIES, STATES, CITIES:
 ATLANTA
CITIES: ATLANTA 82
 See also STATES: GEORGIA
CITIES: B 82
 See also CITIES: BALTIMORE, BERLIN,
 BIRMINGHAM, BOSTON
CITIES: BALTIMORE 83
 See also STATES: MARYLAND
CITIES: BERLIN 83
CITIES: BIRMINGHAM 84
 See also STATES: ALABAMA
CITIES: BOSTON 84
 See also STATES: MASSACHUSETTS
CITIES: C 84
 See also CITIES: CHICAGO, CINCINNATI
CITIES: CHICAGO 85
 See also STATES: ILLINOIS
CITIES: CINCINNATI 86
 See also STATES: OHIO
CITIES: D 86
 See also CITIES: DALLAS, DENVER,
 DETROIT, DUBLIN
CITIES: DALLAS 87
 See also STATES: TEXAS
CITIES: DENVER 87
 See also STATES: COLORADO
CITIES: DETROIT 87
 See also CARS, STATES: MICHIGAN
CITIES: DUBLIN 88
 See also COUNTRIES: IRELAND
CITIES: E 88
CITIES: F 88
CITIES: G 88
CITIES: H 89
 See also CITIES: HOUSTON
CITIES: HOUSTON 89
 See also STATES: TEXAS
CITIES: I 89
CITIES: J 89
CITIES: K 90
 See also CITIES: KANSAS CITY
CITIES: KANSAS CITY 90
 See also STATES: KANSAS, MISSOURI
CITIES: L 90
 See also CITIES: LAS VEGAS, LONDON,
 LOS ANGELES
CITIES: LAS VEGAS 91
 See also GAMBLING, LUCK, STATES:
 NEVADA
CITIES: LONDON 91
 See also COUNTRIES: ENGLAND

COUNTRIES: ENGLAND 149
  See also CITIES: LONDON, COUNTRIES: SCOTLAND
COUNTRIES: FRANCE 150
  See also CITIES: PARIS
COUNTRIES: G 150
COUNTRIES: GERMANY 150
  See also CITIES: BERLIN
COUNTRIES: H 151
COUNTRIES: I 151
COUNTRIES: IRELAND 151
  See also CITIES: DUBLIN
COUNTRIES: JAMAICA 152
COUNTRIES: JAPAN 153
  See also CITIES: TOKYO
COUNTRIES: K 153
COUNTRIES: M 153
COUNTRIES: MEXICO 153
  See also COUNTRIES: S, SPANISH
COUNTRIES: N 154
COUNTRIES: P 154
  See also COUNTRIES: POLAND
COUNTRIES: POLAND 155
COUNTRIES: RUSSIA 155
  See also CITIES: MOSCOW
COUNTRIES: S 156
  See also COUNTRIES: SCOTLAND, SWEDEN, SWITZERLAND
COUNTRIES: SCOTLAND 156
  See also COUNTRIES: ENGLAND
COUNTRIES: SPAIN 156
  See also COUNTRIES: MEXICO; SPANISH
COUNTRIES: SWEDEN 156
COUNTRIES: SWITZERLAND 156
COUNTRIES: T 157
COUNTRIES: U 157
COUNTRIES: V 157
  See also COUNTRIES: VIETNAM
COUNTRIES: VIETNAM 157
  See also POLITICAL CLASSICS, WAR
COUNTRY 157
  See also FARMS, MUSIC
COUNTRY MUSIC *See* COUNTRY 157
COUNTRYSIDE *See* COUNTRY 157
COURAGE *See* FEAR 232
COWBOYS 159
  See also HORSES, REBELS, RODEO
COWGIRLS *See* COWBOYS 159
CRACK *See* DRUGS: COCAINE 214
CRAZY 162
CREEKS *See* RIVERS 508
CRIME 166
  See also FIGHT, LAW & ORDER, POLICE, PRISON, REBELS
CRYING 169
  See also RAIN

D

DADDY *See* FATHERS 229
DANCE 175
  See also MUSIC, PARTY, ROCK
DANCE STYLES *See* DANCE 175
DANGER *See* CHAOS 60
DAWN *See* MORNING 409
DAYS OF THE WEEK: FRIDAY 184
DAYS OF THE WEEK: MONDAY 184
DAYS OF THE WEEK: SATURDAY 185
DAYS OF THE WEEK: SUNDAY 187
DAYS OF THE WEEK: THURSDAY 189
DAYS OF THE WEEK: TUESDAY 189
DAYS OF THE WEEK: WEDNESDAY 190
DEATH 190
  See also CAPITAL PUNISHMENT, HEAVEN, HELL, KILL, LIFE
DEJA VU *See* CIRCLES 78
DELTA *See* RIVERS 508
DETECTIVES *See* POLICE 462
DEVILS 194
  See also HELL, MONSTERS, SPIRITS
DIAMONDS *See* JEWELRY 332
DIARY *See* BOOKS 46
DICE *See* GAMBLING 270
DINOSAURS *See* REPTILES 505
DISASTERS *See* CHAOS 60
DISEASES *See* DOCTORS 196
DISGUISE *See* PRETEND 471
DIVORCE 195
  See also MARRIAGE
DIZZY *See* CRAZY 162
DJs *See* RADIO 492
DOCTORS 196
  See also HEART
DOGS 201
  See also ANIMALS: A-Z
DOLPHINS *See* WHALES 661
DOMESTIC VIOLENCE *See* FIGHT 235
DOORS 203
  See also SECRETS
DRAFT 205
  See also POLITICAL CLASSICS, PROTEST, WAR
DREAMS 205
  See also PRETEND, SLEEP
DRINKING *See* ALCOHOL 13
DRIVING *See* CARS 54
DRUGS 210
  See also ALCOHOL, DRUGS: COCAINE, MARIJUANA
DRUGS: COCAINE 214
DRUGS: MARIJUANA 214
  See also DRUGS, DRUGS: COCAINE

E

EARTH 215
  See also ECOLOGY, STARS
EARTHQUAKE 216
  See also DANCE (SHAKING)
EASTER 216
  See also GOD
EATING *See* FOOD 249
ECHOES 216
  See also REFLECTIONS, SHADOWS
ECLIPSE *See* MOON 406
ECOLOGY 216
  See also NUCLEAR ENERGY, POLITICAL
  CLASSICS
EGO 217
  See also HAPPINESS, JEALOUSY, LIFE
ELECTRICITY *See* ENERGY 222
ENERGY 222
  See also GAS STATIONS, NUCLEAR
  ENERGY
ENVIRONMENT *See* ECOLOGY 216
EVENING *See* NIGHT 434
EYES 223
  See also FINDING, SEARCHING, SEEING

F

FAIRS *See* CARNIVALS 51
FANTASY *See* PRETEND 471
FARMERS *See* FARMS 228
FARMS 228
  See also ANIMALS
FASHION *See* CLOTHES 110
FAT 229
  See also FOOD
FATHERS 229
  See also MEN: GENERAL, MEN'S NAMES
FEAR 232
  See also CHAOS, EGO, HIDING
FEELING GOOD *See* HAPPINESS 285
FEMINISM 234
  See also EGO, WOMEN: GENERAL,
  WORK
FEMINIST INDEPENDENCE *See* FEMINISM
234
FIGHT 235
  See also CRIME, DEATH, POLICE,
  PROTEST, REBELS, WAR
FINDING 237
  See also SEARCHING
FINGERS *See* ANATOMY: HANDS 20
FIRE 238
  See also HOT
FISH 243
  See also FOOD, WHALES
FISHING *See* FISH 243
FLIGHT *See* FLYING 247

FLOWERS 244
  See also ECOLOGY, ROSES, TREES
FLYING 247
  See also AIRPLANES, BIRDS, DRUGS
FLYING IN PLANES *See* AIRPLANES 11
FOG *See* RAIN 494
FOOD 249
  See also ALCOHOL, COFFEE, FISH,
  FRUIT, RESTAURANTS, VEGETABLES
FOOLS 255
  See also INSULTS
FOOTBALL 258
  See also CITIES, FIGHT, SCHOOL,
  SPORTS, STATES
FOWL *See* BIRDS 42
FREEDOM 258
  See also COUNTRIES: AMERICA,
  MONTHS: JULY, PRISON, PROTEST,
  ROYALTY
FREEZING *See* COLD 113
FRIENDS 260
FROGS *See* REPTILES 505
FRUIT 264
  See also FOOD, VEGETABLES
FUN 266
  See also DANCE, HAPPINESS, PARTY,
  SMILE
FUNNY *See* SMILE 575
FUTURE 267
  See also CHAOS, TIME: GENERAL

G

GAMBLING 270
  See also CITIES: LAS VEGAS, LUCK,
  SPORTS, WINNING
GARBAGE *See* TRASH 635
GARDENS *See* FLOWERS 244
GAS STATIONS 272
  See also CARS, ENERGY,
  MOTORCYCLES, TRAVELING, TRUCKS
GEMS *See* JEWELRY 332
GETTING DRUNK *See* ALCOHOL 13
GETTING STONED *See* DRUGS: MARIJUANA
214
GHETTO *See* POVERTY 466
GHOSTS *See* SPIRITS 579
GHOULS *See* SPIRITS 579
GIRLS *See* WOMEN: GENERAL 667
GLASSES *See* CLOTHES 110
GLASSES *See* EYES 223
GOBLINS *See* SPIRITS 579
GOD 272
  See also ANGELS, CHRISTMAS, HEAVEN,
  HELL, MARRIAGE
GOLD 280
GOLDEN *See* GOLD 280
GOODNIGHT *See* NIGHT 434
Good Times *See* FUN 266

GRASS *See* FLOWERS 244
GUNS 282
    See also CRIME, DEATH, FIGHT, KILL,
    POLICE, REBELS, WAR

H

HALLOWEEN *See* MONSTERS 400
HAPPINESS 285
    See also DOCTORS, FUN, PARTY, SMILE
HARBOR, LAKE *See* OCEAN 451
HARD TIMES *See* POVERTY 466
HARLEM *See* CITIES: NEW YORK 98
HATS 290
    See also CLOTHES
HEALING *See* DOCTORS 196
HEAR 291
    See also Various COMMUNICATION
    categories
HEART 293
HEAT *See* HOT 318
HEAVEN 302
    See also ANGELS, DEATH, GOD,
    HAPPINESS, HELL
HELL 304
    See also DEATH, DEVILS, GOD, HEAVEN
HELP 305
HERO 308
    See also WAR, WINNING
HIDING 309
    See also CRIME, FEAR, FINDING, LAW &
    ORDER, PRETEND, REBELS,
    SEARCHING
HIGH CONSCIOUSNESS *See* DRUGS 210
HIGHWAY *See* ROAD 511
HILLS *See* MOUNTAINS 416
HITCHHIKING *See* CARS 54
HOBOS *See* TRAINS 629
HOLLYWOOD 310
    See also CITIES: LOS ANGELES, MOVIES,
    SHOW BIZ
HOME 311
    See also HOUSES, TRAVELING
HOMOSEXUALS 316
    See also SEX
HONKY TONKS *See* BARS 40
HORSE RACING *See* SPORTS 580
HORSES 316
    See also COWBOYS, REBELS, RODEO
HOSPITALS *See* DOCTORS 196
HOT 318
    See also FIRE, HELL
HOTELS 320
HOUSES 322
    See also HOME
HUNGRY *See* FOOD 249
HUNTING *See* GUNS 282
HURRICANES *See* RAIN 494

HURTING *See* DOCTORS 196

I

ICE *See* SNOW 577
IDENTITY *See* EGO 217
IMAGINE *See* PRETEND 471
IMPENDING DOOM *See* CHAOS 60
INDIANS *See* NATIVE AMERICANS 432
INFORMATION *See* COMPUTERS 141
INSECTS 324
INSTRUCTION *See* SCHOOL 529
INSULTS 326
    See also FOOLS
ISLANDS 329
    See also OCEAN, PARADISE

J

JEALOUSY 330
    See also EGO
JESUS CHRIST *See* GOD 272
JEWELRY 332
    See also GOLD, MONEY, ROYALTY
JUKEBOX 334
    See also MUSIC
JUNGLES 335
    See also TREES
JUNK *See* TRASH 635
JUSTICE *See* LAW & ORDER 342

K

KARMA *See* CIRCLES 78
KILL 336
    See also CAPITAL PUNISHMENT, DEATH,
    DRUGS, FIGHT, GUNS, REBELS, WAR
KINGS 338
    See also QUEENS, ROYALTY
KISSING 341
    See also SEX, various ANATOMY
    Categories
KITCHENS *See* FOOD 249

L

LADIES *See* WOMEN: GENERAL 667
LAUGH *See* SMILE 575
LAUNDRY *See* CLOTHES 110
LAW & ORDER 342
    See also CAPITAL PUNISHMENT, CRIME,
    POLICE, PRISON, REBELS
LAWYERS *See* LAW & ORDER 342
LEARNING *See* SCHOOL 529
LETTERS *See* MAIL 363
LIES 344
    See also HIDING, PRETEND

LIFE 346
  See also BABY, CIRCLES, DEATH, WORK
LIGHTNING *See* RAIN 494
LISTEN *See* HEAR 291
LITTLE 355
  See also SMALL for things of small size
LITTLE IN AMOUNT *See* LITTLE 355
LIVING *See* LIFE 346
LOOKING AT *See* SEEING 545
LOOKING FOR... *See* SEARCH 532
LUCK 357
  See also CITIES: LAS VEGAS, GAMBLING

M

MACHINES 358
MAGAZINES *See* NEWS 433
MAGIC 360
  See also MONSTERS, SPIRITS, UFO'S
MAIL 363
MAMA *See* MOTHERS 413
MANHATTAN *See* CITIES: NEW YORK 98
MARDI GRAS *See* CARNIVALS 51
MARDI GRAS *See* CITIES: NEW ORLEANS 97
MARRIAGE 365
  See also DIVORCE
MEALS *See* FOOD 249
MEN'S NAMES: A 380
  See also MEN: GENERAL
MEN'S NAMES: B 381
MEN'S NAMES: C 382
MEN'S NAMES: D 383
MEN'S NAMES: E 383
MEN'S NAMES: F 384
MEN'S NAMES: G 384
MEN'S NAMES: H 384
MEN'S NAMES: I 385
MEN'S NAMES: J 385
  See also GOD (JESUS)
MEN'S NAMES: K 388
MEN'S NAMES: L 388
MEN'S NAMES: M 389
MEN'S NAMES: N 390
MEN'S NAMES: O 390
MEN'S NAMES: P 390
MEN'S NAMES: Q 391
MEN'S NAMES: R 391
MEN'S NAMES: S 392
MEN'S NAMES: T 393
MEN'S NAMES: U 393
MEN'S NAMES: V 393
MEN'S NAMES: W 393
MEN'S NAMES: Z 394
MEN: GENERAL 369
  See also FATHERS, MEN'S NAMES,
  TEENAGERS
MESSAGES *See* MAIL 363
MIDNIGHT 394
  See also NIGHT

MILITARY *See* WAR 654
MIND CONTROL *See* MACHINES 358
MINING 396
  See also GOLD, MOUNTAINS, WORK
MIRACLES *See* MAGIC 360
MIRRORS *See* REFLECTIONS 504
MOM *See* MOTHERS 413
MONEY 396
  See also GOLD, JEWELRY, POVERTY,
  SHOPPING, WORK
MONSTERS 400
  See also CHAOS, HELL, MAGIC, UFO'S
MONTHS & DATES: APRIL 402
  See also SEASONS: SPRING
MONTHS & DATES: AUGUST 402
  See also SEASONS: SUMMER
MONTHS & DATES: DECEMBER 403
  See also CHRISTMAS, COLD, SEASONS:
  WINTER, SNOW
MONTHS & DATES: FEBRUARY 403
  See also SEASONS: WINTER
MONTHS & DATES: JANUARY 403
  See also SEASONS: WINTER
MONTHS & DATES: JULY 403
  See also SEASONS: SUMMER
MONTHS & DATES: JUNE 404
  See also SEASONS: SUMMER
MONTHS & DATES: MARCH 404
  See also SEASONS: SPRING
MONTHS & DATES: MAY 404
  See also SEASONS: SPRING
MONTHS & DATES: NOVEMBER 404
  See also SEASONS: AUTUMN
MONTHS & DATES: OCTOBER 405
  See also MONTHS & DATES: AUTUMN
MONTHS & DATES: SEPTEMBER 405
  See also SEASONS: AUTUMN
MOON 406
MORNING 409
  See also SUN
MOTELS *See* HOTELS 320
MOTHERS 413
  See also WOMEN: GENERAL, WOMEN'S
  NAMES
MOTORCYCLES 416
MOUNTAINS 416
MOVIES 420
  See also HOLLYWOOD, SHOW BIZ,
  TELEVISION
MOVIN' ON *See* TRAVELING 636
MURDER *See* KILL 336
MUSIC 421
  See also DANCE, JUKEBOX, MUSICAL IN-
  STRUMENTS, PARTY, RADIO, RHYTHM
MUSICAL INSTRUMENTS 429
  See also MUSIC
MUSICIANS *See* MUSIC 421

N

NATIVE AMERICANS 432
NATURAL HIGH *See* DRUGS 210
NATURE *See* ECOLOGY 216
NERVOUS *See* CRAZY 162
NEW YEAR'S *See* CHRISTMAS 66
NEWS 433
NEWSPAPERS *See* NEWS 433
NIGHT 434
 See also SATURDAY, SATURDAY NIGHT;
 MIDNIGHT, MOON
NOBLEMEN *See* KINGS 338
NONSENSE WORDS 446
NUCLEAR ENERGY 450
 See also PEACE, POLITICAL CLASSICS,
 WAR
NUCLEAR WAR *See* NUCLEAR ENERGY 450
NUCLEAR WEAPONS *See* NUCLEAR
ENERGY 450

O

OCEAN 451
 See also RIVERS, SAILING, SHIPS,
 SURFING, WATER
OLYMPICS *See* SPORTS 580
OPERATOR *See* TELEPHONE 615
OPPOSITES 454
OUTCAST *See* POVERTY 466
OUTDOORS *See* FLOWERS 244
OUTLAWS *See* REBELS 501

P

PAIN *See* DOCTORS 196
PANIC *See* FEAR 232
PARADES *See* CARNIVALS 51
PARADISE 457
 See also ISLANDS
PARANOIA *See* FEAR 232
PARKS *See* FLOWERS 244
PARTY 458
 See also CARNIVALS, DANCE, FUN,
 HAPPINESS, MUSIC, NIGHT
PEACE 460
 See also FRIENDS, HAPPINESS,
 POLITICAL CLASSICS, WAR
PHILOSOPHY *See* LIFE 346
PHONE NUMBERS *See* TELEPHONE 615
PIGS 462
PILOTS *See* AIRPLANES 11
PIMPS *See* PROSTITUTES 479
PLANETS *See* STARS 582
POLICE 462
 See also CRIME, GUNS, PRISONS, REBELS,
 WAR

POLITICAL CLASSICS 464
 See also ECOLOGY, NUCLEAR ENERGY,
 PEACE, POVERTY, PROTEST, WAR,
 WORLD
POLLUTION *See* ECOLOGY 216
POOR *See* POVERTY 466
PORPOISES *See* WHALES 661
POST OFFICE *See* MAIL 363
POVERTY 466
 See also GAMBLING, LUCK, MONEY,
 ROYALTY, TRAINS
POWER *See* ENERGY 222
PRAYER *See* GOD 272
PRECIOUS STONES *See* JEWELRY 332
PREDICTIONS *See* FUTURE 267
PREGNANT *See* BABY 37
PREJUDICE 470
 See also POLITICAL CLASSICS
PRESIDENTS 471
 See also KINGS, MEN'S NAMES, POLITI-
 CAL CLASSICS, QUEENS, ROYALTY
PRETEND 471
 See also DREAMS, HIDING, LIES
PRIDE *See* EGO 217
PRINCES *See* KINGS 338
PRINCESSES *See* QUEENS 482
PRISON 476
 See also FREEDOM, LAW & ORDER,
 POLICE
PROSTITUTES 479
 See also Sex
PROTEST 481
 See also CRIME, FIGHT, FREEDOM,
 POLITICAL CLASSICS, PREJUDICE, WAR
PSYCHIATRY *See* CRAZY 162
PUPPETS *See* TOYS & GAMES 625

Q

QUEENS *See* CITIES: NEW YORK 98
QUEENS 482
 See also KINGS, ROYALTY
QUESTIONS 484

R

RADIO 492
 See also MUSIC, ROCK
RAIN 494
 See also CHAOS, SKY, SUN
RAINBOWS 500
 See also COLORS (Various), RAIN
RAPE *See* CRIME 166
REBELS 501
 See also COWBOYS, CRIME, LAW &
 ORDER, POLICE, PRISON, TRAVELING
RECORD BUSINESS 504
 See also MUSIC, SHOW BIZ

REFLECTIONS 504
  See also ECHOES, SHADOWS
RELIGION *See* GOD 272
REPTILES 505
  See also ANIMALS: A-Z, FISH
RESCUE *See* HELP 305
RESTAURANTS 506
  See also BARS, COFFEE, FOOD, FRUIT,
  VEGETABLES
REVOLUTION *See* PROTEST 481
RHYTHM 507
  See also DANCE, MUSIC
RICH *See* MONEY 396
RIDING *See* HORSES 316
RIVERS 508
  See also OCEAN, SAILING, SHIPS, WATER
ROAD 511
  See also CARS, TRAVELING, TRUCKS
ROAD ACCIDENTS 516
  See also CARS, DEATH, TRUCKS
ROBOTS *See* MACHINES 358
ROCK 516
  See also DANCE, MOUNTAINS, MUSIC,
  PARTY, RADIO
ROCK & ROLL *See* ROCK 516
ROCKETS *See* SPACE 578
RODEO 523
  See also COWBOYS, HORSES
ROOFS *See* HOUSES 322
ROSES 523
  See also FLOWERS
ROWDY *See* REBELS 501
ROYALTY 526
  See also KINGS, MONEY, POLITICAL
  SONGS, PREJUDICE, QUEENS
RULING CLASS *See* ROYALTY 526
RUNAWAYS *See* REBELS 501
RUNNING *See* TRAVELING 636

S

SAILING 527
  See also OCEAN, RIVERS, SHIPS, WATER
SAILORS *See* SAILING 527
SATAN *See* DEVILS 194
SATELLITES *See* SPACE 578
SAT. NIGHT *See* DAYS OF THE WEEK:
SATURDAY 185
SAVE *See* HELP 305
SCHOOL 529
  See also TEENAGERS
SEA *See* OCEAN 451
SEALS *See* WHALES 661
SEARCH 532
  See also EYES, FINDING, SEEING
SEASONS: AUTUMN 534
  See also MONTHS & DATES: SEPTEMBER,
  OCTOBER, NOVEMBER

SEASONS: GENERAL 536
  See also Other Seasons, MONTHS & DATES
SEASONS: SPRING 536
  See also MONTHS & DATES: MARCH,
  APRIL, MAY
SEASONS: SUMMER 538
  See also HOT; MONTHS & DATES: JUNE,
  JULY, AUGUST; SUN
SEASONS: WINTER 542
  See also CHRISTMAS, MONTHS & DATES:
  DEC., JAN., FEB.; COLD, SNOW
SECRET AGENTS *See* POLICE 462
SECRETS 543
  See also DOORS, HIDING, LIES, PRETEND
SEEING 545
  See also EYES, FINDING, SEARCH
SELF-RESPECT *See* EGO 217
SELLING *See* SHOPPING 559
SEX 548
  See also KISSING, various ANATOMY
  categories
SEXUAL VARIATIONS *See* HOMOSEXUALS
316
SHADOWS 555
  See also ECHOES, REFLECTIONS
SHAKING *See* DANCE 175
SHIPS 556
  See also OCEAN, RIVERS, SAILING,
  WATER
SHIPWRECKS *See* SHIPS 556
SHOES 558
  See also CLOTHES
SHOOTING *See* GUNS 282
SHOPPING 559
  See also MONEY
SHOW BIZ 561
  See also CITIES: NEW YORK (for
  Broadway), HOLLYWOOD, MOVIES
SHUFFLE *See* DANCE 175
SHY *See* FEAR 232
SILENCE *See* HEAR 291
SILVER 563
SINGING *See* MUSIC 421
SINK *See* BATHROOM 41
SKINNY *See* FAT 229
SKY 565
  See also RAIN, SUN
SLAVERY *See* ROYALTY 526
SLEEP 567
  See also DREAMS, SEX
SMALL 570
  See also LITTLE for things of small amount
SMILE 575
  See also FUN, HAPPINESS, PARTY
SMOKE *See* FIRE 238
SMOKING *See* CIGARETTES 77
SNAKES *See* REPTILES 505

SNOW 577
   See also CHRISTMAS, COLD, MONTHS &
   DATES: DECEMBER, SEASONS: WINTER
SOLAR ENERGY *See* ENERGY 222
SOLDIERS *See* WAR 654
SONGS *See* MUSIC 421
SPACE 578
   See also ASTROLOGY, EARTH, MOON,
   STARS, SUN, UFO'S
SPACE PEOPLE *See* UFO'S 651
SPACED OUT *See* CRAZY 162
SPIDERS *See* INSECTS 324
SPIES *See* POLICE 462
SPIRITS 579
   See also ANGELS, DEVILS, MAGIC, UFO'S
SPORTS 580
   See also BASEBALL, COWBOYS, FOOT-
   BALL, RODEO, SURFING, SWIMMING,
   WINNING
STARDOM *See* SHOW BIZ 561
STARS 582
   See also ASTROLOGY, EARTH, MOON,
   SPACE, SUN, UFO's
STATEN ISLAND *See* CITIES: NEW YORK 98
STATES: ALABAMA 585
   See also CITIES: BIRMINGHAM, MOBILE
STATES: ALASKA 586
STATES: ARIZONA 586
STATES: ARKANSAS 586
STATES: CALIFORNIA 587
   See also CITIES: LOS ANGELES, SAN
   FRANCISCO; HOLLYWOOD
STATES: CAROLINAS 588
STATES: COLORADO 588
   See also CITIES: DENVER
STATES: CONNECTICUT 589
STATES: DELAWARE 589
STATES: FLORIDA 589
   See also CITIES: MIAMI
STATES: GEORGIA 589
   See also CITIES: ATLANTA, SAVANNAH
STATES: HAWAII 590
STATES: IDAHO 590
STATES: ILLINOIS 590
   See also CITIES: CHICAGO
STATES: INDIANA 591
STATES: IOWA 591
STATES: KANSAS 591
   See also CITIES: KANSAS CITY
STATES: KENTUCKY 591
STATES: LOUISIANA 592
   See also CITIES: NEW ORLEANS
STATES: MAINE 593
STATES: MARYLAND 593
   See also CITIES: BALTIMORE
STATES: MASSACHUSETTS 593
   See also CITIES: BOSTON
STATES: MICHIGAN 593
   See also CITIES: DETROIT

STATES: MINNESOTA 594
STATES: MISSISSIPPI 594
STATES: MISSOURI 594
   See also CITIES: KANSAS CITY, ST. LOUIS
STATES: MONTANA 594
STATES: NEBRASKA 595
STATES: NEVADA 595
   See also CITIES: LAS VEGAS
STATES: NEW HAMPSHIRE 595
STATES: NEW JERSEY 595
STATES: NEW MEXICO 595
   See also CITIES: SANTA FE
STATES: NEW YORK 595
   See also CITIES: NEW YORK
STATES: NORTH DAKOTA 595
STATES: OHIO 595
   See also CITIES: CINCINNATI
STATES: OKLAHOMA 596
   See also CITIES: TULSA
STATES: OREGON 596
STATES: PENNSYLVANIA 596
   See also CITIES: PHILADELPHIA
STATES: RHODE ISLAND 597
STATES: SOUTH DAKOTA 597
STATES: TENNESSEE 597
   See also CITIES: MEMPHIS, NASHVILLE
STATES: TEXAS 598
   See also CITIES: DALLAS, HOUSTON, SAN
   ANTONIO
STATES: UTAH 601
STATES: VERMONT 601
STATES: VIRGINIA 602
STATES: WASHINGTON 602
STATES: WEST VIRGINIA 602
STATES: WISCONSIN 602
STATES: WYOMING 602
STATIONS *See* TRAINS 629
STEAL *See* CRIME 166
STOP 603
STORIES *See* BOOKS 46
STORMS *See* RAIN 494
STORYBOOK CHARACTERS 604
   See also BOOKS, CARTOON
   CHARACTERS
STREAMS *See* RIVERS 508
STYMIED *See* PRISON 476
SUBWAYS *See* TRAINS 629
SUICIDE 606
   See also DEATH, KILL
SUN 607
   See also HOT, NIGHT, SEASONS:
   SUMMER, SPACE
SUPERNATURAL *See* MAGIC 360
SURFING 611
   See also OCEAN, SPORTS
SURRENDER *See* WAR 654
SURVIVE *See* LIFE 346
SWAMP *See* OCEAN 451

SWIMMING 612
   See also SPORTS

T

TAROT *See* ASTROLOGY 37
TAXES *See* MONEY 396
TAXI 612
   See also CARS, TRAVELING
TEA *See* COFFEE 113
TEACHERS *See* SCHOOL 529
TEARS *See* CRYING 169
TEENAGERS 612
   See also BABY, CHILDREN, REBELS, SCHOOL
TEETH *See* ANATOMY: MOUTH 24
TELEGRAPH *See* TELEPHONE 615
TELEPHONE 615
   See also COMMUNICATION
TELEVISION 617
THIN *See* FAT 229
THINGS OF SMALL SIZE *See* SMALL 570
THUNDER *See* RAIN 494
TIME: GENERAL 620
TIRED *See* SLEEP 567
TOBACCO *See* CIGARETTES 77
TOMORROW *See* FUTURE 267
TONGUE *See* ANATOMY: MOUTH 24
TONIGHT *See* NIGHT 434
TOYS & GAMES 625
   See also CARTOON CHARACTERS, CHILDREN, FUN, STORYBOOK CHARACTERS
TRAINS 629
TRASH 635
TRAVELING 636
   See also BUS, CARS, JOME, PRISON, REBELS, ROAD, TAXI, TRUCKS
TREES 647
   See also ECOLOGY, FLOWERS, JUNGLES
TRUCKIN' *See* TRUCKS 649
TRUCKS 649
   See also CARS, GAS STATIONS, ROAD, TRAVELING

U

UFO'S 651
   See also SPACE, STARS
UNIVERSE *See* SPACE 578
UTOPIA *See* PARADISE 457

V

VALENTINES *See* HEART 293
VALLEYS *See* MOUNTAINS 416
VAMPIRES *See* MONSTERS 400
VEGETABLES 652
   See also FOOD, FRUIT, RESTAURANTS

VEILS *See* HATS 290
VIDEO *See* TELEVISION 617
VIOLENCE *See* FIGHT 235
VOICES *See* COMMUNICATION: CONVERSATION 131
VOLCANOES *See* MOUNTAINS 416
VOODOO *See* MAGIC 360

W

WAITING 653
   See also TIME: GENERAL
WALKING *See* TRAVELING 636
WAR 654
   See also DEATH, DRAFT, GUNS, FIGHT, POLITICAL SONGS
WARM *See* HOT 318
WATER 659
   See also OCEAN, RIVERS, SAILING, SHIPS
WATERFALLS *See* WATER 659
WEALTH *See* MONEY 396
WEDDINGS *See* MARRIAGE 365
WEEKEND 660
   See also DAYS OF THE WEEK, WORK
WHALES 661
   See also ANIMALS: A-Z, ECOLOGY, FISH
WHEELS *See* CIRCLES 78
WILD 662
   See also CHAOS, REBELS
WIND 664
   See also CHAOS, LIFE, RAIN, SKY, SPIRITS
WINE *See* ALCOHOL 13
WINNING 666
   See also GAMBLING, LUCK, MONEY, SPORTS, TOYS & GAMES
WISH *See* PRETEND 471
WITCHES *See* SPIRITS 579
WOMEN'S NAMES: A 685
WOMEN'S NAMES: B 686
WOMEN'S NAMES: C 687
WOMEN'S NAMES: D 688
WOMEN'S NAMES: E 689
WOMEN'S NAMES: F 689
WOMEN'S NAMES: G 689
WOMEN'S NAMES: H 690
WOMEN'S NAMES: I 690
WOMEN'S NAMES: J 690
WOMEN'S NAMES: K 692
WOMEN'S NAMES: L 692
WOMEN'S NAMES: M 693
WOMEN'S NAMES: N 695
WOMEN'S NAMES: O 695
WOMEN'S NAMES: P 695
WOMEN'S NAMES: R 696
   See also ROSES
WOMEN'S NAMES: S 697
WOMEN'S NAMES: T 699
WOMEN'S NAMES: V 699

WOMEN'S NAMES: W **700**
WOMEN'S NAMES: Y **700**
WOMEN: GENERAL **667**
     See also MOTHERS, WOMEN'S NAMES
WONDER *See* PRETEND **471**
WORK **700**
     See also POVERTY, WEEKEND
WORKINGFOLK *See* WORK **700**
WORLD **703**
     See also LIFE, POLITICAL CLASSICS,
     SPACE, STARS
WORRY *See* FEAR **232**
WRITING *See* BOOKS **46**

Z

ZOOS *See* ANIMALS: GENERAL **31**

Notes

Notes

Notes

Notes

Notes

Order More Copies! Be Notified of New Editions!

From TV networks to movie studios, educators and songwriters, thousands of music lovers worldwide agree: *The Green Book Of Songs By Subject* is the unique thematic guide to popular music they can't do without!

Clip the handy form below to order extra copies of *The Green Book,* or to add your name to our mailing list, so we can notify you of future editions.